INTERNATIONAL MONETARY FUND

International Financial Statistics

YEARBOOK
2004

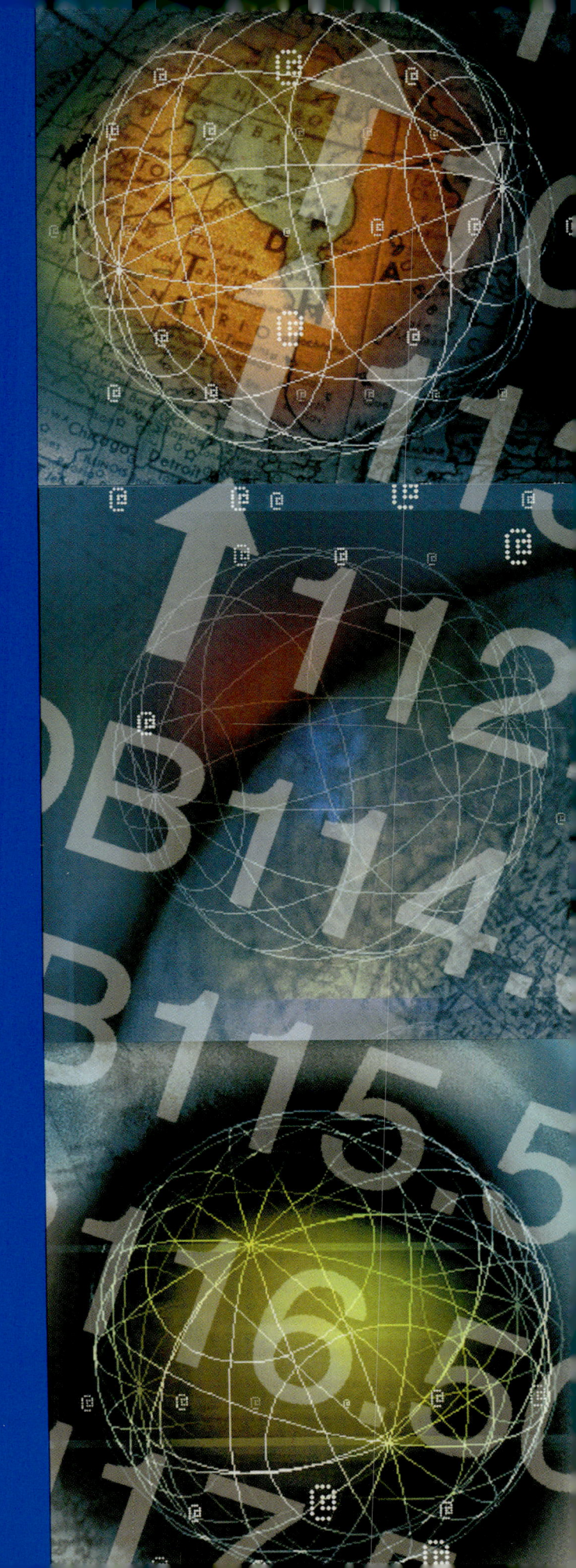

INTERNATIONAL MONETARY FUND

International
Financial Statistics

Yearbook 2004

INTERNATIONAL FINANCIAL STATISTICS

Vol. LVII, 2004
Prepared by the IMF Statistics Department
Robert W. Edwards, Director

For information related to this publication, please:
    fax the Statistics Department at (202) 623-6460,
    or write Statistics Department
        International Monetary Fund
        Washington, D.C. 20431
    or telephone (202) 623-6180.
For copyright inquiries, please fax the Editorial Division at (202) 623-6579.
For purchases only, please contact Publication Services (see information below).

Copyright © 2004, International Monetary Fund

International Financial Statistics (IFS) is a standard source of statistics on all aspects of international and domestic finance. *IFS* publishes, for most countries of the world, current data on exchange rates, international liquidity, international banking, money and banking, interest rates, prices, production, international transactions (including balance of payments and international investment position), government finance, and national accounts. Information is presented in tables for specific countries and in tables for area and world aggregates. *IFS* is published monthly and annually.

Address orders to:
International Monetary Fund
Attention: Publication Services
Washington, D.C. 20431
U.S.A.
Telephone: (202) 623-7430
Telefax: (202) 623-7201
E-mail: publications@imf.org
Internet: http://www.imf.org

ISSN 0250-7463
ISBN 1-58906-381-3

POSTMASTER: Send address changes to International Financial Statistics, Publication Services, 700 19th St., N.W., Washington, D.C. 20431. Postage for periodicals paid at Washington, D.C. USPS 049-610

Recycled paper

# INTERNATIONAL MONETARY FUND

International Financial Statistics

Yearbook 2004
Corrigendum

CONTENTS

World Tables

Fund Account: Position to Date 2
Financing Components: Outstanding Obligations
 to the Fund 5
Purchases 8
Repurchases 10
Loan Disbursements 12
Repayments of Loans 14
Producer Prices/Wholesale Prices 16
Exports, f.o.b. 18
Imports, c.i.f. 21
Terms of Trade 24
Balance of Payments 26
GDP Volume Measures 38

WORLD *and* AREA TABLES

Fund Account: Position to Date

(As of July 31, 2004 and Expressed in Millions of SDRs)

		Quota	Reserve Position in the Fund	Total Fund Credit and Loans Outstanding				Fund Holdings of Currency		SDR Department		
				Total Amount	Percent of Quota	Outstanding Purchases (GRA)	Outstanding Loans	Amount	Percent of Quota	Net Cumulative Allocation	Holdings of SDR	
											Amount	Percent of Allocation
		(1)	(2)	(3)	(4)	(5)	(6)	(7)	(8)	(9)	(10)	(11)
All Countries	010	212,794.0	59,842.4	66,232.4	31.1	59,279.6	6,952.7	212,231.4	99.7	21,433.3	20,557.9	95.9
Industrial Countries	110	130,566.6	47,217.8	—	—	—	—	83,346.1	63.8	14,595.3	15,344.4	105.1
United States	111	37,149.3	13,303.1	—	—	—	—	23,843.0	64.2	4,899.5	8,633.9	176.2
Canada	156	6,369.2	2,241.1	—	—	—	—	4,128.2	64.8	779.3	579.4	74.3
Australia	193	3,236.4	1,172.3	—	—	—	—	2,064.2	63.8	470.5	120.0	25.5
Japan	158	13,312.8	4,724.8	—	—	—	—	8,588.1	64.5	891.7	1,802.4	202.1
New Zealand	196	894.6	329.8	—	—	—	—	564.8	63.1	141.3	20.6	14.6
Austria	122	1,872.3	699.6	—	—	—	—	1,172.7	62.6	179.0	102.3	57.2
Belgium	124	4,605.2	1,669.4	—	—	—	—	2,935.8	63.7	485.2	526.3	108.5
Denmark	128	1,642.8	616.8	—	—	—	—	1,026.0	62.5	178.9	43.5	24.3
Finland	172	1,263.8	463.0	—	—	—	—	800.8	63.4	142.7	151.0	105.8
France	132	10,738.5	3,934.0	—	—	—	—	6,804.4	63.4	1,079.9	537.0	49.7
Germany	134	13,008.2	4,778.9	—	—	—	—	8,229.4	63.3	1,210.8	1,327.9	109.7
Greece	174	823.0	287.6	—	—	—	—	535.4	65.1	103.5	16.0	15.4
Iceland	176	117.6	18.6	—	—	—	—	99.0	84.2	16.4	.1	.4
Ireland	178	838.4	302.9	—	—	—	—	535.5	63.9	87.3	55.2	63.2
Italy	136	7,055.5	2,600.3	—	—	—	—	4,455.3	63.1	702.4	62.0	8.8
Luxembourg	137	279.1	102.2	—	—	—	—	176.9	63.4	17.0	9.0	53.3
Netherlands	138	5,162.4	1,928.2	—	—	—	—	3,234.2	62.6	530.3	500.8	94.4
Norway	142	1,671.7	597.7	—	—	—	—	1,074.0	64.2	167.8	200.2	119.3
Portugal	182	867.4	314.0	—	—	—	—	553.4	63.8	53.3	63.6	119.2
San Marino	135	17.0	4.1	—	—	—	—	12.9	75.9	—	.5	—
Spain	184	3,048.9	1,154.8	—	—	—	—	1,894.1	62.1	298.8	287.0	96.1
Sweden	144	2,395.5	894.0	—	—	—	—	1,501.5	62.7	246.5	101.2	41.0
Switzerland	146	3,458.5	1,253.3	—	—	—	—	2,205.2	63.8	—	2.3	—
United Kingdom	112	10,738.5	3,827.4	—	—	—	—	6,911.1	64.4	1,913.1	202.1	10.6
Developing Countries	200	82,227.4	12,624.6	66,232.4	80.5	59,279.6	6,952.7	128,885.2	156.7	6,838.1	5,213.5	76.2
Africa	605	11,498.1	298.7	5,293.4	46.0	1,312.7	3,980.8	12,512.6	108.8	1,382.5	463.3	33.5
Algeria	612	1,254.7	85.1	490.3	39.1	490.3	—	1,659.9	132.3	128.6	15.7	12.2
Angola	614	286.3	—	—	—	—	….	286.4	100.1	—	.1	—
Benin	638	61.9	2.2	45.2	73.0	—	45.2	59.7	96.5	9.4	.1	.6
Botswana	616	63.0	22.8	—	—	—	—	40.2	63.8	4.4	34.0	778.9
Burkina Faso	748	60.2	7.3	80.5	133.7	—	80.5	52.9	87.9	9.4	.2	1.8
Burundi	618	77.0	.4	26.4	34.3	—	26.4	76.6	99.5	13.7	.2	1.1
Cameroon	622	185.7	.6	225.5	121.4	—	225.5	185.1	99.7	24.5	1.0	4.0
Cape Verde	624	9.6	—	4.9	51.3	—	4.9	9.6	100.0	.6	—	.6
Central African Rep	626	55.7	.2	28.4	51.0	5.6	22.8	61.1	109.7	9.3	1.6	17.7
Chad	628	56.0	.3	66.7	119.2	—	66.7	55.7	99.5	9.4	—	.5
Comoros	632	8.9	.5	—	—	—	—	8.4	93.9	.7	—	1.0
Congo, Dem. Rep. of	636	533.0	—	526.8	98.8	—	526.8	533.0	100.0	86.3	5.1	5.9
Congo, Republic of	634	84.6	.5	13.5	15.9	7.9	5.6	92.0	108.8	9.7	.7	7.6
Côte d'Ivoire	662	325.2	.6	240.3	73.9	—	240.3	324.6	99.8	37.8	.2	.5
Djibouti	611	15.9	1.1	13.6	85.7	—	13.6	14.8	93.1	1.2	.1	4.3
Equatorial Guinea	642	32.6	—	—	—	—	—	32.6	100.0	5.8	.4	7.6
Eritrea	643	15.9	—	—	—	—	—	15.9	100.0	—	—	—
Ethiopia	644	133.7	7.2	111.9	83.7	—	111.9	126.5	94.6	11.2	.3	3.1
Gabon	646	154.3	.2	43.3	28.1	43.3	—	197.4	127.9	14.1	.4	2.7
Gambia, The	648	31.1	1.5	19.4	62.3	—	19.4	29.6	95.2	5.1	.4	7.6
Ghana	652	369.0	—	314.8	85.3	—	314.8	369.0	100.0	63.0	18.3	29.0
Guinea	656	107.1	.1	81.7	76.3	—	81.7	107.0	99.9	17.6	.1	.5
Guinea-Bissau	654	14.2	—	11.3	79.3	.6	10.6	14.8	104.4	1.2	.4	36.9
Kenya	664	271.4	12.7	70.8	26.1	—	70.8	258.7	95.3	37.0	.4	.9
Lesotho	666	34.9	3.5	21.0	60.2	—	21.0	31.4	89.9	3.7	.4	11.0
Liberia	668	71.3	—	223.7	313.7	200.8	22.9	272.1	381.6	21.0	—	—
Madagascar	674	122.2	—	136.8	111.9	—	136.8	122.2	100.0	19.3	.2	.9
Malawi	676	69.4	2.3	63.9	92.0	17.4	46.5	84.5	121.7	11.0	.5	4.5
Mali	678	93.3	9.0	103.9	111.3	—	103.9	84.4	90.4	15.9	.5	3.2
Mauritania	682	64.4	—	62.8	97.5	—	62.8	64.4	100.0	9.7	.1	1.0
Mauritius	684	101.6	21.9	—	—	—	—	79.7	78.5	15.7	17.4	110.3
Morocco	686	588.2	70.4	—	—	—	—	517.8	88.0	85.7	66.0	77.0
Mozambique	688	113.6	—	134.6	118.5	—	134.6	113.6	100.0	—	.1	—
Namibia	728	136.5	.1	—	—	—	—	136.4	100.0	—	—	—
Niger	692	65.8	8.6	90.1	136.9	—	90.1	57.2	87.0	9.4	.3	3.4
Nigeria	694	1,753.2	.1	—	—	—	—	1,753.1	100.0	157.2	.7	.5
Rwanda	714	80.1	—	61.8	77.1	—	61.8	80.1	100.0	13.7	19.8	144.6
São Tomé & Príncipe	716	7.4	—	1.9	25.7	—	1.9	7.4	100.0	.6	—	1.3
Senegal	722	161.8	1.5	142.2	87.9	—	142.2	160.3	99.1	24.5	1.1	4.6
Seychelles	718	8.8	—	—	—	—	—	8.8	100.0	.4	—	.6
Sierra Leone	724	103.7	—	115.4	111.3	—	115.4	103.7	100.0	17.5	19.3	110.6
Somalia	726	44.2	—	112.0	253.4	96.7	15.3	140.9	318.8	13.7	—	—
South Africa	199	1,868.5	.5	—	—	—	—	1,868.0	100.0	220.4	222.8	101.1
Sudan	732	169.7	—	391.8	230.9	332.6	59.2	502.3	296.0	52.2	.3	.5
Swaziland	734	50.7	6.6	—	—	—	—	44.2	87.1	6.4	2.5	38.4
Tanzania	738	198.9	10.0	284.8	143.2	—	284.8	188.9	95.0	31.4	.2	.6
Togo	742	73.4	.3	20.6	28.1	—	20.6	73.1	99.5	11.0	.1	1.0
Tunisia	744	286.5	20.2	—	—	—	—	266.3	93.0	34.2	13.3	38.9
Uganda	746	180.5	—	139.1	77.0	—	139.1	180.5	100.0	29.4	.4	1.3
Zambia	754	489.1	—	576.1	117.8	—	576.1	489.1	100.0	68.3	17.8	26.0
Zimbabwe	698	353.4	.3	195.8	55.4	117.5	78.3	470.6	133.2	10.2	—	.5

2004, International Monetary Fund : *International Financial Statistics Yearbook*

Fund Account: Position to Date

(As of July 31, 2004 and Expressed in Millions of SDRs)

		Quota	Reserve Position in the Fund	Total Fund Credit and Loans Outstanding				Fund Holdings of Currency		SDR Department		
				Total Amount	Percent of Quota	Outstanding Purchases (GRA)	Outstanding Loans	Amount	Percent of Quota	Net Cumulative Allocation	Holdings of SDR	
											Amount	Percent of Allocation
		(1)	(2)	(3)	(4)	(5)	(6)	(7)	(8)	(9)	(10)	(11)
Asia	505	22,046.8	4,966.7	9,242.2	41.9	7,696.1	1,546.1	24,776.7	112.4	2,043.7	1,353.2	66.2
Afghanistan, I.S. of	512	161.9	—	—	—	—	—	161.9	100.0	26.7	.2	.7
Bangladesh	513	533.3	.2	99.0	18.6	—	99.0	533.1	100.0	47.1	1.6	3.3
Bhutan	514	6.3	1.0	—	—	—	—	5.3	83.8	—	.3	—
Brunei Darussalam	516	215.2	58.3	—	—	—	—	157.1	73.0	—	8.3	—
Cambodia	522	87.5	—	65.5	74.9	—	65.5	87.5	100.0	15.4	.2	1.0
China,P.R.: Mainland	924	6,369.2	2,270.4	—	—	—	—	4,098.9	64.4	236.8	773.7	326.7
China,P.R.:Hong Kong	532	....	....	....	....	....	....	....	....	....	....	....
Fiji	819	70.3	15.2	—	—	—	—	55.1	78.4	7.0	5.3	75.6
India	534	4,158.2	887.1	—	—	—	—	3,271.1	78.7	681.2	1.2	.2
Indonesia	536	2,079.3	145.5	6,598.6	317.3	6,598.6	—	8,532.4	410.4	239.0	49.3	20.6
Kiribati	826	5.6	—	—	—	—	....	5.6	100.0	—	—	—
Korea	542	1,633.6	507.7	—	—	—	—	1,125.9	68.9	72.9	17.3	23.8
Lao People's Dem.Rep.	544	52.9	—	26.3	49.8	—	26.3	52.9	100.0	9.4	9.9	105.1
Malaysia	548	1,486.6	550.5	—	—	—	—	936.1	63.0	139.0	123.9	89.1
Maldives	556	8.2	1.6	—	—	—	—	6.6	81.1	.3	.3	110.4
Marshall Islands,Rep.	867	3.5	—	—	—	—	—	3.5	100.0	—	—	—
Micronesia, Fed.Sts.	868	5.1	—	—	—	—	—	5.1	100.0	—	1.2	—
Mongolia	948	51.1	.1	30.8	60.2	—	30.8	51.0	99.8	—	—	—
Myanmar	518	258.4	—	—	—	—	—	258.4	100.0	43.5	.3	.8
Nepal	558	71.3	5.8	7.1	10.0	—	7.1	65.5	91.9	8.1	.5	6.2
Pakistan	564	1,033.7	—	1,355.4	131.1	279.1	1,076.2	1,312.7	127.0	170.0	162.1	95.4
Palau	565	3.1	.1	—	—	—	—	3.1	100.0	—	—	—
Papua New Guinea	853	131.6	.4	62.8	47.7	62.8	—	194.0	147.4	9.3	1.5	16.6
Philippines	566	879.9	87.4	566.8	64.4	566.8	—	1,359.3	154.5	116.6	5.4	4.6
Samoa	862	11.6	.7	—	—	—	—	10.9	94.1	1.1	2.4	211.2
Singapore	576	862.5	285.4	—	—	—	—	577.2	66.9	16.5	184.0	1,116.7
Solomon Islands	813	10.4	.6	—	—	—	—	9.9	94.7	.7	—	.5
Sri Lanka	524	413.4	47.9	227.2	55.0	188.8	38.4	554.4	134.1	70.9	1.9	2.7
Thailand	578	1,081.9	96.7	—	—	—	—	985.2	91.1	84.7	.9	1.1
Timor-Leste	537	8.2	—	—	—	—	—	8.2	100.0	—	—	—
Tonga	866	6.9	1.7	—	—	—	—	5.2	75.3	—	.2	—
Vanuatu	846	17.0	2.5	—	—	—	—	14.5	85.3	—	.9	—
Vietnam	582	329.1	—	202.7	61.6	—	202.7	329.1	100.0	47.7	.4	.8
Europe	170	17,270.1	1,494.7	21,372.8	123.8	20,621.9	750.9	36,397.6	210.8	374.1	484.5	129.5
Albania	914	48.7	3.4	66.0	135.5	—	66.0	45.4	93.1	—	68.0	—
Armenia	911	92.0	—	142.8	155.2	4.2	138.6	96.2	104.6	—	10.7	—
Azerbaijan	912	160.9	—	145.0	90.1	47.0	98.0	207.9	129.2	—	2.4	—
Belarus	913	386.4	—	5.8	1.5	5.8	—	392.2	101.5	—	.1	—
Bosnia & Herzegovina	963	169.1	—	82.8	48.9	82.8	—	251.9	148.9	20.5	1.0	5.0
Bulgaria	918	640.2	32.8	811.3	126.7	811.3	—	1,418.7	221.6	—	49.2	—
Croatia	960	365.1	.2	—	—	—	—	364.9	100.0	44.2	.5	1.1
Cyprus	423	139.6	52.4	—	—	—	—	87.2	62.4	19.4	2.3	11.7
Czech Republic	935	819.3	296.3	—	—	—	—	523.0	63.8	—	1.0	—
Estonia	939	65.2	—	—	—	—	—	65.2	100.0	—	.1	—
Georgia	915	150.3	—	189.8	126.3	6.9	182.8	157.2	104.6	—	3.3	—
Hungary	944	1,038.4	363.8	—	—	—	—	674.6	65.0	—	34.4	—
Kazakhstan	916	365.7	—	—	—	—	—	365.7	100.0	—	.8	—
Kyrgyz Republic	917	88.8	—	144.0	162.2	—	144.0	88.8	100.0	—	14.8	—
Latvia	941	126.8	.1	—	—	—	—	126.8	100.0	—	.1	—
Lithuania	946	144.2	—	21.6	15.0	21.6	—	165.7	114.9	—	.2	—
Macedonia, FYR	962	68.9	—	37.8	54.8	16.9	20.8	85.8	124.6	8.4	2.1	25.2
Malta	181	102.0	40.3	—	—	—	—	61.7	60.5	11.3	30.3	268.1
Moldova	921	123.2	—	85.3	69.3	57.6	27.7	180.8	146.8	—	.1	—
Poland	964	1,369.0	502.1	—	—	—	—	866.9	63.3	—	40.8	—
Romania	968	1,030.2	—	337.0	32.7	337.0	—	1,367.2	132.7	76.0	3.0	4.0
Russia	922	5,945.4	1.8	2,613.5	44.0	2,613.5	—	8,557.1	143.9	—	20.3	—
Serbia & Montenegro	965	467.7	—	650.2	139.0	650.2	—	1,117.9	239.0	56.7	11.1	19.5
Slovak Republic	936	357.5	—	—	—	—	—	357.5	100.0	—	.9	—
Slovenia	961	231.7	88.8	—	—	—	—	142.9	61.7	25.4	6.7	26.2
Tajikistan	923	87.0	—	72.9	83.8	—	72.9	87.0	100.0	—	.1	—
Turkey	186	964.0	112.8	14,823.1	1,537.7	14,823.1	—	15,674.3	1,626.0	112.3	171.7	152.9
Turkmenistan	925	75.2	—	—	—	—	—	75.2	100.0	—	—	—
Ukraine	926	1,372.0	—	1,127.4	82.2	1,127.4	—	2,499.4	182.2	—	8.5	—
Uzbekistan	927	275.6	—	16.6	6.0	16.6	—	292.2	106.0	—	.2	—
Middle East	405	15,478.5	4,180.5	504.5	3.3	283.3	221.2	11,582.1	74.8	986.5	1,311.6	133.0
Bahrain, Kingdom of	419	135.0	70.2	—	—	—	—	64.8	48.0	6.2	.6	10.3
Egypt	469	943.7	—	—	—	—	—	943.7	100.0	135.9	52.0	38.2
Iran, I.R. of	429	1,497.2	—	—	—	—	—	1,497.2	100.0	244.1	273.6	112.1
Iraq	433	504.0	—	—	—	—	—	504.0	100.0	68.5	—	—
Israel	436	928.2	333.4	—	—	—	—	594.8	64.1	106.4	8.0	7.6
Jordan	439	170.5	.1	246.5	144.6	246.5	—	417.0	244.5	16.9	1.9	11.0
Kuwait	443	1,381.1	500.8	—	—	—	—	880.3	63.7	26.7	111.9	418.6
Lebanon	446	203.0	18.8	—	—	—	—	184.2	90.7	4.4	20.9	475.5
Libya	672	1,123.7	395.5	—	—	—	—	728.2	64.8	58.8	468.1	796.4
Oman	449	194.0	64.2	—	—	—	—	129.9	66.9	6.3	8.4	134.1
Qatar	453	263.8	96.6	—	—	—	—	167.2	63.4	12.8	22.6	175.9
Saudi Arabia	456	6,985.5	2,485.6	—	—	—	—	4,499.9	64.4	195.5	311.4	159.3

2004, International Monetary Fund : *International Financial Statistics Yearbook*

Fund Account: Position to Date

(As of July 31, 2004 and Expressed in Millions of SDRs)

		Quota	Reserve Position in the Fund	Total Fund Credit and Loans Outstanding			Fund Holdings of Currency		SDR Department		
				Total Amount	Percent of Quota	Outstanding Purchases (GRA)	Outstanding Loans	Amount	Percent of Quota	Net Qumulative Allocation	Holdings of SDR	
											Amount	Percent of Allocation
		(1)	(2)	(3)	(4)	(5)	(6)	(7)	(8)	(9)	(10)	(11)
Middle East(Cont.)												
Syrian Arab Republic	463	293.6	—	—	—	—	—	293.6	100.0	36.6	.3	.9
United Arab Emirates	466	611.7	215.3	—	—	—	—	397.0	64.9	38.7	2.0	5.0
Yemen, Republic of	474	243.5	—	258.0	105.9	36.8	221.2	280.3	115.1	28.7	29.9	103.9
Western Hemisphere	**205**	**15,933.9**	**1,684.0**	**29,819.5**	**187.1**	**29,365.6**	**453.9**	**43,616.3**	**273.7**	**2,051.3**	**1,601.0**	**78.0**
Antigua and Barbuda	311	13.5	—	—	—	—	—	13.5	100.0	—	—	—
Argentina	213	2,117.1	.1	9,980.4	471.4	9,980.4	—	12,097.4	571.4	318.4	761.1	239.1
Bahamas, The	313	130.3	6.3	—	—	—	—	124.0	95.2	10.2	.1	.5
Barbados	316	67.5	5.1	—	—	—	—	62.4	92.5	8.0	—	.6
Belize	339	18.8	4.2	—	—	—	—	14.6	77.5	—	1.6	—
Bolivia	218	171.5	8.9	184.3	107.5	75.0	109.3	237.7	138.6	26.7	26.3	98.6
Brazil	223	3,036.1	—	17,221.9	567.2	17,221.9	—	20,258.5	667.3	358.7	209.3	58.3
Chile	228	856.1	293.2	—	—	—	—	562.9	65.7	121.9	32.5	26.6
Colombia	233	774.0	285.8	—	—	—	—	488.2	63.1	114.3	114.3	100.0
Costa Rica	238	164.1	20.0	—	—	—	—	144.1	87.8	23.7	.1	.5
Dominica	321	8.2	—	5.6	68.8	3.0	2.7	11.2	136.2	.6	—	6.2
Dominican Republic	243	218.9	—	131.3	60.0	131.3	—	350.2	160.0	31.6	1.5	4.8
Ecuador	248	302.3	17.2	213.9	70.8	213.9	—	499.1	165.1	32.9	10.3	31.4
El Salvador	253	171.3	—	—	—	—	—	171.3	100.0	25.0	25.0	100.0
Grenada	328	11.7	—	2.9	25.0	2.9	—	14.6	125.1	.9	—	3.8
Guatemala	258	210.2	—	—	—	—	—	210.2	100.0	27.7	5.3	19.3
Guyana	336	90.9	—	57.0	62.7	—	57.0	90.9	100.0	14.5	1.4	9.8
Haiti	263	81.9	.1	7.6	9.3	—	7.6	81.8	99.9	13.7	.6	4.2
Honduras	268	129.5	8.6	123.6	95.4	—	123.6	120.9	93.3	19.1	.1	.6
Jamaica	343	273.5	—	2.5	.9	2.5	—	276.1	100.9	40.6	.3	.7
Mexico	273	2,585.8	553.3	—	—	—	—	2,032.5	78.6	290.0	295.0	101.7
Nicaragua	278	130.0	—	153.7	118.3	—	153.7	130.0	100.0	19.5	.2	1.1
Panama	283	206.6	11.9	26.7	12.9	26.7	—	221.4	107.2	26.3	.5	2.0
Paraguay	288	99.9	21.5	—	—	—	—	78.4	78.5	13.7	85.3	622.9
Peru	293	638.4	—	80.3	12.6	80.3	—	718.7	112.6	91.3	1.0	1.1
St. Kitts and Nevis	361	8.9	.1	—	—	—	—	8.8	99.1	—	—	—
St. Lucia	362	15.3	—	—	—	—	—	15.3	100.0	.7	1.5	201.9
St. Vincent & Grens	364	8.3	.5	—	—	—	—	7.8	94.0	.4	—	.8
Suriname	366	92.1	6.1	—	—	—	—	86.0	93.4	7.8	1.3	16.4
Trinidad and Tobago	369	335.6	119.3	—	—	—	—	216.3	64.4	46.2	1.2	2.6
Uruguay	298	306.5	—	1,627.8	531.1	1,627.8	—	1,934.3	631.1	50.0	18.7	37.4
Venezuela, Rep. Bol.	299	2,659.1	321.9	—	—	—	—	2,337.2	87.9	316.9	6.3	2.0
Memorandum Items	**001**											
Oil Exporting Ctys.	999	20,307.3	4,310.6	7,088.9	34.9	7,088.9	—	23,086.4	113.7	1,493.0	1,270.0	85.1
Non-Oil Develop.Ctys.	201	61,920.1	8,314.0	59,143.4	95.5	52,190.7	6,952.7	105,798.8	170.9	5,345.1	3,943.5	73.8

2004, International Monetary Fund : *International Financial Statistics Yearbook*

Financing Components of Members' Outstanding Obligations to the Fund

(As of July 31, 2004 and Expressed in Millions of SDRs)

			Outstanding Purchases (GRA)								Outstanding Loans			
			Ordinary Resources				Borrower Resources				SAF Arrangements	PRGF Arrangements		Trust Fund
	Total Fund Credit and Loans Outstanding	Total Amount	CCFF	STF	Send-by/ Credit Tranche	Extended Fund Facility	Sff	EAR	GAB	NAB	SDA Resources	SDA Resources	PRGF Trust Resources	Administered Accounts
		(1)	(2)	(3)	(4)	(5)	(6)	(7)	(8)	(9)	(10)	(11)	(12)	(13)	(14)
All Countries	010	66,232.4	59,279.6	89.4	110.2	45,452.1	12,736.3	102.0	277.3	512.3	—	64.8	.9	6,798.4	88.6
Industrial Countries	110	—	—	—	....	—	—	—	—	—	—	....	....	....	....
Developing Countries	200	66,232.4	59,279.6	89.4	110.2	45,452.1	12,736.3	102.0	277.3	512.3	—	64.8	.9	6,798.4	88.6
Africa	605	5,293.4	1,312.7	87.7	....	211.5	634.2	102.0	277.3	—	—	64.8	.9	3,826.5	88.6
Algeria	612	490.3	490.3	—	....	—	490.3	....	....	—	—	—	....	—	....
Angola	614	—	—	—	....	....	—	....	....	—	—	—	....	—	—
Benin	638	45.2	—	....	....	....	—	—	—	—	—	—	—	45.2	—
Botswana	616	—	—	—	....	—	—	—	—	—	—	—	....	—	—
Burkina Faso	748	80.5	—	....	....	—	—	—	—	—	—	—	.9	79.5	—
Burundi	618	26.4	—	—	....	—	—	—	—	—	—	—	—	26.4	—
Cameroon	622	225.5	—	—	....	—	—	—	—	—	—	—	—	225.5	—
Cape Verde	624	4.9	—	....	....	....	—	—	—	—	—	—	....	4.9	....
Central African Rep	626	28.4	5.6	—	—	5.6	....	—	—	—	—	—	—	22.8	—
Chad	628	66.7	—	—	—	—	—	—	—	—	—	—	—	66.7	—
Comoros	632	—	—	—	....	—	—	—	—	—	—	—	—	—	....
Congo, Dem. Rep. of	636	526.8	—	—	....	—	—	—	—	—	—	—	—	526.8	—
Congo, Republic of	634	13.5	7.9	—	—	7.9	....	—	—	—	—	—	—	5.6	—
Côte d'Ivoire	662	240.3	—	—	—	—	—	—	—	—	—	—	—	240.3	—
Djibouti	611	13.6	—	....	....	—	—	—	—	—	—	—	....	13.6	....
Equatorial Guinea	642	—	—	—	....	—	—	—	—	—	—	—	—	—	—
Eritrea	643	—	—	—	....	—	—	—	—	—	—	—	—	—	—
Ethiopia	644	111.9	—	—	—	—	....	—	—	—	—	1.4	—	110.5	—
Gabon	646	43.3	43.3	—	....	22.2	21.1	—	—	—	—	—	—	—	....
Gambia, The	648	19.4	—	—	—	—	—	—	—	—	—	—	—	19.4	—
Ghana	652	314.8	—	—	....	—	—	—	—	—	—	—	—	314.8	—
Guinea	656	81.7	—	—	—	—	....	—	—	—	—	—	—	81.7	—
Guinea-Bissau	654	11.3	.6	—	—	.6	....	—	—	—	—	—	—	10.6	....
Kenya	664	70.8	—	—	....	—	—	—	—	—	—	—	—	70.8	—
Lesotho	666	21.0	—	....	....	....	....	—	—	—	—	—	—	21.0	—
Liberia	668	223.7	200.8	34.7	....	45.5	....	36.3	84.3	—	—	—	—	....	22.9
Madagascar	674	136.8	—	—	—	—	—	—	—	—	—	—	—	136.8	—
Malawi	676	63.9	17.4	—	....	17.4	—	—	—	—	—	—	—	46.5	—
Mali	678	103.9	—	—	....	—	—	—	—	—	—	—	—	103.9	—
Mauritania	682	62.8	—	—	—	—	—	—	—	—	—	—	—	62.8	—
Mauritius	684	—	—	—	—	—	—	—	—	—	—	—	—	—	—
Morocco	686	—	—	—	—	—	—	—	—	—	—	—	—	—	—
Mozambique	688	134.6	—	....	....	—	—	—	—	—	—	—	—	134.6	....
Namibia	728	—	—	—	....	—	—	—	—	—	—	—	—	—	—
Niger	692	90.1	—	—	—	—	—	—	—	—	—	—	—	90.1	—
Nigeria	694	—	—	—	....	—	—	—	—	—	—	—	....	—	....
Rwanda	714	61.8	—	—	—	—	—	—	—	—	—	—	—	61.8	—
São Tomé & Príncipe	716	1.9	—	—	—	—	—	—	—	—	—	—	—	1.9	....
Senegal	722	142.2	—	—	—	—	—	—	—	—	—	—	—	142.2	—
Seychelles	718	—	—	—	....	—	—	—	—	—	—	—	....	—	—
Sierra Leone	724	115.4	—	—	—	—	—	—	—	—	—	—	—	115.4	—
Somalia	726	112.0	96.7	28.5	....	12.6	....	—	55.5	—	—	8.8	—	—	6.5
South Africa	199	—	—	—	....	—	—	—	—	—	—	....	....	—	59.2
Sudan	732	391.8	332.6	24.4	—	35.8	69.2	65.6	137.5	—	—	—	—	—	59.2
Swaziland	734	—	—	—	—	—	—	—	—	—	—	—	—	—	—
Tanzania	738	284.8	—	—	—	—	—	—	—	—	—	—	—	284.8	—
Togo	742	20.6	—	—	....	—	—	—	—	—	—	—	—	20.6	—
Tunisia	744	—	—	—	—	—	—	—	—	—	—	—	—	—	....
Uganda	746	139.1	—	—	....	—	....	—	—	—	—	—	—	139.1	—
Zambia	754	576.1	—	—	—	—	—	—	—	—	—	54.5	—	521.6	—
Zimbabwe	698	195.8	117.5	—	....	63.9	53.6	—	—	—	—	—	—	78.3	—
Asia	505	9,242.2	7,696.1	—	—	574.4	7,121.7	—	—	—	—	—	—	1,546.1	—
Afghanistan, I.S. of	512	—	—	—	....	—	—	—	—	—	—	....	....	....	....
Bangladesh	513	99.0	—	—	....	—	....	—	—	—	—	—	....	99.0	—
Bhutan	514	—	—	....	....	....	....	—	—	—	—	—	....	—	—
Brunei Darussalam	516	—	—	—	—	—	—	—	—	—	—	—	—	—	—
Cambodia	522	65.5	—	—	—	—	....	—	—	—	—	—	....	65.5	....
China, People's Rep	924	—	—	—	—	—	—	—	—	—	—	—	....	—	....
Fiji	819	—	—	—	—	—	—	—	—	—	—	—	—	—	—
India	534	—	—	—	....	—	—	—	—	—	—	—	....	—	....
Indonesia	536	6,598.6	6,598.6	—	—	—	6,598.6	....	....	—	—	....	....	—	....
Kiribati	826	—	—	—	—	—	—	—	—	—	—	—	....	—	....
Korea	542	—	—	—	—	—	—	—	—	—	—	—	—	26.3	—
Lao People's Dem.Rep	544	26.3	—	—	—	—	—	—	—	—	—	—	—	26.3	—
Malaysia	548	—	—	—	—	—	—	—	—	—	—	—	....	—	....
Maldives	556	—	—	—	—	—	—	—	—	—	—	—	—	—	—
Marshall Islands,Rep	867	—	—	—	....	—	—	—	—	—	—	—	....	—	—
Micronesia, Fed.Sts	868	—	—	—	—	—	—	—	—	—	—	—	—	—	—
Mongolia	948	30.8	—	—	—	—	—	—	—	—	—	—	....	30.8	—
Myanmar	518	—	—	—	—	—	—	—	—	—	—	—	—	—	—
Nepal	558	7.1	—	—	—	—	—	—	—	—	—	—	—	7.1	—
Pakistan	564	1,355.4	279.1	—	....	195.0	84.1	—	—	—	—	—	—	1,076.2	—

2004, International Monetary Fund : *International Financial Statistics Yearbook*

Financing Components of Members' Outstanding Obligations to the Fund

(As of July 31, 2004 and Expressed in Millions of SDRs)

		Total Fund Credit and Loans Outstanding	\multicolumn{9}{c}{Outstanding Purchases (GRA)}	\multicolumn{3}{c}{Outstanding Loans}	
			\multicolumn{5}{c}{Ordinary Resources}	\multicolumn{4}{c}{Borrower Resources}	SAF Arrangements	PRGF Arrangements	Trust Fund
			Total Amount	CCFF	STF	Send-by/Credit Tranche	Extended Fund Facility	Sff	EAR	GAB	NAB	SDA Resources	SDA Resources	PRGF Trust Resources	Administered Accounts
		(1)	(2)	(3)	(4)	(5)	(6)	(7)	(8)	(9)	(10)	(11)	(12)	(13)	(14)
Asia(Cont.)															
Palau	565	—	—	—	....	—	—	—	—	—	—	—	—	—	—
Papua New Guinea	853	62.8	62.8	—	....	62.8	....	—	—	—	—	....	....	....	—
Philippines	566	566.8	566.8	—	....	148.5	418.3	—	—	—	—	....	....	....	—
Samoa	862	—	—	—	....	—	....	—	—	—	—	....	—	....	—
Singapore	576	—	—	....	....	....	....	—	—	—	—	....	....	....	—
Solomon Islands	813	—	—	—	....	—	....	—	—	—	—	....	—	....	....
Sri Lanka	524	227.2	188.8	—	....	168.1	20.6	—	—	—	—	—	—	38.4	—
Thailand	578	—	—	—	....	—	....	—	—	—	—	....	....	....	—
Tonga	866	—	—	—	....	—	....	—	—	—	—	....	—	....	—
Vanuatu	846	—	—	....	....	....	....	—	—	—	—	....	—	....	—
Vietnam	582	202.7	—	—	....	—	—	—	—	—	—	—	—	202.7	—
Europe	170	21,372.8	20,621.9	1.7	110.2	15,741.0	4,256.6	—	—	512.3	—	—	—	750.9	—
Albania	914	66.0	—	—	—	—	—	—	—	—	—	—	—	66.0	—
Armenia	911	142.8	4.2	—	4.2	—	—	—	—	—	—	—	—	138.6	—
Azerbaijan	912	145.0	47.0	—	12.2	—	34.8	—	—	—	—	—	....	98.0	—
Belarus	913	5.8	5.8	—	5.8	—	—	—	—	—	—	—	—	—	—
Bosnia & Herzegovina	963	82.8	82.8	—	—	82.8	—	—	—	—	—	—	—	—	—
Bulgaria	918	811.3	811.3	—	—	236.0	575.3	—	—	—	—	—	—	—	—
Croatia	960	—	—	—	—	—	—	—	—	—	—	—	—	—	—
Cyprus	423	—	—	—	....	—	....	—	—	—	—	....	....	....	....
Czech Republic	935	—	—	—	—	—	—	—	—	—	—	—	—	—	—
Estonia	939	—	—	—	—	—	—	—	—	—	—	—	—	—	—
Georgia	915	189.8	6.9	—	6.9	—	—	—	—	—	—	—	—	182.8	—
Hungary	944	—	—	—	—	—	—	—	—	—	—	—	—	—	—
Kazakhstan	916	—	—	—	—	—	—	—	—	—	—	—	—	—	—
Kyrgyz Republic	917	144.0	—	—	—	—	—	—	—	—	—	—	—	144.0	—
Latvia	941	—	—	—	—	—	—	—	—	—	—	—	—	—	—
Lithuania	946	21.6	21.6	—	—	—	21.6	—	—	—	—	—	—	—	—
Macedonia, FYR	962	37.8	16.9	1.7	2.1	12.0	1.1	—	—	—	—	—	—	20.8	—
Malta	181	—	—	....	....	....	....	—	—	—	—	....	....	....	—
Moldova	921	85.3	57.6	—	—	—	57.6	—	—	—	—	—	—	27.7	—
Poland	964	—	—	—	—	—	—	—	—	—	—	—	—	—	—
Romania	968	337.0	337.0	—	—	337.0	—	—	—	—	—	—	—	—	—
Russia	922	2,613.5	2,613.5	—	—	—	2,101.2	—	—	512.3	—	—	—	—	—
Serbia & Montenegro	965	650.2	650.2	—	—	250.2	400.0	—	—	—	....	—	—	—	—
Slovak Republic	936	—	—	—	—	—	—	—	—	—	—	—	—	—	—
Slovenia	961	—	—	—	—	—	—	—	—	—	—	—	—	—	—
Tajikistan	923	72.9	—	—	....	—	—	—	—	—	—	—	—	72.9	—
Turkey	186	14,823.1	14,823.1	—	....	14,823.1	....	—	—	—	—	....	....	—	—
Turkmenistan	925	—	—	—	—	—	—	—	—	—	—	....	....	....	—
Ukraine	926	1,127.4	1,127.4	—	62.3	—	1,065.1	—	—	—	—	....	....	—	—
Uzbekistan	927	16.6	16.6	—	16.6	—	—	—	—	—	—	—	—	—	—
Middle East	405	504.5	283.3	—	....	10.7	272.7	....	....	—	—	—	—	221.2	—
Bahrain, Kingdom of	419	—	—	—	....	—	....	—	—	—	—	....	....	....	—
Egypt	469	—	—	—	—	—	—	—	—	—	—	—	—	—	—
Iran, I.R. of	429	—	—	—	....	—	....	—	—	—	—	....	....	....	—
Iraq	433	—	—	—	....	—	....	—	—	—	—	....	....	....	—
Israel	436	—	—	—	—	—	....	—	—	—	—	....	....	....	—
Jordan	439	246.5	246.5	—	....	10.7	235.9	—	—	—	—	....	....	....	—
Kuwait	443	—	—	—	....	—	....	—	—	—	—	....	....	....	—
Lebanon	446	—	—	—	....	—	....	—	—	—	—	....	....	....	—
Libya	672	—	—	—	....	—	....	—	—	—	—	....	....	....	—
Oman	449	—	—	—	....	—	....	—	—	—	—	....	....	....	—
Qatar	453	—	—	—	....	—	....	—	—	—	—	....	....	....	—
Saudi Arabia	456	—	—	—	—	—	—	—	—	—	—	—	—	—	—
Syrian Arab Republic	463	—	—	—	....	—	....	—	—	—	—	....	....	....	—
United Arab Emirates	466	—	—	—	....	—	....	—	—	—	—	....	....	....	—
Yemen, Republic of	474	258.0	36.8	—	—	—	36.8	—	—	—	—	—	—	221.2	—
Western Hemisphere	205	29,819.5	29,365.6	—	....	28,914.6	451.0	—	—	—	—	—	—	453.9	—
Antigua and Barbuda	311	—	—	—	....	—	—	—	—	—	—	....	....	....	—
Argentina	213	9,980.4	9,980.4	—	....	9,638.8	341.6	—	—	—	—	....	....	....	—
Bahamas, The	313	—	—	—	....	—	....	—	—	—	—	....	....	....	—
Barbados	316	—	—	—	—	—	....	—	—	—	—	....	....	....	—
Belize	339	—	—	—	....	—	....	—	—	—	—	....	....	....	—
Bolivia	218	184.3	75.0	—	—	75.0	—	—	—	—	—	—	—	109.3	—
Brazil	223	17,221.9	17,221.9	—	....	17,221.9	—	—	—	—	—	....	....	—	—
Chile	228	—	—	—	....	—	—	—	—	—	—	....	....	....	—
Colombia	233	—	—	—	—	—	—	—	—	—	—	—	—	—	—
Costa Rica	238	—	—	—	—	—	—	—	—	—	—	—	—	—	—
Dominica	321	5.6	3.0	—	....	3.0	—	—	—	—	—	—	—	2.7	—
Dominican Republic	243	131.3	131.3	—	....	131.3	—	—	—	—	—	....	....	—	—
Ecuador	248	213.9	213.9	—	....	213.9	....	—	—	—	—	....	....	....	—
El Salvador	253	—	—	—	....	—	....	....	....	—	—	....	....	....	—
Grenada	328	2.9	2.9	—	....	2.9	....	—	—	—	—	....	....	....	—
Guatemala	258	—	—	—	....	—	....	—	—	—	—	....	....	....	—

2004, International Monetary Fund : *International Financial Statistics Yearbook*

Financing Components of Members' Outstanding Obligations to the Fund

(As of July 31, 2004 and Expressed in Millions of SDRs)

		Total Fund Credit and Loans Outstanding	\multicolumn{5}{c	}{Outstanding Purchases (GRA) Ordinary Resources}	\multicolumn{4}{c	}{Borrower Resources}	SAF Arrangements	PRGF Arrangements	Trust Fund
			Total Amount	CCFF	STF	Send-by/Credit Tranche	Extended Fund Facility	Sff	EAR	GAB	NAB	SDA Resources	SDA Resources	PRGF Trust Resources	Administered Accounts
		(1)	(2)	(3)	(4)	(5)	(6)	(7)	(8)	(9)	(10)	(11)	(12)	(13)	(14)
Western Hemisphere(C															
Guyana	336	57.0	—	—	....	—	—	—	—	—	—	—	—	57.0	—
Haiti	263	7.6	—	—	....	—	—	—	—	—	—	—	....	7.6	—
Honduras	268	123.6	—	—	—	—	—	—	—	—	—	....	—	123.6	—
Jamaica	343	2.5	2.5	—	....	—	2.5	—	—	—	—	....	....	....	....
Mexico	273	—	—	—	....	—	—	—	—	—	—	....	....	....	....
Nicaragua	278	153.7	—	—	....	—	....	....	....	—	—	....	....	153.7	....
Panama	283	26.7	26.7	—	....	—	26.7	—	—	—	—	....	....	....	....
Paraguay	288	—	—	....	....	—	....	....	....	—	—	....	....	....	....
Peru	293	80.3	80.3	—	....	—	80.3	—	—	—	—	....	....	....	....
St. Kitts and Nevis	361	—	—	....	....	—	....	....	....	—	—	—	....	....	....
St. Lucia	362	—	—	....	....	—	....	....	....	—	—	—	....	....	....
St. Vincent & Grens	364	—	—	....	....	—	....	....	....	—	—	—	....	....	....
Suriname	366	—	—	....	....	....	....	....	....	—	—	....	....	....	....
Trinidad and Tobago	369	—	—	—	....	—	....	—	—	—	—	....	....	....	....
Uruguay	298	1,627.8	1,627.8	—	....	1,627.8	....	—	—	—	—	....	....	....	....
Venezuela, Rep. Bol	299	—	—	....	....	—	....	—	—	—	—	....	....	....	....
Memorandum Items	001														
Oil Exporting Ctys	999	7,088.9	7,088.9	—	—	—	7,088.9	....	—	—	—	....	....	....	....
Non-Oil Develop.Ctys.	201	59,143.4	52,190.7	89.4	110.2	45,452.1	5,647.4	102.0	277.3	512.3	—	64.8	.9	6,798.4	88.6

2004, International Monetary Fund : *International Financial Statistics Yearbook*

Purchases

		1992	1993	1994	1995	1996	1997	1998	1999	2000	2001	2002	2003
		\multicolumn{12}{c}{*Expressed in Millions of SDRs*}
World	001	4,791.1	5,042.2	4,979.5	16,967.9	5,271.0	16,112.9	20,586.2	10,010.1	7,178.0	23,761.6	25,237.0	20,323.1
Developing Countries	200	4,791.1	5,042.2	4,979.5	16,967.9	5,271.0	16,112.9	20,586.2	10,010.1	7,178.0	23,761.6	25,237.0	20,323.1
Africa	605	172.7	678.8	761.5	1,038.5	556.9	370.1	313.6	266.9	35.6	—	27.0	9.6
Algeria	612	—	—	587.5	312.8	512.2	337.6	253.3	223.5	—	—	—	—
Angola	614	—	—	—	—	—	—	—	—	—	—	—	—
Benin	638	—	—	—	—	—	—	—	—	—	—	—	—
Burkina Faso	748	—	—	—	—	—	—	—	—	—	—	—	—
Burundi	618	—	—	—	—	—	—	—	—	—	—	9.6	9.6
Cameroon	622	—	—	21.9	8.5	19.7	—	—	—	—	—	—	—
Cape Verde	624	—	—	—	—	—	—	—	—	—	—	—	—
Central African Rep.	626	—	—	10.7	—	—	—	—	—	—	—	—	—
Chad	628	—	—	10.3	—	—	—	—	—	—	—	—	—
Comoros	632	—	—	—	—	—	—	—	—	—	—	—	—
Congo, Dem. Rep. of	636	—	—	—	—	—	—	—	—	—	—	—	—
Congo, Republic of	634	—	—	12.5	—	—	—	—	7.2	—	10.6	—	—
Côte d'Ivoire	662	—	—	—	—	—	—	—	—	—	—	—	—
Djibouti	611	—	—	—	—	2.9	1.1	2.3	1.0	—	—	—	—
Equatorial Guinea	642	—	—	—	—	—	—	—	—	—	—	—	—
Ethiopia	644	—	—	—	—	—	—	—	—	—	—	—	—
Gabon	646	—	—	44.7	37.5	22.1	16.6	—	—	13.2	—	—	—
Gambia, The	648	—	—	—	—	—	—	—	—	—	—	—	—
Ghana	652	—	47.0	—	—	—	—	—	—	—	—	—	—
Guinea	656	—	—	—	—	—	—	—	—	—	—	—	—
Guinea-Bissau	654	—	—	—	—	—	—	—	2.1	1.4	—	—	—
Kenya	664	—	—	—	—	—	—	—	—	—	—	—	—
Lesotho	666	—	—	—	—	—	—	—	—	—	—	—	—
Liberia	668	—	—	—	—	—	—	—	—	—	—	—	—
Madagascar	674	—	—	—	—	—	—	—	—	—	—	—	—
Malawi	676	—	—	12.7	—	—	—	—	—	—	—	17.4	—
Mali	678	—	—	—	—	—	—	—	—	—	—	—	—
Mauritania	682	—	—	—	—	—	—	—	—	—	—	—	—
Mauritius	684	—	—	—	—	—	—	—	—	—	—	—	—
Morocco	686	18.4	—	—	—	—	—	—	—	—	—	—	—
Mozambique	688	—	—	—	—	—	—	—	—	—	—	—	—
Niger	692	—	—	11.1	—	—	—	—	—	—	—	—	—
Nigeria	694	—	—	—	—	—	—	—	—	—	—	—	—
Rwanda	714	—	—	—	8.9	—	14.9	—	—	—	—	—	—
São Tomé & Príncipe	716	—	—	—	—	—	—	—	—	—	—	—	—
Senegal	722	—	—	30.9	—	—	—	—	—	—	—	—	—
Seychelles	718	—	—	—	—	—	—	—	—	—	—	—	—
Sierra Leone	724	—	—	—	—	—	—	11.6	15.6	10.4	—	—	—
Somalia	726	—	—	—	—	—	—	—	—	—	—	—	—
South Africa	199	—	614.4	—	—	—	—	—	—	—	—	—	—
Sudan	732	—	—	—	—	—	—	—	—	—	—	—	—
Swaziland	734	—	—	—	—	—	—	—	—	—	—	—	—
Tanzania	738	—	—	—	—	—	—	—	—	—	—	—	—
Togo	742	—	—	—	—	—	—	—	—	—	—	—	—
Tunisia	744	51.8	—	—	—	—	—	—	—	—	—	—	—
Uganda	746	—	—	—	—	—	—	—	—	—	—	—	—
Zambia	754	—	—	—	651.7	—	—	—	—	—	—	—	—
Zimbabwe	698	102.5	17.4	19.1	19.1	—	—	39.2	24.7	—	—	—	—
Asia	505	1,452.0	755.3	220.2	167.3	109.2	12,801.7	11,259.8	2,236.4	1,267.6	784.7	1,197.6	1,396.9
Afghanistan, I.S. of	512	—	—	—	—	—	—	—	—	—	—	—	—
Bangladesh	513	—	—	—	—	—	—	98.1	—	—	—	—	—
Bhutan	514	—	—	—	—	—	—	—	—	—	—	—	—
Cambodia	522	—	6.3	—	—	—	—	—	—	—	—	—	—
China, People's Rep.	924	—	—	—	—	—	—	—	—	—	—	—	—
Fiji	819	—	—	—	—	—	—	—	—	—	—	—	—
India	534	1,109.0	462.0	—	—	—	—	—	—	—	—	—	—
Indonesia	536	—	—	—	—	—	2,201.5	4,254.3	1,011.0	851.2	309.7	1,101.0	1,376.2
Kiribati	826	—	—	—	—	—	—	—	—	—	—	—	—
Korea	542	—	—	—	—	—	8,200.0	5,850.0	362.5	—	—	—	—
Lao People's Dem.Rep.	544	—	—	—	—	—	—	—	—	—	—	—	—
Malaysia	548	—	—	—	—	—	—	—	—	—	—	—	—
Maldives	556	—	—	—	—	—	—	—	—	—	—	—	—
Micronesia, Fed.Sts.	868	—	—	—	—	—	—	—	—	—	—	—	—
Mongolia	948	2.5	—	—	—	—	—	—	—	—	—	—	—
Myanmar	518	—	—	—	—	—	—	—	—	—	—	—	—
Nepal	558	—	—	—	—	—	—	—	—	—	—	—	—
Pakistan	564	189.6	88.0	123.2	134.0	107.2	91.5	19.0	409.6	150.0	315.0	—	—
Palau	565	—	—	—	—	—	—	—	—	—	—	—	—
Papua New Guinea	853	—	—	—	33.3	2.0	—	—	—	28.9	56.7	—	—
Philippines	566	151.0	126.6	36.5	—	—	508.8	538.3	253.3	237.6	—	—	—
Samoa	862	—	—	—	—	—	—	—	—	—	—	—	—
Solomon Islands	813	—	—	—	—	—	—	—	—	—	—	—	—
Sri Lanka	524	—	—	—	—	—	—	—	—	—	103.4	96.7	20.7
Thailand	578	—	—	—	—	—	1,800.0	500.0	200.0	—	—	—	—
Vietnam	582	—	72.5	60.5	—	—	—	—	—	—	—	—	—

2004, International Monetary Fund: *International Financial Statistics Yearbook*

Purchases

		1992	1993	1994	1995	1996	1997	1998	1999	2000	2001	2002	2003
		Expressed in Millions of SDRs												
Europe	170	1,674.6	1,700.0	3,177.1	5,337.2	3,488.2	2,272.3	5,312.9	1,944.9	3,253.3	9,456.6	10,327.5	1,696.3
Albania	914	9.7	3.4	–	–	–	–	8.8	–	–	–	–	–
Armenia	911	–	–	16.9	30.4	–	–	–	–	–	–	–	–
Azerbaijan	912	–	–	–	67.9	53.8	20.5	15.8	68.6	–	–	–	–
Belarus	913	–	70.1	–	120.1	–	–	–	–	–	–	–	–
Bosnia & Herzegovina	963	–	–	–	30.3	–	–	24.2	29.0	27.2	14.0	31.6	24.0
Bulgaria	918	200.3	31.0	232.5	–	80.0	355.2	228.9	209.2	209.2	104.6	84.0	104.0
Croatia	960	–	–	78.5	65.4	–	28.8	–	–	–	–	–	–
Cyprus	423	–	–	–	–	–	–	–	–	–	–	–	–
Czech Republic	935	–	70.0	–	–	–	–	–	–	–	–	–	–
Czechoslovakia	934	238.6	....	....	....	....	....	....	....	....	....	....	....
Estonia	939	7.8	34.1	–	20.9	–	–	–	–	–	–	–	–
Georgia	915	–	–	27.8	50.0	–	–	–	–	–	–	–	–
Hungary	944	118.4	56.7	–	–	–	–	–	–	–	–	–	–
Kazakhstan	916	–	61.9	136.1	92.8	92.8	–	154.7	–	–	–	–	–
Kyrgyz Republic	917	–	43.9	–	–	–	–	–	–	–	–	–	–
Latvia	941	25.2	52.6	32.0	–	–	–	–	–	–	–	–	–
Lithuania	946	17.3	70.7	46.6	41.4	31.1	41.4	–	–	–	–	–	–
Macedonia, FYR	962	–	–	12.4	24.8	9.9	–	–	13.8	1.1	–	–	12.0
Moldova	921	–	63.0	49.5	42.4	22.5	15.0	–	50.0	–	–	–	–
Poland	964	–	–	640.3	–	–	–	–	–	–	–	–	–
Romania	968	338.5	–	245.1	37.7	–	120.6	–	53.0	86.8	52.0	82.7	165.3
Russia	922	719.0	1,078.3	1,078.3	3,594.3	2,587.9	1,467.3	4,600.0	471.4	–	–	–	–
Serbia & Montenegro	965	–	–	–	–	–	–	–	–	116.9	100.0	200.0	200.0
Slovak Republic	936	–	64.4	96.5	–	–	–	–	–	–	–	–	–
Tajikistan	923	–	–	–	–	15.0	7.5	7.5	–	–	–	–	–
Turkey	186	–	–	235.5	225.0	–	–	–	583.2	2,622.1	8,895.2	9,929.2	1,191.0
Ukraine	926	–	–	249.3	788.0	536.0	207.3	281.8	466.6	190.1	290.8	–	–
Uzbekistan	927	–	–	–	106.0	59.3	–	–	–	–	–	–	–
Middle East	405	288.0	11.1	65.6	75.8	166.2	154.0	32.7	77.4	15.2	37.0	71.6	–
Bahrain, Kingdom of	419	–	–	–	–	–	–	–	–	–	–	–	–
Egypt	469	87.2	–	–	–	–	–	–	–	–	–	–	–
Iran, I.R. of	429	–	–	–	–	–	–	–	–	–	–	–	–
Iraq	433	–	–	–	–	–	–	–	–	–	–	–	–
Israel	436	178.6	–	–	–	–	–	–	–	–	–	–	–
Jordan	439	22.2	11.1	65.6	75.8	82.2	96.7	23.7	55.4	15.2	30.5	71.6	–
Lebanon	446	–	–	–	–	–	–	–	–	–	–	–	–
Syrian Arab Republic	463	–	–	–	–	–	–	–	–	–	–	–	–
Yemen, Republic of	474	–	–	–	–	84.0	57.4	9.0	22.0	–	6.5	–	–
Western Hemisphere	205	1,203.7	1,896.9	755.1	10,349.1	950.6	514.7	3,667.2	5,484.5	2,606.3	13,483.5	13,613.3	17,220.2
Antigua and Barbuda	311	–	–	–	–	–	–	–	–	–	–	–	–
Argentina	213	584.6	1,154.8	612.0	1,559.0	548.2	321.0	–	–	1,587.8	8,168.5	–	4,004.5
Barbados	316	36.8	–	–	–	–	–	–	–	–	–	–	–
Belize	339	–	–	–	–	–	–	–	–	–	–	–	64.3
Bolivia	218	–	–	–	–	–	–	–	–	–	–	–	–
Brazil	223	127.5	–	–	–	–	–	3,419.0	4,450.1	–	5,277.2	12,274.0	12,635.4
Chile	228	–	–	–	–	–	–	–	–	–	–	–	–
Colombia	233	–	–	–	–	–	–	–	–	–	–	–	–
Costa Rica	238	4.0	–	–	–	–	–	–	–	–	–	–	–
Dominica	321	–	–	–	–	–	–	–	–	–	–	2.1	.9
Dominican Republic	243	37.4	53.3	–	–	–	–	39.7	–	–	–	–	87.6
Ecuador	248	–	–	98.9	–	–	–	–	–	113.3	37.8	75.6	60.4
El Salvador	253	–	–	–	–	–	–	–	–	–	–	–	–
Grenada	328	–	–	–	–	–	–	–	–	–	–	–	2.9
Guatemala	258	–	–	–	–	–	–	–	–	–	–	–	–
Guyana	336	–	–	–	–	–	–	–	–	–	–	–	–
Haiti	263	–	–	–	16.4	–	–	15.2	–	–	–	–	–
Honduras	268	51.0	–	–	–	–	–	47.5	–	–	–	–	–
Jamaica	343	41.8	36.4	34.4	7.0	–	–	–	–	–	–	–	–
Mexico	273	233.1	–	–	8,758.0	–	–	–	1,034.4	905.1	–	–	–
Nicaragua	278	–	–	–	–	–	–	–	–	–	–	–	–
Panama	283	71.6	9.9	9.9	8.7	52.4	33.2	30.0	–	–	–	–	–
Paraguay	288	–	–	–	–	–	–	–	–	–	–	–	–
Peru	293	–	642.7	–	–	–	160.5	–	–	–	–	–	–
St. Kitts and Nevis	361	–	–	–	–	–	–	1.6	–	–	–	–	–
St. Lucia	362	–	–	–	–	–	–	–	–	–	–	–	–
St. Vincent & Grens.	364	–	–	–	–	–	–	–	–	–	–	–	–
Suriname	366	–	–	–	–	–	–	–	–	–	–	–	–
Trinidad and Tobago	369	–	–	–	–	–	–	114.2	–	–	–	–	–
Uruguay	298	16.0	–	–	–	–	–	–	–	–	–	1,261.7	364.2
Venezuela, Rep. Bol.	299	–	–	–	–	350.0	–	–	–	–	–	–	–
Memorandum Items													
Oil Exporting Ctys	999	–	–	587.5	312.8	862.2	2,539.1	4,507.6	1,234.5	851.2	309.7	1,101.0	1,376.2
Non-Oil Develop.Ctys	201	4,791.1	5,042.2	4,392.0	16,655.1	4,408.7	13,573.8	16,078.6	8,775.6	6,326.9	23,452.0	24,136.0	18,946.9

2004, International Monetary Fund: *International Financial Statistics Yearbook*

Repurchases

		1992	1993	1994	1995	1996	1997	1998	1999	2000	2001	2002	2003
		\multicolumn{12}{c}{*Expressed in Millions of SDRs*}
World	001	4,201.6	3,814.0	4,572.0	6,650.9	5,071.9	5,681.3	6,694.2	19,398.8	15,249.4	13,274.9	15,113.1	18,892.1
Developing Countries	200	4,201.6	3,814.0	4,572.0	6,650.9	5,071.9	5,681.3	6,694.2	19,398.8	15,249.4	13,274.9	15,113.1	18,892.1
Africa	605	601.3	626.5	423.3	1,522.4	269.2	730.0	827.9	407.3	198.2	241.1	426.4	348.1
Algeria	612	117.7	235.4	136.5	112.5	93.8	254.6	320.8	262.8	70.2	110.5	229.6	313.7
Burkina Faso	748	–	–	–	–	–	–	–	–	–	–	–	–
Burundi	618	–	–	–	–	–	–	–	–	–	–	–	–
Cameroon	622	38.6	33.8	3.9	4.0	4.0	8.2	12.0	13.3	14.1	2.5	–	–
Central African Rep.	626	1.1	.6	.4	–	–	2.7	5.6	2.4	–	–	–	–
Chad	628	–	–	–	–	–	3.9	5.2	1.3	–	–	–	–
Comoros	632	–	–	–	–	–	–	–	–	–	–	–	–
Congo, Dem. Rep. of	636	–	–	3.0	.9	22.7	–	.4	.7	–	–	157.1	–
Congo, Republic of	634	–	.5	2.0	1.5	–	1.6	7.8	3.1	–	.9	3.6	2.7
Côte d'Ivoire	662	65.2	36.5	53.5	56.8	32.8	16.1	–	–	–	–	–	–
Djibouti	611	–	–	–	–	–	–	–	.7	1.7	1.6	1.8	1.3
Equatorial Guinea	642	–	–	–	–	–	–	–	–	–	–	–	–
Ethiopia	644	–	–	–	–	–	–	–	–	–	–	–	–
Gabon	646	25.8	25.7	16.1	34.5	3.8	2.6	16.7	17.9	7.4	8.7	10.1	10.1
Gambia, The	648	1.5	–	–	–	–	–	–	–	–	–	–	–
Ghana	652	45.3	39.3	27.1	13.1	16.8	34.5	24.6	–	–	–	–	–
Guinea	656	.8	–	–	–	–	–	–	–	–	–	–	–
Guinea-Bissau	654	–	–	–	–	–	–	–	–	–	–	.3	1.6
Kenya	664	58.7	41.5	–	–	–	–	–	–	–	–	–	–
Lesotho	666	–	–	–	–	–	–	–	–	–	–	–	–
Liberia	668	–	–	–	.1	–	–	–	–	.2	.3	.2	–
Madagascar	674	11.5	7.4	4.5	.6	–	–	–	–	–	–	–	–
Malawi	676	13.6	4.2	1.2	–	–	–	6.4	6.4	–	–	–	–
Mali	678	4.4	6.3	4.8	1.0	–	–	–	–	–	–	–	–
Mauritania	682	4.6	1.0	–	–	–	–	–	–	–	–	–	–
Mauritius	684	–	–	–	–	–	–	–	–	–	–	–	–
Morocco	686	100.8	112.0	106.1	66.2	32.5	2.3	–	–	–	–	–	–
Niger	692	5.4	3.5	2.0	–	–	4.2	5.6	1.4	–	–	–	–
Nigeria	694	–	–	–	–	–	–	–	–	–	–	–	–
Rwanda	714	–	–	–	–	–	–	–	4.5	6.7	7.4	5.2	–
Senegal	722	28.1	11.0	2.5	–	–	11.6	15.5	3.9	–	–	–	–
Sierra Leone	724	1.4	5.9	42.6	–	–	–	–	–	–	37.5	–	–
Somalia	726	–	–	–	–	–	–	–	–	–	–	–	–
South Africa	199	–	–	–	–	–	307.2	307.2	–	–	–	–	–
Sudan	732	–	–	–	23.0	24.5	25.5	42.2	27.6	41.1	41.1	17.0	18.7
Swaziland	734	–	–	–	–	–	–	–	–	–	–	–	–
Tanzania	738	3.9	–	–	–	–	–	–	–	–	–	–	–
Togo	742	7.1	5.2	2.4	2.0	.2	–	–	–	–	–	–	–
Tunisia	744	20.9	3.8	–	10.2	32.1	36.6	36.6	36.6	30.4	24.7	–	–
Uganda	746	18.7	3.1	–	–	–	–	–	–	–	–	–	–
Zambia	754	26.0	49.8	14.6	1,196.2	–	–	–	–	–	–	–	–
Zimbabwe	698	–	–	–	–	5.9	18.5	21.6	24.8	26.4	5.9	1.5	–
Asia	505	734.3	369.7	1,066.0	1,113.8	1,262.8	831.0	2,514.2	8,330.4	375.5	6,943.9	3,419.1	2,110.8
Afghanistan, I.S. of	512	–	–	–	–	–	–	–	–	–	–	–	–
Bangladesh	513	56.0	35.9	–	–	–	–	–	–	–	–	49.1	49.1
Bhutan	514	–	–	–	–	–	–	–	–	–	–	–	–
Cambodia	522	6.3	6.3	–	–	–	–	1.0	1.0	1.0	1.0	1.0	1.0
China, People's Rep.	924	–	–	–	–	–	–	–	–	–	–	–	–
Fiji	819	–	–	–	–	–	–	–	–	–	–	–	–
India	534	275.0	137.5	821.7	796.5	881.4	495.5	304.9	246.4	38.5	–	–	–
Indonesia	536	115.7	–	–	–	–	–	–	–	–	1,375.9	1,834.6	979.3
Korea	542	–	–	–	–	–	–	2,050.0	7,900.0	–	4,462.5	–	–
Lao People's Dem.Rep.	544	–	–	–	–	–	–	–	–	–	–	–	–
Malaysia	548	–	–	–	–	–	–	–	–	–	–	–	–
Mongolia	948	–	–	–	6.3	6.9	.6	–	–	–	–	–	–
Myanmar	518	–	–	–	–	–	–	–	–	–	–	–	–
Nepal	558	.8	–	–	–	–	–	–	–	–	–	–	–
Pakistan	564	116.1	91.4	34.1	61.2	167.0	138.8	39.7	107.6	161.2	80.8	167.4	351.7
Papua New Guinea	853	–	10.7	21.4	10.7	–	–	3.0	16.7	14.7	1.0	–	3.8
Philippines	566	109.9	46.0	188.7	239.1	207.5	156.9	58.2	39.5	6.1	6.1	313.0	434.4
Samoa	862	.2	–	–	–	–	–	–	–	–	–	–	–
Solomon Islands	813	–	–	–	–	–	–	–	–	–	–	–	–
Sri Lanka	524	54.4	13.6	–	–	–	–	–	–	–	–	–	–
Thailand	578	–	–	–	–	–	–	–	–	150.0	1,012.5	1,050.0	287.5
Vietnam	582	–	28.4	–	–	–	39.3	57.4	19.2	4.0	4.0	4.0	4.0
Europe	170	444.2	244.1	1,325.2	2,010.7	1,047.8	687.5	1,522.7	4,309.1	3,841.5	4,763.9	6,767.4	3,120.3
Albania	914	–	–	–	.8	5.7	5.8	.9	–	–	4.4	4.4	–
Armenia	911	–	–	–	–	–	–	.4	9.6	12.0	5.6	5.6	7.0
Azerbaijan	912	–	–	–	–	–	–	–	11.7	39.0	30.9	35.8	45.3
Belarus	913	–	–	–	–	–	–	17.9	42.5	42.1	23.4	23.4	23.4
Bosnia & Herzegovina	963	–	–	–	18.4	1.4	–	.7	15.2	15.2	6.1	17.6	36.3
Bulgaria	918	60.6	–	48.0	162.3	154.9	64.4	134.7	90.7	105.3	236.2	195.2	76.6
Croatia	960	–	17.2	6.2	3.9	3.1	1.6	6.5	22.9	21.8	24.2	97.2	–
Cyprus	423	–	–	–	–	–	–	–	–	–	–	–	–
Czech Republic	935	–	70.0	780.7	–	–	–	–	–	–	–	–	–

Repurchases

		1992	1993	1994	1995	1996	1997	1998	1999	2000	2001	2002	2003
Expressed in Millions of SDRs
Europe(Cont.)
Czechoslovakia	934	35.0	....	....	....	....	....	....	....	....	....	....	....
Estonia	939	–	–	–	1.0	7.7	14.1	18.7	2.9	3.9	3.9	10.7	–
Georgia	915	–	–	–	–	–	.7	15.7	19.7	9.3	9.3	11.6	
Hungary	944	122.8	36.2	114.7	522.9	140.0	–	118.7	–	–	–	–	–
Kazakhstan	916	–	–	–	–	–	4.6	70.0	128.5	335.1	–	–	–
Kyrgyz Republic	917	–	–	–	–	2.7	7.1	8.5	5.4	5.4	5.4	5.4	4.0
Latvia	941	–	–	–	1.9	17.5	26.7	18.3	11.1	7.6	7.6	7.6	7.6
Lithuania	946	–	–	–	–	16.9	31.1	20.6	12.1	20.7	26.7	31.1	59.1
Macedonia, FYR	962	–	2.2	1.2	.7	.6	.3	1.7	12.4	14.7	6.0	5.9	11.0
Moldova	921	–	–	–	–	5.1	14.6	47.2	47.9	18.6	11.3	13.8	15.8
Poland	964	–	98.9	219.4	918.6	–	–	–	–	–	–	–	–
Romania	968	153.4	–	89.6	245.8	245.4	98.4	92.3	102.0	72.9	91.7	75.7	79.6
Russia	922	–	–	–	–	359.5	359.5	673.9	3,101.1	2,189.5	2,997.9	1,147.6	1,356.1
Serbia & Montenegro	965	–	–	–	–	–	–	–	–	–	–	–	–
Slovak Republic	936	–	–	61.9	132.3	85.6	37.6	49.8	38.1	96.5	–	–	–
Slovenia	961	–	9.9	3.6	2.2	1.8	.9	–	–	–	–	–	–
Tajikistan	923	–	–	–	–	–	–	–	3.8	7.5	9.4	7.5	1.9
Turkey	186	–	–	–	–	–	20.1	164.6	210.2	65.6	867.6	4,916.4	1,223.9
Ukraine	926	–	–	–	–	–	–	77.3	407.0	643.5	361.2	140.7	144.5
Uzbekistan	927	–	–	–	–	–	–	–	18.4	49.4	35.1	16.6	16.6
Yugoslavia, SFR	188	72.4	9.6	–	–	–	–	–	–	....	....	....	....
Middle East	405	**36.3**	**33.1**	**48.4**	**135.2**	**163.2**	**49.4**	**6.8**	**50.7**	**77.9**	**81.7**	**74.6**	**76.3**
Egypt	469	29.0	–	22.5	62.7	58.6	10.9	–	–	–	–	–	–
Iran, I.R. of	429	–	–	–	–	–	–	–	–	–	–	–	–
Iraq	433	–	–	–	–	–	–	–	–	–	–	–	–
Israel	436	–	–	–	67.0	89.3	22.3	–	–	–	–	–	–
Jordan	439	7.3	33.1	25.9	5.6	15.3	16.2	6.8	26.0	23.8	40.2	61.0	71.4
Syrian Arab Republic	463	–	–	–	–	–	–	–	–	–	–	–	–
Yemen, Republic of	474	–	–	–	–	–	–	–	24.8	54.1	41.4	13.6	4.8
Western Hemisphere	205	**2,385.6**	**2,540.5**	**1,709.2**	**1,868.8**	**2,329.0**	**3,383.4**	**1,822.5**	**6,301.3**	**10,756.2**	**1,244.3**	**4,425.6**	**13,236.7**
Argentina	213	637.7	275.1	289.7	319.3	296.5	347.8	484.2	602.5	970.2	927.6	573.6	4,105.8
Barbados	316	–	–	–	11.9	18.4	6.5	–	–	–	–	–	–
Belize	339	–	–	–	–	–	–	–	–	–	–	–	–
Bolivia	218	22.6	17.0	–	–	–	–	–	–	–	–	–	–
Brazil	223	411.3	360.4	93.5	32.3	48.2	23.7	15.5	1,445.9	5,074.2	–	3,588.3	8,898.6
Chile	228	144.4	178.5	147.0	199.5	–	–	–	–	–	–	–	–
Colombia	233	–	–	–	–	–	–	–	–	–	–	–	–
Costa Rica	238	2.8	–	13.8	29.1	15.8	.5	–	–	–	–	–	–
Dominica	321	.4	.1	–	–	–	–	–	–	–	–	–	–
Dominican Republic	243	10.3	7.2	5.6	22.4	41.0	45.3	21.1	–	–	–	19.9	19.9
Ecuador	248	54.9	20.8	14.9	19.0	15.8	2.0	49.5	49.5	–	–	–	24.8
El Salvador	253	–	–	–	–	–	–	–	–	–	–	–	–
Grenada	328	–	–	–	–	–	–	–	–	–	–	–	–
Guatemala	258	22.4	22.4	–	–	–	–	–	–	–	–	–	–
Guyana	336	–	2.4	15.3	15.6	8.1	6.7	1.4	–	–	–	–	–
Haiti	263	–	–	14.8	.3	–	–	6.0	8.2	2.2	–	7.6	7.6
Honduras	268	–	2.1	11.2	28.8	26.1	6.4	–	–	–	–	23.8	23.8
Jamaica	343	55.7	51.9	60.9	62.9	49.5	25.1	12.5	13.9	14.5	14.5	14.5	11.4
Mexico	273	636.1	841.7	841.0	754.1	1,413.6	2,499.2	783.7	3,726.7	4,164.3	–	–	–
Nicaragua	278	–	–	2.1	8.5	6.4	–	–	–	–	–	–	–
Panama	283	141.7	7.3	.9	25.6	35.8	18.8	9.9	17.2	39.3	26.2	6.2	6.7
Paraguay	288	–	–	–	–	–	–	–	–	–	–	–	–
Peru	293	34.7	458.7	–	–	–	53.6	107.1	107.1	107.1	120.5	133.9	80.3
St. Kitts and Nevis	361	–	–	–	–	–	–	–	–	–	–	.8	.8
St. Lucia	362	–	–	–	–	–	–	–	–	–	–	–	–
St. Vincent & Grens	364	–	–	–	–	–	–	–	–	–	–	–	–
Trinidad and Tobago	369	63.7	92.5	50.4	28.7	17.3	13.3	3.1	–	–	–	–	–
Uruguay	298	18.3	10.2	7.4	6.5	8.0	6.0	–	–	–	–	57.1	57.1
Venezuela, Rep. Bol	299	128.6	192.0	140.6	304.2	328.5	328.5	328.5	330.3	384.4	155.6	–	–
Memorandum Items
Oil Exporting Ctys	999	362.0	427.5	277.1	416.7	422.3	583.2	649.3	593.1	454.7	1,642.0	2,064.2	1,292.9
Non-Oil Develop.Ctys	201	3,839.6	3,386.5	4,295.0	6,234.2	4,649.6	5,098.1	6,044.9	18,805.7	14,794.7	11,633.0	13,048.9	17,599.2

2004, International Monetary Fund : *International Financial Statistics Yearbook*

Loan Disbursements

		1992	1993	1994	1995	1996	1997	1998	1999	2000	2001	2002	2003
						Expressed in Millions of SDRs							
World	001	544.3	271.7	910.4	1,431.4	708.6	730.6	896.0	736.8	492.5	872.6	1,344.5	848.4
Developing Countries	200	544.3	271.7	910.4	1,431.4	708.6	730.6	896.0	736.8	492.5	872.6	1,344.5	848.4
Africa	605	273.8	142.1	467.1	1,247.8	404.3	348.3	532.6	334.8	364.8	467.0	922.9	275.5
Benin	638	–	15.7	18.1	9.1	13.6	4.5	–	7.2	6.8	8.1	4.0	6.7
Burkina Faso	748	–	8.8	17.7	17.7	6.6	13.3	13.3	12.2	5.6	16.8	11.2	3.4
Burundi	618	14.9	–	–	–	–	–	–	–	–	–	–	–
Cameroon	622	–	–	–	–	–	27.0	54.0	45.0	52.0	15.9	31.8	15.9
Cape Verde	624	–	–	–	–	–	–	–	–	–	–	2.5	2.5
Central African Rep.	626	–	–	–	–	–	–	8.2	8.2	–	8.0	–	–
Chad	628	–	–	–	8.3	16.5	8.3	8.3	8.3	10.4	13.4	13.4	5.2
Comoros	632	–	–	1.4	–	–	–	–	–	–	–	–	–
Congo, Dem. Rep. of	636	–	–	–	–	–	–	–	–	–	–	420.0	53.4
Congo, Republic of	634	–	–	–	–	13.9	–	–	–	–	–	–	–
Côte d'Ivoire	662	–	–	119.1	119.1	95.3	–	123.9	–	–	–	58.5	–
Djibouti	611	–	–	–	–	–	–	–	2.7	2.7	3.6	4.5	–
Equatorial Guinea	642	–	2.8	1.8	–	–	–	–	–	–	–	–	–
Ethiopia	644	14.1	21.2	14.1	–	14.7	–	14.7	–	–	34.8	34.2	10.4
Gambia, The	648	–	–	–	–	–	–	3.4	3.4	6.9	6.9	2.9	–
Ghana	652	–	–	–	27.4	27.4	–	82.2	44.3	26.8	52.6	52.6	52.7
Guinea	656	8.7	–	8.7	20.3	–	23.6	23.6	7.9	–	20.7	12.9	–
Guinea-Bissau	654	–	–	–	1.6	2.1	4.5	2.4	–	5.1	–	–	–
Kenya	664	–	22.6	22.6	–	24.9	–	–	–	33.6	–	–	25.0
Lesotho	666	5.3	6.8	3.8	–	–	–	–	–	–	7.0	7.0	3.5
Liberia	668	–	–	–	–	–	–	–	–	–	–	–	–
Madagascar	674	–	–	–	–	13.6	13.6	–	13.6	38.0	22.7	11.3	11.3
Malawi	676	–	–	5.6	7.6	15.3	7.6	12.8	7.6	6.4	–	–	6.4
Mali	678	10.2	10.2	29.5	29.5	20.7	20.7	10.3	17.1	6.8	18.2	6.8	12.9
Mauritania	682	8.5	8.5	17.0	14.3	14.3	14.3	–	6.1	6.1	18.2	12.1	.9
Mauritius	684	–	–	–	–	–	–	–	–	–	–	–	–
Morocco	686	–	–	–	–	–	–	–	–	–	–	–	–
Mozambique	688	45.8	15.3	14.7	–	12.6	25.2	25.2	21.0	45.2	8.4	8.4	8.4
Niger	692	–	–	–	–	9.7	19.3	19.3	–	8.5	8.5	16.9	16.9
Rwanda	714	–	–	–	–	–	–	11.9	21.4	19.0	9.5	.6	.6
São Tomé & Príncipe	716	–	–	–	–	–	–	–	–	1.9	–	–	–
Senegal	722	–	–	16.7	54.7	23.8	35.7	35.7	14.3	14.3	23.3	9.0	3.5
Sierra Leone	724	–	–	95.6	13.1	10.2	5.1	–	–	–	46.8	28.0	14.0
Somalia	726	–	–	–	–	–	–	–	–	–	–	–	–
Sudan	732	–	–	–	–	–	–	–	–	–	–	–	–
Swaziland	734	–	–	–	–	–	–	–	–	–	–	–	–
Tanzania	738	64.2	–	–	–	25.7	61.4	35.7	58.8	40.0	40.0	40.0	17.8
Togo	742	7.7	–	10.9	21.7	–	10.9	10.9	–	–	–	–	–
Uganda	746	39.8	–	36.7	36.8	43.5	43.5	36.8	25.7	8.9	8.9	1.5	4.0
Zambia	754	–	–	–	833.4	–	10.0	–	10.0	20.0	74.8	132.7	–
Zimbabwe	698	54.7	30.4	33.4	33.4	–	–	–	–	–	–	–	–
Asia	505	209.7	105.5	358.9	100.1	132.2	125.2	113.7	52.2	14.3	194.3	325.6	460.6
Afghanistan, I.S. of	512	–	–	–	–	–	–	–	–	–	–	–	–
Bangladesh	513	86.3	28.8	–	–	–	–	–	–	–	–	–	49.5
Cambodia	522	–	–	14.0	28.0	–	–	–	8.4	8.4	16.7	16.7	8.4
China,P.R.: Mainland	924	–	–	–	–	–	–	–	–	–	–	–	–
India	534	–	–	–	–	–	–	–	–	–	–	–	–
Lao People's Dem.Rep.	544	5.9	5.9	5.9	11.7	5.9	5.9	–	–	–	4.5	9.1	4.5
Maldives	556	–	–	–	–	–	–	–	–	–	–	–	–
Mongolia	948	–	9.3	14.8	–	5.6	5.6	–	5.9	5.9	4.1	–	8.1
Myanmar	518	–	–	–	–	–	–	–	–	–	–	–	–
Nepal	558	5.6	5.6	5.6	–	–	–	–	–	–	–	–	7.1
Pakistan	564	–	–	202.2	–	–	113.7	113.7	37.9	–	86.2	258.4	344.6
Papua New Guinea	853	–	–	–	–	–	–	–	–	–	–	–	–
Philippines	566	–	–	–	–	–	–	–	–	–	–	–	–
Samoa	862	–	–	–	–	–	–	–	–	–	–	–	–
Solomon Islands	813	–	–	–	–	–	–	–	–	–	–	–	–
Sri Lanka	524	112.0	56.0	56.0	–	–	–	–	–	–	–	–	38.4
Thailand	578	–	–	–	–	–	–	–	–	–	–	–	–
Vietnam	582	–	–	60.4	60.4	120.8	–	–	–	–	82.8	41.4	–
Europe	170	–	8.5	25.0	37.4	105.4	178.4	146.2	107.7	58.9	87.4	83.5	83.0
Albania	914	–	8.5	15.5	7.1	–	–	5.9	15.5	14.3	9.4	4.0	8.0
Armenia	911	–	–	–	–	33.8	16.9	37.8	20.9	–	10.0	20.0	20.0
Azerbaijan	912	–	–	–	–	–	55.6	14.6	11.7	–	8.1	8.1	25.7
Georgia	915	–	–	–	–	55.5	55.5	27.8	33.3	–	27.0	22.5	–
Kyrgyz Republic	917	–	–	9.5	30.3	16.1	32.3	10.8	19.6	14.3	11.7	11.7	21.3
Macedonia, FYR	962	–	–	–	–	–	18.2	9.1	–	1.7	–	–	–
Moldova	921	–	–	–	–	–	–	–	–	–	9.2	9.2	9.2	–
Tajikistan	923	–	–	–	–	–	–	40.3	6.7	19.3	12.0	8.0	8.0
Middle East	405	–	–	–	–	–	44.0	44.0	62.0	–	88.8	–	–
Egypt	469	–	–	–	–	–	–	–	–	–	–	–	–
Yemen, Republic of	474	–	–	–	–	–	44.0	44.0	62.0	–	88.8	–	–

Loan Disbursements

		1992	1993	1994	1995	1996	1997	1998	1999	2000	2001	2002	2003
						Expressed in Millions of SDRs							
Western Hemisphere	205	60.8	15.6	59.4	46.1	66.8	34.8	59.4	180.1	54.5	35.2	12.5	29.2
Bolivia	218	36.3	–	30.4	16.8	33.7	16.8	33.6	16.8	11.2	19.0	–	–
Dominica	321	–	–	–	–	–	–	–	–	–	–	–	2.4
El Salvador	253	–	–	–	–	–	–	–	–	–	–	–	–
Grenada	328	–	–	–	–	–	–	–	–	–	–	–	–
Guyana	336	17.7	8.9	9.0	9.0	17.9	17.9	9.0	9.0	7.0	–	5.6	6.0
Haiti	263	–	–	–	–	15.2	–	–	–	–	–	–	–
Honduras	268	6.8	6.8	–	20.3	–	–	–	76.0	16.2	16.2	–	–
Nicaragua	278	–	–	20.0	–	–	–	16.8	78.3	20.2	–	7.0	20.9
Memorandum Items													
Oil Exporting Ctys	999	....	....	....	....	....	....	....	....	....	....	....	....
Non-Oil Develop.Ctys	201	544.3	271.7	910.4	1,431.4	708.6	730.6	896.0	736.8	492.5	872.6	1,344.5	848.4

Repayments of Loans

Expressed in Millions of SDRs

		1992	1993	1994	1995	1996	1997	1998	1999	2000	2001	2002	2003
World	001	23.6	133.4	223.4	373.8	484.5	606.0	620.9	595.2	605.1	789.6	906.6	842.2
Developing Countries	200	23.6	133.4	223.4	373.8	484.5	606.0	620.9	595.2	605.1	789.6	906.6	842.2
Africa	605	14.0	51.5	145.2	230.6	300.0	338.4	350.0	324.5	320.6	501.5	625.9	532.6
Benin	638	–	–	.6	1.3	1.3	3.1	3.9	6.5	9.5	11.4	11.3	11.4
Burkina Faso	748	–	–	–	–	.6	1.3	2.1	3.9	7.5	10.1	10.8	12.6
Burundi	618	1.7	3.0	4.3	6.0	6.0	6.0	6.8	5.6	3.8	3.8	2.1	–
Cameroon	622	–	–	–	–	–	–	–	–	–	–	–	8.1
Central African Rep.	626	–	.7	2.9	4.9	4.3	2.7	3.9	1.2	.6	–	–	–
Chad	628	–	1.2	1.2	4.6	4.3	4.3	3.1	2.1	.6	2.5	5.8	12.4
Comoros	632	–	–	–	–	–	.2	.2	.3	.5	.5	.3	.3
Congo, Dem. Rep. of	636	–	–	–	–	2.4	–	.2	–	–	–	142.9	–
Congo, Republic of	634	–	–	–	–	–	–	–	–	–	–	2.8	2.8
Côte d'Ivoire	662	–	–	–	–	–	–	–	6.0	29.8	52.4	66.7	75.0
Equatorial Guinea	642	–	–	.4	.7	.8	2.2	2.1	1.8	2.0	2.0	.9	.6
Ethiopia	644	–	–	–	–	–	–	2.8	7.1	9.9	9.9	12.8	10.0
Gambia, The	648	.7	1.7	2.7	4.1	5.1	5.1	4.1	3.1	1.7	.7	–	–
Ghana	652	–	8.2	30.5	57.8	69.4	85.9	77.7	55.4	28.1	51.4	11.0	15.1
Guinea	656	–	2.3	4.1	5.8	5.8	7.5	6.9	5.2	6.1	9.3	8.7	10.5
Guinea-Bissau	654	–	.3	.3	.8	.8	.8	.5	.5	.2	.5	.9	1.9
Kenya	664	–	2.8	9.7	25.8	41.9	48.9	46.1	43.7	32.2	18.6	14.0	14.0
Lesotho	666	–	–	1.1	1.8	2.3	3.1	3.6	4.3	3.9	3.4	2.9	1.8
Liberia	668	–	–	.7	–	–	–	.4	.4	.3	.2	–	–
Madagascar	674	–	2.7	3.9	9.1	11.6	12.9	10.3	9.0	3.8	1.3	2.7	5.4
Malawi	676	–	–	2.8	6.5	10.2	12.3	12.3	10.0	6.9	5.5	5.7	7.2
Mali	678	–	–	2.0	3.6	5.1	5.1	8.1	8.6	13.0	16.9	21.0	21.1
Mauritania	682	1.4	3.4	4.2	5.9	6.8	5.4	5.1	6.8	8.3	10.3	12.5	13.6
Mauritius	684	–	–	–	–	–	–	–	–	–	–	–	–
Morocco	686	–	–	–	–	–	–	–	–	–	–	–	–
Mozambique	688	1.2	4.3	7.3	9.5	22.5	11.0	18.1	22.8	22.2	21.0	17.1	14.8
Niger	692	1.3	3.4	5.1	6.7	8.1	6.7	4.7	3.0	1.3	1.0	2.9	6.8
Rwanda	714	–	–	–	–	.9	1.8	1.8	1.8	1.8	.9	–	1.2
São Tomé & Príncipe	716	–	–	.1	.2	.2	.2	.2	.1	–	–	–	–
Senegal	722	3.4	8.5	17.4	26.8	30.6	34.0	28.9	20.0	17.1	21.1	20.8	27.9
Sierra Leone	724	2.3	–	13.8	2.3	2.3	–	–	9.1	19.1	21.7	24.3	24.8
Somalia	726	–	–	–	–	–	–	–	–	–	–	–	–
Sudan	732	–	–	–	3.0	–	5.2	–	–	–	–	–	–
Swaziland	734	–	–	–	–	–	–	–	–	–	–	–	–
Tanzania	738	–	4.3	10.7	12.8	15.0	22.5	27.8	21.4	19.3	17.1	17.3	17.4
Togo	742	–	.8	2.3	5.4	7.7	8.4	8.4	6.9	7.1	8.1	7.3	9.8
Uganda	746	2.0	4.0	17.1	18.8	34.1	41.8	45.8	37.6	37.1	32.4	31.7	34.1
Zambia	754	–	–	–	6.6	–	–	–	–	–	166.7	167.7	168.7
Zimbabwe	698	–	–	–	–	–	14.0	20.4	27.0	1.0	.9	3.2
Asia	505	5.8	77.8	62.0	123.6	152.1	230.4	224.9	222.7	226.5	223.3	169.9	171.4
Afghanistan, I.S. of	512	–	–	–	–	–	–	–	–	–	–	–	–
Bangladesh	513	5.8	28.8	38.4	40.3	58.9	86.3	77.6	70.9	69.0	50.3	17.3	2.9
Cambodia	522	–	–	–	–	–	–	1.4	4.2	8.4	8.4	8.4
China, People's Rep	924	–	–	–	–	–	–	–	–	–	–	–	–
India	534	–	–	–	–	–	–	–	–	–	–	–	–
Lao People's Dem.Rep.	544	–	–	–	1.2	2.1	3.5	4.7	5.9	5.9	7.3	7.0	6.5
Mongolia	948	–	–	–	–	–	–	.9	2.8	4.8	5.4	5.9	6.1
Myanmar	518	–	–	–	–	–	–	–	–	–	–	–	–
Nepal	558	–	1.5	3.7	5.2	5.2	5.2	4.8	4.3	3.4	3.4	3.4	2.2
Pakistan	564	–	–	10.9	54.6	54.6	87.4	76.5	64.7	62.3	62.3	40.4	74.6
Papua New Guinea	853	–	–	–	–	–	–	–	–	–	–	–	–
Philippines	566	–	–	–	–	–	–	–	–	–	–	–	–
Samoa	862	–	–	–	–	–	–	–	–	–	–	–	–
Solomon Islands	813	–	–	–	–	–	–	–	–	–	–	–	–
Sri Lanka	524	–	4.5	8.9	22.3	31.2	48.0	60.4	72.7	64.9	56.0	39.2	22.4
Thailand	578	–	–	–	–	–	–	–	–	–	–	–	–
Vietnam	582	–	43.1	–	–	–	–	–	–	12.1	30.2	48.3	48.3
Europe	170	–	–	–	–	–	–	–	2.5	8.8	18.6	63.3	82.2
Albania	914	–	–	–	–	–	–	–	2.5	5.5	6.2	6.2	6.8
Armenia	911	–	–	–	–	–	–	–	–	–	1.7	8.4	11.8
Azerbaijan	912	–	–	–	–	–	–	–	–	–	–	2.0	11.1
Georgia	915	–	–	–	–	–	–	–	–	–	2.8	13.9	22.2
Kyrgyz Republic	917	–	–	–	–	–	–	–	–	3.3	8.0	12.8	17.6
Macedonia, FYR	962	–	–	–	–	–	–	–	–	–	–	.9	4.5
Tajikistan	923	–	–	–	–	–	–	–	–	–	–	19.0	8.1
Middle East	405	–	–	–	–	–	–	–	–	–	–	–	8.8
Egypt	469	–	–	–	–	–	–	–	–	–	–	–	–
Yemen, Republic of	474	–	–	–	–	–	–	–	–	–	–	–	8.8
Western Hemisphere	205	3.8	4.0	16.3	19.6	32.4	37.2	46.0	45.5	49.1	46.2	47.5	47.1
Bolivia	218	3.6	3.6	10.4	17.2	21.8	24.9	29.9	24.5	22.4	22.9	21.2	20.5
Dominica	321	.2	.4	.5	.6	.6	.4	.2	–	–	–	–	–
El Salvador	253	–	–	–	–	–	–	–	–	–	–	–	–
Grenada	328	–	–	–	–	–	–	–	–	–	–	–	–

14

2004, International Monetary Fund : *International Financial Statistics Yearbook*

Repayments of Loans

		1992	1993	1994	1995	1996	1997	1998	1999	2000	2001	2002	2003
						Expressed in Millions of SDRs							
Western Hemisphere(Cont.)													
Guyana	336	–	–	–	–	8.3	11.9	14.5	16.3	19.0	12.5	12.5	12.5
Haiti	263	–	–	5.3	1.8	1.8	–	–	–	–	–	3.0	3.0
Honduras	268	–	–	–	–	–	–	1.4	2.7	3.7	6.8	6.8	5.4
Nicaragua	278	–	–	–	–	–	–	–	2.0	4.0	4.0	4.0	5.7
Memorandum Items													
Non-Oil Develop.Ctys	201	23.6	133.4	223.4	373.8	484.5	606.0	620.9	595.2	605.1	789.6	906.6	842.2

2004, International Monetary Fund : *International Financial Statistics Yearbook*

Producer Prices/Wholesale Prices

Percent Change over Previous Year; Calculated from Indices

		1992	1993	1994	1995	1996	1997	1998	1999	2000	2001	2002	2003
World	001	14.29	16.72	27.19	15.31	6.81	4.99	3.95	4.54	7.72	3.48	2.31	5.02
Industrial Countries	110	.75	1.29	1.31	3.15	1.05	.58	−1.46	.18	4.40	.89	−1.29	2.44
United States	111	.59	1.46	1.30	3.58	2.34	−.07	−2.48	.84	5.78	1.11	−2.29	5.35
Canada	156	.47	3.63	6.06	7.43	.42	.86	−.06	1.61	5.05	1.09	.09	−1.12
Australia	193	1.54	2.00	.77	4.19	.31	1.24	−3.97	−.91	7.15	3.06	.21	.48
Japan	158	−.91	−1.52	−1.68	−.83	−1.64	.68	−1.54	−1.48	.05	−2.26	−2.08	−.79
New Zealand	196	2.06	2.44	1.35	.82	.51	.40	.70	.97	7.57	5.96	.35	−.95
Euro Area	163	....	....	....	....	.38	1.06	−.85	−.44	5.31	2.15	−.09	1.54
Austria	122	−.23	−.41	1.34	.31	.01	.37	−.52	−.84	4.05	1.48	−.36	1.62
Belgium	124	−1.80	−2.54	1.60	3.27	2.21	3.68	−1.93	.07	10.55	2.04	−.82	−.40
Finland	172	1.10	2.96	1.34	.66	−.94	1.59	−1.39	−.13	8.27	−.30	−1.21	−.10
France	132	....	....	....	....	....	....	....	....	†4.39	1.22	−.54	.46
Germany	134	....	†.16	.60	1.74	−1.22	1.17	−.40	−1.01	3.29	3.03	−.39	1.71
Greece	174	11.33	11.87	8.71	7.80	6.52	3.48	3.85	1.76	6.55	2.27	2.39	2.07
Ireland	178	.86	4.74	.91	2.15	.52	−.49	1.47	1.10	6.14	2.90	.23	−5.27
Italy	136	1.89	3.76	3.71	7.87	1.89	1.29	.10	−.25	6.02	1.94	−.19	1.60
Luxembourg	137	−2.69	−1.32	1.48	3.92	−3.11	1.48	2.43	−3.13	4.85	1.13	−1.09	1.46
Netherlands	138	1.77	.10	.52	1.53	1.97	1.77	−.15	1.05	4.82	3.00	.78	1.45
Portugal	182	....	....	....	....	....	....	....	....	....	2.75	.41	.82
Spain	184	1.31	2.53	4.27	6.37	1.68	1.03	−.67	.69	5.43	1.71	.69	1.42
Denmark	128	−1.14	−.56	.94	2.77	1.12	1.90	−.59	.50	5.93	1.97	.12	.19
Norway	142	−.44	−.99	1.29	2.56	2.17	1.37	.58	3.07	6.94	−4.68	−5.55	3.55
Sweden	144	−1.28	6.19	4.80	7.72	−1.75	1.19	−.59	1.10	5.84	3.23	.53	−.85
Switzerland	146	.73	.44	−.46	−.09	−1.76	−.73	−1.23	−1.00	.95	.49	−.48	−
United Kingdom	112	3.12	3.93	2.53	4.03	2.60	.89	−	.42	1.52	−.28	.04	1.50
Developing Countries	200	52.73	61.38	87.55	39.46	17.40	12.96	13.88	12.98	14.01	8.35	9.19	9.89
Africa	605	10.34	8.52	8.32	10.08	6.69	5.23	4.87	3.56	7.42	5.81	10.22	.43
Central African Rep.	626	.33	−1.47	....	....	....	....	−.05	1.23	6.36	....	....	....
Morocco	686	2.82	4.46	2.33	6.50	4.43	−1.61	3.48	−1.68	4.16	−.40	2.19	−4.53
South Africa	199	8.18	6.64	8.29	9.50	6.95	7.07	3.51	5.80	9.15	8.49	14.16	1.66
Tunisia	744	3.70	4.67	3.41	5.66	3.74	2.41	3.18	.38	3.33	1.75	2.50	2.42
Zambia	754	121.28	140.82	70.60	72.03	....	....	....	....	....	....	....	....
Zimbabwe	698	52.10	20.47	22.26	20.79	17.09	12.90	31.46	57.18	....	....	....	....
Asia	505	6.99	3.67	7.54	8.85	4.87	4.87	19.18	2.15	5.83	4.02	2.03	4.30
China, P.R.: Hong Kong	532	1.84	.69	2.07	2.75	−.09	−.27	−1.84	−1.58	.20	−1.60	−2.72	−.34
India	534	11.86	7.48	10.54	9.34	4.48	4.53	5.88	3.45	6.55	4.82	2.53	5.42
Indonesia	536	5.16	3.68	5.43	11.39	7.86	8.96	101.80	10.45	12.49	14.15	2.79	2.07
Korea	542	6.17	−2.27	2.71	4.65	3.23	3.81	12.22	−2.07	2.05	−.47	−.29	2.19
Malaysia	548	1.11	1.45	4.88	5.51	2.28	2.62	10.79	−3.27	3.10	−5.03	4.45	5.67
Pakistan	564	7.25	10.25	19.71	12.77	11.09	11.21	7.33	2.31	3.98	4.55	2.98	6.47
Philippines	566	3.72	−.11	8.62	5.50	8.93	.47	11.66	5.77	1.81	2.39	3.61	5.12
Singapore	576	−4.38	−4.35	−.42	.02	.11	−1.15	−3.04	2.10	10.09	−1.59	−1.46	2.00
Sri Lanka	524	8.75	7.60	5.00	8.81	20.49	6.92	6.22	−.40	1.69	11.69	10.73	3.06
Thailand	578	.23	−.42	3.98	8.17	1.83	5.06	12.19	−4.72	3.92	2.50	1.67	4.01
Europe	170	48.55	43.30	199.18	130.84	42.86	33.38	17.41	39.76	34.91	20.56	13.72	12.88
Armenia	911	....	....	....	....	....	....	14.63	5.86	−.41	1.08	3.60	8.87
Belarus	913	....	1,536.33	2,170.84	499.11	34.72	87.55	72.51	355.79	185.63	71.80	40.36	37.53
Bulgaria	918	−60.67	−82.85	1,146.30	55.72	132.68	971.21	16.99	2.81	17.52	3.67	1.29	4.94
Croatia	960	816.67	1,512.42	77.60	.74	1.37	2.28	−1.22	2.56	12.12	1.14	1.83	−.28
Cyprus	423	2.98	2.48	3.32	3.62	2.14	2.79	.51	1.21	7.19	1.59	1.35	2.91
Czech Republic	935	9.93	9.28	5.32	7.53	4.80	4.87	4.91	1.04	4.89	2.82	−.54	−.29
Estonia	939	....	....	....	25.59	14.79	8.38	4.23	−1.23	4.86	4.39	.42	.21
Georgia	915	....	....	....	....	....	....	....	14.28	5.77	3.67	6.02	....
Hungary	944	10.01	13.95	12.25	28.52	21.82	20.34	11.32	5.09	11.72	4.80	−1.39	2.42
Kazakhstan	916	....	....	....	....	23.91	15.52	.83	18.91	37.97	.35	.16	9.31
Kyrgyz Republic	917	....	....	215.26	21.82	22.99	26.26	7.95	53.67	30.70	11.99	4.81	4.59
Latvia	941	....	117.09	16.84	11.89	13.67	4.12	1.88	−4.01	.62	1.72	.93	3.19
Lithuania	946	....	391.88	44.74	28.32	17.26	4.26	−7.40	1.43	17.51	−3.70	−3.63	−.32
Poland	964	27.71	32.25	30.07	25.55	13.20	12.18	7.25	5.54	7.71	1.66	1.16	2.68
Romania	968	203.58	164.98	140.52	35.11	49.87	156.90	33.18	44.53	53.41	41.02	24.65	19.52
Russia	922	....	943.76	337.00	236.46	50.81	15.00	7.03	58.95	46.53	19.17	11.55	15.49
Slovak Republic	936	5.30	17.19	9.98	9.01	4.12	4.49	3.25	3.81	9.80	6.60	2.07	8.31
Slovenia	961	....	21.75	17.69	12.80	6.74	6.10	5.98	2.12	7.69	8.94	5.13	2.55
Turkey	186	62.10	57.97	121.26	86.03	75.94	81.80	71.83	53.06	51.43	61.63	50.11	25.56
Ukraine	926	....	4,619.25	1,143.80	487.94	51.86	7.65	13.21	31.12	20.86	8.65	3.07	7.77
Middle East	405	15.31	12.05	15.98	24.59	14.34	5.49	4.52	7.87	7.04	2.20	5.25	8.14
Egypt	469	12.12	8.55	4.61	6.32	8.32	4.17	1.40	.90	1.79	1.03	6.39	14.38
Iran, I.R. of	429	33.04	25.59	37.62	60.58	32.93	10.69	11.92	19.19	17.83	5.92	8.18	10.58
Israel	436	10.17	8.19	7.89	10.70	8.60	6.29	4.18	7.06	3.64	−.12	3.87	4.33
Jordan	439	4.16	3.40	4.84	−2.40	2.03	1.57	.64	−2.40	−3.58	−1.54	−1.61	....
Kuwait	443	.45	1.79	−.19	1.39	5.16	−1.29	−1.65	−1.22	.45	1.97	3.28	1.95
Saudi Arabia	456	1.32	.56	1.76	7.28	−.25	−	−1.87	.43	.37	−.11	−.02	.86
Syrian Arab Rep.	463	2.63	8.55	14.17	6.90	3.23	2.50	−.61	−1.84	−5.66	−5.00	7.37	....

Producer Prices/Wholesale Prices

		1992	1993	1994	1995	1996	1997	1998	1999	2000	2001	2002	2003
		\multicolumn{12}{c}{*Percent Change over Previous Year; Calculated from Indices*}
Western Hemisphere	205	198.21	289.14	246.39	35.78	18.22	11.81	8.40	12.38	13.50	7.47	17.55	17.93
Argentina	213	....	....	.39	4.31	2.95	−1.06	−3.35	−4.03	3.70	−2.04	78.26	19.61
Brazil	223	987.80	2,050.12	2,311.60	57.53	6.25	10.09	3.55	16.56	18.11	12.61	16.67	27.57
Chile	228	11.72	8.57	7.70	7.57	6.24	1.63	1.89	5.21	11.41	7.80	6.83	6.59
Colombia	233	20.10	14.22	17.15	18.13	15.02	15.43	17.30	9.82	13.20	9.40	5.29	9.13
Costa Rica	238	18.40	5.15	13.11	23.88	16.00	11.60	8.81	10.14	10.97	9.32	7.97	10.57
Ecuador	248	....	....	....	....	31.17	31.17	31.17	102.74	164.32	−.21	6.76	7.28
El Salvador	253	....	....	....	....	....	....	....	....	6.48	.99	−2.16	2.50
Mexico	273	12.34	7.41	6.11	38.64	33.88	17.55	15.98	14.24	7.84	5.02	5.10	7.48
Panama	283	1.85	−.25	2.04	2.98	2.12	−2.24	−3.92	2.68	8.75	−3.21	−3.00	2.21
Paraguay	288	....	....	....	....	....	1.15	14.90	5.30	14.70	5.82	19.89	26.46
Peru	293	57.19	47.55	17.89	10.52	9.44	7.38	7.27	4.91	4.33	1.38	−1.05	1.70
Trinidad and Tobago	369	.77	5.36	5.40	3.58	2.89	1.93	1.44	1.71	1.30	.90	.59	....
Uruguay	298	58.32	33.37	34.20	37.71	25.02	16.36	9.29	−.88	6.84	6.58	31.92	38.92
Venezuela, Rep. Bol	299	23.57	34.96	78.16	57.74	103.24	29.76	22.17	16.21	15.18	13.28	37.28	51.40
Memorandum Items													
Oil Exporting Countries	999	13.56	12.67	20.12	26.68	22.36	10.44	44.98	11.66	12.10	9.32	7.80	9.62
Non-Oil Developing Countries	201	60.71	71.67	100.80	41.51	16.67	13.35	9.78	13.17	14.28	8.22	9.39	9.92

Indices

		1992	1993	1994	1995	1996	1997	1998	1999	2000	2001	2002	2003
		\multicolumn{12}{c}{*Index Numbers: 2000=100*}
World	001	44.5	51.9	66.1	76.2	81.4	85.4	88.8	92.8	100.0	103.5	105.9	111.2
Industrial Countries	110	90.2	91.4	92.6	95.5	96.5	97.0	95.6	95.8	100.0	100.9	99.6	102.0
Developing Countries	200	12.2	19.7	36.9	51.4	60.3	68.2	77.6	87.7	100.0	108.4	118.3	130.0
Africa	605	59.0	64.0	69.4	76.4	81.5	85.7	89.9	93.1	100.0	105.8	116.6	117.1
Asia	505	58.2	60.3	64.8	70.6	74.0	77.6	92.5	94.5	100.0	104.0	106.1	110.7
Europe	170	2.4	3.4	10.3	23.7	33.9	45.2	53.0	74.1	100.0	120.6	137.1	154.8
Middle East	405	42.4	47.5	55.1	68.7	78.6	82.9	86.6	93.4	100.0	102.2	107.6	116.3
Western Hemisphere	205	3.0	11.6	40.3	54.7	64.7	72.3	78.4	88.1	100.0	107.5	126.3	149.0

Exports, f.o.b.

		1992	1993	1994	1995	1996	1997	1998	1999	2000	2001	2002	2003
						Billions of US Dollars							
World	001	3,775.9	3,768.9	4,287.7	5,129.6	5,351.5	5,537.2	5,450.7	5,649.8	6,360.7	6,128.9	6,419.1	7,430.8
Industrial Countries	110	2,662.6	2,598.2	2,915.2	3,471.5	3,565.6	3,644.7	3,674.1	3,746.0	3,998.5	3,873.6	3,989.6	4,561.4
United States	111	448	465	513	585	625	689	682	702	781	731	694	724
Canada	156	134	145	165	192	202	214	214	238	277	260	252	273
Australia	193	43	43	48	53	60	63	56	56	64	63	65	72
Japan	158	340	362	397	443	411	421	388	419	479	403	417	472
New Zealand	196	9.8	10.5	12.2	13.6	14.4	14.2	12.0	12.5	13.3	13.7	14.4	16.5
Austria	122	44.4	40.2	45.0	57.6	57.8	58.6	62.7	†64.1	64.2	66.7	70.9	87.6
Belgium	124	....	126	144	176	175	172	179	†179	188	190	216	255
Belgium-Luxembourg	126	124	120	137	170	166	166	....	....	....	....	....	....
Finland	172	24.0	23.4	29.7	39.6	38.4	39.3	43.0	†41.8	45.5	42.8	44.6	52.5
France	132	236	210	234	285	288	290	306	†302	300	297	312	366
Germany	134	422	382	430	524	524	512	543	†543	550	571	613	751
Greece	174	9.4	9.1	8.8	11.0	11.9	11.1	10.7	10.5	10.7	9.5	10.3	13.2
Ireland	178	28.5	29.3	34.1	44.6	48.7	53.5	64.5	†71.2	77.1	83.0	87.4	92.4
Italy	136	178	169	191	234	252	240	246	†235	240	244	254	294
Luxembourg	137	6	6	7	8	7	7	8	†8	8	8	9	10
Netherlands	138	140	139	156	196	197	195	201	†200	209	216	222	259
Portugal	182	18.4	15.4	18.0	23.2	24.6	24.0	†24.8	†25.2	23.3	24.4	25.5	30.6
Spain	184	64.8	61.0	72.9	91.0	102.0	104.4	109.2	†110.0	113.3	115.2	123.5	156.0
Denmark	128	41.7	38.2	43.1	51.5	51.5	49.1	48.8	50.4	50.4	51.0	56.2	65.7
Iceland	176	1.53	1.40	1.62	1.80	1.64	1.85	2.05	2.00	1.89	2.02	2.23	2.39
Norway	142	35.1	31.8	34.7	42.0	49.6	48.5	40.4	45.5	60.1	59.2	59.7	67.5
Sweden	144	56.1	49.9	61.3	79.8	84.9	82.9	85.0	84.8	86.9	75.8	81.3	101.2
Switzerland	146	†61	59	66	78	76	72	75	76	75	78	84	97
United Kingdom	112	190	181	204	242	262	281	272	268	282	267	276	304
Developing Countries	200	1,113.33	1,170.73	1,372.51	1,658.02	1,785.88	1,892.56	1,776.61	1,903.80	2,362.13	2,255.29	2,429.49	2,869.38
Africa	605	79.62	74.86	79.55	93.38	106.06	107.45	90.87	99.70	125.09	117.58	120.45	146.90
Algeria	612	11.5	10.4	8.9	10.3	13.2	....	....	....	....	....	18.6	....
Angola	614	3.8	2.9	3.0	3.7	5.1	5.0	3.5	5.4	7.7	6.4	7.5	9.2
Benin	638	.34	.38	.40	.42	.65	.42	.41	.42	.39	.37	.45	.54
Botswana	616	1.75	1.76	1.85	2.14	2.54	2.84	1.95	....	....	....	....	....
Burkina Faso	748	.064	.069	.107	.276	.233	.232	.319	.216	.166	.175	.166	....
Burundi	618	.07	.06	.12	.11	.04	.09	.06	.05	.05	.04	.03	.04
Cameroon	622	1.8	1.9	1.5	1.6	1.6	1.7	1.8	1.5	1.5	2.1	2.3	....
Cape Verde	624	—	—	—	.01	.01	.01	.01	.01	.01	.01	....	....
Central African Rep.	626	.11	.11	.15	.17	.15	.16	.15	.15	.16	.14	.15	....
Chad	628	.18	.13	.15	.24	.24	.24	.26	.24	.18	.19	.18	....
Congo, Rep. of	634	1.18	1.07	.96	1.17	1.35	1.67	1.37	1.56	2.49	....	....	....
Côte d'Ivoire	662	2.9	2.5	2.7	3.8	4.4	4.5	4.6	4.7	3.9	3.9	5.3	5.8
Equatorial Guinea	642	.05	.06	.06	.09	.18	.50	.44	.71	1.10	....	....	....
Ethiopia	644	.17	.20	.37	.42	.42	.59	.56	.47	.49	.46	.48	....
Gabon	646	2.1	2.3	2.4	2.7	3.2	3.0	1.9	2.4	2.5	2.6	....	....
Gambia, The	648	.057	.067	.035	.016	.021	.015	.021	.005	.015	.003	.002	....
Ghana	652	1.3	1.0	1.4	1.7	1.7	1.6	1.8	....	....	....	....	....
Guinea	656	....	....	....	.68	.66	.64	.63	.49	.62	.54	....	....
Guinea-Bissau	654	.006	.028	.086	.044	.028	.048	.027	.051	.062	.063	.054	.069
Kenya	664	1.3	1.4	1.6	1.9	2.1	2.1	2.0	1.7	1.7	1.9	2.1	2.4
Lesotho	666	.11	.13	.14	.16	.19	.20	.19	....	....	....	....	....
Madagascar	674	.28	.26	.37	.37	.46	.41	.56	.60	.82	.69	.50	....
Malawi	676	.40	.32	.34	.41	.48	.54	.43	.45	.38	.45	.41	....
Mali	678	.34	.48	.33	.44	.43	.56	.56	.57	.55	.73	.88	.93
Mauritius	684	1.30	1.30	1.35	1.54	1.80	1.59	1.65	1.59	1.56	1.63	1.80	1.94
Morocco	686	4.0	3.1	5.6	6.9	6.9	7.0	7.2	7.4	7.0	7.1	7.9	....
Namibia	728	1.34	1.24	1.31	1.41	1.42	1.34	1.23	1.23	1.32	1.18	....	....
Niger	692	.33	.29	.23	.29	.33	.27	.33	.29	.28	.27	.28	.34
Nigeria	694	12	10	9	†12	16	15	10	14	21	17	15	20
Rwanda	714	.07	.07	.03	.05	.06	.09	.06	.06	.05	.08	.06	.06
São Tomé & Príncipe	716	.005	.005	.006	.005	.005	.005	....	....	....	....	....	....
Senegal	722	.67	.71	.79	.99	.99	.90	.97	1.03	.92	1.00	1.07	1.33
Seychelles	718	.05	.05	.05	.05	.14	.11	.12	.15	.19	.22	.23	.28
Sierra Leone	724	.15	.12	.12	.04	.05	.02	.01	.01	.01	.03	.05	.09
South Africa	199	23.4	24.2	25.3	27.9	29.2	31.0	†26.4	26.7	30.0	29.3	29.7	36.5
Sudan	732	.3	.4	.5	.6	.6	.6	.6	.8	1.8	1.7	....	....
Swaziland	734	.64	.68	.79	.87	.86	.96	.97	.94	.91	1.05	.94	....
Tanzania	738	.42	.45	.52	.68	.78	.75	.59	.54	.66	.78	.87	.65
Togo	742	.27	.14	.33	.38	.44	.42	.42	.39	.36	.36	.43	.62
Tunisia	744	4.0	3.7	4.7	5.5	5.5	5.6	5.7	5.9	5.9	6.6	6.9	8.0
Uganda	746	.14	.18	.41	.46	.59	.55	.50	.52	.46	.46	.44	.56
Zambia	754	.76	.83	.93	1.04	1.04	.92	1.02	.52	.76	....	....	....
Zimbabwe	698	1.44	1.56	1.88	2.11	2.41	2.15	1.73	1.89	3.28	2.28	....	....
Asia *	505	585.86	646.31	768.45	932.71	973.01	1,038.86	986.17	1,051.51	1,266.45	1,182.35	1,297.88	1,547.40
Afghanistan, Islamic State of	512	.09	.18	.02	.03	....	....	....	....	....	....	....	....
Bangladesh	513	2.1	2.3	2.7	3.2	3.3	3.8	3.8	3.9	4.8	4.8	4.6	5.3
Bhutan	514	.1	.1	.1	.1	.1	.1	.1	.1	.1	.1	.1	....
Cambodia	522	....	....	....	....	....	1	1	1	1	1	1	2
China, P.R.: Mainland	924	85	92	121	149	151	183	184	195	249	266	326	438

Exports, f.o.b.

		1992	1993	1994	1995	1996	1997	1998	1999	2000	2001	2002	2003
							Billions of US Dollars						
Asia *(Cont.)													
China, P.R.: Hong Kong	532	119	135	151	174	181	188	174	174	202	190	200	224
China, P.R.: Macao	546	1.77	1.79	1.87	2.00	2.00	2.15	2.14	2.20	2.54	2.30	2.36	2.58
Fiji	819	.37	.38	.45	.54	.59	.52	.45	.48	.48	.44	.55	.68
India	534	19.6	21.6	25.0	30.6	33.1	35.0	33.4	35.7	42.4	43.4	49.3	57.1
Indonesia	536	34.0	36.8	40.1	45.4	49.8	53.4	48.8	48.7	62.1	56.4	58.1	61.1
Korea	542	77	82	96	125	130	136	132	144	172	150	162	194
Lao People's Dem. Rep.	544	.1	.2	.3	.3	.3	.4	.4	.3	.3	.3	.3	.4
Malaysia	548	40.8	47.1	58.8	73.9	78.3	78.7	73.3	84.6	98.2	88.0	93.3	99.4
Maldives	556	–	–	–	–	.1	.1	.1	.1	.1	.1	.1	.1
Mongolia	948	.4	.4	.4	.5	.4	.5	.3	.4	.5	.4	....	....
Myanmar	518	.54	.59	.80	.86	.75	.87	1.08	1.14	1.65	2.38	3.05	2.48
Nepal	558	.368	.384	.362	.345	.385	.406	.474	.602	.804	.737	.568	.662
Pakistan	564	7.3	6.7	7.4	8.0	9.3	8.7	8.5	8.4	9.0	9.2	9.9	11.9
Papua New Guinea	853	1.9	2.6	2.6	2.7	2.5	2.2	1.8	1.9	2.1	1.8	1.5	2.2
Philippines	566	9.8	11.1	13.3	17.5	20.4	24.9	29.4	36.6	39.8	32.7	36.5	37.0
Samoa	862	.006	.006	.004	.009	.010	.015	.015	.020	.014	.016	.014	.015
Singapore	576	63.5	74.0	96.8	118.3	125.0	125.0	109.9	114.7	137.8	121.8	125.2	144.2
Solomon Islands	813	.102	.129	.142	.168	.162	.157	.118	....	....	....	.058	....
Sri Lanka	524	2.46	2.86	3.21	3.80	4.10	4.64	4.81	4.59	5.43	4.82	4.70	5.13
Thailand	578	32	37	45	56	56	57	54	58	69	65	68	81
Tonga	866	.0122	.0158	.0138	.0141	.0114	.0097	.0075	.0124	.0088	.0067	.0146	....
Vanuatu	846	.024	.023	.025	.028	.030	.035	.034	.026	.023	.016	.015	.021
Vietnam	582	....	....	....	....	7	9	9	12	14	15	17	20
*of which:													
Taiwan Province of China	528	81.4	84.6	92.9	111.6	115.7	121.1	110.5	121.5	147.8	122.5	130.5	....
Europe	170	159.84	157.66	201.96	255.78	277.06	286.71	281.09	279.58	340.79	360.68	396.82	509.84
Albania	914	.1	.1	.1	.2	.2	.1	.2	.3	.3	.3	.3	.5
Armenia	911	.08	.16	.22	.27	.29	.23	.22	.23	.29	.34	.51	.68
Azerbaijan	912	1.5	.7	.7	.6	.6	.8	.6	.9	1.7	2.3	....	....
Belarus	913	4	2	3	5	6	7	7	6	7	7	8	10
Bulgaria	918	4	4	4	5	7	5	4	4	5	5	6	8
Croatia	960	4.6	3.9	4.3	4.6	4.5	4.2	4.5	4.3	4.4	4.7	4.9	6.2
Cyprus	423	.99	.87	.97	1.23	1.40	1.10	1.06	1.00	.95	.98	.84	.92
Czech Republic	935	....	†14	†16	†22	22	23	26	26	29	33	38	49
Czechoslovakia	934	11.3	....	....	....	....	....	....	....	....	....	....	....
Estonia	939	....	.8	†1.3	1.8	2.1	2.9	3.1	2.9	3.1	3.3	3.4	4.5
Georgia	915	....	....	156	151	199	240	191	238	331	320	349	....
Hungary	944	10.7	8.9	10.4	12.8	15.6	19.0	23.0	25.0	28.0	30.5	34.5	42.5
Kazakhstan	916	....	3.3	3.2	5.3	5.9	6.5	5.3	5.9	8.8	8.6	9.7	12.9
Kyrgyz Republic	917	....	.3	.3	.4	.5	.6	.5	.5	.5	.5	.5	.6
Latvia	941	1	1	1	1	1	2	2	2	2	2	2	3
Lithuania	946	....	2	2	3	3	4	4	3	4	4	5	7
Macedonia, FYR	962	....	1.1	1.1	1.2	1.1	1.2	1.3	1.2	1.3	1.2	1.1	1.4
Malta	181	1.54	1.36	1.57	1.91	1.73	1.63	1.83	1.98	2.44	1.96	2.23	....
Moldova	921	–	–	1	1	1	1	1	–	–	1	1	1
Poland	964	13	14	17	23	24	26	27	27	32	36	41	54
Romania	968	4.4	4.9	6.2	7.9	8.1	8.4	8.3	8.5	10.4	11.4	13.9	17.6
Russia	922	42	44	†68	83	91	89	75	76	106	103	107	134
Slovak Republic	936	....	5	7	9	9	8	11	10	12	13	14	22
Slovenia	961	†7	6	7	8	8	8	9	9	9	9	10	13
Turkey	186	15	15	18	22	23	26	27	27	28	31	35	47
Ukraine	926	8	8	10	13	14	14	13	12	15	16	18	23
Middle East	405	144.37	135.38	143.04	157.82	183.95	186.00	148.62	183.30	281.08	260.77	281.67	....
Bahrain, Kingdom of	419	3.5	3.7	3.6	4.1	4.7	4.4	3.3	4.4	6.2	5.6	5.8	6.4
Egypt	469	3.1	2.3	3.5	3.4	3.5	3.9	3.1	3.6	4.7	4.1	4.7	6.3
Iran, I.R. of	429	20	18	19	18	22	18	13	21	28	24	28	....
Israel	436	10	15	17	19	21	23	23	26	31	29	29	32
Jordan	439	1.22	1.25	1.42	1.77	1.82	1.84	1.80	1.83	1.90	2.29	2.77	....
Kuwait	443	6.6	10.2	11.3	12.8	14.9	14.2	9.6	12.2	19.4	16.2	15.4	19.4
Lebanon	446	.6	.5	.5	.7	.7	.6	.7	.7	.7	.9	1.0	1.5
Libya	672	11	8	9	8	8	7	5	8	10	9	8	....
Oman	449	5.6	5.4	5.5	6.1	7.3	7.6	5.5	....	....	....	11.2	11.7
Qatar	453	....	....	3.1	3.5	3.8	3.8	4.9	7.1	....	....	....	....
Saudi Arabia	456	50	42	43	50	61	61	39	51	78	68	73	....
Syrian Arab Rep	463	3.1	3.1	3.0	3.6	4.0	3.9	2.9	3.5	†19.3	21.6	28.1	....
United Arab Emirates	466	25	....	....	....	....	....	....	....	....	....	....	....
Yemen, Republic of	474	1	1	1	2	3	3	1	2	4	3	....	....
Western Hemisphere	205	147.60	158.10	182.93	223.54	251.39	278.78	275.67	294.05	353.54	341.23	340.91	351.41
Anguilla	312	.0005	.0010	.0009	.0005	.0016	.0016	.0032	.0026	.0040	.0032	.0043	....
Argentina	213	12	13	16	21	24	26	26	23	26	27	26	29
Aruba	314	....	....	....	–	–	–	–	–	.2	.1	.1	.1
Bahamas, The	313	.2	.2	.2	.2	.2	.2	.3	.5	.6	.4	.4	.4
Barbados	316	.19	.19	.18	.24	.28	.28	.25	.26	.27	.26	.21	.21
Belize	339	.14	.14	.15	.16	.17	.18	.17	.19	.22	.17	.17	.20
Bolivia	218	.7	.7	1.0	1.1	1.1	1.2	1.1	1.1	1.2	1.3	1.3	1.6
Brazil	223	36	39	44	47	48	53	51	48	55	58	60	73
Chile	228	10.0	9.2	11.6	16.0	15.7	17.9	16.3	17.2	19.2	18.3	18.2	21.0
Colombia	233	6.9	7.1	8.4	10.1	10.6	11.5	10.9	11.6	13.0	12.3	11.9	12.7
Costa Rica	238	1.8	2.6	2.9	3.5	3.8	4.3	5.5	6.7	5.8	5.0	5.3	6.1

2004, International Monetary Fund: *International Financial Statistics Yearbook*

Exports, f.o.b.

		1992	1993	1994	1995	1996	1997	1998	1999	2000	2001	2002	2003
						Billions of US Dollars							
Western Hemisphere(Cont.)													
Dominica................	321	.1	–	–	–	.1	.1	.1	.1	.1	–	–	–
Dominican Republic..........	243	.56	.51	.64	.87	.95	1.02	.88	.81	.97	.80	.83	1.04
Ecuador..................	248	3.0	2.9	3.8	4.3	4.9	5.3	4.2	4.5	4.9	4.7	5.0	6.0
El Salvador...............	253	.6	.7	.8	1.0	1.0	1.4	1.3	1.2	1.3	1.2	1.2	1.3
Grenada..................	328	.02	.02	.02	.02	.02	.02	.03	....	....	....	....	....
Guatemala................	258	1.3	1.3	1.5	2.2	2.0	2.3	2.6	2.4	2.7	2.5	2.2	2.5
Guyana...................	336	.29	.41	.46	.45	.52	.64	.48	.52	.50	.48	.49	.63
Haiti.....................	263	.073	.080	.082	.110	.090	.212	.320	.334	.318	.274	.280	.347
Honduras.................	268	.8	.8	.8	1.2	1.3	1.4	1.5	1.2	1.4	1.3	1.3	1.3
Jamaica..................	343	1.05	1.07	1.21	1.43	1.38	1.38	1.31	1.24	1.30	1.22	1.11	1.18
Mexico...................	273	46	52	61	80	96	110	117	136	166	159	161	165
Netherlands Antilles........	353	1.6	1.3	1.4	....	....	....	....	....	1.9	2.3	1.6	....
Nicaragua.................	278	.2	.3	.3	.5	.5	.6	.6	.5	.6	.6	.6	....
Panama...................	283	.50	.55	.58	.63	....	.72	.78	.82	.86	.91	.85	.86
Paraguay.................	288	.7	.7	.8	.9	1.0	1.1	1.0	.7	.9	1.0	....	....
Peru.....................	293	3.5	3.4	4.4	5.5	5.9	6.8	5.8	6.1	7.0	7.0	7.6	9.0
St. Lucia..................	362	.1	.1	.1	.1	.1	.1	.1	.1	–	–	–	....
St. Vincent & Grens........	364	.08	.06	.05	.04	.05	.05	.05	.05	.05	.04	.04	.04
Suriname.................	366	.39	1.19	.45	.48	.54	.56	.51	.46	.51	.40	.47	.64
Trinidad and Tobago........	369	1.7	1.7	1.9	2.5	2.5	2.5	2.3	2.8	4.3	4.3	3.9	....
Uruguay..................	298	1.7	1.6	1.9	2.1	2.4	2.7	2.8	2.2	2.3	2.1	1.9	2.2
Venezuela.................	299	14	15	16	18	23	22	17	20	32	27	24	5
Memorandum Items													
Euro Area.................	163	....	....	....	....	....	....	791.46	†884.59	922.63	936.32	1,006.81	1,170.79
Oil Exporting Countries.....	999	193.72	180.81	187.49	209.58	247.92	250.19	198.25	236.00	349.09	313.54	317.65	....
Non-Oil Developing Countries.	201	918.93	990.35	1,186.02	1,450.01	1,539.17	1,643.87	1,580.38	1,669.57	2,014.29	1,942.57	2,108.94	2,524.06

Imports, c.i.f.

		1992	1993	1994	1995	1996	1997	1998	1999	2000	2001	2002	2003
							Billions of US Dollars						
World	001	3,884.9	3,831.7	4,355.0	5,202.0	5,453.1	5,635.3	5,565.3	5,786.4	6,565.1	6,333.8	6,570.1	7,644.4
Industrial Countries	110	2,711.1	2,558.6	2,906.4	3,436.5	3,559.4	3,636.5	3,739.8	3,931.0	4,338.7	4,159.0	4,266.6	4,917.4
United States	111	554	603	689	771	822	899	944	1,059	1,259	1,179	1,202	1,305
Canada	156	129	139	155	168	175	201	206	220	245	227	227	245
Australia	193	44	46	53	61	65	66	65	69	72	64	73	89
Japan	158	233	242	275	336	349	339	280	311	380	349	337	383
New Zealand	196	9.2	9.6	11.9	14.0	14.7	14.5	12.5	14.3	13.9	13.3	15.0	18.6
Austria	122	54.1	48.6	55.3	66.4	67.3	64.8	68.2	†69.6	69.0	70.4	72.8	88.3
Belgium	124	....	114	130	160	164	157	165	†165	177	179	198	235
Belgium-Luxembourg	126	125	112	126	155	153	155						
Finland	172	21.2	18.0	23.2	28.1	29.3	29.8	32.3	†31.6	33.9	32.1	33.6	41.6
France	132	240	203	235	281	282	272	290	†295	311	302	311	371
Germany	134	402	346	385	464	459	446	471	†474	495	486	492	602
Greece	174	22.8	20.2	21.4	26.8	29.7	27.9	29.4	28.7	29.2	29.9	31.2	44.4
Ireland	178	22.5	22.0	25.9	33.1	35.9	39.2	44.6	†47.2	51.5	51.3	51.5	53.3
Italy	136	189	148	169	206	208	210	218	†220	238	236	246	292
Luxembourg	137	8	8	8	10	10	9	10	†11	11	11	12	14
Netherlands	138	135	125	141	177	181	178	188	†188	198	195	194	232
Portugal	182	30.3	24.3	27.3	33.3	35.2	35.1	†38.5	†39.8	38.2	39.4	38.3	40.8
Spain	184	99.8	79.7	92.2	113.3	121.8	122.7	133.1	†144.4	152.9	153.6	163.5	208.5
Denmark	128	35.5	31.3	36.6	45.7	45.0	44.4	46.3	44.5	44.4	44.3	49.3	56.4
Iceland	176	1.68	1.34	1.47	1.76	2.03	1.99	2.49	2.50	2.59	2.25	2.27	2.79
Norway	142	25.9	24.0	27.3	33.0	35.6	35.7	37.5	34.2	34.4	33.0	34.9	39.5
Sweden	144	50.0	42.7	51.7	64.7	66.9	65.7	68.6	68.8	73.0	63.5	66.7	82.7
Switzerland	146	†62	57	64	77	74	71	74	75	76	77	79	92
United Kingdom	112	221	206	226	265	287	307	314	318	334	321	335	381
Developing Countries	200	1,173.89	1,273.18	1,448.64	1,765.49	1,893.64	1,998.74	1,825.48	1,855.44	2,226.39	2,174.82	2,303.48	2,727.04
Africa	605	78.78	75.82	82.58	101.06	100.45	105.93	104.66	99.97	104.01	108.18	109.81	....
Algeria	612	8.3	8.0	9.2	10.1	9.1	....	....	....	....	....	10.8	....
Benin	638	.58	.57	.43	.75	.65	.68	.74	.75	.61	.55	.68	.76
Botswana	616	1.89	1.77	1.64	1.91	1.72	2.26	2.39	2.21	2.47	1.81	....	....
Burkina Faso	748	.47	.51	.35	.45	.65	.59	.73	.57	.49	.55	.58	....
Burundi	618	.22	.20	.22	.23	.13	.12	.16	.12	.15	.14	.13	.16
Cameroon	622	1.2	1.1	1.1	.9	1.1	1.2	1.5	1.3	1.3	1.6	2.8	....
Cape Verde	624	.18	.15	.21	.25	.23	.24	.23	.25	.23	.23	....	....
Central African Rep.	626	.15	.13	.14	.17	.14	.14	.15	.13	.12	.11	.12	....
Chad	628	.24	.20	.18	.37	.33	.33	.36	.32	.32	.68	1.65	....
Congo, Rep. of	634	.45	.58	.63	.67	1.55	.93	.68	.82	.46	....	....	....
Côte d'Ivoire	662	2.4	2.1	1.9	2.9	2.9	2.8	3.3	2.8	2.4	2.4	2.5	3.3
Djibouti	611	.2	.2	.2	.2	.2	.1	.2	.2	....	....	....	....
Equatorial Guinea	642	.06	.06	.04	.05	.29	.33	.32	.43	.45	....	....	....
Ethiopia	644	.84	.79	1.03	1.15	1.40	....	1.52	1.54	1.26	1.81	1.67	....
Gabon	646	.70	.85	.76	.88	.96	1.10	1.10	.84	.99	.86	....	....
Gambia, The	648	.22	.26	.21	.18	.26	.17	.23	.19	.19	.13	.15	....
Ghana	652	2.2	3.9	2.1	1.9	2.1	2.3	2.6	3.5	3.0	....	....	....
Guinea-Bissau	654	.096	.061	.164	.133	.087	.089	.063	.051	.049	.062	.058	.069
Kenya	664	1.8	1.8	2.1	3.0	2.9	3.3	3.2	2.8	3.1	3.2	3.2	3.7
Lesotho	666	.90	.87	.85	.99	1.00	1.02	.86	.78	.73	.68	.79	1.02
Madagascar	674	.45	.47	.44	.54	.52	.50	.54	.59	.73	.74	.51	....
Malawi	676	.74	.55	.49	.47	.62	.78	.52	.67	.53	.56	.70	....
Mali	678	.61	.63	.59	.77	.77	.74	.76	.61	.59	.73	.74	1.13
Mauritania	682	....	....	.40	....	....	....	....	....	....	....	....	....
Mauritius	684	1.62	1.72	1.93	1.98	2.29	2.19	2.07	2.25	2.09	1.99	2.17	2.38
Morocco	686	7.3	6.7	8.3	10.0	9.7	9.5	10.3	9.9	11.5	11.0	11.9	....
Mozambique	688	....	....	1	1	1	1	1	1	1	....	....	....
Namibia	728	1.28	1.33	1.41	1.62	1.67	1.75	1.65	1.61	1.55	1.55	....	....
Niger	692	.48	.37	.33	.37	.45	.37	.47	.34	.32	.33	.37	.46
Nigeria	694	8.3	5.5	6.6	†8.2	6.4	9.5	9.2	8.6	8.7	11.6	7.5	10.9
Rwanda	714	.29	.33	.12	.24	.26	.30	.28	.25	.21	.25	.20	.25
São Tomé & Príncipe	716	.029	.032	.030	.029	.022	.016	....	....	....	....	....	....
Senegal	722	1.03	1.09	1.02	1.41	1.44	1.33	1.46	1.37	1.34	1.43	1.60	2.03
Seychelles	718	.19	.24	.21	.23	.38	.34	.38	.43	.34	.48	.42	.43
Sierra Leone	724	.15	.15	.15	.13	.21	.09	.09	.08	.15	.18	.26	.30
South Africa	199	20	20	23	31	30	33	†29	27	30	28	29	41
Sudan	732	.8	.9	1.2	†1.2	1.5	1.6	1.9	1.4	1.6	1.6	....	....
Swaziland	734	.87	.79	.84	1.01	1.06	1.07	1.08	1.07	1.05	1.13	.98	....
Tanzania	738	1.5	1.5	1.5	1.7	1.4	1.3	1.5	1.6	1.5	1.7	1.7	1.4
Togo	742	.39	.18	.22	.59	.66	.65	.59	.49	.48	.52	.58	.84
Tunisia	744	6.4	6.2	6.6	7.9	7.7	7.9	8.4	8.5	8.6	9.5	9.5	10.9
Uganda	746	.51	.61	.87	1.06	1.19	1.32	1.42	1.34	1.54	1.59	1.11	1.25
Zambia	754	.80	.81	.59	.70	.84	.82	1.09	.88	1.10	....	....	....
Zimbabwe	698	2.20	1.82	2.24	2.66	2.80	3.28	2.62	2.13	1.81	1.74	....	....
Asia *	505	610.98	686.81	802.57	987.85	1,035.85	1,056.85	878.68	956.55	1,196.45	1,117.67	1,214.43	1,461.13
Afghanistan, Islamic State of	512	.43	.74	.14	.05	....	....	....	....	....	....	....	....
Bangladesh	513	3.7	4.0	4.6	6.5	6.6	6.9	7.0	7.7	8.4	8.3	7.9	9.5
Bhutan	514	.1	.1	.1	.1	.1	.1	.1	.2	.2	.2	.2	....
Cambodia	522	....	....	....	....	....	1	1	1	1	1	2	2

2004, International Monetary Fund : *International Financial Statistics Yearbook*

Imports, c.i.f.

		1992	1993	1994	1995	1996	1997	1998	1999	2000	2001	2002	2003
							Billions of US Dollars						
Asia *(Cont.)													
China, P.R.: Mainland	924	81	104	116	132	139	142	140	166	225	244	295	413
China, P.R.: Hong Kong	532	123	139	162	193	199	209	185	180	213	201	208	232
China, P.R.: Macao	546	1.97	2.03	2.13	2.04	2.00	2.08	1.95	2.04	2.25	2.39	2.53	2.76
Fiji	819	.63	.72	.83	.89	.99	.97	.72	.90	.83	.79	.90	1.17
India	534	23.6	22.8	26.8	34.7	37.9	41.4	43.0	47.0	51.5	50.4	56.5	71.2
Indonesia	536	27.3	28.3	32.0	40.6	42.9	41.7	27.3	24.0	33.5	31.0	31.3	32.6
Korea	542	82	84	102	135	150	145	93	120	160	141	152	179
Lao People's Dem. Rep.	544	.3	.4	.6	.6	.7	.7	.6	.5	.5	.5	.4	.5
Malaysia	548	39.9	45.7	59.6	77.7	78.4	79.0	58.3	65.4	82.0	73.9	79.9	81.9
Maldives	556	.2	.2	.2	.3	.3	.3	.4	.4	.4	.4	.4	.5
Mongolia	948	.4	.4	.3	.4	.5	.5	.5	.5	.6	.6	....	....
Myanmar	518	.66	.82	.89	1.35	1.37	2.06	2.69	2.32	2.40	2.88	2.35	2.09
Nepal	558	.78	.89	1.16	1.33	1.40	1.69	1.25	1.42	1.57	1.47	1.42	1.75
Pakistan	564	9.4	9.5	8.9	11.5	12.1	11.6	9.3	10.2	10.9	10.2	11.2	13.0
Papua New Guinea	853	1.48	1.30	1.52	1.45	1.74	1.71	1.24	1.23	1.15	1.07	1.23	1.30
Philippines	566	15.5	18.7	22.6	28.3	34.1	38.6	31.5	32.6	37.0	34.9	37.2	39.5
Samoa	862	.110	.105	.081	.095	.100	.097	.097	.115	.106	.130	.113	.137
Singapore	576	72	85	103	125	131	132	105	111	135	116	116	128
Solomon Islands	813	.112	.137	.139	.154	.151	.184	.150	....	.093	....	.048	....
Sri Lanka	524	3.50	4.00	4.77	5.31	5.44	5.86	5.91	5.96	7.18	5.97	6.10	6.67
Thailand	578	41	46	54	71	72	63	43	50	62	62	65	76
Tonga	866	.063	.061	.069	.077	.075	.073	.069	.073	.069	.073	.089	....
Vanuatu	846	.082	.079	.089	.095	.098	.094	.088	.096	.087	.102	.089	.105
Vietnam	582	....	....	....	....	11	12	12	12	16	16	19	25
* of which:													
Taiwan Province of China	528	72.2	77.1	85.5	103.7	101.3	113.9	104.9	111.0	139.9	107.3	112.8	....
Europe	**170**	**177.00**	**188.08**	**216.81**	**290.26**	**334.44**	**355.65**	**349.53**	**309.77**	**358.25**	**374.40**	**421.02**	**538.26**
Albania	914	.2	.6	.6	.7	.8	.6	.8	1.1	1.1	1.3	1.5	1.9
Armenia	911	.21	.25	.39	.67	.86	.89	.90	.80	.88	.87	.99	1.27
Azerbaijan	912	.9	.6	.8	.7	1.0	.8	1.1	1.0	1.2	1.4	....	....
Belarus	913	3	3	3	6	7	9	9	7	9	8	9	12
Bulgaria	918	4	5	4	6	7	5	5	5	7	7	8	11
Croatia	960	4.5	4.7	5.2	7.5	7.8	9.1	8.4	7.8	7.9	9.1	10.7	14.1
Cyprus	423	3.31	2.59	3.02	3.69	3.98	3.70	3.69	3.62	3.85	3.92	4.09	4.47
Czech Republic	935	....	† 16	† 18	† 26	29	29	30	29	34	38	43	....
Czechoslovakia	934	13.2	....	....	....	....	....	....	....	....	....	....	....
Estonia	939	....	.9	† 1.7	2.5	3.2	4.4	4.6	4.1	4.2	4.3	4.8	6.5
Georgia	915	....	....	338	392	687	944	887	585	654	684	733	....
Hungary	944	11.1	12.5	14.3	15.4	18.1	21.1	25.7	27.9	32.0	33.7	37.8	47.6
Kazakhstan	916	....	3.9	3.6	3.8	4.2	4.3	4.3	3.7	5.0	6.4	6.6	8.3
Kyrgyz Republic	917	.4	.4	.3	.5	.8	.7	.8	.6	.6	.5	.6	.7
Latvia	941	....	1	1	2	2	3	3	3	3	4	4	5
Lithuania	946	....	2	2	4	5	6	6	5	5	6	8	10
Macedonia, FYR	962	....	1.2	1.5	1.7	1.6	1.8	1.9	1.8	2.1	1.7	1.9	2.2
Malta	181	2.35	2.17	2.44	2.94	2.80	2.55	2.67	2.85	3.40	2.73	2.84	....
Moldova	921	1	1	1	1	1	1	1	1	1	1	....	....
Poland	964	16	19	21	29	37	42	46	46	49	50	55	68
Romania	968	6.3	6.5	7.1	10.3	11.4	11.3	11.8	10.4	13.1	15.6	17.9	24.0
Russia	922	41	36	† 55	69	75	79	64	44	49	59	66	82
Slovak Republic	936	....	7	7	9	11	11	14	12	13	16	17	24
Slovenia	961	† 6	7	7	9	9	9	10	10	10	10	11	14
Turkey	186	23	29	23	36	44	49	46	41	55	41	50	66
Ukraine	926	7	10	11	15	18	17	15	12	14	16	17	23
Middle East	**405**	**136.89**	**135.75**	**128.18**	**142.13**	**154.45**	**160.62**	**158.87**	**162.53**	**184.02**	**202.11**	**211.96**	**....**
Bahrain, Kingdom of	419	4.3	3.9	3.7	3.7	4.3	4.0	3.6	3.7	4.6	4.3	5.0	5.1
Egypt	469	8.3	8.2	10.2	11.8	13.0	13.2	16.2	16.0	14.0	12.8	12.6	11.1
Iran, I.R. of	429	26	21	14	12	15	14	14	13	14	18	21	....
Israel	436	15.5	22.6	25.2	29.6	31.6	30.8	29.3	33.2	31.4	35.4	35.5	36.3
Jordan	439	3.3	3.5	3.4	3.7	4.3	4.1	3.8	3.7	4.6	4.8	5.0	....
Kuwait	443	7.3	7.0	6.7	7.8	8.4	8.2	8.6	7.6	7.2	7.9	9.0	10.8
Lebanon	446	4.2	† 2.2	2.6	5.5	7.5	7.5	7.1	6.2	6.2	7.3	6.4	7.2
Libya	672	5.1	5.6	4.3	4.1	4.4	4.6	4.7	4.2	3.7	4.4	4.4	....
Oman	449	3.77	4.11	3.91	4.25	4.58	5.03	5.68	4.67	5.04	5.80	6.01	6.57
Qatar	453	2.02	1.89	1.93	3.40	2.87	3.32	3.41	2.50	....	....	4.05	....
Saudi Arabia	456	33	28	23	28	28	29	30	28	30	31	32	37
Syrian Arab Rep.	463	3.5	4.1	5.5	4.7	5.4	4.0	3.9	3.8	† 16.7	19.6	21.0	....
United Arab Emirates	466	17	20	21	21	23	30	25	33	38	....	....	....
Yemen, Republic of	474	3	3	2	2	2	2	2	2	2	2	....	....
Western Hemisphere	**205**	**173.08**	**188.88**	**221.43**	**250.24**	**276.66**	**329.44**	**346.37**	**334.47**	**390.75**	**382.64**	**354.87**	**367.33**
Anguilla	312	.0372	.0355	.0364	.0324	.0599	.0616	.0714	.0919	.0945	.0777	.0699	....
Argentina	213	15	17	22	20	24	30	31	26	25	20	9	14
Aruba	314	....	....	....	.6	.6	.6	.8	.8	.8	.8	.8	.8
Bahamas, The	313	1.0	1.0	1.1	1.2	1.4	1.7	1.9	1.8	2.1	1.9	1.7	1.8
Barbados	316	.52	.58	.61	.77	.83	1.00	1.01	1.11	1.16	1.09	1.04	1.13
Belize	339	.27	.28	.26	.26	.26	.29	.30	.37	.52	.52	.52	.55
Bolivia	218	1.1	1.2	1.2	1.4	1.6	1.9	2.0	1.8	1.8	1.7	1.8	1.6
Brazil	223	23	28	36	54	57	65	61	52	59	58	50	51
Chile	228	10.2	11.1	11.8	15.9	19.1	20.8	19.9	16.0	18.5	17.8	17.2	19.4
Colombia	233	6.5	9.8	11.9	13.9	13.7	15.4	14.6	10.7	11.5	12.8	12.7	13.9

Imports, c.i.f.

		1992	1993	1994	1995	1996	1997	1998	1999	2000	2001	2002	2003
						Billions of US Dollars							
Western Hemisphere(Cont.)													
Costa Rica	238	2.4	3.5	3.8	4.1	4.3	5.0	6.2	6.4	6.4	6.6	7.2	7.7
Dominica	321	.1	.1	.1	.1	.1	.1	.1	.1	.1	.1	.1	.1
Dominican Republic	243	2.5	2.4	3.4	3.6	4.1	4.8	5.6	6.0	7.4	....	....	....
Ecuador	248	2.4	2.6	3.6	4.2	3.9	5.0	5.6	3.0	3.7	5.4	6.4	6.5
El Salvador	253	1.7	1.9	2.2	2.9	2.7	3.0	3.1	3.1	3.8	3.9	3.9	4.4
Grenada	328	.11	.12	.12	.12	.15	.17	.20	.20	.25	....	....	....
Guatemala	258	2.5	2.6	2.8	3.3	3.1	3.9	4.7	4.4	4.8	5.6	6.1	6.5
Guyana	336	.44	.48	.51	.53	.60	.63	....	....	....	.58	.56	1.02
Haiti	263	.278	.355	.252	.653	.665	.648	.797	1.025	1.036	1.013	1.130	1.188
Honduras	268	1.0	1.1	1.1	1.6	1.8	2.1	2.5	2.7	2.9	2.9	3.0	3.3
Jamaica	343	1.68	2.13	2.22	2.82	2.97	3.13	3.04	2.90	3.33	3.36	3.53	3.64
Mexico	273	65	68	83	76	94	115	131	149	183	176	177	179
Netherlands Antilles	353	1.9	1.9	1.8	....	....	....	....	....	2.8	2.8	2.2	....
Nicaragua	278	.9	.7	.9	1.0	1.2	1.4	1.5	1.9	1.8	1.8	1.8	....
Panama	283	2.02	2.19	2.40	2.51	2.78	3.00	3.40	3.52	3.38	2.96	2.98	3.09
Paraguay	288	1.4	1.7	2.1	2.8	2.9	3.1	2.5	1.7	2.1	2.0	....	....
Peru	293	4.9	4.9	6.7	9.3	9.4	10.3	9.9	8.2	8.9	....	....	....
St. Lucia	362	.3	.3	.3	.3	.3	.3	.3	.4	.4	.4	.3	....
St. Vincent & Grens	364	.13	.13	.13	.14	.13	.19	.19	.20	.16	.19	.17	.20
Suriname	366	.54	.99	.42	.59	.50	.57	.55	.56	.52	.46	.49	.70
Trinidad and Tobago	369	1.1	1.5	1.1	1.7	2.1	3.0	3.0	2.7	3.3	3.6	3.6	....
Uruguay	298	2.0	2.3	2.8	2.9	3.3	3.7	3.8	3.4	3.5	3.1	2.0	2.2
Venezuela	299	14.1	12.5	9.2	12.6	9.9	14.6	15.8	14.1	16.2	18.0	11.8	9.0
Memorandum Items													
Euro Area	163	....	....	....	....	....	....	709.27	†830.50	911.42	898.96	906.68	1,094.41
Oil Exporting Countries	999	153.17	142.71	132.38	153.21	154.61	168.92	153.83	149.50	171.91	185.61	182.51	....
Non-Oil Developing Countries	201	1,019.81	1,130.75	1,317.31	1,613.78	1,740.93	1,831.68	1,673.37	1,707.85	2,056.94	1,991.24	2,120.14	2,521.18

Terms of Trade

Percent Change over Previous Year; Calculated from Indices

		1992	1993	1994	1995	1996	1997	1998	1999	2000	2001	2002	2003
World	001	.9	.5	–.3	–.2	–.6	–1.0	.9	.4	–3.9	–	1.2	.7
Industrial Countries	110	.6	.7	.1	.3	–.6	–1.1	2.3	–.4	–4.7	1.1	.9	1.2
United States	111	–.7	.8	.4	.5	–.5	1.1	2.9	–2.1	–4.6	2.8	1.5	–1.3
Canada	156	–1.8	–.8	.7	4.1	1.0	–1.1	6.3	7.0	–9.5	–1.0	–2.2	7.0
Australia	193	–2.3	–6.3	–.4	3.7	1.3	1.9	–3.2	–5.0	6.1	4.1	1.7	.1
Japan	158	2.7	2.6	2.9	–2.1	–4.5	–5.2	6.5	–.9	–8.9	.6	.3	–3.3
New Zealand	196	1.4	3.2	–.6	–1.6	–1.0	–1.7	.6	–.7	1.2	7.2	–4.5	.8
Euro Area													
Belgium	124	....	....	–.9	–1.1	–1.1	–.7	1.7	–1.7	–2.3	–.2	1.4	–.6
Belgium-Luxembourg	126	1.9	....	....	....	....	....	....	....	....	....	....	....
Finland	172	–2.9	–3.2	1.8	7.1	–.7	–3.1	3.6	–5.0	–4.5	–1.6	–2.5	–3.7
France	132	2.5	1.9	.2	–.3	–.5	–.2	.1	–.9	–4.7	1.8	1.7	–
Germany	134	2.4	.9	–2.8	–.4	–.2	–2.2	1.8	.3	–6.6	1.9	2.5	2.6
Greece	174	–5.5	–.7	–.5	3.0	4.8	.8	–3.0	–.1	5.6	–1.2	1.4	–1.0
Ireland	178	–.7	2.3	–2.6	–2.3	.6	.6	.3	2.4	–3.1	–1.7	2.2	–.8
Italy	136	1.3	–.3	–.4	–2.7	4.3	–.9	3.7	.7	–7.6	2.2	1.8	....
Netherlands	138	–1.4	3.1	.4	1.6	–.6	.1	–.7	–2.5	2.0	.7	–4.4	1.9
Portugal	182	3.1	–1.3	1.2	–1.7	–3.4	2.4	2.6	–3.0	–3.0	4.5	1.2	–4.0
Spain	184	2.3	–.3	–1.4	2.0	.7	–.4	2.4	–.8	–6.0	3.2	3.5	–.5
Denmark	128	.9	.2	–.1	–1.9	–	–1.6	–1.2	.5	.2	.7	–	1.8
Iceland	176	–2.3	–5.2	–1.2	.8	–4.2	.6	....	....	....	....	....	....
Norway	142	–6.1	–1.3	–4.0	2.5	8.8	3.1	–10.5	18.1	39.9	–5.1	–4.4	–1.0
Sweden	144	–	–3.4	.4	4.6	–1.4	–1.1	.5	–3.4	–3.6	–2.8	–2.1	–.2
Switzerland	146	–2.0	2.2	4.3	.2	1.0	–1.6	3.2	3.4	–2.6	.4	....	....
United Kingdom	112	.9	2.7	–1.3	–2.8	1.2	1.1	.8	.4	–.5	.5	2.9	....
Developing Countries	200	2.1	–1.5	–1.5	–1.8	–.7	–.7	–3.4	3.8	–1.5	–3.7	2.5	–.7
Africa	605	.9	–2.6	–3.8	9.1	3.4	–1.1	.5	–6.2	.7	1.1	1.0	....
Burkina Faso	748	–20.6	–5.4	–20.3	10.2	–5.7	....	....	....	....	....	....	....
Chad	628	–1.6	7.5	....	....	....	....	....	....	....	....	....	....
Kenya	664	–2.5	13.4	12.2	–5.7	–2.8	9.7	–1.5	–13.8	–2.8	....	....	....
Mauritius	684	4.8	–1.8	–2.4	.2	3.9	.9	7.5	–6.4	–4.9	–5.5	3.4	–.9
Morocco	686	.8	–8.9	–13.3	13.1	–.1	4.3	11.6	–1.7	3.1	3.7	–1.9	....
South Africa	199	–.1	1.8	1.7	2.9	1.4	–1.2	–.9	–3.0	–1.8	.1	2.5	....
Togo	742	18.8	18.8	18.8	18.8	337.7	–15.5	–13.7	–32.7	3.4	–62.3	–19.3	–20.0
Uganda	746	....	....	89.2	–3.9	–26.1	8.4	4.6	3.7	....	....	....	....
Asia	505	1.1	.1	–1.2	–.6	–2.6	1.1	–1.9	.3	–3.4	–3.5	–.1	–.8
China, P.R.: Hong Kong	532	.7	.2	–1.2	–1.7	1.0	.7	1.2	–.7	–1.0	.9	1.3	–1.1
India	534	5.8	14.4	5.1	–9.5	–8.4	15.5	2.9	–10.5	–4.5	–2.2	–9.4	....
Korea	542	.1	–1.6	3.4	1.3	–9.4	–2.6	–4.5	–2.2	–12.3	–4.5	–.5	–6.3
Pakistan	564	.2	2.0	–	11.5	.2	–.8	14.9	–13.5	–15.3	–.1	–5.0	–6.5
Philippines	566	–15.9	–1.0	–.6	3.8	1.0	1.8	5.2	17.6	–2.4	3.6	–12.1	....
Singapore	576	–3.3	–.2	–3.1	–1.7	.2	–	–	–1.5	–2.9	–4.1	–1.6	–3.9
Sri Lanka	524	19.9	4.2	–1.0	–.6	1.0	5.3	....	....	....	....	....	....
Thailand	578	1.1	1.0	.3	–3.2	–2.0	.5	–5.4	–1.2	–6.9	–9.2	–1.6	.6
Europe	170	2.0	4.7	.4	–1.5	–2.3	1.8	2.8	–1.7	–4.4	.6	1.0	–.5
Hungary	944	–.7	3.1	.9	1.8	–2.3	1.3	1.3	–1.6	–2.7	–.2	.4	–.5
Poland	964	9.5	7.8	1.2	7.2	–7.8	–.5	2.1	.5	–1.5	2.4	2.7	–3.5
Turkey	186	3.3	3.6	–9.4	–3.6	1.7	4.3	.1	–1.3	–8.5	–2.3	–.6	2.0
Middle East	405	1.3	–7.6	–2.8	–.1	11.7	–.1	–24.7	26.5	30.8	–9.9	....	....
Israel	436	.7	3.9	–3.5	–3.3	.7	3.8	2.6	4.2	–2.9	–2.2	–	–1.4
Jordan	439	2.0	–.6	7.7	2.8	–2.5	–.7	–4.8	–	–6.7	–.9	–2.3	....
Syrian Arab Rep	463	–1.5	3.8	–4.8	11.2	–.4	–7.8	....	....	....	....	....	....
Western Hemisphere	205	11.0	–10.0	–3.7	–13.1	3.8	–11.0	–2.6	21.8	–13.4	–4.9	35.8	5.8
Argentina	213	5.1	2.9	1.1	.2	7.6	–.7	–5.4	–5.9	10.0	–.3	–.7	9.4
Brazil	223	30.3	–10.6	–14.0	–27.3	–.1	–16.2	4.9	3.1	2.4	–4.8	14.2	8.7
Colombia	233	–6.1	1.2	20.0	1.4	–7.6	13.2	–3.5	.3	7.3	–9.3	–1.6	3.0
Costa Rica	238	–4.0	1.8	....	....	....	....	....	....	....	....	....	....
Memorandum Items													
Oil Exporting Countries	999	–2.0	–10.2	–8.4	–9.4	20.1	–7.5	–32.4	14.0	47.1	–13.7	....	....
Non-Oil Developing Countries	201	2.2	–.7	–1.1	–1.9	–2.2	–.5	–.6	2.4	–5.8	–2.7	3.2	–1.6

Terms of Trade

Indices

		1992	1993	1994	1995	1996	1997	1998	1999	2000	2001	2002	2003
							Index Numbers: 2000=100						
World..........................	001	104.4	104.8	104.6	104.3	103.7	102.7	103.7	104.1	100.0	100.0	101.2	102.0
Industrial Countries.............	110	103.6	104.4	104.5	104.8	104.2	103.1	105.4	105.0	100.0	101.1	102.0	103.3
Developing Countries............	200	107.8	106.1	104.5	102.7	102.0	101.3	97.8	101.5	100.0	96.3	98.7	98.0
Africa............................	605	100.8	98.2	94.5	103.0	106.5	105.4	105.9	99.3	100.0	101.1	102.1	....
Asia..............................	505	108.7	108.8	107.5	106.9	104.1	105.2	103.2	103.5	100.0	96.5	96.4	95.6
Europe..........................	170	100.5	105.2	105.7	104.1	101.6	103.5	106.4	104.6	100.0	100.6	101.7	101.2
Middle East.....................	205	139.9	125.9	121.3	105.4	109.4	97.4	94.8	115.5	100.0	95.1	129.2	136.6
Western Hemisphere............	405	80.1	74.0	72.0	71.9	80.4	80.3	60.4	76.5	100.0	90.1	....	....

Balance of Payments

Trade Balance
Expressed in Millions of US Dollars

		1992	1993	1994	1995	1996	1997	1998	1999	2000	2001	2002	2003
All Countries	010	42,700	69,941	94,797	118,183	99,553	114,647	69,572	42,487	11,999	−8,564	33,839	....
Industrial Countries	110	37,101	99,908	94,660	122,300	93,396	96,616	26,637	−111,238	−241,996	−208,671	−206,436	....
United States	111	−95,127	−130,551	−163,781	−172,330	−189,100	−196,164	−244,736	−343,716	−449,784	−424,085	−479,405	−544,300
Canada	156	7,381	10,136	14,834	25,855	31,091	18,565	15,922	28,292	45,047	45,275	36,436	41,513
Australia	193	1,643	−29	−3,277	−4,223	−635	1,849	−5,332	−9,761	−4,813	1,786	−5,431	−15,254
Japan	158	124,764	139,417	144,191	131,787	83,585	101,600	122,389	123,325	116,716	70,214	93,829	106,395
New Zealand	196	1,627	1,719	1,408	971	523	903	912	−371	681	1,471	502	−428
Euro Area													
Austria	122	−7,690	−6,476	−7,914	−6,656	−7,315	−4,274	−3,684	−3,629	−2,737	−1,269	3,572	1,932
Belgium	124	....	....	....	....	....	....	....	....	....	....	8,734	9,532
Belgium-Luxembourg	126	3,700	5,780	6,901	9,555	8,690	7,703	6,981	7,027	2,591	3,707	....	....
Finland	172	4,009	6,449	7,723	12,437	11,314	11,544	12,490	12,168	13,684	12,659	12,882	13,390
France	132	2,371	7,516	7,249	10,998	14,936	26,899	24,940	17,988	−3,618	2,837	6,917	1,042
Germany	134	28,202	41,168	51,028	63,910	69,379	70,119	76,913	70,027	57,452	89,253	128,207	149,367
Greece	174	−11,561	−10,499	−11,273	−14,425	−15,505	−15,375	....	−17,951	−20,239	−19,087	−21,452	−25,606
Ireland	178	7,045	8,175	9,366	13,557	15,754	18,625	25,390	23,587	25,010	27,263	33,447	37,807
Italy	136	−200	28,889	31,568	38,729	54,118	39,878	35,631	23,437	9,549	15,540	16,533	9,700
Luxembourg	137	....	....	....	....	....	....	....	....	....	....	−2,073	−2,463
Netherlands	138	12,309	16,904	18,686	23,812	22,767	20,937	20,430	16,034	17,427	20,840	19,944	26,570
Portugal	182	−9,387	−8,050	−8,321	−8,910	−9,722	−10,342	−12,211	−13,714	−13,853	−13,301	−11,882	−12,444
Spain	184	−30,420	−14,999	−14,892	−18,415	−16,283	−13,407	−20,758	−30,339	−34,820	−32,539	−32,841	−42,923
Denmark	128	7,058	7,719	7,441	6,528	7,532	5,369	3,886	6,399	6,740	7,451	8,308	10,142
Iceland	176	2	181	272	206	19	5	−351	−307	−474	−75	150	−210
Norway	142	8,254	6,966	7,496	8,685	12,972	11,648	2,061	10,723	25,975	26,472	24,339	28,109
Sweden	144	6,720	7,548	9,558	15,978	18,636	17,999	17,632	15,714	15,215	13,832	16,631	18,933
Switzerland	146	−265	1,592	3,346	3,258	1,868	2,738	933	843	2,104	1,563	6,432	....
United Kingdom	112	−23,332	−19,648	−16,947	−19,006	−21,228	−20,203	−36,127	−47,012	−49,850	−58,477	−70,215	−77,296
Developing Countries	200	5,599	−29,967	137	−4,117	6,156	18,030	42,935	153,724	253,995	200,107	240,276	....
Africa	605	8,339	7,197	3,742	3,536	16,510	11,257	−4,657	5,618	31,192	19,364	15,768	....
Algeria	612	....	....	....	....	....	....	....	....	....	....	....	....
Angola	614	1,845	1,438	1,563	2,255	3,055	2,410	1,464	2,047	4,881	3,355	....	....
Benin	638	−215	−168	−54	−203	−32	−153	−158	−214	−124	−180	....	....
Botswana	616	187	267	510	555	750	895	77	675	....	....	....	....
Burkina Faso	748	−222	−243	−129	....	....	....	....	....	−312	−286	....	....
Burundi	618	−105	−99	−92	−63	−60	−9	−59	−42	−59	−69	−73	....
Cameroon	622	893	502	402	627	....	....	....	....	....	....	....	....
Cape Verde	624	−157	−143	−181	−217	−184	−172	−186	−213	−187	−194	−236	−291
Central African Rep.	626	−73	−26	15	....	....	....	....	....	....	....	....	....
Chad	628	−61	−63	−77	....	....	....	....	....	....	....	....	....
Comoros	632	−37	−28	−34	−42	....	....	....	....	....	....	....	....
Congo, Dem. Rep. of	636	....	....	....	....	....	....	....	....	....	....	....	....
Congo, Republic of	634	740	619	346	632	1,068	1,013	809	1,037	2,037	1,374	1,598	....
Côte d'Ivoire	662	995	748	1,289	1,376	1,824	1,793	1,720	1,895	1,486	1,528	2,819	2,524
Djibouti	611	−218	−184	−181	−171	....	....	....	....	....	....	....	....
Equatorial Guinea	642	−6	10	25	−31	−117	....	....	....	....	....	....	....
Eritrea	643	−334	−307	−411	−368	−455	−469	−480	−489	−435	....	....	....
Ethiopia	644	−823	−507	−554	−670	−585	−413	−799	−920	−645	−1,170	−975	....
Gabon	646	1,373	1,481	1,589	1,847	2,373	2,002	744	1,588	....	....	....	....
Gambia, The	648	−31	−57	−57	−40	−98	−87	....	....	....	....	....	....
Ghana	652	−470	−664	−342	−257	−367	−638	−901	−1,274	−830	−1,101	−692	....
Guinea	656	−91	−22	−170	−39	111	118	121	54	79	169	218	....
Guinea-Bissau	654	−77	−38	−21	−35	−35	−14	....	....	....	....	....	....
Kenya	664	−500	−247	−238	−750	−515	−886	−1,012	−975	−1,262	−1,347	−996	....
Lesotho	666	−823	−734	−667	−825	−812	−828	−673	−607	−516	−400	−381	....
Liberia	668	....	....	....	....	....	....	....	....	....	....	....	....
Madagascar	674	−144	−180	−96	−122	−120	−178	−154	−158	−174	−27	−117	....
Malawi	676	−15	−23	−160	−63	−78	−158	39	−127	−59	−44	−151	....
Mali	678	−163	−120	−114	−115	−119	16	−2	−35	−47	−10	163	....
Mauritania	682	−55	3	47	184	134	107	40	....	....	....	....	....
Mauritius	684	−159	−242	−397	−241	−326	−436	−264	−519	−392	−218	−188	....
Morocco	686	−2,463	−2,065	−2,107	−2,482	−2,193	−1,864	−2,319	−2,448	−3,235	−3,022	−3,061	−4,310
Mozambique	688	−630	−727	−767	−536	−478	−454	−491	−806	−682	−271	−536	−348
Namibia	728	−78	−42	−86	−130	−127	−272	−173	−200	−117	−179	−179	....
Niger	692	−49	−12	−44	−18	....	....	....	....	....	....	....	....
Nigeria	694	4,611	3,248	2,948	3,513	9,679	5,706	−240	4,288	....	....	....	....
Rwanda	714	−171	−200	−524	−162	−157	−185	−169	−185	−155	−152	−166	....
São Tomé & Príncipe	716	....	....	....	....	....	−12	−18	−22	−21	−23	....	....
Senegal	722	−331	−350	−203	−250	−276	−271	−313	−346	−417	−425	−537	....
Seychelles	718	−132	−165	−135	−161	−170	−190	−212	−224	−117	−205	−140	....
Sierra Leone	724	11	−69	−73	−127	−180	−56	−57	−81	−124	−136	−195	....
Somalia	726	....	....	....	....	....	....	....	....	....	....	....	....

Balance of Payments

Trade Balance
Expressed in Millions of US Dollars

		1992	1993	1994	1995	1996	1997	1998	1999	2000	2001	2002	2003
Africa(Cont.)													
South Africa	199	6,279	6,232	4,481	2,667	2,695	2,324	2,056	4,156	4,593	5,180	4,631	3,701
Sudan	732	−597	−227	−522	−510	−719	−828	−1,137	−476	440	304	−345	−297
Swaziland	734	−141	−104	−50	−197	−204	−104	−106	−131	−136	−77	−79	....
Tanzania	738	−929	−857	−790	−657	−449	−449	−776	−872	−704	−784	−609	....
Togo	742	−128	−111	−37	−129	−127	−108	−133	−98	−123	−159	....	....
Tunisia	744	−2,037	−2,064	−1,567	−1,989	−1,761	−1,955	−2,152	−2,141	−2,253	−2,369	−2,123	−2,269
Uganda	746	−271	−278	−251	−367	−348	−450	−656	−506	−500	−575	−633	....
Zambia	754	....	....	....	....	....	54	−153	−98	−221	....	....	....
Zimbabwe	698	−255	122	158	....	....	....	....	....	....	....	....	....
Asia*	505	3,684	−10,712	−6,953	−15,725	−23,587	29,133	138,391	135,926	112,634	106,366	129,356	....
Afghanistan, I.S. of	512												
Bangladesh	513	−1,256	−1,113	−1,416	−2,324	−2,275	−1,711	−1,574	−2,077	−1,654	−2,049	−1,678	....
Bhutan	514												
Brunei Darussalam	516	....	....	....	....	....	....	....	....	....	....	....	....
Cambodia	522	−179	−187	−255	−332	−428	−328	−365	−462	−538	−523	−563	....
China,P.R.: Mainland	924	5,183	−10,654	7,290	18,050	19,535	46,222	46,614	35,982	34,474	34,017	44,167	....
China,P.R.:Hong Kong	532							−7,833	−3,159	−8,193	−8,331	−5,053	−5,779
Fiji	819	−189	−282	−229	−242	−168	−283	−186	−116	....	....	....	....
India	534	−2,911	−2,093	−4,150	−6,719	−10,052	−10,028	−10,752	−8,679	−14,632	−12,833	−12,416	....
Indonesia	536	7,022	8,231	7,901	6,533	5,948	10,075	18,429	20,644	25,040	22,695	23,513	....
Kiribati	826	−32	−25	−21	....	....	....	....	....	....	....	....	....
Korea	542	−1,755	2,319	−2,860	−4,444	−14,965	−3,179	41,627	28,371	16,872	13,492	14,180	....
Lao People's Dem.Rep.	544	−100	−150	−214	−316	−321	−283	−165	−190	−205	−217	....	....
Malaysia	548	3,150	3,037	1,577	−103	3,848	3,510	17,505	22,644	20,827	18,383	18,135	....
Maldives	556	−103	−125	−120	−151	−186	−217	−216	−262	−233	−236	−211	....
Mongolia	948	−29	21	34	25	−36	115	−62	−56	−73	−101	−156	....
Myanmar	518	−106	−636	−613	−831	−940	−1,143	−1,401	−887	−504	−271	....	....
Nepal	558	−376	−462	−790	−961	−1,106	−1,278	−757	−882	−814	−765	....	....
Pakistan	564	−2,803	−2,586	−2,239	−2,891	−3,656	−2,399	−1,984	−1,847	−1,157	−610	−596	−100
Papua New Guinea	853	625	1,470	1,326	1,408	1,017	677	695	856	1,095	881	....	....
Philippines	566	−4,695	−6,222	−7,850	−8,944	−11,342	−11,127	−28	4,959	3,814	−743	407	−1,253
Samoa	862	−84	−81	−65	−72	−81	−85	−77	−98	....	....	....	....
Singapore	576	−1,821	−2,724	1,354	4,907	5,653	4,681	14,347	11,976	12,298	14,768	18,549	....
Solomon Islands	813	14	−8	—	14	11	−28	−18	55	....	....	....	....
Sri Lanka	524	−715	−742	−1,085	−985	−800	−640	−505	−769	−1,044	−1,157	−1,406	....
Thailand	578	−4,161	−4,297	−3,726	−7,968	−9,488	1,572	16,238	14,013	11,701	8,543	9,081	11,606
Tonga	866	−39	−41	....	....	....	....	....	....	....	−57	....	....
Vanuatu	846	−49	−47	−50	−51	−51	−44	−42	−59	−50	−58	....	....
Vietnam	582	....	....	....	....	−2,775	−1,247	−989	972	375	481	−1,054	....
of which:													
Taiwan Prov.of China	528	12,718	11,450	11,849	13,235	17,543	13,882	10,316	14,705	13,624	19,864	24,193	24,899
Europe	170	−12,453	−23,072	−3,057	−15,479	−27,847	−41,786	−44,897	−13,805	3,513	8,841	3,924	....
Albania	914	−471	−490	−460	−475	−678	−535	−604	−663	−814	−1,027	−1,155	−1,336
Armenia	911	....	−98	−178	−403	−469	−559	−577	−474	−463	−420	−369	−440
Azerbaijan	912	....	....	....	−373	−694	−567	−1,046	−408	319	614	482	−98
Belarus	913	....	−528	−490	−666	−1,149	−1,407	−1,501	−570	−884	−807	−914	−1,234
Bosnia & Herzegovina	963	....	....	....	....	....	−3,116	−3,297	−2,622	−2,958	−3,340	−3,928	
Bulgaria	918	−212	−885	−17	121	188	380	−381	−1,081	−1,176	−1,580	−1,594	−2,474
Croatia	960	....	−709	−1,278	−3,228	−3,488	−5,383	−4,072	−3,299	−3,204	−4,101	−5,649	−7,921
Cyprus	423	−2,315	−1,507	−1,736	−2,085	−2,183	−2,071	−2,426	−2,309	−2,606	−2,550	−2,859	−3,099
Czech Republic	935	....	−517	−1,408	−3,685	−5,706	−4,938	−2,647	−1,902	−3,095	−3,078	−2,240	....
Czechoslovakia	934	−1,834	....	....	....	....	....	....	....	....	....	....	....
Estonia	939	−90	−145	−356	−666	−1,019	−1,124	−1,115	−878	−768	−789	−1,089	−1,580
Georgia	915	....	....	....	....	....	−786	−695	−534	−512	−550	−483	−636
Hungary	944	−11	−4,021	−3,716	−1,459	−1,673	−1,328	−1,885	−2,170	−2,913	−2,237	−2,119	−3,365
Kazakhstan	916	....	....	....	114	−335	−276	−801	344	2,440	1,320	2,301	4,088
Kyrgyz Republic	917	....	−107	−86	−122	−252	−15	−221	−89	5	40	−54	....
Latvia	941	−40	3	−301	−580	−798	−848	−1,130	−1,027	−1,058	−1,351	−1,444	−1,998
Lithuania	946	....	−155	−205	−698	−896	−1,147	−1,518	−1,405	−1,104	−1,108	−1,315	−1,704
Macedonia, FYR	962	....	....	....	....	−317	−388	−515	−496	−690	−526	−768	....
Malta	181	−513	−568	−603	−810	−838	−721	−673	−663	−753	−566	−414	−689
Moldova	921	....	....	−54	−70	−260	−348	−388	−137	−294	−313	−378	−622
Poland	964	−131	−3,505	−575	−1,646	−7,287	−9,822	−12,836	−15,072	−12,307	−7,661	−7,249	−5,725
Romania	968	−1,194	−1,128	−411	−1,577	−2,470	−1,980	−2,625	−1,092	−1,684	−2,969	−2,611	−4,537
Russia	922	....	....	16,928	19,816	21,591	14,913	16,429	36,012	60,172	48,121	46,335	60,493
Slovak Republic	936	....	−912	61	−229	−2,283	−2,084	−2,351	−1,109	−895	....	−619	−243	−624
Slovenia	961	789	−154	−336	−954	−826	−775	−792	−1,235	−1,139	....	−124	−120
Tajikistan	923												
Turkey	186	−8,190	−14,160	−4,216	−13,212	−10,614	−15,403	−14,264	−10,469	−22,410	−4,543	−8,337	−14,034
Turkmenistan	925	....	....	....	....	304	−231	....	....	....	....	....	....
Ukraine	926	....	....	−2,575	−2,702	−4,296	−4,205	−2,584	244	779	198	710	−269
Uzbekistan	927	....	....	....	....	....	....	....	....	....	....	....	....

2004, International Monetary Fund : *International Financial Statistics Yearbook*

Balance of Payments

Trade Balance
Expressed in Millions of US Dollars

		1992	1993	1994	1995	1996	1997	1998	1999	2000	2001	2002	2003
Middle East	405	12,640	7,399	22,164	24,151	40,348	38,346	−4,387	38,768	107,849	74,378	73,826	....
Bahrain, Kingdom of	419	−527	107	120	626	665	605	−28	894	1,849	1,610	1,190	1,611
Egypt	469	−5,231	−6,378	−5,953	−7,597	−8,390	−8,632	−10,214	−9,928	−8,321	−6,935	−5,762	−4,201
Iran, I.R. of	429	−3,406	−1,207	6,817	5,586	7,402	4,258	−1,168	7,597	13,138	....	....	....
Iraq	433	....	....	....	....	....	....	....	....	....	....	....	....
Israel	436	−4,769	−5,607	−5,486	−7,196	−6,954	−5,008	−3,051	−4,160	−3,034	−3,208	−3,894	−2,177
Jordan	439	−1,780	−1,899	−1,579	−1,518	−2,001	−1,813	−1,602	−1,460	−2,174	−2,007	−1,680	−1,915
Kuwait	443	−689	3,324	4,685	5,579	6,997	6,534	1,903	5,516	13,027	9,192	7,242	11,261
Lebanon	446	....	....	....	....	....	....	....	....	....	....	....	....
Libya	672	2,647	113	945	2,302	2,085	2,249	396	2,974	....	....	....	....
Oman	449	1,928	1,336	1,849	2,015	3,142	3,012	307	2,939	6,726	5,763	....	....
Qatar	453	....	....	....	....	....	....	....	....	....	....	....	....
Saudi Arabia	456	20,039	16,522	21,289	24,390	35,370	34,362	11,287	25,039	49,843	39,418	42,897	61,456
Syrian Arab Republic	463	159	−259	−1,275	−146	−338	454	−178	216	1,423	1,424	2,210	....
United Arab Emirates	466	....	....	....	....	....	....	....	....	....	....	....	....
West Bank and Gaza	487	....	....	....	−1,909	−2,364	−2,443	−2,411	−2,618	−2,303	−1,467	....	....
Yemen, Republic of	474	−862	−971	274	149	−31	−133	−785	358	1,313	766	689	377
Western Hemisphere	205	−6,610	−10,780	−15,760	−600	732	−18,921	−41,515	−12,783	−1,192	−8,842	17,401	....
Argentina	213	−1,396	−2,364	−4,139	2,357	1,760	−2,123	−3,097	−795	2,452	7,385	17,236	16,447
Aruba	314	−377	−392	−311	−425	−308	−387	−353	−592	−28	....	−534	....
Bahamas, The	313	−768	−738	−815	−931	−1,014	−1,116	−1,374	−1,428	−1,371	−1,151	....	....
Barbados	316	−278	−327	−355	−446	−456	−599	−651	−714	−744	−681	−702	....
Belize	339	−104	−119	−75	−66	−58	−90	−105	−124	−191	−214	−190	....
Bolivia	218	−432	−396	−30	−182	−236	−477	−656	−488	−364	−295	−340	54
Brazil	223	15,239	14,329	10,861	−3,157	−5,453	−6,652	−6,603	−1,261	−698	2,650	13,121	24,825
Chile	228	722	−990	732	1,381	−1,072	−1,428	−2,040	2,427	2,119	1,844	2,256	3,015
Colombia	233	1,234	−1,657	−2,229	−2,546	−2,092	−2,638	−2,450	1,775	2,633	579	239	326
Costa Rica	238	−472	−761	−606	−323	−249	−498	−399	580	−210	−820	−1,267	−1,170
Dominican Republic	243	−1,612	−1,443	−1,451	−1,391	−1,674	−1,995	−2,617	−2,904	−3,742	−3,503	−3,673	−2,444
Ecuador	248	1,018	214	149	−66	921	491	−1,132	1,588	1,395	−397	−998	−71
El Salvador	253	−962	−962	−1,170	−1,462	−1,242	−1,143	−1,306	−1,356	−1,740	−1,933	−1,871	−2,274
Guatemala	258	−1,044	−1,021	−997	−875	−643	−940	−1,409	−1,445	−1,657	−2,282	−2,950	....
Guyana	336	−61	−68	−41	−41	−20	−48	−54	−25	−80	−94	−68	....
Haiti	263	−139	−180	−111	−429	−416	−354	−341	....	....	....	....	....
Honduras	268	−151	−204	−250	−141	−287	−294	−323	−753	−658	−833	−836	−987
Jamaica	343	−425	−815	−551	−829	−994	−1,132	−1,131	−1,187	−1,442	−1,618	−1,871	....
Mexico	273	−15,934	−13,481	−18,464	7,089	6,533	623	−7,914	−5,584	−8,003	−9,954	−7,916	−5,624
Netherlands Antilles	353	−836	−838	−921	−1,035	−1,129	−975	−1,048	−1,117	−986	−1,114	−1,027	....
Nicaragua	278	−548	−392	−429	−385	−527	−728	−749	−1,071	−921	−897	−936	−972
Panama	283	−376	−334	−250	−589	−644	−685	−1,365	−1,386	−1,143	−696	−1,037	−1,092
Paraguay	288	9	79	−243	−270	−587	−865	−393	−441	−678	−614	−280	−260
Peru	293	−340	−776	−1,075	−2,241	−1,991	−1,678	−2,437	−655	−411	−195	306	731
Suriname	366	122	84	99	123	−2	36	−27	44	153	140	47	30
Trinidad and Tobago	369	696	547	741	588	382	−529	−741	64	969	718	....	....
Uruguay	298	−122	−387	−706	−563	−687	−704	−772	−897	−927	−775	48	182
Venezuela, Rep. Bol.	299	1,322	3,275	7,625	7,013	13,770	8,954	952	6,471	16,664	7,460	13,034	15,043
ECCU													
Anguilla	312	−33	−33	−37	−46	−51	−53	−60	−78	−79	−65	−57	....
Antigua and Barbuda	311	−187	−208	−242	−238	−271	−275	−283	−315	−293	−283	−291	....
Dominica	321	−37	−43	−47	−53	−64	−65	−53	−66	−76	−71	....	....
Grenada	328	−80	−95	−94	−105	−122	−122	−137	−110	−138	−133	−139	....
Montserrat	351	−28	−22	−27	−22	5	−20	−18	−18	−18	−16	−21	....
St. Kitts and Nevis	361	−51	−63	−70	−81	−93	−85	−87	−90	−121	−112	−113	....
St. Lucia	362	−142	−139	−166	−155	−181	−222	−225	−251	−249	−218	−207	....
St. Vincent & Grens.	364	−38	−61	−67	−57	−75	−105	−120	−127	−93	−109	−117	....
Memorandum Items													
Oil Exporting Ctys.	999	45,882	44,646	60,133	66,033	100,441	92,843	41,365	96,253	193,777	140,612	136,965	....
Non-Oil Develop.Ctys.	201	−40,283	−74,614	−59,996	−70,150	−94,285	−74,812	1,570	57,472	60,217	59,495	103,310	....

Balance of Payments

Current Account Balance
Excluding Exceptional Financing
Expressed in Millions of US Dollars

		1992	1993	1994	1995	1996	1997	1998	1999	2000	2001	2002	2003
All Countries	010	-104,638	-66,164	-63,142	-59,206	-52,292	-4,944	-90,063	-133,989	-153,159	-150,670	-126,248	....
Industrial Countries	110	-38,472	42,329	6,833	42,765	34,227	73,783	-39,795	-184,323	-290,664	-247,300	-274,897	....
United States	111	-47,999	-81,963	-118,062	-109,472	-120,170	-135,979	-209,532	-296,846	-413,442	-385,699	-473,943	-530,664
Canada	156	-21,160	-21,822	-13,024	-4,328	3,378	-8,233	-7,839	1,765	19,622	16,209	14,447	17,268
Australia	193	-11,124	-9,684	-17,146	-19,323	-15,810	-12,384	-18,014	-22,295	-15,481	-8,712	-17,365	-30,554
Japan	158	112,574	131,637	130,255	111,044	65,792	96,814	118,749	114,604	119,660	87,798	112,447	136,215
New Zealand	196	-1,071	-746	-2,384	-3,003	-3,891	-4,304	-2,157	-3,515	-2,460	-1,307	-2,269	-3,531
Euro Area													
Austria	122	-753	-1,013	-2,992	-5,448	-4,890	-5,221	-5,258	-6,655	-4,864	-3,636	575	-2,392
Belgium	124	....	....	....	....	....	....	....	....	....	....	13,305	11,623
Belgium-Luxembourg	126	6,650	11,237	12,571	14,232	13,762	13,914	12,168	14,086	11,381	9,392	....	....
Finland	172	-5,116	-1,135	1,110	5,231	5,003	6,633	7,340	8,045	8,975	8,704	10,148	9,295
France	132	3,893	8,990	7,415	10,840	20,561	37,801	37,699	31,870	18,581	28,759	13,789	4,384
Germany	134	-19,255	-13,817	-29,422	-26,966	-13,793	-9,143	-12,215	-22,695	-25,217	1,707	43,445	53,513
Greece	174	-2,140	-747	-146	-2,864	-4,554	-4,860	....	-7,295	-9,820	-9,400	-10,405	-11,225
Ireland	178	607	1,765	1,577	1,721	2,049	1,866	1,016	245	-516	-690	-1,399	-2,105
Italy	136	-29,217	7,802	13,209	25,076	39,999	32,403	19,998	8,111	-5,781	-652	-6,741	-21,942
Luxembourg	137	....	....	....	....	....	....	....	....	....	....	1,636	2,492
Netherlands	138	6,847	13,203	17,294	25,773	21,502	25,077	13,031	12,996	6,817	7,830	10,116	16,467
Portugal	182	-184	233	-2,196	-132	-5,216	-6,465	-7,833	-9,733	-11,114	-10,403	-8,118	-7,549
Spain	184	-21,537	-5,804	-6,389	792	407	2,512	-3,135	-13,761	-19,237	-16,404	-16,044	-23,676
Denmark	128	4,199	4,832	3,189	1,855	3,090	921	-2,008	2,915	2,412	4,920	4,991	6,139
Iceland	176	-160	37	116	52	-131	-128	-555	-589	-847	-338	-22	-572
Norway	142	4,471	3,522	3,760	5,233	10,969	10,036	6	8,378	25,851	26,171	24,769	28,643
Sweden	144	-8,827	-4,159	743	4,940	5,892	7,406	4,639	5,982	6,617	6,696	12,784	22,844
Switzerland	146	14,247	17,926	17,588	21,804	21,051	26,679	26,775	29,611	34,417	23,898	26,011	....
United Kingdom	112	-23,416	-17,966	-10,234	-14,291	-10,771	-1,562	-6,564	-39,547	-36,219	-32,141	-27,055	-33,457
Developing Countries	200	-66,165	-108,493	-69,975	-101,972	-86,520	-78,727	-50,268	50,334	137,506	96,630	148,649	....
Africa	605	-3,083	-6,299	-8,400	-13,208	2,077	-5,320	-18,534	-9,187	10,715	3,509	-1,816	....
Algeria	612	....	....	....	....	....	....	....	....	....	....	....	....
Angola	614	-735	-669	-340	-295	3,266	-884	-1,867	-1,710	796	-1,431	....	....
Benin	638	-120	-101	-23	-207	-57	-170	-151	-191	-111	-160	....	....
Botswana	616	198	427	212	300	495	721	170	517	....	....	....	....
Burkina Faso	748	-23	-71	15	....	....	....	....	....	-392	-381	....	....
Burundi	618	-60	-28	-17	10	-40	-1	-54	-27	-48	-35	-3	....
Cameroon	622	-397	-565	-56	90	....	....	....	....	....	....	....	....
Cape Verde	624	-12	-24	-46	-62	-35	-30	-59	-74	-58	-56	-72	-77
Central African Rep	626	-83	-13	-25	....	....	....	....	....	....	....	....	....
Chad	628	-86	-117	-38	....	....	....	....	....	....	....	....	....
Comoros	632	-14	10	-7	-19	....	....	....	....	....	....	....	....
Congo, Dem. Rep. of	636	....	....	....	....	....	....	....	....	....	....	....	....
Congo, Republic of	634	-317	-553	-793	-625	-651	-156	-241	-231	648	-28	-34	....
Côte d'Ivoire	662	-1,013	-892	-14	-492	-162	-155	-290	-120	-241	-61	768	353
Djibouti	611	-87	-34	-46	-23	....	....	....	....	....	....	....	....
Equatorial Guinea	642	-11	3	—	-123	-344	....	....	....	....	....	....	....
Eritrea	643	33	35	27	-70	-85	-10	-293	-209	-105	....	....	....
Ethiopia	644	-120	-50	125	39	80	-40	-333	-465	15	-454	-150	....
Gabon	646	-168	-49	317	465	889	531	-596	390	....	....	....	....
Gambia, The	648	37	-5	8	-8	-48	-24	....	....	....	....	....	....
Ghana	652	-377	-559	-255	-144	-324	-550	-522	-965	-386	-325	-33	....
Guinea	656	-263	-57	-248	-216	-177	-91	-184	-215	-155	-102	-46	....
Guinea-Bissau	654	-104	-65	-48	-51	-60	-30	....	....	....	....	....	....
Kenya	664	-180	71	98	-400	-73	-457	-475	-90	-199	-340	-137	....
Lesotho	666	38	29	108	-323	-303	-269	-280	-221	-151	-95	-119	....
Liberia	668	....	....	....	....	....	....	....	....	....	....	....	....
Madagascar	674	-198	-258	-277	-276	-291	-266	-301	-252	-283	-170	-298	....
Malawi	676	-285	-166	-181	-78	-147	-276	-4	-158	-73	-60	-201	....
Mali	678	-241	-189	-163	-284	-261	-178	-164	-252	-237	-310	-149	....
Mauritania	682	-118	-174	-70	22	91	48	77	....	....	....	....	....
Mauritius	684	—	-92	-232	-22	34	-89	3	-124	-37	276	259	....
Morocco	686	-433	-521	-723	-1,296	-58	-169	-146	-171	-501	1,606	1,472	1,603
Mozambique	688	-352	-446	-467	-445	-421	-296	-429	-912	-764	-657	-712	-516
Namibia	728	50	110	85	176	116	90	162	162	164	-6	97	....
Niger	692	-159	-97	-126	-152	....	....	....	....	....	....	....	....
Nigeria	694	2,268	-780	-2,128	-2,578	3,507	552	-4,244	506	....	....	....	....
Rwanda	714	-83	-129	-72	57	-9	-62	-83	-141	-94	-102	-126	....
São Tomé & Príncipe	716	....	....	....	....	....	....	-10	-16	-19	-21	-23	....
Senegal	722	-401	-433	-187	-244	-199	-185	-247	-320	-332	-245	-317	....
Seychelles	718	-7	-7	24	-3	-59	-73	-118	-127	-51	-123	-131	....
Sierra Leone	724	-5	-58	-89	-118	-151	-55	-33	-99	-112	-98	-73	....
Somalia	726	....	....	....	....	....	....	....	....	....	....	....	....

2004, International Monetary Fund: *International Financial Statistics Yearbook*

Balance of Payments

		1992	1993	1994	1995	1996	1997	1998	1999	2000	2001	2002	2003

Current Account Balance
Excluding Exceptional Financing
Expressed in Millions of US Dollars

		1992	1993	1994	1995	1996	1997	1998	1999	2000	2001	2002	2003
Africa(Cont.)													
South Africa	199	1,967	1,503	112	−2,206	−1,842	−2,223	−2,134	−528	−295	56	610	−1,456
Sudan	732	−506	−202	−602	−500	−827	−828	−957	−465	−557	−618	−1,008	−727
Swaziland	734	−41	−64	2	−30	−52	−3	−93	−35	−65	−53	−46	....
Tanzania	738	−714	−1,048	−711	−646	−511	−630	−920	−835	−499	−480	−251	....
Togo	742	−141	−82	−56	−122	−154	−117	−140	−127	−140	−169	....	....
Tunisia	744	−1,104	−1,323	−537	−774	−478	−595	−675	−442	−821	−840	−746	−730
Uganda	746	−100	−224	−208	−339	−252	−367	−503	−711	−825	−802	−421	....
Zambia	754	....	....	....	....	....	−353	−573	−447	−584	....	....	....
Zimbabwe	698	−604	−116	−425	....	....	....	....	....	....	....	....	....
Asia*	505	2,181	−13,271	−3,741	−38,940	−39,830	17,036	114,273	112,206	91,479	94,499	131,792	....
Afghanistan, I.S. of	512	....	....	....	....	....	....	....	....	....	....	....	....
Bangladesh	513	181	359	200	−824	−991	−286	−35	−364	−306	−535	739	....
Bhutan	514	....	....	....	....	....	....	....	....	....	....	....	....
Brunei Darussalam	516	....	....	....	....	....	....	....	....	....	....	....	....
Cambodia	522	−93	−104	−157	−186	−185	−210	−175	−188	−135	−86	−64	....
China,P.R.: Mainland	924	6,401	−11,609	6,908	1,618	7,243	36,963	31,472	21,115	20,518	17,401	35,422	....
China,P.R.:Hong Kong	532	....	....	....	....	....	....	2,529	10,284	7,083	9,941	12,596	16,155
Fiji	819	−61	−138	−113	−113	14	−34	−60	13	....	....	....	....
India	534	−4,485	−1,876	−1,676	−5,563	−5,956	−2,965	−6,903	−3,228	−2,640	1,761	4,656	....
Indonesia	536	−2,780	−2,106	−2,792	−6,431	−7,663	−4,889	4,096	5,785	7,985	6,899	7,823	....
Kiribati	826	−9	−4	1	....	....	....	....	....	....	....	....	....
Korea	542	−3,944	990	−3,867	−8,507	−23,006	−8,167	40,365	24,477	12,241	8,239	6,092	....
Lao People's Dem.Rep.	544	−111	−139	−284	−346	−347	−306	−150	−121	−8	−82	....	....
Malaysia	548	−2,167	−2,991	−4,520	−8,644	−4,462	−5,935	9,529	12,604	8,488	7,287	7,190	....
Maldives	556	−20	−54	−11	−18	−7	−35	−22	−79	−51	−57	−44	....
Mongolia	948	−56	31	46	39	−101	55	−129	−112	−156	−154	−158	....
Myanmar	518	−116	−230	−130	−261	−283	−416	−499	−285	−212	−309	....	....
Nepal	558	−181	−223	−352	−356	−327	−388	−67	−256	−299	−339	....	....
Pakistan	564	−1,877	−2,901	−1,812	−3,349	−4,436	−1,712	−2,248	−920	−85	1,878	3,854	3,597
Papua New Guinea	853	−160	474	402	492	189	−192	−29	95	345	282	....	....
Philippines	566	−1,000	−3,016	−2,950	−1,980	−3,953	−4,351	1,546	7,219	6,258	1,323	4,383	3,347
Samoa	862	−52	−39	6	9	12	9	20	−19	....	....	....	....
Singapore	576	5,915	4,211	11,400	14,800	13,977	14,908	18,544	15,184	13,280	16,137	18,704	....
Solomon Islands	813	−1	−8	−3	8	15	−38	8	21	....	....	....	....
Sri Lanka	524	−451	−382	−757	−770	−683	−395	−228	−561	−1,044	−265	−290	....
Thailand	578	−6,303	−6,364	−8,085	−13,554	−14,691	−3,021	14,243	12,428	9,313	6,192	7,014	7,965
Tonga	866	−	−6	....	....	....	....	....	....	....	−13	....	....
Vanuatu	846	−13	−15	−20	−18	−27	−19	−9	−33	−14	−15	....	....
Vietnam	582	....	....	....	....	−2,020	−1,528	−1,074	1,177	1,106	682	−604	....
*of which:													
Taiwan Prov.of China	528	8,550	7,042	6,498	5,474	10,923	7,051	3,438	7,992	8,851	17,891	25,630	29,202
Europe	170	−7,249	−17,555	4,760	−5,179	−14,271	−28,522	−26,792	−2,949	15,700	16,361	5,641	....
Albania	914	−51	15	−157	−12	−107	−272	−65	−155	−156	−217	−408	−407
Armenia	911	....	−67	−104	−218	−291	−307	−418	−307	−278	−201	−148	−186
Azerbaijan	912	....	....	....	−401	−931	−916	−1,365	−600	−168	−52	−768	−2,021
Belarus	913	....	−435	−444	−458	−516	−859	−1,017	−194	−323	−435	−378	−505
Bosnia & Herzegovina	963	....	....	....	....	....	....	−782	−1,098	−881	−1,217	−1,751	−2,096
Bulgaria	918	−360	−1,099	−32	−26	16	427	−62	−652	−704	−984	−827	−1,666
Croatia	960	....	625	554	−1,592	−1,049	−2,825	−1,468	−1,397	−461	−726	−1,920	−2,099
Cyprus	423	−638	110	74	−164	−466	−338	−603	−217	−456	−395	−517	−282
Czech Republic	935	....	466	−820	−1,374	−4,128	−3,622	−1,308	−1,466	−2,690	−3,273	−4,485	....
Czechoslovakia	934	−31	....	....	....	....	....	....	....	....	....	....	....
Estonia	939	36	22	−166	−158	−398	−562	−478	−295	−294	−339	−717	−1,199
Georgia	915	....	....	....	....	....	−514	−276	−198	−269	−212	−230	−397
Hungary	944	352	−4,262	−4,054	−1,617	−1,150	−684	−2,228	−2,446	−2,900	−1,754	−2,644	−7,364
Kazakhstan	916	....	....	....	−213	−751	−799	−1,225	−171	676	−1,109	−696	−183
Kyrgyz Republic	917	....	−88	−84	−235	−425	−139	−413	−252	−126	−52	−85	....
Latvia	941	191	417	201	−16	−280	−345	−650	−654	−495	−732	−647	−956
Lithuania	946	....	−86	−94	−614	−723	−981	−1,298	−1,194	−675	−574	−721	−1,278
Macedonia, FYR	962	....	....	....	....	−288	−275	−270	−32	−72	−244	−325	....
Malta	181	30	−84	−132	−361	−406	−202	−221	−122	−470	−165	−46	−271
Moldova	921	....	....	−82	−88	−195	−275	−335	−79	−125	−78	−56	−142
Poland	964	−3,104	−5,788	954	854	−3,264	−5,744	−6,901	−12,487	−9,980	−5,371	−5,007	−4,085
Romania	968	−1,506	−1,231	−455	−1,780	−2,579	−2,104	−2,917	−1,297	−1,355	−2,229	−1,525	−3,311
Russia	922	....	....	7,844	6,965	10,847	−80	216	24,611	46,840	33,795	29,116	35,845
Slovak Republic	936	....	−580	671	390	−2,090	−1,961	−2,126	−1,155	−694	....	....	....
Slovenia	961	978	191	575	−75	55	50	−118	−698	−548	31	375	15
Tajikistan	923	....	....	....	....	....	....	....	....	....	....	−15	−5
Turkey	186	−974	−6,433	2,631	−2,338	−2,437	−2,638	1,984	−1,344	−9,819	3,390	−1,521	−6,850
Turkmenistan	925	....	....	....	....	−	−580	....	....	....	....	....	....
Ukraine	926	....	....	−1,163	−1,152	−1,184	−1,335	−1,296	1,658	1,481	1,402	3,174	2,891
Uzbekistan	927	....	....	....	....	....	....	....	....	....	....	....	....

Balance of Payments

		1992	1993	1994	1995	1996	1997	1998	1999	2000	2001	2002	2003

Current Account Balance
Excluding Exceptional Financing
Expressed in Millions of US Dollars

		1992	1993	1994	1995	1996	1997	1998	1999	2000	2001	2002	2003
Middle East	405	−24,273	−25,878	−11,123	−6,736	5,223	4,863	−27,685	7,991	67,189	36,461	30,340	....
Bahrain, Kingdom of	419	−827	−339	−256	237	260	−31	−777	−37	830	227	−513	−68
Egypt	469	2,812	2,299	31	−254	−192	−711	−2,566	−1,635	−971	−388	622	3,743
Iran, I.R. of	429	−6,504	−4,215	4,956	3,358	5,232	2,213	−2,139	6,589	12,645	....	....	....
Iraq	433	....	....	....	....	....	....	....	....	....	....	....	....
Israel	436	−875	−2,480	−3,447	−4,647	−5,124	−3,289	−1,149	−3,335	−2,972	−1,778	−1,320	665
Jordan	439	−835	−629	−398	−259	−222	29	14	405	59	−4	418	1,088
Kuwait	443	−450	2,499	3,243	5,016	7,107	7,935	2,215	5,010	14,672	8,324	4,251	7,567
Lebanon	446	....	....	....	....	....	....	....	....	....	....	....	....
Libya	672	1,407	−1,366	26	1,650	1,220	1,550	−351	2,136	....	....	....	....
Oman	449	−598	−1,190	−805	−801	338	−78	−2,950	−291	3,423	2,315	....	....
Qatar	453	....	....	....	....	....	....	....	....	....	....	....	....
Saudi Arabia	456	−17,740	−17,268	−10,487	−5,325	680	305	−13,150	412	14,336	9,366	11,889	29,701
Syrian Arab Republic	463	55	−203	−791	263	40	461	58	201	1,061	1,221	1,440	....
United Arab Emirates	466	....	....	....	....	....	....	....	....	....	....	....	....
West Bank and Gaza	487	....	....	....	−984	−1,424	−1,548	−1,213	−1,327	−1,023	−641	....	....
Yemen, Republic of	474	−1,126	−1,275	178	144	39	−69	−472	358	1,337	667	538	149
Western Hemisphere	205	−33,742	−45,490	−51,473	−37,910	−39,719	−66,784	−91,530	−57,728	−47,577	−54,201	−17,307	....
Argentina	213	−5,655	−8,163	−11,148	−5,175	−6,822	−12,219	−14,510	−11,948	−8,989	−3,853	9,142	7,838
Aruba	314	44	42	81	−	−69	−196	−19	−333	282	....	−244	....
Bahamas, The	313	36	49	−42	−146	−263	−472	−995	−672	−471	−348	....	....
Barbados	316	140	69	134	43	70	−50	−63	−148	−146	−111	−172	....
Belize	339	−29	−49	−40	−17	−7	−32	−60	−78	−139	−185	−163	....
Bolivia	218	−534	−506	−90	−303	−404	−554	−666	−488	−446	−274	−352	19
Brazil	223	6,089	20	−1,153	−18,136	−23,248	−30,491	−33,829	−25,400	−24,225	−23,215	−7,637	4,063
Chile	228	−957	−2,555	−1,586	−1,350	−3,083	−3,660	−3,918	99	−898	−1,100	−885	−594
Colombia	233	901	−2,102	−3,673	−4,527	−4,641	−5,750	−4,857	671	740	−1,109	−1,451	−1,456
Costa Rica	238	−380	−620	−244	−358	−264	−481	−521	−666	−707	−713	−916	−967
Dominican Republic	243	−708	−533	−283	−183	−213	−163	−338	−429	−1,027	−741	−798	867
Ecuador	248	−122	−849	−898	−1,000	−55	−457	−2,099	918	921	−695	−1,359	−455
El Salvador	253	−195	−123	−18	−262	−169	−98	−91	−239	−431	−150	−412	−734
Guatemala	258	−706	−702	−625	−572	−452	−634	−1,039	−1,026	−1,050	−1,253	−1,193	....
Guyana	336	−139	−140	−125	−135	−69	−111	−102	−78	−115	−134	−111	....
Haiti	263	7	−12	−23	−87	−138	−48	−38	....	....	....	....	....
Honduras	268	−298	−309	−343	−201	−335	−272	−395	−625	−276	−339	−242	−279
Jamaica	343	29	−184	82	−99	−143	−332	−334	−216	−367	−759	−1,119	....
Mexico	273	−24,442	−23,400	−29,662	−1,576	−2,529	−7,696	−16,097	−14,038	−18,212	−18,218	−14,099	−9,247
Netherlands Antilles	353	10	1	−98	128	−254	−65	−137	−277	−51	−206	32	....
Nicaragua	278	−834	−644	−911	−722	−825	−841	−687	−928	−792	−785	−784	−780
Panama	283	−267	−96	16	−471	−201	−507	−1,182	−1,320	−716	−174	−92	−408
Paraguay	288	−57	59	−274	−92	−353	−650	−160	−165	−291	−266	73	146
Peru	293	−1,886	−2,464	−2,701	−4,625	−3,646	−3,367	−3,321	−1,464	−1,559	−1,159	−1,127	−1,061
Suriname	366	25	44	59	73	−64	−68	−155	−29	32	−84	−131	−159
Trinidad and Tobago	369	139	113	218	294	105	−614	−644	31	544	416	....	....
Uruguay	298	−9	−244	−438	−213	−233	−287	−476	−508	−566	−488	322	52
Venezuela, Rep. Bol.	299	−3,749	−1,993	2,541	2,014	8,914	3,732	−4,432	2,112	11,853	1,987	7,423	9,624
ECCU													
Anguilla	312	−16	−13	−11	−9	−20	−19	−19	−51	−54	−36	−35	....
Antigua and Barbuda	311	−10	15	−6	−1	−59	−47	−47	−57	−66	−64	−103	....
Dominica	321	−27	−27	−38	−41	−51	−42	−23	−36	−54	−49	....	....
Grenada	328	−32	−44	−27	−41	−56	−68	−82	−53	−84	−99	−116	....
Montserrat	351	−13	−8	−12	−2	16	−2	3	−1	−7	−6	−8	....
St. Kitts and Nevis	361	−15	−29	−24	−45	−65	−62	−46	−82	−66	−106	−124	....
St. Lucia	362	−56	−50	−48	−33	−58	−78	−60	−97	−79	−75	−104	....
St. Vincent & Grens.	364	−24	−44	−57	−41	−36	−84	−92	−73	−29	−41	−42	....
Memorandum Items													
Oil Exporting Ctys	999	−22,193	−22,243	−4,913	−4,079	24,302	18,524	−20,979	26,615	109,856	62,637	50,064	....
Non-Oil Develop.Ctys	201	−43,972	−86,250	−65,063	−97,893	−110,822	−97,251	−29,289	23,718	27,649	33,993	98,586	....

Balance of Payments

		1992	1993	1994	1995	1996	1997	1998	1999	2000	2001	2002	2003

Capital and Financial Account
Including Net Errors and Omissions, but Excluding Reserve Assets,
Use of Fund Credit, and Exceptional Financing
Expressed in Millions of US Dollars

		1992	1993	1994	1995	1996	1997	1998	1999	2000	2001	2002	2003
All Countries	010	101,579	127,724	123,532	175,999	204,112	71,230	68,122	258,490	311,603	281,749	352,019	....
Industrial Countries	110	32,116	−13,891	28,599	35,365	42,534	−50,296	32,338	224,178	336,037	274,004	341,119	....
United States	111	44,071	83,340	112,712	119,219	113,504	136,991	216,263	288,119	413,737	390,626	477,636	529,135
Canada	156	16,375	22,727	12,632	7,039	2,119	5,840	12,836	4,168	−15,902	−14,037	−14,632	−20,523
Australia	193	6,397	9,642	16,186	19,719	18,282	15,258	15,974	29,001	14,116	9,808	17,487	37,431
Japan	158	−111,954	−104,164	−104,990	−52,433	−30,652	−90,247	−124,914	−38,348	−70,705	−47,311	−66,314	50,938
New Zealand	196	1,202	672	3,117	3,387	5,663	2,862	1,671	3,704	2,317	1,120	3,355	4,313
Euro Area													
Austria	122	3,341	3,214	3,826	6,839	5,965	2,168	8,740	4,484	4,119	1,748	−2,298	356
Belgium	124	....	....	....	....	....	....	....	....	....	....	−13,337	−13,346
Belgium-Luxembourg	126	−6,080	−13,359	−12,351	−13,990	−13,169	−12,858	−14,263	−15,954	−12,340	−7,950	....	....
Finland	172	2,966	1,426	3,603	−5,603	−8,038	−4,329	−7,044	−8,032	−8,624	−8,294	−10,262	−9,802
France	132	−5,469	−13,996	−4,968	−10,128	−20,321	−31,861	−17,883	−33,262	−21,014	−34,325	−17,754	−3,109
Germany	134	56,431	−382	27,386	34,190	12,598	5,391	16,230	8,580	19,995	−7,173	−45,423	−54,197
Greece	174	1,766	4,186	6,455	2,841	8,769	345	....	9,730	12,393	3,701	12,268	6,503
Ireland	178	−2,773	894	−1,752	618	−2,101	−2,974	2,196	−2,218	477	1,085	1,107	215
Italy	136	5,223	−10,938	−11,634	−22,272	−28,092	−19,254	−41,470	−16,162	9,028	64	9,910	23,057
Luxembourg	137	....	....	....	....	....	....	....	....	....	....	−1,600	−2,384
Netherlands	138	−728	−6,562	−16,794	−27,684	−27,197	−27,786	−15,370	−17,607	−6,597	−8,180	−10,248	−17,387
Portugal	182	28	−3,081	765	−168	5,764	7,438	8,341	9,949	11,484	11,256	9,136	1,094
Spain	184	3,728	600	6,426	−7,206	23,871	9,244	−11,220	−9,090	16,356	15,064	19,734	8,189
Denmark	128	−124	−5,399	−5,041	643	474	5,611	−2,231	6,522	−8,061	−1,651	624	−1,465
Iceland	176	239	−96	−266	−48	284	84	587	674	773	290	83	878
Norway	142	−5,203	4,731	−3,507	−4,658	−4,499	−11,234	−6,390	−2,394	−22,165	−28,517	−19,046	−27,092
Sweden	144	15,780	6,689	1,639	−6,604	−12,278	−14,118	−1,386	−4,101	−6,446	−7,744	−12,119	−20,768
Switzerland	146	−9,850	−17,440	−16,579	−21,774	−18,530	−24,525	−25,596	−32,095	−38,421	−23,259	−23,609	....
United Kingdom	112	16,749	23,403	11,735	13,438	10,119	−2,342	6,307	38,511	41,519	27,685	26,421	30,865
Developing Countries	200	69,463	141,615	94,933	140,634	161,579	121,526	35,784	34,312	−24,434	7,745	10,900	....
Africa	605	−13,417	−4,018	−2,478	−3,470	−10,265	3,646	4,983	1,697	−6,945	−912	−2,720	....
Algeria	612	....	....	....	....	....	....	....	....	....	....	....	....
Angola	614	−430	−651	−688	−944	−505	279	755	1,667	−478	645	....	....
Benin	638	53	−56	41	−48	−92	70	65	103	91	114	....	....
Botswana	616	208	−30	−76	−93	16	−86	−126	−146	....	....	....	....
Burkina Faso	748	43	74	−22	....	....	....	....	....	200	194	....	....
Burundi	618	85	44	52	26	5	−8	15	4	24	−17	14	....
Cameroon	622	−909	−320	−495	−74	....	....	....	....	....	....	....	....
Cape Verde	624	35	39	68	30	57	30	69	123	30	39	82	21
Central African Rep.	626	46	−1	38	....	....	....	....	....	....	....	....	....
Chad	628	43	69	43	....	....	....	....	....	....	....	....	....
Comoros	632	8	−2	12	9	....	....	....	....	....	....	....	....
Congo, Dem. Rep. of	636	....	....	....	....	....	....	....	....	....	....	....	....
Congo, Republic of	634	−113	133	639	45	−665	−527	−788	−425	−891	−652	−679	....
Côte d'Ivoire	662	−404	−345	−7	238	−686	−322	−359	−588	−367	−25	−1,047	−1,111
Djibouti	611	72	23	47	−1	....	....	....	....	....	....	....	....
Equatorial Guinea	642	−17	−13	−18	112	339	....	....	....	....	....	....	....
Eritrea	643	−186	−74	−69	29	117	115	133	210	40	....	....	....
Ethiopia	644	−144	82	−126	−145	−544	−388	−28	229	−210	−317	−937	....
Gabon	646	−274	−403	−490	−901	−1,140	−729	−71	−788	....	....	....	....
Gambia, The	648	−18	17	−2	9	62	31	....	....	....	....	....	....
Ghana	652	273	593	508	327	299	627	549	828	201	353	26	....
Guinea	656	88	−40	124	144	117	−40	26	139	92	−14	22	....
Guinea-Bissau	654	53	5	−7	10	17	15	....	....	....	....	....	....
Kenya	664	−77	341	−36	259	460	472	558	56	192	350	120	....
Lesotho	666	12	73	13	421	419	410	396	180	169	261	−7	....
Liberia	668	....	....	....	....	....	....	....	....	....	....	....	....
Madagascar	674	−80	−76	1	−54	197	250	1	148	123	−83	15	....
Malawi	676	238	190	195	3	26	292	−170	191	165	−8	291	....
Mali	678	103	91	98	232	290	169	118	239	299	263	287	....
Mauritania	682	135	−108	−35	−28	−87	−20	−34	....	....	....	....	....
Mauritius	684	43	99	189	131	14	54	−69	314	268	−328	82	....
Morocco	686	1,223	958	1,206	−599	−615	−820	−494	102	−665	−746	−1,524	−2,999
Mozambique	688	−171	−200	−99	58	−3	−183	37	586	347	172	−727	551
Namibia	728	−56	−19	−10	−152	−93	−23	−106	−197	−267	−331	−147	....
Niger	692	64	73	50	134	....	....	....	....	....	....	....	....
Nigeria	694	−7,906	−1,131	190	−195	−4,268	−536	1,371	−4,043	....	....	....	....
Rwanda	714	79	79	78	−5	29	93	76	69	−37	32	105	....
São Tomé & Príncipe	716	....	....	....	....	....	....	4	14	14	20	16	....
Senegal	722	276	292	210	212	−2	90	−1	52	101	51	70	....
Seychelles	718	3	−23	−51	−29	−3	28	44	28	−52	76	−58	....
Sierra Leone	724	22	65	30	119	128	75	35	83	122	128	21	....

2004, International Monetary Fund: *International Financial Statistics Yearbook*

Balance of Payments

		1992	1993	1994	1995	1996	1997	1998	1999	2000	2001	2002	2003

Capital and Financial Account
Including Net Errors and Omissions, but Excluding Reserve Assets,
Use of Fund Credit, and Exceptional Financing
Expressed in Millions of US Dollars

		1992	1993	1994	1995	1996	1997	1998	1999	2000	2001	2002	2003
Africa(Cont.)													
Somalia	726	....	....	....	....	....	....	....	....	....	....	....	....
South Africa	199	−1,464	−2,844	571	3,112	570	6,818	3,054	4,798	759	2,549	1,048	9,218
Sudan	732	347	244	621	563	864	846	1,030	580	681	467	1,253	1,088
Swaziland	734	132	−5	−5	53	44	30	135	38	37	10	46	....
Tanzania	738	510	473	292	288	257	332	410	756	497	611	577	....
Togo	742	−20	−107	−41	−72	129	130	123	159	176	167	....	....
Tunisia	744	1,295	1,390	1,063	871	920	981	538	1,180	616	1,129	885	1,111
Uganda	746	124	99	145	288	243	326	462	255	361	563	274	....
Zambia	754	....	....	....	....	....	−579	−98	−207	64	....	....	....
Zimbabwe	698	409	342	339	....	....	....	....	....	....	....	....	....
Asia*	505	**20,524**	**48,166**	**63,806**	**77,905**	**97,108**	**−11,966**	**−75,690**	**−21,030**	**−33,982**	**4,806**	**22,479**	....
Afghanistan, I.S. of	512	....	....	....	....	....	....	....	....	....	....	....	....
Bangladesh	513	454	338	492	312	577	151	324	175	275	392	−242	....
Bhutan	514	....	....	....	....	....	....	....	....	....	....	....	....
Brunei Darussalam	516	....	....	....	....	....	....	194	233	227	154	230	....
Cambodia	522	106	125	193	212	257	244	−25,224	−12,463	−9,825	30,046	39,795	....
China,P.R.: Mainland	924	−8,461	13,378	23,545	20,851	24,462	−1,106	−9,318	−257	2,961	−5,257	−14,974	−15,161
China,P.R.:Hong Kong	532	....	....	....	....	....	....	−9,318	−257	2,961	−5,257	−14,974	−15,161
Fiji	819	146	125	135	206	65	9	65	−58	....	....	....	....
India	534	5,557	6,087	12,067	4,831	9,914	8,286	9,974	9,892	8,619	10,137	12,212	....
Indonesia	536	4,850	2,700	3,576	8,004	12,166	−3,248	−7,789	−3,813	−4,259	−6,914	−2,865	....
Kiribati	826	−8	−1	−7	....	....	....	....	....	....	....	....	....
Korea	542	7,667	2,019	8,481	15,546	24,421	−14,812	−14,435	8,784	11,549	5,039	5,678	....
Lao People's Dem.Rep	544	−11	2	106	196	188	−64	−104	−212	52	79	....	....
Malaysia	548	8,785	14,341	1,360	6,881	6,975	2,061	489	−7,892	−9,497	−6,287	−3,533	....
Maldives	556	24	52	17	35	36	57	42	88	47	28	52	....
Mongolia	948	−27	−17	−40	−7	13	−49	76	93	71	75	171	....
Myanmar	518	211	152	176	229	258	447	560	239	188	488	....	....
Nepal	558	337	288	414	371	358	557	347	34	222	40	....	....
Pakistan	564	2,268	3,328	3,155	2,145	3,656	2,249	−862	−1,596	−2,542	319	230	−603
Papua New Guinea	853	−166	−727	−572	−531	14	15	−192	30	−241	−153	....	....
Philippines	566	2,689	3,352	5,277	3,215	8,291	1,257	−267	−3,569	−6,634	−1,027	−4,494	−3,431
Samoa	862	40	29	−10	−7	−5	2	−15	26	....	....	....	....
Singapore	576	185	3,367	−6,664	−6,201	−6,581	−6,969	−15,579	−10,991	−6,474	−16,998	−17,362	....
Solomon Islands	813	16	6	1	−9	3	47	9	−26	....	....	−42	....
Sri Lanka	524	652	1,150	1,065	1,009	692	702	451	466	683	6	−42	....
Thailand	578	9,333	10,270	12,254	20,713	16,859	−15,229	−16,938	−11,040	−11,120	−3,916	−1,478	−7,447
Tonga	866	2	4	....	....	....	....	....	....	....	15	....	....
Vanuatu	846	14	18	14	24	22	17	3	10	−5	4	....	....
Vietnam	582	....	....	....	....	2,298	1,856	1,111	133	−996	−476	1,052	....
*of which:													
Taiwan Prov.of China	528	−7,183	−5,501	−1,876	−9,405	−9,821	−7,779	1,389	10,601	−6,374	−538	8,034	7,890
Europe	170	**−9,812**	**5,831**	**−18,414**	**24,230**	**2,882**	**32,015**	**9,259**	**12,718**	**1,598**	**−8,120**	**22,820**	....
Albania	914	15	34	164	32	163	312	118	262	276	364	443	505
Armenia	911	....	80	101	248	245	357	419	312	295	219	212	273
Azerbaijan	912	....	....	....	458	846	1,055	1,305	733	493	125	803	2,145
Belarus	913	....	297	127	380	302	924	697	214	448	356	475	555
Bosnia & Herzegovina	963	....	....	....	....	....	....	350	432	589	1,619	1,251	1,826
Bulgaria	918	629	777	−184	470	−754	718	−32	748	841	1,357	1,542	2,398
Croatia	960	....	−437	−278	1,632	2,066	3,216	1,629	1,807	1,071	2,068	2,746	3,490
Cyprus	423	413	35	173	−199	406	291	520	856	447	1,007	906	94
Czech Republic	935	....	2,575	4,294	8,827	3,302	1,863	3,199	3,105	3,533	5,060	11,103	....
Czechoslovakia	934	−391	....	....	....	....	....	....	....	....	....	....	....
Estonia	939	22	143	184	241	505	778	516	414	422	297	786	1,369
Georgia	915	....	....	....	....	....	452	172	184	275	239	44	349
Hungary	944	418	6,807	3,579	7,014	−88	509	3,179	4,781	3,953	1,670	852	7,700
Kazakhstan	916	....	....	....	512	910	1,348	782	424	−105	1,494	1,231	1,716
Kyrgyz Republic	917	....	58	89	154	405	185	340	203	55	20	74	....
Latvia	941	−154	−119	−145	−17	491	447	712	819	497	1,046	659	1,036
Lithuania	946	....	294	207	783	718	1,206	1,725	1,015	833	933	1,183	1,891
Macedonia, FYR	962	....	....	....	....	193	157	313	174	352	329	203	....
Malta	181	14	219	514	54	321	209	412	360	248	420	333	415
Moldova	921	....	....	95	−88	92	87	−18	−37	123	51	8	99
Poland	964	−1,226	2,560	52	8,981	7,088	8,785	12,825	12,643	10,604	4,944	5,655	5,291
Romania	968	1,368	792	626	1,300	1,997	3,563	2,274	1,536	2,263	3,764	3,316	4,324
Russia	922	....	....	−26,957	−15,291	−28,065	−6,440	−21,594	−26,315	−32,918	−22,529	−17,553	−8,083
Slovak Republic	936	....	594	535	1,401	2,460	2,060	1,649	1,932	1,614	....	1,492	327
Slovenia	961	−346	−66	72	315	535	1,238	276	617	726	1,254	17	33
Tajikistan	923	....	....	....	....	....	....	....	....	....	....	1,307	10,937
Turkey	186	2,458	6,741	−2,428	6,998	6,981	5,981	−1,543	6,698	5,885	−16,278	1,307	10,937
Turkmenistan	925	....	....	....	....	8	978	....	....	....	....	−1,943	−718
Ukraine	926	....	....	−37	−472	581	632	−2,161	−1,842	−908	−409	−1,943	−718
Uzbekistan	927	....	....	....	....	....	....	....	....	....	....	....	....

2004, International Monetary Fund : *International Financial Statistics Yearbook*

Balance of Payments

Capital and Financial Account
Including Net Errors and Omissions, but Excluding Reserve Assets, Use of Fund Credit, and Exceptional Financing
Expressed in Millions of US Dollars

		1992	1993	1994	1995	1996	1997	1998	1999	2000	2001	2002	2003
Middle East	405	23,270	22,609	10,286	12,175	6,391	6,130	23,768	−3,968	−47,876	−26,571	−19,973	....
Bahrain, Kingdom of	419	736	227	208	−68	−267	134	761	62	−630	−104	548	112
Egypt	469	548	−2,281	−1,195	−1,573	−1,533	75	1,179	−2,979	−1,059	−956	−1,426	−4,150
Iran, I.R. of	429	6,343	4,443	−4,048	−572	−2,791	−5,910	1,148	−6,138	−11,562	....	....	....
Iraq	433	....	....	....	....	....	....	....	....	....	....	....	....
Israel	436	−601	2,153	1,337	5,127	6,330	10,365	994	2,296	2,380	2,306	1,203	−2,500
Jordan	439	698	−232	133	87	34	245	−550	844	1,768	629	512	261
Kuwait	443	2,302	−3,976	−3,193	−5,157	−7,132	−7,929	−1,957	−4,092	−12,404	−5,419	−5,224	−9,391
Lebanon	446	....	....	....	....	....	....	....	....	....	....	....	....
Libya	672	371	−351	248	51	1	4	−75	−1,448	....	....	....	....
Oman	449	898	132	144	369	−150	609	2,184	506	−1,160	−1,281	....	....
Qatar	453	....	....	....	....	....	....	....	....	....	....	....	....
Saudi Arabia	456	12,076	18,763	10,341	6,542	5,069	343	12,431	2,403	−11,671	−11,275	−9,153	−28,093
Syrian Arab Republic	463	21	507	1,357	576	947	−12	376	58	−247	−201	−390	....
United Arab Emirates	466	....	....	....	....	....	....	....	....	....	....	....	....
West Bank and Gaza	487	....	....	....	984	1,646	1,706	1,160	1,292	1,107	603	....	....
Yemen, Republic of	474	−176	163	−900	−672	−475	4,087	−109	−284	258	−114	−113	182
Western Hemisphere	205	48,899	69,027	41,732	29,794	65,462	91,701	73,464	44,894	62,770	38,542	−11,707	....
Argentina	213	7,941	19,285	10,474	2,863	10,080	15,549	18,600	13,960	7,813	−17,552	−25,473	−18,558
Aruba	314	−21	−8	−84	43	43	177	70	336	−298	....	277	....
Bahamas, The	313	−64	−30	51	143	256	529	1,115	737	410	318	....	....
Barbados	316	−115	−49	−96	−	17	67	57	184	323	333	147	....
Belize	339	29	34	36	21	27	33	46	90	96	181	155	....
Bolivia	218	402	472	1	395	672	654	791	515	407	238	9	−73
Brazil	223	4,550	6,870	7,751	31,105	31,930	22,240	17,527	8,635	32,206	19,797	−3,630	−477
Chile	228	3,504	2,983	4,737	2,488	5,677	6,979	1,727	−846	1,214	501	1,070	237
Colombia	233	374	2,567	3,855	4,523	6,370	6,028	3,460	−983	121	2,335	1,590	1,268
Costa Rica	238	395	362	141	574	194	288	16	896	365	577	879	748
Dominican Republic	243	644	−11	−228	329	173	254	350	581	978	1,255	244	−1,321
Ecuador	248	146	167	123	−459	−71	−65	1,314	−1,862	−6,618	437	1,138	526
El Salvador	253	61	181	131	410	334	460	394	447	385	−27	288	1,050
Guatemala	258	692	901	632	420	666	863	1,275	901	1,692	1,727	1,214	....
Guyana	336	77	104	119	92	81	110	89	100	156	160	125	....
Haiti	263	−14	−11	−26	225	87	78	73	....	....	....	....	....
Honduras	268	51	−25	273	160	257	454	239	436	119	265	223	77
Jamaica	343	220	294	276	126	414	162	378	80	886	1,624	883	....
Mexico	273	26,187	30,632	12,463	−14,735	4,477	28,156	19,267	18,288	25,338	25,533	21,458	19,064
Netherlands Antilles	353	49	43	22	−67	182	59	162	202	−79	423	27	....
Nicaragua	278	−478	−375	−608	−242	77	548	285	533	336	292	370	279
Panama	283	80	−212	−378	139	467	850	803	1,173	388	818	322	253
Paraguay	288	38	−16	575	137	306	435	177	−136	−49	216	−199	87
Peru	293	964	2,105	4,254	4,034	4,526	5,421	2,080	602	1,428	1,591	2,137	1,622
Suriname	366	−47	−31	−24	49	62	87	163	25	−23	162	112	166
Trinidad and Tobago	369	−243	45	−32	−210	133	807	724	131	−103	86	....	....
Uruguay	298	147	437	547	440	386	687	831	398	733	792	−4,219	906
Venezuela, Rep. Bol.	299	3,087	2,117	−3,485	−3,458	−2,676	−638	1,027	−1,054	−5,895	−3,816	−11,851	−4,170
ECCU													
Anguilla	312	18	14	11	9	22	21	21	53	55	40	37	....
Antigua and Barbuda	311	28	−27	14	14	48	50	56	68	60	80	110	....
Dominica	321	30	28	34	49	53	43	27	47	54	53	....	....
Grenada	328	40	44	32	47	56	75	86	58	91	104	147	....
Montserrat	351	13	8	14	3	−16	5	10	−9	3	8	10	....
St. Kitts and Nevis	361	25	32	24	48	64	65	57	85	62	118	134	....
St. Lucia	362	54	55	45	39	52	83	70	101	84	87	109	....
St. Vincent & Grens.	364	34	43	58	39	36	85	100	77	43	50	36	....
Memorandum Items													
Oil Exporting Ctys.	999	16,497	19,745	−1,414	465	−7,178	−23,371	6,814	−23,101	−71,244	−48,495	−41,388	....
Non-Oil Develop.Ctys.	201	52,966	121,870	96,347	140,168	168,757	144,897	28,970	57,412	46,810	56,240	52,288	....

Balance of Payments

		1992	1993	1994	1995	1996	1997	1998	1999	2000	2001	2002	2003

Overall Balance
Excluding Reserves Assets, Use of Fund Credit, and Exceptional Financing
Expressed in Millions of US Dollars

		1992	1993	1994	1995	1996	1997	1998	1999	2000	2001	2002	2003
All Countries	010	−3,059	61,559	60,390	116,792	151,820	66,285	−21,941	124,501	158,445	131,079	225,771	....
Industrial Countries	110	−6,357	28,438	35,433	78,131	76,761	23,487	−7,457	39,855	45,373	26,704	66,222	....
United States	111	−3,927	1,376	−5,350	9,747	−6,667	1,012	6,731	−8,727	295	4,927	3,692	−1,529
Canada	156	−4,786	904	−392	2,711	5,498	−2,393	4,996	5,933	3,720	2,172	−185	−3,255
Australia	193	−4,726	−42	−960	396	2,471	2,873	−2,040	6,705	−1,365	1,096	122	6,877
Japan	158	620	27,473	25,265	58,611	35,141	6,567	−6,164	76,256	48,955	40,487	46,134	187,153
New Zealand	196	131	−74	733	384	1,772	−1,442	−486	188	−143	−187	1,086	782
Euro Area													
Austria	122	2,588	2,201	834	1,391	1,075	−3,053	3,482	−2,172	−746	−1,888	−1,723	−2,036
Belgium	124	....	....	....	....	....	....	....	....	....	....	−32	−1,723
Belgium-Luxembourg	126	569	−2,122	219	243	593	1,056	−2,095	−1,867	−959	1,442	....	....
Finland	172	−2,150	291	4,714	−372	−3,036	2,304	296	13	351	410	−113	−507
France	132	−1,576	−5,006	2,448	712	239	5,940	19,815	−1,392	−2,433	−5,567	−3,965	1,274
Germany	134	37,176	−14,199	−2,036	7,224	−1,195	−3,751	4,015	−14,115	−5,222	−5,466	−1,979	−684
Greece	174	−374	3,439	6,309	−23	4,215	−4,515	....	2,435	2,573	−5,699	1,863	−4,722
Ireland	178	−2,166	2,660	−176	2,339	−52	−1,109	3,212	−1,973	−39	395	−292	−1,890
Italy	136	−23,993	−3,135	1,575	2,804	11,907	13,150	−21,472	−8,051	3,247	−588	3,169	1,115
Luxembourg	137	....	....	....	....	....	....	....	....	....	....	35	108
Netherlands	138	6,118	6,641	500	−1,911	−5,695	−2,709	−2,339	−4,611	219	−351	−132	−920
Portugal	182	−156	−2,848	−1,430	−300	547	974	508	216	371	852	1,017	−6,455
Spain	184	−17,809	−5,203	36	−6,414	24,279	11,756	−14,355	−22,850	−2,881	−1,340	3,690	−15,487
Denmark	128	4,075	−567	−1,851	2,498	3,563	6,532	−4,239	9,437	−5,649	3,270	5,615	4,674
Iceland	176	79	−59	−150	4	153	−44	32	86	−74	−48	61	307
Norway	142	−732	8,253	253	575	6,470	−1,198	−6,384	5,984	3,686	−2,346	5,723	1,551
Sweden	144	6,953	2,530	2,381	−1,664	−6,386	−6,712	3,254	1,881	170	−1,048	665	2,076
Switzerland	146	4,397	486	1,009	29	2,521	2,154	1,179	−2,484	−4,005	638	2,402	....
United Kingdom	112	−6,667	5,437	1,500	−853	−653	−3,904	−257	−1,036	5,300	−4,456	−635	−2,592
Developing Countries	200	3,298	33,122	24,958	38,662	75,059	42,799	−14,484	84,645	113,072	104,375	159,549	....
Africa	605	−16,500	−10,317	−10,877	−16,678	−8,188	−1,675	−13,551	−7,490	3,770	2,597	−4,536	....
Algeria	612	....	....	....	....	....	....	....	....	....	....	....	....
Angola	614	−1,165	−1,320	−1,028	−1,239	2,761	−604	−1,112	−43	318	−786	....	....
Benin	638	−67	−157	18	−255	−149	−100	−87	−89	−20	−46	....	....
Botswana	616	405	397	135	207	511	635	44	371	....	....	....	....
Burkina Faso	748	20	2	−7	....	....	....	....	....	−192	−187	....	....
Burundi	618	26	16	35	37	−35	−9	−39	−24	−24	−52	11	....
Cameroon	622	−1,305	−885	−551	15	....	....	....	....	....	....	....	....
Cape Verde	624	23	15	22	−32	22	−	11	49	−28	−17	10	−56
Central African Rep.	626	−37	−14	13	....	....	....	....	....	....	....	....	....
Chad	628	−43	−48	6	....	....	....	....	....	....	....	....	....
Comoros	632	−6	8	5	−10	....	....	....	....	....	....	....	....
Congo, Dem. Rep. of	636	....	....	....	....	....	....	....	....	....	....	....	....
Congo, Republic of	634	−430	−420	−155	−581	−1,316	−682	−1,029	−656	−243	−681	−713	....
Côte d'Ivoire	662	−1,417	−1,237	−20	−254	−848	−477	−650	−708	−608	−86	−278	−758
Djibouti	611	−16	−12	1	−24	....	....	....	....	....	....	....	....
Equatorial Guinea	642	−28	−10	−18	−12	−5	....	....	....	....	....	....	....
Eritrea	643	−152	−40	−42	−41	32	106	−160	1	−64	....	....	....
Ethiopia	644	−264	32	−	−105	−465	−429	−360	−236	−196	−771	−1,087	....
Gabon	646	−442	−452	−173	−436	−251	−197	−667	−398	....	....	....	....
Gambia, The	648	19	11	6	1	15	7	....	....	....	....	....	....
Ghana	652	−104	34	253	183	−25	77	28	−136	−186	29	−6	....
Guinea	656	−174	−97	−124	−72	−60	−131	−158	−76	−63	−117	−24	....
Guinea-Bissau	654	−52	−61	−55	−41	−43	−15	....	....	....	....	....	....
Kenya	664	−257	412	62	−142	387	15	83	−34	−7	10	−16	....
Lesotho	666	50	102	121	98	117	141	116	−41	18	166	−125	....
Liberia	668	....	....	....	....	....	....	....	....	....	....	....	....
Madagascar	674	−278	−334	−276	−330	−94	−16	−299	−104	−160	−253	−283	....
Malawi	676	−47	24	14	−75	−122	16	−174	33	91	−68	90	....
Mali	678	−138	−97	−65	−52	29	−10	−46	−13	63	−47	138	....
Mauritania	682	17	−282	−105	−6	4	28	43	....	....	....	....	....
Mauritius	684	43	7	−44	109	48	−35	−65	190	231	−52	341	....
Morocco	686	791	436	483	−1,895	−673	−988	−640	−69	−1,166	861	−52	−1,396
Mozambique	688	−523	−647	−566	−387	−424	−478	−393	−326	−416	−485	−1,439	35
Namibia	728	−7	91	75	24	23	68	56	−35	−103	−337	−50	....
Niger	692	−95	−24	−76	−18	....	....	....	....	....	....	....	....
Nigeria	694	−5,638	−1,911	−1,938	−2,774	−761	15	−2,873	−3,538	....	....	....	....
Rwanda	714	−4	−50	6	53	20	31	−7	−72	−131	−70	−21	....
São Tomé & Príncipe	716	....	....	....	....	....	....	−6	−3	−5	−1	−7	....
Senegal	722	−125	−141	23	−33	−201	−95	−248	−268	−231	−194	−247	....
Seychelles	718	−4	−30	−28	−32	−62	−45	−74	−99	−103	−47	−189	....
Sierra Leone	724	16	8	−59	1	−22	20	2	−16	10	30	−52	....
Somalia	726	....	....	....	....	....	....	....	....	....	....	....	....

2004, International Monetary Fund : *International Financial Statistics Yearbook*

Balance of Payments

Overall Balance
Excluding Reserves Assets, Use of Fund Credit, and Exceptional Financing
Expressed in Millions of US Dollars

		1992	1993	1994	1995	1996	1997	1998	1999	2000	2001	2002	2003
Africa(Cont.)													
South Africa	199	503	−1,341	683	907	−1,272	4,595	920	4,270	464	2,606	1,659	7,762
Sudan	732	−159	42	19	63	38	18	73	115	124	−151	245	362
Swaziland	734	92	−69	−4	24	−8	28	41	3	−28	−43	–	....
Tanzania	738	−204	−575	−419	−359	−254	−297	−509	−79	−1	131	326	....
Togo	742	−160	−190	−97	−194	−25	13	−17	32	37	−2	....	....
Tunisia	744	191	67	527	97	442	386	−138	738	−205	288	139	380
Uganda	746	24	−125	−62	−51	−9	−41	−41	−455	−464	−239	−147	....
Zambia	754	....	....	....	....	....	−932	−671	−654	−520	....	....	....
Zimbabwe	698	−195	226	−86	....	....	....	....	....	....	....	....	....
Asia*	505	22,704	34,895	60,065	38,966	57,278	5,070	38,582	91,176	57,498	99,305	154,271	....
Afghanistan, I.S. of	512	....	....	....	....	....	....	....	....	....	....	....	....
Bangladesh	513	635	698	691	−512	−414	−135	288	−189	−31	−144	497	....
Bhutan	514	....	....	....	....	....	....	....	....	....	....	....	....
Brunei Darussalam	516	....	....	....	....	....	....	....	....	....	....	....	....
Cambodia	522	13	21	36	26	72	34	19	45	92	68	166	....
China,P.R.: Mainland	924	−2,060	1,769	30,453	22,469	31,705	35,857	6,248	8,652	10,693	47,447	75,217	....
China,P.R.:Hong Kong	532	....	....	....	....	....	....	−6,789	10,028	10,044	4,684	−2,377	994
Fiji	819	85	−14	23	93	78	−25	5	−45	....	....	....	....
India	534	1,072	4,211	10,391	−733	3,958	5,321	3,071	6,664	5,979	11,897	16,868	....
Indonesia	536	2,070	594	784	1,573	4,503	−8,137	−3,693	1,972	3,726	−15	4,958	....
Kiribati	826	−17	−5	−6	....	....	....	....	....	....	....	....	....
Korea	542	3,724	3,009	4,614	7,039	1,416	−22,979	25,930	33,260	23,790	13,278	11,770	....
Lao People's Dem.Rep.	544	−122	−137	−178	−151	−158	−369	−254	−333	43	−4	....	....
Malaysia	548	6,618	11,350	−3,160	−1,763	2,513	−3,875	10,018	4,712	−1,009	1,000	3,657	....
Maldives	556	5	−1	5	17	28	22	20	9	−4	−30	8	....
Mongolia	948	−82	15	6	32	−87	7	−53	−19	−86	−79	13	....
Myanmar	518	95	−78	46	−32	−25	31	60	−46	−23	180	....	....
Nepal	558	155	66	63	15	31	169	280	−223	−77	−300	....	....
Pakistan	564	392	428	1,343	−1,204	−780	538	−3,110	−2,516	−2,627	2,197	4,084	2,994
Papua New Guinea	853	−326	−253	−170	−39	202	−177	−221	125	104	129	....	....
Philippines	566	1,689	336	2,327	1,235	4,338	−3,094	1,279	3,650	−376	296	−111	−84
Samoa	862	−13	−9	−4	2	7	11	6	7	....	....	....	....
Singapore	576	6,100	7,578	4,736	8,599	7,396	7,940	2,965	4,194	6,806	−861	1,342	....
Solomon Islands	813	14	−2	−2	−1	18	9	17	−5	....	....	....	....
Sri Lanka	524	202	768	308	239	9	307	224	−95	−361	−259	−331	....
Thailand	578	3,029	3,907	4,169	7,159	2,167	−18,250	−2,696	1,388	−1,806	2,276	5,537	518
Tonga	866	1	−2	....	....	....	....	....	....	....	2	....	....
Vanuatu	846	1	3	−6	5	−5	−2	−7	−23	−19	−10	....	....
Vietnam	582	....	....	....	....	278	328	37	1,310	110	206	448	....
*of which:													
Taiwan Prov.of China	528	1,367	1,541	4,622	−3,931	1,102	−728	4,827	18,593	2,477	17,353	33,664	37,092
Europe	170	−17,061	−11,724	−13,653	19,051	−11,389	3,493	−17,534	9,770	17,298	8,241	28,461	....
Albania	914	−36	49	7	21	56	40	52	107	120	147	36	98
Armenia	911	....	13	−3	30	−45	50	1	5	17	19	64	86
Azerbaijan	912	....	....	....	58	−85	139	−59	133	326	73	34	124
Belarus	913	....	−138	−317	−78	−214	65	−319	20	125	−79	97	50
Bosnia & Herzegovina	963	....	....	....	....	....	−431	−667	−291	402	−499	−270	
Bulgaria	918	269	−322	−216	445	−739	1,145	−94	96	137	373	715	732
Croatia	960	....	188	277	40	1,017	390	161	410	611	1,342	826	1,392
Cyprus	423	−225	145	247	−363	−60	−47	−83	639	−8	612	389	−188
Czech Republic	935	....	3,041	3,474	7,453	−825	−1,758	1,890	1,639	844	1,787	6,618	....
Czechoslovakia	934	−422	....	....	....	....	....	....	....	....	....	....	....
Estonia	939	58	165	17	84	106	216	37	119	128	−42	69	169
Georgia	915	....	....	....	....	....	−62	−103	−14	6	28	−186	−48
Hungary	944	770	2,545	−475	5,398	−1,237	−175	951	2,335	1,052	−84	−1,792	336
Kazakhstan	916	....	....	....	299	159	548	−443	253	570	385	535	1,534
Kyrgyz Republic	917	....	−30	5	−81	−20	46	−73	−50	−70	−32	−11	....
Latvia	941	37	298	57	−33	211	102	63	165	3	314	12	80
Lithuania	946	....	208	113	168	−5	224	427	−179	158	359	463	613
Macedonia, FYR	962	....	....	....	....	−95	−119	43	142	279	86	−122	....
Malta	181	45	135	383	−307	−85	7	191	238	−222	255	288	144
Moldova	921	....	....	13	−175	−103	−188	−353	−116	−2	−27	−49	−43
Poland	964	−4,330	−3,228	1,006	9,835	3,824	3,041	5,924	156	624	−427	648	1,206
Romania	968	−138	−439	171	−480	−582	1,459	−643	239	908	1,535	1,791	1,013
Russia	922	....	....	−19,113	−8,326	−17,218	−6,520	−21,378	−1,704	13,922	11,266	11,563	27,762
Slovak Republic	936	....	14	1,205	1,791	370	99	−478	777	920	....	....	....
Slovenia	961	633	125	647	240	590	1,288	158	−81	178	1,285	1,867	342
Tajikistan	923	....	....	....	....	....	....	....	....	....	....	2	28
Turkey	186	1,484	308	203	4,660	4,544	3,343	441	5,354	−3,934	−12,888	−214	4,087
Turkmenistan	925	....	....	....	....	8	398	....	....	....	....	....	....
Ukraine	926	....	....	−1,200	−1,624	−603	−703	−3,457	−184	573	993	1,231	2,173
Uzbekistan	927	....	....	....	....	....	....	....	....	....	....	....	....

Balance of Payments

Overall Balance
Excluding Reserves Assets, Use of Fund Credit, and Exceptional Financing
Expressed in Millions of US Dollars

		1992	1993	1994	1995	1996	1997	1998	1999	2000	2001	2002	2003
Middle East	405	–1,003	–3,269	–837	5,439	11,614	10,993	–3,916	4,024	19,313	9,890	10,367	....
Bahrain, Kingdom of	419	–90	–113	–48	169	–6	103	–17	25	200	123	35	44
Egypt	469	3,360	18	–1,164	–1,827	–1,725	–635	–1,387	–4,614	–2,030	–1,345	–804	–407
Iran, I.R. of	429	–161	228	908	2,786	2,441	–3,697	–991	451	1,083	....	....	....
Iraq	433	....	....	....	....	....	....	....	....	....	....	....	....
Israel	436	–1,476	–327	–2,111	480	1,206	7,077	–155	–1,039	–592	527	–117	–1,835
Jordan	439	–137	–861	–265	–171	–188	275	–536	1,249	1,827	625	930	1,348
Kuwait	443	1,851	–1,478	50	–141	–25	6	258	918	2,268	2,905	–973	–1,824
Lebanon	446	....	....	....	....	....	....	....	....	....	....	....	....
Libya	672	1,778	–1,716	274	1,701	1,221	1,553	–426	688	....	....	....	....
Oman	449	300	–1,058	–661	–432	189	531	–765	215	2,262	1,034	....	....
Qatar	453	....	....	....	....	....	....	....	....	....	....	....	....
Saudi Arabia	456	–5,664	1,495	–146	1,217	5,749	648	–719	2,815	2,665	–1,909	2,736	1,608
Syrian Arab Republic	463	76	304	566	839	987	449	434	259	814	1,020	1,050	....
United Arab Emirates	466	....	....	....	....	....	....	....	....	....	....	....	....
West Bank and Gaza	487	....	....	....	–	221	158	–53	–35	84	–39	....	....
Yemen, Republic of	474	–1,302	–1,112	–722	–528	–436	4,018	–581	74	1,594	553	425	330
Western Hemisphere	205	15,157	23,537	–9,741	–8,116	25,744	24,917	–18,065	–12,834	15,193	–15,659	–29,014	....
Argentina	213	2,286	11,122	–675	–2,311	3,258	3,331	4,090	2,013	–1,176	–21,405	–16,331	–10,720
Aruba	314	23	33	–3	43	–26	–18	51	3	–16	....	33	....
Bahamas, The	313	–28	19	9	–3	–8	57	119	65	–61	–30	....	....
Barbados	316	25	20	38	42	86	17	–6	36	178	222	–24	....
Belize	339	–	–14	–4	4	21	1	–14	13	–43	–3	–8	....
Bolivia	218	–132	–34	–90	92	268	101	125	27	–39	–36	–343	–55
Brazil	223	10,639	6,890	6,598	12,969	8,682	–8,251	–16,302	–16,765	7,981	–3,418	–11,266	3,586
Chile	228	2,547	428	3,151	1,139	2,594	3,318	–2,191	–747	317	–599	185	–357
Colombia	233	1,274	464	182	–4	1,729	278	–1,398	–312	862	1,225	139	–188
Costa Rica	238	14	–258	–103	216	–69	–193	–504	230	–341	–136	–37	–219
Dominican Republic	243	–64	–544	–511	146	–40	91	11	151	–48	515	–554	–454
Ecuador	248	24	–682	–775	–1,459	–126	–521	–784	–944	–5,697	–258	–221	70
El Salvador	253	–134	59	113	148	165	363	303	208	–45	–178	–123	316
Guatemala	258	–14	200	6	–152	214	230	235	–125	643	474	21	....
Guyana	336	–62	–36	–6	–43	12	–2	–13	22	40	26	15	....
Haiti	263	–6	–23	–50	138	–50	30	34	....	....	....	....	....
Honduras	268	–247	–333	–70	–41	–79	182	–155	–188	–157	–74	–19	–202
Jamaica	343	248	110	358	27	271	–170	44	–136	518	865	–236	....
Mexico	273	1,745	7,232	–17,199	–16,312	1,948	20,460	3,170	4,250	7,126	7,314	7,359	9,817
Netherlands Antilles	353	59	44	–76	60	–72	–6	25	–75	–130	218	60	....
Nicaragua	278	–1,312	–1,019	–1,519	–964	–748	–293	–402	–395	–456	–493	–414	–501
Panama	283	–187	–308	–362	–331	267	343	–380	–148	–327	645	230	–155
Paraguay	288	–19	43	301	45	–47	–216	17	–301	–339	–50	–126	233
Peru	293	–922	–359	1,553	–590	880	2,055	–1,241	–862	–130	432	1,010	561
Suriname	366	–22	13	34	123	–2	19	8	–4	10	78	–19	7
Trinidad and Tobago	369	–104	159	186	84	238	194	80	162	441	502	....	....
Uruguay	298	138	193	109	228	152	400	355	–110	166	304	–3,897	958
Venezuela, Rep. Bol	299	–662	124	–944	–1,444	6,238	3,094	–3,405	1,058	5,958	–1,829	–4,428	5,454
ECCU													
Anguilla	312	1	1	–	–	1	2	2	2	–	4	2	....
Antigua and Barbuda	311	18	–12	8	14	–11	3	9	10	–6	16	8	....
Dominica	321	3	1	–3	8	2	1	4	11	–	5	....	....
Grenada	328	8	–	5	6	–	7	4	5	7	6	31	....
Montserrat	351	–	–	2	1	–	3	14	–11	–4	2	2	....
St. Kitts and Nevis	361	10	3	–1	2	–1	4	11	3	–4	12	10	....
St. Lucia	362	–2	5	–3	6	–6	5	10	4	5	12	5	....
St. Vincent & Grens	364	10	–1	–	–1	–	1	8	4	14	9	–6	....
Memorandum Items													
Oil Exporting Ctys	999	–5,696	–2,498	–6,327	–3,614	17,124	–4,847	–14,165	3,515	38,612	14,142	8,675	....
Non-Oil Develop.Ctys	201	8,994	35,620	31,284	42,276	57,935	47,646	–319	81,131	74,460	90,233	150,874	....

2004, International Monetary Fund : *International Financial Statistics Yearbook*

GDP Volume Measures

Percent Change over Previous Year; Calculated from Indices

		1992	1993	1994	1995	1996	1997	1998	1999	2000	2001	2002	2003
World	001	3.0	2.7	4.6	3.9	4.3	4.1	2.6	3.6	4.6	1.7	1.9	....
Industrial Countries	110	**1.9**	**1.2**	**3.2**	**2.4**	**2.8**	**3.2**	**2.8**	**3.4**	**3.5**	**1.2**	**1.3**	**2.2**
United States	111	3.3	2.7	4.0	2.5	3.7	4.5	4.2	4.4	3.7	.8	1.9	3.0
Canada	156	.9	2.3	4.8	2.8	1.6	4.2	4.1	5.5	5.3	1.9	3.3	1.7
Australia	193	2.0	3.8	4.9	3.5	4.3	3.9	5.2	4.3	3.2	2.5	3.8	3.0
Japan	158	1.0	.2	1.1	1.9	3.5	1.8	−1.2	.2	2.8	.4	−.3	2.5
New Zealand	196	1.0	6.3	5.1	3.7	3.2	2.9	.1	5.2	2.2	4.0	4.1	2.0
Euro Area	163	....	....	....	....	1.3	2.2	2.7	2.4	3.6	3.3	.8	.6
Austria	122	1.3	.5	2.4	1.7	2.0	1.3	3.3	3.6	3.4	.8	1.4	.7
Belgium	124	1.3	−.7	3.3	2.3	.8	3.9	2.1	10.3	3.7	.7	.7	1.1
Finland	172	−3.3	−1.1	4.0	3.8	4.0	6.3	5.3	3.2	5.1	1.1	2.3	1.9
France	132	1.2	−.9	1.8	1.9	1.1	1.9	3.5	3.1	3.8	2.1	1.2	.5
Germany	134	2.2	−1.1	2.3	1.7	.8	1.5	1.8	2.1	2.9	.8	.2	−.1
Greece	174	.7	−1.6	2.0	2.1	2.4	3.6	3.4	3.6	4.1	4.2	3.9	4.3
Ireland	178	3.3	2.7	5.8	9.7	8.0	10.8	8.6	11.6	9.9	6.0	6.1	3.7
Italy	136	.8	−.9	2.2	2.9	1.1	2.0	1.8	1.6	3.0	1.8	.4	.3
Luxembourg	137	....	....	....	....	3.6	9.1	5.9	5.7	9.5	1.6	....	....
Netherlands	138	2.0	.6	6.7	3.0	3.0	3.8	3.1	5.3	3.5	1.2	.2	−.7
Portugal	182	1.9	−1.4	2.5	2.9	3.2	3.5	3.5	8.5	3.7	1.6	.4	−1.4
Spain	184	.7	−1.2	2.3	2.7	2.4	3.5	3.8	4.9	4.2	2.8	2.0	2.4
Denmark	128	.6	—	5.5	2.8	2.5	3.0	2.5	2.6	2.8	1.6	1.0	.5
Iceland	176	−3.3	.8	4.0	.1	5.2	4.7	5.6	4.2	5.6	2.7	−.5	4.0
Norway	142	3.3	2.7	5.3	4.4	5.3	5.2	2.6	2.1	2.8	2.7	1.4	.3
Sweden	144	−1.7	6.8	4.2	4.1	1.3	2.4	3.6	−1.0	4.3	.9	2.1	1.6
Switzerland	146	−.3	−.8	1.0	.1	−.7	−10.3	2.4	1.5	3.2	.9	.2	19.7
United Kingdom	112	.2	2.3	4.4	2.8	2.7	3.3	3.1	2.8	3.8	2.1	1.7	2.1
Developing Countries	200	**4.9**	**5.4**	**6.7**	**6.1**	**6.4**	**5.4**	**2.4**	**3.9**	**5.9**	**2.4**	**2.7**	**....**
Africa	605	−1.3	−.2	2.8	2.3	5.3	2.5	2.7	1.7	2.7	4.0	2.4	3.4
Benin	638	4.0	3.5	4.4	4.6	5.5	5.7	5.0	4.7	5.8	5.0	6.0	....
Botswana	616	6.2	−.2	4.0	3.2	5.6	5.6	8.1	4.1	6.6	8.5	2.2	6.7
Burkina Faso	748	16.4	−1.5	2.1	6.5	9.9	6.8	8.5	3.7	1.6	6.8	4.6	6.5
Burundi	618	1.8	−7.0	−3.1	−7.0	−8.6	.4	4.5	....	....	....	....	....
Cameroon	622	−3.0	−3.2	−2.6	3.3	5.0	5.0	....	....	....	....	....	....
Congo, Dem. Rep. of	636	−10.5	−13.5	−3.9	.7	−1.1	−5.4	−1.7	−4.3	−6.9	.9	....	....
Congo, Rep. of	634	1.7	−1.0	−5.5	2.2	4.3	−.5	3.7	−3.2	8.0	....	....	....
Côte d'Ivoire	662	−.1	−.4	2.0	7.1	6.9	6.6	6.0	....	....	....	....	....
Gambia, The	648	.4	6.6	3.6	−4.1	....	....	....	....	....	....	....	....
Ghana	652	3.9	4.9	3.3	4.0	4.6	4.2	....	....	....	....	....	....
Guinea-Bissau	654	1.8	2.5	5.0	3.7	4.8	4.8	....	....	....	....	....	....
Kenya	664	−.8	.4	2.6	4.4	4.1	3.0	.3	−3.6	7.1	2.4	−8.2	....
Lesotho	666	4.6	3.5	3.4	4.4	10.0	8.1	−4.6	.2	1.3	3.2	3.8	....
Madagascar	674	1.2	2.1	−.1	1.7	2.1	3.7	3.9	4.7	4.7	6.0	−12.7	9.8
Malawi	676	−7.9	10.8	−11.6	13.8	10.4	7.0	2.2	3.6	2.3	....	....	....
Mali	678	8.1	−3.2	2.6	6.6	3.6	....	....	....	....	....	....	....
Mauritius	684	6.2	5.0	4.2	4.4	5.6	5.8	6.0	2.9	9.2	5.3	1.9	4.3
Morocco	686	−4.0	−1.0	10.4	−6.2	11.8	−2.2	7.7	−.1	1.0	6.3	3.2	5.2
Mozambique	688	−8.6	6.8	7.0	3.3	6.8	11.1	12.6	7.5	1.5	13.0	8.3	....
Namibia	728	7.4	−2.0	7.3	4.1	3.2	4.2	3.3	3.4	3.3	....	....	....
Niger	692	.7	1.0	2.5	1.9	3.9	2.4	9.9	−1.6	−.2	5.9	....	....
Nigeria	694	2.9	2.6	1.2	2.2	3.9	3.2	2.3	2.8	3.8	4.2	....	....
Rwanda	714	6.9	−8.4	−49.7	34.2	14.9	14.3	9.2	6.5	6.7	5.9	9.5	2.4
Senegal	722	2.2	−2.2	2.9	5.2	5.1	3.3	4.4	6.2	3.0	4.7	....	....
Seychelles	718	7.2	6.2	−.8	−.8	4.9	4.6	5.5	2.9	1.4	1.0	....	....
Sierra Leone	724	−19.0	1.4	−1.9	−8.0	6.1	−17.6	−.9	−8.1	3.8	5.4	6.6	7.0
South Africa	199	−2.1	1.2	3.2	3.1	4.3	2.6	.8	2.0	3.5	2.7	3.6	1.9
Swaziland	734	1.3	3.3	3.4	3.8	3.9	3.8	3.3	3.5	2.0	1.8	....	....
Tanzania	738	....	....	....	....	....	....	....	....	....	....	....	....
Togo	742	−3.8	−16.6	16.8	6.9	9.7	4.3	−2.2	3.0	−.9	.6	2.9	....
Tunisia	744	7.8	2.2	3.2	2.4	7.1	5.4	4.8	6.1	4.7	4.9	1.7	5.6
Uganda	746	4.6	7.1	10.6	9.6	5.9	....	....	....	....	....	....	....
Zambia	754	−1.7	6.8	−3.5	−2.3	6.5	3.5	....	....	....	....	....	....
Zimbabwe	698	−8.4	2.1	5.8	.2	9.7	1.4	.8	−4.1	−6.8	....	....	....
Asia	505	**8.8**	**8.7**	**9.6**	**8.8**	**8.2**	**6.2**	**2.3**	**6.2**	**6.8**	**....**	**....**	**....**
Bangladesh	513	5.0	4.6	4.1	4.9	4.6	5.4	5.2	4.9	5.9	5.3	4.4	5.3
China, P.R.: Mainland	924	14.2	13.5	12.7	10.5	9.6	8.8	7.8	7.1	8.0	....	....	....
China, P.R.: Hong Kong	532	6.6	6.3	5.5	3.9	4.3	5.1	−5.0	3.4	10.2	.5	1.9	3.2
India	534	5.1	5.9	7.3	7.3	7.8	4.8	6.5	6.1	4.4	5.8	4.0	8.1
Indonesia	536	6.5	6.5	7.5	8.2	7.8	4.7	−13.1	.8	4.9	3.4	3.7	....
Korea	542	5.4	5.5	8.3	8.9	7.0	4.7	−6.9	9.5	8.5	3.8	7.0	3.1
Lao People's Democratic Rep.	544	7.0	4.6	9.5	7.0	6.9	6.9	4.0	7.3	5.8	5.8	5.9	5.9
Malaysia	548	8.9	9.9	9.2	9.8	10.0	7.3	−7.4	6.1	8.3	.4	−.7	10.4
Maldives	556	6.5	5.4	7.5	7.8	9.1	10.2	8.2	7.4	4.6	2.1	....	....
Mongolia	948	−9.5	−3.0	2.3	6.3	2.4	4.0	3.5	3.2	1.1	1.0	4.0	5.0
Myanmar	518	9.7	6.0	7.5	6.9	6.4	5.7	5.8	10.9	6.2	....	....	....
Nepal	558	4.8	2.9	8.3	2.7	5.7	5.0	3.3	4.5	6.1	4.7	−.3	2.7
Pakistan	564	7.8	1.9	3.9	5.1	5.0	−.1	2.6	3.7	4.3	2.4	3.0	5.8
Papua New Guinea	853	13.8	18.2	5.9	−3.3	7.7	−3.9	−1.1	4.6	....	....	....	....

GDP Volume Measures

		1992	1993	1994	1995	1996	1997	1998	1999	2000	2001	2002	2003
Asia(Cont.)													
Philippines	566	.3	2.1	4.4	4.7	5.8	5.2	−.6	3.4	4.0	3.4	5.5	4.9
Samoa	862	−2.3	2.4	−3.7	6.8	6.1	1.6	....	....	....	....	....	....
Singapore	576	6.7	12.3	11.4	8.0	8.1	8.5	−.9	6.8	9.7	−1.9	2.2	1.1
Sri Lanka	524	4.3	6.9	5.6	5.5	3.8	6.3	4.7	4.3	6.0	−1.5	4.0	5.9
Thailand	578	8.1	8.3	9.0	9.2	5.9	−1.4	−10.5	4.4	4.6	1.8	5.4	7.2
Tonga	866	−3.8	−.1	4.8	....	....	....	....	....	....	....	....	....
Vanuatu	846	−.7	4.5	2.5	3.2	8.7	4.9	4.3	−3.2	2.7	−2.1	−2.8	....
Europe	170	**−2.5**	**1.4**	**−**	**5.1**	**4.5**	**4.0**	**2.6**	**.2**	**7.6**	**−**	**4.5**	**4.8**
Armenia	911	....	....	....	6.9	5.9	3.3	7.3	3.3	....	....	....	....
Belarus	913	−9.6	−7.6	−11.7	−10.4	2.8	11.4	8.4	3.4	5.8	4.7	5.0	6.8
Bulgaria	918	−7.3	−1.5	1.8	2.9	−10.1	−6.9	....	....	....	....	....	....
Croatia	960	−11.7	−.9	.6	1.7	4.3	6.8	2.5	−.9	2.9	3.8	5.2	4.3
Kazakhstan	916	....	....	....	−8.2	.5	1.7	−1.9	2.7	9.8	13.5	9.8	9.2
Cyprus	423	9.4	.7	5.9	6.5	1.9	2.3	4.8	4.7	5.0	4.0	2.0	2.0
Czech Republic	935	−.5	.1	2.2	5.9	4.3	−.8	−1.0	.5	3.3	3.1	2.0	2.9
Estonia	939	....	....	−1.6	4.5	4.5	10.5	5.2	−.1	7.8	6.4	7.2	5.1
Hungary	944	−3.1	−.6	2.9	1.5	1.3	4.6	4.9	4.2	5.2	3.8	3.5	2.9
Kyrgyz Republic	917	−13.9	−15.5	−20.1	−5.4	7.1	9.9	2.1	3.6	5.5	5.3	....	6.7
Latvia	941	−34.9	−14.9	.6	−.8	3.8	8.3	4.7	3.3	6.9	8.0	6.4	−.7
Lithuania	946	−21.3	−16.2	−9.8	3.3	4.7	7.0	7.3	−1.7	3.9	6.4	6.8	9.0
Malta	181	4.7	4.2	3.0	9.3	4.0	4.9	3.4	4.1	6.3	−1.1	2.3	−1.7
Poland	964	2.6	3.8	5.2	7.0	6.0	6.8	4.8	4.1	15.8	1.0	1.6	....
Romania	968	−8.7	1.5	3.9	7.1	3.9	−6.1	−4.8	−1.2	2.1	5.7	5.0	4.9
San Marino	135	....	....	....	....	....	....	7.5	9.0	2.2	7.7	−1.7	....
Slovak Republic	936	....	7.2	6.2	5.8	6.1	4.6	4.2	1.5	2.0	3.8	4.4	4.2
Slovenia	961	1.0	2.8	5.3	4.1	3.6	4.8	3.6	5.6	3.9	2.7	3.4	2.3
Turkey	186	6.0	8.0	−5.5	7.2	7.0	7.5	3.1	−4.7	7.2	−7.3	7.8	5.9
Middle East	405	**4.4**	**1.3**	**3.0**	**3.5**	**4.6**	**4.3**	**4.0**	**1.9**	**5.3**	**2.5**	**3.7**	....
Bahrain	419	6.7	12.9	−.3	3.9	4.1	3.1	4.8	4.3	5.3	−	5.2	....
Egypt	469	4.5	2.9	4.0	4.6	5.0	5.5	7.5	6.1	5.4	3.5	3.2	3.2
Iran, I.R. of	429	4.1	−2.1	1.7	3.3	6.7	5.4	2.7	1.9	5.1	3.7	7.5	....
Israel	436	6.6	3.2	6.8	7.1	5.2	3.5	3.7	2.5	8.0	−.9	−.7	1.3
Jordan	439	17.0	4.5	5.0	6.2	2.1	3.3	3.0	3.1	4.2	4.3	....	....
Kuwait	443	−7.3	33.8	8.6	1.4	−2.7	1.2	3.2	−4.9	7.5	−1.0	....	....
Oman	449	8.5	6.1	3.8	4.8	2.9	6.2	2.7	−.2	5.5	9.3	−	....
Saudi Arabia	456	2.8	−.6	.5	.5	1.4	2.6	2.8	−.7	4.9	.5	.1	7.2
Syrian Arab Rep.	463	13.5	5.2	7.7	5.8	7.3	2.5	7.6	−2.0	.6	3.4	3.2	....
United Arab Emirates	466	2.7	....	....	....	....	....	....	....	....	....	....	....
Yemen Republic	474	10.7	7.9	3.0	12.2	8.0	6.3	6.8	2.4	4.7	4.7	3.9	4.0
Western Hemisphere	205	**3.2**	**4.0**	**4.9**	**1.8**	**3.8**	**5.2**	**2.1**	**.2**	**4.0**	**.6**	**−.4**	....
ECCU	309	3.9	2.6	3.0	.7	2.7	3.2	4.0	4.1	2.8	−1.3	.2	....
Antigua and Barbuda	311	.8	5.4	6.3	−4.2	6.6	5.2	3.3	3.7	....	....	....	....
Anguilla	312	7.1	7.5	7.1	−4.1	3.5	9.2	5.2	8.7	−.3	2.1	−3.2	....
Argentina	213	9.6	5.7	5.8	−2.8	5.5	8.1	3.9	−3.4	−.8	−4.4	−10.9	8.7
Bahamas, The	313	−5.8	−2.1	2.0	1.1	....	....	....	....	....	....	....	....
Barbados	316	−7.2	.8	4.5	2.5	3.1	3.3	4.4	3.6	2.4	−3.4	−.4	2.2
Belize	339	8.2	4.3	2.5	4.2	1.2	2.2	4.6	11.6	15.9	2.0	5.5	....
Bolivia	218	1.6	4.3	4.7	4.7	4.4	5.0	5.0	.4	2.3	1.5	2.8	2.5
Brazil	223	−.5	4.9	5.9	4.2	2.7	3.3	.1	.8	4.4	1.3	1.9	....
Chile	228	12.3	7.0	5.7	10.6	7.4	6.6	3.2	−.8	4.5	3.4	2.2	3.3
Colombia	233	4.4	5.7	5.1	5.2	2.1	3.4	.6	−4.2	2.9	1.5	1.8	3.9
Costa Rica	238	9.2	7.4	4.7	3.9	.9	5.6	8.4	8.2	1.8	1.0	2.9	6.5
Dominica	321	4.0	−.3	1.4	2.0	3.5	2.5	3.1	.6	.1	−4.3	....	....
Dominican Republic	243	8.0	3.0	4.7	4.3	7.2	8.2	7.4	8.0	7.3	3.2	4.1	....
Ecuador	248	3.6	2.0	4.3	2.3	2.0	3.4	.4	−7.3	2.8	5.1	3.4	3.5
El Salvador	253	7.5	7.4	6.0	6.4	1.7	4.2	3.7	3.4	2.2	1.7	2.2	1.8
Grenada	328	.6	....	....	....	....	....	....	....	....	....	....	....
Guatemala	258	4.8	3.9	4.0	5.0	2.9	4.4	5.0	3.8	3.6	2.3	2.3	2.1
Guyana	336	7.8	8.2	....	....	....	....	....	....	....	....	....	....
Haiti	263	−13.2	−2.4	−8.3	4.4	2.7	2.7	2.2	2.7	.9	−1.0	−.5	.4
Honduras	268	5.6	6.2	−1.3	4.1	3.6	5.0	2.9	−1.9	5.7	2.6	2.7	3.2
Jamaica	343	2.6	2.4	1.0	2.3	.4	−1.1	−1.2	.9	.8	1.5	1.1	....
Mexico	273	3.6	2.0	4.4	−6.2	5.2	6.8	5.0	3.6	6.6	−	.7	1.2
Montserrat	351	2.7	2.5	.9	−7.6	−21.4	−20.0	−10.1	−12.6	−3.0	−2.8	4.6	....
Nicaragua	278	.4	−.4	3.3	5.9	6.3	4.0	3.7	7.0	4.2	3.0	1.0	2.3
Panama	283	8.2	5.5	2.8	1.8	7.4	6.4	7.4	4.0	2.7	.6	2.2	4.1
Paraguay	288	1.8	4.1	3.1	4.7	1.3	2.6	−.4	.5	−.4	2.7	−2.3	....
Peru	293	−.4	4.8	12.8	8.6	2.5	6.8	−.6	.9	2.8	.3	4.9	....
St. Kitts and Nevis	361	3.3	6.7	5.1	3.7	6.5	6.8	1.1	3.5	3.4	2.2	....	....
St. Lucia	362	6.5	2.6	1.3	1.1	3.1	−1.2	4.7	4.7	−.1	−5.5	....	....
St. Vincent & Grenadines	364	5.9	2.4	−2.0	7.6	1.5	3.7	5.1	4.1	1.9	1.2	....	....
Suriname	366	5.8	−4.5	−.8	....	....	1.3	3.0	−2.6	12.9	−3.6	2.3	3.3
Trinidad and Tobago	369	−1.6	−1.4	3.6	4.0	5.2	6.9	7.7	10.6	11.3	2.6	....	....
Uruguay	298	7.9	2.7	7.3	−1.4	5.6	5.0	4.5	−2.8	−1.4	−3.4	−11.0	2.5
Venezuela, Rep. Bol.	299	6.1	.3	−2.3	4.0	−.2	6.4	.2	−6.1	3.2	2.8	−8.9	....

2004, International Monetary Fund : *International Financial Statistics Yearbook*

GDP Volume Measures

		1992	1993	1994	1995	1996	1997	1998	1999	2000	2001	2002	2003
		Percent Change over Previous Year; Calculated from Indices											
Memorandum Items													
Oil Exporting Countries	999	4.7	2.6	3.5	4.9	5.1	4.6	−4.5	−	4.7	3.1	2.3	....
Non-Oil Developing Countries	201	4.9	5.7	7.2	6.2	6.6	5.5	3.3	4.4	6.1	2.2	2.8	....

Indices

		1992	1993	1994	1995	1996	1997	1998	1999	2000	2001	2002	2003
		Index Numbers: 2000=100											
World	001	74.2	76.2	79.8	82.9	86.4	89.9	92.3	95.6	100.0	101.7	103.6	....
Industrial Countries	110	80.2	81.1	83.7	85.7	88.1	90.9	93.4	96.6	100.0	101.2	102.5	104.8
Developing Countries	200	66.3	69.8	74.5	79.1	84.1	88.7	90.8	94.4	100.0	102.4	105.2	....
Africa	605	82.2	82.1	84.4	86.3	91.0	93.2	95.7	97.4	100.0	104.0	106.4	110.0
Asia	505	57.9	62.9	69.0	75.0	81.2	86.2	88.2	93.7	100.0	....	....	....
Europe	170	78.0	79.1	79.1	83.2	86.9	90.4	92.7	92.9	100.0	100.0	104.4	109.4
Middle East	405	76.0	77.1	79.3	82.2	86.0	89.6	93.3	95.0	100.0	102.5	106.3	....
Western Hemisphere	205	77.5	80.6	84.6	86.1	89.3	94.0	96.0	96.2	100.0	100.6	100.2	....

(THIS PAGE INTENTIONALLY LEFT BLANK)

(THIS PAGE INTENTIONALLY LEFT BLANK)

CONTENTS

Introduction v

World Tables

Exchange Rates (Table A) 2
Exchange Rates (Table D) 3
Fund Account: Position to Date 6
Financing Components: Outstanding Obligations to the Fund 9
Purchases 12
Repurchases 14
Loan Disbursements 16
Repayments of Loans 18
Total Fund Credit & Loans Outstdg. 20
Use of Fund Credit (GRA) 22
Total Reserves minus Gold 24
Nongold Reserves/Imports 27
SDRs 30
Reserve Position in the Fund 33
Foreign Exchange 36
Gold (Million Fine Troy Ounces) 39
Total Reserves 42
Reserve Money 45
Money 48
Money plus Quasi-Money 51
Ratio of Reserve Money to Money plus Quasi-Money 54
Income Velocity of Money plus Quasi-Money .. 57
National Interest Rates 60
International Interest Rates 73
Real Effective Exchange Rate Indices 74
Production and Labor Indices 75
Producer Prices/Wholesale Prices 77
Consumer Prices 79
Exports, f.o.b. 82
Imports, c.i.f. 85
Export Unit Values/Export Prices 88
Import Unit Values/Import Prices 89
Terms of Trade 90
Balance of Payments 92
GDP Volume Measures 113
GDP Deflators 116
Gross Capital Formation as Percentage of GDP 119
Final Consumption Expenditure as Percentage of GDP 121
Commodity Prices 123

Country Tables

Albania 130
Algeria 132
Angola 134
Anguilla 136
Antigua and Barbuda 138
Argentina 140
Armenia 144
Aruba 147
Australia 149
Austria 153
Azerbaijan 157
Bahamas, The 160
Bahrain, Kingdom of 163
Bangladesh 167
Barbados 170
Belarus 173
Belgium 176
Belize 181
Benin 184
Bhutan 187
Bolivia 189
Bosnia & Herzegovina 194
Botswana 196
Brazil 199
Bulgaria 204
Burkina Faso 207
Burundi 210
Cambodia 214
Cameroon 217
Canada 220
Cape Verde 224
CEMAC 227
Central African Rep. 228
Chad 230
Chile 232
China,P.R.- Mainland 236
China,P.R.:Hong Kong 239
China,P.R.:Macao 242
Colombia 244
Comoros 248
Congo, Dem. Rep. of 250
Congo, Republic of 252
Costa Rica 255
Côte d'Ivoire 259
Croatia 262
Cyprus 266
Czech Republic 269
Denmark 272
Djibouti 276
Dominica 278
Dominican Republic 280
ECCU 283
Ecuador 285
Egypt 289
El Salvador 292
Equatorial Guinea 296
Eritrea 298
Estonia 300
Ethiopia 303
Euro Area 306
Fiji 309
Finland 312
France 316
Gabon 320
Gambia, The 322
Georgia 324
Germany 327
Ghana 331
Greece 334
Grenada 338
Guatemala 340
Guinea 343
Guinea-Bissau 345
Guyana 347
Haiti 350
Honduras 353
Hungary 356
Iceland 360
India 363
Indonesia 366
Iran, I.R. of 370
Iraq 373
Ireland 374
Israel 378
Italy 381
Jamaica 385
Japan 388
Jordan 392
Kazakhstan 395
Kenya 398
Korea 401
Kuwait 405
Kyrgyz Republic 408
Lao People's Dem.Rep 411
Latvia 413
Lebanon 416
Lesotho 418
Liberia 421
Libya 422
Lithuania 424
Luxembourg 427
Macedonia, FYR 431
Madagascar 434
Malawi 437
Malaysia 440
Maldives 444
Mali 447
Malta 450
Mauritania 453
Mauritius 455
Mexico 458
Micronesia, Fed.Sts. 462
Moldova 463
Mongolia 466
Montserrat 468
Morocco 470
Mozambique 473
Myanmar 475
Namibia 478
Nepal 482
Netherlands 484
Netherlands Antilles 488
New Zealand 490
Nicaragua 494
Niger 497
Nigeria 499
Norway 502
Oman 506
Pakistan 508
Panama 511
Papua New Guinea 514
Paraguay 517
Peru 521
Philippines 525
Poland 529
Portugal 532
Qatar 536
Romania 538
Russia 541
Rwanda 545
St. Kitts and Nevis 548
St. Lucia 551
St. Vincent & Grens. 553
Samoa 556
San Marino 558
São Tomé & Príncipe 560
Saudi Arabia 562
Senegal 565
Seychelles 568
Sierra Leone 571
Singapore 574
Slovak Republic 578
Slovenia 581
Solomon Islands 585
South Africa 588
Spain 592
Sri Lanka 596
Sudan 599
Suriname 601
Swaziland 603
Sweden 606
Switzerland 610
Syrian Arab Republic 614
Tajikistan 616
Tanzania 618
Thailand 621
Togo 625
Tonga 628
Trinidad and Tobago 631
Tunisia 635
Turkey 639
Uganda 643
Ukraine 646
United Arab Emirates 649
United Kingdom 651
United States 654
Uruguay 659
Vanuatu 663
Venezuela, Rep. Bol. 666
Vietnam 670
WAEMU 672
Yemen, Republic of 674
Zambia 677
Zimbabwe 680

SELECTION OF STATISTICAL PUBLICATIONS

International Financial Statistics (IFS)
Acknowledged as a standard source of statistics on all aspects of international and domestic finance, *IFS* publishes, for most countries of the world, current data on exchange rates, international liquidity, international banking, money and banking, interest rates, prices, production, international transactions (including balance of payments and international investment position), government finance, and national accounts. Information is presented in tables for specific countries and in tables for area and world aggregates. *IFS* is published monthly and annually. *Price:* Subscription price is US$495 a year (US$247 to university faculty and students) for twelve monthly issues and the yearbook. Single copy price is US$65 for a monthly issue and US$95 for a yearbook issue.

Balance of Payments Statistics Yearbook (BOPSY)
Issued in three parts, this annual publication contains balance of payments and international investment position data. Part 1 provides detailed tables on balance of payments statistics for approximately 165 countries and international investment position data for 89 countries. Part 2 presents tables of regional and world totals of major balance of payments components. Part 3 contains descriptions of methodologies, compilation practices, and data sources used by reporting countries Price: US$98.

Direction of Trade Statistics (DOTS)
Quarterly issues of this publication provide, for about 156 countries, tables with current data (or estimates) on the value of imports from and exports to their most important trading partners. In addition, similar summary tables for the world, industrial countries, and developing countries are included. The yearbook provides, for the most recent seven years, detailed trade data by country for approximately 186 countries, the world, and major areas. *Price:* Subscription price is US$155 a year (US$129 to university faculty and students) for the quarterly issues and the yearbook. Price for a quarterly issue only is US$25, the yearbook only is US$70, and a guide only is US$12.50.

Government Finance Statistics Yearbook (GFSY)
This annual publication provides detailed data on transactions in revenue, expense, net acquisition of assets and liabilities, other economic flows, and balances of assets and liabilities of general government and its subsectors. The data are compiled according to the framework of the 2001 *Government Finanace Statistics Manual,* which provides for several summary measures of government fiscal performance. *Price:* US$80.

CD-ROM Subscriptions
International Financial Statistics (IFS), Balance of Payments Statistics (BOPS), Direction of Trade Statistics (DOTS), and *Government Finance Statistics (GFS)* are available on CD-ROM by annual subscription. The CD-ROMs incorporate a Windows-based browser facility, as well as a flat file of the database in scientific notation. *Price of each subscription:* US$450 a year for single-user PC license (US$225 for university faculty and students). Network and redistribution licenses are negotiated on a case-by-case basis. Please contact Publication Services for information.

Subscription Packages

Combined Subscription Package
The combined subscription package includes all issues of *IFS, DOTS, BOPSY, GFSY,* and *Staff Papers,* the Fund's economic journal. *Combined subscription price:* US$749 a year. Airspeed delivery available at additional cost; please inquire.

Combined Statistical Yearbook Subscription
This subscription comprises *BOPSY, GFSY, IFSY,* and *DOTSY* at a combined rate of US$265. Because of different publication dates of the four yearbooks, it may take up to one year to service an order. Airspeed delivery available at additional cost; please inquire.

IFS on the Internet
The Statistics Department of the Fund is pleased to make available to subscribers the *International Financial Statistics (IFS)* database through an easy-to-use online service. The *IFS* database contains time series data beginning in 1948. The browser software provides a familiar and easy-to-use Windows interface for browsing the database, selecting series of interest, displaying the selected series in a spreadsheet format, and saving the selected series for transfer to other software systems, such as Microsoft Excel®. Single user license price for the *IFS Online Service* is $495, and $247 for academic users. Dependent on certain criteria, a range of scaled discounts is available. For full details of qualification for these discounts and online payment, please visit http://www.imfstatistics.org or email us directly at publications@imf.org.

Address orders to
Publication Services, IMF, Washington, DC 20431, USA
Telephone: (202) 623-7430   Telefax: (202) 623-7201   E-mail: publications@imf.org
Internet: http://www.imf.org

Note: Prices include the cost of delivery by surface mail. Enhanced delivery is available for an additional charge.

INTRODUCTION

Table of Contents

1. Overview
2. Exchange rates and exchange rate arrangements
3. Fund accounts
4. International liquidity
5. Money and banking
6. Interest rates
7. Prices, production, and labor
8. International transactions
9. Government finance
10. National accounts and population
11. World tables
12. Country codes and *IFS* line numbers
13. Symbols, conventions, and abbreviations
14. CD-ROM and Internet account subscriptions

1. Overview

The Fund's principal statistical publication, *International Financial Statistics (IFS)*, has been published monthly since January 1948. In 1961, the monthly was supplemented by a yearbook, and in 1991 and 2000, respectively, *IFS* was introduced on CD-ROM and the Internet.

IFS contains country tables for most Fund members, as well as for Aruba, the Central African Economic and Monetary Community (CEMAC), the euro area, the Netherlands Antilles, the West African Economic Monetary Union (WAEMU), and some nonsovereign territorial entities for which statistics are provided internationally on a separate basis. Also, selected series are drawn from the country tables and published in area and world tables. The country tables normally include data on a country's exchange rates, Fund position, international liquidity, money and banking accounts, interest rates, prices, production, international transactions, government accounts, national accounts, and population. Selected series, including data on Fund accounts, international reserves, and international trade, are drawn from the country tables and published in area and world tables as well.

The monthly printed issue of *IFS* reports current monthly, quarterly, and annual data, while the yearbook reports 30 observations of annual data. Most annual data on the CD-ROM and Internet begin in 1948; quarterly and monthly data generally begin in 1957; most balance of payments data begin in 1970.

The following sections describe conceptual and technical aspects of various data published in *IFS*. The reader will find more detailed descriptions—about coverage, deviations from the standard methodologies, and discontinuities in the data—in the footnotes in the individual country and world tables in the monthly and yearbook issues of *IFS*, in the Print_Me file on the CD-ROM, and in the PDF pages on the Internet. (Where references are made in this introduction to notes in monthly issues, they refer to notes files on the CD-ROM and Internet as well.)

2. Exchange Rates and Exchange Rate Arrangements

Exchange rates in *IFS* are classified into three broad categories, reflecting the role of the authorities in determining the rates and/or the multiplicity of the exchange rates in a country. The three categories are the **market rate**, describing an exchange rate determined largely by market forces; the **official rate**, describing an exchange rate determined by the authorities—sometimes in a flexible manner; and the **principal, secondary,** or **tertiary rate**, for countries maintaining multiple exchange arrangements.

In *IFS*, exchange rates are expressed in time series of national currency units per SDR (the unit of account for the Fund) and national currency units per U.S. dollar, or vice versa.

The exchange rates in SDRs are classified and coded as follows:

Series **aa** shows the end-of-period national currency value of the SDR, and series **ac** shows the end-of-period SDR value of the national currency unit.

Series **sa, sb, sc,** and **sd**—provided on the country table for the United States—show the SDR value of U.S. dollars. Series **sa** and **sc** refer to end-of-period values of U.S. dollars per SDR and SDRs per U.S. dollar, respectively, while series **sb** and **sd** are geometric averages of values within the period.

The exchange rates in U.S. dollars are classified and coded as follows:

Series **ae** shows end-of-period national currency units per U.S. dollar, and series **ag** shows end-of-period U.S. dollars per unit of national currency.

Series **rf** shows period-average national currency units per U.S. dollar, and series **rh** shows period-average U.S. dollars per unit of national currency. Series **rf** and **rh** data are the monthly average of market rates or official rates of the reporting country. If those are not available, they are the monthly average rates in New York. Or if the latter are not available, they are estimates based on simple averages of the end-of-month market rates quoted in the reporting country.

The country tables contain two of the U.S. dollar series—either **ae** and **rf** or **ag** and **rh**—depending on the form in which the exchange rate is quoted.

Reciprocal relationships are the following:

The end-of-period rates **aa** and **ac, ae** and **ag,** and **sa** and **sc** are reciprocals of each other. The period-average SDR rates in terms of the U.S. dollar (**sb** and **sd**) are also reciprocals of each other, because they are calculated as geometric averages. Other period average rates (**rf** and **rh**) are calculated as arithmetic averages and are not reciprocals.

The relationship between trade figures in *IFS* and exchange rates is the following:

All trade figures in *IFS* are converted from national currency values to U.S. dollars and from U.S. dollar values to national currency, using series **rf**. Conversions are based on the data available for the shortest period, and these data are summed to obtain data for longer periods. Conversion is based on longer period rates of only the difference, if any, between the longer period data and the sum of the shorter period data. The country table notes in the monthly issues identify the exchange rates used.

For members maintaining dual or multiple exchange rate systems, which often reflect wide ranges of exchange rates in effect in a country, lines **w**, **x**, and **y** are presented. Notes on the tables in the monthly issues for these countries describe the current exchange rate systems and identify the exchange rates shown.

European Currency Unit (ECU) and the Euro

For periods before January 1999, the exchange rate sections in tables for members of the European Union (EU)—Austria, Belgium, Denmark, Finland, France, Germany, Greece, Ireland, Italy, Luxembourg, the Netherlands, Portugal, Spain, Sweden, and the United Kingdom—Norway and the United States contain a time series on the value of the European currency unit (ECU).

The ECU was issued by the European Monetary Institute (EMI)—successor to the European Monetary Cooperation Fund on January 1, 1994—against gold and foreign exchange deposits by the central banks of the EU member states. The ECU was defined as a basket of currencies of the EU member countries. The share of each currency in the basket was based on the gross national product and foreign trade of the country issuing that currency. The equivalent of the ECU was calculated—first in U.S. dollars and then in the currencies of the member countries—by using representative market exchange rates for the U.S. dollar, as reported by the member countries. In *IFS*, series **ea** and **ec** refer to end-of-period values of national currency units per ECU and ECUs per unit of national currency, respectively; series **eb** and **ed** are the arithmetic averages of values within the period.

On January 1, 1999, the euro replaced the ECU, at a rate of one euro per one ECU. Irrevocable conversion factors for the euro, adopted for the eleven countries in the euro area, fixed the central rates between the euro and the currencies participating in the exchange rate mechanism. The irrevocable fixed factors, legally mandated to have six significant digits, are the following: Austria (S 13.7603), Belgium (BF 40.3399), Finland (Fmk 5.94573), France (F 6.55957), Germany (DM 1.95583), Ireland (IR£0.787564), Italy (Lit 1936.27), Luxembourg (Lux F 40.3399), the Netherlands (f. 2.20371), Portugal (Esc 200.482), and Spain (Pta 166.386).

An accord established compulsory intervention rates for the Danish krone (± 2.25 percent around the euro central rate) and the Greek drachma (± 15 percent around the euro central rate) from January 1, 1999 onwards. Greece joined the euro area on January 1, 2001, adopting the euro as its currency, with a conversion factor of 340.750 drachmas per euro.

In addition, from January 1, 1999 onwards, the member countries of the Bank of Central African States and the Central Bank of West African States changed the peg of their currencies from the French franc to the euro, at a rate of CFAF 655.957 per euro. A few other countries also have pegged their currencies to the euro.

On January 1, 2002, euro banknotes and coins were issued. National currencies continued to be accepted in trade for a short transition period that ended in all member countries by the end of February 2002. The statistical treatment of euro banknotes and coins and outstanding national currencies is described in the section *European Economic and Monetary Union* in Section 5—Money and Banking.

Effective Exchange Rates

The country tables, euro area tables, and world tables provide measures of effective exchange rates, compiled by the IMF's Research Department, Policy Development and Review Department, Statistics Department, and area departments.

A **nominal** effective exchange rate index represents the ratio (expressed on the base 2000=100) of an index of a currency's period-average exchange rate to a weighted geometric average of exchange rates for the currencies of selected countries and the euro area. A **real effective** exchange rate index represents a nominal effective exchange rate index adjusted for relative movements in national price or cost indicators of the home country, selected countries, and the euro area.

Line ahx

For ease of comparison between the nominal effective exchange rate index and the real effective exchange rate index, the average exchange rate expressed in terms of U.S. dollars per unit of each of the national currencies (line **ah**) is also given as an index form based on 2000=100 (line **ahx**). In both cases of the indices, an increase in the index reflects an appreciation. Because of certain data-related limits, particularly where Fund estimates have been used, data users need to exercise considerable caution in interpreting movements in nominal and real effective exchange rates.

The Fund publishes calculated effective exchange rates data only for countries that have given their approval. Please note that similar indices that are calculated by country authorities could cause different results.

Lines neu and reu

The nominal effective exchange rate index (line **neu**) and the real effective exchange rate index (line **reu**) are published in the country tables for approximately 18 industrial countries and the euro area, for which data are available for normalized unit labor costs in manufacturing.

For the nominal effective exchange rate index, weights are derived from trade in manufactured goods among industrial countries over the period 1989–91. For the real effective exchange rate index for these countries (excluding Australia and New Zealand) and the euro area (excluding Ireland and Portugal), data are compiled from the nominal effective exchange rate index and from a cost indicator of relative normalized unit labor costs in manufacturing. The **reu** and **neu** indices are discussed more fully in the world table section of this introduction.

A selection of other measures of real effective exchange rates for these countries and the euro area, using alternative measures of costs and prices, is shown in the world table *Real Effective Exchange Rates Indices*.

Lines nec and rec

The country tables for selected other countries include a nominal effective exchange rate index in line **nec**. This index is based on a methodology that takes account of each country's trade in both *manufactured* goods and *primary* products with its partner, or competitor, countries.

For *manufactured* goods, trade by type of good and market is distinguished in the database. So it is possible to allow at a disaggregated level for competition among various exporters in a foreign market (i.e., third-market competition) as well as that arising from bilateral trade links.

For *primary* products, the weights assigned depend principally on a country's role as a global supplier or buyer of the product. Trade in crude petroleum, petroleum, and other energy products is excluded. For some countries that depend heavily on tourism, bilateral exports of tourism services averaged over 1988–90 are also included in calculating the competitiveness weights.

From January 1990 onwards, the line **nec** index is weighted based on disaggregate trade data for manufactured goods and primary products covering the three-year period 1988–90. Before that, the weights are for the three-year span 1980–82. The series based on the old weights and the new weights are linked by splicing at December 1989, and the reference base is shifted to 2000=100.

The real effective exchange rate index in line **rec** is derived from the nominal effective exchange rate index, adjusted for relative changes in consumer prices. Consumer price indices, often available monthly, are used as a measure of domestic costs and prices for these countries. This practice typically reflects the use of consumer prices by the reference and partner, or competitor, countries in compiling these indices.

For countries where multiple exchange rates are in effect, Fund staff estimates of weighted average exchange rates are used in many cases. A weighted average exchange rate is constructed as an average of the various exchange rates, with the weights reflecting the share of trade transacted at each rate. For countries where a weighted average exchange rate cannot be calculated, the principal rate, generally line **ahx**, is used.

The notes to the country tables in the monthly issues provide information about exceptions in the choice of the consumer price index (generally line 64) and the period average exchange rate index (generally line **ahx**). For a relatively small number of countries, notes in the country tables in the monthly issues indicate 1) where alternative price indices, such as the wholesale/producer price index or a weighted average of several price indices, are used; 2) where data constraints have made it necessary to use weighting schemes based on aggregate bilateral non-oil trade data; and 3) where trade in services (such as tourism) has been taken into account.

The world table section of this introduction provides a description of the effective exchange rates tables. In addition, a Fund working paper entitled "A Primer on the IMF's Information Notice System" (WP/97/71), distributed in May 1997, provides background on the concepts and methodology underlying the effective exchange rates.

SDR Value

Before July 1974, the value of the SDR (unit of account for the Fund) was fixed in terms of U.S. dollars. Over time, the value changed as follows: SDR 1 = U.S. dollar 1 through November 1971; SDR 1 = U.S. dollar 1.08571 from December 1971 through January 1973; and SDR 1 = U.S. dollar 1.20635 from February 1973 through June 1974.

Since July 1974, the Fund has determined the value of the SDR daily on the basis of a basket of currencies, with each currency being assigned a weight in the determination of that value. The currencies in the basket are valued at their market exchange rates for the U.S. dollar. The U.S. dollar equivalents of each currency are summed to yield the rate of the SDR in terms of the U.S. dollar. The rates for the SDR in terms of other currencies are derived from the market exchange rates of these currencies for the U.S. dollar and the U.S. dollar rate for the SDR.

Although the method of calculating the U.S. dollar/SDR exchange rate has remained the same, the currencies' number and weight have changed over time. Their amount in the SDR basket is reviewed every five years.

From July 1974 through June 1978, the currencies in the basket were of the countries that averaged more than 1 percent share in world exports of goods and services from 1968–72. This established a basket of 16 currencies. Each currency's relative weight was broadly proportionate to the country's exports but modified for the U.S. dollar to reflect its real weight in the world economy. To preserve the continuity of valuation, the amount of each of the 16 currencies was such that on June 28, 1974 the value of SDR 1 = U.S. dollar 1.20635.

From July 1978 through December 1980, the composition of the basket was changed on the basis of updated data for 1972–76. The weights of some currencies were also changed. The amount of each of the 16 currencies in the revised basket was such as to ensure that the value of the SDR in terms of any currency on June 30, 1978 was exactly the same in the revised valuation as in the previous valuation.

Since January 1, 1981, the value of the SDR has been determined based on the currencies of the five member countries having the largest exports of goods and services during the five-year period ending one year before the date of the latest revision to the valuation basket. Broadly reflecting the currencies' relative importance in international trade and finance, the weights are based on the value of the exports of goods and services of the members issuing these currencies and the balances of their currencies officially held by members of the Fund.

From January 1981 through December 1985, the currencies and currency weights of the five members having the largest exports of goods and services during 1975–79 were the U.S. dollar, 42 percent; deutsche mark, 19 percent; French franc, Japanese yen, and pound sterling, 13 percent each.

From January 1986 through December 1990, reflecting the period 1980–84, the weights had changed to U.S. dollar, 42 percent; deutsche mark, 19 percent; Japanese yen, 15 percent; French franc and pound sterling, 12 percent each.

From January 1991 through December 1995, reflecting the period 1985–89, the weights were U.S. dollar, 40 percent; deutsche mark, 21 percent; Japanese yen, 17 percent; French franc and pound sterling, 11 percent each.

On January 1, 1996, the weights were U.S. dollar, 39 percent; deutsche mark, 21 percent; Japanese yen, 18 percent; French franc and pound sterling, 11 percent each.

On January 1, 1999, the currency amount of deutsche mark and French francs were replaced with equivalent amounts of euros, based on the fixed conversion rates between those currencies and the euro, announced on December 31, 1998 by the European Council. The weights in the SDR basket were changed to U.S. dollar, 39 percent; euro, 32 percent (in replacement of the 21 percent for the deutsche mark and 11 percent for the French franc), Japanese yen, 18 percent; and pound sterling, 11 percent.

As of January 1, 2001, the SDR valuation basket weights are the sum of the values of the amounts of each currency in the following amounts: U.S. dollar, 45 percent; euro, 29 percent; Japanese yen, 15 percent; and pound sterling, 11 percent.

World Tables on Exchange Rates

Tables A, B, C, and D on exchange rates, described below, are presented in *IFS*. Daily exchange rates are not yet provided on the CD-ROM or Internet.

Table A of exchange rates gives the monthly, quarterly, and annual SDR rates in terms of U.S. dollars and reciprocals of these rates.

Table B reports for the latest available month the daily rates and the monthly averages, both in terms of currency units per U.S. dollar (**af**) and U.S. dollars per currency unit (**ah**) of (1) 16 major currencies, other than the U.S. dollar, as quoted in the markets of these countries, (2) the SDR, and (3) the euro.

Table C gives daily rates of currencies in terms of national currency units per SDR for the latest available month.

Table D provides, in terms of national currency units per SDR, end-of-period rates for the currencies of Fund members—including Hong Kong (Special Administrative Region as of 1997)—and the Netherlands Antilles.

Method of Deriving IFS Exchange Rates

For countries that have introduced new currencies, the rates shown in *IFS* for the period before the introduction of the most recent currency may be used as conversion factors—they may be used to convert national currency data in *IFS* to U.S. dollar or SDR data. In such cases, the factors are constructed by chain linking the exchange rates of the old and the new currencies. The basis used is the value of the new currency relative to the old currency, as established by the issuing agency at the time the new currency was introduced. Footnotes about the introduction of new currencies are to be found on individual country tables in the monthly issues of *IFS*.

For countries that are members of the euro area, the exchange rates shown are expressed in national currency units per SDR or per U.S. dollar through 1998, and in euros per SDR or per U.S. dollar thereafter.

A detailed description of the derivation of the exchange rates in *IFS*, as well as technical issues associated with these rates, is contained in the *IFS Supplement on Exchange Rates*, No. 9 (1985).

3. Fund Accounts

Data on members' Fund accounts are presented in the Fund Position section in the country tables and in 12 world tables. Details about Fund Accounts terms and concepts and the time series in the country and world tables follow:

Terms and Concepts in Fund Accounts

Quota

When a country joins the Fund, it is assigned a quota that fits into the structure of existing quotas. Quotas are considered in the light of the member's economic characteristics relative to those of other members of comparable size. The size of the member's quota determines, among other things, the member's voting power, the size of its potential access to Fund resources, and its share in allocations of SDRs.

Quotas are reviewed at intervals of not more than five years. The reviews take account of changes in the relative economic positions of members and the growth of the world economy. Initial subscriptions, and normally subscriptions associated with increases in quotas, are paid mainly in the member's own currency, and a smaller portion, not exceeding 25 percent, is paid in reserve assets (SDRs or other members' currencies that are acceptable to the Fund).

General Resources Account

The General Resources Account (GRA) resources consist of the currencies of Fund member countries, SDRs, and gold. These resources are received in the form of subscriptions (which are equal to quotas), borrowings, charges on the use of the Fund's resources, income from investments, and interest on the Fund's holdings of SDRs. Subscriptions are the main source of funds.

Borrowing Arrangements

Borrowings are regarded as a temporary source of funds. The Fund has the authority to borrow the currency of any member from any source with the consent of the issuer.

General Arrangements to Borrow

The Fund's first borrowings were made under the General Arrangements to Borrow (GAB). The Arrangements were established in 1962 initially for four years but, through successive extensions, have been continuously in force since then. The original Arrangements permitted the Fund to borrow the currencies of ten industrial country members (those forming the Group of Ten) to finance purchases by any of these ten countries.

The Fund also had an agreement with Switzerland, under which Switzerland undertook to consider making loans to the Fund to finance additional purchases by members that made purchases financed by the GAB.

The revised GAB, that became effective in December 1983, permits the Fund under certain circumstances to extend GAB resources to members that are not GAB participants, authorizes participation of the Swiss National Bank, and permits certain borrowing arrangements between the Fund and nonparticipating members to be associated with the GAB. The GAB decision was amended on December 22, 1992 to take account of Switzerland's membership in the Fund.

Temporary Arrangements

The Fund has also entered into borrowing arrangements to finance purchases under its temporary lending facilities.

Oil Facilities: The Fund arranged in 1974 and 1975 to borrow from the principal oil exporting countries and other countries with strong external positions to finance two special facilities—the 1974 and 1975 Oil Facilities. Under these facilities, repayments were completed in May 1983.

Supplementary Financing Facility: In 1977 the Fund initiated bilateral borrowing arrangements with 14 countries or their institutions to finance commitments under the Supplementary Financing Facility. This facility was established in 1979, and its funds were fully committed by March 1981.

Policy on Enlarged Access: The first borrowing agreement under the Policy on Enlarged Access to the Fund's resources was reached in March 1981 between the Fund and the Saudi Arabian Monetary Agency.

Others: Since then, additional agreements have been entered into with central banks and official agencies of a number of countries, and with international agencies. In December 1986 the Fund entered into a borrowing arrangement with the government of Japan, under which resources were made available for use by the Fund in support of members' adjustment programs, including under the Enlarged Access Policy.

All of the above borrowing arrangements were disbursed and used by December 1991, except for the GAB, which remains intact. Meanwhile, in December 1987 the Fund, as "Trustee," was authorized to enter into borrowing arrangements with official lenders from a wide range of countries to finance loans under the Enhanced Structural Adjustment Facility, renamed Poverty Reduction and Growth Facility in November 1999.

New Arrangements to Borrow

The New Arrangements to Borrow (NAB), which became effective on November 17, 1998, is a set of credit arrangements between the Fund and 25 members and institutions to provide supplementary resources to the Fund. These resources are to forestall or cope with an impairment of the international monetary system or to deal with an exceptional situation that poses a threat to the stability of that system. The NAB does not replace the GAB, which remains in force.

The total amount of resources available to the Fund under the NAB and GAB combined will be up to SDR 34 billion, double the amount available under the GAB alone. By strengthening the Fund's ability to support the adjustment efforts of its members and to address their balance of payments difficulties, the NAB is an important element of the Fund's capacity to respond to potential systemic problems. The NAB will be in effect for five years, beginning on November 17, 1998, and may be renewed.

Financing Policies and Facilities

Purchases (.2kk.)

The principal way the Fund makes its resources available to members is to sell to them currencies of other members or SDRs in exchange for their own currencies. Such transactions change the composition, but not the overall size, of the Fund's resources. A member to whom the Fund sells currencies or SDRs is said to make "purchases" (also referred to as "drawings") from the Fund.

The purpose of making the Fund's resources available to members is to meet their balance of payments needs. The Fund's resources are provided through permanent policies for general balance of payments purposes (the tranche policies), permanent facilities for specific purposes (the Buffer Stock Financing Facility, the Extended Fund Facility, the Compensatory and Contingency Financing Facility, and the Supplemental Reserve Facility (SRF)), and temporary facilities (the Oil Facilities, the Supplementary Financing Facility, the Policy on Enlarged Access to the Fund's resources, and the Systemic Transformation Facility (STF)).

Permanent Policies

Reserve Tranche: A member's reserve tranche is the excess of its quota in the Fund over the adjusted Fund holdings of its currency in the GRA. Adjusted Fund holdings of a member's currency are equal to the actual holdings of the currency less holdings arising from outstanding purchases under the Fund's policies and facilities, which are subject to exclusion under Article XXX(c). Reserve tranche purchases, like all other purchases, may be made only to meet a balance of payments need. However, for reserve tranche purchases the Fund does not challenge a member's statement of need. As the reserve tranche is considered a reserve deposit in the Fund, a member using its reserve tranche is not considered to be using Fund credit.

Credit Tranche Policy: The credit tranche policy is often referred to as the Fund's basic financing policy. Credit under this policy is viewed as being available in tranches, each tranche being equivalent to 25 percent of quota. Credit tranche purchases may be made outright or under a stand-by arrangement. The latter, which is like a line of credit, assures the member that during a given period it will be able to use the Fund's resources up to a specified amount, so long as it is observing the terms of the arrangement.

Permanent Facilities

Buffer Stock Financing Facility: The Buffer Stock Financing Facility, established in June 1969, is to assist members with a balance of payments need related to their participation in arrangements to finance approved international buffer stocks of primary products.

Extended Fund Facility (EFF): The EFF, established in September 1974, is to make resources available for longer periods and in larger amounts than under the credit tranche policies. It is to assist members that are experiencing balance of payments difficulties owing to structural imbalances in production, trade, and prices, or that are unable to pursue active development policies because of their weak balance of payments positions.

Compensatory and Contingency Financing Facility (CCFF): The CCFF superseded the Compensatory Financing Facility (CFF) in August 1988. The CCFF keeps the essential elements of the CFF and adds a mechanism for contingency financing to support adjustment programs approved by the Fund.

The CFF, established in February 1963, was to assist members, particularly primary producing countries, experiencing balance of payments difficulties attributable to shortfalls in earnings from merchandise exports. Such difficulties were also attributable to invisibles both temporary and due largely to factors beyond their control.

In May 1981 the Fund decided to extend financial assistance to members facing balance of payments difficulties produced by an excess in the cost of their cereal imports. This assistance was integrated with support available under the compensatory financing facility for temporary shortfalls in export receipts.

Supplemental Reserve Facility (SRF): The SRF, established in December 1997, is to financially assist a member country experiencing exceptional balance of payments difficulties caused by a large short-term financing need. This need resulted from a sudden and disruptive loss of market confidence reflected in pressure on the capital account and the member's reserves.

Financing under the SRF, available in the form of additional resources under a Stand-By or Extended Arrangement, may be committed for up to one year and be generally available in two or more tranches. Purchases under the SRF are included as part of either the Stand-By or the Extended Fund Facility, as indicated in the footnote to the world table "Financing Components of Members' Outstanding Obligations to the Fund."

Access

Under the present guidelines on access limits, adopted on October 24, 1994, member access to the Fund's general resources in the credit tranches and the Extended Facility is subject to an annual limit of 100 percent of quota, and a cumulative limit of 300 percent of quota. This is net of scheduled repurchases and excluding purchases under the Compensatory Financing Facility and the Buffer Stock Financing Facility.

Within these limits, the amount of access in individual cases will vary according to the circumstances of the member. In exceptional circumstances, the Fund may approve Stand-By or Extended Arrangements that provide for amounts over these access limits. The guidelines and access limits are intended to be temporary and are reviewed periodically.

Temporary Facilities

Oil Facilities: The oil facilities, set up in June 1974 and April 1975, were to assist members with balance of payments difficulties owing to the rise in oil prices. Purchases under the facilities were completed in May 1976.

Supplementary Financing Facility (SFF): The SFF, established in February 1979, was to assist members facing payments difficulties that were large in relation to their economies and their Fund quotas. Resources under the facility, which were borrowed and therefore not part of the Fund's ordinary resources, were made available only in connection with an upper credit tranche stand-by arrangement and an extended arrangement. The facility was fully committed by March 1981.

Enlarged Access Policy: The Policy on Enlarged Access to the Fund's resources, which continued the policies of the Supplementary Financing Facility following the full commitment of the latter's resources, became operational in May 1981. Under this policy, resources were provided only under stand-by and extended arrangements. The amount of assistance available to a member under the policy was determined according to guidelines adopted by the Fund from time to time. The policy was discontinued in November 1992 because of the effectiveness of the increases in quotas under the

Ninth Review, which increased the Fund's ordinary resources by 50 percent.

Systemic Transformation Facility (STF): The STF could be accessed between April 1993 and December 1995. It was to help member countries facing balance of payments difficulties owing to severe disruptions of their traditional trade and payments arrangements. The disruptions had arisen during a shift from significant reliance on trading at nonmarket prices to multilateral, market-based trade. Countries eligible to draw on the STF included most of those belonging to the former Council for Mutual Economic Assistance, the Baltic countries, Russia, and other countries of the former Soviet Union (BRO), and a number of other countries experiencing similar transformation.

Access

Except for access to the credit tranches and the Extended Facility, which are now subject to common ceilings, access to resources under one policy or facility is independent of access under any other policies or facilities.

All requests for purchases other than those in the reserve tranche are subject to examination by the Fund to determine whether the proposed use of purchases would be consistent with the provisions of the Articles of Agreement and Fund policies. These provisions call for adequate safeguards to ensure that the member will adopt the policies, take measures to overcome its balance of payments difficulties, and meet scheduled repurchases, thereby ensuring the revolving nature of the Fund's resources.

Repurchases

Because the Fund's resources revolve to finance temporary balance of payments deficits, members that purchase from the Fund must subsequently repurchase their currencies with the currencies of other members or SDRs. A member is required to repurchase Fund holdings of its currency that are subject to charges. These holdings include those that result from purchases of currencies or SDRs, other than reserve tranche purchases, and all adjusted Fund holdings that are more than 100 percent of the member's quota.

Members may repurchase at any time the Fund's holdings of their currencies that are subject to charges. However, if their balance of payments and reserve positions improve, they are expected to repurchase the Fund's holdings of their currencies from purchases.

In any event, they must make repurchases—irrespective of their balance of payments positions—in installments within limits of 3 1/4 to 5 years for purchases under the credit tranche policies, the Compensatory Financing Facility, and the Buffer Stock Financing Facility; 4 1/2 to 10 years for purchases under the Extended Facility and Systemic Transformation Facility financed by ordinary resources; and 3 1/2 to 7 years for purchases under the Policy on Enlarged Access to resources.

Positions in the Fund

The Fund normally determines the currencies that are used in transactions and operations with members. Each quarter, the Fund prepares a financial transactions plan, in which it indicates the amounts of particular currencies and SDRs to be used during the relevant period. The Fund selects the currencies of members with strong balance of payments and reserve positions. It also seeks to promote, over time, balanced **"positions in the Fund."**

The effects of Fund transactions and operations are summarized in the Fund's **holdings of members' currencies** and in two other measures, namely, **reserve position in the Fund** and total **Fund credit and loans outstanding**. (See world table in the monthly printed copy of *IFS* and the yearbook, entitled Fund Accounts: Position to Date, and also the Fund Position section in the country tables.)

These measures are defined as follows:

The Fund's **holdings of a member's currency** reflect, among other things, the transactions and operations of the Fund in that currency. This concept is used in calculating the amounts that a member can draw on the Fund under tranche policies and in respect to certain of its obligations to the Fund.

A member's **reserve position in the Fund** (time series .1c.s), which has the characteristics of a reserve asset, comprises the reserve tranche position and creditor position under the various borrowing arrangements. A reserve tranche position arises from (1) the payment of part of a member's subscription in reserve assets and (2) the Fund's net use of the member's currency. Normally, a member's reserve tranche position is equal to its quota less the adjusted Fund holdings of its currency, less subscriptions receivable, less the balances held in the administrative accounts of the Fund to the extent they are not above 0.1 percent of a member's quota, if positive.

Total Fund credit and loans outstanding (.2tl.) represents the sum of (1) the use of Fund credit within the GRA and (2) outstanding loans under the SAF, PRGF, and the Trust Fund.

Use of Fund credit within the General Resources Account (.2egs) is the sum of a member's outstanding purchases and the Fund's net operational receipts and expenditures in that currency that increase the adjusted Fund holdings above quota. It measures the amount that a member is obligated to repurchase.

Outstanding purchases (.2kk.) are equal to purchases other than reserve tranche purchases, less repurchases, less other members' purchases of that member's currency, and less any other use by the Fund of that member's currency (except administrative expenditures) that the member wishes to attribute to specific outstanding purchases.

Use of Fund credit within the Special Disbursement Account (SDA) relates to outstanding loans under the structural adjustment facility (SAF) and that portion of the enhanced structural adjustment facility (ESAF) loans not financed from the ESAF Trust Account. The SDA is the vehicle for receiving and investing profits from the sale of the IMF's gold (i.e., the net proceeds in excess of the book value of SDR 35 a fine ounce), and for making transfers to other accounts for special purposes authorized in the Articles, in particular for financial assistance to low-income members of the IMF.

Structural Adjustment Facility and Poverty Reduction and Growth Facility

The Structural Adjustment Facility (SAF), established in March 1986, provides additional balance of payments assistance in the form of loans on concessional terms. This assistance is for low-income developing countries that were eligible for International Development Association (IDA) resources, that face protracted balance of payments problems, and that are in need of such assistance.

Resources of the SAF comprise Trust Fund reflows, the interest income on SAF loans, investment income from the resources available for the facility, and amounts not used for the Supplementary Financing Facility (SFF) Subsidy Account, which may be transferred back to the SDA.

The Enhanced Structural Adjustment Facility (ESAF) was established in December 1987 and renamed Poverty Reduction and Growth Facility (PRGF), effective November 22, 1999. It provides additional assistance in the form of loans on concessional terms to low-income developing countries that were eligible for assistance from the SAF.

In contrast to the uniform access limit of 70 percent of quota for SAF loans, individual access limits for PRGF loans are determined on the basis of balance of payments need and the strength of adjustment efforts. The maximum access limit is set at 250 percent of quota, with a provision for higher access in exceptional cases. Repayment of each loan must be made in 10 equal semiannual installments starting 5 1/2 years and finishing 10 years after the date of the disbursement. Outstanding SAF and PRGF loans do not affect a member's access to the Fund's general resources, which remain available under the terms of those policies.

Resources available for disbursement under PRGF arrangements include (1) the resources of the PRGF Trust (previously the ESAF Trust, established in December 1987), which comprise special loans and contributions and are held separately from the property and assets of all other accounts of the Fund, including other administered accounts, (2) amounts available from the SDA that have not been used under SAF arrangements, and (3) amounts made available by associated lenders.

Trust Fund and Supplementary Financing Facility Subsidy Account

The Fund is Trustee for two additional accounts, whose resources are legally separate from the resources of the Fund. These are the Trust Fund and the Supplementary Financing Facility (SFF) Subsidy Account.

The Trust Fund, established in May 1976, provides balance of payments assistance on concessional terms to eligible members and also distributes funds directly to developing members. The resources of the Trust Fund are derived from profits from the sale of about 25 million ounces of the Fund's gold holdings during 1976–80, from income on the investment of these profits, from contributions by members, and from low-interest borrowings.

The SFF Subsidy Account, established in December 1980, reduced the cost for low-income developing countries for using the supplementary financing facility. The SFF Subsidy Account consists of transfers from reflows of Trust Fund loans, donations, loans, and the interest income received from investment of resources held pending disbursement.

SDRs

SDRs are unconditional reserve assets created by the Fund to supplement existing reserve assets. SDRs are allocated to Fund members that participate in the Fund's Operations Division for SDRs and Administered Accounts in proportion to their quotas. Six SDR allocations totaling SDR 21.4 billion have been made by the Fund (in January 1970, January 1971, January 1972, January 1979, January 1980, and January 1981).

The Fund cannot allocate SDRs to itself but receives them from members through various financial transactions and operations. Entities authorized to conduct transactions in SDRs are the Fund itself, participants in the Fund's Operations Division for SDRs and Administered Accounts, and prescribed "other holders."

The SDR can be used for a wide range of transactions and operations, including for acquiring other members' currencies, settling financial obligations, making donations, and extending loans. SDRs may also be used in swap arrangements and as security for the performance of financial obligations. Forward as well as spot transactions may be conducted in SDRs.

World Tables on Fund Accounts

Twelve world tables on Fund Accounts are presented in *IFS*, as described below. The tables on Fund accounts arrangements, position to date, financing components, and borrowing agreements are not yet available on the CD-ROM or Internet.

The world table Fund Accounts: Arrangements reports the current status of stand-by, extended, and poverty reduction and growth (previously, the enhanced structural adjustment) arrangements.

The table Fund Accounts: Position to Date reports latest monthly data on members' Fund positions, including quota, reserve position in the Fund, total Fund credit and loans outstanding, Fund holdings of currencies, and positions in the SDR Department.

The table Financing Components of Members' Outstanding Obligations to the Fund reports latest monthly data on the sources of financing of Fund credit and loans outstanding.

The tables Purchases (.2kk.) and Repurchases (.2lk.) relate to transactions within the General Resources Account (GRA). Purchases exclude reserve tranche purchases.

The table Fund Accounts: Borrowing Agreements reports the current status of the Fund's borrowing activities.

The tables Loan Disbursements (.2kl.) and Repayments of Loans (.2ll.) relate to the Structural Adjustment Facility (SAF), Poverty Reduction and Growth Facility (PRGF; which was previously named Enhanced Structural Adjustment Facility-ESAF), and Trust Fund loans.

The table Total Fund Credit and Loans Outstanding (.2tl.) relates to the outstanding use of Fund resources under the GRA and to outstanding loans under the SAF, PRGF, and Trust Fund.

The table Use of Fund Credit: GRA (.2egs) relates to the outstanding use of the Fund resources under the GRA.

The table SDRs (.1b.s) shows holdings of SDRs by members and includes a foot table showing SDR holdings by all participants, the IMF, other holders, and the world.

The table Reserve Position in the Fund (.1c.s) relates to members' claims on the Fund.

Pamphlet on Fund Accounts

A more detailed description of the Fund accounts is contained in the IMF's *Financial Organization and Operations of the IMF*, Pamphlet No. 45, sixth edition, 2001.

4. International Liquidity

Data on international liquidity are presented in the country tables and in world tables on reserves. The international liquidity section in the country tables comprises lines for total reserves minus gold, gold holdings, other foreign assets and foreign liabilities of the monetary authorities, and foreign accounts of other financial institutions. The euro area section for international liquidity covers assets of the European Central Bank (ECB) and the national central banks (NCBs) of the countries that have adopted the euro (details below).

Total Reserves (Minus Gold) and Gold Holdings

Total Reserves Minus Gold (line 1 l.d) is the sum of the items Foreign Exchange, Reserve Position in the Fund, and the U.S. dollar value of SDR holdings by monetary authorities. Monetary authorities comprise central banks and, to the extent that they perform monetary authorities' functions, currency boards, exchange stabilization funds, and treasuries.

Official Gold Holdings (lines 1ad and 1and) are expressed in millions of fine troy ounces and valued, according to national practice, in U.S. dollars.

Under Total Reserves Minus Gold, the line for Foreign Exchange (1d.d) includes monetary authorities' claims on nonresidents in the form of foreign banknotes, bank deposits, treasury bills, short- and long-term government securities, ECUs (for periods before January 1999), and other claims usable in the event of balance of payments need.

For *IFS* yearbook users, this background information on foreign exchange is particularly useful: Before December 1971, when the U.S. dollar was at par with the SDR, foreign exchange data were compiled and expressed in terms of U.S. dollars at official par values. Conversions from national currencies to U.S. dollars from December 1971 through January 1973 were calculated at the cross rates reflecting the parities and central rates agreed to in December 1971. From February 1973 through June 1974, foreign exchange was valued at the cross rates of parities or central rates for countries having effective parities or central rates, and at market rates for the Canadian dollar, Irish pound, Italian lira, Japanese yen, and pound sterling. Beginning in July 1974, foreign exchange is valued at end-of-month market rates or, in the absence of market rate quotations, at other prevailing official rates.

Total Reserves for the Euro Area

Until December 31, 1998, member countries of the European Union (Austria, Belgium, Denmark, Finland, France, Germany, Greece, Ireland, Italy, Luxembourg, the Netherlands, Portugal, Spain, Sweden, and the United Kingdom) held ECU deposits with the European Monetary Cooperation Fund (EMCF) and/or its successor, the European Monetary Institute. The reserves data for each country excluded, from gold and foreign exchange holdings, the deposits of gold and foreign exchange with the EMCF, but the data included, in foreign exchange holdings, the equivalent amounts of ECU deposits.

These deposits were transferred from the EMCF to the EMI upon its creation on January 1, 1994, and to the European Central Bank (ECB) when it succeeded the EMI on June 1, 1998. Each national central bank (NCB) deposited gold and foreign exchange with the ECB. On January 1, 1999, the euro replaced the ECU at a rate of one euro per one ECU.

Total reserves for the euro area and individual euro area countries are based on the statistical definition of international reserves adopted by the ECB's Statistics Committee in December 1998. Defined on a euro area-wide residency basis, they include reserve assets denominated only in currencies of non-euro area countries. All positions with residents of other euro area countries and with the ECB are excluded from reserve assets.

For the euro area countries, Total Reserves minus Gold (line 1 l.d) is defined in broad accordance with the fifth edition of the *Balance of Payments Manual*. It includes the monetary authorities' holdings of SDRs, reserve position in the Fund, and foreign exchange, including financial derivative claims on non-euro area countries. It excludes claims among euro area countries and all euro-denominated claims on non-euro area countries. Total reserves of the euro area comprise the reserve holdings of the NCBs and ECB. Definitions of reserves at the national and euro area levels are harmonized.

Other Foreign Assets, Foreign Liabilities

Time series, where significant, are also provided in international liquidity sections on other foreign assets and foreign liabilities of the monetary authorities.

Other Assets (line 3..d) usually comprises claims on nonresidents that are of limited usability in the event of balance of payments need, such as balances under bilateral payments agreements and holdings of inconvertible currencies. (Claims on nonresidents under Other Assets (line 3..d) are included in line 11.)

Other Liabilities (line 4..d) comprises foreign liabilities of the monetary authorities other than use of Fund credit (GRA), SAF, PRGF, and Trust Fund loans outstanding. Positions with the Fund are reported separately, in SDRs, in the Fund position section of the country tables.

Foreign Accounts of Other Financial Institutions

Where significant, foreign accounts of financial institutions other than the monetary authorities are reported. The measures provided are normally U.S. dollar equivalents of time series reported in the appropriate money and banking sections as follows: line 7a.d is derived from line 21; line 7b.d is derived from line 26c plus line 26cl; line 7e.d is derived from line 41; and line 7f.d is derived from line 46c plus line 46cl. Sometimes the measures are reported directly in U.S. dollars and may differ slightly in coverage.

In addition for some countries, summary data are provided on the foreign accounts of special or international license banks that operate locally but are not presently covered in the money and banking section. Their foreign assets are reported as line 7k.d, and their foreign liabilities as line 7m.d, when available (although 7m.d is not shown separately if it is equal to line 7k.d).

World Tables on Reserves

World tables on reserves report all country table time series on reserves, other than gold at national valuation, and present totals for countries, country groups, and the world.

Also provided is a table on total reserves, with gold valued at SDR 35 per ounce. A foot table to that table reports total reserves of all countries, including gold valued both at SDR 35 per ounce and at market prices. And the yearbook includes a world table on the ratio of nongold reserves (line 1 l.d) to imports (line 71..d), expressed in terms of the number of weeks of imports covered by the stock of nongold reserves.

Except for the world table on gold holdings in physical terms, world tables on reserves are expressed in SDRs. Foreign exchange holdings are expressed in SDRs by converting the U.S. dollar values shown in the country tables on the basis of the end-period U.S. dollar/SDR rate.

Similarly, a foot table to the world table on gold indicates gold holdings valued at SDR 35 per ounce and at market prices for all countries, the IMF, the ECB, the Bank for International Settlements (BIS), and the world. A simple addition of the gold held by all of these holders would involve double-counting, because most of the gold deposited with the BIS is also included in countries' official gold reserves. *IFS* therefore reports BIS gold holdings net of gold deposits, and negative figures for BIS gold holdings are balanced by forward operations. This foot table also provides data on the U.S. dollar price of gold on the London market, the U.S. dollar/SDR rate, and the end-period derived market price of gold in terms of SDRs.

5. Money and Banking

Statistics on the accounts of monetary and other financial institutions are given in money and banking sections 10 through 50 in the country tables and in world tables, described in the world table section of this introduction.

Monetary Authorities

Monetary authorities' data (section 10) in *IFS* generally consolidate the accounts of the central bank with the accounts of other institutions that undertake monetary functions. These functions include issuing currency, holding international reserves, and conducting Fund account transactions. Data on monetary authorities measure the stock of reserve money comprising currency in circulation, deposits of the deposit money banks, and deposits of other residents, apart from the central government, with the monetary authorities.

Major aggregates of the accounts on the asset side are foreign assets (line 11) and domestic assets (line 12*). Domestic assets are broken down into Claims on Central Government (line 12a), Claims on Deposit Money Banks (line 12e), and, if sizable, Claims on State and Local Governments (line 12b); Claims on Nonfinancial Public Enterprises (line 12c); Claims on the Private Sector (line 12d); Claims on Other Banking Institutions (line 12f), and Claims on Nonbank Financial Institutions (line 12g).

In some countries, where insufficient data are available to provide disaggregations of claims on governmental bodies other than the central government, a classification of Claims on Official Entities (line 12bx) is used. In addition, in countries where insufficient data are available to provide disaggregations of claims on other banking institutions and nonbank financial institutions, a classification of Claims on Other Financial Institutions (line 12f) is used.

The principal liabilities of monetary authorities consist of Reserve Money (line 14); Other Liabilities to Deposit Money Banks (line 14n), comprising liabilities of the central bank to deposit money banks that are excluded from Reserve Money; Liabilities of the Central Bank: Securities (line 16ac); Foreign Liabilities (line 16c); Central Government Deposits (line 16d); and Capital Accounts (line 17a).

Deposit Money Banks

Deposit money banks comprise commercial banks and other financial institutions that accept transferable deposits, such as demand deposits. Deposit money banks' data (section 20) measure the stock of deposit money.

Major aggregates of the accounts on the assets side are Reserves (line 20), comprising domestic currency holdings and deposits with the monetary authorities; Claims on Monetary Authorities: Securities (line 20c), comprising holdings of securities issued by the central bank; Other Claims on Monetary Authorities (line 20n), comprising claims on the central bank that are excluded from Reserves; Foreign Assets (line 21); and Claims on Other Resident Sectors (lines 22*), as described in the preceding section on monetary authorities (lines 12*).

The principal liabilities consist of Demand Deposits (line 24); Time, Savings, and Foreign Currency Deposits (line 25); Money Market Instruments (line 26aa); Bonds (line 26ab); Foreign Liabilities (line 26c); Central Government Deposits (line 26d); Credit from Monetary Authorities (line 26g); Liabilities to Other Banking Institutions (line 26i); Liabilities to Nonbank Financial Institutions (line 26j); and Capital Accounts (line 27a).

Monetary Survey

Monetary authorities' and deposit money banks' data are consolidated into a monetary survey (section 30). The survey measures the stock of narrow Money (line 34), comprising transferable deposits and currency outside deposit money banks, and the Quasi-Money (line 35) liabilities of these institutions, comprising time, savings, and foreign currency deposits.

Standard relationships between the monetary survey lines and the component lines in sections 10 and 20 are as follows:

Foreign Assets (Net) (line 31n) equals the sum of foreign asset lines 11 and 21, less the sum of foreign liability lines 16c and 26c.

Claims on Central Government (Net) (line 32an) equals claims on central government (the sum of lines 12a and 22a), less central government deposits (the sum of lines 16d and 26d), plus, where applicable, the counterpart entries of lines 24..i and 24..r (private sector demand deposits with the postal checking system and with the Treasury).

Claims on State and Local Governments (line 32b) equals the sum of lines 12b and 22b. Note that, for some countries, lack of sufficient data to perform the standard classifications of claims on governmental bodies excluding the central government has resulted in the use of the alternative classification "claims on official entities" (line 32bx), which is the sum of lines 12bx and 22bx. These series may therefore include state and local governments, public financial institutions, and nonfinancial public enterprises.

Claims on Nonfinancial Public Enterprises (line 32c) equals the sum of lines 12c and 22c.

Claims on Private Sector (line 32d) equals the sum of lines 12d and 22d.

Claims on Other Banking Institutions (line 32f) equals the sum of lines 12f and 22f.

Claims on Nonbank Financial Institutions (line 32g) equals the sum of lines 12g and 22g.

Domestic Credit (line 32) is the sum of lines 32an, 32b, 32c, 32d, 32f, and 32g even when, owing to their small size, data for lines 32b, 32c, 32f, and 32g are not published separately. Thus, the data for line 32 may be larger than the sum of its published components.

Money (line 34) equals the sum of currency outside deposit money banks (line 14a) and demand deposits other than those of the central government (lines 14d, 14e, 14f, 14g, and 24) plus, where applicable, lines 24..i and 24..r.

Quasi-Money (line 35) equals the sum of lines 15 and 25, comprising time, savings, and foreign currency deposits of resident sectors other than central government.

The data in line 34 are frequently referred to as M1, while the sum of lines 34 and 35 gives a broader measure of money similar to that which is frequently called M2.

Money Market Instruments (line 36aa) equals the sum of lines 16aa and 26aa.

Bonds (line 36ab) equals the sum of lines 16ab and 26ab.

Liabilities of Central Bank: Securities (line 36ac) equals the outstanding stock of securities issued by the monetary authorities (line 16ac) less the holdings of these securities by deposit money banks (line 20c).

Restricted Deposits (line 36b) equals the sum of lines 16b and 26b.

Long-Term Foreign Liabilities (line 36cl) equals the sum of lines 16cl and 26cl.

Counterpart Funds (line 36e) equals the sum of lines 16e and 26e.

Central Government Lending Funds (line 36f) equals the sum of lines 16f and 26f.

Liabilities to Other Banking Institutions (line 36i) is equal to line 26i.

Liabilities to Nonbank Financial Institutions (line 36j) is equal to line 26j.

Capital Accounts (line 37a) equals the sum of lines 17a and 27a.

These monetary survey lines give the full range of *IFS* standard lines. Some of them are not applicable to every country, whereas others may not be published separately in sections 10 and 20, because the data are small. Unpublished lines are included in Other Items (Net) (lines 17r and 27r) but are classified in the appropriate monetary survey aggregates in section 30.

Exceptions to the standard calculations of monetary survey aggregates are indicated in the notes to the country tables in the monthly issues. Exceptions also exist in the standard presentation of the consolidation of financial institutions, e.g., for Japan, Nicaragua, the United Kingdom, and the United States.

Other Banking Institutions

Section 40 contains data on the accounts of other banking institutions. This subsector comprises institutions that do not accept transferable deposits but that perform financial intermediation by accepting other types of deposits or by issuing securities or other liabilities that are close substitutes for deposits. This subsector covers such institutions as savings and mortgage loan institutions, post-office savings institutions, building and loan associations, finance companies that accept deposits or deposit substitutes, development banks, and offshore banking institutions.

The major aggregates in this section are claims on the various sectors of the economy (lines 42*), as described in the preceding paragraphs, and quasi-monetary liabilities (line 45), largely in the form of time and savings deposits.

Banking Survey

Where reasonably complete data are available for other banking institutions, a banking survey (section 50) is published. It consolidates data for other banking institutions with the monetary survey and thus provides a broader measure of monetary liabilities.

The sectoral classification of assets in the banking survey follows the classification used in the monetary survey, as outlined in the description for that section.

Nonbank Financial Institutions

For a few countries, data are shown on the accounts of nonbank financial institutions, such as insurance companies, pension funds, and superannuation funds. Given the nature of their liabilities, these institutions generally exert minimal impact on the liquidity of a given economy. However, they can play a significant role in distributing credit from the financial sector to the rest of the economy.

European Economic and Monetary Union (Euro Area)

Stage Three of the European Economic and Monetary Union (EMU), beginning in January 1999, created a monetary union among European countries. New definitions of statistics aggregates were created, resulting in a major break in data series for all participating countries. The euro area, an official descriptor of the monetary union, is defined by its membership as of a specified date. The 11 original members were Austria, Belgium, Finland, France, Germany, Ireland, Italy, Luxembourg, Netherlands, Portugal, and Spain. Greece joined in January 2001. In 2002, euro banknotes and coins were issued, and national currency banknotes and coins withdrawn.

The main features of the euro area monetary statistics are described as follows:

Creation of the Eurosystem

In Stage Three of the EMU, the "Eurosystem"—the European Central Bank (ECB) and the national central banks (NCBs) of the euro area member states—executes a single monetary policy for the euro area. The new common currency unit is the euro. Until 2002, national currency circulated, and various types of transactions were denominated in either euros or national currency.

The monetary statistics standards for the euro area countries underwent comprehensive revisions. The revisions permitted compilation of consolidated monetary accounts for the euro area and provided the data needed to execute the single monetary policy. Statistical standards are based on the *European System of Accounts 1995 (1995 ESA)* and additional standards prescribed by ECB regulation. Statistics are collected under a "layered approach," whereby monetary statistics compiled at the country level are forwarded to the ECB for consolidation into euro area totals. NCBs are required to compile monetary statistics according to a single set of standards and a common format for submission of data to the ECB.

Denomination in Euros

Beginning with data for 1999, monetary data for euro area countries presented in *IFS* are denominated in euros, except for Greece whose data are denominated in euros beginning in January 2001. Data for the consolidated euro area table are in euros for all time periods.

Residency Principles

Statistics are compiled on the basis of both national residency criteria, described in the fifth edition of the *Balance of Payments Manual*, and euro area-wide residency criteria, based on the EU membership as of a specified date.

In the application of the latter criteria, all institutional units located in euro area countries are treated as resident, and all units outside the euro area as nonresident. For example, claims on government under the national criteria include only claims on the government of the country, whereas claims on government under the euro area-wide residency criteria include claims on the governments of all euro area countries. Under the euro area-wide residency criteria, the ECB is a resident unit, whereas under the national residency criteria, it is a foreign unit for all countries. Under ECB statistical reporting requirements—concerning the consolidated balance sheet of the monetary financial institutions sector—the ECB is to be classified as a resident unit of the country where it is physically located (Germany).

The monetary statistics in the tables for each euro area country are presented on both national and euro area-wide residency bases.

Euro Banknotes and Coins

On January 1, 2002, euro banknotes and coins were issued. The existing national currencies continued to be accepted in trade for a short transition period that ended in all member countries by the end of February 2002, at the latest. The national currencies and coins can be redeemed with the national authorities for extended periods, or indefinitely, as set by national policy. The changeover to euro banknotes and coins was smooth, and the stock of outstanding national currencies rapidly decreased by 86 percent between January 1 and February 28, 2002. The national currencies still outstanding at the end of each reporting period remained part of the euro area monetary aggregates until year-end 2002. Euro area monetary aggregates are net of banknotes and coins held by monetary financial institutions (other depository corporations) in the euro area.

The euro banknotes are issued by the Eurosystem as a whole, comprising the ECB and the national central banks of the euro area countries. Banknotes are put into circulation by each NCB as demanded and are physically identical regardless of the issuing NCB. According to the accounting regime chosen by the Eurosystem, although the ECB does not put banknotes into circulation, a share of 8 percent of the total value of euro banknotes put into circulation is allocated to the balance sheet of the ECB each month. The balance of the remaining 92 percent is allocated among the NCBs on a monthly basis, whereby each NCB of the Eurosystem records on its balance sheet as "banknotes issued" a share proportional to its share in the ECB's capital. This allocation procedure is referred to as the capital share mechanism–CSM.

For each NCB, the difference between the value of the euro banknotes allocated according to the CSM and the value of euro banknotes it puts into circulation is classified as an "Intra-Eurosystem claim/liability related to banknote issue." Each NCB will have a single claim/liability vis-à-vis the Eurosystem, calculated monthly. Similarly, the ECB will always have an Intra-Eurosystem claim equal to its 8 percent share of banknotes issued.

On the country pages for the euro area countries, Intra-Eurosystem claims/liabilities related to banknote issue are classified by the IMF as part of monetary authorities' Claims on Banking Institutions (line 12e.u)/Liabilities to Banking Institutions (line 14c.u). Intra-Eurosystem claims/liabilities related to banknote issue are also recorded within the memo item Net Claims on Eurosystem (line 12e.s). In contrast, in the Monetary Authorities (Eurosystem) section on the euro area page, the Intra-Eurosystem claims/liabilities of the Eurosystem members are recorded as part of Other Items (Net) (line 17r), where they effectively net to zero.

Euro coins are issued by national authorities. The ECB approves the volume of coins to be issued by each country. All have a common design on the obverse and a national design on the reverse. All revenues associated with coin issuance are retained by national authorities without application to an accounting allocation mechanism such as is used for banknotes.

The euro also has been adopted officially by several small jurisdictions within Europe—Andorra, Monaco, San Marino, and the Vatican. It is also used as the principal currency in several areas that were formerly part of Yugoslavia.

TARGET

Effective with data beginning end-November 2000, changes in the operating procedures of the TARGET (Trans-European Automated Real-Time Gross Settlement Express Transfer) euro clearing system affect monetary authorities' Foreign Assets (line 11), Foreign Liabilities (line 16c), Claims on Banking Institutions (line 12e.u), and Liabilities to Banking Institutions (line 14c.u). (See Recording of TARGET System Positions in the following section.)

Monetary Authorities—Euro Area

In *IFS* country tables, the term monetary authorities refers to the national central bank and other institutional units that perform monetary authorities' functions and are included in the central bank subsector (currency boards, exchange stabilization funds, etc). For the euro area member countries, upon joining the union, the monetary authority consists of the NCB, as defined by its membership within the Eurosystem.

At the Eurosystem level, monetary authority refers to the ECB and the NCBs of the euro area member countries, based on the actual date of membership.

For purposes of comparison with pre-euro area data, "of which" lines show positions with residents of the country.

Beginning in January 1999, Foreign Assets (line 11) and Foreign Liabilities (line 16c) include only positions with non-euro area countries. All positions with residents of other euro area countries, including the ECB, are classified as domestic positions in the data based on euro area residency.

Claims on General Government (line 12a.u) includes claims on the central government and other levels of government, including the social security system. It also includes claims on general government in other euro area countries.

Claims on Banking Institutions (NCBs and Other Monetary Financial Institutions or MFIs) (line 12e.u) and Liabilities to Banking Institutions (NCBs and Other MFIs) (line 14c.u) include all positions with NCBs and Other MFIs in all euro area countries. Before January 1999, positions with NCBs and Other MFIs in other euro area countries were in Foreign Assets and Foreign Liabilities. Other MFIs are monetary institutions other than the NCB and ECB. Other MFIs were previously called deposit money banks (DMBs) and other banking institutions (OBIs). Beginning in January 1999, other MFIs is defined to include money market funds.

Claims on Other Resident Sectors (line 12d) comprises claims on nonbank financial institutions, public nonfinancial corporations, and the private sector.

Net Claims on Eurosystem (line 12e.s) equals gross claims on, less gross liabilities to, the ECB and other NCBs within the Eurosystem. This item comprises euro-denominated claims equivalent to the transfer of foreign currency reserves to the ECB, Intra-Eurosystem claims/liabilities related to banknote issuance, net claims or liabilities within the TARGET clearing system (see description below), and other positions such as contra-entries to the NCBs' holdings of assets acquired in conjunction with open-market or intervention operations. NCBs' issues of securities other than shares and money market paper held by other NCBs, which are not separately identifiable, are included in Liabilities to Banking Institutions (line 14c.u). Before January 1999, positions with the EMI or ECB and other euro area NCBs are included in Foreign Assets and Foreign Liabilities.

Currency Issued (line14a): Until 2002, this line covers national currency in circulation. Beginning in 2002, this series is redefined to include euro banknotes issued by each NCB, euro coins issued by each euro area country, and national currency not yet withdrawn. The amount of euro banknotes recorded as issued by each NCB is the legal allocation recorded on its balance sheet according to the accounting regime (CSM) described above in **Euro Banknotes and Coins.** That amount does not correspond to either the actual amount of euro banknotes put into circulation by the NCB or the actual circulation of euro banknotes within the domestic territory. The actual amount of euro banknotes put into circulation by the NCB is included within Memo: Currency Put into Circulation (line 14m). In addition, this item includes euro coin issued and the national currency not yet withdrawn.

Capital Accounts (line 17a) includes general provisions.

Recording of TARGET System Positions

Effective November 2000, external positions of members of the TARGET (Trans-European Automated Real-Time Gross Settlement Express Transfer) euro clearing system with each other are affected by changes in TARGET's operating procedures. Previously, from January 1999 to October 2000, TARGET positions are on a gross bilateral basis between all members, which results in large external asset and liability positions between the TARGET members. From November 2000 onward, multilateral netting by novation procedures results in each member recording only a single TARGET position vis-à-vis the ECB, which is generally a much smaller value than recorded under the previous arrangement.

This change affects Monetary Authorities' Foreign Assets (line 11) and Foreign Liabilities (line 16c) of all TARGET members. It also affects Monetary Authorities' Claims on Banking Institutions (line 12e.u) and Liabilities to Banking Institutions (line 14c.u) of the euro area TARGET members. The non-euro area TARGET members are not permitted to hold a net liability position against TARGET as a whole; therefore, after November 2000, they do not have any TARGET-related Foreign Liabilities.

Banking Institutions—Euro Area

For comparison with pre-euro area data, "of which" lines show positions with residents of the country.

Beginning in January 1999, this section covers the accounts of other MFIs (monetary financial institutions)—monetary institutions other than the NCB and ECB. Other MFIs were previously called deposit money banks (DMBs) and other banking institutions (OBIs). Beginning in January 1999, other MFIs is defined to include money market funds.

Claims on Monetary Authorities (line 20) comprises banking institutions' holdings of euro banknotes and coins, holdings of national currency, deposits with the NCB, and loans to the NCB.

Claims on Banking Institutions (including ECB) in Other Euro Area Countries (line 20b.u) and Liabilities to Banking Institutions (including ECB) in Other Euro Area Countries (line 26h.u) comprise all positions with the ECB, NCBs, and Other MFIs in other euro area countries. These positions are classified as domestic under the euro area residency criteria. Before January 1999, these accounts were classified under Foreign Assets and Foreign Liabilities. Claims include holdings of currencies issued in other euro area countries.

Beginning in January 1999, Foreign Assets (line 21) and Foreign Liabilities (line 26c) include only positions with non-euro area countries. All positions with residents of other euro area countries, including the ECB, are classified as domestic positions.

Claims on General Government (line 22a.u) includes claims on central government and other levels of government in all euro area countries.

Claims on Other Resident Sectors (line 22d.u) comprises claims on nonbank financial institutions, public nonfinancial corporations, and the private sectors in all euro area countries.

Demand Deposits (line 24.u) includes demand deposits in all currencies by other resident sectors in all euro area countries.

Other Deposits (line 25.u) includes deposits with fixed maturity, deposits redeemable at notice, securities repurchase agreements, and subordinated debt in the form of deposits by other resident sectors of all euro area countries. Before January 1999, subordinated debt was included in Other Items (Net) (line 27r).

Money Market Fund Shares (line 26m.u) include shares/units issued by money market funds.

Bonds and Money Market Instruments (line 26n.u) include subordinated debt in the form of securities, other bonds, and money market paper.

Credit from Monetary Authorities (line 26g) comprises banking institutions' borrowing from the NCBs.

Other Items (Net) (line 27r) includes holdings of shares issued by other MFIs.

Banking Survey (Based on National Residency)—Euro Area

This section consolidates the accounts of the monetary authorities and banking institutions based on national residency criteria.

Foreign Assets (Net) (line 31n) includes positions with nonresidents of the country. Positions with the ECB for all euro area countries are classified in Foreign Assets under the national residency criteria.

Claims on General Government (Net) (line 32an) includes claims on general government minus deposits of central government. Deposits of other levels of government are included in liabilities to other resident sectors.

Until 2002, Currency Issued (line 34a.n) covers national currency in circulation. Beginning in 2002, this series is redefined to include euro banknotes issued by each NCB, euro coins issued by each euro area country, and the amount of national currency not yet withdrawn. Under the accounting regime used by the Eurosystem, the allocation of euro banknotes issued by each NCB is the legal allocation recorded on its balance sheet according to the accounting regime (CSM) described above in **Euro Banknotes and Coins**. The allocation does not correspond to either the actual amount of euro banknotes placed in circulation by the NCB or the actual circulation of banknotes within the domestic territory.

Other Items (Net) (line 37r) includes other MFIs' holdings of shares issued by other MFIs.

Banking Survey (Based on Euro Area-Wide Residency)

This section consolidates the accounts of the monetary authorities and banking institutions based on euro area-wide residency criteria.

Foreign Assets (Net) (line 31n.u) includes all positions with nonresidents of the euro area. Positions with residents of all euro area countries, including the ECB, are classified as domestic positions.

Claims on General Government (Net) (line 32anu) includes claims on central government and all other levels of government of all euro area countries minus deposits of central government of all euro area countries. Deposits of other levels of government are included in liabilities to other resident sectors.

Until 2002, Currency Issued (line 34a.u) covers national currency in circulation. Beginning in 2002, this series is redefined to include euro banknotes issued by each NCB, euro coins issued by each euro area country, and the amount of national currency not yet withdrawn. Under the accounting regime used by the Eurosystem, the allocation of euro banknotes issued by each NCB is the legal allocation recorded on its balance sheet according to the accounting regime (CSM) described above in **Euro Banknotes and Coins**. The allocation does not correspond to either the actual amount of euro banknotes placed in circulation by the NCB or the actual circulation of banknotes within the domestic territory.

Other Items (Net) (line 37r.u) includes other MFIs' holdings of shares issued by other MFIs.

6. Interest Rates

Data are presented in the Interest Rates section in the country tables and in the world tables on national and international interest rates.

Discount Rate/Bank Rate (line 60) is the rate at which the central banks lend or discount eligible paper for deposit money banks, typically shown on an end-of-period basis.

The Eurosystem Marginal Lending Facility Rate (line 60) is the rate at which other MFIs obtain overnight liquidity from NCBs, against eligible assets. The terms and conditions of the lending are identical throughout the euro area. The Eurosystem Refinancing Rate (line 60r) and Interbank Rate (Overnight) (line 60a) are also provided on the euro area table.

Money Market Rate (line 60b) is the rate on short-term lending between financial institutions. Interbank Rate (Three-Month) (line 60b) is shown on the euro area table.

Treasury Bill Rate (line 60c) is the rate at which short-term securities are issued or traded in the market.

Deposit Rate (line 60l) usually refers to rates offered to resident customers for demand, time, or savings deposits. Often, rates for time and savings deposits are classified according to maturity and amounts deposited. In addition, deposit money banks and similar deposit-taking institutions may offer short- and medium-term instruments at specified rates for specific amounts and maturities; these are frequently termed "certificates of deposit." For countries where savings deposits are important, a Savings Rate (line 60k) is also published.

Lending Rate (line 60p) is the bank rate that usually meets the short- and medium-term financing needs of the private sector. This rate is normally differentiated according to creditworthiness of borrowers and objectives of financing.

Government Bond Yield (line 61*) refers to one or more series representing yields to maturity of government bonds or other bonds that would indicate longer term rates.

Interest rates for foreign-currency-denominated instruments are also published for countries where such instruments are important.

Quarterly and annual interest rate data are arithmetic averages of monthly interest rates reported by the countries.

The country notes in the monthly issues carry a brief description of the nature and characteristics of the rates reported and of the financial instrument to which they relate.

A typical series from each of these groups is included in the world tables on national interest rates.

World Table on International Interest Rates

The world table on international interest rates reports London interbank offer rates on deposits denominated in SDRs, U.S. dollars, euros, French francs, deutsche mark, Japanese yen, and Swiss francs and Paris interbank offer rates on deposits denominated in pounds sterling. Monthly data are averages of daily rates. The table includes the premium or discount on three-month forward rates of currencies of the major industrial countries against the U.S. dollar.

This table also reports the SDR interest rate and the rate of remuneration. Monthly data are arithmetic averages of daily rates. Interest is paid on holdings of SDRs, and charges are levied on participants' cumulative allocations. Interest and charges accrue daily at the same rate and are settled quarterly in SDRs. As a result, participants who have SDR holdings above their net cumulative allocations receive net interest, and those with holdings below their net cumulative allocations pay net charges. Other official holders of SDRs—including the Fund's General Resources Account—receive interest on their holdings and pay no charges because they receive no allocations.

The Fund also pays quarterly remuneration to members on their creditor positions arising from the use of their currencies in Fund transactions and operations. This is determined by the positive difference between the remuneration norm and the average daily balances of the member's currency in the General Resources Account.

Effective August 1, 1983, the weekly SDR interest rate has been based on the combined market interest rate. That rate is calculated by applying to the specific amounts of the five currencies included in the SDR valuation basket, converted into SDR equivalents, the market rates on specified short-term money market instruments quoted in the five countries.

As of January 1, 1991, the interest rates used in this calculation are market yield for three-month U.S. treasury bills, three-month interbank deposit rate (line 60bs) in Germany, three-month rate for treasury bills (line 60cs) in France, three-month rate on certificates of deposit (line 60bs) in Japan, and market yield for three-month U.K. treasury bills (line 60cs). These series are shown in the table.

The combined market rate is calculated each Friday and enters into effect each Monday. The interest rate on the SDR is 100 percent of the combined market rate, rounded to two nearest decimal places. The rate of remuneration, effective February 2, 1987, is 100 percent of the rate of interest on the SDR.

7. Prices, Production, and Labor

This section (lines 62 through 67) covers domestic prices, production, and labor market indicators. A more detailed discussion of major price indicators is provided in the *IFS Supplement on Price Statistics*, No. 12 (1986).

The index series are compiled from reported versions of national indices and, for some production and labor series, from absolute data.

There is a wide variation between countries and over time in the selection of base years, depending upon the availability of comprehensive benchmark data that permit an adequate review of weighting patterns. The series are linked by using ratio splicing at the first annual overlap, and the linked series are shifted to a common base period 2000=100.

For industrial production, the data are seasonally adjusted if an appropriate adjusted series is available. Seasonally adjusted series are indicated in the descriptor and also described in the country notes in the monthly issues.

Share Prices

Indices shown for Share Prices (line 62) generally relate to common shares of companies traded on national or foreign stock exchanges. Monthly indices are obtained as simple arithmetic averages of the daily or weekly indices, although in some cases mid-month or end-of-month quotations are included.

All reported indices are adjusted for changes in quoted nominal capital of companies. Indices are, in general, base-weighted arithmetic averages with market value of outstanding shares as weights.

Producer Price Index or Wholesale Price Index

Indices shown for Producer or Wholesale Prices (line 63) are designed to monitor changes in prices of items at the first important commercial transaction. Where a choice is available, preference is given to the Producer Price Index (PPI), because the concept, weighting pattern, and coverage are likely to be more consistent with national accounts and industrial production statistics. In principle, the PPI should include service industries, but in practice it is limited to the domestic agricultural and industrial sectors. The prices should be farm-gate prices for the agricultural sector and ex-factory prices for the industrial sector.

The Wholesale Price Index (WPI), when used, covers a mixture of prices of agricultural and industrial goods at various stages of production and distribution, inclusive of imports and import duties. Preference is given to indices that provide broad coverage of the economy. The indices are computed using the Laspeyres formula, unless otherwise indicated in the country notes in the monthly issues.

Subindices are occasionally included for the PPI or the WPI.

Consumer Price Index

Indices shown for Consumer Prices (line 64) are the most frequently used indicators of inflation and reflect changes in the cost of acquiring a fixed basket of goods and services by the average consumer. Preference is given to series having wider geographical coverage and relating to all income groups, provided they are no less current than more narrowly defined series.

Because the weights are usually derived from household expenditure surveys (which may be conducted infrequently), information on the year to which the weights refer is provided in the country table notes in the monthly issues. The notes also provide information on any limitations in the coverage of commodities for pricing, income groups, or their expenditures in the chosen index. The Laspeyres formula is used unless otherwise indicated in the country notes.

For the European Union (EU) countries, a harmonized index of consumer prices (HICP) (line 64h) is shown. It is compiled according to methodological and sampling standards set by the European Commission. Owing to institutional differences among the EU member countries, the HICP excludes expenditure on certain types of goods and services. Examples are medical care and services of owner-occupied dwellings.

Wage Rates or Earnings

Indices shown for Wages Rates or Earnings (line 65) represent wage rates or earnings per worker employed per specified time period. Where establishment surveys are the source, the indices are likely to have the same coverage as the Industrial Production Index (line 66) and the Industrial Employment Index (line 67). Preference is given to data for earnings that include payments in kind and family allowances and that cover salaried employees as well as wage earners. The indices either are computed from absolute wage data or are as reported directly to the Fund.

Industrial Production

Indices shown for Industrial Production (line 66) are included as indicators of current economic activity. For some countries the indices are supplemented by indicators (such as data on tourism) relevant to a particular country.

Generally, the coverage of industrial production indices comprises mining and quarrying, manufacturing and electricity, and gas and water, according to the UN International Standard Industrial Classification (ISIC). The indices are generally compiled using the Laspeyres formula.

For many developing countries the indices refer to the production of a major primary commodity, such as crude petroleum. For most of the OECD countries, Industrial Production data are sourced from the OECD database, as indicated in the country notes.

Labor

Labor market indicators refer to the levels of the Labor Force (line 67d), Employment (line 67e), Unemployment (line 67c), and the Unemployment Rate (line 67r). Data on labor market statistics cover the economically active civilian population. They are provided by the International Labor Organization (ILO), which publishes these data in its *Yearbook of Labour Statistics* and its quarterly *Bulletin of Labour Statistics* and supplements. The concept of employment and unemployment conforms to the recommendations adopted by the ILO: Thirteenth International Conference of Labor Statisticians, Geneva, 1992. In addition, indices of employment in the industrial sector (line 67) are provided for 49 countries. For the euro area, EUROSTAT provides the data. Supplemental sources are also available on the industrial countries' websites.

8. International Transactions

Summary statistics on the international transactions of a country are given in lines 70 through 79. A section on external trade statistics (lines 70 through 76) provides data on the values (lines 70 and 71), volumes (lines 72 and 73), unit values (lines 74 and 75), and prices (line 76) for exports and imports. A section follows on balance of payments statistics (lines 78 through 79).

External Trade

Merchandise Exports f.o.b. (line 70) and Imports c.i.f. (line 71) are, in general, customs statistics reported under the general trade system, in accordance with the recommendations of the UN International Merchandise Trade Statistics: Concepts and Definitions, 1998. For some countries, data relate to the special trade system. The difference between general and special trade lies mainly in the treatment of the recording of the movement of goods through customs-bonded storage areas (warehouses, free areas, etc.).

Many countries use customs data on exports and imports as the primary source for the recording of exports and imports of goods in the balance of payments. However, customs data and the entries for goods in the balance of payments may not be equal, owing to differences in definition. These differences may relate to the following:

- the coverage of transactions (e.g., the goods item in the balance of payments often includes adjustments for certain goods transactions that may not be recorded by customs authorities, e.g., parcel post),
- the time of recording of transactions (e.g., in the balance of payments, transactions are to be recorded when change of ownership occurs, rather than the moment goods cross the customs border, which generally determines when goods are recorded in customs based trade statistics), and
- some classification differences (e.g., in the balance of payments, repair on goods is part of goods transactions).

The data for Merchandise Imports f.o.b. (line 71.v) are obtained directly from statistical authorities.

Details of commodity exports are presented for commodities that are traded in the international markets and have an impact on world market prices.

Data for petroleum exports are presented only for 12 oil exporting countries. For a number of these countries, data estimated by Fund staff are derived from available data for the volume of production. They are also derived from estimates for prices that are, in part, taken from *Petroleum Intelligence Weekly* and other international sources. The country table notes in the monthly issues provide details of these estimates.

For a number of countries where data are uncurrent or unavailable, additional lines show data, converted from U.S. dollars to national currency, from the Fund's *Direction of Trade Statistics* quarterly publication (*DOTS*). Exports and imports data published in *DOTS* include reported data, updated where necessary with estimates for the current periods. The introduction of *DOTS* gives a description of the nature of the estimates.

Indices for Volume of Exports (line 72) and Volume of Imports (line 73) are either Laspeyres or Paasche. For nine countries, as indicated in the country notes, export volume indices are calculated from reported volume data for individual commodities weighted by reported values.

Indices for Unit Value of Exports (line 74) and Unit Value of Imports (line 75) are Laspeyres, with weights derived from the data for transactions. For about seven countries, also as indicated in the country notes, export unit values are calculated from reported value and volume data for individual commodities. The country indices are unit value indices, except for a few, which are components of wholesale price indices or based on specific price quotations.

Indices for export and import prices are compiled from survey data for wholesale prices or directly from the exporter or importer (called "direct pricing"). They are shown in line 76, where available. In the absence of national sources, data for wholesale prices are taken from world commodity markets and are converted into national currency at period average exchange rates. Indices based on direct pricing are generally considered preferable to unit value indices, because problems of unit value bias are reduced.

A more detailed presentation of trade statistics is presented in the *IFS Supplement on Trade Statistics*, No. 15 (1988).

Balance of Payments Statistics

The balance of payments lines are presented on the basis of the methodology and presentation of the fifth edition of the *Balance of Payments Manual (BPM5)*. Published by the IMF in 1993, the *BPM5* was supplemented and amended by the *Financial Derivatives, a Supplement to the Fifth Edition (1993) of the Balance of Payments Manual*, published in 2000. Before 1995, issues of the *IFS Yearbook* presented balance of payments data based on the fourth edition of the manual (*BPM4*).

Lines for Balance of Payments Statistics

In *IFS*, balance of payments data are shown in an analytic presentation (i.e., the components are classified into five major data categories, which the Fund regards as useful for analyzing balance of payments developments in a uniform manner). In the analytic presentation, the components are arrayed to highlight the financing items (the reserves and related items). The standard presentation, as described in the *BPM5*, provides structural framework within which balance of payments statistics are compiled. Both analytic and standard presentations are published in the *Balance of Payments Statistics Yearbook*.

Current Account, n.i.e. (line 78ald) is the sum of the balance on goods, services and income (line 78aid), plus current transfers, n.i.e.: credit (line 78ajd), plus current transfers: debit (line 78akd) (i.e., line 78aid, plus line 78ajd, plus line 78akd).

Goods: Exports f.o.b. (line 78aad) and Goods: Imports f.o.b. (line 78abd) are both measured on the "free-on-board" (f.o.b.) basis—that is, by the value of the goods at the border of the exporting economy. For imports, this excludes the cost of freight and insurance incurred beyond the border of the exporting economy. The goods item covers general merchandise, goods for processing, repairs on goods, goods procured in ports by carriers, and nonmonetary gold.

Trade Balance (line 78acd) is the balance of exports f.o.b. and imports f.o.b. (line 78aad plus line 78abd). A positive trade balance shows that merchandise exports are larger than merchandise imports, whereas a negative trade balance shows that merchandise imports are larger than merchandise exports.

Services: Credit (line 78add) and Services: Debit (line 78aed) comprise services in transportation, travel, communication, construction, insurance, finance, computer and information, royalties and license fees, other business, personal, cultural and recreational, and government, n.i.e.

Balance on Goods and Services (line 78afd) is the sum of the balance on goods (line 78acd), plus services: credit (line 78add), plus services: debit (line 78aed) (i.e., line 78acd, plus line 78add, plus line 78aed).

Income: Credit (line 78agd) and Income: Debit (line 78ahd) comprise (1) investment income (consisting of direct investment income, portfolio investment income, and other investment income), and (2) compensation of employees.

Balance on Gds., Serv., & Inc. (i.e., Balance on Goods, Services, and Income) (line 78aid) is the sum of the balance on goods and services (line 78afd), plus income: credit (line 78agd), plus income: debit (line 78ahd) (i.e., line 78afd, plus line 78agd, plus line 78ahd).

Current Transfers, n.i.e.: Credit (line 78ajd) comprise all current transfers received by the reporting economy, except those made to the economy to finance its "overall balance" (see line 78cbd description below); therefore, the label "n.i.e." The latter are included in Exceptional Financing (line 79ded) (see below). (Note: Some of the capital and financial account lines shown below are also labeled "n.i.e." This means that Exceptional Financing items have been excluded from specific capital and financial account components.) Current transfers comprise (1) general government transfers and (2) other sector transfers, including workers' remittances.

Current Transfers: Debit (line 78akd) comprise all current transfers paid by the reporting economy.

Capital Account, n.i.e. (line 78bcd) is the balance on the capital account (capital account, n.i.e.: credit, plus capital account: debit). Capital account, n.i.e.: credit (line 78bad) covers (1) transfers linked to the acquisition of a fixed asset and (2) the disposal of nonproduced, nonfinancial assets. It does not include debt forgiveness, which is classified under Exceptional Financing. Capital account: debit (line 78bbd) covers (1) transfers linked to the disposal of fixed assets, and (2) acquisition of nonproduced, nonfinancial assets.

Financial Account, n.i.e. (line 78bjd) is the net sum of direct investment (line 78bdd plus line 78bed), portfolio investment (line 78bfd plus line 78bgd), financial derivatives (line 78bwd plus line 78bxd), and other investment (line 78bhd plus line 78bid).

Direct Investment Abroad (line 78bdd) and Direct Investment in Rep. Econ., n.i.e. (Direct Investment in the Reporting Economy, n.i.e.) (line 78bed) represent the flows of direct investment capital out of the reporting economy and those into the reporting economy, respectively. Direct investment includes equity capital, reinvested earnings, other capital, and financial derivatives associated with various intercompany transactions between affiliated enterprises. Excluded are flows of direct investment capital into the reporting economy for exceptional financing, such as debt-for-equity swaps. Direct investment abroad is usually shown with a negative figure, reflecting an increase in net outward investment by residents, with a corresponding net payment outflow from the reporting economy. Direct investment in the reporting economy is generally shown with a positive figure, reflecting an increase in net inward investment by nonresidents, with a corresponding net payment inflow into the reporting economy.

Portfolio Investment Assets (line 78bfd) and Portfolio Investment Liab., n.i.e. (Portfolio Investment Liabilities) (line 78bgd) include transactions with nonresidents in financial securities of any maturity (such as corporate securities, bonds, notes, and money market instruments) other than those included in direct investment, exceptional financing, and reserve assets.

Equity Securities Assets (line 78bkd) and Equity Securities Liabilities (line 78bmd) include shares, stocks, participation, and similar documents (such as American depository receipts) that usually denote ownership of equity.

Debt Securities Assets (line 78bld) and Debt Securities Liabilities (line 78bnd) cover (1) bonds, debentures, notes, etc., and (2) money market or negotiable debt instruments.

Financial Derivatives Assets (line 78bwd) and Financial Derivatives Liabilities (line 78bxd) cover financial instruments that are linked to other specific financial instruments, indicators, or commodities, and through which specific financial risks (such as interest rate risk, foreign exchange risk, equity and commodity price risks, credit risk, etc.) can, in their own right, be traded in financial markets. The *IFS* presents gross asset and liability information. However, owing to the unique nature of financial derivatives, and the manner in which some institutions record transactions, some countries can provide only net transactions data. While such net data could be included under assets, in the *IFS* it has been decided to include these net transactions, and net positions when reported, under liabilities, because one common source of demand for these instruments is from entities that are hedging cash flows associated with debt liabilities.

Other Investment Assets (line 78bhd) and Other Investment Liabilities, n.i.e. (line 78bid) include all financial transactions not covered in direct investment, portfolio investment, financial derivatives, or reserve assets. Major categories are transactions in currency and deposits, loans, and trade credits.

Net Errors and Omissions (line 78cad) is a residual category needed to ensure that all debit and credit entries in the balance of payments statement sum to zero. It reflects statistical inconsistencies in the recording of the credit and debit entries. In the *IFS* presentation, net errors and omissions is equal to, and opposite in sign to, the total value of the following items: the current account balance (line 78ald), the capital account balance (line 78bcd), the financial account balance (line 78bjd), and reserves and reserve related items (line 79dad). The item is intended as an offset to the overstatement or understatement of the recorded components. Thus, if the balance of those components is a credit, the item for net errors and omissions will be shown as a debit of equal value, and vice versa.

Overall Balance (line 78cbd) is the sum of the balances on the current account (line 78ald), the capital account (line 78bcd), the financial account (line 78bjd), and net errors and omissions (line 78cad) (i.e., line 78ald, plus line 78bcd, plus line 78bjd, plus line 78cad).

Reserves and Related Items (line 79dad) is the sum of transactions in reserve assets (line 79dbd), exceptional financing (line 79ded), and use of Fund credit and loans (line 78dcd) (i.e., line 79dbd, plus line 79ded, plus line 79dcd).

Reserve Assets (line 79dbd) consists of external assets readily available to and controlled by monetary authorities primarily for direct financing of payments imbalances and for indirect regulating of the magnitude of such imbalances through exchange market intervention. Reserve assets comprise monetary gold, special drawing rights, reserve position in the Fund, foreign exchange assets (consisting of currency and deposits and securities), and other claims.

Use of Fund Credit and Loans (line 79dcd) includes purchases and repurchases in the credit tranches of the Fund's General Resource Account, and net borrowings under the Structural Adjustment Facility (SAF), the Poverty Reduction and Growth Facility (PRGF), which was previously named the Enhanced Structural Adjustment Facility (ESAF), and the Trust Fund.

Exceptional Financing (line 79ded) includes any other transactions undertaken by the authorities to finance the "overall balance," as an alternative to, or in conjunction with, the use of reserve assets and the use of Fund credit and loans from the Fund.

A more detailed presentation of balance of payments data for use in cross-country comparisons is published in the *Balance of Payments Statistics Yearbook*.

Lines for International Investment Position

The international investment position (IIP) data are presented in lines 79aad through 79ljd. An economy's IIP is a balance sheet of the stock of external financial assets and liabilities. The coverage of the various components of IIP is similar to that of the corresponding components under the balance of payments. The IIP at the end of a specific period reflects not only the sum of balance of payments transactions over time, but also price changes, exchange rate changes, and other adjustments.

Countries in the early stages of IIP compilation are encouraged to submit partial IIP statements. In general, these partial statements include data on the monetary authorities (including international reserves) and at least one other sector. No totals are shown for partial IIP statements.

9. Government Finance

Section 80 presents summary statistics on government finance. The summary statistics cover operations of the budgetary central government or of the consolidated central government (i.e., operations of budgetary central government, extrabudgetary units, and social security funds). The coverage of consolidated central government may not necessarily include all existing extrabudgetary units and/or social security funds.

Unless otherwise stated in individual country notes in the monthly issues, data are as reported for *IFS*. In some cases, data are derived from unpublished worksheets and are therefore not attributed to a specific source.

Quarterly and monthly data, when available, may not add up to the annual data, owing to differences in coverage and/or methodology. The country notes in the monthly issues will indicate these differences.

More extensive data for use in cross-country comparisons are published in the *Government Finance Statistics Yearbook (GFSY)* and are based on *A Manual on Government Finance Statistics*. When countries do not report data for *IFS* but provide data for the *GFSY*, these data are published in *IFS*.

The data for lines 80 through 87 are flows and are on a cash basis, as follows:

The Deficit or Surplus (line 80) is calculated as the difference between Revenue and, if applicable, Grants Received (lines 81 and 81z) on the one hand and Expenditure and Lending Minus Repayments (lines 82 and 83) on the other. The deficit/surplus is also equal, with the opposite sign, to the sum of the net borrowing by the government plus the net decrease in government cash, deposits, and securities held for liquidity purposes.

Revenue (line 81) comprises all nonrepayable government receipts, whether requited or unrequited, other than grants; revenue is shown net of refunds and other adjustment transactions.

Grants Received (line 81z) comprises all unrequited, nonrepayable, noncompulsory receipts from other governments—domestic or foreign—and international institutions. Grants are grouped with revenue because, like revenue, they provide the means whereby expenditure can be made without incurring a debt for future repayment.

Expenditure (line 82) comprises all nonrepayable payments by government, whether requited or unrequited and whether for current or capital purposes.

Lending Minus Repayments (line 83) comprises government acquisition of claims on others—both loans and equities—for public policy purposes and is net of repayments of lending and sales of equities previously purchased. Line 83 includes both domestic and foreign lending minus repayments. In determining the deficit or surplus, lending minus repayments is grouped with expenditure, because it is presumed to represent a means of pursuing government policy objectives and not to be an action undertaken to manage government liquidity.

The total of the financing items equals the deficit or surplus with a reverse sign. Total Financing is classified according to the residence of the lender. Where this information is not available, the distinction is based on the currency in which the debt instruments are denominated.

For some countries, Total Financing is broken down between Net Borrowing and Use of Cash Balances. Net Borrowing covers the net change in government liabilities to all other sectors. It represents mainly other sectors' direct loans or advances to government or their holding of government securities acquired from the government itself or in transactions with others. Where possible, data for Domestic and Foreign Net Borrowing are classified according to the residence of the lender.

Use of Cash Balances (line 87) is intended to measure changes over a period—resulting from transactions but not revaluations—in government holdings of currency and deposits with the monetary system. It corresponds to changes in IFS lines 16d and 26d. All currency issues are regarded as liabilities of the monetary authorities, rather than government debt. And any proceeds reaching the government are regarded as coming from the monetary authorities.

Data for outstanding Debt (lines 88 and 89) relate to the direct and assumed debt of the central government and exclude loans guaranteed by the government. The distinction between Domestic and Foreign Debt (lines 88a and 89a) is based on residence of the lender, where possible, but otherwise on the currency in which the debt instruments are denominated (lines 88b and 89b).

The euro area table and the tables of the individual euro area countries also present Deficit or Surplus (line 80g) and Debt (line 88g) data for the general government, expressed as percent of harmonized Gross Domestic Product. Both indicators are defined according to the convergence criteria on public finance as laid down in the Maastricht Treaty. Deficit or Surplus corresponds to net lending/borrowing. The data are not comparable with central government Deficit or Surplus (line 80) and Debt (line 88), owing to differences in coverage as well as in definition.

10. National Accounts and Population

The summary data for national accounts are compiled according to the *System of National Accounts (SNA)*. Gross Domestic Product (GDP) is presented in IFS as the sum of final expenditures, following the presentation of the *1993 SNA*, as well as the *European System of Accounts (1995 ESA)*.

The national accounts lines shown in the country tables are as follows:

Household Consumption Expenditure, including Nonprofit Institutions Serving Households (NPISHs) (line 96f), Government Consumption Expenditure (line 91f), Gross Fixed Capital Formation (line 93e), Changes in Inventories (line 93i) (formerly Increase/Decrease(-) in Stocks), Exports of Goods and Services (line 90c), and Imports of Goods and Services (line 98c).

Household Consumption Expenditure, including Nonprofit Institutions Serving Households (NPISHs) (line 96f) consists of the expenditure incurred by resident households and resident NPISHs on individual consumption goods and services. Government Consumption Expenditure (line 91f) consists of expenditure incurred by general government on both individual-consumption goods and services and collective-consumption services.

Gross Fixed Capital Formation (line 93e) is measured by the total value of a producer's acquisitions, less disposals, of fixed assets during the accounting period, plus certain additions to the value of nonproduced assets (such as subsoil assets or major improvements in the quantity, quality, or productivity of land). Changes in Inventories (line 93i) (including work-in-progress) consist of changes in (1) stocks of outputs that are still held by the units that produced them before the outputs are further processed, sold, delivered to other units, or used in other ways and (2) stocks of products acquired from other units that are intended to be used for intermediate consumption or for resale without further processing.

Exports of Goods and Services (line 90c) consist of sales, barter, gifts, or grants of goods and services from residents to nonresidents. Imports of Goods and Services (line 98c) consist of purchases, barter, or receipts of gifts or grants of goods and services by residents from nonresidents. Gross Domestic Product (GDP) (line 99b) is the sum of consumption expenditure (of households, NPISHs, and general government), gross fixed capital formation, changes in inventories, and exports of goods and services, less the value of imports of goods and services.

Net Primary Income from Abroad (line 98.n) is the difference between the total values of the primary incomes receivable from, and payable to, nonresidents. Gross National Income (line 99a) is derived by adding net primary income from abroad to GDP.

Gross National Income (GNI) (line 99a) is derived by adding Net Primary Income from Abroad (line 98.n) to GDP. Gross National Disposable Income (GNDI) (line 99i) is derived by adding Net Current Transfers from Abroad (line 98t) to GNI, and Gross Saving (line 99s) is derived by deducting final consumption expenditure (lines 96f + 91f) from GNDI. Consumption of Fixed Capital (line 99cf) is shown for countries that provide these data.

The country table notes in the monthly issues provide information on which countries have implemented the *1993 SNA* or the *1995 ESA*.

The national accounts lines generally do not explicitly show the statistical discrepancies between aggregate GDP compiled from expenditure flows as against GDP compiled from the production or income accounts (or from a mixture of these accounts). Hence, in some cases, the components of GDP that are shown in IFS may not add up exactly to the total.

For countries that publish quarterly seasonally adjusted data, the data in IFS in the monthly issues are also on a seasonally adjusted basis (codes ending with c or r). For the United States, Japan, Australia, South Africa, Argentina, and Mexico, quarterly data are shown at annual rates, which the country authorities provide as such.

Lines 99b.p and 99b.r are measures of GDP volume at reference year value levels. In the past, these series used a common reference year (e.g., 1990) for publication. With the June 1999 issue, these series are published on the same reference year(s) as reported by the national compilers. The code *p* indicates data that are not seasonally adjusted, whereas code *r* indicates data that are seasonally adjusted.

Lines 99bvp and 99bvr are GDP volume indices that are presented on a standard 2000 reference year and are derived from the GDP volume series reported by national compilers. For this calculation the data series provided by national compilers are linked together (if there is more than one series) to form a single time series. The earliest overlapping year from the different reference year series is used to calculate the link factors.

The GDP Deflator (lines 99bip or 99bir) are not direct measurements of prices but are derived implicitly: the GDP series at current prices is divided by constant price GDP series referenced to

2000. The latter series is constructed by multiplying the 2000 current price GDP level by the GDP volume index (2000=100). The deflator is expressed in index form with 2000=100.

Data on Population are provided by the Population Division of the Department of Economic and Social Affairs of the United Nations. These data represent mid-year estimates and are revised every two years.

11. World Tables

Besides the world tables on exchange rates, members' Fund positions and transactions, international reserves, and interest rates—discussed earlier in this introduction—*IFS* also brings together country data on money, consumer prices, values and unit values of countries' exports and imports, and wholesale prices and unit values (expressed in U.S. dollars) of principal world trade commodities. Tables on balance of payments may be found in the *IFS* yearbook and also in the *Balance of Payments Statistics Yearbook, Part 2*.

Tables showing totals or averages of country series may report data for selected countries only.

Country Groups

Countries whose data are included in **world/all countries'** totals and averages are arrayed into two main groups—industrial countries and developing countries. The **industrial** countries' group also shows separate data for the euro area. The **developing** countries group is further subdivided into area subgroups for Africa, Asia, Europe, the Middle East, and the Western Hemisphere.

The country composition of the world is all countries for which the topic series are available in the *IFS* files. Consequently, the country coverage of some areas, mainly Africa and Asia, differs from topic to topic, and area and world totals or averages may be biased to some extent toward the larger reporting countries.

Data for subgroups oil exporting countries and non-oil developing countries are shown as memorandum items. Oil exporting countries are defined as those countries whose oil exports (net of any imports of crude oil) both represent a minimum of two thirds of their total exports and are at least equivalent to approximately 1 percent of world exports of oil. The calculations presently used to determine which countries meet the above criteria are based on 1976–78 averages.

Area and World Indices

Area and world indices are obtained as weighted averages of country indices. For the area and world indices on unit values of exports and imports—where the country indices are expressed in U.S. dollars—arithmetic means are used. For consumer prices and industrial production, geometric means are used because, unlike arithmetic means, geometric means are not unduly influenced by data for the few countries with extreme growth rates. Geometric means assure that, if all series have constant although different rates of increase, their average will have a constant rate of increase.

The weights are as follows: For the area averages for consumer prices, the country series are weighted by the 2000 purchasing power parity (PPP) value of GDP. (A comparison of PPP-based GDP weights and exchange rate-based GDP weights is presented in *World Economic Outlook*, May 1993, Annex IV.) For the industrial production table, the country series are weighted by value added in industry, as derived from individual countries' national accounts, expressed in U.S. dollars. And for the export unit values and import unit values tables, the country series are weighted by the 2000 value of exports and imports (both in U.S. dollars), respectively.

Weights are normally updated at about five-year intervals—following international practice—to reflect changes in the importance of each country's data with the data of all other countries. The standard weight base years used are 1953, 1958, 1963, 1970, 1975, 1980, 1984–86, 1990, 1995, and 2000. The corresponding time spans to which the weights are applied are 1948–55, 1955–60, 1960–68, 1968–73, 1973–78, 1978–83, 1983–88, 1988–93, 1993–98, and 1998 onward.

Separate averages are calculated for each time span, and the index series are linked by the splicing at overlap years and shifted to the reference base 2000=100.

Calculation of Area Totals and Averages

The calculation of area totals and averages in the world tables takes account of the problem that data for some countries do not run through the end of the period for which world and area data should be calculable. If country data are known that contribute at least 60 percent of the area total or index aggregate during recent periods for which data of all countries of an area are available, then area totals and averages for most topics are estimated for current and for earlier periods.

Area totals or averages are estimated by assuming that the rate of change in the unreported country data is the same as the rate of change in the weighted total or average of the reported country data for that area. These estimates are made for the area totals and averages only; separate country estimates are not calculated.

Except for import unit values, the world totals and averages are made from the calculated and estimated data for the two main groups—industrial countries and developing countries. A world total or average will only be calculated when totals or averages are available for both these country groups.

For import unit values, world data are calculated directly from country data. This is because the number of countries for which the series are available and current is insufficient to allow calculation or estimation of the area averages and because the variability of import unit value indices among countries is judged to be less than that for other topics. World estimates are made when data are available for countries whose combined weights represent at least 80 percent of the total country weights.

For the terms of trade index numbers in the yearbook, the world and area data for export unit values are divided by the corresponding series for import unit values, where possible. Thus terms of trade averages are available only for areas with both export and import unit values. The country coverage within the areas for the export and import unit values is not identical, leading to a small degree of asymmetry in the terms of trade calculation.

Calculation of Individual World Tables

International Reserves: Country series on international reserves begin generally with their appropriate dates and are complete monthly time series; therefore, earlier period estimates are not required. When current data of a few countries of an area are not reported, the area total is estimated by carrying forward the last reported country figure.

Money (and Reserve Money and Money plus Quasi-Money, which are available in the yearbook): Percent changes are based on end-of-year data (over a 12-month period for Money). When there is more than one version or definition of money over time, different time series are chained through a ratio splicing technique. When actual stock data needed for the growth rate calculation are missing, no percent change is shown in the world table.

Ratio of Reserve Money to Money plus Quasi-Money (available in the yearbook): The measures of money used in calculating this ratio are end-of-year data.

Income Velocity of Money plus Quasi-Money: The measure of income in this table is *IFS* data on GDP. The data for money plus quasi-money are annual averages of the highest frequency data available. The ratio is then converted into an index number with a base year of 1995.

Real Effective Exchange Rate Indices: This table shows three real effective exchange rate indices for industrial countries. Two of these comprise alternative measures of costs and prices derived from Relative Unit Labor Costs (line 65um) and Relative Normalized Unit Labor Costs (line reu). They have been applied to the weighting scheme, based on aggregated data for trade in manufactured goods, averaged over the period 1989–91. The weights reflect both the relative importance of a country's trading partners in its direct bilateral trade relations and that resulting from competition in third markets. The measure is expressed as an index 2000=100 in accord with all indices published in *IFS*.

One of the two indices—the index Based on Relative Normalized Unit Labor Costs (line reu)—is also shown in the country tables (except for Ireland), with the Nominal Effective Exchange Rate Index (line neu) from which the measures are drawn.

The third real effective exchange rate index—Based on Relative Consumer Prices (line rec)—is provided as a measure of domestic cost and price developments. It covers trade in manufactured goods and primary products for trading partners—and competitors. It uses the same methodology used to compile nominal and real effective exchange rates for nonindustrial countries, as discussed in the exchange rate and exchange rate arrangements section of this introduction.

Beginning with the October 1992 issue of *IFS*, the data published are from a revised database. The database underwent a comprehensive review and update of the underlying data sources and a change in the method of normalization of output per hour. The method uses the Hodrick-Prescott filter, which smoothes a time series by removing short-run fluctuations while retaining changes of a larger amplitude.

The footnotes to this world table in the monthly issues discuss the data sources used to derive the cost and price indicators for the real effective exchange rates.

Producer/Wholesale Prices (world table available in the yearbook): Data are those prices reported in lines 63* in the country tables. The percent changes are calculated from the index number series.

Consumer Prices: Data are those prices reported in lines 64* in the country tables. The percent changes are calculated from the index number series.

Industrial Production: This table presents non-seasonally adjusted indices on industrial production for 22 industrial countries, together with an aggregate index for the group. The data are those shown in the country tables as either Industrial Production (lines 66..*) or Manufacturing Production (lines 66ey*), the asterisk representing a wildcard.

Wages (world table available in the yearbook): This table presents indices computed either from absolute wage data or from the wage indices reported to the Fund for the industrial sector for 22 industrial countries. The data are those shown in the country tables as Wage Rates or Earnings (line 65).

Employment (world table available in the yearbook): This table presents indices computed from indices of employment or number of persons employed as reported by the countries for the industrial sector for 20 industrial countries. The data are those shown in the country tables as Employment (lines 67 or 67ey).

Exports and *Imports:* Data are published in U.S. dollars, as reported, if available, by the countries. Otherwise, monthly data in national currency, published in the country tables (lines 70... and 71...), are converted to U.S. dollars using the exchange rate rf. For quarterly and annual data, conversions are made using the trade-weighted average of the monthly exchange rates.

Export Unit Values/Export Prices and *Import Unit Values/Import Prices:* Data are the index numbers reported in the country tables expressed in U.S. dollars at rate rf. The country indices are typically unit value data (lines 74 and 75). However, for some countries, they are components of wholesale price indices or are derived from specific price quotations (lines 76, 76.x, and 76aa).

Terms of Trade (world table available in the yearbook): Data are index numbers computed from the export and import unit value indices and shown in the appropriate world table. The percent changes are calculated from the index number series.

Balance of Payments (world tables available in the yearbook): For a precise definition of the concepts used in these tables, the reader is referred to the section in this introduction on international transactions. The concepts and definitions are further described in the fifth edition of the *Balance of Payments Manual*, as supplemented and amended by *Financial Derivatives, a Supplement to the Fifth Edition of the Balance of Payments Manual*.

Trade Balance is the series reported in line 78acd of the country tables. Current Account Balance, Excluding Exceptional Financing is the series reported in line 78ald of the country tables. Capital and Financial Account, Including Net Errors and Omissions but Excluding Reserve Assets, Use of Fund Credit, and Exceptional Financing are the sum of the series reported in lines 78bcd, 78bjd, and 78cad of the country tables. Overall Balance Excluding Reserve Assets, Use of Fund Credit, and Exceptional Financing is the series reported in line 78cbd (calculated as the sum of lines 78ald, 78bcd, 78bjd, and 78cad) of the country tables. Note that in some cases, data published in the country pages may be more current than those in the Balance of Payments world tables due to an earlier cutoff date for calculating these world tables.

GDP Volume Measures (world table available in the yearbook): Data are derived from those series reported in lines 99bvp and 99bvr in the country tables. The percent changes are calculated from index numbers.

GDP Deflator (world table available in the yearbook): Data are derived from those series reported in lines 99bip in the country tables. The percent changes are calculated from index numbers.

Gross Capital Formation as Percentage of GDP (world table available in the yearbook): Data are the percent share of gross capital formation in GDP at current market prices. Gross capital formation comprises Gross Fixed Capital Formation and Increase/Decrease (-) in Stocks (lines 93e and 93i, respectively).

Final Consumption Expenditure as a Percentage of GDP (world table available in the yearbook): Data are the percent share of final consumption expenditure in GDP at current market prices, which comprises Government Consumption and Private Consumption (91f and 96f, respectively).

Commodity Prices: Data are obtained primarily from the Commodities and Special Issues Division of the IMF's Research Department, from *Commodity Price Data* of the World Bank, from

Monthly Commodity Price Bulletin of the UNCTAD, and from a number of countries that produce commodities that are significantly traded in the international markets. Data derived from the last source are reported in the country tables. The market price series (lines 76) are expressed as U.S. dollars per quantity units and refer to values often used in the respective commodity markets. For comparison purposes, indices of unit values (lines 74) at base 2000=100 are provided. The accompanying notes to the table (located in the back of the printed copies) provide information specific to each commodity series, including data sources, grades, and quotation frequency.

12. Country Codes and *IFS* Line Numbers

Each *IFS* time series carries a unique identification code. For publication purposes, the code has been truncated to a three-digit country code and to a five-digit subject code, referred to as the *IFS* line number.

Line numbers apply uniformly across countries—that is, a given line number measures the same economic variable for each country, subject to data availability. The line numbers take the form of two numerics followed by three alphabetic codes (NNaaa). The two numerics are the section and subsection codes, the first two alphabetic codes are the classification codes, and the last alphabetic code is the qualification code. Any of these positions may be blank: for publication purposes, blanks in the first or final positions are omitted, whereas embedded blanks are represented by a period. The line numbers are part of the descriptor stub in the country tables.

Data expressed in units of money (values or prices) are ordinarily expressed in national currency and in natural form, that is, without seasonal adjustment. For these data the qualification code is blank.

Transformation of these data is denoted by various qualification codes. For data that are not seasonally adjusted, qualification codes are *d* for U.S. dollar values, *s* for SDR values, and *p* for constant national currency values. For data that are seasonally adjusted for *IFS*, codes are *f* for U.S. dollar values, *u* for SDR values, and *b* for national currency values. For data that are seasonally adjusted by national compilers, codes are *c* for national currency values and *r* for constant national currency values.

The qualification codes are also used to distinguish separate groups of deposit money banks or other financial institutions when data for separate groups are given.

13. Symbols, Conventions, and Abbreviations

The abbreviation "ff.," often used on the title page of the printed copies of *IFS*, means "following."

Entries printed in bold on the country pages of the monthly book refer to updates and revisions made since the publication of the preceding issue of *IFS*.

Italic midheadings in the middle of the pages of the monthly book and yearbook identify the units in which data are expressed and whether data are stocks (end of period), flows (transactions during a period), or averages (for a period).

(—) Indicates that a figure is zero or less than half a significant digit or that data do not exist.

(....) Indicates a lack of statistical data that can be reported or calculated from underlying observations.

(†) Marks a break in the comparability of data, as explained in the relevant notes in the monthly and yearbook. In these instances, data after the symbol do not form a consistent series with those for earlier dates. The break symbols not explained in the country table notes can show a point of splice, where series having different base years are linked. A case would be the series described in the section of this introduction on prices, production, and labor. They can also point out a change in magnitude for high-inflation countries, as described in the section on electronic products.

(e) In superscript position after the figure marks an observation that is an estimate.

(f) In superscript position after the figure marks an observation that is forecast.

(p) In superscript position after the figure marks that data are in whole or in part provisional or preliminary.

Standard source codes, listed in the footnotes, refer with some exceptions to the following data sources:

(A) Annual report of the central bank
(B) Bulletin of the central bank
(C) Customs department of a country
(E) OECD
(L) International Labor Organization
(M) Ministry or other national source
(N) National bureau or other national source
(S) Statistical office
(U) United Nations
(V) Eurostat

The CD-ROM supports text messages to indicate breaks in the data. The time series observations with footnotes are highlighted in bold blue type within the *IFS* Data Viewer. When the cursor is moved over the footnoted cell, a small window will be displayed with the footnoted text. These footnotes/comments provide meaningful information about the specific observation, e.g., butt splicing, ratio splicing, extrapolation, estimations, etc.

Because of space limits in the phototypesetting of descriptor stubs on the country tables and table headings of world tables, abbreviations are sometimes necessary. While most are self-explanatory, the following abbreviation in the descriptors and table headings should be noted:

n.i.e. = Not included elsewhere.
Of which: Currency Outside DMBs = Of which: Currency Outside Deposit Money Banks.
Househ.Cons.Expend.,incl.NPISHs = Household Consumption Expenditure, including Nonprofit Institutions Serving Households.
Use of Fund Credit (GRA) = Use of Fund Credit (General Resources Account).

Data relating to fiscal years are allocated to calendar years to which most of their months refer. Fiscal years ending June 30 are allocated to that calendar year. For instance, the fiscal year from July 1, 1999 to June 30, 2000 is shown as calendar year 2000.

For countries that have reported semiannual transactions data, the data for the first half of a year may be given in the monthly book in the column for the second quarter of that year. And those for the second half may be given in the column for the fourth quarter. In these instances, no data are shown in the columns for the first and third quarters.

14. CD-ROM and Internet Account Subscriptions

The *IFS* is available on CD-ROM and the Internet. It contains:

(1) all time series appearing on *IFS* country tables;

(2) all series published in the *IFS* world tables, except for the daily exchange rates appearing in the Exchange Rates tables;

(3) the following exchange rate series as available for all Fund members, plus Aruba and the Netherlands Antilles: aa, ac, ae, af, ag, ah, b, c, de, dg, ea, eb, ec, ed, g, rb, rd, rf, rh, sa, sb, sc, sd, wa, wc, we, wf, wg, wh, xe, xf, ye, yf, nec, rec, aat, aet, rbt, rft, neu, reu, and ahx (for an explanation of series af, ah, de, dg, rb, and rd, see *IFS Supplement on Exchange Rates*, No. 9 (1985));

(4) Fund accounts time series, denominated in SDR terms, for all countries for which data are available, though some series are not published in the *IFS* monthly book (2af, 2al, 2ap, 2aq, 2as, 2at 2ej, 2ek, 2en, 2eo, 2f.s, 1c.s, 2tl, 2egs, 2eb, 2h.s, 1bd, 1b.s, 2dus, 2krs, 2ees, 2kxs, 2eu, 2ey, 2eg, 2ens, 2ehs, 2eqs, 2ers, 2ets, 2kk, 2lk, 2kl, 2ll, 1ch, and 1cj) and in percentages (2tlp, 2fz, and 1bf); and

(5) balance of payments series (78aad to 79ded) for all countries for which data are available, though some series are not published in the *IFS* monthly book.

All series in *IFS* contain publication code F except for the euro data lines that contain the code W.

A partner country code may sometimes be included in the control field. When it exists, it usually is shown in the *IFS* printed copy either in the italic midheading (see Real Effective Exchange Rate Indices table) or in the notes (see Commodity Prices table notes). Occasionally, the partner country code attached to a commodity price refers to a market (e.g., the London Metals Exchange) rather than the country of origin.

In the yearbook, data expressed in national currency for countries that have undergone periods of high inflation (e.g., Brazil, Democratic Republic of Congo, and Turkey) are presented in different magnitudes on the same printed line. Users may refer to midheaders on country pages for an indication of the magnitude changes. The practice of expressing different magnitudes on the same line was adopted to prevent early-period data from disappearing from the printed tables. On the CD-ROM and the Internet (CSV format), the data are stored in a scientific notation with six significant digits for all time periods. Therefore, historical as well as current data may be viewed when using the display choices available on the CD-ROM and the Internet.

WORLD
and
AREA TABLES

Exchange Rates

SDR Rates: 1987–2004

	Jan.	Feb.	Mar.	Apr.	May	June	July	Aug.	Sep.	Oct.	Nov.	Dec.	I	II	III	IV	Year
sa US Dollars per SDR (End of Period)																	
1987	1.26759	1.26419	1.28563	1.30626	1.28658	1.27802	1.26723	1.29313	1.27964	1.32109	1.37379	1.41866	1.28563	1.27802	1.27964	1.41866	1.41866
1988	1.36642	1.36101	1.38729	1.38417	1.36483	1.31061	1.29648	1.28818	1.29039	1.34592	1.36637	1.34570	1.38729	1.31061	1.29039	1.34570	1.34570
1989	1.31093	1.32150	1.29271	1.29566	1.24362	1.24639	1.28749	1.24652	1.27981	1.27782	1.28771	1.31416	1.29271	1.24639	1.27981	1.31416	1.31416
1990	1.32559	1.31681	1.30083	1.30247	1.31200	1.32388	1.36564	1.38595	1.39256	1.43078	1.42677	1.42266	1.30083	1.32388	1.39256	1.42266	1.42266
1991	1.43476	1.42053	1.34632	1.34081	1.34084	1.31452	1.33400	1.33698	1.36800	1.36652	1.38072	1.43043	1.34632	1.31452	1.36800	1.43043	1.43043
1992	1.39733	1.38091	1.37174	1.36976	1.39632	1.43117	1.44416	1.48286	1.47284	1.40595	1.37896	1.37500	1.37174	1.43117	1.47284	1.37500	1.37500
1993	1.38188	1.37610	1.39773	1.42339	1.42847	1.40360	1.39072	1.40758	1.41840	1.39293	1.38389	1.37356	1.39773	1.40360	1.41840	1.37356	1.37356
1994	1.38067	1.39930	1.41260	1.42138	1.41733	1.44837	1.44327	1.44770	1.46738	1.48454	1.45674	1.45985	1.41260	1.44837	1.46738	1.45985	1.45985
1995	1.47670	1.49440	1.56050	1.57303	1.57591	1.56876	1.55954	1.49249	1.50632	1.49455	1.48615	1.48649	1.56050	1.56876	1.50632	1.48649	1.48649
1996	1.45169	1.46868	1.46121	1.45006	1.44219	1.44334	1.46554	1.45766	1.43937	1.44623	1.44462	1.43796	1.46121	1.44334	1.43937	1.43796	1.43796
1997	1.39466	1.38494	1.38689	1.36553	1.39179	1.38814	1.35862	1.36358	1.36521	1.38362	1.36184	1.34925	1.38689	1.38814	1.36521	1.34925	1.34925
1998	1.34536	1.35023	1.33589	1.34666	1.33536	1.33154	1.32949	1.34222	1.37132	1.40835	1.38017	1.40803	1.33589	1.33154	1.37132	1.40803	1.40803
1999	1.38977	1.36556	1.35784	1.35123	1.34196	1.33587	1.36421	1.36986	1.38769	1.38072	1.36963	1.37251	1.35784	1.33587	1.38769	1.37251	1.37251
2000	1.35288	1.33928	1.34687	1.31921	1.32002	1.33728	1.31335	1.30480	1.29789	1.27934	1.28197	1.30291	1.34687	1.33728	1.29789	1.30291	1.30291
2001	1.29779	1.29248	1.26065	1.26579	1.25423	1.24565	1.25874	1.28823	1.28901	1.27808	1.26608	1.25673	1.26065	1.24565	1.28901	1.25673	1.25673
2002	1.24204	1.24163	1.24691	1.26771	1.29066	1.33046	1.32248	1.32751	1.32269	1.32163	1.32408	1.35952	1.24691	1.33046	1.32269	1.35952	1.35952
2003	1.37654	1.37085	1.37379	1.38391	1.41995	1.40086	1.39195	1.37727	1.42979	1.43178	1.44878	1.48597	1.37379	1.40086	1.42979	1.48597	1.48597
2004	1.48131	1.48007	1.48051	1.45183	1.46882	1.46622	1.45776						1.48051	1.46622			
sb US Dollars per SDR (Period Average, geometric)																	
1987	1.25112	1.26216	1.26933	1.29153	1.30442	1.28656	1.26932	1.26927	1.29137	1.29530	1.34938	1.38310	1.26085	1.29415	1.27661	1.34210	1.29307
1988	1.37723	1.35556	1.37141	1.38197	1.37595	1.34654	1.30514	1.29206	1.29368	1.31949	1.35659	1.35588	1.36804	1.36807	1.29695	1.34387	1.34392
1989	1.32525	1.31652	1.30486	1.29975	1.26560	1.24062	1.27158	1.26166	1.24703	1.27221	1.27724	1.30191	1.31552	1.26843	1.26005	1.28372	1.28176
1990	1.31850	1.32659	1.30170	1.30135	1.31832	1.31442	1.34402	1.37719	1.39049	1.42846	1.44481	1.42654	1.31556	1.31134	1.37042	1.43325	1.35675
1991	1.42291	1.44058	1.38077	1.35123	1.34351	1.31934	1.32155	1.33571	1.35355	1.36201	1.38487	1.40799	1.41453	1.33796	1.33687	1.38483	1.36816
1992	1.40925	1.39042	1.36599	1.37060	1.38810	1.41173	1.44375	1.45645	1.45767	1.43476	1.38701	1.38883	1.38844	1.39004	1.45261	1.40336	1.40838
1993	1.37705	1.37168	1.38045	1.41266	1.41561	1.40969	1.39025	1.40151	1.41756	1.40746	1.38903	1.38404	1.37639	1.41265	1.40306	1.39347	1.39633
1994	1.37343	1.38750	1.40197	1.40425	1.41500	1.42736	1.45706	1.45439	1.46377	1.47720	1.47121	1.45201	1.38759	1.41550	1.45840	1.46676	1.43170
1995	1.46580	1.47826	1.53602	1.57620	1.55819	1.56369	1.55763	1.51069	1.48396	1.49828	1.49474	1.48532	1.49305	1.56601	1.51712	1.49277	1.51695
1996	1.46779	1.46625	1.46181	1.45086	1.44464	1.44290	1.45003	1.45830	1.44811	1.43968	1.45295	1.43817	1.46528	1.44613	1.45214	1.44359	1.45176
1997	1.41537	1.38421	1.37811	1.37150	1.38518	1.39032	1.37726	1.35396	1.35939	1.36989	1.37399	1.35418	1.39256	1.38231	1.36350	1.36599	1.37602
1998	1.34310	1.35002	1.34421	1.34312	1.34373	1.33354	1.33092	1.32668	1.36482	1.40747	1.39199	1.40211	1.34577	1.34013	1.34070	1.40051	1.35654
1999	1.40441	1.38073	1.36265	1.35485	1.34869	1.34004	1.33924	1.36415	1.37613	1.38943	1.37626	1.37280	1.38249	1.34785	1.35975	1.37948	1.36732
2000	1.37068	1.34485	1.34286	1.33915	1.31082	1.33062	1.32348	1.30836	1.29409	1.28650	1.28276	1.29440	1.35274	1.32681	1.30859	1.28788	1.31879
2001	1.30203	1.29353	1.27989	1.26764	1.26217	1.25028	1.25125	1.27495	1.28593	1.27882	1.26827	1.26279	1.29179	1.26001	1.27062	1.26995	1.27304
2002	1.25276	1.24463	1.25009	1.25669	1.27713	1.30065	1.33033	1.32103	1.32182	1.31765	1.33109	1.34003	1.24915	1.27803	1.32269	1.32960	1.29484
2003	1.36538	1.37045	1.37004	1.36908	1.40825	1.41481	1.39832	1.38494	1.39628	1.43198	1.43391	1.46743	1.36861	1.39658	1.39042	1.43959	1.39883
2004	1.49108	1.49645	1.47301	1.46088	1.45118	1.46565	1.47273						1.48982	1.46100			
sc SDRs per US Dollar (End of Period)																	
1987	.78890	.79102	.77783	.76554	.77725	.78246	.78913	.77332	.78147	.75695	.72791	.70489	.77783	.78246	.78147	.70489	.70489
1988	.73184	.73475	.72083	.72245	.73269	.76300	.77132	.77629	.77496	.74299	.73187	.74311	.72083	.76300	.77496	.74311	.74311
1989	.76282	.75672	.77357	.77181	.80410	.80232	.77670	.80223	.78137	.78258	.77657	.76094	.77357	.80232	.78137	.76094	.76094
1990	.75438	.75941	.76874	.76777	.76219	.75536	.73226	.72153	.71810	.69892	.70089	.70291	.76874	.75536	.71810	.70291	.70291
1991	.69698	.70396	.74277	.74582	.74580	.76074	.74962	.74795	.73100	.73179	.72426	.69909	.74277	.76074	.73100	.69909	.69909
1992	.71565	.72416	.72900	.73006	.71617	.69873	.69244	.67437	.67896	.71127	.72518	.72727	.72900	.69873	.67896	.72727	.72727
1993	.72365	.72669	.71545	.70255	.70005	.71245	.71905	.71044	.70502	.71791	.72260	.72804	.71545	.71245	.70502	.72804	.72804
1994	.72429	.71465	.70792	.70354	.70555	.69043	.69287	.69075	.68149	.67361	.68646	.68500	.70792	.69043	.68149	.68500	.68500
1995	.67719	.66916	.64082	.63572	.63455	.63745	.64121	.67002	.66387	.66910	.67288	.67273	.64082	.63745	.66387	.67273	.67273
1996	.68885	.68088	.68436	.68963	.69339	.69284	.68234	.68603	.69475	.69145	.69222	.69543	.68436	.69284	.69475	.69543	.69543
1997	.71702	.72205	.72104	.73232	.71850	.72039	.73604	.73336	.73249	.72274	.73430	.74115	.72104	.72039	.73249	.74115	.74115
1998	.74330	.74061	.74856	.74258	.74886	.75101	.75217	.74503	.72922	.71005	.72455	.71021	.74856	.75101	.72922	.71021	.71021
1999	.71954	.73230	.73646	.74007	.74518	.74857	.73303	.73000	.72062	.72426	.73013	.72859	.73646	.74857	.72062	.72859	.72859
2000	.73917	.74667	.74246	.75803	.75757	.74779	.76141	.76640	.77048	.78165	.78005	.76751	.74246	.74779	.77048	.76751	.76751
2001	.77054	.77371	.79324	.79002	.79731	.80280	.79445	.77626	.77579	.78243	.78984	.79572	.79324	.80280	.77579	.79572	.79572
2002	.80513	.80403	.80198	.78883	.77480	.75162	.75615	.75329	.75603	.75664	.75524	.73555	.80198	.75162	.75603	.73555	.73555
2003	.72646	.72947	.72791	.72259	.70425	.71385	.71842	.72608	.70614	.69843	.69024	.67296	.72791	.71385	.70614	.67296	.67296
20034	.72646	.72947	.72791	.72259	.70425	.71385	.71842	.72608	.70614	.69843	.69024	.67296	.72791	.71385	.70614	.67296	.67296
sd SDRs per US Dollar (Period Average, geometric)																	
1987	.79928	.79229	.78781	.77427	.76662	.77727	.78782	.78785	.77437	.77202	.74108	.72301	.79312	.77271	.78332	.74510	.77335
1988	.72609	.73770	.72918	.72361	.72677	.74264	.76620	.77396	.77299	.75787	.73714	.73753	.73098	.73096	.77104	.74412	.74409
1989	.75458	.75958	.76637	.76938	.79014	.80605	.78642	.79261	.80191	.78603	.78294	.76810	.76016	.78838	.79362	.77899	.78018
1990	.75844	.75381	.76823	.76843	.75854	.76079	.74404	.72612	.71917	.70006	.69213	.70100	.76014	.76258	.72970	.69772	.73706
1991	.70279	.69417	.72423	.74007	.74432	.75795	.75669	.74867	.73880	.73421	.72209	.71023	.70694	.74741	.74802	.72211	.73091
1992	.70960	.71921	.73207	.72961	.72041	.70835	.69264	.68660	.68603	.69698	.72098	.72003	.72024	.71940	.68842	.71258	.71004
1993	.72619	.72903	.72440	.70788	.70641	.70938	.71930	.71352	.70544	.71050	.71993	.72252	.72654	.70789	.71276	.71763	.71616
1994	.72810	.72072	.71328	.71213	.70671	.70059	.68631	.68757	.68317	.67696	.67971	.68870	.72068	.70646	.68568	.68177	.69847
1995	.68222	.67647	.65104	.63444	.64177	.63951	.64200	.66195	.67387	.66743	.66901	.67326	.66977	.63857	.65914	.66990	.65922
1996	.68130	.68201	.68408	.68925	.69221	.69305	.68964	.68573	.69056	.69460	.68825	.69533	.68246	.69150	.68864	.69272	.68882
1997	.70653	.72243	.72563	.72913	.72193	.71926	.72608	.73857	.73562	.72999	.72781	.73845	.71810	.72344	.73341	.73207	.72673
1998	.74455	.74073	.74393	.74453	.74420	.74988	.75136	.75376	.73270	.71114	.71840	.71321	.73431	.74620	.74588	.71424	.73722
1999	.71204	.72425	.73387	.73809	.74146	.74624	.74669	.73306	.72668	.71972	.72661	.72844	.72333	.74192	.73543	.72491	.73136
2000	.72957	.74358	.74468	.74674	.76288	.75153	.75559	.76431	.77275	.77730	.77957	.77256	.73924	.75369	.76418	.77647	.75827
2001	.76803	.77308	.78132	.78887	.79229	.79982	.79920	.78435	.77765	.78197	.78847	.79189	.77412	.79364	.78702	.78744	.78552
2002	.79824	.80345	.79994	.79574	.78301	.76885	.75169	.75698	.75653	.75893	.75127	.74625	.80054	.78245	.75506	.75213	.77230
2003	.73239	.72969	.72990	.73042	.71010	.70681	.71515	.72205	.71619	.69833	.69739	.68146	.73067	.71618	.71922	.69467	.71517
2004	.67066	.66825	.67888	.68452	.68909	.68229	.67901						.67123	.68449			

Exchange Rates

		1992	1993	1994	1995	1996	1997	1998	1999	2000	2001	2002	2003
		Market, Official, or Principal Rate										
		National Currency Units per SDR: End of Period (aa)										
Industrial Countries													
US dollar	111	1.3750	1.3736	1.4599	1.4865	1.4380	1.3493	1.4080	1.3725	1.3029	1.2567	1.3595	1.4860
Canadian dollar	156	1.7478	1.8186	2.0479	2.0294	1.9694	1.9282	2.1550	1.9809	1.9546	2.0015	2.1475	1.9205
Australian dollar	193	1.9968	2.0286	1.8793	1.9953	1.8053	2.0672	2.2936	2.0993	2.3518	2.4613	2.4011	1.9813
Japanese yen	158	171.53	153.63	145.61	152.86	166.80	175.34	162.77	140.27	149.70	165.64	163.01	159.15
New Zealand dollar	196	2.6735	2.4581	2.2721	2.2754	2.0368	2.3195	2.6723	2.6364	2.9598	3.0246	2.5822	2.2687
EMU Euro	163	....	....	....	....	....	....	....	1.36623	1.40023	1.42600	1.29639	1.17654
Austrian schilling	122	15.612	16.679	16.013	14.996	15.751	17.045	16.540	....	....	....	....	....
Belgium franc	124	45.623	49.599	46.478	43.725	46.022	49.814	48.682	....	....	....	....	....
Finnish markka	172	7.2119	7.9454	6.9244	6.4790	6.6777	7.3139	7.1753	....	....	....	....	....
French franc	132	7.5714	8.0978	7.8044	7.2838	7.5306	8.0794	7.9161	....	....	....	....	....
Deutsche mark	134	2.2193	2.3712	2.2610	2.1309	2.2357	2.4180	2.3556	....	....	....	....	....
Greek drachma	174	295.05	342.32	350.51	352.36	355.20	381.31	397.87	450.79	476.37	....	....	....
Irish pound	178	.84387	.97360	.94360	.92587	.85537	.94327	.94670	....	....	....	....	....
Italian lira	136	2,022.4	2,340.5	2,379.2	2,355.7	2,200.9	2,373.6	2,327.6	....	....	....	....	....
Luxembourg franc	137	45.623	49.599	46.478	43.725	46.022	49.814	48.682	....	....	....	....	....
Netherlands guilder	138	2.4944	2.6659	2.5330	2.3849	2.5072	2.7217	2.6595	....	....	....	....	....
Portuguese escudo	182	201.79	242.86	232.25	222.10	224.88	247.35	241.94	....	....	....	....	....
Spanish peseta	184	157.61	195.34	192.32	180.47	188.77	204.68	200.79	....	....	....	....	....
Danish krone	128	8.601	9.302	8.880	8.244	8.548	9.210	8.992	10.155	10.450	10.568	9.628	8.853
Icelandic krona	176	87.890	99.899	99.708	96.964	96.185	97.389	97.605	99.576	110.356	129.380	109.550	105.489
Norwegian krone	142	9.5212	10.3264	9.8715	9.3393	9.2641	9.8707	10.7010	11.0343	11.5288	11.3251	9.4700	9.9263
Swedish krona	144	9.6841	11.4054	10.8927	9.8973	9.8802	10.6280	11.3501	11.7006	12.4232	13.4062	11.9978	10.6829
Swiss franc	146	2.0020	2.0322	1.9146	1.7102	1.9361	1.9636	1.9382	2.1955	2.1322	2.1079	1.8854	1.8380
Pound sterling	112	.90939	.92733	.93430	.95903	.84686	.81585	.84643	.84912	.87315	.86647	.84348	.83262
Developing Countries													
Africa													
Algerian dinar	612	31.3244	33.1344	62.6166	77.5576	80.7931	78.8150	84.9790	95.1346	98.1649	97.7982	108.3856	107.9004
Angolan kwanza	614	.0008	.0089	.7434	.0085	.2905	.3540	.9807	7.6585	21.9121	40.1517	79.7581	117.5127
Benin, CFA franc	638	378.57	404.89	†780.44	728.38	753.06	807.94	791.61	†896.19	918.49	935.39	850.37	771.76
Botswana pula	616	3.1031	3.5229	3.9670	4.1944	5.2404	5.1400	6.2774	6.3572	6.9861	8.7760	7.4331	6.6014
Burkina Faso, CFA franc	748	378.57	404.89	†780.44	728.38	753.06	807.94	791.61	†896.19	918.49	935.39	850.37	771.76
Burundi franc	618	322.90	362.99	360.78	413.37	462.63	551.56	710.64	860.83	1,014.76	1,090.92	1,451.07	1,618.31
Cameroon, CFA franc	622	378.57	404.89	†780.44	728.38	753.06	807.94	791.61	†896.19	918.49	935.39	850.37	771.76
Cape Verde escudo	624	100.50	118.12	118.45	115.14	122.46	129.85	132.71	150.65	154.40	157.24	142.95	129.74
Cent.African Rep.,CFA franc	626	378.57	404.89	†780.44	728.38	753.06	807.94	791.61	†896.19	918.49	935.39	850.37	771.76
Chad, CFA franc	628	378.57	404.89	†780.44	728.38	753.06	807.94	791.61	†896.19	918.49	935.39	850.37	771.76
Comorian franc	632	378.57	404.89	†585.32	546.28	564.79	605.95	593.70	672.14	688.87	701.54	637.78	578.82
Congo, Dem.Rep., congo franc	636	.009	.481	47.445	.220	1.662	1.430	3.450	6.176	65.146	394.111	519.527	549.200
Congo, Rep., CFA franc	634	378.57	404.89	†780.44	728.38	753.06	807.94	791.61	†896.19	918.49	935.39	850.37	771.76
Côte d'Ivoire, CFA franc	662	378.57	404.89	†780.44	728.38	753.06	807.94	791.61	†896.19	918.49	935.39	850.37	771.76
Djibouti franc	611	244.37	244.11	259.45	264.18	255.56	239.79	250.24	243.92	231.55	223.35	241.62	264.09
Eq. Guinea, CFA franc	642	378.57	404.89	†780.44	728.38	753.06	807.94	791.61	†896.19	918.49	935.39	850.37	771.76
Eritrean nafka	643	6.8750	6.8678	8.6861	9.3946	9.2403	†9.6134	10.6967	13.1761	13.2897	17.3397	19.2117	20.4878
Ethiopian birr	644	6.8750	6.8678	8.6861	9.3946	9.2403	9.2613	10.5644	11.1640	10.8324	10.7555	11.6659	12.8100
Gabon, CFA franc	646	378.57	404.89	†780.44	728.38	753.06	807.94	791.61	†896.19	918.49	935.39	850.37	771.76
Gambian dalasi	648	12.673	13.096	13.983	14.330	14.225	14.207	15.476	15.849	19.397	21.279	31.802	....
Ghanaian cedi	652	716.15e	1,125.87	1,536.68	2,154.33	2,522.74	3,066.48	3,274.49	4,852.02	9,182.45	9,201.70	11,472.74	13,154.28
Guinean franc	656	1,268.31	1,335.67	1,432.15	1,483.49	1,494.23	1,544.82	1,827.67	2,382.68	2,452.43	2,498.79	2,620.18	2,964.24
Guinea-Bissau, CFA franc	654	183.10	242.25	345.18	501.49	772.88	807.94	791.61	896.19	918.49	935.39	850.37	771.76
Kenya shilling	664	49.797	93.626	65.458	83.153	79.118	84.568	87.165	100.098	101.674	98.779	104.781	113.140
Lesotho loti	666	4.1979	4.6667	5.1730	5.4220	6.7332	6.5675	8.2511	8.4471	9.8611	15.2397	11.7463	9.8668
Liberian dollar	668	1.3750	1.3736	1.4599	1.4865	1.4380	1.3493	†60.8973	54.2141	55.6994	62.2081	88.3688	75.0415
Malagasy franc	674	2,626.5	2,695.8	5,651.2	5,088.2	6,224.2	7,130.3	7,606.5	8,980.8	8,534.6	8,333.6	8,748.2	9,061.6
Malawi kwacha	676	6.0442	6.1733	22.3337	22.7479	22.0340	28.6416	61.7894	63.7362	104.3318	84.5705	118.4665	161.3258
Mali, CFA franc	678	378.57	404.89	†780.44	728.38	753.06	807.94	791.61	†896.19	918.49	935.39	850.37	771.76
Mauritanian ouguiya	682	158.26	170.54	187.40	203.81	204.84	227.15	289.74	308.81	328.72	331.93	365.32	394.67
Mauritian rupee	684	23.372	25.625	26.077	26.258	25.842	30.041	34.896	34.955	36.327	38.197	39.694	38.766
Moroccan dirham	686	12.442	13.257	13.080	12.589	12.653	13.107	13.031	13.845	13.836	14.528	13.822	13.002
Mozambique, metical	688	†4,058.2	7,339.2	9,709.5	16,187.9	16,359.7	15,574.4	17,411.7	18,254.4	†22,332.5	29,307.5	32,430.4	35,450.3
Namibia dollar	728	4.19788	4.66667	5.17298	5.42197	6.73325	6.56747	8.25106	8.4471	9.86107	15.23974	11.74625	9.86684
Niger, CFA franc	692	378.57	404.89	†780.44	728.38	753.06	807.94	791.61	†896.19	918.49	935.39	850.37	771.76
Nigerian naira	694	27.014	30.056	32.113	32.534	31.471	29.530	†30.816	134.437	142.734	141.948	171.843	202.835
Rwanda franc	714	201.39	201.39	201.39	445.67	437.37	411.31	450.75	479.24	560.67	572.84	695.88	849.07
São Tomé & Príncipe dobra	716	516.37	709.72	1,730.37	2,611.58	4,074.04	9,403.91	9,694.29	10,019.32	11,218.90	11,335.34	12,496.49	14,051.18
Senegal, CFA franc	722	378.57	404.89	†780.44	728.38	753.06	807.94	791.61	†896.19	918.49	935.39	850.37	771.76
Seychelles rupee	718	7.2345	7.2345	7.2345	7.2345	7.2345	6.9218	7.6699	7.3671	8.1642	7.2226	6.8474	8.1434
Sierra Leonean leone	724	723.68	793.41	894.90	1,402.35	1,307.24	1,799.00	2,239.84	3,123.90	2,171.52	2,716.13	2,979.70	3,807.32
South African rand	199	4.1979	4.6667	5.1730	5.4220	6.7332	6.5675	8.2511	8.4471	9.8611	15.2397	11.7463	9.8668
Sudanese pound	732	18.5811	29.8600	58.3940	78.2363	208.4000	232.3489	334.8307	353.6958	335.3039	328.5469	355.7592	386.5900
Swaziland lilangeni	734	4.1979	4.6667	5.1730	5.4220	6.7332	6.5675	8.2511	8.4471	9.8611	15.2397	11.7463	9.8668
Tanzanian shilling	738	460.63	659.13	764.16	818.10	856.51	842.70	958.87	1,094.34	1,046.58	1,151.54	1,327.30	1,580.51
Togo, CFA franc	742	378.57	404.89	780.44	728.38	753.06	807.94	791.61	†896.19	918.49	935.39	850.37	771.76
Tunisian dinar	744	1.3071	1.4376	1.4470	1.4134	1.4358	1.5483	1.5502	1.7191	1.8049	1.8453	1.8137	1.7955
Uganda shilling	746	1,673.6	1,552.3	1,352.9	1,500.5	1,480.5	1,538.3	1,918.7	2,067.1	2,301.8	2,170.9	2,518.6	2,875.8
Zambian kwacha	754	494.604	686.780	993.095	1,421.278	1,844.457	1,908.973	3,236.948	3,612.707	5,417.278	4,813.779	5,892.703	6,903.044
Zimbabwe dollar	698	7.5384	9.5256	12.2440	13.8407	15.5860	25.1070	52.6170	52.3459	71.7461	69.1651	74.8222	1,224.0280

2004, International Monetary Fund: International Financial Statistics Yearbook

Exchange Rates

Market, Official, or Principal Rate
National Currency Units per SDR: End of Period (aa)

		1992	1993	1994	1995	1996	1997	1998	1999	2000	2001	2002	2003
Asia													
Afghanistan, afghani	512	69.575	69.502	729.925	1,486.490 †	4,313.880	4,047.750	4,224.090	4,117.530	3,908.730	3,770.190	4,078.560	4,457.910
Bangladesh taka	513	53.625	54.736	58.759	60.574	61.041	61.323	68.289	69.998	70.357	71.634	78.716	87.348
Bhutan, ngultrum	514	36.025	43.102	45.810	52.295	51.666	52.999	59.813	59.690	60.911	60.549	65.298	67.768
Cambodian riel	522	2,750.0	3,166.1	3,759.1	3,754.9	3,901.2	4,657.6	5,308.3	5,174.4	5,087.9	4,895.0	5,342.9	5,920.1
Chinese yuan	924	7.9087	7.9666	† 12.3302	12.3637	11.9325	11.1715	11.6567	11.3637	10.7847	10.4017	11.2532	12.2989
Fiji dollar	819	2.1511	2.1164	2.0570	2.1248	1.9900	2.0902	2.7965	2.6981	2.8479	2.9017	2.8072	2.5589
Hong Kong dollar	532	10.6466	10.6121	11.2963	11.4935	11.1241	10.4513	10.9066	10.6658	10.1575	9.7987	10.6015	11.5356
Indian rupee	534	36.025	43.102	45.810	52.295	51.666	52.999	59.813	59.690	60.911	60.549	65.298	67.768
Indonesian rupiah	536	2,835.3	2,898.2	3,211.7	3,430.8	3,426.7	6,274.0	11,299.4	9,724.2	12,501.4	13,070.0	12,154.1	12,578.7
Kiribati, Aust.dollar	826	1.9968	2.0286	1.8793	1.9953	1.8053	2.0672	2.2936	2.0093	2.3518	2.4613	2.4011	1.9813
Korean won	542	1,084.1	1,110.0	1,151.4	1,151.6	1,213.9	2,287.0	1,695.3	1,561.9	1,647.5	1,650.7	1,612.7	1,772.2
Lao P.D. Rep., kip	544	985.88	986.22	1,049.63	† 1,372.03	1,344.49	3,554.60	6,017.92	10,431.08	10,707.31	11,926.37	14,519.67	15,553.65
Macao pataca	546	10.9611	10.9283	11.6352	11.8391	11.4571	10.7690	11.2359	10.9868	10.4672	10.0932	10.9208	11.8832
Malaysian ringgit	548	3.59150	3.71067	3.73722	3.77866	3.63660	5.25115	5.35051	5.21554	4.95106	4.77557	5.16618	5.64669
Maldivian rufiyaa	556	14.486	15.253	17.182	17.496	16.925	15.881	16.573	16.154	15.335	16.086	17.402	19.020
Mongolian togrog	948	55.000	† 544.630	604.509	704.031	997.240	1,097.156	1,270.043	1,471.839	1,429.292	1,384.916	1,529.460	1,735.613
Myanmar kyat	518	8.5085	8.5085	8.5085	8.5085	8.5085	8.5085	8.5085	8.5085	8.5085	8.5085	8.5085	8.5085
Nepalese rupee	558	59.400	67.634	72.817	83.243	82.007	85.408	95.288	94.326	96.806	96.108	106.450	110.021
Pakistan rupee	564	35.338	41.372	44.963	50.912	57.691	59.434	64.608	† 71.075	75.607	76.489	79.578	85.020
Papua New Guinea kina	853	1.3578	1.3479	1.7205	1.9846	1.9366	2.3630	2.9518	3.6995	4.0028	4.7281	5.4643	4.9532
Philippine peso	566	34.507	38.046	35.647	38.967	37.801	53.936	54.996	55.330	65.143	64.601	72.185	82.574
Samoa tala	862	3.5166	3.5816	3.5789	3.7566	3.5004	3.7324	4.2385	4.1428	4.3532	4.4628	4.3729	4.1277
Singapore dollar	576	2.2617	2.2087	2.1324	2.1023	2.0129	2.2607	2.3380	2.2866	2.2560	2.3262	2.3608	2.5273
Solomon Islands dollar	813	4.2622	4.4611	4.8597	5.1668	5.2081	6.4067	6.8417	6.9671	6.6441	6.9935	10.1381	11.1309
Sri Lanka rupee	524	63.250	68.076	72.963	80.341	81.540	82.689	96.164	99.054	107.594	117.075	131.500	143.750
Thai baht	578	35.090	35.081	36.628	37.445	36.826	† 63.748	51.662	51.428	56.374	55.575	58.665	58.831
Tongan pa'anga	866	1.9116	1.8946	1.8371	1.8883	1.7438	1.8377	2.2749	2.2066	2.5754	2.7736	3.0299	3.0020
Vanuatu vatu	846	163.63	165.93	163.62	169.07	159.28	167.73	182.73	176.90	186.07	184.41	181.05	166.15
Vietnamese dong	582	† 14,526.9	14,892.8	16,132.8	16,373.7	16,031.8	16,585.0	19,557.5	19,253.6	18,910.4	18,956.5	20,940.7	23,249.5
Europe													
Albanian lek	914	141.488	135.570	139.547	140.087	148.211	201.227	197.941	185.454	185.847	171.606	181.822	158.375
Armenian dram	911	2.85	103.02	591.98	597.57	625.61	667.85	735.03	718.88	719.44	706.04	795.17	841.06
Azerbaijan manat	912	66.83	162.08	6,105.09	6,600.02	5,892.76	5,245.88	5,477.24	6,008.85	5,947.78	6,000.89	6,652.13	7,315.43
Belarusian rubel	913	.021	.960	15.474	17.095	22.288	41.476	309.767	439.203	1,537.434	1,985.633	2,610.278	3,203.751
Bosnia & Herzegovina conv.marka	963	....	....	....	....	....	2.418	2.356	2.672	2.739	2.789	2.536	2.301
Bulgarian lev	918	.0337	.0449	.0964	.1051	.7008	2.3969	2.3586	2.6721	2.7386	2.7891	2.5627	2.3012
Croatian kuna	960	1.09753	9.01316	8.21706	7.90233	7.96572	8.50446	8.79667	10.49648	10.62568	10.50129	9.71478	9.09192
Cyprus pound	423	.66419	.71398	.69523	.67867	.67567	.70935	.70152	.78862	.80357	.81712	.74344	.69134
Czech Republic koruna	935	....	41.145	40.947	39.544	39.302	46.733	42.037	49.382	49.267	45.568	40.977	38.121
Czechoslovak koruna	934	39.74	....	....	....	....	....	....	....	....	....	....	....
Estonian kroon	939	17.754	19.062	18.088	17.038	17.888	19.343	18.882	21.359	21.915	22.234	20.306	18.440
Georgian lari	915	....	....	....	1.8284	1.8348	1.7594	2.5345	2.6489	2.5732	2.5889	2.8414	3.0834
Hungarian forint	944	115.459	138.317	161.591	207.321	237.163	274.572	308.401	346.586	370.978	350.665	306.110	308.963
Kazakhstani tenge	916	....	8.67	79.21	95.06	105.40	101.94	117.99	189.68	188.27	188.76	210.18	214.31
Kyrgyz som	917	....	11.03	15.55	16.65	24.01	23.44	41.36	62.35	62.94	59.97	62.67	65.67
Latvian lats	941	1.14813	.81727	.80000	.79825	.79951	.79606	.80117	.80017	.79868	.80179	.80755	.80391
Lithuanian litas	946	5.211	5.357	5.839	5.946	5.752	5.397	5.632	5.490	5.212	5.027	4.502	4.104
Macedonian denar	962	....	61.062	59.264	56.456	59.547	74.776	72.987	82.816	86.420	86.930	79.665	72.887
Maltese lira	181	.51450	.54272	.53738	.52384	.51712	.52717	.53141	.56558	.57038	.56812	.54220	.50895
Moldovan lev	921	.5699	4.9998	6.2336	6.6877	6.7215	6.2882	11.7185	15.9077	16.1343	16.4517	18.7913	19.6445
Polish zloty	964	2.1680	2.9317	3.5579	3.6687	4.1349	4.7467	4.9337	5.6936	5.3982	5.0097	5.2189	5.5587
Romanian leu	968	632.5	1,752.7	2,579.6	3,832.2	5,802.2	10,825.0	15,419.3	25,055.2	33,779.2	39,708.9	45,543.9	48,435.2
Russian ruble	922	.5706	1.7128	5.1825	6.8973	7.9951	8.0415	† 29.0758	37.0578	36.6899	37.8778	43.2115	43.7685
Slovak koruna	936	....	45.605	45.660	43.954	45.864	46.930	51.975	58.011	61.744	60.910	54.430	49.000
Slovenian tolar	961	135.713	181.093	184.609	187.283	203.443	228.266	226.974	270.069	296.252	315.371	300.550	281.394
Tajik somoni	923	.006	.019	.058	.436	.472	1.008	1.377	1.971	† 2.866	3.205	4.079	4.393
Turkish lira	186	11,776	19,879	56,534	88,669	154,976	277,413	442,775	743,077	877,360	1,822,418	2,234,642	2,075,362
Ukrainian hryvnia	926	.0088	.1732	1.5212	2.6668	† 2.7163	2.5622	4.8253	7.1594	7.0807	6.6588	7.2495	7.9224
Middle East													
Bahrain, Kingdom of, dinar	419	.51700	.51646	.54890	.55892	.54067	.50732	.52942	.51606	.48989	.47253	.51118	.55873
Egyptian pound	469	4.5906	4.6314	4.9504	5.0392	4.8718	4.5713	4.7704	4.6734	4.8077	5.6427	6.1178	9.1435
Iranian rial	429	92.30	2,415.49	2,534.26	2,597.64	2,515.19	2,366.94	2,465.36	2,405.04	2,948.39	2,200.47 †	10,810.87	12,292.11
Iraqi dinar	433	.42743	.42698	.45381	.46209	.44700	.41942	.43770	.42665	.40502	.39066	.42262	....
Israeli new sheqel	436	3.8005	4.1015	4.4058	4.6601	4.6748	4.7709	5.8588	5.7000	5.2651	5.5497	6.4400	6.5071
Jordan dinar	439	.95011	.96699	1.02336	1.05392	1.01951	.95662	.99829	.97311	.92376	.89102	.96390	1.05355
Kuwaiti dinar	443	.41621	.40990	.43813	.44436	.43123	.41139	.42461	.41749	.39793	.38691	.40726	.43792
Lebanese pound	446	2,527.3	2,350.2	2,404.4	2,372.4	2,231.7	2,060.3	2,123.3	2,069.1	1,964.1	1,894.5	2,049.5	2,240.1
Libyan dinar	672	.41428	.44643	.63412	.63412	.63412	.63412	.63412	.63412	.70403	.81699	1.64474	1.93237
Rial Omani	449	.52869	.52813	.56131	.57156	.55290	.51879	.54139	.52773	.50097	.48321	.52274	.57136
Qatar riyal	453	5.0050	4.9998	5.3139	5.4108	5.2342	4.9113	5.1252	4.9959	4.7426	4.5745	4.9487	5.4089
Saudi Arabian riyal	456	5.1494	5.1440	5.4671	5.5669	5.3852	5.0529	5.2731	5.1400	4.8794	4.7065	5.0914	5.5650
Syrian pound	463	15.434	15.418	16.387	16.686	16.141	15.145	15.805	15.406	14.625	14.107	15.261	16.680
U.A.Emirates dirham	466	5.0476	5.0423	5.3591	5.4569	5.2788	4.9551	5.1710	5.0405	4.7849	4.6153	4.9928	5.4572
Yemen, Rep., Yemeni rial	474	16.514	16.496	17.533	† 74.384	† 182.492	176.023	199.447	218.366	215.749	217.754	243.368	273.879
Western Hemisphere													
Anguilla, E.Caribbean dollar	312	3.7125	3.7086	3.9416	4.0135	3.8825	3.6430	3.8017	3.7058	3.5179	3.3932	3.6707	4.0121
Antigua & Barbuda, E.Car.dollar	311	3.7125	3.7086	3.9416	4.0135	3.8825	3.6430	3.8017	3.7058	3.5179	3.3932	3.6707	4.0121
Argentine peso	213	1.36194	1.37150	1.45912	1.48649	1.43724	1.34858	1.40733	1.37182	1.30226	1.25610	4.51361	4.31674
Aruban florin	314	2.4613	2.4587	2.6131	2.6608	2.5739	2.4152	2.5204	2.4568	2.3322	2.2495	2.4335	2.6599

2004, International Monetary Fund: *International Financial Statistics Yearbook*

Exchange Rates

		1992	1993	1994	1995	1996	1997	1998	1999	2000	2001	2002	2003
						Market, Official, or Principal Rate							
						National Currency Units per SDR: End of Period (aa)							
Western Hemisphere(Cont.)													
Bahamian dollar	313	1.3750	1.3736	1.4599	1.4865	1.4380	1.3493	1.4080	1.3725	1.3029	1.2567	1.3595	1.4860
Barbados dollar	316	2.7500	2.7471	2.9197	2.9730	2.8759	2.6985	2.8161	2.7450	2.6058	2.5135	2.7190	2.9719
Belize dollar	339	2.7500	2.7471	2.9197	2.9730	2.8759	2.6985	2.8161	2.7450	2.6058	2.5135	2.7190	2.9719
Bolivia, boliviano	218	5.63063	6.14668	6.85400	7.33583	7.45582	7.23873	7.94833	8.22133	8.32559	8.57090	10.18280	11.63515
Brazilian real	223	6.19375	.16288	1.23503	1.44635	1.49462	1.50630	1.70189	2.45542	2.54667	2.91612	4.80250	4.29208
Chilean peso	228	525.70	592.06	589.91	605.19	611.09	593.41	667.08	727.53	746.15	824.67	968.49	890.72
Colombian peso	233	1,116.18	1,260.01	1,213.53	1,468.13	1,445.62	1,745.36	2,122.63	2,571.77	2,849.49	2,892.15	3,894.74	4,132.22
Costa Rican colon	238	188.97	208.01	240.98	289.72	316.51	329.61	382.17	409.27	414.35	429.39	514.88	621.92
Dominica, E.Caribbean dollar	321	3.7125	3.7086	3.9416	4.0135	3.8825	3.6430	3.8017	3.7058	3.5179	3.3932	3.6707	4.0121
Dominican peso	243	17.291	17.536	19.071	20.015	20.220	19.383	22.230	22.014	21.725	21.551	28.813	55.352
Ecuadoran sucre	248	2,535.8	2,807.3	3,312.4	4,345.8	5,227.0	5,974.5	9,609.8	27,783.7	32,572.8	31,418.3	33,988.0	37,149.3
Salvadoran colon	253	12.6088	11.9088	12.7737	13.0142	12.5893	11.8127	12.3273	12.0163	11.4070	10.9964	11.8958	13.0022
Grenada, E.Caribbean dollar	328	3.7125	3.7086	3.9416	4.0135	3.8825	3.6430	3.8017	3.7058	3.5179	3.3932	3.6707	4.0121
Guatemalan quetzal	258	7.2522	7.9876	8.2460	8.9810	8.5782	8.3342	9.6425	10.7342	10.0731	10.0544	10.6140	11.9482
Guyana dollar	336	173.250	179.593	208.029	208.852	203.112	194.292	228.453	247.738	240.713	238.150	260.688	288.650
Haitian gourde	263	15.0604	17.5884	18.9001	24.0215	21.7028	23.3569	23.2390	24.6577	29.3470	33.1009	51.1305	62.5369
Honduran lempira	268	8.0163	9.9720	13.7227	15.3751	18.5057	17.6673	19.4415	19.9067	19.7270	20.0068	23.0076	26.3733
Jamaica dollar	343	30.5038	44.6057	48.4692	58.8894	50.1351	49.0326	52.1744	56.6719	59.1715	59.4257	69.0115	89.9266
Mexican peso	273	4.2837	4.2661	7.7737	11.3605	11.2893	10.9064	13.8902	13.0585	12.4717	11.4894	14.0201	16.6964
Montserrat, E.Caribbean dollar	351	3.7125	3.7086	3.9416	4.0135	3.8825	3.6430	3.8017	3.7058	3.5179	3.3932	3.6707	4.0121
Netherlands Antilles guilder	353	2.4613	2.4587	2.6131	2.6608	2.5739	2.4152	2.5204	2.4568	2.3322	2.2495	2.4335	2.6599
Nicaraguan gold córdoba	278	6.875	8.722	10.382	11.840	12.832	13.486	15.761	16.907	17.012	17.394	19.946	23.109
Panamanian balboa	283	1.3750	1.3736	1.4599	1.4865	1.4380	1.3493	1.4080	1.3725	1.3029	1.2567	1.3595	1.4860
Paraguayan guarani	288	2,241.3	2,582.3	2,809.8	2,942.7	3,033.6	3,184.2	3,999.1	4,568.9	4,595.2	5,884.0	9,657.5	9,086.6
Peruvian new sol	293	2.24125	2.96689	3.18247	3.43379	3.73870	3.68345	4.44937	4.81751	4.59536	4.32818	4.77735	5.14591
St.Kitts & Nevis, E.C. dollar	361	3.7125	3.7086	3.9416	4.0135	3.8825	3.6430	3.8017	3.7058	3.5179	3.3932	3.6707	4.0121
St.Lucia, E.Caribbean dollar	362	3.7125	3.7086	3.9416	4.0135	3.8825	3.6430	3.8017	3.7058	3.5179	3.3932	3.6707	4.0121
St. Vinc. & Grens., E. Carib. dollar	364	3.7125	3.7086	3.9416	4.0135	3.8825	3.6430	3.8017	3.7058	3.5179	3.3932	3.6707	4.0121
Surinamese dollar	366	.002	.002	†.598	.605	.577	.541	.565	1.355	2.838	2.738	3.419	†3.901
Trinidad & Tobago dollar	369	5.8438	7.9860	8.6616	8.9146	8.9074	8.5001	9.2881	8.6467	8.2078	7.9051	8.5648	9.3615
Uruguayan peso	298	4.7850	†6.0656	8.1766	10.5704	12.5289	13.5465	15.2307	15.9417	16.3059	18.5594	36.9789	43.5389
Venezuelan bolivar	299	109.244	145.102	†248.175	431.082	685.188	680.359	794.833	889.730	911.711	958.885	1,905.027	2,374.580

2004, International Monetary Fund : *International Financial Statistics Yearbook*

Fund Account: Position to Date

(As of July 31, 2004 and Expressed in Millions of SDRs)

		Quota	Reserve Position in the Fund	Total Fund Credit and Loans Outstanding			Fund Holdings of Currency		SDR Department		
				Total Amount	Percent of Quota	Outstanding Purchases (GRA)	Outstanding Loans	Amount	Percent of Quota	Net Qumulative Allocation	Holdings of SDR	
											Amount	Percent of Allocation
		(1)	(2)	(3)	(4)	(5)	(6)	(7)	(8)	(9)	(10)	(11)
All Countries	010	212,794.0	59,842.4	66,232.4	31.1	59,279.6	6,952.7	212,231.4	99.7	21,433.3	20,557.9	95.9
Industrial Countries	110	130,566.6	47,217.8	ó	ó	ó	ó	83,346.1	63.8	14,595.3	15,344.4	105.1
United States	111	37,149.3	13,303.1	—	—	—	—	23,843.0	64.2	4,899.5	8,633.9	176.2
Canada	156	6,369.2	2,241.1	—	—	—	—	4,128.2	64.8	779.3	579.4	74.3
Australia	193	3,236.4	1,172.3	—	—	—	—	2,064.2	63.8	470.5	120.0	25.5
Japan	158	13,312.8	4,724.8	—	—	—	—	8,588.1	64.5	891.7	1,802.4	202.1
New Zealand	196	894.6	329.8	—	—	—	—	564.8	63.1	141.3	20.6	14.6
Austria	122	1,872.3	699.6	—	—	—	—	1,172.7	62.6	179.0	102.3	57.2
Belgium	124	4,605.2	1,669.4	—	—	—	—	2,935.8	63.7	485.2	526.3	108.5
Denmark	128	1,642.8	616.8	—	—	—	—	1,026.0	62.5	178.9	43.5	24.3
Finland	172	1,263.8	463.0	—	—	—	—	800.8	63.4	142.7	151.0	105.8
France	132	10,738.5	3,934.0	—	—	—	—	6,804.4	63.4	1,079.9	537.0	49.7
Germany	134	13,008.2	4,778.9	—	—	—	—	8,229.4	63.3	1,210.8	1,327.9	109.7
Greece	174	823.0	287.6	—	—	—	—	535.4	65.1	103.5	16.0	15.4
Iceland	176	117.6	18.6	—	—	—	—	99.0	84.2	16.4	.1	.4
Ireland	178	838.4	302.9	—	—	—	—	535.5	63.9	87.3	55.2	63.2
Italy	136	7,055.5	2,600.3	—	—	—	—	4,455.3	63.1	702.4	62.0	8.8
Luxembourg	137	279.1	102.2	—	—	—	—	176.9	63.4	17.0	9.0	53.3
Netherlands	138	5,162.4	1,928.2	—	—	—	—	3,234.2	62.6	530.3	500.8	94.4
Norway	142	1,671.7	597.7	—	—	—	—	1,074.0	64.2	167.8	200.2	119.3
Portugal	182	867.4	314.0	—	—	—	—	553.4	63.8	53.3	63.6	119.2
San Marino	135	17.0	4.1	—	—	—	—	12.9	75.9	—	.5	—
Spain	184	3,048.9	1,154.8	—	—	—	—	1,894.1	62.1	298.8	287.0	96.1
Sweden	144	2,395.5	894.0	—	—	—	—	1,501.5	62.7	246.5	101.2	41.0
Switzerland	146	3,458.5	1,253.3	—	—	—	—	2,205.2	63.8	—	2.3	—
United Kingdom	112	10,738.5	3,827.4	—	—	—	—	6,911.1	64.4	1,913.1	202.1	10.6
Developing Countries	200	82,227.4	12,624.6	66,232.4	80.5	59,279.6	6,952.7	128,885.2	156.7	6,838.1	5,213.5	76.2
Africa	605	11,498.1	298.7	5,293.4	46.0	1,312.7	3,980.8	12,512.6	108.8	1,382.5	463.3	33.5
Algeria	612	1,254.7	85.1	490.3	39.1	490.3	—	1,659.9	132.3	128.6	15.7	12.2
Angola	614	286.3	—	—	—	—	....	286.4	100.1	—	.1	—
Benin	638	61.9	2.2	45.2	73.0	—	45.2	59.7	96.5	9.4	.1	.6
Botswana	616	63.0	22.8	—	—	—	—	40.2	63.8	4.4	34.0	778.9
Burkina Faso	748	60.2	7.3	80.5	133.7	—	80.5	52.9	87.9	9.4	.2	1.8
Burundi	618	77.0	.4	26.4	34.3	—	26.4	76.6	99.5	13.7	.2	1.1
Cameroon	622	185.7	.6	225.5	121.4	—	225.5	185.1	99.7	24.5	1.0	4.0
Cape Verde	624	9.6	—	4.9	51.3	—	4.9	9.6	100.0	.6	—	.6
Central African Rep	626	55.7	.2	28.4	51.0	5.6	22.8	61.1	109.7	9.3	1.6	17.7
Chad	628	56.0	.3	66.7	119.2	—	66.7	55.7	99.5	9.4	—	.5
Comoros	632	8.9	.5	—	—	—	—	8.4	93.9	.7	—	1.0
Congo, Dem. Rep. of	636	533.0	—	526.8	98.8	—	526.8	533.0	100.0	86.3	5.1	5.9
Congo, Republic of	634	84.6	.5	13.5	15.9	7.9	5.6	92.0	108.8	9.7	.7	7.6
Côte d'Ivoire	662	325.2	.6	240.3	73.9	—	240.3	324.6	99.8	37.8	.2	.5
Djibouti	611	15.9	1.1	13.6	85.7	—	13.6	14.8	93.1	1.2	.1	4.3
Equatorial Guinea	642	32.6	—	—	—	—	—	32.6	100.0	5.8	.4	7.6
Eritrea	643	15.9	—	—	—	—	—	15.9	100.0	—	—	—
Ethiopia	644	133.7	7.2	111.9	83.7	—	111.9	126.5	94.6	11.2	.3	3.1
Gabon	646	154.3	.2	43.3	28.1	43.3	—	197.4	127.9	14.1	.4	2.7
Gambia, The	648	31.1	1.5	19.4	62.3	—	19.4	29.6	95.2	5.1	.4	7.6
Ghana	652	369.0	—	314.8	85.3	—	314.8	369.0	100.0	63.0	18.3	29.0
Guinea	656	107.1	.1	81.7	76.3	—	81.7	107.0	99.9	17.6	.1	.5
Guinea-Bissau	654	14.2	—	11.3	79.3	.6	10.6	14.8	104.4	1.2	.4	36.9
Kenya	664	271.4	12.7	70.8	26.1	—	70.8	258.7	95.3	37.0	.4	.9
Lesotho	666	34.9	3.5	21.0	60.2	—	21.0	31.4	89.9	3.7	.4	11.0
Liberia	668	71.3	—	223.7	313.7	200.8	22.9	272.1	381.6	21.0	—	—
Madagascar	674	122.2	—	136.8	111.9	—	136.8	122.2	100.0	19.3	.2	.9
Malawi	676	69.4	2.3	63.9	92.0	17.4	46.5	84.5	121.7	11.0	.5	4.5
Mali	678	93.3	9.0	103.9	111.3	—	103.9	84.4	90.4	15.9	.5	3.2
Mauritania	682	64.4	—	62.8	97.5	—	62.8	64.4	100.0	9.7	.1	.6
Mauritius	684	101.6	21.9	—	—	—	—	79.7	78.5	15.7	17.4	110.3
Morocco	686	588.2	70.4	—	—	—	—	517.8	88.0	85.7	66.0	77.0
Mozambique	688	113.6	—	134.6	118.5	—	134.6	113.6	100.0	—	.1	—
Namibia	728	136.5	.1	—	—	—	—	136.4	100.0	—	—	—
Niger	692	65.8	8.6	90.1	136.9	—	90.1	57.2	87.0	9.4	.3	3.4
Nigeria	694	1,753.2	.1	—	—	—	—	1,753.1	100.0	157.2	.7	.5
Rwanda	714	80.1	—	61.8	77.1	—	61.8	80.1	100.0	13.7	19.8	144.6
São Tomé & Príncipe	716	7.4	—	1.9	25.7	—	1.9	7.4	100.0	.6	—	1.3
Senegal	722	161.8	1.5	142.2	87.9	—	142.2	160.3	99.1	24.5	1.1	4.6
Seychelles	718	8.8	—	—	—	—	—	8.8	100.0	.4	—	.6
Sierra Leone	724	103.7	—	115.4	111.3	—	115.4	103.7	100.0	17.5	19.3	110.6
Somalia	726	44.2	—	112.0	253.4	96.7	15.3	140.9	318.8	13.7	—	—
South Africa	199	1,868.5	.5	—	—	—	—	1,868.0	100.0	220.4	222.8	101.1
Sudan	732	169.7	—	391.8	230.9	332.6	59.2	502.3	296.0	52.2	.3	.5
Swaziland	734	50.7	6.6	—	—	—	—	44.2	87.1	6.4	2.5	38.4
Tanzania	738	198.9	10.0	284.8	143.2	—	284.8	188.9	95.0	31.4	.2	.6
Togo	742	73.4	.3	20.6	28.1	—	20.6	73.1	99.5	11.0	.1	1.0
Tunisia	744	286.5	20.2	—	—	—	—	266.3	93.0	34.2	13.3	38.9
Uganda	746	180.5	—	139.1	77.0	—	139.1	180.5	100.0	29.4	.4	1.3
Zambia	754	489.1	—	576.1	117.8	—	576.1	489.1	100.0	68.3	17.8	26.0
Zimbabwe	698	353.4	.3	195.8	55.4	117.5	78.3	470.6	133.2	10.2	—	.5

2004, International Monetary Fund : *International Financial Statistics Yearbook*

Fund Account: Position to Date

(As of July 31, 2004 and Expressed in Millions of SDRs)

		Quota	Reserve Position in the Fund	Total Fund Credit and Loans Outstanding				Fund Holdings of Currency		SDR Department		
				Total Amount	Percent of Quota	Outstanding Purchases (GRA)	Outstanding Loans	Amount	Percent of Quota	Net Cumulative Allocation	Holdings of SDR	
											Amount	Percent of Allocation
		(1)	(2)	(3)	(4)	(5)	(6)	(7)	(8)	(9)	(10)	(11)
Asia	505	22,046.8	4,966.7	9,242.2	41.9	7,696.1	1,546.1	24,776.7	112.4	2,043.7	1,353.2	66.2
Afghanistan, I.S. of	512	161.9	—	—	—	—	—	161.9	100.0	26.7	.2	.7
Bangladesh	513	533.3	.2	99.0	18.6	—	99.0	533.1	100.0	47.1	1.6	3.3
Bhutan	514	6.3	1.0	—	—	—	—	5.3	83.8	—	.3	—
Brunei Darussalam	516	215.2	58.3	—	—	—	—	157.1	73.0	—	8.3	—
Cambodia	522	87.5	—	65.5	74.9	—	65.5	87.5	100.0	15.4	.2	1.0
China, P.R.: Mainland	924	6,369.2	2,270.4	—	—	—	—	4,098.9	64.4	236.8	773.7	326.7
China, P.R.: Hong Kong	532	...	...	...	...	...	—	...	...	...	...	...
Fiji	819	70.3	15.2	—	—	—	—	55.1	78.4	7.0	5.3	75.6
India	534	4,158.2	887.1	—	—	—	—	3,271.1	78.7	681.2	1.2	.2
Indonesia	536	2,079.3	145.5	6,598.6	317.3	6,598.6	—	8,532.4	410.4	239.0	49.3	20.6
Kiribati	826	5.6	—	—	—	—	...	5.6	100.0	—	—	—
Korea	542	1,633.6	507.7	—	—	—	—	1,125.9	68.9	72.9	17.3	23.8
Lao People's Dem.Rep.	544	52.9	—	26.3	49.8	—	26.3	52.9	100.0	9.4	9.9	105.1
Malaysia	548	1,486.6	550.5	—	—	—	—	936.1	63.0	139.0	123.9	89.1
Maldives	556	8.2	1.6	—	—	—	—	6.6	81.1	.3	.3	110.4
Marshall Islands, Rep.	867	3.5	—	—	—	—	—	3.5	100.0	—	—	—
Micronesia, Fed. Sts.	868	5.1	—	—	—	—	—	5.1	100.0	—	1.2	—
Mongolia	948	51.1	.1	30.8	60.2	—	30.8	51.0	99.8	—	—	—
Myanmar	518	258.4	—	—	—	—	—	258.4	100.0	43.5	.3	.8
Nepal	558	71.3	5.8	7.1	10.0	—	7.1	65.5	91.9	8.1	.5	6.2
Pakistan	564	1,033.7	—	1,355.4	131.1	279.1	1,076.2	1,312.7	127.0	170.0	162.1	95.4
Palau	565	3.1	.1	—	—	—	—	3.1	100.0	—	—	—
Papua New Guinea	853	131.6	.4	62.8	47.7	62.8	—	194.0	147.4	9.3	1.5	16.6
Philippines	566	879.9	87.4	566.8	64.4	566.8	—	1,359.3	154.5	116.6	5.4	4.6
Samoa	862	11.6	.7	—	—	—	—	10.9	94.1	1.1	2.4	211.2
Singapore	576	862.5	285.4	—	—	—	—	577.2	66.9	16.5	184.0	1,116.7
Solomon Islands	813	10.4	.6	—	—	—	—	9.9	94.7	.7	—	.5
Sri Lanka	524	413.4	47.9	227.2	55.0	188.8	38.4	554.4	134.1	70.9	1.9	2.7
Thailand	578	1,081.9	96.7	—	—	—	—	985.2	91.1	84.7	.9	1.1
Timor-Leste	537	8.2	—	—	—	—	—	8.2	100.0	—	—	—
Tonga	866	6.9	1.7	—	—	—	—	5.2	75.3	—	.2	—
Vanuatu	846	17.0	2.5	—	—	—	—	14.5	85.3	—	.9	—
Vietnam	582	329.1	—	202.7	61.6	—	202.7	329.1	100.0	47.7	.4	.8
Europe	170	17,270.1	1,494.7	21,372.8	123.8	20,621.9	750.9	36,397.6	210.8	374.1	484.5	129.5
Albania	914	48.7	3.4	66.0	135.5	—	66.0	45.4	93.1	—	68.0	—
Armenia	911	92.0	—	142.8	155.2	4.2	138.6	96.2	104.6	—	10.7	—
Azerbaijan	912	160.9	—	145.0	90.1	47.0	98.0	207.9	129.2	—	2.4	—
Belarus	913	386.4	—	5.8	1.5	5.8	—	392.2	101.5	—	.1	—
Bosnia & Herzegovina	963	169.1	—	82.8	48.9	82.8	—	251.9	148.9	20.5	1.0	5.0
Bulgaria	918	640.2	32.8	811.3	126.7	811.3	—	1,418.7	221.6	—	49.2	—
Croatia	960	365.1	.2	—	—	—	—	364.9	100.0	44.2	.5	1.1
Cyprus	423	139.6	52.4	—	—	—	—	87.2	62.4	19.4	2.3	11.7
Czech Republic	935	819.3	296.3	—	—	—	—	523.0	63.8	—	1.0	—
Estonia	939	65.2	—	—	—	—	—	65.2	100.0	—	.1	—
Georgia	915	150.3	—	189.8	126.3	6.9	182.8	157.2	104.6	—	3.3	—
Hungary	944	1,038.4	363.8	—	—	—	—	674.6	65.0	—	34.4	—
Kazakhstan	916	365.7	—	—	—	—	—	365.7	100.0	—	.8	—
Kyrgyz Republic	917	88.8	—	144.0	162.2	—	144.0	88.8	100.0	—	14.8	—
Latvia	941	126.8	.1	—	—	—	—	126.8	100.0	—	.1	—
Lithuania	946	144.2	—	21.6	15.0	21.6	—	165.7	114.9	—	.2	—
Macedonia, FYR	962	68.9	—	37.8	54.8	16.9	20.8	85.8	124.6	8.4	2.1	25.2
Malta	181	102.0	40.3	—	—	—	—	61.7	60.5	11.3	30.3	268.1
Moldova	921	123.2	—	85.3	69.3	57.6	27.7	180.8	146.8	—	.1	—
Poland	964	1,369.0	502.1	—	—	—	—	866.9	63.3	—	40.8	—
Romania	968	1,030.2	—	337.0	32.7	337.0	—	1,367.2	132.7	76.0	3.0	4.0
Russia	922	5,945.4	1.8	2,613.5	44.0	2,613.5	—	8,557.1	143.9	—	20.3	—
Serbia & Montenegro	965	467.7	—	650.2	139.0	650.2	—	1,117.9	239.0	56.7	11.1	19.5
Slovak Republic	936	357.5	—	—	—	—	—	357.5	100.0	—	.9	—
Slovenia	961	231.7	88.8	—	—	—	—	142.9	61.7	25.4	6.7	26.2
Tajikistan	923	87.0	—	72.9	83.8	—	72.9	87.0	100.0	—	.1	—
Turkey	186	964.0	112.8	14,823.1	1,537.7	14,823.1	—	15,674.3	1,626.0	112.3	171.7	152.9
Turkmenistan	925	75.2	—	—	—	—	—	75.2	100.0	—	—	—
Ukraine	926	1,372.0	—	1,127.4	82.2	1,127.4	—	2,499.4	182.2	—	8.5	—
Uzbekistan	927	275.6	—	16.6	6.0	16.6	—	292.2	106.0	—	.2	—
Middle East	405	15,478.5	4,180.5	504.5	3.3	283.3	221.2	11,582.1	74.8	986.5	1,311.6	133.0
Bahrain, Kingdom of	419	135.0	70.2	—	—	—	—	64.8	48.0	6.2	.6	10.3
Egypt	469	943.7	—	—	—	—	—	943.7	100.0	135.9	52.0	38.2
Iran, I.R. of	429	1,497.2	—	—	—	—	—	1,497.2	100.0	244.1	273.6	112.1
Iraq	433	504.0	—	—	—	—	—	504.0	100.0	68.5	—	—
Israel	436	928.2	333.4	—	—	—	—	594.8	64.1	106.4	8.0	7.6
Jordan	439	170.5	.1	246.5	144.6	246.5	—	417.0	244.5	16.9	1.9	11.0
Kuwait	443	1,381.1	500.8	—	—	—	—	880.3	63.7	26.7	111.9	418.6
Lebanon	446	203.0	18.8	—	—	—	—	184.2	90.7	4.4	20.9	475.5
Libya	672	1,123.7	395.5	—	—	—	—	728.2	64.8	58.8	468.1	796.4
Oman	449	194.0	64.2	—	—	—	—	129.9	66.9	6.3	8.4	134.1
Qatar	453	263.8	96.6	—	—	—	—	167.2	63.4	12.8	22.6	175.9
Saudi Arabia	456	6,985.5	2,485.6	—	—	—	—	4,499.9	64.4	195.5	311.4	159.3

2004, International Monetary Fund: *International Financial Statistics Yearbook*

Fund Account: Position to Date

(As of July 31, 2004 and Expressed in Millions of SDRs)

		Quota	Reserve Position in the Fund	Total Fund Credit and Loans Outstanding			Fund Holdings of Currency		SDR Department		
				Total Amount	Percent of Quota	Outstanding Purchases (GRA)	Outstanding Loans	Amount	Percent of Quota	Net Qumulative Allocation	Holdings of SDR	
											Amount	Percent of Allocation
		(1)	(2)	(3)	(4)	(5)	(6)	(7)	(8)	(9)	(10)	(11)
Middle East(Cont.)												
Syrian Arab Republic	463	293.6	—	—	—	—	—	293.6	100.0	36.6	.3	.9
United Arab Emirates	466	611.7	215.3	—	—	—	—	397.0	64.9	38.7	2.0	5.0
Yemen, Republic of	474	243.5	—	258.0	105.9	36.8	221.2	280.3	115.1	28.7	29.9	103.9
Western Hemisphere	205	**15,933.9**	**1,684.0**	**29,819.5**	**187.1**	**29,365.6**	**453.9**	**43,616.3**	**273.7**	**2,051.3**	**1,601.0**	**78.0**
Antigua and Barbuda	311	13.5	—	—	—	—	—	13.5	100.0	—	—	—
Argentina	213	2,117.1	.1	9,980.4	471.4	9,980.4	—	12,097.4	571.4	318.4	761.1	239.1
Bahamas, The	313	130.3	6.3	—	—	—	—	124.0	95.2	10.2	.1	.5
Barbados	316	67.5	5.1	—	—	—	—	62.4	92.5	8.0	—	.6
Belize	339	18.8	4.2	—	—	—	—	14.6	77.5	—	1.6	—
Bolivia	218	171.5	8.9	184.3	107.5	75.0	109.3	237.7	138.6	26.7	26.3	98.6
Brazil	223	3,036.1	—	17,221.9	567.2	17,221.9	—	20,258.5	667.3	358.7	209.3	58.3
Chile	228	856.1	293.2	—	—	—	—	562.9	65.7	121.9	32.5	26.6
Colombia	233	774.0	285.8	—	—	—	—	488.2	63.1	114.3	114.3	100.0
Costa Rica	238	164.1	20.0	—	—	—	—	144.1	87.8	23.7	.1	.5
Dominica	321	8.2	—	5.6	68.8	3.0	2.7	11.2	136.2	.6	—	6.2
Dominican Republic	243	218.9	—	131.3	60.0	131.3	—	350.2	160.0	31.6	1.5	4.8
Ecuador	248	302.3	17.2	213.9	70.8	213.9	—	499.1	165.1	32.9	10.3	31.4
El Salvador	253	171.3	—	—	—	—	—	171.3	100.0	25.0	25.0	100.0
Grenada	328	11.7	—	2.9	25.0	2.9	—	14.6	125.1	.9	—	3.8
Guatemala	258	210.2	—	—	—	—	—	210.2	100.0	27.7	5.3	19.3
Guyana	336	90.9	—	57.0	62.7	—	57.0	90.9	100.0	14.5	1.4	9.8
Haiti	263	81.9	.1	7.6	9.3	—	7.6	81.8	99.9	13.7	.6	4.2
Honduras	268	129.5	8.6	123.6	95.4	—	123.6	120.9	93.3	19.1	.1	.6
Jamaica	343	273.5	—	2.5	.9	2.5	—	276.1	100.9	40.6	.3	.7
Mexico	273	2,585.8	553.3	—	—	—	—	2,032.5	78.6	290.0	295.0	101.7
Nicaragua	278	130.0	—	153.7	118.3	—	153.7	130.0	100.0	19.5	.2	1.1
Panama	283	206.6	11.9	26.7	12.9	26.7	—	221.4	107.2	26.3	.5	2.0
Paraguay	288	99.9	21.5	—	—	—	—	78.4	78.5	13.7	85.3	622.9
Peru	293	638.4	—	80.3	12.6	80.3	—	718.7	112.6	91.3	1.0	1.1
St. Kitts and Nevis	361	8.9	.1	—	—	—	—	8.8	99.1	—	—	—
St. Lucia	362	15.3	—	—	—	—	—	15.3	100.0	.7	1.5	201.9
St. Vincent & Grens	364	8.3	.5	—	—	—	—	7.8	94.0	.4	—	.8
Suriname	366	92.1	6.1	—	—	—	—	86.0	93.4	7.8	1.3	16.4
Trinidad and Tobago	369	335.6	119.3	—	—	—	—	216.3	64.4	46.2	1.2	2.6
Uruguay	298	306.5	—	1,627.8	531.1	1,627.8	—	1,934.3	631.1	50.0	18.7	37.4
Venezuela, Rep. Bol.	299	2,659.1	321.9	—	—	—	—	2,337.2	87.9	316.9	6.3	2.0
Memorandum Items	001											
Oil Exporting Ctys.	999	20,307.3	4,310.6	7,088.9	34.9	7,088.9	ó	23,086.4	113.7	1,493.0	1,270.0	85.1
Non-Oil Develop.Ctys.	201	61,920.1	8,314.0	59,143.4	95.5	52,190.7	6,952.7	105,798.8	170.9	5,345.1	3,943.5	73.8

2004, International Monetary Fund : *International Financial Statistics Yearbook*

Financing Components of Members' Outstanding Obligations to the Fund

(As of July 31, 2004 and Expressed in Millions of SDRs)

		Total Fund Credit and Loans Outstanding	\multicolumn{8}{c	}{Outstanding Purchases (GRA)}	\multicolumn{3}{c	}{Outstanding Loans}	Trust Fund
			\multicolumn{5}{c|}{Ordinary Resources}	\multicolumn{3}{c|}{Borrower Resources}	SAF Arrangements	\multicolumn{2}{c|}{PRGF Arrangements}	
			Total Amount	CCFF	STF	Send-by/ Credit Tranche	Extended Fund Facility	Sff	EAR	GAB	NAB	SDA Resources	SDA Resources	PRGF Trust Resources	Administered Accounts
		(1)	(2)	(3)	(4)	(5)	(6)	(7)	(8)	(9)	(10)	(11)	(12)	(13)	(14)
All Countries	010	66,232.4	59,279.6	89.4	110.2	45,452.1	12,736.3	102.0	277.3	512.3	ó	64.8	.9	6,798.4	88.6
Industrial Countries	110	ó	ó	ó	....	ó	ó	ó	....	....	ó	....	....	....	....
Developing Countries	200	66,232.4	59,279.6	89.4	110.2	45,452.1	12,736.3	102.0	277.3	512.3	ó	64.8	.9	6,798.4	88.6
Africa	605	5,293.4	1,312.7	87.7	....	211.5	634.2	102.0	277.3	ó	ó	64.8	.9	3,826.5	88.6
Algeria	612	490.3	490.3	—	....	—	490.3	....	....	—	—	—	—	—	....
Angola	614	—	—	—	....	—	—	....	....	—	—	—	—	—	....
Benin	638	45.2	—	—	....	—	—	....	....	—	—	—	—	45.2	—
Botswana	616	—	—	....	....	—	—	....	....	—	—	—	....	—	....
Burkina Faso	748	80.5	—	—	....	—	—	....	....	—	—	—	.9	79.5	—
Burundi	618	26.4	—	—	....	—	—	....	....	—	—	—	—	26.4	—
Cameroon	622	225.5	—	—	....	—	—	....	....	—	—	—	—	225.5	—
Cape Verde	624	4.9	—	....	....	—	—	....	....	—	—	—	—	4.9	—
Central African Rep.	626	28.4	5.6	—	....	5.6	—	....	....	—	—	—	—	22.8	—
Chad	628	66.7	—	—	....	—	—	....	....	—	—	—	—	66.7	—
Comoros	632	—	—	—	....	—	—	....	....	—	—	—	—	—	—
Congo, Dem. Rep. of	636	526.8	—	—	....	—	—	....	....	—	—	—	—	526.8	—
Congo, Republic of	634	13.5	7.9	—	....	7.9	—	....	....	—	—	—	—	5.6	—
Côte d'Ivoire	662	240.3	—	—	....	—	—	....	....	—	—	—	—	240.3	—
Djibouti	611	13.6	—	—	....	—	—	....	....	—	—	—	....	13.6	—
Equatorial Guinea	642	—	—	—	....	—	—	....	....	—	—	—	—	—	—
Eritrea	643	—	—	—	....	—	—	....	....	—	—	—	—	—	—
Ethiopia	644	111.9	—	—	....	—	....	....	....	—	—	1.4	—	110.5	—
Gabon	646	43.3	43.3	—	....	22.2	21.1	....	....	—	—	—	—	—	....
Gambia, The	648	19.4	—	—	....	—	—	....	....	—	—	—	—	19.4	—
Ghana	652	314.8	—	—	....	—	—	....	....	—	—	—	—	314.8	—
Guinea	656	81.7	—	—	....	—	—	....	....	—	—	—	—	81.7	—
Guinea-Bissau	654	11.3	.6	—	....	.6	—	....	....	—	—	—	—	10.6	—
Kenya	664	70.8	—	—	....	—	—	....	....	—	—	—	—	70.8	—
Lesotho	666	21.0	—	....	....	—	....	....	....	—	—	—	—	21.0	22.9
Liberia	668	223.7	200.8	34.7	....	45.5	—	36.3	84.3	—	—	—	....	—	22.9
Madagascar	674	136.8	—	—	....	—	—	....	....	—	—	—	—	136.8	—
Malawi	676	63.9	17.4	—	....	17.4	—	....	....	—	—	—	—	46.5	—
Mali	678	103.9	—	—	....	—	—	....	....	—	—	—	—	103.9	—
Mauritania	682	62.8	—	—	....	—	—	....	....	—	—	—	—	62.8	—
Mauritius	684	—	—	—	....	—	—	....	....	—	—	—	—	—	—
Morocco	686	—	—	—	....	—	—	....	....	—	—	—	—	—	—
Mozambique	688	134.6	—	—	....	—	—	....	....	—	—	—	—	134.6	....
Namibia	728	—	—	—	....	—	—	....	....	—	—	—	—	—	—
Niger	692	90.1	—	—	....	—	—	....	....	—	—	—	—	90.1	—
Nigeria	694	—	—	—	....	—	—	....	....	—	—	—	....	—	—
Rwanda	714	61.8	—	—	....	—	—	....	....	—	—	—	—	61.8	—
São Tomé & Príncipe	716	1.9	—	—	....	—	—	....	....	—	—	—	—	1.9	....
Senegal	722	142.2	—	—	....	—	—	....	....	—	—	—	—	142.2	....
Seychelles	718	—	—	....	....	—	—	....	....	—	—	—	—	—	—
Sierra Leone	724	115.4	—	—	....	—	—	....	....	—	—	—	—	115.4	—
Somalia	726	112.0	96.7	28.5	....	12.6	....	—	55.5	—	—	8.8	—	—	6.5
South Africa	199	—	—	—	....	—	—	....	....	—	—	....	—	—	—
Sudan	732	391.8	332.6	24.4	....	35.8	69.2	65.6	137.5	—	—	—	—	—	59.2
Swaziland	734	—	—	—	....	—	—	....	....	—	—	—	—	—	—
Tanzania	738	284.8	—	—	....	—	—	....	....	—	—	—	—	284.8	—
Togo	742	20.6	—	—	....	—	—	....	....	—	—	—	—	20.6	—
Tunisia	744	—	—	—	....	—	—	....	....	—	—	—	—	—	....
Uganda	746	139.1	—	—	....	—	—	....	....	—	—	—	—	139.1	—
Zambia	754	576.1	—	—	....	—	—	....	....	—	—	54.5	—	521.6	—
Zimbabwe	698	195.8	117.5	—	....	63.9	53.6	....	....	—	—	—	—	78.3	—
Asia	505	9,242.2	7,696.1	ó	ó	574.4	7,121.7	ó	ó	ó	ó	ó	ó	1,546.1	ó
Afghanistan, I.S. of	512	—	—	—	....	—	....	....	....	—	—	—	....	—	—
Bangladesh	513	99.0	—	—	....	—	—	....	....	—	—	—	—	99.0	....
Bhutan	514	—	—	—	....	—	—	....	....	—	—	—	—	—	—
Brunei Darussalam	516	—	—	—	....	—	—	....	....	—	—	—	—	—	—
Cambodia	522	65.5	—	—	....	—	—	....	....	—	—	—	—	65.5	—
China, People's Rep.	924	—	—	—	....	—	—	....	....	—	—	—	—	—	....
Fiji	819	—	—	—	....	—	—	....	....	—	—	—	—	—	....
India	534	—	—	—	....	—	—	....	....	—	—	—	—	—	—
Indonesia	536	6,598.6	6,598.6	—	....	—	6,598.6	....	....	—	—	—	—	—	—
Kiribati	826	—	—	—	....	—	—	....	....	—	—	—	—	—	—
Korea	542	—	—	—	....	—	—	....	....	—	—	—	—	26.3	—
Lao People's Dem.Rep	544	26.3	—	—	....	—	—	....	....	—	—	—	—	26.3	—
Malaysia	548	—	—	—	....	—	—	....	....	—	—	—	—	—	—
Maldives	556	—	—	....	....	—	—	....	....	—	—	—	—	—	—
Marshall Islands,Rep.	867	—	—	—	....	—	—	....	....	—	—	—	—	—	—
Micronesia, Fed.Sts.	868	—	—	—	....	—	—	....	....	—	—	—	—	—	—
Mongolia	948	30.8	—	—	....	—	—	....	....	—	—	—	—	30.8	—
Myanmar	518	—	—	—	....	—	—	....	....	—	—	—	—	7.1	—
Nepal	558	7.1	—	—	....	—	—	....	....	—	—	—	—	1,076.2	—
Pakistan	564	1,355.4	279.1	—	....	195.0	84.1	....	....	—	—	—	—	1,076.2	—

Financing Components of Members' Outstanding Obligations to the Fund

(As of July 31, 2004 and Expressed in Millions of SDRs)

		Total Fund Credit and Loans Outstanding	Outstanding Purchases (GRA)									Outstanding Loans			
				Ordinary Resources				Borrower Resources				SAF Arrangements	PRGF Arrangements		Trust Fund
			Total Amount	CCFF	STF	Send-by/ Credit Tranche	Extended Fund Facility	Sff	EAR	GAB	NAB	SDA Resources	SDA Resources	PRGF Trust Resources	Administered Accounts
		(1)	(2)	(3)	(4)	(5)	(6)	(7)	(8)	(9)	(10)	(11)	(12)	(13)	(14)
Asia(Cont.)															
Palau	565	—	—	—	....	—	—	....	....	—	—	—	—	—	—
Papua New Guinea	853	62.8	62.8	—	....	62.8	—	....	....	—	—	—	—	—	—
Philippines	566	566.8	566.8	—	....	148.5	418.3	....	....	—	—	—	—	....	—
Samoa	862	—	—	—	....	—	....	....	....	—	—	—	—	—	—
Singapore	576	—	—	....	....	....	....	....	....	—	—	—	—	—	—
Solomon Islands	813	—	—	—	....	—	....	....	....	—	—	—	—	—	....
Sri Lanka	524	227.2	188.8	—	....	168.1	20.6	....	....	—	—	—	—	38.4	....
Thailand	578	—	—	—	....	—	....	....	....	—	—	—	—	—	—
Tonga	866	—	—	—	....	—	....	....	....	—	—	—	—	—	—
Vanuatu	846	—	—	....	....	—	....	....	....	—	—	—	—	—	—
Vietnam	582	202.7	—	....	....	—	....	....	....	—	—	—	—	202.7	—
Europe	170	21,372.8	20,621.9	1.7	110.2	15,741.0	4,256.6	ó	ó	512.3	ó	ó	ó	750.9	ó
Albania	914	66.0	—	—	....	—	—	....	....	—	—	—	—	66.0	—
Armenia	911	142.8	4.2	—	4.2	—	—	....	....	—	—	—	—	138.6	—
Azerbaijan	912	145.0	47.0	—	12.2	—	34.8	....	....	—	—	—	—	98.0	—
Belarus	913	5.8	5.8	—	5.8	—	—	....	....	—	—	—	—	—	—
Bosnia & Herzegovina	963	82.8	82.8	—	—	82.8	—	....	....	—	—	—	—	—	—
Bulgaria	918	811.3	811.3	—	—	236.0	575.3	....	....	—	—	—	—	—	—
Croatia	960	—	—	—	—	—	—	....	....	—	—	—	—	—	—
Cyprus	423	—	—	....	....	....	....	....	....	—	—	—	—	—	—
Czech Republic	935	—	—	—	....	—	....	....	....	—	—	—	—	—	—
Estonia	939	—	—	—	....	—	....	....	....	—	—	—	—	—	—
Georgia	915	189.8	6.9	—	6.9	—	—	....	....	—	—	—	—	182.8	—
Hungary	944	—	—	—	....	—	....	....	....	—	—	—	—	—	—
Kazakhstan	916	—	—	—	....	—	—	....	....	—	—	—	—	—	—
Kyrgyz Republic	917	144.0	—	—	....	—	—	....	....	—	—	—	—	144.0	—
Latvia	941	—	—	—	....	—	—	....	....	—	—	—	—	—	—
Lithuania	946	21.6	21.6	—	—	—	21.6	....	....	—	—	—	—	—	—
Macedonia, FYR	962	37.8	16.9	1.7	2.1	12.0	1.1	....	....	—	—	—	—	20.8	—
Malta	181	—	—	....	....	....	....	....	....	—	—	—	—	—	—
Moldova	921	85.3	57.6	—	....	—	57.6	....	....	—	—	—	—	27.7	—
Poland	964	—	—	—	....	—	—	....	....	—	—	—	—	—	—
Romania	968	337.0	337.0	—	—	337.0	—	....	....	—	—	—	—	—	—
Russia	922	2,613.5	2,613.5	—	—	—	2,101.2	—	—	512.3	—	....	....	—	—
Serbia & Montenegro	965	650.2	650.2	—	—	250.2	400.0	....	....	—	—	....	....	—	—
Slovak Republic	936	—	—	—	—	—	—	....	....	—	—	....	....	—	—
Slovenia	961	—	—	—	....	—	....	....	....	—	—	—	—	—	—
Tajikistan	923	72.9	—	—	....	—	—	....	....	—	—	—	—	72.9	—
Turkey	186	14,823.1	14,823.1	—	....	—	14,823.1	....	....	—	—	—	—	—	—
Turkmenistan	925	—	—	—	....	—	—	....	....	—	—	—	—	—	—
Ukraine	926	1,127.4	1,127.4	—	62.3	—	1,065.1	....	....	—	—	....	....	—	—
Uzbekistan	927	16.6	16.6	—	16.6	—	—	....	....	—	—	—	—	—	—
Middle East	405	504.5	283.3	ó	....	10.7	272.7	....	....	ó	ó	ó	ó	221.2	ó
Bahrain, Kingdom of	419	—	—	....	....	....	....	....	....	—	—	....	....	—	—
Egypt	469	—	—	—	....	—	—	....	....	—	—	—	—	—	—
Iran, I.R. of	429	—	—	—	....	—	....	....	....	—	—	—	—	—	—
Iraq	433	—	—	—	....	—	....	....	....	—	—	—	—	—	—
Israel	436	—	—	....	....	....	....	....	....	—	—	—	—	—	—
Jordan	439	246.5	246.5	—	....	10.7	235.9	....	....	—	—	—	—	—	—
Kuwait	443	—	—	....	....	....	....	....	....	—	—	—	—	—	—
Lebanon	446	—	—	....	....	....	....	....	....	—	—	—	—	—	—
Libya	672	—	—	....	....	....	....	....	....	—	—	—	—	—	—
Oman	449	—	—	....	....	....	....	....	....	—	—	—	—	—	—
Qatar	453	—	—	....	....	....	....	....	....	—	—	—	—	—	—
Saudi Arabia	456	—	—	....	....	....	....	....	....	—	—	—	—	—	—
Syrian Arab Republic	463	—	—	—	....	—	....	....	....	—	—	—	—	—	—
United Arab Emirates	466	—	—	....	....	....	....	....	....	—	—	—	—	—	—
Yemen, Republic of	474	258.0	36.8	—	....	—	36.8	....	....	—	—	—	—	221.2	—
Western Hemisphere	205	29,819.5	29,365.6	ó	....	28,914.6	451.0	ó	ó	ó	ó	ó	ó	453.9	ó
Antigua and Barbuda	311	—	—	....	....	—	....	....	....	—	—	—	—	—	—
Argentina	213	9,980.4	9,980.4	—	....	9,638.8	341.6	....	....	—	—	—	—	—	—
Bahamas, The	313	—	—	....	....	....	....	....	....	—	—	—	—	—	—
Barbados	316	—	—	—	....	—	....	....	....	—	—	—	—	—	—
Belize	339	—	—	—	....	—	....	....	....	—	—	—	—	—	—
Bolivia	218	184.3	75.0	—	....	75.0	—	....	....	—	—	—	—	109.3	—
Brazil	223	17,221.9	17,221.9	—	....	17,221.9	—	....	....	—	—	—	—	—	—
Chile	228	—	—	—	....	—	—	....	....	—	—	—	—	—	—
Colombia	233	—	—	—	....	—	—	....	....	—	—	—	—	—	—
Costa Rica	238	—	—	—	....	—	....	....	....	—	—	—	—	—	—
Dominica	321	5.6	3.0	—	....	3.0	—	....	....	—	—	—	—	2.7	—
Dominican Republic	243	131.3	131.3	—	....	131.3	—	....	....	—	—	—	—	—	—
Ecuador	248	213.9	213.9	—	....	213.9	—	....	....	—	—	—	—	—	—
El Salvador	253	—	—	—	....	—	....	....	....	—	—	—	—	—	—
Grenada	328	2.9	2.9	—	....	2.9	—	....	....	—	—	—	—	—	—
Guatemala	258	—	—	—	....	—	....	....	....	—	—	—	—	....	—

Financing Components of Members' Outstanding Obligations to the Fund

(As of July 31, 2004 and Expressed in Millions of SDRs)

		Outstanding Purchases (GRA)									Outstanding Loans			
	Total Fund Credit and Loans Outstanding	Ordinary Resources					Borrower Resources				SAF Arrangements	PRGF Arrangements		Trust Fund
		Total Amount	CCFF	STF	Send-by/ Credit Tranche	Extended Fund Facility	Sff	EAR	GAB	NAB	SDA Resources	SDA Resources	PRGF Trust Resources	Administered Accounts
	(1)	(2)	(3)	(4)	(5)	(6)	(7)	(8)	(9)	(10)	(11)	(12)	(13)	(14)
Western Hemisphere(C														
Guyana................ 336	57.0	—	—	....	—	—	—	—	—	—	—	—	57.0	—
Haiti..................... 263	7.6	—	—	....	—	—	—	—	—	—	—	....	7.6	—
Honduras............. 268	123.6	—	—	....	—	—	—	—	—	—	....	—	123.6	—
Jamaica............... 343	2.5	2.5	—	....	—	2.5	—	—	—	—	....	....	....	....
Mexico................. 273	—	—	—	....	—	—	—	—	—	—	....	....	....	....
Nicaragua............ 278	153.7	—	—	....	—	....	....	....	—	—	....	....	153.7	....
Panama................ 283	26.7	26.7	—	....	—	26.7	....	....	—	—	....	....	....	....
Paraguay............. 288	—	—	....	....	—	—	....	....	—	—	—	....	....	....
Peru..................... 293	80.3	80.3	—	....	—	80.3	—	—	—	—	....	....	....	....
St. Kitts and Nevis.. 361	—	—	....	....	—	—	....	....	—	—	—	....	....	....
St. Lucia.............. 362	—	—	....	....	—	—	....	....	—	—	—	....	....	....
St. Vincent & Grens.. 364	—	—	....	....	—	—	....	....	—	—	....	....	....	....
Suriname............. 366	—	—	....	....	....	....	....	....	—	—	....	....	....	....
Trinidad and Tobago.. 369	—	—	—	....	—	....	—	—	—	—	....	....	....	....
Uruguay.............. 298	1,627.8	1,627.8	—	....	1,627.8	....	—	—	—	—	....	....	....	....
Venezuela, Rep. Bol.. 299														
Memorandum Items 001														
Oil Exporting Ctys...... 999	7,088.9	7,088.9	ó	ó	ó	7,088.9	....	ó	ó	ó	....	....	....	....
Non-Oil Develop.Ctys. 201	59,143.4	52,190.7	89.4	110.2	45,452.1	5,647.4	102.0	277.3	512.3	ó	64.8	.9	6,798.4	88.6

2004, International Monetary Fund: *International Financial Statistics Yearbook*

Purchases

Expressed in Millions of SDRs

		1992	1993	1994	1995	1996	1997	1998	1999	2000	2001	2002	2003
World	001	4,791.1	5,042.2	4,979.5	16,967.9	5,271.0	16,112.9	20,586.2	10,010.1	7,178.0	23,761.6	25,237.0	20,323.1
Developing Countries	200	4,791.1	5,042.2	4,979.5	16,967.9	5,271.0	16,112.9	20,586.2	10,010.1	7,178.0	23,761.6	25,237.0	20,323.1
Africa	605	172.7	678.8	761.5	1,038.5	556.9	370.1	313.6	266.9	35.6	ñ	27.0	9.6
Algeria	612	–	–	587.5	312.8	512.2	337.6	253.3	223.5	–	–	–	–
Angola	614	–	–	–	–	–	–	–	–	–	–	–	–
Benin	638	–	–	–	–	–	–	–	–	–	–	–	–
Burkina Faso	748	–	–	–	–	–	–	–	–	–	–	–	–
Burundi	618	–	–	–	–	–	–	–	–	–	–	9.6	9.6
Cameroon	622	–	–	21.9	8.5	19.7	–	–	–	–	–	–	–
Cape Verde	624	–	–	–	–	–	–	–	–	–	–	–	–
Central African Rep.	626	–	–	10.7	–	–	–	–	–	–	–	–	–
Chad	628	–	–	10.3	–	–	–	–	–	–	–	–	–
Comoros	632	–	–	–	–	–	–	–	–	–	–	–	–
Congo, Dem. Rep. of	636	–	–	–	–	–	–	–	–	–	–	–	–
Congo, Republic of	634	–	–	12.5	–	–	–	–	7.2	–	10.6	–	–
Côte d'Ivoire	662	–	–	–	–	–	–	–	–	–	–	–	–
Djibouti	611	–	–	–	–	2.9	1.1	2.3	1.0	–	–	–	–
Equatorial Guinea	642	–	–	–	–	–	–	–	–	–	–	–	–
Ethiopia	644	–	–	–	–	–	–	–	–	–	–	–	–
Gabon	646	–	–	44.7	37.5	22.1	16.6	–	–	13.2	–	–	–
Gambia, The	648	–	–	–	–	–	–	–	–	–	–	–	–
Ghana	652	–	47.0	–	–	–	–	–	–	–	–	–	–
Guinea	656	–	–	–	–	–	–	–	–	–	–	–	–
Guinea-Bissau	654	–	–	–	–	–	–	–	2.1	1.4	–	–	–
Kenya	664	–	–	–	–	–	–	–	–	–	–	–	–
Lesotho	666	–	–	–	–	–	–	–	–	–	–	–	–
Liberia	668	–	–	–	–	–	–	–	–	–	–	–	–
Madagascar	674	–	–	–	–	–	–	–	–	–	–	–	–
Malawi	676	–	–	12.7	–	–	–	–	–	–	–	17.4	–
Mali	678	–	–	–	–	–	–	–	–	–	–	–	–
Mauritania	682	–	–	–	–	–	–	–	–	–	–	–	–
Mauritius	684	–	–	–	–	–	–	–	–	–	–	–	–
Morocco	686	18.4	–	–	–	–	–	–	–	–	–	–	–
Mozambique	688	–	–	–	–	–	–	–	–	–	–	–	–
Niger	692	–	–	11.1	–	–	–	–	–	–	–	–	–
Nigeria	694	–	–	–	–	–	–	–	–	–	–	–	–
Rwanda	714	–	–	–	8.9	–	14.9	–	–	–	–	–	–
São Tomé & Príncipe	716	–	–	–	–	–	–	–	–	–	–	–	–
Senegal	722	–	–	30.9	–	–	–	–	–	–	–	–	–
Seychelles	718	–	–	–	–	–	–	–	–	–	–	–	–
Sierra Leone	724	–	–	–	–	–	–	11.6	15.6	10.4	–	–	–
Somalia	726	–	–	–	–	–	–	–	–	–	–	–	–
South Africa	199	–	614.4	–	–	–	–	–	–	–	–	–	–
Sudan	732	–	–	–	–	–	–	–	–	–	–	–	–
Swaziland	734	–	–	–	–	–	–	–	–	–	–	–	–
Tanzania	738	–	–	–	–	–	–	–	–	–	–	–	–
Togo	742	–	–	–	–	–	–	–	–	–	–	–	–
Tunisia	744	51.8	–	–	–	–	–	–	–	–	–	–	–
Uganda	746	–	–	–	–	–	–	–	–	–	–	–	–
Zambia	754	–	–	–	651.7	–	–	–	–	–	–	–	–
Zimbabwe	698	102.5	17.4	19.1	19.1	–	–	39.2	24.7	–	–	–	–
Asia	505	1,452.0	755.3	220.2	167.3	109.2	12,801.7	11,259.8	2,236.4	1,267.6	784.7	1,197.6	1,396.9
Afghanistan, I.S. of	512	–	–	–	–	–	–	–	–	–	–	–	–
Bangladesh	513	–	–	–	–	–	–	98.1	–	–	–	–	–
Bhutan	514	–	–	–	–	–	–	–	–	–	–	–	–
Cambodia	522	–	6.3	–	–	–	–	–	–	–	–	–	–
China, People's Rep.	924	–	–	–	–	–	–	–	–	–	–	–	–
Fiji	819	–	–	–	–	–	–	–	–	–	–	–	–
India	534	1,109.0	462.0	–	–	–	–	–	–	–	–	–	–
Indonesia	536	–	–	–	–	–	2,201.5	4,254.3	1,011.0	851.2	309.7	1,101.0	1,376.2
Kiribati	826	–	–	–	–	–	–	–	–	–	–	–	–
Korea	542	–	–	–	–	–	8,200.0	5,850.0	362.5	–	–	–	–
Lao People's Dem.Rep.	544	–	–	–	–	–	–	–	–	–	–	–	–
Malaysia	548	–	–	–	–	–	–	–	–	–	–	–	–
Maldives	556	–	–	–	–	–	–	–	–	–	–	–	–
Micronesia, Fed.Sts.	868	–	–	–	–	–	–	–	–	–	–	–	–
Mongolia	948	2.5	–	–	–	–	–	–	–	–	–	–	–
Myanmar	518	–	–	–	–	–	–	–	–	–	–	–	–
Nepal	558	–	–	–	–	–	–	–	–	–	–	–	–
Pakistan	564	189.6	88.0	123.2	134.0	107.2	91.5	19.0	409.6	150.0	315.0	–	–
Palau	565	–	–	–	–	–	–	–	–	–	–	–	–
Papua New Guinea	853	–	–	–	33.3	2.0	–	–	–	–	28.9	56.7	–
Philippines	566	151.0	126.6	36.5	–	–	508.8	538.3	253.3	237.6	–	–	–
Samoa	862	–	–	–	–	–	–	–	–	–	–	–	–
Solomon Islands	813	–	–	–	–	–	–	–	–	–	–	–	–
Sri Lanka	524	–	–	–	–	–	–	–	–	–	103.4	96.7	20.7
Thailand	578	–	–	–	–	–	1,800.0	500.0	200.0	–	–	–	–
Vietnam	582	–	72.5	60.5	–	–	–	–	–	–	–	–	–

2004, International Monetary Fund: *International Financial Statistics Yearbook*

Purchases

		1992	1993	1994	1995	1996	1997	1998	1999	2000	2001	2002	2003
		Expressed in Millions of SDRs
Europe	170	1,674.6	1,700.0	3,177.1	5,337.2	3,488.2	2,272.3	5,312.9	1,944.9	3,253.3	9,456.6	10,327.5	1,696.3
Albania	914	9.7	3.4	–	–	–	8.8	–	–	–	–	–	–
Armenia	911	–	–	16.9	30.4	–	–	–	–	–	–	–	–
Azerbaijan	912	–	–	–	67.9	53.8	20.5	15.8	68.6	–	–	–	–
Belarus	913	–	70.1	–	120.1	–	–	–	–	–	–	–	–
Bosnia & Herzegovina	963	–	–	–	30.3	–	–	24.2	29.0	27.2	14.0	31.6	24.0
Bulgaria	918	200.3	31.0	232.5	–	80.0	355.2	228.9	209.2	209.2	104.6	84.0	104.0
Croatia	960	–	–	78.5	65.4	–	28.8	–	–	–	–	–	–
Cyprus	423	–	–	–	–	–	–	–	–	–	–	–	–
Czech Republic	935	–	70.0	–	–	–	–	–	–	–	–	–	–
Czechoslovakia	934	238.6	....	....	–	....	....	....	....	–	–	–	–
Estonia	939	7.8	34.1	–	20.9	–	–	–	–	–	–	–	–
Georgia	915	–	–	27.8	50.0	–	–	–	–	–	–	–	–
Hungary	944	118.4	56.7	–	–	–	–	–	–	–	–	–	–
Kazakhstan	916	–	61.9	136.1	92.8	92.8	–	154.7	–	–	–	–	–
Kyrgyz Republic	917	–	43.9	–	–	–	–	–	–	–	–	–	–
Latvia	941	25.2	52.6	32.0	–	–	–	–	–	–	–	–	–
Lithuania	946	17.3	70.7	46.6	41.4	31.1	41.4	–	–	–	–	–	–
Macedonia, FYR	962	–	–	12.4	24.8	9.9	–	–	13.8	1.1	–	–	12.0
Moldova	921	–	63.0	49.5	42.4	22.5	15.0	–	50.0	–	–	–	–
Poland	964	–	–	640.3	–	–	–	–	–	–	–	–	–
Romania	968	338.5	–	245.1	37.7	–	120.6	–	–	53.0	86.8	52.0	82.7	165.3
Russia	922	719.0	1,078.3	1,078.3	3,594.3	2,587.9	1,467.3	4,600.0	471.4	–	–	–	–
Serbia & Montenegro	965	–	–	–	–	–	–	–	–	116.9	100.0	200.0	200.0
Slovak Republic	936	–	64.4	96.5	–	–	–	–	–	–	–	–	–
Tajikistan	923	–	–	–	–	15.0	7.5	7.5	–	–	–	–	–
Turkey	186	–	–	235.5	225.0	–	–	–	583.2	2,622.1	8,895.2	9,929.2	1,191.0
Ukraine	926	–	–	249.3	788.0	536.0	207.3	281.8	466.6	190.1	290.8	–	–
Uzbekistan	927	–	–	–	106.0	59.3	–	–	–	–	–	–	–
Middle East	405	288.0	11.1	65.6	75.8	166.2	154.0	32.7	77.4	15.2	37.0	71.6	ñ
Bahrain, Kingdom of	419	–	–	–	–	–	–	–	–	–	–	–	–
Egypt	469	87.2	–	–	–	–	–	–	–	–	–	–	–
Iran, I.R. of	429	–	–	–	–	–	–	–	–	–	–	–	–
Iraq	433	–	–	–	–	–	–	–	–	–	–	–	–
Israel	436	178.6	–	–	–	–	–	–	–	–	–	–	–
Jordan	439	22.2	11.1	65.6	75.8	82.2	96.7	23.7	55.4	15.2	30.5	71.6	–
Lebanon	446	–	–	–	–	–	–	–	–	–	–	–	–
Syrian Arab Republic	463	–	–	–	–	–	–	–	–	–	–	–	–
Yemen, Republic of	474	–	–	–	–	84.0	57.4	9.0	22.0	–	6.5	–	–
Western Hemisphere	205	1,203.7	1,896.9	755.1	10,349.1	950.6	514.7	3,667.2	5,484.5	2,606.3	13,483.5	13,613.3	17,220.2
Antigua and Barbuda	311	–	–	–	–	–	–	–	–	–	–	–	–
Argentina	213	584.6	1,154.8	612.0	1,559.0	548.2	321.0	–	–	1,587.8	8,168.5	–	4,004.5
Barbados	316	36.8	–	–	–	–	–	–	–	–	–	–	–
Belize	339	–	–	–	–	–	–	–	–	–	–	–	64.3
Bolivia	218	–	–	–	–	–	–	–	–	–	–	–	–
Brazil	223	127.5	–	–	–	–	–	3,419.0	4,450.1	–	5,277.2	12,274.0	12,635.4
Chile	228	–	–	–	–	–	–	–	–	–	–	–	–
Colombia	233	–	–	–	–	–	–	–	–	–	–	–	–
Costa Rica	238	4.0	–	–	–	–	–	–	–	–	–	2.1	.9
Dominica	321	–	–	–	–	–	–	–	–	–	–	–	87.6
Dominican Republic	243	37.4	53.3	–	–	–	–	39.7	–	–	113.3	37.8	75.6	60.4
Ecuador	248	–	–	98.9	–	–	–	–	–	–	–	–	–
El Salvador	253	–	–	–	–	–	–	–	–	–	–	–	–
Grenada	328	–	–	–	–	–	–	–	–	–	–	–	2.9
Guatemala	258	–	–	–	–	–	–	–	–	–	–	–	–
Guyana	336	–	–	–	–	–	–	–	–	–	–	–	–
Haiti	263	–	–	–	16.4	–	–	15.2	–	–	–	–	–
Honduras	268	51.0	–	–	–	–	–	47.5	–	–	–	–	–
Jamaica	343	41.8	36.4	34.4	7.0	–	–	–	–	–	–	–	–
Mexico	273	233.1	–	–	8,758.0	–	–	–	–	1,034.4	905.1	–	–
Nicaragua	278	–	–	–	–	–	–	–	–	–	–	–	–
Panama	283	71.6	9.9	9.9	8.7	52.4	33.2	30.0	–	–	–	–	–
Paraguay	288	–	–	–	–	–	–	–	–	–	–	–	–
Peru	293	–	642.7	–	–	–	160.5	–	–	–	–	–	–
St. Kitts and Nevis	361	–	–	–	–	–	–	1.6	–	–	–	–	–
St. Lucia	362	–	–	–	–	–	–	–	–	–	–	–	–
St. Vincent & Grens	364	–	–	–	–	–	–	–	–	–	–	–	–
Suriname	366	–	–	–	–	–	–	–	–	–	–	–	–
Trinidad and Tobago	369	–	–	–	–	–	–	114.2	–	–	–	–	–
Uruguay	298	16.0	–	–	–	–	–	–	–	–	–	1,261.7	364.2
Venezuela, Rep. Bol	299	–	–	–	–	350.0	–	–	–	–	–	–	–
Memorandum Items													
Oil Exporting Ctys	999	ñ	ñ	587.5	312.8	862.2	2,539.1	4,507.6	1,234.5	851.2	309.7	1,101.0	1,376.2
Non-Oil Develop.Ctys	201	4,791.1	5,042.2	4,392.0	16,655.1	4,408.7	13,573.8	16,078.6	8,775.6	6,326.9	23,452.0	24,136.0	18,946.9

2004, International Monetary Fund : *International Financial Statistics Yearbook*

Repurchases

		1992	1993	1994	1995	1996	1997	1998	1999	2000	2001	2002	2003
						Expressed in Millions of SDRs							
World	001	4,201.6	3,814.0	4,572.0	6,650.9	5,071.9	5,681.3	6,694.2	19,398.8	15,249.4	13,274.9	15,113.1	18,892.1
Developing Countries	200	4,201.6	3,814.0	4,572.0	6,650.9	5,071.9	5,681.3	6,694.2	19,398.8	15,249.4	13,274.9	15,113.1	18,892.1
Africa	605	601.3	626.5	423.3	1,522.4	269.2	730.0	827.9	407.3	198.2	241.1	426.4	348.1
Algeria	612	117.7	235.4	136.5	112.5	93.8	254.6	320.8	262.8	70.2	110.5	229.6	313.7
Burkina Faso	748	–	–	–	–	–	–	–	–	–	–	–	–
Burundi	618	–	–	–	–	–	–	–	–	–	–	–	–
Cameroon	622	38.6	33.8	3.9	4.0	4.0	8.2	12.0	13.3	14.1	2.5	–	–
Central African Rep	626	1.1	.6	.4	–	–	2.7	5.6	2.4	–	–	–	–
Chad	628	–	–	–	–	–	3.9	5.2	1.3	–	–	–	–
Comoros	632	–	–	–	–	–	–	–	–	–	–	–	–
Congo, Dem. Rep. of	636	–	–	3.0	.9	22.7	–	.4	.7	–	–	157.1	–
Congo, Republic of	634	–	.5	2.0	1.5	–	1.6	7.8	3.1	–	.9	3.6	2.7
Côte d'Ivoire	662	65.2	36.5	53.5	56.8	32.8	16.1	–	–	–	–	–	–
Djibouti	611	–	–	–	–	–	–	–	.7	1.7	1.6	1.8	1.3
Equatorial Guinea	642	–	–	–	–	–	–	–	–	–	–	–	–
Ethiopia	644	–	–	–	–	–	–	–	–	–	–	–	–
Gabon	646	25.8	25.7	16.1	34.5	3.8	2.6	16.7	17.9	7.4	8.7	10.1	10.1
Gambia, The	648	1.5	–	–	–	–	–	–	–	–	–	–	–
Ghana	652	45.3	39.3	27.1	13.1	16.8	34.5	24.6	–	–	–	–	–
Guinea	656	.8	–	–	–	–	–	–	–	–	–	–	–
Guinea-Bissau	654	–	–	–	–	–	–	–	–	–	–	.3	1.6
Kenya	664	58.7	41.5	–	–	–	–	–	–	–	–	–	–
Lesotho	666	–	–	–	–	–	–	–	–	–	–	–	–
Liberia	668	–	–	–	.1	–	–	–	–	.2	.3	.2	–
Madagascar	674	11.5	7.4	4.5	.6	–	–	–	–	–	–	–	–
Malawi	676	13.6	4.2	1.2	–	–	–	6.4	6.4	–	–	–	–
Mali	678	4.4	6.3	4.8	1.0	–	–	–	–	–	–	–	–
Mauritania	682	4.6	1.0	–	–	–	–	–	–	–	–	–	–
Mauritius	684	–	–	–	–	–	–	–	–	–	–	–	–
Morocco	686	100.8	112.0	106.1	66.2	32.5	2.3	–	–	–	–	–	–
Niger	692	5.4	3.5	2.0	–	–	4.2	5.6	1.4	–	–	–	–
Nigeria	694	–	–	–	–	–	–	–	–	–	–	–	–
Rwanda	714	–	–	–	–	–	–	–	4.5	6.7	7.4	5.2	–
Senegal	722	28.1	11.0	2.5	–	–	11.6	15.5	3.9	–	–	–	–
Sierra Leone	724	1.4	5.9	42.6	–	–	–	–	–	–	37.5	–	–
Somalia	726	–	–	–	–	–	–	–	–	–	–	–	–
South Africa	199	–	–	–	–	–	307.2	307.2	–	–	–	–	–
Sudan	732	–	–	–	23.0	24.5	25.5	42.2	27.6	41.1	41.1	17.0	18.7
Swaziland	734	–	–	–	–	–	–	–	–	–	–	–	–
Tanzania	738	3.9	–	–	–	–	–	–	–	–	–	–	–
Togo	742	7.1	5.2	2.4	2.0	.2	–	–	–	–	–	–	–
Tunisia	744	20.9	3.8	–	10.2	32.1	36.6	36.6	36.6	30.4	24.7	–	–
Uganda	746	18.7	3.1	–	–	–	–	–	–	–	–	–	–
Zambia	754	26.0	49.8	14.6	1,196.2	–	–	–	–	–	–	–	–
Zimbabwe	698	–	–	–	–	5.9	18.5	21.6	24.8	26.4	5.9	1.5	–
Asia	505	734.3	369.7	1,066.0	1,113.8	1,262.8	831.0	2,514.2	8,330.4	375.5	6,943.9	3,419.1	2,110.8
Afghanistan, I.S. of	512	–	–	–	–	–	–	–	–	–	–	–	–
Bangladesh	513	56.0	35.9	–	–	–	–	–	–	–	–	49.1	49.1
Bhutan	514	–	–	–	–	–	–	–	–	–	–	–	–
Cambodia	522	6.3	6.3	–	–	–	–	1.0	1.0	1.0	1.0	1.0	1.0
China, People's Rep	924	–	–	–	–	–	–	–	–	–	–	–	–
Fiji	819	–	–	–	–	–	–	–	–	–	–	–	–
India	534	275.0	137.5	821.7	796.5	881.4	495.5	304.9	246.4	38.5	–	–	–
Indonesia	536	115.7	–	–	–	–	–	–	–	–	1,375.9	1,834.6	979.3
Korea	542	–	–	–	–	–	–	2,050.0	7,900.0	–	4,462.5	–	–
Lao People's Dem.Rep	544	–	–	–	–	–	–	–	–	–	–	–	–
Malaysia	548	–	–	–	–	–	–	–	–	–	–	–	–
Mongolia	948	–	–	–	6.3	6.9	.6	–	–	–	–	–	–
Myanmar	518	–	–	–	–	–	–	–	–	–	–	–	–
Nepal	558	.8	–	–	–	–	–	–	–	–	–	–	–
Pakistan	564	116.1	91.4	34.1	61.2	167.0	138.8	39.7	107.6	161.2	80.8	167.4	351.7
Papua New Guinea	853	–	10.7	21.4	10.7	–	–	3.0	16.7	14.7	1.0	–	3.8
Philippines	566	109.9	46.0	188.7	239.1	207.5	156.9	58.2	39.5	6.1	6.1	313.0	434.4
Samoa	862	.2	–	–	–	–	–	–	–	–	–	–	–
Solomon Islands	813	–	–	–	–	–	–	–	–	–	–	–	–
Sri Lanka	524	54.4	13.6	–	–	–	–	–	–	–	–	–	–
Thailand	578	–	–	–	–	–	–	–	–	150.0	1,012.5	1,050.0	287.5
Vietnam	582	–	28.4	–	–	–	39.3	57.4	19.2	4.0	4.0	4.0	4.0
Europe	170	444.2	244.1	1,325.2	2,010.7	1,047.8	687.5	1,522.7	4,309.1	3,841.5	4,763.9	6,767.4	3,120.3
Albania	914	–	–	–	.8	5.7	5.8	.9	–	–	4.4	4.4	–
Armenia	911	–	–	–	–	–	–	.4	9.6	12.0	5.6	5.6	7.0
Azerbaijan	912	–	–	–	–	–	–	–	11.7	39.0	30.9	35.8	45.3
Belarus	913	–	–	–	–	–	–	17.9	42.5	42.1	23.4	23.4	23.4
Bosnia & Herzegovina	963	–	–	–	18.4	1.4	.7	–	15.2	15.2	6.1	17.6	36.3
Bulgaria	918	60.6	–	48.0	162.3	154.9	64.4	134.7	90.7	105.3	236.2	195.2	76.6
Croatia	960	–	17.2	6.2	3.9	3.1	1.6	6.5	22.9	21.8	24.2	97.2	–
Cyprus	423	–	–	–	–	–	–	–	–	–	–	–	–
Czech Republic	935	–	70.0	780.7	–	–	–	–	–	–	–	–	–

Repurchases

		1992	1993	1994	1995	1996	1997	1998	1999	2000	2001	2002	2003
Expressed in Millions of SDRs
Europe(Cont.)
Czechoslovakia	934	35.0	....	....	....	....	....	....	....	....	....	....	....
Estonia	939	—	—	—	1.0	7.7	14.1	18.7	2.9	3.9	3.9	10.7	—
Georgia	915	—	—	—	—	—	—	.7	15.7	19.7	9.3	9.3	11.6
Hungary	944	122.8	36.2	114.7	522.9	140.0	—	118.7	—	—	—	—	—
Kazakhstan	916	—	—	—	—	—	4.6	70.0	128.5	335.1	—	—	—
Kyrgyz Republic	917	—	—	—	—	2.7	7.1	8.5	5.4	5.4	5.4	5.4	4.0
Latvia	941	—	—	—	1.9	17.5	26.7	18.3	11.1	7.6	7.6	7.6	7.6
Lithuania	946	—	—	—	—	16.9	31.1	20.6	12.1	20.7	26.7	31.1	59.1
Macedonia, FYR	962	—	2.2	1.2	.7	.6	.3	1.7	12.4	14.7	6.0	5.9	11.0
Moldova	921	—	—	—	—	5.1	14.6	47.2	47.9	18.6	11.3	13.8	15.8
Poland	964	—	98.9	219.4	918.6	—	—	—	—	—	—	—	—
Romania	968	153.4	—	89.6	245.8	245.4	98.4	92.3	102.0	72.9	91.7	75.7	79.6
Russia	922	—	—	—	—	359.5	359.5	673.9	3,101.1	2,189.5	2,997.9	1,147.6	1,356.1
Serbia & Montenegro	965	—	—	—	—	—	—	—	—	—	—	—	—
Slovak Republic	936	—	—	61.9	132.3	85.6	37.6	49.8	38.1	96.5	—	—	—
Slovenia	961	—	9.9	3.6	2.2	1.8	.9	—	—	—	—	—	—
Tajikistan	923	—	—	—	—	—	—	—	3.8	7.5	9.4	7.5	1.9
Turkey	186	—	—	—	—	—	20.1	164.6	210.2	65.6	867.6	4,916.4	1,223.9
Ukraine	926	—	—	—	—	—	—	77.3	407.0	643.5	361.2	140.7	144.5
Uzbekistan	927	—	—	—	—	—	—	—	18.4	49.4	35.1	16.6	16.6
Yugoslavia, SFR	188	72.4	9.6	—	—	—	—	—	—	—	....	....	....
Middle East	405	36.3	33.1	48.4	135.2	163.2	49.4	6.8	50.7	77.9	81.7	74.6	76.3
Egypt	469	29.0	—	22.5	62.7	58.6	10.9	—	—	—	—	—	—
Iran, I.R. of	429	—	—	—	—	—	—	—	—	—	—	—	—
Iraq	433	—	—	—	—	—	—	—	—	—	—	—	—
Israel	436	—	—	—	67.0	89.3	22.3	—	—	—	—	—	—
Jordan	439	7.3	33.1	25.9	5.6	15.3	16.2	6.8	26.0	23.8	40.2	61.0	71.4
Syrian Arab Republic	463	—	—	—	—	—	—	24.8	54.1	41.4	13.6	4.8	
Yemen, Republic of	474	—	—	—	—	—	—	—	—	—	—	—	—
Western Hemisphere	205	2,385.6	2,540.5	1,709.2	1,868.8	2,329.0	3,383.4	1,822.5	6,301.3	10,756.2	1,244.3	4,425.6	13,236.7
Argentina	213	637.7	275.1	289.7	319.3	296.5	347.8	484.2	602.5	970.2	927.6	573.6	4,105.8
Barbados	316	—	—	—	11.9	18.4	6.5	—	—	—	—	—	—
Belize	339	—	—	—	—	—	—	—	—	—	—	—	—
Bolivia	218	22.6	17.0	—	—	—	—	—	—	—	—	—	—
Brazil	223	411.3	360.4	93.5	32.3	48.2	23.7	15.5	1,445.9	5,074.2	—	3,588.3	8,898.6
Chile	228	144.4	178.5	147.0	199.5	—	—	—	—	—	—	—	—
Colombia	233	—	—	—	—	—	—	—	—	—	—	—	—
Costa Rica	238	2.8	—	13.8	29.1	15.8	.5	—	—	—	—	—	—
Dominica	321	.4	.1	—	—	—	—	—	—	—	—	19.9	19.9
Dominican Republic	243	10.3	7.2	5.6	22.4	41.0	45.3	21.1	—	—	—	—	24.8
Ecuador	248	54.9	20.8	14.9	19.0	15.8	2.0	49.5	49.5	—	—	—	—
El Salvador	253	—	—	—	—	—	—	—	—	—	—	—	—
Grenada	328	—	—	—	—	—	—	—	—	—	—	—	—
Guatemala	258	22.4	22.4	—	—	—	—	—	—	—	—	—	—
Guyana	336	—	2.4	15.3	15.6	8.1	6.7	1.4	—	—	—	7.6	7.6
Haiti	263	—	—	14.8	.3	—	—	6.0	8.2	2.2	—	23.8	23.8
Honduras	268	—	2.1	11.2	28.8	26.1	6.4	—	—	—	—	—	—
Jamaica	343	55.7	51.9	60.9	62.9	49.5	25.1	12.5	13.9	14.5	14.5	14.5	11.4
Mexico	273	636.1	841.7	841.0	754.1	1,413.6	2,499.2	783.7	3,726.7	4,164.3	—	—	—
Nicaragua	278	—	—	2.1	8.5	6.4	—	—	—	—	—	—	—
Panama	283	141.7	7.3	.9	25.6	35.8	18.8	9.9	17.2	39.3	26.2	6.2	6.7
Paraguay	288	—	—	—	—	—	—	—	—	—	—	—	—
Peru	293	34.7	458.7	—	—	—	53.6	107.1	107.1	107.1	120.5	133.9	80.3
St. Kitts and Nevis	361	—	—	—	—	—	—	—	—	—	—	.8	.8
St. Lucia	362	—	—	—	—	—	—	—	—	—	—	—	—
St. Vincent & Grens	364	—	—	—	—	—	—	—	—	—	—	—	—
Trinidad and Tobago	369	63.7	92.5	50.4	28.7	17.3	13.3	3.1	—	—	—	57.1	57.1
Uruguay	298	18.3	10.2	7.4	6.5	8.0	6.0	—	—	—	155.6	—	—
Venezuela, Rep. Bol.	299	128.6	192.0	140.6	304.2	328.5	328.5	328.5	330.3	384.4	—	—	—
Memorandum Items
Oil Exporting Ctys	999	362.0	427.5	277.1	416.7	422.3	583.2	649.3	593.1	454.7	1,642.0	2,064.2	1,292.9
Non-Oil Develop.Ctys	201	3,839.6	3,386.5	4,295.0	6,234.2	4,649.6	5,098.1	6,044.9	18,805.7	14,794.7	11,633.0	13,048.9	17,599.2

2004, International Monetary Fund : *International Financial Statistics Yearbook*

Loan Disbursements

Expressed in Millions of SDRs

		1992	1993	1994	1995	1996	1997	1998	1999	2000	2001	2002	2003
World	001	544.3	271.7	910.4	1,431.4	708.6	730.6	896.0	736.8	492.5	872.6	1,344.5	848.4
Developing Countries	200	544.3	271.7	910.4	1,431.4	708.6	730.6	896.0	736.8	492.5	872.6	1,344.5	848.4
Africa	605	273.8	142.1	467.1	1,247.8	404.3	348.3	532.6	334.8	364.8	467.0	922.9	275.5
Benin	638	–	15.7	18.1	9.1	13.6	4.5	–	7.2	6.8	8.1	4.0	6.7
Burkina Faso	748	–	8.8	17.7	17.7	6.6	13.3	13.3	12.2	5.6	16.8	11.2	3.4
Burundi	618	14.9	–	–	–	–	–	–	–	–	–	–	–
Cameroon	622	–	–	–	–	–	27.0	54.0	45.0	52.0	15.9	31.8	15.9
Cape Verde	624	–	–	–	–	–	–	–	–	–	–	2.5	2.5
Central African Rep.	626	–	–	–	–	–	–	8.2	8.2	–	8.0	–	–
Chad	628	–	–	–	8.3	16.5	8.3	8.3	8.3	10.4	13.4	13.4	5.2
Comoros	632	–	–	1.4	–	–	–	–	–	–	–	–	–
Congo, Dem. Rep. of	636	–	–	–	–	13.9	–	–	–	–	–	–	–
Congo, Republic of	634	–	–	–	–	–	–	–	–	–	–	420.0	53.4
Côte d'Ivoire	662	–	–	119.1	119.1	95.3	–	123.9	–	–	–	58.5	–
Djibouti	611	–	–	–	–	–	–	–	2.7	2.7	3.6	4.5	–
Equatorial Guinea	642	–	2.8	1.8	–	–	–	–	–	–	–	–	–
Ethiopia	644	14.1	21.2	14.1	–	14.7	–	14.7	–	–	34.8	34.2	10.4
Gambia, The	648	–	–	–	–	–	–	3.4	3.4	6.9	6.9	2.9	–
Ghana	652	–	–	–	27.4	27.4	–	82.2	44.3	26.8	52.6	52.6	52.7
Guinea	656	8.7	–	8.7	20.3	–	23.6	23.6	7.9	–	20.7	12.9	–
Guinea-Bissau	654	–	–	–	1.6	2.1	4.5	2.4	–	5.1	–	–	–
Kenya	664	–	22.6	22.6	–	24.9	–	–	–	–	–	–	25.0
Lesotho	666	5.3	6.8	3.8	–	–	–	–	–	33.6	–	–	–
Liberia	668	–	–	–	–	–	–	–	–	–	7.0	7.0	3.5
Madagascar	674	–	–	–	–	13.6	13.6	–	13.6	38.0	22.7	11.3	11.3
Malawi	676	–	–	5.6	7.6	15.3	7.6	12.8	7.6	6.4	–	–	6.4
Mali	678	10.2	10.2	29.5	29.5	20.7	20.7	10.3	17.1	6.8	18.2	6.8	12.9
Mauritania	682	8.5	8.5	17.0	14.3	14.3	14.3	–	6.1	6.1	18.2	12.1	.9
Mauritius	684	–	–	–	–	–	–	–	–	–	–	–	–
Morocco	686	–	–	–	–	–	–	–	–	–	–	–	–
Mozambique	688	45.8	15.3	14.7	–	12.6	25.2	25.2	21.0	45.2	8.4	8.4	8.4
Niger	692	–	–	–	–	9.7	19.3	19.3	–	8.5	8.5	16.9	16.9
Rwanda	714	–	–	–	–	–	–	11.9	21.4	19.0	9.5	.6	.6
São Tomé & Príncipe	716	–	–	–	–	–	–	–	–	1.9	–	–	–
Senegal	722	–	–	16.7	54.7	23.8	35.7	35.7	14.3	14.3	23.3	9.0	3.5
Sierra Leone	724	–	–	95.6	13.1	10.2	5.1	–	–	–	46.8	28.0	14.0
Somalia	726	–	–	–	–	–	–	–	–	–	–	–	–
Sudan	732	–	–	–	–	–	–	–	–	–	–	–	–
Swaziland	734	–	–	–	–	–	–	–	–	–	–	–	–
Tanzania	738	64.2	–	–	–	25.7	61.4	35.7	58.8	40.0	40.0	40.0	17.8
Togo	742	7.7	–	10.9	21.7	–	10.9	10.9	–	–	–	–	–
Uganda	746	39.8	–	36.7	36.8	43.5	43.5	36.8	25.7	8.9	8.9	1.5	4.0
Zambia	754	–	–	–	833.4	–	10.0	–	10.0	20.0	74.8	132.7	–
Zimbabwe	698	54.7	30.4	33.4	33.4	–	–	–	–	–	–	–	–
Asia	505	209.7	105.5	358.9	100.1	132.2	125.2	113.7	52.2	14.3	194.3	325.6	460.6
Afghanistan, I.S. of	512	–	–	–	–	–	–	–	–	–	–	–	49.5
Bangladesh	513	86.3	28.8	–	–	–	–	–	–	–	–	–	–
Cambodia	522	–	–	14.0	28.0	–	–	–	8.4	8.4	16.7	16.7	8.4
China, P.R.: Mainland	924	–	–	–	–	–	–	–	–	–	–	–	–
India	534	–	–	–	–	–	–	–	–	–	–	–	–
Lao People's Dem.Rep.	544	5.9	5.9	5.9	11.7	5.9	5.9	–	–	–	4.5	9.1	4.5
Maldives	556	–	–	–	–	–	–	–	–	–	–	–	–
Mongolia	948	–	9.3	14.8	–	5.6	5.6	–	5.9	5.9	4.1	–	8.1
Myanmar	518	–	–	–	–	–	–	–	–	–	–	–	–
Nepal	558	5.6	5.6	5.6	–	–	–	–	–	–	–	–	7.1
Pakistan	564	–	–	202.2	–	–	113.7	113.7	37.9	–	86.2	258.4	344.6
Papua New Guinea	853	–	–	–	–	–	–	–	–	–	–	–	–
Philippines	566	–	–	–	–	–	–	–	–	–	–	–	–
Samoa	862	–	–	–	–	–	–	–	–	–	–	–	–
Solomon Islands	813	–	–	–	–	–	–	–	–	–	–	–	–
Sri Lanka	524	112.0	56.0	56.0	–	–	–	–	–	–	–	–	–
Thailand	578	–	–	–	–	–	–	–	–	–	–	–	38.4
Vietnam	582	–	–	60.4	60.4	120.8	–	–	–	–	82.8	41.4	–
Europe	170	ñ	8.5	25.0	37.4	105.4	178.4	146.2	107.7	58.9	87.4	83.5	83.0
Albania	914	–	8.5	15.5	7.1	–	–	5.9	15.5	14.3	9.4	4.0	8.0
Armenia	911	–	–	–	–	33.8	16.9	37.8	20.9	–	10.0	20.0	20.0
Azerbaijan	912	–	–	–	–	–	55.6	14.6	11.7	–	8.1	8.1	25.7
Georgia	915	–	–	–	–	55.5	55.5	27.8	33.3	–	27.0	22.5	–
Kyrgyz Republic	917	–	–	9.5	30.3	16.1	32.3	10.8	19.6	14.3	11.7	11.7	21.3
Macedonia, FYR	962	–	–	–	–	–	18.2	9.1	–	1.7	–	–	–
Moldova	921	–	–	–	–	–	–	–	–	9.2	9.2	9.2	–
Tajikistan	923	–	–	–	–	–	–	40.3	6.7	19.3	12.0	8.0	8.0
Middle East	405	ñ	ñ	ñ	ñ	ñ	44.0	44.0	62.0	ñ	88.8	ñ	ñ
Egypt	469	–	–	–	–	–	–	–	–	–	–	–	–
Yemen, Republic of	474	–	–	–	–	–	44.0	44.0	62.0	–	88.8	–	–

Loan Disbursements

		1992	1993	1994	1995	1996	1997	1998	1999	2000	2001	2002	2003
						Expressed in Millions of SDRs							
Western Hemisphere	**205**	**60.8**	**15.6**	**59.4**	**46.1**	**66.8**	**34.8**	**59.4**	**180.1**	**54.5**	**35.2**	**12.5**	**29.2**
Bolivia	218	36.3	–	30.4	16.8	33.7	16.8	33.6	16.8	11.2	19.0	–	–
Dominica	321	–	–	–	–	–	–	–	–	–	–	–	2.4
El Salvador	253	–	–	–	–	–	–	–	–	–	–	–	–
Grenada	328	–	–	–	–	–	–	–	–	–	–	–	–
Guyana	336	17.7	8.9	9.0	9.0	17.9	17.9	9.0	9.0	7.0	–	5.6	6.0
Haiti	263	–	–	–	–	15.2	–	–	–	–	–	–	–
Honduras	268	6.8	6.8	–	20.3	–	–	–	76.0	16.2	16.2	–	–
Nicaragua	278	–	–	20.0	–	–	–	16.8	78.3	20.2	–	7.0	20.9
Memorandum Items													
Oil Exporting Ctys	999	....	....	....	....	....	....	....	....	....	....	....	....
Non-Oil Develop. Ctys	201	544.3	271.7	910.4	1,431.4	708.6	730.6	896.0	736.8	492.5	872.6	1,344.5	848.4

2004, International Monetary Fund : *International Financial Statistics Yearbook*

Repayments of Loans

		1992	1993	1994	1995	1996	1997	1998	1999	2000	2001	2002	2003
						Expressed in Millions of SDRs							
World............................	001	23.6	133.4	223.4	373.8	484.5	606.0	620.9	595.2	605.1	789.6	906.6	842.2
Developing Countries...........	200	23.6	133.4	223.4	373.8	484.5	606.0	620.9	595.2	605.1	789.6	906.6	842.2
Africa............................	605	14.0	51.5	145.2	230.6	300.0	338.4	350.0	324.5	320.6	501.5	625.9	532.6
Benin.............................	638	–	–	.6	1.3	1.3	3.1	3.9	6.5	9.5	11.4	11.3	11.4
Burkina Faso....................	748	–	–	–	–	.6	1.3	2.1	3.9	7.5	10.1	10.8	12.6
Burundi...........................	618	1.7	3.0	4.3	6.0	6.0	6.0	6.8	5.6	3.8	3.8	2.1	–
Cameroon........................	622	–	–	–	–	–	–	–	–	–	–	–	8.1
Central African Rep............	626	–	.7	2.9	4.9	4.3	2.7	3.9	1.2	.6	–	–	–
Chad..............................	628	–	1.2	1.2	4.6	4.3	4.3	3.1	2.1	.6	2.5	5.8	12.4
Comoros.........................	632	–	–	–	–	–	.2	.2	.3	.5	.5	.3	.3
Congo, Dem. Rep. of..........	636	–	–	–	–	2.4	–	.2	–	–	–	142.9	–
Congo, Republic of............	634	–	–	–	–	–	–	–	–	–	–	2.8	2.8
Côte d'Ivoire....................	662	–	–	–	–	–	–	–	6.0	29.8	52.4	66.7	75.0
Equatorial Guinea..............	642	–	–	.4	.7	.8	2.2	2.1	1.8	2.0	2.0	.9	.6
Ethiopia..........................	644	–	–	–	–	–	–	2.8	7.1	9.9	9.9	12.8	10.0
Gambia, The....................	648	.7	1.7	2.7	4.1	5.1	5.1	4.1	3.1	1.7	.7	–	–
Ghana............................	652	–	8.2	30.5	57.8	69.4	85.9	77.7	55.4	28.1	51.4	11.0	15.1
Guinea...........................	656	–	2.3	4.1	5.8	5.8	7.5	6.9	5.2	6.1	9.3	8.7	10.5
Guinea-Bissau..................	654	–	.3	.3	.8	.8	.8	.5	.5	.2	.5	.9	1.9
Kenya............................	664	–	2.8	9.7	25.8	41.9	48.9	46.1	43.7	32.2	18.6	14.0	14.0
Lesotho..........................	666	–	–	1.1	1.8	2.3	3.1	3.6	4.3	3.9	3.4	2.9	1.8
Liberia............................	668	–	–	.7	–	–	–	.4	.4	.3	.2	–	–
Madagascar.....................	674	–	2.7	3.9	9.1	11.6	12.9	10.3	9.0	3.8	1.3	2.7	5.4
Malawi...........................	676	–	–	2.8	6.5	10.2	12.3	12.3	10.0	6.9	5.5	5.7	7.2
Mali...............................	678	–	–	2.0	3.6	5.1	5.1	8.1	8.6	13.0	16.9	21.0	21.1
Mauritania.......................	682	1.4	3.4	4.2	5.9	6.8	5.4	5.1	6.8	8.3	10.3	12.5	13.6
Mauritius........................	684	–	–	–	–	–	–	–	–	–	–	–	–
Morocco.........................	686	–	–	–	–	–	–	–	–	–	–	–	–
Mozambique....................	688	1.2	4.3	7.3	9.5	22.5	11.0	18.1	22.8	22.2	21.0	17.1	14.8
Niger.............................	692	1.3	3.4	5.1	6.7	8.1	6.7	4.7	3.0	1.3	1.0	2.9	6.8
Rwanda..........................	714	–	–	–	–	.9	1.8	1.8	1.8	1.8	.9	–	1.2
São Tomé & Príncipe..........	716	–	–	.1	.2	.2	.2	.2	.1	–	–	–	–
Senegal..........................	722	3.4	8.5	17.4	26.8	30.6	34.0	28.9	20.0	17.1	21.1	20.8	27.9
Sierra Leone....................	724	2.3	–	13.8	2.3	2.3	–	–	9.1	19.1	21.7	24.3	24.8
Somalia..........................	726	–	–	–	–	–	–	–	–	–	–	–	–
Sudan............................	732	–	–	–	3.0	–	5.2	–	–	–	–	–	–
Swaziland.......................	734	–	–	–	–	–	–	–	–	–	–	–	–
Tanzania.........................	738	–	4.3	10.7	12.8	15.0	22.5	27.8	21.4	19.3	17.1	17.3	17.4
Togo..............................	742	–	.8	2.3	5.4	7.7	8.4	8.4	6.9	7.1	8.1	7.3	9.8
Uganda..........................	746	2.0	4.0	17.1	18.8	34.1	41.8	45.8	37.6	37.1	32.4	31.7	34.1
Zambia...........................	754	–	–	–	6.6	–	–	–	–	–	166.7	167.7	168.7
Zimbabwe.......................	698	–	–	–	–	–	–	14.0	20.4	27.0	1.0	.9	3.2
Asia..............................	505	5.8	77.8	62.0	123.6	152.1	230.4	224.9	222.7	226.5	223.3	169.9	171.4
Afghanistan, I.S. of............	512	–	–	–	–	–	–	–	–	–	–	–	–
Bangladesh......................	513	5.8	28.8	38.4	40.3	58.9	86.3	77.6	70.9	69.0	50.3	17.3	2.9
Cambodia........................	522	–	–	–	–	–	–	1.4	4.2	8.4	8.4	8.4	8.4
China, People's Rep...........	924	–	–	–	–	–	–	–	–	–	–	–	–
India..............................	534	–	–	–	–	–	–	–	–	–	–	–	–
Lao People's Dem.Rep........	544	–	–	–	1.2	2.1	3.5	4.7	5.9	5.9	7.3	7.0	6.5
Mongolia.........................	948	–	–	–	–	–	–	.9	2.8	4.8	5.4	5.9	6.1
Myanmar........................	518	–	–	–	–	–	–	–	–	–	–	–	–
Nepal.............................	558	–	1.5	3.7	5.2	5.2	5.2	4.8	4.3	3.4	3.4	3.4	2.2
Pakistan.........................	564	–	–	10.9	54.6	54.6	87.4	76.5	64.7	62.3	62.3	40.4	74.6
Papua New Guinea............	853	–	–	–	–	–	–	–	–	–	–	–	–
Philippines.......................	566	–	–	–	–	–	–	–	–	–	–	–	–
Samoa............................	862	–	–	–	–	–	–	–	–	–	–	–	–
Solomon Islands................	813	–	–	–	–	–	–	–	–	–	–	–	–
Sri Lanka........................	524	–	4.5	8.9	22.3	31.2	48.0	60.4	72.7	64.9	56.0	39.2	22.4
Thailand.........................	578	–	–	–	–	–	–	–	–	–	–	–	–
Vietnam..........................	582	–	43.1	–	–	–	–	–	–	12.1	30.2	48.3	48.3
Europe...........................	170	ñ	ñ	ñ	ñ	ñ	ñ	ñ	2.5	8.8	18.6	63.3	82.2
Albania...........................	914	–	–	–	–	–	–	–	2.5	5.5	6.2	6.2	6.8
Armenia..........................	911	–	–	–	–	–	–	–	–	–	1.7	8.4	11.8
Azerbaijan.......................	912	–	–	–	–	–	–	–	–	–	–	2.0	11.1
Georgia..........................	915	–	–	–	–	–	–	–	–	–	2.8	13.9	22.2
Kyrgyz Republic................	917	–	–	–	–	–	–	–	–	3.3	8.0	12.8	17.6
Macedonia, FYR................	962	–	–	–	–	–	–	–	–	–	–	.9	4.5
Tajikistan........................	923	–	–	–	–	–	–	–	–	–	–	19.0	8.1
Middle East.....................	405	ñ	ñ	ñ	ñ	ñ	ñ	ñ	ñ	ñ	ñ	ñ	8.8
Egypt.............................	469	–	–	–	–	–	–	–	–	–	–	–	–
Yemen, Republic of...........	474	–	–	–	–	–	–	–	–	–	–	–	8.8
Western Hemisphere.........	205	3.8	4.0	16.3	19.6	32.4	37.2	46.0	45.5	49.1	46.2	47.5	47.1
Bolivia............................	218	3.6	3.6	10.4	17.2	21.8	24.9	29.9	24.5	22.4	22.9	21.2	20.5
Dominica........................	321	.2	.4	.5	.6	.6	.4	.2	–	–	–	–	–
El Salvador......................	253	–	–	–	–	–	–	–	–	–	–	–	–
Grenada.........................	328	–	–	–	–	–	–	–	–	–	–	–	–

2004, International Monetary Fund : *International Financial Statistics Yearbook*

Repayments of Loans

		1992	1993	1994	1995	1996	1997	1998	1999	2000	2001	2002	2003
						Expressed in Millions of SDRs							
Western Hemisphere(Cont.)													
Guyana	336	–	–	–	–	8.3	11.9	14.5	16.3	19.0	12.5	12.5	12.5
Haiti	263	–	–	5.3	1.8	1.8	–	–	–	–	–	3.0	3.0
Honduras	268	–	–	–	–	–	–	1.4	2.7	3.7	6.8	6.8	5.4
Nicaragua	278	–	–	–	–	–	–	–	2.0	4.0	4.0	4.0	5.7
Memorandum Items													
Non-Oil Develop.Ctys	201	23.6	133.4	223.4	373.8	484.5	606.0	620.9	595.2	605.1	789.6	906.6	842.2

2004, International Monetary Fund : *International Financial Statistics Yearbook*

Total Fund Credit & Loans Outstdg.

Expressed in Millions of SDRs

		1992	1993	1994	1995	1996	1997	1998	1999	2000	2001	2002	2003
World	001	27,791.1	29,159.1	30,260.9	41,636.1	42,058.6	52,614.7	66,781.7	57,534.1	49,350.2	59,920.0	70,481.7	71,918.9
Developing Countries	200	27,791.1	29,159.1	30,260.9	41,636.1	42,058.6	52,614.7	66,781.7	57,534.1	49,350.2	59,920.0	70,481.7	71,918.9
Africa	605	5,727.2	5,871.5	6,531.6	7,065.3	7,457.3	7,107.3	6,775.7	6,645.5	6,527.1	6,251.5	6,149.0	5,553.4
Algeria	612	578.2	342.7	793.8	994.1	1,412.5	1,495.5	1,428.0	1,388.7	1,318.5	1,208.0	978.4	664.7
Angola	614	—	—	—	—	—	—	—	—	—	—	—	—
Benin	638	15.7	31.3	48.8	56.6	68.9	70.3	66.4	67.1	64.4	61.1	53.9	49.2
Burkina Faso	748	6.3	15.2	32.8	50.5	56.5	68.5	79.6	87.9	86.1	92.7	93.0	83.9
Burundi	618	47.4	44.4	40.1	34.2	28.2	22.2	15.4	9.8	6.0	2.1	9.6	19.3
Cameroon	622	45.7	11.9	29.9	34.4	50.1	68.9	110.9	142.7	180.5	194.0	225.8	233.6
Cape Verde	624	—	—	—	—	—	—	—	—	—	—	2.5	4.9
Central African Rep.	626	22.1	21.0	28.3	23.5	19.2	13.8	12.5	17.1	16.5	24.5	24.5	24.5
Chad	628	21.4	20.2	29.3	33.0	45.2	45.3	45.3	50.2	60.0	70.9	78.5	71.3
Comoros	632	.9	.9	2.3	2.3	2.3	2.1	1.9	1.6	1.1	.7	.4	.1
Congo, Dem. Rep. of	636	330.3	330.3	327.3	326.4	301.3	301.3	300.7	300.0	300.0	300.0	420.0	473.4
Congo, Republic of	634	4.0	3.5	14.0	12.5	26.4	24.8	24.3	21.1	31.7	30.8	24.4	18.9
Côte d'Ivoire	662	194.5	159.1	224.8	287.1	349.6	333.5	457.3	451.4	421.6	369.2	361.1	286.0
Djibouti	611	—	—	—	—	2.9	4.0	6.3	9.3	10.3	12.3	15.1	13.8
Equatorial Guinea	642	9.2	12.0	13.4	12.7	11.9	9.8	7.6	5.8	3.8	1.7	.8	.2
Ethiopia	644	14.1	35.3	49.4	49.4	64.2	64.2	76.1	69.0	59.1	84.0	105.4	105.8
Gabon	646	58.6	32.9	61.4	65.0	83.3	97.2	80.5	62.6	68.4	59.6	49.5	39.4
Gambia, The	648	28.4	26.7	23.9	19.8	14.7	9.6	8.9	9.3	14.4	20.6	23.5	23.5
Ghana	652	537.8	537.3	479.7	436.2	377.3	257.0	236.9	225.8	224.5	225.7	267.3	304.9
Guinea	656	46.3	44.0	48.6	63.1	57.3	73.4	90.0	92.7	86.6	98.1	102.2	91.7
Guinea-Bissau	654	3.8	3.5	3.2	4.0	5.3	9.0	11.0	12.6	19.0	18.4	17.2	13.8
Kenya	664	286.1	264.3	277.3	251.5	234.5	185.6	139.5	95.8	97.2	78.6	64.6	75.6
Lesotho	666	18.1	24.9	27.6	25.8	23.5	20.4	16.8	12.5	8.5	12.1	16.2	17.9
Liberia	668	226.5	226.5	225.8	225.7	225.7	225.7	225.3	224.8	224.4	223.9	223.7	223.7
Madagascar	674	77.1	67.0	58.6	48.9	50.8	51.5	41.2	45.8	80.0	101.4	110.0	115.9
Malawi	676	66.9	62.6	76.9	78.0	83.1	78.4	72.6	63.8	63.4	57.9	69.6	68.8
Mali	678	47.5	51.4	74.1	99.0	114.6	130.2	132.4	140.9	134.7	136.0	121.8	113.6
Mauritania	682	42.0	46.1	58.8	67.1	74.6	83.4	78.3	77.6	75.4	83.2	82.9	70.2
Mauritius	684	—	—	—	—	—	—	—	—	—	—	—	—
Morocco	686	319.1	207.2	101.1	34.8	2.3	—	—	—	—	—	—	—
Mozambique	688	126.9	137.9	145.2	135.8	125.9	140.1	147.2	145.4	168.5	155.9	147.2	140.8
Namibia	728	—	—	—	—	—	—	—	—	—	—	—	—
Niger	692	44.6	37.7	41.8	35.0	36.6	45.0	54.1	49.6	56.8	64.3	78.3	88.4
Nigeria	694	—	—	—	—	—	—	—	—	—	—	—	—
Rwanda	714	8.8	8.8	8.8	17.7	16.8	29.9	40.1	55.3	65.9	67.1	62.5	61.8
São Tomé & Príncipe	716	.8	.8	.7	.6	.4	.2	.1	—	1.9	1.9	1.9	1.9
Senegal	722	197.4	177.8	205.4	233.3	226.5	216.5	207.8	198.2	195.4	197.6	185.8	161.3
Seychelles	718	—	—	—	—	—	—	—	—	—	—	—	—
Sierra Leone	724	67.0	61.0	100.2	110.9	118.8	123.9	135.4	142.0	133.2	120.8	124.5	113.8
Somalia	726	112.0	112.0	112.0	112.0	112.0	112.0	112.0	112.0	112.0	112.0	112.0	112.0
South Africa	199	—	614.4	614.4	614.4	614.4	307.2	—	—	—	—	—	—
Sudan	732	671.6	671.6	671.6	645.7	621.2	590.5	548.4	520.8	479.7	438.6	421.6	402.9
Swaziland	734	—	—	—	—	—	—	—	—	—	—	—	—
Tanzania	738	160.5	156.2	145.5	132.7	143.4	182.4	190.2	227.6	248.3	271.2	293.9	294.3
Togo	742	55.8	49.9	56.0	70.4	62.5	64.9	67.4	60.4	53.3	45.3	38.0	28.2
Tunisia	744	211.1	207.3	207.3	197.1	165.0	128.4	91.8	55.2	24.7	—	—	—
Uganda	746	250.1	243.0	262.6	280.6	290.1	291.7	282.7	270.8	242.6	219.1	188.9	158.8
Zambia	754	615.6	565.8	551.2	833.4	833.4	843.4	843.4	853.4	873.4	781.6	746.6	577.9
Zimbabwe	698	157.2	205.0	257.5	310.0	304.1	285.5	289.2	268.8	215.4	208.4	206.1	202.9
Asia	505	5,952.4	6,365.7	5,816.8	4,846.9	3,673.4	15,538.9	24,173.2	17,908.7	18,588.5	12,400.3	10,334.5	9,909.9
Afghanistan, I.S. of	512	—	—	—	—	—	—	—	—	—	—	—	—
Bangladesh	513	547.7	511.8	473.4	433.1	374.2	287.9	308.4	237.6	168.6	118.3	51.9	49.5
Bhutan	514	—	—	—	—	—	—	—	—	—	—	—	—
Cambodia	522	6.3	6.3	20.3	48.3	48.3	48.3	47.2	53.1	56.2	63.5	70.8	69.7
China, People's Rep.	924	—	—	—	—	—	—	—	—	—	—	—	—
Fiji	819	—	—	—	—	—	—	—	—	—	—	—	—
India	534	3,260.4	3,584.9	2,763.2	1,966.6	1,085.3	589.8	284.9	38.5	—	—	—	—
Indonesia	536	—	—	—	—	—	2,201.5	6,455.8	7,466.8	8,318.0	7,251.7	6,518.1	6,915.1
Kiribati	826	—	—	—	—	—	—	—	—	—	—	—	—
Korea	542	—	—	—	—	—	8,200.0	12,000.0	4,462.5	4,462.5	—	—	—
Lao People's Dem.Rep.	544	20.5	26.4	32.2	42.8	46.6	49.0	44.3	38.4	32.5	29.7	31.8	29.9
Malaysia	548	—	—	—	—	—	—	—	—	—	—	—	—
Maldives	556	—	—	—	—	—	—	—	—	—	—	—	—
Mongolia	948	13.8	23.0	37.9	31.6	30.3	35.2	34.3	37.5	38.6	37.3	31.3	33.4
Myanmar	518	—	—	—	—	—	—	—	—	—	—	—	—
Nepal	558	31.7	35.8	37.7	32.5	27.2	22.0	17.2	12.9	9.5	6.2	2.8	7.7
Pakistan	564	819.9	816.5	1,096.8	1,115.0	1,000.5	979.5	996.0	1,271.2	1,197.7	1,455.8	1,506.4	1,424.6
Palau	565	—	—	—	—	—	—	—	—	—	—	—	—
Papua New Guinea	853	42.8	32.1	10.7	33.3	35.3	35.3	32.4	15.7	29.9	85.5	85.5	81.8
Philippines	566	800.1	880.7	728.6	489.5	281.9	633.8	1,114.0	1,327.7	1,559.2	1,553.1	1,240.2	805.8
Samoa	862	—	—	—	—	—	—	—	—	—	—	—	—
Solomon Islands	813	—	—	—	—	—	—	—	—	—	—	—	—
Sri Lanka	524	337.8	375.7	422.8	400.5	369.2	321.2	260.8	188.1	123.2	170.6	228.0	264.7
Thailand	578	—	—	—	—	—	1,800.0	2,300.0	2,500.0	2,350.0	1,337.5	287.5	—

2004, International Monetary Fund : *International Financial Statistics Yearbook*

Total Fund Credit & Loans Outstdg.

Expressed in Millions of SDRs

		1992	1993	1994	1995	1996	1997	1998	1999	2000	2001	2002	2003
Asia(Cont.)													
Tonga	866	–	–	–	–	–	–	–	–	–	–	–	–
Vietnam	582	71.5	72.5	193.4	253.8	374.6	335.3	277.9	258.7	242.6	291.2	280.2	227.9
Europe	170	**4,695.1**	**6,159.5**	**8,036.4**	**11,400.3**	**13,945.3**	**15,708.5**	**19,644.9**	**17,385.4**	**16,847.3**	**21,608.7**	**25,189.0**	**23,765.9**
Albania	914	9.7	21.6	37.1	43.4	37.7	40.7	45.8	58.7	67.5	66.3	59.6	60.8
Armenia	911	–	–	16.9	47.3	81.0	97.9	135.3	146.6	134.7	137.4	143.3	144.4
Azerbaijan	912	–	–	–	67.9	121.7	197.7	228.1	296.7	257.7	234.9	205.1	174.5
Belarus	913	–	70.1	70.1	190.2	190.2	190.2	172.3	129.7	87.6	64.3	40.9	17.5
Bosnia & Herzegovina	963	–	–	–	32.5	31.0	30.3	54.5	68.4	80.4	88.4	102.4	90.1
Bulgaria	918	428.9	459.9	644.4	482.1	407.2	698.0	792.3	910.7	1,014.6	883.0	771.8	799.2
Croatia	960	–	14.8	87.1	148.6	145.4	172.7	166.1	143.2	121.4	97.2	–	–
Cyprus	423	–	–	–	–	–	–	–	–	–	–	–	–
Czech Republic	935	–	780.7	–	–	–	–	–	–	–	–	–	–
Czechoslovakia	934	1,121.5	....	....	....	....	....	....	....	....	....	....	....
Estonia	939	7.8	41.9	41.9	61.8	54.2	40.0	21.3	18.4	14.5	10.7	–	–
Georgia	915	–	–	27.8	77.7	133.2	188.7	215.8	233.3	213.7	228.7	228.0	194.3
Hungary	944	875.8	896.3	781.6	258.7	118.7	118.7	–	–	–	–	–	–
Kazakhstan	916	–	61.9	198.0	290.8	383.6	379.0	463.7	335.1	–	–	–	–
Kyrgyz Republic	917	–	43.9	53.3	83.6	97.1	122.2	124.4	138.7	144.3	142.7	136.3	135.9
Latvia	941	25.2	77.8	109.8	107.9	90.4	63.7	45.4	34.3	26.7	19.1	11.4	3.8
Lithuania	946	17.3	88.0	134.6	176.0	190.1	200.5	179.8	167.8	147.1	120.3	89.3	30.2
Macedonia, FYR	962	–	2.8	14.0	38.1	47.4	65.3	72.7	74.1	62.3	56.3	49.6	46.0
Moldova	921	–	63.0	112.5	154.9	172.3	172.7	125.6	127.7	118.3	116.3	111.8	95.9
Poland	964	596.6	497.7	918.6	–	–	–	–	–	–	–	–	–
Romania	968	750.9	750.9	906.4	698.3	453.0	475.2	382.8	333.8	347.7	308.0	314.9	400.6
Russia	922	719.0	1,797.3	2,875.6	6,469.8	8,698.2	9,805.9	13,732.0	11,102.3	8,912.8	5,914.8	4,767.3	3,411.2
Serbia & Montenegro	965	–	–	–	–	–	–	–	–	116.9	216.9	416.9	616.9
Slovak Republic	936	–	405.2	439.8	307.5	222.0	184.4	134.6	96.5	–	–	–	–
Slovenia	961	–	8.5	4.9	2.7	.9	–	–	–	–	–	–	–
Tajikistan	923	–	–	–	–	15.0	22.5	70.3	73.2	85.0	87.7	69.2	67.2
Turkey	186	–	–	235.5	460.5	460.5	440.4	275.8	648.8	3,205.3	11,232.9	16,245.7	16,212.8
Ukraine	926	–	–	249.3	1,037.3	1,573.3	1,780.6	1,985.0	2,044.6	1,591.2	1,520.7	1,380.0	1,235.5
Uzbekistan	927	–	–	–	106.0	165.2	165.2	165.2	146.8	97.5	62.3	45.7	29.1
Yugoslavia, SFR	188	142.5	77.4	77.4	56.8	56.1	56.1	56.1	56.6	....	....	....	....
Middle East	405	**407.0**	**385.0**	**409.7**	**350.3**	**353.3**	**502.0**	**571.8**	**660.5**	**597.8**	**641.8**	**638.8**	**553.7**
Bahrain, Kingdom of	419	–	–	–	–	–	–	–	–	–	–	–	–
Egypt	469	147.2	147.2	132.2	69.5	10.9	–	–	–	–	–	–	–
Iran, I.R. of	429	–	–	–	–	–	–	–	–	–	–	–	–
Iraq	433	–	–	–	–	–	–	–	–	–	–	–	–
Israel	436	178.6	178.6	178.6	111.7	22.3	–	–	–	–	–	–	–
Jordan	439	81.2	59.2	98.9	169.2	236.1	316.6	333.4	362.9	354.3	344.5	355.0	283.6
Syrian Arab Republic	463	–	–	–	–	–	–	–	–	–	–	–	–
Yemen, Republic of	474	–	–	–	–	84.0	185.4	238.4	297.6	243.5	297.3	283.8	270.1
Western Hemisphere	205	**11,009.4**	**10,377.5**	**9,466.4**	**17,973.3**	**16,629.2**	**13,758.1**	**15,616.2**	**14,934.0**	**6,789.5**	**19,017.6**	**28,170.4**	**32,136.0**
Antigua and Barbuda	311	–	–	–	–	–	–	–	–	–	–	–	–
Argentina	213	1,682.8	2,562.4	2,884.7	4,124.4	4,376.0	4,349.3	3,865.1	3,262.6	3,880.3	11,121.1	10,547.5	10,446.2
Barbados	316	36.8	36.8	36.8	24.9	6.5	–	–	–	–	–	–	–
Belize	339	–	–	–	–	–	–	–	–	–	–	–	–
Bolivia	218	181.1	160.5	180.5	180.1	192.0	183.9	187.6	180.0	168.8	164.8	143.7	187.5
Brazil	223	581.4	221.0	127.5	95.2	47.0	23.3	3,426.8	6,431.0	1,356.8	6,633.9	15,319.6	19,056.5
Chile	228	525.0	346.5	199.5	–	–	–	–	–	–	–	–	–
Colombia	233	–	–	–	–	–	–	–	–	–	–	–	–
Costa Rica	238	59.3	59.3	45.5	16.3	.5	–	–	–	–	–	2.1	5.3
Dominica	321	2.8	2.3	1.7	1.1	.6	.2	–	–	–	–	19.9	87.6
Dominican Republic	243	89.4	135.5	129.9	107.5	66.5	21.1	39.7	39.7	39.7	39.7	39.7	39.7
Ecuador	248	72.6	51.8	135.7	116.7	100.9	98.9	49.5	–	113.3	151.1	226.7	262.3
El Salvador	253	–	–	–	–	–	–	–	–	–	–	–	–
Grenada	328	–	–	–	–	–	–	–	–	–	–	–	2.9
Guatemala	258	22.4	–	–	–	–	–	–	–	–	–	–	–
Guyana	336	122.2	128.6	122.3	115.6	117.1	116.4	109.5	102.2	90.1	77.7	70.7	64.2
Haiti	263	23.8	23.8	3.8	18.2	31.6	31.6	40.8	32.6	30.4	30.4	19.7	9.1
Honduras	268	81.4	86.0	74.8	66.4	40.3	33.9	80.0	153.3	165.8	175.1	144.6	115.4
Jamaica	343	259.7	244.2	217.6	161.7	112.2	87.1	74.7	60.8	46.3	31.9	17.4	6.0
Mexico	273	4,327.0	3,485.2	2,644.2	10,648.1	9,234.5	6,735.2	5,951.5	3,259.2	–	–	–	–
Nicaragua	278	17.0	17.0	34.9	26.4	20.0	20.0	36.8	113.2	129.3	125.3	128.3	143.5
Panama	283	79.8	82.3	91.3	74.4	91.0	105.4	125.5	108.3	69.1	42.9	36.7	30.0
Paraguay	288	–	–	–	–	–	–	–	–	–	–	–	–
Peru	293	458.7	642.7	642.7	642.7	642.7	749.6	642.5	535.4	428.3	307.8	173.9	93.6
St. Kitts and Nevis	361	–	–	–	–	–	–	–	1.6	1.6	1.6	.8	–
St. Lucia	362	–	–	–	–	–	–	–	–	–	–	–	–
St. Vincent & Grens.	364	–	–	–	–	–	–	–	–	–	–	–	–
Suriname	366	–	–	–	–	–	–	–	–	–	–	–	–
Trinidad and Tobago	369	205.3	112.8	62.4	33.8	16.5	3.1	–	–	–	–	–	–
Uruguay	298	38.1	27.9	20.5	14.0	6.0	–	114.2	114.2	114.2	114.2	1,318.8	1,625.9
Venezuela, Rep. Bol.	299	2,142.8	1,950.7	1,810.2	1,506.0	1,527.4	1,198.9	870.4	540.0	155.6	–	–	–
Memorandum Items													
Oil Exporting Ctys.	999	2,720.9	2,293.5	2,603.9	2,500.0	2,940.0	4,895.9	8,754.2	9,395.6	9,792.1	8,459.7	7,496.5	7,579.8
Non-Oil Develop.Ctys.	201	25,070.2	26,865.6	27,657.0	39,136.1	39,118.6	47,718.8	58,027.5	48,138.5	39,558.2	51,460.3	62,985.2	64,339.1

2004, International Monetary Fund: *International Financial Statistics Yearbook*

Use of Fund Credit (GRA)

		1992	1993	1994	1995	1996	1997	1998	1999	2000	2001	2002	2003
						Expressed in Millions of SDRs							
World	001	23,967.2	25,196.8	25,611.7	35,929.2	36,127.5	46,559.0	60,451.0	51,061.9	42,990.5	53,477.2	63,601.1	65,032.1
Developing Countries	200	23,967.2	25,196.8	25,611.7	35,929.2	36,127.5	46,559.0	60,451.0	51,061.9	42,990.5	53,477.2	63,601.1	65,032.1
Africa	605	3,472.0	3,525.7	3,863.9	3,380.4	3,668.1	3,308.2	2,793.9	2,653.5	2,490.9	2,249.7	1,850.3	1,511.8
Algeria	612	578.2	342.7	793.8	994.1	1,412.5	1,495.5	1,428.0	1,388.7	1,318.5	1,208.0	978.4	664.7
Burkina Faso	748	–	–	–	–	–	–	–	–	–	–	–	–
Burundi	618	–	–	–	–	–	–	–	–	–	–	9.6	19.3
Cameroon	622	45.7	11.9	29.9	34.4	50.1	41.9	29.9	16.6	2.5	–	–	–
Central African Rep.	626	.8	.4	10.7	10.7	10.7	8.0	2.4	–	–	–	–	–
Chad	628	–	–	10.3	10.3	10.3	6.5	1.3	–	–	–	–	–
Comoros	632	–	–	–	–	–	–	–	–	–	–	–	–
Congo, Dem. Rep. of	636	184.8	184.8	181.8	180.9	158.2	158.2	157.8	157.1	157.1	157.1	–	–
Congo, Republic of	634	4.0	3.5	14.0	12.5	12.5	10.9	10.4	7.2	17.8	16.9	13.3	10.6
Côte d'Ivoire	662	194.5	159.1	105.7	48.9	16.1	–	–	–	–	–	–	–
Djibouti	611	–	–	–	–	2.9	4.0	6.3	6.6	4.8	3.2	1.4	.1
Equatorial Guinea	642	–	–	–	–	–	–	–	–	–	–	–	–
Ethiopia	644	–	–	–	–	–	–	–	–	–	–	–	–
Gabon	646	58.6	32.9	61.4	65.0	83.3	97.2	80.5	62.6	68.4	59.6	49.5	39.4
Gambia, The	648	–	–	–	–	–	–	–	–	–	–	–	–
Ghana	652	108.4	116.0	89.0	75.9	59.0	24.6	–	–	–	–	–	–
Guinea	656	–	–	–	–	–	–	–	–	–	–	–	–
Guinea-Bissau	654	–	–	–	–	–	–	–	2.1	3.6	3.6	3.3	1.7
Kenya	664	41.5	–	–	–	–	–	–	–	–	–	–	–
Lesotho	666	–	–	–	–	–	–	–	–	–	–	–	–
Liberia	668	201.6	201.6	201.6	201.5	201.5	201.5	201.5	201.5	201.3	201.0	200.8	200.8
Madagascar	674	12.6	5.2	.6	–	–	–	–	–	–	–	–	–
Malawi	676	5.5	1.2	12.7	12.7	12.7	12.7	6.4	–	–	–	17.4	17.4
Mali	678	12.0	5.7	1.0	–	–	–	–	–	–	–	–	–
Mauritania	682	1.0	–	–	–	–	–	–	–	–	–	–	–
Mauritius	684	–	–	–	–	–	–	–	–	–	–	–	–
Morocco	686	319.1	207.2	101.1	34.8	2.3	–	–	–	–	–	–	–
Niger	692	5.5	2.0	11.1	11.1	11.1	6.9	1.4	–	–	–	–	–
Nigeria	694	–	–	–	–	–	–	–	–	–	–	–	–
Rwanda	714	–	–	–	8.9	8.9	23.8	23.8	19.3	12.6	5.2	–	–
Senegal	722	13.5	2.5	30.9	30.9	30.9	19.3	3.9	–	–	–	–	–
Sierra Leone	724	48.6	42.6	–	–	–	–	11.6	27.1	37.5	–	–	–
Somalia	726	96.7	96.7	96.7	96.7	96.7	96.7	96.7	96.7	96.7	96.7	96.7	96.7
South Africa	199	–	614.4	614.4	614.4	614.4	307.2	–	–	–	–	–	–
Sudan	732	604.3	604.3	604.2	581.3	556.8	531.3	489.1	461.5	420.4	379.4	362.4	343.6
Swaziland	734	–	–	–	–	–	–	–	–	–	–	–	–
Tanzania	738	–	–	–	–	–	–	–	–	–	–	–	–
Togo	742	9.7	4.6	2.2	.2	–	–	–	–	–	–	–	–
Tunisia	744	211.1	207.3	207.3	197.1	165.0	128.4	91.8	55.2	24.7	–	–	–
Uganda	746	3.1	–	–	–	–	–	–	–	–	–	–	–
Zambia	754	609.0	559.2	544.6	–	–	–	–	–	–	–	–	–
Zimbabwe	698	102.5	119.9	139.0	158.1	152.2	133.6	151.3	151.2	124.9	119.0	117.5	117.5
Asia	505	4,638.8	5,024.4	4,178.6	3,232.1	2,078.5	14,049.2	22,794.7	16,700.7	17,592.7	11,433.5	9,212.1	8,498.2
Afghanistan, I.S. of	512	–	–	–	–	–	–	–	–	–	–	–	–
Bangladesh	513	35.9	–	–	–	–	–	98.1	98.1	98.1	98.1	49.1	–
Bhutan	514	–	–	–	–	–	–	–	–	–	–	–	–
Cambodia	522	6.3	6.3	6.3	6.3	6.3	6.3	5.2	4.2	3.1	2.1	1.0	–
China, People's Rep.	924	–	–	–	–	–	–	–	–	–	–	–	–
Fiji	819	–	–	–	–	–	–	–	–	–	–	–	–
India	534	3,260.4	3,584.9	2,763.2	1,966.6	1,085.3	589.8	284.9	38.5	–	–	–	–
Indonesia	536	–	–	–	–	–	2,201.5	6,455.8	7,466.8	8,318.0	7,251.7	6,518.1	6,915.1
Korea	542	–	–	–	–	–	8,200.0	12,000.0	4,462.5	4,462.5	–	–	–
Lao People's Dem.Rep.	544	–	–	–	–	–	–	–	–	–	–	–	–
Malaysia	548	–	–	–	–	–	–	–	–	–	–	–	–
Mongolia	948	13.8	13.8	13.8	7.5	.6	–	–	–	–	–	–	–
Myanmar	518	–	–	–	–	–	–	–	–	–	–	–	–
Nepal	558	–	–	–	–	–	–	–	–	–	–	–	–
Pakistan	564	437.5	434.1	523.2	595.9	536.1	488.8	468.0	770.0	758.8	993.0	825.6	473.9
Palau	565	–	–	–	–	–	–	–	–	–	–	–	–
Papua New Guinea	853	42.8	32.1	10.7	33.3	35.3	35.3	32.4	15.7	29.9	85.5	85.5	81.8
Philippines	566	800.1	880.7	728.6	489.5	281.9	633.8	1,114.0	1,327.7	1,559.2	1,553.1	1,240.2	805.8
Samoa	862	–	–	–	–	–	–	–	–	–	–	–	–
Solomon Islands	813	–	–	–	–	–	–	–	–	–	–	–	–
Sri Lanka	524	13.6	–	–	–	–	–	–	–	–	103.4	200.0	220.7
Thailand	578	–	–	–	–	–	1,800.0	2,300.0	2,500.0	2,350.0	1,337.5	287.5	–
Vietnam	582	28.4	72.5	133.0	133.0	133.0	93.7	36.3	17.1	13.1	9.1	5.0	1.0
Europe	170	4,695.1	6,151.0	8,002.9	11,329.4	13,769.1	15,353.9	19,144.1	16,779.5	16,191.3	20,883.9	24,444.0	23,020.1
Albania	914	9.7	13.1	13.1	12.3	6.6	9.7	8.8	8.8	8.8	4.4	–	–
Armenia	911	–	–	16.9	47.3	47.3	47.3	46.8	37.3	25.3	19.7	14.1	7.0
Azerbaijan	912	–	–	–	67.9	121.7	142.2	157.9	214.8	175.8	144.9	109.2	63.9
Belarus	913	–	70.1	70.1	190.2	190.2	190.2	172.3	129.7	87.6	64.3	40.9	17.5
Bosnia & Herzegovina	963	–	–	–	32.5	31.0	30.3	54.5	68.4	80.4	88.4	102.4	90.1
Bulgaria	918	428.9	459.9	644.4	482.1	407.2	698.0	792.3	910.7	1,014.6	883.0	771.8	799.2
Croatia	960	–	14.8	87.1	148.6	145.4	172.7	166.1	143.2	121.4	97.2	–	–
Cyprus	423	–	–	–	–	–	–	–	–	–	–	–	–

Use of Fund Credit (GRA)

Expressed in Millions of SDRs

		1992	1993	1994	1995	1996	1997	1998	1999	2000	2001	2002	2003
Europe(Cont.)													
Czech Republic	935	–	780.7	–	–	–	–	–	–	–	–	–	–
Czechoslovakia	934	1,121.5	....	....	....	....	....	....	....	....	....	....	....
Estonia	939	7.8	41.9	41.9	61.8	54.2	40.0	21.3	18.4	14.5	10.7	–	–
Georgia	915	–	–	27.8	77.7	77.7	77.7	77.0	61.3	41.6	32.4	23.1	11.6
Hungary	944	875.8	896.3	781.6	258.7	118.7	118.7	–	–	–	–	–	–
Kazakhstan	916	–	61.9	198.0	290.8	383.6	379.0	463.7	335.1	–	–	–	–
Kyrgyz Republic	917	–	43.9	43.9	43.9	41.2	34.1	25.5	20.2	14.8	9.4	4.0	–
Latvia	941	25.2	77.8	109.8	107.9	90.4	63.7	45.4	34.3	26.7	19.1	11.4	3.8
Lithuania	946	17.3	88.0	134.6	176.0	190.1	200.5	179.8	167.8	147.1	120.3	89.3	30.2
Macedonia, FYR	962	–	2.8	14.0	38.1	47.4	47.1	45.4	46.8	33.3	27.3	21.5	22.4
Moldova	921	–	63.0	112.5	154.9	172.3	172.7	125.6	127.7	109.1	97.8	84.1	68.2
Poland	964	596.6	497.7	918.6	–	–	–	–	–	–	–	–	–
Romania	968	750.9	750.9	906.4	698.3	453.0	475.2	382.8	333.8	347.7	308.0	314.9	400.6
Russia	922	719.0	1,797.3	2,875.6	6,469.8	8,698.2	9,805.9	13,732.0	11,102.3	8,912.8	5,914.8	4,767.3	3,411.2
Serbia & Montenegro	965	–	–	–	–	–	–	–	–	116.9	216.9	416.9	616.9
Slovak Republic	936	–	405.2	439.8	307.5	222.0	184.4	134.6	96.5	–	–	–	–
Slovenia	961	–	8.5	4.9	2.7	.9	–	–	–	–	–	–	–
Tajikistan	923	–	–	–	–	15.0	22.5	30.0	26.3	18.8	9.4	1.9	–
Turkey	186	–	–	235.5	460.5	460.5	440.4	275.8	648.8	3,205.3	11,232.9	16,245.7	16,212.8
Ukraine	926	–	–	249.3	1,037.3	1,573.3	1,780.6	1,985.0	2,044.6	1,591.2	1,520.7	1,380.0	1,235.5
Uzbekistan	927	–	–	–	106.0	165.2	165.2	165.2	146.8	97.5	62.3	45.7	29.1
Yugoslavia, SFR	188	142.5	77.4	77.4	56.8	56.1	56.1	56.1	55.6	....	....	....	....
Middle East	405	407.0	385.0	409.7	350.3	353.3	458.0	483.8	510.5	447.8	403.1	400.0	323.7
Egypt	469	147.2	147.2	132.2	69.5	10.9	–	–	–	–	–	–	–
Iran, I.R. of	429	–	–	–	–	–	–	–	–	–	–	–	–
Iraq	433	–	–	–	–	–	–	–	–	–	–	–	–
Israel	436	178.6	178.6	178.6	111.7	22.3	–	–	–	–	–	–	–
Jordan	439	81.2	59.2	98.9	169.2	236.1	316.6	333.4	362.9	354.3	344.5	355.0	283.6
Syrian Arab Republic	463	–	–	–	–	–	–	–	–	–	–	–	–
Yemen, Republic of	474	–	–	–	–	84.0	141.4	150.4	147.6	93.5	58.6	45.0	40.2
Western Hemisphere	205	10,754.3	10,110.8	9,156.6	17,636.9	16,258.5	13,389.8	15,234.5	14,417.7	6,267.8	18,506.9	27,694.7	31,678.3
Argentina	213	1,682.8	2,562.4	2,884.7	4,124.4	4,376.0	4,349.3	3,865.1	3,262.6	3,880.3	11,121.1	10,547.5	10,446.2
Barbados	316	36.8	36.8	36.8	24.9	6.5	–	–	–	–	–	–	–
Belize	339	–	–	–	–	–	–	–	–	–	–	–	64.3
Bolivia	218	17.0	–	–	–	–	–	–	–	–	–	–	–
Brazil	223	581.4	221.0	127.5	95.2	47.0	23.3	3,426.8	6,431.0	1,356.8	6,633.9	15,319.6	19,056.5
Chile	228	525.0	346.5	199.5	–	–	–	–	–	–	–	–	–
Colombia	233	–	–	–	–	–	–	–	–	–	–	–	–
Costa Rica	238	59.3	59.3	45.5	16.3	.5	–	–	–	–	–	–	–
Dominica	321	.1	–	–	–	–	–	–	–	–	–	2.1	3.0
Dominican Republic	243	89.4	135.5	129.9	107.5	66.5	21.1	39.7	39.7	39.7	39.7	19.9	87.6
Ecuador	248	72.6	51.8	135.7	116.7	100.9	98.9	49.5	–	113.3	151.1	226.7	262.3
El Salvador	253	–	–	–	–	–	–	–	–	–	–	–	–
Grenada	328	–	–	–	–	–	–	–	–	–	–	–	2.9
Guatemala	258	22.4	–	–	–	–	–	–	–	–	–	–	–
Guyana	336	49.5	47.1	31.8	16.2	8.1	1.4	–	–	–	–	–	–
Haiti	263	15.0	15.0	.3	16.4	16.4	16.4	25.6	17.4	15.2	15.2	7.6	–
Honduras	268	74.6	72.5	61.3	32.5	6.4	–	47.5	47.5	47.5	47.5	23.8	–
Jamaica	343	259.7	244.2	217.6	161.7	112.2	87.1	74.7	60.8	46.3	31.9	17.4	6.0
Mexico	273	4,327.0	3,485.2	2,644.2	10,648.1	9,234.5	6,735.2	5,951.5	3,259.2	–	–	–	–
Nicaragua	278	17.0	17.0	14.9	6.4	–	–	–	–	–	–	–	–
Panama	283	79.8	82.3	91.3	74.4	91.0	105.4	125.5	108.3	69.1	42.9	36.7	30.0
Paraguay	288	–	–	–	–	–	–	–	–	–	–	–	–
Peru	293	458.7	642.7	642.7	642.7	642.7	749.6	642.5	535.4	428.3	307.8	173.9	93.6
St. Kitts and Nevis	361	–	–	–	–	–	–	1.6	1.6	1.6	1.6	.8	–
St. Lucia	362	–	–	–	–	–	–	–	–	–	–	–	–
St. Vincent & Grens	364	–	–	–	–	–	–	–	–	–	–	–	–
Trinidad and Tobago	369	205.3	112.8	62.4	33.8	16.5	3.1	–	–	–	–	–	–
Uruguay	298	38.1	27.9	20.5	14.0	6.0	–	114.2	114.2	114.2	114.2	1,318.8	1,625.9
Venezuela, Rep. Bol	299	2,142.8	1,950.7	1,810.2	1,506.0	1,527.4	1,198.9	870.4	540.0	155.6	–	–	–
Memorandum Items													
Oil Exporting Ctys	999	2,720.9	2,293.5	2,603.9	2,500.0	2,940.0	4,895.9	8,754.2	9,395.6	9,792.1	8,459.7	7,496.5	7,579.8
Non-Oil Develop.Ctys	201	21,246.2	22,903.4	23,007.7	33,429.1	33,187.5	41,663.2	51,696.8	41,666.3	33,198.5	45,017.5	56,104.6	57,452.2

2004, International Monetary Fund : *International Financial Statistics Yearbook*

Total Reserves minus Gold

Millions of SDRs: End of Period

		1992	1993	1994	1995	1996	1997	1998	1999	2000	2001	2002	2003
All Countries	010	721,295	799,739	860,288	991,304	1,145,651	1,265,414	1,248,151	1,371,157	1,551,442	1,704,458	1,849,058	2,114,629
Industrial Countries	110	396,746	413,531	433,940	487,827	548,944	577,832	545,713	587,706	650,426	683,533	722,672	810,616
United States	111	43,831	45,395	43,350	50,307	44,536	43,659	50,223	44,080	43,442	45,860	49,990	50,401
Canada	156	8,314	9,087	8,416	10,124	14,202	13,209	16,553	20,493	24,502	27,024	27,204	24,376
Australia	193	8,152	8,083	7,730	8,003	10,073	12,485	10,398	15,455	13,906	14,287	15,218	21,662
Japan	158	52,089	71,729	86,214	123,277	150,663	162,793	153,030	209,045	272,392	314,431	339,227	446,368
New Zealand	196	2,239	2,430	2,540	2,967	4,140	3,299	2,986	3,246	2,556	2,394	2,750	3,304
Euro Area (incl. ECB)	163	....	....	....	....	....	....	....	187,088	185,988	186,965	181,678	149,879
Austria	122	9,005	10,637	11,523	12,600	15,901	14,628	22,324	†11,017	10,990	9,954	7,123	5,700
Belgium	124	10,037	8,310	9,505	10,883	11,789	11,999	12,977	†7,969	7,671	8,965	8,720	7,395
Finland	172	3,792	3,939	7,303	6,753	4,810	6,238	6,885	†5,989	6,122	6,352	6,830	7,076
France	132	19,657	16,489	17,986	18,065	18,635	22,922	31,471	†28,926	28,428	25,263	20,864	20,314
Germany	134	66,158	56,525	52,994	57,185	57,844	57,504	52,573	†44,472	43,664	40,903	37,639	34,115
Greece	174	3,486	5,672	9,924	9,943	12,171	9,335	12,399	13,204	10,303	†4,101	5,945	2,935
Ireland	178	2,502	4,314	4,189	5,806	5,706	4,837	6,674	†3,880	4,114	4,445	3,983	2,745
Italy	136	20,104	20,054	22,102	23,482	31,954	41,311	21,227	†16,336	19,623	19,431	21,039	20,435
Luxembourg	137	54	49	52	50	51	47	....	†56	59	84	112	188
Netherlands	138	15,954	22,819	23,655	22,680	18,615	18,429	15,211	†7,203	7,401	7,189	7,034	7,410
Portugal	182	13,912	11,532	10,627	10,663	11,070	11,606	11,239	†6,140	6,838	7,692	8,223	3,954
Spain	184	33,094	29,882	28,459	23,199	40,284	50,694	39,245	†24,127	23,784	23,539	25,403	13,317
Denmark	128	8,032	7,499	6,203	7,411	9,834	14,174	10,841	16,238	11,596	13,615	19,849	24,970
Iceland	176	362	310	201	207	316	284	303	349	298	269	324	533
Norway	142	8,684	14,286	13,033	15,148	18,441	17,343	13,215	14,864	15,476	12,324	15,213	15,476
San Marino	135	....	87	121	134	150	136	121	105	104	106	135	170
Sweden	144	16,454	13,869	15,929	16,180	13,288	8,023	10,013	10,943	11,407	11,122	12,598	13,245
Switzerland	146	24,185	23,760	23,790	24,496	26,727	28,926	29,254	26,463	24,769	25,467	29,536	32,068
United Kingdom	112	26,648	26,775	28,094	28,265	27,745	23,952	22,877	†26,135	33,687	29,668	28,951	28,164
Developing Countries	200	324,549	386,208	426,348	503,478	596,708	687,582	702,438	783,451	901,016	1,020,925	1,126,386	1,304,013
Africa	605	12,535	13,658	16,201	17,727	22,111	32,254	29,372	30,756	42,153	51,819	53,630	61,831
CEMAC (Incl. BEAC hqtrs.)	758	....	....	....	....	....	....	....	....	965	859	1,177	1,220
Cameroon	622	15	2	†2	3	2	1	1	3	163	264	463	430
Central African Republic	626	73	82	144	157	162	132	103	99	102	94	91	89
Chad	628	59	28	52	96	114	101	85	69	85	97	161	126
Congo, Rep. of	634	3	1	34	40	63	44	1	29	170	55	23	23
Equatorial Guinea	642	10	—	—	—	—	4	1	2	18	56	65	160
Gabon	646	52	1	120	100	173	209	11	13	146	8	103	132
WAEMU (Incl. BCEAO hqtrs.)	759	....	....	....	1,708	1,905	2,126	2,247	2,136	2,520	3,008	4,012	4,528
Benin	638	178	178	†177	133	182	188	186	291	352	460	453	343
Burkina Faso	748	248	278	163	234	235	256	265	215	187	207	231	293
Côte d'Ivoire	662	5	2	140	356	421	458	608	459	513	811	1,371	1,501
Guinea Bissau	654	13	10	13	14	8	25	25	26	51	55	76	111
Mali	678	224	242	†152	217	300	308	286	255	293	278	437	611
Niger	692	164	140	76	64	55	39	38	29	62	85	98	77
Senegal	722	9	2	123	183	200	286	306	294	295	356	469	535
Togo	742	198	114	65	88	62	88	84	89	117	101	151	123
Algeria	612	1,060	1,074	1,832	1,349	2,945	5,964	4,862	3,297	9,228	14,388	17,092	22,292
Angola	614	....	....	....	143	384	294	144	361	920	582	276	427
Botswana	616	2,759	2,983	3,015	3,159	3,496	4,206	4,219	4,589	4,849	4,693	4,026	3,593
Burundi	618	127	119	140	141	97	84	47	35	25	14	43	45
Cape Verde	624	55	42	29	25	19	14	6	31	22	36	59	63
Comoros	632	20	28	30	30	35	30	28	27	33	50	59	63
Congo, Dem. Rep. of	636	114	34	83	99	57	....	....	....	....	....	....	....
Djibouti	611	61	55	51	49	54	49	47	51	52	56	54	67
Eritrea	643	....	....	....	27	57	148	16	25	20	32	22	17
Ethiopia	644	169	332	373	519	509	371	363	334	235	345	649	643
Gambia, The	648	68	77	67	71	71	71	76	81	84	84	79	....
Ghana	652	233	298	400	469	576	399	268	331	178	237	397	910
Guinea	656	63	96	60	58	61	90	168	145	114	159	126	....
Kenya	664	39e	295	382	238	519	584	556	577	689	847	786	997
Lesotho	666	115	184	255	307	320	424	408	364	321	308	299	310
Liberia	668	1	2	3	19	—	—	—	—	—	—	2	5
Madagascar	674	61	59	49	73	168	209	122	166	219	317	267	279
Malawi	676	29	41	29	74	157	120	192	183	190	165	121	85
Mauritania	682	44	32	27	57	98	149	144	163	215	226	291	280
Mauritius	684	596	551	512	581	623	514	397	533	689	665	903	1,061
Morocco	686	2,607	2,661	2,981	2,423	2,638	2,959	3,150	4,145	3,702	6,743	7,453	9,321
Mozambique	688	170	136	122	131	239	383	432	475	557	569	603	672
Namibia	728	36	97	139	149	135	186	185	223	200	186	238	219
Nigeria	694	703	999	949	971	2,834	5,619	5,043	3,971	7,607	8,321	5,393	4,797
Rwanda	714	57	35	35	67	74	114	120	127	146	169	179	144
São Tomé & Príncipe	716	....	....	....	3	3	9	7	8	9	12	13	17
Seychelles	718	23	26	21	18	15	20	15	22	34	30	51	45
Sierra Leone	724	14	21	28	23	18	29	31	29	38	41	62	45
South Africa	199	721	742	1,154	1,897	655	3,557	3,094	4,629	4,669	4,810	4,343	4,371
Sudan	732	20	27	54	110	74	60	64	138	†190	94	324	570
Swaziland	734	225	192	203	201	177	219	255	274	270	216	203	187

Total Reserves minus Gold

		1992	1993	1994	1995	1996	1997	1998	1999	2000	2001	2002	2003
1l s						*Millions of SDRs: End of Period*							
Africa(Cont.)													
Tanzania	738	238	148	227	182	306	461	426	565	748	920	1,125	1,372
Tunisia	744	620	622	1,001	1,080	1,320	1,466	1,314	1,648	1,390	1,583	1,685	1,982
Uganda	746	69	107	220	309	367	470	515	556	620	782	687	727
Zambia	754	....	140	184	150	155	177	49	33	188	146	394	167
Zimbabwe	698	162	315	278	401	416	119	93	195	148	51	61	....
Asia *	505	189,134	221,476	262,633	291,111	343,969	384,323	413,513	482,525	548,208	631,748	717,852	839,981
Bangladesh	513	1,327	1,755	2,150	1,574	1,276	1,172	1,353	1,168	1,140	1,015	1,238	1,735
Bhutan	514	62	71	83	†88	132	140	182	213	244	257	261	247
Cambodia	522	....	18	81	129	185	221	230	286	385	467	571	549
China, P.R.: Mainland†	924	†14,997	16,298	36,246	50,708	74,438	105,809	105,955	114,919	129,155	171,560	214,140	274,670
China, P.R.: Hong Kong	532	25,581	31,295	33,737	37,268	44,374	68,782	63,671	70,117	82,540	88,448	82,306	79,652
China, P.R.: Macao	546	947	1,142	1,347	1,518	1,684	1,877	1,749	2,082	2,550	2,792	2,795	2,923
Fiji	819	230	196	187	235	297	267	274	312	316	292	264	285
India	534	4,187	7,425	13,493	12,056	14,027	18,298	19,418	23,801	29,090	36,500	49,772	66,581
Indonesia	536	7,599	8,200	8,311	9,222	12,692	12,293	16,131	19,268	21,876	21,680	22,779	23,528
Korea	542	12,451	14,727	17,563	21,983	23,670	15,096	36,913	53,907	73,781	81,762	89,256	104,500
Lao P. D. Rep.	544	29e	46e	42e	62	118	83	80	74	107	104	141	140
Malaysia	548	12,529	19,838	17,415	15,994	18,783	15,407	18,153	22,286	22,659	24,249	25,172	29,957
Maldives	556	21	19	21	32	53	73	84	93	94	74	98	107
Micronesia, Fed. States of	868	....	....	....	47	62	64	72	68	87	78	86	60
Mongolia	948	12	43	56	79	75	130	67	99	137	164	257	159
Myanmar	518	204	221	289	377	159	185	224	193	171	319	346	370
Nepal	558	340	466	475	395	397	464	537	616	726	826	749	823
Pakistan	564	618	871	2,007	1,166	381	886	730	1,101	1,162	2,896	5,942	7,363
Papua New Guinea	853	174	103	66	176	406	269	137	149	220	336	236	333
Philippines	566	3,202	3,404	4,122	4,287	6,975	5,385	6,552	9,639	10,013	10,686	9,662	9,056
Samoa	862	42	37	35	37	42	48	44	50	49	45	46	56
Singapore†	576	29,007	35,208	39,851	46,213	53,442	52,836	53,215	55,987	61,502	59,977	60,331	64,433
Solomon Islands	813	17	15	12	11	23	27	35	37	25	15	13	25
Sri Lanka	524	674	1,186	1,401	1,404	1,364	1,500	1,406	1,192	797	1,024	1,200	....
Thailand	578	14,806	17,817	20,093	24,206	26,239	19,403	20,472	24,818	24,573	25,745	27,985	27,643
Tonga	866	23	27	24	19	21	20	20	20	21	21	20	29
Vanuatu	846	31	33	30	32	31	28	32	30	30	30	27	29
Vietnam	582	....	....	....	890	1,207	1,472	1,422	2,423	2,622	2,924	3,031	4,189
*of which:													
Taiwan Province of China	528	59,859	60,844	63,331	60,754	61,224	61,888	64,161	77,376	81,926	97,245	118,907	139,055
Europe	170	15,583	25,334	30,530	57,652	61,672	71,931	72,769	79,699	98,363	112,662	139,080	169,915
Albania	914	....	107	140	162	195	229	273	356	473	589	617	679
Armenia	911	1	10	22	67	108	170	230	232	244	255	313	343
Azerbaijan	912	–	–	1	81	147	345	318	490	522	714	531	552
Belarus	913	....	....	†69	254	326	292	499	214	269	311	455	400
Bosnia & Herzegovina	963	....	....	....	....	....	60	124	330	381	972	972	1,208
Bulgaria	918	656	477	686	832	336	1,565	1,907	2,107	2,421	2,619	3,242	4,234
Croatia	960	121	449	962	1,275	1,609	1,882	2,000	2,204	2,705	3,742	4,329	5,512
Cyprus	423	748	798	1,003	751	1,072	1,031	980	1,335	1,336	1,804	2,223	2,192
Czech Republic	935	....	2,759	4,209	9,312	8,590	7,214	8,908	9,330	9,992	11,412	17,326	18,016
Czechoslovakia†	934	†815	....	....	....	....	....	....	....	....	....	....	....
Estonia	939	124	281	304	390	443	562	576	622	707	653	736	924
Georgia	915	....	....	....	131	131	148	87	96	84	127	145	128
Hungary	944	3,218	4,878	4,614	8,055	6,760	6,232	6,618	7,981	8,588	8,536	7,612	8,572
Kazakhstan	916	....	332	574	764	900	1,258	1,038	1,078	1,224	1,589	1,880	2,851
Kyrgyz Republic	917	....	35	18	54	66	126	116	167	183	210	212	245
Latvia	941	....	314	373	340	455	563	569	635	653	914	913	964
Lithuania	946	33	255	360	509	537	749	1,001	871	1,007	1,287	1,728	2,269
Macedonia, FYR	962	....	76	102	173	167	190	217	313	330	593	531	604
Malta	181	922	992	1,267	1,079	1,126	1,103	1,181	1,303	1,128	1,326	1,625	....
Moldova	921	2	56	123	173	217	271	102	135	171	182	198	203
Poland	964	2,981	2,979	4,002	9,939	12,409	15,125	19,407	19,202	20,387	20,409	21,073	21,924
Romania	968	601	725	1,429	1,062	1,462	2,819	2,036	1,958	3,010	4,330	5,304	6,058
Russia	922	....	4,248	2,727	9,676	7,842	9,557	5,541	6,162	18,623	25,895	32,404	49,244
Slovak Republic	936	....	303	1,158	2,263	2,378	2,394	2,037	2,456	3,087	3,295	6,479	7,859
Slovenia	961	520	574	1,027	1,225	1,598	2,457	2,584	2,308	2,453	3,445	5,134	5,718
Tajikistan	923	....	....	....	....	....	27	38	40	71	74	66	75
Turkey	186	4,480	4,566	4,911	8,370	11,430	13,829	13,841	17,010	17,260	15,022	19,910	22,875
Ukraine	926	341	118	446	707	1,363	1,735	541	762	1,038	2,352	3,120	4,530
Middle East	405	43,184	46,757	45,585	50,058	60,551	73,304	72,440	78,426	92,099	98,269	97,426	100,614
Bahrain, Kingdom of	419	1,017	948	801	861	917	956	766	997	1,200	1,340	1,269	1,197
Egypt	469	7,862	9,395	9,234	10,886	12,099	13,833	12,872	10,553	10,068	10,285	9,741	9,145
Israel	436	3,729	4,647	4,653	5,462	7,938	15,069	16,104	16,470	17,869	18,603	17,714	17,709
Jordan	439	558	†1,192	1,159	1,327	1,223	1,631	1,243	1,916	2,557	2,437	2,925	3,496
Kuwait	443	3,743	3,068	2,398	2,395	2,444	2,558	2,803	3,515	5,436	7,875	6,773	5,099
Lebanon	446	1,088	1,646	2,661	3,050	4,125	4,429	4,656	5,665	4,562	3,990	5,328	8,425
Libya	672	4,496	....	....	....	....	....	5,163	5,304	9,564	11,777	10,524	13,179
Oman	449	1,691	1,313	1,128	1,232	1,364	1,534	1,376	2,016	1,827	1,882	2,334	2,418
Qatar	453	497	505	451	500	477	608	741	950	889	1,045	1,152	1,981
Saudi Arabia	456	4,316	5,408	5,054	5,800	†9,959	11,026	10,099	12,384	15,032	14,001	15,160	15,222
United Arab Emirates	466	4,154	4,444	4,561	5,026	5,602	6,205	6,447	7,778	10,379	11,256	11,195	10,154
Yemen, Republic of	474	233	106	175	416	707	892	707	1,072	2,226	2,911	3,244	3,356

2004, International Monetary Fund : *International Financial Statistics Yearbook*

Total Reserves minus Gold

		1992	1993	1994	1995	1996	1997	1998	1999	2000	2001	2002	2003
1l s						*Millions of SDRs: End of Period*							
Western Hemisphere	205	64,113	78,983	71,399	86,929	108,404	125,770	114,344	112,046	120,193	126,427	118,399	131,672
ECCU (incl. ECCB hqtrs.)	309	203	196	179	211	203	228	256	268	297	357	374	366
Anguilla	312	6	7	6	9	10	12	13	15	16	19	19	22
Antigua and Barbuda	311	37	28	31	40	33	38	42	51	49	63	64	77
Dominica	321	15	14	11	15	16	18	20	23	23	25	33	32
Grenada	328	19	20	21	25	25	32	33	37	44	51	65	56
Montserrat	351	5	4	5	6	6	8	18	10	8	10	11	10
St. Kitts and Nevis	361	19	21	22	23	23	27	33	36	35	45	48	44
St. Lucia	362	40	44	40	42	39	45	50	54	61	71	69	72
St. Vincent & Grens	364	24	23	21	20	21	23	28	31	42	49	39	34
Argentina	213	7,265	10,040	9,814	9,612	12,590	16,542	17,579	19,127	19,301	11,580	7,715	9,525
Aruba	314	103	132	122	146	130	128	158	160	160	234	250	199
Bahamas, The	313	113	125	121	121	119	168	246	299	268	254	280	330
Barbados	316	102	110	134	147	201	196	260	220	363	549	492	497
Belize	339	39	28	24	25	41	44	31	52	94	89	84	57
Bolivia	218	132	163	309	444	664	805	674	710	711	705	427	482
Brazil	223	16,379	22,281	25,393	33,440	40,560	37,670	30,241	25,352	24,935	28,438	27,718	33,050
Chile	228	6,667	7,018	8,965	9,512	10,412	13,024	11,271	10,650	11,539	11,442	11,284	10,659
Colombia	233	5,634	5,774	5,474	5,616	6,846	7,265	6,144	5,834	6,843	8,079	7,894	7,257
Costa Rica	238	741	746	612	704	696	935	755	1,064	1,011	1,058	1,101	1,236
Dominican Republic	243	363	474	173	246	244	290	356	506	481	875	345	170
Ecuador	248	631	1,005	1,263	1,095	1,292	1,551	1,150	1,197	727	668	526	547
El Salvador	253	307	390	445	510	652	969	1,146	1,460	1,475	1,385	1,194	1,308
Guatemala	258	557	632	591	472	605	824	948	866	1,340	1,824	1,691	1,907
Guyana	336	137	180	169	181	229	234	196	195	234	229	209	186
Haiti	263	20	23	35	129	150	153	183	192	140	113	60	42
Honduras	268	144	71	117	176	173	430	581	916	1,008	1,126	1,121	962
Jamaica	343	236	304	504	458	612	506	504	404	809	1,512	1,210	804
Mexico	273	13,776	18,281	4,301	11,333	13,514	21,343	22,584	23,156	27,253	35,601	37,215	39,675
Netherlands Antilles	353	160	170	123	137	131	159	176	193	200	240	299	251
Nicaragua	278	95	40	97	92	137	280	249	371	375	302	330	338
Panama	283	367	435	482	526	603	851	678	600	555	869	870	680
Paraguay	288	408	460	706	735	730	619	614	713	585	568	463	652
Peru	293	2,072	2,481	4,790	5,531	7,356	8,140	6,794	6,361	6,427	6,900	6,869	6,579
Suriname	366	13	13	27	89	67	81	75	28	48	95	78	71
Trinidad and Tobago	369	125	150	241	241	378	524	556	689	1,064	1,517	1,491	1,649
Uruguay	298	370	552	663	774	870	1,154	1,472	1,516	1,903	2,464	566	1,402
Venezuela, Rep. Bol.	299	6,954	6,709	5,526	4,227	8,198	10,656	8,466	8,945	10,046	7,352	6,243	10,791
Memorandum Items													
Oil Exporting Countries	999	44,922	45,714	43,434	43,740	60,123	70,933	70,503	77,143	102,277	110,344	108,619	118,610
Non-Oil Developing Countries	201	279,627	340,494	382,914	459,738	536,585	616,649	631,935	706,308	798,740	910,582	1,017,767	1,185,403

Nongold Reserves/Imports

		1992	1993	1994	1995	1996	1997	1998	1999	2000	2001	2002	2003
1rl s							Weeks of Imports						
World	001	13.4	15.0	15.1	14.8	15.8	15.8	16.4	16.9	16.0	17.6	19.9	21.4
Industrial Countries	110	10.5	11.5	11.3	11.0	11.5	11.1	10.7	10.7	10.2	10.7	12.0	12.7
United States	111	5.7	5.4	4.8	5.0	4.1	3.4	3.9	3.0	2.3	2.5	2.9	3.0
Canada	156	4.6	4.7	4.1	4.7	6.1	4.6	5.9	6.6	6.8	7.8	8.5	7.7
Australia	193	13.3	12.7	11.0	10.1	11.5	13.3	11.8	15.9	13.2	14.6	14.8	18.8
Japan	158	16.0	21.2	23.8	28.4	32.3	33.7	39.9	47.9	48.6	58.9	71.1	90.1
New Zealand	196	17.4	18.0	16.2	16.4	21.0	15.9	17.5	16.2	12.5	11.8	12.9	13.8
Euro Area													
Austria	122	11.9	15.6	15.8	14.7	17.7	15.8	17.1	† 11.3	10.8	9.2	6.9	5.0
Belgium	124	...	5.2	5.5	5.3	5.4	5.4	5.8	† 3.5	2.9	3.3	3.1	2.4
Finland	172	12.8	15.6	23.9	18.6	12.3	14.7	15.6	† 13.5	12.2	12.9	14.4	13.1
France	132	5.9	5.8	5.8	5.0	4.9	5.9	7.9	† 7.0	6.2	5.5	4.7	4.2
Germany	134	11.8	11.7	10.4	9.5	9.4	9.1	8.2	† 6.7	6.0	5.5	5.4	4.4
Greece	174	10.9	20.1	35.2	28.7	30.7	23.5	30.9	32.8	23.9	† 9.0	13.5	5.1
Ireland	178	8.0	14.0	12.3	13.6	11.9	8.7	10.9	† 5.9	5.4	5.7	5.5	4.0
Italy	136	7.6	9.7	9.9	8.8	11.5	13.8	7.1	† 5.3	5.6	5.4	6.0	5.4
Luxembourg	137	.5	.5	.5	.4	.4	.4	...	† .4	.4	.5	.7	1.1
Netherlands	138	8.5	13.1	12.7	9.9	7.7	7.3	5.9	† 2.7	2.5	2.4	2.6	2.5
Portugal	182	32.8	33.9	29.5	24.7	23.5	23.2	† 21.4	† 11.0	12.1	12.8	15.2	7.5
Spain	184	23.7	26.8	23.4	15.8	24.7	29.0	21.6	† 11.9	10.5	10.0	11.0	4.9
Denmark	128	16.2	17.1	12.9	12.5	16.3	22.4	17.1	26.0	17.7	20.1	28.5	34.2
Iceland	176	15.4	16.5	10.3	9.1	11.6	10.0	8.9	9.9	7.8	7.8	10.1	14.8
Norway	142	24.0	42.6	36.2	35.5	38.7	34.1	25.8	31.0	30.5	24.4	30.8	30.3
Sweden	144	23.5	23.2	23.4	19.3	14.8	8.6	10.7	11.4	10.6	11.4	13.3	12.4
Switzerland	146	† 28.0	29.9	28.2	24.6	26.8	28.6	29.0	25.0	22.1	21.6	26.4	26.9
United Kingdom	112	8.6	9.3	9.4	8.2	7.2	5.5	5.3	† 5.9	6.8	6.0	6.1	5.7
Developing Countries	200	19.8	21.7	22.3	22.0	23.6	24.1	28.2	30.1	27.4	30.7	34.6	36.8
Africa	605	11.4	12.9	14.9	13.6	16.5	21.4	20.5	22.0	27.5	31.3	34.5	...
CEMAC													
Cameroon	622	.9	.1	† .1	.2	.1	–	–	.2	8.6	10.9	11.5	...
Central African Republic	626	35.8	46.4	78.4	69.8	85.4	66.1	51.7	54.1	59.2	57.7	53.3	...
Chad	628	17.2	10.1	22.3	20.3	25.8	21.2	17.5	15.6	18.3	9.4	6.9	...
Congo, Rep. of	634	.5	.1	4.1	4.6	3.1	3.4	.1	2.5	24.8	...	...	...
Equatorial Guinea	642	12.4	.4	.5	–	.1	.8	.1	.4	2.7	...	...	...
Gabon	646	5.3	–	12.0	8.7	13.5	13.3	.7	1.1	9.9	.6	...	...
WAEMU													
Benin	638	22.1	22.2	† 31.1	13.8	20.8	19.3	18.5	27.8	38.9	54.4	47.2	35.0
Burkina Faso	748	38.1	39.1	35.4	39.7	27.2	30.5	26.5	27.0	25.8	24.5	28.2	...
Côte d'Ivoire	662	.2	.1	5.5	9.4	10.9	11.6	13.3	11.9	14.5	21.9	39.5	34.9
Guinea Bissau	654	9.6	12.0	5.9	7.9	6.9	19.7	29.7	35.9	70.6	58.5	91.5	124.2
Mali	678	26.4	27.3	† 19.5	21.7	29.0	29.2	27.5	30.0	33.5	24.7	41.5	41.8
Niger	692	24.4	26.6	17.5	13.2	9.1	7.4	5.9	6.1	12.9	16.8	18.8	13.0
Senegal	722	.6	.2	9.1	10.0	10.4	15.0	15.4	15.3	14.9	16.3	20.7	20.4
Togo	742	35.9	45.3	22.1	11.4	6.9	9.6	10.4	13.0	16.3	12.7	18.4	11.2
Algeria	612	9.1	9.6	15.2	10.3	24.2	...	...	...	...	...	112.0	...
Botswana	616	104.5	120.7	139.5	127.8	151.7	130.7	129.4	147.9	133.1	169.5	...	...
Burundi	618	40.9	43.2	47.4	46.5	57.1	48.4	21.6	21.1	11.6	6.6	23.6	22.2
Cape Verde	624	21.9	19.5	10.5	7.6	6.1	4.3	1.9	9.0	6.4	10.1	...	...
Comoros	632	20.6	33.8	43.5	37.0	...	...	...	...	...	...	...	...
Congo, Dem. Rep. of	636	19.4	6.5	16.4	19.2	10.1	...	...	...	...	...	...	...
Djibouti	611	19.8	18.5	19.5	21.2	22.4	23.4	21.8	24.1	...	...	...	...
Ethiopia	644	14.4	30.1	27.4	35.0	27.2	...	17.5	15.5	12.6	12.4	27.5	...
Gambia, The	648	22.4	21.1	24.0	30.3	20.6	28.7	24.2	30.1	30.4	41.0	37.6	...
Ghana	652	7.7	5.4	14.4	19.0	20.4	12.0	7.6	6.8	4.1	...	...	...
Kenya	664	1.5e	11.9	13.9	6.1	13.2	12.5	12.7	14.5	15.0	17.3	17.1	20.7
Lesotho	666	9.1	15.1	22.8	24.1	24.0	29.0	34.6	33.2	29.9	29.5	26.9	23.4
Madagascar	674	9.8	9.0	8.5	10.4	24.0	29.4	16.4	20.1	20.3	27.9	37.3	...
Malawi	676	2.8	5.4	4.5	12.1	18.8	10.8	27.2	19.4	24.1	19.1	12.4	...
Mauritania	682	...	...	5.1	...	...	...	...	...	...	...	...	...
Mauritius	684	26.3	22.9	20.1	22.7	20.4	16.5	14.0	16.9	22.3	21.9	29.4	34.5
Morocco	686	25.4	28.2	27.4	18.7	20.3	21.8	22.4	29.8	21.7	39.9	44.4	...
Mozambique	688	...	...	17.3	14.2	23.1	35.7	39.3	29.2	32.6	...	...	...
Namibia	728	2.0	5.2	7.5	7.1	6.0	7.4	8.2	9.9	8.7	7.9	...	...
Nigeria	694	6.1	12.9	10.9	† 9.1	32.9	41.5	40.1	33.0	59.1	46.9	50.5	34.2
Rwanda	714	14.3	7.4	22.0	21.7	21.6	26.8	30.9	36.3	47.0	44.2	62.5	45.5
São Tomé & Príncipe	716	...	...	...	9.1	11.7	40.1	...	...	...	...	8.6	8.2
Seychelles	718	8.5	7.8	7.6	6.1	3.0	4.0	2.9	3.6	6.7	4.1	8.6	11.4
Sierra Leone	724	6.8	10.2	14.0	13.5	6.6	21.6	24.1	25.4	17.1	14.7	16.7	8.2
South Africa	199	2.6	2.7	3.8	4.8	1.6	7.6	† 7.7	12.4	10.7	11.1	10.5	...
Sudan	732	1.7	2.1	3.3	† 7.0	3.6	2.7	2.5	6.9	† 8.3	3.9	...	...
Swaziland	734	18.6	17.5	18.4	15.4	12.4	14.4	17.2	18.3	17.5	12.5	14.6	...
Tanzania	738	11.3	7.1	11.5	8.4	16.5	24.2	21.4	25.9	33.3	35.1	47.1	73.3
Tunisia	744	6.9	7.2	11.5	10.6	12.8	12.9	11.5	13.9	11.0	10.9	12.5	14.0
Uganda	746	9.7	12.4	19.1	22.6	23.1	25.0	26.6	29.6	27.3	32.1	43.7	44.9

2004, International Monetary Fund : *International Financial Statistics Yearbook*

Nongold Reserves/Imports

		1992	1993	1994	1995	1996	1997	1998	1999	2000	2001	2002	2003
1rl s							Weeks of Imports						
Africa(Cont.)													
Zambia	754	....	12.4	23.5	16.5	13.9	15.2	3.3	2.7	11.6	....	....	....
Zimbabwe	698	5.2	12.4	9.4	11.6	11.1	2.5	2.6	6.6	5.5	1.9	....	....
Asia *	505	**22.1**	**23.0**	**24.8**	**22.8**	**24.8**	**25.5**	**34.5**	**36.0**	**31.0**	**36.9**	**41.8**	**44.1**
Bangladesh	513	25.4	31.4	35.5	18.7	14.4	11.9	14.2	10.8	9.2	7.9	11.1	14.1
Bhutan	514	35.4	56.6	68.9	†60.4	77.4	71.6	99.9	83.5	81.5	88.3	111.8	....
Cambodia	522	....	....	....	....	....	13.9	14.9	16.4	18.3	21.0	24.1	24.5
China, P.R.: Mainland	924	†13.3	11.2	23.8	29.7	40.1	52.1	55.3	49.5	38.9	46.0	51.3	51.4
China, P.R.: Hong Kong	532	14.8	16.1	15.8	14.9	16.7	23.1	25.3	27.9	26.3	28.7	28.0	26.5
China, P.R.: Macao	546	34.4	40.3	48.1	57.5	63.0	63.3	65.5	72.9	76.6	76.5	78.1	82.0
Fiji	819	26.1	19.5	17.1	20.4	22.5	19.4	27.8	24.7	26.0	24.0	20.8	18.8
India	534	12.7	23.3	38.2	26.9	27.6	31.0	33.1	36.2	38.3	47.3	62.3	72.2
Indonesia	536	19.9	20.7	19.7	17.5	22.1	20.7	43.2	57.3	44.2	45.7	51.5	43.6
Korea	542	10.9	12.6	13.0	12.6	11.8	7.3	29.0	32.1	31.1	37.9	41.5	45.2
Lao People's Democratic Rep.	544	7.8e	7.6e	5.6e	8.1	12.8	8.3	10.6	10.0	13.5	12.9	23.1	20.7
Malaysia	548	22.5	31.0	22.2	15.9	17.9	13.7	22.8	24.3	18.7	21.5	22.3	28.2
Maldives	556	7.7	7.1	7.3	9.3	13.1	14.7	17.4	16.4	16.4	12.3	17.7	17.6
Mongolia	948	2.0	8.2	16.4	14.7	12.4	19.5	9.7	13.8	15.1	17.0	....	....
Myanmar	518	22.1	19.2	24.6	21.6	8.7	6.3	6.1	5.9	4.8	7.2	10.4	13.7
Nepal	558	31.3	37.4	31.2	22.9	21.2	19.2	31.6	30.9	31.2	36.6	37.3	36.2
Pakistan	564	4.7	6.6	17.1	7.9	2.4	5.4	5.7	7.7	7.2	18.6	37.4	43.6
Papua New Guinea	853	8.4	5.7	3.3	9.4	17.4	11.0	8.1	8.7	13.0	20.5	13.5	19.8
Philippines	566	14.8	13.0	13.8	11.7	15.3	9.8	15.2	21.1	18.3	20.0	18.4	17.7
Samoa	862	27.2	25.2	32.4	30.3	31.5	34.5	33.0	30.7	31.3	22.6	28.8	31.8
Singapore	576	28.7	29.5	29.5	28.7	30.4	28.0	37.2	36.0	31.0	33.8	36.6	38.9
Solomon Islands	813	10.9	7.6	6.5	5.4	11.2	10.3	17.0	....	17.9	....	19.9	....
Sri Lanka	524	13.8	21.2	22.3	20.5	18.7	17.9	17.4	14.3	7.5	11.2	13.9	....
Thailand	578	26.0	27.6	28.0	26.4	27.1	21.7	34.9	35.2	26.9	27.2	30.6	28.2
Tonga	866	26.4	31.4	26.7	19.3	21.3	19.7	21.7	19.1	20.2	18.7	16.2	....
Vanuatu	846	27.0	30.1	25.3	26.4	23.4	20.7	26.4	22.5	23.4	19.3	21.3	....
Vietnam	582	....	....	....	....	8.1	8.9	9.1	14.7	11.4	11.9	11.3	13.0
of which:													
Taiwan Province of China	528	59.3	56.4	56.2	45.3	45.2	38.1	44.8	49.8	39.7	59.2	74.5	....
Europe	170	**6.3**	**9.6**	**10.7**	**15.4**	**13.8**	**14.2**	**15.2**	**18.4**	**18.6**	**19.7**	**23.4**	**24.4**
Albania	914	....	13.4	17.6	17.6	17.4	24.9	24.1	22.3	29.3	28.9	29.0	28.2
Armenia	911	.3	2.8	4.3	7.7	9.5	13.3	18.7	20.7	18.8	19.1	22.3	20.9
Azerbaijan	912	–	–	.1	9.4	11.4	30.5	21.6	33.8	30.2	32.6	....	....
Belarus	913	....	....	†1.7	3.5	3.5	2.4	4.3	2.3	2.1	2.5	3.5	2.7
Bulgaria	918	10.5	7.2	12.2	11.4	3.7	21.0	28.2	27.6	25.2	23.6	28.7	30.0
Croatia	960	1.9	6.9	14.0	13.1	15.5	14.5	17.5	20.2	23.2	26.7	28.6	30.1
Cyprus	423	16.1	22.0	25.2	15.7	20.1	19.6	19.5	26.3	23.5	30.1	38.5	37.9
Czech Republic	935	....	†12.7	†17.5	†27.3	21.9	17.6	21.5	22.6	20.0	19.5	28.6	....
Czechoslovakia	934	†4.4	....	....	....	....	....	....	....	....	....	....	....
Estonia	939	....	22.5	†13.8	11.8	10.3	8.9	9.1	10.8	11.3	9.9	10.8	11.0
Georgia	915	....	....	....	25.7	14.3	11.0	7.2	11.8	8.7	12.1	14.0	....
Hungary	944	20.7	27.9	24.5	40.5	28.0	20.7	18.9	20.4	18.2	16.5	14.2	13.9
Kazakhstan	916	....	6.1	12.2	15.5	15.9	20.5	17.6	21.0	16.4	16.1	20.2	26.5
Kyrgyz Republic	917	....	5.8	4.3	8.1	5.9	12.5	10.1	19.9	22.4	29.3	25.6	26.4
Latvia	941	....	25.7	22.7	14.5	14.7	14.5	13.1	15.4	13.9	17.0	15.9	14.2
Lithuania	946	....	8.0	11.6	10.8	8.8	9.3	12.6	12.9	13.1	13.9	16.2	18.1
Macedonia, FYR	962	....	4.5	5.2	7.8	7.7	7.5	8.3	12.4	10.7	23.1	19.5	20.8
Malta	181	28.1	32.6	39.4	28.3	30.1	30.3	32.4	32.7	22.5	31.8	40.5	....
Moldova	921	.2	6.3	13.3	15.9	15.1	16.2	7.3	16.5	14.9	13.2	....	....
Poland	964	13.6	11.3	14.2	26.4	25.0	25.1	30.6	29.9	28.2	26.5	27.0	24.9
Romania	968	6.9	7.9	15.3	8.0	9.6	17.5	12.6	13.4	15.6	18.2	21.0	19.5
Russia	922	....	8.4	†3.7	10.9	7.8	8.5	6.4	10.1	25.7	28.7	34.6	46.6
Slovak Republic	936	....	3.3	12.9	19.0	15.6	15.6	10.9	14.7	15.6	13.9	26.2	25.6
Slovenia	961	†6.1	6.3	10.7	10.0	12.7	18.4	18.7	16.3	16.4	22.2	33.2	31.9
Turkey	186	14.0	11.1	16.0	18.1	19.6	20.0	22.1	29.8	21.5	23.7	28.3	26.9
Ukraine	926	3.4	.9	3.1	3.5	5.8	7.1	2.7	4.6	5.0	9.7	13.0	15.2
Middle East	405	**22.6**	**24.6**	**27.0**	**27.2**	**29.3**	**32.0**	**33.4**	**34.4**	**33.9**	**31.8**	**32.5**	....
Bahrain	419	17.1	17.6	16.2	17.9	16.0	16.7	15.7	19.3	17.6	20.3	18.0	18.1
Egypt	469	67.5	81.7	68.6	71.6	69.4	73.5	58.3	47.0	48.7	52.7	54.9	63.4
Israel	436	17.2	14.7	14.0	14.3	18.8	34.3	40.2	35.4	38.5	34.3	35.3	37.7
Jordan	439	12.3	†24.1	26.0	27.7	21.3	27.9	23.8	36.8	37.7	32.9	41.2	....
Kuwait	443	36.9	31.1	27.2	23.8	21.8	21.8	23.8	32.9	51.5	65.4	53.2	36.5
Lebanon	446	18.5	†53.1	77.7	43.0	40.9	41.6	48.2	65.1	49.6	35.7	58.4	90.8
Libya	672	63.6e	....	....	....	....	....	80.2	91.0	173.6	175.0	169.2	....
Oman	449	32.1	22.8	21.9	22.4	22.3	21.4	17.7	30.8	24.6	21.2	27.5	28.4
Qatar	453	17.6	19.1	17.7	11.4	12.4	12.8	15.9	27.1	....	....	20.1	....
Saudi Arabia	456	9.3	13.7	16.4	16.0	†26.8	26.9	24.6	31.6	33.7	29.3	33.2	32.1
United Arab Emirates	466	17.1	16.3	16.5	18.5	18.5	14.5	19.1	16.7	18.4	....	....	....
Yemen, Republic of	474	6.4	2.7	6.3	20.4	26.0	31.1	23.9	38.1	64.9	82.3	....	....
Western Hemisphere	205	**26.5**	**29.9**	**24.5**	**26.9**	**29.3**	**26.8**	**24.2**	**23.9**	**20.8**	**21.6**	**23.6**	**27.7**
ECCU (incl. ECCB hqtrs.)	309	....	....	....	....	....	....	....	....	....	....	....	....
Anguilla	312	11.5	13.6	13.1	20.5	12.5	13.8	13.2	11.3	11.2	16.2	19.5	....
Antigua and Barbuda	311	8.4	6.1	7.0	8.9	6.8	7.1	8.0	8.8	....	....	....	....
Dominica	321	10.1	11.1	8.3	9.8	9.2	10.0	10.9	11.9	10.3	12.4	20.5	19.8
Grenada	328	12.6	11.8	13.7	15.5	12.2	12.8	12.2	12.9	12.2	....	....	....

Nongold Reserves/Imports

		1992	1993	1994	1995	1996	1997	1998	1999	2000	2001	2002	2003
1rl s						*Weeks of Imports*							
Western Hemisphere(Cont.)													
Montserrat	351	....	....	....	....	....	....	....	....	....	....	....	....
St. Kitts and Nevis	361	14.3	13.0	13.0	13.1	12.9	14.3	18.6	19.1	13.6	17.6	19.3	....
St. Lucia	362	9.4	10.4	9.9	10.7	9.3	9.5	11.0	10.9	11.5	13.0	15.8	....
St. Vincent & Grens	364	13.1	12.2	12.5	11.4	11.9	8.6	10.5	11.0	17.6	17.2	15.9	13.3
Argentina	213	34.9	42.9	34.5	37.1	39.7	38.2	41.0	53.5	52.0	37.2	60.7	53.3
Aruba	314	....	....	....	19.9	16.9	14.6	14.2	14.6	13.0	18.2	21.0	18.1
Bahamas, The	313	7.8	9.4	8.7	7.5	6.5	7.1	9.6	12.1	8.8	8.7	11.5	14.5
Barbados	316	13.9	13.6	16.6	14.8	18.1	13.8	18.8	14.2	21.3	33.0	33.5	33.9
Belize	339	10.0	7.2	6.9	7.6	11.9	10.8	7.8	10.0	12.2	11.3	11.4	8.0
Bolivia	218	8.7	9.6	19.4	24.1	30.4	30.5	24.9	28.9	26.3	27.0	17.1	22.9
Brazil	223	50.8	57.4	53.5	48.1	53.3	40.7	36.5	35.0	28.8	31.8	39.5	50.4
Chile	228	46.8	45.0	57.6	46.2	40.7	43.9	41.5	47.5	42.2	41.9	46.4	42.4
Colombia	233	61.8	41.9	35.0	31.3	37.4	33.1	30.7	39.1	40.2	41.1	43.8	40.4
Costa Rica	238	21.7	15.1	12.3	13.3	12.0	13.2	8.9	12.0	10.7	10.5	10.8	12.5
Dominican Republic	243	10.4	13.9	3.8	5.2	4.4	4.2	4.6	6.0	4.4	....	....	....
Ecuador	248	18.6	28.0	26.5	20.4	24.6	22.0	15.1	28.3	13.2	8.1	5.8	6.5
El Salvador	253	12.9	14.6	15.0	13.8	18.2	22.8	26.9	33.2	26.3	23.4	21.6	23.1
Guatemala	258	15.7	17.4	16.1	11.1	14.4	15.0	14.9	14.1	19.0	21.3	19.7	22.7
Guyana	336	22.1	26.6	25.4	26.5	28.7	26.0	....	....	....	25.6	26.3	14.1
Haiti	263	5.1	4.7	10.6	15.3	16.9	16.6	16.8	13.4	9.1	7.3	3.8	2.7
Honduras	268	9.9	4.5	8.4	8.3	7.0	14.0	16.8	24.4	23.9	25.0	26.6	22.7
Jamaica	343	10.1	10.2	17.2	12.6	15.4	11.3	12.2	9.9	16.5	29.4	24.2	17.1
Mexico	273	15.1	19.1	3.9	11.5	10.8	13.0	12.6	11.1	10.1	13.2	14.9	17.2
Netherlands Antilles	353	6.1	6.2	5.3	....	....	....	....	....	4.8	5.6	9.5	....
Nicaragua	278	7.9	3.8	8.4	7.1	8.9	13.6	12.2	14.2	14.1	11.1	13.0	....
Panama	283	13.0	14.2	15.2	16.2	16.2	19.9	14.6	12.2	11.1	19.2	20.6	17.0
Paraguay	288	20.5	19.4	25.0	20.4	19.1	14.0	18.2	29.5	19.3	18.7	....	....
Peru	293	30.5	35.8	54.3	46.0	58.3	55.5	50.2	55.7	49.0	....	....	....
Suriname	366	1.7	.9	4.9	11.8	10.0	10.0	10.0	3.5	6.3	13.5	11.2	7.8
Trinidad and Tobago	369	8.1	7.3	16.2	10.9	13.2	12.3	13.6	17.9	21.8	27.8	28.9	....
Uruguay	298	13.0	17.0	18.1	20.9	19.6	21.7	28.3	32.2	37.2	52.6	20.4	49.5
Venezuela, Rep. Bol	299	35.4	38.3	45.7	25.8	62.0	51.2	39.2	45.4	42.0	26.7	37.3	93.1
Memorandum Items													
Oil Exporting Countries	999	21.0	22.9	24.9	22.1	29.1	29.5	33.6	36.8	40.3	38.8	42.1	....
Non-Oil Developing Countries	201	19.6	21.5	22.1	22.0	23.0	23.6	27.7	29.5	26.3	29.9	33.9	36.3

2004, International Monetary Fund : *International Financial Statistics Yearbook*

SDRs

1b s

Millions of SDRs: End of Period

		1992	1993	1994	1995	1996	1997	1998	1999	2000	2001	2002	2003
All Countries	010	12,867.2	14,614.3	15,761.5	19,773.2	18,521.4	20,532.2	20,379.7	18,456.7	18,489.0	19,556.8	19,672.7	19,914.6
Industrial Countries	110	10,468.2	11,454.4	12,485.9	14,998.5	14,521.1	15,511.5	15,844.0	14,726.0	14,411.1	15,967.8	15,791.9	15,305.9
United States	111	6,184.19	6,569.42	6,876.43	7,424.77	7,171.50	7,431.46	7,530.17	7,538.96	8,088.47	8,580.44	8,948.51	8,504.64
Canada	156	755.52	773.46	786.44	791.85	812.37	834.27	779.52	383.75	440.64	488.96	528.84	563.95
Australia	193	69.63	59.66	49.93	36.77	25.39	13.81	12.59	52.64	71.79	86.80	100.26	114.27
Japan	158	795.45	1,123.39	1,426.99	1,821.07	1,837.31	1,955.05	1,891.04	1,935.45	1,870.15	1,891.67	1,856.76	1,861.31
New Zealand	196	.01	.04	.23	.57	.27	.24	1.23	4.97	10.03	12.82	15.89	18.95
Euro Area													
Austria	122	247.64	160.50	193.81	121.69	135.69	124.77	105.87	105.91	102.74	185.33	136.05	121.94
Belgium	124	124.11	124.71	123.44	331.14	346.49	362.69	433.25	197.10	235.81	375.70	407.85	434.12
Finland	172	78.42	83.77	222.66	241.63	201.58	241.71	247.53	211.33	106.46	186.27	147.03	130.98
France	132	118.28	240.78	248.31	642.76	682.07	719.88	786.19	252.67	308.90	391.74	457.85	512.32
Germany	134	611.36	700.15	763.32	1,346.21	1,326.24	1,324.95	1,326.57	1,427.29	1,352.90	1,426.43	1,456.23	1,307.13
Greece	174	.02	.12	.22	.01	.41	.24	.32	3.76	9.19	7.71	11.13	14.43
Ireland	178	90.35	96.58	101.30	107.16	114.87	123.08	137.14	29.23	36.97	43.46	48.60	52.99
Italy	136	173.18	175.38	85.76	.03	20.44	49.57	78.65	122.49	182.43	236.45	79.32	104.85
Luxembourg	137	6.62	6.98	7.22	7.46	7.75	8.04	8.72	1.78	3.22	5.00	6.72	8.29
Netherlands	138	402.61	424.38	441.92	616.41	566.17	586.49	643.85	742.39	501.12	598.28	512.89	523.45
Portugal	182	33.54	41.93	48.32	56.96	68.19	79.43	95.95	32.12	41.22	49.42	55.82	61.13
Spain	184	133.95	157.38	174.50	276.78	313.87	351.26	408.08	189.78	222.63	279.19	260.06	278.04
Denmark	128	66.73	62.38	124.63	106.76	116.72	248.72	245.96	249.94	50.51	223.49	75.87	54.58
Iceland	176	.02	.04	.08	.02	.03	.01	.01	.01	.04	.09	.11	.03
Norway	142	139.08	288.44	266.73	311.47	247.19	257.87	294.08	297.97	235.35	282.06	232.67	225.42
San Marino	135	—	.04	.11	.18	.25	.33	.42	.08	.20	.34	.43	.49
Sweden	144	32.60	42.16	46.40	296.83	198.91	276.70	292.37	227.78	165.25	157.08	132.03	133.13
Switzerland	146	11.73	112.82	161.95	181.27	87.84	170.49	192.32	344.72	124.71	225.00	54.24	24.72
United Kingdom	112	393.15	209.95	335.21	278.72	239.48	350.44	332.17	373.87	250.39	234.07	267.29	254.68
Developing Countries	200	2,398.9	3,159.9	3,275.6	4,774.7	4,000.4	5,020.7	4,535.7	3,730.7	4,077.9	3,589.0	3,880.8	4,608.8
Africa	605	148.6	116.3	119.0	134.0	117.1	122.2	280.2	394.4	404.6	463.5	481.7	491.1
CEMAC (incl. BEAC hqtrs.)	758	5.93	1.02	1.13	1.35	.35	.08	.24	6.50	6.19	5.26	4.13	2.32
Cameroon	622	.20	.06	.03	.03	.11	—	.01	1.90	5.93	.01	.87	.99
Central African Rep.	626	.04	.03	.01	.02	.01	—	.01	.04	—	.01	.01	.01
Chad	628	.02	.01	—	.02	.16	.01	.01	.02	—	—	.01	—
Congo, Rep. of	634	.04	.01	.03	.02	.01	.01	—	.08	.03	.15	2.38	.43
Equatorial Guinea	642	5.52	.28	.01	.01	.01	—	.01	—	.09	.79	.44	.03
Gabon	646	.08	.03	.17	—	.02	—	.01	—	.05	.04	—	.03
WAEMU (incl. BCEAO hqtrs.)	759	6.09	7.28	6.90	10.20	5.78	2.28	1.33	6.62	2.18	8.15	8.94	10.93
Benin	638	.02	.06	.02	.08	.21	.04	.05	.15	.05	.30	.09	.13
Burkina Faso	748	5.58	5.58	5.55	5.52	1.78	1.63	.54	.53	.31	.41	.30	.21
Côte d'Ivoire	662	.19	.77	.11	1.24	.82	.02	.12	2.48	.97	.58	.86	.18
Guinea Bissau	654	—	.01	—	.01	.01	.04	.02	.06	.03	.16	.30	.80
Mali	678	.08	.09	.14	.31	.21	.05	.06	.42	.08	.30	.03	.61
Niger	692	.01	.41	.29	.20	1.33	.12	.14	.98	.02	.25	.50	1.80
Senegal	722	—	.30	.75	2.57	1.18	.35	.36	1.83	.71	5.96	6.68	7.10
Togo	742	.21	.08	.05	.27	.25	.01	.05	.17	—	.18	.19	.10
Algeria	612	.76	4.90	15.66	.78	3.47	.54	1.09	1.38	2.34	9.14	10.18	38.19
Angola	614	.09	.10	.10	.11	.11	.12	.12	.13	.13	.14	.14	.14
Botswana	616	22.46	24.03	25.39	27.06	28.71	30.36	32.41	28.05	29.89	31.53	32.63	33.52
Burundi	618	1.08	.51	.14	.05	.08	.05	.07	.07	.03	.04	.12	.09
Cape Verde	624	.05	.02	.05	.02	.04	.02	.04	.01	.04	.01	—	—
Comoros	632	.02	.07	.03	.07	.04	.10	—	.12	.13	.02	.03	—
Congo, Dem. Rep. of	636	—	—	—	—	—	—	—	—	—	—	6.12	5.35
Djibouti	611	.15	.15	.11	.06	.10	.55	.27	.06	.28	.10	.76	.09
Eritrea	643	—	—	—	—	—	—	—	—	—	—	—	—
Ethiopia	644	.05	.21	.28	.17	.01	.09	.06	.05	—	.15	.11	.06
Gambia, The	648	.45	.23	.18	.09	.20	.09	.30	.49	.17	.01	.01	.02
Ghana	652	3.21	.40	2.88	1.64	1.55	2.50	42.41	13.28	.41	3.19	2.71	31.49
Guinea	656	7.93	8.49	3.79	5.01	.54	1.97	1.02	.94	.19	.63	1.22	.15
Kenya	664	.56	.82	.47	.19	.54	.50	.42	1.71	.21	.78	.61	1.37
Lesotho	666	.48	.41	.33	.24	.92	.89	.86	.85	.51	.46	.44	.42
Liberia	668	—	—	—	—	—	—	—	—	—	—	—	—
Madagascar	674	.02	.10	.02	.02	.04	.05	.03	.11	.04	.09	.03	.02
Malawi	676	.06	.17	4.25	.59	.94	.07	4.84	.29	.36	.67	.07	.32
Mauritania	682	.06	.10	—	.04	.99	.26	.01	—	.28	.16	.15	.09
Mauritius	684	17.64	21.05	21.34	21.68	22.15	22.48	22.84	16.07	16.45	16.81	17.04	17.24
Morocco	686	56.26	25.12	18.04	17.25	5.17	.88	2.34	62.06	91.64	98.14	90.01	75.62
Mozambique	688	.03	.03	.03	.03	.04	.04	.04	.05	.05	.05	.05	.05
Namibia	728	.01	.01	.01	.01	.01	.01	.01	.02	.02	.02	.02	.02
Nigeria	694	.01	.15	—	.45	.43	.44	.52	.14	.24	.53	.11	.15
Rwanda	714	2.43	2.11	1.75	13.65	12.71	19.64	17.36	10.54	.87	9.82	7.48	20.03
São Tomé & Príncipe	716	—	.01	.01	.03	.01	—	—	—	—	—	.01	.02
Seychelles	718	.01	.01	.02	.02	.02	.03	.03	.03	.01	.02	.01	—
Sierra Leone	724	1.22	2.79	6.18	11.48	5.32	8.29	7.36	15.17	4.03	.30	17.69	23.20
Somalia	726	—	—	—	—	—	—	—	—	—	—	—	—
South Africa	199	.07	8.78	.85	3.29	.82	6.81	131.67	209.60	222.40	222.56	222.77	222.79
Sudan	732	—	—	—	—	—	—	—	—	—	—	.13	.23

SDRs

		1992	1993	1994	1995	1996	1997	1998	1999	2000	2001	2002	2003
1b s						Millions of SDRs: End of Period							
Africa(Cont.)													
Swaziland	734	5.84	5.88	5.89	5.90	5.93	5.94	5.96	2.42	2.44	2.45	2.46	2.47
Tanzania	738	.01	.03	–	.05	.10	.08	.25	.20	.11	.39	.08	.34
Tunisia	744	8.77	1.30	1.84	4.72	11.05	12.09	2.07	19.33	2.97	1.34	1.98	1.65
Uganda	746	6.56	.04	2.10	.30	.74	3.98	3.54	1.69	2.72	1.48	2.18	3.22
Zambia	754	–	–	–	8.17	1.41	.79	.57	.05	17.13	53.25	51.73	.32
Zimbabwe	698	.30	.62	.05	.52	6.78	.22	.28	.79	.18	–	.01	–
Asia	505	523.0	683.4	647.5	875.4	925.4	1,530.8	1,298.9	906.1	927.8	973.6	1,045.2	1,226.6
Afghanistan, Islamic State of	512	3.18	2.01	.96	–	–	–	–	–	–	–	–	.40
Bangladesh	513	30.11	16.61	24.64	107.28	76.19	21.65	9.14	.66	.33	.95	1.65	2.16
Bhutan	514	.34	.38	.40	.44	.47	.50	.54	.13	.17	.21	.23	.25
Brunei Darussalam	516	–	–	–	–	.54	1.58	2.75	3.75	5.04	6.24	6.99	7.85
Cambodia	522	–	11.42	10.89	10.21	9.51	8.77	6.95	3.78	.14	.41	.40	.14
China, P.R.: Mainland	924	305.08	352.03	369.13	391.58	427.15	446.53	480.10	539.58	612.71	676.82	734.19	741.38
Fiji	819	5.97	6.26	7.39	7.67	7.99	8.29	8.62	4.10	4.47	4.81	5.02	5.18
India	534	2.80	72.85	1.41	93.33	85.12	57.38	59.02	3.04	1.22	4.15	5.03	1.91
Indonesia	536	.08	.26	.27	.87	1.53	369.98	221.52	.27	24.50	12.64	13.66	2.49
Kiribati	826	.01	.01	.01	.01	.01	.01	.01	.01	.01	.01	.01	.01
Korea	542	30.56	42.29	52.30	65.74	82.34	43.60	8.12	.50	2.70	2.66	8.68	14.18
Lao P. D. Rep	544	.57	1.90	7.46	9.49	7.17	9.31	4.32	.05	.07	2.72	4.47	12.87
Malaysia	548	82.31	87.78	92.71	101.64	115.28	129.88	145.77	60.80	80.81	99.58	111.36	119.95
Maldives	556	.01	.02	.03	.05	.06	.08	.10	.14	.20	.25	.28	.30
Marshall Islands, Rep. of	867	–	–	–	–	–	–	–	–	–	–	–	–
Micronesia, Fed. States of	868	–	.831	.866	.907	.944	.982	1.024	1.060	1.106	1.149	1.176	1.196
Mongolia	948	.01	.02	1.98	1.70	.30	.52	.34	.12	.01	.01	.03	.03
Myanmar	518	.01	.21	.10	.06	.06	.06	.23	.12	.11	.44	.06	.07
Nepal	558	.12	.03	.09	.01	.01	.08	.02	.23	.01	.07	.01	.54
Pakistan	564	.08	.52	.21	9.90	9.18	7.98	.65	.17	10.92	3.09	1.57	166.87
Palau	565	–	–	–	–	–	–	–	–	–	–	–	–
Papua New Guinea	853	.10	.03	.07	.47	.04	.06	.04	.53	9.34	6.93	4.46	2.48
Philippines	566	.38	7.31	16.65	5.36	1.67	1.28	1.36	5.11	1.48	11.15	7.48	1.19
Samoa	862	1.89	1.95	1.99	2.04	2.10	2.14	2.19	2.24	2.29	2.34	2.38	2.40
Singapore	576	49.43	56.92	24.13	33.05	42.48	52.25	64.91	89.23	105.32	119.56	130.19	139.61
Solomon Islands	813	.04	.03	.01	–	.01	–	–	.01	–	.01	–	–
Sri Lanka	524	.05	.28	.24	.62	1.34	.31	.89	.70	.31	.68	1.72	.42
Thailand	578	8.78	15.95	21.84	30.46	41.50	357.56	277.86	188.06	63.43	4.19	3.09	.24
Tonga	866	.38	.44	.49	.04	.08	.11	.15	.03	.10	.15	.19	.22
Vanuatu	846	.68	.15	.22	.29	.36	.44	.53	.60	.70	.79	.84	.89
Vietnam	582	–	4.92	11.03	2.20	11.91	9.44	1.79	1.06	.25	11.59	.03	1.46
Europe	170	103.4	270.1	373.6	636.8	511.5	784.2	730.0	568.0	558.1	480.8	276.4	294.6
Albania	914	.04	.01	.20	.10	.52	.46	43.39	56.06	58.33	64.87	60.02	60.98
Armenia	911	–	–	.19	29.82	28.86	27.63	19.89	29.64	16.54	8.15	22.14	12.67
Azerbaijan	912	–	–	–	.84	14.48	4.14	.08	5.15	5.07	1.98	.51	12.14
Belarus	913	–	3.22	.01	3.05	.10	–	.30	.30	.14	.31	.19	.02
Bosnia and Herzegovina	963	–	–	–	5.05	1.84	–	3.71	5.59	8.18	4.86	2.31	2.29
Bulgaria	918	.32	.83	10.39	20.08	8.31	8.37	21.38	59.53	64.97	1.80	.55	45.54
Croatia	960	–	.82	3.09	94.40	87.31	109.00	164.19	138.07	113.01	85.49	1.10	.03
Cyprus	423	.06	.07	.11	.03	.03	.25	.20	.40	.77	1.13	1.53	1.99
Czech Republic	935	–	5.98	–	.12	–	–	–	–	.16	.68	3.36	6.28
Czechoslovakia	934	30.77	....	....	....	....	....	....	....	....	....	....	....
Estonia	939	7.72	41.56	1.09	.20	.12	.01	.05	.99	.01	.03	.05	.05
Georgia	915	–	–	1.61	1.12	.05	.10	3.69	6.13	2.51	3.15	2.13	3.31
Hungary	944	1.88	2.14	1.08	.58	.35	.13	.52	3.19	8.97	16.36	24.07	31.20
Kazakhstan	916	–	13.98	69.54	154.87	240.19	327.15	275.08	164.24	.01	–	.76	.78
Kyrgyz Republic	917	–	9.37	.65	9.59	5.14	.70	.24	3.71	.54	1.05	.47	6.94
Latvia	941	19.33	71.10	.21	1.49	1.56	1.50	.21	2.24	–	.07	.05	.09
Lithuania	946	.94	54.71	10.38	12.22	7.09	7.95	11.50	3.19	1.01	14.67	39.31	.04
Macedonia, FYR	962	–	.01	.01	.15	.03	.28	.76	.87	.50	1.77	4.50	.19
Malta	181	33.11	35.25	35.62	37.64	39.75	41.91	44.36	22.49	24.51	26.39	28.94	29.84
Moldova	921	–	25.05	14.62	8.81	5.45	.89	.50	.23	.26	.59	.02	.03
Poland	964	.77	.52	1.02	1.51	3.08	3.99	5.02	8.13	13.60	20.54	29.04	36.89
Romania	968	7.90	1.37	38.14	37.72	2.82	76.95	.83	7.34	.75	5.42	1.69	.18
Russia	922	.56	3.65	2.11	78.53	3.13	90.68	.05	.41	.41	2.29	.88	.49
Serbia and Montenegro	965	–	–	–	–	–	–	–	–	15.22	6.81	.70	.26
Slovak Republic	936	–	.25	58.89	39.00	11.24	19.59	1.19	.57	.37	.53	.85	.86
Slovenia	961	–	.03	.04	.04	.09	.05	.17	1.17	2.83	4.00	5.13	6.18
Tajikistan	923	–	–	–	–	2.21	9.06	2.05	.04	6.02	3.86	1.34	.57
Turkey	186	.03	.13	.82	1.93	.98	.58	.97	.06	21.88	3.56	23.01	20.46
Turkmenistan	925	–	–	–	–	–	–	–	–	–	–	–	–
Ukraine	926	–	–	123.73	97.06	46.72	52.70	129.53	47.86	191.19	199.80	20.81	14.27
Uzbekistan	927	–	–	–	.81	.03	.09	.16	.41	.30	.61	.79	.07
Yugoslavia, SFR	188	....	....	....	....	....	....	....	....	....	....	....	....
Middle East	405	765.4	1,014.4	1,090.4	1,165.0	1,397.5	1,556.0	1,424.9	829.9	1,041.1	1,076.7	1,211.3	1,316.5
Bahrain, Kingdom of	419	18.72	10.77	11.01	11.28	11.68	11.90	12.15	.03	1.03	.84	.77	.68
Egypt	469	42.80	50.43	59.19	69.51	85.57	83.92	113.80	30.07	36.94	27.68	67.24	127.01
Iran, I.R. of	429	7.37	104.85	97.91	89.88	239.76	244.62	1.12	101.26	267.49	267.40	267.96	268.41
Iraq	433	–	–	–	–	–	–	–	–	–	–	–	–
Israel	436	.22	.39	.24	.38	.95	.03	.20	.11	.83	1.37	3.36	6.39
Jordan	439	.40	3.99	.46	.82	.57	.14	.55	.19	.47	.93	.63	.75
Kuwait	443	130.35	49.07	55.02	61.28	68.15	74.14	82.51	53.74	69.79	85.90	97.74	107.51
Lebanon	446	9.48	10.51	11.35	12.34	13.34	14.33	15.44	16.38	18.21	19.37	20.10	20.64

2004, International Monetary Fund : *International Financial Statistics Yearbook*

SDRs

		1992	1993	1994	1995	1996	1997	1998	1999	2000	2001	2002	2003
1b s						*Millions of SDRs: End of Period*							
Middle East(Cont.)													
Libya	672	278.28	303.46	324.75	349.69	373.87	398.47	425.79	372.59	412.77	441.19	448.87	461.97
Oman	449	3.39	4.96	6.17	7.49	8.84	10.10	11.47	1.33	3.12	5.02	6.53	7.81
Qatar	453	17.05	18.66	19.88	21.21	22.52	23.76	25.11	10.67	15.85	17.90	19.98	21.75
Saudi Arabia	456	202.02	402.69	415.98	448.24	481.28	512.14	545.95	110.45	146.57	192.27	243.89	289.75
Syrian Arab Rep.	463	–	.02	–	–	.01	.01	.05	.05	.01	.32	.02	.04
United Arab Emirates	466	52.42	54.14	54.99	55.91	57.60	58.36	59.19	4.55	3.08	1.76	1.13	.48
Yemen, Republic of	474	2.88	.47	33.49	37.01	33.34	124.06	131.55	128.48	64.96	14.71	33.04	3.29
Western Hemisphere	205	858.6	1,075.7	1,045.1	1,963.5	1,049.0	1,027.6	801.7	1,032.3	1,146.4	594.5	866.3	1,279.9
ECCU (incl. ECCB hqtrs.)	309	3.24	3.24	3.36	3.47	3.60	3.67	3.80	3.89	3.91	4.02	4.07	4.11
Antigua and Barbuda	311	–	–	–	–	–	–	–	.01	.01	.01	.01	.01
Dominica	321	.07	–	–	–	–	–	–	.01	–	–	–	–
Grenada	328	–	–	.02	.02	.04	–	.03	–	–	–	–	–
St. Kitts and Nevis	361	–	–	–	–	–	–	–	–	–	.01	–	–
St. Lucia	362	1.31	1.34	1.36	1.39	1.42	1.45	1.48	1.50	1.43	1.46	1.48	1.49
St. Vincent & Grens.	364	.09	.09	.09	.08	.07	.07	.07	.06	.06	.03	.02	–
Argentina	213	272.82	329.45	385.68	362.67	277.42	123.58	187.73	100.34	562.21	8.49	69.28	678.68
Bahamas, The	313	.02	.01	.01	.02	.01	.02	.02	.02	.09	.09	.08	.01
Barbados	316	.11	.05	.03	.03	.02	.02	.02	.01	.02	.04	.04	.01
Belize	339	.15	.29	.37	.47	.61	.71	.82	1.01	1.20	1.37	1.48	1.56
Bolivia	218	.06	10.19	16.99	26.88	26.81	26.81	26.81	27.27	27.29	27.32	27.35	27.13
Brazil	223	.80	1.65	.30	.68	.66	.37	1.24	7.32	.27	8.42	202.07	1.54
Chile	228	.47	.92	.45	2.07	1.33	.96	5.86	13.48	18.89	23.02	26.87	30.72
Colombia	233	42.48	114.88	116.38	118.83	122.83	127.64	139.34	95.18	103.32	107.81	113.15	115.19
Costa Rica	238	.17	.12	.12	.04	.01	.02	.05	.59	.33	.07	.06	.04
Dominican Republic	243	.07	10.28	2.53	.35	.29	.23	.19	.21	.27	.35	.21	.09
Ecuador	248	.08	3.15	2.97	2.11	1.87	.41	.20	1.70	.24	1.85	1.38	.67
El Salvador	253	.01	.01	.07	24.99	24.99	24.98	24.98	24.98	24.98	24.98	24.98	24.98
Guatemala	258	11.36	11.43	11.38	10.60	10.15	9.44	8.65	8.36	7.52	6.73	6.06	5.53
Guyana	336	.24	–	.05	.09	.07	.14	.17	.92	7.02	1.96	3.43	3.26
Haiti	263	–	–	–	.36	.03	.06	.39	.62	.05	.41	.37	.23
Honduras	268	.11	.11	.15	.10	.06	.06	.05	.68	.08	.25	.35	.08
Jamaica	343	8.98	9.06	.02	.31	.05	.17	.46	.53	.07	1.19	.66	.04
Mexico	273	398.81	162.65	121.13	1,074.05	178.69	490.13	239.65	575.45	281.23	283.47	288.02	291.64
Nicaragua	278	.06	.03	.01	–	.02	.03	.15	.16	.05	.26	.02	.04
Panama	283	3.33	.09	.03	.55	.03	.37	.10	1.20	.27	1.10	.78	.56
Paraguay	288	62.12	65.08	67.63	70.58	73.30	76.08	79.14	74.81	78.49	81.33	83.25	84.63
Peru	293	.02	.69	.31	.50	.22	.17	1.48	.28	1.15	1.39	.55	.27
Suriname	366	–	–	–	7.75	8.22	8.23	8.25	2.00	1.77	1.56	1.42	1.32
Trinidad and Tobago	369	.24	.24	.08	.15	.03	.10	.08	–	.06	.16	.29	.74
Uruguay	298	.01	.29	.02	2.39	2.75	.03	.53	.71	.36	1.47	4.16	2.52
Venezuela, Rep. Bol.	299	54.61	353.61	316.94	255.38	316.98	135.27	73.73	92.89	27.69	7.92	8.41	6.98
Memorandum Items													
Oil Exporting Countries	999	746.3	1,296.7	1,307.6	1,291.2	1,574.4	1,827.8	1,448.0	749.3	973.4	1,041.7	1,118.5	1,205.5
Non-Oil Developing Countries	201	1,652.6	1,863.1	1,968.0	3,483.5	2,426.0	3,192.9	3,087.7	2,981.4	3,104.5	2,547.4	2,762.4	3,403.3

SDR Holdings

Millions of SDRs: End of Period

		1992	1993	1994	1995	1996	1997	1998	1999	2000	2001	2002	2003
World	001	21,480.1	21,480.9	21,476.9	21,484.5	21,495.2	21,508.2	21,522.1	21,534.8	21,527.5	21,539.5	21,525.8	21,521.2
All Participants	969	12,867.2	14,614.3	15,761.5	19,773.2	18,521.4	20,532.2	20,379.7	18,456.7	18,489.0	19,556.8	19,672.7	19,914.6
IMF	992	8,561.22	6,687.28	5,510.08	652.47	1,726.32	634.78	687.34	2,459.29	2,413.89	1,543.19	1,201.69	1,087.86
Other Holders	970	51.72	179.36	205.33	1,058.87	1,247.41	341.26	455.05	618.86	624.58	439.53	651.43	518.69

Reserve Position in the Fund

Millions of SDRs: End of Period

		1992	1993	1994	1995	1996	1997	1998	1999	2000	2001	2002	2003
All Countries	010	33,902.8	32,802.2	31,725.6	36,673.2	38,005.3	47,078.0	60,630.9	54,785.6	47,377.7	56,861.3	66,064.6	66,507.8
Industrial Countries	110	29,510.6	28,308.8	27,417.0	31,643.8	32,609.8	41,336.5	53,919.2	46,775.8	39,699.5	46,960.1	53,717.1	52,584.4
United States	111	8,552.3	8,589.0	8,240.8	9,854.7	10,733.8	13,393.4	17,124.1	13,092.9	11,377.3	14,219.0	16,166.5	15,164.9
Canada	156	734.92	689.95	629.18	836.15	852.79	1,167.32	1,632.72	2,307.95	1,925.85	2,278.39	2,633.36	2,588.94
Australia	193	419.70	400.48	346.86	337.62	334.89	538.98	892.26	1,189.43	953.89	1,123.59	1,422.89	1,381.33
Japan	158	6,284.31	6,014.52	5,912.26	5,448.95	4,639.25	6,777.41	6,813.09	4,773.53	4,032.09	4,018.95	5,298.43	5,204.18
New Zealand	196	109.08	103.62	100.82	110.33	126.63	131.92	252.82	308.57	245.68	308.25	337.91	433.07
Euro Area													
Austria	122	389.84	381.49	363.86	458.91	562.40	713.73	969.69	698.68	531.46	662.48	705.16	770.73
Belgium	124	586.00	560.17	556.33	675.81	747.30	875.80	1,348.36	1,668.38	1,303.84	1,631.74	1,759.41	1,812.32
Finland	172	240.96	220.39	196.13	259.51	292.84	414.15	594.98	464.32	381.84	438.98	476.83	522.09
France	132	1,804.85	1,681.77	1,626.73	1,853.88	1,874.51	2,119.18	3,161.79	3,949.93	3,470.99	3,893.91	4,249.92	4,241.98
Germany	134	3,083.23	2,876.62	2,760.48	3,504.97	3,802.51	4,406.90	5,698.26	4,676.60	4,191.00	4,695.84	4,924.84	5,152.31
Greece	174	116.85	113.69	113.69	113.69	113.69	113.69	191.49	284.98	227.82	284.31	322.45	334.26
Ireland	178	171.31	155.08	151.93	197.47	226.07	252.15	413.56	302.94	252.37	267.68	345.25	386.68
Italy	136	1,774.07	1,575.39	1,392.80	1,320.60	1,289.87	1,660.68	3,075.29	2,583.58	2,230.13	2,559.73	2,874.12	2,795.77
Luxembourg	137	25.85	23.58	23.61	22.94	23.56	21.75	59.37	54.37	55.47	78.95	104.75	120.26
Netherlands	138	833.97	795.25	802.16	1,169.12	1,275.26	1,625.48	2,112.77	1,879.77	1,524.06	1,871.66	2,095.25	2,055.01
Portugal	182	228.31	219.42	230.80	302.98	320.31	313.36	442.12	274.96	242.38	299.42	329.07	360.82
Spain	184	831.73	750.60	759.53	1,064.90	1,110.30	1,409.46	1,557.62	1,111.18	907.54	1,055.08	1,170.75	1,253.37
Denmark	128	345.71	309.15	294.59	400.00	421.81	467.92	827.45	582.07	440.12	566.83	721.96	686.33
Iceland	176	10.47	10.48	10.48	10.48	10.49	10.49	10.50	18.58	18.58	18.58	18.58	18.58
Norway	142	471.37	425.50	440.93	636.16	643.80	725.52	899.13	621.23	448.09	577.34	729.81	669.50
San Marino	135	—	2.35	2.35	2.35	2.35	2.35	2.35	4.10	4.10	4.10	4.10	4.10
Sweden	144	451.36	451.42	451.42	451.43	451.43	589.10	899.90	862.95	683.33	827.12	1,050.33	988.12
Switzerland	146	580.89	604.54	643.21	981.22	1,064.90	1,407.48	1,828.05	1,218.12	963.67	1,258.68	1,410.04	1,383.44
United Kingdom	112	1,463.6	1,354.4	1,366.1	1,629.5	1,689.1	2,198.2	3,111.3	3,846.7	3,287.9	4,019.5	4,565.4	4,256.3
Developing Countries	200	4,392.1	4,493.4	4,308.6	5,029.4	5,395.4	5,741.5	6,711.7	8,009.8	7,678.1	9,901.1	12,347.5	13,923.4
Africa	605	157.0	157.6	157.6	151.0	152.0	150.5	159.4	335.5	290.0	289.5	291.5	306.0
CEMAC (incl. BEAC hqtrs.)	758	1.17	1.23	1.23	1.28	1.35	1.39	1.43	1.52	1.59	1.65	1.70	1.80
Cameroon	622	.29	.34	.34	.36	.37	.41	.45	.50	.52	.54	.58	.64
Central African Rep.	626	.09	.09	.09	.09	.09	.10	.12	.10	.11	.11	.12	.16
Chad	628	.27	.28	.28	.28	.28	.28	.28	.28	.28	.28	.28	.28
Congo, Rep. of	634	.47	.47	.47	.50	.54	.54	.54	.54	.54	.54	.54	.54
Equatorial Guinea	642	—	—	—	—	—	—	—	—	—	—	—	—
Gabon	646	.05	.05	.05	.05	.07	.07	.07	.11	.15	.18	.18	.18
WAEMU (incl. BCEAO hqtrs.)	759	27.82	28.00	28.07	28.19	28.33	28.46	28.54	28.62	28.71	28.86	29.05	29.29
Benin	638	2.06	2.09	2.10	2.13	2.16	2.18	2.18	2.19	2.19	2.19	2.19	2.19
Burkina Faso	748	7.20	7.20	7.20	7.22	7.22	7.22	7.22	7.22	7.22	7.23	7.26	7.28
Côte d'Ivoire	662	.01	.07	.09	.09	.11	.17	.19	.24	.28	.31	.45	.57
Guinea Bissau	654	—	—	—	—	—	—	—	—	—	—	—	—
Mali	678	8.69	8.73	8.73	8.73	8.76	8.76	8.78	8.78	8.78	8.83	8.83	8.88
Niger	692	8.56	8.56	8.56	8.56	8.56	8.56	8.56	8.56	8.56	8.56	8.56	8.56
Senegal	722	1.05	1.10	1.14	1.20	1.27	1.33	1.35	1.37	1.40	1.44	1.45	1.48
Togo	742	.25	.25	.25	.25	.25	.25	.25	.25	.28	.30	.31	.33
Algeria	612	—	.01	.01	.01	.01	.01	.01	85.08	85.08	85.08	85.08	85.08
Angola	614												
Botswana	616	14.79	16.60	16.34	19.28	19.91	18.13	27.61	22.59	17.74	22.28	23.80	30.32
Burundi	618	5.86	5.86	5.86	5.86	5.86	5.86	5.86	5.86	5.86	.36	.36	.36
Cape Verde	624												
Comoros	632	.50	.50	.52	.54	.54	.54	.54	.54	.54	.54	.54	.54
Congo, Dem. Rep. of	636	—	—	—	—	—	—	—	—	—	—	—	—
Djibouti	611	2.11	—	—	—	—	—	—	1.10	1.10	1.10	1.10	1.10
Eritrea	643				.01	.01	.01	.01	.01	.01	.01	.01	.01
Ethiopia	644	6.93	6.99	7.01	7.03	7.05	7.08	7.10	7.10	7.10	7.12	7.17	7.19
Gambia, The	648	1.48	1.49	1.48	1.48	1.48	1.48	1.48	1.48	1.48	1.48	1.48	1.48
Ghana	652	17.38	17.38	17.38	17.38	17.38	17.38	17.38	41.13	—	—	—	—
Guinea	656	.03	.07	.07	.07	.08	.08	.08	.08	.08	.08	.08	.08
Kenya	664	12.22	12.23	12.31	12.31	12.32	12.36	12.42	12.43	12.45	12.54	12.58	12.68
Lesotho	666	3.51	3.51	3.51	3.51	3.51	3.52	3.53	3.53	3.54	3.54	3.54	3.54
Liberia	668	.03	.03	.03	.03	.03	.03	.03	.03	.03	.03	.03	.03
Madagascar	674			.01	.02	.02	.03	.03	.03	.03	.03	.03	.03
Malawi	676	2.22	2.22	2.22	2.22	2.22	2.22	2.24	2.24	2.24	2.27	2.28	2.29
Mauritania	682												
Mauritius	684	6.22	7.33	7.33	7.34	7.37	7.37	7.38	14.47	14.47	14.47	14.48	21.88
Morocco	686	30.31	30.31	30.31	30.31	30.32	30.32	30.32	70.44	70.44	70.44	70.44	70.44
Mozambique	688	.01	.01	.01	.01	.01	.01	.01	.01	.01	.01	.01	.01
Namibia	728	.01	.01	.01	.02	.03	.03	.04	.04	.04	.04	.05	.05
Nigeria	694	.07	.07	.07	.07	.07	.07	.07	.09	.14	.14	.14	.14
Rwanda	714	10.40	9.79	9.79	—	—	—	—	—	—	—	—	—
São Tomé & Príncipe	716	—	—	—	—	—	—	—	—	—	—	—	—
Seychelles	718	.80	.80	.80	.80	.80	.80	—	—	—	—	—	—
Sierra Leone	724	.02	.02	.02	.02	.02	.02	.02	.02	.02	.02	.02	.02
Somalia	726												
South Africa	199	.05	.05	.05	.06	.10	.10	.11	.11	.27	.35	.42	.50
Sudan	732	.01	.01	.01	.01	.01	.01	.01	.01	.01	.01	.01	.01
Swaziland	734	3.00	3.00	3.00	3.00	3.00	3.00	3.00	6.55	6.55	6.55	6.55	6.55
Tanzania	738	9.98	9.98	9.98	9.98	9.98	9.98	9.98	9.98	9.98	9.98	9.99	10.00

2004, International Monetary Fund: *International Financial Statistics Yearbook*

Reserve Position in the Fund

Millions of SDRs: End of Period

		1992	1993	1994	1995	1996	1997	1998	1999	2000	2001	2002	2003
Africa(Cont.)													
Tunisia	744	.02	.04	.04	.04	.04	.04	.04	20.17	20.17	20.17	20.17	20.20
Uganda	746	–	–	–	–	–	–	–	–	–	–	–	–
Zambia	754	.02	.02	.02	.02	.02	.02	.02	.02	.02	.02	.02	.02
Zimbabwe	698	.05	.07	.07	.10	.11	.15	.19	.27	.31	.33	.33	.33
Asia	505	**2,009.0**	**2,056.7**	**2,173.8**	**2,848.4**	**3,142.2**	**3,201.8**	**3,680.0**	**3,643.0**	**3,355.3**	**4,013.9**	**4,910.5**	**5,359.9**
Afghanistan, Islamic State of	512	4.93	4.93	4.93	4.93	4.93	4.93	4.93	4.93	4.93	4.93	4.93	–
Bangladesh	513	–	.06	.07	.09	.11	.11	.16	.19	.19	.19	.19	.19
Bhutan	514	.57	.57	.57	.57	.57	.57	.57	1.02	1.02	1.02	1.02	1.02
Brunei Darussalam	516	–	–	–	–	35.26	35.26	35.26	35.28	35.28	35.28	51.79	58.29
Cambodia	522	.93	–	–	–	–	–	–	–	–	–	–	–
China, P.R.: Mainland	924	551.18	512.77	517.31	817.78	970.97	1,682.40	2,523.33	1,684.72	1,462.33	2,060.54	2,738.22	2,555.95
China, P.R.: Hong Kong	532	–	–	–	–	–	–	31.34	–	–	–	–	–
Fiji	819	10.43	9.95	9.99	10.00	10.05	10.08	10.12	14.94	14.98	15.00	15.07	15.19
India	534	212.57	212.63	212.63	212.63	212.63	212.63	212.79	488.57	488.64	488.78	488.88	887.01
Indonesia	536	194.40	199.70	213.99	270.00	298.00	–	.05	145.47	145.48	145.48	145.50	145.50
Kiribati	826	–	–	–	–	–	–	–	–	–	–	.02	.01
Korea	542	319.05	339.17	363.61	438.49	474.30	443.72	.06	208.60	208.64	208.83	383.99	507.66
Lao P. D. Rep.	544	–	–	–	–	–	–	–	–	–	–	–	–
Malaysia	548	240.25	229.07	273.70	456.34	478.20	444.68	444.68	608.16	608.16	608.16	581.22	586.19
Maldives	556	.88	.88	.88	.88	.88	.88	.88	1.55	1.55	1.55	1.55	1.55
Marshall Islands, Rep. of	867	–	–	–	–	–	–	–	–	–	–	–	–
Micronesia, Fed. States of	868	–	–	.001	.001	.001	.001	.001	.001	.001	.001	.001	.001
Mongolia	948	.01	.01	–	–	–	–	–	.02	.04	.06	.08	.10
Myanmar	518	–	–	–	–	–	–	–	–	–	–	–	–
Nepal	558	5.71	5.73	5.73	5.73	5.73	5.73	5.73	5.73	5.75	5.75	5.75	5.77
Pakistan	564	.06	.06	.06	.06	.06	.06	.06	.10	.10	.11	.12	–
Palau	565	–	–	–	–	–	–	–	–	–	–	–	.12
Papua New Guinea	853	.04	.05	.05	.05	.05	.05	.05	.05	.18	.30	.36	.40
Philippines	566	87.08	87.10	87.10	87.10	87.10	87.10	87.10	87.10	87.10	87.18	87.28	87.36
Samoa	862	.66	.66	.66	.67	.67	.68	.68	.68	.68	.68	.69	.69
Singapore	576	113.41	157.44	172.84	199.85	204.73	248.42	297.65	303.44	237.71	297.50	351.29	379.27
Solomon Islands	813	.54	.54	.54	.54	.54	.54	.54	.54	.54	.54	.55	.55
Sri Lanka	524	20.19	20.21	20.25	20.25	20.25	20.25	20.25	47.71	47.74	47.79	47.82	47.86
Thailand	578	243.31	271.52	285.15	318.69	333.47	.02	.02	.02	.02	.02	.02	75.02
Tonga	866	1.18	1.19	1.20	1.21	1.21	1.21	1.22	1.70	1.71	1.71	1.71	1.71
Vanuatu	846	1.61	2.49	2.49	2.49	2.49	2.50	2.50	2.50	2.50	2.50	2.50	2.50
Vietnam	582	.01	.01	.01	.01	.01	.01	.01	.01	.01	.01	.01	.01
Europe	170	**255.7**	**262.9**	**262.8**	**264.6**	**268.2**	**269.2**	**302.8**	**653.1**	**665.3**	**1,099.4**	**1,418.3**	**1,662.6**
Albania	914	–	–	–	–	–	–	–	3.4	3.4	3.4	3.4	3.4
Armenia	911	.01	.01	.01	.01	.01	–	–	–	–	–	–	–
Azerbaijan	912	–	.01	.01	.01	.01	.01	.01	.01	.01	.01	.01	.01
Belarus	913	.02	.02	.02	.02	.02	.02	.02	.02	.02	.02	.02	.02
Bosnia and Herzegovina	963	–	–	–	–	–	–	–	–	–	–	–	–
Bulgaria	918	38.73	32.63	32.63	32.63	32.63	32.63	32.63	32.69	32.74	32.78	32.78	32.78
Croatia	960	–	–	–	–	.03	.07	.11	.14	.16	.16	.16	.16
Cyprus	423	25.45	25.45	25.45	25.45	25.45	25.45	25.45	35.36	35.37	35.37	49.11	66.82
Czech Republic	935	–	–	–	–	–	–	–	–	2.35	120.45	173.45	314.61
Czechoslovakia	934	–	–	....	....	....	....	....	....	....	....	....	....
Estonia	939	–	–	.01	.01	.01	.01	.01	.01	.01	.01	.01	.01
Georgia	915	.01	.01	.01	.01	.01	.01	.01	.01	.01	.01	.01	.01
Hungary	944	56.10	56.10	56.10	56.10	56.10	56.10	56.10	176.78	201.78	321.95	437.47	454.95
Kazakhstan	916	.01	.01	.01	.01	.01	.01	.01	.01	.01	.01	.01	.01
Kyrgyz Republic	917	.01	.01	.01	–	–	–	–	–	–	–	–	–
Latvia	941	.01	.01	.01	.01	.01	.01	.01	.01	.06	.06	.06	.06
Lithuania	946	.01	.01	.01	.01	.01	.01	.02	.02	.02	.02	.02	.02
Macedonia, FYR	962	–	–	–	–	–	–	–	–	–	–	–	–
Malta	181	25.32	25.28	25.44	27.26	30.66	31.64	31.64	40.26	40.26	40.26	40.26	40.26
Moldova	921	.01	.01	.01	.01	.01	.01	.01	.01	.01	.01	–	.01
Poland	964	77.13	77.13	77.13	77.13	77.13	77.13	77.13	172.26	172.26	366.84	478.86	537.97
Romania	968	–	–	–	–	–	–	–	–	–	–	–	–
Russia	922	.54	1.01	.84	.77	.93	.93	.93	.93	.93	1.14	1.18	1.43
Serbia and Montenegro	965	–	–	–	–	–	–	–	–	–	–	–	–
Slovak Republic	936	–	–	–	–	–	–	–	–	–	–	–	–
Slovenia	961	–	12.88	12.87	12.88	12.88	12.88	46.46	78.40	63.19	64.16	88.77	97.34
Tajikistan	923	–	–	–	–	–	–	–	–	–	–	–	–
Turkey	186	32.27	32.28	32.27	32.28	32.28	32.28	32.28	112.77	112.78	112.78	112.78	112.78
Turkmenistan	925	–	.01	.01	–	–	–	–	–	–	–	–	–
Ukraine	926	.01	.01	.01	–	–	.01	.01	–	–	–	–	–
Uzbekistan	927	–	.01	.01	.01	.01	.01	.01	.01	.01	.01	.01	.01
Yugoslavia, SFR	188	–	–	–	–	–	–	–	–	–	–	–	–
Middle East	405	**1,667.2**	**1,703.3**	**1,396.5**	**1,399.0**	**1,401.7**	**1,393.2**	**1,500.1**	**2,325.2**	**2,365.1**	**3,474.4**	**4,345.6**	**4,828.7**
Bahrain, Kingdom of	419	31.07	40.90	42.19	43.70	45.09	46.70	48.51	62.37	64.86	67.18	68.62	69.70
Egypt	469	53.75	53.75	53.75	53.75	53.75	53.75	53.75	120.08	120.08	–	–	–
Iran, I.R. of	429	104.63	–	–	–	–	–	–	–	–	–	–	–
Iraq	433	–	–	–	–	–	–	–	–	–	–	–	–
Israel	436	–	–	–	–	–	.01	.01	65.51	89.91	157.36	304.01	354.79
Jordan	439	11.95	–	–	–	–	–	–	–	.01	.05	.05	.05
Kuwait	443	96.65	167.78	142.59	138.95	136.53	167.55	244.76	368.30	373.80	476.07	528.29	522.74
Lebanon	446	18.83	18.83	18.83	18.83	18.83	18.83	18.83	18.83	18.83	18.83	18.83	18.83
Libya	672	318.98	318.98	318.98	318.98	318.98	318.98	318.98	395.51	395.51	395.51	395.51	395.51

2004, International Monetary Fund: *International Financial Statistics Yearbook*

Reserve Position in the Fund

Millions of SDRs: End of Period

		1992	1993	1994	1995	1996	1997	1998	1999	2000	2001	2002	2003
Middle East(Cont.)													
Oman	449	39.36	37.84	35.98	34.47	33.97	31.15	31.15	49.80	49.80	64.96	73.41	77.57
Qatar	453	36.42	33.80	30.65	29.73	29.23	26.40	26.40	44.73	44.73	79.11	99.59	103.46
Saudi Arabia	456	797.3	868.6	604.3	574.7	560.9	532.5	523.8	987.5	1,042.7	2,035.5	2,621.4	3,046.8
Syrian Arab Rep	463	.01	.01	.01	.01	.01	.01	.01	.01	.01	.01	.01	.01
United Arab Emirates	466	158.29	162.82	149.12	185.81	204.37	197.37	233.89	212.55	164.82	179.79	235.83	239.30
Yemen, Republic of	474	.01	.01	.01	.01	.01	.01	.01	.01	.01	.01	.01	.01
Western Hemisphere	205	303.3	313.0	318.0	366.5	431.4	726.8	1,069.3	1,053.0	1,002.5	1,024.0	1,381.6	1,766.2
ECCU (incl. ECCB hqtrs.)	309	.52	.53	.53	.53	.53	.53	.53	.58	.59	.59	.59	.60
Antigua and Barbuda	311	–	–	–	–	–	–	–	–	–	–	–	.01
Dominica	321	.01	.01	.01	.01	.01	.01	.01	.01	.01	.01	.01	.01
Grenada	328	–	–	–	–	–	–	–	–	–	–	–	–
St. Kitts and Nevis	361	.01	.02	.01	.01	.01	.01	.01	.07	.08	.08	.08	.08
St. Lucia	362	–	–	–	–	–	–	–	–	–	–	–	.01
St. Vincent & Grens	364	.50	.50	.50	.50	.50	.50	.50	.50	.50	.50	.50	.50
Argentina	213	–	–	–	–	–	–	–	–	–	–	.02	.06
Bahamas, The	313	6.84	6.24	6.24	6.24	6.24	6.24	6.24	6.24	6.24	6.24	6.24	6.25
Barbados	316	.03	.03	.03	.03	.03	.03	.03	4.68	4.68	4.71	4.85	5.02
Belize	339	2.91	2.91	2.91	2.91	2.91	2.91	2.91	4.24	4.24	4.24	4.24	4.24
Bolivia	218	8.88	8.88	8.87	8.87	8.87	8.87	8.87	8.87	8.87	8.87	8.87	8.87
Brazil	223	–	–	–	–	–	–	–	–	–	–	–	–
Chile	228	.01	.01	.02	.02	35.03	232.03	429.63	299.43	248.82	245.66	360.93	392.29
Colombia	233	69.03	79.81	86.75	135.26	165.06	263.41	408.28	285.80	285.80	285.80	285.80	285.80
Costa Rica	238	8.73	8.73	8.73	8.73	8.73	8.73	8.73	20.00	20.00	20.00	20.00	20.00
Dominican Republic	243	–	–	–	–	–	–	–	–	–	–	–	–
Ecuador	248	17.13	17.13	17.13	17.15	17.15	17.15	17.15	17.15	17.15	17.15	17.15	17.15
El Salvador	253	–	–	–	–	–	–	–	–	–	–	–	–
Guatemala	258	–	–	–	–	–	–	–	–	–	–	–	–
Guyana	336	–	–	–	–	–	–	–	–	–	–	–	–
Haiti	263	.05	.05	.05	.05	.05	.05	.05	.05	.06	.06	.07	.07
Honduras	268	–	–	–	–	–	–	–	8.63	8.63	8.63	8.63	8.63
Jamaica	343	–	–	–	–	–	–	–	–	–	–	–	–
Mexico	273	–	–	–	.03	.12	.12	.21	.27	.32	.39	226.46	526.53
Nicaragua	278	–	–	–	–	–	–	–	–	–	–	–	–
Panama	283	11.86	11.86	11.86	11.86	11.86	11.86	11.86	11.86	11.86	11.86	11.86	11.86
Paraguay	288	16.94	16.48	14.53	14.53	14.53	14.53	14.53	21.48	21.48	21.48	21.48	21.48
Peru	293	–	–	–	–	–	–	–	6.13	6.13	6.13	6.13	6.12
Suriname	366	–	–	–	–	–	–	–	–	–	–	–	–
Trinidad and Tobago	369	.01	.01	.01	.01	.01	.01	.02	.02	.02	24.57	76.37	129.32
Uruguay	298	15.38	15.38	15.38	15.38	15.38	15.38	15.38	35.68	35.68	35.68	–	–
Venezuela, Rep. Bol.	299	144.95	144.95	144.95	144.95	144.95	144.95	144.95	321.90	321.90	321.90	321.90	321.90
Memorandum Items													
Oil Exporting Countries	999	1,891.0	1,934.5	1,640.7	1,697.7	1,727.0	1,418.9	1,524.0	2,610.9	2,623.9	3,783.6	4,506.7	4,938.0
Non-Oil Developing Countries	201	2,501.1	2,558.9	2,667.9	3,331.8	3,668.4	4,322.6	5,187.6	5,398.9	5,054.2	6,117.6	7,840.8	8,985.5

Foreign Exchange

Millions of SDRs: End of Period

		1992	1993	1994	1995	1996	1997	1998	1999	2000	2001	2002	2003
All Countries	010	674,523	752,320	812,798	934,855	1,089,123	1,197,802	1,167,138	1,297,908	1,485,573	1,628,033	1,763,318	2,028,203
Industrial Countries	110	356,767	373,768	394,037	441,184	501,813	520,984	475,950	526,204	596,315	620,605	653,163	742,725
United States	111	29,095	30,237	28,233	33,028	26,631	22,834	25,568	23,448	23,976	23,061	24,875	26,731
Canada	156	6,823	7,623	7,000	8,496	12,537	11,208	14,141	17,801	22,136	24,257	24,042	21,223
Australia	193	7,662	7,623	7,334	7,628	9,713	11,932	9,493	14,213	12,880	13,077	13,694	20,166
Japan	158	45,009	64,591	78,875	116,007	144,187	154,060	144,326	202,336	266,490	308,521	332,072	439,302
New Zealand	196	2,130	2,326	2,439	2,856	4,013	3,167	2,731	2,933	2,300	2,073	2,396	2,852
Euro Area (incl. ECB)	163	....	....	....	....	....	....	....	166,111	167,802	165,440	158,741	126,524
Austria	122	8,368	10,095	10,966	12,020	15,203	13,789	14,856	10,212	10,355	9,106	6,281	4,807
Belgium	124	9,327	7,625	8,826	9,876	10,696	10,761	11,195	†6,104	6,131	6,957	6,553	5,149
Finland	172	3,472	3,635	6,885	6,252	4,315	5,582	6,043	5,313	5,634	5,727	6,206	6,423
France	132	17,734	14,567	16,111	15,568	16,078	20,083	27,523	24,724	24,648	20,978	16,156	15,560
Germany	134	62,463	52,948	49,470	52,334	52,716	51,772	45,548	†38,368	38,120	34,781	31,258	27,656
Greece	174	3,369	5,558	9,810	9,829	12,057	9,221	12,207	12,915	10,066	†3,809	5,612	2,586
Ireland	178	2,240	4,062	3,935	5,501	5,365	4,462	6,123	3,548	3,824	4,134	3,589	2,305
Italy	136	18,157	18,303	20,623	22,161	30,643	39,601	18,073	†13,630	17,210	16,635	18,086	17,534
Luxembourg	137	21	18	21	20	20	18	....	–	–	–	–	60
Netherlands	138	14,718	21,600	22,411	20,895	16,773	16,217	12,455	4,581	5,376	4,719	4,426	4,832
Portugal	182	13,650	11,271	10,348	10,303	10,681	11,214	10,701	†5,833	6,554	7,343	7,838	3,532
Spain	184	32,128	28,974	27,525	21,857	38,860	48,933	37,279	22,826	22,654	22,205	23,972	11,785
Denmark	128	7,619	7,128	5,784	6,904	9,295	13,457	9,767	15,406	11,105	12,825	19,052	24,229
Iceland	176	352	300	190	197	305	274	292	330	280	250	305	515
Norway	142	8,073	13,572	12,325	14,201	17,550	16,360	12,022	13,944	14,793	11,465	14,251	14,581
San Marino	135	....	85	118	131	147	133	118	101	99	102	130	165
Sweden	144	15,970	13,375	15,431	15,432	12,637	7,157	8,820	9,852	10,559	10,137	11,416	12,123
Switzerland	146	23,593	23,042	22,985	23,333	25,574	27,348	27,234	24,900	23,681	23,984	28,072	30,660
United Kingdom	112	24,791	25,210	26,392	26,357	25,816	21,403	19,434	†21,914	30,148	25,414	24,119	23,653
Developing Countries	200	317,756	378,552	418,761	493,670	587,310	676,818	691,188	771,704	889,258	1,007,428	1,110,155	1,285,477
Africa	605	12,229	13,384	15,924	17,441	21,842	31,981	28,932	30,021	41,458	51,062	52,857	61,033
CEMAC (Incl. BEAC hqtrs.)	758	....	....	....	....	....	....	....	....	957	852	1,172	1,216
Cameroon	622	14	1	†1	2	1	–	–	1	156	263	462	429
Central African Republic	626	73	81	144	157	161	132	103	99	102	94	91	89
Chad	628	58	28	52	96	114	100	85	69	85	97	161	126
Congo, Rep. of	634	2	–	34	39	63	44	–	28	170	54	20	22
Equatorial Guinea	642	4	–	–	–	–	4	1	2	18	56	65	160
Gabon	646	52	–	120	100	173	209	11	13	146	8	103	132
WAEMU (Incl. BCEAO hqtrs.)	759	....	....	....	1,669	1,871	2,095	2,217	2,101	2,490	2,971	3,974	4,488
Benin	638	176	175	†175	131	180	185	183	289	349	457	451	341
Burkina Faso	748	235	266	150	221	226	247	257	207	179	200	223	285
Côte d'Ivoire	662	5	1	140	355	420	458	607	457	511	810	1,369	1,500
Guinea Bissau	654	13	10	13	14	8	25	25	26	51	55	75	110
Mali	678	215	233	†143	208	291	299	277	246	284	268	428	602
Niger	692	155	131	67	55	45	31	29	19	53	76	89	66
Senegal	722	8	1	121	179	198	285	304	290	293	348	461	526
Togo	742	198	113	64	87	61	88	83	89	117	100	150	122
Algeria	612	1,059	1,069	1,816	1,348	2,942	5,963	4,861	3,211	9,141	14,293	16,997	22,169
Angola	614	....	....	....	143	383	294	144	361	920	582	276	427
Botswana	616	2,722	2,942	2,973	3,112	3,448	4,158	4,159	4,539	4,802	4,639	3,970	3,530
Burundi	618	120	112	134	135	91	78	41	29	19	14	43	45
Cape Verde	624	55	42	29	25	19	14	6	31	22	36	59	63
Comoros	632	19	28	30	29	35	29	27	26	32	49	58	63
Congo, Dem. Rep. of	636	114	34	83	99	57	....	....	....	....	....	....	....
Djibouti	611	58	55	50	48	53	49	47	50	51	55	52	66
Eritrea	643	....	....	....	27	57	148	16	25	20	32	22	17
Ethiopia	644	162	325	366	512	502	364	356	327	228	337	641	636
Gambia, The	648	66	75	65	70	69	70	74	79	82	83	77	....
Ghana	652	212	280	380	450	557	379	208	276	178	234	394	879
Guinea	656	55	88	56	53	60	88	167	144	113	159	125	....
Kenya	664	26e	282	369	225	506	571	543	563	676	834	772	983
Lesotho	666	111	180	251	304	316	419	404	360	317	304	295	306
Liberia	668	1	2	3	19	–	–	–	–	–	–	2	5
Madagascar	674	61	59	49	73	167	209	122	165	219	317	267	279
Malawi	676	27	39	23	71	154	118	184	180	187	162	119	82
Mauritania	682	44	32	27	57	97	149	144	163	215	226	291	279
Mauritius	684	573	523	483	552	594	484	367	502	658	634	871	1,022
Morocco	686	2,520	2,605	2,933	2,375	2,603	2,928	3,117	4,013	3,540	6,574	7,293	9,175
Mozambique	688	170	136	122	131	239	383	432	475	556	569	602	672
Namibia	728	36	97	139	149	135	186	185	223	200	186	238	219
Nigeria	694	703	999	949	971	2,834	5,619	5,043	3,971	7,606	8,320	5,392	4,797
Rwanda	714	44	23	24	53	62	94	102	116	145	159	172	124
São Tomé & Príncipe	716	....	....	....	3	3	9	7	8	9	12	13	17
Seychelles	718	22	25	20	17	14	19	15	22	34	30	51	45
Sierra Leone	724	13	18	22	12	13	20	24	14	34	41	45	22
South Africa	199	721	734	1,153	1,894	654	3,550	2,963	4,419	4,446	4,587	4,120	4,148
Sudan	732	20	27	54	110	74	60	64	138	†190	94	324	570
Swaziland	734	216	184	195	192	168	210	246	265	261	207	194	178

2004, International Monetary Fund: *International Financial Statistics Yearbook*

Foreign Exchange

Millions of SDRs: End of Period

1d s		1992	1993	1994	1995	1996	1997	1998	1999	2000	2001	2002	2003
Africa(Cont.)													
Tanzania	738	228	138	217	172	296	451	415	555	738	910	1,114	1,361
Tunisia	744	611	620	999	1,075	1,309	1,454	1,312	1,608	1,367	1,561	1,662	1,960
Uganda	746	62	107	218	308	367	466	512	554	617	781	685	724
Zambia	754	....	140	184	142	153	176	49	33	171	93	342	166
Zimbabwe	698	161	314	277	400	410	118	92	194	148	51	61	....
Asia	505	186,602	218,736	259,812	287,387	339,902	379,590	408,535	477,976	543,925	626,760	711,896	833,394
Bangladesh	513	1,297	1,738	2,125	1,467	1,200	1,150	1,344	1,168	1,140	1,013	1,236	1,732
Bhutan	514	61	70	82	†87	131	139	181	212	243	256	260	245
Cambodia	522	....	6	70	119	175	213	223	283	385	467	570	549
China, P.R.: Mainland†	924	†14,140	15,434	35,360	49,498	73,040	103,680	102,952	112,695	127,080	168,823	210,668	271,372
China, P.R.: Hong Kong	532	25,581	31,295	33,737	37,268	44,374	68,782	63,639	70,117	82,540	88,448	82,306	79,652
China, P.R.: Macao	546	947	1,142	1,347	1,518	1,684	1,877	1,749	2,082	2,550	2,792	2,795	2,923
Fiji	819	214	180	170	217	279	249	255	293	297	272	244	265
India	534	3,972	7,140	13,279	11,750	13,729	18,028	19,146	23,309	28,601	36,007	49,278	65,692
Indonesia	536	7,405	8,000	8,097	8,951	12,393	11,923	15,910	19,122	21,706	21,522	22,620	23,380
Korea	542	12,102	14,345	17,147	21,479	23,114	14,608	36,905	53,697	73,570	81,551	88,863	103,978
Lao P. D. Rep.	544	29e	44e	34e	52	111	74	75	74	107	101	136	127
Malaysia	548	12,207	19,522	17,048	15,436	18,190	14,833	17,562	21,617	21,970	23,541	24,479	29,251
Maldives	556	20	18	20	31	52	72	83	91	92	72	96	105
Micronesia, Fed. States of	868	....	....	....	46	61	63	71	66	86	77	85	59
Mongolia	948	12	43	54	77	74	130	66	99	137	164	257	159
Myanmar	518	204	220	289	377	159	185	223	193	171	318	346	370
Nepal	558	334	460	469	389	392	458	531	610	720	820	743	816
Pakistan	564	618	871	2,006	1,156	372	878	729	1,101	1,151	2,893	5,940	7,196
Papua New Guinea	853	173	103	66	175	406	269	137	149	211	329	232	330
Philippines	566	3,115	3,310	4,018	4,194	6,886	5,297	6,464	9,547	9,925	10,587	9,567	8,968
Samoa	862	39	34	32	34	40	45	41	47	46	42	43	53
Singapore†	576	28,845	34,994	39,654	45,980	53,194	52,535	52,852	55,595	61,159	59,560	59,849	63,914
Solomon Islands	813	17	14	11	10	22	26	34	37	24	15	13	24
Sri Lanka	524	654	1,166	1,381	1,384	1,343	1,480	1,385	1,143	749	975	1,150	....
Thailand	578	14,554	17,530	19,786	23,857	25,864	19,045	20,194	24,630	24,509	25,741	27,982	27,568
Tonga	866	22	25	23	18	20	19	19	18	19	19	18	27
Vanuatu	846	29	31	27	30	28	25	29	27	27	27	24	26
Vietnam	582	....	....	....	888	1,195	1,462	1,420	2,422	2,622	2,912	3,031	4,187
Europe	170	15,224	24,801	29,893	56,750	60,893	70,878	71,736	78,478	97,140	111,082	137,385	167,958
Albania	914	....	107	140	162	195	228	229	296	411	521	554	615
Armenia	911	1	10	22	37	79	142	210	202	228	247	290	331
Azerbaijan	912	–	–	1	80	132	341	318	485	517	712	530	540
Belarus	913	....	....	†69	251	326	292	499	214	269	311	455	400
Bosnia & Herzegovina	963	....	....	....	....	....	60	120	324	373	967	970	1,206
Bulgaria	918	617	444	643	779	295	1,524	1,853	2,015	2,324	2,584	3,208	4,155
Croatia	960	121	448	959	1,181	1,522	1,773	1,835	2,066	2,592	3,657	4,327	5,512
Cyprus	423	722	773	978	726	1,047	1,006	954	1,300	1,300	1,768	2,172	2,123
Czech Republic	935	....	2,753	4,209	9,312	8,590	7,214	8,908	9,330	9,990	11,290	17,150	17,695
Czechoslovakia†	934	†784	....	....	....	....	....	....	....	....	....	....	....
Estonia	939	116	240	303	390	443	562	576	621	707	653	736	924
Georgia	915	....	....	....	129	131	148	84	90	81	124	143	125
Hungary	944	3,160	4,820	4,557	7,999	6,703	6,175	6,562	7,801	8,377	8,197	7,150	8,086
Kazakhstan	916	....	318	504	609	660	931	763	914	1,223	1,589	1,879	2,850
Kyrgyz Republic	917	....	26	17	45	61	125	116	164	183	209	212	238
Latvia	941	....	243	373	339	453	562	569	633	653	914	913	964
Lithuania	946	32	200	350	497	530	741	989	867	1,006	1,273	1,689	2,269
Macedonia, FYR	962	....	76	102	173	167	190	217	312	329	591	527	604
Malta	181	864	931	1,206	1,014	1,056	1,029	1,105	1,240	1,064	1,259	1,556	....
Moldova	921	2	31	109	164	211	270	101	135	170	181	198	203
Poland	964	2,903	2,901	3,923	9,860	12,329	15,044	19,325	19,021	20,201	20,021	20,565	21,350
Romania	968	593	723	1,391	1,024	1,459	2,742	2,036	1,950	3,010	4,325	5,303	6,058
Russia	922	....	4,243	2,724	9,596	7,838	9,465	5,540	6,161	18,622	25,891	32,402	49,242
Slovak Republic	936	....	302	1,100	2,224	2,366	2,375	2,036	2,455	3,087	3,295	6,478	7,858
Slovenia	961	520	561	1,014	1,212	1,585	2,444	2,537	2,229	2,387	3,377	5,040	5,615
Tajikistan	923	....	....	....	....	....	18	36	40	65	70	64	75
Turkey	186	4,447	4,533	4,878	8,336	11,397	13,796	13,808	16,897	17,126	14,906	19,775	22,741
Ukraine	926	341	118	322	610	1,316	1,682	411	715	847	2,152	3,099	4,515
Middle East	405	40,752	44,040	43,098	47,494	57,752	70,355	69,515	75,271	88,693	93,718	91,869	94,469
Bahrain, Kingdom of	419	967	896	748	806	860	898	706	935	1,135	1,272	1,200	1,126
Egypt	469	7,765	9,290	9,121	10,762	11,960	13,696	12,704	10,403	9,911	10,258	9,673	9,018
Israel	436	3,729	4,646	4,653	5,462	7,937	15,069	16,103	16,404	17,778	18,444	17,407	17,348
Jordan	439	546	†1,188	1,159	1,326	1,223	1,631	1,243	1,915	2,556	2,436	2,924	3,495
Kuwait	443	3,516	2,851	2,200	2,195	2,240	2,317	2,476	3,092	4,992	7,314	6,147	4,469
Lebanon	446	1,060	1,616	2,630	3,019	4,093	4,396	4,622	5,630	4,525	3,951	5,289	8,386
Libya	672	3,899	....	....	....	....	....	4,418	4,536	8,756	10,940	9,679	12,322
Oman	449	1,648	1,271	1,086	1,190	1,321	1,493	1,334	1,965	1,774	1,812	2,254	2,333
Qatar	453	443	453	400	449	425	558	689	895	828	948	1,033	1,856
Saudi Arabia	456	3,317	4,137	4,033	4,777	†8,917	9,981	9,030	11,286	13,843	11,773	12,295	11,886
United Arab Emirates	466	3,943	4,227	4,357	4,784	5,340	5,949	6,154	7,561	10,211	11,075	10,958	9,914
Yemen, Republic of	474	230	105	141	379	674	768	575	944	2,161	2,896	3,211	3,353

2004, International Monetary Fund : *International Financial Statistics Yearbook*

Foreign Exchange

Millions of SDRs: End of Period

1d s		1992	1993	1994	1995	1996	1997	1998	1999	2000	2001	2002	2003
Western Hemisphere	205	62,950	77,592	70,034	84,597	106,922	124,014	112,471	109,958	118,042	124,806	116,148	128,623
ECCU (incl. ECCB hqtrs.)	309	199	192	175	207	198	224	252	263	292	352	369	361
Anguilla	312	6	7	6	9	10	12	13	15	16	19	19	22
Antigua and Barbuda	311	37	28	31	40	33	38	42	51	49	63	64	77
Dominica	321	15	14	11	15	16	18	20	23	23	25	33	32
Grenada	328	19	20	21	25	25	32	33	37	44	51	65	56
Montserrat	351	5	4	5	6	6	8	18	10	8	10	11	10
St. Kitts and Nevis	361	19	21	22	23	23	27	33	36	35	45	48	44
St. Lucia	362	39	42	38	41	38	44	49	53	59	69	68	70
St. Vincent & Grens.	364	24	22	21	19	20	23	27	30	42	48	39	34
Argentina	213	6,992	9,711	9,428	9,249	12,313	16,419	17,392	19,027	18,738	11,572	7,646	8,846
Aruba	314	103	132	122	146	130	128	158	160	160	234	250	199
Bahamas, The	313	106	119	115	114	113	162	240	293	262	248	274	324
Barbados	316	102	109	134	147	201	196	260	215	358	545	487	492
Belize	339	35	25	20	22	37	40	28	47	89	84	79	51
Bolivia	218	123	144	283	408	628	770	638	674	675	669	391	446
Brazil	223	16,378	22,279	25,392	33,439	40,559	37,670	30,239	25,345	24,935	28,430	27,516	33,048
Chile	228	6,667	7,018	8,965	9,510	10,376	12,791	10,835	10,337	11,272	11,173	10,896	10,236
Colombia	233	5,522	5,579	5,270	5,362	6,559	6,874	5,596	5,454	6,454	7,686	7,495	6,856
Costa Rica	238	732	737	603	695	687	926	746	1,043	991	1,038	1,081	1,216
Dominican Republic	243	363	464	170	246	243	290	356	505	481	875	344	170
Ecuador	248	614	984	1,243	1,076	1,273	1,534	1,133	1,178	709	649	507	529
El Salvador	253	307	390	445	485	627	944	1,121	1,435	1,450	1,360	1,169	1,283
Guatemala	258	545	620	580	462	595	814	940	858	1,333	1,817	1,685	1,901
Guyana	336	137	180	169	181	229	234	196	195	227	227	206	183
Haiti	263	20	23	35	128	150	153	183	192	140	112	60	41
Honduras	268	143	71	117	176	173	430	581	907	999	1,118	1,112	954
Jamaica	343	227	295	504	458	612	505	503	403	809	1,511	1,209	804
Mexico	273	13,377	18,118	4,179	10,259	13,335	20,853	22,344	22,581	26,972	35,317	36,700	38,857
Netherlands Antilles	353	160	170	123	137	131	159	176	193	200	240	299	251
Nicaragua	278	95	40	97	92	137	280	249	371	375	302	330	338
Panama	283	352	423	471	513	591	838	666	587	542	856	857	668
Paraguay	288	329	378	624	650	642	529	520	616	486	465	358	546
Peru	293	2,072	2,480	4,790	5,530	7,356	8,139	6,792	6,361	6,426	6,899	6,869	6,579
Suriname	366	13	13	27	82	59	73	67	20	40	87	71	64
Trinidad and Tobago	369	125	150	241	241	378	523	556	689	1,064	1,493	1,415	1,519
Uruguay	298	355	536	648	756	852	1,138	1,457	1,480	1,867	2,427	562	1,399
Venezuela, Rep. Bol.	299	6,755	6,211	5,064	3,826	7,736	10,376	8,247	8,530	9,696	7,022	5,912	10,462

Memorandum Items

		1992	1993	1994	1995	1996	1997	1998	1999	2000	2001	2002	2003
Oil Exporting Countries	999	42,285	42,483	40,486	40,751	56,821	67,686	67,531	73,782	98,679	105,518	102,994	112,466
Non-Oil Developing Countries	201	275,472	336,069	378,276	452,919	530,489	609,131	623,657	697,921	790,578	901,910	1,007,161	1,173,011

Gold (Million Fine Troy Ounces)

		1992	1993	1994	1995	1996	1997	1998	1999	2000	2001	2002	2003
1ad													
						Millions of Ounces: End of Period							
All Countries	010	928.86	919.72	915.67	907.21	905.38	888.56	968.41	967.07	952.09	942.76	930.56	913.10
Industrial Countries	110	785.24	770.83	768.05	754.97	748.16	732.47	808.67	810.43	796.51	783.55	769.85	754.29
United States	111	261.84	261.79	261.73	261.70	261.66	261.64	261.61	261.67	261.61	262.00	262.00	261.55
Canada	156	9.94	6.05	3.89	3.41	3.09	3.09	2.49	1.81	1.18	1.05	.60	.11
Australia	193	7.93	7.90	7.90	7.90	7.90	2.56	2.56	2.56	2.56	2.56	2.56	2.56
Japan	158	24.23	24.23	24.23	24.23	24.23	24.23	24.23	24.23	24.55	24.60	24.60	24.60
New Zealand	196	–	–	–	–	–	–	–	–	–	–	–	–
Euro Area (incl. ECB)	163	....	....	....	....	....	....	....	402.76	399.54	401.88	399.02	393.54
Austria	122	19.93	18.60	18.34	11.99	10.75	7.87	9.64	13.10	12.14	11.17	10.21	10.21
Belgium	124	25.04	25.04	25.04	20.54	15.32	15.32	9.52	8.30	8.30	8.30	8.29	8.29
Finland	172	2.00	2.00	2.00	1.60	1.60	1.60	2.00	1.58	1.58	1.58	1.58	1.58
France	132	81.85	81.85	81.85	81.85	81.85	81.89	102.37	97.25	97.25	97.25	97.25	97.25
Germany	134	95.18	95.18	95.18	95.18	95.18	95.18	118.98	111.52	111.52	111.13	110.79	110.58
Greece	174	3.43	3.44	3.45	3.46	3.47	3.64	3.62	4.24	4.26	3.94	3.94	3.45
Ireland	178	.36	.36	.36	.36	.36	.36	.45	.18	.18	.18	.18	.18
Italy	136	66.67	66.67	66.67	66.67	66.67	66.67	83.36	78.83	78.83	78.83	78.83	78.83
Luxembourg	137	.34	.31	.31	.31	.31	.31	....	.08	.08	.08	.08	.08
Netherlands	138	43.94	35.05	34.77	34.77	34.77	27.07	33.83	31.57	29.32	28.44	27.38	25.00
Portugal	182	16.06	16.06	16.07	16.07	16.07	16.07	20.09	19.51	19.51	19.51	19.03	16.63
Spain	184	15.62	15.62	15.62	15.63	15.63	15.63	19.54	16.83	16.83	16.83	16.83	16.83
Denmark	128	1.66	1.64	1.63	1.65	1.66	1.69	2.14	2.14	2.14	2.14	2.14	2.14
Iceland	176	.05	.05	.05	.05	.05	.05	.06	.06	.06	.06	.06	.06
Norway	142	1.18	1.18	1.18	1.18	1.18	1.18	1.18	1.18	1.18	1.18	1.18	1.18
San Marino	135	....	....	–	–	–	–	–	–	–	–	–	–
Sweden	144	6.07	6.07	6.07	4.70	4.70	4.72	4.72	5.96	5.96	5.96	5.96	5.96
Switzerland	146	83.28	83.28	83.28	83.28	83.28	83.28	83.28	83.28	77.79	70.68	61.62	52.51
United Kingdom	112	18.61	18.45	18.44	18.43	18.43	18.42	23.00	20.55	15.67	11.42	10.09	10.07
Developing Countries	200	143.62	148.89	147.63	152.24	157.22	156.09	159.74	156.64	155.58	159.22	160.71	158.80
Africa	605	15.22	13.28	12.69	13.84	13.49	14.09	13.98	14.01	15.62	15.20	15.07	13.18
CEMAC (Incl. BEAC hqtrs.)	758	....	....	....	.23	.23	.23	.23	.23	.23	.23	.23	.23
Cameroon	622	.03	.03	.03	.03	.03	.03	.03	.03	.03	.03	.03	.03
Central African Republic	626	.01	.01	.01	.01	.01	.01	.01	.01	.01	.01	.01	.01
Chad	628	.01	.01	.01	.01	.01	.01	.01	.01	.01	.01	.01	.01
Congo, Rep. of	634	.01	.01	.01	.01	.01	.01	.01	.01	.01	.01	.01	.01
Equatorial Guinea	642	....	....	....	....	....	....	....	....	....	....	....	....
Gabon	646	.01	.01	.01	.01	.01	.01	.01	.01	.01	.01	.01	.01
WAEMU (Incl. BCEAO hqtrs.)	759	....	....	....	.80	.86	.90	.96	1.01	1.06	1.12	1.17	1.17
Benin	638	.01	.01	.01	–	–	–	–	–	–	–	–	–
Burkina Faso	748	.01	.01	.01	–	–	–	–	–	–	–	–	–
Côte d'Ivoire	662	.04	.04	.04	–	–	–	–	–	–	–	–	–
Guinea Bissau	654	–	–	–	–	–	–	–	–	–	–	–	–
Mali	678	.02	.02	.02	–	–	–	–	–	–	–	–	–
Niger	692	.01	.01	.01	–	–	–	–	–	–	–	–	–
Senegal	722	.03	.03	.03	–	–	–	–	–	–	–	–	–
Togo	742	.01	.01	.01	–	–	–	–	–	–	–	–	–
Algeria	612	5.58	5.58	5.58	5.58	5.58	5.58	5.58	5.58	5.58	5.58	5.58	5.58
Burundi	618	.02	.02	.02	.02	.02	.02	.02	.02	.02	....	....	....
Comoros	632	–	–	–	–	–	–	–	–	–	–	–	–
Congo, Dem. Rep. of	636	.03	.02	.03	.03	....	.05	....	....	....	....	....	....
Eritrea	643	....	....	....	....	....	.10	.16	.08	.04	.04	–	–
Ethiopia	644	.11	.11	.11	.11	.30	.30	.30	.30	.20	.20	.25	–
Ghana	652	.28	.27	.28	.28	.28	.28	.28	.28	.28	.28	.28	.28
Kenya	664	.08	.08	.08	.08	.08	.08	–	–	–	–	–	–
Malawi	676	.01	.01	.01	.01	.01	.01	.01	.01	.01	.01	.01	.01
Mauritania	682	.01	.01	.01	.01	.01	.01	.01	.01	.01	.01	.01	.01
Mauritius	684	.06	.06	.06	.06	.06	.06	.06	.06	.06	.06	.06	.06
Morocco	686	.70	.70	.70	.70	.70	.70	.70	.70	.71	.71	.71	.71
Mozambique	688	....	....	....	....	....	.07	.07	.06	.07	.05	.06	.02
Namibia	728	–	–	–	–	–	–	–	–	–	–	–	–
Nigeria	694	.69	.69	.69	.69	.69	.69	.69	.69	.69	.69	.69	.69
Rwanda	714	–	–	....	–	–	–	–	–	–	–	–	–
South Africa	199	6.65	4.76	4.20	4.25	3.79	3.99	4.00	3.94	5.90	5.72	5.58	3.98
Tunisia	744	.22	.22	.22	.22	.22	.22	.22	.22	.22	.22	.22	.22
Zambia	754	....	....	....	–	–	–	–	–	–	–	–	....
Zimbabwe	698	.55	.50	.47	.76	.64	.77	.62	.73	.47	.20	.14	....
Asia	505	53.33	53.65	53.70	55.38	56.53	56.76	56.41	56.11	57.00	61.43	65.35	64.92
Bangladesh	513	.09	.09	.09	.09	.09	.10	.11	.11	.11	.11	.11	.11
Cambodia	522	....	–	–	–	–	–	.40	.40	.40	.40	.40	.40
China, P.R.: Mainland†	924	12.70	12.70	12.70	12.70	12.70	12.70	12.70	12.70	12.70	16.10	19.29	19.29
China, P.R.: Hong Kong	532	.23	.07	.07	.07	.07	.07	.07	.07	.07	.07	.07	.07
China, P.R.: Macao	546	–	–	–	–	–	–	–	–	–	–	–	–
Fiji	819	–	–	–	–	–	–	–	–	–	–	–	–
India	534	11.35	11.46	11.80	12.78	12.78	12.74	11.49	11.50	11.50	11.50	11.50	11.50
Indonesia	536	3.10	3.10	3.10	3.10	3.10	3.10	3.10	3.10	3.10	3.10	3.10	3.10
Korea	542	.32	.32	.33	.33	.33	.33	.43	.44	.44	.44	.44	.45

2004, International Monetary Fund : *International Financial Statistics Yearbook*

Gold (Million Fine Troy Ounces)

		1992	1993	1994	1995	1996	1997	1998	1999	2000	2001	2002	2003
1ad						Millions of Ounces: End of Period							
Asia(Cont.)													
Lao People's Democratic Rep.	544	.02	.02	.02	.02	.02	.02	.02	.12	.02	.07	.07	.12
Malaysia	548	2.39	2.39	2.39	2.39	2.39	2.35	2.35	1.18	1.17	1.17	1.17	1.17
Maldives	556	–	–	–	–	–	–	–	–	–	–	–	–
Micronesia, Fed. States of	868	....	....	....	–	–	–	–	–	–	–	–	–
Mongolia	948	.02	.02	.03	.10	.15	.08	.03	–	.08	.18	.14	.02
Myanmar	518	.25	.25	.25	.23	.23	.23	.23	.23	.23	.23	.23	.23
Nepal	558	.15	.15	.15	.15	.15	.15	.15	.15	.15	.15	.15	.15
Pakistan	564	2.02	2.04	2.05	2.05	2.06	2.07	2.08	2.09	2.09	2.09	2.09	2.10
Papua New Guinea	853	.06	.06	.06	.01	.06	.06	.06	.06	.06	.06	.06	.06
Philippines	566	2.80	3.22	2.89	3.58	4.65	4.99	5.43	6.20	7.23	7.98	8.73	8.22
Sri Lanka	524	.16	.06	.06	.06	.06	.06	.06	.06	.06	.06	.06	....
Thailand	578	2.47	2.47	2.47	2.47	2.47	2.47	2.47	2.47	2.37	2.48	2.50	2.60
Europe	170	12.17	23.19	22.00	23.24	27.92	30.72	31.11	30.05	29.46	30.90	29.62	29.56
Albania	914	....	.05	.05	.06	.12	.12	.12	.12	.11	.11	.08	.07
Armenia	911	–	–	.01	.03	.03	.04	.04	.04	.04	.04	.04	–
Azerbaijan	912	–	–	–	–	–	–	–	–	–	–	–	–
Bosnia & Herzegovina	963	....	....	....	....	....	–	–	–	–	–	–	–
Bulgaria	918	1.02	1.02	1.03	1.03	1.03	1.29	1.29	1.28	1.28	1.29	1.28	1.28
Croatia	960	–	–	–	–	–	–	–	–	–	–	–	–
Cyprus	423	.46	.46	.46	.46	.44	.46	.46	.46	.46	.46	.46	.47
Czech Republic	935	....	1.95	2.10	1.99	1.99	1.04	.29	.45	.45	.44	.44	.44
Czechoslovakia	934	3.29	....	....	....	....	....	....	....	....	....	....	....
Estonia	939	.08	.01	.01	.01	.01	.01	.01	.01	.01	.01	.01	.01
Georgia	915	....	....	....	–	–	–	–	–	–	–	–	–
Hungary	944	.10	.11	.11	.11	.10	.10	.10	.10	.10	.10	.10	.10
Kazakhstan	916	....	.65	.99	1.36	1.80	1.81	1.75	1.80	1.84	1.84	1.71	1.74
Kyrgyz Republic	917	....	....	....	....	....	....	.08	.08	.08	.08	.08	.08
Latvia	941	.07	.24	.25	.25	.25	.25	.25	.25	.25	.25	.25	.25
Lithuania	946	.19	.19	.19	.19	.19	.19	.19	.19	.19	.19	.19	.19
Macedonia, FYR	962	.02	.04	.05	.05	.08	.08	.10	.10	.11	.19	.20	.09
Malta	181	.12	.10	.11	.04	.04	.01	.01	.01	–	.01	–	–
Moldova	921	–	–	–	–	–	–	–	–	–	–	–	–
Poland	964	.47	.47	.47	.47	.47	.90	3.31	3.31	3.31	3.31	3.31	3.31
Romania	968	2.31	2.37	2.63	2.70	2.82	3.02	3.22	3.32	3.37	3.38	3.39	3.38
Russia	922	....	10.20	8.42	9.41	13.49	16.30	14.74	13.33	12.36	13.60	12.46	12.55
Slovak Republic	936	....	1.29	1.29	1.29	1.29	1.29	1.29	1.29	1.29	1.13	1.13	1.13
Slovenia	961	–	–	–	–	–	–	–	–	–	.24	.24	.24
Tajikistan	923	....	....	....	....	....	.01	.01	.01	.01	.01	–	.01
Turkey	186	4.05	4.03	3.82	3.75	3.75	3.75	3.75	3.74	3.74	3.73	3.73	3.73
Ukraine	926	–	.01	.04	.05	.03	.06	.11	.16	.45	.48	.50	.50
Middle East	405	34.65	31.48	31.41	30.96	31.55	31.35	35.97	35.20	35.12	35.12	34.84	34.44
Bahrain, Kingdom of	419	.15	.15	.15	.15	.15	.15	.15	.15	.15	.15	.15	.15
Egypt	469	2.43	2.43	2.43	2.43	2.43	2.43	2.43	2.43	2.43	2.43	2.43	2.43
Iran, I.R. of	429	4.34	4.76	4.74	4.84	....	....	....	....	....	....	....	....
Israel	436	.01	.01	.01	.01	.01	.01	–	–	–	–	–	–
Jordan	439	.79	.79	.79	.79	.80	.81	.83	.49	.40	.41	.41	.41
Kuwait	443	2.54	2.54	2.54	2.54	2.54	2.54	2.54	2.54	2.54	2.54	2.54	2.54
Lebanon	446	9.22	9.22	9.22	9.22	9.22	9.22	9.22	9.22	9.22	9.22	9.22	9.22
Libya	672	3.60	....	....	....	....	....	4.62	4.62	4.62	4.62	4.62	4.62
Oman	449	.29	.29	.29	.29	.29	.29	.29	.29	.29	.29	–	–
Qatar	453	.86	.86	.81	.27	.27	.05	.05	.02	.02	.02	.02	.02
Saudi Arabia	456	4.60	4.60	4.60	4.60	4.60	4.60	4.60	4.60	4.60	4.60	4.60	4.60
Syrian Arab Rep.	463	.83	.83	.83	.83	.83	.83	.83	.83	.83	.83	.83	.83
United Arab Emirates	466	.80	.80	.80	.80	.80	.80	.80	.40	.40	.40	.40	–
Yemen, Republic of	474	.05	.05	.05	.05	.05	.05	.05	.05	.05	.05	.05	.05
Western Hemisphere	205	28.24	27.30	27.83	28.81	27.72	23.18	22.26	21.27	18.38	16.57	15.83	16.69
Argentina	213	4.37	4.37	4.37	4.37	4.37	.36	.36	.34	.02	.01	.01	.01
Aruba	314	.10	.10	.10	.10	.10	.10	.10	.10	.10	.10	.10	.10
Bahamas, The	313	–	–	–	–	–	–	–	–	–	–	–	–
Barbados	316	–	–	–	–	–	–	–	–	–	–	–	–
Bolivia	218	.89	.89	.89	.89	.94	.94	.94	.94	.94	.94	.91	.91
Brazil	223	2.23	2.93	3.71	4.58	3.69	3.03	4.60	3.17	1.89	.46	.44	.45
Chile	228	1.87	1.87	1.86	1.86	1.86	1.86	1.22	1.22	.07	.07	.01	.01
Colombia	233	.48	.30	.29	.27	.25	.36	.36	.33	.33	.33	.33	.33
Costa Rica	238	.04	.03	.03	.03	–	–	–	–	–	–	–	–
Dominican Republic	243	.02	.02	.02	.02	.02	.02	.02	.02	.02	.02	.02	.02
Ecuador	248	.44	.41	.41	.41	.41	.41	.41	†.85	.85	.85	.85	.85
El Salvador	253	.47	.47	.47	.47	.47	.47	.47	.47	.47	.47	.47	.47
Guatemala	258	.12	.21	.21	.21	.21	.21	.22	.22	.22	.22	.22	.22
Haiti	263	.02	.02	.02	.02	.02	.02	.02	–	–	–	–	–
Honduras	268	.02	.02	.02	.02	.02	.02	.02	.02	.02	.02	.02	.02
Jamaica	343	–	–	–	–	–	–	–	–	–	–	–	–
Mexico	273	.69	.48	.43	.51	.26	.19	.22	.16	.25	.23	.22	.17
Netherlands Antilles	353	.55	.55	.55	.55	.55	.55	.42	.42	.42	.42	.42	.42
Nicaragua	278	.48	.01	.01	.02	.02	.02	.02	.02	.01	.01	.01	.01
Paraguay	288	.03	.03	.03	.03	.03	.03	.03	.03	.03	.03	.03	.03
Peru	293	1.82	1.30	1.12	1.12	1.11	1.11	1.10	1.10	1.10	1.11	1.11	1.11
Suriname	366	.05	.05	.05	.09	.13	.19	.13	.25	.26	.27	.02	.02
Trinidad and Tobago	369	.05	.06	.05	.05	.05	.06	.06	.06	.06	.06	.06	.06

Gold (Million Fine Troy Ounces)

		1992	1993	1994	1995	1996	1997	1998	1999	2000	2001	2002	2003
1ad						*Millions of Ounces: End of Period*							
Western Hemisphere(Cont.)													
Uruguay...........................	298	2.03	1.70	1.70	1.72	1.74	1.76	1.78	1.80	1.08	.01	.01	.01
Venezuela, Rep. Bol.............	299	11.46	11.46	11.46	11.46	11.46	11.46	9.76	9.76	10.24	10.94	10.56	11.47
Memorandum Items													
Oil Exporting Countries..........	999	42.00	38.82	38.75	38.31	38.89	38.67	41.59	41.16	41.64	42.34	41.67	42.18
Non-Oil Developing Countries.	201	101.62	110.07	108.88	113.93	118.33	117.42	118.15	115.48	113.94	116.87	119.04	116.62
Gold Holdings at SDR 35 per Ounce													
(1a.s)						*Millions of SDRs: End of Period*							
World............................	001	39,595	39,248	39,059	38,906	38,758	38,069	37,739	37,692	37,168	36,839	36,412	35,796
All Countries..................	010	32,510	32,190	32,049	31,752	31,688	31,099	33,894	33,848	33,323	32,997	32,570	31,958
of which: ECB.................	168	....	....	....	....	....	....	....	841	841	863	863	863
IMF.............................	992	3,620	3,620	3,620	3,620	3,620	3,620	3,620	3,620	3,620	3,620	3,620	3,620
EMI.............................	977	3,228	3,135	3,146	3,278	3,219	3,131	....	....	....	....	....	....
BIS..............................	993	237	302	244	255	230	218	224	224	224	222	222	218
Gold Holdings at Market Prices													
(1ams)						*Millions of SDRs: End of Period*							
World............................	001	274,186	318,924	292,970	289,212	284,355	233,944	220,394	227,739	223,691	231,575	262,278	287,182
All Countries..................	010	225,122	261,575	240,389	236,035	232,489	191,113	197,942	204,511	200,553	207,422	234,604	256,391
of which: ECB.................	168	....	....	....	....	....	....	....	5,082	5,062	5,425	6,216	6,923
IMF.............................	992	25,070	29,419	27,156	26,913	26,562	22,248	21,143	21,875	21,789	22,758	26,078	29,045
EMI.............................	977	22,351	25,478	23,594	24,369	23,618	19,240	....	....	....	....	....	....
BIS..............................	993	1,643	2,453	1,831	1,896	1,687	1,343	1,309	1,353	1,349	1,394	1,596	1,746
Gold Prices and SDR Rates:						*End of Period*							
US Dollars per Oz.(London)(c..)......	112	333.25	390.65	383.25	386.75	369.25	290.20	287.80	290.25	274.45	276.50	342.75	417.25
US Dollars per SDR (sa.).............	111	1.3750	1.3736	1.4599	1.4865	1.4380	1.3493	1.4080	1.3725	1.3029	1.2567	1.3595	1.4860
SDRs per Ounce (g..)................	112	242.36	284.41	262.53	260.18	256.79	215.08	204.40	211.47	210.64	220.02	252.11	280.79

Total Reserves

1 s (w/ Gold at SDR 35 per Oz)

Millions of SDRs: End of Period

		1992	1993	1994	1995	1996	1997	1998	1999	2000	2001	2002	2003
All Countries	010	753,805	831,929	892,337	1,023,057	1,177,339	1,296,513	1,282,045	1,405,004	1,584,765	1,737,454	1,881,628	2,146,587
Industrial Countries	110	424,229	440,510	460,821	514,251	575,129	603,469	574,016	616,071	678,303	710,957	749,617	837,016
United States	111	52,995	54,558	52,510	59,467	53,694	52,817	59,379	53,238	52,598	55,030	59,160	59,555
Canada	156	8,662	9,299	8,552	10,243	14,310	13,317	16,640	20,556	24,544	27,061	27,225	24,380
Australia	193	8,429	8,359	8,007	8,279	10,350	12,575	10,487	15,545	13,996	14,377	15,307	21,751
Japan	158	52,937	72,577	87,062	124,125	151,511	163,641	153,878	209,893	273,251	315,292	340,088	447,229
New Zealand	196	2,239	2,430	2,540	2,967	4,140	3,299	2,986	3,246	2,556	2,394	2,750	3,304
Euro Area (incl. ECB)	163	....	....	....	....	....	....	....	201,185	199,971	201,031	195,644	163,653
Austria	122	9,703	11,288	12,165	13,020	16,277	14,903	22,661	† 11,475	11,414	10,345	7,480	6,057
Belgium	124	10,914	9,187	10,382	11,601	12,326	12,535	13,310	† 8,260	7,961	9,255	9,010	7,686
Finland	172	3,862	4,009	7,374	6,809	4,866	6,294	6,955	† 6,044	6,178	6,408	6,885	7,131
France	132	22,522	19,354	20,851	20,930	21,500	25,788	35,054	† 32,330	31,832	28,667	24,268	23,718
Germany	134	69,489	59,856	56,325	60,517	61,176	60,835	56,737	† 48,376	47,567	44,793	41,516	37,986
Greece	174	3,606	5,792	10,045	10,064	12,292	9,462	12,526	13,352	10,452	† 4,239	6,083	3,056
Ireland	178	2,514	4,326	4,201	5,818	5,719	4,849	6,690	† 3,886	4,120	4,451	3,989	2,751
Italy	136	22,438	22,387	24,435	25,815	34,287	43,644	24,144	† 19,095	22,382	22,190	23,798	23,194
Luxembourg	137	66	60	63	61	62	58	....	† 59	61	87	114	191
Netherlands	138	17,492	24,046	24,872	23,897	19,832	19,376	16,395	† 8,308	8,427	8,184	7,993	8,285
Portugal	182	14,474	12,094	11,189	11,225	11,632	12,169	11,942	† 6,823	7,520	8,375	8,889	4,536
Spain	184	33,640	30,429	29,006	23,746	40,831	51,241	39,929	† 24,716	24,373	24,128	25,992	13,906
Denmark	128	8,090	7,557	6,260	7,468	9,892	14,233	10,916	16,313	11,671	13,690	19,924	25,045
Iceland	176	364	312	202	209	317	286	305	351	301	271	326	535
Norway	142	8,725	14,327	13,074	15,190	18,482	17,385	13,256	14,905	15,518	12,366	15,254	15,517
San Marino	135	....	....	121	134	150	136	121	105	104	106	135	170
Sweden	144	16,667	14,081	16,141	16,344	13,452	8,188	10,178	11,151	11,616	11,330	12,807	13,453
Switzerland	146	27,100	26,674	26,704	27,411	29,642	31,840	32,169	29,378	27,492	27,941	31,693	33,906
United Kingdom	112	27,300	27,420	28,739	28,910	28,390	24,596	23,682	† 26,854	34,235	30,067	29,305	28,516
Developing Countries	200	329,576	391,419	431,515	508,806	602,210	693,045	708,029	788,933	906,462	1,026,498	1,132,011	1,309,571
Africa	605	13,067	14,123	16,645	18,212	22,583	32,747	29,862	31,246	42,699	52,351	54,158	62,293
CEMAC (Incl. BEAC hqtrs.)	758	....	....	....	....	....	....	....	....	973	867	1,185	1,228
Cameroon	622	16	3	3	4	3	2	2	4	164	265	464	431
Central African Republic	626	73	82	144	158	162	133	104	100	103	95	91	89
Chad	628	59	29	52	96	115	101	86	70	85	98	161	126
Congo, Rep. of	634	3	1	35	40	64	45	1	29	171	55	24	24
Equatorial Guinea	642	10	–	–	–	–	4	1	2	18	56	65	160
Gabon	646	52	1	120	100	173	210	11	14	146	8	103	133
WAEMU (Incl. BCEAO hqtrs.)	759	....	....	....	1,736	1,935	2,157	2,281	2,172	2,557	3,047	4,053	4,569
Benin	638	179	178	177	133	182	188	186	291	352	460	453	343
Burkina Faso	748	249	279	163	234	235	256	265	215	187	207	231	293
Côte d'Ivoire	662	7	3	141	356	421	458	608	459	513	811	1,371	1,501
Guinea Bissau	654	13	10	13	14	8	25	25	26	51	55	76	111
Mali	678	225	243	152	217	300	308	286	255	293	278	437	611
Niger	692	164	140	76	64	55	39	38	29	62	85	98	77
Senegal	722	10	4	124	183	200	286	306	294	295	356	469	535
Togo	742	199	114	65	88	62	88	84	89	117	101	151	123
Algeria	612	1,255	1,269	2,027	1,544	3,141	6,159	5,057	3,493	9,424	14,583	17,288	22,487
Angola	614	....	....	....	143	384	294	144	361	920	582	276	427
Botswana	616	2,759	2,983	3,015	3,159	3,496	4,206	4,219	4,589	4,849	4,693	4,026	3,593
Burundi	618	127	119	141	142	98	84	47	36	26	14	43	45
Comoros	632	20	28	30	30	35	....	....	....	....	....	....	....
Congo, Dem. Rep. of	636	115	34	84	100	....	....	....	....	....	....	....	....
Djibouti	611	61	55	51	49	54	49	47	51	52	56	54	67
Eritrea	643	....	....	....	....	....	151	22	28	21	33	22	17
Ethiopia	644	173	336	377	523	520	382	374	345	242	352	657	643
Gambia, The	648	68	77	67	71	71	71	76	81	84	84	79	....
Ghana	652	242	308	410	479	586	408	277	340	188	247	407	920
Guinea	656	....	....	....	....	....	....	....	....	....	....	....	....
Kenya	664	41e	298	385	241	522	587	556	577	689	847	786	997
Lesotho	666	115	184	255	307	320	424	408	364	321	308	299	310
Liberia	668	1	2	3	19	–	–	–	–	–	–	2	5
Madagascar	674	61	59	49	73	168	209	122	166	219	317	267	279
Malawi	676	30	42	30	74	157	121	192	183	190	165	122	86
Mauritania	682	45	33	28	58	99	149	144	164	215	227	292	280
Mauritius	684	599	553	514	583	625	516	399	535	691	667	905	1,064
Morocco	686	2,631	2,686	3,006	2,447	2,663	2,984	3,174	4,170	3,727	6,768	7,478	9,346
Mozambique	688	....	....	....	....	....	† 386	435	477	559	571	605	673
Namibia	728	36	97	139	149	135	186	185	223	200	186	238	219
Nigeria	694	727	1,023	973	995	2,858	5,643	5,067	3,995	7,631	8,345	5,417	4,821
Rwanda	714	57	35	....	....	74	114	120	127	146	169	179	144
São Tomé & Príncipe	716	–	–	–	3	3	9	7	8	9	12	13	17
Seychelles	718	23	26	21	18	15	20	15	22	34	30	51	45
Sierra Leone	724	14	21	28	23	18	29	31	29	38	41	62	45
South Africa	199	954	909	1,301	2,046	787	3,697	3,234	4,767	4,875	5,011	4,538	4,510
Sudan	732	20	27	54	110	74	60	64	138	† 190	94	324	570
Swaziland	734	225	192	203	201	177	219	255	274	270	216	203	187
Tanzania	738	238	148	227	182	306	461	426	565	748	920	1,125	1,372
Tunisia	744	627	629	1,009	1,087	1,327	1,474	1,322	1,655	1,398	1,590	1,692	1,990

Total Reserves

Millions of SDRs: End of Period

1 s (w/ Gold at SDR 35 per Oz)

		1992	1993	1994	1995	1996	1997	1998	1999	2000	2001	2002	2003
Africa(Cont.)													
Uganda	746	69	107	220	309	367	470	515	556	620	782	687	727
Zambia	754	....	....	....	150	155	177	49	33	188	146	394	167
Zimbabwe	698	181	332	294	427	439	146	115	221	165	58	66	....
Asia *	505	191,001	223,353	264,513	293,049	345,948	386,309	415,488	484,489	550,203	633,898	720,139	842,253
Bangladesh	513	1,330	1,758	2,153	1,577	1,279	1,176	1,357	1,172	1,144	1,018	1,242	1,739
Bhutan	514	62	71	83	†88	132	140	182	213	244	257	261	247
Cambodia	522	....	18	81	129	185	221	244	300	399	481	585	563
China, P.R.: Mainland†	924	†15,441	16,743	36,691	51,152	74,883	106,253	106,400	115,364	129,600	172,124	214,815	275,345
China, P.R.: Hong Kong	532	25,589	31,298	33,739	37,270	44,376	68,784	63,673	70,119	82,542	88,450	82,308	79,654
China, P.R.: Macao	546	947	1,142	1,347	1,518	1,684	1,877	1,749	2,082	2,550	2,792	2,795	2,923
Fiji	819	230	196	187	235	297	267	274	312	316	292	264	285
India	534	4,584	7,826	13,907	12,504	14,474	18,744	19,820	24,203	29,493	36,902	50,174	66,984
Indonesia	536	7,708	8,308	8,419	9,330	12,801	12,402	16,240	19,376	21,984	21,789	22,888	23,637
Korea	542	12,463	14,738	17,574	21,995	23,682	15,107	36,928	53,922	73,797	81,778	89,272	104,516
Lao People's Democratic Rep	544	29e	46e	42e	62	118	83	80	74	107	104	141	140
Malaysia	548	12,613	19,922	17,498	16,077	18,867	15,489	18,235	22,328	22,700	24,290	25,213	29,998
Maldives	556	21	19	21	32	53	73	84	93	94	74	98	107
Micronesia, Fed. States of	868	....	....	....	47	62	64	72	68	87	78	86	60
Mongolia	948	13	44	57	82	80	133	68	99	140	170	262	159
Myanmar	518	213	229	298	386	167	193	232	202	179	327	354	378
Nepal	558	345	471	480	400	403	469	542	621	731	831	754	828
Pakistan	564	689	943	2,078	1,238	453	958	803	1,174	1,235	2,970	6,015	7,436
Papua New Guinea	853	176	105	68	176	408	271	139	152	222	339	239	335
Philippines	566	3,300	3,517	4,223	4,412	7,138	5,560	6,742	9,856	10,266	10,965	9,967	9,344
Samoa	862	42	37	35	37	42	48	44	50	49	45	46	56
Singapore	576	29,007	35,208	39,851	46,213	53,442	52,836	53,215	55,987	61,502	59,977	60,331	64,433
Solomon Islands	813	17	15	12	11	23	27	35	37	25	15	13	25
Sri Lanka	524	679	1,188	1,404	1,407	1,366	1,502	1,408	1,194	800	1,026	1,202	....
Thailand	578	14,893	17,904	20,179	24,293	26,326	19,490	20,559	24,905	24,655	25,832	28,073	27,734
Tonga	866	23	27	24	19	21	20	20	20	21	21	20	29
Vanuatu	846	31	33	30	32	31	28	32	30	30	30	27	29
of which:													
Taiwan Province of China	528	60,333	61,319	63,806	61,229	61,699	62,362	64,636	77,851	82,400	97,720	119,381	139,532
Europe	170	16,009	26,146	31,300	58,465	62,650	73,007	73,857	80,750	99,394	113,744	140,116	170,950
Albania	914	....	109	142	164	199	233	277	360	476	593	620	682
Armenia	911	1	10	22	68	109	171	232	234	246	257	314	343
Azerbaijan	912	–	–	1	81	147	345	318	490	522	714	531	552
Bosnia & Herzegovina	963	....	....	....	....	....	60	124	330	381	972	972	1,208
Bulgaria	918	692	513	722	868	372	1,610	1,952	2,152	2,466	2,664	3,286	4,278
Croatia	960	121	449	962	1,275	1,609	1,882	2,000	2,204	2,705	3,742	4,329	5,512
Cyprus	423	764	815	1,019	767	1,088	1,048	996	1,352	1,353	1,821	2,239	2,208
Czech Republic	935	....	2,827	4,282	9,382	8,659	7,251	8,918	9,346	10,008	11,427	17,342	18,031
Czechoslovakia	934	†930	....	....	....	....	....	....	....	....	....	....	....
Estonia	939	127	281	304	390	443	562	576	622	707	653	736	924
Georgia	915	....	....	....	131	131	148	87	96	84	127	145	128
Hungary	944	3,222	4,882	4,618	8,059	6,763	6,235	6,622	7,985	8,592	8,539	7,615	8,575
Kazakhstan	916	....	355	608	811	963	1,321	1,099	1,141	1,288	1,654	1,939	2,912
Kyrgyz Republic	917	....	....	....	....	....	....	119	170	186	213	215	248
Latvia	941	....	323	382	349	464	572	578	644	662	923	922	973
Lithuania	946	39	262	366	516	544	755	1,007	877	1,013	1,294	1,735	2,276
Macedonia, FYR	962	....	78	104	175	169	193	221	317	333	600	538	607
Malta	181	927	995	1,271	1,081	1,128	1,103	1,181	1,303	1,129	1,326	1,625	....
Moldova	921	2	56	123	173	217	271	102	135	171	182	198	203
Poland	964	2,998	2,996	4,018	9,955	12,426	15,156	19,522	19,318	20,502	20,525	21,189	22,040
Romania	968	681	808	1,521	1,157	1,561	2,925	2,149	2,074	3,128	4,449	5,423	6,176
Russia	922	....	4,605	3,021	10,005	8,314	10,127	6,056	6,628	19,056	26,370	32,840	49,683
Slovak Republic	936	....	348	1,204	2,308	2,423	2,439	2,083	2,501	3,132	3,335	6,519	7,898
Slovenia	961	520	574	1,027	1,225	1,598	2,457	2,584	2,308	2,453	3,454	5,143	5,727
Tajikistan	923	....	....	....	....	....	27	38	40	71	74	66	76
Turkey	186	4,621	4,707	5,045	8,501	11,561	13,960	13,972	17,141	17,391	15,153	20,041	23,005
Ukraine	926	341	118	447	708	1,364	1,737	545	768	1,054	2,369	3,137	4,547
Middle East	405	44,397	47,859	46,685	51,142	61,655	74,401	73,698	79,658	93,328	99,498	98,645	101,819
Bahrain, Kingdom of	419	1,022	953	806	866	922	962	772	1,003	1,206	1,345	1,275	1,202
Egypt	469	7,947	9,480	9,319	10,971	12,184	13,919	12,957	10,638	10,153	10,370	9,826	9,230
Israel	436	3,729	4,647	4,653	5,462	7,938	15,069	16,104	16,470	17,869	18,603	17,714	17,709
Jordan	439	586	†1,220	1,187	1,355	1,251	1,659	1,272	1,933	2,571	2,451	2,939	3,510
Kuwait	443	3,832	3,157	2,487	2,484	2,533	2,647	2,892	3,603	5,525	7,964	6,862	5,188
Lebanon	446	1,411	1,968	2,983	3,372	4,448	4,752	4,979	5,988	4,885	4,312	5,651	8,748
Libya	672	4,622	....	....	....	....	....	5,325	5,466	9,726	11,939	10,686	13,341
Oman	449	1,701	1,323	1,138	1,242	1,374	1,544	1,386	2,027	1,837	1,892	2,334	2,418
Qatar	453	527	535	479	528	506	620	752	954	893	1,049	1,157	1,987
Saudi Arabia	456	4,477	5,569	5,214	5,961	†10,120	11,187	10,260	12,545	15,193	14,162	15,321	15,383
United Arab Emirates	466	4,182	4,472	4,589	5,054	5,630	6,233	6,474	7,792	10,393	11,270	11,209	10,154
Yemen, Republic of	474	235	108	176	418	709	893	709	1,074	2,228	2,913	3,246	3,358

2004, International Monetary Fund : *International Financial Statistics Yearbook*

Total Reserves

		1992	1993	1994	1995	1996	1997	1998	1999	2000	2001	2002	2003
1 s (w/ Gold at SDR 35 per Oz)						*Millions of SDRs: End of Period*							
Western Hemisphere	205	65,102	79,938	72,373	87,938	109,374	126,581	115,123	112,790	120,837	127,007	118,953	132,256
ECCU (incl. ECCB hqtrs.)	309	203	196	179	211	203	228	256	268	297	357	374	366
Anguilla	312	6	7	6	9	10	12	13	15	16	19	19	22
Antigua and Barbuda	311	37	28	31	40	33	38	42	51	49	63	64	77
Dominica	321	15	14	11	15	16	18	20	23	23	25	33	32
Grenada	328	19	20	21	25	25	32	33	37	44	51	65	56
Montserrat	351	5	4	5	6	6	8	18	10	8	10	11	10
St. Kitts and Nevis	361	19	21	22	23	23	27	33	36	35	45	48	44
St. Lucia	362	40	44	40	42	39	45	50	54	61	71	69	72
St. Vincent & Grens.	364	24	23	21	20	21	23	28	31	42	49	39	34
Argentina	213	7,418	10,193	9,967	9,765	12,743	16,555	17,592	19,139	19,301	11,580	7,716	9,525
Aruba	314	107	135	125	149	134	131	161	164	163	237	253	202
Bahamas, The	313	113	125	121	121	119	168	246	299	268	254	280	330
Barbados	316	102	110	134	147	201	196	260	220	363	549	492	497
Belize	339	39	28	24	25	41	44	31	52	94	89	84	57
Bolivia	218	163	194	340	475	697	838	707	743	744	738	459	514
Brazil	223	16,457	22,383	25,523	33,600	40,689	37,776	30,401	25,463	25,001	28,454	27,734	33,065
Chile	228	6,733	7,084	9,030	9,577	10,477	13,089	11,313	10,692	11,542	11,444	11,284	10,660
Colombia	233	5,651	5,784	5,484	5,626	6,855	7,278	6,157	5,846	6,855	8,091	7,906	7,269
Costa Rica	238	742	747	613	705	696	935	755	1,064	1,011	1,058	1,101	1,236
Dominican Republic	243	364	475	173	247	244	290	357	506	482	876	345	171
Ecuador	248	647	1,019	1,278	1,109	1,307	1,566	1,165	†1,226	756	698	555	576
El Salvador	253	323	407	461	527	668	986	1,162	1,476	1,492	1,402	1,210	1,324
Guatemala	258	561	639	599	480	612	831	956	874	1,348	1,832	1,699	1,914
Guyana	336	137	180	169	181	229	234	196	195	234	229	209	186
Haiti	263	20	24	36	130	151	154	184	192	140	113	60	42
Honduras	268	144	71	118	177	174	431	582	917	1,009	1,127	1,122	963
Jamaica	343	236	304	504	458	612	506	504	404	809	1,512	1,210	804
Mexico	273	13,800	18,298	4,316	11,351	13,523	21,350	22,592	23,162	27,262	35,609	37,223	39,681
Netherlands Antilles	353	179	190	142	156	151	178	191	208	215	254	314	266
Nicaragua	278	....	40	97	92	138	281	249	372	375	303	330	338
Panama	283	367	435	482	526	603	851	678	600	555	869	870	680
Paraguay	288	410	461	707	736	731	621	615	714	587	569	464	653
Peru	293	2,136	2,527	4,829	5,570	7,395	8,179	6,832	6,399	6,466	6,939	6,908	6,618
Suriname	366	14	15	29	93	72	88	80	37	57	104	79	72
Trinidad and Tobago	369	127	152	243	243	380	526	558	691	1,066	1,520	1,494	1,652
Uruguay	298	441	612	723	834	931	1,215	1,535	1,579	1,940	2,465	566	1,402
Venezuela, Rep. Bol.	299	7,356	7,111	5,927	4,628	8,599	11,057	8,807	9,287	10,404	7,735	6,612	11,192
Memorandum Items													
Oil Exporting Countries	999	46,392	47,073	44,790	45,081	61,484	72,286	71,959	78,583	103,734	111,826	110,077	120,086
Non-Oil Developing Countries.	201	283,184	344,346	386,725	463,725	540,727	620,759	636,070	710,350	802,728	914,672	1,021,934	1,189,485
(with Gold at SDR 35 per Ounce) (1..s)													
All Countries	010	....	....	....	....	....	....	....	....	....	....	....	....
(with Gold at Market Prices) (1m.s)						*Millions of SDRs: End of Period*							
All Countries	010	946,417	1,061,314	1,100,677	1,227,339	1,378,140	1,456,527	1,446,093	1,575,667	1,751,995	1,911,880	2,083,662	2,371,020

Reserve Money

		1992	1993	1994	1995	1996	1997	1998	1999	2000	2001	2002	2003
		\multicolumn{12}{c}{Percent Change over Previous Year}
Industrial Countries													
United States	111	8.8	9.1	8.6	4.4	4.7	8.0	6.0	20.0	−6.1	7.8	7.5	5.2
Canada	156	2.3	5.5	2.3	1.4	4.3	3.3	6.6	24.3	−7.4	4.2	5.5	1.0
Australia	193	6.0	6.5	8.1	5.0	61.2	−20.3	5.3	−5.4	—	18.9	1.4	3.7
Japan	158	−3.8	5.8	2.9	7.8	8.5	7.3	3.6	39.3	−18.2	17.3	13.9	....
New Zealand	196	2.2	2.9	11.6	7.1	−2.7	4.9	6.3	76.1	−24.4	9.2	8.6	2.1
Euro Area													
Austria	122	10.3	8.1	4.5	−1.0	6.9	−.7	....	....	....	....	....	....
Belgium	124	−.5	2.9	−6.7	9.2	3.7	2.3	56.2	....	....	....	....	....
Finland	172	5.1	.6	51.1	1.6	−32.8	−7.7	−1.8	....	....	....	....	....
France	132	−12.7	−3.9	.1	8.7	2.2	3.0	22.4	....	....	....	....	....
Germany	134	14.5	−1.3	−1.6	2.0	4.8	−.9	1.1	....	....	....	....	....
Greece	174	9.6	8.5	35.6	3.2	12.1	11.3	34.8	25.1	−16.1	....	....	....
Ireland	178	−8.2	20.5	4.3	26.6	1.1	18.9	....	....	....	....	....	....
Italy	136	4.0	−8.9	−5.0	−6.3	2.4	7.4	−29.0	....	....	....	....	....
Luxembourg	137	−5.3	70.0	—	−11.5	17.1	−.2	....	....	....	....	....	....
Netherlands	138	30.1	7.4	6.0	−12.3	−4.4	10.2	5.4	....	....	....	....	....
Portugal	182	10.6	9.0	−58.8	−2.5	11.2	−1.3	.6	....	....	....	....	....
Spain	184	.5	.8	10.1	4.6	3.3	6.8	3.4	....	....	....	....	....
Denmark	128	−12.3	64.2	.7	13.5	33.3	31.1	−22.6	98.8	†−22.7	−5.6	10.9	8.7
Iceland	176	3.2	−8.9	3.0	−18.1	26.4	11.4	2.2	†55.7	−11.8	−11.7	13.4	....
Norway	142	4.9	10.7	3.3	5.2	53.0	−11.5	−11.0	50.2	−16.3	−.8	49.2	....
Sweden	144	24.2	47.7	22.4	−14.9	−33.1	−25.8	3.8	17.0	−5.0	9.6	−.1	2.2
Switzerland	146	10.1	−1.3	.6	−2.4	5.1	−2.3	7.7	17.0	−10.6	12.5	−6.8	7.9
United Kingdom	112	6.0	6.8	5.3	7.0	3.5	7.1	†4.5	18.6	−.3	.6	4.4	7.9
Developing Countries													
Africa													
CEMAC	758	....	....	....	....	....	....	....	....	5.6	14.3	1.3	
Cameroon	622	−15.3	−23.0	39.3	−21.0	28.3	40.2	10.2	8.2	34.2	22.3	27.7	−11.3
Central African Republic	626	1.5	19.8	84.2	4.5	7.7	−12.4	−20.2	7.7	9.3	−6.2	−6.0	−8.0
Chad	628	−5.0	−20.2	23.5	58.2	31.5	−4.2	−10.2	−6.3	16.3	17.4	34.4	−10.3
Congo, Rep. of	634	15.8	−4.3	35.4	8.3	8.6	11.6	−20.7	34.2	103.1	−23.4	−8.6	7.2
Equatorial Guinea	642	60.7	−20.4	78.0	99.1	14.6	9.8	−19.9	95.3	48.9	85.6	4.6	142.5
Gabon	646	−28.1	−8.2	129.4	−4.2	28.8	1.7	−8.5	−7.9	36.2	−4.2	1.1	14.4
WAEMU	759	....	....	19.5	9.0	2.6	11.2	7.4	3.5	11.6	23.7	20.6	−1.9
Benin	638	22.6	−12.9	1.4	−26.1	9.2	19.9	−4.4	75.7	40.7	23.2	−13.1	−39.0
Burkina Faso	748	6.1	15.4	−.8	24.0	4.7	23.5	−3.6	−14.1	.1	.2	−24.2	34.6
Côte d'Ivoire	662	−11.2	9.1	56.3	11.6	−6.7	11.8	19.1	−7.7	2.0	34.3	40.0	−4.9
Guinea Bissau	654	65.5	32.2	32.3	32.1	38.7	125.8	−13.3	34.5	87.5	15.9	30.5	26.3
Mali	678	−.2	9.1	−19.4	10.3	18.3	7.7	−5.6	12.7	26.5	11.9	46.6	25.6
Niger	692	2.3	−4.3	−24.0	13.0	−5.9	−21.3	−35.7	32.0	3.9	48.6	−4.7	−36.2
Senegal	722	7.2	−30.3	49.2	4.1	−14.2	3.3	6.8	15.9	5.8	34.3	12.2	4.7
Togo	742	−17.9	−32.1	2.4	28.8	−12.6	.8	10.9	14.3	21.1	−6.4	5.9	−31.7
Algeria	612	†22.5	27.6	−5.3	7.6	19.9	16.6	13.1	11.4	22.4	41.8	25.5	43.6
Angola	614	....	....	....	....	3,397.1	92.0	49.8	†419.9	217.7	146.6	117.7	76.0
Botswana	616	−17.2	−6.7	−.9	3.5	11.8	26.2	23.6	14.2	6.1	13.1	8.3	27.5
Burundi	618	11.1	4.9	26.5	−.8	19.1	1.9	2.7	35.6	−2.6	11.1	23.2	10.9
Cape Verde	624	31.4	43.4	−38.9	†22.7	−6.3	.5	9.3	6.7	15.8	7.6	15.3	2.8
Comoros	632	2.2	40.3	14.3	−10.2	36.3	−12.4	†−10.8	19.1	25.9	70.6	18.9	−1.5
Congo, Dem. Rep. of	636	4,342.5	2,608.4	3,264.3	650.3	524.2	106.5	2,690.2	420.3	−38.5	112.7	21.2	29.3
Djibouti	611	23.1	−7.7	5.5	−12.6	−3.7	−2.1	−2.0	4.4	5.4	9.0	31.2	
Eritrea	643	....	....	....	....	86.1	88.5	−34.8	38.3	7.7	−3.4	16.9	13.5
Ethiopia	644	19.1	4.9	10.3	12.6	−16.5	8.8	−12.2	−4.9	38.7	−9.0	34.8	15.1
Gambia, The	648	3.3	11.2	−3.9	25.4	.5	26.8	7.2	14.5	16.8	21.0	34.1	....
Ghana	652	88.4	4.9	78.9	35.1	44.8	33.4	†19.4	38.4	54.5	41.0	46.2	28.1
Guinea	656	11.8	18.9	−10.0	12.3	−1.4	27.2	†4.9	....	....	14.9	21.7	17.8
Kenya	664	53.5	52.5	22.8	31.0	8.2	2.1	−.4	6.0	−.7	−1.0	11.9	−1.1
Lesotho	666	−22.0	21.9	6.6	32.4	5.0	12.3	38.9	32.8	−6.6	−25.4	.3	6.6
Liberia	668	1.2	27.2	5.4	31.3	17.9	8.0	1.9	4.4	†41.3	11.8	6.3	5.3
Madagascar	674	20.8	−6.6	71.9	29.7	48.7	1.1	6.5	26.1	11.8	29.5	4.4	−.2
Malawi	676	17.2	62.6	41.3	89.6	38.5	.2	38.6	32.1	5.8	33.8	26.7	27.6
Mauritania	682	21.5	55.1	−3.7	−5.7	−49.5	−13.1	−7.5	4.5	4.9	5.4	3.2	−.3
Mauritius	684	20.6	18.1	5.1	14.6	−5.2	−2.2	9.4	7.8	11.8	10.4	14.9	9.3
Morocco	686	−8.0	8.6	6.2	5.2	7.6	†7.9	7.1	13.3	3.2	21.4	3.6	16.2
Mozambique	688	73.3	75.8	66.4	31.7	26.6	16.1	−3.7	17.5	25.7	53.0	17.3	21.9
Namibia	728	128.4	5.2	60.2	11.2	22.3	19.9	3.6	43.6	−6.3	8.3	7.8	19.7
Nigeria	694	†90.3	49.4	31.3	20.5	6.1	4.5	16.7	21.7	48.2	34.1	13.1	42.9
Rwanda	714	−3.4	27.9	9.3	38.7	22.6	11.4	−8.8	14.8	−8.3	22.2	−.9	11.5
São Tomé and Príncipe	716	....	....	....	....	81.1	144.9	10.1	−15.2	29.3	74.7	14.3	64.8
Seychelles	718	51.1	23.1	47.7	20.8	13.7	18.7	−49.3	9.4	3.1	7.2	26.7	−19.4
Sierra Leone	724	18.9	3.7	25.4	12.1	†23.9	109.0	−20.4	39.0	9.2	29.4	24.9	22.4
South Africa	199	.2	−8.5	17.8	29.7	13.7	11.4	5.4	41.3	30.7	23.5	33.0	−31.3
Sudan	732	†153.6	64.6	39.9	76.7	81.8	34.3	29.4	35.1	†46.7	4.5	21.3	27.3
Swaziland	734	58.2	−11.3	17.6	2.5	−7.4	5.4	−8.4	11.6	−4.5	−6.4	27.3	27.1
Tanzania	738	60.3	†35.1	48.7	39.1	6.6	8.7	14.7	21.5	9.4	5.0	19.1	12.6
Tunisia	744	7.2	4.8	7.2	9.4	35.8	8.1	−11.8	30.5	−11.4	17.9	−3.1	7.5
Uganda	746	†2.5	23.4	48.1	13.7	11.6	9.1	20.0	15.1	21.8	13.4	10.7	11.0

Reserve Money

		1992	1993	1994	1995	1996	1997	1998	1999	2000	2001	2002	2003
						Percent Change over Previous Year							
Africa(Cont.)													
Zambia	754	....	....	48.0	−14.6	35.4	48.2	16.8	28.5	53.4	45.7	44.7	14.3
Zimbabwe	698	13.3	52.0	23.6	2.5	65.9	37.8	29.9	60.9	16.0	164.9	171.2	394.8
Asia													
Bangladesh	513	21.2	24.0	29.6	−9.3	8.7	9.4	13.4	12.7	14.5	24.1	3.3	6.9
Bhutan	514	−21.1	† 53.7	−33.4	67.1	8.3	9.3	55.4	25.7	21.1	2.3	13.3	19.9
Cambodia	522	....	....	25.4	10.0	43.0	21.2	47.2	15.9	24.9	17.1	45.7	8.5
China, P.R.: Mainland	924	16.3	† 36.2	31.0	20.6	29.5	17.0	2.8	7.6	9.0	10.0	12.5	17.6
China, P.R.: Hong Kong	532	26.3	17.1	9.7	3.9	5.0	6.4	2.2	† 19.6	−8.1	6.7	7.1	18.9
Fiji	819	19.7	−2.9	1.7	8.8	1.9	5.0	6.3	56.8	−18.9	19.3	9.5	31.9
India	534	8.4	21.7	21.7	12.6	9.5	11.2	12.4	11.4	7.7	10.2	9.3	13.8
Indonesia	536	† 19.7	8.3	25.2	17.8	35.8	38.3	77.8	38.8	24.3	16.0	−.9	12.8
Korea	542	10.9	27.5	9.2	16.3	−12.2	−12.5	−8.1	37.6	−.9	16.3	15.7	7.3
Lao People's Democratic Rep.	544	40.6	64.5	22.3	13.4	24.0	43.8	87.7	71.0	59.1	7.3	31.2	23.2
Malaysia	548	† 21.8	−30.6	36.2	24.7	† 35.2	28.4	−56.4	26.3	−9.4	−3.3	6.4	6.9
Maldives	556	34.5	19.0	14.2	1.6	17.7	15.4	10.9	6.9	4.4	9.7	18.7	−1.7
Mongolia	948	142.6	184.5	103.8	29.0	36.4	23.1	18.3	50.4	20.2	6.8	21.9	14.5
Myanmar	518	30.5	20.7	23.1	27.8	32.0	29.5	26.8	18.7	34.5	51.6	34.9	46.1
Nepal	558	15.6	30.1	11.7	8.6	9.9	61.1	−9.3	10.3	19.3	12.0	−.1	2.9
Pakistan	564	8.8	14.2	15.7	17.9	−3.6	14.3	13.0	13.0	−2.1	28.3	8.8	16.5
Papua New Guinea	853	2.6	17.9	11.3	15.3	91.3	−34.3	20.7	73.3	−16.4	5.5	18.0	12.9
Philippines	566	3.9	† 18.0	7.9	12.4	32.5	−6.1	2.0	36.7	−10.6	−11.1	16.3	9.3
Samoa	862	−20.7	−8.0	3.2	4.4	20.5	19.1	−45.7	21.4	8.8	−4.8	20.3	10.7
Singapore	576	10.6	8.4	6.2	9.4	6.7	5.6	−13.3	28.6	−13.7	8.5	−.3	3.4
Solomon Islands	813	−.1	11.7	30.9	23.0	30.4	−6.2	46.0	−.3	14.6	−3.3	16.5	27.3
Sri Lanka	524	12.0	25.9	20.5	15.5	8.8	−2.1	10.9	8.2	4.7	7.0	12.3	11.9
Thailand	578	17.9	16.1	14.5	22.6	13.5	15.8	−4.5	54.8	−12.9	6.2	2.4	26.5
Tonga	866	6.8	−62.8	−4.5	−17.7	43.0	12.3	10.3	7.5	12.6	29.7	20.7	−9.4
Vanuatu	846	−2.6	53.6	−6.8	30.4	−4.2	−.2	5.2	22.3	1.9	−.4	−	8.0
Vietnam	582	....	27.8	....	....	20.1	12.5	8.7	50.5	25.0	16.7	12.4	27.4
Europe													
Albania	914	....	....	....	28.1	14.0	48.1	−1.1	21.6	17.8	18.1	7.7	−2.0
Armenia	911	....	1,375.5	842.0	92.0	42.8	24.8	4.9	−	34.4	11.1	38.4	6.9
Azerbaijan	912	....	1,375.6	642.9	179.8	17.6	41.4	† −24.3	15.9	29.1	† 1.5	14.0	23.5
Belarus	913	....	....	....	287.9	78.1	107.6	162.9	178.5	124.4	103.9	32.1	51.1
Bosnia and Herzegovina	963	....	....	....	....	....	....	38.8	241.7	19.2	164.6	−8.9	12.5
Bulgaria	918	50.7	22.0	55.9	† 81.6	91.5	826.4	10.3	17.7	11.0	26.7	10.1	17.0
Croatia	960	502.8	994.1	109.6	43.1	30.0	18.0	−3.8	3.6	13.6	51.9	29.3	32.8
Cyprus	423	6.9	1.6	12.5	−4.3	−8.8	−.8	16.2	14.8	10.8	7.6	24.8	4.8
Czech Republic	935	....	....	34.4	53.6	.5	† .1	22.5	8.9	6.9	4.9	† −49.6	7.3
Estonia	939	166.1	† 103.3	11.6	19.9	22.2	37.7	6.4	26.7	14.9	−9.8	−1.5	14.6
Georgia	915	....	....	....	....	36.3	32.6	−6.3	18.8	27.0	† 10.4	19.6	14.3
Hungary	944	21.4	2.9	−1.6	17.8	−8.5	29.9	20.6	26.2	17.3	1.7	5.5	10.2
Kazakhstan	916	....	....	623.4	113.5	26.8	† 36.8	−29.4	55.7	6.0	30.6	18.6	52.2
Kyrgyz Republic	917	....	....	....	....	23.9	21.1	7.6	30.7	11.7	11.5	42.7	32.6
Latvia	941	....	....	19.5	1.6	23.0	31.2	6.7	11.6	7.7	13.3	18.4	6.3
Lithuania	946	....	203.7	44.2	35.0	2.2	32.4	28.8	−4.0	−3.3	8.3	20.8	26.6
Macedonia, FYR	962	....	....	71.7	† 30.6	−3.2	22.7	5.6	29.6	46.6	8.1	3.8	7.8
Malta	181	6.3	.2	31.7	−12.2	−4.2	1.5	3.0	6.9	3.5	3.7	4.2	....
Moldova	921	534.0	391.7	128.9	41.3	† 9.5	33.3	−6.6	41.7	32.0	25.9	31.2	18.6
Poland	964	35.8	7.6	22.6	45.0	20.5	34.0	16.9	−1.3	−7.8	30.5	−2.6	6.9
Romania	968	116.3	† 191.5	87.5	56.2	51.4	136.5	20.8	92.4	54.7	59.9	54.7	20.0
Russia	922	....	....	203.5	107.8	27.3	27.6	28.1	65.6	67.2	29.1	31.2	54.1
Slovak Republic	936	....	....	23.9	30.8	28.7	18.2	−5.6	20.0	4.0	22.6	1.7	† −7.3
Slovenia	961	133.1	38.2	56.9	25.2	15.6	23.0	19.7	21.3	1.9	35.5	−1.8	5.4
Turkey	186	78.2	67.9	119.5	79.5	91.5	99.9	80.4	97.5	46.2	78.5	17.6	18.6
Ukraine	926	....	1,560.0	407.4	132.8	39.9	49.0	† 16.6	41.3	43.8	42.5	23.8	30.1
Middle East													
Bahrain	419	−9.0	−20.1	−4.1	34.5	−11.1	12.6	−21.7	45.5	−.6	14.4	13.9	34.8
Egypt	469	10.4	19.2	12.5	9.3	4.2	11.1	19.3	1.6	18.7	17.0	8.7	39.7
Iran, I.R. of	429	13.1	18.8	34.2	48.0	27.1	23.0	18.0	17.1	16.7	6.4	34.8	7.5
Israel	436	6.9	28.1	−6.7	−26.8	34.9	119.3	14.4	23.8	.6	.7	−15.8	−7.5
Jordan	439	6.3	† 5.2	5.1	6.4	−13.4	−2.8	−4.7	12.1	.8	−5.7	3.9	16.9
Kuwait	443	−5.7	−6.3	.1	−6.6	.8	−10.1	5.0	30.0	−8.3	−2.5	13.2	16.9
Lebanon	446	90.2	41.9	76.7	21.2	21.2	50.0	−5.5	5.5	6.6	37.2	10.1	121.7
Libya	672	28.5	−2.4	15.9	7.7	9.0	† 6.6	−1.0	−5.3	−.9	10.0	2.6	11.2
Oman	449	−3.5	−4.8	4.1	3.6	6.4	8.5	7.1	−1.1	8.8	8.8	30.3	5.8
Qatar	453	7.9	4.5	−6.9	5.0	6.1	9.7	3.1	12.2	6.7	11.6	17.0	14.9
Saudi Arabia	456	−1.2	−.2	4.5	−2.3	−1.4	7.6	−1.2	23.5	−4.0	−4.1	9.3	5.1
Syrian Arab Rep.	463	22.3	14.6	8.6	4.7	7.6	4.8	5.0	7.3	15.2	16.9	16.0	10.2
United Arab Emirates	466	21.3	−3.3	25.7	13.1	8.1	.5	.2	30.5	36.5	6.0	−1.9	12.3
Yemen, Republic of	474	21.4	29.8	35.5	19.8	6.9	−12.5	11.2	20.8	14.0	14.0	9.2	21.1
Western Hemisphere													
ECCU	309	19.6	−5.7	2.8	10.7	−5.9	6.8	17.5	6.4	4.3	13.9	8.3	10.7
Anguilla	312	15.1	12.9	−2.1	33.7	14.6	12.5	12.2	11.2	2.7	28.6	1.3	26.2
Antigua and Barbuda	311	32.0	−18.5	15.0	17.5	−17.3	4.6	13.1	14.0	−2.5	20.1	5.3	27.0
Dominica	321	4.3	−7.5	−9.4	17.4	−.7	2.8	11.6	12.4	−2.7	−.8	42.5	−3.4
Grenada	328	27.0	−7.4	6.4	8.5	.3	12.5	6.4	6.0	10.4	11.2	18.7	9.0
Montserrat	351	−.8	−1.3	19.5	9.0	3.0	26.1	115.2	−44.0	−24.9	14.9	13.4	6.1
St. Kitts and Nevis	361	41.4	5.3	7.2	−1.5	−3.3	6.6	19.7	12.9	7.9	10.4	16.4	−2.7

Reserve Money

Percent Change over Previous Year

		1992	1993	1994	1995	1996	1997	1998	1999	2000	2001	2002	2003
Western Hemisphere(Cont.)													
St. Lucia	362	−1.4	4.7	−4.6	11.5	−4.4	1.7	13.9	3.3	3.8	16.4	2.1	12.3
St. Vincent & Grens	364	39.1	−10.7	−3.3	−5.4	−2.6	9.1	20.8	16.8	20.6	9.5	−10.6	4.3
Argentina	213	40.7	36.1	†8.5	−15.4	2.1	13.6	2.6	.8	−8.8	17.9	69.8	66.3
Aruba	314	18.3	10.7	−6.4	18.0	−14.3	−4.2	40.5	6.3	−11.5	32.4	13.7	−5.7
Bahamas, The	313	−2.7	−.4	12.0	2.8	−2.6	14.5	19.7	20.8	−2.2	10.4	11.7	6.4
Barbados	316	13.3	−11.7	−1.9	15.7	34.2	−9.6	9.0	4.2	11.9	15.2	39.2	19.8
Belize	339	21.4	−.7	−2.0	13.4	2.9	5.2	7.8	21.9	22.7	27.1	−22.9	4.1
Bolivia	218	5.4	32.8	4.3	23.3	†15.7	20.1	−20.8	11.3	10.4	12.1	1.5	13.6
Brazil	223	1,148.2	2,424.4	2,241.7	11.9	22.8	34.2	−11.1	7.8	4.8	19.0	145.9	−4.6
Chile	228	34.5	18.5	17.7	21.3	11.5	†7.2	9.8	4.5	−7.0	8.9	5.9	−3.8
Colombia	233	37.6	25.6	28.2	6.8	17.7	16.5	−17.1	39.7	9.1	9.9	20.3	16.4
Costa Rica	238	17.8	9.5	29.6	16.2	21.9	†16.9	11.2	7.4	−4.7	−25.9	4.3	29.8
Dominican Republic	243	12.9	28.3	.5	16.4	10.9	18.9	22.4	15.0	10.3	28.9	−8.7	108.2
Ecuador	248	12.9	47.0	2.5	−9.5	7.0	7.2	†−3.9	†−15.0	−42.7	11.4	†−8.8	9.9
El Salvador	253	1.4	51.7	22.2	12.4	10.0	13.3	8.3	10.2	†−9.7	−29.2	−22.4	52.7
Guatemala	258	8.0	23.3	4.5	3.5	12.8	†22.9	−3.9	2.8	19.3	16.2	18.4	11.1
Guyana	336	51.7	†−23.1	31.4	19.1	5.9	17.1	11.8	−3.9	14.0	10.9	10.0	10.3
Haiti	263	29.5	29.2	23.8	14.7	−4.1	†11.1	.3	29.0	25.9	16.9	23.9	31.4
Honduras	268	44.5	6.8	47.0	23.9	43.5	†91.9	16.1	11.6	9.3	9.8	26.2	6.6
Jamaica	343	88.6	44.6	34.3	29.7	4.0	15.2	22.1	−4.2	7.8	−6.4	−3.2	24.5
Mexico	273	14.4	10.4	21.2	33.4	23.1	†48.4	37.1	38.3	−6.6	23.1	26.6	16.8
Netherlands Antilles	353	29.2	5.5	−6.5	19.9	−14.3	15.6	9.9	−5.9	8.2	36.3	24.9	−6.0
Nicaragua	278	5.7	7.8	52.5	23.6	†34.6	32.5	19.7	5.7	4.7	†41.7	11.0	18.9
Panama	283	−19.5	4.1	−1.8	2.8	39.8	2.8	3.3	−1.5	4.9	.4	−2.0	−.3
Paraguay	288	27.6	13.5	27.3	†26.2	−1.9	7.3	6.5	9.1	−1.0	6.1	2.7	50.9
Peru	293	95.9	59.4	31.0	31.2	37.8	38.7	5.7	15.6	2.0	4.6	8.3	−6.2
Suriname	366	12.6	70.0	207.8	227.0	−10.3	−.4	†65.0	76.3	129.4	13.4	23.2	−8.3
Trinidad and Tobago	369	−9.7	−4.7	56.9	−.7	†8.9	16.1	20.9	3.7	3.1	10.7	−1.4	6.4
Uruguay	298	45.0	42.6	32.4	30.5	32.5	25.0	†14.4	21.2	9.4	26.2	.7	60.6
Venezuela, Rep. Bol.	299	11.5	10.4	64.0	31.7	†96.9	73.9	18.2	33.0	14.8	12.0	19.5	47.2

2004, International Monetary Fund : *International Financial Statistics Yearbook*

Money

		1992	1993	1994	1995	1996	1997	1998	1999	2000	2001	2002	2003
		Percent Change over Previous Year												

Industrial Countries

		1992	1993	1994	1995	1996	1997	1998	1999	2000	2001	2002	2003
United States	111	11.7	9.7	.1	−.9	1.4	3.5	3.5	10.3	−1.7	11.4	2.9	2.0
Canada	156	7.1	8.3	6.6	10.2	12.7	9.2	5.7	10.9	13.0	12.7	5.8	5.9
Australia	193	20.0	17.8	10.9	6.5	14.0	13.3	5.9	9.7	9.3	21.3	....	....
Japan	158	3.9	7.0	4.2	13.1	9.7	8.6	5.0	11.7	3.5	13.7	23.5	....
New Zealand	196	−1.3	7.3	6.1	8.4	2.1	7.2	8.7	18.3	7.2	19.7	6.5	8.4
Euro Area	163	5.2	5.3	4.2	37.1	10.6	12.1	10.1	10.7	5.8	9.2	9.4	11.3
Austria	122	6.1	9.2	8.6	14.8	4.7	4.7	....	....	....	....	....	....
Belgium	124	† −.6	7.5	1.5	4.9	4.2	3.1	....	....	....	....	....	....
Finland	172	3.2	5.1	8.9	14.0	16.4	5.5	4.8	....	....	....	....	....
Germany	134	11.5	8.8	4.9	7.1	12.3	2.1	10.4	....	....	....	....	....
Greece	174	12.4	11.5	23.5	13.6	10.9	14.4	11.9	34.3	−4.0	....	....	....
Ireland	178	.5	12.9	12.5	64.1	8.8	−17.4	25.2	....	....	....	....	....
Italy	136	1.4	6.3	3.9	.4	4.9	6.5	11.1	....	....	....	....	....
Luxembourg	137	1.7	....	....	....	....	3.2	....	....	....	....	....	....
Netherlands	138	4.3	10.5	1.7	13.5	12.1	7.8	....	....	....	....	....	....
Portugal	182	18.5	10.7	6.6	10.9	12.1	12.9	17.0	....	....	....	....	....
Spain	184	−2.0	3.5	7.1	2.9	7.1	14.0	15.8	....	....	....	....	....
Denmark	128	−.9	10.5	−1.4	4.6	11.5	5.7	4.8	5.8	† 1.1	7.5	3.8	8.9
Iceland	176	1.3	5.4	10.7	9.6	8.5	16.4	20.3	† 21.1	2.6	−2.0	19.0	....
Norway	142	26.4	5.2	4.4	1.1	9.5	6.2	19.3	5.6	7.6	16.7	8.2	....
Switzerland	146	4.0	5.8	4.0	6.1	† 27.4	9.0	6.8	9.5	−2.1	8.5	10.2	24.1
United Kingdom	112	† 4.3	9.9	.8	16.7	9.3	25.7	† 9.4	11.1	14.1	11.3	10.1	10.2

Developing Countries
Africa

		1992	1993	1994	1995	1996	1997	1998	1999	2000	2001	2002	2003
CEMAC	758	....	....	....	....	....	....	....	....	....	2.7	14.2	−3.1
Cameroon	622	−27.6	−14.1	35.1	−11.6	−1.6	34.9	14.5	10.8	17.4	12.8	14.3	−5.2
Central African Rep.	626	−3.7	16.4	74.0	7.6	4.9	−8.1	−18.3	12.6	3.2	−2.6	−4.4	−9.8
Chad	628	−8.7	−27.7	31.5	42.7	33.5	−4.7	−8.0	−3.1	17.7	21.8	27.3	−3.1
Congo, Rep. of	634	6.4	−19.7	40.4	.3	13.6	8.7	−13.6	27.8	68.2	−23.1	13.9	−13.3
Equatorial Guinea	642	35.45	−28.55	135.49	58.35	50.13	−4.33	9.72	89.82	34.76	26.04	51.67	56.19
Gabon	646	−27.16	−3.45	41.88	12.35	25.98	8.06	−5.07	−5.12	19.30	3.67	4.35	−.46
WAEMU	759	....	....	54.9	13.6	6.1	8.4	7.9	4.4	6.5	13.3	15.1	1.1
Benin	638	9.9	−13.2	67.3	−13.2	17.2	2.0	−4.7	46.9	35.0	10.0	−8.6	−19.1
Burkina Faso	748	.5	11.6	38.9	25.5	7.0	17.5	−2.6	−1.9	5.3	−3.0	−7.1	17.8
Côte d'Ivoire	662	−4.0	.9	61.7	18.2	2.3	11.7	12.9	−1.7	−3.7	14.8	32.1	−7.1
Guinea Bissau	654	83.1	27.3	58.1	46.9	51.0	236.3	−12.1	22.4	63.7	7.8	22.3	15.4
Mali	678	.9	8.8	47.9	13.8	21.3	6.5	4.5	−.6	9.4	29.6	28.9	21.7
Niger	692	−10.5	11.1	15.4	9.2	−9.5	−19.4	−18.5	15.4	11.8	35.3	−8.2	−22.9
Senegal	722	2.0	−9.0	54.4	3.7	8.5	−.1	15.7	10.8	5.5	14.9	5.8	18.4
Togo	742	−27.2	−18.5	104.6	37.7	−7.8	1.9	6.9	9.9	22.2	−8.7	−8.1	−3.6
Algeria	612	† 16.2	19.4	7.8	7.1	13.4	14.6	20.9	8.9	17.3	18.5	....	....
Angola	614	....	....	....	....	3,392.6	107.5	39.8	† 326.2	342.0	168.1	134.0	108.9
Botswana	616	−1.1	14.7	11.1	7.2	14.7	9.1	45.8	17.3	6.9	23.9	7.4	11.8
Burundi	618	10.3	12.0	28.3	−3.3	12.5	10.5	1.3	41.9	−1.0	16.8	† 25.5	† 19.0
Cape Verde	624	31.4	7.0	8.2	† 16.6	10.6	21.6	−2.0	17.3	11.4	2.6	8.8	1.3
Comoros	632	9.4	4.6	9.8	−5.3	8.1	−18.6	† −5.5	16.4	21.0	62.5	10.4	−2.1
Congo, Dem. Rep. of	636	4,114.6	2,460.6	5,635.4	407.2	....	....	....	....	....	....	41.0	24.6
Djibouti	611	10.5	4.1	3.3	−1.6	−2.9	−9.6	−9.9	3.5	−7.8	2.6	24.0	20.7
Eritrea	643	....	....	....	....	29.9	36.1	18.0	46.4	13.4	28.1	18.8	15.9
Ethiopia	644	15.6	4.4	21.4	2.7	−2.7	20.2	−4.7	14.8	9.6	4.8	19.4	12.3
Gambia, The	648	10.6	6.0	−11.7	15.7	−3.8	38.8	−.5	14.3	37.4	14.4	56.1	....
Ghana	652	53.0	27.9	50.3	33.4	31.7	46.0	† 20.9	15.8	38.2	46.3	59.9	33.2
Guinea	656	19.7	19.4	−3.2	8.5	−.2	21.3	† 8.7	....	....	12.0	21.6	31.1
Kenya	664	47.1	27.4	12.6	3.8	13.9	15.2	3.4	16.4	8.6	6.2	18.5	29.7
Lesotho	666	12.3	23.4	12.3	10.5	19.3	22.7	24.9	−2.6	8.2	24.7	11.5	6.7
Liberia	668	−5.6	59.8	7.6	42.4	6.7	−1.4	128.8	14.9	† −11.5	6.7	38.8	6.1
Madagascar	674	21.6	11.9	56.5	15.2	17.3	22.9	10.9	20.2	13.2	30.3	7.5	4.2
Malawi	676	19.4	34.8	50.5	44.0	24.7	16.5	63.4	33.5	38.9	13.5	26.5	27.1
Mauritania	682	4.3	3.6	−5.4	−8.1	−10.9	8.3	5.3	6.3	22.7	14.8	4.3	11.4
Mauritius	684	8.0	3.0	19.4	8.0	2.7	7.9	9.2	3.6	10.8	16.2	17.5	12.4
Morocco	686	6.1	4.9	11.1	6.0	5.8	† 7.2	7.8	11.6	7.9	15.3	9.0	9.8
Mozambique	688	45.3	52.0	50.5	35.0	20.0	25.1	14.5	24.6	22.3	17.6	14.5	23.8
Namibia	728	22.0	46.3	14.7	8.3	53.6	3.5	27.0	22.2	28.2	9.5	6.1	17.2
Nigeria	694	† 73.2	57.0	43.4	16.3	13.5	16.8	19.0	22.5	62.1	25.7	15.9	29.5
Rwanda	714	24.9	10.7	15.6	41.1	11.7	22.7	−.8	7.0	6.7	1.0	10.4	17.0
São Tomé and Príncipe	716	....	....	....	....	66.5	107.8	−3.3	5.3	23.5	54.3	13.7	48.5
Seychelles	718	10.2	14.5	−2.7	2.6	34.4	44.2	20.3	37.2	6.2	13.5	22.2	5.0
Sierra Leone	724	25.1	11.7	10.0	29.5	† 6.6	57.1	7.3	49.4	4.4	35.4	30.6	18.4
South Africa	199	2.9	6.7	25.1	18.3	32.0	17.4	23.2	21.7	2.4	17.3	12.0	7.4
Sudan	732	† 101.3	76.1	54.6	66.7	86.2	32.5	29.3	27.8	† 42.2	15.7	29.8	30.2
Swaziland	734	20.2	14.2	7.3	16.6	16.5	16.2	1.9	32.3	−.3	14.2	9.5	26.9
Tanzania	738	34.1	† 32.9	33.3	29.9	4.9	9.9	10.5	16.0	9.9	10.2	25.2	16.1
Tunisia	744	7.3	3.6	10.7	9.6	13.0	13.0	7.5	16.0	9.9	10.1	−1.7	5.3
Uganda	746	† 68.0	25.9	36.5	15.4	10.3	13.7	19.5	12.6	16.8	12.8	21.0	12.3
Zambia	754	....	....	44.8	61.1	19.4	31.0	† 16.8	23.6	51.2	34.2	28.6	28.1
Zimbabwe	698	5.8	94.9	18.2	52.4	23.1	53.7	23.5	34.7	53.3	142.8	170.0	485.1

Money

Percent Change over Previous Year

		1992	1993	1994	1995	1996	1997	1998	1999	2000	2001	2002	2003
Asia													
Bangladesh	513	13.6	16.0	24.3	16.7	4.7	7.7	7.4	12.8	18.4	10.7	5.1	7.6
Bhutan	514	12.2	†12.1	27.1	26.6	56.8	4.5	21.2	41.7	5.8	23.1	43.8	−2.9
Cambodia	522	....	....	−1.1	38.1	18.1	17.0	41.2	−2.1	1.4	13.0	33.4	15.1
China, P.R.: Mainland	924	30.3	†21.8	27.2	17.3	19.4	26.3	11.2	21.4	16.1	13.1	17.8	19.0
China, P.R.: Hong Kong	532	24.9	20.9	.1	.3	15.3	−3.8	−4.6	15.4	—	14.3	14.0	34.8
China, P.R.: Macao	546	51.8	−10.3	−9.1	7.3	1.7	−7.1	3.8	−2.6	−7.8	19.6	7.3	38.4
Fiji	819	14.4	15.8	−5.3	12.0	18.2	−2.4	10.9	40.6	−14.5	4.6	14.7	26.5
India	534	7.1	18.7	27.4	11.1	14.1	12.6	11.7	16.9	10.6	10.0	12.5	16.2
Indonesia	536	†7.9	21.9	23.7	15.6	10.0	32.8	25.3	28.8	37.7	8.8	7.4	17.3
Korea	542	13.0	18.1	11.9	19.6	1.7	−11.4	1.6	24.7	5.9	13.8	18.0	3.7
Lao People's Dem. Rep.	544	24.5	48.6	17.4	9.5	12.5	5.8	111.4	29.6	57.3	8.0	57.9	42.5
Malaysia	548	†27.3	35.3	16.8	13.2	†23.7	11.7	−29.4	29.2	6.7	4.0	9.6	14.9
Maldives	556	15.4	49.7	22.5	5.7	17.8	12.9	15.8	14.5	11.1	−5.9	13.9	11.6
Micronesia, Fed.Sts.	868	....	....	....	....	−1.7	10.2	−1.1	−6.5	−5.5	13.0	−7.3	14.1
Mongolia	948	4.5	142.8	78.2	29.0	42.7	25.1	8.5	39.0	13.9	19.4	20.2	13.4
Myanmar	518	34.9	25.2	33.8	28.1	33.4	31.0	28.2	22.6	34.5	50.8	44.0	17.5
Nepal	558	16.0	23.9	20.6	9.9	5.9	44.2	−11.2	21.1	14.4	....	....	....
Pakistan	564	21.5	1.7	15.1	12.8	7.5	32.5	4.6	8.6	10.1	10.1	15.9	24.1
Papua New Guinea	853	4.9	35.9	3.4	14.0	52.0	−5.5	10.3	21.0	2.2	3.2	15.0	16.4
Philippines	566	9.1	†22.3	11.3	21.7	19.8	14.2	7.4	38.3	−1.3	.4	22.0	8.6
Samoa	862	−11.4	14.7	8.1	29.1	−.2	22.5	−10.7	20.7	16.1	−6.9	10.1	23.6
Singapore	576	12.7	23.6	2.3	8.3	6.7	1.7	−1.0	14.2	6.9	8.5	−.7	8.1
Solomon Islands	813	31.9	18.1	31.4	5.0	15.7	7.4	−.2	25.7	−5.8	−1.5	3.5	29.6
Sri Lanka	524	7.4	18.6	18.7	6.7	4.0	9.8	12.1	12.8	9.1	3.2	14.0	16.0
Thailand	578	12.3	18.6	17.0	12.1	9.1	1.5	4.9	64.0	−7.5	−4.9	3.7	28.8
Tonga	866	−12.7	20.5	−5.5	−13.9	3.8	2.6	4.7	22.1	10.6	26.2	32.0	12.7
Vanuatu	846	15.5	12.3	.9	10.1	3.5	1.8	14.4	.2	6.1	−.5	44.3	5.7
Vietnam	582	....	28.9	....	....	25.1	19.5	13.1	51.2	33.1	23.5	11.5	25.3
Europe													
Albania	914	....	....	....	52.8	52.6	1.4	−8.7	23.0	20.4	15.3	6.7	−5.2
Armenia	911	....	1,060.1	907.3	124.3	32.4	10.6	19.6	−.9	36.7	8.3	49.2	6.9
Azerbaijan	912	....	980.1	468.3	130.5	30.4	36.1	†−25.6	17.5	†12.9	†7.6	16.2	27.0
Belarus	913	....	....	....	273.2	†56.7	115.5	139.1	188.4	117.8	84.7	45.4	63.9
Bosnia & Herzegovina	963	....	....	....	....	....	....	11.9	199.4	28.0	89.7	13.1	4.3
Bulgaria	918	53.2	32.2	51.3	†47.2	115.7	908.1	21.7	11.6	20.3	22.8	13.5	22.7
Croatia	960	....	....	112.2	24.6	37.9	21.0	−1.4	1.7	30.1	31.5	30.2	9.8
Cyprus	423	9.5	8.5	4.9	6.2	6.8	7.8	3.7	†42.1	−2.1	−.5	1.1	30.4
Czech Republic	935	....	....	50.2	6.7	4.7	†−7.3	−3.4	10.8	11.4	17.0	†17.0	16.6
Estonia	939	309.9	†75.2	20.9	29.8	37.6	24.0	−6.3	32.1	20.5	19.5	9.3	13.0
Georgia	915	....	....	....	....	37.3	31.1	−10.0	9.9	33.7	†7.2	14.9	14.1
Hungary	944	32.1	11.7	8.0	3.8	22.5	23.5	17.2	19.3	11.4	16.7	18.7	10.4
Kazakhstan	916	....	....	576.0	108.2	20.9	†8.2	−21.3	73.4	14.7	14.3	41.5	25.0
Kyrgyz Republic	917	....	....	....	....	16.6	7.8	2.9	31.0	9.6	20.7	38.1	38.3
Latvia	941	....	....	31.1	.8	20.3	33.3	6.0	6.3	19.6	13.0	21.3	17.7
Lithuania	946	....	....	41.8	40.9	3.5	41.5	9.0	−5.3	7.5	18.9	23.5	26.5
Macedonia, FYR	962	....	....	78.3	†22.7	−3.6	16.2	9.1	32.4	13.1	−50.1	148.2	−2.1
Malta	181	.5	4.0	9.1	†7.6	−1.9	—	7.2	10.6	2.6	6.7	7.0	....
Moldova	921	561.3	304.9	116.5	68.8	†12.4	30.6	†−18.0	38.9	36.7	23.6	42.4	24.0
Poland	964	38.8	31.3	39.7	36.4	39.8	17.9	16.2	23.1	−6.4	14.0	19.9	18.3
Romania	968	41.6	95.0	107.8	57.7	58.7	66.9	17.7	34.6	55.9	39.0	36.2	28.2
Russia	922	....	....	187.0	120.7	27.2	55.6	15.0	53.3	66.9	35.5	25.6	45.6
Slovak Republic	936	....	....	6.2	20.9	15.8	†−4.4	−11.4	4.2	21.5	21.3	8.5	†44.6
Slovenia	961	133.7	41.5	35.1	24.8	18.4	18.1	25.2	26.6	6.1	19.9	47.1	12.8
Tajikistan	923	....	....	....	....	....	....	....	17.6	46.9	25.4	34.4	28.3
Turkey	186	72.5	64.8	81.5	68.3	129.5	69.1	63.1	93.6	57.3	46.3	36.7	43.1
Ukraine	926	....	1,552.5	444.0	151.7	34.9	43.3	†14.1	36.4	47.1	43.1	35.2	31.9
Middle East													
Bahrain, Kingdom of	419	15.4	3.7	−5.5	−3.6	.8	3.7	5.1	16.6	4.6	23.8	17.3	26.9
Egypt	469	8.8	12.1	10.7	8.5	7.2	9.4	20.3	.8	5.3	7.9	13.0	23.4
Iran, I.R. of	429	14.8	30.0	41.6	32.5	33.6	19.9	22.7	21.5	24.7	23.0	29.3	13.6
Israel	436	†33.7	27.9	7.7	15.1	20.4	11.3	12.3	20.4	2.5	21.8	1.5	11.7
Jordan	439	4.2	†7.1	1.3	−.2	−11.8	6.1	−.8	9.5	14.2	3.8	8.5	24.4
Kuwait	443	−7.7	.5	1.1	5.2	4.9	.4	−8.3	19.9	7.0	11.8	25.9	26.4
Lebanon	446	74.0	−4.7	25.7	8.6	12.4	10.0	6.3	10.2	5.7	−1.0	7.6	11.1
Libya	672	16.2	4.5	13.0	6.2	1.2	5.2	.4	4.7	4.5	1.2	6.0	6.3
Oman	449	6.7	4.3	4.7	−.3	6.8	9.2	−8.0	1.1	7.5	27.7	10.0	4.7
Qatar	453	10.0	†4.2	−8.1	−4.9	4.4	6.3	2.1	−.9	6.5	17.3	20.5	79.3
Saudi Arabia	456	†6.4	−1.6	3.4	−.2	6.1	6.1	−.6	11.7	5.7	8.4	12.7	10.2
Syrian Arab Republic	463	17.6	22.0	8.2	8.7	8.6	6.7	8.0	11.1	17.7	13.9	17.8	27.0
United Arab Emirates	466	15.1	21.3	5.6	8.6	6.9	13.9	9.5	8.9	12.6	15.8	19.2	23.8
Yemen, Republic of	474	24.3	31.9	35.1	17.5	−4.5	6.3	8.1	15.2	19.3	14.5	8.2	13.4
Western Hemisphere													
ECCU	309	18.1	2.2	7.5	13.4	−2.5	7.8	14.7	7.9	.4	4.9	7.2	15.7
Anguilla	312	11.1	−21.7	2.8	51.4	−3.8	15.5	5.1	10.7	15.3	−4.3	10.9	9.1
Antigua and Barbuda	311	9.7	−1.8	16.5	28.1	−7.5	2.2	25.1	−1.9	−2.3	8.8	−1.5	18.1
Dominica	321	16.0	−12.7	−5.0	19.6	3.1	1.8	5.8	29.1	−19.9	2.0	25.0	−.1
Grenada	328	18.1	13.5	11.3	5.3	.5	4.9	14.5	4.3	8.4	4.9	16.0	14.8
Montserrat	351	−10.1	5.6	20.4	−.4	−6.8	61.9	3.7	−14.3	−15.3	4.1	1.7	28.3
St. Kitts and Nevis	361	10.1	7.9	−3.4	14.0	7.5	−3.9	24.9	4.0	.4	−6.8	20.9	19.3
St. Lucia	362	25.7	4.9	−.2	7.8	−5.0	7.6	7.9	9.8	−1.0	1.2	3.8	23.3

2004, International Monetary Fund: *International Financial Statistics Yearbook*

Money

		1992	1993	1994	1995	1996	1997	1998	1999	2000	2001	2002	2003
		Percent Change over Previous Year											
Western Hemisphere(Cont.)													
St. Vincent & Grenadines	364	44.4	3.2	18.7	−4.6	7.8	28.0	11.6	22.9	14.9	9.4	1.8	10.3
Argentina	213	49.0	33.0	† 15.7	1.6	14.6	12.8	—	1.6	−9.1	−20.1	78.4	51.9
Aruba	314	5.5	14.1	16.8	.5	.9	5.7	15.6	7.8	1.1	17.5	20.4	16.7
Bahamas, The	313	3.8	.4	9.1	6.8	.5	15.7	14.7	26.1	6.7	−3.9	5.7	9.0
Barbados	316	1.5	−5.1	8.3	−17.0	46.4	−1.1	23.4	20.7	23.5	1.3	2.3	31.0
Belize	339	6.8	7.9	5.7	7.8	5.5	1.3	12.3	33.0	15.7	32.1	−13.5	22.4
Bolivia	218	32.9	30.0	29.3	21.1	† 21.7	19.0	7.1	−5.8	8.8	18.7	−.4	19.3
Brazil	223	981.8	2,017.8	2,195.4	25.7	29.9	22.3	7.5	13.6	18.9	12.8	28.3	4.0
Chile	228	26.4	21.1	15.8	22.3	16.4	† 19.9	−4.6	15.8	7.2	11.4	9.1	11.3
Colombia	233	45.1	28.1	29.0	20.2	23.4	17.4	−7.9	24.2	25.9	9.6	16.9	16.4
Costa Rica	238	37.2	7.0	37.9	−6.0	16.9	† 54.3	17.1	28.6	19.8	13.2	16.4	15.1
Dominican Republic	243	17.1	13.9	7.5	17.3	22.3	19.3	6.2	21.8	−1.1	16.4	6.1	64.5
Ecuador	248	1.9	45.8	19.0	−19.4	4.8	7.4	† −13.6	† −24.8	−.9	45.7	† −1.1	10.6
El Salvador	253	15.4	18.8	4.0	8.8	14.3	.6	8.0	15.1	† −6.7	9.6	−9.0	9.9
Guatemala	258	9.1	20.4	40.1	9.9	13.5	† 29.9	13.5	13.6	21.8	11.8	8.4	18.0
Guyana	336	31.5	† 26.6	10.4	16.7	14.5	10.0	−1.6	23.0	10.4	1.2	7.8	14.2
Haiti	263	27.8	22.7	31.8	31.6	−13.1	† 18.7	.3	26.6	9.5	15.1	27.3	20.2
Honduras	268	22.5	11.9	36.1	21.7	29.4	† 41.0	12.7	18.2	8.2	3.6	14.8	21.3
Jamaica	343	71.3	26.2	25.7	38.0	14.4	2.8	6.4	22.8	6.3	13.0	9.7	6.1
Mexico	273	14.8	17.9	.8	2.4	38.7	† 32.2	21.2	25.8	14.2	13.3	13.1	13.8
Netherlands Antilles	353	8.8	6.5	13.8	7.9	−4.3	—	2.6	3.3	2.1	14.3	15.2	−5.3
Nicaragua	278	11.4	−4.6	36.2	13.2	† 25.9	24.7	23.6	23.5	8.3	† 32.8	3.1	24.9
Panama	283	14.8	10.8	13.5	1.3	3.3	18.3	13.0	1.6	2.9	10.3	2.0	9.6
Paraguay	288	22.5	16.5	30.0	† 28.2	.5	10.4	5.2	9.2	18.2	7.1	.6	37.3
Peru	293	76.9	52.6	28.9	34.2	19.7	69.1	26.3	16.2	−5.4	1.8	2.8	−3.2
Suriname	366	11.6	87.6	245.6	178.2	−2.0	20.2	† 34.6	77.6	88.9	35.2	† 30.4	4.2
Trinidad and Tobago	369	−7.7	16.3	19.5	4.7	† 6.1	21.1	5.8	12.3	6.6	19.6	15.8	−1.4
Uruguay	298	71.2	57.9	40.4	32.3	24.8	16.7	† 14.1	3.1	−3.5	−4.2	3.8	34.3
Venezuela, Rep. Bol.	299	11.1	12.0	139.2	38.0	† 149.2	77.0	4.7	24.5	25.3	15.5	18.2	73.7

Money plus Quasi-Money

		1992	1993	1994	1995	1996	1997	1998	1999	2000	2001	2002	2003
						Percent Change over Previous Year							
Industrial Countries													
United States	111	1.7	1.5	—	5.6	6.1	6.6	10.1	8.2	6.9	14.1	4.3	.7
Canada	156	9.4	11.6	8.0	6.2	5.0	8.6	2.3	5.7	13.9	6.5	5.6	7.0
Australia	193	7.4	5.7	10.0	8.5	10.6	7.3	8.4	11.7	3.8	13.2	....	....
Japan	158	−.1	2.2	3.1	2.7	2.3	3.1	4.1	3.4	1.1	2.2	3.4	....
New Zealand	196	2.6	7.0	7.6	9.3	16.1	5.2	1.8	5.0	2.3	6.8	7.7	10.6
Euro Area	122	6.8	5.5	5.4	5.0	2.8	2.2	....	....	....	....	....	....
Austria	124	†3.3	7.7	2.8	4.9	6.3	7.1	....	....	....	....	....	....
Belgium	172	−1.0	1.5	1.4	6.0	−2.9	2.5	3.7	....	....	....	....	....
Finland	132	−.1	.7	3.3	8.7	—	6.6	....	....	....	....	....	....
France	134	7.7	11.1	2.6	4.4	7.4	2.4	5.9	....	....	....	....	....
Germany	178	5.4	24.8	10.1	52.8	15.6	19.5	17.8	....	....	....	....	....
Ireland	136	5.4	7.5	1.8	2.3	2.2	−5.8	.6	....	....	....	....	....
Italy	137	6.6	....	....	....	....	−4.5	....	....	....	....	....	....
Luxembourg	138	4.9	5.7	.3	6.0	5.6	6.7	....	....	....	....	....	....
Netherlands	182	17.6	10.7	9.1	8.3	5.6	6.8	5.9	....	....	....	....	....
Portugal	184	4.5	9.8	7.1	6.6	2.6	1.4	7.1	....	....	....	....	....
Spain	128	−.7	19.7	−10.0	6.2	8.1	6.8	3.3	−.9	†−5.2	3.6	4.2	6.0
Denmark	176	3.9	6.5	2.0	2.5	6.2	9.4	15.2	†17.3	10.7	14.9	10.9	....
Iceland	142	8.5	−.7	5.0	3.8	6.9	1.4	15.5	1.7	8.7	8.7	7.6	....
Norway	144	3.3	4.2	.7	3.1	8.9	1.1	−.4	8.5	1.9	....	....	....
Sweden	146	2.6	8.9	4.2	4.6	†9.6	6.6	5.1	13.3	−16.9	3.9	5.7	8.4
Switzerland	112	†6.4	4.7	7.7	20.3	14.5	25.6	†6.7	19.1	11.1	8.6	5.0	8.6
Developing Countries													
Africa	758	....	....	....	....	....	....	....	....	6.4	14.9	1.7	
CEMAC	622	−21.9	−9.2	26.5	−6.2	−10.1	18.6	7.8	13.3	19.1	15.1	15.9	1.3
Cameroon	626	−3.8	12.8	78.5	4.3	4.9	−7.7	−16.1	11.1	2.4	−1.1	−4.3	−8.0
Central African Republic	628	−8.9	−28.3	31.4	48.7	27.9	−4.1	−7.7	−2.6	18.5	22.0	26.6	−3.1
Chad	634	5.2	−26.6	28.2	−.1	15.7	9.5	−12.8	19.9	58.5	−22.8	13.1	−2.4
Congo, Rep. of	642	31.0	−25.9	139.5	48.9	42.8	9.3	15.6	68.7	36.2	35.1	53.1	56.7
Equatorial Guinea	646	−21.6	−1.7	37.4	10.1	17.2	11.3	−1.8	−3.0	18.3	7.5	5.7	−1.2
Gabon	759	....	....	39.8	14.1	7.6	7.3	3.5	5.0	7.2	11.8	15.6	3.0
WAEMU	638	18.7	−3.1	47.9	−1.8	13.0	4.6	−3.6	34.8	26.0	12.2	−7.0	−11.3
Benin	748	4.0	8.0	29.4	22.3	5.2	17.7	1.0	2.6	6.2	1.6	.6	19.0
Burkina Faso	662	−1.2	−1.4	46.8	18.1	3.9	8.2	6.0	−1.7	−1.9	12.0	30.0	−6.1
Côte d'Ivoire	654	110.9	40.5	48.5	43.0	48.3	119.4	−11.1	21.5	60.8	7.3	22.8	14.4
Guinea Bissau	678	3.0	8.4	39.2	7.3	24.5	8.9	4.2	1.0	12.2	19.6	27.9	22.7
Mali	692	−1.0	.1	6.7	3.8	−6.6	−21.3	−18.5	15.4	12.4	31.4	−.5	−13.2
Niger	722	3.6	−12.6	38.7	7.4	11.7	3.7	8.5	13.1	10.7	13.6	8.2	14.6
Senegal	742	−18.0	−16.2	44.3	22.3	−6.3	5.3	.1	8.4	15.2	−2.6	−2.2	5.9
Togo	612	†26.1	22.7	13.0	9.2	14.4	18.6	18.9	13.7	13.2	24.8	....	....
Algeria	614	....	....	....	....	4,105.6	71.9	57.6	†564.8	309.0	160.6	158.6	64.6
Angola	616	13.3	−14.4	12.8	12.3	18.8	28.6	39.4	26.3	1.4	31.2	−1.1	15.5
Botswana	618	5.9	8.1	33.3	−11.2	24.3	9.4	−3.7	47.3	4.3	15.7	†29.5	†15.2
Burundi	624	12.9	18.0	12.2	†18.2	9.7	10.9	2.8	14.9	13.7	9.9	13.6	9.0
Cape Verde	632	5.3	3.4	7.3	−6.1	9.8	−4.2	†−14.2	18.5	14.5	46.7	9.2	−1.2
Comoros	636	3,794.4	2,853.1	6,968.9	357.6	....	....	....	....	....	40.0	32.3	
Congo, Dem. Rep. of	611	−5.3	.9	3.7	5.3	−7.4	−4.5	−4.1	−3.8	1.1	7.5	15.7	17.8
Djibouti	643	....	....	....	....	21.0	28.1	20.5	36.1	17.3	32.6	20.6	15.1
Eritrea	644	15.2	8.8	23.2	9.0	9.0	19.8	−1.1	13.7	13.1	9.7	15.9	12.4
Ethiopia	648	13.8	12.8	−3.8	14.2	5.8	23.0	10.2	12.1	34.8	19.4	35.3	....
Gambia, The	652	52.3	33.5	52.6	43.2	39.2	44.1	†17.5	25.4	54.2	31.7	48.9	34.2
Ghana	656	23.3	22.8	−3.4	11.3	3.6	18.2	†6.4	....	....	12.9	19.7	33.2
Guinea	664	39.0	28.0	31.5	24.8	25.4	18.7	2.6	6.0	4.5	2.5	11.7	11.9
Kenya	666	9.8	29.4	10.9	9.8	17.1	14.8	15.5	−5.1	1.4	17.2	8.8	6.0
Lesotho	668	19.6	65.6	11.7	29.5	−11.9	3.5	106.0	11.6	†18.3	12.7	2.0	1.5
Liberia	674	22.3	24.2	52.6	16.2	16.0	20.8	6.2	19.2	17.2	23.8	8.0	8.8
Madagascar	676	15.8	39.9	36.5	56.2	40.0	2.1	67.8	28.0	45.5	23.7	22.6	27.5
Malawi	682	7.2	.7	−.5	−5.1	−5.1	8.0	4.1	2.1	16.1	17.3	8.9	10.5
Mauritania	684	15.9	17.0	12.3	18.7	7.6	16.4	11.2	15.2	9.2	10.9	12.5	10.9
Mauritius	686	9.3	7.9	10.2	7.0	6.6	†8.0	6.0	10.2	8.4	14.1	6.4	8.7
Morocco	688	70.8	67.1	50.4	47.7	19.1	23.9	17.8	31.8	38.3	28.2	21.1	18.3
Mozambique	728	23.5	25.7	25.9	24.2	29.0	6.7	11.3	18.4	13.0	4.5	6.9	20.7
Namibia	694	†59.1	53.8	34.5	19.4	16.2	16.0	22.3	33.1	48.1	27.0	21.6	24.1
Nigeria	714	12.4	2.5	−3.7	69.5	8.6	29.1	3.5	7.9	15.6	11.2	12.6	15.4
Rwanda	716	....	....	....	....	84.5	116.4	2.8	7.7	24.9	40.1	25.0	52.4
São Tomé and Príncipe	718	13.1	20.9	−.8	10.5	14.8	43.1	20.2	21.7	9.1	12.0	14.3	.5
Seychelles	724	33.2	21.9	8.8	19.6	†29.7	47.1	11.3	37.8	12.1	33.7	29.6	21.9
Sierra Leone	199	2.9	6.3	18.3	16.0	14.3	17.8	13.7	10.9	7.2	16.7	18.8	12.5
South Africa	732	†139.8	104.0	51.2	73.3	65.3	37.7	29.9	23.5	37.1	24.7	30.2	30.3
Sudan	734	21.2	13.6	10.9	3.9	16.3	19.4	12.9	15.6	−6.6	10.7	13.1	14.1
Swaziland	738	40.6	†39.2	35.3	33.0	8.4	12.9	10.8	18.6	14.8	17.1	25.1	16.6
Tanzania	744	8.3	6.1	8.1	6.6	13.3	16.5	5.4	18.9	14.1	10.7	4.4	6.4
Tunisia	746	†71.8	57.2	35.8	13.9	19.3	19.4	22.9	13.6	18.1	9.2	25.0	17.9
Uganda													

2004, International Monetary Fund: *International Financial Statistics Yearbook*

Money plus Quasi-Money

		1992	1993	1994	1995	1996	1997	1998	1999	2000	2001	2002	2003
						Percent Change over Previous Year							
Africa(Cont.)													
Zambia	754	....	....	59.2	55.5	35.0	25.1	†25.6	27.7	73.8	13.6	31.1	22.7
Zimbabwe	698	12.6	71.3	35.1	25.5	33.3	41.2	11.3	35.9	68.9	128.5	191.7	430.0
Asia													
Bangladesh	513	12.0	10.5	19.3	12.2	10.7	9.8	11.4	15.5	19.3	14.7	13.3	13.1
Bhutan	514	13.5	†30.0	23.3	35.6	9.0	58.9	13.9	32.0	17.4	7.9	27.9	1.0
Cambodia	522	....	....	35.6	43.6	40.4	16.6	15.7	17.3	26.9	20.4	31.1	14.9
China, P.R.: Mainland	924	30.8	†23.7	31.5	29.5	25.3	20.7	14.9	14.7	12.3	15.0	†19.4	19.7
China, P.R.: Hong Kong	532	8.5	14.5	11.7	10.6	12.5	8.7	11.1	8.3	9.3	−.3	.5	6.3
Fiji	819	14.3	6.7	2.7	4.3	.9	−8.7	−.3	14.2	−2.1	−3.1	7.9	25.2
India	534	16.9	17.0	20.3	11.0	18.7	17.7	18.2	17.1	15.2	14.3	16.8	13.0
Indonesia	536	†19.8	20.1	20.2	27.5	27.1	25.3	62.8	12.2	16.6	12.8	4.5	8.1
Korea	542	14.9	16.6	18.7	15.6	15.8	14.1	27.0	27.4	25.4	13.2	11.0	6.7
Lao People's Democratic Rep.	544	49.0	64.6	31.9	16.4	26.7	65.8	113.3	78.4	46.0	13.7	37.6	20.1
Malaysia	548	†29.2	26.6	12.8	20.9	†25.5	17.4	−1.4	16.9	9.9	2.5	3.1	9.3
Maldives	556	13.0	36.3	24.2	15.6	26.0	23.1	22.8	3.6	4.1	9.0	19.3	14.6
Micronesia, Federal States of	868	....	....	....	....	−5.8	3.8	.7	3.4	−1.0	6.0	−12.0	−3.7
Mongolia	948	31.6	227.6	80.0	32.6	17.2	42.2	−1.7	31.6	17.6	27.9	42.0	49.6
Myanmar	518	33.7	26.9	35.6	36.5	38.9	28.8	34.2	29.7	42.4	43.9	34.6	1.4
Nepal	558	20.7	24.8	18.1	15.6	12.2	29.2	11.1	21.6	18.8	....	....	....
Pakistan	564	29.3	18.1	17.4	13.8	20.1	19.9	7.9	4.3	12.1	11.7	16.8	17.5
Papua New Guinea	853	12.5	17.8	−1.3	13.7	30.7	7.7	2.5	9.2	5.0	1.6	4.0	−.4
Philippines	566	13.1	†28.1	26.7	23.9	23.7	23.1	8.6	16.9	8.1	3.6	10.4	3.6
Samoa	862	.7	1.4	13.9	24.4	6.3	15.2	2.5	15.7	16.3	6.1	10.2	14.0
Singapore	576	8.9	8.5	14.4	8.5	9.8	10.3	30.2	8.5	−2.0	5.9	−.3	8.1
Solomon Islands	813	24.5	15.6	25.1	9.2	15.3	6.7	2.5	7.0	.6	−13.6	6.0	25.4
Sri Lanka	524	16.8	23.3	19.7	35.8	11.3	15.6	13.2	13.4	12.9	13.6	13.4	15.3
Thailand	578	15.6	18.4	12.9	17.0	12.6	16.5	9.7	5.4	3.4	2.4	1.4	6.6
Tonga	866	−4.8	25.0	6.6	.7	5.3	7.8	14.7	11.9	18.8	14.9	7.8	14.4
Vanuatu	846	−2.6	5.0	2.9	13.4	10.1	−.4	12.6	−9.2	5.5	5.7	−1.7	−.8
Vietnam	582	....	12.3	....	....	25.7	24.3	23.5	66.4	35.4	27.3	13.3	33.1
Europe													
Albania	914	....	....	....	51.8	43.8	28.5	20.6	22.3	12.0	19.9	5.9	7.6
Armenia	911	....	1,076.8	740.4	64.3	35.1	29.2	36.7	14.0	38.6	4.3	34.0	10.4
Azerbaijan	912	....	825.8	1,116.5	25.4	17.1	41.4	†−17.4	20.1	†73.4	†−10.6	14.6	30.8
Belarus	913	....	....	....	158.4	†52.4	111.4	276.0	132.7	219.3	62.2	50.3	56.8
Bosnia & Herzegovina	963	....	....	....	....	....	....	22.0	27.5	11.3	90.0	9.4	9.5
Bulgaria	918	53.8	54.6	76.8	†40.3	117.2	353.8	12.4	13.1	32.1	26.8	12.2	19.2
Croatia	960	....	....	74.6	40.4	49.2	38.4	13.0	−1.8	29.1	45.7	9.6	10.7
Cyprus	423	13.9	16.3	12.5	11.4	10.5	11.0	8.3	†20.8	9.7	13.4	9.0	4.0
Czech Republic	935	....	....	20.4	29.3	6.4	†1.7	3.4	2.6	16.0	11.2	†−2.1	7.4
Estonia	939	76.5	†42.8	30.4	27.5	36.8	37.8	4.2	23.7	25.7	23.0	11.2	10.9
Georgia	915	....	....	....	....	41.4	44.0	−1.1	21.1	39.4	†20.5	17.9	22.8
Hungary	944	41.3	17.7	14.2	20.9	22.2	19.7	15.3	16.0	12.5	16.7	14.9	11.2
Kazakhstan	916	....	....	576.0	108.2	20.9	†8.2	−14.1	84.4	45.0	†20.8	30.1	29.3
Kyrgyz Republic	917	....	....	....	....	14.8	32.2	17.5	33.7	11.7	11.3	33.9	33.4
Latvia	941	....	....	50.3	−21.4	19.6	37.0	6.7	8.3	27.0	19.8	19.9	22.1
Lithuania	946	....	....	63.0	28.9	−3.5	34.1	14.5	7.7	16.5	21.4	16.9	18.2
Macedonia, FYR	962	....	....	−57.1	†11.7	−1.0	23.5	13.0	32.0	21.4	32.1	15.7	14.2
Malta	181	9.4	10.5	14.9	†11.8	8.6	8.0	8.1	9.8	4.0	8.4	10.4	....
Moldova	921	358.0	318.8	115.7	65.3	†14.8	34.5	†−8.3	42.9	41.7	35.8	38.6	30.4
Poland	964	57.5	36.0	38.2	35.0	31.0	29.1	25.2	19.4	11.8	15.0	−2.8	5.7
Romania	968	75.4	143.3	138.1	70.1	67.4	105.0	48.9	44.9	38.0	46.2	38.2	23.3
Russia	922	....	....	216.5	112.6	29.6	28.8	37.6	56.7	58.0	36.3	33.8	38.5
Slovak Republic	936	....	....	17.4	18.4	16.2	†8.4	5.0	11.6	15.2	11.9	4.0	†10.0
Slovenia	961	123.0	62.2	44.7	29.8	23.3	23.3	19.5	15.1	18.0	30.4	12.3	6.2
Turkey	186	78.7	64.4	145.3	103.6	117.3	97.5	89.7	100.3	40.5	86.2	29.1	14.2
Ukraine	926	....	1,809.2	567.9	115.5	35.1	33.9	†22.2	40.6	44.5	43.0	42.3	46.9
Middle East													
Bahrain	419	4.9	5.7	6.0	7.4	3.1	7.8	16.8	4.1	10.2	9.2	10.3	6.4
Egypt	469	19.4	13.2	11.2	9.9	10.8	10.8	10.8	5.7	11.6	13.2	12.6	21.3
Iran, I.R. of	429	24.4	30.3	33.3	30.1	32.5	23.7	20.4	21.5	22.4	27.6	27.5	21.9
Israel	436	†25.5	22.0	24.6	21.7	25.0	15.0	19.7	15.5	8.0	9.5	6.9	−.1
Jordan	439	3.3	†9.3	3.3	5.7	−.9	7.6	6.3	15.5	7.6	8.1	8.6	15.1
Kuwait	443	.7	5.6	5.4	9.4	−.6	3.9	−.8	1.6	6.3	12.8	4.8	7.8
Lebanon	446	114.1	33.1	25.3	16.4	26.4	19.6	16.1	11.7	9.8	7.5	7.3	13.2
Libya	672	16.5	5.9	14.0	9.6	1.0	−3.7	3.8	7.4	3.1	4.3	1.1	8.8
Oman	449	3.1	3.2	6.7	7.7	8.1	24.5	4.8	6.4	6.0	9.2	5.2	2.5
Qatar	453	8.0	†5.8	9.1	1.1	5.6	9.9	8.0	11.4	10.7	−	11.8	15.8
Saudi Arabia	456	†2.6	3.4	3.0	3.4	7.3	5.2	3.6	6.8	4.5	5.1	15.2	8.5
Syrian Arab Rep.	463	19.4	30.3	12.2	9.2	10.2	8.2	10.5	13.4	19.0	23.5	18.5	7.8
United Arab Emirates	466	4.6	−1.6	7.9	10.2	6.9	9.0	4.2	11.5	15.3	23.2	11.0	15.5
Yemen, Republic of	474	20.9	31.1	32.5	50.7	8.1	11.2	11.8	13.8	25.3	18.8	17.5	19.7
Western Hemisphere													
ECCU	309	7.7	7.4	7.7	13.5	2.3	8.5	13.3	13.4	9.3	6.5	7.9	8.8
Anguilla	312	4.7	13.2	11.4	26.2	2.8	9.9	20.2	9.2	17.5	12.9	12.9	7.9
Antigua and Barbuda	311	8.2	7.5	8.3	21.4	−3.6	7.3	15.7	26.9	6.3	5.3	5.9	16.1
Dominica	321	11.8	−2.5	3.6	22.2	6.4	4.1	5.8	10.0	−2.1	6.5	10.2	6.4
Grenada	328	6.4	22.1	12.0	9.7	8.3	10.2	11.9	12.8	15.4	10.8	8.4	6.6
Montserrat	351	−2.6	−2.2	20.3	−.7	−8.5	16.3	10.9	−4.3	−7.9	2.8	−.8	11.7

Money plus Quasi-Money

		1992	1993	1994	1995	1996	1997	1998	1999	2000	2001	2002	2003
						Percent Change over Previous Year							
Western Hemisphere(Cont.)													
St. Kitts and Nevis	361	15.6	9.4	1.2	14.9	2.3	13.8	11.5	3.5	26.9	1.1	8.5	13.8
St. Lucia	362	4.1	4.2	6.3	8.5	5.0	4.4	11.1	8.1	5.2	5.6	2.6	8.4
St. Vincent & Grens	364	7.3	9.5	5.5	4.1	6.4	12.6	14.4	16.6	5.6	7.7	4.9	4.5
Argentina	213	62.5	46.5	† 17.6	−2.8	18.8	25.5	10.5	4.1	1.5	−19.4	19.7	29.6
Aruba	314	12.5	5.7	13.9	4.2	4.3	4.0	13.6	10.2	2.0	6.4	10.5	9.0
Bahamas, The	313	5.5	16.1	8.7	8.5	5.6	23.5	16.2	10.6	9.3	4.9	3.0	3.7
Barbados	316	5.0	2.9	8.9	4.9	19.3	8.8	7.6	12.1	9.4	2.4	15.8	6.8
Belize	339	13.0	3.3	8.4	18.2	7.6	11.5	5.9	15.8	12.4	12.3	−1.7	4.7
Bolivia	218	34.5	33.7	24.2	7.7	† 24.2	16.7	12.9	5.7	.4	2.2	−6.9	13.9
Brazil	223	1,606.6	2,936.6	1,211.9	31.9	12.2	18.4	10.0	7.4	4.3	12.1	23.0	4.4
Chile	228	26.1	24.5	11.7	24.3	20.1	† 9.8	10.3	7.8	6.1	2.3	−.3	8.1
Colombia	233	45.6	37.6	39.7	21.7	24.4	41.9	20.9	13.7	14.7	16.0	13.6	10.3
Costa Rica	238	24.5	15.2	22.0	4.8	47.6	† 16.4	26.3	29.0	18.4	10.4	20.9	16.7
Dominican Republic	243	27.0	21.1	12.1	17.8	18.4	24.2	16.6	23.7	17.4	26.9	10.3	63.1
Ecuador	248	4.4	46.8	39.1	6.8	12.4	9.1	† −6.6	† −55.2	47.0	31.8	† −.7	19.0
El Salvador	253	15.5	33.5	40.4	11.9	13.8	10.6	9.0	8.8	† 2.0	3.7	−3.1	2.3
Guatemala	258	31.1	15.1	12.0	15.8	13.8	† 18.4	19.4	12.5	35.5	18.1	11.8	15.0
Guyana	336	62.3	† 19.7	12.5	24.4	19.4	10.1	6.7	10.8	8.4	8.7	5.7	7.8
Haiti	263	30.5	29.2	31.4	27.1	1.1	† 24.8	9.7	23.0	20.1	14.1	22.8	39.0
Honduras	268	22.4	10.4	30.3	29.2	41.2	† 50.5	22.9	24.7	24.4	17.5	13.7	15.8
Jamaica	343	75.8	35.9	40.6	31.8	10.9	13.3	7.7	12.2	13.0	8.6	12.0	10.5
Mexico	273	23.6	16.9	20.1	31.9	27.0	† 33.0	17.4	18.7	−4.5	12.5	8.9	7.2
Netherlands Antilles	353	8.3	9.4	8.7	7.5	−3.5	2.1	4.0	5.6	2.8	14.8	11.5	7.3
Nicaragua	278	20.1	25.2	65.9	35.1	† 40.6	52.5	32.1	18.8	9.4	† 41.0	13.3	12.6
Panama	283	25.0	17.2	15.5	7.9	6.1	15.0	13.0	8.5	10.0	9.6	−.3	4.7
Paraguay	288	40.1	29.0	23.6	† 15.7	14.1	7.7	9.9	18.2	4.8	16.4	3.1	7.6
Peru	293	88.2	71.8	37.2	29.3	37.2	30.8	17.3	14.5	−.4	2.1	5.1	−2.4
Suriname	366	19.4	65.7	204.7	181.5	38.5	19.0	† 37.8	51.2	73.3	26.7	† 107.9	19.9
Trinidad and Tobago	369	−6.9	15.3	16.7	4.0	† 5.8	11.3	14.5	4.2	11.7	6.9	5.7	−.7
Uruguay	298	50.0	37.4	42.1	39.0	36.6	28.4	† 19.3	13.1	7.2	19.0	28.2	12.5
Venezuela, Rep. Bol.	299	17.7	25.5	68.9	36.6	† 70.2	61.1	15.4	20.7	23.1	15.3	15.8	57.6

2004, International Monetary Fund : *International Financial Statistics Yearbook*

Ratio of Reserve Money to Money plus Quasi-Money

		1992	1993	1994	1995	1996	1997	1998	1999	2000	2001	2002	2003
							Percent						
Industrial Countries													
United States	111	9.3	10.0	10.8	10.7	10.6	10.7	10.3	11.4	10.0	9.5	9.8	10.2
Canada	156	7.8	7.4	7.0	6.7	6.6	6.3	6.6	7.7	6.3	6.2	6.2	5.8
Australia	193	8.7	8.7	8.6	8.3	12.1	9.0	8.8	7.4	7.1	7.5	....	....
Japan	158	9.0	9.3	9.3	9.7	10.3	10.7	10.7	14.4	11.6	13.4	14.7	....
New Zealand	196	2.8	2.7	2.8	2.8	2.3	2.3	2.4	4.0	3.0	3.1	3.1	2.8
Euro Area													
Austria	122	10.1	10.4	10.3	9.7	10.1	9.8	....	....	....	....	....	....
Belgium	124	†8.1	7.7	7.0	7.3	7.1	6.8	....	....	....	....	....	....
Finland	172	12.9	12.8	19.1	18.3	12.6	11.4	10.8	....	....	....	....	....
France	132	19.2	18.3	17.8	17.8	18.1	17.5	....	....	....	....	....	....
Germany	134	16.0	14.2	13.6	13.3	13.0	12.6	12.0	....	....	....	....	....
Ireland	178	14.4	13.9	13.2	10.9	9.6	9.5	....	....	....	....	....	....
Italy	136	22.3	18.9	17.6	16.2	16.2	18.5	13.0	....	....	....	....	....
Luxembourg	137	.7	1.1	1.1	.9	1.1	1.1	....	....	....	....	....	....
Netherlands	138	10.9	11.1	11.7	9.7	8.8	9.1	....	....	....	....	....	....
Portugal	182	23.6	23.3	8.8	7.9	8.3	7.7	7.3	....	....	....	....	....
Denmark	128	3.0	4.1	4.6	4.9	6.0	7.4	5.5	11.1	†9.0	8.2	8.8	9.0
Iceland	176	14.5	12.4	12.5	10.0	11.9	12.1	10.8	†14.3	11.4	8.7	8.9	....
Norway	142	8.0	8.9	8.7	8.9	12.7	11.1	8.5	12.6	9.7	8.9	12.3	....
Sweden	144	16.0	22.7	27.6	22.7	14.0	10.3	10.7	11.5	10.7	....	....	....
Switzerland	146	10.2	9.3	9.0	8.4	†8.0	7.4	7.5	7.8	8.4	9.1	8.0	8.0
United Kingdom	112	†5.2	5.3	5.2	4.6	4.2	3.6	†3.5	3.5	3.1	2.9	2.9	2.9
Developing Countries													
Africa													
CEMAC	758	....	....	....	....	....	....	....	....	49.0	48.7	48.4	48.2
Cameroon	622	28.0	23.8	26.2	22.0	31.4	37.1	38.0	36.2	40.8	43.4	47.8	41.8
Central African Republic	626	76.5	81.2	83.8	84.0	86.3	82.0	78.0	75.7	80.8	76.6	75.3	75.3
Chad	628	72.1	80.2	75.4	80.2	82.4	82.3	80.1	77.1	75.6	72.8	77.3	71.6
Congo, Rep. of	634	39.2	51.1	54.0	58.5	54.9	55.9	50.8	56.9	72.9	72.4	58.6	64.3
Equatorial Guinea	642	70.7	75.9	56.4	75.4	60.5	60.8	42.2	48.8	53.4	73.3	50.1	77.5
Gabon	646	26.3	24.6	41.1	35.7	39.3	35.9	33.4	31.7	36.5	32.6	31.2	36.1
WAEMU	759	....	49.5	42.3	40.4	38.6	40.0	41.5	40.9	42.6	47.2	49.3	46.9
Benin	638	70.0	63.0	43.2	32.5	31.4	36.0	35.7	46.5	51.9	57.0	53.3	36.6
Burkina Faso	748	63.1	67.5	51.7	52.4	52.2	54.8	52.3	43.8	41.3	40.7	30.7	34.7
Côte d'Ivoire	662	32.4	35.9	38.2	36.1	37.1	38.3	43.0	40.4	42.0	50.4	54.3	55.0
Guinea Bissau	654	77.9	73.3	65.3	60.3	56.4	58.1	56.7	62.7	73.1	79.0	84.0	92.8
Mali	678	83.8	84.4	48.8	50.2	47.7	47.2	42.8	47.7	53.8	50.3	57.7	59.0
Niger	692	68.9	65.9	46.9	51.1	51.5	51.5	40.6	46.4	42.9	48.5	46.4	34.1
Senegal	722	47.2	37.6	40.5	39.2	30.1	30.0	29.5	30.3	28.9	34.2	35.4	32.4
Togo	742	66.8	54.1	38.4	40.5	37.8	36.1	40.1	42.3	44.4	42.7	46.2	29.8
Algeria	612	†37.1	38.6	32.3	31.9	33.4	32.8	31.2	30.6	33.1	37.5	37.4	42.6
Angola	614	....	....	....	71.9	59.8	66.8	63.5	†49.6	38.6	36.5	30.7	32.9
Botswana	616	17.1	18.6	16.4	15.1	14.2	13.9	12.4	11.2	11.7	10.1	11.0	12.2
Burundi	618	43.5	42.2	40.0	44.7	42.8	39.9	42.6	39.2	36.6	35.1	†33.4	†32.1
Cape Verde	624	62.2	75.5	41.2	†42.7	36.5	33.1	35.2	32.7	33.3	32.6	33.1	31.2
Comoros	632	36.2	49.2	52.4	50.1	62.2	56.9	†59.1	59.4	65.3	75.9	82.7	82.4
Congo, Dem. Rep. of	636	92.4	84.7	40.3	66.1	62.1	19.3	81.1	63.6	5.9	64.3	55.7	54.4
Djibouti	611	21.0	19.2	19.6	16.2	16.9	17.3	17.7	19.2	18.9	18.5	17.4	19.4
Eritrea	643	....	....	....	41.6	64.0	94.2	51.0	51.8	47.6	34.6	33.6	33.1
Ethiopia	644	64.0	61.7	55.3	57.1	43.7	39.7	35.2	29.5	36.1	30.0	34.9	35.7
Gambia, The	648	38.9	38.4	38.3	42.1	40.0	41.2	40.1	40.9	35.4	35.9	35.6	....
Ghana	652	45.1	35.5	41.6	39.2	40.8	37.8	†38.4	42.4	42.5	45.5	44.7	42.6
Guinea	656	64.3	62.3	58.1	58.6	55.8	60.1	†59.2	....	63.0	64.2	65.2	57.7
Kenya	664	32.3	38.5	36.0	37.8	32.6	28.0	27.2	27.2	25.9	25.0	25.0	22.1
Lesotho	666	26.5	25.0	24.0	29.0	26.0	25.4	30.5	42.8	39.4	25.1	23.1	23.2
Liberia	668	96.9	74.4	70.2	71.2	95.2	99.3	49.1	46.0	†54.9	54.5	56.8	58.9
Madagascar	674	46.7	35.1	39.6	44.1	56.6	47.3	47.5	50.2	47.9	50.1	48.5	44.5
Malawi	676	39.0	45.3	46.9	56.9	56.3	55.3	45.7	47.2	34.3	37.1	38.3	38.4
Mauritania	682	53.7	82.7	80.1	79.6	42.4	34.1	30.3	31.0	28.0	25.2	23.8	21.5
Mauritius	684	19.5	19.7	18.4	17.8	15.7	13.2	12.9	12.1	12.4	12.3	12.6	12.4
Morocco	686	28.2	28.3	27.3	26.8	27.1	†27.1	27.4	28.1	26.8	28.5	27.7	29.7
Mozambique	688	33.3	35.0	38.7	34.5	36.7	34.4	28.1	25.0	22.8	27.2	26.3	27.1
Namibia	728	9.3	7.8	9.9	8.9	8.4	9.5	8.8	10.7	8.9	9.2	9.3	9.2
Nigeria	694	†59.9	58.2	56.8	57.3	52.4	47.2	45.0	41.1	41.2	43.5	40.4	46.6
Rwanda	714	37.4	46.7	53.0	43.4	48.9	42.2	37.2	39.6	31.4	34.5	30.3	29.3
São Tomé and Príncipe	716	....	....	....	51.4	50.5	57.1	61.2	48.2	49.9	62.2	56.9	61.5
Seychelles	718	34.1	34.8	51.7	56.6	56.0	46.5	19.6	17.6	16.7	15.9	17.7	14.2
Sierra Leone	724	57.6	49.0	56.5	53.0	†50.6	71.9	51.4	51.8	50.5	48.9	47.1	47.3
South Africa	199	9.6	8.2	8.2	9.2	9.1	8.6	8.0	10.2	12.4	13.1	14.7	9.0
Sudan	732	†67.6	54.6	50.5	51.5	56.6	55.2	55.0	60.2	†64.4	54.0	50.3	49.1
Swaziland	734	30.7	24.0	25.4	25.1	20.0	17.6	14.3	13.8	14.1	11.9	13.4	15.0
Tanzania	738	37.3	†36.2	39.7	41.6	40.9	39.4	40.8	41.8	39.8	35.7	34.0	32.8
Tunisia	744	21.2	21.0	20.8	21.4	25.6	23.8	19.9	21.8	16.9	18.0	16.7	16.9
Uganda	746	†52.5	41.2	44.9	44.8	41.9	38.3	37.4	37.9	39.1	40.6	35.9	33.8
Zambia	754	....	49.0	45.6	25.0	25.1	29.8	†27.7	27.8	24.6	31.5	34.8	32.4
Zimbabwe	698	34.0	30.2	27.6	22.5	28.1	27.4	32.0	37.9	26.0	30.1	28.0	26.2

Ratio of Reserve Money to Money plus Quasi-Money

		1992	1993	1994	1995	1996	1997	1998	1999	2000	2001	2002	2003
							Percent						
Asia													
Bangladesh	513	23.8	26.7	29.0	23.4	23.0	22.9	23.3	22.8	21.9	23.7	21.6	20.4
Bhutan	514	84.1	† 99.4	53.7	66.2	65.8	45.2	61.7	58.7	60.6	57.5	51.0	60.4
Cambodia	522	....	68.4	63.2	48.5	49.3	51.3	65.2	64.5	63.4	61.7	68.6	64.8
China, P.R.: Mainland	924	33.5	† 36.8	36.7	34.2	35.3	34.2	30.6	28.7	27.9	26.7	† 25.1	24.7
China, P.R.: Hong Kong	532	9.8	10.0	9.8	9.2	8.6	8.4	7.7	† 8.5	7.2	7.7	8.2	9.2
Fiji	819	17.5	16.0	15.8	16.5	16.7	19.2	20.4	28.1	23.3	28.6	29.1	30.6
India	534	31.0	32.3	32.6	33.1	30.5	28.9	27.4	26.1	24.4	23.5	22.0	22.2
Indonesia	536	† 14.2	12.8	13.3	12.3	13.1	14.5	15.9	19.6	20.9	21.5	20.4	21.2
Korea	542	18.8	20.6	18.9	19.0	14.4	11.1	8.0	8.7	6.8	7.0	7.3	7.4
Lao People's Democratic Rep	544	48.3	48.2	44.7	43.6	42.6	37.0	32.5	31.2	34.0	32.1	30.6	31.4
Malaysia	548	† 37.5	20.5	24.8	25.6	† 27.6	30.1	13.3	14.4	11.9	11.2	11.6	11.3
Maldives	556	96.2	84.0	77.2	67.9	63.5	59.5	53.7	55.5	55.6	56.0	55.7	47.8
Mongolia	948	38.4	33.4	37.8	36.8	42.8	37.0	44.5	50.9	52.0	43.4	37.3	28.6
Myanmar	518	85.5	81.3	73.8	69.1	65.6	66.0	62.3	57.0	53.8	56.8	56.9	82.0
Nepal	558	40.2	41.9	39.6	37.2	36.5	45.5	37.1	33.6	33.8	....	....	....
Pakistan	564	41.5	40.1	39.6	41.0	32.9	31.4	32.8	35.6	31.1	35.7	33.2	32.9
Papua New Guinea	853	11.8	11.8	13.3	13.5	19.8	12.0	14.2	22.5	17.9	18.6	21.1	23.9
Philippines	566	36.3	† 33.4	28.4	25.8	27.7	21.1	19.8	23.2	19.2	16.5	17.3	18.3
Samoa	862	52.9	48.0	43.5	36.5	41.4	42.8	22.7	23.8	22.3	20.0	21.8	21.2
Singapore	576	17.9	17.9	16.6	16.7	16.2	15.6	10.3	12.3	10.8	11.1	11.1	10.6
Solomon Islands	813	19.5	18.8	19.7	22.2	25.0	22.0	31.3	29.2	33.3	37.3	41.0	41.6
Sri Lanka	524	34.7	35.4	35.6	30.3	29.6	25.1	24.6	23.5	21.8	20.5	20.3	19.7
Thailand	578	11.7	11.5	11.7	12.2	12.3	12.2	10.7	15.7	13.2	13.7	13.8	16.4
Tonga	866	98.3	29.2	26.2	21.4	29.1	30.3	29.2	28.0	26.6	30.0	33.6	26.6
Vanuatu	846	8.4	12.3	11.1	12.8	11.1	11.2	10.4	14.0	13.6	12.8	13.0	14.1
Vietnam	582	56.9	64.8	....	58.2	55.6	50.3	44.3	40.0	36.9	33.9	33.6	32.2
Europe													
Albania	914	....	....	59.4	50.1	39.7	45.8	37.5	37.3	39.2	38.7	39.3	35.8
Armenia	911	43.6	54.6	61.2	71.6	75.7	73.1	56.1	49.2	47.7	50.8	52.5	50.7
Azerbaijan	912	32.1	51.1	31.2	69.7	69.9	69.9	† 64.1	61.8	† 46.0	† 52.3	52.0	49.1
Belarus	913	....	....	25.3	38.0	† 44.4	43.6	30.5	36.5	25.7	32.3	28.4	27.3
Bosnia & Herzegovina	963	....	....	....	....	....	11.4	12.9	34.7	37.2	51.7	43.1	44.3
Bulgaria	918	24.9	19.7	17.3	† 22.4	19.8	40.4	39.6	41.2	34.6	34.6	34.0	33.3
Croatia	960	....	22.5	27.0	27.5	23.9	20.4	17.4	18.3	16.1	16.8	19.9	23.8
Cyprus	423	29.6	25.9	25.9	22.2	18.4	16.4	17.6	† 16.7	16.9	16.0	18.4	18.5
Czech Republic	935	....	21.8	24.3	28.9	27.3	† 26.9	31.8	33.8	31.1	29.4	† 15.1	15.1
Estonia	939	40.7	† 58.0	49.6	46.7	41.7	41.7	42.5	43.6	39.8	29.2	25.9	26.7
Georgia	915	....	....	....	85.0	81.9	75.4	71.5	70.1	63.9	† 58.5	59.3	55.2
Hungary	944	36.3	31.7	27.3	26.6	19.9	21.6	22.6	24.6	25.7	22.4	20.6	20.4
Kazakhstan	916	....	39.5	42.3	43.3	45.5	† 57.5	47.2	39.9	29.2	† 31.5	28.8	33.9
Kyrgyz Republic	917	....	....	....	73.6	79.5	72.8	66.7	65.2	65.2	65.3	69.6	69.2
Latvia	941	....	48.6	38.6	49.9	51.3	49.1	49.2	50.7	43.0	40.6	40.1	34.9
Lithuania	946	....	47.0	41.6	43.5	46.1	45.5	51.2	45.6	37.8	33.7	34.8	37.3
Macedonia, FYR	962	....	8.6	34.4	† 40.2	39.4	39.1	36.5	35.9	43.3	35.5	31.8	30.0
Malta	181	35.8	32.5	37.2	† 29.3	25.8	24.3	23.1	22.5	22.4	21.4	20.2	....
Moldova	921	58.8	69.0	73.3	62.6	† 59.7	59.2	† 60.3	59.8	55.7	51.6	48.9	44.4
Poland	964	36.1	28.6	25.4	27.3	25.1	26.0	24.3	20.1	16.6	18.8	18.8	19.1
Romania	968	37.9	† 45.4	35.6	32.9	29.7	34.3	27.8	36.9	41.4	45.3	50.7	49.3
Russia	922	....	50.1	48.1	47.0	46.2	45.7	42.6	44.9	47.6	45.0	44.2	49.2
Slovak Republic	936	....	15.4	16.2	17.9	19.8	† 21.6	19.4	20.9	18.9	20.7	20.2	17.0
Slovenia	961	13.9	11.9	12.9	12.4	11.6	11.6	11.6	12.3	10.6	11.0	9.6	9.5
Turkey	186	25.1	25.6	22.9	20.2	17.8	18.0	17.1	16.9	17.6	16.8	15.3	15.9
Ukraine	926	70.9	61.6	46.8	50.6	52.3	58.2	† 55.5	55.8	55.6	55.4	48.2	42.7
Middle East													
Bahrain	419	18.9	14.3	12.9	16.2	13.9	14.5	9.7	13.6	12.3	12.9	13.3	16.8
Egypt	469	30.4	32.0	32.3	32.2	30.2	30.3	32.7	31.4	33.4	34.6	33.4	38.4
Iran, I.R. of	429	43.6	39.8	40.1	45.6	43.8	43.5	42.7	41.1	39.2	32.7	34.5	30.5
Israel	436	† 19.8	20.8	15.6	9.4	10.1	19.3	18.4	19.7	18.4	16.9	13.3	12.3
Jordan	439	53.0	† 51.0	51.9	52.2	45.6	41.2	36.9	35.8	33.5	29.3	28.0	28.4
Kuwait	443	8.9	7.9	7.5	6.4	6.5	5.6	5.9	7.6	6.5	5.7	6.1	6.6
Lebanon	446	12.9	13.8	19.4	20.2	19.4	24.3	19.8	18.7	18.1	23.1	23.7	46.5
Libya	672	64.0	58.9	59.9	58.9	63.6	† 70.4	67.1	59.2	56.8	60.0	60.8	62.2
Oman	449	23.5	21.6	21.1	20.3	20.0	17.4	17.8	16.6	17.0	16.9	20.9	21.6
Qatar	453	13.1	† 12.9	11.0	11.4	11.5	11.5	11.0	11.0	10.6	11.9	12.4	12.3
Saudi Arabia	456	† 24.6	23.7	24.1	22.8	20.9	21.4	20.4	23.6	21.6	19.8	18.7	18.2
Syrian Arab Rep	463	66.8	58.7	56.9	54.5	53.2	51.6	49.0	46.3	44.9	42.4	41.5	42.5
United Arab Emirates	466	19.5	19.2	22.4	22.9	23.2	21.4	20.6	24.1	28.5	24.5	21.7	21.1
Yemen, Republic of	474	89.5	88.6	90.6	72.0	71.3	56.1	55.8	59.2	53.9	51.7	48.1	48.7
Western Hemisphere													
ECCU	309	23.0	20.2	19.3	18.8	17.3	17.0	17.7	16.6	15.8	16.9	17.0	17.3
Anguilla	312	13.9	13.9	12.2	13.0	14.4	14.8	13.8	14.1	12.3	14.0	12.6	14.7
Antigua and Barbuda	311	23.5	17.8	18.9	18.3	15.7	15.3	15.0	13.5	12.3	14.1	14.0	15.3
Dominica	321	22.7	21.5	18.8	18.1	16.9	16.7	17.6	18.0	17.9	16.6	21.5	19.5
Grenada	328	27.1	20.6	19.5	19.3	17.9	18.2	17.3	16.3	15.6	15.7	17.2	17.5
Montserrat	351	20.5	20.7	20.6	22.6	25.4	27.6	53.5	31.3	25.5	28.5	32.6	31.0
St. Kitts and Nevis	361	22.5	21.6	22.9	19.7	18.6	17.4	18.7	20.4	17.3	18.9	20.3	17.4
St. Lucia	362	20.9	21.0	18.9	19.4	17.6	17.2	17.6	16.8	16.6	18.3	18.2	18.9
St. Vincent & Grens	364	31.2	25.4	23.3	21.2	19.4	18.8	19.9	19.9	22.7	23.1	19.7	19.7
Argentina	213	35.5	33.0	† 30.4	26.5	22.8	20.6	19.1	18.5	16.7	24.4	34.6	44.3
Aruba	314	22.7	23.7	19.5	22.1	18.1	16.7	20.7	19.9	17.3	21.5	22.1	19.1

2004, International Monetary Fund: *International Financial Statistics Yearbook*

Ratio of Reserve Money to Money plus Quasi-Money

		1992	1993	1994	1995	1996	1997	1998	1999	2000	2001	2002	2003
Western Hemisphere(Cont.)							Percent						
Bahamas, The	313	14.9	12.8	13.2	12.5	11.5	10.7	11.0	12.0	10.7	11.3	12.3	12.6
Barbados	316	20.3	17.4	15.7	17.3	19.5	16.2	16.4	15.2	15.6	17.5	21.0	23.6
Belize	339	25.6	24.6	22.3	21.4	20.4	19.3	19.6	20.6	22.5	25.5	20.0	19.9
Bolivia	218	27.5	27.3	22.9	26.3	†24.5	25.2	17.7	18.6	20.5	22.4	24.5	24.4
Brazil	223	16.7	13.9	24.8	21.1	23.0	26.1	21.1	21.2	21.3	22.6	45.2	41.3
Chile	228	14.9	14.2	15.0	14.6	13.6	†13.3	13.2	12.8	11.2	11.9	12.7	11.3
Colombia	233	53.3	48.7	44.7	39.2	37.0	30.4	20.9	25.6	24.4	23.1	24.5	25.8
Costa Rica	238	51.4	48.9	51.9	57.5	47.5	†47.7	42.0	34.9	28.1	18.9	16.3	18.1
Dominican Republic	243	43.7	46.3	41.5	41.0	38.4	36.8	38.6	35.9	33.7	34.3	28.4	36.2
Ecuador	248	24.9	24.9	18.3	15.6	14.8	14.5	†15.0	†28.4	11.1	9.3	†8.6	7.9
El Salvador	253	24.8	28.1	24.5	24.6	23.8	24.3	24.2	24.5	†21.7	14.8	11.9	17.7
Guatemala	258	50.3	53.9	50.3	45.0	44.6	†46.3	37.3	34.1	30.0	29.5	31.2	30.2
Guyana	336	52.0	†33.4	39.0	37.3	33.1	35.2	36.9	32.0	33.7	34.4	35.8	36.6
Haiti	263	58.8	58.8	55.4	50.0	47.4	†42.2	38.6	40.4	42.3	43.4	43.8	41.4
Honduras	268	29.3	28.4	32.0	30.7	31.2	†39.8	37.6	33.6	29.5	27.6	30.7	28.2
Jamaica	343	37.5	39.9	38.1	37.5	35.1	35.7	40.5	34.6	33.0	28.4	24.6	27.7
Mexico	273	12.9	12.2	12.3	12.4	12.0	†13.4	15.7	18.2	17.9	19.5	22.7	24.8
Netherlands Antilles	353	18.0	17.4	14.9	16.7	14.8	16.7	17.7	15.8	16.6	19.7	22.1	19.3
Nicaragua	278	64.0	55.2	50.7	46.4	†44.4	38.5	34.9	31.1	29.7	†29.9	29.3	30.9
Panama	283	6.6	5.9	5.0	4.8	6.3	5.6	5.1	4.7	4.4	4.1	4.0	3.8
Paraguay	288	32.3	28.5	29.3	†32.0	27.5	27.4	26.6	24.5	23.1	21.1	21.0	29.5
Peru	293	43.8	40.7	38.8	39.4	39.5	41.9	37.8	38.2	39.1	40.0	41.3	39.6
Suriname	366	59.3	60.8	61.5	71.4	46.3	38.7	†46.3	54.0	71.5	64.0	†37.9	29.0
Trinidad and Tobago	369	20.4	16.8	22.7	21.6	†22.3	23.2	24.5	24.4	22.5	23.3	21.7	23.3
Uruguay	298	32.6	33.9	31.6	29.6	28.8	28.0	†26.9	28.8	29.4	31.2	24.5	35.0
Venezuela, Rep. Bol.	299	37.4	32.9	31.9	30.8	†35.6	38.4	39.4	43.4	40.5	39.3	40.6	37.9

Income Velocity of Money plus Quasi-Money

		1992	1993	1994	1995	1996	1997	1998	1999	2000	2001	2002	2003
						Index Numbers: 2000=100							
Industrial Countries													
United States	111	99.7	103.2	109.6	108.5	108.1	107.7	103.1	101.0	100.0	90.5	89.8	93.5
Canada	156	117.0	108.9	106.8	105.8	104.0	101.1	102.4	104.0	100.0	96.6	95.4	93.8
Australia	193	120.0	119.3	114.7	111.3	107.2	105.4	103.0	96.7	100.0	94.1	....	....
Japan	158	116.7	115.0	112.9	111.5	111.9	110.9	105.2	100.3	100.0	96.8	92.2	....
New Zealand	196	111.1	112.3	111.6	108.7	98.2	96.7	96.1	96.5	100.0	101.1	97.5	91.8
Euro Area													
Austria	122	....	....	....	....	....	....	....	....	....	....	....	....
Belgium	124	....	....	....	....	....	....	....	....	....	....	....	....
Finland	172	....	....	....	....	....	....	....	....	....	....	....	....
France	132	....	....	....	....	....	....	....	....	....	....	....	....
Germany	134	....	....	....	....	....	....	....	....	....	....	....	....
Greece	174	108.9	114.7	105.5	106.9	104.3	104.7	106.5	96.4	100.0	....	....	....
Ireland	178	....	....	....	....	....	....	....	....	....	....	....	....
Italy	136	....	....	....	....	....	....	....	....	....	....	....	....
Luxembourg	137	....	....	....	....	....	....	....	....	....	....	....	....
Netherlands	138	....	....	....	....	....	....	....	....	....	....	....	....
Portugal	182	....	....	....	....	....	....	....	....	....	....	....	....
Spain	184	....	....	....	....	....	....	....	....	....	....	....	....
Denmark	128	89.2	75.5	90.0	88.6	86.0	84.8	84.9	89.6	100.0	100.1	98.5	95.5
Iceland	176	117.3	113.5	118.1	118.6	119.9	116.0	111.6	102.0	100.0	97.8	92.3	....
Norway	142	80.6	85.3	85.4	88.3	90.5	96.5	85.2	91.2	100.0	95.5	88.6	....
Sweden	144	88.7	88.5	†93.7	97.8	92.1	94.7	99.4	96.4	100.0	....	....	....
Switzerland	146	115.6	108.5	106.9	103.4	94.8	90.5	88.3	79.5	100.0	97.8	93.6	86.9
United Kingdom	112	177.0	177.7	175.1	153.7	142.4	120.5	119.7	105.6	100.0	96.3	96.3	93.4
Developing Countries													
Africa													
CEMAC	758	....	....	....	....	....	....	....	....	....	....	....	....
Cameroon	622	80.3	87.1	83.3	102.4	126.2	115.9	113.8	108.3	100.0	93.8	86.3	....
Central African Republic	626	102.6	88.1	64.4	72.8	64.3	75.3	100.5	95.7	100.0	102.7	109.4	....
Chad	628	81.1	105.7	127.8	94.2	84.3	97.4	116.2	112.2	100.0	101.6	91.3	103.8
Congo, Rep. of	634	66.8	89.2	89.9	96.7	102.9	98.0	95.3	100.2	100.0	115.8	105.1	105.9
Equatorial Guinea	642	53.7	83.9	47.4	39.7	46.9	94.2	69.1	70.2	100.0	112.3	85.1	53.8
Gabon	646	90.9	95.6	105.8	102.2	102.6	98.4	85.3	95.4	100.0	87.3	....	....
WAEMU	759	....	....	....	....	93.2	101.7	106.9	105.9	100.0	96.7	89.0	....
Benin	638	96.7	104.5	98.5	121.0	120.6	127.5	145.7	115.4	100.0	96.5	117.0	....
Burkina Faso	748	115.6	107.3	106.4	98.1	103.5	94.5	107.5	105.4	100.0	111.3	120.7	110.0
Côte d'Ivoire	662	76.8	77.8	76.5	76.0	81.3	92.6	96.3	100.5	100.0	93.1	74.4	....
Guinea Bissau	654	642.6	513.0	662.4	457.0	337.5	184.6	155.2	144.9	100.0	88.7	74.7	....
Mali	678	99.2	90.4	89.2	100.8	90.0	98.7	103.7	107.4	100.0	97.8	81.9	....
Niger	692	45.5	47.4	54.1	55.2	73.2	97.5	135.3	118.9	100.0	82.8	88.2	....
Senegal	722	104.0	114.6	101.3	112.4	106.3	109.5	109.3	102.9	100.0	95.5	92.8	....
Togo	742	94.1	89.2	95.7	93.7	114.7	127.3	121.5	117.9	100.0	108.1	124.8	....
Algeria	612	82.3	74.3	82.2	101.5	113.8	103.8	88.9	89.4	100.0	82.9	69.2	62.2
Angola	614	....	....	....	46.4	67.2	81.9	75.8	76.6	100.0	82.5	70.2	....
Botswana	616	99.3	126.3	135.6	134.1	130.8	127.0	103.5	87.5	100.0	87.5	98.6	97.3
Burundi	618	113.8	110.3	94.5	98.4	83.3	99.2	120.3	93.0	100.0	93.0	†76.3	†73.8
Congo, Dem. Rep. of	636	....	....	1,192.6	1,052.6	1,251.6	547.4	113.7	95.8	100.0	1,013.7	....	....
Ethiopia	644	†96.9	114.3	98.6	108.1	111.0	110.5	110.7	105.7	100.0	92.8	....	....
Kenya	664	118.0	116.2	106.2	98.9	89.5	88.9	96.5	97.5	100.0	107.7	105.6	107.0
Lesotho	666	92.5	81.2	81.6	84.7	86.7	87.9	79.3	94.6	100.0	94.6	102.2	107.0
Madagascar	674	97.5	90.5	84.0	106.7	110.8	102.0	108.3	104.4	100.0	91.8	85.6	88.8
Malawi	676	88.9	87.9	73.4	100.8	119.7	136.1	109.9	117.8	100.0	....	....	....
Mauritius	684	114.9	112.6	111.5	103.1	107.8	103.1	104.8	98.2	100.0	99.7	95.2	94.9
Morocco	686	127.4	121.1	123.2	116.1	123.5	113.9	116.1	105.8	100.0	94.8	92.5	89.6
Mozambique	688	104.5	99.2	109.6	115.2	153.0	150.3	150.2	126.2	100.0	97.5	93.7	....
Namibia	728	144.7	128.1	126.3	111.9	102.5	107.2	108.0	100.5	100.0	109.8	....	....
Nigeria	694	90.0	74.7	72.4	†131.1	161.1	144.6	115.8	100.3	100.0	91.6	78.3	66.6
Rwanda	714	115.0	117.5	71.8	85.9	100.2	102.6	110.4	103.3	100.0	97.2	94.4	92.7
Seychelles	718	218.6	197.9	201.9	179.8	161.8	127.9	120.4	102.7	100.0	91.5	84.7	....
Sierra Leone	724	132.8	139.9	157.7	162.0	164.8	107.8	122.0	101.9	100.0	83.7	72.0	66.0
South Africa	199	111.3	119.6	114.6	112.1	110.7	104.3	98.9	96.6	100.0	94.9	91.0	87.3
Swaziland	734	64.3	67.9	74.2	86.9	85.9	83.6	83.5	81.5	100.0	102.8	101.8	....
Tanzania	738	87.1	78.8	77.6	76.6	88.2	97.6	104.3	101.6	100.0	97.2	87.9	....
Tunisia	744	118.6	119.6	119.3	120.7	119.1	112.0	114.7	105.5	100.0	97.3	96.9	98.3
Uganda	746	†221.2	153.5	145.3	147.4	137.1	124.8	109.4	109.7	100.0	98.5	83.7	83.2
Zimbabwe	698	154.1	111.1	108.7	95.5	100.7	88.7	108.0	120.0	100.0	....	....	....
Asia													
Bangladesh	513	138.9	131.9	119.4	119.9	118.1	116.9	116.3	110.5	100.0	93.3	88.7	86.2
Bhutan	514	194.7	169.6	164.2	141.8	152.8	116.5	116.7	103.4	100.0	....	....	....
Cambodia	522	....	265.0	204.8	169.4	131.2	123.8	125.1	120.7	100.0	87.5	71.9	....
China, P.R.: Mainland	924	136.5	147.1	151.4	146.6	136.6	124.0	113.9	103.9	100.0	95.9	†83.4	79.4
China, P.R.: Hong Kong	532	139.9	141.0	142.3	136.9	134.5	137.3	117.6	105.7	100.0	98.8	96.6	88.9
Fiji	819	77.0	79.1	81.6	82.0	86.0	97.3	104.8	102.3	100.0	112.9	....	....
India	534	124.6	122.3	119.9	126.6	122.8	116.2	112.4	106.8	100.0	95.5	88.5	87.9
Indonesia	536	139.3	†135.5	130.7	121.8	112.3	105.7	98.9	101.4	100.0	101.5	107.9	....
Korea	542	182.2	176.5	173.3	184.9	179.6	172.2	133.7	114.8	100.0	95.0	94.1	93.0

Income Velocity of Money plus Quasi-Money

Index Numbers: 2000=100

		1992	1993	1994	1995	1996	1997	1998	1999	2000	2001	2002	2003
Asia(Cont.)													
Lao People's Democratic Rep.	544	182.2	124.7	110.1	122.1	116.3	89.5	80.8	110.4	100.0	101.0	86.0	79.1
Malaysia	548	141.6	127.8	128.6	121.1	110.1	104.2	106.2	96.5	100.0	95.2	99.6	99.1
Maldives	556	164.6	141.6	133.2	131.2	117.5	107.8	93.3	98.2	100.0	95.5	85.8	83.6
Nepal	558	156.2	143.5	141.2	134.4	136.1	118.7	114.5	107.1	100.0	....	....	....
Pakistan	564	108.7	101.8	101.6	106.7	100.9	96.4	98.6	103.7	100.0	96.4	87.5	82.4
Philippines	566	169.4	† 144.2	130.6	118.7	109.4	99.2	100.4	95.9	100.0	104.5	103.2	108.2
Singapore	576	114.8	122.9	122.8	124.9	124.3	122.8	91.3	85.7	100.0	91.2	93.8	87.4
Solomon Islands	813	122.4	159.5	141.8	116.7	104.7	105.6	107.2	109.7	100.0	115.8	114.8	....
Sri Lanka	524	126.3	120.3	116.5	98.9	102.3	102.6	103.6	99.3	100.0	98.5	97.7	94.3
Thailand	578	141.1	133.3	135.4	133.5	130.6	115.1	102.5	97.5	100.0	101.8	106.4	109.2
Vietnam	582	196.1	221.6	222.7	225.5	213.2	197.7	184.3	122.6	100.0	85.6	84.2	71.4
Europe													
Albania	914	....	....	158.5	130.1	110.6	104.7	117.0	105.2	100.0	91.3	....	....
Armenia	911	3,712.3	4,302.5	112.3	190.8	178.8	168.4	146.3	132.7	100.0	109.3	94.6	102.1
Belarus	913	....	....	45.3	119.6	124.0	112.2	57.1	105.8	100.0	115.9	117.3	102.9
Bosnia & Herzegovina	963	....	....	....	....	....	114.7	106.9	99.6	100.0	56.0	....	....
Bulgaria	918	47.7	45.9	45.6	54.5	50.2	109.4	125.2	117.5	100.0	87.6	84.9	75.8
Croatia	960	....	198.8	238.1	190.8	140.3	116.2	114.3	119.8	100.0	74.5	73.6	71.6
Cyprus	423	144.1	131.2	130.0	128.1	120.2	113.8	112.9	† 100.0	100.0	93.8	90.7	93.8
Czech Republic	935	....	98.6	94.9	85.7	91.3	96.3	102.0	102.8	100.0	97.4	103.1	96.1
Estonia	939	103.0	125.8	131.9	142.0	134.8	119.5	131.4	110.7	100.0	91.5	92.2	89.5
Hungary	944	79.9	81.8	88.2	93.8	94.2	97.5	99.9	97.3	100.0	96.6	94.8	94.6
Kazakhstan	916	....	45.8	108.7	120.9	129.1	† 141.4	169.6	116.8	100.0	† 99.6	88.9	85.7
Kyrgyz Republic	917	....	....	....	65.8	83.1	82.4	78.1	83.3	100.0	101.6	77.4	64.2
Latvia	941	....	88.9	82.4	132.3	131.9	111.6	114.6	114.5	100.0	92.1	84.5	76.9
Lithuania	946	....	99.6	89.1	104.5	136.7	124.4	122.4	111.0	100.0	87.5	79.9	73.0
Macedonia, FYR	962	....	26.5	153.2	† 158.7	166.8	142.4	132.1	107.3	100.0	74.9	67.5	....
Malta	181	115.4	112.2	106.9	106.5	102.9	102.1	99.8	97.2	100.0	96.5	90.4	....
Moldova	921	51.3	116.3	140.2	116.0	121.6	103.4	115.3	109.0	100.0	87.4	....	....
Poland	964	115.4	115.0	120.2	121.9	117.2	110.5	103.5	100.3	100.0	91.5	96.6	....
Romania	968	75.5	103.1	107.6	91.7	82.7	93.7	93.0	93.7	100.0	99.4	93.2	94.5
Russia	922	....	89.9	101.1	111.2	120.7	109.3	89.1	104.3	100.0	89.8	81.4	72.0
Slovak Republic	936	....	104.2	106.9	105.0	100.1	† 103.1	107.6	104.1	100.0	96.6	100.9	† 100.1
Slovenia	961	180.1	156.5	139.6	137.8	128.4	118.7	110.7	107.6	100.0	85.8	85.3	86.6
Turkey	186	165.2	182.1	144.9	142.8	125.1	123.6	118.0	87.3	100.0	76.9	92.2	105.3
Ukraine	926	36.6	56.4	68.6	144.1	159.4	136.4	122.6	110.9	100.0	84.0	63.8	51.8
Middle East													
Bahrain	419	106.9	110.7	111.8	109.3	110.6	106.7	89.0	91.6	100.0	91.1	80.0	....
Egypt	469	90.8	90.6	90.7	96.2	97.6	98.8	99.6	100.9	100.0	93.2	87.3	78.9
Iran, I.R. of	429	75.9	87.7	85.8	94.0	94.8	90.3	84.3	92.1	100.0	90.4	98.7	....
Israel	436	138.7	131.6	128.2	† 122.9	115.1	113.1	104.5	98.7	100.0	92.7	89.6	91.2
Jordan	439	† 101.6	99.9	108.4	111.0	116.7	113.4	116.4	103.6	100.0	97.5	....	....
Kuwait	443	69.1	81.3	78.7	77.2	91.2	85.5	72.8	83.2	100.0	81.5	79.7	86.0
Libya	672	80.4	74.3	69.6	68.1	76.8	92.7	80.4	83.1	100.0	93.9	131.3	....
Oman	449	118.3	114.9	111.3	110.5	113.1	94.2	80.0	83.8	100.0	91.9	88.9	....
Qatar	453	77.6	68.6	64.8	70.8	74.6	84.7	71.2	77.2	100.0	99.9	90.1	84.6
Saudi Arabia	456	103.7	97.3	96.0	98.5	101.7	101.1	86.3	89.2	100.0	92.4	82.7	86.7
Syrian Arab Rep.	463	116.8	99.7	108.7	112.3	123.4	123.0	118.0	107.8	100.0	85.4	75.5	....
Yemen, Republic of	474	62.7	59.4	58.2	64.2	84.4	91.0	78.1	95.4	100.0	88.4	83.9	81.0
Western Hemisphere													
ECCU	309	136.8	132.4	131.3	119.7	122.6	119.3	112.3	104.9	100.0	94.3	88.5	....
Anguilla	312	163.7	157.8	156.7	123.1	127.6	128.3	115.1	117.3	100.0	89.8	80.4	....
Antigua and Barbuda	311	145.9	146.3	148.1	120.4	136.8	137.0	126.3	104.6	100.0	....	....	....
Dominica	321	110.2	118.1	121.8	102.7	103.3	103.0	103.0	96.7	100.0	91.6	79.8	....
Grenada	328	159.5	130.1	122.0	117.0	115.2	111.6	111.1	106.3	100.0	....	....	....
Montserrat	351	203.4	219.3	191.8	182.6	162.0	118.0	98.4	93.2	100.0	101.2	108.7	....
St. Kitts and Nevis	361	115.3	115.0	127.0	119.1	124.2	122.8	114.7	117.6	100.0	102.8	97.9	89.9
St. Lucia	362	121.7	116.9	114.5	112.8	110.8	107.8	105.6	102.9	100.0	90.6	91.2	....
St. Vincent & Grens	364	140.9	131.7	126.0	133.4	132.2	122.9	116.2	104.0	100.0	95.8	95.3	....
Argentina	213	232.8	† 165.7	153.3	158.1	140.4	120.3	111.2	101.3	100.0	117.4	114.0	105.9
Aruba	314	....	....	....	98.5	98.6	105.2	100.7	94.6	100.0	96.0	87.5	....
Barbados	316	123.3	124.9	120.8	123.7	110.7	112.4	112.5	104.8	100.0	96.8	84.5	....
Belize	339	106.0	112.4	107.9	110.6	108.1	100.2	99.8	95.4	100.0	90.0	98.0	....
Bolivia	218	131.7	109.5	99.6	107.9	101.1	96.1	95.7	93.2	100.0	99.9	113.2	107.0
Brazil	223	50.1	36.3	68.5	96.0	103.2	† 97.4	93.0	92.3	100.0	97.1	88.7	95.6
Chile	228	114.3	109.7	120.9	116.0	106.6	107.9	103.0	97.1	100.0	104.7	112.1	111.4
Colombia	233	148.1	141.5	130.9	134.4	128.9	109.7	104.8	99.4	100.0	93.0	88.3	89.0
Costa Rica	238	114.6	118.2	117.2	142.1	112.5	117.1	112.7	108.7	100.0	99.4	92.3	90.8
Dominican Republic	243	139.5	124.5	125.4	125.6	119.9	113.1	109.2	101.6	100.0	88.5	88.0	....
Ecuador	248	130.7	105.9	93.9	95.7	89.6	91.3	96.2	153.8	100.0	100.1	† 116.6	109.2
El Salvador	253	138.5	125.7	104.9	110.1	105.0	102.5	101.5	96.8	100.0	101.4	108.4	110.7
Guatemala	258	131.9	136.4	141.5	139.4	137.3	131.1	126.2	122.4	100.0	93.2	92.0	86.3
Haiti	263	85.5	87.6	103.7	93.0	121.6	112.8	120.0	107.2	100.0	96.8	86.3	78.2
Honduras	268	158.4	173.1	169.0	170.0	153.3	130.8	122.3	107.3	100.0	94.3	90.6	87.1
Jamaica	343	110.5	113.0	107.5	102.9	110.2	106.0	105.6	100.4	100.0	101.1	99.0	....
Mexico	273	85.4	81.6	76.8	75.3	81.5	77.0	79.5	79.9	100.0	94.1	93.0	93.7
Nicaragua	278	184.9	177.1	198.7	176.6	146.4	109.5	98.0	96.5	100.0	76.4	71.3	69.3
Panama	283	150.4	140.2	129.4	122.6	124.4	117.0	112.3	108.5	100.0	92.7	96.2	....
Paraguay	288	110.9	106.6	107.6	110.0	107.9	105.9	107.9	94.0	100.0	89.7	99.0	....
Peru	293	177.5	159.2	165.2	156.6	129.3	113.6	102.1	93.5	100.0	99.5	99.8	....

Income Velocity of Money plus Quasi-Money

		1992	1993	1994	1995	1996	1997	1998	1999	2000	2001	2002	2003
							Index Numbers: 2000=100						
Western Hemisphere(Cont.)													
Trinidad and Tobago	369	98.6	90.6	93.0	96.7	99.7	92.9	86.1	93.0	100.0	103.0	100.0	....
Uruguay	298	110.3	121.7	127.7	127.7	124.8	121.9	116.8	104.6	100.0	85.5	70.4	75.7
Venezuela, Rep. Bol.	299	68.2	71.7	67.6	78.1	98.6	90.1	94.6	93.5	100.0	96.1	100.7	....

2004, International Monetary Fund: *International Financial Statistics Yearbook*

National Interest Rates

Central Bank Discount Rates (60)
(End of period in percent per annum)

		1992	1993	1994	1995	1996	1997	1998	1999	2000	2001	2002	2003
Industrial Countries													
United States	111	3.00	3.00	4.75	5.25	5.00	5.00	4.50	5.00	6.00	1.25	.75	† 2.00
Canada	156	7.36	4.11	7.43	5.79	3.25	4.50	5.25	5.00	6.00	2.50	3.00	3.00
Australia	193	6.96	5.83	5.75	5.75	....	....	....	....	....	....	....	....
Japan	158	3.25	1.75	1.75	.50	.50	.50	.50	.50	.50	.10	.10	.10
New Zealand	196	9.15	5.70	9.75	9.80	8.80	9.70	5.60	5.00	6.50	4.75	5.75	5.00
Euro Area	163	....	....	....	....	....	....	....	4.00	5.75	4.25	3.75	3.00
Austria	122	8.00	5.25	4.50	3.00	2.50	2.50	2.50	....	....	....	....	....
Belgium	124	7.75	5.25	4.50	3.00	2.50	2.75	2.75	....	....	....	....	....
Finland	172	9.50	5.50	5.25	4.88	4.00	4.00	3.50	....	....	....	....	....
Germany	134	8.25	5.75	4.50	3.00	2.50	2.50	2.50	....	....	....	....	....
Greece	174	19.00	21.50	20.50	18.00	16.50	14.50	....	† 11.81	8.10	....	....	....
Ireland	178	....	7.00	6.25	6.50	6.25	6.75	4.06	....	....	....	....	....
Italy	136	12.00	8.00	7.50	9.00	7.50	5.50	3.00	....	....	....	....	....
Netherlands	138	7.75	5.00	....	....	....	....	....	....	....	....	....	....
Portugal	182	21.96	11.00	8.88	8.50	6.70	5.31	3.00	....	....	....	....	....
Spain	184	13.25	9.00	7.38	9.00	6.25	4.75	3.00	....	....	....	....	....
Denmark	128	9.50	6.25	5.00	4.25	3.25	3.50	3.50	3.00	4.75	3.25	2.86	2.00
Iceland	176	† 16.63	....	4.70	5.93	5.70	6.55	† 8.50	10.00	12.40	12.00	8.20	7.70
Norway	142	11.00	7.00	6.75	6.75	6.00	5.50	10.00	7.50	9.00	8.50	8.50	4.25
Sweden	144	† 10.00	5.00	7.00	7.00	3.50	2.50	2.00	1.50	2.00	2.00	2.00	....
Switzerland	146	6.00	4.00	3.50	1.50	1.00	1.00	1.00	.50	† 3.20	1.59	.50	.11
Developing Countries													
Africa													
CEMAC	758	12.00	11.50	† 7.75	8.60	7.75	7.50	7.00	7.30	7.00	6.50	6.30	6.00
Cameroon	622	12.00	11.50	† 7.75	8.60	7.75	7.50	7.00	7.30	7.00	6.50	6.30	6.00
Central African Rep.	626	12.00	11.50	† 7.75	8.60	7.75	7.50	7.00	7.60	7.00	6.50	6.30	6.00
Chad	628	12.00	11.50	† 7.75	8.60	7.75	7.50	7.00	7.60	7.00	6.50	6.30	6.00
Congo, Republic of	634	12.00	11.50	† 7.75	8.60	7.75	7.50	7.00	7.60	7.00	6.50	6.30	6.00
Equatorial Guinea	642	12.00	11.50	† 7.75	8.60	7.75	7.50	7.00	7.60	7.00	6.50	6.30	6.00
Gabon	646	12.00	11.50	† 7.75	8.60	7.75	7.50	7.00	7.60	7.00	6.50	6.30	6.00
WAEMU	759	....	....	....	6.00	6.00	6.00	6.00	6.00	6.00	6.00	6.00	4.50
Benin	638	12.50	† 6.00	6.00	6.00	6.00	6.00	6.00	6.00	6.00	6.00	6.00	4.50
Burkina Faso	748	12.50	† 6.00	6.00	6.00	6.00	6.00	6.00	6.00	6.00	6.00	6.00	4.50
Côte d'Ivoire	662	12.50	† 6.00	6.00	6.00	6.00	6.00	6.00	6.00	6.00	6.00	6.00	4.50
Guinea-Bissau	654	45.50	† 6.00	6.00	6.00	6.00	6.00	6.00	6.00	6.00	6.00	6.00	4.50
Mali	678	12.50	† 6.00	6.00	6.00	6.00	6.00	6.00	6.00	6.00	6.00	6.00	4.50
Niger	692	12.50	† 6.00	6.00	6.00	6.00	6.00	6.00	6.00	6.00	6.00	6.00	4.50
Senegal	722	12.50	† 6.00	6.00	6.00	6.00	6.00	6.00	6.00	6.00	6.00	6.00	4.50
Togo	742	12.50	† 6.00	6.00	6.00	6.00	6.00	6.00	6.00	6.00	6.00	6.00	4.50
Algeria	612	11.50	11.50	21.00	† 14.00	13.00	11.00	9.50	8.50	6.00	6.00	5.50	4.50
Angola	614	....	....	....	160.00	2.00	48.00	58.00	120.00	150.00	150.00	150.00	150.00
Botswana	616	14.25	14.25	13.50	13.00	13.00	12.50	12.50	13.25	14.25	14.25	15.25	14.25
Burundi	618	11.00	10.00	10.00	10.00	10.00	12.00	12.00	12.00	14.00	14.00	15.50	14.50
Congo, Dem. Rep. of	636	55.00	95.00	145.00	125.00	238.00	13.00	22.00	120.00	120.00	140.00	24.00	8.00
Ethiopia	644	5.25	12.00	12.00	12.00	....	....	....	....	....	....	....	....
Gambia, The	648	17.50	13.50	13.50	14.00	14.00	14.00	12.00	10.50	10.00	13.00	18.00	....
Ghana	652	30.00	35.00	33.00	45.00	45.00	45.00	37.00	27.00	27.00	27.00	24.50	21.50
Guinea	656	19.00	17.00	17.00	18.00	18.00	15.00	....	....	11.50	16.25	16.25	16.25
Kenya	664	20.46	45.50	21.50	24.50	26.88	32.27	17.07	26.46	....	....	....	....
Lesotho	666	15.00	13.50	13.50	15.50	17.00	15.60	19.50	19.00	15.00	13.00	16.19	15.00
Madagascar	674	....	....	....	....	....	....	....	15.00	....	....	....	....
Malawi	676	20.00	25.00	40.00	50.00	27.00	23.00	43.00	47.00	50.23	46.80	40.00	35.00
Mauritius	684	8.30	8.30	13.80	11.40	11.82	10.46	17.19	....	....	....	....	....
Morocco	686	....	....	7.17	....	....	....	6.04	5.42	5.00	4.71	3.79	3.25
Mozambique	688	....	....	69.70	57.75	32.00	12.95	9.95	9.95	9.95	9.95	9.95	9.95
Namibia	728	16.50	14.50	15.50	17.50	17.75	16.00	18.75	11.50	11.25	9.25	12.75	7.75
Nigeria	694	17.50	26.00	13.50	13.50	13.50	13.50	13.50	18.00	14.00	20.50	16.50	15.00
Rwanda	714	11.00	11.00	11.00	16.00	16.00	10.75	11.38	11.19	11.69	13.00	13.00	14.50
São Tomé & Príncipe	716	45.00	30.00	32.00	50.00	35.00	55.00	29.50	17.00	17.00	15.50	15.50	14.50
Seychelles	718	13.53	13.08	12.50	12.83	11.00	11.00	5.50	5.50	5.50	5.50	5.50	4.67
South Africa	199	14.00	12.00	13.00	15.00	17.00	16.00	† 19.32	12.00	12.00	9.50	13.50	8.00
Swaziland	734	12.00	11.00	12.00	15.00	16.75	15.75	18.00	12.00	11.00	9.50	13.50	8.00
Tanzania	738	14.50	14.50	67.50	47.90	19.00	16.20	17.60	20.20	10.70	8.70	9.18	12.34
Tunisia	744	11.38	8.88	8.88	8.88	7.88	....	....	....	....	....	....	....
Uganda	746	41.00	24.00	15.00	13.30	15.85	14.08	9.10	15.75	18.86	8.88	13.08	25.62
Zambia	754	47.00	72.50	20.50	40.20	47.00	17.70	....	32.93	25.67	40.10	27.87	14.35
Zimbabwe	698	29.50	28.50	29.50	29.50	27.00	31.50	† 39.50	74.41	57.84	57.20	29.65	300.00
Asia													
Bangladesh	513	8.50	6.00	5.50	6.00	7.00	8.00	8.00	7.00	7.00	6.00	6.00	5.00
China,P.R.: Mainland	924	7.20	10.08	10.08	10.44	9.00	8.55	4.59	3.24	3.24	3.24	2.70	2.70
China,P.R.:Hong Kong	532	4.00	4.00	5.75	6.25	6.00	7.00	6.25	7.00	8.00	3.25	2.75	2.50
Fiji	819	6.00	6.00	6.00	6.00	6.00	1.88	2.50	2.50	8.00	1.75	1.75	1.75
India	534	12.00	12.00	12.00	12.00	12.00	9.00	9.00	8.00	8.00	6.50	6.25	6.00
Indonesia	536	13.50	8.82	12.44	13.99	12.80	20.00	38.44	12.51	14.53	17.62	12.93	8.31
Korea	542	7.00	5.00	5.00	5.00	5.00	5.00	3.00	3.00	3.00	2.50	2.50	2.50

60   2004, International Monetary Fund : *International Financial Statistics Yearbook*

National Interest Rates

		1992	1993	1994	1995	1996	1997	1998	1999	2000	2001	2002	2003
		\multicolumn{12}{c}{Central Bank Discount Rates (60) *(End of period in percent per annum)*}

Asia (Cont.)

Country	Code	1992	1993	1994	1995	1996	1997	1998	1999	2000	2001	2002	2003
Lao People's Dem.Rep.	544	23.67	25.00	30.00	32.08	35.00	....	35.00	34.89	35.17	35.00	20.00	20.00
Malaysia	548	7.10	5.24	4.51	6.47	7.28	....	....	....	....	....	....	....
Mongolia	948	....	628.80	180.00	150.00	109.00	45.50	23.30	11.40	8.65	8.60	9.90	11.50
Myanmar	518	11.00	11.00	11.00	12.50	15.00	15.00	15.00	12.00	10.00	10.00	10.00	9.00
Nepal	558	13.00	11.00	11.00	11.00	11.00	9.00	9.00	9.00	7.50	6.50	5.50	5.50
Pakistan	564	10.00	10.00	† 15.00	17.00	20.00	18.00	16.50	13.00	13.00	10.00	7.50	7.50
Papua New Guinea	853	7.12	† 6.30	6.55	18.00	10.30	10.20	18.15	12.80	4.41	11.25	13.25	....
Philippines	566	14.30	9.40	8.30	10.83	11.70	14.64	12.40	7.89	13.81	8.30	4.19	5.53
Sri Lanka	524	17.00	17.00	17.00	17.00	17.00	17.00	17.00	16.00	25.00	....	18.00	15.00
Thailand	578	11.00	9.00	9.50	10.50	10.50	12.50	12.50	4.00	4.00	3.75	3.25	2.75
Vanuatu	846	....	....	....	....	....	....	7.00	7.00	7.00	6.50	6.50	6.50
Vietnam	582	....	....	....	....	18.90	10.80	12.00	6.00	6.00	4.80	4.80	5.00

Europe

Country	Code	1992	1993	1994	1995	1996	1997	1998	1999	2000	2001	2002	2003
Albania	914	40.00	34.00	25.00	20.50	24.00	32.00	23.44	18.00	10.82	7.00	8.50	6.50
Armenia	911	30.00	210.00	210.00	77.80	26.00	65.10	....	....	....	....	....	....
Azerbaijan	912	12.00	100.00	200.00	80.00	20.00	12.00	14.00	10.00	10.00	10.00	7.00	7.00
Belarus	913	30.00	210.00	480.00	66.00	8.30	8.90	9.60	23.40	† 80.00	48.00	38.00	28.00
Bulgaria	918	41.00	52.00	† 72.00	34.00	180.00	6.65	5.08	4.46	4.63	4.65	3.31	2.83
Croatia	960	1,889.39	34.49	8.50	8.50	6.50	5.90	5.90	7.90	5.90	5.90	4.50	4.50
Cyprus	423	6.50	6.50	6.50	6.50	† 7.50	7.00	7.00	7.00	7.00	5.50	5.00	4.50
Czech Republic	935	....	8.00	8.50	11.30	12.40	14.75	9.50	5.25	5.25	4.50	2.75	2.00
Hungary	944	21.00	22.00	25.00	28.00	23.00	20.50	17.00	14.50	11.00	9.75	8.50	12.50
Kazakhstan	916	....	170.00	230.00	† 52.50	35.00	18.50	25.00	18.00	14.00	9.00	7.50	7.00
Latvia	941	....	27.00	25.00	24.00	9.50	4.00	4.00	4.00	3.50	3.50	3.00	3.00
Macedonia, FYR	962	....	295.00	33.00	15.00	9.20	8.90	8.90	8.90	7.90	10.70	10.70	6.50
Malta	181	5.50	5.50	5.50	5.50	5.50	5.50	5.50	4.75	4.75	4.25	3.75	....
Poland	964	32.00	29.00	28.00	25.00	22.00	24.50	18.25	19.00	21.50	14.00	7.75	5.75
Russia	922	....	....	....	160.00	48.00	28.00	60.00	55.00	25.00	25.00	21.00	16.00
Slovak Republic	936	....	12.00	12.00	9.75	8.80	8.80	8.80	8.80	8.80	† 7.75	6.50	6.00
Slovenia	961	† 26.00	19.00	17.00	11.00	11.00	11.00	11.00	9.00	11.00	12.00	10.50	7.25
Tajikistan	923	....	....	....	....	....	76.00	36.40	20.10	20.60	20.00	† 24.75	† 15.00
Turkey	186	48.00	48.00	55.00	50.00	50.00	67.00	67.00	60.00	60.00	60.00	55.00	43.00
Ukraine	926	80.00	240.00	252.00	110.00	40.00	35.00	60.00	45.00	27.00	12.50	7.00	7.00

Middle East

Country	Code	1992	1993	1994	1995	1996	1997	1998	1999	2000	2001	2002	2003
Egypt	469	18.40	16.50	14.00	13.50	13.00	12.25	12.00	12.00	12.00	11.00	10.00	10.00
Israel	436	10.39	9.78	17.01	14.19	15.30	13.72	13.47	11.20	8.21	5.67	9.18	5.20
Jordan	439	8.50	8.50	8.50	8.50	8.50	7.75	9.00	8.00	6.50	5.00	4.50	....
Kuwait	443	7.50	5.75	7.00	7.25	7.25	7.50	7.00	6.75	7.25	4.25	3.25	3.25
Lebanon	446	16.00	20.22	16.49	19.01	25.00	30.00	30.00	25.00	20.00	20.00	20.00	20.00
Libya	672	5.00	5.00	....	....	....	....	3.00	5.00	5.00	5.00	5.00	5.00
Syrian Arab Republic	463	5.00	5.00	5.00	5.00	5.00	5.00	5.00	5.00	5.00	5.00	5.00	....

Western Hemisphere

Country	Code	1992	1993	1994	1995	1996	1997	1998	1999	2000	2001	2002	2003
ECCU	309	....	....	9.00	9.00	9.00	8.00	8.00	8.00	8.00	7.00	7.00	6.50
Anguilla	312	....	....	9.00	9.00	9.00	8.00	8.00	8.00	8.00	7.00	7.00	6.50
Antigua and Barbuda	311	....	....	9.00	9.00	9.00	8.00	8.00	8.00	8.00	7.00	7.00	6.50
Dominica	321	....	....	9.00	9.00	9.00	8.00	8.00	8.00	8.00	7.00	7.00	6.50
Grenada	328	....	....	9.00	9.00	9.00	8.00	8.00	8.00	8.00	7.00	7.00	6.50
Montserrat	351	....	....	9.00	9.00	9.00	8.00	8.00	8.00	8.00	7.00	7.00	6.50
St. Kitts and Nevis	361	....	....	9.00	9.00	9.00	8.00	8.00	8.00	8.00	7.00	7.00	6.50
St. Lucia	362	....	....	9.00	9.00	9.00	8.00	8.00	8.00	8.00	7.00	7.00	6.50
St. Vincent & Grens	364	....	....	9.00	9.00	9.00	8.00	8.00	8.00	8.00	7.00	7.00	6.50
Aruba	314	9.50	9.50	9.50	9.50	9.50	9.50	9.50	6.50	6.50	6.50	6.50	5.00
Bahamas, The	313	7.50	7.00	6.50	6.50	6.50	6.50	6.50	5.75	5.75	5.75	5.75	5.75
Barbados	316	12.00	8.00	9.50	12.50	12.50	9.00	9.00	10.00	10.00	7.50	7.50	7.50
Belize	339	12.00	12.00	12.00	12.00	12.00	12.00	12.00	12.00	12.00	12.00	12.00	12.00
Bolivia	218	....	....	....	....	16.50	13.25	14.10	12.50	10.00	8.50	12.50	7.50
Brazil	223	....	....	....	....	25.34	45.09	39.41	21.37	† 18.52	21.43	30.42	23.92
Chile	228	....	7.96	13.89	7.96	11.75	7.96	9.12	7.44	8.73	6.50	3.00	2.45
Colombia	233	34.42	33.49	44.90	40.42	35.05	31.32	42.28	23.05	18.28	16.40	12.73	12.95
Costa Rica	238	29.00	35.00	37.75	38.50	35.00	31.00	37.00	34.00	31.50	28.75	31.25	26.00
Ecuador	248	49.00	33.57	44.88	59.41	46.38	37.46	61.84	64.40	† 13.16	16.44	14.55	11.19
Guyana	336	24.30	17.00	20.25	17.25	12.00	11.00	11.25	13.25	11.75	8.75	6.25	5.50
Honduras	268	26.10	....	....	....	....	....	....	....	....	....	....	....
Netherlands Antilles	353	6.00	5.00	5.00	6.00	6.00	6.00	6.00	6.00	6.00	6.00	6.00	....
Nicaragua	278	15.00	11.75	10.50	....	....	....	....	....	....	....	....	....
Paraguay	288	24.00	27.17	19.15	20.50	15.00	20.00	20.00	20.00	20.00	20.00	20.00	20.00
Peru	293	48.50	28.63	16.08	18.44	18.16	15.94	18.72	17.80	14.00	14.00	4.75	4.25
Trinidad and Tobago	369	13.00	13.00	13.00	13.00	13.00	13.00	13.00	13.00	13.00	13.00	7.25	7.00
Uruguay	298	162.40	164.30	182.30	178.70	160.30	95.50	73.70	66.39	57.26	71.66	316.01	....
Venezuela, Rep. Bol.	299	52.20	71.25	48.00	49.00	45.00	45.00	60.00	38.00	38.00	37.00	40.00	28.50

2004, International Monetary Fund : *International Financial Statistics Yearbook*

National Interest Rates

		1992	1993	1994	1995	1996	1997	1998	1999	2000	2001	2002	2003
Money Market Rates (60b)													
(Period averages in percent per annum)													
Industrial Countries														
United States	111	3.52	3.02	4.20	5.84	5.30	5.46	5.35	4.97	6.24	3.89	1.67	1.13
Canada	156	6.64	4.62	5.05	6.92	4.32	3.26	4.87	4.74	5.52	4.11	2.45	2.93
Australia	193	6.44	5.11	5.18	†7.50	7.20	5.50	4.99	†4.78	5.90	5.06	4.55	4.81
Japan	158	4.58	†3.06	2.20	1.21	.47	.48	.37	.06	.11	.06	.01	—
New Zealand	196	6.63	6.25	6.13	8.91	9.38	7.38	6.86	4.33	6.12	5.76	5.40	5.33
Euro Area	163	....	....	6.53	6.82	5.09	4.38	3.96	2.97	4.39	4.26	3.32	2.34
Austria	122	9.35	7.22	5.03	4.36	3.19	3.27	3.36	....	....	....	....	....
Belgium	124	9.38	8.21	5.72	4.80	3.24	3.46	3.58	....	....	....	....	....
Finland	172	13.25	7.77	5.35	5.75	3.63	3.23	3.57	2.96	4.39	4.26	3.32	2.33
France	132	10.35	8.75	5.69	6.35	3.73	3.24	3.39	....	....	....	....	....
Germany	134	9.42	7.49	5.35	4.50	3.27	3.18	3.41	2.73	4.11	4.37	3.28	2.32
Greece	174	....	....	24.60	16.40	13.80	12.80	13.99	....	....	....	....	....
Ireland	178	15.12	10.49	†5.75	5.45	5.74	6.43	3.23	3.14	4.84	3.31	2.88	2.08
Italy	136	14.02	10.20	8.51	10.46	8.82	6.88	4.99	2.95	4.39	4.26	3.32	2.33
Luxembourg	137	8.93	8.09	5.16	4.26	3.29	3.36	3.48	....	....	....	....	....
Netherlands	138	9.27	7.10	5.14	4.22	2.89	3.07	3.21	....	....	....	....	....
Portugal	182	†17.48	13.25	10.62	8.91	7.38	5.78	4.34	2.71	....	....	....	....
Spain	184	13.01	12.33	7.81	8.98	7.65	5.49	4.34	2.72	4.11	4.36	3.28	2.31
Denmark	128	11.35	†11.49	6.30	6.19	3.98	3.71	4.27	3.37	4.98	....	3.56	2.38
Iceland	176	12.38	8.61	4.96	6.58	6.96	7.38	8.12	9.24	11.61	14.51	11.21	5.16
Norway	142	13.71	7.64	5.70	5.54	4.97	3.77	6.03	6.87	6.72	7.38	7.05	4.45
Sweden	144	18.42	9.08	7.36	8.54	6.28	4.21	4.24	3.14	3.81	4.08	....	....
Switzerland	146	7.47	4.94	3.85	2.89	1.78	1.35	1.22	.93	†3.50	1.65	.44	.09
United Kingdom	112	9.37	5.91	4.88	6.08	5.96	6.61	7.21	5.20	5.77	5.08	3.89	3.59
Developing Countries														
Africa														
WAEMU	759	....	....	....	4.95	4.95	4.95	4.95	4.95	4.95	4.95	4.95	4.95
Benin	638	11.44	....	....	....	....	....	4.81	4.95	4.95	4.95	4.95	4.95
Burkina Faso	748	11.44	....	....	....	....	....	4.81	4.95	4.95	4.95	4.95	4.95
Côte d'Ivoire	662	11.44	....	....	....	....	....	4.81	4.95	4.95	4.95	4.95	4.95
Guinea-Bissau	654	11.45	....	....	....	....	....	4.81	4.95	4.95	4.95	4.95	4.95
Mali	678	11.44	....	....	....	....	....	4.81	4.95	4.95	4.95	4.95	4.95
Niger	692	11.44	....	....	....	....	....	4.81	4.95	4.95	4.95	4.95	4.95
Senegal	722	11.44	....	....	....	....	....	4.81	4.95	4.95	4.95	4.95	4.95
Togo	742	11.44	....	....	....	....	....	4.81	4.95	4.95	4.95	4.95	4.95
Algeria	612	....	....	19.80	†21.05	18.47	11.80	10.40	10.43	6.77	3.35	4.20	3.96
Madagascar	674	15.00	....	—	29.00	10.00	....	11.24	....	16.00	....	....	10.50
Mauritius	684	9.05	7.73	10.23	10.35	9.96	9.43	8.99	10.01	7.66	7.25	6.20	3.22
Morocco	686	....	....	12.29	10.06	8.42	7.89	6.30	5.64	5.41	4.44	2.99	3.22
Mozambique	688	....	....	....	....	....	....	....	9.92	16.12	†25.00	20.40	13.34
Namibia	728	13.87	10.83	10.25	13.08	15.00	15.41	17.14	13.17	9.19	9.53	10.46	10.03
South Africa	199	14.11	10.83	10.24	13.07	15.54	15.59	17.11	13.06	9.54	†8.49	11.11	10.93
Swaziland	734	10.25	9.73	7.01	8.52	9.77	10.35	10.63	8.86	5.54	5.06	7.31	6.98
Tunisia	744	11.73	10.48	8.81	8.81	8.64	6.88	6.89	5.99	5.88	6.04	5.93	5.14
Zimbabwe	698	34.77	34.18	30.90	29.64	26.18	25.15	37.22	53.13	64.98	21.52	32.35	110.05
Asia														
China,P.R.:Hong Kong	532	3.81	4.00	5.44	6.00	5.13	4.50	5.50	5.75	7.13	2.69	1.50	.07
China,P.R.:Macao	546	4.41	3.79	5.91	6.01	5.60	7.54	5.41	5.70	6.29	2.11	1.48	.11
Fiji	819	3.06	2.91	4.10	3.95	2.43	1.91	1.27	1.27	2.58	.79	.92	.86
India	534	15.23	8.64	7.14	15.57	11.04	5.29	....	....	....	....	....	....
Indonesia	536	11.99	8.66	9.74	13.64	13.96	27.82	62.79	23.58	10.32	15.03	13.54	7.76
Korea	542	14.32	12.12	12.45	12.57	12.44	13.24	14.98	5.01	5.16	4.69	4.21	4.00
Malaysia	548	7.92	7.10	4.20	5.60	6.92	7.61	8.46	3.38	2.66	2.79	2.73	2.74
Maldives	556	7.00	5.00	5.00	6.80	6.80	6.80	6.80	6.80	6.80	....	....	....
Pakistan	564	7.51	11.00	8.36	11.52	11.40	12.10	10.76	9.04	8.57	8.49	5.53	2.14
Philippines	566	16.58	13.77	13.99	11.93	12.77	16.16	13.90	10.16	10.84	9.75	7.15	6.97
Singapore	576	2.74	2.50	3.68	2.56	2.93	4.35	5.00	2.04	2.57	1.99	.96	.74
Sri Lanka	524	21.63	25.65	18.54	41.87	24.33	18.42	15.74	16.69	17.30	21.24	12.33	9.68
Thailand	578	6.93	6.54	7.25	10.96	9.23	14.59	13.02	1.77	1.95	2.00	1.76	1.31
Vanuatu	846	5.92	6.00	6.00	6.00	6.00	6.00	8.65	6.99	5.58	5.50	5.50	5.50
Europe														
Armenia	911	....	....	....	....	48.56	36.41	27.84	23.65	18.63	19.40	12.29	7.51
Bulgaria	918	52.39	48.07	66.43	53.09	119.88	66.43	2.48	2.93	3.02	3.74	2.47	1.95
Croatia	960	951.20	1,370.50	26.93	21.13	17.60	9.71	11.16	10.21	6.78	3.42	1.75	3.31
Cyprus	423	....	....	....	....	6.85	4.82	4.80	5.15	5.96	4.93	3.42	3.35
Czech Republic	935	....	8.00	12.65	10.93	12.67	17.50	10.08	5.58	5.42	4.69	2.63	2.08
Estonia	939	....	....	5.67	4.94	3.53	6.45	11.66	5.39	†5.68	5.31	3.88	2.92
Georgia	915	....	....	....	....	43.39	26.58	43.26	34.61	18.17	†17.52	27.69	16.88
Kyrgyz Republic	917	....	....	....	....	....	....	43.98	43.71	24.26	11.92	....	....
Latvia	941	....	....	37.18	22.39	13.08	3.76	4.42	4.72	2.97	5.23	3.01	2.86
Lithuania	946	....	....	69.48	26.73	20.26	9.55	†6.12	6.26	3.60	3.37	2.21	1.79
Moldova	921	....	....	....	....	....	28.10	30.91	32.60	20.77	11.04	5.13	11.51
Poland	964	†29.49	24.51	23.32	25.82	20.63	22.43	20.59	13.58	18.16	16.23	9.39	5.76
Russia	922	....	....	....	190.43	47.65	20.97	50.56	14.79	7.14	10.10	8.19	3.77
Slovak Republic	936	....	....	....	....	....	....	....	....	8.08	7.76	6.33	6.08

National Interest Rates

Money Market Rates (60b)
(Period averages in percent per annum)

		1992	1993	1994	1995	1996	1997	1998	1999	2000	2001	2002	2003
Europe(Cont.)													
Slovenia	961	67.58	39.15	29.08	12.18	13.98	9.71	7.45	6.87	6.95	6.90	4.93	5.59
Turkey	186	65.35	62.83	136.47	72.30	76.24	70.32	74.60	73.53	56.72	91.95	49.51	36.16
Ukraine	926	....	....	....	....	....	22.05	40.41	44.98	18.34	16.57	5.50	7.90
Middle East													
Bahrain, Kingdom of	419	3.99	3.53	5.18	6.24	5.69	....	5.69	5.58	6.89	3.85	2.02	1.24
Kuwait	443	....	7.43	6.31	7.43	6.98	7.05	7.24	6.32	6.82	4.62	2.99	2.47
Libya	672	4.00	4.00	....	....	....	....	4.00	4.00	4.00	4.00	4.00	4.00
Western Hemisphere													
ECCU	309	5.25	5.25	5.25	5.25	5.25	5.25	5.25	5.25	5.25	† 5.64	6.32	6.07
Anguilla	312	5.25	5.25	5.25	5.25	5.25	5.25	5.25	5.25	5.25	† 5.64	6.32	6.07
Antigua and Barbuda	311	5.25	5.25	5.25	5.25	5.25	5.25	5.25	5.25	5.25	† 5.64	6.32	6.07
Dominica	321	5.25	5.25	5.25	5.25	5.25	5.25	5.25	5.25	5.25	† 5.64	6.32	6.07
Grenada	328	5.25	5.25	5.25	5.25	5.25	5.25	5.25	5.25	5.25	† 5.64	6.32	6.07
Montserrat	351	5.25	5.25	5.25	5.25	5.25	5.25	5.25	5.25	5.25	† 5.64	6.32	6.07
St. Kitts and Nevis	361	5.25	5.25	5.25	5.25	5.25	5.25	5.25	5.25	5.25	† 5.64	6.32	6.07
St. Lucia	362	5.25	5.25	5.25	5.25	5.25	5.25	5.25	5.25	5.25	† 5.64	6.32	6.07
St. Vincent & Grens	364	5.25	5.25	5.25	5.25	5.25	5.25	5.25	5.25	5.25	† 5.64	6.32	6.07
Argentina	213	15.11	6.31	7.66	9.46	6.23	6.63	6.81	6.99	8.15	24.90	41.35	3.74
Bolivia	218	....	....	....	22.42	20.27	13.97	12.57	13.49	7.40	6.99	8.41	4.07
Brazil	223	1,574.28	3,284.44	4,820.64	53.37	27.45	25.00	29.50	26.26	17.59	17.47	19.11	23.37
Chile	228	....	....	....	....	....	....	....	....	10.09	6.81	4.08	2.72
Colombia	233	....	....	....	22.40	28.37	23.83	35.00	18.81	10.87	10.43	6.06	6.95
Dominican Republic	243	....	....	....	....	14.70	13.01	16.68	15.30	18.28	13.47	14.50	24.24
El Salvador	253	....	....	....	....	....	10.43	9.43	10.68	6.93	5.28	4.40	3.86
Guatemala	258	....	....	....	....	....	7.77	6.62	9.23	9.33	10.58	9.11	6.65
Mexico	273	18.87	17.39	16.47	† 60.92	33.61	21.91	26.89	24.10	16.96	12.89	8.17	6.83
Panama	283	....	....	....	....	....	....	....	....	....	....	2.22	1.50
Paraguay	288	21.59	22.55	18.64	20.18	16.35	12.48	20.74	17.26	10.70	13.45	13.19	13.02
Uruguay	298	....	....	39.82	36.81	28.47	23.43	20.48	13.96	14.82	22.10	89.37	....
Venezuela, Rep. Bol.	299	....	....	....	....	16.70	12.47	18.58	7.48	8.14	13.33	28.87	13.23

2004, International Monetary Fund : *International Financial Statistics Yearbook*

National Interest Rates

Treasury Bill Rates (60c)
(Period averages in percent per annum)

		1992	1993	1994	1995	1996	1997	1998	1999	2000	2001	2002	2003
Industrial Countries													
United States	111	3.46	3.02	4.27	5.51	5.02	5.07	4.82	4.66	5.84	3.45	1.61	1.01
Canada	156	6.59	4.84	5.54	6.89	4.21	3.26	4.73	4.72	5.49	3.77	2.59	2.87
Australia	193	6.27	5.00	5.69	† 7.64	7.02	5.29	4.84	4.76	5.98	4.80	....	....
New Zealand	196	6.72	6.21	6.69	8.82	9.09	7.53	7.10	4.58	6.39	5.56	5.52	5.21
Belgium	124	9.36	8.52	5.57	4.67	3.19	3.38	3.51	2.72	4.02	4.16	3.17	2.23
France	132	10.49	8.41	5.79	6.58	3.84	3.35	3.45	2.72	4.23	4.26	....	....
Germany	134	8.32	6.22	5.05	4.40	3.30	3.32	3.42	2.88	4.32	3.66	2.97	1.98
Greece	174	22.50	20.25	17.50	14.20	11.20	11.38	10.30	8.30	† 6.22	4.08	3.50	2.34
Iceland	176	† 11.30	8.35	4.95	7.22	6.97	7.04	7.40	8.61	11.12	11.03	8.01	4.93
Ireland	178	....	† 9.06	5.87	6.19	5.36	6.03	5.37	....	....	....	....	....
Italy	136	14.32	10.58	9.17	10.85	8.46	6.33	4.59	3.01	4.53	4.05	3.26	2.19
Portugal	182	12.88	....	....	7.75	5.75	4.43	....	....	....	....	....	....
Spain	184	12.44	10.53	8.11	9.79	7.23	5.02	3.79	3.01	4.61	3.92	3.34	2.21
Sweden	144	12.85	8.35	7.40	8.75	5.79	4.11	4.19	3.12	3.95	....	....	....
Switzerland	146	7.76	4.75	3.97	2.78	1.72	1.45	1.32	1.17	2.93	2.68	.94	.16
United Kingdom	112	8.94	5.21	5.15	6.33	5.78	6.48	6.82	5.04	5.80	4.77	3.86	3.55
Developing Countries													
Africa													
Algeria	612	9.50	9.50	16.50	....	....	....	† 9.96	10.05	7.95	5.69	1.80	1.25
Ethiopia	644	5.25	12.00	12.00	12.00	7.22	3.97	3.48	3.65	2.74	3.06	1.30	1.37
Ghana	652	19.38	30.95	27.72	35.38	41.64	42.77	34.33	26.37	36.28	40.96	25.11	27.25
Kenya	664	16.53	49.80	23.32	18.29	22.25	22.87	22.83	13.87	12.05	12.60	8.95	3.51
Lesotho	666	14.20	† 10.01	9.44	12.40	13.89	14.83	15.47	12.45	9.06	9.49	11.34	11.96
Madagascar	674	....	....	....	....	....	....	....	....	....	10.28	....	11.94
Malawi	676	15.62	23.54	27.68	46.30	30.83	18.31	32.98	42.85	39.52	42.41	41.75	39.32
Mozambique	688	....	....	....	....	....	....	....	....	16.97	24.77	29.55	15.31
Namibia	728	13.88	12.16	11.35	13.91	15.25	15.69	17.24	13.28	10.26	9.29	11.00	10.51
Nigeria	694	17.89	24.50	12.87	12.50	12.25	12.00	12.26	17.82	15.50	17.50	19.03	14.79
Seychelles	718	13.40	13.25	12.50	12.28	11.55	10.50	8.13	5.00	5.00	5.00	5.00	4.61
Sierra Leone	724	78.63	28.64	12.19	14.73	29.25	12.71	22.10	32.42	26.22	13.74	15.15	15.68
South Africa	199	13.77	11.31	10.93	13.53	15.04	15.26	16.53	12.85	10.11	9.68	11.16	10.67
Swaziland	734	12.34	8.25	8.35	10.87	13.68	14.37	13.09	11.19	8.30	7.16	8.59	10.61
Tanzania	738	....	34.00	35.09	40.33	15.30	9.59	11.83	10.05	9.78	4.14	3.55	6.26
Uganda	746	....	† 21.30	12.52	8.75	11.71	10.59	7.77	7.43	13.19	11.00	5.85	16.87
Zambia	754	....	124.03	74.21	39.81	52.78	29.48	24.94	36.19	31.37	44.28	34.54	29.97
Zimbabwe	698	26.16	33.04	29.22	27.98	24.53	22.07	32.78	50.48	64.78	17.60	28.51	52.73
Asia													
China,P.R.:Hong Kong	532	3.83	3.17	5.66	5.55	4.45	7.50	5.04	4.94	5.69	1.69	1.35	−.08
Fiji	819	3.65	2.91	2.69	3.15	2.98	2.60	2.00	2.00	3.63	1.51	1.66	1.06
Lao People's Dem.Rep.	544	....	....	....	20.46	....	....	23.66	30.00	29.94	22.70	21.41	24.87
Malaysia	548	7.66	6.48	3.68	5.50	6.41	6.41	6.86	3.53	2.86	2.79	2.73	2.79
Nepal	558	9.00	4.50	6.50	9.90	11.51	2.52	3.70	4.30	5.30	5.00	3.80	3.85
Pakistan	564	12.47	13.03	11.26	12.49	13.61	† 15.74	....	....	8.38	10.71	6.08	....
Papua New Guinea	853	8.88	6.25	6.85	17.40	14.44	9.94	21.18	22.70	17.00	12.36	10.93	18.68
Philippines	566	16.02	12.45	12.71	11.76	12.34	12.89	15.00	10.00	9.91	9.73	5.49	5.87
Singapore	576	1.73	.92	1.94	1.05	1.38	2.32	2.12	1.12	2.18	1.69	.81	.64
Solomon Islands	813	13.50	12.15	11.25	12.50	12.75	12.88	6.00	6.00	7.05	8.23	6.87	5.85
Sri Lanka	524	16.19	16.52	12.68	16.81	† 17.40	....	12.59	12.51	14.02	17.57	12.47	8.09
Vietnam	582	....	26.40	....	....	....	....	....	....	5.42	5.49	5.92	5.83
Europe													
Albania	914	....	....	....	13.84	17.81	32.59	27.49	17.54	10.80	7.72	9.49	8.81
Armenia	911	....	....	....	37.81	† 43.95	57.54	46.99	55.10	24.40	† 20.59	14.75	11.91
Azerbaijan	912	....	....	....	....	....	12.23	14.10	18.31	16.73	16.51	14.12	8.00
Bulgaria	918	48.11	45.45	57.72	48.27	114.31	78.35	6.02	5.43	4.21	4.57	....	2.81
Cyprus	423	6.00	6.00	6.00	6.00	6.05	5.38	5.59	5.59	6.01	....	....	3.56
Czech Republic	935	....	6.62	6.98	8.99	11.91	11.21	10.51	5.71	5.37	5.06	2.72	2.04
Georgia	915	....	....	....	....	....	....	....	....	....	29.93	43.42	44.26
Hungary	944	22.65	17.22	26.93	32.04	23.96	20.13	17.83	14.68	11.03	10.79	8.91	8.22
Kazakhstan	916	....	....	214.34	48.98	28.91	15.15	23.59	15.63	6.59	5.28	5.20	5.86
Kyrgyz Republic	917	....	....	143.13	34.90	40.10	35.83	43.67	47.19	32.26	19.08	10.15	7.21
Latvia	941	....	....	....	28.24	16.27	4.73	5.27	6.23	† 4.85	5.63	3.52	3.24
Lithuania	946	....	....	....	26.82	20.95	8.64	10.69	11.14	† 9.27	5.68	3.72	2.61
Malta	181	4.58	4.60	4.29	4.65	4.99	5.08	5.41	5.15	4.89	4.93	4.03	....
Moldova	921	....	....	....	52.90	39.01	23.63	30.54	28.49	22.20	14.24	5.89	15.08
Poland	964	44.03	33.16	28.81	25.62	20.32	21.58	19.09	13.14	16.62	....	....	....
Romania	968	....	....	....	....	51.09	85.72	63.99	74.21	51.86	42.18	27.03	....
Russia	922	....	....	....	168.04	86.07	23.43	....	....	12.12	12.45	12.72	5.35
Slovenia	961	....	....	....	....	....	....	....	8.63	10.94	10.88	8.73	6.53
Turkey	186	72.17	....	....	....	....	....	....	....	25.18	85.33	59.50	34.90

National Interest Rates

Treasury Bill Rates (60c)
(Period averages in percent per annum)

		1992	1993	1994	1995	1996	1997	1998	1999	2000	2001	2002	2003
Middle East													
Bahrain, Kingdom of	419	3.78	3.33	4.81	6.07	5.49	5.68	5.53	5.46	6.56	3.78	1.75	1.13
Egypt	469	....	....	....	....	....	8.80	8.80	9.00	9.10	7.20	5.50	6.90
Israel	436	11.79	10.54	11.77	14.37	15.34	13.39	11.33	11.41	8.81	6.50	7.38	7.00
Kuwait	443	....	....	6.32	7.35	6.93	6.98	....	....	....	....	....	....
Lebanon	446	22.40	18.27	15.09	19.40	15.19	13.42	12.70	11.57	11.18	11.18	10.90	....
Western Hemisphere													
Antigua and Barbuda	311	7.00	7.00	7.00	7.00	7.00	7.00	7.00	7.00	7.00	7.00	7.00	7.00
Bahamas, The	313	5.32	3.96	1.88	3.01	4.45	4.35	3.84	1.97	1.03	1.94	2.50	1.78
Barbados	316	10.88	5.44	7.26	8.01	6.85	3.61	5.61	5.83	5.29	3.14	2.10	1.41
Belize	339	5.38	4.59	4.27	4.10	3.78	3.51	3.83	5.91	5.91	5.91	4.59	3.22
Bolivia	218	....	....	17.89	24.51	19.93	13.65	12.33	14.07	10.99	11.48	12.41	9.92
Brazil	223	....	....	....	49.93	25.73	24.79	28.57	26.39	18.51	20.06	19.43	22.10
Dominica	321	6.48	6.40	6.40	6.40	6.40	6.40	6.40	6.40	6.40	6.40	6.40	6.40
Grenada	328	6.50	6.50	6.50	6.50	6.50	6.50	6.50	6.50	6.50	† 7.00	7.00	6.50
Guyana	336	25.75	16.83	17.66	17.51	11.35	8.91	8.33	11.31	9.88	7.78	4.94	3.04
Haiti	263	....	....	....	....	....	14.13	16.21	7.71	12.33	13.53	7.56	20.50
Jamaica	343	34.36	28.85	42.98	27.65	37.95	21.14	25.65	20.75	18.24	16.71	15.54	25.94
Mexico	273	15.62	14.99	14.10	48.44	31.39	19.80	24.76	21.41	15.24	11.31	7.09	6.23
Netherlands Antilles	353	....	4.83	4.48	5.46	5.66	5.77	5.82	6.15	6.15	6.15	4.96	2.80
St. Kitts and Nevis	361	6.50	6.50	6.50	6.50	6.50	6.50	6.50	6.50	6.50	7.50	7.50	7.17
St. Lucia	362	7.00	7.00	7.00	7.00	7.00	7.00	7.00	7.00	7.00	6.80	6.80	6.33
St. Vincent & Grens	364	6.50	6.50	6.50	6.50	6.50	6.50	6.50	6.50	6.50	7.00	7.00	....
Trinidad and Tobago	369	9.26	9.45	10.00	8.41	10.44	9.83	11.93	10.40	10.56	8.55	4.83	4.71
Uruguay	298	....	....	44.60	39.40	29.20	23.18	....	....	....	....	....	....

2004, International Monetary Fund : *International Financial Statistics Yearbook*

National Interest Rates

		1992	1993	1994	1995	1996	1997	1998	1999	2000	2001	2002	2003
						\multicolumn{6}{c}{Deposit Rates (60l)}			
						\multicolumn{6}{c}{except for United States (60lc)}			
						\multicolumn{6}{c}{*(Period averages in percent per annum)*}			

Industrial Countries

Country		1992	1993	1994	1995	1996	1997	1998	1999	2000	2001	2002	2003
United States	111	3.68	3.17	4.63	5.92	5.39	5.62	5.47	5.33	6.46	3.69	1.73	1.15
Canada	156	3.92	3.21	3.98	5.28	3.00	1.90	3.08	2.88	3.48	2.25	.83	1.10
Australia	193	6.32	4.76	5.05	7.33	6.86	5.12	4.67	†3.53	4.12	3.25	2.98	3.31
Japan	158	†3.35	2.14	1.70	.90	.30	.30	.27	.12	.07	.06	.04	.04
New Zealand	196	6.58	6.24	6.38	8.49	8.49	7.26	6.78	4.56	6.36	5.35	5.33	5.10
Euro Area	163	....	....	....	....	4.08	3.41	3.20	2.45	3.45	3.49	2.80	....
Austria	122	3.69	2.98	2.31	2.19	1.71	1.50	†2.65	2.21	....	....	....	....
Belgium	124	6.25	†7.11	4.86	4.04	2.66	2.88	3.01	2.42	3.58	3.40	2.60	1.65
Finland	172	7.50	4.75	3.27	3.19	2.35	2.00	....	1.22	1.63	1.94	1.49	....
France	132	4.50	4.50	4.50	4.50	3.67	3.50	3.21	2.69	2.63	3.00	3.00	2.69
Germany	134	8.01	6.27	4.47	3.85	2.83	2.69	2.88	2.43	3.40	3.56	2.65	....
Greece	174	19.92	19.33	18.92	15.75	13.51	10.11	10.70	8.69	6.13	3.32	2.76	2.48
Ireland	178	5.42	2.27	1.01	.44	.29	.46	.43	.10	.10	.10	.10	.04
Italy	136	7.11	†7.79	6.20	6.45	6.49	4.83	3.16	1.61	1.84	1.96	1.43	.95
Luxembourg	137	6.00	5.33	5.00	5.00	3.54	3.46	3.31	....	....	....	....	....
Netherlands	138	3.20	3.11	†4.70	4.40	3.54	3.18	3.10	2.74	2.89	3.10	2.77	2.49
Portugal	182	14.59	11.06	8.37	8.38	6.32	4.56	3.37	2.40	....	....	....	....
Spain	184	10.43	9.63	6.70	7.68	6.12	3.96	2.92	1.85	2.95	3.08	2.50	....
Denmark	128	7.50	6.52	†3.53	3.85	2.80	2.65	3.08	2.43	3.15	3.30	†2.40	2.40
Iceland	176	5.94	6.63	3.03	3.69	4.25	4.72	4.50	4.82	7.11	6.94	4.69	....
Norway	142	10.69	5.51	5.21	4.95	4.15	3.63	7.24	5.38	6.73	†6.43	6.46	2.12
Sweden	144	†7.80	5.10	4.91	6.16	2.47	2.50	1.91	1.65	2.15	....	....	....
Switzerland	146	5.50	3.50	3.63	1.28	1.34	1.00	.69	1.24	†3.00	1.68	.43	.17
United Kingdom	112	7.46	3.97	3.66	4.11	3.05	3.63	4.48	....	....	....	....	....

Developing Countries

Africa

Country		1992	1993	1994	1995	1996	1997	1998	1999	2000	2001	2002	2003
CEMAC	758	7.50	7.75	5.50	5.50	5.00	5.00	5.00	5.00	5.00	5.00	5.00	5.00
Cameroon	622	7.50	7.75	8.08	5.50	5.38	5.04	5.00	5.00	5.00	5.00	5.00	5.00
Central African Rep.	626	7.50	7.75	8.08	5.50	5.46	5.00	5.00	5.00	5.00	5.00	5.00	5.00
Chad	628	7.50	7.75	8.08	5.50	5.46	5.00	5.00	5.00	5.00	5.00	5.00	5.00
Congo, Republic of	634	7.50	7.75	8.08	5.50	5.46	5.00	5.00	5.00	5.00	5.00	5.00	5.00
Equatorial Guinea	642	7.50	7.75	8.08	5.50	5.46	5.00	5.00	5.00	5.00	5.00	5.00	5.00
Gabon	646	7.50	7.75	8.08	5.50	5.46	5.00	5.00	5.00	5.00	5.00	5.00	5.00
WAEMU	759	....	....	....	3.50	3.50	3.50	3.50	3.50	3.50	3.50	3.50	3.50
Benin	638	7.75	....	....	....	....	....	3.50	3.50	3.50	3.50	3.50	3.50
Burkina Faso	748	7.75	....	....	....	....	....	3.50	3.50	3.50	3.50	3.50	3.50
Côte d'Ivoire	662	7.75	....	....	....	....	....	3.50	3.50	3.50	3.50	3.50	3.50
Guinea-Bissau	654	39.33	53.92	28.67	26.50	47.25	4.63	3.50	3.50	3.50	3.50	3.50	3.50
Mali	678	7.75	....	....	....	....	....	3.50	3.50	3.50	3.50	3.50	3.50
Niger	692	7.75	....	....	....	....	....	3.50	3.50	3.50	3.50	3.50	3.50
Senegal	722	7.75	....	....	....	....	....	3.50	3.50	3.50	3.50	3.50	3.50
Togo	742	7.75	....	....	....	....	....	3.50	3.50	3.50	3.50	3.50	3.50
Algeria	612	8.00	8.00	12.00	†16.00	14.50	9.75	8.50	7.50	7.50	6.25	5.25	5.25
Angola	614	....	....	....	125.92	147.13	29.25	36.88	†36.57	†39.58	47.91	48.69	26.17
Botswana	616	12.50	13.49	10.39	9.98	10.43	9.25	8.72	9.46	10.07	10.15	10.30	10.48
Cape Verde	624	4.00	4.00	4.00	†5.00	5.00	5.04	5.27	4.76	4.34	4.67	4.86	3.93
Congo, Dem. Rep. of	636	....	....	60.00	60.00	60.00	....	....	....	....	....	....	....
Djibouti	611	....	....	....	....	....	....	....	....	....	2.81	1.23	.82
Ethiopia	644	3.63	11.50	11.50	11.46	9.42	7.00	6.00	6.32	6.68	6.97	4.11	3.74
Gambia, The	648	13.83	13.00	12.58	12.50	12.50	12.50	12.50	12.50	12.50	12.50	12.71	....
Ghana	652	16.32	23.63	23.15	28.73	34.50	35.76	32.05	23.56	28.60	30.85	16.21	14.32
Guinea	656	23.00	19.75	18.00	17.50	....	....	6.38	5.67	7.50	8.03	7.40	6.50
Kenya	664	....	....	....	13.60	17.59	16.72	18.40	9.55	8.10	6.64	5.49	4.13
Lesotho	666	10.63	8.06	8.43	13.34	12.73	11.81	10.73	7.45	4.92	4.83	5.19	5.16
Liberia	668	....	....	6.34	6.37	....	6.43	6.22	6.25	6.18	5.94	6.25	5.29
Madagascar	674	20.50	19.50	19.50	18.50	19.00	14.38	8.00	15.33	15.00	12.00	12.00	11.50
Malawi	676	16.50	21.75	25.00	37.27	26.33	10.21	19.06	33.21	33.25	34.96	28.08	25.13
Mauritania	682	5.00	....	....	....	....	....	....	....	....	....	....	8.00
Mauritius	684	10.07	8.40	11.04	12.23	10.77	9.08	9.28	10.92	9.61	9.78	9.88	9.53
Morocco	686	....	....	....	....	....	....	7.26	6.39	5.16	5.04	4.54	3.78
Mozambique	688	....	....	33.38	38.84	18.14	25.43	8.22	7.86	9.70	†15.01	17.99	12.15
Namibia	728	11.36	9.61	9.18	10.84	12.56	12.70	12.94	10.82	7.39	6.79	7.81	8.76
Nigeria	694	18.04	23.24	13.09	13.53	13.06	7.17	10.11	12.81	11.69	15.26	16.67	14.22
Rwanda	714	7.73	5.00	....	....	10.92	9.46	8.50	7.95	8.94	9.22	8.00	8.14
São Tomé & Príncipe	716	35.00	35.00	35.00	35.00	31.00	36.75	38.29	27.00	†21.00	15.00	15.00	12.29
Seychelles	718	9.56	9.37	8.85	9.22	9.90	9.20	7.53	5.13	4.77	4.92	4.93	3.99
Sierra Leone	724	54.67	27.00	11.63	7.03	13.96	9.91	7.12	9.50	9.25	7.67	8.23	8.42
South Africa	199	13.78	11.50	11.11	13.54	14.91	15.38	16.50	12.24	9.20	†9.37	10.77	9.76
Swaziland	734	10.49	7.89	7.54	9.44	11.08	12.00	11.92	9.86	6.53	6.15	8.02	7.59
Tanzania	738	....	....	....	24.63	13.59	7.83	7.75	7.75	†7.39	4.81	3.29	3.05
Uganda	746	35.83	16.26	9.99	7.61	10.62	11.84	11.36	8.73	9.84	8.47	5.56	9.85
Zambia	754	48.50	....	46.14	30.24	42.13	34.48	13.08	20.27	20.24	23.41	23.33	21.95
Zimbabwe	698	28.63	29.45	26.75	25.92	21.58	18.60	29.06	38.51	50.17	13.95	18.38	35.92

National Interest Rates

		1992	1993	1994	1995	1996	1997	1998	1999	2000	2001	2002	2003
						Deposit Rates (60l) except for United States (60lc) (Period averages in percent per annum)							
Asia													
Bangladesh	513	10.47	8.18	6.40	6.04	7.28	8.11	8.42	8.74	8.56	8.50	8.17	7.82
Bhutan	514	8.00	8.00	8.00	8.00	....	....	....	....	....	....	....	....
Cambodia	522	....	....	....	8.71	8.80	8.03	7.80	7.33	6.83	4.36	2.49	2.02
China,P.R.: Mainland	924	7.56	10.98	10.98	10.98	7.47	5.67	3.78	2.25	2.25	2.25	1.98	1.98
China,P.R.:Hong Kong	532	3.07	2.25	3.54	5.63	4.64	5.98	6.62	4.50	4.80	2.38	.35	.07
China,P.R.:Macao	546	3.50	2.75	4.21	5.93	5.23	6.22	7.00	5.30	5.33	2.59	.63	....
Fiji	819	4.10	3.69	3.15	3.18	3.38	3.08	2.17	1.24	.90	.78	.62	.51
Indonesia	536	19.60	14.55	12.53	16.72	17.26	20.01	39.07	25.74	12.50	15.48	15.50	10.59
Korea	542	10.00	8.58	8.50	8.83	7.50	† 10.81	13.29	7.95	7.94	5.79	4.95	4.25
Lao People's Dem.Rep.	544	15.00	13.33	12.00	14.00	16.00	....	17.79	13.42	12.00	6.50	6.00	6.58
Malaysia	548	7.94	7.03	4.89	5.93	7.09	7.78	8.51	4.12	3.36	3.37	3.21	3.07
Maldives	556	....	....	....	....	6.80	6.80	6.80	6.93	6.88	6.97	7.50	7.50
Micronesia, Fed.Sts.	868	....	....	....	5.33	4.58	4.21	3.98	3.72	4.59	3.17	1.47	1.02
Mongolia	948	362.50	280.20	115.71	74.62	44.75	36.37	27.51	23.42	16.80	14.30	13.22	14.00
Myanmar	518	9.00	9.00	9.00	9.75	12.50	12.50	12.50	11.00	9.75	9.50	9.50	9.50
Nepal	558	....	....	8.75	....	9.63	9.79	8.92	7.31	5.96	4.75	....	....
Papua New Guinea	853	7.85	5.03	5.09	12.18	12.19	7.31	13.73	15.46	14.54	8.91	5.80	8.16
Philippines	566	14.27	9.61	10.54	8.39	9.68	10.19	12.11	8.17	8.31	8.74	4.61	5.22
Samoa	862	6.38	5.50	5.50	5.50	5.50	5.50	6.50	6.50	6.46	5.53	5.10	5.10
Singapore	576	2.86	2.30	3.00	3.50	3.41	3.47	4.60	1.68	1.71	1.54	.91	.51
Solomon Islands	813	12.00	9.77	9.00	8.38	6.46	2.42	2.33	2.88	2.54	1.35	.75	.75
Sri Lanka	524	13.74	13.77	13.10	12.13	12.36	11.25	9.56	9.12	9.17	11.01	9.22	6.00
Thailand	578	8.88	8.63	8.46	11.58	10.33	10.52	10.65	4.73	3.29	2.54	1.98	1.33
Tonga	866	5.50	4.25	4.64	4.72	5.53	5.57	5.63	5.42	5.36	5.47	5.47	5.47
Vanuatu	846	4.69	5.00	5.06	3.00	4.50	3.73	3.29	1.60	1.27	1.25	1.00	1.21
Vietnam	582	....	22.04	....	....	....	8.51	9.23	7.37	3.65	5.30	6.45	6.62
Europe													
Albania	914	18.50	† 27.33	19.83	† 15.30	16.78	27.28	22.56	12.95	8.30	7.73	8.54	8.38
Armenia	911	....	....	....	63.18	32.19	26.08	24.94	27.35	18.08	14.90	9.60	6.87
Azerbaijan	912	....	....	....	....	....	....	....	12.08	12.90	8.46	8.66	9.54
Belarus	913	....	65.08	89.60	100.82	32.36	15.64	14.33	23.80	37.55	34.18	26.85	17.44
Bosnia & Herzegovina	963	....	....	....	....	....	....	51.88	9.07	14.67	....	† 4.53	4.03
Bulgaria	918	45.01	42.56	51.14	35.94	74.68	46.83	3.00	3.21	3.10	2.88	2.77	2.89
Croatia	960	658.51	379.31	6.52	5.53	5.59	4.30	4.62	4.31	3.74	3.23	1.89	1.53
Cyprus	423	5.75	5.75	5.75	5.75	† 7.00	6.50	6.50	6.50	6.50	4.65	4.20	3.30
Czech Republic	935	....	7.03	7.07	6.96	6.79	7.71	8.08	4.48	3.42	2.87	2.00	1.33
Estonia	939	....	....	11.51	8.74	6.05	6.19	8.07	4.19	3.76	4.03	2.74	2.40
Georgia	915	....	....	....	....	31.05	13.73	17.00	14.58	10.17	7.75	9.82	9.28
Hungary	944	24.41	15.65	20.31	† 24.36	18.57	16.94	14.42	11.94	9.49	8.40	7.41	10.98
Kyrgyz Republic	917	....	....	....	....	36.37	39.59	35.76	35.58	18.38	12.50	5.91	4.98
Latvia	941	....	34.78	31.68	14.79	11.71	5.90	5.33	5.04	4.38	5.24	3.23	3.02
Lithuania	946	....	88.29	48.43	20.05	13.95	7.89	5.98	4.94	3.86	3.00	1.70	1.27
Macedonia, FYR	962	....	....	117.56	24.07	12.75	11.64	11.68	11.40	11.18	9.97	9.56	7.97
Malta	181	4.50	4.50	4.50	4.50	4.50	4.56	4.64	4.66	4.86	4.84	4.30	....
Moldova	921	....	....	....	....	25.43	23.47	21.68	27.54	24.87	20.93	14.20	12.55
Poland	964	37.75	34.00	† 33.40	26.78	20.02	19.36	18.19	11.22	14.17	11.80	6.21	3.71
Russia	922	....	....	....	101.96	55.05	† 16.77	17.05	13.68	6.51	4.85	4.96	4.48
Slovak Republic	936	....	8.02	9.32	9.01	9.30	13.44	16.25	14.37	8.45	6.46	6.65	5.33
Slovenia	961	153.02	33.04	28.10	15.38	15.08	13.19	10.54	7.24	10.05	9.81	8.24	5.95
Tajikistan	923	....	....	....	....	....	23.93	9.82	5.24	1.26	5.19	† 9.21	9.67
Turkey	186	68.74	64.58	87.79	76.02	80.74	79.49	80.11	78.43	47.16	74.70	50.49	37.68
Ukraine	926	....	148.63	208.63	70.29	33.63	18.21	22.25	20.70	13.72	10.99	7.93	6.98
Middle East													
Bahrain, Kingdom of	419	† 3.63	3.03	4.00	5.70	5.18	5.28	4.74	4.80	5.82	2.71	1.34	....
Egypt	469	12.00	12.00	11.83	10.92	10.54	9.84	9.36	9.22	9.46	9.46	9.33	8.23
Israel	436	11.29	10.44	12.19	14.08	14.48	13.07	10.99	11.34	8.63	6.18	6.03	6.65
Jordan	439	7.20	6.88	7.09	7.68	8.50	9.10	8.21	8.30	6.97	5.81	4.42	....
Kuwait	443	7.59	7.07	5.70	6.53	6.05	5.93	6.32	5.76	5.89	4.47	3.15	2.42
Lebanon	446	17.09	15.56	14.80	16.30	15.54	13.37	13.61	12.50	11.21	10.85	11.03	8.69
Oman	449	6.29	4.17	4.34	6.53	6.85	7.30	8.46	8.12	7.63	4.50	2.89	2.37
Qatar	453	4.75	4.08	4.84	6.19	6.50	6.63	6.56	6.50	....	....	....	....
Saudi Arabia	456	3.65	3.52	5.10	6.18	5.47	5.79	6.21	6.14	6.67	3.92	2.23	1.63
Syrian Arab Republic	463	4.00	4.00	4.00	4.00	4.00	4.00	4.00	4.00	4.00	4.00	4.00	....
Western Hemisphere													
ECCU	309	7.73	7.21	† 3.87	4.06	4.16	4.20	4.30	4.35	4.46	4.37	4.04	4.76
Anguilla	312	1.58	2.25	3.47	3.64	3.74	3.77	3.79	3.78	3.52	3.54	3.25	4.59
Antigua and Barbuda	311	5.75	5.01	4.19	4.02	4.33	4.36	4.34	4.45	5.18	4.49	4.36	4.82
Dominica	321	3.96	4.19	4.50	4.20	4.30	4.27	4.23	4.38	3.87	3.98	3.91	3.66
Grenada	328	3.67	3.88	3.61	3.67	3.74	3.93	4.16	4.30	4.24	4.23	3.59	3.39
Montserrat	351	3.49	3.44	3.25	3.24	3.29	3.02	2.74	3.14	3.35	3.35	3.08	3.06
St. Kitts and Nevis	361	4.35	4.39	3.99	4.52	4.27	4.27	4.22	4.31	4.32	4.23	4.01	4.49
St. Lucia	362	4.31	4.04	3.83	4.43	4.50	4.65	4.80	4.76	4.80	4.88	4.27	5.47
St. Vincent & Grens.	364	3.94	3.90	3.89	4.34	4.14	4.21	4.27	4.46	4.54	4.56	4.35	4.56
Argentina	213	16.78	11.34	8.08	11.90	7.36	6.97	7.56	8.05	8.34	16.16	39.25	10.16
Aruba	314	5.70	4.20	4.40	4.30	4.20	4.40	....	† 6.17	6.20	5.84	5.56	5.33
Bahamas, The	313	6.13	5.19	4.30	4.20	5.14	5.23	5.36	4.57	4.08	4.25	4.25	3.95
Barbados	316	6.68	4.39	4.32	5.11	5.20	4.58	4.20	4.40	4.97	4.04	2.70	2.56
Belize	339	8.15	8.13	8.55	9.37	9.08	9.19	8.76	8.12	7.69	6.35	6.28	6.93

2004, International Monetary Fund : *International Financial Statistics Yearbook*

National Interest Rates

Deposit Rates (60l)
except for United States (60lc)
(Period averages in percent per annum)

		1992	1993	1994	1995	1996	1997	1998	1999	2000	2001	2002	2003
Western Hemisphere(Cont.)													
Bolivia	218	23.22	22.18	18.43	18.87	19.16	14.73	12.82	12.26	10.98	9.82	9.58	11.41
Brazil	223	1,560.18	3,293.50	5,175.24	52.25	26.45	24.35	28.00	26.02	17.20	17.86	19.14	21.97
Chile	228	18.29	18.24	15.12	13.73	13.48	12.02	14.92	8.56	9.20	6.19	3.80	2.73
Colombia	233	26.67	25.84	29.42	32.34	31.15	24.13	32.58	21.33	12.15	12.44	8.94	7.80
Costa Rica	238	15.80	16.90	17.72	23.88	17.29	13.03	12.76	14.31	13.38	11.77	11.46	10.41
Dominican Republic	243	16.70	14.04	13.70	14.94	13.91	13.40	17.65	16.07	17.65	15.61	16.54	20.50
Ecuador	248	46.81	31.97	33.65	43.31	41.50	28.09	39.39	†10.03	8.46	6.58	5.47	5.53
El Salvador	253	11.51	15.27	13.57	14.37	13.98	11.77	10.32	10.75	9.31	....	....	....
Guatemala	258	10.44	12.63	9.69	7.87	7.65	†5.83	5.44	7.96	10.17	8.75	6.92	4.78
Guyana	336	22.51	12.26	11.42	12.90	10.49	8.56	8.10	9.08	8.71	7.63	4.53	3.18
Haiti	263	....	....	....	....	....	10.74	13.06	7.39	11.85	13.66	8.24	13.99
Honduras	268	12.34	11.60	11.56	11.97	16.70	21.28	18.58	19.97	15.93	14.48	13.74	11.48
Jamaica	343	33.63	27.59	36.41	23.21	25.16	13.95	15.61	13.48	11.62	9.64	8.58	8.46
Mexico	273	15.88	16.69	15.03	39.82	26.40	16.36	15.45	11.60	8.26	6.23	3.76	3.09
Netherlands Antilles	353	....	4.33	4.05	3.75	3.67	3.66	3.58	3.59	3.63	3.65	3.62	3.48
Nicaragua	278	12.01	11.61	11.70	11.15	12.35	12.41	10.77	†11.83	10.80	11.56	7.79	5.55
Panama	283	†5.67	5.90	6.11	7.18	7.20	7.03	6.76	6.92	7.07	6.83	4.97	3.98
Paraguay	288	20.15	22.10	23.12	21.16	17.16	13.00	15.95	†19.75	15.72	16.22	22.86	15.83
Peru	293	59.65	44.14	22.35	15.70	14.90	15.01	15.11	16.27	13.29	9.92	4.19	3.83
Suriname	366	4.50	4.75	7.45	21.00	17.83	17.25	16.00	15.60	15.48	11.86	9.00	8.28
Trinidad and Tobago	369	6.99	7.06	6.91	....	....	6.91	7.95	8.51	8.15	7.66	4.76	2.91
Uruguay	298	54.47	39.38	36.98	38.24	28.13	19.61	15.09	14.25	12.11	14.32	....	....
Venezuela, Rep. Bol.	299	35.43	53.75	39.02	24.72	27.58	14.70	34.84	21.28	16.30	15.51	29.00	17.21

National Interest Rates

		1992	1993	1994	1995	1996	1997	1998	1999	2000	2001	2002	2003
		\multicolumn{12}{c}{Lending Rates (60p)}
		\multicolumn{12}{c}{(Period averages in percent per annum)}
Industrial Countries													
United States	111	6.25	6.00	7.14	8.83	8.27	8.44	8.35	7.99	9.23	6.92	4.68	4.12
Canada	156	7.48	5.94	6.88	8.65	6.06	4.96	6.60	6.44	7.27	5.81	4.21	4.69
Australia	193	11.06	9.72	9.55	11.12	11.00	9.31	8.04	7.51	8.78	8.13	7.96	8.41
Japan	158	6.15	†4.41	4.13	3.51	2.66	2.45	2.32	2.16	2.07	1.97	1.86	1.82
New Zealand	196	11.39	10.34	9.69	12.09	12.27	11.35	11.22	8.49	10.22	9.88	9.81	9.80
Euro Area	163	....	....	....	....	8.88	7.58	6.73	5.65	6.60	6.83	6.14	....
Austria	122	....	....	....	....	....	....	6.42	5.64	....	....	....	....
Belgium	124	13.00	11.81	9.42	8.42	7.17	7.06	7.25	6.71	7.98	8.46	7.71	6.89
Finland	172	12.14	9.92	7.91	7.75	6.16	5.29	5.35	4.71	5.61	5.79	4.82	....
France	132	10.00	8.90	7.89	8.12	6.77	6.34	6.55	6.36	6.70	6.98	6.60	6.60
Germany	134	13.59	12.85	11.48	10.94	10.02	9.13	9.02	8.81	9.63	10.01	9.70	....
Greece	174	28.71	28.56	27.44	23.05	20.96	18.92	18.56	15.00	12.32	8.59	7.41	6.79
Ireland	178	†12.66	9.93	6.13	6.56	5.85	6.57	6.22	3.34	4.77	4.84	3.83	2.85
Italy	136	15.76	13.87	11.22	12.47	12.06	9.75	7.88	5.58	6.26	6.53	5.78	5.03
Luxembourg	137	8.75	7.65	6.58	6.50	5.50	5.50	5.27	....	....	....	....	....
Netherlands	138	12.75	10.40	8.29	7.21	5.90	6.13	6.50	†3.46	4.79	5.00	3.96	3.00
Portugal	182	20.43	16.48	15.01	13.80	11.73	9.15	7.24	5.19	....	....	....	....
Spain	184	14.23	12.78	8.95	10.05	8.50	6.08	5.01	3.95	5.18	5.16	4.31	....
Denmark	128	11.78	10.46	†9.95	10.33	8.70	7.73	7.90	7.13	8.08	8.20	†7.10	....
Iceland	176	13.05	14.11	10.57	11.58	12.43	12.89	12.78	13.30	16.80	17.95	15.37	11.95
Norway	142	14.16	10.97	8.40	7.78	7.10	5.95	7.91	8.16	8.22	8.86	8.54	6.15
Sweden	144	†15.20	11.40	10.64	11.11	7.38	7.01	5.94	5.53	5.82	....	....	....
Switzerland	146	7.80	6.40	5.51	5.48	4.97	4.47	4.07	3.90	4.29	4.30	3.93	3.27
United Kingdom	112	9.42	5.92	5.48	6.69	5.96	6.58	7.21	5.33	5.98	5.08	4.00	3.69
Developing Countries													
Africa													
CEMAC	758	17.50	17.50	16.00	16.00	22.00	22.00	22.00	22.00	22.00	18.00	18.00	18.00
Cameroon	622	17.77	17.46	17.50	16.00	22.00	22.00	22.00	22.00	22.00	20.67	18.00	18.00
Central African Rep.	626	17.77	17.46	17.50	16.00	22.00	22.00	22.00	22.00	22.00	20.67	18.00	18.00
Chad	628	17.77	17.46	17.50	16.00	22.00	22.00	22.00	22.00	22.00	20.67	18.00	18.00
Congo, Republic of	634	17.77	17.46	17.50	16.00	22.00	22.00	22.00	22.00	22.00	20.67	18.00	18.00
Equatorial Guinea	642	17.77	17.46	17.50	16.00	22.00	22.00	22.00	22.00	22.00	20.67	18.00	18.00
Gabon	646	17.77	17.46	17.50	16.00	22.00	22.00	22.00	22.00	22.00	20.67	18.00	18.00
Algeria	612	....	....	16.00	†19.00	19.00	12.50	11.00	10.00	10.00	9.50	8.50	8.00
Angola	614	....	....	....	206.25	217.88	37.75	45.00	†80.30	†103.16	95.97	97.34	96.12
Benin	638	16.75	....	....	....	....	....	....	....	....	....	....	....
Botswana	616	14.00	14.92	13.88	14.29	14.50	14.08	13.53	14.63	15.31	15.75	15.96	16.58
Burkina Faso	748	16.75	....	....	....	....	....	....	....	....	....	....	....
Burundi	618	13.66	13.77	14.20	15.26	....	....	....	15.24	15.77	16.82	19.47	18.23
Cape Verde	624	10.00	10.00	10.67	12.00	12.00	12.06	12.51	12.03	11.94	12.85	13.17	12.73
Congo, Dem. Rep. of	636	....	....	398.25	293.88	247.00	134.58	29.00	124.58	165.00	167.92	66.79	....
Côte d'Ivoire	662	16.75	....	....	....	....	....	....	....	....	....	....	....
Djibouti	611	....	....	....	....	....	....	....	....	....	11.46	11.30	11.30
Ethiopia	644	8.00	14.00	14.33	15.08	13.92	10.50	10.50	10.58	10.89	10.87	8.66	8.06
Gambia, The	648	26.75	26.08	25.00	25.04	25.50	25.50	25.38	24.00	24.00	24.00	24.00	....
Guinea	656	27.00	24.50	22.00	21.50	....	....	19.56	19.88	19.38	....	....	....
Guinea-Bissau	654	50.33	63.58	36.33	32.92	51.75	....	....	....	....	....	....	....
Kenya	664	21.07	29.99	36.24	28.80	33.79	30.25	29.49	22.38	22.34	19.67	18.45	16.57
Lesotho	666	18.25	15.83	14.25	16.38	17.71	18.03	20.06	19.06	17.11	16.55	17.11	16.02
Liberia	668	....	....	14.53	15.57	....	16.83	†21.74	16.72	20.53	22.14	20.21	17.06
Madagascar	674	25.00	26.00	30.50	37.50	32.75	30.00	27.00	28.00	26.50	25.25	25.25	24.25
Malawi	676	22.00	29.50	31.00	47.33	45.33	28.25	37.67	53.58	53.13	56.17	50.54	48.92
Mali	678	16.75	....	....	....	....	....	....	....	....	....	....	21.00
Mauritania	682	10.00	....	....	....	....	....	....	....	....	....	....	....
Mauritius	684	17.13	16.58	18.92	20.81	20.81	18.92	19.92	21.63	20.77	21.10	21.00	21.00
Morocco	686	....	....	10.00	....	....	....	13.50	13.50	13.31	13.25	13.13	12.56
Mozambique	688	....	....	....	....	....	....	24.35	19.63	19.04	†22.73	26.71	24.69
Namibia	728	20.21	18.02	17.05	18.51	19.16	20.18	20.72	18.48	15.28	14.53	13.84	14.70
Niger	692	16.75	....	....	....	....	....	....	....	....	....	....	....
Nigeria	694	24.76	31.65	20.48	20.23	19.84	17.80	18.18	20.29	21.27	23.44	24.77	20.71
Rwanda	714	16.67	15.00	....	....	....	....	....	....	....	....	....	....
São Tomé & Príncipe	716	37.00	37.00	30.00	52.00	38.00	51.50	55.58	40.33	†39.67	37.00	37.08	33.79
Senegal	722	16.75	....	....	....	....	....	....	....	....	....	....	....
Seychelles	718	15.56	15.71	15.72	15.76	16.22	14.88	14.39	12.01	11.45	11.14	11.09	11.08
Sierra Leone	724	62.83	50.46	27.33	28.83	32.12	23.87	23.83	26.83	26.25	24.27	22.17	20.00
South Africa	199	18.91	16.16	15.58	17.90	19.52	20.00	21.79	18.00	14.50	13.77	15.75	14.96
Swaziland	734	15.92	14.35	14.25	17.05	18.67	19.50	19.50	17.42	14.00	13.25	15.25	14.63
Tanzania	738	....	31.00	39.00	42.83	†33.97	26.27	22.89	21.89	†21.58	20.26	16.43	14.48
Togo	742	17.50	....	....	....	....	....	....	....	....	....	....	....
Uganda	746	....	....	....	20.16	20.29	21.37	20.86	21.55	22.92	22.66	19.10	18.94
Zambia	754	54.57	113.31	70.56	45.53	53.78	46.69	31.80	40.52	38.80	46.23	45.20	40.57
Zimbabwe	698	19.77	36.33	34.86	34.73	34.23	32.55	42.06	55.39	68.21	38.02	36.48	97.29
Asia													
Bangladesh	513	15.00	15.00	14.50	14.00	14.00	14.00	14.00	14.13	15.50	15.83	16.00	16.00
Bhutan	514	17.00	17.00	16.58	16.00	....	....	....	....	....	16.50	16.23	18.47
Cambodia	522	....	....	....	18.70	18.80	18.40	18.33	17.56	17.34	16.50	16.23	18.47
China, P.R.: Mainland	924	8.64	10.98	10.98	12.06	10.08	8.64	6.39	5.85	5.85	5.85	5.31	5.31

2004, International Monetary Fund: *International Financial Statistics Yearbook*

National Interest Rates

		1992	1993	1994	1995	1996	1997	1998	1999	2000	2001	2002	2003
\multicolumn{14}{c}{Lending Rates (60p) *(Period averages in percent per annum)*}

Asia(Cont.)

		1992	1993	1994	1995	1996	1997	1998	1999	2000	2001	2002	2003
China,P.R.:Hong Kong	532	6.50	6.50	8.50	8.75	8.50	9.50	9.00	8.50	9.50	5.13	5.00	5.00
China,P.R.:Macao	546	7.25	6.50	7.95	9.90	9.56	9.73	10.97	9.46	9.89	7.99	6.11	6.00
Fiji	819	12.35	11.74	11.28	11.06	11.33	11.03	9.66	8.77	8.40	8.34	8.05	7.60
India	534	18.92	16.25	14.75	15.46	15.96	13.83	13.54	12.54	12.29	12.08	11.92	11.46
Indonesia	536	24.03	20.59	17.76	18.85	19.22	21.82	32.15	27.66	18.46	18.55	18.95	16.94
Korea	542	10.00	8.58	8.50	9.00	8.84	†11.88	15.28	9.40	8.55	7.71	6.77	6.24
Lao People's Dem.Rep.	544	26.00	†25.33	24.00	†25.67	27.00	....	29.28	32.00	32.00	26.17	29.33	30.50
Malaysia	548	10.16	10.03	8.76	8.73	9.94	10.63	12.13	8.56	7.67	7.13	6.53	6.30
Maldives	556	....	....	....	....	15.00	15.00	15.00	12.50	13.00	13.00	13.54	14.00
Micronesia, Fed.Sts.	868	....	....	....	15.00	15.00	15.00	15.00	15.17	15.33	15.33	15.28	15.00
Mongolia	948	....	300.00	279.22	134.37	87.91	82.05	46.77	39.29	32.75	30.24	28.38	26.31
Myanmar	518	8.00	....	16.50	16.50	16.50	16.50	16.50	16.13	15.25	15.00	15.00	15.00
Nepal	558	....	....	....	....	12.88	14.54	14.00	11.33	9.46	7.67	....	....
Papua New Guinea	853	14.53	11.29	9.16	13.14	13.30	10.45	17.70	18.90	17.54	16.21	13.89	13.36
Philippines	566	19.48	14.68	15.06	14.68	14.84	16.28	16.78	11.78	10.91	12.40	9.14	9.47
Samoa	862	12.88	12.00	12.00	12.00	12.00	12.00	11.50	11.50	11.00	9.93	9.75	9.75
Singapore	576	5.95	5.39	5.88	6.37	6.26	6.32	7.44	5.80	5.83	5.66	5.37	5.31
Solomon Islands	813	19.75	17.80	15.72	16.59	17.78	15.71	14.84	14.50	15.49	15.72	16.42	16.33
Sri Lanka	524	19.68	20.20	18.13	18.04	18.26	14.69	15.03	14.72	16.16	19.39	13.17	10.34
Thailand	578	12.17	11.17	10.90	13.25	13.40	13.65	14.42	8.98	7.83	7.25	6.88	5.94
Tonga	866	13.50	†9.94	9.48	9.82	10.16	10.02	10.40	10.32	10.35	11.43	11.43	10.15
Vanuatu	846	16.25	16.00	16.00	10.50	10.50	10.50	10.96	10.29	9.85	8.81	7.41	5.90
Vietnam	582	....	32.18	....	....	20.10	14.42	14.40	12.70	10.55	9.42	9.06	9.48

Europe

		1992	1993	1994	1995	1996	1997	1998	1999	2000	2001	2002	2003
Albania	914	20.58	29.58	23.67	†19.65	23.96	....	....	21.62	22.10	19.65	15.30	14.27
Armenia	911	....	....	....	111.86	66.36	54.23	48.49	38.85	31.57	26.69	21.14	20.83
Azerbaijan	912	....	....	....	....	....	....	....	19.48	19.66	19.71	17.37	15.46
Belarus	913	....	71.63	148.50	175.00	62.33	31.80	26.99	51.04	67.67	46.97	36.88	23.98
Bosnia & Herzegovina	963	....	....	....	....	....	....	73.50	24.29	30.50	....	†12.70	10.87
Bulgaria	918	56.67	58.30	72.58	58.98	123.48	83.96	13.30	12.79	11.52	11.11	9.35	8.82
Croatia	960	1,157.79	1,443.61	22.91	20.24	22.52	15.47	15.75	14.94	12.07	9.55	†12.84	11.58
Cyprus	423	9.00	9.00	8.83	8.50	8.50	8.08	8.00	8.00	8.00	†7.52	7.15	6.95
Czech Republic	935	....	14.07	13.12	12.80	12.54	13.20	12.81	8.68	7.16	7.20	6.72	5.95
Estonia	939	30.50	33.66	24.65	19.01	14.87	11.76	15.06	11.09	7.43	7.78	6.70	5.51
Georgia	915	....	....	....	....	58.24	50.64	46.00	33.42	32.75	27.25	31.83	32.27
Hungary	944	33.05	25.43	27.40	32.61	27.31	21.77	19.28	16.34	12.60	12.12	10.17	9.60
Kyrgyz Republic	917	....	....	....	....	65.02	49.38	73.44	60.86	51.90	37.33	24.81	19.13
Latvia	941	....	86.36	55.86	34.56	25.78	15.25	14.29	14.20	11.87	11.17	7.97	5.38
Lithuania	946	....	91.84	62.30	27.08	21.56	14.39	12.21	13.09	12.14	9.63	6.84	5.84
Macedonia, FYR	962	....	....	159.82	45.95	21.58	21.42	21.03	20.45	18.93	19.35	18.36	16.00
Malta	181	8.50	8.50	8.50	†7.38	7.77	7.99	8.09	7.70	7.28	6.90	6.04	....
Moldova	921	....	....	....	....	36.67	33.33	30.83	35.54	33.78	28.69	23.52	19.29
Poland	964	39.00	35.25	32.83	†33.45	26.08	24.96	24.49	16.94	20.01	18.36	12.03	7.30
Russia	922	....	....	....	320.31	146.81	†32.04	41.79	39.72	24.43	17.91	15.71	12.98
Slovak Republic	936	....	14.41	14.56	16.85	13.92	18.65	21.17	21.07	14.89	11.24	10.25	8.46
Slovenia	961	195.11	48.61	38.87	23.36	22.60	20.02	16.09	12.38	15.77	15.05	13.17	10.75
Tajikistan	923	....	....	....	....	....	75.52	50.89	26.24	25.59	21.05	†14.20	16.57
Ukraine	926	....	184.25	250.28	122.70	79.88	49.12	54.50	54.95	41.53	32.28	25.35	17.89

Middle East

		1992	1993	1994	1995	1996	1997	1998	1999	2000	2001	2002	2003
Bahrain, Kingdom of	419	11.85	10.95	10.83	11.83	12.45	12.33	11.92	11.86	11.73	10.81	8.50	....
Egypt	469	20.33	18.30	16.51	16.47	15.58	13.79	13.02	12.97	13.22	13.29	13.79	13.53
Israel	436	19.94	16.44	17.45	20.22	20.68	18.71	16.18	16.36	12.87	10.03	9.89	10.65
Jordan	439	10.16	10.23	10.45	10.66	11.25	12.25	12.61	12.33	11.80	10.92	10.18	....
Kuwait	443	8.00	7.95	7.61	8.37	8.77	8.80	8.93	8.56	8.87	7.88	6.48	5.42
Lebanon	446	40.21	28.53	23.88	24.69	25.21	20.29	....	19.48	18.15	17.19	16.58	13.43
Libya	672	7.00	7.00	....	....	....	....	....	7.00	7.00	7.00	7.00	7.00
Oman	449	9.24	8.49	8.57	9.38	9.23	9.30	10.09	10.32	10.06	9.23	8.55	8.23
Syrian Arab Republic	463	9.00	9.00	9.00	9.00	9.00	9.00	9.00	9.00	9.00	9.00	9.00	....
Qatar	453	8.13	7.20	8.86	....	....	....	....	....	....	....	....	....

Western Hemisphere

		1992	1993	1994	1995	1996	1997	1998	1999	2000	2001	2002	2003
ECCU	309	11.71	11.81	11.71	11.94	11.74	11.77	11.60	11.91	11.98	11.55	11.47	12.94
Anguilla	312	4.36	8.29	12.84	12.60	11.95	11.37	11.16	11.31	11.32	10.74	10.35	11.42
Antigua and Barbuda	311	12.70	12.68	13.15	12.70	12.26	11.98	12.20	12.07	12.17	11.62	11.39	12.56
Dominica	321	11.52	11.92	11.61	11.50	11.43	11.17	11.27	11.40	11.68	11.14	10.97	11.50
Grenada	328	12.02	11.83	11.03	11.08	9.99	11.24	11.73	11.62	11.60	10.19	11.31	12.05
Montserrat	351	11.95	13.12	13.06	12.63	12.37	12.37	12.15	11.52	11.52	11.52	11.34	12.10
St. Kitts and Nevis	361	10.76	10.28	10.94	10.89	10.92	11.16	11.42	11.21	11.10	11.08	10.89	12.22
St. Lucia	362	12.81	11.81	11.06	12.68	12.82	12.68	11.40	12.79	13.06	12.97	12.59	15.00
St. Vincent & Grens.	364	11.30	11.92	11.73	11.07	11.23	11.29	11.31	11.55	11.46	11.63	11.56	11.83
Argentina	213	....	....	10.06	17.85	10.51	9.24	10.64	11.04	11.09	27.71	51.68	19.15
Aruba	314	10.60	10.60	10.60	10.60	10.30	10.00	....	†13.14	12.07	12.10	13.08	11.50
Bahamas, The	313	8.08	7.46	6.88	6.75	6.75	6.75	6.75	6.38	6.00	6.00	6.00	6.00
Barbados	316	13.54	8.92	9.08	10.00	10.00	9.83	9.75	9.40	10.19	9.58	8.50	8.50
Belize	339	14.32	14.37	14.78	15.69	16.30	16.29	16.50	16.27	16.01	15.45	14.83	14.35
Bolivia	218	45.51	53.88	55.57	51.02	55.97	50.05	39.41	35.37	34.60	20.06	20.63	17.66
Brazil	223	....	....	....	....	78.19	86.36	80.44	56.83	57.62	62.88	67.08	
Chile	228	23.97	24.35	20.34	18.16	17.37	15.67	20.17	12.62	14.84	11.89	7.76	6.18
Colombia	233	37.28	35.81	40.47	42.72	41.99	34.22	42.24	†25.77	18.79	20.72	16.33	15.19
Costa Rica	238	28.46	30.02	33.03	36.70	26.27	22.48	22.47	25.74	24.89	23.83	26.42	25.58

2004, International Monetary Fund : *International Financial Statistics Yearbook*

National Interest Rates

Lending Rates (60p)
(Period averages in percent per annum)

Western Hemisphere(Cont.)		1992	1993	1994	1995	1996	1997	1998	1999	2000	2001	2002	2003
Dominican Republic	243	28.34	29.89	28.68	30.68	23.73	21.01	25.64	25.05	26.80	24.26	26.06	31.39
Ecuador	248	60.17	47.83	43.99	55.67	54.50	43.02	49.55	†16.53	16.26	15.46	15.08	13.08
El Salvador	253	16.43	19.42	19.03	19.08	18.57	16.05	14.98	15.46	13.96	....	....	....
Guatemala	258	19.49	24.73	22.93	21.16	22.72	†18.64	16.56	19.51	20.88	18.96	16.86	14.98
Guyana	336	28.69	19.36	18.36	19.22	17.79	17.04	16.77	17.11	17.30	17.01	16.33	14.99
Haiti	263	....	....	....	....	....	21.00	23.62	22.88	25.09	28.63	25.67	30.58
Honduras	268	21.68	22.06	24.68	26.95	29.74	32.07	30.69	30.15	26.82	23.76	22.69	20.80
Jamaica	343	44.81	43.71	49.46	43.58	39.83	32.86	31.59	27.01	23.35	20.61	18.50	18.89
Mexico	273	....	17.73	19.30	59.43	36.39	22.14	26.36	23.74	16.93	12.80	8.20	6.91
Netherlands Antilles	353	....	12.59	12.73	12.93	13.21	13.29	13.58	13.60	9.98	10.44	10.14	11.26
Nicaragua	278	19.32	20.23	20.14	19.89	20.72	21.02	21.63	†17.57	18.14	18.55	18.30	15.55
Panama	283	10.61	10.06	10.15	11.10	10.62	10.63	10.82	10.05	†10.48	10.97	10.58	9.93
Paraguay	288	27.96	30.78	†35.47	33.94	31.88	27.79	30.49	30.21	26.78	28.25	38.66	49.99
Peru	293	173.80	97.37	53.56	27.16	26.07	29.96	30.80	30.79	27.91	20.43	14.73	14.21
Suriname	366	8.93	9.35	15.38	40.18	35.78	33.13	27.50	27.33	28.95	25.73	22.18	21.04
Trinidad and Tobago	369	15.33	15.50	15.98	15.17	15.79	15.33	17.33	17.04	16.50	15.67	12.48	11.17
Uruguay	298	117.77	97.33	95.08	99.10	91.52	71.55	57.93	53.28	49.05	51.71	126.07	....
Venezuela, Rep. Bol.	299	41.33	59.90	54.66	39.74	39.41	23.69	46.35	32.13	25.20	22.45	36.58	25.19

2004, International Monetary Fund : *International Financial Statistics Yearbook*

National Interest Rates

		1992	1993	1994	1995	1996	1997	1998	1999	2000	2001	2002	2003
						Government Bond Yields (61)							
						(Average yields to maturity in percent per annum)							
Industrial Countries													
United States............	111	7.01	5.87	7.08	6.58	6.44	6.35	5.26	5.64	6.03	5.02	4.61	4.02
Canada....................	156	8.77	7.85	8.63	8.28	7.50	6.42	5.47	5.69	5.89	5.78	5.66	5.28
Australia..................	193	9.22	7.28	9.04	9.17	8.17	6.89	5.50	6.08	6.26	5.64	5.82	5.36
Japan......................	158	4.94	3.69	3.71	2.53	2.23	1.69	1.10	† 1.77	1.75	1.33	1.25	1.01
New Zealand...........	196	7.87	6.69	7.48	7.94	8.04	7.21	6.47	6.13	6.85	6.12	6.28	5.51
Euro Area................	163	....	....	8.18	8.73	7.23	5.96	4.70	4.66	5.44	5.03	4.92	4.16
Austria..................	122	8.27	6.64	6.69	6.47	5.30	4.79	4.29	4.09	....	....	....	....
Belgium.................	124	8.64	7.19	7.82	7.45	6.45	5.74	4.72	4.81	5.58	5.13	4.96	4.18
Finland..................	172	....	8.84	9.03	8.78	....	....	....	4.72	5.48	5.04	4.98	4.14
France...................	132	8.60	6.91	7.35	7.59	6.39	5.63	4.72	4.69	5.45	5.05	4.93	4.18
Germany................	134	7.96	6.28	6.67	6.50	5.63	5.08	4.39	4.26	5.24	4.70	4.61	3.81
Greece..................	174	....	....	....	....	....	....	8.48	6.30	6.10	5.30	5.12	4.27
Ireland..................	178	9.11	7.72	8.19	8.30	7.48	6.49	4.99	....	....	....	....	....
Italy......................	136	13.27	11.31	10.56	12.21	9.40	6.86	4.90	4.73	5.58	5.19	5.03	4.25
Luxembourg..........	137	7.90	6.93	6.38	6.05	5.21	5.39	5.29	....	....	....	....	....
Netherlands...........	138	8.10	6.51	7.20	7.20	6.49	5.81	4.87	4.92	5.51	5.17	5.00	4.18
Portugal................	182	15.38	12.45	10.83	10.34	7.25	5.48	4.09	....	....	....	....	....
Spain....................	184	12.17	10.16	9.69	11.04	8.18	5.84	4.55	4.30	5.36	4.87	4.62	3.52
Denmark...................	128	9.47	7.08	7.41	7.58	6.04	5.08	4.59	4.30	5.54	....	4.57	3.53
Iceland.....................	176	7.75	6.80	5.02	7.18	5.61	5.49	4.73	4.28	5.35	5.33	5.23	4.42
Norway....................	142	9.78	6.52	7.13	6.82	5.94	5.13	5.35	5.38	6.38	6.31	6.33	4.50
Sweden....................	144	10.02	8.54	† 9.41	....	....	....	....	....	....	....	....	....
Switzerland..............	146	5.48	4.05	5.23	3.73	3.63	3.08	† 2.71	3.62	3.55	3.56	2.40	2.78
United Kingdom.......	112	9.12	7.87	8.05	8.26	8.10	7.09	5.45	4.70	4.68	4.78	4.83	4.64
Developing Countries													
Africa													
Ethiopia...................	644	7.00	13.00	13.00	13.00	13.00	....	....	....	....	....	....	....
Malawi.....................	676	....	....	23.50	38.58	42.67	39.25	....	....	....	....	....	....
Namibia...................	728	15.44	13.94	14.63	16.11	15.48	14.70	15.10	14.90	13.81	11.39	12.86	12.72
Seychelles................	718	14.80	14.40	14.38	13.25	13.25	11.63	8.96	8.58	8.22	8.13	8.25	5.96
South Africa.............	199	15.44	13.97	14.83	16.11	15.48	14.70	15.12	14.90	13.79	11.41	11.50	9.62
Uganda....................	746	43.50	....	....	....	....	....	....	....	....	....	....	....
Zimbabwe................	698	17.40	....	....	....	....	....	....	....	....	....	....	....
Asia													
Korea.......................	542	15.08	12.08	12.30	12.40	10.90	11.70	12.80	8.72	8.50	6.66	6.47	4.93
Malaysia...................	548	....	6.35	5.11	6.51	6.39	6.87	7.66	5.63	5.11	3.54	3.47	3.60
Myanmar..................	518	....	....	10.50	10.50	13.13	14.00	14.00	† 11.00	9.00	9.00	9.00	9.00
Nepal.......................	558	13.33	....	9.00	3.00	9.00	9.00	9.00	8.75	8.50	8.50	8.25	7.50
Pakistan...................	564	7.67	7.40	7.07	6.63	6.06	5.43	4.79	4.16	....	....	....	....
Philippines...............	566	....	....	13.25	14.25	13.99	13.01	† 17.99	12.33	11.77	13.40	8.69	8.72
Samoa......................	862	13.50	13.50	13.50	13.50	13.50	13.50	13.50	13.50	13.50	13.50	13.50	13.50
Solomon Islands........	813	13.00	13.00	13.00	13.00	11.50	11.75	12.50	12.88	13.00	13.00	13.00	13.00
Sri Lanka..................	524	16.00	16.25	....	....	....	....	....	....	....	....	....	....
Thailand...................	578	10.75	10.75	10.75	10.75	10.75	10.75	10.25	6.69	6.95	5.82	5.07	3.76
Vanuatu....................	846	8.00	8.00	8.00	8.00	8.00	8.00	8.00	8.50	8.50	8.50	8.50	8.50
Europe													
Bulgaria...................	918	....	....	56.86	49.76	....	....	10.10	10.05	7.38	6.70	6.75	....
Czech Republic.........	935	....	....	....	....	....	....	....	....	6.72	4.84	3.17	3.77
Slovak Republic.........	936	....	....	....	....	....	....	....	....	8.34	8.06	6.91	4.99
Western Hemisphere													
Honduras..................	268	10.40	10.40	23.11	27.24	35.55	29.59	20.34	16.04	14.79	15.28	11.97	11.26
Jamaica....................	343	30.50	24.82	26.82	26.85	26.87	26.85	....	....	....	....	....	....
Mexico.....................	273	....	....	....	51.74	32.81	21.44	....	20.11	† 15.81	† 10.28	10.13	8.98
Netherlands Antilles...	353	....	8.14	7.48	8.02	8.25	8.67	8.60	8.75	8.77	9.00	8.20	6.72
Trinidad and Tobago..	369	13.30	....	....	....	....	....	....	....	....	....	....	....
Venezuela, Rep. Bol...	299	31.66	41.03	54.73	53.38	49.09	25.41	47.88	† 31.12	21.03	22.12	38.51	32.15

International Interest Rates

		1992	1993	1994	1995	1996	1997	1998	1999	2000	2001	2002	2003
		\multicolumn{12}{c}{**London Interbank Offer Rates on SDR Deposits**}
		\multicolumn{12}{c}{(99260lsa, 60lsb, 60lsc)}
		\multicolumn{12}{c}{*(Period averages in percent per annum)*}
Three-Month	992	6.27	4.74	3.86	4.60	3.72	3.91	....	....	....	....	....	....
Six-Month	992	6.22	4.64	3.97	4.63	3.79	4.00	....	....	....	....	....	....
One-Year	992	6.34	4.59	4.22	4.72	3.95	4.14	....	....	....	....	....	....
		\multicolumn{12}{c}{**London Interbank Offer Rates on US Dollar Deposits**}
		\multicolumn{12}{c}{(11160lda, 60ldb, 60ldc, 60ldd, 60lde, 60ldf)}
		\multicolumn{12}{c}{*(Period averages in percent per annum)*}
Overnight	111	3.60	3.05	4.24	5.90	5.35	5.54	....	....	....	3.98	1.75	1.19
Seven-Day	111	3.66	3.08	4.31	5.93	5.40	5.58	5.53	5.16	6.36	3.95	1.76	1.20
One-Month	111	3.72	3.16	4.46	5.97	5.44	5.64	5.60	5.25	6.41	3.88	1.76	1.21
Three-Month	111	3.86	3.29	4.74	6.04	5.51	5.76	5.59	5.41	6.53	3.78	1.79	1.22
Six-Month	111	3.90	3.41	5.07	6.10	5.59	5.86	5.56	5.53	6.65	3.73	1.87	1.23
One-Year	111	4.20	3.64	5.59	6.24	5.78	6.08	5.53	5.71	6.83	3.86	2.19	1.36
		\multicolumn{12}{c}{**London Interbank Offer Rates on Three-Month Deposits (60ea)**}
		\multicolumn{12}{c}{*(Pound sterling rates relate to Paris market)*}
		\multicolumn{12}{c}{*(Period averages in percent per annum)*}
French Franc	132	10.37	8.57	5.88	6.68	3.94	3.48	3.64	....	....	....	....	....
Deutsche Mark	134	9.52	7.30	5.36	4.53	3.31	3.37	3.60	2.96	....	....	....	....
Japanese Yen	158	4.46	3.00	2.31	1.27	.63	.63	.71	.22	.28	.15	.08	.06
Netherlands Guilder	138	9.37	6.85	5.23	4.47	3.03	3.37	3.55	....	....	....	....	....
Swiss Franc	146	7.88	4.96	4.16	3.09	2.05	1.71	1.60	1.39	3.10	2.94	1.18	.33
Pound Sterling	112	9.70	6.05	5.54	6.73	6.09	6.90	7.39	5.54	6.19	5.04	4.06	3.73
Euro	163	....	....	....	....	....	....	....	2.96	4.41	4.26	3.32	2.33
		\multicolumn{12}{c}{**London Interbank Offer Rates on Six-Month Deposits (60eb)**}
		\multicolumn{12}{c}{*(Pound sterling rates relate to Paris market)*}
		\multicolumn{12}{c}{*(Period averages in percent per annum)*}
French Franc	132	10.16	7.92	5.95	6.61	4.02	3.54	3.68	....	....	....	....	....
Deutsche Mark	134	9.41	6.95	5.35	4.57	3.31	3.42	3.66	3.05	....	....	....	....
Japanese Yen	158	4.32	2.96	2.36	1.26	.71	.65	.71	.24	.31	.15	.09	.07
Netherlands Guilder	138	9.26	6.57	5.25	4.55	3.08	3.46	3.64	....	....	....	....	....
Swiss Franc	146	7.81	4.76	4.23	3.16	2.09	1.78	1.68	1.55	3.26	2.87	1.24	.38
Pound Sterling	112	9.65	5.93	5.80	6.91	6.13	7.04	7.32	5.62	6.31	5.02	4.16	3.76
Euro	163	....	....	....	....	....	....	....	3.05	4.54	4.15	3.35	2.30
		\multicolumn{12}{c}{**Discounts (−) or Premiums (60f) on Three-Month Forward Exchange Rates**}
		\multicolumn{12}{c}{*(End of period in percent per annum based on end-of-period quotation of*}
		\multicolumn{12}{c}{*the currencies against the US dollar)*}
Canada	156	−3.37	−3.84	−3.99	−.23	22.78	....	....	....	....	....	....	....
Australia	193	−3.93	....	....	....	....	....	....	....	−.65	−2.13	....	....
Japan	158	.03	1.18	3.69	4.86	5.12	5.45	6.25	6.25	5.75	2.78	....	....
Austria	122	−5.14	−2.21	−1.13	−1.67	2.34	1.99	2.32	....	....	....	....	....
Belgium	124	−4.94	−3.54	1.10	1.43	2.44	2.17	1.90	....	....	....	....	....
Denmark	128	−11.80	−3.30	.20	.80	1.85	1.74	.99	2.36	.97	−1.78	−1.72	−1.09
Finland	172	−6.61	−2.61	.43	1.14	2.32	2.12	1.85	....	....	....	....	....
France	132	−6.71	....	....	....	....	....	....	....	....	....	....	....
Germany	134	−5.20	−2.66	1.24	1.81	2.26	2.10	1.89	....	....	....	....	....
Italy	136	−10.37	−7.10	−.87	−4.64	−1.00	−2.62	.51	....	....	....	....	....
Netherlands	138	−4.77	....	....	....	....	....	....	....	−	−	....	....
Norway	142	−9.91	−2.47	.09	−1.08	.89	1.98	1.12	.32	−.99	−4.44	−4.84	−.60
Spain	184	−5.51	−.32	−3.67	−7.31	.79	4.81	3.50	....	....	....	....	....
Sweden	144	−54.41	−1.83	−1.66	−.36	−.37	−.58	.84	2.54	4.07	2.36	1.99	−1.71
Switzerland	146	−2.47	−.95	1.98	3.30	2.50	4.21	3.34	4.65	3.30	−.17	.81	1.26
United Kingdom	112	−3.53	−1.91	−.12	−.86	−.89	−1.77	....	....	....	....	....	....
		\multicolumn{12}{c}{**SDR Interest Rate (99260s) and Rate of Remuneration (99260r)**}
		\multicolumn{12}{c}{*(Period averages in percent per annum)*}
SDR Interest Rate	992	6.2599	4.6394	4.2858	4.5847	3.8998	4.0719	4.1052	3.4759	4.4397	3.4258	2.2416	1.6491
United States (3-Mo.T-Bill Rate)	111	3.51	3.06	4.35	5.65	5.14	5.20	4.90	4.77	6.00	3.48	1.63	1.02
United Kingdom (3-Mo.T-Bill Rate)	112	9.21	5.35	5.18	6.40	5.89	6.62	7.23	5.14	5.83	4.79	3.96	3.55
France (3-Mo.T-Bill Rate)	132	10.49	8.41	5.79	6.58	3.84	3.35	3.45	2.72	4.23	4.26	....	....
Germany (3-Mo. Interbank Rate)	134	9.46	7.24	5.31	4.48	3.27	3.30	3.52	2.94	4.37	4.25	3.30	2.32
Japan (3-Mo.Certif. of Deposits)	158	4.40	2.97	2.24	1.22	.59	.62	.72	.15	.23	....	....	....
Rate of Remuneration	992	6.2599	4.6394	4.2858	4.5847	3.8998	4.0719	4.1052	3.4759	4.4397	3.4258	2.2416	1.6491

2004, International Monetary Fund : *International Financial Statistics Yearbook*

Real Effective Exchange Rate Indices

		1992	1993	1994	1995	1996	1997	1998	1999	2000	2001	2002	2003

(2000=100)
Based on Relative Unit Labor Costs (65um.110)

Industrial Countries

Country		1992	1993	1994	1995	1996	1997	1998	1999	2000	2001	2002	2003
United States	111	89.0	91.4	90.9	84.4	86.6	92.1	95.3	93.5	100.0	111.4	109.9	97.3
Canada	156	113.8	103.7	94.3	94.9	98.6	100.8	97.5	96.8	100.0	93.1	91.3	101.2
Japan	158	84.3	100.6	109.8	110.8	92.8	88.0	84.7	95.2	100.0	90.2	85.9	85.5
Euro Area	163	131.5	128.5	127.7	132.7	131.6	119.3	114.6	109.5	100.0	99.1	100.0	108.6
Austria	122	125.2	124.0	121.2	115.0	110.2	104.2	102.7	100.6	100.0	100.3	100.6	102.6
Belgium	124	114.7	115.1	114.3	116.5	109.8	102.1	102.7	101.6	100.0	101.0	99.3	101.4
Finland	172	135.3	108.3	113.5	126.9	119.0	114.5	113.5	108.5	100.0	101.9	101.5	104.2
France	132	111.8	114.6	111.2	110.6	109.3	102.8	104.6	102.7	100.0	99.4	100.6	102.9
Germany *	134	102.8	111.3	115.9	126.3	123.8	115.6	109.9	107.2	100.0	98.3	97.9	101.2
Ireland	178	200.3	189.0	181.3	164.0	163.0	150.5	124.9	110.6	100.0	101.4	103.4	107.6
Italy	136	118.1	101.1	95.5	86.7	99.1	103.1	102.5	102.5	100.0	99.0	100.0	103.5
Netherlands	138	106.4	108.9	103.8	104.8	101.5	99.5	101.1	100.6	100.0	102.2	104.9	107.7
Spain	184	112.6	101.9	95.0	93.5	96.9	96.2	98.5	99.9	100.0	102.5	104.3	108.8
Denmark	128	106.9	112.7	102.4	104.0	109.0	103.3	104.2	105.7	100.0	102.1	103.9	109.0
Norway	142	79.2	77.5	79.9	83.9	84.9	90.2	90.8	96.0	100.0	105.2	116.3	115.4
Sweden	144	121.6	96.3	92.5	98.2	111.3	103.4	103.8	102.4	100.0	90.0	92.1	97.5
Switzerland	146	87.6	89.1	93.9	98.4	96.3	93.8	98.0	97.7	100.0	105.4	110.7	111.9
United Kingdom	112	74.0	65.8	67.7	67.8	71.8	88.3	95.6	96.0	100.0	97.3	98.9	94.9

(2000=100)
Based on Relative Consumer Prices (..rec)

Country		1992	1993	1994	1995	1996	1997	1998	1999	2000	2001	2002	2003
United States	111	81.1	83.8	82.7	80.0	83.4	89.5	95.9	95.3	100.0	107.4	107.0	98.0
Canada	156	121.9	114.2	104.0	100.6	102.3	103.7	99.1	98.0	100.0	99.2	98.3	106.7
Japan	158	83.4	98.4	103.3	105.0	88.6	83.6	82.2	93.0	100.0	89.5	82.9	81.4
Euro Area	163	127.7	121.2	120.4	126.5	126.2	114.7	117.5	111.9	100.0	103.8	109.2	121.8
Austria	122	103.1	105.8	106.5	110.5	108.2	104.5	104.5	102.5	100.0	101.1	102.1	104.3
Belgium	124	107.0	107.0	108.8	112.7	110.6	105.4	105.2	103.4	100.0	100.8	101.9	105.4
Finland	172	116.0	98.8	105.2	114.7	110.1	105.7	106.8	104.0	100.0	99.9	102.2	106.5
France	132	109.1	110.3	110.0	113.0	112.8	108.0	108.4	105.2	100.0	100.0	101.6	106.4
Germany *	134	109.0	113.6	113.9	119.0	115.1	109.4	110.0	106.4	100.0	100.7	102.1	106.7
Ireland	178	117.1	108.6	108.9	109.6	111.7	111.4	106.4	103.2	100.0	103.7	108.7	117.4
Italy	136	121.1	102.4	99.4	92.6	103.4	104.0	106.3	104.2	100.0	101.4	103.7	109.3
Netherlands	138	103.9	105.7	106.4	110.9	109.1	104.0	104.9	104.1	100.0	103.3	106.6	111.6
Spain	184	122.7	109.4	104.3	106.1	108.4	103.3	103.3	102.5	100.0	101.9	104.5	109.5
Denmark	128	102.8	103.2	102.6	107.0	106.2	103.1	105.1	104.2	100.0	101.6	103.7	108.5
Norway	142	107.6	103.0	101.1	104.0	103.8	105.1	102.1	101.8	100.0	103.8	112.4	110.2
Sweden	144	130.3	107.0	105.4	105.1	113.9	108.5	104.9	102.0	100.0	92.2	94.5	99.8
Switzerland	146	100.4	102.7	107.4	114.4	111.3	102.9	104.2	102.3	100.0	103.1	106.8	106.4
United Kingdom	112	87.5	78.4	78.5	75.7	77.5	91.2	96.9	96.6	100.0	98.3	98.9	95.4

(2000=100)
Based on Relative Normalized Unit Labor Costs (..reu)

Country		1992	1993	1994	1995	1996	1997	1998	1999	2000	2001	2002	2003
United States	111	88.3	90.0	87.9	81.0	83.9	88.7	94.4	93.0	100.0	109.5	108.8	96.6
Canada	156	118.4	111.9	105.0	104.2	105.1	107.8	101.1	100.0	100.0	96.0	95.6	107.2
Japan	158	80.9	95.9	101.8	107.2	91.8	87.6	81.8	93.1	100.0	88.5	80.6	78.6
Euro Area	163	134.6	132.1	129.4	135.2	135.8	122.3	118.1	112.2	100.0	99.6	101.9	111.3
Austria	122	123.3	124.0	121.1	116.7	111.1	105.6	104.0	102.0	100.0	99.7	100.3	102.5
Belgium	124	112.9	114.6	113.5	116.9	111.9	108.0	107.3	103.3	100.0	101.1	100.2	102.6
Finland	172	129.0	109.4	114.7	126.5	117.1	110.3	108.9	104.9	100.0	100.8	99.9	101.9
France	132	112.6	113.5	112.3	113.4	109.9	105.4	105.0	104.1	100.0	98.9	99.7	102.6
Germany *	134	102.7	109.5	112.7	121.0	119.4	112.3	109.5	106.1	100.0	99.2	99.3	102.3
Ireland	178	185.3	169.4	157.4	147.0	139.6	130.8	118.3	110.6	100.0	99.2	99.1	103.9
Italy	136	122.0	104.1	98.4	90.6	103.8	106.1	104.0	103.6	100.0	99.3	100.8	104.8
Netherlands	138	103.6	106.0	107.0	109.6	106.4	101.6	102.9	102.3	100.0	102.0	104.9	108.5
Spain	184	114.1	106.3	99.8	98.9	101.5	99.0	101.0	101.2	100.0	102.2	104.9	109.6
Denmark	128	101.2	104.0	103.1	106.1	104.2	101.7	103.3	103.2	100.0	101.4	103.0	107.5
Norway	142	83.8	82.2	82.0	86.6	88.8	92.6	93.6	98.1	100.0	105.6	118.2	118.1
Sweden	144	118.8	96.3	95.4	95.9	108.2	105.5	103.8	100.6	100.0	90.8	93.0	98.4
Switzerland	146	84.5	84.9	92.1	97.9	98.1	95.1	100.6	100.3	100.0	105.1	110.9	112.0
United Kingdom	112	78.1	71.9	73.5	71.0	73.5	87.6	93.2	94.8	100.0	99.8	101.7	97.7

* Data refer to the former Federal Republic of Germany

Production and Labor Indices

		1992	1993	1994	1995	1996	1997	1998	1999	2000	2001	2002	2003

Industrial Production

Index Numbers (2000=100): (66..i)

		1992	1993	1994	1995	1996	1997	1998	1999	2000	2001	2002	2003
Industrial Countries	110	80.4	79.6	82.8	85.8	87.7	91.9	93.1	95.4	100.0	97.1	96.3	97.2
United States	111	67.8	70.0	73.8	77.3	80.7	86.6	91.8	95.8	100.0	96.6	96.1	96.3
Canada	156	....	....	....	79.0	79.9	84.4	87.3	92.5	100.0	97.1	99.0	99.3
Australia	193	79.2	81.6	85.8	87.1	90.5	92.1	94.6	95.1	100.0	101.4	104.3	104.6
Japan	158	94.1	90.8	92.0	95.5	97.7	101.2	94.5	94.8	100.0	93.7	92.6	95.4
New Zealand	196	67.6	71.8	76.2	95.6	97.5	98.1	94.8	96.4	100.0	99.9	104.0	105.4
Euro Area													
Austria	122	69.3	68.2	70.9	74.5	75.2	80.0	86.6	91.8	100.0	102.8	103.6	105.6
Belgium	124	84.1	79.8	81.5	86.5	87.0	91.0	94.1	94.9	100.0	98.6	99.8	100.6
Finland	172	55.6	58.7	65.3	69.3	71.3	77.5	84.6	89.5	100.0	100.1	102.2	103.0
France	132	85.1	81.9	85.3	87.3	87.2	90.7	94.0	96.3	100.0	101.1	99.8	99.6
Germany	134	83.7	82.8	86.6	84.2	85.9	89.9	90.5	94.3	100.0	95.8	95.6	99.7
Greece	174	87.2	84.3	85.3	87.1	86.8	88.8	96.0	95.2	100.0	101.7	102.9	102.5
Ireland	178	34.8	36.8	41.2	49.6	53.6	63.0	75.5	86.6	100.0	110.2	118.8	126.3
Italy	136	85.0	83.1	88.0	93.0	91.5	95.0	96.2	96.1	100.0	98.8	97.5	97.1
Luxembourg	137	78.6	75.2	79.7	81.3	81.4	86.1	86.0	95.9	100.0	101.8	102.8	105.4
Netherlands	138	87.3	86.3	90.5	90.9	93.1	93.3	95.3	96.6	100.0	100.5	99.5	97.5
Portugal	182	82.1	77.8	77.7	84.7	89.1	91.4	96.6	99.5	100.0	103.1	102.7	102.6
Spain	184	77.9	74.3	80.0	83.9	82.8	88.5	93.4	95.7	100.0	98.5	98.7	100.1
Denmark	128	78.3	75.4	83.2	86.5	87.6	92.0	94.7	94.9	100.0	102.0	103.0	102.5
Norway	142	76.9	79.6	85.2	90.3	95.1	98.5	97.3	97.1	100.0	98.7	99.7	95.6
Sweden	144	83.1	82.5	91.7	84.1	84.7	89.2	92.4	93.8	100.0	99.6	99.9	102.7
Switzerland	146	78.7	77.3	80.6	82.2	82.2	86.0	89.1	92.2	100.0	99.3	94.2	94.2
United Kingdom	112	85.4	87.2	91.8	93.4	94.7	96.0	97.0	98.2	100.0	98.4	96.0	95.8

Wages

Index Numbers (2000=100): (65, 65ey, 65..c)

		1992	1993	1994	1995	1996	1997	1998	1999	2000	2001	2002	2003
Industrial Countries	110	81.8	84.4	86.8	89.0	91.3	93.7	95.5	97.6	100.0	102.0	103.9	105.9
United States	111	79.6	81.7	84.0	86.2	89.0	91.7	93.9	96.7	100.0	103.1	106.8	109.9
Canada	156	86.1	88.2	89.7	90.9	93.6	94.3	96.2	97.5	100.0	101.6	104.4	107.8
Australia	193	74.5	75.8	78.4	82.4	85.6	89.1	92.8	95.3	100.0	104.9	110.3	116.5
Japan	158	90.7	92.4	94.6	96.5	98.3	99.8	99.5	99.8	100.0	99.5	97.9	97.9
New Zealand	196	103.5	†89.1	90.0	91.4	93.1	95.3	97.1	98.5	100.0	101.9	104.2	106.5
Euro Area													
Austria	122	87.5	92.1	95.8	100.0	†90.9	92.9	95.2	98.0	100.0	102.2	104.8	106.8
Belgium	124	82.8	85.4	87.5	89.3	91.1	93.0	95.3	97.9	100.0	102.8	105.4	107.4
Finland	172	78.9	79.5	81.1	84.7	88.2	90.4	93.6	96.1	100.0	104.5	108.2	112.6
France	132	81.3	83.8	86.3	87.0	88.5	91.0	93.6	95.7	100.0	104.4	108.4	112.8
Germany (1990=100)	134	114.8	121.7	123.6	....	....	....	....	....	....	....	....	....
Greece (1995=100)	174	70.7	78.1	88.3	100.0	108.6	118.3	123.9	....	....	....	....	....
Ireland	178	71.4	75.2	77.4	79.1	81.1	85.0	88.5	93.7	100.0	109.1	115.1	122.8
Italy	136	79.0	81.7	84.6	87.2	90.0	93.2	95.8	98.0	100.0	101.7	104.3	....
Netherlands	138	81.5	84.2	85.7	86.6	88.1	90.8	93.7	96.4	100.0	104.2	108.0	110.8
Spain	184	72.4	77.3	80.7	84.6	89.1	92.7	95.3	97.7	100.0	103.8	108.1	112.7
Denmark	128	....	....	79.3	82.3	85.4	88.8	92.6	96.5	100.0	104.2	108.3	112.3
Iceland (1995=100)	176	98.5	96.3	96.8	100.0	....	....	....	....	....	....	....	....
Norway	142	....	....	....	....	....	....	....	91.3	96.1	100.0	104.5	110.0	115.2
Sweden	144	72.7	75.0	78.2	82.4	87.8	91.7	95.0	96.7	100.0	102.9	106.4	109.4
Switzerland	146	....	93.5	94.9	96.2	97.4	97.8	98.5	98.8	100.0	102.5	104.3	105.8
United Kingdom	112	73.0	75.2	77.9	80.4	83.2	86.8	91.3	95.7	100.0	104.4	108.1	....

Employment

Index Numbers (2000=100): (67, 67ey, 67..c, 67e, 67eyc)

		1992	1993	1994	1995	1996	1997	1998	1999	2000	2001	2002	2003
Industrial Countries	110	97.3	96.7	96.8	97.5	97.6	98.4	99.2	99.5	100.0	99.0	96.8	95.5
United States	111	82.5	84.1	86.7	89.0	90.8	93.2	95.5	97.9	100.0	100.0	98.9	98.6
Canada	156	82.9	82.5	84.2	85.8	87.8	91.0	94.0	96.0	100.0	100.0	100.7	100.4
Australia	193	98.9	94.6	97.8	98.8	99.0	100.5	97.2	95.5	100.0	96.7	97.8	95.8
Japan	158	117.0	116.1	113.5	111.4	109.0	107.8	105.9	102.8	100.0	97.0	92.4	89.4
New Zealand	196	90.4	90.4	100.8	104.7	103.6	98.2	102.8	99.2	100.0	103.1	103.2	99.1
Euro Area													
Austria	122	97.5	97.5	98.0	97.9	97.2	97.5	98.1	99.2	100.0	100.5	100.7	101.6
Finland	172	91.8	85.9	86.4	92.5	93.0	93.8	96.2	98.8	100.0	100.7	99.4	95.2
France	132	110.9	105.5	103.3	102.2	99.4	98.7	99.0	98.7	100.0	101.3	99.3	....
Germany	134	100.9	99.4	98.6	98.5	98.3	97.8	98.0	99.4	100.0	100.6	100.0	98.8
Greece	174	92.6	93.5	95.2	96.1	97.3	96.8	100.0	99.7	100.0	99.0	100.7	102.6
Ireland	178	77.3	77.3	80.2	85.1	89.2	94.4	97.1	96.2	100.0	101.0	95.6	90.9
Italy	136	107.1	104.8	102.6	100.3	99.2	98.8	99.8	99.9	100.0	101.0	102.6	....
Luxembourg	137	....	....	....	....	....	....	....	94.7	100.0	105.6	109.0	111.1
Netherlands	138	76.5	76.4	76.7	86.3	88.4	91.1	94.4	97.6	100.0	102.3	103.0	102.4
Spain	184	83.4	80.0	79.4	81.4	83.5	86.3	89.8	94.8	100.0	103.7	105.8	108.6
Denmark	128	97.4	94.9	93.9	95.8	96.5	98.4	98.8	99.5	100.0	100.1	99.8	98.9
Norway	142	88.3	88.3	89.7	91.6	93.9	96.7	99.1	99.5	100.0	100.4	100.7	100.0

2004, International Monetary Fund: *International Financial Statistics Yearbook*

Production and Labor Indices

Industrial Countries(Cont.)		1992	1993	1994	1995	1996	1997	1998	1999	2000	2001	2002	2003
Sweden	144	105.5	97.1	95.6	100.8	101.6	100.5	100.9	100.1	100.0	97.6	93.8	90.9
Switzerland	146	117.7	112.0	107.1	105.7	103.0	100.4	99.9	99.0	100.0	101.4	98.7	95.6
United Kingdom	112	90.2	89.6	90.2	91.3	92.8	94.9	96.7	98.3	100.0	101.1	101.4	101.6

Producer Prices/Wholesale Prices

Percent Change over Previous Year; Calculated from Indices

		1992	1993	1994	1995	1996	1997	1998	1999	2000	2001	2002	2003
World	001	14.29	16.72	27.19	15.31	6.81	4.99	3.95	4.54	7.72	3.48	2.31	5.02
Industrial Countries	110	.75	1.29	1.31	3.15	1.05	.58	ñ1.46	.18	4.40	.89	ñ1.29	2.44
United States	111	.59	1.46	1.30	3.58	2.34	−.07	−2.48	.84	5.78	1.11	−2.29	5.35
Canada	156	.47	3.63	6.06	7.43	.42	.86	−.06	1.61	5.05	1.09	.09	−1.12
Australia	193	1.54	2.00	.77	4.19	.31	1.24	−3.97	−.91	7.15	3.06	.21	.48
Japan	158	−.91	−1.52	−1.68	−.83	−1.64	.68	−1.54	−1.48	.05	−2.26	−2.08	−.79
New Zealand	196	2.06	2.44	1.35	.82	.51	.40	.70	.97	7.57	5.96	.35	−.95
Euro Area	163	....	....	....	....	.38	1.06	−.85	−.44	5.31	2.15	−.09	1.54
Austria	122	−.23	−.41	1.34	.31	.01	.37	−.52	−.84	4.05	1.48	−.36	1.62
Belgium	124	−1.80	−2.54	1.60	3.27	2.21	3.68	−1.93	.07	10.55	2.04	−.82	−.40
Finland	172	1.10	2.96	1.34	.66	−.94	1.59	−1.39	−.13	8.27	−.30	−1.21	−.10
France	132	....	....	....	....	....	....	....	....	†4.39	1.22	−.54	.46
Germany	134	....	†.16	.60	1.74	−1.22	1.17	−.40	−1.01	3.29	3.03	−.39	1.71
Greece	174	11.33	11.87	8.71	7.80	6.52	3.48	3.85	1.76	6.55	2.27	2.39	2.07
Ireland	178	.86	4.74	.91	2.15	.52	−.49	1.47	1.10	6.14	2.90	.23	−5.27
Italy	136	1.89	3.76	3.71	7.87	1.89	1.29	.10	−.25	6.02	1.94	−.19	1.60
Luxembourg	137	−2.69	−1.32	1.48	3.92	−3.11	1.48	2.43	−3.13	4.85	1.13	−1.09	1.46
Netherlands	138	1.77	.10	.52	1.53	1.97	1.77	−.15	1.05	4.82	3.00	.78	1.45
Portugal	182	....	....	....	....	....	....	....	....	....	2.75	.41	.82
Spain	184	1.31	2.53	4.27	6.37	1.68	1.03	−.67	.69	5.43	1.71	.69	1.42
Denmark	128	−1.14	−.56	.94	2.77	1.12	1.90	−.59	.50	5.93	1.97	.12	.19
Norway	142	−.44	−.99	1.29	2.56	2.17	1.37	.58	3.07	6.94	−4.68	−5.55	3.55
Sweden	144	−1.28	6.19	4.80	7.72	−1.75	1.19	−.59	1.10	5.84	3.23	.53	−.85
Switzerland	146	.73	.44	−.46	−.09	−1.76	−.73	−1.23	−1.00	.95	.49	−.48	–
United Kingdom	112	3.12	3.93	2.53	4.03	2.60	.89	–	.42	1.52	−.28	.04	1.50
Developing Countries	200	52.73	61.38	87.55	39.46	17.40	12.96	13.88	12.98	14.01	8.35	9.19	9.89
Africa	605	10.34	8.52	8.32	10.08	6.69	5.23	4.87	3.56	7.42	5.81	10.22	.43
Central African Rep.	626	.33	−1.47	....	....	....	....	−.05	1.23	6.36	....	....	....
Morocco	686	2.82	4.46	2.33	6.50	4.43	−1.61	3.48	−1.68	4.16	−.40	2.19	−4.53
South Africa	199	8.18	6.64	8.29	9.50	6.95	7.07	3.51	5.80	9.15	8.49	14.16	1.66
Tunisia	744	3.70	4.67	3.41	5.66	3.74	2.41	3.18	.38	3.33	1.75	2.50	2.42
Zambia	754	121.28	140.82	70.60	72.03	....	....	....	....	....	....	....	....
Zimbabwe	698	52.10	20.47	22.26	20.79	17.09	12.90	31.46	57.18	....	....	....	....
Asia	505	6.99	3.67	7.54	8.85	4.87	4.87	19.18	2.15	5.83	4.02	2.03	4.30
China, P.R.: Hong Kong	532	1.84	.69	2.07	2.75	−.09	−.27	−1.84	−1.58	.20	−1.60	−2.72	−.34
India	534	11.86	7.48	10.54	9.34	4.48	4.53	5.88	3.45	6.55	4.82	2.53	5.42
Indonesia	536	5.16	3.68	5.43	11.39	7.86	8.96	101.80	10.45	12.49	14.15	2.79	2.07
Korea	542	6.17	−2.27	2.71	4.65	3.23	3.81	12.22	−2.07	2.05	−.47	−.29	2.19
Malaysia	548	1.11	1.45	4.88	5.51	2.28	2.62	10.79	−3.27	3.10	−5.03	4.45	5.67
Pakistan	564	7.25	10.25	19.71	12.77	11.09	11.21	2.31	7.33	3.98	4.55	2.98	6.47
Philippines	566	3.72	−.11	8.62	5.50	8.93	.47	11.66	5.77	1.81	2.39	3.61	5.12
Singapore	576	−4.38	−4.35	−.42	.02	−1.15	−3.04	2.10	10.09	−1.59	−1.46	2.00	
Sri Lanka	524	8.75	7.60	5.00	8.81	20.49	6.92	6.22	−.40	1.69	11.69	10.73	3.06
Thailand	578	.23	−.42	3.98	8.17	1.83	5.06	12.19	−4.72	3.92	2.50	1.67	4.01
Europe	170	48.55	43.30	199.18	130.84	42.86	33.38	17.41	39.76	34.91	20.56	13.72	12.88
Armenia	911	....	....	....	....	....	....	14.63	5.86	−.41	1.08	3.60	8.87
Belarus	913	....	1,536.33	2,170.84	499.11	34.72	87.55	72.51	355.79	185.63	71.80	40.36	37.53
Bulgaria	918	−60.67	−82.85	1,146.30	55.72	132.68	971.21	16.99	2.81	17.52	3.67	1.29	4.94
Croatia	960	816.67	1,512.42	77.60	.74	1.37	2.28	−1.22	2.56	12.12	1.14	1.83	−.28
Cyprus	423	2.98	2.48	3.32	3.62	2.14	2.79	.51	1.21	7.19	1.59	1.35	2.91
Czech Republic	935	9.93	9.28	5.32	7.53	4.80	4.87	4.91	1.04	4.89	2.82	−.54	−.29
Estonia	939	....	....	....	25.59	14.79	8.38	4.23	−1.23	4.86	4.39	.42	.21
Georgia	915	....	....	....	....	....	....	....	14.28	5.77	3.67	6.02	....
Hungary	944	10.01	13.95	12.25	28.52	21.82	20.34	11.32	5.09	11.72	4.80	−1.39	2.42
Kazakhstan	916	....	....	....	....	23.91	15.52	.83	18.91	37.97	.35	.16	9.31
Kyrgyz Republic	917	....	....	215.26	21.82	22.99	26.26	7.95	53.67	30.70	11.99	4.81	4.59
Latvia	941	....	117.09	16.84	11.89	13.67	4.12	1.88	−4.01	.62	1.72	.93	3.19
Lithuania	946	....	391.88	44.74	28.32	17.26	4.26	−7.40	1.43	17.51	−3.70	−3.63	−.32
Poland	964	27.71	32.25	30.07	25.55	13.20	12.18	7.25	5.54	7.71	1.66	1.16	2.68
Romania	968	203.58	164.98	140.52	35.11	49.87	156.90	33.18	44.53	53.41	41.02	24.65	19.52
Russia	922	....	943.76	337.00	236.46	50.81	15.00	7.03	58.95	46.53	19.17	11.55	15.49
Slovak Republic	936	5.30	17.19	9.98	9.01	4.12	4.49	3.25	3.81	9.80	6.60	2.07	8.31
Slovenia	961	....	21.75	17.69	12.80	6.74	6.10	5.98	2.12	7.69	8.94	5.13	2.55
Turkey	186	62.10	57.97	121.26	86.03	75.94	81.80	71.83	53.06	51.43	61.63	50.11	25.56
Ukraine	926	....	4,619.25	1,143.80	487.94	51.86	7.65	13.21	31.12	20.86	8.65	3.07	7.77
Middle East	405	15.31	12.05	15.98	24.59	14.34	5.49	4.52	7.87	7.04	2.20	5.25	8.14
Egypt	469	12.12	8.55	4.61	6.32	8.32	4.17	1.40	.90	1.79	1.03	6.39	14.38
Iran, I.R. of	429	33.04	25.59	37.62	60.58	32.93	10.69	11.92	19.19	17.83	5.92	8.18	10.58
Israel	436	10.17	8.19	7.89	10.70	8.60	6.29	4.18	7.06	3.64	−.12	3.87	4.33
Jordan	439	4.16	3.40	4.84	−2.40	2.03	1.57	.64	−2.40	−3.58	−1.54	−1.61	....
Kuwait	443	.45	1.79	−.19	1.39	5.16	−1.29	−1.65	−1.22	.45	1.97	3.28	1.95
Saudi Arabia	456	1.32	.56	1.76	7.28	−.25	–	−1.87	.43	.37	−.11	−.02	.86
Syrian Arab Rep.	463	2.63	8.55	14.17	6.90	3.23	2.50	−.61	−1.84	−5.66	−5.00	7.37	....

2004, International Monetary Fund: *International Financial Statistics Yearbook*

Producer Prices/Wholesale Prices

		1992	1993	1994	1995	1996	1997	1998	1999	2000	2001	2002	2003
		Percent Change over Previous Year; Calculated from Indices											
Western Hemisphere	205	198.21	289.14	246.39	35.78	18.22	11.81	8.40	12.38	13.50	7.47	17.55	17.93
Argentina	213	....	....	.39	4.31	2.95	−1.06	−3.35	−4.03	3.70	−2.04	78.26	19.61
Brazil	223	987.80	2,050.12	2,311.60	57.53	6.25	10.09	3.55	16.56	18.11	12.61	16.67	27.57
Chile	228	11.72	8.57	7.70	7.57	6.24	1.63	1.89	5.21	11.41	7.80	6.83	6.59
Colombia	233	20.10	14.22	17.15	18.13	15.02	15.43	17.30	9.82	13.20	9.40	5.29	9.13
Costa Rica	238	18.40	5.15	13.11	23.88	16.00	11.60	8.81	10.14	10.97	9.32	7.97	10.57
Ecuador	248	....	....	....	....	31.17	31.17	31.17	102.74	164.32	−.21	6.76	7.28
El Salvador	253									6.48	.99	−2.16	2.50
Mexico	273	12.34	7.41	6.11	38.64	33.88	17.55	15.98	14.24	7.84	5.02	5.10	7.48
Panama	283	1.85	−.25	2.04	2.98	2.12	−2.24	−3.92	2.68	8.75	−3.21	−3.00	2.21
Paraguay	288	....	....	....	....	....	1.15	14.90	5.30	14.70	5.82	19.89	26.46
Peru	293	57.19	47.55	17.89	10.52	9.44	7.38	7.27	4.91	4.33	1.38	−1.05	1.70
Trinidad and Tobago	369	.77	5.36	5.40	3.58	2.89	1.93	1.44	1.71	1.30	.90	.59	....
Uruguay	298	58.32	33.37	34.20	37.71	25.02	16.36	9.29	−.88	6.84	6.58	31.92	38.92
Venezuela, Rep. Bol.	299	23.57	34.96	78.16	57.74	103.24	29.76	22.17	16.21	15.18	13.28	37.28	51.40
Memorandum Items													
Oil Exporting Countries	999	13.56	12.67	20.12	26.68	22.36	10.44	44.98	11.66	12.10	9.32	7.80	9.62
Non-Oil Developing Countries	201	60.71	71.67	100.80	41.51	16.67	13.35	9.78	13.17	14.28	8.22	9.39	9.92

Indices

		1992	1993	1994	1995	1996	1997	1998	1999	2000	2001	2002	2003
		Index Numbers: 2000=100											
World	001	44.5	51.9	66.1	76.2	81.4	85.4	88.8	92.8	100.0	103.5	105.9	111.2
Industrial Countries	110	90.2	91.4	92.6	95.5	96.5	97.0	95.6	95.8	100.0	100.9	99.6	102.0
Developing Countries	200	12.2	19.7	36.9	51.4	60.3	68.2	77.6	87.7	100.0	108.4	118.3	130.0
Africa	605	59.0	64.0	69.4	76.4	81.5	85.7	89.9	93.1	100.0	105.8	116.6	117.1
Asia	505	58.2	60.3	64.8	70.6	74.0	77.6	92.5	94.5	100.0	104.0	106.1	110.7
Europe	170	2.4	3.4	10.3	23.7	33.9	45.2	53.0	74.1	100.0	120.6	137.1	154.8
Middle East	405	42.4	47.5	55.1	68.7	78.6	82.9	86.6	93.4	100.0	102.2	107.6	116.3
Western Hemisphere	205	3.0	11.6	40.3	54.7	64.7	72.3	78.4	88.1	100.0	107.5	126.3	149.0

Consumer Prices

Percent Change over Previous Year; Calculated from Indices

		1992	1993	1994	1995	1996	1997	1998	1999	2000	2001	2002	2003
World	001	17.72	19.01	26.78	15.42	8.69	6.13	5.78	5.39	4.40	4.09	3.42	3.69
Industrial Countries	110	3.09	2.71	2.35	2.44	2.24	2.04	1.41	1.43	2.38	2.18	1.47	1.89
United States	111	3.03	2.95	2.61	2.81	2.93	2.34	1.55	2.19	3.38	2.83	1.59	2.27
Canada	156	1.51	1.84	.19	2.17	1.58	1.62	.99	1.72	2.75	2.53	2.25	2.77
Australia	193	.99	1.81	1.89	4.64	2.61	.25	.85	1.47	4.48	4.38	3.00	2.77
Japan	158	1.73	1.28	.71	−.13	.14	1.73	.66	−.34	−.67	−.73	−.92	−.25
New Zealand	196	1.03	1.42	2.40	3.74	2.30	1.17	1.29	−.12	2.62	2.63	2.68	1.75
Euro Area	163	....	....	....	....	2.15	1.58	1.09	1.12	2.34	2.11	2.25	2.07
Austria	122	4.03	3.63	2.96	2.25	1.84	1.33	.90	.56	2.35	2.66	1.81	1.36
Belgium	124	2.43	2.75	2.38	1.47	2.06	1.63	.95	1.12	2.55	2.47	1.64	1.59
Finland	172	2.60	2.10	1.09	.99	.62	1.20	1.40	1.16	3.37	2.57	1.58	.86
France	132	2.37	2.11	1.66	1.78	2.01	1.20	.67	.50	1.69	1.66	1.92	2.10
Germany	134	....	† 4.43	2.74	1.72	1.45	1.88	.94	.57	1.47	1.98	1.37	1.05
Greece	174	15.87	14.41	10.92	8.94	8.20	5.54	4.77	2.64	3.15	3.37	3.63	3.53
Ireland	178	3.12	1.42	2.37	2.52	1.74	1.40	2.43	1.64	5.56	4.87	4.67	3.48
Italy	136	5.08	4.48	4.03	5.24	3.97	2.04	1.96	1.66	2.54	2.79	2.47	2.67
Luxembourg	137	3.15	3.58	2.20	1.92	1.39	1.37	.96	1.00	3.15	2.67	2.07	2.05
Netherlands	138	3.18	2.58	2.80	2.10	2.02	2.16	1.98	2.21	2.52	4.53	3.47	2.11
Portugal	182	8.94	6.50	5.21	4.12	3.12	2.16	2.72	2.30	2.85	4.39	3.55	3.28
Spain	184	5.93	4.57	4.72	4.67	3.56	1.97	1.83	2.31	3.43	3.59	3.07	3.03
Denmark	128	2.10	1.25	1.99	2.10	2.11	2.20	1.85	2.48	2.92	2.35	2.43	2.09
Iceland	176	3.96	4.08	1.55	1.65	2.30	1.75	1.72	3.22	5.16	6.39	5.17	2.06
Norway	142	2.34	2.27	1.40	2.46	1.26	2.58	2.26	2.33	3.09	3.02	1.29	2.48
Sweden	144	2.38	4.73	2.13	2.45	.55	.66	−.27	.47	.89	2.42	2.17	1.91
Switzerland	146	4.04	3.27	.86	1.80	.82	.52	.02	.82	1.54	.99	.64	.63
United Kingdom	112	3.73	1.56	2.48	3.41	2.45	3.13	3.42	1.56	2.93	1.82	1.63	2.91
Developing Countries	200	44.19	49.91	65.29	33.60	17.26	11.45	11.51	10.19	6.81	6.37	5.75	5.83
Africa	605	51.49	32.68	32.35	32.54	24.12	12.99	8.01	9.72	11.38	12.39	9.03	6.64
CEMAC	758	....	....	....	....	....	....	....	....	....	....	....	....
Cameroon	622	−.02	−3.21	35.09	9.08	3.92	4.78	3.18	1.53	−2.05	4.51	2.80	....
Central African Rep.	626	−1.40	−2.92	24.57	19.19	3.72	1.61	−1.89	−1.41	3.20	3.37	3.39	3.13
Chad	628	−3.14	−7.07	40.43	9.06	12.39	5.62	12.14	−6.80	3.80	12.44	5.19	−1.88
Congo, Rep. of	664	27.33	45.98	28.81	1.55	8.86	11.36	6.72	5.74	9.98	5.74	1.96	9.82
Equatorial Guinea	642	−7.17	3.99	36.42	....	....	....	....	....	....	....	....	....
Gabon	646	−9.54	.53	36.12	9.65	.69	3.97	1.45	−1.94	.50	....	....	....
WAEMU	759	1.08	1.07	29.97	12.05	3.41	3.00	3.69	.19	1.78	4.03	2.93	1.34
Benin	638	....	.44	38.53	14.46	4.91	3.47	5.75	.33	4.17	3.98	2.49	1.49
Burkina Faso	748	−1.99	.55	25.18	7.39	6.17	2.31	5.05	−1.07	−.30	5.01	2.18	2.03
Côte d'Ivoire	662	4.23	2.16	26.08	14.30	2.48	4.02	4.69	.79	2.46	4.28	3.11	3.35
Guinea Bissau	654	69.58	48.11	15.18	45.37	50.73	49.10	6.50	−2.02	8.60	3.17	3.37	−3.52
Mali	678	−6.24	−.26	23.18	13.44	6.81	−.36	4.04	−1.20	−.68	5.19	5.03	−1.35
Niger	692	−4.48	−1.22	36.04	10.56	5.29	2.93	4.55	−2.30	2.90	4.01	2.63	−1.61
Senegal	722	−.11	−.59	32.29	7.86	2.75	1.58	1.16	.83	.73	3.07	2.23	−.03
Togo	742	1.39	−1.01	39.16	16.43	4.69	8.25	.97	−.07	1.89	3.91	3.07	−.96
Algeria	612	31.67	20.54	29.05	29.78	18.68	5.73	4.95	2.65	.34	4.23	1.42	2.58
Angola	614	299.06	1,379.41	948.81	2,671.79	4,145.11	219.18	107.28	248.19	325.00	141.17	118.76	98.23
Botswana	616	16.17	14.33	10.54	10.51	10.08	8.72	6.66	7.75	8.60	6.56	8.03	9.19
Burundi	618	1.82	9.68	14.85	19.26	26.44	31.11	12.50	3.39	24.32	9.24	−5.82	15.96
Cape Verde	624	3.12	5.82	3.34	8.41	6.01	8.57	4.38	4.36	−2.48	3.35	1.88	....
Congo, Dem. Rep. of	636	4,129	1,987	23,773	542	542	176	29	285	514	360	32	....
Ethiopia	644	10.53	3.54	7.59	10.02	−5.07	2.40	2.58	7.87	.65	−8.12	1.55	17.78
Gambia, The	648	9.49	6.46	1.71	6.98	1.10	2.78	3.49	2.16	.19	8.08	4.94	....
Ghana	652	10.06	24.96	24.87	59.46	46.56	27.89	14.62	12.41	25.19	32.91	14.82	26.67
Kenya	664	27.33	45.98	28.81	1.55	8.86	11.36	6.72	5.74	9.98	5.74	1.96	9.82
Lesotho	666	17.21	13.14	8.21	9.27	9.33	8.04	8.04	8.04	6.13	−9.62	33.81	6.67
Madagascar	674	14.57	10.01	38.94	49.06	19.77	4.49	6.21	9.93	12.03	6.94	15.93	−1.22
Malawi	676	23.75	22.77	34.65	83.33	37.60	9.14	29.75	44.80	29.58	22.70	14.74	9.57
Mauritania	682	10.14	9.37	4.13	6.54	4.68	4.63	8.03	4.07	3.25	4.71	3.90	5.15
Mauritius	684	4.64	10.52	7.32	6.03	6.55	6.83	6.81	6.91	4.20	5.39	6.72	4.23
Morocco	686	5.74	5.18	5.14	6.12	2.99	1.04	2.75	.68	1.89	.62	2.80	1.17
Mozambique	688	45.49	42.20	63.18	54.43	48.49	7.37	1.48	2.86	12.72	9.05	16.78	13.43
Namibia	728	17.73	8.53	10.76	10.02	7.98	8.81	6.17	8.64	8.99	9.54	11.35	7.19
Nigeria	694	44.59	57.17	57.03	72.81	29.29	8.21	10.32	4.76	14.52	12.96	12.88	14.03
Rwanda	714	9.56	12.35	41.04	41.04	7.41	12.02	6.21	−2.41	4.29	2.98	2.45	6.94
Seychelles	718	3.25	1.38	1.74	−.24	−1.10	.62	2.58	6.35	6.27	5.97	.18	3.30
Sierra Leone	724	65.50	22.21	24.20	25.99	23.14	14.95	35.53	34.09	−.84	2.09	−3.29	7.60
South Africa	199	13.87	9.72	8.94	8.68	7.35	8.60	6.88	5.18	5.34	5.70	9.16	5.86
Sudan	732	117.62	101.38	115.40	68.38	132.82	46.65	17.11	15.99	5.69	5.85	....	....
Tanzania	738	21.85	25.28	33.09	28.38	20.98	16.09	12.80	7.89	5.92	5.13	4.57	4.43
Tunisia	744	5.82	3.97	4.73	6.24	3.73	3.65	3.13	2.69	2.93	1.98	2.72	2.72
Uganda	746	52.44	6.08	9.73	8.59	7.22	6.93	−.02	6.35	2.83	2.00	−.32	7.83
Zambia	754	165.71	183.31	54.60	34.93	43.07	24.42	24.46	26.79	26.03	21.39	22.23	....
Zimbabwe	698	42.06	27.59	22.26	22.59	21.43	18.74	31.82	58.52	55.86	76.71	140.08	....

2004, International Monetary Fund: *International Financial Statistics Yearbook*

Consumer Prices

Percent Change over Previous Year; Calculated from Indices

		1992	1993	1994	1995	1996	1997	1998	1999	2000	2001	2002	2003
Asia	505	7.78	9.19	14.70	11.81	7.66	4.65	8.04	2.16	1.62	2.38	1.94	2.65
Bangladesh	513	3.63	3.01	5.31	10.20	2.38	5.39	8.40	6.11	2.21	2.01	3.33	5.67
Bhutan	514	15.98	11.21	6.99	9.50	8.79	6.51	10.58	6.78	4.01	3.41	2.48	....
Cambodia	522	....	....	....	1.06	10.07	3.17	14.81	4.01	−.79	−.60	3.21	1.22
China, P.R.: Mainland	924	6.34	14.58	24.24	16.90	8.32	2.81	−.84	−1.41	.26	.46	−.77	1.16
China, P.R.: Hong Kong	532	9.59	8.82	8.78	9.03	6.37	5.78	2.85	−3.96	−3.75	−1.61	−3.04	−2.58
China, P.R.: Macao	546	....	....	....	....	....	....	....	−3.20	−1.61	−1.99	−2.64	−1.56
Fiji	819	4.88	5.21	.82	2.17	3.05	3.37	5.71	1.97	1.09	4.27	.76	4.17
India	564	9.51	9.97	12.37	12.34	10.37	11.38	6.23	4.14	4.37	3.15	3.29	2.91
Indonesia	536	7.53	9.68	8.52	9.43	7.97	6.73	57.64	20.32	9.35	12.55	10.03	5.06
Korea	542	6.31	4.80	6.20	4.44	4.98	4.40	7.54	.82	2.25	4.10	2.69	3.55
Lao People's Dem. Rep.	544	9.86	6.27	6.78	19.59	13.02	27.51	90.98	128.42	25.09	7.81	10.63	15.49
Malaysia	548	4.77	3.54	3.72	3.45	3.49	2.66	5.27	2.74	1.53	1.42	1.81	1.06
Maldives	556	16.85	20.13	3.38	5.49	6.24	7.58	−1.41	2.95	−1.18	.68	.93	−2.87
Mongolia	948	....	268.15	87.58	56.76	46.89	36.56	9.36	7.56	11.60	6.28	.92	5.13
Myanmar	518	21.91	31.83	24.10	25.19	16.28	29.70	51.49	18.40	−.11	21.10	57.07	36.59
Nepal	558	17.15	7.51	8.35	7.62	9.22	4.01	11.24	7.45	2.48	2.69	3.03	5.71
Pakistan	564	9.51	9.97	12.37	12.34	10.37	11.38	6.23	4.14	4.37	3.15	3.29	2.91
Papua New Guinea	853	4.31	4.97	2.85	17.28	11.62	3.96	13.57	14.93	15.60	9.30	11.80	14.71
Philippines	566	8.59	6.88	8.36	8.01	9.03	5.85	9.72	6.71	4.36	6.11	2.97	2.99
Samoa	862	9.03	1.72	12.08	−2.90	5.37	6.86	2.22	.27	.97	3.84	8.05	.12
Singapore	576	2.26	2.29	3.10	1.72	1.38	2.00	−.27	.02	1.36	1.00	−.39	.51
Solomon Islands	813	10.75	9.17	13.26	9.63	11.77	8.08	12.40	8.02	7.06	6.89	10.16	9.96
Sri Lanka	524	11.38	11.75	8.45	7.67	15.94	9.57	9.36	4.69	6.18	14.16	9.55	6.32
Thailand	578	4.07	3.37	5.04	5.80	5.87	5.58	8.08	.31	1.55	1.66	.60	1.82
Tonga	866	7.94	.96	1.02	1.44	3.00	2.12	3.28	4.85	5.91	8.30	10.36	11.62
Vanuatu	846	4.06	3.57	2.30	2.23	.93	2.81	3.29	1.96	2.46	3.65	1.99	3.00
Vietnam	582	....	....	....	....	5.68	3.21	7.27	4.12	−1.71	−.43	3.83	3.10
Europe	170	95.63	85.07	192.81	121.90	44.69	34.17	29.30	49.70	25.07	21.03	15.23	11.28
Albania	914	226.01	85.00	22.57	7.79	12.73	33.18	20.64	.39	.05	3.11	7.77	.48
Armenia	911	....	....	4,962.22	175.97	18.70	13.91	8.67	.66	−.81	3.14	1.10	4.76
Azerbaijan	912	912.30	1,129.04	1,664.53	411.74	19.76	3.60	−.69	−8.59	1.77	1.55	2.81	....
Belarus	913	....	1,190.23	2,221.02	709.35	52.71	63.94	72.87	293.68	168.62	61.13	42.54	28.40
Bulgaria	918	91.30	72.88	96.06	62.05	121.61	1,058.37	18.67	2.57	10.32	7.36	5.81	2.16
Croatia	960	625.00	1,500.00	107.33	3.95	4.30	4.17	6.40	3.46	5.27	4.77	1.70	.12
Cyprus	423	6.51	4.85	4.70	2.62	2.98	3.61	2.23	1.63	4.14	1.98	2.80	4.14
Czech Republic	935	....	....	9.96	9.17	8.80	8.55	10.63	2.14	3.90	4.71	1.79	.10
Czechoslovakia	964	45.33	36.87	33.25	28.07	19.82	15.08	11.73	7.31	10.13	5.51	1.88	.72
Estonia	939	....	89.81	47.65	28.78	23.05	10.58	8.21	3.30	4.03	5.74	3.57	1.34
Georgia	915	....	....	....	162.72	39.36	7.09	3.57	19.19	4.06	4.65	5.56	....
Hungary	944	22.95	22.45	18.87	28.30	23.60	18.28	14.23	10.00	9.80	9.22	5.27	4.64
Kazakhstan	916	....	....	1,877.37	176.16	39.18	17.41	7.15	8.30	13.18	8.35	5.84	6.44
Kyrgyz Republic	917	....	....	....	....	31.95	23.44	10.46	35.90	18.69	6.93	2.13	3.50
Latvia	941	243.27	108.77	35.93	24.98	17.61	8.44	4.66	2.36	2.65	2.49	1.94	2.92
Lithuania	946	....	410.24	72.15	39.66	24.62	8.88	5.07	.75	1.01	1.30	.30	−1.18
Macedonia, FYR	962	....	....	126.58	16.37	2.67	1.09	.54	−1.26	.68	−.75	.07	.08
Malta	181	1.63	4.14	4.13	4.43	2.05	3.11	2.39	2.13	2.37	2.93	2.19	.54
Moldova	921	....	....	....	12.07	20.89	8.01	6.64	45.94	31.29	9.77	5.30	11.75
Poland	964	45.33	36.87	33.25	28.07	19.82	15.08	11.73	7.31	10.13	5.51	1.88	.72
Romania	968	211.21	255.17	136.76	32.24	38.83	154.76	59.10	45.80	45.67	34.47	22.54	15.27
Russia	922	....	874.62	307.63	197.47	47.74	14.77	27.67	85.74	20.78	21.46	15.79	13.67
Slovak Republic	936	....	....	13.41	9.89	5.81	6.11	6.70	10.57	12.04	7.33	3.32	8.55
Slovenia	961	....	32.86	20.99	13.46	9.79	8.38	7.98	6.11	8.87	8.41	7.48	5.58
Turkey	186	70.07	66.10	106.26	88.11	80.35	85.73	84.64	64.87	54.92	54.40	44.96	25.30
Ukraine	926	....	4,734.91	891.19	376.75	80.33	15.94	10.58	22.68	28.20	11.96	.76	5.21
Middle East	405	13.47	11.71	13.78	21.36	12.82	7.61	7.11	7.50	4.98	3.63	5.32	6.47
Bahrain, Kingdom of	419	−.17	2.54	.82	2.70	−.45	2.43	−.22	−1.43	−.70	.24	1.22	....
Egypt	469	13.64	12.09	8.15	15.74	7.19	4.63	3.87	3.08	2.68	2.27	2.74	4.25
Iran, I.R. of	429	25.81	21.20	31.45	49.66	28.94	17.35	17.87	20.07	14.48	11.27	14.34	16.47
Israel	436	11.95	10.94	12.34	10.05	11.27	9.00	5.43	5.20	1.14	1.10	5.64	.72
Jordan	439	4.00	3.32	3.52	2.35	6.50	3.04	3.09	.61	.67	1.79	1.82	2.34
Kuwait	443	−.55	.38	2.53	2.69	3.56	.66	.15	2.99	1.81	1.66	1.40	1.19
Lebanon	446	80.74	15.66	6.80	....	....	....	....	....	....	....	....	....
Oman	449	.96	−.31	.41	2.46	.90	−.52	−.83	.43	−1.14	−1.06	−.66	−.42
Qatar	453	3.06	−.87	1.32	2.96	7.43	2.75	2.60	2.16	1.68	1.44	.24	2.27
Saudi Arabia	456	−.08	1.06	.56	4.87	1.22	.06	−.36	−1.35	−1.13	−1.12	.25	.60
Syrian Arab Republic	463	11.01	13.22	15.33	7.98	8.25	1.89	−.80	−3.70	−3.85	1.89	.97	....
Yemen, Republic of	474	29.41	35.75	49.39	55.08	30.73	2.18	5.98	8.66	4.59	11.91	12.23	10.83
Western Hemisphere	205	150.65	214.73	211.30	40.32	21.35	13.09	9.88	8.95	8.15	6.33	9.09	10.81
ECCU	309	....	....	....	....	....	....	....	....	....	....	....	....
Anguilla	312	2.36	4.27	3.51	1.39	3.58	.11	2.64	2.64	−35.82	2.25	.56	....
Dominica	321	5.47	1.57	.02	1.32	1.68	2.44	1.00	1.19	.86	1.52	.24	1.55
Grenada	328	3.78	2.81	3.77	1.87	2.03	1.24	1.41	.57	2.14	1.67	1.07	....
St. Kitts and Nevis	361	2.86	1.79	1.44	2.96	2.09	8.91	3.45	3.91	2.10	1.50	2.10	....
St. Lucia	362	5.07	1.13	2.53	5.63	.92	−.01	3.20	3.41	3.80	.10	1.60	.94
St. Vincent & Grenadines	364	3.46	4.29	1.01	1.74	4.41	.44	2.14	1.03	.20	.82	.81	.26
Argentina	213	24.90	10.61	4.18	3.38	.16	.53	.92	−1.17	−.94	−1.07	25.87	13.44
Aruba	314	3.87	5.22	6.31	3.36	3.23	3.00	1.87	2.28	4.04	3.11	3.44	3.29
Bahamas, The	313	5.74	2.71	1.41	2.07	1.38	.54	1.34	1.25	1.61	2.04	2.18	3.03
Barbados	316	6.09	1.11	.08	1.88	2.39	7.71	−1.27	1.56	2.44	2.58	.15	1.58
Belize	339	2.42	1.48	2.59	2.89	6.40	1.05	−.87	−1.21	.61	1.16	2.23	2.58

Consumer Prices

		1992	1993	1994	1995	1996	1997	1998	1999	2000	2001	2002	2003
					Percent Change over Previous Year; Calculated from Indices								
Western Hemisphere(Cont.)													
Bolivia	218	12.06	8.53	7.87	10.19	12.43	4.71	7.67	2.16	4.60	1.60	.92	3.34
Brazil	223	951.65	1,927.98	2,075.89	66.01	15.76	6.93	3.20	4.86	7.04	6.84	8.45	14.72
Chile	228	15.43	12.73	11.44	8.24	7.36	6.14	5.11	3.34	3.84	3.57	2.49	2.81
Colombia	233	27.03	22.61	23.84	20.96	20.24	18.46	18.67	10.87	9.22	7.97	6.35	7.13
Costa Rica	238	21.79	9.78	13.53	23.19	17.52	13.23	11.67	10.05	10.99	11.23	9.16	9.45
Dominican Republic	243	4.26	5.25	8.26	12.54	5.40	8.30	4.83	6.47	7.72	8.88	5.22	27.45
Ecuador	248	54.34	45.00	27.44	22.89	24.37	30.64	36.10	52.24	96.09	37.68	12.48	7.93
El Salvador	253	11.22	18.51	10.59	10.03	9.79	4.49	2.55	.51	2.27	3.75	1.87	2.12
Guatemala	258	10.05	11.82	10.86	8.41	11.06	9.23	6.97	4.86	5.98	7.63	8.03	5.48
Guyana	336	....	....	....	12.21	7.09	3.56	4.59	7.54	6.15	2.63	5.34	....
Haiti	263	19.36	29.71	39.33	27.61	20.58	20.56	10.63	8.67	13.71	14.18	9.85	39.28
Honduras	268	8.76	10.75	21.73	29.46	23.84	20.17	13.71	11.65	11.06	9.67	7.70	7.67
Mexico	273	15.51	9.75	6.97	35.00	34.38	20.63	15.93	16.59	9.50	6.36	5.03	4.55
Netherlands Antilles	353	1.39	2.04	1.78	2.80	3.60	3.26	1.13	.37	5.82	1.80	.41	2.03
Nicaragua	278	23.67	20.40	6.71	10.94	11.62	9.22	13.04	11.22	11.55	7.36	3.99	5.15
Panama	283	1.82	.45	1.27	.99	1.26	1.32	.56	1.25	1.50	.31	1.01	1.41
Paraguay	288	15.19	18.21	20.57	13.40	9.81	6.99	11.53	6.75	8.98	7.27	10.51	14.23
Peru	293	73.53	48.58	23.74	11.13	11.54	8.56	7.25	3.47	3.76	1.98	.19	2.26
Suriname	366	43.67	143.51	368.48	235.56	−.70	7.15	18.98	98.93	59.40	38.59	15.53	22.98
Trinidad and Tobago	369	6.44	10.84	8.81	5.18	3.40	3.63	5.61	3.44	3.56	5.54	4.14	3.81
Uruguay	298	68.46	54.10	44.74	42.25	28.34	19.82	10.81	5.66	4.76	4.36	13.97	19.38
Venezuela, Rep. Bol.	299	31.42	38.12	60.82	59.92	99.88	50.04	35.78	23.57	16.20	12.53	22.43	31.09
Memorandum Items													
Oil Exporting Countries	999	16.55	17.10	20.15	25.15	20.44	11.77	27.63	14.31	6.15	8.54	9.76	10.88
Non-Oil Developing Countries	201	48.90	55.79	71.97	34.68	16.87	11.41	9.67	9.73	6.88	6.13	5.32	5.29

Indices

Index Numbers: 2000=100

		1992	1993	1994	1995	1996	1997	1998	1999	2000	2001	2002	2003
World	001	42.8	50.9	64.5	74.5	81.0	85.9	90.9	95.8	100.0	104.1	107.7	111.6
Industrial Countries	110	84.5	86.8	88.9	91.0	93.1	95.0	96.3	97.7	100.0	102.2	103.7	105.6
Developing Countries	200	17.6	26.4	43.6	58.3	68.4	76.2	85.0	93.6	100.0	106.4	112.5	119.0
Africa	605	23.2	30.8	40.8	54.0	67.0	75.8	81.8	89.8	100.0	112.4	122.5	130.7
Asia	505	56.5	61.7	70.8	79.1	85.2	89.2	96.3	98.4	100.0	102.4	104.4	107.1
Europe	170	1.8	3.3	9.6	21.3	30.8	41.3	53.4	80.0	100.0	121.0	139.5	155.2
Middle East	405	44.2	49.3	56.1	68.1	76.9	82.7	88.6	95.3	100.0	103.6	109.1	116.2
Western Hemisphere	205	4.1	12.9	40.1	56.3	68.3	77.2	84.9	92.5	100.0	106.3	116.0	128.5

2004, International Monetary Fund : *International Financial Statistics Yearbook*

Exports, f.o.b.

		1992	1993	1994	1995	1996	1997	1998	1999	2000	2001	2002	2003
		\multicolumn{12}{c}{Billions of US Dollars}
World	001	3,775.9	3,768.9	4,287.7	5,129.6	5,351.5	5,537.2	5,450.7	5,649.8	6,360.7	6,128.9	6,419.1	7,430.8
Industrial Countries	110	2,662.6	2,598.2	2,915.2	3,471.5	3,565.6	3,644.7	3,674.1	3,746.0	3,998.5	3,873.6	3,989.6	4,561.4
United States	111	448	465	513	585	625	689	682	702	781	731	694	724
Canada	156	134	145	165	192	202	214	214	238	277	260	252	273
Australia	193	43	43	48	53	60	63	56	56	64	63	65	72
Japan	158	340	362	397	443	411	421	388	419	479	403	417	472
New Zealand	196	9.8	10.5	12.2	13.6	14.4	14.2	12.0	12.5	13.3	13.7	14.4	16.5
Euro Area													
Austria	122	44.4	40.2	45.0	57.6	57.8	58.6	62.7	†64.1	64.2	66.7	70.9	87.6
Belgium	124	....	126	144	176	175	172	179	†179	188	190	216	255
Belgium-Luxembourg	126	124	120	137	170	166	166	....	....	....	....	....	....
Finland	172	24.0	23.4	29.7	39.6	38.4	39.3	43.0	†41.8	45.5	42.8	44.6	52.5
France	132	236	210	234	285	288	290	306	†302	300	297	312	366
Germany	134	422	382	430	524	524	512	543	†543	550	571	613	751
Greece	174	9.4	9.1	8.8	11.0	11.9	11.1	10.7	10.5	10.7	9.5	10.3	13.2
Ireland	178	28.5	29.3	34.1	44.6	48.7	53.5	64.5	†71.2	77.1	83.0	87.4	92.4
Italy	136	178	169	191	234	252	240	246	†235	240	244	254	294
Luxembourg	137	6	6	7	8	7	7	8	†8	8	8	9	10
Netherlands	138	140	139	156	196	197	195	201	†200	209	216	222	259
Portugal	182	18.4	15.4	18.0	23.2	24.6	24.0	†24.8	†25.2	23.3	24.4	25.5	30.6
Spain	184	64.8	61.0	72.9	91.0	102.0	104.4	109.2	†110.0	113.3	115.2	123.5	156.0
Denmark	128	41.7	38.2	43.1	51.5	51.5	49.1	48.8	50.4	50.4	51.0	56.2	65.7
Iceland	176	1.53	1.40	1.62	1.80	1.64	1.85	2.05	2.00	1.89	2.02	2.23	2.39
Norway	142	35.1	31.8	34.7	42.0	49.6	48.5	40.4	45.5	60.1	59.2	59.7	67.5
Sweden	144	56.1	49.9	61.3	79.8	84.9	82.9	85.0	84.8	86.9	75.8	81.3	101.2
Switzerland	146	†61	59	66	78	76	72	75	76	75	78	84	97
United Kingdom	112	190	181	204	242	262	281	272	268	282	267	276	304
Developing Countries	200	1,113.33	1,170.73	1,372.51	1,658.02	1,785.88	1,892.56	1,776.61	1,903.80	2,362.13	2,255.29	2,429.49	2,869.38
Africa	605	79.62	74.86	79.55	93.38	106.06	107.45	90.87	99.70	125.09	117.58	120.45	146.90
Algeria	612	11.5	10.4	8.9	10.3	13.2	....	....	....	....	....	18.6	....
Angola	614	3.8	2.9	3.0	3.7	5.1	5.0	3.5	5.4	7.7	6.4	7.5	9.2
Benin	638	.34	.38	.40	.42	.65	.42	.41	.42	.39	.37	.45	.54
Botswana	616	1.75	1.76	1.85	2.14	2.54	2.84	1.95	....	....	....	....	....
Burkina Faso	748	.064	.069	.107	.276	.233	.232	.319	.216	.166	.175	.166	....
Burundi	618	.07	.06	.12	.11	.04	.09	.06	.05	.05	.04	.03	.04
Cameroon	622	1.8	1.9	1.5	1.6	1.6	1.7	1.8	1.5	1.5	2.1	2.3	....
Cape Verde	624	–	–	–	.01	.01	.01	.01	.01	.01	.01	....	....
Central African Rep.	626	.11	.11	.15	.17	.15	.16	.15	.15	.16	.14	.15	....
Chad	628	.18	.13	.15	.24	.24	.24	.26	.24	.18	.19	.18	....
Congo, Rep. of	634	1.18	1.07	.96	1.17	1.35	1.67	1.37	1.56	2.49	....	....	....
Côte d'Ivoire	662	2.9	2.5	2.7	3.8	4.4	4.5	4.6	4.7	3.9	3.9	5.3	5.8
Equatorial Guinea	642	.05	.06	.06	.09	.18	.50	.44	.71	1.10	....	....	....
Ethiopia	644	.17	.20	.37	.42	.42	.59	.56	.47	.49	.46	.48	....
Gabon	646	2.1	2.3	2.4	2.7	3.2	3.0	1.9	2.4	2.5	2.6	....	....
Gambia, The	648	.057	.067	.035	.016	.021	.015	.021	.005	.015	.003	.002	....
Ghana	652	1.3	1.0	1.4	1.7	1.7	1.6	1.8	....	....	....	....	....
Guinea	656	....	....	....	.68	.66	.64	.63	.49	.62	.54	....	....
Guinea-Bissau	654	.006	.028	.086	.044	.028	.048	.027	.051	.062	.063	.054	.069
Kenya	664	1.3	1.4	1.6	1.9	2.1	2.1	2.0	1.7	1.7	1.9	2.1	2.4
Lesotho	666	.11	.13	.14	.16	.19	.20	.19	....	....	....	....	....
Madagascar	674	.28	.26	.37	.37	.46	.41	.56	.60	.82	.69	.50	....
Malawi	676	.40	.32	.34	.41	.48	.54	.43	.45	.38	.45	.41	....
Mali	678	.34	.48	.33	.44	.43	.56	.56	.57	.55	.73	.88	.93
Mauritius	684	1.30	1.30	1.35	1.54	1.80	1.59	1.65	1.59	1.56	1.63	1.80	1.94
Morocco	686	4.0	3.1	5.6	6.9	6.9	7.0	7.2	7.4	7.0	7.1	7.9	....
Namibia	728	1.34	1.24	1.31	1.41	1.42	1.34	1.23	1.23	1.32	1.18	....	....
Niger	692	.33	.29	.23	.29	.33	.27	.33	.29	.28	.27	.28	.34
Nigeria	694	12	10	9	†12	16	15	10	14	21	17	15	20
Rwanda	714	.07	.07	.03	.05	.06	.09	.06	.06	.05	.08	.06	.06
São Tomé & Príncipe	716	.005	.005	.006	.005	.005	.005	....	....	....	....	....	....
Senegal	722	.67	.71	.79	.99	.99	.90	.97	1.03	.92	1.00	1.07	1.33
Seychelles	718	.05	.05	.05	.05	.14	.11	.12	.15	.19	.22	.23	.28
Sierra Leone	724	.15	.12	.12	.04	.05	.02	.01	.01	.01	.03	.05	.09
South Africa	199	23.4	24.2	25.3	27.9	29.2	31.0	†26.4	26.7	30.0	29.3	29.7	36.5
Sudan	732	.3	.4	.5	.6	.6	.6	.6	.8	1.8	1.7	....	....
Swaziland	734	.64	.68	.79	.87	.86	.96	.97	.94	.91	1.05	.94	....
Tanzania	738	.42	.45	.52	.68	.78	.75	.59	.54	.66	.78	.87	.65
Togo	742	.27	.14	.33	.38	.44	.42	.42	.39	.36	.36	.43	.62
Tunisia	744	4.0	3.7	4.7	5.5	5.5	5.6	5.7	5.9	5.9	6.6	6.9	8.0
Uganda	746	.14	.18	.41	.46	.59	.55	.50	.52	.46	.46	.44	.56
Zambia	754	.76	.83	.93	1.04	1.04	.92	1.02	.52	.76	....	....	....
Zimbabwe	698	1.44	1.56	1.88	2.11	2.41	2.15	1.73	1.89	3.28	2.28	....	....
Asia *	505	585.86	646.31	768.45	932.71	973.01	1,038.86	986.17	1,051.51	1,266.45	1,182.35	1,297.88	1,547.40
Afghanistan, Islamic State of	512	.09	.18	.02	.03	....	....	....	....	....	....	....	....
Bangladesh	513	2.1	2.3	2.7	3.2	3.3	3.8	3.8	3.9	4.8	4.8	4.6	5.3
Bhutan	514	.1	.1	.1	.1	.1	.1	.1	.1	.1	.1	.1	....
Cambodia	522	....	....	....	....	....	1	1	1	1	1	1	2
China, P.R.: Mainland	924	85	92	121	149	151	183	184	195	249	266	326	438

Exports, f.o.b.

		1992	1993	1994	1995	1996	1997	1998	1999	2000	2001	2002	2003
							Billions of US Dollars						
Asia *(Cont.)													
China, P.R.: Hong Kong	532	119	135	151	174	181	188	174	174	202	190	200	224
China, P.R.: Macao	546	1.77	1.79	1.87	2.00	2.00	2.15	2.14	2.20	2.54	2.30	2.36	2.58
Fiji	819	.37	.38	.45	.54	.59	.52	.45	.48	.48	.44	.55	.68
India	534	19.6	21.6	25.0	30.6	33.1	35.0	33.4	35.7	42.4	43.4	49.3	57.1
Indonesia	536	34.0	36.8	40.1	45.4	49.8	53.4	48.8	48.7	62.1	56.4	58.1	61.1
Korea	542	77	82	96	125	130	136	132	144	172	150	162	194
Lao People's Dem. Rep.	544	.1	.2	.3	.3	.3	.4	.4	.3	.3	.3	.3	.4
Malaysia	548	40.8	47.1	58.8	73.9	78.3	78.7	73.3	84.6	98.2	88.0	93.3	99.4
Maldives	556	—	—	—	—	.1	.1	.1	.1	.1	.1	.1	.1
Mongolia	948	.4	.4	.4	.5	.4	.5	.3	.4	.5	.4	....	....
Myanmar	518	.54	.59	.80	.86	.75	.87	1.08	1.14	1.65	2.38	3.05	2.48
Nepal	558	.368	.384	.362	.345	.385	.406	.474	.602	.804	.737	.568	.662
Pakistan	564	7.3	6.7	7.4	8.0	9.3	8.7	8.5	8.4	9.0	9.2	9.9	11.9
Papua New Guinea	853	1.9	2.6	2.6	2.7	2.5	2.2	1.8	1.9	2.1	1.8	1.5	2.2
Philippines	566	9.8	11.1	13.3	17.5	20.4	24.9	29.4	36.6	39.8	32.7	36.5	37.0
Samoa	862	.006	.006	.004	.009	.010	.015	.015	.020	.014	.016	.014	.015
Singapore	576	63.5	74.0	96.8	118.3	125.0	125.0	109.9	114.7	137.8	121.8	125.2	144.2
Solomon Islands	813	.102	.129	.142	.168	.162	.157	.118	....	....	....	.058	
Sri Lanka	524	2.46	2.86	3.21	3.80	4.10	4.64	4.81	4.59	5.43	4.82	4.70	5.13
Thailand	578	32	37	45	56	56	57	54	58	69	65	68	81
Tonga	866	.0122	.0158	.0138	.0141	.0114	.0097	.0075	.0124	.0088	.0067	.0146	....
Vanuatu	846	.024	.023	.025	.028	.030	.035	.034	.026	.023	.016	.015	.021
Vietnam	582	....	....	....	....	7	9	9	12	14	15	17	20
* of which:													
Taiwan Province of China	528	81.4	84.6	92.9	111.6	115.7	121.1	110.5	121.5	147.8	122.5	130.5	....
Europe	170	159.84	157.66	201.96	255.78	277.06	286.71	281.09	279.58	340.79	360.68	396.82	509.84
Albania	914	.1	.1	.1	.2	.2	.1	.1	.2	.3	.3	.3	.5
Armenia	911	.08	.16	.22	.27	.29	.23	.22	.23	.29	.34	.51	.68
Azerbaijan	912	1.5	.7	.7	.6	.6	.8	.6	.9	1.7	2.3	....	....
Belarus	913	4	2	3	5	6	7	7	6	7	7	8	10
Bulgaria	918	4	4	4	5	7	5	4	4	5	5	6	8
Croatia	960	4.6	3.9	4.3	4.6	4.5	4.2	4.5	4.3	4.4	4.7	4.9	6.2
Cyprus	423	.99	.87	.97	1.23	1.40	1.10	1.06	1.00	.95	.98	.84	.92
Czech Republic	935	....	†14	†16	†22	22	23	26	26	29	33	38	49
Czechoslovakia	934	11.3	....	....	....	....	....	....	....	....	....	....	....
Estonia	939		.8	†1.3	1.8	2.1	2.9	3.1	2.9	3.1	3.3	3.4	4.5
Georgia	915	....	....	156	151	199	240	191	238	331	320	349	
Hungary	944	10.7	8.9	10.4	12.8	15.6	19.0	23.0	25.0	28.0	30.5	34.5	42.5
Kazakhstan	916	....	3.3	3.2	5.3	5.9	6.5	5.3	5.9	8.8	8.6	9.7	12.9
Kyrgyz Republic	917	....	.3	.3	.4	.5	.6	.5	.5	.5	.5	.5	.6
Latvia	941	1	1	1	1	1	2	2	2	2	2	2	3
Lithuania	946	....	2	2	3	3	4	4	3	4	4	5	7
Macedonia, FYR	962	....	1.1	1.1	1.2	1.1	1.2	1.3	1.2	1.3	1.2	1.1	1.4
Malta	181	1.54	1.36	1.57	1.91	1.73	1.63	1.83	1.98	2.44	1.96	2.23	....
Moldova	921	—	—	1	1	1	1	1	—	1	1	1	1
Poland	964	13	14	17	23	24	26	27	27	32	36	41	54
Romania	968	4.4	4.9	6.2	7.9	8.1	8.4	8.3	8.5	10.4	11.4	13.9	17.6
Russia	922	42	44	†68	83	91	89	75	76	106	103	107	134
Slovak Republic	936	....	5	7	9	9	8	11	10	12	13	14	22
Slovenia	961	†7	6	7	8	8	8	9	9	9	9	10	13
Turkey	186	15	15	18	22	23	26	27	27	28	31	35	47
Ukraine	926	8	8	10	13	14	14	13	12	15	16	18	23
Middle East	405	144.37	135.38	143.04	157.82	183.95	186.00	148.62	183.30	281.08	260.77	281.67	....
Bahrain, Kingdom of	419	3.5	3.7	3.6	4.1	4.7	4.4	3.3	4.4	6.2	5.6	5.8	6.4
Egypt	469	3.1	2.3	3.5	3.4	3.5	3.9	3.1	3.6	4.7	4.1	4.7	6.3
Iran, I.R. of	429	20	18	19	18	22	18	13	21	28	24	28	....
Israel	436	10	15	17	19	21	23	23	26	31	29	29	32
Jordan	439	1.22	1.25	1.42	1.77	1.82	1.84	1.80	1.83	1.90	2.29	2.77	....
Kuwait	443	6.6	10.2	11.3	12.8	14.9	14.2	9.6	12.2	19.4	16.2	15.4	19.4
Lebanon	446	.6	.5	.5	.7	.7	.6	.7	.7	.7	.9	1.0	1.5
Libya	672	11	8	9	8	8	7	5	8	10	9	8	
Oman	449	5.6	5.4	5.5	6.1	7.3	7.6	5.5	....	....	....	11.2	11.7
Qatar	453	....	....	3.1	3.5	3.8	3.8	4.9	7.1	....	....	....	....
Saudi Arabia	456	50	42	43	50	61	61	39	51	78	68	73	....
Syrian Arab Rep.	463	3.1	3.1	3.0	3.6	4.0	3.9	2.9	3.5	†19.3	21.6	28.1	....
United Arab Emirates	466	25	....	....	....	....	....	....	....	....	....	....	....
Yemen, Republic of	474	1	1	1	2	3	3	1	2	4	3	....	....
Western Hemisphere	205	147.60	158.10	182.93	223.54	251.39	278.78	275.67	294.05	353.54	341.23	340.91	351.41
Anguilla	312	.0005	.0010	.0009	.0005	.0016	.0016	.0032	.0026	.0040	.0032	.0043	....
Argentina	213	12	13	16	21	24	26	26	23	26	27	26	29
Aruba	314	....	....	....	—	—	—	—	.2	.1	.1	.1	.1
Bahamas, The	313	.2	.2	.2	.2	.2	.2	.3	.5	.6	.4	.4	.4
Barbados	316	.19	.19	.18	.24	.28	.28	.25	.26	.27	.26	.21	.21
Belize	339	.14	.14	.15	.16	.17	.18	.17	.19	.22	.17	.17	.20
Bolivia	218	.7	.7	1.0	1.1	1.1	1.2	1.1	1.1	1.2	1.3	1.3	1.6
Brazil	223	36	39	44	47	48	53	51	48	55	58	60	73
Chile	228	10.0	9.2	11.6	16.0	15.7	17.9	16.3	17.2	19.2	18.3	18.2	21.0
Colombia	233	6.9	7.1	8.4	10.1	10.6	11.5	10.9	11.6	13.0	12.3	11.9	12.7
Costa Rica	238	1.8	2.6	2.9	3.5	3.8	4.3	5.5	6.7	5.8	5.0	5.3	6.1

2004, International Monetary Fund: *International Financial Statistics Yearbook*

Exports, f.o.b.

		1992	1993	1994	1995	1996	1997	1998	1999	2000	2001	2002	2003
						Billions of US Dollars							
Western Hemisphere(Cont.)													
Dominica	321	.1	—	—	—	.1	.1	.1	.1	.1	—	—	—
Dominican Republic	243	.56	.51	.64	.87	.95	1.02	.88	.81	.97	.80	.83	1.04
Ecuador	248	3.0	2.9	3.8	4.3	4.9	5.3	4.2	4.5	4.9	4.7	5.0	6.0
El Salvador	253	.6	.7	.8	1.0	1.0	1.4	1.3	1.2	1.3	1.2	1.2	1.3
Grenada	328	.02	.02	.02	.02	.02	.02	.03	....	....	....	....	....
Guatemala	258	1.3	1.3	1.5	2.2	2.0	2.3	2.6	2.4	2.7	2.5	2.2	2.5
Guyana	336	.29	.41	.46	.45	.52	.64	.48	.52	.50	.48	.49	.63
Haiti	263	.073	.080	.082	.110	.090	.212	.320	.334	.318	.274	.280	.347
Honduras	268	.8	.8	.8	1.2	1.3	1.4	1.5	1.2	1.4	1.3	1.3	1.3
Jamaica	343	1.05	1.07	1.21	1.43	1.38	1.38	1.31	1.24	1.30	1.22	1.11	1.18
Mexico	273	46	52	61	80	96	110	117	136	166	159	161	165
Netherlands Antilles	353	1.6	1.3	1.4	....	....	....	....	....	1.9	2.3	1.6	....
Nicaragua	278	.2	.3	.3	.5	.5	.6	.6	.5	.6	.6	.6	....
Panama	283	.50	.55	.58	.63	....	.72	.78	.82	.86	.91	.85	.86
Paraguay	288	.7	.7	.8	.9	1.0	1.1	1.0	.7	.9	1.0	....	....
Peru	293	3.5	3.4	4.4	5.5	5.9	6.8	5.8	6.1	7.0	7.0	7.6	9.0
St. Lucia	362	.1	.1	.1	.1	.1	.1	.1	.1	—	—	—	....
St. Vincent & Grens	364	.08	.06	.05	.04	.05	.05	.05	.05	.05	.04	.04	.04
Suriname	366	.39	1.19	.45	.48	.54	.56	.51	.46	.51	.40	.47	.64
Trinidad and Tobago	369	1.7	1.7	1.9	2.5	2.5	2.5	2.3	2.8	4.3	4.3	3.9	....
Uruguay	298	1.7	1.6	1.9	2.1	2.4	2.7	2.8	2.2	2.3	2.1	1.9	2.2
Venezuela	299	14	15	16	18	23	22	17	20	32	27	24	5
Memorandum Items													
Euro Area	163	....	....	....	....	....	....	791.46	Ü 884.59	922.63	936.32	1,006.81	1,170.79
Oil Exporting Countries	999	193.72	180.81	187.49	209.58	247.92	250.19	198.25	236.00	349.09	313.54	317.65	....
Non-Oil Developing Countries	201	918.93	990.35	1,186.02	1,450.01	1,539.17	1,643.87	1,580.38	1,669.57	2,014.29	1,942.57	2,108.94	2,524.06

Imports, c.i.f.

		1992	1993	1994	1995	1996	1997	1998	1999	2000	2001	2002	2003
						Billions of US Dollars							
World	001	3,884.9	3,831.7	4,355.0	5,202.0	5,453.1	5,635.3	5,565.3	5,786.4	6,565.1	6,333.8	6,570.1	7,644.4
Industrial Countries	110	2,711.1	2,558.6	2,906.4	3,436.5	3,559.4	3,636.5	3,739.8	3,931.0	4,338.7	4,159.0	4,266.6	4,917.4
United States	111	554	603	689	771	822	899	944	1,059	1,259	1,179	1,202	1,305
Canada	156	129	139	155	168	175	201	206	220	245	227	227	245
Australia	193	44	46	53	61	65	66	65	69	72	64	73	89
Japan	158	233	242	275	336	349	339	280	311	380	349	337	383
New Zealand	196	9.2	9.6	11.9	14.0	14.7	14.5	12.5	14.3	13.9	13.3	15.0	18.6
Euro Area													
Austria	122	54.1	48.6	55.3	66.4	67.3	64.8	68.2	†69.6	69.0	70.4	72.8	88.3
Belgium	124	....	114	130	160	164	157	165	†165	177	179	198	235
Belgium-Luxembourg	126	125	112	126	155	153	155	....	....	....	....	....	....
Finland	172	21.2	18.0	23.2	28.1	29.3	29.8	32.3	†31.6	33.9	32.1	33.6	41.6
France	132	240	203	235	281	282	272	290	†295	311	302	311	371
Germany	134	402	346	385	464	459	446	471	†474	495	486	492	602
Greece	174	22.8	20.2	21.4	26.8	29.7	27.9	29.4	28.7	29.2	29.9	31.2	44.4
Ireland	178	22.5	22.0	25.9	33.1	35.9	39.2	44.6	†47.2	51.5	51.3	51.5	53.3
Italy	136	189	148	169	206	208	210	218	†220	238	236	246	292
Luxembourg	137	8	8	8	10	10	9	10	†11	11	11	12	14
Netherlands	138	135	125	141	177	181	178	188	†188	198	195	194	232
Portugal	182	30.3	24.3	27.3	33.3	35.2	35.1	†38.5	†39.8	38.2	39.4	38.3	40.8
Spain	184	99.8	79.7	92.2	113.3	121.8	122.7	133.1	†144.4	152.9	153.6	163.5	208.5
Denmark	128	35.5	31.3	36.6	45.7	45.0	44.4	46.3	44.5	44.4	44.3	49.3	56.4
Iceland	176	1.68	1.34	1.47	1.76	2.03	1.99	2.49	2.50	2.59	2.25	2.27	2.79
Norway	142	25.9	24.0	27.3	33.0	35.6	35.7	37.5	34.2	34.4	33.0	34.9	39.5
Sweden	144	50.0	42.7	51.7	64.7	66.9	65.7	68.6	68.8	73.0	63.5	66.7	82.7
Switzerland	146	†62	57	64	77	74	71	74	75	76	77	79	92
United Kingdom	112	221	206	226	265	287	307	314	318	334	321	335	381
Developing Countries	200	1,173.89	1,273.18	1,448.64	1,765.49	1,893.64	1,998.74	1,825.48	1,855.44	2,226.39	2,174.82	2,303.48	2,727.04
Africa	605	78.78	75.82	82.58	101.06	100.45	105.93	104.66	99.97	104.01	108.18	109.81	....
Algeria	612	8.3	8.0	9.2	10.1	9.1	....	....	....	....	....	10.8	....
Benin	638	.58	.57	.43	.75	.65	.68	.74	.75	.61	.55	.68	.76
Botswana	616	1.89	1.77	1.64	1.91	1.72	2.26	2.39	2.21	2.47	1.81	.58	....
Burkina Faso	748	.47	.51	.35	.45	.65	.59	.73	.57	.49	.55	.58	....
Burundi	618	.22	.20	.22	.23	.13	.12	.16	.12	.15	.14	.13	.16
Cameroon	622	1.2	1.1	1.1	.9	1.1	1.2	1.5	1.3	1.3	1.6	2.8	....
Cape Verde	624	.18	.15	.21	.25	.23	.24	.23	.25	.23	.23	....	....
Central African Rep	626	.15	.13	.14	.17	.14	.14	.15	.13	.12	.11	.12	....
Chad	628	.24	.20	.18	.37	.33	.33	.36	.32	.32	.68	1.65	....
Congo, Rep. of	634	.45	.58	.63	.67	1.55	.93	.68	.82	.46	....	....	....
Côte d'Ivoire	662	2.4	2.1	1.9	2.9	2.9	2.8	3.3	2.8	2.4	2.4	2.5	3.3
Djibouti	611	.2	.2	.2	.2	.2	.1	.2	.2	....	....	....	....
Equatorial Guinea	642	.06	.06	.04	.05	.29	.33	.32	.43	.45	....	....	....
Ethiopia	644	.84	.79	1.03	1.15	1.40	....	1.52	1.54	1.26	1.81	1.67	....
Gabon	646	.70	.85	.76	.88	.96	1.10	1.10	.84	.99	.86	....	....
Gambia, The	648	.22	.26	.21	.18	.26	.17	.23	.19	.19	.13	.15	....
Ghana	652	2.2	3.9	2.1	1.9	2.1	2.3	2.6	3.5	3.0	....	....	....
Guinea-Bissau	654	.096	.061	.164	.133	.087	.089	.063	.051	.049	.062	.058	.069
Kenya	664	1.8	1.8	2.1	3.0	2.9	3.3	3.2	2.8	3.1	3.2	3.2	3.7
Lesotho	666	.90	.87	.85	.99	1.00	1.02	.86	.78	.73	.68	.79	1.02
Madagascar	674	.45	.47	.44	.54	.52	.50	.54	.59	.73	.74	.51	....
Malawi	676	.74	.55	.49	.47	.62	.78	.52	.67	.53	.56	.70	....
Mali	678	.61	.63	.59	.77	.77	.74	.76	.61	.59	.73	.74	1.13
Mauritania	682	....	....	.40	....	....	....	....	....	....	....	....	....
Mauritius	684	1.62	1.72	1.93	1.98	2.29	2.19	2.07	2.25	2.09	1.99	2.17	2.38
Morocco	686	7.3	6.7	8.3	10.0	9.7	9.5	10.3	9.9	11.5	11.0	11.9	....
Mozambique	688	....	....	1	1	1	1	1	1	1	....	....	....
Namibia	728	1.28	1.33	1.41	1.62	1.67	1.75	1.65	1.61	1.55	1.55	....	....
Niger	692	.48	.37	.33	.37	.45	.37	.47	.34	.32	.33	.37	.46
Nigeria	694	8.3	5.5	6.6	†8.2	6.4	9.5	9.2	8.6	8.7	11.6	7.5	10.9
Rwanda	714	.29	.33	.12	.24	.26	.30	.28	.25	.21	.25	.20	.25
São Tomé & Príncipe	716	.029	.032	.030	.029	.022	.016	....	....	....	....	....	....
Senegal	722	1.03	1.09	1.02	1.41	1.44	1.33	1.46	1.37	1.34	1.43	1.60	2.03
Seychelles	718	.19	.24	.21	.23	.38	.34	.38	.43	.34	.48	.42	.43
Sierra Leone	724	.15	.15	.15	.13	.21	.09	.09	.08	.15	.18	.26	.30
South Africa	199	20	20	23	31	30	33	†29	27	30	28	29	41
Sudan	732	.8	.9	1.2	†1.2	1.5	1.6	1.9	1.4	1.6	1.6	....	....
Swaziland	734	.87	.79	.84	1.01	1.06	1.07	1.08	1.07	1.05	1.13	.98	....
Tanzania	738	1.5	1.5	1.5	1.7	1.4	1.3	1.5	1.6	1.5	1.7	1.7	1.4
Togo	742	.39	.18	.22	.59	.66	.65	.59	.49	.48	.52	.58	.84
Tunisia	744	6.4	6.2	6.6	7.9	7.7	7.9	8.4	8.5	8.6	9.5	9.5	10.9
Uganda	746	.51	.61	.87	1.06	1.19	1.32	1.42	1.34	1.54	1.59	1.11	1.25
Zambia	754	.80	.81	.59	.70	.84	.82	1.09	.88	1.10	....	....	....
Zimbabwe	698	2.20	1.82	2.24	2.66	2.80	3.28	2.62	2.13	1.81	1.74	....	....
Asia *	505	610.98	686.81	802.57	987.85	1,035.85	1,056.85	878.68	956.55	1,196.45	1,117.67	1,214.43	1,461.13
Afghanistan, Islamic State of	512	.43	.74	.14	.05	....	....	....	....	....	....	....	....
Bangladesh	513	3.7	4.0	4.6	6.5	6.6	6.9	7.0	7.7	8.4	8.3	7.9	9.5
Bhutan	514	.1	.1	.1	.1	.1	.1	.1	.2	.2	.2	.2	....
Cambodia	522	....	....	....	....	....	1	1	1	1	1	2	2

Imports, c.i.f.

		1992	1993	1994	1995	1996	1997	1998	1999	2000	2001	2002	2003
							Billions of US Dollars						
Asia *(Cont.)													
China, P.R.: Mainland	924	81	104	116	132	139	142	140	166	225	244	295	413
China, P.R.: Hong Kong	532	123	139	162	193	199	209	185	180	213	201	208	232
China, P.R.: Macao	546	1.97	2.03	2.13	2.04	2.00	2.08	1.95	2.04	2.25	2.39	2.53	2.76
Fiji	819	.63	.72	.83	.89	.99	.97	.72	.90	.83	.79	.90	1.17
India	534	23.6	22.8	26.8	34.7	37.9	41.4	43.0	47.0	51.5	50.4	56.5	71.2
Indonesia	536	27.3	28.3	32.0	40.6	42.9	41.7	27.3	24.0	33.5	31.0	31.3	32.6
Korea	542	82	84	102	135	150	145	93	120	160	141	152	179
Lao People's Dem. Rep.	544	.3	.4	.6	.6	.7	.7	.6	.5	.5	.5	.4	.5
Malaysia	548	39.9	45.7	59.6	77.7	78.4	79.0	58.3	65.4	82.0	73.9	79.9	81.9
Maldives	556	.2	.2	.2	.3	.3	.3	.4	.4	.4	.4	.4	.5
Mongolia	948	.4	.4	.3	.4	.5	.5	.5	.5	.6	.6	....	....
Myanmar	518	.66	.82	.89	1.35	1.37	2.06	2.69	2.32	2.40	2.88	2.35	2.09
Nepal	558	.78	.89	1.16	1.33	1.40	1.69	1.25	1.42	1.57	1.47	1.42	1.75
Pakistan	564	9.4	9.5	8.9	11.5	12.1	11.6	9.3	10.2	10.9	10.2	11.2	13.0
Papua New Guinea	853	1.48	1.30	1.52	1.45	1.74	1.71	1.24	1.23	1.15	1.07	1.23	1.30
Philippines	566	15.5	18.7	22.6	28.3	34.1	38.6	31.5	32.6	37.0	34.9	37.2	39.5
Samoa	862	.110	.105	.081	.095	.100	.097	.097	.115	.106	.130	.113	.137
Singapore	576	72	85	103	125	131	132	105	111	135	116	116	128
Solomon Islands	813	.112	.137	.139	.154	.151	.184	.150	....	.093	....	.048	....
Sri Lanka	524	3.50	4.00	4.77	5.31	5.44	5.86	5.91	5.96	7.18	5.97	6.10	6.67
Thailand	578	41	46	54	71	72	63	43	50	62	62	65	76
Tonga	866	.063	.061	.069	.077	.075	.073	.069	.073	.069	.073	.089	....
Vanuatu	846	.082	.079	.089	.095	.098	.094	.088	.096	.087	.102	.089	.105
Vietnam	582	....	....	....	....	11	12	12	12	16	16	19	25
of which:													
Taiwan Province of China	528	72.2	77.1	85.5	103.7	101.3	113.9	104.9	111.0	139.9	107.3	112.8	....
Europe	170	177.00	188.08	216.81	290.26	334.44	355.65	349.53	309.77	358.25	374.40	421.02	538.26
Albania	914	.2	.6	.6	.7	.8	.6	.8	1.1	1.1	1.3	1.5	1.9
Armenia	911	.21	.25	.39	.67	.86	.89	.90	.80	.88	.87	.99	1.27
Azerbaijan	912	.9	.6	.8	.7	1.0	.8	1.1	1.0	1.2	1.4	....	....
Belarus	913	3	3	3	6	7	9	9	7	9	8	9	12
Bulgaria	918	4	5	4	6	7	5	5	5	7	7	8	11
Croatia	960	4.5	4.7	5.2	7.5	7.8	9.1	8.4	7.8	7.9	9.1	10.7	14.1
Cyprus	423	3.31	2.59	3.02	3.69	3.98	3.70	3.69	3.62	3.85	3.92	4.09	4.47
Czech Republic	935	....	†16	†18	†26	29	29	30	29	34	38	43	....
Czechoslovakia	934	13.2	....	....	....	....	....	....	....	....	....	....	....
Estonia	939	....	.9	†1.7	2.5	3.2	4.4	4.6	4.1	4.2	4.3	4.8	6.5
Georgia	915	....	....	338	392	687	944	887	585	654	684	733	....
Hungary	944	11.1	12.5	14.3	15.4	18.1	21.1	25.7	27.9	32.0	33.7	37.8	47.6
Kazakhstan	916	....	3.9	3.6	3.8	4.2	4.3	4.3	3.7	5.0	6.4	6.6	8.3
Kyrgyz Republic	917	.4	.4	.3	.5	.8	.7	.8	.6	.6	.5	.6	.7
Latvia	941	....	1	1	2	3	3	3	3	3	4	4	5
Lithuania	946	....	2	2	4	5	6	6	5	5	6	8	10
Macedonia, FYR	962	....	1.2	1.5	1.7	1.6	1.8	1.9	1.8	2.1	1.7	1.9	2.2
Malta	181	2.35	2.17	2.44	2.94	2.80	2.55	2.67	2.85	3.40	2.73	2.84	....
Moldova	921	1	1	1	1	1	1	1	1	1	1	....	....
Poland	964	16	19	21	29	37	42	46	46	49	50	55	68
Romania	968	6.3	6.5	7.1	10.3	11.4	11.3	11.8	10.4	13.1	15.6	17.9	24.0
Russia	922	41	36	†55	69	75	79	64	44	49	59	66	82
Slovak Republic	936	....	7	7	9	11	11	14	12	13	16	17	24
Slovenia	961	†6	7	7	9	9	9	10	10	10	10	11	14
Turkey	186	23	29	23	36	44	49	46	41	55	41	50	66
Ukraine	926	7	10	11	15	18	17	15	12	14	16	17	23
Middle East	405	136.89	135.75	128.18	142.13	154.45	160.62	158.87	162.53	184.02	202.11	211.96	....
Bahrain, Kingdom of	419	4.3	3.9	3.7	3.7	4.3	4.0	3.6	3.7	4.6	4.3	5.0	5.1
Egypt	469	8.3	8.2	10.2	11.8	13.0	13.2	16.2	16.0	14.0	12.8	12.6	11.1
Iran, I.R. of	429	26	21	14	12	15	14	14	13	14	18	21	....
Israel	436	15.5	22.6	25.2	29.6	31.6	30.8	29.3	33.2	31.4	35.4	35.5	36.3
Jordan	439	3.3	3.5	3.4	3.7	4.3	4.1	3.8	3.7	4.6	4.8	5.0	....
Kuwait	443	7.3	7.0	6.7	7.8	8.4	8.2	8.6	7.6	7.2	7.9	9.0	10.8
Lebanon	446	4.2	†2.2	2.6	5.5	7.5	7.5	7.1	6.2	6.2	7.3	6.4	7.2
Libya	672	5.1	5.6	4.3	4.1	4.4	4.6	4.7	4.2	3.7	4.4	4.4	....
Oman	449	3.77	4.11	3.91	4.25	4.58	5.03	5.68	4.67	5.04	5.80	6.01	6.57
Qatar	453	2.02	1.89	1.93	3.40	2.87	3.32	3.41	2.50	....	....	4.05	....
Saudi Arabia	456	33	28	23	28	28	29	30	28	30	31	32	37
Syrian Arab Rep.	463	3.5	4.1	5.5	4.7	5.4	4.0	3.9	3.8	†16.7	19.6	21.0	....
United Arab Emirates	466	17	20	21	21	23	30	25	33	38	....	....	....
Yemen, Republic of	474	3	3	2	2	2	2	2	2	2	2	....	....
Western Hemisphere	205	173.08	188.88	221.43	250.24	276.66	329.44	346.37	334.47	390.75	382.64	354.87	367.33
Anguilla	312	.0372	.0355	.0364	.0324	.0599	.0616	.0714	.0919	.0945	.0777	.0699	....
Argentina	213	15	17	22	20	24	30	31	26	25	20	9	14
Aruba	314	....	....	....	.6	.6	.6	.8	.8	.8	.8	.8	.8
Bahamas, The	313	1.0	1.0	1.1	1.2	1.4	1.7	1.9	1.8	2.1	1.9	1.7	1.8
Barbados	316	.52	.58	.61	.77	.83	1.00	1.01	1.11	1.16	1.09	1.04	1.13
Belize	339	.27	.28	.26	.26	.26	.29	.30	.37	.52	.52	.52	.55
Bolivia	218	1.1	1.2	1.2	1.4	1.6	1.9	2.0	1.8	1.8	1.7	1.8	1.6
Brazil	223	23	28	36	54	57	65	61	52	59	58	50	51
Chile	228	10.2	11.1	11.8	15.9	19.1	20.8	19.9	16.0	18.5	17.8	17.2	19.4
Colombia	233	6.5	9.8	11.9	13.9	13.7	15.4	14.6	10.7	11.5	12.8	12.7	13.9

Imports, c.i.f.

		1992	1993	1994	1995	1996	1997	1998	1999	2000	2001	2002	2003
							Billions of US Dollars						
Western Hemisphere(Cont.)													
Costa Rica	238	2.4	3.5	3.8	4.1	4.3	5.0	6.2	6.4	6.4	6.6	7.2	7.7
Dominica	321	.1	.1	.1	.1	.1	.1	.1	.1	.1	.1	.1	.1
Dominican Republic	243	2.5	2.4	3.4	3.6	4.1	4.8	5.6	6.0	7.4	....	....	....
Ecuador	248	2.4	2.6	3.6	4.2	3.9	5.0	5.6	3.0	3.7	5.4	6.4	6.5
El Salvador	253	1.7	1.9	2.2	2.9	2.7	3.0	3.1	3.1	3.8	3.9	3.9	4.4
Grenada	328	.11	.12	.12	.12	.15	.17	.20	.20	.25	....	....	....
Guatemala	258	2.5	2.6	2.8	3.3	3.1	3.9	4.7	4.4	4.8	5.6	6.1	6.5
Guyana	336	.44	.48	.51	.53	.60	.63	....	....	....	.58	.56	1.02
Haiti	263	.278	.355	.252	.653	.665	.648	.797	1.025	1.036	1.013	1.130	1.188
Honduras	268	1.0	1.1	1.1	1.6	1.8	2.1	2.5	2.7	2.9	2.9	3.0	3.3
Jamaica	343	1.68	2.13	2.22	2.82	2.97	3.13	3.04	2.90	3.33	3.36	3.53	3.64
Mexico	273	65	68	83	76	94	115	131	149	183	176	177	179
Netherlands Antilles	353	1.9	1.9	1.8	....	....	....	....	....	2.8	2.8	2.2	....
Nicaragua	278	.9	.7	.9	1.0	1.2	1.4	1.5	1.9	1.8	1.8	1.8	....
Panama	283	2.02	2.19	2.40	2.51	2.78	3.00	3.40	3.52	3.38	2.96	2.98	3.09
Paraguay	288	1.4	1.7	2.1	2.8	2.9	3.1	2.5	1.7	2.1	2.0	....	....
Peru	293	4.9	4.9	6.7	9.3	9.4	10.3	9.9	8.2	8.9	....	....	....
St. Lucia	362	.3	.3	.3	.3	.3	.3	.3	.4	.4	.4	.3	....
St. Vincent & Grens	364	.13	.13	.13	.14	.13	.19	.19	.20	.16	.19	.17	.20
Suriname	366	.54	.99	.42	.59	.50	.57	.55	.56	.52	.46	.49	.70
Trinidad and Tobago	369	1.1	1.5	1.1	1.7	2.1	3.0	3.0	2.7	3.3	3.6	3.6	....
Uruguay	298	2.0	2.3	2.8	2.9	3.3	3.7	3.8	3.4	3.5	3.1	2.0	2.2
Venezuela	299	14.1	12.5	9.2	12.6	9.9	14.6	15.8	14.1	16.2	18.0	11.8	9.0
Memorandum Items													
Euro Area	163	....	....	....	....	....	....	709.27	Ü 830.50	911.42	898.96	906.68	1,094.41
Oil Exporting Countries	999	153.17	142.71	132.38	153.21	154.61	168.92	153.83	149.50	171.91	185.61	182.51	....
Non-Oil Developing Countries	201	1,019.81	1,130.75	1,317.31	1,613.78	1,740.93	1,831.68	1,673.37	1,707.85	2,056.94	1,991.24	2,120.14	2,521.18

2004, International Monetary Fund : *International Financial Statistics Yearbook*

Export Unit Values/Export Prices

Indices of Unit Values (Prices) In Terms of US Dollars: 2000=100

		1992	1993	1994	1995	1996	1997	1998	1999	2000	2001	2002	2003
World	001	113.4	107.7	110.8	121.6	119.4	111.9	105.5	103.9	100.0	96.5	97.0	106.5
Industrial Countries	110	114.8	108.5	111.6	123.1	120.5	111.8	108.1	105.5	100.0	97.6	98.2	109.2
United States	111	96.3	96.9	98.9	103.9	104.5	103.1	99.7	98.4	100.0	99.2	98.2	99.7
Canada	156	92.9	91.0	92.1	98.9	100.2	98.2	97.4	105.7	100.0	97.8	95.1	105.6
Australia	193	108.9	102.2	106.8	116.3	117.7	113.6	100.9	96.2	100.0	98.2	100.0	109.9
Japan	158	104.9	109.9	116.3	123.6	111.9	102.5	96.0	99.2	100.0	91.4	87.6	90.9
New Zealand	196	104.1	107.5	113.2	123.2	124.5	116.4	98.5	98.8	100.0	100.7	99.3	111.0
Euro Area													
Belgium	124	....	104.2	108.9	125.8	122.9	112.1	110.3	105.2	100.0	99.3	103.4	120.4
Belgium-Luxembourg (1995=100	126	93.3	85.8	88.1	100.0	97.1	87.7	....	....	....	....	....	....
Finland	172	122.4	102.1	113.3	145.1	139.1	120.5	117.0	107.1	100.0	92.8	92.3	106.0
France	132	146.6	134.1	†139.8	158.7	154.5	137.2	136.3	113.7	100.0	96.8	98.0	117.5
Germany	134	140.9	127.0	128.3	148.5	138.4	120.5	118.1	111.5	100.0	99.0	101.5	118.3
Greece	174	121.8	112.8	115.8	133.7	138.3	125.7	118.8	123.1	100.0	104.9	112.3	134.8
Ireland	178	116.2	108.5	109.8	119.8	118.9	113.9	109.8	110.0	100.0	98.3	103.2	114.7
Italy	136	121.4	105.9	107.2	115.9	127.7	116.3	115.1	109.7	100.0	101.3	104.5	....
Netherlands	138	120.0	109.9	112.7	130.0	124.2	113.9	108.4	101.3	100.0	100.4	99.2	114.2
Portugal	182	146.1	134.9	132.8	144.2	131.6	119.2	116.2	109.3	100.0	92.9	96.3	112.0
Spain	184	137.8	116.2	115.3	131.9	131.2	117.2	114.9	108.9	100.0	99.7	105.1	124.9
Denmark	128	121.8	111.0	114.4	130.4	128.4	114.9	111.8	107.9	100.0	98.9	102.4	122.2
Norway	142	88.9	78.2	76.1	87.4	92.6	85.6	71.2	77.9	100.0	93.1	93.3	104.3
Sweden	144	124.8	102.2	108.3	130.5	132.0	117.0	111.8	106.5	100.0	90.1	93.8	110.3
Switzerland	146	113.9	108.3	116.2	131.6	127.1	112.2	111.2	108.9	100.0	102.0	....	....
United Kingdom	112	105.9	101.6	105.6	112.2	112.0	111.2	106.6	103.3	100.0	95.3	99.2	....
Developing Countries	200	107.5	104.1	107.3	116.0	115.2	111.1	96.7	98.2	100.0	92.7	92.6	97.0
Africa	605	112.2	104.5	104.8	124.7	119.3	116.3	107.6	101.8	100.0	93.7	96.5	....
Kenya	664	93.1	92.8	98.6	116.8	111.6	127.2	125.2	100.6	100.0	....	....	....
Mauritius	684	108.3	104.1	107.0	117.3	126.4	111.3	111.4	105.4	100.0	91.7	96.6	109.8
Morocco	686	114.1	104.7	103.8	124.1	128.5	118.5	114.5	110.2	100.0	94.4	99.1	....
South Africa	199	108.2	103.7	107.4	123.0	114.5	112.3	103.6	99.9	100.0	93.4	95.6	....
Tunisia (1990=100)	744	94.6	84.2	87.5	....	....	....	....	....	....	....	....	....
Asia	505	111.6	110.0	113.5	121.8	118.9	114.4	99.7	98.6	100.0	91.9	89.5	91.9
China, P.R.: Hong Kong	532	105.2	104.9	106.4	109.8	109.6	107.7	103.6	100.6	100.0	97.6	95.0	93.8
India	534	117.3	112.0	113.6	107.5	102.6	116.8	106.8	101.0	100.0	94.3	91.9	....
Indonesia	536	93.1	91.0	90.3	103.1	109.0	103.6	80.8	64.9	100.0	89.9	95.5	102.7
Korea	542	152.6	146.8	150.6	161.8	140.5	127.9	102.0	99.6	100.0	86.9	83.1	85.1
Malaysia (1995=100)	548	78.8	76.7	84.2	100.0	94.6	90.5	78.8	....	....	....	....	....
Pakistan	564	92.3	89.8	96.7	117.7	114.2	115.0	117.2	109.4	100.0	93.9	89.9	96.2
Papua New Guinea	853	70.2	77.4	87.3	99.0	99.4	97.2	81.2	80.3	100.0	89.4	85.5	....
Philippines	566	138.1	130.9	134.9	139.7	145.3	134.1	104.6	120.2	100.0	82.8	75.9	....
Singapore	576	113.2	111.6	113.2	119.9	119.4	111.7	†97.2	96.2	100.0	92.5	†90.5	89.7
Sri Lanka	524	87.3	86.9	89.1	98.6	102.1	104.5	109.9	100.6	100.0	96.2	90.7	96.2
Thailand	578	101.7	103.0	106.5	116.4	126.7	122.1	106.2	102.1	100.0	98.6	91.5	98.6
Europe	170	112.7	107.9	109.4	119.7	116.2	111.0	109.8	104.2	100.0	99.0	99.7	110.6
Hungary	944	115.9	111.4	114.9	128.7	125.0	117.3	115.4	108.3	100.0	100.7	106.3	121.7
Latvia	941	....	65.5	91.0	112.1	114.1	109.9	108.1	104.9	100.0	99.1	103.4	120.8
Poland	964	114.0	107.8	110.6	125.7	122.1	113.4	115.0	107.9	100.0	101.9	106.8	117.8
Turkey	186	120.8	117.4	†113.9	128.3	122.6	116.8	112.1	104.5	100.0	97.4	95.7	105.3
Middle East	405	77.3	69.9	70.1	76.7	86.7	82.4	59.7	74.7	100.0	89.3	....	....
Israel	436	99.0	99.5	98.0	102.7	†102.7	101.8	98.8	99.9	100.0	†96.4	96.4	100.6
Jordan	439	93.1	92.2	95.8	111.3	116.9	113.5	107.2	104.5	100.0	101.3	101.6	....
Oman	449	67.4	58.4	56.9	61.3	72.7	69.7	44.6	64.9	100.0	86.1	90.9	104.2
Saudi Arabia	456	64.5	56.0	56.3	62.3	73.6	69.6	44.9	65.1	100.0	86.5	....	....
Western Hemisphere	205	98.4	93.7	100.4	107.9	113.6	113.3	100.0	113.7	100.0	94.3	117.6	125.8
Argentina	213	101.8	102.0	104.7	110.6	117.8	114.2	102.4	90.9	100.0	96.6	92.9	101.9
Bolivia	218	147.6	125.3	131.8	141.3	137.6	98.0	86.8	85.8	100.0	91.3	81.0	93.4
Brazil	223	97.4	94.1	98.7	102.9	106.5	112.7	99.8	93.8	100.0	95.0	94.5	101.6
Colombia	233	77.6	77.2	102.9	111.6	104.3	115.0	102.4	95.4	100.0	89.1	85.4	87.3
Costa Rica (1990=100)	238	71.1	68.7	....	....	....	....	....	....	....	....	....	....
Ecuador	248	83.5	68.5	72.8	74.7	87.5	85.7	64.9	77.9	100.0	88.1	94.8	105.4
Guatemala (1990=100)	258	67.0	67.6	68.7	....	....	....	....	....	....	....	....	....
Guyana (1995=100)	336	133.5	102.6	101.2	100.0	166.6	97.1	91.7	....	....	....	....	....
Honduras	268	89.7	91.5	99.5	131.9	118.0	134.7	137.6	103.0	100.0	100.7	95.9	....
Peru	293	88.9	75.0	88.5	107.2	106.8	103.6	83.9	82.7	100.0	83.6	86.6	97.2
Memorandum Items													
Oil Exporting Countries	999	77.4	70.4	70.3	78.6	88.6	84.2	58.9	69.6	100.0	86.8	....	....
Non-Oil Developing Countries	201	111.6	109.0	112.7	121.3	118.7	114.7	102.6	102.6	100.0	93.6	94.1	97.6

Import Unit Values/Import Prices

		1992	1993	1994	1995	1996	1997	1998	1999	2000	2001	2002	2003
		\multicolumn{12}{c}{*Indices of Unit Values (Prices) In Terms of US Dollars: 2000=100*}
World.........................	001	**108.6**	**102.7**	**105.9**	**116.5**	**115.2**	**109.0**	**101.8**	**99.8**	**100.0**	**96.4**	**95.8**	**104.4**
Industrial Countries.........	110	**110.8**	**103.9**	**106.7**	**117.4**	**115.6**	**108.5**	**102.5**	**100.5**	**100.0**	**96.5**	**96.3**	**105.7**
United States..................	111	94.9	94.6	96.2	100.6	101.6	99.1	93.1	93.9	100.0	96.5	94.1	96.9
Canada..........................	156	99.4	98.2	98.6	101.8	102.1	101.2	94.3	95.7	100.0	98.8	98.2	102.0
Australia........................	193	106.0	106.1	111.4	117.0	116.9	110.7	101.6	102.0	100.0	94.3	94.5	103.8
Japan............................	158	94.4	96.4	99.1	107.6	102.1	98.6	86.7	90.4	100.0	90.9	86.8	93.1
New Zealand...................	196	103.5	103.6	109.8	121.4	123.9	117.8	99.0	100.0	100.0	93.9	97.0	107.5
Euro Area													
Belgium........................	124	....	98.0	103.3	120.7	119.2	109.5	106.0	102.7	100.0	99.5	102.2	119.7
Belgium-Luxembourg (1995=100	126	92.5	84.0	86.3	100.0	97.0	88.4	....	....	....	....	....	....
Finland..........................	172	116.7	100.6	109.7	131.2	126.6	113.3	106.2	102.3	100.0	94.3	96.3	114.8
France..........................	132	140.3	125.9	†130.9	149.0	145.9	129.8	128.8	108.4	100.0	95.1	94.7	113.5
Germany.......................	134	128.1	114.4	118.8	138.2	129.0	114.9	110.7	104.2	100.0	97.1	97.2	110.4
Ireland..........................	178	113.9	103.9	108.0	120.7	119.0	113.4	109.0	106.6	100.0	100.0	102.7	115.1
Italy.............................	136	117.1	102.5	104.0	115.7	122.2	112.2	107.2	101.3	100.0	99.1	100.5	....
Netherlands...................	138	123.9	110.1	112.4	127.6	122.7	112.4	107.8	103.3	100.0	99.7	103.0	116.4
Portugal........................	182	137.0	128.1	124.7	137.7	130.0	115.0	109.3	106.0	100.0	88.9	91.0	110.3
Spain............................	184	132.5	112.1	112.7	126.4	124.9	111.9	107.2	102.4	100.0	96.6	98.4	117.5
Denmark.......................	128	117.2	106.6	109.9	127.7	125.7	114.2	112.6	108.1	100.0	98.2	101.6	119.2
Norway.........................	142	143.3	127.6	129.4	144.9	141.2	126.5	117.6	109.0	100.0	98.2	102.8	116.1
Sweden.........................	144	115.6	98.0	103.4	119.2	122.3	109.5	104.2	102.7	100.0	92.7	98.6	116.2
Switzerland....................	146	125.7	117.0	120.3	136.0	130.0	116.7	112.0	106.1	100.0	101.6	....	....
United Kingdom..............	112	107.5	100.4	105.9	115.6	114.1	112.0	106.5	102.8	100.0	94.8	95.9	....
Developing Countries........	200	**99.8**	**98.1**	**102.7**	**112.9**	**112.9**	**109.7**	**98.9**	**96.7**	**100.0**	**96.2**	**93.9**	**99.0**
Africa............................	605	**111.3**	**106.4**	**111.0**	**121.0**	**112.0**	**110.4**	**101.6**	**102.5**	**100.0**	**92.7**	**94.5**	**....**
Kenya...........................	664	98.2	86.4	81.8	102.8	101.1	105.0	104.8	97.8	100.0	....	....	113.4
Mauritius.......................	684	104.5	102.3	107.7	117.8	122.1	106.5	99.1	100.2	100.0	97.0	98.8	....
Morocco........................	686	120.1	121.1	138.3	146.2	151.6	134.0	116.1	113.6	100.0	91.0	97.4	....
South Africa...................	199	109.2	102.8	104.6	116.4	106.9	106.1	98.8	98.2	100.0	93.3	93.2	....
Asia..............................	505	**102.7**	**101.1**	**105.6**	**114.0**	**114.3**	**108.8**	**96.6**	**95.3**	**100.0**	**95.2**	**92.9**	**96.1**
China, P.R.: Hong Kong.....	532	103.6	103.1	105.9	111.2	109.8	107.2	101.9	99.6	100.0	96.8	93.0	92.8
India.............................	534	118.6	99.0	95.6	99.9	104.2	102.7	91.3	96.5	100.0	96.4	103.7	....
Korea............................	542	113.5	111.0	110.1	116.3	112.0	104.7	87.4	87.3	100.0	91.0	87.5	95.6
Pakistan........................	564	87.9	83.8	90.3	98.5	95.5	96.8	85.8	92.6	100.0	94.0	94.8	108.5
Philippines.....................	566	175.2	167.7	174.0	173.6	178.8	162.1	120.1	117.3	100.0	79.9	83.3	....
Singapore......................	576	103.2	101.9	106.7	114.9	114.2	106.8	93.0	93.3	100.0	96.5	95.9	98.9
Thailand........................	578	85.5	85.8	88.4	99.8	110.8	106.2	97.7	95.1	100.0	108.5	102.3	109.5
Europe..........................	170	**112.1**	**102.5**	**103.6**	**115.0**	**114.3**	**107.3**	**103.2**	**99.6**	**100.0**	**98.4**	**98.0**	**109.3**
Hungary........................	944	117.7	109.7	112.1	123.4	122.7	113.8	110.5	105.4	100.0	100.9	106.1	122.1
Poland..........................	964	123.7	108.4	109.9	116.4	122.7	114.6	113.8	106.3	100.0	99.6	101.5	116.1
Turkey..........................	186	104.9	98.4	†105.3	123.0	115.6	105.6	101.2	95.7	100.0	99.7	98.5	106.3
Middle East....................	405	**96.5**	**94.4**	**97.3**	**106.6**	**107.8**	**102.6**	**98.8**	**97.7**	**100.0**	**99.0**	**100.7**	**106.5**
Israel............................	436	104.2	100.7	102.8	111.5	†110.7	105.7	99.9	97.0	100.0	†98.6	98.5	104.4
Jordan..........................	439	88.0	87.8	84.6	95.6	103.0	100.8	99.9	97.5	100.0	102.2	104.9	....
Western Hemisphere........	205	**70.3**	**74.4**	**82.8**	**102.3**	**103.9**	**116.3**	**105.4**	**98.5**	**100.0**	**99.2**	**91.0**	**92.1**
Argentina......................	213	111.1	108.2	109.8	115.7	114.6	111.9	106.0	100.0	100.0	96.9	93.8	94.1
Brazil............................	223	50.4	54.5	66.5	95.4	98.9	124.8	105.3	96.0	100.0	99.8	87.0	86.0
Colombia.......................	233	103.7	102.1	113.3	121.2	122.5	119.4	110.3	102.4	100.0	98.2	95.7	95.0
Memorandum Items													
Oil Exporting Countries.....	999	**72.6**	**73.5**	**80.2**	**99.0**	**92.8**	**95.3**	**98.8**	**102.4**	**100.0**	**100.6**	**101.3**	**112.0**
Non-Oil Developing Countries.	201	**100.4**	**98.6**	**103.2**	**113.2**	**113.3**	**110.0**	**98.9**	**96.6**	**100.0**	**96.1**	**93.8**	**98.8**

2004, International Monetary Fund: *International Financial Statistics Yearbook*

Terms of Trade

		1992	1993	1994	1995	1996	1997	1998	1999	2000	2001	2002	2003
		Percent Change over Previous Year; Calculated from Indices												
World	001	.9	.5	ñ.3	ñ.2	ñ.6	ñ1.0	.9	.4	ñ3.9	ñ	1.2	.7
Industrial Countries	110	.6	.7	.1	.3	ñ.6	ñ1.1	2.3	ñ.4	ñ4.7	1.1	.9	1.2
United States	111	−.7	.8	.4	.5	−.5	1.1	2.9	−2.1	−4.6	2.8	1.5	−1.3
Canada	156	−1.8	−.8	.7	4.1	1.0	−1.1	6.3	7.0	−9.5	−1.0	−2.2	7.0
Australia	193	−2.3	−6.3	−.4	3.7	1.3	1.9	−3.2	−5.0	6.1	4.1	1.7	.1
Japan	158	2.7	2.6	2.9	−2.1	−4.5	−5.2	6.5	−.9	−8.9	.6	.3	−3.3
New Zealand	196	1.4	3.2	−.6	−1.6	−1.0	−1.7	.6	−.7	1.2	7.2	−4.5	.8
Euro Area													
Belgium	124	....	....	−.9	−1.1	−1.1	−.7	1.7	−1.7	−2.3	−.2	1.4	−.6
Belgium-Luxembourg	126	1.9	....	....	....	....	....	....	....	....	....	....	....
Finland	172	−2.9	−3.2	1.8	7.1	−.7	−3.1	3.6	−5.0	−4.5	−1.6	−2.5	−3.7
France	132	2.5	1.9	.2	−.3	−.5	−.2	.1	−.9	−4.7	1.8	1.7	−
Germany	134	2.4	.9	−2.8	−.4	−.2	−2.2	1.8	.3	−6.6	1.9	2.5	2.6
Greece	174	−5.5	−.7	−.5	3.0	4.8	.8	−3.0	−.1	5.6	−1.2	1.4	−1.0
Ireland	178	−.7	2.3	−2.6	−2.3	.6	.6	.3	2.4	−3.1	−1.7	2.2	−.8
Italy	136	1.3	−.3	−.4	−2.7	4.3	−.9	3.7	.7	−7.6	2.2	1.8	....
Netherlands	138	−1.4	3.1	.4	1.6	−.6	.1	−.7	−2.5	2.0	.7	−4.4	1.9
Portugal	182	3.1	−1.3	1.2	−1.7	−3.4	2.4	2.6	−3.0	−3.0	4.5	1.2	−4.0
Spain	184	2.3	−.3	−1.4	2.0	.7	−.4	2.4	−.8	−6.0	3.2	3.5	−.5
Denmark	128	.9	.2	−.1	−1.9	−	−1.6	−1.2	.5	.2	.7	−	1.8
Iceland	176	−2.3	−5.2	−1.2	.8	−4.2	.6	....	....	....	....	....	....
Norway	142	−6.1	−1.3	−4.0	2.5	8.8	3.1	−10.5	18.1	39.9	−5.1	−4.4	−1.0
Sweden	144	−	−3.4	.4	4.6	−1.4	−1.1	.5	−3.4	−3.6	−2.8	−2.1	−.2
Switzerland	146	−2.0	2.2	4.3	.2	1.0	−1.6	3.2	3.4	−2.6	.4	....	....
United Kingdom	112	.9	2.7	−1.3	−2.8	1.2	1.1	.8	.4	−.5	.5	2.9	....
Developing Countries	200	2.1	ñ1.5	ñ1.5	ñ1.8	ñ.7	ñ.7	ñ3.4	3.8	ñ1.5	ñ3.7	2.5	ñ.7
Africa	605	.9	ñ2.6	ñ3.8	9.1	3.4	ñ1.1	.5	ñ6.2	.7	1.1	1.0	....
Burkina Faso	748	−20.6	−5.4	−20.3	10.2	−5.7	....	....	....	....	....	....	....
Chad	628	−1.6	7.5	....	....	....	....	....	....	....	....	....	....
Kenya	664	−2.5	13.4	12.2	−5.7	−2.8	9.7	−1.5	−13.8	−2.8	....	....	....
Mauritius	684	4.8	−1.8	−2.4	.2	3.9	.9	7.5	−6.4	−4.9	−5.5	3.4	−.9
Morocco	686	.8	−8.9	−13.3	13.1	−.1	4.3	11.6	−1.7	3.1	3.7	−1.9	....
South Africa	199	−.1	1.8	1.7	2.9	1.4	−1.2	−.9	−3.0	−1.8	.1	2.5	....
Togo	742	18.8	18.8	18.8	18.8	337.7	−15.5	−13.7	−32.7	3.4	−62.3	−19.3	−20.0
Uganda	746	....	....	89.2	−3.9	−26.1	8.4	4.6	3.7	....	....	....	....
Asia	505	1.1	.1	ñ1.2	ñ.6	ñ2.6	1.1	ñ1.9	.3	ñ3.4	ñ3.5	ñ.1	ñ.8
China, P.R.: Hong Kong	532	.7	.2	−1.2	−1.7	1.0	.7	1.2	−.7	−1.0	.9	1.3	−1.1
India	534	5.8	14.4	5.1	−9.5	−8.4	15.5	2.9	−10.5	−4.5	−2.2	−9.4	....
Korea	542	.1	−1.6	3.4	1.3	−9.4	−2.6	−4.5	−2.2	−12.3	−4.5	−.5	−6.3
Pakistan	564	.2	2.0	−	11.5	.2	−.8	14.9	−13.5	−15.3	−.1	−5.0	−6.5
Philippines	566	−15.9	−1.0	−.6	3.8	1.0	1.8	5.2	17.6	−2.4	3.6	−12.1	....
Singapore	576	−3.3	−.2	−3.1	−1.7	.2	−	−	−1.5	−2.9	−4.1	−1.6	−3.9
Sri Lanka	524	19.9	4.2	−1.0	−.6	1.0	5.3	....	....	....	....	....	....
Thailand	578	1.1	1.0	.3	−3.2	−2.0	.5	−5.4	−1.2	−6.9	−9.2	−1.6	.6
Europe	170	2.0	4.7	.4	ñ1.5	ñ2.3	1.8	2.8	ñ1.7	ñ4.4	.6	1.0	ñ.5
Hungary	944	−.7	3.1	.9	1.8	−2.3	1.3	1.3	−1.6	−2.7	−.2	.4	−.5
Poland	964	9.5	7.8	1.2	7.2	−7.8	−.5	2.1	.5	−1.5	2.4	2.7	−3.5
Turkey	186	3.3	3.6	−9.4	−3.6	1.7	4.3	.1	−1.3	−8.5	−2.3	−.6	2.0
Middle East	405	1.3	ñ7.6	ñ2.8	ñ.1	11.7	ñ.1	ñ24.7	26.5	30.8	ñ9.9	....	....
Israel	436	.7	3.9	−3.5	−3.3	.7	3.8	2.6	4.2	−2.9	−2.2	−	−1.4
Jordan	439	2.0	−.6	7.7	2.8	−2.5	−.7	−4.8	−	−6.7	−.9	−2.3	....
Syrian Arab Rep	463	−1.5	3.8	−4.8	11.2	−.4	−7.8	....	....	....	....	....	....
Western Hemisphere	205	11.0	ñ10.0	ñ3.7	ñ13.1	3.8	ñ11.0	ñ2.6	21.8	ñ13.4	ñ4.9	35.8	5.8
Argentina	213	5.1	2.9	1.1	.2	7.6	−.7	−5.4	−5.9	10.0	−.3	−.7	9.4
Brazil	223	30.3	−10.6	−14.0	−27.3	−.1	−16.2	4.9	3.1	2.4	−4.8	14.2	8.7
Colombia	233	−6.1	1.2	20.0	1.4	−7.6	13.2	−3.5	.3	7.3	−9.3	−1.6	3.0
Costa Rica	238	−4.0	1.8	....	....	....	....	....	....	....	....	....	....
Memorandum Items													
Oil Exporting Countries	999	ñ2.0	ñ10.2	ñ8.4	ñ9.4	20.1	ñ7.5	ñ32.4	14.0	47.1	ñ13.7	....	....
Non-Oil Developing Countries	201	2.2	ñ.7	ñ1.1	ñ1.9	ñ2.2	ñ.5	ñ.6	2.4	ñ5.8	ñ2.7	3.2	ñ1.6

Terms of Trade

Indices

Index Numbers: 2000=100

		1992	1993	1994	1995	1996	1997	1998	1999	2000	2001	2002	2003
World	001	104.4	104.8	104.6	104.3	103.7	102.7	103.7	104.1	100.0	100.0	101.2	102.0
Industrial Countries	110	103.6	104.4	104.5	104.8	104.2	103.1	105.4	105.0	100.0	101.1	102.0	103.3
Developing Countries	200	107.8	106.1	104.5	102.7	102.0	101.3	97.8	101.5	100.0	96.3	98.7	98.0
Africa	605	100.8	98.2	94.5	103.0	106.5	105.4	105.9	99.3	100.0	101.1	102.1	....
Asia	505	108.7	108.8	107.5	106.9	104.1	105.2	103.2	103.5	100.0	96.5	96.4	95.6
Europe	170	100.5	105.2	105.7	104.1	101.6	103.5	106.4	104.6	100.0	100.6	101.7	101.2
Middle East	205	139.9	125.9	121.3	105.4	109.4	97.4	94.8	115.5	100.0	95.1	129.2	136.6
Western Hemisphere	405	80.1	74.0	72.0	71.9	80.4	80.3	60.4	76.5	100.0	90.1	....	....

2004, International Monetary Fund : *International Financial Statistics Yearbook*

Balance of Payments

		1992	1993	1994	1995	1996	1997	1998	1999	2000	2001	2002	2003
						Trade Balance							
						Expressed in Millions of US Dollars							
All Countries	010	42,700	69,941	94,797	118,183	99,553	114,647	69,572	42,487	11,999	ñ8,564	33,839	....
Industrial Countries	110	37,101	99,908	94,660	122,300	93,396	96,616	26,637	ñ111,238	ñ241,996	ñ208,671	ñ206,436	....
United States	111	−95,127	−130,551	−163,781	−172,330	−189,100	−196,164	−244,736	−343,716	−449,784	−424,085	−479,405	−544,300
Canada	156	7,381	10,136	14,834	25,855	31,091	18,565	15,922	28,292	45,047	45,275	36,436	41,513
Australia	193	1,643	−29	−3,277	−4,223	−635	1,849	−5,332	−9,761	−4,813	1,786	−5,431	−15,254
Japan	158	124,764	139,417	144,191	131,787	83,585	101,600	122,389	123,325	116,716	70,214	93,829	106,395
New Zealand	196	1,627	1,719	1,408	971	523	903	912	−371	681	1,471	502	−428
Euro Area													
Austria	122	−7,690	−6,476	−7,914	−6,656	−7,315	−4,274	−3,684	−3,629	−2,737	−1,269	3,572	1,932
Belgium	124	....	....	....	....	....	....	....	....	....	....	8,734	9,532
Belgium-Luxembourg	126	3,700	5,780	6,901	9,555	8,690	7,703	6,981	7,027	2,591	3,707	....	....
Finland	172	4,009	6,449	7,723	12,437	11,314	11,544	12,490	12,168	13,684	12,659	12,882	13,390
France	132	2,371	7,516	7,249	10,998	14,936	26,899	24,940	17,988	−3,618	2,837	6,917	1,042
Germany	134	28,202	41,168	51,028	63,910	69,379	70,119	76,913	70,027	57,452	89,253	128,207	149,367
Greece	174	−11,561	−10,499	−11,273	−14,425	−15,505	−15,375	....	−17,951	−20,239	−19,087	−21,452	−25,606
Ireland	178	7,045	8,175	9,366	13,557	15,754	18,625	25,390	23,587	25,010	27,263	33,447	37,807
Italy	136	−200	28,889	31,568	38,729	54,118	39,878	35,631	23,437	9,549	15,540	16,533	9,700
Luxembourg	137	....	....	....	....	....	....	....	....	....	....	−2,073	−2,463
Netherlands	138	12,309	16,904	18,686	23,812	22,767	20,937	20,430	16,034	17,427	20,840	19,944	26,570
Portugal	182	−9,387	−8,050	−8,321	−8,910	−9,722	−10,342	−12,211	−13,714	−13,853	−13,301	−11,882	−12,444
Spain	184	−30,420	−14,999	−14,892	−18,415	−16,283	−13,407	−20,758	−30,339	−34,820	−32,539	−32,841	−42,923
Denmark	128	7,058	7,719	7,441	6,528	7,532	5,369	3,886	6,399	6,740	7,451	8,308	10,142
Iceland	176	2	181	272	206	19	5	−351	−307	−474	−75	150	−210
Norway	142	8,254	6,966	7,496	8,685	12,972	11,648	2,061	10,723	25,975	26,472	24,339	28,109
Sweden	144	6,720	7,548	9,558	15,978	18,636	17,999	17,632	15,714	15,215	13,832	16,631	18,933
Switzerland	146	−265	1,592	3,346	3,258	1,868	2,738	933	843	2,104	1,563	6,432	....
United Kingdom	112	−23,332	−19,648	−16,947	−19,006	−21,228	−20,203	−36,127	−47,012	−49,850	−58,477	−70,215	−77,296
Developing Countries	200	5,599	ñ29,967	137	ñ4,117	6,156	18,030	42,935	153,724	253,995	200,107	240,276	....
Africa	605	8,339	7,197	3,742	3,536	16,510	11,257	ñ4,657	5,618	31,192	19,364	15,768	....
Algeria	612	....	....	....	....	....	....	....	....	....	....	....	....
Angola	614	1,845	1,438	1,563	2,255	3,055	2,410	1,464	2,047	4,881	3,355	....	....
Benin	638	−215	−168	−54	−203	−32	−153	−158	−214	−124	−180	....	....
Botswana	616	187	267	510	555	750	895	77	675	....	....	....	....
Burkina Faso	748	−222	−243	−129	....	....	....	....	....	−312	−286	....	....
Burundi	618	−105	−99	−92	−63	−60	−9	−59	−42	−59	−69	−73	....
Cameroon	622	893	502	402	627	....	....	....	....	....	....	....	....
Cape Verde	624	−157	−143	−181	−217	−184	−172	−186	−213	−187	−194	−236	−291
Central African Rep.	626	−73	−26	15	....	....	....	....	....	....	....	....	....
Chad	628	−61	−63	−77	....	....	....	....	....	....	....	....	....
Comoros	632	−37	−28	−34	−42	....	....	....	....	....	....	....	....
Congo, Dem. Rep. of	636	....	....	....	....	....	....	....	....	....	....	....	....
Congo, Republic of	634	740	619	346	632	1,068	1,013	809	1,037	2,037	1,374	1,598	....
Côte d'Ivoire	662	995	748	1,289	1,376	1,824	1,793	1,720	1,895	1,486	1,528	2,819	2,524
Djibouti	611	−218	−184	−181	−171	....	....	....	....	....	....	....	....
Equatorial Guinea	642	−6	10	25	−31	−117	....	....	....	....	....	....	....
Eritrea	643	−334	−307	−411	−368	−455	−469	−480	−489	−435	....	....	....
Ethiopia	644	−823	−507	−554	−670	−585	−413	−799	−920	−645	−1,170	−975	....
Gabon	646	1,373	1,481	1,589	1,847	2,373	2,002	744	1,588	....	....	....	....
Gambia, The	648	−31	−57	−57	−40	−98	−87	....	....	....	....	....	....
Ghana	652	−470	−664	−342	−257	−367	−638	−901	−1,274	−830	−1,101	−692	....
Guinea	656	−91	−22	−170	−39	111	118	121	54	79	169	218	....
Guinea-Bissau	654	−77	−38	−21	−35	−35	−14	....	....	....	....	....	....
Kenya	664	−500	−247	−238	−750	−515	−886	−1,012	−975	−1,262	−1,347	−996	....
Lesotho	666	−823	−734	−667	−825	−812	−828	−673	−607	−516	−400	−381	....
Liberia	668	....	....	....	....	....	....	....	....	....	....	....	....
Madagascar	674	−144	−180	−96	−122	−120	−178	−154	−158	−174	−27	−117	....
Malawi	676	−15	−23	−160	−63	−78	−158	39	−127	−59	−44	−151	....
Mali	678	−163	−120	−114	−115	−119	16	−2	−35	−47	−10	163	....
Mauritania	682	−55	3	47	184	134	107	40	....	....	....	....	....
Mauritius	684	−159	−242	−397	−241	−326	−436	−264	−519	−392	−218	−188	....
Morocco	686	−2,463	−2,065	−2,107	−2,482	−2,193	−1,864	−2,319	−2,448	−3,235	−3,022	−3,061	−4,310
Mozambique	688	−630	−727	−767	−536	−478	−454	−491	−806	−682	−271	−536	−348
Namibia	728	−78	−42	−86	−130	−127	−272	−173	−200	−117	−179	−179	....
Niger	692	−49	−12	−44	−18	....	....	....	....	....	....	....	....
Nigeria	694	4,611	3,248	2,948	3,513	9,679	5,706	−240	4,288	....	....	....	....
Rwanda	714	−171	−200	−524	−162	−157	−185	−169	−185	−155	−152	−166	....
São Tomé & Príncipe	716	....	....	....	....	....	....	−12	−18	−22	−21	−23	....
Senegal	722	−331	−350	−203	−250	−276	−271	−313	−346	−417	−425	−537	....
Seychelles	718	−132	−165	−135	−161	−170	−190	−212	−224	−117	−205	−140	....
Sierra Leone	724	11	−69	−73	−127	−180	−56	−57	−81	−124	−136	−195	....
Somalia	726	....	....	....	....	....	....	....	....	....	....	....	....

2004, International Monetary Fund: *International Financial Statistics Yearbook*

Balance of Payments

Trade Balance
Expressed in Millions of US Dollars

		1992	1993	1994	1995	1996	1997	1998	1999	2000	2001	2002	2003
Africa(Cont.)													
South Africa	199	6,279	6,232	4,481	2,667	2,695	2,324	2,056	4,156	4,593	5,180	4,631	3,701
Sudan	732	−597	−227	−522	−510	−719	−828	−1,137	−476	440	304	−345	−297
Swaziland	734	−141	−104	−50	−197	−204	−104	−106	−131	−136	−77	−79	....
Tanzania	738	−929	−857	−790	−657	−449	−449	−776	−872	−704	−784	−609	....
Togo	742	−128	−111	−37	−129	−127	−108	−133	−98	−123	−159	....	....
Tunisia	744	−2,037	−2,064	−1,567	−1,989	−1,761	−1,955	−2,152	−2,141	−2,253	−2,369	−2,123	−2,269
Uganda	746	−271	−278	−251	−367	−348	−450	−656	−506	−500	−575	−633	....
Zambia	754	....	....	....	....	....	54	−153	−98	−221	....	....	....
Zimbabwe	698	−255	122	158	....	....	....	....	....	....	....	....	....
Asia*	505	3,684	ñ10,712	ñ6,953	ñ15,725	ñ23,587	29,133	138,391	135,926	112,634	106,366	129,356	....
Afghanistan, I.S. of	512	....	....	....	....	....	....	....	....	....	....	....	....
Bangladesh	513	−1,256	−1,113	−1,416	−2,324	−2,275	−1,711	−1,574	−2,077	−1,654	−2,049	−1,678	....
Bhutan	514	....	....	....	....	....	....	....	....	....	....	....	....
Brunei Darussalam	516	....	....	....	....	....	....	....	....	....	....	....	....
Cambodia	522	−179	−187	−255	−332	−428	−328	−365	−462	−538	−523	−563	....
China,P.R.: Mainland	924	5,183	−10,654	7,290	18,050	19,535	46,222	46,614	35,982	34,474	34,017	44,167	....
China,P.R.:Hong Kong	532	....	....	....	....	....	....	−7,833	−3,159	−8,193	−8,331	−5,053	−5,779
Fiji	819	−189	−282	−229	−242	−168	−283	−186	−116	....	....	....	....
India	534	−2,911	−2,093	−4,150	−6,719	−10,052	−10,028	−10,752	−8,679	−14,632	−12,833	−12,416	....
Indonesia	536	7,022	8,231	7,901	6,533	5,948	10,075	18,429	20,644	25,040	22,695	23,513	....
Kiribati	826	−32	−25	−21	....	....	....	....	....	....	....	....	....
Korea	542	−1,755	2,319	−2,860	−4,444	−14,965	−3,179	41,627	28,371	16,872	13,492	14,180	....
Lao People's Dem.Rep	544	−100	−150	−214	−316	−321	−283	−165	−190	−205	−217	....	....
Malaysia	548	3,150	3,037	1,577	−103	3,848	3,510	17,505	22,644	20,827	18,383	18,135	....
Maldives	556	−103	−125	−120	−151	−186	−217	−216	−262	−233	−236	−211	....
Mongolia	948	−29	21	34	25	−36	115	−62	−56	−73	−101	−156	....
Myanmar	518	−106	−636	−613	−831	−940	−1,143	−1,401	−887	−504	−271	....	....
Nepal	558	−376	−462	−790	−961	−1,106	−1,278	−757	−882	−814	−765	....	....
Pakistan	564	−2,803	−2,586	−2,239	−2,891	−3,656	−2,399	−1,984	−1,847	−1,157	−610	−596	−100
Papua New Guinea	853	625	1,470	1,326	1,408	1,017	677	695	856	1,095	881	....	....
Philippines	566	−4,695	−6,222	−7,850	−8,944	−11,342	−11,127	−28	4,959	3,814	−743	407	−1,253
Samoa	862	−84	−81	−65	−72	−81	−85	−77	−98	....	....	....	....
Singapore	576	−1,821	−2,724	1,354	4,907	5,653	4,681	14,347	11,976	12,298	14,768	18,549	....
Solomon Islands	813	14	−8	−	14	11	−28	−18	55	....	....	....	....
Sri Lanka	524	−715	−742	−1,085	−985	−800	−640	−505	−769	−1,044	−1,157	−1,406	....
Thailand	578	−4,161	−4,297	−3,726	−7,968	−9,488	1,572	16,238	14,013	11,701	8,543	9,081	11,606
Tonga	866	−39	−41	....	....	....	....	....	....	....	−57	....	....
Vanuatu	846	−49	−47	−50	−51	−51	−44	−42	−59	−50	−58	....	....
Vietnam	582	....	....	....	....	−2,775	−1,247	−989	972	375	481	−1,054	....
of which:													
Taiwan Prov.of China	528	12,718	11,450	11,849	13,235	17,543	13,882	10,316	14,705	13,624	19,864	24,193	24,899
Europe	170	ñ12,453	ñ23,072	ñ3,057	ñ15,479	ñ27,847	ñ41,786	ñ44,897	ñ13,805	3,513	8,841	3,924	....
Albania	914	−471	−490	−460	−475	−678	−535	−604	−663	−814	−1,027	−1,155	−1,336
Armenia	911	....	−98	−178	−403	−469	−559	−577	−474	−463	−420	−369	−440
Azerbaijan	912	....	....	....	−373	−694	−567	−1,046	−408	319	614	482	−98
Belarus	913	....	−528	−490	−666	−1,149	−1,407	−1,501	−570	−884	−807	−914	−1,234
Bosnia & Herzegovina	963	....	....	....	....	....	....	−3,116	−3,297	−2,622	−2,958	−3,340	−3,928
Bulgaria	918	−212	−885	−17	121	188	380	−381	−1,081	−1,176	−1,580	−1,594	−2,474
Croatia	960	....	−709	−1,278	−3,228	−3,488	−5,383	−4,072	−3,299	−3,204	−4,101	−5,649	−7,921
Cyprus	423	−2,315	−1,507	−1,736	−2,085	−2,183	−2,071	−2,426	−2,309	−2,606	−2,550	−2,859	−3,099
Czech Republic	935	....	−517	−1,408	−3,685	−5,706	−4,938	−2,647	−1,902	−3,095	−3,078	−2,240	....
Czechoslovakia	934	−1,834	....	....	....	....	....	....	....	....	....	....	....
Estonia	939	−90	−145	−356	−666	−1,019	−1,124	−1,115	−878	−768	−789	−1,089	−1,580
Georgia	915	....	....	....	....	....	−786	−695	−534	−512	−550	−483	−636
Hungary	944	−11	−4,021	−3,716	−1,459	−1,673	−1,328	−1,885	−2,170	−2,913	−2,237	−2,119	−3,365
Kazakhstan	916	....	....	....	114	−335	−276	−801	344	2,440	1,320	2,301	4,088
Kyrgyz Republic	917	....	−107	−86	−122	−252	−15	−221	−89	5	40	−54	....
Latvia	941	−40	3	−301	−580	−798	−848	−1,130	−1,027	−1,058	−1,351	−1,444	−1,998
Lithuania	946	....	−155	−205	−698	−896	−1,147	−1,518	−1,405	−1,104	−1,108	−1,315	−1,704
Macedonia, FYR	962	....	....	....	....	−317	−388	−515	−496	−690	−526	−768	....
Malta	181	−513	−568	−603	−810	−838	−721	−673	−663	−753	−566	−414	−689
Moldova	921	....	....	−54	−70	−260	−348	−388	−137	−294	−313	−378	−622
Poland	964	−131	−3,505	−575	−1,646	−7,287	−9,822	−12,836	−15,072	−12,307	−7,661	−7,249	−5,725
Romania	968	−1,194	−1,128	−411	−1,577	−2,470	−1,980	−2,625	−1,092	−1,684	−2,969	−2,611	−4,537
Russia	922	....	....	16,928	19,816	21,591	14,913	16,429	36,012	60,172	48,121	46,335	60,493
Slovak Republic	936	....	−912	61	−229	−2,283	−2,084	−2,351	−1,109	−895	....	−243	−624
Slovenia	961	789	−154	−336	−954	−826	−775	−792	−1,235	−1,139	−619	−124	−120
Tajikistan	923	....	....	....	....	....	....	....	....	....	....	−124	−120
Turkey	186	−8,190	−14,160	−4,216	−13,212	−10,614	−15,403	−14,264	−10,469	−22,410	−4,543	−8,337	−14,034
Turkmenistan	925	....	....	....	....	304	−231	....	....	....	....	....	....
Ukraine	926	....	....	−2,575	−2,702	−4,296	−4,205	−2,584	244	779	198	710	−269
Uzbekistan	927	....	....	....	....	....	....	....	....	....	....	....	....

2004, International Monetary Fund : *International Financial Statistics Yearbook*

Balance of Payments

Trade Balance
Expressed in Millions of US Dollars

		1992	1993	1994	1995	1996	1997	1998	1999	2000	2001	2002	2003
Middle East	405	12,640	7,399	22,164	24,151	40,348	38,346	ñ4,387	38,768	107,849	74,378	73,826	....
Bahrain, Kingdom of	419	−527	107	120	626	665	605	−28	894	1,849	1,610	1,190	1,611
Egypt	469	−5,231	−6,378	−5,953	−7,597	−8,390	−8,632	−10,214	−9,928	−8,321	−6,935	−5,762	−4,201
Iran, I.R. of	429	−3,406	−1,207	6,817	5,586	7,402	4,258	−1,168	7,597	13,138	....	....	....
Iraq	433	....	....	....	....	....	....	....	....	....	....	....	....
Israel	436	−4,769	−5,607	−5,486	−7,196	−6,954	−5,008	−3,051	−4,160	−3,034	−3,208	−3,894	−2,177
Jordan	439	−1,780	−1,899	−1,579	−1,518	−2,001	−1,813	−1,602	−1,460	−2,174	−2,007	−1,680	−1,915
Kuwait	443	−689	3,324	4,685	5,579	6,997	6,534	1,903	5,516	13,027	9,192	7,242	11,261
Lebanon	446	....	....	....	....	....	....	....	....	....	....	....	....
Libya	672	2,647	113	945	2,302	2,085	2,249	396	2,974	....	....	....	....
Oman	449	1,928	1,336	1,849	2,015	3,142	3,012	307	2,939	6,726	5,763	....	....
Qatar	453	....	....	....	....	....	....	....	....	....	....	....	....
Saudi Arabia	456	20,039	16,522	21,289	24,390	35,370	34,362	11,287	25,039	49,843	39,418	42,897	61,456
Syrian Arab Republic	463	159	−259	−1,275	−146	−338	454	−178	216	1,423	1,424	2,210	....
United Arab Emirates	466	....	....	....	....	....	....	....	....	....	....	....	....
West Bank and Gaza	487	....	....	....	−1,909	−2,364	−2,443	−2,411	−2,618	−2,303	−1,467	....	....
Yemen, Republic of	474	−862	−971	274	149	−31	−133	−785	358	1,313	766	689	377
Western Hemisphere	205	ñ6,610	ñ10,780	ñ15,760	ñ600	732	ñ18,921	ñ41,515	ñ12,783	ñ1,192	ñ8,842	17,401	....
Argentina	213	−1,396	−2,364	−4,139	2,357	1,760	−2,123	−3,097	−795	2,452	7,385	17,236	16,447
Aruba	314	−377	−392	−311	−425	−308	−387	−353	−592	−28	....	−534	....
Bahamas, The	313	−768	−738	−815	−931	−1,014	−1,116	−1,374	−1,428	−1,371	−1,151	....	....
Barbados	316	−278	−327	−355	−446	−456	−599	−651	−714	−744	−681	−702	....
Belize	339	−104	−119	−75	−66	−58	−90	−105	−124	−191	−214	−190	....
Bolivia	218	−432	−396	−30	−182	−236	−477	−656	−488	−364	−295	−340	54
Brazil	223	15,239	14,329	10,861	−3,157	−5,453	−6,652	−6,603	−1,261	−698	2,650	13,121	24,825
Chile	228	722	−990	732	1,381	−1,072	−1,428	−2,040	2,427	2,119	1,844	2,256	3,015
Colombia	233	1,234	−1,657	−2,229	−2,546	−2,092	−2,638	−2,450	1,775	2,633	579	239	326
Costa Rica	238	−472	−761	−606	−323	−249	−498	−399	580	−210	−820	−1,267	−1,170
Dominican Republic	243	−1,612	−1,443	−1,451	−1,391	−1,674	−1,995	−2,617	−2,904	−3,742	−3,503	−3,673	−2,444
Ecuador	248	1,018	214	149	−66	921	491	−1,132	1,588	1,395	−397	−998	−71
El Salvador	253	−962	−962	−1,170	−1,462	−1,242	−1,143	−1,306	−1,356	−1,740	−1,933	−1,871	−2,274
Guatemala	258	−1,044	−1,021	−997	−875	−643	−940	−1,409	−1,445	−1,657	−2,282	−2,950	....
Guyana	336	−61	−68	−41	−41	−20	−48	−54	−25	−80	−94	−68	....
Haiti	263	−139	−180	−111	−429	−416	−354	−341	....	....	....	....	....
Honduras	268	−151	−204	−250	−141	−287	−294	−323	−753	−658	−833	−836	−987
Jamaica	343	−425	−815	−551	−829	−994	−1,132	−1,131	−1,187	−1,442	−1,618	−1,871	....
Mexico	273	−15,934	−13,481	−18,464	7,089	6,533	623	−7,914	−5,584	−8,003	−9,954	−7,916	−5,624
Netherlands Antilles	353	−836	−838	−921	−1,035	−1,129	−975	−1,048	−1,117	−986	−1,114	−1,027	....
Nicaragua	278	−548	−392	−429	−385	−527	−728	−749	−1,071	−921	−897	−936	−972
Panama	283	−376	−334	−250	−589	−644	−685	−1,365	−1,386	−1,143	−696	−1,037	−1,092
Paraguay	288	9	79	−243	−270	−587	−865	−393	−441	−678	−614	−280	−260
Peru	293	−340	−776	−1,075	−2,241	−1,991	−1,678	−2,437	−655	−411	−195	306	731
Suriname	366	122	84	99	123	−2	36	−27	44	153	140	47	30
Trinidad and Tobago	369	696	547	741	588	382	−529	−741	64	969	718	....	....
Uruguay	298	−122	−387	−706	−563	−687	−704	−772	−897	−927	−775	48	182
Venezuela, Rep. Bol	299	1,322	3,275	7,625	7,013	13,770	8,954	952	6,471	16,664	7,460	13,034	15,043
ECCU													
Anguilla	312	−33	−33	−37	−46	−51	−53	−60	−78	−79	−65	−57	....
Antigua and Barbuda	311	−187	−208	−242	−238	−271	−275	−283	−315	−293	−283	−291	....
Dominica	321	−37	−43	−47	−53	−64	−65	−53	−66	−76	−71	....	....
Grenada	328	−80	−95	−94	−105	−122	−122	−137	−110	−138	−133	−139	....
Montserrat	351	−28	−22	−27	−22	5	−20	−18	−18	−18	−16	−21	....
St. Kitts and Nevis	361	−51	−63	−70	−81	−93	−85	−87	−90	−121	−112	−113	....
St. Lucia	362	−142	−139	−166	−155	−181	−222	−225	−251	−249	−218	−207	....
St. Vincent & Grens	364	−38	−61	−67	−57	−75	−105	−120	−127	−93	−109	−117	....

Memorandum Items

		1992	1993	1994	1995	1996	1997	1998	1999	2000	2001	2002	2003
Oil Exporting Ctys	999	45,882	44,646	60,133	66,033	100,441	92,843	41,365	96,253	193,777	140,612	136,965	....
Non-Oil Develop.Ctys	201	ñ40,283	ñ74,614	ñ59,996	ñ70,150	ñ94,285	ñ74,812	1,570	57,472	60,217	59,495	103,310	....

Balance of Payments

Current Account Balance
Excluding Exceptional Financing
Expressed in Millions of US Dollars

		1992	1993	1994	1995	1996	1997	1998	1999	2000	2001	2002	2003
All Countries	010	ñ104,638	ñ66,164	ñ63,142	ñ59,206	ñ52,292	ñ4,944	ñ90,063	ñ133,989	ñ153,159	ñ150,670	ñ126,248	....
Industrial Countries	110	ñ38,472	42,329	6,833	42,765	34,227	73,783	ñ39,795	ñ184,323	ñ290,664	ñ247,300	ñ274,897	....
United States	111	−47,999	−81,963	−118,062	−109,472	−120,170	−135,979	−209,532	−296,846	−413,442	−385,699	−473,943	−530,664
Canada	156	−21,160	−21,822	−13,024	−4,328	3,378	−8,233	−7,839	1,765	19,622	16,209	14,447	17,268
Australia	193	−11,124	−9,684	−17,146	−19,323	−15,810	−12,384	−18,014	−22,295	−15,481	−8,712	−17,365	−30,554
Japan	158	112,574	131,637	130,255	111,044	65,792	96,814	118,749	114,604	119,660	87,798	112,447	136,215
New Zealand	196	−1,071	−746	−2,384	−3,003	−3,891	−4,304	−2,157	−3,515	−2,460	−1,307	−2,269	−3,531
Euro Area													
Austria	122	−753	−1,013	−2,992	−5,448	−4,890	−5,221	−5,258	−6,655	−4,864	−3,636	575	−2,392
Belgium	124	....	....	....	....	....	....	....	....	....	....	13,305	11,623
Belgium-Luxembourg	126	6,650	11,237	12,571	14,232	13,762	13,914	12,168	14,086	11,381	9,392		
Finland	172	−5,116	−1,135	1,110	5,231	5,003	6,633	7,340	8,045	8,975	8,704	10,148	9,295
France	132	3,893	8,990	7,415	10,840	20,561	37,801	37,699	31,870	18,581	28,759	13,789	4,384
Germany	134	−19,255	−13,817	−29,422	−26,966	−13,793	−9,143	−12,215	−22,695	−25,217	1,707	43,445	53,513
Greece	174	−2,140	−747	−146	−2,864	−4,554	−4,860	....	−7,295	−9,820	−9,400	−10,405	−11,225
Ireland	178	607	1,765	1,577	1,721	2,049	1,866	1,016	245	−516	−690	−1,399	−2,105
Italy	136	−29,217	7,802	13,209	25,076	39,999	32,403	19,998	8,111	−5,781	−652	−6,741	−21,942
Luxembourg	137	....	....	....	....	....	....	....	....	....	....	1,636	2,492
Netherlands	138	6,847	13,203	17,294	25,773	21,502	25,077	13,031	12,996	6,817	7,830	10,116	16,467
Portugal	182	−184	233	−2,196	−132	−5,216	−6,465	−7,833	−9,733	−11,114	−10,403	−8,118	−7,549
Spain	184	−21,537	−5,804	−6,389	792	407	2,512	−3,135	−13,761	−19,237	−16,404	−16,044	−23,676
Denmark	128	4,199	4,832	3,189	1,855	3,090	921	−2,008	2,915	2,412	4,920	4,991	6,139
Iceland	176	−160	37	116	52	−131	−128	−555	−589	−847	−338	−22	−572
Norway	142	4,471	3,522	3,760	5,233	10,969	10,036	6	8,378	25,851	26,171	24,769	28,643
Sweden	144	−8,827	−4,159	743	4,940	5,892	7,406	4,639	5,982	6,617	6,696	12,784	22,844
Switzerland	146	14,247	17,926	17,588	21,804	21,051	26,679	26,775	29,611	34,417	23,898	26,011	....
United Kingdom	112	−23,416	−17,966	−10,234	−14,291	−10,771	−1,562	−6,564	−39,547	−36,219	−32,141	−27,055	−33,457
Developing Countries	200	ñ66,165	ñ108,493	ñ69,975	ñ101,972	ñ86,520	ñ78,727	ñ50,268	50,334	137,506	96,630	148,649	....
Africa	605	ñ3,083	ñ6,299	ñ8,400	ñ13,208	2,077	ñ5,320	ñ18,534	ñ9,187	10,715	3,509	ñ1,816	....
Algeria	612	....	....	....	....	....	....	....	....	....	....	....	....
Angola	614	−735	−669	−340	−295	3,266	−884	−1,867	−1,710	796	−1,431	....	....
Benin	638	−120	−101	−23	−207	−57	−170	−151	−191	−111	−160	....	....
Botswana	616	198	427	212	300	495	721	170	517	....	....	....	....
Burkina Faso	748	−23	−71	15	....	....	....	....	....	−392	−381	....	....
Burundi	618	−60	−28	−17	10	−40	−1	−54	−27	−48	−35	−3	....
Cameroon	622	−397	−565	−56	90	....	....	....	....	....	....	....	....
Cape Verde	624	−12	−24	−46	−62	−35	−30	−59	−74	−58	−56	−72	−77
Central African Rep.	626	−83	−13	−25	....	....	....	....	....	....	....	....	....
Chad	628	−86	−117	−38	....	....	....	....	....	....	....	....	....
Comoros	632	−14	10	−7	−19	....	....	....	....	....	....	....	....
Congo, Dem. Rep. of	636	....	....	....	....	....	....	....	....	....	....	....	....
Congo, Republic of	634	−317	−553	−793	−625	−651	−156	−241	−231	648	−28	−34	....
Côte d'Ivoire	662	−1,013	−892	−14	−492	−162	−155	−290	−120	−241	−61	768	353
Djibouti	611	−87	−34	−46	−23	....	....	....	....	....	....	....	....
Equatorial Guinea	642	−11	3	−	−123	−344	....	....	....	....	....	....	....
Eritrea	643	33	35	27	−70	−85	−10	−293	−209	−105	....	....	....
Ethiopia	644	−120	−50	125	39	80	−40	−333	−465	15	−454	−150	....
Gabon	646	−168	−49	317	465	889	531	−596	390	....	....	....	....
Gambia, The	648	37	−5	8	−8	−48	−24	....	....	....	....	....	....
Ghana	652	−377	−559	−255	−144	−324	−550	−522	−965	−386	−325	−33	....
Guinea	656	−263	−57	−248	−216	−177	−91	−184	−215	−155	−102	−46	....
Guinea-Bissau	654	−104	−65	−48	−51	−60	−30	....	....	....	....	....	....
Kenya	664	−180	71	98	−400	−73	−457	−475	−90	−199	−340	−137	....
Lesotho	666	38	29	108	−323	−303	−269	−280	−221	−151	−95	−119	....
Liberia	668	....	....	....	....	....	....	....	....	....	....	....	....
Madagascar	674	−198	−258	−277	−276	−291	−266	−301	−252	−283	−170	−298	....
Malawi	676	−285	−166	−181	−78	−147	−276	−4	−158	−73	−60	−201	....
Mali	678	−241	−189	−163	−284	−261	−178	−164	−252	−237	−310	−149	....
Mauritania	682	−118	−174	−70	22	91	48	77	....	....	....	....	....
Mauritius	684	−	−92	−232	−22	34	−89	3	−124	−37	276	259	....
Morocco	686	−433	−521	−723	−1,296	−58	−169	−146	−171	−501	1,606	1,472	1,603
Mozambique	688	−352	−446	−467	−445	−421	−296	−429	−912	−764	−657	−712	−516
Namibia	728	50	110	85	176	116	90	162	162	164	−6	97	....
Niger	692	−159	−97	−126	−152	....	....	....	....	....	....	....	....
Nigeria	694	2,268	−780	−2,128	−2,578	3,507	552	−4,244	506	....	....	....	....
Rwanda	714	−83	−129	−72	57	−9	−62	−83	−141	−94	−102	−126	....
São Tomé & Príncipe	716	....	....	....	....	....	....	−10	−16	−19	−21	−23	....
Senegal	722	−401	−433	−187	−244	−199	−185	−247	−320	−332	−245	−317	....
Seychelles	718	−7	−7	24	−3	−59	−73	−118	−127	−51	−123	−131	....
Sierra Leone	724	−5	−58	−89	−118	−151	−55	−33	−99	−112	−98	−73	....
Somalia	726	....	....	....	....	....	....	....	....	....	....	....	....

2004, International Monetary Fund : *International Financial Statistics Yearbook*

Balance of Payments

Current Account Balance
Excluding Exceptional Financing
Expressed in Millions of US Dollars

		1992	1993	1994	1995	1996	1997	1998	1999	2000	2001	2002	2003
Africa(Cont.)													
South Africa	199	1,967	1,503	112	−2,206	−1,842	−2,223	−2,134	−528	−295	56	610	−1,456
Sudan	732	−506	−202	−602	−500	−827	−828	−957	−465	−557	−618	−1,008	−727
Swaziland	734	−41	−64	2	−30	−52	−3	−93	−35	−65	−53	−46	....
Tanzania	738	−714	−1,048	−711	−646	−511	−630	−920	−835	−499	−480	−251	....
Togo	742	−141	−82	−56	−122	−154	−117	−140	−127	−140	−169	....	....
Tunisia	744	−1,104	−1,323	−537	−774	−478	−595	−675	−442	−821	−840	−746	−730
Uganda	746	−100	−224	−208	−339	−252	−367	−503	−711	−825	−802	−421	....
Zambia	754	....	....	....	....	....	−353	−573	−447	−584	....	....	....
Zimbabwe	698	−604	−116	−425	....	....	....	....	....	....	....	....	....
Asia*	505	2,181	ñ13,271	ñ3,741	ñ38,940	ñ39,830	17,036	114,273	112,206	91,479	94,499	131,792	....
Afghanistan, I.S. of	512	....	....	....	....	....	....	....	....	....	....	....	....
Bangladesh	513	181	359	200	−824	−991	−286	−35	−364	−306	−535	739	....
Bhutan	514	....	....	....	....	....	....	....	....	....	....	....	....
Brunei Darussalam	516	....	....	....	....	....	....	....	....	....	....	....	....
Cambodia	522	−93	−104	−157	−186	−185	−210	−175	−188	−135	−86	−64	....
China,P.R.: Mainland	924	6,401	−11,609	6,908	1,618	7,243	36,963	31,472	21,115	20,518	17,401	35,422	....
China,P.R.:Hong Kong	532	....	....	....	....	....	....	2,529	10,284	7,083	9,941	12,596	16,155
Fiji	819	−61	−138	−113	−113	14	−34	−60	13	....	....	....	....
India	534	−4,485	−1,876	−1,676	−5,563	−5,956	−2,965	−6,903	−3,228	−2,640	1,761	4,656	....
Indonesia	536	−2,780	−2,106	−2,792	−6,431	−7,663	−4,889	4,096	5,785	7,985	6,899	7,823	....
Kiribati	826	−9	−4	1	....	....	....	....	....	....	....	....	....
Korea	542	−3,944	990	−3,867	−8,507	−23,006	−8,167	40,365	24,477	12,241	8,239	6,092	....
Lao People's Dem.Rep.	544	−111	−139	−284	−346	−347	−306	−150	−121	−8	−82	....	....
Malaysia	548	−2,167	−2,991	−4,520	−8,644	−4,462	−5,935	9,529	12,604	8,488	7,287	7,190	....
Maldives	556	−20	−54	−11	−18	−7	−35	−22	−79	−51	−57	−44	....
Mongolia	948	−56	31	46	39	−101	55	−129	−112	−156	−154	−158	....
Myanmar	518	−116	−230	−130	−261	−283	−416	−499	−285	−212	−309	....	....
Nepal	558	−181	−223	−352	−356	−327	−388	−67	−256	−299	−339	....	....
Pakistan	564	−1,877	−2,901	−1,812	−3,349	−4,436	−1,712	−2,248	−920	−85	1,878	3,854	3,597
Papua New Guinea	853	−160	474	402	492	189	−192	−29	95	345	282	....	....
Philippines	566	−1,000	−3,016	−2,950	−1,980	−3,953	−4,351	1,546	7,219	6,258	1,323	4,383	3,347
Samoa	862	−52	−39	6	9	12	9	20	−19	....	....	....	....
Singapore	576	5,915	4,211	11,400	14,800	13,977	14,908	18,544	15,184	13,280	16,137	18,704	....
Solomon Islands	813	−1	−8	−3	8	15	−38	8	21	....	....	....	....
Sri Lanka	524	−451	−382	−757	−770	−683	−395	−228	−561	−1,044	−265	−290	....
Thailand	578	−6,303	−6,364	−8,085	−13,554	−14,691	−3,021	14,243	12,428	9,313	6,192	7,014	7,965
Tonga	866	−	−6	....	....	....	....	....	....	....	−13	....	....
Vanuatu	846	−13	−15	−20	−18	−27	−19	−9	−33	−14	−15	....	....
Vietnam	582	....	....	....	....	−2,020	−1,528	−1,074	1,177	1,106	682	−604	....
*of which:													
Taiwan Prov.of China	528	8,550	7,042	6,498	5,474	10,923	7,051	3,438	7,992	8,851	17,891	25,630	29,202
Europe	170	ñ7,249	ñ17,555	4,760	ñ5,179	ñ14,271	ñ28,522	ñ26,792	ñ2,949	15,700	16,361	5,641	....
Albania	914	−51	15	−157	−12	−107	−272	−65	−155	−156	−217	−408	−407
Armenia	911	....	−67	−104	−218	−291	−307	−418	−307	−278	−201	−148	−186
Azerbaijan	912	....	....	....	−401	−931	−916	−1,365	−600	−168	−52	−768	−2,021
Belarus	913	....	−435	−444	−458	−516	−859	−1,017	−194	−323	−435	−378	−505
Bosnia & Herzegovina	963	....	....	....	....	....	....	−782	−1,098	−881	−1,217	−1,751	−2,096
Bulgaria	918	−360	−1,099	−32	−26	16	427	−62	−652	−704	−984	−827	−1,666
Croatia	960	....	625	554	−1,592	−1,049	−2,825	−1,468	−1,397	−461	−726	−1,920	−2,099
Cyprus	423	−638	110	74	−164	−466	−338	−603	−217	−456	−395	−517	−282
Czech Republic	935	....	466	−820	−1,374	−4,128	−3,622	−1,308	−1,466	−2,690	−3,273	−4,485	....
Czechoslovakia	934	−31	....	....	....	....	....	....	....	....	....	....	....
Estonia	939	36	22	−166	−158	−398	−562	−478	−295	−294	−339	−717	−1,199
Georgia	915	....	....	....	....	....	−514	−276	−198	−269	−212	−230	−397
Hungary	944	352	−4,262	−4,054	−1,617	−1,150	−684	−2,228	−2,446	−2,900	−1,754	−2,644	−7,364
Kazakhstan	916	....	....	....	−213	−751	−799	−1,225	−171	676	−1,109	−696	−183
Kyrgyz Republic	917	....	−88	−84	−235	−425	−139	−413	−252	−126	−52	−85	....
Latvia	941	191	417	201	−16	−280	−345	−650	−654	−495	−732	−647	−956
Lithuania	946	....	−86	−94	−614	−723	−981	−1,298	−1,194	−675	−574	−721	−1,278
Macedonia, FYR	962	....	....	....	....	−288	−275	−270	−32	−72	−244	−325	....
Malta	181	30	−84	−132	−361	−406	−202	−221	−122	−470	−165	−46	−271
Moldova	921	....	....	−82	−88	−195	−275	−335	−79	−125	−78	−56	−142
Poland	964	−3,104	−5,788	954	854	−3,264	−5,744	−6,901	−12,487	−9,980	−5,371	−5,007	−4,085
Romania	968	−1,506	−1,231	−455	−1,780	−2,579	−2,104	−2,917	−1,297	−1,355	−2,229	−1,525	−3,311
Russia	922	....	....	7,844	6,965	10,847	−80	216	24,611	46,840	33,795	29,116	35,845
Slovak Republic	936	....	−580	671	390	−2,090	−1,961	−2,126	−1,155	−694	....	....	....
Slovenia	961	978	191	575	−75	55	50	−118	−698	−548	31	375	15
Tajikistan	923	....	....	....	....	....	....	....	....	....	−15	−5	
Turkey	186	−974	−6,433	2,631	−2,338	−2,437	−2,638	1,984	−1,344	−9,819	3,390	−1,521	−6,850
Turkmenistan	925	....	....	....	....	−	−580	....	....	....	....	....	....
Ukraine	926	....	....	−1,163	−1,152	−1,184	−1,335	−1,296	1,658	1,481	1,402	3,174	2,891
Uzbekistan	927	....	....	....	....	....	....	....	....	....	....	....	....

2004, International Monetary Fund: *International Financial Statistics Yearbook*

Balance of Payments

Current Account Balance
Excluding Exceptional Financing
Expressed in Millions of US Dollars

		1992	1993	1994	1995	1996	1997	1998	1999	2000	2001	2002	2003
Middle East	405	ñ24,273	ñ25,878	ñ11,123	ñ6,736	5,223	4,863	ñ27,685	7,991	67,189	36,461	30,340	....
Bahrain, Kingdom of	419	−827	−339	−256	237	260	−31	−777	−37	830	227	−513	−68
Egypt	469	2,812	2,299	31	−254	−192	−711	−2,566	−1,635	−971	−388	622	3,743
Iran, I.R. of	429	−6,504	−4,215	4,956	3,358	5,232	2,213	−2,139	6,589	12,645	....	....	....
Iraq	433	....	....	....	....	....	....	....	....	....	....	....	....
Israel	436	−875	−2,480	−3,447	−4,647	−5,124	−3,289	−1,149	−3,335	−2,972	−1,778	−1,320	665
Jordan	439	−835	−629	−398	−259	−222	29	14	405	59	−4	418	1,088
Kuwait	443	−450	2,499	3,243	5,016	7,107	7,935	2,215	5,010	14,672	8,324	4,251	7,567
Lebanon	446	....	....	....	....	....	....	....	....	....	....	....	....
Libya	672	1,407	−1,366	26	1,650	1,220	1,550	−351	2,136	....	....	....	....
Oman	449	−598	−1,190	−805	−801	338	−78	−2,950	−291	3,423	2,315	....	....
Qatar	453	....	....	....	....	....	....	....	....	....	....	....	....
Saudi Arabia	456	−17,740	−17,268	−10,487	−5,325	680	305	−13,150	412	14,336	9,366	11,889	29,701
Syrian Arab Republic	463	55	−203	−791	263	40	461	58	201	1,061	1,221	1,440	....
United Arab Emirates	466	....	....	....	....	....	....	....	....	....	....	....	....
West Bank and Gaza	487	....	....	....	−984	−1,424	−1,548	−1,213	−1,327	−1,023	−641	....	....
Yemen, Republic of	474	−1,126	−1,275	178	144	39	−69	−472	358	1,337	667	538	149
Western Hemisphere	205	ñ33,742	ñ45,490	ñ51,473	ñ37,910	ñ39,719	ñ66,784	ñ91,530	ñ57,728	ñ47,577	ñ54,201	ñ17,307	....
Argentina	213	−5,655	−8,163	−11,148	−5,175	−6,822	−12,219	−14,510	−11,948	−8,989	−3,853	9,142	7,838
Aruba	314	44	42	81	—	−69	−196	−19	−333	282	....	−244	....
Bahamas, The	313	36	49	−42	−146	−263	−472	−995	−672	−471	−348	....	....
Barbados	316	140	69	134	43	70	−50	−63	−148	−146	−111	−172	....
Belize	339	−29	−49	−40	−17	−7	−32	−60	−78	−139	−185	−163	....
Bolivia	218	−534	−506	−90	−303	−404	−554	−666	−488	−446	−274	−352	19
Brazil	223	6,089	20	−1,153	−18,136	−23,248	−30,491	−33,829	−25,400	−24,225	−23,215	−7,637	4,063
Chile	228	−957	−2,555	−1,586	−1,350	−3,083	−3,660	−3,918	99	−898	−1,100	−885	−594
Colombia	233	901	−2,102	−3,673	−4,527	−4,641	−5,750	−4,857	671	740	−1,109	−1,451	−1,456
Costa Rica	238	−380	−620	−244	−358	−264	−481	−521	−666	−707	−713	−916	−967
Dominican Republic	243	−708	−533	−283	−183	−213	−163	−338	−429	−1,027	−741	−798	867
Ecuador	248	−122	−849	−898	−1,000	−55	−457	−2,099	918	921	−695	−1,359	−455
El Salvador	253	−195	−123	−18	−262	−169	−98	−91	−239	−431	−150	−412	−734
Guatemala	258	−706	−702	−625	−572	−452	−634	−1,039	−1,026	−1,050	−1,253	−1,193	....
Guyana	336	−139	−140	−125	−135	−69	−111	−102	−78	−115	−134	−111	....
Haiti	263	7	−12	−23	−87	−138	−48	−38	....	....	....	....	....
Honduras	268	−298	−309	−343	−201	−335	−272	−395	−625	−276	−339	−242	−279
Jamaica	343	29	−184	82	−99	−143	−332	−334	−216	−367	−759	−1,119	....
Mexico	273	−24,442	−23,400	−29,662	−1,576	−2,529	−7,696	−16,097	−14,038	−18,212	−18,218	−14,099	−9,247
Netherlands Antilles	353	10	1	−98	128	−254	−65	−137	−277	−51	−206	32	....
Nicaragua	278	−834	−644	−911	−722	−825	−841	−687	−928	−792	−785	−784	−780
Panama	283	−267	−96	16	−471	−201	−507	−1,182	−1,320	−716	−174	−92	−408
Paraguay	288	−57	59	−274	−92	−353	−650	−160	−165	−291	−266	73	146
Peru	293	−1,886	−2,464	−2,701	−4,625	−3,646	−3,367	−3,321	−1,464	−1,559	−1,159	−1,127	−1,061
Suriname	366	25	44	59	73	−64	−68	−155	−29	32	−84	−131	−159
Trinidad and Tobago	369	139	113	218	294	105	−614	−644	31	544	416	....	....
Uruguay	298	−9	−244	−438	−213	−233	−287	−476	−508	−566	−488	322	52
Venezuela, Rep. Bol.	299	−3,749	−1,993	2,541	2,014	8,914	3,732	−4,432	2,112	11,853	1,987	7,423	9,624
ECCU													
Anguilla	312	−16	−13	−11	−9	−20	−19	−19	−51	−54	−36	−35	....
Antigua and Barbuda	311	−10	15	−6	−1	−59	−47	−47	−57	−66	−64	−103	....
Dominica	321	−27	−27	−38	−41	−51	−42	−23	−36	−54	−49	....	....
Grenada	328	−32	−44	−27	−41	−56	−68	−82	−53	−84	−99	−116	....
Montserrat	351	−13	−8	−12	−2	16	−2	3	−1	−7	−6	−8	....
St. Kitts and Nevis	361	−15	−29	−24	−45	−65	−62	−46	−82	−66	−106	−124	....
St. Lucia	362	−56	−50	−48	−33	−58	−78	−60	−97	−79	−75	−104	....
St. Vincent & Grens	364	−24	−44	−57	−41	−36	−84	−92	−73	−29	−41	−42	....

Memorandum Items

		1992	1993	1994	1995	1996	1997	1998	1999	2000	2001	2002	2003
Oil Exporting Ctys	999	ñ22,193	ñ22,243	ñ4,913	ñ4,079	24,302	18,524	ñ20,979	26,615	109,856	62,637	50,064	....
Non-Oil Develop.Ctys	201	ñ43,972	ñ86,250	ñ65,063	ñ97,893	ñ110,822	ñ97,251	ñ29,289	23,718	27,649	33,993	98,586	....

2004, International Monetary Fund: *International Financial Statistics Yearbook*

Balance of Payments

		1992	1993	1994	1995	1996	1997	1998	1999	2000	2001	2002	2003

Capital and Financial Account
Including Net Errors and Omissions, but Excluding Reserve Assets,
Use of Fund Credit, and Exceptional Financing
Expressed in Millions of US Dollars

		1992	1993	1994	1995	1996	1997	1998	1999	2000	2001	2002	2003
All Countries	010	101,579	127,724	123,532	175,999	204,112	71,230	68,122	258,490	311,603	281,749	352,019	....
Industrial Countries	110	32,116	ñ13,891	28,599	35,365	42,534	ñ50,296	32,338	224,178	336,037	274,004	341,119	....
United States	111	44,071	83,340	112,712	119,219	113,504	136,991	216,263	288,119	413,737	390,626	477,636	529,135
Canada	156	16,375	22,727	12,632	7,039	2,119	5,840	12,836	4,168	−15,902	−14,037	−14,632	−20,523
Australia	193	6,397	9,642	16,186	19,719	18,282	15,258	15,974	29,001	14,116	9,808	17,487	37,431
Japan	158	−111,954	−104,164	−104,990	−52,433	−30,652	−90,247	−124,914	−38,348	−70,705	−47,311	−66,314	50,938
New Zealand	196	1,202	672	3,117	3,387	5,663	2,862	1,671	3,704	2,317	1,120	3,355	4,313
Euro Area													
Austria	122	3,341	3,214	3,826	6,839	5,965	2,168	8,740	4,484	4,119	1,748	−2,298	356
Belgium	124											−13,337	−13,346
Belgium-Luxembourg	126	−6,080	−13,359	−12,351	−13,990	−13,169	−12,858	−14,263	−15,954	−12,340	−7,950		
Finland	172	2,966	1,426	3,603	−5,603	−8,038	−4,329	−7,044	−8,032	−8,624	−8,294	−10,262	−9,802
France	132	−5,469	−13,996	−4,968	−10,128	−20,321	−31,861	−17,883	−33,262	−21,014	−34,325	−17,754	−3,109
Germany	134	56,431	−382	27,386	34,190	12,598	5,391	16,230	8,580	19,995	−7,173	−45,423	−54,197
Greece	174	1,766	4,186	6,455	2,841	8,769	345		9,730	12,393	3,701	12,268	6,503
Ireland	178	−2,773	894	−1,752	618	−2,101	−2,974	2,196	−2,218	477	1,085	1,107	215
Italy	136	5,223	−10,938	−11,634	−22,272	−28,092	−19,254	−41,470	−16,162	9,028	64	9,910	23,057
Luxembourg	137											−1,600	−2,384
Netherlands	138	−728	−6,562	−16,794	−27,684	−27,197	−27,786	−15,370	−17,607	−6,597	−8,180	−10,248	−17,387
Portugal	182	28	−3,081	765	−168	5,764	7,438	8,341	9,949	11,484	11,256	9,136	1,094
Spain	184	3,728	600	6,426	−7,206	23,871	9,244	−11,220	−9,090	16,356	15,064	19,734	8,189
Denmark	128	−124	−5,399	−5,041	643	474	5,611	−2,231	6,522	−8,061	−1,651	624	−1,465
Iceland	176	239	−96	−266	−48	284	84	587	674	773	290	83	878
Norway	142	−5,203	4,731	−3,507	−4,658	−4,499	−11,234	−6,390	−2,394	−22,165	−28,517	−19,046	−27,092
Sweden	144	15,780	6,689	1,639	−6,604	−12,278	−14,118	−1,386	−4,101	−6,446	−7,744	−12,119	−20,768
Switzerland	146	−9,850	−17,440	−16,579	−21,774	−18,530	−24,525	−25,596	−32,095	−38,421	−23,259	−23,609	....
United Kingdom	112	16,749	23,403	11,735	13,438	10,119	−2,342	6,307	38,511	41,519	27,685	26,421	30,865
Developing Countries	200	69,463	141,615	94,933	140,634	161,579	121,526	35,784	34,312	ñ24,434	7,745	10,900	....
Africa	605	ñ13,417	ñ4,018	ñ2,478	ñ3,470	ñ10,265	3,646	4,983	1,697	ñ6,945	ñ912	ñ2,720	....
Algeria	612	....	....	....	....	....	....	....	....	....	....	....	....
Angola	614	−430	−651	−688	−944	−505	279	755	1,667	−478	645		
Benin	638	53	−56	41	−48	−92	70	65	103	91	114		
Botswana	616	208	−30	−76	−93	16	−86	−126	−146				
Burkina Faso	748	43	74	−22	....					200	194		
Burundi	618	85	44	52	26	5	−8	15	4	24	−17	14	....
Cameroon	622	−909	−320	−495	−74								
Cape Verde	624	35	39	68	30	57	30	69	123	30	39	82	21
Central African Rep.	626	46	−1	38									
Chad	628	43	69	43									
Comoros	632	8	−2	12	9								
Congo, Dem. Rep. of	636												
Congo, Republic of	634	−113	133	639	45	−665	−527	−788	−425	−891	−652	−679	....
Côte d'Ivoire	662	−404	−345	−7	238	−686	−322	−359	−588	−367	−25	−1,047	−1,111
Djibouti	611	72	23	47	−1								
Equatorial Guinea	642	−17	−13	−18	112	339							
Eritrea	643	−186	−74	−69	29	117	115	133	210	40			
Ethiopia	644	−144	82	−126	−145	−544	−388	−28	229	−210	−317	−937	....
Gabon	646	−274	−403	−490	−901	−1,140	−729	−71	−788				
Gambia, The	648	−18	17	−2	9	62	31						
Ghana	652	273	593	508	327	299	627	549	828	201	353	26	....
Guinea	656	88	−40	124	144	117	−40	26	139	92	−14	22	....
Guinea-Bissau	654	53	5	−7	10	17	15						
Kenya	664	−77	341	−36	259	460	472	558	56	192	350	120	....
Lesotho	666	12	73	13	421	419	410	396	180	169	261	−7	....
Liberia	668												
Madagascar	674	−80	−76	1	−54	197	250	1	148	123	−83	15	....
Malawi	676	238	190	195	3	26	292	−170	191	165	−8	291	....
Mali	678	103	91	98	232	290	169	118	239	299	263	287	....
Mauritania	682	135	−108	−35	−28	−87	−20	−34					
Mauritius	684	43	99	189	131	14	54	−69	314	268	−328	82	....
Morocco	686	1,223	958	1,206	−599	−615	−820	−494	102	−665	−746	−1,524	−2,999
Mozambique	688	−171	−200	−99	58	−3	−183	37	586	347	172	−727	551
Namibia	728	−56	−19	−10	−152	−93	−23	−106	−197	−267	−331	−147	....
Niger	692	64	73	50	134								
Nigeria	694	−7,906	−1,131	190	−195	−4,268	−536	1,371	−4,043				
Rwanda	714	79	79	78	−5	29	93	76	69	−37	32	105	....
São Tomé & Príncipe	716						4	14	14	20	16		
Senegal	722	276	292	210	212	−2	90	−1	52	101	51	70	....
Seychelles	718	3	−23	−51	−29	−3	28	44	28	−52	76	−58	....
Sierra Leone	724	22	65	30	119	128	75	35	83	122	128	21	....

2004, International Monetary Fund: *International Financial Statistics Yearbook*

Balance of Payments

		1992	1993	1994	1995	1996	1997	1998	1999	2000	2001	2002	2003

Capital and Financial Account
Including Net Errors and Omissions, but Excluding Reserve Assets, Use of Fund Credit, and Exceptional Financing
Expressed in Millions of US Dollars

		1992	1993	1994	1995	1996	1997	1998	1999	2000	2001	2002	2003
Africa(Cont.)													
Somalia	726	....	....	....	....	....	....	....	....	....	....	....	....
South Africa	199	−1,464	−2,844	571	3,112	570	6,818	3,054	4,798	759	2,549	1,048	9,218
Sudan	732	347	244	621	563	864	846	1,030	580	681	467	1,253	1,088
Swaziland	734	132	−5	−5	53	44	30	135	38	37	10	46	....
Tanzania	738	510	473	292	288	257	332	410	756	497	611	577	....
Togo	742	−20	−107	−41	−72	129	130	123	159	176	167	....	....
Tunisia	744	1,295	1,390	1,063	871	920	981	538	1,180	616	1,129	885	1,111
Uganda	746	124	99	145	288	243	326	462	255	361	563	274	....
Zambia	754	....	....	....	....	....	−579	−98	−207	64	....	....	....
Zimbabwe	698	409	342	339	....	....	....	....	....	....	....	....	....
Asia*	505	20,524	48,166	63,806	77,905	97,108	ñ11,966	ñ75,690	ñ21,030	ñ33,982	4,806	22,479	....
Afghanistan, I.S. of	512	....	....	....	....	....	....	....	....	....	....	....	....
Bangladesh	513	454	338	492	312	577	151	324	175	275	392	−242	....
Bhutan	514	....	....	....	....	....	....	....	....	....	....	....	....
Brunei Darussalam	516	....	....	....	....	....	....	....	....	....	....	....	....
Cambodia	522	106	125	193	212	257	244	194	233	227	154	230	....
China,P.R.: Mainland	924	−8,461	13,378	23,545	20,851	24,462	−1,106	−25,224	−12,463	−9,825	30,046	39,795	....
China,P.R.:Hong Kong	532	....	....	....	....	....	....	−9,318	−257	2,961	−5,257	−14,974	−15,161
Fiji	819	146	125	135	206	65	9	65	−58	....	....	....	....
India	534	5,557	6,087	12,067	4,831	9,914	8,286	9,974	9,892	8,619	10,137	12,212	....
Indonesia	536	4,850	2,700	3,576	8,004	12,166	−3,248	−7,789	−3,813	−4,259	−6,914	−2,865	....
Kiribati	826	−8	−1	−7	....	....	....	....	....	....	....	....	....
Korea	542	7,667	2,019	8,481	15,546	24,421	−14,812	−14,435	8,784	11,549	5,039	5,678	....
Lao People's Dem.Rep	544	−11	2	106	196	188	−64	−104	−212	52	79	....	....
Malaysia	548	8,785	14,341	1,360	6,881	6,975	2,061	489	−7,892	−9,497	−6,287	−3,533	....
Maldives	556	24	52	17	35	36	57	42	88	47	28	52	....
Mongolia	948	−27	−17	−40	−7	13	−49	76	93	71	75	171	....
Myanmar	518	211	152	176	229	258	447	560	239	188	488	....	....
Nepal	558	337	288	414	371	358	557	347	34	222	40	....	....
Pakistan	564	2,268	3,328	3,155	2,145	3,656	2,249	−862	−1,596	−2,542	319	230	−603
Papua New Guinea	853	−166	−727	−572	−531	14	15	−192	30	−241	−153	....	....
Philippines	566	2,689	3,352	5,277	3,215	8,291	1,257	−267	−3,569	−6,634	−1,027	−4,494	−3,431
Samoa	862	40	29	−10	−7	−5	2	−15	26	....	....	....	....
Singapore	576	185	3,367	−6,664	−6,201	−6,581	−6,969	−15,579	−10,991	−6,474	−16,998	−17,362	....
Solomon Islands	813	16	6	1	−9	3	47	9	−26	....	....	....	....
Sri Lanka	524	652	1,150	1,065	1,009	692	702	451	466	683	6	−42	....
Thailand	578	9,333	10,270	12,254	20,713	16,859	−15,229	−16,938	−11,040	−11,120	−3,916	−1,478	−7,447
Tonga	866	2	4	....	....	....	....	....	....	....	15	....	....
Vanuatu	846	14	18	14	24	22	17	3	10	−5	4	....	....
Vietnam	582	....	....	....	....	2,298	1,856	1,111	133	−996	−476	1,052	....
of which:													
Taiwan Prov.of China	528	−7,183	−5,501	−1,876	−9,405	−9,821	−7,779	1,389	10,601	−6,374	−538	8,034	7,890
Europe	170	ñ9,812	5,831	ñ18,414	24,230	2,882	32,015	9,259	12,718	1,598	ñ8,120	22,820	....
Albania	914	15	34	164	32	163	312	118	262	276	364	443	505
Armenia	911	....	80	101	248	245	357	419	312	295	219	212	273
Azerbaijan	912	....	....	....	458	846	1,055	1,305	733	493	125	803	2,145
Belarus	913	....	297	127	380	302	924	697	214	448	356	475	555
Bosnia & Herzegovina	963	....	....	....	....	....	....	350	432	589	1,619	1,251	1,826
Bulgaria	918	629	777	−184	470	−754	718	−32	748	841	1,357	1,542	2,398
Croatia	960	....	−437	−278	1,632	2,066	3,216	1,629	1,807	1,071	2,068	2,746	3,490
Cyprus	423	413	35	173	−199	406	291	520	856	447	1,007	906	94
Czech Republic	935	....	2,575	4,294	8,827	3,302	1,863	3,199	3,105	3,533	5,060	11,103	....
Czechoslovakia	934	−391	....	....	....	....	....	....	....	....	....	....	....
Estonia	939	22	143	184	241	505	778	516	414	422	297	786	1,369
Georgia	915	....	....	....	....	....	452	172	184	275	239	44	349
Hungary	944	418	6,807	3,579	7,014	−88	509	3,179	4,781	3,953	1,670	852	7,700
Kazakhstan	916	....	....	....	512	910	1,348	782	424	−105	1,494	1,231	1,716
Kyrgyz Republic	917	....	58	89	154	405	185	340	203	55	20	74	....
Latvia	941	−154	−119	−145	−17	491	447	712	819	497	1,046	659	1,036
Lithuania	946	....	294	207	783	718	1,206	1,725	1,015	833	933	1,183	1,891
Macedonia, FYR	962	....	....	....	....	193	157	313	174	352	329	203	....
Malta	181	14	219	514	54	321	209	412	360	248	420	333	415
Moldova	921	....	....	95	−88	92	87	−18	−37	123	51	8	99
Poland	964	−1,226	2,560	52	8,981	7,088	8,785	12,825	12,643	10,604	4,944	5,655	5,291
Romania	968	1,368	792	626	1,300	1,997	3,563	2,274	1,536	2,263	3,764	3,316	4,324
Russia	922	....	....	−26,957	−15,291	−28,065	−6,440	−21,594	−26,315	−32,918	−22,529	−17,553	−8,083
Slovak Republic	936	....	594	535	1,401	2,460	2,060	1,649	1,932	1,614	....	....	....
Slovenia	961	−346	−66	72	315	535	1,238	276	617	726	1,254	1,492	327
Tajikistan	923	....	....	....	....	....	....	....	....	....	....	17	33
Turkey	186	2,458	6,741	−2,428	6,998	6,981	5,981	−1,543	6,698	5,885	−16,278	1,307	10,937
Turkmenistan	925	....	....	....	....	8	978	....	....	....	....	....	....
Ukraine	926	....	....	−37	−472	581	632	−2,161	−1,842	−908	−409	−1,943	−718
Uzbekistan	927	....	....	....	....	....	....	....	....	....	....	....	....

2004, International Monetary Fund : *International Financial Statistics Yearbook*

Balance of Payments

Capital and Financial Account
Including Net Errors and Omissions, but Excluding Reserve Assets, Use of Fund Credit, and Exceptional Financing
Expressed in Millions of US Dollars

		1992	1993	1994	1995	1996	1997	1998	1999	2000	2001	2002	2003
Middle East	405	23,270	22,609	10,286	12,175	6,391	6,130	23,768	ñ3,968	ñ47,876	ñ26,571	ñ19,973	....
Bahrain, Kingdom of	419	736	227	208	−68	−267	134	761	62	−630	−104	548	112
Egypt	469	548	−2,281	−1,195	−1,573	−1,533	75	1,179	−2,979	−1,059	−956	−1,426	−4,150
Iran, I.R. of	429	6,343	4,443	−4,048	−572	−2,791	−5,910	1,148	−6,138	−11,562	....	....	....
Iraq	433	....	....	....	....	....	....	....	....	....	....	....	....
Israel	436	−601	2,153	1,337	5,127	6,330	10,365	994	2,296	2,380	2,306	1,203	−2,500
Jordan	439	698	−232	133	87	34	245	−550	844	1,768	629	512	261
Kuwait	443	2,302	−3,976	−3,193	−5,157	−7,132	−7,929	−1,957	−4,092	−12,404	−5,419	−5,224	−9,391
Lebanon	446	....	....	....	....	....	....	....	....	....	....	....	....
Libya	672	371	−351	248	51	1	4	−75	−1,448	....	....	....	....
Oman	449	898	132	144	369	−150	609	2,184	506	−1,160	−1,281	....	....
Qatar	453	....	....	....	....	....	....	....	....	....	....	....	....
Saudi Arabia	456	12,076	18,763	10,341	6,542	5,069	343	12,431	2,403	−11,671	−11,275	−9,153	−28,093
Syrian Arab Republic	463	21	507	1,357	576	947	−12	376	58	−247	−201	−390	....
United Arab Emirates	466	....	....	....	....	....	....	....	....	....	....	....	....
West Bank and Gaza	487	....	....	....	984	1,646	1,706	1,160	1,292	1,107	603	....	....
Yemen, Republic of	474	−176	163	−900	−672	−475	4,087	−109	−284	258	−114	−113	182
Western Hemisphere	205	48,899	69,027	41,732	29,794	65,462	91,701	73,464	44,894	62,770	38,542	ñ11,707	....
Argentina	213	7,941	19,285	10,474	2,863	10,080	15,549	18,600	13,960	7,813	−17,552	−25,473	−18,558
Aruba	314	−21	−8	−84	43	43	177	70	336	−298	....	277	....
Bahamas, The	313	−64	−30	51	143	256	529	1,115	737	410	318	....	....
Barbados	316	−115	−49	−96	−	17	67	57	184	323	333	147	....
Belize	339	29	34	36	21	27	33	46	90	96	181	155	....
Bolivia	218	402	472	1	395	672	654	791	515	407	238	9	−73
Brazil	223	4,550	6,870	7,751	31,105	31,930	22,240	17,527	8,635	32,206	19,797	−3,630	−477
Chile	228	3,504	2,983	4,737	2,488	5,677	6,979	1,727	−846	1,214	501	1,070	237
Colombia	233	374	2,567	3,855	4,523	6,370	6,028	3,460	−983	121	2,335	1,590	1,268
Costa Rica	238	395	362	141	574	194	288	16	896	365	577	879	748
Dominican Republic	243	644	−11	−228	329	173	254	350	581	978	1,255	244	−1,321
Ecuador	248	146	167	123	−459	−71	−65	1,314	−1,862	−6,618	437	1,138	526
El Salvador	253	61	181	131	410	334	460	394	447	385	−27	288	1,050
Guatemala	258	692	901	632	420	666	863	1,275	901	1,692	1,727	1,214	....
Guyana	336	77	104	119	92	81	110	89	100	156	160	125	....
Haiti	263	−14	−11	−26	225	87	78	73	....	....	....	....	....
Honduras	268	51	−25	273	160	257	454	239	436	119	265	223	77
Jamaica	343	220	294	276	126	414	162	378	80	886	1,624	883	....
Mexico	273	26,187	30,632	12,463	−14,735	4,477	28,156	19,267	18,288	25,338	25,533	21,458	19,064
Netherlands Antilles	353	49	43	22	−67	182	59	162	202	−79	423	27	....
Nicaragua	278	−478	−375	−608	−242	77	548	285	533	336	292	370	279
Panama	283	80	−212	−378	139	467	850	803	1,173	388	818	322	253
Paraguay	288	38	−16	575	137	306	435	177	−136	−49	216	−199	87
Peru	293	964	2,105	4,254	4,034	4,526	5,421	2,080	602	1,428	1,591	2,137	1,622
Suriname	366	−47	−31	−24	49	62	87	163	25	−23	162	112	166
Trinidad and Tobago	369	−243	45	−32	−210	133	807	724	131	−103	86	....	....
Uruguay	298	147	437	547	440	386	687	831	398	733	792	−4,219	906
Venezuela, Rep. Bol.	299	3,087	2,117	−3,485	−3,458	−2,676	−638	1,027	−1,054	−5,895	−3,816	−11,851	−4,170
ECCU													
Anguilla	312	18	14	11	9	22	21	21	53	55	40	37	....
Antigua and Barbuda	311	28	−27	14	14	48	50	56	68	60	80	110	....
Dominica	321	30	28	34	49	53	43	27	47	54	53	....	....
Grenada	328	40	44	32	47	56	75	86	58	91	104	147	....
Montserrat	351	13	8	14	3	−16	5	10	−9	3	8	10	....
St. Kitts and Nevis	361	25	32	24	48	64	65	57	85	62	118	134	....
St. Lucia	362	54	55	45	39	52	83	70	101	84	87	109	....
St. Vincent & Grens.	364	34	43	58	39	36	85	100	77	43	50	36	....
Memorandum Items													
Oil Exporting Ctys.	999	16,497	19,745	ñ1,414	465	ñ7,178	ñ23,371	6,814	ñ23,101	ñ71,244	ñ48,495	ñ41,388	....
Non-Oil Develop.Ctys.	201	52,966	121,870	96,347	140,168	168,757	144,897	28,970	57,412	46,810	56,240	52,288	....

Balance of Payments

Overall Balance
Excluding Reserves Assets, Use of Fund Credit, and Exceptional Financing
Expressed in Millions of US Dollars

		1992	1993	1994	1995	1996	1997	1998	1999	2000	2001	2002	2003
All Countries	010	ñ3,059	61,559	60,390	116,792	151,820	66,285	ñ21,941	124,501	158,445	131,079	225,771	....
Industrial Countries	110	ñ6,357	28,438	35,433	78,131	76,761	23,487	ñ7,457	39,855	45,373	26,704	66,222	....
United States	111	–3,927	1,376	–5,350	9,747	–6,667	1,012	6,731	–8,727	295	4,927	3,692	–1,529
Canada	156	–4,786	904	–392	2,711	5,498	–2,393	4,996	5,933	3,720	2,172	–185	–3,255
Australia	193	–4,726	–42	–960	396	2,471	2,873	–2,040	6,705	–1,365	1,096	122	6,877
Japan	158	620	27,473	25,265	58,611	35,141	6,567	–6,164	76,256	48,955	40,487	46,134	187,153
New Zealand	196	131	–74	733	384	1,772	–1,442	–486	188	–143	–187	1,086	782
Euro Area													
Austria	122	2,588	2,201	834	1,391	1,075	–3,053	3,482	–2,172	–746	–1,888	–1,723	–2,036
Belgium	124	....	....	....	....	....	....	....	....	....	....	–32	–1,723
Belgium-Luxembourg	126	569	–2,122	219	243	593	1,056	–2,095	–1,867	–959	1,442	....	....
Finland	172	–2,150	291	4,714	–372	–3,036	2,304	296	13	351	410	–113	–507
France	132	–1,576	–5,006	2,448	712	239	5,940	19,815	–1,392	–2,433	–5,567	–3,965	1,274
Germany	134	37,176	–14,199	–2,036	7,224	–1,195	–3,751	4,015	–14,115	–5,222	–5,466	–1,979	–684
Greece	174	–374	3,439	6,309	–23	4,215	–4,515	....	2,435	2,573	–5,699	1,863	–4,722
Ireland	178	–2,166	2,660	–176	2,339	–52	–1,109	3,212	–1,973	–39	395	–292	–1,890
Italy	136	–23,993	–3,135	1,575	2,804	11,907	13,150	–21,472	–8,051	3,247	–588	3,169	1,115
Luxembourg	137	....	....	....	....	....	....	....	....	....	....	35	108
Netherlands	138	6,118	6,641	500	–1,911	–5,695	–2,709	–2,339	–4,611	219	–351	–132	–920
Portugal	182	–156	–2,848	–1,430	–300	547	974	508	216	371	852	1,017	–6,455
Spain	184	–17,809	–5,203	36	–6,414	24,279	11,756	–14,355	–22,850	–2,881	–1,340	3,690	–15,487
Denmark	128	4,075	–567	–1,851	2,498	3,563	6,532	–4,239	9,437	–5,649	3,270	5,615	4,674
Iceland	176	79	–59	–150	4	153	–44	32	86	–74	–48	61	307
Norway	142	–732	8,253	253	575	6,470	–1,198	–6,384	5,984	3,686	–2,346	5,723	1,551
Sweden	144	6,953	2,530	2,381	–1,664	–6,386	–6,712	3,254	1,881	170	–1,048	665	2,076
Switzerland	146	4,397	486	1,009	29	2,521	2,154	1,179	–2,484	–4,005	638	2,402	....
United Kingdom	112	–6,667	5,437	1,500	–853	–653	–3,904	–257	–1,036	5,300	–4,456	–635	–2,592
Developing Countries	200	3,298	33,122	24,958	38,662	75,059	42,799	ñ14,484	84,645	113,072	104,375	159,549	....
Africa	605	ñ16,500	ñ10,317	ñ10,877	ñ16,678	ñ8,188	ñ1,675	ñ13,551	ñ7,490	3,770	2,597	ñ4,536	....
Algeria	612	....	....	....	....	....	....	....	....	....	....	....	....
Angola	614	–1,165	–1,320	–1,028	–1,239	2,761	–604	–1,112	–43	318	–786	....	....
Benin	638	–67	–157	18	–255	–149	–100	–87	–89	–20	–46	....	....
Botswana	616	405	397	135	207	511	635	44	371	....	–192	–187	....
Burkina Faso	748	20	2	–7	....	....	....	....	....	....	....	....	....
Burundi	618	26	16	35	37	–35	–9	–39	–24	–24	–52	11	....
Cameroon	622	–1,305	–885	–551	15	....	....	....	....	....	....	....	....
Cape Verde	624	23	15	22	–32	22	–	11	49	–28	–17	10	–56
Central African Rep.	626	–37	–14	13	....	....	....	....	....	....	....	....	....
Chad	628	–43	–48	6	....	....	....	....	....	....	....	....	....
Comoros	632	–6	8	5	–10	....	....	....	....	....	....	....	....
Congo, Dem. Rep. of	636	....	....	....	....	....	....	....	....	....	....	....	....
Congo, Republic of	634	–430	–420	–155	–581	–1,316	–682	–1,029	–656	–243	–681	–713	....
Côte d'Ivoire	662	–1,417	–1,237	–20	–254	–848	–477	–650	–708	–608	–86	–278	–758
Djibouti	611	–16	–12	1	–24	....	....	....	....	....	....	....	....
Equatorial Guinea	642	–28	–10	–18	–12	–5	....	....	....	....	....	....	....
Eritrea	643	–152	–40	–42	–41	32	106	–160	1	–64	....	....	....
Ethiopia	644	–264	32	–	–105	–465	–429	–360	–236	–196	–771	–1,087	....
Gabon	646	–442	–452	–173	–436	–251	–197	–667	–398	....	....	....	....
Gambia, The	648	19	11	6	1	15	7	....	....	....	....	....	....
Ghana	652	–104	34	253	183	–25	77	28	–136	–186	29	–6	....
Guinea	656	–174	–97	–124	–72	–60	–131	–158	–76	–63	–117	–24	....
Guinea-Bissau	654	–52	–61	–55	–41	–43	–15	....	....	....	....	....	....
Kenya	664	–257	412	62	–142	387	15	83	–34	–7	10	–16	....
Lesotho	666	50	102	121	98	117	141	116	–41	18	166	–125	....
Liberia	668	....	....	....	....	....	....	....	....	....	....	....	....
Madagascar	674	–278	–334	–276	–330	–94	–16	–299	–104	–160	–253	–283	....
Malawi	676	–47	24	14	–75	–122	16	–174	33	91	–68	90	....
Mali	678	–138	–97	–65	–52	29	–10	–46	–13	63	–47	138	....
Mauritania	682	17	–282	–105	–6	4	28	43	....	....	....	....	....
Mauritius	684	43	7	–44	109	48	–35	–65	190	231	–52	341	....
Morocco	686	791	436	483	–1,895	–673	–988	–640	–69	–1,166	861	–52	–1,396
Mozambique	688	–523	–647	–566	–387	–424	–478	–393	–326	–416	–485	–1,439	35
Namibia	728	–7	91	75	24	23	68	56	–35	–103	–337	–50	....
Niger	692	–95	–24	–76	–18	....	....	....	....	....	....	....	....
Nigeria	694	–5,638	–1,911	–1,938	–2,774	–761	15	–2,873	–3,538	....	....	....	....
Rwanda	714	–4	–50	6	53	20	31	–7	–72	–131	–70	–21	....
São Tomé & Príncipe	716	....	....	....	–33	–201	–95	–6	–3	–5	–1	–7	....
Senegal	722	–125	–141	23	–33	–201	–95	–248	–268	–231	–194	–247	....
Seychelles	718	–4	–30	–28	–32	–62	–45	–74	–99	–103	–47	–189	....
Sierra Leone	724	16	8	–59	1	–22	20	2	–16	10	30	–52	....
Somalia	726	....	....	....	....	....	....	....	....	....	....	....	....

2004, International Monetary Fund: *International Financial Statistics Yearbook*

Balance of Payments

Overall Balance
Excluding Reserves Assets, Use of Fund Credit, and Exceptional Financing
Expressed in Millions of US Dollars

		1992	1993	1994	1995	1996	1997	1998	1999	2000	2001	2002	2003
Africa(Cont.)													
South Africa	199	503	−1,341	683	907	−1,272	4,595	920	4,270	464	2,606	1,659	7,762
Sudan	732	−159	42	19	63	38	18	73	115	124	−151	245	362
Swaziland	734	92	−69	−4	24	−8	28	41	3	−28	−43	−	....
Tanzania	738	−204	−575	−419	−359	−254	−297	−509	−79	−1	131	326	....
Togo	742	−160	−190	−97	−194	−25	13	−17	32	37	−2	....	....
Tunisia	744	191	67	527	97	442	386	−138	738	−205	288	139	380
Uganda	746	24	−125	−62	−51	−9	−41	−41	−455	−464	−239	−147	....
Zambia	754	....	....	....	....	....	−932	−671	−654	−520	....	....	....
Zimbabwe	698	−195	226	−86	....	....							
Asia*	505	22,704	34,895	60,065	38,966	57,278	5,070	38,582	91,176	57,498	99,305	154,271	....
Afghanistan, I.S. of	512	....	....	....	....	....	....	....	....	....	....	....	....
Bangladesh	513	635	698	691	−512	−414	−135	288	−189	−31	−144	497	....
Bhutan	514	....	....	....	....	....	....	....	....	....	....	....	....
Brunei Darussalam	516	....	....	....	....	....	....	....	....	....	....	....	....
Cambodia	522	13	21	36	26	72	34	19	45	92	68	166	....
China,P.R.: Mainland	924	−2,060	1,769	30,453	22,469	31,705	35,857	6,248	8,652	10,693	47,447	75,217	....
China,P.R.:Hong Kong	532							−6,789	10,028	10,044	4,684	−2,377	994
Fiji	819	85	−14	23	93	78	−25	5	−45				
India	534	1,072	4,211	10,391	−733	3,958	5,321	3,071	6,664	5,979	11,897	16,868	....
Indonesia	536	2,070	594	784	1,573	4,503	−8,137	−3,693	1,972	3,726	−15	4,958	
Kiribati	826	−17	−5	−6									
Korea	542	3,724	3,009	4,614	7,039	1,416	−22,979	25,930	33,260	23,790	13,278	11,770	
Lao People's Dem.Rep.	544	−122	−137	−178	−151	−158	−369	−254	−333	43	−4	....	....
Malaysia	548	6,618	11,350	−3,160	−1,763	2,513	−3,875	10,018	4,712	−1,009	1,000	3,657	....
Maldives	556	5	−1	5	17	28	22	20	9	−4	−30	8	....
Mongolia	948	−82	15	6	32	−87	7	−53	−19	−86	−79	13	....
Myanmar	518	95	−78	46	−32	−25	31	60	−46	−23	180	....	....
Nepal	558	155	66	63	15	31	169	280	−223	−77	−300		
Pakistan	564	392	428	1,343	−1,204	−780	538	−3,110	−2,516	−2,627	2,197	4,084	2,994
Papua New Guinea	853	−326	−253	−170	−39	202	−177	−221	125	104	129	....	....
Philippines	566	1,689	336	2,327	1,235	4,338	−3,094	1,279	3,650	−376	296	−111	−84
Samoa	862	−13	−9	−4	2	7	11	6	7	....	....	....	....
Singapore	576	6,100	7,578	4,736	8,599	7,396	7,940	2,965	4,194	6,806	−861	1,342	....
Solomon Islands	813	14	−2	−2	−1	18	9	17	−5	....	....	....	....
Sri Lanka	524	202	768	308	239	9	307	224	−95	−361	−259	−331	....
Thailand	578	3,029	3,907	4,169	7,159	2,167	−18,250	−2,696	1,388	−1,806	2,276	5,537	518
Tonga	866	1	−2	....	....	....	....	....	....	....	2	....	....
Vanuatu	846	1	3	−6	5	−5	−2	−7	−23	−19	−10	....	....
Vietnam	582	....	....	....	....	278	328	37	1,310	110	206	448	....
of which:													
Taiwan Prov.of China	528	1,367	1,541	4,622	−3,931	1,102	−728	4,827	18,593	2,477	17,353	33,664	37,092
Europe	170	ñ17,061	ñ11,724	ñ13,653	19,05	ñ11,389	3,493	ñ17,534	9,770	17,298	8,241	28,461	....
Albania	914	−36	49	7	21	56	40	52	107	120	147	36	98
Armenia	911	....	13	−3	30	−45	50	1	5	17	19	64	86
Azerbaijan	912	....	....	....	58	−85	139	−59	133	326	73	34	124
Belarus	913	....	−138	−317	−78	−214	65	−319	20	125	−79	97	50
Bosnia & Herzegovina	963	....	....	....	....	....	....	−431	−667	−291	402	−499	−270
Bulgaria	918	269	−322	−216	445	−739	1,145	−94	96	137	373	715	732
Croatia	960	....	188	277	40	1,017	390	161	410	611	1,342	826	1,392
Cyprus	423	−225	145	247	−363	−60	−47	−83	639	−8	612	389	−188
Czech Republic	935	....	3,041	3,474	7,453	−825	−1,758	1,890	1,639	844	1,787	6,618	....
Czechoslovakia	934	−422	....	....	....	....	....	....	....	....	....	....	....
Estonia	939	58	165	17	84	106	216	37	119	128	−42	69	169
Georgia	915	....	....	....	....	....	−62	−103	−14	6	28	−186	−48
Hungary	944	770	2,545	−475	5,398	−1,237	−175	951	2,335	1,052	−84	−1,792	336
Kazakhstan	916	....	....	....	299	159	548	−443	253	570	385	535	1,534
Kyrgyz Republic	917	....	−30	5	−81	−20	46	−73	−50	−70	−32	−11	....
Latvia	941	37	298	57	−33	211	102	63	165	3	314	12	80
Lithuania	946	....	208	113	168	−5	224	427	−179	158	359	463	613
Macedonia, FYR	962	....	....	....	....	−95	−119	43	142	279	86	−122	....
Malta	181	45	135	383	−307	−85	7	191	238	−222	255	288	144
Moldova	921	....	....	13	−175	−103	−188	−353	−116	−2	−27	−49	−43
Poland	964	−4,330	−3,228	1,006	9,835	3,824	3,041	5,924	156	624	−427	648	1,206
Romania	968	−138	−439	171	−480	−582	1,459	−643	239	908	1,535	1,791	1,013
Russia	922	....	....	−19,113	−8,326	−17,218	−6,520	−21,378	−1,704	13,922	11,266	11,563	27,762
Slovak Republic	936	....	14	1,205	1,791	370	99	−478	777	920			
Slovenia	961	633	125	647	240	590	1,288	158	−81	178	1,285	1,867	342
Tajikistan	923	....	....	....	....	....	....	....	....	....	....	2	28
Turkey	186	1,484	308	203	4,660	4,544	3,343	441	5,354	−3,934	−12,888	−214	4,087
Turkmenistan	925	....	....	....	....	8	398						
Ukraine	926	....	....	−1,200	−1,624	−603	−703	−3,457	−184	573	993	1,231	2,173
Uzbekistan	927	....	....	....	....	....	....	....	....	....	....	....	....

Balance of Payments

		1992	1993	1994	1995	1996	1997	1998	1999	2000	2001	2002	2003

Overall Balance
Excluding Reserves Assets, Use of Fund Credit, and Exceptional Financing
Expressed in Millions of US Dollars

		1992	1993	1994	1995	1996	1997	1998	1999	2000	2001	2002	2003
Middle East................	405	ñ1,003	ñ3,269	ñ837	5,439	11,614	10,993	ñ3,916	4,024	19,313	9,890	10,367	....
Bahrain, Kingdom of........	419	−90	−113	−48	169	−6	103	−17	25	200	123	35	44
Egypt............................	469	3,360	18	−1,164	−1,827	−1,725	−635	−1,387	−4,614	−2,030	−1,345	−804	−407
Iran, I.R. of..................	429	−161	228	908	2,786	2,441	−3,697	−991	451	1,083	....	....	....
Iraq.............................	433	....	....	....	....	....	....	....	....	....	....	....	....
Israel...........................	436	−1,476	−327	−2,111	480	1,206	7,077	−155	−1,039	−592	527	−117	−1,835
Jordan..........................	439	−137	−861	−265	−171	−188	275	−536	1,249	1,827	625	930	1,348
Kuwait..........................	443	1,851	−1,478	50	−141	−25	6	258	918	2,268	2,905	−973	−1,824
Lebanon........................	446	....	....	....	....	....	....	....	....	....	....	....	....
Libya............................	672	1,778	−1,716	274	1,701	1,221	1,553	−426	688	....	....	....	....
Oman............................	449	300	−1,058	−661	−432	189	531	−765	215	2,262	1,034	....	....
Qatar............................	453	....	....	....	....	....	....	....	....	....	....	....	....
Saudi Arabia..................	456	−5,664	1,495	−146	1,217	5,749	648	−719	2,815	2,665	−1,909	2,736	1,608
Syrian Arab Republic.......	463	76	304	566	839	987	449	434	259	814	1,020	1,050	....
United Arab Emirates......	466	....	....	....	....	....	....	....	....	....	....	....	....
West Bank and Gaza........	487	....	....	....	−	221	158	−53	−35	84	−39	....	....
Yemen, Republic of.........	474	−1,302	−1,112	−722	−528	−436	4,018	−581	74	1,594	553	425	330
Western Hemisphere........	205	15,157	23,537	ñ9,741	ñ8,116	25,744	24,917	ñ18,065	ñ12,834	15,193	ñ15,659	ñ29,014	....
Argentina......................	213	2,286	11,122	−675	−2,311	3,258	3,331	4,090	2,013	−1,176	−21,405	−16,331	−10,720
Aruba...........................	314	23	33	−3	43	−26	−18	51	3	−16	....	33	....
Bahamas, The.................	313	−28	19	9	−3	−8	57	119	65	−61	−30	....	....
Barbados.......................	316	25	20	38	42	86	17	−6	36	178	222	−24	....
Belize...........................	339	−	−14	−4	4	21	1	−14	13	−43	−3	−8	....
Bolivia..........................	218	−132	−34	−90	92	268	101	125	27	−39	−36	−343	−55
Brazil............................	223	10,639	6,890	6,598	12,969	8,682	−8,251	−16,302	−16,765	7,981	−3,418	−11,266	3,586
Chile.............................	228	2,547	428	3,151	1,139	2,594	3,318	−2,191	−747	317	−599	185	−357
Colombia.......................	233	1,274	464	182	−4	1,729	278	−1,398	−312	862	1,225	139	−188
Costa Rica.....................	238	14	−258	−103	216	−69	−193	−504	230	−341	−136	−37	−219
Dominican Republic........	243	−64	−544	−511	146	−40	91	11	151	−48	515	−554	−454
Ecuador........................	248	24	−682	−775	−1,459	−126	−521	−784	−944	−5,697	−258	−221	70
El Salvador....................	253	−134	59	113	148	165	363	303	208	−45	−178	−123	316
Guatemala.....................	258	−14	200	6	−152	214	230	235	−125	643	474	21	....
Guyana.........................	336	−62	−36	−6	−43	12	−2	−13	22	40	26	15	....
Haiti.............................	263	−6	−23	−50	138	−50	30	34	....	....	....	....	....
Honduras.......................	268	−247	−333	−70	−41	−79	182	−155	−188	−157	−74	−19	−202
Jamaica.........................	343	248	110	358	27	271	−170	44	−136	518	865	−236	....
Mexico..........................	273	1,745	7,232	−17,199	−16,312	1,948	20,460	3,170	4,250	7,126	7,314	7,359	9,817
Netherlands Antilles........	353	59	44	−76	60	−72	−6	25	−75	−130	218	60	....
Nicaragua......................	278	−1,312	−1,019	−1,519	−964	−748	−293	−402	−395	−456	−493	−414	−501
Panama.........................	283	−187	−308	−362	−331	267	343	−380	−148	−327	645	230	−155
Paraguay.......................	288	−19	43	301	45	−47	−216	17	−301	−339	−50	−126	233
Peru.............................	293	−922	−359	1,553	−590	880	2,055	−1,241	−862	−130	432	1,010	561
Suriname.......................	366	−22	13	34	123	−2	19	8	−4	10	78	−19	7
Trinidad and Tobago........	369	−104	159	186	84	238	194	80	162	441	502	....	....
Uruguay........................	298	138	193	109	228	152	400	355	−110	166	304	−3,897	958
Venezuela, Rep. Bol........	299	−662	124	−944	−1,444	6,238	3,094	−3,405	1,058	5,958	−1,829	−4,428	5,454
ECCU													
Anguilla.....................	312	1	1	−	−	1	2	2	2	−	4	2	....
Antigua and Barbuda....	311	18	−12	8	14	−11	3	9	10	−6	16	8	....
Dominica....................	321	3	1	−3	8	2	1	4	11	−	5	....	....
Grenada.....................	328	8	−	5	6	−	7	4	5	7	6	31	....
Montserrat..................	351	−	−	2	1	−	3	14	−11	−4	2	2	....
St. Kitts and Nevis........	361	10	3	−1	2	−1	4	11	3	−4	12	10	....
St. Lucia.....................	362	−2	5	−3	6	−6	5	10	4	5	12	5	....
St. Vincent & Grens......	364	10	−1	−	−1	−	1	8	4	14	9	−6	....
Memorandum Items													
Oil Exporting Ctys..........	999	ñ5,696	ñ2,498	ñ6,327	ñ3,614	17,124	ñ4,847	ñ14,165	3,515	38,612	14,142	8,675	....
Non-Oil Develop.Ctys.....	201	8,994	35,620	31,284	42,276	57,935	47,646	ñ319	81,131	74,460	90,233	150,874	....

2004, International Monetary Fund: *International Financial Statistics Yearbook*

Balance of Payments

		1992	1993	1994	1995	1996	1997	1998	1999	2000	2001	2002	2003

Exports of Goods and Services
As percent of GDP

		1992	1993	1994	1995	1996	1997	1998	1999	2000	2001	2002	2003
Industrial Countries													
United States	111	9.7	9.7	9.9	10.7	10.9	11.3	10.7	10.4	10.9	10.0	9.3	9.3
Canada	156	26.9	30.0	33.8	37.2	38.2	39.3	41.2	43.0	45.5	43.5	41.4	37.9
Australia	193	17.7	18.4	18.3	19.3	19.5	20.6	19.9	18.8	21.9	22.4	20.8	18.2
Japan	158	10.1	9.3	9.3	9.4	10.0	11.1	11.1	10.4	11.1	10.8	11.6	....
New Zealand	196	30.6	30.3	30.7	29.7	28.4	27.8	29.3	30.0	34.7	35.4	33.2	29.8
Euro Area													
Austria	122	38.4	36.7	37.4	38.2	39.7	42.9	44.1	45.6	50.4	52.7	53.0	52.5
Belgium	124	....	....	....	....	....	....	....	....	....	....	84.2	82.2
Belgium-Luxembourg	126	....	....	....	....	....	....	....	....	....	....		
Finland	172	26.5	32.5	35.4	37.1	37.5	39.0	38.8	37.9	43.3	40.3	39.0	37.2
France	132	23.7	22.4	22.7	23.3	23.5	26.1	26.7	26.5	28.9	28.5	27.4	26.2
Germany	134	24.7	22.9	23.8	24.6	25.5	28.1	29.3	29.7	33.8	35.5	36.4	36.3
Greece	174	15.0	14.5	14.7	13.2	12.3	12.2	....	19.9	26.0	....	....	....
Ireland	178	59.9	64.6	69.3	74.5	75.2	76.9	110.5	87.6	97.0	97.9	93.7	83.9
Italy	136	19.2	22.3	23.9	26.9	25.8	26.3	25.9	25.0	27.6	27.8	26.5	25.0
Luxembourg	137	....	....	....	....	....	....	....	....	....	....	142.7	139.6
Netherlands	138	52.4	50.9	52.2	58.2	58.8	63.2	62.8	61.5	68.5	66.6	62.8	62.1
Portugal	182	25.3	27.2	28.8	30.8	30.9	32.7	32.2	29.7	31.7	31.0	30.5	30.8
Spain	184	17.3	19.3	22.3	22.9	24.1	26.9	27.4	27.6	30.2	30.1	29.1	28.2
Denmark	128	37.1	35.7	36.5	36.4	36.8	36.8	36.6	40.4	47.0	47.6	48.0	45.8
Iceland	176	30.4	32.7	34.7	35.7	36.4	37.3	35.9	34.9	35.0	40.6	40.0	35.7
Norway	142	37.9	38.0	38.2	37.9	40.8	41.4	37.6	39.3	46.6	45.4	41.2	41.2
Sweden	144	28.1	31.2	34.6	38.5	37.5	40.8	41.6	42.8	44.9	44.8	44.9	44.0
Switzerland	146	41.5	40.9	40.3	40.1	41.1	47.0	46.0	46.5	51.5	50.4	48.5	....
United Kingdom	112	23.6	25.5	26.5	28.3	29.4	28.7	26.8	26.4	28.1	27.4	26.3	25.3
Developing Countries													
Africa													
Algeria	612	....	....	....	....	....	....	....	....	....	....	....	....
Angola	614	–	–	–	76.8	82.2	67.3	56.3	86.3	89.7	75.4	....	....
Benin	638	23.3	25.6	36.1	30.6	29.6	25.2	23.8	25.1	23.4	22.0	....	....
Botswana	616	48.7	50.8	50.1	54.7	55.7	62.4	48.5	65.4	....	....	....	....
Burkina Faso	748	8.7	8.9	12.8	....	....	....	....	....	9.1	9.1	....	....
Burundi	618	8.7	9.1	8.9	12.9	5.9	9.9	8.0	7.6	7.8	7.0	6.2	....
Cameroon	622	19.5	17.2	26.2	23.3	....	....	....	....	....	....	....	....
Cape Verde	624	....	....	....	....	....	....	....	....	....	....	....	....
Central African Rep.	626	11.4	14.2	21.0	....	....	....	....	....	....	....	....	....
Chad	628	12.5	13.7	16.1	....	....	....	....	....	....	....	....	....
Comoros	632	18.4	19.7	20.5	20.4	....	....	....	....	....	....	....	....
Congo, Dem. Rep. of	636	....	....	....	....	....	....	....	....	....	....	....	....
Congo, Republic of	634	42.5	43.8	58.0	64.9	68.7	75.8	76.2	72.5	81.6	78.7	81.3	....
Côte d'Ivoire	662	32.3	30.7	44.4	43.4	46.2	43.0	40.8	41.8	41.2	42.1	50.0	....
Djibouti	611	....	....	....	....	....	....	....	....	....	....	....	....
Equatorial Guinea	642	36.0	40.4	54.6	56.6	65.8	....	....	....	....	....	....	....
Eritrea	643	....	....	....	....	....	....	....	....	....	....	....	....
Ethiopia	644	5.9	8.9	12.9	13.9	13.3	14.5	15.1	15.3	15.7	15.6	....	....
Gabon	646	46.6	48.8	61.7	59.4	62.7	61.3	47.4	59.6	....	....	....	....
Gambia, The	648	68.7	85.8	71.5	....	....	....	....	....	....	....	....	....
Ghana	652	17.8	20.3	25.5	24.5	24.9	24.0	....	....	....	....	....	....
Guinea	656	....	....	....	....	....	....	....	....	....	....	....	....
Guinea-Bissau	654	3.3	6.1	6.1	6.6	8.5	20.3	....	....	....	....	....	....
Kenya	664	26.2	40.4	37.1	32.6	32.6	28.1	24.8	25.5	26.6	26.5	25.8	....
Lesotho	666	18.3	21.0	21.7	21.3	24.3	27.6	27.7	23.7	29.5	41.6	52.9	....
Liberia	668	....	....	....	....	....	....	....	....	....	....	....	....
Madagascar	674	16.7	15.5	22.0	23.7	20.1	22.2	22.2	24.5	30.6	28.2	16.1	....
Malawi	676	23.8	17.1	29.8	32.7	22.9	22.5	31.0	27.9	26.8	....	....	....
Mali	678	16.2	17.8	22.9	22.3	20.3	23.8	21.7	23.1	24.2	29.2	30.9	....
Mauritania	682	38.5	44.8	42.4	47.6	47.3	43.4	....	....	....	....	....	....
Mauritius	684	59.2	58.2	56.4	58.1	62.9	59.6	62.3	61.5	57.6	62.9	62.6	....
Morocco	686	25.1	26.1	24.9	27.4	26.3	28.5	27.8	30.1	31.4	33.0	33.8	32.3
Mozambique	688	15.1	15.1	15.4	18.0	16.5	14.7	13.4	14.2	18.4	28.4	29.1	....
Namibia	728	50.5	53.4	48.6	49.5	49.9	47.4	47.2	44.9	46.1	44.0	....	....
Niger	692	17.3	14.7	18.1	19.2	....	....	....	....	....	....	....	....
Nigeria	694	40.4	34.8	23.6	13.7	13.1	11.9	7.5	38.5	....	....	....	....
Rwanda	714	5.0	5.2	4.3	5.8	6.0	7.7	5.6	6.0	7.4	9.6	7.7	....
São Tomé & Príncipe	716	....	....	....	....	....	....	....	....	....	....	....	....
Senegal	722	22.5	21.4	36.7	33.8	29.8	29.7	30.2	30.7	29.9	30.4	29.9	....
Seychelles	718	55.8	66.5	62.4	65.4	66.3	65.6	60.9	68.0	79.1	83.0	77.7	....
Sierra Leone	724	29.0	23.0	23.7	14.7	11.6	5.6	7.5	4.3	8.7	10.8	12.4	....
Somalia	726	....	....	....	....	....	....	....	....	....	....	....	....
South Africa	199	21.4	21.5	22.2	23.0	24.6	24.6	25.9	25.9	28.8	31.2	33.9	28.3
Sudan	732	8.8	7.2	10.3	8.2	8.2	6.2	....	....	....	....	....	....
Swaziland	734	75.1	75.7	78.9	74.7	71.9	73.4	78.6	73.1	80.5	91.1	91.9	....

Balance of Payments

Exports of Goods and Services
As percent of GDP

		1992	1993	1994	1995	1996	1997	1998	1999	2000	2001	2002	2003
Africa(Cont.)													
Tanzania	738	12.5	18.0	20.8	24.1	21.1	15.7	13.7	13.2	14.3	15.6	....	....
Togo	742	32.8	28.0	40.6	35.5	38.0	34.1	35.0	32.2	35.1	34.8	....	....
Tunisia	744	38.8	39.6	44.2	44.3	41.6	43.2	42.8	42.3	44.2	47.8	45.4	43.8
Uganda	746	5.7	8.7	10.0	10.8	12.4	11.4	11.0	11.2	11.4	11.5	11.9	....
Zambia	754	....	....	....	....	....	31.2	....	....	....	....	....	....
Zimbabwe	698	27.2	30.2	34.0	....	....	....	....	....	....	....	....	....
Asia*													
Afghanistan, I.S. of	512	....	....	....	....	....	....	....	....	....	....	....	....
Bangladesh	513	8.4	9.7	10.5	11.7	11.6	13.4	13.7	13.9	15.9	15.0	14.7	....
Bhutan	514	....	....	....	....	....	....	....	....	....	....	....	....
Brunei Darussalam	516	....	....	....	....	....	....	....	....	....	....	....	....
Cambodia	522	15.9	14.0	19.8	28.6	23.4	26.6	31.5	41.3	50.9	56.4	58.7	....
China,P.R.: Mainland	924	16.8	14.5	22.0	21.0	20.9	22.9	21.7	22.1	25.9	25.1	29.5	....
China,P.R.:Hong Kong	532	....	....	....	....	....	....	126.5	130.1	146.0	141.5	152.1	171.9
Fiji	819	52.4	52.1	56.1	54.4	60.9	56.8	56.4	57.2	....	....	....	....
India	534	8.6	9.6	9.8	10.4	10.6	10.7	10.8	11.4	13.9	13.7	15.3	....
Indonesia	536	26.7	25.7	25.5	26.2	25.0	29.3	57.5	39.9	47.0	44.5	38.1	....
Kiribati	826	....	....	....	....	....	....	....	....	....	....	....	....
Korea	542	27.6	27.5	27.8	28.5	27.5	31.9	45.6	38.5	40.4	37.4	34.9	....
Lao People's Dem.Rep	544	16.5	25.1	25.4	22.9	22.8	24.3	37.9	32.2	29.2	27.2	....	....
Malaysia	548	75.8	78.7	88.9	93.8	91.3	93.1	115.6	121.3	124.6	116.4	114.1	....
Maldives	556	77.0	66.2	76.6	79.7	81.9	79.1	79.0	73.7	73.2	74.3	76.3	....
Mongolia	948	29.6	69.5	60.1	41.4	40.6	58.9	55.6	62.0	....	....	....	....
Myanmar	518	1.6	1.5	1.4	1.2	1.0	.8	.7	.5	....	....	....	....
Nepal	558	18.6	20.7	23.5	24.4	26.1	26.5	23.0	25.3	24.0	20.7	....	....
Pakistan	564	17.6	17.6	17.4	17.3	17.9	16.9	15.6	15.2	17.1	19.2	20.2	21.3
Papua New Guinea	853	52.0	58.5	54.2	65.0	56.8	52.1	55.7	63.7	....	....	....	....
Philippines	566	27.5	29.5	31.6	36.2	40.4	49.0	56.7	51.2	54.4	48.3	48.8	47.7
Samoa	862	27.3	26.5	25.1	33.6	35.3	34.4	....	....	....	....	....	....
Singapore	576	166.0	165.3	171.3	180.8	173.5	167.1	161.7	175.6	184.7	180.6	181.8	....
Solomon Islands	813	48.6	43.7	45.5	57.2	59.2	60.6	65.5	67.4	....	....	....	....
Sri Lanka	524	30.1	33.1	33.8	35.4	35.0	36.5	36.2	35.5	39.1	39.2	36.1	....
Thailand	578	37.1	38.0	38.9	41.8	39.3	48.0	58.9	58.2	66.7	66.0	64.4	65.8
Tonga	866	19.7	22.1	....	....	....	....	....	....	....	....	....	....
Vanuatu	846	46.2	44.1	48.1	46.3	....	....	....	....	....	....	....	....
Vietnam	582	....	....	....	....	38.5	43.6	44.0	48.9	55.0	54.6	56.0	....
*of which:													
Taiwan Prov.of China	528	....	....	....	....	....	....	....	....	....	....	....	....
Europe													
Albania	914	13.4	15.4	11.3	12.3	13.9	9.7	9.6	14.8	18.7	20.4	....	....
Armenia	911	....	.2	35.3	23.3	23.1	20.2	19.0	20.8	23.4	25.5	29.4	31.9
Azerbaijan	912	....	....	....	....	....	....	....	....	....	....	....	....
Belarus	913	....	....	....	50.0	46.2	55.6	46.6	52.7	73.5	68.3	63.5	66.3
Bosnia & Herzegovina	963	....	....	....	....	....	....	26.3	26.2	33.9	32.3	....	....
Bulgaria	918	58.4	45.2	53.5	51.7	63.2	60.6	47.0	44.7	55.6	53.2	51.8	53.4
Croatia	960	....	52.4	48.4	35.8	39.6	39.4	39.4	40.8	47.0	48.5	46.4	51.8
Cyprus	423	50.8	48.5	48.6	47.5	47.7	47.8	44.2	45.2	46.8	47.4	52.5	51.2
Czech Republic	935	....	54.2	51.4	54.2	52.2	55.6	58.9	60.5	64.5	66.3	61.9	....
Czechoslovakia	934	....	....	....	....	....	....	....	....	....	....	....	....
Estonia	939	....	66.0	72.1	68.5	62.8	73.3	74.9	70.9	88.0	83.9	74.6	75.3
Georgia	915	....	....	....	....	....	16.1	18.3	19.5	21.9	25.3	29.2	....
Hungary	944	36.2	28.4	25.9	44.0	48.3	54.8	62.5	65.0	74.6	74.4	65.6	61.8
Kazakhstan	916	....	....	....	34.7	34.6	36.4	32.1	39.4	56.9	48.0	49.0	49.3
Kyrgyz Republic	917	....	....	33.6	30.0	30.8	38.2	36.4	42.2	41.8	36.7	39.6	....
Latvia	941	79.9	73.1	46.0	42.7	46.8	46.8	47.1	40.4	42.3	41.4	41.6	42.5
Lithuania	946	....	83.3	55.3	49.9	52.2	53.1	45.7	39.1	44.9	50.0	53.4	52.4
Macedonia, FYR	962	....	....	....	....	29.5	35.7	40.2	39.8	45.6	40.7	36.0	....
Malta	181	90.9	94.4	96.0	92.4	85.3	83.1	85.7	88.7	100.8	85.8	87.4	83.2
Moldova	921	....	....	....	61.3	54.9	54.8	46.8	52.1	49.8	49.9	....	....
Poland	964	22.2	20.7	25.3	28.1	25.9	27.5	27.2	23.8	28.2	28.0	30.0	....
Romania	968	25.7	21.6	23.9	26.5	27.3	28.2	22.6	27.7	32.7	33.4	35.5	36.3
Russia	922	....	....	27.2	29.7	26.3	24.9	32.0	43.2	44.1	37.0	35.0	35.1
Slovak Republic	936	....	55.3	58.0	56.5	52.3	55.7	58.7	59.3	69.7	....	....	....
Slovenia	961	63.1	59.0	60.1	51.8	52.0	53.6	53.3	49.3	56.0	57.6	57.7	56.9
Tajikistan	923	....	....	....	....	....	....	....	....	....	....	....	....
Turkey	186	15.3	14.6	22.3	21.6	25.1	27.4	27.2	24.7	25.7	34.6	30.0	29.3
Turkmenistan	925	....	....	....	....	....	....	....	....	....	....	....	....
Ukraine	926	....	....	45.3	46.2	45.7	40.6	42.1	54.0	62.4	55.5	56.3	58.6
Uzbekistan	927	....	....	....	....	....	....	....	....	....	....	....	....
Middle East													
Bahrain, Kingdom of	419	84.4	84.1	79.7	82.0	88.0	79.1	64.6	78.9	90.0	83.3	90.5	....
Egypt	469	27.2	24.4	23.4	22.0	20.8	19.6	14.8	16.3	17.2	17.8	19.5	28.3
Iran, I.R. of	429	2.0	24.3	26.6	17.8	16.4	11.7	7.9	8.9	9.0	....	....	....
Iraq	433	....	....	....	....	....	....	....	....	....	....	....	....
Israel	436	29.0	31.1	31.0	30.7	29.9	30.6	31.5	31.9	35.8	32.6	34.6	36.6

2004, International Monetary Fund : *International Financial Statistics Yearbook*

Balance of Payments

Exports of Goods and Services
As percent of GDP

		1992	1993	1994	1995	1996	1997	1998	1999	2000	2001	2002	2003
Middle East(Cont.)													
Jordan	439	50.2	50.3	47.9	51.7	52.9	49.3	45.8	43.4	41.9	42.4	....	....
Kuwait	443	40.5	48.0	51.1	53.6	53.0	53.7	45.3	47.2	57.5	52.6	48.4	54.8
Lebanon	446	....	....	....	....	....	....	....	....	....	....	....	....
Libya	672	30.4	28.0	27.1	29.4	28.5	26.7	19.7	24.1	....	....	....	....
Oman	449	44.7	43.1	43.0	44.0	49.8	50.0	41.8	48.6	59.1	57.3	....	....
Qatar	453	....	....	....	....	....	....	....	....	....	....	....	....
Saudi Arabia	456	39.4	34.6	34.2	37.6	40.3	39.4	29.8	34.8	43.7	39.9	41.2	46.9
Syrian Arab Republic	463	13.2	13.2	11.5	11.3	9.7	8.5	6.8	7.5	8.5	8.8	9.2	....
United Arab Emirates	466	....	....	....	....	....	....	....	....	....	....	....	....
West Bank and Gaza	487	....	....	....	....	....	....	....	....	....	....	....	....
Yemen, Republic of	474	7.7	6.8	7.5	17.1	31.4	36.5	27.0	35.3	42.1	36.9	36.9	37.5
Western Hemisphere													
Argentina	213	6.7	6.9	7.5	9.7	10.4	10.6	10.4	9.8	11.0	11.5	28.2	25.9
Aruba	314	....	....	....	150.9	181.6	166.1	123.5	139.5	194.5	....	135.4	....
Bahamas, The	313	56.2	57.9	56.0	57.6	....	....	....	....	....	....	....	....
Barbados	316	50.9	53.0	57.6	59.4	60.8	56.6	54.4	52.6	53.1	52.1	49.8	....
Belize	339	58.4	53.3	50.3	44.4	43.9	45.5	42.6	44.1	38.5	44.5	45.7	....
Bolivia	218	13.7	15.6	19.7	18.4	17.7	17.8	15.9	15.8	17.5	19.0	19.9	23.9
Brazil	223	10.2	9.9	9.0	7.5	6.8	7.3	7.5	10.3	10.7	13.3	15.2	17.0
Chile	228	27.8	24.6	25.6	27.1	26.7	26.3	25.5	28.8	31.0	32.8	33.4	35.9
Colombia	233	17.7	16.4	13.3	13.3	13.5	13.3	13.6	16.2	18.8	18.3	17.5	19.5
Costa Rica	238	30.1	30.2	31.4	38.0	40.8	41.7	48.8	52.2	48.6	41.6	42.5	46.8
Dominican Republic	243	21.7	49.4	50.1	48.0	46.5	46.9	47.2	46.0	45.7	39.3	38.7	....
Ecuador	248	29.4	25.0	24.8	25.7	26.4	25.6	21.5	32.1	37.6	26.8	25.2	26.2
El Salvador	253	16.4	19.7	20.2	21.5	21.4	26.2	25.4	25.5	27.9	26.0	26.6	26.7
Guatemala	258	18.2	17.8	17.3	19.3	17.7	17.9	18.0	19.0	20.0	18.6	16.2	....
Guyana	336	130.4	113.8	107.1	101.2	102.2	99.7	....	....	....	....	....	....
Haiti	263	7.3	7.5	3.3	8.2	6.4	11.7	12.8	....	....	....	....	....
Honduras	268	30.5	34.9	39.2	41.3	47.1	46.5	46.1	41.1	41.3	37.9	38.1	38.3
Jamaica	343	58.8	49.0	62.2	58.7	51.1	45.8	43.8	45.1	45.2	41.4	38.3	....
Mexico	273	15.3	15.2	16.9	31.2	32.1	30.3	30.7	30.8	31.0	27.5	26.8	28.4
Netherlands Antilles	353	....	....	....	....	....	....	....	....	....	....	....	....
Nicaragua	278	17.3	19.2	16.4	20.8	21.8	26.6	26.4	25.7	27.9	28.1	28.5	31.4
Panama	283	87.0	84.5	87.9	87.9	79.5	83.2	74.9	61.9	67.3	67.7	61.9	....
Paraguay	288	36.6	48.0	48.2	53.3	45.7	41.4	48.6	37.3	36.8	35.7	43.4	....
Peru	293	12.5	12.1	12.2	12.3	13.1	14.2	13.3	14.9	16.1	15.9	16.4	....
Suriname	366	22.7	5.6	76.5	100.4	67.1	54.6	51.5	....	....	....	....	....
Trinidad and Tobago	369	39.4	40.5	42.5	52.5	48.9	52.2	48.5	50.2	59.3	53.6	....	....
Uruguay	298	20.4	18.4	18.6	18.2	18.8	19.4	18.5	17.0	18.2	17.6	21.8	27.3
Venezuela, Rep. Bol.	299	25.7	26.8	30.3	26.8	35.8	28.4	20.0	21.6	28.6	22.2	29.0	....
ECCU													
Anguilla	312	90.3	98.3	102.4	93.0	90.6	94.0	107.0	83.1	80.2	84.3	78.8	....
Antigua and Barbuda	311	96.1	96.2	87.3	81.4	74.5	76.3	75.1	73.2	70.4	....	....	....
Dominica	321	50.9	48.8	46.7	50.6	51.6	56.0	58.4	58.6	53.3	45.4	....	....
Grenada	328	39.7	44.2	48.3	44.8	44.7	44.1	47.3	57.6	57.4	....	....	....
Montserrat	351	43.5	49.4	55.1	71.3	135.8	62.2	43.3	72.3	57.7	48.8	47.9	....
St. Kitts and Nevis	361	64.5	60.6	56.8	51.6	52.1	50.9	50.5	47.9	45.6	45.1	43.9	....
St. Lucia	362	65.1	65.9	65.1	68.5	61.8	61.8	61.8	55.2	56.5	51.9	48.8	....
St. Vincent & Grens.	364	59.2	50.0	46.6	51.3	53.3	50.1	49.7	53.1	53.1	50.3	49.0	....

Balance of Payments

Imports of Goods and Services
As percent of GDP

		1992	1993	1994	1995	1996	1997	1998	1999	2000	2001	2002	2003
Industrial Countries													
United States	111	10.4	10.7	11.3	12.0	12.2	12.6	12.6	13.3	14.8	13.6	13.3	13.8
Canada	156	27.4	30.1	32.7	34.0	34.3	37.4	39.4	39.4	39.8	37.8	37.0	34.0
Australia	193	18.0	18.9	19.6	20.7	19.7	20.2	21.6	21.5	23.1	22.0	22.2	21.3
Japan	158	7.9	7.1	7.3	7.9	9.5	10.0	9.2	8.9	9.7	10.1	10.3	....
New Zealand	196	28.9	27.9	28.8	28.4	28.0	27.4	29.0	31.0	33.6	32.3	31.8	29.6
Euro Area													
Austria	122	37.5	36.1	37.7	39.1	40.9	44.4	44.7	46.4	51.0	52.4	50.9	51.4
Belgium	124	....	....	....	....	....	....	....	....	....	....	79.8	78.4
Belgium-Luxembourg	126	....	....	....	....	....	....	....	....	....	....	....	....
Finland	172	25.5	27.6	29.5	29.2	30.0	30.9	30.0	29.3	33.7	31.7	30.4	30.2
France	132	22.1	20.5	20.8	21.5	21.5	23.0	23.8	24.0	27.7	26.4	25.7	25.3
Germany	134	25.1	22.7	23.5	24.2	24.7	27.0	28.1	29.1	33.7	33.6	32.1	32.2
Greece	174	21.7	20.8	20.6	21.0	20.6	21.1	....	28.4	36.8	....	....	....
Ireland	178	52.5	54.3	59.7	63.5	64.2	64.8	96.0	74.3	84.0	83.0	77.0	68.4
Italy	136	19.2	19.0	20.3	22.8	20.7	22.3	22.6	22.9	26.7	26.3	25.3	24.4
Luxembourg	137	....	....	....	....	....	....	....	....	....	....	120.4	116.5
Netherlands	138	48.8	45.7	46.8	52.2	52.8	56.8	57.0	57.5	64.3	61.8	58.3	57.1
Portugal	182	34.4	35.2	36.9	37.8	38.5	41.5	41.9	40.0	42.9	40.8	37.8	36.6
Spain	184	20.4	20.0	22.3	22.8	23.4	25.8	27.2	28.8	32.5	31.6	30.2	29.6
Denmark	128	30.0	28.6	30.5	32.1	31.7	33.4	34.7	35.8	41.0	41.1	42.0	39.3
Iceland	176	30.4	29.6	29.7	32.0	35.8	36.6	40.5	39.7	42.0	41.5	37.9	38.7
Norway	142	31.0	31.4	32.0	31.7	31.7	33.1	35.8	31.9	29.3	28.4	27.3	27.4
Sweden	144	26.6	27.8	30.6	32.7	31.3	34.3	36.0	37.6	39.9	38.9	38.0	37.1
Switzerland	146	37.8	36.1	35.2	35.4	37.0	41.6	41.2	41.3	45.1	45.2	41.5	....
United Kingdom	112	24.9	26.5	27.2	28.8	29.8	28.6	27.8	28.2	30.1	30.2	29.3	28.2
Developing Countries													
Africa													
Algeria	612	....	....	....	70.5	68.4	68.0	72.5	92.7	62.9	74.9	....	....
Angola	614	–	–	–	....	....	....	....	....	....	....	....	....
Benin	638	34.7	35.0	42.3	44.5	33.9	35.0	32.7	35.6	31.4	31.4	....	....
Botswana	616	48.3	47.3	41.0	46.3	42.4	48.7	52.5	54.0	....	....	....	....
Burkina Faso	748	19.2	20.9	22.7	....	....	....	....	....	25.3	22.8	....	....
Burundi	618	29.4	29.5	24.9	25.9	15.9	14.5	19.4	16.1	21.3	22.1	23.4	....
Cameroon	622	16.2	15.8	22.7	18.4	....	....	....	....	....	....	....	....
Cape Verde	624	....	....	....	....	....	....	....	....	....	....	....	....
Central African Rep.	626	24.2	22.7	28.7	....	....	....	....	....	....	....	....	....
Chad	628	28.0	31.0	34.9	....	....	....	....	....	....	....	....	....
Comoros	632	42.6	37.3	46.9	46.0	....	....	....	....	....	....	....	....
Congo, Dem. Rep. of	636	....	....	....	....	....	....	....	....	....	....	....	....
Congo, Republic of	634	40.1	50.1	90.9	63.6	60.0	60.2	72.6	59.1	37.1	54.9	53.6	....
Côte d'Ivoire	662	30.8	29.8	34.2	38.1	37.5	35.3	34.5	33.6	34.2	34.4	34.1	....
Djibouti	611	....	....	....	....	....	....	....	....	....	....	....	....
Equatorial Guinea	642	56.9	51.7	50.7	117.9	174.2	....	....	....	....	....	....	....
Eritrea	643	....	....	....	....	....	....	....	....	....	....	....	....
Ethiopia	644	18.3	18.8	23.8	26.3	22.6	20.7	28.8	30.2	25.6	34.3	....	....
Gabon	646	32.4	34.6	38.3	35.7	33.0	37.2	48.0	38.1	....	....	....	....
Gambia, The	648	73.8	104.8	82.5	....	....	....	....	....	....	....	....	....
Ghana	652	29.3	36.4	36.8	32.8	34.5	38.3	....	....	....	....	....	....
Guinea	656	....	....	....	....	....	....	....	....	....	....	....	....
Guinea-Bissau	654	20.3	17.7	12.8	20.0	25.7	31.7	....	....	....	....	....	....
Kenya	664	26.5	36.1	34.4	39.1	37.3	35.6	32.4	31.2	36.0	35.6	30.9	....
Lesotho	666	123.6	115.1	104.7	112.2	111.8	106.6	103.2	91.0	89.6	94.8	107.3	....
Liberia	668	....	....	....	....	....	....	....	....	....	....	....	....
Madagascar	674	24.4	24.2	29.4	31.2	25.1	30.5	30.2	32.2	39.2	32.4	22.8	....
Malawi	676	41.9	29.5	53.9	46.0	32.5	35.7	35.9	42.6	38.6	....	....	....
Mali	678	35.1	33.9	43.5	41.7	36.2	33.2	29.5	33.2	34.2	38.5	32.5	....
Mauritania	682	57.7	61.7	53.1	48.1	53.4	48.8	....	....	....	....	....	....
Mauritius	684	62.5	64.2	65.1	60.7	63.8	64.4	63.9	66.5	59.5	58.6	59.2	....
Morocco	686	31.8	32.1	30.9	34.1	29.6	31.8	31.9	33.9	37.6	36.2	36.9	36.4
Mozambique	688	50.6	54.6	56.2	46.1	35.3	29.4	28.6	36.8	39.9	47.0	50.5	....
Namibia	728	64.8	63.9	57.6	59.9	60.5	59.1	56.1	54.4	52.6	51.3	....	....
Niger	692	25.5	21.8	29.7	27.4	....	....	....	....	....	....	....	....
Nigeria	694	28.3	29.5	22.9	14.2	8.7	10.6	10.2	33.5	....	....	....	....
Rwanda	714	17.6	20.7	63.3	29.1	26.5	25.5	21.1	23.5	24.4	26.1	25.4	....
São Tomé & Príncipe	716	....	....	....	....	....	....	....	....	....	....	....	....
Senegal	722	31.0	31.0	45.1	40.9	36.1	36.5	37.4	38.4	39.8	40.0	40.8	....
Seychelles	718	59.3	64.6	55.1	62.5	75.7	76.6	76.7	84.5	78.7	95.7	82.6	....
Sierra Leone	724	29.7	32.3	32.5	29.9	35.5	14.1	19.0	28.0	39.3	36.9	42.5	....
Somalia	726	....	....	....	....	....	....	....	....	....	....	....	....
South Africa	199	17.3	17.8	19.8	22.1	23.2	23.4	24.6	23.1	25.8	27.2	30.2	26.6
Sudan	732	24.2	12.3	21.9	14.9	18.9	15.7	....	....	....	....	....	....
Swaziland	734	100.7	101.7	91.0	93.4	97.9	91.3	99.6	91.6	95.9	102.2	101.0	....

2004, International Monetary Fund: *International Financial Statistics Yearbook*

Balance of Payments

Imports of Goods and Services
As percent of GDP

		1992	1993	1994	1995	1996	1997	1998	1999	2000	2001	2002	2003
Africa(Cont.)													
Tanzania	738	36.4	47.5	40.2	40.7	33.4	25.5	28.1	25.6	22.7	24.1	....	....
Togo	742	44.8	40.5	49.9	51.2	52.6	46.6	49.6	43.4	49.9	52.4	....	....
Tunisia	744	46.7	49.1	48.4	48.9	43.5	46.0	46.1	44.5	47.8	52.2	49.6	47.6
Uganda	746	20.6	22.9	21.8	24.1	26.2	25.7	30.2	23.1	24.3	26.5	27.1	....
Zambia	754	....	....	....	....	....	34.1	....	....	....	....	....	....
Zimbabwe	698	36.2	31.3	36.5	....	....	....	....	....	....	....	....	....
Asia*													
Afghanistan, I.S. of	512	....	....	....	....	....	....	....	....	....	....	....	....
Bangladesh	513	13.5	14.5	16.0	20.0	18.7	19.0	18.6	20.0	21.3	21.3	19.5	....
Bhutan	514	....	....	....	....	....	....	....	....	....	....	....	....
Brunei Darussalam	516	....	....	....	....	....	....	....	....	....	....	....	....
Cambodia	522	25.6	23.9	32.2	40.6	37.4	37.2	44.7	54.6	63.1	65.7	67.2	....
China,P.R.: Mainland	924	15.7	16.4	20.6	19.3	18.8	18.2	17.1	19.1	23.2	22.8	26.5	....
China,P.R.:Hong Kong	532	....	....	....	....	....	....	126.3	125.5	142.4	137.5	144.4	163.2
Fiji	819	55.0	59.5	59.5	58.3	59.3	57.8	58.5	56.1	....	....	....	....
India	534	10.3	10.9	11.7	13.2	14.2	13.9	14.1	14.0	16.5	15.4	16.5	....
Indonesia	536	25.1	24.2	24.7	26.9	26.1	29.1	46.0	30.1	36.9	35.8	30.5	....
Kiribati	826	....	....	....	....	....	....	....	....	....	....	....	....
Korea	542	29.1	27.4	28.9	30.0	31.3	33.2	33.3	32.3	37.6	35.4	33.6	....
Lao People's Dem.Rep	544	25.8	35.6	43.5	42.1	41.1	40.7	46.9	39.8	33.4	31.9	....	....
Malaysia	548	74.4	78.8	90.5	97.8	89.9	92.2	93.5	96.3	104.6	98.0	96.6	....
Maldives	556	76.3	72.9	72.4	78.3	78.5	78.9	76.0	78.4	72.3	72.9	71.2	....
Mongolia	948	34.4	73.0	61.9	42.5	48.6	53.0	69.0	76.8	....	....	....	....
Myanmar	518	1.7	2.4	2.0	1.9	1.6	1.4	1.1	.7	....	....	....	....
Nepal	558	27.9	31.5	36.1	38.5	39.6	39.6	31.5	34.0	33.5	31.1	....	....
Pakistan	564	25.8	25.3	23.3	24.1	26.6	22.7	20.3	19.7	20.5	21.8	20.9	21.9
Papua New Guinea	853	45.9	39.0	36.3	41.4	43.9	49.0	49.8	52.7	....	....	....	....
Philippines	566	31.8	38.0	40.6	45.0	49.9	61.3	60.8	48.3	52.5	52.2	49.6	50.8
Samoa	862	85.9	78.9	52.4	60.1	58.8	60.3	....	....	....	....	....	....
Singapore	576	156.3	157.3	156.4	164.8	158.3	154.3	140.7	157.9	168.9	160.9	157.7	....
Solomon Islands	813	58.4	55.5	58.7	63.1	65.1	78.0	71.3	60.3	....	....	....	....
Sri Lanka	524	39.6	42.6	45.6	45.9	43.9	43.6	42.3	43.3	49.6	45.4	42.9	....
Thailand	578	41.8	42.5	44.1	48.9	45.9	48.0	43.4	45.9	58.5	60.0	58.3	59.6
Tonga	866	50.0	53.5	....	....	....	....	....	....	....	....	....	....
Vanuatu	846	49.3	48.4	50.4	48.3	....	....	....	....	....	....	....	....
Vietnam	582	....	....	....	....	50.0	50.6	49.6	47.4	55.6	54.9	61.2	....
of which:													
Taiwan Prov.of China	528	....	....	....	....	....	....	....	....	....	....	....	....
Europe													
Albania	914	93.2	62.2	37.6	33.7	41.3	35.3	30.8	30.0	40.0	43.2	....	....
Armenia	911	....	.3	67.0	56.4	55.6	58.1	53.6	49.8	50.5	46.2	46.6	49.8
Azerbaijan	912	....	....	....	....	....	....	....	....	....	....	....	....
Belarus	913	....	....	....	54.6	50.2	61.6	53.3	54.8	77.6	72.7	67.1	70.1
Bosnia & Herzegovina	963	....	....	....	....	....	96.8	92.9	88.2	91.7	....	....	....
Bulgaria	918	62.0	53.9	53.5	49.6	60.1	55.3	47.0	50.6	60.9	61.9	58.9	62.8
Croatia	960	....	48.8	47.1	48.4	49.7	57.5	48.7	49.2	52.1	54.4	57.3	59.7
Cyprus	423	60.6	47.5	47.9	49.7	53.0	51.9	50.9	48.0	53.1	51.6	58.9	53.9
Czech Republic	935	....	52.7	53.7	57.7	58.8	61.6	60.2	61.8	67.5	68.8	64.1	....
Czechoslovakia	934	....	....	....	....	....	....	....	....	....	....	....	....
Estonia	939	....	70.0	82.5	76.1	73.6	84.1	84.7	76.4	91.8	87.4	81.7	83.3
Georgia	915	....	....	....	....	....	39.5	36.9	38.9	39.0	40.1	42.4	....
Hungary	944	34.2	38.2	34.5	44.2	47.9	53.9	64.0	67.7	78.4	75.9	67.9	66.1
Kazakhstan	916	....	....	....	35.5	37.6	39.0	37.1	38.4	48.3	48.9	48.1	43.6
Kyrgyz Republic	917	....	....	44.9	48.7	56.5	46.2	56.8	56.5	47.8	37.0	43.4	....
Latvia	941	73.1	57.8	44.4	44.8	54.2	54.6	59.6	49.9	50.3	51.7	51.4	55.2
Lithuania	946	....	91.2	61.4	61.0	61.8	63.4	57.2	49.2	51.2	55.4	58.8	58.4
Macedonia, FYR	962	....	....	....	....	40.2	50.0	56.3	52.2	63.5	56.6	56.9	....
Malta	181	98.9	104.9	106.8	105.5	98.7	91.1	91.8	94.1	111.5	91.3	87.7	88.7
Moldova	921	....	....	....	69.8	73.7	74.3	72.4	67.4	75.5	73.3	....	....
Poland	964	21.5	24.1	23.0	26.6	28.6	32.1	32.6	32.3	34.8	31.8	33.4	....
Romania	968	33.2	26.3	25.9	31.9	35.4	34.9	30.3	32.0	37.9	41.1	41.1	44.1
Russia	922	....	....	23.6	26.4	22.1	22.7	27.5	27.0	23.5	24.3	24.4	23.7
Slovak Republic	936	....	60.1	53.3	54.9	63.1	65.2	69.2	64.5	71.9	....	....	....
Slovenia	961	55.3	57.2	57.9	53.7	53.0	54.4	54.7	53.4	59.6	58.2	56.3	56.9
Tajikistan	923	....	....	....	....	....	....	....	....	....	....	....	....
Turkey	186	16.8	18.7	20.2	23.7	27.3	29.8	27.6	26.3	31.2	31.5	30.2	30.8
Turkmenistan	925	....	....	....	....	....	....	....	....	....	....	....	....
Ukraine	926	....	....	49.0	49.4	48.2	43.6	45.0	48.2	57.4	53.9	51.8	56.0
Uzbekistan	927	....	....	....	....	....	....	....	....	....	....	....	....
Middle East													
Bahrain, Kingdom of	419	96.7	80.7	74.0	70.5	76.2	69.5	63.9	63.0	64.4	60.4	73.2	....
Egypt	469	32.9	32.6	30.3	28.5	27.0	27.6	24.9	23.9	23.4	23.3	23.2	27.7
Iran, I.R. of	429	2.9	31.5	21.2	14.2	12.7	10.5	9.1	6.4	5.3	....	....	....
Iraq	433	....	....	....	....	....	....	....	....	....	....	....	....
Israel	436	35.8	40.0	39.5	39.4	38.0	36.0	34.6	36.8	37.9	35.6	38.5	37.9

2004, International Monetary Fund: *International Financial Statistics Yearbook*

Balance of Payments

Imports of Goods and Services
As percent of GDP

		1992	1993	1994	1995	1996	1997	1998	1999	2000	2001	2002	2003
Middle East(Cont.)													
Jordan	439	81.3	80.1	70.5	72.8	78.2	71.6	65.6	61.3	68.6	67.7	....	....
Kuwait	443	59.5	48.1	44.8	47.6	42.0	43.1	52.8	40.7	30.7	36.4	39.7	38.9
Lebanon	446	....	....	....	....	....	....	....	....	....	....	....	....
Libya	672	25.8	31.3	26.1	22.6	23.8	21.8	21.3	17.4	....	....	....	....
Oman	449	36.6	39.5	35.6	36.5	35.8	38.6	49.0	37.0	31.0	35.0	....	....
Qatar	453	....	....	....	....	....	....	....	....	....	....	....	....
Saudi Arabia	456	45.9	38.1	29.2	31.5	31.5	31.7	30.4	27.7	28.1	26.2	26.3	25.5
Syrian Arab Republic	463	12.2	13.4	13.8	10.9	9.9	7.7	6.8	7.1	6.7	7.0	7.1	....
United Arab Emirates	466	....	....	....	....	....	....	....	....	....	....	....	....
West Bank and Gaza	487	....	....	....	....	....	....	....	....	....	....	....	....
Yemen, Republic of	474	18.1	16.0	8.6	19.5	36.6	45.4	48.0	37.7	34.6	36.0	37.7	40.2
Western Hemisphere													
Argentina	213	8.4	9.3	10.6	10.1	11.1	12.8	13.0	11.6	11.6	10.2	12.9	14.4
Aruba	314	....	....	....	152.8	185.5	177.0	124.4	157.8	177.0	....	140.9	....
Bahamas, The	313	52.5	52.5	53.7	58.5	....	....	....	....	....	....	....	....
Barbados	316	42.6	47.6	49.6	56.3	56.6	58.8	56.9	58.3	58.6	56.5	55.8	....
Belize	339	67.3	64.7	57.9	48.7	45.6	51.5	50.8	52.5	52.3	60.4	58.3	....
Bolivia	218	24.0	25.0	22.6	23.4	23.4	26.0	25.9	24.0	24.8	24.7	26.6	25.5
Brazil	223	7.2	8.0	8.0	9.0	8.5	9.3	9.4	11.8	12.0	14.3	13.4	13.0
Chile	228	26.6	27.1	24.6	25.7	28.1	28.2	28.7	26.5	29.1	31.3	31.0	32.8
Colombia	233	15.4	18.8	17.4	17.3	16.9	17.2	17.6	15.5	17.2	19.4	19.0	21.1
Costa Rica	238	34.1	35.7	34.0	40.3	42.7	44.5	50.0	45.5	45.8	42.2	45.9	48.7
Dominican Republic	243	30.9	57.0	55.7	51.4	51.4	51.7	56.3	53.5	55.4	47.2	47.7	....
Ecuador	248	23.8	26.6	26.4	28.3	24.1	25.8	28.8	25.2	31.5	31.5	32.2	29.0
El Salvador	253	32.3	34.3	35.2	38.2	34.3	37.8	37.5	37.8	42.9	41.8	41.3	43.0
Guatemala	258	27.3	26.1	24.6	25.4	22.4	23.6	26.0	27.4	28.9	28.9	28.5	....
Guyana	336	155.8	135.4	121.9	113.9	108.2	109.4	....	....	....	....	....	....
Haiti	263	16.2	18.7	11.4	34.3	26.3	27.5	27.2	....	....	....	....	....
Honduras	268	36.1	42.7	48.4	46.8	55.2	53.3	53.5	55.5	54.2	53.0	51.8	53.6
Jamaica	343	59.8	56.8	62.7	64.5	59.4	54.7	52.3	52.0	55.8	56.7	57.3	....
Mexico	273	20.4	19.2	22.0	28.7	30.2	30.5	32.9	32.6	33.0	29.8	28.8	30.2
Netherlands Antilles	353	....	....	....	....	....	....	....	....	....	....	....	....
Nicaragua	278	51.3	42.7	32.8	36.1	41.4	50.6	49.8	57.6	54.3	53.5	54.6	57.9
Panama	283	88.0	84.7	86.9	89.7	80.5	85.8	81.7	68.4	69.7	66.0	62.4	....
Paraguay	288	38.0	49.1	53.4	57.7	52.4	50.4	52.6	41.9	43.3	42.3	44.5	....
Peru	293	15.0	15.9	15.7	17.9	17.8	18.4	18.8	17.5	18.3	17.9	17.6	....
Suriname	366	23.2	5.1	64.3	87.7	76.1	61.9	70.1	....	....	....	....	....
Trinidad and Tobago	369	28.6	31.0	29.8	39.6	38.0	56.3	53.8	44.4	45.4	43.5	....	....
Uruguay	298	19.3	19.1	19.9	18.5	19.4	20.2	20.0	19.1	20.9	20.0	20.2	24.2
Venezuela, Rep. Bol.	299	28.4	26.7	22.5	21.8	21.0	21.2	21.7	18.1	17.6	18.9	18.3	....
ECCU													
Anguilla	312	109.2	108.0	103.6	122.5	123.6	115.7	130.6	138.1	143.6	122.7	112.9	....
Antigua and Barbuda	311	91.2	87.3	84.4	88.9	86.5	82.3	79.0	81.4	75.1	....	....	....
Dominica	321	65.2	63.7	62.4	66.6	69.6	70.5	66.2	67.5	67.5	63.1	....	....
Grenada	328	55.2	63.7	61.2	60.9	65.6	67.1	72.2	69.9	75.1	....	....	....
Montserrat	351	85.7	68.6	81.3	94.4	127.4	115.7	122.1	137.1	128.5	134.3	140.0	....
St. Kitts and Nevis	361	71.6	73.9	67.2	75.0	78.9	71.2	67.2	72.4	75.7	70.7	72.9	....
St. Lucia	362	72.4	71.1	71.3	70.9	68.2	71.4	67.7	67.4	64.2	59.2	59.7	....
St. Vincent & Grens	364	69.3	68.2	70.6	65.7	66.5	78.1	78.6	73.5	60.9	61.1	60.2	....

2004, International Monetary Fund : *International Financial Statistics Yearbook*

Balance of Payments

Current Account Balance
Excluding Exceptional Financing
As percent of GDP

		1992	1993	1994	1995	1996	1997	1998	1999	2000	2001	2002	2003
Industrial Countries													
United States	111	−.8	−1.2	−1.7	−1.5	−1.5	−1.6	−2.4	−3.2	−4.2	−3.8	−4.5	−4.8
Canada	156	−3.7	−3.9	−2.3	−.7	.6	−1.3	−1.3	.3	2.7	2.3	2.0	2.0
Australia	193	−3.7	−3.3	−5.1	−5.4	−3.9	−3.1	−5.0	−5.7	−4.1	−2.4	−4.4	−6.0
Japan	158	3.0	3.0	2.7	2.1	1.4	2.2	3.0	2.6	2.5	2.1	2.8	....
New Zealand	196	−2.6	−1.7	−4.6	−4.9	−5.8	−6.5	−4.0	−6.2	−4.8	−2.5	−3.8	−4.6
Euro Area													
Austria	122	−.4	−.6	−1.5	−2.3	−2.1	−2.5	−2.5	−3.2	−2.6	−1.9	.3	−.9
Belgium	124	....	....	....	....	....	....	....	....	....	....	5.4	3.9
Belgium-Luxembourg	126	....	....	....	....	....	....	....	....	....	....		
Finland	172	−4.7	−1.3	1.1	4.0	3.9	5.4	5.7	6.3	7.5	7.2	7.7	5.7
France	132	.3	.7	.5	.7	1.3	2.7	2.6	2.2	1.4	2.2	1.0	.2
Germany	134	−1.0	−.7	−1.4	−1.1	−.6	−.4	−.6	−1.1	−1.3	.1	2.2	2.2
Greece	174	−2.2	−.8	−.1	−2.4	−3.7	−4.0	....	−5.8	−8.7	....	....	....
Ireland	178	1.1	3.5	2.9	2.6	2.8	2.3	1.2	.3	−.5	−.7	−1.2	−1.4
Italy	136	−2.4	.8	1.3	2.3	3.2	2.8	1.7	.7	−.5	−.1	−.6	−1.5
Luxembourg	137	....	....	....	....	....	....	....	....	....	....	7.8	9.5
Netherlands	138	2.0	4.1	4.9	6.2	5.2	6.7	3.3	3.3	1.8	2.0	2.4	3.2
Portugal	182	−.2	.3	−2.5	−.1	−4.8	−6.3	−7.3	−8.5	−10.4	−9.4	−6.7	−5.1
Spain	184	−3.7	−1.2	−1.3	.1	.1	.4	−.5	−2.3	−3.4	−2.8	−2.4	−2.8
Denmark	128	2.9	3.5	2.1	1.0	1.7	.5	−1.2	1.7	1.5	3.1	2.9	2.9
Iceland	176	−2.3	.6	1.8	.7	−1.8	−1.8	−6.9	−7.0	−10.1	−4.4	−.3	−5.4
Norway	142	3.5	3.0	3.0	3.5	6.9	6.4	−	5.3	15.5	15.4	13.0	13.0
Sweden	144	−3.5	−2.1	.3	2.0	2.2	3.0	1.9	2.4	2.8	3.1	5.3	7.6
Switzerland	146	5.9	7.6	6.7	7.1	7.1	10.4	10.2	11.4	14.3	9.7	9.7	....
United Kingdom	112	−2.2	−1.9	−1.0	−1.3	−.9	−.1	−.5	−2.7	−2.5	−2.2	−1.7	−1.9
Developing Countries													
Africa													
Algeria	612	....	....	....	....	....	....	....	....	....	....	....	....
Angola	614	−	−	−	−5.9	50.1	−11.6	−28.7	−27.8	8.7	−16.0	....	....
Benin	638	−5.6	−4.8	−1.5	−10.3	−2.6	−7.9	−6.5	−8.0	−4.9	−6.8	....	....
Botswana	616	5.0	11.3	5.1	6.8	11.6	14.8	3.6	11.1	....	....	....	....
Burkina Faso	748	−.7	−2.2	.7	....	....	....	....	....	−15.1	−13.4	....	....
Burundi	618	−5.5	−2.9	−1.6	1.0	−4.6	−.1	−6.0	−3.3	−6.8	−5.3	−.4	....
Cameroon	622	−3.3	−5.1	−.8	1.0	....	....	....	....	....	....	....	....
Cape Verde	624	....	....	....	....	....	....	....	....	....	....	....	....
Central African Rep.	626	−5.9	−1.0	−2.9	....	....	....	....	....	....	....	....	....
Chad	628	−5.1	−8.0	−3.2	....	....	....	....	....	....	....	....	....
Comoros	632	−5.4	3.6	−3.7	−8.4	....	....	....	....	....	....	....	....
Congo, Dem. Rep. of	636	....	....	....	....	....	....	....	....	....	....	....	....
Congo, Republic of	634	−10.8	−20.6	−44.8	−29.5	−25.6	−6.7	−12.3	−9.8	20.1	−1.0	−1.1	....
Côte d'Ivoire	662	−9.1	−8.6	−.2	−4.9	−1.5	−1.3	−2.3	−1.0	−2.3	−.6	6.6	....
Djibouti	611	....	....	....	....	....	....	....	....	....	....	....	....
Equatorial Guinea	642	−6.6	1.6	−.3	−74.2	−125.7	....	....	....	....	....	....	....
Eritrea	643	....	....	....	....	....	....	....	....	....	....	....	....
Ethiopia	644	−1.6	−.9	2.4	.7	1.3	−.6	−5.3	−7.6	.2	−7.2	....	....
Gabon	646	−3.0	−.9	7.6	9.4	15.6	10.0	−13.3	8.4	....	....	....	....
Gambia, The	648	11.2	−1.9	2.7	....	....	....	....	....	....	....	....	....
Ghana	652	−5.9	−9.4	−4.7	−2.2	−4.7	−8.0	....	....	....	....	....	....
Guinea	656	....	....	....	....	....	....	....	....	....	....	....	....
Guinea-Bissau	654	−19.0	−15.5	−7.5	−11.3	−18.0	−10.8	....	....	....	....	....	....
Kenya	664	−2.2	1.2	1.4	−4.4	−.8	−4.3	−4.1	−.8	−1.9	−3.0	−1.1	....
Lesotho	666	4.6	3.6	12.9	−34.6	−32.1	−26.3	−31.5	−24.2	−17.6	−12.4	−16.1	....
Liberia	668	....	....	....	....	....	....	....	....	....	....	....	....
Madagascar	674	−6.6	−7.7	−9.3	−8.7	−7.3	−7.5	−8.0	−6.8	−7.3	−3.8	−6.8	....
Malawi	676	−15.8	−8.1	−15.4	−5.4	−6.2	−10.7	−.2	−8.8	−4.5	....	....	....
Mali	678	−8.8	−7.5	−9.2	−11.9	−10.1	−6.6	−5.6	−8.6	−9.0	−10.3	−4.4	....
Mauritania	682	−10.7	−18.4	−7.0	2.1	8.4	4.5	....	....	....	....	....	....
Mauritius	684	−	−2.8	−6.5	−.5	.8	−2.1	.1	−2.9	−.8	6.1	5.5	....
Morocco	686	−1.5	−1.9	−2.4	−3.9	−.2	−.5	−.4	−.5	−1.5	4.7	4.1	3.7
Mozambique	688	−17.5	−21.6	−21.2	−19.4	−14.5	−8.6	−10.9	−22.4	−20.4	−19.1	−20.4	....
Namibia	728	1.7	3.9	2.6	5.0	3.3	2.5	4.8	4.8	4.9	−.2	....	....
Niger	692	−6.8	−4.3	−8.9	−9.1	....	....	....	....	....	....	....	....
Nigeria	694	7.1	−2.5	−5.1	−2.9	2.7	.4	−3.2	1.4	....	....	....	....
Rwanda	714	−4.1	−6.6	−6.1	4.5	−.6	−3.3	−4.1	−7.5	−5.4	−6.2	−7.4	....
São Tomé & Príncipe	716	....	....	....	....	....	....	....	....	....	....	....	....
Senegal	722	−6.7	−8.1	−5.6	−5.5	−4.3	−4.3	−5.4	−6.8	−7.6	−5.3	−6.2	....
Seychelles	718	−1.6	−1.6	4.9	−.6	−11.8	−12.9	−19.4	−20.5	−8.3	−20.0	−18.7	....
Sierra Leone	724	−.8	−7.5	−9.8	−13.6	−16.0	−6.5	−4.9	−14.8	−17.7	−13.1	−9.3	....
Somalia	726	....	....	....	....	....	....	....	....	....	....	....	....
South Africa	199	1.5	1.2	.1	−1.5	−1.3	−1.5	−1.6	−.4	−.2	−	.6	−.9
Sudan	732	−12.1	−3.9	−10.4	−6.0	−10.1	−8.1	....	....	....	....	....	....

Balance of Payments

Current Account Balance
Excluding Exceptional Financing
As percent of GDP

		1992	1993	1994	1995	1996	1997	1998	1999	2000	2001	2002	2003
Africa(Cont.)													
Swaziland	734	−4.1	−6.2	.2	−2.2	−3.9	−.2	−6.9	−2.6	−4.7	−4.2	−4.0	....
Tanzania	738	−15.5	−24.6	−15.8	−12.3	−7.9	−8.2	−11.0	−9.7	−5.5	−5.1	....	....
Togo	742	−8.4	−6.6	−5.7	−9.3	−10.5	−7.8	−9.9	−8.9	−11.6	−13.7	....	....
Tunisia	744	−7.1	−9.1	−3.4	−4.3	−2.4	−3.1	−3.4	−2.1	−4.2	−4.2	−3.5	−2.9
Uganda	746	−3.1	−6.7	−3.9	−5.5	−4.0	−5.5	−8.0	−11.7	−14.2	−13.7	−7.0	....
Zambia	754	....	....	....	....	....	−9.0	....	....	....	....	....	....
Zimbabwe	698	−8.9	−1.8	−6.2	....	....	....	....	....	....	....	....	....
Asia*													
Afghanistan, I.S. of	512	....	....	....	....	....	....	....	....	....	....	....	....
Bangladesh	513	.6	1.1	.6	−2.2	−2.5	−.7	−.1	−.8	−.7	−1.2	1.6	....
Bhutan	514	....	....	....	....	....	....	....	....	....	....	....	....
Brunei Darussalam	516	....	....	....	....	....	....	....	....	....	....	....	....
Cambodia	522	−4.7	−4.2	−5.7	−5.5	−5.4	−6.2	−5.6	−5.4	−3.8	−2.3	−1.6	....
China,P.R.: Mainland	924	1.4	−1.9	1.3	.2	.9	4.1	3.3	2.1	1.9	1.5	2.9	....
China,P.R.:Hong Kong	532							1.5	6.4	4.3	6.1	7.9	10.3
Fiji	819	−4.0	−8.4	−6.2	−5.7	.6	−1.6	−3.6	.7	....	....	....	....
India	534	−1.6	−.7	−.5	−1.5	−1.5	−.7	−1.6	−.7	−.6	.4	.9	....
Indonesia	536	−2.0	−1.3	−1.6	−3.2	−3.4	−2.3	4.3	4.1	5.3	4.9	4.5	....
Kiribati	826	....	....	....	....	....	....	....	....	....	....	....	....
Korea	542	−1.3	.3	−1.0	−1.6	−4.1	−1.6	11.7	5.5	2.4	1.7	1.1	....
Lao People's Dem.Rep.	544	−9.4	−10.5	−18.4	−19.5	−18.5	−17.5	−11.7	−8.3	−.5	−4.7	....	....
Malaysia	548	−3.7	−4.5	−6.1	−9.7	−4.4	−5.9	13.2	15.9	9.4	8.3	7.6	....
Maldives	556	−6.9	−16.7	−3.1	−4.5	−1.6	−6.8	−4.0	−13.4	−8.2	−9.2	−6.9	....
Mongolia	948	−4.2	5.5	6.8	3.2	−8.5	5.2	−13.2	−13.1	....	....	....	....
Myanmar	518	−.3	−.4	−.2	−.2	−.2	−.2	−.2	−.1	....	....	....	....
Nepal	558	−5.2	−6.3	−8.7	−8.4	−7.4	−8.0	−1.5	−5.1	−5.6	−6.2	....	....
Pakistan	564	−3.9	−6.1	−3.5	−5.7	−7.5	−2.9	−3.8	−1.5	−.1	3.4	6.3	5.2
Papua New Guinea	853	−3.7	9.5	7.6	10.7	3.6	−3.9	−.8	2.8	....	....	....	....
Philippines	566	−1.9	−5.5	−4.6	−2.7	−4.8	−5.3	2.4	9.5	8.2	1.9	5.7	4.2
Samoa	862	−33.8	−24.3	3.1	4.9	5.8	3.9	....	....	....	....	....	....
Singapore	576	11.9	7.2	16.1	17.6	15.2	15.6	22.6	18.7	14.5	19.0	21.5	....
Solomon Islands	813	−.5	−2.0	−.8	2.3	4.0	−10.1	2.7	6.6	....	....	....	....
Sri Lanka	524	−4.6	−3.7	−6.5	−5.9	−4.9	−2.6	−1.4	−3.6	−6.4	−1.7	−1.8	....
Thailand	578	−5.7	−5.1	−5.6	−8.1	−8.1	−2.0	12.7	10.1	7.6	5.4	5.5	5.6
Tonga	866	−.3	−4.1	....	....	....	....	....	....	....	....	....	....
Vanuatu	846	−6.9	−7.6	−9.2	−7.7	....	....	....	....	....	....	....	....
Vietnam	582	....	....	....	....	−8.2	−5.7	−3.9	4.1	3.5	2.1	−1.7	....
*of which:													
Taiwan Prov.of China	528	....	....	....	....	....	....	....	....	....	....	....	....
Europe													
Albania	914	−7.5	1.2	−8.1	−.5	−4.0	−11.9	−2.1	−4.2	−4.2	−5.3	....	....
Armenia	911	....	−.1	−16.0	−17.0	−18.2	−18.7	−22.1	−16.6	−14.6	−9.5	−6.2	−6.6
Azerbaijan	912	....	....	....	....	....	....	....	....	....	....	....	....
Belarus	913	....	....	....	−4.3	−3.6	−6.1	−6.7	−1.6	−3.1	−3.5	−2.6	−2.9
Bosnia & Herzegovina	963	....	....	....	....	....	....	−19.0	−23.4	−19.5	−26.0	....	....
Bulgaria	918	−4.2	−10.1	−.3	−.2	.2	4.1	−.5	−5.0	−5.6	−7.2	−5.3	−8.4
Croatia	960	....	5.3	3.8	−8.5	−5.3	−13.9	−6.8	−7.0	−2.5	−3.7	−8.4	−7.3
Cyprus	423	−9.2	1.7	1.0	−1.8	−5.2	−4.0	−6.6	−2.3	−5.1	−4.3	−5.1	−2.2
Czech Republic	935	....	1.3	−2.0	−2.6	−7.2	−6.8	−2.3	−2.7	−4.8	−5.4	−6.1	....
Czechoslovakia	934	....	....	....	....	....	....	....	....	....	....	....	....
Estonia	939	....	1.2	−6.9	−4.2	−8.6	−11.4	−8.6	−5.3	−5.4	−5.7	−10.2	−13.2
Georgia	915	....	....	....	....	....	−14.4	−7.6	−7.1	−8.8	−6.6	−6.8	....
Hungary	944	.9	−11.0	−9.8	−3.6	−2.5	−1.5	−4.7	−5.1	−6.2	−3.4	−4.1	−8.9
Kazakhstan	916	....	....	....	−1.2	−3.7	−3.8	−5.8	−1.0	3.7	−5.2	−2.9	−.6
Kyrgyz Republic	917	....	....	−7.6	−15.7	−23.3	−7.8	−25.1	−20.2	−9.2	−3.4	−5.3	....
Latvia	941	14.0	19.2	5.5	−.3	−5.0	−5.6	−9.8	−9.1	−6.4	−8.9	−7.0	−8.6
Lithuania	946	....	−3.2	−2.2	−9.6	−9.0	−10.0	−11.7	−11.0	−5.9	−4.7	−5.1	−7.0
Macedonia, FYR	962	....	....	....	....	−6.5	−7.4	−7.5	−.9	−2.0	−7.1	−8.6	−6.0
Malta	181	1.1	−3.4	−4.8	−11.1	−12.2	−6.1	−6.3	−3.3	−13.2	−4.6	−1.2	−6.0
Moldova	921	....	....	....	−6.1	−11.5	−14.3	−19.7	−6.7	−9.7	−5.3	....	....
Poland	964	−3.7	−6.7	1.0	.7	−2.3	−4.0	−4.3	−7.7	−6.1	−2.9	−2.6	−5.8
Romania	968	−7.7	−4.7	−1.5	−5.0	−7.3	−6.0	−6.9	−3.6	−3.7	−5.5	−3.3	−5.8
Russia	922	....	....	2.8	2.2	2.8	−	.1	12.6	18.0	11.0	8.4	8.3
Slovak Republic	936	....	−4.3	4.3	2.0	−10.0	−9.3	−9.6	−5.7	−3.4	....	....	....
Slovenia	961	7.8	1.5	4.0	−.4	.3	.3	−.6	−3.3	−2.9	.2	1.7	.1
Tajikistan	923	....	....	....	....	....	....	....	....	....	....	....	....
Turkey	186	−.6	−3.6	2.0	−1.4	−1.3	−1.4	1.0	−.7	−4.9	2.3	−.8	−2.9
Turkmenistan	925	....	....	....	....	....	....	....	....	....	....	....	....
Ukraine	926	....	....	−3.2	−3.1	−2.7	−2.7	−3.1	5.3	4.7	3.7	7.7	5.9
Uzbekistan	927	....	....	....	....	....	....	....	....	....	....	....	....
Middle East													
Bahrain, Kingdom of	419	−17.4	−6.5	−4.6	4.1	4.3	−.5	−12.6	−.6	10.4	2.9	−6.7	....
Egypt	469	6.7	4.9	.1	−.4	−.3	−.9	−3.0	−1.8	−1.0	−.4	.7	5.3
Iran, I.R. of	429	−.6	−5.3	6.6	3.2	3.7	1.3	−1.1	2.6	3.8	....	....	....

2004, International Monetary Fund : *International Financial Statistics Yearbook*

Balance of Payments

Current Account Balance
Excluding Exceptional Financing
As percent of GDP

		1992	1993	1994	1995	1996	1997	1998	1999	2000	2001	2002	2003
Middle East(Cont.)													
Iraq	433	....	....	....	....	....	....	....	....	....	....	....	....
Israel	436	−1.3	−3.7	−4.5	−5.2	−5.2	−3.2	−1.1	−3.2	−2.6	−1.6	−1.3	.6
Jordan	439	−15.7	−11.2	−6.4	−3.8	−3.2	.4	.2	5.0	.7	−	....	....
Kuwait	443	−2.3	10.4	13.0	18.9	22.9	26.6	8.8	17.2	39.6	24.4	12.1	18.1
Lebanon	446	....	....	....	....	....	....	....	....	....	....	....	....
Libya	672	4.2	−4.5	.1	6.5	4.4	5.0	−1.3	7.0	....	....	....	....
Oman	449	−4.8	−9.5	−6.2	−5.8	2.2	−.5	−20.9	−1.9	17.2	11.6	....	....
Qatar	453	....	....	....	....	....	....	....	....	....	....	....	....
Saudi Arabia	456	−13.0	−13.1	−7.8	−3.7	.4	.2	−9.0	.3	7.6	5.1	6.3	13.8
Syrian Arab Republic	463	.2	−.6	−1.8	.5	.1	.7	.1	.3	1.3	1.4	1.6	....
United Arab Emirates	466	....	....	....	....	....	....	....	....	....	....	....	....
West Bank and Gaza	487	....	....	....	....	....	....	....	....	....	....	....	....
Yemen, Republic of	474	−7.0	−6.4	.7	1.1	.5	−1.0	−7.6	4.8	14.0	7.0	5.2	1.3
Western Hemisphere													
Argentina	213	−2.5	−3.4	−4.3	−2.0	−2.5	−4.2	−4.9	−4.2	−3.2	−1.4	9.0	6.0
Aruba	314	....	....	....	−	−5.0	−12.8	−1.1	−19.3	15.2	....	−12.8	....
Bahamas, The	313	1.3	1.7	−1.4	−4.8	....	....	....	....	....	....	....	....
Barbados	316	8.8	4.2	7.7	2.3	3.5	−2.3	−2.6	−6.0	−5.6	−4.3	−6.6	....
Belize	339	−5.9	−9.1	−7.3	−2.6	−.9	−4.4	−7.8	−9.1	−13.9	−18.3	−15.0	....
Bolivia	218	−9.5	−8.8	−1.5	−4.5	−5.5	−7.0	−7.8	−5.9	−5.3	−3.4	−4.5	.2
Brazil	223	1.6	−	−.2	−2.6	−3.0	−3.8	−4.3	−4.7	−4.0	−4.6	−1.7	.8
Chile	228	−2.2	−5.4	−2.8	−1.9	−4.1	−4.4	−4.9	.1	−1.2	−1.6	−1.3	−.8
Colombia	233	1.7	−3.5	−4.6	−4.9	−4.8	−5.4	−4.9	.8	.9	−1.4	−1.8	−1.9
Costa Rica	238	−4.4	−6.4	−2.3	−3.1	−2.2	−3.7	−3.7	−4.2	−4.4	−4.3	−5.4	−5.5
Dominican Republic	243	−8.0	−5.5	−2.7	−1.5	−1.6	−1.1	−2.1	−2.5	−5.2	−3.5	−3.7	....
Ecuador	248	−1.0	−5.6	−4.8	−5.0	−.3	−1.9	−9.0	5.5	5.8	−3.3	−5.6	−1.7
El Salvador	253	−3.3	−1.8	−.2	−2.8	−1.6	−.9	−.8	−1.9	−3.3	−1.1	−2.9	−4.9
Guatemala	258	−6.8	−6.2	−4.8	−3.9	−2.9	−3.6	−5.4	−5.6	−5.4	−6.0	−5.1	....
Guyana	336	−37.1	−30.1	−22.9	−21.7	−9.8	−15.0	....	....	....	....	....	....
Haiti	263	.5	−.8	−1.1	−3.7	−4.6	−1.5	−1.0	....	....	....	....	....
Honduras	268	−8.7	−8.8	−10.0	−5.1	−8.2	−5.8	−7.5	−11.5	−4.6	−5.3	−3.7	−4.0
Jamaica	343	.8	−3.8	1.7	−1.7	−2.2	−4.5	−4.3	−2.8	−4.6	−9.4	−13.3	....
Mexico	273	−6.7	−5.8	−7.0	−.6	−.8	−1.9	−3.8	−2.9	−3.1	−2.9	−2.2	−1.5
Netherlands Antilles	353	....	....	....	....	....	....	....	....	....	....	....	....
Nicaragua	278	−46.5	−33.7	−30.6	−22.7	−24.8	−24.8	−19.2	−24.8	−20.0	−19.4	−19.6	−18.9
Panama	283	−3.7	−1.2	.2	−5.4	−2.2	−5.0	−10.8	−11.5	−6.2	−1.5	−.8	....
Paraguay	288	−.9	.9	−3.5	−1.0	−3.7	−6.8	−1.9	−2.1	−3.8	−3.9	1.3	....
Peru	293	−5.2	−7.1	−6.0	−8.6	−6.5	−5.7	−5.9	−2.8	−2.9	−2.2	−2.0	....
Suriname	366	.9	.7	12.2	14.2	−8.5	−7.5	−18.9	....	....	....	....	....
Trinidad and Tobago	369	2.6	2.5	4.4	5.5	1.8	−10.7	−10.6	.4	6.7	4.6	....	....
Uruguay	298	−.1	−1.6	−2.5	−1.1	−1.1	−1.3	−2.1	−2.4	−2.8	−2.6	2.6	.5
Venezuela, Rep. Bol	299	−6.2	−3.3	4.3	2.6	12.6	4.2	−4.6	2.0	9.8	1.6	7.8	....
ECCU													
Anguilla	312	−31.8	−22.6	−18.6	−15.5	−31.1	−26.1	−24.6	−59.2	−63.0	−40.9	−39.9	....
Antigua and Barbuda	311	−2.3	3.3	−1.3	−.1	−11.0	−8.2	−7.5	−8.8	−9.9	....	....	....
Dominica	321	−14.1	−13.7	−17.5	−18.5	−21.7	−17.2	−8.9	−13.4	−19.7	−18.5	....	....
Grenada	328	−12.9	−17.5	−10.3	−14.8	−18.9	−21.6	−23.2	−14.0	−20.5	....	....	....
Montserrat	351	−26.6	−15.2	−22.4	−3.8	37.5	−5.6	10.4	−4.8	−22.2	−18.4	−25.0	....
St. Kitts and Nevis	361	−8.6	−15.4	−11.4	−19.8	−26.6	−22.4	−16.1	−27.1	−20.1	−31.0	−35.1	....
St. Lucia	362	−11.3	−10.1	−9.3	−6.0	−10.1	−13.5	−9.5	−14.6	−11.6	−11.5	−15.5	....
St. Vincent & Grens	364	−10.4	−18.4	−23.8	−15.3	−12.7	−28.7	−29.1	−21.9	−8.8	−11.9	−11.7	....

GDP Volume Measures

Percent Change over Previous Year; Calculated from Indices

		1992	1993	1994	1995	1996	1997	1998	1999	2000	2001	2002	2003
World	001	3.0	2.7	4.6	3.9	4.3	4.1	2.6	3.6	4.6	1.7	1.9	....
Industrial Countries	110	1.9	1.2	3.2	2.4	2.8	3.2	2.8	3.4	3.5	1.2	1.3	2.2
United States	111	3.3	2.7	4.0	2.5	3.7	4.5	4.2	4.4	3.7	.8	1.9	3.0
Canada	156	.9	2.3	4.8	2.8	1.6	4.2	4.1	5.5	5.3	1.9	3.3	1.7
Australia	193	2.0	3.8	4.9	3.5	4.3	3.9	5.2	4.3	3.2	2.5	3.8	3.0
Japan	158	1.0	.2	1.1	1.9	3.5	1.8	−1.2	.2	2.8	.4	−.3	2.5
New Zealand	196	1.0	6.3	5.1	3.7	3.2	2.9	.1	5.2	2.2	4.0	4.1	2.0
Euro Area	163	....	....	....	....	1.3	2.2	2.7	2.4	3.6	3.3	.8	.6
Austria	122	1.3	.5	2.4	1.7	2.0	1.3	3.3	3.6	3.4	.8	1.4	.7
Belgium	124	1.3	−.7	3.3	2.3	.8	3.9	2.1	10.3	3.7	.7	.7	1.1
Finland	172	−3.3	−1.1	4.0	3.8	4.0	6.3	5.3	3.2	5.1	1.1	2.3	1.9
France	132	1.2	−.9	1.8	1.9	1.1	1.9	3.5	3.1	3.8	2.1	1.2	.5
Germany	134	2.2	−1.1	2.3	1.7	.8	1.5	1.8	2.1	2.9	.8	.2	−.1
Greece	174	.7	−1.6	2.0	2.1	2.4	3.6	3.4	3.6	4.1	4.2	3.9	4.3
Ireland	178	3.3	2.7	5.8	9.7	8.0	10.8	8.6	11.6	9.9	6.0	6.1	3.7
Italy	136	.8	−.9	2.2	2.9	1.1	2.0	1.8	1.6	3.0	1.8	.4	.3
Luxembourg	137	....	....	....	....	3.6	9.1	5.9	5.7	9.5	1.6	....	....
Netherlands	138	2.0	.6	6.7	3.0	3.0	3.8	3.1	5.3	3.5	1.2	.2	−.7
Portugal	182	1.9	−1.4	2.5	2.9	3.2	3.5	3.5	8.5	3.7	1.6	.4	−1.4
Spain	184	.7	−1.2	2.3	2.7	2.4	3.5	3.8	4.9	4.2	2.8	2.0	2.4
Denmark	128	.6	−	5.5	2.8	2.5	3.0	2.5	2.6	2.8	1.6	1.0	.5
Iceland	176	−3.3	.8	4.0	.1	5.2	4.7	5.6	4.2	5.6	2.7	−.5	4.0
Norway	142	3.3	2.7	5.3	4.4	5.3	5.2	2.6	2.1	2.8	2.7	1.4	.3
Sweden	144	−1.7	6.8	4.2	4.1	1.3	2.4	3.6	−1.0	4.3	.9	2.1	1.6
Switzerland	146	−.3	−.8	1.0	.1	−.7	−10.3	2.4	1.5	3.2	.9	.2	19.7
United Kingdom	112	.2	2.3	4.4	2.8	2.7	3.3	3.1	2.8	3.8	2.1	1.7	2.1
Developing Countries	200	4.9	5.4	6.7	6.1	6.4	5.4	2.4	3.9	5.9	2.4	2.7	....
Africa	605	ñ1.3	ñ.2	2.8	2.3	5.3	2.5	2.7	1.7	2.7	4.0	2.4	3.4
Benin	638	4.0	3.5	4.4	4.6	5.5	5.7	5.0	4.7	5.8	5.0	6.0	....
Botswana	616	6.2	−.2	4.0	3.2	5.6	5.6	8.1	4.1	6.6	8.5	2.2	6.7
Burkina Faso	748	16.4	−1.5	2.1	6.9	9.9	6.8	8.5	3.7	1.6	6.8	4.6	6.5
Burundi	618	1.8	−7.0	−3.1	−7.0	−8.6	.4	4.5	....	....	....	....	....
Cameroon	622	−3.0	−3.2	−2.6	3.3	5.0	5.0	....	....	....	....	....	....
Congo, Dem. Rep. of	636	−10.5	−13.5	−3.9	.7	−1.1	−5.4	−1.7	−4.3	−6.9	.9	....	....
Congo, Rep. of	634	1.7	−1.0	−5.5	2.2	4.3	−.5	3.7	−3.2	8.0	....	....	....
Côte d'Ivoire	662	−.1	−.4	2.0	7.1	6.9	6.6	6.0	....	....	....	....	....
Gambia, The	648	.4	6.6	3.6	−4.1	....	....	....	....	....	....	....	....
Ghana	652	3.9	4.9	3.3	4.0	4.6	4.2	....	....	....	....	....	....
Guinea-Bissau	654	1.8	2.5	5.0	3.7	4.8	4.8	....	....	....	....	....	....
Kenya	664	−.8	.4	2.6	4.4	4.1	3.0	.3	−3.6	7.1	2.4	−8.2	....
Lesotho	666	4.6	3.5	3.4	4.4	10.0	8.1	−4.6	.2	1.3	3.2	3.8	....
Madagascar	674	1.2	2.1	−.1	1.7	2.1	3.7	3.9	4.7	4.7	6.0	−12.7	9.8
Malawi	676	−7.9	10.8	−11.6	13.8	10.4	7.0	2.2	3.6	2.3	....	....	....
Mali	678	8.1	−3.2	2.6	6.6	3.6	....	....	....	....	....	....	....
Mauritius	684	6.2	5.0	4.2	4.4	5.6	5.8	6.0	2.9	9.2	5.3	1.9	4.3
Morocco	686	−4.0	−1.0	10.4	−6.2	11.8	−2.2	7.7	−.1	1.0	6.3	3.2	5.2
Mozambique	688	−8.6	6.8	7.0	3.3	6.8	11.1	12.6	7.5	1.5	13.0	8.3	....
Namibia	728	7.4	−2.0	7.3	4.1	3.2	4.2	3.3	3.4	3.3	....	....	....
Niger	692	.7	1.0	2.5	1.9	3.9	2.4	9.9	−1.6	−.2	5.9	....	....
Nigeria	694	2.9	2.6	1.2	2.2	3.9	3.2	2.3	2.8	3.8	4.2	....	....
Rwanda	714	6.9	−8.4	−49.7	34.2	14.9	14.3	9.2	6.5	6.7	5.9	9.5	2.4
Senegal	722	2.2	−2.2	2.9	5.2	5.1	3.3	4.4	6.2	3.0	4.7	....	....
Seychelles	718	7.2	6.2	−.8	−.8	4.9	4.6	5.5	2.9	1.4	1.0	....	....
Sierra Leone	724	−19.0	1.4	−1.9	−8.0	6.1	−17.6	−.9	−8.1	3.8	5.4	6.6	7.0
South Africa	199	−2.1	1.2	3.2	3.1	4.3	2.6	.8	2.0	3.5	2.7	3.6	1.9
Swaziland	734	1.3	3.3	3.4	3.8	3.9	3.8	3.3	3.5	2.0	1.8	....	....
Tanzania	738	....	....	....	....	....	....	....	....	....	....	....	....
Togo	742	−3.8	−16.6	16.8	6.9	9.7	4.3	−2.2	3.0	−.9	.6	2.9	....
Tunisia	744	7.8	2.2	3.2	2.4	7.1	5.4	4.8	6.1	4.7	4.9	1.7	5.6
Uganda	746	4.6	7.1	10.6	9.6	5.9	....	....	....	....	....	....	....
Zambia	754	−1.7	6.8	−3.5	−2.3	6.5	3.5	....	....	....	....	....	....
Zimbabwe	698	−8.4	2.1	5.8	.2	9.7	1.4	.8	−4.1	−6.8	....	....	....
Asia	505	8.8	8.7	9.6	8.8	8.2	6.2	2.3	6.2	6.8	....	....	....
Bangladesh	513	5.0	4.6	4.1	4.9	4.6	5.4	5.2	4.9	5.9	5.3	4.4	5.3
China, P.R.: Mainland	924	14.2	13.5	12.7	10.5	9.6	8.8	7.8	7.1	8.0	....	....	....
China, P.R.: Hong Kong	532	6.6	6.3	5.5	3.9	4.3	5.1	−5.0	3.4	10.2	.5	1.9	3.2
India	534	5.1	5.9	7.3	7.3	7.8	4.8	6.5	6.1	4.4	5.8	4.0	8.1
Indonesia	536	6.5	6.5	7.5	8.2	7.8	4.7	−13.1	.8	4.9	3.4	3.7	....
Korea	542	5.4	5.5	8.3	8.9	7.0	4.7	−6.9	9.5	8.5	3.8	7.0	3.1
Lao People's Democratic Rep	544	7.0	4.6	9.5	7.0	6.9	6.9	4.0	7.3	5.8	5.8	5.9	5.9
Malaysia	548	8.9	9.9	9.2	9.8	10.0	7.3	−7.4	6.1	8.3	.4	−.7	10.4
Maldives	556	6.5	5.4	7.5	7.8	9.1	10.2	8.2	7.4	4.6	2.1	....	....
Mongolia	948	−9.5	−3.0	2.3	6.3	2.4	4.0	3.5	3.2	1.1	1.0	4.0	5.0
Myanmar	518	9.7	6.0	7.5	6.9	6.4	5.7	5.8	10.9	6.2	....	....	....
Nepal	558	4.8	2.9	8.3	2.7	5.7	5.0	3.3	4.5	6.1	4.7	−.3	2.7
Pakistan	564	7.8	1.9	3.9	5.1	5.0	−.1	2.6	3.7	4.3	2.4	3.0	5.8
Papua New Guinea	853	13.8	18.2	5.9	−3.3	7.7	−3.9	−1.1	4.6	....	....	....	....

2004, International Monetary Fund: *International Financial Statistics Yearbook*

GDP Volume Measures

		1992	1993	1994	1995	1996	1997	1998	1999	2000	2001	2002	2003
Asia(Cont.)		\multicolumn{12}{c}{*Percent Change over Previous Year; Calculated from Indices*}
Philippines	566	.3	2.1	4.4	4.7	5.8	5.2	–.6	3.4	4.0	3.4	5.5	4.9
Samoa	862	–2.3	2.4	–3.7	6.8	6.1	1.6	....	....	....	....	....	....
Singapore	576	6.7	12.3	11.4	8.0	8.1	8.5	–.9	6.8	9.7	–1.9	2.2	1.1
Sri Lanka	524	4.3	6.9	5.6	5.5	3.8	6.3	4.7	4.3	6.0	–1.5	4.0	5.9
Thailand	578	8.1	8.3	9.0	9.2	5.9	–1.4	–10.5	4.4	4.6	1.8	5.4	7.2
Tonga	866	–3.8	–.1	4.8	....	....	....	....	....	....	....	....	....
Vanuatu	846	–.7	4.5	2.5	3.2	8.7	4.9	4.3	–3.2	2.7	–2.1	–2.8	....
Europe	170	ñ2.5	1.4	ñ	5.1	4.5	4.0	2.6	.2	7.6	ñ	4.5	4.8
Armenia	911	....	....	....	6.9	5.9	3.3	7.3	3.3	....	....	....	....
Belarus	913	–9.6	–7.6	–11.7	–10.4	2.8	11.4	8.4	3.4	5.8	4.7	5.0	6.8
Bulgaria	918	–7.3	–1.5	1.8	2.9	–10.1	–6.9	....	....	....	....	....	....
Croatia	960	–11.7	–.9	.6	1.7	4.3	6.8	2.5	–.9	2.9	3.8	5.2	4.3
Kazakhstan	916	....	....	....	–8.2	.5	1.7	–1.9	2.7	9.8	13.5	9.8	9.2
Cyprus	423	9.4	.7	5.9	6.5	1.9	2.3	4.8	4.7	5.0	4.0	2.0	2.0
Czech Republic	935	–.5	.1	2.2	5.9	4.3	–.8	–1.0	.5	3.3	3.1	2.0	2.9
Estonia	939	....	....	–1.6	4.5	4.5	10.5	5.2	–.1	7.8	6.4	7.2	5.1
Hungary	944	–3.1	–.6	2.9	1.5	1.3	4.6	4.9	4.2	5.2	3.8	3.5	2.9
Kyrgyz Republic	917	–13.9	–15.5	–20.1	–5.4	7.1	9.9	2.1	3.6	5.5	5.3	–	6.7
Latvia	941	–34.9	–14.9	.6	–.8	3.8	8.3	4.7	3.3	6.9	8.0	6.4	–.7
Lithuania	946	–21.3	–16.2	–9.8	3.3	4.7	7.0	7.3	–1.7	3.9	6.4	6.8	9.0
Malta	181	4.7	4.2	3.0	9.3	4.0	4.9	3.4	4.1	6.3	–1.1	2.3	–1.7
Poland	964	2.6	3.8	5.2	7.0	6.0	6.8	4.8	4.1	15.8	1.0	1.6	....
Romania	968	–8.7	1.5	3.9	7.1	3.9	–6.1	–4.8	–1.2	2.1	5.7	5.0	4.9
San Marino	135	....	....	....	....	....	....	7.5	9.0	2.2	7.7	–1.7	....
Slovak Republic	936	....	7.2	6.2	5.8	6.1	4.6	4.2	1.5	2.0	3.8	4.4	4.2
Slovenia	961	1.0	2.8	5.3	4.1	3.6	4.8	3.6	5.6	3.9	2.7	3.4	2.3
Turkey	186	6.0	8.0	–5.5	7.2	7.0	7.5	3.1	–4.7	7.2	–7.3	7.8	5.9
Middle East	405	4.4	1.3	3.0	3.5	4.6	4.3	4.0	1.9	5.3	2.5	3.7	....
Bahrain	419	6.7	12.9	–.3	3.9	4.1	3.1	4.8	4.3	5.3	–	5.2	....
Egypt	469	4.5	2.9	4.0	4.6	5.0	5.5	7.5	6.1	5.4	3.5	3.2	3.2
Iran, I.R. of	429	4.1	–2.1	1.7	3.3	6.7	5.4	2.7	1.9	5.1	3.7	7.5	....
Israel	436	6.6	3.2	6.8	7.1	5.2	3.5	3.7	2.5	8.0	–.9	–.7	1.3
Jordan	439	17.0	4.5	5.0	6.2	2.1	3.3	3.0	3.1	4.2	4.3	....	....
Kuwait	443	–7.3	33.8	8.6	1.4	–2.7	1.2	3.2	–4.9	7.5	–1.0	....	....
Oman	449	8.5	6.1	3.8	4.8	2.9	6.2	2.7	–.2	5.5	9.3	–	....
Saudi Arabia	456	2.8	–.6	.5	.5	1.4	2.6	2.8	–.7	4.9	.5	.1	7.2
Syrian Arab Rep	463	13.5	5.2	7.7	5.8	7.3	2.5	7.6	–2.0	.6	3.4	3.2	....
United Arab Emirates	466	2.7	....	....	....	....	....	....	....	....	....	....	....
Yemen Republic	474	10.7	7.9	3.0	12.2	8.0	6.3	6.8	2.4	4.7	4.7	3.9	4.0
Western Hemisphere	205	3.2	4.0	4.9	1.8	3.8	5.2	2.1	.2	4.0	.6	ñ.4	....
ECCU	309	3.9	2.6	3.0	.7	2.7	3.2	4.0	4.1	2.8	–1.3	.2	....
Antigua and Barbuda	311	.8	5.4	6.3	–4.2	6.6	5.2	3.3	3.7	....	....	....	....
Anguilla	312	7.1	7.5	7.1	–4.1	3.5	9.2	5.2	8.7	–.3	2.1	–3.2	....
Argentina	213	9.6	5.7	5.8	–2.8	5.5	8.1	3.9	–3.4	–.8	–4.4	–10.9	8.7
Bahamas, The	313	–5.8	–2.1	2.0	1.1	....	....	....	....	....	....	....	....
Barbados	316	–7.2	.8	4.5	2.5	3.1	3.3	4.4	3.6	2.4	–3.4	–.4	2.2
Belize	339	8.2	4.3	2.5	4.2	1.2	2.2	4.6	11.6	15.9	2.0	5.5	....
Bolivia	218	1.6	4.3	4.7	4.7	4.4	5.0	5.0	.4	2.3	1.5	2.8	2.5
Brazil	223	–.5	4.9	5.9	4.2	2.7	3.3	.1	.8	4.4	1.3	1.9	....
Chile	228	12.3	7.0	5.7	10.6	7.4	6.6	3.2	–.8	4.5	3.4	2.2	3.3
Colombia	233	4.4	5.7	5.1	5.2	2.1	3.4	.6	–4.2	2.9	1.5	1.8	3.9
Costa Rica	238	9.2	7.4	4.7	3.9	.9	5.6	8.4	8.2	1.8	1.0	2.9	6.5
Dominica	321	4.0	–.3	1.4	2.0	3.5	2.5	3.1	.6	.1	–4.3	....	....
Dominican Republic	243	8.0	3.0	4.7	4.3	7.2	8.2	7.4	8.0	7.3	3.2	4.1	....
Ecuador	248	3.6	2.0	4.3	2.3	2.0	3.4	.4	–7.3	2.8	5.1	3.4	3.5
El Salvador	253	7.5	7.4	6.0	6.4	1.7	4.2	3.7	3.4	2.2	1.7	2.2	1.8
Grenada	328	.6	....	....	....	....	....	....	....	....	....	....	....
Guatemala	258	4.8	3.9	4.0	5.0	2.9	4.4	5.0	3.8	3.6	2.3	2.3	2.1
Guyana	336	7.8	8.2	....	....	....	....	....	....	....	....	....	....
Haiti	263	–13.2	–2.4	–8.3	4.4	2.7	2.7	2.2	2.7	.9	–1.0	–.5	.4
Honduras	268	5.6	6.2	–1.3	4.1	3.6	5.0	2.9	–1.9	5.7	2.6	2.7	3.2
Jamaica	343	2.6	2.4	1.0	2.3	.4	–1.1	–1.2	.9	.8	1.5	1.1	....
Mexico	273	3.6	2.0	4.4	–6.2	5.2	6.8	5.0	3.6	6.6	–	.7	1.2
Montserrat	351	2.7	2.5	.9	–7.6	–21.4	–20.0	–10.1	–12.6	–3.0	–2.8	4.6	....
Nicaragua	278	.4	–.4	3.3	5.9	6.3	4.0	3.7	7.0	4.2	3.0	1.0	2.3
Panama	283	8.2	5.5	2.8	1.8	7.4	6.4	7.4	4.0	2.7	.6	2.2	4.1
Paraguay	288	1.8	4.1	3.1	4.7	1.3	2.6	–.4	.5	–.4	2.7	–2.3	....
Peru	293	–.4	4.8	12.8	8.6	2.5	6.8	–.6	.9	2.8	.3	4.9	....
St. Kitts and Nevis	361	3.3	6.7	5.1	3.7	6.5	6.8	1.1	3.5	3.4	2.2	....	....
St. Lucia	362	6.5	2.6	1.3	1.1	3.1	–1.2	4.7	4.7	–.1	–5.5	....	....
St. Vincent & Grenadines	364	5.9	2.4	–2.0	7.6	1.5	3.7	5.1	4.1	1.9	1.2	....	....
Suriname	366	5.8	–4.5	–.8	....	....	1.3	3.0	–2.6	12.9	–3.6	2.3	3.3
Trinidad and Tobago	369	–1.6	–1.4	3.6	4.0	5.2	6.9	7.7	10.6	11.3	2.6	....	....
Uruguay	298	7.9	2.7	7.3	–1.4	5.6	5.0	4.5	–2.8	–1.4	–3.4	–11.0	2.5
Venezuela, Rep. Bol	299	6.1	.3	–2.3	4.0	–.2	6.4	.2	–6.1	3.2	2.8	–8.9	....

2004, International Monetary Fund: International Financial Statistics Yearbook

GDP Volume Measures

		1992	1993	1994	1995	1996	1997	1998	1999	2000	2001	2002	2003
		Percent Change over Previous Year; Calculated from Indices												
Memorandum Items													
Oil Exporting Countries	999	4.7	2.6	3.5	4.9	5.1	4.6	ñ4.5	ñ	4.7	3.1	2.3	....
Non-Oil Developing Countries	201	4.9	5.7	7.2	6.2	6.6	5.5	3.3	4.4	6.1	2.2	2.8	....

Indices

Index Numbers: 2000=100

		1992	1993	1994	1995	1996	1997	1998	1999	2000	2001	2002	2003
World	001	74.2	76.2	79.8	82.9	86.4	89.9	92.3	95.6	100.0	101.7	103.6	....
Industrial Countries	110	80.2	81.1	83.7	85.7	88.1	90.9	93.4	96.6	100.0	101.2	102.5	104.8
Developing Countries	200	66.3	69.8	74.5	79.1	84.1	88.7	90.8	94.4	100.0	102.4	105.2	....
Africa	605	82.2	82.1	84.4	86.3	91.0	93.2	95.7	97.4	100.0	104.0	106.4	110.0
Asia	505	57.9	62.9	69.0	75.0	81.2	86.2	88.2	93.7	100.0	....	....	....
Europe	170	78.0	79.1	79.1	83.2	86.9	90.4	92.7	92.9	100.0	100.0	104.4	109.4
Middle East	405	76.0	77.1	79.3	82.2	86.0	89.6	93.3	95.0	100.0	102.5	106.3	....
Western Hemisphere	205	77.5	80.6	84.6	86.1	89.3	94.0	96.0	96.2	100.0	100.6	100.2	....

GDP Deflators

Percent Change over Previous Year; Calculated from Indices

		1992	1993	1994	1995	1996	1997	1998	1999	2000	2001	2002	2003
World	001	17.2	19.6	18.8	9.9	6.6	5.2	4.4	3.2	3.8	4.2	4.5	....
Industrial Countries	110	2.9	2.4	1.9	2.2	1.7	1.5	1.2	.9	1.5	1.8	1.6	1.5
United States	111	2.3	2.3	2.1	2.0	1.9	1.7	1.1	1.4	2.2	2.4	1.7	1.8
Canada	156	1.3	1.4	1.1	2.3	1.6	1.2	−.4	1.7	4.0	1.0	1.0	3.4
Australia	193	1.6	1.2	.8	1.8	2.2	1.6	.6	.5	4.1	3.9	2.2	3.0
Japan	158	1.7	.6	.1	−.5	−.8	.3	....	−1.6	−1.9	−1.5	−1.2	−2.4
New Zealand	196	2.1	1.8	1.7	2.6	1.6	.7	1.1	.2	3.8	3.7	−.1	2.1
Euro Area	163	....	....	....	....	3.1	−.1	3.1	2.0	1.6	2.6	2.4	2.1
Austria	122	4.3	2.8	2.8	4.2	1.3	1.2	.7	.1	1.4	2.1	1.4	2.0
Belgium	124	3.5	4.0	2.1	1.3	1.2	1.3	1.7	−5.2	1.3	1.7	1.7	1.7
Finland	172	.9	2.3	2.0	4.1	−.2	2.1	3.0	.2	3.2	3.0	.9	.7
France	132	2.0	2.4	1.9	1.6	1.4	1.2	.9	.5	1.2	1.7	2.3	1.5
Germany	134	5.0	3.7	2.5	2.0	1.0	.8	1.0	.5	−.3	1.3	1.6	1.0
Greece	174	14.8	14.5	11.2	11.2	7.4	6.8	5.2	3.0	3.4	3.5	3.9	4.1
Ireland	178	2.8	5.2	1.7	3.0	2.0	4.3	5.7	4.2	4.8	5.7	4.5	1.6
Italy	136	4.5	3.4	3.9	3.5	5.0	5.3	2.4	2.7	1.6	2.2	2.6	3.1	2.9
Luxembourg	137	5.2	....	....	....	....	....	....	....	....	....	....	....
Netherlands	138	2.3	2.1	−1.0	1.1	1.2	1.9	2.5	.9	3.9	5.4	3.4	2.8
Portugal	182	10.6	7.0	6.1	5.0	3.1	2.8	4.0	3.8	3.2	4.8	4.6	2.3
Spain	184	6.9	4.3	4.0	9.4	3.5	2.8	2.9	2.1	3.5	4.2	4.4	4.2
Denmark	128	2.9	1.4	1.7	1.8	2.5	2.2	1.0	1.8	3.0	2.1	1.6	2.2
Iceland	176	3.3	2.3	2.1	2.9	2.0	1.1	4.9	2.8	2.9	9.4	5.3	−.4
Norway	142	−.6	2.3	−.1	2.9	4.1	2.9	−.7	6.6	15.9	1.1	−1.6	2.4
Sweden	144	1.0	−2.6	2.3	3.4	1.2	1.6	.8	6.4	1.3	2.3	1.4	2.2
Switzerland	146	2.2	2.4	1.5	.8	−.1	−.1	−.3	.7	.8	.6	1.0	1.2
United Kingdom	112	4.0	2.8	1.6	2.6	3.4	2.9	2.8	2.2	1.4	2.4	3.2	3.1
Developing Countries	200	46.0	55.5	47.7	21.9	14.0	10.6	9.3	6.3	6.8	7.4	8.5	....
Africa	605	19.9	14.9	15.4	31.5	23.9	13.0	6.7	15.2	20.1	14.0	8.0	4.4
Benin	638	3.4	1.2	33.5	15.4	6.7	4.7	5.0	2.0	3.3	3.1	6.3	....
Botswana	616	4.2	9.1	16.4	7.6	9.7	18.3	5.2	2.5	8.7	5.8	9.0	6.7
Burkina Faso	748	−2.8	1.7	25.7	5.8	1.0	.7	6.0	−3.1	−.8	5.9	4.3	1.9
Burundi	618	8.2	12.7	17.7	−.5	15.2	29.8	11.7	....	....	....	....	....
Cameroon	622	−1.4	1.7	24.4	11.6	5.5	3.7	....	....	....	....	....	....
Central African Rep.	626	....	....	....	....	....	....	....	....	....	....	....	....
Congo, Dem. Rep. of	636	−100.0	....	....	467.7	638.6	184.9	30.3	442.0	594.5	360.5	....	....
Côte d'Ivoire	662	....	....	....	....	....	....	....	....	....	....	....	....
Ethiopia	644	14.9	13.8	2.6	12.6	.9	3.4	9.6	....	....	....	....	....
Gabon	646	....	....	....	....	....	....	....	....	....	....	....	....
Gambia, The	648	11.6	−19.8	10.6	....	....	....	....	....	....	....	....	....
Ghana	652	11.1	31.7	30.2	43.2	39.8	19.5	....	....	....	....	....	....
Guinea-Bissau	654	−20.0	9.4	82.7	−4.8	4.4	14.5	....	....	....	....	....	....
Kenya	664	18.9	25.7	17.0	11.3	9.0	14.4	11.1	11.1	−	7.7	19.3	....
Lesotho	666	18.6	9.9	7.6	9.3	9.0	7.7	9.3	12.8	5.8	7.4	13.3	....
Madagascar	674	12.5	13.0	41.6	45.1	17.8	7.3	8.5	9.8	7.1	7.3	15.3	2.8
Malawi	676	14.0	24.8	29.0	88.5	50.4	8.5	32.6	32.4	20.9	....	....	....
Mali	678	−3.6	2.0	33.9	13.8	7.3	....	....	....	....	....	....	....
Mauritius	684	5.9	9.2	6.6	5.1	6.6	5.3	6.6	4.9	1.9	5.0	5.4	6.0
Morocco	686	4.4	3.6	1.6	7.6	1.4	2.0	.4	.5	1.5	1.8	.6	−
Mozambique	688	40.1	48.5	55.4	50.3	48.2	9.6	4.6	2.9	8.0	10.6	7.4	....
Namibia	728	9.4	13.6	15.7	5.7	14.5	7.1	8.6	6.5	8.9	....	....	....
Niger	692	−6.1	3.2	18.6	4.0	19.1	2.4	3.0	3.1	−5.2	2.7	....	....
Nigeria	694	64.9	24.3	28.8	111.6	37.5	.8	−4.2	12.1	42.1	11.6	....	....
Rwanda	714	6.0	14.4	16.8	51.2	10.2	15.6	2.0	−5.2	5.0	2.1	−.1	10.7
Senegal	722	.6	−1.4	19.1	13.3	.5	3.4	3.7	.3	4.5	3.6	....	....
Seychelles	718	4.6	3.1	2.0	−.8	−1.5	8.2	7.2	.9	4.8	1.5	....	....
Sierra Leone	724	82.0	26.7	25.1	33.6	24.3	16.8	27.1	25.2	6.0	6.1	4.6	4.4
South Africa	199	14.6	13.1	9.6	10.3	8.1	8.1	7.0	6.2	7.2	7.8	10.1	5.9
Swaziland	734	10.2	16.1	17.2	17.2	10.6	12.0	9.1	9.0	12.4	11.8	....	....
Tanzania	738	34.6	25.5	31.4	26.9	19.7	20.8	13.9	10.2	7.7	7.7	6.6	....
Togo	742	1.8	−4.8	32.6	12.0	4.4	12.0	−2.3	2.1	−1.4	4.5	9.9	....
Tunisia	744	5.7	4.7	4.5	5.4	4.4	4.0	3.0	3.1	3.3	2.7	2.3	2.2
Uganda	746	58.6	1.9	16.2	5.4	5.4	....	....	....	....	....	....	....
Zambia	754	165.5	143.6	56.7	36.9	24.3	25.5	....	....	....	....	....	....
Zimbabwe	698	26.8	21.0	24.9	10.2	28.0	22.7	34.4	57.5	51.0	....	....	....
Asia	505	7.6	11.9	13.4	11.0	6.7	4.4	7.6	.8	1.9	....	....	....
Bangladesh	513	3.0	.3	3.8	7.3	4.2	3.1	5.3	4.7	1.9	....	....	....
Bhutan	514	10.5	6.8	10.7	9.4	12.2	12.0	7.6	9.2	7.9	1.6	3.2	4.4
China, P.R.: Mainland	924	6.4	17.5	20.1	13.4	6.6	.7	−2.1	−2.3	.1	....	....	....
China, P.R.: Hong Kong	532	9.6	8.5	7.0	2.5	5.9	5.7	.2	−5.9	−6.2	−1.9	−3.6	−5.2
Fiji	819	4.9	5.2	.6	2.2	3.1	3.4	5.7	2.0	1.1	4.3	.8	....
India	534	8.7	9.6	9.4	9.0	7.4	6.7	7.9	3.9	3.5	3.9	3.5	3.8
Indonesia	536	6.1	9.7	7.8	9.9	8.7	12.6	75.3	14.2	9.6	10.8	7.2	....
Korea	542	7.6	7.1	7.7	13.2	5.4	5.6	5.8	−.1	.7	3.5	2.8	2.3
Lao People's Democratic Rep.	544	9.3	7.7	6.4	20.6	12.9	19.3	85.2	127.1	25.1	8.6	10.6	4.3
Malaysia	548	2.4	4.0	3.9	3.6	3.7	3.5	8.5	−	5.2	−2.9	8.7	−1.5
Maldives	556	12.9	11.3	8.6	5.6	3.5	2.4	−1.8	1.6	1.3	2.0	....	....
Mongolia	948	176.4	262.3	66.6	82.7	14.8	23.8	−5.1	9.7	8.9	8.5	5.7	5.9

GDP Deflators

Percent Change over Previous Year; Calculated from Indices

		1992	1993	1994	1995	1996	1997	1998	1999	2000	2001	2002	2003
Asia(Cont.)													
Myanmar	518	21.7	36.2	22.1	19.6	23.0	33.7	35.9	22.7	....	....	....	....
Nepal	558	18.5	11.4	7.4	7.1	7.5	7.3	3.8	8.8	4.6	3.4	3.1	4.9
Pakistan	564	9.9	8.5	12.7	13.7	8.2	14.6	7.5	5.9	3.7	5.2	3.0	4.6
Papua New Guinea	853	2.9	−2.5	4.4	13.2	8.5	6.8	11.5	7.7	....	....	....	....
Philippines	566	7.9	6.8	10.0	7.6	7.7	6.2	10.5	8.0	8.3	4.7	3.3	3.5
Samoa	862	14.6	4.3	19.1	−5.2	3.9	11.8	....	....	....	....	....	....
Singapore	576	2.0	3.4	2.7	2.1	1.1	.4	−2.4	−4.7	4.3	−1.6	.4	−.4
Sri Lanka	524	10.0	9.5	9.3	8.4	12.1	8.6	8.4	4.4	6.7	12.4	8.4	5.0
Thailand	578	4.5	3.3	5.2	5.6	4.0	4.1	9.2	−4.0	1.3	2.4	.6	1.9
Vanuatu	846	6.7	5.6	2.4	3.4	−5.4	3.2	4.8	3.2	1.2	3.5	.6	....
Europe	170	**110.9**	**101.1**	**61.0**	**52.2**	**38.3**	**55.5**	**34.7**	**32.5**	**24.9**	**24.0**	**17.5**	**13.7**
Armenia	911	....	....	....	161.2	19.6	17.7	10.7	.1	....	....	....	....
Belarus	913	1,074.1	1,054.0	1,945.1	661.9	53.7	71.6	76.6	317.0	185.3	79.5	44.9	28.8
Bulgaria	918	59.6	51.1	72.7	62.8	122.5	963.2	....	....	....	....	....	....
Croatia	960	629.6	1,506.5	107.7	10.6	5.3	7.4	8.4	3.8	4.7	4.7	2.9	3.2
Cyprus	423	6.1	5.1	5.3	3.0	1.8	2.7	2.5	2.2	4.5	2.3	3.2	5.4
Czech Republic	935	12.4	21.0	13.4	10.2	8.8	8.0	10.6	3.0	9.3	5.0	1.7	−2.8
Estonia	939	....	....	38.9	31.3	24.3	10.5	9.0	4.3	5.3	5.8	4.4	2.4
Hungary	944	21.5	21.3	19.5	26.7	21.2	18.5	12.6	8.4	9.9	8.6	8.9	7.8
Kazakhstan	916	....	....	....	152.1	28.4	16.6	4.9	23.7	13.0	5.9	5.7	14.2
Kyrgyz Republic	917	830.2	754.9	180.9	42.0	35.3	19.3	9.1	37.7	27.0	7.4	2.0	3.8
Latvia	941	975.9	71.5	38.3	27.3	14.9	7.0	4.6	4.8	3.8	2.1	3.4	11.9
Lithuania	946	943.0	306.2	61.6	46.4	20.6	14.0	5.0	−.6	1.0	−.1	−	−.9
Malta	181	3.6	3.1	6.2	1.9	.8	2.3	2.2	2.7	.7	5.8	1.1	3.4
Poland	964	38.5	30.6	37.4	27.9	18.7	14.0	11.8	11.2	−3.8	4.3	1.1	....
Romania	968	199.7	227.3	139.0	35.3	45.3	147.2	55.3	47.7	44.2	37.4	23.4	19.2
San Marino	135	....	....	....	....	....	....	1.8	1.6	2.6	2.8	2.3	....
Slovak Republic	936	....	16.4	13.4	9.9	4.3	6.7	5.2	6.5	8.5	4.2	4.0	4.7
Slovenia	961	188.5	37.1	22.6	23.0	10.9	8.8	7.6	5.9	5.6	9.1	7.9	5.4
Turkey	186	63.7	67.8	106.5	87.2	77.8	81.5	75.7	55.6	50.2	54.5	43.5	23.0
Middle East	405	**17.1**	**19.0**	**13.4**	**18.1**	**15.0**	**6.9**	**.1**	**15.2**	**14.6**	**3.6**	**12.2**	....
Bahrain	419	−3.5	−3.0	7.3	1.1	.2	.9	−7.1	2.6	14.3	−.4	−8.0	....
Egypt	469	18.3	9.9	7.0	11.4	7.1	6.3	3.9	.9	4.9	1.9	2.3	6.2
Iran, I.R. of	429	28.3	53.8	28.3	37.9	25.2	11.8	9.5	30.1	26.4	11.4	29.5	....
Israel	436	13.1	12.1	13.8	8.9	11.2	9.2	6.5	6.5	1.4	2.4	4.1	.4
Jordan	439	8.2	2.8	6.9	1.9	2.1	1.2	6.0	−.2	−.4	1.1	....	....
Kuwait	443	.8	−7.2	−6.0	5.9	20.6	−3.8	−18.1	22.0	19.0	−7.1	....	....
Oman	449	1.2	−5.5	−.4	1.9	7.6	−2.4	−13.4	11.8	19.9	−8.2	1.8	....
Saudi Arabia	456	12.3	−2.4	1.1	5.6	9.2	2.0	−14.0	11.2	11.6	−3.4	2.9	6.1
Syrian Arab Rep	463	5.1	5.9	13.6	6.7	12.7	5.3	−1.5	5.7	9.7	2.1	1.5	....
United Arab Emirates	466	1.6	....	....	....	....	....	....	....	....	....	....	....
Yemen Republic	474	20.1	15.1	26.1	48.3	31.4	12.8	−10.1	35.6	25.4	.3	7.4	11.0
Western Hemisphere	205	**152.5**	**210.2**	**219.4**	**38.4**	**20.5**	**11.4**	**8.1**	**7.9**	**8.9**	**5.8**	**11.4**	....
ECCU	309	3.6	1.3	3.6	2.8	2.0	2.3	2.5	1.8	1.3	1.8	1.0	....
Antigua and Barbuda	311	2.4	2.2	3.0	3.0	2.7	2.2	3.3	1.3	....	....	....	....
Argentina	213	14.4	−1.4	2.8	3.2	−.1	−.5	−1.7	−1.8	1.0	−1.1	30.6	10.7
Anguilla	312	1.3	1.5	3.3	3.3	3.0	1.2	2.5	2.5	.5	−.6	4.5	....
Bahamas, The	313	5.0	2.0	4.9	−.5	....	....	....	....	....	....	....	....
Barbados	316	.8	3.3	.8	4.8	3.5	6.9	3.3	.7	2.0	2.7	1.6	....
Belize	339	3.5	5.0	1.6	16.2	4.0	1.2	.8	−.8	1.6	−.8	1.5	....
Bolivia	218	13.2	6.6	8.0	11.4	11.6	5.7	7.0	2.4	5.3	.7	2.7	5.1
Brazil	223	969.0	1,996.2	2,240.2	77.6	17.4	8.3	4.9	5.7	8.4	7.4	10.2	....
Chile	228	12.9	11.7	16.4	7.9	2.7	4.3	1.9	2.4	4.6	3.6	4.5	3.9
Colombia	233	22.3	24.5	22.9	18.9	16.9	16.8	14.8	12.6	12.1	6.2	6.0	7.0
Costa Rica	238	20.5	10.6	15.5	22.2	15.8	14.9	12.1	15.0	7.0	8.6	9.1	7.8
Dominica	321	2.2	4.8	5.3	1.1	3.5	1.2	2.6	2.5	1.1	1.9	....	....
Dominican Republic	243	8.3	5.0	7.9	13.1	5.4	8.3	4.8	6.5	7.7	8.9	5.2	....
Ecuador	248	4.0	16.6	18.2	6.2	3.3	7.5	−2.0	−22.7	−7.0	25.5	11.8	7.7
El Salvador	253	8.8	12.8	10.5	10.4	6.8	3.5	3.9	.3	3.2	3.4	1.4	2.5
Grenada	328	3.3	....	....	....	....	....	....	....	....	....	....	....
Guatemala	258	8.8	14.5	11.7	8.7	8.9	8.3	9.5	5.1	6.8	7.6	8.0	5.7
Guyana	336	11.3	16.9	....	....	....	....	....	....	....	....	....	....
Haiti	263	21.9	35.8	69.6	9.2	28.8	12.7	14.2	7.0	11.1	11.6	10.1	25.5
Honduras	268	9.1	13.6	28.9	24.9	22.9	22.3	11.6	11.6	9.7	8.0	6.3	7.8
Jamaica	343	65.7	35.8	32.4	23.3	18.4	10.0	8.6	5.7	11.7	8.6	8.3	....
Montserrat	351	2.8	2.8	4.3	2.3	3.4	5.8	2.9	3.7	1.8	7.1	1.8	....
Mexico	273	14.4	9.5	8.3	37.9	30.7	17.7	15.4	15.3	12.2	5.8	7.0	6.7
Nicaragua	278	23.7	20.4	80.1	13.4	9.6	9.8	14.0	9.2	8.8	4.7	4.7	6.9
Panama	283	5.1	3.6	3.7	.5	.3	1.7	1.0	.8	−1.3	1.0	1.2	....
Paraguay	288	14.7	19.1	21.0	13.0	10.5	3.0	12.4	2.5	11.9	1.7	16.4	....
Peru	293	69.2	47.1	26.2	12.9	10.5	7.5	6.2	3.9	3.6	1.3	.6	....
St. Kitts and Nevis	361	7.0	2.2	6.3	3.9	.1	5.4	3.1	2.4	4.4	1.7	....	....
St. Lucia	362	4.3	−2.5	2.8	5.7	.1	2.7	4.0	.7	2.3	1.3	....	....
St. Vincent & Grenadines	364	3.6	−	2.9	2.5	3.9	1.0	2.8	.3	−.4	2.0	....	....
Suriname	366	28.5	125.7	488.4	−87.1	−87.1	11.4	8.7	77.6	43.2	43.2	30.4	24.4
Trinidad and Tobago	369	4.2	7.5	15.6	4.0	3.8	−3.0	−1.5	1.8	7.9	7.3	....	....
Uruguay	298	59.5	47.9	39.0	41.0	26.4	19.3	9.4	4.2	4.0	5.3	18.7	17.9
Venezuela, Rep. Bol.	299	28.2	31.6	62.9	51.8	115.5	38.4	20.9	27.0	27.6	7.8	33.1	....

2004, International Monetary Fund : *International Financial Statistics Yearbook*

GDP Deflators

		1992	1993	1994	1995	1996	1997	1998	1999	2000	2001	2002	2003
Percent Change over Previous Year; Calculated from Indices													
Memorandum Items														
Oil Exporting Countries...........	999	17.9	19.9	18.0	24.8	24.6	12.5	28.4	19.0	18.4	7.9	15.3	....
Non-Oil Developing Countries.	201	50.2	60.8	51.9	21.6	12.7	10.4	7.1	5.0	5.7	7.3	7.5	....

Indices

		1992	1993	1994	1995	1996	1997	1998	1999	2000	2001	2002	2003
Index Numbers: 2000=100													
World...	001	51.1	61.1	72.5	79.7	85.0	89.4	93.4	96.4	100.0	104.2	108.8	....
Industrial Countries.................	110	87.6	89.7	91.4	93.4	95.0	96.4	97.6	98.5	100.0	101.8	103.4	104.9
Developing Countries..............	200	22.8	35.5	52.4	63.9	72.9	80.6	88.1	93.6	100.0	107.4	116.5	....
Africa..	605	27.8	31.9	36.8	48.4	59.9	67.7	72.3	83.2	100.0	114.0	123.1	128.6
Asia..	505	57.7	64.5	73.2	81.3	86.7	90.5	97.4	98.1	100.0	....	....	....
Europe.....................................	170	4.2	8.5	13.7	20.9	28.9	44.9	60.4	80.1	100.0	124.0	145.6	165.6
Middle East.............................	405	38.6	45.9	52.1	61.5	70.8	75.6	75.7	87.2	100.0	103.6	116.3	....
Western Hemisphere.............	205	4.3	13.3	42.3	58.6	70.6	78.7	85.1	91.8	100.0	105.8	117.8	....

Gross Capital Formation as Percentage of GDP

		1992	1993	1994	1995	1996	1997	1998	1999	2000	2001	2002	2003
							Percentages						
World	001	22.83	23.73	23.84	24.17	23.80	23.87	23.36	23.21	23.55	23.00	....	19.83
Industrial Countries	110	20.75	19.98	20.50	20.71	20.70	21.07	21.22	21.54	21.78	20.65	19.82	18.39
United States	111	17.16	17.61	18.64	18.61	19.00	19.77	20.25	20.63	20.78	19.14	18.37	20.15
Canada	156	17.80	17.89	18.86	18.74	18.20	20.73	20.48	20.13	20.26	19.38	19.92	25.39
Australia	193	20.83	21.80	23.28	22.73	22.31	21.85	24.04	24.71	23.08	21.79	23.57	23.99
Japan	158	30.76	29.39	28.16	28.24	29.12	28.66	26.89	26.00	26.27	25.76	23.91	21.72
New Zealand	196	17.54	20.23	21.73	22.74	22.30	21.27	19.46	20.89	20.01	20.67	20.55	19.89
Euro Area	163	21.36	19.40	19.98	20.21	19.33	19.62	21.23	21.42	22.08	21.06	20.16	23.20
Austria	122	22.54	21.55	22.36	23.45	23.33	25.11	25.34	24.30	24.83	23.50	22.30	19.72
Belgium	124	20.92	20.44	20.11	20.08	19.15	20.18	20.51	20.82	21.64	20.40	19.46	18.30
Finland	172	18.64	16.17	17.33	17.50	16.63	18.49	19.33	19.56	20.59	20.60	19.30	19.02
France	132	20.87	18.11	18.98	19.25	18.32	17.87	19.08	19.60	21.03	20.45	19.56	....
Germany	134	22.26	20.77	21.55	21.55	20.51	20.02	19.73	21.65	21.71	19.56	17.95	26.11
Greece	174	20.91	19.83	18.68	18.92	19.79	20.08	21.35	21.43	22.69	23.95	24.03	23.97
Ireland	178	16.25	15.11	16.13	18.11	19.59	21.48	23.37	24.71	25.36	23.77	22.73	19.56
Italy	136	20.78	18.37	18.49	19.34	18.68	18.86	19.30	19.65	20.20	19.64	20.01	20.71
Luxembourg	137	23.99	25.22	21.89	21.61	21.37	22.29	22.66	24.53	22.50	23.72	21.78	22.97
Netherlands	138	19.76	18.06	19.01	19.32	18.45	19.52	19.56	22.65	21.90	21.65	20.11	25.94
Portugal	182	25.94	23.23	23.91	24.41	24.39	25.73	26.50	29.35	30.07	28.96	26.72	19.76
Spain	184	22.63	19.87	20.08	22.33	21.90	22.13	23.22	24.57	25.70	25.71	25.78	21.46
Denmark	128	17.88	16.26	17.46	19.53	18.79	20.61	21.50	19.73	21.03	20.54	20.83	17.62
Iceland	176	19.20	17.92	17.00	17.35	20.18	20.36	24.80	22.58	24.46	21.97	18.68	16.10
Norway	142	20.18	20.76	21.78	22.89	21.49	23.81	27.27	23.73	20.95	19.63	19.42	19.20
Sweden	144	17.83	15.34	16.55	17.19	16.55	16.20	17.23	17.51	18.47	17.75	16.76	16.31
Switzerland	146	23.87	22.43	23.52	23.37	22.53	22.12	23.39	22.41	23.11	22.89	20.04	....
United Kingdom	112	16.15	15.77	16.46	16.94	16.76	17.06	18.15	17.82	17.51	17.11	16.45	....
Developing Countries	200	26.29	28.53	28.12	28.59	27.76	27.46	25.94	25.23	25.70	25.86	....	18.93
Africa	605	17.58	18.11	19.36	18.20	18.32	18.00	18.68	18.22	17.17	17.53	18.26	31.09
Algeria	612	29.76	28.26	31.46	31.57	25.08	23.29	27.34	26.24	23.06	27.09	30.42	29.55
Benin	638	14.64	14.34	18.54	23.51	17.91	18.35	18.84	19.67	19.53	19.86	20.08	19.38
Botswana	616	30.30	30.53	26.57	25.68	23.73	25.95	30.04	36.78	19.92	19.58	26.16	10.61
Burkina Faso	748	18.72	17.30	24.30	21.36	22.36	24.65	21.91	20.51	21.45	19.98	18.67	....
Burundi	618	15.17	15.72	8.70	9.29	12.28	7.20	6.80	7.53	7.55	7.29	13.94	....
Cameroon	622	13.54	16.71	14.08	13.69	15.08	16.15	....	....	....	....	....	....
Central African Rep.	626	12.42	10.58	11.70	14.12	7.26	....	....	....	....	....	....	26.40
Congo, Dem. Rep. of	636	6.38	6.95	7.56	–18.37	16.30	14.99	13.80	12.69	8.87	4.39	....	....
Congo, Rep. of	634	21.62	19.06	46.16	51.68	29.15	24.92	49.79	38.86	23.45	35.78	26.12	....
Côte d'Ivoire	662	5.54	8.29	12.54	14.95	13.24	13.50	11.58	13.24	10.49	10.91	9.65	....
Ethiopia	644	9.19	14.22	15.16	16.44	19.10	17.00	17.20	16.00	15.35	16.50	....	....
Gabon	646	22.24	22.52	20.77	22.06	22.74	24.46	31.84	....	....	....	....	....
Gambia, The	648	....	....	....	....	....	....	....	....	....	....	....	....
Ghana	652	13.84	22.22	23.95	20.02	21.47	24.55	....	....	....	....	23.79	12.93
Guinea-Bissau	654	44.05	25.06	12.94	18.15	19.77	13.06	6.16	10.78	15.19	15.90	13.39	....
Kenya	664	16.89	17.61	19.29	21.80	20.33	18.50	17.30	16.15	15.38	14.61	....	....
Malawi	676	19.39	14.47	29.38	16.93	11.81	12.01	12.78	14.59	15.29	....	20.63	....
Mali	678	21.67	17.36	24.37	24.05	20.88	22.67	19.83	18.74	20.18	25.07	22.01	23.67
Mauritania	682	25.11	18.58	19.12	20.38	17.76	17.26	....	....	....	20.74	22.70	23.77
Mauritius	684	29.16	30.59	31.93	25.62	24.41	29.33	25.42	26.34	25.65	22.89	....	....
Morocco	686	23.21	22.46	21.34	20.73	19.58	20.70	22.16	23.13	23.70	33.95	23.79	....
Mozambique	688	23.08	23.76	24.82	30.63	21.83	20.58	24.22	36.68	26.49	26.49	19.32	....
Namibia	728	21.17	16.46	21.71	21.70	23.12	20.17	25.75	23.28	19.92	23.79	6.89	6.89
Niger	692	11.75	8.14	17.06	14.31	15.57	15.88	16.20	10.22	19.12	21.74	....	....
Nigeria	694	10.72	11.60	9.32	5.81	6.11	7.01	6.72	5.36	3.90	6.89	19.51	....
Rwanda	714	16.98	17.55	10.50	13.13	....	15.20	16.75	20.11	21.62	17.63	....	....
Senegal	722	14.56	13.81	18.45	16.80	17.68	34.36	36.11	....	....	....	....	....
Seychelles	718	21.23	28.67	27.08	30.34	32.14	4.35	5.50	3.47	6.46	14.61	15.88	16.78
Sierra Leone	724	12.94	4.08	8.67	5.49	10.02	16.63	16.59	15.74	15.51	18.09	....	....
South Africa	199	14.76	15.30	16.81	17.98	17.43	20.60	22.36	18.76	19.89	17.00	19.31	....
Swaziland	734	25.81	26.18	21.50	19.95	20.69	14.90	16.20	15.54	17.62	17.87	18.41	....
Tanzania	738	27.23	25.13	24.65	19.79	16.65	26.44	15.28	13.65	16.57	27.87	25.19	25.08
Togo	742	14.50	4.26	14.90	15.64	14.67	14.57	26.90	26.30	27.28	18.98	19.71	21.29
Tunisia	744	29.20	29.24	24.64	24.70	25.01	16.68	18.80	19.73	....	....	20.69	....
Uganda	746	14.69	14.04	13.75	16.39	15.15	38.84	....	....	13.50	....	....	....
Zambia	754	11.88	15.04	19.77	30.16	44.91	18.83	22.25	17.07	13.50	....	....	....
Zimbabwe	698	19.44	17.90	28.98	25.29	17.44	18.83	22.25	17.07	13.50	....	....	....
Asia	505	31.77	34.42	34.16	34.92	33.32	32.46	29.50	29.50	29.75	30.23	....	....
Bangladesh	513	17.31	17.95	18.40	19.12	19.99	20.72	21.63	22.19	23.02	23.09	23.15	23.21
Bhutan	514	46.64	46.06	47.44	46.84	44.68	34.10	38.22	43.07	43.77	....	....	....
China, P.R.: Mainland	924	37.26	43.47	41.25	40.81	39.32	38.00	37.40	37.14	36.37	37.99	....	....
China, P.R.: Hong Kong	532	28.54	27.58	31.76	34.66	32.06	34.52	29.15	25.26	28.08	25.91	23.38	22.84
Fiji	819	12.76	15.97	13.49	13.57	11.37	11.50	15.90	14.94	12.64	14.52	....	....
India	534	23.79	21.25	23.38	26.53	21.77	22.57	21.38	23.66	22.67	22.31	22.83	....
Indonesia	536	35.83	29.48	31.06	31.93	30.69	31.75	16.77	11.37	16.10	17.45	14.27	....
Korea	542	37.34	35.51	36.51	37.67	38.87	35.97	25.00	29.12	31.00	29.33	29.08	29.39
Malaysia	548	35.36	39.18	41.20	43.64	41.48	42.97	26.67	22.38	27.18	23.95	24.45	21.84
Myanmar	518	13.55	12.44	12.37	14.24	12.25	12.50	12.38	13.24	....	....	....	25.83
Nepal	558	21.15	23.14	22.41	25.20	27.33	25.34	24.84	20.48	24.31	24.05	24.08	25.83

2004, International Monetary Fund : *International Financial Statistics Yearbook*

Gross Capital Formation as Percentage of GDP

		1992	1993	1994	1995	1996	1997	1998	1999	2000	2001	2002	2003
						Percentages							
Asia(Cont.)													
Pakistan	564	20.24	20.82	19.54	18.54	18.98	17.92	17.71	15.57	15.86	15.55	14.72	15.45
Papua New Guinea	853	23.30	17.63	21.44	22.06	22.68	21.07	17.91	16.39	....	....	....	....
Philippines	566	21.34	23.98	24.06	22.45	24.02	24.78	20.34	18.75	21.17	18.97	17.56	16.64
Singapore	576	35.80	37.39	33.10	34.17	35.78	39.24	32.33	32.04	32.04	24.86	21.16	13.35
Sri Lanka	524	24.28	25.56	27.03	25.73	24.25	24.39	25.14	27.29	28.04	22.01	21.61	22.44
Thailand	578	39.96	40.01	40.25	42.09	41.82	33.66	20.45	20.50	22.73	23.91	23.84	25.24
Vanuatu	846	28.62	27.82	28.84	32.66	....	....	....	....	....	....	....	....
Europe	**170**	**22.65**	**26.09**	**24.38**	**24.72**	**24.01**	**23.45**	**20.85**	**19.98**	**22.06**	**21.84**	**21.38**	**22.05**
Armenia	911	1.62	9.76	23.45	18.42	20.01	19.07	19.14	18.35	18.64	19.76	21.67	24.68
Belarus	913	31.79	41.03	32.94	24.75	23.52	26.84	26.71	23.71	25.40	23.76	22.18	24.14
Bulgaria	918	19.89	15.28	9.39	15.65	8.12	9.88	16.88	17.92	18.29	20.67	19.81	21.73
Cyprus	423	28.70	24.01	25.43	22.11	22.54	20.13	21.17	20.06	20.02	18.68	20.06	....
Czech Republic	935	26.16	27.29	29.75	34.03	34.25	32.59	30.05	28.08	28.67	29.19	27.62	28.20
Estonia	939	26.74	26.05	27.03	26.63	26.98	30.54	30.22	24.95	27.86	29.20	31.80	31.13
Hungary	944	16.07	19.96	22.19	22.60	25.50	26.57	28.85	28.72	30.91	26.81	25.24	25.11
Kazakhstan	916	31.75	20.87	26.83	22.55	16.89	16.25	16.58	17.08	18.11	27.90	26.54	26.46
Kyrgyz Republic	917	19.92	11.67	9.01	18.34	25.20	21.45	15.16	17.76	19.76	15.49	17.61	16.18
Macedonia, FYR	962	15.60	17.88	15.47	20.76	20.09	20.97	22.26	19.70	22.25	19.08	20.67	....
Malta	181	27.55	29.84	30.66	31.98	28.63	25.57	23.70	24.00	28.42	20.87	16.36	20.40
Moldova	921	59.77	55.80	28.82	24.88	24.25	23.81	25.87	22.88	23.95	20.07	....	....
Poland	964	15.17	15.55	17.62	19.70	21.87	24.56	26.20	25.34	25.03	21.01	19.27	....
Romania	968	31.41	28.93	24.81	24.27	25.85	20.63	17.75	16.08	19.47	22.56	23.52	24.64
Russia	922	34.63	27.01	25.54	25.44	23.67	21.98	14.96	14.83	18.69	21.95	20.18	20.61
Slovak Republic	936	28.29	24.64	20.97	24.83	34.75	34.54	34.00	27.57	26.14	30.00	29.28	25.26
Slovenia	961	17.59	19.35	20.94	22.53	22.38	23.68	24.71	27.27	26.66	23.88	23.63	24.80
Turkey	186	23.86	27.61	21.48	25.47	24.55	25.11	24.18	23.35	24.51	16.78	21.34	22.78
Ukraine	926	34.45	36.29	35.33	26.68	22.67	21.45	20.82	17.44	19.72	21.81	19.07	20.03
Middle East	**405**	**28.45**	**25.48**	**21.37**	**23.20**	**24.77**	**24.64**	**25.26**	**23.20**	**23.14**	**23.83**	**25.46**	**....**
Egypt	469	18.19	16.21	16.57	17.21	16.61	18.16	21.50	21.62	19.55	18.26	18.28	17.11
Iran, I.R. of	429	46.27	33.28	22.74	29.20	35.88	35.75	32.84	29.74	32.98	35.27	39.82	....
Iraq	433	14.65	15.48	....	....	....	....	....	....	....	....	....	....
Israel	436	25.37	25.99	25.27	26.47	25.75	24.20	22.56	22.94	21.65	21.13	18.83	16.90
Jordan	439	33.44	36.62	33.30	32.96	30.48	25.73	21.85	21.62	22.16	20.87	....	....
Kuwait	443	19.87	17.19	16.16	15.11	15.31	13.86	19.05	15.02	7.64	8.71	9.16	8.65
Libya	672	12.16	16.28	16.33	12.16	15.50	12.36	11.96	11.19	13.04	12.98	14.46	....
Oman	449	16.35	17.53	15.74	14.98	13.70	17.65	23.98	14.85	11.93	12.61	12.77	....
Qatar	453	20.63	19.77	24.52	35.08	35.77	35.43	31.97	18.88	20.15	22.69	....	....
Saudi Arabia	456	22.52	24.59	19.85	19.79	18.10	18.30	22.42	21.14	18.71	18.88	19.67	19.41
Syrian Arab Rep.	463	23.17	25.97	29.96	27.23	23.60	20.85	20.55	18.77	17.27	20.88	20.01	....
United Arab Emirates	466	24.18	29.34	29.36	28.52	26.41	28.10	30.08	....	....	....	....	....
Yemen, Republic of	474	22.36	20.18	20.73	21.82	23.29	25.17	32.75	23.75	17.16	17.20	16.20	16.84
Western Hemisphere	**205**	**19.95**	**20.60**	**21.58**	**21.51**	**21.33**	**22.62**	**22.39**	**20.11**	**20.64**	**19.92**	**18.50**	**18.70**
Antigua and Barbuda	311	34.79	31.68	32.40	36.91	39.67	41.32	....	....	....	....	....	....
Argentina	213	16.69	19.69	19.97	18.52	19.64	20.86	21.00	17.88	17.52	15.61	10.98	14.54
Bahamas, The	313	23.22	19.60	21.17	23.21	....	....	....	....	....	....	....	....
Barbados	316	9.48	12.69	13.31	14.08	12.67	15.32	....	....	....	....	....	....
Belize	339	29.11	30.24	24.08	20.12	18.56	18.14	17.12	21.22	26.64	21.30	20.49	....
Bolivia	218	16.71	16.56	14.37	15.24	16.24	19.63	23.61	18.77	18.32	14.25	14.74	11.11
Brazil	223	18.93	20.85	22.15	22.29	20.92	21.50	21.12	20.16	21.54	21.20	19.76	20.07
Chile	228	24.13	26.93	24.29	26.18	27.38	27.72	26.90	20.90	21.86	21.98	21.99	21.76
Colombia	233	14.51	17.79	25.50	25.72	22.05	20.79	19.61	12.77	13.58	14.99	....	....
Costa Rica	238	20.24	20.88	20.05	18.24	15.96	18.08	20.54	17.13	17.01	20.39	22.23	20.22
Dominica	321	28.37	25.47	25.69	31.30	28.78	31.35	27.25	27.70	28.06	24.06	22.06	....
Dominican Republic	243	20.45	23.91	21.38	19.48	18.96	19.79	23.44	24.21	23.96	23.15	23.19	....
Ecuador	248	21.21	20.43	21.87	21.56	19.70	21.46	25.27	14.73	20.11	25.66	27.72	24.66
El Salvador	253	18.53	18.58	19.69	20.04	15.19	15.12	17.55	16.43	16.93	16.67	16.19	16.65
Grenada	328	31.23	33.09	37.80	33.69	36.75	38.25	37.81	41.42	....	....	....	....
Guatemala	258	18.33	17.25	15.68	15.05	12.69	13.68	17.40	17.35	17.84	17.78	18.89	17.04
Guyana	336	53.74	....	....	....	....	....	....	....	....	....	....	....
Honduras	268	25.96	33.56	37.63	31.56	31.13	32.17	30.93	34.67	30.72	29.57	25.62	27.44
Jamaica	343	27.94	28.69	27.19	29.84	29.20	29.34	25.89	24.54	26.84	29.22	32.21	....
Mexico	273	23.29	21.00	21.72	19.82	23.11	25.86	24.32	23.45	23.71	20.91	20.71	19.83
Nicaragua	278	20.93	19.47	20.37	22.00	25.77	31.16	31.03	39.63	32.81	30.96	32.12	31.45
Panama	283	21.63	22.58	24.48	27.65	26.08	26.69	27.42	27.81	24.73	....	....	....
Paraguay	288	22.90	22.95	23.36	23.93	23.40	23.55	22.93	23.04	21.85	19.78	19.09	....
Peru	293	17.31	19.31	22.25	24.83	22.85	24.13	23.69	21.21	20.26	18.64	18.43	....
St. Vincent & Grenadines	364	24.26	25.64	28.51	30.05	28.16	30.81	35.81	34.55	27.28	29.70	30.03	....
Suriname	366	22.79	23.88	43.16	51.77	43.35	41.89	....	....	....	....	....	....
Trinidad and Tobago	369	13.79	14.35	20.20	20.78	24.28	30.11	33.38	21.01	19.98	22.29	....	....
Uruguay	298	15.38	15.64	15.87	15.41	15.24	15.22	15.87	15.14	13.96	13.77	11.52	13.06
Venezuela, Rep. Bol.	299	23.72	18.75	14.16	18.11	16.55	21.04	21.87	18.10	17.22	19.72	13.82	....
Memorandum Items													
Oil Exporting Countries	999	30.62	26.43	24.05	25.67	25.75	26.48	21.74	18.15	19.68	21.46	21.16	....
Non-Oil Developing Countries	201	25.63	28.80	28.65	28.97	28.02	27.59	26.42	26.04	26.39	26.36	....	....

Final Consumption Expenditure as Percentage of GDP

		1992	1993	1994	1995	1996	1997	1998	1999	2000	2001	2002	2003
							Percentages						
World	001	77.28	76.13	75.86	75.67	75.79	75.61	75.79	76.06	75.66	76.46	76.76	....
Industrial Countries	110	78.92	79.34	78.88	78.60	78.56	78.03	78.29	78.79	79.00	79.93	80.72	81.16
United States	111	83.36	83.37	82.68	82.62	82.23	81.45	81.58	82.18	83.09	84.49	85.68	86.13
Canada	156	83.07	82.71	80.36	78.42	78.12	77.57	77.73	75.82	73.46	75.01	75.77	75.78
Australia	193	79.87	78.99	77.97	78.79	77.95	77.75	77.73	78.25	77.89	77.65	77.91	78.05
Japan	158	67.08	68.39	69.83	70.36	70.38	70.24	71.28	72.44	72.30	73.62	74.80	74.40
New Zealand	196	80.03	76.85	76.41	76.50	77.16	78.38	80.22	80.01	78.07	76.34	77.94	77.88
Euro Area	163	78.25	78.75	78.00	77.53	77.95	77.31	76.26	76.83	76.67	77.30	77.37	77.90
Austria	122	75.14	76.39	76.41	76.60	77.46	77.00	76.63	76.64	76.03	76.09	75.39	75.68
Belgium	124	76.51	76.15	75.63	75.50	76.58	75.34	75.40	74.97	75.30	76.30	76.78	77.63
Finland	172	80.35	78.94	76.75	74.58	75.81	73.36	71.85	71.91	70.16	71.09	72.56	74.30
France	132	78.04	79.79	79.10	78.71	79.41	78.57	77.65	77.54	77.06	77.25	77.88	79.13
Germany	134	76.37	77.29	76.43	76.62	77.33	77.07	76.75	77.54	77.92	78.45	77.75	77.87
Greece	174	88.71	89.73	89.05	88.40	88.19	87.27	87.00	85.92	85.24	83.35	82.74	81.98
Ireland	178	77.12	75.34	74.97	70.93	69.74	66.67	64.70	61.60	60.68	60.49	59.93	60.96
Italy	136	79.31	78.39	78.02	76.59	76.39	77.09	77.29	78.29	78.82	78.85	79.05	79.91
Luxembourg	137	70.23	68.28	66.13	66.57	67.20	63.76	62.30	59.02	55.65	58.59	60.83	61.86
Netherlands	138	71.92	72.12	71.07	70.36	70.71	70.32	70.53	73.01	72.57	73.03	74.39	74.57
Portugal	182	86.03	87.24	86.55	85.27	85.37	84.95	85.95	82.06	82.06	81.70	81.66	82.85
Spain	184	80.15	80.69	79.75	77.86	77.58	76.85	76.73	76.68	76.51	75.96	75.99	75.86
Denmark	128	75.28	76.77	77.05	76.24	76.14	75.73	76.31	75.48	73.01	73.01	73.52	73.74
Iceland	176	80.84	78.88	77.80	79.00	79.19	79.07	79.74	82.23	82.64	78.59	79.28	81.91
Norway	142	72.95	72.70	72.04	70.87	69.49	67.90	70.84	68.77	61.71	63.30	66.80	68.76
Sweden	144	80.39	80.93	78.93	76.07	76.85	76.54	76.48	76.33	75.71	75.97	76.78	77.32
Switzerland	146	71.77	71.69	70.91	71.49	72.35	72.33	71.70	71.95	71.12	72.15	72.65	73.44
United Kingdom	112	85.09	85.23	84.24	83.55	83.70	82.80	82.84	83.94	84.54	85.45	86.30	86.46
Developing Countries	200	74.55	72.03	72.01	71.92	72.24	72.52	72.77	72.74	71.60	72.25	71.95	....
Africa	605	84.32	84.33	83.52	82.99	82.13	83.22	85.24	80.87	78.35	80.03	82.42	81.95
Algeria	612	68.21	73.16	74.05	72.57	67.72	67.99	72.79	68.38	55.49	58.28	59.59	56.54
Benin	638	96.05	96.95	90.00	88.87	90.49	91.42	90.02	91.46	89.86	88.94	88.63	....
Botswana	616	61.37	64.45	62.41	63.66	61.40	56.51	57.48	62.79	61.60	59.99	62.21	61.93
Burkina Faso	748	91.63	94.24	85.35	89.77	92.93	89.53	91.97	94.31	94.75	93.70	93.90	92.61
Burundi	618	104.09	104.52	107.06	105.06	97.61	97.39	104.49	100.86	105.92	107.85	103.48	108.18
Cameroon	622	84.41	82.44	73.86	76.02	75.67	73.47	....	....	....	....	....	....
Central African Rep.	626	97.11	94.92	89.91	90.64	96.68	94.92	97.27	93.70	107.86	95.97	96.52	....
Congo, Dem. Rep. of	636	91.70	89.81	87.97	84.01	73.90	87.79	90.55	88.07	85.82	102.00	....	....
Congo, Rep. of	634	80.27	81.16	71.33	47.89	61.96	59.64	46.73	47.74	31.55	40.91	44.50	46.94
Côte d'Ivoire	662	91.35	90.59	77.64	79.66	76.00	76.79	80.20	77.81	81.18	80.59	80.40	....
Ethiopia	644	96.99	94.40	94.97	93.31	93.50	103.50	92.20	98.80	101.00	99.00	....	....
Gabon	646	63.55	62.96	53.23	56.98	50.74	54.46	69.34	....	....	....	....	....
Ghana	652	97.70	93.40	87.40	88.30	88.14	92.19	....	113.96	97.03	89.11	95.48	97.81	....
Guinea-Bissau	654	103.87	101.50	107.50	102.75	102.79	96.93	113.96	97.03	89.11	95.48	97.81	....
Kenya	664	83.20	77.61	77.57	84.11	83.97	88.87	90.32	89.63	94.06	94.90	92.05	91.66
Madagascar	674	97.05	97.85	96.67	96.63	93.65	96.35	95.07	93.11	93.54	89.27	95.64	93.52
Malawi	676	101.50	101.47	107.30	102.32	107.07	99.54	91.94	101.07	95.72	....	....	....
Mali	678	93.78	96.04	95.73	95.42	95.95	85.25	87.84	90.58	90.51	84.24	81.34	....
Mauritania	682	97.05	98.39	91.61	80.13	88.34	89.50	....	....	....	....	....	....
Mauritius	684	74.07	75.44	76.79	76.80	76.28	75.56	75.41	77.16	74.92	73.33	74.93	74.51
Morocco	686	86.86	86.56	87.72	88.99	88.04	86.45	86.12	85.43	87.71	87.11	86.69	86.45
Mozambique	688	117.47	115.01	111.74	109.16	101.83	98.92	93.18	90.97	92.08	87.21	93.78	....
Namibia	728	87.87	90.64	83.31	86.79	87.96	90.87	89.10	89.42	90.01	87.64	....	....
Niger	692	101.87	97.59	92.99	93.54	91.52	91.64	92.81	97.41	89.06	86.82	90.13	....
Nigeria	694	77.23	80.55	85.53	84.25	88.92	88.65	102.78	66.89	55.21	65.60	84.65	84.17
Rwanda	714	95.76	97.24	146.79	109.81	106.23	103.99	100.77	99.84	99.15	99.95	102.21	100.12
Senegal	722	92.50	93.25	91.64	91.78	87.48	86.66	86.65	87.55	88.33	92.15	....	....
Seychelles	718	84.73	80.46	75.30	76.39	77.07	77.71	76.56	....	....	111.16	111.74	111.61
Sierra Leone	724	90.57	95.42	91.80	95.00	91.66	98.27	94.63	95.95	95.99	81.15	80.32	81.07
South Africa	199	83.13	81.89	81.86	80.91	81.34	82.15	82.11	81.63	81.39	81.15	80.32	81.07
Swaziland	734	99.78	102.18	96.51	98.68	105.31	96.66	96.71	96.08	95.47	95.00	....	....
Tanzania	738	102.36	103.15	101.16	99.16	94.63	93.16	95.90	95.11	90.15	89.84	86.49	....
Togo	742	100.45	108.23	94.43	100.09	99.96	97.93	99.27	97.59	98.23	98.41	97.51	....
Tunisia	744	77.73	78.28	78.29	79.20	76.49	76.02	76.45	75.96	76.26	76.65	79.06	78.98
Uganda	746	99.26	98.07	93.45	93.27	91.84	92.04	92.88	92.08	94.65	94.73	94.75	92.63
Zambia	754	93.59	86.96	84.63	74.71	68.26	73.67	....	....	....	....	....	....
Zimbabwe	698	89.81	83.82	72.94	77.38	82.37	87.78	79.44	80.57	87.10	....	....	....
Asia	505	68.81	66.89	65.92	65.82	66.68	66.20	66.18	67.73	67.62	67.40	....	....
Bangladesh	513	86.14	87.70	86.90	86.87	85.10	84.10	82.59	82.29	82.12	82.00	81.84	81.77
Bhutan	514	77.82	66.43	62.35	57.91	64.98	75.37	77.31	74.98	72.59	....	....	....
China, P.R.: Mainland	924	61.68	58.50	57.39	57.49	58.54	58.19	58.74	60.14	61.12	59.78	....	....
China, P.R.: Hong Kong	532	67.09	66.45	67.99	70.87	70.34	69.75	70.60	70.17	68.33	70.40	68.89	68.45
Fiji	819	86.56	83.63	78.68	78.97	78.73	77.63	76.34	70.55	77.11	74.13	....	....
India	534	78.16	78.27	76.31	75.30	76.70	75.78	77.74	78.62	77.73	77.93	76.94	....
Indonesia	536	61.82	67.54	67.80	69.41	69.92	68.52	73.47	80.55	74.44	75.14	78.88	....
Korea	542	63.71	63.97	64.57	63.47	64.27	64.22	62.13	64.23	66.08	68.11	68.62	67.18
Malaysia	548	63.28	60.92	60.40	60.29	57.14	56.11	51.33	52.57	52.84	57.65	58.09	57.07
Myanmar	518	87.16	88.59	88.25	86.63	88.54	88.21	88.19	87.03	....	....	....	....
Nepal	558	89.16	86.48	85.33	85.19	86.17	86.04	86.23	86.39	84.83	85.02	87.98	88.41

2004, International Monetary Fund: *International Financial Statistics Yearbook*

121

Final Consumption Expenditure as Percentage of GDP

		1992	1993	1994	1995	1996	1997	1998	1999	2000	2001	2002	2003
						Percentages							
Asia(Cont.)													
Pakistan	564	82.93	85.32	83.21	84.17	85.52	86.77	83.33	86.05	85.74	85.81	85.65	84.44
Papua New Guinea	853	74.55	66.67	60.23	58.75	68.96	77.58	77.37	86.68	....	....	....	....
Philippines	566	85.07	86.24	85.15	85.47	85.40	85.79	87.60	85.69	82.70	82.88	81.03	80.46
Singapore	576	54.02	54.04	52.10	49.77	49.64	48.90	48.50	50.73	51.69	55.92	55.84	55.08
Sri Lanka	524	84.99	83.99	84.78	84.71	84.68	82.68	80.81	80.49	82.56	84.23	85.52	84.26
Thailand	578	64.67	64.66	63.73	63.07	63.96	64.74	65.21	67.46	67.33	68.44	67.68	66.79
Vanuatu	846	81.94	77.66	76.87	73.94	....	....	....	....	....	....	....	....
Europe	170	78.96	72.19	74.93	75.90	76.44	78.66	78.98	76.66	73.50	75.59	76.05	75.70
Armenia	911	112.15	110.56	105.83	117.45	111.65	114.74	111.15	108.28	108.94	104.84	99.07	94.35
Belarus	913	66.76	74.70	79.90	79.64	80.56	77.38	77.71	78.15	76.39	79.18	80.52	80.94
Bulgaria	918	85.94	92.34	91.23	85.94	86.47	85.54	82.89	87.85	87.06	86.90	86.81	88.07
Cyprus	423	81.51	75.69	74.23	79.51	82.84	84.51	86.37	82.92	84.61	85.75	86.37	....
Czech Republic	935	70.67	71.66	72.93	70.72	72.16	73.36	71.15	73.20	73.90	73.00	72.14	74.13
Estonia	939	71.02	77.52	83.31	82.52	83.80	80.35	79.17	79.24	76.00	75.24	76.03	75.58
Hungary	944	84.19	88.25	84.28	77.45	74.04	72.40	72.58	74.00	73.00	74.73	77.07	79.18
Kazakhstan	916	82.62	88.35	82.57	81.88	83.88	86.38	88.16	80.67	73.33	73.81	69.64	67.34
Kyrgyz Republic	917	92.10	95.98	97.29	94.55	100.62	86.22	106.10	96.77	85.73	82.30	86.15	88.36
Macedonia, FYR	962	95.80	100.83	94.75	89.00	90.25	92.56	92.62	90.28	92.64	94.84	99.52	....
Malta	181	79.55	79.82	79.51	81.68	85.30	82.88	81.85	81.56	82.38	83.94	84.20	85.25
Moldova	921	57.48	55.90	75.43	82.89	94.33	97.35	100.89	90.01	103.02	104.36	....	....
Poland	964	83.30	83.47	80.23	77.95	79.69	79.75	79.04	80.77	81.60	82.72	84.29	....
Romania	968	77.00	76.04	77.26	81.32	82.57	86.44	90.28	88.75	86.16	85.19	82.18	83.27
Russia	922	48.32	62.24	69.10	71.16	71.51	75.82	76.20	68.12	61.28	65.82	68.87	67.51
Slovak Republic	936	75.68	79.66	73.41	72.66	75.76	74.95	76.66	76.78	76.31	78.16	77.71	76.74
Slovenia	961	75.46	79.57	76.87	79.35	78.56	77.05	76.70	76.90	76.89	76.79	74.83	75.22
Turkey	186	80.02	82.12	81.61	81.10	78.84	80.30	81.87	87.42	85.50	86.27	80.71	80.22
Ukraine	926	63.56	64.02	67.83	76.40	79.88	81.61	81.46	77.03	75.25	76.57	76.45	77.24
Middle East	405	75.01	73.99	73.91	73.59	72.18	72.71	78.15	73.76	69.84	71.61	69.87	....
Egypt	469	83.03	83.28	84.86	85.00	87.31	88.10	88.00	86.64	87.06	86.59	86.18	85.54
Iran, I.R. of	429	62.91	59.04	62.15	63.04	59.76	61.16	69.34	64.53	61.53	62.30	57.54	....
Iraq	433	86.87	86.21	....	....	....	....	....	....	....	....	....	....
Israel	436	87.52	89.10	89.02	87.86	87.72	86.04	85.10	84.95	83.86	86.58	89.72	89.04
Jordan	439	98.51	94.00	90.00	88.17	94.81	96.56	97.65	96.29	104.61	104.41	....	....
Kuwait	443	93.88	79.33	74.97	74.25	71.41	72.66	88.42	78.27	65.54	75.14	82.16	75.49
Libya	672	82.72	87.02	82.74	81.08	79.74	82.70	89.55	82.16	67.04	75.13	74.11	....
Oman	449	74.48	77.47	76.04	76.54	72.26	70.88	83.48	73.51	59.96	65.15	66.14	....
Qatar	453	63.87	68.82	64.37	63.92	60.29	52.45	56.90	46.77	34.89	35.75	....	....
Saudi Arabia	456	74.34	74.50	72.17	70.52	68.43	68.49	74.38	67.32	62.54	65.31	62.92	57.77
Syrian Arab Rep.	463	88.20	87.06	82.37	79.66	82.66	80.53	79.82	80.91	75.78	72.59	71.99	....
United Arab Emirates	466	62.09	62.16	63.06	64.41	61.41	63.10	69.90	....	....	....	....	....
Yemen Republic	474	99.50	107.81	97.34	97.82	85.73	83.69	88.23	78.61	75.25	81.95	83.35	87.39
Western Hemisphere	205	79.70	79.65	80.05	79.37	79.17	79.34	80.74	80.95	79.92	81.20	79.56	79.01
Antigua and Barbuda	311	62.40	62.81	66.07	71.83	74.83	69.61	66.63	63.01	67.17	....	....	....
Argentina	213	84.93	82.72	83.11	81.91	81.03	81.39	81.55	83.87	83.12	83.07	74.13	74.70
Bahamas, The	313	83.05	83.91	84.02	83.45	....	....	....	....	....	....	....	....
Barbados	316	82.39	81.56	77.05	81.67	80.28	84.15	83.68	86.14	88.22	86.74	88.93	....
Belize	339	80.13	81.21	82.44	79.88	81.44	81.86	82.88	78.78	73.36	78.70	79.51	....
Bolivia	218	92.31	92.74	91.16	89.39	88.46	88.62	89.28	91.64	91.17	91.58	90.25	90.24
Brazil	223	78.58	77.75	77.50	79.48	80.99	80.87	81.06	81.38	79.97	79.79	78.17	76.20
Chile	228	74.10	75.10	71.98	71.39	74.31	74.40	76.37	76.83	76.28	76.48	75.69	75.09
Colombia	233	68.20	68.15	80.38	80.63	83.49	84.99	86.17	86.58	84.21	85.30	86.09	....
Costa Rica	238	84.39	85.58	85.52	84.57	87.51	85.76	82.22	77.15	80.23	82.77	82.92	81.77
Dominica	321	84.96	86.99	90.40	84.70	89.22	83.22	80.68	81.18	86.17	93.30	91.10	....
Dominican Republic	243	88.74	83.63	84.12	83.90	85.89	84.97	85.56	83.25	85.79	84.63	85.59	....
Ecuador	248	74.97	81.17	79.84	80.97	78.00	78.63	81.60	78.70	73.82	79.08	79.74	80.97
El Salvador	253	97.82	96.17	95.55	96.08	97.67	96.54	94.74	95.92	98.11	99.13	98.60	99.70
Grenada	328	86.08	88.37	77.13	84.05	85.68	85.63	89.57	67.73	82.99	....	....	....
Guatemala	258	91.47	90.77	91.55	91.12	92.09	91.96	90.69	91.00	90.92	92.40	93.31	94.47
Guyana	336	64.00	63.70	63.58	62.30	62.15	65.08	....	....	....	....	....	....
Haiti	263	111.76	107.29	101.21	121.61	98.80	102.14	99.31	....	....	....	....	....
Honduras	268	78.14	75.47	72.39	72.82	73.99	73.46	76.73	80.28	83.15	86.83	89.48	89.21
Jamaica	343	72.94	79.65	79.07	81.48	82.33	83.52	84.11	83.76	84.57	87.13	87.90	....
Mexico	273	81.74	82.93	83.11	77.52	74.83	74.24	77.82	78.16	78.23	81.36	81.17	81.84
Nicaragua	278	115.08	107.96	96.20	93.55	93.46	93.64	92.75	92.95	94.10	94.37	94.21	94.87
Panama	283	66.01	64.99	62.53	61.03	70.60	60.51	62.12	59.63	62.63	....	....	....
Paraguay	288	87.61	87.99	95.22	92.47	92.81	92.66	94.00	90.70	92.90	96.32	93.81	....
Peru	293	85.64	84.55	81.13	80.85	82.10	80.29	81.69	81.12	81.65	83.08	82.48	....
St. Kitts and Nevis	361	67.01	66.12	70.67	77.18	80.79	76.38	72.09	89.29	83.83	72.30	75.85	....
St. Lucia	362	81.57	77.05	77.81	76.14	81.38	83.70	80.95	81.63	82.53	83.50	83.08	....
St. Vincent & Grenadines	364	84.77	92.20	95.77	84.34	85.08	97.25	93.15	86.07	80.97	81.00	82.49	....
Suriname	366	77.57	46.66	38.52	35.80	78.49	87.29	....	....	....	....	....	....
Trinidad and Tobago	369	77.13	80.77	66.96	64.70	65.35	73.10	71.94	73.23	66.16	67.38	....	....
Uruguay	298	83.79	84.79	84.74	84.70	84.95	84.77	84.86	86.12	87.72	87.92	86.52	84.57
Venezuela, Rep. Bol.	299	78.83	81.47	77.28	76.59	68.26	72.29	79.35	76.61	70.65	75.50	73.41	....
Memorandum Items													
Oil Exporting Countries	999	68.71	70.35	70.39	70.65	68.73	69.06	75.90	72.95	66.19	68.84	69.96	....
Non-Oil Developing Countries	201	75.44	72.25	72.22	72.09	72.71	72.97	72.41	72.71	72.22	72.64	72.13	....

Commodity Prices

		1992	1993	1994	1995	1996	1997	1998	1999	2000	2001	2002	2003
Aluminum (US $/MT)													
All Origins (London) *	156	1,256.27	1,139.93	1,475.64	1,805.02	1,506.81	1,599.28	1,357.58	1,359.99	1,551.50	1,446.74	1,351.08	1,432.83
Bananas (US $/MT)													
Latin America (US Ports) *	248	473.08	443.03	439.79	445.10	469.58	522.56	492.19	373.92	422.27	584.70	527.61	375.19
Barley (US $/MT)													
Canada (Winnepeg) *	156	78.68	71.38	72.65	104.01	119.67	97.24	85.05	75.94	77.23	93.94	108.97	104.72
Beef (US cents/pound)													
Australia-NZ (US Ports) *	193	111.34	118.74	105.82	86.50	80.97	84.17	78.30	83.14	87.79	96.54	95.40	89.74
Argentina (frozen)	213	123.41	147.31	111.55	102.34	82.14	87.83	114.38	100.56	99.28	80.58	….	….
Butter (US cents/pound)													
New Zealand	196	91.57	81.65	84.47	99.25	103.17	83.73	80.40	68.96	63.99	67.76	57.06	67.41
Coal (US $/MT)													
Australia	193	38.56	31.33	32.30	39.37	38.07	35.10	29.23	25.89	26.25	32.31	27.06	27.74
Australia	193	41.42	39.38	37.35	40.08	43.14	41.43	37.37	31.60	29.13	33.32	33.65	32.86
South Africa	199	28.83	26.96	28.56	35.23	33.52	31.35	26.84	24.27	26.57	33.86	26.01	29.97
Cocoa Beans (US $/MT)													
New York and London *	652	1,099.42	1,111.27	1,395.68	1,432.54	1,455.25	1,618.74	1,676.00	1,135.05	903.91	1,088.38	1,779.04	1,753.07
Coconut Oil (US $/MT)													
Philippines (New York) *	566	578.06	451.27	606.50	669.58	751.77	656.75	660.29	737.48	450.16	319.24	421.36	467.29
Philippines	566	545.39	416.21	559.83	616.30	719.91	623.44	598.64	716.07	445.89	294.47	373.28	425.55
Coffee (US cents/pound)													
Other Milds (New York) *	386	63.66	69.94	148.53	149.41	120.25	185.02	132.40	101.67	85.05	61.91	60.37	64.05
Brazil (New York)	223	56.26	66.58	143.32	145.98	120.29	166.80	121.81	88.92	79.80	50.50	45.03	50.78
Brazil	223	43.25	50.08	115.54	123.89	100.21	143.38	106.24	79.56	73.16	43.74	34.95	43.16
Uganda (New York) *	799	43.63	53.50	119.82	126.83	82.84	80.70	83.93	67.65	42.16	27.32	30.82	38.38
Copper (US $/MT)													
United Kingdom (London) *	112	2,284.81	1,914.95	2,305.53	2,932.04	2,293.39	2,275.19	1,653.71	1,572.53	1,814.52	1,580.17	1,560.29	1,779.36
Copra (US $/MT)													
Philippines (Europ. Ports)	566	381.85	295.42	416.84	438.50	488.98	433.75	411.03	462.27	308.92	195.55	265.93	299.45
Cotton (US cents/pound)													
Liverpool Index *	111	57.94	58.02	79.72	98.30	80.54	79.23	65.53	53.13	59.05	48.00	46.26	63.44
DAP (US $/MT)													
US Gulf Coast	111	145.16	129.11	172.79	216.59	213.16	199.92	203.42	177.78	154.22	147.73	157.53	179.41
Fish (US $/kilogram)													
Norway *	142	5.90	5.01	5.01	4.78	4.11	3.73	3.72	3.57	3.65	2.89	2.94	2.99
Fish Meal (US $/MT)													
Any Origin (Hamburg) *	293	481.53	364.69	376.66	495.00	586.18	606.25	661.55	392.18	412.74	482.72	597.37	610.50
Iceland	176	522.16	405.15	452.21	528.38	611.03	673.15	724.26	493.31	468.77	….	….	….
Gasoline (US cents/gallon)													
US Gulf Coast	111	57.46	50.86	47.90	50.92	59.65	58.53	41.30	51.84	83.37	73.41	72.05	87.17
Gold (US $/troy ounce)													
United Kingdom (London)	112	343.70	359.53	384.12	384.16	387.82	331.00	294.14	278.87	279.17	271.05	310.04	363.53
Groundnuts (US $/MT)													
Nigeria (London) *	694	799.13	1,092.15	954.80	909.92	962.00	988.42	988.75	834.74	843.93	833.16	753.29	975.70
Groundnut Oil (US $/MT)													
Any Origin (Europe) *	694	609.58	737.88	1,022.64	990.92	897.33	1,010.42	908.58	786.67	712.43	671.80	687.97	1,250.63
Hides (US cents/pound)													
United States (Chicago) *	111	75.86	80.03	86.81	88.14	87.32	88.25	76.69	72.15	80.22	84.60	80.75	68.30
Iron Ore (US cents/DMTU)													
Brazil (North Sea Ports) *	223	33.10	29.09	26.47	28.38	30.00	30.15	31.00	27.59	28.79	29.91	29.33	31.51
Jute (US $/MT)													
Bangladesh (Chitta.-Chalna)	513	279.17	271.25	295.67	365.67	454.25	302.00	259.08	275.67	278.83	329.58	290.75	241.96
Lamb (US cents/pound)													
New Zealand (London) *	196	115.43	124.13	125.66	113.26	145.44	150.28	116.00	115.84	112.85	130.25	146.04	159.81
Lead (US $/MT)													
United Kingdom (London) *	112	543.51	407.34	548.72	629.30	774.13	623.06	526.92	501.77	454.17	476.36	452.25	514.21
Linseed Oil (US $/MT)													
Any Origin	001	396.34	448.50	516.74	657.50	565.83	571.24	707.71	512.54	399.39	382.25	520.21	678.20
Maize (US $/MT)													
United States (US Gulf Pts) *	111	104.21	102.04	107.78	123.45	164.52	117.17	101.62	90.29	88.22	89.61	99.33	105.19
Thailand	578	144.81	134.24	162.64	202.15	297.67	280.16	154.60	143.86	313.34	111.89	181.51	184.73
Natural Gas (US $/000 M)													
Russian Federation	922	85.14	93.54	83.25	97.06	99.00	96.13	80.82	65.05	124.34	139.44	95.99	125.51
Indonesia	536	….	75.69	69.12	74.83	82.11	79.13	57.95	70.33	110.14	98.24	93.14	104.80
United States	111	63.03	76.11	68.94	61.36	96.82	88.57	75.16	81.40	155.07	142.53	120.99	197.83
Newsprint (US $/short ton)													
Finland (1995=100)	172	469.86	377.58	401.99	605.05	650.84	470.85	453.66	….	….	….	….	….
Nickel (US $/MT)													
United Kingdom(N.Europ.Ports)*	156	7,015.48	5,308.17	6,331.93	8,223.56	7,504.09	6,924.72	4,623.59	6,002.51	8,630.52	5,969.63	6,783.31	9,630.29
Olive Oil (US $/MT)													
United Kingdom *	112	3,177.94	2,703.64	3,148.84	4,499.51	5,965.18	4,236.48	3,227.05	3,650.44	2,980.12	2,667.28	2,900.51	3,796.77
Oranges (US $/MT)													
French Import Price *	132	489.24	432.49	411.34	531.47	491.67	458.96	442.40	438.23	363.21	595.50	564.53	683.05
Palm Kernel Oil(US $/MT)													
Malaysia (Rotterdam)	548	581.83	437.84	627.75	677.67	727.97	651.83	686.93	695.03	448.72	308.86	416.47	458.49
Palm Oil (US $/MT)													
Malaysia (N.W.Europe)*	548	393.69	377.73	529.15	628.58	532.03	545.83	671.30	436.31	309.51	286.45	390.06	442.83
Malaysia	548	382.34	383.06	484.21	623.66	509.38	506.51	603.02	424.93	295.36	248.32	359.56	425.80
Pepper (US cents/pound)													
Singapore	576	66.70	104.90	139.41	171.86	167.71	286.88	322.29	309.58	196.93	112.28	104.49	127.71

Market Prices (lines 76) and Unit Values (lines 74) Country of Origin and, for Market Prices, Pricing Point in Parentheses

2004, International Monetary Fund: *International Financial Statistics Yearbook*

Commodity Prices

		1992	1993	1994	1995	1996	1997	1998	1999	2000	2001	2002	2003
		\multicolumn{12}{c}{Market Prices (lines 76) and Unit Values (lines 74) Country of Origin and, for Market Prices, Pricing Point in Parentheses}
Petroleum, spot (US$/barrel)													
Average crude price *	001	19.04	16.79	15.95	17.20	20.37	19.27	13.07	17.98	28.23	24.33	24.95	28.89
Dubai Fateh *	466	17.14	14.91	14.83	16.13	18.54	18.10	12.09	17.08	26.09	22.71	23.73	26.73
U.K. Brent *	112	19.41	17.00	15.83	17.06	20.45	19.12	12.72	17.70	28.31	24.41	25.00	28.85
West Texas Intermediate *	111	20.56	18.46	17.18	18.43	22.13	20.59	14.42	19.17	30.32	25.87	26.12	31.10
Phosphate Rock (US $/MT)													
Morocco (Casablanca)	686	41.75	33.00	33.00	35.00	39.00	40.83	43.00	44.00	43.75	41.84	41.00	40.50
Potash (US $/MT)													
Canada (Vancouver)	156	112.08	107.42	105.72	117.76	116.93	116.53	116.89	121.64	122.50	118.08	113.32	113.28
Poultry (US cents/pound)													
United States (Georgia) *	111	47.97	54.68	55.29	55.48	62.31	60.99	63.16	59.97	59.45	63.63	63.08	66.21
Plywood (US cents/sheet)													
Philippines (Tokyo)	566	380.77	661.42	599.50	584.44	529.52	484.96	374.56	440.56	448.23	409.65	402.75	436.08
Pulp (US $/MT)													
Sweden (North Sea Ports)	144	562.95	423.91	552.46	853.45	574.12	554.87	508.77	500.14	664.63	518.71	452.21	521.42
Rice (US $/MT)													
Thailand (Bangkok) *	578	267.67	237.25	269.46	320.80	338.06	302.47	305.42	248.97	203.69	172.71	191.83	199.46
Thailand	578	291.03	257.18	484.96	314.85	366.67	216.85	321.01	264.11	265.95	205.82	222.39	251.70
Rubber (US cents/pound)													
Malaysia (Singapore) *	548	39.08	37.71	51.07	71.68	63.59	46.16	32.73	28.83	30.30	26.09	34.70	49.12
Malaysia	548	40.55	40.09	49.75	72.17	64.55	47.04	33.06	29.03	31.38	27.40	32.70	45.22
Thailand	578	35.28	35.07	44.08	63.81	59.04	43.30	30.41	23.79	27.02	23.51	28.28	40.75
Shrimp (US $/pound)													
United States (U.S. Gulf Ports) *	111	4.97	5.16	5.93	6.13	5.95	6.70	6.45	6.62	6.92	6.96	4.77	5.21
Silver (US cents/troy ounce)													
United States (New York)	111	393.6	429.8	528.4	519.2	518.3	489.2	553.4	525.0	499.9	438.6	462.5	491.1
Sisal (US $/MT)													
East Africa (Europe)	639	505.58	615.42	604.58	710.42	868.25	777.50	821.33	695.75	628.67	699.00	659.92	698.42
Sorghum (US $/MT)													
United States (US Gulf Ports)	111	102.76	99.03	103.87	118.97	150.03	109.62	98.04	84.39	88.00	95.23	101.75	106.54
Soybeans (US $/MT)													
United States (Rotterdam) *	111	235.50	255.25	252.83	259.25	304.50	295.42	245.42	199.58	211.25	195.50	214.42	264.33
Soybean Meal (US $/MT)													
United States (Rotterdam) *	111	204.33	208.08	192.50	196.92	267.58	275.75	170.33	152.00	189.58	180.00	175.67	211.67
Soybean Oil (US $/MT)													
All Origins (Dutch Ports) *	111	428.66	479.98	616.20	625.17	551.63	564.75	625.92	428.01	338.20	353.59	455.15	555.66
Sugar (US cents/pound)													
EU Import Price *	112	28.48	28.10	28.20	31.21	31.15	28.38	27.13	26.84	25.16	23.88	24.91	27.09
Free Market *	001	9.07	10.02	12.11	13.28	11.96	11.40	8.92	6.27	8.08	8.23	6.24	6.92
U.S. Import Price *	111	21.30	21.61	22.03	23.06	22.36	21.93	22.06	21.14	19.40	21.34	20.94	21.50
Philippines	566	18.91	14.13	15.36	19.72	19.30	22.28	19.21	21.14	16.14	17.64	18.14	18.99
Sunflower Oil (US $/MT)													
EU (NW European ports) *	112	451.85	534.82	636.21	693.17	576.08	581.42	726.85	507.95	390.21	484.45	596.39	592.44
Superphosphate (US $/MT)													
United States (US Gulf Ports)	111	120.74	111.95	132.11	149.63	175.83	171.91	173.67	154.50	137.72	126.88	133.07	149.34
Swine Meat (US cents/pound)													
United States (Iowa) *	111	56.48	64.52	56.41	62.80	92.49	72.86	45.62	44.41	59.29	61.43	47.26	53.40
Tea (US cents/kg)													
Average Auction (London) *	112	199.74	185.64	183.32	164.16	177.17	237.19	238.56	232.36	248.12	198.12	179.19	194.33
Sri Lanka	524	187.03	188.66	184.77	199.64	252.46	268.48	286.82	229.90	239.43	233.78	226.30	237.99
Timber (US $/cubic meter)													
Hardwood Logs													
Malaysia, Sarawak *	548	196.69	388.98	316.32	257.68	253.74	238.21	162.86	187.02	190.06	160.19	162.64	187.12
Hardwood Sawnwood													
Malaysia *	548	607.21	758.24	821.44	740.19	740.89	662.33	484.16	601.11	599.18	488.26	518.38	550.20
Softwood Logs													
United States *	111	152.47	217.94	201.23	193.84	204.07	185.31	159.10	164.55	180.78	157.73	145.92	145.57
Softwood Sawnwood													
United States *	111	234.64	277.44	299.55	300.62	309.91	294.13	279.81	300.55	284.81	282.83	273.25	284.30
Tin (US $/MT)													
Any Origin (London) *	112	6,104.09	5,167.55	5,459.98	6,197.36	6,158.88	5,640.48	5,536.23	5,391.40	5,435.90	4,489.44	4,061.00	4,889.65
Malaysia	548	6,266.29	5,342.31	5,318.29	6,180.62	6,168.86	5,339.01	5,517.63	5,374.75	5,549.34	4,446.94	4,135.67	4,931.50
Bolivia	218	6,038.63	5,495.29	5,459.00	6,210.29	6,145.68	3,842.16	3,692.81	3,673.06	3,684.27	3,362.18	2,794.69	3,165.30
Thailand	578	5,763.54	5,122.65	5,479.86	6,091.70	6,143.43	5,632.28	5,470.51	5,259.14	5,337.72	4,298.25	4,065.75	4,806.09
Tobacco (US $/MT)													
United States (All Markets)	111	3,439.54	2,695.34	2,641.66	2,643.44	3,056.73	3,531.81	3,336.12	3,101.45	2,988.17	2,989.02	2,733.62	....
Uranium (US $/pound)													
Restricted *	001	8.56	10.08	9.42	11.67	15.60	12.10	10.39	10.02	8.29	8.62	9.83	11.24
Urea (US $/MT)													
Ukraine	926	....	....	....	187.21	179.00	114.00	83.08	66.40	101.12	95.32	94.36	138.90
Wheat (US $/MT)													
Australia	193	151.34	136.58	128.75	189.78	214.17	168.79	144.97	129.36	124.72	144.04	152.90	165.55
United States (US Gulf Pts) *	111	151.16	140.21	149.78	176.96	207.14	159.67	126.10	112.05	114.00	126.80	148.53	146.14
Argentina	213	120.37	131.27	131.75	164.37	200.71	158.02	123.00	116.78	110.55	120.56	121.22	152.44
Wool (US cents/kilogram)													
Australia-NZ(UK) 48's *	112	341.20	319.73	399.59	497.14	428.88	442.79	336.39	276.47	280.98	332.43	565.65	658.99
Australia-NZ(UK) 64's *	112	600.08	463.26	745.33	775.31	651.59	759.84	552.81	619.25	733.54	623.44	644.41	702.04
Australia (greasy wool)	193	302.60	240.38	323.18	395.82	325.53	358.97	274.66	238.06	252.51	258.15	373.95	429.00
Zinc (US $/MT)													
United Kingdom (London) *	112	1,241.84	963.96	998.22	1,031.09	1,024.98	1,314.90	1,024.29	1,075.80	1,127.70	886.82	778.90	827.97
Bolivia	218	1,215.76	965.16	982.29	1,032.16	1,012.35	775.45	603.29	631.10	672.37	545.45	463.43	487.86

Commodity Prices

		1992	1993	1994	1995	1996	1997	1998	1999	2000	2001	2002	2003
		\multicolumn{12}{c}{Indices of Market Prices (lines 76) and of Unit Values (lines 74)}
		\multicolumn{12}{c}{2000=100}
All Primary Commodities	001	....	76.8	78.9	86.1	92.0	88.0	68.3	75.4	100.0	91.2	91.0	103.0
Non-Fuel Primary Commodities	001	105.4	103.8	115.2	125.9	123.7	119.8	102.7	95.8	100.0	96.0	96.5	103.4
Food	001	117.1	115.5	119.2	126.7	137.1	124.9	111.2	98.3	100.0	102.3	103.0	109.1
Beverages	001	89.2	93.3	153.4	154.2	131.4	172.2	149.6	117.8	100.0	83.9	97.7	102.5
Agricultural Raw Materials	001	94.1	108.5	119.7	123.7	119.2	113.5	94.6	95.8	100.0	95.1	96.7	100.4
Metals	001	100.5	86.9	100.9	122.1	108.3	109.6	90.1	89.1	100.0	90.2	87.7	98.2
Energy	001	....	61.9	58.8	64.0	74.5	70.4	49.2	64.1	100.0	88.5	88.0	102.8
World Bank LMICs	200	106.1	105.4	128.8	140.8	132.5	135.4	114.2	101.6	100.0	90.9	95.7	105.1
Aluminum (US $/MT)													
All Origins (London) *	156	81.0	73.5	95.1	116.3	97.1	103.1	87.5	87.7	100.0	93.2	87.1	92.4
Bananas (US $/MT)													
Latin America (US Ports) *	248	112.0	104.9	104.1	105.4	111.2	123.7	116.6	88.5	100.0	138.5	124.9	88.9
Barley (US $/MT)													
Canada (Winnepeg) *	156	101.9	92.4	94.1	134.7	154.9	125.9	110.1	98.3	100.0	121.6	141.1	135.6
Beef (US cents/pound)													
Australia-NZ (US Ports) *	193	126.8	135.3	120.5	98.5	92.2	95.9	89.2	94.7	100.0	110.0	108.7	102.2
Argentina (frozen)	213	124.3	148.4	112.4	103.1	82.7	88.5	115.2	101.3	100.0	81.2	....	....
Butter (US cents/pound)													
New Zealand	196	143.1	127.6	132.0	155.1	161.2	130.9	125.6	107.8	100.0	105.9	89.2	105.3
Coal (US $/MT)													
Australia	193	146.9	119.4	123.0	150.0	145.0	133.7	111.4	98.6	100.0	123.1	103.1	105.7
Australia	193	142.2	135.2	128.2	137.6	148.1	142.2	128.3	108.5	100.0	114.4	115.5	112.8
South Africa	199	108.5	101.5	107.5	132.6	126.1	118.0	101.0	91.4	100.0	127.5	97.9	112.8
Cocoa Beans (US $/MT)													
New York and London *	652	121.6	122.9	154.4	158.5	161.0	179.1	185.4	125.6	100.0	120.4	196.8	193.9
Coconut Oil (US $/MT)													
Philippines (New York) *	566	128.4	100.2	134.7	148.7	167.0	145.9	146.7	163.8	100.0	70.9	93.6	103.8
Philippines	566	122.3	93.3	125.6	138.2	161.5	139.8	134.3	160.6	100.0	66.0	83.7	95.4
Coffee (US cents/pound)													
Other Milds (New York) *	386	74.9	82.2	174.6	175.7	141.4	217.6	155.7	119.6	100.0	72.8	71.0	75.3
Brazil (New York)	223	70.5	83.4	179.6	182.9	150.7	209.0	152.6	111.4	100.0	63.3	56.4	63.6
Brazil	223	59.1	68.5	157.9	169.3	137.0	196.0	145.2	108.8	100.0	59.8	47.8	59.0
Uganda (New York) *	799	103.5	126.9	284.2	300.8	196.5	191.4	199.1	160.5	100.0	64.8	73.1	91.0
Copper (US $/MT)													
United Kingdom (London) *	112	125.9	105.5	127.1	161.6	126.4	125.4	91.1	86.7	100.0	87.1	86.0	98.1
Copra (US $/MT)													
Philippines (Europ. Ports)	566	123.6	95.6	134.9	141.9	158.3	140.4	133.1	149.6	100.0	63.3	86.1	96.9
Cotton (US cents/pound)													
Liverpool Index *	111	98.1	98.3	135.0	166.5	136.4	134.2	111.0	90.0	100.0	81.3	78.3	107.4
DAP (US $/MT)													
US Gulf Coast	111	94.1	83.7	112.0	140.4	138.2	129.6	131.9	115.3	100.0	95.8	102.1	116.3
Fish (US $/kilogram)													
Norway *	142	161.9	137.5	137.5	131.0	112.8	102.2	102.0	97.9	100.0	79.3	80.6	82.1
Fish Meal (US $/MT)													
Any Origin (Hamburg) *	293	116.7	88.4	91.3	119.9	142.0	146.9	160.3	95.0	100.0	117.0	144.7	147.9
Iceland	176	111.4	86.4	96.5	112.7	130.3	143.6	154.5	105.2	100.0	....	....	....
Gasoline (US cents/gallon)													
US Gulf Coast	111	68.9	61.0	57.5	61.1	71.5	70.2	49.5	62.2	100.0	88.0	86.4	104.6
Gold (US $/troy ounce)													
United Kingdom (London)	112	123.1	128.8	137.6	137.6	138.9	118.6	105.4	99.9	100.0	97.1	111.1	130.2
Groundnuts (US $/MT)													
Nigeria (London) *	694	94.7	129.4	113.1	107.8	114.0	117.1	117.2	98.9	100.0	98.7	89.3	115.6
Groundnut Oil (US $/MT)													
Any Origin (Europe) *	694	85.6	103.6	143.5	139.1	126.0	141.8	127.5	110.4	100.0	94.3	96.6	175.5
Hides (US cents/pound)													
United States (Chicago) *	111	94.6	99.8	108.2	109.9	108.8	110.0	95.6	89.9	100.0	105.5	100.7	85.1
Iron Ore (US cents/DMTU)													
Brazil (North Sea Ports) *	223	115.0	101.0	91.9	98.6	104.2	104.7	107.7	95.8	100.0	103.9	101.9	109.5
Jute (US $/MT)													
Bangladesh (Chitta.-Chalna)	513	100.1	97.3	106.0	131.1	162.9	108.3	92.9	98.9	100.0	118.2	104.3	86.8
Lamb (US cents/pound)													
New Zealand (London) *	196	102.3	110.0	111.3	100.4	128.9	133.2	102.8	102.7	100.0	115.4	129.4	141.6
Lead (US $/MT)													
United Kingdom (London) *	112	119.7	89.7	120.8	138.6	170.4	137.2	116.0	110.5	100.0	104.9	99.6	113.2
Linseed Oil (US $/MT)													
Any Origin	001	99.2	112.3	129.4	164.6	141.7	143.0	177.2	128.3	100.0	95.7	130.3	169.8
Maize (US $/MT)													
United States (US Gulf Pts) *	111	118.1	115.7	122.2	139.9	186.5	132.8	115.2	102.4	100.0	101.6	112.6	119.2
Thailand	578	46.2	42.8	51.9	64.5	95.0	89.4	49.3	45.9	100.0	35.7	57.9	59.0
Natural Gas (US $/000 M)													
Russian Federation	922	68.5	75.2	67.0	78.1	79.6	77.3	65.0	52.3	100.0	112.1	77.2	100.9
Indonesia	536	....	68.7	62.8	67.9	74.5	71.8	52.6	63.8	100.0	89.2	84.6	95.1
United States	111	40.6	49.1	44.5	39.6	62.4	57.1	48.5	52.5	100.0	91.9	78.0	127.6
Newsprint (US $/short ton)													
Finland	172	77.7	62.4	66.4	100.0	107.6	77.8	75.0	....	....	....	....	....
Nickel (US $/MT)													
United Kingdom(N.Europ.Ports)*	156	81.3	61.5	73.4	95.3	86.9	80.2	53.6	69.5	100.0	69.2	78.6	111.6
Olive Oil (US $/MT)													
United Kingdom *	112	106.6	90.7	105.7	151.0	200.2	142.2	108.3	122.5	100.0	89.5	97.3	127.4

2004, International Monetary Fund : *International Financial Statistics Yearbook*

Commodity Prices

Indices of Market Prices (lines 76) and of Unit Values (lines 74)
2000=100

		1992	1993	1994	1995	1996	1997	1998	1999	2000	2001	2002	2003
Oranges (US $/MT)													
French Import Price *	132	134.7	119.1	113.3	146.3	135.4	126.4	121.8	120.7	100.0	164.0	155.4	188.1
Palm Kernel Oil (US $/MT)													
Malaysia (Rotterdam)	548	129.7	97.6	139.9	151.0	162.2	145.3	153.1	154.9	100.0	68.8	92.8	102.2
Palm Oil (US $/MT)													
Malaysia (N.W.Europe)*	548	127.2	122.0	171.0	203.1	171.9	176.4	216.9	141.0	100.0	92.5	126.0	143.1
Malaysia	548	129.4	129.7	163.9	211.1	172.5	171.5	204.2	143.9	100.0	84.1	121.7	144.2
Pepper (US cents/pound)													
Malaysia (New York)	548	33.9	53.3	70.8	87.3	85.2	145.7	163.7	157.2	100.0	57.0	53.1	64.8
Singapore	576	33.9	53.3	70.8	87.3	85.2	145.7	163.7	157.2	100.0	57.0	53.1	64.8
Petroleum, spot (US$/barrel)													
Average crude price *	001	67.4	59.5	56.5	60.9	72.2	68.2	46.3	63.7	100.0	86.2	88.4	102.3
Dubai Fateh *	466	65.7	57.1	56.9	61.8	71.1	69.4	46.3	65.5	100.0	87.1	91.0	102.5
U.K. Brent *	112	68.6	60.0	55.9	60.3	72.3	67.5	44.9	62.5	100.0	86.2	88.3	101.9
West Texas Intermediate *	111	67.8	60.9	56.7	60.8	73.0	67.9	47.6	63.2	100.0	85.3	86.1	102.6
Phosphate Rock (US $/MT)													
Morocco (Casablanca)	686	95.4	75.4	75.4	80.0	89.1	93.3	98.3	100.6	100.0	95.6	93.7	92.6
Potash (US $/MT)													
Canada (Vancouver)	156	91.5	87.7	86.3	96.1	95.5	95.1	95.4	99.3	100.0	96.4	92.5	92.5
Poultry (US cents/pound)													
United States (Georgia) *	111	80.7	92.0	93.0	93.3	104.8	102.6	106.2	100.9	100.0	107.0	106.1	111.4
Plywood (US cents/sheet)													
Philippines (Tokyo)	566	84.9	147.6	133.7	130.4	118.1	108.2	83.6	98.3	100.0	91.4	89.9	97.3
Pulp (US $/MT)													
Sweden (North Sea Ports)	144	84.7	63.8	83.1	128.4	86.4	83.5	76.5	75.3	100.0	78.0	68.0	78.5
Rice (US $/MT)													
Thailand (Bangkok) *	578	131.4	116.5	132.3	157.5	166.0	148.5	149.9	122.2	100.0	84.8	94.2	97.9
Thailand	578	109.4	96.7	182.3	118.4	137.9	81.5	120.7	99.3	100.0	77.4	83.6	94.6
Rubber (US cents/pound)													
Malaysia (Singapore) *	548	129.0	124.4	168.5	236.6	209.9	152.3	108.0	95.2	100.0	86.1	114.5	162.1
Malaysia	548	129.2	127.7	158.5	230.0	205.7	149.9	105.3	92.5	100.0	87.3	104.2	144.1
Thailand	578	130.6	129.8	163.1	236.1	218.5	160.2	112.5	88.1	100.0	87.0	104.7	150.8
Shrimp (US $/pound)													
United States (U.S. Gulf Ports)*	111	71.8	74.6	85.7	88.6	86.0	96.8	93.2	95.7	100.0	100.6	69.0	75.3
Silver (US cents/troy ounce)													
United States (New York)	111	78.7	86.0	105.7	103.9	103.7	97.9	110.7	105.0	100.0	87.7	92.5	98.2
Sisal (US $/MT)													
East Africa (Europe)	639	80.4	97.9	96.2	113.0	138.1	123.7	130.6	110.7	100.0	111.2	105.0	111.1
Sorghum (US $/MT)													
United States (US Gulf Ports)	111	116.8	112.5	118.0	135.2	170.5	124.6	111.4	95.9	100.0	108.2	115.6	121.1
Soybeans (US $/MT)													
United States (Rotterdam) *	111	111.5	120.8	119.7	122.7	144.1	139.8	116.2	94.5	100.0	92.5	101.5	125.1
Soybean Meal (US $/MT)													
United States (Rotterdam) *	111	107.8	109.8	101.5	103.9	141.1	145.5	89.8	80.2	100.0	94.9	92.7	111.6
Soybean Oil (US $/MT)													
All Origins (Dutch Ports) *	111	126.7	141.9	182.2	184.9	163.1	167.0	185.1	126.6	100.0	104.6	134.6	164.3
Sugar (US cents/pound)													
EU Import Price *	112	113.2	111.7	112.1	124.0	123.8	112.8	107.8	106.7	100.0	94.9	99.0	107.6
Free Market *	001	112.3	124.0	149.9	164.4	148.0	141.1	110.4	77.5	100.0	101.9	77.2	85.7
U.S. Import Price *	111	109.8	111.4	113.6	118.9	115.3	113.1	113.8	109.0	100.0	110.0	108.0	110.8
Philippines	566	117.1	87.6	95.1	122.2	119.6	138.0	119.0	130.9	100.0	109.3	112.4	117.6
Sunflower Oil (US $/MT)													
EU (NW European ports) *	112	115.8	137.1	163.0	177.6	147.6	149.0	186.3	130.2	100.0	124.2	152.8	151.8
Superphosphate (US $/MT)													
United States (US Gulf Ports)	111	87.7	81.3	95.9	108.7	127.7	124.8	126.1	112.2	100.0	92.1	96.6	108.4
Swine Meat (US cents/pound)													
United States (Iowa) *	111	95.3	108.8	95.1	105.9	156.0	122.9	76.9	74.9	100.0	103.6	79.7	90.1
Tea (US cents/kg)													
Average Auction (London) *	112	80.5	74.8	73.9	66.2	71.4	95.6	96.1	93.6	100.0	79.9	72.2	78.3
Sri Lanka	524	78.1	78.8	77.2	83.4	105.4	112.1	119.8	96.0	100.0	97.6	94.5	99.4
Timber (US $/cubic meter)													
Hardwood Logs													
Malaysia, Sarawak *	548	103.5	204.7	166.4	135.6	133.5	125.3	85.7	98.4	100.0	84.3	85.6	98.5
Hardwood Sawnwood													
Malaysia *	548	101.3	126.5	137.1	123.5	123.7	110.5	80.8	100.3	100.0	81.5	86.5	91.8
Softwood Logs													
United States *	111	84.3	120.6	111.3	107.2	112.9	102.5	88.0	91.0	100.0	87.2	80.7	80.5
Softwood Sawnwood													
United States *	111	82.4	97.4	105.2	105.6	108.8	103.3	98.1	105.5	100.0	99.3	95.9	99.8
Tin (US $/MT)													
Any Origin (London) *	112	112.3	95.1	100.4	114.0	113.3	103.8	101.8	99.2	100.0	82.6	74.7	90.0
Malaysia	548	112.9	96.3	95.8	111.4	111.2	96.2	99.4	96.9	100.0	80.1	74.5	88.9
Bolivia	218	163.9	149.2	148.2	168.6	166.8	104.3	100.2	99.7	100.0	91.3	75.9	85.9
Thailand	578	108.0	96.0	102.7	114.1	115.1	105.5	102.5	98.5	100.0	80.5	76.2	90.0
Tobacco (US $/MT)													
United States (All Markets) *	111	115.1	90.2	88.4	88.5	102.3	118.2	111.6	103.8	100.0	100.0	91.5	....
Uranium (US $/pound)													
Restricted *	001	103.3	121.6	113.7	140.8	188.3	146.0	125.4	120.9	100.0	104.0	118.6	135.6
Urea (US $/MT)													
Ukraine	926	....	....	....	185.1	177.0	112.7	82.2	65.7	100.0	94.3	93.3	137.4

Commodity Prices

		1992	1993	1994	1995	1996	1997	1998	1999	2000	2001	2002	2003
Indices of Market Prices (lines 76) and of Unit Values (lines 74) 2000=100													
Wheat (US $/MT)													
Australia	193	121.3	109.5	103.2	152.2	171.7	135.3	116.2	103.7	100.0	115.5	122.6	132.7
United States (US Gulf Pts) *	111	132.6	123.0	131.4	155.2	181.7	140.1	110.6	98.3	100.0	111.2	130.3	128.2
Argentina	213	108.9	118.7	119.2	148.7	181.6	142.9	111.3	105.6	100.0	109.1	109.7	137.9
Wool (US cents/kilogram)													
Australia-NZ(UK) 48's *	112	121.4	113.8	142.2	176.9	152.6	157.6	119.7	98.4	100.0	118.3	201.3	234.5
Australia-NZ(UK) 64's *	112	81.8	63.2	101.6	105.7	88.8	103.6	75.4	84.4	100.0	85.0	87.8	95.7
Australia (greasy wool)	193	119.8	95.2	128.0	156.8	128.9	142.2	108.8	94.3	100.0	102.2	148.1	169.9
Zinc (US $/MT)													
United Kingdom (London) *	112	110.1	85.5	88.5	91.4	90.9	116.6	90.8	95.4	100.0	78.6	69.1	73.4
Bolivia	218	180.8	143.5	146.1	153.5	150.6	115.3	89.7	93.9	100.0	81.1	68.9	72.6

2004, International Monetary Fund : *International Financial Statistics Yearbook*

COUNTRY TABLES

Albania 914

		1992	1993	1994	1995	1996	1997	1998	1999	2000	2001	2002	2003
Exchange Rates						*Leks per SDR: End of Period*							
Market Rate	aa	141.49	135.57	139.55	140.09	148.21	201.23	197.94	185.45	185.85	171.61	181.82	158.37
						Leks per US Dollar: End of Period (ae) Period Average (rf)							
Market Rate	ae	102.90	98.70	95.59	94.24	103.07	149.14	140.58	135.12	142.64	136.55	133.74	106.58
Market Rate	rf	75.03	102.06	94.62	92.70	104.50	148.93	150.63	137.69	143.71	143.48	140.15	121.86
Fund Position						*Millions of SDRs: End of Period*							
Quota	2f.s	35.30	35.30	35.30	35.30	35.30	35.30	35.30	48.70	48.70	48.70	48.70	48.70
SDRs	1b.s	.04	.01	.20	.10	.52	.46	43.39	56.06	58.33	64.87	60.02	60.98
Reserve Position in the Fund	1c.s	.01	.01	.01	.01	.01	.01	.01	3.36	3.36	3.36	3.36	3.35
Total Fund Cred.&Loans Outstg	2tl	9.69	21.60	37.13	43.40	37.70	40.74	45.77	58.69	67.47	66.25	59.63	60.83
International Liquidity						*Millions of US Dollars Unless Otherwise Indicated: End of Period*							
Total Reserves minus Gold	1l.d	....	147.42	204.80	241.05	280.86	308.93	384.22	488.30	615.65	739.90	838.78	1,009.42
SDRs	1b.d	.06	.01	.30	.14	.75	.62	61.10	76.95	76.00	81.52	81.60	90.61
Reserve Position in the Fund	1c.d	.01	.01	.01	.01	.01	.01	.01	4.60	4.37	4.24	4.56	4.99
Foreign Exchange	1d.d	....	147.40	204.50	240.90	280.10	308.30	323.12	406.75	535.27	654.17	752.62	913.83
Gold (Million Fine Troy Ounces)	1ad	....	.05	.05	.06	.12	.12	.12	.12	.11	.11	.08	.07
Gold (National Valuation)	1and	....	19.41	20.85	24.30	42.50	33.40	33.70	34.50	30.40	30.70	27.68	28.86
Monetary Authorities						*Billions of Leks: End of Period*							
Foreign Assets	11	....	....	22.65	46.76	57.02	85.21	91.04	71.08	92.34	104.90	114.63	109.77
Claims on Central Government	12a	....	....	69.33	45.69	52.14	85.48	77.56	74.72	82.49	74.14	78.58	74.30
Claims on Banks	12e	....	....	3.42	3.31	3.37	7.44	7.00	6.69	6.63	6.73	10.72	.42
Reserve Money	14	....	....	42.07	53.88	61.39	90.93	89.89	109.31	128.78	152.14	163.89	160.55
of which: Currency Outside Banks	14a	....	....	27.63	41.91	47.81	72.73	68.32	81.34	99.24	119.08	130.78	125.19
Other Liabilities to Banks	14n	....	....	–	–	–	–	2.44	.79	5.23	–	–	1.21
Foreign Liabilities	16c	....	....	59.41	33.65	36.81	53.85	55.11	24.15	20.48	18.94	19.65	11.45
Central Government Deposits	16d	....	....	3.75	4.27	3.25	5.62	5.39	5.85	7.62	4.20	5.90	8.82
Capital Accounts	17a	....	....	14.26	10.61	16.83	31.43	38.56	14.82	21.52	20.92	27.49	14.31
Other Items (Net)	17r	....	....	–24.08	–6.64	–4.99	–3.00	–15.14	–1.85	–2.10	–10.36	–12.98	–11.85
Banking Institutions						*Billions of Leks: End of Period*							
Reserves	20	....	....	11.93	10.30	12.90	16.44	21.57	28.15	30.16	33.81	32.02	35.21
Other Claims on Monetary Author	20n	....	....	–	–	–	1.40	2.44	.79	5.15	† –	–	1.20
Foreign Assets	21	....	....	16.94	23.47	35.44	38.96	49.97	57.97	65.05	83.36	81.33	77.60
Claims on Central Government	22a	....	....	86.55	108.52	142.51	108.30	125.45	147.34	156.15	† 170.30	175.98	205.43
Claims on Nonfin.Pub.Enterprises	22c	....	....	3.25	3.09	3.41	2.83	2.83	1.67	1.48	1.68	1.16	1.13
Claims on Private Sector	22d	....	....	7.20	8.35	10.89	13.01	14.86	18.22	24.41	34.94	46.17	58.14
Demand Deposits	24	....	....	11.14	17.35	42.59	18.94	15.41	21.67	24.81	23.94	21.90	19.54
Time and Savings Deposits	25a	....	....	18.70	28.12	30.24	70.55	115.53	136.66	140.46	162.25	171.99	204.78
Foreign Currency Deposits	25b	....	....	13.30	20.08	33.91	36.33	40.26	53.21	63.60	88.13	91.96	98.91
Foreign Liabilities	26c	....	....	1.82	1.14	1.22	2.02	2.87	4.83	6.83	12.05	15.49	17.22
Central Government Deposits	26d	....	....	68.05	75.92	80.41	25.80	1.05	.80	1.46	2.25	.82	.86
Credit from Monetary Authorities	26g	....	....	.65	–	1.69	3.64	4.73	1.44	5.81	† 1.05	3.98	.66
Capital Accounts	27a	....	....	10.37	12.01	16.70	21.85	26.46	27.00	34.17	34.43	38.13	38.52
Other Items (Net)	27r	....	....	1.84	–.89	–1.60	1.81	10.80	8.52	5.27	–.02	–7.60	–1.77
Banking Survey						*Billions of Leks: End of Period*							
Foreign Assets (Net)	31n	....	....	–21.63	35.44	54.42	68.30	83.03	100.07	130.08	157.28	160.83	158.71
Domestic Credit	32	....	....	94.52	85.46	125.30	178.20	214.27	235.30	255.45	† 274.61	295.18	329.32
Claims on Central Govt. (Net)	32an	....	....	84.07	74.02	111.00	162.37	196.57	215.41	229.55	† 237.99	247.85	270.05
Claims on Nonfin.Pub.Enterprises	32c	....	....	3.25	3.09	3.41	2.83	2.83	1.67	1.48	1.68	1.16	1.13
Claims on Private Sector	32d	....	....	7.20	8.35	10.89	13.01	14.86	18.22	24.41	34.94	46.17	58.14
Money	34	....	....	38.77	59.25	90.41	91.67	83.73	103.00	124.04	143.03	152.67	144.73
Quasi-Money	35	....	....	32.01	48.20	64.15	106.88	155.80	189.87	204.06	250.39	263.94	303.70
Capital Accounts	37a	....	....	24.62	22.62	33.53	53.29	65.02	41.83	55.69	55.36	65.62	52.83
Other Items (Net)	37r	....	....	–22.50	–9.17	–7.60	–4.63	–6.60	1.25	1.81	† –16.81	–26.23	–13.23
Money plus Quasi-Money	35l	....	....	70.77	107.45	154.55	198.55	239.53	292.87	328.10	393.41	416.62	448.43
Interest Rates						*Percent Per Annum*							
Bank Rate (End of Period)	60	40.00	34.00	25.00	20.50	24.00	32.00	23.44	18.00	10.82	7.00	8.50	6.50
Treasury Bill Rate	60c	....	....	....	13.84	17.81	32.59	27.49	17.54	10.80	7.72	9.49	8.81
Deposit Rate	60l	18.50	† 27.33	19.83	† 15.30	16.78	27.28	22.56	12.95	8.30	7.73	8.54	8.38
Lending Rate	60p	20.58	29.58	23.67	† 19.65	23.96	....	....	21.62	22.10	19.65	15.30	14.27
Prices						*Index Numbers (2000=100): Period Averages*							
Consumer Prices	64	22.5	41.6	51.0	55.0	62.0	82.5	99.6	100.0	100.0	† 103.1	111.1	111.7
						Number in Thousands: Period Averages							
Employment	67e	1,095	1,046	1,162	1,138	1,116	1,108	1,085	1,065	1,068	921	920	926
Unemployment	67c	....	301	262	171	158	194	235	240	215	181	172	166
Unemployment Rate (%)	67r	....	22.0	18.0	12.9	12.3	14.9	17.7	18.4	16.8	16.4	15.8	15.2

2004, International Monetary Fund : *International Financial Statistics Yearbook*

Albania 914

		1992	1993	1994	1995	1996	1997	1998	1999	2000	2001	2002	2003
International Transactions							*Millions of Leks*						
Exports	70	5,707	12,499	13,092	18,712	21,603	21,044	30,656	36,369	37,547	43,771	46,193	55,068
Imports, c.i.f.	71	13,135	58,536	56,732	66,145	87,995	95,021	124,337	157,424	157,219	190,696	210,436	226,056
Balance of Payments						*Millions of US Dollars: Minus Sign Indicates Debit*							
Current Account, n.i.e.	78ald	−50.7	14.9	−157.3	−11.5	−107.3	−272.2	−65.1	−155.4	−156.3	−217.3	−407.5	−406.8
Goods: Exports f.o.b.	78aad	70.0	111.6	141.3	204.9	243.7	158.6	208.0	275.0	255.7	304.5	330.2	447.2
Goods: Imports f.o.b.	78abd	−540.5	−601.5	−601.0	−679.7	−922.0	−693.6	−811.7	−938.0	−1,070.0	−1,331.6	−1,485.4	−1,783.5
Trade Balance	78acd	−470.5	−489.9	−459.7	−474.8	−678.3	−535.0	−603.6	−663.0	−814.3	−1,027.1	−1,155.1	−1,336.3
Services: Credit	78add	20.3	77.6	79.1	98.8	129.2	63.8	86.6	269.4	447.8	534.3	585.0	719.7
Services: Debit	78aed	−89.1	−161.9	−132.5	−156.5	−189.4	−115.2	−129.3	−163.1	−429.3	−444.1	−590.2	−802.6
Balance on Goods & Services	78afd	−539.3	−574.2	−513.1	−532.5	−738.5	−586.4	−646.3	−556.7	−795.8	−936.9	−1,160.3	−1,419.2
Income: Credit	78agd	2.6	64.9	55.1	72.0	83.7	61.4	86.1	85.5	115.9	162.5	148.3	194.8
Income: Debit	78ahd	−37.7	−31.0	−41.3	−28.4	−11.9	−11.8	−8.7	−10.2	−9.3	−13.5	−20.6	−24.4
Balance on Gds, Serv. & Inc.	78aid	−574.4	−540.3	−499.3	−488.9	−666.7	−536.8	−569.0	−481.4	−689.2	−787.9	−1,032.6	−1,248.8
Current Transfers, n.i.e.: Credit	78ajd	524.0	556.9	347.5	521.2	595.9	299.8	560.8	508.9	629.0	647.5	683.7	924.2
Current Transfers: Debit	78akd	−.3	−1.7	−5.5	−43.8	−36.5	−35.2	−56.9	−182.9	−96.1	−76.9	−58.6	−82.3
Capital Account, n.i.e.	78bcd	−	−	−	389.4	4.8	2.0	31.0	22.6	78.0	117.7	121.2	157.0
Capital Account, n.i.e.: Credit	78bad	−	−	−	389.4	4.8	2.0	31.0	22.6	78.0	117.7	121.2	157.0
Capital Account: Debit	78bbd	−	−	−	−	−	−	−	−	−	−	−	−
Financial Account, n.i.e.	78bjd	−32.2	44.1	40.2	−411.0	61.5	151.4	15.4	33.7	188.4	110.0	213.4	200.6
Direct Investment Abroad	78bdd	−	−	−	....	....	....	....	....	....	....	....	....
Dir. Invest. in Rep. Econ., n.i.e.	78bed	20.0	58.0	53.0	70.0	90.1	47.5	45.0	41.2	143.0	207.3	135.0	178.0
Portfolio Investment Assets	78bfd	−	−	−	....	−	−	−	−	−25.0	−23.5	−36.8	−22.5
Equity Securities	78bkd	−	−	−	....	....	....	....	....	−	−	−	−
Debt Securities	78bld	−	−	−	....	....	....	....	....	−25.0	−23.5	−36.8	−22.5
Portfolio Investment Liab., n.i.e.	78bgd	−	−	−	....	....	....	−	−	−	−	−	−
Equity Securities	78bmd	−	−	−	....	....	....	....	....	....	....	....	....
Debt Securities	78bnd	−	−	−	....	....	....	....	....	....	....	....	....
Financial Derivatives Assets	78bwd	....	....	....	....	....	....	....	....	....	....	....	....
Financial Derivatives Liabilities	78bxd	....	....	....	....	....	....	....	....	....	....	....	....
Other Investment Assets	78bhd	−73.2	−78.6	−97.3	−97.0	−138.6	59.8	−126.9	−130.1	−40.2	−197.2	−2.7	−71.6
Monetary Authorities	78bod	....	....	....	−	−	−	−	−	....	−1.8	2.2	.3
General Government	78bpd	−	−	−	−	−	−	−	−	....	....	....	....
Banks	78bqd	−50.0	−25.5	−22.9	−68.4	−110.5	81.5	−91.2	−96.8	−2.5	−132.3	42.2	−45.3
Other Sectors	78brd	−23.2	−53.1	−74.4	−28.6	−28.1	−21.7	−35.7	−33.3	−37.7	−63.1	−47.1	−26.7
Other Investment Liab., n.i.e.	78bid	21.0	64.7	84.5	−384.0	110.0	44.1	97.3	122.6	110.6	123.4	118.0	116.7
Monetary Authorities	78bsd	−	−	−	−9.1	10.4	16.0	10.4	8.9	−.2	−.3	.5	−1.0
General Government	78btd	22.4	50.5	74.6	−404.5	61.3	40.3	81.3	97.9	90.8	86.1	118.2	96.6
Banks	78bud	−1.4	3.4	2.6	−3.3	4.0	−.6	3.5	16.0	5.2	42.1	10.9	19.8
Other Sectors	78bvd	−	10.8	7.3	32.9	34.3	−11.6	2.0	−.2	14.8	−4.5	−11.6	1.4
Net Errors and Omissions	78cad	47.4	−10.3	123.9	53.7	96.9	158.4	71.1	206.2	9.8	136.3	108.5	147.4
Overall Balance	78cbd	−35.5	48.7	6.8	20.6	55.9	39.5	52.4	107.1	119.9	146.7	35.6	98.1
Reserves and Related Items	79dad	35.5	−48.7	−6.8	−20.6	−55.9	−39.5	−52.4	−107.1	−119.9	−146.7	−35.6	−98.1
Reserve Assets	79dbd	−27.4	−114.9	−55.2	−30.5	−47.6	−43.7	−60.0	−124.7	−132.0	−145.1	−28.6	−99.6
Use of Fund Credit and Loans	79dcd	13.9	16.6	22.3	9.9	−8.3	4.2	6.8	17.5	12.1	−1.6	−8.5	1.5
Exceptional Financing	79ded	49.0	49.5	26.1	....	....	....	....	.8	.1	−	−	−
Government Finance						*Millions of Leks: Year Ending December 31*							
Deficit (-) or Surplus	80	....	....	....	−20,157	−34,689	−41,053	−38,972	....	....	....	....	....
Revenue	81	....	....	....	49,068	47,551	53,205	89,145	....	....	....	....	....
Grants Received	81z	....	....	....	598	722	2,304	9,005	....	....	....	....	....
Expenditure	82	....	....	....	69,687	83,553	97,472	137,254	....	....	....	....	....
Lending Minus Repayments	83	....	....	....	136	−591	−910	−132	....	....	....	....	....
Financing													
Domestic	84a	....	....	....	15,919	27,680	36,815	27,464	....	....	....	....	....
Foreign	85a	....	....	....	4,238	7,009	4,238	11,509	....	....	....	....	....
Debt: Domestic	88a	....	....	....	53,876	82,654	120,527	149,439	....	....	....	....	....
Foreign	89a	....	....	....	25,434	42,668	55,432	64,405	....	....	....	....	....
						Millions: Midyear Estimates							
Population	99z	3.28	3.25	3.22	3.19	3.16	3.14	3.12	3.11	3.11	3.12	3.14	3.17

2004, International Monetary Fund: *International Financial Statistics Yearbook*

Algeria 612

		1992	1993	1994	1995	1996	1997	1998	1999	2000	2001	2002	2003
Exchange Rates		\multicolumn{12}{c}{*Dinars per SDR: End of Period*}
Official Rate	aa	31.324	33.134	62.617	77.558	80.793	78.815	84.979	95.135	98.165	97.798	108.386	107.900
		\multicolumn{12}{c}{*Dinars per US Dollar: End of Period (ae) Period Average (rf)*}
Official Rate	ae	22.781	24.123	42.893	52.175	56.186	58.414	60.353	69.314	75.343	77.820	79.723	72.613
Official Rate	rf	21.836	23.345	35.059	47.663	54.749	57.707	58.739	66.574	75.260	77.215	79.682	77.395
		\multicolumn{12}{c}{*Index Numbers (2000=100): Period Averages*}
Nominal Effective Exchange Rate	nec	238.38	247.66	174.72	115.32	102.54	109.03	109.93	100.34	100.00	101.61	94.56	84.24
Real Effective Exchange Rate	rec	105.67	128.27	112.30	93.24	96.89	106.36	111.46	102.58	100.00	102.81	94.85	85.30
Fund Position		\multicolumn{12}{c}{*Millions of SDRs: End of Period*}
Quota	2f.s	914	914	914	914	914	914	914	1,255	1,255	1,255	1,255	1,255
SDRs	1b.s	1	5	16	1	3	1	1	1	2	9	10	38
Reserve Position in the Fund	1c.s	–	–	–	–	–	–	–	85	85	85	85	85
Total Fund Cred.&Loans Outstg	2tl	578	343	794	994	1,413	1,496	1,428	1,389	1,319	1,208	978	665
International Liquidity		\multicolumn{12}{c}{*Millions of US Dollars Unless Otherwise Indicated: End of Period*}
Total Reserves minus Gold	1l.d	1,457	1,475	2,674	2,005	4,235	8,047	6,846	4,526	12,024	18,081	23,238	33,125
SDRs	1b.d	1	7	23	1	5	1	2	2	3	11	14	57
Reserve Position in the Fund	1c.d	–	–	–	–	–	–	–	117	111	107	116	126
Foreign Exchange	1d.d	1,456	1,468	2,651	2,004	4,230	8,046	6,844	4,407	11,910	17,963	23,108	32,942
Gold (Million Fine Troy Ounces)	1ad	5.58	5.58	5.58	5.58	5.58	5.58	5.58	5.58	5.58	5.58	5.58	5.58
Gold (National Valuation)	1and	269	268	285	290	281	264	275	268	255	246	266	290
Monetary Authorities:Other Assets	3..d	13	12	1	4	3	9	7	19	9	9	10	10
Other Liab	4..d	120	464	466	363	291	414	387	364	208	182	248	303
Deposit Money Banks: Assets	7a.d	914	683	1,046	638	576	396	456	402	376	416	....	765
Liabilities	7b.d	7,010	5,201	4,200	2,749	2,088	1,216	1,068	1,015	720	767	....	1,111
Monetary Authorities		\multicolumn{12}{c}{*Billions of Dinars: End of Period*}
Foreign Assets	11	†36.69	38.66	120.39	111.71	252.88	485.04	423.47	329.89	919.47	1,445.97	1,868.63	2,419.76
Claims on Central Government	12a	†162.76	273.80	255.57	243.40	180.87	177.67	174.59	163.48	168.20	144.67	133.77	141.97
Claims on Deposit Money Banks	12e	†78.31	29.39	50.45	188.59	255.13	219.06	226.25	310.80	170.54	–	–	–
Reserve Money	14	†196.28	250.41	237.22	255.17	305.91	356.63	403.47	449.46	550.23	777.84	976.36	1,402.27
of which: Currency Outside DMBs	14a	†184.85	211.31	222.99	249.77	290.88	337.62	390.78	440.26	484.95	577.34	....	781.34
Foreign Liabilities	16c	†20.84	22.55	69.68	96.06	130.45	142.06	144.70	157.34	145.08	132.30	125.80	93.72
Central Government Deposits	16d	†2.31	2.94	9.25	9.80	4.41	21.93	75.32	4.46	324.61	420.96	438.55	606.08
Other Items (Net)	17r	†58.32	65.96	110.26	182.67	248.11	361.16	200.82	192.89	238.28	259.54	461.70	459.66
Deposit Money Banks		\multicolumn{12}{c}{*Billions of Dinars: End of Period*}
Reserves	20	5.86	37.89	7.32	5.58	12.79	18.77	15.85	13.37	42.74	182.94	....	624.51
Foreign Assets	21	20.82	16.47	44.88	33.30	32.38	23.11	27.50	27.89	28.32	32.35	....	55.53
Claims on Central Government	22a	28.33	300.52	204.63	155.64	141.43	273.15	410.39	459.49	600.38	591.50	....	805.90
Claims on Nonfin.Pub.Enterprises	22c	332.07	142.04	208.00	461.00	637.71	632.59	601.86	760.48	530.06	549.31	....	791.37
Claims on Private Sector	22d	†76.00	77.12	96.75	103.47	137.85	108.56	128.86	173.89	245.31	289.05	....	586.56
Demand Deposits	24	140.84	188.93	196.45	210.78	234.03	254.83	334.52	352.71	460.27	551.88	....	719.59
Time Deposits	25	152.02	198.83	247.68	280.46	325.96	409.95	474.19	578.57	617.87	836.18	....	1,655.92
Foreign Liabilities	26c	14.00	12.94	35.14	22.58	20.79	15.71	25.48	30.87	26.66	35.18	....	38.76
Long-Term Foreign Liabilities	26cl	145.70	112.52	145.02	120.88	96.51	55.30	39.00	39.46	27.61	24.50	....	41.88
Central Government Deposits	26d	5.88	90.19	38.82	44.53	97.53	84.36	55.74	56.66	33.51	26.90	....	51.14
Central Govt. Lending Funds	26f	14.00	13.19	13.61	13.79	12.30	12.90	13.69	13.22	20.95	11.13	....	59.76
Credit from Monetary Authorities	26g	†78.66	29.39	50.69	190.29	259.13	219.06	226.25	310.80	170.54	–	–	–
Other Items (Net)	27r	†−88.01	−71.95	−165.83	−124.31	−84.09	4.07	15.58	52.82	89.39	159.39	....	296.81
Post Office: Checking Deposits	24..i	39.83	40.98	48.50	53.74	57.96	71.68	81.05	87.43	89.09	97.00	....	117.19
Treasury: Checking Deposits	24..r	4.20	5.68	7.89	4.82	6.22	7.43	7.33	9.38	7.07	9.44	....	12.94
Monetary Survey		\multicolumn{12}{c}{*Billions of Dinars: End of Period*}
Foreign Assets (Net)	31n	†22.67	19.65	60.45	26.37	134.02	350.38	280.79	169.57	776.05	1,310.85	....	2,342.80
Domestic Credit	32	†639.24	748.09	774.38	968.93	1,061.39	1,164.93	1,273.45	1,593.76	1,282.87	1,234.07	....	1,799.73
Claims on Central Govt. (Net)	32an	†226.93	527.84	468.54	403.29	284.55	423.65	542.30	658.66	506.61	394.74	....	420.79
Claims on Nonfin.Pub.Enterprises	32c	332.07	142.04	208.00	461.00	637.71	632.59	601.86	760.48	530.06	549.31	....	791.37
Claims on Private Sector	32d	†76.05	77.16	96.79	103.50	137.88	108.63	129.18	174.48	245.99	289.80	....	587.25
Money	34	†377.24	450.32	485.65	520.29	589.99	675.96	817.26	889.78	1,044.02	1,237.38	....	1,634.50
Quasi-Money	35	152.02	198.83	247.68	280.46	325.96	409.95	474.19	578.57	617.87	836.18	....	1,655.92
Long-Term Foreign Liabilities	36cl	145.70	112.52	145.02	120.88	96.51	55.30	39.00	39.46	27.61	24.50	....	41.88
Central Govt. Lending Funds	36f	14.00	13.19	13.61	13.79	12.30	12.90	13.69	13.22	20.95	11.13	....	59.76
Other Items (Net)	37r	†−27.04	−7.12	−57.13	59.89	170.65	361.21	210.10	242.26	348.47	435.72	....	750.47
Money plus Quasi-Money	35l	†529.26	649.15	733.33	800.74	915.95	1,085.91	1,291.46	1,468.36	1,661.89	2,073.56	....	3,290.42
Interest Rates		\multicolumn{12}{c}{*Percent Per Annum*}
Discount Rate	60	11.50	11.50	21.00	†14.00	13.00	11.00	9.50	8.50	6.00	6.00	5.50	4.50
Money Market Rate	60b	....	....	19.80	†21.05	18.47	11.80	10.40	10.43	6.77	3.35	4.20	3.96
Treasury Bill Rate	60c	9.50	9.50	16.50	....	....	....	†9.96	10.05	7.95	5.69	1.80	1.25
Deposit Rate	60l	8.00	8.00	12.00	†16.00	14.50	9.75	8.50	7.50	7.50	6.25	5.25	5.25
Lending Rate	60p	....	....	16.00	†19.00	19.00	12.50	11.00	10.00	10.00	9.50	8.50	8.00

Algeria 612

		1992	1993	1994	1995	1996	1997	1998	1999	2000	2001	2002	2003
Prices, Production, Labor						*Index Numbers (2000=100): Period Averages*							
Consumer Prices..................	64	36.5	44.0	56.8	73.7	87.5	92.5	97.1	99.7	100.0	104.2	105.7	108.4
Crude Petroleum Production...........	66aa	98.2	94.6	92.1	95.3	101.4	105.4	102.0	96.0	100.0	101.4	107.2	141.9
						Number in Thousands: Period Averages							
Employment.................................	67e	4,968	5,042	5,154	5,436	5,625	5,815	5,993	6,073	6,240	6,597	6,813	6,684
Unemployment...........................	67c	1,350	1,519	1,660	2,125	2,186	2,257	2,333	2,516	2,610	2,478	....	2,078
Unemployment Rate (%).................	67r	27.0	30.0	32.0	39.0	39.0	39.0	39.0	41.0	42.0	38.0	....	23.7
International Transactions						*Millions of Dinars*							
Exports.......................................	70	149,010	239,552	324,339	498,451	740,811	791,768	599,903	....	....	....	....	....
Imports, c.i.f...............................	71	188,547	205,035	340,142	513,193	498,326	501,598	552,359	610,673	....	....	....	....
Imports, c.i.f., from DOTS.................	71y	188,835	204,533	335,522	513,921	498,523	501,610	552,357	610,673	679,362	752,811	940,941	....
Volume of Exports						*2000=100*							
Petroleum.................................	72a	75.8	81.1	81.5	81.5	90.2	85.4	90.5	93.8	100.0	98.5	108.1	....
Crude Petroleum....................	72aa	61.7	69.7	71.8	72.6	85.2	80.6	88.4	90.0	100.0	94.7	118.0	....
Refined Petroleum.................	72ab	98.0	104.4	96.7	95.5	98.3	93.0	93.8	99.9	100.0	104.7	92.4	....
Export Prices						*2000=100: Index of Prices in US Dollars*							
Crude Petroleum.......................	76aad	70.3	61.4	57.3	61.7	76.1	68.4	45.2	63.1	100.0	87.1	87.9	....
Government Finance						*Millions of Dinars: Year Ending December 31*							
Deficit (-) or Surplus......................	80	....	....	† –65,354	–28,243	75,258	66,126	–108,134	–16,493	398,856	171,015	10,449	....
Revenue...................................	81	....	....	† 434,199	600,847	825,157	926,668	774,511	950,496	1,578,161	1,505,526	1,603,198	....
Expenditure.............................	82	....	....	† 493,626	625,965	749,009	863,196	875,739	961,682	1,178,122	1,321,028	1,550,646	....
Lending Minus Repayments...........	83	....	....	5,927	3,125	890	–2,654	6,906	5,307	1,183	13,483	42,103	....
Financing													
Net Borrowing: Domestic.................	84a	....	....	–120,023	–147,866	–178,249	....	....	....	....	....	....	....
Foreign..................................	85a	....	....	141,376	172,158	100,937	....	....	....	....	....	....	....
Use of Cash Balances....................	87	....	....	44,001	3,951	2,054	....	....	....	....	....	....	....
National Accounts						*Billions of Dinars*							
Househ.Cons.Expend.,incl.NPISHs....	96f	548.3	649.1	837.5	1,114.8	1,335.0	1,430.3	1,556.7	1,670.7	1,714.2	1,847.7	1,971.7	2,121.0
Government Consumption Expend...	91f	184.8	221.2	263.9	340.2	405.4	459.8	503.6	543.6	560.1	624.6	683.2	731.0
Gross Fixed Capital Formation..........	93e	278.0	324.1	407.5	541.8	639.4	638.1	728.8	789.7	879.4	965.5	1,102.2	1,249.0
Changes in Inventories.....................	93i	41.8	12.1	60.4	91.2	5.2	9.3	45.2	60.2	65.6	183.8	253.0	319.0
Exports of Goods and Services..........	90c	266.3	252.3	342.6	533.0	781.7	837.2	652.3	911.6	1,734.7	1,550.9	1,587.7	1,898.0
Imports of Goods and Services (-).....	98c	244.5	269.1	424.5	616.1	596.7	594.7	656.1	737.4	855.2	930.7	1,142.4	1,274.0
Gross Domestic Product (GDP).........	99b	1,074.7	1,189.7	1,487.4	2,005.0	2,570.0	2,780.2	2,830.5	3,238.4	4,098.8	4,241.8	4,455.4	5,044.0
						Millions: Midyear Estimates							
Population...............................	99z	26.22	26.79	27.35	27.88	28.38	28.85	29.30	29.77	30.24	30.75	31.27	31.80

2004, International Monetary Fund: *International Financial Statistics Yearbook*

Angola 614

		1992	1993	1994	1995	1996	1997	1998	1999	2000	2001	2002	2003
Exchange Rates		Kwanzas per Thousands SDRs through 1994; per SDR Thereafter: End of Period											
Market Rate	aa	.0008	.0089	.7434	.0085	.2905	.3540	.9807	†7.6585	21.9121	40.1517	79.7581	117.5127
		Kwanzas per Thous.US$ through 1994; per US$ Thereafter: End of Period: End of Period (ae) Period Average (rf)											
Market Rate	ae	.0006	.0065	.5093	.0057	.2020	.2624	.6965	†5.5799	16.8178	31.9494	58.6664	79.0815
Market Rate	rf	.0003	.0027	.0595	.0028	.1280	.2290	.3928	2.7907	10.0405	22.0579	43.5302	74.6063
Fund Position		Millions of SDRs: End of Period											
Quota	2f.s	207.30	207.30	207.30	207.30	207.30	207.30	207.30	286.30	286.30	286.30	286.30	286.30
SDRs	1b.s	.09	.10	.10	.11	.11	.12	.12	.13	.13	.14	.14	.14
Reserve Position in the Fund	1c.s	–	–	–	–	–	–	–	–	–	–	–	–
Total Fund Cred.&Loans Outstg	2tl	–	–	–	–	–	–	–	–	–	–	–	–
International Liquidity		Millions of US Dollars Unless Otherwise Indicated: End of Period											
Total Reserves minus Gold	1l.d	....	....	....	212.83	551.62	396.43	203.45	496.10	1,198.21	731.87	375.55	634.20
SDRs	1b.d	.12	.14	.15	.16	.16	.16	.17	.18	.17	.17	.19	.21
Reserve Position in the Fund	1c.d	–	–	–	–	–	–	–	–	–	–	–	–
Foreign Exchange	1d.d	....	....	....	212.67	551.46	396.27	203.28	495.93	1,198.04	731.69	375.35	633.99
Monetary Authorities: Other Assets	3..d	....	....	....	143.95	6.86	1.98	.85	–	–	–	–	1.60
Other Liab	4..d	....	....	....	1,901.59	348.01	329.78	444.98	90.53	212.42	247.35	107.88	30.36
Banking Institutions: Assets	7a.d	....	....	....	264.62	523.49	833.30	682.25	747.42	878.08	1,168.78	1,453.84	1,284.30
Liabilities	7b.d	....	....	....	69.68	61.07	137.31	199.46	119.12	49.14	157.42	126.89	90.07
Monetary Authorities		Millions of Kwanzas: End of Period											
Foreign Assets	11	....	....	....	2.1	112.8	104.0	141.7	†2,768.2	20,151.3	23,382.7	22,031.9	50,153.4
Claims on Central Government	12a	....	....	....	4.3	36.2	82.3	330.2	†4,033.1	1,062.1	559.1	26,425.9	25,528.9
Claims on Nonfin.Pub.Enterprises	12c	....	....	....	2.9	2.5	3.7	2.5	†32.4	156.4	272.3	371.3	787.2
Claims on Private Sector	12d	....	....	....	–	–	–	–	†9.0	43.2	247.2	392.2	704.8
Claims on Banking Institutions	12e	....	....	....	–	–	48.8	61.5	†76.7	252.6	330.4	287.2	1.0
Reserve Money	14	....	....	....	2.6	89.9	172.6	258.6	†1,956.0	6,215.2	15,325.7	33,365.3	58,722.7
of which: Currency Outside Banks	14a	....	....	....	1.2	42.2	101.6	165.7	†665.4	2,968.6	8,215.3	20,878.5	35,406.9
Time & Foreign Currency Deposits	15	....	....	....	2.4	58.5	6.8	7.2	†13.5	41.3	–	146.6	240.7
Liabs. of Central Bank: Securities	16ac	....	....	....	–	–	.3	–	†7.0	190.0	3,292.0	5,277.6	11,778.2
Foreign Liabilities	16c	....	....	....	10.8	70.3	86.5	309.9	†505.1	3,572.4	7,902.8	6,328.8	2,401.0
Central Government Deposits	16d	....	....	....	.3	21.3	–	.2	†2,878.4	14,251.9	1,213.0	5,717.2	13,237.4
Capital Accounts	17a	....	....	....	–1.2	18.4	15.1	23.2	†–636.4	–351.9	1,363.0	3,240.8	12,210.7
Other Items (Net)	17r	....	....	....	–5.6	–106.8	–42.4	–63.3	†2,195.7	–2,253.3	–4,304.8	–4,567.7	–21,415.4
Banking Institutions		Millions of Kwanzas: End of Period											
Reserves	20	....	....	....	1.1	47.7	82.3	92.4	†1,044.9	2,964.2	7,509.5	16,099.8	25,390.6
Claims on Mon.Author.:Securities	20c	....	....	....	–	–	–	–	†7.0	175.0	3,292.0	5,277.6	11,778.2
Foreign Assets	21	....	....	....	1.5	105.7	218.6	475.2	†4,170.6	14,767.4	37,341.8	85,291.6	101,564.6
Claims on Central Government	22a	....	....	....	.3	1.0	5.9	55.3	†12.0	3.3	40.4	2,017.1	14,035.0
Claims on Local Government	22b	....	....	....	–	–	–	–	†.4	10.0	23.1	3.7	882.4
Claims on Nonfin. Pub. Enterprises	22c	....	....	....	–	–	–	.2	†61.1	186.7	601.6	1,061.5	3,445.6
Claims on Private Sector	22d	....	....	....	.7	26.5	90.6	90.0	†432.9	1,802.7	7,106.2	22,849.1	53,830.5
Demand Deposits	24	....	....	....	1.2	51.8	93.3	106.6	†516.0	2,037.0	5,449.5	10,961.0	34,444.8
Time, Savings,& Fgn.Currency Dep	25	....	....	....	.4	78.0	194.5	344.9	†2,720.5	10,741.5	27,697.1	74,981.0	108,594.4
of which: Fgn. Currency Deposits	25b	....	....	....	.4	67.7	170.1	330.7	†2,626.3	10,696.1	26,833.9	73,081.0	104,727.5
Money Market Instruments	26aa	....	....	....	–	–	–	–	†–	–	321.3	649.2	2,361.6
Foreign Liabilities	26c	....	....	....	.4	12.3	36.0	138.9	†664.7	826.4	5,029.4	7,444.4	7,123.2
Central Government Deposits	26d	....	....	....	–	5.2	6.8	28.9	†462.8	2,538.1	8,856.9	20,633.7	21,694.9
Credit from Monetary Authorities	26g	....	....	....	–	–	48.0	58.0	†500.6	1,180.8	–	–	–
Capital Accounts	27a	....	....	....	.2	16.1	23.9	100.6	†703.7	2,905.2	8,901.6	17,980.4	38,984.2
Other Items (Net)	27r	....	....	....	1.4	17.7	–5.1	–64.9	†160.6	–319.7	–341.2	–49.4	–2,276.4
Banking Survey		Millions of Kwanzas: End of Period											
Foreign Assets (Net)	31n	....	....	....	–7.6	135.9	200.1	168.0	†5,768.9	30,520.0	47,792.3	93,550.3	142,193.8
Domestic Credit	32	....	....	....	7.9	39.9	175.7	449.0	†1,239.7	–13,525.7	–1,220.1	26,769.9	64,282.0
Claims on Central Govt.(Net)	32an	....	....	....	4.3	10.8	81.4	356.3	†703.9	–15,724.7	–9,470.4	2,092.1	4,631.6
Claims on Local Government	32b	....	....	....	–	–	–	–	†.4	10.0	23.1	3.7	882.4
Claims on Nonfin.Pub.Enterprises	32c	....	....	....	2.9	2.5	3.7	2.7	†93.5	343.1	873.9	1,432.8	4,232.8
Claims on Private Sector	32d	....	....	....	.7	26.5	90.6	90.0	†441.9	1,845.8	7,353.4	23,241.4	54,535.3
Money	34	....	....	....	2.7	93.9	194.9	272.4	†1,206.5	5,332.8	14,298.7	33,459.2	69,888.2
Quasi-Money	35	....	....	....	2.8	136.5	201.3	352.1	†2,734.0	10,782.7	27,697.1	75,127.6	108,835.1
Money Market Instruments	36aa	....	....	....	–	–	–	–	†–	–	321.3	649.2	2,361.6
Liabs. of Central Banks: Securities	36ac	....	....	....	–	–	.3	–	†–	–	15.0	–	–
Capital Accounts	37a	....	....	....	–1.0	34.5	38.9	123.8	†67.3	2,553.4	10,264.6	21,221.2	51,195.0
Other Items (Net)	37r	....	....	....	–4.2	–89.1	–59.6	–131.3	†3,000.8	–1,689.6	–6,009.3	–10,137.0	–25,804.1
Money plus Quasi-Money	35l	....	....	....	5.5	230.4	396.2	624.6	†3,940.5	16,115.5	41,995.8	108,586.8	178,723.3
Interest Rates		Percent Per Annum											
Discount Rate (End of Period)	60	....	....	....	160.00	2.00	48.00	58.00	120.00	150.00	150.00	150.00	150.00
Deposit Rate	60l	....	....	....	125.92	147.13	29.25	36.88	†36.57	†39.58	47.91	48.69	26.17
Lending Rate	60p	....	....	....	206.25	217.88	37.75	45.00	†80.30	†103.16	95.97	97.34	96.12

Angola 614

		1992	1993	1994	1995	1996	1997	1998	1999	2000	2001	2002	2003
Prices		*Index Numbers (2000=100): Period Averages*											
Consumer Prices...................	64	....	....	....	....	1.0	3.3	6.8	23.5	100.0	241.2	527.6	1,045.8
Consumer Prices (2000=1 Million)...	64.a	.1	.8	8.7	240.6	10,213.9	32,600.4	....	....	....	....	....	....
International Transactions		*Millions of US Dollars*											
Exports, f.o.b...................	70..d	3,833.0	2,901.0	3,017.0	3,723.0	5,095.0	5,006.8	3,542.9	5,397.0	7,702.0	6,379.8	7,509.6	9,237.4
Imports, f.o.b...................	71.vd	1,988.0	1,463.0	1,454.0	1,468.0	2,040.5	2,597.0	2,079.4	3,109.1	3,039.5	3,179.2	....	3,406.8
Balance of Payments		*Millions of US Dollars: Minus Sign Indicates Debit*											
Current Account, n.i.e............	78ald	−734.8	−668.5	−339.8	−295.0	3,266.4	−883.5	−1,867.1	−1,710.4	795.7	−1,430.9	....	....
Goods: Exports f.o.b..........	78aad	3,832.8	2,900.5	3,016.6	3,722.7	5,095.0	5,006.8	3,542.9	5,156.5	7,920.7	6,534.3		
Goods: Imports f.o.b..........	78abd	−1,988.0	−1,462.6	−1,454.1	−1,467.7	−2,040.5	−2,597.0	−2,079.4	−3,109.1	−3,039.5	−3,179.2		
Trade Balance................	78acd	1,844.8	1,437.9	1,562.5	2,255.0	3,054.5	2,409.8	1,463.5	2,047.5	4,881.2	3,355.1		
Services: Credit...............	78add	142.9	105.8	150.2	113.1	267.7	138.5	121.8	153.0	267.3	202.5		
Services: Debit................	78aed	−2,042.4	−1,561.9	−1,562.9	−2,051.4	−2,423.3	−2,605.4	−2,635.2	−2,594.6	−2,699.5	−3,518.1		
Balance on Goods & Services.......	78afd	−54.8	−18.2	149.8	316.7	898.9	−57.1	−1,049.8	−394.1	2,449.0	39.5		
Income: Credit................	78agd	15.7	11.3	13.0	15.9	43.3	112.1	34.5	24.1	34.4	23.0		
Income: Debit.................	78ahd	−798.0	−827.4	−747.7	−783.2	−1,516.7	−1,033.1	−1,003.3	−1,396.2	−1,715.2	−1,584.0		
Balance on Gds, Serv. & Inc.....	78aid	−837.0	−834.3	−584.9	−450.6	−574.4	−978.1	−2,018.6	−1,766.2	768.2	−1,521.5		
Current Transfers, n.i.e.: Credit......	78ajd	170.9	253.4	333.2	312.2	3,949.4	176.4	238.2	154.5	123.5	208.3		
Current Transfers: Debit........	78akd	−68.7	−87.6	−88.1	−156.7	−108.6	−81.8	−86.7	−98.7	−96.0	−117.8		
Capital Account, n.i.e............	78bcd	−	−	−	−	−	11.2	8.4	6.8	18.3	3.9		
Capital Account, n.i.e.: Credit......	78bad	−	−	−	−	−	11.2	8.4	6.8	18.3	3.9		
Capital Account: Debit........	78bbd	−	−	−	−	−	−	−	−	−	−		
Financial Account, n.i.e..........	78bjd	−472.9	−274.3	−443.4	−924.8	−654.5	449.9	368.3	1,739.6	−445.6	950.0		
Direct Investment Abroad........	78bdd									−	−		
Dir. Invest. in Rep. Econ., n.i.e.....	78bed	288.0	302.1	170.3	472.4	180.6	411.7	1,114.0	2,471.5	878.6	2,145.5		
Portfolio Investment Assets...........	78bfd									....	....		
Equity Securities..............	78bkd	−	−	−	−	−	−	−	−	....	....		
Debt Securities................	78bld	−	−	−	−	−	−	−	−	....	....		
Portfolio Investment Liab., n.i.e.....	78bgd									....	....		
Equity Securities..............	78bmd	−	−	−	−	−	−	−	−	....	....		
Debt Securities................	78bnd	−	−	−	−	−	−	−	−	....	−		
Financial Derivatives Assets...........	78bwd	....	....	....	....	....	....	....	....	....	....		
Financial Derivatives Liabilities.......	78bxd	....	....	....	....	....	....	....	....	....	....		
Other Investment Assets...........	78bhd	−255.5	−92.9	214.1	−168.4	−327.6	−330.7	−40.8	−186.1	−702.1	−516.6		
Monetary Authorities..............	78bod	....											
General Government...............	78bpd	−52.6	−156.0	−	−	−	−	−	−	−	−		
Banks.......................	78bqd	−	10.0	−	−4.4	−48.8	−	−	−	−	−		
Other Sectors..................	78brd	−202.9	53.1	214.1	−164.1	−278.8	−330.7	−40.8	−186.1	−702.1	−516.6		
Other Investment Liab., n.i.e........	78bid	−505.4	−483.5	−827.8	−1,228.8	−507.4	368.9	−704.8	−545.7	−622.1	−678.9		
Monetary Authorities.............	78bsd	32.8	17.6	−185.9	−114.3	−143.9	−	−303.0	−272.2	17.3	−62.0		
General Government.............	78btd	−430.8	−583.6	−792.6	−778.1	−202.7	−69.0	−478.6	−180.5	−665.3	−483.1		
Banks.......................	78bud	−9.6	.6	−	−	−1.6	4.8	2.4	3.5	−	−		
Other Sectors..................	78bvd	−97.8	81.9	150.7	−336.4	−159.2	433.2	74.4	−96.5	25.9	−133.8		
Net Errors and Omissions............	78cad	43.0	−377.1	−244.5	−19.4	149.2	−181.8	378.5	−78.9	−50.6	−308.6		
Overall Balance...................	78cbd	−1,164.7	−1,319.9	−1,027.7	−1,239.3	2,761.0	−604.3	−1,112.0	−42.9	317.8	−785.6		
Reserves and Related Items...........	79dad	1,164.7	1,319.9	1,027.7	1,239.3	−2,761.0	604.3	1,112.0	42.9	−317.8	785.6		
Reserve Assets................	79dbd	−227.2	192.9	14.2	−30.7	−330.3	162.6	318.0	−530.1	−631.3	466.3		
Use of Fund Credit and Loans........	79dcd	−	−	−	−	−	−	−	−	−	−		
Exceptional Financing.............	79ded	1,391.9	1,127.0	1,013.5	1,270.0	−2,430.7	441.7	794.0	573.0	313.4	319.3		
National Accounts		*Millions of Kwanzas*											
Gross Domestic Product (GDP)........	99b	3.5	26.9	620.2	13.7	835.5	1,752.0	2,556.0	17,171.0	91,666.0	197,111.0	433,553.0	....
GDP Volume 1992 Prices.............	99b.p	3.5	2.6	2.7	3.0	3.4	3.6	3.8	3.9	4.0	4.2	4.9	....
GDP Volume (2000=100).............	99bvp	87.2	65.6	67.3	74.4	83.9	89.1	94.0	96.5	100.0	105.3	121.6	....
		Millions: Midyear Estimates											
Population.....................	99z	9.91	10.24	10.56	10.87	11.16	11.45	11.73	12.04	12.39	12.77	13.18	13.62

Anguilla 312

		1992	1993	1994	1995	1996	1997	1998	1999	2000	2001	2002	2003
Exchange Rates		\multicolumn{12}{c}{E. Caribbean Dollars per SDR: End of Period (aa) E. Caribbean Dollars per US Dollar: End of Period (ae)}
Official Rate	aa	3.7125	3.7086	3.9416	4.0135	3.8825	3.6430	3.8017	3.7058	3.5179	3.3932	3.6707	4.0121
Official Rate	ae	2.7000	2.7000	2.7000	2.7000	2.7000	2.7000	2.7000	2.7000	2.7000	2.7000	2.7000	2.7000
International Liquidity		\multicolumn{12}{c}{Millions of US Dollars Unless Otherwise Indicated: End of Period}
Total Reserves minus Gold	1l.d	8.26	9.33	9.14	12.78	14.45	16.31	18.15	19.91	20.30	24.19	26.20	33.28
Foreign Exchange	1d.d	8.26	9.33	9.14	12.78	14.45	16.31	18.15	19.91	20.30	24.19	26.20	33.28
Monetary Authorities: Other Liab.	4..d	–	–	–	–	–	–	–	–	–	–	–	–
Deposit Money Banks: Assets	7a.d	30.40	39.10	49.34	66.99	74.43	76.65	108.01	89.54	93.14	103.52	129.83	131.97
Liabilities	7b.d	33.74	39.63	38.01	37.47	48.60	49.21	64.12	69.08	75.46	71.52	78.48	91.07
Monetary Authorities		\multicolumn{12}{c}{Millions of E. Caribbean Dollars: End of Period}
Foreign Assets	11	22.31	25.19	24.69	34.53	39.00	44.05	49.01	53.83	54.89	65.51	70.87	89.92
Claims on Central Government	12a	–	–	–	.05	–	–	–	–	–	5.01	.43	–
Claims on Deposit Money Banks	12e	.02	.02	.01	.01	.01	.02	.01	.01	.02	.02	.01	.03
Reserve Money	14	22.32	25.21	24.69	33.00	37.82	42.56	47.77	53.11	54.53	70.13	71.05	89.65
of which: Currency Outside DMBs	14a	5.39	4.87	5.04	7.06	7.32	7.17	8.45	8.72	8.76	8.98	8.25	8.98
Foreign Liabilities	16c	–	–	–	–	–	–	–	–	–	–	–	–
Central Government Deposits	16d	.02	–	.01	1.58	1.19	1.51	1.26	.72	.39	.40	.27	.30
Other Items (Net)	17r	–	–	–	–	–	–	–	–	–	–	–	–
Deposit Money Banks		\multicolumn{12}{c}{Millions of E. Caribbean Dollars: End of Period}
Reserves	20	17.11	20.28	19.20	21.48	30.84	34.40	35.75	44.51	49.27	61.27	62.79	81.50
Foreign Assets	21	82.09	105.56	133.21	180.87	200.95	206.96	291.63	241.76	251.47	279.51	350.54	356.31
Claims on Central Government	22a	3.04	1.34	.73	1.12	.35	1.62	1.76	–	–	–	–	–
Claims on Local Government	22b	1.16	.08	–	–	–	–	–	1.85	12.51	16.11	21.68	23.32
Claims on Nonfin.Pub.Enterprises	22c	–	–	–	–	–	–	7.90	7.89	7.61	7.38	8.20	5.17
Claims on Private Sector	22d	176.40	196.22	193.34	204.82	219.31	245.12	261.08	337.06	424.83	457.66	479.17	540.38
Claims on Nonbank Financial Insts.	22g	.10	.99	.35	.75	.80	1.63	.82	.65	.63	.93	1.04	1.64
Demand Deposits	24	7.33	5.08	5.19	8.43	7.55	9.40	9.63	11.30	14.34	13.13	16.20	17.78
Time, Savings,& Fgn.Currency Dep	25	147.34	171.16	191.60	239.14	246.94	270.47	327.55	357.56	420.57	479.01	541.47	583.99
Foreign Liabilities	26c	91.09	107.01	102.62	101.16	131.21	132.86	173.11	186.53	203.74	193.09	211.90	245.90
Central Government Deposits	26d	15.36	21.20	26.32	31.83	38.22	41.06	45.57	45.87	55.34	62.72	69.07	70.78
Credit from Monetary Authorities	26g	.01	.98	.01	–	.02	–	1.82	.01	3.52	.02	.02	2.22
Capital Accounts	27a	15.92	16.06	21.09	25.82	31.76	37.96	47.13	54.80	62.46	87.72	103.73	110.39
Other Items (Net)	27r	2.85	2.97	–	2.66	–3.44	–2.03	–5.89	–22.34	–13.64	–12.83	–18.97	–22.72
Monetary Survey		\multicolumn{12}{c}{Millions of E. Caribbean Dollars: End of Period}
Foreign Assets (Net)	31n	13.31	23.74	55.27	114.24	108.74	118.15	167.53	109.06	102.62	151.93	209.51	200.34
Domestic Credit	32	165.33	177.43	168.09	173.32	181.05	205.80	224.72	300.85	389.86	423.97	441.18	499.44
Claims on Central Govt. (Net)	32an	–12.33	–19.86	–25.60	–32.25	–39.06	–40.95	–45.06	–46.59	–55.72	–58.11	–68.90	–71.07
Claims on Local Government	32b	1.16	.08	–	–	–	–	–	1.85	12.51	16.11	21.68	23.32
Claims on Nonfin.Pub.Enterprises	32c	–	–	–	–	–	–	7.90	7.89	7.61	7.38	8.20	5.17
Claims on Private Sector	32d	176.40	196.22	193.34	204.82	219.31	245.12	261.08	337.06	424.83	457.66	479.17	540.38
Claims on Nonbank Financial Inst.	32g	.10	.99	.35	.75	.80	1.63	.82	.65	.63	.93	1.04	1.64
Money	34	12.72	9.96	10.23	15.50	14.90	17.21	18.10	20.03	23.10	22.12	24.53	26.76
Quasi-Money	35	147.34	171.16	191.60	239.14	246.94	270.47	327.55	357.56	420.57	479.01	541.47	583.99
Capital Accounts	37a	15.92	16.06	21.09	25.82	31.76	37.96	47.13	54.80	62.46	87.72	103.73	110.39
Other Items (Net)	37r	2.66	3.99	.44	7.11	–3.81	–1.69	–.53	–22.48	–13.65	–12.95	–19.04	–21.35
Money plus Quasi-Money	35l	160.07	181.12	201.83	254.63	261.84	287.68	345.65	377.59	443.67	501.12	566.00	610.74
Money (National Definitions)		\multicolumn{12}{c}{Millions of E. Caribbean Dollars: End of Period}
M1	39ma	10.64	10.48	10.77	15.05	15.50	14.85	17.51	18.53	20.13	20.35	19.51	24.48
M2	39mb	155.95	179.35	199.48	249.45	258.80	283.19	340.99	369.78	432.13	484.25	545.58	586.76
Interest Rates		\multicolumn{12}{c}{Percent Per Annum}
Discount Rate (End of Period)	60	....	....	9.00	9.00	9.00	8.00	8.00	8.00	8.00	7.00	7.00	6.50
Money Market Rate	60b	5.25	5.25	5.25	5.25	5.25	5.25	5.25	5.25	5.25	†5.64	6.32	6.07
Savings Rate	60k	6.29	5.33	4.60	4.96	5.00	5.00	5.00	5.00	5.00	5.00	5.00	†3.23
Deposit Rate	60l	1.58	2.25	3.47	3.64	3.74	3.77	3.79	3.78	3.52	3.54	3.25	4.59
Deposit Rate (Fgn. Currency)	60l.f	....	....	....	....	....	....	....	....	....	....	....	4.65
Lending Rate	60p	4.36	8.29	12.84	12.60	11.95	11.37	11.16	11.31	11.32	10.74	10.35	11.42
Prices, Tourism, Labor		\multicolumn{12}{c}{Index Numbers (2000=100): Period Averages}
Consumer Prices	64	130.4	135.9	140.7	142.6	147.7	147.9	151.8	155.8	100.0	102.3	102.8	....
Number of Tourists	66t	293.0	344.0	399.2	352.0	342.5	394.4	400.8	106.8	100.0	36.5	33.5	51.1
Employment	67e	....	....	759.8	767.6	769.6	765.1	792.6	813.6	809.0	823.3	870.8	926.5
International Transactions		\multicolumn{12}{c}{Millions of E. Caribbean Dollars}
Exports	70	1.4	2.6	2.4	1.4	4.3	4.2	8.6	7.1	10.9	8.6	11.7	....
Imports	71	100.5	96.0	98.2	87.4	161.8	166.3	192.7	248.1	255.2	209.8	188.7	....

Anguilla 312

		1992	1993	1994	1995	1996	1997	1998	1999	2000	2001	2002	2003
Balance of Payments		\multicolumn{12}{c}{*Millions of US Dollars: Minus Sign Indicates Debit*}
Current Account, n.i.e.	78ald	−16.24	−12.61	−11.46	−9.47	−20.26	−18.74	−19.07	−51.05	−54.47	−35.87	−35.38	....
Goods: Exports f.o.b.	78aad	.62	1.14	1.67	1.23	1.76	1.60	3.50	2.90	4.43	3.57	4.38	....
Goods: Imports f.o.b.	78abd	−33.59	−34.36	−39.09	−47.00	−52.86	−54.26	−63.01	−80.86	−83.29	−68.50	−61.63	....
Trade Balance	78acd	−32.97	−33.21	−37.41	−45.78	−51.10	−52.66	−59.51	−77.96	−78.86	−64.93	−57.26	....
Services: Credit	78add	45.46	53.63	61.43	55.56	57.22	66.01	79.44	68.80	64.94	70.43	65.53	....
Services: Debit	78aed	−22.16	−25.78	−24.78	−27.81	−27.59	−28.96	−38.19	−38.30	−40.86	−39.12	−38.53	....
Balance on Goods & Services	78afd	−9.67	−5.36	−.76	−18.03	−21.47	−15.61	−18.26	−47.46	−54.77	−33.62	−30.26	....
Income: Credit	78agd	1.00	1.11	1.47	2.06	2.27	3.28	1.56	3.67	3.97	1.86	1.56	....
Income: Debit	78ahd	−8.08	−9.17	−10.78	−9.60	−8.48	−7.07	−5.43	−6.87	−6.67	−5.39	−6.82	....
Balance on Gds, Serv. & Inc.	78aid	−16.75	−13.41	−10.06	−25.57	−27.67	−19.40	−22.13	−50.65	−57.47	−37.14	−35.52	....
Current Transfers, n.i.e.: Credit	78ajd	6.05	7.28	5.28	21.51	12.63	7.20	9.30	8.25	11.15	9.83	8.54	....
Current Transfers: Debit	78akd	−5.54	−6.48	−6.68	−5.42	−5.22	−6.54	−6.24	−8.64	−8.14	−8.57	−8.40	....
Capital Account, n.i.e.	78bcd	5.37	5.66	6.80	5.40	5.23	2.51	5.60	7.96	9.75	8.81	6.80	....
Capital Account, n.i.e.: Credit	78bad	6.37	6.95	8.11	6.71	6.54	3.87	6.95	9.31	11.10	10.11	8.12	....
Capital Account: Debit	78bbd	−1.00	−1.30	−1.31	−1.31	−1.31	−1.35	−1.35	−1.35	−1.35	−1.30	−1.32	....
Financial Account, n.i.e.	78bjd	12.05	4.44	−1.50	−.95	35.73	19.20	11.60	58.75	41.05	20.23	17.26	....
Direct Investment Abroad	78bdd	−	−	−	−	−	−	−	−	−	−	−	....
Dir. Invest. in Rep. Econ., n.i.e.	78bed	15.42	6.47	11.14	17.58	33.23	21.24	28.06	38.01	38.18	32.72	36.53	....
Portfolio Investment Assets	78bfd	−	.05	−	−.18	−	−	−	−	−	−	−.85	....
Equity Securities	78bkd	....	....	....	....	....	....	....	....	....	....	....	....
Debt Securities	78bld	....	....	....	....	....	....	....	....	....	....	....	....
Portfolio Investment Liab., n.i.e.	78bgd	−	−	−	−	−	−	−.23	−	−	1.15	.01	....
Equity Securities	78bmd	....	....	....	....	....	....	....	....	....	....	....	....
Debt Securities	78bnd	....	....	....	....	....	....	....	....	....	....	....	....
Financial Derivatives Assets	78bwd	....	....	....	....	....	....	....	....	....	....	....	....
Financial Derivatives Liabilities	78bxd	....	....	....	....	....	....	....	....	....	....	....	....
Other Investment Assets	78bhd	−7.56	−.23	−.44	−.75	−1.23	−.61	−.56	−1.29	−.66	−3.49	−.57	....
Monetary Authorities	78bod	....	....	....	....	....	....	....	....	....	....	....	....
General Government	78bpd	....	....	....	....	....	....	....	....	....	....	....	....
Banks	78bqd	....	....	....	....	....	....	....	....	....	....	....	....
Other Sectors	78brd	....	....	....	....	....	....	....	....	....	....	....	....
Other Investment Liab., n.i.e.	78bid	4.19	−1.84	−12.20	−17.60	3.73	−1.43	−15.67	22.03	3.53	−10.15	−17.86	....
Monetary Authorities	78bsd	....	....	....	....	....	....	....	....	....	....	....	....
General Government	78btd	....	....	....	....	....	....	....	....	....	....	....	....
Banks	78bud	....	....	....	....	....	....	....	....	....	....	....	....
Other Sectors	78bvd	....	....	....	....	....	....	....	....	....	....	....	....
Net Errors and Omissions	78cad	.09	3.59	6.16	5.03	−19.26	−1.12	3.70	−13.90	4.05	10.73	13.07	....
Overall Balance	78cbd	1.27	1.07	−	−	1.44	1.86	1.84	1.76	.39	3.90	1.75	....
Reserves and Related Items	79dad	−1.27	−1.07	−	−	−1.44	−1.86	−1.84	−1.76	−.39	−3.90	−1.75	....
Reserve Assets	79dbd	−1.27	−1.07	−	−	−1.44	−1.86	−1.84	−1.76	−.39	−3.90	−1.75	....
Use of Fund Credit and Loans	79dcd	....	....	....	....	....	....	....	....	....	....	....	....
Exceptional Financing	79ded	....	....	....	....	....	....	....	....	....	....	....	....
National Accounts		\multicolumn{12}{c}{*Millions of E. Caribbean Dollars*}
Gross Domestic Product (GDP)	99b	137.8	150.4	166.5	164.9	175.8	194.2	209.2	233.0	233.4	236.9	239.5	....
GDP Volume 1990 Prices	99b.p	130.0	139.7	149.6	143.4	148.4	162.1	170.5	185.2	184.6	188.6	182.5	....
GDP Volume (2000=100)	99bvp	70.4	75.7	81.1	77.7	80.4	87.8	92.3	100.3	100.0	102.1	98.8	....
GDP Deflator (2000=100)	99bip	83.9	85.2	88.0	90.9	93.7	94.8	97.1	99.5	100.0	99.4	103.8	....
		\multicolumn{12}{c}{*Millions: Midyear Estimates*}
Population	99z	.010	.010	.010	.010	.010	.011	.011	.011	.011	.011	.012	.012

Antigua and Barbuda 311

		1992	1993	1994	1995	1996	1997	1998	1999	2000	2001	2002	2003
Exchange Rates													

E. Caribbean Dollars per SDR: End of Period (aa) E. Caribbean Dollars per US Dollar: End of Period (ae)

		1992	1993	1994	1995	1996	1997	1998	1999	2000	2001	2002	2003
Official Rate	aa	3.7125	3.7086	3.9416	4.0135	3.8825	3.6430	3.8017	3.7058	3.5179	3.3932	3.6707	4.0121
Official Rate	ae	2.7000	2.7000	2.7000	2.7000	2.7000	2.7000	2.7000	2.7000	2.7000	2.7000	2.7000	2.7000

Index Numbers (2000=100): Period Averages

		1992	1993	1994	1995	1996	1997	1998	1999	2000	2001	2002	2003
Official Rate	ahx	100.0	100.0	100.0	100.0	100.0	100.0	100.0	100.0	100.0	100.0	100.0	100.0
Nominal Effective Exchange Rate	nec	86.7	92.2	92.2	89.4	90.7	93.6	94.4	95.3	100.0	102.8	100.9	94.2
Real Effective Exchange Rate	rec	98.9	104.7	96.3	92.9	94.4	95.5	97.6	98.0	100.0	103.6	103.0	96.9

Fund Position — *Millions of SDRs: End of Period*

		1992	1993	1994	1995	1996	1997	1998	1999	2000	2001	2002	2003
Quota	2f.s	5.00	8.50	8.50	8.50	8.50	8.50	8.50	13.50	13.50	13.50	13.50	13.50
SDRs	1b.s	–	–	–	–	–	–	–	.01	.01	.01	.01	.01
Reserve Position in the Fund	1c.s	–	–	–	–	–	–	–	–	–	–	–	.01
Total Fund Cred.&Loans Outstg.	2tl	–	–	–	–	–	–	–	–	–	–	–	–

International Liquidity — *Millions of US Dollars: End of Period*

		1992	1993	1994	1995	1996	1997	1998	1999	2000	2001	2002	2003
Total Reserves minus Gold	1l.d	50.52	37.81	45.81	59.44	47.74	50.70	59.37	69.73	63.56	79.72	87.65	113.77
SDRs	1b.d	–	.01	.01	.01	.01	.01	.01	.01	.01	.01	.01	.01
Reserve Position in the Fund	1c.d	–	–	–	–	–	–	–	–	–	–	–	.01
Foreign Exchange	1d.d	50.52	37.80	45.80	59.43	47.73	50.69	59.36	69.72	63.55	79.71	87.64	113.75
Monetary Authorities: Other Liab.	4..d	–	–	–	–	–	–	–	–	–	–	–	–
Deposit Money Banks: Assets	7a.d	53.26	56.76	77.30	77.54	72.02	58.79	71.34	160.10	172.17	187.34	259.14	297.26
Liabilities	7b.d	68.27	54.04	60.72	46.57	78.47	103.51	114.42	129.49	181.85	148.54	208.93	163.61

Monetary Authorities — *Millions of E. Caribbean Dollars: End of Period*

		1992	1993	1994	1995	1996	1997	1998	1999	2000	2001	2002	2003
Foreign Assets	11	137.67	102.05	123.95	159.27	129.36	137.41	161.22	189.29	172.76	216.59	238.44	309.95
Claims on Central Government	12a	36.10	39.48	39.11	32.68	29.28	28.63	26.74	25.27	36.46	34.90	26.37	26.58
Claims on Deposit Money Banks	12e	1.60	1.46	1.33	1.18	1.03	.95	.90	.74	.62	.49	.40	.33
Reserve Money	14	175.26	142.88	164.26	193.00	159.61	166.91	188.77	215.20	209.74	251.86	265.20	336.85
of which: Currency Outside DMBs	14a	64.00	60.78	65.87	77.22	68.06	66.55	79.78	85.01	84.63	78.13	88.20	98.86
Foreign Liabilities	16c	–	–	–	–	–	–	–	–	–	–	–	–
Central Government Deposits	16d	.11	.12	.12	.13	.06	.09	.09	.09	.10	.11	.01	.01
Other Items (Net)	17r	–	–	–	–	–	–	–	–	–	–	–	–

Deposit Money Banks — *Millions of E. Caribbean Dollars: End of Period*

		1992	1993	1994	1995	1996	1997	1998	1999	2000	2001	2002	2003
Reserves	20	105.69	91.66	96.82	116.90	93.87	99.01	115.73	130.99	117.01	190.80	172.61	215.82
Foreign Assets	21	143.80	153.24	208.72	209.36	194.46	158.72	192.61	432.28	464.85	505.83	699.67	802.59
Claims on Central Government	22a	95.19	118.31	124.62	162.83	161.20	192.52	224.83	269.28	283.05	270.51	293.64	289.37
Claims on Local Government	22b	.72	.81	.23	.72	.52	.72	1.43	–	–	.48	.57	.55
Claims on Nonfin.Pub.Enterprises	22c	9.58	9.69	9.53	33.78	33.25	32.44	53.94	77.60	87.36	82.26	75.55	75.53
Claims on Private Sector	22d	607.09	625.30	613.83	706.86	850.34	1,027.00	1,103.30	1,196.01	1,308.10	1,348.71	1,413.70	1,491.61
Claims on Nonbank Financial Insts.	22g	6.00	5.92	21.50	7.78	6.73	6.75	9.34	16.43	8.24	10.13	8.89	47.31
Demand Deposits	24	126.28	125.98	151.77	201.63	189.93	197.19	250.10	238.50	231.42	265.87	250.71	301.33
Time, Savings,& Fgn.Currency Dep.	25	555.04	614.08	649.27	773.57	756.28	824.64	929.91	1,274.88	1,382.59	1,444.39	1,554.36	1,798.06
Foreign Liabilities	26c	184.33	145.92	163.95	125.73	211.88	279.48	308.92	349.62	491.00	401.05	564.11	441.76
Central Government Deposits	26d	51.36	45.22	53.83	65.10	72.77	71.32	69.60	57.57	54.26	55.31	63.45	58.22
Credit from Monetary Authorities	26g	2.12	1.94	1.29	1.17	1.03	4.31	15.63	13.60	10.97	31.50	3.14	4.70
Capital Accounts	27a	71.72	76.01	99.96	107.12	112.55	130.99	147.70	164.56	157.96	174.91	195.26	194.02
Other Items (Net)	27r	−22.77	−4.22	−44.83	−36.09	−4.07	9.24	−20.68	23.87	−59.59	35.70	33.59	124.71

Monetary Survey — *Millions of E. Caribbean Dollars: End of Period*

		1992	1993	1994	1995	1996	1997	1998	1999	2000	2001	2002	2003
Foreign Assets (Net)	31n	97.15	109.37	168.72	242.91	111.94	16.66	44.91	271.95	146.61	321.38	374.00	670.79
Domestic Credit	32	703.20	754.17	754.86	879.42	1,008.49	1,216.65	1,349.89	1,526.93	1,668.85	1,691.55	1,755.25	1,872.73
Claims on Central Govt. (Net)	32an	79.82	112.46	109.78	130.28	117.65	149.73	181.88	236.89	265.15	249.99	256.55	257.72
Claims on Local Government	32b	.72	.81	.23	.72	.52	.72	1.43	–	–	.48	.57	.55
Claims on Nonfin.Pub.Enterprises	32c	9.58	9.69	9.53	33.78	33.25	32.44	53.94	77.60	87.36	82.26	75.55	75.53
Claims on Private Sector	32d	607.09	625.30	613.83	706.86	850.34	1,027.00	1,103.30	1,196.01	1,308.10	1,348.71	1,413.70	1,491.61
Claims on Nonbank Financial Inst.	32g	6.00	5.92	21.50	7.78	6.73	6.75	9.34	16.43	8.24	10.13	8.89	47.31
Money	34	190.39	186.90	217.83	278.95	258.07	263.81	329.93	323.54	316.05	344.00	338.93	400.20
Quasi-Money	35	555.04	614.08	649.27	773.57	756.28	824.64	929.91	1,274.88	1,382.59	1,444.39	1,554.36	1,798.06
Capital Accounts	37a	71.72	76.01	99.96	107.12	112.55	130.99	147.70	164.56	157.96	174.91	195.26	194.02
Other Items (Net)	37r	−16.79	−13.44	−43.48	−37.31	−6.48	13.87	−12.74	35.90	−41.14	49.64	40.71	151.24
Money plus Quasi-Money	35l	745.43	800.98	867.10	1,052.51	1,014.35	1,088.45	1,259.84	1,598.42	1,698.64	1,788.39	1,893.28	2,198.26

Money (National Definitions) — *Millions of E. Caribbean Dollars: End of Period*

		1992	1993	1994	1995	1996	1997	1998	1999	2000	2001	2002	2003
M1	39ma	170.18	174.58	194.92	259.58	233.18	242.39	298.70	302.59	284.33	307.13	308.01	369.52
M2	39mb	687.33	748.45	823.10	998.77	948.94	1,030.10	1,187.53	1,311.71	1,386.99	1,453.58	1,545.09	1,871.10

Interest Rates — *Percent Per Annum*

		1992	1993	1994	1995	1996	1997	1998	1999	2000	2001	2002	2003
Discount Rate (End of Period)	60	....	....	9.00	9.00	9.00	8.00	8.00	8.00	8.00	7.00	7.00	6.50
Money Market Rate	60b	5.25	5.25	5.25	5.25	5.25	5.25	5.25	5.25	5.25	† 5.64	6.32	6.07
Treasury Bill Rate	60c	7.00	7.00	7.00	7.00	7.00	7.00	7.00	7.00	7.00	7.00	7.00	7.00
Savings Rate	60k	7.67	8.00	8.00	8.00	8.00	8.00	8.00	8.00	8.00	8.00	8.00	† 3.65
Deposit Rate	60l	5.75	5.01	4.19	4.02	4.33	4.36	4.34	4.45	5.18	4.49	4.36	4.82
Deposit Rate (Fgn. Currency)	60l.f	....	....	....	....	....	....	....	....	....	....	....	3.52
Lending Rate	60p	12.70	12.68	13.15	12.70	12.26	11.98	12.20	12.07	12.17	11.62	11.39	12.56

Antigua and Barbuda   311

		1992	1993	1994	1995	1996	1997	1998	1999	2000	2001	2002	2003
International Transactions		\multicolumn{12}{c}{*Millions of US Dollars*}
Exports............................	70..d	64.7	62.1	44.4	53.1	37.7	37.9	36.2	37.8	....	....	....	....
Imports, c.i.f.....................	71..d	312.2	323.4	341.5	345.7	365.3	370.4	385.2	414.1	....	....	....	....
Balance of Payments		\multicolumn{12}{c}{*Millions of US Dollars: Minus Sign Indicates Debit*}
Current Account, n.i.e............	78ald	−9.87	15.06	−6.34	−.52	−59.44	−47.37	−46.77	−57.26	−65.78	−64.41	−102.56	....
Goods: Exports f.o.b.............	78aad	75.03	62.08	45.23	53.15	38.88	38.80	37.38	37.43	49.71	38.62	44.80	....
Goods: Imports f.o.b.............	78abd	−261.77	−270.43	−287.50	−291.04	−309.94	−313.86	−320.84	−352.70	−342.39	−321.17	−335.64	....
Trade Balance....................	78acd	−186.74	−208.35	−242.27	−237.89	−271.06	−275.06	−283.46	−315.27	−292.68	−282.55	−290.84	....
Services: Credit..................	78add	332.34	377.09	391.23	348.46	363.64	404.49	428.52	439.21	416.39	402.67	391.84	....
Services: Debit...................	78aed	−124.69	−128.07	−134.42	−147.89	−157.43	−164.43	−169.09	−177.27	−154.32	−171.89	−174.68	....
Balance on Goods & Services....	78afd	20.91	40.67	14.53	−37.32	−64.84	−35.00	−24.02	−53.33	−30.61	−51.77	−73.67	....
Income: Credit....................	78agd	3.70	3.11	4.26	5.21	5.79	3.71	12.89	11.70	15.52	18.69	12.56	....
Income: Debit.....................	78ahd	−33.37	−26.05	−30.81	−32.07	−32.01	−25.86	−33.92	−35.14	−60.04	−40.47	−47.06	....
Balance on Gds, Serv. & Inc.....	78aid	−8.75	17.73	−12.03	−64.18	−91.06	−57.16	−45.06	−76.77	−75.13	−73.55	−108.17	....
Current Transfers, n.i.e.: Credit.	78ajd	8.54	9.07	15.15	78.04	35.19	19.90	12.42	23.61	18.43	22.52	22.97	....
Current Transfers: Debit.........	78akd	−9.66	−11.75	−9.47	−14.38	−3.56	−10.12	−14.13	−4.10	−9.09	−13.38	−17.36	....
Capital Account, n.i.e............	78bcd	5.74	6.81	5.91	6.99	4.36	9.17	156.33	17.62	39.33	11.93	13.92	....
Capital Account, n.i.e.: Credit...	78bad	5.74	6.81	6.53	6.99	4.36	9.17	156.33	17.62	39.33	11.93	13.92	....
Capital Account: Debit...........	78bbd	−	−	−.62	−	−	−	−	−	−	−	−	....
Financial Account, n.i.e..........	78bjd	8.41	−17.47	−19.88	−10.66	54.98	50.54	−56.72	52.10	42.07	60.04	84.64	....
Direct Investment Abroad.......	78bdd	−	−	−	−	−	−	−	−	−	−	−	....
Dir. Invest. in Rep. Econ., n.i.e..	78bed	19.65	15.24	24.79	31.49	19.35	22.94	22.77	32.09	28.11	43.93	47.71	....
Portfolio Investment Assets......	78bfd	−	−	−1.38	1.19	−.78	−	−	−.09	−.01	−.05	−2.92	....
Equity Securities................	78bkd	....	....	....	....	....	....	....	....	....	....	....	....
Debt Securities..................	78bld	....	....	....	....	....	....	....	....	....	....	....	....
Portfolio Investment Liab., n.i.e..	78bgd	−	−	−	−1.28	−.81	−	−.29	2.78	2.35	−2.46	.74	....
Equity Securities................	78bmd	....	....	....	....	....	....	....	....	....	....	....	....
Debt Securities..................	78bnd	....	....	....	....	....	....	....	....	....	....	....	....
Financial Derivatives Assets.....	78bwd	....	....	....	....	....	....	....	....	....	....	....	....
Financial Derivatives Liabilities..	78bxd	....	....	....	....	....	....	....	....	....	....	....	....
Other Investment Assets.........	78bhd	−6.20	−1.17	−23.89	−31.34	−6.68	−2.40	−20.41	74.74	−.39	−3.74	−10.83	....
Monetary Authorities...........	78bod	....	....	....	....	....	....	....	....	....	....	....	....
General Government.............	78bpd	....	....	....	....	....	....	....	....	....	....	....	....
Banks............................	78bqd	....	....	....	....	....	....	....	....	....	....	....	....
Other Sectors...................	78brd	....	....	....	....	....	....	....	....	....	....	....	....
Other Investment Liab., n.i.e.....	78bid	−5.04	−31.54	−19.40	−10.71	43.90	29.99	−58.79	−57.41	12.00	22.36	49.94	....
Monetary Authorities...........	78bsd	−	−	−	−	−	−	−	−	−	−	−	....
General Government.............	78btd	....	....	....	....	....	....	....	....	....	....	....	....
Banks............................	78bud	....	....	....	....	....	....	....	....	....	....	....	....
Other Sectors...................	78bvd	....	....	....	....	....	....	....	....	....	....	....	....
Net Errors and Omissions.........	78cad	13.70	−16.25	28.39	17.78	−11.16	−9.38	−43.96	−2.07	−21.78	8.44	11.72	....
Overall Balance...................	78cbd	17.98	−11.84	8.08	13.59	−11.26	2.96	8.88	10.39	−6.16	15.99	7.72	....
Reserves and Related Items......	79dad	−17.98	11.84	−8.08	−13.59	11.26	−2.96	−8.89	−10.39	6.16	−16.00	−7.73	....
Reserve Assets...................	79dbd	−17.98	11.84	−8.08	−13.59	11.26	−2.96	−8.89	−10.39	6.16	−16.00	−7.73	....
Use of Fund Credit and Loans...	79dcd	....	....	....	....	....	....	....	....	....	....	....	....
Exceptional Financing............	79ded	....	....	....	....	....	....	....	....	....	....	....	....
National Accounts		\multicolumn{12}{c}{*Millions of E. Caribbean Dollars*}
Housh.Cons.Expend.,incl.NPISHs..	96f	504.7	544.1	633.8	672.5	784.0	774.0	750.6	711.3	780.1	....	....	....
Government Consumption Expend...	91f	209.2	230.2	258.2	284.8	307.7	318.1	364.9	396.4	420.0	....	....	....
Gross Fixed Capital Formation....	93e	398.1	390.6	437.4	491.9	578.8	614.6	720.6	793.8	862.4	....	....	....
Exports of Goods and Services....	90c	1,099.6	1,186.1	1,190.0	1,084.3	1,086.8	1,190.2	1,245.6	1,259.8	1,260.3	....	....	....
Imports of Goods and Services (-).	98c	1,067.5	1,118.2	1,169.2	1,201.0	1,298.3	1,328.1	1,407.5	1,403.3	1,536.2	....	....	....
Gross Domestic Product (GDP)....	99b	1,144.2	1,232.7	1,350.2	1,332.7	1,459.0	1,568.8	1,674.2	1,758.1	1,786.6	....	....	....
Net Primary Income from Abroad..	98.n	−80.1	−61.9	−71.7	−72.5	−70.8	−72.8	−80.6	−80.8	−84.7	....	....	....
Gross National Income (GNI).....	99a	1,064.1	1,170.7	1,278.6	1,260.2	1,388.2	1,496.0	1,593.6	1,677.3	1,701.9	....	....	....
Net Current Transf.from Abroad..	98t	−3.0	−7.2	2.4	187.3	85.4	33.1	−2.0	55.7	1.7	....	....	....
Gross Nat'l Disposable Inc.(GNDI).	99i	1,061.1	1,163.5	1,281.0	1,447.5	1,473.6	1,529.1	1,591.7	1,733.0	1,703.6	....	....	....
Gross Saving.....................	99s	347.1	389.3	389.0	490.0	381.9	437.0	476.2	503.6	....	....	....	....
GDP Volume 1990 Prices..........	99b.p	1,087.9	1,146.6	1,219.1	1,168.2	1,245.3	1,310.5	1,353.4	1,403.0	....	....	....	....
GDP Volume (1995=100)..........	99bvp	93.1	98.1	104.4	100.0	106.6	112.2	115.9	120.1	....	....	....	....
GDP Deflator (1995=100).........	99bip	92.2	94.2	97.1	100.0	102.7	104.9	108.4	109.8	....	....	....	....
		\multicolumn{12}{c}{*Millions: Midyear Estimates*}
Population.......................	99z	.06	.07	.07	.07	.07	.07	.07	.07	.07	.07	.07	.07

Argentina 213

		1992	1993	1994	1995	1996	1997	1998	1999	2000	2001	2002	2003
Exchange Rates		\multicolumn{12}{c}{*Pesos per SDR: End of Period*}
Official Rate	aa	1.36194	1.37150	1.45912	1.48649	1.43724	1.34858	1.40733	1.37182	1.30226	1.25610	4.51361	4.31674
		\multicolumn{12}{c}{*Pesos per US Dollar: End of Period (ae) Period Average (rf)*}
Official Rate	ae	.99050	.99850	.99950	1.00000	.99950	.99950	.99950	.99950	.99950	.99950	3.32000	2.90500
Official Rate	rf	.99064	.99895	.99901	.99975	.99966	.99950	.99950	.99950	.99950	.99950	3.06326	2.90063
Fund Position		\multicolumn{12}{c}{*Millions of SDRs: End of Period*}
Quota	2f.s	1,537.1	1,537.1	1,537.1	1,537.1	1,537.1	1,537.1	1,537.1	2,117.1	2,117.1	2,117.1	2,117.1	2,117.1
SDRs	1b.s	272.8	329.5	385.7	362.7	277.4	123.6	187.7	100.3	562.2	8.5	69.3	678.7
Reserve Position in the Fund	1c.s	–	–	–	–	–	–	–	–	–	–	–	.1
Total Fund Cred.&Loans Outstg	2tl	1,682.8	2,562.4	2,884.7	4,124.4	4,376.0	4,349.3	3,865.1	3,262.6	3,880.3	11,121.1	10,547.5	10,446.2
International Liquidity		\multicolumn{12}{c}{*Millions of US Dollars Unless Otherwise Indicated: End of Period*}
Total Reserves minus Gold	1l.d	9,990	13,791	14,327	14,288	18,104	22,320	24,752	26,252	25,147	14,553	10,489	14,153
SDRs	1b.d	375	453	563	539	399	167	264	138	733	11	94	1,008
Reserve Position in the Fund	1c.d	–	–	–	–	–	–	–	–	–	–	–	–
Foreign Exchange	1d.d	9,615	13,339	13,764	13,749	17,705	22,153	24,488	26,114	24,414	14,542	10,395	13,145
Gold (Million Fine Troy Ounces)	1ad	4.373	4.373	4.374	4.374	4.374	.361	.360	.338	.019	.009	.009	.009
Gold (National Valuation)	1and	1,446	1,672	1,651	1,679	1,611	120	124	121	7	3	3	4
Monetary Authorities:Other Assets	3..d	....	....	57	22	30	42	30	13	3	–	–	–
Other Liab	4..d	558	161	–	–	–	–	–	–	–	5	18	34
Deposit Money Banks: Assets	7a.d	3,642	5,153	5,587	6,302	10,011	17,732	16,895	15,007	17,911	7,179	3,627	3,350
Liabilities	7b.d	9,558	9,051	10,995	13,649	15,820	21,048	21,440	22,831	24,170	16,297	12,717	9,334
Other Banking Insts.: Assets	7e.d	12	32	26	31	25	24	17	74	42	35	15	21
Liabilities	7f.d	117	26	39	62	84	148	395	434	405	263	45	17
Monetary Authorities		\multicolumn{12}{c}{*Millions of Pesos: End of Period*}
Foreign Assets	11	11,236	15,448	† 16,035	15,989	19,745	22,806	26,249	27,322	26,925	15,321	35,236	41,544
Claims on Central Government	12a	9,272	11,432	† 8,361	8,499	8,223	7,867	7,170	6,350	7,468	20,495	57,231	62,584
Claims on Deposit Money Banks	12e	23,408	22,527	† 22,463	24,129	2,106	1,794	2,070	2,160	1,930	6,019	24,794	25,098
Claims on Other Banking Insts	12f	5	5	† 4	3	3	–	–	–	–	–	81	91
Reserve Money	14	11,010	14,989	† 16,267	13,769	14,060	15,975	16,392	16,524	15,077	17,768	30,165	50,158
of which: Currency Outside DMBs	14a	7,686	10,067	† 11,229	11,161	11,736	13,331	13,503	13,736	12,571	9,081	16,430	26,649
Foreign Liabilities	16c	2,843	3,677	† 4,211	6,131	6,293	5,868	5,442	4,478	5,056	13,982	48,286	45,652
Central Government Deposits	16d	1,378	1,338	† 764	1,677	2,242	325	1,343	935	1,769	4,366	67	259
Capital Accounts	17a	6,394	7,217	† 3,279	3,583	4,053	4,059	4,604	4,415	4,659	3,542	7,012	4,681
Other Items (Net)	17r	22,296	22,191	† 22,342	23,461	3,430	6,242	7,708	9,480	9,762	2,177	31,811	28,569
Deposit Money Banks		\multicolumn{12}{c}{*Millions of Pesos: End of Period*}
Reserves	20	3,481	5,488	† 5,203	2,637	2,358	2,673	2,905	3,101	2,826	8,429	13,507	23,061
Foreign Assets	21	3,606	5,148	† 5,587	6,302	10,011	17,732	16,895	15,007	17,911	7,179	12,196	9,830
Claims on Central Government	22a	9,871	11,657	† 6,094	10,299	13,013	14,513	17,433	18,982	18,859	20,518	82,709	92,417
Claims on State and Local Govts	22b	....	....	5,008	5,247	5,273	5,950	5,827	8,924	9,585	9,133	11,366	2,507
Claims on Official Entities	22bx	1,103	1,509	† 493	463	565	612	285	276	278	443	259	621
Claims on Private Sector	22d	34,564	42,600	† 51,372	50,780	54,093	63,131	70,525	68,431	65,843	54,159	47,249	39,926
Demand Deposits	24	3,678	5,052	† 5,133	5,458	7,305	8,151	7,986	8,099	7,267	6,763	11,843	16,285
Time, Savings,& Fgn.Currency Dep	25	19,666	30,334	† 37,109	35,352	42,710	56,038	64,162	67,315	70,677	57,078	59,022	70,224
Foreign Liabilities	26c	9,462	9,042	† 10,995	13,649	15,820	21,048	21,440	22,831	24,170	16,297	42,768	27,392
Central Government Deposits	26d	2,958	5,054	† 3,014	2,467	3,054	3,990	4,525	3,602	4,474	2,150	5,255	8,698
Credit from Monetary Authorities	26g	22,967	22,336	† 2,184	2,650	1,375	409	393	308	78	4,478	28,879	28,352
Capital Accounts	27a	10,802	12,503	† 13,519	13,771	15,065	15,806	16,674	16,437	16,726	15,816	25,033	20,964
Other Items (Net)	27r	−16,908	−17,919	† 1,802	2,381	−18	−830	−1,311	−3,868	−8,092	−2,722	−5,513	−3,553
Monetary Survey		\multicolumn{12}{c}{*Millions of Pesos: End of Period*}
Foreign Assets (Net)	31n	2,537	7,877	† 6,416	2,510	7,643	13,623	16,262	15,021	15,610	−7,778	−43,622	−21,669
Domestic Credit	32	50,479	60,811	† 67,554	71,148	75,874	87,759	95,372	98,427	95,790	98,231	193,573	189,190
Claims on Central Govt. (Net)	32an	14,807	16,697	† 10,677	14,654	15,940	18,066	18,735	20,795	20,084	34,496	134,619	146,045
Claims on State and Local Govts	32b	....	....	5,008	5,247	5,273	5,950	5,827	8,924	9,585	9,133	11,366	2,507
Claims on Official Entities	32bx	1,103	1,509	† 493	463	565	612	285	276	278	443	259	621
Claims on Private Sector	32d	34,564	42,600	† 51,372	50,780	54,093	63,131	70,525	68,431	65,843	54,159	47,249	39,926
Claims on Other Banking Insts	32f	5	5	† 4	3	3	–	–	–	–	–	81	91
Money	34	11,364	15,119	† 16,362	16,619	19,042	21,482	21,489	21,836	19,838	15,844	28,272	42,934
Quasi-Money	35	19,666	30,334	† 37,109	35,352	42,710	56,038	64,162	67,315	70,677	57,078	59,022	70,224
Capital Accounts	37a	17,196	19,720	† 16,798	17,354	19,118	19,864	21,279	20,852	21,386	19,358	32,045	25,644
Other Items (Net)	37r	4,790	3,515	† 3,701	4,333	2,647	3,997	4,704	3,446	−501	−1,827	30,612	28,718
Money plus Quasi-Money	35l	31,030	45,453	† 53,471	51,971	61,752	77,520	85,651	89,150	90,515	72,922	87,294	113,158

Argentina 213

		1992	1993	1994	1995	1996	1997	1998	1999	2000	2001	2002	2003
Other Banking Institutions					*Millions of Pesos: End of Period*								
Reserves	40	17	20	†20	14	7	6	7	15	15	89	141	169
Foreign Assets	41	12	32	†26	31	25	24	17	74	42	35	49	61
Claims on Central Government	42a	24	26	†35	37	84	96	114	89	56	18	941	677
Claims on Local and State Govts	42b	....	....	2	2	–	2	–	–	–	–	6	–
Claims on Official Entities	42bx	6	–	†–	–	–	–	–	–	–	2	–	–
Claims on Private Sector	42d	441	644	†838	725	846	1,103	1,681	2,147	2,067	1,821	676	532
Claims on Deposit Money Banks	42e	5	5	†10	13	20	18	22	27	27	22	15	25
Time, Savings,& Fgn.Currency Dep	45	272	412	†501	284	348	320	333	295	344	223	192	215
Foreign Liabilities	46c	116	26	†39	62	84	148	395	434	405	263	153	51
Credit from Monetary Authorities	46g	5	5	†4	3	3	–	–	–	–	–	81	91
Capital Accounts	47a	167	202	†236	210	190	233	367	468	557	667	1,052	981
Other Items (Net)	47r	–55	82	†151	263	357	547	746	1,155	902	833	351	126
Banking Survey					*Millions of Pesos: End of Period*								
Foreign Assets (Net)	51n	2,433	7,883	†6,403	2,480	7,585	13,499	15,884	14,661	15,247	–8,006	–43,726	–21,660
Domestic Credit	52	50,945	61,476	†68,424	71,908	76,802	88,959	97,167	100,663	97,913	100,072	195,116	190,308
Claims on Central Govt. (Net)	52an	14,831	16,723	†10,711	14,691	16,024	18,163	18,850	20,884	20,140	34,514	135,560	146,722
Claims on State and Local Govts	52b	....	....	5,009	5,249	5,273	5,951	5,827	8,924	9,585	9,133	11,372	2,507
Claims on Official Entities	52bx	1,109	1,509	†493	463	565	612	285	276	278	445	259	621
Claims on Private Sector	52d	35,005	43,244	†52,210	51,505	54,939	64,234	72,206	70,578	67,910	55,979	47,924	40,458
Liquid Liabilities	55l	31,285	45,845	†53,952	52,241	62,094	77,835	85,977	89,430	90,844	73,056	87,345	113,204
Capital Accounts	57a	17,363	19,922	†17,034	17,564	19,308	20,098	21,646	21,320	21,942	20,024	33,098	26,625
Other Items (Net)	57r	4,730	3,592	†3,841	4,584	2,984	4,526	5,428	4,573	374	–1,015	30,947	28,820
Interest Rates					*Percent Per Annum*								
Money Market Rate	60b	15.11	6.31	7.66	9.46	6.23	6.63	6.81	6.99	8.15	24.90	41.35	3.74
Money Market Rate (Fgn. Cur.)	60b.f	....	....	....	8.40	5.91	6.39	6.55	6.07	7.53	12.76	13.01	1.64
Deposit Rate	60l	16.78	11.34	8.08	11.90	7.36	6.97	7.56	8.05	8.34	16.16	39.25	10.16
Deposit Rate (Fgn. Currency)	60l.f	....	....	5.68	8.19	6.10	5.87	6.40	6.42	7.03	9.81	4.44	.86
Lending Rate	60p	....	....	10.06	17.85	10.51	9.24	10.64	11.04	11.09	27.71	51.68	19.15
Lending Rate (Fgn. Currency)	60p.f	....	....	8.17	13.88	9.12	7.84	8.95	9.07	9.67	17.67	....	....
Prices, Production, Labor					*Index Numbers (2000=100): Period Averages*								
Share Prices	62	123.3	86.9	114.6	84.0	111.4	149.0	110.6	96.9	100.0	72.6	79.4	145.4
Producer Prices	63	....	97.5	97.9	102.1	105.1	104.0	100.5	96.4	100.0	98.0	174.6	208.9
Consumer Prices	64	84.4	93.3	97.2	100.5	†100.7	101.2	102.1	100.9	100.0	98.9	124.5	141.3
Wages: Monthly(Mfg)('95=100)	65ey	84.6	95.2	101.7	100.0	100.7	....	....	....	....	....	....	....
Manufacturing Prod., Seas.Adj.	66eyc	....	95.7	103.0	96.6	99.1	108.4	110.6	101.4	100.0	74.4	67.0	78.1
Crude Petroleum Production	66aa	72.1	76.9	86.4	93.2	99.5	108.1	109.8	104.1	100.0	100.3	98.0	96.0
					Number in Thousands: Period Averages								
Labor Force	67d	11,462	11,741	11,923	12,306	12,526	12,971	13,077	13,455	13,780	13,914	14,336	....
Employment	67e	10,634	10,675	10,520	10,301	10,453	11,231	11,495	11,641	11,760	11,401	11,827	....
Unemployment	67c	828	1,066	1,402	2,006	2,074	1,740	1,582	1,814	2,019	2,513	2,509	....
Unemployment Rate (%)	67r	7.0	9.0	12.0	16.0	16.6	13.4	12.1	13.5	14.7	18.1	17.5	....
International Transactions					*Millions of US Dollars*								
Exports	70..d	12,235	13,118	15,659	20,967	23,811	26,370	26,441	23,333	26,341	26,543	25,709	29,375
Wheat	70d.d	716	727	665	1,025	1,038	1,331	1,314	1,001	1,221	1,302	1,097	943
Imports, c.i.f.	71..d	14,872	16,703	21,600	20,026	23,722	30,370	31,381	25,507	25,154	20,320	8,990	13,813
Imports, f.o.b.	71.vd	13,589	14,794	19,816	18,077	20,676	27,970	29,498	24,103	23,764	19,158	8,473	13,098
					2000=100								
Volume of Exports	72	45.6	48.8	57.3	71.9	76.5	87.9	97.8	97.4	100.0	104.3	105.1	109.7
Wheat	72d	93.9	51.8	47.0	62.5	53.6	78.8	95.6	80.0	100.0	98.1	82.3	56.0
Volume of Imports	73	52.9	61.3	77.7	68.8	82.2	107.8	117.0	100.9	100.0	82.6	37.9	58.0
					2000=100: Indices of Unit Values in US Dollars								
Unit Value of Exports	74..d	101.8	102.0	104.7	110.6	117.8	114.2	102.4	90.9	100.0	96.6	92.9	101.9
Frozen Beef	74kad	124.3	148.4	112.4	103.1	82.7	88.5	115.2	101.3	100.0	81.2	....	....
Corned Beef (1990=100)	74kdd	90.9	108.7	116.7	....	....	....	....	....	....	....	....	....
Wheat	74d.d	108.9	118.7	119.2	148.7	181.6	142.9	111.3	105.6	100.0	109.1	109.7	137.9
Unit Value of Imports	75..d	111.1	108.2	109.8	115.7	114.6	111.9	106.0	100.0	100.0	96.9	93.8	94.1

2004, International Monetary Fund: *International Financial Statistics Yearbook*

Argentina 213

		1992	1993	1994	1995	1996	1997	1998	1999	2000	2001	2002	2003
Balance of Payments						*Millions of US Dollars: Minus Sign Indicates Debit*							
Current Account, n.i.e.	78ald	−5,655	−8,163	−11,148	−5,175	−6,822	−12,219	−14,510	−11,948	−8,989	−3,853	9,142	7,838
Goods: Exports f.o.b.	78aad	12,399	13,269	16,023	21,162	24,043	26,431	26,434	23,309	26,341	26,543	25,709	29,566
Goods: Imports f.o.b.	78abd	−13,795	−15,633	−20,162	−18,804	−22,283	−28,554	−29,531	−24,103	−23,889	−19,158	−8,473	−13,119
Trade Balance	78acd	−1,396	−2,364	−4,139	2,357	1,760	−2,123	−3,097	−795	2,452	7,385	17,236	16,447
Services: Credit	78add	2,984	3,070	3,362	3,817	4,339	4,534	4,756	4,617	4,808	4,440	3,039	3,989
Services: Debit	78aed	−5,540	−6,394	−7,138	−7,234	−7,865	−8,942	−9,246	−8,768	−9,130	−8,384	−4,697	−5,530
Balance on Goods & Services	78afd	−3,952	−5,688	−7,915	−1,059	−1,767	−6,531	−7,587	−4,946	−1,871	3,441	15,578	14,906
Income: Credit	78agd	2,353	2,592	3,461	4,385	4,440	5,509	6,151	6,109	7,446	5,358	3,052	3,197
Income: Debit	78ahd	−4,826	−5,589	−7,158	−9,054	−9,943	−11,712	−13,538	−13,565	−14,968	−13,083	−10,061	−10,866
Balance on Gds, Serv. & Inc.	78aid	−6,425	−8,685	−11,612	−5,728	−7,270	−12,734	−14,974	−12,402	−9,392	−4,283	8,569	7,237
Current Transfers, n.i.e.: Credit	78ajd	1,032	841	799	823	704	822	790	777	781	838	761	892
Current Transfers: Debit	78akd	−262	−319	−336	−269	−257	−307	−326	−322	−377	−407	−189	−290
Capital Account, n.i.e.	78bcd	16	16	18	14	51	66	73	149	106	157	406	70
Capital Account, n.i.e.: Credit	78bad	24	25	27	25	72	112	92	161	121	165	410	77
Capital Account: Debit	78bbd	−9	−9	−10	−11	−21	−46	−19	−12	−15	−8	−4	−6
Financial Account, n.i.e.	78bjd	7,630	20,328	11,360	4,989	11,713	16,746	18,936	14,448	7,853	−14,971	−23,949	−16,899
Direct Investment Abroad	78bdd	−1,166	−705	−1,013	−1,497	−1,601	−3,653	−2,325	−1,730	−901	−161	627	−774
Dir. Invest. in Rep. Econ., n.i.e.	78bed	4,431	2,793	3,635	5,609	6,949	9,160	7,291	23,988	10,418	2,166	1,093	1,020
Portfolio Investment Assets	78bfd	1,612	−1,555	−1,486	−2,882	−2,381	−1,570	−1,906	−2,005	−1,252	212	477	−95
Equity Securities	78bkd	−295	−1,363	−763	−401	−594	−838	−839	167	−1,455	−931	13	−34
Debt Securities	78bld	1,907	−192	−723	−2,481	−1,787	−733	−1,067	−2,173	203	1,143	464	−61
Portfolio Investment Liab., n.i.e.	78bgd	3,155	35,266	9,843	4,734	12,098	11,666	10,693	−4,780	−1,331	−9,715	−6,886	−8,064
Equity Securities	78bmd	1,120	4,979	3,116	1,090	990	1,391	−210	−10,773	−3,227	31	−116	65
Debt Securities	78bnd	2,035	30,287	6,727	3,643	11,108	10,276	10,903	5,993	1,896	−9,746	−6,770	−8,129
Financial Derivatives Assets	78bwd	....	....	....	....	....	....	....	....	....	....	....	....
Financial Derivatives Liabilities	78bxd	....	....	....	....	....	....	....	....	....	....	....	....
Other Investment Assets	78bhd	−803	−4,721	−3,163	−8,123	−5,217	−7,116	−173	−2,862	−1,368	−1,907	−8,896	−4,448
Monetary Authorities	78bod	330	−	−	−	−	−	−	−	−	−	−	−
General Government	78bpd	−880	−1,548	442	−686	62	−99	111	−1,553	1,056	232	307	−78
Banks	78bqd	−697	−1,727	−297	−603	−3,039	−5,337	613	995	−2,348	8,960	1,896	447
Other Sectors	78brd	444	−1,446	−3,308	−6,834	−2,240	−1,681	−897	−2,304	−76	−11,099	−11,099	−4,818
Other Investment Liab., n.i.e.	78bid	401	−10,750	3,544	7,148	1,865	8,259	5,356	1,838	2,287	−5,566	−10,364	−4,539
Monetary Authorities	78bsd	−173	−3,996	−16	−94	−214	−11	−10	−13	−16	1,130	−341	−634
General Government	78btd	−516	−8,709	535	1,903	−151	311	1,924	1,203	440	1,410	−2,207	167
Banks	78bud	774	1,150	1,098	3,250	443	3,843	621	1,133	898	−6,775	−2,178	−2,917
Other Sectors	78bvd	315	805	1,927	2,089	1,788	4,116	2,822	−486	964	−1,332	−5,638	−1,155
Net Errors and Omissions	78cad	295	−1,059	−904	−2,140	−1,684	−1,263	−409	−637	−146	−2,737	−1,929	−1,729
Overall Balance	78cbd	2,286	11,122	−675	−2,311	3,258	3,331	4,090	2,013	−1,176	−21,405	−16,331	−10,720
Reserves and Related Items	79dad	−2,286	−11,122	675	2,311	−3,258	−3,331	−4,090	−2,013	1,176	21,405	16,331	10,720
Reserve Assets	79bdd	−3,264	−4,279	−685	82	−3,875	−3,293	−3,436	−1,186	403	12,070	4,526	−3,497
Use of Fund Credit and Loans	79dcd	−73	1,211	455	1,924	367	−38	−654	−826	773	9,335	−739	−151
Exceptional Financing	79ded	1,051	−8,054	904	305	250	−	−	−	−	−	12,544	14,368
International Investment Position						*Millions of US Dollars*							
Assets	79aad	72,482	86,913	89,673	102,834	117,398	133,241	140,617	150,380	153,633	132,797	131,983	144,833
Direct Investment Abroad	79abd	7,332	8,086	9,148	10,696	12,374	16,034	18,335	20,118	21,141	21,283	20,618	21,500
Portfolio Investment	79acd	15,126	20,393	19,154	22,539	26,548	28,900	30,270	34,410	35,190	1,225	843	939
Equity Securities	79add	18	53	68	108	102	217	51	31	43	43	30	64
Debt Securities	79aed	15,108	20,340	19,087	22,431	26,447	28,683	30,219	34,379	35,147	1,182	813	875
Financial Derivatives	79ald	−	−	−	−	−	−	−	−	−	−	−	−
Other Investment	79afd	38,658	42,511	44,775	53,097	58,331	65,333	65,498	68,374	69,652	95,365	99,951	107,267
Monetary Authorities	79agd	−	−	−	−	−	−	−	−	−	−	−	−
General Government	79ahd	5,913	6,593	5,252	6,136	6,091	6,075	5,957	7,524	6,377	6,600	6,108	6,330
Banks	79aid	3,353	5,079	5,377	5,980	9,019	13,455	13,742	12,747	15,095	5,888	3,141	2,694
Other Sectors	79ajd	29,392	30,839	34,147	40,981	43,221	44,902	45,799	48,103	48,179	82,877	90,702	98,243
Reserve Assets	79akd	11,366	15,924	16,595	16,502	20,144	22,974	26,513	27,479	27,651	14,923	10,571	15,127
Liabilities	79lad	82,224	102,194	119,555	139,918	159,475	188,157	206,760	218,956	221,785	214,009	172,148	190,936
Dir. Invest. in Rep. Economy	79lbd	16,303	18,520	22,428	27,991	33,589	42,084	47,898	62,088	67,769	69,169	32,394	38,323
Portfolio Investment	79lcd	11,989	49,516	56,945	60,953	73,299	87,297	94,566	91,776	86,682	75,617	67,630	67,110
Equity Securities	79ldd	1,916	10,257	10,102	11,597	13,730	19,070	14,297	8,389	3,636	2,206	862	2,127
Debt Securities	79led	10,073	39,259	46,843	49,356	59,569	68,227	80,269	83,387	83,046	73,411	66,768	64,983
Financial Derivatives	79lld	−	−	−	−	−	−	−	−	−	−	−	−
Other Investment	79lfd	53,932	34,158	40,182	50,974	52,588	58,777	64,296	65,093	67,333	69,223	72,123	85,504
Monetary Authorities	79lgd	6,419	3,619	4,281	6,184	6,331	5,898	5,462	4,493	5,067	13,980	14,466	15,513
General Government	79lhd	37,809	18,706	20,510	23,225	22,054	20,587	22,766	23,334	22,932	23,551	29,977	43,233
Banks	79lid	5,740	6,891	7,988	11,238	11,681	15,524	16,146	17,279	18,177	11,402	9,111	6,967
Other Sectors	79ljd	3,965	4,943	7,403	10,327	12,522	16,768	19,923	19,987	21,158	20,289	18,569	19,790

Argentina 213

		1992	1993	1994	1995	1996	1997	1998	1999	2000	2001	2002	2003
Government Finance		*Millions of Pesos: Year Ending December 31*
Deficit (-) or Surplus	80	−73.0	−1,574.0	−1,885.7	†−1,426.0	−5,233.6	−4,357.3	−4,148.3	−8,125.7	−6,817.6	−8,739.9	−3,463.8	....
Revenue	81	12,889.0	15,555.0	15,591.8	†38,060.9	35,501.0	41,944.1	42,921.1	41,132.2	42,437.9	39,268.4	42,345.7	....
Exp. & Lending Minus Repay	82z	12,962.0	17,129.0	17,477.5	†39,486.9	40,734.6	46,301.4	47,069.4	49,257.9	49,255.5	48,008.3	45,809.5	....
Expenditure	82	....	....	....	40,574.5	41,066.1	46,174.3	47,108.3	49,214.2	49,365.9	48,032.9	45,774.8	....
Lending Minus Repayments	83	....	....	....	−1,087.6	−331.5	127.1	−38.9	43.7	−110.4	−24.6	34.7	....
Total Financing	84	73.0	1,574.0	1,885.7	†1,426.0	5,233.6	4,357.3	4,148.2	8,125.7	6,817.6	8,739.9	3,463.8	....
Net Borrowing: Domestic	84a	895.0	1,740.0	863.2	....	−1,622.4	2,008.2	−576.8	−2,276.1	−1,924.6	....	....	....
Foreign	85a	−118.0	1,283.0	1,256.8	....	....	....	....	....	....	....	....	....
Use of Cash Balances	87	−704.0	−1,449.0	−234.3	†−2,371.3	−344.1	1,262.1	−1,585.9	556.5	−533.9	−2,239.6	9,991.0	....
National Accounts		*Millions of Pesos*
Househ.Cons.Expend.,incl.NPISHs	96f	192,670	†163,676	180,007	176,909	186,487	203,029	206,434	198,869	197,044	185,164	193,482	238,047
Government Consumption Expend	91f	—	†31,953	33,948	34,446	34,023	35,325	37,353	38,908	39,175	38,037	38,245	42,997
Gross Fixed Capital Formation	93e	37,854	†45,069	51,331	46,285	49,211	56,727	59,595	51,074	46,020	38,099	37,387	56,913
Changes in Inventories	93i	—	†1,494	78	1,493	4,251	4,350	3,179	−378	3,766	3,854	−3,076	−2,223
Exports of Goods and Services	90c	15,096	†16,341	19,364	24,897	28,301	30,834	31,046	27,751	30,937	30,977	86,552	93,878
Imports of Goods and Services (-)	98c	18,823	†22,028	27,289	25,998	30,123	37,406	38,659	32,702	32,738	27,434	40,010	53,381
Gross Domestic Product (GDP)	99b	226,847	†236,505	257,440	258,032	272,150	292,859	298,948	283,523	284,204	268,697	312,580	376,232
Net Primary Income from Abroad	98.n	−2,065	†−2,995	−3,697	−4,669	−5,502	−6,218	−7,406	−7,464	−7,470	−7,744	−19,402	....
Gross National Income (GNI)	99a	224,782	†233,510	253,743	253,363	266,648	286,641	291,542	276,059	276,734	260,953	293,178	....
GDP Vol. 1986 Prices	99b.p	11	12	....	....	....	....	....	....	....	....	....	....
GDP Vol. 1993 Prices	99b.p	....	236,505	250,308	243,186	256,626	277,441	288,123	278,369	276,173	263,997	235,236	255,751
GDP Volume (2000=100)	99bvp	81.0	†85.6	90.6	88.1	92.9	100.5	104.3	100.8	100.0	95.6	85.2	92.6
GDP Deflator (2000=100)	99bip	98.5	†97.2	99.9	103.1	103.1	102.6	100.8	99.0	100.0	98.9	129.1	143.0
		Millions: Midyear Estimates
Population	99z	33.42	33.86	34.31	34.77	35.23	35.69	36.15	36.62	37.07	37.53	37.98	38.43

2004, International Monetary Fund : *International Financial Statistics Yearbook*

Armenia 911

		1992	1993	1994	1995	1996	1997	1998	1999	2000	2001	2002	2003
Exchange Rates						*Dram per SDR: End of Period*							
Official Rate	aa	2.85	103.02	591.98	597.57	625.61	667.85	735.03	718.88	719.44	706.04	795.17	841.06
						Dram per US Dollar: End of Period (ae) Period Average (rf)							
Official Rate	ae	2.07	75.00	405.51	402.00	435.07	494.98	522.03	523.77	552.18	561.81	584.89	566.00
Official Rate	rf	....	9.11	288.65	405.91	414.04	490.85	504.92	535.06	539.53	555.08	573.35	578.76
						Index Numbers (2000=100): Period Averages							
Nominal Effective Exchange Rate	nec	....	....	16.94	27.37	60.00	58.06	66.34	93.97	100.00	98.63	97.40	93.88
Real Effective Exchange Rate	rec	....	....	47.16	86.08	104.19	91.32	98.15	105.38	100.00	90.62	82.62	77.07
Fund Position						*Millions of SDRs: End of Period*							
Quota	2f.s	67.50	67.50	67.50	67.50	67.50	67.50	67.50	92.00	92.00	92.00	92.00	92.00
SDRs	1b.s	–	–	.19	29.82	28.86	27.63	19.89	29.64	16.54	8.15	22.14	12.67
Reserve Position in the Fund	1c.s	.01	.01	.01	.01	.01							
Total Fund Cred.&Loans Outstg.	2tl	–	–	16.88	47.25	81.00	97.88	135.25	146.62	134.66	137.35	143.29	144.44
International Liquidity						*Millions of US Dollars Unless Otherwise Indicated: End of Period*							
Total Reserves minus Gold	1l.d	1.29	13.59	32.28	99.58	155.65	228.75	324.00	318.56	318.32	320.82	425.02	510.19
SDRs	1b.d	–	–	.28	44.33	41.50	37.28	28.00	40.68	21.55	10.24	30.10	18.83
Reserve Position in the Fund	1c.d	.01	.01	.01	.01	.01	.01	.01	–	–	–	–	–
Foreign Exchange	1d.d	1.28	13.58	31.99	55.24	114.14	191.46	295.99	277.88	296.77	310.58	394.92	491.36
Gold (Million Fine Troy Ounces)	1ad	–	–	.0100	.0300	.0340	.0361	.0432	.0436	.0446	.0449	.0449	–
Gold (National Valuation)	1and	–	–	2.44	10.46	12.82	10.72	12.37	12.69	12.17	12.41	15.68	–
Monetary Authorities:Other Assets	3..d	99.61	2.93	.20	.10	.52	.25	.10	.05	.11	.01	.01	.03
Other Liab.	4..d	5.82	23.96	2.05	1.19	5.09	5.05	2.54	1.59	2.89	6.51	12.81	15.63
Deposit Money Banks: Assets	7a.d	14.12	22.68	22.03	24.28	18.14	33.28	33.12	70.34	96.07	100.98	125.99	180.76
Liabilities	7b.d	3.82	3.45	12.98	24.59	50.74	73.39	96.10	111.50	119.90	105.29	93.10	102.07
Monetary Authorities						*Millions of Dram: End of Period*							
Foreign Assets	11	209	1,239	14,162	44,278	73,523	118,657	175,652	173,521	182,551	187,222	257,770	288,786
Claims on General Government	12a	54	1,463	9,536	10,624	27,971	16,491	18,083	18,471	10,296	10,190	3,437	1,047
Claims on Deposit Money Banks	12e	81	286	3,629	3,781	3,346	3,345	3,253	1,698	3,332	3,905	10,392	8,700
Reserve Money	14	108	1,593	15,002	28,806	41,140	51,333	53,863	53,853	72,389	80,418	111,272	118,642
of which: Currency Outside DMBs	14a	60	881	10,056	24,601	34,784	37,596	41,370	42,610	59,486	65,037	88,553	91,997
Time,Savings,& Fgn.Currency Dep.	15	–	–	781	556	116	187	491	346	1	1	1	43
Foreign Liabilities	16c	12	1,797	10,823	28,715	52,890	67,863	100,741	106,234	98,480	100,633	121,433	130,334
General Government Deposits	16d	2	76	1,433	423	8,733	8,165	9,851	10,165	2,004	1,922	13,148	32,554
Capital Accounts	17a	4	121	596	1,691	7,214	13,733	16,609	12,079	21,412	22,026	33,427	19,926
Other Items (Net)	17r	218	–599	–1,309	–1,509	–5,254	–2,788	15,431	11,013	1,893	–3,684	–7,680	–2,966
Deposit Money Banks						*Millions of Dram: End of Period*							
Reserves	20	22	529	3,164	3,987	6,083	13,681	12,033	11,082	12,593	14,717	22,092	25,478
Foreign Assets	21	29	1,701	8,933	9,759	7,894	16,472	17,287	36,843	53,048	56,732	73,691	102,308
Claims on General Government	22a	9	199	335	354	5,865	9,198	15,436	12,268	16,890	18,250	26,313	29,179
of which: Claims on Local Govts.	22ab	–	–	–	–	–	–	2	5	–	–	–	–
Claims on Other Sectors	22d	125	353	20,718	37,946	37,181	48,486	70,791	86,188	102,406	91,826	93,478	97,088
Claims on Nonbank Financial Insts.	22g	–	–	–	–	–	–	11,369	4,352	7,137	5,398	4,492	6,559
Demand Deposits	24	55	443	3,188	5,375	4,968	6,372	11,216	9,553	11,743	12,073	26,400	30,618
Time,Savings,& Fgn.Currency Dep.	25	133	1,584	10,310	9,617	14,424	26,005	42,868	56,881	80,258	80,854	96,578	110,503
Money Market Instruments	26aa	–	–	–	–	–	–	–	24	201	–	90	562
Foreign Liabilities	26c	8	259	5,262	9,884	22,074	36,328	50,168	58,399	66,207	59,151	54,453	57,770
General Government Deposits	26d	16	217	1,324	1,748	2,533	2,469	3,662	5,205	15,881	17,121	16,662	12,278
of which: Local Govt. Deposits	26db	11	134	790	857	222	577	349	209	70	58	105	–
Credit from Monetary Authorities	26g	1	4	1,367	4,093	3,539	3,710	3,257	1,701	3,342	3,973	10,601	8,870
Capital Accounts	27a	–40	165	3,646	7,579	12,315	17,835	28,685	36,366	38,151	38,166	35,479	55,148
Other Items (Net)	27r	14	112	8,053	13,750	–2,831	–4,882	–12,966	–17,574	–23,507	–24,504	–20,108	–15,137
Monetary Survey						*Millions of Dram: End of Period*							
Foreign Assets (Net)	31n	218	884	7,010	15,438	6,453	30,938	42,030	45,731	70,912	84,171	155,576	202,990
Domestic Credit	32	182	1,728	27,832	46,753	59,753	63,544	102,167	105,941	119,023	107,305	98,594	89,080
Claims on General Govt. (Net)	32an	46	1,370	7,113	8,807	22,570	15,055	20,005	15,368	9,301	9,396	–60	–14,605
Claims on Other Sectors	32d	125	353	20,718	37,946	37,181	48,486	70,791	86,218	102,586	92,511	94,161	97,126
Claims on Nonbank Financial Insts.	32g	11	5	–	–	3	3	11,372	4,354	7,137	5,398	4,492	6,559
Money	34	115	1,331	13,410	30,078	39,830	44,055	52,678	52,227	71,395	77,297	115,307	123,272
Quasi-Money	35	133	1,584	11,091	10,173	14,540	26,192	43,360	57,227	80,259	80,855	96,579	110,546
Money Market Instruments	36aa	–	–	–	–	–	–	–	24	201	–	90	562
Capital Accounts	37a	–35	286	4,242	9,270	19,530	31,568	45,295	48,445	59,562	60,192	68,906	75,074
Other Items (Net)	37r	188	–590	6,099	12,670	–7,694	–7,333	2,840	–6,428	–21,280	–26,958	–26,623	–17,384
Money plus Quasi-Money	35l	248	2,916	24,501	40,251	54,371	70,247	96,037	109,454	151,653	158,151	211,886	233,818

Armenia 911

		1992	1993	1994	1995	1996	1997	1998	1999	2000	2001	2002	2003
Interest Rates						*Percent Per Annum*							
Discount Rate (End of Period)	60	30.00	210.00	210.00	77.80	26.00	65.10	...	...	...	...	...	7.00
Refinancing Rate (End of Period)	60a	30.00	210.00	210.00	52.00	60.00	54.00	39.00	†43.00	25.00	15.00	13.50	7.00
Money Market Rate	60b	...	...	...	...	48.56	36.41	27.84	23.65	18.63	19.40	12.29	7.51
Treasury Bill Rate	60c	...	...	...	37.81	†43.95	57.54	46.99	55.10	24.40	†20.59	14.75	11.91
Deposit Rate	60l	...	...	...	63.18	32.19	26.08	24.94	27.35	18.08	14.90	9.60	6.87
Lending Rate	60p	...	...	...	111.86	66.36	54.23	48.49	38.85	31.57	26.69	21.14	20.83
Prices, Production, Labor					*Index Numbers (2000=100): Period Averages*								
Producer Prices	63	...	...	...	...	...	82.75	94.85	100.41	100.00	101.08	104.71	114.00
Consumer Prices	64	...	.5	24.7	68.2	80.9	†92.2	100.2	100.8	100.0	103.1	104.3	109.2
Wages: Avg. Month.Earn	65	...	...	...	...	...	55.4	73.7	87.8	100.0	111.2	124.5	...
Industrial Production	66	...	...	...	...	72.5	78.5	82.7	93.5	100.0	...	112.5	...
					Number in Thousands: Period Averages								
Employment	67e	...	...	1,487.6	1,476.4	1,435.6	1,372.2	1,337.3	1,298.2	1,277.7	1,264.9	1,106.4	1,111.6
Unemployment	67c	...	...	91.8	131.7	159.3	174.4	133.8	175.0	153.9	138.4	127.3	118.6
Unemployment Rate (%)	67r	...	...	8.5	10.4	15.2	15.1	13.3	15.0	15.7	14.1	13.1	14.2
International Transactions						*Millions of US Dollars*							
Exports	70..d	82.90	156.20	215.50	270.90	290.30	232.55	220.50	232.20	294.20	342.80	507.20	678.08
Imports, c.i.f.	71..d	205.90	254.20	393.80	673.90	855.80	892.30	902.40	799.70	881.90	874.30	991.00	1,269.44
Imports, f.o.b.	71.vd	185.30	233.80	343.80	625.40	757.50	779.40	794.10	703.60	776.20	751.90	875.70	1,110.17
Balance of Payments					*Millions of US Dollars: Minus Sign Indicates Debit*								
Current Account, n.i.e.	78ald	...	−66.83	−103.78	−218.37	−290.68	−306.51	−417.96	−307.05	−278.34	−200.52	−147.94	−186.43
Goods: Exports f.o.b.	78aad	...	156.19	215.35	270.90	290.44	233.64	228.89	247.31	309.92	353.11	513.78	688.61
Goods: Imports f.o.b.	78abd	...	−254.18	−393.63	−673.87	−759.63	−793.10	−806.29	−721.35	−773.41	−773.34	−882.54	−1,128.32
Trade Balance	78acd	...	−97.99	−178.28	−402.97	−469.19	−559.46	−577.40	−474.04	−463.49	−420.23	−368.76	−439.71
Services: Credit	78add	...	17.28	13.67	28.60	77.71	96.60	130.34	135.81	136.94	186.54	183.83	205.39
Services: Debit	78aed	...	−40.06	−40.70	−52.27	−128.52	−159.38	−208.71	−197.87	−192.75	−204.34	−224.52	−268.26
Balance on Goods & Services	78afd	...	−120.77	−205.31	−426.64	−520.00	−622.24	−655.77	−536.10	−519.30	−438.03	−409.45	−502.58
Income: Credit	78agd	...	...	...	54.63	78.04	138.95	103.91	93.57	103.74	103.08	136.57	163.12
Income: Debit	78ahd	...	−1.30	−4.02	−14.61	−33.31	−40.44	−43.51	−38.64	−50.84	−39.55	−48.41	−71.84
Balance on Gds, Serv. & Inc.	78aid	...	−122.07	−209.33	−386.62	−475.27	−523.73	−595.37	−481.17	−466.40	−374.50	−321.29	−411.30
Current Transfers, n.i.e.: Credit	78ajd	...	56.29	106.33	169.95	198.99	252.41	203.02	200.57	208.52	200.79	199.68	251.41
Current Transfers: Debit	78akd	...	−1.05	−.78	−1.70	−14.40	−35.19	−25.61	−26.45	−20.46	−26.81	−26.33	−26.53
Capital Account, n.i.e.	78bcd	...	5.10	5.74	8.05	13.40	10.88	9.74	12.55	28.31	30.12	68.06	93.47
Capital Account, n.i.e.: Credit	78bad	...	5.10	5.74	8.05	13.40	10.88	9.74	16.85	29.49	32.57	70.18	95.67
Capital Account: Debit	78bbd	...	...	...	...	...	...	−	−4.30	−1.18	−2.45	−2.12	−2.20
Financial Account, n.i.e.	78bjd	...	57.82	89.94	227.48	216.76	334.82	390.43	286.18	249.88	176.86	146.98	156.45
Direct Investment Abroad	78bdd	...	...	...	...	...	...	...	−	...	...	...	.36
Dir. Invest. in Rep. Econ., n.i.e.	78bed	...	.80	8.00	25.32	17.57	51.94	220.83	122.04	104.19	69.87	110.74	120.86
Portfolio Investment Assets	78bfd	...	...	...	...	−.01	−.14	.63	.06	−19.10	−5.76	3.38	.05
Equity Securities	78bkd	...	...	...	...	−.01	−.03	.53	.01	−3.01	−.53	−.86	.05
Debt Securities	78bld	...	...	...	...	...	−.11	.10	.05	−16.09	−5.23	4.24	−
Portfolio Investment Liab., n.i.e.	78bgd	...	...	...	...	7.23	15.90	−16.57	1.58	.25	−.09	−1.85	.22
Equity Securities	78bmd	...	...	...	...	1.88	.46	.72	−.32	.40	.50	−.41	.05
Debt Securities	78bnd	...	...	...	...	5.35	15.44	−17.29	1.90	−.15	−.59	−1.44	.17
Financial Derivatives Assets	78bwd	...	...	...	...	...	...	...	...	...	...	...	...
Financial Derivatives Liabilities	78bxd	...	...	...	...	...	...	...	...	...	...	−	−
Other Investment Assets	78bhd	...	−44.00	35.89	−8.60	35.34	40.76	19.97	2.97	−9.49	−18.23	−88.56	−78.89
Monetary Authorities	78bod	...	−33.40	...	−8.58	−.08	1.36	.07	.06	−.10	.14	−.48	−.02
General Government	78bpd	...	−10.60	−6.24	...	...	...	−43.27	15.56	11.33	12.76	−6.80	2.18
Banks	78bqd	...	...	.27	−.02	7.33	−17.57	6.17	−34.42	−14.11	−19.70	−38.21	−52.70
Other Sectors	78brd	...	...	41.86	...	28.09	56.97	57.00	21.77	−6.61	−11.43	−43.07	−28.35
Other Investment Liab., n.i.e.	78bid	...	101.02	46.05	210.76	156.63	226.36	165.57	159.53	174.03	131.07	123.26	113.85
Monetary Authorities	78bsd	...	28.24	−9.18	.53	4.68	−.04	−2.92	−.93	1.59	3.79	4.44	.25
General Government	78btd	...	99.05	55.26	151.20	44.21	122.86	35.01	80.16	44.28	64.25	45.14	22.90
Banks	78bud	...	−26.27	−.03	.03	26.18	29.04	23.99	11.19	8.78	−3.70	2.38	10.47
Other Sectors	78bvd	...	...	...	59.00	81.56	74.50	109.49	69.11	119.38	66.73	71.31	80.23
Net Errors and Omissions	78cad	...	17.17	4.83	12.35	15.06	10.83	18.39	13.11	17.05	12.14	−3.23	22.94
Overall Balance	78cbd	...	13.26	−3.27	29.51	−45.46	50.02	.60	4.79	16.90	18.60	63.87	86.43
Reserves and Related Items	79dad	...	−13.26	3.27	−29.51	45.46	−50.02	−.60	−4.79	−16.90	−18.60	−63.87	−86.43
Reserve Assets	79dbd	...	−13.26	−21.24	−76.22	−60.35	−73.48	−52.13	−20.79	−19.75	−20.02	−82.91	−60.41
Use of Fund Credit and Loans	79dcd	...	−	24.50	46.71	49.04	23.46	51.53	16.00	−15.91	3.35	8.07	1.78
Exceptional Financing	79ded	...	...	...	...	56.77	...	...	−	18.77	−1.93	10.97	−27.81

2004, International Monetary Fund : *International Financial Statistics Yearbook*

Armenia 911

		1992	1993	1994	1995	1996	1997	1998	1999	2000	2001	2002	2003
International Investment Position							*Millions of US Dollars*						
Assets..................................	79aad	....	....	....	....	....	381.90	417.38	489.43	529.42	542.27	684.10	....
Direct Investment Abroad............	79abd	....	....	....	....	....	–	–	–	.01	.02	.36	....
Portfolio Investment...............	79acd	....	....	....	....	....	.61	.18	.12	19.27	8.90	4.51	....
Equity Securities.................	79add	....	....	....	....	....	.50	.10	.09	3.09	3.60	4.46	....
Debt Securities...................	79aed	....	....	....	....	....	.11	.08	.03	16.18	5.30	.05	....
Financial Derivatives................	79ald	....	....	....	....	....	–	–	–	–	–	–	....
Other Investment..................	79afd	....	....	....	....	....	141.82	124.09	185.77	196.01	203.89	247.96	....
Monetary Authorities............	79agd	....	....	....	....	....	.18	.10	.04	.14	–	.61	....
General Government.............	79ahd	....	....	....	....	....	18.00	61.27	45.71	35.96	23.19	29.99	....
Banks...............................	79aid	....	....	....	....	....	37.77	33.85	70.12	83.37	98.52	131.32	....
Other Sectors......................	79ajd	....	....	....	....	....	85.87	28.87	69.90	76.55	82.18	86.05	....
Reserve Assets......................	79akd	....	....	....	....	....	239.47	293.10	303.53	314.12	329.46	431.26	....
Liabilities...........................	79lad	....	....	....	....	....	949.92	1,332.15	1,607.72	1,829.73	1,975.52	2,197.35	....
Dir. Invest. in Rep. Economy.........	79lbd	....	....	....	....	....	103.44	312.67	421.36	513.10	577.32	684.48	....
Portfolio Investment...............	79lcd	....	....	....	....	....	21.18	3.44	4.47	4.79	5.93	5.84	....
Equity Securities.................	79ldd	....	....	....	....	....	.44	1.09	.75	1.09	1.55	2.94	....
Debt Securities...................	79led	....	....	....	....	....	20.74	2.35	3.72	3.70	4.38	2.90	....
Financial Derivatives................	79lld	....	....	....	....	....	–	–	–	–	–	–	....
Other Investment..................	79lfd	....	....	....	....	....	825.30	1,016.04	1,181.90	1,311.84	1,392.27	1,507.04	....
Monetary Authorities............	79lgd	....	....	....	....	....	137.49	192.94	202.80	178.35	178.93	207.58	....
General Government.............	79lhd	....	....	....	....	....	496.80	538.29	611.83	694.22	757.71	853.16	....
Banks...............................	79lid	....	....	....	....	....	112.51	96.73	111.51	118.48	114.96	94.83	....
Other Sectors......................	79ljd	....	....	....	....	....	78.50	188.08	255.75	320.79	340.66	351.47	....
National Accounts							*Millions of Dram*						
Househ.Cons.Expend.,incl.NPISHs....	96f	....	....	176,885	555,056	664,002	832,638	956,322	951,565	1,001,704	1,100,035	1,213,754	1,364,945
Government Consumption Expend...	91f	....	....	21,086	58,336	74,265	90,220	105,589	117,591	121,791	132,708	136,071	166,602
Gross Fixed Capital Formation.........	93e	....	....	37,855	84,365	118,254	130,336	154,925	162,134	190,130	208,025	287,369	392,096
Changes in Inventories.....................	93i	....	....	6,012	11,859	14,029	23,015	27,900	19,085	2,149	24,304	7,839	8,510
Exports of Goods and Services.........	90c	....	....	73,569	124,965	153,665	163,065	181,552	204,976	241,078	299,477	399,975	516,878
Imports of Goods and Services (-).....	98c	....	....	136,747	324,775	370,208	468,722	504,820	491,769	521,272	542,653	634,733	807,827
Gross Domestic Product (GDP).........	99b	....	....	187,065	522,256	661,209	804,336	955,385	987,444	1,031,338	1,175,877	1,362,472	1,623,336
Statistical Discrepancy.....................	99bs	....	....	8,404	12,451	7,203	33,783	33,917	23,862	−4,241	−46,020	−47,803	−17,867
GDP Volume (1995=100)................	99bvp	....	....	93.6	100.0	105.9	109.4	117.4	121.2	....	....	....	....
GDP Deflator (1995=100)................	99bip	....	....	38.3	100.0	119.6	140.8	155.8	156.0	....	....	....	....
							Millions: Midyear Estimates						
Population..............................	99z	....	3.44	3.38	3.32	3.27	3.22	3.18	3.14	3.11	3.09	3.07	3.06

Aruba 314

		1992	1993	1994	1995	1996	1997	1998	1999	2000	2001	2002	2003
Exchange Rates		\multicolumn{12}{c}{*Aruban Florins per SDR: End of Period*}
Official Rate	aa	2.4613	2.4587	2.6131	2.6608	2.5739	2.4152	2.5204	2.4568	2.3322	2.2495	2.4335	2.6599
		\multicolumn{12}{c}{*Aruban Florins per US Dollar: End of Period (ae) Period Average (rf)*}
Official Rate	ae	1.7900	1.7900	1.7900	1.7900	1.7900	1.7900	1.7900	1.7900	1.7900	1.7900	1.7900	1.7900
Official Rate	rf	1.7900	1.7900	1.7900	1.7900	1.7900	1.7900	1.7900	1.7900	1.7900	1.7900	1.7900	1.7900
International Liquidity		\multicolumn{12}{c}{*Millions of US Dollars: End of Period*}
Total Reserves minus Gold	1l.d	142.11	181.24	177.59	216.67	187.62	172.33	222.19	219.91	208.01	293.71	339.73	295.22
Foreign Exchange	1d.d	142.11	181.24	177.59	216.67	187.62	172.33	222.19	219.91	208.01	293.71	339.73	295.22
Gold (Million Fine Troy Ounces)	1ad	.100	.100	.100	.100	.100	.100	.100	.100	.100	.100	.100	.100
Gold (National Valuation)	1and	25.630	25.630	25.630	26.307	27.978	27.978	22.878	22.900	22.900	30.751	38.118	46.404
Deposit Money Banks: Assets	7a.d	197.89	213.42	222.37	207.98	233.69	257.38	269.57	280.49	299.19	297.19	303.20	354.35
Liabilities	7b.d	143.36	163.04	150.87	161.08	190.85	217.10	190.79	191.93	221.36	228.81	259.06	302.95
Monetary Authorities		\multicolumn{12}{c}{*Millions of Aruban Florins: End of Period*}
Foreign Assets	11	300.25	370.30	363.77	434.93	385.91	358.55	438.67	434.74	417.17	580.79	676.35	611.51
Reserve Money	14	225.48	249.57	233.57	275.54	236.23	226.35	318.08	338.01	299.00	395.80	449.93	424.46
of which: Currency Outside DMBs	14a	76.23	81.66	87.56	93.70	94.87	101.52	104.91	122.44	121.48	125.96	127.84	126.13
Central Government Deposits	16d	23.72	58.57	71.70	99.97	92.55	68.27	65.56	55.64	57.84	96.97	112.16	67.29
Capital Accounts	17a	59.80	58.60	56.02	66.40	70.48	76.12	71.71	65.95	80.62	90.81	124.84	140.68
Other Items (Net)	17r	−8.74	3.57	2.48	−6.98	−13.35	−12.19	−16.67	−24.87	−20.28	−2.80	−10.59	−20.92
Deposit Money Banks		\multicolumn{12}{c}{*Millions of Aruban Florins: End of Period*}
Reserves	20	147.13	168.16	147.44	181.48	154.97	119.11	209.55	224.24	181.36	245.95	314.01	293.31
Foreign Assets	21	354.22	382.02	398.05	372.29	418.30	460.71	482.53	502.08	535.55	531.96	542.73	634.29
Claims on Central Government	22a	36.23	43.16	67.94	36.88	59.43	59.90	55.91	61.44	43.47	62.37	65.86	83.70
Claims on Private Sector	22d	742.74	793.09	946.52	1,017.98	1,121.78	1,185.47	1,248.15	1,376.10	1,502.35	1,581.67	1,783.64	2,012.89
Demand Deposits	24	252.72	293.14	350.09	343.90	346.37	366.07	433.80	458.88	471.23	553.43	705.49	856.30
Time and Savings Deposits	25	663.16	673.52	755.64	795.31	853.93	881.59	991.61	1,105.88	1,133.42	1,138.99	1,188.42	1,230.30
Bonds	26ab	....	....	....	....	12.75	−	5.00	5.00	5.00	5.00	5.00	5.00
Foreign Liabilities	26c	256.62	291.84	270.06	288.33	341.61	388.62	341.52	343.55	396.23	409.58	463.71	542.28
Central Government Deposits	26d	10.57	20.90	37.90	22.95	16.33	15.89	11.28	7.93	9.02	6.41	31.19	59.73
Capital Accounts	27a	62.81	56.56	70.34	85.62	105.49	112.89	105.78	109.64	127.57	146.19	135.59	164.04
Other Items (Net)	27r	34.45	50.48	75.91	72.51	78.00	59.73	107.15	133.00	120.26	162.36	176.82	166.54
Monetary Survey		\multicolumn{12}{c}{*Millions of Aruban Florins: End of Period*}
Foreign Assets (Net)	31n	396.84	448.02	478.10	517.80	461.50	428.18	578.01	593.16	554.17	700.60	746.91	700.92
Domestic Credit	32	744.69	756.79	904.86	931.93	1,072.33	1,160.81	1,227.22	1,373.97	1,478.96	1,540.66	1,706.14	1,969.56
Claims on Central Govt. (Net)	32an	1.95	−36.30	−41.66	−86.05	−49.45	−24.66	−20.93	−2.13	−23.39	−41.01	−77.50	−43.33
Claims on Private Sector	32d	742.74	793.09	946.52	1,017.98	1,121.78	1,185.47	1,248.15	1,376.10	1,502.35	1,581.67	1,783.64	2,012.89
Money	34	331.28	377.89	441.45	443.70	447.47	473.18	547.00	589.73	596.51	701.05	844.41	985.61
Quasi-Money	35	663.66	674.03	756.17	804.74	855.08	881.76	991.78	1,106.06	1,133.60	1,139.18	1,189.11	1,230.99
Bonds	36ab	....	....	....	....	12.75	−	5.00	5.00	5.00	5.00	5.00	5.00
Other Items (Net)	37r	146.59	152.88	185.34	201.30	218.52	234.04	261.45	266.35	298.02	396.02	414.52	448.88
Money plus Quasi-Money	35l	994.94	1,051.93	1,197.62	1,248.44	1,302.55	1,354.94	1,538.78	1,695.79	1,730.11	1,840.23	2,033.52	2,216.59
Interest Rates		\multicolumn{12}{c}{*Percent Per Annum*}
Discount Rate	60	9.5	9.5	9.5	9.5	9.5	9.5	9.5	6.5	6.5	6.5	6.5	5.0
Deposit Rate	60l	5.7	4.2	4.4	4.3	4.2	4.4	....	†6.2	6.2	5.8	5.6	5.3
Lending Rate	60p	10.6	10.6	10.6	10.6	10.3	10.0	....	†13.1	12.1	12.1	13.1	11.5
Prices and Tourism		\multicolumn{12}{c}{*Index Numbers (2000=100): Period Averages*}
Consumer Prices	64	75.0	79.0	83.9	86.8	89.6	92.2	94.0	†96.1	100.0	103.1	106.7	110.2
Number of Tourists	66ta	75.1	77.8	80.7	85.8	88.9	90.1	89.8	94.7	100.0	95.9	89.1	88.9
Number of Tourist Nights	66tb	74.4	76.7	80.7	85.2	89.5	92.3	93.2	98.0	100.0	98.0	92.7	97.1
International Transactions		\multicolumn{12}{c}{*Millions of US Dollars*}
Exports	70..d	....	....	....	14.7	12.5	24.1	29.1	29.2	173.0	148.9	128.4	84.3
Imports, c.i.f.	71..d	....	....	....	566.5	578.3	614.5	814.7	782.1	835.2	841.4	841.4	848.3

Aruba 314

		1992	1993	1994	1995	1996	1997	1998	1999	2000	2001	2002	2003
Balance of Payments					*Millions of US Dollars: Minus Sign Indicates Debit*								
Current Account, n.i.e.	78ald	43.8	41.7	81.1	–.3	–69.1	–195.8	–18.8	–333.2	282.3	....	–244.4	....
Goods: Exports f.o.b.	78aad	1,069.2	1,154.4	1,296.8	1,347.2	1,735.7	1,728.7	1,164.8	1,413.5	2,582.1	....	1,515.8	....
Goods: Imports f.o.b.	78abd	–1,446.7	–1,546.5	–1,607.3	–1,772.5	–2,043.4	–2,115.9	–1,518.2	–2,005.2	–2,610.4	....	–2,049.6	....
Trade Balance	78acd	–377.5	–392.1	–310.6	–425.3	–307.7	–387.2	–353.4	–591.7	–28.3	....	–533.9	....
Services: Credit	78add	571.2	604.1	624.2	645.1	769.9	815.8	892.1	989.7	1,032.0	....	1,072.8	....
Services: Debit	78aed	–159.8	–169.1	–228.7	–245.5	–515.9	–596.1	–553.1	–712.9	–678.7	....	–644.2	....
Balance on Goods & Services	78afd	33.9	42.8	85.0	–25.6	–53.6	–167.5	–14.4	–315.0	325.0	....	–105.3	....
Income: Credit	78agd	14.5	13.4	9.6	16.4	19.2	20.7	40.5	37.4	46.8	....	33.7	....
Income: Debit	78ahd	–21.8	–24.6	–22.3	–24.6	–31.0	–37.9	–40.1	–69.0	–53.5	....	–106.4	....
Balance on Gds, Serv. & Inc.	78aid	26.5	31.6	72.3	–33.8	–65.5	–184.7	–14.0	–346.6	318.3	....	–178.0	....
Current Transfers, n.i.e.: Credit	78ajd	45.9	43.4	47.5	71.5	18.4	18.4	29.3	59.3	46.2	....	36.2	....
Current Transfers: Debit	78akd	–28.7	–33.3	–38.7	–37.9	–22.0	–29.5	–34.1	–45.9	–82.2	....	–102.6	....
Capital Account, n.i.e.	78bcd	–1.5	–1.8	–4.1	–.5	28.0	21.0	5.2	–	9.9	....	19.3	....
Capital Account, n.i.e.: Credit	78bad	.9	.9	.3	3.1	28.7	21.6	10.2	.9	10.5	....	21.5	....
Capital Account: Debit	78bbd	–2.4	–2.8	–4.4	–3.6	–.7	–.6	–5.0	–.9	–.6	....	–2.2	....
Financial Account, n.i.e.	78bjd	–24.1	–8.4	–75.4	41.6	10.7	158.9	64.2	336.4	–314.6	....	263.2	....
Direct Investment Abroad	78bdd	–	–	–	....	–.3	1.7	–1.4	8.9	–11.7	....	–5.8	....
Dir. Invest. in Rep. Econ., n.i.e.	78bed	–37.0	–17.9	–73.2	–5.5	84.5	195.9	83.6	392.1	–227.5	....	238.9	....
Portfolio Investment Assets	78bfd	11.3	10.8	16.5	–16.6	–7.8	–1.6	–44.1	–65.6	–42.9	....	14.4	....
Equity Securities	78bkd	–	–	–	....	....	....	....	....	....	....	....	....
Debt Securities	78bld	11.3	10.8	16.5	–16.6	–7.8	–1.6	–44.1	–65.6	–42.9	....	14.4	....
Portfolio Investment Liab., n.i.e.	78bgd	–18.2	–14.6	–25.8	....	1.6	–17.4	–3.4	12.2	2.1	....	21.6	....
Equity Securities	78bmd	–	–	–	....	....	....	....	....	....	....	....	....
Debt Securities	78bnd	–18.2	–14.6	–25.8	....	1.6	–17.4	–3.4	12.2	2.1	....	21.6	....
Financial Derivatives Assets	78bwd	....	....	....	....	....	....	....	....	....	....	....	....
Financial Derivatives Liabilities	78bxd	....	....	....	....	....	....	....	....	....	....	–.4	....
Other Investment Assets	78bhd	13.6	–25.8	5.8	12.5	–11.3	–49.7	29.2	–15.7	–97.7	....	–43.1	....
Monetary Authorities	78bod	....	....	....	....	....	....	....	....	....	....	....	....
General Government	78bpd	–	–	–.8	....	....	....	....	....	....	....	....	....
Banks	78bqd	–3.5	–15.7	–3.7	15.6	–17.0	–30.7	–11.5	–12.2	–21.1	....	–8.0	....
Other Sectors	78brd	17.2	–10.1	10.4	–3.1	5.7	–19.0	40.7	–3.5	–76.6	....	–35.1	....
Other Investment Liab., n.i.e.	78bid	6.0	39.2	1.3	51.2	–55.9	30.0	.4	4.5	63.1	....	37.6	....
Monetary Authorities	78bsd	–	–	–	....	....	....	....	....	–	....	–	....
General Government	78btd	10.0	.6	.4	.6	–10.6	–8.9	22.2	7.5	34.0	....	27.9	....
Banks	78bud	–10.7	18.5	–8.7	10.7	17.0	37.3	–26.4	.5	29.2	....	26.4	....
Other Sectors	78bvd	6.7	20.1	9.6	39.9	–62.3	1.6	4.6	–3.5	–	....	–16.7	....
Net Errors and Omissions	78cad	4.4	2.0	–4.7	2.0	4.3	–2.5	.6	–.7	6.5	....	–5.3	....
Overall Balance	78cbd	22.6	33.4	–3.2	42.7	–26.1	–18.4	51.3	2.5	–15.9	....	32.7	....
Reserves and Related Items	79dad	–22.6	–33.4	3.2	–42.7	26.1	18.4	–51.3	–2.5	15.9	....	–32.7	....
Reserve Assets	79dbd	–22.6	–33.4	3.2	–42.7	26.1	18.4	–51.3	–2.5	15.9	....	–32.7	....
Use of Fund Credit and Loans	79dcd	–	–	–	....	....	....	....	....	....	....	....	....
Exceptional Financing	79ded	....	....	....	....	....	....	....	....	....	....	–	....
National Accounts					*Millions of Aruban Florins*								
Exports of Goods and Services	90c	....	....	....	2,006.9	2,139.6	2,263.1	2,374.2	2,465.5	2,476.1	2,466.8	2,369.9	....
Government Consumption Expend.	91f	....	....	....	....	....	647.4	655.0	674.0	731.4	804.6	898.5	....
Gross Fixed Capital Formation	93e	....	....	....	....	....	773.6	851.7	899.1	787.0	742.8	765.9	....
Changes in Inventories	93i	....	....	....	....	....	56.0	93.3	53.1	30.8	20.2	32.4	....
Househ.Cons.Expend.,incl.NPISHs	96f	....	....	....	....	....	1,367.0	1,499.5	1,602.4	1,664.2	1,712.1	1,799.8	....
Imports of Goods and Services	98c	....	....	....	2,044.0	2,191.4	2,365.0	2,493.1	2,610.2	2,362.6	2,347.9	2,445.3	....
Gross Domestic Product (GDP)	99b	....	....	....	2,363.7	2,470.1	2,742.2	2,980.5	3,083.8	3,326.9	3,398.7	3,421.2	....
GDP at 1995 Prices	99b.p	....	....	....	2,366.6	2,390.0	2,579.2	2,751.7	2,783.8	2,886.3	2,866.3	2,792.4	....
GDP Volume (2000=100)	99bvp	....	....	....	82.0	82.8	89.4	95.3	96.4	100.0	99.3	96.7	....
GDP Deflator (2000=100)	99bip	....	....	....	86.6	89.7	92.2	94.0	96.1	100.0	102.9	106.3	....
					Millions: Midyear Estimates								
Population	99z	.07	.07	.08	.08	.08	.08	.09	.09	.09	.10	.10	.10

Australia 193

		1992	1993	1994	1995	1996	1997	1998	1999	2000	2001	2002	2003
Exchange Rates		\multicolumn{12}{c}{*SDRs per Australian Dollar: End of Period*}
Market Rate	ac	.5008	.4930	.5321	.5012	.5539	.4838	.4360	.4764	.4252	.4063	.4165	.5047
		\multicolumn{12}{c}{*US Dollars per Australian Dollar: End of Period (ag) Period Average (rh)*}
Market Rate	ag	.6886	.6771	.7768	.7450	.7965	.6527	.6139	.6538	.5540	.5106	.5662	.7500
Market Rate	rh	.7353	.6801	.7317	.7415	.7829	.7441	.6294	.6453	.5823	.5176	.5439	.6519
		\multicolumn{12}{c}{*Index Numbers (2000=100): Period Averages*}
Market Rate	ahx	126.3	116.8	125.6	127.3	134.4	127.8	108.1	110.8	100.0	88.9	93.4	111.9
Nominal Effective Exchange Rate	nec	102.2	100.7	110.6	107.1	117.5	119.0	106.1	107.2	100.0	93.9	97.4	107.2
Real Effective Exchange Rate	rec	111.5	104.4	108.5	106.0	116.5	115.8	102.6	104.4	100.0	96.4	102.0	113.7
Fund Position		\multicolumn{12}{c}{*Millions of SDRs: End of Period*}
Quota	2f.s	2,333	2,333	2,333	2,333	2,333	2,333	2,333	3,236	3,236	3,236	3,236	3,236
SDRs	1b.s	70	60	50	37	25	14	13	53	72	87	100	114
Reserve Position in the Fund	1c.s	420	400	347	338	335	539	892	1,189	954	1,124	1,423	1,381
of which: Outstg.Fund Borrowing	2c	–	–	–	–	–	–	75	–	–	–	–	–
Total Fund Cred.&Loans Outstg	2tl	–	–	–	–	–	–	–	–	–	–	–	–
International Liquidity		\multicolumn{12}{c}{*Millions of US Dollars Unless Otherwise Indicated: End of Period*}
Total Reserves minus Gold	1l.d	11,208	11,102	11,285	11,896	14,485	16,845	14,641	21,212	18,118	17,955	20,689	32,189
SDRs	1b.d	96	82	73	55	37	19	18	72	94	109	136	170
Reserve Position in the Fund	1c.d	577	550	506	502	482	727	1,256	1,633	1,243	1,412	1,934	2,053
Foreign Exchange	1d.d	10,536	10,470	10,706	11,340	13,967	16,099	13,366	19,507	16,782	16,434	18,618	29,966
Gold (Million Fine Troy Ounces)	1ad	7.93	7.90	7.90	7.90	7.90	2.56	2.56	2.56	2.56	2.56	2.56	2.56
Gold (National Valuation)	1and	2,639	3,086	3,023	3,055	2,918	740	737	743	699	709	878	1,070
Monetary Authorities: Other Liab.	4..d	37	26	38	67	50	28	66	55	63	47	78	86
Deposit Money Banks: Assets	7a.d	8,218	9,062	10,601	12,049	14,830	15,735	13,065	18,752	18,560	21,330	....	....
Liabilities	7b.d	37,770	41,840	39,355	49,238	63,521	64,258	73,409	88,291	90,027	98,049	....	....
Monetary Authorities		\multicolumn{12}{c}{*Millions of Australian Dollars: Average of Weekly Figures for Last Month of Period*}
Foreign Assets	11	20,212	21,415	18,344	20,080	22,581	28,325	27,632	38,596	39,820	44,335	44,568	55,222
Claims on Central Government	12a	14,303	14,265	13,446	17,700	30,608	18,374	23,703	14,684	18,834	20,267	20,991	12,200
Reserve Money	14	20,648	21,987	23,777	24,969	40,261	32,081	33,780	31,943	31,930	37,953	38,486	39,911
of which: Currency Outside DMBs	14a	16,326	17,279	18,208	19,092	19,628	21,098	22,784	24,604	26,928	28,471	29,703	31,470
Foreign Liabilities	16c	54	38	49	90	63	43	108	84	114	92	137	115
Central Government Deposits	16d	2,719	2,634	999	3,131	4,197	2,782	4,431	9,801	12,165	9,906	9,799	8,537
Other Items (Net)	17r	11,094	11,022	6,965	9,590	8,668	11,792	13,016	11,452	14,446	16,652	17,138	18,859
Deposit Money Banks		\multicolumn{12}{c}{*Millions of Australian Dollars: Average of Weekly Figures for Last Month of Period*}
Reserves	20	4,265	4,674	5,498	5,830	13,378	8,789	9,052	5,052	4,228	8,532	8,205	7,256
Foreign Assets	21	14,968	16,281	17,210	22,562	27,893	35,887	37,706	45,742	51,810	60,740	....	....
Claims on Central Government	22a	28,405	30,929	28,457	28,072	25,635	19,991	20,182	23,153	13,371	11,756	....	....
Claims on Official Entities	22bx	6,195	4,419	3,233	3,591	3,909	4,659	6,550	11,104	10,593	12,131	....	....
Claims on Private Sector	22d	273,139	290,232	320,032	355,318	388,126	427,280	477,178	532,435	591,739	639,941	....	....
Demand Deposits	24	43,929	53,719	60,496	64,771	75,801	86,965	91,864	101,179	110,660	138,456	....	....
Time, Savings,& Fgn.Currency Dep	25	177,390	180,265	197,542	215,949	236,124	247,668	271,109	305,051	309,634	339,526	....	....
Foreign Liabilities	26c	54,850	61,793	50,663	66,091	79,750	98,450	119,579	135,043	162,504	192,028	....	....
Central Government Deposits	26d	3,566	3,637	2,988	3,523	3,291	3,578	5,721	5,497	5,197	4,399	....	....
Other Items (Net)	27r	47,238	47,120	62,741	65,038	63,975	59,947	62,395	70,717	83,746	58,690	....	....
Monetary Survey		\multicolumn{12}{c}{*Millions of Australian Dollars: Average of Weekly Figures for Last Month of Period*}
Foreign Assets (Net)	31n	−19,724	−24,135	−15,158	−23,540	−29,339	−34,282	−54,348	−50,789	−70,988	−87,045	....	....
Domestic Credit	32	315,758	333,575	361,180	398,027	440,790	463,945	517,460	566,078	617,174	669,791	....	....
Claims on Central Govt. (Net)	32an	36,423	38,924	37,915	39,118	48,755	32,005	33,732	22,539	14,843	17,718	....	....
Claims on Official Entities	32bx	6,195	4,419	3,233	3,591	3,909	4,659	6,550	11,104	10,593	12,131	....	....
Claims on Private Sector	32d	273,139	290,232	320,032	355,318	388,126	427,280	477,178	532,435	591,739	639,941	....	....
Money	34	60,294	71,026	78,762	83,899	95,641	108,352	114,794	125,945	137,720	167,035	....	....
Quasi-Money	35	177,390	180,265	197,542	215,949	236,124	247,668	271,109	305,051	309,634	339,526	....	....
Other Items (Net)	37r	58,350	58,149	69,718	74,640	79,686	73,644	77,210	84,294	98,833	76,185	....	....
Money plus Quasi-Money	35l	237,683	251,291	276,304	299,848	331,765	356,020	385,903	430,996	447,353	506,560	....	....
Money (National Definitions)		\multicolumn{12}{c}{*Millions of Australian Dollars: Average of Weekly Figures for Last Month of Period*}
Money Base	19ma	20,637	21,980	23,765	24,958	33,043	29,962	31,926	29,733	31,189	37,017	37,513	38,844
M1	59ma	60,300	71,026	78,762	83,898	95,466	108,137	114,737	125,832	137,621	166,942	151,348	164,456
M1, Seasonally Adjusted	59mac	58,121	68,421	75,987	80,916	92,058	104,062	110,454	121,148	133,856	162,756	147,724	160,729
M3	59mb	224,371	237,660	262,064	286,243	313,435	333,599	358,762	394,886	412,854	473,374	507,434	568,176
M3, Seasonally Adjusted	59mbc	221,363	234,318	258,598	282,588	309,350	328,895	353,878	389,521	409,429	469,664	504,416	563,654
Broad Money	59mc	277,190	288,532	313,938	341,113	372,700	400,461	434,029	463,700	493,040	549,174	580,037	639,064
Broad Money, Seasonally Adjusted	59mcc	274,101	285,220	310,546	337,538	368,702	395,837	429,130	458,271	490,076	546,094	577,698	634,401

2004, International Monetary Fund : *International Financial Statistics Yearbook*

Australia 193

		1992	1993	1994	1995	1996	1997	1998	1999	2000	2001	2002	2003
Interest Rates		\multicolumn{12}{c}{*Percent Per Annum*}
Discount Rate	60	6.96	5.83	5.75	5.75	....	....	....	....	....	....	....	....
Money Market Rate	60b	6.44	5.11	5.18	†7.50	7.20	5.50	4.99	†4.78	5.90	5.06	4.55	4.81
Treasury Bill Rate	60c	6.27	5.00	5.69	†7.64	7.02	5.29	4.84	4.76	5.98	4.80	....	....
Deposit Rate	60l	6.32	4.76	5.05	7.33	6.86	5.12	4.67	†3.53	4.12	3.25	2.98	3.31
Lending Rate	60p	11.06	9.72	9.55	11.12	11.00	9.31	8.04	7.51	8.78	8.13	7.96	8.41
Govt. Bond Yield: Short-Term	61a	7.25	5.63	†8.19	8.42	7.53	6.00	5.02	5.55	6.18	4.97	5.30	4.90
Long-Term	61	9.22	7.28	9.04	9.17	8.17	6.89	5.50	6.08	6.26	5.64	5.82	5.36
Prices, Production, Labor		\multicolumn{12}{c}{*Index Numbers (2000=100): Period Averages*}
Share Prices	62	49.1	57.3	64.3	63.9	71.6	80.0	83.9	92.7	100.0	103.2	100.2	96.0
Prices: Manufacturing Output	63	90.19	92.00	92.70	96.58	96.88	98.08	94.19	93.33	100.00	103.06	103.28	103.77
Consumer Prices	64	83.8	85.3	86.9	90.9	93.3	93.5	94.3	95.7	100.0	104.4	107.5	110.5
Wages, Weekly Earnings	65	74.5	75.8	78.4	82.4	85.6	89.1	92.8	95.3	100.0	104.9	110.3	116.5
Industrial Production	66	79.2	81.6	85.8	87.1	90.5	92.1	94.6	95.1	100.0	101.4	104.3	104.6
Manufacturing Empl., Seas. Adj.	67eyc	98.9	94.6	97.8	98.8	99.0	100.5	97.2	95.5	100.0	96.7	97.8	95.8
		\multicolumn{12}{c}{*Number in Thousands: Period Averages*}
Labor Force	67d	8,557	8,613	8,771	8,995	9,115	9,204	9,339	9,466	9,678	9,817	9,983	10,112
Employment	67e	7,660	7,699	7,942	8,256	8,364	8,444	8,618	8,785	9,043	9,157	9,334	....
Unemployment	67c	897	914	829	739	751	760	721	658	611	660	629	611
Unemployment Rate (%)	67r	10.5	10.6	9.5	8.2	8.2	8.3	7.8	7.0	6.3	6.7	6.3	5.9
International Transactions		\multicolumn{12}{c}{*Millions of Australian Dollars*}
Exports	70	58,363	62,839	64,904	71,657	76,978	84,786	88,977	86,895	110,464	122,664	119,483	109,811
Wheat	70d	1,501	2,217	2,283	1,765	3,987	4,407	3,514	3,311	3,813	4,330	4,136	2,426
Coal	70vr	7,245	7,707	6,700	7,380	7,758	8,784	9,823	8,391	9,340	12,482	12,843	10,890
Greasy Wool	70ha	2,461	1,951	2,394	2,242	2,108	2,446	1,715	1,494	2,103	2,304	2,482	1,790
Imports, c.i.f.	71	59,732	67,027	72,882	82,673	83,543	88,884	102,905	107,154	123,461	123,539	133,424	136,577
Imports, f.o.b.	71.v	55,513	62,385	68,087	77,467	78,402	83,364	96,723	101,446	116,840	117,357	126,457	129,884
		\multicolumn{12}{c}{*2000=100*}
Volume of Exports	72	57.8	61.4	66.6	68.7	76.7	87.5	86.5	91.0	100.0	103.1	103.9	101.5
Wheat	72d	41.1	62.3	73.1	38.9	82.2	109.3	85.9	93.2	100.0	87.7	82.9	53.6
Coal	72vr	68.9	71.3	70.3	73.1	75.4	84.5	88.6	91.8	100.0	103.8	111.2	115.7
Greasy Wool	72ha	123.3	113.8	111.8	86.6	104.5	104.5	81.0	83.5	100.0	95.3	74.4	56.1
Volume of Imports	73	47.7	50.4	58.0	63.5	68.9	77.3	83.7	92.4	100.0	94.6	108.2	121.2
Export Prices	76	86.0	87.1	84.7	90.9	87.2	88.7	93.1	†86.4	100.0	110.0	106.7	98.3
Wheat (1995=100)	76d	101.5	85.2	83.1	100.0	109.0	94.7	92.6	....	....	....	....	....
Coal (Unit Value)	74vr	112.6	115.8	102.1	108.1	110.2	111.3	118.7	97.9	100.0	128.7	123.7	100.8
Greasy Wool (Unit Value)	74ha	94.9	81.5	101.9	123.1	95.9	111.3	100.6	85.1	100.0	115.0	158.6	151.8
Import Prices	76.x	83.7	90.5	88.3	91.5	86.6	86.4	93.7	†91.6	100.0	105.7	100.8	92.8

Australia 193

		1992	1993	1994	1995	1996	1997	1998	1999	2000	2001	2002	2003
Balance of Payments							*Millions of US Dollars: Minus Sign Indicates Debit*						
Current Account, n.i.e.	78ald	−11,124	−9,684	−17,146	−19,323	−15,810	−12,384	−18,014	−22,295	−15,481	−8,712	−17,365	−30,554
Goods: Exports f.o.b.	78aad	42,816	42,637	47,371	53,220	60,397	64,893	55,884	56,096	64,052	63,676	65,099	70,596
Goods: Imports f.o.b.	78abd	−41,173	−42,666	−50,648	−57,443	−61,032	−63,044	−61,215	−65,857	−68,865	−61,890	−70,530	−85,850
Trade Balance	78acd	1,643	−29	−3,277	−4,223	−635	1,849	−5,332	−9,761	−4,813	1,786	−5,431	−15,254
Services: Credit	78add	11,200	11,942	14,185	16,156	18,531	18,488	16,181	17,399	18,677	16,698	17,906	21,204
Services: Debit	78aed	−13,767	−13,412	−15,458	−17,110	−18,606	−18,844	−17,272	−18,330	−18,388	−16,948	−18,107	−21,514
Balance on Goods & Services	78afd	−924	−1,500	−4,550	−5,177	−710	1,493	−6,422	−10,692	−4,524	1,536	−5,632	−15,565
Income: Credit	78agd	3,774	4,179	4,462	5,258	6,027	7,162	6,532	7,394	8,984	8,063	8,154	9,579
Income: Debit	78ahd	−13,892	−12,268	−16,829	−19,294	−21,220	−21,000	−17,842	−18,968	−19,893	−18,332	−19,823	−24,490
Balance on Gds, Serv. & Inc.	78aid	−11,042	−9,589	−16,917	−19,213	−15,903	−12,345	−17,732	−22,266	−15,433	−8,733	−17,301	−30,476
Current Transfers, n.i.e.: Credit	78ajd	2,139	2,101	2,206	2,364	2,699	2,765	2,651	3,003	2,622	2,242	2,310	2,767
Current Transfers: Debit	78akd	−2,221	−2,196	−2,434	−2,474	−2,606	−2,805	−2,933	−3,032	−2,669	−2,221	−2,373	−2,845
Capital Account, n.i.e.	78bcd	1,050	260	323	558	964	903	670	819	615	591	443	764
Capital Account, n.i.e.: Credit	78bad	1,572	780	908	1,250	1,674	1,606	1,315	1,535	1,406	1,320	1,298	1,694
Capital Account: Debit	78bbd	−522	−519	−586	−692	−710	−703	−646	−716	−791	−729	−855	−931
Financial Account, n.i.e.	78bjd	5,023	10,203	15,897	18,632	16,070	16,820	15,117	27,808	12,771	8,601	17,307	36,238
Direct Investment Abroad	78bdd	−5,145	−1,942	−2,817	−3,267	−7,052	−6,368	−3,368	966	−829	−12,228	−7,393	−17,115
Dir. Invest. in Rep. Econ., n.i.e.	78bed	5,699	4,318	5,001	12,026	6,181	7,631	6,046	4,733	12,884	4,667	16,141	8,601
Portfolio Investment Assets	78bfd	−4,115	−3,947	1,503	−2,842	−3,307	−79	−3,127	−10,521	−12,465	−9,767	−16,400	−8,911
Equity Securities	78bkd	−1,573	−2,358	−543	−1,175	−2,416	−567	−2,882	−6,481	−9,748	−8,079	−13,364	−4,595
Debt Securities	78bld	−2,542	−1,589	2,045	−1,668	−892	489	−245	−4,040	−2,717	−1,688	−3,036	−4,316
Portfolio Investment Liab., n.i.e.	78bgd	3,301	12,023	14,593	15,200	23,738	13,219	6,917	24,321	15,588	20,735	17,007	50,692
Equity Securities	78bmd	798	7,004	8,120	2,585	2,068	8,775	10,776	11,060	−648	11,918	624	10,515
Debt Securities	78bnd	2,503	5,020	6,473	12,615	21,670	4,444	−3,859	13,261	16,236	8,817	16,383	40,177
Financial Derivatives Assets	78bwd	—	—	1,004	2,801	974	−470	−382	290	−1,165	161	2,243	3,553
Financial Derivatives Liabilities	78bxd	—	—	−632	−2,217	−681	1,092	−636	1,089	291	336	−2,041	−3,459
Other Investment Assets	78bhd	1,033	−1,008	−1,597	−3,223	−5,613	−6,735	−243	−3,077	−4,347	555	−2,955	−6,295
Monetary Authorities	78bod	—	—	—	—	−246	−414	−180	−327	133	275	411	110
General Government	78bpd	222	17	137	−57	−94	−840	−412	−214	−22	−153	−85	−104
Banks	78bqd	873	−47	−2,438	−2,824	−4,618	−4,233	−609	−2,441	−1,147	−2,854	−3,612	−6,010
Other Sectors	78brd	−61	−978	704	−342	−656	−1,248	956	−95	−3,312	3,288	330	−291
Other Investment Liab., n.i.e.	78bid	4,250	758	−1,158	154	1,829	8,530	9,909	10,006	2,815	4,141	10,705	9,173
Monetary Authorities	78bsd	11	13	−4	27	−29	−3	9	61	−70	3	7	37
General Government	78btd	25	−9	157	133	103	−91	129	−228	75	−125	—	—
Banks	78bud	3,965	2,622	−1,375	2,998	2,717	7,207	7,654	7,927	4,286	2,967	9,691	9,406
Other Sectors	78bvd	248	−1,868	64	−3,004	−963	1,417	2,116	2,246	−1,476	1,295	1,007	−270
Net Errors and Omissions	78cad	324	−821	−34	529	1,248	−2,466	188	374	730	616	−263	430
Overall Balance	78cbd	−4,726	−42	−960	396	2,471	2,873	−2,040	6,705	−1,365	1,096	122	6,877
Reserves and Related Items	79dad	4,726	42	960	−396	−2,471	−2,873	2,040	−6,705	1,365	−1,096	−122	−6,877
Reserve Assets	79dbd	4,726	42	960	−396	−2,471	−2,873	2,040	−6,705	1,365	−1,096	−122	−6,877
Use of Fund Credit and Loans	79dcd	—	—	—	—	—	—	—	—	....	....	....	....
Exceptional Financing	79ded	....	....	....	....	....	....	....	....	....	....	....	....
International Investment Position							*Millions of US Dollars*							
Assets	79aad	87,569	100,894	119,962	133,885	161,821	173,545	185,349	232,599	230,378	239,043	266,811	381,174
Direct Investment Abroad	79abd	34,539	40,510	47,774	53,010	66,816	71,936	78,635	89,556	83,443	90,646	91,707	127,091
Portfolio Investment	79acd	24,160	30,247	29,375	35,658	42,023	42,451	48,651	72,847	77,169	79,406	91,056	128,620
Equity Securities	79add	17,092	21,428	22,538	27,029	31,518	32,947	36,652	57,043	61,035	63,710	70,792	100,324
Debt Securities	79aed	7,067	8,819	6,837	8,629	10,506	9,504	11,999	15,804	16,134	15,696	20,264	28,296
Financial Derivatives	79ald	—	—	8,924	7,679	6,733	8,058	9,282	10,756	12,593	14,780	19,521	32,848
Other Investment	79afd	15,022	15,950	19,581	22,589	28,847	34,006	33,404	37,485	38,356	35,547	42,960	59,357
Monetary Authorities	79agd	—	—	—	—	—	491	766	953	875	536	136	—
General Government	79ahd	1,212	1,173	1,201	1,208	1,377	4,044	4,283	4,677	4,223	4,155	4,508	5,551
Banks	79aid	6,994	7,099	9,232	11,905	16,989	18,892	18,470	21,626	20,563	21,775	27,957	41,156
Other Sectors	79ajd	6,816	7,678	9,148	9,476	10,481	10,578	9,886	10,229	12,695	9,081	10,359	12,651
Reserve Assets	79akd	13,848	14,188	14,308	14,949	17,402	17,094	15,377	21,956	18,817	18,664	21,567	33,258
Liabilities	79lad	233,727	264,564	309,880	335,211	388,362	360,313	380,429	451,510	425,857	432,436	507,631	733,601
Dir. Invest. in Rep. Economy	79lbd	75,777	82,891	95,519	104,074	116,724	101,043	105,944	120,589	109,288	106,112	131,958	182,647
Portfolio Investment	79lcd	114,250	137,835	162,325	181,223	218,728	203,158	208,590	254,691	242,535	253,089	279,243	412,401
Equity Securities	79ldd	18,945	35,916	46,544	51,314	61,123	60,297	72,987	100,761	84,987	94,710	93,313	146,181
Debt Securities	79led	95,304	101,919	115,780	129,909	157,605	142,861	135,603	153,930	157,548	158,379	185,930	266,220
Financial Derivatives	79lld	—	—	7,564	7,250	8,275	9,884	9,862	12,550	13,318	12,778	20,487	36,440
Other Investment	79lfd	43,700	43,838	44,472	42,665	44,636	46,227	56,034	63,679	60,717	60,457	75,942	102,113
Monetary Authorities	79lgd	32	43	46	71	45	33	36	100	18	19	28	81
General Government	79lhd	216	202	397	439	573	237	360	153	210	64	71	89
Banks	79lid	21,741	24,229	23,637	25,010	27,883	30,851	37,522	46,949	47,543	47,849	60,766	83,695
Other Sectors	79ljd	21,711	19,363	20,392	17,145	16,134	15,106	18,116	16,477	12,946	12,524	15,077	18,249

2004, International Monetary Fund: *International Financial Statistics Yearbook*

Australia 193

		1992	1993	1994	1995	1996	1997	1998	1999	2000	2001	2002	2003
Government Finance		\multicolumn{12}{c}{*Millions of Australian Dollars: Year Ending June 30*}
Deficit (-) or Surplus	80	−9,511	−13,500	−13,637	−11,641	−4,840	2,062	16,368	†−3,398	13,283	4,194	−8,297	....
Revenue	81	96,436	99,204	104,559	114,234	125,092	134,579	142,036	†151,934	167,700	161,200	164,432	....
Expenditure	82	108,007	115,239	121,561	127,358	135,130	139,857	140,887	†149,023	154,936	156,296	165,946	....
Lending Minus Repayments	83	−2,060	−2,535	−3,365	−1,483	−5,198	−7,340	−15,209	†6,309	−519	710	6,783	....
Financing (by Residence of Lender)													
Domestic	84a	11,422	11,122	10,024	8,349	−3,123	−3,978	−11,213	....	....	....	....	....
Foreign	85a	−1,911	3,325	3,612	3,292	7,963	1,916	−5,155	....	....	....	....	....
Debt: Domestic	88a	43,080	58,025	71,334	79,489	78,892	73,510	60,094	....	....	....	....	....
Foreign	89a	16,794	21,376	22,869	28,012	36,482	42,610	39,355	....	....	....	....	....
National Accounts		\multicolumn{12}{c}{*Billions of Australian Dollars*}
Househ.Cons.Expend.,incl.NPISHs	96f.c	250.62	260.54	273.29	292.60	307.46	325.12	344.36	364.97	388.68	414.79	440.23	466.45
Government Consumption Expend.	91f.c	80.62	83.64	85.79	89.58	95.53	99.18	104.60	109.09	117.88	123.05	131.86	141.35
Gross Fixed Capital Formation	93e.c	87.86	93.40	105.44	109.36	113.88	123.28	135.57	144.01	148.83	150.95	174.24	192.81
Changes in Inventories	93i.c	−1.47	1.59	1.79	.87	1.45	−4.03	3.25	5.72	1.27	−.01	−1.17	4.94
Exports of Goods and Services	90c.c	73.46	80.28	84.11	93.71	100.61	112.00	114.78	113.69	142.78	155.55	152.56	141.33
Imports of Goods and Services (-)	98c.c	74.73	82.41	90.08	100.61	101.66	110.22	124.83	130.27	150.30	152.42	162.45	164.71
Gross Domestic Product (GDP)	99b.c	414.70	435.71	460.55	485.04	516.96	545.72	577.56	605.84	650.32	692.67	734.26	778.76
Net Primary Income from Abroad	98.nc	−13.75	−11.80	−16.92	−18.97	−19.30	−18.72	−18.08	−17.91	−18.86	−19.79	−21.58	−23.10
Gross National Income (GNI)	99a.c	400.95	423.91	443.63	466.07	497.67	527.00	559.48	587.93	631.47	672.87	712.68	755.66
Net Current Transf.from Abroad	98t.c	−.55	−.95	1.06	1.18	.80	.41	.27	−1.68	1.82	−.16	.93	1.00
Gross Nat'l Disposable Inc.(GNDI)	99i.c	400.40	422.96	444.69	467.25	498.46	527.41	559.75	586.25	633.28	672.72	713.61	756.66
Gross Saving	99s.c	69.17	78.79	85.62	85.07	95.48	103.12	110.80	112.19	126.73	134.87	141.52	148.86
Consumption of Fixed Capital	99cfc	68.10	71.81	75.10	77.46	79.24	82.99	88.59	94.43	102.10	110.65	118.24	125.62
GDP Vol. 2001/02 Ref.,Chained	99b.r	493.64	512.51	537.44	556.28	580.01	602.41	633.94	661.47	682.40	699.75	726.00	747.75
GDP Volume (2000=100)	99bvr	72.3	75.1	78.8	81.5	85.0	88.3	92.9	96.9	100.0	102.5	106.4	109.6
GDP Deflator (2000=100)	99bir	88.2	89.2	89.9	91.5	93.5	95.1	95.6	96.1	100.0	103.9	106.1	109.3
		\multicolumn{12}{c}{*Millions: Midyear Estimates*}
Population	99z	17.37	17.61	17.84	18.07	18.30	18.52	18.74	18.95	19.15	19.35	19.54	19.73

2004, International Monetary Fund : *International Financial Statistics Yearbook*

Austria 122

		1992	1993	1994	1995	1996	1997	1998	1999	2000	2001	2002	2003
Exchange Rates					*Schillings per SDR through 1998, Euros per SDR Thereafter: End of Period*								
Official Rate	aa	15.612	16.679	16.013	14.996	15.751	17.045	16.540	1.3662	1.4002	1.4260	1.2964	1.1765
				Schillings per US Dollar through 1998, Euros per US Dollar Thereafter: End of Period (ae) Period Average (rf)									
Official Rate	ae	11.354	12.143	10.969	10.088	10.954	12.633	11.747	.9954	1.0747	1.1347	.9536	.7918
Official Rate	rf	10.989	11.632	11.422	10.081	10.587	12.204	12.379	.9386	1.0854	1.1175	1.0626	.8860
				Schillings per ECU: End of Period (ea) Period Average (eb)									
ECU Rate	ea	13.7486	13.5998	13.4923	13.2581	13.7253	13.9495	13.7058	....	....	....	....	....
ECU Rate	eb	14.2511	13.6360	13.5755	13.1880	13.4234	13.8403	13.8648	....	....	....	....	....
				Index Numbers (2000=100): Period Averages									
Official Rate (1995=100)	ahx	91.9	86.6	88.4	100.0	95.2	82.6	81.5	....	100.0	100.4	100.8	102.7
Nominal Effective Exchange Rate	neu	101.5	104.2	104.1	107.1	105.4	103.0	103.3	102.2	100.0	99.7	100.3	102.5
Real Effective Exchange Rate	reu	123.3	124.0	121.1	116.7	111.1	105.6	104.0	102.0	100.0	99.7	100.3	102.5
Fund Position					*Millions of SDRs: End of Period*								
Quota	2f.s	1,188	1,188	1,188	1,188	1,188	1,188	1,188	1,872	1,872	1,872	1,872	1,872
SDRs	1b.s	248	161	194	122	136	125	106	106	103	185	136	122
Reserve Position in the Fund	1c.s	390	381	364	459	562	714	970	699	531	662	705	771
of which: Outstg.Fund Borrowing	2c	–	–	–	–	–	–	38	–	–	–	–	–
International Liquidity					*Millions of US Dollars Unless Otherwise Indicated: End of Period*								
Total Res.Min.Gold (Eurosys.Def)	1l.d	12,383	14,610	16,822	18,730	22,865	19,736	22,432	†15,120	14,319	12,509	9,683	8,470
SDRs	1b.d	341	220	283	181	195	168	149	145	134	233	185	181
Reserve Position in the Fund	1c.d	536	524	531	682	809	963	1,365	959	692	833	959	1,145
Foreign Exchange	1d.d	11,506	13,866	16,008	17,867	21,861	18,605	20,918	14,016	13,492	11,444	8,540	7,144
o/w:Fin.Deriv.Rel.to Reserves	1ddd	....	....	....	....	....	....	....	–	–	–	–	–
Other Reserve Assets	1e.d	....	....	....	....	....	....	....					
Gold (Million Fine Troy Ounces)	1ad	19.93	18.60	18.34	11.99	10.75	7.87	9.64	13.10	12.14	11.17	10.21	10.21
Gold (Eurosystem Valuation)	1and	3,291	2,871	3,135	2,223	1,805	1,168	2,795	3,803	3,331	3,089	3,499	4,259
Memo:Euro Cl. on Non-EA Res	1dgd	....	....	....	....	....	....	....	2,146	1,453	985	3,588	4,389
Non-Euro Cl. on EA Res	1dhd	....	....	....	....	....	....	....					
Mon. Auth.: Other Foreign Assets	3..d	....	....	....	....	....	....	....					
Foreign Liabilities	4..d	15	9	18	19	8	107	....	†1,584	845	925	613	472
Banking Insts.: Foreign Assets	7a.d	66,763	68,418	77,885	92,040	89,538	....	....	†62,990	69,678	74,777	91,219	122,766
Foreign Liab	7b.d	77,427	74,089	84,321	99,148	102,739	....	....	†49,417	49,932	58,520	56,534	70,378
Monetary Authorities					*Billions of Schillings through 1998; Billions of Euros Beginning 1999: End of Period*								
Fgn. Assets (Cl.on Non-EA Ctys)	11	177.5	211.6	217.4	237.0	268.3	263.4	....	21.95	20.48	19.01	16.44	13.69
Claims on General Government	12a.u	....	....	....	....	....	....	....	1.43	1.06	1.45	3.19	3.22
o/w: Claims on Gen.Govt.in Cty	12a	8.8	9.2	9.6	9.6	10.6	11.6	....	.22	.26	.40	.43	.59
Claims on Banking Institutions	12e.u	....	....	....	....	....	....	....	16.20	10.45	6.42	8.81	8.09
o/w: Claims on Bank.Inst.in Cty	12e	70.8	64.0	62.0	47.6	47.2	74.2	....	5.57	7.08	1.73	3.13	3.60
Claims on Other Resident Sectors	12d.u	....	....	....	....	....	....	....	2.33	2.42	2.32	2.58	2.43
o/w: Cl. on Oth.Res.Sect.in Cty	12d	....	....	....	....	....	....	....	.86	.90	.99	1.13	.94
Currency Issued	14a	141.2	149.8	158.3	168.6	176.7	178.8	....	13.92	14.54	10.69	11.01	12.29
Liabilities to Banking Insts	14c.u	....	....	....	....	....	....	....	16.21	8.76	6.87	11.04	7.40
o/w: Liabs to Bank.Inst.in Cty	14c	48.5	55.2	55.9	43.5	50.1	46.3	....	3.28	3.40	6.56	3.54	4.26
Demand Dep. of Other Res.Sect	14d.u	....	....	....	....	....	....	....	.01	.01	.01	.01	–
o/w:D.Dep.of Oth.Res.Sect.in Cty	14d	....	....	....	....	....	....	....	.01	.01	.01	.01	–
Other Dep. of Other Res.Sect	15..u	....	....	....	....	....	....	....	–	–	–	–	–
o/w:O.Dep.of Oth.Res.Sect.in Cty	15	....	....	....	....	....	....	....	–	–	–	–	–
Bonds & Money Mkt. Instruments	16n.u	....	....	....	....	....	....	....					
o/w: Held by Resid. of Cty	16n	....	....	....	....	....	....	....	1.58	.91	1.05	.59	.37
Foreign Liab. (to Non-EA Ctys)	16c	.2	.1	.2	.2	.1	1.3	....	.01	.01	.03	.02	.02
Central Government Deposits	16d.u	....	....	....	....	....	....	....	.01	.01	.03	.02	.02
o/w: Cent.Govt.Dep. in Cty	16d	.2	.3	.3	.2	.3	.2	....	.01	.01	.03	.02	.02
Other Items (Net)	17r	67.0	79.5	74.4	81.6	98.9	122.5	....	10.18	10.18	10.56	8.36	7.36
Memo: Net Claims on Eurosystem	12e.s	....	....	....	....	....	....	....	–5.55	–3.84	3.04	–3.36	–.35
Currency Put into Circ	14m	....	....	....	....	....	....	....	....	....	....	18.41	15.35

2004, International Monetary Fund : *International Financial Statistics Yearbook*

Austria 122

		1992	1993	1994	1995	1996	1997	1998	1999	2000	2001	2002	2003
Banking Institutions		*Billions of Schillings through 1998; Billions of Euros Beginning 1999: End of Period*
Claims on Monetary Authorities	20	69.8	77.4	80.5	74.0	80.1	77.5	....	3.31	3.88	7.98	3.73	4.86
Claims on Bk.Inst.in Oth.EA Ctys	20b.u	....	....	....	....	....	....	....	31.09	38.65	44.68	39.15	43.61
Fgn. Assets (Cl.on Non-EA Ctys)	21	758.0	830.8	854.3	928.5	980.8	....	....	62.70	74.88	84.85	86.98	97.20
Claims on General Government	22a.u	....	....	....	....	....	....	....	52.70	51.69	48.80	49.72	51.10
o/w: Claims on Gen.Govt.in Cty	22a	641.7	676.8	805.6	†833.1	823.9	783.4	....	49.85	48.51	43.72	41.85	41.56
Claims on Other Resident Sectors	22d.u	....	....	....	....	....	....	....	208.29	227.15	240.55	246.66	253.34
o/w: Cl. on Oth.Res.Sect.in Cty	22d	1,934.4	2,018.6	2,086.2	†2,228.8	2,376.9	2,595.9	....	197.09	213.04	224.07	229.50	234.89
Demand Deposits	24..u	....	....	....	....	....	....	....	44.60	45.05	51.04	54.07	63.44
o/w:D.Dep.of Oth.Res.Sect.in Cty	24	162.0	181.2	201.1	244.0	255.2	273.5	....	42.15	42.69	48.41	51.45	60.66
Other Deposits	25..u	....	....	....	....	....	....	....	130.22	132.01	139.87	137.19	139.75
o/w:O.Dep.of Oth.Res.Sect.in Cty	25	1,567.3	1,643.1	1,721.0	1,770.9	1,812.1	1,840.7	....	123.21	124.96	132.12	129.78	130.51
Money Market Fund Shares	26m.u	....	....	....	....	....	....	....	–	–	–	–	–
Bonds & Money Mkt. Instruments	26n.u	....	....	....	....	....	....	....	94.14	114.39	128.43	135.36	142.45
o/w: Held by Resid.of Cty	26n	419.7	491.9	538.7	596.8	607.9	630.2	....	....	....	....	....	....
Foreign Liab. (to Non-EA Ctys)	26c	879.1	899.7	924.9	1,000.2	1,125.4	....	....	49.19	53.66	66.40	53.91	55.72
Central Government Deposits	26d.u	....	....	....	....	....	....	....	1.61	1.90	3.26	3.36	2.89
o/w: Cent.Govt.Dep. in Cty	26d	59.6	55.2	74.0	77.4	77.7	69.7	....	1.61	1.90	3.25	3.36	2.88
Credit from Monetary Authorities	26g	70.8	64.0	62.0	47.6	47.2	74.2	....	5.19	7.50	1.98	3.41	4.07
Liab. to Bk.Inst.in Oth. EA Ctys	26h.u	....	....	....	....	....	....	....	27.81	31.89	28.08	26.98	26.69
Capital Accounts	27a	194.7	211.4	226.6	238.4	254.7	275.7	....	25.50	27.25	29.30	30.93	33.96
Other Items (Net)	27r	50.7	57.0	78.3	89.0	81.6	....	....	−19.96	−17.40	−21.51	−18.98	−18.86
Banking Survey (Nat'l Residency)		*Billions of Schillings through 1998; Billions of Euros Beginning 1999: End of Period*
Foreign Assets (Net)	31n	56.3	142.6	146.6	165.1	123.6	....	....	42.55	56.15	71.50	78.90	93.62
Domestic Credit	32	2,525.1	2,649.0	2,827.2	†2,993.8	3,133.4	3,321.0	....	246.41	260.79	265.88	269.53	275.07
Claims on General Govt. (Net)	32an	590.8	630.5	740.9	†765.0	756.5	725.1	....	48.46	46.85	40.83	38.90	39.25
Claims on Other Resident Sectors	32d	1,934.4	2,018.6	2,086.2	†2,228.8	2,376.9	2,595.9	....	197.96	213.94	225.05	230.63	235.83
Currency Issued	34a.n	141.2	149.8	158.3	168.6	176.7	178.8	....	13.92	14.54	10.69	11.01	12.29
Demand Deposits	34b.n	162.0	181.2	201.1	244.0	255.2	273.5	....	42.16	42.70	48.42	51.46	60.66
Other Deposits	35..n	1,567.3	1,643.1	1,721.0	1,770.9	1,812.1	1,840.7	....	123.21	124.96	132.12	129.78	130.51
Money Market Fund Shares	36m	....	....	....	....	....	....	....	–	–	–	–	–
Bonds & Money Mkt. Instruments	36n	419.7	491.9	538.7	596.8	607.9	630.2	....	94.14	114.39	128.43	135.36	142.45
o/w: Over Two Years	36na	....	....	....	....	....	....	....	87.95	104.01	118.57	128.15	135.12
Other Items (Net)	37r	291.2	325.7	354.7	378.6	405.1	....	....	15.54	20.35	17.73	20.82	22.79
Banking Survey (EA-Wide Residency)		*Billions of Euros: End of Period*
Foreign Assets (Net)	31n.u	....	....	....	....	....	....	....	33.88	40.79	36.41	48.93	54.79
Domestic Credit	32..u	....	....	....	....	....	....	....	263.33	280.41	289.83	298.77	307.19
Claims on General Govt. (Net)	32anu	....	....	....	....	....	....	....	52.72	50.84	46.96	49.53	51.42
Claims on Other Resident Sect	32d.u	....	....	....	....	....	....	....	210.62	229.57	242.87	249.24	255.78
Currency Issued	34a.u	....	....	....	....	....	....	....	13.92	14.54	10.69	11.01	12.29
Demand Deposits	34b.u	....	....	....	....	....	....	....	44.61	45.06	51.05	54.08	63.44
Other Deposits	35..u	....	....	....	....	....	....	....	130.22	132.01	139.87	137.19	139.75
o/w: Other Dep. Over Two Yrs	35abu	....	....	....	....	....	....	....	49.83	50.09	50.65	49.07	51.34
Money Market Fund Shares	36m.u	....	....	....	....	....	....	....	–	–	–	–	–
Bonds & Money Mkt. Instruments	36n.u	....	....	....	....	....	....	....	94.14	114.39	128.43	135.36	142.45
o/w: Over Two Years	36nau	....	....	....	....	....	....	....	87.95	104.01	118.57	128.15	135.12
Other Items (Net)	37r.u	....	....	....	....	....	....	....	14.33	15.21	−3.79	10.05	4.05
Money (National Definitions)		*Billions of Schillings: End of Period*
Central Bank Money	19ma	189.88	205.24	214.47	212.37	227.13	225.38	....	....	....	....	....	....
Extended Monetary Base	19mb	216.26	224.39	235.17	250.84	260.35	265.81	....	....	....	....	....	....
Money, M1	39m	301.81	334.64	355.58	409.19	431.15	452.30	....	....	....	....	....	....
Interest Rates		*Percent Per Annum*
Discount Rate (End of Period)	60	8.00	5.25	4.50	3.00	2.50	2.50	2.50	....	....	....	....	....
Money Market Rate	60b	9.35	7.22	5.03	4.36	3.19	3.27	3.36	....	....	....	....	....
Deposit Rate	60l	3.69	2.98	2.31	2.19	1.71	1.50	†2.65	2.21	....	....	....	....
Lending Rate	60p	....	....	....	....	....	....	6.42	5.64	....	....	....	....
Government Bond Yield	61	8.27	6.64	6.69	6.47	5.30	4.79	4.29	4.09	....	....	....	....
Prices, Production, Labor		*Index Numbers (2000=100): Period Averages*
Share Prices (1995=100)	62	103.0	100.9	115.3	100.0	105.2	119.9	135.2	....	....	....	....	....
Wholesale Prices	63	95.9	95.5	96.8	97.1	97.1	97.4	96.9	96.1	100.0	101.5	101.1	102.7
Consumer Prices	64	85.5	88.6	91.3	93.3	†95.0	96.3	97.2	97.7	100.0	†102.7	104.5	105.9
Harmonized CPI	64h	....	....	....	94.0	95.7	96.8	97.6	98.1	100.0	102.3	104.0	105.4
Wages: Monthly Earnings (1995=10	65	87.5	92.1	95.8	100.0	....	....	....	....	....	....	....	....
Wages (1996=100)	65a	....	....	....	....	90.9	92.9	95.2	98.0	100.0	102.2	104.8	106.8
Industrial Production	66	69.3	68.2	70.9	74.5	75.2	80.0	86.6	91.8	100.0	102.8	103.6	105.6
Employment	67	97.5	97.5	98.0	97.9	97.2	97.5	98.1	99.2	100.0	100.5	100.7	101.6
		Number in Thousands: Period Averages
Labor Force	67d	3,679	3,734	3,881	....	3,870	3,884	3,888	3,909	3,918	3,940	3,997	....
Employment	67e	3,547	†3,576	3,742	3,759	3,710	3,719	3,723	3,762	3,777	3,148	3,155	3,185
Unemployment	67c	193	222	215	216	231	233	238	222	194	204	224	240
Unemployment Rate (%)	67r	5.9	6.8	6.5	6.6	7.0	7.1	7.2	6.7	5.8	6.1	6.9	7.0

2004, International Monetary Fund : *International Financial Statistics Yearbook*

Austria 122

		1992	1993	1994	1995	1996	1997	1998	1999	2000	2001	2002	2003
International Transactions		\multicolumn{8}{l}{Billions of Schillings through 1998; Billions of Euros Beginning 1999}				
Exports	70	487.56	467.66	511.89	580.01	612.19	715.02	774.74	†60.27	69.69	74.45	75.05	77.44
Imports, c.i.f.	71	593.92	565.56	629.42	668.03	712.76	790.25	842.13	†65.32	74.94	78.66	77.19	78.10
						1990=100							
Volume of Exports	72	110.8	108.0	....	....	....	....	....	....	....	....	....	....
Volume of Imports	73	106.6	105.8	....	....	....	....	....	....	....	....	....	....
Export Prices	76	94.8	90.6	....	....	....	....	....	....	....	....	....	....
Import Prices	76.x	98.8	95.5	....	....	....	....	....	....	....	....	....	....
Balance of Payments		\multicolumn{12}{l}{Millions of US Dollars: Minus Sign Indicates Debit}
Current Account, n.i.e.	78ald	−753	−1,013	−2,992	−5,448	−4,890	−5,221	−5,258	−6,655	−4,864	−3,636	575	−2,392
Goods: Exports f.o.b.	78aad	44,516	40,271	45,175	57,695	57,937	58,662	63,299	64,422	64,684	66,900	73,667	89,102
Goods: Imports f.o.b.	78abd	−52,205	−46,747	−53,089	−64,352	−65,252	−62,936	−66,983	−68,051	−67,421	−68,169	−70,096	−87,170
Trade Balance	78acd	−7,690	−6,476	−7,914	−6,656	−7,315	−4,274	−3,684	−3,629	−2,737	−1,269	3,572	1,932
Services: Credit	78add	27,326	26,725	28,019	32,211	33,977	29,605	29,759	31,306	31,342	33,352	35,198	43,667
Services: Debit	78aed	−17,956	−19,186	−20,743	−27,703	−29,331	−28,569	−27,398	−29,421	−29,653	−31,437	−34,498	−42,893
Balance on Goods & Services	78afd	1,680	1,064	−639	−2,149	−2,669	−3,239	−1,323	−1,745	−1,048	646	4,272	2,706
Income: Credit	78agd	6,998	7,237	7,074	8,900	9,852	10,393	9,957	12,673	11,992	12,031	13,173	15,358
Income: Debit	78ahd	−8,414	−8,310	−8,344	−10,498	−10,291	−10,682	−11,958	−15,552	−14,456	−15,111	−15,255	−18,136
Balance on Gds, Serv. & Inc.	78aid	264	−9	−1,909	−3,746	−3,107	−3,527	−3,325	−4,624	−3,512	−2,435	2,190	−72
Current Transfers, n.i.e.: Credit	78ajd	1,308	1,266	1,370	2,972	3,145	2,912	2,940	2,925	2,914	3,267	4,004	4,363
Current Transfers: Debit	78akd	−2,326	−2,270	−2,453	−4,674	−4,928	−4,605	−4,874	−4,956	−4,267	−4,468	−5,619	−6,683
Capital Account, n.i.e.	78bcd	−50	−448	−68	−62	78	26	−347	−265	−432	−529	−571	−127
Capital Account, n.i.e.: Credit	78bad	247	246	676	540	591	590	483	555	530	483	815	761
Capital Account: Debit	78bbd	−297	−694	−744	−602	−513	−564	−831	−820	−962	−1,013	−1,386	−887
Financial Account, n.i.e.	78bjd	2,378	3,970	4,311	7,365	5,325	1,666	9,535	4,789	3,407	1,795	−4,950	1,647
Direct Investment Abroad	78bdd	−1,693	−1,189	−1,256	−1,134	−1,848	−1,984	−2,794	−3,306	−5,599	−3,132	−5,501	−7,139
Dir. Invest. in Rep. Econ., n.i.e.	78bed	1,442	1,129	2,117	1,901	4,485	2,624	4,661	3,008	8,523	5,906	886	6,916
Portfolio Investment Assets	78bfd	−2,676	−1,912	−4,475	−2,836	−8,296	−10,157	−11,210	−29,216	−27,145	−10,955	−22,964	−17,604
Equity Securities	78bkd	−178	−618	−842	−545	−1,146	−2,405	−5,280	−5,281	−15,387	35	−3,087	−2,445
Debt Securities	78bld	−2,498	−1,294	−3,633	−2,291	−7,150	−7,752	−5,930	−23,935	−11,757	−10,990	−19,878	−15,160
Portfolio Investment Liab., n.i.e.	78bgd	9,164	7,912	4,253	12,292	5,607	10,956	17,942	26,364	30,360	16,699	18,599	23,516
Equity Securities	78bmd	158	1,182	1,304	1,262	2,652	2,610	1,005	2,131	3,436	−4,538	2,473	2,447
Debt Securities	78bnd	9,006	6,729	2,949	11,030	2,955	8,345	16,937	24,232	26,924	21,237	16,126	21,069
Financial Derivatives Assets	78bwd	7	−20	−85	−133	215	−191	303	−517	−441	−143	−484	−690
Financial Derivatives Liabilities	78bxd	....	....	....	....	....	223	−99	100	254	95	8	−77
Other Investment Assets	78bhd	−7,301	−5,099	−2,545	−9,923	719	−5,208	−690	−11,592	−16,334	−8,680	11,238	−14,575
Monetary Authorities	78bod	....	....	−17	−131	131	—	−115	−3,561	1,760	538	−139	353
General Government	78bpd	259	70	−183	−231	324	−647	−512	331	−1,003	−286	745	−246
Banks	78bqd	−5,955	−5,176	−1,307	−10,848	2,292	−3,873	924	−5,242	−13,593	−6,790	11,979	−13,108
Other Sectors	78brd	−1,605	7	−1,039	1,287	−2,027	−687	−988	−3,121	−3,498	−2,143	−1,347	−1,573
Other Investment Liab., n.i.e.	78bid	3,434	3,149	6,303	7,199	4,442	5,403	1,423	19,948	13,790	2,005	−6,733	11,301
Monetary Authorities	78bsd	—	—	—	—	—	—	−1	6,684	−647	−6,130	−1,443	959
General Government	78btd	242	−492	1,558	467	−715	−319	526	101	157	1,417	−364	44
Banks	78bud	1,887	3,088	4,584	6,077	5,142	5,695	1,695	10,740	11,721	5,812	−9,149	7,933
Other Sectors	78bvd	1,305	553	160	655	15	27	−797	2,422	2,559	905	4,223	2,365
Net Errors and Omissions	78cad	1,013	−308	−417	−464	562	476	−447	−40	1,143	482	3,223	−1,164
Overall Balance	78cbd	2,588	2,201	834	1,391	1,075	−3,053	3,482	−2,172	−746	−1,888	−1,723	−2,036
Reserves and Related Items	79dad	−2,588	−2,201	−834	−1,391	−1,075	3,053	−3,482	2,172	746	1,888	1,723	2,036
Reserve Assets	79dcd	−2,588	−2,201	−834	−1,391	−1,075	3,053	−3,482	2,172	746	1,888	1,723	2,036
Use of Fund Credit and Loans	79dcd	—	—	—	—	—	—	—	—	—	—	—	—
Exceptional Financing	79ded	....	....	....	....	....	....	....	....	....	....	....	....
International Investment Position		\multicolumn{12}{l}{Millions of US Dollars}
Assets	79aad	117,479	122,090	137,955	160,211	161,785	166,135	194,856	225,924	261,554	267,909	331,959	....
Direct Investment Abroad	79abd	6,817	8,112	9,390	11,707	11,868	15,159	18,726	20,458	26,262	29,934	40,788	....
Portfolio Investment	79acd	16,866	17,096	22,673	27,389	33,303	44,051	58,747	93,299	115,680	112,458	152,135	....
Equity Securities	79add	3,435	3,722	4,941	5,868	6,454	11,502	17,225	28,936	42,698	31,190	30,182	....
Debt Securities	79aed	13,431	13,374	17,732	21,521	26,849	32,549	41,522	64,363	72,982	81,268	121,953	....
Financial Derivatives	79ald	—	74	109	169	219	201	—	—	—	—	—	....
Other Investment	79afd	74,696	75,113	82,040	95,054	89,730	84,853	90,959	93,236	101,985	109,906	125,855	....
Monetary Authorities	79agd	—	—	—	—	—	12	189	4,355	2,383	1,765	2,220	....
General Government	79ahd	2,686	2,528	1,021	1,209	1,607	2,039	2,828	2,078	2,853	2,934	2,576	....
Banks	79aid	62,780	62,645	70,380	83,267	77,716	73,651	77,267	74,447	80,897	87,993	99,475	....
Other Sectors	79ajd	9,230	9,940	10,639	10,577	10,407	9,150	10,676	12,357	15,852	17,214	21,584	....
Reserve Assets	79akd	19,099	21,695	23,742	25,893	26,666	21,871	26,423	18,931	17,627	15,611	13,181	....
Liabilities	79lad	127,955	133,600	155,538	189,790	189,264	198,918	236,547	262,994	299,033	315,205	382,285	....
Dir. Invest. in Rep. Economy	79lbd	11,221	11,398	13,246	17,536	18,258	19,694	23,837	23,991	31,280	35,164	42,691	....
Portfolio Investment	79lcd	55,813	61,896	69,469	89,473	87,676	97,091	121,674	139,054	161,082	171,393	224,539	....
Equity Securities	79ldd	2,633	3,591	5,379	6,989	9,056	15,662	15,623	14,745	19,569	14,920	19,510	....
Debt Securities	79led	53,179	58,305	64,090	82,484	78,620	81,430	106,052	124,309	141,512	156,473	205,030	....
Financial Derivatives	79lld	—	—	119	129	110	12	—	—	—	—	—	....
Other Investment	79lfd	60,921	60,306	72,705	82,653	83,221	82,121	91,036	99,949	106,672	108,648	115,054	....
Monetary Authorities	79lgd	—	—	18	20	9	—	—	6,141	5,639	−562	−2,392	....
General Government	79lhd	1,409	1,359	3,045	4,074	3,478	2,955	3,719	3,564	3,412	4,319	4,451	....
Banks	79lid	50,167	49,543	57,681	65,385	68,267	68,669	76,438	79,628	84,906	91,597	93,422	....
Other Sectors	79ljd	9,345	9,405	11,961	13,174	11,466	10,496	10,879	10,616	12,715	13,294	19,574	....

2004, International Monetary Fund: *International Financial Statistics Yearbook*

Austria 122

		1992	1993	1994	1995	1996	1997	1998	1999	2000	2001	2002	2003
Government Finance													
Federal Government		*Billions of Schillings through 1998; Millions of Euros Beginning 1999: Year Ending December 31*											
Deficit (-) or Surplus	80	−75.48	−107.14	−128.81	....	....	....	....	....	....	....	....	....
Revenue	81	747.39	777.75	815.10	†859.52	903.03	951.21	979.97	....	....	....	....	....
Grants Received	81z	3.45	3.59	4.03	†23.93	16.36	6.14	8.46	....	....	....	....	....
Expenditure	82	805.16	875.99	917.14	†993.55	1,013.35	978.86	1,058.29	....	....	....	....	....
Lending Minus Repayments	83	21.16	12.49	30.80	....	....	....	....	....	....	....	....	....
Financing													
Net Borrowing	84	68.09	107.42	136.38	....	....	....	....	....	....	....	....	....
Net Borrowing: Domestic	84a	46.73	82.11	89.13	....	....	....	....	....	....	....	....	....
Net Borrowing: Foreign	85a	21.36	25.31	47.25	....	....	....	....	....	....	....	....	....
Use of Cash Balances	87	7.39	−.28	−7.57	....	....	....	....	....	....	....	....	....
Debt: Domestic	88a	828.70	899.56	975.25	†1,053.73	1,120.66	1,190.76	†1,384.46	....	....	....	....	....
Debt: Foreign	89a	172.14	212.86	260.94	†296.63	296.47	304.93	†188.43	....	....	....	....	....
General Government		*As Percent of Gross Domestic Product*											
Deficit (-) or Surplus	80g	−2.0	−4.2	−5.0	−5.1	−3.8	−1.7	−2.4	−2.2	−1.5	.1	....	....
Debt	88g	58.0	62.7	65.4	69.4	68.3	64.7	63.9	64.9	63.6	61.7	....	....
National Accounts		*Billions of Schillings through 1998; Billions of Euros Beginning 1999*											
House.Cons.Expend.,incl.NPISHs	96f	1,147.7	1,194.1	1,255.1	†1,331.3	1,400.6	1,440.9	1,490.2	†112.0	117.4	121.6	123.9	127.7
Government Consumption Expend	91f	398.3	429.6	455.0	†484.6	497.2	494.5	513.4	†39.0	39.7	40.1	40.7	41.9
Gross Fixed Capital Formation	93e	455.4	455.2	501.6	†552.2	571.2	589.8	615.1	†46.3	49.7	49.3	48.3	51.0
Changes in Inventories	93i	8.2	2.7	−1.1	3.8	.5	41.4	47.4	†1.6	1.7	.7	.4	1.0
Exports of Goods and Services	90c	791.6	786.5	838.8	†903.7	969.9	1,074.3	1,137.7	†89.6	103.9	111.6	115.2	116.2
Imports of Goods and Services (-)	98c	772.0	772.6	843.0	†922.7	997.3	1,113.1	1,153.3	†91.3	105.2	111.0	110.4	115.6
Gross Domestic Product (GDP)	99b	2,057.3	2,125.3	2,237.9	†2,370.7	2,450.0	2,513.5	2,614.7	†197.1	206.7	212.5	218.3	224.1
Net Primary Income from Abroad	98.n	−12.6	−15.6	−18.0	−34.7	−17.2	−26.8	−28.7	−3.0	−3.2	−3.8	−2.0	−2.5
Gross National Income (GNI)	99a	2,037.6	2,111.4	2,242.1	2,338.3	2,428.9	2,528.8	2,617.9	†194.0	203.5	208.7	216.3	221.6
Net Current Transf.from Abroad	98t	....	....	....	....	....	....	....	†−1.1	−.9	−.8	−1.7	−1.6
Gross Nat'l Disposable Inc.(GNDI)	99i	....	....	....	....	....	....	....	†192.9	202.6	207.9	214.6	220.0
Gross Saving	99s	....	....	....	....	....	....	....	†41.8	45.5	46.2	50.0	50.3
Consumption of Fixed Capital	99cf	1,532.1	1,573.5	1,641.6	1,716.3	1,763.5	1,828.6	1,897.4	....	....	....	....	....
GDP Volume 1983 Prices	99b.p	1,556.4	1,564.4	1,601.7	†1,628.7	....	....	....	....	....	....	....	....
GDP Volume 1995 Prices	99b.p	....	....	....	2,370.7	2,418.2	2,450.5	2,530.2	†190.5	197.0	198.5	201.2	202.5
GDP Volume (2000=100)	99bvp	83.6	84.0	86.0	†87.5	89.2	90.4	93.3	†96.7	100.0	100.8	102.1	102.8
GDP Deflator (2000=100)	99bip	86.6	89.0	91.5	†95.3	96.6	97.8	98.5	†98.6	100.0	102.1	103.4	105.5
						Millions: Midyear Estimates							
Population	99z	7.86	7.93	8.00	8.05	8.08	8.09	8.10	8.10	8.10	8.11	8.11	8.12

Azerbaijan 912

		1992	1993	1994	1995	1996	1997	1998	1999	2000	2001	2002	2003
Exchange Rates			*Manats per SDR: End of Period*
Official Rate	aa	66.83	162.08	6,105.09	6,600.02	5,892.76	5,245.88	5,477.24	6,008.85	5,947.78	6,000.89	6,652.13	7,315.43
			*Manats per US Dollar: End of Period (ae) Period Average (rf)*
Official Rate	ae	48.60	118.00	4,182.00	4,440.00	4,098.00	3,888.00	3,890.00	4,378.00	4,565.00	4,775.00	4,893.00	4,923.00
Official Rate	rf	54.20	99.98	1,570.23	4,413.54	4,301.26	3,985.38	3,869.00	4,120.17	4,474.15	4,656.58	4,860.82	4,910.73
Fund Position			*Millions of SDRs: End of Period*
Quota	2f.s	78.00	117.00	117.00	117.00	117.00	117.00	117.00	160.90	160.90	160.90	160.90	160.90
SDRs	1b.s	–	–	–	.84	14.48	4.14	.08	5.15	5.07	1.98	.51	12.14
Reserve Position in the Fund	1c.s	–	.01	.01	.01	.01	.01	.01	.01	.01	.01	.01	.01
Total Fund Cred.&Loans Outstg.	2tl	–	–	–	67.86	121.68	197.73	228.14	296.73	257.73	234.90	205.11	174.47
International Liquidity			*Millions of US Dollars Unless Otherwise Indicated: End of Period*
Total Reserves minus Gold	1l.d	–	.59	2.03	120.88	211.28	466.09	447.33	672.59	679.61	896.70	721.51	820.85
SDRs	1b.d	–	–	–	1.25	20.82	5.59	.11	7.07	6.60	2.49	.70	18.03
Reserve Position in the Fund	1c.d	–	.01	.01	.01	.01	.01	.01	.01	.01	.01	.01	.01
Foreign Exchange	1d.d	–	.58	2.02	119.62	190.45	460.49	447.20	665.50	672.99	894.20	720.80	802.80
Gold (Million Fine Troy Ounces)	1ad	–	–	–	–	–	–	–	–	–	–	–	–
Gold (National Valuation)	1and	–	–	–	–	2.38	1.38	1.37	–	–	–	–	–
Monetary Authorities:Other Assets	3..d	80.06	54.28	1.93	1.57	1.91	1.53	1.16	1.03	.05	–	.17	–
Other Liab.	4..d	124.66	63.09	2.87	1.75	1.33	1.37	13.28	12.34	12.01	.30	1.31	.87
Deposit Money Banks: Assets	7a.d	66.15	257.48	135.30	167.69	156.17	154.48	97.27	152.11	379.46	193.13	211.78	226.59
Liabilities	7b.d	96.79	152.74	41.05	33.95	75.89	53.16	56.08	69.32	96.54	92.58	110.60	109.46
Monetary Authorities			*Billions of Manats: End of Period*
Foreign Assets	11	3.89	6.47	16.59	543.70	883.38	1,823.46	†1,739.58	2,948.81	3,102.63	†4,270.19	3,549.44	3,954.69
Claims on Central Government	12a	2.42	25.73	428.87	333.46	416.73	360.26	†1,903.93	2,563.34	2,518.48	†790.17	722.57	652.74
Claims on Nonfin.Pub.Enterprises	12c	.19	.13	1.02	8.48	8.93	8.76	†3.50	3.44	–	†–	–	–
Claims on Deposit Money Banks	12e	2.63	23.93	141.69	1,052.40	893.67	865.45	†750.15	746.24	701.25	†101.00	86.41	236.58
Reserve Money	14	2.97	43.84	325.69	911.14	1,071.06	1,514.08	†1,181.57	1,369.42	1,767.31	†1,797.40	2,049.62	2,530.55
of which: Currency Outside DMBs	14a	2.72	43.18	276.13	602.40	865.44	1,170.51	†926.05	1,135.84	1,349.81	†1,468.99	1,668.73	2,040.88
Time, Savings,& Fgn.Currency Dep.	15	–	–	.88	–	.03	.04	†–	–	–	†2.05	10.03	53.46
Foreign Liabilities	16c	6.06	7.44	12.02	455.63	722.52	1,042.60	†1,301.25	1,837.03	1,587.77	†1,411.05	1,370.81	1,280.56
Central Government Deposits	16d	.29	5.75	235.86	447.68	334.46	367.65	†1,817.21	2,837.37	2,556.29	†1,488.12	612.61	590.51
Capital Accounts	17a	.09	4.08	44.87	405.19	400.30	1,128.62	†196.15	240.35	333.32	†368.47	324.18	431.81
Other Items (Net)	17r	–.28	–4.85	–31.14	–281.61	–325.66	–995.06	†–99.02	–22.34	77.67	†94.28	–8.83	–42.88
Deposit Money Banks			*Billions of Manats: End of Period*
Reserves	20	.98	6.65	43.89	303.17	242.76	301.94	204.07	177.85	†391.51	†318.49	361.20	491.92
Foreign Assets	21	3.21	30.38	565.81	744.55	639.97	600.62	378.37	665.95	†1,732.24	†922.21	1,036.26	1,115.49
Claims on Central Government	22a	1.69	.33	51.49	12.49	32.03	52.69	30.04	69.44	†275.99	†324.61	366.05	333.57
Claims on Nonfin.Pub.Enterprises	22c	13.95	53.43	623.57	1,403.59	1,719.82	1,635.51	1,658.84	1,722.20	†1,391.76	†1,327.53	468.48	491.92
Claims on Private Sector	22d	2.61	15.08	62.46	126.52	159.32	386.81	530.06	559.69	†3.24	†1.97	1,662.15	2,353.97
Claims on Nonbank Financial Insts.	22g	.01	.02	.06	–	–	–	–	–	†3.24	†1.97	.56	100.64
Demand Deposits	24	3.29	22.00	93.70	251.29	250.08	323.80	203.02	215.83	†218.21	†218.73	292.74	458.18
Time,Savings,& Fgn.Currency Dep.	25	3.23	20.59	674.36	455.53	418.73	651.71	662.47	826.07	†2,273.28	†1,743.55	1,961.90	2,601.40
Restricted Deposits	26b	–	–	–	–	–	–	–	–	†–	†152.01	213.54	167.25
Foreign Liabilities	26c	4.70	18.02	171.66	150.75	311.00	206.69	218.15	303.46	†440.72	†442.07	541.17	538.86
Central Government Deposits	26d	4.70	7.19	101.60	98.20	222.31	30.20	82.23	84.95	†185.40	†51.27	25.88	62.67
Credit from Monetary Authorities	26g	3.99	27.06	56.53	893.23	782.36	838.02	615.87	592.89	†654.22	†96.45	86.31	236.06
Liab. to Nonbank Financial Insts.	26j	.06	.20	.45	2.84	7.44	6.84	5.55	2.17	†–	†15.87	27.36	105.62
Capital Accounts	27a	1.16	12.84	121.45	355.30	640.98	831.83	1,020.01	1,152.11	†732.21	†670.34	790.98	898.05
Other Items (Net)	27r	1.32	–2.02	127.51	383.18	160.99	88.51	–5.92	17.67	†108.32	†1.15	–45.17	–180.57
Monetary Survey			*Billions of Manats: End of Period*
Foreign Assets (Net)	31n	–3.66	11.39	398.73	681.87	489.83	1,174.80	†598.55	1,474.27	†2,806.39	†3,339.29	2,673.73	3,250.76
Domestic Credit	32	15.88	81.77	830.00	1,338.66	1,780.06	2,046.19	†2,226.93	1,995.80	†2,265.39	†1,401.51	2,581.69	3,281.87
Claims on Central Govt. (Net)	32an	–.88	13.12	142.89	–199.93	–108.00	15.11	†34.53	–289.53	†52.78	†–424.60	450.13	333.12
Claims on Nonfin.Pub.Enterprises	32c	14.14	53.56	624.59	1,412.07	1,728.75	1,644.27	†1,662.34	1,725.64	†817.62	†496.61	468.48	491.92
Claims on Private Sector	32d	2.61	15.08	62.46	126.52	159.32	386.81	†530.06	559.69	†1,391.76	†1,327.53	1,662.52	2,356.19
Claims on Nonbank Fin. Insts.	32g	.01	.02	.06	–	–	–	†–	–	†3.24	†1.97	.56	100.64
Money	34	6.07	65.52	372.38	858.38	1,119.74	1,524.08	†1,183.26	1,390.08	†1,569.81	†1,693.10	1,967.27	2,499.09
Quasi-Money	35	3.24	20.59	675.23	455.53	418.76	651.75	†662.47	826.07	†2,273.28	†1,745.60	1,971.93	2,654.85
Restricted Deposits	36b	–	–	–	–	–	–	†–	–	†–	†152.01	213.54	167.25
Liab. to Nonbank Financial Insts.	36j	.06	.20	.45	2.84	7.44	6.84	†5.55	2.17	†–	†15.87	27.36	105.62
Capital Accounts	37a	1.24	16.92	166.33	760.50	1,041.28	1,960.45	†1,216.16	1,392.46	†1,065.53	†1,038.81	1,115.16	1,329.86
Other Items (Net)	37r	1.62	–10.07	14.34	–56.72	–317.33	–922.14	†–241.95	–140.72	†163.16	†95.42	–39.84	–224.04
Money plus Quasi-Money	35l	9.30	86.11	1,047.62	1,313.92	1,538.50	2,175.83	†1,845.73	2,216.15	†3,843.09	†3,438.71	3,939.20	5,153.95
Money (National Definitions)			*Billions of Manats: End of Period*
Reserve Money	19ma	....	....	....	736.30	985.40	1,339.30	1,057.10	1,256.60	1,541.90	1,680.60	1,871.90	2,316.00
M1	59ma	....	....	....	924.99	1,173.68	1,537.82	1,202.45	1,390.04	1,609.50	1,469.00	1,967.40	2,499.10
M2	59mb	....	....	....	957.59	1,204.18	1,556.27	1,218.50	1,404.32	1,661.10	1,687.50	2,032.10	2,592.20

2004, International Monetary Fund : *International Financial Statistics Yearbook*

Azerbaijan 912

		1992	1993	1994	1995	1996	1997	1998	1999	2000	2001	2002	2003
Interest Rates						*Percent Per Annum*							
Refinancing Rate	60	12.00	100.00	200.00	80.00	20.00	12.00	14.00	10.00	10.00	10.00	7.00	7.00
Treasury Bill Rate	60c	....	....	....	....	....	12.23	14.10	18.31	16.73	16.51	14.12	8.00
Deposit Rate	60l	....	....	....	....	....	....	....	12.08	12.90	8.46	8.66	9.54
Deposit Rate (Foreign Currency)	60l.f	....	....	....	....	....	....	....	10.75	11.12	9.51	9.34	8.83
Lending Rate	60p	....	....	....	....	....	....	....	19.48	19.66	19.71	17.37	15.46
Lending Rate (Foreign Currency)	60p.f	....	....	....	....	....	....	....	16.27	17.98	18.67	18.69	18.64
Prices and Labor						*Percent Change over Previous Period*							
Consumer Prices	64.xx	912.3	1,129.0	1,664.5	411.7	19.8	3.6	–.7	–8.6	1.8	1.5	2.8	....
						Number in Thousands: Period Averages							
Employment	67e	3,722.0	3,714.6	3,631.3	3,613.0	3,686.7	3,694.1	3,701.5	3,702.8	3,704.5	3,715.0	....	....
Unemployment	67c	....	19.5	23.6	28.3	31.9	38.3	42.3	45.2	43.7	....	....	....
Unemployment Rate (%)	67r	....	.5	.7	.8	.9	1.0	1.1	1.2	1.2	....	....	....
International Transactions						*Millions of US Dollars*							
Exports	70..d	1,484.0	724.7	652.7	637.2	631.2	781.3	606.2	929.7	1,745.2	2,314.3	....	....
Imports, cif	71..d	939.9	628.8	777.9	667.7	960.6	794.3	1,076.5	1,035.9	1,172.1	1,430.9	....	....
Balance of Payments						*Millions of US Dollars: Minus Sign Indicates Debit*							
Current Account, n.i.e	78ald	....	....	....	–400.7	–931.2	–915.8	–1,364.5	–599.7	–167.8	–51.8	–768.4	–2,020.9
Goods: Exports f.o.b	78aad	....	....	....	612.3	643.7	808.3	677.8	1,025.2	1,858.3	2,078.9	2,304.9	2,624.6
Goods: Imports f.o.b	78abd	....	....	....	–985.4	–1,337.6	–1,375.2	–1,723.9	–1,433.4	–1,539.0	–1,465.1	–1,823.3	–2,723.1
Trade Balance	78acd	....	....	....	–373.1	–693.9	–566.9	–1,046.2	–408.2	319.3	613.9	481.6	–98.5
Services: Credit	78add	....	....	....	172.4	149.3	341.8	331.7	256.8	259.8	289.8	362.1	432.0
Services: Debit	78aed	....	....	....	–304.6	–440.9	–726.0	–700.8	–485.1	–484.5	–664.9	–1,297.7	–2,046.5
Balance on Goods & Services	78afd	....	....	....	–505.4	–985.6	–951.1	–1,415.2	–636.5	94.6	238.8	–454.0	–1,713.0
Income: Credit	78agd	....	....	....	9.9	15.1	22.8	38.3	11.0	55.9	41.5	37.1	52.6
Income: Debit	78ahd	....	....	....	–16.0	–27.2	–32.3	–51.6	–56.0	–391.4	–408.7	–421.8	–494.7
Balance on Gds, Serv., & Inc.	78aid	....	....	....	–511.4	–997.7	–960.6	–1,428.5	–681.5	–240.9	–128.4	–838.7	–2,155.0
Current Transfers, n.i.e.: Credit	78ajd	....	....	....	129.3	107.2	95.7	145.0	134.5	135.0	176.5	228.2	225.1
Current Transfers: Debit	78akd	....	....	....	–18.5	–40.7	–50.9	–80.9	–52.8	–62.0	–99.9	–157.9	–90.9
Capital Account, n.i.e	78bcd	....	....	....	–1.6	–	–10.2	–.7	....	....	....	–28.7	–23.1
Capital Account, n.i.e.: Credit	78bad	....	....	....	....	....	....	....	....	....	....	18.4	15.0
Capital Account: Debit	78bbd	....	....	....	–1.6	....	–10.2	–.7	....	....	....	–47.1	–38.1
Financial Account, n.i.e	78bjd	....	....	....	400.3	822.5	1,092.1	1,326.0	690.2	493.4	126.0	918.7	2,279.7
Direct Investment Abroad	78bdd	....	....	....	–	–	–	–	–	–.8	–	–325.6	–933.3
Dir. Invest. in Rep. Econ., n.i.e	78bed	....	....	....	330.1	627.3	1,114.8	1,023.0	510.3	129.9	226.5	1,392.4	3,285.0
Portfolio Investment Assets	78bfd	....	....	....	–1.7	–	1.1	–	....	....	....	.4	–
Equity Securities	78bkd	....	....	....	....	....	....	....	....	....	....	....	....
Debt Securities	78bld	....	....	....	–1.7	....	1.1	–	....	....	....	.4	–
Portfolio Investment Liab., n.i.e	78bgd	....	....	....	–	–	–	.4	....	....	....	....	....
Equity Securities	78bmd	....	....	....	....	....	....	....	....	....	....	....	....
Debt Securities	78bnd	....	....	....	–	–	–	.4	....	....	....	....	....
Financial Derivatives Assets	78bwd	....	....	....	....	....	....	....	....	....	....	....	....
Financial Derivatives Liabilities	78bxd	....	....	....	....	....	....	....	....	....	....	....	–
Other Investment Assets	78bhd	....	....	....	–22.1	–216.8	–102.6	22.3	–81.0	–114.2	–394.0	–302.9	–169.2
Monetary Authorities	78bod	....	....	....	....	....	....	....	....	....	....	....	....
General Government	78bpd	....	....	....	....	....	....	....	....	....	–220.5	–200.7	–109.4
Banks	78bqd	....	....	....	–19.6	–136.9	5.3	62.4	–44.2	7.1	–77.7	–18.3	–16.7
Other Sectors	78brd	....	....	....	–2.5	–79.8	–107.9	–40.1	–36.8	–121.2	–95.8	–83.9	–43.2
Other Investment Liab., n.i.e	78bid	....	....	....	94.1	412.0	78.8	280.4	260.9	478.4	293.5	154.4	97.2
Monetary Authorities	78bsd	....	....	....	–	–	–	–	–	–	–	–	–
General Government	78btd	....	....	....	30.0	–	70.8	75.6	161.6	246.2	138.6	30.3	34.4
Banks	78bud	....	....	....	–.3	26.5	–18.8	–1.7	–.1	–22.9	3.0	17.2	32.4
Other Sectors	78bvd	....	....	....	64.3	385.5	26.8	206.5	99.3	255.0	151.9	16.9	–.2
Net Errors and Omissions	78cad	....	....	....	59.7	23.6	–27.0	–20.1	42.4	–	–.9	90.0	30.5
Overall Balance	78cbd	....	....	....	57.8	–85.0	139.2	–59.2	132.9	325.6	73.4	–87.4	–111.8
Reserves and Related Items	79dad	....	....	....	–57.8	85.0	–139.2	59.2	–132.9	–325.6	–73.4	34.2	123.8
Reserve Assets	79dbd	....	....	....	–161.6	7.1	–244.2	18.7	–228.5	–274.2	–44.1	–34.2	–123.8
Use of Fund Credit and Loans	79dcd	....	....	....	103.8	77.9	105.0	40.5	95.6	–51.4	–29.3	5.0	–82.0
Exceptional Financing	79ded	....	....	....	....	....	....	....	....	....	....	–39.2	–41.8

Azerbaijan 912

		1992	1993	1994	1995	1996	1997	1998	1999	2000	2001	2002	2003
International Investment Position							*Millions of US Dollars*						
Assets	79aad	....	....	....	....	....	....	....	....	....	....	2,084.8	3,185.3
Direct Investment Abroad	79abd	....	....	....	....	....	....	....	....	–	.8	.8	326.4	1,259.7
Portfolio Investment	79acd	....	....	....	....	....	....	....	–	–	–	.4	.4
Equity Securities	79add	....	....	....	....	....	....	....	....	....	–	–	–
Debt Securities	79aed	....	....	....	....	....	....	....	....	....	–	.4	.4
Financial derivatives	79ald	....	....	....	....	....	....	....	....	....	....	....	....
Other Investment	79afd	....	....	....	....	....	....	....	385.1	282.4	827.5	1,037.5	1,122.4
Monetary Authorities	79agd	....	....	....	....	....	....	....	....	....	–	–	–
General Government	79ahd	....	....	....	....	....	....	....	....	....	491.5	692.2	801.6
Banks	79aid	....	....	....	....	....	....	....	....	....	190.7	209.3	225.6
Other Sectors	79ajd	....	....	....	....	....	....	....	....	....	145.3	136.0	95.2
Reserve Assets	79akd	....	....	....	....	....	....	....	675.8	950.8	725.4	720.5	802.8
Liabilities	79lad	....	....	....	....	....	....	....	....	....	....	7,221.9	10,733.7
Dir. Invest. in Rep. Economy	79lbd	....	....	....	....	....	....	....	3,099.5	3,735.2	3,961.7	5,354.1	8,639.1
Portfolio Investment	79lcd	....	....	....	....	....	....	....	–	–	–	–	–
Equity Securities	79ldd	....	....	....	....	....	....	....	....	....	–	–	–
Debt Securities	79led	....	....	....	....	....	....	....	....	....	–	–	–
Financial Derivatives	79lld	....	....	....	....	....	....	....	....	....	....	–	–
Other Investment	79lfd	....	....	....	....	....	....	....	1,616.4	1,497.1	1,797.9	1,867.8	2,094.6
Monetary Authorities	79lgd	....	....	....	....	....	....	....	....	....	446.9	453.9	476.9
General Government	79lhd	....	....	....	....	....	....	....	....	....	56.8	87.3	131.4
Banks	79lid	....	....	....	....	....	....	....	....	....	98.2	115.2	112.5
Other Sectors	79ljd	....	....	....	....	....	....	....	....	....	1,196.0	1,211.4	1,373.8
Government Finance						*Billions of Manats: Year Ending December 31*							
Deficit(-)/ or Surplus	80	....	....	–209.21	–545.03	–405.89	–341.84	–623.00	–479.46	....	....	....	....
Total Revenue and Grants	81y	....	....	479.70	1,920.25	1,960.77	2,402.03	3,143.02	3,380.17	....	....	....	....
Revenue	81	....	....	479.70	1,920.25	1,881.02	2,350.03	3,076.02	3,316.97	....	....	....	....
Grants	81z	....	....	–	–	79.76	52.00	67.00	63.20	....	....	....	....
Exp. & Lending Minus Repay	82z	....	....	688.91	2,465.27	2,366.67	2,743.88	3,766.02	3,859.64	....	....	....	....
Expenditure	82	....	....	688.91	2,254.33	2,283.64	3,028.57	3,993.14	4,260.94	....	....	....	....
Lending Minus Repayments	83	....	....	–	210.94	83.03	–284.70	–227.12	–401.31	....	....	....	....
Total Financing	80h	....	....	209.21	545.03	405.90	341.84	623.00	479.46	....	....	....	....
						Millions: Midyear Estimates							
Population	99z	7.44	7.57	7.68	7.79	7.88	7.96	8.03	8.09	8.16	8.23	8.30	8.37

2004, International Monetary Fund : *International Financial Statistics Yearbook*

Bahamas, The 313

		1992	1993	1994	1995	1996	1997	1998	1999	2000	2001	2002	2003
Exchange Rates			*Bahamian Dollars per SDR: End of Period*
Principal Rate........aa=.......	wa	1.3750	1.3736	1.4599	1.4865	1.4380	1.3493	1.4080	1.3725	1.3029	1.2567	1.3595	1.4860
			*Bahamian Dollars per US Dollar: End of Period (we and xe) Period Average (xf)*
Principal Rate........ae=.......	we	1.0000	1.0000	1.0000	1.0000	1.0000	1.0000	1.0000	1.0000	1.0000	1.0000	1.0000	1.0000
Secondary Rate....................	xe	1.2250	1.2250	1.2250	1.2250	1.2250	1.2250	1.2250	1.2250	1.2250	1.2250	1.2250	1.2250
Secondary Rate....................	xf	1.2250	1.2250	1.2250	1.2250	1.2250	1.2250	1.2250	1.2250	1.2250	1.2250	1.2250	1.2250
			*Index Numbers (2000=100): Period Averages*
Principal Rate....................	ahx	100.0	100.0	100.0	100.0	100.0	100.0	100.0	100.0	100.0	100.0	100.0	100.0
Nominal Effective Exchange Rate......	nec	86.6	89.8	88.2	87.9	89.8	93.0	94.8	97.2	100.0	102.8	102.0	97.4
Real Effective Exchange Rate..........	rec	95.9	97.7	94.2	91.0	91.5	93.5	95.2	97.4	100.0	102.5	102.8	99.3
Fund Position			*Millions of SDRs: End of Period*
Quota.................................	2f.s	94.9	94.9	94.9	94.9	94.9	94.9	94.9	130.3	130.3	130.3	130.3	130.3
SDRs..................................	1b.s	–	–	–	–	–	–	–	–	.1	.1	.1	–
Reserve Position in the Fund...........	1c.s	6.8	6.2	6.2	6.2	6.2	6.2	6.2	6.2	6.2	6.2	6.2	6.2
Total Fund Cred.&Loans Outstg.......	2tl	–	–	–	–	–	–	–	–	–	–	–	–
International Liquidity			*Millions of US Dollars Unless Otherwise Indicated: End of Period*
Total Reserves minus Gold..........	1l.d	155.3	172.3	176.6	179.2	171.4	227.0	346.5	410.5	349.6	319.3	380.6	491.1
SDRs..................................	1b.d	–	–	–	–	–	–	–	–	.1	.1	.1	–
Reserve Position in the Fund..........	1c.d	9.4	8.6	9.1	9.3	9.0	8.4	8.8	8.6	8.1	7.8	8.5	9.3
Foreign Exchange....................	1d.d	145.9	163.7	167.5	169.9	162.4	218.6	337.7	401.9	341.4	311.3	372.1	481.8
Deposit Money Banks: Assets.........	7a.d	32,319	35,688	42,817	35,144	41,384	41,310	46,329	58,682	77,649	103,669	136,339	89,838
Liabilities...........	7b.d	33,951	35,958	43,219	35,542	41,796	41,662	47,053	59,127	78,346	104,136	136,804	90,451
Other Banking Insts.: Assets...........	7e.d	2,266	1,911	2,232	2,450	2,646	2,836	2,685	2,785	2,907	2,293	2,490	2,411
Liabilities...........	7f.d	1,988	1,541	1,802	1,881	2,084	2,384	2,498	2,626	2,644	2,036	2,130	2,077
Branches of US Banks: Assets..........	7k.d	87,983	87,620	....	....	....	....	....	....	....	....	....	....
Liab...........	7m.d	90,049	89,058	....	....	....	....	....	....	....	....	....	....
Monetary Authorities			*Millions of Bahamian Dollars: End of Period*
Foreign Assets........................	11	144	163	170	171	163	219	339	404	343	312	373	484
Claims on Central Government.........	12a	137	115	144	149	153	141	62	73	129	190	182	115
Claims on Deposit Money Banks......	12e	1	–	–	–	–	1	–	–	–	–	–	–
Claims on Nonbank Financial Insts...	12g	2	3	3	4	3	4	5	8	9	8	8	8
Reserve Money....................	14	206	205	230	236	230	264	315	381	373	411	459	489
of which: Currency Outside DMBs..	14a	84	84	89	93	97	110	126	149	152	154	155	160
Central Government Deposits..........	16d	7	3	14	8	8	17	4	14	11	9	12	24
Capital Accounts.....................	17a	72	74	77	78	80	84	87	90	98	95	97	96
Other Items (Net).....................	17r	–2	–1	–3	2	2	1	–	–	–1	–5	–5	–2
Deposit Money Banks			*Millions of Bahamian Dollars: End of Period*
Reserves.............................	20	101	105	123	128	118	146	183	226	208	250	292	318
Foreign Assets.......................	21	32,319	35,688	42,817	35,144	41,384	41,310	46,329	58,682	77,649	103,669	136,339	89,838
Claims on Central Government........	22a	225	330	296	303	313	356	458	489	454	493	547	487
Claims on Official Entities.............	22bx	106	89	73	77	82	79	128	158	126	133	203	347
Claims on Private Sector.............	22d	1,215	1,400	1,592	1,777	1,953	2,488	2,767	3,072	3,511	3,782	3,926	3,948
Claims on Other Banking Insts.........	22f	6	11	20	18	16	27	29	25	33	54	65	65
Demand Deposits....................	24	274	280	309	336	334	398	460	588	630	605	644	714
Time, Savings,& Fgn.Currency Dep...	25	1,000	1,221	1,326	1,447	1,551	1,950	2,275	2,423	2,668	2,870	2,934	2,999
Bonds...............................	26ab	10	18	7	7	5	3	1	4	1	5	5	1
Foreign Liabilities....................	26c	33,951	35,958	43,219	35,542	41,796	41,662	47,053	59,127	78,346	104,136	136,804	90,451
Central Government Deposits..........	26d	29	30	36	44	59	65	66	68	71	58	72	94
Credit from Monetary Authorities.....	26g	1	–	–	–	–	1	–	1	1	1	1	1
Liabilities to Other Banking Insts......	26i	30	29	27	40	43	43	42	34	37	48	43	43
Capital Accounts....................	27a	–1,332	79	–16	13	41	271	–9	432	266	678	921	971
Other Items (Net).....................	27r	8	8	14	21	38	13	5	–25	–38	–20	–53	–271
Monetary Survey			*Millions of Bahamian Dollars: End of Period*
Foreign Assets (Net).................	31n	–1,488	–107	–231	–227	–248	–133	–385	–41	–355	–154	–92	–129
Domestic Credit.....................	32	1,654	1,914	2,078	2,277	2,454	3,014	3,379	3,743	4,180	4,594	4,847	4,852
Claims on Central Govt. (Net).........	32an	326	412	390	401	399	415	450	481	501	617	646	485
Claims on Official Entities.............	32bx	106	89	73	77	82	79	128	158	126	133	203	347
Claims on Private Sector.............	32d	1,215	1,400	1,592	1,777	1,953	2,488	2,767	3,072	3,511	3,782	3,926	3,948
Claims on Other Banking Insts.......	32f	6	11	20	18	16	27	29	25	33	54	65	65
Claims on Nonbank Financial Inst..	32g	2	3	3	4	3	4	5	8	9	8	8	8
Money..............................	34	380	382	416	445	447	517	593	748	798	767	811	884
Quasi-Money........................	35	1,000	1,221	1,326	1,447	1,551	1,950	2,275	2,423	2,668	2,870	2,934	2,999
Bonds...............................	36ab	10	18	7	7	5	3	1	4	1	5	5	1
Liabilities to Other Banking Insts......	36i	30	29	27	40	43	43	42	34	37	48	43	43
Capital Accounts....................	37a	–1,260	152	60	91	120	355	78	523	364	773	1,018	1,068
Other Items (Net).....................	37r	5	5	9	22	39	13	5	–30	–42	–23	–56	–271
Money plus Quasi-Money..............	35l	1,380	1,603	1,743	1,892	1,998	2,467	2,868	3,171	3,466	3,637	3,745	3,883

Bahamas, The 313

		1992	1993	1994	1995	1996	1997	1998	1999	2000	2001	2002	2003
Other Banking Institutions		*Millions of Bahamian Dollars End of Period*											
Reserves............................	40	17	13	13	13	13	3	3	4	5	4	5	6
Foreign Assets..................	41	2,266	1,911	2,232	2,450	2,646	2,836	2,685	2,785	2,907	2,293	2,490	2,411
Claims on Central Government.......	42a	34	24	22	22	22	3	3	4	4	3	3	4
Claims on Private Sector..............	42d	364	268	267	283	297	63	69	87	108	120	144	147
Claims on Deposit Money Banks......	42e	30	25	27	32	43	45	43	59	32	47	40	46
Demand Deposits...............	44	9	8	8	11	12	4	5	5	8	8	9	12
Time, Savings,& Fgn.Currency Dep...	45	326	245	243	248	260	39	41	66	78	71	84	97
Foreign Liabilities............	46c	1,988	1,541	1,802	1,881	2,084	2,384	2,498	2,626	2,644	2,036	2,130	2,077
Central Government Deposits.........	46d	3	—	—	—	—	—	—	—	—	—	—	—
Credit from Monetary Authorities.....	46g	—	—	—	—	—	10	15	—	10	—	—	—
Credit from Deposit Money Banks....	46h	1	4	13	11	12	23	26	17	25	46	56	48
Capital Accounts...............	47a	302	316	323	323	292	253	233	255	320	360	407	386
Other Items (Net)............	47r	81	126	172	328	362	237	−14	−28	−28	−53	−5	−6
Banking Survey		*Millions of Bahamian Dollars: End of Period*											
Foreign Assets (Net)............	51n	−1,210	262	198	343	314	319	−198	119	−92	103	269	205
Domestic Credit..................	52	2,044	2,195	2,346	2,564	2,757	3,053	3,423	3,809	4,259	4,663	4,929	4,938
Claims on Central Govt. (Net)........	52an	356	435	412	423	421	419	453	485	506	620	649	489
Claims on Official Entities............	52bx	106	89	73	77	82	79	128	158	126	133	203	347
Claims on Private Sector.............	52d	1,580	1,668	1,859	2,060	2,250	2,551	2,837	3,159	3,619	3,902	4,070	4,095
Claims on Nonbank Financial Inst..	52g	2	3	3	4	3	4	5	8	9	8	8	8
Liquid Liabilities................	55l	1,699	1,844	1,981	2,137	2,256	2,507	2,911	3,238	3,547	3,711	3,834	3,986
Bonds............................	56ab	10	18	7	7	5	3	1	4	1	5	5	1
Capital Accounts.............	57a	−958	468	384	413	413	608	311	778	684	1,133	1,426	1,453
Other Items (Net)............	57r	82	128	174	349	397	254	1	−91	−65	−83	−67	−297
Interest Rates		*Percent Per Annum*											
Bank Rate (End of Period).............	60	7.50	7.00	6.50	6.50	6.50	6.50	6.50	5.75	5.75	5.75	5.75	5.75
Treasury Bill Rate.............	60c	5.32	3.96	1.88	3.01	4.45	4.35	3.84	1.97	1.03	1.94	2.50	1.78
Savings Rate................	60k	4.32	3.79	3.34	3.15	3.30	3.65	3.72	3.31	3.07	3.03	2.77	2.66
Deposit Rate..................	60l	6.13	5.19	4.30	4.20	5.14	5.23	5.36	4.57	4.08	4.25	4.25	3.95
Lending Rate................	60p	8.08	7.46	6.88	6.75	6.75	6.75	6.75	6.38	6.00	6.00	6.00	6.00
Prices, Production, Labor		*Index Numbers (2000=100): Period Averages*											
Consumer Prices.................	64	88.5	90.9	92.2	†94.1	95.4	95.9	97.2	98.4	100.0	102.0	104.3	107.4
Tourist Arrivals..................	66t	87.8	86.1	81.4	77.0	81.1	82.0	78.4	86.7	100.0	99.5	104.8	109.3
		Number in Thousands: Period Averages											
Labor Force..................	67d	135	....	137	....	....	....	296	....	....	153	153	155
Employment...................	67e	115	119	120	127	130	135	144	145	....	....	....	....
Unemployment...............	67c	20	18	18	16	17	15	12	....	....	....	....	....
Unemployment Rate (%).........	67r	14.8	13.1	13.3	10.9	11.5	9.8	7.7	....	....	....	....	....
International Transactions		*Millions of Bahamian Dollars*											
Exports..............................	70	192	162	167	176	180	181	300	462	576	423	446	425
Imports, c.i.f.....................	71	1,038	954	1,056	1,243	1,366	1,666	1,873	1,757	2,074	1,912	1,728	1,762

2004, International Monetary Fund : *International Financial Statistics Yearbook*

Bahamas, The 313

Balance of Payments

Millions of US Dollars: Minus Sign Indicates Debit

		1992	1993	1994	1995	1996	1997	1998	1999	2000	2001	2002	2003
Current Account, n.i.e.	78ald	35.8	48.7	−42.2	−145.9	−263.3	−472.1	−995.4	−671.9	−471.3	−348.0	....	....
Goods: Exports f.o.b.	78aad	216.6	192.2	198.5	225.4	273.3	295.0	362.9	379.9	805.3	614.1	....	....
Goods: Imports f.o.b.	78abd	−984.3	−930.2	−1,013.8	−1,156.7	−1,287.4	−1,410.7	−1,737.1	−1,808.1	−2,176.4	−1,764.7	....	....
Trade Balance	78acd	−767.7	−738.0	−815.3	−931.3	−1,014.1	−1,115.7	−1,374.2	−1,428.2	−1,371.1	−1,150.6	....	....
Services: Credit	78add	1,389.6	1,459.0	1,510.6	1,542.3	1,578.2	1,592.9	1,533.0	1,811.2	2,036.6	1,889.7	....	....
Services: Debit	78aed	−515.5	−567.7	−627.2	−639.1	−715.8	−836.0	−990.9	−953.8	−1,007.2	−939.1	....	....
Balance on Goods & Services	78afd	106.4	153.3	68.1	−28.1	−151.7	−358.8	−832.1	−570.8	−341.7	−200.0	....	....
Income: Credit	78agd	103.3	112.2	61.2	75.1	84.6	105.7	147.9	229.6	212.0	94.0	....	....
Income: Debit	78ahd	−185.9	−240.6	−198.8	−210.8	−233.4	−258.3	−345.4	−367.2	−385.0	−283.8	....	....
Balance on Gds, Serv. & Inc.	78aid	23.8	24.9	−69.5	−163.8	−300.5	−511.4	−1,029.6	−708.4	−514.7	−389.8	....	....
Current Transfers, n.i.e.: Credit	78ajd	19.9	33.1	33.1	25.1	45.9	50.0	45.0	49.0	53.8	52.7	....	....
Current Transfers: Debit	78akd	−7.9	−9.3	−5.8	−7.2	−8.7	−10.7	−10.8	−12.5	−10.5	−10.9	....	....
Capital Account, n.i.e.	78bcd	−9.8	−9.4	−11.6	−12.5	−24.4	−12.9	−11.7	−14.5	−16.4	−20.3	....	....
Capital Account, n.i.e.: Credit	78bad	−	−	−	−	−	−	−	−	−	−	....	....
Capital Account: Debit	78bbd	−9.8	−9.4	−11.6	−12.5	−24.4	−12.9	−11.7	−14.5	−16.4	−20.3	....	....
Financial Account, n.i.e.	78bjd	−4.4	9.3	66.8	104.6	181.1	412.0	817.7	611.4	429.3	279.8	....	....
Direct Investment Abroad	78bdd	−.3	−.1	.1	−.1	.3	−.4	−1.0	−.2	−	−	....	....
Dir. Invest. in Rep. Econ., n.i.e.	78bed	.3	27.1	23.4	106.8	87.8	210.0	146.9	144.6	249.7	100.8	....	....
Portfolio Investment Assets	78bfd	....	....	....	....	....	....	....	....	....	....	....	....
Equity Securities	78bkd	....	....	....	....	....	....	....	....	....	....	....	....
Debt Securities	78bld	....	....	....	....	....	....	....	....	....	....	....	....
Portfolio Investment Liab., n.i.e.	78bgd	....	....	....	....	....	....	....	....	....	....	....	....
Equity Securities	78bmd	....	....	....	....	....	....	....	....	....	....	....	....
Debt Securities	78bnd	....	....	....	....	....	....	....	....	....	....	....	....
Financial Derivatives Assets	78bwd	....	....	....	....	....	....	....	....	....	....	....	....
Financial Derivatives Liabilities	78bxd	....	....	....	....	....	....	....	....	....	....	....	....
Other Investment Assets	78bhd	−5,520.5	−3,009.4	−7,455.9	7,436.6	−6,428.8	−80.7	−4,872.0	−12,487.1	−19,067.2	−25,411.7	....	....
Monetary Authorities	78bod	−	−	−	−	−	−	−	−	−	−	....	....
General Government	78bpd	−	−	−	−	−	−	−	−	−	−	....	....
Banks	78bqd	−5,520.5	−3,009.4	−7,455.9	7,436.6	−6,428.8	−80.7	−4,872.0	−12,487.1	−19,067.2	−25,411.7	....	....
Other Sectors	78brd	−	−	−	−	−	−	−	−	−	−	....	....
Other Investment Liab., n.i.e.	78bid	5,516.1	2,991.7	7,499.2	−7,438.7	6,521.8	283.1	5,543.8	12,954.1	19,246.9	25,590.7	....	....
Monetary Authorities	78bsd	−	−	−	−	−	−	−	−	−	−	....	....
General Government	78btd	−4.7	−16.4	−5.8	−26.9	−25.2	19.2	−5.9	11.7	−11.2	....	....	....
Banks	78bud	5,474.1	3,010.7	7,459.6	−7,417.9	6,451.8	141.9	4,901.8	12,578.9	19,039.1	25,533.1	....	....
Other Sectors	78bvd	46.7	−2.6	45.4	6.1	95.2	122.0	647.9	363.5	218.9	57.6	....	....
Net Errors and Omissions	78cad	−49.6	−30.0	−3.9	50.9	99.0	129.5	308.6	140.2	−2.6	58.6	....	....
Overall Balance	78cbd	−28.0	18.6	9.1	−2.9	−7.6	56.5	119.2	65.2	−61.0	−29.9	....	....
Reserves and Related Items	79dad	28.0	−18.6	−9.1	2.9	7.6	−56.5	−119.2	−65.2	61.0	29.9	....	....
Reserve Assets	79dbd	28.0	−18.6	−9.1	2.9	7.6	−56.5	−119.2	−65.2	61.0	29.9	....	....
Use of Fund Credit and Loans	79dcd	−	−	−	−	−	−	−	−	−	−	....	....
Exceptional Financing	79ded	....	....	....	....	....	....	....	....	....	....	....	....

Government Finance

Millions of Bahamian Dollars: Year Ending December 31

		1992	1993	1994	1995	1996	1997	1998	1999	2000	2001	2002	2003
Deficit (-) or Surplus	80	−88.1	† −85.1	−20.0	−23.2	−63.5	−136.3	−80.9	−51.7	−14.3	−95.2	−134.3	−207.9
Revenue	81	534.6	† 537.1	618.2	660.2	685.8	728.1	760.9	868.8	937.2	920.2	888.9	901.8
Grants Received	81z	....	....	....	....	.5	.5						
Expenditure	82	597.8	† 584.0	604.5	657.3	719.7	829.4	806.4	885.2	917.7	955.9	1,018.2	1,067.7
Lending Minus Repayments	83	24.9	† 38.2	33.7	26.1	30.1	35.5	35.4	35.3	33.8	59.5	5.0	42.0
Financing													
Net Borrowing: Domestic	84a	85.0	† 93.8	47.3	10.1	94.8	130.4	72.1	38.2	16.8	65.8	167.1	30.8
Net borrowing: Foreign	85a	−4.7	† −14.6	−9.6	14.8	−13.7	19.4	−3.1	11.4	5.5	7.3	−21.6	196.0
Use of Cash Balances	87	7.8	† 5.9	−17.7	−1.7	−17.5	−14.3	11.5	1.7	−8.0	22.1	−11.3	−18.8
Debt: Domestic	88a	777.1	† 954.1	1,032.9	1,074.9	1,158.0	1,281.7	1,342.7	1,407.9	1,404.1	1,486.1	1,710.5	1,647.6
Debt: Foreign	89a	125.2	† 110.6	100.4	90.9	77.0	96.4	93.2	104.7	110.2	117.5	96.1	293.1

National Accounts

Millions of Bahamian Dollars

		1992	1993	1994	1995	1996	1997	1998	1999	2000	2001	2002	2003
Househ.Cons.Expend.,incl.NPISHs	96f	1,938.2	1,986.0	2,054.1	2,077.4	....	....	....	....	....	....	....	....
Government Consumption Expend.	91f	434.7	408.4	511.0	483.9	....	....	....	....	....	....	....	....
Gross Fixed Capital Formation	93e	650.3	526.4	614.0	698.5	....	....	....	....	....	....	....	....
Changes in Inventories	93i	13.0	32.8	32.4	13.8	....	....	....	....	....	....	....	....
Exports of Goods and Services	90c	1,462.3	1,517.4	1,569.3	1,680.1	....	....	....	....	....	....	....	....
Imports of Goods and Services (-)	98c	1,503.8	1,477.4	1,633.3	1,819.6	....	....	....	....	....	....	....	....
Statistical Discrepancy	99bs	−137.5	−140.1	−94.3	−64.7	....	....	....	....	....	....	....	....
Gross Domestic Product (GDP)	99b	2,857.1	2,853.6	3,053.1	3,069.4	....	....	....	....	....	....	....	....
Net Primary Income from Abroad	98.n	−58.0	−74.5	−89.3	−96.9	....	....	....	....	....	....	....	....
Gross National Income (GNI)	99a	2,799.1	2,779.1	2,963.8	2,972.5	....	....	....	....	....	....	....	....
Net Current Transf.from Abroad	98t	13.4	14.5	15.7	5.4	....	....	....	....	....	....	....	....
Gross Nat'l Disposable Inc.(GNDI)	99i	2,812.5	2,793.6	2,979.5	2,977.9	....	....	....	....	....	....	....	....
Gross Saving	99s	439.7	399.1	423.4	416.6	....	....	....	....	....	....	....	....
GDP Volume 1991 Prices	99b.p	2,720.9	2,664.8	2,716.8	2,746.1	....	....	....	....	....	....	....	....
GDP Volume (1995=100)	99bvp	99.1	97.0	98.9	100.0	....	....	....	....	....	....	....	....
GDP Deflator (1995=100)	99bip	93.9	95.8	100.5	100.0	....	....	....	....	....	....	....	....

Millions: Midyear Estimates

		1992	1993	1994	1995	1996	1997	1998	1999	2000	2001	2002	2003
Population	99z	.27	.27	.28	.28	.29	.29	.30	.30	.30	.31	.31	.31

Bahrain, Kingdom of 419

		1992	1993	1994	1995	1996	1997	1998	1999	2000	2001	2002	2003
Exchange Rates						*SDRs per Dinar: End of Period*							
Official Rate	ac	1.9343	1.9363	1.8218	1.7892	1.8495	1.9711	1.8889	1.9377	2.0413	2.1163	1.9563	1.7898
						US Dollars per Dinar: End of Period (ag) Period Average (rh)							
Official Rate	ag	2.6596	2.6596	2.6596	2.6596	2.6596	2.6596	2.6596	2.6596	2.6596	2.6596	2.6596	2.6596
Official Rate	rh	2.6596	2.6596	2.6596	2.6596	2.6596	2.6596	2.6596	2.6596	2.6596	2.6596	2.6596	2.6596
						Index Numbers (2000=100): Period Averages							
Official Rate	ahx	100.0	100.0	100.0	100.0	100.0	100.0	100.0	100.0	100.0	100.0	100.0	100.0
Nominal Effective Exchange Rate	nec	85.6	90.1	88.3	84.1	86.1	91.4	94.7	94.5	100.0	104.2	101.7	92.7
Real Effective Exchange Rate	rec	94.6	99.4	96.0	91.4	91.1	98.5	100.2	97.4	100.0	102.2	101.1	92.6
Fund Position						*Millions of SDRs: End of Period*							
Quota	2f.s	48.9	82.8	82.8	82.8	82.8	82.8	82.8	135.0	135.0	135.0	135.0	135.0
SDRs	1b.s	18.7	10.8	11.0	11.3	11.7	11.9	12.1	–	1.0	.8	.8	.7
Reserve Position in the Fund	1c.s	31.1	40.9	42.2	43.7	45.1	46.7	48.5	62.4	64.9	67.2	68.6	69.7
International Liquidity						*Millions of US Dollars Unless Otherwise Indicated: End of Period*							
Total Reserves minus Gold	1l.d	1,398.5	1,302.2	1,169.7	1,279.9	1,318.4	1,290.3	1,079.2	1,369.0	1,564.1	1,684.0	1,725.7	1,778.4
SDRs	1b.d	25.7	14.8	16.1	16.8	16.8	16.1	17.1	–	1.3	1.1	1.1	1.0
Reserve Position in the Fund	1c.d	42.7	56.2	61.6	65.0	64.8	63.0	68.3	85.6	84.5	84.4	93.3	103.6
Foreign Exchange	1d.d	1,330.0	1,231.2	1,092.0	1,198.2	1,236.8	1,211.2	993.8	1,283.4	1,478.3	1,598.5	1,631.4	1,673.8
Monetary Agency	1dad	1,079.6	980.4	841.5	947.3	985.9	960.5	743.0	1,032.9	1,227.4	1,348.5	1,381.4	1,423.8
Government	1dbd	250.4	250.8	250.5	250.9	250.9	250.7	250.8	250.5	250.9	250.0	250.0	250.0
Gold (Million Fine Troy Ounces)	1ad	.150	.150	.150	.150	.150	.150	.150	.150	.150	.150	.150	.150
Gold (National Valuation)	1and	6.6	6.6	6.6	6.6	6.6	6.6	6.6	6.6	6.6	6.6	6.6	6.6
Monetary Authorities: Other Liab.	4..d	–	–	–	–	–	–	–	–	–	–	–	–
Deposit Money Banks: Assets	7a.d	1,855.1	2,272.9	2,761.7	2,592.0	2,557.2	2,863.0	3,164.1	3,410.6	3,419.9	3,327.9	3,387.9	3,719.1
Liabilities	7b.d	675.5	977.1	1,486.2	1,136.4	1,042.3	1,583.2	1,522.1	2,305.3	1,672.9	1,480.6	1,536.0	1,949.3
OBU: Foreign Assets	7k.d	67,142	57,673	62,363	61,061	64,435	69,382	....	....	....	....	54,847	....
Foreign Liabilities	7m.d	66,569	57,180	61,875	60,579	64,068	68,644	....	....	....	....	53,458	....
Monetary Authorities						*Millions of Dinars: End of Period*							
Foreign Assets	11	475.9	433.5	417.2	481.5	478.0	514.7	509.5	518.5	592.1	634.5	653.1	672.8
Claims on Central Government	12a	22.7	48.4	41.9	14.7	16.7	43.7	40.4	12.4	20.7	41.7	113.5	116.3
Reserve Money	14	227.1	181.5	173.9	234.0	208.0	234.1	183.2	266.5	264.9	303.0	345.1	465.3
of which: Currency Outside DMBs	14a	99.9	103.8	105.5	103.3	102.9	104.6	93.3	113.0	120.7	122.9	142.0	155.8
Time and Savings Deposits	15	5.0	10.0	10.0	20.0	24.5	23.5	35.9	48.4	26.3	40.3	146.1	46.0
Foreign Liabilities	16c	–	–	–	–	–	–	–	–	–	–	–	–
Central Government Deposits	16d	117.7	118.9	120.3	131.4	124.5	122.2	137.5	124.4	133.0	125.1	128.1	130.6
Capital Accounts	17a	198.4	213.3	206.1	240.3	251.0	270.8	291.5	296.5	313.2	332.9	347.1	353.8
Other Items (Net)	17r	–49.6	–41.8	–51.1	–129.3	–113.0	–92.2	–98.2	–204.9	–124.7	–125.1	–199.8	–206.5
Deposit Money Banks						*Millions of Dinars: End of Period*							
Reserves	20	116.5	73.3	66.3	124.6	99.0	126.6	89.4	153.7	139.1	177.9	204.1	303.7
Foreign Assets	21	697.5	854.6	1,038.4	974.6	961.5	1,076.5	1,189.7	1,282.4	1,285.9	1,251.3	1,273.9	1,398.4
Claims on Central Government	22a	156.6	132.1	138.5	150.7	166.6	172.1	223.3	323.8	322.3	333.5	311.7	412.7
Claims on Private Sector	22d	676.4	818.5	915.0	947.8	954.7	1,074.3	1,164.2	1,302.5	1,380.5	1,411.3	1,606.6	1,754.2
Demand Deposits	24	252.0	261.1	239.2	229.2	232.4	243.1	272.3	313.2	325.1	429.1	505.2	665.6
Time and Savings Deposits	25	845.6	896.5	992.7	1,095.0	1,132.6	1,238.3	1,477.7	1,482.1	1,684.6	1,763.7	1,806.3	1,897.4
Foreign Liabilities	26c	254.0	367.4	558.8	427.3	391.9	595.3	572.3	866.8	629.0	556.7	577.6	732.9
Central Government Deposits	26d	284.2	337.0	416.7	358.0	433.3	443.1	409.9	431.0	436.7	426.3	439.4	513.2
Capital Accounts	27a	155.7	169.1	194.6	185.5	191.5	199.4	254.9	259.6	294.1	312.1	357.5	387.9
Other Items (Net)	27r	–144.6	–152.8	–243.7	–97.4	–200.0	–269.8	–320.4	–290.2	–241.7	–313.9	–289.7	–328.1
Monetary Survey						*Millions of Dinars: End of Period*							
Foreign Assets (Net)	31n	919.4	920.7	896.8	1,028.8	1,047.6	995.9	1,126.9	934.1	1,249.0	1,329.1	1,349.4	1,338.3
Domestic Credit	32	453.8	543.1	558.4	623.8	580.2	724.8	880.5	1,083.3	1,153.8	1,235.1	1,464.2	1,639.4
Claims on Central Govt. (Net)	32an	–222.6	–275.4	–356.6	–324.0	–374.5	–349.5	–283.7	–219.2	–226.7	–176.2	–142.3	–114.8
Claims on Private Sector	32d	676.4	818.5	915.0	947.8	954.7	1,074.3	1,164.2	1,302.5	1,380.5	1,411.3	1,606.6	1,754.2
Money	34	351.9	364.9	344.7	332.5	335.3	347.7	365.6	426.2	445.8	552.0	647.2	821.4
Quasi-Money	35	850.6	906.5	1,002.7	1,115.0	1,157.1	1,261.8	1,513.6	1,530.5	1,710.9	1,804.0	1,952.4	1,943.4
Other Items (Net)	37r	170.6	192.2	108.0	205.2	135.6	111.1	128.3	60.8	246.0	208.2	214.0	212.8
Money plus Quasi-Money	35l	1,202.5	1,271.4	1,347.4	1,447.5	1,492.4	1,609.5	1,879.2	1,956.7	2,156.7	2,356.0	2,599.6	2,764.8

2004, International Monetary Fund : *International Financial Statistics Yearbook*

Bahrain, Kingdom of 419

		1992	1993	1994	1995	1996	1997	1998	1999	2000	2001	2002	2003
Other Banking Institutions						*Millions of Dinars: End of Period*							
Reserves.............................	40	....	....	....	....	....	....	....	....	....	....	....	....
Claims on Mon.Author.:Securities....	40c	....	....	....	....	....	....	....	....	....	....	....	....
Foreign Assets.........................	41	25,535.8	21,879.0	23,637.0	23,312.5	24,699.8	26,667.8	32,591.7	32,964.2	34,407.4	32,933.0	22,040.8	31,083.6
Claims on Central Government.........	42a	.2	.2	.2	.2	.3	.3	15.5	24.7	24.4	39.4	49.2	106.9
Claims on Local Government...........	42b	....	....	....	....	....	....	....	....	....	....	....	....
Claims on Private Sector...............	42d	420.7	365.8	369.0	313.5	278.1	349.5	299.8	298.4	262.4	273.4	284.1	315.9
Other Claims on Dep.Money Banks..	42e	....	....	....	....	....	....	....	....	....	....	....	....
Time and Saving Deposits...............	45	....	....	....	....	....	....	....	....	....	....	....	....
Liquid Liabilities..........................	45l	288.4	152.3	178.4	206.2	317.8	434.5	439.6	391.6	282.3	229.2	239.8	261.9
Money Market Instruments............	46aa	....	....	....	....	....	....	....	....	....	....	....	....
Foreign Liabilities........................	46c	24,846.0	21,371.2	23,613.8	22,799.6	23,993.5	25,852.6	31,798.4	32,042.1	33,712.0	32,206.7	21,286.7	30,244.7
Central Government Deposits...........	46d	268.5	103.4	174.5	369.3	375.4	243.7	190.0	177.5	185.6	228.2	197.6	269.2
Credit from Monetary Authorities.....	46g	....	....	....	....	....	....	....	....	....	....	....	....
Credit from Deposit Money Banks....	46h	....	....	....	....	....	....	....	....	....	....	....	....
Capital Accounts.........................	47a	....	....	....	....	....	....	....	....	....	....	....	....
Other Items (Net)........................	47r	....	....	....	....	....	....	....	....	....	....	....	....
Banking Survey						*Millions of Dinars: End of Period*							
Foreign Assets (Net).....................	51n	....	....	....	....	....	....	....	....	....	....	....	....
Domestic Credit..........................	52	....	....	....	....	....	....	....	....	....	....	....	....
Claims on Central Govt. (Net).......	52an	....	....	....	....	....	....	....	....	....	....	....	....
Claims on Local Government.........	52	....	....	....	....	....	....	....	....	....	....	....	....
Claims on Private Sector..............	52d	....	....	....	....	....	....	....	....	....	....	....	....
Liquid Liabilities.........................	55l	....	....	....	....	....	....	....	....	....	....	....	....
Money Market Instruments...........	56a	....	....	....	....	....	....	....	....	....	....	....	....
Capital Accounts........................	57a	....	....	....	....	....	....	....	....	....	....	....	....
Other Items (Net).......................	57r	....	....	....	....	....	....	....	....	....	....	....	....
Interest Rates						*Percent Per Annum*							
Money Market Rate.....................	60b	4.0	3.5	5.2	6.2	5.7	....	5.7	5.6	6.9	3.9	2.0	1.2
Treasury Bill Rate.......................	60c	3.8	3.3	4.8	6.1	5.5	5.7	5.5	5.5	6.6	3.8	1.8	1.1
Deposit Rate.............................	60l	†3.6	3.0	4.0	5.7	5.2	5.3	4.7	4.8	5.8	2.7	1.3	....
Lending Rate.............................	60p	11.9	11.0	10.8	11.8	12.5	12.3	11.9	11.9	11.7	10.8	8.5	....
Prices, Production, Labor						*Index Numbers (2000=100): Period Averages*							
Consumer Prices.........................	64	94.6	97.0	97.8	100.4	100.0	†102.4	102.2	100.7	100.0	100.2	101.5	....
Refined Petroleum Production.........	66ab	99.9	95.4	96.0	97.3	101.2	97.4	96.4	102.0	100.0	93.2	96.5	98.7
						Number in Thousands: Period Averages							
Labor Force...............................	67d	....	....	....	....	....	....	295	....	....	....	....	....
Employment..............................	67e	103	110	116	....	....	124	....	148	149	157	165	....
Unemployment..........................	67c	3	4	4	5	....	6	4	4	6	....	....	....
International Transactions						*Millions of Dinars*							
Exports....................................	70	1,302.6	1,400.0	1,359.9	1,546.4	1,768.0	1,648.2	1,229.6	1,640.4	2,329.3	2,096.9	2,175.4	2,393.0
Imports, c.i.f.............................	71	1,602.9	1,450.6	1,409.2	1,397.1	1,606.6	1,513.6	1,340.9	1,390.3	1,742.2	1,619.0	1,874.5	1,923.7

Bahrain, Kingdom of 419

		1992	1993	1994	1995	1996	1997	1998	1999	2000	2001	2002	2003
Balance of Payments					*Millions of US Dollars: Minus Sign Indicates Debit*								
Current Account, n.i.e.	78ald	−826.6	−339.4	−255.6	237.4	260.4	−31.1	−777.4	−36.9	830.2	227.0	−513.3	−68.4
Goods: Exports f.o.b.	78aad	3,465.4	3,723.4	3,617.0	4,114.4	4,702.1	4,383.0	3,270.2	4,362.8	6,242.7	5,657.1	5,887.3	6,689.8
Goods: Imports f.o.b.	78abd	−3,992.3	−3,616.2	−3,497.3	−3,488.3	−4,037.0	−3,778.2	−3,298.7	−3,468.3	−4,393.6	−4,047.2	−4,697.3	−5,079.3
Trade Balance	78acd	−526.9	107.2	119.7	626.1	665.2	604.8	−28.5	894.5	1,849.1	1,609.9	1,190.0	1,610.5
Services: Credit	78add	542.8	651.9	818.6	683.2	666.2	637.2	724.7	858.9	933.5	950.4	1,068.1	1,067.8
Services: Debit	78aed	−604.0	−581.9	−621.8	−634.0	−612.8	−634.8	−651.9	−700.5	−738.5	−747.6	−926.6	−870.8
Balance on Goods & Services	78afd	−588.0	177.1	316.5	675.3	718.6	607.2	44.4	1,053.0	2,044.1	1,812.6	1,331.5	1,807.6
Income: Credit	78agd	2,525.3	2,283.8	3,112.5	4,086.9	3,815.1	4,271.0	4,764.0	5,118.5	6,327.9	3,794.4	1,678.8	1,206.7
Income: Debit	78ahd	−2,493.1	−2,477.7	−3,355.1	−4,145.8	−3,840.3	−4,507.1	−4,926.0	−5,388.9	−6,551.5	−4,115.9	−2,203.8	−1,742.7
Balance on Gds, Serv. & Inc.	78aid	−555.9	−16.8	73.9	616.4	693.4	371.1	−117.6	782.6	1,820.4	1,491.0	806.5	1,271.6
Current Transfers, n.i.e.: Credit	78ajd	64.9	73.1	101.1	120.7	126.3	232.7	65.2	36.7	22.4	22.9	14.7	...
Current Transfers: Debit	78akd	−335.6	−395.7	−430.6	−499.7	−559.3	−634.8	−725.0	−856.2	−1,012.7	−1,286.9	−1,334.4	−1,340.0
Capital Account, n.i.e.	78bcd	101.1	202.1	319.1	156.9	50.0	125.0	100.0	100.0	50.0	100.0	101.6	50.0
Capital Account, n.i.e.: Credit	78bad	101.1	202.1	319.1	156.9	50.0	125.0	100.0	100.0	50.0	100.0	101.6	50.0
Capital Account: Debit	78bbd	....	....	....	....	....	....	−	−	−	−	−	−
Financial Account, n.i.e.	78bjd	397.3	593.9	1,176.9	−1,726.7	−510.2	15.1	22.5	229.9	−29.8	−417.1	−1,234.2	−252.9
Direct Investment Abroad	78bdd	−52.9	−38.8	−198.7	16.1	−304.8	−47.6	−180.8	−163.4	−9.6	−216.0	−190.0	−741.4
Dir. Invest. in Rep. Econ., n.i.e.	78bed	868.6	−275.0	208.2	430.6	2,048.2	329.3	179.5	453.7	363.6	80.4	217.0	516.7
Portfolio Investment Assets	78bfd	−1,398.1	−1,335.4	−454.0	−113.3	−779.9	−1,150.9	−1,206.7	−2,105.8	−88.3	−1,448.0	−5,140.1	−3,064.4
Equity Securities	78bkd	−	−	....	....	−	−	−	−	−119.9	−161.1	−389.0	−1,143.5	−489.0
Debt Securities	78bld	−1,398.1	−1,335.4	−454.0	−113.3	−779.9	−1,150.9	−1,206.7	−1,985.9	72.8	−1,059.0	−3,996.6	−2,575.4
Portfolio Investment Liab., n.i.e.	78bgd	−	....	....	....	−	−	−	194.8	112.8	282.5	−30.7	915.2	688.4
Equity Securities	78bmd	−	....	....	....	−	−	−	−	−	−	1.2	366.0	238.5
Debt Securities	78bnd	−	....	....	....	−	−	−	194.8	112.8	282.5	−31.9	549.2	449.9
Financial Derivatives Assets	78bwd	....	....	....	....	....	....	....	....	....	....	....	....
Financial Derivatives Liabilities	78bxd	....	....	....	....	....	....	....	....	....	....	....	....
Other Investment Assets	78bhd	−14,709.8	10,672.3	−4,527.1	1,124.5	−2,579.8	−4,342.1	−14,677.8	966.9	−3,833.9	5,623.2	33,425.4	−20,786.6
Monetary Authorities	78bod	....	....	....	....	....	....	....	....	....	....	....	....
General Government	78bpd	−5.3	−5.3	−8.0	−5.3	−8.0	−8.0	−5.1	−7.7	−5.9	−6.9	−7.2	−10.4
Banks	78bqd	−14,704.5	10,677.7	−4,519.1	1,129.8	−2,571.8	−4,334.1	−14,672.7	974.6	−3,828.0	5,629.1	33,427.2	−20,777.7
Other Sectors	78brd	−	−	−	−	−	−	−	−	−	1.0	5.3	1.6
Other Investment Liab., n.i.e.	78bid	15,689.6	−8,429.3	6,148.4	−3,184.5	1,106.2	5,226.5	15,713.5	965.6	3,255.8	−4,426.0	−30,461.7	23,134.3
Monetary Authorities	78bsd	....	....	....	....	....	....	....	....	−	−	−	−
General Government	78btd	.8	4.5	4.0	11.0	1.4	52.3	44.0	54.8	59.1	34.6	102.7	168.5
Banks	78bud	15,009.3	−8,660.1	6,268.4	−2,901.9	1,056.3	5,175.5	15,394.5	875.7	3,249.2	−4,289.7	−29,734.7	23,793.4
Other Sectors	78bvd	679.5	226.3	−123.9	−293.6	48.4	−1.3	275.0	35.1	−52.4	−170.9	−829.7	−827.5
Net Errors and Omissions	78cad	238.1	−569.2	−1,288.0	1,501.3	193.4	−6.3	638.3	−267.8	−650.3	213.6	1,680.6	314.9
Overall Balance	78cbd	−90.1	−112.5	−47.5	168.9	−6.4	102.8	−16.6	25.3	200.1	123.5	34.8	43.7
Reserves and Related Items	79dad	90.1	112.5	47.5	−168.9	6.4	−102.8	16.6	−25.3	−200.1	−123.5	−34.8	−43.7
Reserve Assets	79dbd	90.1	112.5	47.5	−168.9	6.4	−102.8	16.6	−25.3	−200.1	−123.5	−34.8	−43.7
Use of Fund Credit and Loans	79dcd	−	−	−	−	−	−	−	−	....	....	....	....
Exceptional Financing	79ded	−	....	....	....	....	....	....	....	....	....	....	....
International Investment Position							*Millions of US Dollars*							
Assets	79aad	71,035.4	61,614.0	66,735.3	65,872.8	69,518.5	75,156.1	91,569.9	92,887.3	97,291.7	93,445.4	65,416.1	90,081.9
Direct Investment Abroad	79abd	822.3	861.2	1,059.9	1,043.8	1,348.6	1,396.3	1,579.2	1,742.6	1,752.1	1,968.1	2,158.1	2,899.5
Portfolio Investment	79acd	4,870.3	6,201.1	6,647.5	6,760.6	7,538.9	8,696.9	10,268.2	12,373.7	12,719.2	14,166.7	19,338.0	22,433.7
Equity Securities	79add	....	....	−	−	−	−	1,342.6	1,462.4	1,840.2	2,229.2	3,372.7	3,861.7
Debt Securities	79aed	4,870.3	6,201.1	6,647.5	6,760.6	7,538.9	8,696.9	8,925.6	10,911.3	10,879.0	11,937.4	15,965.3	18,572.0
Financial Derivatives	79ald	....	....	....	....	....	....	....	....	....	....	....	....
Other Investment	79afd	64,076.9	53,398.6	57,917.8	56,788.0	59,359.8	63,693.9	78,366.6	77,392.1	81,245.7	75,615.6	42,183.1	62,959.2
Monetary Authorities	79agd	....	....	....	....	....	....	....	....	....	....	....	....
General Government	79ahd	....	....	....	....	....	....	....	....	....	....	....	....
Banks	79aid	....	....	57,917.8	56,788.0	59,359.8	63,693.9	78,366.6	77,392.1	81,220.0	75,590.9	42,163.7	62,941.4
Other Sectors	79ajd	....	....	....	....	....	....	....	....	25.7	24.7	19.4	17.8
Reserve Assets	79akd	1,265.8	1,153.2	1,110.1	1,280.4	1,271.3	1,355.9	1,379.0	1,574.7	1,695.1	1,736.9	1,789.4
Liabilities	79lad	66,979.9	58,049.1	64,529.7	62,081.8	65,187.7	70,744.6	86,515.4	88,016.3	92,136.4	87,929.8	59,426.0	84,599.9
Dir. Invest. in Rep. Economy	79lbd	2,039.6	1,764.6	1,972.8	2,403.4	4,451.6	4,780.9	4,960.3	5,414.0	5,905.8	5,986.1	6,203.1	6,719.8
Portfolio Investment	79lcd	....	....	−	−	−	−	194.8	307.6	615.9	585.3	1,500.5	2,188.9
Equity Securities	79ldd	....	....	−	−	−	−	−	−	25.8	27.1	393.0	631.5
Debt Securities	79led	....	....	−	−	−	−	194.8	307.6	590.1	558.2	1,107.4	1,557.4
Financial Derivatives	79lld	....	....	....	....	....	....	....	....	....	....	....	....
Other Investment	79lfd	64,940.0	56,284.5	62,556.8	59,678.5	60,736.2	65,963.7	81,360.3	82,294.6	85,614.7	81,358.4	51,722.4	75,691.2
Monetary Authorities	79lgd	....	....	....	....	....	....	229.2	287.8	345.8	378.8	478.3	653.0
General Government	79lhd	....	....	....	....	....	....	....	....	....	....	....	....
Banks	79lid	....	....	62,406.6	59,504.7	60,561.1	65,736.6	81,131.1	82,006.8	85,256.0	80,966.3	51,231.6	75,025.0
Other Sectors	79ljd	....	....	....	....	....	....	−	−	12.9	13.3	12.4	13.2

2004, International Monetary Fund: *International Financial Statistics Yearbook*

Bahrain, Kingdom of 419

		1992	1993	1994	1995	1996	1997	1998	1999	2000	2001	2002	2003
Government Finance						*Millions of Dinars: Year Ending December 31*							
Deficit (-) or Surplus	80	−115.2	−1.9	−58.3	−126.6	−55.0	−125.2	−116.5	−133.6	66.0	−30.9	....	....
Revenue	81	464.8	544.8	476.3	526.6	615.5	633.2	516.6	653.5	1,065.9	969.3	....	....
Grants Received	81z	37.6	18.8	37.6	37.6	18.8	46.9	37.6	37.6	18.8	37.6	....	....
Expenditure	82	548.8	593.4	623.4	594.1	581.3	620.0	644.6	699.3	777.0	826.6	....	....
Lending Minus Repayments	83	68.8	−27.9	−51.2	96.7	108.0	185.3	26.1	125.4	241.7	211.2	....	....
Financing													
Total Financing	80h	115.2	1.9	58.3	126.6	55.0	125.3	116.5	133.6	−66.0	30.9	....	....
Domestic	84a	114.2	−.4	56.6	122.5	54.5	125.1	99.9	113.4	−87.6	19.1	....	....
Foreign	85a	1.0	2.3	1.7	4.1	.5	.2	16.6	20.2	21.6	11.8	....	....
Debt: Domestic	88a	328.5	323.6	318.8	314.0	297.0	319.5	404.5	482.0	747.9	773.6	....	....
Foreign	89a	52.0	54.7	55.5	59.6	65.8	85.4	87.6	107.8	129.4	141.2	....	....
National Accounts						*Millions of Dinars*							
Househ.Cons.Expend.,incl.NPISHs	96f	1,055.8	1,095.3	1,123.4	1,165.5	1,229.3	1,277.4	1,327.6	1,378.4	1,411.8	1,415.7	1,338.0	....
Government Consumption Expend	91f	426.2	435.5	440.0	458.5	464.3	465.1	482.8	518.2	526.2	550.6	579.9	....
Gross Fixed Capital Formation	93e	386.2	454.2	417.5	381.3	284.1	285.9	326.2	338.0	404.6	397.7	355.0	....
Changes in Inventories	93i	139.3	−96.3	−6.5	−59.8	46.4	130.6	171.9	−36.1	100.0	−23.3	150.0	....
Exports of Goods and Services	90c	1,507.1	1,645.1	1,667.8	1,803.9	2,018.5	1,887.6	1,502.1	1,921.9	2,641.3	2,407.8	2,343.4	....
Imports of Goods and Services (-)	98c	1,728.2	1,578.5	1,548.8	1,550.0	1,748.3	1,659.3	1,485.4	1,547.5	1,901.3	1,765.1	1,877.6	....
Gross Domestic Product (GDP)	99b	1,786.3	1,955.4	2,093.4	2,199.4	2,294.3	2,387.3	2,325.1	2,489.3	2,996.9	2,983.5	2,888.7	....
Net Primary Income from Abroad	98.n	12.0	−72.9	−91.0	−22.2	−9.5	−88.8	−60.9	−101.6	−84.1	−124.8	....	....
Gross National Income (GNI)	99a	1,798.3	1,882.5	2,002.4	2,177.2	2,284.8	2,298.5	2,264.3	2,387.7	2,912.8	2,858.7	....	....
Consumption of Fixed Capital	99cf	262.8	307.5	326.7	332.6	328.6	332.3	343.5	358.5	364.8	346.2	....	....
Net National Income	99e	1,535.5	1,575.0	1,675.7	1,844.6	1,956.2	1,966.2	1,920.8	2,029.2	2,548.1	2,512.5	....	....
GDP Volume 1989 Prices	99b.p	1,800.6	2,032.5	2,027.4	2,107.0	2,193.4	2,261.5	2,369.7	2,471.9	2,603.3	2,603.3	2,739.0	....
GDP Volume (2000=100)	99bvp	69.2	78.1	77.9	80.9	84.3	86.9	91.0	95.0	100.0	100.0	105.2	....
GDP Deflator (2000=100)	99bip	86.2	83.6	89.7	90.7	90.9	91.7	85.2	87.5	100.0	99.6	91.6	....
						Millions: Midyear Estimates							
Population	99z	.53	.55	.57	.59	.61	.62	.64	.66	.68	.69	.71	.72

Bangladesh 513

		1992	1993	1994	1995	1996	1997	1998	1999	2000	2001	2002	2003
Exchange Rates						*Taka per SDR: End of Period*							
Official Rate........aa=.......	wa	53.625	54.736	58.759	60.574	61.041	61.323	68.289	69.998	70.357	71.634	78.716	87.348
						Taka per US Dollar: End of Period (we) Period Average (wf)							
Official Rate........ae=.......	we	39.000	39.850	40.250	40.750	42.450	45.450	48.500	51.000	54.000	57.000	57.900	58.782
Official Rate........rf=.......	wf	38.951	39.567	40.212	40.278	41.794	43.892	46.906	49.085	52.142	55.807	57.888	58.150
Fund Position						*Millions of SDRs: End of Period*							
Quota..........................	2f.s	392.5	392.5	392.5	392.5	392.5	392.5	392.5	533.3	533.3	533.3	533.3	533.3
SDRs...........................	1b.s	30.1	16.6	24.6	107.3	76.2	21.6	9.1	.7	.3	.9	1.7	2.2
Reserve Position in the Fund.....	1c.s	–	.1	.1	.1	.1	.1	.2	.2	.2	.2	.2	.2
Total Fund Cred.&Loans Outstg...	2tl	547.7	511.8	473.4	433.1	374.2	287.9	308.4	237.6	168.6	118.3	51.9	49.5
International Liquidity						*Millions of US Dollars Unless Otherwise Indicated: End of Period*							
Total Reserves minus Gold........	1l.d	1,824.6	2,410.8	3,138.7	2,339.7	1,834.6	1,581.5	1,905.4	1,603.6	1,486.0	1,275.0	1,683.2	2,577.9
SDRs.........................	1b.d	41.4	22.8	36.0	159.5	109.6	29.2	12.9	.9	.4	1.2	2.2	3.2
Reserve Position in the Fund.....	1c.d	–	.1	.1	.1	.2	.1	.2	.3	.2	.2	.3	.3
Foreign Exchange.............	1d.d	1,783.2	2,387.9	3,102.6	2,180.1	1,724.9	1,552.1	1,892.3	1,602.5	1,485.3	1,273.6	1,680.7	2,574.4
Gold (Million Fine Troy Ounces)...	1ad	.087	.092	.094	.094	.094	.101	.105	.106	.109	.111	.112	.112
Gold (National Valuation)........	1and	22.7	25.9	27.2	26.9	28.0	25.3	22.3	19.6	29.6	30.6	39.2	46.3
Monetary Authorities: Other Liab..	4..d	38.6	100.2	124.0	171.8	160.9	127.5	257.4	137.6	151.9	289.5	186.6	226.8
Deposit Money Banks: Assets.....	7a.d	356.5	402.5	703.4	730.6	771.6	827.9	794.9	917.0	1,203.4	1,081.0	916.2	772.8
Liabilities.............	7b.d	242.0	241.7	283.7	327.0	399.7	510.7	437.3	463.7	571.4	673.5	633.6	444.8
Monetary Authorities						*Millions of Taka: End of Period*							
Foreign Assets..................	11	76,772	101,190	130,167	97,949	80,687	73,398	93,361	82,779	81,907	74,715	100,019	154,540
Claims on Central Government.....	12a	10,426	5,366	5,697	22,783	38,576	36,371	47,968	72,915	81,529	130,336	85,570	56,217
Claims on Nonfin.Pub.Enterprises...	12c	649	597	594	591	590	590	2,140	2,140	1,570	1,321	1,013	688
Claims on Deposit Money Banks...	12e	27,399	24,409	26,275	29,139	34,551	36,220	40,993	41,282	43,852	45,836	47,814	48,124
Claims on Other Financial Insts.....	12f	8,231	11,721	13,153	11,555	11,521	11,493	11,724	12,617	12,507	11,477	11,467	8,736
Reserve Money..................	14	70,950	87,967	114,017	103,458	112,457	122,988	139,489	157,166	180,023	223,476	230,752	246,755
of which: Currency Outside DMBs..	14a	37,990	44,987	57,248	64,523	68,195	76,074	80,756	93,870	116,877	127,863	133,895	144,556
Liabs. of Central Bank: Securities.....	16ac	900	1,450	4,000	2,755	7,361	–	–	–	–	–	–	–
Foreign Liabilities................	16c	30,875	32,005	32,807	33,237	29,670	23,454	33,547	23,647	20,063	24,972	14,892	17,654
Central Government Deposits.....	16d	3,670	9,717	4,868	3,986	9	13	14	10	11	10	10	12
Central Govt. Lending Funds.....	16f	16,661	13,272	18,977	14,128	11,263	8,452	18,209	22,120	10,516	9,129	10,728	10,971
Capital Accounts................	17a	5,966	6,346	6,726	6,665	7,345	8,025	8,705	9,385	12,454	13,041	13,903	14,833
Other Items (Net)................	17r	–5,545	–7,474	–5,509	–2,212	–2,179	–4,860	–3,778	–595	–1,702	–6,942	–24,403	–21,919
Deposit Money Banks						*Millions of Taka: End of Period*							
Reserves.......................	20	35,787	46,874	56,221	43,333	45,882	48,678	64,661	63,584	65,494	96,995	94,687	104,787
Claims on Mon.Author.:Securities....	20c	900	1,450	3,994	2,741	7,358	–	–	–	–	–	–	–
Foreign Assets..................	21	13,903	16,039	28,313	29,770	32,753	37,628	38,554	46,766	64,985	61,619	53,048	45,429
Claims on Central Government.....	22a	47,353	54,135	64,899	64,283	63,790	81,206	99,534	117,884	142,606	130,277	181,406	191,745
Claims on Nonfin.Pub.Enterprises...	22c	43,412	45,951	33,731	31,717	39,426	42,900	40,712	40,431	46,111	52,784	60,644	59,831
Claims on Private Sector..........	22d	173,881	191,744	220,332	318,484	359,202	411,731	465,130	509,760	577,077	667,883	779,577	852,312
Claims on Other Financial Insts.....	22f	11,543	11,614	14,644	18,114	20,234	19,231	20,312	25,019	26,986	31,434	30,250	35,840
Demand Deposits................	24	42,452	48,294	58,717	70,819	73,481	76,559	83,214	91,055	102,074	114,572	120,705	129,272
Time Deposits..................	25	218,159	236,578	277,489	305,996	347,091	383,813	433,586	504,965	603,882	701,196	814,259	935,128
Foreign Liabilities................	26c	8,873	9,122	11,064	12,993	16,782	23,112	21,115	23,554	30,762	38,299	36,290	25,692
Central Government Deposits.....	26d	23,726	26,845	32,200	34,509	31,250	39,571	50,076	52,881	59,785	54,802	61,510	63,528
Central Govt. Lending Funds.....	26f	4,952	5,341	5,423	6,443	5,869	7,164	7,174	6,391	6,065	5,431	5,832	6,125
Credit from Monetary Authorities.....	26g	30,019	27,192	28,781	30,843	37,623	39,047	43,789	44,463	47,049	48,552	48,137	48,898
Capital Accounts................	27a	13,101	18,515	21,068	21,768	24,551	28,660	30,769	36,644	41,889	46,465	53,093	62,972
Other Items (Net)................	27r	–14,503	–4,080	–12,608	25,071	31,998	43,448	59,180	43,491	31,753	31,675	59,786	18,329
Monetary Survey						*Millions of Taka: End of Period*							
Foreign Assets (Net)..............	31n	50,927	76,102	114,609	81,489	66,989	64,460	77,253	82,344	96,067	73,064	101,884	156,624
Domestic Credit.................	32	268,099	284,566	315,982	429,032	502,080	563,938	637,430	735,469	836,297	980,024	1,099,209	1,153,834
Claims on Central Govt. (Net).....	32an	30,383	22,939	33,528	48,571	71,107	77,993	97,412	137,908	164,339	205,801	205,456	184,422
Claims on Nonfin.Pub.Enterprises...	32c	44,061	46,548	34,325	32,308	40,016	43,490	42,852	42,571	47,681	54,105	61,657	60,519
Claims on Private Sector........	32d	173,881	191,744	220,332	318,484	359,202	411,731	465,130	517,354	584,784	677,207	790,379	864,317
Claims on Other Financial Insts......	32f	19,774	23,335	27,797	29,669	31,755	30,724	32,036	37,636	39,493	42,911	41,717	44,576
Money.........................	34	80,442	93,281	115,965	135,342	141,676	152,633	163,970	184,925	218,951	242,437	254,717	274,021
Quasi-Money..................	35	218,159	236,578	277,489	305,996	347,091	383,813	433,586	504,965	603,882	701,196	814,259	935,128
Central Govt. Lending Funds.....	36f	21,613	18,613	24,400	20,571	17,132	15,616	25,383	28,511	16,581	14,560	16,560	17,096
Capital Accounts................	37a	19,067	24,861	27,794	28,433	31,896	36,685	39,474	46,029	54,343	59,506	66,996	77,805
Other Items (Net)................	37r	–20,255	–12,665	–15,057	20,179	31,274	39,651	52,270	53,383	38,607	35,389	48,561	6,408
Money plus Quasi-Money.........	35l	298,601	329,859	393,454	441,338	488,767	536,446	597,556	689,890	822,833	943,633	1,068,976	1,209,149
Interest Rates						*Percent Per Annum*							
Discount Rate (End of Period).....	60	8.50	6.00	5.50	6.00	7.00	8.00	8.00	7.00	7.00	6.00	6.00	5.00
Deposit Rate....................	60l	10.47	8.18	6.40	6.04	7.28	8.11	8.42	8.74	8.56	8.50	8.17	7.82
Lending Rate...................	60p	15.00	15.00	14.50	14.00	14.00	14.00	14.00	14.13	15.50	15.83	16.00	16.00

2004, International Monetary Fund : *International Financial Statistics Yearbook*

Bangladesh 513

		1992	1993	1994	1995	1996	1997	1998	1999	2000	2001	2002	2003
Prices, Production, Labor						*Index Numbers (2000=100): Period Averages*							
Share Prices............................	62	58.3	68.5	123.2	139.0	251.2	190.5	107.8	89.1	100.0	117.6	138.6	141.8
Consumer Prices......................	64	65.9	67.9	71.5	78.8	80.7	85.1	92.2	97.8	100.0	102.0	105.4	111.4
Industrial Production.................	66	†55.6	63.6	68.7	73.4	78.0	85.2	88.7	91.8	100.0	102.6	110.1	....
						Number in Thousands: Period Averages							
Labor Force.............................	67d	....	....	....	50,337	....	....	....	....	....	....	....	....
Employment.............................	67e	....	....	....	....	54,597	....	....	....	51,764	....	....	....
Unemployment..........................	67c	....	....	....	....	1,417	....	....	....	....	....	....	....
Unemployment Rate..................	67r	....	....	....	....	2.5	....	....	....	....	....	....	....
International Transactions						*Millions of Taka*							
Exports....................................	70	81,724	90,183	107,013	127,782	137,944	166,087	179,614	192,571	249,860	269,150	264,295	306,090
Imports, c.i.f.............................	71	145,328	158,123	185,098	261,878	276,838	302,942	327,575	377,496	436,450	465,607	458,119	553,235
Imports, f.o.b............................	71.v	137,000	142,055	166,246	235,502	248,932	265,565	298,386	342,064	394,340	421,415	....	....
Balance of Payments						*Millions of US Dollars: Minus Sign Indicates Debit*							
Current Account, n.i.e................	78ald	180.8	359.3	199.6	−823.9	−991.4	−286.3	−35.2	−364.4	−305.8	−535.4	739.3	....
Goods: Exports f.o.b................	78aad	2,097.9	2,544.7	2,934.4	3,733.3	4,009.3	4,839.9	5,141.4	5,458.3	6,399.2	6,084.7	6,102.4	....
Goods: Imports f.o.b................	78abd	−3,353.8	−3,657.3	−4,350.5	−6,057.4	−6,284.6	−6,550.7	−6,715.7	−7,535.5	−8,052.9	−8,133.4	−7,780.1	....
Trade Balance........................	78acd	−1,255.9	−1,112.6	−1,416.1	−2,324.1	−2,275.3	−1,710.8	−1,574.3	−2,077.2	−1,653.7	−2,048.7	−1,677.8	....
Services: Credit.......................	78add	483.4	529.4	589.8	698.2	604.8	687.3	723.9	777.7	815.1	752.2	848.7	....
Services: Debit........................	78aed	−788.8	−932.2	−1,025.0	−1,531.2	−1,166.0	−1,283.7	−1,237.1	−1,396.7	−1,620.2	−1,521.5	−1,405.7	....
Balance on Goods & Services...	78afd	−1,561.4	−1,515.3	−1,851.3	−3,157.1	−2,836.5	−2,307.2	−2,087.4	−2,696.3	−2,458.9	−2,818.0	−2,234.8	....
Income: Credit.........................	78agd	100.1	100.1	150.5	270.1	129.4	86.6	91.5	94.3	78.4	76.6	56.8	....
Income: Debit..........................	78ahd	−166.0	−175.8	−188.7	−201.8	−193.1	−198.0	−206.1	−258.5	−344.8	−361.9	−322.0	....
Balance on Gds, Serv. & Inc.....	78aid	−1,627.3	−1,591.0	−1,889.6	−3,088.8	−2,900.2	−2,418.6	−2,202.1	−2,860.4	−2,725.3	−3,103.3	−2,500.1	....
Current Transfers, n.i.e.: Credit..	78ajd	1,808.8	1,951.8	2,091.4	2,266.7	1,912.8	2,136.5	2,172.9	2,501.4	2,426.5	2,572.8	3,245.4	....
Current Transfers: Debit............	78akd	−.7	−1.5	−2.2	−1.8	−4.0	−4.3	−5.9	−5.3	−7.0	−4.9	−6.0	....
Capital Account, n.i.e.................	78bcd	–	–	–	–	371.2	366.8	238.7	364.1	248.7	235.4	363.7	....
Capital Account, n.i.e.: Credit.....	78bad	–	–	–	–	371.2	366.8	238.7	364.1	248.7	235.4	363.7	....
Capital Account: Debit...............	78bbd	–	–	–	–	–	–	–	–	....	....	....	....
Financial Account, n.i.e..............	78bjd	538.4	268.9	748.8	178.8	92.4	−140.2	−116.0	−446.9	−256.0	262.1	−256.2	....
Direct Investment Abroad..........	78bdd	–	–	–	–	–	−3.1	−3.0	−.1	....	....	−2.7	....
Dir. Invest. in Rep. Econ., n.i.e...	78bed	3.7	14.0	11.1	1.9	13.5	139.4	190.1	179.7	280.4	78.5	52.3	....
Portfolio Investment Assets.......	78bfd	–	–	–	–	–	–	–	−.2	–	.1	−1.2	....
Equity Securities.....................	78bkd	–	–	–	–	–	–	–	−.2	–	−.2	−1.2	....
Debt Securities.......................	78bld	–	–	–	–	–	–	–	–	–	.3	–	....
Portfolio Investment Liab., n.i.e...	78bgd	8.7	8.4	105.9	−15.2	−117.0	−9.9	−4.1	−1.1	1.3	−3.5	−1.4	....
Equity Securities.....................	78bmd	8.7	8.4	105.9	−15.2	−117.0	−9.9	−4.2	−1.1	1.2	−3.5	−1.4	....
Debt Securities.......................	78bnd	–	–	–	–	–	–	.1	–	.1	....	....	....
Financial Derivatives Assets.......	78bwd	–	–	–	–	–	–	–	–	–	....	....	....
Financial Derivatives Liabilities...	78bxd	–	–	–	–	–	–	–	–	–	....	....	....
Other Investment Assets............	78bhd	−196.0	−178.4	−1.6	−243.9	−426.7	−677.8	−859.7	−1,143.7	−1,246.8	−433.8	−560.4	....
Monetary Authorities...............	78bod	....	....	....	....	–	–	–	–	–	–	–	....
General Government................	78bpd	–	−.7	−.1	–	–	–	–	–	–	–	–	....
Banks.....................................	78bqd	−196.0	−177.7	−1.5	−243.9	−41.1	−70.2	−38.1	−131.4	−315.7	151.7	143.7	....
Other Sectors.........................	78brd	–	–	–	–	−385.6	−607.6	−821.6	−1,012.3	−931.0	−585.5	−704.0	....
Other Investment Liab., n.i.e......	78bid	722.0	424.8	633.4	436.1	622.6	411.2	560.7	518.4	709.1	620.7	257.1	....
Monetary Authorities...............	78bsd	−.9	−.2	15.0	58.3	−4.3	−25.5	126.6	−118.9	35.2	132.7	−99.9	....
General Government................	78btd	667.6	379.3	718.5	374.2	511.3	294.1	404.6	524.7	537.9	413.7	138.2	....
Banks.....................................	78bud	14.5	–	−116.3	−34.2	83.0	118.4	2.6	30.7	105.7	29.0	58.4	....
Other Sectors.........................	78bvd	40.8	45.8	16.2	37.9	32.7	24.2	26.9	82.0	30.4	45.3	160.4	....
Net Errors and Omissions..........	78cad	−84.0	69.4	−257.1	133.3	113.5	−75.5	201.0	258.0	282.4	−106.0	−349.3	....
Overall Balance.........................	78cbd	635.2	697.6	691.3	−511.7	−414.3	−135.1	288.5	−189.2	−30.7	−143.9	497.4	....
Reserves and Related Items......	79dad	−635.2	−697.6	−691.3	511.7	414.3	135.1	−288.5	189.2	30.7	143.9	−497.4	....
Reserve Assets.........................	79dbd	−670.1	−647.0	−636.2	572.8	499.9	253.8	−319.1	286.0	121.0	207.9	−411.8	....
Use of Fund Credit and Loans....	79dcd	34.9	−50.6	−55.1	−61.0	−85.6	−118.7	30.6	−96.8	−90.3	−64.0	−85.6	....
Exceptional Financing................	79ded	–	–	–	–	–	....	....	....	....	....	....	....

Bangladesh 513

		1992	1993	1994	1995	1996	1997	1998	1999	2000	2001	2002	2003
International Investment Position						*Millions of US Dollars*							
Assets...	79aad	....	....	....	....	....	....	....	....	2,715.4	1,997.6	....	....
Direct Investment Abroad...............	79abd	....	....	....	–	–	–	–	–	–	–	–	....
Portfolio Investment.........................	79acd	....	....	....	–	–	–	–	–	.6	.7	–	....
Equity Securities...........................	79add	....	....	....	–	–	–	–	–	.6	.7	–	....
Debt Securities.............................	79aed	....	....	....	–	–	–	–	–	–	–	–	....
Financial Derivatives.......................	79ald	....	....	....	....	....	....	....	....	....	....	....	....
Other Investment.............................	79afd	....	....	....	730.6	771.6	827.9	794.9	917.0	1,203.4	691.1	568.4	....
Monetary Authorities...................	79agd	....	....	....	–	–	–	–	–	–	–	–	....
General Government.....................	79ahd	....	....	....	–	–	–	–	–	–	–	–	....
Banks..	79aid	....	....	....	730.6	771.6	827.9	794.9	917.0	1,203.4	691.1	568.4	....
Other Sectors...............................	79ajd	....	....	....	–	–	–	–	–	–	–	–	....
Reserve Assets.................................	79akd	....	....	....	2,337.2	1,842.4	1,558.2	1,920.8	1,617.6	1,511.4	1,305.7	1,724.7	....
Liabilities...	79lad	....	....	....	....	....	....	....	....	18,988.4	17,813.2	....	....
Dir. Invest. in Rep. Economy............	79lbd	....	....	....	–	–	–	–	–	2,202.0	2,246.3	–	....
Portfolio Investment.........................	79lcd	....	....	....	–	–	–	–	–	22.2	17.2	–	....
Equity Securities...........................	79ldd	....	....	....	–	–	–	–	–	19.8	15.2	–	....
Debt Securities.............................	79led	....	....	....	–	–	–	–	–	2.4	2.0	–	....
Financial Derivatives.......................	79lld	....	....	....	....	....	....	....	....	....	....	....	....
Other Investment.............................	79lfd	....	....	....	17,018.2	15,509.7	15,462.1	14,569.4	15,267.0	16,764.2	15,549.7	16,728.4	....
Monetary Authorities...................	79lgd	....	....	....	643.8	538.1	388.5	434.3	326.1	219.6	148.6	70.6	....
General Government.....................	79lhd	....	....	....	16,055.5	14,576.3	14,565.1	13,699.8	14,479.1	15,974.9	14,926.1	16,205.5	....
Banks..	79lid	....	....	....	318.8	395.3	508.5	435.4	461.8	569.7	475.0	452.3	....
Other Sectors...............................	79ljd	....	....	....	–	–	–	–	–	–	–	–	....
National Accounts						*Billions of Taka: Year Ending June 30*							
Househ.Cons.Expend.,incl.NPISHs....	96f	976.5	1,037.4	1,110.6	1,254.4	1,342.2	1,440.8	1,558.6	1,707.1	1,838.5	1,964.9	2,099.2	2,308.0
Government Consumption Expend...	91f	53.2	62.1	66.1	70.6	73.3	78.9	94.7	100.8	108.4	114.3	136.6	149.0
Gross Fixed Capital Formation..........	93e	206.9	225.0	249.2	291.6	332.5	374.5	433.0	487.6	545.9	585.4	632.4	697.4
Changes in Inventories......................	93i	–	–	–	–	–	–	–	–	–	–	–	–
Exports of Goods and Services..........	90c	90.7	113.1	121.9	165.7	184.4	216.7	266.8	289.9	331.5	390.0	390.0	398.2
Imports of Goods and Services (-).....	98c	147.6	176.8	187.7	263.5	310.9	325.6	365.9	409.9	455.9	545.1	520.4	565.2
Gross Domestic Product (GDP).........	99b	1,195.4	1,253.7	1,354.1	1,525.2	1,663.2	1,807.0	2,001.8	2,197.0	2,370.9	2,535.5	2,732.0	3,004.9
Net Primary Income from Abroad.....	98.n	29.0	34.1	42.3	46.5	49.5	58.5	65.0	75.5	87.1	88.4	125.4	140.4
Gross National Income (GNI)............	99a	1,224.4	1,287.8	1,396.5	1,571.7	1,712.8	1,865.5	2,066.7	2,272.5	2,458.0	2,623.9	2,857.4	3,145.3
Consumption of Fixed Capital..........	99cf	105.3	110.9	120.2	134.1	146.9	158.9	176.0	175.3	187.8	203.0	218.1	239.8
GDP Volume 1995/96 Prices............	99b.p	1,392.0	1,455.7	1,515.1	1,589.8	1,663.2	1,752.9	1,844.5	1,934.3	2,049.3	2,157.4	2,252.6	2,372.6
GDP Volume (2000=100).................	99bvp	67.9	71.0	73.9	77.6	81.2	85.5	90.0	94.4	100.0	105.3	109.9	115.8
GDP Deflator (2000=100)................	99bip	74.2	74.4	77.3	82.9	86.4	89.1	93.8	98.2	100.0	101.6	104.8	109.5
						Millions: Midyear Estimates							
Population......................................	99z	114.88	117.70	120.54	123.41	126.29	129.19	132.10	135.02	137.95	140.88	143.81	146.74

Barbados 316

		1992	1993	1994	1995	1996	1997	1998	1999	2000	2001	2002	2003
Exchange Rates		*Barbados Dollars per SDR: End of Period (aa) Barbados Dollars per US Dollar: End of Period (ae)*											
Official Rate	aa	2.7500	2.7471	2.9197	2.9730	2.8759	2.6985	2.8161	2.7450	2.6058	2.5135	2.7190	2.9719
Official Rate	ae	2.0000	2.0000	2.0000	2.0000	2.0000	2.0000	2.0000	2.0000	2.0000	2.0000	2.0000	2.0000
Fund Position		*Millions of SDRs: End of Period*											
Quota	2f.s	48.90	48.90	48.90	48.90	48.90	48.90	48.90	67.50	67.50	67.50	67.50	67.50
SDRs	1b.s	.11	.05	.03	.03	.02	.02	.02	.01	.02	.04	.04	.01
Reserve Position in the Fund	1c.s	.03	.03	.03	.03	.03	.03	.03	4.68	4.68	4.71	4.85	5.02
Total Fund Cred.&Loans Outstg	2tl	36.84	36.84	36.84	24.94	6.52	–	–	–	–	–	–	–
International Liquidity		*Millions of US Dollars Unless Otherwise Indicated: End of Period*											
Total Reserves minus Gold	1l.d	139.96	150.45	195.77	219.10	289.69	264.92	365.95	301.94	472.69	690.37	668.51	737.94
SDRs	1b.d	.15	.07	.04	.04	.03	.03	.03	.01	.02	.05	.06	.01
Reserve Position in the Fund	1c.d	.04	.03	.04	.04	.04	.03	.04	6.42	6.09	5.92	6.60	7.46
Foreign Exchange	1d.d	139.77	150.35	195.69	219.02	289.62	264.85	365.88	295.52	466.58	684.40	661.86	730.47
Monetary Authorities	1dad	133.14	143.21	188.28	212.75	280.06	227.62	298.66	226.13	373.25	568.41	515.28	552.37
Government	1dbd	6.63	7.14	7.41	6.27	9.56	37.23	67.22	69.39	93.33	115.99	146.58	178.10
Gold (Million Fine Troy Ounces)	1ad	–	–	–	–	–	–	–	–	–	–	–	–
Gold (National Valuation)	1and	–	–	–	–	–	–	–	–	–	–	–	–
Monetary Authorities: Other Liab	4..d	71.79	55.93	38.20	28.12	16.47	8.72	7.72	6.81	–	–	–	–
Deposit Money Banks: Assets	7a.d	90.95	95.65	126.53	204.00	341.07	309.48	277.73	338.78	263.09	335.70	527.73	617.71
Liabilities	7b.d	143.43	152.56	173.11	274.86	402.14	382.40	400.97	450.04	373.02	440.94	607.94	566.85
Monetary Authorities		*Millions of Barbados Dollars: End of Period*											
Foreign Assets	11	315.2	335.8	442.2	502.6	641.5	592.1	571.8	628.7	967.6	1,396.9	1,342.3	1,468.4
Claims on Central Government	12a	239.4	225.3	219.2	117.6	90.3	64.1	50.0	83.1	15.6	.6	.6	.6
Claims on Deposit Money Banks	12e	31.2	5.0	–	6.0	–	–	23.5	15.0	–	–	–	–
Claims on Other Banking Insts	12f	62.3	25.3	10.1	10.1	9.0	9.0	9.0	9.0	9.0	9.0	9.0	9.0
Reserve Money	14	367.6	324.6	318.4	368.5	494.4	446.8	486.9	507.4	567.8	654.2	910.8	1,091.2
of which: Currency Outside DMBs	14a	176.8	177.0	189.6	200.3	220.1	239.6	268.2	302.7	310.7	312.4	337.5	329.0
Foreign Liabilities	16c	244.9	213.1	184.0	130.4	51.7	17.4	15.4	13.6	–	–	–	–
Central Government Deposits	16d	112.3	110.1	212.0	197.8	255.5	266.7	244.5	261.6	471.5	757.7	474.4	405.7
Capital Accounts	17a	34.1	34.1	35.5	35.9	35.1	33.7	34.6	34.1	32.9	32.2	33.9	35.9
Other Items (Net)	17r	–110.7	–90.5	–78.3	–96.3	–95.9	–99.4	–127.1	–80.9	–80.1	–37.6	–67.2	–54.8
Deposit Money Banks		*Millions of Barbados Dollars: End of Period*											
Reserves	20	167.4	129.3	114.1	144.9	243.8	166.5	217.2	195.8	255.7	328.1	533.4	748.1
Foreign Assets	21	181.9	191.3	253.1	408.0	682.1	619.0	555.5	677.6	526.2	671.4	1,055.5	1,235.4
Claims on Central Government	22a	555.1	594.9	603.4	713.5	915.3	981.6	922.9	880.6	1,067.7	1,169.1	1,346.6	1,567.2
Claims on Private Sector	22d	1,121.0	1,128.9	1,268.1	1,470.6	1,536.1	1,839.1	2,138.1	2,445.4	2,508.2	2,504.3	2,583.9	2,578.1
Claims on Other Banking Insts	22f	66.7	83.7	159.3	39.4	41.2	91.6	108.5	94.1	109.2	111.5	178.4	180.6
Demand Deposits	24	305.1	280.8	309.6	208.4	370.0	350.1	493.3	615.6	825.7	837.1	842.3	1,211.7
Time, Savings,& Fgn.Currency Dep	25	1,311.0	1,389.0	1,514.5	1,701.6	1,913.3	2,144.3	2,209.2	2,411.4	2,508.0	2,582.0	3,146.4	3,073.8
Foreign Liabilities	26c	286.9	305.1	346.2	549.7	804.3	764.8	801.9	900.1	746.0	881.9	1,215.9	1,133.7
Central Government Deposits	26d	125.5	101.3	173.5	215.3	245.8	330.1	287.7	249.8	270.8	391.7	337.3	434.2
Credit from Monetary Authorities	26g	38.3	19.7	10.1	24.7	28.7	12.2	22.5	38.5	19.6	29.6	26.4	25.6
Capital Accounts	27a	43.5	46.5	92.2	101.0	105.4	117.1	117.6	137.4	134.0	154.0	288.4	539.9
Other Items (Net)	27r	–18.2	–14.4	–48.2	–24.6	–48.9	–20.8	10.0	–59.4	–37.1	–91.9	–159.0	–109.4
Monetary Survey		*Millions of Barbados Dollars: End of Period*											
Foreign Assets (Net)	31n	–34.7	8.9	165.0	230.5	467.7	428.9	309.9	392.6	747.8	1,186.4	1,181.9	1,570.1
Domestic Credit	32	1,806.7	1,846.5	1,874.6	1,938.0	2,090.7	2,388.7	2,696.3	3,000.8	2,967.4	2,645.1	3,306.7	3,495.7
Claims on Central Govt. (Net)	32an	556.7	608.7	437.0	417.9	504.4	449.0	440.8	452.3	341.0	20.4	535.4	728.0
Claims on Private Sector	32d	1,121.0	1,128.9	1,268.1	1,470.6	1,536.1	1,839.1	2,138.1	2,445.4	2,508.2	2,504.3	2,583.9	2,578.1
Claims on Other Banking Insts	32f	129.0	109.0	169.4	49.5	50.2	100.6	117.5	103.1	118.2	120.5	187.4	189.6
Money	34	502.3	476.6	516.3	428.5	627.2	620.6	765.7	924.4	1,141.2	1,156.3	1,182.3	1,549.2
Quasi-Money	35	1,311.0	1,389.0	1,514.5	1,701.6	1,913.3	2,144.3	2,209.2	2,411.4	2,508.0	2,582.0	3,146.4	3,073.8
Capital Accounts	37a	77.6	80.5	127.7	136.9	140.5	150.8	152.2	171.5	167.0	186.2	322.2	575.8
Other Items (Net)	37r	–118.9	–90.8	–118.9	–98.6	–122.6	–98.1	–120.9	–113.9	–101.0	–92.9	–162.3	–133.0
Money plus Quasi-Money	35l	1,813.28	1,865.60	2,030.76	2,130.12	2,540.47	2,764.86	2,974.90	3,335.75	3,649.22	3,738.32	4,328.66	4,623.02
Other Banking Institutions		*Millions of Barbados Dollars: End of Period*											
Claims on Central Government	42a	.4	7.1	.5	5.5	4.9	1.3	1.7	1.9	3.2	3.7	3.7	.6
Claims on Private Sector	42d	387.1	403.5	417.5	424.7	443.0	381.8	433.4	378.6	423.0	446.4	442.3	440.6
Claims on Deposit Money Banks	42e	15.9	8.6	2.1	6.3	14.8	19.5	14.0	13.9	53.6	21.3	57.4	43.5
Time Deposits	45	306.9	339.4	301.8	308.8	326.5	258.8	297.1	241.4	273.2	255.2	340.2	321.7
Central Government Deposits	46d	49.8	26.2	34.5	37.7	44.0	31.5	7.5	40.0	50.2	90.7	76.8	54.8
Credit from Deposit Money Banks	46h	4.6	6.3	46.8	49.2	43.8	70.7	92.6	63.4	94.9	54.3	15.4	52.2
Capital Accounts	47a	4.8	5.0	5.1	5.1	5.1	7.9	10.9	18.9	18.9	18.9	18.9	18.9
Other Items (Net)	47r	37.2	42.4	32.0	35.8	43.3	33.7	40.9	30.7	42.6	52.4	52.1	37.2

Barbados 316

		1992	1993	1994	1995	1996	1997	1998	1999	2000	2001	2002	2003
Banking Survey		\multicolumn{12}{c}{*Millions of Barbados Dollars: End of Period*}
Foreign Assets (Net)	51n	−34.7	8.9	165.0	230.5	467.7	428.9	310.0	392.7	747.8	1,186.4	1,181.9	1,570.1
Domestic Credit	52	2,015.3	2,122.0	2,088.7	2,281.0	2,444.5	2,639.6	3,006.4	3,238.1	3,225.1	2,884.0	3,488.6	3,692.5
Claims on Central Govt. (Net)	52an	507.3	589.7	403.0	385.7	465.3	418.7	435.0	414.1	294.0	−66.6	462.4	673.8
Claims on Private Sector	52d	1,508.0	1,532.3	1,685.7	1,895.2	1,979.1	2,220.9	2,571.4	2,824.0	2,931.1	2,950.6	3,026.2	3,018.7
Liquid Liabilities	55l	2,120.1	2,205.0	2,332.5	2,438.9	2,867.0	3,023.6	3,271.9	3,577.0	3,920.1	3,992.9	4,667.7	4,944.5
Capital Accounts	57a	82.4	85.5	132.8	142.0	145.6	158.7	163.1	190.4	185.9	205.1	341.1	594.7
Other Items (Net)	57r	−221.9	−159.6	−211.6	−69.5	−100.4	−113.8	−118.6	−136.6	−133.1	−127.6	−338.3	−276.6
Interest Rates		\multicolumn{12}{c}{*Percent Per Annum*}
Bank Rate (End of Period)	60	12.00	8.00	9.50	12.50	12.50	9.00	9.00	10.00	10.00	7.50	7.50	7.50
Treasury Bill Rate	60c	10.88	5.44	7.26	8.01	6.85	3.61	5.61	5.83	5.29	3.14	2.10	1.41
Savings Rate	60k	6.50	4.17	4.25	5.00	5.00	4.33	4.00	4.17	4.83	4.38	3.29	3.00
Deposit Rate	60l	6.68	4.39	4.32	5.11	5.20	4.58	4.20	4.40	4.97	4.04	2.70	2.56
Lending Rate	60p	13.54	8.92	9.08	10.00	10.00	9.83	9.75	9.40	10.19	9.58	8.50	8.50
Prices, Production, Labor		\multicolumn{12}{c}{*Index Numbers (2000=100): Period Averages*}
Consumer Prices	64	85.6	86.6	†86.7	88.3	90.4	97.4	96.1	97.6	100.0	†102.6	102.7	104.4
Industrial Production	66	82.1	86.7	89.1	90.6	92.1	96.4	102.7	100.8	100.0	93.8	94.4	94.0
		\multicolumn{12}{c}{*Number in Thousands: Period Averages*}
Labor Force	67d	132	133	135	137	136	136	136	137	139	145	143	145
Employment	67e	102	101	106	110	115	118	122	125	129	129	129	129
Unemployment	67c	29	31	28	27	21	20	17	14	13	14	15	....
Unemployment Rate (%)	67r	26.1	27.6	26.4	23.2	19.3	17.8	16.3	13.2	11.4	11.9	12.2	12.6
International Transactions		\multicolumn{12}{c}{*Millions of Barbados Dollars*}
Exports	70	380.3	374.0	363.0	477.8	561.2	565.9	503.1	527.6	544.7	518.7	412.8	419.9
Imports, c.i.f.	71	1,048.5	1,154.1	1,228.6	1,541.2	1,667.3	1,991.0	2,019.6	2,216.1	2,312.1	2,173.3	2,078.3	2,266.0
Balance of Payments		\multicolumn{12}{c}{*Millions of US Dollars: Minus Sign Indicates Debit*}
Current Account, n.i.e.	78ald	140.0	68.8	133.6	42.6	69.7	−50.0	−63.0	−148.1	−145.5	−111.1	−171.7	....
Goods: Exports f.o.b.	78aad	189.9	187.8	190.0	245.4	286.7	289.0	270.1	275.3	286.4	271.2	253.0	....
Goods: Imports f.o.b.	78abd	−467.7	−514.3	−544.7	−691.1	−743.0	−887.7	−920.7	−989.4	−1,030.3	−952.3	−955.0	....
Trade Balance	78acd	−277.8	−326.6	−354.7	−445.8	−456.3	−598.7	−650.6	−714.1	−743.9	−681.1	−702.0	....
Services: Credit	78add	619.1	689.5	813.6	866.6	926.9	959.3	1,023.6	1,029.4	1,090.2	1,068.5	1,041.3	....
Services: Debit	78aed	−209.4	−272.6	−319.0	−363.2	−387.1	−409.5	−432.3	−458.3	−487.4	−498.5	−494.9	....
Balance on Goods & Services	78afd	131.9	90.4	140.0	57.7	83.6	−48.9	−59.3	−143.0	−141.1	−111.1	−155.7	....
Income: Credit	78agd	37.6	40.1	46.1	48.4	54.2	60.5	63.5	66.7	70.2	73.0	72.2	....
Income: Debit	78ahd	−66.5	−81.0	−86.8	−96.1	−106.3	−108.2	−119.4	−138.1	−152.5	−166.4	−174.0	....
Balance on Gds, Serv. & Inc.	78aid	103.0	49.4	99.3	10.0	31.4	−96.6	−115.2	−214.4	−223.4	−204.5	−257.5	....
Current Transfers, n.i.e.: Credit	78ajd	51.7	41.8	54.5	56.2	64.8	71.7	78.4	94.0	108.9	125.6	120.1	....
Current Transfers: Debit	78akd	−14.7	−22.5	−20.2	−23.6	−26.6	−25.1	−26.2	−27.7	−31.0	−32.3	−34.3	....
Capital Account, n.i.e.	78bcd	–	–	–	–	.4	–	.7	.7	1.8	1.3	....	....
Capital Account, n.i.e.: Credit	78bad	–	–	–	–	.4	–	.7	.7	1.8	1.3	....	....
Capital Account: Debit	78bbd	–	–	–	–	–	–	–	–	–	–	....	....
Financial Account, n.i.e.	78bjd	−80.3	.6	−5.9	−26.4	−21.8	19.9	55.1	120.3	289.2	284.8	34.8	....
Direct Investment Abroad	78bdd	−.9	−2.6	−1.1	−3.3	−3.6	−1.2	−1.0	−1.3	−1.1	−1.1	−.5	....
Dir. Invest. in Rep. Econ., n.i.e.	78bed	14.5	9.4	13.0	11.8	13.3	14.8	15.8	17.4	19.4	18.6	17.4	....
Portfolio Investment Assets	78bfd	−7.0	−9.9	−1.9	−3.1	−16.5	−17.3	−29.1	−29.8	−29.2	−30.5	−36.5	....
Equity Securities	78bkd	−7.0	−9.9	−13.4	−7.6	−8.7	−11.3	−18.3	−16.3	−14.2	−14.8	−21.2	....
Debt Securities	78bld	–	–	11.5	4.6	−7.8	−6.0	−10.8	−13.5	−15.0	−15.7	−15.3	....
Portfolio Investment Liab., n.i.e.	78bgd	−7.8	1.5	48.7	40.4	−1.6	−25.5	−25.6	44.9	100.3	150.2	−8.9	....
Equity Securities	78bmd	–	.9	–	–	–	−.1	−.1	−.1	....	....	1.1	....
Debt Securities	78bnd	−7.8	.6	48.7	40.4	−1.6	−25.4	−25.6	45.0	100.3	150.2	−10.0	....
Financial Derivatives Assets	78bwd	....	....	....	....	....	....	....	....	....	....	....	....
Financial Derivatives Liabilities	78bxd	....	....	....	....	....	....	....	....	....	....	....	....
Other Investment Assets	78bhd	−16.4	−8.2	−88.9	−167.0	−210.9	−12.1	−12.6	−92.9	52.9	−56.7	−252.7	....
Monetary Authorities	78bod	....	....	....	....	....	....	....	....	....	....	....	....
General Government	78bpd	−.6	−1.4	−7.7	−9.3	−7.1	−14.1	−6.7	−4.4	−4.3	−5.4	−5.4	....
Banks	78bqd	−11.1	−14.9	−32.6	−87.5	−154.1	24.5	21.5	−72.5	66.9	−83.1	−273.3	....
Other Sectors	78brd	−4.8	8.0	−48.6	−70.3	−49.8	−22.5	−27.4	−16.1	−9.7	31.8	26.1	....
Other Investment Liab., n.i.e.	78bid	−62.7	10.4	24.3	94.9	197.4	61.1	107.5	182.1	146.9	204.4	315.9	....
Monetary Authorities	78bsd	9.5	−1.9	−5.2	−8.5	−6.7	−6.7	–	–	–	–	–	....
General Government	78btd	−31.3	−25.2	−40.6	−34.3	9.8	7.9	23.8	5.0	18.6	11.5	−2.2	....
Banks	78bud	13.9	11.2	16.6	101.4	127.3	−19.8	18.6	49.1	−77.0	67.9	167.0	....
Other Sectors	78bvd	−54.8	26.3	53.5	36.3	67.1	79.6	65.2	128.0	205.2	125.0	151.1	....
Net Errors and Omissions	78cad	−34.4	−49.7	−89.9	25.9	38.1	47.5	1.2	63.4	32.1	47.4	112.5	....
Overall Balance	78cbd	25.3	19.6	37.8	42.1	86.4	17.4	−6.1	36.3	177.6	222.4	−24.4	....
Reserves and Related Items	79dad	−25.3	−19.6	−37.8	−42.1	−86.4	−17.4	6.1	−36.3	−177.6	−222.4	24.4	....
Reserve Assets	79dbd	−80.3	−21.1	−59.1	−25.0	−61.1	−9.1	5.5	−37.0	−178.1	−222.9	23.9	....
Use of Fund Credit and Loans	79dcd	51.5	–	–	−18.1	−26.8	−9.0	–	–	–	–	–	....
Exceptional Financing	79ded	3.4	1.5	21.3	1.0	1.5	.7	.6	.8	.5	.6	.5	....

2004, International Monetary Fund: *International Financial Statistics Yearbook*

Barbados 316

		1992	1993	1994	1995	1996	1997	1998	1999	2000	2001	2002	2003
Government Finance		\multicolumn{12}{c}{*Millions of Barbados Dollars: Year Ending December 31*}
Deficit (-) or Surplus	80	−32.23	−86.31	−81.17	26.85	−129.65	−39.05	−39.21	−118.39	−76.69	−179.65	−309.34	....
Total Revenue and Grants	81y	985.05	1,022.79	1,017.43	1,140.52	1,194.44	1,424.53	1,526.78	1,545.31	1,694.00	1,731.94	1,698.20	....
Revenue	81	985.05	1,022.79	1,017.43	1,140.52	1,194.44	1,424.53	1,526.78	1,545.31	1,694.00	1,731.94	1,698.20	....
Grants	81z	–	–	–	–	–	–	–	–	–	–	–	....
Exp. & Lending Minus Repay.	82z	1,017.28	1,109.10	1,098.60	1,113.67	1,324.09	1,463.58	1,565.99	1,663.70	1,770.69	1,911.59	2,007.54	....
Expenditure	82	1,003.95	1,103.97	1,070.34	1,125.78	1,324.26	1,458.02	1,573.67	1,660.81	1,767.40	1,890.98	2,006.40	....
Lending Minus Repayments	83	13.33	5.13	28.26	−12.10	−.17	5.56	−7.68	2.89	3.29	20.81	1.14	....
Statistical Discrepancy	80xx	....	....	−31.79	1.43	−47.47	−10.65	−14.07	28.95	−67.61	10.70	−235.07	....
Total Financing	80h	....	....	112.99	−28.28	177.13	49.70	53.29	89.44	144.30	168.95	544.41	....
Domestic	84a	....	....	69.58	−19.30	162.93	83.98	104.99	6.69	−97.41	−163.37	551.49	....
Foreign	85a	....	....	43.41	−8.98	14.20	−34.28	−51.70	82.75	237.95	332.13	−7.08	....
Total Debt by Residence	88	1,991.7	2,322.6	2,492.2	2,479.9	2,721.1	2,737.1	2,796.2	2,897.5	3,246.3	3,722.5	3,950.7	....
Domestic	88a	1,236.7	1,618.0	1,777.8	1,762.2	1,967.0	2,036.9	2,121.4	2,108.6	2,204.1	2,333.4	2,605.4	....
Foreign	89a	755.0	704.6	714.4	717.7	754.1	700.2	674.9	788.9	1,028.6	1,353.3	1,345.3	....
National Accounts		\multicolumn{12}{c}{*Millions of Barbados Dollars*}
Househ.Cons.Expend.,incl.NPISHs	96f	1,978	1,967	1,978	2,305	2,359	2,786	2,998	3,249	3,488	3,316	3,402	....
Government Consumption Expend	91f	640	732	707	752	848	927	982	1,027	1,084	1,143	1,219	....
Gross Capital Formation	93	301	420	464	527	506	676	....	....	....	....	....	....
Exports of Goods and Services	90c	1,588	1,727	1,980	2,177	2,380	2,438	2,522	2,546	2,583	2,593	2,480	....
Imports of Goods and Services (-)	98c	1,330	1,537	1,684	2,059	2,200	2,530	2,620	2,823	2,919	2,735	2,740	....
Gross Domestic Product (GDP)	99b	3,176	3,309	3,485	3,742	3,995	4,413	4,755	4,963	5,183	5,140	5,197	....
GDP Volume 1974 Prices	99b.p	784.1	790.5	825.8	846.5	873.1	901.9	941.3	975.3	998.7	964.4	960.1	981.3
GDP Volume (2000=100)	99bvp	78.5	79.2	82.7	84.8	87.4	90.3	94.3	97.7	100.0	96.6	96.1	98.3
GDP Deflator (2000=100)	99bip	78.1	80.7	81.3	85.2	88.2	94.3	97.3	98.1	100.0	102.7	104.3	....
		\multicolumn{12}{c}{*Millions: Midyear Estimates*}
Population	99z	.26	.26	.26	.26	.26	.26	.27	.27	.27	.27	.27	.27

Belarus 913

		1992	1993	1994	1995	1996	1997	1998	1999	2000	2001	2002	2003
Exchange Rates		\multicolumn{12}{c}{*Rubels per SDR: End of Period*}
Official Rate	aa	.021	.960	15.474	17.095	22.288	41.476	309.767	439.203	1,537.434	1,985.633	2,610.278	3,203.751
		\multicolumn{12}{c}{*Rubels per US Dollar: End of Period (ae) Period Average (rf)*}
Official Rate	ae	.015	.699	10.600	11.500	15.500	30.740	106.000	320.000	1,180.000	1,580.000	1,920.000	2,156.000
Official Rate	rf	....	....	....	11.521	13.230	26.021	46.128	249.295	876.750	1,390.000	1,790.917	2,053.583
Fund Position		\multicolumn{12}{c}{*Millions of SDRs: End of Period*}
Quota	2f.s	187.00	280.40	280.40	280.40	280.40	280.40	280.40	386.40	386.40	386.40	386.40	386.40
SDRs	1b.s	—	3.22	.01	3.05	.10	—	.30	.30	.14	.31	.19	.02
Reserve Position in the Fund	1c.s	.02	.02	.02	.02	.02	.02	.02	.02	.02	.02	.02	.02
Total Fund Cred.&Loans Outstg.	2tl	—	70.10	70.10	190.20	190.20	190.20	172.27	129.74	87.62	64.26	40.89	17.52
International Liquidity		\multicolumn{12}{c}{*Millions of US Dollars Unless Otherwise Indicated: End of Period*}
Total Reserves minus Gold	1l.d	....	....	†100.99	377.02	469.15	393.70	702.76	294.27	350.50	390.68	618.81	594.81
SDRs	1b.d	—	4.43	.01	4.54	.14	—	.42	.42	.18	.40	.26	.03
Reserve Position in the Fund	1c.d	.03	.03	.03	.03	.03	.03	.03	.03	.03	.03	.03	.03
Foreign Exchange	1d.d	....	....	†100.95	372.45	468.98	393.67	702.31	293.82	350.29	390.26	618.52	594.75
Monetary Authorities: Other Liab.	4..d	....	....	7.53	11.88	144.97	61.87	78.90	77.31	94.29	137.08	253.69	275.63
Dep.Money Banks: Assets Conv.	7axd	....	....	280.29	261.71	†246.78	276.63	290.03	308.20	280.54	249.61	215.34	272.12
Assets Nonconv.	7ayd	....	....	40.66	27.90	†82.98	93.25	18.54	28.73	49.55	47.20	48.47	61.54
Dep.Money Banks: Liab. Conv.	7bxd	....	....	51.69	88.05	†84.25	89.30	134.49	108.07	99.16	142.17	202.86	329.25
Liab. Nonconv.	7byd	....	....	36.49	31.68	†58.55	70.10	4.71	7.78	14.90	45.92	70.48	66.34
Monetary Authorities		\multicolumn{12}{c}{*Millions of Rubels: End of Period*}
Foreign Assets	11	....	....	1,226	4,594	7,411	12,333	76,465	98,355	423,560	706,179	1,439,903	1,946,823
Claims on Central Government	12a	....	....	1,679	4,876	8,591	14,448	54,930	153,755	302,799	504,345	190,416	643,263
Claims on Local Government	12b	....	....	—	—	—	—	22	—	—	—	—	—
Claims on Nonfin.Pub.Enterprises	12c	....	....	12	88	112	101	22	44	23	—	8,170	12,069
Claims on Private Sector	12d	....	....	7	38	32	71	343	2,041	7,524	12,577	8,849	11,452
Claims on Banks	12e	....	....	1,435	2,325	6,719	17,046	51,229	60,226	107,082	180,557	255,447	332,130
Reserve Money	14	....	....	1,757	6,817	12,143	25,214	66,300	184,680	414,335	844,955	1,116,294	1,686,787
of which: Currency Outside DMBs	14a	....	....	736	3,779	6,199	12,300	27,074	86,852	238,796	512,211	650,020	926,438
Time, Savings,& Fgn.Currency Dep.	15	....	....	15	19	20	23	81	139	306	757	—	190
Foreign Liabilities	16c	....	....	1,263	3,388	6,486	9,791	70,720	81,722	245,979	344,175	593,814	650,394
Central Government Deposits	16d	....	....	379	342	1,107	2,010	6,490	15,072	41,741	35,099	22,569	126,677
Capital Accounts	17a	....	....	301	637	1,402	3,694	5,968	24,895	129,194	185,695	311,865	474,978
Other Items (Net)	17r	....	....	643	718	1,708	3,266	33,430	7,912	9,433	−7,023	−141,758	6,712
Deposit Money Banks		\multicolumn{12}{c}{*Millions of Rubels: End of Period*}
Reserves	20	....	....	951	2,842	†5,693	11,889	35,688	92,002	158,118	324,836	389,797	675,582
Foreign Assets	21	....	....	3,691	3,331	†5,111	11,370	67,886	107,816	389,506	468,964	506,519	719,353
Claims on Central Government	22a	....	....	9	640	†2,273	6,084	21,956	53,796	176,938	302,612	550,196	849,632
Claims on Local Government	22b	....	....	—	—	†4	22	143	358	815	468	81,519	194,244
Claims on Nonfin.Pub.Enterprises	22c	....	....	2,866	6,571	†9,232	18,565	84,059	170,553	677,713	1,138,159	1,663,793	2,049,489
Claims on Private Sector	22d	....	....	3,127	7,360	†12,303	30,292	112,999	279,701	802,505	1,400,762	2,320,546	4,283,530
Claims on Nonbank Financial Insts.	22g	....	....	....	....	302	498	480	1,278	1,310	7,938	11,648	21,695
Demand Deposits	24	....	....	1,877	6,132	†9,240	21,052	52,487	140,714	259,602	425,663	714,285	1,311,184
Time, Savings,& Fgn. Currency Dep.	25	....	....	4,238	7,889	†11,609	23,904	136,239	271,888	1,104,976	1,677,831	2,569,986	3,933,105
Foreign Liabilities	26c	....	....	1,014	1,377	†2,213	4,900	30,622	37,073	134,597	297,179	524,803	852,903
Central Government Deposits	26d	....	....	238	1,000	†2,848	5,799	20,991	44,722	177,905	443,511	347,220	314,727
Credit from Monetary Authorities	26g	....	....	1,243	2,122	†6,486	15,931	48,371	53,471	84,391	142,487	152,101	180,334
Capital Accounts	27a	....	....	1,107	4,620	†5,277	8,925	25,545	147,109	431,902	567,361	1,160,144	2,016,223
Other Items (Net)	27r	....	....	926	−2,396	†−2,753	−1,792	8,955	10,527	13,532	89,708	55,476	185,048
Monetary Survey		\multicolumn{12}{c}{*Millions of Rubels: End of Period*}
Foreign Assets (Net)	31n	....	....	2,640	3,160	†3,823	9,012	43,008	87,376	432,490	533,790	827,804	1,162,879
Domestic Credit	32	....	....	7,083	18,232	†28,896	62,271	247,452	601,732	1,749,981	2,888,252	4,465,347	7,623,971
Claims on Central Govt. (Net)	32an	....	....	1,071	4,175	†6,909	12,723	49,405	147,757	260,091	328,347	370,822	1,051,490
Claims on Local Government	32b	....	....	—	—	†4	22	143	358	815	468	81,519	194,244
Claims on Nonfin.Pub.Enterprises	32c	....	....	2,878	6,659	†9,344	18,665	84,081	170,598	677,736	1,138,159	1,671,962	2,061,558
Claims on Private Sector	32d	....	....	3,134	7,398	†12,335	30,363	113,343	281,741	810,029	1,413,339	2,329,395	4,294,982
Claims on Nonbank Financ. Insts.	32g	....	....	....	....	302	498	480	1,278	1,310	7,938	11,648	21,695
Money	34	....	....	2,687	10,027	†15,708	33,852	80,932	233,415	508,432	939,179	1,365,668	2,238,376
Quasi-Money	35	....	....	4,253	7,908	†11,629	23,927	136,320	272,027	1,105,282	1,678,588	2,569,986	3,933,295
Capital Accounts	37a	....	....	1,407	5,257	†6,678	12,619	31,513	172,005	561,096	753,056	1,472,009	2,491,201
Other Items (Net)	37r	....	....	1,375	−1,800	†−1,297	885	41,694	11,661	7,660	51,219	−114,513	123,978
Money plus Quasi-Money	35l	....	....	6,940	17,934	†27,337	57,779	217,252	505,442	1,613,714	2,617,766	3,935,654	6,171,671
Interest Rates		\multicolumn{12}{c}{*Percent Per Annum*}
Refinancing Rate (End of Per.)	60	30.0	210.0	480.0	66.0	8.3	8.9	9.6	23.4	†80.0	48.0	38.0	28.0
Deposit Rate	60l	....	65.1	89.6	100.8	32.4	15.6	14.3	23.8	37.6	34.2	26.9	17.4
Lending Rate	60p	....	71.6	148.5	175.0	62.3	31.8	27.0	51.0	67.7	47.0	36.9	24.0

2004, International Monetary Fund: *International Financial Statistics Yearbook*

Belarus 913

		1992	1993	1994	1995	1996	1997	1998	1999	2000	2001	2002	2003
Prices and Labor						*Percent Change over Previous Period*							
Producer Prices	63.xx	....	1,536.3	2,170.8	499.1	34.7	87.5	72.5	355.8	185.6	71.8	40.4	37.5
Consumer Prices	64.xx	....	1,190.2	2,221.0	709.3	52.7	63.9	72.9	293.7	168.6	61.1	42.5	28.4
Wages	65.xx	....	1,106.8	1,504.4	668.9	60.5	87.3	104.2	322.4	200.9	108.8	53.8	7.9
						Number in Thousands: Period Averages							
Employment	67e	4,981	4,828	4,701	4,410	4,365	4,370	4,417	4,442	4,441	4,417	4,381	....
Unemployment	67c	24	66	101	131	183	126	106	95	96	....	....	....
Unemployment Rate (%)	67r	.5	1.4	2.1	2.7	3.9	2.8	2.3	2.1	2.1	....	....	....
International Transactions						*Millions of US Dollars*							
Exports	70..d	3,559	1,970	2,510	4,803	5,652	7,301	7,070	5,909	7,326	7,451	8,021	9,964
Imports, c.i.f.	71..d	3,495	2,539	3,066	5,564	6,939	8,689	8,549	6,674	8,646	8,286	9,092	11,505
Balance of Payments						*Millions of US Dollars: Minus Sign Indicates Debit*							
Current Account, n.i.e.	78ald	....	−435.0	−443.8	−458.3	−515.9	−859.2	−1,016.5	−193.7	−323.1	−434.9	−377.5	−505.3
Goods: Exports f.o.b.	78aad	....	1,970.1	2,510.0	4,803.0	5,790.1	6,918.7	6,172.3	5,646.4	6,640.5	7,334.1	7,964.7	10,091.6
Goods: Imports f.o.b.	78abd	....	−2,498.0	−2,999.8	−5,468.7	−6,938.6	−8,325.7	−7,673.4	−6,216.4	−7,524.6	−8,140.8	−8,879.0	−11,326.0
Trade Balance	78acd	....	−527.9	−489.8	−665.7	−1,148.5	−1,407.0	−1,501.1	−570.0	−884.1	−806.7	−914.3	−1,234.4
Services: Credit	78add	....	184.9	251.4	466.1	908.0	918.8	925.1	753.3	1,015.6	1,101.8	1,299.8	1,500.4
Services: Debit	78aed	....	−136.8	−199.3	−283.7	−335.9	−364.8	−443.2	−438.8	−562.6	−841.3	−908.0	−943.6
Balance on Goods & Services	78afd	....	−479.8	−437.7	−483.3	−576.4	−853.0	−1,019.2	−255.5	−431.1	−546.2	−522.5	−677.6
Income: Credit	78agd	....	.1	.5	1.9	74.1	31.2	26.8	20.8	25.7	27.0	44.5	65.6
Income: Debit	78ahd	....	−7.5	−29.3	−52.9	−104.9	−115.8	−119.7	−62.8	−72.4	−69.8	−73.1	−93.6
Balance on Gds, Serv. & Inc.	78aid	....	−487.2	−466.5	−534.3	−607.2	−937.6	−1,112.1	−297.5	−477.8	−589.0	−551.1	−705.6
Current Transfers, n.i.e.: Credit	78ajd	....	64.6	50.9	107.2	135.5	106.1	120.9	137.0	177.1	202.6	235.1	285.2
Current Transfers: Debit	78akd	....	−12.4	−28.2	−31.2	−44.2	−27.7	−25.3	−33.2	−22.4	−48.5	−61.5	−84.9
Capital Account, n.i.e.	78bcd	....	−	23.8	7.3	101.1	133.2	170.1	60.4	69.4	56.3	52.7	68.9
Capital Account, n.i.e.: Credit	78bad	....	−	23.8	7.3	257.2	248.0	261.3	131.1	125.6	132.3	119.8	133.2
Capital Account: Debit	78bbd	....	....	....	....	−156.1	−114.8	−91.2	−70.7	−56.2	−76.0	−67.1	−64.3
Financial Account, n.i.e.	78bjd	....	294.1	144.6	204.0	378.7	738.1	354.8	399.5	140.1	265.0	482.5	361.8
Direct Investment Abroad	78bdd	....	....	....	....	....	−2.1	−2.3	−.8	−.2	−.3	206.2	−1.5
Dir. Invest. in Rep. Econ., n.i.e.	78bed	....	17.6	10.5	14.7	104.5	351.6	203.2	444.0	118.8	95.8	247.1	170.5
Portfolio Investment Assets	78bfd	....	....	....	....	−17.7	−61.6	28.0	−15.4	−5.7	25.5	−2.4	.8
Equity Securities	78bkd	....	....	....	....	....	−.6	.3	−7.3	.5	.7	6.9	−1.1
Debt Securities	78bld	....	....	....	....	−17.7	−61.0	27.7	−8.1	−6.2	24.8	−9.3	1.9
Portfolio Investment Liab., n.i.e.	78bgd	....	....	....	....	3.2	41.8	−13.4	−5.2	50.1	−45.4	−6.7	5.3
Equity Securities	78bmd	....	....	....	....	....	....	2.7	....	.5	2.5	.7	3.3
Debt Securities	78bnd	....	....	....	....	3.2	41.8	−16.1	−5.2	49.6	−47.9	−7.4	2.0
Financial Derivatives Assets	78bwd	....	....	....	....	....	....	....	....	....	....	....	....
Financial Derivatives Liabilities	78bxd	....	....	....	....	....	....	....	....	....	....	....	....
Other Investment Assets	78bhd	....	−118.1	−232.5	−155.4	−131.5	49.9	199.4	−36.7	41.7	−139.2	−309.4	−61.0
Monetary Authorities	78bod	....	....	....	....	....	1.5	−.9	1.1	−.2	−99.3	−215.1	−10.0
General Government	78bpd	....	−	−	14.0	....	....	....	....	....	....	....	....
Banks	78bqd	....	−60.6	−94.2	58.6	−40.2	−12.6	19.0	−16.4	8.4	17.5	19.1	−61.1
Other Sectors	78brd	....	−57.5	−138.3	−228.0	−91.3	61.0	181.3	−21.4	33.5	−57.4	−113.4	10.1
Other Investment Liab., n.i.e.	78bid	....	394.6	366.6	344.7	420.2	358.5	−60.1	13.6	−64.6	328.6	347.7	247.7
Monetary Authorities	78bsd	....	−	−.3	3.7	133.1	−86.8	6.8	.7	−21.2	20.2	20.4	−4.1
General Government	78btd	....	243.9	239.4	81.7	33.4	62.4	24.7	−28.5	−37.2	44.9	9.3	−43.2
Banks	78bud	....	−4.8	34.9	24.1	23.1	16.6	−20.3	−24.1	1.9	81.4	90.8	118.7
Other Sectors	78bvd	....	155.5	92.6	235.2	230.6	366.3	−71.3	65.5	−8.1	182.1	227.2	176.3
Net Errors and Omissions	78cad	....	3.4	−41.6	168.6	−178.1	53.0	172.3	−246.3	238.9	35.1	−60.6	124.6
Overall Balance	78cbd	....	−137.5	−317.0	−78.4	−214.2	65.1	−319.3	19.9	125.3	−78.5	97.1	49.9
Reserves and Related Items	79dad	....	137.5	317.0	78.4	214.2	−65.1	319.3	−19.9	−125.3	78.5	−97.1	−49.9
Reserve Assets	79dbd	....	12.5	−58.6	−283.7	−78.6	75.3	54.6	34.6	−75.7	5.2	−100.9	13.8
Use of Fund Credit and Loans	79dcd	....	98.2	−	177.8	−	−	−24.4	−58.1	−55.8	−29.8	−30.2	−32.3
Exceptional Financing	79ded	....	26.8	375.6	184.3	292.8	−140.4	289.1	3.6	6.2	103.1	33.9	−31.5

Belarus 913

		1992	1993	1994	1995	1996	1997	1998	1999	2000	2001	2002	2003
International Investment Position						\multicolumn{7}{c}{*Millions of US Dollars*}				
Assets	79aad	....	....	....	....	1,335.4	1,273.7	991.3	1,004.2	996.9	1,171.2	1,561.7	1,680.0
Direct Investment Abroad	79abd	....	....	....	....	–	2.1	4.4	5.2	5.5	20.1	3.7	6.2
Portfolio Investment	79acd	....	....	....	....	21.5	83.1	55.1	69.0	57.5	31.6	16.3	16.3
Equity Securities	79add	....	....	....	....	2.3	2.9	2.6	9.8	9.3	8.3	.8	1.8
Debt Securities	79aed	....	....	....	....	19.2	80.2	52.5	59.2	48.2	23.3	15.5	14.5
Financial Derivatives	79ald	....	....	....	....	–	–	–	–	–	–	–	–
Other Investment	79afd	....	....	....	....	844.8	794.9	592.8	625.4	577.1	760.1	1,066.1	1,161.9
Monetary Authorities	79agd	....	....	....	....	9.0	7.5	8.4	7.4	2.2	148.4	361.0	401.1
General Government	79ahd	....	....	....	....	–	–	–	–	–	–	–	–
Banks	79aid	....	....	....	....	291.7	304.3	285.4	298.2	288.9	268.6	247.8	311.9
Other Sectors	79ajd	....	....	....	....	544.1	483.1	299.0	319.8	286.0	343.1	457.3	448.9
Reserve Assets	79akd	....	....	....	....	469.1	393.6	339.0	304.6	356.8	359.4	475.6	495.6
Liabilities	79lad	....	....	....	....	2,064.7	2,656.7	3,086.9	3,419.6	3,436.8	3,855.3	4,523.8	5,028.3
Dir. Invest. in Rep. Economy	79lbd	....	....	....	....	154.3	505.9	709.1	1,153.1	1,305.5	1,397.2	1,645.9	1,897.3
Portfolio Investment	79lcd	....	....	....	....	34.6	76.4	63.0	44.7	78.6	36.1	20.3	24.0
Equity Securities	79ldd	....	....	....	....	5.5	5.5	8.2	8.2	8.8	11.4	9.8	11.7
Debt Securities	79led	....	....	....	....	29.1	70.9	54.8	36.5	69.8	24.7	10.5	12.3
Financial Derivatives	79lld	....	....	....	....	–	–	–	–	–	–	–	–
Other Investment	79lfd	....	....	....	....	1,875.8	2,074.4	2,314.8	2,221.8	2,052.7	2,422.0	2,857.6	3,107.0
Monetary Authorities	79lgd	....	....	....	....	409.9	303.4	298.6	230.1	142.4	194.8	281.8	280.6
General Government	79lhd	....	....	....	....	639.5	683.0	386.3	375.9	346.0	353.3	361.7	340.9
Banks	79lid	....	....	....	....	142.8	159.4	139.1	112.4	114.1	188.1	273.4	395.6
Other Sectors	79ljd	....	....	....	....	683.6	928.6	1,490.8	1,503.4	1,450.2	1,685.8	1,940.7	2,089.9
Government Finance						\multicolumn{7}{c}{*Billions of Rubels: Year Ending December 31*}				
Deficit (-) or Surplus	80	–	–.04	–.33	–3.22	–3.46	–5.72	–5.99	–60.22	7.30	–235.68	....	....
Total Revenue and Grants	81y	.03	.38	6.01	37.10	58.99	117.87	206.59	876.23	2,646.10	4,938.20	....	....
Revenue	81	.03	.38	6.01	37.10	58.99	117.87	206.59	876.23	2,646.00	4,938.20	....	....
Grants	81z	–	–	–	–	–	–	–	–	.10	–	....	....
Exp. & Lending Minus Repay	82z	.03	.42	6.34	40.33	62.46	123.59	212.58	936.45	2,638.80	5,173.88	....	....
Expenditure	82	.03	.42	6.34	40.33	62.51	121.79	213.22	933.87	2,639.80	5,080.21	....	....
Lending Minus Repayments	83	–	–	–	–	–.06	1.80	–.64	2.58	–1.00	93.67	....	....
Total Financing	80h	–	.04	.33	3.22	3.46	5.72	5.99	60.22	–7.30	235.68	....	....
Domestic	84a	–	–	–.13	2.79	3.69	4.11	7.97	84.65	42.90	–19.56	....	....
Foreign	85a	–	.04	.45	.43	–.22	1.61	–1.98	–24.43	–50.20	255.24	....	....
Total Debt by Residence	88	.02	.05	13.51	20.49	22.10	44.65	141.70	....	....	....	....	....
Domestic	88a	.01	.05	.51	3.04	7.42	14.63	33.56	....	....	....	....	....
Foreign	89a	.01	–	13.01	17.46	14.68	30.02	108.14	....	....	....	....	....
National Accounts						\multicolumn{7}{c}{*Billions of Rubels*}				
Househ.Cons.Expend.,incl.NPISHs	96f	–	.6	10.6	71.7	115.1	209.3	406.2	1,774.6	5,198.1	9,895.9	15,549.9	21,406.6
Government Consumption Expend	91f	–	.2	3.6	24.9	39.4	74.5	139.5	590.2	1,779.1	3,701.3	5,496.7	7,674.4
Gross Fixed Capital Formation	93e	–	.3	5.9	30.0	40.4	92.6	182.1	796.7	2,301.9	3,893.0	5,746.4	8,484.7
Changes in Inventories	93i	–	.1	–.1	.1	4.7	5.9	5.5	–79.3	18.0	187.5	50.2	189.5
Exports of Goods and Services	90c	.1	.7	12.7	60.3	88.9	219.6	414.6	1,791.5	6,321.6	11,462.7	16,631.2	23,855.2
Imports of Goods and Services (-)	98c	.1	.8	15.0	65.6	96.7	240.8	448.7	1,865.0	6,612.7	12,072.3	17,610.6	25,280.9
Statistical Discrepancy	99bs	....	....	....	....	....	5.8	3.0	17.4	127.8	105.1	274.5	–399.3
Gross Domestic Product (GDP)	99b	.1	1.0	17.8	121.4	191.8	366.8	702.2	3,026.1	9,133.8	17,173.2	26,138.3	35,930.2
Net Primary Income from Abroad	98.n	....	–	–	–.1	.2	–.5	–.4	2.8	11.2	29.3	21.7	....
Gross National Income (GNI)	99a	.1	1.0	17.8	121.4	192.0	366.3	701.8	3,028.9	9,145.0	17,202.5	26,160.0	....
Net Current Transf.from Abroad	98t	–	–	–	.8	1.2	2.1	4.5	31.2	118.1	217.9	309.9	....
Gross Nat'l Disposable Inc.(GNDI)	99i	.1	1.0	17.8	122.2	193.2	368.4	706.3	3,060.1	9,263.1	17,420.4	26,469.9	....
Gross Saving	99s	–	.3	3.6	25.5	38.7	84.5	160.7	695.3	2,285.9	3,823.2	5,423.3	....
GDP Volume 1995 Ref., Chained	99b.p	166.2	153.5	135.6	121.4	124.8	139.0	150.7	155.8	164.8	....	....	....
GDP Volume 2000 Ref., Chained	99b.p	....	....	....	....	....	....	....	....	9,133.8	9,565.4	10,048.0	10,727.3
GDP Volume (2000=100)	99bvp	100.9	93.1	82.2	73.7	75.7	84.4	91.4	94.5	†100.0	104.7	110.0	117.4
GDP Deflator (2000=100)	99bip	–	–	.2	1.8	2.8	4.8	8.4	35.1	100.0	179.5	260.1	334.9
						\multicolumn{7}{c}{*Millions: Midyear Estimates*}				
Population	99z	10.29	10.29	10.28	10.25	10.22	10.18	10.13	10.08	10.03	9.99	9.94	9.90

2004, International Monetary Fund : *International Financial Statistics Yearbook*

Belgium 124

		1992	1993	1994	1995	1996	1997	1998	1999	2000	2001	2002	2003
Exchange Rates		Francs per SDR through 1998, Euros per SDR Thereafter: End of Period											
Market Rate......aa=	aa	45.623	49.599	46.478	43.725	46.022	49.814	48.682	1.3662	1.4002	1.4260	1.2964	1.1765
		Francs per US Dollar through 1998, Euros per US Dollar Thereafter: End of Period (we) Period Average (wf)											
Market Rate......ae=	we	33.180	36.110	31.838	29.415	32.005	36.920	34.575	....	....	....	....	....
Market Rate......rf=	wf	32.150	34.597	33.456	29.480	30.962	35.774	36.299	....	....	....	....	....
		Francs per ECU: End of Period (ea) Period Average (eb)											
ECU Rate	ea	40.178	40.287	39.161	38.698	40.102	40.771	40.340	....	....	....	....	....
ECU Rate	eb	41.604	40.466	39.662	38.537	39.290	40.529	40.623	....	....	....	....	....
		Index Numbers (2000=100): Period Averages											
Market Rate (1995=100)	ahx	91.8	85.2	88.2	100.0	95.1	82.4	81.2	....	....	....	....	....
Nominal Effective Exchange Rate	neu	103.5	104.7	106.6	111.0	108.6	104.2	104.2	103.0	100.0	100.5	101.2	104.2
Real Effective Exchange Rate	reu	112.9	114.6	113.5	116.9	111.9	108.0	107.3	103.3	100.0	101.1	100.2	102.6
Fund Position		Millions of SDRs: End of Period											
Quota	2f.s	3,102	3,102	3,102	3,102	3,102	3,102	3,102	4,605	4,605	4,605	4,605	4,605
SDRs	1b.s	124	125	123	331	346	363	433	197	236	376	408	434
Reserve Position in the Fund	1c.s	586	560	556	676	747	876	1,348	1,668	1,304	1,632	1,759	1,812
of which: Outstg.Fund Borrowing	2c	–	–	–	–	–	–	140	–	–	–	–	–
International Liquidity		Millions of US Dollars Unless Otherwise Indicated: End of Period											
Total Res.Min.Gold (Eurosys.Def)	1l.d	13,801	11,415	13,876	16,177	16,953	16,190	18,272	†10,938	9,994	11,266	11,855	10,989
SDRs	1b.d	171	171	180	492	498	489	610	271	307	472	554	645
Reserve Position in the Fund	1c.d	806	769	812	1,005	1,075	1,182	1,899	2,290	1,699	2,051	2,392	2,693
Foreign Exchange	1d.d	12,825	10,474	12,884	14,680	15,380	14,519	15,763	†8,377	7,988	8,743	8,909	7,651
o/w:Fin.Deriv.Rel.to Reserves	1ddd	....	....	....	....	....	....	....	–	–	–	–	–
Other Reserve Assets	1e.d	....	....	....	....	....	....	....	–	–	–	–	–
Gold (Million Fine Troy Ounces)	1ad	25.04	25.04	25.04	20.54	15.32	15.32	9.52	8.30	8.30	8.30	8.29	8.29
Gold (Eurosystem Valuation)	1and	8,321	9,955	8,482	7,306	6,171	5,140	2,565	2,408	2,277	2,294	2,843	3,459
Memo:Euro Cl. on Non-EA Res	1dgd	....	....	....	....	....	....	....	257	....	....	....	....
Non-Euro Cl. on EA Res	1dhd	....	....	....	....	....	....	....	139	427	704	313	405
Mon. Auth.: Other Foreign Assets	3..d	165	140	115	113	100	91	97	†–	–	–	–	–
Foreign Liabilities	4..d	241	341	477	629	144	81	382	†7,341	1,081	1,719	1,141	1,646
Banking Insts.: Foreign Assets	7a.d	†197,574	211,230	238,602	273,058	267,758	262,470	....	†112,048	108,165	126,964	164,254	194,301
Foreign Liab.	7b.d	†231,022	228,782	263,337	302,856	293,657	280,033	....	†181,820	163,882	176,325	199,014	236,369
Monetary Authorities		Billions of Francs through 1998; Millions of Euros Beginning 1999: End of Period											
Fgn. Assets (Cl.on Non-EA Ctys)	11	716.9	764.7	729.1	692.6	741.4	793.7	712.1	13,303	12,737	15,024	13,675	11,321
Claims on General Government	12a.u	....	....	....	....	....	....	....	3,683	3,630	3,668	2,937	2,960
o/w: Claims on Gen.Govt.in Cty	12a	71.6	90.3	79.3	86.3	91.0	94.1	47.0	1,123	1,220	1,158	805	666
Claims on Banking Institutions	12e.u	....	....	....	....	....	....	....	25,795	17,312	9,699	18,118	30,707
o/w: Claims on Bank.Inst.in Cty	12e	82.5	155.4	128.3	151.3	151.4	150.5	185.0	20,457	15,481	7,672	10,953	16,891
Claims on Other Resident Sectors	12d.u	....	....	....	....	....	....	....	92	24	59	45	18
o/w: Cl. on Oth.Res.Sect.in Cty	12d	....	....	....	....	....	....	....	3	3	2	2	2
Currency Issued	14a	448.0	459.3	431.4	465.9	486.2	501.1	505.8	13,535	13,496	9,081	12,715	14,877
Liabilities to Banking Insts	14c.u	....	....	....	....	....	....	....	17,500	13,675	11,116	17,401	26,226
o/w: Liabs to Bank.Inst.in Cty	14c	3.8	5.5	2.3	7.6	4.7	1.2	279.0	3,509	7,130	5,945	4,482	8,325
Demand Dep. of Other Res.Sect	14d.u	....	....	....	....	....	....	....	19	12	7	6	9
o/w:D.Dep.of Oth.Res.Sect.in Cty	14d	....	....	....	....	....	....	....	19	12	7	6	8
Other Dep. of Other Res.Sect.	15..u	....	....	....	....	....	....	....	–	–	–	–	–
o/w:O.Dep.of Oth.Res.Sect.in Cty	15	....	....	....	....	....	....	....	–	–	–	–	–
Bonds & Money Mkt. Instruments	16n.u	....	....	....	....	....	....	....	–	–	–	–	–
o/w: Bonds Held by Resid.of Cty	16n	–	–	–	–	230.0	230.0	–	....	....	....	....	....
Foreign Liab. (to Non-EA Ctys)	16c	8.4	12.3	15.2	18.5	4.6	3.0	13.2	7,307	1,162	1,950	1,088	1,303
Central Government Deposits	16d.u	....	....	....	....	....	....	....	64	62	118	115	152
o/w: Cent.Govt.Dep. in Cty	16d	–	1.3	1.0	.5	.7	.1	.4	64	62	118	115	152
Capital Accounts	17a	40.0	43.6	46.5	48.6	50.6	53.1	53.6	5,369	5,816	6,108	4,724	4,265
Other Items (Net)	17r	370.8	488.5	440.2	389.1	206.9	249.8	92.3	–921	–520	72	–1,272	–1,824
Memo: Net Claims on Eurosystem	12e.s	....	....	....	....	....	....	....	–8,690	–5,103	–3,736	–6,655	–5,325
Currency Put into Circ.	14m	....	....	....	....	....	....	....	....	....	....	7,887	3,807

Belgium 124

		1992	1993	1994	1995	1996	1997	1998	1999	2000	2001	2002	2003
Banking Institutions		\multicolumn{12}{c}{*Billions of Francs through 1998; Millions of Euros Beginning 1999: End of Period*}
Claims on Monetary Authorities.......	20	†35.4	34.3	35.1	37.9	245.8	228.6	....	3,509	7,130	5,945	4,482	8,325
Claims on Bk.Inst.in Oth.EA Ctys......	20b.u	....	....	....	....	....	....	....	97,105	91,411	90,488	105,573	147,521
Fgn. Assets (Cl.on Non-EA Ctys)........	21	†6,555.5	7,627.5	7,596.5	8,032.0	8,569.6	9,690.4	....	111,535	116,244	144,064	156,626	153,841
Claims on General Government........	22a.u	....	....	....	....	....	....	....	175,991	160,255	180,779	166,928	172,616
o/w: Claims on Gen.Govt.in Cty......	22a	†5,267.1	5,528.2	6,101.4	6,215.7	6,296.0	6,236.2	....	134,534	119,713	111,147	102,045	96,484
Claims on Other Resident Sectors.....	22d.u	....	....	....	....	....	....	....	218,724	225,662	230,712	234,954	241,271
o/w: Cl. on Oth.Res.Sect.in Cty.......	22d	†5,695.7	5,794.3	5,979.9	6,099.0	6,402.6	6,749.2	....	192,349	196,554	197,316	198,894	203,822
Demand Deposits.........................	24..u	....	....	....	....	....	....	....	53,554	58,499	61,397	62,067	69,449
o/w:D.Dep.of Oth.Res.Sect.in Cty...	24	†966.4	1,060.6	1,111.3	1,152.7	1,200.0	1,237.0	....	50,428	53,682	56,546	57,877	64,171
Other Deposits...........................	25..u	....	....	....	....	....	....	....	188,347	182,139	199,536	212,803	230,927
o/w:O.Dep.of Oth.Res.Sect.in Cty...	25	†4,148.9	4,560.7	4,706.0	4,936.3	5,490.4	5,915.4	....	157,750	154,139	167,216	176,584	193,044
Money Market Fund Shares............	26m.u	....	....	....	....	....	....	....	1,029	804	1,191	1,609	1,815
Bonds & Money Mkt. Instruments....	26n.u	....	....	....	....	....	....	....	80,682	85,516	79,747	75,651	66,741
o/w: Held by Resid.of Cty..............	26n	†3,422.9	3,583.8	3,703.8	3,691.3	3,593.6	3,291.5	....	....	....	....	....	....
Foreign Liab. (to Non-EA Ctys)........	26c	†7,665.3	8,261.3	8,384.0	8,908.5	9,398.5	10,338.8	....	180,987	176,122	200,074	189,772	187,149
Central Government Deposits.........	26d.u	....	....	....	....	....	....	....	1,222	763	1,109	917	746
o/w: Cent.Govt.Dep. in Cty...........	26d	238.1	270.3	217.0	78.8	60.6	245.6	....	863	586	868	789	628
Credit from Monetary Authorities.....	26g	66.1	139.0	123.8	106.7	121.7	75.5	....	20,457	15,481	7,672	10,953	16,891
Liab. to Bk.Inst.in Oth. EA Ctys........	26h.u	....	....	....	....	....	....	....	58,685	56,463	73,442	77,142	108,305
Capital Accounts..........................	27a	728.8	787.6	856.8	894.7	1,621.1	2,077.7	....	29,525	32,448	34,027	36,300	36,436
Other Items (Net)........................	27r	†317.0	321.3	609.7	615.3	27.9	−277.3	....	−7,627	−7,532	−6,209	1,346	5,115
Banking Survey (Nat'l Residency)		\multicolumn{12}{c}{*Billions of Francs through 1998; Millions of Euros Beginning 1999: End of Period*}
Foreign Assets (Net)......................	31n	†−401.3	118.6	−73.6	−202.4	−92.1	142.3	....	10,450	29,696	49,596	74,985	94,362
Domestic Credit..........................	32	†10,796.3	11,141.2	11,942.6	12,321.7	12,728.3	12,833.8	....	327,082	316,842	308,637	300,842	300,194
Claims on General Govt. (Net)........	32an	†5,100.6	5,346.9	5,962.7	6,222.7	6,325.7	6,084.6	....	134,730	120,285	111,319	101,946	96,370
Claims on Other Resident Sectors.....	32d	†5,695.7	5,794.3	5,979.9	6,099.0	6,402.6	6,749.2	....	192,352	196,557	197,318	198,896	203,824
Currency Issued..............................	34a.n	448.0	459.3	431.4	465.9	486.2	501.1	505.8	13,535	13,496	9,081	12,715	14,877
Demand Deposits..........................	34b.n	†966.4	1,060.6	1,111.3	1,152.7	1,200.0	1,237.0	....	50,447	53,694	56,553	57,883	64,179
Other Deposits............................	35..n	†4,148.9	4,560.7	4,706.0	4,936.3	5,490.4	5,915.4	....	157,750	154,139	167,216	176,584	193,044
Money Market Fund Shares............	36m	....	....	....	....	....	....	....	1,029	804	1,191	1,609	1,815
Bonds & Money Mkt. Instruments....	36n	†3,422.9	3,583.8	3,703.8	3,691.3	3,823.6	3,521.5	....	80,682	85,516	79,747	75,651	66,741
o/w: Over Two Years...................	36na	....	....	....	....	....	....	....	66,704	66,949	64,789	62,698	55,598
Capital Accounts..........................	37a	†768.8	831.2	903.3	943.3	1,671.7	2,130.8	....	34,894	38,264	40,135	41,024	40,701
Other Items (Net)........................	37r	†639.8	764.6	1,012.6	929.5	−36.0	−329.9	....	−808	626	4,310	10,360	13,201
Banking Survey (EA-Wide Residency)		\multicolumn{12}{c}{*Millions of Euros: End of Period*}
Foreign Assets (Net)......................	31n.u	....	....	....	....	....	....	....	−63,456	−48,303	−42,936	−20,559	−23,290
Domestic Credit..........................	32..u	....	....	....	....	....	....	....	397,204	388,746	413,991	403,832	415,967
Claims on General Govt. (Net)........	32anu	....	....	....	....	....	....	....	178,388	163,060	183,220	168,833	174,678
Claims on Other Resident Sect.......	32d.u	....	....	....	....	....	....	....	218,816	225,686	230,771	234,999	241,289
Currency Issued..............................	34a.u	....	....	....	....	....	....	....	13,535	13,496	9,081	12,715	14,877
Demand Deposits..........................	34b.u	....	....	....	....	....	....	....	53,573	58,511	61,404	62,073	69,458
Other Deposits............................	35..u	....	....	....	....	....	....	....	188,347	182,139	199,536	212,803	230,927
o/w: Other Dep. Over Two Yrs........	35abu	....	....	....	....	....	....	....	19,642	21,591	23,859	24,343	27,340
Money Market Fund Shares............	36m.u	....	....	....	....	....	....	....	1,029	804	1,191	1,609	1,815
Bonds & Money Mkt. Instruments....	36n.u	....	....	....	....	....	....	....	80,682	85,516	79,747	75,651	66,741
o/w: Over Two Years...................	36nau	....	....	....	....	....	....	....	66,704	66,949	64,789	62,698	55,598
Capital Accounts..........................	37a	....	....	....	....	....	....	....	34,894	38,264	40,135	41,024	40,701
Other Items (Net)........................	37r.u	....	....	....	....	....	....	....	−38,315	−38,286	−20,039	−22,603	−31,840
Interest Rates		\multicolumn{12}{c}{*Percent Per Annum*}
Discount Rate (End of Period)..........	60	7.75	5.25	4.50	3.00	2.50	2.75	2.75	....	....	....	....	....
Money Market Rate......................	60b	9.38	8.21	5.72	4.80	3.24	3.46	3.58	....	....	....	....	....
Treasury Bill Rate.........................	60c	9.36	8.52	5.57	4.67	3.19	3.38	3.51	2.72	4.02	4.16	3.17	2.23
Deposit Rate...............................	60l	6.25	†7.11	4.86	4.04	2.66	2.88	3.01	2.42	3.58	3.40	2.60	1.65
Lending Rate...............................	60p	13.00	11.81	9.42	8.42	7.17	7.06	7.25	6.71	7.98	8.46	7.71	6.89
Government Bond Yield.................	61	8.64	7.19	7.82	7.45	6.45	5.74	4.72	4.81	5.58	5.13	4.96	4.18
Prices, Production, Labor		\multicolumn{12}{c}{*Index Numbers (2000=100): Period Averages*}
Industrial Share Prices...................	62	89	93	106	100	....	....	....	....	....	....	....	....
Producer Prices													
Home and Import Goods.............	63	85.1	82.9	84.2	87.0	88.9	92.2	90.4	90.5	100.0	102.0	101.2	100.8
Industrial Production Prices...........	63b	89.0	88.1	89.3	†91.4	91.9	93.4	92.3	91.9	100.0	100.8	102.2	102.9
Consumer Prices...........................	64	86.3	88.7	90.8	92.1	†94.0	95.5	96.4	97.5	100.0	102.5	104.2	105.8
Harmonized CPI...........................	64h	....	....	....	92.4	94.0	95.4	96.3	97.4	100.0	102.4	104.0	105.6
Wages.......................................	65	82.8	85.4	87.5	89.3	91.1	93.0	95.3	97.9	100.0	102.8	105.4	107.4
Industrial Production....................	66	84.1	79.8	81.5	86.5	87.0	91.0	94.1	94.9	100.0	98.6	99.8	100.6
		\multicolumn{12}{c}{*Number in Thousands: Period Averages*}
Labor Force.................................	67d	4,237	....	4,160	4,185	4,196	4,214	4,241	4,382	4,401	....	4,402	....
Employment................................	67e	3,773	3,746	3,755	3,794	3,792	3,839	3,858	†4,007	4,092	4,051	4,070	....
Unemployment............................	67c	473	550	589	597	588	570	541	508	474	470	....	538
Unemployment Rate (%).................	67r	11.2	12.9	13.9	14.1	13.8	13.3	12.6	11.7	10.9	10.8	....	12.3

Belgium 124

		1992	1993	1994	1995	1996	1997	1998	1999	2000	2001	2002	2003
International Transactions (For Belgium Only)					*Billions of Francs through 1998; Billions of Euros Beginning 1999*								
Exports	70	....	4,349.1	4,792.7	5,177.8	5,430.2	6,142.9	6,491.3	†168.10	203.94	212.55	228.58	225.56
Imports, c.i.f.	71	....	3,953.5	4,339.7	4,702.0	5,065.8	5,619.2	5,967.9	†154.62	192.18	199.49	209.73	207.60
							2000=100						
Volume of Exports	72	....	66	72	77	78	84	88	91	100	103	111	114
Volume of Imports	73	....	69	75	78	82	85	91	91	100	104	113	116
Unit Value of Exports	74	....	82	83	85	87	92	91	91	100	102	101	98
Unit Value of Imports	75	....	77	79	81	84	89	88	89	100	102	100	98
Import Price (1990=100)	76.x	96	....	....	....	....	....	....	....	....	....	....	....
(BLEU: Country Code 126)							*Billions of Francs*						
Exports	70	3,969.8	4,129.0	4,579.0	4,996.1	5,133.1	5,916.2	....	....	....	....	....	....
Imports, c.i.f.	71	4,023.3	3,875.0	4,192.0	4,568.4	4,729.1	5,554.4	....	....	....	....	....	....
							1995=100						
Volume of Exports	72	77	†84	93	100	103	110	....	....	....	....	....	....
Volume of Imports	73	82	†83	95	100	106	111	....	....	....	....	....	....
Unit Value of Exports	74	102	†101	100	100	102	106	....	....	....	....	....	....
Unit Value of Imports	75	101	†99	98	100	102	107	....	....	....	....	....	....

Belgium 124

		1992	1993	1994	1995	1996	1997	1998	1999	2000	2001	2002	2003
Balance of Payments		\multicolumn{12}{c}{*Millions of US Dollars: Minus Sign Indicates Debit*}
(For Belgium-Luxembourg (126)													
Current Account, n.i.e.	78ald	6,650	11,237	12,571	14,232	13,762	13,914	12,168	14,086	11,381	9,392	....	....
Goods: Exports f.o.b.	78aad	116,841	106,302	122,795	155,219	154,695	149,497	153,558	161,263	164,677	163,498	....	....
Goods: Imports f.o.b.	78abd	−113,141	−100,522	−115,895	−145,664	−146,004	−141,794	−146,577	−154,237	−162,086	−159,790	....	....
Trade Balance	78acd	3,700	5,780	6,901	9,555	8,690	7,703	6,981	7,027	2,591	3,707	....	....
Services: Credit	78add	33,658	33,366	40,440	35,466	34,702	35,503	38,081	45,291	49,789	50,314	....	....
Services: Debit	78aed	−30,999	−29,995	−36,500	−33,134	−32,069	−31,664	−34,411	−39,167	−41,868	−43,316	....	....
Balance on Goods & Services	78afd	6,359	9,151	10,841	11,887	11,322	11,542	10,651	13,151	10,512	10,705	....	....
Income: Credit	78agd	88,295	83,011	89,403	74,798	62,884	58,237	65,251	71,892	75,673	78,906	....	....
Income: Debit	78ahd	−85,309	−78,138	−84,166	−67,990	−55,838	−51,882	−59,315	−66,125	−70,625	−75,999	....	....
Balance on Gds, Serv. & Inc.	78aid	9,345	14,024	16,078	18,695	18,368	17,896	16,588	18,918	15,560	13,612	....	....
Current Transfers, n.i.e.: Credit	78ajd	4,368	4,198	4,501	7,822	7,474	7,142	7,006	7,041	7,014	7,316	....	....
Current Transfers: Debit	78akd	−7,063	−6,986	−8,009	−12,285	−12,081	−11,124	−11,426	−11,872	−11,193	−11,535	....	....
Capital Account, n.i.e.	78bcd	—	—	....	378	179	403	−113	−54	−213	26	....	....
Capital Account, n.i.e.: Credit	78bad	—	—	....	734	673	783	323	449	222	480	....	....
Capital Account: Debit	78bbd	—	—	....	−356	−494	−379	−436	−503	−436	−454	....	....
Financial Account, n.i.e.	78bjd	−7,806	−13,563	−10,182	−12,912	−12,257	−12,091	−16,043	−13,470	−9,233	−7,978	....	....
Direct Investment Abroad	78bdd	−11,407	−4,904	−1,371	−11,603	−8,026	−7,252	−28,845	−130,012	−207,472	−86,091	....	....
Dir. Invest. in Rep. Econ., n.i.e.	78bed	11,286	10,750	8,514	10,689	14,064	11,998	22,690	142,703	214,941	73,635	....	....
Portfolio Investment Assets	78bfd	−62,887	−58,431	−40,963	−29,472	−48,409	−62,657	−100,234	−161,521	−122,814	−125,068	....	....
Equity Securities	78bkd	−115	−9,465	−10,649	−3,525	−3,582	−21,006	−29,087	−60,678	−103,290	−57,427	....	....
Debt Securities	78bld	−62,773	−48,966	−30,314	−25,946	−44,827	−41,651	−71,147	−100,842	−19,524	−67,642	....	....
Portfolio Investment Liab., n.i.e.	78bgd	59,016	50,472	17,445	4,649	36,666	54,047	59,253	135,837	132,547	140,588	....	....
Equity Securities	78bmd	56,272	46,838	22,489	6,505	34,243	47,207	58,418	92,372	82,908	97,662	....	....
Debt Securities	78bnd	2,743	3,634	−5,043	−1,856	2,423	6,840	835	43,466	49,639	42,926	....	....
Financial Derivatives Assets	78bwd	—	—	....	1,213	−970	−330	489	884	−3,653	−5,089	....	....
Financial Derivatives Liabilities	78bxd	—	—	....	630	483	444	302	1,142	1,252	942	....	....
Other Investment Assets	78bhd	−49,920	−51,772	11,269	−23,445	−14,977	−48,692	7,467	−58,713	−39,033	−70,053	....	....
Monetary Authorities	78bod	—	—	....	—	—	—	−147	−991	−342	13	....	....
General Government	78bpd	−536	−802	−294	−72	−372	−306	371	−1,848	−236	−137	....	....
Banks	78bqd	−49,107	−45,916	9,829	−16,926	9,164	−28,220	3,886	−12,806	−22,296	−58,086	....	....
Other Sectors	78brd	−277	−5,054	1,734	−6,447	−23,769	−20,166	3,357	−43,067	−16,159	−11,843	....	....
Other Investment Liab., n.i.e.	78bid	46,107	40,321	−5,076	34,426	8,913	40,352	22,836	56,210	14,999	63,158	....	....
Monetary Authorities	78bsd	—	—	—	223	−458	−50	193	23,578	−1,386	−3,903	....	....
General Government	78btd	−2,887	10,758	−5,233	322	−40	−161	203	1,405	−1,279	415	....	....
Banks	78bud	32,419	19,043	64	42,121	6,469	31,211	18,087	6,702	7,139	67,159	....	....
Other Sectors	78bvd	16,575	10,520	93	−8,240	2,941	9,352	4,352	24,525	10,524	−513	....	....
Net Errors and Omissions	78cad	1,726	204	−2,169	−1,456	−1,091	−1,171	1,893	−2,430	−2,894	3	....	....
Overall Balance	78cbd	569	−2,122	219	243	593	1,056	−2,095	−1,867	−959	1,442	....	....
Reserves and Related Items	79dad	−569	2,122	−219	−243	−593	−1,056	2,095	1,867	959	−1,442	....	....
Reserve Assets	79dbd	−569	2,122	−219	−243	−593	−1,056	2,095	1,867	959	−1,442	....	....
Use of Fund Credit and Loans	79dcd	—	—	—	—	—	—	....	....	....	....	....	....
Exceptional Financing	79ded	—	—	—	....	....	....	....	....	....	....	....	....
Balance of Payments		\multicolumn{12}{c}{*Millions of US Dollars: Minus Sign Indicates Debit*}
(For Belgium Only)													
Current Account, n.i.e.	78ald	....	....	....	....	....	....	....	....	....	....	13,305	11,623
Goods: Exports f.o.b.	78aad	....	....	....	....	....	....	....	....	....	....	168,192	203,299
Goods: Imports f.o.b.	78abd	....	....	....	....	....	....	....	....	....	....	−159,459	−193,767
Trade Balance	78acd	....	....	....	....	....	....	....	....	....	....	8,734	9,532
Services: Credit	78add	....	....	....	....	....	....	....	....	....	....	37,776	44,742
Services: Debit	78aed	....	....	....	....	....	....	....	....	....	....	−35,727	−42,823
Balance on Goods & Services	78afd	....	....	....	....	....	....	....	....	....	....	10,783	11,451
Income: Credit	78agd	....	....	....	....	....	....	....	....	....	....	35,845	37,165
Income: Debit	78ahd	....	....	....	....	....	....	....	....	....	....	−29,003	−30,335
Balance on Gds, Serv. & Inc.	78aid	....	....	....	....	....	....	....	....	....	....	17,625	18,281
Current Transfers, n.i.e.: Credit	78ajd	....	....	....	....	....	....	....	....	....	....	5,288	6,523
Current Transfers: Debit	78akd	....	....	....	....	....	....	....	....	....	....	−9,608	−13,181
Capital Account, n.i.e.	78bcd	....	....	....	....	....	....	....	....	....	....	−661	−968
Capital Account, n.i.e.: Credit	78bad	....	....	....	....	....	....	....	....	....	....	197	252
Capital Account: Debit	78bbd	....	....	....	....	....	....	....	....	....	....	−858	−1,220
Financial Account, n.i.e.	78bjd	....	....	....	....	....	....	....	....	....	....	−13,857	726
Direct Investment Abroad	78bdd	....	....	....	....	....	....	....	....	....	....	−11,442	−23,302
Dir. Invest. in Rep. Econ., n.i.e.	78bed	....	....	....	....	....	....	....	....	....	....	13,772	33,768
Portfolio Investment Assets	78bfd	....	....	....	....	....	....	....	....	....	....	−5,007	−3,190
Equity Securities	78bkd	....	....	....	....	....	....	....	....	....	....	−3,533	−5,557
Debt Securities	78bld	....	....	....	....	....	....	....	....	....	....	−1,474	2,367
Portfolio Investment Liab., n.i.e.	78bgd	....	....	....	....	....	....	....	....	....	....	19,683	5,739
Equity Securities	78bmd	....	....	....	....	....	....	....	....	....	....	−459	3,181
Debt Securities	78bnd	....	....	....	....	....	....	....	....	....	....	20,143	2,559
Financial Derivatives Assets	78bwd	....	....	....	....	....	....	....	....	....	....	−3,864	−7,417
Financial Derivatives Liabilities	78bxd	....	....	....	....	....	....	....	....	....	....	1,921	3,568
Other Investment Assets	78bhd	....	....	....	....	....	....	....	....	....	....	−44,556	−80,013
Monetary Authorities	78bod	....	....	....	....	....	....	....	....	....	....	185	−107
General Government	78bpd	....	....	....	....	....	....	....	....	....	....	−1	919
Banks	78bqd	....	....	....	....	....	....	....	....	....	....	−40,291	−69,456
Other Sectors	78brd	....	....	....	....	....	....	....	....	....	....	−4,392	−11,018
Other Investment Liab., n.i.e.	78bid	....	....	....	....	....	....	....	....	....	....	15,636	71,572
Monetary Authorities	78bsd	....	....	....	....	....	....	....	....	....	....	6,695	6,664

2004, International Monetary Fund: International Financial Statistics Yearbook

Belgium 124

		1992	1993	1994	1995	1996	1997	1998	1999	2000	2001	2002	2003
Balance of Payments(Cont.)													
General Government	78btd	....	....	....	....	....	....	....	....	....	....	−1,200	−628
Banks	78bud	....	....	....	....	....	....	....	....	....	....	6,683	57,492
Other Sectors	78bvd	....	....	....	....	....	....	....	....	....	....	3,458	8,044
Net Errors and Omissions	78cad	....	....	....	....	....	....	....	....	....	....	1,181	−13,104
Overall Balance	78cbd	....	....	....	....	....	....	....	....	....	....	−32	−1,723
Reserves and Related Items	79dad	....	....	....	....	....	....	....	....	....	....	32	1,723
Reserve Assets	79dbd	....	....	....	....	....	....	....	....	....	....	32	1,723
Use of Fund Credit and Loans	79dcd	....	....	....	....	....	....	....	....	....	....	−	−
Exceptional Financing	79ded	....	....	....	....	....	....	....	....	....	....	....	....
International Investment Position						*Millions of US Dollars*							
(For Belgium Only)													
Assets	79aad	439,946	469,094	533,478	602,052	609,439	608,200	702,972	762,666	757,673	771,750	910,115	....
Direct Investment Abroad	79abd	55,636	62,642	69,541	80,690	87,311	94,734	134,982	151,795	179,773	181,459	201,461	....
Portfolio Investment	79acd	124,141	145,694	161,256	190,573	194,879	199,743	250,060	312,632	297,202	320,225	348,829	....
Equity Securities	79add	42,616	59,319	59,804	63,767	64,571	64,661	94,142	125,274	124,687	110,226	104,777	....
Debt Securities	79aed	81,525	86,375	101,453	126,806	130,308	135,081	155,918	187,358	172,515	209,999	244,052	....
Financial Derivatives	79ald	−	−	−	653	1,362	1,869	2,383	3,516	4,187	6,564	5,000	....
Other Investment	79afd	237,342	238,244	279,199	306,655	302,837	290,473	295,043	281,414	264,269	249,933	340,127	....
Monetary Authorities	79agd	784	775	597	1,625	1,028	141	416	1,708	1,861	1,756	1,905	....
General Government	79ahd	2,140	2,049	1,947	7,952	7,277	6,333	6,375	5,425	5,025	4,815	405	....
Banks	79aid	177,366	178,926	203,816	219,643	207,834	199,252	197,284	183,264	162,845	172,133	263,025	....
Other Sectors	79ajd	57,052	56,494	72,839	77,435	86,698	84,748	90,968	91,017	94,539	71,228	74,791	....
Reserve Assets	79akd	22,827	22,514	23,482	23,482	23,050	21,382	20,503	13,310	12,242	13,569	14,698	....
Liabilities	79lad	416,667	437,690	495,611	554,101	542,475	528,266	604,018	617,628	615,340	653,214	804,743	....
Dir. Invest. in Rep. Economy	79lbd	75,678	94,295	105,881	112,960	123,883	128,728	180,492	179,924	195,219	203,537	238,270	....
Portfolio Investment	79lcd	80,530	93,603	103,808	106,724	97,497	89,423	91,255	112,113	126,455	127,152	162,140	....
Equity Securities	79ldd	5,937	8,253	9,737	10,012	11,173	12,099	17,843	15,471	14,237	15,663	18,067	....
Debt Securities	79led	74,593	85,350	94,071	96,713	86,324	77,324	73,412	96,643	112,218	111,489	144,073	....
Financial Derivatives	79lld	−	−	−	568	940	1,268	1,909	3,516	4,746	4,421	4,083	....
Other Investment	79lfd	260,458	249,792	285,921	333,849	320,154	308,847	330,362	322,075	288,920	318,103	400,251	....
Monetary Authorities	79lgd	663	665	848	1,132	522	452	847	17,279	7,165	6,274	14,649	....
General Government	79lhd	573	305	942	864	694	385	411	1,808	651	888	3,891	....
Banks	79lid	227,818	219,247	251,590	310,283	296,380	284,299	297,515	272,146	245,931	276,091	347,698	....
Other Sectors	79ljd	31,404	29,576	32,540	21,571	22,559	23,711	31,589	30,841	35,173	34,850	34,014	....
Government Finance													
Central Government				*Billions of Francs through 1998; Millions of Euros Beginning 1999: Year Ending December 31*									
Deficit (-) or Surplus	80	−486.1	−450.2	−324.9	−259.1	†−210.2	−165.1	−162.1	†−3,644.0	−550.4	−1,856.9	−1,778.4	−728.4
Revenue	81	3,094.5	3,263.4	3,476.4	3,567.5	†3,685.2	3,820.1	3,986.1	†39,405.1	42,181.4	42,278.1	45,189.6	50,387.4
Grants Received	81z	5.8	4.6	5.7	11.1	†5.0	20.3	6.8	....	....	....	....	....
Expenditure	82	3,575.3	3,699.5	3,821.3	3,885.6	†3,909.5	4,032.3	4,152.3	†43,049.1	42,731.8	44,135.0	46,968.0	51,115.8
Lending Minus Repayments	83	11.1	18.7	−14.3	−47.9	†−9.1	−26.8	2.7	....	....	....	....	....
Financing													
Net Borrowing: National Currency	84a	619.5	112.3	360.1	380.1	†612.9	104.7	273.1	†7,990.6	2,283.1	3,763.1	4,767.8	3,556.7
Net borrowing: Foreign Currency	85a	−107.6	454.9	−152.4	−262.0	†−334.1	−1.0	−79.6	†−4,345.7	−1,727.9	−1,911.2	−2,989.8	−2,828.4
Use of Cash Balances	87	−25.8	−117.0	117.2	141.0	†−68.6	61.4	−31.4	....	....	....	....	....
Debt: National Currency	88a	7,899.7	8,075.9	8,623.7	9,063.4	†9,576.7	9,702.8	9,717.7	†236,314.4	242,454.7	250,084.9	257,288.0	259,294.0
Debt: Foreign Currency	89a	1,010.5	1,519.9	1,349.5	1,085.3	†734.0	784.4	701.7	†10,441.3	8,606.9	7,079.8	5,464.0	3,724.0
General Government						*As Percent of Gross Domestic Product*							
Deficit (-) or Surplus	80g	−6.9	−7.1	−4.9	−4.0	−3.7	−1.9	−.8	−.6	.1	.2	....	....
Debt	88g	129.0	135.2	133.2	132.2	128.3	125.3	119.3	115.0	109.3	107.5	....	....
National Accounts						*Billions of Francs through 1998; Billions of Euros Beginning 1999*							
Househ.Cons.Expend.,incl.NPISHs	96f	4,006	4,093	4,288	4,424	4,567	4,744	4,938	†127	134	139	142	147
Government Consumption Expend	91f	1,529	1,596	1,670	1,739	1,810	1,857	1,917	†50	52	55	58	61
Gross Fixed Capital Formation	93e	1,495	1,498	1,534	1,625	1,647	1,790	1,880	†49	53	53	52	52
Changes in Inventories	93i	19	29	51	13	−52	−22	−15	†−	1	−1	−1	1
Exports of Goods and Services	90c	4,848	4,819	5,321	5,653	5,893	6,542	6,833	†178	212	218	218	220
Imports of Goods and Services (-)	98c	4,662	4,565	4,985	5,293	5,537	6,149	6,460	†168	204	210	208	212
Gross Domestic Product (GDP)	99b	7,234	7,471	7,878	8,161	8,327	8,761	9,093	†236	248	254	260	267
Net Primary Income from Abroad	98.n	39	114	182	168	166	173	194	†5	5	4	6	5
Gross National Income (GNI)	99a	7,273	7,585	8,061	8,330	8,493	8,934	9,287	†241	252	258	266	273
Net Current Transf.from Abroad	98t	−47	−51	−61	−56	−83	−83	−95	†−2	−2	−2	−2	−2
Gross Nat'l Disposable Inc.(GNDI)	99i	7,241	7,529	7,989	8,268	8,434	8,852	9,185	†238	250	256	264	271
Gross Saving	99s	1,705	1,838	2,035	2,101	2,057	2,252	2,331	†61	64	62	64	63
Consumption of Fixed Capital	99cf	1,000	1,053	1,108	1,178	1,242	1,299	1,362	†36	38	39	40	42
GDP Volume 1995 Prices	99b.p	7,777	7,724	7,980	8,162	8,231	8,551	8,728	†222.8	231.4	232.8	234.5	....
GDP Volume 2000 Prices	99b.p	....	....	....	....	....	....	....	†238.7	247.7	249.4	251.1	253.8
GDP Volume (2000=100)	99bvp	77.8	77.3	79.9	81.7	82.4	85.6	87.4	†96.4	100.0	100.7	101.4	102.5
GDP Deflator (2000=100)	99bip	93.0	96.7	98.7	99.9	101.1	102.4	104.1	†98.7	100.0	101.7	103.5	105.3
Population						*Millions: Midyear Estimates*							
	99z	10.03	10.07	10.11	10.14	10.16	10.19	10.21	10.23	10.25	10.27	10.30	10.32

Belize 339

		1992	1993	1994	1995	1996	1997	1998	1999	2000	2001	2002	2003
Exchange Rates		\multicolumn{12}{c}{*Belize Dollars per SDR: End of Period (aa) Belize Dollars per US Dollar: End of Period (ae)*}
Official Rate	aa	2.7500	2.7471	2.9197	2.9730	2.8759	2.6985	2.8161	2.7450	2.6058	2.5135	2.7190	2.9719
Official Rate	ae	2.0000	2.0000	2.0000	2.0000	2.0000	2.0000	2.0000	2.0000	2.0000	2.0000	2.0000	2.0000
		\multicolumn{12}{c}{*Index Numbers (2000=100): Period Averages*}
Official Rate	ahx	100.0	100.0	100.0	100.0	100.0	100.0	100.0	100.0	100.0	100.0	100.0	100.0
Nominal Effective Exchange Rate	nec	75.3	81.8	85.7	86.0	88.7	92.8	95.4	96.3	100.0	103.2	102.2	96.4
Real Effective Exchange Rate	rec	94.1	99.2	95.6	93.5	98.3	101.4	101.1	98.6	100.0	101.5	101.3	95.9
Fund Position		\multicolumn{12}{c}{*Millions of SDRs: End of Period*}
Quota	2f.s	13.50	13.50	13.50	13.50	13.50	13.50	13.50	18.80	18.80	18.80	18.80	18.80
SDRs	1b.s	.15	.29	.37	.47	.61	.71	.82	1.01	1.20	1.37	1.48	1.56
Reserve Position in the Fund	1c.s	2.91	2.91	2.91	2.91	2.91	2.91	2.91	4.24	4.24	4.24	4.24	4.24
Total Fund Cred.&Loans Outstg	2tl	–	–	–	–	–	–	–	–	–	–	–	–
International Liquidity		\multicolumn{12}{c}{*Millions of US Dollars Unless Otherwise Indicated: End of Period*}
Total Reserves minus Gold	1l.d	52.94	38.75	34.52	37.61	58.40	59.42	44.09	71.31	122.90	112.04	114.51	84.68
SDRs	1b.d	.21	.39	.54	.70	.88	.96	1.16	1.39	1.56	1.72	2.01	2.32
Reserve Position in the Fund	1c.d	4.00	4.00	4.25	4.34	4.19	3.93	4.10	5.82	5.52	5.33	5.76	6.30
Foreign Exchange	1d.d	48.74	34.35	29.72	32.58	53.34	54.53	38.82	64.10	115.82	104.99	106.74	76.07
Monetary Authorities: Other Liab.	4..d	8.79	6.81	6.21	5.31	1.77	3.64	1.61	1.04	.84	1.47	2.99	2.90
Deposit Money Banks: Assets	7a.d	12.31	23.64	24.27	26.21	38.45	35.84	37.94	45.64	71.64	69.17	58.95	62.09
Liabilities	7b.d	23.60	49.15	51.68	39.59	41.40	43.71	50.69	43.06	59.83	71.64	71.35	101.82
Other Banking Insts.: Assets	7e.d	.01	–	–	–	–	–	–	–	–	–	–	–
Liabilities	7f.d	15.53	14.11	14.20	14.33	13.64	17.88	17.97	21.11	64.25	108.18	126.07	95.90
Monetary Authorities		\multicolumn{12}{c}{*Millions of Belize Dollars: End of Period*}
Foreign Assets	11	105.86	77.27	68.94	75.24	116.85	118.89	88.23	142.90	245.85	224.15	229.98	169.43
Claims on Central Government	12a	31.40	61.47	67.54	81.72	110.78	89.86	94.89	67.38	62.49	78.03	63.59	165.37
Claims on Deposit Money Banks	12e	10.00	8.50	7.84	7.06	6.39	4.18	2.25	1.00	84.19	84.00	15.00	15.12
Reserve Money	14	105.38	104.63	102.50	116.21	119.64	125.81	135.57	165.22	202.80	257.79	198.86	207.09
of which: Currency Outside DMBs	14a	50.98	54.19	56.74	61.42	63.61	66.45	70.38	84.15	95.96	105.17	106.80	103.27
Foreign Liabilities	16c	17.58	13.62	12.41	10.62	3.54	7.29	3.22	2.08	1.67	2.94	5.99	5.79
Central Government Deposits	16d	13.30	15.06	17.88	19.42	65.93	47.31	21.48	25.87	91.92	31.48	83.08	123.06
Capital Accounts	17a	19.85	17.18	17.78	18.50	19.30	20.19	20.82	21.30	21.52	21.72	22.18	22.49
Other Items (Net)	17r	–8.85	–3.25	–6.24	–.73	25.62	12.35	4.29	–3.19	74.62	72.25	–1.54	–8.51
Deposit Money Banks		\multicolumn{12}{c}{*Millions of Belize Dollars: End of Period*}
Reserves	20	53.40	49.95	45.13	53.77	54.71	58.68	64.85	59.02	101.45	103.28	84.42	100.36
Foreign Assets	21	24.62	47.28	48.53	52.42	76.90	71.68	75.89	91.27	143.27	138.34	117.90	124.18
Claims on Central Government	22a	60.75	48.93	52.99	63.88	39.77	61.92	58.39	80.11	87.12	87.87	62.98	54.98
Claims on Local Government	22b	.02	.01	.11	–	.05	.01	.23	1.38	1.16	2.17	2.49	3.27
Claims on Official Entities	22bx	1.16	.31	.27	2.73	2.81	5.18	9.36	4.99	9.03	10.72	6.90	5.31
Claims on Private Sector	22d	372.01	385.99	405.27	436.44	478.03	540.03	610.72	641.14	679.71	771.03	884.12	1,010.75
Demand Deposits	24	74.45	81.65	86.81	93.32	99.12	99.03	115.85	141.86	185.99	225.05	214.13	295.42
Time, Savings,& Fgn.Currency Dep	25	285.11	288.57	316.35	388.84	421.56	486.98	504.93	552.39	612.72	631.29	665.59	638.57
Foreign Liabilities	26c	47.21	98.30	103.36	79.18	82.79	87.42	101.39	86.12	119.67	143.27	142.70	203.64
Central Government Deposits	26d	74.24	49.30	43.86	23.59	27.78	26.89	40.68	21.56	24.31	20.93	27.47	20.50
Credit from Monetary Authorities	26g	7.98	5.32	1.66	1.48	1.28	1.09	.88	.63	.41	.16	–	5.12
Capital Accounts	27a	28.41	31.00	31.04	39.40	43.54	49.77	51.73	69.71	71.33	89.16	112.06	154.42
Other Items (Net)	27r	–5.45	–21.66	–30.78	–16.57	–23.81	–13.69	4.00	5.64	7.31	3.55	–3.14	–18.82
Monetary Survey		\multicolumn{12}{c}{*Millions of Belize Dollars: End of Period*}
Foreign Assets (Net)	31n	65.70	12.64	1.70	37.85	95.86	107.43	59.51	145.97	267.79	216.28	199.19	84.18
Domestic Credit	32	377.78	432.35	464.44	541.76	537.72	622.80	711.44	747.57	723.29	897.41	909.53	1,096.12
Claims on Central Govt. (Net)	32an	4.60	46.03	58.80	102.59	56.83	77.58	91.13	100.07	33.38	113.50	16.02	76.80
Claims on Local Government	32b	.02	.01	.11	–	.05	.01	.23	1.38	1.16	2.17	2.49	3.27
Claims on Official Entities	32bx	1.16	.31	.27	2.73	2.81	5.18	9.36	4.99	9.03	10.72	6.90	5.31
Claims on Private Sector	32d	372.01	385.99	405.27	436.44	478.03	540.03	610.72	641.14	679.71	771.03	884.12	1,010.75
Money	34	126.33	136.35	144.18	155.47	164.02	166.17	186.65	248.24	287.32	379.65	328.47	402.17
Quasi-Money	35	285.11	288.57	316.35	388.84	421.56	486.98	504.93	552.39	612.72	631.29	665.59	638.57
Capital Accounts	37a	48.26	48.18	48.82	57.90	62.84	69.95	72.55	91.00	92.85	110.88	134.24	176.91
Other Items (Net)	37r	–16.23	–28.11	–43.20	–22.59	–3.28	–4.45	6.83	1.92	–1.82	–8.12	–19.59	–37.35
Money plus Quasi-Money	35l	411.45	424.92	460.53	544.31	585.58	653.15	691.58	800.62	900.04	1,010.93	994.07	1,040.74
Other Banking Institutions		\multicolumn{12}{c}{*Millions of Belize Dollars: End of Period*}
Reserves	40	2.38	1.28	1.41	2.47	.93	3.17	1.58	11.35	10.17	20.68	8.36	5.85
Foreign Assets	41	.02	–	–	–	–	–	–	–	–	–	–	–
Claims on Central Government	42a	–	–	–	–	–	–	–	–	–	–	–	–
Claims on Official Entities	42bx	.17	.17	–	–	–	–	–	–	–	–	–	–
Claims on Private Sector	42d	36.59	40.66	45.70	47.03	53.75	60.78	65.96	61.92	199.33	266.63	216.41	224.24
Foreign Liabilities	46c	31.05	28.22	28.41	28.66	27.29	35.77	35.93	42.22	128.50	216.35	252.14	191.81
Central Government Deposits	46d	.26	.80	1.23	1.40	1.07	1.20	2.71	27.06	6.10	3.35	8.81	85.36
Credit from Monetary Authorities	46g	–	3.08	3.35	4.07	6.30	6.02	5.77	5.36	4.45	85.27	16.57	11.10
Capital Accounts	47a	–1.52	–.26	1.21	3.48	8.69	10.68	11.88	13.80	15.84	23.90	29.13	31.55
Other Items (Net)	47r	9.36	10.29	12.90	11.89	11.34	10.29	11.25	–15.17	54.61	–41.57	–81.88	–89.72

2004, International Monetary Fund: International Financial Statistics Yearbook

Belize 339

		1992	1993	1994	1995	1996	1997	1998	1999	2000	2001	2002	2003
Banking Survey						*Millions of Belize Dollars: End of Period*							
Foreign Assets (Net)	51n	34.66	−15.58	−26.70	9.20	80.14	60.09	23.58	103.75	139.29	−.07	−52.96	−107.63
Domestic Credit	52	414.29	472.39	508.91	587.39	590.40	682.38	774.70	782.43	916.52	1,160.69	1,117.13	1,235.00
Claims on Central Govt. (Net)	52an	4.35	45.24	57.57	101.20	55.76	76.38	88.42	73.01	27.29	110.15	7.21	−8.56
Claims on Local Government	52b	.02	.01	.11	—	.05	.01	.23	1.38	1.16	2.17	2.49	3.27
Claims on Official Entities	52bx	1.33	.48	.27	2.73	2.81	5.18	9.36	4.99	9.03	10.72	6.90	5.31
Claims on Private Sector	52d	408.60	426.66	450.97	483.47	531.79	600.81	676.69	703.06	879.03	1,037.66	1,100.53	1,234.99
Liquid Liabilities	55l	409.07	423.64	459.12	541.85	584.65	649.98	690.00	789.27	889.87	990.25	985.71	1,034.89
Capital Accounts	57a	46.75	47.92	50.04	61.38	71.53	80.63	84.43	104.80	108.69	134.78	163.37	208.46
Other Items (Net)	57r	−6.87	−14.74	−26.95	−6.63	14.36	11.86	23.86	−7.89	57.24	35.58	−84.90	−115.97
Interest Rates						*Percent Per Annum*							
Discount Rate (End of Period)	60	12.00	12.00	12.00	12.00	12.00	12.00	12.00	12.00	12.00	12.00	12.00	12.00
Treasury Bill Rate	60c	5.38	4.59	4.27	4.10	3.78	3.51	3.83	5.91	5.91	5.91	4.59	3.22
Savings Rate	60k	5.40	5.40	5.32	5.30	5.30	5.35	5.43	5.42	5.43	5.44	5.10	5.05
Deposit Rate	60l	8.15	8.13	8.55	9.37	9.08	9.19	8.76	8.12	7.69	6.35	6.28	6.93
Lending Rate	60p	14.32	14.37	14.78	15.69	16.30	16.29	16.50	16.27	16.01	15.45	14.83	14.35
Prices						*Index Numbers (2000=100): Period Averages*							
Consumer Prices	64	88.1	89.4	91.8	94.4	100.4	101.5	100.6	99.4	100.0	101.2	103.4	106.1
						Number in Thousands: Period Averages							
Labor Force	67d	....	....	70	....	....	....	....	....	....	....	....	....
Employment	67e	....	62	62	63	65	71	73	78	....	....	....	....
Unemployment	67c	....	7	8	....	....	....	....	....	....	86	85	....
Unemployment Rate (%)	67r	....	9.8	11.1	....	....	....	....	....	....	....	....	....
International Transactions						*Millions of Belize Dollars*							
Exports	70	281.01	272.97	301.98	323.25	335.27	352.95	344.26	372.08	436.95	337.29	337.11	409.11
Imports, c.i.f.	71	548.06	561.92	519.86	514.43	510.97	572.42	590.32	739.82	1,048.57	1,033.65	1,049.03	1,103.33
Balance of Payments						*Millions of US Dollars: Minus Sign Indicates Debit*							
Current Account, n.i.e.	78ald	−28.6	−48.5	−40.1	−17.2	−6.6	−31.9	−59.8	−77.5	−139.5	−184.9	−162.7	....
Goods: Exports f.o.b.	78aad	140.6	132.0	156.5	164.6	171.3	193.4	186.2	213.2	212.3	275.0	310.4	....
Goods: Imports f.o.b.	78abd	−244.5	−250.5	−231.9	−230.6	−229.5	−282.9	−290.9	−337.5	−403.7	−488.7	−500.3	....
Trade Balance	78acd	−103.9	−118.5	−75.4	−66.1	−58.2	−89.5	−104.7	−124.3	−191.4	−213.7	−189.9	....
Services: Credit	78add	142.6	150.5	121.1	132.8	137.9	137.8	140.5	161.6	172.4	174.6	184.1	....
Services: Debit	78aed	−81.6	−92.5	−88.0	−94.9	−91.3	−91.7	−99.0	−108.2	−119.8	−121.8	−130.7	....
Balance on Goods & Services	78afd	−42.9	−60.5	−42.2	−28.1	−11.7	−43.3	−63.3	−70.8	−138.8	−161.0	−136.5	....
Income: Credit	78agd	6.7	5.9	2.9	2.8	6.3	7.5	7.2	2.7	4.8	11.1	7.1	....
Income: Debit	78ahd	−22.8	−23.4	−28.2	−25.1	−32.4	−30.8	−39.3	−46.6	−58.9	−83.2	−79.2	....
Balance on Gds, Serv. & Inc.	78aid	−59.0	−78.0	−67.5	−50.4	−37.8	−66.7	−95.4	−114.7	−192.9	−233.1	−208.7	....
Current Transfers, n.i.e.: Credit	78ajd	35.4	33.8	34.4	38.3	34.2	38.2	38.4	40.6	56.6	50.0	48.0	....
Current Transfers: Debit	78akd	−5.0	−4.3	−6.9	−5.2	−3.1	−3.4	−2.8	−3.5	−3.2	−1.8	−2.1	....
Capital Account, n.i.e.	78bcd	—	—	—	—	−2.2	−3.4	−1.9	−2.0	.5	.5	7.5	....
Capital Account, n.i.e.: Credit	78bad	—	—	—	—	—	—	—	.5	.9	2.1	9.6	....
Capital Account: Debit	78bbd	—	—	—	—	−2.2	−3.4	−1.9	−2.4	−.5	−1.7	−2.1	....
Financial Account, n.i.e.	78bjd	22.4	32.8	3.6	−1.0	11.0	27.6	23.5	91.5	88.4	171.5	143.7	....
Direct Investment Abroad	78bdd	—	—	—	—	−5.7	−3.9	−4.5	—	....	....	....	....
Dir. Invest. in Rep. Econ., n.i.e.	78bed	15.6	9.2	15.4	21.1	16.6	12.0	17.7	47.4	17.7	59.9	25.0	....
Portfolio Investment Assets	78bfd	—	—	—	—	—	—	—	—	....	....	—	....
Equity Securities	78bkd	—	—	—	—	—	—	—	—	....	....	—	....
Debt Securities	78bld	—	—	—	—	—	—	—	—	....	....	—	....
Portfolio Investment Liab., n.i.e.	78bgd	.2	7.0	6.1	3.5	10.1	10.2	12.5	32.9	26.9	−14.9	110.0	....
Equity Securities	78bmd	—	—	—	—	—	—	....	....	....	....	—	....
Debt Securities	78bnd	.2	7.0	6.1	3.5	10.1	10.2	12.5	32.9	26.9	−14.9	110.0	....
Financial Derivatives Assets	78bwd	....	....	....	....	....	....	....	....	....	....	—	....
Financial Derivatives Liabilities	78bxd	....	....	....	....	....	....	....	....	....	—	.8	....
Other Investment Assets	78bhd	3.7	−11.6	−17.1	−14.1	−12.2	2.8	—	−8.9	−39.4	−2.4	−1.4	....
Monetary Authorities	78bod	....	....	....	....	....	....	....	....	....	....	—	....
General Government	78bpd	—	—	—	—	—	—	—	....	....	−11.1	−3.1	−8.0	....
Banks	78bqd	3.7	−11.6	−3.3	−1.7	−12.2	2.8	—	−6.3	−26.3	2.5	9.3	....
Other Sectors	78brd	—	—	−13.8	−12.4	—	—	—	−2.7	−2.1	−1.9	−2.7	....
Other Investment Liab., n.i.e.	78bid	3.0	28.2	−.8	−11.5	2.2	6.5	−2.2	20.2	83.3	129.0	9.4	....
Monetary Authorities	78bsd	—	—	—	—	—	—	—	−.6	41.8	−.6	−33.0	....
General Government	78btd	6.1	16.3	8.9	−2.6	19.7	11.5	8.8	14.9	46.1	122.6	11.6	....
Banks	78bud	9.1	18.7	−9.3	−12.1	−6.3	4.8	7.2	−8.9	15.5	11.6	−1.4	....
Other Sectors	78bvd	−12.2	−6.8	−.3	3.2	−11.2	−9.8	−18.2	14.8	−20.2	−4.6	32.2	....
Net Errors and Omissions	78cad	6.3	1.5	32.8	22.4	18.4	9.1	24.5	.9	7.3	9.4	3.8	....
Overall Balance	78cbd	.1	−14.2	−3.6	4.1	20.6	1.4	−13.7	12.9	−43.3	−3.5	−7.7	....
Reserves and Related Items	79dad	−.1	14.2	3.6	−4.1	−20.6	−1.4	13.7	−12.9	43.3	3.5	7.7	....
Reserve Assets	79dbd	−.1	14.2	3.6	−4.1	−20.6	−1.4	13.7	−27.5	−51.8	3.2	5.5	....
Use of Fund Credit and Loans	79dcd	—	—	—	—	—	—	—	—	—	—	—	....
Exceptional Financing	79ded	—	—	—	—	—	—	....	14.6	95.2	.3	2.2	....

Belize 339

		1992	1993	1994	1995	1996	1997	1998	1999	2000	2001	2002	2003
Government Finance		*Thousands of Belize Dollars: Year Beginning April 1*											
Deficit (-) or Surplus	80	−44,411	−82,365	−70,802	−39,698	−15,671	−32,588f	....	....	....	....	....	....
Revenue	81	245,281	247,864	258,978	261,658	288,256	283,357f	....	....	....	....	....	....
Grants Received	81z	9,848	6,953	13,264	1,079	4,076	41,191f	....	....	....	....	....	....
Expenditure	82	332,438	342,935	348,953	306,090	317,781	362,261f	....	....	....	....	....	....
Lending Minus Repayments	83	−32,898	−5,753	−5,909	−3,655	−9,778	−5,125f	....	....	....	....	....	....
Financing													
Domestic	84a	5,348	42,583	45,433	41,604	−33,262	....	....	....	....	....	....	....
Foreign	85a	39,063	39,782	25,369	−1,906	48,933	....	....	....	....	....	....	....
Debt: Domestic	88a	113,070	136,104	145,985	167,747	168,330	....	....	....	....	....	....	....
Foreign	89a	228,555	259,453	285,800	282,610	329,798	....	....	....	....	....	....	....
National Accounts						*Millions of Belize Dollars*							
Househ.Cons.Expend.,incl.NPISHs	96f	630.3	690.2	723.7	891.6	964.6	1,000.9	1,074.3	1,139.8	1,252.1	1,362.4	1,470.5	....
Government Consumption Expend	91f	146.4	171.4	186.8	177.1	181.4	190.2	197.5	197.9	215.3	229.3	250.4	....
Gross Fixed Capital Formation	93e	276.0	318.9	254.3	269.2	260.6	261.0	259.0	360.4	477.0	436.9	420.6	....
Changes in Inventories	93i	6.2	1.9	11.7	−	.5	3.0	3.8	−.1	55.9	−6.2	23.0	....
Exports of Goods and Services	90c	568.3	565.9	579.2	594.9	641.4	690.7	724.6	806.8	865.8	881.3	974.2	....
Imports of Goods and Services (-)	98c	651.6	685.5	639.4	609.1	644.8	729.0	784.5	987.1	1,226.0	1,204.9	1,233.4	....
Gross Domestic Product (GDP)	99b	969.3	1,061.0	1,104.5	1,338.0	1,407.2	1,455.1	1,534.5	1,698.1	2,000.3	2,022.5	2,164.6	....
Net Primary Income from Abroad	98.n	−33.5	−37.4	−43.8	−45.2	−52.8	−46.8	−58.2	−83.4	−109.0	130.2	....	....
Gross National Income (GNI)	99a	935.8	1,023.5	1,060.7	1,129.2	1,158.6	1,188.2	1,201.0	1,292.6	1,437.0	1,479.7	....	....
Consumption of Fixed Capital	99cf	59.4	70.4	53.9	60.1	59.5	60.1	996.1	1,098.3	1,183.7	....	....	....
GDP Volume 2000 Prices	99b.p	....	....	....	1,430.8	1,447.3	1,478.9	1,546.6	1,726.1	2,000.3	2,039.7	2,151.4	....
GDP Volume (2000=100)	99bvp	64.2	67.0	68.6	†71.5	72.4	73.9	77.3	86.3	100.0	102.0	107.6	....
GDP Deflator (2000=100)	99bip	75.4	79.2	80.5	93.5	97.2	98.4	99.2	98.4	100.0	99.2	100.6	....
						Millions: Midyear Estimates							
Population	99z	.20	.20	.21	.21	.22	.22	.23	.23	.24	.25	.25	.26

2004, International Monetary Fund: *International Financial Statistics Yearbook*

Benin 638

		1992	1993	1994	1995	1996	1997	1998	1999	2000	2001	2002	2003
Exchange Rates						*Francs per SDR: End of Period*							
Official Rate	aa	378.57	404.89	†780.44	728.38	753.06	807.94	791.61	†896.19	918.49	935.39	850.37	771.76
					Francs per US Dollar: End of Period (ae) Period Average (rf)								
Official Rate	ae	275.33	294.78	†534.60	490.00	523.70	598.81	562.21	†652.95	704.95	744.31	625.50	519.36
Official Rate	rf	264.69	283.16	†555.20	499.15	511.55	583.67	589.95	†615.70	711.98	733.04	696.99	581.20
Fund Position						*Millions of SDRs: End of Period*							
Quota	2f.s	45.3	45.3	45.3	45.3	45.3	45.3	45.3	61.9	61.9	61.9	61.9	61.9
SDRs	1b.s	–	.1	–	.1	.2	–	–	.2	.1	.3	.1	.1
Reserve Position in the Fund	1c.s	2.1	2.1	2.1	2.1	2.2	2.2	2.2	2.2	2.2	2.2	2.2	2.2
Total Fund Cred.&Loans Outstg	2tl	15.7	31.3	48.8	56.6	68.9	70.3	66.4	67.1	64.4	61.1	53.9	49.2
International Liquidity					*Millions of US Dollars Unless Otherwise Indicated: End of Period*								
Total Reserves minus Gold	1l.d	245.2	244.0	†258.2	197.9	261.8	253.1	261.5	400.1	458.1	578.1	615.7	509.8
SDRs	1b.d	–	.1	–	.1	.3	.1	.1	.2	.1	.4	.1	.2
Reserve Position in the Fund	1c.d	2.8	2.9	3.1	3.2	3.1	2.9	3.1	3.0	2.9	2.7	3.0	3.3
Foreign Exchange	1d.d	242.4	241.0	†255.1	194.7	258.4	250.1	258.4	396.9	455.2	574.9	612.6	506.3
Gold (Million Fine Troy Ounces)	1ad	.011	.011	.011	–	–	–	–	–	–	–	–	–
Gold (National Valuation)	1and	3.8	4.1	4.1	–	–	–	–	–	–	–	–	–
Monetary Authorities: Other Liab	4..d	4.7	13.6	3.8	6.1	10.9	12.8	2.6	2.0	1.7	–2.5	2.8	6.3
Deposit Money Banks: Assets	7a.d	72.7	96.2	143.9	239.3	278.8	265.0	288.9	253.9	214.2	239.7	271.8	283.8
Liabilities	7b.d	56.2	50.7	30.4	50.2	102.0	53.1	89.5	107.3	88.2	99.0	100.3	151.5
Monetary Authorities						*Billions of Francs: End of Period*							
Foreign Assets	11	67.5	71.9	138.1	97.0	137.1	151.5	147.0	261.2	322.9	430.3	385.1	264.8
Claims on Central Government	12a	28.7	23.2	28.3	41.9	42.6	55.1	52.0	52.7	52.8	51.1	45.5	41.9
Claims on Deposit Money Banks	12e	50.3	50.3	–	–	2.0	1.0	–	–	–	–	–	–
Reserve Money	14	123.3	107.4	108.9	80.5	87.9	105.4	100.7	177.0	249.1	306.8	266.7	162.8
of which: Currency Outside DMBs	14a	51.7	25.5	77.3	50.6	68.9	80.8	70.4	160.3	211.8	222.3	167.9	80.0
Foreign Liabilities	16c	7.2	16.7	40.1	44.2	57.6	64.5	54.1	61.4	60.4	55.3	47.6	41.2
Central Government Deposits	16d	11.6	17.4	18.7	15.1	37.0	31.1	36.7	71.1	63.4	112.8	91.6	87.7
Other Items (Net)	17r	4.4	3.9	–1.4	–.9	–.8	6.6	7.5	4.4	2.9	6.5	24.8	14.9
Deposit Money Banks						*Billions of Francs: End of Period*							
Reserves	20	71.0	93.2	30.9	32.4	17.1	31.9	31.5	16.5	37.1	77.0	86.3	78.0
Foreign Assets	21	20.0	28.4	76.9	117.3	146.0	158.7	162.4	165.8	151.0	178.4	170.0	147.4
Claims on Central Government	22a	6.4	7.1	44.4	40.6	44.2	32.9	30.7	25.9	25.8	23.1	20.6	23.8
Claims on Private Sector	22d	69.4	67.7	75.0	80.4	102.4	71.7	100.1	161.7	194.0	192.8	222.2	293.8
Claims on Other Financial Insts	22f	–	–	1.0	1.0	–	–	–	–	–	–	–	–
Demand Deposits	24	72.9	84.6	106.3	107.8	114.8	107.5	108.4	104.2	146.7	167.2	191.3	208.8
Time Deposits	25	47.9	59.3	66.1	86.0	90.5	99.6	98.3	110.2	114.6	136.8	133.3	146.9
Foreign Liabilities	26c	14.9	14.0	14.9	24.1	52.8	31.0	49.6	67.6	59.8	72.9	61.4	76.2
Long-Term Foreign Liabilities	26cl	.6	.9	1.3	.5	.6	.8	.7	2.4	2.3	.9	1.4	2.5
Central Government Deposits	26d	19.7	25.6	35.0	34.0	35.1	39.8	56.1	74.4	79.4	84.5	95.0	81.9
Credit from Monetary Authorities	26g	50.3	50.3	–	–	4.0	1.0	–	–	–	–	–	–
Other Items (Net)	27r	–39.4	–38.4	4.5	19.3	12.0	15.5	11.6	10.9	5.2	9.2	16.9	26.8
Treasury Claims: Private Sector	22d.i	–	–	–	–	–	–	–	–	–	–	–	–
Post Office: Checking Deposits	24..i	1.9	.6	2.0	2.8	5.3	4.4	4.7	5.1	5.8	9.6	7.3	7.4
Monetary Survey						*Billions of Francs: End of Period*							
Foreign Assets (Net)	31n	65.4	69.5	159.9	146.0	172.7	214.7	205.7	298.0	353.8	480.5	446.2	294.7
Domestic Credit	32	75.2	55.7	97.0	117.7	122.4	93.2	94.7	99.9	135.7	79.3	109.1	197.4
Claims on Central Govt. (Net)	32an	5.8	–12.1	21.0	36.3	20.0	21.5	–5.4	–61.7	–58.3	–113.5	–113.2	–96.5
Claims on Private Sector	32d	69.4	67.7	75.0	80.4	102.4	71.7	100.1	161.7	194.0	192.8	222.2	293.8
Claims on Other Financial Insts	32f	–	–	1.0	1.0	–	–	–	–	–	–	–	–
Money	34	128.2	111.3	186.2	161.7	189.5	193.4	184.2	270.6	365.4	401.8	367.3	297.3
Quasi-Money	35	47.9	59.3	66.1	86.0	90.5	99.6	98.3	110.2	114.6	136.8	133.3	146.9
Long-Term Foreign Liabilities	36cl	.6	.9	1.3	.5	.6	.8	.7	2.4	2.3	.9	1.4	2.5
Other Items (Net)	37r	–36.1	–46.3	3.3	15.4	14.5	14.2	17.2	14.6	7.2	20.5	53.3	45.4
Money plus Quasi-Money	35l	176.1	170.6	252.3	247.7	280.0	293.0	282.5	380.8	480.0	538.5	500.6	444.2
Interest Rates						*Percent Per Annum*							
Bank Rate (End of Period)	60	12.50	†6.00	6.00	6.00	6.00	6.00	6.00	6.00	6.00	6.00	6.00	4.50
Money Market Rate	60b	11.44	....	....	....	....	....	4.81	4.95	4.95	4.95	4.95	4.95
Deposit Rate	60l	7.75	....	....	....	....	....	3.50	3.50	3.50	3.50	3.50	3.50
Lending Rate	60p	16.75	....	....	....	....	....	....	....	....	....	....	....
Prices						*Index Numbers (2000=100): Period Averages*							
Consumer Prices	64	52.3	52.6	72.8	83.4	87.5	†90.5	95.7	96.0	100.0	104.0	106.6	108.2
						Number in Thousands: Period Averages							
Labor Force	67d	2,085	....	....	....	3,211	....	....	....	....	....	....	....
Employment	67e	56	....	....	....	....	....	....	....	....	....	....	....
International Transactions						*Billions of Francs*							
Exports	70	88.80	108.60	220.90	209.60	334.70	243.40	240.40	259.50	279.40	273.90	312.10	314.20
Imports, c.i.f	71	153.02	161.78	239.35	372.20	334.70	397.90	434.00	464.58	433.30	405.40	473.10	440.50

Benin 638

		1992	1993	1994	1995	1996	1997	1998	1999	2000	2001	2002	2003
Balance of Payments		\multicolumn{12}{c}{*Millions of US Dollars: Minus Sign Indicates Debit*}
Current Account, n.i.e.	78ald	−120.1	−101.0	−23.2	−206.6	−57.4	−169.9	−151.5	−191.4	−111.0	−160.5	....	....
Goods: Exports f.o.b.	78aad	345.1	393.5	397.9	419.9	527.7	424.0	414.3	421.5	392.4	373.5	....	....
Goods: Imports f.o.b.	78abd	−560.5	−561.4	−451.5	−622.5	−559.7	−576.9	−572.6	−635.2	−516.1	−553.0	....	....
Trade Balance	78acd	−215.5	−167.9	−53.6	−202.5	−32.0	−152.9	−158.3	−213.7	−123.7	−179.5	....	....
Services: Credit	78add	156.0	146.6	142.2	194.3	126.1	116.0	142.3	176.9	136.1	147.1	....	....
Services: Debit	78aed	−186.2	−175.1	−181.4	−272.2	−188.8	−172.3	−191.4	−215.3	−191.7	−191.9	....	....
Balance on Goods & Services	78afd	−245.6	−196.4	−92.8	−280.4	−94.7	−209.2	−207.4	−252.2	−179.4	−224.3	....	....
Income: Credit	78agd	34.1	37.8	18.8	24.0	29.6	24.4	27.8	27.7	28.0	29.4	....	....
Income: Debit	78ahd	−27.1	−32.8	−21.7	−25.1	−50.6	−44.4	−41.2	−39.1	−40.3	−42.9	....	....
Balance on Gds, Serv. & Inc.	78aid	−238.6	−191.4	−95.7	−281.5	−115.6	−229.2	−220.8	−263.6	−191.6	−237.7	....	....
Current Transfers, n.i.e.: Credit	78ajd	146.5	118.5	98.5	105.4	92.4	77.8	102.0	87.1	91.3	87.3	....	....
Current Transfers: Debit	78akd	−28.1	−28.1	−25.9	−30.5	−34.2	−18.5	−32.7	−14.9	−10.7	−10.0	....	....
Capital Account, n.i.e.	78bcd	79.3	75.5	75.2	85.6	6.4	84.5	66.6	69.9	73.3	70.0	....	....
Capital Account, n.i.e.: Credit	78bad	79.3	75.5	75.2	85.6	6.4	84.5	66.6	69.9	73.4	70.0	....	....
Capital Account: Debit	78bbd	−	−	−	−	−	−	−	−	−.1	−	....	....
Financial Account, n.i.e.	78bjd	−35.7	−123.3	−17.6	−132.9	−104.2	−21.3	−8.9	25.4	10.8	40.5	....	....
Direct Investment Abroad	78bdd	−	−	−	−.6	−15.0	−12.1	−1.9	−1.4	−8.1	−2.3	....	....
Dir. Invest. in Rep. Econ., n.i.e.	78bed	77.6	1.4	13.6	7.4	28.6	26.0	34.7	39.3	64.3	43.9	....	....
Portfolio Investment Assets	78bfd	−5.6	−9.1	−26.4	−64.2	−7.7	−7.8	1.2	−1.4	5.7	3.1	....	....
Equity Securities	78bkd	−	−	−	−	1.4	−	.1	−.9	.9	−1.1	....	....
Debt Securities	78bld	−5.6	−9.1	−26.4	−64.2	−9.1	−7.7	1.1	−.5	4.7	4.2	....	....
Portfolio Investment Liab., n.i.e.	78bgd	−	−	−	.3	2.5	2.0	1.2	2.0	.1	−.4	....	....
Equity Securities	78bmd	−	−	−	.3	2.5	2.0	1.2	2.0	.1	−.4	....	....
Debt Securities	78bnd	−	−	−	−	−	−	−	−	−	−	....	....
Financial Derivatives Assets	78bwd	....	....	....	....	−	−	....	−.1	−	−.2	....	....
Financial Derivatives Liabilities	78bxd	....	....	....	....	−	−	−	8.6	−	−	....	....
Other Investment Assets	78bhd	−83.6	−73.9	−52.2	−62.1	−4.0	−12.4	−9.6	−58.3	25.1	−34.4	....	....
Monetary Authorities	78bod	−	−	−	−	−	−	−	....	....	−	....	....
General Government	78bpd	−.4	−2.2	11.9	−6.9	−	−.1	−	−26.7	1.8	−46.6	....	....
Banks	78bqd	−23.5	−48.9	−50.8	−44.2	11.8	−41.1	12.4	−31.6	23.4	12.2	....	....
Other Sectors	78brd	−59.7	−22.9	−13.3	−10.9	−15.8	28.8	−22.0	36.8	−76.2	30.8	....	....
Other Investment Liab., n.i.e.	78bid	−24.1	−41.7	47.4	−13.7	−108.6	−17.0	−34.4	36.8	−76.2	30.8	....	....
Monetary Authorities	78bsd	−2.2	8.6	.6	−2.7	5.2	4.7	−5.4	.3	−1.4	.8	....	....
General Government	78btd	−23.8	−68.0	−28.1	−36.0	−129.4	−26.8	−29.7	−33.6	−49.2	−30.9	....	....
Banks	78bud	2.3	35.0	9.8	−.5	4.5	−11.6	21.1	33.3	−21.0	13.6	....	....
Other Sectors	78bvd	−.3	−17.2	65.1	25.4	11.1	16.7	−20.4	36.8	−4.7	47.4	....	....
Net Errors and Omissions	78cad	9.1	−8.1	−16.3	−1.0	6.3	6.7	7.1	7.3	6.7	3.6	....	....
Overall Balance	78cbd	−67.4	−156.9	18.1	−254.9	−149.0	−100.0	−86.7	−88.7	−20.3	−46.4	....	....
Reserves and Related Items	79dad	67.4	156.9	−18.1	254.9	149.0	100.0	86.7	88.7	20.3	46.4	....	....
Reserve Assets	79dbd	−67.3	−15.4	−117.7	81.9	−78.3	−24.5	7.0	−40.2	−87.3	−147.4	....	....
Use of Fund Credit and Loans	79dcd	−	21.9	24.9	12.2	18.0	1.9	−5.3	1.1	−3.6	−4.1	....	....
Exceptional Financing	79ded	134.7	150.4	74.6	160.7	209.3	122.6	85.0	127.8	111.2	197.9	....	....
International Investment Position		\multicolumn{12}{c}{*Millions of US Dollars*}
Assets	79aad	....	....	....	....	613.1	664.5	598.7	726.4	737.4	904.9	....	....
Direct Investment Abroad	79abd	....	....	....	....	13.7	−2.3	5.3	5.6	10.5	12.6	....	....
Portfolio Investment	79acd	....	....	....	....	75.9	75.2	94.4	81.4	67.6	63.2	....	....
Equity Securities	79add	....	....	....	....	.2	−	2.5	1.7	3.2	3.2	....	....
Debt Securities	79aed	....	....	....	....	75.8	75.2	91.9	79.7	64.4	60.0	....	....
Financial Derivatives	79afd	....	....	....	....	.1	−	−	.1	−	.2	....	....
Other Investment	79afd	....	....	....	....	261.6	338.4	236.9	239.2	200.5	249.2	....	....
Monetary Authorities	79agd	....	....	....	....	−	−	−	−	−	−	....	....
General Government	79ahd	....	....	....	....	.1	.1	.1	.1	.1	.1	....	....
Banks	79aid	....	....	....	....	166.9	186.2	185.1	170.0	155.3	187.8	....	....
Other Sectors	79ajd	....	....	....	....	94.6	152.2	51.7	69.2	45.1	61.3	....	....
Reserve Assets	79akd	....	....	....	....	261.8	253.1	262.2	400.1	458.8	579.7	....	....
Liabilities	79lad	....	....	....	....	1,802.5	1,628.9	1,776.1	1,748.1	1,842.2	1,900.9	....	....
Dir. Invest. in Rep. Economy	79lbd	....	....	....	....	62.3	46.9	67.0	73.5	213.2	173.8	....	....
Portfolio Investment	79lcd	....	....	....	....	81.7	62.2	91.2	95.1	16.3	11.5	....	....
Equity Securities	79ldd	....	....	....	....	2.5	3.5	6.3	6.5	6.1	4.8	....	....
Debt Securities	79led	....	....	....	....	79.2	58.7	84.9	88.6	10.2	6.6	....	....
Financial Derivatives	79lld	....	....	....	....	.8	−	−	8.1	−	−	....	....
Other Investment	79lfd	....	....	....	....	1,657.8	1,519.7	1,618.0	1,571.4	1,612.7	1,715.6	....	....
Monetary Authorities	79lgd	....	....	....	....	115.1	109.1	102.1	99.6	89.3	82.2	....	....
General Government	79lhd	....	....	....	....	1,368.5	1,165.8	1,288.4	1,204.2	1,291.5	1,310.0	....	....
Banks	79lid	....	....	....	....	3.2	34.6	59.0	83.7	70.7	88.7	....	....
Other Sectors	79ljd	....	....	....	....	171.0	210.2	168.4	183.9	161.2	234.6	....	....

Benin 638

		1992	1993	1994	1995	1996	1997	1998	1999	2000	2001	2002	2003
National Accounts						*Billions of Francs*							
Househ.Cons.Expend.,incl.NPISHs	96f	481.1	508.9	657.8	791.2	913.9	1,028.8	1,117.2	1,215.6	1,305.7	1,400.3	1,569.6	....
Government Consumption Expend	91f	65.9	69.4	90.1	100.1	108.3	113.8	122.5	128.9	136.9	145.9	166.7	....
Gross Fixed Capital Formation	93e	79.8	89.4	144.1	190.0	196.7	223.1	250.3	274.7	302.8	333.7	380.3	....
Changes in Inventories	93i	3.6	−3.9	10.0	45.8	5.6	6.2	9.1	14.5	10.7	11.5	13.0	....
Exports of Goods and Services	90c	138.1	144.7	248.9	269.9	300.2	315.2	317.1	336.8	345.4	367.3	373.7	....
Imports of Goods and Services (−)	98c	199.0	212.0	319.9	394.0	395.1	437.3	439.1	500.5	496.1	520.4	544.1	....
Gross Domestic Product (GDP)	99b	569.5	596.4	831.1	1,002.9	1,129.5	1,249.8	1,377.1	1,470.0	1,605.4	1,738.4	1,959.0	....
Net Primary Income from Abroad	98.n	−6.9	−1.8	−14.5	−22.1	....	....	....	....	....	....	....	....
Gross National Income (GNI)	99a	562.6	594.6	816.6	980.8	....	....	....	....	....	....	....	....
GDP Volume 1985 Prices	99b.p	533.9	552.7	576.9	603.5	636.9	673.3	706.8	740.0	782.7	822.0	871.3	....
GDP Volume (2000=100)	99bvp	68.2	70.6	73.7	77.1	81.4	86.0	90.3	94.5	100.0	105.0	111.3	....
GDP Deflator (2000=100)	99bip	52.0	52.6	70.2	81.0	86.5	90.5	95.0	96.8	100.0	103.1	109.6	....
						Millions: Midyear Estimates							
Population	99z	4.97	5.14	5.31	5.47	5.62	5.77	5.92	6.07	6.22	6.39	6.56	6.74

Bhutan 514

		1992	1993	1994	1995	1996	1997	1998	1999	2000	2001	2002	2003
Exchange Rates						*Ngultrum per SDR: End of Period*							
Official Rate	aa	36.025	43.102	45.810	52.295	51.666	52.999	59.813	59.690	60.911	60.549	65.298	67.768
						Ngultrum per US Dollar: End of Period (ae) Period Average (rf)							
Official Rate	ae	26.200	31.380	31.380	35.180	35.930	39.280	42.480	43.490	46.750	48.180	48.030	45.605
Official Rate	rf	25.918	30.493	31.374	32.427	35.433	36.313	41.259	43.055	44.942	47.186	48.610	46.583
Fund Position						*Millions of SDRs: End of Period*							
Quota	2f.s	4.500	4.500	4.500	4.500	4.500	4.500	4.500	6.300	6.300	6.300	6.300	6.300
SDRs	1b.s	.340	.376	.405	.438	.471	.504	.541	.134	.174	.211	.235	.252
Reserve Position in the Fund	1c.s	.570	.570	.570	.570	.570	.570	.570	1.020	1.020	1.020	1.020	1.020
Total Fund Cred.&Loans Outstg	2tl	–	–	–	–	–	–	–	–	–	–	–	–
International Liquidity						*Millions of US Dollars Unless Otherwise Indicated: End of Period*							
Total Reserves minus Gold	1l.d	85.12	97.96	121.40	†130.46	190.07	188.72	256.80	292.29	317.63	323.36	354.95	366.60
SDRs	1b.d	.47	.52	.59	.65	.68	.68	.76	.18	.23	.27	.32	.37
Reserve Position in the Fund	1c.d	.78	.78	.83	.85	.82	.77	.80	1.40	1.33	1.28	1.39	1.52
Foreign Exchange	1d.d	83.87	96.66	119.98	†128.96	188.57	187.27	255.24	290.70	316.08	321.81	353.24	364.71
of which: Convertible Currency	1dxd	82.55	94.77	116.56	†127.17	150.95	155.27	189.55	214.66	236.69	230.94	258.16	286.30
Deposit Money Banks: Assets	7a.d	8.11	13.84	8.88	7.17	43.01	38.86	72.22	93.24	100.88	105.45	110.45	107.53
Liabilities	7b.d	13.63	18.09	–	–	–	–	–	–	–	20.20	–	–
Monetary Authorities						*Millions of Ngultrum End of Period*							
Foreign Assets	11	2,027	†2,945	3,533	4,341	5,289	6,069	8,030	8,850	10,362	10,718	12,004	11,865
Claims on Central Government	12a	....	74	–	50	–	51	–	–	–	–	127	56
Claims on Deposit Money Banks	12e	....	108	7	3	308	3	1,193	1,188	893	293	194	303
Claims on Other Financial Insts	12f	44	†–	55	5	5	5	–	–	–	–	–	–
Reserve Money	14	1,257	†1,931	1,287	2,149	2,328	2,545	3,954	4,971	6,022	6,161	6,982	8,368
of which: Currency Outside DMBs	14a	345	†335	348	433	423	721	769	969	1,270	1,610	1,648	1,802
Liabs.of Central Bank:Securities	16ac	....	–	600	550	1,000	681	560	487	410	410	1,100	–
Foreign Liabilities	16c	....	–	617	161	250	250	250	–	–	–	–	–
Central Government Deposits	16d	20	†25	30	29	334	28	1,207	1,234	918	338	141	357
Other Items (Net)	17r	794	†1,170	1,062	1,510	1,690	2,624	3,252	3,344	3,905	4,102	4,101	3,499
of which: Valuation Adjustment	17rv	....	....	....	1,451	1,653	2,013	1,905	1,610	1,780	1,705	2,077	1,197
Deposit Money Banks						*Millions of Ngultrum End of Period*							
Reserves	20	828	†1,001	829	1,850	1,490	2,338	2,475	3,215	4,375	4,519	5,385	6,342
Claims on Mon.Author.:Securities	20c	....	–	588	532	595	671	426	460	295	405	1,089	–
Foreign Assets	21	213	†434	279	252	1,545	1,526	3,068	4,055	4,716	5,081	5,305	4,904
Claims on Central Government	22a	3	†2	5	2	100	201	50	50	50	370	974	1,213
Claims on Nonfin.Pub.Enterprises	22c	770	†796	561	535	484	449	411	372	333	315	252	252
Claims on Private Sector	22d	426	†489	724	751	748	1,472	1,472	1,490	1,748	2,420	3,147	4,249
Demand Deposits	24	496	†487	697	890	1,652	1,447	1,860	2,755	2,669	3,238	5,323	4,968
Time & Foreign Currency Deposits	25	746	†1,120	1,351	1,926	1,465	3,458	3,782	4,741	5,996	5,868	6,732	7,076
Foreign Liabilities	26c	357	†568	–	–	–	–	–	–	–	973	–	–
Central Government Deposits	26d	200	†311	140	344	459	209	322	914	631	1,288	1,415	1,951
Capital Accounts	27a	534	†330	324	371	371	539	561	633	756	958	1,194	1,735
Other Items (Net)	27r	–95	†–90	473	390	1,016	1,007	1,365	599	1,463	784	1,487	1,231
Monetary Survey						*Millions of Ngultrum: End of Period*							
Foreign Assets (Net)	31n	1,883	†2,811	3,195	4,432	6,584	7,346	10,848	12,905	15,078	14,825	17,309	16,769
Domestic Credit	32	1,022	†1,024	1,175	969	545	1,941	404	–236	581	1,479	2,943	3,462
Claims on Central Govt. (Net)	32an	–218	†–261	–165	–321	–692	15	–1,480	–2,098	–1,499	–1,256	–456	–1,038
Claims on Nonfin.Pub.Enterprises	32c	770	†796	561	535	484	449	411	372	333	315	252	252
Claims on Private Sector	32d	426	†489	724	751	748	1,472	1,472	1,490	1,748	2,420	3,147	4,249
Claims on Other Financial Insts	32f	44	†–	55	5	5	5	–	–	–	–	–	–
Money	34	841	†822	1,044	1,322	2,074	2,168	2,629	3,724	3,939	4,849	6,971	6,770
Quasi-Money	35	746	†1,120	1,351	1,926	1,465	3,458	3,782	4,741	5,996	5,868	6,732	7,076
Liabs.of Central Bank:Securities	36ac	....	–	12	18	405	11	134	26	115	6	11	–
Other Items (Net)	37r	1,317	†1,897	1,962	2,135	3,185	3,652	4,696	4,176	5,609	5,582	6,537	6,385
Money plus Quasi-Money	35l	1,587	†1,942	2,395	3,249	3,540	5,626	6,410	8,465	9,935	10,716	13,703	13,846
Interest Rates						*Percent Per Annum*							
Deposit Rate	60l	8.0	8.0	8.0	8.0	....	....	....	....	....	....	....	....
Lending Rate	60p	17.0	17.0	16.6	16.0	....	....	....	....	....	....	....	....
Prices and Tourism						*Index Numbers (2000=100): Period Averages*							
Consumer Prices	64	53.9	60.0	64.2	70.3	76.4	81.4	90.0	96.1	100.0	103.4	106.0	....
Tourist Arrivals	66ta	37.8	39.7	52.5	63.1	68.0	71.7	81.6	94.8	100.0	84.6	69.5	....
International Transactions						*Millions of Ngultrum: Year Ending June 30*							
Exports	70	1,715.2	1,991.7	2,082.7	3,350.1	3,553.8	4,274.2	4,455.6	4,988.0	4,615.8	4,994.7	5,261.8	....
Imports, c.i.f	71	3,238.8	2,745.3	2,876.4	3,641.9	4,525.2	4,977.9	5,516.4	7,834.9	9,106.3	8,990.2	8,023.7	....

Bhutan 514

		1992	1993	1994	1995	1996	1997	1998	1999	2000	2001	2002	2003
Government Finance		\multicolumn{12}{c}{*Millions of Ngultrum: Year Ending June 30*}
Deficit (-) or Surplus............	80	−247.3	312.2	−45.1	7.8	238.6	−300.9	143.4	−304.9	−764.6	−2,490.8	−1,756.7p	....
Revenue......................	81	1,207.5	1,650.9	1,666.3	1,877.4	2,127.7	2,424.2	3,133.1	3,656.9	4,585.4	4,975.7	5,140.6p	....
Grants Received............	81z	785.9	1,230.1	1,456.2	1,773.2	2,363.6	2,232.1	1,816.3	3,262.6	3,274.1	3,711.0	2,918.4p	....
Expenditure.................	82	2,138.9	2,397.3	2,891.0	3,655.6	4,152.6	4,630.6	4,588.4	7,284.0	8,334.2	10,716.5	9,813.7p	....
Lending Minus Repayments......	83	101.8	171.5	276.6	−12.8	100.1	326.6	217.6	−59.6	289.9	461.0	2.0p	....
Financing													
Total Financing.............	84	247.4	−312.2	45.1	−7.8	−238.6	300.9	−143.3	304.9	764.6	2,490.8	1,756.7p	....
Domestic.....................	84a	157.0	−334.7	21.0	−1.1	−211.8	176.6	−479.5	−248.8	158.0	1,434.1	1,047.1p	....
Foreign......................	85a	90.4	22.5	24.1	−6.7	−26.8	124.3	336.2	553.7	606.6	1,056.7	709.6p	....
Debt: Domestic..............	88a	226.3	19.3	64.9	28.4	107.4	−	−	−	−	....	....	....
Foreign......................	89a	2,730.2	2,801.8	2,733.3	2,634.0	3,962.1	4,084.9	4,661.2	6,205.3	7,721.8	15,723.8	....	....
National Accounts		\multicolumn{12}{c}{*Millions of Ngultrum: Calendar Year*}
Househ.Cons.Expend.,incl.NPISHs....	96f	3,730	3,537	3,770	3,428	5,171	7,138	9,322	10,067	11,329	....	....	....
Government Consumption Expend...	91f	1,215	1,241	1,585	2,400	2,502	3,651	3,308	4,271	4,422	....	....	....
Gross Fixed Capital Formation......	93e	2,624	3,374	3,945	4,487	5,094	5,514	6,200	8,127	9,447	....	....	....
Changes in Inventories.............	93i	340	−60	129	228	182	−632	45	108	49	....	....	....
Exports of Goods and Services......	90c	2,079	2,264	2,508	3,712	3,979	4,771	5,148	5,714	6,456	....	....	....
Imports of Goods and Services (-)....	98c	3,634	3,163	3,349	4,190	5,120	6,128	7,686	9,164	10,004	....	....	....
Gross Domestic Product (GDP)......	99b	6,354	7,193	8,589	10,064	11,808	14,314	16,337	19,122	21,698	....	....	....
Net Primary Income from Abroad....	98.n	−734	−734	−634	−1,208	−1,247	−1,141	−2,323	−3,083	−3,458	....	....	....
Gross National Income (GNI)........	99a	5,619	6,458	7,954	8,856	10,562	13,173	14,013	16,040	18,240	....	....	....
GDP at Factor Cost.................	99ba	6,178	7,008	8,238	9,707	11,449	13,808	15,791	18,514	21,127	....	....	....
GDP at Fac.Cost,Vol.1980 Prices.....	99bap	2,405	2,555	2,713	2,921	3,070	3,306	3,514	3,773	3,989	....	....	....
GDP Volume (2000=100)............	99bvp	60.3	64.1	68.0	73.2	77.0	82.9	88.1	94.6	100.0	....	....	....
GDP Deflator (2000=100)..........	99bip	48.5	51.8	57.3	62.7	70.4	78.9	84.8	92.6	100.0	....	....	....
		\multicolumn{12}{c}{*Millions: Midyear Estimates*}
Population.........................	99z	1.74	1.76	1.78	1.81	1.85	1.90	1.95	2.00	2.06	2.12	2.19	2.26

Bolivia 218

		1992	1993	1994	1995	1996	1997	1998	1999	2000	2001	2002	2003
Exchange Rates		*Bolivianos per SDR: End of Period*
Market Rate	aa	5.6306	6.1467	6.8540	7.3358	7.4558	7.2387	7.9483	8.2213	8.3256	8.5709	10.1828	11.6351
		Bolivianos per US Dollar: End of Period (ae) Period Average (rf)
Market Rate	ae	4.0950	4.4750	4.6950	4.9350	5.1850	5.3650	5.6450	5.9900	6.3900	6.8200	7.4900	7.8300
Market Rate	rf	3.9005	4.2651	4.6205	4.8003	5.0746	5.2543	5.5101	5.8124	6.1835	6.6069	7.1700	7.6592
		Index Numbers (2000=100): Period Averages
Market Rate	ahx	158.60	145.02	133.82	128.78	121.78	117.66	112.21	106.38	100.00	93.60	86.27	80.72
Nominal Effective Exchange Rate	nec	38.75	60.53	96.58	98.68	96.93	99.56	99.20	102.05	100.00	101.23	102.53	91.17
Real Effective Exchange Rate	rec	92.58	91.98	87.28	84.98	89.22	92.90	97.56	100.52	100.00	99.79	98.07	86.13
Fund Position		*Millions of SDRs: End of Period*
Quota	2f.s	126.2	126.2	126.2	126.2	126.2	126.2	126.2	171.5	171.5	171.5	171.5	171.5
SDRs	1b.s	.1	10.2	17.0	26.9	26.8	26.8	26.8	27.3	27.3	27.3	27.3	27.1
Reserve Position in the Fund	1c.s	8.9	8.9	8.9	8.9	8.9	8.9	8.9	8.9	8.9	8.9	8.9	8.9
Total Fund Cred.&Loans Outstg.	2tl	181.1	160.5	180.5	180.1	192.0	183.9	187.6	180.0	168.8	164.8	143.7	187.5
International Liquidity		*Millions of US Dollars Unless Otherwise Indicated: End of Period*
Total Reserves minus Gold	1l.d	181.8	223.4	451.0	660.0	955.0	1,086.6	948.5	974.9	926.4	886.4	580.5	716.8
SDRs	1b.d	.1	14.0	24.8	40.0	38.5	36.2	37.7	37.4	35.6	34.3	37.2	40.3
Reserve Position in the Fund	1c.d	12.2	12.2	13.0	13.2	12.8	12.0	12.5	12.2	11.6	11.2	12.1	13.2
Foreign Exchange	1d.d	169.5	197.2	413.2	606.8	903.7	1,038.5	898.3	925.3	879.3	840.9	531.2	663.3
Gold (Million Fine Troy Ounces)	1ad	.894	.894	.893	.893	.939	.939	.939	.943	.939	.939	.911	.911
Gold (National Valuation)	1and	37.8	39.6	37.7	37.7	39.6	39.6	234.9	235.7	244.8	259.6	316.4	379.4
Monetary Authorities: Other Liab.	4..d	486.9	432.1	503.9	545.9	419.3	370.1	323.9	297.1	283.0	237.3	56.9	52.4
Deposit Money Banks: Assets	7a.d	79.3	72.2	84.5	103.6	124.4	137.9	409.8	471.8	552.8	693.9	604.1	550.8
Liabilities	7b.d	189.0	318.1	476.8	544.0	540.9	721.4	879.7	744.6	461.3	214.7	181.1	107.2
Other Banking Insts.: Assets	7e.d	–	–	–	–	3.8	6.6	46.9	55.9	63.4	74.3	35.7	78.9
Liabilities	7f.d	4.1	4.1	4.1	–	2.5	2.4	8.1	13.3	16.5	15.0	19.1	28.3
Monetary Authorities		*Millions of Bolivianos: End of Period*
Foreign Assets	11	2,343	2,917	3,702	4,538	† 7,032	7,735	8,217	8,905	9,161	9,651	8,940	11,090
Claims on Central Government	12a	5,906	4,700	5,009	4,328	† 3,889	3,475	3,598	4,123	4,731	5,436	6,492	7,253
Claims on State and Local Govts.	12b	150	20	18	–	† –	–	–	–	–	–	–	–
Claims on Nonfin.Pub.Enterprises	12c	1,461	814	891	113	† 119	–	–	–	–	–	–	–
Claims on Private Sector	12d	–	–	–	–	† 2	2	2	2	3	4	3	4
Claims on Deposit Money Banks	12e	1,789	1,392	2,405	3,032	† 3,394	3,427	3,444	3,506	2,873	3,028	2,671	2,750
Claims on Other Banking Insts.	12f	–	–	–	–	† 107	66	72	42	52	64	–	–
Claims on Nonbank Financial Insts.	12g	84	91	108	119	† –	–	–	206	220	235	–	–
Reserve Money	14	1,925	2,557	2,668	3,291	† 4,194	5,036	3,989	4,441	4,905	5,497	5,582	6,338
of which: Currency Outside DMBs	14a	886	1,034	1,406	1,694	† 1,802	2,061	2,193	2,173	2,189	2,422	2,707	3,231
Time, Savings,& Fgn.Currency Dep.	15	570	568	1,682	897	† 547	452	451	994	542	624	441	581
of which: Fgn. Currency Deposits	15b	284	244	1,235	522	† 573	442	446	990	530	597	435	571
Foreign Liabilities	16c	786	606	800	753	† 1,430	1,330	1,490	1,477	1,403	1,414	1,463	2,179
Long-Term Foreign Liabilities	16cl	1,641	1,674	1,898	2,217	† 2,175	1,987	1,830	1,782	1,811	1,617	426	413
Central Government Deposits	16d	6,220	2,524	2,589	3,565	† 4,460	3,591	3,489	3,642	3,679	3,750	3,237	3,659
Central Govt. Lending Funds	16f	1,741	2,238	2,684	1,240	† 1,081	919	989	999	972	936	728	813
Capital Accounts	17a	205	1,075	1,673	2,516	† 1,057	1,441	3,287	3,857	4,381	5,246	6,906	7,915
Other Items (Net)	17r	–1,355	–1,307	–1,861	–2,347	† –403	–52	–192	–407	–653	–667	–678	–803
Deposit Money Banks		*Millions of Bolivianos: End of Period*
Reserves	20	1,030	1,539	1,133	1,450	† 2,788	3,588	1,426	1,459	1,797	1,827	1,753	1,789
Foreign Assets	21	325	323	397	511	† 645	740	2,313	2,826	3,532	4,732	4,525	4,313
Claims on Central Government	22a	114	29	103	572	† 1,522	1,590	1,322	924	1,053	1,530	1,919	1,765
Claims on State and Local Govts.	22b	–	–	–	–	† –	–	–	–	–	–	–	–
Claims on Nonfin.Pub.Enterprises	22c	–	–	–	–	† –	5	1	2	2	39	28	53
Claims on Private Sector	22d	7,599	10,740	13,452	15,152	† 17,568	21,017	26,103	27,331	26,403	24,152	23,753	23,721
Claims on Other Banking Insts.	22f	–	–	–	–	† –	–	11	10	–	6	54	2
Claims on Nonbank Financial Insts.	22g	–	–	–	–	† 153	131	309	291	263	407	451	482
Demand Deposits	24	1,037	1,466	1,826	2,219	† 867	1,036	1,124	1,031	1,150	1,353	1,271	1,385
Time, Savings,& Fgn.Currency Dep.	25	5,167	7,175	7,809	8,887	† 13,542	15,916	18,237	19,203	19,424	19,130	17,651	19,779
of which: Fgn. Currency Deposits	25b	5,039	7,036	7,568	8,700	† 13,201	15,546	17,799	18,737	18,947	18,601	17,229	19,190
Money Market Instruments	26aa	–	–	–	–	† –	–	70	68	891	1,576	2,235	34
Foreign Liabilities	26c	402	1,028	1,570	1,955	† 2,088	2,717	3,364	2,868	1,869	527	683	243
Long-Term Foreign Liabilities	26cl	372	396	669	730	† 717	1,153	1,602	1,592	1,079	937	674	597
Central Government Deposits	26d	38	49	74	179	† 935	1,319	260	97	117	139	97	72
Credit from Monetary Authorities	26g	1,297	1,334	2,260	2,984	† 3,830	3,721	3,499	3,920	3,914	3,802	3,767	3,661
Liabilities to Other Banking Insts.	26i	–	–	–	–	† –	–	95	93	103	103	127	163
Liab. to Nonbank Financial Insts.	26j	–	–	–	–	† –	310	520	894	927	2,069	2,332	2,158
Capital Accounts	27a	1,283	1,577	1,899	2,043	† 2,352	2,821	3,822	4,626	5,252	5,732	6,608	6,978
Other Items (Net)	27r	–527	–393	–1,023	–1,312	† –1,655	–1,921	–1,108	–1,550	–1,676	–2,676	–2,962	–2,944

2004, International Monetary Fund : *International Financial Statistics Yearbook*

Bolivia 218

		1992	1993	1994	1995	1996	1997	1998	1999	2000	2001	2002	2003
Monetary Survey						*Millions of Bolivianos: End of Period*							
Foreign Assets (Net)	31n	1,480	1,607	1,730	2,341	† 4,158	4,428	5,676	7,386	9,422	12,441	11,319	12,981
Domestic Credit	32	9,056	13,821	16,917	16,541	† 17,964	21,377	27,669	29,192	28,931	27,984	29,366	29,548
Claims on Central Govt. (Net)	32an	−238	2,156	2,449	1,156	† 16	155	1,171	1,308	1,988	3,078	5,076	5,287
Claims on State and Local Govts.	32b	150	20	18	−	† −	−	−	−	−	−	−	−
Claims on Nonfin.Pub.Enterprises	32c	1,461	814	891	113	† 119	5	1	2	2	39	28	53
Claims on Private Sector	32d	7,599	10,740	13,452	15,152	† 17,570	21,019	26,105	27,333	26,406	24,156	23,757	23,725
Claims on Other Banking Insts.	32f	−	−	−	−	† 107	66	83	52	52	70	54	2
Claims on Nonbank Financial Inst.	32g	84	91	108	119	† 153	131	309	497	483	642	451	482
Money	34	1,923	2,499	3,232	3,913	† 3,055	3,636	3,895	3,670	3,995	4,743	4,725	5,636
Quasi-Money	35	5,737	7,743	9,490	9,784	† 14,089	16,368	18,688	20,197	19,966	19,754	18,093	20,360
Money Market Instruments	36aa	−	−	−	−	† −	−	70	68	891	1,576	2,235	34
Long-Term Foreign Liabilities	36cl	2,013	2,069	2,567	2,947	† 2,892	3,140	3,432	3,374	2,890	2,554	1,100	1,010
Central Govt. Lending Funds	36f	1,901	2,238	2,684	1,240	† 1,081	919	989	999	972	936	728	813
Liabilities to Other Banking Insts.	36i	−	−	−	−	† −	−	95	93	103	103	127	163
Liab. to Nonbank Financial Insts.	36j	−	−	−	−	† −	310	520	894	927	2,069	2,332	2,158
Capital Accounts	37a	1,488	2,652	3,573	4,559	† 3,409	4,263	7,109	8,483	9,633	10,978	13,514	14,893
Other Items (Net)	37r	−2,525	−1,773	−2,899	−3,560	† −2,405	−2,831	−1,452	−1,201	−1,025	−2,288	−2,169	−2,537
Money plus Quasi-Money	35l	7,660	10,242	12,722	13,697	† 17,145	20,004	22,583	23,867	23,961	24,497	22,818	25,996
Other Banking Institutions						*Millions of Bolivianos: End of Period*							
Reserves	40	−	−	1	−	† 160	192	80	84	135	178	400	177
Foreign Assets	41	−	−	−	−	† 20	35	265	335	405	507	268	618
Claims on Central Government	42a	2	3	3	3	† 106	91	118	14	150	529	497	785
Claims on State and Local Govts	42b	−	−	−	−	† −	−	−	−	−	−	−	−
Claims on Nonfin.Pub.Enterprises	42c	−	−	−	−	† −	−	−	−	−	−	4	−
Claims on Private Sector	42d	393	389	349	386	† 2,226	3,249	3,885	3,703	4,087	4,552	5,007	5,784
Claims on Deposit Money Banks	42e	−	−	−	−	† −	−	140	86	346	414	416	337
Claims on Nonbank Financial Insts.	42g	−	−	−	−	† 4	4	26	57	88	164	35	58
Demand Deposits	44	−	−	−	−	† −	1	1	1	11	4	5	6
Time, Savings,& Fgn.Currency Dep.	45	1	1	1	−	† 2,305	3,185	3,693	3,480	4,132	5,132	5,044	6,300
of which: Fgn. Currency Deposits	45b	1	1	1	−	† 2,251	3,114	3,619	3,429	4,075	5,073	4,981	6,210
Money Market Instruments	46aa	−	−	−	−	† −	−	−	−	68	208	364	−
Foreign Liabilities	46c	−	−	−	−	† 2	6	12	6	−	1	12	7
Long-Term Foreign Liabilities	46cl	17	18	19	−	† 11	7	34	74	106	101	131	214
Central Government Deposits	46d	1	1	1	−	† 6	14	16	8	21	13	15	17
Credit from Monetary Authorities	46g	307	292	272	548	† 4	6	8	11	21	80	67	54
Credit from Deposit Money Banks	46h	−	−	−	−	† 86	100	72	55	39	47	29	30
Liabs. to Nonbank Financial Insts.	46j	−	−	−	−	† 245	303	294	301	299	325	368	384
Capital Accounts	47a	73	34	21	−289	† 447	579	775	819	986	1,188	1,416	1,649
Other Items (Net)	47r	−5	46	40	130	† −592	−630	−391	−476	−470	−756	−823	−902
Banking Survey						*Millions of Bolivianos: End of Period*							
Foreign Assets (Net)	51n	1,480	1,607	1,730	2,341	† 4,176	4,457	5,929	7,715	9,827	12,947	11,574	13,592
Domestic Credit	52	9,450	14,211	17,269	16,930	† 20,187	24,641	31,599	32,907	33,184	33,145	34,841	36,156
Claims on Central Govt. (Net)	52an	−237	2,158	2,452	1,160	† 116	232	1,273	1,314	2,117	3,593	5,559	6,055
Claims on State and Local Govts	52b	150	20	18	−	† −	−	−	−	−	−	−	−
Claims on Nonfin.Pub.Enterprises	52c	1,461	814	891	113	† 119	5	1	2	2	39	32	53
Claims on Private Sector	52d	7,992	11,128	13,801	15,538	† 19,796	24,268	29,991	31,037	30,493	28,708	28,764	29,508
Claims on Nonbank Financial Inst.	52g	84	91	108	119	† 157	135	335	554	572	806	486	540
Liquid Liabilities	55l	7,661	10,243	12,723	13,697	† 19,291	22,998	26,198	27,265	27,969	29,456	27,467	32,124
Money Market Instruments	56aa	−	−	−	−	† −	−	70	68	959	1,784	2,599	34
Long-Term Foreign Liabilities	56cl	2,029	2,087	2,587	2,947	† 2,903	3,147	3,465	3,448	2,996	2,655	1,231	1,224
Central Govt. Lending Funds	56f	2,023	2,238	2,684	1,240	† 1,081	919	989	999	972	936	728	813
Liab. to Nonbank Financial Insts.	56j	−	−	−	−	† 245	613	813	1,195	1,227	2,394	2,699	2,542
Capital Accounts	57a	1,561	2,686	3,593	4,270	† 3,856	4,842	7,884	9,302	10,619	12,166	14,930	16,542
Other Items (Net)	57r	−2,344	−1,435	−2,588	−2,882	† −3,014	−3,421	−1,892	−1,655	−1,730	−3,299	−3,239	−3,531
Money (National Definitions)						*Millions of Bolivianos: End of Period*							
Reserve Money	19ma	1,776	2,352	2,760	3,105	3,963	4,731	3,560	3,685	4,104	4,455	4,790	5,186
M1	59ma	1,236	1,417	1,890	2,333	2,580	3,061	3,276	3,153	3,287	3,709	3,908	4,532
M'1	59mb	1,924	2,499	3,232	3,913	4,768	5,738	6,342	5,893	6,406	7,533	8,115	9,206
M2	59mc	1,312	1,499	1,997	2,425	2,791	3,355	3,589	3,480	3,617	4,151	4,291	5,051
M'2	59md	2,646	3,544	4,534	5,460	8,028	10,219	11,533	11,212	12,678	15,367	15,439	18,219
M3	59me	1,364	1,555	2,132	2,520	2,983	3,526	3,766	3,646	3,798	4,295	4,408	5,220
M'3	59mf	7,092	9,675	11,767	12,880	18,430	22,039	25,118	25,777	27,264	29,160	28,473	29,912
M4	59mg	1,364	1,555	2,136	2,523	3,106	3,532	3,782	3,646	3,803	4,332	4,432	5,261
M'4	59mh	7,092	9,675	12,036	13,330	18,948	22,408	25,552	26,162	28,013	31,341	29,971	31,832

Bolivia 218

		1992	1993	1994	1995	1996	1997	1998	1999	2000	2001	2002	2003
Interest Rates						*Percent Per Annum*							
Discount Rate (End of Period)	60	....	....	....	....	16.50	13.25	14.10	12.50	10.00	8.50	12.50	7.50
Discount Rate (Fgn.Cur.)(End per)	60..f	....	....	....	....	9.89	8.58	9.30	9.04	7.41	5.69	5.58	6.38
Money Market Rate	60b	....	....	....	22.42	20.27	13.97	12.57	13.49	7.40	6.99	8.41	4.07
Money Market Rate (Fgn. Cur.)	60b.f	....	....	....	14.16	9.54	7.85	9.26	8.29	5.68	3.57	2.96	2.12
Treasury Bill Rate	60c	....	....	17.89	24.51	19.93	13.65	12.33	14.07	10.99	11.48	12.41	9.92
Treasury Bill Rate (Fgn.Currency)	60c.f	....	....	8.22	13.20	9.89	7.15	7.48	7.84	7.02	4.19	3.56	2.53
Savings Rate	60k	20.28	20.92	17.46	16.52	16.43	14.30	12.08	10.79	9.39	6.57	6.20	5.52
Savings Rate (Fgn.Currency)	60k.f	8.14	7.97	7.16	7.03	7.20	6.60	5.93	5.50	4.76	2.68	1.10	.73
Deposit Rate	60l	23.22	22.18	18.43	18.87	19.16	14.73	12.82	12.26	10.98	9.82	9.58	11.41
Deposit Rate (Fgn.Currency)	60l.f	11.40	11.19	9.89	10.36	10.13	8.32	7.96	8.78	7.84	5.21	2.82	2.01
Lending Rate	60p	45.51	53.88	55.57	51.02	55.97	50.05	39.41	35.37	34.60	20.06	20.63	17.66
Lending Rate (Fgn.Currency)	60p.f	19.13	18.46	16.46	16.86	17.64	16.48	15.66	16.03	15.68	14.46	12.11	10.30
Prices, Production, Labor						*Index Numbers (2000=100): Period Averages*							
Consumer Prices	64	†57.2	62.1	67.0	73.8	83.0	86.9	93.6	95.6	100.0	101.6	102.5	106.0
Crude Petroleum Production	66aa	67.4	70.6	81.6	90.0	92.9	95.4	119.7	103.0	100.0	113.6	115.2	125.5
						Number in Thousands: Period Averages							
Labor Force	67d	2,365	....	....	....	1,369	3,645	....	....	3,824	....	....	....
Employment	67e	1,016	1,091	1,195	1,257	†1,849	1,878	....	2,017	2,096	....	....	....
Unemployment	67c	59	70	39	47	†74	71	....	157	168	....	....	....
Unemployment Rate (%)	67r	5.5	6.0	3.1	3.6	†3.8	3.7	....	7.2	7.4	....	....	....
International Transactions						*Millions of US Dollars*							
Exports	70..d	710.1	727.5	1,032.4	1,100.7	1,137.1	1,166.5	1,103.9	1,051.2	1,229.5	1,284.8	1,298.7	1,573.4
Tin	70q.d	107.3	83.3	91.1	88.6	85.5	75.1	59.9	65.3	70.5	52.6	53.2	66.0
Zinc	70t.d	173.0	119.5	105.3	151.3	153.4	119.3	92.3	91.4	101.3	71.6	66.5	73.2
Imports, c.i.f.	71..d	1,090.3	1,205.9	1,209.0	1,423.8	1,635.0	1,850.9	1,983.0	1,755.1	1,829.7	1,707.7	1,770.1	1,630.5
Imports, f.o.b.	71.vd	1,005.0	1,111.6	1,121.7	1,263.2	1,450.5	1,698.1	1,824.4	1,539.1	1,604.5	1,497.5	1,552.3	1,519.5
						2000=100							
Volume of Exports	72	103.3	91.0	89.4	95.6	97.6	101.6	96.2	87.7	100.0	107.3	129.1	139.4
Tin	72q	126.5	114.8	120.9	102.1	100.6	103.1	81.9	92.2	100.0	78.9	101.2	110.5
Zinc	72t	94.5	82.2	71.2	97.3	100.6	102.1	101.6	96.2	100.0	87.2	95.2	99.7
						2000=100: Indices of Unit Values in US Dollars							
Unit Value of Exports	74..d	147.6	125.3	131.8	141.3	137.6	98.0	86.8	85.8	100.0	91.3	81.0	93.4
Tin	74q.d	163.9	149.2	148.2	168.6	166.8	104.3	100.2	99.7	100.0	91.3	75.9	85.9
Zinc	74t.d	180.8	143.5	146.1	153.5	150.6	115.3	89.7	93.9	100.0	81.1	68.9	72.6

2004, International Monetary Fund : *International Financial Statistics Yearbook*

Bolivia 218

		1992	1993	1994	1995	1996	1997	1998	1999	2000	2001	2002	2003
Balance of Payments		*Millions of US Dollars: Minus Sign Indicates Debit*										
Current Account, n.i.e.	78ald	−533.9	−505.5	−90.2	−302.5	−404.3	−553.5	−666.1	−488.0	−446.3	−274.0	−351.9	18.9
Goods: Exports f.o.b.	78aad	608.4	715.5	985.1	1,041.4	1,132.0	1,166.6	1,104.0	1,051.2	1,246.1	1,284.8	1,298.7	1,573.4
Goods: Imports f.o.b.	78abd	−1,040.8	−1,111.7	−1,015.3	−1,223.7	−1,368.0	−1,643.6	−1,759.5	−1,539.0	−1,610.2	−1,580.0	−1,639.0	−1,519.4
Trade Balance	78acd	−432.4	−396.2	−30.2	−182.3	−236.0	−477.0	−655.5	−487.8	−364.1	−295.2	−340.3	54.0
Services: Credit	78add	164.6	181.4	196.0	192.4	180.9	247.2	251.2	259.4	224.0	235.9	256.6	305.9
Services: Debit	78aed	−311.0	−321.7	−337.5	−350.2	−363.4	−418.7	−440.5	−449.7	−467.7	−399.4	−432.9	−485.5
Balance on Goods & Services	78afd	−578.8	−536.5	−171.7	−340.1	−418.5	−648.5	−844.8	−678.1	−607.8	−458.7	−516.6	−125.6
Income: Credit	78agd	17.7	9.2	18.7	28.3	28.6	98.2	127.4	157.3	139.7	121.2	103.2	71.7
Income: Debit	78ahd	−215.4	−215.1	−201.2	−234.9	−236.8	−294.7	−289.3	−353.3	−365.0	−332.5	−307.9	−373.4
Balance on Gds, Serv. & Inc.	78aid	−776.5	−742.4	−354.2	−546.7	−626.7	−845.0	−1,006.7	−874.1	−833.1	−670.1	−721.3	−427.4
Current Transfers, n.i.e.: Credit	78ajd	246.3	241.0	269.2	248.0	226.2	300.3	352.3	414.7	420.0	431.6	407.8	486.2
Current Transfers: Debit	78akd	−3.7	−4.1	−5.2	−3.8	−3.8	−8.8	−11.7	−28.6	−33.2	−35.5	−38.4	−39.9
Capital Account, n.i.e.	78bcd	.6	1.0	1.2	2.0	2.8	25.3	9.9	–	–	–	–	–
Capital Account, n.i.e.: Credit	78bad	.6	1.0	1.2	2.0	2.8	25.3	9.9	–	–	–	–	–
Capital Account: Debit	78bbd	–	–	–	–	–	–	–	–	–	–	–	–
Financial Account, n.i.e.	78bjd	367.4	347.1	315.3	505.2	701.0	889.9	1,181.6	868.2	461.8	440.7	649.7	206.0
Direct Investment Abroad	78bdd	−2.0	−2.0	−2.2	−2.0	−2.1	−2.4	−2.8	−2.8	−2.8	−2.5	−2.5	−2.5
Dir. Invest. in Rep. Econ., n.i.e.	78bed	93.1	123.8	130.2	392.7	474.1	730.6	949.3	1,010.5	736.4	705.8	676.6	171.3
Portfolio Investment Assets	78bfd	–	–	–	–	.3	−53.2	−74.5	−44.4	55.4	−23.0	−19.3	−68.4
Equity Securities	78bkd	–	–	–	–	–	–	–	–	–	–	–	–
Debt Securities	78bld	–	–	–	–	.3	−53.2	−74.5	−44.4	55.4	−23.0	−19.3	−68.4
Portfolio Investment Liab., n.i.e.	78bgd	–	–	–	–	–	–	–	−16.9	–	–	–	–
Equity Securities	78bmd	–	–	–	–	–	–	–	–	–	–	–	–
Debt Securities	78bnd	–	–	–	–	–	–	–	−16.9	–	–	–	–
Financial Derivatives Assets	78bwd	....	....	....	....	....	–	–	....	....	....	....	....
Financial Derivatives Liabilities	78bxd	....	....	....	....	....	–	–	....	....	....	....	....
Other Investment Assets	78bhd	−13.0	17.1	−104.0	−38.4	12.2	−19.9	−13.2	−47.7	−146.1	−166.7	−193.7	−177.6
Monetary Authorities	78bod	....	....	....	....	–	–	−8.4	−9.2	−1.2	–	–	–
General Government	78bpd	−6.4	−6.1	–	–	−.2	–	–	–	−7.9	−15.7	−17.1	−18.2
Banks	78bqd	−14.3	−6.4	−104.0	−38.4	12.4	−19.9	66.1	−24.2	−94.4	−157.0	49.8	46.3
Other Sectors	78brd	7.7	29.6	–	–	–	–	−70.9	−14.3	−42.6	6.1	−226.5	−205.8
Other Investment Liab., n.i.e.	78bid	289.3	208.2	291.3	152.9	216.5	234.8	322.8	−30.5	−181.1	−72.9	188.7	283.2
Monetary Authorities	78bsd	75.2	42.5	40.8	78.0	11.7	1.5	−46.0	−11.6	−23.7	−20.3	−17.7	−2.4
General Government	78btd	−42.6	−23.7	−16.9	−41.0	206.9	199.7	149.4	123.1	131.4	226.1	310.8	279.9
Banks	78bud	86.5	124.4	206.3	78.8	2.8	169.7	137.9	−138.1	−280.1	−247.7	−35.4	−80.9
Other Sectors	78bvd	170.2	65.0	61.1	37.1	−4.9	−136.1	81.5	−3.9	−8.7	−31.0	−69.0	86.6
Net Errors and Omissions	78cad	34.3	123.6	−315.8	−112.3	−31.6	−260.7	−400.7	−353.2	−54.8	−202.7	−640.5	−279.5
Overall Balance	78cbd	−131.6	−33.7	−89.5	92.4	268.0	101.0	124.7	27.0	−39.4	−36.0	−342.7	−54.6
Reserves and Related Items	79dad	131.6	33.7	89.5	−92.4	−268.0	−101.0	−124.7	−27.0	39.4	36.0	342.7	54.6
Reserve Assets	79dbd	−41.2	−81.7	−26.4	−147.4	−310.1	−89.6	−133.0	−31.9	38.8	32.5	303.0	−152.0
Use of Fund Credit and Loans	79dcd	14.7	−28.7	28.7	−1.1	17.1	−11.4	5.7	−10.9	−14.5	−5.3	−27.7	60.0
Exceptional Financing	79ded	158.1	144.2	87.3	56.1	25.1	–	2.6	15.8	15.1	8.8	67.3	146.5
International Investment Position		*Millions of US Dollars*										
Assets	79aad	....	....	....	....	....	2,058.0	2,520.5	2,606.6	2,647.4	2,834.7	2,953.3	3,424.3
Direct Investment Abroad	79abd	....	....	....	....	....	21.9	24.4	26.9	29.4	31.9	34.4	36.9
Portfolio Investment	79acd	....	....	....	....	....	293.7	689.2	733.6	662.9	685.9	837.0	905.4
Equity Securities	79add	....	....	....	....	....	–	–	–	–	–	–	–
Debt Securities	79aed	....	....	....	....	....	293.7	689.2	733.6	662.9	685.9	837.0	905.4
Financial Derivatives	79ald	....	....	....	....	....	–	–	–	–	–	–	–
Other Investment	79afd	....	....	....	....	....	428.1	479.4	485.7	650.2	831.9	1,033.1	1,229.1
Monetary Authorities	79agd	....	....	....	....	....	139.4	167.3	176.5	123.7	124.9	134.3	152.1
General Government	79ahd	....	....	....	....	....	–	–	–	61.9	88.5	104.0	121.6
Banks	79aid	....	....	....	....	....	128.7	141.1	165.2	271.7	428.7	378.9	332.6
Other Sectors	79ajd	....	....	....	....	....	160.0	171.0	144.0	192.9	189.8	415.9	622.9
Reserve Assets	79akd	....	....	....	....	....	1,314.3	1,327.5	1,360.4	1,304.9	1,285.0	1,048.8	1,252.9
Liabilities	79lad	....	....	....	....	....	7,822.9	9,277.4	10,056.1	10,400.0	11,175.3	11,706.0	12,634.5
Dir. Invest. in Rep. Economy	79lbd	....	....	....	....	....	2,414.7	3,440.8	4,451.3	5,187.7	5,893.5	6,570.0	6,732.7
Portfolio Investment	79lcd	....	....	....	....	....	15.0	36.9	20.0	20.0	–	–	–
Equity Securities	79ldd	....	....	....	....	....	–	–	–	–	–	–	–
Debt Securities	79led	....	....	....	....	....	15.0	36.9	20.0	20.0	–	–	–
Financial Derivatives	79lld	....	....	....	....	....	–	–	–	–	–	–	–
Other Investment	79lfd	....	....	....	....	....	5,393.2	5,799.7	5,584.8	5,192.3	5,281.8	5,135.9	5,901.8
Monetary Authorities	79lgd	....	....	....	....	....	733.1	707.1	667.8	597.7	342.4	335.4	424.9
General Government	79lhd	....	....	....	....	....	3,304.7	3,490.1	3,454.8	3,434.5	3,774.3	3,773.7	4,426.3
Banks	79lid	....	....	....	....	....	847.6	1,006.8	854.2	579.5	312.3	301.0	235.4
Other Sectors	79ljd	....	....	....	....	....	507.8	595.7	608.0	580.6	852.9	725.8	815.2
Government Finance		*Millions of Bolivianos: Year Ending December 31*										
Deficit (-) or Surplus	80	....	†−1,161	−902	−697	−869	−1,783	−1,917	−1,969	−2,317	−3,915	−5,484	−4,543
Revenue	81	....	†5,273	6,532	7,687	9,014	9,884	11,699	12,131	13,048	12,906	13,524	14,717
Expenditure	82	....	†6,434	7,434	8,384	9,883	11,667	13,615	14,100	15,365	16,821	19,008	19,259
Financing													
Domestic	84a	....	†259	165	−327	−355	602	646	860	1,314	2,373	2,023	721
Foreign	85a	....	†903	737	1,024	1,224	1,181	1,271	1,109	1,003	1,543	3,461	3,821

Bolivia 218

		1992	1993	1994	1995	1996	1997	1998	1999	2000	2001	2002	2003
National Accounts							*Millions of Bolivianos*						
Househ.Cons.Expend.,incl.NPISHs	96f	17,489	19,413	21,444	24,440	28,201	31,113	35,144	37,002	39,706	40,475	41,840	44,389
Government Consumption Expend	91f	2,833	3,270	3,750	4,375	5,003	5,790	6,658	7,126	7,595	8,071	8,638	9,980
Gross Fixed Capital Formation	93e	3,592	4,076	4,104	5,007	6,072	7,899	10,841	9,197	9,290	7,687	8,885	7,971
Changes in Inventories	93i	86	−25	−133	−93	23	276	212	−157	213	−135	−642	−1,274
Exports of Goods and Services	90c	4,413	4,667	5,987	7,269	8,476	8,791	9,223	8,129	9,301	10,436	12,264	14,286
Imports of Goods and Services (-)	98c	6,398	6,943	7,516	8,764	10,238	12,226	15,256	13,141	14,222	13,525	15,052	15,101
Gross Domestic Product (GDP)	99b	22,014	24,459	27,636	32,235	37,537	41,644	46,822	48,156	51,884	53,010	55,933	60,252
GDP Volume 1990 Prices	99b.p	16,524	17,230	18,034	18,877	19,701	20,677	21,717	21,809	22,306	22,642	23,266	23,837
GDP Volume (2000=100)	99bvp	74.1	77.2	80.8	84.6	88.3	92.7	97.4	97.8	100.0	101.5	104.3	106.9
GDP Deflator (2000=100)	99bip	57.3	61.0	65.9	73.4	81.9	86.6	92.7	94.9	100.0	100.7	103.4	108.7
						Millions: Midyear Estimates							
Population	99z	6.98	7.15	7.31	7.48	7.65	7.82	7.98	8.15	8.32	8.48	8.65	8.81

2004, International Monetary Fund : *International Financial Statistics Yearbook*

Bosnia & Herzegovina 963

		1992	1993	1994	1995	1996	1997	1998	1999	2000	2001	2002	2003
Exchange Rates						*Convertible Marka per SDR: End of Period*							
Official Rate	aa	....	....	....	....	....	2.418	2.356	2.672	2.739	2.789	2.536	2.301
					Convertible Marka per US Dollar: End of Period (ae) Period Average (rf)									
Official Rate	ae	....	....	....	....	....	1.792	1.673	1.947	2.102	2.219	1.865	1.549
Official Rate	rf	....	....	....	....	....	1.734	1.760	1.836	2.123	2.186	2.078	1.733
Fund Position						*Millions of SDRs: End of Period*							
Quota	2f.s	–	–	–	121.2	121.2	121.2	121.2	169.1	169.1	169.1	169.1	169.1
SDRs	1b.s	–	–	–	5.0	1.8	–	3.7	5.6	8.2	4.9	2.3	2.3
Reserve Position in the Fund	1c.s	–	–	–	–	–	–	–	–	–	–	–	–
Total Fund Cred.&Loans Outstg	2tl	–	–	–	32.5	31.0	30.3	54.5	68.4	80.4	88.4	102.4	90.1
International Liquidity					*Millions of US Dollars Unless Otherwise Indicated: End of Period*								
Total Reserves minus Gold	1l.d	....	....	....	....	....	80	175	452	497	1,221	1,321	1,796
SDRs	1b.d	–	–	–	8	3	–	5	8	11	6	3	3
Reserve Position in the Fund	1c.d	–	–	–	–	–	–	–	–	–	–	–	–
Foreign Exchange	1d.d	....	....	....	....	....	80	169	445	486	1,215	1,318	1,792
Monetary Authorities						*Millions of Convertible Marka End of Period*							
Foreign Assets	11	....	....	....	....	....	144	292	881	1,044	2,737	2,492	2,808
Reserve Money	14	....	....	....	....	....	170	236	807	961	2,544	2,318	2,608
of which: Currency Outside Banks	14a	....	....	....	....	....	113	162	515	652	1,674	1,734	1,601
Foreign Liabilities	16c	....	....	....	....	....	73	128	183	220	276	261	208
Central Government Deposits	16d	....	....	....	....	....	–	7	9	10	49	27	19
Capital Accounts	17a	....	....	....	....	....	1	30	34	58	121	181	215
Other Items (Net)	17r	....	....	....	....	....	–101	–109	–151	–207	–253	–295	–241
Deposit Money Banks						*Millions of Convertible Marka End of Period*							
Reserves	20	....	....	....	....	....	71	90	275	287	872	595	1,005
Foreign Assets	21	....	....	....	....	....	1,299	1,172	1,134	1,246	1,364	1,469	1,562
Claims on State Government	22ab	....	....	....	....	....	129	106	26	24	11	29	24
Claims on Local Government	22b	....	....	....	....	....	4	7	11	9	22	23	21
Claims on Other Resident Sectors	22d	....	....	....	....	....	3,835	4,193	4,129	4,368	3,306	4,220	5,076
Demand Deposits	24	....	....	....	....	....	134	147	566	730	957	1,221	1,442
Time & Savings Deposits	25a	....	....	....	....	....	10	8	22	78	140	272	462
Foreign Currency Deposits	25b	....	....	....	....	....	907	1,219	1,039	970	1,827	1,786	1,914
Foreign Liabilities	26c	....	....	....	....	....	3,428	3,375	3,289	3,347	1,527	1,794	2,437
Central Government Deposits	26d	....	....	....	....	....	–	1	9	18	28	81	77
State Government Deposits	26da	....	....	....	....	....	331	288	183	158	318	365	471
Capital Accounts	27a	....	....	....	....	....	1,043	1,305	1,257	1,096	1,119	1,214	1,305
Other Items (Net)	27r	....	....	....	....	....	–514	–775	–791	–462	–341	–395	–421
Monetary Survey						*Millions of Convertible Marka End of Period*							
Foreign Assets (Net)	31n	....	....	....	....	....	–2,058	–2,040	–1,457	–1,277	2,298	1,906	1,725
Domestic Credit	32	....	....	....	....	....	3,969	4,297	4,148	4,373	3,262	4,165	5,026
Claims on Central Govt. (Net)	32an	....	....	....	....	....	–	–8	–18	–28	–77	–107	–95
Claims on State Government	32ab	....	....	....	....	....	129	106	26	24	11	29	24
Claims on Local Government	32b	....	....	....	....	....	4	7	11	9	22	23	21
Claims on Other Resident Sectors	32d	....	....	....	....	....	3,835	4,193	4,129	4,368	3,306	4,220	5,076
Money	34	....	....	....	....	....	343	384	1,149	1,471	2,790	3,154	3,289
Quasi-Money	35	....	....	....	....	....	1,152	1,440	1,177	1,117	2,126	2,224	2,601
Capital Accounts	37a	....	....	....	....	....	1,045	1,335	1,291	1,155	1,240	1,394	1,520
Other Items (Net)	37r	....	....	....	....	....	–629	–901	–926	–647	–596	–701	–660
Money plus Quasi-Money	35l	....	....	....	....	....	1,495	1,824	2,326	2,588	4,916	5,378	5,891
Interest Rates						*Percent Per Annum*							
Deposit Rate	60l	....	....	....	....	....	....	51.88	9.07	14.67	....	† 4.53	4.03
Lending Rate	60p	....	....	....	....	....	....	73.50	24.29	30.50	....	† 12.70	10.87
International Transactions						*Millions of Convertible Marka*							
Exports	70	....	....	....	....	....	....	1,043	1,376	2,265	2,256	2,089	2,363
Imports, f.o.b.	71	....	....	....	....	....	....	5,120	6,048	6,583	7,331	8,048	8,223

Bosnia & Herzegovina 963

		1992	1993	1994	1995	1996	1997	1998	1999	2000	2001	2002	2003
Balance of Payments		*Millions of US Dollars: Minus Sign Indicates Debit*												
Current Account, n.i.e.	78ald	....	....	....	....	....	....	−781.9	−1,098.1	−880.9	−1,216.8	−1,750.6	−2,096.0
Goods: Exports f.o.b.	78aad	....	....	....	....	....	....	663.8	831.8	1,173.6	1,134.2	1,109.7	1,498.0
Goods: Imports f.o.b.	78abd	....	....	....	....	....	....	−3,779.4	−4,128.7	−3,795.8	−4,092.0	−4,449.4	−5,425.9
Trade Balance	78acd	....	....	....	....	....	....	−3,115.6	−3,296.9	−2,622.2	−2,957.8	−3,339.7	−3,927.9
Services: Credit	78add	....	....	....	....	....	....	420.0	394.5	359.8	376.2	382.0	487.5
Services: Debit	78aed	....	....	....	....	....	....	−206.8	−226.4	−197.1	−202.6	−240.5	−296.8
Balance on Goods & Services	78afd	....	....	....	....	....	....	−2,902.4	−3,128.9	−2,459.6	−2,784.2	−3,198.2	−3,737.2
Income: Credit	78agd	....	....	....	....	....	....	481.2	455.0	392.1	396.3	339.4	349.3
Income: Debit	78ahd	....	....	....	....	....	....	−53.7	−64.9	−73.3	−80.6	−86.5	−106.6
Balance on Gds, Serv. & Inc.	78aid	....	....	....	....	....	....	−2,474.9	−2,738.8	−2,140.8	−2,468.5	−2,945.4	−3,494.6
Current Transfers, n.i.e.: Credit	78ajd	....	....	....	....	....	....	1,695.8	1,643.6	1,263.1	1,255.6	1,223.1	1,440.4
Current Transfers: Debit	78akd	....	....	....	....	....	....	−2.8	−2.9	−3.2	−3.9	−28.4	−41.8
Capital Account, n.i.e.	78bcd	....	....	....	....	....	....	490.3	606.9	524.7	382.9	392.0	478.8
Capital Account, n.i.e.: Credit	78bad	....	....	....	....	....	....	490.3	606.9	524.7	382.9	392.0	478.8
Capital Account: Debit	78bbd	....	....	....	....	....	....						
Financial Account, n.i.e.	78bjd	....	....	....	....	....	....	−429.9	−471.1	−243.5	1,010.9	695.4	931.9
Direct Investment Abroad	78bdd	....	....	....	....	....	....	−	−	−	−	−	−
Dir. Invest. in Rep. Econ., n.i.e.	78bed	....	....	....	....	....	....	66.7	176.8	146.1	118.5	267.8	381.8
Portfolio Investment Assets	78bfd	....	....	....	....	....	....	−	−	−	−	−	−
Equity Securities	78bkd	....	....	....	....	....	....	−	−	−	−	−	−
Debt Securities	78bid	....	....	....	....	....	....	−	−	−	−	−	−
Portfolio Investment Liab., n.i.e.	78bgd	....	....	....	....	....	....	−	−	−	−	−	−
Equity Securities	78bmd	....	....	....	....	....	....	−	−	−	−	−	−
Debt Securities	78bnd	....	....	....	....	....	....	−	−	−	−	−	−
Financial Derivatives Assets	78bwd	....	....	....	....	....	....	−	−	−	−	−	−
Financial Derivatives Liabilities	78bxd	....	....	....	....	....	....	−	−	−	−	−	−
Other Investment Assets	78bhd	....	....	....	....	....	....	−443.8	−552.5	−417.3	906.2	314.7	135.9
Monetary Authorities	78bod	....	....	....	....	....	....	....	....	....	....	....	....
General Government	78bpd	....	....	....	....	....	....	71.9	21.1	−52.9	−185.6	−40.5	−72.4
Banks	78bqd	....	....	....	....	....	....	−515.6	−573.7	−364.4	1,091.9	355.2	208.2
Other Sectors	78brd	....	....	....	....	....	....	−52.9	−95.3	27.7	−13.8	112.9	414.2
Other Investment Liab., n.i.e.	78bid	....	....	....	....	....	....		−	−	13.6	−13.4	−.1
Monetary Authorities	78bsd	....	....	....	....	....	....	−	−36.9	−27.9	−24.4	−62.6	−96.3
General Government	78btd	....	....	....	....	....	....	−29.8	−47.1	27.2	−22.5	130.8	382.2
Banks	78bud	....	....	....	....	....	....	−23.1	−11.4	27.8	19.5	58.0	128.4
Other Sectors	78bvd	....	....	....	....	....	....	290.1	295.8	308.2	225.5	164.0	414.9
Net Errors and Omissions	78cad	....	....	....	....	....	....	−431.4	−666.5	−291.5	402.5	−499.3	−270.4
Overall Balance	78cbd	....	....	....	....	....	....	431.4	666.5	291.5	−402.5	499.3	270.4
Reserves and Related Items	79dad	....	....	....	....	....	....	−84.0	−319.4	−76.5	−761.6	109.6	−196.6
Reserve Assets	79dbd	....	....	....	....	....	....	32.3	18.2	15.5	9.9	19.0	−17.1
Use of Fund Credit and Loans	79dcd	....	....	....	....	....	....	483.1	967.7	352.5	349.2	370.7	484.1
Exceptional Financing	79ded												
National Accounts		*Millions of Convertible Marka*												
Gross Domestic Product (GDP)	99b	....	....	....	....	4,192	6,367	7,244	8,990	10,050	10,960	11,650	12,170
		Millions: Midyear Estimates												
Population	99z	3.95	3.72	3.52	3.42	3.43	Ü 3.53	3.68	3.85	3.98	4.07	4.13	4.16

2004, International Monetary Fund : *International Financial Statistics Yearbook*

Botswana 616

		1992	1993	1994	1995	1996	1997	1998	1999	2000	2001	2002	2003
Exchange Rates						*Pula per SDR: End of Period*							
Official Rate	aa	3.1031	3.5229	3.9670	4.1944	5.2404	5.1400	6.2774	6.3572	6.9861	8.7760	7.4331	6.6014
					Pula per US Dollar: End of Period (ae) Period Average (rf)								
Official Rate	ae	2.2568	2.5648	2.7174	2.8217	3.6443	3.8095	4.4583	4.6318	5.3619	6.9832	5.4675	4.4425
Official Rate	rf	2.1097	2.4231	2.6846	2.7722	3.3242	3.6508	4.2259	4.6244	5.1018	5.8412	6.3278	4.9499
Fund Position						*Millions of SDRs: End of Period*							
Quota	2f.s	36.60	36.60	36.60	36.60	36.60	36.60	36.60	63.00	63.00	63.00	63.00	63.00
SDRs	1b.s	22.46	24.03	25.39	27.06	28.71	30.36	32.41	28.05	29.89	31.53	32.63	33.52
Reserve Position in the Fund	1c.s	14.79	16.60	16.34	19.28	19.91	18.13	27.61	22.59	17.74	22.28	23.80	30.32
Total Fund Cred.&Loans Outstg.	2tl	–	–	–	–	–	–	–	–	–	–	–	–
International Liquidity					*Millions of US Dollars Unless Otherwise Indicated: End of Period*								
Total Reserves minus Gold	1l.d	3,793.42	4,097.34	4,401.47	4,695.48	5,027.66	5,675.00	5,940.67	6,298.72	6,318.21	5,897.25	5,473.92	5,339.78
SDRs	1b.d	30.88	33.00	37.07	40.22	41.28	40.96	45.63	38.50	38.94	39.62	44.36	49.81
Reserve Position in the Fund	1c.d	20.34	22.79	23.86	28.66	28.63	24.46	38.87	31.00	23.11	28.00	32.36	45.05
Foreign Exchange	1d.d	3,742.20	4,041.54	4,340.54	4,626.60	4,957.75	5,609.58	5,856.17	6,229.21	6,256.16	5,829.63	5,397.20	5,244.92
Monetary Authorities: Other Liab.	4..d	–	–	–	–	–	–	–	–	–	–	–	–
Deposit Money Banks: Assets	7a.d	64.91	61.17	63.42	69.60	124.51	211.33	317.73	290.52	267.62	319.47	284.37	398.85
Liabilities	7b.d	19.40	54.32	24.22	35.05	41.61	31.61	38.49	34.79	41.93	52.65	53.33	94.76
Monetary Authorities						*Millions of Pula: End of Period*							
Foreign Assets	11	8,561	10,506	10,567	12,115	18,356	21,637	26,502	28,867	33,900	41,211	29,984	23,887
Reserve Money	14	424	395	392	405	453	572	707	808	857	970	1,050	1,338
of which: Currency Outside DMBs	14a	163	180	195	223	247	276	353	404	427	481	470	533
Time Deposits	15	605	38	46	48	47	63	26	172	183	184	286	231
Liabs. of Central Bank: Securities	16ac	344	1,201	1,451	1,964	2,816	3,308	3,246	4,230	3,712	5,148	7,663	8,739
Foreign Liabilities	16c	–	–	–	–	–	–	–	–	–	–	–	–
Central Government Deposits	16d	5,058	5,586	6,689	6,469	7,221	15,362	19,072	20,086	24,026	27,719	16,433	10,514
Capital Accounts	17a	1,365	2,167	2,935	2,942	6,107	1,888	3,229	3,415	4,384	6,668	4,107	2,758
Other Items (Net)	17r	767	1,119	–945	288	1,713	444	223	156	737	524	445	307
Deposit Money Banks						*Millions of Pula: End of Period*							
Reserves	20	124	194	160	166	177	271	331	353	229	263	311	397
Claims on Mon.Author.:Securities	20c	344	361	493	832	1,192	1,572	1,322	1,718	1,197	1,874	1,732	2,229
Foreign Assets	21	146	157	172	196	454	805	1,417	1,346	1,435	2,231	1,555	1,772
Claims on Central Government	22a	–	–	2	–	–	–	–	–	–	–	–	–
Claims on Local Government	22b	2	3	2	3	2	2	14	15	2	1	–	–
Claims on Nonfin.Pub.Enterprises	22c	76	94	148	95	70	61	267	528	458	480	462	381
Claims on Private Sector	22d	1,285	1,434	1,600	1,560	1,626	1,775	2,461	3,518	4,344	4,915	6,155	6,821
Claims on Other Financial Insts.	22f	35	32	95	122	100	61	231	130	123	64	4	–
Demand Deposits	24	444	516	579	607	704	762	1,160	1,371	1,470	1,869	2,054	2,290
Time and Savings Deposits	25	1,267	1,386	1,573	1,809	2,192	3,003	4,183	5,282	5,248	7,082	6,698	7,924
Foreign Liabilities	26c	44	139	66	99	152	120	172	161	225	368	292	421
Central Government Deposits	26d	9	31	16	19	40	36	29	66	107	61	58	148
Capital Accounts	27a	221	244	308	337	402	464	568	732	843	1,042	1,102	1,346
Other Items (Net)	27r	27	–43	131	103	131	162	–70	–5	–103	–594	16	–529
Monetary Survey						*Millions of Pula: End of Period*							
Foreign Assets (Net)	31n	8,664	10,524	10,673	12,213	18,658	22,321	27,747	30,051	35,110	43,075	31,247	25,238
Domestic Credit	32	–3,669	–4,054	–4,859	–4,709	–5,463	–13,499	–16,128	–15,961	–19,205	–22,320	–9,870	–3,460
Claims on Central Govt. (Net)	32an	–5,067	–5,617	–6,703	–6,488	–7,261	–15,398	–19,101	–20,152	–24,133	–27,779	–16,491	–10,662
Claims on Local Government	32b	2	3	2	3	2	2	14	15	2	1	–	–
Claims on Nonfin.Pub.Enterprises	32c	76	94	148	95	70	61	267	528	458	480	462	381
Claims on Private Sector	32d	1,285	1,434	1,600	1,560	1,626	1,775	2,461	3,518	4,344	4,915	6,155	6,821
Claims on Other Financial Insts.	32f	35	32	95	122	100	61	231	130	123	64	4	–
Money	34	607	696	774	829	951	1,038	1,513	1,775	1,897	2,351	2,524	2,822
Quasi-Money	35	1,871	1,424	1,619	1,856	2,239	3,066	4,209	5,454	5,432	7,266	6,984	8,155
Liabs. of Central Bank: Securities	36ac	–	840	958	1,132	1,623	1,736	1,924	2,513	2,515	3,274	5,931	6,510
Capital Accounts	37a	1,585	2,412	3,243	3,279	6,509	2,352	3,797	4,147	5,227	7,710	5,209	4,104
Other Items (Net)	37r	931	1,097	–778	407	1,873	631	177	202	835	155	730	187
Money plus Quasi-Money	35l	2,478	2,121	2,392	2,686	3,190	4,104	5,722	7,228	7,328	9,617	9,508	10,977
Interest Rates						*Percent Per Annum*							
Bank Rate (End of Period)	60	14.25	14.25	13.50	13.00	13.00	12.50	12.50	13.25	14.25	14.25	15.25	14.25
Deposit Rate	60l	12.50	13.49	10.39	9.98	10.43	9.25	8.72	9.46	10.07	10.15	10.30	10.48
Lending Rate	60p	14.00	14.92	13.88	14.29	14.50	14.08	13.53	14.63	15.31	15.75	15.96	16.58
Prices, Production, Labor						*Index Numbers (2000=100): Period Averages*							
Consumer Prices	64	47.9	54.8	60.6	66.9	†73.7	80.1	85.5	92.1	100.0	106.6	115.1	125.7
Mining Production (1995=100)	66zx	96.4	89.3	94.0	100.0	....	....	....	....	....	....	....	....
					Number in Thousands: Period Averages								
Labor Force	67d	....	....	....	437	439	....	....	....	....	....	....	....
Employment	67e	85	86	87	88	90	87	91	97	100	102	105	....

Botswana 616

		1992	1993	1994	1995	1996	1997	1998	1999	2000	2001	2002	2003
International Transactions		\multicolumn{12}{c}{*Millions of Pula*}
Exports	70	3,675.0	4,270.9	4,965.0	5,941.5	8,133.4	10,390.7	8,696.9	12,227.8	13,834.7	14,306.5	....	....
Imports, c.i.f.	71	3,970.1	4,285.0	4,407.3	5,305.1	5,742.9	8,250.0	9,803.8	10,164.4	12,646.8	10,556.9	....	....
Balance of Payments		\multicolumn{12}{c}{*Millions of US Dollars: Minus Sign Indicates Debit*}
Current Account, n.i.e.	78ald	197.7	426.9	211.6	299.7	495.0	721.5	170.1	516.8	....	....	....	....
Goods: Exports f.o.b.	78aad	1,743.9	1,722.2	1,874.3	2,160.2	2,217.5	2,819.8	2,060.6	2,671.0	....	....	....	....
Goods: Imports f.o.b.	78abd	–1,556.6	–1,455.4	–1,364.3	–1,605.4	–1,467.7	–1,924.4	–1,983.1	–1,996.5	....	....	....	....
Trade Balance	78acd	187.3	266.8	510.0	554.8	749.8	895.4	77.5	674.5	....	....	....	....
Services: Credit	78add	189.2	191.3	186.1	260.4	163.0	210.2	255.3	372.6	....	....	....	....
Services: Debit	78aed	–360.1	–325.6	–322.0	–444.2	–343.6	–440.7	–522.4	–515.9	....	....	....	....
Balance on Goods & Services	78afd	16.4	132.5	374.2	370.9	569.2	664.9	–189.6	531.2	....	....	....	....
Income: Credit	78agd	542.1	554.5	230.8	483.2	501.7	622.1	622.7	429.8	....	....	....	....
Income: Debit	78ahd	–429.7	–260.9	–455.1	–515.6	–754.8	–766.9	–503.1	–696.0	....	....	....	....
Balance on Gds, Serv. & Inc.	78aid	128.8	426.1	149.9	338.5	316.1	520.1	–70.0	265.1	....	....	....	....
Current Transfers, n.i.e.: Credit	78ajd	344.5	275.9	356.8	330.7	355.4	456.8	460.9	474.4	....	....	....	....
Current Transfers: Debit	78akd	–275.6	–275.1	–295.1	–369.5	–176.6	–255.5	–220.8	–222.6	....	....	....	....
Capital Account, n.i.e.	78bcd	53.2	84.9	19.2	14.4	6.2	16.9	31.8	20.6	....	....	....	....
Capital Account, n.i.e.: Credit	78bad	53.8	86.1	19.6	15.4	18.0	29.4	44.2	33.5	....	....	....	....
Capital Account: Debit	78bbd	–.5	–1.3	–.4	–.9	–11.9	–12.5	–12.4	–12.9	....	....	....	....
Financial Account, n.i.e.	78bjd	275.8	–40.3	41.1	–33.9	42.4	5.6	–202.4	–175.2	....	....	....	....
Direct Investment Abroad	78bdd	–9.9	–9.5	–9.5	–40.9	1.1	–4.1	–3.5	–1.5	....	....	....	....
Dir. Invest. in Rep. Econ., n.i.e.	78bed	–1.6	–286.9	–14.2	70.4	71.2	100.1	95.3	36.7	....	....	....	....
Portfolio Investment Assets	78bfd	....	....	....	–36.2	–35.5	–28.5	–42.8	–22.8	....	....	....	....
Equity Securities	78bkd	....	....	....	–30.8	–26.7	–33.1	–16.9	6.5	....	....	....	....
Debt Securities	78bld	....	....	....	–5.4	–8.9	4.7	–25.9	–29.3	....	....	....	....
Portfolio Investment Liab., n.i.e.	78bgd	.1	.2	–.1	5.5	28.9	10.8	–14.1	–7.5	....	....	....	....
Equity Securities	78bmd	....	....	....	5.5	28.7	10.8	–14.1	–7.5	....	....	....	....
Debt Securities	78bnd	.1	.2	–.1	–	.2	–	–	–	....	....	....	....
Financial Derivatives Assets	78bwd	....	....	....	–.2	–	–15.4	5.2	–4.6	....	....	....	....
Financial Derivatives Liabilities	78bxd	....	....	....	.3	2.1	–	–	–	....	....	....	....
Other Investment Assets	78bhd	148.9	63.4	15.8	–88.7	–95.6	–166.5	–310.8	–206.1	....	....	....	....
Monetary Authorities	78bod	....	....	....	....	....	....	....	....	....	....	....	....
General Government	78bpd	139.9	56.1	19.7	–46.1	–28.7	–78.0	–101.1	–17.8	....	....	....	....
Banks	78bqd	–7.0	14.3	.4	–8.7	–35.1	–76.9	–139.7	–154.7	....	....	....	....
Other Sectors	78brd	16.1	–6.9	–4.3	–34.0	–31.8	–11.6	–70.0	–33.7	....	....	....	....
Other Investment Liab., n.i.e.	78bid	138.2	192.5	49.0	55.9	70.3	109.3	68.2	30.7	....	....	....	....
Monetary Authorities	78bsd	–	–	–	–	–	–	–	–	....	....	....	....
General Government	78btd	54.4	67.0	6.5	–12.3	–19.6	51.3	22.2	–16.1	....	....	....	....
Banks	78bud	–5.6	23.1	–2.8	–2.5	17.8	–3.4	–3.5	1.4	....	....	....	....
Other Sectors	78bvd	89.4	102.4	45.3	70.7	72.1	61.4	49.5	45.4	....	....	....	....
Net Errors and Omissions	78cad	–121.4	–74.5	–136.7	–73.6	–32.9	–108.9	44.6	8.7	....	....	....	....
Overall Balance	78cbd	405.3	397.0	135.2	206.6	510.7	635.1	44.2	371.0	....	....	....	....
Reserves and Related Items	79dad	–405.3	–397.0	–135.2	–206.6	–510.7	–635.1	–44.2	–371.0	....	....	....	....
Reserve Assets	79dbd	–405.3	–397.0	–135.2	–206.6	–510.7	–635.1	–44.2	–371.0	....	....	....	....
Use of Fund Credit and Loans	79dcd	–	–	–	–	–	–	–	–	....	....	....	....
Exceptional Financing	79ded	....	....	....	....	....	....	....	....	....	....	....	....
International Investment Position		\multicolumn{12}{c}{*Millions of US Dollars*}
Assets	79aad	....	....	5,084.0	5,643.9	6,001.0	6,510.5	6,855.1	7,356.3	....	....	....	....
Direct Investment Abroad	79abd	....	....	484.5	650.1	576.7	404.5	257.5	596.9	....	....	....	....
Portfolio Investment	79acd	....	....	26.9	61.5	139.1	132.2	214.6	148.2	....	....	....	....
Equity Securities	79add	....	....	16.1	45.8	105.8	81.7	73.6	120.2	....	....	....	....
Debt Securities	79aed	....	....	10.9	15.8	33.3	50.5	141.0	28.0	....	....	....	....
Financial Derivatives	79ald	....	....	....	.2	–	17.1	9.6	–	....	....	....	....
Other Investment	79afd	....	....	171.3	239.1	253.1	280.3	433.0	382.4	....	....	....	....
Monetary Authorities	79agd	....	....	–	–	–	–	–	–	....	....	....	....
General Government	79ahd	....	....	–	–	–	–	–	–	....	....	....	....
Banks	79aid	....	....	63.3	69.5	99.9	186.2	291.5	289.9	....	....	....	....
Other Sectors	79ajd	....	....	107.9	169.6	153.3	94.2	141.5	92.5	....	....	....	....
Reserve Assets	79akd	....	....	4,401.3	4,693.0	5,032.1	5,676.5	5,940.3	6,228.8	....	....	....	....
Liabilities	79lad	....	....	2,005.3	1,995.1	1,941.9	2,151.9	2,248.7	2,514.8	....	....	....	....
Dir. Invest. in Rep. Economy	79lbd	....	....	998.5	1,126.4	1,058.1	1,172.9	1,294.8	1,387.3	....	....	....	....
Portfolio Investment	79lcd	....	....	10.9	15.9	50.4	60.5	34.2	24.0	....	....	....	....
Equity Securities	79ldd	....	....	10.9	15.9	50.4	60.0	33.4	22.7	....	....	....	....
Debt Securities	79led	....	....	–	–	–	.5	.8	1.3	....	....	....	....
Financial Derivatives	79lld	....	....	–	.2	1.9	–	–	–	....	....	....	....
Other Investment	79lfd	....	....	996.0	852.6	831.5	918.5	919.7	1,103.5	....	....	....	....
Monetary Authorities	79lgd	....	....	–	–	–	–	–	–	....	....	....	....
General Government	79lhd	....	....	496.9	495.8	387.9	483.1	482.6	523.6	....	....	....	....
Banks	79lid	....	....	38.9	35.1	27.4	23.7	16.8	15.3	....	....	....	....
Other Sectors	79ljd	....	....	460.1	321.7	416.2	411.7	420.3	564.6	....	....	....	....

2004, International Monetary Fund : *International Financial Statistics Yearbook*

Botswana 616

		1992	1993	1994	1995	1996	1997	1998	1999	2000	2001	2002	2003
Government Finance						*Millions of Pula: Year Beginning April 1*							
Deficit (-) or Surplus	80	881.40	878.30	195.60	269.90	1,302.40	875.19	−1,387.80	1,535.58	2,578.56	−961.96	−1,392.32	128.60
Total Revenue and Grants	81y	4,652.30	5,359.50	4,472.50	5,464.40	7,394.80	8,281.29	7,677.62	11,963.09	14,115.04	12,708.89	14,311.02	15,992.06
Revenue	81	4,552.20	5,172.90	4,396.80	5,427.30	7,311.80	8,169.20	7,539.93	11,837.04	14,050.51	12,649.73	14,226.62	15,913.19
Grants	81z	100.10	186.60	75.70	37.10	83.00	112.09	137.69	126.05	64.53	59.16	84.40	78.87
Exp. & Lending Minus Repay	82z	3,770.90	4,481.20	4,276.90	5,194.50	6,092.40	7,406.10	9,065.42	10,427.51	11,536.48	13,670.85	15,703.34	16,206.67
Expenditure	82	3,422.30	4,291.90	4,389.10	5,181.60	6,283.50	7,188.10	9,199.78	10,608.94	11,637.69	13,783.06	15,791.25	17,257.97
Lending Minus Repayments	83	348.60	189.30	−112.20	12.90	−191.10	218.00	−134.36	−181.43	−101.21	−112.21	−87.91	−1,051.30
Total Financing	80h	−881.30	−878.30	−195.70	−269.80	−1,302.30	−875.14	1,387.80	−1,535.58	−2,578.57	961.96	1,392.34	−128.60
Total Net Borrowing	84	−62.20	90.90	69.50	89.80	−8,148.70	13,467.36	1,098.16	−216.47	513.19	−1,752.62	−6,340.24	−2,663.87
Net Domestic	84a	−142.50	46.00	91.20	135.80	−8,233.80	13,380.80	1,118.38	−151.90	690.14	−1,568.98	−6,090.24	−2,504.85
Net Foreign	85a	80.30	44.90	−21.70	−46.00	85.10	86.56	−20.22	−64.57	−176.95	−183.64	−250.00	−159.02
Use of Cash Balances	87	−819.10	−969.20	−265.20	−359.60	6,846.40	−14,342.50	289.64	−1,319.11	−3,091.76	2,714.58	7,732.58	2,535.27
Total Debt by Currency	88	1,096.20	1,267.80	1,377.70	1,439.90	1,791.20	1,996.90	2,422.80	2,425.30	2,426.20	2,917.50	2,194.70	2,194.50
Domestic	88b	−	−	−	−	−	−	−	−	−	−	−	−
Foreign	89b	1,096.20	1,267.80	1,377.70	1,439.90	1,791.20	1,996.90	2,422.80	2,425.30	2,426.20	2,917.50	2,194.70	2,194.50
National Accounts						*Millions of Pula: Year Ending June 30*							
Househ.Cons.Expend.,incl.NPISHs	96f	3,123.9	3,282.2	3,843.0	4,258.5	4,714.7	5,314.7	6,136.1	6,936.8	7,841.1	8,438.6	9,307.6	10,336.0
Government Consumption Expend	91f	2,016.4	2,595.2	3,048.1	3,546.7	4,006.7	4,711.0	5,452.9	6,578.8	7,524.5	8,741.8	10,552.7	12,167.5
Gross Fixed Capital Formation	93e	2,551.3	2,618.7	2,729.2	3,135.2	3,632.4	4,275.9	5,170.1	6,263.3	6,751.0	6,898.2	7,743.2	8,735.7
Changes in Inventories	93i	−13.3	165.3	204.3	13.7	−261.4	328.0	885.9	1,653.8	−1,782.9	−1,291.2	607.6	2,002.2
Exports of Goods and Services	90c	4,346.6	4,082.8	5,421.8	6,071.4	7,411.6	9,881.6	11,392.8	10,051.6	15,318.5	17,555.0	15,564.3	16,132.4
Imports of Goods and Services (-)	98c	3,648.3	3,625.0	4,260.3	4,772.5	5,300.1	6,711.1	8,875.3	9,960.6	10,422.4	10,805.9	11,737.9	12,690.3
Gross Domestic Product (GDP)	99b	8,376.5	9,119.2	11,041.4	12,261.7	14,203.9	17,740.1	20,162.5	21,523.8	24,943.1	28,636.5	31,922.4	36,338.5
Consumption of Fixed Capital	99cf	1,156.8	1,195.1	1,496.4	1,652.7	1,944.3	....	....	....	....	....	....	....
GDP Volume 1993/94 Prices	99b.p	10,634.3	10,612.1	11,041.4	11,396.8	12,029.5	12,703.7	13,728.7	14,295.6	15,238.8	16,535.3	16,905.8	18,038.1
GDP Volume (2000=100)	99bvp	69.8	69.6	72.5	74.8	78.9	83.4	90.1	93.8	100.0	108.5	110.9	118.4
GDP Deflator (2000=100)	99bip	48.1	52.5	61.1	65.7	72.1	85.3	89.7	92.0	100.0	105.8	115.4	123.1
						Millions: Midyear Estimates							
Population	99z	**1.43**	**1.47**	**1.51**	**1.55**	**1.59**	**1.63**	**1.66**	**1.70**	**1.73**	**1.75**	**1.77**	**1.79**

Brazil 223

		1992	1993	1994	1995	1996	1997	1998	1999	2000	2001	2002	2003
Exchange Rates		Reais per Thousands SDR through 1992, per SDR Thereafter: End of Period											
Principal Rate	aa	†6.194	.163	†1.235	1.446	1.495	1.506	1.702	2.455	2.547	2.916	4.803	4.292
		Reais per Thousands US$ through 1992, per US$ Thereafter: End of Period (ae) Period Average (rf)											
Principal Rate	ae	†4.505	.119	†.846	.973	1.039	1.116	1.209	1.789	1.955	2.320	3.533	2.888
Principal Rate	rf	1.641	.032	.639	.918	1.005	1.078	1.161	1.815	1.830	2.358	2.921	3.077
Fund Position						Millions of SDRs: End of Period							
Quota	2f.s	2,171	2,171	2,171	2,171	2,171	2,171	2,171	3,036	3,036	3,036	3,036	3,036
SDRs	1b.s	1	2	–	1	1	–	1	7	–	8	202	2
Reserve Position in the Fund	1c.s	–	–	–	–	–	–	–	–	–	–	–	–
Total Fund Cred.&Loans Outstg	2tl	581	221	128	95	47	23	3,427	6,431	1,357	6,634	15,320	19,056
International Liquidity					Millions of US Dollars Unless Otherwise Indicated: End of Period								
Total Reserves minus Gold	1l.d	22,521	30,604	37,070	49,708	58,323	50,827	42,580	34,796	32,488	35,739	37,683	49,111
SDRs	1b.d	1	2	–	1	1	1	2	10	–	11	275	2
Reserve Position in the Fund	1c.d	–	–	–	–	–	–	–	–	–	–	–	–
Foreign Exchange	1d.d	22,520	30,602	37,069	49,707	58,322	50,826	42,578	34,786	32,488	35,729	37,409	49,108
Other Liquid Foreign Assets	1e.d	486	501	319	365	467	503	585	618	–	–	–	–
Gold (Million Fine Troy Ounces)	1ad	2.23	2.93	3.71	4.58	3.69	3.03	4.60	3.17	1.89	.46	.44	.45
Gold (National Valuation)	1and	747	1,107	1,418	1,767	1,381	903	1,358	929	523	127	153	186
Monetary Authorities:Other Assets	3..d	2,331	2,056	1,851	4,077	5,050	4,935	5,456	5,334	6,110	–	–	–
Other Liab	4..d	47,253	48,399	6,888	5,614	3,239	2,948	8,284	5,288	2,419	1,255	4,735	9,435
Deposit Money Banks: Assets	7a.d	11,763	15,196	20,855	18,682	20,345	19,550	17,621	16,754	15,878	16,525	12,697	19,237
Liabilities	7b.d	21,472	31,054	36,771	42,494	51,432	54,756	50,580	41,890	40,646	39,837	31,651	30,795
Other Banking Insts.: Assets	7e.d	141	702	1,504	393	177	143	74	65	207	152	230	428
Liabilities	7f.d	2,242	2,527	2,224	2,247	3,211	4,398	9,406	6,282	7,975	8,532	8,872	9,651
Monetary Authorities				Thousands of Reais through 1992; Millions of Reais Beginning 1993: End of Period									
Foreign Assets	11	111,731	†3,968	35,326	55,218	69,829	61,745	55,053	69,273	76,097	82,026	133,291	150,909
Claims on Central Government	12a	363,345	†7,941	26,509	31,221	27,713	41,233	136,916	121,463	130,779	189,786	284,115	290,363
Claims on State and Local Govts	12b	172	†9	–	–	–	–	–	–	–	–	–	–
Claims on Nonfin.Pub.Enterprises	12c	–	†–	–	–	–	–	–	–	–	–	–	–
Claims on Private Sector	12d	2	†–	3	5	5	5	–	–	–	–	–	–
Claims on Deposit Money Banks	12e	17,299	†120	20,557	34,576	67,642	68,012	40,368	33,755	38,604	20,679	2,924	226
Claims on Other Banking Insts	12f	163	†1	5	5	3	902	–	–	–	1,764	–	–
Claims on Nonbank Financial Insts	12g	5	†–	–	–	6	7	1,926	2,036	1,373	1,456	1,070	606
Reserve Money	14	61,120	†1,543	36,130	40,430	49,638	66,636	59,213	63,849	66,901	79,639	195,807	186,708
of which: Currency Outside DMBs	14a	14,564	†340	8,700	12,517	15,316	18,141	21,185	25,978	28,641	32,625	42,351	43,064
Money Market Instruments	16aa	–	†–	–	–	–	–	3,290	4,708	6,347	6,297	9,587	8,527
Liabs. of Central Bank: Securities	16ac	94,933	†867	39,289	52,457	83,106	65,724	104,709	62,468	85,839	126,524	67,021	30,619
Restricted Deposits	16b	5,014	†75	306	190	125	12	10	13	13	15	23	18
Foreign Liabilities	16c	28,125	†807	895	478	143	167	7,723	15,942	3,509	19,405	73,689	81,890
Long-Term Foreign Liabilities	16cl	188,322	†4,968	5,075	5,116	3,292	3,157	8,111	9,297	4,675	2,844	16,612	27,154
Central Government Deposits	16d	42,889	†1,023	12,094	22,239	25,143	41,135	50,403	75,779	88,380	82,516	89,151	120,264
Capital Accounts	17a	70,673	†1,838	998	1,408	4,190	4,198	3,809	–4,496	–8,312	6,814	–12,032	8,788
Other Items (Net)	17r	1,642	†918	–12,387	–1,293	–438	–9,125	–3,005	–1,034	–500	–28,342	–18,457	–21,865
Deposit Money Banks				Thousands of Reais through 1992; Millions of Reais Beginning 1993: End of Period									
Reserves	20	30,779	†901	22,956	22,126	22,035	42,494	32,716	38,029	38,341	46,389	153,456	142,886
Claims on Mon.Author.:Securities	20c	46,131	†320	5,192	6,578	18,932	11,603	37,545	29,240	52,258	61,524	36,468	19,022
Blocked Financial Assets	20d	1	†–	–	–	–	–	–	–	–	–	–	–
Foreign Assets	21	52,983	†1,802	17,602	18,159	21,130	21,810	21,284	29,960	31,035	38,331	44,851	55,563
Claims on Central Government	22a	27,547	†1,027	7,850	17,966	29,225	92,066	74,107	118,083	138,772	201,663	215,431	258,622
Claims on State and Local Govts	22b	57,656	†1,522	27,482	25,986	56,061	39,447	38,228	19,000	4,274	2,752	2,477	2,538
Claims on Nonfin.Pub.Enterprises	22c	42,715	†1,158	10,245	12,399	18,736	5,716	12,542	15,169	3,703	1,467	2,268	2,104
Claims on Private Sector	22d	348,163	†11,589	174,660	210,488	220,655	254,585	296,921	301,955	315,948	345,315	386,930	437,392
Claims on Other Banking Insts	22f	3,046	†79	873	770	1,078	3,353	3,678	3,122	3,339	3,718	1,380	3,547
Claims on Nonbank Financial Insts	22g	–	†–	–	–	–	–	5,910	985	794	3,671	2,143	190
Demand Deposits	24	24,073	†497	13,979	14,034	14,320	27,912	29,059	36,251	45,060	50,880	64,680	65,879
Time and Savings Deposits	25	312,748	†9,980	119,979	159,901	173,714	203,992	225,619	238,851	240,116	268,522	325,910	340,530
Money Market Instruments	26aa	9,140	†283	3,320	4,744	7,029	10,283	12,684	13,377	22,880	32,788	20,371	35,860
Restricted Deposits	26b	18	†–	98	1,806	227	–	–	–	414	249	–	–
Foreign Liabilities	26c	70,000	†2,568	21,212	28,209	37,441	38,539	31,974	49,786	56,007	62,167	79,848	65,966
Long-Term Foreign Liabilities	26cl	26,719	†1,115	9,823	13,095	15,976	22,547	29,122	25,121	23,440	30,239	31,960	22,983
Central Government Deposits	26d	44,638	†1,411	18,288	14,670	16,074	17,939	11,776	7,394	9,430	11,201	7,600	12,223
Credit from Monetary Authorities	26g	16,508	†146	20,455	23,407	39,025	30,272	11,623	3,159	8,568	23,975	3,433	233
Liabilities to Other Banking Insts	26i	31,305	†1,081	11,914	9,396	22,017	21,973	27,590	30,632	31,344	43,214	52,545	59,442
Liab. to Nonbank Financial Insts	26j	442	†1	92	111	60	234	22,200	25,256	41,412	46,122	93,620	115,198
Capital Accounts	27a	143,861	†4,069	44,094	57,704	74,127	95,976	115,114	132,225	133,957	163,177	192,426	227,765
Other Items (Net)	27r	–70,431	†–2,752	3,606	–12,605	–12,157	1,407	6,169	–6,508	–24,163	–27,703	–26,988	–24,215

Brazil 223

		1992	1993	1994	1995	1996	1997	1998	1999	2000	2001	2002	2003
Monetary Survey		*Thousands of Reais through 1992; Millions of Reais Beginning 1993: End of Period*											
Foreign Assets (Net)	31n	66,589	† 2,395	30,821	44,690	53,375	44,849	36,640	33,504	47,615	38,785	24,606	58,616
Domestic Credit	32	755,285	† 20,892	217,245	261,931	312,266	378,240	508,048	498,641	501,173	657,875	799,063	862,876
Claims on Central Govt. (Net)	32an	303,364	† 6,535	3,977	12,278	15,721	74,225	148,844	156,373	171,741	297,732	402,795	416,498
Claims on State and Local Govts	32b	57,828	† 1,531	27,482	25,986	56,061	39,447	38,228	19,000	4,274	2,752	2,477	2,538
Claims on Nonfin.Pub.Enterprises	32c	42,715	† 1,158	10,245	12,399	18,736	5,716	12,542	15,169	3,703	1,467	2,268	2,104
Claims on Private Sector	32d	348,165	† 11,589	174,663	210,493	220,660	254,590	296,921	301,955	315,948	345,315	386,930	437,392
Claims on Other Banking Insts	32f	3,209	† 79	878	775	1,081	4,255	3,678	3,122	3,339	5,482	1,380	3,547
Claims on Nonbank Financial Inst	32g	5	† –	–	–	6	7	7,836	3,021	2,167	5,127	3,213	797
Money	34	52,539	† 1,113	25,540	32,094	41,683	50,999	54,819	62,287	74,081	83,550	107,208	111,541
Quasi-Money	35	312,748	† 9,980	119,979	159,901	173,714	203,992	225,619	238,851	240,116	268,522	325,910	340,530
Money Market Instruments	36aa	9,140	† 283	3,320	4,744	7,029	10,283	15,974	18,085	29,227	39,085	29,958	44,387
Liabs. of Central Bank: Securities	36ac	48,802	† 547	34,097	45,879	64,174	54,121	67,164	33,228	33,581	65,000	30,553	11,597
Restricted Deposits	36b	5,032	† 75	404	1,996	352	12	10	13	427	264	23	18
Long-Term Foreign Liabilities	36cl	215,041	† 6,083	14,898	18,211	19,268	25,704	37,233	34,418	28,115	33,083	48,572	50,137
Liabilities to Other Banking Insts	36i	31,305	† 1,081	11,914	9,396	22,017	21,973	27,590	30,632	31,344	43,214	52,545	59,442
Liab. to Nonbank Financial Insts	36j	442	† 1	92	111	60	234	22,200	25,256	41,412	46,122	93,620	115,198
Capital Accounts	37a	214,533	† 5,908	45,092	59,112	78,317	100,174	118,923	127,729	125,645	169,991	180,394	236,553
Other Items (Net)	37r	−67,706	† −1,783	−7,270	−24,823	−40,973	−44,403	−24,844	−38,354	−55,160	−52,169	−45,114	−47,912
Money plus Quasi-Money	35l	365,286	† 11,092	145,519	191,995	215,397	254,991	280,438	301,138	314,197	352,072	433,118	452,071
Other Banking Institutions		*Thousands of Reais through 1992; Millions of Reais Beginning 1993: End of Period*											
Reserves	40	2,064	† 53	1,526	611	768	1,174	881	224	546	246	393	3,074
Claims on Mon.Author.:Securities	40c	829	† 15	113	459	1,195	3,015	734	211	662	1,281	687	525
Blocked Financial Assets	40d	–	† –	–	–	–	–	–	–	–	–	–	–
Foreign Assets	41	634	† 83	1,269	382	184	159	89	117	404	353	812	1,237
Claims on Central Government	42a	2,965	† 95	525	1,633	1,644	3,801	9,204	2,044	2,335	3,205	4,597	6,970
Claims on State and Local Govts	42b	5,852	† 156	918	1,890	1,164	2,441	2,550	3,102	2,964	2,965	4,033	4,927
Claims on Nonfin.Pub.Enterprises	42c	15,257	† 355	2,705	6,674	3,560	2,859	3,192	1,863	1,727	1,625	3,264	4,122
Claims on Private Sector	42d	82,942	† 1,981	28,159	30,310	29,336	33,368	33,153	47,596	65,993	65,361	81,772	87,452
Claims on Deposit Money Banks	42e	31,115	† 1,025	11,491	15,627	19,344	22,533	27,749	38,889	50,190	62,870	87,184	87,015
Claims on Nonbank Financial Insts	42g	–	† –	–	–	–	–	265	23	284	175	–	–
Demand Deposits	44	–	† –	–	–	–	–	–	–	–	–	–	–
Time and Savings Deposits	45	25,462	† 684	7,865	5,298	6,339	7,281	7,505	4,528	4,160	3,978	4,481	6,050
Money Market Instruments	46aa	427	† 9	179	143	563	497	359	447	836	850	813	697
Restricted Deposits	46b	4	† –	–	–	–	–	–	–	–	–	–	–
Foreign Liabilities	46c	1,068	† 39	239	43	699	550	398	816	978	879	1,369	2,817
Long-Term Foreign Liabilities	46cl	9,032	† 261	1,638	2,141	2,636	4,356	10,964	10,417	14,609	18,912	29,973	25,058
Central Government Deposits	46d	40,373	† 1,086	10,432	12,308	14,607	16,443	20,649	23,841	25,818	24,414	34,639	37,514
Credit from Monetary Authorities	46g	2,537	† 57	778	1,035	1,065	2,020	354	385	287	1,967	289	266
Credit from Deposit Money Banks	46h	7,865	† 145	958	1,162	1,152	3,804	1,667	1,372	1,151	1,862	1,337	3,527
Liab. to Nonbank Financial Insts	46j	–	† –	–	–	–	–	224	194	529	710	924	2,402
Capital Accounts	47a	54,101	† 1,382	16,756	21,323	18,350	19,931	19,697	20,936	22,515	65,269	81,988	89,045
Other Items (Net)	47r	788	† 100	7,861	14,132	11,784	14,467	16,001	31,132	54,221	19,241	26,930	27,947
Banking Survey		*Thousands of Reais through 1992; Millions of Reais Beginning 1993: End of Period*											
Foreign Assets (Net)	51n	66,155	† 2,440	31,851	45,029	52,860	44,458	36,331	32,805	47,041	38,259	24,049	57,036
Domestic Credit	52	818,719	† 22,314	238,243	289,354	332,282	400,011	532,086	526,305	545,319	701,310	856,711	925,285
Claims on Central Govt. (Net)	52an	265,956	† 5,545	−5,930	1,603	2,759	61,583	137,399	134,576	148,258	276,524	372,754	385,954
Claims on State and Local Govts	52b	63,679	† 1,687	28,400	27,875	57,225	41,889	40,778	22,103	7,238	5,717	6,510	7,465
Claims on Nonfin.Pub.Enterprises	52c	57,972	† 1,513	12,950	19,073	22,296	8,575	15,735	17,032	5,430	3,092	5,532	6,226
Claims on Private Sector	52d	431,107	† 13,570	202,822	240,803	249,996	287,958	330,074	349,551	381,941	410,676	468,703	524,843
Claims on Nonbank Financial Inst	52g	5	† –	–	–	6	7	8,101	3,044	2,451	5,302	3,213	797
Liquid Liabilities	55l	388,684	† 11,724	151,858	196,682	220,968	261,098	287,062	305,442	317,811	355,804	437,206	455,047
Money Market Instruments	56aa	9,567	† 292	3,499	4,887	7,592	10,780	16,333	18,532	30,063	39,935	30,771	45,084
Liabs. of Central Bank: Securities	56ac	47,972	† 532	33,984	45,420	62,979	51,106	66,430	33,017	32,919	63,718	29,866	11,072
Restricted Deposits	56b	5,035	† 75	404	1,996	352	12	10	13	427	264	23	18
Long-Term Foreign Liabilities	56cl	224,073	† 6,344	16,536	20,352	21,904	30,060	48,197	44,835	42,724	51,995	78,545	75,195
Liab. to Nonbank Financial Insts	56j	442	† 1	92	111	60	234	22,424	25,450	41,942	46,831	94,544	117,600
Capital Accounts	57a	268,634	† 7,289	61,848	80,435	96,667	120,105	138,620	148,665	148,160	235,260	262,382	325,598
Other Items (Net)	57r	−59,534	† −1,503	1,873	−15,500	−25,380	−28,926	−10,659	−16,844	−21,686	−54,237	−52,577	−47,293

Brazil 223

		1992	1993	1994	1995	1996	1997	1998	1999	2000	2001	2002	2003
Nonbank Financial Institutions		\multicolumn{12}{c}{*Thousands of Reais through 1992; Millions of Reais Beginning 1993: End of Period*}
Reserves	40..n	353	† –	3	6	31	14	3	4	4	5	106	7
Claims on Mon.Author.:Securities	40c.n	2,804	† 8	405	154	350	364	667	333	1,085	1,523	1,128	423
Blocked Financial Assets	40d.n	1	† –	–	–	–	–	–	–	–	–	–	–
Foreign Assets	41..n	277	† 11	76	87	93	45	44	104	118	18	37	30
Claims on Central Government	42a.n	1,528	† 65	17	55	1,090	1,229	1,103	2,275	2,063	2,048	1,842	2,036
Claims on State and Local Govt	42b.n	547	† 26	360	348	408	103	617	23	18	17	3	1
Claims on Nonfin.Pub.Enterprises	42c.n	1,775	† 4	36	14	14	14	13	7	11	47	102	152
Claims on Private Sector	42d.n	1,515	† 91	11,228	15,870	10,231	11,404	12,526	12,201	16,125	15,179	13,906	12,767
Claims on Deposit Money Banks	42e.n	6,165	† 178	1,327	1,737	2,824	2,421	10,735	4,400	4,731	4,820	3,486	5,323
Claims on Other Banking Insts	42f.n	13	† 1	14	5	12	35	100	88	74	40	27	116
Money Market Instruments	46aan	3,919	† 131	1,181	3,901	5,482	8,307	9,247	7,033	7,428	6,253	6,721	9,934
Restricted Deposits	46b.n	8	† –	–	–	–	–	–	–	–	–	–	–
Foreign Liabilities	46c.n	–	† –	–	–	22	176	182	630	685	811	757	619
Long-Term Foreign Liabilities	46cln	4,757	† 170	1,529	2,293	2,972	3,552	4,041	4,483	4,176	3,262	3,868	2,625
Central Government Deposits	46d.n	5	† –	–	–	1	1	3	4	4	4	–	–
Credit from Monetary Authorities	46g.n	–	† –	–	–	–	–	–	–	–	98	75	130
Cred. from Deposit Money Banks	46h.n	–	† –	–	–	–	–	6,488	1,062	830	3,646	356	187
Liabilities to Other Banking Insts	46i.n	2,873	† 118	1,517	1,619	3,670	4,093	5,440	4,643	2,307	1,065	703	831
Capital Accounts	47a.n	15,086	† 444	5,767	8,783	10,848	11,187	13,141	16,465	16,750	20,005	22,588	23,038
Other Items (Net)	47r.n	–11,669	† –479	3,472	1,680	–7,942	–11,687	–12,734	–14,886	–7,952	–11,446	–14,431	–16,508
Money (National Definitions)		\multicolumn{12}{c}{*Thousands of Reais through 1992; Millions of Reais Beginning 1993: End of Period*}
Reserve Money	19ma	25,167	† 517	17,685	21,682	19,796	31,828	39,184	48,430	47,686	53,256	73,302	73,219
M1	59ma	38,027	† 848	22,773	28,493	29,807	47,363	50,707	62,744	74,352	83,707	107,846	109,648
M2	59mb	332,740	† 10,223	132,558	178,755	188,735	239,777	254,965	274,770	283,785	321,612	397,503	412,895
M3	59mc	389,877	† 11,759	154,544	225,008	285,942	340,210	376,015	468,728	556,577	625,057	688,269	838,386
M4	59md	447,583	† 13,938	176,449	261,176	336,148	405,946	459,308	551,092	652,093	756,181	807,523	960,061
BA	19maa	....	....	80,734	122,291	184,050	280,070	352,345	447,132	538,693	646,672	788,034	886,894
B2	19mab	....	....	101,902	156,428	231,898	318,599	374,282	458,567	540,894	649,254	789,960	889,265
M2A	59mba	....	....	60,443	72,380	60,084	63,353	63,170	271,790	356,298	....	....	....
M3A	59mca	....	....	119,882	143,410	142,159	173,436	185,294	386,382	468,390	....	....	....
M4A	59mda	....	....	174,523	259,381	342,305	422,306	480,202	575,666	677,021	....	....	....
Interest Rates		\multicolumn{12}{c}{*Percent Per Annum*}
Discount Rate (End of Period)	60	....	....	....	....	25.34	45.09	39.41	21.37	† 18.52	21.43	30.42	23.92
Money Market Rate	60b	1,574.28	3,284.44	4,820.64	53.37	27.45	25.00	29.50	26.26	17.59	17.47	19.11	23.37
Treasury Bill Rate	60c	....	....	....	49.93	25.73	24.79	28.57	26.39	18.51	20.06	19.43	22.10
Treasury Bill Rate (Fgn.Currency)	60c.f	....	....	....	17.78	15.13	11.60	15.04	....	....	11.46	....	....
Savings Rate	60k	1,254.90	2,743.33	4,206.04	40.26	16.39	16.62	14.48	12.31	8.44	8.66	9.27	11.26
Deposit Rate	60l	1,560.18	3,293.50	5,175.24	52.25	26.45	24.35	28.00	26.02	17.20	17.86	19.14	21.97
Lending Rate	60p	....	....	....	....	....	78.19	86.36	80.44	56.83	57.62	62.88	67.08
Prices, Production, Labor		\multicolumn{12}{c}{*Index Numbers (2000=100): Period Averages*}
Share Prices	62	–	.7	20.8	24.4	37.0	64.3	57.0	71.0	100.0	87.0	71.7	91.8
Wholesale Prices	63	.1	1.6	38.1	60.0	63.7	70.1	72.6	84.7	100.0	112.6	131.4	167.6
Consumer Prices	64	.1	† 1.9	42.0	69.7	80.7	86.3	89.1	93.4	100.0	106.8	115.9	132.9
Industrial Production, Seas. Adj	66..c	77.5	83.4	89.8	91.6	† 92.4	96.3	94.4	93.8	100.0	101.6	104.0	† 104.5
		\multicolumn{12}{c}{*Number in Thousands: Period Averages*}
Labor Force	67d	66,139	67,159	....	70,539	70,182	75,213	76,886	79,315	....	83,243	....	....
Employment	67e	† 65,395	66,570	....	69,629	67,920	69,332	69,963	71,676	76,159	75,458	78,180	....
Unemployment	67c	† 4,574	4,396	....	4,510	5,076	5,882	6,923	7,639	....	....	....	....
Unemployment Rate (%)	67r	† 6.5	† 6.2	5.1	6.1	7.0	7.8	9.0	9.6	....	....	....	....
International Transactions		\multicolumn{12}{c}{*Millions of US Dollars*}
Exports	70..d	35,793	38,555	43,545	46,506	47,747	52,994	51,140	48,011	55,086	58,223	60,362	73,084
Coffee	70e.d	970	1,065	2,219	1,970	1,719	2,746	2,332	2,230	1,559	1,208	1,195	1,302
Imports, c.i.f	71..d	23,068	27,740	35,997	53,783	56,947	64,995	60,652	51,759	58,631	58,351	49,603	50,665
Imports, f.o.b	71.vd	20,554	25,256	33,079	49,972	53,346	59,744	57,763	49,295	55,839	55,572	47,241	48,253
		\multicolumn{12}{c}{*2000=100*}
Volume of Exports	72	68.4	74.7	79.8	82.1	81.5	85.4	94.1	93.5	100.0	111.4	120.8	131.3
Coffee	72e	105.3	99.8	90.1	74.6	80.5	89.9	103.0	131.5	100.0	129.5	160.4	141.6
Volume of Imports	73	73.1	83.8	87.6	95.3	96.6	94.2	98.2	92.2	100.0	100.0	97.5	100.3
		\multicolumn{12}{c}{*2000=100: Indices of Unit Values in US Dollars*}
Unit Value of Exports	74..d	97.4	94.1	98.7	102.9	106.5	112.7	99.8	93.8	100.0	95.0	94.5	101.6
Coffee (Unit Value)	74e.d	59.1	68.5	157.9	169.3	137.0	196.0	145.2	108.8	100.0	59.8	47.8	59.0
Coffee (Wholesale Price)	76ebd	70.5	83.4	179.6	182.9	150.7	209.0	152.6	111.4	100.0	63.3	56.4	63.6
Unit Value of Imports	75..d	50.4	54.5	66.5	95.4	98.9	124.8	105.3	96.0	100.0	99.8	87.0	86.0

2004, International Monetary Fund : *International Financial Statistics Yearbook*

Brazil 223

		1992	1993	1994	1995	1996	1997	1998	1999	2000	2001	2002	2003
Balance of Payments						*Millions of US Dollars: Minus Sign Indicates Debit*							
Current Account, n.i.e.	78ald	6,089	20	−1,153	−18,136	−23,248	−30,491	−33,829	−25,400	−24,225	−23,215	−7,637	4,063
Goods: Exports f.o.b.	78aad	35,793	39,630	44,102	46,506	47,851	53,189	51,136	48,011	55,086	58,223	60,362	73,084
Goods: Imports f.o.b.	78abd	−20,554	−25,301	−33,241	−49,663	−53,304	−59,841	−57,739	−49,272	−55,783	−55,572	−47,240	−48,260
Trade Balance	78acd	15,239	14,329	10,861	−3,157	−5,453	−6,652	−6,603	−1,261	−698	2,650	13,121	24,825
Services: Credit	78add	4,088	3,965	4,908	6,135	4,655	5,989	7,631	7,189	9,498	9,322	9,551	10,483
Services: Debit	78aed	−7,430	−9,555	−10,254	−13,630	−12,714	−15,298	−16,676	−14,172	−16,660	−17,081	−14,509	−15,559
Balance on Goods & Services	78afd	11,897	8,739	5,515	−10,652	−13,512	−15,961	−15,648	−8,244	−7,860	−5,109	8,164	19,749
Income: Credit	78agd	1,118	1,308	2,202	3,457	5,350	5,344	4,914	3,936	3,621	3,280	3,295	3,339
Income: Debit	78ahd	−9,115	−11,630	−11,293	−14,562	−17,527	−21,688	−24,531	−22,780	−21,507	−23,023	−21,486	−21,891
Balance on Gds, Serv. & Inc.	78aid	3,900	−1,583	−3,576	−21,757	−25,689	−32,305	−35,265	−27,088	−25,746	−24,852	−10,026	1,197
Current Transfers, n.i.e.: Credit	78ajd	2,260	1,704	2,577	3,861	2,699	2,130	1,795	1,969	1,828	1,934	2,627	3,132
Current Transfers: Debit	78akd	−71	−101	−154	−240	−258	−316	−359	−281	−307	−296	−237	−265
Capital Account, n.i.e.	78bcd	54	81	173	352	494	482	375	339	273	−36	433	498
Capital Account, n.i.e.: Credit	78bad	54	86	175	363	507	519	488	361	300	328	464	535
Capital Account: Debit	78bbd	—	−5	−2	−11	−13	−37	−113	−22	−28	−364	−31	−37
Financial Account, n.i.e.	78bjd	5,889	7,604	8,020	29,306	33,428	24,918	20,063	8,056	29,376	20,331	−3,909	−184
Direct Investment Abroad	78bdd	−137	−491	−1,037	−1,384	467	−1,042	−2,721	−1,690	−2,282	2,258	−2,482	−249
Dir. Invest. in Rep. Econ., n.i.e.	78bed	2,061	1,292	3,072	4,859	11,200	19,650	31,913	28,576	32,779	22,457	16,590	10,144
Portfolio Investment Assets	78bfd	—	−606	−3,052	−936	−257	−335	−594	258	−1,696	−795	−321	179
Equity Securities	78bkd	—	−607	—	−168	−49	−306	−553	−865	−1,953	−1,121	−389	−258
Debt Securities	78bld	—	1	−3,052	−768	−208	−29	−41	1,123	258	326	67	437
Portfolio Investment Liab., n.i.e.	78bgd	7,366	12,928	47,784	10,171	21,089	10,393	19,013	3,542	8,651	872	−4,797	5,129
Equity Securities	78bmd	1,704	6,570	7,280	2,775	5,785	5,099	−1,768	2,572	3,076	2,481	1,981	2,973
Debt Securities	78bnd	5,662	6,358	40,504	7,396	15,304	5,294	20,781	970	5,575	−1,609	−6,778	2,156
Financial Derivatives Assets	78bwd	....	—	—	....	....	....	....	642	386	567	933	683
Financial Derivatives Liabilities	78bxd	....	....	....	....	....	....	....	−729	−583	−1,038	−1,289	−834
Other Investment Assets	78bhd	−99	−2,696	−4,368	−1,783	−3,327	2,251	−5,992	−4,399	−2,989	−6,586	−3,211	−9,483
Monetary Authorities	78bod	—	−34	—	....	−44	−67	−84	1,668	−18	2,430	2	—
General Government	78bpd	−44	29	—	....	....	2,146	60	−880	193	−1,085	−979	−1,101
Banks	78bqd	−37	−2,980	−4,077	−228	−4,610	5,133	3,383	−121	1,551	−3,561	4,335	−6,999
Other Sectors	78brd	−18	289	−291	−1,555	1,327	−4,961	−9,351	−5,066	−4,715	−4,370	−6,569	−1,383
Other Investment Liab., n.i.e.	78bid	−3,302	−2,823	−34,379	18,379	4,256	−5,999	−21,556	−18,144	−4,890	2,596	−9,331	−5,752
Monetary Authorities	78bsd	−277	−140	−545	−1,652	−3,773	−1,698	−1,704	−6,671	−201	−171	−156	−162
General Government	78btd	−1,968	−2,622	−35,609	....	....	....	....	934	1,540	−26	−493	−1,561
Banks	78bud	1,167	−2,269	−1,439	7,071	6,450	−897	−8,570	−5,059	1,718	−741	−3,835	348
Other Sectors	78bvd	−2,224	2,208	3,214	12,960	1,579	−3,404	−11,282	−7,348	−7,946	3,534	−4,847	−4,377
Net Errors and Omissions	78cad	−1,393	−815	−442	1,447	−1,992	−3,160	−2,911	240	2,557	−498	−154	−791
Overall Balance	78cbd	10,639	6,890	6,598	12,969	8,682	−8,251	−16,302	−16,765	7,981	−3,418	−11,266	3,586
Reserves and Related Items	79dad	−10,639	−6,890	−6,598	−12,969	−8,682	8,251	16,302	16,765	−7,981	3,418	11,266	−3,586
Reserve Assets	79bdd	−14,670	−8,709	−7,215	−12,920	−8,326	8,284	6,990	7,783	2,260	−3,311	−314	−8,479
Use of Fund Credit and Loans	79dcd	−399	−504	−133	−49	−70	−33	4,773	4,059	−6,795	6,729	11,580	4,893
Exceptional Financing	79ded	4,430	2,323	750	—	−286	—	4,539	4,924	−3,446	—	—	—
International Investment Position						*Millions of US Dollars*							
Assets	79aad	....	....	....	....	....	....	....	....	....	107,086	112,914	134,384
Direct Investment Abroad	79abd	....	....	....	....	....	....	....	....	....	49,689	54,423	54,462
Portfolio Investment	79acd	....	....	....	....	....	....	....	....	....	6,402	5,845	6,504
Equity Securities	79add	....	....	....	....	....	....	....	....	....	3,001	2,388	2,555
Debt Securities	79aed	....	....	....	....	....	....	....	....	....	3,401	3,457	3,950
Financial Derivatives	79ald	....	....	....	....	....	....	....	....	....	42	105	437
Other Investment	79afd	....	....	....	....	....	....	....	....	....	15,087	14,705	23,684
Monetary Authorities	79agd	....	....	....	....	....	....	....	....	....	1,383	1,357	1,231
General Government	79ahd	....	....	....	....	....	....	....	....	....	—	—	—
Banks	79aid	....	....	....	....	....	....	....	....	....	5,521	4,052	11,052
Other Sectors	79ajd	....	....	....	....	....	....	....	....	....	8,183	9,296	11,401
Reserve Assets	79akd	....	....	....	....	....	....	....	....	....	35,866	37,837	49,296
Liabilities	79lad	....	....	....	....	....	....	....	....	....	372,052	343,450	406,759
Dir. Invest. in Rep. Economy	79lbd	....	....	....	....	....	....	....	....	....	121,948	100,847	132,799
Portfolio Investment	79lcd	....	....	....	....	....	....	....	....	....	151,741	137,355	166,095
Equity Securities	79ldd	....	....	....	....	....	....	....	....	....	36,910	27,249	53,138
Debt Securities	79led	....	....	....	....	....	....	....	....	....	114,831	110,106	112,957
Financial Derivatives	79lld	....	....	....	....	....	....	....	....	....	45	250	125
Other Investment	79lfd	....	....	....	....	....	....	....	....	....	98,317	104,999	107,740
Monetary Authorities	79lgd	....	....	....	....	....	....	....	....	....	9,250	21,729	28,965
General Government	79lhd	....	....	....	....	....	....	....	....	....	—	—	—
Banks	79lid	....	....	....	....	....	....	....	....	....	7,777	8,731	8,500
Other Sectors	79ljd	....	....	....	....	....	....	....	....	....	81,291	74,538	70,276
Government Finance			*Thousands of Reais through 1992; Millions of Reais Beginning 1993: Year Ending December 31*											
Deficit (−) or Surplus	80	−24,389	† −1,315	−21,270	....	....	−63,664	−70,880	....	....	....	....	....
Revenue	81	173,586	† 4,272	108,280	....	....	213,409	237,116	....	....	....	....	....
Grants Received	81z	115	† 2	125	....	....	9	71	....	....	....	....	....
Expenditure	82	187,242	† 5,250	117,906	....	....	213,484	245,032	....	....	....	....	....
Lending Minus Repayments	83	10,848	† 338	11,769	....	....	63,597	63,034	....	....	....	....	....

Brazil 223

		1992	1993	1994	1995	1996	1997	1998	1999	2000	2001	2002	2003
National Accounts		*Thousands of Reais through 1992; Millions of Reais Beginning 1993*											
Househ.Cons.Expend.,incl.NPISHs....	96f	394,313	†8,470	208,256	386,910	486,813	545,698	566,192	606,701	670,702	725,760	781,174	862,447
Government Consumption Expend...	91f	109,367	†2,490	62,388	126,652	144,001	158,502	174,847	185,828	209,953	230,741	270,965	291,920
Gross Fixed Capital Formation.........	93e	118,086	†2,718	72,453	132,753	150,050	172,939	179,982	184,098	212,384	233,384	246,606	273,321
Changes in Inventories....................	93i	3,277	†220	4,880	11,274	12,903	14,248	13,074	12,238	24,871	20,753	19,348	30,656
Exports of Goods and Services.........	90c	69,661	†1,481	33,220	49,917	54,430	65,356	67,862	100,136	117,423	158,501	208,489	255,385
Imports of Goods and Services (-)....	98c	53,745	†1,282	31,993	61,314	69,311	86,000	87,769	115,154	134,079	170,403	180,554	198,805
Gross Domestic Product (GDP)........	99b	640,959	†14,097	349,205	646,192	778,887	870,743	914,188	973,846	1,101,255	1,198,736	1,346,028	1,514,924
Net Primary Income from Abroad.....	98.n	−12,358	†−355	−5,913	−10,154	−12,228	−17,436	−21,241	−34,107	−32,597	−45,284	−51,944	....
Gross National Income (GNI)...........	99a	629,000	†13,742	343,292	636,038	766,659	853,307	892,947	939,739	1,068,658	1,153,452	1,294,084	....
GDP Vol.1990 Prices.......................	99b.p	11,605	†12	13	13	14	14	14	14	15	15	15	....
GDP Volume (2000=100)................	99bvp	77.4	81.2	85.9	89.5	91.9	94.9	95.1	95.8	100.0	101.3	103.3	....
GDP Deflator (2000=100)................	99bip	.1	1.6	36.9	65.5	76.9	83.3	87.3	92.3	100.0	107.4	118.4	....
						Millions: Midyear Estimates							
Population....................................	99z	153.63	155.96	158.26	160.54	162.82	165.07	167.32	169.56	171.80	174.03	176.26	178.47

Bulgaria 918

		1992	1993	1994	1995	1996	1997	1998	1999	2000	2001	2002	2003
Exchange Rates						*Leva per SDR: End of Period*							
Official Rate	aa	.0337	.0449	.0964	.1051	.7008	2.3969	2.3586	2.6721	2.7386	2.7891	2.5627	2.3012
						Leva per US Dollar: End of Period (ae) Period Average (rf)							
Official Rate	ae	.0245	.0327	.0660	.0707	.4874	1.7765	1.6751	1.9469	2.1019	2.2193	1.8850	1.5486
Official Rate	rf	.0233	.0276	.0541	.0672	.1779	1.6819	1.7604	1.8364	2.1233	2.1847	2.0770	1.7327
						Index Numbers (2000=100): Period Averages							
Nominal Effective Exchange Rate	nec	1,897.03	2,671.51	1,910.87	1,647.66	941.10	92.26	90.28	99.05	100.00	105.05	109.73	118.76
Real Effective Exchange Rate	rec	50.29	76.43	69.04	79.34	68.30	82.02	93.66	98.04	100.00	104.82	109.50	115.63
Fund Position						*Millions of SDRs: End of Period*							
Quota	2f.s	464.90	464.90	464.90	464.90	464.90	464.90	464.90	640.20	640.20	640.20	640.20	640.20
SDRs	1b.s	.32	.83	10.39	20.08	8.31	8.37	21.38	59.53	64.97	1.80	.55	45.54
Reserve Position in the Fund	1c.s	38.73	32.63	32.63	32.63	32.63	32.63	32.63	32.69	32.74	32.78	32.78	32.78
Total Fund Cred.&Loans Outstg	2tl	428.90	459.90	644.41	482.12	407.25	698.02	792.27	910.74	1,014.62	883.00	771.75	799.16
International Liquidity						*Millions of US Dollars Unless Otherwise Indicated: End of Period*							
Total Reserves minus Gold	1l.d	902.19	655.16	1,001.80	1,236.45	483.57	2,111.52	2,684.71	2,892.12	3,154.93	3,290.77	4,407.06	6,291.01
SDRs	1b.d	.44	1.14	15.16	29.84	11.95	11.29	30.10	81.70	84.65	2.26	.74	67.67
Reserve Position in the Fund	1c.d	53.25	44.82	47.63	48.50	46.92	44.03	45.95	44.87	42.66	41.19	44.56	48.71
Foreign Exchange	1d.d	848.50	609.20	939.00	1,158.10	424.70	2,056.20	2,608.65	2,765.54	3,027.63	3,247.32	4,361.76	6,174.64
Gold (Million Fine Troy Ounces)	1ad	1.017	1.017	1.031	1.031	1.031	1.288	1.293	1.284	1.284	1.285	1.282	1.282
Gold (National Valuation)	1and	305.00	305.00	309.37	309.37	309.37	†362.57	371.67	329.65	305.33	289.56	339.98	413.76
Monetary Authorities:Other Liab	4..d	350.40	355.41	635.08	†657.61	689.55	—	—	—	—	—	—	—
Deposit Money Banks: Assets	7a.d	....	....	....	1,063	973	1,360	1,469	1,492	1,942	2,102	2,018	1,939
Liabilities	7b.d	....	....	....	579	402	103	127	172	260	314	474	968
Monetary Authorities						*Millions of Leva: End of Period*							
Foreign Assets	11	31.9	33.9	124.6	†154.0	618.0	4,684.5	5,259.0	6,428.7	7,441.7	7,946.5	8,948.8	10,383.6
Claims on Central Government	12a	23.5	34.8	54.2	†100.7	410.9	1,632.1	1,665.9	2,203.2	2,560.9	2,314.6	1,926.4	1,838.9
Claims on Nonfin.Pub.Enterprises	12c	—	—	—	.3	.5	.6	1.4	2.1	2.3	2.3	70.6	71.7
Claims on Deposit Money Banks	12e	20.7	32.1	54.8	†42.2	240.7	51.8	4.3	2.1	.4	.4	.2	—
Reserve Money	14	44.7	54.5	85.0	†129.1	247.3	2,291.2	2,526.1	2,972.5	3,299.7	4,180.0	4,603.6	5,386.0
of which: Currency Outside Banks	14a	18.3	25.2	38.5	61.6	126.5	1,316.2	1,743.0	1,961.6	2,374.1	3,081.0	3,334.9	3,874.1
Other Liab. to Dep. Money Banks	14n	—	.4	3.8	25.2	82.5	—	—	—	—	—	—	—
Time, Savings,& Fgn.Currency Dep	15	.8	.3	—	—	3.6	1.5	10.9	.3	957.4	822.1	862.8	1,352.5
Restricted Deposits	16b	—	—	—	—	.1	16.2	17.8	—	17.8	13.4	36.0	41.0
Foreign Liabilities	16c	23.0	32.3	104.0	†97.2	621.4	1,673.1	1,868.6	2,433.6	2,778.6	2,462.7	1,977.8	1,839.0
Central Government Deposits	16d	10.5	11.8	42.2	†51.0	192.4	1,592.8	1,807.8	2,445.7	2,029.6	1,778.9	2,177.7	2,347.3
Capital Accounts	17a	17.2	30.5	91.3	102.2	307.3	961.7	916.3	1,019.5	1,190.6	1,229.8	1,371.3	1,455.7
Other Items (Net)	17r	−20.1	−28.9	−92.7	†−107.6	−184.7	−167.4	−216.9	−235.7	−268.4	−223.0	−83.1	−127.3
Deposit Money Banks						*Millions of Leva: End of Period*							
Reserves	20	26.7	24.6	43.5	†67.6	118.6	800.2	643.8	745.3	598.1	864.4	1,071.2	1,388.2
Other Claims on Dep.Money Banks	20n	....	....	....	25.2	82.5	—	—	—	—	—	—	—
Foreign Assets	21	37.1	43.5	109.5	†75.2	474.2	2,416.7	2,459.9	2,904.5	4,081.9	4,665.3	3,803.1	3,002.7
Claims on Central Government	22a	82.8	179.6	283.6	†226.1	615.1	2,168.4	1,526.3	1,202.7	1,068.0	1,338.0	1,945.5	2,024.0
Claims on Local Government	22b	1.4	2.4	2.8	†.1	—	—	17.0	30.3	30.6	39.6	12.5	27.0
Claims on Nonfin.Pub.Enterprises	22c	138.7	187.5	239.1	†161.0	462.4	679.6	563.0	396.3	183.9	199.9	263.1	269.2
Claims on Private Sector	22d	11.6	11.1	19.8	†185.4	622.0	938.2	1,790.6	2,459.4	3,147.2	4,181.2	5,960.5	8,892.5
Claims on Other Financial Insts	22f	....	....	....	4.7	24.2	8.1	11.8	16.7	29.1	59.5	100.5	251.6
Demand Deposits	24	19.6	23.2	36.6	†50.0	114.8	991.8	1,079.0	1,096.0	1,322.9	1,654.8	2,086.1	2,807.2
Time, Savings,& Fgn.Currency Dep	25	111.1	181.3	334.0	†463.5	1,004.7	3,237.0	3,403.3	3,903.0	4,591.6	6,371.2	7,148.3	8,000.4
Money Market Instruments	26aa	3.4	4.2	8.9	.1	.3	4.3	7.6	56.0	65.3	60.7	35.1	75.6
Restricted Deposits	26b	3.4	4.2	8.9	†13.0	67.3	255.4	246.4	271.0	248.6	271.0	342.3	551.6
Foreign Liabilities	26c	288.0	385.2	236.2	†41.0	196.1	183.1	212.5	334.5	547.2	696.8	893.6	1,498.4
Central Government Deposits	26d	5.1	5.8	13.6	†21.2	28.4	207.0	265.7	224.6	223.3	347.6	447.5	778.7
Credit from Central Bank	26g	6.4	9.6	28.7	†34.5	106.1	58.0	7.5	.8	1.6	.3	.3	.3
Capital Accounts	27a	22.0	36.1	79.0	†87.1	771.6	795.5	1,134.8	1,283.5	1,493.1	1,637.3	1,921.6	2,270.3
Other Items (Net)	27r	−157.3	−196.6	−38.8	†34.9	109.7	1,279.1	655.8	585.8	646.3	308.2	281.5	−127.4
Monetary Survey						*Millions of Leva: End of Period*							
Foreign Assets (Net)	31n	−242.0	−340.1	−106.1	†91.1	274.7	5,244.9	5,637.8	6,565.1	8,197.7	9,452.3	9,880.6	10,048.9
Domestic Credit	32	242.4	397.9	543.7	†605.9	1,914.2	3,627.3	3,502.6	3,640.4	4,770.2	6,008.6	7,656.4	10,251.4
Claims on Central Govt. (Net)	32an	90.7	196.9	282.1	†254.5	805.2	2,000.8	1,118.7	735.6	1,377.1	1,526.1	1,246.7	736.9
Claims on Local Government	32b	1.4	2.4	2.8	†.1	—	—	17.0	30.3	30.6	39.6	12.5	27.0
Claims on Nonfin.Pub.Enterprises	32c	138.7	187.5	239.1	†161.2	462.9	680.2	564.4	398.4	186.2	202.2	333.7	340.9
Claims on Private Sector	32d	11.6	11.1	19.8	†185.4	622.0	938.2	1,790.6	2,459.4	3,147.2	4,181.2	5,960.5	8,892.5
Claims on Other Financial Insts	32f	—	—	—	†4.7	24.2	8.1	11.8	16.7	29.1	59.5	103.0	254.1
Money	34	38.0	50.3	76.0	†111.9	241.4	2,433.1	2,960.7	3,305.2	3,976.0	4,883.2	5,542.3	6,801.0
Quasi-Money	35	112.0	181.6	334.0	†463.5	1,008.4	3,238.6	3,414.2	3,903.4	5,548.9	7,193.3	8,011.1	9,353.0
Money Market Instruments	36aa	—	—	—	.1	.3	4.3	7.6	56.0	65.3	60.7	35.1	75.6
Restricted Deposits	36b	3.4	4.2	8.9	†13.0	67.4	271.6	264.2	271.1	266.4	284.4	378.3	592.6
Capital Accounts	37a	39.2	66.7	170.3	†189.4	1,079.0	1,757.2	2,051.1	2,303.0	2,683.7	2,867.2	3,292.8	3,726.0
Other Items (Net)	37r	−192.2	−244.9	−151.6	†−80.8	−207.5	1,167.5	442.6	366.8	427.6	172.1	277.3	−247.9
Money plus Quasi-Money	35l	150.0	231.9	410.0	†575.4	1,249.7	5,671.6	6,374.9	7,208.5	9,524.9	12,076.5	13,553.4	16,154.0

Bulgaria 918

		1992	1993	1994	1995	1996	1997	1998	1999	2000	2001	2002	2003
Money (National Definitions)					*Millions of Leva: End of Period*								
M3	39mc	....	....	....	588.4	1,317.4	5,947.5	6,646.7	7,535.6	9,856.6	12,400.5	13,857.3	16,566.5
Interest Rates					*Percent Per Annum*								
Bank Rate (End of Period)	60	41.00	52.00	†72.00	34.00	180.00	6.65	5.08	4.46	4.63	4.65	3.31	2.83
Money Market Rate	60b	52.39	48.07	66.43	53.09	119.88	66.43	2.48	2.93	3.02	3.74	2.47	1.95
Treasury Bill Yield	60c	48.11	45.45	57.72	48.27	114.31	78.35	6.02	5.43	4.21	4.57	....	2.81
Deposit Rate	60l	45.01	42.56	51.14	35.94	74.68	46.83	3.00	3.21	3.10	2.88	2.77	2.89
Lending Rate	60p	56.67	58.30	72.58	58.98	123.48	83.96	13.30	12.79	11.52	11.11	9.35	8.82
Government Bond Yield	61	....	....	56.86	49.76	....	....	10.10	10.05	7.38	6.70	6.75	....
Prices and Labor					*Index Numbers (2000=100): Period Averages*								
Producer Prices	63	.9	.1	1.8	2.8	6.6	70.7	82.8	85.1	100.0	103.7	105.0	110.2
Consumer Prices	64	.5	.9	1.8	2.9	6.4	74.5	88.4	90.6	100.0	107.4	113.6	116.0
Industrial Production	66	....	....	....	....	....	....	....	....	100.0	102.2	106.9	123.3
					Number in Thousands: Period Averages								
Labor Force	67d	3,240	2,856	2,521	2,265	2,721	2,679	2,527	2,489	2,323	2,563	2,520	....
Employment	67e	2,663	2,267	2,032	1,910	2,242	2,155	2,086	1,994	1,901	1,900	1,906	....
Unemployment	67c	577	626	488	424	479	524	465	611	567	663	592	449
Unemployment Rate (%)	67r	15.3	16.4	12.4	11.1	12.5	13.7	12.2	16.0	16.9	19.8	17.8	13.7
International Transactions					*Millions of Leva*								
Exports	70	91.5	102.9	216.2	359.7	859.8	8,281.4	7,391.1	7,302.6	10,247.1	11,176.1	11,857.9	13,041.9
Imports, c.i.f.	71	104.3	131.5	227.0	380.0	892.1	8,268.5	8,709.4	10,052.8	13,856.8	15,896.6	16,450.9	18,796.6
Balance of Payments					*Millions of US Dollars: Minus Sign Indicates Debit*								
Current Account, n.i.e.	78ald	−359.9	−1,098.8	−31.8	−25.8	15.7	426.9	−61.9	−652.1	−703.7	−984.0	−826.7	−1,666.3
Goods: Exports f.o.b.	78aad	3,956.4	3,726.5	3,935.1	5,345.0	4,890.2	4,939.6	4,193.5	4,006.4	4,824.6	5,112.9	5,692.1	7,438.5
Goods: Imports f.o.b.	78abd	−4,168.7	−4,611.9	−3,951.9	−5,224.0	−4,702.6	−4,559.3	−4,574.2	−5,087.4	−6,000.2	−6,693.4	−7,286.6	−9,912.3
Trade Balance	78acd	−212.3	−885.4	−16.8	121.0	187.6	380.3	−380.7	−1,081.0	−1,175.5	−1,580.5	−1,594.4	−2,473.7
Services: Credit	78ascd	1,070.3	1,171.3	1,256.9	1,431.4	1,366.0	1,337.4	1,787.8	1,788.4	2,175.2	2,123.4	2,364.9	3,163.5
Services: Debit	78aed	−1,165.2	−1,229.3	−1,246.1	−1,277.9	−1,245.9	−1,171.0	−1,415.2	−1,474.1	−1,669.6	−1,721.3	−1,883.4	−2,563.1
Balance on Goods & Services	78afd	−307.2	−943.4	−6.0	274.5	307.7	546.7	−8.0	−766.7	−670.0	−1,178.4	−1,112.9	−1,873.4
Income: Credit	78agd	125.1	92.6	84.6	149.7	181.0	210.8	306.3	265.4	320.8	352.0	319.7	328.0
Income: Debit	78ahd	−220.7	−284.9	−277.1	−581.9	−577.2	−567.4	−590.2	−450.5	−644.2	−656.0	−580.9	−812.6
Balance on Gds, Serv. & Inc.	78aid	−402.8	−1,135.7	−198.5	−157.7	−88.5	190.1	−291.9	−951.9	−993.4	−1,482.3	−1,374.1	−2,358.0
Current Transfers, n.i.e.: Credit	78ajd	114.1	285.9	357.1	256.8	231.8	275.5	261.5	328.7	354.1	598.5	653.6	862.9
Current Transfers: Debit	78akd	−71.2	−249.0	−190.4	−124.9	−127.6	−38.7	−31.5	−29.0	−64.3	−100.2	−106.2	−171.2
Capital Account, n.i.e.	78bcd	–	–	763.3	–	65.9	–	–	−2.4	24.9	−.1	−.1	−.2
Capital Account, n.i.e.: Credit	78bad	–	–	763.3	–	65.9	–	–	–	25.0	–	–	–
Capital Account: Debit	78bbd	–	–	–	–	....	–	–	−2.4	−.1	−.1	−.1	−.2
Financial Account, n.i.e.	78bjd	613.9	759.0	−1,018.7	326.6	−715.0	462.0	266.8	720.9	781.3	662.8	1,750.2	1,852.9
Direct Investment Abroad	78bdd	–	–	–	8.0	28.5	1.7	−.1	−17.1	−3.3	−9.7	−28.3	−21.8
Dir. Invest. in Rep. Econ., n.i.e.	78bed	41.5	40.0	105.4	90.4	109.0	504.8	537.3	818.8	1,001.5	812.9	904.7	1,419.4
Portfolio Investment Assets	78bfd	–	–	−222.0	9.7	−7.1	−13.7	−129.4	−207.4	−62.2	−40.3	218.3	−72.0
Equity Securities	78bkd	–	–	–	9.7	−7.1	−8.5	−10.6	–	−8.2	−33.5	−16.8	−7.9
Debt Securities	78bld	–	–	−222.0	–	–	−5.2	−118.8	−207.4	−54.0	−6.8	235.1	−64.1
Portfolio Investment Liab., n.i.e.	78bgd	–	–	−9.8	−75.4	−122.2	146.5	−112.0	8.0	−114.7	105.1	−302.1	−134.6
Equity Securities	78bmd	–	–	–	–	2.0	52.0	19.3	1.9	4.9	−8.6	−22.9	−25.6
Debt Securities	78bnd	–	–	−9.8	−75.4	−124.2	94.5	−131.3	6.2	−119.6	113.7	−279.1	−109.0
Financial Derivatives Assets	78bwd	....	....	–	–	–	–	–	–	−1.8	17.5	6.8	−1.1
Financial Derivatives Liabilities	78bxd	....	....	....	....	....	....	....	....	....			
Other Investment Assets	78bhd	244.3	338.4	−209.2	404.2	−568.1	−53.9	222.3	−52.3	−332.1	−100.4	283.0	147.5
Monetary Authorities	78bod	....	....	–	–	–	–	–	–	–	.9	−2.1	2.1	–
General Government	78bpd	307.7	285.5	90.1	292.6	293.7	106.5	−19.8	−17.5	−9.1	−20.7	10.1	−1.8
Banks	78bqd	−63.4	52.9	−299.3	111.6	113.7	−440.6	102.9	25.7	−495.8	−129.8	263.1	263.8
Other Sectors	78brd	–	–	–	–	−975.5	280.2	139.1	−60.5	171.9	52.2	7.6	−114.6
Other Investment Liab., n.i.e.	78bid	328.1	380.6	−683.1	−110.3	−155.1	−123.4	−251.2	170.9	293.8	−122.3	667.9	515.4
Monetary Authorities	78bsd	89.9	3.0	–	–	–	–	–	–	–	–	–	–
General Government	78btd	–	−59.6	−951.0	−1.9	44.0	−82.1	−213.8	−104.9	−223.9	−310.0	−130.6	−105.5
Banks	78bud	−279.8	10.2	−39.2	−94.8	−179.7	−52.3	−65.2	10.1	108.4	102.9	256.3	389.2
Other Sectors	78bvd	518.0	427.0	307.1	−13.6	−19.4	11.0	27.8	265.8	409.3	84.8	542.2	231.6
Net Errors and Omissions	78cad	14.7	18.1	71.6	143.8	−105.3	256.4	−299.2	29.9	34.5	694.7	−208.3	545.6
Overall Balance	78cbd	268.7	−321.7	−215.6	444.6	−738.7	1,145.3	−94.3	96.2	137.0	373.4	715.2	732.0
Reserves and Related Items	79dad	−268.7	321.7	215.6	−444.6	738.7	−1,145.3	94.3	−96.2	−137.0	−373.4	−715.2	−732.0
Reserve Assets	79dbd	−637.0	247.0	−341.6	−233.7	750.9	−1,641.3	−461.4	−527.6	−408.9	−275.4	−586.3	−932.3
Use of Fund Credit and Loans	79dcd	196.1	42.7	262.4	−245.9	−108.7	396.9	129.4	161.9	136.0	−168.5	−142.3	36.4
Exceptional Financing	79ded	172.2	32.0	294.8	35.0	96.5	99.1	426.3	269.5	136.0	70.5	13.4	164.0

2004, International Monetary Fund: *International Financial Statistics Yearbook*

Bulgaria 918

		1992	1993	1994	1995	1996	1997	1998	1999	2000	2001	2002	2003
International Investment Position							*Millions of US Dollars*						
Assets	79aad	....	....	....	....	....	....	7,869.6	8,138.1	8,829.4	9,045.4	....	....
Direct Investment Abroad	79abd	....	....	....	....	....	....	74.5	90.0	87.0	96.7	....	....
Portfolio Investment	79acd	....	....	....	....	....	....	521.9	677.6	728.2	677.5	....	....
Equity Securities	79add	....	....	....	....	....	....	20.6	20.6	28.7	.4	....	....
Debt Securities	79aed	....	....	....	....	....	....	501.4	657.0	699.5	677.1	....	....
Financial Derivatives	79ald	....	....	....	....	....	....	–	–	1.8	19.2	....	....
Other Investment	79afd	....	....	....	....	....	....	4,216.8	4,148.8	4,552.2	4,671.7	....	....
Monetary Authorities	79agd	....	....	....	....	....	....	3.1	2.5	2.3	2.2	....	....
General Government	79ahd	....	....	....	....	....	....	2,348.2	2,389.9	2,416.7	2,446.7	....	....
Banks	79aid	....	....	....	....	....	....	1,524.5	1,397.4	1,806.1	1,848.7	....	....
Other Sectors	79ajd	....	....	....	....	....	....	341.0	359.0	327.1	374.1	....	....
Reserve Assets	79akd	....	....	....	....	....	....	3,056.4	3,221.7	3,460.3	3,580.3	....	....
Liabilities	79lad	....	....	....	....	....	....	12,539.8	13,086.6	13,216.1	13,011.1	....	....
Dir. Invest. in Rep. Economy	79lbd	....	....	....	....	....	....	1,596.6	2,402.6	2,257.3	2,757.7	....	....
Portfolio Investment	79lcd	....	....	....	....	....	....	5,173.1	5,195.3	5,193.6	5,083.3	....	....
Equity Securities	79ldd	....	....	....	....	....	....	113.4	97.9	99.8	95.3	....	....
Debt Securities	79led	....	....	....	....	....	....	5,059.7	5,097.5	5,093.8	4,988.0	....	....
Financial Derivatives	79lld	....	....	....	....	....	....	–	–	–	–	....	....
Other Investment	79lfd	....	....	....	....	....	....	5,770.1	5,488.6	5,765.2	5,170.1	....	....
Monetary Authorities	79lgd	....	....	....	....	....	....	1,118.0	1,252.9	1,325.1	1,112.0	....	....
General Government	79lhd	....	....	....	....	....	....	2,968.8	2,271.7	2,260.7	1,970.9	....	....
Banks	79lid	....	....	....	....	....	....	440.8	325.3	396.2	373.7	....	....
Other Sectors	79ljd	....	....	....	....	....	....	1,242.5	1,638.8	1,783.2	1,713.6	....	....
Government Finance						*Millions of Leva: Year Ending December 31*							
Deficit (-) or Surplus	80	–9.9	–36.1	†–24.5	–46.2	–332.8	353.3	599.2	348.7	154.9	556.2	–9.8	255.4
Total Revenue and Grants	81y	71.8	100.0	†209.3	315.5	703.3	5,662.1	7,530.6	8,219.9	9,340.1	10,268.4	10,637.4	12,057.2
Revenue	81	71.6	99.9	†209.3	314.6	699.1	5,558.0	7,380.3	8,015.0	9,124.7	9,874.4	10,229.5	11,760.6
Grants	81z	.2	.1	†–	.9	4.2	104.1	150.3	204.9	215.4	394.0	407.9	296.7
Exp. & Lending Minus Repay	82z	81.7	136.1	†233.8	361.7	1,036.1	5,308.8	6,931.4	7,871.1	9,185.2	9,712.2	10,647.2	11,801.8
Expenditure	82	81.6	133.9	†235.9	360.6	1,040.9	5,733.2	7,227.6	8,122.6	9,444.9	10,212.5	10,820.2	11,993.6
Lending Minus Repayments	83	.1	2.2	†–2.1	1.1	–4.8	–424.4	–296.2	–251.5	–259.7	–500.3	–173.0	–191.8
Total Financing	80h	9.9	36.1	†24.5	46.2	332.8	–353.3	–599.3	–348.9	–154.9	–556.2	9.9	–255.4
Total Net Borrowing	84	16.5	35.5	†53.0	58.7	295.5	1,261.0	–213.3	227.3	–434.0	–276.4	633.5	275.2
Net Domestic	84a	13.6	38.3	†44.6	65.5	331.3	1,204.3	–65.8	49.9	–3.9	–224.3	129.8	294.8
Net Foreign	85a	2.9	–2.8	†8.4	–6.8	–35.8	56.7	–147.5	177.4	–430.1	–52.1	503.7	–19.6
Use of Cash Balances	87	–6.6	.6	†–28.5	–12.5	37.3	–1,614.3	–386.0	–576.2	279.1	–279.8	–623.6	–530.6
Total Debt by Residence	88	....	....	....	....	....	....	....	....	....	....	....	....
Domestic	88a	39.8	112.0	†275.1	345.4	1,052.8	....	....	....	....	....	....	....
Foreign	89a	....	....	....	....	....	....	....	....	....	....	....	....
National Accounts							*Millions of Leva*						
Househ.Cons.Expend.,incl.NPISHs	96f	132	220	389	622	1,313	12,724	15,144	16,964	18,506	20,642	22,238	23,772
Government Consumption Expend	91f	41	56	90	134	210	2,188	3,440	3,937	4,786	5,177	5,832	6,532
Gross Fixed Capital Formation	93e	33	39	72	134	238	1,914	2,920	3,600	4,206	5,415	5,909	6,733
Changes in Inventories	93i	7	7	–23	4	–95	–191	865	662	688	726	497	743
Exports of Goods and Services	90c	95	114	237	393	976	10,155	10,553	10,601	14,902	16,510	17,180	18,314
Imports of Goods and Services (-)	98c	106	137	240	407	881	9,358	10,501	11,974	16,334	18,760	19,321	21,670
Gross Domestic Product (GDP)	99b	201	299	526	880	1,761	17,433	22,421	23,790	26,753	29,709	32,335	34,410
Statistical Discrepancy	99bs	....	....	–	–	–	–	–	–	–	–	–	–13
Net Primary Income from Abroad	98.n	–3	–5	–11	–29	–69	–589	–510	–327	–671	–664	–489	–858
Gross National Income (GNI)	99a	198	294	515	852	1,692	16,844	21,911	23,464	26,082	29,045	31,777	33,552
Net Current Transf.from Abroad	98t	–	–	1	1	17	399	404	552	618	1,099	1,109	....
Gross Nat'l Disposable Inc.(GNDI)	99i	198	294	516	853	1,709	17,242	22,315	24,016	26,701	30,144	32,944	....
Gross Saving	99s	25	18	37	96	186	2,330	3,731	3,115	3,409	4,325	4,712	....
GDP Volume (1995=100)	99bvp	†96.9	†95.5	†97.2	†100.0	†89.9	83.7	....	....	....	....	....	....
GDP Deflator (1995=100)	99bip	23.5	35.6	61.4	100.0	222.5	2,366.0	....	....	....	....	....	....
						Millions: Midyear Estimates							
Population	99z	8.59	8.53	8.47	8.41	8.34	8.28	8.22	8.16	Ü 8.10	8.03	7.96	7.90

Burkina Faso 748

		1992	1993	1994	1995	1996	1997	1998	1999	2000	2001	2002	2003
Exchange Rates						*Francs per SDR: End of Period*							
Official Rate	aa	378.57	404.89	†780.44	728.38	753.06	807.94	791.61	†896.19	918.49	935.39	850.37	771.76
					Francs per US Dollar: End of Period (ae) Period Average (rf)								
Official Rate	ae	275.32	294.77	†534.60	490.00	523.70	598.81	562.21	†652.95	704.95	744.31	625.50	519.36
Official Rate	rf	264.69	283.16	†555.20	499.15	511.55	583.67	589.95	†615.70	711.98	733.04	696.99	581.20
Fund Position						*Millions of SDRs: End of Period*							
Quota	2f.s	44.2	44.2	44.2	44.2	44.2	44.2	44.2	60.2	60.2	60.2	60.2	60.2
SDRs	1b.s	5.6	5.6	5.6	5.5	1.8	1.6	.5	.5	.3	.4	.3	.2
Reserve Position in the Fund	1c.s	7.2	7.2	7.2	7.2	7.2	7.2	7.2	7.2	7.2	7.2	7.3	7.3
Total Fund Cred.&Loans Outstg.	2tl	6.3	15.2	32.8	50.5	56.5	68.5	79.6	87.9	86.1	92.7	93.0	83.9
International Liquidity					*Millions of US Dollars Unless Otherwise Indicated: End of Period*								
Total Reserves minus Gold	1l.d	341.3	382.3	237.2	347.4	338.6	344.8	373.3	295.0	243.6	260.5	313.4	434.8
SDRs	1b.d	7.7	7.7	8.1	8.2	2.6	2.2	.8	.7	.4	.5	.4	.3
Reserve Position in the Fund	1c.d	9.9	9.9	10.5	10.7	10.4	9.7	10.2	9.9	9.4	9.1	9.9	10.8
Foreign Exchange	1d.d	323.7	364.7	218.6	328.4	325.6	332.9	362.4	284.4	233.8	250.9	303.1	423.6
Gold (Million Fine Troy Ounces)	1ad	.011	.011	.011	–	–	–	–	–	–	–	–	–
Gold (National Valuation)	1and	3.8	4.1	4.1	–	–	–	–	–	–	–	–	–
Monetary Authorities: Other Liab.	4..d	32.5	29.8	14.9	4.1	5.8	29.0	43.9	29.3	37.8	22.6	20.1	41.9
Deposit Money Banks: Assets	7a.d	48.6	53.1	155.5	253.5	212.8	167.5	167.5	232.9	212.6	188.8	203.0	249.1
Liabilities	7b.d	43.1	42.5	39.7	58.7	44.0	54.5	67.0	129.1	105.3	119.5	111.2	176.4
Monetary Authorities						*Billions of Francs: End of Period*							
Foreign Assets	11	94.0	112.7	126.8	170.2	177.3	206.5	209.9	192.6	171.7	193.9	196.0	225.8
Claims on Central Government	12a	22.6	26.3	44.8	55.7	59.3	80.1	92.9	103.7	104.4	110.7	112.5	103.3
Claims on Deposit Money Banks	12e	9.0	9.0	–	2.5	4.0	14.6	24.7	3.9	10.3	3.3	–	–
Claims on Other Financial Insts.	12f	1.0	.9	.4	.3	.4	.7	1.1	1.1	1.1	1.1	1.1	1.0
Reserve Money	14	105.2	121.4	120.4	149.3	156.3	193.1	186.2	160.0	160.2	160.5	121.7	163.8
of which: Currency Outside DMBs	14a	65.8	78.5	94.9	123.5	139.6	170.1	165.0	142.5	136.6	120.9	83.2	91.0
Foreign Liabilities	16c	11.3	14.9	33.6	38.8	45.6	72.7	87.7	97.9	105.7	103.6	91.7	86.5
Central Government Deposits	16d	6.0	8.4	19.5	37.4	37.3	29.5	48.4	45.0	22.9	41.4	79.9	65.3
Other Items (Net)	17r	3.9	4.1	–1.4	3.2	1.7	6.6	6.2	–1.6	–1.3	3.5	16.3	14.5
Deposit Money Banks						*Billions of Francs: End of Period*							
Reserves	20	37.7	41.0	20.9	17.7	9.1	15.7	14.4	19.8	18.1	35.4	30.1	61.8
Foreign Assets	21	13.4	15.7	83.1	124.2	111.5	100.3	94.2	152.1	149.9	140.5	127.0	129.4
Claims on Central Government	22a	14.0	13.5	35.3	27.3	26.1	28.1	32.7	26.1	21.4	15.0	20.6	31.3
Claims on Private Sector	22d	94.9	87.6	72.3	79.0	89.9	163.2	180.9	186.5	217.6	247.9	293.6	338.6
Claims on Other Financial Insts.	22f	1.2	.3	.3	–	–	–	–	–	–	–	–	–
Demand Deposits	24	41.4	42.0	69.8	81.5	80.2	90.7	89.5	107.7	126.0	135.7	152.9	183.3
Time Deposits	25	56.8	57.4	62.6	71.0	70.7	83.7	94.3	108.5	117.5	131.7	152.6	184.6
Foreign Liabilities	26c	6.4	6.9	12.2	19.7	23.1	30.5	33.0	77.2	68.4	82.5	60.7	82.3
Long-Term Foreign Liabilities	26cl	5.4	5.6	9.0	9.1	–	2.1	4.7	7.1	5.8	6.4	8.8	9.3
Central Government Deposits	26d	50.9	47.8	59.0	61.3	54.6	57.5	58.0	60.5	60.1	57.1	74.0	78.9
Credit from Monetary Authorities	26g	9.0	9.0	–	2.5	–	14.6	25.2	4.4	10.3	3.3	–	–
Other Items (Net)	27r	–8.8	–10.5	–.7	3.1	7.9	28.3	17.6	19.2	18.8	22.1	22.2	22.8
Treasury Claims: Private Sector	22d.i	2.2	.9	1.7	1.6	1.6	1.8	1.4	1.1	.4	.5	.9	1.3
Post Office: Checking Deposits	24..i	1.7	1.6	2.4	2.7	2.7	2.1	2.3	2.3	2.3	1.9	2.5	3.1
Monetary Survey						*Billions of Francs: End of Period*							
Foreign Assets (Net)	31n	89.6	106.5	164.2	236.0	220.1	203.5	183.4	169.6	147.5	148.4	170.5	186.5
Domestic Credit	32	78.4	74.1	77.0	66.3	86.5	187.3	203.5	214.2	263.7	278.0	276.4	333.1
Claims on Central Govt. (Net)	32an	–20.9	–15.7	2.4	–14.6	–5.4	21.5	20.1	25.4	44.7	28.5	–19.2	–7.8
Claims on Private Sector	32d	97.1	88.5	73.9	80.6	91.5	165.0	182.3	187.6	217.9	248.4	294.5	339.9
Claims on Other Financial Insts.	32f	2.2	1.2	.6	.3	.4	.7	1.1	1.1	1.1	1.1	1.1	1.0
Money	34	109.9	122.6	170.3	213.7	228.7	268.9	261.9	256.9	270.4	262.3	243.7	287.2
Quasi-Money	35	56.8	57.4	62.6	71.0	70.7	83.7	94.3	108.5	117.5	131.7	152.6	184.6
Long-Term Foreign Liabilities	36cl	5.4	5.6	9.0	9.1	–	2.1	4.7	7.1	5.8	6.4	8.8	9.3
Other Items (Net)	37r	–4.2	–5.0	–.8	8.5	7.2	36.2	26.0	11.4	17.5	26.0	41.8	38.5
Money plus Quasi-Money	35l	166.7	180.0	232.9	284.7	299.4	352.5	356.2	365.3	387.9	394.0	396.3	471.8
Other Banking Institutions						*Billions of Francs: End of Period*							
Savings Deposits	45	10.17	….	….	….	….	….	….	….	….	….	….	….
Interest Rates						*Percent Per Annum*							
Bank Rate (End of Period)	60	12.50	†6.00	6.00	6.00	6.00	6.00	6.00	6.00	6.00	6.00	6.00	4.50
Money Market Rate	60b	11.44	….	….	….	….	….	4.81	4.95	4.95	4.95	4.95	4.95
Deposit Rate	60l	7.75	….	….	….	….	….	3.50	3.50	3.50	3.50	3.50	3.50
Lending Rate	60p	16.75	….	….	….	….	….	….	….	….	….	….	….
Prices and Labor					*Index Numbers (2000=100): Period Averages*								
Consumer Prices	64	65.7	66.1	82.7	88.9	94.3	†96.5	101.4	100.3	100.0	105.0	107.3	109.5
					Number in Thousands: Period Averages								
Employment	67e	163	….	….	….	….	….	….	….	….	….	….	….
Unemployment	67c	30	30	27	14	13	9	9	8	7	….	….	….

2004, International Monetary Fund : *International Financial Statistics Yearbook*

Burkina Faso 748

		1992	1993	1994	1995	1996	1997	1998	1999	2000	2001	2002	2003
International Transactions							**Billions of Francs**						
Exports	70	16.83	19.66	59.22	138.00	119.04	133.62	190.44	132.19	115.97	126.26	114.66	....
Imports, c.i.f.	71	123.36	144.02	193.70	227.00	330.96	342.35	430.33	350.77	351.88	405.46	398.41	....
							1995=100						
Unit Value of Exports	74	67.3	64.7	84.8	100.0	97.8	....	....	....	....	....	....	....
Unit Value of Imports	75	55.9	56.8	93.5	100.0	103.7	....	....	....	....	....	....	....
Balance of Payments						**Millions of US Dollars: Minus Sign Indicates Debit**							
Current Account, n.i.e.	78ald	−23.0	−71.1	14.9	....	....	....	....	....	−392.0	−380.8	....	....
Goods: Exports f.o.b.	78aad	237.2	226.1	215.6	....	....	....	....	....	205.6	223.5	....	....
Goods: Imports f.o.b.	78abd	−458.9	−469.1	−344.3	....	....	....	....	....	−517.7	−509.3	....	....
Trade Balance	78acd	−221.7	−243.0	−128.7	....	....	....	....	....	−312.1	−285.8	....	....
Services: Credit	78add	64.5	64.6	56.3	....	....	....	....	....	31.4	36.5	....	....
Services: Debit	78aed	−207.7	−209.0	−138.3	....	....	....	....	....	−139.9	−141.2	....	....
Balance on Goods & Services	78afd	−364.9	−387.4	−210.7	....	....	....	....	....	−420.6	−390.5	....	....
Income: Credit	78agd	21.7	21.5	8.7	....	....	....	....	....	13.5	15.2	....	....
Income: Debit	78ahd	−19.1	−28.6	−38.1	....	....	....	....	....	−33.6	−39.7	....	....
Balance on Gds, Serv. & Inc	78aid	−362.3	−394.5	−240.1	....	....	....	....	....	−440.7	−414.9	....	....
Current Transfers, n.i.e.: Credit	78ajd	419.2	389.6	308.0	....	....	....	....	....	87.6	72.0	....	....
Current Transfers: Debit	78akd	−79.9	−66.3	−53.0	....	....	....	....	....	−38.9	−37.9	....	....
Capital Account, n.i.e.	78bcd	−	−	−	....	....	....	....	....	175.9	165.2	....	....
Capital Account, n.i.e.: Credit	78bad	−	−	−	....	....	....	....	....	175.9	165.2	....	....
Capital Account: Debit	78bbd	−	−	−	....	....	....	....	....	−	−	....	....
Financial Account, n.i.e.	78bjd	34.7	69.1	−13.9	....	....	....	....	....	19.2	25.2	....	....
Direct Investment Abroad	78bdd	−	....	....	....	....	....	....	....	−.2	−.6	....	....
Dir. Invest. in Rep. Econ., n.i.e.	78bed	−	−	−	....	....	....	....	....	23.2	8.8	....	....
Portfolio Investment Assets	78bfd	−	−	....	....	....	....	....	....	6.2	10.0	....	....
Equity Securities	78bkd	−	−	....	....	....	....	....	....	.4	−2.1	....	....
Debt Securities	78bld	−	−	....	....	....	....	....	....	5.8	12.2	....	....
Portfolio Investment Liab., n.i.e.	78bgd	−	−	....	....	....	....	....	....	−2.6	.7	....	....
Equity Securities	78bmd	−	−	....	....	....	....	....	....	−	−	....	....
Debt Securities	78bnd	−	−	....	....	....	....	....	....	−2.6	.7	....	....
Financial Derivatives Assets	78bwd	....	....	....	....	....	....	....	....	−	−	....	....
Financial Derivatives Liabilities	78bxd	....	....	....	....	....	....	....	....	−	−	....	....
Other Investment Assets	78bhd	−45.2	24.2	−139.2	....	....	....	....	....	−9.7	5.6	....	....
Monetary Authorities	78bod	....	....	....	....	....	....	....	....	....	....	....	....
General Government	78bpd	−	−	−	....	....	....	....	....	−2.1	−.5	....	....
Banks	78bqd	−21.7	24.2	−135.2	....	....	....	....	....	−3.0	16.4	....	....
Other Sectors	78brd	−23.4	−	−4.0	....	....	....	....	....	−4.6	−10.3	....	....
Other Investment Liab., n.i.e.	78bid	79.9	44.9	125.3	....	....	....	....	....	2.2	.6	....	....
Monetary Authorities	78bsd	−6.6	−	−	....	....	....	....	....	5.7	.7	....	....
General Government	78btd	100.0	84.4	29.3	....	....	....	....	....	−	−	....	....
Banks	78bud	−12.1	−47.1	41.9	....	....	....	....	....	−13.7	−4.2	....	....
Other Sectors	78bvd	−1.3	7.7	54.0	....	....	....	....	....	10.2	4.2	....	....
Net Errors and Omissions	78cad	8.3	4.6	−8.3	....	....	....	....	....	5.1	3.4	....	....
Overall Balance	78cbd	20.0	2.5	−7.3	....	....	....	....	....	−191.8	−187.0	....	....
Reserves and Related Items	79dad	−20.0	−2.5	7.3	....	....	....	....	....	191.8	187.0	....	....
Reserve Assets	79dbd	−15.9	−53.5	−17.4	....	....	....	....	....	30.6	−31.0	....	....
Use of Fund Credit and Loans	79dcd	−	12.5	25.5	....	....	....	....	....	−2.4	8.5	....	....
Exceptional Financing	79ded	−4.2	38.5	−.7	....	....	....	....	....	163.6	209.6	....	....
International Investment Position						**Millions of US Dollars**							
Assets	79aad	....	....	....	....	....	....	....	....	457.2	428.8	....	....
Direct Investment Abroad	79abd	....	....	....	....	....	....	....	....	.4	.7	....	....
Portfolio Investment	79acd	....	....	....	....	....	....	....	....	84.0	51.8	....	....
Equity Securities	79add	....	....	....	....	....	....	....	....	1.3	3.1	....	....
Debt Securities	79aed	....	....	....	....	....	....	....	....	82.7	48.7	....	....
Financial Derivatives	79ald	....	....	....	....	....	....	....	....	−	−	....	....
Other Investment	79afd	....	....	....	....	....	....	....	....	130.1	115.8	....	....
Monetary Authorities	79agd	....	....	....	....	....	....	....	....	−	−	....	....
General Government	79ahd	....	....	....	....	....	....	....	....	3.7	7.2	....	....
Banks	79aid	....	....	....	....	....	....	....	....	125.0	102.2	....	....
Other Sectors	79ajd	....	....	....	....	....	....	....	....	1.3	6.3	....	....
Reserve Assets	79akd	....	....	....	....	....	....	....	....	242.6	260.5	....	....
Liabilities	79lad	....	....	....	....	....	....	....	....	1,815.3	1,513.9	....	....
Dir. Invest. in Rep. Economy	79lbd	....	....	....	....	....	....	....	....	27.8	15.9	....	....
Portfolio Investment	79lcd	....	....	....	....	....	....	....	....	4.3	2.9	....	....
Equity Securities	79ldd	....	....	....	....	....	....	....	....	1.5	1.6	....	....
Debt Securities	79led	....	....	....	....	....	....	....	....	2.8	1.3	....	....
Financial Derivatives	79lld	....	....	....	....	....	....	....	....	−	−	....	....
Other Investment	79lfd	....	....	....	....	....	....	....	....	1,783.2	1,495.1	....	....
Monetary Authorities	79lgd	....	....	....	....	....	....	....	....	149.5	119.3	....	....
General Government	79lhd	....	....	....	....	....	....	....	....	....	....	....	....
Banks	79lid	....	....	....	....	....	....	....	....	98.7	85.1	....	....
Other Sectors	79ljd	....	....	....	....	....	....	....	....	....	....	....	....

Burkina Faso 748

		1992	1993	1994	1995	1996	1997	1998	1999	2000	2001	2002	2003
Government Finance						*Millions of Francs: Year Ending December 31*							
Deficit (-) or Surplus	80	−34,620	−37,540	−46,806	−37,971	−23,579	−50,500	−50,300	−63,800	−67,500	−61,796	−55,628	−88,801
Total Revenue and Grants	81y	128,000	139,800	189,669	225,178	223,280	279,200	303,100	377,600	363,000	313,231	335,183	434,302
Revenue	81	93,000	100,800	114,325	137,183	160,812	181,400	199,400	236,500	219,300	227,966	258,897	300,971
Grants	81z	35,000	39,000	75,344	87,995	62,468	97,800	103,700	141,100	143,700	85,265	76,286	133,331
Exp. & Lending Minus Repay	82z	164,400	181,940	225,115	244,859	229,859	323,200	347,900	432,100	431,500	387,948	422,519	507,014
Expenditure	82	164,400	183,940	227,449	247,053	231,552	325,700	348,500	431,800	428,400	389,841	422,606	483,510
Lending Minus Repayments	83	—	−2,000	−2,334	−2,194	−1,693	−2,500	−600	300	3,100	−1,893	−87	23,504
Adjustment to Cash Basis	80x	1,780	4,600	−11,360	−18,290	−17,000	−6,500	−5,500	−9,300	1,000	12,921	31,708	−16,089
Total Financing	80h	34,620	37,540	46,806	37,971	23,579	50,500	50,300	63,800	67,500	61,796	55,628	88,801
National Accounts						*Billions of Francs*							
Househ.Cons.Expend.,incl.NPISHs	96f	627.1	647.0	726.6	887.4	1,041.0	1,074.0	1,300.9	1,301.6	1,312.5	1,491.5	1,639.7	1,774.3
Government Consumption Expend	91f	214.4	220.2	281.1	306.9	330.9	347.6	378.1	428.4	438.8	467.2	501.2	516.3
Gross Fixed Capital Formation	93e	171.6	167.7	271.6	267.0	298.4	346.2	370.2	386.1	404.3	448.0	449.9	459.1
Changes in Inventories	93i	.3	−8.5	15.3	17.2	31.7	45.2	29.8	−9.8	−7.8	−30.3	−24.2	20.3
Exports of Goods and Services	90c	78.6	81.1	149.4	168.0	139.8	154.5	211.9	176.7	168.7	190.1	202.1	221.5
Imports of Goods and Services (-)	98c	173.5	187.3	263.4	316.0	365.4	380.1	465.5	448.6	468.2	476.1	488.9	518.2
Gross Domestic Product (GDP)	99b	918.4	920.2	1,180.7	1,330.4	1,476.2	1,587.8	1,825.5	1,834.3	1,848.4	2,090.4	2,279.9	2,473.3
Net Primary Income from Abroad	98.n	58.2	65.0	92.5	115.8	111.7	102.4	118.7	93.9	90.2	92.5	101.6	141.1
Gross National Income (GNI)	99a	976.6	985.2	1,273.2	1,446.2	1,587.9	1,690.2	1,944.2	1,928.2	1,938.7	2,182.9	2,381.5	2,614.3
GDP Volume 1985 Prices	99b.p	963.5	948.8	968.6	1,031.4	1,133.2	1,210.6	1,313.2	1,362.4	1,383.8	1,477.3	1,545.1	1,645.0
GDP Volume (2000=100)	99bvp	69.6	68.6	70.0	74.5	81.9	87.5	94.9	98.5	100.0	106.8	111.7	118.9
GDP Deflator (2000=100)	99bip	71.4	72.6	91.3	96.6	97.5	98.2	104.1	100.8	100.0	105.9	110.5	112.6
						Millions: Midyear Estimates							
Population	99z	9.45	9.73	10.01	10.30	10.60	10.91	Ü 11.23	11.56	11.91	12.26	12.62	13.00

2004, International Monetary Fund : *International Financial Statistics Yearbook*

Burundi 618

		1992	1993	1994	1995	1996	1997	1998	1999	2000	2001	2002	2003
Exchange Rates						*Francs per SDR: End of Period*							
Official Rate	aa	322.90	362.99	360.78	413.37	462.63	551.56	710.64	860.83	1,014.76	1,090.92	1,451.07	1,618.31
					Francs per US Dollar: End of Period (ae) Period Average (rf)								
Official Rate	ae	236.55	264.38	246.94	277.92	322.35	408.38	505.16	628.58	778.20	864.20	1,071.23	1,093.00
Official Rate	rf	208.30	242.78	252.66	249.76	302.75	352.35	447.77	563.56	720.67	830.35	930.75	1,082.62
					Index Numbers (2000=100): Period Averages								
Official Rate	ahx	343.4	294.3	282.6	286.5	236.6	203.2	160.5	127.2	100.0	86.2	77.5	65.9
Nominal Effective Exchange Rate	nec	160.2	173.0	193.2	196.2	170.9	161.4	133.5	114.6	100.0	90.3	80.1	61.2
Real Effective Exchange Rate	rec	90.4	89.0	92.7	102.0	107.2	127.5	114.9	96.1	100.0	94.3	80.0	65.5
Fund Position						*Millions of SDRs: End of Period*							
Quota	2f.s	57.20	57.20	57.20	57.20	57.20	57.20	57.20	57.20	77.00	77.00	77.00	77.00
SDRs	1b.s	1.08	.51	.14	.05	.08	.05	.07	.07	.03	.04	.12	.09
Reserve Position in the Fund	1c.s	5.86	5.86	5.86	5.86	5.86	5.86	5.86	5.86	5.86	.36	.36	.36
Total Fund Cred.&Loans Outstg.	2tl	47.39	44.40	40.13	34.16	28.18	22.20	15.37	9.82	5.98	2.13	9.63	19.25
International Liquidity					*Millions of US Dollars Unless Otherwise Indicated: End of Period*								
Total Reserves minus Gold	1l.d	174.17	162.98	204.70	209.45	139.60	113.04	65.52	47.98	32.92	17.71	58.78	66.97
SDRs	1b.d	1.49	.70	.21	.07	.11	.06	.09	.10	.04	.06	.16	.14
Reserve Position in the Fund	1c.d	8.06	8.05	8.56	8.71	8.43	7.91	8.25	8.04	7.64	.45	.49	.54
Foreign Exchange	1d.d	164.63	154.23	195.94	200.67	131.06	105.07	57.18	39.84	25.24	17.20	58.13	66.29
Gold (Million Fine Troy Ounces)	1ad	.017	.017	.017	.017	.017	.017	.017	.017	.017	.001	.001	.001
Gold (National Valuation)	1and	5.79	6.66	6.59	6.66	6.36	4.99	4.95	5.00	4.74	.27	.34	.40
Monetary Authorities: Other Liab.	4..d	81.06	74.82	71.02	60.59	48.11	36.17	28.35	19.60	14.16	7.78	37.34	36.41
Deposit Money Banks: Assets	7a.d	6.00	10.00	19.00	17.00	24.00	12.00	5.00	13.00	18.00	14.00	18.00	39.33
Liabilities	7b.d	8.00	9.00	13.00	11.00	8.00	8.00	8.00	8.00	14.00	19.00	22.00	30.59
Other Banking Insts.: Assets	7e.d	–	–	–	–	–	–	–	–	–	–	–	–
Liabilities	7f.d	12.24	14.00	18.21	18.41	16.20	13.72	12.25	10.35	9.14	8.41	9.48	10.90
Monetary Authorities						*Millions of Francs: End of Period*							
Foreign Assets	11	43,387	46,912	54,230	61,439	48,407	49,620	37,711	33,642	33,702	20,573	64,415	75,336
Claims on Central Government	12a	11,885	9,170	8,698	10,504	12,443	20,702	27,498	41,685	59,106	69,082	75,991	103,781
Claims on Nonfin.Pub.Enterprises	12c	25	25	25	25	25	25	25	25	25	25	25	25
Claims on Private Sector	12d	325	421	420	1,486	1,563	1,181	1,220	703	827	1,191	1,414	1,578
Claims on Deposit Money Banks	12e	550	3,355	2,538	2,210	9,239	3,838	15,460	13,983	23,028	15,532	26,093	10,220
Claims on Other Financial Insts.	12f	1,616	1,487	634	1,307	761	162	781	117	1,660	4,914	9,233	1,411
Reserve Money	14	16,797	17,617	22,292	22,114	26,346	26,854	27,566	37,387	36,398	40,431	49,820	55,246
of which: Currency Outside DMBs	14a	12,933	14,440	19,073	19,495	23,974	23,693	24,180	32,087	31,300	34,058	42,752	†44,515
Nonfin.Pub.Ent. Deps.	14e	990	1,118	649	577	371	749	860	710	1,044	347	449	1,158
Bonds	16ab	2,743	2,174	2,701	2,329	2,531	2,400	1,915	3,924	3,689	1,278	2,159	4,353
Restricted Deposits	16b	1,123	1,019	842	1,164	540	2,230	3,014	1,752	5,035	2,941	609	1,053
Stabilization Fund	16bb	452	4	4	74	16	20	–	4	47	51	19	15
Foreign Liabilities	16c	19,174	19,782	17,537	16,840	15,508	14,770	14,320	12,319	11,023	6,724	40,001	39,793
Central Government Deposits	16d	6,966	8,299	7,710	10,764	7,290	6,062	7,629	7,108	31,081	21,893	42,267	48,245
Capital Accounts	17a	11,654	12,490	12,744	15,926	17,531	20,418	20,262	22,482	24,206	22,068	24,087	25,568
Other Items (Net)	17r	–1,122	–15	2,714	7,762	2,675	2,773	7,987	5,179	6,870	15,932	18,210	18,079
Deposit Money Banks													
Commercial Banks						*Millions of Francs: End of Period*							
Reserves	20	2,469	1,761	2,171	1,290	1,716	2,852	2,839	4,754	3,625	6,289	†6,720	†9,308
Foreign Assets	21	1,539	2,553	4,773	4,760	7,907	4,898	2,650	8,427	14,352	12,334	†16,878	†42,990
Claims on Central Government	22a	†460	2,441	5,311	6,799	8,824	10,524	10,879	9,888	220	4,361	†6,387	†3,107
Claims on Nonfin.Pub.Enterprises	22c	5,793	1,591	2,749	1,322	1,673	2,213	3,515	4,538	3,230	4,634	†5,297	†6,930
Claims on Private Sector	22d	23,862	31,557	34,022	29,162	35,886	39,516	52,948	69,385	101,356	110,418	†143,552	†158,978
Claims on Other Financial Insts.	22f	†127	114	142	284	1,748	104	106	105	265	273	†1,350	†96
Demand Deposits	24	13,525	14,721	19,095	18,730	18,038	22,235	22,180	34,296	34,860	44,244	†55,838	†71,331
Savings Deposits	25	10,695	10,135	14,951	10,681	16,373	17,038	15,955	26,144	30,976	35,126	†48,691	†53,090
Foreign Liabilities	26c	1,872	1,969	3,155	3,048	2,447	3,019	3,796	4,848	11,115	16,579	†22,887	†33,431
Central Government Deposits	26d	25	526	76	192	14	–	180	150	773	476	†340	†13,921
Credit from Monetary Authorities	26g	1,134	4,044	2,602	806	8,020	1,128	14,518	13,199	22,338	14,663	†24,867	†9,743
Capital Accounts	27a	5,111	7,085	8,281	8,221	11,446	12,625	14,510	17,470	21,297	24,892	†31,872	†47,623
Other Items (Net)	27r	1,888	1,536	1,008	1,939	1,414	4,064	1,798	989	1,689	2,328	†–2,163	†–7,751
Other Monetary Institutions						*Millions of Francs: End of Period*							
Reserves	20..h	4	169	72	....	7	342	....	....	....	....	....	....
Claims on Central Government	22a.h	506	1,052	1,355	....	1,262	1,531	1,602	2,203	1,373	1,437	1,494	†2,114
Claims on Nonfin.Pub.Enterprises	22c.h	1,379	1,286	1,071	....	†1,896	1,312	....	....	....	....	....	....
Claims on Private Sector	22d.h	530	1,404	1,675	....	2,690	2,133	....	....	....	....	....	....
Claims on Other Financial Insts.	22f.h	6	6	6	....	6	6	....	....	....	....	....	....
Demand Deposits	24..h	506	1,021	1,329	....	1,259	1,527	1,595	2,200	1,369	1,431	1,487	1,857
Time and Savings Deposits	25..h	2	347	598	....	1,484	2,052	2	2	2	2	2	2
Foreign Liabilities	26c.h	41	66	43	....	29	29	....	....	....	....	....	....
Central Government Deposits	26d.h	2,186	1,779	1,811	....	639	500	....	....	....	....	....	....
Cred.from Monetary Authorities	26g.h	469	749	303	....	1,195	1,172	....	....	....	....	....	....
Other Items (Net)	27r.h	–157	–7	115	....	1,256	69	4	1	2	3	5	5

Burundi 618

		1992	1993	1994	1995	1996	1997	1998	1999	2000	2001	2002	2003
Monetary Survey						*Millions of Francs: End of Period*							
Foreign Assets (Net)........................	31n	23,839	27,648	38,267	46,311	38,330	36,699	22,244	24,902	25,916	9,604	†18,405	†45,102
Domestic Credit...........................	32	39,515	41,721	48,316	39,933	61,466	73,341	90,764	121,389	136,209	173,966	†202,135	†215,853
Claims on Central Govt. (Net)........	32an	5,860	3,838	7,578	6,347	15,225	26,695	32,169	46,517	28,846	52,510	†41,265	†46,835
Claims on Nonfin.Pub.Enterprises...	32c	7,197	2,902	3,844	1,347	3,593	3,550	3,540	4,563	3,255	4,659	†5,322	†6,955
Claims on Private Sector.................	32d	24,717	33,381	36,117	30,648	40,138	42,830	54,168	70,087	102,183	111,609	†144,965	†160,556
Claims on Other Financial Insts......	32f	1,743	1,601	776	1,591	2,510	267	887	222	1,925	5,188	†10,583	†1,507
Money..	34	27,955	31,300	40,146	38,802	43,642	48,203	48,816	69,293	68,573	80,080	†100,527	†118,861
Quasi-Money.................................	35	10,697	10,482	15,549	10,681	17,857	19,089	15,957	26,146	30,978	35,128	†48,693	†53,092
Other Items (Net)...........................	37r	29,595	32,883	36,348	44,703	45,033	51,035	57,943	59,304	68,639	70,689	73,904	†88,732
Money plus Quasi-Money..................	35l	38,652	41,782	55,695	49,482	61,499	67,292	64,773	95,439	99,551	115,209	†149,220	†171,954
Other Banking Institutions						*Millions of Francs: End of Period*							
Cash...	40..f	49	....	132	123	191	†478	102	291	†799	178	†145	†255
Foreign Assets................................	41..f	–	–	–	–	–	–	–	–	....	–	–	–
Claims on Central Government........	42a.f	208	73	52	111	87	†405	1,057	1,491	†618	2,121	†2,675	†1,198
Claims on Private Sector.................	42d.f	11,610	....	12,577	13,319	14,304	†15,376	16,637	18,068	†21,256	25,902	†29,972	†20,466
Bonds..	46abf	4,129	....	3,347	2,324	3,224	†2,829	2,561	2,980	†3,981	5,198	†4,873	†1,521
Long-Term Foreign Liabilities............	46clf	2,896	....	4,496	5,117	5,222	†6,057	6,641	6,962	†7,717	8,091	†10,814	12,386
Central Govt. Lending Funds............	46f.f	1,213	....	1,151	1,185	1,045	914	1,371	1,340	1,280	1,772	2,390	2,574
Credit from Monetary Authorities......	46g.f	1,347	....	228	1,043	599	–	623	118	972	3,331	6,645	†722
Credit from Depos. Money Banks.....	46h.f	–	....	–	4	375	–	1	–	†–	–	†–	†–
Capital Accounts............................	47a.f	2,897	....	2,990	3,589	4,357	†7,125	7,834	10,142	†10,737	12,494	†13,910	†12,496
Other Items (Net)...........................	47r.f	–624	....	548	290	–242	†–667	–1,235	–1,692	†–2,015	–2,686	†–5,840	†–7,781
Banking Survey						*Millions of Francs: End of Period*							
Foreign Assets (Net)........................	51n	23,839	34,621	38,267	46,311	38,330	36,699	22,244	24,902	25,916	9,604	†18,405	†45,102
Domestic Credit...........................	52	48,373	....	58,377	....	72,709	85,811	103,539	135,963	149,216	187,112	†215,072	†236,010
Claims on Central Govt. (Net)........	52an	4,850	2,168	5,840	....	14,674	26,625	32,526	47,248	†29,464	54,631	†43,940	†48,033
Claims on Nonfin.Pub.Enterprises...	52c	7,197	2,902	3,844	1,347	3,593	3,550	3,540	4,563	3,255	4,659	†5,322	†6,955
Claims on Private Sector.................	52d	36,326	....	48,693	43,967	54,442	55,637	67,473	84,152	†123,439	137,511	†174,937	180,855
Liquid Liabilities.............................	55l	38,948	....	55,563	....	61,308	66,815	64,671	95,148	†98,753	115,030	†149,075	†171,699
Other Items (Net)...........................	57r	33,264	....	41,081	54,331	49,731	55,695	61,113	65,716	†82,444	84,013	†84,402	†109,413
Interest Rates						*Percent Per Annum*							
Discount Rate (End of Period)..........	60	11.00	10.00	10.00	10.00	10.00	12.00	12.00	12.00	14.00	14.00	15.50	14.50
Lending Rate.................................	60p	13.66	13.77	14.20	15.26	....	....	....	15.24	15.77	16.82	19.47	18.23
Prices and Labor						*Index Numbers (2000=100): Period Averages*							
Consumer Prices...........................	64	27.8	†30.5	35.0	41.7	52.7	69.2	77.8	80.4	100.0	109.2	102.9	119.3
International Transactions						*Millions of Francs*							
Exports..	70	15,355	15,019	30,034	25,982	11,372	30,767	28,635	30,971	35,223	31,978	28,867	40,698
Imports, c.i.f...................................	71	46,106	47,435	56,511	58,186	37,332	43,250	70,274	66,308	106,059	115,249	121,028	169,742

2004, International Monetary Fund : *International Financial Statistics Yearbook*

Burundi 618

		1992	1993	1994	1995	1996	1997	1998	1999	2000	2001	2002	2003
Balance of Payments						*Millions of US Dollars: Minus Sign Indicates Debit*							
Current Account, n.i.e.	78ald	−59.6	−28.1	−16.9	10.4	−40.0	−.3	−51.4	−23.0	−53.2	−39.0	−10.2	−37.3
Goods: Exports f.o.b.	78aad	77.0	73.9	80.7	112.9	40.4	87.5	64.0	55.0	49.1	39.2	31.0	37.5
Goods: Imports f.o.b.	78abd	−181.8	−172.8	−172.6	−175.6	−100.0	−96.1	−123.5	−97.3	−107.9	−108.3	−104.8	−130.0
Trade Balance	78acd	−104.8	−99.0	−91.9	−62.7	−59.6	−8.6	−59.5	−42.3	−58.8	−69.1	−73.8	−92.5
Services: Credit	78add	17.5	14.6	14.9	16.4	10.5	5.2	4.5	4.4	4.0	5.2	6.3	5.6
Services: Debit	78aed	−137.3	−114.8	−93.9	−83.3	−38.4	−35.5	−41.6	−25.3	−42.8	−37.9	−43.2	−45.0
Balance on Goods & Services	78afd	−224.7	−199.2	−170.9	−129.6	−87.4	−38.8	−96.6	−63.2	−97.6	−101.8	−110.7	−131.9
Income: Credit	78agd	14.0	11.2	8.1	10.4	6.4	4.3	3.6	1.9	2.4	1.9	.9	1.3
Income: Debit	78ahd	−27.6	−22.2	−19.5	−22.9	−20.4	−16.8	−11.9	−11.3	−14.5	−15.8	−12.6	−18.6
Balance on Gds, Serv. & Inc.	78aid	−238.2	−210.2	−182.3	−142.1	−101.4	−51.4	−104.9	−72.6	−109.7	−115.7	−122.4	−149.3
Current Transfers, n.i.e.: Credit	78ajd	180.6	183.8	167.0	154.7	62.5	55.6	56.8	51.4	58.3	79.6	115.5	115.5
Current Transfers: Debit	78akd	−1.9	−1.8	−1.6	−2.1	−1.1	−4.5	−3.3	−1.8	−1.8	−2.9	−3.3	−3.5
Capital Account, n.i.e.	78bcd	−.8	−1.2	−.2	−.8	−.3	−.1	−	−	−	−	−.5	−.9
Capital Account, n.i.e.: Credit	78bad	−	−	−	−	−	−	−	−	−	−	−	−
Capital Account: Debit	78bbd	−.8	−1.2	−.2	−.8	−.3	−.1	−	−	−	−	−.5	−.9
Financial Account, n.i.e.	78bjd	98.7	52.5	31.1	21.1	14.1	−12.3	−7.8	−6.5	−7.5	−4.0	−40.5	−50.0
Direct Investment Abroad	78bdd	−	−.1	−.1	−.6	−	−	−	−.5	−	−	−	−
Dir. Invest. in Rep. Econ., n.i.e.	78bed	.6	.5	−	2.0	−	−	−	.2	11.7	−	−	−
Portfolio Investment Assets	78bfd	−	−	−	−	−	−	−	−	−	−	−	....
Equity Securities	78bkd	−	−	−	−	−	−	−	−	−	−	−	−
Debt Securities	78bld	−	−	−	−	−	−	−	−	−	−	−	....
Portfolio Investment Liab., n.i.e.	78bgd	−	−	−	−	−	−	−	−	−	−	−	....
Equity Securities	78bmd	−	−	−	−	−	−	−	−	−	−	−	−
Debt Securities	78bnd	−	−	−	−	−	−	−	−	−	−	−	....
Financial Derivatives Assets	78bwd	....	....	....	....	....	−	−	−	−	−	−	....
Financial Derivatives Liabilities	78bxd	....	....	....	....	....	−	−	−	−	−	−	....
Other Investment Assets	78bhd	−1.0	−1.5	−1.6	8.2	6.6	15.3	10.7	14.2	6.8	24.0	−4.3	−19.9
Monetary Authorities	78bod	....	....	....	....	....	−	−	−	−	−	−	−
General Government	78bpd	−.6	−.3	−.8	−.4	−.3	−.4	−.3	−.3	−	−	−	−
Banks	78bqd	−1.3	−4.2	−8.8	.1	−10.4	8.5	5.0	−10.3	−8.2	2.4	−7.7	−22.2
Other Sectors	78brd	1.0	3.0	7.9	8.6	17.3	7.1	6.0	24.7	15.0	21.6	3.4	2.3
Other Investment Liab., n.i.e.	78bid	99.1	53.6	32.9	11.5	7.6	−27.6	−18.5	−20.4	−25.9	−28.0	−36.2	−30.1
Monetary Authorities	78bsd	−	−	−	−	−	−	−	−	−	−	−	−
General Government	78btd	90.8	47.2	25.2	4.9	7.3	−34.0	−21.4	−23.4	−35.8	−34.6	−42.9	−41.0
Banks	78bud	1.1	.4	4.7	−.4	−2.0	1.6	1.7	1.9	8.7	6.6	6.8	10.0
Other Sectors	78bvd	7.1	6.0	3.0	7.0	2.2	4.8	1.1	1.1	1.2	.1	−.1	.9
Net Errors and Omissions	78cad	−12.7	−7.2	21.1	5.9	−9.2	−27.8	−18.8	−19.0	−34.2	−31.2	3.9	−12.6
Overall Balance	78cbd	25.5	16.0	35.2	36.7	−35.3	−40.5	−78.1	−48.6	−94.8	−74.3	−47.2	−100.9
Reserves and Related Items	79dad	−25.5	−16.0	−35.2	−36.7	35.3	40.5	78.1	48.6	94.8	74.3	47.2	100.9
Reserve Assets	79dbd	−44.0	−11.9	−29.0	−27.6	44.0	−2.0	28.7	8.8	1.2	16.1	−46.9	−9.6
Use of Fund Credit and Loans	79dcd	18.5	−4.1	−6.1	−9.0	−8.7	−8.3	−9.3	−7.6	−5.0	−4.8	9.9	13.6
Exceptional Financing	79ded	....	....	....	....	....	50.8	58.6	47.4	98.7	63.0	84.3	97.0
International Investment Position						*Millions of US Dollars*							
Assets	79aad	....	....	....	....	....	....	....	88.4	75.6	....	....	....
Direct Investment Abroad	79abd	....	....	....	....	....	−	−	−.4	−	−	−	−
Portfolio Investment	79acd	....	....	....	....	....	−	−	−	−	−	−	−
Equity Securities	79add	....	....	....	....	....	−	−	−	−	−	−	−
Debt Securities	79aed	....	....	....	....	....	−	−	−	−	−	−	−
Financial Derivatives	79ald	....	....	....	....	....	−	−	−	−	....	....	....
Other Investment	79afd	....	....	....	....	....	17.8	10.3	35.3	32.3	35.0	21.0	42.0
Monetary Authorities	79agd	....	....	....	....	....	....	−	−	−	−	−	−
General Government	79ahd	....	....	....	....	....	−	−.3	−.3	−	−	−.1	−.1
Banks	79aid	....	....	....	....	....	12.0	5.2	13.4	18.4	14.3	18.2	39.8
Other Sectors	79ajd	....	....	....	....	....	6.2	5.3	22.2	13.9	20.7	2.9	2.3
Reserve Assets	79akd	....	....	....	....	....	121.5	74.7	53.5	43.3	23.8	65.5	73.8
Liabilities	79lad	....	....	....	....	....	....	....	22.5	63.9	....	....	....
Dir. Invest. in Rep. Economy	79lbd	....	....	....	....	....	−	−	.2	10.8	−	−	−
Portfolio Investment	79lcd	....	....	....	....	....	−	−	−	−	−	−	−
Equity Securities	79ldd	....	....	....	....	....	−	−	−	−	−	−	−
Debt Securities	79led	....	....	....	....	....	−	−	−	−	−	−	−
Financial Derivatives	79lld	....	....	....	....	....	−	−	−	−	−	−	−
Other Investment	79lfd	....	....	....	....	....	34.6	43.6	22.3	53.0	8.0	43.3	77.0
Monetary Authorities	79lgd	....	....	....	....	....	....	21.6	13.4	7.8	2.7	13.0	28.5
General Government	79lhd	....	....	....	....	....	....	13.5	.2	29.8	−14.0	8.8	16.7
Banks	79lid	....	....	....	....	....	7.4	7.5	7.7	14.3	19.2	21.4	30.8
Other Sectors	79ljd	....	....	....	....	....	....	1.0	1.0	1.2	.1	.1	1.0

Burundi 618

		1992	1993	1994	1995	1996	1997	1998	1999	2000	2001	2002	2003
Government Finance						*Millions of Francs: Year Ending December 31*							
Deficit (-) or Surplus	80	†−20,130.1	−12,476.6	−13,305.2	−6,638.4	−21,154.4	−16,561.9	−14,635.9	−15,017.4	−11,778.9	8,678.1	−178.0	−16,973.5
Total Revenue and Grants	81y	†54,307.8	63,024.4	68,493.8	58,743.4	47,086.9	52,933.3	73,963.7	99,142.6	112,997.9	160,945.2	176,565.8	202,211.3
Revenue	81	†38,326.7	38,679.8	40,335.6	44,074.2	37,754.0	42,662.8	63,489.4	87,788.0	97,123.1	118,953.9	113,550.4	136,927.8
Grants	81z	†15,981.1	24,344.6	28,158.2	14,669.2	9,332.9	10,270.5	10,474.3	11,354.6	15,874.8	41,991.3	63,015.4	65,283.5
Exp. & Lending Minus Repay	82z	†74,437.9	75,501.0	81,799.0	65,381.8	68,241.3	69,495.2	88,599.6	114,160.0	124,776.8	152,267.1	176,743.8	219,184.8
Expenditure	82	†71,949.0	74,780.1	81,898.7	65,152.6	67,556.6	70,717.0	89,938.0	115,142.4	128,540.0	156,954.2	178,083.5	220,557.8
Lending Minus Repayments	83	†2,488.9	720.9	−99.7	229.2	684.7	−1,221.8	−1,338.4	−982.4	−3,763.2	−4,687.1	−1,339.7	−1,373.0
Total Financing	80h	†20,130.1	12,476.6	13,305.2	6,638.4	21,154.4	16,561.9	14,635.9	15,017.4	11,778.9	−8,678.1	178.2	16,973.5
Domestic	84a	†2,114.1	224.7	4,675.6	−38.6	5,057.6	7,529.6	−682.4	2,842.9	−39,053.9	−29,472.5	−43,025.1	416.5
Foreign	85a	†18,016.0	12,251.9	8,629.6	6,677.0	16,096.8	9,032.3	15,318.3	12,174.5	50,832.8	20,794.4	43,203.3	16,557.0
Total Debt by Residence	88	†235,360	272,667	278,631	323,864	380,437	465,172	605,411	740,305	912,989	968,564	1,269,334	1,487,783
Domestic	88a	†15,644	13,694	13,502	17,695	27,357	39,989	49,659	64,528	60,480	80,294	95,081	117,255
Foreign	89a	†219,716	258,973	265,129	306,169	353,080	425,183	555,752	675,777	852,509	888,270	1,174,253	1,370,528
National Accounts						*Millions of Francs*							
Househ.Cons.Expend.,incl.NPISHs	96f	190,669	217,092	256,656	228,920	216,869	283,525	359,511	395,805	465,739	512,657	505,882	580,060
Government Consumption Expend	91f	44,429	30,280	32,459	33,600	39,911	50,299	58,630	63,547	75,577	80,479	99,050	124,851
Gross Fixed Capital Formation	93e	36,425	36,193	23,446	23,419	32,712	21,975	24,000	34,314	38,564	40,073	55,787	69,130
Changes in Inventories	93i	−2,158	1,002	53	−199	−400	2,700	3,200	–	–	–	25,700	–
Exports of Goods and Services	90c	15,346	21,370	24,029	32,298	15,426	33,760	32,019	34,507	39,761	38,236	36,035	48,700
Imports of Goods and Services (-)	98c	58,854	69,261	66,592	68,173	41,443	49,473	77,193	72,730	108,601	121,464	137,849	171,120
Gross Domestic Product (GDP)	99b	225,857	236,676	270,051	249,865	263,075	342,786	400,166	455,443	511,039	549,981	584,605	651,590
Net Primary Income from Abroad	98.n	−2,845	−2,674	−2,876	−3,152	−4,003	−4,416	−3,699	−5,315	−8,698	−11,545	−10,906	−18,778
Gross National Income (GNI)	99a	223,012	234,002	267,175	246,713	259,072	338,370	396,467	450,128	502,341	538,436	573,699	632,812
GDP Volume 1980 Prices	99b.p	137,284	127,635	123,698	115,013	105,113	105,512	110,249	....	....	....	....	....
GDP Volume (1995=100)	99bvp	119.4	111.0	107.6	100.0	91.4	91.7	95.9	....	....	....	....	....
GDP Deflator (1995=100)	99bip	75.7	85.4	100.5	100.0	115.2	149.5	167.1	....	....	....	....	....
						Millions: Midyear Estimates							
Population	99z	5.82	5.90	5.97	6.02	6.06	6.08	6.11	6.17	6.27	6.41	6.60	6.83

2004, International Monetary Fund : *International Financial Statistics Yearbook*

Cambodia 522

		1992	1993	1994	1995	1996	1997	1998	1999	2000	2001	2002	2003
Exchange Rates						*Riels per SDR: End of Period*							
Official Rate	aa	2,750.0	3,166.1	3,759.1	3,754.9	3,901.2	4,657.6	5,308.3	5,174.4	5,087.9	4,895.0	5,342.9	5,920.1
					Riels per US Dollar: End of Period (ae) Period Average (rf)								
Official Rate	ae	2,000.0	2,305.0	2,575.0	2,526.0	2,713.0	3,452.0	3,770.0	3,770.0	3,905.0	3,895.0	3,930.0	3,984.0
Official Rate	rf	1,266.6	2,689.0	2,545.3	2,450.8	2,624.1	2,946.3	3,744.4	3,807.8	3,840.8	3,916.3	3,912.1	3,973.3
Fund Position						*Millions of SDRs: End of Period*							
Quota	2f.s	25.00	25.00	65.00	65.00	65.00	65.00	65.00	87.50	87.50	87.50	87.50	87.50
SDRs	1b.s	–	11.42	10.89	10.21	9.51	8.77	6.95	3.78	.14	.41	.40	.14
Reserve Position in the Fund	1c.s	.93	–	–	–	–	–	–	–	–	–	–	–
Total Fund Cred.&Loans Outstg	2tl	6.25	6.25	20.25	48.25	48.25	48.25	47.21	53.12	56.24	63.51	70.78	69.70
International Liquidity					*Millions of US Dollars Unless Otherwise Indicated: End of Period*								
Total Reserves minus Gold	1l.d	....	24.18	118.50	191.98	265.78	298.63	324.38	393.19	501.68	586.81	776.15	815.53
SDRs	1b.d		15.68	15.90	15.18	13.68	11.83	9.78	5.19	.18	.51	.55	.20
Reserve Position in the Fund	1c.d	1.28	–	–	–	–	–	–	–	–	–	–	–
Foreign Exchange	1d.d	....	8.50	102.60	176.80	252.10	286.80	314.60	388.00	501.50	586.30	775.60	815.33
Gold (Million Fine Troy Ounces)	1ad	....	–	–	–	–	–	.3998	.3998	.3998	.3998	.3998	.3998
Gold (National Valuation)	1and	....	–	–	–	–	–	114.85	116.27	109.21	110.75	137.54	166.40
Deposit Money Banks: Assets	7a.d	....	103.69	126.75	161.57	186.57	162.08	139.55	154.43	167.33	216.74	173.28	209.50
Liabilities	7b.d	....	68.43	63.93	65.78	59.55	58.03	59.51	56.88	44.23	50.27	41.61	79.88
Monetary Authorities						*Billions of Riels: End of Period*							
Foreign Assets	11	....	56.44	305.09	484.88	720.91	1,033.02	1,675.22	1,923.51	2,388.61	2,740.07	3,598.33	3,906.16
Claims on Central Government	12a	....	206.26	215.02	217.11	213.58	211.28	288.55	283.04	271.83	271.14	269.05	269.39
Claims on Private Sector	12d	....	3.93	2.70	–	–	–	–	–	–	–	–	–
Claims on Deposit Money Banks	12e	....	32.49	34.20	10.09	9.48	6.19	8.10	4.94	15.81	53.19	13.19	17.09
Reserve Money	14	....	228.09	285.91	314.53	449.83	545.33	802.61	929.87	1,161.01	1,359.61	1,980.66	2,149.95
of which: Currency Outside DMBs	14a	....	189.72	176.30	250.92	299.84	356.06	509.06	489.86	494.60	577.78	765.98	906.39
Restricted Deposits	16b	....	16.23	26.17	24.55	70.93	42.94	68.67	75.52	84.40	98.21	94.13	107.48
Foreign Liabilities	16c	....	19.79	76.12	181.17	188.23	224.73	250.59	274.88	286.14	310.89	378.19	412.63
Central Government Deposits	16d	....	5.59	70.12	62.36	81.86	153.49	106.11	176.26	268.08	346.16	429.09	488.04
Capital Accounts	17a	....	57.61	127.42	115.87	200.71	391.54	839.59	870.19	1,000.17	1,035.12	1,134.32	1,228.70
Other Items (Net)	17r	....	−28.17	−28.74	13.60	−47.61	−107.53	−95.70	−115.22	−123.55	−85.58	−135.81	−194.17
Deposit Money Banks						*Billions of Riels: End of Period*							
Reserves	20	....	11.67	88.75	88.15	178.43	199.15	346.00	503.74	737.13	866.85	1,270.85	1,329.73
Foreign Assets	21	....	239.01	326.39	408.14	506.15	559.51	526.10	582.19	653.43	844.19	680.99	834.64
Claims on Central Government	22a	....	.07	.01	.31	.31	.31	.31	.31	.31	.01	40.91	90.81
Claims on Nonfin.Pub.Enterprises	22c	....	6.21	6.00	5.11	5.22	5.93	5.86	10.14	2.65	6.55	2.03	.01
Claims on Private Sector	22d	....	157.67	234.39	293.40	434.55	636.79	654.60	763.23	898.46	936.11	1,058.91	1,336.62
Demand Deposits	24	....	11.77	20.94	27.29	29.09	28.70	34.21	42.09	45.04	31.94	47.30	29.47
Time and Savings Deposits	25a	....	8.51	17.80	5.07	7.85	13.21	19.77	31.71	45.89	55.50	74.31	81.87
Foreign Currency Deposits	25b	....	121.13	232.57	365.55	574.84	664.90	667.03	878.84	1,244.97	1,538.65	2,000.83	2,301.09
Restricted Deposits	26b	....	10.30	3.22	4.04	11.45	4.23	3.97	4.04	1.87	1.48	1.41	1.43
Foreign Liabilities	26c	....	157.74	164.61	166.15	161.56	200.32	224.37	214.45	172.73	195.82	163.54	318.26
Central Government Deposits	26d	....	25.43	1.75	7.14	4.38	4.26	4.20	4.15	.71	.01	–	.07
Credit from Monetary Authorities	26g	....	3.03	2.96	4.81	3.51	6.55	5.87	7.52	6.04	8.11	8.74	67.39
Capital Accounts	27a	....	121.81	356.49	356.11	454.98	602.77	689.78	767.43	791.25	923.56	808.64	839.90
Other Items (Net)	27r	....	−45.08	−144.79	−141.05	−123.00	−123.26	−116.42	−90.62	−16.53	−101.37	−51.09	−47.68
Monetary Survey						*Billions of Riels: End of Period*							
Foreign Assets (Net)	31n	....	117.93	390.75	545.70	877.28	1,167.48	1,726.36	2,016.37	2,583.18	3,077.55	3,737.59	4,009.90
Domestic Credit	32	....	343.14	386.25	446.43	567.41	696.95	839.01	876.31	904.45	867.64	941.81	1,208.72
Claims on Central Govt. (Net)	32an	....	175.32	143.16	147.92	127.64	53.84	178.55	102.95	3.34	−75.02	−119.13	−127.92
Claims on Nonfin.Pub.Enterprises	32c	....	6.21	6.00	5.11	5.22	5.93	5.86	10.14	2.65	6.55	2.03	.01
Claims on Private Sector	32d	....	161.61	237.09	293.40	434.55	636.79	654.60	763.23	898.46	936.11	1,058.91	1,336.62
Money	34	....	203.82	201.68	278.49	328.93	384.76	543.27	531.95	539.64	609.72	813.28	935.86
Quasi-Money	35	....	129.65	250.37	370.62	582.69	678.11	686.80	910.55	1,290.87	1,594.15	2,075.14	2,382.96
Capital Accounts	37a	....	179.42	483.91	471.98	655.70	994.31	1,529.37	1,637.62	1,791.41	1,958.69	1,942.95	2,068.60
Other Items (Net)	37r	....	−51.82	−158.95	−128.96	−122.63	−193.15	−194.15	−187.44	−134.30	−217.37	−151.98	−168.80
Money plus Quasi-Money	35l	....	333.47	452.05	649.11	911.62	1,062.87	1,230.07	1,442.50	1,830.51	2,203.87	2,888.43	3,318.82
Interest Rates						*Percent Per Annum*							
Deposit Rate	60l	....	....	....	8.7	8.8	8.0	7.8	7.3	6.8	4.4	2.5	2.0
Lending Rate	60p	....	....	....	18.7	18.8	18.4	18.3	17.6	17.3	16.5	16.2	18.5
Prices and Labor						*Index Numbers (2000=100): Period Averages*							
Consumer Prices	64	....	....	73.6	74.3	81.8	84.4	96.9	100.8	100.0	†99.4	102.6	103.8
						Number in Thousands: Period Averages							
Labor Force	67d	3,964	4,010	....	....	4,680	....	5,119	....	....	....	....	....
International Transactions						*Millions of US Dollars*							
Exports	70..d	....	....	....	....	....	626	933	1,040	1,123	1,296	1,489	1,771
Imports, c.i.f	71..d	....	....	....	....	....	1,116	1,129	1,243	1,424	1,456	1,675	1,732

Cambodia 522

		1992	1993	1994	1995	1996	1997	1998	1999	2000	2001	2002	2003
Balance of Payments					*Millions of US Dollars: Minus Sign Indicates Debit*								
Current Account, n.i.e.	78ald	−93.0	−103.9	−156.6	−185.7	−184.9	−209.9	−175.2	−187.8	−135.4	−85.8	−64.0	....
Goods: Exports f.o.b.	78aad	264.5	283.7	489.9	855.2	643.6	736.0	800.5	1,129.3	1,401.1	1,571.2	1,750.1	....
Goods: Imports f.o.b.	78abd	−443.4	−471.1	−744.4	−1,186.8	−1,071.8	−1,064.0	−1,165.8	−1,591.0	−1,939.3	−2,094.0	−2,313.5	....
Trade Balance	78acd	−178.9	−187.4	−254.5	−331.6	−428.2	−328.0	−365.3	−461.6	−538.2	−522.8	−563.5	....
Services: Credit	78add	49.7	63.9	54.5	114.0	162.8	160.4	177.3	293.8	428.4	524.6	600.2	....
Services: Debit	78aed	−63.6	−120.5	−139.6	−187.9	−214.8	−188.0	−220.5	−291.5	−327.9	−347.3	−379.6	....
Balance on Goods & Services	78afd	−192.8	−244.0	−339.6	−405.5	−480.2	−355.6	−408.5	−459.4	−437.7	−345.5	−342.8	....
Income: Credit	78agd	....	.5	2.1	9.7	12.6	16.0	47.9	51.4	67.1	57.5	50.7	....
Income: Debit	78ahd	−20.6	−16.6	−49.1	−66.9	−98.3	−58.5	−108.0	−150.2	−189.6	−193.4	−219.2	....
Balance on Gds, Serv. & Inc.	78aid	−213.4	−260.1	−386.6	−462.7	−565.9	−398.1	−468.6	−558.2	−560.2	−481.4	−511.2	....
Current Transfers, n.i.e.: Credit	78ajd	120.4	156.4	230.0	277.9	383.4	188.5	299.0	378.0	432.0	403.8	456.5	....
Current Transfers: Debit	78akd	....	−.2	−	−.9	−2.4	−.3	−5.6	−7.6	−7.3	−8.3	−9.3	....
Capital Account, n.i.e.	78bcd	126.3	123.4	73.2	78.0	75.8	65.2	−4.8	10.9	35.6	44.9	13.3	....
Capital Account, n.i.e.: Credit	78bad	126.3	123.4	73.2	78.0	75.8	65.2	89.5	78.7	79.8	102.8	76.7	....
Capital Account: Debit	78bbd	....	....	....	....	....	−	−94.3	−67.7	−44.2	−58.0	−63.4	....
Financial Account, n.i.e.	78bjd	13.9	.2	54.0	122.4	259.1	219.8	230.0	191.8	175.2	133.3	266.5	....
Direct Investment Abroad	78bdd	....	....	....	....	....	....	−19.8	−9.1	−6.6	−7.3	−6.0	....
Dir. Invest. in Rep. Econ., n.i.e.	78bed	33.0	54.1	68.9	150.8	293.6	203.7	242.9	230.3	148.5	148.1	53.8	....
Portfolio Investment Assets	78bfd	....	....	....	....	....	....	−13.5	−7.8	−7.2	−7.7	−7.5	....
Equity Securities	78bkd	....	....	....	....	....	....	....	....	....	....	....	....
Debt Securities	78bld	....	....	....	....	....	....	....	....	....	....	....	....
Portfolio Investment Liab., n.i.e.	78bgd	....	....	....	....	....	....	....	....	....	....	....	....
Equity Securities	78bmd	....	....	....	....	....	....	....	....	....	....	....	....
Debt Securities	78bnd	....	....	....	....	....	....	....	....	....	....	....	....
Financial Derivatives Assets	78bwd	....	....	....	....	....	....	....	....	....	....	....	....
Financial Derivatives Liabilities	78bxd	....	....	....	....	....	....	....	....	....	....	....	....
Other Investment Assets	78bhd	−24.1	−51.1	−46.8	−103.4	−118.0	−23.6	−70.2	−59.2	−183.7	−118.2	−11.9	....
Monetary Authorities	78bod	....	....	....	....	....	....	....	....	....	....	....	....
General Government	78bpd	....	−.4	....	−39.8	−23.6	23.6	23.2	−15.0	−13.6	−48.8	44.2	....
Banks	78bqd	....	−25.6	−	−63.6	−94.4	−47.2	−93.4	−44.2	−170.1	−69.4	−56.1	....
Other Sectors	78brd	−24.1	−25.1	−46.8	−63.6	−94.4	−47.2	−93.4	−44.2	224.2	118.4	238.1	....
Other Investment Liab., n.i.e.	78bid	5.0	−2.8	31.9	75.0	83.5	39.7	90.6	37.6	224.2	118.4	238.1	....
Monetary Authorities	78bsd	−								−5.5	−10.7	−10.9	....
General Government	78btd	−2.1	3.2	51.4	73.1	89.7	41.2	42.7	43.6	74.6	77.7	145.7	....
Banks	78bud	7.1	−6.0	−19.5	1.9	−6.2	−1.5	1.5	−2.6	−6.7	.1	−8.6	....
Other Sectors	78bvd	....	....	....	....	....	....	46.5	−3.4	161.8	51.3	111.9	....
Net Errors and Omissions	78cad	−34.0	1.1	65.6	11.5	−78.0	−41.2	−31.3	29.9	16.6	−24.2	−50.2	....
Overall Balance	78cbd	13.2	20.8	36.2	26.2	72.0	33.9	18.7	44.8	92.0	68.1	165.7	....
Reserves and Related Items	79dad	−13.2	−20.8	−36.2	−26.2	−72.0	−33.9	−18.7	−44.8	−92.0	−68.1	−165.7	....
Reserve Assets	79dbd	−4.5	−23.0	−71.2	−73.2	−68.9	−34.3	−29.3	−65.1	−108.7	−90.2	−187.7	....
Use of Fund Credit and Loans	79dcd	−8.7	−	19.8	42.3	−	−3.1	.4	−1.4	8.3	4.0	9.3	9.3	....
Exceptional Financing	79ded	....	2.2	15.2	4.7	....	....	12.0	12.0	12.8	12.8	12.8	....
International Investment Position						*Millions of US Dollars*							
Assets	79aad	....	....	....	374.3	711.9	798.5	1,811.5	1,995.5	2,343.5	2,622.6	2,918.4	....
Direct Investment Abroad	79abd	....	....	....	....	....	....	159.0	176.9	193.2	211.0	228.5	....
Portfolio Investment	79acd	....	....	....	....	....	....	164.8	181.7	198.8	217.4	236.8	....
Equity Securities	79add	....	....	....	....	....	....	164.8	181.7	198.8	217.4	236.8	....
Debt Securities	79aed	....	....	....	....	....	....	−	−	−	−	−	....
Financial Derivatives	79ald	....	....	....	....	....	....	−	−	−	−	−	....
Other Investment	79afd	....	....	....	182.3	206.9	223.2	1,040.8	1,127.4	1,340.8	1,491.6	1,539.0	....
Monetary Authorities	79agd	....	....	....	−	−	−	−	−	−	−	−	....
General Government	79ahd	....	....	....	163.3	186.9	163.2	140.0	155.1	168.6	217.4	173.2	....
Banks	79aid	....	....	....	19.0	20.0	60.0	900.8	972.3	1,172.2	1,274.2	1,365.8	....
Other Sectors	79ajd	....	....	....	192.1	504.1	575.2	446.9	509.5	610.7	702.6	914.1	....
Reserve Assets	79akd	....	....	....	1,108.0	1,351.2	1,210.5	2,294.1	2,579.9	2,976.1	3,274.6	3,606.6	....
Liabilities	79lad	....	....	....	498.1	677.6	580.4	1,199.1	1,429.2	1,577.6	1,725.9	1,779.7	....
Dir. Invest. in Rep. Economy	79lbd	....	....	....	....	....	....	−	−	−	−	−	....
Portfolio Investment	79lcd	....	....	....	−	−	−	−	−	−	−	−	....
Equity Securities	79ldd	....	....	....	−	−	−	−	−	−	−	−	....
Debt Securities	79led	....	....	....	−	−	−	−	−	−	−	−	....
Financial Derivatives	79lld	....	....	....	−	−	−	−	−	−	−	−	....
Other Investment	79lfd	....	....	....	609.9	673.6	630.1	1,095.0	1,150.7	1,398.5	1,548.7	1,826.9	....
Monetary Authorities	79lgd	....	....	....	71.7	69.4	65.1	66.5	72.9	73.3	79.8	96.2	....
General Government	79lhd	....	....	....	472.5	544.7	506.9	627.2	682.5	774.9	867.3	1,025.8	....
Banks	79lid	....	....	....	65.7	59.6	58.1	59.5	56.9	50.2	50.2	41.6	....
Other sectors	79ljd	....	....	....	−	−	−	341.8	338.4	500.1	551.4	663.3	....
Government Finance						*Trillions of Riels: Year Ending December 31*							
Deficit (-) or Surplus	80	....	....	....	....	....	....	....	....	....	−439.86	−577.04	....
Revenue	81	....	....	....	....	....	....	....	....	....	1,521.19	1,729.37	....
Grants	81z	....	....	....	....	....	....	....	....	....	500.73	452.97	....
Expenditure	82	....	....	....	....	....	....	....	....	....	2,461.77	2,759.38	....
Financing													
Domestic	84a	....	....	....	....	....	....	....	....	....	51.22	−30.89	....
Foreign	85a	....	....	....	....	....	....	....	....	....	388.64	607.94	....

2004, International Monetary Fund: *International Financial Statistics Yearbook*

Cambodia 522

National Accounts		1992	1993	1994	1995	1996	1997	1998	1999	2000	2001	2002	2003
							Billions of Riels						
Househ.Cons.Expend.,incl.NPISHs....	96f	2,066	6,896	6,750	8,100	8,990	9,183	11,096	11,865	12,132	12,338	12,860	....
Government Consumption Expend...	91f	255	306	493	413	529	553	563	661	737	828	913	....
Gross Fixed Capital Formation.........	93e	245	733	760	1,174	1,166	1,361	1,463	2,031	2,576	2,787	3,550	....
Changes in Inventories.....................	93i	....	17	73	37	164	137	−83	202	−191	299	−69	....
Exports of Goods and Services.........	90c	127	1,094	1,833	2,630	2,334	3,411	3,727	4,994	7,028	7,915	9,275	....
Imports of Goods and Services (-).....	98c	185	2,186	2,751	4,001	4,042	4,625	5,254	6,716	8,695	9,375	10,558	....
Statistical Discrepancy.....................	99bs	....	−195	−171	−60	−117	−92	96	95	221	−247	−305	....
Gross Domestic Product (GDP).........	99b	2,508	6,666	6,986	8,294	9,024	9,927	11,609	13,131	13,810	14,544	15,667	....
GDP Volume 2000 Prices................	99b.p	....	8,594	9,371	10,017	10,514	11,231	11,647	12,903	13,810	14,593	15,392	....
GDP Volume (2000=100)................	99bvp	59.8	†62.2	67.9	72.5	76.1	81.3	84.3	93.4	100.0	105.7	111.5	....
GDP Deflator (2000=100)................	99bip	30.4	77.6	74.5	82.8	85.8	88.4	99.7	101.8	100.0	99.7	101.8	....
						Millions: Midyear Estimates							
Population................................	99z	10.44	10.79	11.14	11.48	11.82	12.16	Ü 12.49	12.82	13.15	13.48	13.81	14.14

Cameroon 622

		1992	1993	1994	1995	1996	1997	1998	1999	2000	2001	2002	2003
Exchange Rates						*Francs per SDR: End of Period*							
Official Rate	aa	378.57	404.89	†780.44	728.38	753.06	807.94	791.61	†896.19	918.49	935.39	850.37	771.76
					Francs per US Dollar: End of Period (ae) Period Average (rf)								
Official Rate	ae	275.33	294.78	†534.60	490.00	523.70	598.81	562.21	†652.95	704.95	744.31	625.50	519.36
Official Rate	rf	264.69	283.16	†555.20	499.15	511.55	583.67	589.95	†615.70	711.98	733.04	696.99	581.20
					Index Numbers (2000=100): Period Averages								
Official Rate	ahx	268.8	250.9	128.1	142.3	138.8	121.8	120.5	115.5	100.0	96.9	102.2	122.4
Nominal Effective Exchange Rate	nec	155.1	172.4	96.3	104.8	105.5	101.4	103.7	105.8	100.0	101.6	104.8	111.8
Real Effective Exchange Rate	rec	152.0	140.9	90.7	104.7	106.3	101.4	106.8	111.6	100.0	103.2	106.9	112.3
Fund Position					*Millions of SDRs: End of Period*								
Quota	2f.s	135.10	135.10	135.10	135.10	135.10	135.10	135.10	185.70	185.70	185.70	185.70	185.70
SDRs	1b.s	.20	.06	.03	.03	.11	–	.01	1.90	5.93	.01	.87	.99
Reserve Position in the Fund	1c.s	.29	.34	.34	.36	.37	.41	.45	.50	.52	.54	.58	.64
Total Fund Cred.&Loans Outstg.	2tl	45.66	11.86	29.91	34.41	50.11	68.91	110.94	142.65	180.50	193.96	225.80	233.60
International Liquidity				*Millions of US Dollars Unless Otherwise Indicated: End of Period*									
Total Reserves minus Gold	1l.d	20.37	2.45	†2.26	3.79	2.77	.86	1.29	4.43	212.00	331.83	629.66	639.64
SDRs	1b.d	.28	.09	.05	.04	.16	–	.02	2.61	7.73	.02	1.18	1.47
Reserve Position in the Fund	1c.d	.40	.47	.49	.53	.53	.55	.63	.69	.67	.68	.79	.96
Foreign Exchange	1d.d	19.70	1.90	†1.72	3.22	2.08	.31	.64	1.13	203.60	331.14	627.70	637.21
Gold (Million Fine Troy Ounces)	1ad	.030	.030	.030	.030	.030	.030	.030	.030	.030	.030	.030	.030
Gold (National Valuation)	1and	9.95	11.91	†11.33	11.56	11.04	8.72	8.61	†8.69	8.17	8.33	10.27	12.52
Monetary Authorities: Other Liab.	4..d	637.31	762.34	650.63	713.03	537.11	300.24	238.09	188.63	62.45	57.36	63.77	72.18
Deposit Money Banks: Assets	7a.d	98.99	88.27	135.55	131.07	90.23	105.23	122.82	163.34	163.10	153.17	248.67	317.31
Liabilities	7b.d	90.26	125.49	50.01	81.98	71.50	62.51	85.92	84.52	70.75	67.43	96.10	114.56
Monetary Authorities					*Billions of Francs: End of Period*								
Foreign Assets	11	8.35	4.17	7.37	7.53	7.25	5.70	5.57	8.57	155.21	253.18	400.27	338.70
Claims on Central Government	12a	331.57	319.09	340.51	338.23	340.59	338.61	358.64	403.25	434.19	499.81	518.28	490.23
Claims on Deposit Money Banks	12e	51.63	52.06	27.07	21.41	4.93	4.07	13.51	2.17	1.12	.15	–	–
Claims on Other Banking Insts.	12f	–	–	–	–	–	–	–	–	–	–	–	–
Reserve Money	14	168.61	129.79	180.77	142.77	183.17	256.74	282.83	305.91	410.67	502.29	641.32	568.66
of which: Currency Outside DMBs	14a	149.02	116.13	136.33	102.29	95.32	180.28	205.76	237.40	264.96	296.14	333.74	298.02
Foreign Liabilities	16c	192.75	229.52	371.17	374.45	319.02	235.47	221.67	251.01	209.81	224.12	231.90	217.78
Central Government Deposits	16d	23.62	14.85	44.83	63.03	59.71	49.52	63.96	57.54	171.12	213.39	208.32	193.84
Capital Accounts	17a	12.16	13.59	22.17	20.38	21.00	22.19	21.45	25.24	26.74	27.89	26.06	23.87
Other Items (Net)	17r	–5.58	–12.43	–243.99	–233.45	–230.12	–215.54	–212.19	–224.75	–227.82	–214.54	–189.05	–175.21
Deposit Money Banks					*Billions of Francs: End of Period*								
Reserves	20	17.22	12.39	42.57	37.49	82.48	70.57	68.60	62.66	141.59	201.24	301.04	260.33
Foreign Assets	21	27.25	26.02	72.46	64.22	47.25	63.01	69.05	106.65	114.98	114.01	155.54	164.80
Claims on Central Government	22a	†126.05	154.08	185.76	187.67	159.72	171.59	173.66	173.85	168.57	165.04	156.99	139.34
Claims on Nonfin.Pub.Enterprises	22c	77.03	52.68	39.45	42.06	36.26	39.76	53.95	54.35	89.19	82.95	84.92	97.12
Claims on Private Sector	22d	400.06	368.81	369.54	371.39	385.89	348.14	428.82	481.46	543.95	605.78	676.26	740.15
Claims on Other Banking Insts.	22f	–	.01	.03	.19	.05	.06	.19	.08	–	.04	.01	–
Claims on Nonbank Financial Insts	22g	3.06	3.05	4.43	8.83	9.16	11.95	14.57	5.41	4.56	7.20	10.87	8.11
Demand Deposits	24	159.94	150.06	223.09	213.97	213.45	237.72	271.06	294.49	361.99	410.94	473.35	462.88
Time and Savings Deposits	25	290.32	278.67	329.79	329.30	268.89	267.45	259.81	306.43	374.62	445.75	528.07	588.18
Bonds	26ab	6.22	5.01	3.85	3.85	.90	5.30	.90	.90	–	–	–	.28
Foreign Liabilities	26c	22.92	32.58	17.44	36.08	34.84	34.74	43.80	47.21	39.18	47.73	58.15	47.36
Long-Term Foreign Liabilities	26cl	1.93	4.41	9.30	4.09	2.60	2.69	4.50	7.98	10.70	2.46	1.96	12.14
Central Government Deposits	26d	†82.24	77.65	97.04	94.00	109.15	55.43	85.19	101.56	117.74	113.66	159.38	122.65
Credit from Monetary Authorities	26g	51.63	52.06	27.07	21.41	4.93	4.07	13.51	2.17	1.12	.15	–	–
Capital Accounts	27a	77.27	75.87	84.39	62.25	102.79	112.58	129.23	150.84	154.45	175.85	195.08	206.98
Other Items (Net)	27r	†–41.80	–59.27	–77.72	–53.09	–16.75	–14.91	.84	–27.10	3.03	–20.28	–30.35	–30.62
Monetary Survey					*Billions of Francs: End of Period*								
Foreign Assets (Net)	31n	–181.99	–236.32	–318.07	–342.86	–301.96	–204.18	–195.36	–190.98	10.49	92.89	263.80	226.23
Domestic Credit	32	†831.91	805.22	797.85	791.34	762.82	806.10	881.16	959.54	952.03	1,033.83	1,079.63	1,158.46
Claims on Central Govt. (Net)	32an	†351.76	380.67	384.40	368.88	331.46	405.25	383.15	418.00	313.90	337.80	307.57	313.08
Claims on Nonfin.Pub.Enterprises	32c	77.03	52.68	39.45	42.06	36.26	39.76	53.95	54.35	89.19	82.95	84.92	97.12
Claims on Private Sector	32d	400.06	368.81	369.54	371.39	385.89	348.14	428.82	481.46	543.95	605.78	676.26	740.15
Claims on Other Banking Insts.	32f	–	.01	.03	.19	.05	.06	.19	.08	–	.04	.01	–
Claims on Nonbank Financial Inst.	32g	3.06	3.05	4.43	8.83	9.16	12.89	15.06	5.64	4.99	7.26	10.87	8.11
Money	34	311.33	267.46	361.29	319.24	314.14	423.90	485.29	537.73	631.06	711.98	813.63	771.21
Quasi-Money	35	290.32	278.67	329.79	329.30	268.89	267.45	259.81	306.43	374.62	445.75	528.07	588.18
Bonds	36ab	6.22	5.01	3.85	3.85	.90	5.30	.90	.90	–	–	–	.28
Other Items (Net)	37r	†42.05	17.76	–215.15	–203.91	–123.08	–94.74	–60.19	–75.54	–43.16	–31.02	1.74	25.03
Money plus Quasi-Money	35l	601.65	546.13	691.08	648.55	583.03	691.35	745.09	844.17	1,005.69	1,157.74	1,341.70	1,359.38
Interest Rates						*Percent Per Annum*							
Discount Rate (End of Period)	60	12.00	11.50	†7.75	8.60	7.75	7.50	7.00	7.30	7.00	6.50	6.30	6.00
Deposit Rate	60l	7.50	7.75	8.08	5.50	5.38	5.04	5.00	5.00	5.00	5.00	5.00	5.00
Lending Rate	60p	17.77	17.46	17.50	16.00	22.00	22.00	22.00	22.00	22.00	20.67	18.00	18.00

2004, International Monetary Fund : *International Financial Statistics Yearbook*

Cameroon 622

		1992	1993	1994	1995	1996	1997	1998	1999	2000	2001	2002	2003
Prices						*Index Numbers (2000=100): Period Averages*							
Consumer Prices	64	62.8	60.7	†82.1	89.5	93.0	97.5	100.6	102.1	100.0	104.5	107.4	....
International Transactions						*Billions of Francs*							
Exports	70	487.13	533.24	825.20	811.02	821.61	982.81	1,084.15	939.59	1,092.20	1,540.20	1,586.50	....
Imports, c.i.f.	71	307.79	311.96	601.50	464.73	572.62	708.17	874.61	816.83	910.68	1,157.80	1,978.90	....
Balance of Payments						*Millions of US Dollars: Minus Sign Indicates Debit*							
Current Account, n.i.e.	78ald	−396.6	−565.4	−56.1	89.9	....	....	....	....	....	....	....	....
Goods: Exports f.o.b.	78aad	1,934.1	1,507.7	1,454.2	1,735.9	....	....	....	....	....	....	....	....
Goods: Imports f.o.b.	78abd	−1,041.4	−1,005.3	−1,052.3	−1,109.0	....	....	....	....	....	....	....	....
Trade Balance	78acd	892.7	502.4	401.9	626.9	....	....	....	....	....	....	....	....
Services: Credit	78add	407.5	390.9	330.8	304.4	....	....	....	....	....	....	....	....
Services: Debit	78aed	−907.3	−741.1	−493.2	−498.6	....	....	....	....	....	....	....	....
Balance on Goods & Services	78afd	392.8	152.2	239.6	432.6	....	....	....	....	....	....	....	....
Income: Credit	78agd	41.8	17.0	19.9	12.4	....	....	....	....	....	....	....	....
Income: Debit	78ahd	−823.9	−669.5	−336.4	−424.6	....	....	....	....	....	....	....	....
Balance on Gds, Serv. & Inc.	78aid	−389.3	−500.3	−76.9	20.4	....	....	....	....	....	....	....	....
Current Transfers, n.i.e.: Credit	78ajd	141.0	65.2	83.8	100.7	....	....	....	....	....	....	....	....
Current Transfers: Debit	78akd	−148.3	−130.2	−63.0	−31.2	....	....	....	....	....	....	....	....
Capital Account, n.i.e.	78bcd	17.0	6.3	14.1	20.4	....	....	....	....	....	....	....	....
Capital Account, n.i.e.: Credit	78bad	17.1	6.4	14.1	21.1	....	....	....	....	....	....	....	....
Capital Account: Debit	78bbd	−.1	−.1	−	−.7	....	....	....	....	....	....	....	....
Financial Account, n.i.e.	78bjd	−342.9	−310.0	−626.4	43.3	....	....	....	....	....	....	....	....
Direct Investment Abroad	78bdd	−33.1	−22.1	−.4	−.6	....	....	....	....	....	....	....	....
Dir. Invest. in Rep. Econ., n.i.e.	78bed	29.2	5.1	−9.0	7.3	....	....	....	....	....	....	....	....
Portfolio Investment Assets	78bfd	−46.5	−106.3	−74.6	−26.2	....	....	....	....	....	....	....	....
Equity Securities	78bkd	53.4	8.0	6.4	−	....	....	....	....	....	....	....	....
Debt Securities	78bld	−99.9	−114.4	−81.1	−26.2	....	....	....	....	....	....	....	....
Portfolio Investment Liab., n.i.e.	78bgd	−	−	−	−	....	....	....	....	....	....	....	....
Equity Securities	78bmd	−	−	−	−	....	....	....	....	....	....	....	....
Debt Securities	78bnd	−	−	−	−	....	....	....	....	....	....	....	....
Financial Derivatives Assets	78bwd	....	....	....	....	....	....	....	....	....	....	....	....
Financial Derivatives Liabilities	78bxd	....	....	....	....	....	....	....	....	....	....	....	....
Other Investment Assets	78bhd	16.8	105.5	138.4	−146.8	....	....	....	....	....	....	....	....
Monetary Authorities	78bod	....	....	....	....	....	....	....	....	....	....	....	....
General Government	78bpd	.1	−	−	−	....	....	....	....	....	....	....	....
Banks	78bqd	26.0	42.8	−27.9	6.6	....	....	....	....	....	....	....	....
Other Sectors	78brd	−9.2	62.6	166.3	−153.4	....	....	....	....	....	....	....	....
Other Investment Liab., n.i.e.	78bid	−309.4	−292.2	−680.7	209.6	....	....	....	....	....	....	....	....
Monetary Authorities	78bsd	3.5	−5.4	−181.3	666.9	....	....	....	....	....	....	....	....
General Government	78btd	−175.8	−22.5	−272.3	−457.0	....	....	....	....	....	....	....	....
Banks	78bud	−41.3	−104.1	−76.2	17.0	....	....	....	....	....	....	....	....
Other Sectors	78bvd	−95.8	−160.1	−150.9	−17.3	....	....	....	....	....	....	....	....
Net Errors and Omissions	78cad	−582.6	−16.2	117.0	−138.1	....	....	....	....	....	....	....	....
Overall Balance	78cbd	−1,305.2	−885.3	−551.3	15.4	....	....	....	....	....	....	....	....
Reserves and Related Items	79dad	1,305.2	885.3	551.3	−15.4	....	....	....	....	....	....	....	....
Reserve Assets	79dbd	20.9	14.9	.4	14.5	....	....	....	....	....	....	....	....
Use of Fund Credit and Loans	79dcd	−54.6	−47.4	25.3	6.7	....	....	....	....	....	....	....	....
Exceptional Financing	79ded	1,338.9	917.8	525.6	−36.6	....	....	....	....	....	....	....	....
Government Finance						*Billions of Francs: Year Ending June 30*							
Deficit (−) or Surplus	80	†−81.16	−54.74	−99.05	†8.25	....	....	83.71	7.16	....	....	....	....
Revenue	81	†498.47	448.41	385.90	†536.54	....	....	862.31	867.46	....	....	....	....
Grants Received	81z	†−	−	−	†−	....	....	−	−	....	....	....	....
Expenditure	82	†578.43	501.15	483.49	†525.27	....	....	777.60	859.80	....	....	....	....
Lending Minus Repayments	83	†1.20	2.00	1.46	†3.02	....	....	1.00	.50	....	....	....	....
Financing													
Domestic	84a	†14.27	12.45	−13.09	†−13.17	....	....	−19.40	−14.90	....	....	....	....
Foreign	85a	†106.73	61.16	120.84	†14.42	....	....	−63.10	8.50	....	....	....	....
Adj. to Total Financing	84x	†−39.84	−18.87	−8.70	†−9.50	....	....	−1.21	−.76	....	....	....	....
Debt: Domestic	88a	†377.90	374.16	1,179.18	†1,419.89	....	....	1,391.38	1,224.04	....	....	....	....
Foreign	89a	†1,496.02	1,852.61	4,084.80	†4,343.87	....	....	4,261.53	4,432.12	....	....	....	....

Cameroon 622

		1992	1993	1994	1995	1996	1997	1998	1999	2000	2001	2002	2003
National Accounts						*Billions of Francs: Year Ending June 30*							
Househ.Cons.Expend.,incl.NPISHs....	96f	2,292.4	2,233.6	2,538.9	3,018.9	3,354.8	3,537.2	....	....	....	....	....	....
Government Consumption Expend...	91f	387.1	343.0	257.5	299.9	305.0	332.1	....	....	....	....	....	....
Gross Fixed Capital Formation..........	93e	457.1	492.5	533.0	597.5	729.3	850.5	....	....	....	....	....	....
Changes in Inventories.....................	93i	−27.3	29.8	–	–	–	–	....	....	....	....	....	....
Exports of Goods and Services..........	90c	649.5	531.3	768.5	1,068.3	1,116.3	1,335.8	....	....	....	....	....	....
Imports of Goods and Services (-).....	98c	584.4	504.7	681.8	834.5	950.4	1,038.2	....	....	....	....	....	....
Gross Domestic Product (GDP).........	99b	3,174.3	3,125.6	3,786.0	4,365.5	4,836.5	5,266.5	5,572.0	6,010.6	6,611.0	7,136.7	7,609.3	....
Net Primary Income from Abroad.....	98.n	−174.6	−198.9	−190.0	−168.5	−284.0	−299.0	....	....	....	....	....	....
Gross National Income (GNI)............	99a	2,999.7	2,926.6	3,226.0	3,981.7	4,271.0	4,718.4	....	....	....	....	....	....
GDP Volume 1985 Prices.................	99b.p	3,158.7	3,058.3	2,977.6	3,075.9	3,229.7	3,391.1	....	....	....	....	....	....
GDP Volume (1995=100)................	99bvp	102.7	99.4	96.8	100.0	105.0	110.2	....	....	....	....	....	....
GDP Deflator (1995=100)................	99bip	70.8	72.0	89.6	100.0	105.5	109.4	....	....	....	....	....	....
						Millions: Midyear Estimates							
Population...............................	99z	12.35	12.71	13.06	13.41	13.77	14.11	14.46	14.79	15.12	15.43	15.73	16.02

2004, International Monetary Fund : *International Financial Statistics Yearbook*

Canada 156

		1992	1993	1994	1995	1996	1997	1998	1999	2000	2001	2002	2003
Exchange Rates		\multicolumn{12}{c}{*Canadian Dollars per SDR: End of Period*}												
Market Rate	aa	1.7478	1.8186	2.0479	2.0294	1.9694	1.9282	2.1550	1.9809	1.9546	2.0015	2.1475	1.9205
		Canadian Dollars per US Dollar: End of Period (ae) Period Average (rf)											
Market Rate	ae	1.2711	1.3240	1.4028	1.3652	1.3696	1.4291	1.5305	1.4433	1.5002	1.5926	1.5796	1.2924
Market Rate	rf	1.2087	1.2901	1.3656	1.3724	1.3635	1.3846	1.4835	1.4857	1.4851	1.5488	1.5693	1.4011
		Index Numbers (2000=100): Period Averages											
Market Rate	ahx	122.9	115.1	108.7	108.2	108.9	107.2	100.2	99.9	100.0	95.9	94.6	106.3
Nominal Effective Exchange Rate	neu	119.7	112.9	105.9	103.8	105.6	105.8	99.5	98.8	100.0	97.0	95.3	104.6
Real Effective Exchange Rate	reu	118.4	111.9	105.0	104.2	105.1	107.8	101.1	100.0	100.0	96.0	95.6	107.2
Fund Position		*Millions of SDRs: End of Period*											
Quota	2f.s	4,320	4,320	4,320	4,320	4,320	4,320	4,320	6,369	6,369	6,369	6,369	6,369
SDRs	1b.s	756	773	786	792	812	834	780	384	441	489	529	564
Reserve Position in the Fund	1c.s	735	690	629	836	853	1,167	1,633	2,308	1,926	2,278	2,633	2,589
of which: Outstg.Fund Borrowing	2c	–	–	–	–	–	–	204	–	–	–	–	–
International Liquidity		*Millions of US Dollars Unless Otherwise Indicated: End of Period*											
Total Reserves minus Gold	1l.d	11,431	12,481	12,286	15,049	20,422	17,823	23,308	28,126	31,924	33,962	36,984	36,222
SDRs	1b.d	1,039	1,062	1,148	1,177	1,168	1,126	1,098	527	574	614	719	838
Reserve Position in the Fund	1c.d	1,011	948	919	1,243	1,226	1,575	2,299	3,168	2,509	2,863	3,580	3,847
Foreign Exchange	1d.d	9,382	10,471	10,219	12,629	18,028	15,122	19,911	24,432	28,841	30,484	32,685	31,537
of which: US Dollars	1dxd	7,864	9,950	9,693	12,127	17,521	14,630	15,907	18,838	21,692	19,748	17,946	15,576
Gold (Million Fine Troy Ounces)	1ad	9.94	6.05	3.89	3.41	3.09	3.09	2.49	1.81	1.18	1.05	.60	.11
Gold (National Valuation)	1and	478	292	198	178	155	146	122	524	323	291	205	45
Monetary Authorities: Other Liab.	4..d	307	276	355	349	139	99	64	187	65	67	134	85
Deposit Money Banks: Assets	7a.d	46,851	41,114	54,614	64,061	76,144	84,432	86,453	79,191	91,441	102,502	105,719	122,185
Liabilities	7b.d	73,613	67,151	80,507	77,143	87,951	108,978	111,723	92,325	94,728	109,353	116,856	127,172
Monetary Authorities		*Billions of Canadian Dollars: End of Period*											
Foreign Assets	11	15.14	16.91	17.51	20.79	28.18	25.68	35.86	40.72	47.97	54.16	58.47	46.82
Claims on Central Government	12a	27.83	29.63	30.41	30.09	31.03	31.81	32.41	41.68	36.98	40.08	41.89	43.22
Reserve Money	14	29.31	30.93	31.65	32.08	33.46	34.58	36.86	45.83	42.45	44.24	46.66	47.11
of which: Currency Outside DMBs	14a	23.60	25.57	27.30	27.99	28.78	30.15	32.32	38.72	36.34	38.66	41.13	42.35
Foreign Liabilities	16c	.39	.37	.50	.48	.19	.14	.10	.27	.10	.11	.21	.11
Central Government Deposits	16d	12.58	14.41	15.01	17.69	25.01	22.09	30.83	35.85	43.95	49.85	52.73	41.70
Other Items (Net)	17r	.69	.83	.76	.64	.56	.68	.47	.45	−1.55	.05	.76	1.12
Deposit Money Banks		*Billions of Canadian Dollars: End of Period*											
Reserves	20	5.88	5.92	5.04	4.67	5.24	4.79	4.89	8.56	6.87	6.07	5.96	5.10
Foreign Assets	21	57.44	51.74	73.94	83.18	97.07	109.86	122.51	105.26	127.80	149.15	152.51	147.77
Claims on Central Government	22a	50.68	69.59	78.33	84.20	81.50	72.55	71.89	70.75	85.79	100.16	100.04	103.31
Claims on Local Government	22b	8.90	9.67	13.15	13.01	12.91	14.80	15.24	15.95	16.37	17.58	23.10	22.65
Claims on Private Sector	22d	372.22	415.63	450.77	474.89	531.94	607.32	617.22	643.28	714.84	757.17	799.48	841.99
Demand Deposits	24	84.73	91.87	97.84	109.89	126.60	139.61	147.04	160.24	188.58	214.89	227.04	241.67
Savings & Fgn Currency Deposits	25	266.81	301.19	326.97	342.32	348.69	377.66	380.37	392.79	449.05	464.64	490.02	527.38
Foreign Liabilities	26c	87.68	82.23	105.94	97.52	113.51	146.31	160.94	122.40	129.33	157.69	170.59	149.86
Central Government Deposits	26d	1.41	2.44	2.78	6.19	4.22	6.63	5.89	11.59	4.17	4.12	2.26	3.48
Other Items (Net)	27r	54.50	74.83	87.70	104.04	135.63	139.12	137.51	156.78	180.54	188.79	191.17	198.44
Monetary Survey		*Billions of Canadian Dollars: End of Period*											
Foreign Assets (Net)	31n	−15.49	−13.94	−14.99	5.98	11.55	−10.91	−2.67	23.31	46.35	45.52	40.18	44.63
Domestic Credit	32	445.64	507.67	554.86	578.31	628.15	697.75	700.04	724.22	805.85	861.02	909.52	966.00
Claims on Central Govt. (Net)	32an	64.52	82.36	90.94	90.41	83.30	75.64	67.58	64.99	74.64	86.26	86.94	101.35
Claims on Local Government	32b	8.90	9.67	13.15	13.01	12.91	14.80	15.24	15.95	16.37	17.58	23.10	22.65
Claims on Private Sector	32d	372.22	415.63	450.77	474.89	531.94	607.32	617.22	643.28	714.84	757.17	799.48	841.99
Money	34	108.54	117.58	125.32	138.07	155.56	169.92	179.58	199.24	225.19	253.75	268.50	284.39
Quasi-Money	35	266.81	301.19	326.97	342.32	348.69	377.66	380.37	392.79	449.05	464.64	490.02	527.38
Other Items (Net)	37r	54.80	74.96	87.58	103.90	135.45	139.27	137.42	155.51	177.96	188.14	191.17	198.86
Money plus Quasi-Money	35l	375.35	418.77	452.29	480.40	504.25	547.57	559.95	592.03	674.24	718.40	758.52	811.76
Other Banking Institutions		*Billions of Canadian Dollars: End of Period*											
Reserves	40	16.80	14.95	14.94	16.77	16.57	15.45	16.93	19.56	20.98	12.55	12.72	14.33
Claims on Central Government	42a	8.96	7.55	6.74	7.41	7.58	5.18	5.47	6.49	1.35	3.30	3.12	4.14
Claims on State and Local Govts	42b	3.04	2.13	1.63	1.48	1.33	1.26	.94	.84	1.02	3.26	3.32	4.17
Claims on Private Sector	42d	177.59	148.62	141.24	140.10	144.18	132.09	133.94	135.34	103.52	113.07	121.40	133.47
Demand Deposits	44	11.45	9.47	8.96	8.37	8.69	7.87	8.07	8.11	.13	.19	.11	.11
Time and Savings Deposits	45	178.95	148.27	141.95	143.53	145.42	131.64	136.34	141.39	116.16	125.00	133.21	144.82
Money Market Instruments	46aa	1.00	.80	1.01	1.29	3.07	1.63	2.06	2.57	.03	.04	.08	.11
Capital Accounts	47a	11.22	10.27	9.40	9.54	9.84	9.60	9.91	10.18	9.32	10.16	10.81	12.08
Other Items (Net)	47r	3.76	4.43	3.22	3.03	2.63	3.23	.91	−.03	1.22	−3.21	−3.66	−1.01

Canada 156

		1992	1993	1994	1995	1996	1997	1998	1999	2000	2001	2002	2003
Banking Survey						*Billions of Canadian Dollars: End of Period*							
Foreign Assets (Net)	51n	−15.49	−13.94	−14.99	5.98	11.55	−10.91	−2.67	23.31	46.35	45.52	40.18	44.63
Domestic Credit	52	635.23	665.97	704.48	727.30	781.23	836.28	840.38	866.88	911.74	980.65	1,037.36	1,107.78
Claims on Central Govt. (Net)	52an	73.47	89.91	97.68	97.82	90.88	80.82	73.05	71.48	75.99	89.56	90.06	105.49
Claims on State and Local Govts	52b	11.95	11.80	14.79	14.49	14.23	16.06	16.18	16.79	17.39	20.85	26.42	26.82
Claims on Private Sector	52d	549.81	564.25	592.01	614.99	676.11	739.40	751.15	778.62	818.35	870.24	920.87	975.46
Liquid Liabilities	55l	548.96	561.57	588.27	615.53	641.79	671.64	687.42	721.97	769.56	831.03	879.12	942.36
Money Market Instruments	56aa	1.00	.80	1.01	1.29	3.07	1.63	2.06	2.57	.03	.04	.08	.11
Other Items (Net)	57r	69.78	89.66	100.21	116.47	147.92	152.11	148.24	165.65	188.51	195.09	198.32	209.93
Nonbank Financial Institutions						*Billions of Canadian Dollars: End of Period*							
Reserves	40..n	1.82	2.19	2.42	3.63	3.72	3.78	3.86	†4.57	6.00	6.89	5.88	9.34
Claims on Central Government	42a.n	17.98	22.24	25.50	29.43	28.56	30.05	31.33	†32.20	29.22	29.83	32.35	33.58
Claims on State & Local Govts	42b.n	13.96	16.80	17.51	20.60	23.41	23.68	24.43	†26.68	31.98	33.50	35.79	41.11
Claims on Private Sector	42d.n	121.48	123.86	126.46	131.93	137.89	154.64	164.51	†196.09	211.66	219.16	226.03	244.17
Claims on Deposit Money Banks	42e.n	2.08	2.32	2.43	2.17	3.83	4.73	5.42	†7.39	8.74	9.36	9.13	9.88
Money Market Instruments	46aan	6.73	6.20	8.50	8.89	10.57	16.71	18.80	†29.01	27.13	18.78	19.34	18.52
Bonds	46abn	8.94	8.83	9.45	11.12	11.41	16.83	23.41	†32.79	35.52	40.13	41.08	45.13
Cred. from Deposit Money Banks	46h.n	.30	.34	.30	.28	.21	.36	.36	†3.34	5.04	5.54	6.69	7.03
Capital Accounts	47a.n	154.13	165.31	173.06	183.54	190.49	201.44	212.41	†239.75	262.42	267.33	283.77	310.63
Other Items (Net)	47r.n	−12.78	−13.27	−16.99	−16.06	−15.27	−18.45	−25.44	†−37.96	−42.52	−33.04	−41.71	−43.23
Interest Rates						*Percent Per Annum*							
Bank Rate (End of Period)	60	7.36	4.11	7.43	5.79	3.25	4.50	5.25	5.00	6.00	2.50	3.00	3.00
Money Market Rate	60b	6.64	4.62	5.05	6.92	4.32	3.26	4.87	4.74	5.52	4.11	2.45	2.93
Corporate Paper Rate	60bc	6.74	4.97	5.66	7.22	4.35	3.61	5.05	4.94	5.71	3.87	2.66	2.94
Treasury Bill Rate	60c	6.59	4.84	5.54	6.89	4.21	3.26	4.73	4.72	5.49	3.77	2.59	2.87
Savings Rate	60k	2.27	.77	.50	.50	.50	.50	.24	.10	.10	.10	.05	.05
Deposit Rate	60l	3.92	3.21	3.98	5.28	3.00	1.90	3.08	2.88	3.48	2.25	.83	1.10
Lending Rate	60p	7.48	5.94	6.88	8.65	6.06	4.96	6.60	6.44	7.27	5.81	4.21	4.69
Govt. Bond Yield: Med.-Term	61a	7.43	6.46	7.79	7.64	6.21	5.33	5.16	5.50	5.99	4.88	4.44	3.88
Long-Term	61	8.77	7.85	8.63	8.28	7.50	6.42	5.47	5.69	5.89	5.78	5.66	5.28
Prices, Production, Labor						*Index Numbers (2000=100): Period Averages*							
Industrial Share Prices	62	35.4	40.6	44.6	46.1	54.8	67.2	70.3	73.5	100.0	80.5	73.2	74.5
Prices: Industry Selling	63	78.4	81.2	86.1	92.5	92.9	93.7	93.7	95.2	100.0	101.1	101.2	100.0
Consumer Prices	64	88.1	89.7	89.8	†91.8	93.2	94.7	95.7	97.3	100.0	102.5	104.8	107.7
Wages: Hourly Earnings (Mfg)	65ey	86.1	88.2	89.7	90.9	93.6	94.3	96.2	97.5	100.0	101.6	104.4	107.8
Industrial Production	66	....	....	....	79.0	79.9	84.4	87.3	92.5	100.0	97.1	99.0	99.3
Gold Production (1995=100)	66kr	105.7	100.9	97.8	100.0	....	....	....	....	....	....	....	....
Manufacturing Employment	67ey	82.9	82.5	84.2	85.8	87.8	91.0	94.0	96.0	100.0	100.0	100.7	100.4
						Number in Thousands: Period Averages							
Labor Force	67d	....	13,946	14,832	14,928	15,145	15,354	15,632	15,721	15,999	16,246	....	....
Employment	67e	12,842	13,015	13,292	†13,506	13,676	13,941	14,326	14,531	14,910	15,077	15,412	....
Unemployment	67c	1,640	1,649	1,541	†1,422	1,469	1,414	1,305	1,216	1,103	1,170	1,278	1,301
Unemployment Rate (%)	67r	11.3	11.2	10.4	†9.6	9.7	9.2	8.3	†7.6	6.8	7.2	....	7.6
International Transactions						*Millions of Canadian Dollars*							
Exports	70	162,596	187,346	225,908	263,697	274,884	296,928	317,903	354,108	410,994	402,172	396,020	381,655
Imports, f.o.b	71.v	152,435	175,049	206,626	224,977	232,672	271,422	298,076	319,008	354,728	343,311	348,198	334,331
						2000=100							
Volume of Exports	72	†47.6	53.4	59.8	65.8	69.8	†75.6	82.0	91.2	100.0	96.1	96.1	94.5
Volume of Imports	73	†48.5	53.0	58.9	63.5	66.9	†79.3	86.1	95.8	100.0	94.5	95.9	99.4
Unit Value of Exports	74	†75.6	79.1	84.7	91.4	92.0	†91.6	97.3	105.7	100.0	102.0	100.5	99.6
Unit Value of Imports	75	†80.9	85.3	90.7	94.1	93.7	†94.3	94.2	95.7	100.0	103.0	103.8	96.2

2004, International Monetary Fund : *International Financial Statistics Yearbook*

Canada 156

		1992	1993	1994	1995	1996	1997	1998	1999	2000	2001	2002	2003
Balance of Payments		\multicolumn{12}{c}{*Millions of US Dollars: Minus Sign Indicates Debit*}
Current Account, n.i.e.	78ald	−21,160	−21,822	−13,024	−4,328	3,378	−8,233	−7,839	1,765	19,622	16,209	14,447	17,268
Goods: Exports f.o.b.	78aad	135,153	147,418	166,990	193,373	205,443	219,063	220,539	248,494	289,022	271,803	263,754	285,794
Goods: Imports f.o.b.	78abd	−127,772	−137,281	−152,155	−167,517	−174,352	−200,498	−204,617	−220,203	−243,975	−226,528	−227,318	−244,281
Trade Balance	78acd	7,381	10,136	14,834	25,855	31,091	18,565	15,922	28,292	45,047	45,275	36,436	41,513
Services: Credit	78add	20,785	21,868	23,958	26,128	29,243	31,596	33,836	36,117	40,230	39,225	40,748	42,934
Services: Debit	78aed	−30,868	−32,446	−32,530	−33,473	−35,906	−38,013	−38,156	−40,573	−44,118	−43,880	−45,129	−50,661
Balance on Goods & Services	78afd	−2,702	−442	6,262	18,510	24,428	12,148	11,602	23,836	41,159	40,620	32,055	33,786
Income: Credit	78agd	11,413	10,697	15,443	18,888	19,204	23,998	21,830	22,158	24,746	16,742	19,881	23,500
Income: Debit	78ahd	−28,925	−31,499	−34,382	−41,609	−40,755	−44,878	−41,815	−44,777	−47,036	−42,181	−38,133	−40,238
Balance on Gds, Serv. & Inc.	78aid	−20,214	−21,243	−12,676	−4,211	2,877	−8,732	−8,383	1,216	18,868	15,181	13,803	17,047
Current Transfers, n.i.e.: Credit	78ajd	2,564	2,593	2,625	2,878	3,594	3,634	3,407	3,796	4,122	4,501	4,429	4,796
Current Transfers: Debit	78akd	−3,510	−3,172	−2,973	−2,995	−3,092	−3,135	−2,863	−3,247	−3,368	−3,473	−3,785	−4,575
Capital Account, n.i.e.	78bcd	7,105	8,292	7,498	4,950	5,833	5,429	3,336	3,400	3,581	3,741	3,177	2,836
Capital Account, n.i.e.: Credit	78bad	7,470	8,908	7,876	5,666	6,262	5,862	3,794	3,862	4,045	4,191	3,599	3,454
Capital Account: Debit	78bbd	−365	−617	−378	−716	−429	−433	−457	−462	−464	−451	−422	−618
Financial Account, n.i.e.	78bjd	6,244	19,505	5,159	−1,277	−9,277	3,394	4,944	−5,968	−14,500	−11,483	−11,606	−21,592
Direct Investment Abroad	78bdd	−3,547	−5,711	−9,303	−11,490	−13,107	−23,069	−34,112	−17,262	−44,487	−36,229	−26,461	−22,240
Dir. Invest. in Rep. Econ., n.i.e.	78bed	4,777	4,749	8,224	9,319	9,635	11,523	22,742	24,789	66,144	27,529	20,940	6,273
Portfolio Investment Assets	78bfd	−9,800	−13,784	−6,587	−5,328	−14,183	−8,568	−15,106	−15,579	−42,975	−24,374	−15,928	−9,139
Equity Securities	78bkd	−8,586	−9,886	−6,898	−4,570	−12,661	−3,777	−10,428	−13,910	−40,229	−23,120	−11,965	−3,467
Debt Securities	78bld	−1,214	−3,898	311	−759	−1,522	−4,792	−4,678	−1,669	−2,746	−1,254	−3,963	−5,672
Portfolio Investment Liab., n.i.e.	78bgd	20,506	41,352	17,155	18,402	13,718	11,692	16,590	2,653	10,259	24,631	13,365	13,160
Equity Securities	78bmd	830	9,334	4,718	−3,077	5,900	5,461	9,645	9,722	24,239	2,713	−914	9,546
Debt Securities	78bnd	19,676	32,018	12,437	21,479	7,818	6,230	6,945	−7,069	−13,980	21,918	14,279	3,614
Financial Derivatives Assets	78bwd	....	....	....	....	....	....	....	....	....	....	....	....
Financial Derivatives Liabilities	78bxd	....	....	....	....	....	....	....	....	....	....	....	....
Other Investment Assets	78bhd	−3,536	−415	−20,378	−8,328	−21,064	−16,167	9,400	10,235	−4,195	−10,544	−8,531	−20,555
Monetary Authorities	78bod	....	....	....	....	....	....	....	....	....	....	....	....
General Government	78bpd	−403	−230	−436	−336	−119	−515	−579	−305	−232	−131	−19	248
Banks	78bqd	−59	5,848	−12,575	−8,314	−13,847	−5,419	969	13,368	−7,301	−2,268	2,302	−15,347
Other Sectors	78brd	−3,074	−6,033	−7,366	322	−7,098	−10,233	9,010	−2,828	3,338	−8,145	−10,813	−5,456
Other Investment Liab., n.i.e.	78bid	−2,156	−6,686	16,049	−3,852	15,724	27,983	5,430	−10,804	754	7,506	5,009	10,910
Monetary Authorities	78bsd	−	−	−	−	−	−	−	−	−	−	−	−
General Government	78btd	−278	−179	586	−484	−508	−321	−270	−318	−350	−237	−126	−527
Banks	78bud	−3,202	−6,649	15,233	−4,579	12,707	24,630	953	−16,273	−626	15,314	8,527	12,532
Other Sectors	78bvd	1,324	142	230	1,211	3,525	3,673	4,747	5,788	1,730	−7,571	−3,392	−1,096
Net Errors and Omissions	78cad	3,025	−5,070	−26	3,366	5,563	−2,983	4,555	6,736	−4,984	−6,295	−6,204	−1,767
Overall Balance	78cbd	−4,786	904	−392	2,711	5,498	−2,393	4,996	5,933	3,720	2,172	−185	−3,255
Reserves and Related Items	79dad	4,786	−904	392	−2,711	−5,498	2,393	−4,996	−5,933	−3,720	−2,172	185	3,255
Reserve Assets	79dbd	4,786	−904	392	−2,711	−5,498	2,393	−4,996	−5,933	−3,720	−2,172	185	3,255
Use of Fund Credit and Loans	79dcd	−	−	−	−	−	−	−	−	−	−	−	−
Exceptional Financing	79ded	....	....	....	....	....	....	....	....	....	....	....	....
International Investment Position		\multicolumn{12}{c}{*Millions of US Dollars*}
Assets	79aad	234,853	246,426	282,944	324,692	371,736	419,480	448,443	497,023	551,469	577,406	622,538	708,662
Direct Investment Abroad	79abd	87,870	92,468	104,302	118,105	132,329	152,969	171,780	201,434	235,402	244,669	273,372	308,146
Portfolio Investment	79acd	45,380	53,200	59,601	66,487	79,054	91,222	102,845	124,558	141,516	151,030	164,052	182,272
Equity Securities	79add	35,204	39,982	46,543	52,700	63,529	72,619	81,118	103,263	118,289	127,755	138,756	149,545
Debt Securities	79aed	10,175	13,218	13,057	13,787	15,525	18,603	21,728	21,294	23,226	23,275	25,296	32,727
Financial Derivatives	79ald	−	−	−	−	−	−	−	−	−	−	−	−
Other Investment	79afd	89,696	88,007	106,564	124,885	139,761	157,305	150,351	142,298	142,686	148,219	149,492	182,907
Monetary Authorities	79agd	−	−	−	−	−	−	−	−	−	−	−	−
General Government	79ahd	15,341	14,966	15,419	15,656	15,868	16,759	18,716	20,835	21,983	22,857	23,396	23,525
Banks	79aid	43,015	37,279	49,976	60,268	73,657	76,024	74,550	61,364	68,306	70,262	68,053	87,892
Other Sectors	79ajd	31,339	35,762	41,170	48,961	50,236	64,522	57,084	60,099	52,397	55,100	58,043	71,490
Reserve Assets	79akd	11,908	12,751	12,476	15,216	20,591	17,984	23,467	28,732	31,866	33,488	35,622	35,338
Liabilities	79lad	469,385	490,942	520,374	562,156	599,081	622,564	644,239	665,852	682,677	696,340	739,003	868,027
Dir. Invest. in Rep. Economy	79lbd	108,503	106,868	110,204	123,181	132,978	135,944	143,344	174,990	205,033	209,491	221,188	276,793
Portfolio Investment	79lcd	234,585	266,961	281,767	309,774	323,661	321,742	334,129	336,824	324,502	324,590	343,468	390,635
Equity Securities	79ldd	14,083	17,685	22,001	27,170	34,537	35,968	42,041	47,856	57,999	46,545	46,643	60,942
Debt Securities	79led	220,502	249,276	259,766	282,604	289,125	285,774	292,088	288,968	266,502	278,045	296,825	329,694
Financial Derivatives	79lld	−	−	−	−	−	−	−	−	−	−	−	−
Other Investment	79lfd	126,297	117,113	128,403	129,201	142,442	164,879	166,766	154,038	153,142	162,259	174,347	200,599
Monetary Authorities	79lgd	−	−	−	−	−	−	−	−	−	−	−	−
General Government	79lhd	3,819	3,889	4,568	4,059	3,334	2,790	2,648	2,530	2,011	1,609	1,638	1,299
Banks	79lid	75,630	68,757	83,691	79,735	92,486	115,623	118,008	100,131	98,443	113,639	123,028	141,637
Other Sectors	79ljd	46,849	44,468	40,145	45,407	46,622	46,466	46,110	51,377	52,689	47,011	49,682	57,663

Canada 156

		1992	1993	1994	1995	1996	1997	1998	1999	2000	2001	2002	2003
Government Finance						*Billions of Canadian Dollars: Year Beginning April 1*							
Deficit (-) or Surplus	80	-42.68	-42.28	-36.70	-29.22	-15.55	5.33	3.10	9.14	13.39	14.38	....	....
Revenue	81	149.89	148.33	157.60	164.25	174.51	188.91	195.82	209.54	228.76	226.83	....	....
Grants Received	81z	.46	.54	.53	.52	.54	.52	.50	.56	.57	.61	....	....
Expenditure	82	191.39	191.20	196.04	199.90	190.91	186.95	193.92	201.68	213.48	212.61	....	....
Lending Minus Repayments	83	1.63	-.04	-1.20	-5.91	-.31	-2.85	-.70	-.72	2.46	.45	....	....
Financing													
Total Net Borrowing	84	38.64	43.76	35.59	40.04	19.43	-6.95	8.56	2.92	3.83	-15.55	....	....
Net Domestic	84a	44.66	47.55	42.91	29.10	22.10	-1.53	5.61	-12.75	-12.50	-20.44	....	....
Net Foreign	85a	-6.03	-3.79	-7.32	10.94	-2.67	-5.42	2.95	15.67	16.33	4.89	....	....
Use of Cash Balances	87	4.05	-1.48	1.11	-10.81	-3.88	1.63	-11.66	-12.05	-17.22	1.17	....	....
Total Debt	88z	514.36	557.60	595.88	634.94	651.12	645.73	648.39	648.21	644.90	629.09	....	....
Domestic	88a	506.39	544.60	577.02	616.22	626.32	616.73	610.73	614.22	610.25	600.69	....	....
Foreign	89a	7.97	13.00	18.86	18.71	24.81	28.99	37.65	33.99	34.65	28.41	....	....
National Accounts						*Billions of Canadian dollars*							
Househ.Cons.Expend.,incl.NPISHs	96f.c	412.94	430.16	447.75	462.87	482.37	512.86	534.39	561.57	594.09	623.17	656.18	689.42
Government Consumption Expend	91f.c	168.93	171.27	171.73	172.65	171.35	171.88	176.84	183.29	196.00	207.51	218.90	231.00
Gross Fixed Capital Formation	93e.c	131.23	131.07	144.96	143.00	149.94	174.84	181.62	193.83	209.94	219.85	227.19	237.19
Changes in Inventories	93i.c	-6.56	-.95	.45	8.91	2.34	8.18	5.79	3.91	8.00	-5.24	2.87	7.56
Exports of Goods and Services	90c.c	189.78	219.66	262.13	302.48	321.25	348.60	377.35	418.54	484.33	482.07	474.30	459.56
Imports of Goods and Services (-)	98c.c	192.39	219.67	253.01	276.62	287.55	331.27	360.26	386.03	428.93	418.81	423.99	409.99
Gross Domestic Product (GDP)	99b.c	700.48	727.18	770.87	810.43	836.86	882.73	914.97	982.44	1,075.57	1,107.46	1,154.95	1,214.60
Net Primary Income from Abroad	98.nc	-25.40	-25.17	-27.99	-28.55	-28.33	-27.70	-30.04	-29.51	-22.37	-29.61	-27.39	-25.06
Gross National Income (GNI)	99a.c	677.00	704.41	744.83	783.91	810.73	857.32	885.83	945.75	1,042.63	1,077.85	1,127.56	1,189.54
Gross Nat'l Disposable Inc.(GNDI)	99i.c	675.86	703.67	744.36	783.75	811.42	858.02	886.60	946.88	1,044.10	1,079.53	1,128.92	1,190.09
Gross Saving	99s.c	....	....	....	....	....	182.81	187.46	198.21	219.51	213.52	229.56	244.30
Consumption of Fixed Capital	99cfc	89.57	94.04	99.63	105.02	110.82	116.57	122.30	127.72	135.78	146.80	155.00	164.03
GDP Volume 1997 Ref., Chained	99b.r	755.85	773.53	810.70	833.46	846.95	882.73	918.91	969.75	1,020.79	1,040.39	1,074.52	1,092.89
GDP Volume (2000=100)	99bvr	74.0	75.8	79.4	81.6	83.0	86.5	90.0	95.0	100.0	101.9	105.3	107.1
GDP Deflator (2000=100)	99bir	88.0	89.2	90.2	92.3	93.8	94.9	94.5	96.1	100.0	101.0	102.0	105.5
						Millions: Midyear Estimates							
Population	99z	28.40	28.73	29.04	29.35	29.66	29.95	30.23	30.51	30.77	31.02	31.27	31.51

2004, International Monetary Fund : *International Financial Statistics Yearbook*

Cape Verde 624

		1992	1993	1994	1995	1996	1997	1998	1999	2000	2001	2002	2003
Exchange Rates						*Escudos per SDR: End of Period*							
Official Rate	aa	100.497	118.115	118.452	115.136	122.464	129.845	132.714	150.654	154.403	157.245	142.952	129.737
				Escudos per US Dollar: End of Period (ae) Period Average (rf)									
Official Rate	ae	73.089	85.992	81.140	77.455	85.165	96.235	94.255	109.765	118.506	125.122	105.149	87.308
Official Rate	rf	68.018	80.427	81.891	76.853	82.591	93.177	98.158	103.502	119.687	123.228	117.168	97.703
Fund Position						*Millions of SDRs: End of Period*							
Quota	2f.s	7.00	7.00	7.00	7.00	7.00	7.00	7.00	9.60	9.60	9.60	9.60	9.60
SDRs	1b.s	.05	.02	.05	.02	.04	.02	.04	.01	.04	.01	–	–
Reserve Position in the Fund	1c.s	–	–	–	–	–	–	–	–	–	–	–	–
Total Fund Cred.&Loans Outstg	2tl	–	–	–	–	–	–	–	–	–	–	2.46	4.92
International Liquidity					*Millions of US Dollars Unless Otherwise Indicated: End of Period*								
Total Reserves minus Gold	1l.d	75.76	57.69	42.08	36.89	27.57	19.32	8.32	42.62	28.26	45.43	79.80	93.61
SDRs	1b.d	.07	.03	.07	.03	.06	.03	.06	.02	.05	.02	–	–
Reserve Position in the Fund	1c.d	–	–	–	–	–	–	–	–	–	–	.01	.01
Foreign Exchange	1d.d	75.69	57.66	42.01	36.86	27.50	19.29	8.26	42.59	28.21	45.40	79.79	93.60
Monetary Authorities: Other Liab	4..d	2.90	.80	.60	6.47	3.51	2.60	.94	1.09	1.35	1.36	1.42	.97
Deposit Money Banks: Assets	7a.d	....	14.47	31.60	10.62	32.35	23.89	33.41	30.10	42.45	42.95	44.76	52.87
Liabilities	7b.d	....	2.47	3.38	6.32	5.73	9.95	11.16	15.21	16.41	14.08	19.09	25.75
Monetary Authorities						*Millions of Escudos: End of Period*							
Foreign Assets	11	5,536.9	4,999.9	3,483.1	†5,154.8	4,838.5	4,521.9	3,584.9	8,203.7	4,221.8	6,561.2	9,135.4	8,817.8
Claims on Central Government	12a	4,118.6	5,068.2	4,446.4	†4,964.4	4,315.8	6,001.6	5,615.2	5,865.2	9,209.4	9,024.0	9,469.0	9,977.4
Claims on Local Government	12b	68.8	27.6	–	†–	–	–	–	–	–	–	–	–
Claims on Nonfin.Pub.Enterprises	12c	3,694.1	2,136.9	119.7	†118.8	113.9	.1	–	86.8	82.3	82.3	72.3	72.3
Claims on Private Sector	12d	4,731.8	2,005.7	1,091.2	†1,099.4	2,049.4	1,151.9	1,142.7	1,100.8	1,074.9	1,106.3	1,111.9	1,107.1
Claims on Deposit Money Banks	12e	–	612.8	592.1	†632.7	630.3	519.8	361.6	331.4	1,098.9	438.4	274.5	409.8
Claims on Other Banking Insts	12f	301.4	–	–	†–	–	–	–	–	–	–	–	–
Claims on Nonbank Financial Insts	12g	....	....	....	–	–	–	–	5.5	5.5	–	–	–
Reserve Money	14	9,906.6	14,205.4	8,685.9	†10,655.6	9,982.8	10,035.2	10,971.4	11,701.4	13,552.2	14,580.5	16,812.2	17,288.5
of which: Currency Outside DMBs	14a	3,191.3	3,549.4	3,929.7	†4,635.1	4,513.0	4,853.6	5,059.8	6,026.1	6,458.2	6,702.9	6,459.3	6,515.6
Time & Foreign Currency Deposits	15	6,730.7	–	173.9	†101.4	–	–	–	–	–	–	–	32.8
Foreign Liabilities	16c	211.8	69.2	48.7	†500.9	298.8	249.8	88.8	119.7	159.6	170.0	500.7	722.9
Central Government Deposits	16d	803.9	–	–	†245.9	230.8	944.7	516.6	2,446.1	607.7	675.1	1,199.7	948.5
Capital Accounts	17a	3,002.9	2,190.4	2,069.3	†2,338.7	2,739.2	3,114.5	3,051.5	2,376.6	2,917.5	2,999.7	2,447.4	2,483.4
Other Items (Net)	17r	–2,204.3	–1,613.9	–1,245.3	†–1,872.4	–1,303.7	–2,149.0	–3,918.4	–1,050.4	–1,549.7	–1,213.1	–896.9	–1,026.2
Deposit Money Banks						*Millions of Escudos: End of Period*							
Reserves	20	....	10,604.3	4,803.9	†5,987.1	5,472.5	5,701.4	5,820.3	5,648.0	7,111.0	7,869.1	9,760.4	10,796.5
Foreign Assets	21	....	1,244.4	2,563.7	†822.3	2,754.7	2,299.1	3,149.0	3,303.5	5,031.1	5,373.5	4,706.1	4,615.9
Claims on Central Government	22a	....	–	6,046.7	†7,557.0	8,944.3	10,357.8	10,347.4	10,036.0	14,472.6	14,961.6	17,677.1	18,157.5
Claims on Local Government	22b	....	48.7	76.2	†97.1	109.1	.2	10.7	238.0	289.3	260.9	266.4	239.3
Claims on Nonfin.Pub.Enterprises	22c	....	433.9	432.7	†545.0	378.5	24.2	21.4	425.3	73.3	132.9	157.8	107.6
Claims on Private Sector	22d	....	5,495.8	6,473.9	†9,292.1	10,159.8	13,540.5	15,308.7	17,289.2	18,252.2	21,099.2	23,778.0	27,619.1
Claims on Nonbank Financial Insts	22g	....	....	....	–	–	–	–	–	–	7.0	5.5	3.9
Demand Deposits	24	....	7,049.3	7,542.3	†7,232.4	8,609.7	11,106.4	10,573.4	12,216.4	13,966.4	14,247.6	16,337.9	16,574.9
Time, Savings,& Fgn.Currency Dep	25	....	9,039.4	10,394.4	†12,974.5	14,251.9	14,386.0	15,557.7	17,494.4	20,301.7	23,826.3	28,050.8	32,342.0
Restricted Deposits	26b	....	300.9	203.8	†257.6	491.7	398.1	710.0	242.6	502.8	210.4	187.4	192.5
Foreign Liabilities	26c	....	212.8	274.3	†489.7	488.3	957.1	1,051.5	1,669.6	1,944.8	1,761.9	2,007.4	2,248.1
Central Government Deposits	26d	....	847.8	1,035.7	†2,401.0	2,539.4	2,038.2	2,100.4	1,165.9	1,324.8	1,621.4	1,164.0	1,693.0
Counterpart Funds	26e	....	....	....	–	–	2.0	3.4	–	–	–	–	–
Credit from Monetary Authorities	26g	....	612.8	592.1	†573.5	551.4	519.8	361.6	331.4	1,098.9	438.4	274.5	409.8
Liab. to Nonbank Financial Insts	26j	....	3.4	20.3	†181.1	298.7	125.6	36.2	306.0	257.0	276.3	188.4	184.6
Capital Accounts	27a	....	1,292.9	1,638.8	†2,833.5	3,433.6	4,426.3	5,365.6	5,954.5	7,007.2	7,903.9	8,340.4	8,871.8
Other Items (Net)	27r	....	–1,532.2	–1,304.6	†–2,642.8	–2,845.9	–2,036.3	–1,102.3	–2,440.8	–1,174.1	–582.0	–199.5	–976.9
Monetary Survey						*Millions of Escudos: End of Period*							
Foreign Assets (Net)	31n	5,325.1	5,962.3	5,723.8	†4,986.5	6,806.0	5,614.0	5,593.6	9,717.9	7,148.5	10,002.8	11,333.5	10,462.7
Domestic Credit	32	12,110.8	14,369.0	17,651.1	†21,026.9	23,300.6	28,093.4	29,834.6	31,434.8	41,521.5	44,377.7	50,174.3	54,675.5
Claims on Central Govt. (Net)	32an	3,314.7	4,220.4	9,457.4	†9,874.5	10,489.9	13,376.5	13,345.6	12,289.2	21,749.5	21,689.1	24,782.4	25,493.4
Claims on Local Government	32b	68.8	76.3	76.2	†97.1	109.1	.2	10.7	238.0	289.3	260.9	266.4	239.3
Claims on Nonfin.Pub.Enterprises	32c	3,694.1	2,570.8	552.4	†663.8	492.4	24.3	21.4	512.1	155.6	215.2	230.1	179.9
Claims on Private Sector	32d	4,731.8	7,501.5	7,565.1	†10,391.5	12,209.2	14,692.4	16,451.4	18,390.0	19,327.1	22,205.5	24,889.9	28,726.2
Claims on Other Banking Insts	32f	301.4	–	–	†–	–	–	–	–	–	–	–	–
Claims on Nonbank Financial Inst	32g	....	....	....	–	–	–	–	5.5	5.5	–	7.0	5.5	36.7
Money	34	9,906.6	10,598.7	11,472.0	†11,867.5	13,122.7	15,960.0	15,633.2	18,332.6	20,425.3	20,951.3	22,798.3	23,090.9
Quasi-Money	35	6,730.7	9,039.4	10,568.3	†13,075.9	14,251.9	14,386.0	15,557.7	17,494.4	20,301.7	23,826.3	28,050.8	32,342.0
Restricted Deposits	36b	142.5	300.9	203.8	†257.6	491.7	398.1	710.0	242.6	502.8	210.4	187.4	192.5
Counterpart Funds	36e	....	....	....	–	–	2.0	3.4	–	–	–	–	–
Liab. to Nonbank Financial Insts	36j	....	3.4	20.3	†181.1	298.7	125.6	36.2	306.0	257.0	276.3	188.4	184.6
Capital Accounts	37a	3,002.9	3,483.3	3,708.1	†5,172.2	6,172.8	7,540.8	8,417.1	8,331.1	9,924.7	10,903.6	10,787.8	11,355.2
Other Items (Net)	37r	–2,346.8	–3,094.4	–2,597.6	†–4,541.0	–4,231.2	–4,705.1	–4,929.4	–3,554.0	–2,741.5	–1,787.4	–505.0	–2,027.1
Money plus Quasi-Money	35l	16,637.3	19,638.1	22,040.3	†24,943.4	27,374.6	30,346.0	31,190.9	35,827.0	40,727.0	44,777.6	50,849.1	55,432.9

Cape Verde 624

		1992	1993	1994	1995	1996	1997	1998	1999	2000	2001	2002	2003
Other Banking Institutions					*Millions of Escudos: End of Period*								
Cash	40	74.6	....	....	....	....	....	....	....	....	....	....	....
Foreign Assets	41	.2	....	....	....	....	....	....	....	....	....	....	....
Claims on Private Sector	42d	1,126.4	....	....	....	....	....	....	....	....	....	....	....
Time, Savings,& Fgn.Currency Dep.	45	623.8	....	....	....	....	....	....	....	....	....	....	....
Credit from Monetary Authorities	46g	301.4	....	....	....	....	....	....	....	....	....	....	....
Capital Accounts	47a	–	....	....	....	....	....	....	....	....	....	....	....
Other Items (Net)	47r	276.0	....	....	....	....	....	....	....	....	....	....	....
Banking Survey					*Millions of Escudos: End of Period*								
Foreign Assets (Net)	51n	5,325.3	....	....	....	....	....	....	....	....	....	....	....
Domestic Credit	52	12,935.8	....	....	....	....	....	....	....	....	....	....	....
Claims on Central Govt. (Net)	52an	3,314.7	....	....	....	....	....	....	....	....	....	....	....
Claims on Local Government	52b	68.8	....	....	....	....	....	....	....	....	....	....	....
Claims on Nonfin.Pub.Enterprises	52c	3,694.1	....	....	....	....	....	....	....	....	....	....	....
Claims on Private Sector	52d	5,858.2	....	....	....	....	....	....	....	....	....	....	....
Liquid Liabilities	55l	17,186.5	....	....	....	....	....	....	....	....	....	....	....
Restricted Deposits	56b	142.5	....	....	....	....	....	....	....	....	....	....	....
Capital Accounts	57a	3,002.9	....	....	....	....	....	....	....	....	....	....	....
Other Items (Net)	57r	–2,070.8	....	....	....	....	....	....	....	....	....	....	....
Interest Rates							*Percent Per Annum*							
Deposit Rate	60l	4.00	4.00	4.00	†5.00	5.00	5.04	5.27	4.76	4.34	4.67	4.86	3.93
Lending Rate	60p	10.00	10.00	10.67	12.00	12.00	12.06	12.51	12.03	11.94	12.85	13.17	12.73
Prices and Labor					*Index Numbers (2000=100): Period Averages*								
Consumer Prices	64	†69	73	75	82	87	94	98	103	100	103	105	....
International Transactions						*Millions of Escudos*								
Exports	70	301	312	355	640	1,046	1,309	1,024	1,185	1,272	1,212	....	....
Imports, c.i.f.	71	12,234	12,387	17,113	19,394	19,355	21,936	22,395	25,484	27,517	28,694	....	....
Balance of Payments					*Millions of US Dollars: Minus Sign Indicates Debit*								
Current Account, n.i.e	78ald	–12.15	–23.93	–45.73	–61.62	–35.04	–29.72	–58.51	–74.18	–58.03	–55.73	–71.52	–77.25
Goods: Exports f.o.b	78aad	11.39	9.05	14.16	16.58	23.88	43.24	32.69	26.03	38.30	37.17	41.76	52.83
Goods: Imports f.o.b	78abd	–168.50	–151.95	–195.26	–233.63	–207.52	–215.10	–218.81	–239.03	–225.66	–231.52	–278.02	–343.95
Trade Balance	78acd	–157.12	–142.90	–181.10	–217.05	–183.64	–171.87	–186.13	–213.00	–187.36	–194.35	–236.26	–291.11
Services: Credit	78add	39.31	40.09	47.01	66.90	77.52	91.31	86.45	105.06	107.58	129.68	152.83	224.08
Services: Debit	78aed	–25.34	–29.39	–34.52	–60.50	–70.03	–71.90	–90.59	–115.82	–100.24	–119.01	–142.08	–203.25
Balance on Goods & Services	78afd	–143.14	–132.20	–168.61	–210.65	–176.15	–152.46	–190.27	–223.76	–180.01	–183.68	–225.51	–270.29
Income: Credit	78agd	5.68	4.81	4.22	4.00	2.98	4.87	2.51	1.90	5.03	7.53	6.41	13.14
Income: Debit	78ahd	–4.40	–3.85	–4.56	–6.57	–7.38	–8.46	–8.07	–10.41	–17.67	–12.66	–18.26	–29.79
Balance on Gds, Serv. & Inc	78aid	–141.86	–131.24	–168.95	–213.22	–180.55	–156.05	–195.83	–232.27	–192.66	–188.81	–237.36	–286.93
Current Transfers, n.i.e.: Credit	78ajd	133.81	110.41	125.55	155.96	148.38	129.91	142.46	167.12	146.28	155.55	181.57	228.99
Current Transfers: Debit	78akd	–4.09	–3.11	–2.33	–4.36	–2.87	–3.58	–5.15	–9.04	–11.66	–22.47	–15.73	–19.30
Capital Account, n.i.e	78bcd	9.17	19.02	20.07	20.88	12.83	6.30	19.01	4.47	10.76	24.36	8.64	21.07
Capital Account, n.i.e.: Credit	78bad	9.17	19.02	20.07	20.88	12.83	6.30	19.01	4.47	10.76	24.36	8.64	21.09
Capital Account: Debit	78bbd	–	–	–	–	–	–	....	....	....	....	....	–.02
Financial Account, n.i.e	78bjd	16.82	17.52	39.60	44.51	46.00	44.06	36.99	127.77	31.53	38.53	80.67	5.55
Direct Investment Abroad	78bdd	–1.20	–.66	–.42	–.57	–.26	–.05	....	–.42	–1.36	–.52	....	....
Dir. Invest. in Rep. Econ., n.i.e	78bed	.45	3.64	2.13	26.18	28.53	11.58	9.04	53.32	33.42	9.11	14.81	14.78
Portfolio Investment Assets	78bfd	....	....	....	....	....	....	....	....	–.12	1.45	....	....
Equity Securities	78bkd	–	....	....	....	....	....	....	....	....	1.56	....	....
Debt Securities	78bld	–	....	....	....	....	....	....	....	–.12	–.11	....	....
Portfolio Investment Liab., n.i.e	78bgd	–	....	....	....	....	....	....	2.98	....	....	....	....
Equity Securities	78bmd	–	....	....	....	....	....	....	2.98	....	....	....	....
Debt Securities	78bnd	–	....	....	....	....	....	....	....	....	....	....	....
Financial Derivatives Assets	78bwd	....	....	....	....	....	....	....	....	....	....	....	....
Financial Derivatives Liabilities	78bxd	....	....	....	....	....	....	....	....	....	....	....	....
Other Investment Assets	78bhd	.57	–6.75	1.61	–1.67	–2.25	–1.79	–22.44	–13.91	–22.01	–3.30	–2.02	–7.24
Monetary Authorities	78bod	.57	–6.75	1.61	2.32	–2.34	–1.84	4.02	5.19	....	–.10	–.07	1.01
General Government	78bpd	–	–	–	....	....	....	–28.39	–18.54	–21.33	....	....	–4.29
Banks	78bqd	–	–	–	–3.99	.09	.05	3.02	–.05	–.68	–1.64	–1.95	–3.95
Other Sectors	78brd	–	–	–	....	....	....	–1.09	–.51	....	–1.56	....	....
Other Investment Liab., n.i.e	78bid	17.01	21.29	36.28	20.57	19.99	34.33	50.39	85.79	21.60	31.79	67.89	–2.00
Monetary Authorities	78bsd	.68	.88	–1.21	–.93	–.12	–.12	–.01	.17	....	.03	2.97	....
General Government	78btd	18.16	19.69	22.74	17.57	22.88	19.79	28.49	42.98	9.68	2.98	9.58	–21.89
Banks	78bud	–	2.65	1.11	2.38	.02	4.94	8.00	27.18	18.83	26.93	35.96	33.10
Other Sectors	78bvd	–1.84	–1.93	13.64	1.55	–2.80	9.72	13.91	15.45	–6.91	1.85	19.37	–13.21
Net Errors and Omissions	78cad	8.71	2.38	8.31	–35.64	–1.34	–20.40	13.28	–8.74	–12.03	–23.91	–7.67	–5.35
Overall Balance	78cbd	22.55	14.99	22.24	–31.87	22.46	.24	10.76	49.31	–27.77	–16.74	10.13	–55.98
Reserves and Related Items	79dad	–22.55	–14.99	–22.24	31.87	–22.46	–.24	–10.76	–49.31	27.77	16.74	–10.13	55.98
Reserve Assets	79dbd	–18.46	–11.50	–20.78	30.93	–19.76	9.84	–8.50	–41.86	10.27	23.37	.17	9.92
Use of Fund Credit and Loans	79dcd	–	–	–	–	–	–	–	–	–	–	3.19	3.52
Exceptional Financing	79ded	–4.09	–3.49	–1.46	.95	–2.70	–10.08	–2.26	–7.45	17.49	–6.63	–13.49	42.54

2004, International Monetary Fund : *International Financial Statistics Yearbook*

Cape Verde 624

		1992	1993	1994	1995	1996	1997	1998	1999	2000	2001	2002	2003
National Accounts						*Millions of Escudos*							
GDP Volume 1980 Prices	99b.p	9,954	10,682	11,422	12,278	....	....	....	....	....	....	....	....
GDP Volume (1995=100)	99bvp	81.1	87.0	93.0	100.0	....	....	....	....	....	....	....	....
						Millions: Midyear Estimates							
Population	99z	.37	.37	.38	.39	.40	.41	.42	.43	.44	.44	.45	.46

CEMAC 758

		1992	1993	1994	1995	1996	1997	1998	1999	2000	2001	2002	2003
Exchange Rates						*Francs per SDR: End of Period*							
Official Rate	aa	378.57	404.89	†780.44	728.38	753.06	807.94	791.61	†896.19	918.49	935.39	850.37	771.76
					Francs per US Dollar: End of Period (ae) Period Average (rf)								
Official Rate	ae	275.32	294.77	†534.60	490.00	523.70	598.81	562.21	†652.95	704.95	744.31	625.50	519.36
Official Rate	rf	264.69	283.16	†555.20	499.15	511.55	583.67	589.95	†615.70	711.98	733.04	696.99	581.20
Fund Position						*Millions of SDRs: End of Period*							
Quota	2f.s	410.10	410.10	410.10	410.10	410.10	410.10	410.10	568.90	568.90	568.90	568.90	568.90
SDRs	1b.s	5.93	1.02	1.13	1.35	.35	.08	.24	6.50	6.19	5.26	4.13	2.32
Reserve Position in the Fund	1c.s	1.17	1.23	1.23	1.28	1.35	1.39	1.43	1.52	1.59	1.65	1.70	1.80
Total Fund Cred.&Loans Outstg.	2tl	160.92	101.37	176.40	181.00	236.12	259.81	281.17	299.45	360.80	381.52	403.55	387.88
International Liquidity						*Millions of US Dollars Unless Otherwise Indicated: End of Period*							
Total Reserves minus Gold	1l.d	....	....	....	....	....	....	....	....	1,256.72	1,079.10	1,600.67	1,812.80
SDRs	1b.d	8.15	1.40	1.64	2.01	.51	.11	.33	8.93	8.06	6.61	5.62	3.45
Reserve Position in the Fund	1c.d	1.61	1.69	1.80	1.91	1.94	1.87	2.01	2.09	2.07	2.07	2.31	2.68
Foreign Exchange	1d.d	....	....	....	....	....	....	....	....	1,246.59	1,070.41	1,592.75	1,806.67
Gold (Million Fine Troy Ounces)	1ad	....	....	....	.229	.229	.229	.229	.229	.229	.229	.229	.229
Gold (National Valuation)	1and	....	....	....	†87.89	83.93	66.29	65.59	†66.23	62.21	63.61	78.40	95.59
Monetary Authorities: Other Liab.	4..d	....	....	....	....	....	....	....	....	.49	.49	.56	.61
Deposit Money Banks: Assets	7a.d	....	....	....	....	....	....	....	....	.44	.30	.53	.53
Liabilities	7b.d	....	....	....	....	....	....	....	....	.13	.15	.28	.28
Monetary Authorities						*Billions of Francs: End of Period*							
Foreign Assets	11	....	....	....	....	....	....	....	....	929.77	849.75	1,049.72	991.10
Claims on Central Government	12a	....	....	....	....	....	....	....	....	864.55	1,070.37	1,090.21	1,037.75
Claims on Deposit Money Banks	12e	....	....	....	....	....	....	....	....	11.43	12.34	12.84	12.86
Claims on Other Banking Insts.	12f	....	....	....	....	....	....	....	....	4.00	3.00	—	—
Reserve Money	14	....	....	....	....	....	....	....	....	1,054.43	1,113.04	1,271.89	1,288.55
of which: Currency Outside DMBs	14a	....	....	....	....	....	....	....	....	690.21	760.84	814.94	770.56
Foreign Liabilities	16c	....	....	....	....	....	....	....	....	342.03	365.31	353.04	315.71
Central Government Deposits	16d	....	....	....	....	....	....	....	....	245.77	274.38	337.84	268.43
Capital Accounts	17a	....	....	....	....	....	....	....	....	229.01	235.80	233.13	232.73
Other Items (Net)	17r	....	....	....	....	....	....	....	....	−61.49	−53.06	−43.14	−63.71
Deposit Money Banks						*Billions of Francs: End of Period*							
Reserves	20	....	....	....	....	....	....	....	....	344.42	331.88	437.54	492.77
Foreign Assets	21	....	....	....	....	....	....	....	....	311.88	224.25	333.37	274.16
Claims on Central Government	22a	....	....	....	....	....	....	....	....	293.33	288.30	308.11	283.71
Claims on Nonfin.Pub.Enterprises	22c	....	....	....	....	....	....	....	....	144.46	141.79	135.29	150.33
Claims on Private Sector	22d	....	....	....	....	....	....	....	....	1,101.02	1,198.05	1,309.97	1,389.40
Claims on Other Banking Insts.	22f	....	....	....	....	....	....	....	....	.82	.64	.65	.59
Claims on Nonbank Financial Insts.	22g	....	....	....	....	....	....	....	....	29.95	30.37	37.69	33.55
Demand Deposits	24	....	....	....	....	....	....	....	....	807.44	776.84	944.44	928.62
Time and Savings Deposits	25	....	....	....	....	....	....	....	....	633.03	729.59	849.46	948.82
Bonds	26ab	....	....	....	....	....	....	....	....	2.65	2.25	1.85	1.34
Foreign Liabilities	26c	....	....	....	....	....	....	....	....	86.86	107.35	166.65	124.77
Long-Term Foreign Liabilities	26cl	....	....	....	....	....	....	....	....	8.04	5.90	10.70	22.92
Central Government Deposits	26d	....	....	....	....	....	....	....	....	301.53	257.65	303.63	249.50
Credit from Monetary Authorities	26g	....	....	....	....	....	....	....	....	11.43	12.34	12.84	12.86
Capital Accounts	27a	....	....	....	....	....	....	....	....	383.06	385.38	390.82	430.38
Other Items (Net)	27r	....	....	....	....	....	....	....	....	−8.16	−62.01	−117.77	−94.70
Monetary Survey						*Billions of Francs: End of Period*							
Foreign Assets (Net)	31n	....	....	....	....	....	....	....	....	804.72	595.44	852.70	801.85
Domestic Credit	32	....	....	....	....	....	....	....	....	1,891.26	2,200.56	2,240.44	2,377.40
Claims on Central Govt. (Net)	32an	....	....	....	....	....	....	....	....	610.57	826.64	756.84	803.53
Claims on Nonfin.Pub.Enterprises	32c	....	....	....	....	....	....	....	....	144.46	141.79	135.29	150.33
Claims on Private Sector	32d	....	....	....	....	....	....	....	....	1,101.02	1,198.05	1,309.97	1,389.40
Claims on Other Banking Insts.	32f	....	....	....	....	....	....	....	....	4.82	3.64	.65	.59
Claims on Nonbank Financial Inst.	32g	....	....	....	....	....	....	....	....	30.38	30.44	37.69	33.55
Money	34	....	....	....	....	....	....	....	....	1,517.45	1,558.00	1,778.79	1,724.41
Quasi-Money	35	....	....	....	....	....	....	....	....	633.03	729.59	849.46	948.82
Bonds	36ab	....	....	....	....	....	....	....	....	2.65	2.25	1.85	1.34
Other Items (Net)	37r	....	....	....	....	....	....	....	....	542.84	506.17	463.04	504.69
Money plus Quasi-Money	35l	....	....	....	....	....	....	....	....	2,150.48	2,287.59	2,628.25	2,673.23
Interest Rates						*Percent Per Annum*							
Discount Rate (End of Period)	60	12.00	11.50	†7.75	8.60	7.75	7.50	7.00	7.30	7.00	6.50	6.30	6.00
Deposit Rate	60l	7.50	7.75	5.50	5.50	5.00	5.00	5.00	5.00	5.00	5.00	5.00	5.00
Lending Rate	60p	17.50	17.50	16.00	16.00	22.00	22.00	22.00	22.00	22.00	18.00	18.00	18.00

Central African Rep. 626

		1992	1993	1994	1995	1996	1997	1998	1999	2000	2001	2002	2003
Exchange Rates						*Francs per SDR: End of Period*							
Official Rate	aa	378.57	404.89	†780.44	728.38	753.06	807.94	791.61	†896.19	918.49	935.39	850.37	771.76
					Francs per US Dollar: End of Period (ae) Period Average (rf)								
Official Rate	ae	275.32	294.77	†534.60	490.00	523.70	598.81	562.21	†652.95	704.95	744.31	625.50	519.36
Official Rate	rf	264.69	283.16	†555.20	499.15	511.55	583.67	589.95	†615.70	711.98	733.04	696.99	581.20
					Index Numbers (2000=100): Period Averages								
Official Rate	ahx	268.8	250.9	128.1	142.3	138.8	121.8	120.5	115.5	100.0	96.9	102.2	122.4
Nominal Effective Exchange Rate	nec	126.4	139.8	87.7	94.9	99.6	99.1	100.2	99.9	100.0	105.3	108.9	113.5
Real Effective Exchange Rate	rec	161.7	151.6	95.0	112.1	114.5	110.9	108.1	102.4	100.0	103.3	107.0	114.4
Fund Position						*Millions of SDRs: End of Period*							
Quota	2f.s	41.20	41.20	41.20	41.20	41.20	41.20	41.20	55.70	55.70	55.70	55.70	55.70
SDRs	1b.s	.04	.03	.01	.02	.01	–	.01	.04	–	.01	.01	.01
Reserve Position in the Fund	1c.s	.09	.09	.09	.09	.10	.10	.10	.10	.11	.11	.12	.16
Total Fund Cred.&Loans Outstg.	2tl	22.09	20.96	28.34	23.48	19.22	13.80	12.47	17.09	16.48	24.48	24.48	24.48
International Liquidity					*Millions of US Dollars Unless Otherwise Indicated: End of Period*								
Total Reserves minus Gold	1l.d	100.12	111.98	210.01	233.64	232.24	178.56	145.70	136.28	133.26	118.75	123.24	132.41
SDRs	1b.d	.06	.04	.01	.02	.01	–	.01	.05	–	.01	.01	.01
Reserve Position in the Fund	1c.d	.12	.13	.14	.14	.14	.13	.13	.13	.15	.14	.16	.24
Foreign Exchange	1d.d	99.94	111.81	209.86	233.48	232.09	178.43	145.56	136.10	133.11	118.60	123.06	132.17
Gold (Million Fine Troy Ounces)	1ad	.011	.011	.011	.011	.011	.011	.011	.011	.011	.011	.011	.011
Gold (National Valuation)	1and	3.70	4.42	†4.21	4.29	4.10	3.24	3.20	†3.23	3.03	3.09	3.81	4.65
Monetary Authorities: Other Liab.	4..d	21.20	12.45	12.57	12.79	12.43	11.87	12.90	17.24	16.36	16.85	17.14	18.64
Deposit Money Banks: Assets	7a.d	9.12	6.85	11.45	6.39	4.41	4.99	5.91	10.48	7.96	4.52	5.84	6.33
Liabilities	7b.d	14.34	12.04	12.10	7.93	7.35	6.36	7.43	8.81	9.39	8.10	9.64	15.10
Monetary Authorities						*Billions of Francs: End of Period*							
Foreign Assets	11	28.59	34.29	114.56	116.59	123.77	108.86	83.71	91.10	96.08	90.69	79.47	71.19
Claims on Central Government	12a	28.23	28.34	41.99	36.97	37.69	32.76	32.28	37.86	41.62	44.43	46.54	47.48
Claims on Deposit Money Banks	12e	2.18	3.66	–	1.60	1.24	.50	5.00	4.79	3.14	2.25	3.34	1.82
Claims on Other Banking Insts.	12f	–	–	–	–	–	–	–	–	–	–	–	–
Reserve Money	14	43.80	52.46	96.65	101.04	108.82	95.35	76.11	81.96	89.59	84.01	78.96	72.64
of which: Currency Outside DMBs	14a	43.36	52.16	88.53	98.97	104.00	92.96	75.25	81.12	88.62	82.57	77.43	70.37
Foreign Liabilities	16c	14.20	12.16	28.84	23.37	20.98	18.25	17.13	26.57	26.67	35.44	31.54	28.58
Central Government Deposits	16d	.63	1.69	1.89	1.58	2.82	1.36	.91	3.45	2.36	6.00	.85	.87
Capital Accounts	17a	.99	1.27	1.01	.83	.90	.65	.64	.97	1.32	1.72	1.58	1.74
Other Items (Net)	17r	–.62	–1.28	28.16	28.35	29.18	26.51	26.20	20.81	20.90	10.21	16.43	16.66
Deposit Money Banks						*Billions of Francs: End of Period*							
Reserves	20	.44	.30	8.11	2.07	4.82	2.38	.86	.84	.96	1.44	1.53	2.27
Foreign Assets	21	2.51	2.02	6.12	3.13	2.31	2.99	3.32	6.84	5.61	3.37	3.66	3.29
Claims on Central Government	22a	†4.22	5.21	5.07	4.35	3.33	4.47	3.50	3.96	10.68	11.79	8.32	8.06
Claims on Nonfin.Pub.Enterprises	22c	4.25	4.54	5.84	7.65	7.14	6.37	7.97	14.71	7.99	7.95	8.06	8.44
Claims on Private Sector	22d	16.85	15.93	18.70	23.16	23.25	24.17	27.95	27.77	30.90	34.52	41.32	40.98
Claims on Other Banking Insts.	22f	–	–	–	–	–	–	–	–	–	–	–	–
Claims on Nonbank Financial Insts.	22g	–	–	–	–	–	–	–	.92	.02	–	–	–
Demand Deposits	24	7.68	7.26	14.86	12.27	12.64	14.22	12.33	17.53	13.21	16.58	17.31	15.06
Time and Savings Deposits	25	6.20	5.16	11.89	8.98	9.42	9.14	9.97	9.69	9.08	10.54	10.19	11.08
Foreign Liabilities	26c	3.53	3.18	5.80	3.45	3.43	3.45	3.52	5.66	6.61	6.03	5.78	6.15
Long-Term Foreign Liabilities	26cl	.42	.37	.66	.44	.42	.36	.66	.10	.01	.01	.25	1.69
Central Government Deposits	26d	†2.41	1.98	3.55	7.22	7.77	7.04	4.73	6.25	10.44	5.82	6.86	4.93
Credit from Monetary Authorities	26g	2.18	3.66	–	1.60	1.24	.50	5.00	4.79	3.14	2.25	3.34	1.82
Capital Accounts	27a	8.01	8.10	8.70	9.35	7.78	7.44	8.20	13.35	15.49	18.92	22.42	22.21
Other Items (Net)	27r	†–2.15	–1.71	–1.62	–2.94	–1.85	–1.77	–.79	–2.31	–1.82	–1.08	–3.25	.09
Monetary Survey						*Billions of Francs: End of Period*							
Foreign Assets (Net)	31n	12.95	20.60	85.38	92.47	101.25	89.79	65.73	65.62	68.40	52.58	45.55	38.05
Domestic Credit	32	†50.52	50.35	66.15	63.33	60.82	59.38	66.06	75.53	78.41	86.88	96.55	99.16
Claims on Central Govt. (Net)	32an	†29.41	29.88	41.61	32.52	30.44	28.84	30.14	32.13	39.51	44.41	47.16	49.74
Claims on Nonfin.Pub.Enterprises	32c	4.25	4.54	5.84	7.65	7.14	6.37	7.97	14.71	7.99	7.95	8.06	8.44
Claims on Private Sector	32d	16.85	15.93	18.70	23.16	23.25	24.17	27.95	27.77	30.90	34.52	41.32	40.98
Claims on Other Banking Insts.	32f	–	–	–	–	–	–	–	–	–	–	–	–
Claims on Nonbank Financial Inst.	32g	–	–	–	–	–	–	–	.92	.02	–	–	–
Money	34	51.05	59.42	103.40	111.24	116.64	107.19	87.58	98.64	101.83	99.15	94.74	85.44
Quasi-Money	35	6.20	5.16	11.89	8.98	9.42	9.14	9.97	9.69	9.08	10.54	10.19	11.08
Other Items (Net)	37r	†6.23	6.38	36.25	35.58	36.00	32.84	34.25	32.81	35.90	29.77	37.17	40.70
Money plus Quasi-Money	35l	57.24	64.58	115.29	120.22	126.07	116.33	97.54	108.34	110.91	109.69	104.93	96.51
Interest Rates						*Percent Per Annum*							
Discount Rate (End of Period)	60	12.00	11.50	†7.75	8.60	7.75	7.50	7.00	7.60	7.00	6.50	6.30	6.00
Deposit Rate	60l	7.50	7.75	8.08	5.50	5.46	5.00	5.00	5.00	5.00	5.00	5.00	5.00
Lending Rate	60p	17.77	17.46	17.50	16.00	22.00	22.00	22.00	22.00	22.00	20.67	18.00	18.00

Central African Rep. 626

		1992	1993	1994	1995	1996	1997	1998	1999	2000	2001	2002	2003
Prices and Labor					*Index Numbers (2000=100): Period Averages*								
Wholesale Prices..................	63	61.2	60.2	....	....	....	92.9	92.9	94.0	100.0	....	....	....
Consumer Prices..................	64	65.9	64.0	79.7	95.0	98.6	100.2	98.3	96.9	100.0	103.4	106.9	110.2
					Number in Thousands: Period Averages								
Employment.........................	67e	14	....	....	....	....	....	....	....	....	....	....	....
Unemployment......................	67c	6	6	10	8	....	....	....	....	....	....	....	....
International Transactions						*Millions of Francs*							
Exports................................	70	28,328	31,079	83,900	85,300	75,100	94,850	89,309	90,136	114,414	104,299	102,292	....
Imports, c.i.f........................	71	38,469	35,559	77,300	86,900	72,300	82,039	86,375	80,689	83,290	78,464	83,795	....
Balance of Payments					*Millions of US Dollars: Minus Sign Indicates Debit*								
Current Account, n.i.e............	78ald	−83.1	−13.0	−24.7	....	....	....	....	....	....	....	....	....
Goods: Exports f.o.b..............	78aad	115.9	132.5	145.9	....	....	....	....	....	....	....	....	....
Goods: Imports f.o.b.............	78abd	−189.0	−158.1	−130.6	....	....	....	....	....	....	....	....	....
Trade Balance...................	78acd	−73.2	−25.7	15.3	....	....	....	....	....	....	....	....	....
Services: Credit....................	78add	45.1	49.3	33.1	....	....	....	....	....	....	....	....	....
Services: Debit.....................	78aed	−152.7	−131.9	−113.8	....	....	....	....	....	....	....	....	....
Balance on Goods & Services..	78afd	−180.7	−108.3	−65.4	....	....	....	....	....	....	....	....	....
Income: Credit......................	78agd	6.4	4.5	−	....	....	....	....	....	....	....	....	....
Income: Debit.......................	78ahd	−22.2	−23.2	−22.7	....	....	....	....	....	....	....	....	....
Balance on Gds, Serv. & Inc...	78aid	−196.5	−127.1	−88.1	....	....	....	....	....	....	....	....	....
Current Transfers, n.i.e.: Credit....	78ajd	151.0	152.4	92.6	....	....	....	....	....	....	....	....	....
Current Transfers: Debit........	78akd	−37.6	−38.3	−29.2	....	....	....	....	....	....	....	....	....
Capital Account, n.i.e............	78bcd	−	....	....	....	....	....	....	....	....	....	....	....
Capital Account, n.i.e.: Credit....	78bad	−	....	....	....	....	....	....	....	....	....	....	....
Capital Account: Debit..........	78bbd	−	....	....	....	....	....	....	....	....	....	....	....
Financial Account, n.i.e.........	78bjd	20.3	−7.1	52.8	....	....	....	....	....	....	....	....	....
Direct Investment Abroad......	78bdd	−5.9	−5.3	−7.2	....	....	....	....	....	....	....	....	....
Dir. Invest. in Rep. Econ., n.i.e....	78bed	−10.7	−10.0	3.6	....	....	....	....	....	....	....	....	....
Portfolio Investment Assets....	78bfd	−	....	....	....	....	....	....	....	....	....	....	....
Equity Securities................	78bkd	−	....	....	....	....	....	....	....	....	....	....	....
Debt Securities..................	78bld	−	....	....	....	....	....	....	....	....	....	....	....
Portfolio Investment Liab., n.i.e....	78bgd	−	....	....	....	....	....	....	....	....	....	....	....
Equity Securities................	78bmd	−	....	....	....	....	....	....	....	....	....	....	....
Debt Securities..................	78bnd	−	....	....	....	....	....	....	....	....	....	....	....
Financial Derivatives Assets...	78bwd	....	....	....	....	....	....	....	....	....	....	....	....
Financial Derivatives Liabilities...	78bxd	....	....	....	....	....	....	....	....	....	....	....	....
Other Investment Assets........	78bhd	−33.2	−18.2	8.1	....	....	....	....	....	....	....	....	....
Monetary Authorities..........	78bod	....	....	....	....	....	....	....	....	....	....	....	....
General Government...........	78bpd	−	....	....	....	....	....	....	....	....	....	....	....
Banks................................	78bqd	−	2.5	−	....	....	....	....	....	....	....	....	....
Other Sectors....................	78brd	−33.2	−20.7	8.1	....	....	....	....	....	....	....	....	....
Other Investment Liab., n.i.e....	78bid	70.0	26.4	48.3	....	....	....	....	....	....	....	....	....
Monetary Authorities..........	78bsd	1.6	−8.4	−	....	....	....	....	....	....	....	....	....
General Government...........	78btd	57.7	23.2	43.9	....	....	....	....	....	....	....	....	....
Banks................................	78bud	1.2	3.2	5.9	....	....	....	....	....	....	....	....	....
Other Sectors....................	78bvd	9.4	8.4	−1.6	....	....	....	....	....	....	....	....	....
Net Errors and Omissions......	78cad	26.2	6.3	−15.0	....	....	....	....	....	....	....	....	....
Overall Balance.................	78cbd	−36.6	−13.7	13.1	....	....	....	....	....	....	....	....	....
Reserves and Related Items....	79dad	36.6	13.7	−13.1	....	....	....	....	....	....	....	....	....
Reserve Assets..................	79dbd	−2.8	−20.1	−56.0	....	....	....	....	....	....	....	....	....
Use of Fund Credit and Loans....	79dcd	−1.7	−1.6	10.3	....	....	....	....	....	....	....	....	....
Exceptional Financing.........	79ded	41.0	35.4	32.6	....	....	....	....	....	....	....	....	....
National Accounts						*Billions of Francs*							
Househ.Cons.Expend.,incl.NPISHs....	96f	299	289	347	422	432	449	518	514	568	592	617	....
Government Consumption Expend...	91f	64	55	78	83	67	80	89	105	193	96	88	....
Gross Fixed Capital Formation.....	93e	45	36	56	73	35	43	61	72	63	60	59	....
Changes in Inventories.........	93i	1	3	−1	6	3	....	....	....	....	....	....	....
Exports of Goods and Services.....	90c	68	63	62	111	115	144	123	117	136	117	113	....
Imports of Goods and Services (-).....	98c	99	83	118	146	132	158	167	148	165	149	146	....
Gross Domestic Product (GDP).....	99b	374	362	473	557	516	558	624	660	706	717	730	....
					Millions: Midyear Estimates								
Population..........................	99z	3.10	3.19	3.27	3.35	3.43	Ü 3.51	3.58	3.65	3.71	3.77	3.82	3.86

2004, International Monetary Fund : *International Financial Statistics Yearbook*

Chad 628

		1992	1993	1994	1995	1996	1997	1998	1999	2000	2001	2002	2003
Exchange Rates													
		*Francs per SDR: End of Period*											
Official Rate	aa	378.57	404.89	†780.44	728.38	753.06	807.94	791.61	†896.19	918.49	935.39	850.37	771.76
		*Francs per US Dollar: End of Period (ae) Period Average (rf)*											
Official Rate	ae	275.33	294.78	†534.60	490.00	523.70	598.81	562.21	†652.95	704.95	744.31	625.50	519.36
Official Rate	rf	264.69	283.16	†555.20	499.15	511.55	583.67	589.95	†615.70	711.98	733.04	696.99	581.20
Fund Position													
		*Millions of SDRs: End of Period*											
Quota	2f.s	41.30	41.30	41.30	41.30	41.30	41.30	41.30	56.00	56.00	56.00	56.00	56.00
SDRs	1b.s	.02	.01	–	.02	.16	.01	.01	.02	–	–	.01	–
Reserve Position in the Fund	1c.s	.27	.28	.28	.28	.28	.28	.28	.28	.28	.28	.28	.28
Total Fund Cred.&Loans Outstg	2tl	21.42	20.20	29.30	45.20	45.31	45.34	50.17	59.96	70.88	78.50	71.28	
International Liquidity													
		*Millions of US Dollars Unless Otherwise Indicated: End of Period*											
Total Reserves minus Gold	1l.d	80.48	38.94	76.01	142.52	164.48	135.82	120.09	95.02	110.70	122.37	218.70	187.10
SDRs	1b.d	.03	.01	–	.03	.24	.01	.01	.03	–	–	.01	–
Reserve Position in the Fund	1c.d	.37	.38	.41	.42	.40	.38	.40	.39	.37	.35	.38	.42
Foreign Exchange	1d.d	80.08	38.54	75.60	142.07	163.84	135.44	119.68	94.60	110.33	122.02	218.31	186.68
Gold (Million Fine Troy Ounces)	1ad	.011	.011	.011	.011	.011	.011	.011	.011	.011	.011	.011	.011
Gold (National Valuation)	1and	3.70	4.42	†4.21	4.29	4.10	3.24	3.20	†3.23	3.03	3.09	3.81	4.65
Monetary Authorities: Other Liab	4..d	18.94	.01	.75	.44	1.10	16.61	12.47	18.56	21.07	18.28	18.42	21.03
Deposit Money Banks: Assets	7a.d	31.02	8.55	11.09	9.91	10.55	32.35	24.20	39.72	27.66	42.53	41.20	38.59
Liabilities	7b.d	28.40	26.43	22.36	17.37	8.83	14.78	8.59	14.56	12.96	15.53	29.48	34.04
Monetary Authorities													
		*Billions of Francs: End of Period*											
Foreign Assets	11	23.18	12.75	42.93	75.53	88.29	83.26	69.31	64.15	80.18	93.39	139.18	99.59
Claims on Central Government	12a	29.91	33.79	48.48	49.71	61.94	65.56	64.83	73.94	89.78	101.14	106.76	93.50
Claims on Deposit Money Banks	12e	13.18	9.69	.50	1.00	7.66	5.20	10.70	4.05	.50	4.50	1.50	10.43
Claims on Other Banking Insts	12f	–	–	–	–	–	1.50	3.85	3.30	4.00	3.00	–	–
Reserve Money	14	47.94	38.25	47.24	74.73	98.29	94.13	84.51	79.22	92.11	108.15	145.39	130.48
of which: Currency Outside DMBs	14a	46.95	35.84	39.69	61.98	89.36	78.81	73.62	68.25	81.27	94.77	116.80	110.92
Foreign Liabilities	16c	13.32	8.18	23.27	24.23	34.62	46.55	42.91	57.08	69.92	79.91	78.28	65.93
Central Government Deposits	16d	.44	.56	3.61	10.78	6.99	3.40	9.87	3.27	6.16	9.86	13.57	6.15
Capital Accounts	17a	4.58	5.06	8.38	8.44	8.81	9.03	8.94	9.93	10.42	10.78	10.05	9.41
Other Items (Net)	17r	−.02	4.12	9.41	8.06	9.18	2.40	2.46	−4.06	−4.16	−6.66	.16	−8.45
Deposit Money Banks													
		*Billions of Francs: End of Period*											
Reserves	20	.86	1.98	6.17	10.08	7.39	12.77	10.13	10.35	9.89	12.89	28.59	19.54
Foreign Assets	21	8.54	2.52	5.93	4.86	5.52	19.37	13.61	25.94	19.50	31.65	25.77	20.04
Claims on Central Government	22a	5.71	6.37	7.98	8.19	2.22	2.49	1.88	1.60	3.08	7.40	8.81	12.49
Claims on Nonfin.Pub.Enterprises	22c	12.95	6.71	7.13	7.25	17.24	20.77	19.95	15.05	19.49	21.97	22.51	29.88
Claims on Private Sector	22d	31.22	20.86	23.75	27.79	29.95	29.16	34.03	33.89	34.31	43.29	56.48	67.08
Claims on Other Banking Insts	22f	–	–	–	–	–	–	–	–	–	–	–	–
Claims on Nonbank Financial Insts	22g	.03	–	–	–	–	–	.36	.27	.02	.16	.14	1.13
Demand Deposits	24	15.79	9.19	18.73	20.68	22.98	27.11	25.38	27.80	31.60	43.43	59.79	60.23
Time and Savings Deposits	25	3.62	2.20	2.86	7.87	5.36	5.87	5.77	6.11	7.95	9.92	11.61	11.16
Foreign Liabilities	26c	3.14	7.58	11.22	8.42	4.62	8.79	4.83	7.52	6.87	9.70	16.07	13.41
Long-Term Foreign Liabilities	26cl	4.67	.21	.73	.09	–	.06	–	1.99	2.27	1.86	2.37	4.27
Central Government Deposits	26d	8.14	6.53	4.91	10.84	13.27	24.60	21.36	23.71	22.77	20.20	29.59	25.51
Credit from Monetary Authorities	26g	9.83	5.88	.50	1.00	7.66	5.20	10.70	4.05	.50	4.50	1.50	10.43
Capital Accounts	27a	27.43	10.64	11.95	11.57	13.45	15.52	15.83	17.83	27.35	39.23	27.68	30.59
Other Items (Net)	27r	−13.35	−3.79	.06	−2.30	−5.01	−2.60	−3.90	−1.91	−13.03	−11.47	−6.29	−5.43
Monetary Survey													
		*Billions of Francs: End of Period*											
Foreign Assets (Net)	31n	10.58	−.70	13.64	47.64	54.57	47.23	35.18	23.50	20.61	33.57	68.24	36.02
Domestic Credit	32	71.24	60.64	78.82	71.33	91.09	91.48	93.68	101.07	121.75	146.90	151.56	172.42
Claims on Central Govt. (Net)	32an	27.03	33.07	47.94	36.28	43.90	40.06	35.48	48.57	63.93	78.49	72.42	74.33
Claims on Nonfin.Pub.Enterprises	32c	12.95	6.71	7.13	7.25	17.24	20.77	19.95	15.05	19.49	21.97	22.51	29.88
Claims on Private Sector	32d	31.22	20.86	23.75	27.79	29.95	29.16	34.03	33.89	34.31	43.29	56.48	67.08
Claims on Other Banking Insts	32f	–	–	–	–	–	1.50	3.85	3.30	4.00	3.00	–	–
Claims on Nonbank Financial Inst	32g	.03	–	–	–	–	–	.36	.27	.02	.16	.14	1.13
Money	34	62.86	45.47	59.79	85.33	113.88	108.47	99.75	96.67	113.82	138.69	176.59	171.17
Quasi-Money	35	3.62	2.20	2.86	7.87	5.36	5.87	5.77	6.11	7.95	9.92	11.61	11.16
Other Items (Net)	37r	15.30	12.22	29.80	25.76	26.43	24.36	23.33	21.79	20.58	31.86	31.59	26.11
Money plus Quasi-Money	35l	66.48	47.67	62.66	93.20	119.23	114.35	105.52	102.78	121.78	148.61	188.21	182.33
Interest Rates													
		*Percent Per Annum*											
Discount Rate (End of Period)	60	12.00	11.50	†7.75	8.60	7.75	7.50	7.00	7.60	7.00	6.50	6.30	6.00
Deposit Rate	60l	7.50	7.75	8.08	5.50	5.46	5.00	5.00	5.00	5.00	5.00	5.00	5.00
Lending Rate	60p	17.77	17.46	17.50	16.00	22.00	22.00	22.00	22.00	22.00	20.67	18.00	18.00
Prices and Labor													
		*Index Numbers (2000=100): Period Averages*											
Consumer Prices	64	54.6	50.7	71.2	77.7	87.3	92.2	103.4	96.3	100.0	112.4	118.3	116.0
		*Number in Thousands: Period Averages*											
Labor Force	67d	....	....	....	....	....	....	....	....	....	....	....	....
Employment	67e	....	....	....	....	....	....	....	....	....	....	....	....

Chad 628

		1992	1993	1994	1995	1996	1997	1998	1999	2000	2001	2002	2003
International Transactions						*Millions of Francs*							
Exports.................................	70	48,250	37,330	82,160	121,273	121,895	138,130	154,455	149,635	130,200	138,300	128,685	....
Imports, c.i.f..........................	71	64,320	56,910	98,310	182,400	169,733	194,732	210,207	194,523	224,386	497,417	1,146,934	....
Balance of Payments					*Millions of US Dollars: Minus Sign Indicates Debit*								
Current Account, n.i.e..............	78ald	−85.7	−116.6	−37.7	....	....	....	....	....	....	....	....	....
Goods: Exports f.o.b................	78aad	182.3	151.8	135.3	....	....	....	....	....	....	....	....	....
Goods: Imports f.o.b...............	78abd	−243.0	−215.2	−212.1	....	....	....	....	....	....	....	....	....
Trade Balance....................	78acd	−60.7	−63.5	−76.8	....	....	....	....	....	....	....	....	....
Services: Credit......................	78add	26.7	47.1	54.8	....	....	....	....	....	....	....	....	....
Services: Debit.......................	78aed	−224.1	−235.1	−199.4	....	....	....	....	....	....	....	....	....
Balance on Goods & Services....	78afd	−258.1	−251.4	−221.4	....	....	....	....	....	....	....	....	....
Income: Credit........................	78agd	17.5	4.3	5.0	....	....	....	....	....	....	....	....	....
Income: Debit.........................	78ahd	−14.9	−15.7	−12.4	....	....	....	....	....	....	....	....	....
Balance on Gds, Serv. & Inc.....	78aid	−255.5	−262.9	−228.7	....	....	....	....	....	....	....	....	....
Current Transfers, n.i.e.: Credit......	78ajd	222.3	192.4	209.4	....	....	....	....	....	....	....	....	....
Current Transfers: Debit..............	78akd	−52.5	−46.2	−18.4	....	....	....	....	....	....	....	....	....
Capital Account, n.i.e...............	78bcd	−	−	−	....	....	....	....	....	....	....	....	....
Capital Account, n.i.e.: Credit.....	78bad	−	−	−	....	....	....	....	....	....	....	....	....
Capital Account: Debit.............	78bbd	−	−	−	....	....	....	....	....	....	....	....	....
Financial Account, n.i.e............	78bjd	33.7	68.8	76.3	....	....	....	....	....	....	....	....	....
Direct Investment Abroad.........	78bdd	−13.8	−10.9	−.6	....	....	....	....	....	....	....	....	....
Dir. Invest. in Rep. Econ., n.i.e....	78bed	2.0	15.2	27.1	....	....	....	....	....	....	....	....	....
Portfolio Investment Assets...........	78bfd	−	−	−	....	....	....	....	....	....	....	....	....
Equity Securities.................	78bkd	−	−	−	....	....	....	....	....	....	....	....	....
Debt Securities...................	78bld	−	−	−	....	....	....	....	....	....	....	....	....
Portfolio Investment Liab., n.i.e.....	78bgd	−	−	−	....	....	....	....	....	....	....	....	....
Equity Securities.................	78bmd	−	−	−	....	....	....	....	....	....	....	....	....
Debt Securities...................	78bnd	−	−	−	....	....	....	....	....	....	....	....	....
Financial Derivatives Assets...........	78bwd	....	....	....	....	....	....	....	....	....	....	....	....
Financial Derivatives Liabilities.......	78bxd	....	....	....	....	....	....	....	....	....	....	....	....
Other Investment Assets.............	78bhd	3.9	42.1	.6	....	....	....	....	....	....	....	....	....
Monetary Authorities............	78bod	....	....	....	....	....	....	....	....	....	....	....	....
General Government.............	78bpd	−	−	−	....	....	....	....	....	....	....	....	....
Banks.................................	78bqd	−1.8	31.0	−4.8	....	....	....	....	....	....	....	....	....
Other Sectors.......................	78brd	5.7	11.0	5.4	....	....	....	....	....	....	....	....	....
Other Investment Liab., n.i.e..........	78bid	41.6	22.5	49.2	....	....	....	....	....	....	....	....	....
Monetary Authorities............	78bsd	−6.3	−5.2	−.1	....	....	....	....	....	....	....	....	....
General Government.............	78btd	71.3	102.1	49.8	....	....	....	....	....	....	....	....	....
Banks.................................	78bud	5.0	−	−	....	....	....	....	....	....	....	....	....
Other Sectors.......................	78bvd	−28.3	−74.4	−.6	....	....	....	....	....	....	....	....	....
Net Errors and Omissions...........	78cad	9.2	−.1	−33.0	....	....	....	....	....	....	....	....	....
Overall Balance.......................	78cbd	−42.8	−47.9	5.5	....	....	....	....	....	....	....	....	....
Reserves and Related Items.........	79dad	42.8	47.9	−5.5	....	....	....	....	....	....	....	....	....
Reserve Assets......................	79dbd	32.9	39.4	−30.7	....	....	....	....	....	....	....	....	....
Use of Fund Credit and Loans.....	79dcd	−	−1.7	12.7	....	....	....	....	....	....	....	....	....
Exceptional Financing..............	79ded	9.9	10.2	12.4	....	....	....	....	....	....	....	....	....
Government Finance						*Millions of Francs: Year Ending December 31*							
Deficit (-) or Surplus.................	80	−63,670	−22,954	−82,198	−45,532	−97,696	−65,653	−65,161	−56,178	−47,612	3,653	....	....
Total Revenue and Grants..........	81y	71,072	79,116	87,592	98,502	110,407	128,747	115,415	107,489	136,732	145,106	....	....
Revenue...............................	81	31,421	29,150	31,964	44,834	59,790	72,359	77,347	79,289	88,750	96,867	....	....
Grants..................................	81z	39,651	49,966	55,628	53,668	50,617	56,388	38,068	28,200	47,982	48,239	....	....
Exp. & Lending Minus Repay........	82z	134,742	102,070	169,790	144,034	208,103	194,400	180,576	163,667	184,344	141,453	....	....
Expenditure.........................	82	124,952	104,840	148,300	130,304	151,794	159,400	153,028	163,667	184,344	141,453	....	....
Lending Minus Repayments.......	83	9,790	−2,770	21,490	13,730	56,309	35,000	27,548	−	−	−	....	....
Statistical Discrepancy...............	80xx	−9,536	−4,428	−1,341	31,313	22,600	46,377	13,208	32,642	−23,310	34,390	....	....
Total Financing.......................	80h	54,134	18,526	80,857	76,845	120,296	112,030	78,369	88,820	24,302	30,737	....	....
Domestic..............................	84a	19,927	9,916	−460	−5,817	14,546	28,432	5,041	32,650	9,658	1,141	....	....
Foreign................................	85a	34,207	8,610	81,317	82,662	105,750	83,598	73,328	56,170	14,644	29,596	....	....
Total Debt by Residence.............	88	196,019	225,936	423,574	435,728	489,035	546,857	525,691	642,939	800,014	862,293	....	....
Domestic..............................	88a	3,119	4,236	6,503	5,481	4,236	7,108	7,310	24,000	65,113	66,300	....	....
Foreign................................	89a	192,900	221,700	417,071	430,247	484,799	539,749	518,381	618,939	734,901	795,993	....	....
National Accounts						*Billions of Francs*							
Gross Domestic Product (GDP).........	99b	441.0	412.0	655.0	717.8	822.0	911.0	1,003.0	943.0	996.0	1,235.0	1,405.0	1,548.0
						Millions: Midyear Estimates							
Population.............................	99z	6.17	6.35	6.53	6.73	6.94	7.16	7.39	7.62	7.86	8.10	8.35	8.60

Chile 228

		1992	1993	1994	1995	1996	1997	1998	1999	2000	2001	2002	2003
Exchange Rates						*Pesos per SDR: End of Period*							
Market Rate	aa	525.70	592.06	589.91	605.19	611.09	593.41	667.08	727.53	746.15	824.67	968.49	890.72
					Pesos per US Dollar: End of Period (ae) Period Average (rf)								
Market Rate	ae	382.33	431.04	404.09	407.13	424.97	439.81	473.77	530.07	572.68	656.20	712.38	599.42
Market Rate	rf	362.58	404.17	420.18	396.77	412.27	419.30	460.29	508.78	539.59	634.94	688.94	691.43
					Index Numbers (2000=100): Period Averages								
Market Rate	ahx	148.7	133.3	128.2	135.9	130.6	128.4	117.0	106.0	100.0	85.3	78.3	79.2
Nominal Effective Exchange Rate	nec	75.7	85.8	101.7	107.4	107.2	113.3	107.9	100.6	100.0	90.2	85.0	78.0
Real Effective Exchange Rate	rec	85.1	87.1	89.7	95.1	97.6	106.7	105.5	100.0	100.0	91.1	85.7	78.5
Fund Position						*Millions of SDRs: End of Period*							
Quota	2f.s	621.7	621.7	621.7	621.7	621.7	621.7	621.7	856.1	856.1	856.1	856.1	856.1
SDRs	1b.s	.5	.9	.5	2.1	1.3	1.0	5.9	13.5	18.9	23.0	26.9	30.7
Reserve Position in the Fund	1c.s	–	–	–	–	35.0	232.0	429.6	299.4	248.8	245.7	360.9	392.3
Total Fund Cred.&Loans Outstg.	2tl	525.0	346.5	199.5	–	–	–	–	–	–	–	–	–
International Liquidity				*Millions of US Dollars Unless Otherwise Indicated: End of Period*									
Total Reserves minus Gold	1l.d	9,167.7	9,640.3	13,087.6	14,139.8	14,972.6	17,573.2	15,869.3	14,616.6	15,034.9	14,379.0	15,341.1	15,839.6
SDRs	1b.d	.6	1.3	.7	3.1	1.9	1.3	8.3	18.5	24.6	28.9	36.5	45.7
Reserve Position in the Fund	1c.d	–	–	–	–	50.4	313.1	604.9	411.0	324.2	308.7	490.7	582.9
Foreign Exchange	1d.d	9,167.0	9,639.0	13,086.9	14,136.7	14,920.3	17,258.9	15,256.1	14,187.1	14,686.1	14,041.3	14,813.9	15,211.0
Gold (Million Fine Troy Ounces)	1ad	1.867	1.865	1.864	1.861	1.859	1.858	1.222	1.220	.074	.074	.008	.008
Gold (National Valuation)	1and	574.0	612.0	652.0	642.8	637.4	533.0	321.9	316.9	318.3	18.6	2.3	2.7
Monetary Authorities: Other Liab.	4..d	2,283.6	2,100.5	2,573.3	1,596.2	7.9	353.6	330.6	488.6	316.9	274.1	235.3	235.3
Banking Institutions: Assets	7a.d	559.2	525.5	549.1	491.7	605.2	1,522.0	2,441.5	5,638.7	5,162.5	4,096.0	2,494.0	1,962.4
Liabilities	7b.d	3,895.9	3,793.2	4,258.3	3,962.0	3,634.1	2,151.7	2,267.5	1,505.2	1,214.0	1,991.3	3,317.2	4,841.0
Nonbank Financial Insts.: Assets	7e.d	–	89.8	199.3	51.6	148.4	351.9	1,748.5	4,572.9	3,871.8	4,684.3	5,781.5	11,697.8
Monetary Authorities						*Billions of Pesos: End of Period*							
Foreign Assets	11	4,115.5	4,749.6	5,999.0	6,439.5	7,230.9	†8,062.0	7,784.1	8,097.1	8,770.8	9,608.7	11,000.7	9,668.5
Claims on Central Government	12a	3,432.4	3,814.8	3,597.8	3,805.1	3,817.6	†3,863.8	3,890.8	4,099.6	4,546.3	5,046.6	5,067.1	4,085.6
Claims on Nonfin.Pub.Enterprises	12c	–	–	–	–	–	† –	–	–	–	–	–	–
Claims on Private Sector	12d	146.7	167.5	188.0	200.8	224.8	†837.6	846.3	863.5	878.5	880.8	892.6	924.3
Claims on Banking Institutions	12e	2,449.1	2,535.3	2,440.7	2,454.6	2,257.2	†635.1	482.4	567.9	578.0	681.1	132.3	101.7
Reserve Money	14	713.0	844.8	994.5	1,206.7	1,345.4	†1,824.3	2,003.4	2,093.2	1,945.7	2,118.5	2,242.8	2,158.5
of which: Currency Outside DMBs	14a	480.5	582.1	667.3	784.2	859.5	†978.5	969.5	1,167.9	1,113.7	1,214.7	1,301.5	1,379.7
Time, Savings,& Fgn.Currency Dep.	15	287.8	285.7	258.9	110.9	62.7	†3.3	1.7	4.3	.4	.2	.8	–
Liabs. of Central Bank: Securities	16ac	5,162.8	5,814.2	7,045.3	7,951.2	9,267.6	†10,540.3	10,018.5	10,793.9	12,151.4	12,414.1	13,313.6	12,417.9
Foreign Liabilities	16c	305.3	222.0	155.4	1.1	1.8	†15.6	19.2	125.2	50.2	56.3	21.1	23.2
Long-Term Foreign Liabilities	16cl	843.8	888.6	1,002.2	648.8	1.6	†139.9	137.5	133.8	131.3	123.5	146.5	117.8
Central Government Deposits	16d	1,200.6	1,371.0	1,573.3	1,753.7	2,011.3	†2,131.2	1,919.9	1,326.0	966.3	621.5	430.2	87.8
Capital Accounts	17a	802.5	520.7	–113.3	374.1	268.3	†–1,319.0	–1,796.6	–1,535.9	–1,432.3	–206.9	615.6	–819.4
Other Items (Net)	17r	827.8	1,320.4	1,309.1	853.5	571.9	†62.9	700.2	687.8	960.5	1,089.9	322.0	794.3
Banking Institutions						*Billions of Pesos: End of Period*							
Reserves	20	527.4	575.7	713.0	719.9	750.9	†664.8	911.5	916.0	880.3	948.6	931.2	1,523.0
Claims on Mon.Author.:Securities	20c	1,845.4	1,691.1	2,077.6	2,293.0	2,405.1	†3,115.3	2,714.2	3,649.1	4,163.7	4,913.2	6,135.3	5,206.3
Foreign Assets	21	207.9	225.7	221.0	199.4	256.5	†669.4	1,156.7	2,988.9	2,956.5	2,687.8	1,776.7	1,176.3
Claims on Central Government	22a	27.8	51.3	56.6	84.0	137.0	†320.2	264.8	247.2	315.0	335.3	432.3	331.7
Claims on Local Government	22b	.4	.4	.4	.5	.5	†.4	.3	.3	.3	.7	.7	.6
Claims on Nonfin.Pub.Enterprises	22c	174.7	170.5	124.6	95.4	88.7	†133.5	550.0	128.2	73.3	247.5	61.3	160.8
Claims on Private Sector	22d	7,141.9	9,324.2	10,953.1	13,871.5	16,675.1	†18,745.3	20,470.3	21,995.4	24,876.8	26,569.0	29,186.1	30,750.0
Claims on Nonbank Financial Insts.	22g	–	–	–	–	–	†697.9	617.2	760.7	407.4	829.8	240.0	434.8
Demand Deposits	24	859.9	1,040.6	1,212.7	1,515.5	1,816.9	†2,101.0	1,967.1	2,233.9	2,531.3	2,847.6	3,129.3	3,551.0
Time, Savings,& Fgn.Currency Dep.	25	4,404.0	5,603.9	6,250.2	8,021.0	9,788.5	†10,676.7	12,233.3	12,947.6	13,701.5	13,680.2	13,262.8	14,189.5
Money Market Instruments	26aa	302.8	415.4	559.9	674.9	833.9	†5,898.9	5,280.2	6,543.8	7,475.6	8,196.2	9,644.1	9,105.5
Bonds	26ab	794.0	1,049.5	1,554.9	2,229.2	2,894.2	†639.0	750.7	1,057.7	1,252.5	1,338.1	1,335.5	1,200.2
Foreign Liabilities	26c	1,173.1	1,316.6	1,359.4	1,155.6	1,020.0	†338.3	440.2	160.4	274.5	752.7	974.9	1,453.1
Long-Term Foreign Liabilities	26cl	316.1	318.4	361.3	457.5	524.4	†608.1	634.1	637.5	420.7	554.0	1,388.3	1,448.7
Central Government Deposits	26d	358.5	426.0	490.2	708.7	686.2	†816.5	664.3	898.9	774.4	1,090.4	1,170.7	1,258.9
Credit from Monetary Authorities	26g	694.8	542.1	443.3	361.7	326.5	†228.4	176.8	119.9	140.3	561.5	262.8	699.0
Liabs. to Nonbank Financial Insts.	26j	270.6	287.2	437.4	425.3	323.1	†2,408.1	3,126.5	4,215.0	4,951.3	5,599.9	7,439.8	6,202.3
Capital Accounts	27a	1,302.8	1,652.7	2,334.5	3,133.0	3,743.7	†2,509.0	2,848.2	3,075.7	3,492.9	3,781.1	4,069.5	4,343.8
Other Items (Net)	27r	–551.3	–613.6	–857.5	–1,418.6	–1,643.7	†–1,877.0	–1,436.5	–1,203.9	–1,341.8	–1,869.9	–3,914.2	–3,868.6

Chile 228

		1992	1993	1994	1995	1996	1997	1998	1999	2000	2001	2002	2003
Banking Survey						*Billions of Pesos: End of Period*							
Foreign Assets (Net)	31n	2,844.9	3,436.8	4,705.3	5,482.2	6,465.7	†8,377.5	8,481.5	10,800.4	11,402.6	11,487.4	11,781.4	9,368.5
Domestic Credit	32	9,364.7	11,731.5	12,856.9	15,595.1	18,246.2	†21,651.1	24,055.5	25,870.2	29,356.8	32,197.9	34,279.0	35,341.1
Claims on Central Govt. (Net)	32an	1,901.0	2,069.1	1,590.8	1,426.8	1,257.1	†1,236.3	1,571.4	2,122.0	3,120.5	3,670.1	3,898.4	3,070.6
Claims on Local Government	32b	.4	.4	.4	.5	.5	†.4	.3	.3	.3	.7	.7	.6
Claims on Nonfin.Pub.Enterprises	32c	174.7	170.5	124.6	95.4	88.7	†133.5	550.0	128.2	73.3	247.5	61.3	160.8
Claims on Private Sector	32d	7,288.6	9,491.6	11,141.1	14,072.3	16,899.9	†19,582.9	21,316.6	22,859.0	25,755.3	27,449.8	30,078.7	31,674.3
Claims on Nonbank Financial Insts.	32g	—	—	—	—	—	†697.9	617.2	760.7	407.4	829.8	240.0	434.8
Money	34	1,340.7	1,623.1	1,880.2	2,300.0	2,677.0	†3,079.5	2,936.5	3,401.2	3,645.2	4,062.3	4,430.8	4,930.7
Quasi-Money	35	4,691.7	5,889.5	6,509.1	8,131.9	9,851.2	†10,680.0	12,235.1	12,951.9	13,701.9	13,680.4	13,263.7	14,189.5
Money Market Instruments	36aa	302.8	415.4	559.9	674.9	833.9	†5,898.9	5,280.2	6,543.8	7,475.6	8,196.2	9,644.1	9,105.5
Bonds	36ab	794.0	1,049.5	1,554.9	2,229.2	2,894.2	†639.0	750.7	1,057.7	1,252.5	1,338.1	1,335.5	1,200.2
Liabs. of Central Bank: Securities	36ac	3,317.4	4,123.0	4,967.7	5,658.2	6,862.5	†7,424.9	7,304.3	7,144.8	7,987.6	7,500.9	7,178.3	7,211.5
Long-Term Foreign Liabilities	36cl	1,160.2	1,207.0	1,363.5	1,106.3	526.0	†748.0	771.5	771.3	552.0	677.5	1,534.8	1,566.5
Liabs. to Nonbank Financial Insts.	36j	270.6	287.2	437.4	425.3	323.1	†2,408.1	3,126.5	4,215.0	4,951.3	5,599.9	7,439.8	6,202.3
Capital Accounts	37a	2,105.3	2,173.3	2,221.2	3,507.1	4,012.0	†1,190.0	1,051.6	1,539.8	2,060.6	3,574.2	4,685.1	3,524.4
Other Items (Net)	37r	−1,773.0	−1,599.9	−1,931.8	−2,955.6	−3,268.0	†−2,039.7	−919.4	−954.7	−867.5	−944.3	−3,451.7	−3,221.2
Money plus Quasi-Money	35l	6,032.4	7,512.6	8,389.3	10,431.9	12,528.1	†13,759.5	15,171.6	16,353.1	17,347.1	17,742.7	17,694.5	19,120.3
Nonbank Financial Institutions						*Billions of Pesos End of Period*							
Claims on Mon.Author.:Securities	40c.p	1,904.5	2,656.8	3,462.9	3,883.0	4,538.6	4,937.3	5,521.9	5,670.3	6,566.5	6,958.9	6,224.2	5,646.4
Foreign Assets	41..p	—	38.7	80.5	21.0	63.1	154.8	828.4	2,423.9	2,217.3	3,073.8	4,118.6	7,011.9
Claims on Central Government	42a.p	35.5	32.8	108.3	195.7	384.5	428.7	505.2	655.9	790.0	1,172.1	1,428.8	1,641.1
Claims on Private Sector	42d.p	1,601.7	2,693.5	3,536.8	3,848.1	3,832.4	3,924.8	3,114.6	3,339.1	3,616.8	4,293.7	4,706.1	7,085.5
Claims on Banking Institutions	42e.p	1,195.8	1,415.5	1,807.2	2,391.5	2,872.4	4,083.6	4,715.4	6,163.9	7,333.3	7,680.9	8,944.0	8,052.5
Reserve Funds and Capital	47a.p	4,736.5	6,831.4	8,983.6	10,231.0	11,555.6	13,405.8	14,552.5	18,093.0	20,343.4	22,956.0	25,227.1	29,176.6
Other Items (Net)	47r.p	.9	5.9	12.2	108.3	135.4	123.2	133.0	160.1	180.4	223.5	194.6	261.0
Interest Rates						*Percent Per Annum*							
Discount Rate (End of Period)	60	....	7.96	13.89	7.96	11.75	7.96	9.12	7.44	8.73	6.50	3.00	2.45
Money Market Rate	60b	....	....	....	....	....	....	....	....	10.09	6.81	4.08	2.72
Savings Rate	60k	3.51	3.52	3.53	3.53	3.51	3.50	3.50	3.50	3.50	2.39	.69	.26
Deposit Rate	60l	18.29	18.24	15.12	13.73	13.48	12.02	14.92	8.56	9.20	6.19	3.80	2.73
Deposit Rate (Foreign Currency)	60l.f	4.21	3.96	4.05	5.45	5.24	5.02	4.41	4.39	5.48	3.51	1.59	1.39
Lending Rate	60p	23.97	24.35	20.34	18.16	17.37	15.67	20.17	12.62	14.84	11.89	7.76	6.18
Lending Rate (Foreign Currency)	60p.f	6.77	6.76	8.42	9.96	9.27	9.49	8.73	7.38	7.76	5.50	3.83	3.37
Prices, Production, Labor						*Index Numbers (2000=100): Period Averages*							
Industrial Share Prices	62	68.7	77.7	108.1	137.6	122.8	111.3	83.3	90.3	100.0	106.6	104.2	131.4
Prices: Home & Import Goods	63	61.6	66.9	72.1	77.5	82.4	83.7	85.3	89.8	100.0	107.8	115.2	122.8
Home Goods	63a	60.9	65.8	71.2	77.8	83.0	85.1	86.0	89.5	100.0	105.9	112.4	120.2
Consumer Prices	64	57.2	64.5	71.9	77.8	83.5	88.7	93.2	96.3	100.0	103.6	106.1	109.1
Wages, Hourly	65a	....	56.3	59.2	66.7	76.6	83.2	89.7	95.0	100.0	105.2	110.0	114.2
Manufacturing Production	66ey	80.6	82.4	84.5	88.6	91.9	96.4	96.5	96.5	100.0	101.9	102.6	106.4
Mining Production	66zx	46.7	48.5	51.6	57.2	70.2	76.6	81.6	94.8	100.0	101.6	98.0	104.4
Copper Production	66c	42.5	45.3	47.9	53.9	67.2	73.9	79.6	95.4	100.0	102.6	99.6	105.7
Employment	67	86.7	93.7	94.8	95.9	97.2	99.3	101.2	98.9	100.0	100.3	101.4	104.5
						Number in Thousands: Period Averages							
Labor Force	67d	4,990	5,219	5,300	5,274	5,601	5,684	5,852	5,934	5,871	5,949	6,000	6,128
Employment	67e	4,773	4,986	†4,988	5,026	†5,299	5,380	5,432	5,405	5,382	5,479	5,531	5,675
Unemployment	67c	217	234	†427	402	350	344	384	572	536	535	529	515
Unemployment Rate (%)	67r	4.4	4.5	†5.9	4.7	5.4	5.3	7.2	8.9	8.3	7.9	7.8	7.4
International Transactions						*Millions of US Dollars*							
Exports	70..d	10,007	9,199	11,604	16,024	15,657	17,902	16,323	17,162	19,210	18,272	18,177	21,046
Imports, c.i.f.	71..d	10,183	11,134	11,820	15,900	19,123	20,825	19,880	15,988	18,507	17,832	17,196	19,413
Imports, f.o.b.	71.vd	9,285	10,189	10,872	14,643	17,699	19,298	18,363	14,735	17,091	16,428	15,921	18,031
						1995=100							
Import Prices	76.x	82.5	91.7	97.5	100.0	110.2	....	....	....	....	....	....	....

2004, International Monetary Fund: *International Financial Statistics Yearbook*

Chile 228

		1992	1993	1994	1995	1996	1997	1998	1999	2000	2001	2002	2003
Balance of Payments		\multicolumn{12}{c}{*Millions of US Dollars: Minus Sign Indicates Debit*}
Current Account, n.i.e.	78ald	−957	−2,555	−1,586	−1,350	−3,083	−3,660	−3,918	99	−898	−1,100	−885	−594
Goods: Exports f.o.b.	78aad	10,007	9,199	11,604	16,025	16,627	17,870	16,323	17,162	19,210	18,272	18,177	21,046
Goods: Imports f.o.b.	78abd	−9,285	−10,189	−10,872	−14,644	−17,699	−19,298	−18,363	−14,735	−17,091	−16,428	−15,921	−18,031
Trade Balance	78acd	722	−990	732	1,381	−1,072	−1,428	−2,040	2,427	2,119	1,844	2,256	3,015
Services: Credit	78add	2,360	2,513	2,840	3,333	3,588	3,892	3,952	3,869	4,083	4,138	4,332	4,805
Services: Debit	78aed	−2,536	−2,742	−2,990	−3,657	−3,589	−4,028	−4,404	−4,606	−4,802	−4,983	−4,988	−5,571
Balance on Goods & Services	78afd	546	−1,219	582	1,057	−1,073	−1,563	−2,492	1,690	1,400	999	1,600	2,249
Income: Credit	78agd	558	502	556	869	842	1,170	1,196	912	1,598	1,458	1,046	1,114
Income: Debit	78ahd	−2,438	−2,158	−3,056	−3,582	−3,359	−3,787	−3,085	−3,145	−4,453	−3,985	−3,960	−4,394
Balance on Gds, Serv. & Inc.	78aid	−1,335	−2,875	−1,917	−1,657	−3,590	−4,180	−4,381	−543	−1,456	−1,527	−1,315	−1,031
Current Transfers, n.i.e.: Credit	78ajd	536	536	449	482	665	835	810	841	765	713	792	748
Current Transfers: Debit	78akd	−158	−216	−118	−175	−158	−315	−348	−198	−207	−286	−362	−310
Capital Account, n.i.e.	78bcd	–	–	–	–	–	–	–	–	–	–	–	–
Capital Account, n.i.e.: Credit	78bad	–	–	–	–	–	–	–	–	–	–	–	–
Capital Account: Debit	78bbd	–	–	–	–	–	–	–	–	–	–	–	–
Financial Account, n.i.e.	78bjd	3,132	2,995	5,294	2,357	5,660	6,742	1,967	238	788	1,362	2,097	−630
Direct Investment Abroad	78bdd	−398	−434	−911	−752	−1,133	−1,463	−1,483	−2,558	−3,987	−1,610	−294	−1,395
Dir. Invest. in Rep. Econ., n.i.e.	78bed	935	1,034	2,583	2,957	4,815	5,271	4,628	8,761	4,860	4,200	1,888	2,982
Portfolio Investment Assets	78bfd	–	−90	−351	−14	−135	−989	−3,311	−5,795	766	−1,386	−3,083	−5,327
Equity Securities	78bkd	–	−90	−351	−14	−43	−743	−2,518	−3,474	821	−2,094	−2,922	−5,176
Debt Securities	78bld	–	–	–	–	−92	−246	−792	−2,321	−55	708	−161	−151
Portfolio Investment Liab., n.i.e.	78bgd	458	820	1,259	48	1,269	2,614	842	2,578	−127	1,525	999	1,701
Equity Securities	78bmd	338	816	1,259	−249	700	1,720	580	524	−427	−217	−320	312
Debt Securities	78bnd	120	4	–	297	569	894	262	2,054	300	1,742	1,319	1,390
Financial Derivatives Assets	78bwd	–	–	–	–	–	–	–	....	....	....	....	....
Financial Derivatives Liabilities	78bxd	–	–	–	–	−22	165	−59	−6	2	−86	−124	118
Other Investment Assets	78bhd	−323	726	−152	−309	−855	−457	−1,953	−3,369	−2,065	−1,326	1,624	−387
Monetary Authorities	78bod	−15	−4	−57	10	–	–	–	–	–	–	–	−60
General Government	78bpd	47	–	–	–	–	–	–	–	–	–	–	1
Banks	78bqd	−21	7	−26	57	−87	−547	−381	−1,642	653	145	879	299
Other Sectors	78brd	−334	723	−70	−376	−768	90	−1,572	−1,727	−2,717	−1,471	745	−627
Other Investment Liab., n.i.e.	78bid	2,460	939	2,865	427	1,721	1,600	3,303	627	1,338	44	1,087	1,678
Monetary Authorities	78bsd	10	−240	−99	−402	−73	−24	−74	−65	36	−47	−2	−2
General Government	78btd	157	−119	−99	−1,323	−545	−386	−171	−101	−128	−132	−294	−117
Banks	78bud	1,589	61	407	−322	−444	−1,498	−36	−840	−278	771	1,305	1,604
Other Sectors	78bvd	704	1,237	2,656	2,474	2,784	3,508	3,584	1,633	1,707	−548	77	193
Net Errors and Omissions	78cad	372	−12	−557	132	16	237	−239	−1,083	426	−861	−1,027	866
Overall Balance	78cbd	2,547	428	3,151	1,139	2,594	3,318	−2,191	−747	317	−599	185	−357
Reserves and Related Items	79dad	−2,547	−428	−3,151	−1,139	−2,594	−3,318	2,191	747	−317	599	−185	357
Reserve Assets	79dbd	−2,344	−170	−2,918	−740	−1,119	−3,318	2,191	747	−317	599	−185	357
Use of Fund Credit and Loans	79dcd	−203	−249	−210	−298	–	–	–	–	–	–	–	–
Exceptional Financing	79ded	–	−9	−22	−101	−1,475	–	–	–	–	–	–	–
International Investment Position						\multicolumn{8}{c}{*Millions of US Dollars*}
Assets	79aad	....	....	....	....	....	35,654	40,771	51,381	52,350	53,177	56,168	64,278
Direct Investment Abroad	79abd	....	....	....	....	–	5,110	6,735	9,000	11,154	11,905	12,508	13,812
Portfolio Investment	79acd	....	....	....	....	–	1,176	4,717	11,402	9,876	10,662	12,988	19,668
Equity Securities	79add	....	....	....	....	–	902	3,411	7,670	6,911	7,870	10,500	16,977
Debt Securities	79aed	....	....	....	....	–	274	1,306	3,732	2,965	2,792	2,488	2,690
Financial Derivatives	79ald	....	....	....	....	....	–	–	–	–	–	268	514
Other Investment	79afd	....	....	....	....	598	11,094	13,027	16,027	16,207	16,200	15,053	14,433
Monetary Authorities	79agd	....	....	....	....	–	–	–	–	–	–	–	62
General Government	79ahd	....	....	....	....	–	–	–	–	–	–	–	–
Banks	79aid	....	....	....	....	598	1,055	1,284	2,741	2,486	2,341	1,706	1,402
Other Sectors	79ajd	....	....	....	....	–	10,040	11,743	13,286	13,721	13,859	13,347	12,968
Reserve Assets	79akd	....	....	....	....	15,660	18,273	16,292	14,952	15,114	14,410	15,352	15,852
Liabilities	79lad	....	....	....	....	....	66,974	71,588	80,231	82,219	82,250	81,703	99,332
Dir. Invest. in Rep. Economy	79lbd	....	....	....	....	–	34,523	37,630	43,498	45,753	44,685	42,928	54,900
Portfolio Investment	79lcd	....	....	....	....	6,417	9,172	7,966	10,611	9,187	10,302	10,527	14,322
Equity Securities	79ldd	....	....	....	....	5,223	7,111	5,704	6,451	4,701	3,770	2,304	3,940
Debt Securities	79led	....	....	....	....	1,194	2,061	2,262	4,159	4,486	6,532	8,223	10,382
Financial Derivatives	79lld	....	....	....	....	–	–	–	–	–	–	102	222
Other Investment	79lfd	....	....	....	....	21,367	23,279	25,992	26,122	27,278	27,263	28,146	29,888
Monetary Authorities	79lgd	....	....	....	....	189	166	92	26	62	15	13	10
General Government	79lhd	....	....	....	....	2,653	2,284	2,183	2,094	1,920	1,742	1,467	1,392
Banks	79lid	....	....	....	....	3,599	2,106	2,185	1,438	1,158	1,927	3,229	4,834
Other Sectors	79ljd	....	....	....	....	14,926	18,724	21,533	22,564	24,138	23,579	23,437	23,652

Chile 228

		1992	1993	1994	1995	1996	1997	1998	1999	2000	2001	2002	2003
Government Finance		\multicolumn{12}{c}{*Billions of Pesos: Year Ending December 31*}
Deficit (-) or Surplus	80	346.3	356.6	361.9	667.7	657.8	623.3	131.8	−502.4	56.4	....	....	....
Total Revenue and Grants	81y	3,491.0	4,172.7	4,822.8	5,747.7	6,626.3	7,358.9	7,726.9	7,737.8	8,976.1	....	....	....
Revenue	81	3,491.0	4,172.7	4,822.8	5,747.7	6,626.3	7,358.9	7,726.9	7,737.8	8,976.1	....	....	....
Grants	81z	–	–	–	–	–	–	–	–	–	....	....	....
Exp. & Lending Minus Repay.	82z	3,144.7	3,816.1	4,460.9	5,080.1	5,968.5	6,735.6	7,595.1	8,240.2	8,919.7	....	....	....
Expenditure	82	3,152.0	3,842.7	4,482.0	5,137.1	5,982.8	6,695.3	7,575.8	8,235.4	8,853.3	....	....	....
Lending Minus Repayments	83	−7.3	−26.6	−21.1	−57.0	−14.3	40.3	19.3	4.8	66.4	....	....	....
Total Debt by Residence	88	5,162.6	5,686.4	5,477.7	5,056.4	4,719.1	4,588.0	4,657.6	5,159.4	5,606.9	....	....	....
Domestic	88a	2,981.6	3,431.6	3,305.6	3,432.1	3,392.0	3,476.5	3,491.6	3,684.3	4,129.2	....	....	....
Foreign	89a	2,181.0	2,254.8	2,172.1	1,624.3	1,327.1	1,111.5	1,165.9	1,475.1	1,477.7	....	....	....
National Accounts		\multicolumn{12}{c}{*Billions of Pesos*}
Househ.Cons.Expend.,incl.NPISHs	96f	10,330.3	12,458.9	14,648.7	17,270.3	19,785.0	21,972.0	23,703.6	23,927.9	25,897.2	27,743.0	29,184.7	31,123.6
Government Consumption Expend	91f	1,617.5	2,017.9	2,420.1	2,938.5	3,426.1	3,860.5	4,197.1	4,603.8	5,053.9	5,480.8	5,942.1	6,288.0
Gross Fixed Capital Formation	93e	3,742.5	5,001.7	5,649.2	7,117.9	8,240.7	9,414.2	9,545.7	7,740.1	8,410.7	9,382.3	9,846.9	10,543.9
Changes in Inventories	93i	148.3	189.7	110.3	294.9	312.9	211.8	281.7	22.8	457.4	167.6	359.2	296.5
Exports of Goods and Services	90c	4,806.6	5,132.0	6,544.1	8,295.4	8,520.5	9,404.2	9,608.6	10,992.3	12,820.2	14,501.0	15,749.8	18,141.1
Imports of Goods and Services (-)	98c	4,541.8	5,516.7	6,158.5	7,672.6	9,047.9	10,140.1	10,801.9	10,148.4	12,064.1	13,833.3	14,671.4	16,573.8
Gross Domestic Product (GDP)	99b	16,123.2	19,276.5	23,714.7	28,309.2	31,237.3	34,722.6	36,534.9	37,138.5	40,575.3	43,441.4	46,411.3	49,819.3
Net Primary Income from Abroad	98.n	−696.4	−689.7	−1,072.3	−1,106.4	−1,033.0	−1,104.5	−869.6	−1,132.6	−1,552.5	−1,588.0	−2,012.3	−2,248.1
Gross National Income (GNI)	99a	14,489.1	17,285.2	20,322.9	24,769.3	30,204.3	33,618.1	35,665.3	36,005.9	38,022.8	41,853.4	44,399.0	47,571.2
Consumption of Fixed Capital	99cf	1,432.6	1,692.7	1,957.3	2,269.8	4,122.4	4,424.2	4,644.6	5,007.2	5,257.3	5,704.2	6,228.9	....
Net National Income	99e	14,634.2	17,414.7	20,461.7	24,892.5	30,414.1	33,837.0	35,879.9	36,410.1	39,151.9	40,860.7	....	....
GDP Vol.1996 Prices	99b.p	23,242.0	24,868.7	26,289.6	29,084.5	31,237.3	33,300.7	34,376.6	34,115.0	35,646.5	36,854.9	37,670.2	38,900.4
GDP Volume (2000=100)	99bvp	65.2	69.8	73.8	81.6	87.6	93.4	96.4	95.7	100.0	103.4	105.7	109.1
GDP Deflator (2000=100)	99bip	60.9	68.1	79.2	85.5	87.9	91.6	93.4	95.6	100.0	103.6	108.2	112.5
		\multicolumn{12}{c}{*Millions: Midyear Estimates*}
Population	99z	13.55	13.77	13.99	14.21	14.42	14.63	14.83	15.03	15.22	15.42	15.61	15.81

2004, International Monetary Fund: *International Financial Statistics Yearbook*

China, P.R.: Mainland 924

		1992	1993	1994	1995	1996	1997	1998	1999	2000	2001	2002	2003
Exchange Rates		Yuan per SDR: End of Period										
Market Rate......aa=......	wa	7.9087	7.9666	12.3302	12.3637	11.9325	11.1715	11.6567	11.3637	10.7847	10.4017	11.2532	12.2989
		Yuan per US Dollar: End of Period (we) Period Average (wf)										
Market Rate......ae=......	we	5.7518	5.8000	8.4462	8.3174	8.2982	8.2798	8.2787	8.2795	8.2774	8.2768	8.2773	8.2767
Market Rate......rf=......	wf	5.5146	5.7620	8.6187	8.3514	8.3142	8.2898	8.2790	8.2783	8.2785	8.2771	8.2770	8.2770
		Index Numbers (2000=100): Period Averages										
Nominal Effective Exchange Rate.....	nec	119.26	95.75	86.68	85.63	89.25	95.11	99.45	97.31	100.00	104.49	103.59	96.47
Real Effective Exchange Rate..........	rec	78.90	69.81	75.90	84.57	92.76	98.84	100.81	97.51	100.00	104.32	102.64	96.68
Fund Position		Millions of SDRs: End of Period										
Quota..................	2f.s	3,385	3,385	3,385	3,385	3,385	3,385	3,385	4,687	4,687	6,369	6,369	6,369
SDRs...................	1b.s	305	352	369	392	427	447	480	540	613	677	734	741
Reserve Position in the Fund..........	1c.s	551	513	517	818	971	1,682	2,523	1,685	1,462	2,061	2,738	2,556
Total Fund Cred.&Loans Outstg......	2tl	–	–	–	–	–	–	–	–	–	–	–	–
International Liquidity		Millions of US Dollars Unless Otherwise Indicated: End of Period										
Total Reserves Minus Gold..............	1l.d	†20,620	22,387	52,914	75,377	107,039	142,762	149,188	157,728	168,278	215,605	291,128	408,151
SDRs.....................	1b.d	419	484	539	582	614	602	676	741	798	851	998	1,102
Reserve Position in the Fund..........	1c.d	758	704	755	1,216	1,396	2,270	3,553	2,312	1,905	2,590	3,723	3,798
Foreign Exchange..............	1d.d	†19,443	21,199	51,620	73,579	105,029	139,890	144,959	154,675	165,574	212,165	286,407	403,251
Gold (Million Fine Troy Ounces)........	1ad	12.7	12.7	12.7	12.7	12.7	12.7	12.7	12.7	12.7	16.1	19.3	19.3
Gold (National Valuation)................	1and	610	612	646	660	637	601	624	608	578	3,093	4,074	4,074
Banking Institutions: Liabilities..........	7b.d	19,398	†39,230	44,890	50,370	55,990	59,035	54,685	47,057	49,536	37,477	47,317	53,221
Monetary Authorities		Billions of Yuan: End of Period										
Foreign Assets.....................	11	133.04	†154.95	445.13	666.95	956.22	1,345.21	1,376.17	1,485.75	1,558.28	1,986.04	2,324.29	3,114.18
Claims on Central Government........	12a	124.11	158.27	168.77	158.28	158.28	158.28	158.28	158.28	158.28	282.13	286.38	290.10
Claims on Other Sectors.........	12d	53.39	†68.23	72.83	68.01	65.87	17.10	10.38	10.15	11.02	19.55	20.67	20.63
Claims on Deposit Money Banks.......	12e	678.02	†960.95	1,045.10	1,151.03	1,451.84	1,435.79	1,305.75	1,537.39	1,351.92	1,131.16	998.26	1,061.95
Claims on Other Banking Insts........	12f	20.11	25.17	26.99	18.16	11.77	207.23	296.28	383.31	860.04	854.73	†230.51	136.33
Claims on Nonbank Financial Insts...	12g	....	....	....	....	....	....	....	....	....	....	724.03	725.60
Reserve Money......................	14	922.80	†1,314.70	1,721.78	2,075.98	2,688.85	3,145.45	3,233.94	3,478.81	3,791.38	4,171.30	4,692.18	5,517.17
Of which Curr.Outside Banking Inst	14a	432.94	†577.65	728.44	788.19	879.89	1,017.46	1,120.07	1,345.21	1,464.99	1,568.73	1,727.80	1,974.60
Bonds...........................	16ab	....	–	–	19.71	–	11.89	11.89	11.89	–	–	148.75	303.16
Foreign Liabilities................	16c	–	–	–	–	–	22.29	20.14	39.90	39.39	50.91	42.31	48.26
Central Government Deposits...........	16d	23.06	†47.34	83.33	97.34	122.54	†66.42	72.20	61.73	167.81	98.93	130.19	262.44
Capital Accounts..................	17a	68.27	32.92	29.49	40.04	39.51	39.27	39.44	39.37	38.23	37.98	24.64	24.89
Other Items (Net).......................	17r	–5.47	†–27.39	–75.78	–170.64	–206.92	–121.70	–230.76	–56.82	–97.26	–85.50	–453.93	–807.12
Banking Institutions		Billions of Yuan: End of Period										
Reserves.....................	20	367.80	†594.32	768.59	1,006.41	1,387.00	1,645.68	1,511.15	1,610.78	1,619.32	1,817.14	2,041.32	2,428.93
Foreign Assets..............	21	147.05	†294.87	440.47	390.50	428.68	531.95	600.90	646.58	903.57	1,017.55	1,284.31	1,147.86
Claims on Central Government........	22a	....	7.45	47.82	105.73	182.30	151.98	498.79	607.94	739.31	1,104.51	1,355.36	1,523.22
Claims on Other Sectors...........	22d	2,295.48	†3,388.68	4,104.28	5,097.18	6,358.26	7,693.40	8,951.61	9,986.66	11,132.41	12,180.33†	14,280.97	17,249.40
Claims on Nonbank Financial Insts...	22g	....	....	....	....	....	....	....	....	....	....	903.62	1,314.89
Demand Deposits..................	24	669.14	†969.29	1,238.99	1,520.16	1,876.49	2,381.03	2,648.57	3,235.62	3,846.88	4,414.01	5,356.21	6,431.42
Savings Deposits..................	25aa	214.06	†1,458.29	2,051.60	2,804.55	3,637.34	4,363.52	5,020.57	5,580.51	5,975.44	6,785.08	7,954.16	9,463.32
Time Deposits.....................	25ab	154.83	218.88	194.31	332.42	504.19	673.85	830.19	947.68	1,126.11	1,418.01	1,643.38	2,094.04
Foreign Currency Deposits..........	25b	....	....	....	....	....	....	....	....	....	....	1,215.91	1,188.43
Other Deposits.......................	25e	....	214.80	292.13	377.70	401.74	315.07	383.55	496.20	586.97	679.86	804.18	1,021.00
Bonds................................	26ab	....	24.79	21.30	18.91	29.98	354.18	520.38	635.46	742.89	844.80	1,010.24	1,165.40
Foreign Liabilities...............	26c	111.57	†227.53	379.15	418.95	464.61	488.80	452.72	389.61	410.03	310.19	391.66	440.50
Credit from Monetary Authorities.....	26g	670.99	†971.56	1,034.44	1,119.78	1,423.29	1,403.85	1,206.98	828.92	913.44	964.67	1,243.39	1,086.14
Liabilities to Nonbank Fin. Insts........	26j	....	....	....	....	....	....	....	....	....	....	856.73	995.55
Capital Accounts..................	27a	131.30	†283.72	343.25	351.58	411.37	428.59	658.27	626.34	739.67	765.98	877.22	1,072.93
Other Items (Net)......................	27r	14.31	†–83.62	–194.06	–344.23	–392.77	–385.88	–158.78	111.64	53.18	–63.07	–1,487.51	–1,294.43
Banking Survey		Billions of Yuan: End of Period										
Foreign Assets (Net)................	31n	168.52	†222.29	506.45	638.50	920.29	1,366.07	1,504.20	1,702.82	2,012.43	2,642.48	3,174.63	3,773.29
Domestic Credit..................	32	2,449.92	†3,575.29	4,310.37	5,331.86	6,642.17	7,954.34	9,546.87	10,701.30	11,873.21	13,487.60	17,440.83	20,861.40
Claims on Central Govt. (Net)........	32an	101.05	†118.38	133.26	166.67	218.04	243.84	584.88	704.49	729.79	1,287.71	1,511.55	1,550.89
Claims on Other Sectors............	32d	2,348.87	†3,456.91	4,177.11	5,165.19	6,424.13	7,710.50	8,961.99	9,996.82	11,143.43	12,199.89†	14,301.64	17,270.02
Claims on Nonbank Financial Insts.	32g	....	....	....	....	....	....	....	....	....	....	1,627.64	2,040.49
Money..............................	34	1,171.43	†1,546.94	1,967.43	2,308.35	2,756.38	3,480.65	3,869.05	4,697.64	5,454.10	6,168.85	7,266.54	8,644.89
Quasi-Money......................	35	1,261.30	†2,021.14	2,724.60	3,766.00	4,853.15	5,706.13	6,686.96	7,406.57	8,141.93	9,472.34†	11,412.52	13,710.43
Foreign Currency Deposits............	35b	....	....	....	....	....	....	....	....	....	....	1,215.91	1,188.43
Bonds............................	36ab	....	24.79	21.30	38.62	29.98	356.31	526.40	642.69	742.12	844.23	1,079.66	1,173.93
Capital Accounts.................	37a	199.57	†316.64	372.74	391.62	450.88	467.86	697.71	665.70	777.90	803.96	901.86	1,097.82
Other Items (Net).....................	37r	–13.87	†–112.04	–269.25	–532.70	–528.11	–690.53	–729.05	–1,008.46	–1,230.39	–1,159.30†	–1,261.02	–1,180.80
Money plus Quasi-Money..........	35l	2,432.73	†3,568.08	4,692.03	6,074.35	7,609.53	9,186.78	10,556.01	12,104.21	13,596.02	15,641.19†	18,679.05	22,355.32
Interest Rates		Percent per Annum										
Bank Rate........................	60	7.20	10.08	10.08	10.44	9.00	8.55	4.59	3.24	3.24	3.24	2.70	2.70
Deposit Rate..................	60l	7.56	10.98	10.98	10.98	7.47	5.67	3.78	2.25	2.25	2.25	1.98	1.98
Lending Rate..................	60p	8.64	10.98	10.98	12.06	10.08	8.64	6.39	5.85	5.85	5.85	5.31	5.31

China,P.R.: Mainland 924

		1992	1993	1994	1995	1996	1997	1998	1999	2000	2001	2002	2003
Prices, Production, Labor		*Percent Change over Corresponding Period of Previous Year*											
Consumer Prices	64..x	6.3	14.6	24.2	16.9	8.3	2.8	–.8	–1.4	.3	.5	–.8	1.2
Industrial Production	66..x	21.2	....	21.4	16.1	15.1	13.2	9.6	9.8	11.2	9.9	....	....
		Number in Thousands: Period Averages											
Employment	67e	655,540	663,730	674,550	680,650	689,500	698,200	706,370	713,940	720,850	730,250	737,400	....
Unemployment	67c	3,603	4,201	4,764	5,196	5,528	5,768	5,710	5,750	5,950	....	....	....
Unemployment Rate (%)	67r	2.3	2.6	2.8	2.9	3.0	3.0	3.1	3.1	3.1	....	....	....
International Transactions		*Millions of US Dollars*											
Exports	70..d	84,940	91,744	121,006	148,780	151,048	182,792	183,712	194,931	249,203	266,098	325,591	437,899
Imports, c.i.f.	71..d	80,585	103,959	115,614	132,084	138,833	142,370	140,237	165,699	225,094	243,553	295,171	413,062
Balance of Payments		*Millions of US Dollars: Minus Sign Indicates Debit*											
Current Account, n.i.e.	78ald	6,401	–11,609	6,908	1,618	7,243	36,963	31,472	21,115	20,518	17,401	35,422	....
Goods: Exports f.o.b.	78aad	69,568	75,659	102,561	128,110	151,077	182,670	183,529	194,716	249,131	266,075	325,651	....
Goods: Imports f.o.b.	78abd	–64,385	–86,313	–95,271	–110,060	–131,542	–136,448	–136,915	–158,734	–214,657	–232,058	–281,484	....
Trade Balance	78acd	5,183	–10,654	7,290	18,050	19,535	46,222	46,614	35,982	34,474	34,017	44,167	....
Services: Credit	78add	9,249	11,193	16,620	19,130	20,601	24,569	23,895	26,248	30,430	33,334	39,745	....
Services: Debit	78aed	–9,434	–12,036	–16,299	–25,223	–22,585	–27,967	–26,672	–31,589	–36,031	–39,267	–46,528	....
Balance on Goods & Services	78afd	4,998	–11,497	7,611	11,958	17,551	42,824	43,837	30,641	28,874	28,084	37,383	....
Income: Credit	78agd	5,595	4,390	5,737	5,191	7,318	5,710	5,584	8,330	12,550	9,388	8,344	....
Income: Debit	78ahd	–5,347	–5,674	–6,775	–16,965	–19,755	–16,715	–22,228	–22,800	–27,216	–28,563	–23,289	....
Balance on Gds, Serv. & Inc.	78aid	5,246	–12,781	6,573	184	5,114	31,819	27,193	16,171	14,207	8,909	22,438	....
Current Transfers, n.i.e.: Credit	78ajd	1,206	1,290	1,269	1,827	2,368	5,477	4,661	5,368	6,861	9,125	13,795	....
Current Transfers: Debit	78akd	–51	–118	–934	–392	–239	–333	–382	–424	–550	–633	–811	....
Capital Account, n.i.e.	78bcd	–	–	–	–	–	–21	–47	–26	–35	–54	–50	....
Capital Account, n.i.e.: Credit	78bad	–	–	–	–	–	–	–	–	....	....	....	....
Capital Account: Debit	78bbd	–	–	–	–	–	–21	–47	–26	–35	–54	–50	....
Financial Account, n.i.e.	78bjd	–250	23,474	32,645	38,674	39,966	21,037	–6,275	5,204	1,958	34,832	32,341	....
Direct Investment Abroad	78bdd	–4,000	–4,400	–2,000	–2,000	–2,114	–2,563	–2,634	–1,775	–916	–6,884	–2,518	....
Dir. Invest. in Rep. Econ., n.i.e.	78bed	11,156	27,515	33,787	35,849	40,180	44,237	43,751	38,753	38,399	44,241	49,308	....
Portfolio Investment Assets	78bfd	–450	–597	–380	79	–628	–899	–3,830	–10,535	–11,307	–20,654	–12,095	....
Equity Securities	78bkd	–	–	–	–	–	–	–	–	–	32	–	....
Debt Securities	78bld	–450	–597	–380	79	–628	–899	–3,830	–10,535	–11,307	–20,686	–12,095	....
Portfolio Investment Liab., n.i.e.	78bgd	393	3,646	3,923	710	2,372	7,842	98	–699	7,317	1,249	1,752	....
Equity Securities	78bmd	–	–	–	....	....	5,657	765	612	6,912	849	2,249	....
Debt Securities	78bnd	393	3,646	3,923	710	2,372	2,185	–667	–1,311	405	400	–497	....
Financial Derivatives Assets	78bwd	....	....	....	....	....	....	....	....	....	....	....	....
Financial Derivatives Liabilities	78bxd	....	....	....	....	....	....	....	....	....	....	....	....
Other Investment Assets	78bhd	–3,267	–2,114	–1,189	–1,081	–1,126	–39,608	–35,041	–24,394	–43,864	20,813	–3,077	....
Monetary Authorities	78bod	....	....	....	....	....	–7,977	–2,417	–5,715	–7,261	–5,387	–	....
General Government	78bpd	–3,351	–1,741	–1,136	–367	–1,102	....	....	....	....	....	....	....
Banks	78bqd	–	–	....	....	....	–12,572	2,841	6,075	–21,430	16,800	–10,258	....
Other Sectors	78brd	84	–373	–53	–714	–24	–19,059	–35,465	–24,754	–15,173	9,400	7,181	....
Other Investment Liab., n.i.e.	78bid	–4,082	–576	–1,496	5,116	1,282	12,028	–8,619	3,854	12,329	–3,933	–1,029	....
Monetary Authorities	78bsd	140	175	1,004	1,154	1,256	–2,037	–5,441	–3,936	–	–	–	....
General Government	78btd	–18	1,564	5,178	6,021	4,995	–	–	3,233	3,153	1,124	40	....
Banks	78bud	–786	–415	–5,222	–4,045	–5,959	6,968	–3,150	–5,021	–8,281	–1,305	–1,725	....
Other Sectors	78bvd	–3,418	–1,900	–2,456	1,986	990	7,097	–28	9,578	17,457	–3,752	655	....
Net Errors and Omissions	78cad	–8,211	–10,096	–9,100	–17,823	–15,504	–22,122	–18,902	–17,641	–11,748	–4,732	7,504	....
Overall Balance	78cbd	–2,060	1,769	30,453	22,469	31,705	35,857	6,248	8,652	10,693	47,447	75,217	....
Reserves and Related Items	79dad	2,060	–1,769	–30,453	–22,469	–31,705	–35,857	–6,248	–8,652	–10,693	–47,447	–75,217	....
Reserve Assets	79dbd	2,060	–1,769	–30,453	–22,469	–31,705	–35,857	–6,248	–8,652	–10,693	–47,447	–75,217	....
Use of Fund Credit and Loans	79dcd	–	–	–	–	–	–	–	–	–	–	–	....
Exceptional Financing	79ded	....	....	....	....	....	....	....	....	....	....	–	....
Government Finance		*Billions of Yuan: Year Ending December 31*											
Deficit (-) or Surplus	80	–70.38	–70.46	–94.07	–90.93	–86.70	–92.70	–125.57	–203.39	–277.03	–438.29f	–309.78	–291.69
Total Revenue and Grants	81y	348.34	434.90	521.81	624.22	740.80	865.11	987.60	1,144.40	1,339.50	1,476.00f	1,917.35	2,191.71
Exp. & Lending Minus Repay.	82z	418.72	505.36	615.88	715.15	827.50	957.81	1,113.17	1,347.79	1,616.53	1,914.29	2,227.13	2,483.40
Financing													
Domestic	84a	33.91	33.36	63.64	69.96	55.35	56.44	95.25	188.26	260.49	256.90	319.33	315.69
Foreign	85a	–8.03	–4.02	3.06	–3.68	6.53	–.60	.56	–9.10	–.45	3.61	–9.53	4.61
Use of Cash Balances	87	–	–	–9.25	–8.13	–7.93	–	–3.58	–4.80	–10.56	....	....	....

2004, International Monetary Fund: *International Financial Statistics Yearbook*

China,P.R.: Mainland 924

		1992	1993	1994	1995	1996	1997	1998	1999	2000	2001	2002	2003
National Accounts						**Billions of Yuan**							
Househ.Cons.Expend.,incl.NPISHs	96f	1,246.0	1,568.2	2,081.0	2,694.5	3,215.2	3,485.5	3,692.1	3,933.4	4,291.1	4,592.3	....	....
Government Consumption Expend...	91f	349.2	450.0	598.6	669.1	785.2	872.5	948.5	1,038.8	1,170.5	1,302.9	....	....
Gross Fixed Capital Formation	93e	831.7	1,298.0	1,685.6	2,030.1	2,333.6	2,515.4	2,763.1	2,947.6	3,262.4	3,681.3	....	....
Changes in Inventories	93i	131.9	201.8	240.4	357.7	353.1	330.3	191.5	122.6	−12.4	64.8	....	....
Exports (Net)	90n	27.6	−67.9	63.4	99.9	145.9	285.7	305.2	244.9	224.0	220.5	....	....
Gross Domestic Product (GDP)	99b	2,586.4	3,450.1	4,669.1	5,851.1	6,833.0	7,489.4	7,900.3	8,267.3	8,935.7	9,731.4	10,517.2	11,689.8
Net Primary Income from Abroad	98.n	1.4	−7.4	−8.9	−98.3	....	....	....	....	....	....	....	....
Gross National Income (GNI)	99a	2,587.7	3,442.7	4,660.1	5,752.7	....	....	....	....	....	....	....	....
GDP Volume 1995 Prices	99b.p	4,141.1	4,699.7	5,294.8	5,851.1	6,412.0	6,976.5	7,520.9	8,055.9	8,700.4	....	....	....
GDP Volume (2000=100)	99bvp	47.6	54.0	60.9	67.3	73.7	80.2	86.4	92.6	100.0	....	....	....
GDP Deflator (2000=100)	99bip	60.8	71.5	85.9	97.4	103.8	104.5	102.3	99.9	100.0	....	....	....
						Millions: Midyear Estimates							
Population	99z	1,183.3	1,195.7	1,207.7	1,219.4	1,231.1	1,242.6	1,253.9	1,264.8	1,275.2	1,285.2	1,294.9	1,304.2

China, P.R.: Hong Kong 532

		1992	1993	1994	1995	1996	1997	1998	1999	2000	2001	2002	2003
Exchange Rates						*Hong Kong Dollars per SDR: End of Period*							
Market Rate	aa	10.647	10.612	11.296	11.494	11.124	10.451	10.907	10.666	10.157	9.799	10.602	11.536
					Hong Kong Dollars per US Dollar: End of Period (ae) Period Average (rf)								
Market Rate	ae	7.743	7.726	7.738	7.732	7.736	7.746	7.746	7.771	7.796	7.797	7.798	7.763
Market Rate	rf	7.741	7.736	7.728	7.736	7.734	7.742	7.745	7.758	7.791	7.799	7.799	7.787
					Index Numbers (2000=100) Period Averages								
Nominal Effective Exchange Rate	nec	86.42	92.45	92.59	88.28	91.36	96.28	101.77	98.95	100.00	104.37	103.76	98.16
Fund Position						*Millions of SDRs: End of Period*							
Reserve Position in the Fund	1c.s	–	–	–	–	–	–	31.34	–	–	–	–	–
of which: Outstg.Fund Borrowing	2c	–	–	–	–	–	–	31.34	–	–	–	–	–
International Liquidity					*Billions of US Dollars Unless Otherwise Indicated: End of Period*								
Total Reserves minus Gold	1l.d	35.17	42.99	49.25	55.40	63.81	92.80	89.65	96.24	107.54	111.16	111.90	118.36
Reserve Position in the Fund	1c.d							.04					
Foreign Exchange	1d.d	35.17	42.99	49.25	55.40	63.81	†92.80	†89.61	96.24	107.54	111.16	111.90	118.36
Gold (Million Fine Troy Ounces)	1ad	.228	.068	.068	.067	.067	.067	.067	.067	.067	.067	.067	.067
Gold (National Valuation)	1and	.076	.026	.026	.026	.025	.019	.019	.019	.018	.019	.023	.028
Banking Institutions: Assets	7a.d	507.32	518.78	614.80	655.58	608.62	600.63	501.17	475.78	450.48	405.22	394.41	440.28
Liabilities	7b.d	463.87	477.58	582.33	620.40	579.85	597.32	447.35	371.87	319.15	264.39	244.74	267.03
Monetary Authorities						*Billions of Hong Kong Dollars: End of Period*							
Foreign Assets	11	199.10	290.52	297.27	376.59	463.89	549.97	672.68	691.27	803.69	822.50	832.87	868.65
Reserve Money	14	62.17	72.79	79.88	82.96	87.12	92.71	94.77	†234.39	215.40	229.74	246.11	292.67
of which: Currency Outside Banks	14a	51.70	62.89	67.31	70.87	76.05	80.34	80.92	99.27	91.51	101.38	112.98	127.61
Foreign Liabilities	16c	.02	.03	1.54	.03	.32	.04	.04	.27	.04	19.82	42.08	1.67	1.01
Government Deposits	16d	96.15	115.68	131.24	125.92	145.90	237.63	424.56	392.21	417.16	380.60	301.67	252.30
Capital Accounts	17a	106.64	127.54	125.77	160.13	172.86	190.21	242.22	290.86	307.10	302.59	327.17	384.88
Other Items (Net)	17r	–65.88	–25.52	–41.17	7.56	57.69	29.38	–89.15	–226.22	–155.79	–132.51	–43.75	–62.21
Banking Institutions						*Billions of Hong Kong Dollars: End of Period*							
Reserves	20	10.47	9.91	12.57	12.09	11.07	12.37	13.85	32.67	14.34	12.53	11.91	41.18
Foreign Assets	21	3,928.17	4,008.11	4,757.31	5,068.93	4,708.31	4,652.49	3,882.07	3,697.31	3,511.95	3,159.51	3,075.65	3,417.93
Claims on Government	22a	29.72	56.77	106.77	57.25	104.74	143.61	140.34	166.64	201.19	212.75	234.12	220.67
Claims on Other Sectors	22d	1,045.40	1,256.02	1,506.39	1,671.93	1,935.32	2,324.36	2,181.93	1,964.83	2,010.95	1,968.19	1,890.33	1,837.65
Demand Deposits	24	72.85	87.71	83.38	80.32	98.33	87.44	79.07	85.35	93.05	109.51	127.39	196.44
Time, Savings,& Fgn.Currency Dep	25	1,193.40	1,357.87	1,534.82	1,713.81	1,923.57	2,113.05	2,374.65	2,560.47	2,816.59	2,781.96	2,768.92	2,874.11
Money Market Instruments	26aa	38.51	46.83	71.26	82.62	107.13	118.16	116.51	110.77	103.79	107.79	143.08	170.67
Foreign Liabilities	26c	3,591.78	3,689.75	4,506.08	4,796.95	4,485.74	4,626.87	3,465.16	2,889.78	2,488.13	2,061.42	1,908.48	2,072.93
Government Deposits	26d	11.30	26.60	18.87	14.43	19.09	5.16	6.15	3.78	2.93	1.46	2.51	2.38
Capital Accounts	27a	90.86	104.85	113.03	132.61	153.91	170.34	153.67	154.03	164.10	204.27	207.72	188.87
Other Items (Net)	27r	15.04	17.20	55.58	–10.56	–28.33	11.78	22.98	57.27	69.84	86.58	53.91	12.02
Banking Survey						*Billions of Hong Kong Dollars: End of Period*							
Foreign Assets (Net)	31n	535.47	608.86	546.96	648.53	686.14	575.54	1,089.32	1,498.76	1,807.70	1,878.52	1,998.37	2,212.64
Domestic Credit	32	967.68	1,170.50	1,463.04	1,588.84	1,875.07	2,225.17	1,891.55	1,735.49	1,792.05	1,798.88	1,820.27	1,803.65
Claims on Government (net)	32an	–77.73	–85.51	–43.34	–83.10	–60.25	–99.18	–290.38	–229.34	–218.90	–169.31	–70.06	–34.00
Claims on Other Sectors	32d	1,045.40	1,256.02	1,506.39	1,671.93	1,935.32	2,324.36	2,181.93	1,964.83	2,010.95	1,968.19	1,890.33	1,837.65
Money	34	124.55	150.60	150.70	151.19	174.38	167.78	159.99	184.62	184.56	210.88	240.37	324.06
Quasi-Money	35	1,193.40	1,357.87	1,534.82	1,713.81	1,923.57	2,113.05	2,374.65	2,560.47	2,816.59	2,781.96	2,768.92	2,874.11
Money Market Instruments	36aa	38.51	46.83	71.26	82.62	107.13	118.16	116.51	110.77	103.79	107.79	143.08	170.67
Capital Accounts	37a	197.50	232.39	238.81	292.75	326.77	360.55	395.89	444.89	471.20	506.86	534.90	573.75
Other Items (Net)	37r	–50.83	–8.32	14.40	–3.00	29.36	41.16	–66.17	–66.49	23.61	69.90	131.37	73.70
Money plus Quasi-Money	35l	1,317.95	1,508.46	1,685.52	1,865.00	2,097.95	2,280.84	2,534.64	2,745.08	3,001.15	2,992.84	3,009.29	3,198.17
Interest Rates						*Percent Per Annum*							
Discount Rate (End of Period)	60	4.00	4.00	5.75	6.25	6.00	7.00	6.25	7.00	8.00	3.25	2.75	2.50
Money Market Rate	60b	3.81	4.00	5.44	6.00	5.13	4.50	5.50	5.75	7.13	2.69	1.50	.07
Treasury Bill Rate	60c	3.83	3.17	5.66	5.55	4.45	7.50	5.04	4.94	5.69	1.69	1.35	–.08
Deposit Rate	60l	3.07	2.25	3.54	5.63	4.64	5.98	6.62	4.50	4.80	2.38	.35	.07
Lending Rate	60p	6.50	6.50	8.50	8.75	8.50	9.50	9.00	8.50	9.50	5.13	5.00	5.00
Prices, Production, Labor						*Index Numbers (2000=100): Period Averages*							
Share Prices	62	34.2	46.5	59.4	56.2	71.6	83.4	58.8	79.1	100.0	78.4	65.2	64.1
Producer Prices	63	98.2	98.8	100.9	103.7	103.6	103.3	101.4	99.8	100.0	98.4	95.7	95.4
Consumer Prices	64	72.4	78.8	85.7	93.5	99.4	105.2	108.2	103.9	100.0	98.4	95.4	92.9
Wages:Avg.Earnings(Mfg)	65	....	....	72.4	80.2	†86.3	93.4	99.3	98.6	100.0	102.1	100.9	97.8
Wage Rates (Manufacturing)	65a	†68.6	75.5	81.6	86.2	92.7	98.4	98.4	97.8	100.0	102.7	101.1	97.3
Manufacturing Production	66ey	123.0	122.2	121.9	123.1	118.5	†117.6	107.4	100.5	100.0	95.6	86.3	78.3
						Number in Thousands: Period Averages							
Labor Force	67d	....	2,873	2,972	3,001	3,094	3,216	3,359	....	3,383	3,427	3,488	....
Employment	67e	2,738	2,800	2,873	2,905	†3,073	3,164	3,122	3,112	3,207	3,252	3,232	3,223
Unemployment	67c	55	56	56	96	†87	71	154	208	167	175	256	278
Unemployment Rate (%)	67r	2.0	2.0	1.9	3.2	†2.8	2.2	4.7	6.3	5.0	5.1	7.3	7.9

2004, International Monetary Fund : *International Financial Statistics Yearbook*

China,P.R.: Hong Kong 532

		1992	1993	1994	1995	1996	1997	1998	1999	2000	2001	2002	2003
International Transactions							**Billions of US Dollars**						
Exports	70..d	119.49	135.24	151.40	173.75	180.75	188.06	174.00	173.89	201.86	189.89	200.09	223.76
Imports, c.i.f.	71..d	123.41	138.65	161.84	192.75	198.55	208.61	184.52	179.52	212.81	201.08	207.64	231.90
							2000=100						
Volume of Exports	72	55.2	62.6	69.1	77.4	81.1	86.1	82.4	85.4	100.0	96.7	104.9	119.6
Volume of Imports	73	55.6	62.8	71.6	81.4	84.9	91.0	84.5	84.7	100.0	98.0	105.7	119.2
Unit Value of Exports	74	104.5	104.1	105.6	109.1	108.8	107.0	103.0	100.2	100.0	97.7	95.1	93.8
Unit Value of Imports	75	103.0	102.4	105.1	110.4	109.0	106.5	101.3	99.2	100.0	96.9	93.1	92.8
Balance of Payments						**Millions of US Dollars Minus Sign Indicates Debit**							
Current Account, n.i.e.	78ald	....	....	....	....	....	....	2,529	10,284	7,083	9,941	12,596	16,155
Goods: Exports f.o.b.	78aad	....	....	....	....	....	....	175,833	174,719	202,698	190,926	200,300	224,656
Goods: Imports f.o.b.	78abd	....	....	....	....	....	....	−183,666	−177,878	−210,891	−199,257	−205,353	−230,435
Trade Balance	78acd	....	....	....	....	....	....	−7,833	−3,159	−8,193	−8,331	−5,053	−5,779
Services: Credit	78add	....	....	....	....	....	....	33,235	34,226	38,735	39,449	43,008	44,624
Services: Debit	78aed	....	....	....	....	....	....	−24,991	−23,725	−24,584	−24,677	−25,603	−25,185
Balance on Goods & Services	78afd	....	....	....	....	....	....	412	7,342	5,958	6,441	12,352	13,659
Income: Credit	78agd	....	....	....	....	....	....	46,831	47,031	53,494	49,315	43,223	42,198
Income: Debit	78ahd	....	....	....	....	....	....	−43,117	−42,548	−50,699	−44,036	−41,083	−37,813
Balance on Gds, Serv. & Inc.	78aid	....	....	....	....	....	....	4,125	11,824	8,753	11,721	14,492	18,044
Current Transfers, n.i.e.: Credit	78ajd	....	....	....	....	....	....	669	570	538	605	777	574
Current Transfers: Debit	78akd	....	....	....	....	....	....	−2,265	−2,109	−2,208	−2,385	−2,673	−2,463
Capital Account, n.i.e.	78bcd	....	....	....	....	....	....	−2,382	−1,780	−1,546	−1,174	−2,011	−1,016
Capital Account, n.i.e.: Credit	78bad	....	....	....	....	....	....	377	103	57	41	31	123
Capital Account: Debit	78bbd	....	....	....	....	....	....	−2,759	−1,883	−1,602	−1,215	−2,042	−1,139
Financial Account, n.i.e.	78bjd	....	....	....	....	....	....	−8,476	1,061	4,165	−6,626	−19,751	−17,453
Direct Investment Abroad	78bdd	....	....	....	....	....	....	−16,985	−19,369	−59,352	−11,345	−17,463	−3,747
Dir. Invest. in Rep. Econ., n.i.e.	78bed	....	....	....	....	....	....	14,765	24,578	61,924	23,776	9,682	13,538
Portfolio Investment Assets	78bfd	....	....	....	....	....	....	25,492	−25,440	−22,022	−40,133	−37,702	−31,458
Equity Securities	78bkd	....	....	....	....	....	....	8,507	−30,337	−17,606	−22,682	−15,756	−8,537
Debt Securities	78bld	....	....	....	....	....	....	16,985	4,897	−4,416	−17,452	−21,946	−22,921
Portfolio Investment Liab., n.i.e.	78bgd	....	....	....	....	....	....	−3,407	58,525	46,508	−1,161	−1,084	991
Equity Securities	78bmd	....	....	....	....	....	....	−2,106	60,470	46,976	−855	1,391	5,537
Debt Securities	78bnd	....	....	....	....	....	....	−1,301	−1,944	−468	−305	−2,475	−4,546
Financial Derivatives Assets	78bwd	....	....	....	....	....	....	10,837	21,224	8,445	17,971	20,035	25,435
Financial Derivatives Liabilities	78bxd	....	....	....	....	....	....	−7,538	−11,011	−8,240	−12,888	−13,424	−15,224
Other Investment Assets	78bhd	....	....	....	....	....	....	119,830	42,963	18,279	59,137	46,617	−22,181
Monetary Authorities	78bod	....	....	....	....	....	....	....	....	....	....	....	....
General Government	78bpd	....	....	....	....	....	....	....	....	....	....	....	....
Banks	78bqd	....	....	....	....	....	....	101,774	34,181	23,857	61,452	46,037	−18,705
Other Sectors	78brd	....	....	....	....	....	....	18,057	8,781	−5,578	−2,315	580	−3,476
Other Investment Liab., n.i.e.	78bid	....	....	....	....	....	....	−151,470	−90,410	−41,375	−41,985	−26,412	15,193
Monetary Authorities	78bsd	....	....	....	....	....	....	....	....	....	....	....	....
General Government	78btd	....	....	....	....	....	....	....	....	....	....	....	....
Banks	78bud	....	....	....	....	....	....	−148,616	−85,768	−44,259	−42,888	−20,937	12,209
Other Sectors	78bvd	....	....	....	....	....	....	−2,854	−4,642	2,884	903	−5,475	2,984
Net Errors and Omissions	78cad	....	....	....	....	....	....	1,539	462	341	2,543	6,788	3,308
Overall Balance	78cbd	....	....	....	....	....	....	−6,789	10,028	10,044	4,684	−2,377	994
Reserves and Related Items	79dad	....	....	....	....	....	....	6,789	−10,028	−10,044	−4,684	2,377	−994
Reserve Assets	79dbd	....	....	....	....	....	....	6,789	−10,028	−10,044	−4,684	2,377	−994
Use of Fund Credit and Loans	79dcd	....	....	....	....	....	....	....	....	....	....	....	....
Exceptional Financing	79ded	....	....	....	....	....	....	....	....	....	....	....	....
International Investment Position						**Millions of US Dollars**							
Assets	79aad	....	....	....	....	....	....	....	....	1,141,521	1,071,005	1,030,103	1,175,434
Direct Investment Abroad	79abd	....	....	....	....	....	235,763	223,811	321,635	388,380	352,602	309,430	336,098
Portfolio Investment	79acd	....	....	....	....	....	....	....	....	178,851	205,600	244,068	331,773
Equity Securities	79add	....	....	....	....	....	....	....	....	88,325	94,615	95,721	152,047
Debt Securities	79aed	....	....	....	....	....	....	....	....	90,526	110,984	148,347	179,726
Financial Derivatives	79ald	....	....	....	....	....	....	....	....	16,812	17,529	22,521	21,561
Other Investment	79afd	....	....	....	....	....	....	....	−	449,880	384,088	342,158	367,606
Monetary Authorities	79agd	....	....	....	....	....	....	....	....	....	....	....	....
General Government	79ahd	....	....	....	....	....	....	....	....	....	−	....	....
Banks	79aid	....	....	....	....	....	....	....	....	393,157	318,398	275,831	299,645
Other Sectors	79ajd	....	....	....	....	....	....	....	....	56,723	65,690	66,327	67,961
Reserve Assets	79akd	....	....	....	....	....	92,855	89,639	96,287	107,599	111,187	111,927	118,396
Liabilities	79lad	....	....	....	....	....	....	....	....	919,670	805,779	686,763	777,710
Dir. Invest. in Rep. Economy	79lbd	....	....	....	....	....	249,360	225,078	405,266	455,469	419,348	336,278	375,048
Portfolio Investment	79lcd	....	....	....	....	....	....	....	....	153,217	117,031	93,544	125,088
Equity Securities	79ldd	....	....	....	....	....	....	....	....	138,078	102,833	79,289	115,520
Debt Securities	79led	....	....	....	....	....	....	....	....	15,139	14,198	14,255	9,568
Financial Derivatives	79lld	....	....	....	....	....	....	....	....	12,517	12,059	21,198	21,261
Other Investment	79lfd	....	....	....	....	....	−	−	−	298,467	257,342	235,742	256,313
Monetary Authorities	79lgd	....	....	....	....	....	....	....	....	....	....	....	....
General Government	79lhd	....	....	....	....	....	....	....	....	....	−	....	....
Banks	79lid	....	....	....	....	....	....	....	....	279,017	231,182	213,161	230,063
Other Sectors	79ljd	....	....	....	....	....	....	....	....	19,451	26,160	22,581	26,251

China,P.R.: Hong Kong 532

		1992	1993	1994	1995	1996	1997	1998	1999	2000	2001	2002	2003
National Accounts		\multicolumn{12}{c}{*Billions of Hong Kong Dollars*}
Househ.Cons.Expend.,incl.NPISHs....	96f	467	534	617	683	748	825	787	754	760	765	728	705
Government Consumption Expend...	91f	64	72	83	94	104	113	117	120	120	129	131	130
Gross Fixed Capital Formation..........	93e	218	249	306	334	378	452	389	325	347	333	286	269
Changes in Inventories.....................	93i	8	2	21	46	10	12	−16	−11	14	−4	6	9
Exports of Goods and Services..........	90c	1,101	1,246	1,392	1,585	1,670	1,729	1,605	1,615	1,875	1,789	1,898	2,096
Imports of Goods and Services (-).....	98c	1,067	1,191	1,390	1,645	1,699	1,786	1,602	1,558	1,828	1,742	1,801	1,990
Gross Domestic Product (GDP).........	99b	791	913	1,030	1,096	1,211	1,345	1,280	1,246	1,288	1,270	1,247	1,220
Net Primary Income from Abroad.....	98.n	....	13	12	21	−	10	29	35	22	41	17	34
Gross National Income (GNI)............	99a	....	926	1,042	1,117	1,211	1,355	1,309	1,281	1,310	1,311	1,264	1,254
Net Current Transf.from Abroad.......	98t	....	....	....	....	....	−12	−12	−12	−13	−14	−15	−15
Gross Nat'l Disposable Inc.(GNDI)....	99i	....	....	....	....	....	1,343	1,296	1,269	1,297	1,297	1,249	1,239
Gross Saving....................................	99s	....	....	....	....	....	405	393	395	417	403	390	404
GDP Volume 1995 Prices.................	99b.p	932	991	1,045	1,086	1,133	1,190	1,131	1,169	1,288	1,294	1,319	1,361
GDP Volume (2000=100)................	99bvp	72.3	76.9	81.1	84.3	87.9	92.4	87.8	90.8	100.0	100.5	102.4	105.6
GDP Deflator (2000=100)...............	99bip	84.9	92.1	98.5	101.0	106.9	113.0	113.2	106.6	100.0	98.1	94.6	89.6
		\multicolumn{12}{c}{*Millions: Midyear Estimates*}
Population..............................	99z	5.86	5.96	6.07	6.18	6.31	6.44	6.57	6.70	6.81	6.90	6.98	7.05

China,P.R.: Macao 546

		1992	1993	1994	1995	1996	1997	1998	1999	2000	2001	2002	2003
Exchange Rates		*Patacas Per SDR: End of Period*
Market Rate	aa	10.961	10.928	11.635	11.839	11.457	10.769	11.236	10.987	10.467	10.093	10.921	11.883
		Patacas per US Dollar: End of Period (ae) Period Average (rf)
Market Rate	ae	7.972	7.956	7.970	7.965	7.968	7.982	7.980	8.005	8.034	8.031	8.033	7.997
Market Rate	rf	7.972	7.968	7.960	7.968	7.966	7.975	7.979	7.992	8.026	8.034	8.033	8.021
International Liquidity		*Billions of US Dollars Unless Otherwise Indicated: End of Period*
Total Reserves minus Gold	1l.d	1.30	1.57	1.97	2.26	2.42	2.53	2.46	2.86	3.32	3.51	3.80	4.34
Foreign Exchange	1d.d	1.30	1.57	1.97	2.26	2.42	2.53	2.46	2.86	3.32	3.51	3.80	4.34
Gold (Million Fine Troy Ounces)	1ad	–	–	–	–	–	–	–	–	–	–	–	–
Gold (National Valuation)	1and	–	–	–	–	–	–	–	–	–	–	–	–
Banking Institutions: Assets	7a.d	5.20	6.61	6.08	6.77	10.83	10.75	†12.63	7.83	8.58	9.30	10.65	11.72
Liabilities	7b.d	2.46	4.62	3.96	4.10	7.82	7.92	†8.30	3.30	3.06	2.85	2.98	2.69
Monetary Authorities		*Millions of Patacas: End of Period*
Foreign Assets	11	10,377.0	12,483.6	15,672.0	17,972.4	19,298.9	20,215.3	19,651.1	22,873.1	30,646.3	33,431.6	36,380.5	42,483.7
Claims on Government	12a	49.8	132.6	67.2	69.2	85.5	115.0	143.3	190.9	188.6	181.5	191.6	206.4
Claims on Deposit Money Banks	12e	59.5	45.1	59.6	42.3	55.7	53.6	37.7	515.4	6,284.9	5,013.8	3,596.8	2,685.1
Reserve Money	14	2,015.9	2,138.7	2,405.7	2,735.1	2,909.6	3,047.8	3,239.1	3,957.9	3,665.3	3,871.6	4,208.8	4,885.1
of which: Currency Outside Banks	14a	968.8	1,080.9	1,197.8	1,280.1	1,426.7	1,518.3	1,554.6	1,819.4	1,717.2	1,895.8	2,053.0	2,361.8
Liab. of Central Bank: Securities	16ac	5,701.2	5,876.5	8,686.3	11,242.7	11,207.2	10,942.6	11,803.9	15,086.4	17,530.0	16,927.7	15,837.5	17,076.1
Foreign Liabilities	16c	.1	.1	.9	.1	103.1	.1	.2	–	–	4.9	–	.1
Government Deposits	16d	2,159.8	3,761.2	4,246.0	3,160.3	4,555.6	5,744.6	3,835.0	3,450.8	14,320.4	15,662.8	17,596.8	20,643.9
Capital Accounts	17a	889.0	1,216.7	1,071.2	1,569.6	1,693.1	1,979.1	2,437.9	2,333.9	2,878.0	3,077.5	3,286.1	3,439.1
Other Items (Net)	17r	–279.7	–337.1	–611.2	–624.1	–1,028.6	–1,330.2	–1,483.8	–1,249.8	–1,274.0	–917.7	–760.4	–669.1
Banking Institutions		*Millions of Patacas: End of Period*
Reserves	20	1,047.1	1,057.8	1,207.9	1,455.0	1,482.9	1,529.5	1,684.5	2,138.5	1,948.1	1,975.8	2,155.8	2,523.3
Claims on Mon.Author.: Securities	20c	5,701.2	5,876.7	8,686.3	11,242.7	11,207.2	10,942.6	11,803.9	15,086.4	17,530.0	16,927.7	15,837.5	17,076.1
Foreign Assets	21	41,419.1	52,554.5	48,434.0	53,955.6	86,316.3	85,763.6†	100,793.3	62,680.8	68,927.7	74,657.0	85,554.1	93,722.5
Claims on Government	22a	279.3	214.5	143.0	71.5	–	.3	2.2	–	–	–	–	–
Claims on Nonfin.Pub. Enterprises	22c	....	....	....	....	....	....	....	....	....	1,438.7	2,008.4	1,951.8
Claims on Other Sectors	22d	25,882.3	35,997.1	39,707.3	41,694.5	44,492.5	48,890.5	†42,808.1	42,111.3	39,127.6	34,897.7	32,321.9	31,895.7
Demand Deposits	24	5,454.8	4,679.7	4,038.6	4,337.6	4,289.2	3,790.7	†3,954.1	3,543.7	3,228.2	4,020.9	4,297.8	6,427.8
Time & Savings Deposits	25	44,378.6	48,552.9	55,976.9	63,825.8	68,616.8	72,873.9	†75,118.9	80,733.2	79,972.4	85,633.3	92,608.6	102,300.6
Foreign Liabilities	26c	19,644.5	36,786.8	31,533.0	32,685.2	62,316.5	63,178.3	†66,239.9	26,433.7	24,598.4	22,861.4	23,974.1	21,488.8
Government Deposits	26d	1,305.4	1,208.3	1,161.6	1,439.4	1,677.6	2,275.6	4,244.5	2,784.9	4,447.9	3,943.1	4,468.7	4,686.0
Credit from Monetary Authorities	26g	59.5	45.1	59.6	42.3	55.7	53.6	37.7	515.4	6,284.9	5,013.8	3,596.8	2,685.1
Capital Accounts	27a	3,215.6	3,938.7	4,812.2	5,005.5	5,561.0	6,222.5	6,330.2	5,707.4	6,593.4	7,000.4	7,733.3	8,523.1
Other Items (Net)	27r	271.7	490.3	596.6	1,083.4	982.2	–1,268.1	1,166.7	2,298.8	2,408.5	1,424.0	1,198.2	1,058.3
Banking Survey		*Millions of Patacas: End of Period*
Foreign Assets (Net)	31n	32,151.5	28,251.2	32,572.1	39,242.7	43,195.6	42,800.5	†54,204.3	59,120.2	74,975.6	85,222.3	97,960.5	114,717.3
Domestic Credit	32	22,746.2	31,374.7	34,509.9	37,235.5	38,344.8	40,985.6	†34,874.1	36,066.5	20,547.9	16,912.0	12,456.4	8,724.0
Claims on Government (net)	32an	–3,136.1	–4,622.4	–5,197.4	–4,459.0	–6,147.7	–7,904.9	–7,934.0	–6,044.8	–18,579.7	–19,424.4	–21,873.9	–25,123.5
Claims on Nonfin.Pub. Enterprises	32c	....	....	....	....	....	....	....	....	....	1,438.7	2,008.4	1,951.8
Claims on Other Sectors	32d	25,882.3	35,997.1	39,707.3	41,694.5	44,492.5	48,890.5	†42,808.1	42,111.3	39,127.6	34,897.7	32,321.9	31,895.7
Money	34	6,423.6	5,760.6	5,236.4	5,617.7	5,715.9	5,309.0	†5,508.7	5,363.1	4,945.4	5,916.7	6,350.8	8,789.6
Quasi-Money	35	44,378.6	48,552.9	55,976.9	63,825.8	68,616.8	72,873.9	†75,118.9	80,733.2	79,972.4	85,633.3	92,608.6	102,300.6
Capital Accounts	37a	4,104.6	5,155.4	5,883.4	6,575.1	7,254.1	8,201.6	8,768.1	8,041.3	9,471.4	10,077.9	11,019.4	11,962.2
Other Items (Net)	37r	–8.0	153.0	–14.6	459.3	–46.4	–2,598.3	–317.1	1,049.0	1,134.5	506.3	437.8	389.2
Money plus Quasi-Money	35l	50,802.2	54,313.5	61,213.3	69,443.5	74,332.7	78,182.9	†80,627.6	86,096.3	84,917.8	91,550.0	98,959.4	111,090.2
Interest Rates		*Percent Per Annum*
Interbank Rate (End of Period)	60b	4.41	3.79	5.91	6.01	5.60	7.54	5.41	5.70	6.29	2.11	1.48	.11
Deposit Rate	60l	3.50	2.75	4.21	5.93	5.23	6.22	7.00	5.30	5.33	2.59	.63	....
Lending Rate	60p	7.25	6.50	7.95	9.90	9.56	9.73	10.97	9.46	9.89	7.99	6.11	6.00
Prices and Labor		*Index Numbers (2000=100): Period Averages*
Consumer Prices	64	....	....	....	....	....	....	105.0	101.6	100.0	98.0	95.4	93.9
		Number in Thousands: Period Averages
Labor Force	67d	173	175	177	187	202	202	206	209	210	217	214	216
Employment	67e	169	171	173	180	194	196	197	196	195	203	201	203
Unemployment	67c	4	4	4	7	9	7	10	13	14	14	13	13
Unemployment Rate (%)	67r	2.2	2.1	2.5	3.6	4.3	3.2	4.6	6.3	6.8	6.4	6.3	6.0
International Transactions		*Millions of US Dollars*
Exports	70..d	1,766.4	1,786.6	1,866.0	1,997.3	1,995.8	2,147.8	2,141.1	2,199.6	2,539.0	2,299.5	2,355.8	2,580.8
Imports, c.i.f	71..d	1,967.6	2,025.5	2,126.2	2,041.6	1,999.8	2,081.8	1,954.9	2,039.5	2,254.7	2,386.3	2,529.8	2,755.2

China,P.R.: Macao   546

		1992	1993	1994	1995	1996	1997	1998	1999	2000	2001	2002	2003
Balance of Payments						*Millions of US Dollars Minus Sign Indicates Debit*							
Current Account, n.i.e.	78ald	....	....	....	....	....	....	....	....	....	....	2,565	....
Goods: Exports f.o.b.	78aad	....	....	....	....	....	....	....	....	....	....	2,357	....
Goods: Imports f.o.b.	78abd	....	....	....	....	....	....	....	....	....	....	−3,191	....
Trade Balance	78acd	....	....	....	....	....	....	....	....	....	....	−833	....
Services: Credit	78add	....	....	....	....	....	....	....	....	....	....	4,467	....
Services: Debit	78aed	....	....	....	....	....	....	....	....	....	....	−1,050	....
Balance on Goods & Services	78afd	....	....	....	....	....	....	....	....	....	....	2,584	....
Income: Credit	78agd	....	....	....	....	....	....	....	....	....	....	449	....
Income: Debit	78ahd	....	....	....	....	....	....	....	....	....	....	−469	....
Balance on Gds, Serv. & Inc.	78aid	....	....	....	....	....	....	....	....	....	....	2,564	....
Current Transfers, n.i.e.: Credit	78ajd	....	....	....	....	....	....	....	....	....	....	99	....
Current Transfers: Debit	78akd	....	....	....	....	....	....	....	....	....	....	−97	....
Capital Account, n.i.e.	78bcd	....	....	....	....	....	....	....	....	....	....	128	....
Capital Account, n.i.e.: Credit	78bad	....	....	....	....	....	....	....	....	....	....	161	....
Capital Account: Debit	78bbd	....	....	....	....	....	....	....	....	....	....	−33	....
Financial Account, n.i.e.	78bjd	....	....	....	....	....	....	....	....	....	....	−1,080	....
Direct Investment Abroad	78bdd	....	....	....	....	....	....	....	....	....	....	−60	....
Dir. Invest. in Rep. Econ., n.i.e.	78bed	....	....	....	....	....	....	....	....	....	....	418	....
Portfolio Investment Assets	78bfd	....	....	....	....	....	....	....	....	....	....	−903	....
Equity Securities	78bkd	....	....	....	....	....	....	....	....	....	....	−291	....
Debt Securities	78bld	....	....	....	....	....	....	....	....	....	....	−612	....
Portfolio Investment Liab., n.i.e.	78bgd	....	....	....	....	....	....	....	....	....	....	1	....
Equity Securities	78bmd	....	....	....	....	....	....	....	....	....	....	1	....
Debt Securities	78bnd	....	....	....	....	....	....	....	....	....	....	....	....
Financial Derivatives Assets	78bwd	....	....	....	....	....	....	....	....	....	....	118	....
Financial Derivatives Liabilities	78bxd	....	....	....	....	....	....	....	....	....	....	....	....
Other Investment Assets	78bhd	....	....	....	....	....	....	....	....	....	....	−866	....
Monetary Authorities	78bod	....	....	....	....	....	....	....	....	....	....	−15	....
General Government	78bpd	....	....	....	....	....	....	....	....	....	....	−1,004	....
Banks	78bqd	....	....	....	....	....	....	....	....	....	....	153	....
Other Sectors	78brd	....	....	....	....	....	....	....	....	....	....	213	....
Other Investment Liab., n.i.e.	78bid	....	....	....	....	....	....	....	....	....	....	....	....
Monetary Authorities	78bsd	....	....	....	....	....	....	....	....	....	....	−	....
General Government	78btd	....	....	....	....	....	....	....	....	....	....	246	....
Banks	78bud	....	....	....	....	....	....	....	....	....	....	−33	....
Other Sectors	78bvd	....	....	....	....	....	....	....	....	....	....	−1,320	....
Net Errors and Omissions	78cad	....	....	....	....	....	....	....	....	....	....	293	....
Overall Balance	78cbd	....	....	....	....	....	....	....	....	....	....	−293	....
Reserves and Related Items	79dad	....	....	....	....	....	....	....	....	....	....	−293	....
Reserve Assets	79dbd	....	....	....	....	....	....	....	....	....	....	−293	....
Use of Fund Credit and Loans	79dcd	....	....	....	....	....	....	....	....	....	....	....	....
Exceptional Financing	79ded	....	....	....	....	....	....	....	....	....	....	....	....
Government Finance						*Millions of Patacas: Year Ending December 31*							
Deficit (-) or Surplus	80	....	....	....	....	25.4	882.2	−457.3	−452.8	777.3	....	....	....
Total Revenue and Grants	81y	....	....	....	....	9,491.9	10,934.6	10,098.8	10,749.4	9,809.6	....	....	....
Revenue	81	....	....	....	....	9,491.6	10,934.3	10,098.7	10,749.4	9,809.6	....	....	....
Grants	81z	....	....	.3	....	.3	.3	.1	−	−	....	....	....
Exp. & Lending Minus Repay	82z	....	....	....	....	9,466.5	10,052.4	10,556.1	11,202.2	9,032.3	....	....	....
Expenditure	82	....	....	....	....	8,817.8	9,530.9	10,071.0	11,033.7	9,004.5	....	....	....
Lending Minus Repayments	83	....	....	....	....	648.7	521.5	485.1	168.5	27.8	....	....	....
National Accounts						*Millions of Patacas*							
Househ.Cons.Expend.,incl.NPISHs	96f	13,144.1	14,912.0	16,863.9	18,609.9	20,202.2	20,996.5	20,684.6	20,402.9	20,376.4	20,646.4	21,179.7	21,900.2
Government Consumption Expend	91f	3,036.7	3,500.4	4,056.4	4,673.1	5,204.1	5,732.1	6,029.4	6,771.8	5,900.7	5,968.6	6,189.1	6,600.2
Gross Capital Formation	93	13,472.9	15,481.5	17,101.4	16,043.7	11,791.3	11,836.5	9,667.2	8,668.3	5,918.7	5,132.8	5,580.0	8,412.2
Changes in Inventories	93i	350.6	421.6	585.3	253.6	540.7	112.8	−71.8	83.3	73.7	28.9	239.7	262.0
Exports of Goods and Services	90c	31,813.6	33,991.0	36,530.6	41,044.0	41,806.8	42,355.6	39,780.0	39,237.0	46,708.6	48,746.2	54,540.9	62,469.8
Imports of Goods and Services (-)	98c	22,298.5	23,113.6	25,023.6	25,291.2	24,251.5	25,139.2	24,187.6	26,142.2	29,236.1	30,660.7	33,434.6	36,279.0
Gross Domestic Product (GDP)	99b	39,519.4	45,193.0	50,114.0	55,333.2	55,293.5	55,894.3	51,901.7	49,021.1	49,742.0	49,862.2	54,294.7	63,365.4
GDP Volume 1996 Prices	99b.p	49,019.4	51,561.6	53,754.6	55,526.3	55,293.5	55,139.1	52,618.8	51,021.4	53,380.6	54,560.2	60,031.7	69,409.6
GDP Volume (2000=100)	99bvp	91.8	96.6	100.7	104.0	103.6	103.3	98.6	95.6	100.0	102.2	112.5	130.0
GDP Deflator (2000=100)	99bip	86.5	94.1	100.0	106.9	107.3	108.8	105.9	103.1	100.0	98.1	97.1	98.0
						Millions: Midyear Estimates							
Population	99z	.39	.40	.40	.41	.42	.43	.44	.44	.45	.46	.46	.46

Colombia 233

		1992	1993	1994	1995	1996	1997	1998	1999	2000	2001	2002	2003
Exchange Rates						*Pesos per SDR: End of Period*							
Principal Rate	aa	1,116.18	1,260.01	1,213.53	1,468.13	1,445.62	1,745.36	2,122.63	2,571.77	2,849.49	2,892.15	3,894.74	4,132.22
					Pesos per US Dollar: End of Period (ae) Period Average (rf)								
Principal Rate	ae	811.77	917.33	831.27	987.65	1,005.33	1,293.58	1,507.52	1,873.77	2,187.02	2,301.33	2,864.79	2,780.82
Principal Rate	rf	759.28	863.06	844.84	912.83	1,036.69	1,140.96	1,426.04	1,756.23	2,087.90	2,299.63	2,504.24	2,877.65
					Index Numbers (2000=100): Period Averages								
Principal Rate	ahx	273.7	241.6	247.0	229.0	201.0	183.8	146.6	119.6	100.0	90.6	82.4	72.4
Nominal Effective Exchange Rate	nec	171.5	177.2	198.9	180.7	168.6	165.2	136.4	113.9	100.0	94.7	86.8	71.6
Real Effective Exchange Rate	rec	86.7	91.3	102.9	104.6	111.9	124.5	118.7	107.4	100.0	100.2	95.2	82.0
Fund Position						*Millions of SDRs: End of Period*							
Quota	2f.s	561	561	561	561	561	561	561	774	774	774	774	774
SDRs	1b.s	42	115	116	119	123	128	139	95	103	108	113	115
Reserve Position in the Fund	1c.s	69	80	87	135	165	263	408	286	286	286	286	286
Total Fund Cred.&Loans Outstg	2tl	–	–	–	–	–	–	–	–	–	–	–	–
International Liquidity					*Millions of US Dollars Unless Otherwise Indicated: End of Period*								
Total Reserves minus Gold	1l.d	7,746	7,930	7,991	8,349	9,845	9,803	8,651	8,008	8,916	10,154	10,732	10,784
SDRs	1b.d	58	158	170	177	177	172	196	131	135	135	154	171
Reserve Position in the Fund	1c.d	95	110	127	201	237	355	575	392	372	359	389	425
Foreign Exchange	1d.d	7,593	7,663	7,694	7,971	9,431	9,275	7,880	7,485	8,409	9,659	10,190	10,188
Gold (Million Fine Troy Ounces)	1ad	.484	.302	.293	.267	.252	.358	.358	.328	.328	.327	.327	.327
Gold (National Valuation)	1and	172	119	112	119	94	104	103	95	89	91	112	136
Monetary Authorities:Other Assets	3..d	382	378	425	420	420	419	422	418	448	412	452	464
Other Liab.	4..d	800	602	383	473	355	249	237	212	187	184	133	129
Deposit Money Banks: Assets	7a.d	425	544	506	443	484	1,031	944	552	458	357	341	516
Liabilities	7b.d	1,019	1,655	1,854	2,136	2,654	3,316	2,868	1,712	1,365	1,120	1,122	793
Other Banking Insts.: Assets	7e.d	73	149	169	134	257	199	162	211	133	164	121	133
Liabilities	7f.d	1,785	2,271	3,182	3,476	4,241	3,834	3,352	2,837	1,860	1,287	1,221	847
Monetary Authorities						*Billions of Pesos: End of Period*							
Foreign Assets	11	6,047.5	6,709.4	7,073.1	8,760.5	10,402.8	13,295.7	13,841.5	15,953.9	20,665.9	24,660.9	31,824.1	31,941.6
Claims on Central Government	12a	777.3	679.6	711.1	565.0	725.0	574.3	951.6	2,397.2	2,767.5	2,034.3	2,384.3	3,210.7
Claims on Nonfin.Pub.Enterprises	12c	9.7	9.3	–	–	–	–	–	–	–	–	–	–
Claims on Private Sector	12d	4.5	6.2	52.2	81.6	105.8	128.3	538.8	541.4	397.6	203.0	200.8	181.6
Claims on Deposit Money Banks	12e	117.1	75.6	66.3	239.9	62.6	416.3	905.8	2,508.5	1,536.3	919.2	1,807.4	3,206.1
Claims on Other Banking Insts.	12f	290.1	322.6	339.0	436.9	264.9	286.0	377.9	481.5	853.9	374.3	544.7	484.8
Claims on Nonbank Financial Insts.	12g	–	–	–	–	133.1	408.8	579.5	681.6	802.7	893.2	1,000.9	1,050.5
Reserve Money	14	3,665.9	4,605.8	5,902.5	6,301.1	7,415.6	8,640.7	7,165.0	10,012.5	10,922.4	12,003.0	14,441.8	16,816.9
of which: Currency Outside DMBs	14a	1,438.6	1,804.4	2,373.3	2,994.3	3,536.0	4,453.0	4,997.3	6,505.9	7,676.6	8,653.6	10,188.5	12,196.6
Time, Savings,& Fgn.Currency Dep	15	28.5	31.7	49.6	9.9	14.0	.8	120.4	101.3	7.9	2.0	1.3	1.0
Money Market Instruments	16aa	1,627.2	1,231.7	392.2	214.7	723.0	.5	15.8	–	–	–	–	–
Restricted Deposits	16b	.4	.4	.4	.4	.4	.3	.4	.3	.3	–	–	–
Foreign Liabilities	16c	7.7	22.1	83.8	131.2	43.8	3.9	1.1	4.3	4.3	123.0	10.2	16.2
Long-Term Foreign Liabilities	16cl	582.4	461.4	234.0	335.1	312.3	316.7	357.4	392.2	403.5	338.0	365.1	344.8
Central Government Deposits	16d	589.4	414.3	475.6	128.4	247.3	349.0	236.8	235.5	339.6	402.6	283.3	341.2
Capital Accounts	17a	498.2	1,104.3	1,388.1	3,110.2	3,231.1	6,120.0	9,644.1	12,089.9	15,696.9	16,963.9	23,484.6	23,470.6
Other Items (Net)	17r	246.5	–69.0	–284.5	–147.1	–293.3	–322.6	–345.9	–271.8	–351.0	–747.5	–824.2	–915.2
Deposit Money Banks						*Billions of Pesos: End of Period*							
Reserves	20	1,791.6	2,461.1	2,937.1	2,736.3	2,890.2	3,544.7	2,157.1	3,242.9	3,008.2	3,201.2	4,112.9	4,459.3
Foreign Assets	21	313.6	437.3	419.9	437.0	485.9	1,326.9	1,427.0	1,033.9	1,001.5	893.9	961.0	1,449.4
Claims on Central Government	22a	158.1	337.8	430.9	463.7	617.1	1,441.0	2,454.1	2,167.1	5,525.5	9,616.7	13,179.7	17,560.4
Claims on Local Government	22b	233.0	347.3	1,009.7	1,407.0	1,715.4	3,214.1	3,498.4	3,577.6	3,373.2	3,746.1	3,783.4	3,544.5
Claims on Nonfin.Pub.Enterprises	22c	50.0	8.1	68.7	100.0	89.1	136.4	301.4	295.5	450.3	395.3	427.6	335.4
Claims on Private Sector	22d	4,902.7	7,701.0	11,266.6	15,162.0	18,547.0	26,167.9	33,048.8	31,334.5	32,452.5	36,215.7	40,461.1	44,234.3
Claims on Other Banking Insts.	22f	581.2	560.7	1,081.2	1,581.3	2,714.1	2,970.9	3,125.2	6,597.7	7,243.4	7,015.5	6,336.9	6,192.3
Demand Deposits	24	2,164.1	2,883.8	3,626.1	4,271.9	5,272.6	6,251.6	5,673.3	6,533.1	8,825.6	9,622.9	11,256.3	12,737.1
Time, Savings,& Fgn.Currency Dep	25	2,777.6	4,217.7	6,447.3	8,005.4	10,036.5	16,709.5	23,452.4	25,587.6	27,956.5	33,498.9	37,454.3	40,028.3
Money Market Instruments	26aa	191.5	221.5	294.7	247.4	185.1	122.9	103.7	56.9	45.2	48.3	40.1	27.4
Bonds	26ab	40.5	69.7	670.5	823.2	1,715.6	2,772.2	2,826.9	1,684.7	1,406.3	1,467.1	1,384.4	1,219.7
Restricted Deposits	26b	8.2	5.8	18.5	21.8	25.6	32.6	37.9	29.8	140.8	84.0	142.6	263.3
Foreign Liabilities	26c	745.3	1,283.3	1,448.5	2,003.0	2,557.8	3,889.9	4,048.0	3,009.3	1,689.0	1,905.6	2,679.0	1,892.2
Long-Term Foreign Liabilities	26cl	6.5	46.6	88.7	104.6	106.4	377.8	285.4	195.7	1,295.3	901.9	477.9	335.2
Central Government Deposits	26d	589.8	816.7	1,015.3	1,319.0	1,666.7	2,333.0	2,457.4	2,243.1	2,615.1	3,526.4	3,443.9	5,193.3
Credit from Monetary Authorities	26g	138.5	119.6	122.9	119.4	104.0	73.3	934.0	2,471.6	1,538.5	904.9	1,908.4	3,106.7
Liabilities to Other Banking Insts.	26i	1,026.1	1,484.5	1,878.4	2,474.4	2,708.5	3,011.4	4,250.2	3,586.7	4,308.9	3,970.3	4,063.5	4,500.4
Capital Accounts	27a	1,076.4	1,719.5	2,676.0	3,558.6	4,808.3	6,159.0	5,179.0	6,120.2	6,201.0	6,477.8	7,131.9	8,322.9
Other Items (Net)	27r	–734.3	–1,015.4	–1,072.8	–1,061.4	–2,128.5	–2,931.3	–3,236.2	–3,269.5	–2,967.8	–1,323.7	–719.6	149.1

Colombia 233

		1992	1993	1994	1995	1996	1997	1998	1999	2000	2001	2002	2003
Monetary Survey		*Billions of Pesos: End of Period*											
Foreign Assets (Net)	31n	5,608.1	5,841.3	5,960.7	7,063.2	8,287.1	10,728.8	11,219.4	13,974.2	19,974.2	23,526.2	30,095.8	31,482.6
Domestic Credit	32	5,827.4	8,741.6	13,468.5	18,350.1	22,997.5	32,645.6	42,181.5	45,595.6	50,911.8	56,565.0	64,592.1	71,260.2
Claims on Central Govt. (Net)	32an	−243.8	−213.6	−348.9	−418.7	−571.9	−666.7	711.5	2,085.8	5,338.3	7,722.0	11,836.7	15,236.6
Claims on Local Government	32b	233.0	347.3	1,009.7	1,407.0	1,715.4	3,214.1	3,498.4	3,577.6	3,373.2	3,746.1	3,783.4	3,544.5
Claims on Nonfin.Pub.Enterprises	32c	59.7	17.4	68.7	100.0	89.1	136.4	301.4	295.5	450.3	395.3	427.6	335.4
Claims on Private Sector	32d	4,907.2	7,707.2	11,318.6	15,243.6	18,652.8	26,296.2	33,587.6	31,875.9	32,850.1	36,418.6	40,662.0	44,415.9
Claims on Other Banking Insts.	32f	871.3	883.3	1,420.2	2,018.2	2,979.0	3,256.9	3,503.1	7,079.3	8,097.3	7,389.8	6,881.6	6,677.1
Claims on Nonbank Financial Inst.	32g	–	–	–	–	133.1	408.8	579.5	681.6	802.7	893.2	1,000.9	1,050.5
Money	34	4,067.0	5,211.3	6,722.4	8,078.5	9,966.0	11,697.9	10,772.0	13,376.7	16,837.0	18,450.6	21,576.4	25,108.9
Quasi-Money	35	2,806.1	4,249.4	6,496.9	8,015.3	10,050.5	16,710.3	23,572.8	25,688.9	27,964.4	33,500.9	37,455.6	40,029.3
Money Market Instruments	36aa	1,818.7	1,453.2	686.9	462.1	908.1	123.4	119.5	56.9	45.2	48.3	40.1	27.4
Bonds	36ab	40.5	69.7	670.5	823.2	1,715.6	2,772.2	2,826.9	1,684.7	1,406.3	1,467.1	1,384.4	1,219.7
Restricted Deposits	36b	8.6	6.2	18.9	22.2	26.0	32.9	38.3	30.2	141.2	84.0	142.6	263.3
Long-Term Foreign Liabilities	36cl	588.9	508.0	322.7	439.7	418.7	694.5	642.8	587.9	1,698.9	1,239.9	843.0	680.0
Liabilities to Other Banking Insts.	36i	1,026.1	1,484.5	1,878.4	2,474.4	2,708.5	3,011.4	4,250.2	3,586.7	4,308.9	3,970.3	4,063.5	4,500.4
Capital Accounts	37a	1,574.6	2,823.8	4,064.1	6,668.8	8,039.4	12,279.0	14,823.1	18,210.1	21,897.9	23,441.7	30,616.6	31,793.4
Other Items (Net)	37r	−495.0	−1,223.2	−1,431.6	−1,570.8	−2,548.2	−3,947.3	−3,644.7	−3,652.2	−3,413.8	−2,111.6	−1,434.2	−879.6
Money plus Quasi-Money	35l	6,873.1	9,460.7	13,219.3	16,093.8	20,016.5	28,408.2	34,344.8	39,065.6	44,801.4	51,951.5	59,032.0	65,138.2
Other Banking Institutions		*Billions of Pesos: End of Period*											
Reserves	40	513.4	548.5	702.0	988.1	1,282.4	1,103.8	334.8	641.8	481.5	269.9	131.6	188.2
Foreign Assets	41	53.7	120.0	140.2	132.0	258.5	256.7	244.9	394.2	289.8	411.0	339.6	372.3
Claims on Central Government	42a	172.7	202.0	273.7	131.1	155.7	265.2	1,306.3	3,607.2	3,519.3	3,519.0	3,956.9	4,827.9
Claims on Local Government	42b	13.1	30.8	783.2	1,294.4	1,472.6	1,256.2	870.9	649.1	630.1	465.1	398.8	375.4
Claims on Nonfin.Pub.Enterprises	42c	1,191.3	1,329.9	676.7	765.9	974.7	1,329.3	2,244.4	1,759.3	1,853.6	1,777.9	1,944.3	1,520.4
Claims on Private Sector	42d	5,122.1	7,623.3	10,207.6	13,978.3	17,955.1	19,457.4	18,014.6	18,975.6	13,836.5	11,240.7	10,202.0	8,552.1
Claims on Deposit Money Banks	42e	1,234.2	1,560.4	2,271.5	2,993.6	3,275.9	3,466.2	4,692.0	4,633.3	5,169.5	5,336.4	5,566.9	8,440.4
Demand Deposits	44	6.8	–	–	–	–	–	–	–	–	–	–	–
Time, Savings,& Fgn.Currency Dep.	45	4,360.4	6,064.6	9,501.0	12,870.1	15,339.3	15,222.5	13,657.5	15,000.6	11,166.5	8,457.3	5,537.4	7,435.8
Money Market Instruments	46aa	16.3	15.2	89.4	35.0	15.1	13.1	16.9	1.5	1.6	1.4	1.3	–
Bonds	46ab	625.3	869.0	578.8	1,052.1	3,379.5	3,577.5	2,976.2	2,534.3	1,447.4	1,194.8	1,029.3	968.7
Restricted Deposits	46b	28.4	7.6	7.1	6.4	5.9	.7	.7	3.1	3.3	22.3	–	.4
Foreign Liabilities	46c	387.6	741.6	1,380.0	1,456.9	1,709.9	1,951.6	1,942.3	1,710.0	492.7	810.1	1,199.2	785.8
Long-Term Foreign Liabilities	46cl	929.4	1,083.3	1,258.9	1,973.4	2,548.4	2,983.2	3,122.8	3,600.9	3,572.7	2,417.3	2,236.7	1,592.3
Central Government Deposits	46d	215.5	261.5	322.8	390.7	357.4	266.1	420.8	598.8	584.0	378.3	228.7	87.1
Credit from Monetary Authorities	46g	215.5	250.2	280.5	232.4	209.5	96.6	362.7	533.7	976.5	375.5	407.5	400.1
Credit from Deposit Money Banks	46h	437.4	628.0	1,112.2	1,632.2	1,617.5	2,176.8	2,505.6	5,695.9	6,519.5	7,440.2	8,065.0	8,127.7
Capital Accounts	47a	1,544.8	1,985.7	2,874.4	4,034.8	5,214.9	6,004.5	7,076.0	7,952.5	7,991.1	7,788.8	7,953.2	6,084.8
Other Items (Net)	47r	−466.9	−491.8	−2,350.2	−3,400.7	−5,022.6	−5,157.8	−4,373.4	−6,970.7	−6,974.7	−5,866.1	−4,118.1	−1,206.1
Banking Survey		*Billions of Pesos: End of Period*											
Foreign Assets (Net)	51n	5,274.2	5,219.7	4,720.9	5,738.3	6,835.8	9,033.8	9,521.9	12,658.4	19,771.4	23,127.0	29,236.2	31,069.1
Domestic Credit	52	11,239.8	16,782.8	23,666.7	32,110.9	40,219.2	51,430.7	60,693.8	62,908.8	62,070.2	65,799.6	73,983.9	79,771.7
Claims on Central Govt. (Net)	52an	−286.6	−273.1	−398.0	−678.3	−773.6	−667.6	1,597.0	5,094.2	8,273.6	10,862.6	15,564.9	19,977.4
Claims on Local Government	52b	246.1	378.1	1,792.9	2,701.4	3,188.0	4,470.3	4,369.3	4,226.8	4,003.3	4,211.3	4,182.2	3,919.9
Claims on Nonfin.Pub.Enterprises	52c	1,251.0	1,347.3	745.4	865.9	1,063.8	1,465.7	2,545.8	2,054.8	2,303.9	2,173.2	2,371.9	1,855.8
Claims on Private Sector	52d	10,029.3	15,330.5	21,526.4	29,221.9	36,608.0	45,753.6	51,602.2	50,851.5	46,686.7	47,659.3	50,864.0	52,968.0
Claims on Nonbank Financial Inst.	52g	–	–	–	–	133.1	408.8	579.5	681.6	802.7	893.2	1,000.9	1,050.5
Liquid Liabilities	55l	10,726.9	14,976.8	22,018.3	27,975.8	34,073.4	42,527.0	47,667.6	53,424.3	55,486.4	60,138.9	64,437.8	72,385.8
Money Market Instruments	56aa	1,835.0	1,468.4	776.3	497.1	923.2	136.5	136.4	58.4	46.8	49.7	41.3	27.5
Bonds	56ab	665.8	938.7	1,249.3	1,875.3	5,095.1	6,349.7	5,803.1	4,219.0	2,853.7	2,661.9	2,413.7	2,188.4
Restricted Deposits	56b	37.0	13.8	26.0	28.6	31.9	33.6	38.9	33.2	144.4	106.4	142.6	263.7
Long-Term Foreign Liabilities	56cl	1,518.3	1,591.3	1,581.6	2,413.1	2,967.2	3,677.6	3,765.5	4,188.8	5,271.6	3,657.2	3,079.7	2,272.2
Capital Accounts	57a	3,119.4	4,809.5	6,938.5	10,703.6	13,254.3	18,283.5	21,899.1	26,162.6	29,889.0	31,230.5	38,569.8	37,878.3
Other Items (Net)	57r	−1,388.4	−1,796.0	−4,202.4	−5,644.3	−9,290.1	−10,543.4	−9,094.8	−12,519.0	−11,850.4	−8,917.9	−5,464.8	−4,175.1
Money (National Definitions)		*Billions of Pesos: End of Period*											
Reserve Money	19ma	3,312.5	4,419.0	5,634.4	6,267.1	6,627.6	8,287.1	6,923.1	9,739.6	10,710.4	11,647.9	14,107.4	16,441.5
M1	39ma	3,941.8	5,124.8	6,419.0	7,717.8	8,992.8	10,948.0	10,526.5	12,814.0	16,720.8	18,737.0	21,635.6	24,918.3
M2	59ma	11,179.6	15,817.3	22,569.1	28,961.3	34,815.5	43,794.6	48,558.1	53,670.5	56,178.6	62,158.4	66,672.2	74,758.4
M3	59mb	11,956.3	17,222.7	24,623.9	31,900.8	41,299.2	52,528.2	56,638.6	60,574.0	62,276.3	68,572.5	74,199.6	83,153.9
Interest Rates		*Percent Per Annum*											
Discount Rate (End of Period)	60	34.42	33.49	44.90	40.42	35.05	31.32	42.28	23.05	18.28	16.40	12.73	12.95
Money Market Rate	60b	....	....	....	22.40	28.37	23.83	35.00	18.81	10.87	10.43	6.06	6.95
Deposit Rate	60l	26.67	25.84	29.42	32.34	31.15	24.13	32.58	21.33	12.15	12.44	8.94	7.80
Lending Rate	60p	37.28	35.81	40.47	42.72	41.99	34.22	42.24	†25.77	18.79	20.72	16.33	15.19

Colombia 233

		1992	1993	1994	1995	1996	1997	1998	1999	2000	2001	2002	2003
Prices, Production, Labor		*Index Numbers (2000=100): Period Averages*											
Share Prices	62	56.0	62.9	114.7	95.5	100.0	148.8	129.4	115.6	100.0	106.2	148.6	234.8
Producer Prices	63	32.7	37.3	43.7	51.6	59.4	68.6	80.4	88.3	100.0	109.4	115.2	125.7
Consumer Prices	64	26.6	32.6	40.4	48.9	†58.7	69.6	82.6	91.6	100.0	108.0	114.8	123.0
Manufacturing Production	66ey	98.6	101.5	105.0	107.2	104.4	106.9	105.3	....	100.0	102.0	102.3	106.1
Vol. of Gold Produced(1990=100)	66kr	108.8	92.8	71.1	....	....	....	....	....	....	....	....	....
Crude Petroleum Prod.	66aa	63.1	65.1	65.1	83.8	90.2	91.5	104.9	115.4	100.0	87.7	82.3	77.1
		Number in Thousands: Period Averages											
Labor Force	67d	5,286	....	5,261	....	6,153	6,452	6,653	7,056	7,436	....	....	....
Employment	67e	5,053	5,333	5,408	5,494	5,451	5,702	5,655	5,641	5,910	†16,498	16,620	....
Unemployment	67c	505	447	442	522	735	782	998	1,415	1,526	2,942	3,098	2,878
Unemployment Rate (%)	67r	9.2	7.8	7.6	8.7	11.9	12.1	15.0	20.1	20.5	....	....	....
International Transactions		*Millions of US Dollars*											
Exports	70..d	6,916.5	7,115.9	8,418.5	10,056.2	10,587.0	11,522.4	10,890.1	11,575.4	13,043.3	12,289.9	11,911.0	12,671.0
Coffee	70e.d	1,258.9	1,139.7	1,990.1	1,831.8	1,576.5	2,259.0	1,891.0	1,324.0	1,080.3	764.2	772.0	806.5
Imports, c.i.f.	71..d	6,516.4	9,831.5	11,882.9	13,852.9	13,683.6	15,377.7	14,634.5	10,658.6	11,538.8	12,833.6	12,737.7	13,892.4
Imports, f.o.b.	71.vd	5,980.2	9,085.7	11,039.3	12,921.2	12,793.7	14,408.9	13,726.2	9,990.1	10,783.6	12,009.8	11,911.2	13,034.9
Volume of Exports							*2000=100*						
Coffee	72e	179.4	146.9	127.5	105.9	114.5	119.0	121.7	108.2	100.0	118.6	126.1	125.3
Export Prices in Pesos	76	28.2	31.9	41.6	48.8	†51.8	62.8	70.0	80.3	100.0	98.1	102.4	120.3
Import Prices in Pesos	76.x	37.7	42.2	45.9	53.0	†60.8	65.2	75.3	86.1	100.0	108.2	114.8	131.0
Export Prices		*2000=100: Indices of Prices in US Dollars*											
Coffee	76e.d	62.2	70.4	129.0	158.7	128.5	196.6	142.9	116.5	100.0	69.4	63.0	64.0
Balance of Payments		*Millions of US Dollars: Minus Sign Indicates Debit*											
Current Account, n.i.e.	78ald	901	−2,102	−3,673	−4,527	−4,641	−5,750	−4,857	671	740	−1,109	−1,451	−1,456
Goods: Exports f.o.b.	78aad	7,263	7,429	9,059	10,593	10,966	12,065	11,480	12,037	13,722	12,848	12,316	13,584
Goods: Imports f.o.b.	78abd	−6,029	−9,086	−11,288	−13,139	−13,058	−14,703	−13,930	−10,262	−11,090	−12,269	−12,077	−13,258
Trade Balance	78acd	1,234	−1,657	−2,229	−2,546	−2,092	−2,638	−2,450	1,775	2,633	579	239	326
Services: Credit	78add	1,983	2,520	1,571	1,701	2,192	2,156	1,955	1,941	2,049	2,190	1,866	1,792
Services: Debit	78aed	−2,028	−2,321	−2,626	−2,885	−3,385	−3,656	−3,416	−3,144	−3,328	−3,618	−3,332	−3,343
Balance on Goods & Services	78afd	1,189	−1,458	−3,284	−3,730	−3,284	−4,138	−3,911	572	1,354	−849	−1,227	−1,225
Income: Credit	78agd	449	561	702	678	716	920	949	923	1,051	914	711	548
Income: Debit	78ahd	−2,471	−2,344	−2,161	−2,274	−2,778	−3,246	−2,646	−2,278	−3,337	−3,529	−3,559	−3,995
Balance on Gds, Serv. & Inc.	78aid	−833	−3,240	−4,742	−5,326	−5,347	−6,464	−5,608	−783	−933	−3,463	−4,076	−4,672
Current Transfers, n.i.e.: Credit	78ajd	1,871	1,350	1,262	1,033	924	931	912	1,703	1,911	2,656	2,928	3,450
Current Transfers: Debit	78akd	−137	−212	−193	−234	−218	−217	−162	−248	−238	−302	−304	−234
Capital Account, n.i.e.	78bcd	−	−	−	−	−	−	−	−	−	−	−	−
Capital Account, n.i.e.: Credit	78bad	−	−	−	−	−	−	−	−	−	−	−	−
Capital Account: Debit	78bbd	−	−	−	−	−	−	−	−	−	−	−	−
Financial Account, n.i.e.	78bjd	183	2,701	3,393	4,560	6,683	6,587	3,307	−551	71	2,484	1,309	877
Direct Investment Abroad	78bdd	−50	−240	−149	−256	−328	−809	−796	−116	−325	−16	−857	−923
Dir. Invest. in Rep. Econ., n.i.e.	78bed	729	959	1,446	968	3,112	5,562	2,829	1,508	2,395	2,525	2,115	1,746
Portfolio Investment Assets	78bfd	−	−	−1,381	395	−586	−769	286	−1,345	−1,173	−3,460	2,029	−1,741
Equity Securities	78bkd	....	....	−	−	−	−	−	−	−	−	−	−
Debt Securities	78bld	−	−	−1,381	395	−586	−769	286	−1,345	−1,173	−3,460	2,029	−1,741
Portfolio Investment Liab., n.i.e.	78bgd	126	498	1,593	1,042	2,270	1,701	916	720	1,453	3,453	−933	130
Equity Securities	78bmd	....	....	478	165	292	278	47	−27	17	−42	17	−52
Debt Securities	78bnd	126	498	1,115	877	1,978	1,424	869	747	1,436	3,495	−950	181
Financial Derivatives Assets	78bwd	....	....	−	−	−	−	−	−	−	−	−	−
Financial Derivatives Liabilities	78bxd	....	....	−	−	−	295	−39	101	−104	−113	−82	−45
Other Investment Assets	78bhd	−637	160	55	−3	−1,015	−1,656	−801	−789	−551	231	283	1,651
Monetary Authorities	78bod	....	−40	−	−	−	−	−7	5	−8	7	−	−4
General Government	78bpd	−346	267	−31	−23	−20	−19	−15	−23	−40	−35	−30	−30
Banks	78bqd	−110	−74	−68	70	−41	−231	−177	118	145	102	57	−149
Other Sectors	78brd	−182	7	155	−50	−954	−1,407	−603	−889	−648	157	255	1,834
Other Investment Liab., n.i.e.	78bid	15	1,325	1,828	2,414	3,230	2,263	912	−630	−1,623	−136	−1,246	59
Monetary Authorities	78bsd	−131	−99	−177	51	14	−18	−22	−11	−15	−12	−13	−12
General Government	78btd	−78	−329	−384	−80	−266	−54	347	910	340	226	−203	2,180
Banks	78bud	785	710	727	588	417	487	−861	−1,208	−1,149	−331	−376	−531
Other Sectors	78bvd	−561	1,043	1,663	1,854	3,066	1,848	1,448	−321	−799	−18	−654	−1,578
Net Errors and Omissions	78cad	191	−135	463	−37	−313	−559	153	−432	50	−150	282	391
Overall Balance	78cbd	1,274	464	182	−4	1,729	278	−1,398	−312	862	1,225	139	−188
Reserves and Related Items	79dad	−1,274	−464	−182	4	−1,729	−278	1,398	312	−862	−1,225	−139	188
Reserve Assets	79dbd	−1,274	−464	−182	4	−1,729	−278	1,398	312	−862	−1,225	−139	188
Use of Fund Credit and Loans	79dcd	−	−	−	−	−	−	−	−	−	−	−	−
Exceptional Financing	79ded	....	....	−	−	−	−	−	−	−	−	−	−

Colombia 233

		1992	1993	1994	1995	1996	1997	1998	1999	2000	2001	2002	2003
International Investment Position						*Millions of US Dollars*							
Assets	79aad	9,212	12,701	15,149	16,445	17,652	20,839	20,928	22,490	25,409	29,856	28,749	29,755
Direct Investment Abroad	79abd	472	592	744	1,028	1,096	1,893	2,648	2,703	2,989	2,952	3,553	4,375
Portfolio Investment	79acd	–	–	447	1,171	2,453	3,221	2,936	4,281	5,454	8,914	6,885	8,626
Equity Securities	79add	–	–	447	1,171	–	–	–	–	–	–	–	–
Debt Securities	79aed	–	–	–	–	2,453	3,221	2,936	4,281	5,454	8,914	6,885	8,626
Financial Derivatives	79ald	–	–	–	–	–	–	–	–	–	–	–	–
Other Investment	79afd	927	4,163	5,845	5,786	4,165	5,816	6,611	7,405	7,971	7,749	7,468	5,840
Monetary Authorities	79agd	–	40	40	40	477	472	473	473	501	502	503	530
General Government	79ahd	–	561	1,545	1,052	109	128	142	165	205	240	270	300
Banks	79aid	554	1,109	1,150	1,051	263	493	670	552	407	305	248	397
Other Sectors	79ajd	373	2,452	3,110	3,643	3,316	4,723	5,326	6,215	6,858	6,701	6,446	4,613
Reserve Assets	79akd	7,813	7,946	8,114	8,462	9,939	9,908	8,733	8,102	8,995	10,242	10,843	10,914
Liabilities	79lad	23,047	24,937	30,129	35,297	44,193	56,267	54,408	50,897	47,707	54,916	55,727	59,258
Dir. Invest. in Rep. Economy	79lbd	6,152	5,779	6,916	8,563	11,773	19,694	16,645	13,424	10,991	15,194	17,830	20,511
Portfolio Investment	79lcd	419	741	2,026	2,591	5,945	7,984	8,278	8,413	9,621	13,008	12,307	12,841
Equity Securities	79ldd	–	215	693	858	942	1,553	880	586	397	325	325	289
Debt Securities	79led	419	525	1,333	1,733	5,003	6,432	7,398	7,827	9,224	12,683	11,982	12,551
Financial Derivatives	79lld	–	–	–	–	–	–	295	256	356	253	141	16
Other Investment	79lfd	16,476	18,417	21,187	24,144	26,475	28,294	29,230	28,704	26,841	26,573	25,529	25,890
Monetary Authorities	79lgd	650	452	231	301	329	252	236	211	186	199	134	130
General Government	79lhd	5,589	5,202	5,102	5,144	4,723	4,516	5,000	5,864	6,580	6,878	6,876	9,357
Banks	79lid	1,628	3,741	4,518	5,169	5,547	6,004	4,950	3,886	2,714	2,335	1,962	1,377
Other Sectors	79ljd	8,609	9,023	11,336	13,530	15,876	17,523	19,045	18,743	17,362	17,160	16,556	15,025
Government Finance						*Billions of Pesos: Year Ending December 31*							
Deficit (-) or Surplus	80	–1,117.3	–329.2	–1,027.2	–1,939.8	–3,780.2	–4,504.0	–6,940.6	–8,888.9	–11,945.5	–11,169.7	–11,516.4	–11,128.2
Total Revenue and Grants	81y	4,113.0	5,715.3	7,656.1	9,521.2	12,007.3	15,282.6	16,880.2	20,144.0	23,285.3	28,941.6	31,459.1	35,798.3
Revenue	81	....	....	7,656.1	9,521.2	12,007.3	15,282.6	16,880.2	20,144.0	23,285.3	28,941.6	31,459.1	35,798.3
Grants	81z			–	–	–	–	–	–	–	–	–	–
Exp. & Lending Minus Repay	82z	5,230.2	6,044.6	8,683.3	11,461.0	15,787.5	19,786.6	23,820.8	29,032.9	35,230.8	40,111.3	42,975.5	46,926.4
Expenditure	82	....	....	8,553.8	11,289.5	15,610.9	19,583.6	23,492.0	28,153.8	34,444.4	38,640.9	41,789.6	46,061.6
Lending Minus Repayments	83	....	....	129.5	171.5	176.6	203.0	328.8	879.1	786.4	1,470.4	1,185.9	864.8
Total Financing	80h	1,117.3	329.1	1,027.2	1,939.8	3,780.2	4,504.0	6,940.6	8,888.9	11,945.5	11,169.7	11,372.5	11,128.2
Domestic	84a	1,093.2	809.8	907.7	1,717.5	2,516.5	3,140.4	4,522.0	4,569.7	7,137.8	5,242.1	8,355.4	6,358.2
Foreign	85a	24.1	–480.6	119.5	222.3	1,263.7	1,363.6	2,418.6	4,319.2	4,807.7	5,927.6	3,017.1	4,769.9
National Accounts						*Billions of Pesos*							
Househ.Cons.Expend.,incl.NPISHs	96f	23,133	30,513	44,510	55,462	65,966	79,194	92,501	97,631	110,217	122,929	133,076	....
Government Consumption Expend	91f	3,965	5,108	9,774	12,622	18,123	24,246	28,548	33,588	37,057	37,910	42,046	....
Gross Fixed Capital Formation	93e	5,212	8,251	15,727	18,911	21,750	24,592	26,603	20,079	21,952	26,593	29,960	....
Changes in Inventories	93i	552	1,049	1,497	2,806	462	708	941	–725	1,793	1,671	....	....
Exports of Goods and Services	90c	6,563	7,937	10,129	12,272	15,308	18,063	21,083	27,807	37,606	38,477	39,150	48,399
Imports of Goods and Services (-)	98c	6,791	10,973	14,127	17,701	20,993	25,261	29,363	26,983	33,926	39,308	41,284	50,865
Gross Domestic Product (GDP)	99b	39,731	52,272	67,533	84,439	100,711	121,708	140,483	151,565	174,896	188,559	203,430	226,330
Net Primary Income from Abroad	98.n	–6,320	–8,128	–1,200	–1,442	–2,128	–2,706	–2,510	–2,663	–4,835	....	....	....
Gross National Income (GNI)	99a	33,411	44,143	66,333	82,997	98,583	119,002	137,973	148,902	170,062	....	....	....
Net Current Transf.from Abroad	98t	1,180	1,552	3,458	4,536	3,958	3,681	4,547	2,856	3,625	....	....	....
Gross Nat'l Disposable Inc.(GNDI)	99i	33,411	44,143	69,791	87,534	102,541	123,147	142,128	151,758	172,107	....	....	....
Gross Saving	99s	6,369	8,582	15,506	19,450	18,453	19,707	20,556	20,540	22,136	....	....	....
GDP Volume 1994 Prices	99b.p	60,758	64,227	67,533	71,046	72,507	74,994	75,421	72,251	74,364	75,458	76,789	79,820
GDP Volume (2000=100)	99bvp	81.7	86.4	90.8	95.5	97.5	100.8	101.4	97.2	100.0	101.5	103.3	107.3
GDP Deflator (2000=100)	99bip	27.8	34.6	42.5	50.5	59.1	69.0	79.2	89.2	100.0	106.2	112.6	120.6
						Millions: Midyear Estimates							
Population	99z	36.38	37.10	37.82	38.54	39.26	39.98	40.70	41.41	42.12	42.83	43.53	44.22

Comoros 632

		1992	1993	1994	1995	1996	1997	1998	1999	2000	2001	2002	2003
Exchange Rates						*Francs per SDR: End of Period (aa)*							
Official Rate	aa	378.57	404.89	†585.32	546.28	564.79	605.95	593.70	672.14	688.87	701.54	637.78	578.82
					Francs per US Dollar: End of Period (ae) Period Average (rf)								
Official Rate	ae	275.32	294.77	†400.95	367.50	392.77	449.10	421.65	489.72	528.71	558.23	469.12	389.52
Official Rate	rf	264.69	283.16	416.40	374.36	383.66	437.75	442.46	461.77	533.98	549.78	522.74	435.90
Fund Position						*Millions of SDRs: End of Period*							
Quota	2f.s	6.50	6.50	6.50	6.50	6.50	6.50	6.50	8.90	8.90	8.90	8.90	8.90
SDRs	1b.s	.02	.07	.03	.07	.04	.10	–	.12	.13	.02	.03	–
Reserve Position in the Fund	1c.s	.50	.50	.52	.54	.54	.54	.54	.54	.54	.54	.54	.54
Total Fund Cred.&Loans Outstg.	2tl	.90	.90	2.25	2.25	2.25	2.07	1.89	1.58	1.13	.68	.41	.14
International Liquidity						*Millions of US Dollars Unless Otherwise Indicated: End of Period*							
Total Reserves minus Gold	1l.d	27.09	38.63	44.03	44.48	50.55	40.48	39.14	37.15	43.21	62.32	79.94	94.30
SDRs	1b.d	.03	.09	.05	.11	.05	.13	.01	.16	.16	.02	.04	.01
Reserve Position in the Fund	1c.d	.69	.69	.76	.80	.78	.73	.76	.74	.70	.68	.73	.81
Foreign Exchange	1d.d	26.38	37.85	43.22	43.58	49.72	39.62	38.37	36.24	42.34	61.62	79.17	93.48
Gold (Million Fine Troy Ounces)	1ad	.001	.001	.001	.001	.001	.001	....	....	....	....	....	....
Gold (National Valuation)	1and	.19	.22	.22	.22	.21	.18	.17	.17	.16	.15	.20	.24
Deposit Money Banks: Assets	7a.d	4.35	2.73	.29	2.42	2.16	4.29	†2.04	8.10	5.69	8.71	6.78	4.34
Liabilities	7b.d	4.76	2.66	.01	.25	.02	–	†1.99	2.45	4.35	4.18	4.81	4.46
Monetary Authorities						*Millions of Francs: End of Period*							
Foreign Assets	11	7,512	11,475	17,729	16,422	19,950	18,305	†16,581	18,295	23,017	34,879	38,796	37,860
Claims on Central Government	12a	2,510	2,648	3,483	3,589	3,569	3,646	†3,806	3,814	3,858	3,654	3,930	3,120
Claims on Private Sector	12d	....	....	....	....	....	....	57	49	64	70	81	65
Claims on Other Banking Insts.	12f	....	....	....	....	....	....	50	75	75	75	75	75
Reserve Money	14	6,085	8,539	9,756	8,760	11,936	10,454	†9,326	11,104	13,980	23,851	28,358	27,940
of which: Currency Outside DMBs	14a	4,082	4,402	5,100	5,672	5,639	5,433	†5,418	6,310	7,564	12,355	12,503	11,505
Foreign Liabilities	16c	505	524	1,428	1,421	1,393	1,385	†1,183	1,171	915	1,393	397	223
Central Government Deposits	16d	657	2,287	1,743	1,278	1,723	1,515	†542	518	508	712	582	1,126
Counterpart Funds	16e	....	....	....	....	....	....	56	49	49	49	49	49
Central Govt. Lending Funds	16f	....	....	....	....	....	....	504	314	316	1,374	1,191	465
Capital Accounts	17a	2,976	2,971	8,491	8,673	8,670	8,770	†9,241	9,277	11,120	11,056	12,056	12,567
Other Items (Net)	17r	–201	–198	–206	–121	–203	–173	†–359	–199	126	245	250	–1,249
Deposit Money Banks						*Millions of Francs: End of Period*							
Reserves	20	1,599	2,972	3,082	1,631	4,719	4,024	†5,195	3,796	5,257	8,806	12,547	13,214
Foreign Assets	21	1,198	804	115	889	848	1,927	†859	3,966	3,009	4,864	3,182	1,690
Claims on Central Government	22a	–	–	–	–	415	94	†358	554	300	301	301	300
Claims on Private Sector	22d	9,998	8,829	8,579	9,452	6,712	8,458	†6,948	8,600	9,480	9,223	10,278	11,379
Demand Deposits	24	3,866	3,710	3,954	4,170	4,487	4,518	†4,250	4,386	5,626	8,955	10,655	11,075
Time and Savings Deposits	25a	5,720	5,781	5,910	5,442	6,167	7,771	†5,737	6,974	7,237	8,363	8,874	8,952
Foreign Currency Deposits	25b	....	....	....	....	....	....	21	62	63	125	110	151
Restricted Deposits	26b	....	....	....	....	....	....	260	618	111	482	1,348	767
Foreign Liabilities	26c	1,311	783	3	93	8	–	†840	1,200	2,298	2,331	2,257	1,738
Central Government Deposits	26d	–	377	–	167	132	209	†362	240	378	509	501	690
Credit From Monetary Authorities	26g	–	87	122	–	–	–	†–	–	–	–	–	–
Capital Accounts	27a	1,405	1,586	1,850	2,194	2,022	2,235	†2,667	3,368	3,504	3,904	3,947	4,281
Other Items (Net)	27r	493	281	–63	–94	–122	–230	†–777	68	–1,171	–1,475	–1,384	–1,072
Monetary Survey						*Millions of Francs: End of Period*							
Foreign Assets (Net)	31n	6,894	10,972	16,413	15,797	19,397	18,847	†15,417	19,890	22,813	36,019	39,324	37,587
Domestic Credit	32	14,403	11,465	12,497	12,450	10,213	10,474	†10,315	12,342	12,891	12,103	13,590	13,133
Claims on Central Govt. (Net)	32an	4,316	2,566	3,822	2,925	3,422	2,016	†3,260	3,610	3,272	2,733	3,148	1,604
Claims on Private Sector	32d	10,087	8,899	8,675	9,525	6,791	8,458	†7,005	8,649	9,544	9,294	10,359	11,444
Claims on Other Banking Insts.	32f	....	....	....	....	....	....	50	83	75	76	83	86
Money	34	11,069	11,575	12,714	12,040	13,021	10,603	†10,015	11,662	14,115	22,937	25,323	24,793
Quasi-Money	35	5,720	5,781	5,910	5,442	6,167	7,771	†5,758	7,036	7,300	8,487	8,984	9,102
Restricted Deposits	36b	....	....	....	....	....	....	260	618	111	482	1,348	767
Counterpart Funds	36e	....	....	....	....	....	....	56	49	49	49	49	49
Central Govt. Lending Funds	36f	....	....	....	....	....	....	504	314	316	1,374	1,191	465
Other Items (Net)	37r	4,508	5,081	10,286	10,765	10,422	10,947	†9,139	12,553	13,813	14,793	16,020	15,545
Money plus Quasi-Money	35l	16,789	17,356	18,624	17,482	19,188	18,374	†15,773	18,698	21,415	31,424	34,307	33,896

Comoros 632

		1992	1993	1994	1995	1996	1997	1998	1999	2000	2001	2002	2003
Other Banking Institutions		*Millions of Francs: End of Period*											
Reserves	40	511	697	1,340	1,250	856	88	†475	1,060	947	1,484	2,013	1,578
Foreign Assets	41	2	2	4	2	5	–	†89	96	9	10	11	11
Claims on Central Government	42a	–	526	11	–	–	–	†–	–	–	–	–	–
Claims on Private Sector	42d	1,991	1,916	1,985	2,200	3,029	4,022	†4,038	3,329	3,334	2,928	2,293	2,594
Time Deposits	45	472	473	387	267	694	760	†709	768	837	963	1,070	1,223
Central Government Deposits	46d	–	–	–	–	–	–	†263	153	749	146	146	633
Long-Term Foreign Liabilities	46cl	1,284	1,551	1,838	1,964	1,588	1,633	†845	688	527	364	197	104
Central Govt. Lending Funds	46f	235	233	230	296	317	306	†883	896	280	809	979	394
Capital Accounts	47a	854	887	918	1,018	1,399	1,494	†2,090	1,971	1,988	1,978	1,950	2,292
Other Items (Net)	47r	–341	–3	–33	–93	–108	–83	†–188	9	–91	161	–26	–463
Banking Survey		*Millions of Francs: End of Period*											
Foreign Assets (Net)	51n	5,612	9,423	14,579	13,835	17,814	17,214	†14,661	19,298	22,295	35,666	39,138	37,494
Domestic Credit	52	16,394	13,907	14,493	14,650	13,242	14,496	†14,040	15,435	15,401	14,809	15,654	15,009
Claims on Central Govt. (Net)	52an	4,316	3,092	3,833	2,925	3,422	2,016	†2,997	3,457	2,523	2,587	3,002	971
Claims on Private Sector	52d	12,078	10,815	10,660	11,725	9,820	12,480	†11,043	11,978	12,878	12,221	12,652	14,039
Liquid Liabilities	55l	16,781	17,172	17,704	16,525	19,002	19,114	†16,166	18,522	21,360	30,812	33,257	33,113
Money	54	10,589	10,918	11,407	10,816	12,141	10,583	†9,699	10,718	13,223	21,362	23,202	22,788
Quasi-Money	55	6,192	6,254	6,297	5,709	6,861	8,531	†6,467	7,804	8,137	9,450	10,054	10,325
Restricted Deposits	56b	....	....	....	....	....	....	260	618	111	482	1,348	767
Counterpart Funds	56e	....	....	....	....	....	....	56	49	49	49	49	49
Central Govt. Lending Funds	56f	585	583	230	296	317	306	†1,387	1,210	596	2,183	2,170	859
Other Items (Net)	57r	4,640	5,575	11,138	11,664	11,737	12,290	†10,832	14,334	15,580	16,949	17,969	17,716
Liquid Liabilities	55l	16,781	17,172	17,704	16,525	19,002	19,114	†16,166	18,522	21,360	30,812	33,257	33,113
International Transactions		*Millions of Francs*											
Exports	70	5,847	6,189	4,688	4,236	....	....	....	....	....	....	....	....
Imports, c.i.f.	71	18,139	16,817	21,929	23,411	....	....	....	....	....	....	....	....
Balance of Payments		*Millions of US Dollars: Minus Sign Indicates Debit*											
Current Account, n.i.e.	78ald	–14.19	9.57	–7.22	–18.96	....	....	....	....	....	....	....	....
Goods: Exports f.o.b.	78aad	21.43	21.58	10.79	11.32	....	....	....	....	....	....	....	....
Goods: Imports f.o.b.	78abd	–58.27	–49.54	–44.94	–53.50	....	....	....	....	....	....	....	....
Trade Balance	78acd	–36.84	–27.96	–34.16	–42.18	....	....	....	....	....	....	....	....
Services: Credit	78add	26.59	31.06	28.84	34.51	....	....	....	....	....	....	....	....
Services: Debit	78aed	–52.97	–49.87	–45.59	–49.85	....	....	....	....	....	....	....	....
Balance on Goods & Services	78afd	–63.22	–46.77	–50.91	–57.53	....	....	....	....	....	....	....	....
Income: Credit	78agd	3.49	3.30	2.62	3.40	....	....	....	....	....	....	....	....
Income: Debit	78ahd	.46	–1.27	–2.69	–2.39	....	....	....	....	....	....	....	....
Balance on Gds, Serv. & Inc.	78aid	–59.27	–44.74	–50.98	–56.52	....	....	....	....	....	....	....	....
Current Transfers, n.i.e.: Credit	78ajd	56.11	59.83	49.95	41.06	....	....	....	....	....	....	....	....
Current Transfers: Debit	78akd	–11.04	–5.52	–6.19	–3.50	....	....	....	....	....	....	....	....
Capital Account, n.i.e.	78bcd	–	–	–	–	....	....	....	....	....	....	....	....
Capital Account, n.i.e.: Credit	78bad	–	–	–	–	....	....	....	....	....	....	....	....
Capital Account: Debit	78bbd	–	–	–	–	....	....	....	....	....	....	....	....
Financial Account, n.i.e.	78bjd	13.48	4.05	18.54	10.87	....	....	....	....	....	....	....	....
Direct Investment Abroad	78bdd	–	–	–	–	....	....	....	....	....	....	....	....
Dir. Invest. in Rep. Econ., n.i.e.	78bed	–1.45	.19	.18	.89	....	....	....	....	....	....	....	....
Portfolio Investment Assets	78bfd	–	–	–	–	....	....	....	....	....	....	....	....
Equity Securities	78bkd	–	–	–	–	....	....	....	....	....	....	....	....
Debt Securities	78bld	–	–	–	–	....	....	....	....	....	....	....	....
Portfolio Investment Liab., n.i.e.	78bgd	–	–	–	–	....	....	....	....	....	....	....	....
Equity Securities	78bmd	–	–	–	–	....	....	....	....	....	....	....	....
Debt Securities	78bnd	–	–	–	–	....	....	....	....	....	....	....	....
Financial Derivatives Assets	78bwd	....	....	....	....	....	....	....	....	....	....	....	....
Financial Derivatives Liabilities	78bxd	....	....	....	....	....	....	....	....	....	....	....	....
Other Investment Assets	78bhd	.24	–1.45	1.66	–1.83	....	....	....	....	....	....	....	....
Monetary Authorities	78bod	....	....	....	....	....	....	....	....	....	....	....	....
General Government	78bpd	–	–	–	–	....	....	....	....	....	....	....	....
Banks	78bqd	.24	–1.45	1.66	–1.83	....	....	....	....	....	....	....	....
Other Sectors	78brd	–	–	–	–	....	....	....	....	....	....	....	....
Other Investment Liab., n.i.e.	78bid	14.69	5.30	16.70	11.81	....	....	....	....	....	....	....	....
Monetary Authorities	78bsd	–.29	2.99	7.93	2.02	....	....	....	....	....	....	....	....
General Government	78btd	12.03	2.06	10.63	8.72	....	....	....	....	....	....	....	....
Banks	78bud	–	–	–	–	....	....	....	....	....	....	....	....
Other Sectors	78bvd	2.96	.25	–1.86	1.06	....	....	....	....	....	....	....	....
Net Errors and Omissions	78cad	–5.32	–5.84	–6.33	–1.77	....	....	....	....	....	....	....	....
Overall Balance	78cbd	–6.03	7.78	4.99	–9.86	....	....	....	....	....	....	....	....
Reserves and Related Items	79dad	6.03	–7.78	–4.99	9.86	....	....	....	....	....	....	....	....
Reserve Assets	79dbd	–.39	–14.00	–14.97	3.37	....	....	....	....	....	....	....	....
Use of Fund Credit and Loans	79dcd	–	–	1.89	–	....	....	....	....	....	....	....	....
Exceptional Financing	79ded	6.42	6.22	8.09	6.49	....	....	....	....	....	....	....	....
National Accounts		*Billions of Francs*											
Gross Domestic Product (GDP)	99b	69.1	75.5	80.4	84.1	....	....	....	....	....	....	....	....
		Millions: Midyear Estimates											
Population	99z	.56	.57	.59	.61	.63	.65	.67	.68	.71	.73	.75	.77

Congo, Dem. Rep. of   636

		1992	1993	1994	1995	1996	1997	1998	1999	2000	2001	2002	2003
Exchange Rates		\multicolumn{12}{l}{*Congo Francs per Thousand SDRs through 1994, per SDR Thereafter: End of Period*}
Market Rate	aa	.009	.481	47.445	.220	1.662	1.430	†3.450	6.176	65.146	394.111	519.527	549.200
		\multicolumn{12}{l}{*Congo Francs per Thousand US$ 1992-95, per US$ Thereafter: End of Period (ae) Period Average (rf)*}
Market Rate	ae	.007	.350	32.500	.148	1.156	1.060	†2.450	4.500	50.000	313.600	382.140	369.590
Market Rate	rf	.002	.025	11.941	.070	.502	1.313	1.607	4.018	21.818	206.618	346.485	405.340
		\multicolumn{12}{l}{*Index Numbers (2000=100): Period Averages*}
Market Rate	ahx	.3	–	–	100.0	13.8	4.1	924.1	363.6	100.0	12.9	4.0	3.4
Nominal Effective Exchange Rate	nec	.3	–	–	–	–	–	–	–	–	–	–	–
Real Effective Exchange Rate	rec	40.7	53.9	40.9	36.0	35.8	43.9	45.6	122.4	100.0	89.6	39.3	35.1
Fund Position		\multicolumn{12}{l}{*Millions of SDRs: End of Period*}
Quota	2f.s	291.00	291.00	291.00	291.00	291.00	291.00	291.00	291.00	291.00	291.00	533.00	533.00
SDRs	1b.s	–	–	–	–	–	–	–	–	–	–	6.12	5.35
Reserve Position in the Fund	1c.s	–	–	–	–	–	–	–	–	–	–	–	–
Total Fund Cred.&Loans Outstg	2tl	330.31	330.31	327.27	326.37	301.26	301.26	300.71	300.03	300.02	300.02	420.00	473.37
International Liquidity		\multicolumn{12}{l}{*Millions of US Dollars Unless Otherwise Indicated: End of Period*}
Total Reserves minus Gold	1l.d	156.73	46.20	120.69	146.60	82.50	....	....	....	....	....	....	....
SDRs	1b.d	–	–	–	–	–	–	–	–	–	–	8.32	7.96
Reserve Position in the Fund	1c.d	–	–	–	–	–	–	–	–	–	–	–	–
Foreign Exchange	1d.d	156.73	46.20	120.69	146.60	82.50	....	....	....	....	....	....	....
Gold (Million Fine Troy Ounces)	1ad	.028	.022	.028	.028	....	.054	....	....	....	....	....	....
Gold (National Valuation)	1and	9.32	8.59	10.71	10.83	....	15.80	....	....	....	....	....	....
Monetary Authorities: Other Liab	4..d	290.50	272.40	280.95	331.50	244.16	205.15	5,841.57	5,423.52	–49.34	–38.34	139.49	192.99
Deposit Money Banks: Assets	7a.d	68.00	62.37	81.18	69.18	....	....	....	....	....	93.42	95.64	181.79
Liabilities	7b.d	27.72	27.31	31.29	16.75	35.04	....	....	....	....	48.77	41.96	84.68
Monetary Authorities		\multicolumn{12}{l}{*Congo Francs through 1993; Thousands of Congo Francs 1994–95; Millions Beginning 1996: End of Period*}
Foreign Assets	11	1,219	66,820	†5,148	25,276	†107	67	1,834	4,125	2,571	20,163	28,663	36,414
Claims on Central Government	12a	2,434	41,830	†1,675	1,675	†54	332	6,416	37,068	16,415	20,142	13,089	29,835
Claims on Nonfin.Pub.Enterprises	12c	5	20	†5	323	†7	6	149	272	301	1,895	–	–
Claims on Private Sector	12d	28	800	†34	705	†7	14	170	460	524	899	1,283	1,943
Claims on Deposit Money Banks	12e	4	1,270	†163	8,234	†17	9	150	526	132	425	2,799	3,901
Claims on Other Banking Insts	12f	–	70	†10	931	†–	–	–	–	3	–	–	–
Reserve Money	14	2,584	69,990	†2,355	17,668	†110	228	6,353	33,057	20,314	43,205	52,376	67,728
of which: Currency Outside DMBs	14a	1,214	46,930	†2,771	16,839	†83	152	5,145	29,445	18,180	36,110	49,757	63,148
Time & Foreign Currency Deposits	15	33	6,880	†707	1,522	†8	9	195	436	470	2,524	5,333	3,964
Restricted Deposits	16b	202	12,620	†1,005	4,870	†38	29	703	1,526	1,224	6,936	3,650	3,459
Foreign Liabilities	16c	4,940	254,135	†24,658	121,116	†783	648	15,349	26,259	17,078	106,216	271,507	331,302
Central Government Deposits	16d	33	340	†298	660	†8	60	1,025	5,513	2,393	6,759	20,335	24,085
Counterpart Funds	16e	–	–	†–	–	†–	–	–	–	–	–	–	–
Capital Accounts	17a	1,070	45,370	†4,124	24,842	†128	449	4,760	6,104	4,150	17,043	–317,454	–360,408
Other Items (Net)	17r	–5,227	137,605	†–25,179	–46,070	†–891	–995	–19,667	–30,445	–24,224	–138,495	10,085	1,965
Deposit Money Banks		\multicolumn{12}{l}{*Congo Francs through 1993; Thousands of Congo Francs 1994–95; Millions Beginning 1996: End of Period*}
Reserves	20	1,312	21,220	†265	643	....	....	....	....	....	4,359	3,072	5,912
Foreign Assets	21	451	21,830	†2,638	10,260	....	....	....	....	....	29,295	36,548	67,188
Claims on Central Government	22a	1	230	†180	80	....	....	....	....	....	1,253	593	14,361
Claims on Nonfin.Pub.Enterprises	22c	2	80	†76	170	....	....	....	....	....	395	827	228
Claims on Private Sector	22d	135	2,460	†700	3,510	....	....	....	....	....	9,644	11,842	17,704
Claims on Other Banking Insts	22f	–	–	†–	–	....	....	....	....	....	903	–	1
Demand Deposits	24	1,264	16,180	†919	1,870	....	....	....	....	....	7,922	7,956	8,606
Time & Foreign Currency Deposits	25	227	10,770	†1,407	6,304	....	....	....	....	....	18,497	30,863	48,429
Restricted Deposits	26b	25	1,940	†63	208	....	....	....	....	....	1,101	1,094	2,157
Foreign Liabilities	26c	184	9,560	†1,017	2,484	....	....	....	....	....	15,295	16,036	31,295
Central Government Deposits	26d	47	1,000	†–	–	....	....	....	....	....	2,092	3,737	8,008
Counterpart Funds	26e	–	–	†–	–	....	....	....	....	....	–	–	–
Credit from Monetary Authorities	26g	4	1,270	†163	8,234	†17	9	150	526	132	622	1,533	3,218
Capital Accounts	27a	103	1,140	†201	4,125	....	....	....	....	....	9,860	12,445	16,717
Other Items (Net)	27r	51	5,230	†253	–327	....	....	....	....	....	–9,541	–20,784	–13,035
Post Office: Checking Deposits	24..i	–	–	†–	–	....	....	....	....	....	....	....	....

Congo, Dem. Rep. of 636

		1992	1993	1994	1995	1996	1997	1998	1999	2000	2001	2002	2003
Monetary Survey		*Congo Francs through 1993; Thousands of Congo Francs 1994–95; Millions Beginning 1996: End of Period*											
Foreign Assets (Net)	31n	−3,454	−175,045	†−17,889	−88,064	....	....	....	....	....	−72,052	−222,333	−258,995
Domestic Credit	32	2,526	44,150	†2,383	6,733	....	....	....	....	....	26,224	3,561	31,982
Claims on Central Govt. (Net)	32an	2,355	40,720	†1,557	1,095	....	....	....	....	....	12,488	−10,391	12,104
Claims on Nonfin.Pub.Enterprises	32c	8	100	†81	493	....	....	....	....	....	2,290	827	228
Claims on Private Sector	32d	164	3,260	†735	4,214	....	....	....	....	....	10,543	13,125	19,648
Claims on Other Banking Insts.	32f	–	70	†10	931	....	....	....	....	....	903	–	1
Money	34	2,536	64,950	†3,725	18,895	....	....	....	....	....	41,064	57,893	72,110
Quasi-Money	35	261	17,650	†2,114	7,826	....	....	....	....	....	26,134	36,196	52,393
of which: Fgn. Currency Deposits	35x	261	17,650	†2,114	7,826	....	....	....	....	....	21,021	36,196	52,393
Restricted Deposits	36b	227	14,560	†1,068	5,077	....	....	....	....	....	8,037	4,744	5,616
Counterpart Funds	36e	–	–	†–		....	....	....	....	....			
Capital Accounts	37a	1,173	46,510	†4,324	28,967	....	....	....	....	....	26,903	−305,008	−343,691
Revaluation Accounts	37ar	−2,872	−115,720	†−14,351	−68,579	....	....	....	....	....	−105,946	–	–
Other Items (Net)	37r	−2,249	−157,575	†−12,223	−65,283	....	....	....	....	....	−41,500	−12,597	−13,441
Money plus Quasi-Money	35l	2,797	82,600	†5,839	26,721	....	....	....	....	....	67,198	94,089	124,503
Interest Rates		*Percent Per Annum*											
Discount Rate (End of Period)	60	55.0	95.0	145.0	125.0	238.0	13.0	22.0	120.0	120.0	140.0	24.0	8.0
Deposit Rate	60l	....	....	60.0	60.0	60.0	....	....	....	....	....	....	....
Lending Rate	60p	....	....	398.3	293.9	247.0	134.6	29.0	124.6	165.0	167.9	66.8	....
Prices		*Index Numbers (2000=100): Period Averages*											
Consumer Prices	64	†–	–	–	†.2	1.2	3.3	4.2	16.3	100.0	459.9	604.9	....
Mining Production(1980=100)	66zx	....	....	....	....	....	....	....	....	....	....	....	....
International Transactions		*Millions of US Dollars*											
Exports	70..d	426	368	419	438	592	....	....	....	....	....	....	....
Imports, c.i.f.	71..d	420	372	382	397	424	....	....	....	....	....	....	....
Government Finance		*Congo Francs through 1993; Thousands of Congo Francs 1994–95; Millions Beginning 1996: Year Ending December 31*											
Deficit (-) or Surplus	80	†−2,650	−36,940	†−1,228	80	†−9	−63	....	....	....	....	....	....
Revenue	81	†590	12,160	†2,084	21,200	†157	404	....	....	....	....	....	....
Grants Received	81z	†60	300	†168	11,770	†171	323	....	....	....	....	....	....
Expenditure	82	†3,060	48,310	†3,312	32,890	†337	790	....	....	....	....	....	....
Lending Minus Repayments	83	†240	1,090	†168	–	†–	–	....	....	....	....	....	....
Financing													
Domestic	84a	†2,544	35,960	†1,060	−80	†9	63	....	....	....	....	....	....
Foreign	85a	†110	990	†168	–	†–	–	....	....	....	....	....	....
Debt: Domestic	88a	†2,355	40,722	†1,557	1,750	†37	304	....	....	....	....	....	....
Foreign	89a	†20,385	239,254	†116,448	921,660	†7,019	11,871	....	....	....	....	....	....
National Accounts		*Thousands of Congo Francs through 1995; Millions of Congo Francs Beginning 1996*											
Househ.Cons.Expend.,incl.NPISHs	96f	....	....	†58,901	320,731	†2,009	6,351	8,491	43,025	272,306	1,518,353	....	....
Government Consumption Expend	91f	....	....	†2,100	12,300	†131	501	554	2,619	15,124	68,887	....	....
Gross Fixed Capital Formation	93e	....	....	†5,223	38,270	†450	666	731	3,832	28,031	66,054	....	....
Changes in Inventories	93i	....	....	†21	−111,102	†22	....	....	2,746	1,677	2,211	....	....
Exports of Goods and Services	90c	....	....	†16,888	112,910	†895	1,876	2,494	3,427	19,427	1,406	....	....
Imports of Goods and Services (-)	98c	....	....	†14,724	94,056	†659	1,758	2,621	3,310	20,027	209,719	....	....
Gross Domestic Product (GDP)	99b	....	....	†69,342	396,421	†2,896	7,804	9,990	51,824	334,926	1,556,120	....	....
Net Primary Income from Abroad	98.n	....	....	†−60,259	−19,076	†−132	−98	−133	−2,060	−8,756	−85,541	....	....
Gross National Income (GNI)	99a	....	....	†67,900	443,900	†3,213	7,937	10,100	52,338	316,539	1,447,192	....	....
Consumption of Fixed Capital	99cf	....	....	†−2,100	−11,900	†−87	−234	−300	−1,555	−10,048	−2,642	....	....
Net National Income	99e	....	....	†67,900	448,800	†3,255	8,157	10,155	52,156	317,258	1,444,550	....	....
GDP Vol.1987 Prices	99b.p	....	....	†181,300	182,570	†181	171	168	161	150	151	....	....
GDP Volume (2000=100)	99bvp	145.9	126.2	121.3	122.1	120.8	114.2	112.3	107.5	100.0	100.9	....	....
GDP Deflator (2000=100)	99bip	–	–	–	.1	.7	2.0	2.7	14.4	100.0	460.5	....	....
		Millions: Midyear Estimates											
Population	99z	Ü 40.24	41.76	43.17	44.38	45.35	46.13	46.82	47.60	48.57	49.79	51.20	52.77

2004, International Monetary Fund : *International Financial Statistics Yearbook*

Congo, Republic of 634

		1992	1993	1994	1995	1996	1997	1998	1999	2000	2001	2002	2003
Exchange Rates					*Francs per SDR: End of Period*								
Official Rate	aa	378.57	404.89	†780.44	728.38	753.06	807.94	791.61	†896.19	918.49	935.39	850.37	771.76
				Francs per US Dollar: End of Period (ae) Period Average (rf)									
Official Rate	ae	275.32	294.77	†534.60	490.00	523.70	598.81	562.21	†652.95	704.95	744.31	625.50	519.36
Official Rate	rf	264.69	283.16	†555.20	499.15	511.55	583.67	589.95	†615.70	711.98	733.04	696.99	581.20
Fund Position					*Millions of SDRs: End of Period*								
Quota	2f.s	57.90	57.90	57.90	57.90	57.90	57.90	57.90	84.60	84.60	84.60	84.60	84.60
SDRs	1b.s	.04	.01	.03	.02	.01	.01	–	.08	.03	.15	2.38	.43
Reserve Position in the Fund	1c.s	.47	.47	.47	.50	.54	.54	.54	.54	.54	.54	.54	.54
Total Fund Cred.&Loans Outstg	2tl	4.00	3.50	14.00	12.50	26.40	24.83	24.26	21.14	31.71	30.81	24.41	18.91
International Liquidity				*Millions of US Dollars Unless Otherwise Indicated: End of Period*									
Total Reserves minus Gold	1l.d	4.01	1.34	50.36	59.30	90.99	59.92	.84	39.35	222.01	68.91	31.63	34.80
SDRs	1b.d	.06	.02	.05	.03	.02	.01	.01	.11	.04	.19	3.23	.64
Reserve Position in the Fund	1c.d	.65	.64	.68	.75	.77	.72	.75	.74	.70	.67	.73	.80
Foreign Exchange	1d.d	3.31	.68	49.63	58.52	90.20	59.19	.08	38.51	221.27	68.05	27.67	33.36
Gold (Million Fine Troy Ounces)	1ad	.011	.011	.011	.011	.011	.011	.011	.011	.011	.011	.011	.011
Gold (National Valuation)	1and	3.70	4.42	†4.21	4.29	4.10	3.24	3.20	†3.23	3.03	3.09	3.81	4.65
Monetary Authorities: Other Liab	4..d	43.48	38.71	17.20	18.62	16.48	13.53	35.97	25.10	24.66	22.97	27.65	28.74
Deposit Money Banks: Assets	7a.d	68.00	82.84	41.43	33.16	33.17	27.79	29.01	34.07	140.68	21.84	130.81	42.62
Liabilities	7b.d	96.22	58.86	50.04	28.91	25.81	14.13	41.82	39.17	17.98	17.79	68.69	39.94
Monetary Authorities					*Billions of Francs: End of Period*								
Foreign Assets	11	2.12	1.67	29.21	31.17	49.81	37.81	2.27	27.80	158.64	53.60	22.18	20.49
Claims on Central Government	12a	73.25	72.61	77.25	80.75	92.48	110.27	123.14	120.76	128.71	173.15	171.64	195.30
Claims on Deposit Money Banks	12e	6.84	1.51	1.54	4.26	3.70	5.01	7.16	6.20	6.45	2.44	–	.61
Claims on Other Banking Insts	12f	–	–	–	–	–	–	–	–	–	–	–	–
Reserve Money	14	66.33	63.50	85.97	93.09	101.08	112.80	89.44	120.07	243.82	186.79	170.80	183.09
of which: Currency Outside DMBs	14a	59.32	53.71	69.49	81.58	87.35	93.26	73.26	102.34	123.87	142.91	129.00	131.92
Foreign Liabilities	16c	13.49	12.83	20.12	18.23	28.51	28.17	39.43	35.33	46.51	45.91	38.05	29.52
Central Government Deposits	16d	4.01	4.95	22.34	15.87	24.01	19.59	11.33	12.77	21.03	12.90	7.69	13.25
Capital Accounts	17a	5.44	6.10	9.35	8.51	8.68	8.99	8.50	9.82	10.89	11.20	10.56	9.76
Other Items (Net)	17r	–7.06	–11.58	–29.78	–19.53	–16.30	–16.46	–16.13	–23.24	–28.45	–27.61	–33.28	–19.21
Deposit Money Banks					*Billions of Francs: End of Period*								
Reserves	20	4.42	9.68	12.05	7.41	8.99	15.08	13.85	12.72	105.99	30.07	29.34	37.44
Foreign Assets	21	18.72	24.42	22.15	16.25	17.37	16.64	16.31	22.25	99.17	16.25	81.82	22.13
Claims on Central Government	22a	†36.78	17.84	30.76	28.91	29.45	25.74	28.74	20.12	26.43	15.07	24.86	16.81
Claims on Nonfin.Pub.Enterprises	22c	26.78	11.28	10.17	13.75	13.96	13.35	16.16	13.98	10.65	6.98	4.81	5.12
Claims on Private Sector	22d	122.33	66.02	75.62	85.68	98.09	106.53	112.01	158.00	109.59	101.03	60.62	75.06
Claims on Other Banking Insts	22f	.41	.06	.01	.02	.01	.30	.13	.78	.08	–	–	–
Claims on Nonbank Financial Insts	22g	.26	.40	.60	.84	1.05	1.16	1.33	.63	.05	.98	.98	1.57
Demand Deposits	24	57.40	41.94	60.57	49.16	61.08	68.85	68.39	76.68	171.74	81.36	129.77	89.50
Time and Savings Deposits	25	49.86	28.48	24.78	24.34	31.00	35.14	31.94	26.84	24.70	19.93	20.46	49.44
Foreign Liabilities	26c	24.81	17.18	26.75	14.04	13.51	8.45	23.51	25.57	12.67	13.24	42.97	20.74
Long-Term Foreign Liabilities	26cl	1.68	.17	–	.13	.01	.01	–	–	–	–	–	–
Central Government Deposits	26d	†18.08	2.61	6.10	11.03	12.65	10.95	17.44	25.53	56.16	11.83	15.48	15.14
Credit from Monetary Authorities	26g	6.84	1.51	1.54	4.26	3.70	5.01	7.16	6.20	6.45	2.44	–	.61
Capital Accounts	27a	57.41	36.24	41.05	54.40	59.64	62.30	45.04	62.95	36.19	48.65	9.42	12.23
Other Items (Net)	27r	†–6.38	1.57	–9.42	–4.51	–12.65	–11.91	–4.96	4.70	44.04	–7.08	–15.66	–30.19
Monetary Survey					*Billions of Francs: End of Period*								
Foreign Assets (Net)	31n	–19.13	–4.09	4.49	15.02	25.15	17.82	–44.36	–10.86	198.63	10.70	22.99	–7.64
Domestic Credit	32	†237.72	160.65	165.98	183.04	198.39	226.80	252.73	275.96	198.32	272.48	239.75	265.46
Claims on Central Govt. (Net)	32an	†87.94	82.89	79.58	82.75	85.27	105.46	123.10	102.58	77.94	163.49	173.34	183.73
Claims on Nonfin.Pub.Enterprises	32c	26.78	11.28	10.17	13.75	13.96	13.35	16.16	13.98	10.65	6.98	4.81	5.12
Claims on Private Sector	32d	122.33	66.02	75.62	85.68	98.09	106.53	112.01	158.00	109.59	101.03	60.62	75.06
Claims on Other Banking Insts	32f	.41	.06	.01	.02	.01	.30	.13	.78	.08	–	–	–
Claims on Nonbank Financial Inst	32g	.26	.40	.60	.84	1.05	1.16	1.33	.63	.05	.98	.98	1.57
Money	34	119.32	95.76	134.49	134.85	153.18	166.56	143.98	184.03	309.58	238.08	271.24	235.15
Quasi-Money	35	49.86	28.48	24.78	24.34	31.00	35.14	31.94	26.84	24.70	19.93	20.46	49.44
Other Items (Net)	37r	†49.41	32.32	11.20	38.87	39.37	42.92	32.45	54.23	62.67	25.16	–28.96	–27.42
Money plus Quasi-Money	35l	169.17	124.24	159.27	159.19	184.17	201.70	175.92	210.87	334.28	258.01	291.69	284.59
Interest Rates					*Percent Per Annum*								
Discount Rate (End of Period)	60	12.00	11.50	†7.75	8.60	7.75	7.50	7.00	7.60	7.00	6.50	6.30	6.00
Deposit Rate	60l	7.50	7.75	8.08	5.50	5.46	5.00	5.00	5.00	5.00	5.00	5.00	5.00
Lending Rate	60p	17.77	17.46	17.50	16.00	22.00	22.00	22.00	22.00	22.00	20.67	18.00	18.00
Prices and Production					*Index Numbers (2000=100): Period Averages*								
Wholesale Prices (1990=100)	63	98.03	101.01	....	....	....	....	....	....	....	....	....	....
Consumer Prices	64	47.2	49.5	70.5	77.1	84.8	....	95.7	100.9	100.0	100.1	104.7	103.8
Crude Petroleum Production	66aa	67.9	75.0	71.0	72.8	81.6	91.1	96.4	100.3	100.0	92.1	91.3	149.2

Congo, Republic of 634

		1992	1993	1994	1995	1996	1997	1998	1999	2000	2001	2002	2003
International Transactions						*Billions of Francs*							
Exports	70	312.00	302.63	532.40	585.30	688.10	973.70	806.90	960.50	1,772.20	....	....	....
Imports, c.i.f.	71	119.48	164.79	350.41	334.18	793.31	540.65	401.29	505.22	330.94	....	....	....
Imports, f.o.b.	71.v	97.22	134.08	340.20	324.50	770.20	524.90	329.40	429.80	321.30	....	....	....
Balance of Payments						*Millions of US Dollars: Minus Sign Indicates Debit*							
Current Account, n.i.e.	78ald	−316.6	−552.7	−793.4	−625.2	−650.9	−155.8	−240.6	−230.6	648.1	−28.4	−34.5	....
Goods: Exports f.o.b.	78aad	1,178.7	1,119.1	958.9	1,286.6	1,654.9	1,661.5	1,367.8	1,560.1	2,491.8	2,055.3	2,288.8	....
Goods: Imports f.o.b.	78abd	−438.2	−500.1	−612.7	−654.2	−587.2	−648.8	−558.4	−522.7	−455.3	−681.3	−691.1	....
Trade Balance	78acd	740.5	619.1	346.2	632.4	1,067.7	1,012.7	809.4	1,037.4	2,036.5	1,373.9	1,597.7	....
Services: Credit	78add	66.1	56.2	67.0	87.4	91.9	99.7	117.6	146.0	136.5	143.8	164.8	....
Services: Debit	78aed	−737.5	−845.5	−995.8	−691.7	−936.0	−748.5	−857.4	−868.6	−738.3	−852.2	−926.9	....
Balance on Goods & Services	78afd	69.1	−170.2	−582.7	28.2	223.5	363.9	69.6	314.9	1,434.7	665.6	835.6	....
Income: Credit	78agd	12.5	11.3	2.0	8.6	9.3	5.9	4.0	29.6	14.0	15.2	6.2	....
Income: Debit	78ahd	−379.7	−384.9	−291.1	−703.8	−914.7	−527.7	−311.1	−569.8	−819.3	−694.0	−866.4	....
Balance on Gds, Serv. & Inc.	78aid	−298.1	−543.9	−871.8	−667.0	−681.9	−157.9	−237.6	−225.3	629.3	−13.2	−24.7	....
Current Transfers, n.i.e.: Credit	78ajd	54.8	50.5	111.3	52.0	54.5	9.0	10.0	14.9	38.9	18.3	12.9	....
Current Transfers: Debit	78akd	−73.3	−59.3	−33.0	−10.3	−23.5	−6.9	−13.0	−20.2	−20.1	−33.5	−22.7	....
Capital Account, n.i.e.	78bcd	−	−	−	18.9	10.9	17.5	−.2	10.2	8.4	12.7	5.3	....
Capital Account, n.i.e.: Credit	78bad	−	−	−	18.9	11.6	17.5	−	10.3	8.9	13.3	5.3	....
Capital Account: Debit	78bbd	−	−	−	−	−.7	−	−.2	−.1	−.6	−.7	....	....
Financial Account, n.i.e.	78bjd	−153.8	−111.2	605.4	80.6	−663.4	−604.5	−715.9	−336.2	−821.8	−653.1	−464.3	....
Direct Investment Abroad	78bdd	−	−	−	−1.6	.4	−3.5	8.1	−19.3	−3.8	−5.9	−4.2	....
Dir. Invest. in Rep. Econ., n.i.e.	78bed	−	−	−	125.0	72.6	79.2	32.8	538.2	165.9	77.2	331.2	....
Portfolio Investment Assets	78bfd	−	−	−	−2.0	−1.0	−5.2	−13.5	−17.5	−4.5	−11.5	−7.0	....
Equity Securities	78bkd	−	−	−	−2.5	−4.4	−3.8	−14.2	.6	−3.9	−10.2	−3.8	....
Debt Securities	78bld	−	−	−	.5	3.4	−1.4	.8	−18.2	−.6	−1.3	−3.2	....
Portfolio Investment Liab., n.i.e.	78bgd	−	−	−	−	.1	.1	.7	−.2	−.1	....	....	....
Equity Securities	78bmd	−	−	−	−	−	.1	....	−.2	−.1	....	....	....
Debt Securities	78bnd	−	−	−	−	.1	−	.7	−	−	....	....	....
Financial Derivatives Assets	78bwd	....	....	....	....	....	....	....	....	....	....	....	....
Financial Derivatives Liabilities	78bxd	....	....	....	....	....	....	....	....	....	....	....	....
Other Investment Assets	78bhd	−24.9	−22.6	35.5	115.5	33.8	−19.9	49.5	84.3	−73.8	−41.1	−25.0	....
Monetary Authorities	78bod	....	....	....	....	....	....	....	....	....	....	....	....
General Government	78bpd	−	−	−	−	−	−	....	....	....	....	....	....
Banks	78bqd	−18.5	−14.8	33.9	13.1	−2.9	1.3	−5.5	−3.8	−20.4	27.1	31.9	....
Other Sectors	78brd	−6.4	−7.8	1.6	102.4	36.7	−21.1	55.0	88.1	−53.5	−68.2	−56.8	....
Other Investment Liab., n.i.e.	78bid	−128.8	−88.6	569.9	−156.3	−769.2	−655.2	−793.5	−921.7	−905.4	−671.8	−759.3	....
Monetary Authorities	78bsd	−	−	−	1.1	−1.5	13.3	20.5	−6.2	1.4	−.4	−47.2	....
General Government	78btd	−257.3	−288.9	88.4	−457.9	−906.0	−586.4	−812.3	−459.6	−365.2	−606.8	−418.8	....
Banks	78bud	−	−	−	−25.4	−1.3	−8.7	14.8	13.6	−12.5	1.3	14.5	....
Other Sectors	78bvd	128.5	200.2	481.4	325.9	139.5	−73.4	−16.7	−469.5	−529.2	−65.9	−307.8	....
Net Errors and Omissions	78cad	40.4	244.0	33.1	−54.9	−12.8	60.5	−72.0	−99.0	−77.6	−11.8	−219.7	....
Overall Balance	78cbd	−429.9	−420.0	−154.9	−580.7	−1,316.1	−682.4	−1,028.6	−655.6	−242.8	−680.6	−713.1	....
Reserves and Related Items	79dad	429.9	420.0	154.9	580.7	1,316.1	682.4	1,028.6	655.6	242.8	680.6	713.1	....
Reserve Assets	79dbd	−26.8	−1.7	−55.5	−4.3	−36.3	20.2	60.0	−40.9	−183.7	143.5	91.1	....
Use of Fund Credit and Loans	79dcd	−	−.7	15.0	−2.3	20.1	−2.1	−1.0	−4.2	13.6	−1.1	−8.2	....
Exceptional Financing	79ded	456.8	422.4	195.4	587.3	1,332.2	664.3	969.6	700.7	413.0	538.3	630.3	....
Government Finance						*Billions of Francs: Year Ending December 31*							
Deficit (−) or Surplus	80	−109.7	−95.9	−129.9	−86.3	−24.5	−109.6	−226.0	−81.4	26.5	117.5p	....	....
Total Revenue and Grants	81y	174.4	183.2	230.6	260.4	362.1	401.6	266.8	394.1	611.3	642.4p	....	....
Revenue	81	174.4	183.1	220.2	249.7	357.8	400.2	263.2	387.8	604.5	637.4p	....	....
Grants	81z	−	.1	10.4	10.7	4.3	1.4	3.6	6.3	6.8	5.0p	....	....
Exp. & Lending Minus Repay.	82z	284.1	279.1	360.5	346.6	386.6	511.2	492.8	475.5	584.8	524.9p	....	....
Expenditure	82	276.3	279.1	360.5	346.6	386.6	511.2	492.8	475.5	584.8	524.9p	....	....
Lending Minus Repayments	83	7.8	−	−	−	−	−	−	−	−	−p	....	....
Total Financing	80h	....	125.9	129.9	86.2	24.5	109.6	226.0	81.5	−26.5	....	....	....
Domestic	84a	....	91.4	12.9	15.9	−51.1	−77.3	39.7	−4.0	−71.8	....	....	....
Foreign	85a	....	34.5	117.0	70.3	75.6	186.9	186.3	85.4	45.3	....	....	....
Total Debt by Residence	88	....	....	....	....	....	....	....	4,112.3	3,681.5	....	....	....
Domestic	88a	....	....	....	....	....	....	....	390.0	433.6	....	....	....
Foreign	89a	1,154.0	1,295.7	2,875.4	2,839.4	3,318.7	3,468.4	3,770.4	3,722.4	3,247.9	....	....	....

2004, International Monetary Fund: *International Financial Statistics Yearbook*

Congo, Republic of 634

		1992	1993	1994	1995	1996	1997	1998	1999	2000	2001	2002	2003
National Accounts						**Billions of Francs**							
Househ.Cons.Expend.,incl.NPISHs	96f	430.1	434.7	499.9	372.2	671.5	551.3	373.3	506.7	507.4	632.8	663.6	757.1
Government Consumption Expend...	91f	192.4	182.3	200.8	133.6	133.8	257.2	164.1	185.3	215.9	205.2	272.2	213.0
Gross Fixed Capital Formation	93e	159.8	140.7	439.6	521.8	364.9	329.3	557.6	512.3	534.5	682.9	599.2	555.7
Changes in Inventories	93i	7.9	4.2	13.8	24.0	13.9	8.6	15.0	51.0	3.0	50.0	−50.0	−10.2
Exports of Goods and Services	90c	323.1	323.5	557.6	682.9	894.8	1,024.9	875.5	1,050.5	1,881.8	1,602.9	1,706.4	1,582.0
Imports of Goods and Services (-)	98c	336.9	325.3	725.4	666.7	779.1	815.6	835.3	856.6	849.8	1,125.4	1,088.4	1,031.1
Gross Domestic Product (GDP)	99b	775.5	760.2	982.3	1,056.2	1,299.7	1,355.7	1,150.1	1,449.4	2,292.5	2,048.3	2,103.0	2,066.6
Net Primary Income from Abroad	98.n	−97.4	−105.8	−160.5	−352.9	−463.2	−304.5	−181.2	−332.6	−573.8	−497.5	−599.6	−546.1
Gross National Income (GNI)	99a	684.9	662.6	780.9	703.3	836.5	1,051.2	968.9	1,116.8	1,718.7	1,550.8	1,503.4	1,520.5
GDP Volume 1978 Prices	99b.p	428.7	424.5	401.3	410.1	....	....	....	....	....	....	....	....
GDP Volume (2000=100)	99bvp	92.9	92.0	86.9	†88.8	92.6	92.2	95.7	92.6	100.0	....	....	....
GDP Deflator (2000=100)	99bip	36.4	36.1	49.3	51.9	61.2	64.1	52.4	68.3	100.0	....	....	....
						Millions: Midyear Estimates							
Population	99z	2.66	2.75	2.84	2.94	3.04	3.14	3.24	3.35	3.45	3.54	3.63	3.72

Costa Rica

		1992	1993	1994	1995	1996	1997	1998	1999	2000	2001	2002	2003
Exchange Rates						*Colones per SDR: End of Period*							
Market Rate	aa	188.97	208.01	240.98	289.72	316.51	329.61	382.17	409.27	414.35	429.39	514.88	621.92
						Colones per US Dollar: End of Period (ae) Period Average (rf)							
Market Rate	ae	137.43	151.44	165.07	194.90	220.11	244.29	271.42	298.19	318.02	341.67	378.72	418.53
Market Rate	rf	134.51	142.17	157.07	179.73	207.69	232.60	257.23	285.68	308.19	328.87	359.82	398.66
						Index Numbers (2000=100): Period Averages							
Market Rate	ahx	229.1	216.9	196.3	171.8	148.6	132.6	119.9	107.9	100.0	93.7	85.7	77.3
Nominal Effective Exchange Rate	nec	149.3	161.2	164.4	145.0	130.3	121.9	113.8	104.4	100.0	96.8	88.7	76.6
Real Effective Exchange Rate	rec	89.9	92.4	91.7	93.5	94.1	96.5	98.0	96.7	100.0	104.5	102.2	94.2
Fund Position						*Millions of SDRs: End of Period*							
Quota	2f.s	119.00	119.00	119.00	119.00	119.00	119.00	119.00	164.10	164.10	164.10	164.10	164.10
SDRs	1b.s	.17	.12	.12	.04	.01	.02	.05	.59	.33	.07	.06	.04
Reserve Position in the Fund	1c.s	8.73	8.73	8.73	8.73	8.73	8.73	8.73	20.00	20.00	20.00	20.00	20.00
Total Fund Cred.&Loans Outstg	2tl	59.28	59.28	45.46	16.32	.50	—	—	—	—	—	—	—
International Liquidity						*Millions of US Dollars Unless Otherwise Indicated: End of Period*							
Total Reserves minus Gold	1l.d	1,018.65	1,024.03	893.20	1,046.64	1,000.23	1,261.82	1,063.39	1,460.40	1,317.76	1,329.82	1,496.55	1,836.27
SDRs	1b.d	.23	.16	.18	.06	.01	.03	.07	.81	.43	.09	.09	.05
Reserve Position in the Fund	1c.d	12.00	11.98	12.74	12.97	12.55	11.77	12.29	27.45	26.06	25.13	27.19	29.72
Foreign Exchange	1d.d	1,006.41	1,011.89	880.28	1,033.61	987.67	1,250.02	1,051.04	1,432.14	1,291.27	1,304.59	1,469.27	1,806.49
Gold (Million Fine Troy Ounces)	1ad	.040	.035	.034	.034	.002	.002	.002	.002	.002	.002	.002	.002
Gold (National Valuation)	1and	95.97	13.46	....	....	....	.03	.02	.02	.02	.02	.02	.02
Monetary Authorities: Other Liab.	4..d	1,533.13	1,452.73	1,294.60	1,217.58	1,115.12	1,047.67	1,078.46	1,013.79	917.51	811.13	671.21	574.96
Deposit Money Banks: Assets	7a.d	200.90	151.99	199.11	203.90	248.10	251.59	324.56	284.38	330.69	362.78	335.19	384.00
Liabilities	7b.d	49.73	90.29	102.24	166.96	200.85	293.53	333.73	387.96	529.25	651.69	727.40	901.48
Other Banking Insts.: Liabilities	7f.d	4.21	3.81	3.58	....	....	....	....	....	....	....	....	....
Monetary Authorities						*Billions of Colones: End of Period*							
Foreign Assets	11	148.6	162.3	155.9	196.7	203.7	†364.0	370.6	556.3	536.1	534.6	636.8	819.4
Claims on Central Government	12a	42.8	52.0	71.5	100.2	283.4	†359.7	416.8	312.1	234.5	82.8	83.6	90.2
Claims on Nonfin.Pub.Enterprises	12c	34.3	28.8	23.5	23.4	25.4	†8.7	9.3	9.9	10.0	9.9	9.9	9.6
Claims on Deposit Money Banks	12e	28.8	30.9	62.7	38.3	43.4	†22.0	20.8	22.9	18.7	17.6	16.2	16.2
Claims on Other Banking Insts	12f	3.5	3.5	3.3	3.1	3.3	†1.0	.9	.8	.7	.7	.6	.5
Reserve Money	14	190.3	208.4	270.0	313.7	382.2	†446.8	497.0	533.5	508.5	376.6	392.9	510.0
of which: Currency Outside DMBs	14a	47.9	54.7	74.9	84.8	91.7	†106.8	124.2	152.6	141.4	156.5	169.7	186.9
Time, Savings,& Fgn.Currency Dep.	15	9.2	8.9	4.8	4.7	8.2	†4.2	4.3	3.7	3.2	3.3	1.8	—
Liabs. of Central Bank: Securities	16ac	39.6	45.5	78.9	128.5	46.8	†196.4	184.2	379.4	406.9	496.2	696.5	906.8
Restricted Deposits	16b	—	—	—	—	—	†.3	.3	.3	.3	.3	—	—
Foreign Liabilities	16c	17.7	14.3	11.6	4.9	.3	†8.5	9.2	14.5	8.4	24.1	3.2	2.8
Long-Term Foreign Liabilities	16cl	204.2	218.0	213.0	237.1	245.3	†247.4	283.5	287.8	283.4	253.0	251.0	237.8
Central Government Deposits	16d	11.7	14.1	9.3	28.5	111.9	†63.2	60.8	80.4	32.1	77.4	71.5	65.4
Counterpart Funds	16e						†8.6	10.8	2.5	2.3	5.0	.6	.6
Capital Accounts	17a	24.5	25.1	26.8	29.0	126.9	†126.5	105.6	−221.0	−280.4	−559.8	−675.7	−811.7
Other Items (Net)	17r	−239.2	−256.8	−297.5	−384.8	−362.4	†−346.5	−337.5	−179.1	−164.7	−30.6	5.3	24.3
of which: Valuation Adjustment	17rv	−274.6	−293.3	−335.0	−415.0	−401.3	†−353.0	−346.5	−196.6	−107.2	−41.9	−4.4	−2.3
Deposit Money Banks						*Billions of Colones: End of Period*							
Reserves	20	142.1	155.7	196.2	232.3	289.9	†248.8	282.5	294.0	282.1	275.2	288.5	325.7
Claims on Mon.Author.:Securities	20c	2.6	1.5	7.7	36.1	30.3	†109.4	36.7	171.9	203.6	181.6	263.9	284.0
Foreign Assets	21	27.6	23.0	32.9	39.7	54.6	†61.5	88.1	84.8	105.2	124.0	126.9	160.7
Claims on Central Government	22a	7.8	6.6	34.6	28.4	89.7	†130.1	133.1	134.4	162.0	228.5	356.4	453.1
Claims on Nonfin.Pub.Enterprises	22c	2.6	2.6	2.8	2.4	2.5	†7.3	7.0	9.8	23.4	11.1	11.5	11.1
Claims on Private Sector	22d	138.7	190.3	222.9	223.0	329.9	†434.3	670.6	914.3	1,180.0	1,493.3	1,824.4	2,176.4
Claims on Other Banking Insts	22f	2.8	2.9	2.6	.1		†9.6	26.4	9.5	20.5	19.4	21.8	32.3
Demand Deposits	24	61.1	62.4	86.6	67.0	84.9	†243.7	279.6	350.5	479.7	542.3	662.6	779.0
Time, Savings,& Fgn.Currency Dep.	25	252.3	301.3	355.1	389.7	620.7	†578.1	763.8	989.1	1,164.7	1,267.6	1,567.7	1,845.2
Bonds	26ab	—	—	—	—	—	†7.0	16.3	37.2	35.5	35.3	39.6	39.0
Restricted Deposits	26b						†.3	.1			.1	.1	.1
Foreign Liabilities	26c	3.1	8.6	7.3	13.4	22.2	†64.3	75.7	100.2	148.2	201.0	253.7	330.9
Long-Term Foreign Liabilities	26cl	3.7	5.1	9.6	19.1	22.1	†7.4	14.9	15.5	20.1	21.7	21.8	46.4
Central Government Deposits	26d	5.0	5.6	41.4	15.0	3.4	†—	—	—	—	—	—	—
Credit from Monetary Authorities	26g	18.7	17.4	45.8	14.5	11.0	†9.2	7.9	7.5	4.9	7.7	4.6	2.8
Capital Accounts	27a	35.5	43.0	31.8	63.7	95.5	†185.6	229.1	306.7	370.6	486.8	589.6	738.7
Other Items (Net)	27r	−55.4	−60.8	−78.0	−20.6	−62.7	†−94.6	−143.0	−187.8	−246.8	−229.3	−246.3	−338.8

2004, International Monetary Fund: *International Financial Statistics Yearbook*

Costa Rica 238

		1992	1993	1994	1995	1996	1997	1998	1999	2000	2001	2002	2003
Monetary Survey						**Billions of Colones: End of Period**							
Foreign Assets (Net)	31n	155.4	162.4	169.8	218.1	235.8	†352.6	373.9	526.4	484.7	433.4	506.9	646.5
Domestic Credit	32	215.7	267.0	310.5	336.9	618.9	†887.5	1,203.4	1,310.4	1,599.0	1,768.2	2,236.7	2,707.9
Claims on Central Govt. (Net)	32an	33.8	38.8	55.4	85.0	257.8	†426.6	489.1	366.0	364.3	233.9	368.6	478.0
Claims on Nonfin.Pub.Enterprises	32c	36.9	31.4	26.3	25.8	27.9	†16.0	16.4	19.7	33.4	21.0	21.4	20.7
Claims on Private Sector	32d	138.7	190.3	222.9	223.0	329.9	†434.3	670.6	914.3	1,180.0	1,493.3	1,824.4	2,176.4
Claims on Other Banking Insts.	32f	6.3	6.4	5.9	3.1	3.3	†10.6	27.3	10.3	21.3	20.1	22.4	32.8
Money	34	109.5	117.2	161.6	151.9	177.5	†354.6	415.4	534.1	639.7	724.2	843.1	970.1
Quasi-Money	35	261.5	310.2	359.8	394.4	628.8	†582.3	768.1	992.7	1,167.9	1,270.9	1,569.5	1,845.3
Bonds	36ab	—	—	—	—	—	†7.0	16.3	37.2	35.5	35.3	39.6	39.0
Liabs. of Central Bank: Securities	36ac	37.0	44.0	71.2	92.4	16.5	†87.0	147.5	207.5	203.3	314.6	432.6	622.8
Restricted Deposits	36b	—	—	—	—	—	†.5	.4	.3	.3	.4	.1	.1
Long-Term Foreign Liabilities	36cl	207.9	223.1	222.6	256.2	267.3	†254.8	298.5	303.3	303.5	274.7	272.8	284.3
Counterpart Funds	36e	—	—	—	—	—	†8.6	10.8	2.5	2.3	5.0	.6	.6
Capital Accounts	37a	60.0	68.1	58.6	92.7	222.3	†312.1	335.0	85.7	90.2	−73.0	−86.0	−73.0
Other Items (Net)	37r	−304.9	−333.2	−393.5	−432.7	−457.7	†−366.9	−414.6	−326.4	−359.1	−350.3	−328.7	−334.7
Money plus Quasi-Money	35l	371.06	427.40	521.41	546.34	806.33	†936.91	1,183.52	1,526.83	1,807.62	1,995.06	2,412.60	2,815.39
Other Banking Institutions						**Billions of Colones: End of Period**							
Cash	40	—	.1	—	....	....	....	....	....	....	....	....	....
Claims on Central Government	42a	.6	.8	.4	....	....	....	....	....	....	....	....	....
Claims on Official Entities	42bx	—	—	—	....	....	....	....	....	....	....	....	....
Claims on Private Sector	42d	4.8	5.0	7.3	....	....	....	....	....	....	....	....	....
Demand Deposits	44	—	—	—	....	....	....	....	....	....	....	....	....
Time, Savings,& Fgn.Currency Dep.	45	.5	.4	.5	....	....	....	....	....	....	....	....	....
Bonds	46ab	1.4	2.0	2.1	....	....	....	....	....	....	....	....	....
Long-Term Foreign Liabilities	46cl	.6	.6	.6	....	....	....	....	....	....	....	....	....
Central Government Deposits	46d	—	—	—	....	....	....	....	....	....	....	....	....
Credit from Monetary Authorities	46g	.7	.7	2.4	....	....	....	....	....	....	....	....	....
Credit from Deposit Money Banks	46h	2.1	2.3	2.2	....	....	....	....	....	....	....	....	....
Capital Accounts	47a	.2	.1	.2	....	....	....	....	....	....	....	....	....
Other Items (Net)	47r	−.1	−.3	−.1	....	....	....	....	....	....	....	....	....
Banking Survey						**Billions of Colones: End of Period**							
Foreign Assets (net)	51n	155.4	162.4	169.8	....	....	....	....	....	....	....	....	....
Domestic Credit	52	214.8	266.3	312.1	....	....	....	....	....	....	....	....	....
Claims on Central Govt. (Net)	52an	34.5	39.6	55.8	....	....	....	....	....	....	....	....	....
Claims on Official Entities	52bx	36.9	31.4	26.3	....	....	....	....	....	....	....	....	....
Claims on Private Sector	52d	143.5	195.3	230.2	....	....	....	....	....	....	....	....	....
Liquid Liabilities	55l	371.6	427.8	521.8	....	....	....	....	....	....	....	....	....
Bonds	56ab	38.4	46.0	73.3	....	....	....	....	....	....	....	....	....
Long-Term Foreign Liabilities	56cl	208.5	223.7	223.2	....	....	....	....	....	....	....	....	....
Capital Accounts	57a	60.1	68.2	58.8	....	....	....	....	....	....	....	....	....
Other Items (Net)	57r	−308.4	−336.9	−395.0	....	....	....	....	....	....	....	....	....
Interest Rates						**Percent Per Annum**							
Discount Rate (End of Period)	60	29.00	35.00	37.75	38.50	35.00	31.00	37.00	34.00	31.50	28.75	31.25	26.00
Deposit Rate	60l	15.80	16.90	17.72	23.88	17.29	13.03	12.76	14.31	13.38	11.77	11.46	10.41
Lending Rate	60p	28.46	30.02	33.03	36.70	26.27	22.48	22.47	25.74	24.89	23.83	26.42	25.58
Prices and Labor						**Index Numbers (2000=100): Period Averages**							
Producer Prices	63	39.42	41.45	46.88	58.08	67.37	75.19	81.82	90.11	100.00	109.32	118.04	130.51
Consumer Prices	64	35.9	39.4	†44.7	55.1	64.8	73.3	81.9	90.1	100.0	111.2	121.4	132.9
					Number in Thousands: Period Averages								
Labor Force	67d	1,063	1,119	1,160	....	1,199	1,277	1,377	1,383	1,391	....	....	....
Employment	67e	1,043	1,096	1,138	1,174	1,145	1,227	1,300	1,300	1,319	1,553	1,587	1,640
Unemployment	67c	44	47	49	64	76	74	77	83	72	....	....	....
Unemployment Rate (%)	67r	4.1	4.1	4.2	5.2	6.2	5.7	5.6	6.0	5.2	....	....	....
International Transactions						**Millions of US Dollars**							
Exports	70..d	1,840.8	2,625.5	2,878.2	3,475.9	3,758.4	4,334.5	5,525.6	6,662.4	5,849.7	5,021.4	5,263.5	6,102.2
Imports, c.i.f.	71..d	2,440.7	3,515.1	3,788.5	4,090.0	4,326.6	4,969.6	6,238.7	6,354.6	6,388.5	6,568.6	7,187.9	7,662.6

Costa Rica 238

		1992	1993	1994	1995	1996	1997	1998	1999	2000	2001	2002	2003
Balance of Payments		\multicolumn{12}{c}{*Millions of US Dollars: Minus Sign Indicates Debit*}
Current Account, n.i.e.	78ald	−380.4	−620.2	−244.0	−358.1	−263.7	−480.9	−520.8	−666.4	−706.8	−712.7	−916.1	−967.0
Goods: Exports f.o.b.	78aad	1,739.1	1,866.8	2,122.0	3,481.8	3,774.1	4,220.6	5,538.3	6,576.4	5,813.4	4,923.2	5,269.9	6,124.7
Goods: Imports f.o.b.	78abd	−2,210.9	−2,627.6	−2,727.8	−3,804.4	−4,023.3	−4,718.2	−5,937.4	−5,996.1	−6,023.8	−5,743.3	−6,537.1	−7,294.4
Trade Balance	78acd	−471.8	−760.8	−605.8	−322.6	−249.2	−497.6	−399.0	580.3	−210.5	−820.1	−1,267.2	−1,169.6
Services: Credit	78add	841.3	1,039.3	1,195.0	969.1	1,053.5	1,128.6	1,343.4	1,666.1	1,936.3	1,900.6	1,869.9	2,027.0
Services: Debit	78aed	−710.6	−816.4	−860.1	−913.0	−1,033.3	−988.4	−1,109.8	−1,195.1	−1,273.5	−1,168.9	−1,182.1	−1,188.4
Balance on Goods & Services	78afd	−341.1	−537.9	−270.9	−266.5	−228.9	−357.4	−165.5	1,051.2	452.3	−88.4	−579.5	−331.0
Income: Credit	78agd	112.8	111.2	154.6	146.4	142.5	185.4	182.7	198.2	242.8	196.0	317.9	213.3
Income: Debit	78ahd	−315.4	−336.6	−283.0	−371.9	−326.7	−434.4	−651.2	−2,019.8	−1,495.2	−975.6	−835.2	−1,061.9
Balance on Gds, Serv. & Inc.	78aid	−543.7	−763.3	−399.3	−492.0	−413.2	−606.4	−634.0	−770.4	−800.1	−867.9	−1,096.8	−1,179.6
Current Transfers, n.i.e.: Credit	78ajd	168.9	149.3	164.5	165.2	192.7	191.2	190.5	201.4	203.8	266.4	296.9	368.6
Current Transfers: Debit	78akd	−5.6	−6.2	−9.2	−31.3	−43.2	−65.7	−77.3	−97.5	−110.5	−111.1	−116.2	−156.0
Capital Account, n.i.e.	78bcd	−	−	−	−	28.2	....	....	−	8.9	12.4	5.7	26.1
Capital Account, n.i.e.: Credit	78bad	−	−	−	−	28.2	....	....	−	8.9	12.4	5.7	26.1
Capital Account: Debit	78bbd	−	−	−	−	....	....	....	−	−	−	−	−
Financial Account, n.i.e.	78bjd	192.8	62.8	−108.4	517.3	47.5	129.7	199.0	683.1	−34.6	320.4	844.8	653.4
Direct Investment Abroad	78bdd	−4.4	−2.3	−4.7	−5.5	−5.7	−4.4	−4.8	−5.0	−5.0	−11.1	−34.1	−26.9
Dir. Invest. in Rep. Econ., n.i.e.	78bed	226.0	246.7	297.6	336.9	427.0	408.2	613.1	619.5	408.6	453.6	661.9	576.7
Portfolio Investment Assets	78bfd	−	−	−	−.4	....	−22.5	−33.9	−11.0	−18.5	−81.2	28.4	−91.6
Equity Securities	78bkd	−	−	−	−.4	....	−22.5	−33.9	−28.1	−4.0	−21.9	4.6	−1.5
Debt Securities	78bld	−	−	−	−	....	....	....	17.1	−14.4	−59.2	23.8	−90.1
Portfolio Investment Liab., n.i.e.	78bgd	−16.9	−5.1	−1.2	−24.4	−21.5	−190.8	−296.0	−123.2	−67.5	−57.9	−125.8	−304.5
Equity Securities	78bmd	−	−	−	−	....	....	....	−	−	−	−	−
Debt Securities	78bnd	−16.9	−5.1	−1.2	−24.4	−21.5	−190.8	−296.0	−123.2	−67.5	−57.9	−125.8	−304.5
Financial Derivatives Assets	78bwd	....	....	....	....	....	....	....	....	....	....	....	....
Financial Derivatives Liabilities	78bxd	....	....	....	....	....	....	....	....	....	....	....	....
Other Investment Assets	78bhd	84.8	54.5	−76.2	16.8	−159.3	−267.4	−95.6	156.1	−344.3	106.2	217.5	170.6
Monetary Authorities	78bod	....	....	....	.1	−6.3	−.1	....	−.1	−.2	−.2	−.2	−27.6
General Government	78bpd	−8.5	34.9	−4.4	−	....	....	....	....	....	....	....	....
Banks	78bqd	−	−	−	−9.8	−17.8	43.3	−29.8	43.6	−76.3	54.4	.6	−28.3
Other Sectors	78brd	93.3	19.6	−71.8	26.5	−135.2	−310.6	−65.8	112.7	−267.8	52.0	217.0	226.5
Other Investment Liab., n.i.e.	78bid	−96.7	−231.0	−323.9	193.9	−192.9	206.7	16.2	46.8	−7.8	−89.2	96.9	329.1
Monetary Authorities	78bsd	−76.6	−256.8	−216.1	−94.4	−104.0	−118.6	−98.5	−93.7	−175.3	−135.2	−76.7	−47.4
General Government	78btd	−47.8	−25.7	−106.2	12.9	−85.2	−64.1	−60.7	−77.9	−74.6	−65.3	−57.7	−86.5
Banks	78bud	7.1	27.7	−18.8	23.0	48.7	73.7	37.3	49.0	142.9	144.6	59.2	219.3
Other Sectors	78bvd	20.6	23.8	17.2	252.4	−52.3	315.7	138.1	169.4	99.1	−33.4	172.1	243.8
Net Errors and Omissions	78cad	201.9	299.0	249.1	57.1	118.7	157.8	−182.5	213.1	391.0	243.9	28.2	68.0
Overall Balance	78cbd	14.3	−258.4	−103.3	216.2	−69.3	−193.3	−504.3	229.7	−341.4	−136.0	−37.4	−219.5
Reserves and Related Items	79dad	−14.3	258.4	103.3	−216.2	69.3	193.3	504.3	−229.7	341.4	136.0	37.4	219.5
Reserve Assets	79dbd	−176.8	59.6	65.5	−179.2	77.3	−215.7	149.6	−481.0	152.9	−13.0	−163.0	−338.9
Use of Fund Credit and Loans	79dcd	1.7	−	−20.3	−44.4	−23.1	−.7	−	−	−	−	−	−
Exceptional Financing	79ded	160.8	198.8	58.1	7.4	15.0	409.7	354.7	251.3	188.4	149.0	200.4	558.3
International Investment Position		\multicolumn{12}{c}{*Millions of US Dollars*}
Assets	79aad	....	....	....	....	3,367.6	3,887.1	3,817.3	4,103.8	4,337.1	4,241.5	4,166.6	4,422.0
Direct Investment Abroad	79abd	....	....	....	....	60.0	65.7	71.4	81.1	89.5	100.8	132.4	157.0
Portfolio Investment	79acd	....	....	....	....	86.2	108.7	105.8	90.1	108.5	142.5	131.1	222.7
Equity Securities	79add	....	....	....	....	19.0	41.5	38.6	40.0	44.0	7.4	2.7	4.3
Debt Securities	79aed	....	....	....	....	67.2	67.2	67.2	50.1	64.5	135.1	128.3	218.4
Financial Derivatives	79ald	....	....	....	....	....	....	....	....	....	....	....	....
Other Investment	79afd	....	....	....	....	2,212.6	2,488.9	2,565.2	2,377.1	2,737.9	2,585.0	2,324.9	2,122.7
Monetary Authorities	79agd	....	....	....	....	132.6	132.7	132.7	132.8	133.0	133.2	133.3	160.9
General Government	79ahd	....	....	....	....	−	−	−	−	−	−	−	−
Banks	79aid	....	....	....	....	247.6	204.4	245.2	201.6	277.9	223.6	223.0	251.2
Other Sectors	79ajd	....	....	....	....	1,832.3	2,151.9	2,187.3	2,042.6	2,327.0	2,228.3	1,968.6	1,710.5
Reserve Assets	79akd	....	....	....	....	1,008.8	1,223.8	1,074.9	1,555.6	1,401.1	1,413.2	1,578.3	1,919.7
Liabilities	79lad	....	....	....	....	5,369.5	6,067.8	6,700.8	7,461.2	7,553.9	8,051.9	8,718.7	9,786.8
Dir. Invest. in Rep. Economy	79lbd	....	....	....	....	836.1	1,221.5	1,759.0	2,364.6	2,709.1	3,177.8	3,737.9	4,198.7
Portfolio Investment	79lcd	....	....	....	....	674.2	776.4	726.2	821.4	771.1	860.9	937.3	1,033.5
Equity Securities	79ldd	....	....	....	....	−	−	−	−	−	−	−	−
Debt Securities	79led	....	....	....	....	674.2	776.4	726.2	821.4	771.1	860.9	937.3	1,033.5
Financial Derivatives	79lld	....	....	....	....	....	....	....	....	....	....	....	....
Other Investment	79lfd	....	....	....	....	3,859.2	4,069.9	4,215.7	4,275.1	4,073.7	4,013.2	4,043.6	4,554.6
Monetary Authorities	79lgd	....	....	....	....	659.5	548.4	557.0	491.7	417.5	316.6	260.7	373.1
General Government	79lhd	....	....	....	....	1,026.0	975.7	942.3	865.1	819.4	807.1	757.1	703.1
Banks	79lid	....	....	....	....	191.6	277.1	306.7	363.2	505.6	649.8	713.4	932.2
Other Sectors	79ljd	....	....	....	....	1,982.1	2,268.7	2,409.7	2,555.1	2,331.3	2,239.8	2,312.3	2,546.2

Costa Rica   238

		1992	1993	1994	1995	1996	1997	1998	1999	2000	2001	2002	2003
Government Finance						*Millions of Colones: Year Ending December 31*							
Deficit (-) or Surplus	80	−16,047	−24,131	−85,361	−84,575	−95,471	−81,769	−89,435	−98,989	−140,173	−144,246	−239,767	....
Total Revenue and Grants	81y	142,671	166,065	191,247	253,699	302,497	363,540	444,486	547,435	599,101	704,131	781,797	....
Revenue	81	142,671	166,065	191,247	253,699	302,497	363,540	444,486	547,435	599,101	704,131	781,797	....
Grants	81z	−	−	−	−	−	−	−	−	−	−	−	....
Exp. & Lending Minus Repay.	82z	158,718	190,196	276,608	338,274	397,968	445,309	533,921	646,424	739,274	848,377	1,021,564	....
Expenditure	82	158,718	190,196	276,608	338,274	397,968	445,309	533,921	646,424	739,274	848,377	1,021,564	....
Lending Minus Repayments	83	−	−	−	−	−	−	−	−	−	−	−	....
Total Financing	80h	16,047	24,131	85,361	84,575	95,472	81,769	89,436	98,991	140,175	144,246	239,767	....
Domestic	84a	13,919	33,742	88,498	101,350	120,983	106,561	39,827	34,517	69,303	89,679	....	....
Foreign	85a	2,128	−9,611	−3,138	−16,775	−25,511	−24,792	49,609	64,474	70,872	54,567	....	....
Total Debt by Residence	88	338,524	398,135	506,771	671,357	922,811	1,080,891	1,283,354	1,599,430	1,797,993	2,140,538	2,593,277	....
Domestic Debt	88a	176,706	228,678	320,272	463,933	697,676	706,375	977,150	1,235,767	1,343,884	1,547,216	1,796,466	....
Foreign Debt	89a	161,818	169,457	186,499	207,424	225,135	374,516	306,204	363,663	454,109	593,322	796,811	....
National Accounts							*Millions of Colones*						
Househ.Cons.Expend.,incl.NPISHs	96f	829,736	992,516	1,189,292	1,496,157	1,822,342	2,168,885	2,510,880	2,916,434	3,290,353	3,689,866	4,117,134	4,670,299
Government Consumption Expend	91f	143,472	180,214	228,887	284,636	330,455	390,087	469,886	565,207	652,654	772,575	900,615	1,010,580
Gross Fixed Capital Formation	93e	227,467	280,900	324,161	399,983	421,650	538,478	740,341	811,325	873,951	987,278	1,146,091	1,370,526
Changes in Inventories	93i	5,892	5,270	8,282	−15,918	−29,099	1,161	4,137	−38,188	−37,903	112,225	199,308	34,043
Exports of Goods and Services	90c	406,115	490,201	589,686	790,800	967,130	1,215,914	1,716,713	2,330,567	2,384,640	2,227,964	2,564,249	3,244,430
Imports of Goods and Services (-)	98c	459,477	578,808	682,071	849,971	1,052,522	1,330,505	1,816,627	2,072,582	2,249,196	2,398,443	2,875,929	3,382,288
Gross Domestic Product (GDP)	99b	1,153,205	1,370,292	1,658,236	2,105,687	2,459,957	2,984,020	3,625,330	4,512,763	4,914,498	5,391,466	6,051,467	6,947,590
Net Primary Income from Abroad	98.n	−28,745	−34,039	−21,837	−40,473	−38,353	−57,912	−120,500	−520,932	−385,150	−262,112	−248,837	−312,656
Gross National Income (GNI)	99a	1,124,460	1,336,253	1,636,400	2,065,214	2,421,604	2,926,108	3,504,830	3,991,831	4,529,348	5,129,354	5,802,630	6,634,934
Consumption of Fixed Capital	99cf	66,942	78,649	92,123	115,025	138,579	168,727	201,867	264,890	284,228	319,926	368,334	422,878
GDP Volume 1991 Prices	99b.p	957,166	1,028,127	1,076,753	1,118,971	1,128,892	1,191,864	1,291,955	1,398,182	1,423,344	1,438,186	1,480,210	1,576,252
GDP Volume (2000=100)	99bvp	67.2	72.2	75.6	78.6	79.3	83.7	90.8	98.2	100.0	101.0	104.0	110.7
GDP Deflator (2000=100)	99bip	34.9	38.6	44.6	54.5	63.1	72.5	81.3	93.5	100.0	108.6	118.4	127.7
						Millions: Midyear Estimates							
Population	99z	3.23	3.31	3.39	3.47	3.56	3.66	3.75	3.84	3.93	4.01	4.09	4.17

Côte d'Ivoire 662

		1992	1993	1994	1995	1996	1997	1998	1999	2000	2001	2002	2003
Exchange Rates						*Francs per SDR: End of Period*							
Official Rate	aa	378.57	404.89	†780.44	728.38	753.06	807.94	791.61	†896.19	918.49	935.39	850.37	771.76
					Francs per US Dollar: End of Period (ae) Period Average (rf)								
Official Rate	ae	275.32	294.77	†534.60	490.00	523.70	598.81	562.21	†652.95	704.95	744.31	625.50	519.36
Official Rate	rf	264.69	283.16	†555.20	499.15	511.55	583.67	589.95	†615.70	711.98	733.04	696.99	581.20
					Index Numbers (2000=100): Period Averages								
Official Rate	ahx	268.8	250.9	128.1	142.3	138.8	121.8	120.5	115.5	100.0	96.9	102.2	122.4
Nominal Effective Exchange Rate	nec	153.5	172.1	99.5	105.9	106.6	102.7	107.3	106.1	100.0	102.0	105.0	112.1
Real Effective Exchange Rate	rec	146.9	144.8	89.2	103.1	103.6	101.9	108.7	106.5	100.0	103.5	107.6	115.8
Fund Position						*Millions of SDRs: End of Period*							
Quota	2f.s	238.2	238.2	238.2	238.2	238.2	238.2	238.2	325.2	325.2	325.2	325.2	325.2
SDRs	1b.s	.2	.8	.1	1.2	.8	–	.1	2.5	1.0	.6	.9	.2
Reserve Position in the Fund	1c.s	–	.1	.1	.1	.1	.2	.2	.2	.3	.3	.4	.6
Total Fund Cred.&Loans Outstg	2tl	194.5	159.1	224.8	287.1	349.6	333.5	457.3	451.4	421.6	369.2	361.1	286.0
International Liquidity					*Millions of US Dollars Unless Otherwise Indicated: End of Period*								
Total Reserves minus Gold	1l.d	6.9	2.3	204.3	529.0	605.8	618.4	855.5	630.4	667.9	1,019.0	1,863.3	2,230.5
SDRs	1b.d	.3	1.1	.2	1.8	1.2	–	.2	3.4	1.3	.7	1.2	.3
Reserve Position in the Fund	1c.d	–	.1	.1	.1	.2	.2	.3	.3	.4	.4	.6	.8
Foreign Exchange	1d.d	6.7	1.1	204.0	527.0	604.4	618.1	855.0	626.6	666.2	1,017.9	1,861.5	2,229.3
Gold (Million Fine Troy Ounces)	1ad	.045	.045	.045	–	–	–	–	–	–	–	–	–
Gold (National Valuation)	1and	15.4	16.6	16.6	–	–	–	–	–	–	–	–	–
Monetary Authorities: Other Liab	4..d	1,519.8	1,382.4	1.7	9.6	7.8	10.6	14.4	8.1	.5	6.6	16.3	8.9
Deposit Money Banks: Assets	7a.d	206.9	176.5	202.1	352.6	268.5	266.8	311.3	351.9	252.5	222.3	364.6	290.1
Liabilities	7b.d	449.6	486.4	299.8	400.6	312.0	295.4	363.0	389.7	317.2	345.8	258.3	240.0
Monetary Authorities						*Billions of Francs: End of Period*							
Foreign Assets	11	1.9	.7	109.2	259.2	317.2	370.3	481.0	412.0	475.1	766.6	1,165.5	1,158.8
Claims on Central Government	12a	239.1	273.2	433.2	382.6	439.8	449.3	572.3	596.4	538.3	491.1	497.6	432.6
Claims on Deposit Money Banks	12e	533.6	506.6	130.0	140.8	125.8	104.7	114.6	99.8	75.3	36.8	14.7	.5
Claims on Other Financial Insts	12f	9.3	10.6	5.1	12.3	14.4	13.4	14.7	14.2	12.7	9.7	7.9	5.2
Reserve Money	14	271.1	295.8	462.4	516.0	550.8	615.7	733.1	676.7	690.1	926.9	1,297.5	1,233.8
of which: Currency Outside DMBs	14a	252.1	272.5	392.6	451.4	473.2	571.8	652.1	615.5	620.7	774.7	1,146.7	1,049.9
Foreign Liabilities	16c	492.1	471.9	176.3	213.8	267.3	275.8	370.2	409.8	387.6	350.3	317.2	225.4
Central Government Deposits	16d	8.2	13.1	45.8	43.0	49.5	27.8	51.1	56.7	39.3	40.8	44.2	97.8
Other Items (Net)	17r	12.5	10.3	−6.9	22.0	29.5	18.4	28.2	−20.8	−15.6	−13.9	26.7	40.2
Deposit Money Banks						*Billions of Francs: End of Period*							
Reserves	20	22.1	20.6	66.6	58.1	74.7	45.4	67.2	60.7	64.7	96.1	106.4	172.4
Foreign Assets	21	57.0	52.0	108.0	172.8	140.6	159.8	175.0	229.8	178.0	165.5	228.1	150.7
Claims on Central Government	22a	226.8	224.7	314.9	371.1	413.4	415.9	412.6	382.8	325.4	302.5	292.8	300.5
Claims on Private Sector	22d	928.9	878.5	828.2	997.1	1,016.0	1,147.4	1,186.7	1,084.5	1,136.2	1,192.3	1,192.3	1,073.3
Claims on Other Financial Insts	22f	11.2	6.2	5.8	1.7	–	–	–	–	–	–	–	–
Demand Deposits	24	234.5	219.2	403.3	490.7	489.0	502.8	562.0	576.7	526.7	507.8	571.6	563.3
Time Deposits	25	346.9	331.0	412.1	485.3	519.6	527.7	485.1	477.7	489.3	515.3	641.1	618.6
Foreign Liabilities	26c	78.1	95.8	112.5	160.1	128.2	153.8	172.3	207.1	192.4	185.3	145.1	109.3
Long-Term Foreign Liabilities	26cl	45.7	47.6	47.8	36.2	35.2	23.1	31.7	47.4	31.3	72.1	16.4	15.3
Central Government Deposits	26d	74.9	92.5	171.1	183.1	243.3	278.9	325.7	234.4	267.3	287.6	262.3	214.6
Credit from Monetary Authorities	26g	524.7	497.3	134.4	152.2	124.3	104.7	116.0	91.0	76.8	37.0	14.7	.5
Other Items (Net)	27r	−58.9	−101.3	42.3	93.0	105.0	177.6	148.7	123.5	120.5	151.2	168.4	175.2
Treasury Claims: Private Sector	22d.i	17.5	17.8	26.7	19.0	22.7	22.0	–	16.0	13.4	21.2	16.3	14.2
Post Office: Checking Deposits	24..i	2.5	1.7	2.1	1.5	2.4	3.6	2.0	3.0	3.9	3.6	4.7	6.1
Monetary Survey						*Billions of Francs: End of Period*							
Foreign Assets (Net)	31n	−511.3	−515.0	−71.5	58.1	62.3	100.5	113.5	24.8	73.2	396.4	931.2	974.8
Domestic Credit	32	1,334.6	1,289.3	1,372.4	1,540.1	1,593.1	1,722.9	1,811.5	1,789.8	1,709.8	1,670.6	1,688.8	1,505.2
Claims on Central Govt. (Net)	32an	367.7	376.1	506.5	510.1	540.0	540.1	610.1	675.1	547.6	447.5	472.3	412.5
Claims on Private Sector	32d	946.4	896.3	854.9	1,016.0	1,038.7	1,169.4	1,186.7	1,100.5	1,149.5	1,213.5	1,208.6	1,087.5
Claims on Other Financial Insts	32f	20.5	16.9	10.9	13.9	14.4	13.4	14.7	14.2	12.7	9.7	7.9	5.2
Money	34	489.4	494.0	798.8	944.5	966.4	1,080.0	1,219.3	1,198.0	1,154.0	1,324.8	1,750.5	1,626.3
Quasi-Money	35	346.9	331.0	412.1	485.3	519.6	527.7	485.1	477.7	489.3	515.3	641.1	618.6
Long-Term Foreign Liabilities	36cl	45.7	47.6	47.8	36.2	35.2	23.1	31.7	47.4	31.3	72.1	16.4	15.3
Other Items (Net)	37r	−58.7	−98.3	42.1	132.0	134.2	192.6	188.9	91.6	108.5	154.9	212.0	219.7
Money plus Quasi-Money	35l	836.4	825.0	1,210.9	1,429.9	1,486.0	1,607.7	1,704.4	1,675.7	1,643.3	1,840.1	2,391.6	2,245.0
Interest Rates						*Percent Per Annum*							
Bank Rate (End of Period)	60	12.50	†6.00	6.00	6.00	6.00	6.00	6.00	6.00	6.00	6.00	6.00	4.50
Money Market Rate	60b	11.44	....	....	....	....	....	4.81	4.95	4.95	4.95	4.95	4.95
Deposit Rate	60l	7.75	....	....	....	....	....	3.50	3.50	3.50	3.50	3.50	3.50
Lending Rate	60p	16.75	....	....	....	....	....	....	....	....	....	....	....

2004, International Monetary Fund: *International Financial Statistics Yearbook*

Côte d'Ivoire 662

		1992	1993	1994	1995	1996	1997	1998	1999	2000	2001	2002	2003
Prices, Production, Labor		\multicolumn{12}{c}{*Index Numbers (2000=100): Period Averages*}
Consumer Prices	64	58.9	†60.2	75.9	86.8	†88.9	92.5	96.8	97.6	100.0	104.3	107.5	111.1
Industrial Production	66	67.4	66.7	68.8	74.8	84.8	94.9	105.5	108.5	100.0	96.1	92.2	85.1
		\multicolumn{12}{c}{*Number in Thousands: Period Averages*}
Unemployment	67c	172	175	186	216	238	....	....	....	....	....	....	....
Unemployment Rate	67r	26.3	27.7	30.0	35.6	38.8	....	....	....	....	....	....	....
International Transactions		\multicolumn{12}{c}{*Billions of Francs*}
Exports	70	751.70	713.20	1,522.50	1,899.70	2,274.40	2,598.10	2,717.60	2,870.10	2,768.20	2,892.70	3,676.60	3,396.50
Imports, c.i.f.	71	613.17	599.00	1,064.60	1,463.00	1,484.50	1,623.10	1,973.77	1,703.10	1,710.00	1,772.30	1,711.60	1,929.60
Balance of Payments		\multicolumn{12}{c}{*Millions of US Dollars: Minus Sign Indicates Debit*}
Current Account, n.i.e.	78ald	−1,012.7	−891.7	−13.8	−492.4	−162.3	−154.7	−290.2	−119.5	−241.3	−61.3	768.2	352.8
Goods: Exports f.o.b	78aad	2,946.8	2,518.7	2,895.9	3,805.9	4,446.1	4,451.2	4,606.4	4,661.5	3,888.0	3,945.9	5,274.8	5,844.1
Goods: Imports f.o.b	78abd	−1,952.1	−1,770.4	−1,606.8	−2,430.3	−2,622.4	−2,658.4	−2,886.4	−2,766.0	−2,401.8	−2,417.7	−2,455.6	−3,320.0
Trade Balance	78acd	994.7	748.3	1,289.1	1,375.5	1,823.7	1,792.8	1,720.0	1,895.5	1,486.2	1,528.2	2,819.3	2,524.0
Services: Credit	78add	649.2	675.9	507.7	530.9	565.7	579.6	614.5	586.5	482.4	577.8	585.3	712.5
Services: Debit	78aed	−1,477.2	−1,331.7	−1,011.1	−1,375.7	−1,440.3	−1,478.6	−1,524.1	−1,459.0	−1,226.9	−1,271.3	−1,544.7	−1,727.7
Balance on Goods & Services	78afd	166.8	92.5	785.7	530.7	949.1	893.8	810.4	1,022.9	741.7	834.8	1,859.9	1,508.9
Income: Credit	78agd	18.9	97.8	133.8	189.5	170.7	161.2	169.0	162.6	141.6	137.3	141.2	167.0
Income: Debit	78ahd	−1,099.8	−887.8	−817.5	−976.1	−939.5	−829.2	−876.1	−919.2	−794.5	−723.1	−770.9	−854.1
Balance on Gds, Serv. & Inc.	78aid	−914.1	−697.5	102.0	−255.8	180.2	225.8	103.4	266.3	88.8	249.0	1,230.2	821.7
Current Transfers, n.i.e.: Credit	78ajd	404.6	270.9	246.8	277.7	204.1	137.7	148.2	136.8	79.4	88.5	131.9	150.7
Current Transfers: Debit	78akd	−503.2	−465.1	−362.6	−514.3	−546.6	−518.3	−541.7	−522.6	−409.4	−398.7	−593.8	−619.6
Capital Account, n.i.e.	78bcd	−	−	527.6	291.3	47.1	40.6	25.6	13.8	8.4	10.0	8.3	5.5
Capital Account, n.i.e.: Credit	78bad	−	−	527.6	291.3	49.8	50.5	35.9	17.4	9.9	11.5	9.1	8.0
Capital Account: Debit	78bbd	−	−	−	−	−2.7	−9.9	−10.3	−3.6	−1.4	−1.4	−.8	−2.5
Financial Account, n.i.e.	78bjd	−450.7	−356.0	−523.1	−88.6	−717.8	−323.0	−417.1	−577.5	−362.6	−66.0	−1,032.3	−1,099.2
Direct Investment Abroad	78bdd	−	−	−	−	−.4	−	−	....	....	....	....	....
Dir. Invest. in Rep. Econ., n.i.e.	78bed	−230.8	87.9	78.0	211.5	269.2	415.3	380.0	323.7	234.7	272.7	212.6	179.9
Portfolio Investment Assets	78bfd	−	7.4	−27.4	−8.4	−16.0	−26.9	−29.8	−28.8	−12.5	−12.0	−21.1	−35.0
Equity Securities	78bkd	−	7.4	7.7	1.2	−1.6	.2	−1.7	−1.6	−1.3	−1.3	−2.0	−
Debt Securities	78bld	−	−	−35.1	−9.6	−14.5	−27.1	−28.2	−27.2	−11.2	−10.7	−19.1	−35.0
Portfolio Investment Liab., n.i.e.	78bgd	−	−	−.7	10.0	25.0	19.2	19.5	13.4	4.5	4.0	49.8	52.1
Equity Securities	78bmd	−	−	1.1	1.2	10.2	8.6	8.6	5.6	1.2	2.4	3.6	4.0
Debt Securities	78bnd	−	−	−1.8	8.8	14.9	10.6	10.8	7.8	3.4	1.6	46.2	48.2
Financial Derivatives Assets	78bwd	....	−	−	−	−	−	−3.2	−3.1	−2.6	−3.8	−6.0	−
Financial Derivatives Liabilities	78bxd	....	−	−	−	−3.3	−3.1	−	−	−	−	−	−
Other Investment Assets	78bhd	169.6	51.9	−39.6	−323.2	−256.5	−304.8	−317.6	−350.6	−182.4	−129.1	−439.0	−413.0
Monetary Authorities	78bod	....	−	−	−	....	....	....	....	....	....	....	....
General Government	78bpd	−	−	−11.9	−14.2	−22.3	−9.9	−7.7	−5.2	−4.5	−5.1	−7.8	−4.1
Banks	78bqd	63.8	72.7	−95.3	−33.1	35.2	−25.7	−16.4	−49.1	2.8	37.7	−89.8	....
Other Sectors	78brd	105.8	−20.8	67.5	−275.9	−269.4	−269.2	−293.5	−296.3	−180.7	−161.8	−341.5	−408.9
Other Investment Liab., n.i.e.	78bid	−389.5	−503.2	−533.3	21.4	−735.8	−422.7	−465.9	−532.1	−404.3	−197.8	−828.6	−883.1
Monetary Authorities	78bsd	−33.2	−44.1	−726.6	1.8	−1.2	4.3	3.1	−5.2	−.7	−14.4	10.5	−
General Government	78btd	−207.4	−444.6	249.8	−105.8	−621.6	−473.6	−597.3	−583.6	−523.3	−487.3	−737.2	−678.8
Banks	78bud	−134.9	7.8	75.1	77.1	−38.5	64.9	37.3	42.0	23.1	46.1	−136.4	−
Other Sectors	78bvd	−14.0	−22.2	−131.7	48.3	−74.5	−18.3	91.0	14.7	96.7	257.9	34.5	−204.4
Net Errors and Omissions	78cad	46.6	11.1	−11.1	35.6	−15.4	−39.6	32.1	−24.6	−12.9	31.1	−22.6	−17.1
Overall Balance	78cbd	−1,416.9	−1,236.6	−20.3	−254.2	−848.4	−476.6	−649.6	−707.9	−608.3	−86.1	−278.4	−757.9
Reserves and Related Items	79dad	1,416.9	1,236.6	20.3	254.2	848.4	476.6	649.6	707.9	608.3	86.1	278.4	757.9
Reserve Assets	79dbd	−84.4	4.4	−194.5	−302.5	−113.4	−95.4	−179.8	109.8	−89.0	−386.6	−584.1	−17.2
Use of Fund Credit and Loans	79dcd	−91.9	−49.0	94.3	94.9	90.3	−22.3	168.8	−8.2	−38.8	−66.4	−13.5	−106.4
Exceptional Financing	79ded	1,593.2	1,281.2	120.5	461.8	871.5	594.3	660.6	606.3	736.1	539.1	876.1	881.6

Côte d'Ivoire 662

		1992	1993	1994	1995	1996	1997	1998	1999	2000	2001	2002	2003
International Investment Position							*Millions of US Dollars*						
Assets	79aad	....	....	....	....	....	....	2,768.3	2,640.9	2,735.7	3,114.5	4,876.3	6,393.2
Direct Investment Abroad	79abd	....	....	–	–	–	–	–	–	–	–	–	–
Portfolio Investment	79acd	....	....	–	–	–	–	158.9	166.9	169.9	176.4	240.2	328.5
Equity Securities	79add	....	....	–	–	–	–	10.5	10.5	11.1	11.8	16.3	19.6
Debt Securities	79aed	....	....	–	–	–	–	148.4	156.3	158.7	164.6	223.9	309.0
Financial Derivatives	79ald	....	....	....	....	....	....	–	–	–	–	–	–
Other Investment	79afd	....	....	337.4	378.6	268.3	266.9	1,757.3	1,843.7	1,891.9	1,919.1	2,772.8	3,801.5
Monetary Authorities	79agd	....	....	....	....	....	....	–	–	–	–	–	–
General Government	79ahd	....	....	....	....	....	....	–	–	–	–	–	–
Banks	79aid	....	....	230.5	249.8	81.0	100.7	–	–	–	–	–	–
Other Sectors	79ajd	....	....	....	....	....	....	1,757.3	1,843.7	1,891.9	1,919.1	2,772.8	3,801.5
Reserve Assets	79akd	....	....	204.4	531.0	607.0	623.0	852.1	630.4	673.9	1,019.0	1,863.3	2,263.2
Liabilities	79lad	....	....	....	....	....	....	18,731.5	16,581.2	15,907.8	12,696.6	15,390.7	18,627.4
Dir. Invest. in Rep. Economy	79lbd	....	....	–	–	–	–	1,858.2	1,905.1	2,001.6	2,164.4	2,812.4	3,588.3
Portfolio Investment	79lcd	....	....	–	–	–	–	244.4	223.1	211.2	205.8	299.3	418.8
Equity Securities	79ldd	....	....	–	–	–	–	–	–	–	–	–	–
Debt Securities	79led	....	....	–	–	–	–	244.4	223.1	211.2	205.8	299.3	418.8
Financial Derivatives	79lld	....	....	....	....	....	....	–	–	–	–	–	–
Other Investment	79lfd	....	....	15,272.6	17,009.2	16,101.1	14,046.3	16,628.9	14,453.0	13,695.0	10,326.5	12,279.0	14,620.3
Monetary Authorities	79lgd	....	....	329.8	436.8	510.7	461.3	644.0	619.5	549.3	464.0	490.9	425.0
General Government	79lhd	....	....	....	....	....	....	14,790.1	12,756.1	12,027.6	8,518.3	10,291.1	11,885.0
Banks	79lid	....	....	743.5	522.9	266.2	295.4	437.8	429.2	454.9	511.8	507.1	1,118.1
Other Sectors	79ljd	....	....	....	....	....	....	756.9	648.2	663.2	832.3	990.0	1,192.3
Government Finance							*Billions of Francs: Year Ending December 31*						
Deficit (-) or Surplus	80	....	....	−280.1	−147.3	−57.7	23.2	−84.0	−11.0	....	....	....	....
Total Revenue and Grants	81y	....	....	878.7	1,142.2	1,274.5	1,374.2	1,442.7	1,482.1	....	....	....	....
Revenue	81	....	....	849.0	1,107.2	1,234.0	1,330.2	1,392.2	1,442.1	....	....	....	....
Grants	81z	....	....	29.7	35.0	40.5	44.1	50.5	40.0	....	....	....	....
Exp. & Lending Minus Repay	82z	....	....	1,158.8	1,289.5	1,332.2	1,351.0	1,526.7	1,493.1	....	....	....	....
Expenditure	82	....	....	1,166.0	1,322.6	1,385.2	1,494.5	1,557.3	1,533.1	....	....	....	....
Lending Minus Repayments	83	....	....	−7.2	−33.1	−53.0	−143.5	−30.6	−40.0	....	....	....	....
Total Financing	80h	....	....	280.1	147.3	57.7	−23.2	84.0	11.0	....	....	....	....
Domestic	84a	....	....	−153.1	−61.6	−107.5	−85.0	36.3	−104.2	....	....	....	....
Foreign	85a	....	....	433.2	208.9	165.2	61.8	47.7	115.2	....	....	....	....
Total Debt by Residence	88	....	....	9,148.6	9,392.7	9,606.0	10,056.3	7,620.7	....	....	....	....	....
Domestic	88a	....	....	1,320.4	1,230.7	1,137.8	1,070.6	1,039.5	....	....	....	....	....
Foreign	89a	....	....	7,828.2	8,162.0	8,468.2	8,985.7	6,581.2	....	....	....	....	....
National Accounts							*Billions of Francs*						
Househ.Cons.Expend.,incl.NPISHs	96f	2,220.5	2,185.0	2,749.2	3,379.0	3,502.3	4,535.0	4,916.0	4,868.0	5,076.6	5,241.7	5,275.8	....
Government Consumption Expend	91f	473.2	484.0	555.0	594.0	714.4	713.2	1,132.0	1,150.0	1,050.0	1,100.5	1,290.6	....
Gross Fixed Capital Formation	93e	210.0	230.9	473.0	641.2	846.5	959.8	1,167.3	1,124.1	821.8	760.8	852.7	....
Changes in Inventories	93i	−46.6	13.3	60.8	104.6	−112.0	−37.2	−294.3	−100.1	−30.0	98.0	−65.0	....
Exports of Goods and Services	90c	857.3	847.0	1,827.0	2,051.0	2,533.0	2,737.8	2,835.0	3,074.0	3,010.0	3,163.0	3,390.8	....
Imports of Goods and Services (-)	98c	810.5	814.0	1,409.0	394.5	1,960.7	2,074.3	2,215.0	2,382.0	2,381.9	2,494.5	2,578.0	....
Gross Domestic Product (GDP)	99b	2,948.8	2,946.2	4,256.0	4,987.7	5,548.2	6,834.4	7,541.1	7,734.1	7,546.5	7,869.5	8,166.9	....
							Millions: Midyear Estimates						
Population	99z	13.29	13.66	14.02	14.36	14.69	14.99	15.27	15.55	15.83	16.10	16.37	16.63

2004, International Monetary Fund: *International Financial Statistics Yearbook*

Croatia 960

		1992	1993	1994	1995	1996	1997	1998	1999	2000	2001	2002	2003
Exchange Rates						*Kuna per SDR: End of Period*							
Official Rate	aa	1.098	9.013	8.217	7.902	7.966	8.504	8.797	10.496	10.626	10.501	9.715	9.092
						Kuna per US Dollar: End of Period (ae) Period Average (rf)							
Official Rate	ae	.798	6.562	5.629	5.316	5.540	6.303	6.248	7.648	8.155	8.356	7.146	6.119
Official Rate	rf	....	3.577	5.996	5.230	5.434	6.101	6.362	7.112	8.277	8.340	7.869	6.704
						Index Numbers (2000=100): Period Averages							
Nominal Effective Exchange Rate	nec	2,547.37	248.15	98.89	105.67	106.05	107.89	105.96	100.16	100.00	103.66	105.22	104.83
Real Effective Exchange Rate	rec	65.57	83.46	98.57	100.99	100.13	101.55	101.99	98.03	100.00	104.46	105.00	103.38
Fund Position						*Millions of SDRs: End of Period*							
Quota	2f.s	–	261.6	261.6	261.6	261.6	261.6	261.6	365.1	365.1	365.1	365.1	365.1
SDRs	1b.s	–	.8	3.1	94.4	87.3	109.0	164.2	138.1	113.0	85.5	1.1	–
Reserve Position in the Fund	1c.s	–	–	–	–	–	.1	.1	.1	.2	.2	.2	.2
Total Fund Cred.&Loans Outstg	2tl	–	14.8	87.1	148.6	145.4	172.7	166.1	143.2	121.4	97.2	–	–
International Liquidity						*Millions of US Dollars Unless Otherwise Indicated: End of Period*							
Total Reserves minus Gold	1l.d	166.8	616.2	1,405.0	1,895.7	2,314.0	2,539.1	2,815.7	3,025.0	3,524.4	4,703.2	5,884.9	8,190.5
SDRs	1b.d	–	1.1	4.5	140.3	125.6	147.1	231.2	189.5	147.2	107.4	1.5	–
Reserve Position in the Fund	1c.d	–	–	–	–	–	.1	.2	.2	.2	.2	.2	.2
Foreign Exchange	1d.d	166.8	615.1	1,400.5	1,755.4	2,188.4	2,391.9	2,584.4	2,835.3	3,376.9	4,595.6	5,883.2	8,190.2
Gold (Million Fine Troy Ounces)	1ad	–	–	–	–	–	–	–	–	–	–	–	–
Gold (National Valuation)	1and	–	–	–	–	–	–	–	–	–	–	–	–
Monetary Authorities: Other Liab.	4..d	–	.1	.1	.2	.3	.5	.7	22.2	41.8	68.5	27.0	457.3
Deposit Money Banks: Assets	7a.d	....	946.7	1,258.3	1,748.8	2,265.4	2,567.9	2,042.9	1,621.4	2,416.9	3,926.2	3,635.4	5,782.9
Liabilities	7b.d	....	1,838.9	2,333.5	2,849.8	2,250.6	2,190.5	2,589.3	2,250.3	2,183.8	2,615.8	4,901.3	8,160.8
Monetary Authorities						*Millions of Kuna: End of Period*							
Foreign Assets	11	133.2	4,026.5	7,908.3	10,077.7	12,818.8	16,005.6	17,592.6	23,135.7	28,743.7	39,306.1	42,057.0	50,118.5
Claims on Central Government	12a	52.7	535.1	250.6	390.1	218.8	–	3.8	24.1	–	–	.5	1.4
Claims on Private Sector	12d	.1	.3	.7	.9	1.1	24.4	1.0	276.1	289.5	229.2	110.6	93.6
Claims on Deposit Money Banks	12e	107.7	191.6	223.8	220.2	213.9	33.5	1,043.7	1,139.4	329.9	18.5	17.9	972.0
Reserve Money	14	205.5	2,248.9	4,714.2	6,744.1	8,770.3	10,346.2	9,954.3	10,309.9	11,717.2	17,803.3	23,027.9	30,586.2
of which: Currency Outside DMBs	14a	130.8	1,367.0	2,658.2	3,365.1	4,366.2	5,319.6	5,730.1	5,958.9	6,636.7	8,507.4	9,680.9	10,573.1
Restricted Deposits	16b	.1	1.4	40.3	212.2	243.2	101.1	119.1	380.6	315.0	325.4	49.0	12.6
Foreign Liabilities	16c	–	133.9	716.2	1,175.2	1,160.4	1,471.4	1,465.4	1,672.9	1,630.8	1,593.1	192.8	2,798.0
Central Government Deposits	16d	–	–	793.8	395.5	557.6	1,032.7	434.8	397.2	1,157.4	1,752.1	768.1	1,551.1
Capital Accounts	17a	114.4	2,366.0	2,066.0	2,019.4	1,900.1	2,361.8	2,902.1	4,535.5	5,216.6	6,425.2	5,354.7	5,039.0
Other Items (Net)	17r	−26.4	3.2	52.9	142.5	621.0	750.4	3,765.3	7,279.1	9,326.2	11,654.8	12,793.4	11,198.6
Deposit Money Banks						*Millions of Kuna: End of Period*							
Reserves	20	....	862.1	2,039.7	3,508.3	4,573.9	5,056.7	5,908.1	8,987.9	10,588.9	15,002.7	20,373.5	26,783.7
Foreign Assets	21	....	6,212.1	7,082.5	9,296.6	12,549.6	16,185.8	12,763.1	12,400.0	19,710.4	32,807.7	25,977.8	35,382.9
Claims on Central Government	22a	....	† 19,971.9	17,837.0	17,188.1	16,693.4	15,238.8	14,864.2	16,264.4	19,055.5	20,059.8	21,917.7	21,543.6
Claims on Local Government	22b	....	11.4	112.9	147.1	145.4	308.8	654.0	905.6	1,174.9	1,280.0	1,422.4	1,563.1
Claims on Nonfin.Pub.Enterprises	22c	....	1,802.4	2,141.4	1,896.2	1,943.8	2,182.5	2,291.8	1,794.2	2,413.4	3,180.0	3,813.3	4,083.0
Claims on Private Sector	22d	....	† 18,447.9	25,344.4	30,674.5	31,600.7	46,100.9	56,650.9	52,699.9	56,775.7	69,823.7	90,982.7	104,728.2
Claims on Other Banking Insts	22f	....	10.2	–	–	–	–	.4	45.4	68.7	170.2	219.5	431.8
Claims on Nonbank Financial Insts	22g	....	15.7	62.1	100.8	140.2	246.8	193.9	154.0	161.7	281.4	915.3	761.8
Demand Deposits	24	....	1,758.7	3,969.7	4,870.0	7,007.5	8,423.8	7,808.9	7,891.5	11,386.0	15,180.6	21,166.2	23,315.0
Time, Savings,& Fgn.Currency Dep.	25	....	6,878.3	10,828.8	16,257.4	25,204.1	36,876.9	43,654.7	42,363.6	54,552.7	82,050.0	85,055.7	94,406.1
Money Market Instruments	26aa	....	3.3	1.5	.2	.9	7.0	4.5	1.4	–	–	5.1	–
Bonds	26ab	....	45.0	207.0	130.5	127.2	126.6	149.7	435.4	478.2	317.8	211.2	598.4
Restricted Deposits	26b	....	14,261.5	12,087.7	10,662.4	8,223.6	5,852.3	4,196.0	3,434.2	2,549.6	1,600.8	1,680.5	1,709.0
Foreign Liabilities	26c	....	12,066.4	13,134.8	15,150.0	12,467.4	13,807.1	16,176.8	17,209.2	17,809.8	21,857.8	35,023.5	49,932.0
Central Government Deposits	26d	....	1,437.8	1,675.0	2,025.6	1,720.9	6,874.7	7,298.3	5,828.6	6,730.5	5,634.7	6,094.9	5,283.3
Credit from Monetary Authorities	26g	....	275.2	224.6	182.6	267.7	33.7	1,049.2	1,138.7	328.8	16.6	17.6	968.9
Capital Accounts	27a	....	11,203.3	13,883.6	15,392.4	15,441.8	17,023.6	19,786.8	21,975.4	24,953.1	25,455.1	26,323.2	27,389.5
Other Items (Net)	27r	....	† −595.9	−1,392.6	−1,859.2	−2,813.9	−3,705.5	−6,798.4	−7,026.5	−8,839.6	−9,507.9	−9,955.6	−8,324.2

Croatia 960

		1992	1993	1994	1995	1996	1997	1998	1999	2000	2001	2002	2003
Monetary Survey						*Millions of Kuna: End of Period*							
Foreign Assets (Net)	31n	....	−1,961.7	1,139.8	3,049.2	11,740.6	16,912.9	12,713.5	16,653.6	29,013.5	48,662.9	32,818.4	32,771.3
Domestic Credit	32	....	† 39,357.0	43,280.3	47,976.5	48,464.9	56,194.8	66,937.0	65,937.9	72,051.5	87,637.5	112,518.9	126,372.0
Claims on Central Govt. (Net)	32an	....	† 19,069.1	15,618.7	15,157.1	14,633.7	7,331.4	7,134.9	10,062.7	11,167.6	12,673.0	15,055.2	14,710.6
Claims on Local Government	32b	....	11.4	112.9	147.1	145.4	308.8	654.0	905.6	1,174.9	1,280.0	1,422.4	1,563.1
Claims on Nonfin.Pub.Enterprises	32c	....	1,802.4	2,141.4	1,896.2	1,943.8	2,182.5	2,291.8	1,794.2	2,413.4	3,180.0	3,813.3	4,083.0
Claims on Private Sector	32d	....	† 18,448.2	25,345.1	30,675.3	31,601.8	46,125.3	56,651.9	52,976.0	57,065.2	70,052.9	91,093.2	104,821.7
Claims on Other Banking Insts.	32f	....	10.2	—	—	—	—	10.5	45.4	68.7	170.2	219.5	431.8
Claims on Nonbank Financial Inst.	32g	....	15.7	62.1	100.8	140.2	246.8	193.9	154.0	161.7	281.4	915.3	761.8
Money	34	....	3,133.9	6,648.8	8,283.6	11,419.6	13,814.3	13,621.1	13,858.9	18,030.2	23,703.6	30,869.8	33,888.7
Quasi-Money	35	....	6,878.3	10,828.8	16,257.4	25,204.1	36,876.9	43,654.7	42,363.6	54,552.7	82,050.0	85,055.7	94,406.1
Money Market Instruments	36aa	....	3.3	1.5	.2	.9	7.0	4.5	1.4	—	—	5.1	—
Bonds	36ab	....	45.0	207.0	130.5	127.2	126.6	149.7	435.4	478.2	317.8	211.2	598.4
Restricted Deposits	36b	....	14,262.9	12,128.0	10,874.6	8,466.8	5,953.4	4,315.1	3,814.8	2,864.6	1,926.2	1,729.5	1,721.6
Capital Accounts	37a	....	13,569.3	15,949.6	17,411.8	17,341.9	19,385.4	22,688.9	26,510.9	30,169.7	31,880.3	31,677.8	32,428.5
Other Items (Net)	37r	....	† −497.5	−1,343.4	−1,932.0	−2,354.7	−3,055.9	−4,783.5	−4,393.5	−5,030.4	−3,577.4	−4,211.7	−3,900.0
Money plus Quasi-Money	35l	....	10,012.2	17,477.6	24,541.0	36,623.7	50,691.2	57,275.8	56,222.5	72,582.9	105,753.6	115,925.5	128,294.7
Interest Rates						*Percent Per Annum*							
Discount Rate (End of Period)	60	1,889.39	34.49	8.50	8.50	6.50	5.90	5.90	7.90	5.90	5.90	4.50	4.50
Money Market Rate	60b	951.20	1,370.50	26.93	21.13	17.60	9.71	11.16	10.21	6.78	3.42	1.75	3.31
Deposit Rate	60l	658.51	379.31	6.52	5.53	5.59	4.30	4.62	4.31	3.74	3.23	1.89	1.53
Lending Rate	60p	1,157.79	1,443.61	22.91	20.24	22.52	15.47	15.75	14.94	12.07	9.55	† 12.84	11.58
Prices, Production, Labor						*Index Numbers (2000=100): Period Averages*							
Wholesale Prices	63	2.94	47.46	84.28	84.91	86.07	88.03	86.96	89.19	100.00	101.14	103.00	102.71
Consumer Prices	64	2.3	36.9	76.4	79.4	82.8	86.3	91.8	95.0	100.0	104.8	106.5	106.7
Wages	65	10.0	15.8	37.5	54.7	61.1	71.5	80.6	91.9	100.0	106.5	111.8	118.4
Industrial Production	66	95.1	89.5	87.1	87.3	90.1	96.4	99.8	98.4	100.0	106.0	111.8	116.4
Total Employment	67	110.4	107.9	107.2	105.7	99.2	97.8	103.4	101.7	100.0	100.5	101.3	103.9
						Number in Thousands: Period Averages							
Employment	67e	1,159	1,108	1,061	1,027	1,028	1,004	1,275	1,269	1,256	1,257	1,272	....
Unemployment	67c	267	251	243	241	261	278	288	322	358	380	390	330
Unemployment Rate (%)	67r	15.3	14.8	14.5	14.5	16.4	17.5	17.2	19.1	21.1	22.0	22.3	19.2
International Transactions						*Millions of US Dollars*							
Exports	70..d	4,597.5	3,903.8	4,260.4	4,632.7	4,511.8	4,170.7	4,541.1	4,302.5	4,431.6	4,665.9	4,898.7	6,161.6
Imports, c.i.f.	71..d	4,460.7	4,666.4	5,229.3	7,509.9	7,787.9	9,104.0	8,383.1	7,798.6	7,886.5	9,147.1	10,713.5	14,136.3

Croatia 960

		1992	1993	1994	1995	1996	1997	1998	1999	2000	2001	2002	2003
Balance of Payments						*Millions of US Dollars: Minus Sign Indicates Debit*							
Current Account, n.i.e.	78ald	....	624.9	554.1	−1,591.8	−1,049.1	−2,825.4	−1,468.0	−1,397.2	−460.8	−725.8	−1,920.1	−2,098.6
Goods: Exports f.o.b.	78aad	....	3,910.4	4,402.8	4,517.3	4,677.5	4,021.1	4,580.6	4,394.7	4,567.2	4,758.7	5,003.6	6,285.2
Goods: Imports f.o.b.	78abd	....	−4,619.6	−5,681.2	−7,744.8	−8,165.5	−9,404.1	−8,652.1	−7,693.3	−7,770.9	−8,860.0	−10,652.2	−14,206.3
Trade Balance	78acd	....	−709.2	−1,278.4	−3,227.5	−3,488.0	−5,383.0	−4,071.5	−3,298.6	−3,203.8	−4,101.3	−5,648.6	−7,921.0
Services: Credit	78add	....	2,215.9	2,660.6	2,223.4	3,193.2	3,984.6	3,949.1	3,723.0	4,095.9	4,875.5	5,567.4	8,621.4
Services: Debit	78aed	....	−1,089.8	−1,190.3	−1,361.1	−1,707.0	−2,273.9	−1,887.1	−2,097.8	−1,828.0	−1,948.1	−2,412.7	−2,979.9
Balance on Goods & Services	78afd	....	416.9	191.9	−2,365.2	−2,001.8	−3,672.3	−2,009.5	−1,673.4	−935.9	−1,173.9	−2,493.9	−2,279.5
Income: Credit	78agd	....	128.0	149.0	218.8	269.9	363.7	394.8	254.8	345.8	418.9	428.4	487.4
Income: Debit	78ahd	....	−247.5	−313.2	−247.7	−339.7	−386.1	−559.1	−611.1	−753.9	−936.4	−930.5	−1,700.3
Balance on Gds, Serv. & Inc.	78aid	....	297.4	27.7	−2,394.1	−2,071.6	−3,694.7	−2,173.8	−2,029.7	−1,343.9	−1,691.5	−2,996.0	−3,492.3
Current Transfers, n.i.e.: Credit	78ajd	....	507.5	669.2	971.2	1,173.3	963.8	919.1	967.4	1,101.0	1,174.5	1,358.1	1,727.2
Current Transfers: Debit	78akd	....	−180.0	−142.8	−168.9	−150.8	−94.5	−213.3	−335.0	−217.8	−208.8	−282.3	−333.5
Capital Account, n.i.e.	78bcd	....	−	−	−	16.2	21.3	19.1	24.9	20.9	133.0	443.4	83.6
Capital Account, n.i.e.: Credit	78bad	....	−	−	−	18.0	23.5	24.1	28.2	24.4	137.6	450.1	95.3
Capital Account: Debit	78bbd	....	−	−	−	−1.8	−2.2	−5.0	−3.4	−3.6	−4.6	−6.7	−11.7
Financial Account, n.i.e.	78bjd	....	−156.4	16.4	1,135.3	2,996.3	3,020.8	1,610.3	2,913.1	1,827.0	2,515.1	3,085.4	4,612.9
Direct Investment Abroad	78bdd	....	−18.5	−6.7	−5.5	−24.4	−186.1	−97.5	−47.2	−3.9	−154.6	−532.9	−80.5
Dir. Invest. in Rep. Econ., n.i.e.	78bed	....	120.3	116.9	114.3	510.8	532.8	932.3	1,467.2	1,089.4	1,558.7	1,124.0	1,955.9
Portfolio Investment Assets	78bfd	....	−.4	1.0	.3	6.2	11.2	−.1	−38.3	−22.7	−129.3	−626.5	155.1
Equity Securities	78bkd	....	−.4	1.0	.3	6.2	.2	−.1	−.3	−.2	.3	−69.4	−65.7
Debt Securities	78bld	....	−	−	−	−	11.0	−	−38.0	−22.5	−129.6	−557.2	220.8
Portfolio Investment Liab., n.i.e.	78bgd	....	.4	9.9	4.5	622.0	565.7	15.1	570.8	730.3	730.0	396.8	854.4
Equity Securities	78bmd	....	.4	9.9	4.5	−6.8	15.9	1.3	−18.6	−.2	13.6	64.3	20.3
Debt Securities	78bnd	....	−	−	−	628.8	549.8	13.8	589.4	730.5	716.4	332.5	834.0
Financial Derivatives Assets	78bwd	....	....	....	....	....	....	....	....	....	....	....	....
Financial Derivatives Liabilities	78bxd	....	....	....	....	....	....	....	....	....	....	....	....
Other Investment Assets	78bhd	....	−165.8	−15.9	419.5	794.5	171.2	348.8	−15.4	−966.0	360.4	358.8	−2,520.6
Monetary Authorities	78bod	....	....	....	....	....	....	....	....	....	....	....	....
General Government	78bpd	....	−5.2	−.2	−15.5	−33.4	30.7	−22.3	15.1	−25.8	−19.2	−30.5	26.3
Banks	78bqd	....	−205.4	−189.3	−451.6	−589.2	−371.8	406.1	168.6	−899.1	−1,611.2	1,323.9	−2,311.1
Other Sectors	78brd	....	44.8	173.6	886.6	1,417.1	512.3	−35.0	−199.1	−41.2	1,990.8	−934.7	−235.8
Other Investment Liab., n.i.e.	78bid	....	−92.4	−88.8	602.2	1,087.2	1,926.0	411.7	976.0	999.9	149.9	2,365.2	4,248.7
Monetary Authorities	78bsd	....	−	−	−	−	−	−	21.6	18.5	25.6	−56.1	374.5
General Government	78btd	....	−119.3	−131.5	−47.2	268.8	95.7	−61.3	187.0	297.6	−188.7	390.2	573.0
Banks	78bud	....	−20.6	52.6	492.5	226.2	670.3	135.7	29.9	−3.5	328.3	1,225.3	2,480.1
Other Sectors	78bvd	....	47.5	−9.9	156.9	592.2	1,160.0	337.3	737.5	687.4	−15.3	805.8	821.1
Net Errors and Omissions	78cad	....	−280.2	−294.0	496.9	−946.1	173.7	−.9	−1,130.7	−776.4	−580.3	−782.8	−1,206.4
Overall Balance	78cbd	....	188.3	276.5	40.4	1,017.3	390.4	160.5	410.0	610.7	1,342.1	825.9	1,391.6
Reserves and Related Items	79dad	....	−188.3	−276.5	−40.4	−1,017.3	−390.4	−160.5	−410.0	−610.7	−1,342.1	−825.9	−1,391.6
Reserve Assets	79dbd	....	−466.4	−742.8	−443.2	−533.4	−428.0	−151.7	−378.5	−582.1	−1,311.2	−697.0	−1,391.6
Use of Fund Credit and Loans	79dcd	....	19.8	107.0	97.1	−4.5	37.5	−8.9	−31.5	−28.6	−30.8	−128.9	−
Exceptional Financing	79ded	....	258.3	359.3	305.7	−479.4	−	−	−	−	−	−	−
International Investment Position						*Millions of US Dollars*							
Assets	79aad	....	....	....	....	....	....	7,020.7	7,142.9	8,353.4	11,082.5	12,245.0	17,906.9
Direct Investment Abroad	79abd	....	....	....	....	....	....	1,002.4	881.7	875.1	967.1	1,818.1	2,294.6
Portfolio Investment	79acd	....	....	....	....	....	....	29.7	26.0	14.3	22.5	26.3	60.3
Equity Securities	79add	....	....	....	....	....	....	29.7	26.0	14.3	22.5	26.3	60.3
Debt Securities	79aed	....	....	....	....	....	....	−	−	−	−	−	−
Financial Derivatives	79ald	....	....	....	....	....	....	....	....	....	....	....	....
Other Investment	79afd	....	....	....	....	....	....	3,172.9	3,210.2	3,942.3	5,389.6	4,515.7	7,361.5
Monetary Authorities	79agd	....	....	....	....	....	....	−	−	−	−	−	−
General Government	79ahd	....	....	....	....	....	....	70.0	49.7	72.5	88.9	126.4	108.9
Banks	79aid	....	....	....	....	....	....	1,978.6	1,657.7	2,510.9	3,988.0	2,966.1	5,787.7
Other Sectors	79ajd	....	....	....	....	....	....	1,124.3	1,502.8	1,358.9	1,312.7	1,423.2	1,464.9
Reserve Assets	79akd	....	....	....	....	....	....	2,815.7	3,025.0	3,521.8	4,703.3	5,884.9	8,190.5
Liabilities	79lad	....	....	....	....	....	....	11,332.6	12,339.1	14,096.9	15,536.4	21,113.5	32,084.4
Dir. Invest. in Rep. Economy	79lbd	....	....	....	....	....	....	1,902.6	2,578.1	3,560.3	4,706.4	6,710.7	10,123.8
Portfolio Investment	79lcd	....	....	....	....	....	....	2,145.3	2,700.0	3,288.4	3,880.0	4,694.6	6,312.6
Equity Securities	79ldd	....	....	....	....	....	....	87.3	128.3	108.8	148.2	169.8	188.1
Debt Securities	79led	....	....	....	....	....	....	2,058.0	2,571.8	3,179.6	3,731.8	4,524.8	6,124.5
Financial Derivatives	79lld	....	....	....	....	....	....	....	....	....	....	....	....
Other Investment	79lfd	....	....	....	....	....	....	7,284.7	7,060.9	7,248.2	6,949.9	9,708.2	15,647.9
Monetary Authorities	79lgd	....	....	....	....	....	....	233.9	196.6	158.2	122.2	−	−
General Government	79lhd	....	....	....	....	....	....	1,346.0	1,454.2	1,687.2	1,455.5	1,989.2	2,807.9
Banks	79lid	....	....	....	....	....	....	2,498.6	2,187.9	2,086.5	2,299.5	3,979.9	7,393.1
Other Sectors	79ljd	....	....	....	....	....	....	3,206.2	3,222.3	3,316.3	3,072.8	3,739.0	5,447.0

Croatia 960

		1992	1993	1994	1995	1996	1997	1998	1999	2000	2001	2002	2003
Government Finance						*Millions of Kuna: Year Ending December 31*							
Deficit (-) or Surplus..................	80	....	....	543.9	−715.4	−133.8	−1,160.2	1,256.7	−2,522.0	−6,107.9	−3,758.5	−3,872.0	....
Total Revenue and Grants..........	81y	....	....	22,817.3	27,485.1	30,813.1	33,702.4	42,376.2	40,277.9	41,774.7	49,156.8	69,870.2	....
Revenue................................	81	....	....	22,817.3	27,385.1	30,813.1	33,702.4	42,376.2	40,277.9	41,774.7	49,156.8	69,870.2	....
Grants..................................	81z	....	....	−	100.0	−	−	−	−	−	−	−	....
Exp. & Lending Minus Repay......	82z	....	....	22,273.4	28,200.5	30,946.9	34,862.5	41,119.6	42,799.9	47,882.6	52,915.3	73,742.2	....
Expenditure..........................	82	....	....	22,282.8	28,475.6	30,971.2	34,395.2	41,390.4	47,379.6	49,567.5	56,386.7	72,186.2	....
Lending Minus Repayments......	83	....	....	−9.3	−275.1	−24.3	467.4	−270.8	−4,579.7	−1,684.9	−3,471.4	1,556.0	....
Total Financing...........................	80h	....	....	−543.9	715.3	134.0	1,160.2	−1,256.7	2,521.9	6,107.8	3,758.5	3,872.0	....
Domestic...............................	84a	....	....	−591.2	29.3	−669.9	−1,825.7	−1,247.6	−2,093.1	−813.6	−353.9	1,597.7	....
Foreign.................................	85a	....	....	47.3	686.0	804.0	2,985.9	−9.1	4,615.0	6,921.4	4,112.4	2,274.3	....
Total Debt by Residence...............	88	....	....	....	27,739.7	29,814.0	32,760.0	....	....	....	....	....	....
Domestic...............................	88a	17,218.4	20,768.6	17,284.7	16,405.4	16,533.7	14,501.6	13,697.5	13,944.0	14,549.8	21,944.3	23,596.6	....
Foreign.................................	89a	....	....	....	11,334.3	13,280.3	18,258.4	....	....	....	....	....	....
National Accounts						*Millions of Kuna:*							
Househ.Cons.Expend.,incl.NPISHs....	96f	....	....	46,575	60,476	65,367	77,028	81,067	81,545	89,637	98,054	107,427	113,396
Government Consumption Expend...	91f	....	....	25,738	18,437	18,533	32,183	36,642	39,341	39,816	37,956	37,741	39,789
Gross Fixed Capital Formation.........	93e	....	....	12,210	15,398	22,089	29,936	32,066	33,025	33,281	36,984	44,114	53,168
Changes in Inventories.................	93i	....	....	2,982	1,916	1,599	4,143	982	−404	−2,421	2,665	6,822	5,508
Exports of Goods and Services.........	90c	....	....	40,086	37,951	43,402	50,873	54,546	57,920	71,899	80,246	81,375	90,927
Imports of Goods and Services (-).....	98c	....	....	40,149	48,681	53,630	70,351	67,700	69,731	79,693	90,265	98,089	109,721
Gross Domestic Product (GDP).........	99b	2,628	41,833	87,441	98,382	107,981	123,811	137,604	141,579	152,519	165,639	179,390	193,067
GDP Volume 1997 Prices.................	99b.p	....	....	....	....	....	123,811	126,936	125,843	129,438	134,318	141,339	147,356
GDP Volume (2000=100)................	99bvp	84.7	84.0	84.5	85.9	89.6	†95.7	98.1	97.2	100.0	103.8	109.2	113.8
GDP Deflator (2000=100)................	99bip	2.0	32.7	67.8	75.1	79.0	84.9	92.0	95.5	100.0	104.7	107.7	111.2
						Millions: Midyear Estimates							
Population.............................	99z	4.73	4.62	4.52	4.45	4.42	4.41	4.42	4.44	4.45	4.45	4.44	4.43

2004, International Monetary Fund : *International Financial Statistics Yearbook*

Cyprus 423

		1992	1993	1994	1995	1996	1997	1998	1999	2000	2001	2002	2003
Exchange Rates						*SDRs per Pound: End of Period*							
Official Rate	ac	1.5056	1.4006	1.4384	1.4735	1.4800	1.4097	1.4255	1.2680	1.2444	1.2238	1.3451	1.4465
					US Dollars per Pound: End of Period (ag) Period Average (rh)								
Official Rate	ag	2.0702	1.9238	2.0998	2.1903	2.1282	1.9021	2.0071	1.7404	1.6214	1.5380	1.8287	2.1494
Official Rate	rh	2.2212	2.0120	2.0347	2.2113	2.1446	1.9476	1.9342	1.8440	1.6107	1.5559	1.6431	1.9356
					Index Numbers (2000=100): Period Averages								
Official Rate	ahx	137.9	124.9	126.3	137.3	133.1	120.9	120.1	114.5	100.0	96.6	102.0	120.2
Nominal Effective Exchange Rate	nec	90.1	91.0	94.3	97.9	99.8	100.6	106.0	103.7	100.0	103.8	106.5	111.1
Real Effective Exchange Rate	rec	98.9	99.3	102.5	103.5	103.7	103.6	107.0	102.6	100.0	102.5	104.9	110.9
Fund Position						*Millions of SDRs: End of Period*							
Quota	2f.s	100.0	100.0	100.0	100.0	100.0	100.0	100.0	139.6	139.6	139.6	139.6	139.6
SDRs	1b.s	.1	.1	.1	–	–	.2	.2	.4	.8	1.1	1.5	2.0
Reserve Position in the Fund	1c.s	25.5	25.5	25.5	25.5	25.5	25.5	25.5	35.4	35.4	35.4	49.1	66.8
Total Fund Cred.&Loans Outstg	2tl	–	–	–	–	–	–	–	–	–	–	–	–
International Liquidity					*Millions of US Dollars Unless Otherwise Indicated: End of Period*								
Total Reserves minus Gold	1l.d	1,027.9	1,096.7	1,464.5	1,116.9	1,541.9	1,391.6	1,379.7	1,832.9	1,741.1	2,267.8	3,022.0	3,256.7
SDRs	1b.d	.1	.1	.2	–	–	.3	.3	.5	1.0	1.4	2.1	3.0
Reserve Position in the Fund	1c.d	35.0	35.0	37.2	37.8	36.6	34.3	35.8	48.5	46.1	44.4	66.8	99.3
Foreign Exchange	1d.d	992.8	1,061.6	1,427.2	1,079.0	1,505.3	1,356.9	1,343.6	1,783.8	1,694.0	2,221.9	2,953.2	3,154.5
Gold (Million Fine Troy Ounces)	1ad	.459	.460	.459	.460	.440	.462	.462	.464	.464	.464	.465	.465
Gold (National Valuation)	1and	15.0	14.2	15.6	16.7	170.2	133.9	132.9	142.6	127.6	127.6	149.2	196.2
Monetary Authorities: Other Liab.	4..d	77.2	53.9	55.7	89.6	56.4	73.2	57.1	49.7	40.5	24.5	15.5	15.9
Deposit Money Banks: Assets	7a.d	1,396.6	1,554.3	1,915.4	3,083.3	3,255.1	3,612.4	3,519.3	†3,880.2	5,377.6	6,191.7	6,348.5	8,686.2
Liabilities	7b.d	2,010.5	2,187.8	2,697.5	3,738.3	4,302.8	4,694.4	4,790.3	†5,273.4	6,579.1	7,683.4	8,621.3	10,328.6
Other Banking Insts.: Liabilities	7f.d	1,647.7	1,722.9	2,052.7	2,257.4	3,189.6	13,090.6	8,607.2	8,060.5	10,564.4	10,161.4	....	....
Monetary Authorities						*Millions of Pounds: End of Period*							
Foreign Assets	11	504.3	578.1	705.6	518.2	805.2	802.7	754.4	1,135.8	1,153.3	1,558.4	1,734.9	1,607.2
Claims on Central Government	12a	415.2	407.3	398.5	607.2	570.5	558.4	596.7	534.9	770.7	696.5	992.4	968.5
Claims on Deposit Money Banks	12e	34.2	13.4	12.4	22.4	6.5	.1	104.6	.1	3.1	–	–	8.0
Reserve Money	14	763.6	775.6	872.4	834.6	761.5	755.5	878.0	1,008.3	1,117.0	1,201.5	1,498.8	1,571.4
of which: Currency Outside DMBs	14a	215.1	229.4	246.6	257.1	265.8	276.3	290.1	313.6	333.3	356.5	392.8	467.2
Foreign Liabilities	16c	37.3	28.0	26.6	40.9	26.5	38.5	28.4	28.5	15.1	26.3	8.5	7.4
Central Government Deposits	16d	131.7	154.8	175.2	227.3	342.9	339.5	325.7	316.4	451.2	559.5	598.8	754.2
Other Items (Net)	17r	21.1	40.4	42.4	45.1	251.3	227.7	223.6	317.4	343.8	467.6	621.3	250.8
Deposit Money Banks						*Millions of Pounds: End of Period*							
Reserves	20	542.0	538.0	612.4	555.1	479.7	452.9	455.4	†681.3	761.0	941.3	1,481.3	1,128.5
Foreign Assets	21	674.6	807.9	912.2	1,407.7	1,529.5	1,899.1	1,753.4	†2,229.5	3,316.6	4,025.8	3,471.6	4,041.2
Claims on Central Government	22a	342.5	519.9	566.5	463.7	722.1	834.5	854.0	†983.3	902.4	1,409.2	1,415.9	1,765.4
Claims on Private Sector	22d	2,158.9	2,436.7	2,754.3	3,225.3	3,667.0	4,109.7	4,635.2	†5,543.9	6,344.0	7,136.9	7,726.6	8,122.5
Demand Deposits	24	289.3	317.2	326.1	353.9	386.5	427.2	439.2	†723.5	681.5	653.4	613.3	864.5
Time and Savings Deposits	25	2,064.1	2,440.9	2,785.4	3,131.2	3,487.3	3,890.0	4,243.3	†4,971.3	5,575.0	6,462.9	7,143.6	7,158.8
Foreign Liabilities	26c	971.2	1,137.3	1,284.6	1,706.8	2,021.8	2,468.0	2,386.7	†3,030.0	4,057.7	4,995.7	4,714.4	4,805.4
Central Government Deposits	26d	36.4	38.1	38.4	42.7	40.7	44.8	50.3	†63.8	76.8	72.2	71.2	73.0
Credit from Monetary Authorities	26g	34.2	13.4	12.4	22.4	6.5	.1	5.6	†.1	3.1	–	–	8.0
Other Items (Net)	27r	322.8	355.5	398.5	394.8	455.5	466.2	573.1	†649.4	929.9	1,329.1	1,552.9	2,147.9
Monetary Survey						*Millions of Pounds: End of Period*							
Foreign Assets (Net)	31n	170.4	220.8	306.6	178.3	286.4	195.4	92.7	†306.7	397.1	562.2	483.6	835.7
Domestic Credit	32	2,797.6	3,225.9	3,579.3	4,108.1	4,670.8	5,229.1	5,847.5	†6,840.1	7,661.1	8,794.1	9,642.4	10,207.5
Claims on Central Govt. (Net)	32an	589.6	734.2	751.5	800.9	908.9	1,008.6	1,074.8	†1,137.9	1,145.1	1,474.1	1,738.3	1,906.8
Claims on Local Government	32b	34.5	37.5	42.9	46.8	55.6	65.4	79.3	†90.9	92.4	127.5	132.6	142.4
Claims on Nonfin.Pub.Enterprises	32c	12.0	14.9	28.1	34.8	38.9	45.0	57.9	†66.8	78.9	55.7	44.9	35.8
Claims on Private Sector	32d	2,161.5	2,439.2	2,756.8	3,225.7	3,667.4	4,110.0	4,635.6	†5,544.6	6,344.7	7,136.9	7,726.6	8,122.5
Money	34	506.3	549.1	576.2	612.2	653.5	704.5	730.3	†1,037.6	1,015.3	1,010.6	1,021.6	1,332.6
Quasi-Money	35	2,070.2	2,448.0	2,794.3	3,142.2	3,495.6	3,900.4	4,255.6	†4,986.8	5,595.2	6,483.3	7,143.6	7,158.8
Other Items (Net)	37r	391.5	449.5	515.4	532.0	808.1	819.6	954.4	†1,122.5	1,447.6	1,862.4	1,960.9	2,551.8
Money plus Quasi-Money	35l	2,576.5	2,997.1	3,370.5	3,754.4	4,149.1	4,604.9	4,985.9	†6,024.4	6,610.5	7,493.9	8,165.2	8,491.5
Other Banking Institutions						*Millions of Pounds: End of Period*							
Reserves	40	10.1	18.3	27.0	25.1	20.6	32.3	39.6	35.2	76.3	90.1	....	....
Foreign Assets	41	795.1	894.9	977.1	1,030.2	1,498.4	6,901.6	4,290.9	4,647.4	6,527.0	6,615.8	....	....
Claims on Private Sector	42d	1,235.1	1,405.8	1,599.8	1,826.0	2,056.5	2,244.4	2,431.6	2,747.0	2,868.3	2,987.5	....	....
Liquid Liabilities	45l	1,276.6	1,475.7	1,685.0	1,897.6	2,095.8	2,327.6	2,582.7	2,754.2	3,072.8	3,428.0	....	....
Foreign Liabilities	46c	795.9	895.6	977.6	1,030.6	1,498.7	6,882.2	4,288.4	4,631.4	6,515.6	6,606.9	....	....
Capital Accounts	47a	34.9	38.3	41.9	39.9	42.9	43.8	48.6	80.0	90.3	92.5	....	....
Other Items (Net)	47r	−67.0	−90.6	−100.6	−86.8	−62.0	−75.2	−157.6	−36.0	−207.0	−434.1	....	....

Cyprus 423

		1992	1993	1994	1995	1996	1997	1998	1999	2000	2001	2002	2003
Banking Survey						*Millions of Pounds: End of Period*							
Foreign Assets (Net)	51n	169.6	220.1	306.1	177.8	286.0	214.8	95.2	322.7	408.5	571.0	....	....
Domestic Credit	52	4,035.8	4,635.8	5,182.2	5,940.0	6,737.5	7,482.1	8,292.5	9,578.6	10,523.7	11,710.9	....	....
Claims on Central Govt. (Net)	52an	595.3	740.9	757.2	807.2	919.5	1,017.5	1,088.5	1,137.9	1,145.1	1,371.3	....	....
Claims on Local Government	52b	34.5	37.5	42.9	46.8	55.6	65.4	79.3	86.5	90.6	122.8	....	....
Claims on Nonfin.Pub.Enterprises	52c	12.0	14.9	28.1	34.8	38.9	45.0	57.9	63.3	75.8	92.4	....	....
Claims on Private Sector	52d	3,394.0	3,842.5	4,354.1	5,051.3	5,723.5	6,354.1	7,066.8	8,290.9	9,212.3	10,124.4	....	....
Monetary Liabilities	54	503.8	539.8	560.1	601.7	644.7	685.1	708.3	1,024.7	1,038.9	1,016.0	....	....
Quasi-Monetary Liabilities	55	3,339.3	3,915.3	4,468.6	5,026.2	5,580.0	6,214.4	6,822.0	7,722.7	8,644.1	9,885.2	....	....
Other Items (Net)	57r	362.3	400.8	459.6	489.9	798.7	797.4	857.5	1,184.3	1,398.7	1,654.7	....	....
Liquid Liabilities	55l	3,843.0	4,454.6	5,028.4	5,626.9	6,224.4	6,900.2	7,529.1	8,743.9	9,684.9	10,902.7	....	....
Interest Rates						*Percent Per Annum*							
Discount Rate (End of Period)	60	6.50	6.50	6.50	6.50	†7.50	7.00	7.00	7.00	7.00	5.50	5.00	4.50
Money Market Rate	60b	....	....	....	....	6.85	4.82	4.80	5.15	5.96	4.93	3.42	3.35
Treasury Bill Rate	60c	6.00	6.00	6.00	6.00	6.05	5.38	5.59	5.59	6.01			3.56
Deposit Rate	60l	5.75	5.75	5.75	5.75	†7.00	6.50	6.50	6.50	6.50	4.65	4.20	3.30
Lending Rate	60p	9.00	9.00	8.83	8.50	8.50	8.08	8.00	8.00	8.00	†7.52	7.15	6.95
Prices, Production, Labor						*Index Numbers (2000=100): Period Averages*							
Wholesale Prices	63	79.6	81.6	84.3	87.4	89.2	91.7	92.2	93.3	100.0	101.6	103.0	106.0
Wholesale Prices: Home Goods	63a	....	....	....	†86.2	88.7	91.6	93.7	95.1	100.0	101.9	105.6	110.3
Consumer Prices	64	†76.9	80.6	84.4	86.6	89.2	92.4	†94.5	96.0	100.0	102.0	104.8	109.2
Industrial Production	66	96.1	90.0	93.1	94.6	91.8	91.5	94.1	†95.7	†100.0	101.8	105.8	108.2
Mining Production	66zx	61.3	74.9	81.0	74.6	76.4	76.5	90.2	†96.3	†100.0	95.4	105.4	108.4
						Number in Thousands: Period Averages							
Labor Force	67d	287	....	....	302	306	308	311	318	325	330	....	....
Employment	67e	267	267	271	284	286	286	289	279	289	310	315	327
Unemployment	67c	5	8	8	8	9	10	10	11	11	10	11	12
Unemployment Rate (%)	67r	1.8	2.6	2.7	2.6	3.1	3.4	3.4	3.6	3.4	3.0	....	....
International Transactions						*Millions of Pounds*							
Exports	70	443.72	431.40	474.99	554.91	651.01	563.89	551.13	541.79	590.35	628.90	514.66	476.81
Imports, c.i.f.	71	1,490.77	1,288.29	1,481.66	1,670.41	1,857.53	1,899.37	1,904.84	1,970.92	2,401.96	2,526.73	2,486.63	2,304.05
Balance of Payments						*Millions of US Dollars: Minus Sign Indicates Debit*							
Current Account, n.i.e.	78ald	−638.2	109.8	74.4	−164.0	−465.6	−338.2	−602.9	−217.3	−455.6	−394.8	−517.1	−281.6
Goods: Exports f.o.b	78aad	985.9	867.7	967.5	1,228.7	1,392.4	1,245.8	1,064.6	1,000.3	951.0	976.5	843.6	927.2
Goods: Imports f.o.b.	78abd	−3,301.1	−2,374.5	−2,703.0	−3,314.2	−3,575.7	−3,317.2	−3,490.4	−3,309.5	−3,556.5	−3,526.9	−3,702.7	−4,026.1
Trade Balance	78acd	−2,315.2	−1,506.8	−1,735.5	−2,085.5	−2,183.3	−2,071.4	−2,425.7	−2,309.2	−2,605.5	−2,550.4	−2,859.2	−3,098.8
Services: Credit	78add	2,521.4	2,335.1	2,646.7	2,991.2	2,872.3	2,827.6	2,954.7	3,190.0	3,206.4	3,352.9	4,481.2	5,657.5
Services: Debit	78aed	−884.0	−765.0	−862.1	−1,105.8	−1,160.6	−1,109.4	−1,132.6	−1,147.3	−1,160.0	−1,185.2	−2,265.4	−2,910.9
Balance on Goods & Services	78afd	−677.8	63.3	49.2	−200.0	−471.6	−353.2	−603.7	−266.5	−559.1	−382.7	−643.3	−352.3
Income: Credit	78agd	156.8	131.9	121.5	371.1	359.2	382.2	416.7	418.5	508.5	563.8	512.5	451.0
Income: Debit	78ahd	−234.9	−198.4	−211.1	−363.8	−386.4	−393.1	−445.3	−456.6	−530.8	−597.6	−452.2	−531.8
Balance on Gds, Serv. & Inc.	78aid	−755.9	−3.2	−40.4	−192.7	−498.8	−364.1	−632.3	−304.6	−581.5	−416.4	−583.0	−433.1
Current Transfers, n.i.e.: Credit	78ajd	123.2	118.4	125.0	46.4	43.1	40.9	49.6	113.6	153.3	49.3	226.6	375.6
Current Transfers: Debit	78akd	−5.6	−5.4	−10.2	−17.7	−9.9	−15.0	−20.3	−26.3	−27.5	−27.7	−160.6	−224.2
Capital Account, n.i.e.	78bcd	....	....	....	....	....	....	....	....	....	....	−5.5	22.9
Capital Account, n.i.e.: Credit	78bad	....	....	....	....	....	....	....	....	....	....	22.1	43.9
Capital Account: Debit	78bbd	....	....	....	....	....	....	....	....	....	....	−27.6	−21.1
Financial Account, n.i.e.	78bjd	323.4	−3.8	185.7	−140.8	419.0	383.7	657.9	1,006.4	263.5	845.7	850.7	65.8
Direct Investment Abroad	78bdd	−14.7	−12.3	−6.1	−27.6	−48.3	−32.7	−68.9	−146.2	−202.4	−217.7	−299.1	−345.5
Dir. Invest. in Rep. Econ., n.i.e.	78bed	107.4	83.4	75.2	85.8	54.3	75.9	68.7	121.4	162.6	163.3	613.6	838.4
Portfolio Investment Assets	78bfd	−5.1	−18.9	−244.6	−44.4	−117.5	−125.9	−106.2	−474.8	−292.7	−443.2	−635.6	−663.7
Equity Securities	78bkd	....	....	....	....	−	−	....	....	....	....	−32.4	160.6
Debt Securities	78bld	−5.1	−18.9	−244.6	−44.4	−117.5	−125.9	−106.2	−474.8	−292.7	−443.2	−603.2	−824.3
Portfolio Investment Liab., n.i.e.	78bgd	57.6	−33.4	84.5	−27.4	69.7	268.3	303.0	476.5	89.3	524.0	161.4	806.8
Equity Securities	78bmd	....	....	....	2.0	2.8	3.1	−12.0	139.2	177.1	15.5	−2.1	5.4
Debt Securities	78bnd	57.6	−33.4	84.5	−29.4	66.9	265.2	315.0	337.2	−87.7	508.5	163.5	801.3
Financial Derivatives Assets	78bwd	....	....	....	....	....	....	....	....	....	....	−3.5	32.0
Financial Derivatives Liabilities	78bxd	....	....	....	....	....	....	....	....	....	....	−46.9	−13.6
Other Investment Assets	78bhd	−321.2	−231.2	56.3	−1,075.5	−158.0	−700.5	659.1	−389.7	−1,388.6	−540.5	2,161.3	−2,550.4
Monetary Authorities	78bod	....	....	....	....	....	....	....	....	....	....	−	−
General Government	78bpd	57.4	10.1	1.0	−11.9	−7.7	−22.8	32.4	.6	−4.5	−9.2	27.1	4.9
Banks	78bqd	−395.5	−246.1	55.3	−1,063.6	−150.3	−677.8	626.7	−390.3	−1,384.1	−531.3	2,119.6	−2,563.9
Other Sectors	78brd	16.9	4.8	....	....	....	....	....	....	....	....	14.5	8.7
Other Investment Liab., n.i.e.	78bid	499.4	208.5	220.4	948.5	618.9	898.6	−197.7	1,419.3	1,895.4	1,359.8	−1,100.3	1,961.9
Monetary Authorities	78bsd	9.8	−23.1	.4	29.2	−36.2	20.6	−24.3	−5.7	−20.1	16.0	−19.0	9.9
General Government	78btd	−169.1	−155.0	−228.6	−147.2	−95.4	−112.9	−7.1	−39.6	31.8	−113.7	−42.9	244.6
Banks	78bud	463.4	331.3	301.5	964.4	693.3	872.0	−125.7	1,411.0	1,742.6	1,489.3	−1,123.9	1,718.8
Other Sectors	78bvd	195.3	55.3	147.1	102.1	57.3	118.9	−40.6	53.6	141.1	−31.9	85.5	−11.4
Net Errors and Omissions	78cad	89.9	38.8	−13.1	−58.2	−13.3	−92.5	−137.6	−150.0	184.0	161.4	60.8	5.3
Overall Balance	78cbd	−224.9	144.8	246.9	−363.1	−59.8	−47.0	−82.5	639.0	−8.2	612.3	389.0	−187.6
Reserves and Related Items	79dad	224.9	−144.8	−246.9	363.1	59.8	47.0	82.5	−639.0	8.2	−612.3	−389.0	187.6
Reserve Assets	79dbd	224.9	−144.8	−246.9	363.1	59.8	47.0	82.5	−639.0	8.2	−612.3	−389.0	187.6
Use of Fund Credit and Loans	79dcd	−	−	−	−	−	−	−	−	−	−	−	−
Exceptional Financing	79ded	....	....	....	....	....	....	....	....	....	....	−	−

2004, International Monetary Fund : *International Financial Statistics Yearbook*

Cyprus 423

		1992	1993	1994	1995	1996	1997	1998	1999	2000	2001	2002	2003
International Investment Position						*Millions of US Dollars*							
Assets	79aad	....	....	....	....	....	....	....	....	....	....	22,959.5	....
Direct Investment Abroad	79abd	....	....	....	....	....	....	....	....	....	....	1,231.8	....
Portfolio Investment	79acd	....	....	....	....	....	....	....	....	1,088.3	1,590.3	4,990.5	....
Equity Securities	79add	....	....	....	....	....	....	....	....	.3	129.3	1,122.8	....
Debt Securities	79aed	....	....	....	....	....	....	....	....	1,088.0	1,460.9	3,867.7	....
Financial Derivatives	79ald	....	....	....	....	....	....	....	....	....	....	2.7	....
Other Investment	79afd	....	....	....	....	....	....	....	....	3,951.0	4,269.6	13,561.9	....
Monetary Authorities	79agd	....	....	....	....	....	....	....	....	....	....	15.4	....
General Government	79ahd	....	....	....	....	....	....	....	....	....	....	−5.5	....
Banks	79aid	....	....	....	....	....	....	....	....	3,951.0	4,268.9	9,048.9	....
Other Sectors	79ajd	....	....	....	....	....	....	....	....	....	....	4,503.1	....
Reserve Assets	79akd	....	....	....	....	....	....	....	....	1,869.9	2,396.4	3,172.7	....
Liabilities	79lad	....	....	....	....	....	....	....	....	....	....	22,416.3	....
Dir. Invest. in Rep. Economy	79lbd	....	....	....	....	....	....	....	....	....	....	4,856.3	....
Portfolio Investment	79lcd	....	....	....	....	....	....	....	....	979.3	1,445.1	2,234.2	....
Equity Securities	79ldd	....	....	....	....	....	....	....	....	−	−	383.6	....
Debt Securities	79led	....	....	....	....	....	....	....	....	979.3	1,445.1	1,850.5	....
Financial Derivatives	79lld	....	....	....	....	....	....	....	....	....	....	3.0	....
Other Investment	79lfd	....	....	....	....	....	....	....	....	8,691.0	9,367.7	15,322.9	....
Monetary Authorities	79lgd	....	....	....	....	....	....	....	....	.2	.2	41.9	....
General Government	79lhd	....	....	....	....	....	....	....	....	403.9	279.9	306.3	....
Banks	79lid	....	....	....	....	....	....	....	....	6,723.5	7,568.0	13,319.7	....
Other Sectors	79ljd	....	....	....	....	....	....	....	....	1,563.5	1,519.5	1,655.0	....
Government Finance						*Millions of Pounds: Year Ending December 31*							
Deficit (−) or Surplus	80	−147.56	−77.82	−51.85	−39.90	−142.08	−231.22	−257.58	−201.27	−150.46	....	....	....
Revenue	81	873.99	987.93	1,140.55	1,266.90	1,321.30	1,373.39	1,473.17	1,590.06	1,863.05	....	....	....
Grants Received	81z	1.14	3.75	3.97	3.90	2.35	1.64	.74	.94	2.51	....	....	....
Expenditure	82	1,007.37	1,053.83	1,192.36	1,306.10	1,462.72	1,603.53	1,731.70	1,787.73	2,005.59	....	....	....
Lending Minus Repayments	83	15.32	15.67	4.01	4.60	3.01	2.72	−.21	4.54	10.43	....	....	....
Financing													
Net Borrowing: Domestic	84a	249.03	219.76	106.87	117.40	203.91	143.13	109.31	52.57	185.30	....	....	....
Foreign	85a	−54.63	−91.04	−65.02	−77.50	−61.83	88.08	148.28	148.70	−34.84	....	....	....
Use of Cash Balances	87	−46.84	−50.90	10.00	−	−	−	−.01	−	−	....	....	....
Debt: Domestic	88a	1,075.44	1,295.36	1,402.51	1,583.40	1,837.56	1,987.35	2,130.72	2,165.40	2,467.70	....	....	....
Foreign	89a	665.27	627.81	556.65	479.27	402.95	515.33	664.77	850.68	820.82	....	....	....
National Accounts						*Millions of Pounds*							
Househ.Cons.Expend.,incl.NPISHs	96f	1,938.6	1,934.3	2,111.0	2,551.8	2,704.3	2,879.6	3,160.3p	3,316.3p	3,764.1	4,011.6	4,208.6	....
Government Consumption Expend	91f	590.7	552.5	608.1	644.7	748.9	821.6	902.5	860.3	911.0	1,027.6	1,137.0	....
Gross Fixed Capital Formation	93e	795.9	741.2	751.5	778.6	861.2	847.1	925.2	935.4	981.7	1,037.7	1,169.1	....
Changes in Inventories	93i	94.6	47.6	180.0	110.3	78.3	34.5	70.9	75.0	124.3	60.0	72.3	....
Exports of Goods and Services	90c	1,544.4	1,555.2	1,741.1	2,226.3	2,324.1	2,470.7	2,523.5	2,758.3	3,137.0	3,359.4	3,189.6	....
Imports of Goods and Services (−)	98c	1,881.6	1,569.4	1,755.5	2,368.5	2,601.3	2,705.9	2,882.3	2,908.7	3,425.8	3,619.5	3,637.3	....
Gross Domestic Product (GDP)	99b	3,102.9	3,285.4	3,663.2	4,020.0	4,168.3	4,379.6	4,704.2	5,037.1	5,525.3	5,876.9	6,189.0	6,654.7
Net Primary Income from Abroad	98.n	39.6	36.6	28.8	70.0	61.6	66.5	57.1	53.3	60.4	53.6	76.7	....
Gross National Income (GNI)	99a	3,142.5	3,322.0	3,692.0	4,090.0	4,229.9	4,446.1	4,761.3p	5,090.4p	5,585.7	5,930.5	6,265.7	....
Consumption of Fixed Capital	99cf	330.0	348.8	387.7	429.5	444.1	466.8	499.9p	534.5p	586.5	622.7	657.9	....
GDP Volume 1995 Prices	99b.p	3,538.7	3,563.5	3,773.7	4,020.0	4,096.3	4,190.5	4,391.3	4,598.7	4,828.0	5,021.1	5,123.0	5,225.5
GDP Volume (2000=100)	99bvp	†73.3	73.8	78.2	83.3	84.8	86.8	91.0	95.3	100.0	104.0	106.1	108.2
GDP Deflator (2000=100)	99bip	76.6	80.6	84.8	87.4	88.9	91.3	93.6	95.7	100.0	102.3	105.6	111.3
						Millions: Midyear Estimates							
Population	99z	.70	.72	.73	.74	.75	.76	.77	.78	.78	.79	.80	.80

Czech Republic 935

		1992	1993	1994	1995	1996	1997	1998	1999	2000	2001	2002	2003
Exchange Rates						*Koruny per SDR: End of Period*							
Official Rate	aa	....	41.145	40.947	39.544	39.302	46.733	42.037	49.382	49.267	45.568	40.977	38.121
					Koruny per US Dollar: End of Period (ae) Period Average (rf)								
Official Rate	ae	....	29.955	28.049	26.602	27.332	34.636	29.855	35.979	37.813	36.259	30.141	25.654
Official Rate	rf	....	29.153	28.785	26.541	27.145	31.698	32.281	34.569	38.598	38.035	32.739	28.209
					Index Numbers (2000=100): Period Averages								
Nominal Effective Exchange Rate	nec	92.27	97.43	99.75	99.75	101.65	98.14	98.82	98.95	100.00	104.68	115.82	117.00
Real Effective Exchange Rate	rec	68.93	80.14	84.17	87.01	92.76	93.47	101.12	99.74	100.00	105.71	116.59	114.22
Fund Position						*Millions of SDRs: End of Period*							
Quota	2f.s	–	589.6	589.6	589.6	589.6	589.6	589.6	819.3	819.3	819.3	819.3	819.3
SDRs	1b.s	–	6.0	–	.1	–	–	–	–	.2	.7	3.4	6.3
Reserve Position in the Fund	1c.s	–	–	–	–	–	–	–	–	2.4	120.5	173.5	314.6
Total Fund Cred.&Loans Outstg	2tl	–	780.7	–	–	–	–	–	–	–	–	–	–
International Liquidity				*Millions of US Dollars Unless Otherwise Indicated: End of Period*									
Total Reserves minus Gold	1l.d	....	3,789	6,145	13,843	12,352	9,734	12,542	12,806	13,019	14,341	23,556	26,771
SDRs	1b.d	–	8	–	–	–	–	–	–	–	1	5	9
Reserve Position in the Fund	1c.d	–	–	–	–	–	–	–	–	3	151	236	468
Foreign Exchange	1d.d	....	3,781	6,145	13,843	12,352	9,734	12,542	12,806	13,016	14,189	23,315	26,294
Gold (Million Fine Troy Ounces)	1ad	....	1.950	2.098	1.990	1.985	1.041	.288	.446	.446	.444	.442	.442
Gold (National Valuation)	1and	....	129	140	141	137	57	18	23	22	23	28	32
Monetary Authorities:Other Assets	3..d	....	2,264	1,043	1,084	1,161	843	946	1,285	378	435	†309	118
Other Liab.	4..d	....	2,905	1,791	1,802	658	696	381	849	366	407	†157	120
Deposit Money Banks: Assets	7a.d	....	2,802	3,203	3,783	5,767	8,585	11,793	13,302	13,259	15,609	†14,598	15,336
Liabilities	7b.d	....	1,459	2,464	6,428	9,048	9,124	10,799	9,678	8,419	7,714	†7,664	10,094
Monetary Authorities						*Billions of Koruny: End of Period*							
Foreign Assets	11	....	185.20	205.53	400.83	373.08	368.28	403.23	507.82	507.43	536.61	†720.12	690.65
Claims on Central Government	12a	....	44.98	39.73	12.63	.32	–	–	–	–	11.65	†10.69	9.68
Claims on Other Resident Sectors	12d	....	2.16	1.33	1.51	5.10	†22.14	48.50	61.11	42.43	40.77	†38.52	36.89
Claims on Banking Institutions	12e	....	78.40	77.71	74.84	84.88	100.49	74.91	50.47	37.10	20.52	†.13	.11
Reserve Money	14	....	166.12	223.23	342.77	344.40	†344.60	422.24	459.98	491.57	515.76	†260.14	279.08
of which: Currency Outside BIs	14a	....	59.04	83.58	104.27	118.90	118.74	127.16	157.90	171.82	180.38	†197.81	221.36
Other Liabs. to Banking Insts	14n	....	....	....	....	....	....	....	....	....	....	455.20	439.50
Other Deposits	15	....	.14	9.22	52.68	40.27	†.68	.79	.85	.70	.70	†.72	.66
Foreign Liabilities	16c	....	119.15	50.25	47.93	17.98	24.11	11.38	30.55	13.83	14.74	†4.73	3.09
Central Government Deposits	16d	....	33.41	51.86	41.15	43.09	†68.46	63.07	62.44	57.97	84.25	†82.26	73.28
Capital Accounts	17a	....	†9.90	18.00	27.34	29.56	60.56	39.07	82.84	36.83	8.25	†–22.32	–40.40
Other Items (Net)	17r	....	†–17.98	–28.26	–22.05	–11.91	–7.51	–9.92	–17.06	–13.93	–14.19	†–11.27	–17.88
Banking Institutions						*Billions of Koruny: End of Period*							
Reserves	20	....	71.45	80.78	160.93	158.50	214.94	288.85	296.54	310.93	333.32	†60.20	56.56
Other Claims on Monetary Author.	20n	....	....	....	....	....	....	....	....	....	....	455.20	439.50
Foreign Assets	21	....	83.95	89.84	100.64	157.64	297.34	352.08	478.59	501.35	565.97	†440.00	393.42
Claims on Central Government	22a	....	78.18	94.64	130.94	103.86	62.05	73.66	93.76	117.90	270.78	†433.78	520.96
Claims on Other General Govt	22b	....	....	....	....	....	....	....	....	....	....	21.81	24.26
Claims on Other Resident Sectors	22d	....	731.67	904.27	1,036.60	1,153.91	†1,250.40	1,176.26	1,098.47	1,029.89	916.37	†720.70	782.40
Demand Deposits	24	....	201.96	307.64	310.89	317.46	297.24	275.68	288.88	326.53	402.50	†626.31	741.80
Other Deposits	25	....	428.21	426.43	601.90	663.78	755.75	809.54	797.54	945.94	1,022.98	†890.51	880.24
Money Market Fund Shares	26m	....	....	....	....	....	....	....	....	....	....	....	....
Bonds	26n	....	3.78	21.21	46.68	60.88	81.58	113.38	189.74	93.39	76.74	†48.58	52.05
Foreign Liabilities	26c	....	43.70	69.12	170.99	247.29	316.01	322.40	348.22	318.35	279.70	†231.01	258.96
Central Government Deposits	26d	....	78.73	90.33	92.38	88.19	51.87	55.31	54.59	50.83	80.54	†101.89	48.63
Credit from Monetary Authorities	26g	....	76.35	77.71	74.01	79.82	96.93	52.76	33.68	18.27	4.66	†2.74	.12
Capital Accounts	27a	....	160.75	185.37	195.88	204.28	†348.20	395.15	411.80	405.39	291.53	†291.86	282.69
Other Items (Net)	27r	....	–28.25	–8.29	–63.62	–87.77	–122.85	–133.39	–157.09	–198.63	–72.20	†–61.23	–47.39
Banking Survey						*Billions of Koruny: End of Period*							
Foreign Assets (Net)	31n	....	106.29	176.00	282.55	265.44	325.50	421.52	607.64	676.60	808.14	†924.38	822.03
Domestic Credit	32	....	744.85	897.77	1,048.15	1,131.92	†1,214.25	1,180.04	1,136.31	1,081.43	1,074.78	†1,041.33	1,252.27
Claims on Central Govt. (Net)	32an	....	11.03	–7.82	10.04	–27.10	†–58.28	–44.71	–23.27	9.10	117.65	†260.31	408.72
Claims on Other General Govt	32b	....	....	....	....	....	....	....	....	....	....	21.81	24.26
Claims on Other Resident Sectors	32d	....	733.83	905.59	1,038.12	1,159.02	†1,272.53	1,224.76	1,159.58	1,072.33	957.13	†759.22	819.29
Money	34	....	268.98	403.97	431.08	451.55	†418.39	404.00	447.81	498.96	583.55	†827.04	964.18
Quasi-Money	35	....	428.35	435.65	654.58	704.05	†756.44	810.33	798.39	946.64	1,023.72	†891.23	880.90
Money Market Fund Shares	36m	....	....	....	....	....	....	....	....	....	....	....	....
Bonds	36n	....	3.78	21.21	46.68	60.88	81.58	113.38	189.74	93.39	76.74	†48.58	52.05
Capital Accounts	37a	....	170.10	202.22	221.26	231.06	†408.76	434.22	494.64	442.22	299.78	†269.54	242.29
Other Items (Net)	37r	....	–20.61	9.57	–24.86	–52.94	–125.41	–160.39	–186.63	–223.18	–100.87	†–70.67	–65.12
Money plus Quasi-Money	35l	....	697.33	839.62	1,085.66	1,155.59	†1,174.83	1,214.33	1,246.20	1,445.60	1,607.27	†1,718.27	1,845.08

Czech Republic 935

		1992	1993	1994	1995	1996	1997	1998	1999	2000	2001	2002	2003
Interest Rates							*Percent Per Annum*						
Bank Rate (End of Period)	60	….	8.00	8.50	11.30	12.40	14.75	9.50	5.25	5.25	4.50	2.75	2.00
Money Market Rate	60b	….	8.00	12.65	10.93	12.67	17.50	10.08	5.58	5.42	4.69	2.63	2.08
Treasury Bill Rate	60c	….	6.62	6.98	8.99	11.91	11.21	10.51	5.71	5.37	5.06	2.72	2.04
Deposit Rate	60l	….	7.03	7.07	6.96	6.79	7.71	8.08	4.48	3.42	2.87	2.00	1.33
Lending Rate	60p	….	14.07	13.12	12.80	12.54	13.20	12.81	8.68	7.16	7.20	6.72	5.95
Government Bond Yield	61	….	….	….	….	….	….	….	….	6.72	4.84	3.17	3.77
Prices, Production, Labor						*Index Numbers (2000=100): Period Averages*							
Producer Prices	63	66.13	72.26	76.11	81.84	85.77	89.94	94.36	95.34	100.00	102.82	102.26	101.97
Consumer Prices	64	….	†60.1	66.1	72.1	78.5	85.2	94.2	96.2	100.0	104.7	106.6	106.7
Wages	65	….	43.4	51.4	61.0	72.2	79.3	86.7	94.0	100.0	108.7	116.5	124.3
Industrial Production	66	….	89.3	91.2	90.5	92.3	96.4	98.0	94.9	100.0	106.5	116.6	123.4
Industrial Employment	67	….	120.8	115.1	103.1	98.2	111.1	110.6	104.3	100.0	100.5	98.7	96.2
					Number in Thousands: Period Averages								
Labor Force	67d	….	….	….	….	5,199	5,215	5,233	5,236	5,181	5,171	5,139	….
Employment	67e	….	4,932	4,943	4,995	†4,980	4,927	4,853	4,764	4,732	4,728	4,765	….
Unemployment	67c	….	200	202	181	206	248	336	454	455	418	457	523
Unemployment Rate (%)	67r	….	3.8	3.9	3.5	4.0	4.8	6.5	8.7	8.8	8.1	8.8	9.9
International Transactions							*Millions of Koruny*						
Exports	70	248,090	†421,601	466,403	574,722	594,630	722,501	850,240	908,756	1,121,099	1,269,634	1,254,394	1,371,337
Imports, f.o.b.	71.v	293,399	†426,084	501,549	670,445	752,343	861,770	926,559	973,169	1,241,924	1,386,319	1,325,717	1,440,733
Balance of Payments						*Millions of US Dollars: Minus Sign Indicates Debit*							
Current Account, n.i.e.	78ald	….	466	−820	−1,374	−4,128	−3,622	−1,308	−1,466	−2,690	−3,273	−4,265	−5,661
Goods: Exports f.o.b.	78aad	….	14,231	15,964	21,477	21,950	22,319	25,886	26,259	29,019	33,404	38,480	48,736
Goods: Imports f.o.b.	78abd	….	−14,748	−17,372	−25,162	−27,656	−27,257	−28,532	−28,161	−32,114	−36,482	−40,720	−51,242
Trade Balance	78acd	….	−517	−1,408	−3,685	−5,706	−4,938	−2,647	−1,902	−3,095	−3,078	−2,240	−2,505
Services: Credit	78add	….	4,721	5,167	6,725	8,181	7,132	7,665	7,048	6,839	7,092	7,083	7,789
Services: Debit	78aed	….	−3,709	−4,685	−4,882	−6,264	−5,389	−5,750	−5,850	−5,436	−5,567	−6,439	−7,320
Balance on Goods & Services	78afd	….	496	−926	−1,842	−3,789	−3,196	−731	−704	−1,692	−1,554	−1,597	−2,035
Income: Credit	78agd	….	548	791	1,197	1,170	1,405	1,713	1,859	1,952	2,233	2,052	2,643
Income: Debit	78ahd	….	−664	−812	−1,301	−1,892	−2,197	−2,806	−3,209	−3,323	−4,422	−5,632	−6,809
Balance on Gds, Serv. & Inc.	78aid	….	379	−947	−1,945	−4,512	−3,987	−1,825	−2,053	−3,063	−3,743	−5,177	−6,201
Current Transfers, n.i.e.: Credit	78ajd	….	242	298	664	617	866	1,067	1,310	948	959	1,465	1,655
Current Transfers: Debit	78akd	….	−154	−171	−92	−233	−501	−550	−722	−575	−489	−553	−1,115
Capital Account, n.i.e.	78bcd	….	−563	—	7	1	11	2	−2	−5	−9	−4	−3
Capital Account, n.i.e.: Credit	78bad	….	208	—	12	1	17	14	18	6	2	7	7
Capital Account: Debit	78bbd	….	−771	—	−5	—	−5	−12	−21	−11	−11	−11	−10
Financial Account, n.i.e.	78bjd	….	3,043	4,504	8,225	4,202	1,122	2,908	3,080	3,835	4,569	10,621	5,855
Direct Investment Abroad	78bdd	….	−90	−116	−37	−155	−28	−125	−90	−43	−165	−211	−242
Dir. Invest. in Rep. Econ., n.i.e.	78bed	….	654	878	2,568	1,435	1,286	3,700	6,313	4,987	5,641	8,497	2,514
Portfolio Investment Assets	78bfd	….	−232	−47	−325	−50	−159	−44	−1,882	−2,236	125	−2,373	−3,006
Equity Securities	78bkd	….	−232	−47	−325	−50	3	119	−1,409	−1,167	247	−231	188
Debt Securities	78bld	….	….	….	….	….	−162	−163	−473	−1,069	−121	−2,142	−3,194
Portfolio Investment Liab., n.i.e.	78bgd	….	1,840	893	1,695	771	1,152	1,146	499	482	798	814	1,753
Equity Securities	78bmd	….	1,125	497	1,236	601	378	1,096	120	619	616	−265	1,104
Debt Securities	78bnd	….	715	396	460	170	774	49	380	−137	181	1,079	649
Financial Derivatives Assets	78bwd	….	….	….	….	….	….	….	….	−129	−254	−476	257
Financial Derivatives Liabilities	78bxd	….	….	….	….	….	….	….	….	89	168	347	−114
Other Investment Assets	78bhd	….	−2,867	−2,437	−2,492	−2,370	−4,427	−1,552	−2,688	984	−1,199	4,015	2,279
Monetary Authorities	78bod	….	….	….	….	….	….	….	—	—	—	—	—
General Government	78bpd	….	−3,054	−2,362	−2,138	48	16	20	28	76	180	651	277
Banks	78bqd	….	36	−163	−224	−2,317	−4,161	−1,652	−2,642	1,011	−1,299	3,844	1,469
Other Sectors	78brd	….	151	88	−130	−101	−281	80	−74	−102	−80	−480	533
Other Investment Liab., n.i.e.	78bid	….	3,738	5,333	6,816	4,571	3,298	−217	927	−300	−544	9	2,414
Monetary Authorities	78bsd	….	106	−47	40	−2	−11	−7	−57	—	1	−1	−2
General Government	78btd	….	3,037	2,821	1,657	−295	−360	−364	−185	−49	−129	−45	372
Banks	78bud	….	4	888	3,310	2,858	1,638	387	886	−974	−1,152	−282	1,335
Other Sectors	78bvd	….	591	1,671	1,809	2,011	2,030	−234	283	723	735	338	709
Net Errors and Omissions	78cad	….	95	−210	596	−901	730	288	27	−296	499	266	251
Overall Balance	78cbd	….	3,041	3,474	7,453	−825	−1,758	1,890	1,639	844	1,787	6,618	442
Reserves and Related Items	79dad	….	−3,041	−3,474	−7,453	825	1,758	−1,890	−1,639	−844	−1,787	−6,618	−442
Reserve Assets	79dbd	….	−3,039	−2,357	−7,453	825	1,758	−1,890	−1,639	−844	−1,787	−6,618	−442
Use of Fund Credit and Loans	79dcd	….	−3	−1,117	—	—	—	—	—	—	—	—	—
Exceptional Financing	79ded	….	….	….	….	….	….	….	….	….	….	—	—

Czech Republic 935

		1992	1993	1994	1995	1996	1997	1998	1999	2000	2001	2002	2003
International Investment Position							**Millions of US Dollars**						
Assets	79aad	....	17,950	20,471	29,396	30,629	29,779	36,426	37,465	38,304	42,609	52,419	59,550
Direct Investment Abroad	79abd	....	181	300	345	498	548	804	698	738	1,136	1,473	1,912
Portfolio Investment	79acd	....	276	433	755	1,372	1,032	1,202	2,900	4,772	5,106	9,102	13,404
Equity Securities	79add	....	264	334	693	748	417	449	1,843	2,439	1,894	2,869	1,845
Debt Securities	79aed	....	12	99	62	624	615	752	1,057	2,333	3,212	6,233	11,558
Financial Derivatives	79ald	....	—	—	—	—	—	—	—	168	435	1,036	941
Other Investment	79afd	....	13,621	13,494	14,273	16,323	18,425	21,804	21,042	19,488	21,469	17,098	16,337
Monetary Authorities	79agd	....	820	876	984	956	754	875	—	10	10	22	22
General Government	79ahd	....	6,469	6,278	5,987	5,931	5,923	5,902	5,843	5,839	5,813	3,301	3,103
Banks	79aid	....	2,837	2,944	3,469	5,622	8,308	11,263	11,841	10,305	12,116	9,349	8,859
Other Sectors	79ajd	....	3,495	3,396	3,833	3,814	3,440	3,763	3,358	3,335	3,530	4,427	4,353
Reserve Assets	79akd	....	3,872	6,243	14,023	12,435	9,774	12,617	12,825	13,139	14,464	23,710	26,957
Liabilities	79lad	....	14,123	18,088	27,182	33,151	32,863	40,361	40,548	43,378	49,340	65,598	83,549
Dir. Invest. in Rep. Economy	79lbd	....	3,423	4,547	7,350	8,572	9,234	14,375	17,552	21,644	27,092	38,669	47,527
Portfolio Investment	79lcd	....	1,956	2,910	4,696	5,298	4,880	5,564	4,602	4,353	4,974	6,673	9,698
Equity Securities	79ldd	....	1,101	1,331	2,642	3,398	3,028	3,793	2,724	3,059	3,551	4,250	6,469
Debt Securities	79led	....	855	1,579	2,054	1,900	1,853	1,771	1,878	1,294	1,423	2,423	3,229
Financial Derivatives	79lld	....	—	—	—	—	—	—	—	140	317	752	758
Other Investment	79lfd	....	8,744	10,631	15,136	19,280	18,749	20,422	18,394	17,242	16,957	19,504	25,566
Monetary Authorities	79lgd	....	1,272	62	98	85	64	64	6	5	6	5	5
General Government	79lhd	....	2,748	2,910	2,031	1,619	1,098	801	580	521	261	314	875
Banks	79lid	....	1,283	2,402	6,007	8,964	9,009	10,640	9,682	8,219	7,286	7,954	10,524
Other Sectors	79ljd	....	3,442	5,257	6,999	8,612	8,577	8,916	8,126	8,497	9,405	11,230	14,162
Government Finance							**Billions of Koruny: Year Ending December 31**						
Deficit (-) or Surplus	80	....	1.1	10.4	7.2	−1.8	−15.9	−29.2	−29.7	−46.1	−67.9	−45.6	−109.1
Total Revenue and Grants	81y	....	349.0	381.3	440.4	476.4	500.8	530.6	563.3	583.1	623.2	683.4	697.3
Revenue	81	....	349.0	381.3	440.4	476.4	500.8	530.6	563.3	583.1	623.2	657.7	691.3
Grants	81z	....	—	—	—	—	—	—	—	—	—	25.7	6.0
Exp. & Lending Minus Repay	82z	....	347.9	370.9	433.2	478.2	516.7	559.8	593.0	629.2	691.1	729.0	806.4
Expenditure	82	....	351.9	373.1	433.9	480.6	521.2	561.6	593.8	629.5	688.2	746.2	806.1
Lending Minus Repayments	83	....	−4.0	−2.2	−.7	−2.4	−4.5	−1.8	−.8	−.3	2.9	−17.3	.3
Total Financing	80h	....	−1.1	−10.4	−7.2	1.7	15.9	29.3	29.6	46.1	67.8	45.6	109.1
Domestic	84a	....	−1.1	−10.4	−7.2	1.7	15.9	29.3	29.6	46.1	67.8	45.6	109.1
Foreign	85a	....	—	—	—	—	—	—	—	—	—	—	—
Total Debt by Residence	88	....	158.9	161.7	154.4	155.2	167.2	194.5	228.3	289.3	345.0	395.9	493.2
Domestic	88a	....	86.5	90.2	101.3	110.9	128.9	169.9	207.1	259.5	323.7	371.5	453.9
Foreign	89a	....	72.4	71.5	53.1	44.3	38.3	24.6	21.2	29.8	21.3	24.4	39.3
National Accounts							**Billions of Koruny**						
Househ.Cons.Expend.,incl.NPISHs	96f	....	509.5	607.0	†701.7	817.7	899.9	966.1	1,019.2	1,117.3	1,187.5	1,200.6	1,267.8
Government Consumption Expend	91f	....	221.6	255.5	†275.0	313.0	332.5	342.4	373.3	468.6	508.3	536.7	518.9
Gross Fixed Capital Formation	93e	....	289.6	339.8	†442.5	500.6	514.5	535.5	528.3	588.2	639.0	624.0	627.7
Changes in Inventories	93i	....	−11.2	12.2	†27.6	36.0	32.9	17.1	5.8	27.2	39.0	41.2	51.8
Exports of Goods and Services	90c	....	559.5	597.1	†740.8	823.3	949.7	1,080.9	1,152.6	1,385.9	1,539.3	1,481.6	1,591.0
Imports of Goods and Services (-)	98c	....	551.5	628.8	†806.5	923.7	1,049.7	1,103.0	1,176.9	1,452.2	1,598.0	1,534.6	1,647.1
Gross Domestic Product (GDP)	99b	....	1,020.3	1,182.8	1,381.0	1,567.0	1,679.9	1,839.1	1,902.3	2,146.2	2,323.1	2,408.4	2,410.1
Net Primary Income from Abroad	98.n	....	−4.3	−.8	−7.1	−17.3	−20.2	−35.1	−46.7	−53.0	−83.5	−97.5	−116.7
Gross National Income (GNI)	99a	....	1,016.0	1,181.9	1,373.9	1,549.7	1,659.7	1,804.0	1,855.6	2,093.2	2,239.5	2,284.7	2,293.5
Net Current Transf.from Abroad	98t	....	3.2	3.6	15.2	10.4	11.3	16.7	20.4	14.4	17.8	28.7	15.6
Gross Nat'l Disposable Inc.(GNDI)	99i	....	1,003.0	1,185.6	1,389.1	1,560.1	1,671.0	1,820.7	1,876.0	1,946.2	2,109.5	2,206.8	2,309.1
Gross Saving	99s	....	285.3	323.0	412.4	429.4	438.6	512.1	483.5	483.8	517.8	519.1	522.3
GDP Volume 1995 Prices	99b.p	....	1,275.3	1,303.6	1,381.0	1,440.4	1,429.3	1,414.4	1,421.0	1,467.3	1,512.6	1,542.2	1,587.2
GDP Volume (2000=100)	99bvp	....	86.9	88.8	94.1	98.2	97.4	96.4	96.8	100.0	103.1	105.1	108.2
GDP Deflator (2000=100)	99bip	....	54.7	62.0	68.4	74.4	80.4	88.9	91.5	100.0	105.0	106.8	103.8
							Millions: Midyear Estimates						
Population	99z	....	10.33	10.33	10.33	10.32	10.31	10.30	10.28	10.27	10.26	10.25	10.24

2004, International Monetary Fund : *International Financial Statistics Yearbook*

Denmark 128

		1992	1993	1994	1995	1996	1997	1998	1999	2000	2001	2002	2003
Exchange Rates						*Kroner per SDR: End of Period*							
Market Rate	aa	8.601	9.302	8.880	8.244	8.548	9.210	8.992	10.155	10.450	10.568	9.628	8.853
						Kroner per US Dollar: End of Period (ae) Period Average (rf)							
Market Rate	ae	6.256	6.773	6.083	5.546	5.945	6.826	6.387	7.399	8.021	8.410	7.082	5.958
Market Rate	rf	6.036	6.484	6.361	5.602	5.799	6.604	6.701	6.976	8.083	8.323	7.895	6.588
					Kroner per ECU through 1998; Kroner per Euro Beginning 1999: End of Period (ea) Period Average (eb)								
Euro Rate	ea	7.5748	7.5508	7.4823	7.2940	7.4466	7.5312	7.4488	†7.4432	7.4631	7.4357	7.4243	7.4450
Euro Rate	ag	....	....	....	....	....	....	....	1.0046	.9305	.8813	1.0487	1.2630
Euro Rate	eb	7.8119	7.5916	7.5415	7.3271	7.3598	7.4830	7.4999	†7.4356	7.4529	7.4521	7.4301	7.4306
Euro Rate	rh	....	....	....	....	....	....	....	1.0668	.9240	.8956	.9444	1.1308
						Index Numbers (2000=100): Period Averages							
Market Rate	ahx	133.9	124.5	127.0	144.0	139.0	122.2	120.4	115.7	100.0	96.9	102.4	122.6
Nominal Effective Exchange Rate	neu	100.5	104.7	104.7	108.8	107.3	104.3	105.0	103.8	100.0	101.5	102.1	105.2
Real Effective Exchange Rate	reu	101.2	104.0	103.1	106.1	104.2	101.7	103.3	103.2	100.0	101.4	103.0	107.5
Fund Position						*Millions of SDRs: End of Period*							
Quota	2f.s	1,069.9	1,069.9	1,069.9	1,069.9	1,069.9	1,069.9	1,069.9	1,642.8	1,642.8	1,642.8	1,642.8	1,642.8
SDRs	1b.s	66.7	62.4	124.6	106.8	116.7	248.7	246.0	249.9	50.5	223.5	75.9	54.6
Reserve Position in the Fund	1c.s	345.7	309.1	294.6	400.0	421.8	467.9	827.5	582.1	440.1	566.8	722.0	686.3
of which: Outstg.Fund Borrowing	2c	–	–	–	–	–	–	34.2	–	–	–	–	–
International Liquidity						*Millions of US Dollars Unless Otherwise Indicated: End of Period*							
Total Reserves minus Gold	1l.d	11,044	10,301	9,056	11,016	14,140	19,124	15,264	22,287	15,108	17,110	26,986	37,105
SDRs	1b.d	92	86	182	159	168	336	346	343	66	281	103	81
Reserve Position in the Fund	1c.d	475	425	430	595	607	631	1,165	799	573	712	982	1,020
Foreign Exchange	1d.d	10,477	9,791	8,444	10,262	13,366	18,157	13,753	21,145	14,469	16,117	25,901	36,004
Gold (Million Fine Troy Ounces)	1ad	2	2	2	2	2	2	2	2	2	2	2	2
Gold (National Valuation)	1and	580	478	703	714	590	545	677	531	569	557	703	872
Monetary Authorities: Other Liab.	4..d	4,609	117	253	397	275	124	196	297	381	421	400	481
Banking Institutions: Assets	7a.d	45,629	57,272	50,945	56,593	62,392	65,675	76,754	68,432	†71,009	60,469	72,054	102,896
Liabilities	7b.d	36,845	27,128	30,141	33,246	40,172	50,347	61,484	63,340	62,554	58,799	75,582	110,390
Monetary Authorities						*Billions of Kroner: End of Period*							
Foreign Assets	11	72.32	70.88	63.18	69.34	86.25	129.49	101.85	169.06	†120.86	152.26	199.74	227.62
Claims on Central Government	12a	6.79	10.04	20.05	14.83	15.47	15.19	15.50	14.80	†14.97	16.47	18.33	17.15
Claims on Banking Institutions	12e	24.86	79.21	57.28	45.33	40.72	31.57	36.96	70.19	†52.72	89.99	106.94	73.65
Claims on Other Banking Insts	12f	28.90	30.95	24.99	19.97	21.26	20.24	22.95	24.56	....	....	....	....
Claims on Other Resident Sectors	12d	1.40	.24	2.86	1.64	6.14	3.44	1.67	2.50	†1.85	1.93	.23	.51
Reserve Money	14	38.18	62.70	63.15	71.69	95.55	125.31	97.00	192.86	†58.28	54.99	60.96	66.28
of which: Currency Outside BIs	14a	24.97	25.72	28.93	30.59	30.94	33.25	34.49	36.86	†37.43	39.21	38.98	40.99
Money Market Instruments	16m	....	....	....	....	....	....	....	....	51.87	113.62	160.66	157.28
Foreign Liabilities	16c	28.78	.79	1.54	2.20	1.63	.88	1.25	2.43	†3.37	3.89	3.70	3.09
Central Government Deposits	16d	31.27	89.57	56.91	35.44	31.65	30.73	34.03	36.49	†35.32	40.56	47.06	40.89
Capital Accounts	17a	....	....	....	....	....	....	....	....	49.45	50.90	58.01	55.05
Other Items (Net)	17r	36.04	38.26	46.77	41.78	41.00	43.00	46.66	49.33	†–7.91	–3.32	–5.15	–3.67
Banking Institutions						*Billions of Kroner: End of Period*							
Reserves	20	16.31	35.33	32.69	39.57	51.62	70.63	54.20	96.26	†23.82	17.37	32.47	18.91
Claims on Mon.Author.:Securities	20c	....	....	....	....	....	....	....	....	50.56	113.88	151.14	156.66
Foreign Assets	21	285.43	387.88	309.90	313.87	370.89	448.30	490.19	506.32	†569.52	508.52	510.30	613.02
Claims on Central Government	22a	103.49	70.18	124.60	99.53	85.34	69.80	71.14	65.37	†89.38	112.10	119.04	102.18
Claims on Other General Govt	22b	....	....	....	....	....	....	....	....	57.95	61.17	66.27	75.03
Claims on Other Banking Insts	22f	46.51	136.53	108.44	125.15	157.66	181.52	218.24	191.46	....	....	....	....
Claims on Other Resident Sectors	22d	361.76	317.67	297.74	312.89	331.06	357.73	405.37	420.62	†1,750.73	1,904.42	1,999.09	2,122.47
Demand Deposits	24	229.77	255.44	248.31	259.86	287.09	304.47	321.44	336.34	†346.55	373.20	391.63	427.72
Other Deposits	25	246.11	318.06	262.20	282.89	296.17	320.02	325.42	298.27	†258.93	253.06	265.42	269.11
Money Market Instruments	26m	....	....	....	....	....	....	....	....	2.22	8.55	2.17	2.11
Bonds	26n	....	....	....	....	....	....	....	....	1,173.61	1,268.87	1,363.06	1,417.13
Foreign Liabilities	26c	230.49	183.73	183.35	184.38	238.80	343.67	392.67	468.64	†501.72	494.47	535.28	657.66
Central Government Deposits	26d	....	....	....	....	....	....	....	....	5.23	17.04	18.62	16.54
Credit from Monetary Authorities	26g	26.50	80.56	58.66	45.94	35.73	21.46	34.03	34.01	†30.19	69.62	86.34	57.00
Capital Accounts	27a	86.11	72.13	79.54	75.37	77.42	82.25	87.64	91.43	†221.46	212.55	207.06	235.80
Other Items (Net)	27r	–5.48	37.67	41.31	42.58	61.35	56.11	77.93	51.34	†2.28	20.12	8.69	5.16

Denmark 128

		1992	1993	1994	1995	1996	1997	1998	1999	2000	2001	2002	2003
Banking Survey						*Billions of Kroner: End of Period*							
Foreign Assets (Net)	31n	98.49	274.24	188.19	196.62	216.70	233.24	198.12	204.31	†185.29	162.42	171.06	179.88
Domestic Credit	32	523.25	482.44	528.22	545.50	592.83	629.40	714.58	697.55	†1,874.33	2,038.48	2,137.28	2,259.90
Claims on Central Govt. (Net)	32an	79.00	−9.36	87.74	78.91	69.16	54.26	52.62	43.68	†63.80	70.96	71.69	61.89
Claims on Other General Govt.	32b	5.67	6.40	6.44	6.93	7.56	12.22	13.73	14.74	†57.95	61.17	66.27	75.03
Claims on Other Banking Insts.	32f	75.41	167.48	133.43	145.13	178.91	201.75	241.19	216.02	....	....	....	....
Claims on Other Resident Sectors	32d	363.16	317.91	300.61	314.53	337.19	361.17	407.04	423.12	†1,752.58	1,906.35	1,999.32	2,122.98
Money	34	256.00	283.00	279.05	291.98	325.52	344.05	360.74	381.77	†385.98	414.85	430.82	469.15
Quasi-Money	35	246.11	318.06	262.20	282.89	296.17	320.02	325.42	298.27	†258.93	253.06	265.42	269.11
Money Market Instruments	36m	....	....	....	....	....	....	....	....	3.53	8.30	11.70	2.73
Bonds	36n	....	....	....	....	....	....	....	....	1,148.73	1,244.30	1,340.38	1,394.52
Capital Accounts	37a	....	....	....	....	....	....	....	....	270.91	263.45	265.08	290.85
Other Items (Net)	37r	119.62	155.62	175.16	167.25	187.84	198.57	226.54	221.82	†−8.24	16.96	−5.08	13.38
Money plus Quasi-Money	35l	502.11	601.06	541.25	574.87	621.69	664.08	686.16	680.04	†644.91	667.91	696.24	738.27
Money (National Definitions)						*Billions of Kroner: End of Period*							
Broad Money	39m	373.90	416.42	394.03	410.01	439.74	462.66	476.23	495.94	505.91	546.18	604.71	680.56
Interest Rates						*Percent Per Annum*							
Discount Rate (End of Period)	60	9.50	6.25	5.00	4.25	3.25	3.50	3.50	3.00	4.75	3.25	2.86	2.00
Money Market Rate	60b	11.35	†11.49	6.30	6.19	3.98	3.71	4.27	3.37	4.98	....	3.56	2.38
Deposit Rate	60l	7.5	6.5	†3.5	3.9	2.8	2.7	3.1	2.4	3.2	3.3	†2.4	2.4
Lending Rate	60p	11.8	10.5	†10.0	10.3	8.7	7.7	7.9	7.1	8.1	8.2	†7.1	....
Government Bond Yield	61	9.47	7.08	7.41	7.58	6.04	5.08	4.59	4.30	5.54	....	4.57	3.53
Mortgage Bond Yield	61a	10.14	8.17	8.34	8.97	7.84	7.14	6.04	6.08	7.06	....	6.13	5.16
Prices, Production, Labor						*Index Numbers (2000=100): Period Averages*							
Share Prices: Industrial	62a	33	34	40	40	49	65	70	62	100	....	....	....
Shipping	62b	26	30	33	30	37	66	68	77	100	....	....	....
Prices: Home & Import Goods	63	88.89	88.40	89.23	91.70	92.72	94.49	93.93	94.40	100.00	101.97	102.10	102.29
Home Goods	63a	89.2	†88.7	....	91.6	93.0	94.8	94.2	95.1	†100.0	102.8	103.5	104.8
Consumer Prices	64	84.6	85.7	87.4	89.2	91.1	93.1	94.8	97.2	100.0	102.4	104.8	107.0
Harmonized CPI	64h	....	....	....	90.5	92.4	94.1	95.4	97.3	100.0	102.3	104.7	106.8
Wages: Hourly Earnings	65..c	....	....	79.3	82.3	85.4	88.8	92.6	96.5	100.0	104.2	108.3	112.3
Industrial Production	66	78.3	75.4	83.2	86.5	87.6	92.0	94.7	94.9	100.0	102.0	103.0	102.5
Agricultural Production (1995=100)	66bx	96.4	†101.7	101.1	100.0	100.2	101.0	104.6	104.8	....	....	....	....
						Number in Thousands: Period Averages							
Labor Force	67d	....	2,893	2,777	....	2,822	2,856	2,848	....	2,853	2,862	2,849	....
Employment	67e	2,652	2,584	†2,555	2,607	2,627	2,678	2,691	2,708	2,722	2,725	2,715	2,693
Unemployment	67c	318	349	343	288	246	220	183	158	151	135	138	160
Unemployment Rate (%)	67r	11.3	12.4	12.2	10.3	8.8	7.9	6.6	5.7	5.4	4.8	4.9	5.7
International Transactions						*Millions of Kroner*							
Exports	70	251,025	247,750	273,163	288,186	298,535	324,254	326,434	351,916	408,054	424,484	442,163	432,053
Imports, c.i.f.	71	214,153	203,061	231,832	256,198	261,049	293,110	309,897	310,714	358,972	368,470	387,818	370,936
						2000=100							
Volume of Exports	72	66	64	69	†78	80	84	86	92	100	103	109	108
Volume of Imports	73	66	61	69	†81	82	88	93	93	100	102	108	107
Unit Value of Exports	74	91	89	90	†90	92	94	93	93	100	102	100	100
Unit Value of Imports	75	87	85	86	†88	90	93	93	93	100	101	99	97
Import Prices	76.x	88	†87	90	92	92	94	93	93	100	101	100	....

Denmark 128

		1992	1993	1994	1995	1996	1997	1998	1999	2000	2001	2002	2003
Balance of Payments						*Millions of US Dollars: Minus Sign Indicates Debit*							
Current Account, n.i.e.	78ald	4,199	4,832	3,189	1,855	3,090	921	−2,008	2,915	2,412	4,920	4,991	6,139
Goods: Exports f.o.b.	78aad	40,504	36,948	41,741	50,348	50,735	48,103	47,908	49,932	50,183	50,502	55,586	65,202
Goods: Imports f.o.b.	78abd	−33,446	−29,229	−34,300	−43,821	−43,203	−42,734	−44,021	−43,533	−43,443	−43,051	−47,279	−55,060
Trade Balance	78acd	7,058	7,719	7,441	6,528	7,532	5,369	3,886	6,399	6,740	7,451	8,308	10,142
Services: Credit	78add	14,083	12,564	13,661	15,307	16,502	14,044	15,212	20,090	24,107	25,367	27,182	32,104
Services: Debit	78aed	−10,736	−10,467	−12,067	−14,040	−14,771	−13,727	−15,779	−18,517	−21,488	−22,485	−25,116	−28,293
Balance on Goods & Services	78afd	10,405	9,816	9,035	7,795	9,263	5,685	3,319	7,972	9,360	10,333	10,374	13,952
Income: Credit	78agd	15,956	23,091	22,743	28,433	37,626	18,774	10,401	9,100	11,815	10,892	12,270	9,257
Income: Debit	78ahd	−21,282	−27,480	−27,385	−32,982	−42,235	−22,203	−14,247	−11,426	−15,749	−13,888	−15,040	−13,238
Balance on Gds, Serv. & Inc.	78aid	5,079	5,427	4,394	3,246	4,655	2,256	−527	5,646	5,426	7,337	7,603	9,972
Current Transfers, n.i.e.: Credit	78ajd	2,136	2,442	2,261	2,580	2,398	3,633	3,443	4,156	3,395	3,877	4,120	4,300
Current Transfers: Debit	78akd	−3,016	−3,037	−3,466	−3,970	−3,963	−4,968	−4,924	−6,888	−6,410	−6,294	−6,731	−8,133
Capital Account, n.i.e.	78bcd	–	–	....	....	....	128	50	1,083	−14	−25	101	−45
Capital Account, n.i.e.: Credit	78bad	–	–	....	....	....	128	81	1,331	320	253	351	296
Capital Account: Debit	78bbd	–	–	....	....	....	....	−31	−248	−334	−278	−251	−341
Financial Account, n.i.e.	78bjd	423	−6,545	−5,647	−432	1,882	8,496	−1,489	6,247	−3,830	−5,146	2,525	−4,495
Direct Investment Abroad	78bdd	−2,236	−1,373	−4,162	−2,969	−2,510	−4,355	−4,215	−17,039	−28,355	−13,327	−5,152	−1,314
Dir. Invest. in Rep. Econ., n.i.e.	78bed	1,017	1,713	5,006	4,139	773	2,792	6,675	16,076	35,847	10,236	6,410	2,908
Portfolio Investment Assets	78bfd	1,420	2	−1,175	−1,171	−2,349	−6,239	−7,563	−9,719	−23,723	−14,819	−4,362	−21,938
Equity Securities	78bkd	–					....	....	....	....	....	....	−3,458
Debt Securities	78bld	1,420	2	−1,175	−1,171	−2,349	....	....	....	....	....	....	−18,480
Portfolio Investment Liab., n.i.e.	78bgd	8,707	12,659	−10,596	7,487	7,865	11,186	−2,598	7,014	5,783	10,510	4,843	6,012
Equity Securities	78bmd	–					....	....	....	....	....	....	1,388
Debt Securities	78bnd	8,707	12,659	−10,596	7,487	7,865	....	....	....	....	....	....	4,623
Financial Derivatives Assets	78bwd	....	....	....	....	....	....	....	....	....	....	....	−12
Financial Derivatives Liabilities	78bxd	....	....	....	....	....	....	....	325	326	685	617	....
Other Investment Assets	78bhd	432	−14,812	12,136	−1,330	−9,339	−8,033	−1,797	−1,188	−2,143	10,013	−6,307	−9,983
Monetary Authorities	78bod	....	....	....	....	....	....	....	....	....	....	....	56
General Government	78bpd	–	–	....	....	....	....	....	....	....	....	....	365
Banks	78bqd	432	−14,812	12,136	−1,330	−9,339	....	....	....	....	....	....	−12,577
Other Sectors	78brd	–	–	....	....	....	−8,033	−1,797	....	....	....	....	2,155
Other Investment Liab., n.i.e.	78bid	−8,918	−4,734	−6,856	−6,589	7,442	13,145	8,009	10,778	8,435	−8,444	6,476	19,832
Monetary Authorities	78bsd	4,301	−4,419	122	133	−108	....	....	....	....	....	....	−27
General Government	78btd	1,309	8,648	−4,058	−3,380	−1,563	....	....	....	....	....	....	−437
Banks	78bud	−9,476	−6,497	414	15	9,343	....	....	....	....	....	....	24,560
Other Sectors	78bvd	−5,052	−2,467	−3,333	−3,357	−231	13,145	8,009	....	....	....	....	−4,264
Net Errors and Omissions	78cad	−547	1,146	606	1,075	−1,408	−3,012	−792	−808	−4,217	3,520	−2,001	3,075
Overall Balance	78cbd	4,075	−567	−1,851	2,498	3,563	6,532	−4,239	9,437	−5,649	3,270	5,615	4,674
Reserves and Related Items	79dad	−4,075	567	1,851	−2,498	−3,563	−6,532	4,239	−9,437	5,649	−3,270	−5,615	−4,674
Reserve Assets	79dbd	−4,075	567	1,851	−2,498	−3,563	−6,532	4,239	−9,437	5,649	−3,270	−5,615	−4,674
Use of Fund Credit and Loans	79dcd	–	–	–	–	–	....	....	....	....	....	....	....
Exceptional Financing	79ded	....	....	....	....	....	....	....	....	....	....	....	....
International Investment Position						*Millions of US Dollars*							
Assets	79aad	104,156	111,991	109,111	123,004	145,614	156,402	187,516	219,613	249,021	241,767	....	....
Direct Investment Abroad	79abd	16,306	15,799	19,892	24,702	27,589	28,128	34,664	44,841	65,890	69,760	....	....
Portfolio Investment	79acd	16,625	17,866	17,261	22,899	29,944	37,064	51,792	70,762	84,973	82,938	....	....
Equity Securities	79add	6,394	7,973	8,877	10,819	16,149	22,414	32,623	50,132	56,480	46,845	....	....
Debt Securities	79aed	10,231	9,893	8,384	12,081	13,794	14,650	19,169	20,630	28,493	36,093	....	....
Financial Derivatives	79ald	–							2,502	9,285	14,093	11,201	....
Other Investment	79afd	59,628	67,183	62,798	63,469	73,513	71,931	82,423	72,054	69,009	59,784	....	....
Monetary Authorities	79agd	–	–	–	–	–	–	–	–	–	–	....	....
General Government	79ahd	2,718	2,362	2,795	2,524	2,187	2,051	2,524	2,621	3,396	3,422	....	....
Banks	79aid	39,965	51,384	46,359	49,766	55,177	56,255	64,534	54,775	51,786	42,099	....	....
Other Sectors	79ajd	16,945	13,437	13,645	11,179	16,149	13,624	15,365	14,658	13,827	14,262	....	....
Reserve Assets	79akd	11,597	11,142	9,160	11,933	14,569	19,279	16,136	22,670	15,056	18,084	....	....
Liabilities	79lad	154,104	155,186	151,734	170,934	187,737	197,480	235,320	241,569	272,052	268,174	....	....
Dir. Invest. in Rep. Economy	79lbd	14,387	14,618	18,083	23,801	22,205	22,268	31,055	41,225	66,459	65,827	....	....
Portfolio Investment	79lcd	65,063	84,016	72,826	88,713	101,607	106,505	117,215	105,272	104,119	112,111	....	....
Equity Securities	79ldd	2,398	3,248	6,740	8,294	12,448	20,363	20,556	20,740	26,023	22,853	....	....
Debt Securities	79led	62,665	80,768	66,086	80,418	89,158	86,141	96,658	84,532	78,095	89,258	....	....
Financial Derivatives	79lld	–	–	–	–	–	–	2,159	8,453	13,363	10,828	....	....
Other Investment	79lfd	74,654	56,552	60,825	58,420	63,925	68,708	84,891	86,619	88,111	79,408	....	....
Monetary Authorities	79lgd	4,476	148	329	361	336	146	204	328	420	463	....	....
General Government	79lhd	2,877	2,067	3,123	1,983	1,178	732	1,265	949	468	474	....	....
Banks	79lid	30,853	22,444	27,289	29,210	35,159	42,631	53,475	52,813	60,547	56,584	....	....
Other Sectors	79ljd	36,448	31,894	30,084	26,866	27,252	25,198	29,948	32,530	26,675	21,887	....	....
Government Finance						*Millions of Kroner: Year Ending December 31*							
Deficit (−) or Surplus	80	−16,116	−21,935	−26,398	−23,692	−3,081	12,661p	19,479p	6,296p	20,804f	....	....	....
Revenue	81	339,246	358,056	385,593	391,286	417,948	434,423p	449,490p	462,510p	470,916f	....	....	....
Grants Received	81z	4,766	5,973	5,546	3,873	3,771	4,583p	4,826p	4,665p	5,507f	....	....	....
Expenditure	82	356,044	381,805	412,967	417,654	423,596	425,124p	434,285p	443,021p	452,939f	....	....	....
Lending Minus Repayments	83	4,083	4,157	4,570	1,195	1,202	1,222p	554p	17,857p	2,677f	....	....	....

Denmark 128

		1992	1993	1994	1995	1996	1997	1998	1999	2000	2001	2002	2003
National Accounts							*Billions of Kroner*						
Househ.Cons.Expend.,incl.NPISHs	96f	439.3	450.2	493.8	509.6	533.2	560.9	581.3	599.5	610.5	624.5	641.9	659.3
Government Consumption Expend...	91f	229.2	240.9	250.3	260.3	274.6	284.5	300.5	312.1	323.3	343.3	358.5	371.8
Gross Fixed Capital Formation	93e	159.0	154.3	167.0	187.9	196.8	218.8	238.3	238.8	256.3	269.2	280.9	277.8
Changes in Inventories	93i	−.2	−7.9	1.6	9.3	2.5	11.2	10.1	−.5	12.6	3.1	2.5	−1.6
Exports of Goods and Services	90c	324.2	318.6	342.6	357.5	379.4	406.9	413.4	460.2	564.0	592.1	603.3	606.8
Imports of Goods and Services (−)	98c	265.6	257.3	291.0	316.1	327.2	367.7	390.1	402.4	487.8	506.5	526.4	515.0
Gross Domestic Product (GDP)	99b	887.9	900.2	965.7	1,009.8	1,060.9	1,116.3	1,155.4	1,207.7	1,279.0	1,325.5	1,360.7	1,398.3
Net Primary Income from Abroad	98.n	−22.3	−16.0	−16.0	−12.7	−14.0	−16.0	−12.1	−10.1	−26.8	−18.3	−20.7	−19.4
Gross National Income (GNI)	99a	865.5	884.2	949.7	997.1	1,046.9	1,100.3	1,143.3	1,197.7	1,252.1	1,307.2	1,340.0	1,378.9
Net Current Transf.from Abroad	98t	−17.3	−20.1	−20.8	−21.5	−22.8	−18.7	−21.4	−26.6	−30.7	−26.7	−28.6	−32.0
Gross Nat'l Disposable Inc.(GNDI)	99i	848.3	864.1	928.9	975.6	1,024.1	1,081.6	1,121.9	1,171.1	1,221.4	1,280.5	1,311.4	1,346.9
Gross Saving	99s	179.9	173.0	184.8	205.8	216.3	236.2	240.1	259.5	287.6	312.7	311.0	315.9
Consumption of Fixed Capital	99cf	141.9	143.5	146.0	152.1	168.8	177.4	183.3	189.7	199.6	211.3	218.5	222.2
GDP Volume 1995 Prices	99b.p	931.8	931.8	982.7	1,009.8	1,035.2	1,065.9	1,092.2	1,121.0	1,152.8	1,170.7	1,182.6	1,188.6
GDP Volume (2000=100)	99bvp	80.8	80.8	85.2	87.6	89.8	92.5	94.7	97.2	100.0	101.6	102.6	103.1
GDP Deflator (2000=100)	99bip	85.9	87.1	88.6	90.1	92.4	94.4	95.3	97.1	100.0	102.1	103.7	106.0
							Millions: Midyear Estimates						
Population	99z	5.17	5.19	5.21	5.23	5.25	5.27	5.29	5.31	5.32	5.34	5.35	5.36

2004, International Monetary Fund : *International Financial Statistics Yearbook*

Djibouti 611

		1992	1993	1994	1995	1996	1997	1998	1999	2000	2001	2002	2003
Exchange Rates						*Francs per SDR: End of Period (aa)*							
Official Rate	aa	244.37	244.11	259.45	264.18	255.56	239.79	250.24	243.92	231.55	223.35	241.62	264.09
						Francs per US Dollar: End of Period (ae) Period Average (rf)							
Official Rate	ae	177.72	177.72	177.72	177.72	177.72	177.72	177.72	177.72	177.72	177.72	177.72	177.72
Official Rate	rf	177.72	177.72	177.72	177.72	177.72	177.72	177.72	177.72	177.72	177.72	177.72	177.72
Fund Position						*Millions of SDRs: End of Period*							
Quota	2f.s	11.50	11.50	11.50	11.50	11.50	11.50	11.50	15.90	15.90	15.90	15.90	15.90
SDRs	1b.s	.15	.15	.11	.06	.10	.55	.27	.06	.28	.10	.76	.09
Reserve Position in the Fund	1c.s	2.11	–	–	–	–	–	–	1.10	1.10	1.10	1.10	1.10
Total Fund Cred.&Loans Outstg	2tl	–	–	–	–	2.88	3.98	6.30	9.28	10.29	12.32	15.06	13.75
International Liquidity						*Millions of US Dollars Unless Otherwise Indicated: End of Period*							
Total Reserves minus Gold	1l.d	83.40	75.10	73.76	72.16	76.97	66.57	66.45	70.61	67.80	70.31	73.71	100.13
SDRs	1b.d	.21	.21	.16	.09	.15	.75	.38	.09	.36	.13	1.03	.14
Reserve Position in the Fund	1c.d	2.90	–	–	–	–	–	–	1.51	1.43	1.38	1.50	1.63
Foreign Exchange	1d.d	80.29	74.89	73.60	72.07	76.82	65.82	66.07	69.01	66.01	68.80	71.18	98.36
Deposit Money Banks: Assets	7a.d	200.09	219.26	211.53	209.96	173.31	167.22	169.95	178.25	166.03	201.85	251.41	296.17
Liabilities	7b.d	84.45	84.81	88.65	91.10	89.01	83.33	88.47	45.30	50.12	38.75	43.04	36.37
Other Banking Insts.: Liabilities	7f.d	3.62	4.01	3.43	3.21	3.26	....	....	....	....	....	....	....
Monetary Authorities						*Millions of Francs: End of Period*							
Foreign Assets	11	14,822	13,347	13,990	12,688	13,683	12,064	11,518	12,507	12,051	12,498	13,215	17,915
Claims on Central Government	12a	–	307	534	534	1,275	1,487	2,176	2,928	2,832	3,234	3,177	4,331
Claims on Deposit Money Banks	12e	39	40	40	42	44	44	44	–	–	–	–	–
Reserve Money	14	12,187	11,250	11,869	10,370	9,989	9,783	9,588	10,011	9,932	10,467	11,409	14,965
of which: Currency Outside DMBs	14a	11,331	10,401	10,693	9,367	9,686	9,450	9,112	9,289	9,207	9,370	10,188	11,113
Central Government Deposits	16d	114	716	797	1,074	284	106	676	1,152	514	319	115	792
Capital Accounts	17a	1,436	1,425	1,390	1,712	1,729	1,872	2,361	2,537	2,713	2,786	2,807	2,834
Other Items (Net)	17r	1,124	303	511	108	3,000	1,889	1,125	1,735	1,724	2,161	2,062	3,656
Deposit Money Banks						*Millions of Francs: End of Period*							
Reserves	20	868	925	1,148	1,065	638	778	575	743	718	1,056	1,221	3,854
Foreign Assets	21	35,561	38,967	37,594	37,314	30,801	29,719	30,204	31,679	29,507	35,873	44,681	52,636
Claims on Central Government	22a	–	446	2,525	2,144	1,569	1,678	724	214	111	74	1,478	1,318
Claims on Nonfin.Pub.Enterprises	22c	444	483	419	464	599	778	2,115	2,309	1,540	1,758	1,374	1,259
Claims on Private Sector	22d	34,712	32,057	33,382	37,783	38,826	38,469	42,098	27,491	31,413	26,898	25,629	24,967
Demand Deposits	24	21,595	22,209	21,814	21,157	18,738	17,506	20,146	20,985	18,704	19,275	25,327	31,737
Time Deposits	25	22,986	22,094	23,030	26,841	23,185	23,943	24,845	21,747	24,697	27,924	29,922	34,207
Foreign Liabilities	26c	15,008	15,073	15,755	16,191	15,819	14,810	15,723	8,051	8,908	6,886	7,650	6,464
Central Government Deposits	26d	929	925	2,089	727	568	605	877	233	87	31	3	12
Credit From Monetary Authorities	26g	39	40	40	40	52	406	40	–	–	–	–	–
Capital Accounts	27a	7,466	8,082	9,854	10,051	10,053	9,609	9,814	8,730	7,550	7,646	7,676	7,643
Other Items (Net)	27r	3,562	4,456	2,485	3,763	4,021	4,544	4,271	2,690	3,342	3,896	3,804	3,970
Monetary Survey						*Millions of Francs: End of Period*							
Foreign Assets (Net)	31n	35,358	37,222	35,815	33,794	27,904	25,959	24,336	33,720	29,979	38,410	47,230	59,918
Domestic Credit	32	36,168	35,446	39,075	45,598	48,918	47,223	45,560	31,557	35,295	31,614	31,540	31,071
Claims on Central Govt. (Net)	32an	739	2,158	5,180	7,233	9,384	7,873	1,347	1,757	2,342	2,958	4,537	4,845
Claims on Nonfin.Pub.Enterprises	32c	444	483	419	464	599	778	2,115	2,309	1,540	1,758	1,374	1,259
Claims on Private Sector	32d	34,985	32,805	33,476	37,901	38,935	38,572	42,098	27,491	31,413	26,898	25,629	24,967
Money	34	34,981	36,404	37,608	36,998	35,925	32,478	29,258	30,274	27,911	28,645	35,515	42,850
Quasi-Money	35	22,986	22,094	23,030	26,841	23,185	23,943	24,845	21,747	24,697	27,924	29,922	34,207
Other Items (Net)	37r	13,559	14,171	14,254	15,553	17,715	16,817	15,805	13,256	12,665	13,455	13,333	13,932
Money plus Quasi-Money	35l	57,967	58,498	60,638	63,839	59,110	56,421	54,103	52,021	52,608	56,569	65,437	77,057
Other Banking Institutions						*Millions of Francs: End of Period*							
Reserves	40	251	261	167	80	30	....	....	....	....	....	....	....
Claims on Private Sector	42d	4,202	4,472	4,277	4,126	3,537	....	....	....	....	....	....	....
Long-Term Foreign Liabilities	46cl	644	712	610	570	580	....	....	....	....	....	....	....
Central Govt. Lending Funds	46f	1,999	1,788	1,542	1,533	1,180	....	....	....	....	....	....	....
Capital Accounts	47a	1,529	1,557	1,557	1,817	1,696	....	....	....	....	....	....	....
Other Items (Net)	47r	281	676	735	286	111	....	....	....	....	....	....	....
Interest Rates						*Percent Per Annum*							
Deposit Rate	60l	....	....	....	....	....	....	....	....	....	2.81	1.23	.82
Lending Rate	60p	....	....	....	....	....	....	....	....	....	11.46	11.30	11.30
International Transactions						*Millions of Francs*							
Exports	70	2,800	2,151	2,151	2,414	2,439	1,917	2,195	2,168	....	....	....	....
Imports	71	38,860	37,499	34,908	31,395	31,805	26,322	28,120	27,131	....	....	....	....
						1995=100							
Volume of Imports	73	95.5	115.7	107.0	100.0	90.8	75.9	88.2	99.3	....	....	....	....
Import Prices	76.x	125.5	101.4	100.6	100.0	110.5	102.1	103.8	95.3	....	....	....	....

Djibouti 611

		1992	1993	1994	1995	1996	1997	1998	1999	2000	2001	2002	2003
Balance of Payments		*Millions of US Dollars: Minus Sign Indicates Debit*
Current Account, n.i.e.	78ald	−87.5	−34.3	−46.1	−23.0	....	....	....	....	....	....	....	....
Goods: Exports f.o.b.	78aad	53.2	71.2	56.4	33.5	....	....	....	....	....	....	....	....
Goods: Imports f.o.b.	78abd	−271.0	−255.1	−237.1	−205.0	....	....	....	....	....	....	....	....
Trade Balance	78acd	−217.8	−183.9	−180.7	−171.5	....	....	....	....	....	....	....	....
Services: Credit	78add	145.1	156.9	152.3	151.4	....	....	....	....	....	....	....	....
Services: Debit	78aed	−109.3	−110.8	−89.7	−87.2	....	....	....	....	....	....	....	....
Balance on Goods & Services	78afd	−182.0	−137.8	−118.1	−107.3	....	....	....	....	....	....	....	....
Income: Credit	78agd	29.4	30.3	23.7	25.9	....	....	....	....	....	....	....	....
Income: Debit	78ahd	−9.4	−7.2	−7.0	−8.7	....	....	....	....	....	....	....	....
Balance on Gds, Serv. & Inc.	78aid	−162.0	−114.8	−101.4	−90.0	....	....	....	....	....	....	....	....
Current Transfers, n.i.e.: Credit	78ajd	90.7	96.6	73.7	85.4	....	....	....	....	....	....	....	....
Current Transfers: Debit	78akd	−16.3	−16.1	−18.3	−18.4	....	....	....	....	....	....	....	....
Capital Account, n.i.e.	78bcd	−	−	−	−	....	....	....	....	....	....	....	....
Capital Account, n.i.e.: Credit	78bad	−	−	−	−	....	....	....	....	....	....	....	....
Capital Account: Debit	78bbd	−	−	−	−	....	....	....	....	....	....	....	....
Financial Account, n.i.e.	78bjd	74.0	16.6	39.0	−2.1	....	....	....	....	....	....	....	....
Direct Investment Abroad	78bdd	−	−	−	−	....	....	....	....	....	....	....	....
Dir. Invest. in Rep. Econ., n.i.e.	78bed	2.3	1.4	1.4	3.2	....	....	....	....	....	....	....	....
Portfolio Investment Assets	78bfd	−	−	−	−	....	....	....	....	....	....	....	....
Equity Securities	78bkd	−	−	−	−	....	....	....	....	....	....	....	....
Debt Securities	78bld	−	−	−	−	....	....	....	....	....	....	....	....
Portfolio Investment Liab., n.i.e.	78bgd	−	−	−	−	....	....	....	....	....	....	....	....
Equity Securities	78bmd	−	−	−	−	....	....	....	....	....	....	....	....
Debt Securities	78bnd	−	−	−	−	....	....	....	....	....	....	....	....
Financial Derivatives Assets	78bwd	....	....	....	....	....	....	....	....	....	....	....	....
Financial Derivatives Liabilities	78bxd	....	....	....	....	....	....	....	....	....	....	....	....
Other Investment Assets	78bhd	−	−	−	−	....	....	....	....	....	....	....	....
Monetary Authorities	78bod	....	....	....	....	....	....	....	....	....	....	....	....
General Government	78bpd	−	−	−	−	....	....	....	....	....	....	....	....
Banks	78bqd	−	−	−	−	....	....	....	....	....	....	....	....
Other Sectors	78brd	−	−	−	−	....	....	....	....	....	....	....	....
Other Investment Liab., n.i.e.	78bid	71.7	15.2	37.6	−5.4	....	....	....	....	....	....	....	....
Monetary Authorities	78bsd	−	−	−	−	....	....	....	....	....	....	....	....
General Government	78btd	8.1	15.9	12.0	−9.4	....	....	....	....	....	....	....	....
Banks	78bud	37.6	−18.8	11.6	4.0	....	....	....	....	....	....	....	....
Other Sectors	78bvd	26.0	18.1	14.1	.1	....	....	....	....	....	....	....	....
Net Errors and Omissions	78cad	−2.0	6.0	7.9	.7	....	....	....	....	....	....	....	....
Overall Balance	78cbd	−15.5	−11.7	.8	−24.5	....	....	....	....	....	....	....	....
Reserves and Related Items	79dad	15.5	11.7	−.8	24.5	....	....	....	....	....	....	....	....
Reserve Assets	79dbd	15.5	11.3	−3.4	7.3	....	....	....	....	....	....	....	....
Use of Fund Credit and Loans	79dcd	−	−	−	−	....	....	....	....	....	....	....	....
Exceptional Financing	79ded	−	.4	2.6	17.2	....	....	....	....	....	....	....	....
		Millions: Midyear Estimates
Population	99z	.55	.55	.56	.57	.58	.60	.63	.65	.67	.68	.69	.70

2004, International Monetary Fund : *International Financial Statistics Yearbook*

Dominica 321

		1992	1993	1994	1995	1996	1997	1998	1999	2000	2001	2002	2003
Exchange Rates		E.Caribbean Dollars per SDR: End of Period (aa) E.Caribbean Dollars per US Dollar: End of Period (ae)
Official Rate	aa	3.7125	3.7086	3.9416	4.0135	3.8825	3.6430	3.8017	3.7058	3.5179	3.3932	3.6707	4.0121
Official Rate	ae	2.7000	2.7000	2.7000	2.7000	2.7000	2.7000	2.7000	2.7000	2.7000	2.7000	2.7000	2.7000
		Index Numbers (2000=100): Period Averages
Nominal Effective Exchange Rate	nec	76.19	83.09	87.09	84.46	86.93	91.96	97.54	96.64	100.00	104.62	103.36	96.72
Real Effective Exchange Rate	rec	94.32	96.98	93.53	88.06	89.26	94.09	98.67	97.77	100.00	103.29	100.66	93.98
Fund Position		Millions of SDRs: End of Period
Quota	2f.s	6.00	6.00	6.00	6.00	6.00	6.00	6.00	8.20	8.20	8.20	8.20	8.20
SDRs	1b.s	.07	—	—	—	—	—	—	.01	—	—	—	—
Reserve Position in the Fund	1c.s	.01	.01	.01	.01	.01	.01	.01	.01	.01	.01	.01	.01
Total Fund Cred.&Loans Outstg	2tl	2.78	2.26	1.71	1.15	.59	.19	.03	—	—	—	2.05	5.33
International Liquidity		Millions of US Dollars Unless Otherwise Indicated: End of Period
Total Reserves minus Gold	1l.d	20.41	19.92	15.41	22.12	22.89	23.89	27.67	31.57	29.37	31.22	45.50	47.74
SDRs	1b.d	.10	—	—	—	—	—	—	.01	—	—	—	—
Reserve Position in the Fund	1c.d	.01	.01	.01	.01	.01	.01	.01	.01	.01	.01	.01	.01
Foreign Exchange	1d.d	20.30	19.90	15.40	22.11	22.88	23.88	27.65	31.55	29.36	31.21	45.48	47.72
Monetary Authorities: Other Liab.	4..d	—	—	—	—	—	—	—	—	—	—	—	—
Deposit Money Banks: Assets	7a.d	28.13	24.13	26.62	28.14	38.81	43.08	51.84	60.28	44.68	51.24	77.01	101.93
Liabilities	7b.d	27.30	30.77	39.49	34.45	35.63	43.28	46.01	45.66	49.75	46.32	48.05	38.83
Monetary Authorities		Millions of E. Caribbean Dollars: End of Period
Foreign Assets	11	57.83	53.71	41.74	60.65	62.71	64.67	74.87	85.34	79.41	84.38	122.96	129.09
Claims on Central Government	12a	27.85	24.04	26.16	19.74	14.78	13.31	11.30	11.07	11.41	10.71	17.09	30.51
Claims on Deposit Money Banks	12e	.02	.37	2.04	.01	.01	.03	.03	.01	3.92	.01	.02	.01
Reserve Money	14	75.37	69.74	63.21	74.20	73.69	75.76	84.55	95.02	92.46	91.69	130.64	126.16
of which: Currency Outside DMBs	14a	31.13	27.85	24.49	29.16	28.53	28.21	29.13	34.09	35.45	34.61	35.51	34.18
Foreign Liabilities	16c	10.32	8.38	6.72	4.60	2.28	.68	.10	—	—	—	7.52	21.39
Central Government Deposits	16d	—	—	—	.79	.72	.75	.74	.57	1.46	2.56	1.08	11.24
Other Items (Net)	17r	—	—	—	.82	.82	.82	.82	.82	.82	.86	.83	.83
Deposit Money Banks		Millions of E. Caribbean Dollars: End of Period
Reserves	20	41.68	42.78	33.46	45.86	46.52	44.93	56.16	68.92	56.53	58.48	98.16	85.59
Foreign Assets	21	75.95	65.16	71.88	75.98	104.78	116.31	139.96	162.76	120.63	138.34	207.93	275.20
Claims on Central Government	22a	42.17	53.46	66.56	77.86	79.34	87.40	87.73	94.14	102.78	110.20	103.78	91.55
Claims on Local Government	22b	.01	.05	.23	.17	.17	.12	.09	.06	.05	.02	.01	.02
Claims on Nonfin.Pub.Enterprises	22c	21.40	26.40	29.07	29.13	19.27	21.77	23.05	24.25	27.82	24.29	23.37	22.21
Claims on Private Sector	22d	263.99	289.57	312.48	344.63	358.48	386.35	409.97	419.77	454.09	439.58	433.34	420.62
Claims on Nonbank Financial Insts	22g	1.62	1.29	.42	.46	1.57	1.48	1.52	1.22	3.11	2.86	2.05	2.39
Demand Deposits	24	59.47	51.27	50.66	60.67	63.94	66.18	70.60	94.56	67.69	70.63	96.06	97.23
Time, Savings,& Fgn.Currency Dep	25	241.38	244.57	260.18	319.00	342.74	358.88	379.83	398.90	413.50	444.86	474.59	513.27
Foreign Liabilities	26c	73.71	83.08	106.61	93.02	96.20	116.85	124.23	123.29	134.32	125.06	129.72	104.85
Central Government Deposits	26d	29.81	43.14	57.29	56.21	48.45	61.70	70.32	65.29	57.56	38.84	69.12	82.54
Credit from Monetary Authorities	26g	—	9.68	2.00	—	—	—	2.80	.85	5.30	—	—	—
Capital Accounts	27a	36.79	40.92	45.93	49.60	51.31	50.39	51.60	62.70	67.02	78.37	76.55	80.81
Other Items (Net)	27r	5.67	6.06	−8.56	−4.49	7.50	4.36	19.10	25.53	19.61	16.02	22.60	18.89
Monetary Survey		Millions of E. Caribbean Dollars: End of Period
Foreign Assets (Net)	31n	49.75	27.42	.29	39.01	69.01	63.65	90.50	124.81	65.72	97.67	193.64	278.06
Domestic Credit	32	327.23	351.67	377.63	415.00	424.45	447.99	462.60	484.64	540.23	546.28	509.44	473.52
Claims on Central Govt. (Net)	32an	40.21	34.36	35.44	40.60	44.95	38.27	27.97	39.34	55.17	79.53	50.67	28.28
Claims on Local Government	32b	.01	.05	.23	.17	.17	.12	.09	.06	.05	.02	.01	.02
Claims on Nonfin.Pub.Enterprises	32c	21.40	26.40	29.07	29.13	19.27	21.77	23.05	24.25	27.82	24.29	23.37	22.21
Claims on Private Sector	32d	263.99	289.57	312.48	344.63	358.48	386.35	409.97	419.77	454.09	439.58	433.34	420.62
Claims on Nonbank Financial Inst.	32g	1.62	1.29	.42	.46	1.57	1.48	1.52	1.22	3.11	2.86	2.05	2.39
Money	34	90.72	79.19	75.23	89.97	92.73	94.45	99.89	128.92	103.23	105.32	131.64	131.54
Quasi-Money	35	241.38	244.57	260.18	319.90	343.56	359.70	380.64	399.72	414.32	445.72	475.42	514.10
Capital Accounts	37a	38.98	43.10	48.26	51.97	53.61	52.55	53.86	64.89	69.11	80.38	78.72	83.19
Other Items (Net)	37r	5.90	12.22	−5.75	−7.83	3.57	4.74	18.71	15.92	19.30	12.52	17.31	22.75
Money plus Quasi-Money	35l	332.09	323.76	335.41	409.87	436.29	454.14	480.54	528.64	517.54	551.04	607.06	645.64
Money (National Definitions)		Millions of E. Caribbean Dollars: End of Period
M1	39ma	71.69	64.58	62.29	72.88	71.43	74.70	85.45	106.82	90.33	91.58	106.65	107.88
M2	39mb	297.26	281.94	293.30	361.01	368.10	380.95	424.32	468.30	471.05	505.99	549.25	554.47
Interest Rates		Percent Per Annum
Discount Rate (End of Period)	60	....	....	9.00	9.00	9.00	8.00	8.00	8.00	8.00	7.00	7.00	6.50
Money Market Rate	60b	5.25	5.25	5.25	5.25	5.25	5.25	5.25	5.25	5.25	†5.64	6.32	6.07
Treasury Bill Rate	60c	6.48	6.40	6.40	6.40	6.40	6.40	6.40	6.40	6.40	6.40	6.40	6.40
Savings Rate	60k	6.08	5.00	5.46	5.50	5.50	5.50	5.50	5.50	5.50	5.50	5.00	†3.38
Deposit Rate	60l	3.96	4.19	4.50	4.20	4.30	4.27	4.23	4.38	3.87	3.98	3.91	3.66
Lending Rate	60p	11.52	11.92	11.61	11.50	11.43	11.17	11.27	11.40	11.68	11.14	10.97	11.50

Dominica 321

		1992	1993	1994	1995	1996	1997	1998	1999	2000	2001	2002	2003
Prices		\multicolumn{12}{c}{*Index Numbers (2000=100): Period Averages*}
Consumer Prices	64	90.5	91.9	91.9	93.1	94.7	97.0	†98.0	99.2	100.0	101.5	101.8	103.3
International Transactions		\multicolumn{12}{c}{*Millions of E. Caribbean Dollars*}
Exports	70	144.35	131.67	127.30	121.81	138.46	143.01	167.45	150.45	144.67	117.17	113.01	105.37
Imports, c.i.f.	71	284.69	252.99	260.10	316.66	350.85	336.31	356.99	373.23	400.24	353.84	311.36	339.04
Balance of Payments		\multicolumn{12}{c}{*Millions of US Dollars: Minus Sign Indicates Debit*}
Current Account, n.i.e.	78ald	−27.12	−27.48	−37.55	−40.73	−51.16	−42.25	−23.01	−35.88	−53.53	−48.86	....	....
Goods: Exports f.o.b.	78aad	55.31	49.29	48.33	50.27	52.91	53.77	63.19	56.01	54.75	44.40	....	....
Goods: Imports f.o.b.	78abd	−92.79	−91.96	−95.76	−103.21	−117.20	−118.71	−116.35	−121.57	−130.39	−115.29	....	....
Trade Balance	78acd	−37.48	−42.68	−47.43	−52.94	−64.29	−64.94	−53.16	−65.56	−75.64	−70.89	....	....
Services: Credit	78add	42.36	48.54	51.59	61.36	68.94	83.39	88.41	100.79	89.74	75.75	....	....
Services: Debit	78aed	−32.21	−35.66	−37.76	−43.72	−47.17	−54.14	−55.31	−59.03	−52.69	−51.65	....	....
Balance on Goods & Services	78afd	−27.33	−29.80	−33.60	−35.30	−42.53	−35.70	−20.06	−23.79	−38.59	−46.79	....	....
Income: Credit	78agd	2.50	2.97	3.08	3.29	2.85	3.60	4.65	4.63	4.67	3.64	....	....
Income: Debit	78ahd	−9.78	−9.34	−14.10	−16.59	−21.66	−20.51	−20.34	−30.27	−37.68	−23.18	....	....
Balance on Gds, Serv. & Inc	78aid	−34.61	−36.18	−44.62	−48.59	−61.33	−52.61	−35.75	−49.44	−71.59	−66.33	....	....
Current Transfers, n.i.e.: Credit	78ajd	10.87	12.42	14.86	16.26	17.83	17.44	19.92	20.46	25.09	24.77	....	....
Current Transfers: Debit	78akd	−3.38	−3.72	−7.79	−8.39	−7.66	−7.09	−7.18	−6.90	−7.02	−7.30	....	....
Capital Account, n.i.e.	78bcd	9.80	9.72	6.90	24.54	25.30	22.52	14.75	11.76	8.18	17.97	....	....
Capital Account, n.i.e.: Credit	78bad	11.28	11.20	9.37	24.65	25.42	22.64	14.87	12.06	9.70	18.10	....	....
Capital Account: Debit	78bbd	−1.48	−1.48	−2.47	−.11	−.12	−.12	−.13	−.30	−1.52	−.13	....	....
Financial Account, n.i.e.	78bjd	22.28	19.65	30.00	42.15	6.10	25.83	−1.70	37.29	46.43	27.51	....	....
Direct Investment Abroad	78bdd	−	−	−	−	−	−	−	−	−	−	....	....
Dir. Invest. in Rep. Econ., n.i.e.	78bed	20.41	13.20	22.60	54.09	17.80	21.11	6.51	17.96	10.82	11.90	....	....
Portfolio Investment Assets	78bfd	−	−	.01	−7.96	−	−	−	−1.70	−.40	.01	....	....
Equity Securities	78bkd	....	....	....	....	....	....	....	....	....	....	....	....
Debt Securities	78bld	....	....	....	....	....	....	....	....	....	....	....	....
Portfolio Investment Liab., n.i.e.	78bgd	−	−	−	−	.46	−.18	1.30	30.44	14.03	−.24	....	....
Equity Securities	78bmd	....	....	....	....	....	....	....	....	....	....	....	....
Debt Securities	78bnd	....	....	....	....	....	....	....	....	....	....	....	....
Financial Derivatives Assets	78bwd	....	....	....	....	....	....	....	....	....	....	....	....
Financial Derivatives Liabilities	78bxd	....	....	....	....	....	....	....	....	....	....	....	....
Other Investment Assets	78bhd	−6.61	2.10	−4.31	−3.60	−5.79	−3.01	−5.37	−3.92	−10.42	−5.03	....	....
Monetary Authorities	78bod	....	....	....	....	....	....	....	....	....	....	....	....
General Government	78bpd	....	....	....	....	....	....	....	....	....	....	....	....
Banks	78bqd	....	....	....	....	....	....	....	....	....	....	....	....
Other Sectors	78brd	....	....	....	....	....	....	....	....	....	....	....	....
Other Investment Liab., n.i.e.	78bid	8.48	4.34	11.71	−.38	−6.37	7.90	−4.14	−5.49	32.40	20.88	....	....
Monetary Authorities	78bsd	−	−	−	−	−	−	−	−	−	−	....	....
General Government	78btd	....	....	....	....	....	....	....	....	....	....	....	....
Banks	78bud	....	....	....	....	....	....	....	....	....	....	....	....
Other Sectors	78bvd	....	....	....	....	....	....	....	....	....	....	....	....
Net Errors and Omissions	78cad	−1.59	−.97	−2.71	−17.62	21.99	−5.46	13.51	−2.14	−.60	7.91	....	....
Overall Balance	78cbd	3.36	.92	−3.35	8.34	2.24	.64	3.54	11.03	.48	4.54	....	....
Reserves and Related Items	79dad	−3.36	−.92	3.35	−8.34	−2.24	−.64	−3.54	−11.03	−.48	−4.54	....	....
Reserve Assets	79dbd	−2.60	−.19	4.15	−7.48	−1.43	−.09	−3.32	−10.99	−.48	−4.54	....	....
Use of Fund Credit and Loans	79dcd	−.76	−.73	−.80	−.86	−.81	−.55	−.22	−.04	−	−	....	....
Exceptional Financing	79ded	....	....	....	....	....	....	....	....	....	....	....	....
National Accounts		\multicolumn{12}{c}{*Millions of E. Caribbean Dollars*}
Househ.Cons.Expend.,incl.NPISHs	96f	336.7	358.5	404.9	381.4	440.2	407.5	412.2	427.6	470.3	513.3	476.8	....
Government Consumption Expend	91f	103.2	112.2	117.4	123.2	128.9	143.1	153.0	159.3	160.6	152.8	147.3	....
Gross Fixed Capital Formation	93e	146.9	137.8	148.4	186.4	183.6	207.4	190.9	200.3	205.4	171.8	151.2	....
Exports of Goods and Services	90c	269.1	262.8	272.2	301.4	329.0	370.3	409.3	423.4	390.1	326.9	317.0	....
Imports of Goods and Services (−)	98c	338.1	330.2	365.1	396.7	443.8	466.7	464.9	487.6	494.3	450.9	407.2	....
Gross Domestic Product (GDP)	99b	517.8	541.1	577.8	595.6	637.9	661.6	700.5	722.8	732.2	713.9	685.2	....
Net Primary Income from Abroad	98.n	−19.9	−17.2	−29.8	−35.9	−50.8	−45.7	−41.1	−69.1	−97.0	−65.4	−69.8	....
Gross National Income (GNI)	99a	497.9	523.9	548.0	559.7	587.1	616.0	659.4	653.7	635.1	648.5	615.4	....
Net Current Transf.from Abroad	98t	20.2	23.5	19.1	21.2	27.5	28.0	34.4	36.6	48.8	47.2	48.4	....
Gross Nat'l Disposable Inc.(GNDI)	99i	518.1	547.4	567.1	581.0	614.5	643.9	693.8	690.3	683.9	695.7	663.9	....
Gross Saving	99s	78.3	76.7	44.8	76.4	45.5	93.3	128.6	103.5	53.0	29.6	39.7	....
GDP Volume 1990 Prices	99b.p	470.0	468.8	475.5	484.9	501.9	514.5	530.7	534.1	534.9	512.0	....	....
GDP Volume (2000=100)	99bvp	87.9	87.6	88.9	90.7	93.8	96.2	99.2	99.9	100.0	95.7	....	....
GDP Deflator (2000=100)	99bip	80.5	84.3	88.8	89.7	92.8	93.9	96.4	98.9	100.0	101.9	....	....
		\multicolumn{12}{c}{*Millions: Midyear Estimates*}
Population	99z	.07	.07	.07	.08	.08	.08	.08	Ü .08	.08	.08	.08	.08

2004, International Monetary Fund : *International Financial Statistics Yearbook*

Dominican Republic 243

		1992	1993	1994	1995	1996	1997	1998	1999	2000	2001	2002	2003
Exchange Rates						*Pesos per SDR: End of Period*							
Market Rate...........aa=	wa	17.291	17.536	19.071	20.015	20.220	19.383	22.230	22.014	21.725	21.551	28.813	55.352
					Pesos per US Dollar: End of Period (we) Period Average (wf)								
Market Rate...........ae=	we	12.575	12.767	13.064	13.465	14.062	14.366	15.788	16.039	16.674	17.149	21.194	37.250
Market Rate...........rf=	wf	12.774	12.676	13.160	13.597	13.775	14.265	15.267	16.033	16.415	16.952	18.610	30.831
					Index Numbers (2000=100): Period Averages								
Market Rate	ahx	128.5	129.5	124.7	120.7	119.2	115.0	107.3	102.4	100.0	96.8	88.6	55.2
Nominal Effective Exchange Rate	nec	97.1	106.4	114.2	109.4	109.7	108.9	105.3	99.7	100.0	100.1	92.2	56.0
Real Effective Exchange Rate	rec	80.5	84.0	87.8	90.4	92.3	96.7	96.1	95.2	100.0	106.3	101.1	74.7
Fund Position						*Millions of SDRs: End of Period*							
Quota	2f.s	158.8	158.8	158.8	158.8	158.8	158.8	158.8	218.9	218.9	218.9	218.9	218.9
SDRs	1b.s	.1	10.3	2.5	.3	.3	.2	.2	.2	.3	.3	.2	.1
Reserve Position in the Fund	1c.s	–	–	–	–	–	–	–	–	–	–	–	–
Total Fund Cred.&Loans Outstg.	2tl	89.4	135.5	129.9	107.5	66.5	21.1	39.7	39.7	39.7	39.7	19.9	87.6
International Liquidity					*Millions of US Dollars Unless Otherwise Indicated: End of Period*								
Total Reserves minus Gold	1l.d	499.8	651.2	252.1	365.6	350.3	391.0	501.9	694.0	627.2	1,099.5	468.4	253.1
SDRs	1b.d	.1	14.1	3.7	.5	.4	.3	.3	.3	.4	.4	.3	.1
Reserve Position in the Fund	1c.d	–	–	–	–	–	–	–	–	–	–	–	–
Foreign Exchange	1d.d	499.7	637.1	248.4	365.0	349.8	390.7	501.6	693.7	626.8	1,099.0	468.1	253.0
Gold (Million Fine Troy Ounces)	1ad	.018	.018	.018	.018	.018	.018	.018	.018	.018	.018	.018	.018
Gold (National Valuation)	1and	6.1	6.9	6.8	6.8	6.7	5.5	5.3	5.2	5.0	5.1	5.2	7.6
Monetary Authorities: Other Liab.	4..d	1,277.2	1,259.3	916.0	967.7	975.1	938.2	881.2	865.5	879.3	838.7	668.0	643.6
Deposit Money Banks: Assets	7a.d	232.5	191.8	189.4	183.8	174.5	236.7	307.0	322.5	416.4	527.0	515.5	648.8
Liabilities	7b.d	218.2	184.0	183.3	55.0	97.6	188.6	401.4	458.9	739.3	684.5	924.5	517.1
Other Banking Insts.: Liabilities	7f.d	49.3	62.7	91.2	8.4	10.9	6.3	17.2	22.7	24.3	27.2	36.5	26.9
Monetary Authorities						*Millions of Pesos: End of Period*							
Foreign Assets	11	7,128	9,008	4,804	6,577	6,962	7,696	10,071	13,599	13,128	22,364	13,208	15,926
Claims on Central Government	12a	1,953	938	558	605	1,236	1,537	1,632	2,416	4,026	4,023	4,631	75
Claims on Nonfin.Pub.Enterprises	12c	585	738	2,959	1,609	1,632	1,665	1,987	2,520	2,631	2,676	2,638	3,105
Claims on Private Sector	12d	550	550	45	45	45	45	5	5	2	1	–	–
Claims on Deposit Money Banks	12e	1,383	1,343	2,075	2,092	3,108	2,161	2,917	2,992	2,874	3,510	9,896	105,493
Claims on Other Banking Insts.	12f	1,087	923	292	307	320	388	384	375	345	347	231	36
Reserve Money	14	11,602	14,889	14,956	17,412	19,306	22,963	28,110	32,328	35,667	45,980	41,961	87,367
of which: Currency Outside DMBs	14a	5,913	6,905	7,679	8,892	9,635	11,534	12,568	16,889	15,076	16,628	18,265	29,631
Liabs.of Centl.Bank: Securities	16ac	518	196	743	1,991	4,099	4,357	3,499	5,135	4,369	3,276	6,905	60,008
Foreign Liabilities	16c	1,873	2,661	3,663	3,529	2,602	1,682	1,684	1,549	2,106	2,420	2,073	4,847
Long-Term Foreign Liabilities	16cl	15,734	15,793	10,780	11,652	12,454	12,205	13,110	13,207	13,418	12,818	12,656	23,973
Central Government Deposits	16d	2,308	2,179	151	344	400	351	424	479	414	1,838	834	4,113
Counterpart Funds	16e	–	–	–	–	–	–	–	–	–	–	–	–
Capital Accounts	17a	−17,126	−18,805	−16,906	−18,443	−20,241	−21,519	−23,395	−25,126	−26,960	−27,817	−28,456	−56,803
of which: Revaluation of Reserves	17rv	−17,627	−17,883	−16,415	−16,961	−17,326	−17,376	−17,872	−18,169	−18,315	−18,315	−18,632	–
Other Items (Net)	17r	−2,223	−3,412	−2,653	−5,249	−5,318	−6,547	−6,435	−5,665	−6,008	−5,594	−5,369	1,130
Deposit Money Banks						*Millions of Pesos: End of Period*							
Reserves	20	7,438	8,992	9,214	10,654	10,761	12,964	16,947	17,331	26,692	30,404	28,653	58,047
Claims on Mon.Author.:Securities	20c	28	15	180	914	2,264	2,118	675	1,443	215	26	2,121	19,758
Foreign Assets	21	2,924	2,449	2,474	2,475	2,453	3,400	4,846	5,172	6,943	9,037	10,925	24,167
Claims on Central Government	22a	465	371	540	505	536	1,934	1,998	4,144	4,813	11,678	14,091	17,386
Claims on Local Government	22b	3	5	6	29	4	6	4	14	29	32	1	142
Claims on Nonfin.Pub.Enterprises	22c	1,396	1,417	1,290	1,453	2,221	2,308	3,263	3,271	2,521	2,540	2,943	4,539
Claims on Private Sector	22d	15,806	19,442	22,166	27,688	34,500	44,404	52,744	66,877	82,120	101,941	123,242	165,620
Claims on Other Banking Insts.	22f	965	805	799	554	778	764	957	760	593	928	1,081	2,290
Demand Deposits	24	7,221	8,104	8,470	10,064	13,540	16,081	16,782	18,884	20,290	24,529	25,341	41,736
Time, Savings,& Fgn.Currency Dep.	25	13,322	17,092	19,854	23,458	27,022	34,725	43,380	54,211	70,282	92,908	104,184	169,315
Bonds	26ab	–	133	122	80	138	76	17	398	112	2	14	27
Foreign Liabilities	26c	2,743	2,349	2,394	740	1,372	2,710	6,337	7,361	12,328	11,738	19,594	19,261
Central Government Deposits	26d	2,774	2,568	1,746	2,533	2,594	3,076	2,500	3,578	3,192	6,566	6,076	7,268
Credit from Monetary Authorities	26g	1,103	902	1,334	1,310	1,220	1,532	2,222	2,449	2,931	3,226	7,971	72,091
Capital Accounts	27a	3,028	3,388	4,050	4,581	5,203	6,524	8,220	10,224	12,667	16,707	19,901	−9,773
Other Items (Net)	27r	−1,165	−1,042	−1,301	1,506	2,428	3,175	1,975	1,907	2,124	911	−26	−7,975

Dominican Republic 243

		1992	1993	1994	1995	1996	1997	1998	1999	2000	2001	2002	2003
Monetary Survey						*Millions of Pesos: End of Period*							
Foreign Assets (Net)...............	31n	5,435	6,447	1,221	4,784	5,441	6,704	6,896	9,862	5,638	17,242	2,465	15,985
Domestic Credit.....................	32	17,729	20,442	26,759	29,919	38,278	49,624	60,051	76,324	93,474	115,762	141,948	181,813
Claims on Central Govt. (Net)........	32an	−2,665	−3,438	−798	−1,766	−1,221	43	706	2,503	5,233	7,296	11,812	6,080
Claims on Local Government..........	32b	3	5	6	29	4	6	4	14	29	32	1	142
Claims on Nonfin.Pub.Enterprises...	32c	1,982	2,155	4,249	3,062	3,853	3,973	5,250	5,791	5,152	5,216	5,582	7,644
Claims on Private Sector................	32d	16,356	19,992	22,211	27,733	34,545	44,449	52,749	66,881	82,122	101,942	123,242	165,620
Claims on Other Banking Insts.......	32f	2,053	1,728	1,091	861	1,098	1,152	1,342	1,135	938	1,275	1,313	2,326
Money...................................	34	13,231	15,065	16,198	18,996	23,225	27,703	29,416	35,840	35,445	41,258	43,765	72,013
Quasi-Money..........................	35	13,322	17,092	19,854	23,458	27,022	34,725	43,380	54,211	70,282	92,908	104,184	169,315
Bonds....................................	36ab	–	133	122	80	138	76	17	398	112	2	14	27
Liabs.of Centl.Bank: Securities........	36ac	490	182	564	1,078	1,835	2,239	2,825	3,692	4,154	3,250	4,784	40,250
Long-Term Foreign Liabilities............	36cl	15,734	15,793	10,780	11,652	12,454	12,205	13,110	13,207	13,418	12,818	12,656	23,973
Capital Accounts........................	37a	−14,098	−15,416	−12,857	−13,863	−15,038	−14,996	−15,175	−14,902	−14,293	−11,111	−8,555	−66,576
Other Items (Net)......................	37r	−5,515	−5,959	−6,682	−6,698	−5,917	−5,625	−6,625	−6,259	−10,008	−6,121	−12,434	−41,205
Money plus Quasi-Money............	35l	26,553	32,157	36,052	42,454	50,247	62,428	72,795	90,051	105,727	134,166	147,948	241,328
Other Banking Institutions						*Millions of Pesos: End of Period*							
Reserves................................	40	415	316	329	332	353	429	483	796	951	1,037	1,315	3,072
Claims on Mon.Author.:Securities....	40c	–	–	–	–	–	1,080	1,153	1,483	1,596	1,772	3,781	4,532
Claims on Central Government........	42a	277	474	522	774	569	452	837	971	971	699	872	893
Claims on Nonfin.Pub.Enterprises.....	42c	11	10	12	19	18	18	19	19	19	28	31	30
Claims on Private Sector................	42d	10,088	10,365	12,263	12,513	13,797	16,324	19,797	24,375	30,407	34,552	36,922	43,819
Claims on Deposit Money Banks......	42e	2,589	3,388	2,358	3,097	3,674	3,223	4,216	4,950	6,149	10,353	6,776	8,843
Time, Savings,& Fgn.Currency Dep...	45	3,581	3,881	4,112	4,396	4,628	5,682	7,387	7,691	8,433	9,545	10,531	11,240
Bonds..................................	46ab	6,310	6,589	7,290	8,474	9,418	11,295	13,120	17,634	22,433	27,956	27,359	32,854
Long-Term Foreign Liabilities............	46cl	620	800	1,192	113	153	90	271	364	405	467	774	1,003
Credit from Monetary Authorities......	46g	1,216	1,641	1,623	1,464	1,434	1,360	1,298	1,112	1,118	1,092	931	921
Credit from Deposit Money Banks....	46h	354	429	424	460	478	457	539	458	513	495	569	584
Capital Accounts........................	47a	2,554	2,543	2,667	2,818	2,855	3,390	4,430	5,889	7,572	9,200	12,083	17,161
Other Items (Net)......................	47r	−1,256	−1,330	−1,824	−990	−558	−748	−542	−554	−380	−315	−2,550	−2,573
Banking Survey						*Millions of Pesos: End of Period*							
Foreign Assets (Net).................	51n	5,435	6,447	1,221	4,784	5,441	6,704	6,896	9,862	5,638	17,242	2,465	15,985
Domestic Credit......................	52	26,052	29,563	38,464	42,364	51,564	65,266	79,362	100,554	123,933	149,764	178,461	224,229
Claims on Central Govt. (Net)........	52an	−2,388	−2,964	−276	−992	−652	496	1,543	3,474	6,205	7,995	12,684	6,973
Claims on Local Government..........	52b	3	5	6	29	4	6	4	14	29	32	1	142
Claims on Nonfin.Pub.Enterprises...	52c	1,993	2,165	4,261	3,081	3,871	3,991	5,269	5,810	5,171	5,243	5,612	7,674
Claims on Private Sector................	52d	26,444	30,356	34,474	40,246	48,342	60,772	72,545	91,256	112,529	136,494	160,164	209,439
Liquid Liabilities......................	55l	29,719	35,722	39,835	46,518	54,522	67,681	79,699	96,946	113,209	142,674	157,164	249,496
Bonds...................................	56ab	6,310	6,722	7,412	8,554	9,556	11,371	13,137	18,032	22,545	27,958	27,373	32,881
Liabs.of Centl.Bank: Securities........	56ac	490	182	564	1,078	1,835	1,158	1,672	2,208	2,558	1,478	1,003	35,718
Long-Term Foreign Liabilities............	56cl	16,354	16,593	11,972	11,765	12,607	12,295	13,381	13,571	13,823	13,285	13,430	24,976
Capital Accounts.......................	57a	−11,545	−12,873	−10,190	−11,045	−12,182	−11,606	−10,745	−9,013	−6,720	−1,911	3,528	−49,415
Other Items (Net).....................	57r	−9,842	−10,335	−9,907	−9,721	−9,333	−8,931	−10,886	−11,327	−15,843	−16,478	−21,573	−53,442
Interest Rates						*Percent Per Annum*							
Money Market Rate................	60b	....	....	....	....	14.70	13.01	16.68	15.30	18.28	13.47	14.50	24.24
Savings Rate.........................	60k	5.58	5.00	4.87	4.66	5.00	4.74	4.51	4.54	4.29	4.29	4.30	4.26
Savings Rate (Foreign Currency)........	60k.f	....	....	....	....	4.67	4.29	3.62	3.58	4.16	4.00	3.81	3.83
Deposit Rate.........................	60l	16.70	14.04	13.70	14.94	13.91	13.40	17.65	16.07	17.65	15.61	16.54	20.50
Deposit Rate (Foreign Currency).......	60l.f					6.69	6.98	6.50	6.66	7.57	6.88	6.37	6.55
Lending Rate.........................	60p	28.34	29.89	28.68	30.68	23.73	21.01	25.64	25.05	26.80	24.26	26.06	31.39
Lending Rate (Foreign Currency).......	60p.f	....	....	....	....	13.87	12.75	11.95	11.73	11.56	11.17	10.27	10.58
Prices and Labor						*Index Numbers (2000=100): Period Averages*							
Consumer Prices....................	64	56.8	59.8	64.7	72.9	76.8	83.2	†87.2	92.8	100.0	108.9	114.6	146.0
						Number in Thousands: Period Averages							
Labor Force..........................	67d	....	....	....	3,008	2,920	3,594	....	....	....	....	....	....
Employment.........................	67e	2,406	2,417	2,401	2,401	2,523	2,652	....	....	....	....	....	....
Unemployment......................	67c	612	599	457	452	†506	504	....	....	....	....	....	....
Unemployment Rate (%)..........	67r	20.3	19.9	16.0	15.9	†16.7	15.9	....	....	....	....	....	....
International Transactions						*Millions of US Dollars*							
Exports...............................	70..d	562.4	511.0	644.0	872.1	945.5	1,017.4	880.2	805.2	966.2	804.8	833.7	1,040.7
Imports, f.o.b.......................	71.vd	2,174.6	2,118.4	2,991.7	3,164.2	3,580.7	4,192.0	4,896.6	5,206.8	6,416.1	5,936.9	6,037.3	5,265.8
						1995=100							
Volume of Exports..................	72	95	99	96	100	106	109	103	....	....	....	....	....
						1995=100: Indices of Unit Values in US Dollars							
Unit Value of Exports..............	74..d	90	69	88	100	101	105	82	....	....	....	....	....

2004, International Monetary Fund: *International Financial Statistics Yearbook*

Dominican Republic 243

		1992	1993	1994	1995	1996	1997	1998	1999	2000	2001	2002	2003
Balance of Payments		\multicolumn{12}{c}{*Millions of US Dollars: Minus Sign Indicates Debit*}
Current Account, n.i.e.	78ald	−707.9	−532.9	−283.0	−182.8	−212.7	−163.0	−338.4	−429.2	−1,026.5	−740.8	−797.9	867.1
Goods: Exports f.o.b.	78aad	562.5	3,211.0	3,452.5	3,779.5	4,052.8	4,613.7	4,980.5	5,136.7	5,736.7	5,276.3	5,165.0	5,439.4
Goods: Imports f.o.b.	78abd	−2,174.3	−4,654.2	−4,903.2	−5,170.4	−5,727.0	−6,608.7	−7,597.3	−8,041.1	−9,478.5	−8,779.3	−8,837.7	−7,883.4
Trade Balance	78acd	−1,611.8	−1,443.2	−1,450.7	−1,390.9	−1,674.2	−1,995.0	−2,616.8	−2,904.4	−3,741.8	−3,503.0	−3,672.7	−2,444.0
Services: Credit	78add	1,348.6	1,537.1	1,787.9	1,951.3	2,140.0	2,446.6	2,501.5	2,850.3	3,227.6	3,110.3	3,070.8	3,435.3
Services: Debit	78aed	−555.1	−823.8	−921.1	−966.4	−1,121.4	−1,171.3	−1,319.5	−1,248.0	−1,373.3	−1,283.9	−1,313.5	−1,216.1
Balance on Goods & Services	78afd	−818.3	−729.9	−583.9	−406.0	−655.6	−719.7	−1,434.8	−1,302.1	−1,887.5	−1,676.6	−1,915.4	−224.8
Income: Credit	78agd	54.7	103.6	101.4	128.1	130.3	140.4	168.2	218.3	299.7	271.2	300.4	343.7
Income: Debit	78ahd	−376.1	−800.6	−783.3	−897.1	−855.1	−935.8	−1,058.3	−1,193.2	−1,341.0	−1,362.9	−1,452.2	−1,587.3
Balance on Gds, Serv. & Inc.	78aid	−1,139.7	−1,426.9	−1,265.8	−1,175.0	−1,380.4	−1,515.1	−2,324.9	−2,277.0	−2,928.8	−2,768.3	−3,067.2	−1,468.4
Current Transfers, n.i.e.: Credit	78ajd	431.8	908.4	996.8	1,007.7	1,187.6	1,373.1	2,016.9	1,997.1	2,095.6	2,232.0	2,451.9	2,510.3
Current Transfers: Debit	78akd	−	−14.4	−14.0	−15.5	−19.9	−21.0	−30.4	−149.3	−193.3	−204.5	−182.6	−174.8
Capital Account, n.i.e.	78bcd	−	−	−	−	−	−	....	....	−	−	−	−
Capital Account, n.i.e.: Credit	78bad	−	−	−	−	−	−	....	....	−	−	−	−
Capital Account: Debit	78bbd	−	−	−	−	−	−	....	....	−	−	−	−
Financial Account, n.i.e.	78bjd	74.8	−226.6	368.0	253.6	64.1	447.6	688.1	1,061.0	1,596.6	1,707.4	383.0	−853.4
Direct Investment Abroad	78bdd						....	....	....	....			
Dir. Invest. in Rep. Econ., n.i.e.	78bed	179.7	189.3	206.8	414.3	96.5	420.6	699.8	1,337.8	952.9	1,079.1	916.8	309.9
Portfolio Investment Assets	78bfd	−	−	−38.9	−2.9	−7.3	−5.6	−17.5	−433.0	268.4	123.5	−14.0	−20.1
Equity Securities	78bkd	....	....	....	....	−4.0	−2.1	−13.7	−428.9	270.6	128.2	−2.5	−7.1
Debt Securities	78bld	....	....	−38.9	−2.9	−3.3	−3.5	−3.8	−4.1	−2.2	−4.7	−11.5	−13.0
Portfolio Investment Liab., n.i.e.	78bgd	....	....	....	....	....	−1.9	−3.8	−3.8	−3.9	480.2	−11.7	552.6
Equity Securities	78bmd	....	....	....	....	....	....	....	....	....	....	....	....
Debt Securities	78bnd	....	....	....	....	....	−1.9	−3.8	−3.8	−3.9	480.2	−11.7	552.6
Financial Derivatives Assets	78bwd	....	....	....	....	....	....	....	....	....	−	−	−
Financial Derivatives Liabilities	78bxd	....	....	....	....	....	....	....	....	....	−	−	−
Other Investment Assets	78bhd	128.8	−49.2	176.8	−263.1	42.3	−220.1	−66.4	−53.4	−165.0	−155.5	−1,402.2	−1,535.2
Monetary Authorities	78bod	....	....	−15.2	−.6	−.9	−.9	−1.0	−1.0	−1.2	−.8	−3.9	1.9
General Government	78bpd	....	....	....	....	....	....	....	....	....	....	....	....
Banks	78bqd	−1.2	−26.7	18.0	−39.0	17.0	−40.7	−53.2	−18.8	−64.4	−94.9	11.0	−121.2
Other Sectors	78brd	130.0	−22.5	174.0	−223.5	26.2	−178.5	−12.2	−33.6	−99.4	−59.8	−1,409.3	−1,415.9
Other Investment Liab., n.i.e.	78bid	−233.7	−366.7	23.3	105.3	−67.4	254.6	76.0	213.4	544.2	180.1	894.1	−160.6
Monetary Authorities	78bsd	−131.6	−465.2	31.1	27.1	−22.8	−17.3	−88.7	−24.7	72.0	−22.3	91.0	−222.9
General Government	78btd	−66.2	−75.9	−59.5	−18.8	−35.3	−64.2	−38.5	124.2	119.1	119.3	252.6	672.4
Banks	78bud	−12.7	−9.5	45.4	32.1	89.7	172.3	218.5	106.9	234.2	−37.0	115.6	−172.2
Other Sectors	78bvd	−23.2	183.9	6.3	64.9	−99.0	163.8	−15.3	7.0	118.9	120.1	434.9	−437.9
Net Errors and Omissions	78cad	569.0	215.1	−596.0	75.3	108.8	−193.7	−338.6	−480.4	−618.5	−451.9	−139.3	−468.1
Overall Balance	78cbd	−64.0	−544.4	−511.0	146.1	−39.8	90.9	11.1	151.4	−48.4	514.7	−554.2	−454.4
Reserves and Related Items	79dad	64.0	544.4	511.0	−146.1	39.8	−90.9	−11.1	−151.4	48.4	−514.7	554.2	454.4
Reserve Assets	79dbd	−63.5	−153.5	384.7	−131.2	15.2	−39.5	−98.2	−193.6	69.9	−518.2	526.0	351.7
Use of Fund Credit and Loans	79dcd	37.3	63.9	−8.1	−34.0	−59.4	−62.4	26.8	−	−	−	−25.7	94.5
Exceptional Financing	79ded	90.2	634.0	134.4	19.1	84.1	11.0	60.3	42.2	−21.5	3.5	53.9	8.2
Government Finance		\multicolumn{12}{c}{*Millions of Pesos: Year Ending December 31*}
Deficit (−) or Surplus	80	3,763.3	288.1	−690.6	1,720.3	540.6	2,038.0	2,109.8	−1,267.2	3,449.5	....	216.0	....
Total Revenue and Grants	81y	17,842.0	20,188.0	21,499.9	24,890.8	27,133.6	34,729.1	38,867.3	43,947.3	51,651.8	....	67,593.2	....
Revenue	81	17,572.0	19,776.1	21,482.3	24,890.8	26,921.3	34,729.1	38,564.8	43,483.6	51,271.3	....	67,077.5	....
Grants	81z	270.0	411.9	17.6	−	212.3	−	302.5	463.7	380.5	....	515.7	....
Exp. & Lending Minus Repay	82z	14,078.7	19,899.9	22,190.5	23,170.5	26,593.0	32,691.1	36,757.5	45,214.5	48,202.3	....	67,377.2	....
Expenditure	82	14,078.7	19,899.9	22,190.5	23,170.5	26,593.0	32,691.1	36,757.5	45,164.5	48,202.3	....	67,377.2	....
Lending Minus Repayments	83	−	−	−	−	−	−	−	50.0	−	....	....	....
Total Financing	80h	−3,763.3	−288.1	690.6	−1,720.3	−540.6	−2,038.4	−2,110.0	1,217.1	−3,449.7	....	−216.0	....
Domestic	84a	−2,225.7	1,708.5	2,522.1	1.8	1,289.3	379.2	−8.4	1,862.4	6.4	....	3,569.5	....
Foreign	85a	−1,537.6	−1,996.6	−1,831.5	−1,722.1	−1,829.9	−2,417.6	−2,101.6	−645.4	−3,456.1	....	−3,785.5	....
National Accounts		\multicolumn{12}{c}{*Millions of Pesos*}
Househ.Cons.Expend.,incl.NPISHs	96f	96,532	96,467	109,023	127,819	147,082	166,162	187,591	209,244	248,930	273,148	300,799	....
Government Consumption Expend.	91f	3,480	5,398	6,692	8,331	10,413	16,403	19,449	22,467	27,140	32,847	38,231	....
Gross Fixed Capital Formation	93e	22,723	28,771	29,020	31,146	34,230	41,906	56,024	66,593	76,164	82,653	90,727	....
Changes in Inventories	93i	325	351	396	468	528	619	697	802	927	1,042	1,142	....
Exports of Goods and Services	90c	24,175	59,703	67,847	77,150	84,621	100,513	113,793	127,887	146,094	141,583	152,286	....
Imports of Goods and Services (−)	98c	34,537	68,883	75,412	82,632	93,513	110,739	135,577	148,646	177,473	169,704	187,068	....
Gross Domestic Product (GDP)	99b	112,698	121,808	137,566	162,283	183,361	214,864	241,977	278,347	321,783	361,569	396,117	....
Net Primary Income from Abroad	98.n	−4,069	−8,761	−8,851	−10,405	−9,966	−11,342	−13,550	−15,616	−17,047	−18,439	−21,041	....
Gross National Income (GNI)	99a	108,629	113,047	128,715	151,878	173,395	203,521	228,427	262,730	304,736	343,130	375,076	....
Consumption of Fixed Capital	99cf	6,762	7,309	8,254	9,737	11,002	12,892	14,519	16,701	19,307	21,694	23,767	....
GDP Volume 1970 Prices	99b.p	4,073	4,194	4,390	4,579	4,907	5,308	5,702	6,161	6,611	6,823	7,105	....
GDP Volume (2000=100)	99bvp	61.6	63.4	66.4	69.3	74.2	80.3	86.3	93.2	100.0	103.2	107.5	....
GDP Deflator (2000=100)	99bip	56.8	59.7	64.4	72.8	76.8	83.2	87.2	92.8	100.0	108.9	114.5	....
Population		\multicolumn{12}{c}{*Millions: Midyear Estimates*}
Population	99z	7.30	7.43	7.56	7.69	7.82	7.95	8.09	8.22	8.35	8.49	8.62	8.74

2004, International Monetary Fund: *International Financial Statistics Yearbook*

ECCU 309

		1992	1993	1994	1995	1996	1997	1998	1999	2000	2001	2002	2003
Exchange Rates			E. Caribbean Dollars per SDR: End of Period (aa) E. Caribbean Dollars per US Dollar: End of Period (ae)
Official Rate	aa	3.7125	3.7086	3.9416	4.0135	3.8825	3.6430	3.8017	3.7058	3.5179	3.3932	3.6707	4.0121
Official Rate	ae	2.7000	2.7000	2.7000	2.7000	2.7000	2.7000	2.7000	2.7000	2.7000	2.7000	2.7000	2.7000
Fund Position			Millions of SDRs: End of Period
Quota	2f.s	43.00	46.50	46.50	46.50	46.50	46.50	46.50	63.60	65.90	65.90	65.90	65.90
SDRs	1b.s	3.24	3.24	3.36	3.47	3.60	3.67	3.80	3.89	3.91	4.02	4.07	4.11
Reserve Position in the Fund	1c.s	.52	.53	.53	.53	.53	.53	.53	.58	.59	.59	.59	.60
Total Fund Cred.&Loans Outstg	2tl	2.78	2.26	1.71	1.15	.59	.19	1.65	1.63	1.63	1.63	2.86	8.26
International Liquidity			Millions of US Dollars: End of Period
Total Reserves minus Gold	1l.d	279.26	269.13	261.52	312.93	291.36	307.84	360.76	367.63	386.41	448.54	508.25	543.73
SDRs	1b.d	4.46	4.46	4.91	5.16	5.17	4.95	5.36	5.34	5.10	5.05	5.54	6.11
Reserve Position in the Fund	1c.d	.72	.72	.77	.78	.76	.71	.74	.80	.77	.75	.81	.90
Foreign Exchange	1d.d	274.08	263.95	255.84	306.99	285.43	302.19	354.66	361.49	380.55	442.74	501.91	536.72
Monetary Authorities: Other Liab.	4..d	12.86	6.57	9.46	8.71	9.50	5.97	3.67	6.34	8.23	7.55	4.89	4.96
Deposit Money Banks: Assets	7a.d	230.77	246.58	270.67	304.74	312.47	321.14	402.51	495.69	478.78	618.11	746.99	961.50
Liabilities	7b.d	214.82	239.82	263.29	263.56	335.81	381.54	388.92	447.97	476.56	525.38	577.00	602.51
Monetary Authorities			Millions of E. Caribbean Dollars: End of Period
Foreign Assets	11	754.00	726.64	706.09	844.91	786.67	831.17	974.05	992.59	1,043.32	1,211.06	1,370.68	1,466.13
Claims on Central Government	12a	127.69	122.69	116.46	105.54	109.13	95.34	89.32	94.20	96.60	91.07	72.75	89.36
Claims on Private Sector	12d	—	—	—	7.36	8.13	9.88	10.64	10.94	12.94	14.65	14.01	12.47
Claims on Deposit Money Banks	12e	3.15	2.38	7.22	1.33	1.10	1.08	1.09	.90	19.75	.61	.54	.52
Claims on Nonbank Financial Insts.	12g	—	.64	1.62	5.12	5.99	6.60	7.58	7.86	10.93	12.90	12.73	13.17
Reserve Money	14	753.23	710.46	730.35	808.81	760.96	812.36	954.70	1,016.00	1,060.05	1,207.38	1,308.01	1,448.23
of which: Currency Outside DMBs	14a	275.28	272.73	285.55	311.58	298.36	315.31	347.02	391.46	389.47	375.92	395.72	429.61
Foreign Liabilities	16c	45.04	26.13	32.28	28.13	27.93	16.80	16.18	23.15	27.95	25.89	23.70	46.55
Central Government Deposits	16d	33.36	47.26	46.64	46.52	64.88	59.02	73.98	66.62	65.94	56.06	70.04	57.08
Capital Accounts	17a	106.60	114.30	82.62	133.13	105.15	105.01	110.92	84.98	112.99	122.58	148.93	131.35
Other Items (Net)	17r	−53.39	−45.81	−60.51	−52.33	−47.90	−49.11	−73.10	−84.25	−83.38	−81.61	−79.97	−101.56
Deposit Money Banks			Millions of E. Caribbean Dollars: End of Period
Reserves	20	450.80	462.40	448.45	475.41	454.93	503.49	625.33	652.56	670.63	845.93	919.40	981.19
Foreign Assets	21	623.07	665.76	730.82	822.79	843.68	867.07	1,086.77	1,338.36	1,292.71	1,668.90	2,016.87	2,596.05
Claims on Central Government	22a	357.72	386.36	410.53	519.58	567.50	625.09	749.90	853.94	1,063.19	1,086.18	1,195.31	1,198.57
Claims on Local Government	22b	14.90	10.32	9.83	11.59	9.57	9.73	16.16	21.85	46.65	57.92	69.20	84.52
Claims on Nonfin.Pub.Enterprises	22c	138.54	165.99	202.93	253.66	270.23	281.12	311.51	363.39	415.04	470.05	498.18	507.99
Claims on Private Sector	22d	2,743.64	3,067.80	3,187.72	3,511.33	3,940.59	4,471.39	4,839.12	5,333.95	5,892.00	6,017.45	6,251.22	6,282.97
Claims on Nonbank Financial Insts.	22g	22.24	33.17	62.49	61.87	75.76	69.66	89.36	120.92	119.22	133.72	147.24	217.02
Demand Deposits	24	540.99	561.67	610.96	697.19	691.63	751.45	877.41	928.40	935.39	1,013.16	1,097.32	1,287.98
Time, Savings,& Fgn.Currency Dep.	25	2,456.17	2,678.95	2,885.29	3,276.61	3,401.37	3,695.73	4,172.08	4,798.86	5,363.40	5,735.46	6,195.26	6,637.84
Foreign Liabilities	26c	580.02	647.51	710.90	711.61	906.69	1,030.16	1,050.09	1,209.51	1,286.72	1,418.52	1,557.91	1,626.79
Central Government Deposits	26d	478.20	528.17	593.72	678.28	763.19	849.00	1,007.02	1,078.17	1,167.22	1,231.14	1,335.81	1,425.20
Credit from Monetary Authorities	26g	3.63	25.72	16.66	8.12	12.88	11.71	34.07	23.63	48.95	105.35	64.78	30.80
Capital Accounts	27a	287.97	319.29	376.16	415.02	431.08	489.34	539.75	655.66	698.11	829.14	937.38	1,003.80
Other Items (Net)	27r	3.93	30.49	−140.92	−130.59	−44.58	.16	37.73	−9.28	−.33	−52.63	−91.05	−144.08
Monetary Survey			Millions of E. Caribbean Dollars: End of Period
Foreign Assets (Net)	31n	752.02	718.76	693.74	927.96	695.72	651.29	994.55	1,098.29	1,021.37	1,435.54	1,805.94	2,388.85
Domestic Credit	32	2,893.16	3,211.55	3,351.44	3,751.26	4,158.82	4,660.80	5,032.59	5,662.48	6,423.43	6,596.74	6,854.78	6,923.80
Claims on Central Govt. (Net)	32an	−26.16	−66.39	−113.38	−99.68	−151.44	−187.59	−241.77	−196.66	−73.37	−109.96	−137.80	−194.33
Claims on Local Government	32b	14.90	10.32	9.83	11.59	9.57	9.73	16.16	21.85	46.65	57.92	69.20	84.52
Claims on Nonfin.Pub.Enterprises	32c	138.54	165.99	203.17	253.66	270.23	281.12	311.51	363.62	415.04	470.05	498.18	507.99
Claims on Private Sector	32d	2,743.64	3,067.80	3,187.72	3,518.69	3,948.71	4,481.27	4,849.75	5,344.89	5,904.96	6,032.10	6,265.23	6,295.44
Claims on Nonbank Financial Inst.	32g	22.24	33.81	64.11	67.00	81.75	76.26	96.94	128.78	130.15	146.63	159.98	230.19
Money	34	817.13	835.02	897.56	1,017.74	992.09	1,069.05	1,226.51	1,322.91	1,327.77	1,393.48	1,493.96	1,729.10
Quasi-Money	35	2,456.17	2,678.95	2,885.29	3,277.43	3,402.19	3,696.55	4,173.90	4,800.68	5,365.22	5,737.33	6,197.10	6,638.67
Capital Accounts	37a	394.57	433.60	458.79	548.16	536.23	594.35	650.66	740.64	811.09	951.71	1,086.31	1,135.16
Other Items (Net)	37r	−22.69	−17.26	−196.45	−164.11	−75.95	−47.87	−23.93	−103.46	−59.29	−50.24	−116.65	−190.28
Money plus Quasi-Money	35l	3,273.29	3,513.97	3,782.84	4,295.17	4,394.28	4,765.60	5,400.40	6,123.59	6,692.99	7,130.81	7,691.05	8,367.77
Money (National Definitions)			Millions of E. Caribbean Dollars: End of Period
M1	39ma	719.92	747.98	793.20	912.86	882.90	963.94	1,091.06	1,193.49	1,214.24	1,248.49	1,321.66	1,508.13
M2	39mb	2,870.73	3,148.04	3,395.26	3,874.39	3,948.43	4,325.35	4,881.69	5,399.32	5,971.19	6,322.12	6,736.98	7,379.32
Interest Rates			Percent Per Annum
Discount Rate (End of Period)	60	....	....	9.00	9.00	9.00	8.00	8.00	8.00	8.00	7.00	7.00	6.50
Money Market Rate	60b	5.25	5.25	5.25	5.25	5.25	5.25	5.25	5.25	5.25	†5.64	6.32	6.07
Savings Rate	60k	7.71	8.00	8.00	8.00	8.00	8.00	8.00	8.00	8.00	8.00	8.00	†3.90
Deposit Rate	60l	7.73	7.21	†3.87	4.06	4.16	4.20	4.30	4.35	4.46	4.37	4.04	4.76
Deposit Rate (Fgn. Currency)	60l.f	....	....	....	....	....	....	....	....	....	....	....	4.06
Lending Rate	60p	11.71	11.81	11.71	11.94	11.74	11.77	11.60	11.91	11.98	11.55	11.47	12.94

2004, International Monetary Fund: *International Financial Statistics Yearbook*

ECCU 309

		1992	1993	1994	1995	1996	1997	1998	1999	2000	2001	2002	2003
Balance of Payments						*Millions of US Dollars: Minus Sign Indicates Debit*							
Current Account, n.i.e.	78ald	−193.4	−190.6	−212.3	−215.4	−329.3	−402.7	−365.8	−450.4	−438.3	−475.8	−570.6	....
Goods: Exports f.o.b.	78aad	396.7	350.8	300.9	350.3	337.8	298.2	316.1	327.4	359.2	303.1	310.4	....
Goods: Imports f.o.b.	78abd	−993.0	−1,006.0	−1,040.2	−1,106.7	−1,190.8	−1,245.8	−1,298.6	−1,383.2	−1,425.5	−1,309.9	−1,315.2	....
Trade Balance	78acd	−596.3	−655.2	−739.3	−756.4	−853.0	−947.6	−982.5	−1,055.8	−1,066.3	−1,006.8	−1,004.8	....
Services: Credit	78add	850.0	939.1	1,026.4	1,010.5	1,064.0	1,156.5	1,256.5	1,306.0	1,285.5	1,209.9	1,169.4	....
Services: Debit	78aed	−401.4	−422.7	−456.0	−508.8	−537.3	−580.4	−627.2	−663.6	−614.3	−615.2	−642.7	....
Balance on Goods & Services	78afd	−147.7	−138.8	−168.8	−254.6	−326.3	−371.5	−353.2	−413.4	−395.0	−412.1	−478.1	....
Income: Credit	78agd	23.8	19.6	24.6	32.7	26.7	25.1	35.3	37.5	43.3	38.8	33.9	....
Income: Debit	78ahd	−122.0	−122.8	−142.1	−157.7	−153.7	−156.8	−181.8	−207.5	−250.7	−215.9	−235.7	....
Balance on Gds, Serv. & Inc.	78aid	−245.9	−242.0	−286.3	−379.6	−453.3	−503.1	−499.7	−583.4	−602.4	−589.2	−679.9	....
Current Transfers, n.i.e.: Credit	78ajd	98.2	107.3	127.1	219.4	175.1	157.6	193.9	185.1	227.5	189.2	192.6	....
Current Transfers: Debit	78akd	−45.7	−55.9	−53.2	−55.2	−51.1	−57.2	−60.0	−52.1	−63.4	−75.7	−83.4	....
Capital Account, n.i.e.	78bcd	66.1	56.8	67.8	94.3	73.5	89.2	255.3	108.6	122.3	134.2	132.2	....
Capital Account, n.i.e.: Credit	78bad	70.9	62.1	77.0	100.2	91.8	98.0	264.4	118.0	133.9	142.2	140.4	....
Capital Account: Debit	78bbd	−4.8	−5.4	−9.1	−6.0	−18.3	−8.8	−9.1	−9.4	−11.6	−8.0	−8.1	....
Financial Account, n.i.e.	78bjd	176.2	149.4	152.6	137.3	260.5	362.1	194.2	406.9	378.6	345.9	434.8	....
Direct Investment Abroad	78bdd	−	−	−	−	−	−	−	−	−	−.1	−	....
Dir. Invest. in Rep. Econ., n.i.e.	78bed	150.0	139.3	179.8	210.0	183.3	261.3	312.9	335.2	306.8	281.1	316.3	....
Portfolio Investment Assets	78bfd	−.2	2.5	−2.0	−5.7	−.4	−	−.4	−10.5	−1.7	−5.7	−27.4	....
Equity Securities	78bkd	....	....	....	....	....	....	....	....	....	....	....	....
Debt Securities	78bld	....	....	....	....	....	....	....	....	....	....	....	....
Portfolio Investment Liab., n.i.e.	78bgd	.7	.6	1.1	−.4	6.1	20.2	6.0	58.9	69.7	54.4	195.1	....
Equity Securities	78bmd	....	....	....	....	....	....	....	....	....	....	....	....
Debt Securities	78bnd	....	....	....	....	....	....	....	....	....	....	....	....
Financial Derivatives Assets	78bwd	....	....	....	....	....	....	....	....	....	....	....	....
Financial Derivatives Liabilities	78bxd	....	....	....	....	....	....	....	....	....	....	....	....
Other Investment Assets	78bhd	−20.2	−12.3	−18.3	−51.0	−31.3	−16.2	−49.2	19.3	−61.7	−54.3	−52.2	....
Monetary Authorities	78bod	....	....	....	....	....	....	....	....	....	....	....	....
General Government	78bpd	....	....	....	....	....	....	....	....	....	....	....	....
Banks	78bqd	....	....	....	....	....	....	....	....	....	....	....	....
Other Sectors	78brd	....	....	....	....	....	....	....	....	....	....	....	....
Other Investment Liab., n.i.e.	78bid	45.8	19.3	−8.0	−15.7	102.7	96.8	−75.1	4.0	65.5	70.6	2.9	....
Monetary Authorities	78bsd	−	−	−	−	−	−	−	−	−	−	−	....
General Government	78btd	....	....	....	....	....	....	....	....	....	....	....	....
Banks	78bud	....	....	....	....	....	....	....	....	....	....	....	....
Other Sectors	78bvd	....	....	....	....	....	....	....	....	....	....	....	....
Net Errors and Omissions	78cad	56.8	−18.2	−16.9	35.5	−23.7	−25.3	−32.3	−43.5	−50.3	61.6	61.4	....
Overall Balance	78cbd	105.7	−2.7	−8.8	51.6	−19.0	23.3	51.5	21.6	12.3	66.0	57.8	....
Reserves and Related Items	79dad	−59.9	2.7	8.8	−51.6	19.0	−23.3	−51.5	−21.6	−12.3	−66.0	−57.8	....
Reserve Assets	79dbd	−59.2	3.4	9.6	−50.8	19.9	−22.8	−53.5	−21.6	−12.3	−66.0	−59.5	....
Use of Fund Credit and Loans	79dcd	−.8	−.7	−.8	−.9	−.8	−.6	2.1	−	−	−	1.7	....
Exceptional Financing	79ded	....	....	....	....	....	....	....	....	....	....	....	....
National Accounts						*Millions of E. Caribbean Dollars*							
Gross Domestic Product (GDP)	99b	4,322.6	4,491.8	4,795.5	4,963.1	5,199.6	5,490.4	5,854.0	6,204.5	6,461.6	6,493.1	6,569.9	....
GDP Volume 1990 Prices	99b.p	3,965.5	4,066.7	4,188.8	4,216.2	4,328.9	4,469.2	4,647.3	4,837.6	4,973.8	4,909.0	4,918.2	....
GDP Volume (2000=100)	99bvp	79.7	81.8	84.2	84.8	87.0	89.9	93.4	97.3	100.0	98.7	98.9	....
GDP Deflator (2000=100)	99bip	83.9	85.0	88.1	90.6	92.5	94.6	97.0	98.7	100.0	101.8	102.8	....
						Millions: Midyear Estimates							
Population	99z	.522	.526	.531	.534	.536	.537	.538	.539	.540	.542	.544	.546

Ecuador 248

		1992	1993	1994	1995	1996	1997	1998	1999	2000	2001	2002	2003
Exchange Rates		*Sucres per SDR: End of Period*											
Principal Rate	aa	2,535.8	2,807.3	3,312.4	4,345.8	5,227.0	5,974.5	9,609.8	27,783.7	32,572.8	31,418.3	33,988.0	37,149.3
		Sucres per US Dollar: End of Period (ae) Period Average (rf)											
Principal Rate	ae	1,844.3	2,043.8	2,269.0	2,923.5	3,635.0	4,428.0	6,825.0	20,243.0	25,000.0	25,000.0	25,000.0	25,000.0
Principal Rate	rf	1,534.0	1,919.1	2,196.7	2,564.5	3,189.5	3,998.3	5,446.6	11,786.8	24,988.4	25,000.0	25,000.0	25,000.0
		Index Numbers (2000=100): Period Averages											
Principal Rate	ahx	1,670.7	1,297.5	1,139.3	977.7	796.5	624.6	468.0	228.7	100.0	100.0	100.0	100.0
Nominal Effective Exchange Rate	nec	861.4	849.8	911.7	789.9	656.9	555.6	426.1	216.9	100.0	104.6	106.1	99.6
Real Effective Exchange Rate	rec	110.9	129.2	138.3	136.1	135.2	145.1	147.1	109.8	100.0	139.9	155.7	153.4
Fund Position		*Millions of SDRs: End of Period*											
Quota	2f.s	219.2	219.2	219.2	219.2	219.2	219.2	219.2	302.3	302.3	302.3	302.3	302.3
SDRs	1b.s	.1	3.2	3.0	2.1	1.9	.4	.2	1.7	.2	1.8	1.4	.7
Reserve Position in the Fund	1c.s	17.1	17.1	17.1	17.2	17.2	17.2	17.2	17.2	17.2	17.2	17.2	17.2
Total Fund Cred.&Loans Outstg.	2tl	72.6	51.8	135.7	116.7	100.9	98.9	49.5	—	113.3	151.1	226.7	262.3
International Liquidity		*Millions of US Dollars Unless Otherwise Indicated: End of Period*											
Total Reserves minus Gold	1l.d	868.2	1,379.9	1,844.2	1,627.6	1,858.5	2,092.8	1,619.7	1,642.4	946.9	839.8	714.6	812.6
SDRs	1b.d	.1	4.3	3.1	2.7	.5	.3	2.3	.3	2.3	1.9	1.0
Reserve Position in the Fund	1c.d	23.6	23.5	25.0	25.5	24.7	23.1	24.2	23.5	22.3	21.6	23.3	25.5
Foreign Exchange	1d.d	844.5	1,352.1	1,814.9	1,599.0	1,831.1	2,069.1	1,595.3	1,616.5	924.3	815.9	689.4	786.1
Gold (Million Fine Troy Ounces)	1ad	.443	.414	.414	.414	.414	.414	.414	† .845	.845	.845	.845	.845
Gold (National Valuation)	1and	165.7	165.6	165.6	166.6	166.6	166.7	166.7	245.4	232.7	233.8	293.3	348.0
Monetary Authorities: Other Liab.	4..d	871.1	4,079.9	4,052.7	196.1	178.3	147.5	310.6	673.6	400.6	375.5	154.4	53.5
Banking Institutions: Assets	7a.d	162.0	180.1	355.4	398.4	561.1	938.3	972.3	748.9	819.4	1,013.1	1,367.1	1,985.7
Liabilities	7b.d	424.9	390.5	847.8	1,074.6	1,229.4	1,795.2	1,527.0	862.0	595.3	512.3	452.5	476.1
Nonbank Financial Insts.: Assets	7e.d	....	....	....	....	....	....	20.1	16.8	26.7	41.5	32.6	35.8
Liabilities	7f.d	....	....	....	....	....	....	523.3	383.2	321.4	274.5	.3	.1
Monetary Authorities		*Millions of US Dollars: End of Period*											
Foreign Assets	11	229.7	1,489.3	1,986.6	1,746.7	1,992.2	2,254.8	† 1,663.1	† 1,527.7	1,538.6	1,563.0	† 1,522.2	1,715.9
Claims on Central Government	12a	671.1	3,924.6	4,021.3	194.7	166.1	129.0	† 303.0	† 1,479.2	1,425.0	1,278.8	† 1,145.0	1,244.3
Claims on State & Local Govts.	12b	—	—	—	—	—	—	†—	†—	—	—	†—	1.5
Claims on Nonfin.Pub.Enterprises	12c	.2	.1	.1	—	—	—	†—	†—	—	—	†—	—
Claims on Private Sector	12d	14.3	14.6	21.2	6.1	8.2	7.2	† 18.4	† 1.8	3.6	2.9	† 16.8	15.2
Claims on Banking Institutions	12e	103.9	77.9	15.7	185.8	267.4	44.8	† 944.0	† 424.4	314.4	348.5	† 272.7	100.1
Claims on Nonbank Financial Insts.	12g	—	—	—	—	—	—	†—	†—	24.6	25.3	† 26.7	18.3
Reserve Money	14	821.4	1,207.2	1,237.8	1,120.3	1,198.6	1,285.0	† 1,053.3	† 828.6	474.6	528.7	† 426.3	468.7
of which: Currency Outside Banks	14a	323.2	417.1	493.6	469.6	516.6	537.5	† 426.6	† 576.3	31.7	21.8	† 39.6	49.7
Time and Savings Deposits	15	43.3	125.5	175.6	130.9	121.1	111.9	†—	† 86.1	115.0	98.2	† 97.3	125.3
Liabs. of Central Bank: Securities	16ac	69.0	88.5	36.0	19.8	9.4	.4	† 319.8	† 341.8	6.2	54.7	† 8.7	43.7
Foreign Liabilities	16c	970.9	4,151.0	4,250.9	369.6	323.4	280.9	† 380.2	† 673.6	548.2	565.4	† 462.7	443.3
Central Government Deposits	16d	413.0	627.0	816.1	634.1	699.4	600.5	† 391.2	† 388.7	887.9	818.0	† 864.1	1,076.7
Capital Accounts	17a	57.1	303.1	344.6	331.8	533.1	448.8	† 1,169.7	† 1,243.2	1,542.2	1,571.6	† 1,363.4	1,432.8
Other Items (Net)	17r	–1,355.5	–995.7	–816.1	–473.2	–451.1	–291.8	† –385.7	† –128.8	–268.0	–418.1	† –239.0	–495.3
Banking Institutions		*Millions of US Dollars: End of Period*											
Reserves	20	341.1	423.9	413.4	444.9	539.0	566.6	† 686.5	† 180.8	243.5	250.7	† 326.3	259.7
Claims on Mon.Author.:Securities	20c	47.0	37.0	36.0	19.8	9.4	.4	† .1	† 117.9	2.1	8.7	† 4.2	12.0
Foreign Assets	21	162.0	180.1	355.4	398.4	561.1	938.3	† 972.3	† 748.9	819.4	1,013.1	† 1,367.1	1,985.7
Claims on Central Government	22a	11.4	33.4	64.3	129.3	221.3	387.8	† 892.9	† 490.1	399.0	568.0	† 527.7	364.5
Claims on State & Local Govts.	22b	—	—	—	—	—	—	†—	†—	—	—	†—	11.1
Claims on Nonfin.Pub.Enterprises	22c	8.7	21.3	—	—	—	—	†—	†—	—	—	†—	1.5
Claims on Private Sector	22d	1,762.7	2,871.2	4,648.0	5,387.6	5,591.5	6,740.6	† 6,126.3	† 4,400.6	4,766.7	5,861.5	† 5,150.0	5,423.0
Claims on Nonbank Financial Insts.	22g	—	—	.1	.1	21.2	24.4	† 45.5	†—	—	—	† 131.4	352.5
Demand Deposits	24	556.4	804.5	977.4	765.9	819.1	883.3	† 951.3	† 614.9	996.7	1,552.7	† 1,629.1	1,793.0
Time, Savings,& Fgn.Currency Dep.	25	1,317.4	1,881.3	2,905.3	3,606.4	4,186.3	4,611.2	† 3,701.0	† 1,239.2	2,434.3	3,087.3	† 3,073.6	3,799.3
Bonds	26ab	83.4	59.9	61.7	161.5	508.2	687.8	† 661.7	† 347.0	233.6	171.7	†—	—
Restricted Deposits	26b	41.3	58.5	84.5	121.4	162.7	174.9	†—	† 1,057.5	364.8	159.0	† 25.8	27.4
Foreign Liabilities	26c	424.9	390.5	847.8	1,074.6	1,229.4	1,795.2	† 1,527.0	† 862.0	595.3	512.3	† 452.5	476.1
Central Government Deposits	26d	—	—	—	2.6	4.1	6.5	† 131.2	† 48.0	128.6	1,007.0	† 1,120.1	1,290.3
Credit from Monetary Authorities	26g	95.2	89.5	26.1	162.8	132.9	6.8	† 652.5	† 311.1	136.4	169.1	† 71.2	54.4
Liab. to Nonbank Financial Insts.	26j	19.3	72.3	165.9	237.7	18.3	13.8	† 34.3	† 88.7	135.1	139.4	† 67.6	74.3
Capital Accounts	27a	572.6	895.9	1,306.8	1,614.0	1,685.5	1,937.0	† 1,719.8	† –95.8	–365.0	–875.2	† –985.9	–733.5
Other Items (Net)	27r	–777.5	–685.4	–858.1	–1,366.8	–1,803.0	–1,458.4	† –655.1	† 1,465.7	1,570.9	1,778.7	† 2,052.8	1,628.5

2004, International Monetary Fund: International Financial Statistics Yearbook

Ecuador 248

		1992	1993	1994	1995	1996	1997	1998	1999	2000	2001	2002	2003
Banking Survey						*Millions of US Dollars: End of Period*							
Foreign Assets (Net)	31n	−1,004.1	−2,872.2	−2,756.6	700.9	1,000.5	1,117.0	†728.3	†741.1	1,214.6	1,498.4	†1,974.2	2,782.2
Domestic Credit	32	2,055.3	6,238.4	7,938.8	5,081.0	5,304.8	6,681.9	†6,863.7	†5,935.0	5,602.3	5,911.4	†5,013.4	5,064.8
Claims on Central Govt. (Net)	32an	269.5	3,331.0	3,269.5	−312.7	−316.1	−90.3	†673.5	†1,532.6	807.5	21.7	†−311.5	−758.1
Claims on State and Local Govts.	32b	—	—	—	—	—	—	†−	†−	—	—	†−	12.5
Claims on Nonfin.Pub.Enterprises	32c	8.9	21.4	.1	—	—	—	†−	†−	—	—	†−	1.5
Claims on Private Sector	32d	1,776.9	2,885.9	4,669.2	5,393.7	5,599.8	6,747.7	†6,144.8	†4,402.4	4,770.2	5,864.4	†5,166.8	5,438.2
Claims on Nonbank Financial Insts.	32g	—	.1	.1	—	21.2	24.4	†45.5	†−	24.6	25.3	†158.1	370.7
Money	34	986.7	1,438.2	1,711.2	1,379.3	1,445.1	1,551.8	†1,546.7	†1,255.9	1,245.2	1,814.1	†1,794.8	1,985.3
Quasi-Money	35	1,360.7	2,006.8	3,080.8	3,737.2	4,307.4	4,723.1	†3,701.0	†1,325.4	2,549.3	3,185.4	†3,170.9	3,924.7
Bonds	36ab	83.4	59.9	61.7	161.5	508.2	687.8	†661.7	†347.0	233.6	171.7	†−	—
Liabs. of Central Bank: Securities	36ac	21.9	51.4	—	—	—	—	†319.7	†223.8	4.0	45.9	†4.4	31.7
Restricted Deposits	36b	41.7	58.8	84.7	121.6	162.8	175.0	†−	†1,057.5	364.8	159.0	†25.8	27.4
Liab. to Nonbank Financial Insts.	36j	19.3	72.3	165.9	237.7	18.3	13.8	†34.3	†88.7	135.1	139.4	†67.6	74.3
Capital Accounts	37a	629.7	1,199.0	1,651.3	1,945.8	2,218.7	2,385.8	†2,889.5	†1,147.4	1,177.3	696.4	†377.5	699.3
Other Items (Net)	37r	−2,092.0	−1,520.3	−1,573.5	−1,801.2	−2,355.1	−1,738.4	†−1,560.9	†1,230.4	1,107.7	1,197.8	†1,546.5	1,104.3
Money plus Quasi-Money	35l	2,347.3	3,445.0	4,792.0	5,116.6	5,752.5	6,274.9	†5,247.6	†2,581.2	3,794.5	4,999.5	†4,965.7	5,909.9
Nonbank Financial Institutions						*Millions of US Dollars: End of Period*							
Reserves	40	....	....	....	....	....	....	2.0	†1.3	5.0	8.3	†1.2	3.5
Claims on Mon.Author.:Securities	40c	....	....	....	....	....	....	—	†−	—	—	†.7	—
Foreign Assets	41	....	....	....	....	....	....	20.1	†16.8	26.7	41.5	†32.6	35.8
Claims on Central Government	42a	....	....	....	....	....	....	8.1	†257.5	227.9	151.6	†125.1	109.0
Claims on State & Local Govts.	42b	....	....	....	....	....	....	—	†−	—	—	†−	—
Claims on Nonfin.Pub.Enterprises	42c	....	....	....	....	....	....	—	†−	—	—	†−	—
Claims on Private Sector	42d	....	....	....	....	....	....	994.1	†738.6	420.2	383.8	†21.6	10.5
Claims on Banking Institutions	42e	....	....	....	....	....	....	8.1	†40.7	332.9	6.7	†195.6	225.8
Restricted Deposits	46b	....	....	....	....	....	....	17.9	†11.1	20.6	15.3	†−	—
Foreign Liabilities	46c	....	....	....	....	....	....	523.3	†383.2	321.4	274.5	†.3	.1
Central Government Deposits	46d	....	....	....	....	....	....	92.6	†80.0	104.1	106.8	†98.6	98.3
Credit from Monetary Authorities	46g	....	....	....	....	....	....	232.0	†176.8	125.0	75.9	†32.1	20.1
Credit from Banking Institutions	46h	....	....	....	....	....	....	.7	†−	1.2	16.8	†3.1	2.3
Capital Accounts	47a	....	....	....	....	....	....	149.0	†134.8	133.3	80.2	†160.9	167.9
Other Items (Net)	47r	....	....	....	....	....	....	17.0	†269.0	307.0	22.5	†82.0	95.8
Interest Rates						*Percent Per Annum*							
Discount Rate (End of Period)	60	49.00	33.57	44.88	59.41	46.38	37.46	61.84	64.40	†13.16	16.44	14.55	11.19
Savings Rate	60k	31.12	19.22	16.71	21.64	19.90	16.62	16.25	†4.91	4.47	3.49	2.45	2.24
Deposit Rate	60l	46.81	31.97	33.65	43.31	41.50	28.09	39.39	†10.03	8.46	6.58	5.47	5.53
Lending Rate	60p	60.17	47.83	43.99	55.67	54.50	43.02	49.55	†16.53	16.26	15.46	15.08	13.08
Prices, Production, Labor						*Index Numbers (2000=100): Period Averages*							
Producer Prices	63	....	....	....	8.3	10.8	14.2	18.7	37.8	100.0	99.8	106.5	114.3
Consumer Prices	64	6.7	9.7	12.3	†15.1	18.8	24.6	33.5	51.0	100.0	137.7	154.9	167.1
Crude Petroleum Production	66aa	79.9	85.7	94.7	95.9	96.1	96.9	93.7	93.2	100.0	101.6	98.0	104.3
						Number in Thousands: Period Averages							
Labor Force	67d	2,957	2,892	2,905	3,104	3,169	3,326	3,560	3,770	3,709	4,124	3,801	....
Employment	67e	2,693	2,651	2,698	2,892	2,889	3,062	3,151	3,226	3,376	3,673	3,459	....
Unemployment	67c	263	241	207	213	335	312	409	543	333	451	351	....
Unemployment Rate (%)	67r	8.9	8.3	7.1	6.9	10.4	9.2	11.5	14.4	9.0	10.4	8.6	9.8
International Transactions						*Millions of US Dollars*							
Exports	70..d	3,007.4	2,903.7	3,819.9	4,307.2	4,899.9	5,264.4	4,202.9	4,451.0	4,926.5	4,678.4	5,041.6	6,038.5
Imports, c.i.f.	71..d	2,431.0	2,562.2	3,622.0	4,152.6	3,934.5	4,954.9	5,575.7	3,017.3	3,721.1	5,362.9	6,431.2	6,534.6
Imports, f.o.b.	71.vd	1,975.5	2,223.0	3,252.5	3,774.8	3,570.9	4,520.1	5,012.7	2,736.9	3,400.9	4,936.0	5,953.3	6,071.2
						2000=100							
Volume of Exports	72	75.0	80.2	89.1	99.7	102.1	101.8	96.4	92.6	100.0	100.8	99.4	104.2
Volume of Imports	73	73.5	49.3	74.7	100.1	96.4	132.8	166.2	95.7	100.0	124.5	156.9	170.7
Unit Value of Exports	74..d	83.5	68.5	72.8	74.7	87.5	85.7	64.9	77.9	100.0	88.1	94.8	105.4

Ecuador 248

		1992	1993	1994	1995	1996	1997	1998	1999	2000	2001	2002	2003
Balance of Payments		\multicolumn{12}{c}{*Millions of US Dollars: Minus Sign Indicates Debit*}
Current Account, n.i.e.	78ald	−122	−849	−898	−1,000	−55	−457	−2,099	918	921	−695	−1,359	−455
Goods: Exports f.o.b.	78aad	3,101	3,136	3,936	4,468	4,929	5,360	4,326	4,615	5,137	4,781	5,198	6,197
Goods: Imports f.o.b.	78abd	−2,083	−2,922	−3,787	−4,535	−4,008	−4,869	−5,458	−3,028	−3,743	−5,179	−6,196	−6,268
Trade Balance	78acd	1,018	214	149	−66	921	491	−1,132	1,588	1,395	−397	−998	−71
Services: Credit	78add	617	636	676	728	683	686	678	730	849	862	923	898
Services: Debit	78aed	−933	−1,089	−1,107	−1,173	−1,110	−1,230	−1,241	−1,181	−1,269	−1,434	−1,632	−1,590
Balance on Goods & Services	78afd	702	−240	−283	−512	494	−52	−1,695	1,136	975	−969	−1,707	−763
Income: Credit	78agd	35	32	61	98	80	128	119	75	70	48	30	27
Income: Debit	78ahd	−979	−896	−999	−1,029	−1,121	−1,154	−1,290	−1,383	−1,476	−1,412	−1,335	−1,492
Balance on Gds, Serv. & Inc.	78aid	−242	−1,104	−1,221	−1,442	−547	−1,078	−2,865	−171	−431	−2,333	−3,012	−2,227
Current Transfers, n.i.e.: Credit	78ajd	134	318	391	506	616	738	933	1,188	1,437	1,686	1,712	1,794
Current Transfers: Debit	78akd	−14	−62	−69	−64	−124	−117	−166	−99	−85	−47	−58	−22
Capital Account, n.i.e.	78bcd	−	5	18	17	14	11	14	2	−1	−63	20	25
Capital Account, n.i.e.: Credit	78bad	....	8	21	21	18	17	23	11	8	21	24	26
Capital Account: Debit	78bbd	....	−3	−3	−4	−4	−6	−9	−9	−10	−84	−4	−1
Financial Account, n.i.e.	78bjd	361	−44	332	−43	103	−14	1,448	−1,344	−6,602	775	1,122	316
Direct Investment Abroad	78bdd	−	....	....	....	....	....	....	....	....	−	−	−
Dir. Invest. in Rep. Econ., n.i.e.	78bed	178	474	576	452	500	724	870	648	720	1,330	1,275	1,555
Portfolio Investment Assets	78bfd	−	....	....	....	....	....	....	....	....	−	−	−
Equity Securities	78bkd	−	....	....	....	....	....	....	....	....	−	−	−
Debt Securities	78bld	−	....	....	....	....	....	....	....	....	−	−	−
Portfolio Investment Liab., n.i.e.	78bgd	−	1	6	3	−4	−242	−34	−46	−5,583	−148	−	8
Equity Securities	78bmd	−	1	6	13	6	22	5	1	−	1	1	9
Debt Securities	78bnd	−	....	....	−10	−10	−264	−40	−47	−5,583	−149	−1	−1
Financial Derivatives Assets	78bwd	....	....	....	....	....	....	....	....	....	....	....	....
Financial Derivatives Liabilities	78bxd	....	....	....	....	....	....	....	....	....	....	....	....
Other Investment Assets	78bhd	−	−140	−177	−668	−302	−560	−54	−725	−1,274	−1,275	−1,394	−904
Monetary Authorities	78bod	−	....	....	....	....	....	....	....	....	−	−	−
General Government	78bpd	−	....	....	....	....	....	....	....	....	−	−	−
Banks	78bqd	−	....	....	....	....	....	....	....	....	−	−	−
Other Sectors	78brd	−	−140	−177	−668	−302	−560	−54	−725	−1,274	−1,275	−1,394	−904
Other Investment Liab., n.i.e.	78bid	183	−380	−75	170	−91	64	666	−1,221	−465	868	1,240	−343
Monetary Authorities	78bsd	−4	−119	83	−54	−48	−18	230	−76	−135	−144	−138	−17
General Government	78btd	−678	−640	−727	−692	127	−190	−37	117	206	188	−22	−10
Banks	78bud	−	27	26	31	95	26	−24	−72	−37	−108	−19	−22
Other Sectors	78bvd	865	351	544	885	−265	245	497	−1,190	−499	932	1,418	−295
Net Errors and Omissions	78cad	−215	206	−226	−433	−189	−62	−147	−521	−15	−276	−4	184
Overall Balance	78cbd	24	−682	−775	−1,459	−126	−521	−784	−944	−5,697	−258	−221	70
Reserves and Related Items	79dad	−24	682	775	1,459	126	521	784	944	5,697	258	221	−70
Reserve Assets	79bdd	54	−442	−578	174	−247	−253	461	489	−307	105	68	−150
Use of Fund Credit and Loans	79dcd	−77	−29	122	−29	−23	−3	−67	−68	151	48	95	48
Exceptional Financing	79ded	−	1,153	1,231	1,314	396	777	391	523	5,853	105	58	32
International Investment Position		\multicolumn{12}{c}{*Millions of US Dollars*}
Assets	79aad	....	1,641	2,442	2,388	2,650	2,942	2,387	1,319	1,904	2,451	2,709	3,709
Direct Investment Abroad	79abd	....	−	−	−	−	−	−	−	−	−	−	−
Portfolio Investment	79acd	....	−	−	−	−	−	−	−	−	−	−	−
Equity Securities	79add	....	−	−	−	−	−	−	−	−	−	−	−
Debt Securities	79aed	....	−	−	−	−	−	−	−	−	−	−	−
Financial Derivatives	79ald	....	−	−	−	−	−	−	−	−	−	−	−
Other Investment	79afd	....	317	538	658	674	715	619	445	724	1,377	1,701	2,549
Monetary Authorities	79agd	....	−	−	−	−	−	−	−	−	−	−	−
General Government	79ahd	....	−	−	−	−	−	−	−	−	−	−	−
Banks	79aid	....	317	538	658	674	715	619	445	724	1,377	1,701	2,549
Other Sectors	79ajd	....	−	−	−	−	−	−	−	−	−	−	−
Reserve Assets	79akd	....	1,324	1,904	1,730	1,976	2,227	1,768	874	1,180	1,074	1,008	1,161
Liabilities	79lad	....	16,410	18,366	18,391	19,442	20,912	23,255	23,416	21,335	24,063	26,924	28,274
Dir. Invest. in Rep. Economy	79lbd	....	2,590	3,166	3,619	4,118	4,842	5,712	6,361	7,081	8,410	9,686	11,240
Portfolio Investment	79lcd	....	1	199	6,019	6,039	6,382	6,437	6,465	4,017	4,134	4,134	4,142
Equity Securities	79ldd	....	1	8	20	26	48	53	54	54	55	56	66
Debt Securities	79led	....	−	191	5,999	6,013	6,334	6,383	6,411	3,963	4,079	4,078	4,077
Financial Derivatives	79lld	....	−	−	−	−	−	−	−	−	−	−	−
Other Investment	79lfd	....	13,819	15,001	8,753	9,284	9,688	11,106	10,590	10,238	11,519	13,104	12,892
Monetary Authorities	79lgd	....	511	729	669	591	549	721	665	681	579	572	528
General Government	79lhd	....	11,202	11,526	4,408	4,578	4,274	4,670	5,109	5,204	5,352	5,577	5,870
Banks	79lid	....	515	856	1,142	1,137	1,364	1,674	1,298	1,158	1,601	1,159	968
Other Sectors	79ljd	....	1,590	1,891	2,534	2,979	3,501	4,041	3,517	3,194	3,987	5,796	5,526
Government Finance		\multicolumn{12}{c}{*Millions of US Dollars: Year Ending December 31*}
Deficit (−) or Surplus	80	300.5	287.0	52.4	−163.8	−88.7	−291.4	68.7	−99.0	90.0	98.9	135.1	108.7
Revenue	81	1,961.3	2,248.2	2,570.9	3,131.4	3,334.1	3,380.3	3,280.3	2,705.1	3,056.6	3,873.7	4,205.3	4,709.7
Expenditure	82	1,660.8	1,961.3	2,518.5	3,295.2	3,422.7	3,671.7	3,211.6	2,804.1	2,966.6	3,774.8	4,070.2	4,601.0
Financing													
Domestic	84a	19.5	−30.9	237.5	365.4	150.2	824.4	−68.8	32.3	−269.4	−22.3	17.4	−216.5
Foreign	85a	−320.0	−256.0	−290.0	−201.6	−61.5	−533.0	.1	66.8	179.4	−76.9	−152.7	107.6

2004, International Monetary Fund: *International Financial Statistics Yearbook*

Ecuador 248

		1992	1993	1994	1995	1996	1997	1998	1999	2000	2001	2002	2003
National Accounts						*Millions of US Dollars*							
Househ.Cons.Expend.,incl.NPISHs	96f	8,571	10,454	12,592	13,827	14,022	15,682	16,120	11,035	10,199	14,491	16,837	18,873
Government Consumption Expend...	91f	917	1,767	2,237	2,525	2,567	2,902	2,857	2,088	1,564	2,134	2,550	3,061
Gross Fixed Capital Formation	93e	2,467	2,857	3,521	3,797	3,852	4,234	4,623	2,826	3,265	4,541	5,549	6,192
Changes in Inventories	93i	217	219	540	557	338	838	1,253	−371	−60	854	1,191	488
Exports of Goods and Services	90c	3,989	3,778	4,576	5,196	5,612	6,058	4,997	5,257	5,906	5,613	5,829	6,111
Imports of Goods and Services (-)	98c	3,506	4,018	4,894	5,707	5,124	6,078	6,595	4,161	4,939	6,608	7,644	7,637
Gross Domestic Product (GDP)	99b	12,656	15,057	18,573	20,196	21,268	23,636	23,255	16,675	15,934	21,024	24,311	27,088
Net Primary Income from Abroad	98.n	−607	−572	−1,279	−1,262	−1,304	−1,422	−1,625	−1,741	−2,229	−1,911	....	....
Gross National Income (GNI)	99a	12,049	13,732	15,327	16,677	17,736	18,347	18,098	11,948	11,698	15,208	....	....
Net National Income	99e	10,089	11,456	12,887	14,104	14,214	....	....	....	....	....	....	....
GDP Volume 2000 Prices	99b.p	....	14,270	14,942	15,203	15,568	16,199	16,541	15,499	15,934	16,749	17,321	17,918
GDP Volume (2000=100)	99bvp	91.0	92.8	96.8	99.1	101.1	104.5	104.9	†97.3	100.0	105.1	108.7	112.5
GDP Deflator (2000=100)	99bip	87.3	101.8	120.4	127.9	132.1	142.0	139.1	107.6	100.0	125.5	140.4	151.2
						Millions: Midyear Estimates							
Population	99z	10.73	10.96	11.18	11.40	11.62	11.82	12.02	12.22	12.42	12.62	12.81	13.00

2004, International Monetary Fund : *International Financial Statistics Yearbook*

Egypt

		1992	1993	1994	1995	1996	1997	1998	1999	2000	2001	2002	2003
Exchange Rates						*Pounds per SDR: End of Period*							
Market Rate......aa=	wa	4.5906	4.6314	4.9504	5.0392	4.8718	4.5713	4.7704	4.6734	4.8077	5.6427	6.1178	9.1435
						Pounds per US Dollar: End of Period							
Market Rate......ae=	we	3.3386	3.3718	3.3910	3.3900	3.3880	3.3880	3.3880	3.4050	3.6900	4.4900	4.5000	6.1532
Fund Position						*Millions of SDRs: End of Period*							
Quota................	2f.s	678	678	678	678	678	678	678	944	944	944	944	944
SDRs................	1b.s	43	50	59	70	86	84	114	30	37	28	67	127
Reserve Position in the Fund.........	1c.s	54	54	54	54	54	54	54	120	120	–	–	–
Total Fund Cred.&Loans Outstg.......	2tl	147	147	132	70	11	–	–	–	–	–	–	–
International Liquidity						*Millions of US Dollars Unless Otherwise Indicated: End of Period*							
Total Reserves minus Gold............	1l.d	10,810	12,904	13,481	16,181	17,398	18,665	18,124	14,484	13,118	12,926	13,242	13,589
SDRs................	1b.d	59	69	86	103	123	113	160	41	48	35	91	189
Reserve Position in the Fund.........	1c.d	74	74	78	80	77	73	76	165	156	–	–	–
Foreign Exchange................	1d.d	10,677	12,761	13,316	15,998	17,198	18,479	17,888	14,278	12,913	12,891	13,151	13,400
Gold (Million Fine Troy Ounces)......	1ad	2.432	2.432	2.432	2.432	2.432	2.432	2.432	2.432	2.432	2.432	2.432	2.432
Gold (National Valuation)............	1and	616	616	694	704	695	609	541	475	511	488	571	631
Monetary Authorities:Other Assets...	3..d	1,280	1,274	1,293	1,131	1,003	938	874	811	762	715	668	629
Other Liab...........	4..d	12,457	11,842	12,551	13,298	12,324	11,384	11,873	11,296	11,091	10,569	11,866	13,061
Deposit Money Banks: Assets..........	7a.d	11,326.8	10,786.5	11,432.3	11,070.3	10,736.2	9,153.2	7,815.1	7,441.1	7,297.1	5,915.0	6,279.5	7,782.2
Liabilities.............	7b.d	2,343.2	1,782.0	1,465.3	1,500.2	1,844.2	3,555.7	4,995.3	4,318.3	4,232.6	4,268.9	4,264.0	3,553.2
Other Banking Insts.: Assets........	7e.d	42.9	51.2	29.5	29.8	22.0	16.9	14.8	7.3	7.0	10.3	7.7	24.7
Liabilities.............	7f.d	436.1	486.5	457.1	275.5	255.4	267.4	219.9	215.1	240.8	161.5	173.2	166.9
Monetary Authorities						*Millions of Pounds: End of Period*							
Foreign Assets............	11	45,911	55,894	60,529	61,901	65,189	68,799	66,782	52,923	52,478	61,332	63,203	88,391
Claims on Central Government........	12a	56,993	52,849	50,978	51,615	47,015	44,368	61,209	75,447	95,715	116,392	131,068	177,255
Claims on Nonfin.Pub.Enterprises.....	12c	823	820	799	799	900	849	817	1,029	1,177	1,330	1,661	2,103
Claims on Deposit Money Banks......	12e	8,279	11,655	12,224	12,892	12,700	12,438	8,359	6,462	6,577	7,094	6,621	7,048
Claims on Other Banking Insts........	12f	1,974	2,134	2,040	2,095	2,147	2,261	2,275	3,336	2,846	2,901	2,319	2,509
Reserve Money................	14	35,712	42,554	47,888	52,357	54,562	60,610	72,336	73,522	87,271	102,094	111,002	155,065
of which: Currency Outside DMBs..	14a	15,241	17,818	20,612	22,750	24,954	28,215	31,502	35,310	37,902	40,548	45,281	52,475
Foreign Liabilities............	16c	42,264	40,609	43,215	45,430	41,807	38,570	40,224	38,464	40,926	47,454	53,398	80,365
Central Government Deposits..........	16d	35,109	38,481	33,617	29,661	28,476	26,738	22,296	23,298	27,676	42,862	43,420	59,364
Other Items (Net)............	17r	894	1,707	1,851	1,855	3,105	2,797	4,586	3,913	2,920	–3,359	–2,948	–17,487
Deposit Money Banks						*Millions of Pounds: End of Period*							
Reserves............	20	19,540	23,097	25,402	28,094	28,146	30,241	33,262	34,636	46,432	61,180	62,156	104,221
Foreign Assets............	21	37,722	36,370	38,767	37,528	36,374	31,011	26,477	25,337	26,926	26,559	28,258	47,886
Claims on Central Government........	22a	40,681	41,262	42,398	41,882	47,567	54,479	47,244	40,363	47,276	54,991	80,056	91,095
Claims on Nonfin.Pub.Enterprises.....	22c	23,928	29,283	29,998	33,180	37,481	38,643	38,801	42,109	38,141	42,062	42,655	45,896
Claims on Private Sector........	22d	30,978	36,885	48,831	66,777	83,810	105,545	133,799	159,958	176,693	197,038	207,089	225,023
Claims on Other Banking Insts........	22f	1,250	1,432	1,284	1,630	2,424	2,988	4,251	2,958	3,429	4,918	6,186	5,459
Demand Deposits............	24	13,985	14,940	15,919	17,282	18,026	18,920	19,335	20,506	21,747	23,515	27,021	36,627
Time, Savings,& Fgn.Currency Dep...	25	86,761	98,598	109,810	121,175	135,764	150,966	162,512	174,713	198,421	228,053	256,045	308,286
Bonds................	26ab	–	–	–	–	800	1,675	1,675	2,238	2,238	2,238	1,563	1,263
Restricted Deposits............	26b	7,076	8,239	9,182	10,858	12,513	14,081	15,771	18,113	17,502	19,658	20,161	22,750
Foreign Liabilities............	26c	7,804	6,009	4,969	5,086	6,248	12,047	16,924	14,704	15,618	19,167	19,188	21,864
Central Government Deposits..........	26d	10,206	6,907	7,805	11,016	13,638	14,670	18,906	23,889	28,596	34,429	40,488	51,498
Credit from Monetary Authorities.....	26g	9,613	15,598	17,571	20,842	20,648	20,938	11,244	7,256	7,464	7,547	7,475	7,675
Other Items (Net)............	27r	18,654	18,040	21,423	22,832	28,165	29,609	37,468	43,943	47,310	52,141	54,461	69,616
Monetary Survey						*Millions of Pounds: End of Period*							
Foreign Assets (Net)............	31n	33,566	45,646	51,111	48,914	53,508	49,194	36,111	25,092	22,860	21,270	18,875	34,049
Domestic Credit............	32	111,311	119,278	134,906	157,300	179,230	207,724	247,195	278,013	309,006	342,342	387,126	438,479
Claims on Central Govt. (Net)........	32an	52,358	48,724	51,953	52,820	52,467	57,439	67,252	68,623	86,720	94,091	127,216	157,489
Claims on Nonfin.Pub.Enterprises...	32c	24,751	30,103	30,797	33,979	38,381	39,492	39,618	43,138	39,318	43,393	44,316	47,999
Claims on Private Sector............	32d	30,978	36,885	48,831	66,777	83,810	105,545	133,799	159,958	176,693	197,038	207,089	225,023
Claims on Other Banking Insts.......	32f	3,224	3,566	3,324	3,724	4,571	5,248	6,526	6,294	6,275	7,820	8,505	7,968
Money................	34	30,832	34,571	38,275	41,540	44,521	48,708	58,577	59,066	62,195	67,078	75,781	93,520
of which: Foreign Currency Deps....	34a	10,253	10,918	9,892	10,980	10,260	9,332	10,225	11,148	17,493	31,330	32,734	52,864
Quasi-Money................	35	86,762	98,602	109,834	121,227	135,882	151,129	162,795	174,844	198,804	228,413	257,031	310,114
of which: Fgn. Currency Deposits...	35a	27,608	25,964	30,851	33,335	32,015	31,792	33,271	37,435	47,102	60,149	65,939	95,788
Bonds................	36ab	–	–	–	–	800	1,675	1,675	2,238	2,238	2,238	1,563	1,263
Restricted Deposits............	36b	7,076	8,239	9,182	10,858	12,513	14,081	15,771	18,113	17,502	19,658	20,161	22,750
Other Items (Net)............	37r	20,207	23,512	28,727	32,590	39,021	41,325	44,489	48,845	51,125	46,226	51,466	44,880
Money plus Quasi-Money................	35l	117,594	133,174	148,109	162,766	180,404	199,837	221,372	233,909	260,999	295,491	332,813	403,634

2004, International Monetary Fund: *International Financial Statistics Yearbook*

Egypt

		1992	1993	1994	1995	1996	1997	1998	1999	2000	2001	2002	2003
Other Banking Institutions													
Specialized Banks						*Millions of Pounds: End of Period*							
Cash	40	134	184	169	262	288	300	467	382	583	912	1,338	2,725
Foreign Assets	41	143	173	100	101	74	57	50	25	26	46	35	152
Claims on Nonfin.Pub.Enterprises	42c	1,881	1,961	2,067	2,130	2,170	2,112	2,073	2,397	2,246	2,262	2,720	2,447
Claims on Private Sector	42d	5,458	6,361	7,425	8,785	11,355	13,814	17,607	20,657	22,884	25,728	27,614	30,261
Demand Deposits	44	575	722	912	1,195	1,434	2,010	2,366	652	660	774	753	1,058
Time and Savings Deposits	45	1,330	1,705	2,322	2,751	3,464	4,297	5,703	8,835	9,807	11,304	13,382	16,360
Restricted Deposits	46b	19	32	20	32	36	42	59	53	43	14	13	36
Foreign Liabilities	46c	1,456	1,640	1,550	934	865	906	745	732	889	725	779	1,027
Central Government Deposits	46d	427	592	713	893	1,614	1,980	1,712	1,860	2,058	2,146	2,133	2,274
Credit from Monetary Authorities	46g	2,008	2,067	2,043	2,112	2,155	2,279	2,299	3,375	3,372	3,435	2,856	3,042
Credit from Deposit Money Banks	46h	1,236	1,410	1,021	1,500	2,292	2,790	3,932	2,442	2,911	4,496	5,324	4,899
Other Items (Net)	47r	565	509	1,180	1,861	2,027	1,980	3,381	5,513	5,999	6,054	6,465	6,890
Post Office: Savings Deposits	45..i	1,046	1,335	1,866	2,591	3,524	4,877	6,680	8,783	11,322	14,584	18,902	24,037
Banking Survey						*Millions of Pounds: End of Period*							
Foreign Assets (Net)	51n	32,253	44,178	49,661	48,081	52,717	48,346	35,416	24,384	21,997	20,591	18,130	33,174
Domestic Credit	52	116,128	124,880	142,295	166,797	190,938	222,041	266,064	301,818	337,171	374,998	425,773	486,385
Claims on Central Govt. (Net)	52an	53,060	49,570	53,175	55,127	55,223	61,079	72,968	75,668	96,030	106,577	144,035	180,655
Claims on Nonfin.Pub.Enterprises	52c	26,632	32,064	32,864	36,108	40,551	41,603	41,691	45,535	41,564	45,655	47,035	50,446
Claims on Private Sector	52d	36,436	43,246	56,256	75,562	95,164	119,359	151,406	180,615	199,577	222,766	234,703	255,283
Liquid Liabilities	55l	120,411	136,752	153,040	169,041	188,538	210,721	235,654	251,797	282,205	321,241	364,512	442,364
Bonds	56ab	–	–	–	–	800	1,675	1,675	2,238	2,238	2,238	1,563	1,263
Restricted Deposits	56b	7,095	8,271	9,202	10,890	12,550	14,123	15,830	18,166	17,546	19,672	20,174	22,786
Other Items (Net)	57r	20,876	24,035	29,714	34,948	41,768	43,868	48,322	54,003	57,178	52,439	57,657	53,146
Interest Rates						*Percent Per Annum*							
Discount Rate (End of Period)	60	18.40	16.50	14.00	13.50	13.00	12.25	12.00	12.00	12.00	11.00	10.00	10.00
Treasury Bill Rate	60c	...	...	...	...	...	8.8	8.8	9.0	9.1	7.2	5.5	6.9
Deposit Rate	60l	12.0	12.0	11.8	10.9	10.5	9.8	9.4	9.2	9.5	9.5	9.3	8.2
Lending Rate	60p	20.3	18.3	16.5	16.5	15.6	13.8	13.0	13.0	13.2	13.3	13.8	13.5
Prices and Labor						*Index Numbers (2000=100): Period Averages*							
Industrial Share Price	62	...	...	...	...	...	63.80	67.43	83.34	100.00	109.41	119.62	133.56
Wholesale Prices	63	70.48	76.51	80.04	85.09	92.17	96.02	97.36	98.24	100.00	101.03	107.49	122.94
Consumer Prices	64	57.8	64.8	70.1	†81.1	86.9	91.0	†94.5	97.4	100.0	102.3	105.1	109.5
						Number in Thousands: Period Averages							
Labor Force	67d	15,862	16,494	17,174	17,365	...	18,027	18,616	...	...	...	...	...
Employment	67e	14,399	†14,703	15,241	15,344	...	15,830	16,183	16,750	17,203	17,557	...	...
Unemployment	67c	1,416	1,801	1,877	1,917	...	†1,446	1,448	1,481	...	...	...	...
Unemployment Rate (%)	67r	9.0	10.9	11.0	11.3	...	†8.4	8.2	8.1	...	...	...	...
International Transactions						*Millions of Pounds*							
Exports	70	10,173.4	7,558.8	11,767.9	11,703.8	12,004.1	13,285.9	10,605.9	12,086.1	16,273.8	16,343.3	21,183.5	36,822.9
Suez Canal Dues	70.s	6,187.9	6,628.4	6,998.1	6,692.9	6,381.4	6,072.5	6,108.9	6,015.3	6,223.1	7,545.6	8,978.4	15,158.6
Imports, c.i.f.	71	27,656.1	27,553.8	34,598.9	39,892.0	44,218.0	44,769.0	54,771.0	54,399.0	48,645.0	50,660.0	56,480.0	65,082.0

Egypt 469

		1992	1993	1994	1995	1996	1997	1998	1999	2000	2001	2002	2003
Balance of Payments			*Millions of US Dollars: Minus Sign Indicates Debit*
Current Account, n.i.e.	78ald	2,812	2,299	31	−254	−192	−711	−2,566	−1,635	−971	−388	622	3,743
Goods: Exports f.o.b.	78aad	3,670	3,545	4,044	4,670	4,779	5,525	4,403	5,237	7,061	7,025	7,118	8,987
Goods: Imports f.o.b.	78abd	−8,901	−9,923	−9,997	−12,267	−13,169	−14,157	−14,617	−15,165	−15,382	−13,960	−12,879	−13,189
Trade Balance.	78acd	−5,231	−6,378	−5,953	−7,597	−8,390	−8,632	−10,214	−9,928	−8,321	−6,935	−5,762	−4,201
Services: Credit.	78add	7,716	7,895	8,070	8,590	9,271	9,380	8,141	9,494	9,803	9,042	9,320	11,073
Services: Debit.	78aed	−4,867	−5,367	−5,645	−4,873	−5,084	−6,770	−6,492	−6,452	−7,513	−7,037	−6,629	−6,474
Balance on Goods & Services.	78afd	−2,382	−3,850	−3,528	−3,880	−4,203	−6,021	−8,565	−6,886	−6,031	−4,929	−3,071	398
Income: Credit.	78agd	915	1,110	1,330	1,578	1,901	2,122	2,030	1,788	1,871	1,468	698	578
Income: Debit.	78ahd	−2,797	−1,967	−2,114	−1,983	−1,556	−1,185	−1,075	−1,045	−983	−885	−965	−832
Balance on Gds, Serv. & Inc.	78aid	−4,264	−4,707	−4,312	−4,285	−3,858	−5,085	−7,610	−6,143	−5,143	−4,346	−3,338	145
Current Transfers, n.i.e.: Credit.	78ajd	7,076	7,006	4,622	4,284	3,888	4,738	5,166	4,564	4,224	4,056	4,002	3,708
Current Transfers: Debit.	78akd	–	–	−279	−253	−222	−363	−122	−55	−52	−98	−42	−109
Capital Account, n.i.e.	78bcd	–	–	–	–	–	....	....	....	–	....	–	....
Capital Account, n.i.e.: Credit.	78bad	–	–	–	–	–	....	....	....	....	....	–	....
Capital Account: Debit.	78bbd	–	–	–	–	–	....	....	....	....	....	....	....
Financial Account, n.i.e.	78bjd	−168	−762	−1,450	−1,845	−1,459	1,958	1,901	−1,421	−1,646	190	−3,333	−5,725
Direct Investment Abroad.	78bdd	−4	–	−43	−93	−5	−129	−45	−38	−51	−12	−28	−21
Dir. Invest. in Rep. Econ., n.i.e.	78bed	459	493	1,256	598	636	891	1,076	1,065	1,235	510	647	237
Portfolio Investment Assets.	78bfd	6	–	–	–	–	–	−63	−22	−3	−2	−6	−25
Equity Securities.	78bkd	–	–	–	....	–	–	−63	−22	−3	−2	−6	−25
Debt Securities.	78bld	6	–	–	–	–	....	....	....	....	....	....	....
Portfolio Investment Liab., n.i.e.	78bgd	–	4	3	20	545	816	−537	617	269	1,463	−672	−18
Equity Securities.	78bmd	–	–	–	....	–	515	−160	658	269	39	−217	37
Debt Securities.	78bnd	–	4	3	20	545	301	−377	−41	....	1,424	−455	−55
Financial Derivatives Assets.	78bwd	....	....	–	....	–	....	....	....	....	....	....	....
Financial Derivatives Liabilities.	78bxd	....	....	–	....	–	....	....	....	....	....	....	....
Other Investment Assets.	78bhd	1,183	319	−905	−396	−565	−170	39	−1,805	−2,991	−1,261	−2,943	−4,651
Monetary Authorities.	78bod	−13	−21	−25	65	65	37	24	−14	−21	−73	29	−38
General Government.	78bpd	−104	−4	–	....	–	....	....	....	....	....	....	....
Banks.	78bqd	1,300	523	−634	371	338	1,599	1,357	372	257	1,369	−331	−1,682
Other Sectors.	78brd	–	−179	−246	−832	−968	−1,806	−1,342	−2,163	−3,227	−2,556	−2,641	−2,931
Other Investment Liab., n.i.e.	78bid	−1,812	−1,578	−1,761	−1,974	−2,070	551	1,431	−1,240	−105	−509	−331	−1,248
Monetary Authorities.	78bsd	−42	629	−5	−21	−4	−19	−204	−3	−5	104	5	6
General Government.	78btd	−1,175	−1,761	−1,536	−1,783	−2,578	−1,506	−946	−989	−1,109	−1,157	−1,358	−1,673
Banks.	78bud	−383	−202	−256	−148	324	1,715	1,393	−692	−129	−56	−9	−601
Other Sectors.	78bvd	−212	−244	36	−22	188	361	1,188	444	1,138	601	1,031	1,020
Net Errors and Omissions.	78cad	716	−1,519	255	272	−74	−1,882	−722	−1,558	587	−1,146	1,906	1,575
Overall Balance.	78cbd	3,360	18	−1,164	−1,827	−1,725	−635	−1,387	−4,614	−2,030	−1,345	−804	−407
Reserves and Related Items.	79dad	−3,360	−18	1,164	1,827	1,725	635	1,387	4,614	2,030	1,345	804	407
Reserve Assets.	79dbd	−6,330	−2,809	−1,193	−409	−1,010	−1,185	535	4,027	1,306	507	−57	−395
Use of Fund Credit and Loans.	79dcd	81	–	−22	−95	−85	−15	–	–	–	–	–	–
Exceptional Financing.	79ded	2,889	2,791	2,379	2,331	2,820	1,836	852	587	724	838	861	801
Government Finance			*Millions of Pounds: Year Ending June 30*
Deficit (−) or Surplus.	80	−4,831	2,681	589	1,828	†−4,411	−5,178	−2,591	....	....	....	....	....
Revenue.	81	49,678	59,443	67,828	73,654	†69,233	72,782	69,091	....	....	....	....	....
Grants Received.	81z	3,337	3,269	2,811	2,056	†1,954	1,392	1,689	....	....	....	....	....
Expenditure.	82	54,649	56,143	65,382	68,689	†74,400	78,503	72,048	....	....	....	....	....
Lending Minus Repayments.	83	3,197	3,888	4,668	5,193	†1,198	849	1,323	....	....	....	....	....
Financing													
Domestic.	84a	6,708	−1,319	1,454	−60	†5,844	6,785	4,397	....	....	....	....	....
Foreign.	85a	−1,877	−1,362	−2,043	−1,768	†−1,433	−1,607	−1,806	....	....	....	....	....
National Accounts			*Millions of Pounds: Year Ending June 30*
Househ.Cons.Expend.,incl.NPISHs.	96f	101,000	115,000	130,500	151,900	176,490	200,500	220,400	230,800	258,000	270,000	279,000	303,000
Government Consumption Expend.	91f	14,500	16,000	18,000	21,500	23,800	26,100	32,500	35,700	38,100	40,600	47,200	52,000
Gross Fixed Capital Formation.	93e	26,500	25,500	29,000	33,100	36,760	47,700	61,300	64,000	64,400	63,600	67,500	68,100
Changes in Inventories.	93i	−1,200	–	–	2,000	1,340	−1,000	500	2,500	2,100	1,900	1,700	2,900
Exports of Goods and Services.	90c	39,500	40,100	39,500	45,990	47,620	50,100	46,600	46,300	55,100	62,700	69,500	90,000
Imports of Goods and Services (−).	98c	43,000	48,700	50,100	58,290	61,100	66,200	73,900	71,700	77,600	80,100	86,400	101,000
Gross Domestic Product (GDP).	99b	139,100	157,300	175,000	204,000	229,400	257,200	287,400	307,600	340,100	358,700	378,500	415,000
GDP Volume 1986/87 Prices.	99b.p	63,650	....	....	....	....	....	....	....	....	....	....	....
GDP Volume 1991/92 Prices.	99b.p	139,100	143,140	148,820	155,730	163,500	172,480	....	....	....	....	....	....
GDP Volume 1996/97 Prices.	99b.p	....	....	....	....	....	257,200	276,600	293,500	309,300	320,200	330,400	....
GDP Volume 2001/02.	99b.p	....	....	....	....	....	....	....	....	....	....	378,500	390,600
GDP Volume (2000=100).	99bvp	†67.1	69.0	71.7	75.1	78.8	†83.2	89.4	94.9	100.0	103.5	†106.8	110.2
GDP Deflator (2000=100).	99bip	61.0	67.0	71.7	79.9	85.6	90.9	94.5	95.3	100.0	101.9	104.2	110.7
			*Millions: Midyear Estimates*
Population.	99z	58.13	59.30	60.46	61.64	62.82	64.02	65.24	66.49	67.78	Ü 69.12	70.51	71.93

2004, International Monetary Fund : *International Financial Statistics Yearbook*

El Salvador 253

		1992	1993	1994	1995	1996	1997	1998	1999	2000	2001	2002	2003
Exchange Rates			*Colones per SDR: End of Period (aa) Colones per US Dollar: End of Period (ae)*
Market Rate	aa	12.609	11.909	12.774	13.014	12.589	11.813	12.327	12.016	11.407	10.996	11.896	13.002
Market Rate	ae	9.170	8.670	8.750	8.755	8.755	8.755	8.755	8.755	8.755	8.750	8.750	8.750
Fund Position						*Millions of SDRs: End of Period*							
Quota	2f.s	125.6	125.6	125.6	125.6	125.6	125.6	125.6	171.3	171.3	171.3	171.3	171.3
SDRs	1b.s	–	–	.1	25.0	25.0	25.0	25.0	25.0	25.0	25.0	25.0	25.0
Reserve Position in the Fund	1c.s	–	–	–	–	–	–	–	–	–	–	–	–
Total Fund Cred.&Loans Outstg	2tl	–	–	–	–	–	–	–	–	–	–	–	–
International Liquidity					*Millions of US Dollars Unless Otherwise Indicated: End of Period*								
Total Reserves minus Gold	1l.d	422.1	536.2	649.4	758.3	936.9	1,307.9	1,613.1	2,003.8	1,922.4	1,741.0	1,622.8	1,942.9
SDRs	1b.d	–	–	.1	37.1	35.9	33.7	35.2	34.3	32.6	31.4	34.0	37.1
Reserve Position in the Fund	1c.d	–	–	–	–	–	–	–	–	–	–	–	–
Foreign Exchange	1d.d	422.1	536.2	649.3	721.2	901.0	1,274.2	1,577.9	1,969.5	1,889.8	1,709.6	1,588.8	1,905.8
Gold (Million Fine Troy Ounces)	1ad	.469	.469	.469	.469	.469	.469	.469	.469	.469	.469	.469	.469
Gold (National Valuation)	1and	144.9	181.1	179.8	181.5	173.2	152.5	152.5	152.4	120.7	117.8	117.8	117.8
Monetary Authorities: Other Liab.	4..d	368.1	293.1	158.6	175.6	217.9	244.4	169.5	166.5	190.9	159.5	130.8	299.0
Banking Institutions: Assets	7a.d	81.1	94.0	59.6	69.9	106.2	113.4	121.3	125.3	280.0	793.8	867.0	975.9
Liabilities	7b.d	31.4	48.5	142.3	361.7	404.6	534.9	514.4	549.7	671.2	949.9	1,085.1	1,573.5
Nonbank Financial Insts.:Assets	7e.d	....	....	....	....	....	....	....	....	2.1	27.3	43.7	86.2
Liabs	7f.d	....	....	....	....	....	....	....	....	60.0	73.1	91.1	153.7
Monetary Authorities						*Millions of US Dollars: End of Period*							
Foreign Assets	11	555.5	736.5	854.1	937.9	1,110.3	1,452.9	1,776.8	1,971.2	†1,992.6	1,810.7	1,689.8	2,007.5
Claims on Central Government	12a	748.9	787.2	721.6	708.2	663.9	649.7	614.9	637.2	†678.6	692.4	708.8	708.7
Claims on Local Government	12b	1.3	1.3	1.3	1.3	1.2	1.1	.9	.8	†.7	.6	.5	.3
Claims on Nonfin.Pub.Enterprises	12c	1.4	–	–	–	–	–	–	–	†–	–	–	–
Claims on Private Sector	12d	–	–	–	–	–	–	–	–	†5.9	5.9	13.7	13.7
Claims on Banking Institutions	12e	205.1	227.7	262.0	340.3	401.0	421.1	476.0	518.7	†119.8	105.5	88.0	87.1
Claims on Nonbank Financial Insts.	12g	–	–	–	–	–	–	–	–	†698.2	658.2	625.8	588.8
Reserve Money	14	663.6	1,006.9	1,229.9	1,382.2	1,520.6	1,722.9	1,866.3	2,056.4	†1,318.3	932.9	723.9	1,105.4
of which: Currency Outside Banks	14a	265.4	306.3	339.4	357.6	355.0	369.7	403.0	538.4	†451.5	220.2	60.6	36.4
Time, Savings,& Fgn.Currency Dep.	15	75.6	98.4	96.1	101.3	37.4	8.4	6.4	2.9	†5.2	20.1	25.5	31.7
Liabs. of Central Bank: Securities	16ac	320.1	386.0	324.1	210.7	294.8	427.3	478.9	596.2	†1,155.4	1,327.6	1,287.9	1,223.2
Restricted Deposits	16b	–	.1	–	.1	–	–	–	–	†.8	.8	.8	.8
Foreign Liabilities	16c	60.1	34.6	7.2	9.0	3.0	2.9	–	2.8	†4.9	3.5	2.1	4.9
Long-Term Foreign Liabilities	16cl	308.0	258.6	151.4	166.5	214.9	241.6	169.5	163.6	†186.0	156.0	128.7	294.1
Central Government Deposits	16d	238.0	186.2	235.7	204.0	140.3	141.1	469.6	529.3	†634.2	613.5	691.0	467.5
Capital Accounts	17a	218.3	248.7	255.5	227.2	226.0	230.8	249.4	266.3	†249.7	172.7	185.3	188.0
Other Items (Net)	17r	–371.7	–466.7	–461.1	–313.5	–260.6	–250.2	–371.4	–489.6	†–58.8	46.2	81.4	90.4
Banking Institutions						*Millions of US Dollars: End of Period*							
Reserves	20	365.1	581.2	858.9	967.1	1,094.6	1,222.4	1,337.9	1,464.9	†782.2	712.2	660.2	987.7
Claims on Mon.Author.:Securities	20c	98.5	150.2	182.8	137.8	106.3	138.4	61.7	357.3	†627.9	984.4	1,063.2	936.0
Foreign Assets	21	81.1	94.0	59.6	69.9	106.2	113.4	121.3	125.3	†280.0	793.8	867.0	975.9
Claims on Central Government	22a	83.4	116.4	157.3	157.0	170.4	144.0	90.3	128.3	†364.8	590.4	409.2	454.6
Claims on Local Government	22b	–	–	–	–	–	1.9	2.8	8.0	†–	–	–	–
Claims on Private Sector	22d	1,337.7	1,661.4	2,634.0	3,378.7	3,828.7	4,520.6	5,039.4	5,475.9	†5,857.3	5,456.3	5,639.5	6,115.1
Claims on Nonbank Financial Insts.	22g	–	–	–	–	–	–	–	–	†151.6	350.0	380.5	341.6
Demand Deposits	24	333.5	404.4	404.4	449.3	570.6	562.1	601.7	618.7	†630.2	977.7	1,027.1	1,085.6
Time, Savings,& Fgn.Currency Dep.	25	1,222.1	1,722.4	2,723.2	3,078.6	3,577.8	4,080.8	4,459.0	4,791.7	†4,976.7	5,082.5	4,990.4	5,013.8
Money Market Instruments	26aa	16.4	12.9	20.6	65.0	127.4	187.6	191.6	241.3	†327.4	322.6	339.8	415.9
Foreign Liabilities	26c	31.4	48.5	133.8	332.0	328.1	402.7	300.9	286.9	†359.3	676.8	616.7	900.7
Long-Term Foreign Liabilities	26cl	–	–	8.5	29.7	76.5	132.2	213.5	262.8	†311.9	273.2	468.4	672.7
Central Government Deposits	26d	59.0	64.8	138.0	205.9	215.3	242.7	324.0	303.3	†335.5	416.5	457.8	479.2
Credit from Monetary Authorities	26g	135.0	151.9	2.0	–	–	26.9	81.2	148.1	†92.5	106.1	87.6	86.9
Liab. to Nonbank Financial Insts.	26j	62.6	71.0	77.1	79.3	88.7	138.0	129.2	80.8	†473.0	414.3	353.8	313.0
Capital Accounts	27a	88.3	99.2	272.3	345.8	445.4	489.1	570.5	609.0	†640.4	694.2	762.5	836.6
Other Items (Net)	27r	17.7	28.0	112.6	124.6	–123.6	–121.4	–218.1	217.2	†–83.0	–76.6	–84.7	6.3

El Salvador 253

		1992	1993	1994	1995	1996	1997	1998	1999	2000	2001	2002	2003
Banking Survey						*Millions of US Dollars: End of Period*							
Foreign Assets (Net)...............	31n	545.2	747.5	772.7	666.7	885.4	1,160.7	1,597.2	1,806.8	†1,908.4	1,924.3	1,938.1	2,077.8
Domestic Credit.....................	32	1,875.6	2,315.4	3,140.4	3,835.2	4,308.6	4,933.5	4,954.8	5,422.3	†6,787.5	6,723.8	6,629.1	7,276.0
Claims on Central Govt. (Net)......	32an	535.2	652.6	505.1	455.3	478.7	409.9	−88.4	−67.1	†73.7	252.8	−30.9	216.5
Claims on Local Government......	32b	1.3	1.3	1.3	1.3	1.2	3.0	3.8	8.8	†.7	.6	.5	.3
Claims on Nonfin.Pub.Enterprises...	32c	1.4	–	–	–	–	–	–	4.7	†–	–	–	–
Claims on Private Sector............	32d	1,337.7	1,661.4	2,634.0	3,378.7	3,828.7	4,520.6	5,039.4	5,475.9	†5,863.2	5,462.2	5,653.1	6,128.8
Claims on Nonbank Financial Insts.	32g	–	–	–	–	–	–	–	–	†849.8	1,008.2	1,006.4	930.3
Money...............................	34	604.6	718.2	746.5	812.0	927.7	933.1	1,007.7	1,160.2	†1,093.0	1,198.1	1,090.4	1,198.6
Quasi-Money.......................	35	1,297.7	1,820.8	2,819.3	3,180.0	3,615.1	4,089.2	4,465.4	4,794.6	†4,981.9	5,102.6	5,015.9	5,045.6
Money Market Instruments...........	36aa	16.4	12.9	20.6	65.0	127.4	187.6	191.6	241.3	†327.4	322.6	339.8	415.9
Liabs. of Central Bank: Securities.....	36ac	221.5	235.8	141.4	72.9	188.5	288.9	417.2	238.8	†527.6	343.2	224.7	287.3
Restricted Deposits.................	36b	–	.1	–	.1	–	–	–	–	†.8	.8	.8	.8
Long-Term Foreign Liabilities.........	36cl	308.0	258.6	160.0	196.2	291.4	373.8	383.0	426.5	†497.9	429.1	597.1	966.9
Liab. to Nonbank Financial Insts.......	36j	62.6	71.0	77.1	79.3	88.7	138.0	129.2	80.8	†473.0	414.3	353.8	313.0
Capital Accounts.....................	37a	306.6	347.9	527.8	573.0	671.5	719.9	819.9	875.2	†890.1	866.9	947.8	1,024.6
Other Items (Net)...................	37r	−396.6	−402.4	−579.6	−476.5	−716.3	−636.3	−862.0	−588.4	†−95.8	−29.6	−3.4	101.1
Money plus Quasi-Money...........	35l	1,902.3	2,539.0	3,565.8	3,991.9	4,542.9	5,022.3	5,473.1	5,954.9	†6,074.9	6,300.6	6,106.4	6,244.2
Nonbank Financial Institutions						*Millions of US Dollars: End of Period*							
Reserves............................	40	....	....	....	....	....	....	....	....	8.3	–	2.6	68.5
Claims on Mon.Author.:Securities.....	40c	....	....	....	....	....	....	....	....	148.9	133.0	158.8	133.0
Foreign Assets......................	41	....	....	....	....	....	....	....	....	2.1	27.3	43.7	86.2
Claims on Banking Institutions........	42e	....	....	....	....	....	....	....	....	354.6	369.1	304.3	243.2
Foreign Liabilities...................	46c	....	....	....	....	....	....	....	....	60.0	73.1	91.1	153.7
Credit from Monetary Authorities.....	46g	....	....	....	....	....	....	....	....	451.5	419.4	388.3	357.5
Capital Accounts....................	47a	....	....	....	....	....	....	....	....	31.3	35.9	43.8	47.8
Other Items (Net)..................	47r	....	....	....	....	....	....	....	....	−29.0	1.1	−13.8	−28.0
Interest Rates						*Percent Per Annum*							
Money Market Rate.................	60b	....	....	....	....	....	10.43	9.43	10.68	6.93	5.28	4.40	3.86
Deposit Rate.......................	60l	11.51	15.27	13.57	14.37	13.98	11.77	10.32	10.75	9.31	....	....	....
Deposit Rate (Fgn. Currency)...........	60l.f	....	....	....	....	8.38	7.68	6.86	6.61	6.50	5.48	3.41	3.37
Lending Rate......................	60p	16.43	19.42	19.03	19.08	18.57	16.05	14.98	15.46	13.96	....	....	....
Lending Rate (Fgn. Currency)...........	60p.f	....	....	....	....	12.53	10.82	9.93	10.38	10.74	9.60	7.14	6.56
Prices and Labor						*Index Numbers (2000=100): Period Averages*							
Producer Prices (2000=100)...........	63	....	....	....	....	....	....	....	93.9	100.0	101.0	98.8	101.3
Wholesale Prices...................	63a	77.1	82.9	89.4	98.7	103.5	104.5	98.3	96.8	100.0	98.4	94.3	96.6
Consumer Prices...................	64	†57.3	68.0	75.2	82.7	90.8	94.9	97.3	97.8	100.0	103.8	105.7	107.9
						Number in Thousands: Period Averages							
Labor Force.......................	67d	1,683	....	2,010	2,051	2,140	2,188	2,403	2,445	....	....	....	2,520
Employment.......................	67e	†1,782	....	1,951	1,973	2,056	2,076	2,228	2,275	2,323	2,451	2,413	....
Unemployment...................	67c	81	†109	162	163	171	180	176	170	174	184	160	....
Unemployment Rate (%).............	67r	7.9	†9.9	7.7	7.7	7.7	8.0	7.3	7.0	7.0	7.0	6.2	....
International Transactions						*Millions of US Dollars*							
Exports.............................	70..d	597.5	731.7	843.9	998.0	1,024.4	1,371.1	1,256.4	1,176.6	1,332.3	1,213.5	1,238.1	1,255.0
Imports, c.i.f.......................	71..d	1,698.5	1,912.2	2,248.7	2,853.3	2,670.9	2,980.5	3,121.4	3,140.0	3,794.7	3,866.0	3,909.4	4,381.8

2004, International Monetary Fund : *International Financial Statistics Yearbook*

El Salvador 253

		1992	1993	1994	1995	1996	1997	1998	1999	2000	2001	2002	2003
Balance of Payments						*Millions of US Dollars: Minus Sign Indicates Debit*							
Current Account, n.i.e.	78ald	−195.1	−122.8	−18.0	−261.6	−169.0	−97.8	−90.7	−239.3	−430.5	−150.3	−411.8	−733.6
Goods: Exports f.o.b.	78aad	598.1	1,031.8	1,252.3	1,651.1	1,787.4	2,437.1	2,459.5	2,534.3	2,963.2	2,891.6	3,020.8	3,162.4
Goods: Imports f.o.b.	78abd	−1,560.5	−1,994.0	−2,422.3	−3,113.5	−3,029.7	−3,580.3	−3,765.2	−3,890.4	−4,702.8	−4,824.1	−4,891.7	−5,436.0
Trade Balance	78acd	−962.3	−962.3	−1,170.0	−1,462.3	−1,242.3	−1,143.2	−1,305.7	−1,356.1	−1,739.6	−1,932.5	−1,870.9	−2,273.6
Services: Credit	78add	377.1	335.5	387.2	388.6	414.4	475.8	588.5	640.4	698.4	703.6	781.9	824.1
Services: Debit	78aed	−364.7	−386.7	−428.9	−509.8	−504.6	−628.0	−737.3	−822.9	−933.3	−954.0	−1,022.2	−993.5
Balance on Goods & Services	78afd	−949.9	−1,013.4	−1,211.7	−1,583.5	−1,332.5	−1,295.4	−1,454.5	−1,538.6	−1,974.5	−2,182.9	−2,111.2	−2,443.0
Income: Credit	78agd	31.7	30.8	35.5	54.0	44.1	75.1	111.4	112.9	141.3	168.9	159.1	140.4
Income: Debit	78ahd	−128.9	−142.4	−130.1	−120.7	−134.4	−238.3	−274.4	−395.1	−394.4	−434.6	−482.5	−548.1
Balance on Gds, Serv. & Inc.	78aid	−1,047.1	−1,125.0	−1,306.4	−1,650.2	−1,422.8	−1,458.6	−1,617.5	−1,820.8	−2,227.6	−2,448.6	−2,434.6	−2,850.7
Current Transfers, n.i.e.: Credit	78ajd	852.8	1,004.7	1,290.9	1,393.2	1,258.6	1,363.6	1,534.1	1,590.5	1,830.3	2,373.5	2,110.6	2,197.1
Current Transfers: Debit	78akd	−.7	−2.5	−2.5	−4.6	−4.8	−2.7	−7.3	−9.0	−33.2	−75.2	−87.8	−80.0
Capital Account, n.i.e.	78bcd	−	−	−	−	−	11.6	28.6	78.6	109.0	198.9	208.9	112.9
Capital Account, n.i.e.: Credit	78bad	−	−	−	−	−	11.6	28.9	78.8	109.4	199.3	209.4	113.4
Capital Account: Debit	78bbd	−	−	−	−	....	−	−.3	−.2	−.4	−.4	−.5	−.5
Financial Account, n.i.e.	78bjd	−4.3	73.9	115.8	438.3	358.1	653.2	1,034.3	574.5	287.5	230.3	686.9	1,089.5
Direct Investment Abroad	78bdd	−	−	−	−	−2.4	−	−1.0	−53.8	5.0	9.7	25.7	−18.6
Dir. Invest. in Rep. Econ., n.i.e.	78bed	15.3	16.4	−	38.0	−4.8	59.0	1,103.7	215.9	173.4	278.9	470.0	103.7
Portfolio Investment Assets	78bfd	−	−	−	−	.5	−	−	−1.7	−8.9	−126.5	−289.2	−263.7
Equity Securities	78bkd	−	−	−	−	.5	−	−	−	−	−	−	−
Debt Securities	78bld	−	−	−	−	....	−	−	−1.7	−8.9	−126.5	−289.2	−263.7
Portfolio Investment Liab., n.i.e.	78bgd	−	−	−	68.5	150.0	115.9	−226.4	75.2	−16.8	155.5	554.8	452.7
Equity Securities	78bmd	−	−	−	−	....	−	−	−	−	2.4	−2.4	−
Debt Securities	78bnd	−	−	−	68.5	150.0	115.9	−226.4	75.2	−16.8	153.1	557.2	452.7
Financial Derivatives Assets	78bwd	....	....	....	....	....	....	....	....	....	....	....	....
Financial Derivatives Liabilities	78bxd	....	....	....	....	....	....	....	....	....	....	....	....
Other Investment Assets	78bhd	−	18.5	−8.7	24.2	4.7	−19.9	12.2	−126.9	−245.2	−629.1	−224.8	19.8
Monetary Authorities	78bod	....	14.4	−	35.0	−	−	−	−	−	−	−	−
General Government	78bpd	−	−	−	−	−	−	−	−	−	−	−	−
Banks	78bqd	−	4.1	−8.7	−10.2	−	2.1	−8.0	−4.6	−146.4	−391.3	−83.1	133.7
Other Sectors	78brd	−	−	−	−.6	4.7	−21.9	20.2	−122.3	−98.8	−237.8	−141.7	−113.9
Other Investment Liab., n.i.e.	78bid	−19.6	39.0	124.5	307.5	210.2	498.2	145.7	465.8	380.0	541.8	150.4	795.6
Monetary Authorities	78bsd	−92.8	−91.1	−147.2	38.2	51.2	27.9	−72.2	−2.1	−19.5	−30.8	−27.7	76.7
General Government	78btd	42.2	115.4	177.0	46.4	162.8	154.6	162.9	51.4	83.3	201.0	217.6	33.2
Banks	78bud	−	14.7	94.7	219.9	−3.2	130.8	−20.4	35.0	120.0	278.3	139.2	493.3
Other Sectors	78bvd	31.0	−	−	3.1	−.6	184.9	75.5	381.5	196.2	93.3	−178.7	192.4
Net Errors and Omissions	78cad	65.6	107.6	15.4	−28.4	−24.2	−204.4	−668.9	−206.0	−11.5	−456.6	−607.5	−152.6
Overall Balance	78cbd	−133.8	58.6	113.3	148.3	164.8	362.7	303.3	207.8	−45.5	−177.7	−123.5	316.2
Reserves and Related Items	79dad	133.8	−58.6	−113.3	−148.3	−164.8	−362.7	−303.3	−207.8	45.5	177.7	123.5	−316.2
Reserve Assets	79dbd	−91.6	−111.9	−113.3	−148.3	−164.8	−362.7	−303.3	−207.8	45.5	177.7	123.5	−316.2
Use of Fund Credit and Loans	79dcd	−	−	−	−	−	−	−	−	−	−	−	−
Exceptional Financing	79ded	225.5	53.3	−	−	−	−	−	−	−	−	−	−
International Investment Position						*Millions of US Dollars*							
Assets	79aad	....	....	....	....	1,771.3	2,153.8	2,445.6	2,832.4	3,004.0	3,309.9	3,697.7	4,462.1
Direct Investment Abroad	79abd	....	−	−	−	55.7	55.7	56.7	110.5	103.9	64.3	38.6	146.3
Portfolio Investment	79acd	....	−	−	−	−	−	−	2.1	11.0	152.5	441.6	859.5
Equity Securities	79add	....	....	....	....	−	−	−	−	−	17.8	316.8	260.4
Debt Securities	79aed	....	....	....	....	−	−	−	2.1	11.0	134.7	124.8	599.1
Financial Derivatives	79ald	....	....	....	....	−	−	−	−	−	−	−	−
Other Investment	79afd	....	51.4	59.9	70.1	615.9	635.8	623.5	747.5	995.8	1,381.5	1,626.1	1,546.2
Monetary Authorities	79agd	....	....	....	....	−	−	−	−	−	−	−	−
General Government	79ahd	....	....	....	....	22.0	22.0	22.0	22.0	22.0	−	−	−
Banks	79aid	....	....	....	....	115.8	113.8	121.8	123.5	273.1	658.5	741.6	608.5
Other Sectors	79ajd	....	....	....	....	478.0	500.0	479.7	602.0	700.7	723.0	884.5	937.7
Reserve Assets	79akd	....	707.3	812.9	959.6	1,099.7	1,462.3	1,765.4	1,972.3	1,893.2	1,711.6	1,591.4	1,910.1
Liabilities	79lad	....	....	....	....	4,335.6	4,990.5	6,025.5	6,854.7	7,358.3	8,340.2	9,368.1	11,214.6
Dir. Invest. in Rep. Economy	79lbd	....	−	−	−	421.2	480.3	1,583.9	1,815.2	2,000.6	2,240.9	2,448.8	3,220.0
Portfolio Investment	79lcd	....	−	−	−	241.0	357.0	130.5	205.0	202.8	352.6	948.3	1,402.5
Equity Securities	79ldd	....	....	....	....	−	−	−	−	−	2.4	−	−
Debt Securities	79led	....	....	....	....	241.0	357.0	130.5	205.0	202.8	350.2	948.3	1,402.5
Financial Derivatives	79lld	....	....	....	....	−	−	−	−	−	−	−	−
Other Investment	79lfd	....	2,042.7	2,198.1	2,530.1	3,673.3	4,153.3	4,311.1	4,834.5	5,154.9	5,746.7	5,971.0	6,592.1
Monetary Authorities	79lgd	....	....	....	....	220.4	237.5	165.4	202.4	181.9	153.6	126.0	202.3
General Government	79lhd	....	....	....	....	2,075.8	2,194.9	2,350.1	2,423.2	2,448.3	2,678.0	2,943.4	2,629.0
Banks	79lid	....	....	....	....	406.2	531.0	516.5	548.3	673.8	950.0	1,084.5	1,598.0
Other Sectors	79ljd	....	....	....	....	970.9	1,189.9	1,279.1	1,660.6	1,850.9	1,965.1	1,817.1	2,162.8

El Salvador 253

		1992	1993	1994	1995	1996	1997	1998	1999	2000	2001	2002	2003
Government Finance						*Millions of Colones: Year Ending December 31*							
Deficit (-) or Surplus	80	−1,839.3	−1,284.4	†−521.8	−455.2	−1,841.3	−1,102.1	−1,920.9	−2,456.0	−2,658.6	....	....	....
Total Revenue and Grants	81y	5,715.6	7,215.7	†9,529.7	11,436.9	12,248.9	12,204.7	13,202.2	12,570.2	13,857.3	....	....	....
Revenue	81	....	....	....	....	....	....	13,104.2	12,471.4	13,030.6	....	....	....
Grants	81z	....	....	....	....	....	....	98.0	98.8	826.7	....	....	....
Exp. & Lending Minus Repay	82z	7,554.9	8,500.1	†10,051.5	11,892.1	14,090.2	13,306.8	15,123.1	15,026.2	16,515.9	....	....	....
Expenditure	82	7,253.7	8,314.0	†9,970.9	11,755.7	14,070.3	13,533.6	15,227.1	15,094.3	16,628.1	....	....	....
Lending Minus Repayments	83	301.2	186.1	†80.6	136.4	19.9	−226.8	−104.0	−68.1	−112.2	....	....	....
Total Financing	80h	....	....	†521.9	455.2	1,841.3	1,102.1	1,920.1	2,456.0	2,658.7	....	....	....
Domestic	84a	....	....	†−844.2	−542.3	−86.2	−553.4	2,159.8	1,296.7	1,300.6	....	....	....
Foreign	85a	....	1,305.0	†1,366.1	997.5	1,927.5	1,655.5	−239.7	1,159.3	1,358.1	....	....	....
Use of Cash Balances	87	....	....	....	−527.8	−313.6	....	....	....	....	....	....	....
Total Debt by Residence	88	25,142.3	25,292.0	†21,305.8	22,066.6	23,968.0	24,759.7	24,663.7	27,714.1	30,634.4	....	....	....
Domestic	88a	9,494.8	9,995.6	†8,463.0	8,226.3	7,883.7	7,460.9	7,119.9	8,015.2	10,687.0	....	....	....
Foreign	89a	15,647.5	15,296.4	†12,842.8	13,840.3	16,084.3	17,298.8	17,543.8	19,698.9	19,947.4	....	....	....
National Accounts						*Millions of Colones*							
Househ.Cons.Expend.,incl.NPISHs	96f	44,082	52,854	61,658	72,683	79,719	85,218	89,305	93,686	101,059	107,136	110,374	116,760
Government Consumption Expend	91f	4,670	5,196	5,942	7,184	8,438	8,842	10,243	10,928	11,690	12,677	13,097	13,587
Gross Fixed Capital Formation	93e	8,561	10,737	13,067	15,557	14,266	15,663	17,517	17,522	19,460	19,857	20,596	21,762
Changes in Inventories	93i	673	478	865	1,106	−559	−936	927	394	−8	292	−324	−
Exports of Goods and Services	90c	8,019	11,683	14,126	17,987	19,023	25,228	26,048	27,197	31,490	31,220	33,014	34,882
Imports of Goods and Services (-)	98c	16,166	20,588	24,909	31,388	30,627	36,586	38,965	40,661	48,767	50,320	51,527	56,258
Gross Domestic Product (GDP)	99b	49,839	60,359	70,748	83,130	90,261	97,428	105,074	109,066	114,924	120,862	125,230	130,733
Net Primary Income from Abroad	98.n	−901	−979	−804	−839	−1,062	−1,429	−1,426	−2,468	−2,215	−2,325	−2,830	−3,567
Gross National Income (GNI)	99a	48,938	59,380	69,944	82,291	89,199	95,999	103,647	106,597	112,709	118,537	122,400	127,166
GDP Volume 1990 Prices	99b.p	40,643	43,638	46,278	49,238	50,078	52,204	54,162	56,030	57,236	58,214	59,512	60,603
GDP Volume (2000=100)	99bvp	71.0	76.2	80.9	86.0	87.5	91.2	94.6	97.9	100.0	101.7	104.0	105.9
GDP Deflator (2000=100)	99bip	61.1	68.9	76.1	84.1	89.8	92.9	96.6	96.9	100.0	103.4	104.8	107.4
						Millions: Midyear Estimates							
Population	99z	5.32	5.43	5.55	5.67	5.78	5.89	6.00	6.10	6.21	6.31	6.42	6.52

2004, International Monetary Fund : *International Financial Statistics Yearbook*

Equatorial Guinea 642

		1992	1993	1994	1995	1996	1997	1998	1999	2000	2001	2002	2003
Exchange Rates							*Francs per SDR: End of Period*						
Official Rate	aa	378.57	404.89	†780.44	728.38	753.06	807.94	791.61	†896.19	918.49	935.39	850.37	771.76
					Francs per US Dollar: End of Period(ae)Period Average(rf)									
Official Rate	ae	275.32	294.77	†534.60	490.00	523.70	598.81	562.21	†652.95	704.95	744.31	625.50	519.36
Official Rate	rf	264.69	283.16	†555.20	499.15	511.55	583.67	589.95	†615.70	711.98	733.04	696.99	581.20
					Index Numbers (2000=100): Period Averages									
Nominal Effective Exchange Rate	nec	156.58	166.22	103.40	108.20	107.70	104.29	106.11	104.59	100.00	100.71	102.65	107.12
Real Effective Exchange Rate	rec	109.97	115.97	83.21	97.78	98.57	96.40	103.55	100.41	100.00	105.91	114.38	128.28
Fund Position						*Millions of SDRs: End of Period*								
Quota	2f.s	24.30	24.30	24.30	24.30	24.30	24.30	24.30	32.60	32.60	32.60	32.60	32.60
SDRs	1b.s	5.52	.28	.01	.01	.01	–	.01	–	.09	.79	.44	.03
Reserve Position in the Fund	1c.s	–	–	–	–	–	–	–	–	–	–	–	–
Total Fund Cred.&Loans Outstg	2tl	9.20	11.96	13.43	12.70	11.93	9.75	7.64	5.80	3.77	1.75	.83	.18
International Liquidity					*Millions of US Dollars Unless Otherwise Indicated: End of Period*									
Total Reserves minus Gold	1l.d	13.41	.48	.39	.04	.52	4.93	.80	3.35	23.01	70.85	88.54	237.69
SDRs	1b.d	7.59	.38	.02	.01	.01	–	.01	–	.12	.99	.60	.04
Reserve Position in the Fund	1c.d	–	–	–	–	–	–	–	–	–	–	–	–
Foreign Exchange	1d.d	5.82	.10	.37	.03	.51	4.93	.79	3.35	22.89	69.86	87.94	237.65
Monetary Authorities: Other Liab	4..d	28.89	11.02	9.16	2.97	.12	.11	4.80	7.46	7.52	6.94	7.53	10.19
Deposit Money Banks: Assets	7a.d	6.08	4.07	5.78	5.08	4.92	2.38	18.07	39.45	27.51	41.56	106.01	73.28
Liabilities	7b.d	2.96	2.17	2.67	3.56	1.96	6.18	5.22	19.31	14.82	21.88	18.71	4.73
Monetary Authorities						*Billions of Francs: End of Period*								
Foreign Assets	11	3.69	.14	.21	.02	.27	2.95	.45	2.19	16.22	52.74	55.38	123.45
Claims on Central Government	12a	9.71	12.18	17.84	17.42	17.33	15.86	14.03	20.90	14.24	3.90	2.50	1.44
Claims on Deposit Money Banks	12e	–	–	–	–	–	–	–	–	–	–	–	–
Claims on Other Banking Insts	12f	–	–	–	–	–	–	–	–	–	–	–	–
Reserve Money	14	3.09	2.46	4.38	8.72	9.99	10.97	8.79	17.17	25.57	47.45	49.61	120.29
of which: Currency Outside DMBs	14a	1.62	1.21	3.77	6.78	8.50	6.59	5.79	12.06	15.20	17.63	25.95	35.12
Foreign Liabilities	16c	11.44	8.09	15.38	10.70	9.05	7.94	8.74	10.07	8.77	6.80	5.42	5.43
Central Government Deposits	16d	.35	.17	.06	.07	.08	.48	1.08	1.19	1.92	7.44	6.61	4.03
Capital Accounts	17a	2.42	2.55	4.82	4.53	4.63	4.95	4.83	5.56	5.91	6.22	5.90	5.56
Other Items (Net)	17r	–3.87	–.95	–6.58	–6.58	–6.15	–5.54	–8.96	–10.90	–11.71	–11.26	–9.66	–10.42
Deposit Money Banks						*Billions of Francs: End of Period*								
Reserves	20	1.47	1.25	.62	1.95	1.49	4.38	3.00	5.11	10.37	29.02	22.86	84.37
Foreign Assets	21	1.67	1.20	3.09	2.49	2.57	1.43	10.16	25.76	19.39	30.93	66.31	38.06
Claims on Central Government	22a	2.76	.05	.23	.25	.51	1.63	.94	.46	1.89	.30	4.14	2.09
Claims on Nonfin.Pub.Enterprises	22c	.29	.44	.72	.72	.96	.80	.72	.03	–	.40	1.45	.86
Claims on Private Sector	22d	7.57	1.99	2.25	3.40	6.20	12.02	14.13	21.29	27.06	36.49	52.77	50.76
Claims on Other Banking Insts	22f	–	–	–	–	–	–	–	–	–	–	–	–
Claims on Nonbank Financial Insts	22g	–	–	–	–	–	–	–	–	–	–	–	–
Demand Deposits	24	1.95	1.34	2.24	2.73	5.78	7.07	9.19	16.39	23.14	29.88	46.52	78.53
Time and Savings Deposits	25	.80	.69	1.76	2.05	2.23	4.38	5.86	6.72	9.58	16.42	25.81	40.79
Foreign Liabilities	26c	.56	.41	1.24	1.60	.92	3.67	2.94	12.61	9.90	15.97	11.56	2.46
Long-Term Foreign Liabilities	26cl	.25	.23	.19	.14	.11	.03	–	–	.55	.31	.15	–
Central Government Deposits	26d	1.05	.53	.46	.88	1.86	3.10	6.12	10.76	6.49	24.82	50.83	33.85
Credit from Monetary Authorities	26g	–	–	–	–	–	–	–	–	–	–	–	–
Capital Accounts	27a	9.63	1.67	1.36	2.30	1.26	3.02	5.26	6.67	7.69	13.44	16.02	21.43
Other Items (Net)	27r	–.13	.07	–.33	–.91	–.43	–1.03	–.42	–.50	1.37	–3.70	–3.36	–.92
Monetary Survey						*Billions of Francs: End of Period*								
Foreign Assets (Net)	31n	–6.89	–7.39	–13.51	–9.94	–7.23	–7.26	–1.07	5.27	16.40	60.58	104.57	153.62
Domestic Credit	32	18.93	13.96	20.52	20.83	23.05	26.72	22.66	30.73	34.78	8.84	3.41	17.27
Claims on Central Govt. (Net)	32an	11.07	11.53	17.55	16.72	15.90	13.90	7.78	9.41	7.72	–28.05	–50.81	–34.35
Claims on Nonfin.Pub.Enterprises	32c	.29	.44	.72	.72	.96	.80	.72	.03	–	.40	1.45	.86
Claims on Private Sector	32d	7.57	1.99	2.25	3.40	6.20	12.02	14.13	21.29	27.06	36.49	52.77	50.76
Claims on Other Banking Insts	32f	–	–	–	–	–	–	–	–	–	–	–	–
Claims on Nonbank Financial Inst	32g	–	–	–	–	–	–	.03	–	–	–	–	–
Money	34	3.57	2.55	6.01	9.51	14.28	13.66	14.99	28.45	38.33	48.31	73.28	114.45
Quasi-Money	35	.80	.69	1.76	2.05	2.23	4.38	5.86	6.72	9.58	16.42	25.81	40.79
Other Items (Net)	37r	8.05	3.34	–.73	–.66	–.68	1.59	.75	.84	3.27	4.69	8.90	15.65
Money plus Quasi-Money	35l	4.37	3.24	7.76	11.56	16.51	18.04	20.85	35.16	47.91	64.73	99.08	155.24
Interest Rates						*Percent Per Annum*								
Discount Rate (End of Period)	60	12.00	11.50	†7.75	8.60	7.75	7.50	7.00	7.60	7.00	6.50	6.30	6.00
Deposit Rate	60l	7.50	7.75	8.08	5.50	5.46	5.00	5.00	5.00	5.00	5.00	5.00	5.00
Lending Rate	60p	17.77	17.46	17.50	16.00	22.00	22.00	22.00	22.00	22.00	20.67	18.00	18.00
Prices						*Index Numbers (1990=100): Period Averages*								
Consumer Prices	64	†89.90	†93.49	127.54	....	....	....	....	....	....	....	....	....

Equatorial Guinea 642

		1992	1993	1994	1995	1996	1997	1998	1999	2000	2001	2002	2003
International Transactions		\multicolumn{12}{c}{*Millions of Francs*}											
Exports	70	13,306	16,060	34,420	42,683	89,682	289,204	258,957	436,735	780,819	....	....	....
Imports, c.i.f.	71	14,824	17,000	20,514	24,897	149,384	192,800	187,167	261,784	320,800	....	....	....
Balance of Payments		\multicolumn{12}{c}{*Millions of US Dollars: Minus Sign Indicates Debit*}											
Current Account, n.i.e.	78ald	−10.57	2.84	−.38	−123.40	−344.04	....	....	....	....	....	....	....
Goods: Exports f.o.b.	78aad	49.54	61.06	62.00	89.93	175.31	....	....	....	....	....	....	....
Goods: Imports f.o.b.	78abd	−56.00	−51.03	−36.95	−120.57	−292.04	....	....	....	....	....	....	....
Trade Balance	78acd	−6.47	10.03	25.05	−30.64	−116.73	....	....	....	....	....	....	....
Services: Credit	78add	8.15	8.99	3.36	4.18	4.88	....	....	....	....	....	....	....
Services: Debit	78aed	−35.17	−38.53	−23.82	−75.54	−184.58	....	....	....	....	....	....	....
Balance on Goods & Services	78afd	−33.49	−19.51	4.59	−102.00	−296.43	....	....	....	....	....	....	....
Income: Credit	78agd	1.32	–	–	.10	.16	....	....	....	....	....	....	....
Income: Debit	78ahd	−4.92	−9.30	−8.75	−25.03	−45.18	....	....	....	....	....	....	....
Balance on Gds, Serv. & Inc.	78aid	−37.09	−28.80	−4.16	−126.93	−341.44	....	....	....	....	....	....	....
Current Transfers, n.i.e.: Credit	78ajd	33.63	37.76	5.67	6.83	4.03	....	....	....	....	....	....	....
Current Transfers: Debit	78akd	−7.11	−6.11	−1.89	−3.30	−6.62	....	....	....	....	....	....	....
Capital Account, n.i.e.	78bcd	–	–	–	–	–	....	....	....	....	....	....	....
Capital Account, n.i.e.: Credit	78bad	–	–	–	–	–	....	....	....	....	....	....	....
Capital Account: Debit	78bbd	....	....	....	....	....	....	....	....	....	....	....	....
Financial Account, n.i.e.	78bjd	−16.08	13.95	−15.04	101.56	313.75	....	....	....	....	....	....	....
Direct Investment Abroad	78bdd	–	–	–	–	–	....	....	....	....	....	....	....
Dir. Invest. in Rep. Econ., n.i.e.	78bed	6.02	22.30	17.00	126.92	376.18	....	....	....	....	....	....	....
Portfolio Investment Assets	78bfd	–	–	–	–	–	....	....	....	....	....	....	....
Equity Securities	78bkd	–	–	–	–	–	....	....	....	....	....	....	....
Debt Securities	78bld	–	–	–	–	–	....	....	....	....	....	....	....
Portfolio Investment Liab., n.i.e.	78bgd	–	–	–	–	–	....	....	....	....	....	....	....
Equity Securities	78bmd	–	–	–	–	–	....	....	....	....	....	....	....
Debt Securities	78bnd	–	–	–	–	–	....	....	....	....	....	....	....
Financial Derivatives Assets	78bwd	....	....	....	....	....	....	....	....	....	....	....	....
Financial Derivatives Liabilities	78bxd	....	....	....	....	....	....	....	....	....	....	....	....
Other Investment Assets	78bhd	–	–	–	–	–	....	....	....	....	....	....	....
Monetary Authorities	78bod	–	....	....	....	....	....	....	....	....	....	....	....
General Government	78bpd	–	–	–	–	–	....	....	....	....	....	....	....
Banks	78bqd	–	–	–	–	–	....	....	....	....	....	....	....
Other Sectors	78brd	–	–	–	–	–	....	....	....	....	....	....	....
Other Investment Liab., n.i.e.	78bid	−22.09	−8.35	−32.04	−25.36	−62.43	....	....	....	....	....	....	....
Monetary Authorities	78bsd	–	–	–	–	–	....	....	....	....	....	....	....
General Government	78btd	1.17	−3.12	−7.32	−13.95	−3.84	....	....	....	....	....	....	....
Banks	78bud	.01	1.05	−1.98	1.84	−1.57	....	....	....	....	....	....	....
Other Sectors	78bvd	−23.28	−6.28	−22.73	−13.25	−57.02	....	....	....	....	....	....	....
Net Errors and Omissions	78cad	−1.13	−27.17	−2.93	10.33	24.82	....	....	....	....	....	....	....
Overall Balance	78cbd	−27.78	−10.38	−18.36	−11.52	−5.46	....	....	....	....	....	....	....
Reserves and Related Items	79dad	27.78	10.38	18.36	11.52	5.46	....	....	....	....	....	....	....
Reserve Assets	79dbd	4.36	−1.02	−.92	−8.98	−3.59	....	....	....	....	....	....	....
Use of Fund Credit and Loans	79dcd	–	3.79	2.08	−1.11	−1.11	....	....	....	....	....	....	....
Exceptional Financing	79ded	23.42	7.61	17.20	21.61	10.17	....	....	....	....	....	....	....
National Accounts		\multicolumn{12}{c}{*Millions of Francs*}											
Househ.Cons.Expend.,incl.NPISHs	96f	31,042	25,150	24,300	18,646	49,826	157,939	....	....	....	....	....	....
Government Consumption Expend	91f	5,294	7,996	6,938	10,791	18,274	27,811	....	....	....	....	....	....
Gross Fixed Capital Formation	93e	15,885	17,620	55,126	64,528	176,141	197,359	....	....	....	....	....	....
Changes in Inventories	93i	−987	531	−20	−9	−11	−13	....	....	....	....	....	....
Exports of Goods and Services	90c	15,269	19,837	36,308	45,088	105,083	292,158	....	....	....	....	....	....
Imports of Goods and Services (-)	98c	24,133	25,361	42,332	59,662	211,429	358,965	....	....	....	....	....	....
Gross Domestic Product (GDP)	99b	42,400	49,100	66,500	83,000	140,000	307,000	260,200	445,700	865,500	1,312,700	1,523,900	1,507,800
GDP Volume 1985 Prices	99b.p	42,311	46,323	53,358	61,956	89,995	182,536	....	....	....	....	....	....
GDP Volume (1995=100)	99bvp	68.3	74.8	86.1	100.0	145.3	294.6	....	....	....	....	....	....
GDP Deflator (1995=100)	99bip	74.8	79.1	93.0	100.0	116.1	125.5	....	....	....	....	....	....
		\multicolumn{12}{c}{*Millions: Midyear Estimates*}											
Population	99z	.37	.38	.39	.40	.41	.42	.43	.44	.46	.47	.48	.49

2004, International Monetary Fund : *International Financial Statistics Yearbook*

Eritrea 643

		1992	1993	1994	1995	1996	1997	1998	1999	2000	2001	2002	2003
Exchange Rates					*Nakfa per SDR: End of Period*								
Official Rate	aa	6.8750	6.8678	8.6861	9.3946	9.2403	†9.6134	10.6967	13.1761	13.2897	17.3397	19.2117	20.4878
					Nakfa per US Dollar: End of Period (ae) Period Average (rf)								
Official Rate	ae	5.0000	5.0000	5.9500	6.3200	6.4260	†7.1250	7.5969	9.6000	10.2000	13.7975	14.1313	13.7875
Official Rate	rf	2.8052	5.0047	5.4702	6.1642	6.3577	†6.8373	7.3619	8.1526	9.6250	11.3095	13.9582	13.8779
Fund Position					*Millions of SDRs: End of Period*								
Quota	2f.s	–	–	11.5	11.5	11.5	11.5	11.5	15.9	15.9	15.9	15.9	15.9
SDRs	1b.s	–	–	–	–	–	–	–	–	–	–	–	–
Reserve Position in the Fund	1c.s	–	–	–	–	–	–	–	–	–	–	–	–
Total Fund Cred.&Loans Outstg.	2tl	–	–	–	–	–	–	–	–	–	–	–	–
International Liquidity					*Millions of US Dollars Unless Otherwise Indicated: End of Period*								
Total Reserves minus Gold	1l.d	....	....	....	40.5	81.3	199.4	23.1	34.2	25.5	39.8	30.3	24.7
SDRs	1b.d	–	–	–	–	–	–	–	–	–	–	–	–
Reserve Position in the Fund	1c.d	–	–	–	–	–	–	–	–	–	–	–	–
Foreign Exchange	1d.d	....	....	....	40.5	81.3	199.4	23.1	34.2	25.5	39.7	30.3	24.7
Gold (Million Fine Troy Ounces)	1ad	....	....	....	....	....	.104	.157	.085	.039	.039	–	–
Gold (National Valuation)	1and	....	....	....	20.9	27.2	42.6	44.7	19.7	10.4	10.5	–	–
Monetary Authorities:Other Assets	3..d	....	....	....	43.7	36.1	2.5	1.0	1.6	1.5	1.4	1.3	1.9
Other Liab.	4..d	....	....	....	19.0	18.8	16.3	16.3	30.1	33.6	28.9	26.9	44.5
Banking Institutions: Assets	7a.d	....	....	....	317.9	309.3	50.0	72.6	88.9	89.5	153.3	187.2	227.8
Liabilities	7b.d	....	....	....	4.4	2.4	2.6	2.2	1.7	13.5	7.1	2.9	3.0
Monetary Authorities					*Millions of Nakfa: End of Period*								
Foreign Assets	11	....	....	....	664	930	1,742	522	534	383	713	452	366
Claims on Central Government	12a	....	....	....	1,013	1,820	2,009	1,788	3,794	4,155	4,043	5,450	7,232
Claims on Private Sector	12d	....	....	....	40	60	102	75	95	161	117	188	155
Claims on Banking Institutions	12e	....	....	....	–	100	235	381	371	448	653	887	236
Reserve Money	14	....	....	....	1,340	2,494	4,701	3,065	4,239	4,563	4,407	5,152	5,849
of which: Currency Outside Banks	14a	....	....	....	–	–	574	825	1,138	1,468	1,868	2,279	2,765
Foreign Currency Deposits	15	....	....	....	157	157	22	23	77	100	108	48	20
Foreign Liabilities	16c	....	....	....	13	15	13	11	113	139	194	193	310
Central Government Deposits	16d	....	....	....	131	203	401	369	926	604	806	912	991
Capital Accounts	17a	....	....	....	117	148	213	350	470	796	718	752	844
Other Items (Net)	17r	....	....	....	–41	–108	–1,261	–1,051	–1,030	–1,056	–707	–80	–23
Banking Institutions					*Millions of Nakfa: End of Period*								
Reserves	20	....	....	....	1,340	2,494	4,049	2,154	2,897	3,055	2,447	2,827	2,973
Foreign Assets	21	....	....	....	2,009	1,987	356	551	854	913	2,115	2,679	3,141
Claims on Central Government	22a	....	....	....	–	–	135	2,262	3,207	4,639	5,397	6,076	5,714
Claims on State and Local Govts	22b	....	....	....	–	–	–	–	–	–	–	–	–
Claims on Nonfin.Pub.Enterprises	22c	....	....	....	461	459	385	265	697	402	349	365	392
Claims on Private Sector	22d	....	....	....	592	1,468	1,639	2,475	1,775	1,823	2,367	2,726	3,372
Demand Deposits	24	....	....	....	1,135	1,474	1,355	1,456	2,133	2,425	3,081	3,667	4,036
Time, Savings,& Fgn.Currency Dep.	25	....	....	....	1,927	2,264	2,961	3,624	4,641	5,566	7,579	9,316	10,708
Foreign Liabilities	26c	....	....	....	28	15	19	17	16	138	98	42	41
Central Government Deposits	26d	....	....	....	121	196	244	378	362	372	435	379	435
Credit from Monetary Authorities	26g	....	....	....	–	100	235	362	364	474	760	886	147
Capital Accounts	27a	....	....	....	159	245	169	253	297	353	413	441	844
Other Items (Net)	27r	....	....	....	1,032	2,114	1,581	1,619	1,614	1,504	308	–59	–618
Banking Survey					*Millions of Nakfa: End of Period*								
Foreign Assets (Net)	31n	....	....	....	2,632	2,886	2,067	1,046	1,258	1,018	2,536	2,896	3,157
Domestic Credit	32	....	....	....	1,853	3,407	3,625	6,120	8,304	10,230	11,042	13,514	15,441
Claims on Central Govt. (Net)	32an	....	....	....	760	1,421	1,499	3,304	5,713	7,818	8,200	10,235	11,521
Claims on State and Local Govts.	32b	....	....	....	–	–	–	–	–	–	–	–	–
Claims on Nonfin.Pub.Enterprises	32c	....	....	....	461	459	385	265	697	402	349	365	392
Claims on Private Sector	32d	....	....	....	632	1,528	1,740	2,551	1,870	1,985	2,483	2,913	3,528
Money	34	....	....	....	1,135	1,474	2,007	2,367	3,465	3,930	5,035	5,982	6,932
Quasi-Money	35	....	....	....	2,084	2,422	2,983	3,646	4,718	5,666	7,686	9,364	10,728
Capital Accounts	37a	....	....	....	276	392	382	604	767	1,149	1,131	1,193	1,688
Other Items (Net)	37r	....	....	....	991	2,006	321	549	612	502	–275	–129	–750
Money plus Quasi-Money	35l	....	....	....	3,219	3,896	4,989	6,013	8,184	9,596	12,721	15,347	17,659
Money (National Definitions)					*Millions of Nakfa: End of Period*								
Monetary Base	19ma	....	....	....	1,340	2,494	4,701	3,065	4,239	4,563	4,407	5,152	5,844
M1	39ma	....	....	....	1,135	1,474	2,007	2,365	3,348	3,915	5,027	5,982	6,927
M2	39mb	....	....	....	3,013	3,622	4,693	5,636	7,437	8,712	10,941	13,146	14,841

Eritrea 643

		1992	1993	1994	1995	1996	1997	1998	1999	2000	2001	2002	2003
Balance of Payments		\<td colspan="12"\> *Millions of US Dollars: Minus Sign Indicates Debit*
Current Account, n.i.e.	78ald	188.2	107.2	123.7	−31.6	−59.8	5.1	−292.7	−208.8	−104.7	....	....	....
Goods: Exports f.o.b.	78aad	16.4	41.9	78.0	86.0	98.0	56.8	28.1	20.7	36.8	....	....	....
Goods: Imports f.o.b.	78abd	−350.8	−348.9	−488.9	−453.5	−552.8	−525.3	−508.3	−510.2	−471.4	....	....	....
Trade Balance	78acd	−334.4	−307.0	−410.9	−367.5	−454.8	−468.5	−480.2	−489.5	−434.6	....	....	....
Services: Credit	78add	72.7	107.7	89.9	48.6	104.9	159.2	81.8	47.6	60.9	....	....	....
Services: Debit	78aed	....	−1.0	−7.7	−44.7	−53.7	−100.3	−187.1	−104.6	−28.4	....	....	....
Balance on Goods & Services	78afd	−261.6	−200.4	−328.7	−363.7	−403.6	−409.6	−585.5	−546.5	−402.0	....	....	....
Income: Credit	78agd	....	....	3.6	7.8	8.3	10.8	11.6	8.5	9.1	....	....	....
Income: Debit	78ahd	....	....	....	....	−15.6	−14.4	−7.3	−2.1	−10.5	....	....	....
Balance on Gds, Serv. & Inc.	78aid	−261.6	−200.4	−325.1	−355.9	−410.9	−413.2	−581.2	−540.2	−403.4	....	....	....
Current Transfers, n.i.e.: Credit	78ajd	450.9	307.7	465.3	324.9	354.6	423.5	293.3	346.5	306.1	....	....	....
Current Transfers: Debit	78akd	−1.1	−.1	−16.5	−.6	−3.5	−5.3	−4.9	−15.1	−7.3	....	....	....
Capital Account, n.i.e.	78bcd	....	....	....	....	....	....	2.7	.6	....	....	....	....
Capital Account, n.i.e.: Credit	78bad	....	....	....	....	....	....	2.7	.6	....	....	....	....
Capital Account: Debit	78bbd	....	....	....	....	....	....	....	....	....	....	....	....
Financial Account, n.i.e.	78bjd	−135.1	−105.9	−7.9	69.2	181.4	255.4	197.0	196.3	63.2	....	....	....
Direct Investment Abroad	78bdd	....	....	....	....	....	....	....	....	....	....	....	....
Dir. Invest. in Rep. Econ., n.i.e.	78bed	....	....	....	....	36.7	41.1	148.5	83.2	27.9	....	....	....
Portfolio Investment Assets	78bfd	....	....	....	....	....	....	....	....	....	....	....	....
Equity Securities	78bkd	....	....	....	....	....	....	....	....	....	....	....	....
Debt Securities	78bld	....	....	....	....	....	....	....	....	....	....	....	....
Portfolio Investment Liab., n.i.e.	78bgd	....	....	....	....	....	....	....	....	....	....	....	....
Equity Securities	78bmd	....	....	....	....	....	....	....	....	....	....	....	....
Debt Securities	78bnd	....	....	....	....	....	....	....	....	....	....	....	....
Financial Derivatives Assets	78bwd	....	....	....	....	....	....	....	....	....	....	....	....
Financial Derivatives Liabilities	78bxd	....	....	....	....	....	....	....	....	....	....	....	....
Other Investment Assets	78bhd	−194.0	−108.4	−39.8	60.8	137.3	184.5	−20.0	−26.2	−25.9	....	....	....
Monetary Authorities	78bod	....	....	....	....	....	....	....	....	....	....	....	....
General Government	78bpd	....	....	....	....	....	....	....	....	....	....	....	....
Banks	78bqd	−194.0	−108.4	−39.8	60.8	137.3	184.5	−15.3	−23.9	−25.1	....	....	....
Other Sectors	78brd	....	....	....	....	....	....	−4.7	−2.4	−.8	....	....	....
Other Investment Liab., n.i.e.	78bid	58.9	2.5	31.9	8.4	7.4	29.9	68.5	139.3	61.2	....	....	....
Monetary Authorities	78bsd	−	−	−	−	−	−	−	−	−	....	....	....
General Government	78btd	−	2.5	32.9	8.4	7.4	29.9	59.3	128.9	52.3	....	....	....
Banks	78bud	....	....	....	....	....	....	10.1	10.4	8.8	....	....	....
Other Sectors	78bvd	58.9	−	−1.0	−	−	−	−.9	....	−	....	....	....
Net Errors and Omissions	78cad	−50.5	31.7	−61.5	−40.5	−64.5	−140.4	−66.5	12.8	−22.9	....	....	....
Overall Balance	78cbd	2.6	33.1	54.3	−2.9	57.1	120.1	−159.5	.9	−64.3	....	....	....
Reserves and Related Items	79dad	−2.6	−33.1	−54.3	2.9	−57.1	−120.1	159.5	−.9	64.3	....	....	....
Reserve Assets	79dbd	−2.6	−33.1	−54.3	2.9	−57.1	−120.1	159.5	−.9	61.2	....	....	....
Use of Fund Credit and Loans	79dcd	−	−	−	−	−	−	−	−	−	....	....	....
Exceptional Financing	79ded	....	....	....	....	....	....	....	....	3.2	....	....	....
		\<td colspan="12"\> *Millions: Midyear Estimates*
Population	99z	3.15	3.15	3.16	3.19	3.24	3.31	3.41	3.52	3.67	3.82	....	....

2004, International Monetary Fund : *International Financial Statistics Yearbook*

Estonia 939

		1992	1993	1994	1995	1996	1997	1998	1999	2000	2001	2002	2003
Exchange Rates						*Krooni per SDR: End of Period*							
Official Rate	aa	17.754	19.062	18.088	17.038	17.888	19.343	18.882	21.359	21.915	22.234	20.306	18.440
						Krooni per US Dollar: End of Period (ae) Period Average (rf)							
Official Rate	ae	12.912	13.878	12.390	11.462	12.440	14.336	13.410	15.562	16.820	17.692	14.936	12.410
Official Rate	rf	....	13.223	12.991	11.465	12.038	13.882	14.075	14.678	16.969	17.478	16.612	13.856
Fund Position						*Millions of SDRs: End of Period*							
Quota	2f.s	46.50	46.50	46.50	46.50	46.50	46.50	46.50	65.20	65.20	65.20	65.20	65.20
SDRs	1b.s	7.72	41.56	1.09	.20	.12	.01	.05	.99	.01	.03	.05	.05
Reserve Position in the Fund	1c.s	–	–	.01	.01	.01	.01	.01	.01	.01	.01	.01	.01
Total Fund Cred.&Loans Outstg.	2tl	7.75	41.85	41.85	61.81	54.15	40.01	21.31	18.41	14.53	10.66	–	–
International Liquidity						*Millions of US Dollars Unless Otherwise Indicated: End of Period*							
Total Reserves minus Gold	1l.d	170.18	386.12	443.35	579.91	636.82	757.72	810.60	853.49	920.64	820.24	1,000.42	1,373.36
SDRs	1b.d	10.62	57.08	1.58	.29	.17	.01	.07	1.36	.02	.03	.07	.08
Reserve Position in the Fund	1c.d	–	–	.01	.01	.01	.01	.01	.01	.01	.01	.01	.01
Foreign Exchange	1d.d	159.56	329.04	441.76	579.61	636.64	757.70	810.53	852.12	920.62	820.20	1,000.34	1,373.27
Gold (Million Fine Troy Ounces)	1ad	.0820	.0080	.0080	.0080	.0080	.0080	.0080	.0080	.0080	.0080	.0080	.0080
Gold (National Valuation)	1and	25.36	3.22	3.61	3.19	3.03	2.39	2.37	2.38	2.25	2.29	2.83	3.44
Monetary Authorities:Other Liab.	4..d	42.44	65.89	60.88	65.84	48.52	24.75	1.02	.63	3.29	1.04	7.03	39.11
Banks: Assets	7a.d	122.81	103.10	243.80	322.58	320.69	563.45	483.29	563.67	615.88	874.72	1,104.93	1,375.84
Liabilities	7b.d	7.95	14.34	55.98	140.83	337.97	913.11	884.58	879.19	976.66	989.70	1,582.58	2,808.67
Monetary Authorities						*Millions of Krooni: End of Period*							
Foreign Assets	11	3,596.7	† 5,418.0	5,540.6	6,688.0	7,954.2	10,900.8	10,908.7	13,334.3	15,539.2	14,573.2	14,995.0	17,194.7
Claims on Central Government	12a	–	† 45.2	–	3.0	48.5	4.1	3.0	3.1	3.4	1.3	.2	.2
Claims on Nonfin.Pub.Enterprises	12c	–	† 63.5	14.8	.8	–	–	–	–	–	–	–	–
Claims on Private Sector	12d	–	† 4.6	8.2	14.5	44.2	44.1	57.2	66.5	69.5	74.8	78.8	75.4
Claims on Banks	12e	583.7	† 473.7	480.9	194.0	168.0	82.4	280.3	267.3	9.8	8.0	9.0	–
Reserve Money	14	1,862.8	† 3,786.6	4,225.1	5,066.7	6,190.9	8,526.7	9,070.3	11,496.0	13,207.1	11,910.2	11,732.1	13,450.4
of which: Currency Outside Banks	14a	1,040.7	† 2,380.6	3,071.3	3,803.6	4,268.5	4,588.5	4,538.6	5,711.3	6,201.3	6,951.9	6,994.9	7,139.7
Foreign Liabilities	16c	685.6	† 1,712.2	1,511.2	1,807.7	1,572.3	1,128.8	416.1	403.0	373.8	255.4	104.9	485.3
Central Government Deposits	16d	.3	† 5.1	.2	.1	.3	355.5	6.4	27.1	7.2	7.8	5.6	5.1
Capital Accounts	17a	1,672.7	† 1,342.2	1,256.1	1,223.2	1,325.9	1,881.1	2,276.5	2,141.3	2,424.1	2,889.7	3,377.5	3,512.0
Other Items (Net)	17r	−41.0	† −841.1	−948.0	−1,197.4	−874.7	−860.7	−520.1	−396.2	−390.3	−405.8	−137.1	−182.4
Banking Institutions						*Millions of Krooni: End of Period*							
Reserves	20	835.0	1,437.7	1,208.4	1,293.1	1,922.5	3,885.3	4,509.5	5,790.9	6,787.1	4,896.6	4,678.0	6,243.0
Foreign Assets	21	1,585.7	1,430.8	3,020.7	3,697.4	3,989.4	8,077.7	6,480.9	8,771.9	10,358.9	15,475.5	16,503.6	17,073.6
Claims on Central Government	22a	1.8	293.2	297.0	345.4	614.0	561.1	303.6	404.5	445.4	445.5	480.2	538.1
Claims on Local Government	22b	12.7	1.5	108.3	303.9	159.9	547.2	651.5	767.6	822.9	1,296.9	1,959.1	2,311.9
Claims on Nonfin.Pub.Enterprises	22c	644.4	416.7	346.0	334.5	304.6	328.6	225.8	372.5	262.7	141.8	245.0	221.4
Claims on Private Sector	22d	986.1	2,409.8	4,176.0	6,041.3	10,088.3	16,908.5	18,532.4	19,810.4	22,134.0	26,246.5	31,433.7	41,693.3
Claims on Nonbank Financial Insts.	22g	–	8.7	12.2	628.9	2,036.4	5,127.7	6,336.8	6,489.2	12,370.2	16,106.6	22,644.3	27,104.3
Demand Deposits	24	1,813.8	2,847.4	3,248.6	4,399.6	7,019.6	9,357.2	8,577.3	11,600.5	14,456.8	17,967.9	20,225.5	23,603.3
Time, Savings,& Fgn.Currency Dep.	25	1,242.9	1,241.0	2,088.8	2,616.6	3,560.9	6,467.6	8,208.1	9,024.3	12,292.5	15,855.1	18,099.7	19,497.4
Money Market Instruments	26aa	–	.6	220.2	11.5	–	44.8	85.9	266.3	296.5	508.9	999.2	280.7
Bonds	26ab	–	–	40.0	82.5	67.5	70.0	65.6	113.0	41.5	14.1	310.2	612.9
Foreign Liabilities	26c	102.6	199.0	693.5	1,614.2	4,204.4	13,090.4	11,862.2	13,682.0	16,427.2	17,509.9	23,638.1	34,854.5
Central Government Deposits	26d	35.1	527.8	1,180.9	1,894.8	1,735.4	2,472.6	1,881.5	1,345.4	2,342.5	2,311.4	3,268.3	3,006.8
Counterpart Funds	26e	51.5	114.3	112.0	102.0	–	–	–	–	–	–	–	–
Government Lending Funds	26f	9.8	151.8	487.1	819.5	987.7	739.7	555.2	540.7	450.9	306.4	240.4	222.4
Credit from Monetary Authorities	26g	271.0	337.9	401.7	88.6	47.9	23.2	14.5	11.4	8.4	6.3	6.6	7.5
Capital Accounts	27a	493.9	776.8	994.4	1,834.9	2,519.4	5,372.5	7,845.3	8,459.5	8,340.0	10,432.5	11,239.7	12,195.2
Other Items (Net)	27r	45.1	−198.5	−298.6	−819.7	−1,027.6	−2,202.0	−2,055.1	−2,636.0	−1,475.3	−303.2	−83.8	905.0
Banking Survey						*Millions of Krooni: End of Period*							
Foreign Assets (Net)	31n	4,394.2	† 4,937.5	6,356.5	6,963.5	6,166.8	4,759.3	5,111.3	8,021.2	9,097.1	12,283.4	7,755.6	−1,071.5
Domestic Credit	32	1,609.6	† 2,813.3	3,781.4	5,777.4	11,663.5	20,796.6	24,222.7	26,541.6	33,758.5	41,994.3	53,567.5	68,933.1
Claims on Central Govt. (Net)	32an	−33.6	† −194.5	−884.1	−1,546.6	−1,073.3	−2,262.9	−1,581.4	−964.9	−1,901.0	−1,872.4	−2,793.4	−2,473.4
Claims on Local Government	32b	12.7	† 1.5	108.3	303.9	159.9	547.2	651.5	767.6	822.9	1,296.9	1,959.1	2,311.9
Claims on Nonfin.Pub.Enterprises	32c	644.4	† 480.1	360.8	335.3	304.6	328.6	225.8	372.5	262.7	141.8	245.0	221.4
Claims on Private Sector	32d	986.1	† 2,414.5	4,184.3	6,055.8	10,132.5	16,952.7	18,589.7	19,876.9	22,203.5	26,321.2	31,512.5	41,768.7
Claims on Nonbank Financial Inst.	32g	–	† 111.7	12.2	628.9	2,139.7	5,231.0	6,337.1	6,489.5	12,370.5	16,106.7	22,644.3	27,104.5
Money	34	2,854.6	† 5,228.2	6,319.9	8,203.2	11,289.7	13,998.0	13,119.8	17,335.5	20,884.1	24,948.2	27,274.5	30,806.6
Quasi-Money	35	1,242.9	† 1,301.0	2,191.8	2,650.5	3,562.9	6,467.6	8,208.1	9,054.3	12,292.5	15,855.1	18,099.7	19,497.4
Money Market Instruments	36aa	–	† .6	220.2	11.5	–	44.8	85.9	266.3	296.5	508.9	999.2	280.7
Bonds	36ab	–	† –	40.0	82.5	67.5	70.0	65.6	113.0	41.5	14.1	310.2	612.9
Counterpart Funds	36e	51.5	† 114.3	112.0	102.0	–	–	–	–	–	–	–	–
Government Lending Funds	36f	9.8	† 151.8	487.1	819.5	987.7	739.7	555.2	540.7	450.9	306.4	240.4	222.4
Capital Accounts	37a	2,166.6	† 2,119.1	2,250.4	3,058.1	3,845.3	7,253.6	10,121.8	10,600.8	10,764.1	13,322.2	14,617.2	15,707.2
Other Items (Net)	37r	−321.6	† −1,164.3	−1,483.5	−2,186.4	−1,922.7	−3,017.9	−2,822.4	−3,347.7	−1,873.9	−677.1	−218.2	734.3
Money plus Quasi-Money	35l	4,097.5	† 6,529.2	8,511.7	10,853.7	14,852.6	20,465.6	21,327.9	26,389.9	33,176.6	40,803.2	45,374.2	50,304.0

Estonia 939

		1992	1993	1994	1995	1996	1997	1998	1999	2000	2001	2002	2003
Interest Rates							*Percent Per Annum*						
Money Market Rate	60b	....	....	5.67	4.94	3.53	6.45	11.66	5.39	†5.68	5.31	3.88	2.92
Deposit Rate	60l	....	....	11.51	8.74	6.05	6.19	8.07	4.19	3.76	4.03	2.74	2.40
Lending Rate	60p	30.50	33.66	24.65	19.01	14.87	11.76	15.06	11.09	7.43	7.78	6.70	5.51
Prices and Labor						*Index Numbers (2000=100): Period Averages*							
Producer Prices	63	....	....	59.29	74.45	85.47	92.63	96.55	95.36	100.00	104.39	104.83	105.05
Consumer Prices	64	17.5	†33.2	49.1	63.2	77.8	†86.0	93.1	96.1	100.0	105.7	109.5	111.0
						Number in Thousands: Period Averages							
Labor Force	67d	....	....	....	734	....	708	711	....	705	661	653	....
Employment	67e	766	708	693	656	646	†648	640	579	572	578	586	594
Unemployment	67c	29	50	56	68	68	†66	66	81	90	83	67	66
Unemployment Rate (%)	67r	3.7	6.5	7.6	9.7	9.9	†9.7	9.8	12.2	13.6	12.6	10.3	10.0
International Transactions							*Millions of Krooni*						
Exports	70	5,549	10,642	†16,941	21,040	25,024	40,662	43,952	43,178	53,324	57,528	56,920	62,523
Imports, c.i.f.	71	5,128	11,848	†21,525	29,101	38,887	61,610	64,897	60,248	72,309	75,163	79,468	89,709
Imports, f.o.b.	71.v	4,736	10,944	†19,883	26,881	35,920	56,909	59,945	55,651	66,792	69,428	....	....
Balance of Payments						*Millions of US Dollars: Minus Sign Indicates Debit*							
Current Account, n.i.e.	78ald	36.2	21.6	−166.3	−157.8	−398.2	−561.7	−478.4	−294.6	−294.0	−338.8	−716.6	−1,199.2
Goods: Exports f.o.b.	78aad	460.7	811.7	1,225.0	1,696.3	1,811.8	2,289.6	2,690.1	2,453.1	3,311.4	3,359.7	3,532.2	4,603.4
Goods: Imports f.o.b.	78abd	−551.1	−956.6	−1,581.4	−2,362.3	−2,830.6	−3,413.7	−3,805.4	−3,330.6	−4,079.5	−4,148.4	−4,621.3	−6,183.0
Trade Balance	78acd	−90.4	−144.9	−356.5	−666.0	−1,018.8	−1,124.1	−1,115.2	−877.5	−768.1	−788.7	−1,089.2	−1,579.5
Services: Credit	78add	203.1	334.6	515.3	876.8	1,107.9	1,318.0	1,479.6	1,489.7	1,499.0	1,649.3	1,712.7	2,233.6
Services: Debit	78aed	−160.4	−259.4	−410.2	−497.7	−589.6	−726.6	−910.1	−917.6	−936.3	−1,069.2	−1,126.1	−1,382.9
Balance on Goods & Services	78afd	−47.7	−69.7	−251.3	−286.9	−500.6	−532.7	−545.7	−305.4	−205.4	−208.6	−502.5	−728.8
Income: Credit	78agd	.5	26.9	37.3	63.6	112.2	115.1	133.5	133.8	117.6	171.3	203.1	244.9
Income: Debit	78ahd	−13.6	−40.8	−66.9	−60.8	−110.3	−260.8	−214.5	−235.5	−321.7	−453.5	−530.2	−821.6
Balance on Gds, Serv. & Inc.	78aid	−60.8	−83.6	−280.9	−284.1	−498.7	−678.4	−626.7	−407.1	−409.6	−490.8	−829.6	−1,305.5
Current Transfers, n.i.e.: Credit	78ajd	97.4	108.4	120.3	134.5	116.7	135.3	172.9	153.7	144.7	181.4	174.3	207.7
Current Transfers: Debit	78akd	−.3	−3.2	−5.7	−8.2	−16.3	−18.6	−24.6	−41.3	−29.1	−29.4	−61.3	−101.4
Capital Account, n.i.e.	78bcd	27.4	−	−.6	−.8	−.7	−.2	1.8	1.2	16.5	5.1	19.0	39.7
Capital Account, n.i.e.: Credit	78bad	27.4	−	.5	1.4	.2	.7	2.1	1.4	16.8	5.5	20.1	47.9
Capital Account: Debit	78bbd	−	−	−1.1	−2.2	−.8	−.9	−.3	−.2	−.2	−.4	−1.0	−8.2
Financial Account, n.i.e.	78bjd	−1.3	188.9	167.2	233.4	540.8	802.8	508.1	418.2	392.9	269.4	751.5	1,337.4
Direct Investment Abroad	78bdd	−1.9	−6.2	−2.4	−2.5	−40.0	−136.6	−6.3	−82.9	−63.4	−200.1	−131.9	−148.2
Dir. Invest. in Rep. Econ., n.i.e.	78bed	82.3	162.2	214.4	201.5	150.2	266.2	580.5	305.2	387.3	542.5	284.5	890.8
Portfolio Investment Assets	78bfd	−	−.4	−22.5	−33.2	−52.7	−165.0	−10.9	−132.3	15.5	−118.8	−192.0	−394.3
Equity Securities	78bkd	−	−.4	−14.5	5.1	−15.0	−87.8	35.1	12.9	3.5	14.3	.3	−75.5
Debt Securities	78bld	−	−	−8.0	−38.2	−37.6	−77.2	−46.0	−145.2	12.1	−133.2	−192.3	−318.8
Portfolio Investment Liab., n.i.e.	78bgd	−	.2	8.4	11.1	198.0	427.5	1.1	153.3	75.6	84.7	344.9	558.2
Equity Securities	78bmd	−	.1	8.4	9.9	172.2	127.8	25.7	235.4	−28.5	31.9	53.3	107.6
Debt Securities	78bnd	−	.1	−	1.2	25.7	299.7	−24.6	−82.1	104.1	52.8	291.6	450.6
Financial Derivatives Assets	78bwd	....	....	....	....	....	....	....	....	−4.7	−.1	−2.6	−9.9
Financial Derivatives Liabilities	78bxd	....	....	....	....	....	....	....	....	5.4	−2.1	−1.4	8.1
Other Investment Assets	78bhd	−122.4	−144.7	−146.7	−98.9	−7.2	−334.2	−168.5	−110.3	−166.7	−220.3	50.5	−127.3
Monetary Authorities	78bod	−72.8	5.7	.1	.1	.1	−	−	−18.3	−9.6	−11.3	−2.8	.1
General Government	78bpd	−	−17.1	.4	−.4	−3.3	−24.7	−61.9	−60.1	43.1	35.9	−23.4	40.1
Banks	78bqd	−48.5	−44.7	−102.8	−41.1	20.9	−195.9	61.3	−53.8	−77.0	−219.3	−28.3	−87.0
Other Sectors	78brd	−1.1	−88.6	−44.4	−57.5	−24.9	−113.5	−167.9	22.5	−123.3	−25.6	105.1	−80.5
Other Investment Liab., n.i.e.	78bid	40.7	177.8	115.9	155.4	292.5	744.8	112.1	285.2	143.8	183.6	399.4	560.0
Monetary Authorities	78bsd	8.1	14.9	6.2	−13.5	−6.7	−2.5	−1.1	7.3	1.7	−5.4	32.5	43.5
General Government	78btd	11.1	77.3	19.8	61.0	31.2	−3.3	4.4	9.8	−17.2	−7.3	−53.1	30.8
Banks	78bud	7.2	7.2	37.5	82.2	173.6	492.4	−17.3	188.3	76.8	59.4	344.1	336.3
Other Sectors	78bvd	14.3	78.4	52.3	25.7	94.3	258.2	126.0	79.8	82.5	136.9	75.9	149.4
Net Errors and Omissions	78cad	−4.4	−45.9	17.2	8.7	−35.6	−25.1	5.9	−5.5	12.2	22.3	15.3	−8.6
Overall Balance	78cbd	57.9	164.6	17.5	83.5	106.3	215.9	37.3	119.3	127.6	−41.9	69.3	169.4
Reserves and Related Items	79dad	−57.9	−164.6	−17.5	−83.5	−106.3	−215.9	−37.3	−119.3	−127.6	41.9	−69.3	−169.4
Reserve Assets	79dbd	−69.2	−212.4	−17.5	−112.9	−95.2	−196.4	−11.7	−115.3	−122.4	46.9	−55.2	−169.4
Use of Fund Credit and Loans	79dcd	11.3	47.7	−	29.4	−11.1	−19.4	−25.6	−4.0	−5.2	−4.9	−14.0	−
Exceptional Financing	79ded	....	....	....	....	....	....	....	....	....	....	....	....

Estonia 939

		1992	1993	1994	1995	1996	1997	1998	1999	2000	2001	2002	2003
International Investment Position						*Millions of US Dollars*							
Assets...............................	79aad	....	....	....	....	1,344.1	2,045.5	2,300.4	2,415.1	2,614.0	2,920.5	4,078.2	6,015.5
Direct Investment Abroad........	79abd	....	....	....	....	107.7	215.3	198.4	281.2	259.1	441.8	676.0	1,020.8
Portfolio Investment...............	79acd	....	....	....	....	121.0	249.3	211.2	305.2	271.8	262.1	824.1	1,487.5
Equity Securities................	79add	....	....	....	....	26.1	98.5	31.5	12.4	26.4	22.5	36.8	153.5
Debt Securities..................	79aed	....	....	....	....	94.9	150.9	179.7	292.9	245.4	239.6	787.3	1,334.0
Financial Derivatives..............	79ald	....	....	....	....	–	–	–	–	9.1	8.7	13.0	26.9
Other Investment..................	79afd	....	....	....	....	475.9	820.4	1,077.4	972.4	1,151.0	1,385.3	1,561.8	2,095.6
Monetary Authorities............	79agd	....	....	....	....	–	–	–	–	1.0	6.9	.9	.9
General Government.............	79ahd	....	....	....	....	4.6	26.7	97.7	129.6	87.5	98.0	52.7	30.1
Banks................................	79aid	....	....	....	....	246.9	392.8	360.9	374.4	411.8	601.1	782.6	1,043.4
Other Sectors.....................	79ajd	....	....	....	....	224.3	400.8	618.7	468.4	650.8	679.2	725.5	1,021.2
Reserve Assets.....................	79akd	....	....	....	....	639.6	760.5	813.5	856.2	922.9	822.5	1,003.2	1,384.7
Liabilities...............................	79lad	....	....	....	....	1,974.9	3,757.8	4,451.9	5,199.6	5,389.5	6,017.7	8,488.0	12,956.0
Dir. Invest. in Rep. Economy.....	79lbd	....	....	....	....	824.6	1,147.9	1,821.7	2,467.3	2,644.7	3,159.9	4,226.4	6,510.5
Portfolio Investment...............	79lcd	....	....	....	....	117.4	954.2	702.9	771.8	761.4	764.3	1,378.9	2,373.4
Equity Securities................	79ldd	....	....	....	....	76.3	572.9	301.2	500.7	431.6	403.0	634.9	949.6
Debt Securities..................	79led	....	....	....	....	41.1	381.3	401.7	271.2	329.8	361.3	744.0	1,423.9
Financial Derivatives..............	79lld	....	....	....	....	–	–	–	–	10.2	6.3	5.9	16.8
Other Investment..................	79lfd	....	....	....	....	1,033.0	1,655.6	1,927.4	1,960.4	1,973.1	2,087.2	2,876.7	4,055.3
Monetary Authorities............	79lgd	....	....	....	....	151.4	55.7	30.8	25.8	22.1	14.4	17.1	39.1
General Government.............	79lhd	....	....	....	....	175.3	161.4	173.6	178.6	153.6	155.6	113.9	171.1
Banks................................	79lid	....	....	....	....	299.1	747.1	692.7	778.2	809.0	827.8	1,362.5	1,971.1
Other Sectors.....................	79ljd	....	....	....	....	407.1	691.5	1,030.3	977.8	988.6	1,089.5	1,383.3	1,874.1
Government Finance						*Millions of Krooni: Year Ending December 31*							
Deficit (-) or Surplus..............	80	163.3	–458.5	416.8	–233.6	–433.7	1,632.4	–42.3	–120.9	137.4	2,492.0	....	....
Revenue.............................	81	2,994.8	6,320.3	10,566.8	14,649.3	17,544.8	22,360.5	24,006.5	23,397.4	26,474.5	29,602.4	....	....
Grants Received..................	81z	219.9	243.7	–	132.0	–	25.0	124.0	302.5	258.5	624.0	....	....
Expenditure........................	82	3,024.0	6,088.5	9,590.3	14,523.5	17,713.7	20,551.8	24,103.3	26,815.5	27,373.3	29,236.5	....	....
Lending Minus Repayments.....	83	27.4	934.0	559.7	491.4	264.8	201.3	69.5	–2,994.7	–777.7	–1,502.1	....	....
Financing													
Domestic...........................	84a	–172.1	....	....	–150.2	49.3	–974.0	524.0	469.7	–87.4	–2,177.9	....	....
Foreign..............................	85a	8.8	....	....	383.8	384.4	–658.4	–481.7	–348.8	–50.0	–314.1	....	....
Total Debt													
Domestic...........................	88a	....	....	....	....	682.1	572.5	413.4	338.8	210.0	180.0	....	....
Foreign..............................	89a	....	....	....	....	2,584.6	2,770.9	2,715.6	3,175.1	2,505.6	2,411.1	....	....
National Accounts						*Millions of Krooni*							
Househ.Cons.Expend.,incl.NPISHs....	96f	7,261	12,592	18,145	23,837	32,915	39,552	45,124	46,726	52,060	58,674	66,898	71,240
Government Consumption Expend...	91f	2,084	5,203	7,992	11,711	13,983	15,349	16,895	17,962	18,407	19,832	21,956	23,858
Gross Fixed Capital Formation.........	93e	2,755	5,440	8,299	11,168	14,535	18,984	23,366	20,239	23,769	28,134	33,555	35,750
Changes in Inventories.............	93i	763	541	181	305	564	1,882	311	132	2,060	2,336	3,610	3,423
Exports of Goods and Services.........	90c	7,893	15,197	22,486	29,451	35,186	50,213	58,590	58,947	81,832	87,534	86,613	94,348
Imports of Goods and Services (-).....	98c	7,121	16,125	25,739	32,736	41,229	57,633	66,267	62,703	85,401	91,157	94,932	104,449
Gross Domestic Product (GDP).........	99b	13,158	22,956	31,374	43,078	55,967	68,328	78,341	81,640	92,717	104,338	116,869	125,832
Net Primary Income from Abroad.....	98.n	....	–185	–378	28	26	–2,011	–1,164	–1,506	–3,483	–4,926	–5,423	–7,937
Gross National Income (GNI).....	99a	....	22,771	30,996	43,106	55,993	66,317	77,177	80,134	89,234	99,412	111,446	117,895
Net Current Transf.from Abroad.......	98t	....	1,392	1,486	1,446	1,210	1,620	2,080	1,654	1,959	2,660	2,377	1,475
Gross Nat'l Disposable Inc.(GNDI)....	99i	....	24,163	32,482	44,553	57,203	67,937	79,258	81,787	91,193	102,072	113,304	119,370
Gross Saving.......................	99s	....	6,368	6,345	9,005	10,305	13,036	17,240	17,100	20,726	23,566	24,451	24,272
Consumption of Fixed Capital.........	99cf	....	4,130	5,275	7,046	8,655	10,718	13,366	14,817	16,594	18,290	18,691	20,211
GDP Volume 2000 Prices..........	99b.p	....	68,853	67,748	70,824	74,022	81,811	86,071	86,005	92,717	98,645	105,791	111,234
GDP Volume (2000=100)........	99bvp	....	74.3	73.1	76.4	79.8	88.2	92.8	92.8	100.0	106.4	114.1	120.0
GDP Deflator (2000=100)........	99bip	....	33.3	46.3	60.8	75.6	83.5	91.0	94.9	100.0	105.8	110.5	113.1
						Millions: Midyear Estimates							
Population...........................	99z	1.54	1.51	1.47	1.45	1.42	1.41	1.39	1.38	1.37	1.35	1.34	1.32

Ethiopia   644

		1992	1993	1994	1995	1996	1997	1998	1999	2000	2001	2002	2003
Exchange Rates		\multicolumn{12}{c}{*Birr per SDR: End of Period*}											
Official Rate	aa	6.8750	6.8678	8.6861	9.3946	9.2403	9.2613	10.5644	11.1640	10.8324	10.7555	11.6659	12.8100
		\multicolumn{12}{c}{*Birr per US Dollar: End of Period (ae) Period Average (rf)*}											
Official Rate	ae	5.0000	5.0000	5.9500	6.3200	6.4260	6.8640	7.5030	8.1340	8.3140	8.5583	8.5809	8.6206
Official Rate	rf	2.8025	5.0000	5.4650	6.1583	6.3517	6.7093	7.1159	7.9423	8.2173	8.4575	8.5678	8.5997
Fund Position		\multicolumn{12}{c}{*Millions of SDRs: End of Period*}											
Quota	2f.s	98.3	98.3	98.3	98.3	98.3	98.3	98.3	133.7	133.7	133.7	133.7	133.7
SDRs	1b.s	.1	.2	.3	.2	–	.1	.1	–	–	.1	.1	.1
Reserve Position in the Fund	1c.s	6.9	7.0	7.0	7.0	7.1	7.1	7.1	7.1	7.1	7.1	7.2	7.2
Total Fund Cred.&Loans Outstg.	2tl	14.1	35.3	49.4	49.4	64.2	64.2	76.1	69.0	59.1	84.0	105.4	105.8
International Liquidity		\multicolumn{12}{c}{*Millions of US Dollars Unless Otherwise Indicated: End of Period*}											
Total Reserves minus Gold	1l.d	232.4	455.8	544.2	771.5	732.2	501.1	511.1	458.5	306.3	433.2	881.7	955.6
SDRs	1b.d	.1	.3	.4	.3	–	.1	.1	.1	–	.2	.1	.1
Reserve Position in the Fund	1c.d	9.5	9.6	10.2	10.5	10.1	9.5	10.0	9.7	9.2	9.0	9.7	10.7
Foreign Exchange	1d.d	222.8	445.9	533.6	760.8	722.0	491.4	501.0	448.7	297.1	424.1	871.9	944.8
Gold (Million Fine Troy Ounces)	1ad	.113	.113	.113	.113	.301	.301	.303	.303	.205	.205	.246	–
Gold (National Valuation)	1and	11.4	11.4	11.4	11.4	.4	.4	.4	.3	.3	.3	.3	–
Monetary Authorities: Other Liab.	4..d	178.2	252.2	319.0	286.3	300.6	24.1	41.9	41.3	38.8	81.0	133.6	153.2
Deposit Money Banks: Assets	7a.d	193.5	236.2	533.3	454.2	435.9	680.8	652.9	542.1	597.3	624.4	698.9	862.3
Liabilities	7b.d	47.6	68.6	108.3	192.3	221.5	225.4	218.4	250.2	227.0	180.8	187.5	210.6
Other Banking Insts.: Assets	7e.d	2.2	1.0	3.5	2.5	8.6	9.3	9.2	6.8	5.7	.6	1.3	2.6
Liabilities	7f.d	55.5	58.9	52.8	45.0	39.0	36.9	27.2	28.1	29.5	28.9	29.5	29.5
Monetary Authorities		\multicolumn{12}{c}{*Millions of Birr: End of Period*}											
Foreign Assets	11	1,172.4	2,680.0	3,413.5	4,891.8	4,722.6	3,456.1	3,893.3	3,666.4	2,535.9	3,614.8	7,682.8	9,134.2
Claims on Central Government	12a	5,724.1	8,244.0	8,443.5	8,182.1	7,694.6	8,549.3	9,218.4	10,301.1	13,896.5	12,524.9	15,100.4	15,665.4
Claims on Other Financial Insts.	12f	2,101.7	457.8	464.0	465.1	465.1	465.1	465.1	466.1	395.3	395.3	395.3	395.3
Reserve Money	14	6,119.6	6,421.1	7,084.0	7,976.6	6,664.0	7,249.7	6,362.5	6,050.6	8,394.9	7,639.8	10,301.8	11,858.5
of which: Currency Outside DMBs	14a	4,708.8	4,776.0	5,380.4	5,718.0	5,401.5	4,964.3	3,977.7	4,506.8	4,590.8	4,870.3	5,686.3	6,874.3
Foreign Liabilities	16c	988.1	1,503.3	2,327.4	2,273.5	2,388.0	622.9	806.4	777.6	643.6	906.1	1,261.7	1,357.0
Central Government Deposits	16d	728.3	2,141.6	2,082.8	2,229.8	2,294.8	2,544.4	2,630.9	3,086.5	2,812.4	4,381.9	7,165.9	6,966.0
Central Government Lending Funds	16f	–	–	–	–	–	792.3	1,041.6	1,650.7	1,381.3	460.4	584.8	436.8
Capital Accounts	17a	446.7	478.4	728.4	879.5	1,159.7	1,198.1	1,272.5	1,422.3	1,646.1	2,100.5	2,674.5	2,992.3
Other Items (Net)	17r	715.5	837.5	98.0	179.6	375.9	63.1	1,462.9	1,445.9	1,949.4	1,046.2	1,189.8	1,584.4
Deposit Money Banks		\multicolumn{12}{c}{*Millions of Birr: End of Period*}											
Reserves	20	1,413.5	1,634.8	1,665.7	2,197.1	1,227.7	2,173.1	2,312.2	1,314.6	3,197.1	2,213.0	3,833.2	4,913.9
Foreign Assets	21	967.5	1,180.9	3,173.0	2,870.6	2,801.3	4,673.0	4,899.0	4,409.5	4,965.7	5,344.1	5,997.4	7,433.3
Claims on Central Government	22a	2,617.1	2,617.1	2,617.2	2,773.0	2,612.7	2,361.0	2,629.4	5,233.7	5,556.2	7,499.5	9,242.8	10,992.2
Claims on Nonfin.Pub.Enterprises	22c	825.2	1,515.2	1,630.0	1,630.0	1,794.6	1,589.7	1,612.2	798.3	775.5	851.8	646.8	829.5
Claims on Private Sector	22d	624.4	1,349.7	1,988.1	3,706.0	6,448.6	8,007.1	8,693.6	11,216.2	11,836.2	12,187.0	12,057.4	12,946.0
Claims on Other Financial Insts.	22f	–	–	–	–	279.0	248.0	217.0	486.5	435.0	389.5	369.5	407.2
Demand Deposits	24	2,534.8	2,788.0	3,803.5	3,711.4	3,761.7	5,967.2	6,501.2	7,143.8	8,004.3	8,484.8	10,185.4	11,659.4
Time, Savings,& Fgn.Currency Dep.	25	2,325.2	2,845.0	3,637.4	4,549.7	6,069.6	7,241.7	7,554.9	8,474.9	10,001.9	11,609.8	12,976.3	14,612.6
Foreign Liabilities	26c	238.1	343.2	644.4	1,215.6	1,423.5	1,547.3	1,638.5	2,035.0	1,883.9	1,535.6	1,594.2	1,800.6
Long-Term Foreign Liabilities	26cl	–	–	–	–	–	–	–	–	–	3.2	11.7	14.5	14.6
Central Government Deposits	26d	243.2	411.8	619.2	810.1	736.7	91.9	75.9	56.3	72.2	57.4	86.8	107.4
Central Government Lending Funds	26f	–	–	–	–	43.4	51.1	21.0	44.2	34.6	45.5	45.7	33.1
Capital Accounts	27a	123.5	330.2	439.2	567.4	1,270.0	1,351.4	1,808.8	1,939.5	2,235.6	2,553.8	2,528.8	2,801.7
Other Items (Net)	27r	982.8	1,579.4	1,930.2	2,322.4	1,859.0	2,801.2	2,763.1	3,765.1	4,528.3	4,186.3	4,715.5	6,492.7
Monetary Survey		\multicolumn{12}{c}{*Millions of Birr: End of Period*}											
Foreign Assets (Net)	31n	913.6	2,014.4	3,614.7	4,273.2	3,712.3	5,958.9	6,347.3	5,263.2	4,974.1	6,517.3	10,824.2	13,409.9
Domestic Credit	32	10,921.0	11,630.5	12,440.8	13,716.4	16,263.1	18,583.8	20,128.9	25,359.2	30,010.1	29,408.6	30,559.6	34,162.3
Claims on Central Govt. (Net)	32an	7,369.7	8,307.7	8,358.7	7,915.3	7,275.8	8,273.9	9,140.9	12,392.0	16,568.1	15,585.0	17,090.6	19,584.2
Claims on Nonfin.Pub.Enterprises	32c	825.2	1,515.2	1,630.0	1,630.0	1,794.6	1,589.7	1,612.2	798.3	775.5	851.8	646.8	829.5
Claims on Private Sector	32d	624.4	1,349.7	1,988.1	3,706.0	6,448.6	8,007.1	8,693.6	11,216.2	11,836.2	12,187.0	12,057.4	12,946.0
Claims on Other Financial Insts.	32f	2,101.7	457.8	464.0	465.1	744.1	713.1	682.1	952.6	830.3	784.8	764.8	802.5
Money	34	7,243.6	7,564.1	9,184.0	9,429.5	9,174.0	11,024.0	10,511.0	12,067.0	13,225.7	13,865.2	16,557.9	18,595.1
Quasi-Money	35	2,325.2	2,845.0	3,637.4	4,549.7	6,069.6	7,241.7	7,554.9	8,474.9	10,001.9	11,609.8	12,976.3	14,612.6
Long-Term Foreign Liabilities	36cl	–	–	–	–	–	–	–	–	3.2	11.7	14.5	14.6
Central Government Lending Funds	36f	–	–	–	–	43.4	843.4	1,062.6	1,694.9	1,417.6	505.9	630.5	469.9
Capital Accounts	37a	570.1	808.6	1,167.6	1,447.0	2,429.6	2,549.5	3,081.3	3,361.7	3,881.7	4,654.3	5,203.3	5,794.0
Other Items (Net)	37r	1,695.7	2,427.2	2,066.5	2,563.5	2,258.8	2,884.2	4,266.5	5,023.8	6,454.1	5,279.0	6,001.3	8,086.0
Money plus Quasi-Money	35l	9,568.8	10,409.1	12,821.4	13,979.2	15,243.6	18,265.6	18,065.9	20,541.9	23,227.5	25,475.0	29,534.2	33,207.6

2004, International Monetary Fund : *International Financial Statistics Yearbook*

Ethiopia   644

		1992	1993	1994	1995	1996	1997	1998	1999	2000	2001	2002	2003
Other Banking Institutions		\multicolumn{12}{c}{*Millions of Birr: End of Period*}
Reserves	40	297.3	369.3	233.7	9.7	8.1	22.7	8.1	57.6	28.4	17.4	18.0	31.4
Foreign Assets	41	10.8	5.1	20.7	15.9	55.4	63.5	69.1	55.3	47.1	4.9	11.2	22.0
Claims on Central Government	42a	46.6	131.6	123.2	–	–	–	–	42.5	42.5	34.0	34.0	104.6
Claims on Nonfin.Pub.Enterprises	42c	–	–	–	492.4	574.8	396.7	299.7	257.9	226.0	200.8	197.4	175.7
Claims on Private Sector	42d	2,701.0	954.3	1,205.7	701.4	1,173.4	1,773.5	2,475.8	3,222.0	3,540.1	2,401.7	2,036.3	1,966.4
Claims on Deposit Money Banks	42e	–	–	–	–	–	–	–	170.3	110.4	83.4	118.4	146.6
Demand Deposits	44	–	–	–	9.5	22.2	31.3	15.8	26.0	11.4	5.6	3.4	6.3
Time and Savings Deposits	45	497.0	529.9	538.1	48.6	2.1	234.4	681.4	734.6	717.4	678.3	742.3	711.7
Foreign Liabilities	46c	277.5	294.6	314.4	284.6	250.4	253.5	204.3	228.2	245.6	247.5	253.1	254.2
Central Govt. Lending Funds	46f	29.2	100.0	54.1	13.8	13.8	13.8	13.8	13.8	13.8	13.8	83.8	72.6
Credit from Monetary Authorities	46g	2,101.7	457.8	464.0	465.1	465.1	465.1	465.1	387.8	387.8	387.8	387.8	381.4
Credit from Deposit Money Banks	46h	97.0	97.0	116.1	414.6	685.5	958.1	894.5	1,410.1	1,646.7	456.3	369.5	408.2
Capital Accounts	47a	–40.7	–106.4	101.1	176.9	390.8	361.2	380.5	397.4	415.0	429.3	425.9	524.9
Other Items (Net)	47r	94.0	87.4	–4.5	–193.7	–18.2	–61.0	197.3	607.7	557.0	523.6	149.6	87.4
Banking Survey		\multicolumn{12}{c}{*Millions of Birr: End of Period*}
Foreign Assets (Net)	51n	646.9	1,724.9	3,321.0	4,004.5	3,517.3	5,768.9	6,212.1	5,090.4	4,775.6	6,274.6	10,582.4	13,177.8
Domestic Credit	52	11,566.9	12,258.6	13,305.7	14,445.1	17,267.2	20,040.9	22,222.3	27,928.9	32,988.5	31,260.3	32,062.4	35,606.3
Claims on Central Government(Net	52an	7,416.3	8,439.3	8,481.9	7,915.3	7,275.8	8,273.9	9,140.9	12,434.5	16,610.6	15,619.0	17,124.6	19,688.8
Claims on Nonfin. Pub. Enterprises	52c	825.2	1,515.2	1,630.0	2,122.4	2,369.4	1,986.4	1,911.9	1,056.2	1,001.6	1,052.6	844.2	1,005.2
Claims on Private Sector	52d	3,325.4	2,304.0	3,193.8	4,407.4	7,622.0	9,780.6	11,169.4	14,438.3	15,376.3	14,588.7	14,093.7	14,912.4
Liquid Liabilities	55l	9,768.5	10,569.7	13,125.8	14,027.6	15,259.8	18,508.6	18,755.0	21,245.0	23,927.9	26,141.4	30,261.9	33,894.2
Long-Term Foreign Liabilities	56cl	–	–	–	–	–	–	–	–	3.2	11.7	14.5	14.6
Central Government Lending Funds	56f	29.2	100.0	54.1	13.8	57.2	857.2	1,076.4	1,708.7	1,431.4	519.7	714.3	542.5
Capital Accounts	57a	529.4	702.2	1,268.7	1,623.9	2,820.4	2,910.7	3,461.8	3,759.2	4,296.7	5,083.6	5,629.2	6,318.9
Other Items (Net)	57r	1,886.7	2,611.6	2,178.1	2,784.4	2,647.1	3,533.3	5,141.3	6,306.5	8,104.9	5,778.4	6,025.0	8,013.9
Interest Rates		\multicolumn{12}{c}{*Percent Per Annum*}
Discount Rate	60	5.25	12.00	12.00	12.00	....	....	....	....	....	....	....	....
Treasury Bill Rate	60c	5.25	12.00	12.00	12.00	7.22	3.97	3.48	3.65	2.74	3.06	1.30	1.37
Deposit Rate	60l	3.63	11.50	11.50	11.46	9.42	7.00	6.00	6.32	6.68	6.97	4.11	3.74
Lending Rate	60p	8.00	14.00	14.33	15.08	13.92	10.50	10.50	10.58	10.89	10.87	8.66	8.06
Government Bond Yield	61	7.00	13.00	13.00	13.00	13.00	....	....	....	....	....	....	....
Prices and Labor		\multicolumn{12}{c}{*Index Numbers (2000=100): Period Averages*}
Consumer Prices	64	75.4	78.0	83.9	92.4	†87.7	89.8	†92.1	99.3	100.0	91.9	93.3	109.9
		\multicolumn{12}{c}{*Number in Thousands: Period Averages*}
Labor Force	67d	....	....	....	....	....	26,408	....	27,272	....	....	....	....
Employment	67e	....	683	....	....	....	....	....	....	....	....	....	....
Unemployment	67c	71	63	65	23	28	35	29	26	....	....	....	....
Unemployment Rate (%)	67r	70.9	62.9	....	....	....	....	....	....	....	....	....	....
International Transactions		\multicolumn{12}{c}{*Millions of Birr*}
Exports	70	448.4	994.2	2,062.4	2,602.9	2,650.6	3,941.3	3,967.0	3,711.0	3,991.0	3,850.0	4,115.0	....
Imports, c.i.f	71	2,604.3	3,936.7	5,658.0	7,052.5	8,899.2	....	10,792.0	12,274.0	10,368.0	15,347.0	14,272.0	....

Ethiopia   644

		1992	1993	1994	1995	1996	1997	1998	1999	2000	2001	2002	2003
Balance of Payments		\multicolumn{12}{c}{*Millions of US Dollars: Minus Sign Indicates Debit*}
Current Account, n.i.e.	78ald	−120.0	−50.0	125.4	39.4	79.6	−40.3	−332.6	−465.2	14.6	−454.3	−149.5	....
Goods: Exports f.o.b.	78aad	169.9	198.8	372.0	423.0	417.5	588.3	560.3	467.4	486.0	455.6	480.2	....
Goods: Imports f.o.b.	78abd	−992.7	−706.0	−925.7	−1,092.8	−1,002.8	−1,001.6	−1,359.8	−1,387.2	−1,131.4	−1,625.8	−1,455.0	....
Trade Balance	78acd	−822.9	−507.1	−553.7	−669.8	−585.3	−413.4	−799.4	−919.8	−645.4	−1,170.3	−974.8	....
Services: Credit	78add	267.6	277.2	294.6	344.5	377.2	390.7	391.5	473.6	506.2	522.9	585.4	....
Services: Debit	78aed	−368.3	−299.0	−310.4	−352.8	−349.8	−394.2	−455.6	−466.3	−490.7	−525.6	−582.6	....
Balance on Goods & Services	78afd	−923.5	−528.9	−569.5	−678.1	−557.9	−416.9	−863.5	−912.5	−629.8	−1,172.9	−972.0	....
Income: Credit	78agd	22.3	25.9	42.9	68.4	41.2	24.2	21.0	16.6	16.2	16.3	14.3	....
Income: Debit	78ahd	−104.1	−78.4	−74.6	−87.1	−75.2	−65.5	−64.2	−50.4	−52.0	−48.3	−36.9	....
Balance on Gds, Serv. & Inc.	78aid	−1,005.3	−581.4	−601.1	−696.9	−591.8	−458.2	−906.7	−946.3	−665.7	−1,204.9	−994.6	....
Current Transfers, n.i.e.: Credit	78ajd	887.4	532.6	728.5	737.3	679.0	425.5	589.8	500.7	697.9	774.6	865.5	....
Current Transfers: Debit	78akd	−2.0	−1.2	−2.0	−1.1	−7.5	−7.6	−15.7	−19.7	−17.6	−24.0	−20.5	....
Capital Account, n.i.e.	78bcd	−	−	3.7	2.6	.9	−	1.4	1.8	....	....	....	....
Capital Account, n.i.e.: Credit	78bad	−	−	3.7	2.6	.9	−	1.4	1.8	....	....	....	....
Capital Account: Debit	78bbd	−	−	−	....	....	....	....	....	....	....	....	....
Financial Account, n.i.e.	78bjd	−62.9	97.7	−199.0	−24.9	−499.6	241.2	−21.3	−180.1	22.8	−175.2	−79.0	....
Direct Investment Abroad	78bdd	−	−	−	−	....	....	....	....	....	....	....	....
Dir. Invest. in Rep. Econ., n.i.e.	78bed	−	−	−	−	....	....	....	....	....	....	....	....
Portfolio Investment Assets	78bfd	−	−	−	−	....	....	....	....	....	....	....	....
Equity Securities	78bkd	−	−	−	−	....	....	....	....	....	....	....	....
Debt Securities	78bld	−	−	−	−	....	....	....	....	....	....	....	....
Portfolio Investment Liab., n.i.e.	78bgd	−	−	−	−	....	....	....	....	....	....	....	....
Equity Securities	78bmd	−	−	−	−	....	....	....	....	....	....	....	....
Debt Securities	78bnd	−	−	−	−	....	....	....	....	....	....	....	....
Financial Derivatives Assets	78bwd	....	....	....	....	....	....	....	....	....	....	....	....
Financial Derivatives Liabilities	78bxd	....	....	....	....	....	....	....	....	....	....	....	....
Other Investment Assets	78bhd	−87.1	−31.7	−318.5	57.7	−306.8	318.5	59.8	−85.3	116.1	25.1	−4.1	....
Monetary Authorities	78bod	−	....	....	....	....	....	....	....	....	....	....	....
General Government	78bpd	−	−	....	....	....	....	....	....	....	−	....	....
Banks	78bqd	−26.7	−40.2	−358.5	44.7	−283.0	350.7	26.3	−69.6	23.2	29.7	75.2	....
Other Sectors	78brd	−60.4	8.4	40.0	13.1	−23.8	−32.2	33.5	−15.8	92.8	−4.7	−79.3	....
Other Investment Liab., n.i.e.	78bid	24.2	129.4	119.5	−82.6	−192.8	−77.3	−81.0	−94.7	−93.2	−200.3	−75.0	....
Monetary Authorities	78bsd	37.3	−50.9	25.4	.4	−7.8	−.1	−.4	.4	47.0	−54.6	5.7	....
General Government	78btd	1.0	209.1	82.4	−145.1	−131.5	−91.0	−79.9	−125.7	−178.3	−107.9	−88.4	....
Banks	78bud	1.1	26.5	55.3	91.2	205.6	15.0	2.4	62.2	4.1	−70.5	6.7	....
Other Sectors	78bvd	−15.2	−55.2	−43.6	−29.1	−259.0	−1.2	−3.1	−31.6	34.0	32.7	1.0	....
Net Errors and Omissions	78cad	−81.2	−15.2	69.5	−122.4	−45.8	−629.5	−7.9	407.2	−233.0	−141.7	−858.4	....
Overall Balance	78cbd	−264.0	32.4	−.4	−105.2	−464.8	−428.6	−360.4	−236.3	−195.6	−771.3	−1,087.0	....
Reserves and Related Items	79dad	264.0	−32.4	.4	105.2	464.8	428.6	360.4	236.3	195.6	771.3	1,087.0	....
Reserve Assets	79dbd	−95.9	−296.2	−124.7	−204.8	20.0	192.1	179.0	−49.7	−84.5	117.2	438.7	....
Use of Fund Credit and Loans	79dcd	19.9	29.7	20.8	−	21.2	−	16.9	−9.7	−13.0	31.8	27.1	....
Exceptional Financing	79ded	340.0	234.0	104.3	310.0	423.6	236.5	164.5	295.7	293.0	622.2	621.2	....
Government Finance		\multicolumn{12}{c}{*Millions of Birr: Year Ending July 7*}
Deficit (-) or Surplus	80	†−1,454.3	−1,465.3	−2,814.8	−1,379.3	−749.2	−635.8	−1,786.5	−2,524.3	....	....	....	....
Total Revenue and Grants	81y	†2,751.0	3,733.5	5,060.7	6,874.1	7,824.0	9,381.4	9,673.5	8,265.5	....	....	....	....
Revenue	81	†2,208.0	3,206.6	3,842.6	5,839.2	6,817.3	7,877.4	8,400.2	7,847.0	....	....	....	....
Grants	81z	543.0	526.9	1,218.1	1,034.9	1,006.7	1,504.0	1,273.3	418.5	....	....	....	....
Exp. & Lending Minus Repay	82z	†4,205.3	5,198.8	7,875.5	8,253.4	8,573.2	10,017.2	11,460.0	10,789.8	....	....	....	....
Total Financing	80h	1,454.3	1,465.3	2,814.8	1,379.3	749.2	635.8	1,786.5	2,524.5	....	....	....	....
Domestic	84a	1,155.1	750.8	709.6	60.0	−652.6	−92.1	1,007.0	1,175.8	....	....	....	....
Foreign	85a	299.2	714.5	2,105.2	1,319.3	1,401.8	727.9	779.5	1,348.7	....	....	....	....
Use of Cash Balances	87	299.2	714.5	2,105.2	1,319.3	1,401.8	727.9	779.5	1,348.7	....	....	....	....
Total Debt by Residence	88	13,051.0	27,645.6	37,063.1	39,599.8	38,967.1	38,748.5	41,947.3	49,485.0	....	....	....	....
Domestic	88a	8,691.4	9,474.5	11,778.3	11,654.8	11,950.8	12,359.0	13,339.0	14,700.3	....	....	....	....
Foreign	89a	4,359.6	18,171.1	25,284.8	27,945.0	27,016.3	26,389.5	28,608.3	34,784.7	....	....	....	....
National Accounts		\multicolumn{12}{c}{*Millions of Birr: Year Ending July 7*}
Househ.Cons.Expend.,incl.NPISHs	96f	†18,059	22,359	23,748	27,942	31,299	41,665	35,110	38,999	40,566	43,416	....	....
Government Consumption Expend	91f	†2,108	2,819	3,155	3,675	4,173	5,157	6,233	9,105	12,029	9,065	....	....
Gross Capital Formation	93	†1,911	3,792	4,294	5,569	7,246	7,691	7,713	7,790	7,995	8,747	....	....
Exports of Goods and Services	90c	†937	2,223	3,223	4,852	5,240	6,780	7,382	7,258	8,086	8,106	....	....
Imports of Goods and Services (-)	98c	†2,223	4,521	6,091	8,154	9,284	10,663	11,767	14,884	16,105	16,335	....	....
Gross Domestic Product (GDP)	99b	†20,792	26,671	28,329	33,885	37,938	45,238	44,840	48,688	52,074	53,011	....	....
Net Primary Income from Abroad	98.n	†−179	−414	−460	−378	−275	−224	−178	....	....	....	....	....
Gross National Income (GNI)	99a	†20,613	26,257	27,869	33,508	37,662	41,241	44,857	....	....	....	....	....
GDP at Factor Cost	99ba	†19,897	25,209	26,283	31,434	35,093	38,189	41,358	....	....	....	....	....
GDP Fact.Cost,Vol.'80/81 Prices	99bap	10,535	11,724	11,910	12,645	13,987	14,714	14,543	15,461	16,303	17,583	....	....
GDP Volume (2000=100)	99bvp	64.6	71.9	73.1	77.6	85.8	90.3	89.2	94.8	100.0	107.9	....	....
GDP Deflator (1995=100)	99bip	†76.0	86.5	88.8	100.0	100.9	104.4	114.4	....	....	....	....	....
		\multicolumn{12}{c}{*Millions: Midyear Estimates*}
Population	99z	52.20	53.93	55.65	57.35	59.02	60.67	62.30	63.94	65.59	67.27	68.96	70.68

2004, International Monetary Fund : *International Financial Statistics Yearbook*

Euro Area 163

		1992	1993	1994	1995	1996	1997	1998	1999	2000	2001	2002	2003
Exchange Rates							*Euros per SDR: End of Period*						
Market Rate	aa	....	....	....	....	....	....	....	1.36623	1.40023	1.42600	1.29639	1.17654
						Euros per US Dollar: End of Period (ae) Period Average (rf)								
Market Rate	ae	....	....	....	....	....	....	....	.99542	1.07469	1.13469	.95356	.79177
Market Rate	rf	....	....	....	....	....	....	....	.93863	1.08540	1.11751	1.06255	.88603
						Index Numbers (2000=100): Period Averages								
Nominal Effective Exchange Rate	neu	128.30	123.61	121.36	126.79	126.91	115.72	115.66	110.44	100.00	101.51	104.00	114.57
Real Effective Exchange Rate	reu	134.62	132.14	129.35	135.15	135.81	122.26	118.10	112.21	100.00	99.64	101.90	111.32
International Liquidity						*Millions of US Dollars Unless Otherwise Indicated: End of Period*								
Tot.Res.minus Gold (Eurosyst.Def)	1l.d	....	....	....	....	....	....	....	256,780	242,325	234,965	246,995	222,716
SDRs	1b.d	2,778	3,039	3,519	5,572	5,440	5,359	6,015	4,546	4,032	4,757	4,866	5,275
Reserve Position in the Fund	1c.d	13,709	12,691	12,941	16,100	16,572	18,637	27,364	24,245	19,662	22,294	26,317	29,431
Foreign Exchange	1d.d	....	....	....	....	....	....	....	227,989	218,631	207,914	215,811	188,011
of which: Fin.Deriv.rel.to Res.	1ddd	....	....	....	....	....	....	....	−209	679	346	456	865
Other Reserve Assets	1e.d	....	....	....	....	....	....	....	–	–	–	–	–
Gold (Million Fine Troy Ounces)	1ad	....	....	....	....	....	....	....	402.76	399.54	401.88	399.02	393.54
Gold (Eurosystem Valuation)	1and	....	....	....	....	....	....	....	116,901	109,653	111,119	136,765	164,206
Memo:Euro Cl. on Non-EA Res.	1dgd	....	....	....	....	....	....	....	....	....	....	....	....
Non-Euro Cl. on EA Res.	1dhd	....	....	....	....	....	....	....	14,691	14,685	21,797	23,451	25,674
Mon. Auth.: Other Foreign Assets	3..d	....	....	....	....	....	....	....	....	....	....	....	....
Foreign Liabilities	4..d	....	....	....	....	....	....	....	49,993	27,856	31,417	34,461	34,777
Banking Insts: Foreign Assets	7a.d	....	....	....	....	....	....	....	1,727,480	1,885,360	2,122,864	2,585,591	3,242,118
Foreign Liabs.	7b.d	....	....	....	....	....	....	....	1,878,975	2,139,671	2,368,396	2,720,500	3,295,949
Monetary Authorities (Eurosyst.)						*Billions of Euros: End of Period*								
Foreign Assets (on Non-EA Ctys)	11	....	....	....	....	....	323.7	322.3	400.6	380.7	399.0	374.0	317.9
Claims on General Government	12a.u	....	....	....	....	....	132.9	106.6	105.8	110.7	127.5	110.2	144.1
Claims on EA Banking Sector	12e.u	....	....	....	....	....	216.2	205.7	426.3	429.9	390.2	399.0	458.8
Claims on Other Resident Sectors	12d.u	....	....	....	....	....	4.5	4.4	11.5	12.7	11.1	9.9	10.3
Currency in Circulation	14a	....	....	....	....	....	355.0	359.1	393.3	390.2	285.9	392.9	450.5
Liabilities to EA Banking Sector	14c.u	....	....	....	....	....	92.4	94.2	279.3	270.4	342.4	283.3	285.8
Deposits of Other Resident Sect.	15..u	....	....	....	....	....	3.4	3.5	8.8	9.8	14.4	15.6	16.9
Bonds & Money Mkt. Instruments	16n.u	....	....	....	....	....	28.2	13.8	7.9	3.8	4.6	3.6	1.6
Foreign Liabs. (to Non-EA Ctys)	16c	....	....	....	....	....	32.8	18.6	49.8	29.9	35.6	32.9	27.5
Central Government Deposits	16d.u	....	....	....	....	....	51.7	54.4	53.4	47.1	35.1	29.5	21.3
Capital Accounts	17a	....	....	....	....	....	106.0	97.1	174.3	197.5	209.8	165.9	143.8
Other Items (Net)	17r	....	....	....	....	....	7.8	−1.6	−22.7	−14.6	–	−30.6	−16.2
Banking Institutions (Oth.MFIs)						*Billions of Euros: End of Period*								
Claims on EA Banking Sector	20..u	....	....	....	....	....	3,639.7	3,972.3	4,359.4	4,561.8	4,917.0	5,188.2	5,469.5
Foreign Assets (on Non-EA Ctys)	21	....	....	....	....	....	1,599.5	1,591.8	1,719.6	2,026.2	2,408.8	2,465.5	2,567.0
Claims on General Government	22a.u	....	....	....	....	....	1,874.9	1,934.0	1,952.1	1,813.7	1,899.4	1,948.0	2,065.0
Claims on Oth. Resident Sectors	22d.u	....	....	....	....	....	5,130.7	5,652.6	6,203.4	6,866.5	7,413.2	7,711.1	8,142.4
Demand (Overnight) Deposits	24..u	568.9	600.1	621.7	949.9	1,072.7	1,233.0	1,387.1	1,537.6	1,648.9	1,936.9	2,041.0	2,254.1
Deposits with Agreed Maturity	25a.u	....	....	....	....	....	1,901.9	1,929.1	2,043.2	2,159.8	2,257.5	2,264.7	2,295.2
Deposits Redeemable at Notice	25b.u	....	....	....	....	....	1,328.4	1,392.6	1,331.5	1,276.9	1,350.2	1,421.7	1,519.7
Repurchase Agreements	25f.u	....	....	....	....	....	205.4	176.5	143.9	174.9	218.5	226.9	208.7
Money Market Fund Shares	26m.u	....	....	....	....	....	252.2	241.4	293.4	323.3	436.5	532.8	649.1
Bonds & Money Mkt. Instruments	26n.u	....	....	....	....	....	2,063.5	2,261.5	2,531.1	2,712.9	2,882.9	2,992.6	3,158.8
Foreign Liabs. (to Non-EA Ctys)	26c	....	....	....	....	....	1,381.3	1,507.0	1,870.4	2,299.5	2,687.4	2,594.2	2,609.6
Central Government Deposits	26d.u	....	....	....	....	....	102.1	95.4	88.6	117.4	103.9	106.9	132.3
Credit fr. EA Banking Sector	26g.u	....	....	....	....	....	3,009.6	3,305.3	3,590.9	3,679.3	3,829.6	4,136.6	4,362.6
Capital Accounts	27a	....	....	....	....	....	688.4	754.6	849.1	940.5	1,041.9	1,108.7	1,151.1
Other Items (Net)	27r	....	....	....	....	....	78.8	100.1	−45.2	−65.1	−107.0	−113.3	−97.4
Banking Survey						*Billions of Euros: End of Period*								
Foreign Assets (Net)	31n.u	....	....	....	....	....	509.1	388.5	200.0	77.5	84.7	212.5	247.8
Domestic Credit	32..u	....	....	....	....	....	6,989.1	7,547.7	8,130.8	8,639.2	9,312.3	9,642.8	10,208.2
Claims on General Govt. (Net)	32anu	....	....	....	....	....	1,853.9	1,890.8	1,915.9	1,760.0	1,887.9	1,921.8	2,055.5
Claims on Oth. Resident Sectors	32d.u	....	....	....	....	....	5,135.2	5,656.9	6,214.9	6,879.3	7,424.4	7,721.0	8,152.7
Currency in Circulation	34a.u	264.7	277.1	292.2	303.8	313.3	320.6	323.4	350.8	348.4	239.7	341.2	397.9
Demand (Overnight) Deposits	34b.u	570.8	602.9	624.5	952.6	1,075.7	1,236.4	1,390.5	1,546.4	1,658.7	1,951.0	2,056.3	2,270.8
Deposits with Agreed Maturity	35a.u	....	....	....	....	....	1,901.9	1,929.1	2,043.2	2,159.8	2,257.9	2,265.0	2,295.4
of which: Over 2-Yr. Maturity	35abu	....	....	....	....	....	1,004.1	1,033.0	1,160.9	1,168.3	1,169.1	1,189.5	1,256.5
Deposits Redeemable at Notice	35b.u	....	....	....	....	....	1,328.4	1,392.6	1,331.5	1,276.9	1,350.2	1,421.7	1,519.7
of which: Over 3-Mos Notice	35bbu	....	....	....	....	....	219.5	214.4	112.2	125.4	115.8	105.6	92.2
Repurchase Agreements	35f.u	....	....	....	....	....	205.4	176.5	143.9	174.9	218.5	226.9	208.7
Money Market Fund Shares	36m.u	....	....	....	....	....	244.3	231.1	280.0	300.0	398.0	470.5	581.8
Bonds & Money Mkt. Instruments	36n.u	....	....	....	....	....	1,361.0	1,456.5	1,591.8	1,662.8	1,760.8	1,818.2	1,873.7
of which: Over 2-Yr. Maturity	36nau	....	....	....	....	....	1,230.5	1,312.3	1,446.1	1,525.3	1,613.6	1,689.3	1,785.5
Capital Accounts	37a	....	....	....	....	....	700.2	681.4	807.7	893.5	995.2	1,006.4	1,010.8
Other Items (Net)	37r.u	....	....	....	....	....	199.9	355.0	235.5	241.7	225.7	249.2	297.3

Euro Area 163

		1992	1993	1994	1995	1996	1997	1998	1999	2000	2001	2002	2003
Money (Eurosystem Definition)						**Billions of Euros: End of Period**							
M1	39mau	1,215.3	1,287.9	1,343.1	1,423.1	1,528.5	1,626.9	1,785.4	1,971.4	2,084.6	2,279.0	2,499.4	2,729.4
M2	39mbu	2,939.9	3,150.3	3,243.8	3,397.5	3,562.5	3,687.2	3,920.2	4,141.5	4,299.8	4,684.4	4,981.4	5,298.0
M3	39mcu	3,433.2	3,651.8	3,735.8	3,937.4	4,090.3	4,267.3	4,472.0	4,707.9	4,910.5	5,446.8	5,806.4	6,176.2
Nonmonetary Liabs. of MFIs	39mdu	1,824.7	2,018.4	2,125.9	2,472.7	2,775.4	3,154.4	3,241.0	3,526.9	3,712.5	3,893.8	3,990.8	4,144.9
Interest Rates							**Percent Per Annum**						
Eurosyst.Marg.Lending Fac.Rate	60	....	....	....	....	....	....	....	4.00	5.75	4.25	3.75	3.00
Eurosyst. Refinancing Rate	60r	....	....	....	....	....	....	....	2.71	....	†4.30	3.29	2.32
Eurosyst. Deposit Facility Rate	60x	....	....	....	....	....	....	....	1.71	3.06	3.23	2.21	1.25
Interbank Rate (Overnight)	60a	....	....	6.18	6.09	4.58	4.02	3.73	2.74	4.12	4.38	3.28	2.32
Interbank Rate (3-Mos Maturity)	60b	....	....	6.53	6.82	5.09	4.38	3.96	2.97	4.39	4.26	3.32	2.34
Deposit Rate	60l	....	....	....	....	4.08	3.41	3.20	2.45	3.45	3.49	2.80	....
Lending Rate	60p	....	....	....	....	8.88	7.58	6.73	5.65	6.60	6.83	6.14	....
Government Bond Yield	61	....	....	8.18	8.73	7.23	5.96	4.70	4.66	5.44	5.03	4.92	4.16
Prices, Production, Labor					**Index Numbers (2000=100): Period Averages**								
Producer Prices	63	....	....	....	94.8	95.2	96.2	95.4	95.0	100.0	102.2	102.1	103.6
Harmonized CPI (hcpi)	64h	....	....	....	....	....	....	96.6	97.7	100.0	102.1	104.4	106.6
Wages/Labor Costs	65..c	....	....	....	....	91.4	93.7	95.2	97.3	100.0	103.2	107.1	....
Industrial Production (Seas. Adjustec	66..c	....	....	....	....	....	....	†93.1	95.0	100.0	100.4	99.9	100.2
Employment	67..c	....	....	....	....	....	....	....	97.9	100.0	101.4	101.8	....
						Number in Thousands: Period Averages							
Unemployment	67c.c	....	....	....	....	....	....	....	12,253	11,092	11,042	11,654	12,334
Unemployment Rate (%)	67r.c	....	....	....	....	....	....	....	9	8	8	8	9
International Transactions					**Billions of Ecus through 1998; Billions of Euros beginning 1999**								
Exports	70	....	....	....	....	....	....	791.5	†831.8	1,003.0	1,046.4	1,065.6	1,035.0
Imports, c.i.f.	71	....	....	....	....	....	....	709.3	†780.5	990.5	1,003.9	960.6	968.2
								2000=100					
Volume of Exports	72	....	....	....	....	....	....	†87.0	88.9	100.0	105.1	107.8	....
Volume of Imports	73	....	....	....	....	....	....	†89.0	94.5	100.0	99.0	98.6	....
Unit Value of Exports	74	....	....	....	....	....	....	†90.5	92.4	100.0	101.0	100.3	....
Unit Value of Imports	75	....	....	....	....	....	....	†79.4	82.0	100.0	100.2	97.8	....
Balance of Payments					**Billions of US Dollars Minus Sign Indicates Debit**								
Current Account, n.i.e.	78ald	....	....	....	....	....	....	30.53	−22.26	−61.90	−14.90	52.43	28.84
Goods: Exports f.o.b.	78aad	....	....	....	....	....	....	878.68	870.88	911.06	925.46	1,004.34	1,172.06
Goods: Imports f.o.b.	78abd	....	....	....	....	....	....	−756.38	−790.35	−882.16	−859.81	−877.54	−1,048.74
Trade Balance	78acd	....	....	....	....	....	....	122.29	80.52	28.89	65.65	126.80	123.32
Services: Credit	78add	....	....	....	....	....	....	258.92	260.85	261.61	287.62	312.32	368.83
Services: Debit	78aed	....	....	....	....	....	....	−265.56	−277.70	−277.20	−288.20	−299.36	−351.00
Balance on Goods & Services	78afd	....	....	....	....	....	....	115.65	63.68	13.30	65.07	139.76	141.14
Income: Credit	78agd	....	....	....	....	....	....	222.34	220.55	246.20	246.86	222.83	250.33
Income: Debit	78ahd	....	....	....	....	....	....	−254.42	−257.77	−271.67	−281.24	−264.24	−299.02
Balance on Gds, Serv. & Inc.	78aid	....	....	....	....	....	....	83.57	26.45	−12.17	30.70	98.35	92.45
Current Transfers, n.i.e.: Credit	78ajd	....	....	....	....	....	....	70.06	69.68	62.26	70.94	79.83	90.56
Current Transfers: Debit	78akd	....	....	....	....	....	....	−123.10	−118.40	−111.99	−116.54	−125.75	−154.17
Capital Account, n.i.e.	78bcd	....	....	....	....	....	....	13.92	13.58	9.05	5.88	10.28	15.53
Capital Account, n.i.e.: Credit	78bad	....	....	....	....	....	....	19.85	20.31	16.81	15.56	17.96	26.50
Capital Account: Debit	78bbd	....	....	....	....	....	....	−5.93	−6.73	−7.76	−9.68	−7.68	−10.97
Financial Account, n.i.e.	78bjd	....	....	....	....	....	....	−86.05	4.66	47.61	−45.95	−65.03	−90.37
Direct Investment Abroad	78bdd	....	....	....	....	....	....	−195.08	−338.23	−404.90	−283.07	−141.87	−133.88
Dir. Invest. in Rep. Econ., n.i.e.	78bed	....	....	....	....	....	....	101.63	209.68	404.82	182.49	138.21	117.88
Portfolio Investment Assets	78bfd	....	....	....	....	....	....	−403.37	−330.49	−385.17	−252.78	−162.59	−321.80
Equity Securities	78bkd	....	....	....	....	....	....	−129.30	−165.52	−267.56	−91.00	−35.54	−78.76
Debt Securities	78bld	....	....	....	....	....	....	−274.06	−164.97	−117.61	−161.79	−127.04	−243.04
Portfolio Investment Liab., n.i.e.	78bgd	....	....	....	....	....	....	280.04	282.86	270.75	311.26	273.72	342.72
Equity Securities	78bmd	....	....	....	....	....	....	117.31	97.05	37.89	206.20	81.50	119.64
Debt Securities	78bnd	....	....	....	....	....	....	162.73	185.81	232.86	105.06	192.22	223.09
Financial Derivatives Assets	78bwd	....	....	....	....	....	....	−9.74	3.53	−8.91	−.94	−10.93	−14.84
Financial Derivatives Liabilities	78bxd	....	....	....	....	....	....	−86.08	−31.00	−166.16	−243.97	−224.19	−265.74
Other Investment Assets	78bhd	....	....	....	....	....	....	−.84	−2.05	−.98	.55	−1.07	−.93
Monetary Authorities	78bod	....	....	....	....	....	....	−.76	3.56	−2.43	2.70	.11	−1.27
General Government	78bpd	....	....	....	....	....	....	−21.81	17.77	−118.37	−208.87	−162.54	−174.08
Banks	78bqd	....	....	....	....	....	....	−63.19	−50.27	−44.38	−38.35	−60.70	−89.46
Other Sectors	78brd	....	....	....	....	....	....	226.54	208.30	337.17	241.06	62.62	185.29
Other Investment Liab., n.i.e.	78bid	....	....	....	....	....	....	4.02	7.23	.54	3.82	18.23	13.45
Monetary Authorities	78bsd	....	....	....	....	....	....	−6.82	−14.03	.01	−.68	−7.49	−3.91
General Government	78btd	....	....	....	....	....	....	211.64	174.23	272.79	215.68	25.40	151.12
Banks	78bud	....	....	....	....	....	....	16.88	40.88	63.84	22.24	26.48	24.63
Other Sectors	78bvd	....	....	....	....	....	....	29.29	−7.56	−10.91	38.46	4.96	10.94
Net Errors and Omissions	78cad	....	....	....	....	....	....	−12.32	−11.58	−16.15	−16.51	2.64	−35.07
Overall Balance	78cbd	....	....	....	....	....	....	12.32	11.58	16.15	16.51	−2.64	35.07
Reserves and Related Items	79dad	....	....	....	....	....	....	12.32	11.58	16.15	16.51	−2.64	35.07
Reserve Assets	79dbd	....	....	....	....	....	....	−	....	....	....	....	....
Use of Fund Credit and Loans	79dcd	....	....	....	....	....	....	−	....	....	....	....	....
Exceptional Financing	79ded	....	....	....	....	....	....	....	....	....	....	....	....

2004, International Monetary Fund: *International Financial Statistics Yearbook*

Euro Area 163

		1992	1993	1994	1995	1996	1997	1998	1999	2000	2001	2002	2003
International Investment Position						*Billions of US Dollars*							
Assets..	79aad	....	....	....	....	....	....	....	5,823.55	6,287.26	6,642.47	7,632.22	....
Direct Investment Abroad.................	79abd	....	....	....	....	....	....	....	1,180.11	1,511.14	1,671.80	2,031.87	....
Portfolio Investment........................	79acd	....	....	....	....	....	....	....	2,089.99	2,218.47	2,222.06	2,381.02	....
Equity Securities...........................	79add	....	....	....	....	....	....	....	1,020.25	1,102.68	989.16	904.14	....
Debt Securities.............................	79aed	....	....	....	....	....	....	....	1,069.73	1,115.80	1,232.90	1,476.88	....
Financial Derivatives........................	79ald	....	....	....	....	....	....	....	111.62	98.39	95.50	128.60	....
Other Investment............................	79afd	....	....	....	....	....	....	....	2,067.96	2,107.96	2,307.13	2,706.97	....
Monetary Authorities....................	79agd	....	....	....	....	....	....	....	2.91	3.29	2.71	3.60	....
General Government.....................	79ahd	....	....	....	....	....	....	....	126.11	124.59	112.21	126.42	....
Banks...	79aid	....	....	....	....	....	....	....	1,318.79	1,353.95	1,512.12	1,800.60	....
Other Sectors...............................	79ajd	....	....	....	....	....	....	....	620.15	626.12	680.09	776.35	....
Reserve Assets................................	79akd	....	....	....	....	....	....	....	373.88	351.29	345.99	383.76	....
Liabilities..	79lad	....	....	....	....	....	....	....	6,104.19	6,596.47	6,809.66	7,936.06	....
Dir. Invest. in Rep. Economy............	79lbd	....	....	....	....	....	....	....	805.10	1,088.22	1,234.35	1,586.11	....
Portfolio Investment........................	79lcd	....	....	....	....	....	....	....	2,940.54	2,896.80	2,831.35	3,174.14	....
Equity Securities...........................	79ldd	....	....	....	....	....	....	....	1,694.62	1,488.05	1,394.22	1,392.95	....
Debt Securities.............................	79led	....	....	....	....	....	....	....	1,245.93	1,408.75	1,437.13	1,781.19	....
Financial Derivatives........................	79lld	....	....	....	....	....	....	....	95.53	96.53	94.20	137.06	....
Other Investment............................	79lfd	....	....	....	....	....	....	....	2,263.02	2,514.92	2,649.77	3,038.75	....
Monetary Authorities....................	79lgd	....	....	....	....	....	....	....	39.27	38.94	35.84	60.90	....
General Government.....................	79lhd	....	....	....	....	....	....	....	51.44	48.29	54.27	64.02	....
Banks...	79lid	....	....	....	....	....	....	....	1,830.21	2,012.37	2,126.67	2,385.41	....
Other Sectors...............................	79ljd	....	....	....	....	....	....	....	342.09	415.32	433.00	528.43	....
National Accounts						*Billions of Ecus through 1998; Billions of Euros beginning 1999*							
Househ.Cons.Expend.,incl.NPISHs.....	96f.c	....	....	....	....	....	....	3,309.5	†3,482.2	3,664.4	3,918.1	4,033.5	4,149.4
Government Consumption Expend...	91f.c	....	....	....	....	....	....	1,168.0	†1,229.8	1,283.2	1,369.3	1,431.6	1,501.3
Gross Fixed Capital Formation..........	93e.c	....	....	....	....	....	....	1,186.8	†1,291.4	1,387.0	1,437.4	1,427.6	1,434.9
Changes in Inventories......................	93i.c	....	....	....	....	....	....	59.9	†22.3	37.9	2.8	–3.4	8.1
Exports of Goods and Services..........	90c.c	....	....	....	....	....	....	1,925.5	†2,052.7	2,410.3	2,556.1	2,571.2	2,582.4
Imports of Goods and Services (-).....	98c.c	....	....	....	....	....	....	1,778.2	†1,951.1	2,342.4	2,443.7	2,397.0	2,422.0
Gross Domestic Product (GDP).........	99b.c	....	....	....	....	....	....	5,871.3	†6,132.8	6,453.1	6,840.1	7,063.5	7,254.1
Net Primary Income from Abroad.....	98.nc	....	....	....	....	....	....	–35.6	–39.1	....	....	....	....
GDP Volume 1995 Prices..................	99b.r	....	....	....	....	....	....	5,647.3	5,819.7	6,029.9	6,227.3	6,279.4	6,317.5
GDP Volume (2000=100).................	99bvr	....	....	....	....	....	....	94.2	†96.5	100.0	103.3	104.1	104.8
GDP Deflator (2000=100)................	99bir	....	....	....	....	....	....	96.6	†98.5	100.0	102.6	105.1	107.3

Fiji

		1992	1993	1994	1995	1996	1997	1998	1999	2000	2001	2002	2003
Exchange Rates						*Fiji Dollars per SDR: End of Period*							
Official Rate	aa	2.1511	2.1164	2.0570	2.1248	1.9900	2.0902	2.7965	2.6981	2.8479	2.9017	2.8072	2.5589
					Fiji Dollars per US Dollar: End of Period (ae) Period Average (rf)								
Official Rate	ae	1.5645	1.5408	1.4090	1.4294	1.3839	1.5492	1.9861	1.9658	2.1858	2.3089	2.0648	1.7221
Official Rate	rf	1.5030	1.5418	1.4641	1.4063	1.4033	1.4437	1.9868	1.9696	2.1286	2.2766	2.1869	1.8958
					Index Numbers (2000=100): Period Averages								
Official Rate	ahx	141.4	137.8	145.2	151.1	151.4	147.3	107.0	107.9	100.0	93.3	97.3	112.3
Nominal Effective Exchange Rate	nec	119.3	120.8	122.9	121.9	123.5	127.6	101.8	100.9	100.0	98.9	100.1	103.3
Real Effective Exchange Rate	rec	113.2	117.2	116.5	114.3	116.4	122.0	101.4	101.6	100.0	100.3	100.9	106.6
Fund Position						*Millions of SDRs: End of Period*							
Quota	2f.s	51.10	51.10	51.10	51.10	51.10	51.10	51.10	70.30	70.30	70.30	70.30	70.30
SDRs	1b.s	5.97	6.26	7.39	7.67	7.99	8.29	8.62	4.10	4.47	4.81	5.02	5.18
Reserve Position in the Fund	1c.s	10.43	9.95	9.99	10.00	10.05	10.08	10.12	14.94	14.98	15.00	15.07	15.19
Total Fund Cred.&Loans Outstg	2tl	—	—	—	—	—	—	—	—	—	—	—	—
International Liquidity					*Millions of US Dollars Unless Otherwise Indicated: End of Period*								
Total Reserves minus Gold	1l.d	316.87	269.46	273.14	349.03	427.24	360.29	385.67	428.69	411.79	366.39	358.82	423.62
SDRs	1b.d	8.21	8.59	10.79	11.41	11.49	11.18	12.14	5.63	5.82	6.04	6.83	7.70
Reserve Position in the Fund	1c.d	14.34	13.67	14.58	14.87	14.45	13.60	14.25	20.50	19.52	18.85	20.49	22.57
Foreign Exchange	1d.d	294.32	247.19	247.77	322.76	401.30	335.51	359.29	402.55	386.45	341.50	331.50	393.35
Gold (Million Fine Troy Ounces)	1ad	.001	.001	.001	.001	.001	.001	.001	.001	.001	.001	.001	.001
Gold (National Valuation)	1and	.28	.33	.32	.32	.31	.24	.24	.24	.23	.23	.29	.35
Monetary Authorities: Other Liab.	4..d	—	—	—	—	—	—	—	—	—	—	—	—
Deposit Money Banks: Assets	7a.d	44.47	58.69	62.91	50.13	78.07	89.31	136.34	200.07	81.06	84.21	93.30	147.74
Liabilities	7b.d	67.17	64.30	65.66	73.89	124.33	123.48	108.04	159.49	114.08	120.65	148.10	181.70
Monetary Authorities						*Millions of Fiji Dollars: End of Period*							
Foreign Assets	11	498.0	414.8	384.9	498.9	591.2	558.1	765.5	842.7	900.1	846.0	741.2	729.5
Claims on Central Government	12a	—	6.7	—	—	—	—	—	50.7	56.1	66.2	59.0	90.4
Claims on Official Entities	12bx	.1	2.2	.1	.1	—	—	—	—	—	—	—	—
Reserve Money	14	226.4	219.9	223.6	243.4	247.9	260.4	276.8	434.2	352.2	420.0	460.1	606.8
of which: Currency Outside DMBs	14a	103.1	112.4	115.6	117.8	125.4	134.0	159.8	189.9	163.3	181.7	202.6	226.2
Liabs.of Central Bank: Securities	16ac	163.9	108.9	126.6	220.5	253.3	210.7	252.9	255.8	415.7	338.6	219.9	119.1
Foreign Liabilities	16c												
Central Government Deposits	16d	21.8	14.3	14.8	6.8	47.2	40.0	22.3	42.6	22.5	17.3	6.0	8.0
Capital Accounts	17a	82.8	62.7	45.8	49.3	42.3	50.5	197.1	169.0	136.5	115.3	103.1	90.6
Other Items (Net)	17r	3.3	17.9	−25.8	−21.0	.4	−3.4	16.4	−8.3	29.2	21.0	11.1	−4.7
Deposit Money Banks						*Millions of Fiji Dollars: End of Period*							
Reserves	20	123.3	107.5	107.9	125.5	120.2	126.4	111.5	237.3	174.2	233.3	243.9	372.7
Claims on Mon.Author.:Securities	20c	60.2	44.6	44.0	104.1	106.0	60.4	44.4	54.5	43.7	17.1	29.8	54.2
Foreign Assets	21	69.6	90.4	88.6	71.7	108.0	138.4	270.8	393.3	177.2	194.4	192.7	254.4
Claims on Central Government	22a	91.6	88.9	80.7	65.4	78.8	87.0	107.0	117.8	95.3	129.9	164.2	222.8
Claims on Official Entities	22bx	118.4	141.9	144.4	137.7	145.8	164.5	154.4	137.1	138.7	120.0	97.7	100.1
Claims on Private Sector	22d	880.4	994.4	1,080.9	1,112.2	1,165.0	1,013.9	963.8	997.0	1,145.9	1,081.8	1,136.1	1,326.4
Demand Deposits	24	211.0	251.4	229.0	268.3	328.7	311.3	328.6	497.6	415.7	434.2	495.8	666.0
Time Deposits	25	977.4	1,013.7	1,069.7	1,089.6	1,032.1	913.2	859.9	851.6	920.1	846.2	870.6	1,080.5
Foreign Liabilities	26c	105.1	99.1	92.5	105.6	172.1	191.3	214.6	313.5	249.3	278.6	305.8	312.9
Central Government Deposits	26d	6.8	21.5	40.5	40.1	21.0	37.8	78.6	122.5	54.6	56.1	59.2	68.9
Other Items (Net)	27r	43.2	81.9	114.7	112.8	170.1	136.9	170.2	151.8	135.1	161.6	133.0	202.3
Monetary Survey						*Millions of Fiji Dollars: End of Period*							
Foreign Assets (Net)	31n	462.5	406.2	381.0	464.9	527.2	505.2	821.7	922.5	827.9	761.8	628.0	671.0
Domestic Credit	32	1,061.9	1,198.2	1,250.7	1,268.3	1,321.3	1,187.6	1,124.3	1,137.5	1,358.8	1,324.6	1,391.7	1,662.9
Claims on Central Govt. (Net)	32an	63.0	59.8	25.3	18.4	10.5	9.1	6.1	3.3	74.2	122.8	158.0	236.4
Claims on Official Entities	32bx	118.5	144.1	144.5	137.8	145.8	164.5	154.4	137.1	138.7	120.0	97.7	100.1
Claims on Private Sector	32d	880.4	994.4	1,080.9	1,112.2	1,165.0	1,013.9	963.8	997.0	1,145.9	1,081.8	1,136.1	1,326.4
Money	34	314.1	363.8	344.6	386.2	456.3	445.3	493.9	694.5	593.7	620.9	712.0	900.6
Quasi-Money	35	977.4	1,013.7	1,069.7	1,089.6	1,032.1	913.2	859.9	851.6	920.1	846.2	870.6	1,080.5
Liabs.of Central Bank: Securities	36ac	103.7	64.4	82.5	116.4	147.3	150.3	208.4	201.3	372.0	321.4	190.1	64.9
Capital Accounts	37a	82.8	62.7	45.8	49.3	42.3	50.5	197.1	169.0	136.5	115.3	103.1	90.6
Other Items (Net)	37r	46.4	99.8	89.0	91.8	170.5	133.4	186.6	143.5	164.3	182.5	144.1	197.2
Money plus Quasi-Money	35l	1,291.5	1,377.5	1,414.4	1,475.7	1,488.4	1,358.5	1,353.8	1,546.1	1,513.9	1,467.1	1,582.5	1,981.1
Nonbank Financial Institutions						*Millions of Fiji Dollars: End of Period*							
Claims on Central Government	42a.l	55.6	55.3	58.1	58.2	77.4	127.7	127.0	134.8	146.8	164.2	186.2	201.0
Claims on Local Government	42b.l	14.1	14.9	20.6	26.8	26.9	—	—	—	—	—	—	—
Claims on Nonfin.Pub.Enterprises	42c.l	14.2	15.2	26.7	36.2	54.4	—	—	—	—	—	—	—
Claims on Private Sector	42d.l	37.6	42.6	59.0	68.3	73.8	93.5	100.5	119.8	126.7	134.5	139.2	153.4
Incr.in Total Assets(Within Per.)	49z.l	19.9	22.1	23.2	27.6	15.1	−14.4	14.8	28.7	25.9	34.0	31.2	34.4

2004, International Monetary Fund: *International Financial Statistics Yearbook*

Fiji 819

		1992	1993	1994	1995	1996	1997	1998	1999	2000	2001	2002	2003
Interest Rates						**Percent Per Annum**							
Bank Rate (End of Period)	60	6.00	6.00	6.00	6.00	6.00	1.88	2.50	2.50	8.00	1.75	1.75	1.75
Money Market Rate	60b	3.06	2.91	4.10	3.95	2.43	1.91	1.27	1.27	2.58	.79	.92	.86
Treasury Bill Rate	60c	3.65	2.91	2.69	3.15	2.98	2.60	2.00	2.00	3.63	1.51	1.66	1.06
Deposit Rate	60l	4.10	3.69	3.15	3.18	3.38	3.08	2.17	1.24	.90	.78	.62	.51
Lending Rate	60p	12.35	11.74	11.28	11.06	11.33	11.03	9.66	8.77	8.40	8.34	8.05	7.60
Prices, Production, Labor						**Index Numbers (2000=100): Period Averages**							
Consumer Prices	64	79.5	†83.6	84.3	86.2	88.8	91.8	97.0	98.9	100.0	104.3	105.1	109.5
Wage Rates	65	83.9	90.9	93.7	94.9	106.6	98.8	94.6	99.0	100.0	104.3	105.2	109.5
Industrial Production	66	80.6	85.3	89.5	92.0	84.6	83.7	98.1	116.7	100.0	101.9	98.2	....
Tourist Arrivals	66.t	94.7	97.8	108.4	108.3	115.5	122.2	126.3	139.4	100.0	118.3	135.3	146.5
Industrial Employment(1995=100)	67	83.7	93.8	86.3	88.0	99.6	102.2	101.8	100.6	100.0	104.1	106.8	108.6
						Number in Thousands: Period Averages							
Labor Force	67d	265	269	....	....	298	....	320	331	341	....	....	....
Employment	67e	92	94	95	97	111	113	113	114	....	....	....	....
Unemployment	67c	14	16	16	15	....	....	....	....	....	....	....	....
Unemployment Rate (%)	67r	5.4	5.9	5.7	5.4	....	....	....	....	....	....	....	....
International Transactions						**Millions of Fiji Dollars**							
Exports	70	554.78	588.39	657.04	764.48	821.07	758.13	905.64	947.64	1,025.53	1,007.81	1,192.08	1,273.07
Imports, c.i.f.	71	947.11	1,109.81	1,209.85	1,253.83	1,384.46	1,392.66	1,434.17	1,778.71	1,756.39	1,807.86	1,953.22	2,214.59
Imports, f.o.b.	71.v	809.80	1,006.50	1,053.70	1,070.80	1,178.70	1,182.20	1,221.00	....	1,756.40	1,808.00	1,953.32	1,953.31
Balance of Payments						**Millions of US Dollars: Minus Sign Indicates Debit**							
Current Account, n.i.e.	78ald	−61.3	−138.1	−112.8	−112.7	13.5	−34.1	−59.9	12.7	....	....	....	....
Goods: Exports f.o.b.	78aad	349.8	370.9	490.2	519.6	672.2	535.6	428.9	537.7	....	....	....	....
Goods: Imports f.o.b.	78abd	−538.8	−652.8	−719.7	−761.4	−839.9	−818.9	−614.6	−653.3	....	....	....	....
Trade Balance	78acd	−189.0	−281.9	−229.5	−241.8	−167.7	−283.2	−185.6	−115.6	....	....	....	....
Services: Credit	78add	453.2	481.1	534.7	564.1	612.6	667.9	503.2	525.1	....	....	....	....
Services: Debit	78aed	−303.7	−321.1	−366.0	−398.6	−412.9	−405.6	−352.0	−389.8	....	....	....	....
Balance on Goods & Services	78afd	−39.5	−121.8	−60.8	−76.3	31.9	−20.9	−34.4	19.7	....	....	....	....
Income: Credit	78agd	52.3	52.1	49.2	55.4	63.6	61.7	54.6	47.3	....	....	....	....
Income: Debit	78ahd	−79.8	−80.4	−105.7	−94.6	−91.6	−99.2	−110.6	−82.8	....	....	....	....
Balance on Gds, Serv. & Inc.	78aid	−66.9	−150.1	−117.3	−115.5	4.0	−58.4	−90.4	−15.8	....	....	....	....
Current Transfers, n.i.e.: Credit	78ajd	34.9	40.2	38.1	36.0	44.1	54.6	45.3	42.7	....	....	....	....
Current Transfers: Debit	78akd	−29.3	−28.2	−33.5	−33.1	−34.6	−30.3	−14.7	−14.2	....	....	....	....
Capital Account, n.i.e.	78bcd	72.5	57.1	43.4	87.0	70.8	48.5	60.6	14.0	....	....	....	....
Capital Account, n.i.e.: Credit	78bad	96.7	83.7	76.0	120.1	114.5	88.9	100.6	59.3	....	....	....	....
Capital Account: Debit	78bbd	−24.2	−26.7	−32.6	−33.1	−43.8	−40.5	−40.0	−45.3	....	....	....	....
Financial Account, n.i.e.	78bjd	84.0	45.1	61.0	88.3	3.6	−15.1	28.7	−104.0	....	....	....	....
Direct Investment Abroad	78bdd	−25.8	−28.9	.3	2.8	−9.8	−30.0	−62.6	−53.0	....	....	....	....
Dir. Invest. in Rep. Econ., n.i.e.	78bed	103.6	91.2	67.5	69.5	2.4	15.6	107.0	−33.2	....	....	....	....
Portfolio Investment Assets	78bfd	−	−	−	−	−	−	−	....	....	....	....	....
Equity Securities	78bkd	−	−	−	−	−	−	−	....	....	....	....	....
Debt Securities	78bld	−	−	−	−	−	−	−	....	....	....	....	....
Portfolio Investment Liab., n.i.e.	78bgd	−	−	−	−	−	−	−	....	....	....	....	....
Equity Securities	78bmd	−	−	−	−	−	−	−	....	....	....	....	....
Debt Securities	78bnd	−	−	−	−	−	−	−	....	....	....	....	....
Financial Derivatives Assets	78bwd	−	−	−	−	−	−	−	....	....	....	....	....
Financial Derivatives Liabilities	78bxd	−	−	−	−	−	−	−	....	....	....	....	....
Other Investment Assets	78bhd	2.6	−13.5	1.2	12.0	−25.9	−21.1	−66.6	−62.2	....	....	....	....
Monetary Authorities	78bod	−	−	−	−	−	−	−	....	....	....	....	....
General Government	78bpd	−	−	−	−	−	−	−	....	....	....	....	....
Banks	78bqd	2.6	−13.5	1.2	12.0	−25.9	−21.1	−66.6	−62.2	....	....	....	....
Other Sectors	78brd	−	−	−	−	−	−	−	....	....	....	....	....
Other Investment Liab., n.i.e.	78bid	3.7	−3.8	−8.1	3.9	36.8	20.4	51.0	44.4	....	....	....	....
Monetary Authorities	78bsd	−	−	−	−	−	−	−	−	....	....	....	....
General Government	78btd	−	−	−	−	−	−	−	−	....	....	....	....
Banks	78bud	3.7	−3.8	−8.1	3.9	36.8	20.4	51.0	44.4	....	....	....	....
Other Sectors	78bvd	−	−	−	−	−	−	−	−	....	....	....	....
Net Errors and Omissions	78cad	−10.6	22.4	30.9	30.4	−9.7	−24.3	−24.6	32.5	....	....	....	....
Overall Balance	78cbd	84.6	−13.6	22.5	93.0	78.1	−25.1	4.9	−44.9	....	....	....	....
Reserves and Related Items	79dad	−84.6	13.6	−22.5	−93.0	−78.1	25.1	−4.9	44.9	....	....	....	....
Reserve Assets	79dbd	−59.3	45.2	10.7	−76.6	−71.1	29.7	−27.4	−30.5	....	....	....	....
Use of Fund Credit and Loans	79dcd	−	−	−	−	−	−	−	−	....	....	....	....
Exceptional Financing	79ded	−25.3	−31.7	−33.2	−16.4	−7.0	−4.6	22.5	75.3	....	....	....	....

Fiji 819

		1992	1993	1994	1995	1996	1997	1998	1999	2000	2001	2002	2003
Government Finance		*Millions of Fiji Dollars: Year Ending December 31*											
Deficit (-) or Surplus	80	−112.1	−158.7	−114.6	−92.7	−211.4	−281.9	−104.3	....	....	....	....	....
Total Revenue and Grants	81y	602.5	654.0	697.9	718.9	743.6	803.4	1,141.2	....	....	....	....	....
Revenue	81	595.3	649.9	693.4	712.6	736.3	798.5	1,138.6	....	....	....	....	....
Grants	81z	7.2	4.1	4.5	6.3	7.3	4.9	2.6	....	....	....	....	....
Exp. & Lending Minus Repay.	82z	714.6	812.7	812.5	811.6	955.0	1,085.3	1,245.5	....	....	....	....	....
Expenditure	82	708.3	799.1	794.4	803.6	945.2	1,081.8	1,231.5	....	....	....	....	....
Lending Minus Repayments	83	6.3	13.6	18.1	8.0	9.8	3.5	14.0	....	....	....	....	....
Total Financing	80h	112.1	158.7	114.6	92.7	211.4	281.9	104.3	....	....	....	....	....
Domestic	84a	100.7	146.9	83.6	71.5	193.9	273.2	93.5	....	....	....	....	....
Foreign	85a	11.4	11.8	31.0	21.2	17.5	8.7	10.8	....	....	....	....	....
Total Debt by Residence	88	843.5	923.7	981.8	1,001.8	1,133.5	1,356.3	1,454.9	....	....	....	....	....
Domestic	88a	638.1	733.3	792.2	807.3	942.8	1,156.1	1,060.6	....	....	....	....	....
Foreign	89a	205.4	190.4	189.6	194.5	190.7	200.2	394.3	....	....	....	....	....
National Accounts						*Millions of Fiji Dollars*							
Househ.Cons.Expend.,incl.NPISHs	96f	1,578.8	1,643.0	1,666.0	1,764.7	1,858.2	1,868.8	1,934.3	1,976.2	2,069.0	2,188.0	....	....
Government Consumption Expend	91f	414.7	466.5	437.2	446.4	474.1	507.5	572.6	607.7	633.7	655.4	....	....
Gross Fixed Capital Formation	93e	263.9	364.9	320.5	350.0	296.8	312.2	482.2	507.2	403.1	516.8	....	....
Changes in Inventories	93i	30.0	38.0	40.0	30.0	40.0	40.0	40.0	40.0	40.0	40.0	....	....
Exports of Goods and Services	90c	1,195.3	1,320.7	1,507.8	1,532.2	1,771.4	1,765.1	1,837.5	2,210.3	2,092.2	2,136.0	....	....
Imports of Goods and Services (-)	98c	1,264.3	1,499.0	1,588.8	1,630.6	1,758.3	1,766.7	1,918.3	2,349.5	2,355.0	2,327.0	....	....
Gross Domestic Product (GDP)	99b	2,303.2	2,522.5	2,673.1	2,799.9	2,962.3	3,060.9	3,283.8	3,662.3	3,504.8	3,835.8	....	....
Net National Income	99e	2,078.6	....	....	2,553.0	2,719.3	2,803.0	2,857.5	3,179.8	3,196.3	3,339.1	....	....
GDP at Factor Cost	99ba	2,009.8	2,169.3	2,293.4	2,402.0	2,552.8	2,617.1	2,807.2	3,136.8	3,070.9	3,300.3	3,462.9	....
Net Primary Income from Abroad	98.n	84.9	75.6	54.1	81.6	70.2	67.6	152.0	100.9	76.1	202.4	....	....
Gross National Income (GNI)	99a	2,261.9	2,478.9	2,590.3	2,744.7	2,923.0	3,006.8	3,172.4	3,511.0	3,459.5	3,676.6	....	....
Consumption of Fixed Capital	99cf	183	183	183	192	204	204	315	331	263	337	....	....
GDP at Fact.Cost,Vol.'89 Prices	99bap	1,664.2	1,707.5	1,794.4	1,838.9	1,895.6	1,879.4	1,907.3	2,089.4	2,023.1	2,084.7	2,170.1	....
GDP Volume (2000=100)	99bvp	82.3	84.4	88.7	90.9	93.7	92.9	94.3	103.3	100.0	103.0	107.3	....
GDP Deflator (2000=100)	99bip	79.6	83.7	84.2	86.1	88.7	91.7	97.0	98.9	100.0	104.3	105.1	....
						Millions: Midyear Estimates							
Population	99z	.74	.75	.76	.77	.78	.79	.80	.80	.81	.82	.83	.84

2004, International Monetary Fund : *International Financial Statistics Yearbook*

Finland 172

		1992	1993	1994	1995	1996	1997	1998	1999	2000	2001	2002	2003
Exchange Rates		\multicolumn{12}{c}{*Markkaa per SDR through 1998, Euros per SDR Thereafter: End of Period*}
Official Rate	aa	7.2119	7.9454	6.9244	6.4790	6.6777	7.3139	7.1753	1.3662	1.4002	1.4260	1.2964	1.1765
		\multicolumn{12}{c}{*Markkaa per US Dollar through 1998; Euros per US Dollar Thereafter: End of Period (ae) Period Average (rf)*}
Official Rate	ae	5.2450	5.7845	4.7432	4.3586	4.6439	5.4207	5.0960	.9954	1.0747	1.1347	.9536	.7918
Official Rate	rf	4.4794	5.7123	5.2235	4.3667	4.5936	5.1914	5.3441	.9386	1.0854	1.1175	1.0626	.8860
		\multicolumn{12}{c}{*Markkaa per ECU: End of Period (ea) Period Average (eb)*}
ECU Rate	ea	6.3512	6.4785	5.8343	5.7282	5.8188	5.9856	5.9458	....	....	....	....	....
ECU Rate	eb	5.8090	6.6963	6.2084	5.7122	5.8245	5.8874	5.9855	....	....	....	....	....
		\multicolumn{12}{c}{*Index Numbers (2000=100): Period Averages*}
Official Rate (1995=100)	ahx	97.8	76.4	83.9	100.0	95.0	84.1	81.7	....	....	....	....	....
Nominal Effective Exchange Rate	neu	109.3	95.6	103.2	113.6	109.8	107.0	106.2	104.3	100.0	101.9	102.5	106.2
Real Effective Exchange Rate	reu	129.0	109.4	114.7	126.5	117.1	110.3	108.9	104.9	100.0	100.8	99.9	101.9
Fund Position		\multicolumn{12}{c}{*Millions of SDRs: End of Period*}
Quota	2f.s	861.8	861.8	861.8	861.8	861.8	861.8	861.8	1,263.8	1,263.8	1,263.8	1,263.8	1,263.8
SDRs	1b.s	78.4	83.8	222.7	241.6	201.6	241.7	247.5	211.3	106.5	186.3	147.0	131.0
Reserve Position in the Fund	1c.s	241.0	220.4	196.1	259.5	292.8	414.2	595.0	464.3	381.8	439.0	476.8	522.1
of which: Outstg.Fund Borrowing	2c	–	–	–	–	–	–	31.3	–	–	–	–	–
Total Fund Cred.&Loans Outstg	2tl	–	–	–	–	–	–	–	–	–	–	–	–
International Liquidity		\multicolumn{12}{c}{*Millions of US Dollars Unless Otherwise Indicated: End of Period*}
Total Res.Min.Gold (Eurosys.Def)	1l.d	5,213.4	5,410.8	10,662.0	10,038.3	6,916.3	8,416.6	9,694.5	†8,219.7	7,976.9	7,983.3	9,285.0	10,514.9
SDRs	1b.d	107.8	115.1	325.1	359.2	289.9	326.1	348.5	290.1	138.7	234.1	199.9	194.6
Reserve Position in the Fund	1c.d	331.3	302.7	286.3	385.8	421.1	558.5	837.8	637.3	497.5	551.7	648.3	775.8
Foreign Exchange	1d.d	4,774.3	4,993.0	10,050.6	9,293.4	6,205.3	7,531.7	8,508.2	7,292.4	7,340.7	7,197.6	8,436.8	9,544.5
o/w:Fin.Deriv.Rel.to Reserves	1ddd	....	....	....	....	....	....	....	–	–	–	1.05	7.58
Other Reserve Assets	1e.d	....	....	....	....	....	....	....	....	....	....	....	....
Gold (Million Fine Troy Ounces)	1ad	2.002	2.002	2.003	1.600	1.600	1.600	2.002	1.577	1.577	1.577	1.577	1.577
Gold (Eurosystem Valuation)	1and	415.6	376.9	459.6	399.7	375.1	321.4	427.8	457.7	432.8	436.0	540.5	658.0
Memo:Euro Cl. on Non-EA Res	1dgd	....	....	....	....	....	....	....	2,686	–	–	30	254
Non-Euro Cl. on EA Res	1dhd	....	....	....	....	....	....	....	682	812	653	733	976
Mon. Auth.: Other Foreign Assets	3..d	....	....	....	....	....	....	....	†–	–	–	733.0	975.1
Foreign Liabilities	4..d	452.7	33.4	27.5	278.6	201.2	107.8	143.9	†437.0	458.7	97.8	4.2	314.5
Banking Insts.: Foreign Assets	7a.d	21,499	21,608	22,295	24,169	26,986	21,364	21,845	†15,715	19,914	35,258	41,884	47,589
Foreign Liab.	7b.d	40,169	31,854	30,679	29,269	25,884	17,916	19,991	†9,372	15,472	28,041	26,341	25,284
Monetary Authorities		\multicolumn{12}{c}{*Millions of Markkaa through 1998; Millions of Euros Beginning 1999: End of Period*}
Fgn. Assets (Cl.on Non-EA Ctys)	11	29,928	33,478	52,752	48,916	36,461	51,505	51,999	10,926	8,897	9,419	9,398	9,002
Claims on General Government	12a.u	....	....	....	....	....	....	....	91	107	142	111	115
o/w: Claims on Gen.Govt.in Cty	12a	2,447	1,788	1,806	1,882	1,907	2,015	2,074	–	–	–	–	–
Claims on Banking Institutions	12e.u	....	....	....	....	....	....	....	4,565	1,654	2,327	6,820	7,269
o/w: Claims on Bank.Inst.in Cty	12e	11,547	7,575	1,718	8,415	13,301	2,837	19	1,513	471	1,294	2,970	2,850
Claims on Other Resident Sectors	12d.u	....	....	....	....	....	....	....	535	429	361	385	349
o/w: Cl. on Oth.Res.Sect.in Cty	12d	2,921	4,404	3,951	3,302	2,462	1,877	1,541	234	171	106	34	7
Currency Issued	14a	14,508	14,994	14,315	15,611	16,891	17,817	17,689	3,350	3,336	2,687	6,258	7,215
Liabilities to Banking Insts.	14c.u	....	....	....	....	....	....	....	8,238	2,646	5,007	5,923	4,918
o/w: Liabs to Bank.Inst.in Cty	14c	23,295	23,037	43,148	42,766	22,359	18,412	17,888	4,884	2,475	4,111	3,759	2,146
Demand Dep. of Other Res.Sect.	14d.u	....	....	....	....	....	....	....	–	–	–	–	–
o/w:D.Dep.of Oth.Res.Sect.in Cty	14d	–	–	–	–	–	–	–	–	–	–	–	–
Other Dep. of Other Res.Sect.	15..u	....	....	....	....	....	....	....	1	–	–	–	–
o/w:O.Dep.of Oth.Res.Sect.in Cty	15	3,362	2,087	1,549	994	574	32	6	1	–	–	–	–
Bonds & Money Mkt. Instruments	16n.u	....	....	....	....	....	....	....	....	....	....	....	....
o/w: Held by Resid.of Cty	16n	....	....	....	....	....	....	....	....	....	....	....	....
Foreign Liab. (to Non-EA Ctys)	16c	2,375	193	130	1,214	934	584	733	435	493	111	4	249
Central Government Deposits	16d.u	....	....	....	....	....	....	....	–	–	–	–	–
o/w: Cent.Govt.Dep. in Cty	16d	90	784	93	75	–	–	–	–	–	–	–	–
Capital Accounts	17a	6,790	6,895	6,749	6,691	6,716	6,810	6,785	4,552	5,061	5,332	5,342	4,654
Other Items (Net)	17r	–3,577	–745	–5,756	–4,836	6,658	14,579	12,533	–459	–449	–890	–812	–302
Memo: Currency Put into Circ.	14m	....	....	....	....	....	....	....	....	....	....	3,446	3,918

Finland 172

		1992	1993	1994	1995	1996	1997	1998	1999	2000	2001	2002	2003
Banking Institutions			*Millions of Markkaa through 1998; Millions of Euros Beginning 1999: End of Period*
Claims on Monetary Authorities	20	29,983	27,638	46,653	45,976	25,604	21,711	20,774	4,884	2,475	4,111	3,759	2,146
Claims on Bk.Inst.in Oth.EA Ctys	20b.u	....	....	....	....	....	....	....	5,775	7,515	3,951	2,866	2,853
Fgn. Assets (Cl.on Non-EA Ctys)	21	112,765	124,993	105,751	105,344	125,320	115,806	111,320	15,643	21,401	40,007	39,939	37,679
Claims on General Government	22a.u	....	....	....	....	....	....	....	8,690	9,017	11,543	10,356	11,742
o/w: Claims on Gen.Govt.in Cty	22a	7,568	11,117	15,630	37,442	30,796	37,738	41,067	7,792	7,738	9,842	8,005	10,432
Claims on Other Resident Sectors	22d.u	....	....	....	....	....	....	....	65,481	70,733	78,285	84,208	92,632
o/w: Cl. on Oth.Res.Sect.in Cty	22d	437,016	398,932	360,408	350,038	347,768	337,266	358,798	64,975	70,091	77,784	83,773	92,050
Demand Deposits	24..u	....	....	....	....	....	....	....	38,335	37,129	39,014	40,952	44,445
o/w:D.Dep.of Oth.Res.Sect.in Cty	24	125,425	131,365	143,547	163,521	191,188	201,557	211,632	38,277	37,033	38,866	40,807	44,372
Other Deposits	25..u	....	....	....	....	....	....	....	22,246	23,873	25,103	27,418	26,439
o/w:O.Dep.of Oth.Res.Sect.in Cty	25	154,861	153,618	145,670	142,710	104,963	102,154	103,542	22,209	23,823	24,980	27,213	26,167
Money Market Fund Shares	26m.u	....	....	....	....	....	....	....	360	1,524	2,906	4,668	7,026
Bonds & Money Mkt. Instruments	26n.u	....	....	....	....	....	....	....	24,953	23,708	25,475	28,218	31,509
o/w: Held by Resid.of Cty	26n	....	....	....	....	....	....	....	....	....	....	....	....
Foreign Liab. (to Non-EA Ctys)	26c	210,685	184,260	145,519	127,572	120,204	97,118	101,876	9,329	16,628	31,818	25,118	20,019
Central Government Deposits	26d.u	....	....	....	....	....	....	....	2,553	4,368	1,697	1,424	2,824
o/w: Cent.Govt.Dep. in Cty	26d	9,843	10,174	11,250	19,057	19,881	27,569	17,951	2,552	4,368	1,696	1,423	2,823
Credit from Monetary Authorities	26g	13,132	7,576	1,718	8,415	13,301	2,837	19	1,514	455	1,293	2,970	2,850
Liab. to Bk.Inst.in Oth. EA Ctys	26h.u	....	....	....	....	....	....	....	3,153	1,964	2,397	2,387	2,616
Capital Accounts	27a	38,497	38,496	31,789	31,579	29,799	34,003	34,113	6,763	8,156	16,986	17,304	18,648
Other Items (Net)	27r	34,890	37,190	48,948	45,947	50,152	47,285	62,826	−8,733	−6,665	−8,790	−9,329	−9,320
Banking Survey (Nat'l Residency)			*Millions of Markkaa through 1998; Millions of Euros Beginning 1999: End of Period*
Foreign Assets (Net)	31n	−70,367	−25,982	12,854	25,474	40,643	69,609	60,710	20,912	21,967	21,602	29,347	30,370
Domestic Credit	32	440,018	405,283	370,451	373,532	363,052	351,327	385,529	70,449	73,632	86,036	90,389	99,666
Claims on General Govt. (Net)	32an	81	1,947	6,092	20,192	12,821	12,184	25,190	5,240	3,370	8,146	6,582	7,609
Claims on Other Resident Sectors	32d	439,937	403,335	364,359	353,340	350,231	339,143	360,339	65,209	70,262	77,890	83,807	92,057
Currency Issued	34a.n	14,508	14,994	14,315	15,611	16,891	17,817	17,689	3,350	3,336	2,687	6,258	7,215
Demand Deposits	34b.n	125,425	131,365	143,547	163,521	191,188	201,557	211,632	38,277	37,033	38,866	40,807	44,372
Other Deposits	35..n	158,223	155,705	147,218	143,704	105,537	102,186	103,548	22,210	23,823	24,980	27,213	26,167
Money Market Fund Shares	36m	....	....	....	....	....	....	....	360	1,524	2,906	4,668	7,026
Bonds & Money Mkt. Instruments	36n	....	....	....	....	....	....	....	24,953	23,708	25,475	28,218	31,509
o/w: Over Two Years	36na	....	....	....	....	....	....	....	4,985	8,682	9,419	10,048	10,600
Capital Accounts	37a	45,287	45,391	38,538	38,270	36,514	40,813	40,897	11,315	13,217	22,318	22,646	23,302
Other Items (Net)	37r	26,209	31,846	39,688	37,901	53,564	58,563	72,473	−9,104	−7,043	−9,594	−10,071	−9,552
Banking Survey (EA-Wide Residency)			*Millions of Euros: End of Period*
Foreign Assets (Net)	31n.u	....	....	....	....	....	....	....	16,805	13,177	17,497	24,215	26,413
Domestic Credit	32..u	....	....	....	....	....	....	....	72,244	75,918	88,634	93,636	102,014
Claims on General Govt. (Net)	32anu	....	....	....	....	....	....	....	6,228	4,756	9,988	9,043	9,033
Claims on Other Resident Sect.	32d.u	....	....	....	....	....	....	....	66,016	71,162	78,646	84,593	92,981
Currency Issued	34a.u	....	....	....	....	....	....	....	3,350	3,336	2,687	6,258	7,215
Demand Deposits	34b.u	....	....	....	....	....	....	....	38,335	37,129	39,014	40,952	44,445
Other Deposits	35..u	....	....	....	....	....	....	....	22,247	23,873	25,103	27,418	26,439
o/w: Other Dep. Over Two Yrs	35abu	....	....	....	....	....	....	....	2,088	2,631	2,230	3,094	2,423
Money Market Fund Shares	36m.u	....	....	....	....	....	....	....	360	1,524	2,906	4,668	7,026
Bonds & Money Mkt. Instruments	36n.u	....	....	....	....	....	....	....	24,953	23,708	25,475	28,218	31,509
o/w: Over Two Years	36nau	....	....	....	....	....	....	....	4,985	8,682	9,419	10,048	10,600
Capital Accounts	37a	....	....	....	....	....	....	....	11,315	13,217	22,318	22,646	23,302
Other Items (Net)	37r.u	....	....	....	....	....	....	....	−11,511	−13,693	−11,372	−12,306	−11,506
Interest Rates			*Percent Per Annum*
Discount Rate (End of Period)	60	9.50	5.50	5.25	4.88	4.00	4.00	3.50	....	....	....	....	....
Money Market Rate	60b	13.25	7.77	5.35	5.75	3.63	3.23	3.57	2.96	4.39	4.26	3.32	2.33
Deposit Rate	60l	7.50	4.75	3.27	3.19	2.35	2.00		1.22	1.63	1.94	1.49	....
Lending Rate	60p	12.14	9.92	7.91	7.75	6.16	5.29	5.35	4.71	5.61	5.79	4.82	....
Government Bond Yield	61	....	8.8	9.0	8.8	....	....	....	4.7	5.5	5.0	5.0	4.1
Prices, Production, Labor			*Index Numbers (2000=100): Period Averages*
Industrial Share Prices	62	6.3	10.7	16.5	18.3	16.2	21.5	30.4	52.3	100.0	57.5	44.5	38.1
Prices: Domestic Supply	63	88.7	91.4	92.6	93.2	92.3	93.8	92.5	92.4	100.0	99.7	98.5	98.4
Producer, Manufacturing	63ey	87.1	90.3	91.7	94.8	†94.9	96.1	94.7	93.7	100.0	97.8	94.8	92.8
Consumer Prices	64	88.9	90.7	91.7	†92.6	93.2	94.3	95.6	96.7	†100.0	102.6	104.2	105.1
Harmonized CPI	64h	....	....	....	92.5	93.5	94.6	95.9	97.1	100.0	102.7	104.7	106.1
Wages: Hourly Earnings	65ey	78.9	79.5	81.1	84.7	88.2	90.4	93.6	96.1	†100.0	104.5	108.2	112.6
Industrial Production	66	55.6	58.7	65.3	69.3	71.3	77.5	84.6	89.5	100.0	100.1	102.2	103.0
Industrial Employment, Seas.Adj	67eyc	91.8	85.9	86.4	92.5	93.0	93.8	96.2	98.8	100.0	100.7	99.4	95.2
			*Number in Thousands: Period Averages*
Labor Force	67d	....	2,507	....	2,481	2,490	2,484	2,507	2,557	2,609	2,626	2,630	2,620
Employment	67e	2,233	†2,099	2,080	2,128	2,158	†2,194	2,247	2,317	2,355	2,388	2,393	2,385
Unemployment	67c	328	444	456	382	448	†409	372	348	321	302	294	277
Unemployment Rate (%)	67r	13.0	17.9	18.4	17.2	17.9	†16.4	14.7	13.9	12.6	11.7	11.3	10.6

Finland 172

		1992	1993	1994	1995	1996	1997	1998	1999	2000	2001	2002	2003
International Transactions		*Millions of Markkaa through 1998 Millions of Euros Beginning 1999*										
Exports	70	107,471	133,962	153,690	172,380	176,592	204,202	229,233	†39,306	49,485	47,768	47,245	46,378
Newsprint	70ul	2,656	2,955	2,915	3,187	3,342	3,169	3,205	†593	594	....	....	....
Imports, c.i.f	71	94,984	103,162	119,897	122,428	134,422	154,681	172,315	†29,691	36,837	35,845	35,611	36,775
						1995=100							
Volume of Exports	72	69.3	82.1	93.3	100.0	105.6	118.4	....	....	....	....	....	....
Newsprint	72ul	104.6	113.6	115.1	100.0	92.7	107.5	109.6	111.7	....	....	....	....
Volume of Imports	73	79.4	77.3	92.9	100.0	107.8	117.0	....	....	....	....	....	....
Unit Value of Exports	74	88.2	92.5	94.1	100.0	100.0	101.6	....	....	....	....	....	....
Newsprint	74ul	79.7	81.6	79.5	100.0	113.2	92.5	91.8	....	....	....	....	....
Unit Value of Imports	75	92.4	103.8	100.6	100.0	101.9	105.1	....	....	....	....	....	....
Export Prices (2000=100)	76	85.0	90.4	91.7	98.2	99.0	97.0	96.9	†92.6	†100.0	95.6	90.4	86.5
Import Prices (2000=100)	76.x	81.0	89.0	88.8	88.8	90.1	91.1	87.9	†88.4	†100.0	97.1	94.3	93.7
Balance of Payments		*Millions of US Dollars: Minus Sign Indicates Debit*										
Current Account, n.i.e	78ald	−5,116	−1,135	1,110	5,231	5,003	6,633	7,340	8,045	8,975	8,704	10,148	9,295
Goods: Exports f.o.b	78aad	24,101	23,587	29,881	40,558	40,725	41,148	43,393	41,983	45,703	42,980	44,856	52,487
Goods: Imports f.o.b	78abd	−20,093	−17,138	−22,158	−28,121	−29,411	−29,604	−30,903	−29,815	−32,019	−30,321	−31,974	−39,097
Trade Balance	78acd	4,009	6,449	7,723	12,437	11,314	11,544	12,490	12,168	13,684	12,659	12,882	13,390
Services: Credit	78add	4,656	4,412	5,490	7,415	7,129	6,640	6,698	6,522	6,177	5,832	6,490	7,775
Services: Debit	78aed	−7,577	−6,637	−7,335	−9,584	−8,817	−8,235	−7,767	−7,615	−8,440	−8,105	−8,009	−9,743
Balance on Goods & Services	78afd	1,088	4,225	5,878	10,268	9,627	9,949	11,421	11,075	11,421	10,386	11,363	11,423
Income: Credit	78agd	1,536	1,154	1,789	2,879	2,868	4,136	4,237	5,664	7,265	8,568	8,657	9,293
Income: Debit	78ahd	−6,946	−6,086	−6,103	−7,318	−6,503	−6,600	−7,320	−7,712	−8,989	−9,573	−9,259	−10,408
Balance on Gds, Serv. & Inc	78aid	−4,322	−707	1,564	5,828	5,992	7,485	8,338	9,026	9,698	9,381	10,761	10,307
Current Transfers, n.i.e.: Credit	78ajd	427	475	410	1,536	1,253	1,210	1,523	1,658	1,611	1,562	1,732	2,052
Current Transfers: Debit	78akd	−1,221	−903	−863	−2,133	−2,242	−2,062	−2,521	−2,640	−2,334	−2,239	−2,344	−3,065
Capital Account, n.i.e	78bcd	−	−	−	66	56	247	91	49	103	83	89	108
Capital Account, n.i.e.: Credit	78bad	−	−	−	114	130	247	91	85	111	93	93	113
Capital Account: Debit	78bbd	−	−	−	−48	−74	−	−	−36	−7	−10	−4	−5
Financial Account, n.i.e	78bjd	3,071	374	4,093	−4,284	−7,718	−2,976	−1,722	−6,414	−8,841	−10,942	−8,603	−6,329
Direct Investment Abroad	78bdd	757	−1,401	−4,354	−1,494	−3,583	−5,260	−18,698	−6,739	−23,898	−8,458	−7,801	7,538
Dir. Invest. in Rep. Econ., n.i.e	78bed	396	864	1,496	1,044	1,118	2,129	12,029	4,649	9,125	3,739	8,156	2,899
Portfolio Investment Assets	78bfd	−622	−604	775	204	−4,186	−4,600	−3,906	−15,699	−18,920	−11,594	−13,432	−9,872
Equity Securities	78bkd	−10	−151	−78	−209	−736	−1,694	−2,099	−5,527	−7,164	−5,153	−5,387	−5,463
Debt Securities	78bld	−612	−452	853	414	−3,450	−2,906	−1,807	−10,173	−11,756	−6,441	−8,045	−4,410
Portfolio Investment Liab., n.i.e	78bgd	8,243	6,836	6,180	−1,779	1,153	3,843	3,866	13,550	17,116	5,985	8,899	8,943
Equity Securities	78bmd	89	2,216	2,541	2,027	1,915	4,023	7,931	10,279	10,114	3,960	2,527	−831
Debt Securities	78bnd	8,154	4,620	3,640	−3,807	−761	−181	−4,065	3,271	7,002	2,025	6,372	9,774
Financial Derivatives Assets	78bwd	−	−	51	38	38	−72	89	−	−	−	−	−
Financial Derivatives Liabilities	78bxd	−	−	5	600	325	114	−725	−419	−630	38	−325	1,716
Other Investment Assets	78bhd	−3,285	−1,832	−668	−2,863	−4,683	−2,201	331	−3,324	−5,636	−10,117	−1,328	−16,164
Monetary Authorities	78bod	−416	−29	99	146	27	94	145	−343	−129	77	−53	−55
General Government	78bpd	−275	−344	−445	−366	−719	−609	−126	−224	−171	−966	−617	−3,515
Banks	78bqd	−896	−987	−511	−1,926	−3,815	−1,725	41	−1,566	−4,107	−8,197	1,204	−10,283
Other Sectors	78brd	−1,698	−472	189	−717	−175	39	270	−1,191	−1,229	−1,032	−1,863	−2,312
Other Investment Liab., n.i.e	78bid	−2,418	−3,488	607	−35	2,099	3,072	5,292	1,567	14,001	9,465	−2,773	−1,389
Monetary Authorities	78bsd	1,244	−298	−107	92	−96	−173	−180	−872	1,433	282	1,127	988
General Government	78btd	255	983	965	−331	764	1,478	394	−420	−1,272	467	343	2,143
Banks	78bud	−5,034	−4,970	−1,088	869	−626	1,876	3,607	−154	4,098	8,762	−4,665	−3,460
Other Sectors	78bvd	1,117	796	837	−666	2,056	−110	1,471	3,014	9,742	−47	422	−1,060
Net Errors and Omissions	78cad	−105	1,053	−489	−1,384	−375	−1,600	−5,412	−1,667	114	2,565	−1,747	−3,582
Overall Balance	78cbd	−2,150	291	4,714	−372	−3,036	2,304	296	13	351	410	−113	−507
Reserves and Related Items	79dad	2,150	−291	−4,714	372	3,036	−2,304	−296	−13	−351	−410	113	507
Reserve Assets	79dbd	2,150	−291	−4,714	372	3,036	−2,304	−296	−13	−351	−410	113	507
Use of Fund Credit and Loans	79dcd	−	−	−	−	−	−	−	−	−	−	−	−
Exceptional Financing	79ded	−	−	....	....	....	....	....	−	−	−	−	−

Finland 172

		1992	1993	1994	1995	1996	1997	1998	1999	2000	2001	2002	2003
International Investment Position							*Millions of US Dollars*						
Assets	79aad	39,957	40,838	51,570	57,970	65,385	71,091	85,854	109,967	148,094	161,069	202,570	286,626
Direct Investment Abroad	79abd	8,565	9,178	12,534	14,993	17,666	20,297	29,407	33,850	52,109	52,226	63,924	68,702
Portfolio Investment	79acd	3,257	4,067	3,417	3,572	7,713	11,659	16,825	33,621	51,125	55,905	76,017	107,389
Equity Securities	79add	89	308	418	738	1,564	3,245	5,271	13,670	20,263	20,157	22,939	36,470
Debt Securities	79aed	3,168	3,758	2,999	2,835	6,149	8,414	11,554	19,951	30,862	35,748	53,078	70,919
Financial Derivatives	79ald	–	77	103	41	–5	259	151	3,469	2,816	2,110	4,069	26,131
Other Investment	79afd	22,510	21,729	24,395	28,153	32,173	29,385	29,684	30,348	33,637	42,407	48,736	73,230
Monetary Authorities	79agd	928	874	969	911	830	617	1,078	821	887	767	997	1,260
General Government	79ahd	1,521	1,841	2,481	2,966	3,636	3,497	3,611	3,670	3,460	4,352	5,740	10,583
Banks	79aid	11,301	10,933	12,021	14,203	17,872	18,430	18,004	18,169	20,957	31,303	33,145	47,794
Other Sectors	79ajd	8,759	8,081	8,924	10,073	9,835	6,842	6,992	7,688	8,334	5,986	8,854	13,592
Reserve Assets	79akd	5,626	5,788	11,122	11,210	7,839	9,490	9,787	8,679	8,408	8,420	9,824	11,173
Liabilities	79lad	83,423	85,949	107,281	111,245	118,245	119,705	186,126	325,521	329,900	261,959	256,656	332,758
Dir. Invest. in Rep. Economy	79lbd	3,689	4,217	6,714	8,465	8,797	9,530	15,320	16,455	18,320	24,272	24,071	34,007	46,400
Portfolio Investment	79lcd	44,974	53,875	69,508	69,408	75,311	76,436	131,124	266,119	253,376	178,121	158,592	197,152
Equity Securities	79ldd	979	5,251	12,767	14,625	23,457	28,870	79,722	219,531	204,361	128,039	89,176	99,672
Debt Securities	79led	43,995	48,624	56,741	54,782	51,855	47,566	51,403	46,587	49,015	50,083	69,416	97,480
Financial Derivatives	79lld	–	–1,055	–1,092	354	723	1,153	229	2,965	1,925	1,678	3,102	26,020
Other Investment	79lfd	34,760	28,913	32,151	33,018	33,414	32,586	38,317	38,118	50,327	58,089	60,955	63,185
Monetary Authorities	79lgd	1,301	908	996	1,176	1,018	713	734	–690	614	887	2,274	3,816
General Government	79lhd	1,689	2,767	4,016	3,886	4,299	5,340	6,133	5,575	4,040	4,273	5,221	6,775
Banks	79lid	19,348	12,708	12,620	13,824	12,527	13,003	16,135	14,484	17,825	31,785	29,773	27,963
Other Sectors	79ljd	12,423	12,530	14,519	14,133	15,570	13,530	15,316	18,749	27,848	21,144	23,687	24,632
Government Finance													
Central Government				*Millions of Markkaa through 1998; Millions of Euros Beginning 1999: Year Ending December 31*									
Deficit (–) or Surplus	80	–70,346	–64,554	–58,781	–53,599	–36,571	–15,523	–1,904	–3,283	3,920	–291	2,362	30
Total Revenue and Grants	81y	161,995	165,820	173,827	187,954	199,273	205,870	226,344	32,853	37,936	37,345	37,301	36,996
Revenue	81	156,114	160,235	168,307	178,584	192,955	199,126	221,033	32,853	37,936	37,345	37,301	36,996
Grants	81z	5,881	5,585	5,520	9,370	6,318	6,744	5,311	–	–	–	–	–
Exp. & Lending Minus Repay	82z	232,341	230,374	232,608	241,553	235,844	221,394	228,250	36,136	34,016	37,637	34,939	36,966
Expenditure	82	203,201	218,612	223,119	232,883	231,425	219,527	230,509	36,353	36,646	35,574	34,352	34,612
Lending Minus Repayments	83	29,140	11,762	9,489	8,670	4,419	1,867	–2,259	–217	–2,630	2,063	588	2,354
Total Financing	80h	70,346	64,554	58,751	53,599	36,571	15,524	1,906	–3,236	–3,920	292	–2,362	–30
Total Net Borrowing	84	....	....	58,781	53,599	36,571	15,524	1,906	–3,413	–4,141	–1,701	–2,529	3,827
Net Domestic	84a	19,449	15,431	26,024	53,823	36,203	34,420	9,721	–3,413	–4,141	–1,701	–2,529	3,827
Net foreign	85a	....	....	32,727	–224	368	–18,896	–7,815	–	–	–	–	–
Use of Cash Balances	87	....	....	....	....	....	....	....	–3,500	221	1,992	167	–3,857
Total Debt by Currency	88	171,930	272,778	314,285	362,202	396,718	419,346	421,390	68,052	63,435	61,760	59,253	63,320
Domestic	88b	....	....	123,434	174,874	196,836	210,088	211,413	57,008	53,844	52,678	51,456	62,079
Foreign	89b	....	....	190,851	187,328	199,882	209,258	209,977	11,044	9,590	9,082	7,797	1,241
General Government							*As Percent of Gross Domestic Product*						
Deficit (–) or Surplus	80g	–5.9	–8.0	–6.4	–4.6	–3.2	–1.5	1.3	1.9	7.0	4.9	....	....
Debt	88g	41.5	58.0	59.6	58.1	57.1	54.1	48.8	46.8	44.0	43.6	....	....
National Accounts				*Billions of Markkaa through 1998; Billions of Euros Beginning in 1999*									
Househ.Cons.Expend.,incl.NPISHs	96f	267.38	269.14	278.70	292.12	308.50	323.56	346.02	†60.35	64.45	67.92	71.14	74.92
Government Consumption Expend	91f	123.89	119.72	122.15	128.91	135.63	142.64	149.43	†25.93	26.87	28.39	30.30	31.65
Gross Fixed Capital Formation	93e	96.92	80.62	80.85	91.97	99.73	114.30	128.91	†23.49	25.75	27.73	26.57	25.85
Changes in Inventories	93i	–6.16	–.99	9.67	6.82	–2.32	3.18	4.34	†–.02	1.00	.10	.40	.40
Exports of Goods and Services	90c	128.77	159.92	183.33	209.14	219.91	248.31	267.47	†45.35	55.95	54.07	54.12	53.07
Imports of Goods and Services (–)	98c	123.87	135.80	152.39	164.40	175.59	196.46	206.65	†35.11	43.91	42.78	42.37	42.99
Gross Domestic Product (GDP)	99b	486.92	492.61	522.31	564.57	585.87	635.53	689.52	†119.99	130.15	135.47	139.80	143.42
Net Primary Income from Abroad	98.n	–24.19	–28.08	–22.75	–20.45	–16.55	–12.36	–16.30	†–1.80	–1.63	–.85	–.22	–.82
Gross National Income (GNI)	99a	462.73	464.53	499.55	543.93	568.97	622.83	672.69	†118.19	128.51	134.62	139.58	142.60
Net Current Transf.from Abroad	98t	–3.51	–2.45	–2.42	–.75	–3.78	–3.61	–5.43	†–1.01	–1.00	–1.07	–1.19	–1.39
Gross Nat'l Disposable Inc.(GNDI)	99i	459.22	462.08	497.13	543.18	565.18	619.22	668.89	†117.18	127.52	133.54	138.39	141.22
Gross Saving	99s	67.96	73.21	96.29	122.15	121.05	152.93	171.82	†30.90	36.20	37.23	36.95	34.65
Consumption of Fixed Capital	99cf	97.40	99.26	101.49	102.84	104.47	108.28	113.68	†19.85	21.19	22.35	22.59	22.75
GDP Volume 1995 Prices	99b.p	529.24	523.16	543.85	564.57	587.20	624.15	657.45	†114.14	119.98	121.26	124.02	126.35
GDP Volume (2000=100)	99bvp	74.2	73.3	76.2	79.1	82.3	87.5	92.2	†95.1	100.0	101.1	103.4	105.3
GDP Deflator (2000=100)	99bip	84.8	86.8	88.5	92.2	93.0	93.9	96.7	†96.9	100.0	103.0	103.9	104.7
							Millions: Midyear Estimates						
Population	99z	5.03	5.06	5.09	5.11	5.13	5.14	5.15	5.17	5.18	5.19	5.20	5.21

2004, International Monetary Fund : International Financial Statistics Yearbook

France 132

		1992	1993	1994	1995	1996	1997	1998	1999	2000	2001	2002	2003
Exchange Rates													
		\multicolumn{12}{c}{*Francs per SDR through 1998, Euros per SDR Thereafter: End of Period*}
Market Rate	aa	7.5714	8.0978	7.8044	7.2838	7.5306	8.0794	7.9161	1.3662	1.4002	1.4260	1.2964	1.1765
		Francs per US Dollar through 1998, Euros per US Dollar Thereafter: End of Period (ae) Period Average (rf)											
Market Rate	ae	5.5065	5.8955	5.3460	4.9000	5.2370	5.9881	5.6221	.9954	1.0747	1.1347	.9536	.7918
Market Rate	rf	5.2938	5.6632	5.5520	4.9915	5.1155	5.8367	5.8995	.9386	1.0854	1.1175	1.0626	.8860
		Francs per ECU: End of Period (ea) Period Average (eb)											
ECU Rate	ea	6.6678	6.5742	6.5758	6.4458	6.5619	6.6135	6.5596	....	....	....	....	....
ECU Rate	eb	6.8496	6.6334	6.5796	6.5250	6.4928	6.6122	6.6015	....	....	....	....	....
		Index Numbers (2000=100): Period Averages											
Market Rate (1995=100)	ahx	94.4	88.2	90.0	100.0	97.5	85.6	84.7	....	....	....	....	....
Nominal Effective Exchange Rate	neu	100.3	103.9	104.7	107.9	107.8	104.3	104.9	103.4	100.0	100.4	101.2	104.7
Real Effective Exchange Rate	reu	112.6	113.5	112.3	113.4	109.9	105.4	105.0	104.1	100.0	98.9	99.7	102.6
Fund Position													
		Millions of SDRs: End of Period											
Quota	2f.s	7,415	7,415	7,415	7,415	7,415	7,415	7,415	10,739	10,739	10,739	10,739	10,739
SDRs	1b.s	118	241	248	643	682	720	786	253	309	392	458	512
Reserve Position in the Fund	1c.s	1,805	1,682	1,627	1,854	1,875	2,119	3,162	3,950	3,471	3,894	4,250	4,242
of which: Outstg.Fund Borrowing	2c	–	–	–	–	–	–	382	–	–	–	–	–
International Liquidity													
		Millions of US Dollars Unless Otherwise Indicated: End of Period											
Total Res.Min.Gold (Eurosys.Def)	1l.d	27,028	22,649	26,257	26,853	26,796	30,927	44,312	†39,701	37,039	31,749	28,365	30,186
SDRs	1b.d	163	331	362	955	981	971	1,107	347	402	492	622	761
Reserve Position in the Fund	1c.d	2,482	2,310	2,375	2,756	2,695	2,859	4,452	5,421	4,522	4,894	5,778	6,303
Foreign Exchange	1d.d	24,384	20,008	23,520	23,142	23,120	27,097	38,753	33,933	32,114	26,363	21,965	23,122
o/w:Fin.Deriv.Rel.to Reserves	1ddd	....	....	....	....	....	....	....	....	....	....	....	....
Other Reserve Assets	1e.d	....	....	....	....	....	....	....	–	–	–	–	–
Gold (Million Fine Troy Ounces)	1ad	81.85	81.85	81.85	81.85	81.85	81.89	102.37	97.25	97.25	97.25	97.25	97.25
Gold (Eurosystem Valuation)	1and	26,313	30,729	30,730	31,658	30,368	25,002	29,871	28,225	26,689	26,888	33,331	40,576
Memo:Euro Cl. on Non-EA Res	1dgd	....	....	....	....	....	....	....	–	–	–	–	–
Non-Euro Cl. on EA Res	1dhd	....	....	....	....	....	....	....	3,330	3,870	3,562	3,861	3,035
Mon. Auth.: Other Foreign Assets	3..d	....	....	....	....	....	....	....	....	....	....	....	....
Foreign Liabilities	4..d	29,541	20,553	11,650	11,649	†796	618	1,014	†7,678	1,007	3,233	1,838	4,801
Banking Insts.: Foreign Assets	7a.d	512,485	581,393	599,906	705,082	684,056	736,795	....	†427,935	435,469	447,009	538,479	635,130
Foreign Liab	7b.d	526,214	523,077	592,630	662,469	671,759	694,578	....	†331,659	384,416	399,215	464,826	547,132
Monetary Authorities													
		Billions of Francs through 1998; Millions of Euros Beginning 1999: End of Period											
Fgn. Assets (Cl.on Non-EA Ctys)	11	345	351	372	346	†309	335	420	68,150	68,300	66,406	58,388	55,979
Claims on General Government	12a.u	....	....	....	....	....	....	....	4,051	4,044	3,691	3,314	5,029
o/w: Claims on Gen.Govt.in Cty	12a	95	75	72	59	58	52	51	4,051	4,044	3,691	3,314	5,029
Claims on Banking Institutions	12e.u	....	....	....	....	....	....	....	65,188	42,512	44,767	81,628	84,513
o/w: Claims on Bank.Inst.in Cty	12e	294	372	200	147	143	125	167	48,448	29,013	16,413	16,107	11,084
Claims on Other Resident Sectors	12d.u	....	....	....	....	....	....	....	380	361	341	323	294
o/w: Cl. on Oth.Res.Sect.in Cty	12d	4	4	4	6	18	19	20	380	361	341	323	294
Currency Issued	14a	271	267	270	275	278	283	287	49,282	49,187	34,575	74,153	84,978
Liabilities to Banking Insts	14c.u	....	....	....	....	....	....	....	51,345	28,083	29,467	34,591	27,774
o/w: Liabs to Bank.Inst.in Cty	14c	22	14	10	30	33	36	129	24,371	28,083	29,467	34,591	27,774
Demand Dep. of Other Res.Sect	14d.u	....	....	....	....	....	....	....	1,573	801	846	811	752
o/w:D.Dep.of Oth.Res.Sect.in Cty	14d	3	3	3	4	4	4	4	1,573	801	846	811	752
Other Dep. of Other Res.Sect	15..u	....	....	....	....	....	....	....	–	–	–	–	–
o/w:O.Dep.of Oth.Res.Sect.in Cty	15	....	....	....	....	....	....	....	–	–	–	–	–
Bonds & Money Mkt. Instruments	16n.u	....	....	....	....	....	....	....	–	–	–	–	–
o/w: Held by Resid.of Cty	16n	....	....	....	....	....	....	....	....	....	....	....	....
Foreign Liab. (to Non-EA Ctys)	16c	163	121	62	57	†4	4	6	7,643	1,082	3,669	1,753	3,801
Central Government Deposits	16d.u	....	....	....	....	....	....	....	1,057	1,982	2,455	811	280
o/w: Cent.Govt.Dep. in Cty	16d	148	198	123	58	20	43	89	1,057	1,982	2,455	811	280
Capital Accounts	17a	182	225	201	177	191	201	168	35,675	39,750	44,024	39,842	36,766
Other Items (Net)	17r	–51	–26	–23	–44	–3	–39	–25	–8,807	–5,668	169	–7,972	–8,535
Memo: Currency Put into Circ	14m	....	....	....	....	....	....	....	....	....	....	41,636	43,250

France 132

		1992	1993	1994	1995	1996	1997	1998	1999	2000	2001	2002	2003
Banking Institutions		*Billions of Francs through 1998; Millions of Euros Beginning 1999: End of Period*											
Claims on Monetary Authorities	20	34	27	26	47	51	48	....	24,371	28,083	29,467	34,591	27,774
Claims on Bk.Inst.in Oth.EA Ctys	20b.u	....	....	....	....	....	....	....	192,393	186,176	211,491	231,399	262,766
Fgn. Assets (Cl.on Non-EA Ctys)	21	2,822	3,428	3,207	3,455	3,582	4,412	....	425,976	467,995	507,215	513,473	502,874
Claims on General Government	22a.u	....	....	....	....	....	....	....	386,731	338,623	336,930	375,275	402,395
o/w: Claims on Gen.Govt.in Cty	22a	699	798	1,074	1,275	1,566	1,729	....	312,415	267,985	269,527	279,124	299,509
Claims on Other Resident Sectors	22d.u	....	....	....	....	....	....	....	1,156,145	1,276,367	1,380,548	1,402,545	1,499,829
o/w: Cl. on Oth.Res.Sect.in Cty	22d	6,930	6,712	6,589	6,745	6,653	6,785	....	1,111,777	1,225,372	1,314,276	1,325,885	1,403,834
Demand Deposits	24..u	....	....	....	....	....	....	....	246,895	269,174	305,546	295,536	350,139
o/w:D.Dep.of Oth.Res.Sect.in Cty	24	1,349	1,364	1,415	1,557	1,554	1,670	....	242,376	264,944	300,271	290,917	344,061
Other Deposits	25..u	....	....	....	....	....	....	....	649,980	654,675	684,583	710,793	752,835
o/w:D.Dep.of Oth.Res.Sect.in Cty	25	2,619	2,776	3,012	3,374	3,582	3,855	....	632,781	636,781	666,151	691,318	731,410
Money Market Fund Shares	26m.u	....	....	....	....	....	....	....	179,867	210,662	255,856	297,874	324,445
Bonds & Money Mkt. Instruments	26n.u	....	....	....	....	....	....	....	478,806	502,177	554,152	561,360	593,490
o/w: Held by Resid.of Cty	26n	2,586	2,673	2,538	2,548	2,266	2,151	....	....	....	....	....	....
Foreign Liab. (to Non-EA Ctys)	26c	2,898	3,084	3,168	3,246	3,518	4,159	....	330,140	413,128	452,984	443,240	433,200
Central Government Deposits	26d.u	....	....	....	....	....	....	....	10,109	5,865	4,937	12,110	39,745
o/w: Cent.Govt.Dep. in Cty	26d	96	50	55	124	156	152	....	9,844	5,637	4,403	11,666	38,999
Credit from Monetary Authorities	26g	294	372	200	147	143	125	167	48,448	29,013	16,413	16,107	11,084
Liab. to Bk.Inst.in Oth. EA Ctys	26h.u	....	....	....	....	....	....	....	150,237	139,026	149,425	170,842	173,576
Capital Accounts	27a	1,105	1,240	1,293	1,284	1,288	1,320	....	245,031	249,326	270,482	284,117	294,879
Other Items (Net)	27r	−462	−595	−785	−759	−654	−459	....	−153,897	−175,799	−228,727	−234,696	−277,755
Banking Survey (Nat'l Residency)		*Billions of Francs through 1998; Millions of Euros Beginning 1999: End of Period*											
Foreign Assets (Net)	31n	106	573	349	497	†369	584	....	293,233	292,794	326,850	412,206	467,022
Domestic Credit	32	7,484	7,342	7,560	7,903	8,118	8,390	....	1,417,722	1,490,143	1,580,977	1,596,169	1,669,387
Claims on General Govt. (Net)	32an	550	626	968	1,152	1,447	1,586	....	305,565	264,410	266,360	269,961	265,259
Claims on Other Resident Sectors	32d	6,934	6,716	6,593	6,751	6,671	6,804	....	1,112,157	1,225,733	1,314,617	1,326,208	1,404,128
Currency Issued	34a.n	271	267	270	275	278	283	287	49,282	49,187	34,575	74,153	84,978
Demand Deposits	34b.n	1,352	1,368	1,418	1,561	1,557	1,674	....	243,949	265,745	301,117	291,728	344,813
Other Deposits	35..n	2,619	2,776	3,012	3,374	3,582	3,855	....	632,781	636,781	666,151	691,318	731,410
Money Market Fund Shares	36m	....	....	....	....	....	....	....	179,867	210,662	255,856	297,874	324,445
Bonds & Money Mkt. Instruments	36n	2,586	2,673	2,538	2,548	2,266	2,151	....	478,806	502,177	554,152	561,360	593,490
o/w: Over Two Years	36na	....	....	....	....	....	....	....	322,255	338,332	357,016	354,893	375,237
Capital Accounts	37a	1,287	1,465	1,494	1,462	1,479	1,521	....	280,706	289,076	314,506	323,959	331,645
Other Items (Net)	37r	−525	−633	−824	−819	−675	−509	....	−154,437	−170,688	−218,530	−231,681	−274,371
Banking Survey (EA-Wide Residency)							*Millions of Euros: End of Period*						
Foreign Assets (Net)	31n.u	....	....	....	....	....	....	....	156,343	122,085	116,968	126,868	121,852
Domestic Credit	32..u	....	....	....	....	....	....	....	1,536,141	1,611,548	1,714,118	1,768,536	1,867,522
Claims on General Govt. (Net)	32anu	....	....	....	....	....	....	....	379,616	334,820	333,229	365,668	367,399
Claims on Other Resident Sect.	32d.u	....	....	....	....	....	....	....	1,156,525	1,276,728	1,380,889	1,402,868	1,500,123
Currency Issued	34a.u	....	....	....	....	....	....	....	49,282	49,187	34,575	74,153	84,978
Demand Deposits	34b.u	....	....	....	....	....	....	....	248,468	269,975	306,392	296,347	350,891
Other Deposits	35..u	....	....	....	....	....	....	....	649,980	654,675	684,583	710,793	752,835
o/w: Other Dep. Over Two Yrs	35abu	....	....	....	....	....	....	....	299,588	281,832	279,539	285,760	303,383
Money Market Fund Shares	36m.u	....	....	....	....	....	....	....	179,867	210,662	255,856	297,874	324,445
Bonds & Money Mkt. Instruments	36n.u	....	....	....	....	....	....	....	478,806	502,177	554,152	561,360	593,490
o/w: Over Two Years	36nau	....	....	....	....	....	....	....	322,255	338,332	357,016	354,893	375,237
Capital Accounts	37a	....	....	....	....	....	....	....	280,706	289,076	314,506	323,959	331,645
Other Items (Net)	37r.u	....	....	....	....	....	....	....	−194,626	−242,116	−318,978	−368,746	−448,909
Money (National Definitions)						*Billions of Francs: End of Period*							
M1	39ma	1,603	1,626	1,671	1,800	1,815	1,933	1,993	....	....	....	....	....
M1, Seasonally Adjusted	39mac	1,521	1,513	1,559	1,581	1,666	1,735	1,884	....	....	....	....	....
M2	39mb	2,807	2,854	3,003	3,246	3,363	3,624	3,781	....	....	....	....	....
M2, Seasonally Adjusted	39mbc	2,719	2,696	2,806	2,935	3,143	3,356	3,641	....	....	....	....	....
M3	39mc	5,287	5,134	5,225	5,463	5,281	5,385	5,532	....	....	....	....	....
M3, Seasonally Adjusted	39mcc	5,138	5,217	5,083	5,283	5,318	5,263	5,492	....	....	....	....	....
M4	39md	5,343	5,184	5,296	5,541	5,364	5,511	5,622	....	....	....	....	....
M4, Seasonally Adjusted	39mdc	5,190	5,273	5,142	5,360	5,409	5,369	5,590	....	....	....	....	....
Interest Rates							*Percent Per Annum*						
Repurchase of Agreements	60a	9.56	7.60	5.44	4.96	3.60	3.15	3.28	....	....	....	....	....
Money Market Rate	60b	10.35	8.75	5.69	6.35	3.73	3.24	3.39	....	....	....	....	....
Treasury Bill Rate	60c	10.49	8.41	5.79	6.58	3.84	3.35	3.45	2.72	4.23	4.26	....	....
Deposit Rate	60l	4.50	4.50	4.50	4.50	3.67	3.50	3.21	2.69	2.63	3.00	3.00	2.69
Lending Rate	60p	10.00	8.90	7.89	8.12	6.77	6.34	6.55	6.36	6.70	6.98	6.60	6.60
Government Bond Yield	61	8.60	6.91	7.35	7.59	6.39	5.63	4.72	4.69	5.45	5.05	4.93	4.18

2004, International Monetary Fund : *International Financial Statistics Yearbook*

France 132

		1992	1993	1994	1995	1996	1997	1998	1999	2000	2001	2002	2003
Prices, Production, Labor						*Index Numbers (2000=100): Period Averages*							
Share Prices	62	29.7	32.7	32.7	29.6	33.7	44.4	59.8	74.0	100.0	80.1	60.4	....
Producer Prices	63	....	....	....	....	....	....	....	†95.8	100.0	101.2	100.7	101.1
Intermediate Indust. Goods	63a	97.2	†94.4	95.5	†101.3	98.6	98.0	97.1	95.8	100.0	101.2	100.7	101.1
Imported Raw Materials	63b	†71.0	68.0	82.1	89.0	79.5	89.6	76.2	77.4	100.0	92.9	86.8	81.8
Consumer Prices	64	89.1	91.0	92.5	94.1	96.0	97.2	†97.8	98.3	100.0	101.7	103.6	105.8
Harmonized CPI	64h	....	....	....	93.8	95.8	97.0	97.7	98.2	100.0	101.8	103.7	106.0
Labor Costs	65	81.3	83.8	86.3	87.0	88.5	91.0	93.6	95.7	100.0	104.4	108.4	112.8
Industrial Production	66	85.1	81.9	85.3	†87.3	87.2	90.7	94.0	96.3	100.0	101.1	99.8	99.6
Industrial Employment, Seas. Adj.	67..c	110.9	105.5	103.3	102.2	99.4	98.7	99.0	98.7	100.0	101.3	99.3	....
						Number in Thousands: Period Averages							
Labor Force	67d	....	25,756	....	26,803	26,404	26,404	....	....	26,226	26,385	26,653	....
Employment	67e	†21,609	†20,705	21,875	20,233	22,311	20,413	22,479	20,864	23,262	23,759	23,942	....
Unemployment	67c	2,911	3,172	3,329	†2,893	3,063	3,102	2,977	2,772	2,338	2,152	2,259	2,396
Unemployment Rate (%)	67r	†10.1	11.1	12.4	11.6	12.1	12.3	11.8	11.7	9.5	8.8	....	....
International Transactions					*Billions of Francs through 1998; Billions of Euros Beginning 1999*								
Exports	70	1,248.83	1,190.46	1,294.81	1,420.27	1,471.64	1,692.65	1,801.93	†284.13	325.71	331.79	330.55	323.02
Imports, c.i.f.	71	1,268.37	1,149.13	1,298.43	1,403.80	1,441.62	1,585.34	1,708.92	†277.03	337.67	336.78	330.17	327.57
Imports, f.o.b.	71.v	1,217.81	1,101.03	1,244.07	1,357.60	1,394.18	1,521.75	1,638.34	†269.83	329.91	330.96	324.69	322.01
						2000=100							
Volume of Exports	72	†50.2	51.1	55.1	59.5	61.7	68.0	74.9	88.8	100.0	106.6	111.8	109.9
Volume of Imports	73	†49.7	51.3	55.6	59.0	60.5	64.9	74.1	64.8	100.0	108.8	112.7	112.0
Unit Value of Exports	74	109.0	106.7	109.0	111.2	111.0	112.5	112.9	98.3	100.0	99.7	96.0	95.9
Unit Value of Imports	75	104.3	100.1	102.1	104.5	104.8	106.4	106.7	93.7	100.0	97.9	92.7	92.6
Balance of Payments					*Billions of US Dollars: Minus Sign Indicates Debit*								
Current Account, n.i.e.	78ald	3.89	8.99	7.42	10.84	20.56	37.80	37.70	31.87	18.58	28.76	13.79	4.38
Goods: Exports f.o.b.	78aad	227.44	199.04	230.81	278.63	281.85	286.07	303.02	300.05	298.20	294.62	307.66	361.87
Goods: Imports f.o.b.	78abd	−225.07	−191.53	−223.56	−267.63	−266.91	−259.17	−278.08	−282.06	−301.82	−291.78	−300.74	−360.83
Trade Balance	78acd	2.37	7.52	7.25	11.00	14.94	26.90	24.94	17.99	−3.62	2.84	6.92	1.04
Services: Credit	78add	91.77	86.38	75.52	84.09	83.53	80.79	84.96	82.39	80.92	82.30	86.56	99.73
Services: Debit	78aed	−72.65	−69.54	−57.67	−66.12	−67.28	−64.16	−67.73	−64.45	−61.04	−56.86	−69.29	−84.80
Balance on Goods & Services	78afd	21.49	24.36	25.10	28.97	31.19	43.52	42.17	35.93	16.25	28.27	24.19	15.98
Income: Credit	78agd	87.60	98.99	41.56	45.18	47.55	57.13	66.66	64.96	72.39	74.11	64.84	88.57
Income: Debit	78ahd	−96.21	−108.16	−48.32	−54.15	−50.25	−50.04	−58.00	−56.19	−56.81	−59.04	−60.86	−80.98
Balance on Gds, Serv. & Inc.	78aid	12.87	15.19	18.34	20.01	28.48	50.62	50.83	44.69	31.84	43.34	28.17	23.57
Current Transfers, n.i.e.: Credit	78ajd	20.73	16.74	18.22	22.01	22.76	19.61	19.65	18.88	17.87	17.28	19.88	23.57
Current Transfers: Debit	78akd	−29.71	−22.94	−29.15	−31.17	−30.68	−32.43	−32.79	−31.70	−31.13	−31.86	−34.26	−42.75
Capital Account, n.i.e.	78bcd	.66	.03	−4.18	.51	1.23	1.48	1.47	1.57	1.39	−.31	−.19	−8.24
Capital Account, n.i.e.: Credit	78bad	.93	.30	.99	1.16	1.88	2.41	2.10	1.89	1.92	1.10	.91	1.93
Capital Account: Debit	78bbd	−.27	−.28	−5.16	−.66	−.65	−.93	−.63	−.31	−.53	−1.41	−1.10	−10.17
Financial Account, n.i.e.	78bjd	−8.04	−16.67	10.18	−7.52	−22.64	−37.60	−29.29	−36.13	−32.55	−33.25	−23.84	−.69
Direct Investment Abroad	78bdd	−31.27	−20.60	−24.44	−15.82	−30.36	−35.49	−45.70	−119.49	−174.32	−86.98	−49.68	−57.42
Dir. Invest. in Rep. Econ., n.i.e.	78bed	21.84	20.75	15.80	23.74	21.97	23.05	29.52	46.63	42.37	50.36	49.44	47.75
Portfolio Investment Assets	78bfd	−19.51	−31.16	−21.96	−7.42	−46.63	−60.79	−105.22	−126.81	−97.44	−85.48	−84.65	−147.53
Equity Securities	78bkd	−1.55	−2.52	−1.02	1.78	−1.08	−9.67	−24.46	−20.73	−32.54	−19.15	−16.35	−29.99
Debt Securities	78bld	−17.96	−28.64	−20.94	−9.20	−45.55	−51.12	−80.76	−106.08	−64.90	−66.34	−68.30	−117.55
Portfolio Investment Liab., n.i.e.	78bgd	52.50	34.52	−27.90	13.08	−15.35	35.32	59.75	117.52	132.33	106.90	67.89	136.16
Equity Securities	78bmd	5.41	13.58	5.26	6.82	12.20	11.97	17.21	49.35	49.97	13.65	−4.37	16.39
Debt Securities	78bnd	47.09	20.94	−33.16	6.26	−27.56	23.36	42.54	68.17	82.36	93.25	72.26	119.77
Financial Derivatives Assets	78bwd	1.04	−.34	−	−	−6.47	−	−	−	−	−	−	−
Financial Derivatives Liabilities	78bxd	....			1.00	7.81	4.10	−.44	−2.23	4.78	2.29	5.31	−7.06
Other Investment Assets	78bhd	−61.09	−13.38	23.05	−40.16	26.31	−53.64	26.11	−26.62	.63	−59.15	−36.41	−20.01
Monetary Authorities	78bod	−	−	−.24	.50	.13	−.43	−.05	−10.31	−6.00	−12.50	−4.63	−
General Government	78bpd	−4.96	−3.91	3.08	−.64	1.11	1.18	.86	.74	−.08	.14	1.04	−2.43
Banks	78bqd	−65.09	−46.69	22.72	−43.19	28.59	−46.82	41.70	−11.66	7.08	−46.96	−35.17	−6.82
Other Sectors	78brd	8.96	37.22	−2.50	3.18	−3.52	−7.57	−16.40	−5.39	−.37	.18	2.34	−10.76
Other Investment Liab., n.i.e.	78bid	28.44	−6.46	45.63	18.06	20.08	49.85	6.70	74.88	59.09	38.82	24.27	47.42
Monetary Authorities	78bsd	22.02	−1.07	.55	.25	−.78	.13	.31	28.86	−23.39	1.15	−1.28	2.11
General Government	78btd	.11	.23	3.16	1.10	−.01	4.67	.15	2.14	2.69	1.32	.25	−.43
Banks	78bud	10.39	−5.69	32.11	13.13	15.83	39.05	2.26	43.89	55.65	42.81	29.18	41.90
Other Sectors	78bvd	−4.08	.07	9.81	3.59	5.04	6.00	3.98	−.01	24.14	−6.46	−3.89	3.83
Net Errors and Omissions	78cad	1.90	2.65	−10.97	−3.12	1.09	4.26	9.94	1.30	10.14	−.77	6.28	5.82
Overall Balance	78cbd	−1.58	−5.01	2.45	.71	.24	5.94	19.82	−1.39	−2.43	−5.57	−3.97	1.27
Reserves and Related Items	79dad	1.58	5.01	−2.45	−.71	−.24	−5.94	−19.82	1.39	2.43	5.57	3.97	−1.27
Reserve Assets	79dbd	1.58	5.01	−2.45	−.71	−.24	−5.94	−19.82	1.39	2.43	5.57	3.97	−1.27
Use of Fund Credit and Loans	79dcd	−	−	−	−	−	−	−	−	−	−	−	−
Exceptional Financing	79ded	....	....	....	....	....	−	−	−	−	−	−	−

France 132

		1992	1993	1994	1995	1996	1997	1998	1999	2000	2001	2002	2003
International Investment Position							*Billions of US Dollars*						
Assets	79aad	844.10	927.97	1,202.25	1,383.08	1,482.34	1,698.37	2,052.67	2,319.06	2,481.26	2,455.31	2,678.91	3,513.03
Direct Investment Abroad	79abd	158.87	159.13	300.86	374.96	482.74	598.65	747.30	912.98	1,054.72	931.09	855.21	1,173.96
Portfolio Investment	79acd	97.72	130.47	184.92	203.62	248.12	340.21	489.01	590.20	663.73	710.33	880.91	1,249.23
Equity Securities	79add	43.23	51.97	53.74	58.36	73.52	99.13	143.05	190.67	210.01	201.73	196.84	300.22
Debt Securities	79aed	54.49	78.51	131.17	145.25	174.60	241.09	345.96	399.53	453.71	508.60	684.07	949.02
Financial Derivatives	79ald	—	—	24.78	31.33	34.71	42.62	76.07	110.00	95.00	109.81	108.12	125.29
Other Investment	79afd	530.38	583.10	633.73	714.57	659.48	661.24	670.19	637.82	604.27	645.38	773.00	893.83
Monetary Authorities	79agd	—	—	1.23	.92	.75	1.88	2.09	11.55	16.10	27.94	37.33	43.70
General Government	79ahd	—	—	31.28	34.80	33.33	29.79	31.63	28.73	27.17	26.26	29.26	36.75
Banks	79aid	—	—	469.32	530.27	484.61	498.42	487.70	457.70	429.70	453.16	541.55	620.89
Other Sectors	79ajd	530.38	583.10	131.89	148.59	140.79	131.15	148.77	139.84	131.29	138.01	164.86	192.48
Reserve Assets	79akd	57.13	55.27	57.96	58.61	57.30	55.65	70.09	68.05	63.55	58.70	61.67	70.72
Liabilities	79lad	890.25	989.90	1,227.25	1,418.35	1,438.55	1,543.08	1,919.90	2,254.32	2,312.01	2,302.84	2,547.50	3,380.80
Dir. Invest. in Rep. Economy	79lbd	130.05	135.38	301.83	341.10	359.21	399.73	548.62	648.87	598.50	529.84	534.21	748.58
Portfolio Investment	79lcd	292.19	366.99	366.66	456.61	460.09	518.04	671.45	865.56	949.20	976.57	1,074.39	1,512.95
Equity Securities	79ldd	72.53	103.82	102.21	120.76	155.32	208.58	300.44	482.21	502.10	415.97	339.15	502.17
Debt Securities	79led	219.66	263.17	264.45	335.86	304.77	309.46	371.01	383.36	447.11	560.59	735.24	1,010.78
Financial Derivatives	79lld	—	—	20.24	32.94	38.32	45.24	81.09	105.08	98.26	104.79	112.32	134.26
Other Investment	79lfd	468.01	487.53	538.52	587.69	580.93	580.07	618.74	634.81	666.05	691.64	826.59	985.01
Monetary Authorities	79lgd	—	—	1.72	2.00	2.26	2.30	2.68	28.03	2.33	3.35	2.20	4.42
General Government	79lhd	—	—	9.45	11.24	10.64	16.33	15.05	14.47	15.82	17.01	20.34	23.74
Banks	79lid	—	—	435.09	466.41	468.95	472.90	501.82	500.79	530.29	548.26	662.04	787.10
Other Sectors	79ljd	468.01	487.53	92.26	108.04	99.08	88.53	99.18	91.52	117.62	123.03	141.99	169.75
Government Finance													
Central Government					*Billions of Francs through 1998; Millions of Euros Beginning 1999: Year Ending December 31*								
Deficit (-) or Surplus	80	−274.0	−402.0	−412.0	−502.6	−413.3	−284.4	....	....	....	....	....	....
Revenue	81	2,845.5	2,871.3	2,983.5	3,116.5	3,271.2	3,438.7	....	....	....	....	....	....
Grants Received	81z	47.2	50.2	48.8	53.0	46.6	51.8	....	....	....	....	....	....
Exp. & Lending Minus Repay	82z	3,159.0	3,319.0	3,429.8	3,662.0	3,740.9	3,797.3	....	....	....	....	....	....
Expenditure	82	3,154.7	3,336.9	3,458.2	3,564.7	3,687.2	3,789.2	....	....	....	....	....	....
Lending Minus Repayments	83	4.3	−17.9	−28.4	97.3	53.7	8.1	....	....	....	....	....	....
Overall Adj. to Cash Basis	80x	−7.7	−4.5	−14.5	−10.1	9.8	22.4	....	....	....	....	....	....
Financing													
Net Borrowing	84	328.8	460.3	326.7	451.5	364.9	....	....	....	....	....	....	....
Domestic	84a	293.9	420.5	375.9	396.1	350.0	....	....	....	....	....	....	....
Foreign	85a	34.9	39.8	−49.2	55.4	14.9	....	....	....	....	....	....	....
Use of Cash Balances	87	−54.8	−58.3	85.3	51.1	48.4	....	....	....	....	....	....	....
Debt: Francs	88b	2,056.6	2,417.1	2,859.2	3,214.2	3,506.8	3,738.2	3,977.9	....	....	....	....	....
Foreign Currency	89b	55.4	57.9	62.6	58.6	57.1	56.4	49.8	....	....	....	....	....
General Government					*As Percent of Gross Domestic Product*								
Deficit (-) or Surplus	80g	−3.9	−5.8	−5.8	−4.9	−4.2	−3.0	−2.7	−1.6	−1.3	−1.4	....	....
Debt	88g	39.8	45.3	48.5	52.8	57.1	59.3	59.5	58.5	57.4	57.2	....	....
National Accounts					*Billions of Francs through 1998; Billions of Euros Beginning 1999*								
Househ.Cons.Expend.,incl.NPISHs	96f.c	3,912.1	3,994.1	4,118.1	†4,255.8	4,392.9	4,459.9	4,646.1	†734.3	765.3	797.3	825.9	854.7
Government Consumption Expend	91f.c	1,643.8	1,769.1	1,809.1	†1,851.8	1,922.0	1,985.6	2,007.2	†315.7	330.2	342.8	364.3	378.5
Gross Fixed Capital Formation	93e.c	1,491.0	1,397.8	1,428.7	†1,458.8	1,470.7	1,472.6	1,578.9	†259.9	287.2	297.2	296.4	298.9
Changes in Inventories	93i.c	−5.2	−89.9	−6.6	†34.8	−13.8	−6.6	55.8	†5.5	11.8	4.6	2.6	−2.4
Exports of Goods and Services	90c.c	1,530.3	1,494.9	1,610.4	†1,746.8	1,831.4	2,092.5	2,236.2	†350.1	406.1	413.2	413.4	402.9
Imports of Goods and Services (-)	98.c.c	1,487.1	1,385.4	1,509.4	†1,633.3	1,698.9	1,851.1	2,007.9	†319.8	387.5	389.2	384.3	384.7
Gross Domestic Product (GDP)	99b.c	7,119.8	7,223.4	7,493.0	†7,760.0	7,952.2	8,203.4	8,568.8	†1,354.1	1,421.7	1,475.9	1,528.3	1,558.5
Net Primary Income from Abroad	98.nc	−25.8	−6.4	−28.7	−41.0	−4.6	19.0	39.9	†15.6	10.1	11.2	−.5	−2.3
Gross National Income (GNI)	99a.c	7,100.2	7,220.1	7,471.0	7,711.5	7,946.8	8,226.1	8,605.7	†1,369.7	1,431.8	1,487.1	1,527.8	1,556.2
Net Current Transf.from Abroad	98t.c	−18.6	−26.0	−28.9	−18.2	−31.9	−34.3	−40.1	†−9.8	−11.3	−12.3	−14.4	−9.2
Gross Nat'l Disposable Inc.(GNDI)	99i.c	7,059.5	7,170.8	7,418.0	7,666.5	7,892.3	8,170.9	8,542.0	†1,359.9	1,420.5	1,474.9	1,513.4	1,547.6
Gross Saving	99s.c	1,461.5	1,370.8	1,440.5	1,512.2	1,528.7	1,673.8	1,837.3	†301.8	317.4	324.6	317.2	311.3
Consumption of Fixed Capital	99cfc	983.1	1,009.2	1,037.9	1,064.9	1,110.1	1,141.3	1,172.2	†185.0	196.5	205.5	214.5	228.8
GDP Vol. 1995 Ref., Chained	99b.r	7,548.2	7,480.8	7,615.4	7,758.9	7,841.5	7,990.3	8,268.1	†1,299.5	1,348.8	1,377.1	1,393.4	1,399.9
GDP Volume (2000=100)	99bvr	85.3	84.6	86.1	87.7	88.6	90.3	93.5	†96.3	100.0	102.1	103.3	103.8
GDP Deflator (2000=100)	99bir	89.5	91.6	93.3	†94.9	96.2	97.4	98.3	†98.9	100.0	101.7	104.1	105.6
					Millions: Midyear Estimates								
Population	99z	57.32	57.60	57.88	58.14	58.38	58.60	58.82	59.05	59.30	59.56	59.85	60.14

2004, International Monetary Fund : *International Financial Statistics Yearbook*

Gabon 646

		1992	1993	1994	1995	1996	1997	1998	1999	2000	2001	2002	2003
Exchange Rates		\multicolumn{12}{c}{*Francs per SDR: End of Period*}
Official Rate	aa	378.57	404.89	†780.44	728.38	753.06	807.94	791.61	†896.19	918.49	935.39	850.37	771.76
		\multicolumn{12}{c}{*Francs per US Dollar: End of Period (ae) Period Average (rf)*}
Official Rate	ae	275.32	294.77	†534.60	490.00	523.70	598.81	562.21	†652.95	704.95	744.31	625.50	519.36
Official Rate	rf	264.69	283.16	†555.20	499.15	511.55	583.67	589.95	†615.70	711.98	733.04	696.99	581.20
		\multicolumn{12}{c}{*Index Numbers (2000=100): Period Averages*}
Official Rate	ahx	268.8	250.9	128.1	142.3	138.8	121.8	120.5	115.5	100.0	96.9	102.2	122.4
Nominal Effective Exchange Rate	nec	189.3	195.3	104.7	109.1	109.6	105.9	108.5	105.8	100.0	101.4	103.7	109.0
Real Effective Exchange Rate	rec	154.3	149.7	101.0	111.5	110.2	108.6	112.3	107.4	100.0	101.4	101.9	107.8
Fund Position		\multicolumn{12}{c}{*Millions of SDRs: End of Period*}
Quota	2f.s	110.30	110.30	110.30	110.30	110.30	110.30	110.30	154.30	154.30	154.30	154.30	154.30
SDRs	1b.s	.08	.03	.17	–	.02	–	.01	–	.05	.04	–	–
Reserve Position in the Fund	1c.s	.05	.05	.05	.05	.07	.07	.07	.11	.15	.18	.18	.18
Total Fund Cred.&Loans Outstg	2tl	58.55	32.89	61.42	64.95	83.26	97.20	80.52	62.60	68.38	59.64	49.53	39.42
International Liquidity		\multicolumn{12}{c}{*Millions of US Dollars Unless Otherwise Indicated: End of Period*}
Total Reserves minus Gold	1l.d	71.21	.75	175.19	148.09	248.72	282.60	15.41	17.95	190.09	9.85	139.65	196.57
SDRs	1b.d	.10	.03	.25	–	.03	–	.01	.01	.07	.06	–	–
Reserve Position in the Fund	1c.d	.07	.07	.08	.08	.09	.09	.09	.15	.19	.23	.24	.27
Foreign Exchange	1d.d	71.04	.64	174.86	148.01	248.59	282.51	15.30	17.79	189.83	9.57	139.40	196.30
Gold (Million Fine Troy Ounces)	1ad	.013	.013	.013	.013	.013	.013	.013	.013	.013	.013	.013	.013
Gold (National Valuation)	1and	4.28	5.11	†4.85	4.95	4.73	3.74	3.69	†3.73	3.50	3.57	4.40	5.36
Monetary Authorities: Other Liab.	4..d	45.95	35.48	33.67	34.56	33.52	53.73	34.62	46.34	44.91	41.61	48.64	64.32
Deposit Money Banks: Assets	7a.d	61.55	53.13	82.23	75.69	159.03	64.55	71.56	74.88	239.68	132.33	115.94	166.73
Liabilities	7b.d	117.45	89.15	41.28	79.93	94.16	50.58	56.73	77.78	91.62	81.39	131.84	138.52
Monetary Authorities		\multicolumn{12}{c}{*Billions of Francs: End of Period*}
Foreign Assets	11	20.78	1.70	96.30	74.99	132.74	171.45	10.74	14.15	136.47	9.99	90.10	104.88
Claims on Central Government	12a	58.00	62.47	95.83	101.92	123.60	87.49	211.13	200.78	157.33	248.21	231.47	196.78
Claims on Deposit Money Banks	12e	23.54	19.82	.16	3.74	.75	–	8.11	11.63	.22	3.00	8.00	–
Claims on Other Banking Insts.	12f	3.11	–	–	–	–	–	–	–	–	–	–	–
Reserve Money	14	63.58	58.38	133.91	128.24	165.20	167.93	153.60	141.52	192.68	184.59	186.61	213.40
of which: Currency Outside DMBs	14a	56.79	50.47	76.93	100.69	110.88	121.03	124.72	105.26	116.18	128.19	132.02	124.22
Foreign Liabilities	16c	34.82	23.78	65.94	64.24	80.26	110.71	83.21	86.36	94.46	86.76	72.54	63.83
Central Government Deposits	16d	7.97	3.11	18.51	10.67	32.35	16.13	12.14	26.10	43.18	24.57	100.81	50.30
Capital Accounts	17a	6.97	7.59	12.49	11.53	11.89	12.32	11.87	13.76	14.46	15.24	14.52	13.35
Other Items (Net)	17r	−7.90	−8.87	−38.56	−34.03	−32.61	−48.15	−30.85	−41.17	−50.75	−49.97	−44.90	−39.23
Deposit Money Banks		\multicolumn{12}{c}{*Billions of Francs: End of Period*}
Reserves	20	5.94	7.86	56.87	27.06	48.32	44.10	27.47	34.75	75.73	56.10	54.19	88.82
Foreign Assets	21	16.95	15.66	43.96	37.09	83.28	38.65	40.23	48.89	168.96	98.49	72.52	86.59
Claims on Central Government	22a	†105.35	99.25	172.94	161.16	152.37	143.46	135.76	137.99	92.91	88.71	104.98	104.94
Claims on Nonfin.Pub.Enterprises	22c	8.78	9.88	10.17	9.49	13.60	26.91	23.20	22.32	17.11	21.39	13.53	8.92
Claims on Private Sector	22d	162.01	157.91	157.20	196.08	191.93	269.89	285.12	286.06	313.79	375.04	415.74	380.53
Claims on Other Banking Insts.	22f	–	–	.88	.88	.91	1.39	.60	.74	.74	.60	.63	.59
Claims on Nonbank Financial Insts.	22g	4.65	4.22	7.07	10.22	7.99	7.66	7.55	10.53	25.30	22.05	25.70	22.74
Demand Deposits	24	84.71	86.92	117.96	117.90	159.11	174.41	156.99	161.85	203.51	203.74	214.27	220.52
Time and Savings Deposits	25	99.11	99.87	130.98	139.87	144.78	169.98	176.47	177.21	206.85	234.47	252.33	246.66
Bonds	26ab	.90	1.20	.30	.23	.15	.08	3.09	5.55	2.65	2.25	1.85	.41
Foreign Liabilities	26c	19.86	19.37	13.73	36.34	46.79	28.24	22.66	38.99	56.61	58.85	74.03	57.40
Long-Term Foreign Liabilities	26cl	12.48	6.91	8.34	2.83	2.52	2.05	9.24	11.80	7.98	1.72	8.44	14.54
Central Government Deposits	26d	†22.88	16.72	32.21	15.35	20.93	20.62	21.82	29.67	112.30	71.32	41.42	47.38
Credit from Monetary Authorities	26g	23.54	19.82	.16	3.74	.75	–	8.11	11.63	.22	3.00	8.00	–
Capital Accounts	27a	54.68	54.55	133.44	128.50	123.58	115.89	122.47	120.48	85.73	107.75	120.20	136.94
Other Items (Net)	27r	†−14.49	−10.58	11.97	−2.78	−.21	20.78	−.92	−15.89	18.68	−20.73	−33.25	−30.72
Monetary Survey		\multicolumn{12}{c}{*Billions of Francs: End of Period*}
Foreign Assets (Net)	31n	−29.43	−32.70	52.25	8.68	86.45	69.10	−64.14	−74.10	146.38	−38.86	7.62	55.70
Domestic Credit	32	†311.04	313.90	393.36	453.74	437.12	500.04	629.38	602.65	451.70	660.10	649.82	616.82
Claims on Central Govt. (Net)	32an	†132.50	141.89	218.05	237.06	222.68	194.19	312.92	283.00	94.76	241.03	194.22	204.04
Claims on Nonfin.Pub.Enterprises	32c	8.78	9.88	10.17	9.49	13.60	26.91	23.20	22.32	17.11	21.39	13.53	8.92
Claims on Private Sector	32d	162.01	157.91	157.20	196.08	191.93	269.89	285.12	286.06	313.79	375.04	415.74	380.53
Claims on Other Banking Insts.	32f	3.11	–	.88	.88	.91	1.39	.60	.74	.74	.60	.63	.59
Claims on Nonbank Financial Inst.	32g	4.65	4.22	7.07	10.22	7.99	7.66	7.55	10.53	25.30	22.05	25.70	22.74
Money	34	142.35	137.44	195.01	219.09	276.00	298.25	283.12	268.61	320.46	332.22	346.69	345.10
Quasi-Money	35	99.11	99.87	130.98	139.87	144.78	169.98	176.47	177.21	206.85	234.47	252.33	246.66
Bonds	36ab	.90	1.20	.30	.23	.15	.08	3.09	5.55	2.65	2.25	1.85	.41
Other Items (Net)	37r	†39.26	42.69	119.33	103.23	102.64	100.84	102.57	77.17	68.12	52.30	56.56	80.34
Money plus Quasi-Money	35l	241.46	237.31	325.98	358.96	420.78	468.22	459.59	445.82	527.31	566.69	599.03	591.76
Interest Rates		\multicolumn{12}{c}{*Percent Per Annum*}
Discount Rate (End of Period)	60	12.00	11.50	†7.75	8.60	7.75	7.50	7.00	7.60	7.00	6.50	6.30	6.00
Deposit Rate	60l	7.50	7.75	8.08	5.50	5.46	5.00	5.00	5.00	5.00	5.00	5.00	5.00
Lending Rate	60p	17.77	17.46	17.50	16.00	22.00	22.00	22.00	22.00	22.00	20.67	18.00	18.00

2004, International Monetary Fund : *International Financial Statistics Yearbook*

Gabon 646

		1992	1993	1994	1995	1996	1997	1998	1999	2000	2001	2002	2003
Prices and Production		*Index Numbers (2000=100): Period Averages*											
Consumer Prices	64	63.7	64.0	87.1	95.5	96.2	100.0	101.5p	99.5p	100.0p	....	....	....
Crude Petroleum	66aa	88.4	87.4	97.8	101.1	106.7	108.8	107.6	101.3	100.0	86.1	79.1	81.9
International Transactions		*Billions of Francs*											
Exports	70	551.10	649.80	1,304.90	1,354.40	1,628.70	1,765.20	1,130.20	1,473.80	1,753.00	1,942.00	....	....
Imports, c.i.f.	71	185.20	239.30	420.00	440.20	489.30	644.30	650.80	518.00	708.00	629.50	....	....
Imports, c.i.f., from DOTS	71y	256.43	259.86	392.82	464.29	459.63	719.62	645.74	963.12	993.69	1,071.32	797.63	....
Balance of Payments		*Millions of US Dollars: Minus Sign Indicates Debit*											
Current Account, n.i.e.	78ald	−168.1	−49.1	317.4	464.7	888.6	531.4	−595.5	390.4	....	....	....	....
Goods: Exports f.o.b.	78aad	2,259.2	2,326.2	2,365.3	2,727.8	3,334.2	3,032.7	1,907.6	2,498.8	....	....	....	....
Goods: Imports f.o.b.	78abd	−886.3	−845.1	−776.7	−880.9	−961.6	−1,030.6	−1,163.2	−910.5	....	....	....	....
Trade Balance	78acd	1,372.9	1,481.1	1,588.6	1,846.9	2,372.5	2,002.1	744.4	1,588.3	....	....	....	....
Services: Credit	78add	347.6	311.1	219.6	217.1	233.9	232.9	219.6	280.9	....	....	....	....
Services: Debit	78aed	−924.8	−1,022.7	−826.7	−891.6	−917.8	−952.7	−991.0	−867.0	....	....	....	....
Balance on Goods & Services	78afd	795.6	769.5	981.4	1,172.4	1,688.6	1,282.3	−27.0	1,002.2	....	....	....	....
Income: Credit	78agd	47.2	32.1	11.9	35.0	42.8	39.0	57.5	84.2	....	....	....	....
Income: Debit	78ahd	−868.9	−658.3	−509.9	−700.5	−805.8	−755.5	−572.5	−653.1	....	....	....	....
Balance on Gds, Serv. & Inc.	78aid	−26.1	143.4	483.4	507.0	925.6	565.8	−542.1	433.3	....	....	....	....
Current Transfers, n.i.e.: Credit	78ajd	51.4	48.0	18.7	58.0	65.2	62.7	36.6	42.6	....	....	....	....
Current Transfers: Debit	78akd	−193.4	−240.5	−184.8	−100.3	−102.1	−97.1	−90.0	−85.6	....	....	....	....
Capital Account, n.i.e.	78bcd	−	−	−	4.8	5.1	5.8	1.8	5.4	....	....	....	....
Capital Account, n.i.e.: Credit	78bad	−	−	−	5.6	9.6	7.5	3.6	5.7	....	....	....	....
Capital Account: Debit	78bbd	−	−	....	−.8	−4.5	−1.7	−1.8	−.3	....	....	....	....
Financial Account, n.i.e.	78bjd	−218.7	−389.2	−745.0	−724.7	−1,047.6	−626.2	−165.8	−686.8	....	....	....	....
Direct Investment Abroad	78bdd	−25.7	−2.5	−	−35.0	−2.3	−21.0	−33.2	−73.9	....	....	....	....
Dir. Invest. in Rep. Econ., n.i.e.	78bed	126.9	−113.7	−99.6	−314.5	−489.1	−311.3	146.6	−156.6	....	....	....	....
Portfolio Investment Assets	78bfd	−	−	....	−29.8	−21.1	260.1	19.2	22.4	....	....	....	....
Equity Securities	78bkd	−	−	....	−45.0	−16.7	311.3	19.2	44.0	....	....	....	....
Debt Securities	78bld	−	−	....	15.2	−4.4	−51.2	−	−21.6	....	....	....	....
Portfolio Investment Liab., n.i.e.	78bgd	−	−	....	80.3	4.6	−20.7	−.2	−.7	....	....	....	....
Equity Securities	78bmd	−	−	−	−	−7.5	−	−.2	−	....	....	....	....
Debt Securities	78bnd	−	−	....	80.3	12.1	−20.7	−	−.7	....	....	....	....
Financial Derivatives Assets	78bwd	....	....	....	....	....	....	....	....	....	....	....	....
Financial Derivatives Liabilities	78bxd	....	....	....	....	....	....	....	....	....	....	....	....
Other Investment Assets	78bhd	−27.2	−7.8	−258.6	−39.9	−215.1	18.3	−220.7	−109.0	....	....	....	....
Monetary Authorities	78bod	....	....	....	−2.1	1.2	25.0	−21.5	17.5	....	....	....	....
General Government	78bpd	−	−	−	−	−	−	−	−	....	....	....	....
Banks	78bqd	6.8	4.6	−22.9	13.8	−90.3	76.5	−2.7	−14.0	....	....	....	....
Other Sectors	78brd	−34.0	−12.4	−235.8	−51.5	−126.0	−83.2	−196.4	−112.5	....	....	....	....
Other Investment Liab., n.i.e.	78bid	−292.8	−265.2	−386.7	−385.7	−324.7	−551.6	−77.5	−369.1	....	....	....	....
Monetary Authorities	78bsd	1.9	−6.4	−203.9	−	−	−	−	−	....	....	....	....
General Government	78btd	−236.1	−174.1	−133.1	−280.3	−208.4	−251.7	−276.0	−268.5	....	....	....	....
Banks	78bud	−2.6	1.8	−54.9	34.3	19.8	−32.6	2.7	30.7	....	....	....	....
Other Sectors	78bvd	−55.9	−86.5	5.2	−139.7	−136.1	−267.3	195.8	−131.3	....	....	....	....
Net Errors and Omissions	78cad	−55.1	−13.6	254.6	−181.1	−97.4	−108.4	92.5	−106.7	....	....	....	....
Overall Balance	78cbd	−442.0	−451.9	−173.0	−436.3	−251.2	−197.4	−667.0	−397.8	....	....	....	....
Reserves and Related Items	79dad	442.0	451.9	173.0	436.3	251.2	197.4	667.0	397.8	....	....	....	....
Reserve Assets	79dbd	246.3	67.5	−173.8	42.2	−112.8	−66.8	272.2	−4.9	....	....	....	....
Use of Fund Credit and Loans	79dcd	−36.3	−35.9	40.9	5.0	26.4	19.4	−22.7	−24.5	....	....	....	....
Exceptional Financing	79ded	232.0	420.3	306.0	389.1	337.6	244.8	417.5	427.3	....	....	....	....
National Accounts		*Billions of Francs*											
Househ.Cons.Expend.,incl.NPISHs	96f	717.3	729.5	959.6	1,119.3	1,169.1	1,348.2	1,408.6	....	....	....	....	....
Government Consumption Expend.	91f	223.4	234.3	278.9	291.0	308.8	345.0	425.7	....	....	....	....	....
Gross Capital Formation	93	329.2	344.7	483.2	546.0	662.4	760.6	842.1	....	....	....	....	....
Exports of Goods and Services	90c	692.4	750.4	1,451.7	1,455.8	1,853.5	1,920.4	1,362.3	....	....	....	....	....
Imports of Goods and Services (-)	98c	493.2	521.2	865.2	952.4	1,133.5	1,266.9	1,310.7	....	....	....	....	....
Gross Domestic Product (GDP)	99b	1,480.3	1,530.8	2,326.7	2,475.2	2,912.6	3,109.0	2,645.2	2,870.8	3,558.3	3,340.3	....	....
Net Primary Income from Abroad	98.n	−264.3	−190.6	−308.2	−376.8	−400.7	−395.8	−416.7	....	....	....	....	....
Gross National Income (GNI)	99a	1,210.8	1,347.1	2,000.0	2,082.9	2,459.4	2,711.5	2,311.3	....	....	....	....	....
Consumption of Fixed Capital	99cf	192.5	216.6	243.7	274.2	308.5	347.1	390.5	....	....	....	....	....
		Millions: Midyear Estimates											
Population	99z	1.01	1.05	1.08	1.11	1.14	1.17	1.20	1.23	1.26	1.28	1.31	1.33

Gambia, The 648

		1992	1993	1994	1995	1996	1997	1998	1999	2000	2001	2002	2003
Exchange Rates		\multicolumn{12}{c}{*Dalasis per SDR: End of Period*}
Market Rate	aa	12.673	13.096	13.983	14.330	14.225	14.207	15.476	15.849	19.397	21.279	31.802	....
		\multicolumn{12}{c}{*Dalasis per US Dollar: End of Period (ae) Period Average (rf)*}
Market Rate	ae	9.217	9.535	9.579	9.640	9.892	10.530	10.991	11.547	14.888	16.932	23.392	....
Market Rate	rf	8.888	9.129	9.576	9.546	9.789	10.200	10.643	11.395	12.788	15.687	19.918	....
		\multicolumn{12}{c}{*Index Numbers (2000=100): Period Averages*}
Market Rate	ahx	142.82	139.51	132.84	133.29	130.02	124.81	119.59	111.74	100.00	81.26	64.54	....
Nominal Effective Exchange Rate	nec	92.21	105.18	110.40	105.39	106.15	110.25	109.05	103.83	100.00	85.90	66.50	41.60
Real Effective Exchange Rate	rec	109.32	118.28	109.80	105.81	104.68	109.88	107.54	105.19	100.00	87.77	72.34	52.12
Fund Position		\multicolumn{12}{c}{*Millions of SDRs: End of Period*}
Quota	2f.s	17.10	22.90	22.90	22.90	22.90	22.90	22.90	31.10	31.10	31.10	31.10	31.10
SDRs	1b.s	.45	.23	.18	.09	.20	.09	.30	.49	.17	.01	.01	.02
Reserve Position in the Fund	1c.s	1.48	1.49	1.48	1.48	1.48	1.48	1.48	1.48	1.48	1.48	1.48	1.48
Total Fund Cred.&Loans Outstg	2tl	28.39	26.68	23.94	19.84	14.71	9.58	8.91	9.26	14.42	20.61	23.50	23.50
International Liquidity		\multicolumn{12}{c}{*Millions of US Dollars Unless Otherwise Indicated: End of Period*}
Total Reserves minus Gold	1l.d	94.03	105.75	98.02	106.15	102.13	96.04	106.36	111.25	109.43	106.01	106.88	....
SDRs	1b.d	.62	.31	.26	.13	.29	.11	.42	.67	.23	.02	.02	.03
Reserve Position in the Fund	1c.d	2.04	2.04	2.17	2.21	2.14	2.00	2.09	2.04	1.93	1.87	2.02	2.21
Foreign Exchange	1d.d	91.38	103.40	95.59	103.81	99.71	93.92	103.85	108.54	107.27	104.13	104.84	....
Monetary Authorities: Other Liab	4..d	33.69	29.54	26.15	22.03	17.38	11.69	12.22	12.71	18.79	25.90	31.95	....
Deposit Money Banks: Assets	7a.d	12.47	2.81	3.59	5.64	3.43	10.68	6.54	10.92	9.23	.92	24.28	....
Liabilities	7b.d	1.35	4.05	3.03	2.52	6.28	14.52	12.93	17.01	8.88	10.38	18.20	....
Monetary Authorities		\multicolumn{12}{c}{*Millions of Dalasis: End of Period*}
Foreign Assets	11	869.92	1,020.68	948.01	1,030.19	1,011.63	1,010.13	1,163.67	1,277.17	1,626.32	1,793.06	2,499.12	....
Claims on Central Government	12a	258.76	270.72	297.93	253.65	259.73	240.84	239.90	239.39	223.20	250.52	405.91	....
Claims on Official Entities	12bx	–	–	–	–	–	–	–	–	–	–	–	....
Claims on Private Sector	12d	13.97	15.02	17.02	20.45	21.54	21.08	20.86	21.91	22.71	24.13	23.72	....
Claims on Deposit Money Banks	12e	–	–	–	–	–	–	–	–	–	56.98	31.35	....
Reserve Money	14	287.44	319.64	307.08	385.02	386.85	490.42	525.60	601.65	702.68	850.40	1,140.53	....
of which: Currency Outside DMBs	14a	207.08	224.49	207.36	247.97	255.03	360.51	347.55	379.72	540.26	600.75	797.37	....
Restricted Deposits	16b	–	–	–	–	–	–	–	–	–	–	–	....
Foreign Liabilities	16c	453.55	407.04	354.07	284.26	209.19	136.05	137.85	146.82	279.79	438.56	747.34	....
Central Government Deposits	16d	383.29	553.08	597.69	559.54	669.41	718.02	782.05	808.47	984.40	767.72	750.76	....
Capital Accounts	17a	71.12	73.70	75.50	83.59	80.87	81.34	85.33	86.76	91.53	107.09	122.05	....
Other Items (Net)	17r	–52.75	–47.04	–71.38	–8.11	–53.42	–153.78	–106.39	–105.23	–186.16	–39.09	199.43	....
of which: Valuation Adjustment	17rv	250.37	199.18	217.07	249.70	231.01	129.79	154.75	390.50	306.25	95.79	599.47	....
Deposit Money Banks		\multicolumn{12}{c}{*Millions of Dalasis: End of Period*}
Reserves	20	83.15	98.01	97.09	117.71	128.16	129.91	178.05	221.93	162.43	249.65	367.65	....
Foreign Assets	21	114.93	26.80	34.41	54.36	33.94	112.47	71.90	126.06	137.47	15.51	568.05	....
Claims on Central Government	22a	168.52	135.74	100.50	228.00	355.70	447.25	516.62	587.86	819.73	1,078.99	913.64	....
Claims on Official Entities	22bx	1.54	3.81	.10	.18	.43	1.11	3.86	9.20	11.86	75.79	74.69	....
Claims on Private Sector	22d	222.85	361.90	385.44	342.35	341.89	425.26	489.76	591.41	652.18	873.21	1,203.05	....
Demand Deposits	24	228.09	236.89	200.17	223.50	198.46	268.90	279.02	336.32	443.27	524.66	959.40	....
Time and Savings Deposits	25	303.15	371.17	393.49	443.45	514.30	560.66	685.01	754.26	998.82	1,241.90	1,445.75	....
Restricted Deposits	26b	–	–	–	–	–	–	–	–	–	–	–	....
Foreign Liabilities	26c	12.47	38.65	28.98	24.25	62.10	152.86	142.17	196.46	132.14	175.83	425.63	....
Central Government Deposits	26d	3.96	3.96	3.96	3.96	3.96	3.96	3.96	3.96	3.96	3.96	3.96	....
Credit from Monetary Authorities	26g	–	–	–	–	–	–	–	–	–	–	–	....
Capital Accounts	27a	49.71	68.77	72.28	77.98	88.13	113.08	126.34	188.41	246.75	315.19	491.54	....
Other Items (Net)	27r	–6.39	–93.18	–81.34	–30.54	–6.83	16.54	23.69	57.05	–41.27	31.61	–199.20	....
Monetary Survey		\multicolumn{12}{c}{*Millions of Dalasis: End of Period*}
Foreign Assets (Net)	31n	518.83	601.79	599.37	776.05	774.28	833.70	955.55	1,059.95	1,351.87	1,194.18	1,894.21	....
Domestic Credit	32	278.39	230.15	199.34	281.13	305.92	413.56	484.99	637.34	741.32	1,530.96	1,866.29	....
Claims on Central Govt. (Net)	32an	40.03	–150.58	–203.22	–81.85	–57.94	–33.89	–29.49	14.82	54.57	557.83	564.83	....
Claims on Official Entities	32bx	1.54	3.81	.10	.18	.43	1.11	3.86	9.20	11.86	75.79	74.69	....
Claims on Private Sector	32d	236.82	376.92	402.46	362.80	363.43	446.34	510.62	613.32	674.89	897.34	1,226.77	....
Money	34	435.17	461.38	407.53	471.47	453.49	629.41	626.57	716.04	983.53	1,125.41	1,756.77	....
Quasi-Money	35	303.15	371.17	393.49	443.45	514.30	560.66	685.01	754.26	998.82	1,241.90	1,445.75	....
Restricted Deposits	36b	–	–	–	–	–	–	–	–	–	–	–	....
Capital Accounts	37a	120.83	142.47	147.78	161.57	169.00	194.42	211.67	275.17	338.28	422.28	613.59	....
Other Items (Net)	37r	–61.93	–143.08	–150.09	–19.31	–56.59	–137.24	–82.70	–48.18	–227.44	–64.46	–55.62	....
Money plus Quasi-Money	35l	738.32	832.55	801.02	914.92	967.79	1,190.07	1,311.58	1,470.30	1,982.35	2,367.31	3,202.52	....
Interest Rates		\multicolumn{12}{c}{*Percent Per Annum*}
Discount Rate (End of Period)	60	17.50	13.50	13.50	14.00	14.00	14.00	12.00	10.50	10.00	13.00	18.00	....
Deposit Rate	60l	13.83	13.00	12.58	12.50	12.50	12.50	12.50	12.50	12.50	12.50	12.71	....
Lending Rate	60p	26.75	26.08	25.00	25.04	25.50	25.50	25.38	24.00	24.00	24.00	24.00	....
Prices		\multicolumn{12}{c}{*Index Numbers (2000=100): Period Averages*}
Consumer Prices	64	78.4	83.5	84.9	90.9	91.8	94.4	97.7	99.8	100.0	108.1	113.4	....

Gambia, The 648

		1992	1993	1994	1995	1996	1997	1998	1999	2000	2001	2002	2003
International Transactions						*Millions of Dalasis*							
Exports	70	510.52	604.73	337.80	155.23	209.15	149.82	221.51	51.45	195.00	47.76	37.94	....
Imports, c.i.f.	71	1,944.94	2,372.27	2,032.75	1,741.26	2,527.62	1,773.80	2,426.44	2,186.82	2,394.93	2,106.96	2,974.04	....
Balance of Payments					*Millions of US Dollars: F.Y. Ending June 30: Minus Sign Indicates Debit*								
Current Account, n.i.e.	78ald	37.16	−5.32	8.17	−8.19	−47.70	−23.56	....	....	....	....	....	....
Goods: Exports f.o.b.	78aad	146.95	157.03	124.97	122.96	118.75	119.61	....	....	....	....	....	....
Goods: Imports f.o.b.	78abd	−177.76	−214.46	−181.62	−162.53	−217.10	−207.09	....	....	....	....	....	....
Trade Balance	78acd	−30.81	−57.43	−56.65	−39.57	−98.35	−87.48	....	....	....	....	....	....
Services: Credit	78add	80.86	79.57	90.47	53.71	101.21	109.35	....	....	....	....	....	....
Services: Debit	78aed	−66.93	−74.56	−67.04	−69.25	−77.03	−74.67	....	....	....	....	....	....
Balance on Goods & Services	78afd	−16.89	−52.42	−33.22	−55.11	−74.17	−52.81	....	....	....	....	....	....
Income: Credit	78agd	4.85	5.82	4.87	4.37	6.01	3.73	....	....	....	....	....	....
Income: Debit	78ahd	−7.31	−5.11	−5.14	−9.58	−9.28	−11.30	....	....	....	....	....	....
Balance on Gds, Serv. & Inc.	78aid	−19.35	−51.71	−33.50	−60.32	−77.44	−60.38	....	....	....	....	....	....
Current Transfers, n.i.e.: Credit	78ajd	60.51	49.99	45.85	55.81	35.10	45.04	....	....	....	....	....	....
Current Transfers: Debit	78akd	−4.00	−3.60	−4.18	−3.68	−5.35	−8.22	....	....	....	....	....	....
Capital Account, n.i.e.	78bcd	−	−	−	−	8.52	5.74	....	....	....	....	....	....
Capital Account, n.i.e.: Credit	78bad	−	−	−	−	8.52	5.74	....	....	....	....	....	....
Capital Account: Debit	78bbd	−	−	−	−	....	....	....	....	....	....	....	....
Financial Account, n.i.e.	78bjd	18.71	39.39	33.13	24.77	58.59	39.44	....	....	....	....	....	....
Direct Investment Abroad	78bdd	−	−	−	−	....	....	....	....	....	....	....	....
Dir. Invest. in Rep. Econ., n.i.e.	78bed	6.16	11.07	9.81	7.78	10.80	11.98	....	....	....	....	....	....
Portfolio Investment Assets	78bfd	−	−	−	....	....	....	....	....	....	....	....	....
Equity Securities	78bkd	−	−	−	....	....	....	....	....	....	....	....	....
Debt Securities	78bld	−	−	−	....	....	....	....	....	....	....	....	....
Portfolio Investment Liab., n.i.e.	78bgd	−	−	−	....	....	....	....	....	....	....	....	....
Equity Securities	78bmd	−	−	−	....	....	....	....	....	....	....	....	....
Debt Securities	78bnd	−	−	−	....	....	....	....	....	....	....	....	....
Financial Derivatives Assets	78bwd	....	....	....	....	....	....	....	....	....	....	....	....
Financial Derivatives Liabilities	78bxd	....	....	....	....	....	....	....	....	....	....	....	....
Other Investment Assets	78bhd	−1.52	1.40	3.79	−3.66	5.62	10.28	....	....	....	....	....	....
Monetary Authorities	78bod	....	....	....	....	....	....	....	....	....	....	....	....
General Government	78bpd	−	−	−	....	....	....	....	....	....	....	....	....
Banks	78bqd	−1.52	1.40	3.79	−3.66	4.71	7.14	....	....	....	....	....	....
Other Sectors	78brd	−	−	−	....	.91	3.14	....	....	....	....	....	....
Other Investment Liab., n.i.e.	78bid	14.07	26.92	19.54	20.65	42.18	17.19	....	....	....	....	....	....
Monetary Authorities	78bsd	−	−	−	−	34.01	3.00	....	....	....	....	....	....
General Government	78btd	13.82	23.12	17.79	22.60	3.11	10.49	....	....	....	....	....	....
Banks	78bud	.47	3.80	1.75	−1.95	−.26	.13	....	....	....	....	....	....
Other Sectors	78bvd	−.22	−	−	....	5.32	3.57	....	....	....	....	....	....
Net Errors and Omissions	78cad	−36.74	−22.70	−35.13	−15.67	−4.89	−14.21	....	....	....	....	....	....
Overall Balance	78cbd	19.12	11.37	6.17	.91	14.52	7.40	....	....	....	....	....	....
Reserves and Related Items	79dad	−19.12	−11.37	−6.17	−.91	−14.52	−7.40	....	....	....	....	....	....
Reserve Assets	79dbd	−35.28	−8.95	−3.29	4.26	−7.48	−.15	....	....	....	....	....	....
Use of Fund Credit and Loans	79dcd	.32	−2.42	−2.88	−5.18	−7.04	−7.25	....	....	....	....	....	....
Exceptional Financing	79ded	15.84	−	−	−	....	....	....	....	....	....	....	....
Government Finance					*Millions of Dalasis: Year Ending June 30*								
Deficit (-) or Surplus	80	140.84p	120.69p	....	....	....	....	....	....	....	....	....	....
Revenue	81	644.46p	791.77p	....	....	....	....	....	....	....	....	....	....
Grants Received	81z	45.81p	8.14p	....	....	....	....	....	....	....	....	....	....
Expenditure	82	563.60p	695.14p	....	....	....	....	....	....	....	....	....	....
Lending Minus Repayments	83	−14.17p	−15.92p	....	....	....	....	....	....	....	....	....	....
Financing													
Domestic	84a	−280.05p	−219.12p	....	....	....	....	....	....	....	....	....	....
Foreign	85a	139.21p	98.43p	....	....	....	....	....	....	....	....	....	....
National Accounts					*Millions of Dalasis: Year Ending June 30*								
Gross Domestic Product (GDP)	99b	2,947.6	2,518.5	2,886.3	....	....	....	....	....	....	....	....	....
GDP Volume 1976 Prices	99b.p	566.8	604.0	626.1	600.4	....	....	....	....	....	....	....	....
GDP Volume (1995=100)	99bvp	94.4	100.6	104.3	100.0	....	....	....	....	....	....	....	....
GDP Deflator (1990=100)	99bip	117.6	94.3	104.3	....	....	....	....	....	....	....	....	....
					Millions: Midyear Estimates								
Population	99z	Ü 1.01	1.04	1.08	1.11	1.15	1.19	1.23	1.27	1.31	1.35	1.39	1.43

Georgia 915

		1992	1993	1994	1995	1996	1997	1998	1999	2000	2001	2002	2003
Exchange Rates						*Lari per SDR: End of Period*							
Official Rate	aa	....	....	....	1.8284	1.8348	1.7594	2.5345	2.6489	2.5732	2.5889	2.8414	3.0834
					Lari per US Dollar: End of Period (ae) Period Average (rf)								
Official Rate	ae	....	....	....	1.2300	1.2760	1.3040	1.8000	1.9300	1.9750	2.0600	2.0900	2.0750
Official Rate	rf	....	....	....	....	1.2628	1.2975	1.3898	2.0245	1.9762	2.0730	2.1957	2.1457
					Index Numbers (2000=100): Period Averages								
Nominal Effective Exchange Rate	nec	....	....	158.36	100.00	117.88	138.71	159.99	....	....	....	....	....
Real Effective Exchange Rate	rec	....	....	44.73	100.00	129.37	136.48	135.73	....	....	....	....	....
Fund Position					*Millions of SDRs: End of Period*								
Quota	2f.s	111.00	111.00	111.00	111.00	111.00	111.00	111.00	150.30	150.30	150.30	150.30	150.30
SDRs	1b.s	–	–	1.61	1.12	.05	.10	3.69	6.13	2.51	3.15	2.13	3.31
Reserve Position in the Fund	1c.s	.01	.01	.01	.01	.01	.01	.01	.01	.01	.01	.01	.01
Total Fund Cred.& Loans Outstg	2tl	–	–	27.75	77.70	133.20	188.70	215.76	233.33	213.68	228.65	228.03	194.26
International Liquidity					*Millions of US Dollars Unless Otherwise Indicated: End of Period*								
Total Reserves minus Gold	1l.d	....	....	....	194.01	188.91	199.80	122.99	132.39	109.41	159.37	197.55	190.72
SDRs	1b.d	–	–	2.35	1.66	.07	.13	5.20	8.42	3.27	3.96	2.89	4.91
Reserve Position in the Fund	1c.d	.01	.01	.01	.01	.01	.01	.01	.01	.01	.01	.01	.01
Foreign Exchange	1d.d	....	....	....	192.33	188.83	199.66	117.78	123.96	106.13	155.40	194.64	185.79
Gold(Millions Fine Troy Ounces)	1ad	....	....	....	–	–	–	–	–	–	–	–	–
Gold (National Valuation)	1and	....	....	....	–	–	–	–	–	–	–	–	–
Monetary Authorities:Other Assets	3..d	....	....	....	.11	–	–	–	–	–	–	–	–
Other Liab	4..d	....	....	....	.06	.06	27.75	36.68	41.18	38.79	40.27	46.60	55.98
Deposit Money Banks: Assets	7a.d	....	....	....	26.88	33.88	39.10	46.41	48.57	54.11	84.53	94.32	114.47
Liabilities	7b.d	....	....	....	49.26	4.80	11.95	35.99	46.94	57.64	70.58	87.89	97.43
Monetary Authorities					*Millions of Lari: End of Period*								
Foreign Assets	11	....	....	....	238.75	241.15	260.50	221.53	255.50	216.12	† 337.19	422.35	407.02
Claims on General Government	12a	....	....	....	112.45	296.72	437.52	541.78	717.82	802.49	† 767.62	776.87	816.53
Claims on Nonfin. Pub. Enterprises	12c	....	....	....	–	–	–	–	–	–	† 79.04	95.28	114.18
Claims on Private Sector	12d	....	....	....	–	–	36.67	66.67	80.86	77.88	† 1.17	1.59	2.01
Claims on Deposit Money Banks	12e	....	....	....	3.66	14.30	5.26	6.56	1.86	4.49	† 1.76	.25	6.81
Reserve Money	14	....	....	....	153.28	208.96	277.07	259.72	308.47	391.66	† 431.78	516.38	590.36
of which: Currency Outside DMBs	14a	....	....	....	124.78	176.76	239.87	212.19	244.00	315.18	† 348.85	390.79	441.54
Time, Savings,& Fgn. Currency Dep	15	....	....	....	–	–	–	–	–	–	† 1.82	1.52	1.01
Foreign Liabilities	16c	....	....	....	142.14	244.47	368.19	612.84	697.55	626.45	† 674.90	745.30	715.14
General Government Deposits	16d	....	....	....	57.17	87.86	52.08	41.94	21.74	20.26	† 28.60	20.95	33.62
Counterpart Funds	16e	....	....	....	–	–	–	4.41	.75	–	† –	–	–
Capital Accounts	17a	....	....	....	14.88	18.53	94.02	–14.88	182.32	176.07	† 74.20	54.89	49.03
Other Items (Net)	17r	....	....	....	–12.61	–7.65	–51.41	–67.49	–154.79	–113.47	† –24.51	–42.70	–42.61
Deposit Money Banks					*Millions of Lari: End of Period*								
Reserves	20	....	....	....	38.00	30.39	39.62	45.01	56.37	76.65	† 82.45	126.13	148.91
Foreign Assets	21	....	....	....	33.06	43.23	50.99	83.55	93.73	106.86	† 174.12	197.13	237.52
Claims on General Government	22a	....	....	....	1.47	1.27	4.86	1.12	1.70	5.72	† 17.02	37.35	53.17
of which: Claims on Local Govt	22ab	....	....	....	1.42	1.26	1.09	1.12	–	.30	† 2.04	2.87	10.61
Claims on Nonfin. Pub. Enterprises	22c	....	....	....	–	–	–	–	–	–	† 25.00	39.62	39.33
Claims on Private Sector	22d	....	....	....	148.71	127.80	175.06	239.95	339.74	446.96	† 496.38	602.46	743.93
Claims on Nonbank Fin. Insts	22g	....	....	....	.31	.06	–	–	–	–	† –	–	–
Demand Deposits	24	....	....	....	30.02	35.78	38.67	38.38	31.51	53.20	† 45.33	62.01	75.32
Time,Savings,& Fgn.Currency Dep	25	....	....	....	28.51	46.69	94.82	118.63	171.44	254.51	† 341.94	415.86	550.92
Money Market Instruments	26aa	....	....	....	–	–	–	–	–	–	† .02	.11	.02
Foreign Liabilities	26c	....	....	....	60.59	6.12	15.58	64.79	90.59	113.84	† 145.40	183.70	202.16
General Government Deposits	26d	....	....	....	14.27	18.30	9.08	15.61	10.71	11.15	† 26.46	74.28	66.87
of which: Local Govt. Deposits	26db	....	....	....	4.91	4.72	3.50	4.69	3.88	4.54	† 6.45	59.50	54.53
Counterpart Funds	26e	....	....	....	–	10.26	10.37	8.10	1.33	.24	† .36	.36	.36
Central Govt. Lending Funds	26f	....	....	....	–	–	–	–	3.52	6.29	† 6.29	6.94	6.69
Credit from Monetary Authorities	26g	....	....	....	–	–	–	–	–	–	† 1.21	.61	7.12
Liab. to Nonbank Financial Insts	26j	....	....	....	–	–	–	–	–	–	† .15	–	–
Capital Accounts	27a	....	....	....	61.09	90.82	145.14	200.17	280.27	376.61	† 471.60	495.13	578.09
Other Items (Net)	27r	....	....	....	27.08	–5.22	–43.12	–76.05	–97.82	–179.64	† –243.80	–236.30	–264.69

Georgia 915

		1992	1993	1994	1995	1996	1997	1998	1999	2000	2001	2002	2003
Monetary Survey						*Millions of Lari: End of Period*							
Foreign Assets (Net)	31n	....	....	....	69.09	33.79	−72.29	−372.55	−438.90	−417.31	†−308.98	−309.52	−272.77
Domestic Credit	32	....	....	....	191.50	319.69	592.96	791.97	1,107.67	1,301.63	†1,331.16	1,457.94	1,668.67
Claims on General Govt. (Net)	32an	....	....	....	42.48	191.83	381.22	485.35	687.07	776.79	†729.58	718.98	769.21
Claims on Nonfin.Pub. Enterprises	32c	....	....	....	−	−	−	−	−	−	†104.04	134.90	153.51
Claims on Private Sector	32d	....	....	....	148.71	127.80	211.73	306.62	420.60	524.84	†497.55	604.06	745.95
Claims on Nonbank Fin. Insts	32g	....	....	....	.31	.06	−	−	−	−	†−	−	−
Money	34	....	....	....	154.80	212.54	278.54	250.58	275.50	368.37	†394.23	452.84	516.92
Quasi-Money	35	....	....	....	28.51	46.69	94.82	118.63	171.44	254.51	†343.76	417.38	551.93
Money Market Instruments	36aa	....	....	....	−	−	−	−	−	−	†.02	.11	.02
Counterpart Funds	36e	....	....	....	−	10.26	10.37	12.50	2.08	.24	†.36	.36	.36
Central Govt. Lending Funds	36f	....	....	....	−	−	−	−	3.52	6.29	†6.29	6.94	6.69
Liab. to Nonbank Financial Insts	36j	....	....	....	−	−	−	−	−	−	†.15	−	−
Capital Accounts	37a	....	....	....	75.97	109.35	239.16	185.30	462.58	552.68	†545.80	550.01	627.12
Other Items (Net)	37r	....	....	....	1.31	−25.36	−102.21	−147.58	−246.36	−297.77	†−268.44	−279.22	−307.15
Money plus Quasi-Money	35l	....	....	....	183.31	259.23	373.36	369.20	446.94	622.88	†737.99	870.22	1,068.85
Interest Rates						*Percent Per Annum*							
Money Market Rate	60b				....	43.39	26.58	43.26	34.61	18.17	†17.52	27.69	16.88
Treasury Bill Rate	60c				....	....	....	....	....	....	29.93	43.42	44.26
Deposit Rate	60l				....	31.05	13.73	17.00	14.58	10.17	7.75	9.82	9.28
Deposit Rate (Foreign Currency)	60l.f				....	24.55	19.11	15.75	14.58	12.00	10.42	10.23	9.19
Lending Rate	60p				....	58.24	50.64	46.00	33.42	32.75	27.25	31.83	32.27
Lending Rate (Foreign Currency)	60p.f				....	51.92	54.16	46.75	42.92	36.58	32.17	29.27	27.62
Prices						*Index Numbers (2000=100): Period Averages*							
Producer Prices	63	....	....	....	....	....	....	82.7	94.5	100.0	103.7	109.9	....
Consumer Prices	64	....	....	19.9	52.2	72.7	77.8	80.6	96.1	100.0	104.6	110.5	....
						Number in Thousands: Period Averages							
Labor Force	67d	....	....	....	....	....	1,999	2,026	2,010	2,052	2,113	2,104	....
Employment	67e	....	....	....	....	....	1,848	1,731	1,733	1,839	1,878	1,839	1,814
Unemployment	67c	....	....	....	....	....	152	295	277	212	236	265	....
Unemployment Rate (%)	67r	....	....	....	....	....	7.6	14.5	13.8	10.3	11.1	12.6	....
International Transactions						*Millions of Lari*							
Exports	70	....	....	163	194	251	312	267	481	653	662	765	....
Imports, c.i.f.	71	....	....	288	507	868	1,224	1,229	1,184	1,292	1,418	1,609	....
Imports, f.o.b.	71.v	....	....	259	456	781	1,103	1,107	....	....	....	....	....

2004, International Monetary Fund : *International Financial Statistics Yearbook*

Georgia 915

		1992	1993	1994	1995	1996	1997	1998	1999	2000	2001	2002	2003
Balance of Payments		*Millions of US Dollars: Minus Sign Indicates Debit*											
Current Account, n.i.e.	78ald	....	....	....	....	....	−514.2	−275.7	−198.4	−269.0	−211.7	−230.0	−397.1
Goods: Exports f.o.b.	78aad	....	....	....	....	....	376.5	299.9	329.5	459.0	496.1	601.7	830.6
Goods: Imports f.o.b.	78abd	....	....	....	....	....	−1,162.9	−994.5	−863.4	−970.5	−1,045.6	−1,084.7	−1,466.6
Trade Balance	78acd	....	....	....	....	....	−786.4	−694.6	−533.9	−511.5	−549.5	−483.0	−636.0
Services: Credit	78add	....	....	....	....	....	198.0	365.3	216.9	206.4	314.1	391.6	442.0
Services: Debit	78aed	....	....	....	....	....	−249.7	−345.2	−224.0	−216.3	−236.9	−356.7	−389.5
Balance on Goods & Services	78afd	....	....	....	....	....	−838.1	−674.5	−541.0	−521.4	−472.3	−448.1	−583.5
Income: Credit	78agd	....	....	....	....	....	186.6	243.4	211.4	178.6	97.7	166.1	179.3
Income: Debit	78ahd	....	....	....	....	....	−59.2	−52.7	−64.5	−61.1	−65.4	−127.4	−145.0
Balance on Gds, Serv. & Inc.	78aid	....	....	....	....	....	−710.7	−483.8	−394.1	−403.9	−440.0	−409.3	−549.2
Current Transfers, n.i.e.: Credit	78ajd	....	....	....	....	....	205.5	219.9	228.7	163.2	246.4	213.3	193.5
Current Transfers: Debit	78akd	....	....	....	....	....	−9.0	−11.8	−33.0	−28.3	−18.1	−34.0	−41.5
Capital Account, n.i.e.	78bcd	....	....	....	....	....	−6.5	−6.1	−7.1	−4.8	−5.2	18.4	19.9
Capital Account, n.i.e.: Credit	78bad	....	....	....	....	....	−	−	−	−	....	27.1	27.9
Capital Account: Debit	78bbd	....	....	....	....	....	−6.5	−6.1	−7.1	−4.8	−5.2	−8.6	−8.0
Financial Account, n.i.e.	78bjd	....	....	....	....	....	322.7	348.8	135.5	92.8	209.7	19.2	323.0
Direct Investment Abroad	78bdd	....	....	....	....	....	−	−	−1.0	.5	.1	−4.1	−3.8
Dir. Invest. in Rep. Econ., n.i.e.	78bed	....	....	....	....	....	242.5	265.3	82.3	131.1	109.8	167.4	337.9
Portfolio Investment Assets	78bfd	....	....	....	....	....	....	....	....	2.7	−.1	−	−
Equity Securities	78bkd	....	....	....	....	....	....	....	....	2.7	....	−	−
Debt Securities	78bld	....	....	....	....	....	....	....	....	....	....	....	....
Portfolio Investment Liab., n.i.e.	78bgd	....	....	....	....	....	2.4	−	6.2	−	....	....	....
Equity Securities	78bmd	....	....	....	....	....	2.4	−	6.2	−	....	....	....
Debt Securities	78bnd	....	....	....	....	....	....	....	....	....	....	....	....
Financial Derivatives Assets	78bwd	....	....	....	....	....	....	....	....	....	....	−	−
Financial Derivatives Liabilities	78bxd	....	....	....	....	....	....	....	....	....	....	−	−
Other Investment Assets	78bhd	....	....	....	....	....	−24.8	−86.9	9.3	−7.7	−24.6	−72.8	−6.1
Monetary Authorities	78bod	....	....	....	....	....	....	....	....	....	....	....	....
General Government	78bpd	....	....	....	....	....	−	−45.0	−	−	....	−5.0	−5.0
Banks	78bqd	....	....	....	....	....	−15.0	−23.2	9.3	−7.7	−24.6	−59.3	.5
Other Sectors	78brd	....	....	....	....	....	−9.8	−18.7	−	−	−	−8.5	−1.7
Other Investment Liab., n.i.e.	78bid	....	....	....	....	....	102.6	170.4	38.7	−33.8	124.5	−71.3	−5.0
Monetary Authorities	78bsd	....	....	....	....	....	−	−	−	−	−	−	−.5
General Government	78btd	....	....	....	....	....	90.0	141.5	17.6	−41.1	99.1	−132.6	−55.2
Banks	78bud	....	....	....	....	....	7.4	37.4	26.3	7.3	25.4	16.3	4.1
Other Sectors	78bvd	....	....	....	....	....	5.2	−8.5	−5.2	−	−	45.1	46.5
Net Errors and Omissions	78cad	....	....	....	....	....	136.0	−170.5	55.7	187.4	34.9	6.0	6.6
Overall Balance	78cbd	....	....	....	....	....	−62.0	−103.5	−14.3	6.4	27.7	−186.4	−47.7
Reserves and Related Items	79dad	....	....	....	....	....	62.0	103.5	14.3	−6.4	−27.7	186.4	47.7
Reserve Assets	79dbd	....	....	....	....	....	−14.1	67.6	−9.6	19.8	−47.0	−37.7	6.0
Use of Fund Credit and Loans	79dcd	....	....	....	....	....	76.1	35.8	23.9	−26.2	19.4	−.1	−47.4
Exceptional Financing	79ded	....	....	....	....	....	....	....	....	....	....	224.1	89.1
Government Finance		*Millions of Lari: Year Ending December 31*											
Deficit (−) or Surplus	80	....	....	....	....	....	....	−175.39	−128.46	−193.61	−103.96	−185.15	−153.85
Total Revenue and Grants	81y	....	....	....	....	....	....	621.87	723.96	640.26	740.34	818.01	914.76
Revenue	81	....	....	....	....	....	....	591.43	674.62	625.93	692.26	795.41	866.35
Grants	81z	....	....	....	....	....	....	30.44	49.35	14.33	48.08	22.60	48.41
Exp.& Lending Minus Repayments	82z	....	....	....	....	....	....	797.25	852.42	833.87	844.30	1,003.16	1,068.60
Expenditure	82	....	....	....	....	....	....	761.51	849.12	737.78	726.57	834.12	927.88
Lending Minus Repayments	83	....	....	....	....	....	....	35.74	3.30	96.09	117.73	169.04	140.72
Total Financing	80h	....	....	....	....	....	....	175.39	128.46	193.61	103.96	185.13	153.85
Domestic	84a	....	....	....	....	....	....	145.47	109.77	149.18	2.21	53.05	63.15
Foreign	85a	....	....	....	....	....	....	29.91	18.69	44.44	101.75	132.08	90.70
Total Debt by Residence	88	....	....	....	....	....	....	2,857.83	4,077.92	4,192.54	4,449.53	4,843.33	4,608.05
Domestic	88a	....	....	....	....	....	....	556.52	1,343.49	1,497.97	1,492.41	1,520.35	1,567.90
Foreign	89a	....	....	....	....	....	....	2,301.30	2,734.43	2,694.56	2,957.12	3,322.98	3,040.15
National Accounts		*Millions of Lari*											
Househ.Cons.Expend.,incl.NPISHs	96f	....	....	....	3,368	4,007	4,545	4,258	4,648	5,332	5,464	6,087	....
Government Consumption Expend	91f	....	....	....	295	298	463	557	603	516	644	732	....
Gross Fixed Capital Formation	93e	....	....	....	714	416	519	755	1,252	1,308	1,374	1,575	....
Changes in Inventories	93i	....	....	....	173	46	49	81	14	73	67	73	....
Exports of Goods and Services	90c	....	....	....	516	516	711	827	1,080	1,390	1,633	2,045	....
Imports of Goods and Services (−)	98c	....	....	....	1,053	1,252	1,920	1,864	2,160	2,397	2,594	2,917	....
Gross Domestic Product (GDP)	99b	....	....	....	3,694	3,846	4,639	5,040	5,665	6,013	6,638	7,457	....
		Millions: Midyear Estimates											
Population	99z	5.44	5.41	5.38	5.35	5.33	5.32	5.31	5.29	5.26	5.22	5.18	5.13

Germany 134

		1992	1993	1994	1995	1996	1997	1998	1999	2000	2001	2002	2003
Exchange Rates			*Deutsche Mark per SDR through 1998, Euros per SDR Thereafter: End of Period*
Market Rate	aa	2.2193	2.3712	2.2610	2.1309	2.2357	2.4180	2.3556	1.3662	1.4002	1.4260	1.2964	1.1765
			*Deutsche Mark per US Dollar through 1998, Euros per US Dollar Thereafter: End of Period (ae) Period Average (rf)*
Market Rate	ae	1.6140	1.7263	1.5488	1.4335	1.5548	1.7921	1.6730	.9954	1.0747	1.1347	.9536	.7918
Market Rate	rf	1.5617	1.6533	1.6228	1.4331	1.5048	1.7341	1.7597	.9386	1.0854	1.1175	1.0626	.8860
			*Deutsche Mark per ECU: End of Period (ea) Period Average (eb)*
ECU Rate	ea	1.9556	1.9357	1.9053	1.8840	1.9465	1.9763	1.9558	....	....	....	....	....
ECU Rate	eb	2.0210	1.9368	1.9248	1.8736	1.9096	1.9642	1.9692	....	....	....	....	....
			*Index Numbers (2000=100): Period Averages*
Market Rate (1995=100)	ahx	91.9	86.6	88.4	100.0	95.2	82.7	81.5	....	....	....	....	....
Nominal Effective Exchange Rate	neu	104.3	108.4	108.7	114.3	111.3	106.2	106.4	104.3	100.0	100.7	101.7	105.9
Real Effective Exchange Rate	reu	102.7	109.5	112.7	121.0	119.4	112.3	109.5	106.1	100.0	99.2	99.3	102.3
Fund Position			*Millions of SDRs: End of Period*
Quota	2f.s	8,242	8,242	8,242	8,242	8,242	8,242	8,242	13,008	13,008	13,008	13,008	13,008
SDRs	1b.s	611	700	763	1,346	1,326	1,325	1,327	1,427	1,353	1,426	1,456	1,307
Reserve Position in the Fund	1c.s	3,083	2,877	2,760	3,505	3,803	4,407	5,698	4,677	4,191	4,696	4,925	5,152
of which: Outstg.Fund Borrowing	2c	–	–	–	–	–	–	530	–	–	–	–	–
International Liquidity			*Millions of US Dollars Unless Otherwise Indicated: End of Period*
Total Res.Min.Gold (Eurosys.Def)	1l.d	90,967	77,640	77,363	85,005	83,178	77,587	74,024	†61,039	56,890	51,404	51,171	50,694
SDRs	1b.d	841	962	1,114	2,001	1,907	1,788	1,868	1,959	1,763	1,793	1,980	1,942
Reserve Position in the Fund	1c.d	4,239	3,951	4,030	5,210	5,468	5,946	8,023	6,419	5,460	5,901	6,695	7,656
Foreign Exchange	1d.d	85,887	72,727	72,219	77,794	75,803	69,853	64,133	†52,661	49,667	43,710	42,495	41,095
o/w:Fin.Deriv.Rel.to Reserves	1ddd	....	....	....	....	....	....	....					
Other Reserve Assets	1e.d	....	....	....	....	....	....	....					
Gold (Million Fine Troy Ounces)	1ad	95.18	95.18	95.18	95.18	95.18	95.18	118.98	111.52	111.52	111.13	110.79	110.58
Gold (Eurosystem Valuation)	1and	8,481	7,929	8,838	9,549	8,804	7,638	10,227	32,368	30,606	30,728	37,972	46,141
Memo:Euro Cl. on Non-EA Res	1dgd	....	....	....	....	....	....	....	9,191	279	264	315	379
Non-Euro Cl. on EA Res	1dhd								–	–	–	–	–
Mon. Auth.: Other Foreign Assets	3..d	1,637	1,548	1,539	1,371	944	559	680	†9,204	291	276	327	394
Foreign Liabilities	4..d	16,423	22,909	15,620	11,435	10,035	9,436	9,551	†6,195	6,125	7,670	9,409	13,178
Banking Insts.: Foreign Assets	7a.d	386,841	461,962	484,892	578,196	606,018	650,287	828,893	†513,967	579,527	641,339	774,425	1,015,356
Foreign Liab	7b.d	264,432	286,135	378,834	482,236	490,213	561,585	760,827	†491,336	559,069	571,750	630,474	719,227
Monetary Authorities			*Billions of Deutsche Mark through 1998; Billions of Euros Beginning 1999: End of Period*
Fgn. Assets (Cl.on Non-EA Ctys)	11	152.0	134.5	128.7	132.9	132.2	129.7	135.1	102.2	94.1	93.5	85.3	77.0
Claims on General Government	12a.u	....	....	....	....	....	....	....	4.4	4.4	4.4	4.4	4.4
o/w: Claims on Gen.Govt.in Cty	12a	33.2	27.7	26.6	24.7	24.0	24.2	24.3	4.4	4.4	4.4	4.4	4.4
Claims on Banking Institutions	12e.u	....	....	....	....	....	....	....	135.9	151.5	135.3	145.1	181.4
o/w: Claims on Bank.Inst.in Cty	12e	188.9	257.5	217.7	213.1	226.2	235.2	216.0	90.6	139.2	123.0	127.9	164.3
Claims on Other Resident Sectors	12d.u	....	....	....	....	....	....	....	–	–	–	–	–
o/w: Cl. on Oth.Res.Sect.in Cty	12d	....	....	....	....	....	....	....	–	–	–	–	–
Currency Issued	14a	227.3	238.6	250.9	263.5	275.7	276.2	271.0	148.2	142.2	82.8	112.2	125.9
Liabilities to Banking Insts	14c.u	....	....	....	....	....	....	....	48.8	53.9	88.4	74.0	89.4
o/w: Liabs to Bank.Inst.in Cty	14c	88.9	73.4	56.2	49.7	51.9	48.7	57.7	41.9	47.0	57.4	44.8	44.7
Demand Dep. of Other Res.Sect	14d.u	....	....	....	....	....	....	....	.5	.4	1.0	.6	.6
o/w:D.Dep.of Oth.Res.Sect.in Cty	14d	.8	.8	.7	.7	1.3	1.1	1.0	.5	.4	1.0	.6	.5
Other Dep. of Other Res.Sect	15..u	....	....	....	....	....	....	....	–	–	–	–	–
o/w:O.Dep.of Oth.Res.Sect.in Cty	15	....	....	....	....	....	....	....	–	–	–	–	–
Bonds & Money Mkt. Instruments	16n.u	....	....	....	....	....	....	....	–	–	–	–	–
Foreign Liab. (to Non-EA Ctys)	16c	26.5	23.2	19.6	16.4	15.6	16.9	16.0	6.2	6.6	8.7	9.0	10.4
Central Government Deposits	16d.u	....	....	....	....	....	....	....	–	–	–	–	–
o/w: Cent.Govt.Dep. in Cty	16d	.4	13.4	.2	.1	.4	.3	.2	–	–	–	–	–
Capital Accounts	17a	18.8	21.1	23.1	22.4	23.1	24.6	21.5	41.7	46.0	48.4	40.8	35.5
Other Items (Net)	17r	11.5	49.2	22.2	17.9	14.4	21.3	8.0	–2.8	1.0	3.9	–1.6	1.1
Memo: Net Claims on Eurosystem	12e.s	....	....	....	....	....	....	....	38.5	5.4	–18.6	–12.1	–27.9
Currency Put into Circ	14m	....	....	....	....	....	....	....	....	....	....	141.3	170.5

2004, International Monetary Fund : *International Financial Statistics Yearbook*

Germany 134

		1992	1993	1994	1995	1996	1997	1998	1999	2000	2001	2002	2003
Banking Institutions		*Billions of Deutsche Mark through 1998; Billions of Euros Beginning 1999: End of Period*
Claims on Monetary Authorities	20	115.0	102.0	86.5	87.0	88.6	89.5	92.1	45.6	51.0	56.4	45.6	46.9
Claims on Bk.Inst.in Oth.EA Ctys	20b.u	....	....	....	....	....	....	....	203.1	244.4	286.3	346.8	375.5
Fgn. Assets (Cl.on Non-EA Ctys)	21	624.4	797.5	751.0	828.8	942.2	1,165.4	1,386.7	511.6	622.8	727.7	738.5	803.9
Claims on General Government	22a.u	....	....	....	....	....	....	....	735.7	720.4	708.8	709.4	702.3
o/w: Claims on Gen.Govt.in Cty	22a	746.2	849.3	937.4	1,078.7	1,161.4	1,223.7	1,251.8	632.1	616.9	587.8	586.4	585.6
Claims on Other Resident Sectors	22d.u	....	....	....	....	....	....	....	2,391.7	2,529.4	2,608.3	2,630.8	2,630.9
o/w: Cl. on Oth.Res.Sect.in Cty	22d	2,939.1	3,206.4	3,451.4	3,630.7	3,900.1	4,137.6	4,471.9	2,326.4	2,445.7	2,497.1	2,505.8	2,497.4
Demand Deposits	24..u	....	....	....	....	....	....	....	426.0	448.2	532.7	582.9	631.4
o/w:D.Dep.of Oth.Res.Sect.in Cty	24	439.6	484.8	505.3	545.4	631.8	650.0	747.7	419.5	441.4	525.0	574.8	622.1
Other Deposits	25..u	....	....	....	....	....	....	....	1,541.7	1,533.6	1,557.2	1,542.8	1,551.3
o/w:O.Dep.of Oth.Res.Sect.in Cty	25	1,337.9	1,500.9	1,523.6	1,572.2	1,649.6	1,692.4	1,752.4	1,435.6	1,432.3	1,457.8	1,461.6	1,474.1
Money Market Fund Shares	26m.u	....	....	....	....	....	....	....	20.8	19.3	32.6	36.7	36.7
Bonds & Money Mkt. Instruments	26n.u	....	....	....	....	....	....	....	1,348.1	1,455.8	1,488.3	1,517.5	1,531.1
o/w: Held by Resid.of Cty	26n	1,370.0	1,467.6	1,612.5	1,786.9	1,948.0	2,075.8	2,196.0	....	....	....	....	....
Foreign Liab. (to Non-EA Ctys)	26c	426.8	494.0	586.7	691.3	762.2	1,006.4	1,272.9	489.1	600.8	648.8	601.2	569.5
Central Government Deposits	26d.u	....	....	....	....	....	....	....	46.6	69.9	49.1	47.7	45.9
o/w: Cent.Govt.Dep. in Cty	26d	237.5	242.9	249.5	245.4	248.1	248.4	251.3	45.9	67.6	46.9	45.6	44.2
Credit from Monetary Authorities	26g	188.9	257.5	217.7	213.1	226.2	235.2	216.0	92.1	139.3	125.0	125.4	162.8
Liab. to Bk.Inst.in Oth. EA Ctys	26h.u	....	....	....	....	....	....	....	166.3	190.5	215.9	242.4	241.6
Capital Accounts	27a	352.1	391.6	410.1	438.1	463.9	507.0	544.9	237.0	258.5	275.7	291.7	294.4
Other Items (Net)	27r	71.8	116.1	120.7	132.8	162.7	201.0	221.4	−480.0	−547.8	−537.5	−517.3	−505.0
Banking Survey (Nat'l Residency)		*Billions of Deutsche Mark through 1998; Billions of Euros Beginning 1999: End of Period*
Foreign Assets (Net)	31n	323.1	414.9	273.3	254.0	296.6	271.7	233.0	266.1	271.3	361.9	486.0	591.6
Domestic Credit	32	3,480.6	3,827.2	4,165.6	4,488.6	4,837.1	5,137.0	5,496.5	2,917.1	2,999.4	3,042.3	3,051.0	3,043.3
Claims on General Govt. (Net)	32an	541.6	620.7	714.2	857.8	937.0	999.4	1,024.6	590.6	553.8	545.3	545.2	545.9
Claims on Other Resident Sectors	32d	2,939.1	3,206.4	3,451.4	3,630.7	3,900.1	4,137.6	4,471.9	2,326.4	2,445.7	2,497.1	2,505.8	2,497.4
Currency Issued	34a.n	227.3	238.6	250.9	263.5	275.7	276.2	271.0	148.2	142.2	82.8	112.2	125.9
Demand Deposits	34b.n	440.4	485.6	506.1	546.2	633.0	651.1	748.7	420.0	441.8	526.0	575.4	622.6
Other Deposits	35..n	1,337.9	1,500.9	1,523.6	1,572.2	1,649.6	1,692.4	1,752.4	1,435.6	1,432.3	1,457.8	1,461.6	1,474.1
Money Market Fund Shares	36m	....	....	....	....	....	....	....	20.8	19.3	32.6	36.7	36.7
Bonds & Money Mkt. Instruments	36n	1,370.0	1,467.6	1,612.5	1,786.9	1,948.0	2,075.8	2,196.0	1,348.1	1,455.8	1,488.3	1,517.5	1,531.1
o/w: Over Two Years	36na	....	....	....	....	....	....	....	1,226.2	1,303.8	1,316.1	1,326.4	1,355.6
Capital Accounts	37a	370.9	412.6	433.2	460.5	487.0	531.6	566.4	278.7	304.5	324.1	332.5	329.9
Other Items (Net)	37r	57.2	136.7	112.7	113.3	140.3	181.5	194.9	−468.2	−525.1	−507.3	−498.8	−485.3
Banking Survey (EA-Wide Residency)		*Billions of Euros: End of Period*
Foreign Assets (Net)	31n.u	....	....	....	....	....	....	....	118.6	109.5	163.8	213.6	301.0
Domestic Credit	32..u	....	....	....	....	....	....	....	3,085.2	3,184.4	3,272.4	3,296.9	3,291.8
Claims on General Govt. (Net)	32anu	....	....	....	....	....	....	....	693.5	655.0	664.1	666.1	660.8
Claims on Other Resident Sect	32d.u	....	....	....	....	....	....	....	2,391.7	2,529.4	2,608.3	2,630.8	2,630.9
Currency Issued	34a.u	....	....	....	....	....	....	....	148.2	142.2	82.8	112.2	125.9
Demand Deposits	34b.u	....	....	....	....	....	....	....	426.7	448.7	533.7	583.5	631.9
Other Deposits	35..u	....	....	....	....	....	....	....	1,541.7	1,533.6	1,557.2	1,542.8	1,551.3
o/w: Other Dep. Over Two Yrs	35abu	....	....	....	....	....	....	....	664.4	674.0	672.8	670.2	683.7
Money Market Fund Shares	36m.u	....	....	....	....	....	....	....	20.8	19.3	32.6	36.7	36.7
Bonds & Money Mkt. Instruments	36n.u	....	....	....	....	....	....	....	1,348.1	1,455.8	1,488.3	1,517.5	1,531.1
o/w: Over Two Years	36nau	....	....	....	....	....	....	....	1,226.2	1,303.8	1,316.1	1,326.4	1,355.6
Capital Accounts	37a	....	....	....	....	....	....	....	278.7	304.5	324.1	332.5	329.9
Other Items (Net)	37r.u	....	....	....	....	....	....	....	−560.3	−610.1	−582.4	−614.6	−614.1
Money (National Definitions)		*Billions of Deutsche Mark: End of Period*
Central Bank Money,Seas. Adj	19m.c	205.7	229.8	249.7	258.8	274.3	282.5	281.8	....	....	....	....	....
M1, Seasonally Adjusted	39mac	586.3	641.2	703.0	729.0	805.0	872.9	930.6	....	....	....	....	....
M2, Seasonally Adjusted	39mbc	1,108.9	1,204.1	1,279.2	1,206.5	1,224.6	1,265.7	1,322.1	....	....	....	....	....
M3, Seasonally Adjusted	39mcc	1,596.5	1,720.8	1,875.1	1,885.6	2,026.1	2,151.3	2,245.2	....	....	....	....	....
Extended Money M3,Seas.Adj	39mdc	1,802.0	1,986.0	2,179.7	2,215.8	2,341.6	2,460.5	2,569.4	....	....	....	....	....
Interest Rates		*Percent Per Annum*
Discount Rate (End of Period)	60	8.25	5.75	4.50	3.00	2.50	2.50	2.50	....	....	....	....	....
Money Market Rate	60b	9.42	7.49	5.35	4.50	3.27	3.18	3.41	2.73	4.11	4.37	3.28	2.32
Treasury Bill Rate	60c	8.32	6.22	5.05	4.40	3.30	3.32	3.42	2.88	4.32	3.66	2.97	1.98
Deposit Rate	60l	8.01	6.27	4.47	3.85	2.83	2.69	2.88	2.43	3.40	3.56	2.65	....
Lending Rate	60p	13.59	12.85	11.48	10.94	10.02	9.13	9.02	8.81	9.63	10.01	9.70	....
Government Bond Yield	61	7.96	6.28	6.67	6.50	5.63	5.08	4.39	4.26	5.24	4.70	4.61	3.81
Prices, Production, Labor		*Index Numbers (2000=100): Period Averages*
Share Prices	62	32.7	35.0	39.7	38.7	44.1	60.4	77.3	80.1	100.0	76.2	57.6	45.5
Producer Prices	63	†95.85	96.00	96.58	98.26	97.06	98.20	97.81	96.81	100.00	103.03	102.63	104.38
Consumer Prices	64	86.1	89.9	92.3	93.9	95.3	97.1	98.0	98.6	100.0	102.0	103.4	104.5
Harmonized CPI	64h	....	....	....	94.2	95.3	96.8	97.3	98.0	100.0	101.2	102.6	103.7
Industrial Production	66	83.7	82.8	86.6	84.2	85.9	89.9	90.5	94.3	100.0	95.8	95.6	99.7
		Number in Thousands: Period Averages
Labor Force	67d	39,044	39,139	39,218	40,083	39,455	39,694	39,709	39,905	39,731	39,966	40,022	....
Employment	67e	36,940	36,380	†36,075	36,048	35,982	35,805	35,860	36,402	36,604	36,816	36,586	36,172
Unemployment	67c	2,621	3,443	3,693	3,612	3,980	4,400	4,266	4,093	3,887	3,852	4,071	4,380
Unemployment Rate (%)	67r	....	9.8	10.6	10.4	11.5	12.7	12.3	11.7	10.7	10.4	10.9	11.7

Germany 134

		1992	1993	1994	1995	1996	1997	1998	1999	2000	2001	2002	2003
International Transactions		*Billions of Deutsche Mark through 1998; Billions of Euros Beginning 1999*											
Exports	70	658.47	632.22	694.69	749.54	788.94	888.64	954.67	†510.01	597.48	638.27	648.31	664.18
Imports, c.i.f.	71	628.19	571.91	622.92	664.23	690.40	772.33	828.29	†444.80	538.34	542.77	520.60	531.97
Imports, f.o.b.	71.v	612.56	556.41	605.96	646.14	671.59	751.29	805.72	†432.68	523.68	527.99	506.42	516.81
						1995=100							
Volume of Exports	72	87.8	84.0	96.0	†100.0	107.6	120.7	130.5	136.4	....	....	....	....
Volume of Imports	73	100.0	90.3	98.4	†100.0	106.0	115.5	126.9	132.9	....	....	....	....
						2000=100							
Unit Value of Exports	74	103.7	98.9	98.0	†100.2	98.1	98.4	97.9	96.4	†100.0	101.9	99.3	96.6
Unit Value of Imports	75	94.2	89.1	90.8	†93.3	91.5	93.9	91.7	90.1	†100.0	100.0	95.1	90.1
Export Prices	76	93.6	93.6	94.5	95.8	95.8	97.2	97.2	96.6	100.0	101.0	100.9	100.9
Import Prices	76.x	90.1	88.7	89.5	89.7	90.1	93.3	90.4	89.9	100.0	100.6	98.1	96.3
Balance of Payments		*Billions of US Dollars: Minus Sign Indicates Debit*											
Current Account, n.i.e.	78ald	−19.25	−13.81	−29.42	−26.96	−13.73	−8.66	−11.65	−22.69	−25.22	1.71	43.44	53.51
Goods: Exports f.o.b.	78aad	430.48	382.68	430.55	523.58	522.58	510.02	542.62	542.72	549.83	570.54	617.50	750.32
Goods: Imports f.o.b.	78abd	−402.28	−341.51	−379.52	−459.67	−453.20	−439.90	−465.71	−472.69	−492.38	−481.28	−489.30	−600.95
Trade Balance	78acd	28.20	41.17	51.03	63.91	69.38	70.12	76.91	70.03	57.45	89.25	128.21	149.37
Services: Credit	78add	68.32	63.67	65.71	80.23	83.85	82.73	84.50	83.89	83.10	88.36	104.63	123.00
Services: Debit	78aed	−104.72	−101.98	−112.17	−132.52	−134.35	−129.65	−135.12	−141.00	−137.25	−141.93	−147.33	−172.48
Balance on Goods & Services	78afd	−8.20	2.86	4.57	11.62	18.87	23.21	26.29	12.91	3.29	35.68	85.51	99.89
Income: Credit	78agd	79.50	79.01	70.01	82.76	81.58	80.43	83.43	86.80	98.40	93.43	90.39	110.55
Income: Debit	78ahd	−57.74	−62.36	−67.09	−82.57	−80.36	−81.92	−91.03	−95.82	−100.87	−102.91	−106.09	−124.40
Balance on Gds, Serv. & Inc.	78aid	13.56	19.51	7.49	11.81	20.09	21.72	18.69	3.89	.82	26.20	69.81	86.04
Current Transfers, n.i.e.: Credit	78ajd	14.90	13.18	13.63	16.44	17.50	15.95	15.96	17.07	14.98	14.83	15.37	18.43
Current Transfers: Debit	78akd	−47.71	−46.50	−50.54	−55.21	−51.32	−46.33	−46.30	−43.66	−41.01	−39.32	−41.74	−50.96
Capital Account, n.i.e.	78bcd	−1.26	−1.15	−1.67	−2.73	−2.18	−	.72	−.16	6.19	−.33	−.23	.36
Capital Account, n.i.e.: Credit	78bad	1.12	1.38	1.56	1.68	2.76	2.83	3.31	3.00	9.41	1.87	2.09	3.23
Capital Account: Debit	78bbd	−2.38	−2.53	−3.23	−4.41	−4.94	−2.82	−2.59	−3.16	−3.22	−2.20	−2.32	−2.87
Financial Account, n.i.e.	78bjd	48.03	12.84	34.34	44.09	16.12	1.19	17.84	−28.12	28.99	−23.80	−70.20	−62.72
Direct Investment Abroad	78bdd	−18.73	−17.14	−18.94	−39.10	−50.75	−42.73	−89.93	−109.62	−59.74	−36.50	−9.29	−1.52
Dir. Invest. in Rep. Econ., n.i.e.	78bed	−2.12	.40	7.29	11.99	6.43	12.80	23.64	55.63	210.09	20.83	35.55	11.27
Portfolio Investment Assets	78bfd	−44.72	−25.33	−41.48	−18.05	−30.89	−90.02	−145.49	−190.26	−191.55	−111.55	−60.36	−37.59
Equity Securities	78bkd	−40.45	−16.80	−20.97	.28	−17.52	−42.62	−78.33	−87.57	−127.50	−27.53	−10.39	2.73
Debt Securities	78bld	−4.27	−8.53	−20.51	−18.33	−13.38	−47.39	−67.17	−102.69	−64.04	−84.03	−49.97	−40.32
Portfolio Investment Liab., n.i.e.	78bgd	76.93	145.72	10.64	53.15	93.91	91.03	150.91	177.86	40.88	133.14	101.76	103.52
Equity Securities	78bmd	−2.80	7.54	3.92	−1.51	12.98	12.87	56.77	28.71	−27.96	76.89	13.62	27.08
Debt Securities	78bnd	79.73	138.18	6.72	54.66	80.92	78.16	94.14	149.15	68.84	56.24	88.13	76.44
Financial Derivatives Assets	78bwd	−	−	−	−	−	−	−	−	−	−	−	−
Financial Derivatives Liabilities	78bxd	−.28	−.66	.81	−.56	−5.73	−8.70	−7.99	−2.10	−11.44	6.05	−1.08	−.70
Other Investment Assets	78bhd	−7.29	−131.42	−.71	−61.28	−39.77	−83.53	−86.02	−70.85	−80.17	−102.40	−164.47	−153.36
Monetary Authorities	78bod	−.02	−.01	.17	.28	.35	.29	−.11	−51.70	39.37	20.70	−33.41	−.21
General Government	78bpd	−6.36	−7.07	2.46	−6.72	−.34	−2.33	−.63	8.46	−17.98	14.84	6.70	1.43
Banks	78bqd	3.69	−88.30	14.90	−55.17	−39.13	−80.40	−79.22	−46.32	−92.60	−118.47	−126.98	−135.11
Other Sectors	78brd	−4.61	−36.05	−18.24	.34	−.64	−1.09	−6.06	18.71	−8.97	−19.48	−10.78	−19.48
Other Investment Liab., n.i.e.	78bid	44.23	41.28	76.72	97.94	42.93	122.34	172.73	111.24	120.93	66.64	27.69	15.68
Monetary Authorities	78bsd	−9.53	−1.57	−2.04	−2.65	−1.17	−.39	2.16	−2.21	.37	2.35	.53	2.13
General Government	78btd	−1.19	3.73	2.12	3.84	3.45	−7.75	.10	−12.29	.29	.68	−1.37	4.04
Banks	78bud	48.01	35.36	69.32	83.74	36.62	120.20	159.94	103.54	109.95	52.86	25.88	10.31
Other Sectors	78bvd	6.93	3.76	7.32	13.01	4.03	10.29	10.53	22.21	10.32	10.76	2.66	−.80
Net Errors and Omissions	78cad	9.65	−12.08	−5.29	−7.17	−1.41	3.71	−2.90	36.86	−15.19	16.95	25.01	8.16
Overall Balance	78cbd	37.18	−14.20	−2.04	7.22	−1.20	−3.75	4.02	−14.11	−5.22	−5.47	−1.98	−.68
Reserves and Related Items	79dad	−37.18	14.20	2.04	−7.22	1.20	3.75	−4.02	14.11	5.22	5.47	1.98	.68
Reserve Assets	79dbd	−37.18	14.20	2.04	−7.22	1.20	3.75	−4.02	14.11	5.22	5.47	1.98	.68
Use of Fund Credit and Loans	79dcd	−	−	−	−	−	−	−	−	−	−	−	−
Exceptional Financing	79ded	....	....	....	....	....	....	....	....	....	....	....	....

2004, International Monetary Fund : *International Financial Statistics Yearbook*

Germany 134

		1992	1993	1994	1995	1996	1997	1998	1999	2000	2001	2002	2003
International Investment Position						*Billions of US Dollars*							
Assets..............................	79aad	1,172.60	1,285.19	1,431.95	1,663.83	1,699.68	1,749.43	2,208.94	2,389.48	2,593.54	2,698.48	3,217.65	....
Direct Investment Abroad........	79abd	148.46	156.70	188.32	234.13	250.14	296.28	365.22	411.94	484.86	545.17	654.95	....
Portfolio Investment............	79acd	246.49	279.91	320.00	385.42	413.69	502.70	724.01	893.30	1,001.95	987.74	1,087.56	....
Equity Securities............	79add	94.61	115.20	145.79	165.97	187.49	241.39	370.57	507.08	572.72	494.35	440.89	....
Debt Securities.............	79aed	151.88	164.70	174.22	219.45	226.20	261.31	353.44	386.21	429.24	493.39	646.67	....
Financial Derivatives...........	79ald	–	–	–	–	–	–	–	–	–	–	–	....
Other Investment................	79afd	690.08	778.99	850.27	959.66	958.95	879.65	1,039.60	990.77	1,019.43	1,083.41	1,386.00	....
Monetary Authorities.........	79agd	1.62	1.52	1.52	1.36	.93	.54	.64	49.14	6.46	−15.04	19.87	....
General Government.........	79ahd	43.37	48.60	52.34	62.62	59.52	55.32	61.63	44.38	61.13	44.84	44.92	....
Banks........................	79aid	346.69	413.31	426.96	504.96	516.49	545.60	662.82	625.10	679.04	768.13	996.21	....
Other Sectors................	79ajd	298.40	315.56	369.45	390.72	382.01	278.19	314.50	272.15	272.80	285.48	324.99	....
Reserve Assets....................	79akd	87.58	69.59	73.35	84.62	76.90	70.79	80.11	93.48	87.30	82.16	89.14	....
Liabilities.........................	79lad	909.26	1,079.71	1,236.60	1,534.68	1,610.14	1,675.87	2,215.51	2,309.64	2,539.26	2,534.73	2,987.53	....
Dir. Invest. in Rep. Economy....	79lbd	75.48	71.17	85.72	101.48	101.73	188.88	250.34	288.56	460.64	404.50	510.23	....
Portfolio Investment............	79lcd	326.07	486.93	493.72	636.90	705.19	756.01	1,023.21	1,083.63	1,040.02	1,060.26	1,250.82	....
Equity Securities............	79ldd	69.46	93.61	99.51	110.78	140.29	186.98	289.98	375.41	299.72	295.50	214.42	....
Debt Securities.............	79led	256.61	393.32	394.21	526.13	564.90	569.04	733.23	708.22	740.30	764.76	1,036.39	....
Financial Derivatives...........	79lld	–	–	–	–	–	–	–	–	–	–	–	....
Other Investment................	79lfd	507.72	521.62	657.16	796.29	803.22	730.97	941.97	937.46	1,038.61	1,069.97	1,226.48	....
Monetary Authorities.........	79lgd	25.00	22.01	22.13	20.88	18.88	16.02	19.31	14.59	13.90	15.07	9.44	....
General Government.........	79lhd	26.82	28.17	33.51	46.24	45.54	32.26	34.55	18.42	17.64	17.49	18.99	....
Banks........................	79lid	263.47	285.75	380.24	485.00	493.21	564.48	760.33	780.21	844.91	863.22	983.43	....
Other Sectors................	79ljd	192.43	185.69	221.29	244.18	245.59	118.21	127.78	124.24	162.16	174.19	214.62	....
Government Finance													
Central Government		*Billions of Deutsche Mark through 1998; Millions of Euros Beginning 1999: Year Ending December 31*											
Deficit (-) or Surplus...........	80	†−73.39	−78.79	−44.85	−61.83	−74.19	−48.97p	−35.12p	....	....	....	....	....
Revenue.........................	81	†985.18	1,017.55	1,099.41	1,124.66	1,133.06	1,160.25	1,188.14	....	....	....	....	....
Grants Received.................	81z	†4.52	5.11	5.24	6.10	6.70	6.44	6.31	....	....	....	....	....
Expenditure.....................	82	†1,045.45	1,084.30	1,142.81	1,188.04	1,213.20	1,214.65	1,233.89	....	....	....	....	....
Lending Minus Repayments........	83	†13.83	12.10	15.84	3.60	3.02	−3.01	−17.98	....	....	....	....	....
Overall Cash Adjustment........	80x	†−3.81	−5.05	9.15	−.95	2.27	−4.02	−13.66	....	....	....	....	....
Financing													
Net Borrowing...................	84	†56.40	91.49	34.23	46.86	70.19	50.41	35.73	25.10	....	....	....	....
Net borrowing: Domestic.....	84a	†1.78	−16.45	57.19	−11.61	15.91	−29.50	−44.59	2.16	....	....	....	....
Net borrowing: Foreign......	85a	†54.62	107.94	−22.96	58.47	54.28	79.91	80.32	22.94	....	....	....	....
Use of Cash Balances...........	87	†16.99	−12.70	10.62	14.97	4.00	−1.44	−.61	−6.30	....	....	....	....
Debt............................	88	†801.86	902.71	1,004.15	1,289.81	1,373.07	1,423.68	1,461.87	772.44	....	....	....	....
Debt: Domestic.................	88a	†504.03	496.94	610.53	762.27	791.26	758.67	716.52	368.41	....	....	....	....
Debt: Foreign..................	89a	†297.83	405.77	393.62	527.54	581.81	665.01	745.35	404.03	....	....	....	....
General Government						*As Percent of Gross Domestic Product*							
Deficit (-) or Surplus...........	80g	−2.6	−3.2	−2.4	−3.3	−3.4	−2.7	−2.2	−1.6	1.2	−2.7	....	....
Debt............................	88g	44.1	48.0	50.2	58.3	59.8	60.9	60.9	61.3	60.3	59.8	....	....
National Accounts						*Billions of Deutsche Mark: through 1998; Billions of Euros Beginning 1999*							
Househ.Cons.Expend.,incl.NPISHs....	96f.c	1,786.0	1,857.5	1,925.1	2,001.6	2,055.4	2,113.0	2,170.7	†1,156.0	1,196.2	1,232.7	1,236.5	1,247.1
Government Consumption Expend...	91f.c	623.6	643.0	669.2	697.8	717.5	712.9	722.8	†378.2	385.6	394.1	404.4	410.9
Gross Fixed Capital Formation........	93e.c	709.4	689.2	729.7	751.1	741.2	732.7	726.7	†426.4	440.0	420.7	392.0	377.7
Changes in Inventories............	93i.c	−7.0	−17.3	1.9	8.1	−5.6	1.3	17.2	†2.1	.7	−15.0	−13.2	....
Exports of Goods and Services........	90c.c	774.0	736.5	800.1	862.3	908.8	1,025.2	1,092.1	†586.4	686.1	731.5	757.6	761.0
Imports of Goods and Services (-).....	98c.c	779.8	729.5	787.1	837.4	869.5	974.4	1,037.7	†570.4	678.6	690.2	667.0	670.5
Gross Domestic Product (GDP)........	99b.c	3,155.2	3,235.4	3,394.4	3,523.0	3,586.0	3,666.6	3,769.9	†1,978.6	2,030.0	2,073.7	2,110.4	2,129.2
Net Primary Income from Abroad......	98.nc	15.5	13.4	−13.8	−18.6	−15.7	−17.8	−27.3	†−13.5	−9.7	−8.1	−1.6	−11.1
Gross National Income (GNI).........	99a.c	3,170.6	3,248.9	3,380.6	3,504.4	3,570.9	3,648.6	3,758.6	†1,965.1	2,020.3	2,065.6	2,108.8	2,118.2
Net Current Transf.from Abroad........	98t.c	−31.7	−37.5	−39.7	−32.7	−33.3	−36.3	−39.5	†−19.1	−21.0	−21.0	−23.5	−24.9
Gross Nat'l Disposable Inc.(GNDI).....	99i.c	3,139.7	3,212.3	3,341.6	3,471.8	3,537.6	3,612.6	3,719.4	†1,946.7	1,998.3	1,723.7	1,757.3	....
Gross Saving....................	99s.c	728.2	710.5	745.1	770.2	764.8	787.1	819.1	†411.9	417.5	417.9	444.4	435.3
Consumption of Fixed Capital........	99cfc	451.1	482.5	502.4	521.2	532.3	544.6	557.8	†291.4	302.4	311.1	317.7	319.7
GDP Volume 1995 Prices............	99b.r	3,421.0	3,383.8	3,463.2	3,523.0	3,549.6	3,601.1	3,666.5	†1,914.8	1,969.5	1,986.2	1,989.7	1,987.7
GDP Volume (2000=100)............	99bvr	88.8	87.8	89.9	91.5	92.1	93.5	95.2	†97.2	100.0	100.8	101.0	100.9
GDP Deflator (2000=100)...........	99bir	89.5	92.8	95.1	97.0	98.0	98.8	99.8	†100.3	100.0	101.3	102.9	103.9
						Millions: Midyear Estimates							
Population........................	99z	80.41	80.89	81.32	81.66	81.91	82.07	82.16	82.22	82.28	82.35	82.41	82.48

Ghana 652

		1992	1993	1994	1995	1996	1997	1998	1999	2000	2001	2002	2003
Exchange Rates		\multicolumn{12}{c}{*Cedis per SDR: End of Period*}
Market Rate............................	aa	716.15e	1,125.87	1,536.68	2,154.33	2,522.74	3,066.48	3,274.49	4,852.02	9,182.45	9,201.70	11,472.74	13,154.28
		\multicolumn{12}{c}{*Cedis per US Dollar: End of Period (ae) Period Average (rf)*}
Market Rate............................	ae	520.83e	819.67	1,052.63	1,449.28	1,754.39	2,272.73	2,325.58	3,535.14	7,047.65	7,321.94	8,438.82	8,852.32
Market Rate............................	rf	437.09	649.06	956.71	1,200.43	1,637.23	2,050.17	2,314.15	2,669.30	5,455.06	7,170.76	7,932.70	8,677.37
		\multicolumn{12}{c}{*Index Numbers (2000=100): Period Averages*}
Nominal Effective Exchange Rate.....	nec	789.88	621.79	454.71	347.85	262.39	222.97	205.51	186.37	100.00	75.99	67.08	55.21
Real Effective Exchange Rate............	rec	153.29	133.49	107.98	124.52	134.59	142.65	154.29	155.05	100.00	100.65	100.00	101.40
Fund Position		\multicolumn{12}{c}{*Millions of SDRs: End of Period*}
Quota...................................	2f.s	274.0	274.0	274.0	274.0	274.0	274.0	274.0	369.0	369.0	369.0	369.0	369.0
SDRs.....................................	1b.s	3.2	.4	2.9	1.6	1.6	2.5	42.4	13.3	.4	3.2	2.7	31.5
Reserve Position in the Fund............	1c.s	17.4	17.4	17.4	17.4	17.4	17.4	17.4	41.1	–	–	–	–
Total Fund Cred.&Loans Outstg........	2tl	537.8	537.3	479.7	436.2	377.3	257.0	236.9	225.8	224.5	225.7	267.3	304.9
International Liquidity		\multicolumn{12}{c}{*Millions of US Dollars Unless Otherwise Indicated: End of Period*}
Total Reserves minus Gold...............	1l.d	319.9	409.7	583.9	697.5	828.7	537.8	377.0	453.8	232.1	298.2	539.7	1,352.8
SDRs.....................................	1b.d	4.4	.5	4.2	2.4	2.2	3.4	59.7	18.2	.5	4.0	3.7	46.8
Reserve Position in the Fund..........	1c.d	23.9	23.9	25.4	25.8	25.0	23.4	24.5	56.5	–	–	–	–
Foreign Exchange........................	1d.d	291.6	385.3	554.3	669.2	801.5	511.0	292.8	379.1	231.5	294.2	536.1	1,306.0
Gold (Million Fine Troy Ounces)........	1ad	.275	.275	.275	.275	.275	.275	.277	.279	.280	.281	.281	.281
Gold (National Valuation)................	1and	78.1	77.2	77.2	77.4	77.2	77.3	78.8	78.9	79.3	78.9	96.5	116.1
Monetary Authorities:Other Assets...	3..d	41.7	33.5	36.6	52.4	55.4	47.0	47.8	48.7	48.9	37.5	37.8	38.1
Monetary Authorities: Other Liab.....	4..d	67.6	56.3	96.5	34.8	45.4	126.7	53.3	41.0	119.0	38.0	46.9	48.2
Banking Institutions: Assets.............	7a.d	311.1	313.8	405.4	327.9	396.7	392.3	242.9	194.4	168.6	181.4	207.5	331.1
Liabilities...................	7b.d	21.1	35.3	32.4	45.8	62.8	75.7	26.1	140.4	116.3	51.7	66.3	140.5
Monetary Authorities		\multicolumn{12}{c}{*Billions of Cedis: End of Period*}
Foreign Assets............................	11	192.2	380.0	663.2	1,079.9	1,182.1	1,337.6	† 1,464.0	1,382.3	2,522.4	2,865.4	5,728.2	12,967.2
Claims on Central Government........	12a	482.6	850.6	893.0	1,405.5	1,553.3	2,001.7	† 10,999.6	15,242.7	24,281.3	2,480.3	30,939.8	7,520.0
Claims on Nonfin.Pub.Enterprises.....	12c	3.8	44.8	148.8	151.9	135.8	71.9	† 37.5	54.6	23.8	4.4	283.4	3.4
Claims on Private Sector................	12d	–	–	–	–	–	–	† 26.8	32.2	42.5	52.7	72.5	70.1
Claims on Banking Institutions.........	12e	4.2	6.8	6.7	8.3	9.4	33.0	† 50.3	465.9	842.8	1,398.4	1,136.1	597.1
Claims on Nonbank Financial Insts...	12g	–	–	–	37.2	10.7	4.6	† .9	.9	.3	.3	.3	4.7
Reserve Money............................	14	245.8	257.9	461.3	623.1	902.2	1,203.1	† 1,518.0	2,101.6	3,247.1	4,580.0	6,696.0	8,578.1
of which: Currency Outside Banks..	14a	183.5	222.2	368.8	546.3	724.0	981.8	† 1,164.6	1,585.9	2,637.6	3,089.0	4,671.6	6,337.8
Other Liabs. to Banking Insts...........	14n	–	–	–	–	–	–	† 56.6	124.6	328.9	87.5	598.5	2,273.2
Time, Savings,& Fgn.Ccy. Deposits...	15	–	–	–	–	–	–	† 8.8	135.7	546.8	30.2	32.8	181.1
Liabs. of Central Bank: Securities......	16ac	148.1	334.5	479.5	722.4	518.2	182.6	† –	–	–	–	–	1,817.3
Restricted Deposits........................	16b	.9	.9	.9	.9	.9	–	† –	–	–	–	–	–
Foreign Liabilities........................	16c	420.4	651.1	838.7	990.3	1,031.5	1,076.0	† 899.6	1,240.6	2,900.1	2,354.7	3,462.6	4,438.0
Central Government Deposits...........	16d	104.2	237.2	318.1	494.3	324.5	484.7	† 9,945.0	13,768.5	21,704.2	525.5	28,127.8	5,086.5
Capital Accounts...........................	17a	48.4	88.5	127.1	296.7	351.1	626.1	† 419.8	500.3	815.7	797.5	1,163.1	1,044.7
Other Items (Net)............................	17r	–285.0	–287.8	–514.0	–444.9	–237.2	–123.7	† –268.6	–692.6	–1,829.8	–1,574.0	–1,920.6	–2,256.4
Banking Institutions		\multicolumn{12}{c}{*Billions of Cedis: End of Period*}
Reserves..................................	20	78.7	41.6	88.8	106.8	194.1	219.3	† 365.3	559.0	779.1	1,398.0	1,576.2	2,325.4
Claims on Mon.Author.:Securities....	20c	82.6	293.9	410.5	614.8	512.1	182.6	† –	–	–	–	–	1,033.2
Other Claims on Monetary Author....	20n	–	–	–	–	–	–	† 56.6	124.6	259.8	65.6	598.5	584.1
Foreign Assets............................	21	162.0	257.2	426.8	475.3	695.9	891.7	† 564.9	687.2	1,188.3	1,328.4	1,751.3	2,930.9
Claims on Central Government........	22a	.3	.3	.3	.3	74.1	752.3	† 1,444.5	2,413.5	2,913.6	4,481.3	5,603.6	6,214.0
Claims on Local Government..........	22b	2.2	–	–	–	–	–	† –	–	–	.2	–	–
Claims on Nonfin.Pub.Enterprises.....	22c	75.7	44.1	29.5	44.5	57.4	144.0	† 263.8	373.2	1,225.6	1,805.4	949.7	2,003.1
Claims on Private Sector................	22d	138.5	187.3	273.3	393.3	680.9	1,156.6	† 1,591.9	2,553.0	3,751.1	4,460.5	5,813.2	7,759.7
Claims on Nonbank Financial Insts...	22g	.3	.1	.2	1.7	–	–	† 26.7	77.7	392.5	343.6	801.1	74.6
Demand Deposits........................	24	174.8	235.3	320.9	371.1	485.0	788.5	† 981.8	892.1	791.7	1,930.3	3,339.5	4,342.8
Time, Savings,& Fgn.Ccy. Deposits...	25	214.6	306.7	478.3	752.4	1,116.8	1,585.7	† 1,793.4	2,332.3	3,659.5	5,006.2	6,909.9	9,218.4
Money Market Instruments...............	26aa	–	–	–	–	–	–	† –	11.5	.1	93.6	137.6	–
Restricted Deposits........................	26b	–	–	–	–	–	–	† 120.9	141.2	727.7	1,186.3	603.6	588.1
Foreign Liabilities........................	26c	11.0	28.9	34.1	66.3	110.2	172.0	† 60.6	496.3	819.7	378.8	559.7	1,243.9
Central Government Deposits..........	26d	22.5	63.5	69.2	76.0	105.4	45.9	† 197.4	286.2	256.1	406.7	743.0	1,460.0
Credit from Monetary Authorities.....	26g	5.0	5.8	19.8	50.9	40.1	48.2	† 87.7	514.7	931.5	1,114.1	850.4	650.9
Liab. to Nonbank Financial Insts.......	26j	–	–	–	–	–	–	† 16.9	56.2	167.0	284.6	431.9	221.3
Capital Accounts...........................	27a	93.8	135.5	257.2	276.2	363.7	534.2	† 608.3	879.2	1,419.3	1,923.2	2,359.0	3,077.7
Other Items (Net)............................	27r	18.5	48.8	49.9	43.7	–6.5	171.9	† 446.7	1,178.5	1,737.5	1,559.3	1,158.9	2,121.8

2004, International Monetary Fund : *International Financial Statistics Yearbook*

Ghana 652

		1992	1993	1994	1995	1996	1997	1998	1999	2000	2001	2002	2003
Banking Survey						*Billions of Cedis: End of Period*							
Foreign Assets (Net)	31n	−77.1	−42.8	217.1	498.6	736.3	981.3	†1,068.7	332.5	−9.1	1,460.3	3,457.1	10,216.2
Domestic Credit	32	576.6	826.6	957.7	1,464.1	2,082.3	3,600.4	†4,249.3	6,693.2	10,670.3	12,696.5	15,592.7	17,103.3
Claims on Central Govt. (Net)	32an	356.2	550.3	506.0	835.5	1,197.5	2,223.3	†2,301.8	3,601.5	5,234.5	6,029.4	7,672.6	7,187.5
Claims on Local Government	32b	2.2	–	–	–	–	–	†–	–	–	.2	–	–
Claims on Nonfin.Pub.Enterprises	32c	79.5	88.9	178.3	196.4	193.2	215.9	†301.3	427.8	1,249.3	1,809.8	1,233.1	2,006.5
Claims on Private Sector	32d	138.5	187.3	273.3	393.3	680.9	1,156.6	†1,618.7	2,585.3	3,793.6	4,513.2	5,885.7	7,829.9
Claims on Nonbank Financial Insts.	32g	.3	.1	.2	38.9	10.7	4.6	†27.6	78.6	392.8	343.9	801.4	79.3
Money	34	360.7	461.3	693.5	925.3	1,218.6	1,779.3	†2,151.2	2,490.2	3,441.5	5,035.0	8,048.6	10,723.4
Quasi-Money	35	214.6	306.7	478.3	752.4	1,116.8	1,585.7	†1,802.2	2,468.0	4,206.3	5,036.4	6,942.7	9,399.6
Money Market Instruments	36aa	–	–	–	–	–	–	†–	11.5	.1	93.6	137.6	–
Liabs. of Central Bank: Securities	36ac	65.5	40.6	69.0	107.6	6.1	–	†–	–	–	–	–	784.1
Restricted Deposits	36b	.9	.9	.9	.9	.9	–	†120.9	141.2	727.7	1,186.3	603.6	588.1
Liab. to Nonbank Financial Insts.	36j	–	–	–	–	–	–	†16.9	56.2	167.0	284.6	431.9	221.3
Capital Accounts	37a	142.2	223.9	384.3	572.9	714.7	1,160.3	†1,028.1	1,379.5	2,234.9	2,720.7	3,522.1	4,122.4
Other Items (Net)	37r	−284.4	−249.7	−451.2	−396.5	−238.5	56.5	†198.8	479.1	−116.3	−199.8	−636.7	1,480.4
Money plus Quasi-Money	35l	575.3	768.0	1,171.8	1,677.7	2,335.3	3,364.9	†3,953.4	4,958.3	7,647.8	10,071.4	14,991.3	20,123.0
Interest Rates						*Percent Per Annum*							
Discount Rate (End of Period)	60	30.00	35.00	33.00	45.00	45.00	45.00	37.00	27.00	27.00	27.00	24.50	21.50
Treasury Bill Rate	60c	19.38	30.95	27.72	35.38	41.64	42.77	34.33	26.37	36.28	40.96	25.11	27.25
Deposit Rate	60l	16.32	23.63	23.15	28.73	34.50	35.76	32.05	23.56	28.60	30.85	16.21	14.32
Prices and Labor						*Index Numbers (2000=100): Period Averages*							
Consumer Prices	64	13.3	16.6	20.7	33.1	48.5	†62.0	71.1	79.9	100.0	132.9	152.6	193.3
						Number in Thousands: Period Averages							
Unemployment	67c	31	39	37	41	….	….	….	….	….	….	….	….
International Transactions						*Billions of Cedis*							
Exports	70	547	632	1,359	2,070	2,733	3,353	4,151	….	….	….	….	….
Cocoa Beans	70r	118	162	266	457	791	826	1,437	1,422	2,170	….	….	….
Imports, c.i.f.	71	951	2,439	2,029	2,289	3,452	4,769	5,932	9,347	16,171	….	….	….
Volume of Exports						*1995=100*							
Cocoa Beans	72r	88.6	101.6	94.2	100.0	142.6	10.3	129.6	152.1	….	….	….	….
Export Prices													
Cocoa Beans (Unit Value)	74r	29.2	34.9	61.8	100.0	121.4	1,748.6	242.8	204.6	….	….	….	….

Ghana 652

		1992	1993	1994	1995	1996	1997	1998	1999	2000	2001	2002	2003
Balance of Payments		\multicolumn{12}{c}{*Millions of US Dollars: Minus Sign Indicates Debit*}
Current Account, n.i.e.	78ald	−377.0	−558.8	−254.6	−143.7	−306.9	−403.5	−521.7	−964.3	−386.5	−324.6	−31.8	254.9
Goods: Exports f.o.b.	78aad	986.3	1,063.6	1,237.7	1,431.2	1,570.0	1,489.9	2,090.8	2,005.5	1,936.3	1,867.1	2,015.2	2,562.4
Goods: Imports f.o.b.	78abd	−1,456.5	−1,728.0	−1,579.9	−1,687.8	−1,950.7	−2,143.7	−2,991.6	−3,279.9	−2,766.6	−2,968.5	−2,707.0	−3,276.1
Trade Balance	78acd	−470.2	−664.4	−342.2	−256.6	−380.7	−653.9	−900.8	−1,274.4	−830.3	−1,101.4	−691.8	−713.7
Services: Credit	78add	154.4	144.7	147.5	150.6	156.8	164.9	440.9	467.8	504.2	531.7	554.9	630.0
Services: Debit	78aed	−425.3	−445.3	−420.8	−431.7	−424.8	−468.7	−659.4	−646.0	−583.7	−606.1	−620.9	−903.7
Balance on Goods & Services	78afd	−741.1	−965.0	−615.5	−537.7	−648.7	−957.7	−1,119.3	−1,452.6	−909.8	−1,175.8	−757.8	−987.4
Income: Credit	78agd	−15.4	−6.2	−3.0	13.7	23.5	26.7	26.7	15.0	15.6	16.3	14.7	21.4
Income: Debit	78ahd	−90.8	−105.1	−107.9	−142.9	−163.4	−32.6	−163.0	−146.8	−123.2	−124.1	−188.9	−178.3
Balance on Gds, Serv. & Inc.	78aid	−847.3	−1,076.3	−726.4	−666.9	−788.6	−963.6	−1,255.6	−1,584.4	−1,017.4	−1,283.6	−932.0	−1,144.3
Current Transfers, n.i.e.: Credit	78ajd	484.8	532.0	487.3	538.9	497.9	576.5	751.0	637.9	649.3	978.4	912.4	1,408.4
Current Transfers: Debit	78akd	−14.5	−14.5	−15.5	−15.7	−16.2	−16.4	−17.1	−17.8	−18.4	−19.4	−12.2	−9.2
Capital Account, n.i.e.	78bcd	−.1	−.1	−.1	−	−	−	−	−	−	−	−	−
Capital Account, n.i.e.: Credit	78bad	−	−	−	−	−	−	−	−	−	−	−	−
Capital Account: Debit	78bbd	−.1	−.1	−.1	−	−	−	−	−	−	−	−	−
Financial Account, n.i.e.	78bjd	275.9	642.6	481.7	304.4	285.5	492.8	560.9	746.0	369.3	392.2	−38.7	347.3
Direct Investment Abroad	78bdd	−	−	−	−	−	−	−	−	−	−	−	−
Dir. Invest. in Rep. Econ., n.i.e.	78bed	22.5	125.0	233.0	106.5	120.0	81.8	167.4	243.7	165.9	89.3	58.9	136.7
Portfolio Investment Assets	78bfd	−	−	−	−	−	−	−	−	−	−	−	−
Equity Securities	78bkd	−	−	−	−	−	−	−	−	−	−	−	−
Debt Securities	78bld	−	−	−	−	−	−	−	−	−	−	−	−
Portfolio Investment Liab., n.i.e.	78bgd	−	−	−	−	−	−	−	−	−	−	−	−
Equity Securities	78bmd	−	−	−	−	−	−	−	−	−	−	−	−
Debt Securities	78bnd	−	−	−	−	−	−	−	−	−	−	−	−
Financial Derivatives Assets	78bwd	....	....	....	−	−	−	−	−	−	−	−	−
Financial Derivatives Liabilities	78bxd	....	....	....	−	−	−	−	−	−	−	−	−
Other Investment Assets	78bhd	−49.8	5.8	−119.6	75.7	50.0	−	45.0	47.5	70.0	65.0	94.7	68.0
Monetary Authorities	78bod	−	−	−	−	−	−	−	−	−	−	−	−
General Government	78bpd	−	−	−	.7	−	−	−	47.5	70.0	−	14.7	−
Banks	78bqd	−5.1	−1.2	−93.3	−	−	−	−	−	−	−	−	−
Other Sectors	78brd	−44.7	7.0	−26.3	75.0	50.0	−	45.0	−	−	65.0	80.0	68.0
Other Investment Liab., n.i.e.	78bid	303.2	511.8	368.3	122.2	115.5	411.0	348.5	454.8	133.4	237.9	−192.3	142.6
Monetary Authorities	78bsd	−33.4	32.2	−19.4	−	−	−	−	−	−	−	−	−
General Government	78btd	386.5	370.2	295.3	135.5	313.9	404.5	327.2	144.8	81.7	45.6	−115.2	62.7
Banks	78bud	−16.2	44.8	64.8	−54.2	−148.4	32.9	88.0	186.4	40.8	144.3	−123.8	9.7
Other Sectors	78bvd	−33.7	64.6	27.6	40.9	−50.0	−26.4	−66.7	123.6	10.9	48.0	46.7	70.2
Net Errors and Omissions	78cad	−3.0	−49.9	26.1	22.1	−3.7	−12.1	−11.5	81.9	−168.6	−189.1	195.1	−46.9
Overall Balance	78cbd	−104.2	33.8	253.1	182.8	−25.0	77.2	27.6	−136.4	−185.8	−121.5	124.6	555.3
Reserves and Related Items	79dad	104.2	−33.8	−253.1	−182.8	25.0	−77.2	−27.6	136.4	185.8	121.5	−124.6	−555.3
Reserve Assets	79dbd	167.6	−32.7	−170.2	−117.5	110.3	88.5	−1.5	89.4	161.0	−80.3	−294.1	−785.1
Use of Fund Credit and Loans	79dcd	−63.4	−1.1	−82.9	−65.2	−85.3	−165.8	−26.1	−15.0	−2.3	.8	51.4	54.6
Exceptional Financing	79ded	−	−	−	−	−	−	−	62.0	27.0	201.0	118.0	175.2
Government Finance		\multicolumn{12}{c}{*Billions of Cedis: Year Ending December 31*}
Deficit (-) or Surplus	80	−144.4	−97.3	111.7	70.3	−335.5	−297.6	−1,048.8	....	....	....	....	....
Revenue	81	333.6	657.6	1,221.8	1,691.0	2,191.0	2,549.9	3,276.1	....	....	....	....	....
Grants Received	81z	32.7	66.6	39.5	93.8	77.5	66.6	161.9	....	....	....	....	....
Expenditure	82	498.8	813.5	1,141.3	1,698.7	2,515.2	2,908.9	4,513.2	....	....	....	....	....
Lending Minus Repayments	83	11.9	8.0	8.3	15.8	88.8	5.2	−26.4	....	....	....	....	....
Financing													
Domestic	84a	144.1	45.4	−26.7	−27.7	531.1	728.0	672.6	....	....	....	....	....
Foreign	85a	.3	51.9	−85.0	−42.6	−195.7	−430.3	376.2	....	....	....	....	....
National Accounts		\multicolumn{12}{c}{*Billions of Cedis: End of Period*}
Househ.Cons.Expend.,incl.NPISHs	96f	2,338.4	3,048.7	3,834.9	5,909.9	8,629.0	11,267.0	....	....	....	....	....	....
Government Consumption Expend	91f	400.1	568.2	714.3	935.9	1,365.6	1,743.8	....	....	....	....	....	....
Gross Fixed Capital Formation	93e	386.1	921.3	1,174.5	1,638.0	2,332.0	3,338.2	....	....	....	....	....	....
Changes in Inventories	93i	1.9	−60.7	72.2	−85.9	102.2	127.3	....	....	....	....	....	....
Exports of Goods and Services	90c	482.9	693.3	1,171.5	1,898.9	2,827.3	2,794.6	....	....	....	....	....	....
Imports of Goods and Services (-)	98c	806.4	1,298.3	1,762.2	2,544.2	3,916.9	5,157.5	....	....	....	....	....	....
Gross Domestic Product (GDP)	99b	2,802.9	3,872.5	5,205.2	7,752.6	11,339.2	14,113.4	....	....	....	....	....	....
Net Primary Income from Abroad	98.n	−46.4	72.9	106.1	155.1	220.0	273.9	....	....	....	....	....	....
Gross National Income (GNI)	99a	2,756.5	3,799.6	5,099.1	7,597.5	11,119.2	13,839.5	....	....	....	....	....	....
Consumption of Fixed Capital	99cf	156.3	329.0	411.2	514.0	800.8	996.7	....	....	....	....	....	....
GDP Volume 1975 Prices	99b.p	7.5	7.9	....	....	....	....	....	....	....	....	....	....
GDP Volume 1993 Prices	99b.p	....	3,872.5	3,999.1	4,160.0	4,351.2	4,533.0	....	....	....	....	....	....
GDP Volume (1995=100)	99bvp	88.7	†93.1	96.1	100.0	104.6	109.0	....	....	....	....	....	....
GDP Deflator (1995=100)	99bip	40.8	53.7	69.8	100.0	139.8	167.1	....	....	....	....	....	....
		\multicolumn{12}{c}{*Millions: Midyear Estimates*}
Population	99z	16.16	16.62	17.07	17.51	17.93	18.35	18.76	19.17	19.59	20.03	20.47	20.92

Greece 174

		1992	1993	1994	1995	1996	1997	1998	1999	2000	2001	2002	2003
Exchange Rates		*Drachmas per SDR Through 2000, Euros per SDR Thereafter End of Period*											
Market Rate............................	aa	295.05	342.32	350.51	352.36	355.20	381.31	397.87	450.79	476.37	1.4260	1.2964	1.1765
		Drachmas per US Dollar through 2000, Euros per US Dollar Thereafter: End of Period (ae) Period Average (rf)											
Market Rate............................	ae	214.58	249.22	240.10	237.04	247.02	282.61	282.57	328.44	365.62	1.1347	.9536	.7918
Market Rate............................	rf	190.62	229.25	242.60	231.66	240.71	273.06	295.53	305.65	365.40	1.1175	1.0626	.8860
		Drachmas per ECU through 1998; Drachmas per Euro through 2000: End of Period (ea) Period Average (eb)											
Euro Rate...............................	ea	260.20	278.20	294.78	303.76	306.83	312.12	330.01	†330.35	340.75	....	....	....
Euro Rate...............................	eb	246.60	267.99	287.21	299.54	301.48	308.51	331.50	†325.76	336.66	....	....	....
		Index Numbers (2000=100): Period Averages											
Market Rate............................	ahx	191.7	159.1	150.0	157.3	151.3	133.5	123.4	119.0	100.0	....	....	....
Nominal Effective Exchange Rate.....	neu	141.5	130.4	121.5	117.9	115.9	113.5	106.7	106.2	100.0	99.3	99.9	102.6
Real Effective Exchange Rate.........	reu	92.1	92.1	93.8	99.5	102.2	106.0	102.4	103.2	100.0	100.5	103.6	108.4
Fund Position		*Millions of SDRs: End of Period*											
Quota....................................	2f.s	587.6	587.6	587.6	587.6	587.6	587.6	587.6	823.0	823.0	823.0	823.0	823.0
SDRs.....................................	1b.s	–	.1	.2	–	.4	.2	.3	3.8	9.2	7.7	11.1	14.4
Reserve Position in the Fund..........	1c.s	116.9	113.7	113.7	113.7	113.7	113.7	191.5	285.0	227.8	284.3	322.5	334.3
Total Fund Cred.&Loans Outstg......	2tl	–	–	–	–	–	–	–	–	–	–	–	–
International Liquidity		*Millions of US Dollars Unless Otherwise Indicated: End of Period*											
Total Res.Min.Gold(Eurosys.Def.)....	1l.d	4,793.6	7,790.3	14,487.9	14,780.0	17,501.4	12,594.8	17,458.4	18,122.3	13,424.3	†5,154.2	8,082.8	4,361.4
SDRs.....................................	1b.d	–	.2	.3	–	.6	.3	.5	5.2	12.0	9.7	15.1	21.4
Reserve Position in the Fund..........	1c.d	160.7	156.2	166.0	169.0	163.5	153.4	269.6	391.1	296.8	357.3	438.4	496.7
Foreign Exchange......................	1d.d	4,632.9	7,634.0	14,321.6	14,611.0	17,337.3	12,441.1	17,188.3	17,726.0	13,115.5	†4,787.2	7,629.3	3,843.3
o/w:Fin.Deriv.Rel.to Reserves........	1ddd	....	....	....	....	....	....	....	....	....	....	....	....
Other Reserve Assets..................	1e.d	....	....	....	....	....	....	....	....	....	....	....	....
Gold (Million Fine Troy Ounces)......	1ad	3.433	3.443	3.448	3.461	3.469	3.644	3.623	4.237	4.262	3.942	3.935	3.451
Gold (Eurosystem Valuation)..........	1and	746.5	856.3	850.9	871.7	833.2	684.5	685.3	781.8	753.2	1,090.0	1,348.7	1,439.9
Memo:Euro Cl. on Non-EA Res.......	1dgd	....	....	....	....	....	....	....	....	....	61.0	–	–
Non-Euro Cl. on EA Res..............	1dhd	....	....	....	....	....	....	....	....	....	5,566.3	4,014.4	2,979.4
Mon. Auth.: Other Foreign Assets....	3..d	....	....	....	....	....	....	....	....	....	....	....	....
Foreign Liabilities.......................	4..d	1,055.1	731.4	777.5	860.4	795.5	1,336.5	888.4	733.4	179.1	665.4	713.1	764.1
Banking Insts.: Foreign Assets........	7a.d	4,707.1	5,358.7	6,051.3	8,962.9	12,656.1	15,994.8	15,550.7	13,848.5	12,627.4	†16,386.0	21,765.8	32,368.2
Foreign Liab....................	7b.d	18,126.7	18,235.5	26,410.3	34,286.1	38,540.2	42,278.6	46,854.1	41,732.5	39,645.4	†9,636.1	18,557.8	27,716.5
Monetary Authorities		*Billions of Drachmas through 2000; Billions of Euros Beginning 2001: End of Period*											
Fgn. Assets (Cl.on Non-EA Ctys).......	11	1,736.7	2,975.5	4,463.9	4,333.9	5,253.9	4,020.3	5,414.0	6,434.2	4,961.0	6.97	9.00	5.10
Claims on General Government........	12a.u	....	....	....	....	....	....	....	....	....	18.45	19.13	19.60
o/w: Claims on Gen.Govt.in Cty......	12a	4,555.9	†7,966.2	7,352.3	7,059.4	6,457.6	6,012.1	5,757.9	5,911.7	5,759.1	17.23	17.02	15.25
Claims on Banking Institutions........	12e.u	....	....	....	....	....	....	....	....	....	5.16	5.19	6.49
o/w: Claims on Bank.Inst.in Cty......	12e	1,059.7	580.3	377.8	461.4	332.8	791.9	447.2	54.4	299.3	.65	3.02	4.42
Claims on Other Resident Sectors.....	12d.u	....	....	....	....	....	....	....	....	....	.17	.20	.23
o/w: Cl. on Oth.Res.Sect.in Cty......	12d	4.2	3.8	4.8	14.1	19.9	21.9	24.6	27.3	37.5	.17	.20	.23
Currency Issued.........................	14a	1,529.7	1,641.6	1,839.8	2,061.0	2,251.1	2,451.5	2,519.4	3,154.1	3,097.3	8.71	9.21	10.65
Liabilities to Banking Insts.............	14c.u	....	....	....	....	....	....	....	....	....	15.79	19.89	18.50
o/w: Liabs to Bank.Inst.in Cty........	14c	3,620.9	4,236.5	5,364.8	5,084.2	5,406.7	5,189.2	6,634.0	7,033.2	5,955.8	7.70	1.71	2.41
Demand Dep. of Other Res.Sect.......	14d.u	....	....	....	....	....	....	....	....	....	.42	.34	.31
o/w:D.Dep.of Oth.Res.Sect.in Cty....	14d	76.0	63.9	27.3	47.3	29.7	5.2	4.5	165.8	60.8	.42	.34	.31
Other Dep. of Other Res.Sect..........	15..u	....	....	....	....	....	....	....	....	....	.36	.30	.19
o/w:O.Dep.of Oth.Res.Sect.in Cty...	15	....	....	....	....	....	....	....	....	....	.36	.30	.19
Bonds & Money Mkt. Instruments....	16n.u	....	....	....	....	....	....	....	....	....	1.68	1.56	.55
o/w:Bonds Held by Resid.of Cty......	16n	2,482.5	3,626.6	3,342.7	2,742.2	2,102.0	1,533.9	1,065.9	1,015.0	606.0	....	....	....
Foreign Liab. (to Non-EA Ctys)........	16c	226.4	182.3	186.7	203.9	196.5	377.7	251.0	240.9	65.5	.76	.68	.61
Central Government Deposits..........	16d.u	....	....	....	....	....	....	....	....	....	.44	.08	.07
o/w: Cent.Govt.Dep. in Cty............	16d	102.0	259.6	237.6	621.2	672.5	443.4	345.5	128.9	194.6	.44	.08	.07
Capital Accounts........................	17a	57.0	62.7	69.5	71.8	74.1	166.2	196.1	290.0	293.1	2.53	2.51	1.68
Other Items (Net).......................	17r	–738.0	1,452.7	1,130.5	1,037.1	1,331.6	679.1	627.4	399.7	783.8	.08	–1.04	–1.12
Memo: Net Claims on Eurosystem...	12e.s	....	....	....	....	....	....	....	....	....	–7.06	–17.16	–15.05
Currency Put into Circ.................	14m	....	....	....	....	....	....	....	....	....	....	9.98	11.38

Greece 174

		1992	1993	1994	1995	1996	1997	1998	1999	2000	2001	2002	2003
Banking Institutions		\multicolumn{12}{c}{Billions of Drachmas through 2000; Billions of Euros Beginning 2001: End of Period}
Claims on Monetary Authorities	20	2,125.9	2,531.4	2,905.2	5,000.4	5,080.2	5,583.7	7,464.1	8,196.2	7,034.8	11.52	4.84	2.48
Claims on Bk.Inst.in Oth.EA Ctys.	20b.u	....	....	....	....	....	....	....	....	....	9.42	10.80	12.13
Fgn. Assets (Cl.on Non-EA Ctys)	21	1,010.0	1,335.5	1,452.9	2,124.6	3,126.3	4,520.3	4,394.2	4,548.4	4,616.8	18.59	20.76	25.63
Claims on General Government	22a.u										45.94	46.13	40.00
o/w: Claims on Gen.Govt.in Cty	22a	7,039.6	8,957.3	9,522.7	10,448.8	11,082.1	11,565.5	11,354.2	12,447.7	14,506.2	45.87	45.24	36.96
Claims on Other Resident Sectors	22d.u										84.80	97.28	113.03
o/w: Cl. on Oth.Res.Sect.in Cty	22d	6,356.1	6,644.9	7,531.6	9,142.9	10,371.1	11,902.0	13,721.5	17,734.0	21,775.7	83.13	94.47	110.44
Demand Deposits	24..u										70.39	71.37	79.14
o/w:D.Dep.of Oth.Res.Sect.in Cty	24	883.2	1,126.5	1,619.7	1,874.6	2,340.2	2,699.4	3,104.6	4,337.2	4,287.4	70.19	71.18	78.96
Other Deposits	25..u										59.04	55.49	49.47
o/w:O.Dep.of Oth.Res.Sect.in Cty	25	9,066.3	9,760.5	11,925.5	13,684.8	15,339.1	16,704.7	16,564.0	17,975.3	19,164.2	57.93	54.53	48.96
Money Market Fund Shares	26m.u										9.66	10.72	15.73
Bonds & Money Mkt. Instruments	26n.u										.29	.43	.73
o/w: Held by Resid.of Cty	26n	673.8	703.5	838.4	570.5	59.8	126.7	163.6	78.7	85.3	....	....	....
Foreign Liab. (to Non-EA Ctys)	26c	3,889.6	4,544.7	6,341.1	8,127.2	9,520.2	11,948.4	13,239.6	13,706.6	14,495.2	10.93	17.70	21.95
Central Government Deposits	26d.u										1.38	2.32	2.48
o/w: Cent.Govt.Dep. in Cty	26d	....	....	....	....	....	....	....	....	....	1.38	2.32	2.48
Credit from Monetary Authorities	26g	1,244.5	2,166.2	486.3	551.0	409.4	826.6	1,771.1	3,342.1	3,930.6	.71	2.15	4.43
Liab. to Bk.Inst.in Oth. EA Ctys	26h.u										4.67	6.40	5.43
Capital Accounts	27a	1,294.8	1,510.2	1,481.2	1,740.7	1,881.7	2,217.3	2,860.2	5,157.3	5,876.1	19.49	19.88	17.49
Other Items (Net)	27r	−520.4	−342.5	−1,279.8	167.7	109.4	−951.6	−769.2	−1,670.9	94.8	−6.29	−6.63	−3.58
Banking Survey (Nat'l Residency)		\multicolumn{12}{c}{Billions of Drachmas through 2000; Billions of Euros Beginning 2001: End of Period}
Foreign Assets (Net)	31n	−1,369.3	−416.0	−611.0	−1,872.7	−1,336.5	−3,785.5	−3,682.5	−2,965.0	−4,982.8	17.17	4.90	10.62
Domestic Credit	32	17,853.9	†23,312.6	24,173.8	26,044.0	27,258.3	29,058.1	30,512.8	35,991.7	41,884.0	144.58	154.54	160.33
Claims on General Govt. (Net)	32an	11,493.6	†16,663.9	16,637.4	16,887.0	16,867.2	17,134.2	16,766.7	18,230.5	20,070.7	61.28	59.87	49.67
Claims on Other Resident Sectors	32d	6,360.3	6,648.7	7,536.5	9,157.0	10,391.0	11,924.0	13,746.1	17,761.3	21,813.3	83.30	94.67	110.67
Currency Issued	34a.n	1,529.7	1,641.6	1,839.8	2,061.0	2,251.1	2,451.5	2,519.4	3,154.1	3,097.3	8.71	9.21	10.65
Demand Deposits	34b.n	959.2	1,190.3	1,647.0	1,921.9	2,369.9	2,704.5	3,109.1	4,503.0	4,348.3	70.61	71.52	79.27
Other Deposits	35..n	9,066.3	9,760.5	11,925.5	13,684.8	15,339.1	16,704.7	16,564.0	17,975.3	19,164.2	58.29	54.83	49.15
Money Market Fund Shares	36m										9.66	10.72	15.73
Bonds & Money Mkt. Instruments	36n	3,156.3	4,330.1	4,181.1	3,313.0	2,161.9	1,660.6	1,229.5	1,093.7	691.4	1.96	1.98	1.28
o/w: Over Two Years	36na										1.79	1.67	.80
Capital Accounts	37a	1,351.9	1,573.0	1,550.7	1,812.5	1,955.7	2,383.5	3,056.3	5,447.3	6,169.2	22.02	22.39	19.17
Other Items (Net)	37r	421.4	4,401.2	2,418.7	1,378.1	1,844.1	−632.1	352.0	853.5	3,431.0	−9.49	−11.21	−4.29
Banking Survey (EA-Wide Residency)		\multicolumn{12}{c}{Billions of Euros: End of Period}
Foreign Assets (Net)	31n.u										13.87	11.38	8.18
Domestic Credit	32..u										147.54	160.35	170.31
Claims on General Govt. (Net)	32anu										62.57	62.87	57.05
Claims on Other Resident Sect.	32d.u										84.97	97.49	113.25
Currency Issued	34a.u										8.71	9.21	10.65
Demand Deposits	34b.u										70.81	71.71	79.45
Other Deposits	35..u										59.40	55.79	49.65
o/w: Other Dep. Over Two Yrs.	35abu										2.10	2.87	3.26
Money Market Fund Shares	36m.u										9.66	10.72	15.73
Bonds & Money Mkt. Instruments	36n.u										1.96	1.98	1.28
o/w: Over Two Years	36nau										1.79	1.67	.80
Capital Accounts	37a										22.02	22.39	19.17
Other Items (Net)	37r.u										−11.14	−.06	2.56
Interest Rates		\multicolumn{12}{c}{Percent Per Annum}
Central Bank Rate	60	19.0	21.5	20.5	18.0	16.5	14.5		†11.8	8.1	....	....	....
Money Market Rate	60b	....	....	24.60	16.40	13.80	12.80	13.99	....	....	....	....	....
Treasury Bill Rate	60c	22.5	20.3	17.5	14.2	11.2	11.4	10.3	8.3	†6.2	4.1	3.5	2.3
Deposit Rate	60l	19.92	19.33	18.92	15.75	13.51	10.11	10.70	8.69	6.13	3.32	2.76	2.48
Lending Rate	60p	28.71	28.56	27.44	23.05	20.96	18.92	18.56	15.00	12.32	8.59	7.41	6.79
Government Bond Yield	61	....	....	....	....	....	....	8.48	6.30	6.10	5.30	5.12	4.27
Prices, Production, Labor		\multicolumn{12}{c}{Index Numbers (2000=100): Period Averages}
Wholesale Prices	63	61.5	68.8	74.7	80.6	85.8	88.8	92.2	93.9	100.0	102.3	104.7	106.9
Home and Import Goods	63a	62.0	69.5	75.5	†81.1	86.2	89.3	93.0	94.9	100.0	102.4	105.0	107.9
Consumer Prices	64	57.1	65.3	†72.5	79.0	85.4	†90.2	94.5	96.9	100.0	103.4	107.1	110.9
Harmonized CPI	64h	....	....	....	80.0	86.3	91.0	95.2	97.2	100.0	103.7	107.7	111.4
Wages: Hourly Earnings (1995=100)	65	70.7	78.1	88.3	100.0	108.6	118.3	123.9	....	....	....	....	....
Manufacturing Production	66ey	87.2	84.3	85.3	†87.1	86.8	88.8	96.0	95.2	100.0	101.7	102.9	102.5
		\multicolumn{12}{c}{Number in Thousands: Period Averages}
Labor Force	67d	4,034	4,112	4,188	4,249	4,314	4,294	4,470	4,500	4,475	4,403	4,450	4,503
Employment	67e	3,685	3,720	3,790	3,824	3,872	3,854	3,978	3,968	3,979	3,941	4,006	4,084
Unemployment	67c	350	398	404	425	446	440	†492	532	495	462	445	420
Unemployment Rate (%)	67r	8.7	9.7	9.6	10.0	10.3	10.3	†10.8	11.8	11.1	10.5	10.0	9.3

2004, International Monetary Fund : *International Financial Statistics Yearbook*

Greece 174

		1992	1993	1994	1995	1996	1997	1998	1999	2000	2001	2002	2003
International Transactions		\multicolumn{12}{c}{*Millions of US Dollars*}
Exports	70..d	9,439.3	9,092.7	8,807.6	10,960.8	11,948.2	11,127.7	10,731.9	10,475.1	10,747.0	9,483.3	10,315.2	13,195.2
Imports, c.i.f	71..d	22,818.0	20,200.3	21,381.3	26,795.2	29,672.4	27,898.7	29,388.1	28,719.5	29,221.4	29,927.7	31,164.4	44,375.2
						1995=100							
Volume of Exports	72	89.5	87.1	90.7	100.0	106.8	118.7	134.9	143.7	....	....	....	....
Volume of Imports	73	79.8	87.5	92.3	100.0	109.0	110.7	134.5	141.9	....	....	....	....
Unit Value of Exp	74	86.9	89.2	99.3	100.0	105.2	100.7	93.3	92.7	....	....	....	....
Unit Value of Imp	75	98.4	99.6	98.3	100.0	105.4	112.3	109.7	109.0	....	....	....	....
						2000=100							
Export Prices	76	58.6	65.2	70.8	†78.1	83.9	86.6	88.5	89.0	100.0	100.7	102.6	102.6
Import Prices	76.x	64.4	72.2	78.9	†84.4	86.6	88.6	93.4	94.0	100.0	101.9	102.3	103.4
Balance of Payments		\multicolumn{12}{c}{*Millions of US Dollars: Minus Sign Indicates Debit*}
Current Account, n.i.e	78ald	−2,140	−747	−146	−2,864	−4,554	−4,860	....	−7,295	−9,820	−9,400	−10,405	−11,225
Goods: Exports f.o.b	78aad	6,076	5,112	5,338	5,918	5,890	5,576	....	8,545	10,202	10,615	9,868	12,578
Goods: Imports f.o.b	78abd	−17,637	−15,611	−16,611	−20,343	−21,395	−20,951	....	−26,496	−30,440	−29,702	−31,320	−38,184
Trade Balance	78acd	−11,561	−10,499	−11,273	−14,425	−15,505	−15,375	....	−17,951	−20,239	−19,087	−21,452	−25,606
Services: Credit	78add	8,697	8,214	9,213	9,605	9,348	9,287	....	16,506	19,239	19,456	20,223	24,286
Services: Debit	78aed	−3,701	−3,521	−3,774	−4,368	−4,238	−4,650	....	−9,251	−11,286	−11,589	−10,677	−11,253
Balance on Goods & Services	78afd	−6,565	−5,806	−5,834	−9,188	−10,395	−10,738	....	−10,696	−12,286	−11,220	−11,906	−12,573
Income: Credit	78agd	555	927	1,099	1,312	1,156	1,208	....	2,577	2,807	1,885	1,530	1,769
Income: Debit	78ahd	−2,605	−2,367	−2,347	−2,996	−3,337	−2,840	....	−3,248	−3,692	−3,652	−3,487	−4,693
Balance on Gds, Serv. & Inc	78aid	−8,615	−7,246	−7,082	−10,872	−12,576	−12,370	....	−11,367	−13,171	−12,987	−13,863	−15,497
Current Transfers, n.i.e.: Credit	78ajd	6,489	6,516	6,964	8,039	8,053	7,538	....	4,957	4,116	4,592	4,901	7,202
Current Transfers: Debit	78akd	−14	−17	−28	−31	−31	−28	....	−884	−764	−1,005	−1,443	−2,930
Capital Account, n.i.e	78bcd	−	−	−	−	−	−	....	2,211	2,112	2,153	1,522	1,411
Capital Account, n.i.e.: Credit	78bad	−	−	−	−	−	−	....	2,318	2,244	2,320	1,692	1,585
Capital Account: Debit	78bbd	−	−	−	−	−	−	....	−107	−131	−167	−170	−174
Financial Account, n.i.e	78bjd	2,619	4,817	6,903	3,162	8,658	119	....	7,478	10,830	537	11,574	6,168
Direct Investment Abroad	78bdd	−	−	−	−	−	−	....	−542	−2,099	−611	−669	−9
Dir. Invest. in Rep. Econ., n.i.e	78bed	1,144	977	981	1,053	1,058	984	....	567	1,083	1,585	53	717
Portfolio Investment Assets	78bfd	−	−	−	−	−	−	....	−858	−1,184	−474	−1,893	−9,807
Equity Securities	78bkd	−	−	−	−	−	−	....	−166	−846	−1,020	−314	−507
Debt Securities	78bld	−	−	−	−	−	−	....	−692	−338	546	−1,579	−9,300
Portfolio Investment Liab., n.i.e	78bgd	−	−	−	−	−	−	....	6,754	9,262	9,012	12,315	23,456
Equity Securities	78bmd	−	−	−	−	−	−	....	−2,589	1,637	1,829	1,381	2,569
Debt Securities	78bnd	−	−	−	−	−	−	....	9,343	7,625	7,183	10,935	20,887
Financial Derivatives Assets	78bwd	....	....	....	....	....	....	....	....	....	....	....	....
Financial Derivatives Liabilities	78bxd	....	....	....	....	....	....	....	419	348	74	−176	111
Other Investment Assets	78bhd	−	−	−	−	−	980	....	−2,913	6,970	−1,539	−6,953	−4,413
Monetary Authorities	78bod	....	....	....	....	....	....	....	....	....	....	....	....
General Government	78bpd	−	−	−	−	−	980	....	−2,913	6,970	−1,539	−6,953	−4,413
Banks	78bqd	−	−	−	−	−	−	....	....	....	....	....	....
Other Sectors	78brd	−	−	−	−	−	−	....	....	....	....	....	....
Other Investment Liab., n.i.e	78bid	1,475	3,840	5,922	2,109	7,600	−1,845	....	4,050	−3,551	−7,511	8,896	−3,887
Monetary Authorities	78bsd	1,460	2,584	−1,791	−2,385	−2,194	−2,570	....	−	−	−	−	−
General Government	78btd	−1,773	884	4,703	3,441	3,530	7,101	....	....	....	....	....	....
Banks	78bud	−2	78	89	−2,110	−598	−3,348	....	1,644	−3,425	−6,989	11,197	2,256
Other Sectors	78bvd	1,790	294	2,921	3,163	6,862	−3,028	....	2,406	−126	−522	−2,301	−6,143
Net Errors and Omissions	78cad	−853	−631	−448	−321	111	226	....	42	−550	1,011	−828	−1,076
Overall Balance	78cbd	−374	3,439	6,309	−23	4,215	−4,515	....	2,435	2,573	−5,699	1,863	−4,722
Reserves and Related Items	79dad	374	−3,439	−6,309	23	−4,215	4,515	....	−2,435	−2,573	5,699	−1,863	4,722
Reserve Assets	79dbd	188	−3,019	−6,309	23	−4,215	4,515	....	−2,435	−2,573	5,699	−1,863	4,722
Use of Fund Credit and Loans	79dcd	−	−	−	−	−	−	....	−	−	−	−	−
Exceptional Financing	79ded	186	−420	−	−	−	−	....	....	....	....	....	....

Greece 174

		1992	1993	1994	1995	1996	1997	1998	1999	2000	2001	2002	2003
International Investment Position							*Millions of US Dollars*						
Assets...	79aad	....	....	....	....	....	....	55,491	59,106	57,427	57,652	82,336	109,631
Direct Investment Abroad...............	79abd	....	....	....	....	....	....	2,792	3,809	6,085	7,020	9,001	11,114
Portfolio Investment.........................	79acd	....	....	....	....	....	....	4,503	4,778	3,848	8,028	15,714	30,474
Equity Securities............................	79add	....	....	....	....	....	....	1,177	1,147	1,346	1,406	1,602	2,625
Debt Securities...............................	79aed	....	....	....	....	....	....	3,326	3,631	2,502	6,622	14,111	27,849
Financial Derivatives........................	79ald	....	....	....	....	....	....	12	13	12	88	315	326
Other Investment..............................	79afd	....	....	....	....	....	....	38,726	40,361	35,227	36,347	47,874	61,916
Monetary Authorities.....................	79agd	....	....	....	....	....	....	7,239	6,134	477	3,067	1,290	1,398
General Government......................	79ahd	....	....	....	....	....	....	–	–	–	–	–	–
Banks...	79aid	....	....	....	....	....	....	18,712	20,881	20,908	19,649	28,117	36,890
Other Sectors.................................	79ajd	....	....	....	....	....	....	12,775	13,346	13,841	13,631	18,468	23,628
Reserve Assets..................................	79akd	....	....	....	....	....	....	9,458	10,145	12,255	6,169	9,432	5,801
Liabilities...	79lad	....	....	....	....	....	....	91,539	102,665	108,301	116,557	164,112	228,275
Dir. Invest. in Rep. Economy...........	79lbd	....	....	....	....	....	....	13,084	15,386	14,091	13,941	15,561	20,966
Portfolio Investment.........................	79lcd	....	....	....	....	....	....	45,330	52,758	57,294	59,610	78,524	121,402
Equity Securities............................	79ldd	....	....	....	....	....	....	12,001	15,211	9,584	7,711	8,425	16,140
Debt Securities...............................	79led	....	....	....	....	....	....	33,329	37,547	47,710	51,899	70,098	105,262
Financial Derivatives........................	79lld	....	....	....	....	....	....	....	....	....	....	....	....
Other Investment..............................	79lfd	....	....	....	....	....	....	33,125	34,521	36,917	43,006	70,028	85,907
Monetary Authorities.....................	79lgd	....	....	....	....	....	....	–	–	–	7,132	18,259	19,391
General Government......................	79lhd	....	....	....	....	....	....	8,071	7,949	8,837	10,101	11,922	14,523
Banks...	79lid	....	....	....	....	....	....	15,384	16,551	18,846	14,879	26,537	35,565
Other Sectors.................................	79ljd	....	....	....	....	....	....	9,670	10,021	9,233	10,894	13,310	16,428
Government Finance							*Billions of Drachmas: Year Ending December 31*						
Budgetary Central Government													
Deficit (-) or Surplus.........................	80	–1,358.4	–2,431.7	–5,050.3	–3,252.2	–2,904.2	–2,505.4	–2,125.5	–1,930.0	....	....	....	....
Total Revenue and Grants...............	81y	4,821.6	5,281.7	6,191.7	7,113.6	7,956.4	9,185.4	10,412.5	11,603.0	....	....	....	....
Revenue...	81	4,617.6	4,989.1	5,883.4	6,753.5	7,306.9	....	....	....	....	....	....	....
Grants Received............................	81z	204.0	292.6	308.3	360.1	649.5	....	....	....	....	....	....	....
Expenditure.......................................	82	6,180.0	7,713.4	11,242.0	10,365.8	10,860.6	11,690.8	12,538.0	13,533.0	....	....	....	....
Financing													
Net Borrowing.................................	84	1,358.4	2,431.7	5,050.3	3,252.2	2,904.2	2,505.4	2,125.5	1,930.0	....	....	....	....
Borrowing: Domestic.....................	84c	2,892.3	3,385.9	6,439.2	5,111.7	5,180.4	....	....	....	....	....	....	....
Borrowing: Foreign.......................	85c	649.0	649.8	1,138.0	914.0	1,362.0	....	....	....	....	....	....	....
Amortization..................................	84y	–2,182.9	–1,604.0	–2,526.9	–2,773.5	–3,638.2	–3,589.4	–3,536.4	–3,362.3	....	....	....	....
General Government							*As Percent of Gross Domestic Product*						
Deficit (-) or Surplus.........................	80g	....	....	....	....	....	....	–2.4	–1.7	–.8	.1	....	....
Debt...	88g	....	....	....	....	....	....	105.0	103.8	102.8	99.7	....	....
National Accounts						*Billions of Drachmas through 2000; Billions of Euros Beginning 2001*							
House.Cons.Expend.,incl.NPISHs....	96f	14,033.5	15,900.9	18,012.1	†19,901.6	22,050.8	23,901.9	25,850.0	27,157.0	28,884.9	†89.2	94.8	102.2
Government Consumption Expend...	91f	2,613.9	3,063.3	3,345.4	†4,174.1	4,348.0	5,013.3	5,506.8	5,879.9	6,408.4	†20.0	22.1	23.6
Gross Fixed Capital Formation..........	93e	3,983.8	4,267.1	4,453.5	†5,066.0	5,828.1	6,558.7	7,615.1	8,346.6	9,377.6	†31.3	33.8	40.0
Changes in Inventories......................	93i	–60.4	–75.5	25.8	†85.7	96.5	93.2	79.7	–106.6	17.5	†.1	.2	.1
Exports of Goods and Services..........	90c	3,174.5	3,355.5	3,904.0	†4,800.2	5,245.6	6,523.7	7,150.6	7,893.2	10,343.4	†31.2	29.5	30.3
Imports of Goods and Services (-).....	98c	4,979.2	5,375.6	5,757.2	†6,792.4	7,633.9	8,958.1	10,160.0	10,720.9	13,633.7	†40.8	39.1	42.7
Gross Domestic Product (GDP).........	99b	18,766.1	21,135.7	23,983.6	27,235.2	29,935.1	33,132.7	36,042.2	38,449.2	41,406.7	†131.0	141.3	153.5
Net Primary Income from Abroad.....	98.n	249.8	137.8	212.8	861.8	835.2	897.5	976.6	510.8	356.8	†.1	.1	–.4
Gross National Income (GNI)............	99a	19,015.9	21,273.5	24,195.7	†28,096.9	30,770.3	34,060.9	37,018.7	39,208.5	42,051.0	†131.1	141.5	153.0
Net Current Transf.from Abroad.......	98t	....	....	....	....	....	....	....	....	....	†1.4	2.1	2.7
Gross Nat'l Disposable Inc.(GNDI)....	99i	....	....	....	....	....	....	....	....	....	†132.6	143.6	155.7
Gross Saving.....................................	99s	....	....	....	....	....	....	....	....	....	†23.4	26.6	29.9
Consumption of Fixed Capital..........	99cf	1,640.0	1,847.7	2,117.2	2,469.1	2,737.6	2,976.8	3,260.0	3,475.7	....	†11.6	12.5	13.4
GDP Volume 1995 Prices..................	99b.p	26,577.1	26,151.9	26,674.9	27,235.2	27,877.5	28,891.4	29,863.2	30,939.7	32,217.2	†98.5	102.3	106.7
GDP Volume (2000=100)................	99bvp	82.5	81.2	82.8	84.5	86.5	89.7	92.7	96.0	100.0	104.2	108.2	112.8
GDP Deflator (2000=100)................	99bip	54.9	62.9	70.0	†77.8	83.5	89.2	93.9	96.7	100.0	103.5	107.5	111.9
							Millions: Midyear Estimates						
Population......................................	99z	10.26	10.31	10.38	10.45	10.54	10.64	10.74	10.83	10.90	10.95	10.97	10.98

2004, International Monetary Fund : *International Financial Statistics Yearbook*

Grenada 328

		1992	1993	1994	1995	1996	1997	1998	1999	2000	2001	2002	2003
Exchange Rates		\multicolumn{12}{c}{E.Caribbean Dollars per SDR: End of Period (aa) E.Caribbean Dollars per US Dollar: End of Period (ae)}
Official Rate	aa	3.7125	3.7086	3.9416	4.0135	3.8825	3.6430	3.8017	3.7058	3.5179	3.3932	3.6707	4.0121
Official Rate	ae	2.7000	2.7000	2.7000	2.7000	2.7000	2.7000	2.7000	2.7000	2.7000	2.7000	2.7000	2.7000
		\multicolumn{12}{c}{Index Numbers (2000=100): Period Averages}
Official Rate	ahx	100.0	100.0	100.0	100.0	100.0	100.0	100.0	100.0	100.0	100.0	100.0	100.0
Nominal Effective Exchange Rate	nec	64.7	76.9	87.9	87.0	88.9	92.5	93.9	96.0	100.0	103.4	102.6	96.4
Real Effective Exchange Rate	rec	89.6	94.5	94.9	91.6	92.4	94.8	95.8	96.4	100.0	103.9	102.3	96.7
Fund Position		\multicolumn{12}{c}{Millions of SDRs: End of Period}
Quota	2f.s	8.50	8.50	8.50	8.50	8.50	8.50	8.50	11.70	11.70	11.70	11.70	11.70
SDRs	1b.s	–	–	.02	.02	.04	–	.03	–	–	–	–	–
Reserve Position in the Fund	1c.s	–	–	–	–	–	–	–	–	–	–	–	–
Total Fund Cred.&Loans Outstg	2tl	–	–	–	–	–	–	–	–	–	–	–	2.93
International Liquidity		\multicolumn{12}{c}{Millions of US Dollars Unless Otherwise Indicated: End of Period}
Total Reserves minus Gold	1l.d	25.88	26.90	31.23	36.73	35.73	42.67	46.84	50.84	57.66	63.94	87.84	83.23
SDRs	1b.d	–	–	.03	.02	.06	.01	.04	–	–	–	–	–
Reserve Position in the Fund	1c.d	–	–	–	–	–	–	–	–	–	–	–	–
Foreign Exchange	1d.d	25.88	26.90	31.20	36.71	35.67	42.66	46.80	50.84	57.66	63.94	87.84	83.22
Monetary Authorities: Other Liab	4..d	–	–	–	–	–	–	–	–	–	–	–	–
Deposit Money Banks: Assets	7a.d	27.93	35.68	51.88	59.06	61.88	57.07	54.97	72.71	69.81	113.23	137.94	174.69
Liabilities	7b.d	29.70	37.26	41.15	38.98	50.55	68.25	69.12	74.01	76.85	99.94	104.39	107.89
Monetary Authorities		\multicolumn{12}{c}{Millions of E. Caribbean Dollars: End of Period}
Foreign Assets	11	73.21	72.71	84.27	99.27	96.50	115.30	126.52	137.20	155.57	173.02	237.88	225.95
Claims on Central Government	12a	35.02	28.34	24.30	21.70	20.82	18.69	18.64	16.33	13.84	11.17	5.63	26.77
Claims on Deposit Money Banks	12e	.64	–	.48	.27	.09	.01	.02	.03	.02	.04	.01	.02
Reserve Money	14	108.87	100.82	107.30	116.40	116.77	131.40	139.75	148.10	163.52	181.87	215.94	235.46
of which: Currency Outside DMBs	14a	46.68	46.56	52.96	53.83	53.18	58.35	64.08	64.75	71.14	70.20	75.15	84.68
Foreign Liabilities	16c	–	–	–	–	–	–	–	–	–	–	–	11.76
Central Government Deposits	16d	–	.71	1.54	4.66	.55	2.61	5.44	5.66	5.92	2.33	27.57	5.52
Other Items (Net)	17r	–	–	–	–	–	–	–	–.22	–	–	–	–
Deposit Money Banks		\multicolumn{12}{c}{Millions of E. Caribbean Dollars: End of Period}
Reserves	20	55.55	53.14	56.10	56.87	59.35	73.43	76.10	92.36	98.26	107.62	138.17	149.50
Foreign Assets	21	75.42	96.33	140.08	159.47	167.09	154.08	148.42	196.32	188.48	305.73	372.43	471.66
Claims on Central Government	22a	34.62	38.39	42.98	46.44	55.93	74.32	80.49	64.91	84.37	101.89	115.60	143.93
Claims on Local Government	22b	–	–	.06	–	–	–	–	–	.79	3.51	–	–
Claims on Nonfin.Pub.Enterprises	22c	9.38	9.74	6.71	6.12	16.07	20.92	25.88	26.13	46.43	65.79	75.83	28.18
Claims on Private Sector	22d	315.02	413.64	414.60	437.29	495.26	587.95	684.68	767.87	878.39	886.41	896.24	923.68
Claims on Nonbank Financial Insts	22g	2.22	4.32	4.24	6.06	10.31	10.09	15.59	23.33	31.50	39.30	55.85	29.87
Demand Deposits	24	64.49	79.58	87.26	93.77	95.43	97.51	114.34	121.25	130.47	141.41	169.92	197.21
Time, Savings,& Fgn.Currency Dep	25	290.62	364.42	409.15	455.19	504.59	564.27	627.50	722.76	846.61	949.71	1,013.31	1,059.95
Foreign Liabilities	26c	80.19	100.60	111.11	105.24	136.50	184.29	186.63	199.83	207.51	269.84	281.85	291.31
Central Government Deposits	26d	17.03	20.35	24.37	30.55	41.02	42.04	56.74	71.04	71.67	65.49	95.51	99.86
Credit from Monetary Authorities	26g	.79	.58	.25	.07	.02	.02	2.72	.02	.03	.01	–	1.86
Capital Accounts	27a	36.94	46.56	50.00	50.47	54.27	60.91	64.96	74.66	83.00	95.94	119.35	144.83
Other Items (Net)	27r	2.14	3.46	−17.38	−23.04	−27.81	−28.23	−21.73	−18.62	−11.05	−12.15	−25.82	−48.18
Monetary Survey		\multicolumn{12}{c}{Millions of E. Caribbean Dollars: End of Period}
Foreign Assets (Net)	31n	68.44	68.44	113.24	153.50	127.09	85.10	88.31	133.70	136.54	208.91	328.45	394.54
Domestic Credit	32	379.23	473.36	466.97	482.40	556.82	667.32	763.09	822.09	977.73	1,040.25	1,026.07	1,047.06
Claims on Central Govt. (Net)	32an	52.61	45.65	41.36	32.93	35.18	48.36	36.96	4.54	20.62	45.24	−1.86	65.32
Claims on Local Government	32b	–	–	.06	–	–	–	–	–	.79	3.51	–	–
Claims on Nonfin.Pub.Enterprises	32c	9.38	9.74	6.71	6.12	16.07	20.92	25.88	26.35	46.43	65.79	75.83	28.18
Claims on Private Sector	32d	315.02	413.64	414.60	437.29	495.26	587.95	684.68	767.87	878.39	886.41	896.24	923.68
Claims on Nonbank Financial Inst	32g	2.22	4.32	4.24	6.06	10.31	10.09	15.59	23.33	31.50	39.30	55.85	29.87
Money	34	111.18	126.14	140.36	147.85	148.63	155.87	178.41	186.00	201.71	211.67	245.51	281.93
Quasi-Money	35	290.62	364.42	409.15	455.19	504.59	564.27	627.50	722.76	846.61	949.71	1,013.31	1,059.95
Capital Accounts	37a	40.40	50.01	53.67	54.20	57.88	64.30	68.50	78.10	86.27	99.09	122.76	148.56
Other Items (Net)	37r	5.48	1.23	−22.97	−21.33	−27.19	−32.02	−23.00	−31.08	−20.32	−11.32	−27.06	−48.84
Money plus Quasi-Money	35l	401.79	490.56	549.51	603.03	653.22	720.14	805.91	908.76	1,048.32	1,161.38	1,258.82	1,341.88
Money (National Definitions)		\multicolumn{12}{c}{Millions of E. Caribbean Dollars: End of Period}
M1	39ma	100.95	109.66	124.16	131.65	131.44	144.51	159.41	175.15	182.38	192.34	211.98	241.08
M2	39mb	376.34	453.99	504.52	550.69	600.74	671.52	750.44	854.56	985.84	1,090.37	1,167.38	1,260.37
Interest Rates		\multicolumn{12}{c}{Percent Per Annum}
Discount Rate (End of Period)	60	....	....	9.00	9.00	9.00	8.00	8.00	8.00	8.00	7.00	7.00	6.50
Money Market Rate	60b	5.25	5.25	5.25	5.25	5.25	5.25	5.25	5.25	5.25	†5.64	6.32	6.07
Treasury Bill Rate	60c	6.50	6.50	6.50	6.50	6.50	6.50	6.50	6.50	6.50	†7.00	7.00	6.50
Savings Rate	60k	5.00	5.00	5.46	5.00	5.00	5.33	6.00	6.00	6.00	6.00	5.83	†3.25
Deposit Rate	60l	3.67	3.88	3.61	3.67	3.74	3.93	4.16	4.30	4.24	4.23	3.59	3.39
Deposit Rate (Fgn. Currency)	60l.f	....	....	....	....	....	....	....	....	....	....	....	3.69
Lending Rate	60p	12.02	11.83	11.03	11.08	9.99	11.24	11.73	11.62	11.60	10.19	11.31	12.05

Grenada 328

		1992	1993	1994	1995	1996	1997	1998	1999	2000	2001	2002	2003
Prices		\multicolumn{12}{c}{*Index Numbers (2000=100): Period Averages*}
Consumer Prices................	64	85.5	87.9	91.2	92.9	94.8	†96.0	97.3	97.9	100.0	101.7	102.8	....
International Transactions		\multicolumn{12}{c}{*Millions of E. Caribbean Dollars*}
Exports.................................	70	53.90	55.10	64.30	58.70	54.00	61.50	72.50	....	....	....	....	....
Imports, c.i.f........................	71	287.80	319.60	320.60	333.80	411.10	468.20	540.40	....	....	....	....	....
Balance of Payments		\multicolumn{12}{c}{*Millions of US Dollars: Minus Sign Indicates Debit*}
Current Account, n.i.e........	78ald	−32.39	−43.68	−26.93	−40.84	−55.54	−67.87	−81.51	−53.04	−84.33	−98.54	−116.22	....
Goods: Exports f.o.b.........	78aad	23.53	22.74	25.24	24.57	24.96	32.80	45.95	74.30	82.96	63.60	41.99	....
Goods: Imports f.o.b.........	78abd	−103.18	−118.13	−119.45	−129.78	−147.44	−154.90	−183.01	−184.57	−220.94	−196.83	−181.42	....
Trade Balance.................	78acd	−79.65	−95.38	−94.21	−105.21	−122.48	−122.10	−137.06	−110.28	−137.98	−133.23	−139.43	....
Services: Credit.................	78add	76.04	87.68	101.53	99.19	106.70	106.14	119.77	143.72	152.76	133.34	133.04	....
Services: Debit..................	78aed	−35.45	−41.19	−41.26	−38.46	−45.78	−56.48	−70.16	−79.86	−87.41	−82.22	−88.16	....
Balance on Goods & Services...	78afd	−39.06	−48.89	−33.94	−44.48	−61.56	−72.44	−87.45	−46.41	−72.63	−82.10	−94.56	....
Income: Credit...................	78agd	3.41	2.68	3.61	4.91	4.71	4.70	4.13	4.33	5.08	3.73	4.13	....
Income: Debit....................	78ahd	−8.74	−11.16	−12.43	−18.36	−20.10	−21.65	−27.38	−30.15	−36.89	−41.81	−48.92	....
Balance on Gds, Serv. & Inc....	78aid	−44.40	−57.37	−42.76	−57.92	−76.94	−89.39	−110.70	−72.23	−104.43	−120.18	−139.35	....
Current Transfers, n.i.e.: Credit.	78ajd	14.26	16.10	19.75	21.58	25.47	25.53	34.19	26.76	30.35	31.00	31.83	....
Current Transfers: Debit.........	78akd	−2.25	−2.41	−3.92	−4.50	−4.07	−4.01	−5.00	−7.57	−10.25	−9.36	−8.70	....
Capital Account, n.i.e............	78bcd	16.38	16.89	21.67	25.84	31.42	31.78	28.58	31.18	32.13	42.36	31.83	....
Capital Account, n.i.e.: Credit...	78bad	17.76	18.27	23.04	27.28	31.42	33.42	30.36	33.10	34.21	44.39	33.87	....
Capital Account: Debit............	78bbd	−1.38	−1.38	−1.38	−1.44	—	−1.64	−1.78	−1.92	−2.08	−2.04	−2.04	....
Financial Account, n.i.e..........	78bjd	16.30	17.74	4.06	3.10	27.39	59.16	55.77	27.56	63.74	47.26	108.25	....
Direct Investment Abroad......	78bdd	—											....
Dir. Invest. in Rep. Econ., n.i.e.	78bed	22.58	20.25	19.31	19.98	16.95	33.50	48.69	41.55	37.41	58.75	57.61	....
Portfolio Investment Assets.....	78bfd	−.16	.20	−.38	−.87	—	−.04	.04	−.36	−.07	−.42	−1.69	....
Equity Securities................	78bkd	....	....	....	....	....	....	....	....	....	....	....	....
Debt Securities.................	78bld	....	....	....	....	....	....	....	....	....	....	....	....
Portfolio Investment Liab., n.i.e.	78bgd	—	—	—	—	—	—	−.01	.75	19.52	.17	109.42	....
Equity Securities...............	78bmd	....	....	....	....	....	....	....	....	....	....	....	....
Debt Securities.................	78bnd	....	....	....	....	....	....	....	....	....	....	....	....
Financial Derivatives Assets....	78bwd	....	....	....	....	....	....	....	....	....	....	....	....
Financial Derivatives Liabilities.	78bxd	....	....	....	....	....	....	....	....	....	....	....	....
Other Investment Assets.......	78bhd	−12.51	−9.95	−23.59	−11.02	−3.70	−5.89	−3.80	−12.39	−11.07	−5.31	−14.21	....
Monetary Authorities..........	78bod	....	....	....	....	....	....	....	....	....	....	....	....
General Government...........	78bpd	....	....	....	....	....	....	....	....	....	....	....	....
Banks...............................	78bqd	....	....	....	....	....	....	....	....	....	....	....	....
Other Sectors...................	78brd	....	....	....	....	....	....	....	....	....	....	....	....
Other Investment Liab., n.i.e....	78bid	6.38	7.24	8.72	−4.99	14.15	31.59	10.85	−2.00	17.96	−5.93	−42.89	....
Monetary Authorities..........	78bsd	—									—	—	....
General Government...........	78btd	....	....	....	....	....	....	....	....	....	....	....	....
Banks...............................	78bud	....	....	....	....	....	....	....	....	....	....	....	....
Other Sectors...................	78bvd	....	....	....	....	....	....	....	....	....	....	....	....
Net Errors and Omissions......	78cad	7.82	9.49	5.88	17.94	−2.83	−16.14	1.26	−1.04	−4.95	14.77	7.36	....
Overall Balance...................	78cbd	8.10	.44	4.68	6.03	.45	6.93	4.09	4.66	6.60	5.84	31.22	....
Reserves and Related Items.....	79dad	−8.10	−.44	−4.68	−6.03	−.45	−6.93	−4.09	−4.66	−6.60	−5.84	−31.22	....
Reserve Assets....................	79dbd	−8.10	−.44	−4.68	−6.03	−.45	−6.93	−4.09	−4.66	−6.60	−5.84	−31.22	....
Use of Fund Credit and Loans...	79dcd	—	—	—	—	—	—	—	—	—	—	—	....
Exceptional Financing............	79ded	—	—	—	—	....	....	....	....	....	....	....	....
Government Finance		\multicolumn{12}{c}{*Millions of E. Caribbean Dollars: Year Ending December 31*}
Deficit (−) or Surplus.............	80	1.18	−1.42	−7.86	16.79	....	....	....	....	....	....	....	....
Revenue............................	81	165.59	178.27	194.26	205.00	....	....	....	....	....	....	....	....
Grants Received.................	81z	14.15	16.33	26.50	21.48	....	....	....	....	....	....	....	....
Expenditure.......................	82	178.56	196.02	228.62	209.69	....	....	....	....	....	....	....	....
Lending Minus Repayments...	83	—	—	—	—	....	....	....	....	....	....	....	....
National Accounts		\multicolumn{12}{c}{*Millions of E. Caribbean Dollars*}
House.Cons.Expend.,incl.NPISHs...	96f	455.6	472.9	420.2	503.3	551.4	590.5	697.1	544.1	758.6	....	....	....
Government Consumption Expend...	91f	127.5	123.7	126.6	123.7	130.3	137.5	150.8	147.5	161.4	....	....	....
Gross Fixed Capital Formation.....	93e	199.5	210.5	253.8	239.3	280.4	311.2	343.9	408.9	453.8	....	....	....
Exports of Goods and Services.....	90c	268.2	297.7	342.3	334.2	355.1	381.7	448.8	636.8	674.0	....	....	....
Imports of Goods and Services (−)...	98c	373.4	429.7	433.9	454.5	521.6	570.7	694.0	716.2	939.2	....	....	....
Gross Domestic Product (GDP).....	99b	677.5	675.1	708.9	746.0	795.6	850.2	946.7	1,021.1	1,108.5	....	....	....
Net Primary Income from Abroad...	98.n	−14.4	−22.6	−23.8	−36.3	−41.6	−46.8	−64.2	−80.2	−90.9	....	....	....
Gross National Income (GNI).......	99a	663.1	652.5	685.1	709.7	754.0	803.4	882.5	940.9	1,017.7	....	....	....
Net Current Transf.from Abroad...	98t	32.4	37.0	42.7	46.1	51.2	53.9	78.9	75.6	78.0	....	....	....
Gross Nat'l Disposable Inc.(GNDI)...	99i	695.5	689.5	727.9	755.8	805.2	857.3	961.4	1,016.5	1,095.6	....	....	....
Gross Saving......................	99s	112.3	92.9	181.1	128.8	123.5	129.3	113.4	325.0	175.6	....	....	....
GDP Volume 1984 Prices........	99b.p	317.5	....	....	....	....	....	....	....	....	....	....	....
GDP Volume (1990=100).......	99bvp	103.5	....	....	....	....	....	....	....	....	....	....	....
GDP Deflator (1990=100)......	99bip	109.6	....	....	....	....	....	....	....	....	....	....	....
		\multicolumn{12}{c}{*Millions: Midyear Estimates*}
Population..........................	99z	.08	.08	.08	.08	.08	.08	.08	.08	.08	.08	.08	.08

Guatemala 258

		1992	1993	1994	1995	1996	1997	1998	1999	2000	2001	2002	2003
Exchange Rates													
						Quetzales per SDR: End of Period							
Market Rate......aa=	wa	7.2522	7.9876	8.2460	8.9810	8.5782	8.3342	9.6425	10.7342	10.0731	10.0544	10.6140	11.9482
					Quetzales per US Dollar: End of Period (we) Period Average (wf)								
Market Rate......ae=	we	5.2743	5.8152	5.6485	6.0418	5.9656	6.1769	6.8482	7.8208	7.7312	8.0005	7.8072	8.0407
Market Rate......rf=	wf	5.1706	5.6354	5.7512	5.8103	6.0495	6.0653	6.3947	7.3856	7.7632	7.8586	7.8216	7.9408
Secondary Rate	xe	1.00	1.00	1.00	1.00	1.00	1.00	1.00	1.00	1.00	....	....	....
Secondary Rate	xf	1.00	1.00	1.00	1.00	1.00	1.00	1.00	1.00	1.00	....	....	....
Fund Position						*Millions of SDRs: End of Period*							
Quota	2f.s	153.8	153.8	153.8	153.8	153.8	153.8	153.8	210.2	210.2	210.2	210.2	210.2
SDRs	1b.s	11.4	11.4	11.4	10.6	10.2	9.4	8.7	8.4	7.5	6.7	6.1	5.5
Reserve Position in the Fund	1c.s	–	–	–	–	–	–	–	–	–	–	–	–
of which: Outstg.Fund Borrowing	2c	–	–	–	–	–	–	–	–	–	–	–	–
Total Fund Cred.&Loans Outstg	2tl	22.4	–	–	–	–	–	–	–	–	–	–	–
International Liquidity					*Millions of US Dollars Unless Otherwise Indicated: End of Period*								
Total Reserves minus Gold	1l.d	765.2	867.8	863.1	702.0	869.7	1,111.1	1,335.1	1,189.2	1,746.4	2,292.2	2,299.1	2,833.2
SDRs	1b.d	15.6	15.7	16.6	15.8	14.6	12.7	12.2	11.5	9.8	8.5	8.2	8.2
Reserve Position in the Fund	1c.d	–	–	–	–	–	–	–	–	–	–	–	–
Foreign Exchange	1d.d	749.6	852.1	846.5	686.2	855.1	1,098.4	1,322.9	1,177.7	1,736.6	2,283.7	2,290.9	2,825.0
Gold (Million Fine Troy Ounces)	1ad	.122	.209	.209	.210	.212	.213	.215	.215	.216	.217	.216	.220
Gold (National Valuation)	1and	5.1	8.8	8.8	8.9	8.9	9.0	9.1	9.1	9.1	9.2	9.1	9.3
Monetary Authorities: Other Liab	4..d	115.1	89.6	66.5	55.4	48.1	184.3	152.3	126.4	102.3	90.1	79.1	69.1
Deposit Money Banks: Assets	7a.d	6.8	8.6	17.7	66.3	81.2	72.6	65.6	84.1	123.6	203.4	245.2	293.5
Liabilities	7b.d	48.4	113.1	373.3	266.2	375.4	413.4	500.9	452.5	613.8	656.6	689.2	732.1
Other Banking Insts.: Assets	7e.d	–	.1	4.1	4.3	4.5	1.8	12.1	4.3	3.2	6.1	22.8	30.1
Liabilities	7f.d	79.4	79.9	100.2	515.8	554.3	592.0	615.8	633.7	654.1	526.0	534.3	552.4
Monetary Authorities						*Millions of Quetzales: End of Period*							
Foreign Assets	11	1,149.3	1,307.4	1,292.5	1,157.7	1,341.6	†7,566.2	10,109.3	10,521.1	15,038.3	19,265.5	18,920.6	24,029.8
Claims on Central Government	12a	452.4	112.5	357.6	187.4	698.0	†78.7	.2	.2	.2	.2	.2	.2
Claims on Local Government	12b	–	2.6	2.0	1.3	.6	†.3	–	–	–	–	–	–
Claims on Nonfin.Pub.Enterprises	12c	7.4	7.4	7.4	7.4	–	†–	–	–	–	–	–	–
Claims on Private Sector	12d	–	–	–	–	–	†29.7	30.0	29.9	30.6	31.5	32.2	33.2
Claims on Deposit Money Banks	12e	184.6	184.8	61.3	123.3	97.5	†81.9	228.5	652.6	793.8	2,227.2	2,146.5	2,081.3
Claims on Other Banking Insts	12f	284.3	245.2	188.3	148.4	97.1	†44.1	12.8	41.7	7.5	7.4	.4	.4
Reserve Money	14	4,263.2	5,255.3	5,494.3	5,689.3	6,418.2	†10,746.6	10,324.2	10,608.5	12,653.6	14,702.7	17,403.2	19,340.6
of which: Currency Outside DMBs	14a	2,712.6	3,097.3	3,714.6	4,018.9	4,179.1	†4,890.2	5,632.5	7,752.8	7,298.2	8,360.7	8,729.4	10,608.8
Time and Foreign Currency Deposits	15	1,141.9	2,460.9	3,845.6	4,600.0	6,582.4	†665.2	1,103.4	1,995.1	6,872.7	8,083.6	8,997.9	9,925.3
Liabs. of Central Bank: Securities	16ac	970.1	670.7	372.9	76.0	50.3	†212.7	67.5	60.9	58.4	57.1	53.8	53.9
Foreign Liabilities	16c	506.1	323.5	338.3	352.6	359.5	†13.4	9.2	8.4	4.9	3.5	2.6	2.2
Long-Term Foreign Liabilities	16cl	462.1	451.6	277.6	236.2	202.1	†1,125.2	1,034.0	980.2	785.9	717.7	615.1	553.8
Central Government Deposits	16d	1,555.4	1,421.5	1,566.3	1,439.6	1,872.3	†5,293.5	7,586.1	6,405.8	5,527.8	9,162.1	6,446.5	8,700.0
Liabilities to Other Banking Insts	16i	–	–	–	–	–	†2.0	–	–	–	–	1.4	.5
Capital Accounts	17a	333.7	354.1	363.5	384.6	372.1	†330.2	366.4	396.6	3,595.0	3,958.3	2,924.3	2,824.8
Other Items (Net)	17r	–7,154.6	–9,077.7	–10,349.5	–11,152.8	–13,622.1	†–10,587.9	–10,110.0	–9,210.0	–13,627.9	–15,153.2	–15,344.9	–15,256.2
Deposit Money Banks						*Millions of Quetzales: End of Period*							
Reserves	20	2,346.5	2,815.2	2,175.5	4,019.2	4,794.7	†5,731.3	4,823.0	3,121.7	5,132.4	6,120.3	9,051.8	7,879.7
Foreign Assets	21	35.7	50.0	100.1	400.8	484.2	†448.4	449.5	657.4	955.4	1,627.4	1,914.5	2,360.2
Claims on Central Government	22a	1,732.4	1,794.1	2,869.7	1,292.5	1,676.9	†2,870.0	2,389.0	2,277.1	3,361.2	4,654.9	4,799.2	5,104.9
Claims on Local Government	22b	–	–	–	–	–	†81.3	14.4	14.6	38.1	30.4	67.4	–
Claims on Nonfin.Pub.Enterprises	22c	–	–	–	–	–	†–	–	–	63.1	–	–	–
Claims on Private Sector	22d	6,624.8	7,434.4	9,156.9	13,898.6	15,446.7	†16,603.7	21,142.4	24,115.9	26,416.0	30,155.3	32,502.5	35,350.6
Claims on Other Banking Insts	22f	–	–	–	–	–	†2,116.8	2,482.6	2,034.7	2,155.3	2,174.0	1,854.3	1,530.5
Demand Deposits	24	1,475.4	1,928.0	3,336.2	3,728.4	4,617.5	†6,856.2	7,866.9	7,614.1	11,271.5	12,512.2	13,930.4	16,188.0
Time, Savings,& Fgn.Currency Dep	25	8,912.8	8,893.9	7,450.0	8,900.3	8,802.5	†10,535.8	12,976.8	13,682.8	16,506.1	20,722.1	23,935.5	27,270.2
Bonds	26ab	–	–	–	–	–	†5,139.9	4,480.2	4,266.1	4,286.1	3,917.4	3,655.9	2,699.8
Foreign Liabilities	26c	255.5	657.9	2,108.7	1,608.2	2,239.3	†2,385.2	3,261.9	3,318.0	4,659.8	5,068.2	5,232.4	5,749.7
Long-Term Foreign Liabilities	26cl	–	–	–	–	–	†168.4	168.6	221.0	85.3	184.8	148.0	137.0
Central Government Deposits	26d	63.3	76.7	71.0	171.5	194.4	†410.7	677.9	1,197.0	2,675.4	3,722.9	4,739.6	3,853.0
Credit from Monetary Authorities	26g	187.0	185.9	66.0	123.5	97.6	†7.4	162.7	804.6	755.1	2,195.8	2,102.0	2,063.8
Liabilities to Other Banking Insts	26i	–	–	–	–	–	†478.9	575.9	578.0	658.0	1,277.6	1,013.7	900.1
Capital Accounts	27a	1,056.3	1,293.0	1,586.7	1,821.9	2,019.8	†2,315.5	2,775.7	3,810.3	4,464.9	2,834.7	3,077.5	3,315.1
Other Items (Net)	27r	–1,210.9	–941.7	–316.4	3,257.3	4,431.4	†–446.5	–1,645.7	–3,207.4	–7,303.8	–7,673.4	–7,645.3	–9,950.9

Guatemala 258

		1992	1993	1994	1995	1996	1997	1998	1999	2000	2001	2002	2003
Monetary Survey						*Millions of Quetzales: End of Period*							
Foreign Assets (Net)	31n	423.4	376.0	−1,054.4	−402.3	−773.0	†5,616.0	7,287.7	7,852.1	11,329.0	15,821.2	15,600.2	20,638.1
Domestic Credit	32	7,482.6	8,098.0	10,944.6	13,924.5	15,852.6	†16,120.4	17,807.4	20,974.4	23,805.7	24,168.7	28,070.2	29,466.8
Claims on Central Govt. (Net)	32an	566.1	408.4	1,590.0	−131.2	308.2	†−2,755.5	−5,874.8	−5,325.5	−4,841.8	−8,229.9	−6,386.7	−7,447.8
Claims on Local Government	32b	–	2.6	2.0	1.3	.6	†81.6	14.4	14.6	38.1	30.4	67.4	–
Claims on Nonfin.Pub.Enterprises	32c	7.4	7.4	7.4	7.4	–	†–	–	63.1	–	–	–	–
Claims on Private Sector	32d	6,624.8	7,434.4	9,156.9	13,898.6	15,446.7	†16,633.4	21,172.4	24,145.8	26,446.6	30,186.8	32,534.7	35,383.7
Claims on Other Banking Insts	32f	284.3	245.2	188.3	148.4	97.1	†2,160.9	2,495.4	2,076.4	2,162.8	2,181.4	1,854.7	1,530.9
Money	34	4,193.2	5,048.1	7,073.6	7,771.8	8,822.4	†11,997.5	13,613.5	15,467.6	18,832.2	21,059.0	22,835.7	26,937.7
Quasi-Money	35	10,054.7	11,354.8	11,295.6	13,500.3	15,384.9	†11,201.0	14,080.2	15,677.9	23,378.8	28,805.7	32,933.4	37,195.5
Bonds	36ab	–	–	–	–	–	†5,139.9	4,480.2	4,266.1	4,286.1	3,917.4	3,655.9	2,699.8
Liabs. of Central Bank: Securities	36ac	970.1	670.7	372.9	76.0	50.3	†212.7	67.5	60.9	58.4	57.1	53.8	53.9
Long-Term Foreign Liabilities	36cl	462.1	451.6	277.6	236.2	202.1	†1,293.6	1,202.6	1,201.2	871.2	902.5	763.1	690.9
Liabilities to Other Banking Insts	36i					–	†480.9	575.9	578.0	658.0	1,277.6	1,015.1	900.6
Capital Accounts	37a	1,390.0	1,647.1	1,950.2	2,206.5	2,391.9	†2,645.7	3,142.1	4,206.9	8,059.9	6,793.0	6,001.8	6,139.9
Other Items (Net)	37r	−9,164.2	−10,698.3	−11,079.8	−10,268.6	−11,772.0	†−11,234.9	−12,066.9	−12,632.1	−21,009.9	−22,822.4	−23,588.5	−24,513.3
Money plus Quasi-Money	35l	14,247.9	16,402.9	18,369.2	21,272.1	24,207.3	−23,198.5	27,693.7	31,145.5	42,211.0	49,864.7	55,769.1	64,133.2
Other Banking Institutions						*Millions of Quetzales: End of Period*							
Reserves	40	51.7	66.1	31.5	48.3	69.6	†14.9	120.8	45.8	30.2	50.6	49.5	70.0
Foreign Assets	41	.2	.4	23.4	26.2	26.6	†10.9	83.2	33.9	24.7	48.6	177.6	242.1
Claims on Central Government	42a	36.0	36.2	48.4	42.6	111.5	†77.0	120.0	88.7	155.6	220.0	235.6	385.3
Claims on Nonfin.Pub.Enterprises	42c							13.2	.2	.2	.2	.2	–
Claims on Private Sector	42d	1,188.9	1,489.9	2,055.3	2,512.4	2,655.5	†3,388.5	4,310.1	3,859.8	3,181.8	2,813.0	2,185.7	2,209.3
Claims on Deposit Money Banks	42e	186.2	331.7	309.3	458.5	443.5	†555.7	550.1	453.8	540.5	567.2	556.4	267.0
Time, Savings,& Fgn.Currency Dep	45	–	–	–	–	–	†3.8	201.4	4.5	3.3	5.9	4.0	4.4
Bonds	46ab	942.2	1,326.4	1,710.5	1,176.0	1,378.7	†2,298.6	2,692.3	2,192.6	2,314.7	2,171.6	1,843.1	1,476.8
Foreign Liabilities	46c	9.0	26.4	99.7	146.1	157.7	†–	–	–	–	–	–	–
Long-Term Foreign Liabilities	46cl	409.9	438.0	466.4	2,970.0	3,149.1	†3,656.5	4,216.9	4,956.2	5,057.0	4,208.6	4,171.5	4,441.6
Credit from Monetary Authorities	46g	295.6	259.3	195.4	144.2	102.3	†–	–	–	–	–	–	–
Credit from Deposit Money Banks	46h	431.2	523.5	877.6	1,637.1	1,689.4	†1,584.0	1,925.9	2,110.8	1,629.1	1,436.3	1,264.7	1,473.1
Capital Accounts	47a	−107.0	−142.8	−107.4	−2,559.7	−2,667.4	†−2,849.0	−3,329.4	−4,019.0	−4,242.2	−3,414.7	−3,417.2	−3,641.6
Other Items (Net)	47r	−517.9	−506.5	−774.3	−425.7	−503.1	†−633.7	−522.7	−762.9	−828.9	−708.1	−661.1	−580.5
Banking Survey						*Millions of Quetzales: End of Period*							
Foreign Assets (Net)	51n	414.6	350.0	−1,130.7	−522.2	−904.1	†5,626.9	7,370.9	7,886.0	11,353.7	15,869.8	15,777.8	20,880.2
Domestic Credit	52	8,423.2	9,378.9	12,860.0	16,331.1	18,522.5	†17,438.2	19,743.0	22,853.3	24,980.5	25,020.5	28,640.8	30,530.6
Claims on Central Govt. (Net)	52an	602.1	444.6	1,638.4	−88.6	419.7	†−2,678.5	−5,754.8	−5,236.8	−4,686.2	−8,009.9	−6,151.0	−7,062.5
Claims on Local Government	52b	–	2.6	2.0	1.3	.6	†81.6	15.1	21.2	38.1	30.4	71.2	–
Claims on Nonfin.Pub.Enterprises	52c	7.4	7.4	7.4	7.4	–	†13.2	.2	63.3	.2	.2	.2	–
Claims on Private Sector	52d	7,813.7	8,924.3	11,212.0	16,411.0	18,102.2	†20,021.9	25,482.5	28,005.6	29,628.4	32,999.8	34,720.5	37,593.1
Liquid Liabilities	55l	14,196.2	16,336.8	18,337.7	21,223.8	24,137.7	†23,186.8	27,912.3	31,097.0	42,176.7	49,815.0	55,709.7	64,064.3
Bonds	56ab	942.2	1,326.4	1,710.5	1,176.0	1,378.7	†7,438.5	7,172.5	6,458.7	6,600.8	6,089.0	5,499.0	4,176.6
Liabs. of Central Bank: Securities	56ac	970.1	670.7	372.9	76.0	50.3	†212.7	67.5	60.9	58.4	57.1	53.8	53.9
Long-Term Foreign Liabilities	56cl	872.0	889.6	744.0	3,206.2	3,351.2	†4,950.1	5,419.5	6,157.4	5,928.2	5,111.1	4,934.6	5,132.4
Capital Accounts	57a	1,283.0	1,504.3	1,842.8	−353.2	−275.5	†−203.3	−187.3	187.9	3,817.7	3,378.3	2,584.6	2,498.2
Other Items (Net)	57r	−9,425.8	−10,998.9	−11,278.7	−9,519.9	−11,024.0	†−12,519.7	−13,270.6	−13,222.6	−22,247.6	−23,560.2	−24,363.1	−24,514.7
Interest Rates						*Percent Per Annum*							
Money Market Rate	60b	….	….	….	….	….	7.77	6.62	9.23	9.33	10.58	9.11	6.65
Savings Rate	60k	….	….	….	….	….	5.13	4.50	5.19	5.41	4.51	3.31	2.09
Deposit Rate	60l	10.44	12.63	9.69	7.87	7.65	†5.83	5.44	7.96	10.17	8.75	6.92	4.78
Lending Rate	60p	19.49	24.73	22.93	21.16	22.72	†18.64	16.56	19.51	20.88	18.96	16.86	14.98
Prices and Labor						*Index Numbers (2000=100): Period Averages*							
Consumer Prices	64	51.6	57.7	64.0	69.3	77.0	84.1	90.0	94.4	†100.0	107.6	116.3	122.6
						Number in Thousands: Period Averages							
Labor Force	67d	….	….	2,326	….	….	….	….	3,982	4,208	….	….	….
Employment	67e	796	823	830	856	831	….	….	….	….	….	….	….
Unemployment	67c	2	1	1	1	….	….	….	….	….	….	….	….
International Transactions						*Millions of US Dollars*							
Exports	70..d	1,295.3	1,340.4	1,521.5	2,155.5	2,030.7	2,344.1	2,581.6	2,397.5	2,695.6	2,466.0	2,231.6	2,488.9
Imports, c.i.f.	71..d	2,531.5	2,599.3	2,781.4	3,292.5	3,146.1	3,851.9	4,651.1	4,381.7	4,790.9	5,606.8	6,078.0	6,488.0
Imports, f.o.b.	71.vd	2,330.7	2,384.0	2,425.7	3,032.5	2,880.3	3,542.8	4,164.5	4,010.5	4,423.3	5,234.2	5,580.3	5,963.2

2004, International Monetary Fund: *International Financial Statistics Yearbook*

Guatemala 258

		1992	1993	1994	1995	1996	1997	1998	1999	2000	2001	2002	2003
Balance of Payments					*Millions of US Dollars: Minus Sign Indicates Debit*								
Current Account, n.i.e.	78ald	−705.9	−701.7	−625.3	−572.0	−451.5	−633.5	−1,039.1	−1,025.9	−1,049.6	−1,252.9	−1,193.0	....
Goods: Exports f.o.b.	78aad	1,283.7	1,363.2	1,550.1	2,157.5	2,236.9	2,602.9	2,846.9	2,780.6	3,085.1	2,859.8	2,628.4	....
Goods: Imports f.o.b.	78abd	−2,327.8	−2,384.0	−2,546.6	−3,032.6	−2,880.3	−3,542.7	−4,255.7	−4,225.7	−4,742.0	−5,142.0	−5,578.4	....
Trade Balance	78acd	−1,044.1	−1,020.8	−996.5	−875.1	−643.4	−939.8	−1,408.8	−1,445.1	−1,656.9	−2,282.2	−2,950.0	....
Services: Credit	78add	614.0	660.4	697.5	665.9	559.0	588.8	639.9	699.5	777.0	1,044.8	1,140.1	....
Services: Debit	78aed	−525.3	−586.1	−644.9	−694.9	−659.7	−650.5	−791.8	−790.7	−825.4	−927.9	−1,043.8	....
Balance on Goods & Services	78afd	−955.4	−946.5	−943.9	−904.1	−744.1	−1,001.5	−1,560.7	−1,536.3	−1,705.3	−2,165.3	−2,853.6	....
Income: Credit	78agd	69.1	61.1	63.6	46.6	40.2	72.4	91.4	76.2	214.4	317.5	151.1	....
Income: Debit	78ahd	−210.1	−179.5	−193.6	−205.7	−270.1	−311.1	−275.1	−280.7	−424.0	−401.9	−448.9	....
Balance on Gds, Serv. & Inc.	78aid	−1,096.4	−1,064.9	−1,073.9	−1,063.2	−974.0	−1,240.2	−1,744.4	−1,740.8	−1,914.9	−2,249.7	−3,151.4	....
Current Transfers, n.i.e.: Credit	78ajd	406.2	371.4	456.4	508.2	537.1	628.8	742.9	754.4	908.2	1,024.3	2,059.9	....
Current Transfers: Debit	78akd	−15.7	−8.2	−7.8	−17.0	−14.6	−22.1	−37.6	−39.5	−42.9	−27.5	−101.5	....
Capital Account, n.i.e.	78bcd	−	−	−	61.6	65.0	85.0	71.0	68.4	85.5	93.4	129.8	....
Capital Account, n.i.e.: Credit	78bad	−	−	−	61.6	65.0	85.0	71.0	68.4	85.5	93.4	129.8	....
Capital Account: Debit	78bbd	−	−	−	....	....	....	....	....	....	....	....	....
Financial Account, n.i.e.	78bjd	610.5	816.2	655.2	494.8	672.3	737.4	1,136.7	637.5	1,520.7	1,546.7	1,172.7	....
Direct Investment Abroad	78bdd	−	−	....	....	....	....	....	....	....	....	....	....
Dir. Invest. in Rep. Econ., n.i.e.	78bed	94.1	142.5	65.2	75.2	76.9	84.4	672.8	154.6	229.9	455.5	110.2	....
Portfolio Investment Assets	78bfd	1.8	112.4	−9.8	−22.2	−11.5	−18.1	−11.6	−26.0	−36.3	−45.0	−38.3	....
Equity Securities	78bkd	−	−	....	....	....	....	....	....	....	....	....	....
Debt Securities	78bld	1.8	112.4	−9.8	−22.2	−11.5	−18.1	−11.6	−26.0	−36.3	−45.0	−38.3	....
Portfolio Investment Liab., n.i.e.	78bgd	9.6	−27.0	7.1	5.9	−4.5	249.7	65.8	136.5	78.9	175.3	−107.8	....
Equity Securities	78bmd	−	−	....	....	....	....	....	....	....	....	....	....
Debt Securities	78bnd	9.6	−27.0	7.1	5.9	−4.5	249.7	65.8	136.5	78.9	175.3	−107.8	....
Financial Derivatives Assets	78bwd	....	....	−	−	−	−	−	−	−	−	−	....
Financial Derivatives Liabilities	78bxd	....	....	−	−	−	−	−	−	−	−	−	....
Other Investment Assets	78bhd	57.2	−3.0	116.8	125.1	199.2	221.2	241.7	199.9	213.2	156.7	196.4	....
Monetary Authorities	78bod	....	....	−	....	....	....	....	....	....	....	−	....
General Government	78bpd	−	−45.9	−49.2	....	....	....	....	....	....	....	−	....
Banks	78bqd	....	....	−	....	....	....	....	....	....	....	−	....
Other Sectors	78brd	57.2	42.9	166.0	125.1	199.2	221.2	241.7	199.9	213.2	156.7	196.4	....
Other Investment Liab., n.i.e.	78bid	447.8	591.3	475.9	310.8	412.2	200.2	168.0	172.5	1,035.0	804.0	1,012.3	....
Monetary Authorities	78bsd	.6	−44.1	−63.9	−78.3	−56.3	−108.6	−54.2	−25.6	−24.0	−11.2	−11.3	....
General Government	78btd	−16.3	−51.3	132.7	11.8	91.1	89.5	252.4	295.9	92.7	42.6	172.7	....
Banks	78bud	14.4	−	−	7.3	19.4	−4.6	3.2	23.0	−17.4	21.8	−	....
Other Sectors	78bvd	449.1	686.7	407.1	370.0	358.0	223.9	−33.4	−120.8	983.7	750.9	850.9	....
Net Errors and Omissions	78cad	81.8	85.2	−23.6	−136.2	−71.7	40.7	66.8	195.0	86.1	87.2	−88.3	....
Overall Balance	78cbd	−13.6	199.7	6.3	−151.8	214.1	229.6	235.4	−125.0	642.7	474.4	21.2	....
Reserves and Related Items	79dad	13.6	−199.7	−6.3	151.8	−214.1	−229.6	−235.4	125.0	−642.7	−474.4	−21.2	....
Reserve Assets	79dbd	51.6	−120.5	−47.3	157.3	−199.0	−257.7	−263.0	125.0	−642.7	−474.4	−21.2	....
Use of Fund Credit and Loans	79dcd	−31.7	−31.3	−	−	−	−	−	−	−	−	−	....
Exceptional Financing	79ded	−6.4	−47.9	41.0	−5.5	−15.1	28.1	27.6	....	....	−	−	....
Government Finance					*Millions of Quetzales: Year Ending December 31*								
Deficit (−) or Surplus	80	407.0	−1,064.5	†−938.7	−218.4	−268.0	−2,244.3	−2,708.9	−3,804.2	−2,709.8	−3,105.0	−1,351.8	−4,646.8
Revenue	81	5,575.0	5,645.8	†5,712.3	7,227.7	8,605.1	9,730.3	12,714.0	14,735.7	16,050.5	17,656.4	20,503.5	21,387.5
Grants Received	81z	....	....	†74.3	39.1	53.0	55.1	94.2	188.2	348.5	565.7	377.8	299.1
Exp. & Lending Minus Repay.	82z	....	....	†6,725.3	7,485.2	8,926.1	12,029.7	15,517.1	18,728.1	19,108.8	21,327.1	22,233.1	26,333.4
Expenditure	82	5,168.0	6,710.3	†6,592.2	7,512.4	8,378.5	11,408.0	15,517.1	18,728.1	19,108.8	21,327.1	22,233.1	26,333.4
Lending Minus Repayments	83	....	....	†237.8	308.4	235.9	−	−	−	−	−	−	−
Adjustment to Cash Basis	82x	....	....	†−104.7	−335.6	311.7	621.7	−	−	−	−	−	−
Financing (by Residence of Lender)													
Domestic	84a	....	....	†−187.5	433.0	−54.7	92.9	1,306.7	1,541.9	2,058.4	−129.2	156.4	2,061.9
Foreign	85a	....	....	†1,126.2	−214.6	322.7	2,151.4	1,402.2	2,262.3	651.4	3,234.2	1,195.4	2,584.9
Debt: Domestic	88a	....	....	4,854.7	4,485.2	5,093.0	5,862.2	6,259.8	7,807.1	8,629.7	9,281.1	8,169.9	11,036.7
Foreign	89a	....	....	887.8	1,203.5	1,308.2	1,491.3	1,693.8	2,034.4	2,058.0	2,350.1	2,956.4	3,396.5
Financing (by Currency)													
Net Borrowing: Quetzales	84b	80.9	551.7	....	....	....	....	....	....	....	....	....	....
Foreign Currency	85b	−11.2	−84.9	....	....	....	....	....	....	....	....	....	....
Use of Cash Balances	87	−476.7	597.7	....	....	....	....	....	....	....	....	....	....
National Accounts					*Millions of Quetzales*								
Househ.Cons.Expend.,incl.NPISHs	96f	45,899	54,165	63,893	72,899	83,072	93,804	105,429	114,554	125,661	139,917	156,815	171,424
Government Consumption Expend.	91f	3,482	4,151	4,468	4,692	4,851	5,391	7,041	8,552	10,486	12,420	13,005	14,105
Gross Fixed Capital Formation	93e	8,445	10,335	10,622	12,360	12,727	16,302	20,645	24,205	24,147	25,486	28,465	28,894
Changes in Inventories	93i	1,448	745	1,087	460	−614	−1,540	929	−728	2,560	3,822	5,905	4,567
Exports of Goods and Services	90c	9,483	11,613	13,170	16,400	17,005	19,370	22,537	25,711	30,241	30,999	29,622	31,902
Imports of Goods and Services (−)	98c	14,771	16,765	18,571	21,656	21,562	25,454	32,559	37,008	43,351	47,774	51,816	54,495
Gross Domestic Product (GDP)	99b	53,985	64,243	74,669	85,157	95,479	107,873	124,022	135,287	149,743	164,870	181,996	196,396
Net Primary Income from Abroad	98.n	−426	−854	−856	−926	−1,400	−1,451	−979	−1,480	−1,751	−899	−2,442	−3,366
Gross National Income (GNI)	99a	53,560	63,389	73,813	84,231	94,079	106,422	123,043	133,807	147,992	163,972	179,554	193,031
Consumption of Fixed Capital	99cf	1,108	1,362	1,672	1,990	2,361	2,742	3,231	3,850	4,576	5,300	6,065	6,918
GDP Volume 1958 Prices	99b.p	3,684	3,828	3,983	4,180	4,303	4,491	4,716	4,897	5,074	5,192	5,309	5,421
GDP Volume (2000=100)	99bvp	72.6	75.4	78.5	82.4	84.8	88.5	93.0	96.5	100.0	102.3	104.6	106.8
GDP Deflator (2000=100)	99bip	49.7	56.9	63.5	69.0	75.2	81.4	89.1	93.6	100.0	107.6	116.2	122.8
					Millions: Midyear Estimates								
Population	99z	9.21	9.46	9.71	9.98	10.25	10.53	10.82	11.12	11.42	11.73	12.04	12.35

Guinea 656

		1992	1993	1994	1995	1996	1997	1998	1999	2000	2001	2002	2003
Exchange Rates						*Francs per SDR: End of Period*							
Official Rate	aa	1,268.3	1,335.7	1,432.1	1,483.5	1,494.2	1,544.8	1,827.7	2,382.7	2,452.4	2,498.8	2,620.2	2,964.2
					Francs per US Dollar: End of Period (ae) Period Average (rf)								
Official Rate	ae	922.4	972.4	981.0	998.0	1,039.1	1,145.0	1,298.0	1,736.0	1,882.3	1,988.3	1,976.0	2,000.0
Official Rate	rf	902.0	955.5	976.6	991.4	1,004.0	1,095.3	1,236.8	1,387.4	1,746.9	1,950.6	1,975.8	1,984.9
Fund Position						*Millions of SDRs: End of Period*							
Quota	2f.s	78.70	78.70	78.70	78.70	78.70	78.70	78.70	107.10	107.10	107.10	107.10	107.10
SDRs	1b.s	7.93	8.49	3.79	5.01	.54	1.97	1.02	.94	.19	.63	1.22	.15
Reserve Position in the Fund	1c.s	.03	.07	.07	.07	.08	.08	.08	.08	.08	.08	.08	.08
Total Fund Cred.&Loans Outstg	2tl	46.32	44.00	48.64	63.11	57.32	73.39	90.05	92.71	86.63	98.08	102.23	91.70
International Liquidity					*Millions of US Dollars Unless Otherwise Indicated: End of Period*								
Total Reserves minus Gold	1l.d	86.96	132.12	87.85	86.76	87.34	121.63	236.71	199.68	147.91	200.23	171.40	....
SDRs	1b.d	10.90	11.67	5.53	7.45	.77	2.66	1.43	1.29	.25	.80	1.66	.22
Reserve Position in the Fund	1c.d	.04	.09	.10	.10	.11	.10	.11	.10	.10	.09	.10	.11
Foreign Exchange	1d.d	76.01	120.36	82.22	79.21	86.46	118.88	235.17	198.29	147.56	199.34	169.64	....
Monetary Authorities: Other Liab.	4..d	15.88	5.50	6.70	5.30	44.61	10.13	10.51	....	7.78	21.94	7.62	11.09
Deposit Money Banks: Assets	7a.d	87.24	85.47	86.27	90.89	81.05	73.08	85.27	77.53	80.32	68.46	73.85	68.11
Liabilities	7b.d	45.68	46.81	52.39	79.93	70.17	53.86	58.75	62.70	40.88	27.33	38.68	34.73
Monetary Authorities						*Millions of Francs: End of Period*							
Foreign Assets	11	139,668	185,522	155,011	185,089	201,116	254,054	319,566	....	303,361	407,345	332,610	268,660
Claims on Central Government	12a	168,089	183,958	225,807	332,922	429,007	532,766	662,569	....	802,821	1,421,713	842,762	1,130,869
Claims on Nonfin.Pub.Enterprises	12c	2,359	2,352	3,059	3,685	4,063	4,659	31,740	....	33,048	33,236	2,670	2,688
Claims on Private Sector	12d	445	42	129	108	159	3,362	5,763	....	5,313	12,924	26,619	33,503
Claims on Deposit Money Banks	12e	9,890	8,211	8,587	8,632	8,196	26,227	6,701	....	8,090	3,043	4,349	1,557
Claims on Other Banking Insts.	12f	–	–	48	493	–	–	439	....	193	78	–	–
Reserve Money	14	165,178	196,468	176,724	198,442	195,681	248,968	†262,015	....	385,183	442,501	538,658	634,343
of which: Currency Outside DMBs	14a	133,028	166,609	154,748	167,144	154,420	191,635	209,682	....	288,468	310,063	349,781	478,133
Foreign Liabilities	16c	73,396	64,127	76,223	98,912	132,011	124,978	178,215	....	227,096	288,707	282,906	293,998
Central Government Deposits	16d	93,479	129,003	151,170	249,942	313,926	444,141	590,113	....	576,045	1,170,909	407,441	574,870
Capital Accounts	17a	41,609	51,848	57,608	55,460	51,645	52,291	55,559	....	74,939	91,303	54,101	111,184
Other Items (Net)	17r	–53,217	–61,361	–69,088	–71,830	–50,726	–49,316	–59,124	....	–110,436	–115,080	–74,095	–177,118
Deposit Money Banks						*Millions of Francs: End of Period*							
Reserves	20	17,591	20,458	15,380	28,310	31,930	46,130	50,064	59,859	66,492	101,186	138,767	116,171
Foreign Assets	21	80,474	83,110	84,630	90,710	84,220	83,670	110,678	134,586	151,182	136,119	145,935	136,221
Claims on Central Government	22a	20	12,596	13,210	29,910	38,500	46,750	44,054	39,287	18,037	46,993	134,114	285,888
Claims on Nonfin.Pub.Enterprises	22c	59	124	10	270	430	260	273	54	185	60	9,964	3,891
Claims on Private Sector	22d	106,487	130,322	144,410	181,410	188,270	184,070	156,383	178,654	203,379	210,107	215,213	255,654
Demand Deposits	24	76,665	86,763	94,430	104,060	112,590	130,430	144,030	139,940	177,997	226,047	300,520	386,359
Time, Savings,& Fgn.Currency Dep.	25	38,624	54,794	52,180	64,950	77,710	83,430	81,176	99,528	111,339	129,777	144,302	206,281
Foreign Liabilities	26c	42,135	45,523	51,400	79,770	72,920	61,670	76,257	108,851	76,944	54,341	76,439	69,457
Central Government Deposits	26d	13,934	15,267	17,100	16,490	15,800	19,960	23,575	25,296	23,108	27,527	30,135	40,470
Credit from Monetary Authorities	26g	10,622	9,601	10,360	11,580	10,360	10,660	7,239	7,822	8,995	4,775	15,456	6,407
Capital Accounts	27a	39,613	47,601	46,400	50,870	38,980	49,600	34,986	43,293	53,695	53,017	81,611	71,187
Other Items (Net)	27r	–16,962	–12,939	–14,230	2,920	14,960	5,120	–5,811	–12,290	–12,803	–1,019	–4,470	17,664
Monetary Survey						*Millions of Francs: End of Period*							
Foreign Assets (Net)	31n	104,610	158,982	112,018	97,118	80,405	151,077	175,772	....	150,503	200,416	119,201	41,426
Domestic Credit	32	170,046	185,124	218,403	282,366	330,703	307,766	287,534	....	466,370	526,693	794,387	1,098,650
Claims on Central Govt. (Net)	32an	60,696	52,284	70,747	96,400	137,781	115,415	92,935	....	221,705	270,270	539,300	801,417
Claims on Nonfin.Pub.Enterprises	32c	2,418	2,476	3,069	3,955	4,493	4,919	32,013	....	33,233	33,296	12,634	6,579
Claims on Private Sector	32d	106,932	130,364	144,539	181,518	188,429	187,432	162,146	....	208,692	223,031	241,832	289,157
Claims on Other Banking Insts.	32f	–	–	48	493	–	–	439	....	193	78	–	–
Money	34	218,445	260,854	252,582	274,125	273,465	331,666	†361,469	....	499,885	559,993	681,228	893,055
Quasi-Money	35	38,624	54,794	52,180	64,950	77,710	83,430	81,176	99,528	111,339	129,777	144,302	206,281
Capital Accounts	37a	81,222	99,449	104,008	106,330	90,625	101,891	90,545	....	128,634	144,320	135,712	182,371
Other Items (Net)	37r	–63,640	–70,991	–78,353	–65,895	–30,726	–58,161	–69,885	....	–122,984	–106,980	–47,654	–141,631
Money plus Quasi-Money	35l	257,069	315,648	304,762	339,075	351,175	415,096	†442,645	....	611,224	689,770	825,530	1,099,336
Interest Rates						*Percent Per Annum*							
Refinancing Rate (End of Period)	60	19.00	17.00	17.00	18.00	18.00	15.00	....	....	11.50	16.25	16.25	16.25
Savings Rate	60k	21.00	17.00	16.00	15.50	....	....	6.38	5.67	7.50	8.03	7.40	....
Deposit Rate	60l	23.00	19.75	18.00	17.50	....	....	19.56	19.88	19.38	....	....	....
Lending Rate	60p	27.00	24.50	22.00	21.50	....	....	19.56	19.88	19.38	....	....	....

2004, International Monetary Fund: *International Financial Statistics Yearbook*

Guinea 656

		1992	1993	1994	1995	1996	1997	1998	1999	2000	2001	2002	2003
Balance of Payments					*Millions of US Dollars: Minus Sign Indicates Debit*								
Current Account, n.i.e.	78ald	−262.7	−56.8	−248.0	−216.5	−177.3	−91.1	−183.6	−214.7	−155.2	−102.4	−46.0	....
Goods: Exports f.o.b.	78aad	517.2	561.1	515.7	582.8	636.5	630.1	693.0	635.7	666.3	731.0	886.0	....
Goods: Imports f.o.b.	78abd	−608.4	−582.7	−685.4	−621.7	−525.3	−512.5	−572.0	−581.7	−587.1	−561.9	−668.4	....
Trade Balance	78acd	−91.2	−21.6	−169.7	−39.0	111.2	117.6	121.0	53.9	79.3	169.1	217.7	....
Services: Credit	78add	159.7	186.8	152.9	117.5	124.1	110.7	110.8	113.1	68.0	102.8	90.4	....
Services: Debit	78aed	−322.6	−334.8	−366.0	−389.3	−422.2	−321.6	−382.7	−364.5	−284.8	−319.0	−330.7	....
Balance on Goods & Services	78afd	−254.0	−169.6	−382.9	−310.8	−186.8	−93.3	−150.9	−197.4	−137.5	−47.1	−22.6	....
Income: Credit	78agd	7.9	9.3	6.5	12.9	12.8	7.8	9.0	24.7	23.5	11.3	6.1	....
Income: Debit	78ahd	−148.9	−92.6	−79.8	−97.5	−105.7	−121.3	−133.5	−106.9	−101.1	−113.6	−75.3	....
Balance on Gds, Serv. & Inc.	78aid	−395.0	−252.9	−456.1	−395.5	−279.8	−206.9	−275.5	−279.6	−215.2	−149.4	−91.8	....
Current Transfers, n.i.e.: Credit	78ajd	193.5	260.3	280.6	258.3	137.8	131.4	116.2	80.0	88.6	91.5	70.6	....
Current Transfers: Debit	78akd	−61.2	−64.2	−72.5	−79.3	−35.3	−15.6	−24.3	−15.1	−28.5	−44.5	−24.8	....
Capital Account, n.i.e	78bcd	8.0	5.0	–	–	–	–	–	–	–	–	–	....
Capital Account, n.i.e.: Credit	78bad	8.0	5.0	–	–	–	–	–	–	–	–	–	....
Capital Account: Debit	78bbd	....	....	....	....	....	....	–	–	–	–	–	....
Financial Account, n.i.e.	78bjd	61.7	62.6	84.2	109.2	47.5	−89.3	8.0	116.5	8.2	−12.1	13.8	....
Direct Investment Abroad	78bdd	....	....	....	....	−.5	–	–	–	–	–	–	....
Dir. Invest. in Rep. Econ., n.i.e.	78bed	19.7	2.7	.2	.8	23.8	17.3	17.8	63.4	9.9	1.6	–	....
Portfolio Investment Assets	78bfd	....	....	....	....	....	....	−82.7	−20.0	8.7	4.6	5.1	....
Equity Securities	78bkd	....	....	....	....	....	....	....	....	....	....	....	....
Debt Securities	78bld	....	....	....	....	....	....	−82.7	−20.0	8.7	4.6	5.1	....
Portfolio Investment Liab., n.i.e.	78bgd	....	....	....	....	....	....	....	–	–	–	–	....
Equity Securities	78bmd	....	....	....	....	....	....	....	–	–	–	–	....
Debt Securities	78bnd	....	....	....	....	....	....	....	–	–	–	–	....
Financial Derivatives Assets	78bwd	....	....	....	....	....	....	....	....	....	....	....	....
Financial Derivatives Liabilities	78bxd	....	....	....	....	....	....	....	....	....	....	....	....
Other Investment Assets	78bhd	−27.5	−20.1	−14.5	−73.7	−19.8	−99.1	−14.6	.1	−17.0	11.7	−4.5	....
Monetary Authorities	78bod	....	....	−6.5	9.0	6.0	2.4	1.2	−1.5	−13.7	1.5	−7.3	....
General Government	78bpd	−4.1	2.2	....	....	....	....	–	–	–	–	–	....
Banks	78bqd	−5.0	–	−2.2	−4.6	9.0	9.3	−12.5	7.6	−1.3	9.5	4.8	....
Other Sectors	78brd	−18.4	−22.3	−5.8	−78.2	−34.7	−110.8	−3.3	−6.0	−2.0	.6	−2.0	....
Other Investment Liab., n.i.e.	78bid	69.6	80.0	98.5	182.2	44.0	−7.5	87.5	73.0	6.6	−30.0	13.2	....
Monetary Authorities	78bsd	−5.7	−.1	.1	−.5	39.1	−35.3	−3.0	.2	−.8	13.4	11.7	....
General Government	78btd	15.4	54.6	79.6	106.5	−14.4	48.2	37.6	84.1	61.5	26.5	34.8	....
Banks	78bud	−6.5	.1	8.3	26.0	−9.8	−18.1	6.7	3.8	−23.1	−12.4	11.1	....
Other Sectors	78bvd	66.4	25.4	10.5	50.2	29.0	−2.3	46.2	−15.1	−30.9	−57.5	−44.5	....
Net Errors and Omissions	78cad	18.6	−107.5	39.7	34.8	69.9	49.8	17.8	22.3	84.0	−2.1	8.5	....
Overall Balance	78cbd	−174.4	−96.7	−124.1	−72.5	−59.9	−130.6	−157.8	−75.9	−62.9	−116.5	−23.7	....
Reserves and Related Items	79dad	174.4	96.7	124.1	72.5	59.9	130.6	157.8	75.9	62.9	116.5	23.7	....
Reserve Assets	79dbd	1.6	−49.9	32.4	−43.8	−6.5	−20.3	60.7	60.6	50.5	−3.9	−76.0	....
Use of Fund Credit and Loans	79dcd	11.0	−3.2	7.0	22.1	−8.4	22.4	22.8	3.7	−7.9	14.8	5.7	....
Exceptional Financing	79ded	161.8	149.9	84.7	94.2	74.9	128.5	74.3	11.5	20.4	105.7	94.0	....
Government Finance					*Millions of Francs: Year Ending December 31*								
Deficit (−) or Surplus	80	−83,585	....	....	....	....	....	−192,650	−116,309f	....	....	....	....
Revenue	81	357,889	....	....	....	....	....	497,293	574,901f	....	....	....	....
Grants Received	81z	117,300	....	....	....	....	....	106,481	320,500f	....	....	....	....
Expenditure	82	559,854	....	....	....	....	....	792,554	1,010,060f	....	....	....	....
Lending Minus Repayments	83	−1,080	....	....	....	....	....	3,870	1,650f	....	....	....	....
Financing													
Domestic	84a	−26,108	....	....	....	....	....	−2,610	8,249f	....	....	....	....
Foreign	85a	109,693	....	....	....	....	....	195,260	108,060f	....	....	....	....
					Millions: Midyear Estimates								
Population	99z	6.59	6.85	7.10	7.32	7.52	7.69	7.84	7.98	8.12	8.24	8.36	8.48

Guinea-Bissau 654

		1992	1993	1994	1995	1996	1997	1998	1999	2000	2001	2002	2003
Exchange Rates		\multicolumn{12}{c}{*Francs per SDR: End of Period*}
Official Rate	aa	183.10	242.25	345.18	501.49	772.88	807.94	791.61	896.19	918.49	935.39	850.37	771.76
		\multicolumn{12}{c}{*Francs per US Dollar: End of Period (ae) Period Average (rf)*}
Official Rate	ae	133.16	176.37	236.45	337.37	537.48	598.81	562.21	652.95	704.95	744.31	625.50	519.36
Official Rate	rf	106.68	155.11	198.34	278.04	405.75	583.67	589.95	†615.70	711.98	733.04	696.99	581.20
Fund Position		\multicolumn{12}{c}{*Millions of SDRs: End of Period*}
Quota	2f.s	10.50	10.50	10.50	10.50	10.50	10.50	10.50	14.20	14.20	14.20	14.20	14.20
SDRs	1b.s	–	.01	–	.01	.01	.04	.02	.06	.03	.16	.30	.80
Reserve Position in the Fund	1c.s	–	–	–	–	–	–	–	–	–	–	–	–
Total Fund Cred.&Loans Outstg	2tl	3.75	3.45	3.15	3.98	5.33	9.04	10.95	12.63	18.97	18.45	17.24	13.78
International Liquidity		\multicolumn{12}{c}{*Millions of US Dollars Unless Otherwise Indicated: End of Period*}
Total Reserves minus Gold	1l.d	17.75	14.17	18.43	20.27	11.53	33.70	35.76	35.28	66.73	69.47	102.71	164.38
SDRs	1b.d	–	.01	–	.01	.01	.06	.03	.08	.04	.20	.40	1.18
Reserve Position in the Fund	1c.d	–	–	–	–	–	–	–	–	–	–	–	–
Foreign Exchange	1d.d	17.75	14.16	18.43	20.26	11.52	33.65	35.73	35.21	66.69	69.28	102.31	163.20
Monetary Authorities: Other Liab	4..d	53.1	48.3	42.6	38.6	18.2	1.8	.7	1.4	–.6	1.0	–.1	–.7
Deposit Money Banks: Assets	7a.d	12.1	10.8	12.1	18.7	16.7	19.2	19.3	16.6	2.3	3.8	8.7	11.6
Liabilities	7b.d	1.7	.7	7.2	6.9	7.5	11.7	12.9	11.1	13.7	11.5	13.5	–
Monetary Authorities		\multicolumn{12}{c}{*Millions of Francs: End of Period*}
Foreign Assets	11	2,364	2,499	4,357	6,837	6,196	20,183	20,105	23,038	47,044	51,711	64,246	85,374
Claims on Central Government	12a	2,857	3,197	4,144	4,728	7,679	10,690	12,453	13,081	20,343	20,288	20,214	17,885
Claims on Other Financial Insts	12f	–	–	–	–	–	–	–	–	–	–	–	–
Reserve Money	14	3,031	4,005	5,300	6,998	9,709	21,922	19,011	25,561	47,936	55,559	72,528	91,623
of which: Currency Outside DMBs	14a	1,603	2,039	3,015	4,278	6,370	20,137	17,642	24,186	44,245	53,054	70,223	89,569
Foreign Liabilities	16c	7,752	9,360	11,157	15,012	13,878	8,359	9,055	12,251	17,006	18,019	14,565	10,271
Central Government Deposits	16d	2,487	2,642	4,915	7,722	9,080	6,110	8,148	2,994	3,567	3,742	492	1,929
Other Items (Net)	17r	–4,808	–5,985	–8,542	–13,840	–18,793	–5,518	–3,655	–4,686	–1,122	–5,320	–3,049	–564
Deposit Money Banks		\multicolumn{12}{c}{*Millions of Francs: End of Period*}
Reserves	20	1,484	2,052	2,420	3,362	2,614	4,392	2,728	2,728	6,256	2,397	1,667	2,027
Foreign Assets	21	1,610	1,912	2,856	6,295	8,989	11,479	10,827	10,827	1,621	2,850	5,470	6,032
Claims on Central Government	22a	624	544	576	567	77	21	21	21	–	–	–	456
Claims on Private Sector	22d	1,751	2,859	4,617	4,612	5,305	7,651	9,859	9,859	12,121	4,436	4,211	2,651
Claims on Other Financial Insts	22f	–	–	–	–	–	–	–	–	–	–	–	–
Demand Deposits	24	834	1,050	1,855	2,880	4,507	16,431	14,476	14,476	19,985	16,261	14,623	8,319
Time & Foreign Currency Deposits	25	1,452	2,361	3,207	4,395	6,320	1,132	1,355	1,355	1,037	794	1,282	564
Foreign Liabilities	26c	228	114	1,700	2,330	3,999	6,984	7,220	7,220	2,924	543	439	2
Long-Term Foreign Liabilities	26cl	3	4	6	8	13	14	14	14	6,744	8,001	8,001	–
Central Government Deposits	26d	232	132	47	14	561	820	1,014	1,014	1,066	1,144	1,156	1,286
Credit from Monetary Authorities	26g	3,223	4,328	4,328	4,328	97	–	–	–	–	–	–	–
Other Items (Net)	27r	–502	–622	–674	881	1,489	–1,838	–644	–644	–11,758	–17,061	–14,153	995
Monetary Survey		\multicolumn{12}{c}{*Millions of Francs: End of Period*}
Foreign Assets (Net)	31n	–4,006	–5,064	–5,644	–4,211	–2,692	16,318	14,657	14,394	28,735	35,999	54,712	81,132
Domestic Credit	32	2,514	3,825	4,374	2,171	3,420	11,432	13,172	18,954	27,831	19,838	22,777	17,777
Claims on Central Govt. (Net)	32an	62	–542	–2,302	–3,959	–3,923	331	613	9,095	15,709	15,402	18,566	15,126
Claims on Private Sector	32d	2,452	4,368	6,677	6,129	7,343	11,101	12,559	9,859	12,121	4,436	4,211	2,651
Claims on Other Financial Insts	32f	–	–	–	–	–	–	–	–	–	–	–	–
Money	34	2,440	3,105	4,910	7,211	10,891	36,625	32,194	39,420	64,524	69,535	85,074	98,209
Quasi-Money	35	1,452	2,361	3,207	4,395	6,320	1,132	1,355	1,355	1,037	794	1,282	564
Long-Term Foriegn Liabilities	36cl	3	4	6	8	13	14	14	14	6,744	8,001	8,001	–
Other Items (Net)	37r	–6,775	–8,598	–11,538	–16,195	–19,639	–10,020	–5,733	–7,440	–15,739	–22,493	–16,868	137
Money plus Quasi-Money	35l	3,891	5,466	8,116	11,606	17,212	37,757	33,548	40,774	65,561	70,329	86,356	98,773
Interest Rates		\multicolumn{12}{c}{*Percent Per Annum*}
Bank Rate (End of Period)	60	45.50	†6.00	6.00	6.00	6.00	6.00	6.00	6.00	6.00	6.00	6.00	4.50
Money Market Rate	60b	11.45	....	....	....	....	....	4.81	4.95	4.95	4.95	4.95	4.95
Deposit Rate	60l	39.33	53.92	28.67	26.50	47.25	4.63	3.50	3.50	3.50	3.50	3.50	3.50
Lending Rate	60p	50.33	63.58	36.33	32.92	51.75	....	....	....	....	....	....	....
Prices		\multicolumn{12}{c}{*Index Numbers (2000=100): Period Averages*}
Consumer Prices	64	15.8	23.5	27.0	39.3	59.2	88.2	†94.0	92.1	100.0	103.2	106.6	102.9
International Transactions		\multicolumn{12}{c}{*Millions of Francs*}
Exports	70	690	4,360	16,580	12,310	11,030	28,300	15,800	31,500	44,300	46,100	37,800	39,900
Imports, c.i.f	71	10,181	9,541	32,530	36,990	35,240	51,800	37,000	31,500	35,000	45,300	40,700	40,000

2004, International Monetary Fund : *International Financial Statistics Yearbook*

Guinea-Bissau 654

		1992	1993	1994	1995	1996	1997	1998	1999	2000	2001	2002	2003
Balance of Payments		\multicolumn{12}{c}{*Millions of US Dollars: Minus Sign Indicates Debit*}
Current Account, n.i.e.	78ald	−104.18	−65.48	−47.63	−50.65	−60.43	−30.28	....	....	....	....	....	....
Goods: Exports f.o.b.	78aad	6.47	15.96	33.21	23.90	21.61	48.86	....	....	....	....	....	....
Goods: Imports f.o.b.	78abd	−83.51	−53.82	−53.80	−59.34	−56.80	−62.49	....	....	....	....	....	....
Trade Balance	78acd	−77.04	−37.86	−20.59	−35.44	−35.19	−13.63	....	....	....	....	....	....
Services: Credit	78add	11.56	9.76	5.61	5.69	6.96	8.00	....	....	....	....	....	....
Services: Debit	78aed	−27.56	−21.14	−27.11	−29.91	−29.25	−26.15	....	....	....	....	....	....
Balance on Goods & Services	78afd	−93.04	−49.24	−42.09	−59.66	−57.48	−31.78	....	....	....	....	....	....
Income: Credit	78agd	−	−	−	−	−	−	....	....	....	....	....	....
Income: Debit	78ahd	−27.78	−28.98	−26.27	−21.09	−18.65	−14.30	....	....	....	....	....	....
Balance on Gds, Serv. & Inc.	78aid	−120.82	−78.22	−68.36	−80.75	−76.13	−46.08	....	....	....	....	....	....
Current Transfers, n.i.e.: Credit	78ajd	17.28	14.39	21.79	31.42	15.70	15.80	....	....	....	....	....	....
Current Transfers: Debit	78akd	−.64	−1.65	−1.06	−1.32	−	−	....	....	....	....	....	....
Capital Account, n.i.e.	78bcd	28.49	36.57	44.42	49.20	40.70	32.20	....	....	....	....	....	....
Capital Account, n.i.e.: Credit	78bad	28.49	36.57	44.42	49.20	40.70	32.20	....	....	....	....	....	....
Capital Account: Debit	78bbd	−	−	−	−	−	−	....	....	....	....	....	....
Financial Account, n.i.e.	78bjd	2.13	−15.82	−26.98	−28.25	−12.30	2.03	....	....	....	....	....	....
Direct Investment Abroad	78bdd	−	−	....	....	....	....	....	....	....	....	....	....
Dir. Invest. in Rep. Econ., n.i.e.	78bed	−	−	....	....	....	....	....	....	....	....	....	....
Portfolio Investment Assets	78bfd	−	−	....	....	....	....	....	....	....	....	....	....
Equity Securities	78bkd	−	−	....	....	....	....	....	....	....	....	....	....
Debt Securities	78bld	−	−	....	....	....	....	....	....	....	....	....	....
Portfolio Investment Liab., n.i.e.	78bgd	−	−	....	....	....	....	....	....	....	....	....	....
Equity Securities	78bmd	−	−	....	....	....	....	....	....	....	....	....	....
Debt Securities	78bnd	−	−	....	....	....	....	....	....	....	....	....	....
Financial Derivatives Assets	78bwd	....	....	....	....	....	....	....	....	....	....	....	....
Financial Derivatives Liabilities	78bxd	....	....	....	....	....	....	....	....	....	....	....	....
Other Investment Assets	78bhd	−	−	....	....	....	−5.80	....	....	....	....	....	....
Monetary Authorities	78bod	....	....	....	....	....	....	....	....	....	....	....	....
General Government	78bpd	−	−	....	....	....	....	....	....	....	....	....	....
Banks	78bqd	−	−	....	....	....	−5.80	....	....	....	....	....	....
Other Sectors	78brd	−	−	....	....	....	....	....	....	....	....	....	....
Other Investment Liab., n.i.e.	78bid	2.13	−15.82	−26.98	−28.25	−12.30	7.83	....	....	....	....	....	....
Monetary Authorities	78bsd	−	−2.27	−	−6.88	−	.43	....	....	....	....	....	....
General Government	78btd	2.13	−13.55	−26.98	−21.37	−12.30	7.40	....	....	....	....	....	....
Banks	78bud	−	−	−	−	−	−	....	....	....	....	....	....
Other Sectors	78bvd	−	−	....	....	....	....	....	....	....	....	....	....
Net Errors and Omissions	78cad	22.01	−15.97	−24.34	−10.90	−11.47	−19.19	....	....	....	....	....	....
Overall Balance	78cbd	−51.55	−60.70	−54.53	−40.60	−43.50	−15.24	....	....	....	....	....	....
Reserves and Related Items	79dad	51.55	60.70	54.53	40.60	43.50	15.24	....	....	....	....	....	....
Reserve Assets	79dbd	−5.10	9.02	6.24	−3.64	−8.90	−35.15	....	....	....	....	....	....
Use of Fund Credit and Loans	79dcd	−	−.42	−.43	1.19	1.94	5.11	....	....	....	....	....	....
Exceptional Financing	79ded	56.65	52.10	48.72	43.05	50.46	45.28	....	....	....	....	....	....
Government Finance		\multicolumn{12}{c}{*Millions of Francs: Year Ending December 31*}
Deficit (−) or Surplus	80	−3,655.8p	....	....	....	....	....	....	....	....	....	....	....
Revenue	81	2,592.2p	....	....	....	....	....	....	....	....	....	....	....
Grants Received	81z	3,328.3p	....	....	....	....	....	....	....	....	....	....	....
Expenditure	82	8,552.3p	....	....	....	....	....	....	....	....	....	....	....
Lending Minus Repayments	83	1,024.0p	....	....	....	....	....	....	....	....	....	....	....
Financing													
Domestic	84a	452.2p	....	....	....	....	....	....	....	....	....	....	....
Foreign	85a	3,203.2p	....	....	....	....	....	....	....	....	....	....	....
Unallocated Financing	84xx	.6p	....	....	....	....	....	....	....	....	....	....	....
National Accounts		\multicolumn{12}{c}{*Millions of Francs*}
Househ.Cons.Expend.,incl.NPISHs	96f	51,017	58,010	119,594	117,485	128,800	144,600	127,500	119,200	115,300	121,900	124,200	....
Government Consumption Expend	91f	9,748	8,573	15,645	10,033	10,891	13,500	11,300	14,900	21,400	17,400	23,400	....
Gross Fixed Capital Formation	93e	22,078	15,255	23,302	22,373	21,248	21,278	....	....	....	....	....	....
Changes in Inventories	93i	3,694	1,182	−7,021	154	5,624	27	....	....	....	....	....	....
Exports of Goods and Services	90c	4,669	7,149	23,222	16,051	17,304	33,700	18,100	53,900	62,100	51,900	41,000	....
Imports of Goods and Services (−)	98c	32,537	24,490	48,871	42,122	47,932	62,500	42,600	64,700	68,700	68,500	73,600	....
Gross Domestic Product (GDP)	99b	58,500	65,600	125,800	124,100	135,900	163,100	121,800	138,200	153,400	145,900	150,900	....
Net Primary Income from Abroad	98.n	14	−131	....	....	....	....	....	....	....	....	....	....
Gross National Income (GNI)	99a	23,553	36,264	....	....	....	....	....	....	....	....	....	....
GDP Volume 1986 Prices	99b.p	96,200	98,600	103,500	107,300	112,500	117,900	....	....	....	....	....	....
GDP Volume (1995=100)	99bvp	89.7	91.9	96.5	100.0	104.8	109.9	....	....	....	....	....	....
GDP Deflator (1995=100)	99bip	52.6	57.5	105.1	100.0	104.4	119.6	....	....	....	....	....	....
		\multicolumn{12}{c}{*Millions: Midyear Estimates*}
Population	99z	1.08	1.12	1.15	1.19	1.22	1.26	1.29	1.33	1.37	1.41	1.45	1.49

Guyana 336

		1992	1993	1994	1995	1996	1997	1998	1999	2000	2001	2002	2003
Exchange Rates		\multicolumn{12}{c}{*Guyana Dollars per SDR: End of Period*}
Market Rate	aa	173.3	179.6	208.0	208.9	203.1	194.3	228.5	247.7	240.7	238.2	260.7	288.6
		\multicolumn{12}{c}{*Guyana Dollars per US Dollar: End of Period (ae) Period Average (rf)*}
Market Rate	ae	126.0	130.8	142.5	140.5	141.3	144.0	162.3	180.5	184.8	189.5	191.8	194.3
Market Rate	rf	125.0	126.7	138.3	142.0	140.4	142.4	150.5	178.0	182.4	187.3	190.7	193.9
		\multicolumn{12}{c}{*Index Numbers (2000=100): Period Averages*}
Market Rate	ahx	145.3	144.0	132.1	128.6	129.9	127.9	121.5	102.6	100.0	97.4	95.7	94.1
Nominal Effective Exchange Rate	nec	97.1	111.3	113.7	108.4	112.4	117.1	114.8	98.2	100.0	101.8	98.9	90.2
Real Effective Exchange Rate	rec	83.0	90.6	89.9	91.5	98.8	104.1	104.7	94.8	100.0	101.1	95.0	83.2
Fund Position		\multicolumn{12}{c}{*Millions of SDRs: End of Period*}
Quota	2f.s	67.20	67.20	67.20	67.20	67.20	67.20	67.20	90.90	90.90	90.90	90.90	90.90
SDRs	1b.s	.24	–	.05	.09	.07	.14	.17	.92	7.02	1.96	3.43	3.26
Reserve Position in the Fund	1c.s	–	–	–	–	–	–	–	–	–	–	–	–
Total Fund Cred.&Loans Outstg	2tl	122.17	128.60	122.25	115.60	117.11	116.44	109.50	102.15	90.12	77.67	70.73	64.18
International Liquidity		\multicolumn{12}{c}{*Millions of US Dollars Unless Otherwise Indicated: End of Period*}
Total Reserves minus Gold	1l.d	188.08	247.45	247.13	268.94	329.68	315.51	276.60	268.28	304.96	287.26	284.47	276.39
SDRs	1b.d	.33	–	.08	.14	.11	.20	.24	1.27	9.15	2.47	4.66	4.84
Reserve Position in the Fund	1c.d	–	–	–	–	–	–	–	–	–	–	–	–
Foreign Exchange	1d.d	187.75	247.45	247.05	268.80	329.57	315.31	276.36	267.01	295.81	284.79	279.81	271.55
Monetary Authorities: Other Liab.	4..d	729.66	715.25	656.62	725.00	448.57	286.86	222.56	187.68	186.51	179.00	69.17	61.43
Deposit Money Banks: Assets	7a.d	29.83	24.40	24.88	27.03	26.55	24.29	23.91	40.13	38.77	46.36	63.06	92.70
Liabilities	7b.d	14.64	15.92	20.57	20.52	25.62	34.47	31.93	22.23	20.66	17.55	25.94	25.43
Other Banking Insts.: Assets	7e.d	.72	.94	1.21	1.28	1.38	2.38	1.98	2.59	7.32	7.67	11.73	8.39
Liabilities	7f.d	–	.04	–	7.30	1.03	1.12	.69	.46	3.42	5.38	5.06	5.00
Monetary Authorities		\multicolumn{12}{c}{*Millions of Guyana Dollars: End of Period*}
Foreign Assets	11	23,488	† 31,557	35,741	38,398	46,466	43,578	40,149	44,590	54,645	53,979	53,634	52,731
Claims on Central Government	12a	100,839	† 109,080	118,849	125,918	96,232	76,959	67,904	71,686	72,208	70,613	50,267	50,956
Claims on Nonfin.Pub.Enterprises	12c	898	† 762	1,098	811	2,441	3,238	3,320	4,709	4,710	4,710	4,710	4,710
Reserve Money	14	15,647	† 12,523	16,453	19,603	20,760	24,314	27,179	26,128	29,794	33,043	36,359	40,112
of which: Currency Outside DMBs	14a	5,095	† 6,480	8,167	8,967	9,959	11,210	11,334	13,394	14,495	15,138	15,410	17,888
Time, Savings,& Fgn.Currency Dep	15	278	† 378	335	561	489	749	694	1,219	1,146	921	565	692
Restricted Deposits	16b	84	† –	–	–	–	–	–	–	–	–	–	–
Foreign Liabilities	16c	86,008	† 89,751	91,358	95,914	63,243	44,406	45,418	46,547	43,511	40,968	21,650	21,827
Long-Term Foreign Liabilities	16cl	27,094	† 26,864	27,641	30,091	23,903	19,525	15,708	12,636	12,640	11,449	10,052	8,630
Central Government Deposits	16d	1,260	† 15,220	22,623	21,335	30,256	27,147	22,066	34,594	39,130	37,965	37,399	36,750
Capital Accounts	17a	2,522	† –1,455	2,345	3,253	2,567	3,449	5,184	5,891	6,822	7,290	6,636	6,889
Other Items (Net)	17r	–7,669	† –1,882	–5,068	–5,631	3,921	4,187	–4,875	–6,030	–1,482	–2,334	–4,049	–6,503
Deposit Money Banks		\multicolumn{12}{c}{*Millions of Guyana Dollars: End of Period*}
Reserves	20	10,548	5,503	8,171	10,326	10,781	13,315	16,070	12,419	15,510	18,340	21,031	21,883
Foreign Assets	21	3,759	3,190	3,546	3,798	3,750	3,497	3,880	7,243	7,163	8,786	12,091	18,006
Claims on Central Government	22a	12,282	20,064	15,651	14,847	17,251	18,028	15,851	13,346	20,264	20,766	23,959	32,249
Claims on Local Government	22b	28	36	–	36	1	4	500	48	39	1	7	62
Claims on Nonfin.Pub.Enterprises	22c	835	471	188	410	254	216	410	683	420	852	807	822
Claims on Private Sector	22d	8,735	10,254	13,900	21,107	36,309	44,863	51,838	55,823	58,341	58,943	59,200	48,594
Claims on Other Banking Insts	22f	5	28	13	73	183	118	195	569	660	464	724	855
Demand Deposits	24	3,897	4,902	4,941	6,336	7,565	8,064	7,639	9,949	11,286	10,945	12,700	14,223
Time, Savings,& Fgn.Currency Dep	25	21,483	25,271	28,764	36,661	44,708	49,032	53,981	57,049	61,514	69,109	72,942	76,696
Restricted Deposits	26b	517	368	334	330	330	318	307	70	66	56	56	58
Foreign Liabilities	26c	1,845	2,081	2,931	2,883	3,619	4,964	5,181	4,012	3,816	3,325	4,975	4,940
Central Government Deposits	26d	1,612	3,161	3,246	2,071	2,920	5,662	5,782	3,857	7,284	5,488	7,375	8,361
Liabilities to Other Banking Insts	26i	3,200	2,895	1,356	1,827	2,757	3,778	5,898	5,796	8,455	8,009	9,222	10,934
Capital Accounts	27a	4,045	3,660	3,968	5,392	13,712	15,054	19,385	21,477	22,277	22,722	22,308	14,667
Other Items (Net)	27r	–409	–2,792	–4,072	–4,903	–7,079	–6,828	–9,429	–12,081	–12,302	–11,501	–11,759	–7,407
Monetary Survey		\multicolumn{12}{c}{*Millions of Guyana Dollars: End of Period*}
Foreign Assets (Net)	31n	–60,606	† –57,085	–55,003	–56,600	–16,646	–2,294	–6,570	1,274	14,480	18,472	39,101	43,971
Domestic Credit	32	120,749	† 122,314	123,830	139,796	119,495	110,619	112,172	108,412	110,227	112,896	94,900	93,137
Claims on Central Govt. (Net)	32an	110,249	† 110,763	108,630	117,360	80,307	62,178	55,908	46,581	46,058	47,927	29,452	38,094
Claims on Local Government	32b	28	† 36	–	36	1	4	500	48	39	1	7	62
Claims on Nonfin.Pub.Enterprises	32c	1,733	† 1,232	1,286	1,220	2,695	3,455	3,730	5,392	5,129	5,562	5,518	5,532
Claims on Private Sector	32d	8,735	† 10,254	13,900	21,107	36,309	44,863	51,838	55,823	58,341	58,943	59,200	48,594
Claims on Other Banking Insts	32f	5	† 28	13	73	183	118	195	569	660	464	724	855
Money	34	8,999	† 11,881	13,115	15,310	17,531	19,281	18,980	23,350	25,788	26,089	28,116	32,117
Quasi-Money	35	21,762	† 25,649	29,100	37,222	45,197	49,780	54,675	58,268	62,660	70,029	73,507	77,389
Restricted Deposits	36b	601	† 368	334	330	330	318	307	70	66	56	56	58
Long-Term Foreign Liabilities	36cl	27,094	† 26,864	27,641	30,091	23,903	19,525	15,708	12,636	12,640	11,449	10,052	8,630
Liabilities to Other Banking Insts	36i	3,200	† 2,895	1,356	1,827	2,757	3,778	5,898	5,796	8,455	8,009	9,222	10,934
Capital Accounts	37a	6,567	† 2,205	6,313	8,645	16,278	18,503	24,569	27,368	29,099	30,013	28,944	21,556
Other Items (Net)	37r	–8,080	† –4,634	–9,032	–10,231	–3,146	–2,860	–14,536	–17,803	–14,000	–14,277	–15,896	–13,575
Money plus Quasi-Money	35l	30,760	† 37,531	42,214	52,532	62,727	69,061	73,655	81,618	88,448	96,119	101,624	109,506

2004, International Monetary Fund : *International Financial Statistics Yearbook*

Guyana 336

		1992	1993	1994	1995	1996	1997	1998	1999	2000	2001	2002	2003
Other Banking Institutions					*Millions of Guyana Dollars: End of Period*								
Cash.................................	40	6	129	9	21	50	29	44	184	331	464	623	666
Foreign Assets...................	41	91	123	172	180	195	342	321	467	1,353	1,454	2,248	1,630
Claims on Central Government..	42a	2,146	2,611	3,444	3,410	4,339	5,055	5,226	4,725	5,227	7,020	7,872	9,668
Claims on Local Government...	42b	12	18	17	17	–	–	–	–	–	–	–	–
Claims on Private Sector.........	42d	1,300	2,102	2,446	3,615	5,335	6,609	8,718	14,759	15,939	18,034	19,185	21,667
Claims on Deposit Money Banks..	42e	437	530	131	555	460	233	287	255	1,168	1,790	2,594	2,757
Time, Savings,& Fgn.Currency Dep...	45	3,435	4,339	5,254	6,360	8,450	10,477	12,065	13,352	15,641	19,648	23,099	25,098
Foreign Liabilities................	46c	–	5	–	1,025	145	162	111	83	632	1,020	970	971
Capital Accounts.................	47a	343	581	778	1,078	1,990	2,658	3,515	4,721	5,358	5,828	5,735	6,567
Other Items (Net)................	47r	214	588	188	−665	−205	−1,027	−1,095	2,234	2,386	2,265	2,718	3,751
Banking Survey					*Millions of Guyana Dollars: End of Period*								
Foreign Assets (Net)..............	51n	−60,515	†−56,967	−54,831	−57,445	−16,595	−2,114	−6,360	1,658	15,201	18,905	40,380	44,630
Domestic Credit..................	52	124,202	†127,017	129,724	146,764	128,986	122,165	125,921	127,328	130,733	137,487	121,232	123,615
Claims on Central Govt. (Net)..	52an	112,395	†113,374	112,074	120,769	84,646	67,234	61,134	51,306	51,285	54,947	37,323	47,761
Claims on Local Government...	52b	40	†55	17	53	1	4	500	48	39	1	7	62
Claims on Nonfin.Pub.Enterprises..	52c	1,733	†1,232	1,286	1,220	2,695	3,455	3,730	5,392	5,129	5,562	5,518	5,532
Claims on Private Sector........	52d	10,035	†12,356	16,346	24,722	41,644	51,472	60,556	70,583	74,280	76,977	78,385	70,260
Liquid Liabilities..................	55l	34,189	†41,741	47,459	58,871	71,128	79,509	85,676	94,786	103,758	115,303	124,100	133,938
Restricted Deposits...............	56b	601	†368	334	330	330	318	307	70	66	56	56	58
Long-Term Foreign Liabilities....	56cl	27,094	†26,864	27,641	30,091	23,903	19,525	15,708	12,636	12,640	11,449	10,052	8,630
Capital Accounts.................	57a	6,910	†2,786	7,091	9,723	18,268	21,161	28,084	32,089	34,457	35,841	34,679	28,122
Other Items (Net)................	57r	−5,107	†−1,709	−7,633	−9,697	−1,238	−461	−10,215	−10,596	−4,987	−6,257	−7,274	−2,503
Money (National Definitions)					*Millions of Guyana Dollars: End of Period*								
Base Money.......................	19ma	....	....	....	....	....	....	11,334	13,394	14,495	15,138	15,410	17,888
Reserve Money...................	19mb	....	....	....	....	....	....	27,173	26,122	29,788	33,037	36,352	40,105
M1.................................	39ma	....	....	....	....	....	....	17,821	21,548	24,827	24,807	26,365	30,793
M2.................................	39mb	....	....	....	....	....	....	68,696	76,980	85,445	93,035	98,147	106,259
Interest Rates					*Percent Per Annum*								
Discount Rate (End of Period)...	60	24.30	17.00	20.25	17.25	12.00	11.00	11.25	13.25	11.75	8.75	6.25	5.50
Treasury Bill Rate.................	60c	25.75	16.83	17.66	17.51	11.35	8.91	8.33	11.31	9.88	7.78	4.94	3.04
Savings Rate......................	60k	20.47	10.88	9.94	10.95	8.75	7.48	7.16	7.73	7.65	7.09	5.02	3.84
Deposit Rate......................	60l	22.51	12.26	11.42	12.90	10.49	8.56	8.10	9.08	8.71	7.63	4.53	3.18
Lending Rate.....................	60p	28.69	19.36	18.36	19.22	17.79	17.04	16.77	17.11	17.30	17.01	16.33	14.99
Prices					*Index Numbers (2000=100): Period Averages*								
Consumer Prices.................	64	....	....	67.3	75.5	80.9	83.8	87.6	94.2	100.0	102.6	108.1	....
International Transactions					*Millions of Guyana Dollars*								
Exports............................	70	36,567.2	52,506.9	63,389.8	64,581.3	72,597.9	91,808.7	73,336.3	93,138.0	90,830.4	89,593.4	93,938.0	123,048.2
Imports, c.i.f......................	71	55,319.8	61,376.0	70,000.6	74,911.5	83,895.0	89,746.8	....	....	....	109,362.4	107,273.7	198,001.4
							2000=100						
Volume of Exports...............	72	65	80	86	104	73	101	96	104	100	33	90	31,834

Guyana 336

Balance of Payments

Millions of US Dollars: Minus Sign Indicates Debit

		1992	1993	1994	1995	1996	1997	1998	1999	2000	2001	2002	2003
Current Account, n.i.e.	78ald	−138.5	−140.2	−124.9	−134.8	−69.1	−111.4	−102.0	−78.2	−115.3	−133.8	−110.6	....
Goods: Exports f.o.b.	78aad	381.7	415.5	463.4	495.7	574.8	593.4	547.0	525.0	505.2	490.3	494.9	....
Goods: Imports f.o.b.	78abd	−442.7	−483.8	−504.0	−536.5	−595.0	−641.6	−601.2	−550.2	−585.4	−584.1	−563.1	....
Trade Balance	78acd	−61.0	−68.3	−40.6	−40.8	−20.2	−48.2	−54.2	−25.2	−80.2	−93.8	−68.2	....
Services: Credit	78add	105.9	115.3	120.7	133.5	146.1	148.1	141.8	147.0	169.2	172.0	172.3	....
Services: Debit	78aed	−139.8	−148.1	−160.9	−171.8	−168.6	−171.3	−173.9	−178.1	−193.2	−192.4	−195.8	....
Balance on Goods & Services	78afd	−95.0	−101.1	−80.8	−79.2	−42.7	−71.4	−86.3	−56.3	−104.2	−114.2	−91.7	....
Income: Credit	78agd	4.9	5.1	8.7	12.2	11.6	12.5	11.9	11.3	11.7	10.1	7.8	....
Income: Debit	78ahd	−101.5	−106.8	−114.8	−129.9	−79.0	−92.5	−71.6	−72.2	−69.8	−73.7	−66.7	....
Balance on Gds, Serv. & Inc.	78aid	−191.6	−202.9	−186.9	−196.8	−110.1	−151.4	−146.0	−117.2	−162.3	−177.8	−150.6	....
Current Transfers, n.i.e.: Credit	78ajd	62.9	70.0	68.1	67.4	69.1	67.1	74.3	76.1	100.8	98.1	128.7	....
Current Transfers: Debit	78akd	−9.9	−7.4	−6.2	−5.3	−28.1	−27.1	−30.3	−37.1	−53.8	−54.1	−88.7	....
Capital Account, n.i.e.	78bcd	1.6	4.4	8.3	9.5	—	23.7	13.1	15.5	16.3	31.9	33.7	....
Capital Account, n.i.e.: Credit	78bad	3.4	6.6	11.0	12.5	—	23.7	13.1	15.5	16.3	31.9	33.7	....
Capital Account: Debit	78bbd	−1.8	−2.2	−2.7	−3.0	....	....	....	....	....	....	....	....
Financial Account, n.i.e.	78bjd	63.1	88.7	126.9	71.1	69.5	96.9	64.0	87.3	114.6	101.9	89.5	....
Direct Investment Abroad	78bdd	....	....	....	....	....	....	....	....	....	....	....	....
Dir. Invest. in Rep. Econ., n.i.e.	78bed	146.6	69.5	106.7	74.4	59.0	52.0	44.0	46.0	67.1	56.0	43.6	....
Portfolio Investment Assets	78bfd	....	....	....	....	−.4	−2.3	−.8	16.6	−3.4	9.7	17.8	....
Equity Securities	78bkd	....	....	....	....	....	....	....	....	....	....	....	....
Debt Securities	78bld	....	....	....	....	−.4	−2.3	−.8	16.6	−3.4	9.7	17.8	....
Portfolio Investment Liab., n.i.e.	78bgd	2.8	3.6	15.8	3.2	4.8	9.2	−3.1	−9.2	−1.5	−3.2	8.4	....
Equity Securities	78bmd	....	....	....	....	....	....	....	....	....	....	....	....
Debt Securities	78bnd	2.8	3.6	15.8	3.2	4.8	9.2	−3.1	−9.2	−1.5	−3.2	8.4	....
Financial Derivatives Assets	78bwd	....	....	....	....	....	....	....	....	....	....	....	....
Financial Derivatives Liabilities	78bxd	....	....	....	....	....	....	....	....	....	....	....	....
Other Investment Assets	78bhd	−19.9	8.8	−5.8	−8.9	40.2	67.0	59.7	47.4	66.1	65.8	45.3	....
Monetary Authorities	78bod	....	....	....	....	....	....	....	....	....	....	....	....
General Government	78bpd	−3.4	1.4	1.3	−2.2	40.2	67.0	59.7	47.4	66.1	65.8	45.3	....
Banks	78bqd	−6.4	3.2	4.2	−2.8	....	....	....	....	....	....	....	....
Other Sectors	78brd	−10.2	4.2	−11.2	−3.9	....	....	....	....	....	....	....	....
Other Investment Liab., n.i.e.	78bid	−66.4	6.7	10.2	2.3	−34.1	−29.0	−35.8	−13.5	−13.7	−26.4	−25.6	....
Monetary Authorities	78bsd	−4.7	−13.9	1.3	18.6	—	—	—	—	—	—	—	....
General Government	78btd	−73.6	27.3	−1.0	−5.4	−34.1	−29.0	−45.8	−23.5	−23.7	−26.4	−25.6	....
Banks	78bud	−5.5	−4.9	−2.9	−.4	....	....	....	....	....	....	....	....
Other Sectors	78bvd	17.4	−1.8	12.9	−10.5	....	....	10.0	10.0	10.0	....	....	....
Net Errors and Omissions	78cad	12.2	11.0	−16.3	11.2	11.5	−10.8	11.9	−3.0	24.6	26.2	2.1	....
Overall Balance	78cbd	−61.6	−36.1	−6.0	−43.0	11.9	−1.6	−13.0	21.6	40.2	26.2	14.7	....
Reserves and Related Items	79dad	61.6	36.1	6.0	43.0	−11.9	1.6	13.0	−21.6	−40.2	−26.2	−14.7	....
Reserve Assets	79dbd	−67.1	−57.1	−21.8	.8	−13.9	2.9	22.6	−11.4	−24.0	−10.4	−5.9	....
Use of Fund Credit and Loans	79dcd	24.8	9.1	−8.8	−9.7	2.0	−1.3	−9.6	−10.2	−16.2	−15.8	−8.9	....
Exceptional Financing	79ded	103.9	84.2	36.6	52.0	—	....	....	....	....	....	....	....

Government Finance

Millions of Guyana Dollars: Year Ending December 31

		1992	1993	1994	1995	1996	1997						
Deficit (−) or Surplus	80	−7,994	−4,001	−5,092	−2,886	−3,115	−6,611	....	....	....	....	....	....
Total Revenue and Grants	81y	19,464	23,901	29,133	32,428	37,180	39,071	....	....	....	....	....	....
Revenue	81	18,913	23,191	28,138	30,823	34,666	36,006	....	....	....	....	....	....
Grants	81z	551	710	995	1,605	2,515	3,065	....	....	....	....	....	....
Exp. & Lending Minus Repay	82z	27,457	27,902	34,226	35,314	40,295	45,682	....	....	....	....	....	....
Expenditure	82	27,457	27,902	34,226	35,314	40,295	45,682	....	....	....	....	....	....
Lending Minus Repayments	83	—	—	—	—	—	—	....	....	....	....	....	....
Total Financing	80h	7,994	4,001	5,092	2,886	3,115	6,611	....	....	....	....	....	....
Total Net Borrowing	84	4,715	−5,398	−699	2,826	−931	4,310	....	....	....	....	....	....
Net Domestic	84a	1,183	−6,573	−4,394	1,627	−7,298	−162	....	....	....	....	....	....
Net Foreign	85a	3,532	1,175	3,695	1,199	6,367	4,473	....	....	....	....	....	....
Use of Cash Balances	87	3,278	9,399	5,791	60	4,046	2,301	....	....	....	....	....	....
Total Debt	88	265,920	283,213	316,419	322,444	249,167	258,325	....	....	....	....	....	....
Domestic	88a	18,053	27,793	31,490	33,252	37,478	35,888	....	....	....	....	....	....
Foreign	89a	247,867	255,420	284,929	289,191	211,688	222,436	....	....	....	....	....	....

National Accounts

Millions of Guyana Dollars

		1992	1993	1994	1995	1996	1997						
Househ.Cons.Expend.,incl.NPISHs	96f	23,525	29,134	36,131	40,897	44,224	47,147	....	....	....	....	....	....
Government Consumption Expend	91f	6,383	8,529	11,817	14,092	17,330	21,747	....	....	....	....	....	....
Gross Fixed Capital Formation	93e	25,113	30,745	34,348	40,077	43,436	47,099	....	....	....	....	....	....
Exports of Goods and Services	90c	47,689	52,518	59,185	70,315	82,155	84,375	....	....	....	....	....	....
Imports of Goods and Services (−)	98c	55,310	64,370	64,370	74,912	83,895	91,749	....	....	....	....	....	....
Gross Domestic Product (GDP)	99b	46,734	59,124	75,412	88,271	99,038	105,859	....	....	....	....	....	....
Net Primary Income from Abroad	98.n	−13,800	−11,912	−11,473	−12,203	−7,319	−10,406	....	....	....	....	....	....
Gross National Income (GNI)	99a	32,934	47,212	63,939	76,068	91,719	95,399	....	....	....	....	....	....
Net National Income	99e	32,934	47,212	63,939	76,068	91,719	95,399	....	....	....	....	....	....
GDP Volume 1988 Prices	99b.p	3,792	4,104	....	....	....	....	....	....	....	....	....	....
GDP Volume (1990=100)	99bvp	114.3	123.7	....	....	....	....	....	....	....	....	....	....
GDP Deflator (1990=100)	99bip	261.1	305.2	....	....	....	....	....	....	....	....	....	....

Millions: Midyear Estimates

		1992	1993	1994	1995	1996	1997	1998	1999	2000	2001	2002	2003
Population	99z	.73	.73	.74	.74	.74	.75	.75	.76	.76	.76	.76	.77

2004, International Monetary Fund : *International Financial Statistics Yearbook*

Haiti 263

		1992	1993	1994	1995	1996	1997	1998	1999	2000	2001	2002	2003
Exchange Rates													
						Gourdes per SDR: End of Period							
Market Rate	aa	15.060	17.588	18.900	24.022	21.703	23.357	23.239	24.658	29.347	33.101	51.130	62.537
						Gourdes per US Dollar: End of Period (ae) Period Average (rf)							
Market Rate	ae	10.953	12.805	12.947	16.160	15.093	17.311	16.505	17.965	22.524	26.339	37.609	42.085
Market Rate	rf	9.802	12.823	15.040	15.110	15.701	16.655	16.766	16.938	21.171	24.429	29.250	42.367
Fund Position						*Millions of SDRs: End of Period*							
Quota	2f.s	44.1	44.1	44.1	60.7	60.7	60.7	60.7	60.7	60.7	60.7	60.7	81.9
SDRs	1b.s	–	–	–	.4	–	.1	.4	.6	.1	.4	.4	.2
Reserve Position in the Fund	1c.s	.1	–	–	–	–	–	–	–	–	.1	.1	.1
Total Fund Cred.&Loans Outstg	2tl	23.8	23.8	3.8	18.2	31.6	31.6	40.8	32.6	30.4	30.4	19.7	9.1
International Liquidity						*Millions of US Dollars Unless Otherwise Indicated: End of Period*							
Total Reserves minus Gold	1l.d	27.1	32.1	51.1	191.6	216.1	207.1	258.2	264.0	182.1	141.4	81.7	62.0
SDRs	1b.d	–	–	–	.5	.1	.1	.5	.9	.1	.5	.5	.3
Reserve Position in the Fund	1c.d	.1	.1	.1	.1	.1	.1	.1	.1	.1	.1	.1	.1
Foreign Exchange	1d.d	27.0	32.0	51.0	191.0	216.0	206.9	257.6	263.1	182.0	140.8	81.1	61.6
Gold (Million Fine Troy Ounces)	1ad	.019	.019	.019	.019	.019	.020	.020	.001	.001	.001	.001	.001
Monetary Authorities: Other Liab	4..d	9.0	9.7	48.3	20.6	82.1	59.6	60.4	60.7	61.4	62.2	61.1	63.8
Deposit Money Banks: Assets	7a.d	54.0	78.3	96.1	98.1	114.9	133.1	124.4	150.7	199.1	177.0	137.8	237.1
Liabilities	7b.d	–	–	.8	4.9	6.9	17.9	8.3	16.7	21.8	18.7	20.8	26.7
Monetary Authorities						*Millions of Gourdes: End of Period*							
Foreign Assets	11	152.9	236.8	834.0	3,073.7	3,988.0	†4,757.2	5,308.4	5,916.0	5,549.2	6,988.4	7,274.7	8,684.2
Claims on Central Government	12a	3,985.1	4,394.6	5,860.7	7,074.0	7,238.8	†7,668.1	8,273.3	10,302.3	11,802.0	13,846.8	17,920.5	22,663.1
Claims on Local Government	12b	–	–	–	–	12.9	†8.5	5.0	1.7	.6	–	–	–
Claims on Nonfin.Pub.Enterprises	12c	348.7	426.5	328.1	152.1	80.8	†50.9	85.5	84.5	1,820.3	1,996.3	2,155.5	2,162.9
Claims on Private Sector	12d	–	–	–	–	141.2	†163.5	233.1	304.2	358.8	452.9	543.7	721.9
Claims on Deposit Money Banks	12e	331.9	754.6	415.6	65.0	70.2	†129.2	106.2	264.6	228.5	93.1	423.7	813.5
Claims on Other Banking Insts	12f	–	–	–	28.6	–	†–	–	–	–	–	–	–
Claims on Nonbank Financial Insts	12g	–	–	–	–	4.7	†22.4	19.8	13.9	12.0	9.8	7.7	5.2
Reserve Money	14	4,346.1	5,616.6	6,954.9	7,975.8	7,645.1	†7,653.3	7,672.5	9,894.3	12,452.2	14,556.2	18,038.3	23,702.1
of which: Currency Outside DMBs	14a	2,074.5	2,668.8	3,029.5	3,536.7	3,435.7	†3,935.4	3,905.4	4,927.1	5,807.2	6,584.3	8,687.5	9,843.2
Time, Savings,& Fgn.Currency Dep	15	–	–	–	–	–	†8.4	37.3	55.9	84.0	101.8	122.0	36.7
Liabs. of Central Bank: Securities	16ac	....	....	....	....	....	857.0	1,980.0	2,335.0	944.0	2,432.0	2,563.0	4,996.0
Foreign Liabilities	16c	456.9	543.7	136.0	555.9	1,595.1	†737.5	954.0	802.6	890.9	1,004.8	1,008.7	569.4
Long-Term Foreign Liabilities	16cl	–	–	560.6	212.8	–	†1,030.9	990.4	1,091.0	1,383.0	1,638.3	2,298.3	2,683.6
Central Government Deposits	16d	457.3	481.3	892.7	1,983.0	1,617.2	†1,514.2	1,647.6	1,895.3	1,125.1	1,093.7	1,440.9	2,005.7
Capital Accounts	17a	411.4	472.2	564.0	1,139.1	857.2	†1,266.5	1,313.1	1,566.8	3,974.8	4,143.9	4,504.9	3,656.1
Other Items (Net)	17r	–853.1	–1,301.3	–1,669.8	–1,473.3	–178.0	†–268.1	–563.6	–753.7	–1,082.6	–1,583.5	–1,650.2	–2,598.8
Deposit Money Banks						*Millions of Gourdes: End of Period*							
Reserves	20	2,420.8	3,059.1	3,718.1	3,608.0	3,979.8	†3,323.6	3,411.0	4,394.1	6,297.4	7,713.6	8,805.2	12,936.4
Claims on Mon.Author.:Securities	20c	....	....	....	....	....	857.0	1,980.0	2,335.0	944.0	2,432.0	2,563.0	4,996.0
Foreign Assets	21	592.0	1,002.7	1,243.6	1,584.9	1,734.2	†2,303.9	2,053.8	2,706.8	4,484.6	4,662.5	5,183.1	9,979.6
Claims on Central Government	22a	11.5	8.0	114.1	11.3	6.5	†6.5	6.5	169.3	164.3	99.3	59.3	–
Claims on Private Sector	22d	2,100.2	2,516.3	3,253.2	5,072.4	5,825.0	†8,511.2	9,156.2	10,128.9	12,074.3	12,914.0	16,785.7	20,448.6
Claims on Other Banking Insts	22f	....	....	....	....	–	†–	–	–	170.0	–	–	–
Demand Deposits	24	1,199.9	1,429.6	1,578.0	2,372.7	2,211.1	†2,435.2	2,544.2	3,241.3	3,251.2	3,749.2	4,394.7	6,142.5
Time, Savings,& Fgn.Currency Dep	25	3,671.8	4,944.8	6,486.8	8,018.7	9,064.7	†11,499.7	13,209.8	15,997.4	20,102.3	22,847.1	27,582.9	41,036.9
Bonds	26ab	....	....	....	....	....	46.1	44.9	21.9	113.6	148.2	385.2	481.9
Foreign Liabilities	26c	.5	.3	10.7	78.6	104.5	†310.3	136.4	299.8	490.4	492.9	782.1	1,124.7
Central Government Deposits	26d	26.3	27.0	27.6	37.5	54.5	†514.7	475.1	402.9	257.2	157.5	80.3	361.9
Credit from Monetary Authorities	26g	–	–	–	72.6	81.9	†49.0	42.8	134.7	72.1	32.1	293.0	33.0
Capital Accounts	27a	269.7	320.9	395.7	525.7	946.2	†1,373.9	1,692.9	1,811.2	2,432.1	2,878.4	3,257.6	4,409.6
Other Items (Net)	27r	–43.7	–136.5	–169.8	–829.1	–917.4	†–1,226.7	–1,538.6	–2,175.1	–2,584.1	–2,483.9	–3,379.5	–5,229.8
Monetary Survey						*Millions of Gourdes: End of Period*							
Foreign Assets (Net)	31n	287.5	695.5	1,930.9	4,024.1	4,022.6	†6,013.4	6,271.8	7,520.4	8,652.5	10,153.2	10,667.0	16,969.8
Domestic Credit	32	5,961.9	6,837.1	8,440.9	10,317.9	11,638.2	†14,402.1	15,656.7	18,706.6	25,020.0	28,067.9	35,951.2	43,634.2
Claims on Central Govt. (Net)	32an	3,513.0	3,894.3	4,861.4	5,064.8	5,573.6	†5,645.7	6,157.1	8,173.4	10,584.0	12,694.9	16,458.6	20,295.6
Claims on Local Government	32b	–	–	–	–	12.9	†8.5	5.0	1.7	.6	–	–	–
Claims on Nonfin.Pub.Enterprises	32c	348.7	426.5	326.3	152.1	80.8	†50.9	85.5	84.5	1,820.3	1,996.3	2,155.5	2,162.9
Claims on Private Sector	32d	2,100.2	2,516.3	3,253.2	5,072.4	5,966.2	†8,674.6	9,389.3	10,433.0	12,433.1	13,367.0	17,329.4	21,170.5
Claims on Other Banking Insts	32f	–	–	–	28.6	–	†–	–	–	170.0	–	–	–
Claims on Nonbank Financial Inst	32g	–	–	–	–	4.7	†22.4	19.8	13.9	12.0	9.8	7.7	5.2
Money	34	3,150.1	3,866.4	5,095.5	6,703.9	5,823.9	†6,633.5	6,650.9	8,422.8	9,220.2	10,610.2	13,501.5	16,222.1
Quasi-Money	35	3,671.8	4,944.8	6,486.8	8,018.7	9,064.7	†11,508.1	13,247.1	16,053.3	20,186.3	22,948.9	27,704.8	41,073.6
Bonds	36ab	....	....	....	....	....	46.1	44.9	21.9	113.6	148.2	385.2	481.9
Long-Term Foreign Liabilities	36cl	–	–	560.6	212.8	–	†1,030.9	990.4	1,091.0	1,383.0	1,638.3	2,298.3	2,683.6
Capital Accounts	37a	681.1	793.1	959.7	1,664.7	1,803.4	†2,640.4	3,006.0	3,378.0	6,406.8	7,022.3	7,762.4	8,065.7
Other Items (Net)	37r	–1,253.6	–2,071.7	–2,730.8	–2,258.1	–1,031.3	†–1,443.5	–2,010.8	–2,740.1	–3,637.3	–4,146.8	–5,034.0	–7,923.0
Money plus Quasi-Money	35l	6,821.9	8,811.2	11,582.3	14,722.5	14,888.6	†18,141.5	19,898.0	24,476.2	29,406.4	33,559.1	41,206.3	57,295.7

Haiti 263

		1992	1993	1994	1995	1996	1997	1998	1999	2000	2001	2002	2003
Interest Rates							*Percent per Annum*						
Treasury Bill Rate...............	60c	....	....	....	....	....	14.13	16.21	7.71	12.33	13.53	7.56	20.50
Savings Rate.......................	60k	....	....	....	....	....	5.36	5.50	3.51	3.57	3.35	2.52	3.01
Savings Rate (Foreign Currency).......	60k.f	....	....	....	....	....	....	....	....	....	1.73	1.47	1.38
Deposit Rate.......................	60l	....	....	....	....	....	10.74	13.06	7.39	11.85	13.66	8.24	13.99
Deposit Rate (Foreign Currency).......	60l.f	....	....	....	....	....	....	....	....	....	4.66	2.83	3.39
Lending Rate.......................	60p	....	....	....	....	....	21.00	23.62	22.88	25.09	28.63	25.67	30.58
Lending Rate (Foreign Currency).......	60p.f	....	....	....	....	....	....	....	....	....	14.76	12.23	13.92
Prices						*Index Numbers (2000=100): Period Averages*							
Consumer Prices..................	64	†21.8	28.3	39.4	50.3	60.7	73.1	80.9	87.9	100.0	114.2	125.4	174.7
International Transactions						*Millions of Gourdes*							
Exports.............................	70	719.4	1,029.3	1,236.7	1,666.5	1,413.9	3,537.1	5,365.0	5,661.3	6,725.3	6,700.7	8,203.0	14,682.2
Imports, c.i.f......................	71	2,727.9	4,555.7	3,783.6	9,866.2	10,448.2	10,792.1	13,365.6	17,366.9	21,936.2	24,745.7	33,060.7	50,323.7
Balance of Payments					*Millions of US Dollars: F.Y. Ending Sept 30; Minus Sign Indicates Debit*								
Current Account, n.i.e............	78ald	7.3	−11.8	−23.4	−87.1	−137.7	−47.7	−38.1	....	....	....	....	....
Goods: Exports f.o.b.............	78aad	73.4	80.3	60.3	88.3	82.5	205.4	299.3	....	....	....	....	....
Goods: Imports f.o.b.............	78abd	−212.5	−260.5	−171.5	−517.2	−498.6	−559.6	−640.7	....	....	....	....	....
Trade Balance...................	78acd	−139.1	−180.2	−111.2	−428.9	−416.1	−354.2	−341.4	....	....	....	....	....
Services: Credit...................	78add	38.5	35.8	6.7	104.1	109.1	173.7	180.0	....	....	....	....	....
Services: Debit....................	78aed	−35.2	−30.2	−63.9	−284.5	−283.3	−331.5	−380.6	....	....	....	....	....
Balance on Goods & Services......	78afd	−135.8	−174.6	−168.4	−609.3	−590.3	−512.0	−542.0	....	....	....	....	....
Income: Credit....................	78agd	1.0	2.0	−	....	....	....	....	....	....	....	....	....
Income: Debit.....................	78ahd	−12.9	−12.6	−11.2	−30.6	−9.9	−13.6	−11.7	....	....	....	....	....
Balance on Gds, Serv. & Inc.......	78aid	−147.7	−185.2	−179.6	−639.9	−600.2	−525.6	−553.7	....	....	....	....	....
Current Transfers, n.i.e.: Credit..	78ajd	155.0	173.4	156.2	552.9	462.5	477.9	515.6	....	....	....	....	....
Current Transfers: Debit.........	78akd	−	−	−	....	....	....	....	....	....	....	....	....
Capital Account, n.i.e..............	78bcd	−	−	−	....	....	....	....	....	....	....	....	....
Capital Account, n.i.e.: Credit.......	78bad	−	−	−	....	....	....	....	....	....	....	....	....
Capital Account: Debit.............	78bbd	−	−	−	....	....	....	....	....	....	....	....	....
Financial Account, n.i.e...........	78bjd	−22.8	−46.5	−15.8	99.2	67.9	61.5	193.1	....	....	....	....	....
Direct Investment Abroad........	78bdd	−	−	−	....	....	....	....	....	....	....	....	....
Dir. Invest. in Rep. Econ., n.i.e....	78bed	−2.2	−2.8	−	7.4	4.1	4.0	10.8	....	....	....	....	....
Portfolio Investment Assets.......	78bfd	−	−	−	....	....	....	....	....	....	....	....	....
Equity Securities................	78bkd	−	−	−	....	....	....	....	....	....	....	....	....
Debt Securities...................	78bld	−	−	−	....	....	....	....	....	....	....	....	....
Portfolio Investment Liab., n.i.e...	78bgd	−	−	−	....	....	....	....	....	....	....	....	....
Equity Securities................	78bmd	−	−	−	....	....	....	....	....	....	....	....	....
Debt Securities..................	78bnd	−	−	−	....	....	....	....	....	....	....	....	....
Financial Derivatives Assets......	78bwd	....	....	....	....	....	....	....	....	....	....	....	....
Financial Derivatives Liabilities...	78bxd	....	....	....	....	....	....	....	....	....	....	....	....
Other Investment Assets.........	78bhd	−12.6	−30.6	−5.5	−11.2	−4.6	21.6	86.8	....	....	....	....	....
Monetary Authorities.............	78bod	−	−	−	....	....	....	....	....	....	....	....	....
General Government.............	78bpd	−	−	−	....	....	....	....	....	....	....	....	....
Banks..............................	78bqd	−12.6	−30.6	−5.5	−11.2	−4.6	3.6	2.8	....	....	....	....	....
Other Sectors....................	78brd	−	−	−	−	−	18.0	84.0	....	....	....	....	....
Other Investment Liab., n.i.e.....	78bid	−8.0	−13.1	−10.3	103.1	68.4	35.9	95.5	....	....	....	....	....
Monetary Authorities.............	78bsd	2.9	2.2	2.1	−	−	−	−	....	....	....	....	....
General Government............	78btd	−10.9	−15.3	−12.4	112.5	68.8	37.7	43.0	....	....	....	....	....
Banks.............................	78bud	−	−	−	.4	−.4	12.3	−4.5	....	....	....	....	....
Other Sectors...................	78bvd	−	−	−	−9.8	.1	−14.1	57.0	....	....	....	....	....
Net Errors and Omissions........	78cad	9.2	35.3	−10.5	125.9	19.5	16.1	−120.6	....	....	....	....	....
Overall Balance...................	78cbd	−6.3	−23.0	−49.7	138.1	−50.4	29.9	34.4	....	....	....	....	....
Reserves and Related Items.......	79dad	6.3	23.0	49.7	−138.1	50.4	−29.9	−34.4	....	....	....	....	....
Reserve Assets....................	79dbd	−11.3	−19.1	12.8	−175.6	48.5	−50.6	−29.1	....	....	....	....	....
Use of Fund Credit and Loans.....	79dcd	−	−	−	−6.6	−2.6	20.6	−5.3	....	....	....	....	....
Exceptional Financing............	79ded	17.6	42.1	36.9	44.1	4.4	....	....	....	....	....	....	....
Government Finance						*Millions of Gourdes: Year Ending September 30*							
Deficit (−) or Surplus.............	80	−590.2	−506.9	−947.1	−986.1	−329.5	−320.5	−776.5	−1,647.7	−1,774.1	−1,887.0	−2,542.3	−3,508.4
Revenue...........................	81	1,234.7	1,284.2	874.8	2,456.0	3,436.1	4,781.8	5,330.0	6,211.2	6,169.4	6,332.2	7,721.7	10,502.5
Grants Received...................	81z	14.0	1.1	2.2	696.7	354.3	694.6	644.7	47.0	197.2	369.8	112.7	283.3
Expenditure.......................	82	1,838.9	1,792.2	1,824.1	4,138.8	4,119.9	5,796.9	6,751.2	7,905.9	8,140.7	8,589.0	10,376.7	14,294.2
Financing													
Net Domestic Borrowing..........	84a	625.4	516.9	1,109.6	885.7	650.4	223.7	431.5	1,900.1	1,529.9	2,143.8	2,874.7	3,452.8
Monetary Authorities..............	84aa	618.7	516.9	1,109.6	885.7	650.4	223.7	591.5	1,799.6	1,566.1	2,148.0	2,912.3	3,778.4
Other.............................	84ac	6.7	−	−	−	−	−	−160.0	100.5	−36.2	−4.2	−37.6	−325.6
Net Foreign Borrowing...........	85a	1.1	−	−	1,031.3	−260.7	−272.0	−421.7	−577.5	−389.5	−309.6	−277.2	−745.3
Use of Cash Balances.............	87	−32.2	39.1	−88.1	−975.8	−28.4	−327.3	85.5	−544.4	371.5	233.3	−20.8	117.3
Adjustment to Financing.........	84x	−4.1	−49.1	−74.4	44.9	−31.8	696.1	681.2	869.5	262.2	−180.5	−34.3	683.6

2004, International Monetary Fund : *International Financial Statistics Yearbook*

Haiti 263

		1992	1993	1994	1995	1996	1997	1998	1999	2000	2001	2002	2003
National Accounts		\multicolumn{12}{c}{*Millions of Gourdes: Year Ending September 30*}
Househ.Cons.Expend.,incl.NPISHs....	96f	15,321	21,344	31,310	38,167	41,719	49,393	57,148	62,157	72,446	83,921	92,375	117,891
Gross Fixed Capital Formation..........	93e	1,376	1,467	1,857	4,867	13,122	13,247	16,382	19,182	21,208	22,158	23,425	36,704
Changes in Inventories.....................	93i	....	....	....	....	....	....	....	....	....	....	....	....
Exports of Goods and Services..........	90c	1,346	1,912	1,942	3,845	5,284	5,646	6,237	8,482	9,849	10,594	11,403	19,389
Imports of Goods and Services (-).....	98c	3,022	4,849	4,173	11,634	13,479	14,280	16,770	20,568	25,923	30,973	33,363	55,815
Gross Domestic Product (GDP).........	99b	15,020	19,894	30,936	35,265	46,647	54,005	62,997	69,254	77,580	85,700	93,840	118,169
Net Primary Income from Abroad.....	98.n	−153	−211	−584	....	....	....	....	....	....	....	....	....
Gross National Income (GNI).............	99a	14,871	....	....	....	....	....	....	....	....	....	....	....
GDP Volume 1976 Prices.................	99b.p	4,638	4,525	4,150	4,334	4,451	....	....	....	....	....	....	....
GDP Volume 1987 Prices.................	99b.p	....	....	....	....	12,083	12,410	12,681	13,025	13,138	13,001	12,930	12,976
GDP Volume (2000=100).................	99bvp	95.8	93.5	85.8	89.6	†92.0	94.5	96.5	99.1	100.0	99.0	98.4	98.8
GDP Deflator (2000=100).................	99bip	20.2	27.4	46.5	50.8	65.4	73.7	84.1	90.0	100.0	111.6	122.9	154.2
		\multicolumn{12}{c}{*Millions: Midyear Estimates*}
Population...................................	99z	7.16	7.27	7.38	7.49	7.59	7.69	7.80	7.90	8.01	8.11	8.22	8.33

2004, International Monetary Fund: *International Financial Statistics Yearbook*

Honduras 268

		1992	1993	1994	1995	1996	1997	1998	1999	2000	2001	2002	2003
Exchange Rates						*Lempiras per SDR: End of Period*							
Market Rate	aa	8.0163	9.9720	13.7227	15.3751	18.5057	17.6673	19.4415	19.9067	19.7270	20.0068	23.0076	26.3733
					Lempiras per US Dollar: End of Period (ae) Period Average (rf)								
Market Rate	ae	5.8300	7.2600	9.4001	10.3432	12.8694	13.0942	13.8076	14.5039	15.1407	15.9197	16.9233	17.7482
Market Rate	rf	5.4979	6.4716	8.4088	9.4710	11.7053	13.0035	13.3850	14.2132	14.8392	15.4737	16.4334	17.3453
Fund Position						*Millions of SDRs: End of Period*							
Quota	2f.s	95.00	95.00	95.00	95.00	95.00	95.00	95.00	129.50	129.50	129.50	129.50	129.50
SDRs	1b.s	.11	.11	.15	.10	.06	.06	.05	.68	.08	.25	.35	.08
Reserve Position in the Fund	1c.s	–	–	–	–	–	–	–	8.63	8.63	8.63	8.63	8.63
Total Fund Cred.&Loans Outstg.	2tl	81.35	86.01	74.81	66.36	40.28	33.90	80.04	153.33	165.75	175.12	144.59	115.42
International Liquidity					*Millions of US Dollars Unless Otherwise Indicated: End of Period*								
Total Reserves minus Gold	1l.d	197.45	97.15	171.01	261.45	249.19	580.37	818.07	1,257.58	1,313.04	1,415.56	1,524.00	1,430.03
SDRs	1b.d	.15	.15	.21	.15	.09	.07	.07	.94	.10	.32	.47	.11
Reserve Position in the Fund	1c.d	–	–	–	–	–	–	–	11.84	11.24	10.84	11.73	12.82
Foreign Exchange	1d.d	197.30	97.00	170.80	261.30	249.10	580.30	818.00	1,244.80	1,301.70	1,404.40	1,511.80	1,417.10
Gold (Million Fine Troy Ounces)	1ad	.021	.021	.021	.021	.021	.021	.021	.021	.021	.021	.021	.021
Gold (National Valuation)	1and	7.79	8.47	8.30	8.41	8.03	6.43	6.25	6.28	5.99	6.05	7.11	9.26
Monetary Authorities: Other Liab.	4..d	588.14	560.88	599.86	595.09	509.27	379.96	361.89	443.44	427.88	412.08	400.10	396.09
Deposit Money Banks: Assets	7a.d	66.52	75.65	84.32	123.47	209.97	228.00	275.70	379.81	451.94	487.77	565.46	551.08
Liabilities	7b.d	16.95	28.71	68.89	103.20	154.84	271.39	344.95	297.64	272.02	228.04	230.62	221.51
Other Banking Insts.: Assets	7e.d	6.50	8.79	10.20	9.29	12.39	8.06	6.80	7.67	11.77	11.42	10.01	8.25
Liabilities	7f.d	17.51	13.93	15.80	16.49	13.01	15.80	17.19	9.84	38.26	56.86	39.01	23.75
Monetary Authorities						*Millions of Lempiras: End of Period*							
Foreign Assets	11	1,343	954	1,930	3,058	3,641	†10,437	14,282	21,375	23,151	25,978	29,586	29,402
Claims on Central Government	12a	1,555	2,023	1,512	1,284	1,220	†1,462	1,534	1,014	1,109	935	919	2,296
Claims on Local Government	12b	67	63	60	53	92	†48	45	42	39	36	33	29
Claims on Private Sector	12d	42	59	58	64	58	†1	1	1	1	1	–	–
Claims on Deposit Money Banks	12e	665	665	678	616	721	†136	99	60	33	215	5	269
Claims on Other Banking Insts.	12f	532	547	569	572	555	†157	108	108	97	74	61	49
Reserve Money	14	1,734	1,852	2,723	3,373	4,842	†9,045	10,501	11,720	12,813	14,071	17,762	18,935
of which: Currency Outside DMBs	14a	1,141	1,448	1,995	2,111	2,630	†3,315	3,744	4,714	4,727	5,166	5,549	6,448
Time, Savings,& Fgn.Currency Dep	15	39	52	86	318	219	†791	503	1,582	3,599	5,979	6,662	7,501
Foreign Liabilities	16c	2,428	3,103	4,274	4,438	4,216	†960	1,618	3,190	3,361	3,582	3,375	3,082
Long-Term Foreign Liabilities	16cl	1,599	1,692	2,206	2,216	2,456	†4,015	4,302	4,188	4,054	3,928	3,943	3,948
Central Government Deposits	16d	1,390	1,751	1,229	1,562	2,042	†2,878	4,766	7,409	6,112	4,834	5,081	5,222
Capital Accounts	17a	891	1,116	1,422	1,762	1,930	†1,623	908	945	973	1,080	1,136	1,457
Other Items (Net)	17r	–3,876	–5,255	–7,133	–8,022	–9,419	†–7,072	–6,528	–6,432	–6,483	–6,236	–7,353	–8,099
Deposit Money Banks						*Millions of Lempiras: End of Period*							
Reserves	20	648	423	668	1,118	1,968	†5,021	6,018	6,374	7,134	8,091	11,269	11,042
Foreign Assets	21	388	549	793	1,277	2,702	†2,985	3,807	5,509	6,843	7,765	9,570	9,781
Claims on Central Government	22a	1,045	968	1,287	1,205	867	†275	77	41	370	732	935	1,260
Claims on Local Government	22b	5	2	1	1	10	†54	147	125	136	79	255	354
Claims on Private Sector	22d	4,341	5,009	6,364	7,711	10,966	†16,744	23,247	28,014	32,021	35,524	38,001	45,208
Claims on Other Banking Insts.	22f	6	6	37	55	29	†26	43	473	195	280	391	3,674
Demand Deposits	24	1,276	1,313	1,761	2,368	3,074	†4,287	4,841	5,666	6,180	6,344	7,658	9,315
Time, Savings,& Fgn.Currency Dep	25	3,151	3,432	4,287	5,626	8,721	†13,657	18,094	22,228	27,819	32,585	37,027	42,288
Bonds	26ab	19	16	14	29	33	†61	90	58	50	42	33	66
Foreign Liabilities	26c	66	74	256	459	759	†1,294	1,314	878	961	822	1,083	1,069
Long-Term Foreign Liabilities	26cl	33	135	392	609	1,234	†2,259	3,449	3,439	3,158	2,808	2,819	2,862
Central Government Deposits	26d	649	349	300	270	331	†1,059	2,004	2,846	2,457	2,103	2,651	2,491
Credit from Monetary Authorities	26g	679	704	691	619	760	†156	90	60	33	215	11	269
Liabilities to Other Banking Insts.	26i	....	....	....	....	....	833	1,453	2,575	2,897	3,421	3,205	5,266
Capital Accounts	27a	876	1,234	1,670	2,224	2,846	†3,885	4,876	5,958	7,168	8,343	8,888	9,860
Other Items (Net)	27r	–315	–302	–222	–829	–1,212	†–2,385	–2,872	–3,173	–4,024	–4,212	–2,956	–2,168
Monetary Survey						*Millions of Lempiras: End of Period*							
Foreign Assets (Net)	31n	–763	–1,673	–1,807	–562	1,368	†11,168	15,156	22,816	25,672	29,339	34,698	35,031
Domestic Credit	32	5,554	6,577	8,359	9,122	11,427	†14,830	18,432	19,563	25,397	30,724	32,863	45,158
Claims on Central Govt. (Net)	32an	561	890	1,270	657	–287	†–2,200	–5,158	–9,200	–7,091	–5,271	–5,877	–4,157
Claims on Local Government	32b	72	66	61	63	107	†102	192	168	175	116	288	383
Claims on Private Sector	32d	4,383	5,068	6,422	7,775	11,024	†16,745	23,247	28,015	32,021	35,525	38,001	45,208
Claims on Other Banking Insts.	32f	538	553	606	627	583	†183	151	581	292	354	452	3,723
Money	34	2,523	2,825	3,845	4,678	6,053	†8,294	9,349	11,050	11,954	12,388	14,224	17,251
Quasi-Money	35	3,190	3,485	4,374	5,945	8,941	†14,448	18,597	23,810	31,418	38,564	43,689	49,789
Bonds	36ab	19	16	14	29	33	†61	90	58	50	42	33	66
Long-Term Foreign Liabilities	36cl	1,632	1,826	2,597	2,825	3,690	†6,274	7,751	7,626	7,212	6,737	6,762	6,810
Liabilities to Other Banking Insts.	36i	....	....	....	....	....	833	1,453	2,575	2,897	3,421	3,205	5,266
Capital Accounts	37a	1,767	2,350	3,093	3,986	4,775	†5,509	5,784	6,903	8,141	9,423	10,024	11,317
Other Items (Net)	37r	–4,340	–5,599	–7,370	–8,902	–10,697	†–9,420	–9,436	–9,643	–10,602	–10,512	–10,375	–10,310
Money plus Quasi-Money	35l	5,713	6,309	8,219	10,623	14,994	†22,742	27,946	34,860	43,371	50,952	57,913	67,040

Honduras 268

		1992	1993	1994	1995	1996	1997	1998	1999	2000	2001	2002	2003
Other Banking Institutions		\multicolumn{12}{c}{*Millions of Lempiras: End of Period*}
Reserves	40	58	75	139	124	121	†661	759	654	1,057	945	1,089	1,507
Foreign Assets	41	38	64	96	96	160	†106	94	111	178	182	169	146
Claims on Central Government	42a	76	79	110	137	156	†294	79	54	46	209	304	2,090
Claims on Local Government	42b	76	80	86	93	95	†136	131	112	110	99	55	51
Claims on Private Sector	42d	981	1,094	1,261	1,529	1,507	†3,044	3,337	3,969	4,363	5,282	5,904	4,085
Claims on Deposit Money Banks	42e	7	20	27	38	34	†881	1,462	2,597	2,918	3,463	3,300	5,321
Demand Deposits	44	17	19	21	19	20	†26	18	40	38	41	34	49
Time, Savings,& Fgn.Currency Dep	45	557	675	744	938	1,063	†3,387	3,154	3,504	3,531	4,121	4,435	2,805
Bonds	46ab	1	1	1	1	–	†17	7	–	–	–	–	105
Foreign Liabilities	46c	1	–	6	18	1	†30	14	1	17	4	4	41
Long-Term Foreign Liabilities	46cl	101	101	143	153	166	†177	224	142	563	901	656	381
Central Government Deposits	46d	194	217	326	425	407	†636	1,091	1,462	1,851	1,685	1,729	1,924
Credit from Monetary Authorities	46g	589	579	647	586	584	†177	110	112	102	74	61	49
Credit from Deposit Money Banks	46h	4	5	36	54	28	†70	92	527	186	213	315	3,655
Capital Accounts	47a	345	301	407	449	497	†2,058	2,087	2,866	3,479	4,378	4,783	4,977
Other Items (Net)	47r	−574	−487	−611	−623	−693	†−1,456	−935	−1,157	−1,094	−1,237	−1,196	−787
Banking Survey		\multicolumn{12}{c}{*Millions of Lempiras: End of Period*}
Foreign Assets (Net)	51n	−726	−1,610	−1,717	−484	1,527	†11,244	15,237	22,926	25,833	29,516	34,863	35,137
Domestic Credit	52	5,954	7,059	8,884	9,830	12,195	†17,484	20,737	21,655	27,774	34,276	36,945	45,736
Claims on Central Govt. (Net)	52an	442	752	1,054	369	−537	†−2,542	−6,171	−10,609	−8,896	−6,746	−7,303	−3,991
Claims on Local Government	52b	148	146	146	156	202	†238	323	280	285	215	344	434
Claims on Private Sector	52d	5,364	6,161	7,683	9,305	12,530	†19,788	26,584	31,983	36,384	40,807	43,905	49,293
Liquid Liabilities	55l	6,229	6,928	8,845	11,455	15,956	†25,494	30,359	37,749	45,883	54,170	61,293	68,388
Bonds	56ab	20	17	14	30	33	†78	97	58	50	42	34	171
Long-Term Foreign Liabilities	56cl	1,733	1,927	2,740	2,977	3,856	†6,451	7,974	7,768	7,775	7,637	7,418	7,191
Capital Accounts	57a	2,111	2,652	3,500	4,434	5,272	†7,566	7,870	9,769	11,620	13,802	14,806	16,294
Other Items (Net)	57r	−4,865	−6,074	−7,932	−9,550	−11,396	†−10,861	−10,328	−10,764	−11,721	−11,859	−11,742	−11,171
Money (National Definitions)		\multicolumn{12}{c}{*Millions of Lempiras: End of Period*}
Reserve Money (M0)	19ma	....	....	....	....	4,627	8,102	9,281	10,079	10,353	9,790	10,992	11,945
M1	59ma	2,444	2,762	3,783	4,474	5,690	7,609	8,577	10,450	10,943	11,515	13,192	15,807
M2	59mb	6,270	6,822	8,537	10,224	12,560	20,344	23,706	28,723	33,482	36,253	40,336	45,881
M3	59mc	6,592	7,517	9,834	12,173	16,727	25,716	30,395	37,155	43,924	50,115	56,733	64,767
Interest Rates		\multicolumn{12}{c}{*Percent Per Annum*}
Discount Rate (End of Period)	60	26.10	....	....	....	....	....	....	....	....	....	....	....
Savings Rate	60k	9.55	9.20	9.44	10.02	9.93	12.56	12.27	12.05	10.88	9.96	8.26	6.60
Savings Rate (Fgn.Currency)	60k.f	....	....	....	....	....	4.66	4.53	3.99	3.67	3.18	1.95	1.29
Deposit Rate	60l	12.34	11.60	11.56	11.97	16.70	21.28	18.58	19.97	15.93	14.48	13.74	11.48
Deposit Rate (Fgn.Currency)	60l.f	....	....	....	....	....	9.89	9.53	9.09	7.53	6.36	4.05	2.80
Lending Rate	60p	21.68	22.06	24.68	26.95	29.74	32.07	30.69	30.15	26.82	23.76	22.69	20.80
Lending Rate (Fgn.Currency)	60p.f	....	....	....	....	....	12.88	12.53	12.60	12.91	12.68	11.48	10.00
Government Bond Yield	61	10.40	10.40	23.11	27.24	35.55	29.59	20.34	16.04	14.79	15.28	11.97	11.26
Prices and Labor		\multicolumn{12}{c}{*Index Numbers (2000=100): Period Averages*}
Consumer Prices	64	27.3	30.2	36.8	47.7	59.0	†70.9	80.6	90.0	100.0	109.7	118.1	127.2
		\multicolumn{12}{c}{*Number in Thousands: Period Averages*}
Labor Force	67d	....	....	....	1,777	1,977	2,053	2,135	2,388	....	....	....	....
Employment	67e	1,675	....	....	1,806	1,985	2,088	2,135	2,299	....	2,335	....	....
Unemployment	67c	54	....	....	59	89	69	88	89	....	103	....	....
Unemployment Rate (%)	67r	3.1	....	....	3.2	4.3	3.2	3.9	3.7	....	4.0	....	....
International Transactions		\multicolumn{12}{c}{*Millions of US Dollars*}
Exports	70..d	801.5	814.0	842.0	1,220.2	1,316.0	1,445.7	1,532.8	1,164.4	1,380.0	1,324.4	1,321.2	1,332.3
Imports, c.i.f	71..d	1,036.6	1,130.0	1,055.9	1,642.7	1,839.9	2,148.6	2,534.8	2,676.1	2,854.7	2,941.6	2,981.2	3,275.6
Imports, f.o.b	71.vd	938.1	1,022.6	955.6	1,486.6	1,665.1	1,944.4	2,293.9	2,421.8	2,583.5	2,662.1	2,697.9	2,964.4
		\multicolumn{12}{c}{*2000=100*}
Volume of Exports	72	82.0	76.5	70.9	70.0	79.7	60.1	77.1	69.9	100.0	133.1	117.5	....
Export Prices	74..d	89.7	91.5	99.5	131.9	118.0	134.7	137.6	103.0	100.0	100.7	95.9	....

Honduras 268

		1992	1993	1994	1995	1996	1997	1998	1999	2000	2001	2002	2003
Balance of Payments			*Millions of US Dollars: Minus Sign Indicates Debit*
Current Account, n.i.e.	78ald	−298.2	−308.7	−343.3	−200.9	−335.4	−272.2	−394.8	−624.6	−275.8	−339.1	−242.3	−279.2
Goods: Exports f.o.b.	78aad	839.3	999.6	1,101.5	1,377.2	1,638.4	1,856.5	2,047.9	1,756.3	2,011.6	1,935.5	1,973.6	2,078.2
Goods: Imports f.o.b.	78abd	−990.2	−1,203.1	−1,351.1	−1,518.6	−1,925.8	−2,150.4	−2,370.5	−2,509.6	−2,669.6	−2,768.1	−2,809.2	−3,065.4
Trade Balance	78acd	−150.9	−203.5	−249.6	−141.4	−287.4	−293.9	−322.6	−753.3	−658.0	−832.6	−835.6	−987.2
Services: Credit	78add	202.0	223.9	242.4	257.6	283.3	334.9	377.1	474.1	478.9	487.2	530.3	576.2
Services: Debit	78aed	−243.2	−294.7	−311.0	−333.7	−327.8	−360.9	−446.8	−502.4	−597.5	−626.6	−601.9	−653.2
Balance on Goods & Services	78afd	−192.1	−274.3	−318.2	−217.5	−331.9	−319.9	−392.3	−781.6	−776.6	−972.0	−907.2	−1,064.2
Income: Credit	78agd	61.4	16.6	24.0	32.3	61.2	70.0	59.5	80.5	110.1	88.0	66.8	56.7
Income: Debit	78ahd	−343.4	−215.3	−238.1	−258.2	−292.0	−281.8	−263.6	−235.7	−256.8	−259.2	−249.7	−240.0
Balance on Gds, Serv. & Inc.	78aid	−474.1	−473.0	−532.3	−443.4	−562.7	−531.7	−596.4	−936.8	−923.3	−1,143.2	−1,090.0	−1,247.5
Current Transfers, n.i.e.: Credit	78ajd	186.1	165.5	190.2	243.7	271.7	306.8	241.7	354.6	717.9	894.0	946.6	1,072.2
Current Transfers: Debit	78akd	−10.2	−1.2	−1.2	−1.2	−44.4	−47.3	−40.1	−42.4	−70.4	−89.9	−98.9	−104.0
Capital Account, n.i.e.	78bcd	–	–	–	–	28.5	14.6	29.4	110.9	30.1	36.7	23.6	21.0
Capital Account, n.i.e.: Credit	78bad	–	–	–	–	29.2	15.3	29.4	110.9	30.1	36.7	23.6	21.0
Capital Account: Debit	78bbd	–	–	–	–	−.7	−.7	–	–	–	–	–	–
Financial Account, n.i.e.	78bjd	22.0	22.8	157.5	114.6	70.2	243.3	113.9	203.4	−29.5	160.1	139.3	−20.0
Direct Investment Abroad	78bdd	–	–	–	–	–	–	–	–	–	–	–	–
Dir. Invest. in Rep. Econ., n.i.e.	78bed	47.6	26.7	34.8	50.0	90.9	121.5	99.0	237.3	282.0	189.5	175.5	198.0
Portfolio Investment Assets	78bfd	.1	–	–	–	16.0	–	–	−72.4	−59.4	−3.6	−3.8	−4.1
Equity Securities	78bkd	.1	–	....	....	16.0	–	–	–	–	–	–	–
Debt Securities	78bld	–	–	–	–	....	....	–	−72.4	−59.4	−3.6	−3.8	−4.1
Portfolio Investment Liab., n.i.e.	78bgd	–	–	–	–	....	....	–	–	−1.2	–	–	–
Equity Securities	78bmd	–	–	–	–	....	....	–	–	–	–	–	–
Debt Securities	78bnd	–	–	–	–	....	....	–	–	−1.2	–	–	–
Financial Derivatives Assets	78bwd	....	....	....	....	....	....	–	–	–	–	–	–
Financial Derivatives Liabilities	78bxd	....	....	....	....	....	....	−25.8	−16.1	–	–	–	–
Other Investment Assets	78bhd	−63.4	−139.6	8.9	−12.8	−89.4	−53.4	−61.7	−132.2	−203.8	−102.3	24.2	−77.6
Monetary Authorities	78bod	....	3.9	3.3	11.7	....	....	–	–	–	–	–	–
General Government	78bpd	−26.3	−132.0	14.4	14.4	....	....	–	–	−97.9	−65.1	−83.5	12.5
Banks	78bqd	−37.1	−11.5	−8.8	−38.9	−89.4	−53.4	−61.7	−132.2	–	–	–	–
Other Sectors	78brd	–	–	–	–	–	–	–	–	−105.9	−37.2	107.7	−90.1
Other Investment Liab., n.i.e.	78bid	37.7	135.7	113.8	77.4	52.7	175.2	102.4	186.8	−47.1	76.5	−56.6	−136.3
Monetary Authorities	78bsd	−84.8	−73.6	−60.7	−73.1	−180.1	−24.1	−27.2	−22.2	−32.4	−20.5	−23.1	−15.7
General Government	78btd	104.7	224.8	96.2	101.7	141.9	−48.4	−30.3	168.8	10.5	127.3	−6.2	3.0
Banks	78bud	−7.3	1.7	−2.2	6.3	34.5	113.8	51.1	−11.5	−40.5	−45.9	−13.7	−9.4
Other Sectors	78bvd	25.1	−17.2	80.5	42.5	56.4	133.9	108.8	51.7	15.3	15.6	−13.6	−114.2
Net Errors and Omissions	78cad	29.2	−47.5	115.5	45.0	157.9	196.5	96.1	122.0	118.7	68.3	60.5	76.1
Overall Balance	78cbd	−247.0	−333.4	−70.3	−41.3	−78.8	182.2	−155.4	−188.3	−156.6	−74.0	−18.8	−202.1
Reserves and Related Items	79dad	247.0	333.4	70.3	41.3	78.8	−182.2	155.4	188.3	156.6	74.0	18.8	202.1
Reserve Assets	79dbd	−92.0	99.6	−74.1	−90.3	12.7	−307.9	−229.8	−441.9	−32.3	−85.6	−91.9	100.3
Use of Fund Credit and Loans	79dcd	80.7	6.4	−16.1	−13.7	−38.0	−8.8	64.8	99.5	16.4	12.0	−39.7	−41.1
Exceptional Financing	79ded	258.3	227.4	160.4	145.3	104.1	134.5	320.4	530.6	172.5	147.6	150.5	143.0
Government Finance			*Millions of Lempiras: Year Ending December 31*
Deficit (−) or Surplus	80	−860.6	−1,447.7	−1,458.6	−1,326.1	−1,516.1	−1,260.2	−277.5	−1,115.4	−3,847.6	....	....	−6,526.7
Total Revenue and Grants	81y	3,772.1	4,453.1	4,952.1	7,296.6	8,512.4	11,091.2	14,012.5	16,395.1	17,128.1	....	....	23,562.1
Revenue	81	3,500.5	4,182.2	4,809.8	7,139.5	8,256.8	10,773.8	13,641.8	15,136.2	15,872.0	....	....	22,233.9
Grants	81z	271.6	270.9	142.3	157.1	255.6	317.4	370.7	1,258.9	1,256.1	....	....	1,328.2
Exp. & Lending Minus Repay	82z	4,632.7	5,900.8	6,410.7	8,622.7	10,028.5	12,351.4	14,290.0	17,510.5	20,975.7	....	....	30,088.8
Expenditure	82	4,414.6	5,888.7	6,030.7	7,780.4	9,778.8	12,727.6	14,583.9	16,312.8	20,477.8	....	....	29,417.2
Lending Minus Repayments	83	218.1	12.1	380.0	842.3	249.7	−376.2	−293.9	1,197.7	497.9	....	....	671.6
Total Financing	80h	860.6	1,447.7	1,458.6	1,326.1	1,516.1	1,260.2	277.5	1,115.4	3,847.6	....	....	6,526.7
Domestic	84a	−170.0	−322.8	505.2	−134.8	337.4	129.0	−685.8	−3,282.5	1,722.4	....	....	3,980.3
Foreign	85a	1,030.6	1,770.5	953.4	1,460.9	1,178.7	1,131.2	963.3	4,397.9	2,125.2	....	....	2,546.4
Total Debt by Residence	88	16,955.2	22,597.0	30,997.1	36,435.5	44,360.1	46,672.5	50,721.6	56,112.1	58,646.1	....	....	84,726.4
Domestic	88a	3,065.8	3,460.8	3,570.3	3,711.7	3,875.5	4,424.1	3,970.4	3,280.2	3,825.0	....	....	9,035.6
Foreign	89a	13,889.4	19,136.2	27,426.8	32,723.8	40,484.6	42,248.4	46,751.2	52,831.9	54,821.1	....	....	75,690.8
Memorandum Item:													
Intragovernmental Debt	88s	−100.7	−67.3	−332.2	−347.8	−394.1	−304.4	−330.2	−163.4	−20.3	....	....	....
National Accounts			*Millions of Lempiras*
Househ.Cons.Expend.,incl.NPISHs	96f	12,520	14,718	18,113	23,819	30,782	39,626	46,930	53,168	63,119	72,200	81,825	91,136
Government Consumption Expend	91f	2,171	2,405	2,780	3,495	4,556	5,422	7,117	8,726	11,218	13,792	14,925	16,209
Gross Fixed Capital Formation	93e	4,202	6,535	8,110	8,994	11,468	15,732	19,874	23,045	23,372	23,525	23,992	28,114
Changes in Inventories	93i	679	1,079	2,751	2,842	3,400	3,994	1,910	3,687	4,095	5,756	3,710	4,897
Exports of Goods and Services	90c	6,048	7,869	11,498	16,390	22,378	28,322	32,699	31,627	36,959	37,479	41,137	46,054
Imports of Goods and Services (−)	98c	6,820	9,916	14,391	18,033	24,821	31,775	38,092	43,157	49,362	53,720	57,466	66,088
Gross Domestic Product (GDP)	99b	18,800	22,689	28,862	37,507	47,763	61,322	70,438	77,096	89,401	99,032	108,124	120,322
Net Primary Income from Abroad	98.n	−1,859	−1,498	−1,843	−2,532	−3,069	−2,812	−2,845	−2,335	−2,325	−2,811	−3,179	−3,404
Gross National Income (GNI)	99a	16,941	21,191	27,019	34,975	44,694	58,510	67,593	74,761	87,076	96,221	104,945	116,918
Consumption of Fixed Capital	99cf	1,214	1,372	1,707	2,258	2,845	3,528	4,086	4,645	5,269	5,908	6,507	7,180
GDP Volume 1978 Prices	99b.p	5,634	5,985	5,907	6,148	6,368	6,686	6,880	6,750	7,138	7,324	7,523	7,767
GDP Volume (2000=100)	99bvp	78.9	83.8	82.8	86.1	89.2	93.7	96.4	94.6	100.0	102.6	105.4	108.8
GDP Deflator (2000=100)	99bip	26.6	30.3	39.0	48.7	59.9	73.2	81.7	91.2	100.0	108.0	114.8	123.7
			*Millions: Midyear Estimates*
Population	99z	5.17	5.32	5.48	5.64	5.80	5.96	6.13	6.29	6.46	6.62	6.78	6.94

2004, International Monetary Fund: *International Financial Statistics Yearbook*

Hungary 944

		1992	1993	1994	1995	1996	1997	1998	1999	2000	2001	2002	2003
Exchange Rates		\multicolumn{12}{c}{*Forint per SDR: End of Period*}											
Official Rate	aa	115.459	138.317	161.591	207.321	237.163	274.572	308.401	346.586	370.978	350.665	306.110	308.963
		\multicolumn{12}{c}{*Forint per US Dollar: End of Period (ae) Period Average (rf)*}											
Official Rate	ae	83.970	100.700	110.690	139.470	164.930	203.500	219.030	252.520	284.730	279.030	225.160	207.920
Official Rate	rf	78.988	91.933	105.160	125.681	152.647	186.789	214.402	237.146	282.179	286.490	257.887	224.307
		\multicolumn{12}{c}{*Index Numbers (2000=100): Period Averages*}											
Official Rate	ahx	356.0	306.8	267.5	224.8	184.4	151.0	131.2	118.7	100.0	98.2	109.4	125.4
Nominal Effective Exchange Rate	nec	239.0	229.0	202.8	158.1	135.5	125.9	112.3	105.8	100.0	101.9	109.4	109.3
Real Effective Exchange Rate	rec	88.3	96.0	95.0	91.3	93.7	98.5	97.7	99.3	100.0	105.8	117.3	121.7
Fund Position		\multicolumn{12}{c}{*Millions of SDRs: End of Period*}											
Quota	2f.s	755	755	755	755	755	755	755	1,038	1,038	1,038	1,038	1,038
SDRs	1b.s	2	2	1	1	–	–	1	3	9	16	24	31
Reserve Position in the Fund	1c.s	56	56	56	56	56	56	56	177	202	322	437	455
Total Fund Cred.&Loans Outstg.	2tl	876	896	782	259	119	119	–	–	–	–	–	–
International Liquidity		\multicolumn{12}{c}{*Millions of US Dollars Unless Otherwise Indicated: End of Period*}											
Total Reserves minus Gold	1l.d	4,425	6,700	6,735	11,974	9,720	8,408	9,319	10,954	11,190	10,727	10,348	12,737
SDRs	1b.d	3	3	2	1	–	–	1	4	12	21	33	46
Reserve Position in the Fund	1c.d	77	77	82	83	81	76	79	243	263	405	595	676
Foreign Exchange	1d.d	4,345	6,620	6,652	11,890	9,639	8,332	9,239	10,707	10,915	10,302	9,721	12,015
Gold (Million Fine Troy Ounces)	1ad	.102	.114	.110	.111	.101	.101	.101	.101	.101	.101	.101	.101
Gold (National Valuation)	1and	33	45	42	43	37	29	29	29	28	28	35	42
Monetary Authorities:Other Liabs.	4..d	14,974	17,244	19,191	20,836	16,239	11,647	11,677	9,847	8,537	6,614	5,338	4,393
Deposit Money Banks: Assets	7a.d	1,504	1,331	1,030	921	1,679	2,495	3,306	3,594	2,745	4,445	4,369	5,974
Liabilities	7b.d	1,831	1,783	2,379	2,878	3,092	4,482	5,464	5,577	5,514	5,980	7,490	12,642
Monetary Authorities		\multicolumn{12}{c}{*Billions of Forint: End of Period*}											
Foreign Assets	11	385.2	689.8	784.0	1,680.7	1,614.9	1,723.3	2,054.3	2,992.4	3,463.4	3,336.2	2,469.2	2,834.2
Claims on Consolidated Cent.Govt.	12a	1,841.9	2,166.9	2,558.3	3,144.7	2,902.9	2,854.0	2,930.0	2,488.2	2,202.4	1,664.6	1,216.3	910.2
Other Claims on Residents	12d	3.8	4.4	4.4	3.8	.6	.7	.8	.7	.7	.7	.8	3.3
Claims on Banking Institutions	12e	293.4	368.8	405.8	302.6	231.4	185.3	178.4	126.6	93.8	46.9	22.8	12.5
Reserve Money	14	606.7	624.2	614.1	723.5	662.0	860.3	1,037.5	1,309.7	1,535.9	1,562.6	1,648.6	1,816.0
of which: Currency Outside DMBs	14a	322.3	371.2	410.7	443.9	497.7	562.6	669.0	855.3	883.9	1,037.6	1,181.8	1,346.8
Other Liabilities to Banks	14n	281.1	387.0	533.9	748.4	920.8	835.4	820.5	1,075.0	774.8	526.9	648.0	387.5
Time & Foreign Currency Deposits	15	2.6	3.5	6.1	7.3	5.7	6.4	19.8	14.0	11.5	6.4	6.7	7.2
Money Market Instruments	16aa	–	–	–	–	–	68.9	152.2	–	349.7	402.7	.1	.5
Bonds	16ab	5.6	7.6	6.4	5.2	3.5	2.3	–	–	–	–	–	–
Liabs. of Central Bank: Securities	16ac	–	8.0	21.0	44.2	76.2	272.5	340.7	242.7	305.8	248.6	142.4	105.5
Foreign Liabilities	16c	111.5	140.6	148.3	104.9	57.8	138.2	42.6	137.0	334.4	268.3	121.4	127.6
Long-Term Foreign Liabilities	16cl	1,247.0	1,719.9	2,102.3	2,854.7	2,648.7	2,264.7	2,515.1	2,349.6	2,096.3	1,577.2	1,080.5	785.7
Consolidated Centr.Govt.Deposits	16d	255.3	341.1	316.6	561.8	389.9	328.4	194.1	555.8	434.4	745.1	197.7	297.8
Capital Accounts	17a	39.5	46.1	31.6	55.2	59.3	72.7	128.2	74.0	65.0	65.0	40.9	12.7
Other Items (Net)	17r	−25.1	−48.1	−28.0	26.5	−74.1	−86.3	−87.2	−184.6	−147.5	−354.2	−177.3	219.7
Banking Institutions		\multicolumn{12}{c}{*Billions of Forint: End of Period*}											
Reserves	20	274.7	234.6	194.1	273.7	154.0	291.1	365.6	447.5	646.9	520.1	460.7	407.2
Claims on Mon.Author.:Securities	20c	–	8.0	21.0	44.2	76.2	272.5	340.7	242.7	309.4	250.3	145.3	108.5
Other Claims on Monetary Author.	20n	281.1	387.0	533.9	748.4	920.8	835.4	820.5	1,075.0	774.6	526.9	648.3	430.9
Foreign Assets	21	126.3	134.1	114.0	128.5	276.9	507.7	724.0	907.5	781.5	1,240.2	983.8	1,242.2
Claims on Consolidated Cent.Govt	22a	263.2	601.8	649.7	732.7	910.4	944.7	1,127.1	1,053.7	1,149.6	1,441.5	1,901.4	2,020.3
Claims on Local Government	22b	13.0	22.6	47.6	49.9	38.5	30.3	44.4	50.3	57.6	73.2	115.9	147.9
Other Claims on Residents	22d	979.7	1,003.8	1,152.9	1,263.1	1,520.7	†2,076.9	2,440.4	2,968.0	4,247.5	5,026.7	5,989.7	7,986.5
Demand Deposits	24	475.7	512.4	553.9	561.5	730.8	961.3	1,121.4	1,277.2	1,494.3	1,738.3	2,113.5	2,288.3
Time, Savings,& Fgn.Currency Dep	25	861.1	1,061.6	1,266.0	1,696.7	2,074.9	2,437.2	2,782.5	3,172.5	3,592.8	4,193.3	4,715.4	5,267.7
Bonds	26ab	71.4	41.8	26.7	15.8	30.8	36.8	29.6	51.0	70.7	114.2	401.0	1,040.7
Foreign Liabilities	26c	83.0	90.6	134.3	196.0	307.9	593.3	689.2	746.7	725.8	614.6	576.1	1,044.0
Long-Term Foreign Liabilities	26cl	70.8	89.0	129.1	205.4	202.1	318.8	507.5	661.7	844.0	1,054.1	1,110.3	1,584.5
Consolidated Centr.Govt.Deposits	26d	14.4	16.1	31.1	13.0	10.0	7.6	5.0	4.7	23.3	28.6	27.8	29.0
Credit from Monetary Authorities	26g	293.4	368.8	405.8	302.6	231.4	185.3	178.4	126.6	91.5	44.6	21.1	11.6
Capital Accounts	27a	277.5	174.0	230.8	316.7	382.9	559.8	596.7	662.9	817.6	962.6	1,047.0	1,273.9
Other Items (Net)	27r	−209.2	37.6	−64.5	−67.0	−73.2	−141.6	−47.6	41.5	307.1	328.5	232.8	−196.4

Hungary 944

		1992	1993	1994	1995	1996	1997	1998	1999	2000	2001	2002	2003
Banking Survey		\multicolumn{12}{c}{*Billions of Forint End of Period*}
Foreign Assets (Net)	31n	317.1	592.7	615.4	1,508.3	1,526.2	1,499.5	2,046.6	3,016.2	3,184.6	3,693.6	2,755.5	2,904.7
Domestic Credit	32	2,831.8	3,442.3	4,064.9	4,619.4	4,973.3	†5,570.6	6,343.5	6,000.5	7,200.2	7,432.9	8,998.5	10,741.4
Claims on Cons.Cent.Govt.(Net)	32an	1,835.4	2,411.4	2,860.1	3,302.6	3,413.5	3,462.7	3,857.9	2,981.4	2,894.3	2,332.4	2,892.1	2,603.8
Claims on Local Government	32b	13.0	22.6	47.6	49.9	38.5	30.3	44.4	50.3	57.6	73.2	115.9	147.9
Other Claims on Residents	32d	983.4	1,008.2	1,157.2	1,266.9	1,521.4	†2,077.6	2,441.2	2,968.8	4,248.3	5,027.4	5,990.5	7,989.8
Money	34	807.7	901.9	973.9	1,011.3	1,238.8	1,530.4	1,793.3	2,139.3	2,382.3	2,779.0	3,298.1	3,640.0
Quasi-Money	35	863.7	1,065.1	1,272.1	1,704.0	2,080.6	2,443.7	2,802.3	3,186.5	3,604.3	4,199.7	4,722.1	5,275.0
Money Market Instruments	36aa	–	–	–	–	–	68.9	152.2	–	349.7	402.7	.1	.5
Bonds	36ab	76.9	49.4	33.1	21.0	34.4	39.0	29.6	51.0	70.7	114.2	401.0	1,040.7
Long-Term Foreign Liabilities	36cl	1,317.8	1,808.9	2,231.3	3,060.1	2,850.9	2,583.4	3,022.6	3,011.3	2,940.3	2,631.3	2,190.9	2,370.2
Capital Accounts	37a	317.0	220.1	262.4	371.8	442.2	632.5	724.9	736.9	882.6	1,027.5	1,087.8	1,286.6
Other Items (Net)	37r	−234.3	−10.5	−92.5	−40.5	−147.3	−227.9	−134.8	−143.1	155.0	−27.9	54.0	33.2
Money plus Quasi-Money	35l	1,671.4	1,967.0	2,246.0	2,715.3	3,319.4	3,974.1	4,582.8	5,314.4	5,976.4	6,972.3	8,013.5	8,907.7
Money (National Definition)		\multicolumn{12}{c}{*Billions of Forint: End of Period*}
Monetary Base	19m	593.9	599.8	621.0	749.6	859.1	994.6	1,244.0	1,465.8	1,649.1	1,608.5	1,763.9	2,091.9
M1	39ma	807.7	882.6	1,038.1	1,166.4	1,374.8	1,703.3	1,987.4	2,358.4	2,653.8	3,113.3	3,655.0	4,027.7
M2	39mb	1,671.4	1,879.2	2,148.6	2,590.2	3,162.5	3,787.3	4,373.4	5,063.0	5,680.6	6,634.2	7,547.0	8,575.0
M3	39mc	1,748.3	1,892.1	2,157.2	2,605.4	3,196.7	3,923.1	4,585.2	5,187.3	6,129.5	7,177.7	7,858.5	8,790.8
M4	39md	1,820.1	2,223.5	2,628.1	3,285.5	4,170.2	5,293.9	6,352.9	7,557.1	8,690.1	10,058.9	11,397.5	13,151.2
Interest Rates		\multicolumn{12}{c}{*Percent Per Annum*}
Discount Rate (End of Period)	60	21.0	22.0	25.0	28.0	23.0	20.5	17.0	14.5	11.0	9.8	8.5	12.5
Treasury Bill Rate	60c	22.7	17.2	26.9	32.0	24.0	20.1	17.8	14.7	11.0	10.8	8.9	8.2
Deposit Rate	60l	24.4	15.7	20.3	†24.4	18.6	16.9	14.4	11.9	9.5	8.4	7.4	11.0
Lending Rate	60p	33.1	25.4	27.4	32.6	27.3	21.8	19.3	16.3	12.6	12.1	10.2	9.6
Prices, Production, Labor		\multicolumn{12}{c}{*Index Numbers (2000=100): Period Averages*}
Producer Prices: Industry	63	31.8	36.2	40.6	52.2	63.6	76.5	85.2	89.5	100.0	104.8	103.3	105.8
Consumer Prices	64	†26.5	32.5	38.6	†49.6	61.3	72.5	82.8	91.1	100.0	109.2	115.0	120.3
Wages: Avg. Earnings	65	26.7	31.9	40.0	46.4	54.6	67.7	79.1	88.7	100.0	113.2	130.2	146.8
Industrial Production	66	46.7	48.5	53.2	59.4	61.4	68.2	76.7	84.6	100.0	103.6	106.4	113.2
Industrial Employment	67	128.5	116.2	108.3	102.5	97.1	96.4	97.9	98.7	100.0	99.3	97.3	95.3
		\multicolumn{12}{c}{*Number in Thousands: Period Averages*}
Labor Force	67d	4,242	....	4,144	4,095	4,048	3,995	4,011	4,096	4,112	4,102	4,109	4,167
Employment	67e	4,083	3,827	3,752	3,679	3,648	3,646	3,698	3,811	3,849	3,868	3,871	3,922
Unemployment	67c	444	519	449	417	400	349	313	285	263	234	239	245
Unemployment Rate (%)	67r	9.8	11.9	10.7	10.2	9.9	8.7	7.8	7.0	6.4	5.7	5.8	5.9
International Transactions		\multicolumn{12}{c}{*Billions of Forint*}
Exports	70	842.5	819.9	1,101.4	1,622.1	2,392.1	3,567.0	4,934.4	5,938.6	7,942.8	8,748.3	8,874.0	9,528.6
Imports, c.i.f.	71	878.6	1,153.5	1,505.7	1,936.1	2,764.0	3,961.0	5,511.4	6,645.6	9,064.0	9,665.0	9,704.1	10,662.8
Imports, f.o.b.	71.v	878.6	1,162.5	1,518.1	1,913.1	2,735.5	3,919.9	5,451.0	6,558.0	8,958.4	9,534.9	9,578.8	10,513.7
		\multicolumn{12}{c}{*2000=100*}
Volume of Exports	72	38.8	33.6	39.3	42.6	44.5	†57.8	70.9	82.2	100.0	107.8	114.1	124.1
Volume of Imports	73	32.8	39.6	45.3	43.5	45.9	†58.0	72.4	82.8	100.0	104.0	109.3	120.3
Export Prices	76	32.4	36.3	42.8	57.3	67.6	77.7	87.7	91.0	100.0	102.2	97.1	96.7
Import Prices	76.x	32.9	35.7	41.8	55.0	66.4	75.3	83.9	88.6	100.0	102.5	96.9	97.0

Hungary 944

		1992	1993	1994	1995	1996	1997	1998	1999	2000	2001	2002	2003
Balance of Payments		\multicolumn{12}{c}{*Millions of US Dollars: Minus Sign Indicates Debit*}
Current Account, n.i.e.	78ald	352	−4,262	−4,054	−1,617	−1,150	−684	−2,228	−2,446	−2,900	−1,754	−2,644	−7,364
Goods: Exports f.o.b.	78aad	10,097	8,119	7,648	14,619	15,966	19,284	23,698	25,608	28,762	31,080	34,792	43,229
Goods: Imports f.o.b.	78abd	−10,108	−12,140	−11,364	−16,078	−17,640	−20,611	−25,583	−27,778	−31,675	−33,318	−36,911	−46,594
Trade Balance	78acd	−11	−4,021	−3,716	−1,459	−1,673	−1,328	−1,885	−2,170	−2,913	−2,237	−2,119	−3,365
Services: Credit	78add	3,405	2,836	3,117	5,057	5,866	5,793	5,723	5,613	6,046	7,479	7,807	7,974
Services: Debit	78aed	−2,641	−2,620	−2,958	−3,647	−3,979	−4,049	−4,539	−4,740	−4,926	−6,017	−7,193	−8,171
Balance on Goods & Services	78afd	753	−3,805	−3,557	−49	213	416	−701	−1,297	−1,793	−775	−1,506	−3,562
Income: Credit	78agd	424	465	676	970	1,323	1,539	1,258	924	1,123	1,307	1,215	1,330
Income: Debit	78ahd	−1,684	−1,655	−2,082	−2,741	−2,683	−2,842	−3,028	−2,469	−2,549	−2,644	−2,801	−5,785
Balance on Gds, Serv. & Inc.	78aid	−506	−4,995	−4,963	−1,820	−1,147	−887	−2,471	−2,842	−3,218	−2,112	−3,092	−8,017
Current Transfers, n.i.e.: Credit	78ajd	2,866	2,694	2,871	482	270	463	510	672	634	734	1,001	1,278
Current Transfers: Debit	78akd	−2,008	−1,961	−1,961	−279	−272	−260	−266	−277	−316	−376	−554	−625
Capital Account, n.i.e.	78bcd	–	–	–	60	156	117	189	29	270	317	179	−77
Capital Account, n.i.e.: Credit	78bad	–	–	–	80	266	266	408	509	458	417	225	189
Capital Account: Debit	78bbd	–	–	–	−20	−110	−149	−219	−480	−188	−101	−46	−267
Financial Account, n.i.e.	78bjd	416	6,083	3,370	5,794	−1,357	196	2,980	5,140	3,862	1,577	127	7,311
Direct Investment Abroad	78bdd	–	−11	−49	−46	2	−442	−496	−268	−547	−340	−264	−1,598
Dir. Invest. in Rep. Econ., n.i.e.	78bed	1,479	2,350	1,144	4,878	2,363	2,224	2,084	2,019	1,694	2,595	854	2,506
Portfolio Investment Assets	78bfd	–	−8	6	−1	−35	−134	−93	−75	831	−149	−47	35
Equity Securities	78bkd	–	–	−10	–	−15	−32	−45	16	−151	−55	−57	−38
Debt Securities	78bld	–	−8	16	–	−20	−102	−48	−91	982	−95	10	73
Portfolio Investment Liab., n.i.e.	78bgd	–	3,927	2,458	2,213	−396	−914	1,925	2,065	−187	1,523	1,838	2,900
Equity Securities	78bmd	–	46	224	−62	359	1,004	556	1,191	−416	134	−137	266
Debt Securities	78bnd	–	3,881	2,234	2,275	−754	−1,918	1,369	874	229	1,389	1,976	2,633
Financial Derivatives Assets	78bwd	....	....	....	157	17	12	185	852	753	582	1,917	2,929
Financial Derivatives Liabilities	78bxd	....	....	....	102	−1	−4	−38	−899	−692	−459	−2,123	−2,893
Other Investment Assets	78bhd	−421	881	362	−1,083	−2,013	−1,095	−573	−598	−193	−2,693	−1,574	−2,606
Monetary Authorities	78bod	....	....	....	−17	14	1	4	–	−1,148	4	36	−1,049
General Government	78bpd	−899	811	156	27	44	189	75	30	64	30	19	198
Banks	78bqd	616	−127	191	125	−1,129	−789	−333	−430	755	−1,463	515	−951
Other Sectors	78brd	−138	198	15	−1,218	−942	−496	−318	−198	136	−1,265	−2,144	−804
Other Investment Liab., n.i.e.	78bid	−642	−1,055	−551	−427	−1,294	549	−13	2,046	2,204	519	−473	6,039
Monetary Authorities	78bsd	174	54	17	−906	−1,875	−659	−15	286	613	−644	−622	588
General Government	78btd	−787	−1,541	−1,761	−438	−331	−106	−288	235	−225	−47	766	319
Banks	78bud	−29	−69	365	323	394	1,123	619	522	401	294	647	3,986
Other Sectors	78bvd	–	501	828	595	518	190	−329	1,002	1,414	916	−1,264	1,145
Net Errors and Omissions	78cad	2	724	209	1,161	1,113	196	9	−388	−180	−224	546	466
Overall Balance	78cbd	770	2,545	−475	5,398	−1,237	−175	951	2,335	1,052	−84	−1,792	336
Reserves and Related Items	79dad	−770	−2,545	475	−5,398	1,237	175	−951	−2,335	−1,052	84	1,792	−336
Reserve Assets	79dbd	−763	−2,574	640	−4,612	1,441	175	−791	−2,335	−1,052	84	1,792	−336
Use of Fund Credit and Loans	79dcd	−7	30	−165	−785	−203	–	−160	–	–	–	–	–
Exceptional Financing	79ded	....	....	....	....	....	–	–	–	–	–	–	–
International Investment Position		\multicolumn{12}{c}{*Millions of US Dollars*}
Assets	79aad	....	....	....	....	....	15,139	17,422	20,384	20,261	23,314	24,653	32,386
Direct Investment Abroad	79abd	....	....	....	....	....	898	1,301	1,524	1,976	2,260	2,745	3,921
Portfolio Investment	79acd	....	....	....	....	....	171	293	367	667	814	936	1,026
Equity Securities	79add	....	....	....	....	....	32	87	73	221	271	363	424
Debt Securities	79aed	....	....	....	....	....	139	206	294	447	543	573	602
Financial Derivatives	79ald	....	....	....	....	....	–	9	880	859	1,165	909	1,604
Other Investment	79afd	....	....	....	....	....	5,634	6,472	6,629	5,542	8,320	9,680	13,055
Monetary Authorities	79agd	....	....	....	....	....	32	23	20	75	55	20	1,107
General Government	79ahd	....	....	....	....	....	593	505	468	381	353	340	360
Banks	79aid	....	....	....	....	....	2,323	3,083	3,387	2,559	4,040	3,862	5,313
Other Sectors	79ajd	....	....	....	....	....	2,686	2,860	2,754	2,527	3,872	5,457	6,275
Reserve Assets	79akd	....	....	....	....	....	8,437	9,348	10,983	11,217	10,755	10,383	12,780
Liabilities	79lad	....	....	....	....	....	41,432	45,881	50,134	50,177	54,434	66,496	97,221
Dir. Invest. in Rep. Economy	79lbd	....	....	....	....	....	16,325	18,811	19,542	20,009	23,099	28,717	42,915
Portfolio Investment	79lcd	....	....	....	....	....	12,496	14,534	16,934	14,839	15,721	20,943	27,499
Equity Securities	79ldd	....	....	....	....	....	2,582	2,317	4,335	3,014	2,935	3,825	5,310
Debt Securities	79led	....	....	....	....	....	9,914	12,217	12,599	11,825	12,786	17,118	22,189
Financial Derivatives	79lld	....	....	....	....	....	450	11	164	276	483	624	2,000
Other Investment	79lfd	....	....	....	....	....	12,161	12,524	13,494	15,053	15,132	16,212	24,808
Monetary Authorities	79lgd	....	....	....	....	....	1,216	1,094	1,322	1,863	1,165	574	1,240
General Government	79lhd	....	....	....	....	....	1,635	1,380	1,532	1,246	1,167	2,118	2,806
Banks	79lid	....	....	....	....	....	4,290	5,185	5,297	5,476	5,581	6,784	11,993
Other Sectors	79ljd	....	....	....	....	....	5,019	4,866	5,343	6,468	7,218	6,735	8,769

Hungary 944

		1992	1993	1994	1995	1996	1997	1998	1999	2000	2001	2002	2003
Government Finance						**Billions of Forint: Year Ending December 31**							
Deficit (-) or Surplus...............	80	−214.6	−202.9	−310.8	−355.5	−213.1	−383.6	−631.5	−420.0	−449.3	−444.8	−1,569.0	−1,062.9
Total Revenue and Grants..........	81y	1,411.1	1,716.1	2,085.4	2,393.6	2,908.9	3,205.9	4,072.5	4,663.1	5,228.1	5,831.5	6,191.5	6,942.8
Revenue.........................	81	1,411.1	1,716.1	2,085.2	2,393.4	2,908.5	3,205.3	4,065.5	4,649.9	5,193.7	5,801.1	6,152.8	6,902.4
Grants............................	81z	−	−	.2	.2	.4	.6	7.0	13.2	34.4	30.4	38.7	40.4
Exp. & Lending Minus Repay........	82z	1,625.7	1,919.0	2,396.2	2,749.1	3,122.0	3,589.5	4,704.0	5,083.1	5,677.4	6,276.3	7,760.5	8,005.7
Expenditure.....................	82	1,623.1	1,985.6	2,390.9	2,734.4	3,122.1	3,644.0	4,671.6	5,070.0	5,682.5	6,273.3	7,672.0	8,040.6
Lending Minus Repayments.......	83	2.6	−66.6	5.3	14.7	−.1	−54.5	32.4	13.1	−5.1	3.0	88.5	−34.9
Total Financing................	80h	214.6	203.0	310.8	355.5	213.2	....	....	....	....	444.8	1,569.0	1,062.9
Total Net Borrowing............	84	218.4	221.8	203.9	204.4	380.6	....	....	....	....	635.9	1,279.1	1,062.8
Net Domestic..................	84a	217.7	216.7	202.4	198.5	373.7	....	....	....	....	408.0	1,028.2	476.2
Net Foreign...................	85a	.7	5.1	1.5	5.9	6.9	....	....	....	....	227.9	250.9	586.6
Use of Cash Balances...........	87	−3.8	−18.8	106.9	151.1	−167.4	....	....	....	....	−191.1	289.9	.1
Total Debt by Residence..........	88	2,310.8	3,181.6	3,801.0	4,781.6	4,959.1	5,405.7	6,161.5	6,890.5	7,228.7	7,721.6	9,223.7	10,588.1
Domestic........................	88a	2,176.9	2,978.9	3,564.5	4,461.7	4,669.2	5,055.4	5,867.3	5,940.0	6,144.2	6,486.1	7,806.0	8,494.4
Foreign.........................	89a	133.9	202.7	236.5	319.9	289.9	350.3	294.2	950.5	1,084.5	1,235.5	1,417.7	2,093.7
Memorandum Item:													
Privatization Receipts...........	83a	20.0	7.2	31.0	150.0	219.9	161.9	13.0	4.0	.9	....	....	....
National Accounts						**Billions of Forint**							
Househ.Cons.Expend.,incl.NPISHs....	96f	2,141.1	2,639.9	3,151.7	3,730.3	4,400.4	5,283.0	6,297.2	7,274.2	8,342.1	9,583.8	11,088.7	12,673.7
Government Consumption Expend...	91f	336.4	491.4	527.1	617.7	703.6	900.8	1,024.6	1,156.7	1,273.3	1,513.7	1,813.1	2,034.0
Gross Fixed Capital Formation.........	93e	584.7	670.0	878.5	1,125.4	1,475.5	1,898.9	2,384.6	2,724.5	3,099.1	3,493.0	3,916.9	4,086.1
Changes in Inventories............	93i	−111.7	38.1	90.1	143.4	282.5	370.6	526.0	548.0	971.8	487.9	309.2	577.6
Exports of Goods and Services.........	90c	925.3	937.0	1,262.5	2,505.2	3,341.8	4,709.2	6,247.0	7,329.0	9,738.3	10,803.4	10,709.3	11,472.0
Imports of Goods and Services (-).....	98c	933.2	1,228.1	1,545.1	2,507.9	3,310.0	4,621.8	6,392.0	7,639.0	10,252.5	11,032.0	11,096.8	12,269.5
Gross Domestic Product (GDP).........	99b	2,942.7	3,548.3	4,364.8	5,614.0	6,893.9	8,540.7	10,087.4	11,393.5	13,172.3	14,849.8	16,740.4	18,574.0
GDP Volume 1991 Prices..........	99b.p	2,421.8	2,407.8	2,478.8	2,515.7	....	....	....	....	....	....	....	....
GDP Volume 2000 Prices............	99b.p	....	....	....	10,820.8	10,963.6	11,464.2	12,021.4	12,520.7	13,172.3	13,679.4	14,157.9	14,573.9
GDP Volume (2000=100)..........	99bvp	79.1	78.6	80.9	† 82.1	83.2	87.0	91.3	95.1	100.0	103.8	107.5	110.6
GDP Deflator (2000=100)............	99bip	28.2	34.3	40.9	51.9	62.9	74.5	83.9	91.0	100.0	108.6	118.2	127.4
						Millions: Midyear Estimates							
Population................	99z	10.30	10.27	10.25	10.21	10.18	10.14	10.10	10.06	10.01	9.97	9.92	9.88

2004, International Monetary Fund: *International Financial Statistics Yearbook*

Iceland 176

		1992	1993	1994	1995	1996	1997	1998	1999	2000	2001	2002	2003
Exchange Rates		\multicolumn{12}{c}{*Kronur per SDR: End of Period*}
Official Rate	aa	87.890	99.899	99.708	96.964	96.185	97.389	97.605	99.576	110.356	129.380	109.550	105.489
		\multicolumn{12}{c}{*Kronur per US Dollar: End of Period (ae) Period Average (rf)*}
Official Rate	ae	63.920	72.730	68.300	65.230	66.890	72.180	69.320	72.550	84.700	102.950	80.580	70.990
Official Rate	rf	57.546	67.603	69.944	64.692	66.500	70.904	70.958	72.335	78.616	97.425	91.662	76.709
		\multicolumn{12}{c}{*Index Numbers (2000=100): Period Averages*}
Official Rate	ahx	136.3	116.2	112.0	121.1	117.7	110.4	110.4	108.3	100.0	80.8	85.8	102.1
Nominal Effective Exchange Rate	nec	100.4	95.4	94.3	95.4	95.6	97.8	100.3	99.9	100.0	84.7	87.0	91.7
Real Effective Exchange Rate	rec	104.8	97.2	91.3	91.0	91.4	93.3	95.7	97.3	100.0	88.2	93.8	99.0
Fund Position		\multicolumn{12}{c}{*Millions of SDRs: End of Period*}
Quota	2f.s	85.3	85.3	85.3	85.3	85.3	85.3	85.3	117.6	117.6	117.6	117.6	117.6
SDRs	1b.s	–	–	.1	–	–	–	–	–	–	.1	.1	–
Reserve Position in the Fund	1c.s	10.5	10.5	10.5	10.5	10.5	10.5	10.5	18.6	18.6	18.6	18.6	18.6
Total Fund Cred.&Loans Outstg.	2tl	–	–	–	–	–	–	–	–	–	–	–	–
International Liquidity		\multicolumn{12}{c}{*Millions of US Dollars Unless Otherwise Indicated: End of Period*}
Total Reserves minus Gold	1l.d	498.3	426.4	292.9	308.1	453.7	383.7	426.4	478.4	388.9	338.2	440.1	792.3
SDRs	1b.d	–	.1	.1	–	–	–	–	–	–	.1	.1	–
Reserve Position in the Fund	1c.d	14.4	14.4	15.3	15.6	15.1	14.2	14.8	25.5	24.2	23.3	25.3	27.6
Foreign Exchange	1d.d	483.9	412.0	277.5	292.5	438.6	369.5	411.6	452.9	364.6	314.8	414.7	764.6
Gold (Million Fine Troy Ounces)	1ad	.049	.049	.049	.049	.049	.049	.056	.056	.059	.062	.063	.063
Gold (National Valuation)	1and	2.4	2.4	2.5	2.6	2.7	2.6	2.8	†17.0	16.4	17.0	21.4	26.4
Monetary Authorities: Other Liab.	4..d	12.4	36.8	137.5	176.5	75.5	75.1	130.9	67.5	186.1	145.5	204.8	....
Deposit Money Banks: Assets	7a.d	70.8	94.0	118.7	79.9	108.9	153.4	162.7	188.8	243.7	290.8	562.1	....
Liabilities	7b.d	682.4	593.0	464.1	419.4	639.0	875.8	1,477.8	1,989.9	2,649.4	2,503.0	3,102.3	....
Monetary Authorities		\multicolumn{12}{c}{*Millions of Kronur: End of Period*}
Foreign Assets	11	32,017	31,318	24,347	25,961	36,151	33,274	35,136	†37,139	34,495	36,819	37,376	....
Claims on Central Government	12a	6,751	12,865	24,546	18,476	10,534	12,852	5,011	†3,988	4,579	2,466	1,841	....
Claims on Private Sector	12d	380	330	408	413	487	142	113	†86	52	28	41	....
Claims on Deposit Money Banks	12e	3,983	2,630	2,226	5,353	1,878	6,496	19,600	†29,520	38,978	54,053	69,141	....
Claims on Other Financial Insts.	12f	531	639	4,490	3,380	3,443	3,472	7,770	†9,672	13,074	22,774	8,227	....
Reserve Money	14	22,328	20,333	20,949	17,164	21,691	24,153	24,690	†38,442	33,921	29,942	33,961	....
of which: Currency Outside DMBs	14a	3,593	3,906	4,641	5,169	5,475	5,751	6,322	†7,125	7,151	7,406	7,666	....
Foreign Liabilities	16c	792	2,678	9,389	11,513	5,049	5,418	9,073	†4,900	15,763	14,979	16,499	....
Central Government Deposits	16d	5,512	7,350	7,419	6,177	6,850	6,438	13,176	†15,550	16,594	33,488	22,667	....
Capital Accounts	17a	13,733	16,135	16,656	16,849	17,613	19,217	19,652	†20,320	23,422	36,456	40,629	....
Other Items (Net)	17r	1,298	1,286	1,602	1,879	1,290	1,009	1,039	†1,192	1,477	1,275	2,869	....
Deposit Money Banks		\multicolumn{12}{c}{*Millions of Kronur: End of Period*}
Reserves	20	14,474	11,747	11,540	10,325	13,418	14,100	13,990	29,026	25,731	20,701	23,099	....
Foreign Assets	21	4,524	6,835	8,105	5,213	7,285	11,076	11,276	13,699	20,641	29,939	45,291	....
Claims on Central Government	22a	20,577	26,746	19,168	11,432	13,241	10,578	6,287	7,271	4,126	13,077	9,037	....
Claims on Private Sector	22d	187,675	193,643	196,262	208,982	236,720	348,883	376,255	461,004	663,599	772,541	778,622	....
Claims on Other Financial Insts.	22f	3,162	4,265	4,485	1,750	1,167	1,680	375	934	2,486	2,167	–	....
Demand Deposits	24	26,351	27,663	30,313	33,146	36,081	42,660	51,852	63,346	65,117	63,413	76,624	....
Savings Deposits	25	124,088	132,526	132,482	133,341	140,725	150,977	171,434	198,763	225,879	271,691	295,508	....
Bonds	26a	20,589	22,699	22,337	24,095	32,166	40,731	53,419	62,938	169,070	196,279	203,497	....
Restricted Deposits	26b	–	–	–	6	2	5	2	–	–	–	–	....
Foreign Liabilities	26c	43,616	43,127	31,697	27,356	42,741	63,215	102,438	144,370	224,406	257,682	249,986	....
Credit from Monetary Authorities	26g	2,520	1,600	4,833	4,860	1,954	6,480	21,000	30,797	39,016	54,194	33,211	....
Capital Accounts	27a	18,729	22,446	23,186	23,296	27,617	28,907	35,604	42,424	66,448	95,709	96,083	....
Other Items (Net)	27r	–7,519	–8,757	–7,623	–8,278	–9,330	53,400	–27,551	–30,706	–73,352	–100,540	–98,860	....
Monetary Survey		\multicolumn{12}{c}{*Millions of Kronur: End of Period*}
Foreign Assets (Net)	31n	–7,867	–7,652	–8,635	–7,695	–4,354	–24,282	–65,099	†–98,432	–185,033	–205,903	–183,819	....
Domestic Credit	32	213,565	231,138	241,940	238,256	258,943	371,168	382,635	†467,406	671,321	779,565	775,100	....
Claims on Central Govt. (Net)	32an	21,816	32,260	36,295	23,731	16,925	16,991	–1,878	†–4,291	–7,889	–17,946	–11,789	....
Claims on Private Sector	32d	188,055	193,973	196,670	209,395	237,207	349,025	376,368	†461,090	663,651	772,569	778,662	....
Claims on Other Financial Inst.	32f	3,693	4,904	8,975	5,130	4,610	5,152	8,145	†10,606	15,560	24,942	8,227	....
Money	34	29,944	31,569	34,954	38,315	41,556	48,351	58,174	†70,471	72,268	70,819	84,290	....
Quasi-Money	35	124,088	132,526	132,482	133,341	140,725	150,977	171,434	198,763	225,879	271,691	295,508	....
Bonds	36a	20,589	22,699	22,337	24,095	32,166	40,731	53,419	62,938	169,070	196,279	203,497	....
Capital Accounts	37a	32,462	38,581	39,842	40,145	45,230	48,124	55,256	†62,744	89,870	132,165	136,712	....
Other Items (Net)	37r	–3,423	–3,821	1,354	–5,215	–5,163	58,700	–20,732	†–25,944	–70,798	–97,289	–128,725	....
Money plus Quasi-Money	35l	154,032	164,095	167,436	171,656	182,281	199,328	229,608	†269,234	298,147	342,510	379,798	....

Iceland 176

		1992	1993	1994	1995	1996	1997	1998	1999	2000	2001	2002	2003
Interest Rates		\multicolumn{12}{c}{*Percent Per Annum*}
Discount Rate (End of Period)	60	†16.63	....	4.70	5.93	5.70	6.55	†8.50	10.00	12.40	12.00	8.20	7.70
Money Market Rate	60b	12.38	8.61	4.96	6.58	6.96	7.38	8.12	9.24	11.61	14.51	11.21	5.16
Treasury Bill Rate	60c	†11.30	8.35	4.95	7.22	6.97	7.04	7.40	8.61	11.12	11.03	8.01	4.93
Deposit Rate	60l	5.94	6.63	3.03	3.69	4.25	4.72	4.50	4.82	7.11	6.94	4.69	....
Housing Bond Rate	60m	....	....	5.75	5.80	5.78	5.30	4.71	4.78	6.31	6.07	5.18	4.60
Lending Rate	60p	13.05	14.11	10.57	11.58	12.43	12.89	12.78	13.30	16.80	17.95	15.37	11.95
Government Bond Yield	61	7.75	6.80	5.02	7.18	5.61	5.49	4.73	4.28	5.35	5.33	5.23	4.42
Prices, Production, Labor		\multicolumn{12}{c}{*Index Numbers (2000=100): Period Averages*}
Consumer Prices	64	81.0	84.3	85.6	87.0	89.0	90.6	92.1	95.1	100.0	106.4	111.9	114.2
Wages, Hourly (1995=100)	65	98.5	96.3	96.8	100.0	....	....	....	....	....	....	....	....
Total Fish Catch	66al	91.7	100.3	86.2	92.0	117.4	133.5	91.5	86.1	100.0	117.0	126.2	117.6
		\multicolumn{12}{c}{*Number in Thousands: Period Averages*}
Labor Force	67d	143	144	145	149	148	148	152	157	160	163	162	....
Employment	67e	137	137	138	142	142	142	148	153	156	159	157	....
Unemployment	67c	4	6	6	7	6	5	4	3	2	2	4	5
Unemployment Rate (%)	67r	3.0	4.3	4.7	4.9	4.4	3.9	2.8	1.9	1.4	1.4	2.5	3.3
International Transactions		\multicolumn{12}{c}{*Millions of Kronur*}
Exports	70	87,833	94,711	113,279	116,613	108,977	131,228	145,008	145,132	148,516	196,803	204,078	182,960
Fish	70al	42,599	45,754	54,644	50,535	46,030	46,712	54,722	60,028	57,442	66,986	72,691	68,422
Fishmeal	70z	4,415	5,015	4,757	4,789	8,792	9,460	9,896	7,404	9,299	12,906	18,064	13,044
Imports, c.i.f.	71	96,895	90,775	102,499	113,388	135,165	141,355	176,521	181,321	203,847	218,296	207,632	213,590
		\multicolumn{12}{c}{*1995=100*}
Volume of Exports	72	86.8	91.3	102.3	100.0	109.0	111.1	107.9	....	....	....	....	....
Volume of Imports	73	101.4	87.4	93.9	100.0	116.5	123.7	154.2	....	....	....	....	....
Unit Value of Exports	74	88.3	91.3	95.4	100.0	98.4	99.6	....	....	....	....	....	....
Unit Value of Imports	75	83.3	90.9	96.1	100.0	102.7	103.4	....	....	....	....	....	....
Balance of Payments		\multicolumn{12}{c}{*Millions of US Dollars: Minus Sign Indicates Debit*}
Current Account, n.i.e.	78ald	−160	37	116	52	−131	−128	−555	−589	−847	−338	−22	−572
Goods: Exports f.o.b.	78aad	1,529	1,399	1,560	1,804	1,890	1,855	1,927	2,009	1,902	2,016	2,240	2,386
Goods: Imports f.o.b.	78abd	−1,527	−1,218	−1,288	−1,598	−1,871	−1,850	−2,279	−2,316	−2,376	−2,091	−2,090	−2,596
Trade Balance	78acd	2	181	272	206	19	5	−351	−307	−474	−75	150	−210
Services: Credit	78add	590	601	619	691	768	843	953	930	1,044	1,086	1,154	1,372
Services: Debit	78aed	−590	−592	−577	−642	−741	−802	−965	−1,027	−1,164	−1,074	−1,131	−1,477
Balance on Goods & Services	78afd	2	190	314	255	46	47	−363	−404	−595	−63	172	−315
Income: Credit	78agd	97	85	72	82	104	101	120	129	147	170	190	225
Income: Debit	78ahd	−255	−235	−262	−280	−274	−272	−298	−304	−390	−437	−398	−467
Balance on Gds, Serv. & Inc.	78aid	−156	40	124	56	−124	−125	−541	−579	−837	−329	−36	−556
Current Transfers, n.i.e.: Credit	78ajd	18	18	12	15	10	17	4	5	6	8	36	12
Current Transfers: Debit	78akd	−22	−21	−21	−20	−17	−20	−18	−15	−16	−17	−22	−28
Capital Account, n.i.e.	78bcd	−4	−1	−6	−4	−	−	−5	−1	−3	4	−1	−5
Capital Account, n.i.e.: Credit	78bad	11	11	6	12	10	11	9	17	17	15	14	15
Capital Account: Debit	78bbd	−15	−12	−12	−17	−10	−11	−14	−18	−21	−12	−15	−20
Financial Account, n.i.e.	78bjd	241	−48	−291	2	318	203	683	864	846	169	172	758
Direct Investment Abroad	78bdd	−6	−15	−23	−25	−64	−57	−75	−125	−375	−331	−228	−169
Dir. Invest. in Rep. Econ., n.i.e.	78bed	−13	−	−1	−9	83	148	150	65	155	162	124	147
Portfolio Investment Assets	78bfd	−4	−31	−72	−64	−51	−202	−303	−448	−667	−64	−337	−593
Equity Securities	78bkd	−4	−12	−24	−44	−68	−180	−253	−369	−651	−67	−287	−531
Debt Securities	78bld	−	−19	−48	−20	17	−22	−51	−79	−16	3	−50	−62
Portfolio Investment Liab., n.i.e.	78bgd	286	305	242	215	175	−39	68	1,030	1,142	665	577	3,696
Equity Securities	78bmd	−	−	−	1	1	−1	14	56	−44	43	22	−34
Debt Securities	78bnd	286	305	242	214	174	−38	54	974	1,186	622	555	3,730
Financial Derivatives Assets	78bwd	7	−	−49	−17	−1	−1	−1	59	15	−	−	−
Financial Derivatives Liabilities	78bxd	−7	−	55	16	−	−	−	−57	−16	−	−	−
Other Investment Assets	78bhd	29	−28	−31	25	−30	−162	2	−173	−79	−475	−336	−1,978
Monetary Authorities	78bod	−	−	−	−	−	−	−	−	−	−	−	−
General Government	78bpd	−	−	−	−	−	−	−	−	−	−	−	−
Banks	78bqd	13	−28	−17	49	−37	−86	28	−92	−71	−216	−380	−2,064
Other Sectors	78brd	16	−	−15	−24	7	−76	−26	−81	−8	−259	43	86
Other Investment Liab., n.i.e.	78bid	−50	−280	−412	−139	206	517	843	511	671	213	373	−345
Monetary Authorities	78bsd	1	22	41	21	−99	−	55	−3	142	−33	48	−206
General Government	78btd	−116	−46	−76	60	−17	34	81	43	27	79	41	−76
Banks	78bud	−10	−69	−158	−54	288	307	420	441	332	−104	296	−37
Other Sectors	78bvd	75	−187	−219	−166	34	176	287	31	170	271	−12	−26
Net Errors and Omissions	78cad	3	−47	31	−45	−33	−119	−91	−189	−70	117	−87	126
Overall Balance	78cbd	79	−59	−150	4	153	−44	32	86	−74	−48	61	307
Reserves and Related Items	79dad	−79	59	150	−4	−153	44	−32	−86	74	48	−61	−307
Reserve Assets	79dbd	−79	59	150	−4	−153	44	−32	−86	74	48	−61	−307
Use of Fund Credit and Loans	79dcd	−	−	−	−	−	−	−	−	−	−	−	−
Exceptional Financing	79ded	−	−	−	−	−	−	−	−	−	−	−	....

Iceland 176

		1992	1993	1994	1995	1996	1997	1998	1999	2000	2001	2002	2003
International Investment Position						*Millions of US Dollars*							
Assets...	79aad	784	787	872	1,009	1,306	1,599	2,199	3,374	3,738	4,094	4,934	9,243
Direct Investment Abroad...............	79abd	98	114	149	180	241	272	342	456	665	842	1,113	1,382
Portfolio Investment.......................	79acd	9	41	118	198	264	488	967	1,902	2,205	1,971	1,982	3,404
Equity Securities........................	79add	9	22	48	103	183	398	830	1,718	2,128	1,830	1,853	3,185
Debt Securities.........................	79aed	–	19	71	95	81	90	137	185	78	141	129	219
Financial Derivatives......................	79ald	4	4	59	81	80	76	78	16	–	–	–	–
Other Investment............................	79afd	176	201	248	235	259	376	384	506	463	925	1,378	3,639
Monetary Authorities.................	79agd	–	–	–	–	–	–	–	–	–	–	–	–
General Government...................	79ahd	–	–	–	–	–	–	–	–	–	–	–	–
Banks..	79aid	61	94	119	80	115	164	142	184	229	442	1,101	3,420
Other Sectors............................	79ajd	114	107	129	155	144	211	243	321	233	483	278	218
Reserve Assets................................	79akd	497	428	298	315	461	386	427	495	405	355	462	819
Liabilities...	79lad	4,133	4,125	4,245	4,478	4,720	5,024	6,371	7,553	9,050	9,789	11,961	17,107
Dir. Invest. in Rep. Economy............	79lbd	123	117	127	129	200	336	466	482	492	675	763	880
Portfolio Investment.......................	79lcd	1,251	1,550	1,882	2,128	2,213	2,039	2,200	3,127	4,105	4,546	5,811	10,631
Equity Securities........................	79ldd	–	–	–	–	1	–	14	66	15	55	98	83
Debt Securities.........................	79led	1,251	1,550	1,882	2,128	2,212	2,039	2,186	3,061	4,090	4,492	5,713	10,548
Financial Derivatives......................	79lld	4	4	56	74	74	74	74	16	–	–	–	–
Other Investment............................	79lfd	2,755	2,454	2,180	2,146	2,233	2,575	3,631	3,928	4,454	4,567	5,387	5,596
Monetary Authorities.................	79lgd	12	33	81	103	2	1	57	51	187	145	205	2
General Government...................	79lhd	395	333	287	377	334	345	446	444	456	520	631	612
Banks..	79lid	676	592	459	421	660	903	1,427	1,814	2,273	2,097	3,039	3,349
Other Sectors............................	79ljd	1,673	1,495	1,352	1,246	1,238	1,326	1,701	1,618	1,538	1,804	1,513	1,633
Government Finance						*Millions of Kronur: Year Ending December 31*							
Deficit (-) or Surplus........................	80	–12,490	–16,844	–21,972	–20,270	–4,389	1,863	†16,284	20,435	9,548	–25,714	–4,133	11,843
Total Revenue and Grants...............	81y	122,859	122,810	130,008	135,715	150,816	155,200	†167,388	194,993	207,561	219,748	230,510	249,606
Revenue.......................................	81	122,284	122,285	129,409	135,715	150,816	155,200	†166,529	194,250	206,993	219,029	229,815	248,201
Grants..	81z	575	525	599	–	–	–	†859	743	568	719	695	1,405
Exp. & Lending Minus Repay...........	82z	135,349	139,655	151,980	155,985	155,205	153,337	†151,104	174,558	198,013	245,462	234,643	237,763
Expenditure.................................	82	133,466	135,537	142,756	146,826	156,454	152,990	†159,651	177,964	195,411	221,305	246,810	268,714
Lending Minus Repayments.........	83	1,883	4,117	9,224	9,159	–1,248	347	†–8,547	–3,406	2,602	24,157	–12,167	–30,951
Financing													
Total Financing................................	80h	....	....	....	....	....	....	†–16,284	–20,435	–9,548	25,714	4,134	–11,842
Total Net Borrowing.......................	84	12,489	16,844	21,972	20,270	4,389	–1,863	†–10,498	–20,691	–9,246	26,539	–4,292	–13,452
Net Domestic...............................	84a	2,118	13,866	10,493	5,185	–2,254	4,660	†48	–19,586	–17,443	–4,840	–492	10,308
Net Foreign.................................	85a	10,371	2,979	11,479	15,085	6,643	–6,523	†–10,546	–1,105	8,197	31,379	–3,800	–23,760
Use of Cash Balances.....................	87	....	....	....	....	....	....	†–5,786	256	–302	–825	8,426	1,610
Total Debt by Residence..................	88	153,412	181,030	197,106	213,575	225,677	226,111	†209,020	190,693	187,972	242,353	279,055	255,697
Domestic......................................	88a	66,139	78,725	83,473	86,314	93,459	99,483	†92,938	74,480	61,643	69,160	70,336	89,749
Foreign...	89a	87,273	102,305	113,633	127,261	132,218	126,628	†116,082	116,213	126,329	173,193	208,719	165,948
National Accounts						*Millions of Kronur*							
Househ.Cons.Expend.,incl.NPISHs....	96f	240,278	237,402	247,821	258,215	278,656	293,247	325,847	358,731	389,061	407,733	418,778	448,000
Government Consumption Expend...	91f	83,927	88,618	93,823	98,961	105,563	112,776	127,752	142,430	157,934	176,656	198,410	212,563
Gross Fixed Capital Formation..........	93e	76,885	71,776	74,398	75,386	97,867	104,419	140,163	137,493	159,436	165,471	145,567	174,545
Changes in Inventories.....................	93i	122	2,307	260	3,052	25	102	906	120	2,494	–2,084	–182	–1,501
Exports of Goods and Services..........	90c	121,597	135,694	157,436	161,250	176,836	190,653	204,214	212,166	231,632	303,067	308,802	284,457
Imports of Goods and Services (-).....	98c	121,784	122,466	134,631	144,725	173,755	187,717	230,055	241,482	278,637	307,279	292,909	311,624
Gross Domestic Product (GDP).........	99b	401,025	413,331	439,108	452,139	485,192	513,480	568,827	609,457	661,920	743,563	778,466	806,439
Net Primary Income from Abroad.....	98.n	–9,086	–10,108	–13,659	–12,829	–11,317	–12,116	–12,647	–12,567	–19,353	–25,244	–19,284	–17,373
Gross National Income (GNI)............	99a	391,939	403,223	425,449	439,310	473,875	501,364	556,180	596,890	642,567	718,319	759,182	789,066
Consumption of Fixed Capital..........	99cf	56,875	61,028	63,427	64,960	67,526	70,897	75,053	81,397	87,000	101,953	112,000	117,600
GDP Volume 1990 Prices..................	99b.p	359,030	361,876	376,465	376,770	396,438	414,939	....	....	....	....	....	....
GDP Volume 1997 Prices...................	99b.p	....	....	....	....	....	107,743	114,469	118,538	126,967	128,909	126,472	132,639
GDP Volume (2000=100).................	99bvp	74.5	75.1	78.1	78.2	82.2	†86.1	90.9	94.7	100.0	102.7	102.1	106.2
GDP Deflator (2000=100).................	99bip	81.3	83.2	84.9	87.4	89.1	90.1	94.5	97.2	100.0	109.4	115.2	114.7
						Millions: Midyear Estimates							
Population................................	99z	.26	.26	.26	.27	.27	.27	.28	.28	.28	.28	.29	.29

India 534

		1992	1993	1994	1995	1996	1997	1998	1999	2000	2001	2002	2003
Exchange Rates						*Rupees per SDR: End of Period*							
Market Rate	aa	36.025	43.102	45.810	52.295	51.666	52.999	59.813	59.690	60.911	60.549	65.298	67.768
					Rupees per US Dollar: End of Period (ae) Period Average (rf)								
Market Rate	ae	26.200	31.380	31.380	35.180	35.930	39.280	42.480	43.490	46.750	48.180	48.030	45.605
Market Rate	rf	25.918	30.493	31.374	32.427	35.433	36.313	41.259	43.055	44.942	47.186	48.610	46.583
Fund Position						*Millions of SDRs: End of Period*							
Quota	2f.s	3,056	3,056	3,056	3,056	3,056	3,056	3,056	4,158	4,158	4,158	4,158	4,158
SDRs	1b.s	3	73	1	93	85	57	59	3	1	4	5	2
Reserve Position in the Fund	1c.s	213	213	213	213	213	213	213	489	489	489	489	887
Total Fund Cred.&Loans Outstg.	2tl	3,260	3,585	2,763	1,967	1,085	590	285	39	—	—	—	—
International Liquidity					*Millions of US Dollars Unless Otherwise Indicated: End of Period*								
Total Reserves minus Gold	1l.d	5,757	10,199	19,698	17,922	20,170	24,688	27,341	32,667	37,902	45,870	67,665	98,938
SDRs	1b.d	4	100	2	139	122	77	83	4	2	5	7	3
Reserve Position in the Fund	1c.d	292	292	310	316	306	287	300	671	637	614	665	1,318
Foreign Exchange	1d.d	5,461	9,807	19,386	17,467	19,742	24,324	26,958	31,992	37,264	45,251	66,994	97,617
Gold (Million Fine Troy Ounces)	1ad	11.348	11.457	11.800	12.780	12.781	12.740	11.487	11.502	11.502	11.502	11.502	11.502
Gold (National Valuation)	1and	2,908	3,325	3,355	3,669	3,614	2,880	2,492	2,403	2,252	2,329	2,712	3,323
Monetary Authorities						*Billions of Rupees: Last Friday of Period*							
Foreign Assets	11	230.6	413.0	721.3	749.0	847.8	1,058.1	1,256.4	1,525.2	1,876.8	2,326.0	3,379.6	4,612.5
Claims on Central Government	12a	1,020.6	1,155.7	1,034.9	1,128.0	1,360.6	1,373.8	1,571.3	1,631.0	1,538.5	1,553.0	1,190.3	565.4
Claims on Deposit Money Banks	12e	37.7	13.2	25.2	60.1	7.9	12.7	31.9	26.8	68.0	70.8	.7	.1
Claims on Other Financial Insts.	12f	105.4	103.8	120.7	125.2	124.0	134.9	146.2	158.6	210.4	194.9	107.4	67.7
Reserve Money	14	1,042.2	1,268.0	1,543.8	1,737.8	1,903.2	2,116.1	2,378.7	2,649.3	2,854.2	3,145.1	3,438.3	3,911.5
of which: Currency Outside DMBs.	14a	645.8	783.3	948.5	1,136.2	1,295.2	1,443.0	1,624.4	1,925.0	2,038.5	2,296.9	2,609.8	3,004.8
Foreign Liabilities	16c	117.5	154.5	126.6	102.8	56.1	31.3	17.0	2.3	—	—	—	—
Central Government Deposits	16d	.6	.7	.7	.7	.6	.6	.6	1.4	1.4	1.4	1.4	1.4
Capital Accounts	17a	148.1	152.9	154.8	159.2	158.8	166.8	167.4	164.3	161.7	157.5	111.5	113.2
Other Items (Net)	17r	86.0	109.5	76.4	61.7	221.5	264.7	442.0	524.2	676.2	840.7	1,126.8	1,219.5
Deposit Money Banks						*Billions of Rupees: Last Friday of Period*							
Reserves	20	379.9	483.9	628.8	646.9	568.7	604.3	783.7	661.7	747.4	769.8	733.6	799.5
Claims on Central Government	22a	761.2	922.1	1,223.3	1,291.1	1,545.9	1,896.4	2,237.7	2,768.1	3,333.8	4,082.5	5,097.4	6,358.9
Claims on Private Sector	22d	1,880.0	2,087.7	2,429.9	2,713.9	3,264.2	3,640.0	4,196.4	5,054.7	6,064.3	6,626.1	8,052.8	8,831.7
Demand Deposits	24	466.4	530.6	710.8	686.2	808.5	933.1	1,039.1	1,203.4	1,435.5	1,523.9	1,689.0	1,984.2
Time Deposits	25	2,239.4	2,601.5	3,034.0	3,366.2	4,084.4	4,914.7	5,963.3	6,991.9	8,197.5	9,522.0	11,283.7	12,617.0
Credit from Monetary Authorities	26g	37.4	16.2	77.6	138.4	18.1	7.7	63.1	25.5	66.9	69.9	.7	.3
Other Items (Net)	27r	277.9	345.3	459.7	461.1	467.8	285.2	152.3	263.6	445.6	362.6	910.3	1,388.5
Monetary Survey						*Billions of Rupees: Last Friday of Period*							
Foreign Assets (Net)	31n	113.2	258.4	594.8	646.2	791.7	1,026.8	1,239.3	1,522.9	1,876.8	2,326.0	3,379.6	4,612.5
Domestic Credit	32	3,766.6	4,268.6	4,808.2	5,257.5	6,294.0	7,044.4	8,151.0	9,610.9	11,145.5	12,455.1	14,446.4	15,822.2
Claims on Central Govt. (Net)	32an	1,781.2	2,077.1	2,257.6	2,418.4	2,905.9	3,269.6	3,808.4	4,397.6	4,870.8	5,634.1	6,286.2	6,922.8
Claims on Private Sector	32d	1,880.0	2,087.7	2,429.9	2,713.9	3,264.2	3,640.0	4,196.4	5,054.7	6,064.3	6,626.1	8,052.8	8,831.7
Claims on Other Financial Insts.	32f	105.4	103.8	120.7	125.2	124.0	134.9	146.2	158.6	210.4	194.9	107.4	67.7
Money	34	1,120.9	1,330.2	1,695.0	1,883.5	2,148.9	2,419.3	2,703.5	3,161.2	3,495.9	3,846.0	4,324.9	5,026.0
Quasi-Money	35	2,239.4	2,601.5	3,034.0	3,366.2	4,084.4	4,914.7	5,963.3	6,991.9	8,197.5	9,522.0	11,283.7	12,617.0
Other Items (Net)	37r	519.5	595.3	673.9	653.9	852.4	737.3	723.6	980.7	1,328.9	1,413.1	2,217.4	2,791.7
Money plus Quasi-Money	35l	3,360.3	3,931.8	4,729.0	5,249.7	6,233.4	7,334.0	8,666.8	10,153.0	11,693.4	13,368.0	15,608.6	17,643.0
Interest Rates						*Percent Per Annum*							
Bank Rate (End of Period)	60	12.00	12.00	12.00	12.00	12.00	9.00	9.00	8.00	8.00	6.50	6.25	6.00
Money Market Rate	60b	15.23	8.64	7.14	15.57	11.04	5.29	....	....	....	....	....	....
Lending Rate	60p	18.92	16.25	14.75	15.46	15.96	13.83	13.54	12.54	12.29	12.08	11.92	11.46
Prices, Production, Labor						*Index Numbers (2000=100): Period Averages*							
Share Prices	62	64.5	55.4	88.2	72.8	73.3	82.4	72.4	89.9	100.0	75.5	70.7	117.6
Wholesale Prices	63	60.40	64.91	71.76	78.46	81.97	85.68	90.72	93.85	100.00	104.82	107.47	113.29
Consumer Prices	64	53.8	57.2	63.0	69.5	75.7	81.1	91.9	96.1	100.0	103.7	108.2	112.4
Industrial Production	66	58.2	59.3	64.9	†73.1	79.4	83.7	86.5	93.1	100.0	102.1	107.3	114.2
					Number in Thousands: Period Averages								
Employment	67e	27,056	27,177	27,375	27,987	27,941	28,245	28,166	28,113	27,960	27,789	27,206	....
Unemployment	67c	†36,758	36,276	36,692	36,742	37,430	39,140	40,090	40,371	41,344	41,996	41,171	....
International Transactions						*Billions of Rupees*							
Exports	70	509	657	785	995	1,172	1,271	1,379	1,536	1,907	2,045	2,394	2,656
Imports, c.i.f.	71	611	694	842	1,127	1,344	1,505	1,772	2,024	2,317	2,378	2,747	3,313
						2000=100							
Unit Value of Exports	74	68	76	79	78	81	94	98	97	100	99	99	....
Unit Value of Imports	75	68	67	67	72	82	83	84	92	100	101	112	....

India 534

		1992	1993	1994	1995	1996	1997	1998	1999	2000	2001	2002	2003
Balance of Payments		\multicolumn{12}{c}{*Millions of US Dollars: Minus Sign Indicates Debit*}
Current Account, n.i.e.	78ald	−4,485	−1,876	−1,676	−5,563	−5,956	−2,965	−6,903	−3,228	−2,640	1,761	4,656	....
Goods: Exports f.o.b.	78aad	20,019	22,016	25,523	31,239	33,737	35,702	34,076	36,877	45,636	45,399	52,743	....
Goods: Imports f.o.b.	78abd	−22,931	−24,108	−29,673	−37,957	−43,789	−45,730	−44,828	−45,556	−60,268	−58,232	−65,159	....
Trade Balance	78acd	−2,911	−2,093	−4,150	−6,719	−10,052	−10,028	−10,752	−8,679	−14,632	−12,833	−12,416	....
Services: Credit	78add	4,934	5,107	6,038	6,775	7,238	9,111	11,691	14,509	19,175	20,886	24,859	....
Services: Debit	78aed	−6,735	−6,497	−8,200	−10,268	−11,171	−12,443	−14,540	−17,271	−16,654	−16,253	−18,691	....
Balance on Goods & Services	78afd	−4,712	−3,482	−6,312	−10,212	−13,984	−13,360	−13,601	−11,441	−12,111	−8,200	−6,248	....
Income: Credit	78agd	377	375	821	1,486	1,411	1,484	1,806	1,919	2,405	2,777	2,298	....
Income: Debit	78ahd	−4,289	−4,121	−4,370	−5,219	−4,667	−5,002	−5,443	−5,629	−6,290	−5,461	−6,184	....
Balance on Gds, Serv. & Inc.	78aid	−8,624	−7,228	−9,861	−13,945	−17,240	−16,878	−17,238	−15,151	−15,996	−10,883	−10,134	....
Current Transfers, n.i.e.: Credit	78ajd	4,157	5,375	8,208	8,410	11,350	13,975	10,402	11,958	13,434	12,712	15,156	....
Current Transfers: Debit	78akd	−18	−23	−23	−27	−66	−62	−67	−35	−78	−68	−366	....
Capital Account, n.i.e.	78bcd	....	....	....	....	....	−	−	....	−296	162	3,480	....
Capital Account, n.i.e.: Credit	78bad	....	....	....	....	....	−	−	....	4,059	3,662	6,369	....
Capital Account: Debit	78bbd	....	....	....	....	....	−	−	....	−4,355	−3,500	−2,889	....
Financial Account, n.i.e.	78bjd	4,075	7,074	10,576	3,861	11,848	9,635	8,584	9,579	9,391	9,378	8,065	....
Direct Investment Abroad	78bdd	....	−	−83	−117	−239	−113	−48	−79	−424	−697	−453	....
Dir. Invest. in Rep. Econ., n.i.e.	78bed	277	550	973	2,144	2,426	3,577	2,635	2,169	2,657	4,334	3,030	....
Portfolio Investment Assets	78bfd	....	....	....	....	....	−	−	....	−173	−70	−36	....
Equity Securities	78bkd	....	....	....	....	....	−	−	....	−173	−70	−36	....
Debt Securities	78bld	....	....	....	....	....	−	−	....	....	....	....	....
Portfolio Investment Liab., n.i.e.	78bgd	284	1,369	5,491	1,590	3,958	2,556	−601	2,317	2,774	2,041	967	....
Equity Securities	78bmd	284	1,369	5,491	1,590	3,958	2,556	−601	2,317	2,774	2,041	967	....
Debt Securities	78bnd	....	....	....	....	....	−	−	....	....	....	....	....
Financial Derivatives Assets	78bwd	....	....	....	....	....	−	−	....	....	....	....	....
Financial Derivatives Liabilities	78bxd	....	....	....	....	....	−	−	....	....	....	....	....
Other Investment Assets	78bhd	929	1,830	1,170	−1,179	−4,710	−4,743	−3,239	−450	−1,519	2,205	4,790	....
Monetary Authorities	78bod	1	3	1	....	....	−	−	−498	−	....	....	....
General Government	78bpd	−791	309	9	−29	−5	67	11	33	−18	−88	−32	....
Banks	78bqd	1,732	−148	−1,029	−92	−1,642	−2,156	−1,355	1,140	−1,507	2,289	4,813	....
Other Sectors	78brd	−13	1,667	2,189	−1,058	−3,063	−2,653	−1,896	−1,126	5	4	9	....
Other Investment Liab., n.i.e.	78bid	2,587	3,325	3,024	1,423	10,413	8,357	9,837	5,623	6,075	1,566	−234	....
Monetary Authorities	78bsd	407	81	142	−65	45	233	122	1,344	−81	207	296	....
General Government	78btd	−1,345	141	92	1,483	1,698	397	−72	237	−194	696	−2,874	....
Banks	78bud	1,947	2,045	1,307	266	2,989	1,098	1,739	2,458	2,386	3,157	3,077	....
Other Sectors	78bvd	1,578	1,058	1,483	−261	5,680	6,629	8,047	1,584	3,965	−2,494	−732	....
Net Errors and Omissions	78cad	1,482	−987	1,492	970	−1,934	−1,348	1,390	313	−475	597	666	....
Overall Balance	78cbd	1,072	4,211	10,391	−733	3,958	5,321	3,071	6,664	5,979	11,897	16,868	....
Reserves and Related Items	79dad	−1,072	−4,211	−10,391	733	−3,958	−5,321	−3,071	−6,664	−5,979	−11,897	−16,868	....
Reserve Assets	79dbd	−2,253	−4,663	−9,238	1,956	−2,676	−4,637	−2,659	−6,327	−5,928	−11,897	−16,868	....
Use of Fund Credit and Loans	79dcd	1,181	451	−1,153	−1,223	−1,282	−684	−412	−337	−52	−	−	....
Exceptional Financing	79ded	....	....	....	....	....	−	−	....	....	....	....	....
International Investment Position		\multicolumn{12}{c}{*Millions of US Dollars*}
Assets	79aad	....	....	....	....	....	37,782	41,636	46,826	54,692	62,474	73,699	....
Direct Investment Abroad	79abd	....	....	....	....	....	617	706	1,707	1,859	2,615	4,006	....
Portfolio Investment	79acd	....	....	....	....	....	282	275	130	121	505	670	....
Equity Securities	79add	....	....	....	....	....	172	165	25	21	270	356	....
Debt Securities	79aed	....	....	....	....	....	110	111	105	100	235	314	....
Financial Derivatives	79ald	....	....	....	....	....	−	−	−	−	−	−	....
Other Investment	79afd	....	....	....	....	....	10,097	10,906	11,832	14,043	16,456	14,256	....
Monetary Authorities	79agd	....	....	....	....	....	−	−	−	−	−	−	....
General Government	79ahd	....	....	....	....	....	1,057	1,026	1,002	1,011	1,032	1,061	....
Banks	79aid	....	....	....	....	....	7,269	7,688	7,680	10,599	12,648	10,801	....
Other Sectors	79ajd	....	....	....	....	....	1,771	2,192	3,150	2,432	2,777	2,394	....
Reserve Assets	79akd	....	....	....	....	....	26,785	29,749	33,157	38,670	42,898	54,767	....
Liabilities	79lad	....	....	....	....	....	118,246	121,938	125,615	131,538	138,626	142,469	....
Dir. Invest. in Rep. Economy	79lbd	....	....	....	....	....	10,630	14,065	15,426	17,517	20,326	25,408	....
Portfolio Investment	79lcd	....	....	....	....	....	18,744	20,410	23,105	25,009	31,295	31,540	....
Equity Securities	79ldd	....	....	....	....	....	13,631	14,109	13,080	15,734	17,414	18,614	....
Debt Securities	79led	....	....	....	....	....	5,113	6,301	10,026	9,275	13,882	12,927	....
Financial Derivatives	79lld	....	....	....	....	....	−	−	−	−	−	−	....
Other Investment	79lfd	....	....	....	....	....	88,872	87,462	87,083	89,012	87,005	85,521	....
Monetary Authorities	79lgd	....	....	....	....	....	1,319	886	584	361	282	386	....
General Government	79lhd	....	....	....	....	....	47,828	45,408	45,244	45,991	43,330	42,863	....
Banks	79lid	....	....	....	....	....	17,154	16,169	16,111	17,294	19,595	20,197	....
Other Sectors	79ljd	....	....	....	....	....	22,571	24,999	25,144	25,366	23,798	22,075	....

India 534

		1992	1993	1994	1995	1996	1997	1998	1999	2000	2001	2002	2003
Government Finance		\multicolumn{12}{c}{*Billions of Rupees: Year Beginning April 1*}
Deficit (-) or Surplus	80	−399.1	−605.3	−567.5	−598.5	−668.8	−741.9	−917.2	−1,061.5	−1,087.1p	−1,079.2f	....	....
Revenue	81	1,004.6	1,011.7	1,283.2	1,488.8	1,717.1	1,864.5	2,015.3	2,349.7	2,696.9p	3,093.7f	....	....
Grants Received	81z	9.2	9.9	10.4	11.4	11.9	10.2	9.9	11.1	7.3p	7.0f	....	....
Expenditure	82	1,189.3	1,363.7	1,540.6	1,763.1	2,010.6	2,305.8	2,610.5	3,013.1	3,486.8p	3,953.1f	....	....
Lending Minus Repayments	83	223.5	263.2	320.5	335.6	387.2	310.7	331.9	409.1	304.5p	226.8f	....	....
Financing													
Net Borrowing: Domestic	84a	340.5	564.8	519.4	611.8	634.3	740.1	900.4	1,041.0	1,055.3p	1,060.6f	....	....
Foreign	85a	53.2	50.7	35.8	3.2	29.9	10.9	19.2	11.8	5.7p	18.7f	....	....
Use of Cash Balances	87	5.4	−10.2	12.3	−16.6	4.6	−9.1	−2.4	8.6	26.1p	−f	....	....
Debt: Domestic	88a	3,359.0	4,060.7	4,586.9	5,213.0	5,835.2	7,229.6	8,345.5	9,625.9	11,052.1p	12,563.6f	....	....
Foreign	89a	422.7	473.5	509.3	512.5	542.4	553.3	572.5	584.4	584.3p	595.9f	....	....
National Accounts		\multicolumn{12}{c}{*Billions of Rupees: Year Beginning April 1*}
Househ.Cons.Expend.,incl.NPISHs	96f	5,009.8	5,747.7	6,641.6	7,658.0	9,036.5	9,816.7	11,394.1	12,715.6	13,600.2	14,940.5	15,911.3	....
Government Consumption Expend	91f	839.6	977.3	1,086.4	1,288.2	1,457.3	1,721.9	2,140.3	2,511.1	2,642.4	2,843.1	3,088.3	....
Gross Fixed Capital Formation	93e	1,679.7	1,842.9	2,222.4	2,894.1	3,118.5	3,304.2	3,743.4	4,219.0	4,597.9	5,004.1	5,552.2	....
Changes in Inventories	93i	100.5	−16.7	145.5	257.7	−139.9	132.9	−21.3	363.6	138.3	86.5	86.0	....
Exports of Goods and Services	90c	673.1	861.5	1,016.1	1,307.3	1,448.5	1,652.0	1,952.8	2,277.0	2,901.8	3,075.8	3,758.7	....
Imports of Goods and Services (-)	98c	730.0	860.0	1,047.1	1,449.5	1,610.2	1,843.3	2,247.5	2,657.0	3,060.9	3,218.0	3,852.7	....
Gross Domestic Product (GDP)	99b	7,483.7	8,592.2	10,127.7	11,880.1	13,682.1	15,225.5	17,409.9	19,368.3	20,895.0	22,821.4	24,695.6	27,721.9
Net Primary Income from Abroad	98.n	−116.5	−120.8	−130.8	−134.8	−130.8	−132.1	−149.7	−154.3	−172.9	−120.9	−192.2	....
Gross National Income (GNI)	99a	7,367.2	8,471.4	9,996.9	11,745.3	13,551.3	15,093.4	17,260.2	19,214.0	20,722.1	22,700.6	24,503.4	....
Gross Nat'l Disposable Inc.(GNDI)	99i	6,734.4	7,803.0	9,271.1	10,787.1	12,625.9	14,011.1	16,012.5	17,851.2	19,474.4	21,270.5	....	....
Gross Saving	99s	1,629.1	1,936.2	2,514.6	2,987.5	3,172.6	3,521.8	3,749.3	4,686.8	4,959.9	5,351.8	5,977.0	....
Consumption of Fixed Capital	99cf	745.1	833.5	979.9	1,179.3	1,365.0	1,520.0	1,680.7	1,823.6	1,979.0	2,177.5	2,350.4	....
GDP at Factor Cost	99ba	6,732.2	7,813.5	9,170.6	10,732.7	12,435.5	13,901.5	15,981.3	17,618.4	19,030.0	20,909.6	22,494.9	25,238.7
GDP Vol.,fact.cost,93/94 Prices	99bap	7,377.9	7,813.5	8,380.3	8,995.6	9,700.8	10,166.0	10,827.5	11,483.7	11,985.9	12,678.3	13,183.2	14,245.1
GDP Volume 1993/94 Prices	99b.p	8,193.2	8,592.2	9,244.6	9,939.5	10,674.5	11,152.5	11,820.2	12,662.8	13,162.0	13,840.1	14,476.0	15,600.1
GDP Volume (2000=100)	99bvp	62.2	65.3	70.2	75.5	81.1	84.7	89.8	96.2	100.0	105.2	110.0	118.5
GDP Deflator (2000=100)	99bip	57.5	63.0	68.9	75.1	80.7	86.1	93.0	96.6	100.0	103.9	107.5	111.6
		\multicolumn{12}{c}{*Millions: Midyear Estimates*}
Population	99z	880.17	897.14	914.20	931.35	948.59	965.88	983.11	1,000.16	1,016.94	1,033.39	1,049.55	1,065.46

Indonesia 536

		1992	1993	1994	1995	1996	1997	1998	1999	2000	2001	2002	2003
Exchange Rates		\multicolumn{12}{c}{*Rupiah per SDR: End of Period*}
Market Rate	aa	2,835.3	2,898.2	3,211.7	3,430.8	3,426.7	6,274.0	11,299.4	9,724.2	12,501.4	13,070.0	12,154.1	12,578.7
		\multicolumn{12}{c}{*Rupiah per US Dollar: End of Period (ae) Period Average (rf)*}
Market Rate	ae	2,062.0	2,110.0	2,200.0	2,308.0	2,383.0	4,650.0	8,025.0	7,085.0	9,595.0	10,400.0	8,940.0	8,465.0
Market Rate	rf	2,029.9	2,087.1	2,160.8	2,248.6	2,342.3	2,909.4	10,013.6	7,855.2	8,421.8	10,260.9	9,311.2	8,577.1
Fund Position		\multicolumn{12}{c}{*Millions of SDRs: End of Period*}
Quota	2f.s	1,498	1,498	1,498	1,498	1,498	1,498	1,498	2,079	2,079	2,079	2,079	2,079
SDRs	1b.s	–	–	–	1	2	370	222	–	24	13	14	2
Reserve Position in the Fund	1c.s	194	200	214	270	298	–	–	145	145	145	145	145
Total Fund Cred.&Loans Outstg	2tl	–	–	–	–	–	2,201	6,456	7,467	8,318	7,252	6,518	6,915
International Liquidity		\multicolumn{12}{c}{*Millions of US Dollars Unless Otherwise Indicated: End of Period*}
Total Reserves minus Gold	1l.d	10,449	11,263	12,133	13,708	18,251	16,587	22,713	26,445	28,502	27,246	30,969	34,962
SDRs	1b.d	–	–	–	1	2	499	312	–	32	16	19	4
Reserve Position in the Fund	1c.d	267	274	312	401	429	–	–	200	190	183	198	216
Foreign Exchange	1d.d	10,181	10,988	11,820	13,306	17,820	16,088	22,401	26,245	28,280	27,048	30,753	34,742
Gold (Million Fine Troy Ounces)	1ad	3.101	3.101	3.101	3.101	3.101	3.101	3.101	3.101	3.101	3.101	3.101	3.101
Gold (National Valuation)	1and	946	1,092	1,067	1,079	1,030	809	803	812	766	772	1,077	1,291
Monetary Authorities: Other Liab.	4..d	26	22	20	21	21	419	3,374	3,586	2,260	2,151	2,136	2,146
Deposit Money Banks: Assets	7a.d	6,337	5,374	5,852	7,407	8,737	10,067	14,412	16,967	10,649	10,555	10,084	9,136
Liabilities	7b.d	7,894	9,691	11,311	11,678	12,482	15,147	12,192	14,167	9,659	6,577	5,805	3,716
Monetary Authorities		\multicolumn{12}{c}{*Billions of Rupiah: End of Period*}
Foreign Assets	11	†34,753	39,949	38,405	43,642	60,607	99,716	194,054	194,325	294,112	304,982	293,802	313,585
Claims on Central Government	12a	†7,976	9,013	7,510	4,672	4,269	5,470	35,700	248,095	233,669	267,464	304,058	260,629
Claims on Nonfin.Pub.Enterprises	12c	†19	13	8	4	–	–	–	–	–	–	–	–
Claims on Private Sector	12d	†51	256	196	218	197	205	265	1,230	6,382	6,194	6,295	6,280
Claims on Deposit Money Banks	12e	†10,899	9,950	13,333	15,722	14,438	58,624	113,543	14,437	18,790	17,907	16,861	15,065
Claims on Nonbank Financial Insts.	12g	†161	935	274	734	744	8,535	53,356	28,984	29,571	30,015	30,365	30,852
Reserve Money	14	†16,997	18,414	23,053	27,160	36,895	51,013	90,690	125,848	156,420	181,508	179,896	202,870
of which: Currency Outside DMBs	14a	†11,465	14,430	18,634	20,807	22,486	28,423	41,393	58,352	72,370	76,342	80,659	94,539
Foreign Currency Deposits	15	†–	–	–	–	–	–	–	–	192	126	129	25
Liabs. of Central Bank: Securities	16ac	†20,595	23,339	15,051	11,851	18,553	14,885	49,590	63,049	60,076	55,742	77,654	107,025
Restricted Deposits	16b	†382	534	497	461	436	267	660	244	290	505	299	175
Foreign Liabilities	16c	†54	46	43	49	50	15,761	100,025	98,018	125,676	117,149	98,319	105,147
Central Government Deposits	16d	†11,206	13,016	13,536	15,558	16,856	33,472	35,438	83,990	96,820	93,138	114,581	73,070
Capital Accounts	17a	†5,917	4,889	7,399	8,807	7,421	56,851	122,284	84,687	118,814	127,678	123,943	97,017
Other Items (Net)	17r	†–1,291	–122	147	1,106	45	301	–1,770	31,235	24,237	50,715	56,560	41,082
Deposit Money Banks		\multicolumn{12}{c}{*Billions of Rupiah: End of Period*}
Reserves	20	†4,112	4,591	5,051	7,371	14,896	24,172	50,229	68,479	66,537	93,357	94,633	105,650
Claims on Mon.Author.:Securities	20c	†11,782	14,799	7,619	5,152	11,225	6,318	44,964	63,049	58,700	55,742	76,859	102,259
Foreign Assets	21	†13,009	11,340	12,874	17,096	20,820	46,810	115,657	120,209	102,179	109,774	90,147	77,340
Claims on Central Government	22a	†3,541	4,004	2,843	4,165	5,727	8,571	10,230	274,551	439,177	423,735	393,338	361,397
Claims on State and Local Govts	22b	†1,032	256	113	276	290	292	319	214	376	446	310	2,718
Claims on Nonfin.Pub.Enterprises	22c	†6,000	6,492	6,866	8,423	9,248	11,036	15,128	11,854	10,343	10,748	15,946	11,107
Claims on Private Sector	22d	†128,521	161,273	198,311	243,067	295,195	381,741	508,558	225,236	270,301	298,901	352,378	426,685
Claims on Other Banking Insts	22f	97	190	236	312	370	364	277	100	101	130	194	353
Claims on Nonbank Financial Insts.	22g	†1,934	1,276	2,329	2,785	4,897	6,353	5,763	1,998	2,554	4,025	5,602	7,214
Demand Deposits	24	†15,147	19,979	24,135	28,639	31,766	43,879	49,185	57,646	82,241	97,746	106,558	125,329
Time, Savings,& Fgn. Currency Dep.	25	†91,570	109,402	130,280	171,257	226,097	279,073	481,350	525,227	587,730	669,789	695,181	734,197
Money Market Instruments	26aa	1,730	2,435	2,437	4,162	3,353	4,306	3,223	2,986	2,253	1,847	1,962	6,273
Restricted Deposits	26b	†1,370	1,699	1,541	1,779	2,099	1,419	2,417	1,659	4,783	7,966	5,075	3,096
Foreign Liabilities	26c	†16,206	20,448	24,885	26,952	29,744	70,434	97,842	100,375	92,675	68,406	51,895	31,458
Central Government Deposits	26d	†6,501	10,761	8,919	9,407	10,975	13,282	19,701	21,017	43,106	39,963	36,509	38,970
Central Govt. Lending Funds	26f	–	3,307	3,801	3,871	5,029	1,653	1,416	4,508	9,178	9,450	514	628
Credit from Monetary Authorities	26g	†10,554	16,237	11,432	10,394	11,622	23,008	112,947	33,360	16,547	15,225	12,694	10,971
Liab. to Nonbank Financial Insts.	26j	10,974	1,153	1,326	1,564	2,533	7,536	39,332	14,725	14,690	2,845	4,652	4,860
Capital Accounts	27a	†15,196	21,973	26,775	36,506	42,523	53,408	–94,556	–17,346	52,327	66,988	93,823	113,081
Other Items (Net)	27r	†780	–3,173	711	–5,884	–3,073	–12,341	38,268	21,533	44,739	16,632	20,545	25,863

Indonesia 536

		1992	1993	1994	1995	1996	1997	1998	1999	2000	2001	2002	2003
Monetary Survey					*Billions of Rupiah: End of Period*								
Foreign Assets (Net)	31n	†31,502	30,795	26,351	33,737	51,633	60,331	111,844	116,141	177,941	229,202	233,736	254,321
Domestic Credit	32	†131,625	159,931	196,231	239,691	293,106	375,813	574,457	687,255	852,548	908,557	957,396	995,197
Claims on Central Govt. (Net)	32an	†−6,190	−10,760	−12,102	−16,128	−17,835	−32,713	−9,209	417,639	532,919	558,098	546,305	509,987
Claims on State and Local Govts.	32b	†1,032	256	113	276	290	292	319	214	376	446	310	2,718
Claims on Nonfin.Pub.Enterprises	32c	†6,019	6,505	6,874	8,427	9,248	11,036	15,128	11,854	10,343	10,748	15,946	11,107
Claims on Private Sector	32d	†128,572	161,529	198,507	243,285	295,392	381,946	508,823	226,466	276,683	305,095	358,673	432,965
Claims on Other Banking Insts.	32f	97	190	236	312	370	364	277	100	101	130	194	353
Claims on Nonbank Financial Inst.	32g	†2,095	2,211	2,603	3,519	5,641	14,888	59,119	30,982	32,125	34,039	35,968	38,066
Money	34	†28,426	34,661	42,887	49,572	54,534	72,431	90,768	116,880	160,923	175,110	188,008	220,552
Quasi-Money	35	†91,570	109,402	130,280	171,257	226,097	279,073	481,350	525,227	587,922	669,916	695,310	734,223
Money Market Instruments	36aa	1,730	2,435	2,437	4,162	3,353	4,306	3,223	2,986	2,253	1,847	1,962	6,273
Liabs. of Central Bank: Securities	36ac	†8,813	8,540	7,432	6,699	7,328	8,567	4,626	–	1,376	–	796	4,766
Restricted Deposits	36b	†1,752	2,233	2,038	2,240	2,535	1,686	3,077	1,903	5,073	8,472	5,374	3,271
Central Govt. Lending Funds	36f	–	3,307	3,801	3,871	5,029	1,653	1,416	4,508	9,178	9,450	514	628
Liab. to Nonbank Financial Insts.	36j	10,974	1,153	1,326	1,564	2,533	7,536	39,332	14,725	14,690	2,845	4,652	4,860
Capital Accounts	37a	†21,113	26,862	34,174	45,313	49,944	110,259	27,728	67,341	171,141	194,666	217,766	210,098
Other Items (Net)	37r	†−1,250	2,133	−1,793	−11,250	−6,613	−49,367	34,780	69,826	77,934	75,454	76,750	64,847
Money plus Quasi-Money	35l	†119,996	144,063	173,167	220,829	280,631	351,504	572,118	642,107	748,845	845,026	883,318	954,775
Money (National Definitions)					*Billions of Rupiah: End of Period*								
Base Money	19ma	....	....	....	25,852	34,405	46,086	75,120	101,790	125,615	127,796	138,250	166,474
M1	39ma	....	....	....	52,677	64,089	78,343	101,197	124,633	162,186	177,731	191,939	223,799
M2	39mb	....	....	....	222,638	288,632	355,643	577,381	646,205	747,028	844,053	883,908	955,692
Interest Rates					*Percent Per Annum*								
Discount Rate (End of Period)	60	13.50	8.82	12.44	13.99	12.80	20.00	38.44	12.51	14.53	17.62	12.93	8.31
Money Market Rate	60b	11.99	8.66	9.74	13.64	13.96	27.82	62.79	23.58	10.32	15.03	13.54	7.76
Deposit Rate	60l	19.60	14.55	12.53	16.72	17.26	20.01	39.07	25.74	12.50	15.48	15.50	10.59
Deposit Rate (Foreign Currency)	60l.f	....	....	....	....	....	....	....	7.45	5.56	5.37	3.26	2.17
Lending Rate	60p	24.03	20.59	17.76	18.85	19.22	21.82	32.15	27.66	18.46	18.55	18.95	16.94
Lending Rate (Foreign Currency)	60p.f	....	....	....	....	....	....	....	....	....	8.95	7.38	6.52
Prices, Production, Labor					*Index Numbers (2000=100): Period Averages*								
Share Prices	62	....	....	....	101.0	119.2	121.5	84.8	110.0	100.0	82.1	91.6	104.3
Wholesale Prices: Incl. Petroleum	63	27.9	28.9	30.5	33.9	36.6	39.9	80.5	88.9	100.0	114.2	117.3	119.8
Excl. Petroleum	63a	28.8	30.9	34.1	38.9	41.3	44.5	80.2	†94.6	100.0	117.1	124.2	126.2
Consumer Prices	64	†32.1	35.2	38.2	41.8	†45.2	48.2	76.0	91.5	100.0	112.5	123.8	†130.1
Crude Petroleum Production	66aa	106.4	107.8	113.7	113.4	112.8	83.6	103.9	95.8	100.0	94.7	88.6	80.0
					Number in Thousands: Period Averages								
Labor Force	67d	....	....	....	....	88,187	89,603	94,735	95,793	....	....	....	....
Employment	67e	78,104	79,201	80,110	82,038	85,702	87,050	87,674	88,817	89,838	90,807	91,647	....
Unemployment	67c	2,199	2,246	3,738	....	3,625	4,197	5,063	6,030	5,813	8,005	....	....
Unemployment Rate (%)	67r	2.7	2.8	4.4	....	4.0	4.7	5.5	6.4	6.1	8.1	....	....
International Transactions					*Millions of US Dollars*								
Exports	70..d	33,967	36,823	40,055	45,417	49,814	53,443	48,848	48,665	62,124	56,447	58,120	61,058
Crude Petroleum & Products	70a.d	5,850	5,009	6,006	6,441	7,243	6,822	4,264	3,855	7,761	6,916	6,544	7,167
Crude Petroleum	70aad	4,648	4,259	5,072	5,146	5,712	5,479	3,349	3,162	6,090	5,715	5,205	5,579
Imports, c.i.f.	71..d	27,280	28,328	31,983	40,630	42,929	41,694	27,337	24,003	33,515	31,010	31,289	32,610
					2000=100								
Volume of Exports	72	67.6	70.8	78.0	81.5	85.6	110.0	102.3	84.0	100.0	121.0	99.7	97.0
Crude Petroleum	72aa	117.5	98.8	149.5	139.2	130.8	133.4	125.8	218.6	100.0	112.4	99.6	89.3
Export Prices					*2000=100: Indices of Unit Values in US Dollars*								
Exports (Unit Value)	74..d	93.1	91.0	90.3	103.1	109.0	103.6	80.8	64.9	100.0	89.9	95.5	102.7
Crude Petroleum (Unit Value)	74aad	66.8	63.6	58.0	87.4	92.4	87.8	60.9	55.0	100.0	1,000.9	1,036.4	306.4
Crude Petroleum (Ofc.Price)	76aad	66.3	61.2	56.3	61.0	71.3	66.7	43.2	61.7	100.0	84.1	88.0	101.8

2004, International Monetary Fund : *International Financial Statistics Yearbook*

Indonesia 536

		1992	1993	1994	1995	1996	1997	1998	1999	2000	2001	2002	2003
Balance of Payments					*Millions of US Dollars: Minus Sign Indicates Debit*								
Current Account, n.i.e.	78ald	−2,780	−2,106	−2,792	−6,431	−7,663	−4,889	4,096	5,785	7,985	6,899	7,823	....
Goods: Exports f.o.b.	78aad	33,796	36,607	40,223	47,454	50,188	56,298	50,371	51,242	65,406	57,364	59,165	....
Goods: Imports f.o.b.	78abd	−26,774	−28,376	−32,322	−40,921	−44,240	−46,223	−31,942	−30,598	−40,366	−34,669	−35,652	....
Trade Balance	78acd	7,022	8,231	7,901	6,533	5,948	10,075	18,429	20,644	25,040	22,695	23,513	....
Services: Credit	78add	3,391	3,959	4,797	5,469	6,599	6,941	4,479	4,599	5,213	5,500	6,661	....
Services: Debit	78aed	−8,100	−9,846	−11,416	−13,540	−15,139	−16,607	−11,961	−11,573	−15,011	−15,880	−17,054	....
Balance on Goods & Services	78afd	2,313	2,344	1,282	−1,538	−2,592	409	10,947	13,670	15,242	12,315	13,120	....
Income: Credit	78agd	818	1,028	1,048	1,306	1,210	1,855	1,910	1,891	2,456	2,004	1,318	....
Income: Debit	78ahd	−6,482	−6,015	−5,741	−7,180	−7,218	−8,187	−10,099	−11,690	−11,529	−8,940	−8,366	....
Balance on Gds, Serv. & Inc.	78aid	−3,351	−2,643	−3,411	−7,412	−8,600	−5,923	2,758	3,871	6,169	5,379	6,072	....
Current Transfers, n.i.e.: Credit	78ajd	571	537	619	981	937	1,034	1,338	1,914	1,816	1,520	2,255	....
Current Transfers: Debit	78akd	–	–	–	–	–	–	–	–	–	–	−504	....
Capital Account, n.i.e.	78bcd	–	–	–	–	–	–	–	–	–	–	–	....
Capital Account, n.i.e.: Credit	78bad	–	–	–	–	–	–	–	–	–	–	–	....
Capital Account: Debit	78bbd	–	–	–	–	–	–	–	–	–	–	–	....
Financial Account, n.i.e.	78bjd	6,129	5,632	3,839	10,259	10,847	−603	−9,638	−5,941	−7,896	−7,614	−1,173	....
Direct Investment Abroad	78bdd	–	−356	−609	−603	−600	−178	–	–	–	–	–	....
Dir. Invest. in Rep. Econ., n.i.e.	78bed	1,777	2,004	2,109	4,346	6,194	4,677	−356	−2,745	−4,550	−3,278	145	....
Portfolio Investment Assets	78bfd	–	–	....	....	....	....	....	....	....	....	....	....
Equity Securities	78bkd	–	–	....	....	....	....	....	....	....	....	....	....
Debt Securities	78bld	–	–	....	....	....	....	....	....	....	....	....	....
Portfolio Investment Liab., n.i.e.	78bgd	−88	1,805	3,877	4,100	5,005	−2,632	−1,878	−1,792	−1,909	−243	1,222	....
Equity Securities	78bmd	–	1,805	1,900	1,493	1,819	−4,987	−4,371	−782	−1,020	443	877	....
Debt Securities	78bnd	−88	–	1,977	2,607	3,186	2,355	2,493	−1,010	−889	−686	345	....
Financial Derivatives Assets	78bwd	....	....	....	....	....	....	....	....	....	....	....	....
Financial Derivatives Liabilities	78bxd	....	....	....	....	....	....	....	....	....	....	....	....
Other Investment Assets	78bhd	–	–	–	....	–	–	−44	−72	−150	−125	−500	....
Monetary Authorities	78bod	....	....	....	....	....	....	....	....	....	....	....	....
General Government	78bpd	–	–	–	....	....	....	....	....	....	....	....	....
Banks	78bqd	....	....	....	....	....	....	....	....	....	....	....	....
Other Sectors	78brd	–	–	–	....	–	–	−44	−72	−150	−125	−500	....
Other Investment Liab., n.i.e.	78bid	4,440	2,179	−1,538	2,416	248	−2,470	−7,360	−1,332	−1,287	−3,968	−2,040	....
Monetary Authorities	78bsd	–	–	–	–	–	–	–	–	–	–	–	....
General Government	78btd	858	552	137	6	−663	−265	4,209	3,979	2,093	636	457	....
Banks	78bud	–	1,357	527	1,953	−758	−276	−2,270	126	−1,420	−1,867	−1,217	....
Other Sectors	78bvd	3,582	270	−2,202	457	1,669	−1,929	−9,299	−5,437	−1,960	−2,737	−1,280	....
Net Errors and Omissions	78cad	−1,279	−2,932	−263	−2,255	1,319	−2,645	1,849	2,128	3,637	700	−1,692	....
Overall Balance	78cbd	2,070	594	784	1,573	4,503	−8,137	−3,693	1,972	3,726	−15	4,958	....
Reserves and Related Items	79dad	−2,070	−594	−784	−1,573	−4,503	8,137	3,693	−1,972	−3,726	15	−4,958	....
Reserve Assets	79dbd	−1,909	−594	−784	−1,573	−4,503	5,113	−2,090	−3,342	−4,851	1,370	−4,010	....
Use of Fund Credit and Loans	79dcd	−161	–	–	–	–	3,025	5,782	1,371	1,125	−1,356	−948	....
Exceptional Financing	79ded	....	....	....	....	....	....	....	....	....	....	....	....
International Investment Position						*Millions of US Dollars*							
Assets	79aad	....	....	....	....	....	....	....	....	....	....	48,398	....
Direct Investment Abroad	79abd	....	....	....	....	....	....	....	....	....	....	159	....
Portfolio Investment	79acd	....	....	....	....	....	....	....	....	....	....	7,198	....
Equity Securities	79add	....	....	....	....	....	....	....	....	....	....	23	....
Debt Securities	79aed	....	....	....	....	....	....	....	....	....	....	7,176	....
Financial Derivatives	79ald	....	....	....	....	....	....	....	....	....	....	84	....
Other Investment	79afd	....	....	....	....	....	....	....	....	....	....	8,916	....
Monetary Authorities	79agd	....	....	....	....	....	....	....	....	....	....	1,265	....
General Government	79ahd	....	....	....	....	....	....	....	....	....	....	44	....
Banks	79aid	....	....	....	....	....	....	....	....	....	....	3,536	....
Other Sectors	79ajd	....	....	....	....	....	....	....	....	....	....	4,072	....
Reserve Assets	79akd	....	....	....	....	....	....	....	....	....	....	32,042	....
Liabilities	79lad	....	....	....	....	....	....	....	....	....	....	152,782	....
Dir. Invest. in Rep. Economy	79lbd	....	....	....	....	....	....	....	....	....	....	11,641	....
Portfolio Investment	79lcd	....	....	....	....	....	....	....	....	....	....	14,332	....
Equity Securities	79ldd	....	....	....	....	....	....	....	....	....	....	6,452	....
Debt Securities	79led	....	....	....	....	....	....	....	....	....	....	7,881	....
Financial Derivatives	79lld	....	....	....	....	....	....	....	....	....	....	63	....
Other Investment	79lfd	....	....	....	....	....	....	....	....	....	....	126,745	....
Monetary Authorities	79lgd	....	....	....	....	....	....	....	....	....	....	10,768	....
General Government	79lhd	....	....	....	....	....	....	....	....	....	....	63,429	....
Banks	79lid	....	....	....	....	....	....	....	....	....	....	6,858	....
Other Sectors	79ljd	....	....	....	....	....	....	....	....	....	....	45,690	....

Indonesia 536

		1992	1993	1994	1995	1996	1997	1998	1999	2000	2001	2002	2003
Government Finance						*Billions of Rupiah: Year Beginning April 1*							
Deficit (-) or Surplus..................	80	−1,096	2,018	3,581	10,085	6,180	−4,211	−28,191	†−12,645	....	−17,340p	....	....
Revenue.............................	81	50,645	56,318	69,402	80,427	90,298	113,882	157,412	†198,673	....	307,876p	....	....
Grants Received..................	81z	–	–	67	–	–	–	–	–	....	52p	....	....
Expenditure.......................	82	52,200	54,983	61,866	66,723	77,964	112,893	174,097	225,874	....	359,039p	....	....
Lending Minus Repayments....	83	−459	−683	4,022	3,619	6,154	5,200	11,506	−14,556	....	−33,771p	....	....
Financing													
Net Borrowing: Domestic........	84a	−1,225	444	−4,295	....	−3,058	5,210	9,593	−9,446	....	12,578p	....	....
Net borrowing: Foreign.........	85a	1,159	−451	−303	−1,677	−2,659	−4,674	49,705	15,942	....	6,722p	....	....
Use of Cash Balances............	87	1,162	−2,011	1,017	....	−463	3,676	−31,106	6,149	....	−1,960p	....	....
Debt: Domestic....................	88a	5,449	4,861	939	3,229	83	4,097	13,481	6,481	....	....	....	....
Debt: Foreign......................	89a	105,546	118,797	138,841	136,781	127,324	450,890	514,134	490,685	....	....	....	....
National Accounts						*Billions of Rupiah*							
Househ.Cons.Expend.,incl.NPISHs....	96f	147,709	†192,958	228,119	279,876	332,094	387,171	647,824	813,183	850,819	975,731	1,137,763	....
Government Consumption Expend...	91f	26,879	†29,757	31,014	35,584	40,299	42,952	54,416	72,631	90,780	113,416	132,219	....
Gross Fixed Capital Formation.........	93e	76,965	86,667	105,381	129,218	157,653	177,686	243,043	221,472	275,881	316,179	325,334	....
Changes in Inventories....................	93i	24,229	10,546	13,326	15,900	5,800	21,615	−82,716	−96,461	−72,236	−63,282	−95,614	....
Exports of Goods and Services.........	90c	83,050	†88,231	101,332	119,593	137,533	174,871	506,245	390,560	542,992	612,482	569,942	....
Imports of Goods and Services (-)....	98c	76,438	†78,383	96,953	125,657	140,812	176,600	413,058	301,654	423,318	505,128	459,631	....
Gross Domestic Product (GDP).........	99b	282,395	†329,776	382,220	454,514	532,568	627,695	955,754	1,099,732	1,264,919	1,684,280	1,897,800	2,086,760
Net Primary Income from Abroad.....	98.n	−12,447	†−12,553	−10,248	−13,366	−14,272	−18,355	−53,894	−83,764	−92,162	−58,079	−77,816	....
Gross National Income (GNI)............	99a	269,947	†296,095	348,072	413,661	489,377	571,512	895,379	998,017	1,210,577	1,359,894	1,461,009	....
Consumption of Fixed Capital..........	99cf	13,045	16,489	19,111	22,725	26,629	31,385	47,788	54,987	63,246	72,470	80,501	....
GDP Volume 1983 Prices.................	99b.p	131,185	139,707	....	....	....	....	....	....	....	....	....	....
GDP Volume 1993 Prices.................	99b.p	....	329,776	354,641	383,792	413,798	433,246	376,375	379,353	398,017	411,691	426,741	....
GDP Volume 2000 Prices.................	99b.p	....	....	....	....	....	....	....	....	....	....	1,504,380	1,572,160
GDP Volume (2000=100)................	99bvp	77.8	†82.9	89.1	96.4	104.0	108.9	94.6	95.3	100.0	103.4	107.2	112.0
GDP Deflator (2000=100)................	99bip	28.7	†31.5	33.9	37.3	40.5	45.6	79.9	91.2	100.0	128.7	140.0	147.3
						Millions: Midyear Estimates							
Population.............................	99z	188.26	191.28	194.27	197.22	200.15	203.04	Ü 205.90	208.74	211.56	214.36	217.13	219.88

2004, International Monetary Fund : *International Financial Statistics Yearbook*

Iran, I.R. of 429

		1992	1993	1994	1995	1996	1997	1998	1999	2000	2001	2002	2003
Exchange Rates		\multicolumn{12}{c}{*Rials per SDR: End of Period*}
Official Rate	aa	92.30	2,415.49	2,534.26	2,597.64	2,515.19	2,366.94	2,465.36	2,405.04	2,948.39	2,200.47 †	10,810.87	12,292.11
		\multicolumn{12}{c}{*Rials per US Dollar: End of Period (ae) Period Average (rf)*}
Official Rate	ae	67.04	1,758.56	1,735.97	1,747.50	1,749.14	1,754.26	1,750.93	1,752.29	2,262.93	1,750.95 †	7,951.98	8,272.11
Official Rate	rf	65.55	1,267.77	1,748.75	1,747.93	1,750.76	1,752.92	1,751.86	1,752.93	1,764.43	1,753.56 †	6,906.96	8,193.89
		\multicolumn{12}{c}{*Rials per US Dollar: End of Period*}
Market Rate	aea	....	....	....	....	....	4,645	5,721	8,135	7,909	7,924	....	....
		\multicolumn{12}{c}{*Rials per US Dollar: Months Ending the 20th*}
Weighted Average	yf	655	890	1,222	1,726	2,194	2,780	3,206	4,172	5,731	6,163	....	....
		\multicolumn{12}{c}{*Index Numbers (2000=100): Period Averages*}
Nominal Effective Exchange Rate	nec	447.28	307.93	222.78	128.05	128.20	143.50	138.78	98.43	100.00	111.22	109.38	93.28
Real Effective Exchange Rate	rec	129.10	97.38	81.93	65.52	80.45	100.26	108.68	89.21	100.00	118.57	128.57	124.09
Fund Position		\multicolumn{12}{c}{*Millions of SDRs: End of Period*}
Quota	2f.s	1,079	1,079	1,079	1,079	1,079	1,079	1,079	1,497	1,497	1,497	1,497	1,497
SDRs	1b.s	7	105	98	90	240	245	1	101	267	267	268	268
Reserve Position in the Fund	1c.s	105	–	–	–	–	–	–	–	–	–	–	–
Total Fund Cred.&Loans Outstg.	2tl	–	–	–	–	–	–	–	–	–	–	–	–
International Liquidity		\multicolumn{12}{c}{*Millions of US Dollars Unless Otherwise Indicated: End of Period*}
SDRs	1b.d	10	144	143	134	345	330	2	139	349	336	364	399
Reserve Position in the Fund	1c.d	144	–	–	–	–	–	–	–	–	–	–	–
Gold (Million Fine Troy Ounces)	1ad	4.343	4.765	4.740	4.842	....	....	....	....	....	....	....	....
Gold (National Valuation)	1and	209	229	242	252	....	....	....	....	....	....	....	....
Monetary Authorities:Other Assets	3..d	....	....	....	....	....	....	....	....	....	....	....	....
Deposit Money Banks: Assets	7a.d	3,070	1,459	3,321	3,354	4,319	4,403	4,648	2,258	3,112	6,298	7,244	8,903
Liabilities	7b.d	4,053	3,397	5,589	4,015	2,668	2,128	2,771	3,410	3,486	6,695	8,657	13,749
Other Banking Insts.: Liabilities	7f.d	227	71	53	118	110	66	136	250	266	403	409	522
Monetary Authorities		\multicolumn{12}{c}{*Billions of Rials: Months Ending the 20th*}
Foreign Assets	11	1,349	7,916	9,681	14,413	19,454	15,669	9,827	11,413	24,478	28,151	154,928	188,442
Claims on Central Government	12a	14,651	16,002	28,169	32,648	42,461	42,624	55,710	61,731	60,207	64,673	101,692	111,341
Claims on Official Entities	12bx	2,520	3,792	5,549	10,704	18,826	15,618	18,842	19,794	23,189	16,287	19,200	21,897
Claims on Deposit Money Banks	12e	742	3,751	1,967	10,462	2,056	11,162	9,565	13,392	17,567	18,589	17,732	23,823
Reserve Money	14	13,901	16,511	22,165	32,805	41,708	51,298	60,533	70,911	82,726	88,015	111,487	127,554
of which: Currency Outside DMBs	14a	4,088	4,925	6,199	7,949	9,598	11,271	14,050	16,652	20,020	21,840	25,945	30,809
Nonfin.Pub.Ent. Deps.	14e	559	862	1,604	2,020	2,639	2,642	4,662	5,304	7,859	4,552	5,401	6,800
Restricted Deposits	16b	352	1,158	4,004	7,085	8,764	6,789	3,810	4,066	3,351	4,133	1,182	1,415
Foreign Liabilities	16c	166	2,924	2,883	2,679	3,466	5,057	8,012	6,562	7,094	13,991	83,330	77,087
Central Government Deposits	16d	3,077	4,965	6,752	9,738	13,035	13,837	13,814	18,275	28,645	37,312	57,194	60,139
Capital Accounts	17a	294	801	903	989	1,004	1,003	1,012	1,097	1,064	1,235	3,225	3,991
Other Items (Net)	17r	1,472	5,104	8,658	14,929	14,820	7,089	6,763	5,420	2,561	-16,986	37,132	75,318
Deposit Money Banks		\multicolumn{12}{c}{*Billions of Rials: Months Ending the 20th*}
Reserves	20	9,134	10,586	14,179	22,519	28,865	36,563	40,385	47,190	51,536	58,559	72,743	82,353
Foreign Assets	21	206	2,566	5,766	5,861	7,555	7,724	8,138	3,957	7,043	11,027	57,605	73,648
Claims on Central Government	22a	1,343	1,236	1,232	1,827	1,823	1,821	1,821	7,494	5,800	5,648	7,187	15,856
Claims on Private Sector	22d	16,665	22,131	27,535	32,938	41,043	52,579	63,716	85,701	112,986	155,268	206,970	291,624
Demand Deposits	24	9,434	12,519	18,120	24,373	33,628	41,064	48,732	59,996	74,291	99,275	123,963	147,018
Time and Savings Deposits	25	17,770	23,181	29,377	37,599	49,426	62,881	74,438	90,435	108,884	143,689	181,022	234,086
Foreign Liabilities	26c	272	5,973	9,703	7,016	4,667	3,734	4,851	5,975	7,890	11,723	68,837	113,736
Credit from Monetary Authorities	26g	742	3,751	1,967	10,462	2,056	11,162	9,565	13,392	17,567	18,589	17,732	23,823
Capital Accounts	27a	134	3,719	3,724	3,724	3,724	3,724	3,724	3,764	3,764	8,564	8,564	8,564
Other Items (Net)	27r	-1,003	-12,625	-14,180	-20,030	-14,215	-23,878	-27,250	-29,220	-35,031	-51,338	-55,612	-63,745
Monetary Survey		\multicolumn{12}{c}{*Billions of Rials: Months Ending the 20th*}
Foreign Assets (Net)	31n	1,118	1,585	2,860	10,578	18,876	14,603	5,102	2,833	16,538	13,465	60,366	71,268
Domestic Credit	32	33,915	43,385	59,484	74,426	101,566	115,511	151,740	187,227	211,234	246,942	319,626	416,605
Claims on Central Govt. (Net)	32an	12,816	12,211	22,556	24,674	31,026	30,370	43,463	48,057	34,512	30,557	39,216	45,566
Claims on Official Entities	32bx	4,434	9,043	9,393	16,814	29,498	32,562	44,561	53,469	63,736	61,117	73,440	79,415
Claims on Private Sector	32d	16,665	22,131	27,535	32,938	41,043	52,579	63,716	85,701	112,986	155,268	206,970	291,624
Money	34	14,081	18,305	25,923	34,342	45,865	54,977	67,444	81,952	102,170	125,667	155,309	184,627
Quasi-Money	35	17,770	23,181	29,377	37,599	49,426	62,881	74,438	90,435	108,884	143,689	181,022	234,086
Restricted Deposits	36b	352	1,158	4,004	7,085	8,764	6,789	3,810	4,066	3,351	4,133	1,182	1,415
Other Items (Net)	37r	2,829	2,327	3,040	5,977	16,387	5,467	11,150	13,608	13,367	-13,082	42,479	67,746
Money plus Quasi-Money	35l	31,851	41,486	55,299	71,941	95,291	117,858	141,883	172,387	211,054	269,356	336,331	418,712

Iran, I.R. of 429

		1992	1993	1994	1995	1996	1997	1998	1999	2000	2001	2002	2003
Other Banking Institutions						*Billions of Rials: Months Ending the 20th*							
Cash....................................	40	147	166	218	361	671	912	1,549	1,901	3,417	3,094	7,449	7,667
Claims on Central Government........	42a	2	2	2	2	2	2	2	941	1,249	1,755	1,846	3,522
Claims on Official Entities................	42bx	58	113	141	90	163	591	1,002	195	208	222	909	885
Claims on Private Sector...................	42d	5,134	6,159	7,504	9,831	13,506	18,611	25,812	36,411	51,503	66,108	88,257	105,605
Demand Deposits...........................	44	476	767	870	1,287	2,129	3,325	4,002	4,001	6,023	6,948	11,435	14,789
Private Sector............................	44x	476	767	870	1,287	2,129	3,325	4,002	4,001	6,023	6,948	11,435	14,784
Official Entities............................	44y	–	–	–	–	–	–	–	–	–	–	–	5
Time and Savings Deposits...............	45	729	914	1,409	2,367	3,327	5,591	9,157	12,584	15,831	24,110	35,582	46,604
Foreign Liabilities............................	46c	15	125	91	207	192	116	238	438	601	705	3,253	4,319
Central Government Deposits..........	46d	138	139	114	124	175	158	106	69	87	112	557	2,986
Credit from Monetary Authorities.....	46g	509	215	795	3,437	8,126	3,518	4,635	5,895	9,358	652	2,025	4,410
Capital Accounts............................	47a	567	870	1,928	1,928	1,940	1,940	1,940	1,940	2,960	6,385	6,409	6,409
Other Items (Net)............................	47r	2,907	3,409	2,658	935	–1,548	5,469	8,287	14,522	21,517	32,267	39,201	38,170
Liquid Liabilities...............................	55l	32,908	43,002	57,360	75,232	100,077	125,862	153,493	187,070	229,491	297,320	375,899	472,437
Prices and Production						*Index Numbers (2000=100)*							
Share Prices...................................	62	19.1	16.9	18.3	36.8	76.9	73.8	65.2	70.1	100.0	133.8	178.7	....
Wholesale Prices.............................	63	15.6	19.6	26.9	43.2	57.5	63.6	71.2	84.9	100.0	105.9	114.6	126.7
Home Goods................................	63a	15.5	19.5	26.8	41.1	53.8	60.2	70.4	†84.4	100.0	107.3	118.0	132.1
Consumer Prices..............................	64	17.1	20.7	27.3	40.8	52.6	61.7	72.8	87.4	100.0	111.3	127.2	148.2
Crude Petroleum Production............	66aa	91.4	97.0	95.6	95.7	97.6	96.4	95.4	93.2	100.0	96.8	90.9	99.3
International Transactions						*Millions of US Dollars Year Ending March 20*							
Exports..	70..d	19,868	18,080	19,434	18,360	22,391	18,381	13,118	21,030	28,461	23,904	28,186	....
Imports, c.i.f...................................	71..d	25,860	21,427	13,774	12,313	15,117	14,196	14,323	12,683	14,347	17,626	21,180	....
Imports, f.o.b..................................	71.vd	22,293	18,472	11,874	10,615	13,032	12,238	12,347	10,934	12,368	....	....	....
Volume of Exports						*2000=100*							
Petroleum.................................	72a	110.6	104.6	103.5	108.0	108.8	108.0	97.6	95.8	100.0	....	....	....
Crude Petroleum....................	72aa	122.1	112.7	110.0	111.6	111.6	107.1	105.2	95.1	100.0	....	....	....
Export Prices..................................	76	....	....	....	178.7	169.5	127.2	79.9	110.6	100.0	....	....	....
Import Prices..................................	76.x	....	....	....	102.5	118.8	107.3	145.0	114.1	100.0	....	....	....
Balance of Payments						*Millions of US$: Year Beginning March 21: Minus Sign Indicates Debit*							
Current Account, n.i.e.....................	78ald	–6,504	–4,215	4,956	3,358	5,232	2,213	–2,139	6,589	12,645	....	....	....
Goods: Exports f.o.b......................	78aad	19,868	18,080	19,434	18,360	22,391	18,381	13,118	21,030	28,345	....	....	....
Goods: Imports f.o.b......................	78abd	–23,274	–19,287	–12,617	–12,774	–14,989	–14,123	–14,286	–13,433	–15,207	....	....	....
Trade Balance............................	78acd	–3,406	–1,207	6,817	5,586	7,402	4,258	–1,168	7,597	13,138	....	....	....
Services: Credit............................	78add	559	1,084	438	593	860	1,192	1,793	1,216	1,382	....	....	....
Services: Debit.............................	78aed	–5,783	–5,600	–3,226	–2,339	–3,083	–3,371	–2,760	–2,457	–2,296	....	....	....
Balance on Goods & Services.......	78afd	–8,630	–5,723	4,029	3,840	5,179	2,079	–2,135	6,356	12,224	....	....	....
Income: Credit............................	78agd	287	151	142	316	488	466	230	181	404	....	....	....
Income: Debit.............................	78ahd	–157	–143	–413	–794	–898	–725	–731	–473	–604	....	....	....
Balance on Gds, Serv. & Inc.......	78aid	–8,500	–5,715	3,758	3,362	4,769	1,820	–2,636	6,064	12,024	....	....	....
Current Transfers, n.i.e.: Credit......	78ajd	1,996	1,500	1,200	–	471	400	500	508	539	....	....	....
Current Transfers: Debit.................	78akd	–	–	–2	–4	–8	–7	–3	17	82	....	....	....
Capital Account, n.i.e.	78bcd										....	....	....
Capital Account, n.i.e.: Credit........	78bad	–	–	–	–	–	–	–	–	–	....	....	....
Capital Account: Debit...................	78bbd	–	–	–	–	–	–	–	–	–	....	....	....
Financial Account, n.i.e..................	78bjd	4,703	5,563	–346	–774	–5,508	–4,822	2,270	–5,894	–10,189	....	....	....
Direct Investment Abroad..............	78bdd										....	....	....
Dir. Invest. in Rep. Econ., n.i.e.......	78bed	–	–	2	17	26	53	24	35	39	....	....	....
Portfolio Investment Assets............	78bfd										....	....	....
Equity Securities.........................	78bkd	–	–	–	–	–	–	–	–	–	....	....	....
Debt Securities...........................	78bld	–	–	–	–	–	–	–	–	–	....	....	....
Portfolio Investment Liab., n.i.e......	78bgd	–	–	–	–	–	–	–	–	–	....	....	....
Equity Securities.........................	78bmd	–	–	–	–	–	–	–	–	–	....	....	....
Debt Securities...........................	78bnd	–	–	–	–	–	–	–	–	–	....	....	....
Financial Derivatives Assets...........	78bwd	....	....	....	....	....	....	–	–	–	....	....	....
Financial Derivatives Liabilities.......	78bxd	....	....	....	....	....	....	–	–	–	....	....	....
Other Investment Assets................	78bhd	1,000	1,250	–1,258	–419	–1,305	2,293	963	–1,650	–8,257	....	....	....
Monetary Authorities..................	78bod	....	....	....	....	....	....	–	–	–	....	....	....
General Government....................	78bpd	342	44	–42	235	–48	–99	–21	–6	–5,932	....	....	....
Banks...	78bqd	658	1,206	–1,216	–654	–1,257	2,392	984	–1,638	–1,783	....	....	....
Other Sectors..............................	78brd	–	–	–	–	–	–	–	–6	–542	....	....	....
Other Investment Liab., n.i.e...........	78bid	3,703	4,313	910	–372	–4,229	–7,168	1,283	–4,279	–1,971	....	....	....
Monetary Authorities...................	78bsd	63	68	–252	–64	–283	179	93	–5,517	–1,410	....	....	....
General Government....................	78btd	4,556	–1,358	10,447	1,684	–4,523	–4,035	–489	104	–621	....	....	....
Banks...	78bud	–	–	–	–	–	–	–	–	–	....	....	....
Other Sectors..............................	78bvd	–916	5,603	–9,285	–1,992	577	–3,312	1,679	1,134	60	....	....	....
Net Errors and Omissions.................	78cad	1,640	–1,120	–3,702	202	2,717	–1,088	–1,122	–244	–1,373	....	....	....
Overall Balance............................	78cbd	–161	228	908	2,786	2,441	–3,697	–991	451	1,083	....	....	....
Reserves and Related Items..............	79dad	161	–228	–908	–2,786	–2,441	3,697	991	–451	–1,083	....	....	....
Reserve Assets............................	79dbd	161	–228	–908	–2,786	–2,441	3,697	991	–451	–1,083	....	....	....
Use of Fund Credit and Loans.........	79dcd	–	–	–	–	–	–	–	–	–	....	....	....
Exceptional Financing.....................	79ded	....	....	....	....	....	....	–	–	–	....	....	....

Iran, I.R. of 429

		1992	1993	1994	1995	1996	1997	1998	1999	2000	2001	2002	2003
Government Finance						*Billions of Rials: Year Beginning March 21*							
Deficit (-) or Surplus	80	−872	−636	332	245	493	−2,869	−17,208	−691	−3,675	−3,150	....	....
Revenue	81	9,885	20,251	29,245	41,575	57,276	62,569	53,762	92,470	104,641	125,479	....	....
Grants	81z	−	†−	−	−	−	−	−	−	−	−	....	....
Exp. & Lending Minus Repay	82z	....	....	....	....	....	....	....	....	....	....	....	....
Expenditure	82	10,757	20,887	28,912	41,331	56,783	65,438	70,970	93,161	108,316	128,860	....	....
Lending Minus Repayments	83	....	....	....	....	....	....	....	....	....	....	....	....
Total Financing	80h	872	638	−331	−244	−492	2,869	17,208	691	1,311	3,381	....	....
Total Net Borrowing	84	....	....	....	....	....	....	....	....	....	....	....	....
Net Domestic	84a	....	....	....	....	....	....	....	....	....	....	....	....
Net Foreign	85a	....	....	....	....	....	....	....	....	....	....	....	....
Debt: Domestic	88a	....	....	....	....	....	....	....	....	....	....	....	....
National Accounts						*Billions of Rials: Year Beginning March 21*							
Househ.Cons.Expend.,incl.NPISHs	96f	34,490	43,550	60,138	87,496	113,240	140,807	181,172	225,770	276,612	323,659	405,033	....
Government Consumption Expend	91f	7,319	15,517	21,005	29,708	35,174	38,207	47,037	55,998	80,554	93,734	131,464	....
Gross Fixed Capital Formation	93e	19,396	24,858	28,819	38,954	65,626	83,765	96,051	124,202	153,462	194,140	259,143	....
Changes in Inventories	93i	11,352	8,435	866	15,329	23,485	20,855	12,044	5,670	37,958	42,138	112,117	....
Exports of Goods and Services	90c	9,645	27,420	39,632	40,362	51,746	51,007	44,857	93,509	131,811	141,420	247,973	....
Imports of Goods and Services (-)	98c	17,700	19,847	17,024	24,386	37,160	44,728	51,567	64,931	101,190	126,201	218,202	....
Gross Domestic Product (GDP)	99b	66,455	100,047	130,565	185,928	248,348	292,678	329,134	436,625	580,473	669,997	932,373	....
Net Primary Income from Abroad	98.n	146	−1,390	−2,267	−1,346	−1,649	−491	380	−532	278	1,455	−4,695	....
Gross National Income (GNI)	99a	66,601	98,657	128,298	184,582	246,699	292,170	329,466	436,008	580,153	671,452	927,678	....
GDP Volume 1990 Prices	99b.p	41,079	40,220	40,913	42,260	45,088	47,507	....	....	....	....	....	....
GDP Volume 1997 Prices	99b.p	....	....	....	....	....	292,678	300,699	306,514	322,278	334,049	359,047	....
GDP Volume (2000=100)	99bvp	78.5	76.9	78.2	80.8	86.2	†90.8	93.3	95.1	100.0	103.7	111.4	....
GDP Deflator (2000=100)	99bip	14.6	22.4	28.8	39.6	49.6	55.5	60.8	79.1	100.0	111.4	144.2	....
						Millions: Midyear Estimates							
Population	99z	59.27	60.39	61.42	62.38	63.27	64.10	64.89	65.66	66.44	67.24	68.07	68.92

Iraq 433

		1992	1993	1994	1995	1996	1997	1998	1999	2000	2001	2002	2003
Exchange Rates						*SDRs per Dinar: End of Period*							
Principal Rate............	ac	2.3396	2.3420	2.2036	2.1641	2.2371	2.3842	2.2847	2.3438	2.4690	2.5597	2.3662	....
					US Dollars per Dinar: End of Period (ag) Period Average (rh)								
Principal Rate............	ag	3.2169	3.2169	3.2169	3.2169	3.2169	3.2169	3.2169	3.2169	3.2169	3.2169	3.2169	....
Principal Rate............	rh	3.2169	3.2169	3.2169	3.2169	3.2169	3.2169	3.2169	3.2169	3.2169	3.2169	3.2169	....
					Index Numbers (2000=100): Period Averages								
Principal Rate............	ahx	100.0	100.0	100.0	100.0	100.0	100.0	100.0	100.0	100.0	100.0	100.0	....
Nominal Effective Exchange Rate.....	nec	47.2	56.1	64.5	63.9	69.0	78.8	83.8	89.5	100.0	109.8	109.5	98.7
Fund Position					*Millions of SDRs: End of Period*								
Quota............	2f.s	504.0	504.0	504.0	504.0	504.0	504.0	504.0	504.0	504.0	504.0	504.0	504.0
SDRs............	1b.s	–	–	–	–	–	–	–	–	–	–	–	–
Reserve Position in the Fund............	1c.s	–	–	–	–	–	–	–	--	–	–	–	–
Total Fund Cred.&Loans Outstg........	2tl	–	–	–	–	–	–	–	–	–	–	–	–
International Liquidity					*Millions of US Dollars Unless Otherwise Indicated: End of Period*								
SDRs............	1b.d	–	–	–	–	–	–	–	–	–	–	–	–
Reserve Position in the Fund............	1c.d	–	–	–	–	–	–	–	–	–	–	–	–
Production					*Index Numbers (2000=100): Period Averages*								
Crude Petroleum............	66aa	17.0	23.2	23.2	23.2	24.4	47.0	76.6	93.6	100.0	93.0	73.4	51.6
International Transactions						*Millions of Dinars*							
Imports, c.i.f., from DOTS............	71y	187.3	165.6	155.0	206.9	176.7	353.2	576.0	656.0	1,064.8	1,751.4	1,810.7	....
National Accounts						*Millions of Dinars*							
Househ.Cons.Expend.,incl.NPISHs....	96f	40,929.8	81,106.0	....	....	....	....	....	....	....	....	....	....
Government Consumption Expend...	91f	8,898.0	15,576.3	....	....	....	....	....	....	....	....	....	....
Gross Fixed Capital Formation..........	93e	10,782.0	16,258.7	....	....	....	....	....	....	....	....	....	....
Changes in Inventories............	93i	–2,379.0	1,102.0	....	....	....	....	....	....	....	....	....	....
Exports of Goods and Services..........	90c	670.3	1,474.0	....	....	....	....	....	....	....	....	....	....
Imports of Goods and Services (-).....	98c	1,540.6	3,375.0	....	....	....	....	....	....	....	....	....	....
Gross Domestic Product (GDP).........	99b	57,360.5	112,142.0	....	....	....	....	....	....	....	....	....	....
					Millions: Midyear Estimates								
Population............	99z	18.42	19.00	19.61	20.21	20.80	21.40	21.99	22.60	23.22	23.86	24.51	25.17

2004, International Monetary Fund : *International Financial Statistics Yearbook*

Ireland 178

		1992	1993	1994	1995	1996	1997	1998	1999	2000	2001	2002	2003
Exchange Rates		\multicolumn{12}{c}{*SDRs per Pound through 1998, SDRs per Euro Thereafter: End of Period*}
Market Rate	ac	1.1850	1.0271	1.0598	1.0801	1.1691	1.0601	1.0563	.7319	.7142	.7013	.7714	.8499
		\multicolumn{12}{c}{*US Dollars per Pound through 1998, US Dollars per Euro Thereafter: End of Period (ag) Period Average (rh)*}
Market Rate	ag	1.6294	1.4108	1.5471	1.6055	1.6811	1.4304	1.4873	1.0046	.9305	.8813	1.0487	1.2630
Market Rate	rh	1.7053	1.4671	1.4978	1.6038	1.6006	1.5180	1.4257	1.0668	.9240	.8956	.9444	1.1308
		\multicolumn{12}{c}{*ECUs per Pound: End of Period (ec) Period Average (ed)*}
ECU Rate	ec	1.3456	1.2630	1.2578	1.2218	1.3417	1.2960	1.2697	....	....	....	....	....
ECU Rate	ed	1.3146	1.2514	1.2604	1.2263	1.2611	1.3380	1.2717	....	....	....	....	....
		\multicolumn{12}{c}{*Index Numbers (2000=100): Period Averages*}
Market Rate (1995=100)	ahx	106.3	91.5	93.4	100.0	99.8	94.7	88.9	....	....	....	....	....
Nominal Effective Exchange Rate	neu	117.53	112.39	111.78	112.38	114.72	115.04	109.04	105.84	100.00	100.85	102.26	108.68
Fund Position		\multicolumn{12}{c}{*Millions of SDRs: End of Period*}
Quota	2f.s	525	525	525	525	525	525	525	838	838	838	838	838
SDRs	1b.s	90	97	101	107	115	123	137	29	37	43	49	53
Reserve Position in the Fund	1c.s	171	155	152	197	226	252	414	303	252	268	345	387
Total Fund Cred.&Loans Outstg.	2tl	–	–	–	–	–	–	–	–	–	–	–	–
International Liquidity		\multicolumn{12}{c}{*Millions of US Dollars Unless Otherwise Indicated: End of Period*}
Total Res.Min.Gold (Eurosys.Def)	1l.d	3,440	5,925	6,115	8,630	8,205	6,526	9,397	†5,325	5,360	5,587	5,415	4,079
SDRs	1b.d	124	133	148	159	165	166	193	40	48	55	66	79
Reserve Position in the Fund	1c.d	236	213	222	294	325	340	582	416	329	336	469	575
Foreign Exchange	1d.d	3,080	5,579	5,745	8,178	7,715	6,020	8,622	4,869	4,983	5,196	4,879	3,425
o/w:Fin.Deriv.Rel.to Reserves	1ddd	....	....	....	....	....	....	....	–	–	–	–	–
Other Reserve Assets	1e.d	....	....	....	....	....	....	....	–	–	–	–	–
Gold (Million Fine Troy Ounces)	1ad	.360	.360	.360	.361	.361	.361	.451	.176	.176	.176	.176	.176
Gold (Eurosystem Valuation)	1and	109	123	141	137	143	116	132	51	48	49	60	73
Memo:Euro Cl. on Non-EA Res.	1dgd	....	....	....	....	....	....	....	43.17	19.54	185.07	372.29	1,207.43
Non-Euro Cl. on EA Res	1dhd	....	....	....	....	....	....	....	94.34	275.49	357.68	292.01	318.05
Mon. Auth.: Other Foreign Assets	3..d	....	....	....	....	....	....	....	–	–	–	–	–
Foreign Liabilities	4..d	1,167	–	–	–	–	–	–	†1,389	573	78	91	110
Banking Insts.: Foreign Assets	7a.d	18,428	21,381	30,088	46,679	70,324	101,447	142,089	†78,106	135,339	173,199	236,529	324,806
Foreign Liab.	7b.d	18,727	19,146	28,127	49,100	70,169	99,225	142,772	†77,733	141,507	191,246	255,228	338,470
Monetary Authorities		\multicolumn{12}{c}{*Millions of Pounds through 1998; Millions of Euros Beginning 1999: End of Period*}
Fgn. Assets (Cl.on Non-EA Ctys)	11	2,158	4,283	4,173	5,471	4,959	4,634	6,445	5,411	6,333	6,617	5,601	4,296
Claims on General Government	12a.u	....	....	....	....	....	....	....	2,109	2,183	2,029	1,650	2,958
o/w: Claims on Gen.Govt.in Cty.	12a	361	315	254	183	132	132	132	279	229	29	–	21
Claims on Banking Institutions	12e.u	....	....	....	....	....	....	....	8,662	9,012	13,977	11,939	18,947
o/w: Claims on Bank.Inst.in Cty.	12e	....	....	....	....	....	....	....	5,062	8,407	13,201	11,158	17,535
Claims on Other Resident Sectors	12d.u	....	....	....	....	....	....	....	–	–	–	–	7
o/w: Cl. on Oth.Res.Sect.in Cty	12d	....	....	–	–	–	–	–	–	–	–	–	7
Currency Issued	14a	1,604	1,776	1,907	2,092	2,287	2,619	3,040	4,848	5,368	4,704	4,278	4,650
Liabilities to Banking Insts	14c.u	....	....	....	....	....	....	....	4,228	6,426	8,619	10,405	17,702
o/w: Liabs to Bank.Inst.in Cty.	14c	457	709	685	1,188	1,030	1,326	2,258	2,074	2,426	3,506	4,509	3,815
Demand Dep. of Other Res.Sect.	14d.u	....	....	....	....	....	....	....	–	–	–	–	–
o/w:D.Dep.of Oth.Res.Sect.in Cty	14d	....	....	....	....	....	....	....	–	–	–	–	–
Other Dep. of Other Res.Sect.	15..u	....	....	....	....	....	....	....	–	–	–	–	–
o/w:O.Dep.of Oth.Res.Sect.in Cty	15	....	....	....	....	....	....	....	–	–	–	–	–
Bonds & Money Mkt. Instruments	16n.u	....	....	....	....	....	....	....	–	–	–	–	–
o/w: Held by Resid.of Cty	16n	....	....	....	....	....	....	....	....	....	....	....	....
Foreign Liab. (to Non-EA Ctys)	16c	716	–	–	–	–	–	–	1,383	616	89	87	87
Central Government Deposits	16d.u	....	....	....	....	....	....	....	3,546	2,139	5,151	3,826	3,529
o/w: Cent.Govt.Dep. in Cty	16d	639	1,426	836	1,082	1,178	1,191	1,674	3,546	2,139	5,151	3,826	3,529
Capital Accounts	17a	999	1,366	1,416	1,264	841	1,265	1,248	2,593	2,923	3,073	2,069	1,838
Other Items (Net)	17r	–1,897	–679	–417	28	–245	–1,635	–1,642	–416	58	985	–1,475	–1,596
Memo: Currency Put into Circ.	14m	....	....	....	....	....	....	....	....	....	....	6,583	8,197

Ireland 178

		1992	1993	1994	1995	1996	1997	1998	1999	2000	2001	2002	2003
Banking Institutions			*Millions of Pounds through 1998; Millions of Euros Beginning 1999: End of Period*
Claims on Monetary Authorities	20	642	775	675	1,436	1,348	1,686	2,706	2,486	....	4,324	4,909	4,303
Claims on Bk.Inst.in Oth.EA Ctys.	20b.u	....	....	....	....	....	....	....	34,495	49,609	63,850	75,392	94,066
Fgn. Assets (Cl.on Non-EA Ctys)	21	11,310	15,155	19,448	29,074	41,832	70,922	95,535	77,748	145,448	196,527	225,545	257,170
Claims on General Government	22a.u	....	....	....	....	....	....	....	29,909	30,698	38,230	40,400	60,322
o/w: Claims on Gen.Govt.in Cty.	22a	3,260	3,196	3,581	4,637	4,049	4,220	4,676	6,335	5,465	5,363	5,017	5,279
Claims on Other Resident Sectors	22d.u	....	....	....	....	....	....	....	109,999	136,032	161,126	175,193	199,215
o/w: Cl. on Oth.Res.Sect.in Cty.	22d	14,321	14,835	16,571	29,106	33,978	44,058	54,020	91,795	110,652	129,079	142,382	160,220
Demand Deposits	24..u	....	....	....	....	....	....	....	12,711	15,117	18,871	19,671	49,721
o/w:D.Dep.of Oth.Res.Sect. in Cty.	24	2,783	3,103	3,539	6,808	7,552	5,199	6,802	12,649	15,032	18,768	19,624	48,828
Other Deposits	25..u	....	....	....	....	....	....	....	67,614	76,097	81,626	93,246	75,417
o/w:O.Dep.of Oth.Res.Sect.in Cty.	25	9,744	12,693	13,848	20,494	24,324	32,890	38,108	59,223	67,035	71,694	80,225	62,017
Money Market Fund Shares	26m.u	....	....	....	....	....	....	....	–	7,742	9,504	15,681	17,646
Bonds & Money Mkt. Instruments	26n.u	....	....	....	....	....	....	....	24,237	28,224	41,322	43,636	65,518
o/w: Held by Resid.of Cty	26n	....	....	....	....	....	....	....					
Foreign Liab. (to Non-EA Ctys)	26c	11,493	13,571	18,180	30,582	41,740	69,369	95,994	77,377	152,076	217,004	243,376	267,989
Central Government Deposits	26d.u	....	....	....	....	....	....	....	1,274	1,970	1,471	790	1,747
o/w: Cent.Govt.Dep. in Cty	26d	121	119	360	239	248	299	332	1,274	1,970	1,454	790	747
Credit from Monetary Authorities	26g	2,065	737	403	37	261	1,637	1,755	5,245	....	13,316	11,290	17,738
Liab. to Bk.Inst.in Oth. EA Ctys.	26h.u	....	....	....	....	....	....	....	44,248	44,476	50,923	63,083	86,853
Capital Accounts	27a	3,934	4,322	4,854	6,486	7,249	10,280	12,881	22,091	26,993	31,133	33,664	37,769
Other Items (Net)	27r	–607	–584	–909	–394	–167	1,211	1,067	–158	....	–1,113	–2,996	–5,321
Banking Survey (Nat'l Residency)			*Millions of Pounds through 1998; Millions of Euros Beginning 1999: End of Period*
Foreign Assets (Net)	31n	1,258	5,867	5,440	3,963	5,051	6,187	5,986	31,539	....	52,094	54,300	72,185
Domestic Credit	32	17,182	16,801	19,210	32,604	36,733	46,920	56,822	93,589	112,237	127,866	142,783	161,251
Claims on General Govt. (Net)	32an	2,861	1,966	2,639	3,498	2,755	2,862	2,802	1,794	1,585	–1,213	401	1,024
Claims on Other Resident Sectors	32d	14,321	14,835	16,571	29,106	33,978	44,058	54,020	91,795	110,652	129,079	142,382	160,227
Currency Issued	34a.n	1,604	1,776	1,907	2,092	2,287	2,619	3,040	5,528	5,368	4,704	4,278	4,650
Demand Deposits	34b.n	2,783	3,103	3,539	6,808	7,552	5,199	6,802	12,649	15,032	18,768	19,624	48,828
Other Deposits	35..n	9,744	12,693	13,848	20,494	24,324	32,890	38,108	59,223	67,035	71,694	80,225	62,017
Money Market Fund Shares	36m	....	....	....	....	....	....	....	–	7,742	9,504	15,681	17,646
Bonds & Money Mkt. Instruments	36n	....	....	....	....	....	....	....	24,237	28,224	41,322	43,636	65,518
o/w: Over Two Years	36na	....	....	....	....	....	....	....	10,200	11,038	12,563	14,377	32,411
Capital Accounts	37a	4,934	5,688	6,271	7,750	8,090	11,545	14,129	24,684	29,916	34,206	35,733	39,607
Other Items (Net)	37r	–625	–591	–914	–577	–469	853	732	–1,191	....	–240	–2,092	–4,827
Banking Survey (EA-Wide Residency)			*Millions of Euros: End of Period*
Foreign Assets (Net)	31n.u	....	....	....	....	....	....	....	4,399	–911	–13,949	–12,317	–6,610
Domestic Credit	32..u	....	....	....	....	....	....	....	137,197	164,804	194,763	212,627	257,226
Claims on General Govt. (Net)	32anu	....	....	....	....	....	....	....	27,198	28,772	33,637	37,434	58,004
Claims on Other Resident Sect.	32d.u	....	....	....	....	....	....	....	109,999	136,032	161,126	175,193	199,222
Currency Issued	34a.u	....	....	....	....	....	....	....	5,528	5,368	4,704	4,278	4,650
Demand Deposits	34b.u	....	....	....	....	....	....	....	12,711	15,117	18,871	19,671	49,721
Other Deposits	35..u	....	....	....	....	....	....	....	67,614	76,097	81,626	93,246	75,417
o/w: Other Dep. Over Two Yrs.	35abu	....	....	....	....	....	....	....	7,633	8,496	9,904	13,499	16,643
Money Market Fund Shares	36m.u	....	....	....	....	....	....	....	–	7,742	9,504	15,681	17,646
Bonds & Money Mkt. Instruments	36n.u	....	....	....	....	....	....	....	24,237	28,224	41,322	43,636	65,518
o/w: Over Two Years	36nau	....	....	....	....	....	....	....	10,200	11,038	12,563	14,377	32,411
Capital Accounts	37a	....	....	....	....	....	....	....	24,684	29,916	34,206	35,733	39,607
Other Items (Net)	37r.u	....	....	....	....	....	....	....	6,824	1,431	–9,421	–11,933	–1,940
Nonbank Financial Institutions			*Millions of Pounds: End of Period*
Cash	40..k	915	1,559	1,676	† 18	6	5	5	....	....	....	....	....
Foreign Assets	41..k	112	241	704	† 2	5	8	11	....	....	....	....	....
Claims on Central Government	42a.k	2,147	1,801	1,777	† 717	762	786	819	....	....	....	....	....
Claims on Private Sector	42d.k	6,836	7,634	8,438	† 644	703	878	1,051	....	....	....	....	....
Quasi-Monetary Liabilities	45..k	7,927	8,682	9,274	† 917	1,039	1,154	1,237	....	....	....	....	....
Foreign Liabilities	46c.k	1,456	1,690	2,233	† 2	5	8	10	....	....	....	....	....
Cred.from Deposit Money Banks	46h.k	653	1,009	1,285	† 394	339	448	564	....	....	....	....	....
Capital Accounts	47a.k	607	795	928	† 35	78	53	56	....	....	....	....	....
Other Items (Net)	47r.k	–634	–941	–1,125	† 33	15	15	18	....	....	....	....	....
Interest Rates			*Percent Per Annum*
Discount Rate (End of Period)	60	....	7.00	6.25	6.50	6.25	6.75	4.06	....	....	....	....	....
Money Market Rate	60b	15.12	10.49	† 5.75	5.45	5.74	6.43	3.23	3.14	4.84	3.31	2.88	2.08
Treasury Bill Rate	60c	....	† 9.06	5.87	6.19	5.36	6.03	5.37	....	....	....	....	....
Deposit Rate	60l	5.42	2.27	.33	.44	.29	.46	.43	.10	.10	.10	.10	.04
Lending Rate	60p	† 12.66	9.93	6.13	6.56	5.85	6.57	6.22	3.34	4.77	4.84	3.83	2.85
Government Bond Yield	61	9.11	7.72	8.19	8.30	7.48	6.49	4.99	....	....	....	....	....

2004, International Monetary Fund : *International Financial Statistics Yearbook*

Ireland 178

		1992	1993	1994	1995	1996	1997	1998	1999	2000	2001	2002	2003
Prices, Production, Labor		*Index Numbers (2000=100): Period Averages*											
Share Prices	62	24.4	30.5	34.8	38.1	47.6	64.6	90.9	93.6	100.0	108.2	87.2	81.9
Wholesale Prices	63	85.0	89.1	89.9	91.8	92.3	91.8	93.2	94.2	100.0	102.9	103.1	97.7
Output Manufacturing Industry	63a	85.6	89.5	90.5	92.8	93.4	92.9	93.7	94.6	†100.0	101.7	100.5	92.4
Consumer Prices	64	†82.9	84.0	86.0	88.2	89.7	91.0	93.2	94.7	100.0	†104.9	109.8	113.6
Harmonized CPI	64h	….	….	….	87.8	89.7	90.8	92.7	95.0	100.0	104.0	108.9	113.2
Wages: Weekly Earnings	65ey	71.4	75.2	77.4	79.1	81.1	85.0	88.5	93.7	†100.0	109.1	115.1	122.8
Industrial Production	66	34.8	36.8	41.2	49.6	53.6	63.0	75.5	86.6	100.0	110.2	118.8	126.3
Manufacturing Employment	67ey	77.3	77.3	80.2	85.1	89.2	94.4	97.1	96.2	100.0	101.0	95.6	90.9
		Number in Thousands: Period Averages											
Labor Force	67d	….	….	….	1,443	1,494	1,539	1,621	1,688	….	1,782	1,847	1,899
Employment	67e	1,165	1,183	1,221	†1,282	1,329	1,380	1,521	1,616	1,692	1,741	1,765	1,811
Unemployment	67c	283	294	282	277	279	254	202	165	116	144	162	172
Unemployment Rate (%)	67r	16.3	16.7	15.1	14.1	11.8	10.1	7.1	5.3	4.1	4.0	4.4	4.7
International Transactions		*Millions of Pounds through 1998; Millions of Euros Beginning 1999*											
Exports	70	16,744	19,830	22,753	27,825	30,407	35,336	45,145	†66,956	83,889	92,730	92,893	81,639
Imports, c.i.f.	71	13,195	14,885	17,283	20,619	22,429	25,882	31,278	†44,327	55,909	57,230	54,805	47,107
		2000=100											
Volume of Exports	72	30.2	33.2	38.2	45.8	50.4	57.9	72.0	83.8	100.0	105.0	104.3	99.2
Volume of Imports	73	38.4	41.1	46.5	53.2	58.5	67.2	79.3	85.9	100.0	99.4	97.3	90.0
Unit Value of Exports	74	79.9	85.9	85.9	87.4	86.9	87.9	90.2	95.1	100.0	101.2	101.0	93.7
Unit Value of Imports	75	78.3	82.3	84.5	88.0	87.0	87.5	89.5	92.2	100.0	103.0	100.5	93.9
Balance of Payments		*Millions of US Dollars: Minus Sign Indicates Debit*											
Current Account, n.i.e.	78ald	607	1,765	1,577	1,721	2,049	1,866	1,016	245	−516	−690	−1,399	−2,105
Goods: Exports f.o.b.	78aad	28,107	28,728	33,642	44,423	49,184	55,293	78,562	67,831	73,530	77,623	84,216	89,570
Goods: Imports f.o.b.	78abd	−21,062	−20,553	−24,275	−30,866	−33,430	−36,668	−53,172	−44,244	−48,520	−50,360	−50,769	−51,763
Trade Balance	78acd	7,045	8,175	9,366	13,557	15,754	18,625	25,390	23,587	25,010	27,263	33,447	37,807
Services: Credit	78add	4,054	3,769	4,319	5,017	5,749	6,186	16,735	15,688	18,538	23,465	28,600	38,008
Services: Debit	78aed	−7,084	−6,760	−8,452	−11,303	−13,448	−15,195	−29,626	−26,534	−31,272	−35,339	−41,963	−52,314
Balance on Goods & Services	78afd	4,015	5,185	5,233	7,270	8,055	9,616	12,499	12,741	12,276	15,389	20,084	23,501
Income: Credit	78agd	3,282	2,780	3,513	5,110	5,576	7,353	25,430	24,442	27,613	28,850	27,281	32,191
Income: Debit	78ahd	−8,827	−8,116	−8,919	−12,435	−13,772	−17,059	−38,800	−38,191	−41,160	−45,202	−49,464	−58,333
Balance on Gds, Serv. & Inc.	78aid	−1,530	−151	−173	−55	−141	−90	−870	−1,008	−1,271	−962	−2,099	−2,641
Current Transfers, n.i.e.: Credit	78ajd	3,033	2,858	2,850	3,009	3,538	3,083	7,428	5,308	4,143	7,400	7,719	7,159
Current Transfers: Debit	78akd	−896	−941	−1,100	−1,233	−1,349	−1,128	−5,543	−4,055	−3,388	−7,128	−7,018	−6,623
Capital Account, n.i.e.	78bcd	787	775	387	817	785	871	1,218	593	1,074	635	512	442
Capital Account, n.i.e.: Credit	78bad	889	863	477	914	881	962	1,327	674	1,167	719	656	617
Capital Account: Debit	78bbd	−102	−89	−90	−96	−96	−91	−108	−81	−93	−84	−144	−175
Financial Account, n.i.e.	78bjd	−3,962	−901	−3,963	−33	−2,780	−7,484	4,686	−4,185	7,912	16	1,866	951
Direct Investment Abroad	78bdd	−215	−220	−438	−820	−727	−1,008	−4,955	−6,102	−4,641	−4,103	−8,524	−3,528
Dir. Invest. in Rep. Econ., n.i.e.	78bed	1,442	1,121	838	1,447	2,618	2,743	11,035	18,323	25,501	9,573	29,131	26,599
Portfolio Investment Assets	78bfd	−439	−272	−1,019	−1,056	−183	−716	−66,738	−82,813	−83,075	−111,347	−105,302	−161,319
Equity Securities	78bkd	–	–	–	–	–	–	−27,624	−36,357	−28,849	−23,808	−27,179	−26,839
Debt Securities	78bld	−439	−272	−1,019	−1,056	−183	−716	−39,114	−46,457	−54,226	−87,539	−78,123	−134,480
Portfolio Investment Liab., n.i.e.	78bgd	−2,750	2,723	−379	771	982	−2,505	54,735	67,377	77,906	89,085	68,812	106,389
Equity Securities	78bmd	–	–	–	–	–	–	47,948	52,061	69,606	79,352	68,780	77,218
Debt Securities	78bnd	−2,750	2,723	−379	771	982	−2,505	6,787	15,316	8,300	9,733	33	29,172
Financial Derivatives Assets	78bwd	….	….	….	….	….	….	….	….	416	−576	1,996	−2,297
Financial Derivatives Liabilities	78bxd	–	–	–	–	–	–	….	….	−42	957	−19	−58
Other Investment Assets	78bhd	−8,489	−10,642	−4,483	−16,572	−22,162	−48,337	−25,211	−38,545	−37,036	−21,431	−33,267	−48,864
Monetary Authorities	78bod	–	–	–	–	–	–	….	….	−16	−121	−583	−1,576
General Government	78bpd	–	–	−76	76	–	–	….	….	−2,057	725	3,327	−148
Banks	78bqd	−6,414	−9,486	−2,919	−14,083	−19,623	−43,421	….	….	−12,563	−5,348	−20,722	−35,545
Other Sectors	78brd	−2,075	−1,157	−1,489	−2,565	−2,539	−4,916	….	….	−22,400	−16,687	−15,290	−11,596
Other Investment Liab., n.i.e.	78bid	6,489	6,389	1,519	16,197	16,691	42,340	35,820	37,576	28,882	37,859	49,038	84,028
Monetary Authorities	78bsd	1,376	−1,255	–	–	–	–	–	–	3,493	922	−1,583	7,461
General Government	78btd	1,142	−580	−1,585	−808	−947	−812	….	….	−160	−2	−34	−286
Banks	78bud	3,972	8,224	3,103	17,005	17,639	43,152	….	….	19,637	18,656	32,823	62,399
Other Sectors	78bvd	–	–	–	–	–	–	….	….	5,913	18,283	17,833	14,455
Net Errors and Omissions	78cad	402	1,021	1,823	−167	−106	3,639	−3,708	1,373	−8,509	434	−1,271	−1,178
Overall Balance	78cbd	−2,166	2,660	−176	2,339	−52	−1,109	3,212	−1,973	−39	395	−292	−1,890
Reserves and Related Items	79dad	2,166	−2,660	176	−2,339	52	1,109	−3,212	1,973	39	−395	292	1,890
Reserve Assets	79dbd	2,166	−2,660	176	−2,339	52	1,109	−3,212	1,973	−121	−395	292	1,890
Use of Fund Credit and Loans	79dcd	–	–	–	–	–	–	–	–	–	–	–	–
Exceptional Financing	79ded	….	….	….	….	….	….	….	….	160	….	….	….

Ireland 178

		1992	1993	1994	1995	1996	1997	1998	1999	2000	2001	2002	2003
International Investment Position		\multicolumn{12}{c}{*Millions of US Dollars*}
Assets...	79aad	....	....	....	....	....	....	....	....	....	739,269	919,145	....
Direct Investment Abroad..............	79abd	....	....	....	....	....	....	....	....	....	34,338	34,770	....
Portfolio Investment......................	79acd	....	....	....	....	....	....	....	....	....	434,872	565,495	....
Equity Securities.........................	79add	....	....	....	....	....	....	....	....	....	136,389	150,121	....
Debt Securities...........................	79aed	....	....	....	....	....	....	....	....	....	298,483	415,373	....
Financial Derivatives.....................	79ald	....	....	....	....	....	....	....	....	....	8,204	7,889	....
Other Investment...........................	79afd	....	....	....	....	....	....	....	....	....	256,213	305,510	....
Monetary Authorities..................	79agd	....	....	....	....	....	....	....	....	....	669	−2,277	....
General Government...................	79ahd	....	....	....	....	....	....	....	....	....	3,412	5,688	....
Banks..	79aid	....	....	....	....	....	....	....	....	....	115,042	137,197	....
Other Sectors.............................	79ajd	....	....	....	....	....	....	....	....	....	137,091	164,902	....
Reserve Assets..............................	79akd	....	....	....	....	....	....	....	....	....	5,641	5,481	....
Liabilities...	79lad	....	....	....	....	....	....	....	....	....	758,216	949,017	....
Dir. Invest. in Rep. Economy..........	79lbd	....	....	....	....	....	....	....	....	....	143,952	184,702	....
Portfolio Investment......................	79lcd	....	....	....	....	....	....	....	....	....	353,181	431,817	....
Equity Securities.........................	79ldd	....	....	....	....	....	....	....	....	....	272,175	348,252	....
Debt Securities...........................	79led	....	....	....	....	....	....	....	....	....	81,006	83,565	....
Financial Derivatives.....................	79lld	....	....	....	....	....	....	....	....	....	3,766	5,512	....
Other Investment...........................	79lfd	....	....	....	....	....	....	....	....	....	257,318	326,986	....
Monetary Authorities..................	79lgd	....	....	....	....	....	....	....	....	....	4,635	3,905	....
General Government...................	79lhd	....	....	....	....	....	....	....	....	....	501	541	....
Banks..	79lid	....	....	....	....	....	....	....	....	....	153,142	206,556	....
Other Sectors.............................	79ljd	....	....	....	....	....	....	....	....	....	99,040	115,983	....
Government Finance		\multicolumn{12}{c}{*Millions of Pounds through 1998; Millions of Euros Beginning 1999: Year Ending December 31*}
Central Government													
Deficit (−) or Surplus.....................	80	−700.5	−260.4	−322.6	−259.5	102.0	289.7	1,226.2	†1,513.0	3,171.2	649.7	94.9	....
Revenue......................................	81	9,812.9	10,872.8	11,676.6	12,423.4	13,422.3	15,108.6	17,175.6	†29,441.7	29,865.1	30,204.1	32,610.5	....
Expenditure................................	82	10,513.4	11,133.2	11,999.2	12,682.9	13,320.3	14,818.9	15,949.4	†27,928.7	26,693.9	29,554.4	32,515.6	....
Financing													
Net Borrowing.............................	84	−440.0	850.2	−18.6	535.0	164.5	−109.3	−881.8	†−1,686.3	−3,177.3	−80.9	−742.6	....
Use of Cash Balances.................	87	1,140.5	−589.8	341.2	−275.5	−266.5	−180.4	−344.4	†173.3	6.1	−569.0	647.7	....
General Government		\multicolumn{12}{c}{*As Percent of Gross Domestic Product*}
Deficit (−) or Surplus.....................	80g	−2.5	−2.4	−1.7	−2.1	−.6	.7	2.3	2.3	4.5	1.7	....	....
Debt...	88g	92.3	96.3	88.2	78.9	74.1	65.1	55.1	49.6	39.0	36.6	....	....
National Accounts		\multicolumn{12}{c}{*Millions of Pounds through 1998; Millions of Euros Beginning in 1999*}
Househ.Cons.Expend.,incl.NPISHs....	96f	19,161	20,162	21,621	23,192	25,311	27,900	31,219	†43,721	49,488	54,349	59,019	62,935
Government Consumption Expend...	91f	5,155	5,495	5,838	6,177	6,514	7,274	7,978	†11,383	13,050	15,474	17,692	19,232
Gross Fixed Capital Formation..........	93e	5,211	5,259	6,043	7,072	8,512	10,650	13,275	†21,712	25,321	27,056	28,983	31,816
Changes in Inventories.....................	93i	−87	−112	−135	428	427	683	886	†391	819	377	114	498
Exports of Goods and Services..........	90c	19,179	22,475	25,923	31,679	35,453	42,121	52,585	†79,096	100,719	113,642	119,701	112,759
Imports of Goods and Services (−).....	98c	16,775	18,860	22,301	26,936	30,142	35,442	45,678	†66,816	87,110	96,301	98,508	91,981
Statistical Discrepancy......................	99bs	−316	−364	−365	−202	−440	−426	318	†−31	777	835	990	−473
Gross Domestic Product (GDP)........	99b	31,529	34,054	36,624	41,409	45,634	52,760	60,582	†89,457	103,065	115,432	127,992	134,786
Net Primary Income from Abroad.....	98.n	−3,537	−3,671	−3,716	−4,685	−5,147	−6,332	−7,389	†−13,098	−14,910	−18,327	−23,518	−23,115
Gross National Income (GNI)............	99a	27,992	30,383	32,908	36,725	40,487	46,428	53,193	†76,359	88,155	97,105	104,474	111,671
Net National Income.......................	99e	25,094	27,037	29,170	32,366	35,618	40,392	46,109	†68,540	78,130	85,575	91,999	98,011
GDP Volume 1995 Prices................	99b.p	34,746	35,682	37,736	41,409	44,719	49,564	53,830	†76,261	83,824	88,860	94,309	97,756
GDP Volume (2000=100)................	99bvp	52.6	54.0	57.2	62.7	67.7	75.1	81.5	†91.0	100.0	106.0	112.5	116.6
GDP Deflator (2000=100)................	99bip	73.8	77.6	78.9	81.3	83.0	86.6	91.5	†95.4	100.0	105.7	110.4	112.1
		\multicolumn{12}{c}{*Millions: Midyear Estimates*}
Population......................................	99z	3.53	3.55	3.58	3.61	3.64	3.68	3.73	3.77	3.82	3.87	3.91	3.96

2004, International Monetary Fund : *International Financial Statistics Yearbook*

Israel 436

		1992	1993	1994	1995	1996	1997	1998	1999	2000	2001	2002	2003
Exchange Rates		\multicolumn{12}{c}{*New Sheqalim per SDR: End of Period*}
Market Rate	aa	3.8005	4.1015	4.4058	4.6601	4.6748	4.7709	5.8588	5.7000	5.2651	5.5497	6.4400	6.5071
		\multicolumn{12}{c}{*New Sheqalim per US Dollar: End of Period (ae) Period Average (rf)*}
Market Rate	ae	2.7640	2.9860	3.0180	3.1350	3.2510	3.5360	4.1610	4.1530	4.0410	4.4160	4.7370	4.3790
Market Rate	rf	2.4591	2.8301	3.0111	3.0113	3.1917	3.4494	3.8001	4.1397	4.0773	4.2057	4.7378	4.5541
		\multicolumn{12}{c}{*Index Numbers (2000=100): Period Averages*}
Nominal Effective Exchange Rate	nec	136.40	125.27	115.79	108.70	105.82	106.06	99.26	91.63	100.00	100.67	87.07	80.95
Real Effective Exchange Rate	rec	87.49	86.42	87.34	88.05	93.21	99.72	96.77	92.37	100.00	100.35	90.32	83.18
Fund Position		\multicolumn{12}{c}{*Millions of SDRs: End of Period*}
Quota	2f.s	666.2	666.2	666.2	666.2	666.2	666.2	666.2	928.2	928.2	928.2	928.2	928.2
SDRs	1b.s	.2	.4	.2	.4	1.0	–	.2	.1	.8	1.4	3.4	6.4
Reserve Position in the Fund	1c.s	–	–	–	–	–	–	–	65.5	89.9	157.4	304.0	354.8
Total Fund Cred.&Loans Outstg.	2tl	178.6	178.6	178.6	111.7	22.3	–	–	–	–	–	–	–
International Liquidity		\multicolumn{12}{c}{*Millions of US Dollars Unless Otherwise Indicated: End of Period*}
Total Reserves minus Gold	1l.d	5,127.4	6,382.6	6,792.4	8,119.3	11,414.6	20,332.1	22,674.3	22,604.9	23,281.2	23,378.6	24,082.9	26,315.1
SDRs	1b.d	.3	.5	.4	.6	1.4	–	.3	.2	1.1	1.7	4.6	9.5
Reserve Position in the Fund	1c.d	–	–	–	–	–	–	–	89.9	117.1	197.8	413.3	527.2
Foreign Exchange	1d.d	5,127.1	6,382.1	6,792.0	8,118.7	11,413.2	†20,332.0	22,674.0	22,514.8	23,163.0	23,179.1	23,665.0	25,778.4
Gold (Million Fine Troy Ounces)	1ad	.009	.009	.009	.009	.009	.009	–	–	–	–	–	–
Gold (National Valuation)	1and	.4	.4	.4	.5	.4	.4	–	–	–	–	–	–
Monetary Authorities: Other Liab.	4..d	37.7	38.5	37.8	38.6	38.1	30.0	21.9	17.8	18.1	17.0	16.0	15.5
Deposit Money Banks: Assets	7a.d	10,608.7	10,137.7	11,330.0	12,055.9	12,945.4	10,823.5	12,746.6	14,146.6	16,095.4	15,644.9	14,475.2	17,936.1
Liabilities	7b.d	12,093.0	12,159.1	13,098.9	14,514.4	15,113.4	16,738.3	18,334.0	20,452.0	21,872.6	22,106.4	21,821.6	21,796.1
Monetary Authorities		\multicolumn{12}{c}{*Millions of New Sheqalim: End of Period*}
Foreign Assets	11	14,186	19,065	20,508	25,578	37,130	70,970	94,326	93,878	94,084	103,248	114,102	115,275
Claims on Central Government	12a	10,419	10,338	9,976	10,818	12,304	12,199	12,288	12,416	12,530	12,204	11,056	10,048
Claims on Deposit Money Banks	12e	11,053	16,972	15,555	4,503	1,236	1,519	838	810	787	802	3,006	2,727
Reserve Money	14	21,901	28,051	26,166	19,157	25,838	56,659	64,802	80,218	80,706	81,237	68,440	63,312
of which: Currency Outside DMBs	14a	†4,113	4,852	5,467	6,731	7,772	8,767	10,051	12,178	12,347	14,580	15,580	16,184
Foreign Cur.Deps.	14cf	15,893	20,203	16,413	10,119	7,982	7,633	7,931	10,741	9,100	10,773	7,066	2,624
Foreign Liabilities	16c	783	848	901	641	228	106	91	74	73	75	76	68
Central Government Deposits	16d	11,694	16,165	17,456	19,325	23,013	26,509	39,407	32,242	37,369	39,290	51,914	62,643
Other Items (Net)	17r	1,280	1,311	1,516	1,775	1,591	1,414	3,152	–5,430	–10,747	–4,348	7,734	2,027
Deposit Money Banks		\multicolumn{12}{c}{*Millions of New Sheqalim: End of Period*}
Reserves	20	†17,854	23,223	20,743	12,425	18,085	48,103	54,578	68,029	67,882	65,788	52,630	46,825
Foreign Assets	21	29,322	30,271	34,194	37,795	42,086	38,272	53,038	58,751	65,041	69,088	68,569	78,542
Claims on Central Government	22a	†62,094	65,080	66,289	69,960	77,542	66,136	63,806	61,984	44,464	43,883	45,563	49,349
Claims on Private Sector	22d	†94,092	121,800	154,285	185,123	219,842	254,886	303,434	347,382	390,938	439,228	480,467	462,949
Demand Deposits	24	†6,324	8,526	8,946	9,870	12,227	13,502	14,937	17,933	18,536	23,053	22,619	26,483
Time and Savings Deposits	25	†89,564	104,678	139,899	171,485	217,117	251,747	306,960	352,568	381,425	412,502	451,051	439,538
Restricted Deposits	26b	†29,879	28,775	28,730	22,979	21,481	19,368	17,063	13,593	11,002	6,489	8,147	6,366
Foreign Liabilities	26c	33,425	36,307	39,533	45,503	49,134	59,187	76,288	84,937	88,387	97,622	103,369	95,445
Central Government Deposits	26d	†15,147	19,604	23,211	26,684	27,590	28,190	24,286	24,300	21,082	22,058	25,412	23,391
Credit from Monetary Authorities	26g	†11,053	16,896	15,569	4,212	1,186	1,506	835	814	787	806	3,004	2,725
Other Items (Net)	27r	†17,972	25,587	19,621	24,570	28,821	33,895	34,486	42,001	47,106	55,462	33,631	43,715
Monetary Survey		\multicolumn{12}{c}{*Millions of New Sheqalim: End of Period*}
Foreign Assets (Net)	31n	9,300	12,181	14,268	17,229	29,854	49,949	70,986	67,618	70,665	74,639	79,226	98,304
Domestic Credit	32	†139,765	161,448	189,882	219,891	259,086	278,521	315,834	365,240	389,482	433,967	459,760	436,312
Claims on Central Govt. (Net)	32an	†45,673	39,649	35,598	34,768	39,244	23,635	12,401	17,858	–1,457	–5,261	–20,707	–26,637
Claims on Private Sector	32d	†94,092	121,800	154,285	185,123	219,842	254,886	303,434	347,382	390,938	439,228	480,467	462,949
Money	34	†10,541	13,486	14,523	16,716	20,131	22,401	25,145	30,263	31,030	37,796	38,364	42,838
Quasi-Money	35	†100,085	121,441	153,587	187,829	235,519	271,480	326,491	376,013	407,831	442,567	475,268	470,048
Restricted Deposits	36b	†29,879	28,775	28,730	22,979	21,481	19,368	17,063	13,593	11,002	6,489	8,147	6,366
Other Items (Net)	37r	†8,560	9,928	7,310	9,596	11,809	15,221	18,120	12,990	10,283	21,759	17,211	15,362
Money plus Quasi-Money	35l	†110,626	134,926	168,109	204,545	255,650	293,881	351,636	406,276	438,862	480,363	513,632	512,886
Interest Rates		\multicolumn{12}{c}{*Percent Per Annum*}
Discount Rate	60	10.4	9.8	17.0	14.2	15.3	13.7	13.5	11.2	8.2	5.7	9.2	5.2
Treasury Bill Rate	60c	11.8	10.5	11.8	14.4	15.3	13.4	11.3	11.4	8.8	6.5	7.4	7.0
Deposit Rate	60l	11.3	10.4	12.2	14.1	14.5	13.1	11.0	11.3	8.6	6.2	6.0	6.6
Lending Rate	60p	19.9	16.4	17.4	20.2	20.7	18.7	16.2	16.4	12.9	10.0	9.9	10.7

Israel 436

		1992	1993	1994	1995	1996	1997	1998	1999	2000	2001	2002	2003
Prices, Production, Labor		\multicolumn{12}{c}{*Index Numbers (2000=100): Period Averages*}
Share Prices....................	62	43.7	61.6	37.3	42.6	42.9	58.4	60.0	99.5	100.0	93.1	74.3	115.7
Prices: Industrial Products...........	63	58.0	62.8	67.7	74.9	81.4	86.5	90.1	96.5	100.0	99.9	103.8	108.2
Consumer Prices.................	64	53.6	†59.5	66.8	73.5	81.8	89.1	94.0	98.9	†100.0	101.1	†106.8	107.6
Wages: Daily Earnings.............	65	43.3	47.7	52.8	60.5	68.9	79.2	87.1	94.1	100.0	108.6	109.7	111.9
Industrial Production, Seas. Adj.....	66..c	66.3	70.4	†75.8	81.7	85.9	87.6	90.0	91.1	100.0	95.6	93.4	93.0
Industrial Employment............	67	89.8	93.6	†96.9	100.6	102.2	101.1	100.2	98.7	100.0	97.2	93.3	91.0
		\multicolumn{12}{c}{*Number in Thousands: Period Averages*}
Labor Force.....................	67d	1,858	1,946	2,030	†2,110	2,157	2,210	†2,266	2,345	2,435	2,499	2,547	2,610
Employment...................	67e	1,650	1,751	1,871	†1,965	2,013	2,040	†2,073	2,137	2,221	2,261	2,283	2,330
Unemployment.................	67c	208	195	158	†145	144	170	†193	208	214	233	262	280
Unemployment Rate (%)...........	67r	11.2	10.0	7.8	†6.9	6.7	7.7	†8.6	8.9	8.8	9.3	10.3	10.7
International Transactions		\multicolumn{12}{c}{*Millions of US Dollars*}
Exports........................	70..d	10,019	14,826	16,884	19,046	20,610	22,503	22,993	25,794	31,404	29,048	29,347	31,577
Imports, c.i.f...................	71..d	15,535	22,624	25,237	29,579	31,620	30,781	29,342	33,166	31,404	35,449	35,517	36,282
Imports,c.i.f.,excl. Military Gds.....	71.md	18,814	20,518	23,776	28,287	29,951	29,084	27,470	31,090	35,750	33,303	33,106	34,213
		\multicolumn{12}{c}{*2000=100*}
Volume of Exports...............	72	42.0	47.2	54.6	58.6	†63.0	69.4	73.6	79.7	100.0	†95.9	96.9	99.7
Volume of Imports...............	73	50.4	56.9	64.5	70.9	†75.6	76.6	76.8	88.0	100.0	†92.6	93.4	91.9
Unit Value of Exports(US$)........	74..d	99.0	99.5	98.0	102.7	†102.7	101.8	98.8	99.9	100.0	†96.4	96.4	100.6
Unit Value of Imports(US$)........	75..d	104.2	100.7	102.8	111.5	†110.7	105.7	99.9	97.0	100.0	†98.6	98.5	104.4
Balance of Payments		\multicolumn{12}{c}{*Millions of US Dollars: Minus Sign Indicates Debit*}
Current Account, n.i.e.............	78ald	−875	−2,480	−3,447	−4,647	−5,124	−3,289	−1,149	−3,335	−2,972	−1,778	−1,320	665
Goods: Exports f.o.b.............	78aad	13,621	14,926	17,242	19,694	21,515	22,867	23,190	25,882	31,012	27,795	27,326	30,155
Goods: Imports f.o.b.............	78abd	−18,389	−20,533	−22,728	−26,890	−28,469	−27,875	−26,241	−30,042	−34,045	−31,003	−31,219	−32,333
Trade Balance.................	78acd	−4,769	−5,607	−5,486	−7,196	−6,954	−5,008	−3,051	−4,160	−3,034	−3,208	−3,894	−2,177
Services: Credit.................	78add	5,811	5,967	6,579	7,788	8,027	8,734	9,490	7,246	10,339	9,205	8,780	10,227
Services: Debit..................	78aed	−5,545	−6,397	−7,590	−8,401	−9,107	−9,299	−9,636	−8,142	−9,702	−9,482	−8,952	−9,404
Balance on Goods & Services......	78afd	−4,502	−6,037	−6,497	−7,808	−8,034	−5,573	−3,197	−5,056	−2,397	−3,485	−4,065	−1,354
Income: Credit..................	78agd	1,599	1,295	1,160	1,751	1,832	2,068	2,508	2,815	3,683	2,574	2,464	2,214
Income: Debit..................	78ahd	−3,651	−3,344	−3,711	−4,263	−5,058	−5,834	−6,537	−7,407	−10,740	−7,560	−6,485	−6,573
Balance on Gds, Serv. & Inc......	78aid	−6,553	−8,087	−9,048	−10,320	−11,260	−9,339	−7,226	−9,648	−9,455	−8,470	−8,086	−5,712
Current Transfers, n.i.e.: Credit.....	78ajd	6,002	5,911	5,850	5,941	6,440	6,377	6,683	7,122	7,468	7,799	8,128	7,499
Current Transfers: Debit..........	78akd	−324	−304	−250	−268	−304	−328	−606	−809	−985	−1,107	−1,362	−1,122
Capital Account, n.i.e.............	78bcd	1,070	863	786	609	576	552	397	569	455	679	151	458
Capital Account, n.i.e.: Credit......	78bad	1,070	863	786	609	576	552	397	569	455	679	151	458
Capital Account: Debit...........	78bbd	–	–	–	–	–	–	–	–	–	–	–	–
Financial Account, n.i.e............	78bjd	−451	1,041	−959	4,206	4,537	7,207	−172	2,875	3,165	1,241	−1,527	−2,527
Direct Investment Abroad.........	78bdd	−580	−615	−742	−820	−815	−923	−1,125	−959	−3,465	−630	−1,116	−1,773
Dir. Invest. in Rep. Econ., n.i.e.....	78bed	589	605	442	1,351	1,398	1,635	1,737	3,112	5,012	3,548	1,723	3,672
Portfolio Investment Assets........	78bfd	−1,183	−812	−1,772	98	368	215	106	−674	−2,805	−1,623	−2,686	−3,078
Equity Securities..............	78bkd	−926	80	303	16	160	166	154	385	−1,536	−421	−583	−838
Debt Securities................	78bld	−257	−891	−2,075	82	208	49	−47	−1,058	−1,270	−1,201	−2,102	−2,240
Portfolio Investment Liab., n.i.e......	78bgd	−40	276	481	978	1,438	1,712	423	1,461	4,408	567	441	384
Equity Securities..............	78bmd	−32	284	469	991	1,440	1,719	476	1,502	4,408	567	441	384
Debt Securities...............	78bnd	−8	−7	13	−13	−2	−7	−53	−41	–	–	–	–
Financial Derivatives Assets........	78bwd	–	–	–	–	–	–	–	−122	663	510	193	339
Financial Derivatives Liabilities.....	78bxd	–	–	–	–	–	–	–	–	–	–	–	–
Other Investment Assets..........	78bhd	−1,143	1,003	−1,063	−586	845	1,600	−1,595	−2,095	−2,126	−2,649	−1,063	−1,634
Monetary Authorities...........	78bod	....	....	....	....	....	....	....	−458	−1	−561	110	−14
General Government...........	78bpd	78	261	−28	−1,230	864	−19	−13	−736	−1,189	−392	340	−1,255
Banks.......................	78bqd	−1,657	940	−1,736	−216	−1,165	1,686	−1,808	−902	−936	−1,696	−1,514	−365
Other Sectors.................	78brd	436	−197	701	860	1,146	−66	225	2,152	1,478	1,517	982	−438
Other Investment Liab., n.i.e.......	78bid	1,907	583	1,695	3,185	1,303	2,969	282	–	–	–	–	–
Monetary Authorities...........	78bsd	–	–	–	–	–	–	–	329	−75	122	13	184
General Government...........	78btd	905	225	−64	215	77	−272	−383	2,343	1,657	1,271	117	−558
Banks.......................	78bud	692	280	1,000	1,219	612	2,352	1,525	−520	−104	124	853	−63
Other Sectors.................	78bvd	310	78	760	1,751	615	889	−859	−1,147	−1,240	386	2,579	−432
Net Errors and Omissions.........	78cad	−1,220	249	1,510	312	1,218	2,606	769	−1,039	−592	527	−117	−1,835
Overall Balance................	78cbd	−1,476	−327	−2,111	480	1,206	7,077	−155	1,039	592	−527	117	1,835
Reserves and Related Items........	79dad	1,476	327	2,111	−480	−1,206	−7,077	155	−94	−33	−86	−190	−74
Reserve Assets.................	79dbd	1,444	−1,533	−124	−1,123	−3,413	−9,378	−1,880	–	–	–	–	–
Use of Fund Credit and Loans......	79dcd	245	–	–	−101	−129	−31	–	1,133	624	−441	308	1,909
Exceptional Financing............	79ded	−212	1,861	2,235	745	2,336	2,332	2,036	1,133	624	−441	308	1,909

2004, International Monetary Fund : International Financial Statistics Yearbook

Israel 436

		1992	1993	1994	1995	1996	1997	1998	1999	2000	2001	2002	2003
International Investment Position						*Millions of US Dollars*							
Assets	79aad	19,720	21,944	26,345	30,754	34,751	44,602	50,536	60,484	69,192	72,296	77,965	87,628
Direct Investment Abroad	79abd	–	–	–	2,867	3,283	5,223	5,376	6,417	9,353	9,461	10,622	12,132
Portfolio Investment	79acd	1,219	2,518	2,866	2,801	2,609	2,711	3,027	4,983	7,281	7,975	10,162	13,844
Equity Securities	79add	–	–	374	430	356	447	499	1,432	2,506	2,024	1,747	2,949
Debt Securities	79aed	1,219	2,518	2,492	2,371	2,253	2,264	2,528	3,551	4,775	5,951	8,415	10,895
Financial Derivatives	79ald	–	–	–	–	–	–	–	–	–	–	–	–
Other Investment	79afd	13,168	12,656	16,315	16,698	17,211	16,264	19,384	26,409	29,201	31,397	33,009	35,028
Monetary Authorities	79agd	–	–	–	–	–	–	–	–	–	–	–	–
General Government	79ahd	–	–	–	222	104	242	387	656	515	409	347	626
Banks	79aid	8,935	7,776	9,789	10,262	11,223	9,155	11,070	11,571	12,613	12,887	12,900	14,710
Other Sectors	79ajd	4,233	4,880	6,526	6,214	5,884	6,867	7,927	14,182	16,073	18,101	19,762	19,693
Reserve Assets	79akd	5,333	6,770	7,164	8,387	11,648	20,404	22,749	22,675	23,357	23,463	24,172	26,625
Liabilities	79lad	39,086	40,969	47,586	58,088	64,169	74,593	77,755	107,229	118,026	107,330	104,466	123,025
Dir. Invest. in Rep. Economy	79lbd	353	402	474	5,741	7,096	9,315	10,507	20,586	24,319	25,115	24,807	31,752
Portfolio Investment	79lcd	5,461	7,315	12,437	14,998	19,427	25,754	27,047	43,805	49,786	37,051	32,455	43,319
Equity Securities	79ldd	–	–	2,893	4,706	6,806	10,789	9,912	25,658	31,117	18,970	13,826	22,323
Debt Securities	79led	5,461	7,315	9,544	10,292	12,621	14,965	17,135	18,147	18,669	18,081	18,629	20,996
Financial Derivatives	79lld	–	–	–	–	–	–	–	–	–	–	–	–
Other Investment	79lfd	33,272	33,253	34,676	37,350	37,647	39,524	40,201	42,838	43,921	45,164	47,204	47,954
Monetary Authorities	79lgd	284	284	317	235	98	30	21	17	17	16	16	16
General Government	79lhd	12,946	13,023	12,944	13,335	13,289	12,724	12,614	12,845	12,676	12,754	12,904	13,098
Banks	79lid	11,986	12,211	13,500	14,958	15,428	17,470	19,129	21,218	22,668	23,790	24,505	24,745
Other Sectors	79ljd	8,057	7,736	7,915	8,822	8,832	9,300	8,436	8,759	8,559	8,604	9,779	10,096
Government Finance						*Millions of New Sheqalim: Year Ending December 31*							
Deficit (-) or Surplus	80	†–6,949	–4,675	–6,882	–11,971	–13,253	1,017	–5,519	–8,698	4,019	–17,270	....	....
Revenue	81	†63,295	73,482	88,559	108,032	123,796	145,110	159,911	173,187	194,736	195,376	....	....
Grants Received	81z	†9,074	8,229	7,927	6,340	12,953	11,437	12,158	12,327	11,957	11,534	....	....
Expenditure	82	†78,163	86,273	102,350	125,369	149,571	165,250	183,046	197,954	208,603	224,287	....	....
Lending Minus Repayments	83	†1,155	113	1,018	974	431	–9,720	–5,458	–3,742	–5,929	–107	....	....
Financing													
Domestic	84a	†4,864	–273	655	12,615	7,431	–5,091	538	11,602	–1,783	17,750	....	....
Foreign	85a	†2,085	4,948	6,227	–644	5,822	4,074	4,981	–2,904	–2,236	–480	....	....
Debt: Domestic	88a	168,248	188,706	211,726	240,333	277,034	292,401	318,398	330,062	328,534	348,388	....	....
Foreign	89a	54,742	64,112	71,069	75,083	83,673	92,523	114,261	113,472	111,644	121,212	....	....
National Accounts						*Millions of New Sheqalim*							
Househ.Cons.Expend.,incl.NPISHs	96f	97,926	116,158	141,769	†157,290	182,397	201,913	220,881	240,541	262,194	272,252	288,794	295,385
Government Consumption Expend	91f	46,138	53,486	64,081	†79,683	94,358	104,943	114,544	124,669	132,581	141,411	154,182	151,606
Gross Fixed Capital Formation	93e	39,633	44,759	55,333	†68,596	79,270	83,894	85,763	92,225	93,032	90,739	90,914	88,485
Changes in Inventories	93i	2,122	4,736	3,094	†2,796	1,983	2,411	3,140	6,402	8,905	10,230	2,057	–3,668
Exports of Goods and Services	90c	49,899	61,021	73,553	†83,071	94,462	109,236	124,176	155,163	186,731	167,357	182,796	192,762
Imports of Goods and Services (-)	98c	71,104	89,753	106,579	†121,717	136,975	145,745	154,368	189,082	212,710	204,191	225,035	222,586
Gross Domestic Product (GDP)	99b	164,614	190,407	231,251	†269,719	315,495	356,651	394,136	429,918	470,733	477,797	493,707	501,984
Net Primary Income from Abroad	98.n	–3,267	–3,306	–3,722	†4,387	6,799	9,899	12,416	15,584	25,749	17,251	15,269	14,903
Gross National Income (GNI)	99a	161,347	187,101	227,529	†265,332	308,696	346,752	381,720	414,334	444,984	460,546	478,438	487,081
Consumption of Fixed Capital	99cf	22,472	26,814	31,886	†39,305	45,086	52,128	59,257	67,373	70,043	75,003	85,906	87,952
Net National Income	99e	138,875	160,287	195,643	†226,027	263,610	294,624	322,463	346,961	374,941	385,543	392,532	399,129
GDP Volume 1990 Prices	99b.p	119,157	122,965	131,280	140,540	....	....	....	....	....	....	....	....
GDP Volume 2000 Prices	99b.p	....	....	....	†376,496	396,148	409,975	425,289	435,787	470,730	466,514	463,128	469,114
GDP Volume (2000=100)	99bvp	67.8	70.0	74.7	†80.0	84.2	87.1	90.3	92.6	100.0	99.1	98.4	99.7
GDP Deflator (2000=100)	99bip	51.6	57.8	65.8	†71.6	79.6	87.0	92.7	98.7	100.0	102.4	106.6	107.0
						Millions: Midyear Estimates							
Population	99z	4.82	5.00	5.18	5.35	5.50	5.65	5.78	5.91	6.04	6.17	6.30	6.43

Italy 136

		1992	1993	1994	1995	1996	1997	1998	1999	2000	2001	2002	2003
Exchange Rates		Lire per SDR through 1998, Euros per SDR Thereafter: End of Period											
Market Rate	aa	2,022.4	2,340.5	2,379.2	2,355.7	2,200.9	2,373.6	2,327.6	1.3662	1.4002	1.4260	1.2964	1.1765
		Lire per US Dollar through 1998, Euros per US Dollar Thereafter: End of Period (ae) Period Average (rf)											
Market Rate	ae	1,470.9	1,704.0	1,629.7	1,584.7	1,530.6	1,759.2	1,653.1	.9954	1.0747	1.1347	.9536	.7918
Market Rate	rf	1,232.4	1,573.7	1,612.4	1,628.9	1,542.9	1,703.1	1,736.2	.9386	1.0854	1.1175	1.0626	.8860
		Lire per ECU: End of Period (ea) Period Average (eb)											
ECU Rate	ea	1,787.4	1,908.4	1,997.5	2,082.7	1,913.7	1,940.7	1,936.3	....	....	....	....	....
ECU Rate	eb	1,587.5	1,841.6	1,913.9	2,131.3	1,958.6	1,929.7	1,943.7	....	....	....	....	....
		Index Numbers (2000=100): Period Averages											
Market Rate (1995=100)	ahx	132.7	103.6	101.1	100.0	105.5	95.7	93.9	....	....	....	....	....
Nominal Effective Exchange Rate	neu	132.2	111.2	106.4	95.9	104.9	105.6	105.2	103.3	100.0	100.4	101.2	104.6
Real Effective Exchange Rate	reu	122.0	104.1	98.4	90.6	103.8	106.1	104.0	103.6	100.0	99.3	100.8	104.8
Fund Position		Millions of SDRs: End of Period											
Quota	2f.s	4,591	4,591	4,591	4,591	4,591	4,591	4,591	7,056	7,056	7,056	7,056	7,056
SDRs	1b.s	173	175	86	–	20	50	79	122	182	236	79	105
Reserve Position in the Fund	1c.s	1,774	1,575	1,393	1,321	1,290	1,661	3,075	2,584	2,230	2,560	2,874	2,796
of which: Outstg.Fund Borrowing	2c	–	–	–	–	–	–	257	–	–	–	–	–
Total Fund Cred.&Loans Outstg.	2tl	–	–	–	–	–	–	–					
International Liquidity		Millions of US Dollars Unless Otherwise Indicated: End of Period											
Total Res.Min.Gold (Eurosys.Def)	1l.d	27,643	27,545	32,265	34,905	45,948	55,739	29,888	†22,422	25,567	24,419	28,603	30,366
SDRs	1b.d	238	241	125	–	29	67	111	168	238	297	108	156
Reserve Position in the Fund	1c.d	2,439	2,164	2,033	1,963	1,855	2,241	4,330	3,546	2,906	3,217	3,907	4,154
Foreign Exchange	1d.d	24,966	25,140	30,107	32,942	44,064	53,431	25,447	†18,708	22,423	20,905	24,588	26,056
o/w:Fin.Deriv.Rel.to Reserves	1ddd	....	....	....	....	....	....	....	–	–	–	–	–
Other Reserve Assets	1e.d	....	....	....	....	....	....	....					
Gold (Million Fine Troy Ounces)	1ad	66.67	66.67	66.67	66.67	66.67	66.67	83.36	78.83	78.83	78.83	78.83	78.83
Gold (Eurosystem Valuation)	1and	23,175	23,593	26,342	25,570	25,369	21,806	24,711	22,880	21,635	21,796	27,019	32,891
Memo:Euro Cl. on Non-EA Res.	1dgd	....	....	....	....	....	....	....	1	476	451	537	125
Non-Euro Cl. on EA Res.	1dhd	....	....	....	....	....	....	....	3,620	2,812	4,814	5,556	8,145
Mon. Auth.: Other Foreign Assets	3..d	....	....	....	....	....	....	....					
Foreign Liabilities	4..d	6,282	1,543	1,510	2,598	1,249	1,123	1,045	†6,315	235	2,198	3,078	509
Banking Insts.: Foreign Assets	7a.d	112,306	134,425	123,919	145,842	193,215	177,149	193,743	†90,837	85,886	75,040	94,258	118,060
Foreign Liab.	7b.d	249,851	217,128	230,505	216,808	237,872	223,249	236,896	†136,369	146,783	150,863	153,427	202,998
Monetary Authorities		Trillions of Lire through 1998; Billions of Euros Beginning 1999: End of Period											
Fgn. Assets (Cl.on Non-EA Ctys)	11	76.54	86.57	93.90	95.59	108.65	135.62	90.33	45.80	50.49	52.42	52.74	49.88
Claims on General Government	12a.u	....	....	....	....	....	....	....	60.12	63.25	65.06	44.49	53.72
o/w: Claims on Gen.Govt.in Cty.	12a	161.75	170.23	195.88	196.42	168.95	174.17	156.37	60.12	63.25	65.06	44.49	53.72
Claims on Banking Institutions	12e.u	....	....	....	....	....	....	....	51.35	36.49	33.51	19.96	22.48
o/w: Claims on Bank.Inst.in Cty.	12e	49.28	44.94	42.50	41.04	50.03	32.30	11.04	36.01	26.53	10.70	7.76	9.72
Claims on Other Resident Sectors	12d.u	....	....	....	....	....	....	....	7.36	8.29	6.75	5.28	5.75
o/w: Cl. on Oth.Res.Sect.in Cty.	12d	.10	4.35	.56	2.64	–	–	–	7.13	8.06	6.49	5.25	5.74
Currency Issued	14a	90.85	95.23	101.86	105.22	108.16	116.27	124.88	71.96	76.42	65.89	65.49	76.09
Liabilities to Banking Insts.	14c.u	....	....	....	....	....	....	....	24.84	25.52	26.28	18.43	18.03
o/w: Liabs to Bank.Inst.in Cty.	14c	127.97	104.19	87.54	72.30	73.69	79.08	13.78	9.23	7.75	26.28	10.45	10.30
Demand Dep. of Other Res.Sect.	14d.u	....	....	....	....	....	....	....	.39	.08	.23	.01	.08
o/w:D.Dep.of Oth.Res.Sect.in Cty.	14d	....	....	....	....	....	....	....	.39	.08	.23	.01	.08
Other Dep. of Other Res.Sect.	15..u	....	....	....	....	....	....	....	–	–	–	–	–
o/w:O.Dep.of Oth.Res.Sect.in Cty.	15	....	....	....	....	....	....	....	–	–	–	–	–
Bonds & Money Mkt. Instruments	16n.u	....	....	....	....	....	....	....	....	....	....	....	....
o/w: Bonds Held by Resid.of Cty.	16n	1.30	1.22	1.47	1.99	1.66	1.20	.92					
Foreign Liab. (to Non-EA Ctys)	16c	9.24	2.63	2.46	4.12	1.91	1.98	1.73	6.29	.25	2.49	2.94	.40
Central Government Deposits	16d.u	....	....	....	....	....	....	....	29.08	19.37	23.46	21.32	13.30
o/w: Cent.Govt.Dep. in Cty.	16d	–	30.67	63.94	72.13	54.76	57.78	42.21	29.08	19.37	23.46	21.32	13.30
Capital Accounts	17a	69.80	84.36	90.66	94.79	99.84	98.93	75.85	35.37	40.44	41.46	25.26	25.02
Other Items (Net)	17r	−11.51	−12.21	−15.09	−14.85	−12.39	−13.15	−1.61	−3.30	−3.56	−2.09	−10.98	−1.08
Memo: Net Claims on Eurosystem	12e.s	....	....	....	....	....	....	....	−3.85	−10.31	18.16	−6.15	−5.95
Currency Put into Circ	14m	....	....	....	....	....	....	....	....	....	....	71.23	81.78

2004, International Monetary Fund : *International Financial Statistics Yearbook*

Italy 136

		1992	1993	1994	1995	1996	1997	1998	1999	2000	2001	2002	2003
Banking Institutions		*Trillions of Lire through 1998; Billions of Euros Beginning 1999: End of Period*											
Claims on Monetary Authorities.......	20	133.29	109.65	93.29	79.31	81.70	87.81	23.65	9.90	8.16	25.73	10.34	10.38
Claims on Bk.Inst.in Oth.EA Ctys......	20b.u	....	....	....	....	....	....	....	67.89	69.20	62.36	86.55	91.85
Fgn. Assets (Cl.on Non-EA Ctys).......	21	165.19	229.06	201.96	231.12	295.73	311.64	320.28	90.42	92.30	85.15	89.88	93.48
Claims on General Government........	22a.u	....	....	....	....	....	....	....	243.13	211.34	211.95	207.66	237.55
o/w: Claims on Gen.Govt.in Cty.....	22a	355.88	404.16	434.80	413.46	442.92	408.43	395.40	240.00	206.65	207.15	201.86	219.97
Claims on Other Resident Sectors....	22d.u	....	....	....	....	....	....	....	811.05	926.19	997.04	1,063.70	1,148.02
o/w: Cl. on Oth.Res.Sect.in Cty.........	22d	942.92	969.94	983.66	1,027.70	1,060.42	1,123.53	1,224.36	788.23	896.82	966.60	1,030.75	1,110.72
Demand Deposits...........................	24..u	....	....	....	....	....	....	....	386.95	410.65	449.75	492.52	519.67
o/w:D.Dep.of Oth.Res.Sect.in Cty...	24	426.20	454.92	471.38	471.06	498.87	531.72	601.15	384.91	407.91	446.12	488.03	515.70
Other Deposits................................	25..u	....	....	....	....	....	....	....	194.71	194.55	192.43	205.83	181.74
o/w:O.Dep.of Oth.Res.Sect.in Cty...	25	430.86	469.88	458.91	476.50	469.39	359.51	287.75	190.61	190.26	190.54	201.04	177.08
Money Market Fund Shares.............	26m.u	....	....	....	....	....	....	....	13.06	10.04	26.10	41.69	106.70
Bonds & Money Mkt. Instruments....	26n.u	....	....	....	....	....	....	....	271.55	302.48	334.67	367.97	399.14
o/w: Held by Resid.of Cty............	26n	265.77	289.91	303.38	341.95	399.97	510.23	544.00	....	....	....	....	....
Foreign Liab. (to Non-EA Ctys).......	26c	367.50	369.98	375.66	343.58	364.08	392.74	391.61	135.75	157.75	171.18	146.30	160.73
Central Government Deposits.........	26d.u	....	....	....	....	....	....	....	7.96	7.00	7.51	7.12	7.75
o/w: Cent.Govt.Dep. in Cty...........	26d	10.73	13.40	13.23	9.29	11.15	12.73	13.40	7.92	6.96	7.21	7.11	7.73
Credit from Monetary Authorities.....	26g	49.28	44.94	42.50	41.04	50.03	32.30	11.04	33.29	26.46	10.81	7.62	9.16
Liab. to Bk.Inst.in Oth. EA Ctys......	26h.u	....	....	....	....	....	....	....	98.65	107.61	109.57	111.65	117.40
Capital Accounts............................	27a	189.99	206.02	219.39	232.44	250.19	257.05	280.93	118.27	123.93	133.63	146.17	156.87
Other Items (Net)..........................	27r	−143.06	−136.25	−170.74	−164.29	−162.91	−164.86	−166.20	−37.79	−33.28	−53.44	−68.74	−77.88
Post Office: Checking Deposits.......	24..i	9.34	9.48	8.16	8.49	7.28	6.67	1.66	....	....	....	....	....
Post Office: Savings Deposits........	25..i	29.06	30.86	39.15	43.94	46.26	52.00	58.33	....	....	....	....	....
Savings Certif..................	26abi	66.58	72.16	87.05	97.77	110.61	117.35	121.65	....	....	....	....	....
Banking Survey (Nat'l Residency)		*Trillions of Lire through 1998; Billions of Euros Beginning 1999: End of Period*											
Foreign Assets (Net)......................	31n	−135.01	−56.99	−82.27	−20.99	38.39	52.54	17.26	−11.03	−27.51	−23.60	9.43	13.91
Domestic Credit.............................	32	1,554.88	1,617.11	1,672.10	1,708.99	1,770.52	1,811.64	1,902.18	1,058.49	1,148.44	1,214.62	1,253.91	1,369.13
Claims on General Govt. (Net)......	32an	611.86	642.82	687.88	678.65	710.10	688.11	677.82	263.13	243.56	241.53	217.92	252.66
Claims on Other Resident Sectors.....	32d	943.01	974.29	984.22	1,030.34	1,060.42	1,123.53	1,224.36	795.36	904.89	973.09	1,036.00	1,116.46
Currency Issued.............................	34a.n	100.19	104.71	110.02	113.71	115.44	122.94	126.54	71.96	76.42	65.89	65.49	76.09
Demand Deposits..........................	34b.n	426.20	454.92	471.38	471.06	498.87	531.72	601.15	385.30	407.99	446.35	488.03	515.78
Other Deposits...............................	35..n	459.92	500.75	498.06	520.44	515.65	411.52	346.08	190.61	190.26	190.54	201.04	177.08
Money Market Fund Shares.............	36m	....	....	....	....	....	....	....	13.06	10.04	26.10	41.69	106.70
Bonds & Money Mkt. Instruments....	36n	333.65	363.30	391.90	441.72	512.24	628.77	666.57	271.55	302.48	334.67	367.97	399.14
o/w: Over Two Years.................	36na	....	....	....	....	....	....	....	259.05	289.12	322.13	353.93	387.97
Capital Accounts............................	37a	259.79	290.37	310.05	327.22	350.03	355.99	356.78	153.63	164.37	175.10	171.43	181.89
Other Items (Net)..........................	37r	−159.89	−153.92	−191.58	−186.14	−183.31	−186.74	−177.68	−38.66	−30.63	−47.64	−72.32	−73.64
Banking Survey (EA-Wide Residency)		*Billions of Euros: End of Period*											
Foreign Assets (Net)......................	31n.u	....	....	....	....	....	....	....	−5.81	−15.21	−36.11	−6.62	−17.77
Domestic Credit.............................	32..u	....	....	....	....	....	....	....	1,084.62	1,182.69	1,249.82	1,292.69	1,424.00
Claims on General Govt. (Net)......	32anu	....	....	....	....	....	....	....	266.21	248.22	246.04	223.71	270.23
Claims on Other Resident Sect.......	32d.u	....	....	....	....	....	....	....	818.41	934.47	1,003.78	1,068.98	1,153.77
Currency Issued.............................	34a.u	....	....	....	....	....	....	....	71.96	76.42	65.89	65.49	76.09
Demand Deposits..........................	34b.u	....	....	....	....	....	....	....	387.33	410.74	449.98	492.53	519.75
Other Deposits...............................	35..u	....	....	....	....	....	....	....	194.71	194.55	192.43	205.83	181.74
o/w: Other Dep. Over Two Yrs...	35abu	....	....	....	....	....	....	....	17.00	11.49	6.41	4.07	4.42
Money Market Fund Shares.............	36m.u	....	....	....	....	....	....	....	13.06	10.04	26.10	41.69	106.70
Bonds & Money Mkt. Instruments....	36n.u	....	....	....	....	....	....	....	271.55	302.48	334.67	367.97	399.14
o/w: Over Two Years.................	36nau	....	....	....	....	....	....	....	259.05	289.12	322.13	353.93	387.97
Capital Accounts............................	37a	....	....	....	....	....	....	....	153.63	164.37	175.10	171.43	181.89
Other Items (Net)..........................	37r.u	....	....	....	....	....	....	....	−13.44	8.89	−30.46	−58.87	−59.07
Money (National Definitions)		*Trillions of Lire: End of Period*											
M2..	39m	814.20	841.32	847.42	834.15	863.29	930.99	975.34	....	....	....	....	....
Interest Rates		*Percent Per Annum*											
Discount Rate (End of Period).........	60	12.00	8.00	7.50	9.00	7.50	5.50	3.00	....	....	....	....	....
Money Market Rate.......................	60b	14.02	10.20	8.51	10.46	8.82	6.88	4.99	2.95	4.39	4.26	3.32	2.33
Treasury Bill Rate..........................	60c	14.32	10.58	9.17	10.85	8.46	6.33	4.59	3.01	4.53	4.05	3.26	2.19
Deposit Rate.................................	60l	7.11	† 7.79	6.20	6.45	6.49	4.83	3.16	1.61	1.84	1.96	1.43	.95
Lending Rate................................	60p	15.76	13.87	11.22	12.47	12.06	9.75	7.88	5.58	6.26	6.53	5.78	5.03
Govt Bond Yield (Long-Term)..........	61	13.27	11.31	10.56	12.21	9.40	6.86	4.90	4.73	5.58	5.19	5.03	4.25
Govt Bond Yield (Medium-Term)......	61b	13.67	11.21	10.57	11.98	8.93	6.47	4.55	4.04	5.29	4.64	4.48	3.36

Italy 136

		1992	1993	1994	1995	1996	1997	1998	1999	2000	2001	2002	2003
Prices, Production, Labor		*Index Numbers (2000=100): Period Averages*											
Share Prices	62	23.2	27.4	34.2	31.4	31.5	43.2	69.1	77.0	100.0	81.1	64.3	58.1
Producer Prices	63	78.85	81.82	84.85	91.53	93.26	94.46	94.56	94.33	100.00	101.94	101.75	103.38
Consumer Prices	64	77.5	81.0	84.3	†88.7	92.2	94.1	95.9	97.5	100.0	102.8	105.3	108.1
Harmonized CPI	64h	....	....	....	88.8	92.3	94.0	95.9	97.5	100.0	102.3	105.0	107.9
Wages: Contractual	65ey	79.0	81.7	84.6	87.2	90.0	93.2	95.8	98.0	100.0	101.7	104.3	....
Industrial Production	66	85.0	83.1	88.0	93.0	91.5	95.0	96.2	96.1	100.0	98.8	97.5	97.1
Industrial Employment	67	107.1	104.8	102.6	100.3	99.2	98.8	99.8	99.9	100.0	101.0	102.6	....
		Number in Thousands: Period Averages											
Labor Force	67d	....	....	22,680	22,734	22,849	22,889	23,363	23,361	23,720	23,900	24,086	....
Employment	67e	21,609	†20,705	20,373	20,233	20,320	20,413	20,618	20,864	21,225	21,634	21,922	22,133
Unemployment	67c	2,799	†2,299	2,508	2,638	2,654	2,688	2,744	2,670	2,495	2,267	2,163	2,096
Unemployment Rate (%)	67r	11.4	†9.6	11.1	11.7	11.7	11.8	11.8	11.5	10.6	9.6	9.0	8.7
International Transactions		*Billions of Lire through 1998; Millions of Euros Beginning 1999*											
Exports	70	219,436	266,213	308,045	381,175	388,885	409,128	426,182	†221,040	260,414	272,990	269,064	259,346
Imports, c.i.f.	71	232,200	232,991	272,382	335,661	321,286	357,587	378,784	†207,016	258,507	263,756	261,226	258,462
		2000=100											
Volume of Exports	72	61.4	66.8	74.7	84.6	†82.7	86.6	89.3	89.6	100.0	100.8	100.1	....
Volume of Imports	73	67.8	60.9	68.4	75.1	†71.6	78.6	85.5	91.3	100.0	100.1	101.4	....
Unit Value of Exports	74	71.2	79.3	82.2	89.9	†93.7	94.2	95.1	94.8	100.0	104.3	102.3	....
Unit Value of Imports	75	68.7	76.7	79.8	89.7	†89.7	90.9	88.5	87.6	100.0	102.1	98.4	....
Balance of Payments		*Millions of US Dollars: Minus Sign Indicates Debit*											
Current Account, n.i.e.	78ald	−29,217	7,802	13,209	25,076	39,999	32,403	19,998	8,111	−5,781	−652	−6,741	−21,942
Goods: Exports f.o.b.	78aad	178,155	169,153	191,421	233,998	252,039	240,404	242,572	235,856	240,473	244,931	253,680	293,264
Goods: Imports f.o.b.	78abd	−178,355	−140,264	−159,854	−195,269	−197,921	−200,527	−206,941	−212,420	−230,925	−229,392	−237,147	−283,565
Trade Balance	78acd	−200	28,889	31,568	38,729	54,118	39,878	35,631	23,437	9,549	15,540	16,533	9,700
Services: Credit	78add	58,545	52,284	53,681	61,619	65,660	66,991	67,549	58,788	56,556	57,676	60,251	73,855
Services: Debit	78aed	−58,134	−48,939	−48,238	−55,050	−57,605	−59,227	−63,379	−57,707	−55,601	−57,753	−63,542	−75,237
Balance on Goods & Services	78afd	211	32,235	37,011	45,299	62,173	47,642	39,801	24,517	10,504	15,463	13,243	8,319
Income: Credit	78agd	28,757	31,844	28,599	34,168	40,142	45,734	51,319	46,361	38,671	38,574	43,303	52,819
Income: Debit	78ahd	−50,644	−49,062	−45,289	−49,812	−55,101	−56,936	−63,636	−57,411	−50,680	−48,911	−57,854	−74,921
Balance on Gds, Serv. & Inc.	78aid	−21,676	15,017	20,321	29,655	47,213	36,440	27,483	13,467	−1,506	5,127	−1,307	−13,784
Current Transfers, n.i.e.: Credit	78ajd	14,198	12,925	12,254	14,287	14,320	15,552	14,402	16,776	15,797	16,136	20,872	20,530
Current Transfers: Debit	78akd	−21,739	−20,140	−19,366	−18,866	−21,535	−19,588	−21,887	−22,132	−20,073	−21,915	−26,305	−28,688
Capital Account, n.i.e.	78bcd	807	1,659	1,026	1,671	66	3,434	2,358	2,964	2,879	846	736	3,110
Capital Account, n.i.e.: Credit	78bad	2,266	2,807	2,213	2,797	1,414	4,582	3,359	4,572	4,172	2,098	2,060	5,018
Capital Account: Debit	78bbd	−1,459	−1,149	−1,187	−1,125	−1,348	−1,148	−1,001	−1,608	−1,293	−1,252	−1,323	−1,909
Financial Account, n.i.e.	78bjd	11,550	5,260	−14,207	−2,889	−7,982	−6,878	−18,074	−17,415	7,504	−3,570	11,192	19,377
Direct Investment Abroad	78bdd	−4,148	−7,329	−5,239	−7,024	−8,697	−10,414	−12,407	−6,723	−12,077	−21,758	−17,247	−9,871
Dir. Invest. in Rep. Econ., n.i.e.	78bed	3,105	3,749	2,199	4,842	3,546	3,700	2,635	6,943	13,176	14,874	14,699	17,285
Portfolio Investment Assets	78bfd	−16,827	12,187	−37,718	−4,938	−25,598	−61,857	−109,064	−129,624	−80,263	−36,167	−15,265	−58,515
Equity Securities	78bkd	3,699	385	−3,360	1,014	−1,036	−15,116	−26,570	−63,277	−77,036	−9,988	−5,198	−14,918
Debt Securities	78bld	−20,526	11,802	−34,358	−5,952	−24,562	−46,741	−82,493	−66,347	−3,227	−26,179	−10,067	−43,597
Portfolio Investment Liab., n.i.e.	78bgd	25,237	62,107	29,895	45,583	74,655	73,375	111,987	104,607	57,020	29,329	32,928	61,388
Equity Securities	78bmd	−432	4,133	−1,395	5,358	9,331	9,414	14,423	−4,537	−2,426	−245	−6,268	−2,251
Debt Securities	78bnd	25,670	57,974	31,290	40,225	65,324	63,962	97,563	109,144	59,446	29,573	39,197	63,639
Financial Derivatives Assets	78bwd	−148	−8	87	−852	−1,009	−1,118	−850	161	744	−2,277	−6,137	−10,247
Financial Derivatives Liabilities	78bxd	−108	−221	628	1,079	1,272	1,273	1,041	1,709	1,588	1,839	3,431	4,816
Other Investment Assets	78bhd	−28,863	−44,197	2,092	−28,947	−68,358	−25,541	−21,232	−33,573	242	2,032	4,164	−29,790
Monetary Authorities	78bod	....	....	....	....	....	....	....	5,396	3,034	−27,626	13,536	−65
General Government	78bpd	−1,820	−1,539	−2,023	−2,148	−1,112	−62	−1,101	−163	−649	−355	1,247	1,279
Banks	78bqd	−16,090	−33,300	22,599	−18,689	−45,046	−1,602	−7,052	−9,643	2,388	12,091	−34,000	8,891
Other Sectors	78brd	−10,953	−9,358	−18,483	−8,110	−22,199	−23,877	−13,078	−29,163	−4,532	17,921	23,381	−39,895
Other Investment Liab., n.i.e.	78bid	33,301	−21,027	−6,152	−12,632	16,206	13,703	9,816	39,085	27,074	8,560	−5,383	44,310
Monetary Authorities	78bsd	7,198	−4,602	−95	1,062	−1,269	−48	−128	916	−690	1,928	869	−2,548
General Government	78btd	1,423	765	−1,812	4,893	−2,583	−1,798	−5,739	−3,255	−3,549	−759	−534	−982
Banks	78bud	17,005	−16,752	−1,527	−22,716	26,613	6,861	12,780	1,109	24,875	12,783	−6,123	34,525
Other Sectors	78bvd	7,675	−439	−2,719	4,129	−6,555	8,688	2,903	40,315	6,438	−5,392	405	13,314
Net Errors and Omissions	78cad	−7,133	−17,856	1,547	−21,054	−20,176	−15,810	−25,754	−1,711	−1,355	2,787	−2,018	571
Overall Balance	78cbd	−23,993	−3,135	1,575	2,804	11,907	13,150	−21,472	−8,051	3,247	−588	3,169	1,115
Reserves and Related Items	79dad	23,993	3,135	−1,575	−2,804	−11,907	−13,150	21,472	8,051	−3,247	588	−3,169	−1,115
Reserve Assets	79dbd	23,992	3,135	−1,575	−2,804	−11,907	−13,150	21,472	8,051	−3,247	588	−3,169	−1,115
Use of Fund Credit and Loans	79dcd	−	−	−	−	−	−	−	−	−	−	−	−
Exceptional Financing	79ded	1	....	....	....	....	....	....	....	....	....	....	....

2004, International Monetary Fund : *International Financial Statistics Yearbook*

Italy 136

		1992	1993	1994	1995	1996	1997	1998	1999	2000	2001	2002	2003
International Investment Position							*Millions of US Dollars*						
Assets	79aad	410,960	450,985	516,329	597,810	727,498	809,597	1,002,865	1,081,092	1,119,394	1,078,391	1,201,342	1,548,820
Direct Investment Abroad	79abd	71,004	81,892	91,097	109,176	113,251	130,668	165,412	181,852	180,275	182,375	194,496	238,885
Portfolio Investment	79acd	111,125	130,670	150,426	171,793	192,351	257,494	394,501	546,903	590,753	552,028	595,922	780,120
Equity Securities	79add	12,170	11,723	14,015	13,982	16,915	26,600	37,690	210,929	285,553	239,473	247,462	329,911
Debt Securities	79aed	98,954	118,947	136,411	157,811	175,436	230,894	356,811	335,974	305,200	312,555	348,460	450,209
Financial Derivatives	79ald	–	–	–	–	–	–	–	2,951	3,533	4,315	11,050	22,704
Other Investment	79afd	176,794	187,620	217,192	256,520	350,907	344,344	388,310	304,085	297,775	293,458	344,253	443,850
Monetary Authorities	79agd	–	–	–	–	–	–	–	–4,190	–6,715	20,629	8,944	12,244
General Government	79ahd	13,455	13,641	16,459	19,542	21,777	20,180	22,567	20,417	23,316	23,057	25,403	28,924
Banks	79aid	106,045	116,107	121,726	146,945	214,524	198,520	225,089	138,717	140,447	119,177	181,173	225,428
Other Sectors	79ajd	57,294	57,872	79,006	90,034	114,606	125,644	140,653	149,141	140,727	130,595	128,732	177,254
Reserve Assets	79akd	52,037	50,803	57,615	60,321	70,989	77,091	54,642	45,302	47,058	46,215	55,622	63,262
Liabilities	79lad	521,563	535,352	587,612	650,102	761,656	807,436	1,022,771	1,027,672	1,072,544	1,051,312	1,272,220	1,643,720
Dir. Invest. in Rep. Economy	79lbd	50,730	54,538	60,955	65,980	74,640	83,158	105,397	108,638	113,047	108,007	126,480	173,598
Portfolio Investment	79lcd	101,229	160,403	188,595	237,861	333,422	385,388	544,602	549,251	570,236	561,024	704,422	913,328
Equity Securities	79ldd	7,724	11,123	11,118	16,434	27,245	35,500	65,833	53,380	53,182	35,743	29,505	31,090
Debt Securities	79led	93,504	149,280	177,477	221,427	306,177	349,888	478,769	495,871	517,054	525,281	674,917	882,238
Financial Derivatives	79lld	–	–	–	–	–	–	–	3,244	2,641	4,522	8,919	15,896
Other Investment	79lfd	369,604	320,411	338,063	346,261	353,593	338,891	372,772	366,538	386,620	377,760	432,399	540,897
Monetary Authorities	79lgd	5,316	578	485	1,554	239	175	56	950	235	2,197	3,078	633
General Government	79lhd	21,579	21,506	21,551	26,328	22,187	21,470	15,595	8,881	7,272	6,062	6,341	6,511
Banks	79lid	242,770	213,524	229,119	228,859	247,732	239,171	268,935	241,669	265,040	260,561	296,676	386,976
Other Sectors	79ljd	99,939	84,803	86,907	89,521	83,436	78,075	88,186	115,039	114,073	108,939	126,303	146,778
Government Finance													
Central Government					*Trillions of Lire through 1998; Billions of Euros Beginning 1999: Year Ending December 31*								
Deficit (-) or Surplus	80	–162.8	†–157.8	–152.9	–122.6	–136.1	–31.0	–47.9	.3	–14.6	–40.8	....	....
Revenue	81	499.1	†470.1	477.1	524.8	549.7	621.3	594.7	353.1	350.6	351.7	....	....
Expenditure	82	651.4	†610.3	601.8	619.3	652.8	602.6	611.3	327.5	341.3	372.8	....	....
Lending Minus Repayments	83	10.4	†17.6	28.2	28.0	32.9	49.7	31.3	25.3	24.0	19.7	....	....
Financing	80h	164.1	164.8	153.0	122.7	136.1	31.3	48.0	–.4	14.7	40.9	....	....
Domestic	84a	....	....	109.5	61.6	34.4	–72.3	–91.9	–92.9	–34.4	28.8	....	....
Foreign	85a	....	....	43.5	61.1	101.7	103.6	139.9	92.5	49.1	12.1	....	....
Total Debt by Residence	88	1,595.1	1,765.5	†1,931.8	2,073.7	2,206.1	2,250.8	2,290.5	1,188.0	1,212.8	1,255.1	....	....
Debt: Domestic	88a	....	....	1,621.8	1,720.3	1,769.8	1,719.1	1,630.0	756.0	742.5	775.8	....	....
Foreign	89a	....	....	310.0	353.4	436.3	531.7	660.5	432.0	470.3	479.3	....	....
Net Borrowing: Lire	84b	163.8	150.3	147.5	100.9	129.9	....	....	....	....	....	....	....
Net Borrowing: Foreign Currency	85b	.2	14.4	9.2	25.8	12.9	....	....	....	....	....	....	....
Monetary Operations	86c	.1	.1	.1	.1	.1	....	....	....	....	....	....	....
General Government						*As Percent of Gross Domestic Product*							
Deficit (-) or Surplus	80g	–9.6	–9.5	–9.2	–7.7	–7.1	–2.7	–2.8	–1.8	–.5	–1.4	....	....
Debt	88g	108.7	119.1	124.9	125.3	122.1	120.1	116.4	114.5	110.6	109.4	....	....
National Accounts						*Trillions of Lire through 1998; Billions of Euros Beginning 1999*							
Househ.Cons.Expend.,incl.NPISHs	96f.c	892.5	906.8	966.5	1,041.9	1,101.2	1,162.0	1,223.5	†667.9	706.2	731.3	757.4	786.2
Government Consumption Expend	91f.c	311.0	318.6	323.5	326.9	352.0	369.9	382.2	†199.5	213.3	229.5	238.9	253.4
Gross Fixed Capital Formation	93e.c	310.7	288.2	297.6	327.9	348.8	362.3	384.8	†210.6	230.9	240.6	249.3	248.8
Changes in Inventories	93i.c	4.7	–1.1	8.1	17.8	6.4	12.0	16.1	†7.1	4.7	–1.2	2.9	5.7
Exports of Goods and Services	90c.c	289.2	347.9	394.4	483.2	491.1	524.1	548.1	†283.0	330.0	345.9	340.2	330.2
Imports of Goods and Services (-)	98c.c	290.4	297.2	336.8	410.5	397.3	443.6	477.3	†260.3	318.6	328.4	327.9	323.3
Gross Domestic Product (GDP)	99b.c	1,517.6	1,563.3	1,653.4	1,787.3	1,902.3	1,987.2	2,077.4	†1,108.0	1,166.5	1,218.5	1,260.4	1,300.9
Net Primary Income from Abroad	98.n	–26.8	–26.7	–26.6	–25.5	–22.7	–18.2	–19.7	†–7.3	–9.5	–8.8	–9.6	–14.0
Gross National Income (GNI)	99a	1,490.8	1,536.6	1,626.8	1,761.7	1,879.5	1,968.9	2,057.6	†1,100.7	1,157.0	1,209.7	1,250.8	1,286.9
Net Current Transf.from Abroad	98t	–6.7	–8.5	–5.7	–2.4	–6.6	–7.1	–9.4	†–4.4	–3.9	–5.3	–6.6	–8.4
Gross Nat'l Disposable Inc.(GNDI)	99i	1,481.0	1,525.2	1,615.7	1,754.5	1,869.5	1,961.8	2,044.8	†1,096.3	1,153.1	1,204.4	1,244.2	1,278.5
Gross Saving	99s	277.4	299.7	325.7	385.7	416.3	429.9	439.1	†228.8	233.6	243.6	247.9	238.9
Consumption of Fixed Capital	99cfc	196.3	208.4	219.5	234.2	246.4	257.2	268.6	†144.1	152.3	160.4	168.9	176.0
GDP Volume 1995 Prices	99b.r	1,714.1	1,699.0	1,736.5	1,787.3	1,806.8	1,843.4	1,876.8	†985.3	1,015.1	1,033.0	1,036.7	1,039.4
GDP Volume (2000=100)	99bvr	87.2	86.4	88.4	90.9	91.9	93.8	95.5	†97.1	100.0	101.8	102.1	102.4
GDP Deflator (2000=100)	99bir	77.0	80.1	82.9	87.0	91.6	93.8	96.3	†97.9	100.0	102.6	105.8	108.9
						Millions: Midyear Estimates							
Population	99z	56.93	57.06	57.19	57.30	57.39	57.46	57.50	57.53	57.54	57.52	57.48	57.42

Jamaica 343

		1992	1993	1994	1995	1996	1997	1998	1999	2000	2001	2002	2003
Exchange Rates						Jamaica Dollars per SDR: End of Period							
Market Rate......aa=	wa	30.504	44.606	48.469	58.889	50.135	49.033	52.174	56.672	59.172	59.426	69.012	89.927
				Jamaica Dollars per US Dollar: End of Period (we) Period Average (wf)									
Market Rate......ae=	we	22.185	32.475	33.202	39.616	34.865	36.341	37.055	41.291	45.415	47.286	50.762	60.517
Market Rate......rf=	wf	22.960	24.949	33.086	35.142	37.120	35.404	36.550	39.044	42.701	45.996	48.416	57.741
Fund Position						Millions of SDRs: End of Period							
Quota	2f.s	200.9	200.9	200.9	200.9	200.9	200.9	200.9	273.5	273.5	273.5	273.5	273.5
SDRs	1b.s	9.0	9.1	–	.3	–	.2	.5	.5	.1	1.2	.7	–
Reserve Position in the Fund	1c.s	–	–	–	–	–	–	–	–	–	–	–	–
Total Fund Cred.&Loans Outstg.	2tl	259.7	244.2	217.6	161.7	112.2	87.1	74.7	60.8	46.3	31.9	17.4	6.0
International Liquidity					Millions of US Dollars Unless Otherwise Indicated: End of Period								
Total Reserves minus Gold	1l.d	324.1	417.0	735.9	681.3	880.0	682.1	709.5	554.5	1,053.7	1,900.5	1,645.1	1,194.9
SDRs	1b.d	12.3	12.4	–	.5	.1	.2	.7	.7	.1	1.5	.9	.1
Reserve Position in the Fund	1c.d	–	–	–	–	–	–	–	–	–	–	–	–
Foreign Exchange	1d.d	311.8	404.6	735.9	680.8	879.9	681.9	708.8	553.8	1,053.6	1,899.0	1,644.2	1,194.8
Other Official Insts.: Assets	3b.d	14.9	17.5	8.3	7.7	8.0	1.1	1.0	3.2	3.1	6.6	2.9	4.3
Monetary Authorities: Other Liab.	4..d	109.8	65.1	58.2	–36.5	–100.1	–73.9	–68.8	–61.5	–45.3	–30.6	–15.0	–1.1
Deposit Money Banks: Assets	7a.d	307.0	292.6	449.5	489.0	464.6	542.0	457.9	571.8	593.8	811.8	898.8	941.6
Liabilities	7b.d	253.4	238.3	393.2	336.2	370.2	371.6	328.0	267.2	219.7	368.7	360.2	432.9
Other Banking Insts.: Assets	7e.d	7.6	1.8	34.1	7.0	9.1	16.7	23.8	33.7	37.8	133.7	348.8	378.5
Liabilities	7f.d	.1	3.9	53.8	47.0	43.5	11.7	6.4	5.4	12.9	53.5	215.9	270.9
Monetary Authorities						Millions of Jamaica Dollars: End of Period							
Foreign Assets	11	6,912	12,618	24,486	27,084	30,663	24,739	26,280	22,850	47,664	89,818	83,151	72,171
Claims on Central Government	12a	2,562	7,055	7,466	15,702	20,751	39,777	51,219	57,268	54,930	56,038	57,270	78,188
Claims on Deposit Money Banks	12e	–	–	–	–	–	–	–	–	–	–	–	–
Reserve Money	14	12,859	18,588	24,969	32,381	33,668	38,770	47,324	45,343	48,887	45,735	44,292	55,127
of which: Currency Outside DMBs	14a	3,741	5,228	7,118	9,516	10,760	12,449	13,504	17,821	17,607	18,783	20,399	23,186
Foreign Liabilities	16c	10,357	13,007	12,480	8,077	2,136	1,588	1,345	906	685	448	441	469
Central Government Deposits	16d	12,682	17,255	26,512	28,948	37,755	41,571	45,837	48,058	64,072	110,622	98,225	86,452
Capital Accounts	17a	1,243	1,815	1,972	2,396	2,060	2,015	2,143	2,326	2,427	2,437	2,827	3,656
Other Items (Net)	17r	–27,668	–30,993	–33,981	–29,015	–24,205	–19,427	–19,150	–16,515	–13,477	–13,386	–5,363	4,654
Deposit Money Banks						Millions of Jamaica Dollars: End of Period							
Reserves	20	11,113	13,681	18,794	25,623	23,568	29,167	30,812	26,972	32,236	40,378	44,099	46,530
Foreign Assets	21	6,810	9,501	14,924	19,373	16,197	19,697	16,966	23,608	26,967	38,388	45,624	56,983
Claims on Central Government	22a	8,134	7,580	16,967	13,716	22,281	23,898	23,280	30,373	34,886	93,576	80,134	87,205
Claims on Nonfin.Pub.Enterprises	22c	159	730	1,016	2,081	1,902	3,326	3,462	3,236	4,269	6,094	15,869	17,967
Claims on Private Sector	22d	14,358	23,326	32,164	44,408	52,006	57,482	74,777	84,593	102,602	42,312	56,047	76,845
Claims on Other Banking Insts	22f	488	281	686	803	380	512	342	579	1,059	42	284	132
Demand Deposits	24	9,650	11,675	14,134	19,804	22,788	22,022	23,160	27,221	30,289	35,359	39,020	39,871
Time and Savings Deposits	25	20,908	29,725	44,300	57,075	62,243	74,017	80,138	86,054	100,215	106,772	120,730	136,079
Foreign Liabilities	26c	5,622	7,740	13,055	13,319	12,905	13,504	12,153	11,031	9,978	17,436	18,284	26,201
Central Government Deposits	26d	1,814	2,304	6,529	6,945	6,690	8,086	5,736	8,075	15,816	11,261	12,286	10,863
Credit from Monetary Authorities	26g	442	38	283	3,721	8,120	5,239	101	1,527	3,044	83	135	168
Capital Accounts	27a	3,902	5,139	8,615	10,613	14,140	16,469	33,180	32,567	30,751	31,232	31,761	35,434
Other Items (Net)	27r	–1,275	–1,522	–2,363	–5,474	–10,554	–5,254	–4,830	2,887	11,925	18,647	19,842	37,047
Monetary Survey						Millions of Jamaica Dollars: End of Period							
Foreign Assets (Net)	31n	–2,257	1,372	13,876	25,061	31,818	29,345	29,748	34,521	63,967	110,322	110,051	102,484
Domestic Credit	32	11,378	19,442	25,492	41,074	53,129	75,593	101,760	120,167	118,003	76,315	99,217	163,137
Claims on Central Govt. (Net)	32an	–3,800	–4,924	–8,608	–6,475	–1,413	14,019	22,926	31,508	9,928	27,732	26,893	68,078
Claims on Local Government	32b	–	–	6	6	2	3	1	–	–	–	–	3
Claims on Nonfin.Pub.Enterprises	32c	159	730	1,016	2,081	1,902	3,326	3,462	3,236	4,269	6,094	15,869	17,967
Claims on Private Sector	32d	14,531	23,355	32,391	44,660	52,258	57,734	75,029	84,845	102,747	42,447	56,171	76,957
Claims on Other Banking Insts	32f	488	281	686	803	380	512	342	579	1,059	42	284	132
Money	34	13,391	16,903	21,252	29,320	33,548	34,470	36,664	45,042	47,897	54,142	59,419	63,057
Quasi-Money	35	20,908	29,725	44,300	57,075	62,243	74,017	80,138	86,054	100,215	106,772	120,730	136,079
Capital Accounts	37a	5,145	6,954	10,587	13,009	16,200	18,484	35,323	34,893	33,178	33,669	34,587	39,090
Other Items (Net)	37r	–30,322	–32,768	–36,771	–33,269	–27,043	–22,033	–20,618	–11,299	680	–7,946	–5,468	27,395
Money plus Quasi-Money	35l	34,299	46,628	65,552	86,396	95,791	108,487	116,803	131,095	148,112	160,914	180,149	199,136

Jamaica 343

		1992	1993	1994	1995	1996	1997	1998	1999	2000	2001	2002	2003
Other Banking Institutions		\multicolumn{12}{c}{*Millions of Jamaica Dollars: End of Period*}
Reserves............................	40	870	1,396	1,276	1,287	1,390	1,233	1,279	765	454	828	744	495
Foreign Assets.....................	41	168	59	1,133	277	318	608	882	1,393	1,718	6,322	17,706	22,904
Claims on Central Government........	42a	832	312	1,681	2,818	4,404	4,281	1,894	1,500	2,004	4,167	2,612	9,333
Claims on Private Sector.................	42d	6,902	7,468	7,627	9,890	10,662	7,069	5,781	4,354	2,855	3,372	3,572	5,954
Claims on Deposit Money Banks......	42e	1,019	686	1,148	932	865	1,442	379	299	143	251	370	85
Demand Deposits........................	44	–	–	–	–	–	–	–	–	–	–	–	–
Time and Savings Deposits.............	45	6,580	7,306	6,998	7,077	6,996	6,862	5,759	4,938	3,966	7,290	8,368	9,330
Foreign Liabilities........................	46c	–	–	–	–	–	15	24	–	–	–	–	–
Long-Term Foreign Liabilities...........	46cl	2	127	1,786	1,863	1,516	410	213	224	586	2,531	10,959	16,395
Credit from Deposit Money Banks.....	46h	843	949	1,312	1,096	5,463	4,098	1,120	–	170	160	196	50
Capital Accounts........................	47a	1,189	1,738	2,521	2,924	3,013	1,688	2,946	4,259	2,820	4,117	4,760	4,943
Other Items (Net).......................	47r	1,177	−200	249	2,244	649	1,559	153	−1,111	−367	844	720	8,052
Banking Survey		\multicolumn{12}{c}{*Millions of Jamaica Dollars: End of Period*}
Foreign Assets (Net)...................	51n	−2,090	1,432	15,009	25,339	32,136	29,937	30,606	35,914	65,686	116,644	127,757	125,388
Domestic Credit.......................	52	18,624	26,940	34,114	52,979	67,815	86,431	109,094	125,442	121,804	83,813	105,117	178,292
Claims on Central Govt. (Net)........	52an	−2,968	−4,612	−6,927	−3,658	2,991	18,299	24,821	33,008	11,932	31,899	29,505	77,411
Claims on Local Government.........	52b	–	–	6	6	2	3	1	–	–	–	–	3
Claims on Nonfin.Pub.Enterprises...	52c	159	730	1,016	2,081	1,902	3,326	3,462	3,236	4,269	6,094	15,869	17,967
Claims on Private Sector..............	52d	21,433	30,823	40,018	54,550	62,920	64,803	80,810	89,198	105,603	45,819	59,743	82,912
Liquid Liabilities.......................	55l	40,008	52,538	71,273	92,186	101,398	114,116	121,282	135,267	151,624	167,375	187,772	207,972
Long-Term Foreign Liabilities.........	56cl	2	127	1,786	1,863	1,516	410	213	224	586	2,531	10,959	16,395
Capital Accounts......................	57a	6,334	8,692	13,108	15,933	19,213	20,172	38,270	39,152	35,999	37,786	39,347	44,033
Other Items (Net).....................	57r	−29,810	−32,986	−37,045	−31,663	−22,175	−18,330	−20,066	−13,288	−718	−7,236	−5,205	35,281
Interest Rates		\multicolumn{12}{c}{*Percent Per Annum*}
Treasury Bill Rate.....................	60c	34.36	28.85	42.98	27.65	37.95	21.14	25.65	20.75	18.24	16.71	15.54	25.94
Savings Rate..........................	60k	15.00	15.00	15.00	15.00	15.00	10.96	9.69	8.75	8.50	7.75	7.50	5.21
Deposit Rate..........................	60l	33.63	27.59	36.41	23.21	25.16	13.95	15.61	13.48	11.62	9.64	8.58	8.46
Lending Rate.........................	60p	44.81	43.71	49.46	43.58	39.83	32.86	31.59	27.01	23.35	20.61	18.50	18.89
Government Bond Yield..............	61	30.50	24.82	26.82	26.85	26.87	26.85	....	....	....	....	....	....
Prices, Production, Labor		\multicolumn{12}{c}{*Index Numbers (2000=100): Period Averages*}
Industrial Share Prices................	62	40.9	73.7	50.2	60.2	48.9	58.6	73.8	69.3	100.0	110.6	134.1	184.7
Consumer Prices......................	64	29.3	35.8	48.3	57.9	73.2	80.3	87.3	92.4	100.0	107.0	114.6	126.4
		\multicolumn{12}{c}{*Number in Thousands: Period Averages*}
Labor Force...........................	67d	1,075	1,083	1,140	1,150	1,143	1,134	1,129	1,119	1,105	1,105	1,125	....
Employment..........................	67e	906	906	923	963	960	956	954	937	936	942	942	....
Unemployment.......................	67c	169	177	167	187	183	187	175	176	171	166	170	....
Unemployment Rate (%)..............	67r	15.7	16.3	15.4	16.2	16.0	16.5	15.5	15.7	15.5	15.0	15.1	....
International Transactions		\multicolumn{12}{c}{*Millions of Jamaica Dollars*}
Exports................................	70	24,099	26,421	40,121	49,916	51,513	48,971	47,940	48,425	55,621	56,061	53,897	67,931
Imports, c.i.f..........................	71	38,267	53,737	73,631	99,418	109,687	110,932	110,926	113,472	141,987	154,526	171,201	209,852
		\multicolumn{12}{c}{*2000=100*}
Volume of Exports....................	72	91.2	91.0	96.8	90.9	100.1	101.4	104.7	103.2	100.0	104.1	106.7	108.3

Jamaica 343

		1992	1993	1994	1995	1996	1997	1998	1999	2000	2001	2002	2003
Balance of Payments		*Millions of US Dollars: Minus Sign Indicates Debit*											
Current Account, n.i.e.	78ald	28.5	−184.0	81.6	−98.9	−142.6	−332.2	−333.8	−216.3	−367.4	−758.8	−1,119.3	....
Goods: Exports f.o.b.	78aad	1,116.5	1,105.4	1,548.0	1,796.0	1,721.0	1,700.3	1,613.4	1,499.1	1,562.8	1,454.4	1,309.1	....
Goods: Imports f.o.b.	78abd	−1,541.1	−1,920.5	−2,099.2	−2,625.3	−2,715.2	−2,832.6	−2,743.9	−2,685.6	−3,004.3	−3,072.6	−3,179.6	....
Trade Balance	78acd	−424.6	−815.1	−551.2	−829.3	−994.2	−1,132.3	−1,130.5	−1,186.5	−1,441.5	−1,618.2	−1,870.5	....
Services: Credit	78add	1,104.0	1,260.7	1,480.2	1,597.9	1,601.9	1,698.9	1,770.4	1,978.4	2,025.7	1,897.0	1,919.6	....
Services: Debit	78aed	−714.4	−823.5	−955.3	−1,103.8	−1,149.2	−1,231.7	−1,293.6	−1,323.0	−1,422.5	−1,513.9	−1,648.7	....
Balance on Goods & Services	78afd	−35.0	−377.9	−26.3	−335.2	−541.5	−665.1	−653.7	−531.1	−838.3	−1,235.1	−1,599.6	....
Income: Credit	78agd	75.0	117.0	104.6	146.6	141.8	147.3	156.3	165.8	193.1	218.2	220.8	....
Income: Debit	78ahd	−368.9	−312.9	−456.6	−517.3	−366.5	−439.2	−464.4	−498.3	−543.0	−656.0	−826.4	....
Balance on Gds, Serv. & Inc.	78aid	−328.9	−573.8	−378.3	−705.9	−766.2	−957.0	−961.8	−863.6	−1,188.2	−1,672.9	−2,205.2	....
Current Transfers, n.i.e.: Credit	78ajd	387.2	415.9	504.2	669.6	709.3	705.7	727.6	757.9	969.4	1,090.7	1,336.9	....
Current Transfers: Debit	78akd	−29.8	−26.1	−44.3	−62.6	−85.7	−80.9	−99.6	−110.6	−148.6	−176.6	−251.0	....
Capital Account, n.i.e.	78bcd	−17.6	−12.9	10.4	10.5	16.6	−11.6	−8.7	−10.9	2.2	−22.3	−16.9	....
Capital Account, n.i.e.: Credit	78bad	−	−	33.2	34.5	42.5	21.7	20.3	19.1	29.6	15.2	18.9	....
Capital Account: Debit	78bbd	−17.6	−12.9	−22.8	−24.0	−25.9	−33.3	−29.0	−30.0	−27.4	−37.5	−35.8	....
Financial Account, n.i.e.	78bjd	297.3	257.1	256.1	108.3	388.6	163.5	337.3	94.8	853.9	1,660.5	867.1	....
Direct Investment Abroad	78bdd	−	−	−52.7	−66.3	−93.3	−56.6	−82.0	−94.9	−74.3	−89.0	−73.9	....
Dir. Invest. in Rep. Econ., n.i.e.	78bed	142.4	77.9	129.7	147.4	183.7	203.3	369.1	523.7	468.3	613.9	481.1	....
Portfolio Investment Assets	78bfd	−	−	−	−	−	−	−3.9	−3.7	−70.0	−39.3	−351.3	....
Equity Securities	78bkd	−	−	....	....	....	....	−	−	−	−	−	....
Debt Securities	78bld	−	−	−	−	−	−	−3.9	−3.7	−70.0	−39.3	−351.3	....
Portfolio Investment Liab., n.i.e.	78bgd	−	−	−	−	−	5.7	10.9	8.6	5.9	69.7	155.8	....
Equity Securities	78bmd	−	−	....	....	....	....	−	−	−	−	−	....
Debt Securities	78bnd	−	−	−	−	−	5.7	10.9	8.6	5.9	69.7	155.8	....
Financial Derivatives Assets	78bwd	....	....	....	....	....	....	−	−	−	−	−	....
Financial Derivatives Liabilities	78bxd	....	....	....	....	....	....	−	−	−	−	−	....
Other Investment Assets	78bhd	10.2	1.1	−141.3	−148.8	−13.8	−113.2	−59.1	−122.7	−95.5	−215.5	−184.5	....
Monetary Authorities	78bod	....	....	−	−	−	−	−	−	−	−	−	....
General Government	78bpd	−1.0	−1.4	−	−	−	−	−	−	−	−	−	....
Banks	78bqd	11.2	2.5	−177.9	−199.2	−88.1	−186.9	−142.3	−215.1	−181.5	−282.9	−227.0	....
Other Sectors	78brd	−	−	36.6	50.4	74.3	73.7	83.2	92.4	86.0	67.4	42.5	....
Other Investment Liab., n.i.e.	78bid	144.7	178.1	320.4	176.0	312.0	124.3	102.3	−216.2	619.5	1,320.7	839.9	....
Monetary Authorities	78bsd	−50.8	−35.9	−	−	−	−	−	−	−	−	−	....
General Government	78btd	−10.0	37.8	−127.4	−97.0	−144.7	43.1	−41.3	−331.4	383.6	653.4	77.1	....
Banks	78bud	−46.4	−6.0	142.2	74.7	130.7	156.7	205.5	122.2	167.9	250.5	166.3	....
Other Sectors	78bvd	251.9	182.2	305.6	198.3	326.0	−75.5	−61.9	−7.0	68.0	416.8	596.5	....
Net Errors and Omissions	78cad	−59.9	49.7	9.6	7.1	8.8	9.9	49.1	−4.0	29.7	−14.4	32.9	....
Overall Balance	78cbd	248.3	109.9	357.7	27.0	271.4	−170.4	43.9	−136.4	518.4	865.0	−236.2	....
Reserves and Related Items	79dad	−248.3	−109.9	−357.7	−27.0	−271.4	170.4	−43.9	136.4	−518.4	−865.0	236.2	....
Reserve Assets	79dbd	−192.2	−92.9	−321.0	55.8	−201.7	205.0	−26.9	155.3	−499.4	−846.6	255.0	....
Use of Fund Credit and Loans	79dcd	−19.4	−21.3	−38.2	−84.6	−71.9	−34.6	−17.0	−18.9	−19.0	−18.3	−18.9	....
Exceptional Financing	79ded	−36.7	4.4	1.5	1.9	2.2	−	−	−	−	−	−	....
National Accounts		*Millions of Jamaica Dollars*											
Househ.Cons.Expend.,incl.NPISHs	96f	55,618	82,116	110,993	142,950	166,340	179,309	190,205	205,124	232,467	264,686	283,690	....
Government Consumption Expend.	91f	7,587	13,876	16,469	22,635	32,476	40,235	47,156	46,926	53,971	59,635	74,647	....
Gross Fixed Capital Formation	93e	23,953	33,781	43,499	57,901	70,023	76,493	72,660	73,531	90,338	108,324	130,653	....
Changes in Inventories	93i	262	790	333	699	500	619	405	319	589	440	674	....
Exports of Goods and Services	90c	50,552	57,835	83,815	103,215	106,090	103,466	114,038	124,754	146,163	144,614	147,948	....
Imports of Goods and Services (-)	98c	51,319	67,883	93,908	124,175	133,943	137,264	142,266	149,721	184,815	205,484	229,947	....
Gross Domestic Product (GDP)	99b	86,653	113,054	150,856	188,828	224,520	245,396	262,854	281,190	316,581	348,877	381,074	....
Net Primary Income from Abroad	98.n	−6,843	−4,689	−7,952	−8,575	−4,852	−4,655	−9,847	−12,543	−14,058	−20,277	−28,872	....
Gross National Income (GNI)	99a	79,810	115,826	153,249	194,650	236,634	258,203	272,351	288,390	324,655	351,988	378,792	....
GDP Volume 1996 Prices	99b.p	211,533	216,572	218,738	223,682	224,520	222,130	219,491	221,486	223,245	226,635	229,195	....
GDP Volume (2000=100)	99bvp	94.8	97.0	98.0	100.2	100.6	99.5	98.3	99.2	100.0	101.5	102.7	....
GDP Deflator (2000=100)	99bip	27.0	36.8	48.6	59.5	70.5	77.9	84.5	89.5	100.0	108.6	117.3	....
		Millions: Midyear Estimates											
Population	99z	2.41	2.43	2.45	2.47	2.49	2.51	2.54	2.56	2.58	2.60	2.63	2.65

2004, International Monetary Fund : *International Financial Statistics Yearbook*

Japan 158

		1992	1993	1994	1995	1996	1997	1998	1999	2000	2001	2002	2003
Exchange Rates						*Yen per SDR: End of Period*							
Market Rate	aa	171.53	153.63	145.61	152.86	166.80	175.34	162.77	140.27	149.70	165.64	163.01	159.15
					Yen per US Dollar: End of Period (ae) Period Average (rf)								
Market Rate	ae	124.75	111.85	99.74	102.83	116.00	129.95	115.60	102.20	114.90	131.80	119.90	107.10
Market Rate	rf	126.65	111.20	102.21	94.06	108.78	120.99	130.91	113.91	107.77	121.53	125.39	115.93
					Index Numbers (2000=100): Period Averages								
Market Rate	ahx	85.1	97.2	105.6	115.2	99.1	89.2	82.7	94.6	100.0	88.7	86.1	93.1
Nominal Effective Exchange Rate	neu	74.0	88.8	95.7	100.4	87.3	82.1	76.9	89.8	100.0	90.3	85.7	85.9
Real Effective Exchange Rate	reu	80.9	95.9	101.8	107.2	91.8	87.6	81.8	93.1	100.0	88.5	80.6	78.6
Fund Position						*Millions of SDRs: End of Period*							
Quota	2f.s	8,242	8,242	8,242	8,242	8,242	8,242	8,242	13,313	13,313	13,313	13,313	13,313
SDRs	1b.s	795	1,123	1,427	1,821	1,837	1,955	1,891	1,935	1,870	1,892	1,857	1,861
Reserve Position in the Fund	1c.s	6,284	6,015	5,912	5,449	4,639	6,777	6,813	4,774	4,032	4,019	5,298	5,204
of which: Outstg.Fund Borrowing	2c	2,985	2,985	2,913	1,137	–	–	508	–	–	–	–	–
International Liquidity					*Millions of US Dollars Unless Otherwise Indicated: End of Period*								
Total Reserves minus Gold	1l.d	71,623	98,524	125,860	183,250	216,648	219,648	215,471	286,916	354,902	395,155	461,186	663,289
SDRs	1b.d	1,094	1,543	2,083	2,707	2,642	2,638	2,663	2,656	2,437	2,377	2,524	2,766
Reserve Position in the Fund	1c.d	8,641	8,261	8,631	8,100	6,671	9,144	9,593	6,552	5,253	5,051	7,203	7,733
Foreign Exchange	1d.d	61,888	88,720	115,146	172,443	207,335	207,866	203,215	277,708	347,212	387,727	451,458	652,790
Gold (Million Fine Troy Ounces)	1ad	24.23	24.23	24.23	24.23	24.23	24.23	24.23	24.23	24.55	24.60	24.60	24.60
Gold (National Valuation)	1and	1,166	1,165	1,238	1,260	1,219	1,144	1,194	1,164	1,119	1,082	1,171	1,280
Deposit Money Banks: Assets	7a.d	879,191	918,559	1,007,605	1,217,867	1,123,529	1,217,900	1,252,700	1,193,000	1,198,200	1,159,300	1,231,900	....
Liabilities	7b.d	708,623	688,436	723,697	738,324	695,848	705,100	708,200	542,300	564,900	522,100	555,900	....
Monetary Authorities						*Trillions of Yen: End of Period*							
Foreign Assets (Net)	11	3.40	6.73	7.25	11.54	17.49	16.86	14.47	21.56	33.01	42.25	50.48	....
Claims on Central Government	12a	19.13	21.40	21.98	25.08	31.30	32.87	37.93	50.06	44.42	71.86	85.27	....
Claims on Deposit Money Banks	12e	20.01	14.13	12.92	11.62	9.91	13.80	15.28	14.60	8.11	21.33	28.55	....
Reserve Money	14	45.40	48.03	49.44	53.32	57.84	62.09	64.34	89.62	73.27	85.96	97.91	....
of which: Currency Outside DMBs	14a	38.10	40.85	42.35	46.23	49.08	52.73	54.31	59.40	61.95	66.68	71.33	72.46
Central Government Deposits	16d	5.61	1.97	5.03	5.85	7.64	3.79	7.65	8.08	14.29	13.93	22.01	....
Other Items (Net)	17r	–8.47	–7.73	–12.31	–10.93	–6.77	–2.35	–4.31	–11.48	–2.03	35.54	44.38	....
Deposit Money Banks						*Trillions of Yen: End of Period*							
Reserves	20	7.29	7.18	7.09	7.09	8.75	9.36	10.03	30.22	11.33	19.28	26.59	....
Foreign Assets	21	77.99	102.29	98.89	110.01	104.51	128.73	109.07	77.75	84.90	93.38	90.81	....
Claims on Central Government	22a	40.25	42.89	40.14	38.50	37.04	37.68	44.39	67.07	102.47	99.11	102.85	....
Claims on Local Government	22b	12.01	14.95	17.38	19.78	20.72	21.39	23.75	24.79	24.33	25.27	25.67	....
Claims on Nonfin.Pub.Enterprises	22c	13.58	13.47	12.55	11.57	10.06	9.01	8.34	8.06	8.99	10.58	11.56	....
Claims on Private Sector	22d	564.98	558.67	559.81	569.20	575.88	578.79	583.35	570.91	559.37	538.91	510.32	....
Demand Deposits	24	98.04	104.77	109.31	125.31	139.06	151.55	160.09	180.13	185.91	215.11	276.65	291.14
Time Deposits	25	370.66	372.57	382.44	377.04	373.00	374.11	387.86	383.27	381.76	361.53	317.22	313.35
Certificates of Deposit	26aa	8.69	8.65	7.32	10.22	14.16	19.10	19.23	15.21	20.24	27.95	18.39	17.91
Bonds	26ab	65.89	64.39	63.90	62.22	62.10	53.56	43.31	43.13	38.28	33.47	26.84	....
Foreign Liabilities	26c	89.01	77.24	71.58	75.53	80.07	92.26	80.18	54.54	61.29	68.73	67.30	....
Credit from Monetary Authorities	26g	20.01	14.13	12.92	11.62	9.91	13.80	15.28	14.60	8.11	21.33	28.55	....
Other Items (Net)	27r	63.81	97.69	88.38	94.19	78.67	80.58	76.65	89.14	103.29	71.25	48.51	....
Monetary Survey						*Trillions of Yen: End of Period*							
Foreign Assets (Net)	31n	–7.62	31.78	34.56	46.01	41.94	53.33	43.36	44.77	56.61	66.90	73.99	....
Domestic Credit	32	644.34	649.41	646.82	658.28	667.36	675.96	690.11	712.82	725.30	731.79	713.65	....
Claims on Central Govt. (Net)	32an	53.77	62.32	57.09	57.73	60.70	66.76	74.67	109.06	132.60	157.03	166.12	....
Claims on Local Government	32b	12.01	14.95	17.38	19.78	20.72	21.39	23.75	24.79	24.33	25.27	25.67	....
Claims on Nonfin.Pub.Enterprises	32c	13.58	13.47	12.55	11.57	10.06	9.01	8.34	8.06	8.99	10.58	11.56	....
Claims on Private Sector	32d	564.98	558.67	559.81	569.20	575.88	578.79	583.35	570.91	559.37	538.91	510.32	....
Money	34	136.14	145.61	151.67	171.54	188.15	204.28	214.40	239.54	247.86	281.79	347.98	....
Quasi-Money	35	370.66	372.57	382.44	377.04	373.00	374.11	387.86	383.27	381.76	361.53	317.22	313.35
Certificates of Deposit	36aa	8.69	8.65	7.32	10.22	14.16	19.10	19.23	15.21	20.24	27.95	18.39	17.91
Bonds	36ab	65.89	64.39	63.90	62.22	62.10	53.56	43.31	43.13	38.28	33.47	26.84	....
Other Items (Net)	37r	55.34	89.96	76.07	83.27	71.90	78.23	72.34	77.66	101.26	106.79	92.89	....
Money plus Quasi-Money	35l	506.79	518.19	534.10	548.59	561.14	578.39	602.26	622.80	629.62	643.31	665.20	....
Other Banking Institutions						*Trillions of Yen: End of Period*							
Cash	40	76.47	82.85	76.56	82.47	87.21	84.43	....	....	....	....	....	....
Claims on Central Government	42a	111.09	117.65	126.45	142.11	151.55	170.24	....	....	....	....	....	....
Claims on Local Government	42b	69.31	74.34	82.91	89.40	100.50	110.58	....	....	....	....	....	....
Claims on Nonfin.Pub.Enterprises	42c	39.17	43.44	47.27	50.76	54.46	57.78	....	....	....	....	....	....
Claims on Private Sector	42d	289.22	307.76	324.62	327.79	339.87	332.09	....	....	....	....	....	....
Demand and Time Deposits	45a	401.74	430.84	456.40	479.69	502.71	531.44	....	....	....	....	....	....
Deposits with Trust Fund Bureau	46b	138.86	147.58	153.18	150.65	155.69	153.94	....	....	....	....	....	....
Insurance Reserves	47d	62.81	71.34	79.86	88.88	88.16	95.68	....	....	....	....	....	....
Other Items (Net)	47r	–18.16	–23.73	–31.64	–26.70	–12.97	–25.93	....	....	....	....	....	....

2004, International Monetary Fund : *International Financial Statistics Yearbook*

Japan 158

		1992	1993	1994	1995	1996	1997	1998	1999	2000	2001	2002	2003
Nonbank Financial Institutions							*Trillions of Yen: End of Period*						
Cash................................	40..s	24.62	27.30	30.88	33.05	27.86	33.77	....	....	....	....	....	....
Claims on Central Government.........	42a.s	10.39	14.86	20.86	29.58	29.72	31.36	....	....	....	....	....	....
Claims on Local Government............	42b.s	2.19	2.98	4.44	6.78	7.90	8.79	....	....	....	....	....	....
Claims on Nonfin.Pub.Enterprises.....	42c.s	4.38	3.62	4.42	4.44	4.83	5.20	....	....	....	....	....	....
Claims on Private Sector................	42d.s	105.59	111.33	114.86	112.66	120.58	108.74	....	....	....	....	....	....
Insurance and Pension Reserves.......	47d.s	171.50	186.38	199.49	210.48	226.01	230.02	....	....	....	....	....	....
Other Items (Net).........................	47r.s	−24.34	−26.30	−24.04	−23.99	−35.12	−42.17	....	....	....	....	....	....
Financial Survey							*Trillions of Yen: End of Period*						
Foreign Assets (Net)......................	51n	−7.62	31.78	34.56	46.01	41.94	†90.22	109.48	103.15	110.55	123.25	116.68	....
Domestic Credit............................	52	1,275.67	1,325.38	1,372.64	1,421.79	1,476.78	†1,524.71	1,551.73	1,632.01	1,622.45	1,604.30	1,564.85	....
Claims on Central Govt. (Net)........	52an	175.25	194.82	204.40	229.42	241.97	†287.42	317.87	363.67	392.86	408.45	433.89	....
Claims on Local Government.........	52b	83.51	92.27	104.72	115.95	129.13	†127.42	135.38	144.48	150.40	154.06	159.81	....
Claims on Nonfin.Pub.Enterprises...	52c	57.12	60.53	64.24	66.77	69.35	†111.30	92.31	92.85	93.94	95.44	93.13	....
Claims on Private Sector................	52d	959.79	977.75	999.29	1,009.65	1,036.33	†998.58	1,006.17	1,031.01	985.26	946.35	878.01	....
Liquid Liabilities............................	55l	868.82	900.42	945.09	976.19	1,019.37	†920.87	955.29	983.02	989.24	1,002.50	1,009.00	....
Bonds..	56ab	65.89	64.39	63.90	62.22	62.10	†121.12	116.88	121.41	117.09	111.78	85.94	....
Deposits with Fiscal Loan Fund........	56b	138.86	147.58	153.18	150.65	155.69	†147.35	152.85	156.60	159.19	147.35	129.52	....
Insurance and Pension Reserves.......	57d	234.31	257.73	279.35	299.37	314.17	†360.26	373.34	384.24	396.87	400.74	401.63	....
Other Items (Net)..........................	57r	−39.84	−12.96	−34.33	−20.64	−32.62	†69.39	67.44	93.23	75.61	65.18	55.45	....
Interest Rates							*Percent Per Annum*						
Discount Rate (End of Period)...........	60	3.25	1.75	1.75	.50	.50	.50	.50	.50	.50	.10	.10	.10
Money Market Rate.......................	60b	4.58	†3.06	2.20	1.21	.47	.48	.37	.06	.11	.06	.01	−
Private Bill Rate.............................	60bs	4.40	2.97	2.24	1.22	.59	.62	.72	.15	.23	....	....	....
Deposit Rate.................................	60l	†3.35	2.14	1.70	.90	.30	.30	.27	.12	.07	.06	.04	.04
Lending Rate.................................	60p	6.15	†4.41	4.13	3.51	2.66	2.45	2.32	2.16	2.07	1.97	1.86	1.82
Government Bond Yield..................	61	4.94	3.69	3.71	2.53	2.23	1.69	1.10	†1.77	1.75	1.33	1.25	1.01
Prices, Production, Labor							*Index Numbers (2000=100): Period Averages*						
Share Prices.................................	62	88.2	98.5	103.4	89.3	103.8	90.2	76.2	89.6	100.0	77.3	62.7	59.4
Wholesale Prices...........................	63	108.4	106.7	104.9	104.1	102.4	103.0	101.5	100.0	100.0	97.7	95.7	95.0
Consumer Prices............................	64	96.7	97.9	98.6	98.5	98.6	100.4	101.0	100.7	100.0	99.3	98.4	98.1
Wages: Monthly Earnings................	65	90.7	92.4	94.6	96.5	98.3	99.8	99.5	99.8	100.0	99.5	97.9	97.9
Industrial Production......................	66	94.1	90.8	92.0	95.5	97.7	101.2	94.5	94.8	100.0	93.7	92.6	95.4
Mfg. Employment, Seas. Adj............	67eyc	117.0	116.1	113.5	111.4	109.0	107.8	105.9	102.8	100.0	97.0	92.4	89.4
							Number in Thousands: Period Averages						
Labor Force..................................	67d	65,780	66,150	66,450	66,660	67,110	67,870	67,930	67,790	67,660	67,520	66,890	....
Employment..................................	67e	64,360	64,500	64,530	64,570	64,860	65,570	65,140	64,623	64,464	64,121	63,303	63,160
Unemployment..............................	67c	1,420	1,656	1,920	2,098	2,250	2,303	2,787	3,171	3,198	3,395	3,588	3,504
Unemployment Rate (%).................	67r	2.2	2.5	2.9	3.2	3.4	3.4	4.1	4.7	4.7	5.0	5.4	5.3
International Transactions							*Billions of Yen*						
Exports...	70	43,011	40,200	40,470	41,532	44,729	50,938	50,644	47,549	51,649	49,010	52,109	54,549
Imports, c.i.f.................................	71	29,527	26,824	28,051	31,534	37,992	40,956	36,653	35,270	40,915	42,402	42,177	44,319
							2000=100						
Volume of Exports.........................	72	78.6	76.6	78.0	†80.5	81.1	90.7	89.5	91.5	100.0	89.9	97.4	....
Volume of Imports.........................	73	61.9	63.7	72.4	†81.4	85.4	86.9	82.3	90.2	100.0	98.7	100.2	....
Unit Value of Exports.....................	74	106.0	101.6	100.6	†100.0	106.8	108.8	109.6	100.9	100.0	105.6	103.7	....
Unit Value of Imports.....................	75	116.6	103.2	95.0	†94.8	108.7	115.3	109.0	95.7	100.0	105.1	103.0	....
Export Prices.................................	76	123.3	113.4	110.3	†107.9	113.0	115.1	116.6	104.9	100.0	103.0	101.9	97.8
Import Prices.................................	76.x	111.0	99.5	94.0	†93.9	103.0	110.7	105.3	95.5	100.0	102.5	101.0	100.1

2004, International Monetary Fund : *International Financial Statistics Yearbook*

Japan 158

		1992	1993	1994	1995	1996	1997	1998	1999	2000	2001	2002	2003
Balance of Payments						*Billions of US Dollars: Minus Sign Indicates Debit*							
Current Account, n.i.e.	78ald	112.57	131.64	130.26	111.04	65.79	96.81	118.75	114.60	119.66	87.80	112.45	136.22
Goods: Exports f.o.b.	78aad	332.56	352.66	385.70	428.72	400.29	409.24	374.04	403.69	459.51	383.59	395.58	449.12
Goods: Imports f.o.b.	78abd	−207.79	−213.24	−241.51	−296.93	−316.70	−307.64	−251.66	−280.37	−342.80	−313.38	−301.75	−342.72
Trade Balance	78acd	124.76	139.42	144.19	131.79	83.58	101.60	122.39	123.32	116.72	70.21	93.83	106.40
Services: Credit	78add	49.07	53.22	58.30	65.27	67.71	69.30	62.41	61.00	69.24	64.52	65.71	77.62
Services: Debit	78aed	−93.03	−96.30	−106.36	−122.63	−129.99	−123.45	−111.83	−115.16	−116.86	−108.25	−107.94	−111.53
Balance on Goods & Services	78afd	80.80	96.33	96.13	74.43	21.31	47.45	72.97	69.16	69.09	26.48	51.60	72.49
Income: Credit	78agd	142.87	147.83	155.19	192.45	112.44	111.83	100.33	92.05	97.20	103.09	91.48	95.21
Income: Debit	78ahd	−107.27	−107.42	−114.96	−148.16	−58.95	−53.63	−45.71	−34.47	−36.80	−33.87	−25.71	−23.97
Balance on Gds, Serv. & Inc.	78aid	116.41	136.74	136.36	118.72	74.80	105.65	127.59	126.74	129.49	95.70	117.37	143.73
Current Transfers, n.i.e.: Credit	78ajd	1.67	1.58	1.83	1.98	6.02	6.01	5.53	6.21	7.38	6.15	10.04	6.51
Current Transfers: Debit	78akd	−5.50	−6.68	−7.94	−9.66	−15.03	−14.84	−14.37	−18.35	−17.21	−14.06	−14.96	−14.02
Capital Account, n.i.e.	78bcd	−1.30	−1.46	−1.85	−2.23	−3.29	−4.05	−14.45	−16.47	−9.26	−2.87	−3.32	−4.00
Capital Account, n.i.e.: Credit	78bad	−	−	−	.01	1.22	1.52	1.57	.75	.78	.99	.91	.39
Capital Account: Debit	78bbd	−1.30	−1.46	−1.85	−2.24	−4.51	−5.57	−16.02	−17.21	−10.04	−3.86	−4.24	−4.39
Financial Account, n.i.e.	78bjd	−100.28	−102.21	−85.11	−63.98	−28.02	−120.51	−114.82	−38.85	−78.31	−48.16	−63.38	71.92
Direct Investment Abroad	78bdd	−17.39	−13.83	−18.09	−22.51	−23.45	−26.06	−24.62	−22.27	−31.53	−38.50	−32.02	−28.77
Dir. Invest. in Rep. Econ., n.i.e.	78bed	2.76	.12	.91	.04	.21	3.20	3.27	12.31	8.23	6.19	9.09	6.24
Portfolio Investment Assets	78bfd	−33.95	−63.74	−91.97	−86.05	−100.61	−47.06	−95.24	−154.41	−83.36	−106.79	−85.93	−176.29
Equity Securities	78bkd	2.98	−15.28	−14.00	.07	−8.17	−13.73	−14.00	−32.40	−19.72	−11.28	−37.28	−4.47
Debt Securities	78bld	−36.93	−48.46	−77.97	−86.11	−92.43	−33.34	−81.24	−122.01	−63.64	−95.51	−48.65	−171.82
Portfolio Investment Liab., n.i.e.	78bgd	9.57	−6.11	64.53	59.79	66.79	79.19	56.06	126.93	47.39	60.50	−20.04	81.18
Equity Securities	78bmd	8.88	19.86	48.95	50.60	49.45	27.00	16.11	103.89	−1.29	39.10	−16.69	87.78
Debt Securities	78bnd	.70	−25.97	15.58	9.19	17.34	52.19	39.95	23.04	48.67	21.40	−3.35	−6.59
Financial Derivatives Assets	78bwd	−.61	−.49	.43	−1.20	98.70	86.17	90.75	83.80	106.74	102.79	77.25	64.96
Financial Derivatives Liabilities	78bxd	−1.97	−.54	−.20	−9.12	−105.95	−92.02	−89.65	−86.43	−111.41	−101.40	−74.77	−59.38
Other Investment Assets	78bhd	46.56	15.07	−35.12	−102.24	5.21	−191.96	37.94	266.34	−4.15	46.59	36.41	149.89
Monetary Authorities	78bod	....	....	....	....	....	....	....	....	....	....	....	....
General Government	78bpd	−9.51	−7.80	−8.76	−8.66	−5.28	−9.12	−15.50	−11.56	−1.89	−3.95	.92	4.49
Banks	78bqd	49.64	27.73	−10.67	−85.62	75.57	−140.18	54.14	239.40	36.51	15.59	1.59	140.78
Other Sectors	78brd	6.42	−4.85	−15.69	−7.96	−65.08	−42.66	−.70	38.50	−38.77	34.95	33.90	4.62
Other Investment Liab., n.i.e.	78bid	−105.24	−32.70	−5.60	97.30	31.08	68.03	−93.33	−265.12	−10.21	−17.55	26.63	34.10
Monetary Authorities	78bsd	−	−	−	−	−	−	−	−	−	−	−	−
General Government	78btd	1.28	−.10	−2.00	1.18	−2.12	−.11	−1.30	.55	−.93	7.01	.06	5.14
Banks	78bud	−119.86	−37.90	4.87	17.27	−9.06	43.34	−23.75	−189.16	28.22	4.99	22.46	−26.22
Other Sectors	78bvd	13.34	5.30	−8.47	78.86	42.27	24.80	−68.28	−76.50	−37.49	−29.54	4.11	55.17
Net Errors and Omissions	78cad	−10.38	−.50	−18.03	13.78	.65	34.31	4.36	16.97	16.87	3.72	.39	−16.99
Overall Balance	78cbd	.62	27.47	25.27	58.61	35.14	6.57	−6.16	76.26	48.95	40.49	46.13	187.15
Reserves and Related Items	79dad	−.62	−27.47	−25.27	−58.61	−35.14	−6.57	6.16	−76.26	−48.95	−40.49	−46.13	−187.15
Reserve Assets	79dbd	−.62	−27.47	−25.27	−58.61	−35.14	−6.57	6.16	−76.26	−48.95	−40.49	−46.13	−187.15
Use of Fund Credit and Loans	79dcd	−	−	−	−	−	−	−	−	−	−	−	−
Exceptional Financing	79ded	....	....	....	....	....	....	....	....	....	....	....	....
International Investment Position						*Billions of US Dollars*							
Assets	79aad	2,035.24	2,180.88	2,424.24	2,632.86	2,652.61	2,737.45	2,986.33	3,013.60	2,969.59	2,881.51	3,052.08	3,599.80
Direct Investment Abroad	79abd	248.06	259.80	275.57	238.45	258.61	271.90	270.04	248.78	278.44	300.11	304.23	335.50
Portfolio Investment	79acd	715.45	771.11	858.69	855.07	933.20	902.26	1,056.49	1,242.37	1,306.48	1,289.75	1,394.52	1,721.32
Equity Securities	79add	....	....	....	146.26	154.90	158.77	209.38	285.34	262.25	227.35	210.82	274.46
Debt Securities	79aed	....	....	....	708.81	778.30	743.49	847.11	957.04	1,044.23	1,062.40	1,183.70	1,446.86
Financial Derivatives	79ald	....	....	....	3.21	3.97	4.41	5.09	4.46	3.31	3.00	3.37	4.90
Other Investment	79afd	998.94	1,050.29	1,162.87	1,351.31	1,239.23	1,338.08	1,438.88	1,230.34	1,020.36	888.23	882.34	865.03
Monetary Authorities	79agd	−	−	−	−	−	−	−	−	−	−	−	−
General Government	79ahd	123.40	142.22	165.01	184.05	170.47	162.32	196.16	230.91	210.17	191.93	206.97	228.79
Banks	79aid	690.32	701.47	752.12	911.23	773.14	861.44	876.07	630.02	529.23	467.46	486.66	447.35
Other Sectors	79ajd	185.22	206.60	245.74	256.02	295.63	314.32	366.65	369.41	280.96	228.84	188.71	188.88
Reserve Assets	79akd	72.79	99.68	127.10	184.82	217.61	220.81	215.83	287.66	360.99	400.41	467.62	673.06
Liabilities	79lad	1,520.39	1,568.84	1,733.92	1,815.26	1,761.59	1,778.72	1,832.69	2,184.48	1,811.65	1,521.42	1,589.92	1,986.18
Dir. Invest. in Rep. Economy	79lbd	15.51	16.89	19.17	33.51	29.94	27.08	26.07	46.12	50.32	50.32	78.14	89.73
Portfolio Investment	79lcd	513.10	545.32	630.67	545.42	556.25	582.48	632.76	1,165.44	884.32	665.79	610.42	867.17
Equity Securities	79ldd	124.59	171.17	250.88	306.28	315.65	279.53	304.33	833.43	550.23	376.05	339.93	561.02
Debt Securities	79led	388.51	374.15	379.79	239.14	240.60	302.95	328.43	332.01	334.09	289.75	270.49	306.14
Financial Derivatives	79lld	−	−	−	2.85	2.72	4.10	4.54	3.10	3.19	3.54	3.71	6.79
Other Investment	79lfd	991.78	1,006.63	1,084.08	1,233.48	1,172.69	1,165.06	1,169.32	969.83	873.82	801.77	897.65	1,022.50
Monetary Authorities	79lgd	54.72	65.52	99.85	−	−	−	−	−	−	−	−	−
General Government	79lhd	−	−	−	14.96	11.35	10.12	9.65	11.62	9.68	8.15	5.26	5.14
Banks	79lid	696.71	673.58	694.94	745.42	701.56	714.28	751.47	570.71	603.99	568.40	631.12	660.40
Other Sectors	79ljd	240.35	267.53	289.29	473.10	459.78	440.66	408.20	387.50	260.15	225.21	261.27	356.96

Japan 158

		1992	1993	1994	1995	1996	1997	1998	1999	2000	2001	2002	2003
Government Finance						*Billions of Yen: Year Beginning April 1*							
Deficit (-) or Surplus	80	1,473p	-7,318p	....	....	....	....	....	....	....	....	....	....
Revenue	81	99,412p	99,866p	....	....	....	....	....	....	....	....	....	....
Grants Received	81z	3,278p	3,498p	....	....	....	....	....	....	....	....	....	....
Expenditure	82	100,642p	112,655p	....	....	....	....	....	....	....	....	....	....
Lending Minus Repayments	83	575p	-1,973p	....	....	....	....	....	....	....	....	....	....
Financing													
Domestic	84a	-1,473p	7,318p	....	....	....	....	....	....	....	....	....	....
Foreign Currency	85b	....	....	....	....	....	....	....	....	....	....	....	....
Use of Cash Balances	87	....	....	....	....	....	....	....	....	....	....	....	....
Debt: Domestic	88a	196,194p	212,474p	....	....	....	....	....	....	....	....	....	....
Foreign	89a	....	....	....	....	....	....	....	....	....	....	....	....
National Accounts						*Billions of Yen*							
Househ.Cons.Expend.,incl.NPISHs	96f.c	258,052	264,149	272,646	276,844	283,433	288,788	288,210	286,605	285,750	285,966	284,797	283,215
Government Consumption Expend	91f.c	64,249	67,014	69,510	72,789	75,491	77,094	78,582	80,843	84,019	86,419	87,973	87,191
Gross Fixed Capital Formation	93e.c	146,782	142,008	138,676	138,099	145,022	146,161	138,331	133,596	134,739	130,311	120,430	119,049
Changes in Inventories	93i.c	1,011	298	-710	2,233	3,499	3,137	29	-1,711	-361	-22	-1,336	391
Exports of Goods and Services	90c.c	47,288	44,109	44,270	45,230	49,561	56,074	55,051	51,144	55,256	52,567	55,829	58,882
Imports of Goods and Services (-)	98c.c	36,891	33,344	34,387	38,272	47,022	50,316	45,607	43,251	47,940	49,393	49,417	50,907
Gross Domestic Product (GDP)	99b.c	480,492	484,234	490,005	496,922	509,984	520,937	514,595	507,224	511,462	505,847	498,276	497,821
Net Primary Income from Abroad	98.nc	3,990	4,163	3,812	3,836	5,471	6,758	6,940	6,384	6,421	8,321	8,193	8,524
Gross National Income (GNI)	99a.c	484,482	488,397	493,818	500,758	515,455	527,695	521,535	513,608	517,884	514,168	506,469	506,345
Net Current Transf.from Abroad	98t.c	-10,551	-11,841	-13,570	-14,672	-10,509	-15,397	-19,818	-19,913	-18,762	....	....	....
Gross Nat'l Disposable Inc.(GNDI)	99i.c	475,019	478,840	482,076	486,901	505,762	513,220	502,955	499,001	499,494	....	....	....
Gross Saving	99s.c	159,463	155,365	150,179	148,959	157,999	157,300	147,390	139,993	140,110	....	....	....
Consumption of Fixed Capital	99cf	81,736	84,602	86,676	88,950	92,051	94,234	96,149	95,681	97,841	99,095	....	....
GDP Volume 1995 Prices	99b.r	481,087	482,049	487,519	496,922	514,292	523,621	517,366	518,200	532,677	534,956	533,216	546,509
GDP Volume (2000=100)	99bvr	90.3	90.5	91.5	93.3	96.5	98.3	97.1	97.3	100.0	100.4	100.1	102.6
GDP Deflator (2000=100)	99bir	104.0	104.6	104.7	104.1	103.3	103.6	103.6	101.9	100.0	98.5	97.3	94.9
						Millions: Midyear Estimates							
Population	99z	124.37	124.75	125.12	125.47	125.82	126.15	126.47	126.77	127.03	127.27	127.48	127.65

2004, International Monetary Fund : *International Financial Statistics Yearbook*

Jordan 439

		1992	1993	1994	1995	1996	1997	1998	1999	2000	2001	2002	2003
Exchange Rates			*SDRs per Dinar: End of Period*
Official Rate...............................	ac	1.0525	1.0341	.9772	.9488	.9809	1.0454	1.0017	1.0276	1.0825	1.1223	1.0375	.9492
			*US Dollars per Dinar: End of Period (ag) Period Average (rh)*
Official Rate...............................	ag	1.4472	1.4205	1.4265	1.4104	1.4104	1.4104	1.4104	1.4104	1.4104	1.4104	1.4104	1.4104
Official Rate...............................	rh	1.4712	1.4434	1.4312	1.4276	1.4104	1.4104	1.4104	1.4104	1.4104	1.4105	1.4104	1.4104
Fund Position			*Millions of SDRs: End of Period*
Quota......................................	2f.s	121.7	121.7	121.7	121.7	121.7	121.7	121.7	170.5	170.5	170.5	170.5	170.5
SDRs.......................................	1b.s	.4	4.0	.5	.8	.6	.1	.6	.2	.5	.9	.6	.7
Reserve Position in the Fund............	1c.s	12.0	–	–	–	–	–	–	–	.1	.1	.1	.1
Total Fund Cred.&Loans Outstg........	2tl	81.2	59.2	98.9	169.2	236.1	316.6	333.4	362.9	354.3	344.5	355.0	283.6
International Liquidity			*Millions of US Dollars Unless Otherwise Indicated: End of Period*
Total Reserves minus Gold..............	1l.d	767.2	†1,637.4	1,692.6	1,972.9	1,759.3	2,200.3	1,750.4	2,629.1	3,331.3	3,062.2	3,975.9	5,194.3
SDRs.....................................	1b.d	.6	5.5	.7	1.2	.8	.2	.8	.3	.6	1.2	.9	1.1
Reserve Position in the Fund..........	1c.d	16.4	–	–	–	–	–	–	–	.1	.1	.1	.1
Foreign Exchange.....................	1d.d	750.2	†1,631.9	1,691.9	1,971.7	1,758.5	2,200.1	1,749.6	2,628.8	3,330.6	3,061.0	3,975.0	5,193.1
Gold (Million Fine Troy Ounces)........	1ad	.789	.791	.794	.793	.800	.812	.827	.486	.401	.405	.410	.411
Gold (National Valuation)................	1and	101.4	99.8	198.5	195.9	197.7	200.7	204.3	120.0	99.1	112.2	141.2	171.3
Monetary Authorities: Other Liab.....	4..d	.8	125.6	117.5	82.3	71.3	43.8	32.8	230.6	177.6	181.3	180.3	176.1
Deposit Money Banks: Assets..........	7a.d	2,137.9	2,216.3	2,399.3	2,655.3	2,845.0	3,077.5	3,607.1	4,101.5	5,235.2	6,104.3	6,336.7	6,180.3
Liabilities...................	7b.d	2,310.5	2,166.6	2,518.5	2,926.5	3,100.7	3,084.7	3,079.7	3,285.2	3,819.1	4,213.5	4,718.0	4,549.2
Other Banking Insts.: Liabilities........	7f.d	98.0	112.3	120.6	130.3	117.0	126.0	124.7	120.9	114.9	....	....	....
Monetary Authorities			*Millions of Dinars: End of Period*
Foreign Assets...........................	11	999.7	†1,688.7	1,904.3	2,185.2	2,253.9	2,557.1	2,297.7	2,889.6	3,267.4	3,064.2	3,694.0	4,571.1
Claims on Central Government.........	12a	688.9	772.5	905.3	867.1	930.9	989.4	1,033.4	1,015.8	1,125.7	1,097.0	1,007.1	938.8
Reserve Money...........................	14	1,771.3	†2,236.0	2,349.5	2,498.9	2,164.4	2,104.0	2,005.0	2,246.9	2,264.8	2,135.7	2,218.9	2,593.6
of which: Currency Outside DMBs..	14a	1,003.9	1,047.9	1,072.6	1,050.9	952.1	987.6	952.8	1,106.6	1,239.9	1,202.4	1,252.7	1,443.7
Foreign Liabilities.........................	16c	77.7	†145.7	183.6	236.7	291.3	333.9	356.1	516.6	453.2	435.5	470.0	423.6
Central Government Deposits...........	16d	137.6	101.3	225.1	163.5	323.7	321.0	137.7	145.9	420.7	401.6	401.9	190.8
Other Items (Net).........................	17r	−297.9	†−21.8	51.4	153.1	405.4	787.5	832.3	995.9	1,254.4	1,188.4	1,610.2	2,301.9
Deposit Money Banks			*Millions of Dinars: End of Period*
Reserves..................................	20	1,584.9	1,477.1	1,576.9	1,799.6	1,854.9	2,163.8	2,015.9	2,389.2	2,518.1	2,383.3	2,826.5	3,586.7
Foreign Assets...........................	21	1,477.3	1,560.3	1,681.9	1,882.6	2,017.1	2,182.0	2,557.5	2,907.9	3,711.7	4,328.0	4,492.7	4,381.8
Claims on Central Government.........	22a	457.9	358.7	307.0	240.0	238.1	163.0	412.5	618.5	733.0	902.5	1,087.9	887.7
Claims on Private Sector.................	22d	2,013.7	2,310.5	2,763.4	3,192.5	3,354.9	3,526.5	3,803.2	4,050.2	4,230.7	4,709.9	4,833.4	5,000.4
Demand Deposits.........................	24	685.9	†669.6	666.0	664.7	578.1	636.1	648.5	658.0	774.2	888.4	1,019.2	1,382.1
Time and Savings Deposits..............	25	2,448.8	†2,510.0	2,782.4	3,040.5	3,209.8	3,469.3	3,734.4	4,212.9	4,651.9	4,963.3	5,430.2	5,965.1
Foreign Liabilities.........................	26c	1,596.5	1,525.3	1,765.5	2,074.9	2,198.4	2,187.1	2,183.5	2,329.2	2,707.7	2,987.4	3,345.1	3,225.4
Central Government Deposits...........	26d	91.5	†424.8	499.8	550.9	634.6	736.3	848.3	1,011.0	1,062.8	1,071.4	914.8	692.5
Capital Accounts.........................	27a	348.5	492.6	582.8	701.7	771.0	1,047.7	1,181.3	1,316.6	1,377.9	1,436.2	1,545.1	1,623.2
Other Items (Net)..........................	27r	362.7	†84.3	32.9	82.0	73.2	−41.3	193.2	438.0	619.1	976.9	986.1	968.4
Monetary Survey			*Millions of Dinars: End of Period*
Foreign Assets (Net)......................	31n	802.7	†1,578.0	1,637.2	1,756.2	1,781.3	2,218.1	2,315.6	2,951.7	3,818.2	3,969.3	4,371.6	5,303.9
Domestic Credit...........................	32	3,220.9	†3,324.8	3,723.1	4,089.0	4,114.2	4,184.4	4,780.0	4,925.6	5,016.0	5,613.0	5,961.8	6,310.1
Claims on Central Govt. (Net)..........	32an	917.8	†605.1	487.4	392.7	210.8	95.1	459.9	477.3	375.2	526.4	778.2	943.2
Claims on Nonfin.Pub.Enterprises...	32c	235.0	†296.8	341.9	362.2	408.9	425.3	381.2	307.9	316.9	284.3	261.3	278.0
Claims on Private Sector................	32d	2,018.1	2,316.1	2,769.9	3,200.1	3,363.0	3,535.2	3,812.7	4,062.1	4,243.9	4,723.6	4,847.9	5,015.5
Money.....................................	34	1,716.0	†1,719.4	1,741.6	1,738.7	1,532.8	1,626.1	1,612.6	1,766.1	2,017.4	2,094.8	2,273.2	2,827.0
Quasi-Money.............................	35	2,479.0	†2,664.7	2,788.6	3,051.0	3,213.3	3,482.7	3,818.8	4,507.2	4,734.3	5,204.0	5,652.5	6,294.9
Other Items (Net).........................	37r	−171.4	†518.8	830.1	1,055.6	1,149.4	1,293.6	1,664.1	1,603.9	2,082.6	2,283.5	2,407.7	2,492.1
Money plus Quasi-Money...............	35l	4,195.0	†4,384.1	4,530.2	4,789.7	4,746.1	5,108.8	5,431.4	6,273.3	6,751.7	7,298.7	7,925.7	9,121.9
Other Banking Institutions			*Millions of Dinars: End of Period*
Cash.......................................	40	49.8	†70.6	59.9	63.3	54.3	53.0	41.2	22.5	71.2	....	....	....
Claims on Private Sector.................	42d	256.2	†294.9	284.8	306.2	315.0	334.9	349.3	362.2	343.0	....	....	....
Deposits..................................	45	44.9	†66.5	47.4	32.7	24.5	17.0	11.8	8.8	9.5	....	....	....
Foreign Liabilities.........................	46c	67.5	†79.0	84.6	92.4	83.0	89.3	88.4	85.7	81.5	....	....	....
Central Govt. Lending Funds............	46f	.9	†17.1	16.2	16.2	15.0	14.3	13.7	13.1	50.3	....	....	....
Capital Accounts........................	47a	104.0	†90.9	91.6	111.5	132.0	153.2	164.5	177.4	186.4	....	....	....
Other Items (Net).........................	47r	88.7	†111.9	104.9	116.8	114.9	114.2	112.0	99.7	86.4	....	....	....
Liquid Liabilities...........................	55l	4,190.1	†4,380.0	4,517.8	4,759.1	4,716.3	5,072.7	5,402.0	6,259.6	6,690.0	....	....	....
Interest Rates			*Percent Per Annum*
Discount Rate (End of Period)...........	60	8.50	8.50	8.50	8.50	8.50	7.75	9.00	8.00	6.50	5.00	4.50	....
Deposit Rate (Period Average)..........	60l	7.20	6.88	7.09	7.68	8.50	9.10	8.21	8.30	6.97	5.81	4.42	....
Lending Rate (Period Average).........	60p	10.16	10.23	10.45	10.66	11.25	12.25	12.61	12.33	11.80	10.92	10.18	....
Prices and Production			*Index Numbers (2000=100): Period Averages*
Wholesale Prices........................	63	96.3	99.6	104.4	101.9	103.9	105.6	106.3	103.7	100.0	98.5	96.9	....
Consumer Prices........................	64	†79.7	82.4	85.3	87.3	93.0	†95.8	98.7	99.3	100.0	101.8	103.6	106.1
Industrial Production.....................	66	†73.3	79.0	†83.4	93.8	89.0	92.1	94.0	96.2	100.0	109.6	121.8	114.3

Jordan 439

		1992	1993	1994	1995	1996	1997	1998	1999	2000	2001	2002	2003
International Transactions						*Millions of Dinars*							
Exports	70	829.3	864.7	995.2	1,241.1	1,288.2	1,301.4	1,277.9	1,298.8	1,346.6	1,625.7	1,963.9	....
Imports, c.i.f.	71	2,214.0	2,453.6	2,362.6	2,590.3	3,043.6	2,908.1	2,714.4	2,635.2	3,259.4	3,434.5	3,559.0	....
							2000=100						
Volume of Exports	72	67.2	72.6	†77.7	84.5	82.2	87.8	90.3	92.9	100.0	123.3	141.8	....
Volume of Imports	73	82.9	90.4	†88.1	85.4	92.0	89.9	84.9	84.0	100.0	104.6	105.6	....
Unit Value of Exports	74	89.2	90.1	†94.4	109.9	116.9	113.5	107.2	104.5	100.0	101.3	101.6	....
Unit Value of Imports	75	84.4	85.8	†83.4	94.4	103.0	100.8	99.9	97.5	100.0	102.1	104.9	....
Balance of Payments					*Millions of US Dollars: Minus Sign Indicates Debit*								
Current Account, n.i.e.	78ald	−835.2	−629.1	−398.0	−258.6	−221.9	29.3	14.1	404.9	58.5	−4.2	418.2	1,087.6
Goods: Exports f.o.b.	78aad	1,218.9	1,246.3	1,424.5	1,769.6	1,816.9	1,835.5	1,802.4	1,831.9	1,899.3	2,294.4	2,770.0	3,081.5
Goods: Imports f.o.b.	78abd	−2,998.7	−3,145.2	−3,003.8	−3,287.8	−3,818.1	−3,648.5	−3,403.9	−3,292.0	−4,073.6	−4,301.4	−4,450.4	−4,996.5
Trade Balance	78acd	−1,779.7	−1,898.8	−1,579.4	−1,518.2	−2,001.1	−1,813.0	−1,601.6	−1,460.1	−2,174.3	−2,006.9	−1,680.4	−1,915.0
Services: Credit	78add	1,449.2	1,573.7	1,562.0	1,709.2	1,846.3	1,736.8	1,825.1	1,701.7	1,636.7	1,481.7	1,512.6	1,493.4
Services: Debit	78aed	−1,324.7	−1,347.2	−1,392.7	−1,614.9	−1,597.7	−1,537.2	−1,783.8	−1,698.0	−1,722.6	−1,725.2	−1,789.9	−1,753.3
Balance on Goods & Services	78afd	−1,655.2	−1,672.3	−1,410.1	−1,424.0	−1,752.6	−1,613.4	−1,560.2	−1,456.4	−2,260.2	−2,250.4	−1,957.7	−2,174.9
Income: Credit	78agd	112.4	99.0	72.7	115.7	111.7	248.2	306.9	467.6	670.1	648.5	484.1	492.8
Income: Debit	78ahd	−460.0	−409.4	−387.5	−394.5	−412.7	−457.0	−445.0	−479.7	−535.4	−461.4	−372.3	−370.7
Balance on Gds, Serv. & Inc.	78aid	−2,002.8	−1,982.8	−1,724.9	−1,702.8	−2,053.6	−1,822.1	−1,698.3	−1,468.5	−2,125.5	−2,063.2	−1,845.9	−2,052.8
Current Transfers: n.i.e.: Credit	78ajd	1,263.6	1,441.1	1,447.4	1,591.8	1,970.2	2,096.1	1,984.3	2,154.9	2,461.5	2,365.9	2,524.4	3,404.7
Current Transfers: Debit	78akd	−96.1	−87.4	−120.5	−147.6	−138.5	−244.6	−271.9	−281.4	−277.4	−306.9	−260.2	−264.3
Capital Account, n.i.e.	78bcd	−	−	−	197.2	157.7	163.8	81.1	90.3	64.9	21.6	68.4	93.5
Capital Account, n.i.e.: Credit	78bad	−	−	−	197.2	157.7	163.8	81.1	90.3	64.9	21.6	68.4	93.5
Capital Account: Debit	78bbd	−	−	−	....	....	....	....	....	....	....	....	....
Financial Account, n.i.e.	78bjd	615.1	−530.0	188.9	230.0	233.9	242.3	−177.3	725.1	1,387.6	526.2	441.2	−247.5
Direct Investment Abroad	78bdd	3.4	53.0	23.1	27.3	43.3	−	−	−4.5	−4.7	−9.3	−25.1	....
Dir. Invest. in Rep. Econ., n.i.e.	78bed	40.7	−33.5	2.9	13.3	15.5	360.9	310.0	158.0	786.6	100.3	55.9	376.0
Portfolio Investment Assets	78bfd	−	−	−	....	....	....	....	32.2	−	−	−191.8	−118.9
Equity Securities	78bkd	−	−	−	....	....	....	....	32.2	....	....	−191.8	−118.9
Debt Securities	78bld	−	−	−	....	....	....	....	....	....	....	....	....
Portfolio Investment Liab., n.i.e.	78bgd	−	−	−	....	....	....	....	−28.1	−140.9	−171.7	−52.2	−349.2
Equity Securities	78bmd	−	−	−	....	....	....	....	21.9	−16.8	−145.1	−52.2	−58.0
Debt Securities	78bnd	−	−	−	....	....	....	....	−49.9	−124.1	−26.5	−	−291.3
Financial Derivatives Assets	78bwd	....	....	....	....	....	....	....	....	....	....	....	....
Financial Derivatives Liabilities	78bxd	....	....	....	....	....	....	....	....	....	....	....	....
Other Investment Assets	78bhd	609.2	384.8	62.5	−313.4	−5.9	16.4	−80.3	−41.9	146.4	26.8	11.0	283.1
Monetary Authorities	78bod	−113.6	−94.9	−163.5	−313.4	−5.9	16.4	−80.3	−40.5	148.4	30.6	130.5	38.4
General Government	78bpd	−	−.3	−	....	....	....	....	−1.4	−2.0	−3.8	−3.0	−3.7
Banks	78bqd	−	−	−	....	....	....	....	....	....	....	−116.5	248.4
Other Sectors	78brd	722.8	480.0	225.9	....	....	....	....	....	....	....	....	....
Other Investment Liab., n.i.e.	78bid	−38.3	−934.3	100.4	502.8	181.0	−135.0	−407.1	609.4	600.1	580.1	643.4	−438.5
Monetary Authorities	78bsd	.6	.7	−8.7	−34.4	−11.0	−27.6	−11.0	183.5	−69.8	4.7	23.4	−188.2
General Government	78btd	−532.1	−675.8	−235.4	96.8	17.8	−91.4	−391.0	277.3	15.7	146.7	68.1	−152.3
Banks	78bud	495.1	−257.5	344.5	440.5	174.2	−15.9	−5.1	205.5	533.9	394.5	466.1	−99.4
Other Sectors	78bvd	−1.9	−1.7	−	....	....	....	....	−56.8	120.5	34.3	85.8	1.4
Net Errors and Omissions	78cad	83.1	298.0	−55.8	−339.9	−357.9	−160.8	−454.0	28.7	315.6	81.7	2.2	414.7
Overall Balance	78cbd	−137.1	−861.1	−264.9	−171.3	−188.2	274.6	−536.1	1,249.0	1,826.6	625.3	930.0	1,348.2
Reserves and Related Items	79dad	137.1	861.1	264.9	171.3	188.2	−274.6	536.1	−1,249.0	−1,826.6	−625.3	−930.0	−1,348.2
Reserve Assets	79dbd	−432.0	402.9	−216.8	−371.5	−280.7	−677.1	−83.4	−1,288.7	−1,815.4	−613.1	−942.5	−1,248.2
Use of Fund Credit and Loans	79dcd	21.1	−31.0	57.6	106.5	97.6	110.3	22.4	39.7	−11.2	−12.1	12.5	−100.0
Exceptional Financing	79ded	548.0	489.1	424.1	436.3	371.4	292.2	597.0	−	−	−	−	....
International Investment Position					*Millions of US Dollars*								
Assets	79aad	....	....	....	....	....	....	....	....	....	....	....	....
Direct Investment Abroad	79abd	....	....	....	....	....	....	....	....	....	....	....	....
Portfolio Investment	79acd	....	....	....	....	118.9	188.6	190.0	184.6	229.9	457.8	642.7	761.9
Equity Securities	79add	....	....	....	....	89.1	110.6	109.7	93.1	102.0	136.0	146.7	143.1
Debt Securities	79aed	....	....	....	....	29.8	78.0	80.3	91.5	127.9	321.9	496.1	618.8
Financial Derivatives	79ald	....	....	....	....	....	....	....	....	....	....	....	....
Other Investment	79afd	....	....	....	....	3,992.5	4,139.2	4,748.0	5,288.4	6,228.6	6,840.2	6,826.1	6,566.6
Monetary Authorities	79agd	....	....	....	....	1,221.9	1,205.6	1,286.0	1,326.5	1,178.1	1,147.5	1,092.9	1,081.7
General Government	79ahd	....	....	....	....	−	−	−	−	−	−	−	−
Banks	79aid	....	....	....	....	2,770.7	2,933.6	3,461.9	3,961.9	5,050.5	5,692.7	5,733.2	5,484.9
Other Sectors	79ajd	....	....	....	....	−	−	−	−	−	−	−	−
Reserve Assets	79akd	....	....	....	....	1,957.0	2,401.0	1,954.8	2,749.1	3,430.5	3,174.3	4,117.1	5,365.7
Liabilities	79lad	....	....	....	....	....	....	....	....	....	....	....	....
Dir. Invest. in Rep. Economy	79lbd	....	....	....	....	....	....	....	....	....	....	....	....
Portfolio Investment	79lcd	....	....	....	....	622.6	588.9	456.8	456.8	350.9	320.2	320.2	−
Equity Securities	79ldd	....	....	....	....	−	−	−	−	−	−	−	−
Debt Securities	79led	....	....	....	....	622.6	588.9	456.8	456.8	350.9	320.2	320.2	−
Financial Derivatives	79lld	....	....	....	....	....	....	....	....	....	....	....	....
Other Investment	79lfd	....	....	....	....	9,833.2	9,611.8	10,169.3	10,830.1	10,757.9	11,084.0	12,126.9	12,159.2
Monetary Authorities	79lgd	....	....	....	....	410.9	470.9	502.2	728.6	639.2	614.2	662.9	597.5
General Government	79lhd	....	....	....	....	6,321.6	6,056.1	6,587.6	6,816.4	6,299.9	6,256.3	6,746.0	7,182.8
Banks	79lid	....	....	....	....	3,100.7	3,084.8	3,079.6	3,285.1	3,818.9	4,213.5	4,718.1	4,378.9
Other Sectors	79ljd	....	....	....	....	−	−	−	−	−	−	−	−

Jordan 439

		1992	1993	1994	1995	1996	1997	1998	1999	2000	2001	2002	2003
Government Finance		*Millions of Dinars: Year Ending December 31*											
Deficit (-) or Surplus	80	180.9	141.7	45.2	49.3	−66.3	−163.4	−327.1	−140.4	−119.8	−155.5	....	....
Revenue	81	1,109.4	1,191.6	1,162.4	1,332.6	1,366.9	1,312.6	1,422.4	1,530.5	1,506.6	1,578.7	....	....
Grants Received	81z	137.5	163.3	175.6	182.8	219.9	205.0	172.2	198.5	240.2	249.4	....	....
Expenditure	82	1,081.2	1,235.1	1,312.8	1,471.5	1,666.9	1,681.9	1,876.8	1,804.1	1,868.6	2,027.7	....	....
Lending Minus Repayments	83	−15.2	−21.9	−20.0	−5.4	−13.8	−.9	44.9	65.3	−2.0	−44.1	....	....
Financing													
Net Borrowing: Dinars	84b	−51.2	−47.7	−15.5	−18.3	−15.2	−11.6	−7.3	−2.8	−33.2	−110.7	....	....
Foreign Currency	85b	208.6	−133.2	75.4	287.8	302.1	84.3	−12.3	55.7	−103.3	−5.8	....	....
Use of Cash Balances	87	−338.3	39.2	−105.1	−318.8	−220.6	90.7	346.7	87.5	....	....	....	....
Debt: Domestic	88a	1,004.19	1,106.50	1,098.70	838.60	831.50	822.70	1,006.90	889.00	1,119.80	1,260.30	....	....
Foreign	89a	4,505.30	3,772.70	3,975.20	4,114.80	4,386.30	4,334.40	4,668.70	4,883.90	4,501.60	4,491.10	....	....
National Accounts		*Millions of Dinars*											
Househ.Cons.Expend.,incl.NPISHs	96f	†2,771.0	2,793.0	2,936.0	3,046.0	3,453.0	3,648.0	4,111.0	4,166.0	4,843.0	5,130.0	....	....
Government Consumption Expend	91f	†791.0	858.0	986.0	1,111.0	1,204.0	1,313.0	1,367.0	1,387.0	1,422.0	1,458.0	....	....
Gross Fixed Capital Formation	93e	†1,049.2	1,303.5	1,391.0	1,395.0	1,445.3	1,325.1	1,190.0	1,354.0	1,263.0	1,238.0	....	....
Changes in Inventories	93i	†160.0	119.0	60.0	159.0	52.0	−3.0	36.0	−107.0	64.0	79.0	....	....
Exports of Goods and Services	90c	†1,820.0	1,962.0	2,093.0	2,439.0	2,597.0	2,533.0	2,516.0	2,505.0	2,507.0	2,677.0	....	....
Imports of Goods and Services (-)	98c	†2,974.7	3,151.7	3,107.6	3,435.2	3,839.9	3,676.7	3,608.7	3,538.0	4,110.0	4,273.0	....	....
Gross Domestic Product (GDP)	99b	†3,616.0	3,884.0	4,358.0	4,715.0	4,912.0	5,138.0	5,610.0	5,767.0	5,989.0	6,310.0	....	....
Net Primary Income from Abroad	98.n	†−186.2	−149.1	−151.4	−116.8	−112.3	−47.0	−5.8	−9.0	96.0	133.0	....	....
Gross National Income (GNI)	99a	†3,430.0	3,735.0	4,207.0	4,598.0	4,800.0	5,090.0	5,604.0	5,759.0	6,085.0	6,443.0	....	....
Net National Income	99e	†3,106.0	3,383.0	3,817.0	4,164.0	4,282.0	4,525.0	4,988.0	5,083.0	5,414.0	5,752.0	....	....
GDP Volume 1994 Prices	99b.p	3,972.9	4,151.2	4,358.0	4,627.7	4,723.7	4,880.7	5,027.9	5,181.4	5,399.9	5,629.4	....	....
GDP Volume (2000=100)	99bvp	†73.6	76.9	80.7	85.7	87.5	90.4	93.1	96.0	100.0	104.3	....	....
GDP Deflator (2000=100)	99bip	†82.1	84.4	90.2	91.9	93.8	94.9	100.6	100.4	100.0	101.1	....	....
		Millions: Midyear Estimates											
Population	99z	3.63	3.84	4.05	4.25	4.43	4.59	4.74	4.89	5.04	5.18	5.33	5.47

Kazakhstan 916

		1992	1993	1994	1995	1996	1997	1998	1999	2000	2001	2002	2003
Exchange Rates						*Tenge per SDR: End of Period*							
Official Rate	aa	....	8.67	79.21	95.06	105.40	101.94	117.99	189.68	188.27	188.76	210.18	214.31
					Tenge per US Dollar: End of Period (ae) Period Average (rf)								
Official Rate	ae	....	6.31	54.26	63.95	73.30	75.55	83.80	138.20	144.50	150.20	154.60	144.22
Official Rate	rf	....	....	35.54	60.95	67.30	75.44	78.30	119.52	142.13	146.74	153.28	149.58
Fund Position						*Millions of SDRs: End of Period*							
Quota	2f.s	247.50	247.50	247.50	247.50	247.50	247.50	247.50	365.70	365.70	365.70	365.70	365.70
SDRs	1b.s	–	13.98	69.54	154.87	240.19	327.15	275.08	164.24	.01	–	.76	.78
Reserve Position in the Fund	1c.s	.01	.01	.01	.01	.01	.01	.01	.01	.01	.01	.01	.01
Total Fund Cred.&Loans Outstg	2tl	–	61.88	198.00	290.82	383.60	378.96	463.66	335.15	–	–	–	–
International Liquidity					*Millions of US Dollars Unless Otherwise Indicated: End of Period*								
Total Reserves minus Gold	1l.d	....	455.7	837.5	1,135.6	1,294.7	1,697.1	1,461.2	1,479.2	1,594.1	1,997.2	2,555.3	4,236.2
SDRs	1b.d	–	19.2	101.5	230.2	345.4	441.4	387.3	225.4	–	–	1.0	1.2
Reserve Position in the Fund	1c.d	.01	.01	.01	.01	.01	.01	.01	.01	.01	.01	.01	.01
Foreign Exchange	1d.d	....	436.5	736.0	905.3	949.3	1,255.7	1,073.9	1,253.8	1,594.1	1,997.2	2,554.2	4,235.0
Gold (Million Fine Troy Ounces)	1ad	....	.65	.99	1.36	1.80	1.81	1.75	1.80	1.84	1.84	1.71	1.74
Gold (National Valuation)	1and	....	255.5	378.0	524.3	949.3	523.9	503.6	522.8	501.5	510.7	585.6	725.9
Monetary Authorities:Other Assets	3..d	....	825.2	1,117.5	1,432.0	1,425.4	†1,848.1	1,577.6	1,776.8	2,096.5	3,767.1	5,096.5	8,607.4
Other liab	4..d	....	336.6	15.9	59.4	76.0	†50.0	19.6	18.3	2.0	2.3	2.5	45.4
Deposit Money Banks: Assets	7a.d	....	345.6	271.9	440.9	330.1	273.8	344.6	570.6	383.5	556.0	1,331.9	2,052.0
Liabilities	7b.d	....	563.5	1,195.8	414.2	138.1	207.5	390.5	232.2	379.6	982.2	1,802.5	3,957.0
Monetary Authorities						*Millions of Tenge: End of Period*							
Foreign Assets	11	....	5,328	66,143	106,300	129,801	†172,971	164,663	276,713	302,950	565,816	788,081	1,241,532
Claims on Central Government	12a	....	1,696	20,236	39,467	39,265	†77,078	87,931	109,304	41,568	19,134	19,230	2,946
Claims on Rest of the Economy	12d	....	197	760	332	16,906	†620	7,277	12,657	2,146	3,587	4,060	6,349
Claims on Deposit Money Banks	12e	....	6,095	13,355	10,487	9,059	†8,248	2,084	4,634	2,774	1,810	3,758	3,150
Reserve Money	14	....	4,309	31,171	66,550	84,354	†115,389	81,427	126,749	134,416	175,551	208,171	316,872
of which: Currency Outside Banks	14a	....	2,273	20,255	47,998	62,811	†92,796	68,728	103,486	106,428	131,175	161,701	238,730
Other Deposits	15	....	127	738	445	3,068	†18	47	1,107	702	750	138	82
Liabs. of Central Bank:Securities	16ac	....	....	....	....	....	6,855	12,046	6,206	49,180	17,796	65,166	205,681
Foreign Liabilities	16c	....	2,660	16,548	31,444	46,001	†42,409	56,354	66,097	286	345	390	6,543
Central Government Deposits	16d	....	2,016	8,337	14,641	13,908	†53,647	59,766	93,898	57,507	256,768	356,425	570,924
Capital Accounts	17a	....	2,744	47,653	62,822	64,993	†52,611	63,480	121,957	118,963	134,375	179,834	167,299
Other Items (Net)	17r	....	1,460	−3,953	−19,317	−17,293	†−12,012	−11,167	−12,707	−11,615	4,762	5,005	−13,424
Deposit Money Banks						*Millions of Tenge: End of Period*							
Reserves	20	....	1,914	8,638	14,771	16,891	†22,361	12,144	21,793	24,359	42,343	45,362	75,970
Claims on Central Bank: Securities	20c	....	....	....	....	....	....	2,018	4,235	41,591	7,182	25,119	85,164
Other Claims on Central Bank	20n	....	....	....	....	....	....	–	6,390	3,700	16,748	1	3,608
Foreign Assets	21	....	2,181	14,755	28,197	24,196	†20,685	28,874	78,863	55,410	83,512	205,913	295,942
Claims on Central Government	22a	....	514	426	5,104	8,691	†25,303	21,184	34,752	59,512	†75,847	107,424	106,217
Claims on Local Government	22b	....	....	....	....	....	....	....	....	....	5,205	1,792	2,993
Claims on Nonfin.Pub.Enterprises	22c	....	....	....	....	....	....	....	....	....	14,564	12,795	30,109
Claims on Rest of the Economy	22d	....	14,310	111,747	71,988	72,448	†85,866	102,887	153,534	288,856	†515,735	699,030	1,007,393
Claims on Nonbank Financial Insts	22g	....	....	....	....	....	....	2,195	2,904	3,703	16,079	22,795	31,872
Demand Deposits	24	....	5,593	32,894	63,930	71,938	†57,998	49,511	101,050	126,124	137,014	219,423	237,201
Other Deposits	25	....	....	....	....	....	†22,073	29,767	66,844	160,150	†285,867	341,811	458,218
Bonds	26ab	....	–	92	1,902	119	†30	–	32	1,173	1,613	6,675	12,730
Restricted Deposits	26b	....	....	....	....	....	....	....	....	....	19,397	41,011	34,078
Foreign Liabilities	26c	....	3,556	64,883	26,485	10,120	†15,674	32,727	32,087	54,857	147,524	278,665	570,675
Central Government Deposits	26d	....	111	1,494	5,416	11,494	†26,484	10,986	15,178	17,242	†14,699	17,708	6,336
Liabilities to Local Government	26db	....	....	....	....	....	....	....	....	....	2,627	3,457	3,116
Credit from Central Bank	26g	....	6,049	14,204	5,883	11,482	†8,208	5,092	4,699	2,915	1,888	5,347	9,139
Capital Accounts	27a	....	1,091	14,662	29,259	39,289	†40,183	59,735	89,539	107,159	159,897	179,516	256,334
Other Items (Net)	27r	....	2,521	7,338	−12,815	−22,216	†−16,436	−18,517	−6,957	7,509	6,690	26,616	51,444
Monetary Survey						*Millions of Tenge: End of Period*							
Foreign Assets (Net)	31n	....	1,293	−533	76,568	97,876	†135,572	104,455	257,392	303,217	501,460	714,938	960,257
Domestic Credit	32	....	14,590	123,338	96,834	111,908	†108,737	150,721	204,074	321,036	376,057	489,536	607,504
Claims on Central Govt. (Net)	32an	....	83	10,831	24,514	22,554	†22,250	38,363	34,979	26,331	†−176,487	−247,478	−468,096
Claims on Local Government	32b	....	....	....	....	....	....	....	....	....	2,578	−1,666	−123
Claims on Nonfin.Pub.Enterprises	32c	....	....	....	....	....	....	....	....	....	14,564	12,795	30,109
Claims on Rest of the Economy	32d	....	14,507	112,507	72,320	89,354	†86,487	110,163	166,191	291,002	†519,321	703,090	1,013,742
Claims on Nonbank Fin. Insts	32g	....	....	....	....	....	....	2,195	2,904	3,703	16,079	22,795	31,872
Money	34	....	8,198	55,417	115,384	139,452	†150,908	118,735	205,929	236,163	270,009	381,975	477,519
Quasi-Money	35	....	....	....	....	....	†22,091	29,815	67,951	160,852	†286,617	341,949	458,300
Bonds	36ab	....	–	92	1,902	119	†30	–	32	1,173	1,613	6,675	12,730
Liabs. of Central Bank: Securities	36ac	....	–	92	1,902	119	6,855	†10,028	1,971	7,589	10,614	40,047	120,517
Restricted Deposits	36b	....	....	....	....	....	....	....	....	....	19,397	41,011	34,078
Capital Accounts	37a	....	3,835	62,315	92,081	104,282	†92,794	123,215	211,495	226,122	294,271	359,350	423,633
Other Items (Net)	37r	....	3,852	4,982	−35,966	−34,069	†−28,369	−26,617	−25,912	−7,647	−5,006	33,466	40,984
Money plus Quasi-Money	35l	....	8,198	55,417	115,384	139,452	†172,999	148,549	273,880	397,015	†556,626	723,925	935,819

Kazakhstan 916

		1992	1993	1994	1995	1996	1997	1998	1999	2000	2001	2002	2003
Interest Rates						*Percent Per Annum*							
Refinancing Rate (End of Per.)	60	....	170.00	230.00	†52.50	35.00	18.50	25.00	18.00	14.00	9.00	7.50	7.00
Treasury Bill Rate	60c	....	....	214.34	48.98	28.91	15.15	23.59	15.63	6.59	5.28	5.20	5.86
Prices and Labor					*Index Numbers (2000=100): Period Averages*								
Producer Prices	63	....	....	....	42.2	52.3	60.4	61.00	72.5	100.0	100.3	100.5	109.9
Consumer Prices	64	....	.9	16.9	46.6	†64.9	76.1	81.6	88.4	100.0	108.4	114.7	122.1
Wages: Monthly Earnings	65	....	.9	12.5	34.7	49.5	61.9	70.1	80.7	100.0	125.6	147.5	168.8
Total Employment	67	....	227.4	212.7	185.5	178.7	148.3	124.9	111.1	100.0	102.3	105.9	....
					Number in Thousands: Period Averages								
Employment	67e	7,356	6,565	5,853	5,329	4,794	3,874	3,071	2,744	....	6,699	6,710	6,968
Unemployment	67c	34	41	70	140	282	258	252	251	231	780	691	671
Unemployment Rate (%)	67r	.4	.6	1.1	2.1	4.2	3.8	3.7	3.9	3.7	10.5	9.4	8.8
International Transactions						*Millions of US Dollars*							
Exports	70..d	....	3,277.0	3,230.8	5,250.2	5,911.0	6,497.0	5,334.1	5,871.6	8,812.2	8,639.1	9,709.1	12,900.4
Imports, c.i.f.	71..d	....	3,887.4	3,561.2	3,806.7	4,241.1	4,300.8	4,313.9	3,655.1	5,040.0	6,446.0	6,584.0	8,327.0
Balance of Payments					*Millions of US Dollars: Minus Sign Indicates Debit*								
Current Account, n.i.e.	78ald	....	....	....	−213.1	−751.0	−799.3	−1,224.9	−171.0	675.5	−1,108.9	−695.8	−182.5
Goods: Exports f.o.b.	78aad	....	....	....	5,440.0	6,291.6	6,899.3	5,870.5	5,988.7	9,288.1	8,927.8	10,027.6	13,232.6
Goods: Imports f.o.b.	78abd	....	....	....	−5,325.9	−6,626.7	−7,175.7	−6,671.7	−5,645.0	−6,848.2	−7,607.3	−7,726.3	−9,144.5
Trade Balance	78acd	....	....	....	114.1	−335.1	−276.4	−801.2	343.7	2,439.9	1,320.5	2,301.2	4,088.2
Services: Credit	78add	....	....	....	535.1	674.4	841.9	904.3	932.5	1,133.3	1,306.8	1,587.5	1,700.8
Services: Debit	78aed	....	....	....	−775.8	−928.3	−1,124.4	−1,154.1	−1,104.2	−2,004.3	−2,824.6	−3,667.2	−4,066.0
Balance on Goods & Services	78afd	....	....	....	−126.6	−589.0	−558.9	−1,051.0	172.0	1,568.9	−197.3	221.5	1,723.0
Income: Credit	78agd	....	....	....	44.6	56.7	73.8	95.5	108.6	138.8	224.8	233.8	256.8
Income: Debit	78ahd	....	....	....	−190.1	−277.1	−388.8	−391.8	−608.3	−1,281.2	−1,368.4	−1,264.6	−1,997.7
Balance on Gds, Serv. & Inc.	78aid	....	....	....	−272.1	−809.4	−873.9	−1,347.3	−327.7	426.5	−1,340.9	−809.3	−17.9
Current Transfers, n.i.e.: Credit	78ajd	....	....	....	79.9	83.4	104.7	141.4	174.7	352.2	394.4	425.6	278.6
Current Transfers: Debit	78akd	....	....	....	−20.9	−25.0	−30.1	−19.0	−18.0	−103.2	−162.4	−312.2	−443.3
Capital Account, n.i.e.	78bcd	....	....	....	−380.6	−315.5	−439.8	−369.1	−234.0	−290.6	−194.0	−119.9	−28.8
Capital Account, n.i.e.: Credit	78bad	....	....	....	116.7	87.9	58.3	65.9	61.1	66.3	92.4	109.7	122.7
Capital Account: Debit	78bbd	....	....	....	−496.7	−403.4	−498.1	−435.0	−295.1	−356.9	−286.5	−229.6	−151.5
Financial Account, n.i.e.	78bjd	....	....	....	1,162.5	2,005.1	2,901.6	2,229.1	1,299.2	1,308.1	2,613.7	1,357.3	2,728.9
Direct Investment Abroad	78bdd	....	....	....	−.3	....	−1.4	−8.1	−3.6	−4.4	25.6	−426.3	119.6
Dir. Invest. in Rep. Econ., n.i.e.	78bed	....	....	....	964.2	1,137.0	1,321.4	1,151.4	1,587.0	1,282.5	2,835.0	2,583.3	2,068.5
Portfolio Investment Assets	78bfd	....	....	....	−	....	−1.2	−5.3	−5.6	−85.5	−1,348.9	−1,077.6	−2,073.3
Equity Securities	78bkd	....	....	....	....	....	−1.2	−.4	−1.8	.7	−10.4	−376.4	−312.6
Debt Securities	78bld	....	....	....	−	....	....	−4.9	−3.8	−86.2	−1,338.5	−701.3	−1,760.7
Portfolio Investment Liab., n.i.e.	78bgd	....	....	....	7.2	223.5	405.4	66.2	−39.9	30.7	31.4	−182.9	212.3
Equity Securities	78bmd	....	....	....	....	....	....	....	....	....	19.4	55.4	39.3	87.7
Debt Securities	78bnd	....	....	....	7.2	223.5	405.4	66.2	−39.9	11.3	−23.9	−222.1	124.7
Financial Derivatives Assets	78bwd	....	....	....	....	....	....	....	....	....	−	−	−
Financial Derivatives Liabilities	78bxd	....	....	....	....	....	....	....	....	....	....	....	15.9
Other Investment Assets	78bhd	....	....	....	−657.4	243.8	−139.5	−220.5	−778.4	43.6	464.8	−1,098.0	−873.5
Monetary Authorities	78bod	....	....	....	21.3	2.1	....	....	−.3	−.4	.3	−1.7	−43.3
General Government	78bpd	....	....	....	−	27.8	.3	−41.1	16.3	−.3	209.7	321.2	210.0
Banks	78bqd	....	....	....	−152.3	174.4	−66.0	−67.9	−205.8	154.4	−63.6	−624.7	−313.0
Other Sectors	78brd	....	....	....	−526.4	39.5	−73.8	−111.5	−588.6	−110.1	318.5	−792.8	−727.2
Other Investment Liab., n.i.e.	78bid	....	....	....	848.8	400.8	1,316.9	1,245.4	539.7	41.2	605.7	1,558.7	3,259.4
Monetary Authorities	78bsd	....	....	....	−4.9	12.1	−5.0	−37.7	−	−2.6	.4	.2	−.1
General Government	78btd	....	....	....	331.3	323.4	317.2	673.3	291.5	88.2	51.3	1.7	55.5
Banks	78bud	....	....	....	−251.5	−125.7	161.4	60.2	−20.2	165.1	432.8	935.7	2,146.7
Other Sectors	78bvd	....	....	....	773.9	191.0	843.3	549.6	268.4	−209.5	121.2	621.1	1,057.4
Net Errors and Omissions	78cad	....	....	....	−270.1	−780.0	−1,114.1	−1,078.4	−641.6	−1,122.7	−926.1	−6.5	−984.1
Overall Balance	78cbd	....	....	....	298.7	158.6	548.4	−443.3	252.6	570.3	384.7	535.1	1,533.5
Reserves and Related Items	79dad	....	....	....	−298.7	−158.6	−548.4	443.3	−252.6	−570.3	−384.7	−535.1	−1,533.5
Reserve Assets	79dbd	....	....	....	−440.1	−293.7	−542.0	321.7	−77.1	−129.2	−384.7	−535.1	−1,533.5
Use of Fund Credit and Loans	79dcd	....	....	....	141.4	135.1	−6.4	121.6	−175.5	−441.0	−	−	−
Exceptional Financing	79ded	....	....	....	....	....	....	....	....	−	−	−	−

Kazakhstan 916

		1992	1993	1994	1995	1996	1997	1998	1999	2000	2001	2002	2003
International Investment Position							*Millions of US Dollars*						
Assets	79aad	....	....	....	....	....	2,629.1	2,391.8	2,598.4	4,612.9	6,117.0	9,288.7	14,122.7
Direct Investment Abroad	79abd	....	....	....	....	....	2.6	3.1	3.1	15.5	−9.7	415.4	304.8
Portfolio Investment	79acd	....	....	....	....	....	2.0	4.2	1.0	69.7	1,430.8	2,423.2	4,564.3
Equity Securities	79add	....	....	....	....	....	−	−	−	3.4	15.2	310.8	642.3
Debt Securities	79aed	....	....	....	....	....	2.0	4.2	1.0	66.3	1,415.6	2,112.3	3,922.0
Financial Derivatives	79ald	....	....	....	....	....	−	2.0	−	−	−	−	−
Other Investment	79afd	....	....	....	....	....	335.3	417.7	592.2	2,432.1	2,187.8	3,309.3	4,291.5
Monetary Authorities	79agd	....	....	....	....	....	.3	.1	.3	.7	.3	2.0	97.7
General Government	79ahd	....	....	....	....	....	46.8	46.8	46.8	852.3	636.1	314.9	104.9
Banks	79aid	....	....	....	....	....	288.2	370.8	545.1	359.8	423.0	1,048.3	1,338.7
Other Sectors	79ajd	....	....	....	....	....	−	−	−	1,219.3	1,128.4	1,944.1	2,750.2
Reserve Assets	79akd	....	....	....	....	....	2,289.2	1,964.8	2,002.1	2,095.7	2,508.2	3,140.8	4,962.1
Liabilities	79lad	....	....	....	....	....	2,595.3	3,594.3	3,678.4	15,726.9	19,192.4	23,013.2	28,855.4
Dir. Invest. in Rep. Economy	79lbd	....	....	....	....	....	50.1	122.3	115.9	10,077.7	12,916.6	15,453.3	17,566.9
Portfolio Investment	79lcd	....	....	....	....	....	623.9	663.4	617.2	695.9	725.0	337.8	603.6
Equity Securities	79ldd	....	....	....	....	....	53.9	49.9	37.7	101.6	146.9	142.0	246.4
Debt Securities	79led	....	....	....	....	....	570.0	613.5	579.5	594.3	578.1	195.7	357.2
Financial Derivatives	79lld	....	....	....	....	....	−	−	−	−	−	−	40.9
Other Investment	79lfd	....	....	....	....	....	1,921.3	2,808.6	2,945.3	4,953.3	5,550.8	7,222.2	10,644.1
Monetary Authorities	79lgd	....	....	....	....	....	553.0	655.4	462.6	1.9	2.3	2.5	2.4
General Government	79lhd	....	....	....	....	....	1,175.3	1,896.4	2,231.3	2,277.0	2,249.0	2,294.1	2,423.2
Banks	79lid	....	....	....	....	....	193.0	256.8	251.4	392.2	859.3	1,790.6	3,948.5
Other Sectors	79ljd	....	....	....	....	....	−	−	−	2,282.3	2,440.2	3,135.1	4,270.0
Government Finance							*Millions of Tenge: Year Ending December 31*						
Deficit (−) or Surplus	80	....	....	−30,382	−25,181	−59,564	−63,998	−72,073	−69,830	−3,279	−12,998	−13,004	−40,354
Total Revenue and Grants	81y	....	....	79,474	178,347	306,943	405,624	379,521	395,580	590,236	733,893	807,853	1,004,565
Revenue	81	....	....	79,413	178,347	306,943	405,342	379,311	392,951	587,039	733,659	807,853	1,004,565
Grants Received	81z	....	....	61	−	−	282	210	2,629	3,197	234	−	−
Exp. & Lending Minus Repay	82z	....	....	109,856	203,528	366,507	469,622	451,594	465,410	593,515	746,891	820,857	1,044,919
Expenditure	82	....	....	109,672	210,603	381,602	439,476	426,142	447,426	576,182	726,015	801,071	1,021,768
Lending Minus Repayments	83	....	....	184	−7,075	−15,095	30,146	25,452	17,984	17,333	20,876	19,786	23,151
Total Financing													
Domestic	84a	....	....	....	....	....	17,170	20,504	20,671	−28,515	2,591	64,929	35,065
Foreign	85a	....	....	....	....	....	46,828	51,569	49,159	31,794	10,407	−51,925	5,289
National Accounts							*Billions of Tenge*						
Househ.Cons.Expend.,incl.NPISHs	96f	....	20.85	328.85	721.13	952.79	1,179.14	1,270.02	1,460.12	1,595.38	1,875.58	2,094.92	2,541.71
Government Consumption Expend	91f	....	4.09	45.23	137.75	182.79	207.02	186.87	232.71	313.99	436.04	435.88	511.05
Gross Fixed Capital Formation	93e	....	8.21	110.65	233.81	243.88	271.77	272.44	326.26	450.26	771.39	847.18	1,062.24
Changes in Inventories	93i	....	−2.32	10.90	2.69	−15.28	−10.94	1.49	32.19	21.34	102.26	117.35	137.19
Exports of Goods and Services	90c	....	11.15	156.96	395.27	499.32	583.86	525.95	856.23	1,481.10	1,511.49	1,799.14	2,240.36
Imports of Goods and Services (−)	98c	....	13.75	199.53	441.67	509.74	626.10	604.22	808.94	1,258.20	1,565.11	1,700.23	1,959.38
Gross Domestic Product (GDP)	99b	....	28.23	453.07	1,048.99	1,353.75	1,604.76	1,652.55	2,098.57	2,603.86	3,131.63	3,634.24	4,533.17
Net Primary Income from Abroad	98.n	....	−.07	−2.17	−9.11	−12.28	−23.38	−23.33	−62.78	−162.36	−163.76	−158.30	−261.73
Gross National Income (GNI)	99a	....	29.35	421.30	1,005.08	1,403.47	1,648.76	1,709.93	1,953.68	2,437.54	3,083.33	3,617.98	4,188.07
Net Current Transf.from Abroad	98t	....	.34	7.36	7.88	9.81	5.63	6.11	18.38	35.45	33.96	17.33	−24.51
Gross Nat'l Disposable Inc.(GNDI)	99i	....	29.69	428.66	1,012.96	1,413.29	1,654.40	1,716.05	1,972.06	2,472.99	3,117.29	3,635.31	4,163.56
Gross Saving	99s	....	4.75	54.58	154.09	277.71	268.23	259.16	279.23	559.27	798.76	994.37	1,136.44
Consumption of Fixed Capital	99cf	....	5.29	84.31	154.42	228.04	253.96	238.76	286.95	420.52	498.16	576.88	....
GDP, Production Based	99bp	....	29.42	423.47	1,014.19	1,415.75	1,672.14	1,733.26	2,016.46	2,599.90	3,250.59	3,776.28	4,449.80
Statistical Discrepancy	99bs	....	1.19	−29.60	−34.80	61.99	67.39	80.71	−82.11	−8.30	88.46	71.15	−39.03
GDP Volume (2000=100)	99bvp	....	....	†96.3	88.4	88.9	90.4	88.7	91.1	100.0	113.5	124.7	136.2
GDP Deflator (2000=100)	99bip	....	....	†18.1	45.6	58.5	68.2	71.6	88.5	100.0	105.9	112.0	127.9
							Millions: Midyear Estimates						
Population	99z	16.85	16.79	16.69	16.56	16.39	16.19	15.98	15.79	15.64	15.53	15.47	15.43

Kenya 664

		1992	1993	1994	1995	1996	1997	1998	1999	2000	2001	2002	2003
Exchange Rates													
						Shillings per SDR: End of Period							
Principal Rate................	aa	49.797	93.626	65.458	83.153	79.118	84.568	87.165	100.098	101.674	98.779	104.781	113.140
						Shillings per US Dollar: End of Period (ae) Period Average (rf)							
Principal Rate................	ae	36.216	68.163	44.839	55.939	55.021	62.678	61.906	72.931	78.036	78.600	77.072	76.139
Principal Rate................	rf	32.217	58.001	56.051	51.430	57.115	58.732	60.367	70.326	76.176	78.563	78.749	75.936
Fund Position						*Millions of SDRs: End of Period*							
Quota.......................	2f.s	199.4	199.4	199.4	199.4	199.4	199.4	199.4	271.4	271.4	271.4	271.4	271.4
SDRs........................	1b.s	.6	.8	.5	.2	.5	.5	.4	1.7	.2	.8	.6	1.4
Reserve Position in the Fund...	1c.s	12.2	12.2	12.3	12.3	12.3	12.4	12.4	12.4	12.5	12.5	12.6	12.7
Total Fund Cred.&Loans Outstg..	2tl	286.1	264.3	277.3	251.5	234.5	185.6	139.5	95.8	97.2	78.6	64.6	75.6
International Liquidity						*Millions of US Dollars Unless Otherwise Indicated: End of Period*							
Total Reserves minus Gold.......	1l.d	53.0e	405.6	557.6	353.4	746.5	787.9	783.1	791.6	897.7	1,064.9	1,068.0	1,481.9
SDRs........................	1b.d	.8	1.1	.7	.3	.8	.7	.6	2.4	.3	1.0	.8	2.0
Reserve Position in the Fund...	1c.d	16.8	16.8	18.0	18.3	17.7	16.7	17.5	17.1	16.2	15.8	17.1	18.8
Foreign Exchange..............	1d.d	35.4e	387.7	538.9	334.8	728.0	770.6	765.0	772.2	881.2	1,048.1	1,050.0	1,461.0
Gold (Million Fine Troy Ounces)..	1ad	.080	.080	.080	.080	.080	.080	–	–	–	–	.001	.001
Gold (National Valuation).......	1and	12.2	14.3	15.2	15.4	14.8	23.1	–	–	.1	.1	.2	.2
Monetary Authorities: Other Liab.	4..d	203.0	232.0	278.1	265.7	261.6	205.8	174.8	126.5	127.9	99.2	88.1	125.4
Deposit Money Banks: Assets.....	7a.d	108.2	348.9	425.4	439.6	444.2	594.2	501.6	313.6	500.7	395.0	546.6	408.6
Liabilities....................	7b.d	53.1	49.8	293.1	103.8	103.3	165.2	195.8	218.2	173.0	162.3	142.1	107.4
Other Banking Insts.: Liabilities..	7f.d	13.4	10.2	11.0	8.7	7.0	18.9	1.2	.8	.5	.4	.2	–
Monetary Authorities						*Millions of Shillings: End of Period*							
Foreign Assets................	11	6,315	34,527	28,227	25,683	47,266	44,499	47,103	57,816	71,245	83,499	82,304	112,771
Claims on Central Government....	12a	16,074	49,275	53,857	98,401	57,287	47,905	43,585	39,028	36,742	37,421	40,947	40,836
Claims on Deposit Money Banks...	12e	12,717	11,484	10,072	9,766	9,056	9,124	1,140	904	4,884	1,362	7,484	674
Reserve Money................	14	31,230	47,628	58,472	76,610	82,903	84,621	84,269	89,341	88,758	87,859	98,311	97,205
of which: Currency Outside DMBs..	14a	17,205	21,355	24,817	28,887	30,390	36,178	38,713	42,963	43,466	45,349	53,895	55,550
Foreign Liabilities..............	16c	14,287	24,771	18,252	20,923	18,590	15,715	12,244	9,653	9,982	7,796	6,790	9,549
Long-Term Foreign Liabilities.....	16cl	81	83	25	21	14	5	2	2	–	–	–	–
Central Government Deposits.....	16d	–	38,289	32,920	55,239	27,349	11,698	17,172	18,922	26,526	28,537	25,886	42,237
Counterpart Funds.............	16e	73	73	127	6	–	–	–	–	–	–	–	–
Capital Accounts...............	17a	2,278	720	813	1,079	1,892	2,484	4,057	5,097	5,561	5,968	9,672	10,620
Other Items (Net)...............	17r	–12,843	–16,279	–18,454	–20,028	–17,139	–12,995	–25,916	–25,267	–17,956	–7,878	–9,924	–5,331
Deposit Money Banks						*Millions of Shillings: End of Period*							
Reserves......................	20	8,956	20,870	31,790	35,316	42,460	39,736	34,970	36,081	31,762	37,062	34,165	31,588
Foreign Assets................	21	3,919	23,783	19,073	24,594	24,440	37,240	31,051	22,871	39,072	31,049	42,126	31,113
Claims on Central Government....	22a	18,010	21,136	38,088	26,417	42,576	46,121	70,550	68,415	71,206	89,091	98,549	137,614
Claims on Local Government.....	22b	148	219	249	304	358	582	595	895	1,143	659	687	658
Claims on Nonfin.Pub.Enterprises..	22c	4,003	3,885	5,174	4,987	5,290	7,572	6,922	6,479	7,013	6,839	7,846	6,403
Claims on Private Sector........	22d	58,587	61,705	78,809	117,351	145,926	182,253	182,976	202,657	210,268	201,934	207,549	215,162
Claims on Other Financial Insts...	22f	4,809	3,793	6,835	11,347	14,620	16,255	32,507	50,317	53,116	53,500	63,059	71,149
Demand Deposits..............	24	26,621	33,664	39,294	38,994	43,094	46,258	47,273	56,849	65,206	76,220	86,651	129,286
Time & Foreign Currency Deposits..	25	50,003	64,332	95,755	133,520	175,401	210,888	215,615	218,788	224,051	225,233	242,968	245,313
Foreign Liabilities..............	26c	1,922	3,392	13,144	5,807	5,681	10,356	12,122	15,914	13,501	12,756	10,954	8,176
Central Government Deposits.....	26d	3,078	4,790	4,950	5,531	3,822	4,226	9,592	8,754	8,385	5,310	4,333	7,922
Credit from Monetary Authorities..	26g	4,921	252	–	–	–	448	4,335	1,614	3,635	2,974	2,673	740
Credit from Other Financial Insts...	26i	–	–	–	2	–	–	–	–	–	–	–	–
Capital Accounts...............	27a	17,398	24,328	31,942	45,104	56,111	72,324	78,930	91,311	79,289	80,284	83,831	94,115
Other Items (Net)...............	27r	–5,510	4,634	–5,068	–8,643	–8,439	–14,740	–8,298	–5,513	19,513	17,357	22,572	8,134
Monetary Survey						*Millions of Shillings: End of Period*							
Foreign Assets (Net)............	31n	–5,975	30,146	15,903	23,546	47,434	55,669	53,787	55,121	86,833	93,996	106,687	126,160
Domestic Credit................	32	98,554	96,935	145,142	198,876	236,037	285,817	311,661	341,495	345,964	357,093	390,088	423,482
Claims on Central Govt. (Net).....	32an	31,007	27,332	54,075	64,048	68,693	78,101	87,370	79,767	73,037	92,665	109,277	128,290
Claims on Local Government.....	32b	148	219	249	304	358	582	595	895	1,143	659	687	658
Claims on Nonfin.Pub.Enterprises...	32c	4,003	3,885	5,174	4,987	5,290	7,572	6,922	6,479	7,013	6,839	7,846	6,403
Claims on Private Sector.........	32d	58,587	61,705	78,809	118,189	147,077	183,306	184,267	204,037	211,654	203,430	209,219	216,981
Claims on Other Financial Insts...	32f	4,809	3,793	6,835	11,347	14,620	16,255	32,507	50,317	53,116	53,500	63,059	71,149
Money........................	34	46,577	59,322	66,792	69,333	78,995	91,037	94,092	109,506	118,968	126,332	149,712	194,119
Quasi-Money..................	35	50,003	64,332	95,755	133,520	175,401	210,888	215,615	218,788	224,051	225,233	242,968	245,313
Long-Term Foreign Liabilities.....	36cl	81	83	25	21	14	5	2	2	–	–	–	–
Counterpart Funds.............	36e	73	73	127	6	–	–	–	–	–	–	–	–
Capital Accounts...............	37a	19,675	25,048	32,756	46,183	58,004	74,808	82,987	96,408	84,850	86,252	93,503	104,735
Other Items (Net)...............	37r	–23,830	–21,778	–34,409	–26,641	–28,941	–35,252	–27,248	–28,087	4,928	13,272	10,592	5,474
Money plus Quasi-Money........	35l	96,579	123,654	162,547	202,853	254,395	301,924	309,707	328,293	343,019	351,565	392,680	439,432

Kenya 664

		1992	1993	1994	1995	1996	1997	1998	1999	2000	2001	2002	2003
Other Banking Institutions		\multicolumn{12}{c}{*Millions of Shillings: End of Period*}
Cash	40	5,502	5,781	8,762	12,988	11,937	5,148	6,900	4,920	4,671	2,325	1,738	2,607
Claims on Central Government	42a	8,915	20,933	24,065	10,748	7,193	8,826	7,163	8,122	9,323	10,454	11,268	4,577
Claims on Local Government	42b	47	39	35	35	16	7	8	8	–	–	–	–
Claims on Nonfin.Pub.Enterprises	42c	434	348	1,031	48	34	10	6	6	6	–	–	–
Claims on Private Sector	42d	33,557	35,734	37,808	40,629	36,398	27,632	28,723	24,378	25,860	16,460	17,575	15,340
Claims on Deposit Money Banks	42e	92	150	446	27	423	–	–	4	30	7	1	1
Claims on Other Financial Insts	42f	2,083	578	1,024	541	151	124	106	96	114	97	24	58
Demand Deposits	44	6,062	7,763	12,738	6,687	3,276	2,432	2,261	1,921	1,726	1,605	1,499	1,694
Time and Savings Deposits	45	32,764	37,939	43,266	42,335	36,447	22,385	24,752	23,335	23,586	20,349	20,450	13,996
Foreign Liabilities	46c	484	697	494	487	384	1,185	75	58	41	33	17	–
Central Government Deposits	46d	511	403	908	572	459	667	661	775	775	486	308	51
Credit from Deposit Money Banks	46h	1,687	661	674	1,672	2,417	1,327	1,442	229	469	160	–	–
Capital Accounts	47a	4,154	6,315	7,773	7,148	6,423	4,347	4,278	4,410	3,556	2,343	2,339	2,318
Other Items (Net)	47r	4,968	9,785	7,318	6,114	6,744	9,405	9,437	6,806	9,852	4,367	5,994	4,525
Banking Survey		\multicolumn{12}{c}{*Millions of Shillings: End of Period*}
Foreign Assets (Net)	51n	–6,458	29,449	15,411	23,067	47,060	54,493	53,771	55,064	86,929	93,973	106,682	126,222
Domestic Credit	52	143,079	154,164	208,196	250,305	279,369	321,748	347,007	373,330	380,492	383,619	418,646	443,406
Claims on Central Govt. (Net)	52an	39,411	47,862	77,232	74,224	75,427	86,260	93,872	87,114	81,585	102,633	120,237	132,817
Claims on Local Government	52b	195	258	284	339	374	589	603	903	1,143	659	687	658
Claims on Nonfin.Pub.Enterprises	52c	4,438	4,233	6,204	5,035	5,324	7,582	6,928	6,485	7,019	6,839	7,846	6,403
Claims on Private Sector	52d	92,144	97,440	116,617	158,818	183,475	210,938	212,990	228,415	237,514	219,890	226,794	232,322
Claims on Nonbank Financial Inst	52f	6,892	4,371	7,859	11,889	14,770	16,379	32,613	50,413	53,230	53,597	63,083	71,206
Liquid Liabilities	55l	129,903	163,575	209,789	238,888	282,181	321,592	329,821	348,628	363,660	371,193	412,890	452,515
Long-Term Foreign Liabilities	56cl	81	83	25	21	14	5	2	2	–	–	–	–
Counterpart Funds	56e	73	73	127	6	–	–	–	–	–	–	–	–
Capital Accounts	57a	23,830	31,364	40,529	53,331	64,427	79,155	87,265	100,818	88,406	88,595	95,842	107,053
Other Items (Net)	57r	–17,267	–11,481	–26,863	–18,874	–20,192	–24,511	–16,311	–21,054	15,356	17,803	16,596	10,060
Interest Rates		\multicolumn{12}{c}{*Percent Per Annum*}
Discount Rate (End of Period)	60	20.46	45.50	21.50	24.50	26.88	32.27	17.07	26.46	....	....	....	....
Treasury Bill Rate	60c	16.53	49.80	23.32	18.29	22.25	22.87	22.83	13.87	12.05	12.60	8.95	3.51
Deposit Rate	60l	....	....	....	13.60	17.59	16.72	18.40	9.55	8.10	6.64	5.49	4.13
Lending Rate	60p	21.07	29.99	36.24	28.80	33.79	30.25	29.49	22.38	22.34	19.67	18.45	16.57
Prices, Production, Labor		\multicolumn{12}{c}{*Index Numbers (2000=100): Period Averages*}
Consumer Prices	64	34.8	50.8	65.4	66.5	72.4	†80.6	86.0	90.9	100.0	105.7	107.8	118.4
Industrial Production (1995=100)	66	70.0	73.8	83.2	100.0	90.7	....	....	....	....	....	....	....
		\multicolumn{12}{c}{*Number in Thousands: Period Averages*}
Employment	67e	1,463	1,475	1,506	1,557	1,607	1,647	....	....	....	....	....	....
International Transactions		\multicolumn{12}{c}{*Millions of Shillings*}
Exports	70	43,756	77,919	87,142	97,284	118,226	119,960	121,252	122,067	132,183	152,712	166,635	183,121
Imports, c.i.f	71	59,097	101,128	115,080	155,168	168,486	190,674	193,032	198,313	236,613	250,782	255,569	282,616
		\multicolumn{12}{c}{*2000=100*}
Volume of Exports (1995=100)	72	66	73	83	100	....	....	....	....	....	....	....	....
Volume of Imports	73	57	62	77	90	89	95	96	87	100	....	....	....
Export Prices	74	39	71	73	79	84	98	99	93	100	....	....	....
Unit Value of Imports	75	42	66	60	69	76	81	83	90	100	....	....	....

Kenya 664

		1992	1993	1994	1995	1996	1997	1998	1999	2000	2001	2002	2003
Balance of Payments		*Millions of US Dollars: Minus Sign Indicates Debit*											
Current Account, n.i.e.	78ald	−180.2	71.2	97.9	−400.4	−73.5	−456.8	−475.3	−89.6	−199.4	−339.8	−136.6	....
Goods: Exports f.o.b.	78aad	1,108.5	1,262.6	1,537.0	1,923.7	2,083.3	2,062.6	2,017.0	1,756.7	1,782.2	1,891.4	2,162.5	....
Goods: Imports f.o.b.	78abd	−1,608.7	−1,509.6	−1,775.3	−2,673.9	−2,598.2	−2,948.4	−3,028.7	−2,731.8	−3,043.9	−3,238.2	−3,159.0	....
Trade Balance	78acd	−500.2	−247.0	−238.4	−750.1	−514.8	−885.9	−1,011.7	−975.1	−1,261.7	−1,346.9	−996.5	....
Services: Credit	78add	1,042.2	1,063.5	1,117.3	1,024.5	936.2	914.5	830.4	934.5	993.4	1,089.4	1,018.1	....
Services: Debit	78aed	−563.7	−569.4	−686.8	−868.1	−854.0	−826.0	−694.7	−570.4	−718.7	−765.8	−645.9	....
Balance on Goods & Services	78afd	−21.7	247.0	192.2	−593.7	−432.6	−797.4	−876.0	−611.0	−987.0	−1,023.3	−624.2	....
Income: Credit	78agd	1.7	3.3	20.9	25.6	21.4	23.0	41.2	31.7	45.0	46.1	35.4	....
Income: Debit	78ahd	−359.6	−392.2	−385.7	−350.5	−242.2	−254.9	−214.7	−190.9	−178.1	−167.3	−178.2	....
Balance on Gds, Serv. & Inc.	78aid	−379.6	−141.8	−172.6	−918.6	−653.4	−1,029.4	−1,049.4	−770.2	−1,120.2	−1,144.5	−767.1	....
Current Transfers, n.i.e.: Credit	78ajd	392.9	276.0	333.7	563.6	585.4	572.5	578.6	685.3	926.6	804.8	632.1	....
Current Transfers: Debit	78akd	−193.5	−63.0	−63.2	−45.5	−5.4	−	−4.5	−4.7	−5.8	−	−1.6	....
Capital Account, n.i.e.	78bcd	83.1	28.1	−.4	−.4	−.4	76.8	84.3	55.4	49.6	51.5	81.2	....
Capital Account, n.i.e.: Credit	78bad	83.5	28.5	−	....	....	76.8	84.3	55.4	49.6	51.5	82.1	....
Capital Account: Debit	78bbd	−.4	−.4	−.4	−.4	−.4	....	....	....	−	−	−.9	....
Financial Account, n.i.e.	78bjd	−270.1	55.1	−41.7	247.9	589.1	362.6	562.1	165.7	269.8	148.1	−173.9	....
Direct Investment Abroad	78bdd	−	−	−	....	.5	−2.1	....	....	−	−	−7.4	....
Dir. Invest. in Rep. Econ., n.i.e.	78bed	6.4	1.6	3.7	32.5	12.7	19.7	11.4	13.8	110.9	5.3	27.6	....
Portfolio Investment Assets	78bfd	−	−	−	....	....	....	....	....	−10.9	−6.9	−10.0	....
Equity Securities	78bkd	−	−	−	....	....	....	....	....	−.5	−.9	−2.0	....
Debt Securities	78bld	−	−	−	....	....	....	....	....	−10.4	−6.0	−8.1	....
Portfolio Investment Liab., n.i.e.	78bgd	−	−	−	6.0	7.5	34.2	1.3	−8.0	−3.5	5.5	5.3	....
Equity Securities	78bmd	−	−	−	6.0	7.5	26.9	1.3	−8.0	−6.0	2.4	3.0	....
Debt Securities	78bnd	−	−	−	....	....	7.3	....	....	2.5	3.1	2.3	....
Financial Derivatives Assets	78bwd	....	....	....	....	....	....	....	....	....	....	....	....
Financial Derivatives Liabilities	78bxd	....	....	....	....	....	....	....	....	....	....	....	....
Other Investment Assets	78bhd	−125.0	−31.4	171.1	277.1	628.2	−53.6	−58.6	−89.8	−55.7	−86.4	−132.6	....
Monetary Authorities	78bod	....	....	....	....	....	....	....	....	....	....	....	....
General Government	78bpd	−4.3	−	−	....	....	−4.7	....	....	....	....	....	....
Banks	78bqd	−117.5	−310.7	−61.2	−	−	−44.2	−44.4	−74.3	−5.3	−6.6	−7.8	....
Other Sectors	78brd	−3.2	279.3	232.3	277.1	628.2	−4.7	−14.3	−15.5	−50.4	−79.8	−124.9	....
Other Investment Liab., n.i.e.	78bid	−151.5	85.0	−216.5	−67.7	−59.9	364.6	608.0	249.7	228.9	230.6	−56.7	....
Monetary Authorities	78bsd	−	−	−	−	−	−	−	−	−	−	−	....
General Government	78btd	−64.8	152.7	−113.3	−5.7	5.0	−110.9	−109.4	−257.4	243.8	−158.4	−133.7	....
Banks	78bud	13.8	25.4	32.1	....	....	....	22.6	31.0	−232.0	92.0	−169.0	....
Other Sectors	78bvd	−100.5	−93.0	−135.3	−61.9	−64.9	475.5	694.8	476.1	217.1	297.0	246.0	....
Net Errors and Omissions	78cad	110.3	257.5	5.8	11.4	−128.2	32.8	−88.6	−165.5	−127.1	150.1	212.9	....
Overall Balance	78cbd	−256.9	411.8	61.6	−141.6	387.0	15.5	82.6	−34.0	−7.2	10.0	−16.4	....
Reserves and Related Items	79dad	256.9	−411.8	−61.6	141.6	−387.0	−15.5	−82.6	34.0	7.2	−10.0	16.4	....
Reserve Assets	79dbd	−27.4	−477.3	−95.3	174.2	−378.1	70.8	5.4	−9.2	−107.1	−167.8	−1.7	....
Use of Fund Credit and Loans	79dcd	−82.9	−30.6	19.3	−39.1	−24.6	−67.3	−62.8	−59.5	1.3	−23.6	−18.4	....
Exceptional Financing	79ded	367.1	96.2	14.4	6.5	15.8	−19.0	−25.2	102.7	113.0	181.4	36.5	....
Government Finance		*Millions of Shillings: Year Ending June 30*											
Deficit (−) or Surplus	80	−3,443	−14,931	−23,415	−6,172	6,228	†−13,605	−5,304	−5,189	7,196	−14,705	−26,990	−35,769
Total Revenue and Grants	81y	67,321	78,469	112,413	138,181	156,804	†156,167	179,055	201,177	188,350	216,393	205,546	225,692
Revenue	81	58,580	69,661	103,250	125,312	145,558	†150,384	173,783	196,257	184,103	192,313	198,723	210,750
Grants	81z	8,741	8,808	9,163	12,869	11,246	5,783	5,272	4,920	4,247	24,080	6,823	14,942
Expenditure	82	70,764	93,400	135,828	144,353	150,576	†169,772	184,359	206,366	181,154	231,098	232,536	261,461
Statistical Discrepancy	80xx	....	....	....	....	−	†−1,048	64	2,740	266	1,600	532	989
Total Financing	80h	3,443	14,931	23,415	6,172	−6,228	†14,653	5,240	2,449	−7,462	13,105	26,458	34,780
Domestic	84a	4,958	8,571	21,962	16,977	−5,437	†21,287	12,441	11,194	11,876	616	39,769	46,923
Foreign	85a	−1,515	6,360	1,453	−10,805	−791	−6,634	−7,201	−8,745	−19,338	12,489	−13,311	−12,143
Total Debt	88	....	....	....	....	....	463,507	441,561	455,050	550,185	†605,791	613,739	689,013
Domestic	88a	....	....	....	....	....	145,810	145,541	150,499	163,405	†211,813	235,991	289,377
Foreign	89a	....	....	....	....	....	317,697	296,020	304,551	386,780	393,978	377,748	399,636
National Accounts		*Millions of Shillings*											
Househ.Cons.Expend.,incl.NPISHs	96f	178,571	210,596	250,098	322,622	359,442	453,173	513,249	540,400	609,862	665,208	701,822	805,163
Government Consumption Expend.	91f	41,475	48,307	60,719	69,057	84,523	100,712	113,568	125,943	139,159	168,731	184,337	195,467
Gross Fixed Capital Formation	93e	43,777	56,505	75,616	99,497	104,470	109,873	113,879	112,961	116,369	123,079	124,313	136,567
Changes in Inventories	93i	898	2,245	1,683	2,020	3,000	5,400	6,210	7,142	6,142	5,282	4,542	4,588
Exports of Goods and Services	90c	69,287	134,918	148,225	152,596	172,459	174,846	171,895	189,265	211,433	234,176	250,429	271,785
Imports of Goods and Services (−)	98c	69,041	118,958	135,641	180,139	195,155	220,769	224,772	232,233	286,621	317,745	302,758	321,929
Gross Domestic Product (GDP)	99b	264,475	333,616	400,700	465,654	528,740	623,235	694,029	743,479	796,343	878,731	962,686	1,091,640
Net Primary Income from Abroad	98.n	−12,548	−24,380	−23,074	−19,832	−15,837	−13,623	−10,468	−11,196	−10,140	−9,524	−11,250	−6,696
Gross National Income (GNI)	99a	252,419	309,233	377,626	445,821	512,130	609,730	681,652	732,283	786,203	869,207	951,436	1,046,959
GDP Volume 1982 Prices	99b.p	100,057	100,411	103,054	107,595	112,058	115,418	115,736	111,573	119,454	122,338	112,357	....
GDP Volume (2000=100)	99bvp	83.8	84.1	86.3	90.1	93.8	96.6	96.9	93.4	100.0	102.4	94.1	....
GDP Deflator (2000=100)	99bip	39.6	49.8	58.3	64.9	70.8	81.0	90.0	100.0	100.0	107.7	128.5	....
		Millions: Midyear Estimates											
Population	99z	25.15	Ü 25.92	26.67	27.39	28.09	Ü 28.76	29.39	29.99	30.55	31.06	31.54	31.99

Korea 542

		1992	1993	1994	1995	1996	1997	1998	1999	2000	2001	2002	2003
Exchange Rates		\multicolumn{12}{c}{*Won per SDR: End of Period*}
Market Rate	aa	1,084.05	1,109.97	1,151.38	1,151.58	1,213.93	2,286.98	1,695.27	1,561.92	1,647.53	1,650.71	1,612.66	1,772.17
		\multicolumn{12}{c}{*Won per US Dollar: End of Period (ae) Period Average (rf)*}
Market Rate	ae	788.40	808.10	788.70	774.70	844.20	1,695.00	1,204.00	1,138.00	1,264.50	1,313.50	1,186.20	1,192.60
Market Rate	rf	780.65	802.67	803.45	771.27	804.45	951.29	1,401.44	1,188.82	1,130.96	1,290.99	1,251.09	1,191.61
Fund Position		\multicolumn{12}{c}{*Millions of SDRs: End of Period*}
Quota	2f.s	799.6	799.6	799.6	799.6	799.6	799.6	799.6	1,633.6	1,633.6	1,633.6	1,633.6	1,633.6
SDRs	1b.s	30.6	42.3	52.3	65.7	82.3	43.6	8.1	.5	2.7	2.7	8.7	14.2
Reserve Position in the Fund	1c.s	319.1	339.2	363.6	438.5	474.3	443.7	.1	208.6	208.6	208.8	384.0	507.7
Total Fund Cred.&Loans Outstg.	2tl	–	–	–	–	–	8,200.0	12,000.0	4,462.5	4,462.5			
International Liquidity		\multicolumn{12}{c}{*Millions of US Dollars Unless Otherwise Indicated: End of Period*}
Total Reserves minus Gold	1l.d	17,120.6	20,228.2	25,639.3	32,677.7	34,037.1	20,367.9	51,974.5	73,987.3	96,130.5	102,753.3	121,345.2	155,284.2
SDRs	1b.d	42.0	58.1	76.3	97.7	118.4	58.8	11.4	.7	3.5	3.3	11.8	21.1
Reserve Position in the Fund	1c.d	438.7	465.9	530.8	651.8	682.0	598.7	.1	286.3	271.8	262.4	522.0	754.4
Foreign Exchange	1d.d	16,639.9	19,704.2	25,032.1	31,928.2	33,236.7	19,710.4	51,963.0	73,700.3	95,855.1	102,487.5	120,811.4	154,508.8
Gold (Million Fine Troy Ounces)	1ad	.323	.324	.325	.327	.327	.335	.435	.437	.439	.442	.444	.449
Gold (National Valuation)	1and	32.6	33.3	33.6	34.4	36.0	36.9	66.3	67.1	67.6	68.3	69.2	70.9
Monetary Authorities: Other Liab.	4..d	46.4	95.4	442.4	158.6	381.1	140.1	160.9	307.6	286.1	4,877.1	8,371.9	6,952.5
Deposit Money Banks: Assets	7a.d	12,905.0	16,211.0	20,938.0	27,806.0	33,136.0	32,749.0	34,310.0	34,748.0	34,562.0	28,086.0	25,851.0	30,923.2
Liabilities	7b.d	14,652.6	14,795.8	21,170.3	31,446.0	43,181.5	27,975.3	29,455.3	27,546.5	24,804.8	21,289.5	36,680.7	43,689.0
Other Banking Insts.: Assets	7e.d	1,963.0	5,365.0	7,897.0	4,136.0	7,144.0	10,761.0	10,027.0	8,975.0	11,926.0	13,058.0	17,371.0	….
Liabilities	7f.d	9,780.0	15,834.0	21,692.0	21,816.0	26,857.0	29,661.0	22,466.0	18,033.0	15,222.0	13,387.0	16,521.0	….
Monetary Authorities		\multicolumn{12}{c}{*Billions of Won: End of Period*}
Foreign Assets	11	13,684	16,672	20,880	25,390	28,173	29,227	64,832	85,342	121,558	142,589	155,362	194,033
Claims on Central Government	12a	2,333	2,659	2,628	1,951	2,235	5,562	5,961	6,382	4,958	5,570	5,091	6,110
Claims on Official Entities	12bx	570	570	570	570	370	2,370	8,640	2,370	2,370	2,370	2,370	1,370
Claims on Deposit Money Banks	12e	25,571	29,169	28,971	28,076	24,378	62,442	37,830	26,003	15,563	11,637	6,849	8,117
Reserve Money	14	18,107	23,080	25,204	29,306	25,723	22,519	20,703	28,487	28,238	32,827	37,987	40,749
of which: Currency Outside DMBs	14a	8,581	12,109	13,127	15,061	15,453	15,448	13,670	19,475	17,636	18,702	19,863	20,111
Bonds	16ab	23,614	27,148	29,114	29,598	29,068	26,701	53,580	61,389	79,142	93,120	104,929	133,938
Foreign Liabilities	16c	37	77	349	123	322	18,991	20,537	7,320	7,714	6,406	9,931	8,292
Central Government Deposits	16d	4,524	5,059	6,477	6,917	6,684	5,410	5,917	9,126	10,608	7,347	11,178	5,482
Other Items (Net)	17r	–4,124	–6,293	–8,095	–9,956	–6,640	25,980	16,526	13,775	18,747	22,466	5,647	21,170
Deposit Money Banks		\multicolumn{12}{c}{*Billions of Won: End of Period*}
Reserves	20	9,399	10,836	11,947	14,092	10,181	6,798	6,610	8,958	10,434	14,063	17,904	20,427
Claims on Mon.Author.:Securities	20c	7,068	8,865	12,700	15,775	18,419	20,996	29,559	27,375	33,073	36,238	43,515	51,019
Foreign Assets	21	10,174	13,100	16,514	21,542	28,627	55,509	41,309	39,543	43,704	36,891	30,665	36,879
Claims on Central Government	22a	4,921	4,912	5,196	5,373	4,897	6,341	13,564	21,372	23,677	22,959	24,369	29,538
Claims on Private Sector	22d	128,230	144,828	173,903	200,769	240,936	293,812	318,667	383,884	457,258	520,733	628,230	684,192
Demand Deposits	24	16,182	17,344	19,593	23,672	24,221	19,331	21,569	25,139	29,193	34,918	43,265	45,226
Time, Savings,& Fgn.Currency Dep.	25	71,660	83,178	100,668	115,072	138,769	168,482	222,926	284,916	366,041	414,031	455,741	488,084
Bonds	26ab	1,896	2,270	2,923	4,782	6,167	5,954	17,072	11,287	14,699	19,920	45,236	54,005
Restricted Deposits	26b	1,693	635	792	904	988	1,214	772	803	1,030	908	974	1,159
Foreign Liabilities	26c	11,552	11,957	16,697	24,361	36,454	47,418	35,464	31,348	31,366	27,964	43,511	52,104
Central Government Deposits	26d	400	424	286	948	1,632	3,290	4,499	5,493	9,442	10,446	12,743	18,968
Central Govt. Lending Funds	26f	7,708	9,234	11,032	13,493	14,828	23,193	26,703	29,946	29,182	29,340	25,461	25,323
Credit from Monetary Authorities	26g	25,874	29,420	29,256	28,429	24,460	63,076	38,738	26,242	17,191	13,515	10,591	12,682
Capital Accounts	27a	15,641	17,110	20,406	22,523	24,877	22,673	21,891	28,152	29,883	34,792	38,696	41,158
Other Items (Net)	27r	7,186	10,970	18,605	23,366	30,663	28,825	20,075	37,807	40,120	45,051	68,465	83,347
Monetary Survey		\multicolumn{12}{c}{*Billions of Won: End of Period*}
Foreign Assets (Net)	31n	12,269	17,739	20,347	22,448	20,024	18,327	50,140	86,217	126,182	145,110	132,585	170,517
Domestic Credit	32	139,463	157,358	186,520	213,688	255,240	314,581	351,179	412,126	479,780	546,056	645,391	705,594
Claims on Central Govt. (Net)	32an	2,329	2,089	1,061	–541	–1,183	3,204	9,108	13,135	8,585	10,736	5,539	11,198
Claims on Official Entities	32bx	570	570	570	570	370	2,370	8,640	2,370	2,370	2,370	2,370	1,370
Claims on Private Sector	32d	136,564	154,699	184,888	213,658	256,054	309,008	333,431	396,621	468,825	532,951	637,482	693,025
Money	34	24,586	29,041	32,511	38,873	39,542	35,036	35,583	44,375	46,997	53,506	63,151	65,481
Quasi-Money	35	71,672	83,178	100,668	115,073	138,770	168,495	222,956	284,943	366,052	414,072	455,754	488,102
Bonds	36ab	18,442	20,553	19,338	18,606	16,817	11,659	41,092	45,301	60,767	76,802	106,650	136,924
Restricted Deposits	36b	1,693	635	792	904	988	1,214	772	803	1,030	908	974	1,159
Central Govt. Lending Funds	36f	7,713	9,234	11,032	13,493	14,828	23,193	26,703	29,946	29,182	29,340	25,461	25,323
Other Items (Net)	37r	27,625	32,455	42,526	49,187	64,320	93,311	74,214	92,975	101,934	116,539	125,986	159,121
Money plus Quasi-Money	35l	96,259	112,219	133,179	153,946	178,312	203,532	258,538	329,317	413,049	467,577	518,904	553,583

2004, International Monetary Fund: *International Financial Statistics Yearbook*

Korea 542

		1992	1993	1994	1995	1996	1997	1998	1999	2000	2001	2002	2003
Other Banking Institutions													
Development Institutions						*Billions of Won: End of Period*							
Claims on Private Sector	42d	21,102	23,874	26,771	30,616	35,600	48,097	55,361	55,283	58,351	55,843	51,933	56,062
Bonds	46ab	10,412	13,921	16,617	19,639	23,764	34,782	36,096	34,666	35,251	34,317	32,620	35,584
Counterpart Funds	46e	1	1	1	1	1	1	1	1	–	–	–	–
Central Govt. Lending Funds	46f	3,121	3,045	2,967	3,018	3,336	3,822	14,549	15,380	16,889	14,533	13,644	10,199
Credit from Deposit Money Banks	46h	4,910	5,110	5,450	5,710	5,564	2,130	2,397	1,358	704	1,594	560	662
Capital Accounts	47a	1,285	1,382	1,615	1,614	1,814	2,909	4,486	6,247	3,773	6,931	6,926	7,688
Other Items (Net)	47r	1,372	414	121	634	1,122	4,454	−2,168	−2,367	1,734	−1,532	−1,817	1,929
Trust Accounts of Coml. Banks						*Billions of Won: End of Period*							
Claims on Private Sector	42d.g	79,724	112,416	143,539	182,319	216,569	253,305	307,920	273,872	178,537	181,683	197,589	152,187
Claims on Deposit Money Banks	42e.g	1,259	1,000	1,118	1,475	1,982	2,797	8,570	9,366	6,787	10,967	5,972	10,671
Quasi-Monetary Liabilities	45..g	53,022	71,319	93,415	124,891	151,093	171,456	138,941	115,360	77,594	81,330	73,713	58,135
Other Items (Net)	47r.g	27,961	42,096	51,242	58,903	67,458	84,646	177,549	167,878	107,730	111,319	129,848	104,723
Postal Savings Deposits	45..h	3,578	4,078	5,948	5,321	6,421	7,280	11,491	14,980	22,150	26,111	29,400	35,985
Nonbank Financial Institutions						*Billions of Won: End of Period*							
Cash	40..s	4,496	3,186	3,633	5,984	8,310	12,071	7,906	5,836	6,638	6,602	3,686	3,511
Claims on Central Government	42a.s	401	452	269	107	123	163	510	1,677	2,571	4,536	12,202	18,850
Claims on Private Sector	42d.s	28,656	33,091	38,931	43,207	51,210	55,510	43,442	42,937	53,578	58,010	65,418	70,299
Real Estate	42h.s	3,333	3,842	4,504	5,124	6,173	7,333	8,703	9,752	10,113	9,757	9,435	9,313
Incr.in Total Assets(Within Per.)	49z.s	6,528	5,607	7,230	10,951	13,101	12,461	357	15,997	13,896	16,280	25,095	20,435
Liquid Liabilities	55l	148,364	184,430	228,909	278,174	327,515	370,197	401,064	453,822	506,155	568,417	618,332	644,192
Interest Rates						*Percent Per Annum*							
Discount Rate (End of Period)	60	7.0	5.0	5.0	5.0	5.0	5.0	3.0	3.0	3.0	2.5	2.5	2.5
Money Market Rate	60b	14.3	12.1	12.5	12.6	12.4	13.2	15.0	5.0	5.2	4.7	4.2	4.0
Corporate Bond Rate	60bc	†16.2	12.6	12.9	13.8	11.8	13.4	15.1	8.9	9.4	7.1	6.6	5.4
Deposit Rate	60l	10.0	8.6	8.5	8.8	7.5	†10.8	13.3	7.9	7.9	5.8	4.9	4.3
Lending Rate	60p	10.0	8.6	8.5	9.0	8.8	†11.9	15.3	9.4	8.5	7.7	6.8	6.2
Government Bond Yield	61	15.1	12.1	12.3	12.4	10.9	11.7	12.8	8.7	8.5	6.7	6.5	4.9
Prices, Production, Labor						*Index Numbers (2000=100): Period Averages*							
Share Prices	62	80.2	100.2	132.2	125.8	113.6	89.2	55.8	109.5	100.0	78.3	103.5	92.9
Producer Prices	63	79.2	77.4	79.5	83.2	85.9	89.2	100.1	98.0	100.0	99.5	99.2	101.4
Consumer Prices	64	70.8	74.2	78.8	82.3	86.4	90.2	97.0	97.8	100.0	104.1	106.9	110.7
Wages: Monthly Earnings	65ey	50.9	56.5	65.2	71.7	80.5	84.6	81.9	92.1	100.0	105.8	118.5	128.7
Industrial Production	66	50.0	52.2	58.0	64.9	70.4	73.7	69.0	85.6	100.0	100.7	108.8	114.4
Manufacturing Employment	67ey	116.1	109.9	110.8	112.2	110.1	105.7	91.2	93.8	100.0	99.4	98.8	97.9
						Number in Thousands: Period Averages							
Labor Force	67d	19,499	19,806	20,353	20,845	21,288	21,782	21,428	21,666	22,069	22,417	22,877	....
Employment	67e	18,961	19,253	19,837	20,379	20,764	21,048	19,926	20,281	21,061	21,362	22,169	....
Unemployment	67c	465	550	489	419	425	557	1,463	1,353	913	845	710	777
Unemployment Rate (%)	67r	2.4	2.8	2.4	2.0	2.0	2.6	6.8	6.3	4.1	3.8	3.1	3.4
International Transactions						*Millions of US Dollars*							
Exports	70..d	76,632	82,236	96,013	125,058	129,715	136,164	132,313	143,686	172,268	150,439	162,471	193,817
Imports, c.i.f	71..d	81,775	83,800	102,348	135,119	150,339	144,616	93,282	119,725	160,481	141,098	152,126	178,827
								2000=100					
Volume of Exports	72	29.0	33.2	37.7	46.1	54.1	62.1	74.0	82.9	100.0	100.7	114.1	133.4
Volume of Imports	73	45.7	48.5	59.4	73.7	85.2	86.9	65.1	84.0	100.0	97.7	109.7	117.7
Unit Value of Exports	74	105.3	104.2	107.0	110.3	99.9	107.6	126.4	104.7	100.0	99.2	91.9	89.7
Unit Value of Imports	75	78.3	78.8	78.2	79.7	79.7	88.1	108.3	91.8	100.0	103.9	96.8	100.7
Export Prices	76	87.0	89.1	91.6	92.9	89.0	94.8	124.5	101.0	100.0	96.2	89.5	87.5
Import Prices	76.x	65.7	68.0	70.7	74.8	75.3	82.4	105.7	92.9	100.0	103.5	97.1	98.9

Korea 542

		1992	1993	1994	1995	1996	1997	1998	1999	2000	2001	2002	2003
Balance of Payments		*Millions of US Dollars: Minus Sign Indicates Debit*											
Current Account, n.i.e.	78ald	−4,095	821	−4,024	−8,665	−23,120	−8,287	40,371	24,522	12,251	8,033	5,394	12,321
Goods: Exports f.o.b.	78aad	76,210	82,098	94,983	124,934	130,038	138,731	132,251	145,375	176,221	151,478	163,414	197,637
Goods: Imports f.o.b.	78abd	−78,117	−79,948	−98,000	−129,298	−145,115	−141,986	−90,586	−116,912	−159,267	−137,990	−148,637	−175,476
Trade Balance	78acd	−1,907	2,150	−3,017	−4,365	−15,077	−3,256	41,665	28,463	16,954	13,488	14,777	22,161
Services: Credit	78add	10,722	12,950	16,805	22,827	23,412	26,301	25,565	26,529	30,534	29,055	28,388	32,702
Services: Debit	78aed	−13,605	−15,076	−18,606	−25,806	−29,592	−29,502	−24,541	−27,180	−33,381	−32,927	−36,585	−40,313
Balance on Goods & Services	78afd	−4,791	24	−4,818	−7,343	−21,257	−6,456	42,689	27,812	14,106	9,616	6,580	14,550
Income: Credit	78agd	2,450	2,509	2,835	3,486	3,665	3,878	2,675	3,245	6,375	6,650	6,900	7,111
Income: Debit	78ahd	−2,845	−2,900	−3,322	−4,788	−5,480	−6,333	−8,313	−8,404	−8,797	−7,848	−6,467	−6,515
Balance on Gds, Serv. & Inc.	78aid	−5,187	−367	−5,305	−8,646	−23,071	−8,910	37,051	22,653	11,685	8,418	7,012	15,146
Current Transfers, n.i.e.: Credit	78ajd	3,239	3,382	3,672	4,104	4,279	5,288	6,737	6,421	6,500	6,687	7,314	7,879
Current Transfers: Debit	78akd	−2,147	−2,194	−2,392	−4,123	−4,328	−4,665	−3,416	−4,552	−5,934	−7,072	−8,932	−10,703
Capital Account, n.i.e.	78bcd	−407	−475	−437	−488	−598	−608	171	−389	−615	−731	−1,087	−1,402
Capital Account, n.i.e.: Credit	78bad	5	2	8	15	19	17	464	95	98	42	47	53
Capital Account: Debit	78bbd	−412	−477	−445	−502	−617	−624	−293	−484	−713	−773	−1,133	−1,455
Financial Account, n.i.e.	78bjd	6,994	3,216	10,732	17,273	23,924	−9,195	−8,381	12,709	12,725	3,025	7,338	14,530
Direct Investment Abroad	78bdd	−1,162	−1,340	−2,461	−3,552	−4,670	−4,449	−4,740	−4,198	−4,999	−2,420	−2,617	−3,429
Dir. Invest. in Rep. Econ., n.i.e.	78bed	728	588	809	1,776	2,325	2,844	5,412	9,333	9,283	3,528	2,392	3,222
Portfolio Investment Assets	78bfd	76	−986	−2,481	−2,907	−6,413	1,076	−1,999	1,282	−520	−5,521	−5,032	−4,333
Equity Securities	78bkd	8	−204	−382	−238	−653	−320	42	−271	−480	−492	−1,460	−1,993
Debt Securities	78bld	68	−781	−2,098	−2,669	−5,760	1,395	−2,041	1,553	−40	−5,029	−3,571	−2,340
Portfolio Investment Liab., n.i.e.	78bgd	5,875	11,088	8,713	14,619	21,514	13,308	775	7,908	12,697	12,227	5,378	22,653
Equity Securities	78bmd	2,482	6,615	3,614	4,219	5,954	2,525	3,856	12,072	13,094	10,266	395	14,213
Debt Securities	78bnd	3,392	4,473	5,099	10,400	15,561	10,783	−3,081	−4,164	−397	1,962	4,983	8,439
Financial Derivatives Assets	78bwd	773	448	452	623	414	932	412	401	532	463	1,288	888
Financial Derivatives Liabilities	78bxd	−921	−535	−565	−744	−331	−1,021	−1,066	−915	−711	−586	−926	−1,248
Other Investment Assets	78bhd	−3,299	−4,592	−7,369	−13,991	−13,487	−13,568	6,693	−2,606	−2,289	7,085	2,557	−3,496
Monetary Authorities	78bod	−24	−42	−72	−36	—	−86	−36	−164	−44	−38	−40	−48
General Government	78bpd	−213	−625	−296	−156	−543	−149	−46	−169	−155	−509	−311	−27
Banks	78bqd	−3,291	−3,993	−5,061	−9,199	−8,173	−8,336	6,970	−203	−1,219	8,755	3,087	−3,918
Other Sectors	78brd	228	68	−1,940	−4,600	−4,770	−4,996	−194	−2,071	−871	−1,124	−179	496
Other Investment Liab., n.i.e.	78bid	4,924	−1,455	13,632	21,450	24,571	−8,317	−13,868	1,502	−1,268	−11,751	4,297	274
Monetary Authorities	78bsd	7	15	−2	−10	−29	23	25	148	28	63	−52	−35
General Government	78btd	−700	−1,842	−335	−593	−493	4,671	4,628	3,309	110	−397	−1,436	−5,239
Banks	78bud	1,820	720	7,368	11,389	9,952	−9,785	−6,233	1,418	−4,538	−4,147	6,257	2,561
Other Sectors	78bvd	3,798	−348	6,600	10,664	15,142	−3,226	−12,288	−3,372	3,132	−7,271	−473	2,988
Net Errors and Omissions	78cad	1,232	−553	−1,657	−1,081	1,209	−4,889	−6,231	−3,581	−571	2,951	124	342
Overall Balance	78cbd	3,724	3,009	4,614	7,039	1,416	−22,979	25,930	33,260	23,790	13,278	11,769	25,791
Reserves and Related Items	79dad	−3,724	−3,009	−4,614	−7,039	−1,416	22,979	−25,930	−33,260	−23,790	−13,278	−11,769	−25,791
Reserve Assets	79dbd	−3,724	−3,009	−4,614	−7,039	−1,416	11,875	−30,968	−22,989	−23,790	−7,586	−11,769	−25,791
Use of Fund Credit and Loans	79dcd	—	—	—	—	—	11,104	5,038	−10,271	—	−5,692	—	—
Exceptional Financing	79ded	....	....	....	....	....	....	....	....	....	....	....	....
International Investment Position		*Millions of US Dollars*											
Assets	79aad	38,068	46,762	60,612	....	....	....	....	....	....	184,872	....	....
Direct Investment Abroad	79abd	4,499	5,555	7,630	....	....	....	....	....	....	19,967	....	....
Portfolio Investment	79acd	225	522	992	....	....	....	....	....	....	8,798	....	....
Equity Securities	79add	—	—	—	....	....	....	....	....	....	1,301	....	....
Debt Securities	79aed	225	522	992	....	....	....	....	....	....	7,497	....	....
Financial Derivatives	79ald	—	—	—	....	....	....	....	....	....	414	....	....
Other Investment	79afd	16,192	20,423	26,317	....	....	....	....	....	....	52,871	....	....
Monetary Authorities	79agd	—	—	—	....	....	....	....	....	....	771	....	....
General Government	79ahd	—	—	—	....	....	....	....	....	....	959	....	....
Banks	79aid	12,081	15,389	19,944	....	....	....	....	....	....	41,706	....	....
Other Sectors	79ajd	4,111	5,034	6,373	....	....	....	....	....	....	9,436	....	....
Reserve Assets	79akd	17,152	20,262	25,673	....	....	....	....	....	....	102,822	....	....
Liabilities	79lad	41,508	53,706	69,830	....	....	....	....	....	....	249,968	....	....
Dir. Invest. in Rep. Economy	79lbd	6,482	6,984	7,715	....	....	....	....	....	....	50,160	....	....
Portfolio Investment	79lcd	11,416	22,438	29,714	....	....	....	....	....	....	105,259	....	....
Equity Securities	79ldd	3,030	9,316	11,796	....	....	....	....	....	....	70,080	....	....
Debt Securities	79led	8,386	13,122	17,918	....	....	....	....	....	....	35,179	....	....
Financial Derivatives	79lld	—	—	—	....	....	....	....	....	....	417	....	....
Other Investment	79lfd	23,610	24,284	32,401	....	....	....	....	....	....	94,133	....	....
Monetary Authorities	79lgd	193	208	207	....	....	....	....	....	....	502	....	....
General Government	79lhd	—	—	—	....	....	....	....	....	....	17,966	....	....
Banks	79lid	23,417	24,076	32,194	....	....	....	....	....	....	28,917	....	....
Other Sectors	79ljd	—	—	—	....	....	....	....	....	....	46,747	....	....

Korea 542

		1992	1993	1994	1995	1996	1997	1998	1999	2000	2001	2002	2003
Government Finance						*Billions of Won: Year Ending December 31*							
Deficit (-) or Surplus	80	-1,188	1,704	984	1,035	431	-5,747	....	....	....	....	....	....
Revenue	81	43,805	50,750	61,109	72,087	84,272	91,979	....	....	....	....	....	....
Grants Received	81z	–	–	–	–	–	–	....	....	....	....	....	....
Expenditure	82	40,776	45,010	53,887	62,320	72,600	79,004	....	....	....	....	....	....
Lending Minus Repayments	83	4,217	4,036	6,238	8,732	11,241	18,722	....	....	....	....	....	....
Financing													
Domestic	84a	1,499	-1,257	-589	-678	-136	-1,214	....	....	....	....	....	....
Foreign	85a	-311	-447	-395	-357	-295	6,961	....	....	....	....	....	....
Debt	88	27,737	28,998	30,466	31,537	33,687	47,045	....	....	....	....	....	....
Domestic	88a	22,216	23,504	24,800	26,296	28,636	31,724	....	....	....	....	....	....
Foreign	89a	5,521	5,494	5,666	5,241	5,051	15,321	....	....	....	....	....	....
National Accounts							*Billions of Won*						
Househ.Cons.Expend.,incl.NPISHs	96f	130,028	148,264	175,970	208,462	236,194	258,636	238,811	274,934	312,301	343,417	381,063	388,417
Government Consumption Expend	91f	26,506	29,250	32,857	44,687	52,138	56,749	61,981	65,174	70,098	80,298	88,512	96,180
Gross Fixed Capital Formation	93e	90,809	100,354	116,436	148,820	168,157	174,961	146,914	157,407	179,908	183,792	199,047	213,844
Changes in Inventories	93i	931	-1,804	1,636	1,410	6,225	1,706	-25,903	-3,199	-494	-1,315	-41	-1,868
Exports of Goods and Services	90c	67,942	76,423	89,986	114,978	124,988	159,091	223,481	206,842	236,210	235,187	241,209	275,316
Imports of Goods and Services (-)	98c	71,600	76,278	93,668	119,336	140,574	162,056	161,180	171,437	217,979	220,914	231,765	257,118
Statistical Discrepancy	99bs	1,084	1,287	190	-183	1,468	2,049	-1	-221	-1,377	1,657	6,238	6,575
Gross Domestic Product (GDP)	99b	245,700	277,497	323,407	398,838	448,596	491,135	484,103	529,500	578,665	622,123	684,263	721,346
Net Primary Income from Abroad	98.n	-312	-389	-596	-1,379	-1,740	-2,677	-7,857	-6,144	-2,505	-1,095	806	1,010
Gross National Income (GNI)	99a	245,388	277,108	322,812	397,459	446,856	488,457	476,245	523,355	576,160	621,028	685,069	722,356
Consumption of Fixed Capital	99cf	25,005	28,721	32,278	48,131	56,784	66,147	74,349	79,006	83,416	88,113	91,113	99,068
GDP Volume 1995 Prices	99b.p	303,384	320,044	346,448	377,350	....	....	....	....	....	....	....	....
GDP Volume 2000 Prices	99b.p	....	....	....	467,099	499,790	523,035	487,184	533,399	578,665	600,866	642,748	662,474
GDP Volume (2000=100)	99bvp	64.9	68.5	74.1	†80.7	86.4	90.4	84.2	92.2	100.0	103.8	111.1	114.5
GDP Deflator (2000=100)	99bip	65.4	70.0	75.4	85.4	89.8	93.9	99.4	99.3	100.0	103.5	106.5	108.9
						Millions: Midyear Estimates							
Population	99z	43.74	44.19	44.62	45.04	45.44	45.81	46.17	46.51	46.84	47.14	47.43	47.70

Kuwait 443

		1992	1993	1994	1995	1996	1997	1998	1999	2000	2001	2002	2003
Exchange Rates		\multicolumn{12}{c}{*SDRs per Dinar: End of Period*}
Official Rate	ac	2.4026	2.4396	2.2824	2.2504	2.3190	2.4308	2.3551	2.3953	2.5130	2.5846	2.4554	2.2835
		\multicolumn{12}{c}{*US Dollars per Dinar: End of Period (ag) Period Average (rh)*}
Official Rate	ag	3.3036	3.3510	3.3320	3.3453	3.3346	3.2798	3.3161	3.2875	3.2742	3.2481	3.3382	3.3933
Official Rate	rh	3.4087	3.3147	3.3600	3.3509	3.3399	3.2966	3.2814	3.2850	3.2600	3.2607	3.2906	3.3557
Fund Position		\multicolumn{12}{c}{*Millions of SDRs: End of Period*}
Quota	2f.s	635.3	995.2	995.2	995.2	995.2	995.2	995.2	1,381.1	1,381.1	1,381.1	1,381.1	1,381.1
SDRs	1b.s	130.4	49.1	55.0	61.3	68.2	74.1	82.5	53.7	69.8	85.9	97.7	107.5
Reserve Position in the Fund	1c.s	96.7	167.8	142.6	139.0	136.5	167.5	244.8	368.3	373.8	476.1	528.3	522.7
of which: Outstg.Fund Borrowing	2c	—	—	—	—	—	—	31.8	—	—	—	—	—
International Liquidity		\multicolumn{12}{c}{*Millions of US Dollars Unless Otherwise Indicated: End of Period*}
Total Reserves minus Gold	1l.d	5,146.9	4,214.1	3,500.7	3,560.8	3,515.1	3,451.8	3,947.1	4,823.7	7,082.4	9,897.3	9,208.1	7,577.0
SDRs	1b.d	179.2	67.4	80.3	91.1	98.0	100.0	116.2	73.8	90.9	108.0	132.9	159.8
Reserve Position in the Fund	1c.d	132.9	230.5	208.2	206.6	196.3	226.1	344.6	505.5	487.0	598.3	718.2	776.8
Foreign Exchange	1d.d	4,834.8	3,916.3	3,212.2	3,263.2	3,220.8	3,125.7	3,486.3	4,244.4	6,504.4	9,191.1	8,357.0	6,640.5
Gold (Million Fine Troy Ounces)	1ad	2.539	2.539	2.539	2.539	2.539	2.539	2.539	2.539	2.539	2.539	2.539	2.539
Gold (National Valuation)	1and	104.7	106.2	105.6	106.0	105.7	104.0	105.1	104.2	103.9	103.1	105.9	107.6
Deposit Money Banks: Assets	7a.d	5,449.0	5,946.6	6,419.1	7,127.7	7,230.3	6,945.2	5,928.5	5,873.8	6,444.9	6,582.6	8,148.5	8,240.5
Liabilities	7b.d	1,936.9	1,803.2	2,377.0	2,239.0	2,536.6	4,009.2	3,595.3	3,971.0	3,913.3	5,101.3	6,782.3	6,542.2
Other Financial Insts.: Assets	7e.d	4,115.3	3,772.2	3,706.5	3,666.7	3,556.0	4,339.1	5,498.4	6,013.2	7,184.2	6,795.5	7,001.5	8,235.2
Liab	7f.d	2,381.2	1,790.8	1,533.7	1,584.6	1,592.9	2,330.6	3,504.4	3,693.2	4,582.2	4,628.6	4,637.1	5,182.6
Monetary Authorities		\multicolumn{12}{c}{*Millions of Dinars: End of Period*}
Foreign Assets	11	1,564.5	1,151.4	1,168.2	1,124.1	1,112.0	1,108.7	1,186.3	1,476.1	2,157.3	3,037.7	2,748.0	2,216.5
Claims on Central Government	12a	152.9	87.1	59.2	2.3	41.2	39.3	.1	45.1	—	—	—	—
Claims on Deposit Money Banks	12e	77.6	142.4	90.8	—	—	6.0	—	—	14.0	—	—	—
Reserve Money	14	537.4	503.4	504.0	470.9	474.7	426.9	448.4	582.9	534.6	521.4	590.2	690.0
of which: Currency Outside DMBs	14a	379.1	355.2	351.3	311.5	350.1	345.3	348.7	442.9	416.6	401.2	442.2	494.1
Central Government Deposits	16d	863.9	497.2	368.8	163.9	265.7	298.7	229.0	450.8	547.8	602.3	381.9	440.7
Capital Accounts	17a	208.0	210.3	209.7	193.7	188.5	189.6	186.1	186.5	188.0	187.5	195.9	218.5
Other Items (Net)	17r	186.0	170.0	236.1	298.0	224.2	238.9	322.9	301.0	900.9	1,726.5	1,580.0	867.2
Deposit Money Banks		\multicolumn{12}{c}{*Millions of Dinars: End of Period*}
Reserves	20	160.9	146.0	151.8	158.1	123.0	79.0	98.0	141.2	119.3	119.5	143.7	199.4
Foreign Assets	21	1,649.4	1,774.6	1,926.5	2,130.7	2,168.3	2,117.6	1,787.8	1,786.7	1,968.4	2,026.6	2,441.0	2,428.5
Claims on Central Government	22a	7,111.6	5,989.9	5,881.7	5,760.3	4,901.3	4,782.8	4,641.5	4,619.6	4,246.8	4,127.4	4,118.2	4,009.7
Claims on Private Sector	22d	1,032.7	1,240.9	1,703.2	2,436.1	3,173.1	4,324.2	4,801.6	5,015.1	5,251.7	6,125.3	6,953.4	8,501.9
Demand Deposits	24	729.4	758.8	774.7	873.5	892.5	902.2	794.7	928.5	1,051.1	1,240.2	1,624.6	2,117.4
Time and Savings Deposits	25	4,950.0	5,282.5	5,616.9	6,189.8	6,088.3	6,368.5	6,413.1	6,306.6	6,695.5	7,567.1	7,579.6	7,789.7
Foreign Liabilities	26c	586.3	538.1	713.4	669.3	760.7	1,222.4	1,084.2	1,207.9	1,195.2	1,570.5	2,031.7	1,928.0
Central Government Deposits	26d	613.5	555.9	421.3	459.4	374.1	343.6	256.8	195.0	185.1	230.9	299.4	315.2
Credit from Monetary Authorities	26g	1,384.2	196.4	112.0	6.0	—	6.0	.7	—	14.0	—	—	—
Capital Accounts	27a	977.1	1,059.8	1,090.1	1,201.5	1,259.0	1,407.8	1,469.9	1,511.9	1,776.3	1,681.9	1,763.4	2,008.7
Other Items (Net)	27r	714.3	760.0	935.0	1,086.2	991.2	1,053.1	1,309.7	1,412.4	669.0	108.1	357.6	980.5
Monetary Survey		\multicolumn{12}{c}{*Millions of Dinars: End of Period*}
Foreign Assets (Net)	31n	2,627.6	2,387.9	2,381.3	2,585.5	2,519.6	2,003.9	1,889.9	2,054.9	2,930.5	3,493.8	3,157.2	2,717.0
Domestic Credit	32	6,820.0	6,264.8	6,854.0	7,575.6	7,475.8	8,504.0	8,957.4	9,034.0	8,765.6	9,419.5	10,390.3	11,755.7
Claims on Central Govt. (Net)	32an	5,787.3	5,023.9	5,150.8	5,139.3	4,302.7	4,179.8	4,155.8	4,018.9	3,513.9	3,294.2	3,437.0	3,253.9
Claims on Private Sector	32d	1,032.7	1,240.9	1,703.2	2,436.1	3,173.1	4,324.2	4,801.6	5,015.1	5,251.7	6,125.3	6,953.4	8,501.9
Money	34	1,108.5	1,114.0	1,126.0	1,185.0	1,242.6	1,247.5	1,143.4	1,371.4	1,467.7	1,641.4	2,066.7	2,611.5
Quasi-Money	35	4,950.0	5,282.5	5,616.9	6,189.8	6,088.3	6,368.5	6,413.1	6,306.6	6,695.5	7,567.1	7,579.6	7,789.7
Other Items (Net)	37r	3,389.4	2,256.3	2,493.0	2,786.7	2,664.5	2,892.0	3,291.0	3,410.6	3,532.9	3,704.8	3,901.3	4,071.4
Money plus Quasi-Money	35l	6,058.5	6,396.5	6,742.9	7,374.8	7,330.9	7,616.0	7,556.5	7,678.0	8,163.2	9,208.5	9,646.3	10,401.2
Other Financial Institutions		\multicolumn{12}{c}{*Millions of Dinars: End of Period*}
Cash	40	141.6	132.6	120.5	95.7	125.8	153.9	258.7	207.8	154.1	167.7	133.6	135.9
Foreign Assets	41	1,245.7	1,125.7	1,112.4	1,096.1	1,066.4	1,323.0	1,658.1	1,829.1	2,194.2	2,092.1	2,097.4	2,426.9
Claims on Private Sector	42d	878.8	713.1	596.6	632.9	707.6	904.0	1,244.9	931.7	766.0	852.1	970.3	1,499.9
Foreign Liabilities	46c	720.8	534.4	460.3	473.7	477.7	710.6	1,056.8	1,123.4	1,399.5	1,425.0	1,389.1	1,527.3
Central Government Deposits	46d	267.3	181.0	119.9	101.1	142.7	94.5	84.8	7.5	7.0	7.5	.3	63.8
Credit from Deposit Money Banks	46h	230.7	186.5	134.7	185.5	158.5	206.9	296.1	207.7	239.8	392.6	416.9	572.0
Capital Accounts	47a	594.0	609.7	686.0	769.1	861.6	1,018.3	1,325.5	1,255.0	1,294.7	1,005.4	1,029.5	1,285.1
Other Items (Net)	47r	453.3	460.0	428.5	295.3	259.4	350.8	398.6	374.9	173.8	281.4	365.5	614.4
Interest Rates		\multicolumn{12}{c}{*Percent Per Annum*}
Discount Rate (End of Period)	60	7.50	5.75	7.00	7.25	7.25	7.50	7.00	6.75	7.25	4.25	3.25	3.25
Money Market Rate	60b	....	7.43	6.31	7.43	6.98	7.05	7.24	6.32	6.82	4.62	2.99	2.47
Treasury Bill Rate	60c	....	....	6.32	7.35	6.93	6.98	....	....	....	....	....	....
Deposit Rate	60l	7.59	7.07	5.70	6.53	6.05	5.93	6.32	5.76	5.89	4.47	3.15	2.42
Lending Rate	60p	8.00	7.95	7.61	8.37	8.77	8.80	8.93	8.56	8.87	7.88	6.48	5.42

2004, International Monetary Fund : *International Financial Statistics Yearbook*

Kuwait 443

		1992	1993	1994	1995	1996	1997	1998	1999	2000	2001	2002	2003
Prices, Production, Labor		\multicolumn{12}{c}{*Index Numbers (2000=100): Period Averages*}
Wholesale Prices	63	95.84	97.56	97.37	98.72	103.81	102.47	100.78	99.56	100.00	101.97	105.31	107.36
Consumer Prices	64	86.4	86.8	89.0	91.4	94.6	95.2	95.4	98.2	100.0	101.7	103.1	†104.3
Crude Petroleum Production	66aa	57.0	103.4	112.3	112.7	114.2	115.2	115.3	104.5	100.0	93.4	88.3	88.5
		\multicolumn{12}{c}{*Number in Thousands: Period Averages*}
Labor Force	67d	....	....	....	748	....	....	....	....	....	....	....	....
International Transactions		\multicolumn{12}{c}{*Millions of Dinars*}
Exports	70	1,931.1	3,091.2	3,342.3	3,814.5	4,458.0	4,314.3	2,911.6	3,702.8	5,962.7	4,969.7	4,666.2	5,772.7
Oil Exports	70a	1,824.9	2,929.6	3,112.7	3,597.1	4,231.3	4,085.4	2,581.8	3,356.4	5,578.3	4,590.8	4,272.8	5,663.5
Imports, c.i.f.	71	2,129.2	2,123.8	1,988.2	2,323.1	2,507.2	2,501.6	2,626.2	2,318.3	2,195.4	2,413.3	2,735.6	3,216.8
Balance of Payments		\multicolumn{12}{c}{*Millions of US Dollars: Minus Sign Indicates Debit*}
Current Account, n.i.e.	78ald	−450	2,499	3,243	5,016	7,107	7,935	2,215	5,010	14,672	8,324	4,251	7,567
Goods: Exports f.o.b.	78aad	6,548	10,264	11,284	12,833	14,946	14,281	9,618	12,223	19,478	16,238	15,366	20,959
Goods: Imports f.o.b.	78abd	−7,237	−6,940	−6,600	−7,254	−7,949	−7,747	−7,714	−6,708	−6,451	−7,046	−8,124	−9,698
Trade Balance	78acd	−689	3,324	4,685	5,579	6,997	6,534	1,903	5,516	13,027	9,192	7,242	11,261
Services: Credit	78add	1,494	1,242	1,415	1,401	1,520	1,760	1,762	1,560	1,822	1,663	1,648	1,916
Services: Debit	78aed	−4,590	−4,589	−4,531	−5,381	−5,100	−5,129	−5,542	−5,171	−4,920	−5,354	−5,837	−6,557
Balance on Goods & Services	78afd	−3,786	−23	1,569	1,598	3,417	3,165	−1,877	1,905	9,929	5,500	3,053	6,621
Income: Credit	78agd	5,907	4,489	4,174	6,125	6,409	7,744	7,163	6,094	7,315	5,426	3,708	3,611
Income: Debit	78ahd	−662	−663	−1,004	−1,243	−1,229	−1,467	−1,296	−985	−616	−525	−365	−285
Balance on Gds, Serv. & Inc.	78aid	1,460	3,804	4,739	6,480	8,597	9,441	3,990	7,013	16,628	10,401	6,397	9,946
Current Transfers, n.i.e.: Credit	78ajd	17	109	94	54	53	79	98	99	85	52	49	67
Current Transfers: Debit	78akd	−1,927	−1,415	−1,590	−1,518	−1,543	−1,586	−1,874	−2,102	−2,041	−2,129	−2,195	−2,446
Capital Account, n.i.e.	78bcd	....	−205	−205	−194	−204	−96	79	703	2,217	2,931	1,672	1,429
Capital Account, n.i.e.: Credit	78bad	....	−	−	−	3	115	289	716	2,236	2,951	1,708	1,463
Capital Account: Debit	78bbd	....	−205	−205	−194	−207	−211	−210	−13	−20	−20	−36	−34
Financial Account, n.i.e.	78bjd	11,067	421	3,304	157	−7,632	−6,211	−2,920	−5,706	−13,773	−6,313	−5,163	−11,332
Direct Investment Abroad	78bdd	−1,211	−653	1,519	1,022	−1,740	969	1,867	−23	303	−365	155	4,990
Dir. Invest. in Rep. Econ., n.i.e.	78bed	....	13	−	7	347	20	59	72	16	−147	7	−67
Portfolio Investment Assets	78bfd	−3	−931	394	−2,064	−788	−6,926	−4,768	−2,638	−12,923	−7,366	−3,425	−13,379
Equity Securities	78bkd	....	−	−	−	−	−	−	−	−	−	−	−
Debt Securities	78bld	−3	−931	394	−2,064	−788	−6,926	−4,768	−2,638	−12,923	−7,366	−3,425	−13,379
Portfolio Investment Liab., n.i.e.	78bgd	276	−	−	−50	27	−	−	79	254	−78	161	336
Equity Securities	78bmd	....	−	−	−	−	−	−	−	−	−	−	−
Debt Securities	78bnd	276	−	−	−50	27	−	−	79	254	−78	161	336
Financial Derivatives Assets	78bwd	....	−	−	−	−	−	−	−	−	−	−	−
Financial Derivatives Liabilities	78bxd	....	−	−	−	−	−	−	−	−	−	−	−
Other Investment Assets	78bhd	11,261	−669	529	−221	−745	3,356	646	−3,512	−1,108	505	−3,754	−2,812
Monetary Authorities	78bod	10,490	−	−	−	−	−	−	−	−	−	−	−
General Government	78bpd	−634	−523	825	724	−1,122	2,993	−10	−3,288	−284	900	−3,879	−2,752
Banks	78bqd	1,385	−301	−401	−734	−23	260	929	−161	−1,004	241	−599	−17
Other Sectors	78brd	20	156	104	−211	401	102	−272	−62	179	−636	724	−44
Other Investment Liab., n.i.e.	78bid	743	2,660	862	1,464	−4,733	−3,629	−725	315	−316	1,138	1,695	−399
Monetary Authorities	78bsd	−	7	−3	−54	−17	3	−10	−	7	−	26	30
General Government	78btd	....	3,429	525	1,541	−5,371	−6,290	−1,316	−115	−838	−33	401	−181
Banks	78bud	720	−159	589	−97	304	1,523	−456	302	−297	1,301	1,356	−540
Other Sectors	78bvd	24	−616	−249	74	351	1,134	1,057	128	812	−130	−89	292
Net Errors and Omissions	78cad	−8,765	−4,192	−6,292	−5,120	704	−1,623	885	912	−847	−2,038	−1,733	511
Overall Balance	78cbd	1,851	−1,478	50	−141	−25	6	258	918	2,268	2,905	−973	−1,824
Reserves and Related Items	79dad	−1,851	1,478	−50	141	25	−6	−258	−918	−2,268	−2,905	973	1,824
Reserve Assets	79dbd	−1,851	1,478	−50	141	25	−6	−258	−918	−2,268	−2,905	973	1,824
Use of Fund Credit and Loans	79dcd	−	−	−	−	−	−	−	−	−	−	−	−
Exceptional Financing	79ded	....	−	−	−	−	−	−	−	−	−	−	−
Government Finance		\multicolumn{12}{c}{*Millions of Dinars: Year Ending December 31*}
Deficit (-) or Surplus	80	....	....	−977	−656	1,031	1,050	−456	385	3,055	1,855	1,534	2,521
Total Revenue and Grants	81y	....	....	2,787	3,076	4,198	4,179	2,859	3,710	6,434	5,632	5,632	6,801
Revenue	81	....	....	2,787	3,076	4,198	4,179	2,859	3,710	6,434	5,632	5,632	6,801
Grants	81z	....	....	−	−	−	−	−	−	−	−	−	−
Exp. & Lending Minus Repay.	82z	....	....	3,763	3,732	3,167	3,129	3,315	3,325	3,379	3,778	4,098	4,279
Expenditure	82	....	....	3,763	3,732	3,167	3,129	3,315	3,325	3,379	3,778	4,098	4,279
Lending Minus Repayments	83	....	....	−	−	−	−	−	−	−	−	−	−

2004, International Monetary Fund: *International Financial Statistics Yearbook*

Kuwait 443

		1992	1993	1994	1995	1996	1997	1998	1999	2000	2001	2002	2003
National Accounts						*Millions of Dinars*							
Househ.Cons.Expend.,incl.NPISHs	96f	2,233	3,143	3,029	3,272	4,073	4,131	4,358	4,490	4,958	5,320	5,855	6,169
Government Consumption Expend	91f	3,237	2,593	2,503	2,612	2,570	2,451	2,412	2,463	2,485	2,529	2,929	3,224
Gross Capital Formation	93	1,158	1,243	1,192	1,197	1,424	1,256	1,459	1,335	868	910	979	1,076
Gross Fixed Capital Formation	93e	1,013	1,094	982	1,100	1,318	1,240	1,448	1,335	868	910	979	1,076
Changes in Inventories	93i	145	149	210	97	106	15	11	....	....	....	....	....
Exports of Goods and Services	90c	2,358	3,454	3,753	4,248	4,930	4,866	3,468	4,212	6,534	5,490	5,171	6,817
Imports of Goods and Services (-)	98c	3,159	3,202	3,098	3,405	3,695	3,645	4,040	3,616	3,488	3,803	4,243	4,844
Gross Domestic Product (GDP)	99b	5,826	7,231	7,380	7,925	9,303	9,060	7,656	8,884	11,357	10,446	10,691	12,441
Net Primary Income from Abroad	98.n	1,538	1,155	941	1,457	1,551	1,904	1,788	1,555	2,055	1,503	1,016	991
Gross National Income (GNI)	99a	7,364	8,386	8,321	9,382	10,854	10,964	9,444	10,439	13,412	11,949	11,707	13,432
Consumption of Fixed Capital	99cf	532	571	639	711	671	701	768	614	399	419	450	479
GDP Volume 1984 Prices	99b.p	6,506	8,702	9,453	9,583	9,324	9,435	9,733	9,255	9,946	9,844	....	....
GDP Volume (2000=100)	99bvp	65.4	87.5	95.0	96.4	93.7	94.9	97.9	93.1	100.0	99.0	....	....
GDP Deflator (2000=100)	99bip	78.4	72.8	68.4	72.4	87.4	84.1	68.9	84.1	100.0	92.9	....	....
						Millions: Midyear Estimates							
Population	99z	1.98	1.84	1.74	1.70	1.73	1.83	1.97	2.12	2.25	Ü 2.35	2.44	2.52

Kyrgyz Republic 917

		1992	1993	1994	1995	1996	1997	1998	1999	2000	2001	2002	2003
Exchange Rates					*Soms per SDR: End of Period*								
Official Rate	aa	....	11.030	15.547	16.649	24.014	23.443	41.362	62.352	62.936	59.969	62.667	65.665
					Soms per US Dollar: End of Period (ae) Period Average (rf)								
Official Rate	ae	....	8.030	10.650	11.200	16.700	17.375	29.376	45.429	48.304	47.719	46.095	44.190
Official Rate	rf	....	....	10.842	10.822	12.810	17.362	20.838	39.008	47.704	48.378	46.937	43.648
Fund Position					*Millions of SDRs: End of Period*								
Quota	2f.s	64.5	64.5	64.5	64.5	64.5	64.5	64.5	88.8	88.8	88.8	88.8	88.8
SDRs	1b.s	–	9.4	.7	9.6	5.1	.7	.2	3.7	.5	1.1	.5	6.9
Reserve Position in the Fund	1c.s	–	–	–	–	–	–	–	–	–	–	–	–
Total Fund Cred.&Loans Outstg.	2tl	–	43.9	53.3	83.6	97.1	122.2	124.4	138.7	144.3	142.7	136.3	135.9
International Liquidity					*Millions of US Dollars Unless Otherwise Indicated: End of Period*								
Total Reserves minus Gold	1l.d	....	48.2	26.2	81.0	94.6	170.2	163.8	229.7	239.0	263.5	288.8	364.6
SDRs	1b.d	–	12.9	1.0	14.3	7.4	.9	.3	5.1	.7	1.3	.6	10.3
Reserve Position in the Fund	1c.d	–	–	–	–	–	–	–	–	–	–	–	–
Foreign Exchange	1d.d	....	35.4	25.2	66.7	87.2	169.3	163.4	224.6	238.3	262.2	288.2	354.3
Gold (Million Fine Troy Ounces)	1ad	....	....	....	....	....	....	.0831	.0831	.0831	.0831	.0831	.0831
Gold (National Valuation)	1and	....	....	....	43.22	28.13	29.08	23.88	24.17	22.80	22.97	28.48	34.67
Monetary Authorities: Other Liab.	4..d	....	....	....	73.5	65.8	59.2	39.7	44.1	55.5	57.4	58.1	57.5
Banking Institutions: Assets	7a.d	....	....	....	19.6	13.1	34.3	17.1	15.8	18.0	32.8	72.6	124.0
Liabilities	7b.d	....	....	....	2.8	1.8	13.1	8.3	1.8	3.0	3.4	36.4	71.9
Monetary Authorities					*Millions of Soms: End of Period*								
Foreign Assets	11	....	....	....	1,393	2,035	3,368	5,517	11,338	12,687	13,632	14,620	17,197
Claims on General Government	12a	....	....	....	2,049	3,911	4,473	4,940	5,787	6,144	6,186	7,090	6,752
Claims on Banking Institutions	12e	....	....	....	1,153	124	92	333	543	609	506	490	421
Reserve Money	14	....	....	....	2,044	2,533	3,069	3,303	4,317	4,821	5,375	7,670	10,171
of which: Currency Outside Banks	14a	....	....	....	1,938	2,416	2,678	2,829	3,578	4,102	5,016	6,866	9,302
Other Liabilities to DMBs	14n	....	....	....	–	–	200	36	243	189	–	–	147
Foreign Liabilities	16c	....	....	....	2,216	3,430	3,893	6,314	10,652	11,763	11,296	11,218	11,461
General Government Deposits	16d	....	....	....	28	174	305	322	1,239	1,185	2,235	2,172	1,835
Capital Accounts	17a	....	....	....	136	243	506	949	1,118	989	1,096	1,518	1,105
Other Items (Net)	17r	....	....	....	171	–311	–40	–133	98	493	323	–378	–350
Banking Institutions					*Millions of Soms: End of Period*								
Reserves	20	....	....	....	113	110	381	449	739	700	343	792	773
Other Claims on Monetary Author.	20n	....	....	....	–	–	162	107	172	172	3	8	180
Foreign Assets	21	....	....	....	219	219	596	503	719	870	1,563	3,344	5,478
Claims on General Government	22a	....	....	....	83	93	323	378	150	202	487	597	746
Claims on Rest of the Economy	22d	....	....	....	2,024	2,026	1,047	1,804	2,448	2,679	2,780	3,098	3,963
Demand Deposits	24	....	....	....	545	478	442	379	624	504	542	811	1,314
Time & Foreign Currency Deposits	25	....	....	....	295	295	1,095	1,745	2,418	2,791	2,676	3,346	4,085
Foreign Liabilities	26c	....	....	....	31	31	228	245	84	143	164	1,680	3,179
General Government Deposits	26d	....	....	....	–	–	30	45	64	49	71	107	188
Credit from Monetary Authorities	26g	....	....	....	1,188	1,188	118	318	605	619	597	575	543
Capital Accounts	27a	....	....	....	120	149	735	980	1,125	1,229	1,802	2,134	2,365
Other Items (Net)	27r	....	....	....	261	307	–138	–471	–694	–712	–676	–813	–535
Banking Survey					*Millions of Soms: End of Period*								
Foreign Assets (Net)	31n	....	....	....	–635	–1,207	–157	–539	1,321	1,651	3,736	5,067	8,034
Domestic Credit	32	....	....	....	4,129	5,856	5,528	6,780	7,120	7,831	7,196	8,557	9,487
Claims on General Govt. (Net)	32an	....	....	....	2,105	3,830	4,462	4,951	4,634	5,112	4,367	5,408	5,475
Claims on Rest of the Economy	32d	....	....	....	2,024	2,026	1,066	1,828	2,487	2,720	2,829	3,149	4,012
Money	34	....	....	....	2,482	2,893	3,119	3,208	4,203	4,606	5,558	7,677	10,616
Quasi-Money	35	....	....	....	295	295	1,095	1,745	2,418	2,791	2,676	3,346	4,085
Capital Accounts	37a	....	....	....	256	392	1,242	1,929	2,243	2,218	2,898	3,651	3,470
Other Items (Net)	37r	....	....	....	461	1,069	–85	–641	–423	–131	–200	–1,051	–650
Money plus Quasi-Money	35l	....	....	....	2,777	3,188	4,214	4,953	6,621	7,397	8,234	11,024	14,701
Interest Rates					*Percent per Annum*								
Lombard Rate	60.a	....	265.5	94.1	64.1	43.1	43.2	54.0	51.6	32.8	10.7	6.8	4.0
Money Market Rate	60b	....	....	....	....	....	....	44.0	43.7	24.3	11.9	....	....
Treasury Bill Rate	60c	....	....	143.1	34.9	40.1	35.8	43.7	47.2	32.3	19.1	10.2	7.2
Deposit Rate	60l	....	....	....	....	36.7	39.6	35.8	35.6	18.4	12.5	5.9	5.0
Lending Rate	60p	....	....	....	....	65.0	49.4	73.4	60.9	51.9	37.3	24.8	19.1
Prices and Labor					*Index Numbers (2000=100): Period Averages*								
Producer Prices	63	....	7.7	24.4	29.7	36.5	46.1	49.8	76.5	100.0	112.0	117.4	122.8
Consumer Prices	64	....	....	....	34.5	45.5	56.1	62.0	84.3	100.0	106.9	109.2	113.0
Wages: Average Earnings	65	....	7.1	19.8	31.3	41.8	57.8	71.4	89.2	100.0	118.4	137.5	....
					Number in Thousands: Period Averages								
Employment	67e	1,836	1,681	1,645	1,642	1,652	1,689	1,705	1,764	1,768	1,787	....	....
Unemployment	67c	....	3	13	50	77	55	56	55	....	....	....	....
Unemployment Rate	67r	....	.2	.8	3.0	4.5	3.1	3.2	3.0	3.1	3.2	....	....

Kyrgyz Republic 917

		1992	1993	1994	1995	1996	1997	1998	1999	2000	2001	2002	2003
International Transactions						*Millions of US Dollars*							
Exports	70..d	....	339.7	340.0	408.9	505.4	603.8	513.6	453.8	504.5	476.1	485.5	581.7
Imports, c.i.f.	71..d	418.0	429.5	315.9	522.3	837.7	709.3	841.5	599.7	554.1	467.2	586.7	717.0
Balance of Payments					*Millions of US Dollars: Minus Sign Indicates Debit*								
Current Account, n.i.e.	78ald	....	−87.6	−84.0	−234.7	−424.8	−138.5	−412.5	−252.4	−125.8	−51.5	−85.1	....
Goods: Exports f.o.b.	78aad	....	339.6	340.0	408.9	531.2	630.8	535.1	462.6	510.9	480.3	498.1	....
Goods: Imports f.o.b.	78abd	....	−446.7	−426.1	−531.0	−782.9	−646.1	−755.7	−551.1	−506.4	−440.3	−552.0	....
Trade Balance	78acd	....	−107.1	−86.1	−122.0	−251.7	−15.3	−220.7	−88.5	4.6	40.0	−53.9	....
Services: Credit	78add	....	8.7	32.7	39.2	31.5	45.0	62.8	65.0	61.8	80.3	138.4	....
Services: Debit	78aed	....	−50.7	−71.1	−195.1	−249.0	−171.2	−175.7	−154.4	−148.8	−124.7	−145.5	....
Balance on Goods & Services	78afd	....	−149.1	−124.6	−278.0	−469.2	−141.4	−333.6	−177.9	−82.4	−4.4	−61.0	....
Income: Credit	78agd	....	....	....	3.7	4.4	6.8	12.6	10.9	17.0	11.9	6.0	....
Income: Debit	78ahd	....	−5.7	−22.0	−39.2	−43.9	−71.4	−91.7	−85.4	−100.9	−77.4	−65.7	....
Balance on Gds, Serv. & Inc.	78aid	....	−154.8	−146.6	−313.4	−508.7	−206.1	−412.7	−252.4	−166.3	−70.0	−120.6	....
Current Transfers, n.i.e.: Credit	78ajd	....	68.0	63.4	80.4	85.9	69.8	2.2	1.2	43.0	21.6	39.9	....
Current Transfers: Debit	78akd	....	−.8	−.8	−1.7	−1.9	−2.2	−2.0	−1.2	−2.4	−3.2	−4.3	....
Capital Account, n.i.e.	78bcd	....	−107.1	−62.4	−29.0	−15.9	−8.4	−8.1	−15.2	−11.3	−32.0	−27.9	....
Capital Account, n.i.e.: Credit	78bad	....	....	.3	2.2	9.0	6.2	3.9	14.6	22.8	9.2	15.1	....
Capital Account: Debit	78bbd	....	−107.1	−62.7	−31.3	−25.0	−14.6	−12.0	−29.8	−34.2	−41.2	−43.0	....
Financial Account, n.i.e.	78bjd	....	199.1	85.7	260.1	362.5	250.4	284.6	220.8	56.9	31.6	94.1	....
Direct Investment Abroad	78bdd	....	....	....	....	....	....	−22.6	−6.1	−4.5	−6.1	....	....
Dir. Invest. in Rep. Econ., n.i.e.	78bed	....	10.0	38.2	96.1	47.2	83.8	109.2	44.4	−2.4	5.0	4.8	....
Portfolio Investment Assets	78bfd	....	....	....	−.1	.1	.6	−.2	−	−1.6	1.2	−2.5	....
Equity Securities	78bkd	....	....	....	....	....	....	....	....	....	....	....	....
Debt Securities	78bld	....	....	....	−.1	.1	.6	−.2	−	−1.6	1.2	−2.5	....
Portfolio Investment Liab., n.i.e.	78bgd	....	....	....	1.8	−1.8	5.0	−4.1	.1	.3	−	....	....
Equity Securities	78bmd	....	....	....	....	....	....	....	.2	.3	....	....	....
Debt Securities	78bnd	....	....	....	1.8	−1.8	5.0	−4.1	−.1	−	−	....	....
Financial Derivatives Assets	78bwd	....	....	....	....	....	19.0	30.6	26.4	25.8	17.6	−5.1	....
Financial Derivatives Liabilities	78bxd	....	....	....	....	....	....	....	....	....	....	....	....
Other Investment Assets	78bhd	....	−53.0	−43.2	11.9	1.9	−43.1	−84.1	−.7	−27.3	−3.9	21.5	....
Monetary Authorities	78bod	....	....	....	−1.0	....	−3.0	−2.0	....	....	....	....	....
General Government	78bpd	....	....	−1.7	−2.1	13.3	....	−57.4	−6.9	−31.9	−6.7	14.8	....
Banks	78bqd	....	−13.4	1.3	−1.2	1.6	−18.7	9.6	−1.4	−1.6	−16.5	−42.3	....
Other Sectors	78brd	....	−39.6	−42.9	16.2	−13.0	−21.5	−34.3	7.6	6.1	19.2	49.0	....
Other Investment Liab., n.i.e.	78bid	....	242.1	90.8	150.4	315.1	185.1	255.8	156.6	66.6	17.9	75.5	....
Monetary Authorities	78bsd	....	35.8	−35.4	.5	.2	....	....	....	....	....	....	....
General Government	78btd	....	179.5	110.9	102.0	104.7	137.2	177.1	224.5	96.8	86.5	58.5	....
Banks	78bud	....	5.7	3.6	−3.3	−2.1	14.0	1.0	−2.8	−.4	3.9	32.7	....
Other Sectors	78bvd	....	21.1	11.7	51.2	212.2	33.9	77.7	−65.0	−29.8	−72.5	−15.6	....
Net Errors and Omissions	78cad	....	−34.1	65.7	−77.1	58.4	−57.4	63.4	−3.0	9.8	19.9	7.9	....
Overall Balance	78cbd	....	−29.6	5.0	−80.7	−19.8	46.2	−72.7	−49.7	−70.4	−32.0	−11.0	....
Reserves and Related Items	79dad	....	29.6	−5.0	80.7	19.8	−46.2	72.7	49.7	70.4	32.0	11.0	....
Reserve Assets	79dbd	....	−35.5	−31.9	.1	−18.6	−82.8	5.9	−61.3	−21.3	−17.7	−43.0	....
Use of Fund Credit and Loans	79dcd	....	62.1	13.8	46.3	19.6	34.1	2.8	19.4	7.4	−2.1	−8.0	....
Exceptional Financing	79ded	....	3.0	13.1	34.4	18.8	2.6	64.1	91.7	84.3	51.8	62.0	....
International Investment Position							*Millions of US Dollars*						
Assets	79aad	....	118.5	190.1	202.4	203.9	341.3	366.2	405.2	479.6	519.5	601.2	....
Direct Investment Abroad	79abd	−	−	−	−	−	−	22.6	28.7	33.2	39.3	39.3	....
Portfolio Investment	79acd	−	−	−	.1	.6	−	.2	.2	1.6	3.7	12.1	....
Equity Securities	79add	−	−	−	−	−	−	−	−	−	−	−	....
Debt Securities	79aed	−	−	−	.1	.6	−	.2	.2	1.6	3.7	12.1	....
Financial Derivatives	79ald	....	−	−	−	−	31.7	7.8	7.3	19.5	17.2	−	....
Other Investment	79afd	32.0	55.1	92.2	88.6	75.8	113.7	146.9	120.3	164.1	174.2	233.1	....
Monetary Authorities	79agd	−	−	−	−	−	−	−	−	−	−	−	....
General Government	79ahd	24.2	33.9	72.4	67.7	56.3	42.7	69.1	53.2	75.2	82.4	108.9	....
Banks	79aid	7.8	21.2	19.9	20.9	19.5	38.1	29.2	30.8	59.9	64.4	124.2	....
Other Sectors	79ajd	−	−	−	−	−	32.9	48.7	36.3	29.1	27.4	−	....
Reserve Assets	79akd	−	63.5	97.9	113.7	127.5	195.9	188.6	248.8	261.1	285.2	316.7	....
Liabilities	79lad	....	350.9	528.4	913.8	1,301.3	1,711.7	1,962.5	2,125.9	2,134.5	2,125.0	2,514.2	....
Dir. Invest. in Rep. Economy	79lbd	−	10.0	48.2	144.3	191.0	274.1	383.3	427.7	438.6	427.3	476.2	....
Portfolio Investment	79lcd	−	−	−	1.8	−	5.0	.9	.8	1.2	2.3	.2	....
Equity Securities	79ldd	−	−	−	−	−	−	−	−	−	−	−	....
Debt Securities	79led	−	−	−	1.8	−	5.0	.9	.8	1.2	2.3	.2	....
Financial Derivatives	79lld	....	−	−	−	−	−	−	−	−	−	29.7	....
Other Investment	79lfd	34.1	340.9	480.2	767.8	1,110.3	1,432.6	1,578.3	1,697.3	1,694.8	1,695.3	2,008.1	....
Monetary Authorities	79lgd	−	60.2	77.8	124.3	139.6	164.9	175.2	190.3	188.0	179.3	185.2	....
General Government	79lhd	34.1	274.9	393.1	547.8	673.7	839.9	979.4	1,195.3	1,279.8	1,354.4	1,582.1	....
Banks	79lid	−	5.7	9.3	6.0	4.0	17.9	18.9	16.1	1.7	5.6	40.9	....
Other Sectors	79ljd	−	−	−	89.7	293.0	409.9	404.8	295.6	225.2	155.9	199.9	....

2004, International Monetary Fund : International Financial Statistics Yearbook

Kyrgyz Republic 917

		1992	1993	1994	1995	1996	1997	1998	1999	2000	2001	2002	2003
Government Finance						*Millions of Soms: Year Ending December 31*							
Deficit (-) or Surplus............	80	....	–377.9	–921.6	–1,864.6	–1,269.3	–1,605.4	–1,035.8	–1,213.5	–1,244.8	286.7	–798.1	–681.0
Total Revenue and Grants........	81y	....	847.9	1,891.2	2,745.9	3,933.1	5,090.3	6,262.6	7,828.7	10,039.6	12,543.6	14,392.1	16,214.9
Exp. & Lending Minus Repay......	82z	....	1,225.8	2,812.8	4,610.5	5,202.4	6,695.7	7,298.4	9,042.2	11,284.4	12,256.9	15,190.2	16,895.9
Financing													
Domestic........................	84a	....	297.8	406.5	995.5	604.8	287.9	68.7	–379.6	–334.1	–377.5	–52.5	–96.7
Foreign.........................	85a	....	80.0	515.1	851.1	664.5	1,317.5	966.8	1,593.1	1,579.0	90.8	850.6	777.8
National Accounts						*Millions of Soms*							
Househ.Cons.Expend.,incl.NPISHs....	96f	524	† 4,053	9,422	12,111	19,212	21,151	30,163	37,848	42,930	47,893	50,897	59,332
Government Consumption Expend...	91f	158	† 1,086	2,272	3,155	4,333	5,307	6,103	9,320	13,099	12,912	14,033	14,378
Gross Fixed Capital Formation......	93e	108	† 715	1,493	3,338	5,296	3,802	4,404	7,663	11,782	10,721	12,418	12,556
Changes in Inventories..............	93i	40	† –90	–409	–377	600	2,781	780	993	1,136	724	852	940
Exports of Goods and Services.....	90c	264	† 1,796	4,058	4,758	7,193	11,749	12,471	20,571	27,351	27,133	29,831	31,726
Imports of Goods and Services (-)....	98c	353	† 2,205	4,816	6,839	13,234	14,174	19,834	27,782	31,099	27,353	32,664	35,238
Statistical Discrepancy............	99bs	....	....	....	....	....	....	....	....	–	–	–504	–273
Gross Domestic Product (GDP)......	99b	741	† 5,355	12,019	16,145	23,399	30,686	34,181	48,744	65,358	73,883	75,367	83,421
Net Primary Income from Abroad....	98.n	–4	† –68	–190	–200	–485	–1,004	–1,748	–2,940	–3,848	–3,139	–2,825	....
Gross National Income (GNI).......	99a	737	† 5,286	11,830	15,945	22,914	29,682	32,433	45,804	61,510	70,744	72,542	....
Net Current Transf.from Abroad.....	98t	40	521	665	820	1,438	1,161	1,043	1,969	3,911	2,507	5,487	....
Gross Nat'l Disposable Inc.(GNDI)....	99i	777	5,808	12,495	16,765	24,352	30,843	33,476	47,773	65,421	73,251	78,028	....
Gross Saving.....................	99s	94	668	801	1,500	807	4,385	–2,790	605	9,393	12,446	13,099	....
GDP Volume 1995 Prices...........	99b.p	25,278	† 21,360	17,067	16,145	17,289	19,003	19,406	20,101	21,215	22,329	22,327	23,817
GDP Volume (2000=100)...........	99bvp	119.2	† 100.7	80.4	76.1	81.5	89.6	91.5	94.7	100.0	105.3	105.2	112.3
GDP Deflator (2000=100).........	99bip	1.0	† 8.1	22.9	32.5	43.9	52.4	57.2	78.7	100.0	107.4	109.6	113.7
						Millions: Midyear Estimates							
Population....................	99z	4.47	4.49	4.52	4.56	4.62	4.69	4.76	4.84	4.92	4.99	5.07	5.14

Lao People's Dem.Rep 544

		1992	1993	1994	1995	1996	1997	1998	1999	2000	2001	2002	2003
Exchange Rates						*Kip per SDR: End of Period*							
Official Rate	aa	985.88	986.22	1,049.63	†1,372.03	1,344.49	3,554.60	6,017.92	10,431.08	10,707.31	11,926.37	14,519.67	15,553.65
					Kip per US Dollar: End of Period (ae) Period Average (rf)								
Official Rate	ae	717.00	718.00	719.00	†923.00	935.00	2,634.50	4,274.00	7,600.00	8,218.00	9,490.00	10,680.00	10,467.00
Official Rate	rf	716.08	716.25	717.67	†804.69	921.02	1,259.98	3,298.33	7,102.03	7,887.64	8,954.58	10,056.33	10,569.04
Fund Position						*Millions of SDRs: End of Period*							
Quota	2f.s	39.10	39.10	39.10	39.10	39.10	39.10	39.10	39.10	39.10	52.90	52.90	52.90
SDRs	1b.s	.57	1.90	7.46	9.49	7.17	9.31	4.32	.05	.07	2.72	4.47	12.87
Reserve Position in the Fund	1c.s	–	–	–	–	–	–	–	–	–	–	–	–
Total Fund Cred.&Loans Outstg	2tl	20.51	26.38	32.24	42.80	46.61	48.96	44.27	38.41	32.55	29.75	31.77	29.85
International Liquidity					*Millions of US Dollars Unless Otherwise Indicated: End of Period*								
Total Reserves minus Gold	1l.d	40.31e	62.96e	60.93e	92.11	169.50	112.18	112.21	101.19	138.97	130.93	191.59	208.59
SDRs	1b.d	.78	2.61	10.89	14.10	10.31	12.56	6.09	.07	.10	3.42	6.07	19.13
Reserve Position in the Fund	1c.d	–	–	–	–	–	–	–	–	–	–	–	–
Foreign Exchange	1d.d	39.52e	60.34e	50.03e	78.01	159.19	99.62	106.13	101.12	138.87	127.51	185.51	189.46
Gold (Million Fine Troy Ounces)	1ad	.0171	.0171	.0171	.0171	.0171	.0171	.0171	.1171	.0169	.0723	.0723	.1171
Gold (National Valuation)	1and	.60	.60	.60	.60	.60	.60	.60	4.10	.59	2.53	2.53	4.10
Deposit Money Banks: Assets	7a.d	.04	.09	.10	.10	.11	.07	.11	.15	.13	.09	.15	.16
Liabilities	7b.d	.01	.01	.03	.04	.05	.03	.04	.04	.04	.04	.08	.07
Monetary Authorities						*Billions of Kip: End of Period*							
Foreign Assets	11	29.06	45.36	43.96	85.18	158.64	295.70	479.76	799.78	1,146.86	1,265.54	2,069.17	2,226.69
Claims on Central Government	12a	10.83	8.96	12.16	4.25	4.25	4.70	91.27	198.83	158.51	184.98	239.27	234.17
Claims on Nonfin.Pub.Enterprises	12c	1.44	.86	1.86	6.98	10.87	59.54	112.80	223.71	346.10	488.49	566.64	523.51
Claims on Private Sector	12d	1.15	3.01	6.83	10.40	13.90	38.22	72.05	143.25	143.23	150.82	175.88	153.24
Claims on Deposit Money Banks	12e	15.18	34.62	37.05	46.59	52.37	57.94	80.35	301.90	445.60	347.66	218.07	137.63
Reserve Money	14	36.90	60.70	74.23	84.17	104.37	150.09	281.75	481.75	766.65	822.49	1,079.11	1,329.94
of which: Currency Outside DMBs	14a	22.83	33.24	38.61	41.95	42.97	53.31	63.16	77.79	67.83	113.08	228.81	399.10
Foreign Liabilities	16c	20.22	26.01	33.84	58.72	62.67	174.04	266.43	400.67	348.51	354.80	461.31	464.28
Central Government Deposits	16d	.81	8.59	13.52	7.45	64.82	52.74	77.51	235.23	505.77	281.32	650.15	608.53
Government Lending Funds	16f	16.31	18.34	12.07	16.17	18.04	31.09	54.37	87.33	211.05	346.68	428.12	323.82
Capital Accounts	17a	14.38	13.85	15.23	26.44	25.21	91.25	172.61	456.94	463.05	706.21	838.10	896.94
Other Items (Net)	17r	–30.97	–34.68	–47.02	–39.56	–35.08	–43.10	–16.43	5.55	–54.73	–73.99	–187.77	–348.27
Deposit Money Banks						*Billions of Kip: End of Period*							
Reserves	20	13.75	30.66	36.45	44.16	59.24	77.70	212.42	402.96	688.77	714.46	939.28	1,109.01
Foreign Assets	21	31.78	62.82	69.79	91.20	107.47	180.35	452.00	1,142.98	1,075.88	865.78	1,577.12	1,713.16
Claims on Central Government	22a	–	–	26.81	19.38	39.18	40.78	37.86	11.35	7.64	29.74	69.16	324.36
Claims on Nonfin.Pub.Enterprises	22c	16.40	17.47	15.57	20.69	26.06	60.88	110.75	221.69	296.54	528.24	566.40	402.59
Claims on Private Sector	22d	36.54	62.90	92.02	118.46	141.79	247.35	460.77	728.69	1,074.91	1,354.49	1,329.22	1,318.96
Demand Deposits	24	12.05	18.99	22.73	25.22	32.59	26.62	105.82	141.19	272.23	256.88	358.15	437.29
Time, Savings,& Fgn.Currency Dep	25	41.32	73.61	104.69	126.09	169.37	326.07	696.95	1,325.52	1,911.25	2,193.15	2,942.40	3,401.38
Foreign Liabilities	26c	3.96	9.28	21.51	39.76	46.87	77.24	169.34	281.96	349.38	376.08	863.70	752.28
Central Government Deposits	26d	9.32	9.79	12.69	15.41	21.60	36.34	103.46	247.16	79.93	51.42	37.20	80.71
Credit from Monetary Authorities	26g	10.84	29.57	35.04	41.93	49.12	51.46	81.67	314.49	489.84	383.78	252.38	165.62
Capital Accounts	27a	14.80	33.83	47.45	56.55	66.51	126.78	215.97	457.31	519.69	574.10	487.44	201.02
Other Items (Net)	27r	6.18	–1.23	–3.47	–11.05	–12.31	–37.46	–99.42	–259.97	–478.79	–342.73	–460.11	–170.23
Monetary Survey						*Billions of Kip: End of Period*							
Foreign Assets (Net)	31n	36.66	72.89	58.40	77.90	156.57	224.77	496.00	1,260.13	1,524.85	1,400.44	2,321.28	2,723.29
Domestic Credit	32	56.22	74.82	129.04	157.30	149.62	362.39	704.53	1,045.12	1,441.22	2,404.02	2,259.22	2,267.59
Claims on Central Govt. (Net)	32an	.69	–9.42	12.77	.78	–43.00	–43.61	–51.84	–272.21	–419.56	–118.02	–378.92	–130.71
Claims on Nonfin.Pub.Enterprises	32c	17.84	18.33	17.43	27.67	36.93	120.42	223.55	445.39	642.63	1,016.73	1,133.04	926.10
Claims on Private Sector	32d	37.68	65.91	98.85	128.86	155.69	285.58	532.82	871.94	1,218.14	1,505.31	1,505.10	1,472.20
Money	34	35.14	52.24	61.34	67.18	75.56	79.94	168.98	218.98	344.35	371.84	587.00	836.54
Quasi-Money	35	41.32	73.61	104.69	126.09	169.37	326.07	696.95	1,325.52	1,911.25	2,193.15	2,942.40	3,401.38
Other Items (Net)	37r	16.41	21.87	21.41	41.93	61.27	181.15	334.60	760.75	710.46	1,239.46	1,051.07	752.95
Money plus Quasi-Money	35l	76.46	125.85	166.03	193.27	244.93	406.00	865.93	1,544.50	2,255.60	2,564.99	3,529.40	4,237.92
Interest Rates						*Percent Per Annum*							
Bank Rate (End of Period)	60	23.67	25.00	30.00	32.08	35.00	….	35.00	34.89	35.17	35.00	20.00	20.00
Treasury Bill Rate	60c	….	….	….	20.46	….	….	23.66	30.00	29.94	22.70	21.41	24.87
Deposit Rate	60l	15.00	13.33	12.00	14.00	16.00	….	17.79	13.42	12.00	6.50	6.00	6.58
Lending Rate	60p	26.00	†25.33	24.00	†25.67	27.00	….	29.28	32.00	32.00	26.17	29.33	30.50
Prices						*Index Numbers (2000=100): Period Averages*							
Consumer Prices	64	9.4	10.0	10.6	12.7	†14.4	18.3	35.0	†79.9	100.0	107.8	119.3	137.7
International Transactions						*Millions of US Dollars*							
Exports	70..d	132.6	241.0	300.5	311.0	322.8	359.0	369.5	310.8	330.3	331.3	297.7	378.1
Imports, c.i.f	71..d	270.0	432.0	564.1	588.8	689.6	706.0	552.8	524.8	535.3	527.9	431.1	524.2

2004, International Monetary Fund : *International Financial Statistics Yearbook*

Lao People's Dem.Rep 544

		1992	1993	1994	1995	1996	1997	1998	1999	2000	2001	2002	2003
Balance of Payments						*Millions of US Dollars: Minus Sign Indicates Debit*							
Current Account, n.i.e.	78ald	−111.3	−139.2	−284.0	−346.2	−346.8	−305.5	−150.1	−121.1	−8.5	−82.4	....	....
Goods: Exports f.o.b.	78aad	132.6	247.9	305.5	310.9	322.8	318.3	342.1	338.2	330.3	311.1	....	....
Goods: Imports f.o.b.	78abd	−232.8	−397.4	−519.2	−626.8	−643.7	−601.3	−506.8	−527.7	−535.3	−527.9	....	....
Trade Balance	78acd	−100.2	−149.5	−213.7	−315.9	−320.9	−283.0	−164.7	−189.5	−205.0	−216.8	....	....
Services: Credit	78add	61.4	85.2	87.0	96.8	104.4	105.8	145.0	130.0	175.7	166.1	....	....
Services: Debit	78aed	−71.3	−75.9	−152.1	−121.6	−126.0	−110.5	−95.5	−51.8	−43.1	−31.6	....	....
Balance on Goods & Services	78afd	−110.1	−140.2	−278.8	−340.7	−342.5	−287.7	−115.2	−111.3	−72.4	−82.3	....	....
Income: Credit	78agd	5.6	8.6	7.2	7.4	9.2	11.1	6.9	10.5	7.3	5.8	....	....
Income: Debit	78ahd	−4.6	−5.6	−9.2	−12.9	−13.5	−28.9	−41.8	−49.9	−59.7	−39.6	....	....
Balance on Gds, Serv. & Inc	78aid	−109.1	−137.2	−280.8	−346.2	−346.8	−305.5	−150.1	−150.7	−124.7	−116.1	....	....
Current Transfers, n.i.e.: Credit	78ajd	–	–	–	–	–	–	–	80.2	116.3	33.7	....	....
Current Transfers: Debit	78akd	−2.2	−2.0	−3.2	–	–	–	–	−50.6	....	....	....	....
Capital Account, n.i.e.	78bcd	8.6	9.5	9.5	13.2	35.0	33.4	43.1	–	....	....	....	....
Capital Account, n.i.e.: Credit	78bad	8.6	9.5	9.5	21.7	44.9	40.3	49.4	–	....	....	....	....
Capital Account: Debit	78bbd	–	–	–	−8.5	−9.9	−6.9	−6.3	–	....	....	....	....
Financial Account, n.i.e.	78bjd	−3.0	−21.0	24.3	90.0	135.7	3.5	−43.4	−46.9	126.1	135.7	....	....
Direct Investment Abroad	78bdd	–	–	–	–	....	–	–	–	–	–	....	....
Dir. Invest. in Rep. Econ., n.i.e.	78bed	7.8	29.9	59.2	95.1	159.8	–	–	–	33.9	23.9	....	....
Portfolio Investment Assets	78bfd	–	–	–	–	....	–	–	–	....	....	....	....
Equity Securities	78bkd	–	–	–	–	....	–	–	–	....	....	....	....
Debt Securities	78bld	–	–	–	–	....	–	–	–	....	....	....	....
Portfolio Investment Liab., n.i.e.	78bgd	1.2	–	–	–	–	–	–	–	....	....	....	....
Equity Securities	78bmd	1.2	–	–	–	–	–	–	–	....	....	....	....
Debt Securities	78bnd	–	–	–	–	....	–	–	–	....	....	....	....
Financial Derivatives Assets	78bwd	....	....	....	....	....	....	....	....	....	....	....	....
Financial Derivatives Liabilities	78bxd	....	....	....	....	....	....	....	....	....	....	....	....
Other Investment Assets	78bhd	−16.1	−43.2	−9.6	−1.5	−14.1	39.5	−22.8	−43.2	18.8	25.2	....	....
Monetary Authorities	78bod	....	....	....	....	....	....	....	....	....	....	....	....
General Government	78bpd	–	–	–	–	....	–	–	–	....	....	....	....
Banks	78bqd	−16.1	−43.2	−9.6	−1.5	−14.1	39.5	−22.8	−43.2	18.8	25.2	....	....
Other Sectors	78brd	–	–	–	....	....	–	–	–	....	....	....	....
Other Investment Liab., n.i.e.	78bid	4.1	−7.7	−25.3	−3.6	−10.0	−36.0	−20.6	−3.7	73.3	86.6	....	....
Monetary Authorities	78bsd	–	–	–	−15.4	−17.5	−18.2	−25.3	–	–	–	....	....
General Government	78btd	−9.0	−9.3	−8.3	–	–	–	–	–	67.2	79.0	....	....
Banks	78bud	−1.2	−7.4	−17.0	11.8	7.5	−17.8	4.7	−3.7	6.2	7.6	....	....
Other Sectors	78bvd	14.3	9.0	–	–	....	–	–	–	....	....	....	....
Net Errors and Omissions	78cad	−16.3	13.2	71.8	92.4	17.7	−100.5	−103.8	−165.1	−74.2	−57.2	....	....
Overall Balance	78cbd	−122.0	−137.5	−178.4	−150.6	−158.4	−369.1	−254.2	−333.1	43.4	−3.9	....	....
Reserves and Related Items	79dad	122.0	137.5	178.4	150.6	158.4	369.1	254.2	333.1	−43.4	3.9	....	....
Reserve Assets	79dbd	−12.8	−24.1	−5.6	−73.0	−70.7	25.4	28.1	12.4	−35.7	7.4	....	....
Use of Fund Credit and Loans	79dcd	8.1	8.3	8.1	15.6	5.5	3.3	−6.4	−8.0	−7.7	−3.6	....	....
Exceptional Financing	79ded	126.7	153.3	175.9	208.0	223.6	340.4	232.5	328.7	....	....	....	....
National Accounts						*Billions of Kip*							
Gross Domestic Product (GDP)	99b	844.4	951.0	1,107.8	1,430.4	1,725.7	2,201.0	4,240.0	10,329.0	13,669.0	15,702.0	18,390.0	20,307.0
GDP Volume 1990 Prices	99b.p	681.7	712.8	780.7	835.7	893.3	955.0	993.1	1,065.4	1,127.0	1,192.0	1,262.0	1,336.0
GDP Volume (2000=100)	99bvp	60.5	63.3	69.3	74.2	79.3	84.7	88.1	94.5	100.0	105.8	112.0	118.5
GDP Deflator (2000=100)	99bip	10.2	11.0	11.7	14.1	15.9	19.0	35.2	79.9	100.0	108.6	120.1	125.3
						Millions: Midyear Estimates							
Population	99z	4.35	4.46	4.57	4.69	4.80	4.92	5.04	5.16	5.28	5.40	5.53	5.66

Latvia 941

		1992	1993	1994	1995	1996	1997	1998	1999	2000	2001	2002	2003
Exchange Rates						*Lats per SDR: End of Period*							
Official Rate	aa	1.148	.817	.800	.798	.800	.796	.801	.800	.799	.802	.808	.804
					Lats per US Dollar: End of Period (ae) Period Average (rf)								
Official Rate	ae	.835	.595	.548	.537	.556	.590	.569	.583	.613	.638	.594	.541
Official Rate	rf	.736	.675	.560	.528	.551	.581	.590	.585	.607	.628	.618	.571
Fund Position						*Millions of SDRs: End of Period*							
Quota	2f.s	91.50	91.50	91.50	91.50	91.50	91.50	91.50	126.80	126.80	126.80	126.80	126.80
SDRs	1b.s	19.33	71.10	.21	1.49	1.56	1.50	.21	2.24	–	.07	.05	.09
Reserve Position in the Fund	1c.s	.01	.01	.01	.01	.01	.01	.01	.01	.06	.06	.06	.06
Total Fund Cred.&Loans Outstg	2tl	25.16	77.78	109.80	107.89	90.36	63.67	45.37	34.31	26.69	19.06	11.44	3.81
International Liquidity					*Millions of US Dollars Unless Otherwise Indicated: End of Period*								
Total Reserves minus Gold	1l.d	....	431.55	545.18	505.70	654.07	760.20	801.23	872.00	850.91	1,148.74	1,241.42	1,432.44
SDRs	1b.d	26.58	97.66	.31	2.22	2.25	2.03	.29	3.07	.01	.09	.07	.14
Reserve Position in the Fund	1c.d	.01	.01	.01	.01	.01	.01	.01	.01	.07	.07	.08	.08
Foreign Exchange	1d.d	....	333.88	544.86	503.47	651.81	758.17	800.93	868.92	850.83	1,148.59	1,241.27	1,432.22
Gold (Million Fine Troy Ounces)	1ad	.0675	.2428	.2492	.2492	.2493	.2491	.2493	.2493	.2487	.2486	.2486	.2486
Gold (National Valuation)	1and	20.20	72.80	74.80	74.77	74.78	73.13	71.44	72.41	68.38	69.66	85.90	102.67
Monetary Authorities:Other Assets	3..d	....	.01	–	–	–	–	.01	.01	.01	.01	.01	.01
Other Liab	4..d	....	.01	–	–	–	–	–	–	.01	.01	.01	.02
Deposit Money Banks: Assets	7a.d	....	229.93	664.25	599.56	1,021.16	1,546.56	1,258.96	1,489.19	2,112.97	2,271.57	3,019.08	4,071.00
Liabilities	7b.d	....	92.26	448.07	452.38	852.57	1,297.97	1,342.03	1,767.48	2,141.32	2,649.83	3,735.76	5,454.74
Monetary Authorities						*Millions of Lats: End of Period*							
Foreign Assets	11	....	307.13	341.98	313.52	407.63	461.47	461.23	535.64	568.45	780.39	793.51	836.43
Claims on Central Government	12a	....	–	6.59	39.38	22.33	72.88	81.00	57.70	73.47	43.33	76.13	65.29
Claims on Banks	12e	....	13.31	21.40	22.04	20.22	7.55	52.04	63.32	42.53	18.83	30.69	59.32
Reserve Money	14	....	225.56	269.43	273.62	336.66	441.74	471.45	526.28	566.72	641.88	759.87	807.63
of which: Currency Outside Banks	14a	....	152.75	213.06	209.54	264.00	332.65	340.19	377.41	427.66	485.19	543.13	601.05
Foreign Liabilities	16c	....	67.11	88.46	86.56	72.55	51.17	36.66	31.54	28.35	21.58	15.63	12.19
Central Government Deposits	16d	....	3.08	10.78	3.62	35.40	24.91	42.03	79.03	45.93	119.59	62.08	80.25
Capital Accounts	17a	....	14.70	8.02	11.00	20.89	36.60	47.22	47.23	52.02	61.64	82.76	83.17
Other Items (Net)	17r	....	10.00	–6.71	.15	–15.32	–12.52	–3.09	–27.40	–8.56	–2.13	–19.99	–22.20
Banking Institutions						*Millions of Lats: End of Period*							
Reserves	20	....	69.31	57.29	64.15	71.69	107.23	129.93	144.46	135.11	153.25	213.73	204.90
Foreign Assets	21	....	136.81	364.01	321.96	567.77	912.47	716.35	868.20	1,295.25	1,449.26	1,793.32	2,202.41
Claims on Central Government	22a	....	520.53	† 97.14	120.81	140.09	113.01	71.41	114.01	138.36	170.10	180.33	273.65
Claims on Local Government	22b	....	–	6.66	11.51	15.52	2.66	4.41	15.77	36.22	51.71	42.70	67.84
Claims on Nonfin.Pub.Enterprises	22c	....	16.94	39.59	24.99	17.71	28.15	23.82	30.61	52.53	81.21	112.50	87.42
Claims on Private Sector	22d	....	253.97	335.67	184.13	202.99	344.28	533.10	612.18	804.74	1,100.54	1,506.83	2,189.49
Claims on Nonbank Financial Insts	22g	....	–	–	–	–	19.24	25.34	25.90	56.69	190.68	254.59	294.93
Demand Deposits	24	....	115.03	138.08	144.24	156.36	232.76	259.75	257.52	332.97	374.97	501.36	630.02
Time, Savings,& Fgn.Currency Dep	25	....	196.49	346.82	195.06	230.50	331.56	357.60	398.73	554.19	716.43	847.19	1,081.23
Money Market Instruments	26aa	....	–	–	–	–	–	–	–	–	–	.61	–
Foreign Liabilities	26c	....	54.90	245.54	242.93	474.03	765.80	763.61	1,030.44	1,312.63	1,690.59	2,219.04	2,951.02
Central Government Deposits	26d	....	520.57	† 13.92	36.98	6.31	50.33	32.83	18.10	10.14	31.37	55.07	22.80
Government Lending Funds	26f	....	16.94	61.43	39.68	22.00	19.66	16.73	22.48	22.55	21.26	9.94	6.80
Credit from Central Bank	26g	....	–	1.44	3.52	4.32	6.94	54.94	63.18	42.53	18.83	30.69	59.32
Capital Accounts	27a	....	73.52	96.79	77.58	118.67	117.56	62.05	40.07	230.18	314.26	389.68	493.07
Other Items (Net)	27r	....	20.12	–3.64	–12.44	3.58	2.43	–43.16	–19.39	13.70	29.04	50.45	76.39
Banking Survey						*Millions of Lats: End of Period*							
Foreign Assets (Net)	31n	....	321.94	371.98	306.00	428.82	556.97	377.31	341.86	522.72	517.48	352.18	75.64
Domestic Credit	32	....	267.79	† 460.96	340.22	356.93	504.98	664.22	759.05	1,105.94	1,486.61	2,055.94	2,875.56
Claims on Central Govt. (Net)	32an	....	–3.12	† 79.04	119.59	120.71	110.66	77.55	74.60	155.77	62.46	139.31	235.88
Claims on Local Government	32b	....	–	6.66	11.51	15.52	2.66	4.41	15.77	36.22	51.71	42.70	67.84
Claims on Nonfin.Pub.Enterprises	32c	....	16.94	39.59	24.99	17.71	28.15	23.82	30.61	52.53	81.21	112.50	87.42
Claims on Private Sector	32d	....	253.97	335.67	184.13	202.99	344.28	533.10	612.18	804.74	1,100.54	1,506.83	2,189.49
Claims on Nonbank Fin. Insts	32g	....	–	–	–	–	19.24	25.34	25.90	56.69	190.68	254.59	294.93
Money	34	....	267.78	351.13	353.78	425.65	567.27	601.27	639.34	764.57	863.59	1,047.50	1,232.74
Quasi-Money	35	....	196.49	346.82	195.06	230.50	331.56	357.60	398.73	554.19	716.43	847.19	1,081.23
Money Market Instruments	36aa	....	–	–	–	–	–	–	–	–	–	.61	–
Government Lending Funds	36f	....	16.94	61.43	39.68	22.00	19.66	16.73	22.48	22.55	21.26	9.94	6.80
Capital Accounts	37a	....	88.23	104.81	88.58	139.56	154.16	109.27	87.30	282.19	375.89	472.43	576.24
Other Items (Net)	37r	....	20.30	–31.24	–30.88	–31.97	–10.69	–43.34	–46.94	5.14	26.91	30.46	54.19
Money plus Quasi-Money	35l	....	464.27	697.95	548.84	656.15	898.83	958.87	1,038.07	1,318.77	1,580.02	1,894.69	2,313.97
Interest Rates						*Percent Per Annum*							
Discount Rate (End of Period)	60	....	27.00	25.00	24.00	9.50	4.00	4.00	4.00	3.50	3.50	3.00	3.00
Money Market Rate	60b	....	....	37.18	22.39	13.08	3.76	4.42	4.72	2.97	5.23	3.01	2.86
Treasury Bill Rate	60c	....	....	....	28.24	16.27	4.73	5.27	6.23	† 4.85	5.63	3.52	3.24
Deposit Rate	60l	....	34.78	31.68	14.79	11.71	5.90	5.33	5.04	4.38	5.24	3.23	3.02
Lending Rate	60p	....	86.36	55.86	34.56	25.78	15.25	14.29	14.20	11.87	11.17	7.97	5.38

2004, International Monetary Fund : *International Financial Statistics Yearbook*

Latvia 941

		1992	1993	1994	1995	1996	1997	1998	1999	2000	2001	2002	2003
Prices, Production, Labor						*Index Numbers (2000=100): Period Averages*							
Share Prices	62	....	....	....	....	....	345.8	181.4	72.4	100.0	136.1	149.1	172.2
Producer Prices	63	30.25	65.67	76.73	85.86	97.60	101.62	103.53	99.38	100.00	101.72	102.66	105.93
Consumer Prices	64	†20.1	42.0	57.1	71.3	83.9	90.9	95.2	97.4	100.0	†102.5	104.5	107.5
Wages: Average Earnings	65	14.9	31.5	50.5	62.6	71.9	87.5	93.2	96.9	100.0	104.9	111.5	121.6
Industrial Employment	67	200.2	128.2	110.6	104.9	104.7	102.0	107.5	99.9	100.0	97.2	96.5	99.3
						Number in Thousands: Period Averages								
Labor Force	67d	1,367	1,320	1,300	....	1,182	1,186	1,168	1,157	1,132	1,106	1,124	....
Employment	67e	1,294	1,205	1,083	1,046	1,018	1,037	1,043	1,038	1,038	1,037	1,006	....
Unemployment	67c	31	77	84	83	91	85	111	110	93	92	....	119
Unemployment Rate (%)	67r	2.3	5.8	6.5	6.6	7.2	7.0	9.2	9.1	7.8	7.7	....	10.6
International Transactions						*Millions of Lats*								
Exports	70	573	676	553	688	795	972	1,069	1,008	1,131	1,256	1,409	1,651
Imports, c.i.f.	71	....	....	....	960	1,278	1,582	1,881	1,724	1,934	2,202	2,497	2,989
Imports, f.o.b.	71.v	....	639	695	923	1,223	1,513	1,796	1,652	....	....	....	....
						(2000=100) Period Averages								
Volume of Exports	72	....	76.7	52.0	59.1	63.9	84.7	85.7	87.3	100.0	102.5	112.2	121.5
Unit Value of Exports	74	....	72.9	84.0	97.5	103.6	105.2	105.1	101.2	†100.0	102.6	105.4	113.8
Balance of Payments						*Millions of US Dollars: Minus Sign Indicates Debit*								
Current Account, n.i.e.	78ald	191	417	201	−16	−280	−345	−650	−654	−495	−732	−647	−956
Goods: Exports f.o.b.	78aad	800	1,054	1,022	1,368	1,488	1,838	2,011	1,889	2,058	2,216	2,576	3,171
Goods: Imports f.o.b.	78abd	−840	−1,051	−1,322	−1,947	−2,286	−2,686	−3,141	−2,916	−3,116	−3,566	−4,020	−5,169
Trade Balance	78acd	−40	3	−301	−580	−798	−848	−1,130	−1,027	−1,058	−1,351	−1,444	−1,998
Services: Credit	78add	291	533	657	720	1,126	1,033	1,108	1,024	1,212	1,189	1,252	1,527
Services: Debit	78aed	−156	−205	−297	−246	−742	−662	−806	−689	−770	−693	−708	−944
Balance on Goods & Services	78afd	94	332	60	−106	−414	−477	−827	−691	−616	−854	−900	−1,414
Income: Credit	78agd	3	17	51	71	140	177	207	158	215	278	289	365
Income: Debit	78ahd	−1	−10	−42	−53	−99	−122	−154	−214	−191	−234	−296	−424
Balance on Gds, Serv. & Inc.	78aid	95	339	68	−87	−373	−422	−774	−747	−592	−810	−907	−1,473
Current Transfers, n.i.e.: Credit	78ajd	97	81	136	75	98	91	137	114	203	221	537	912
Current Transfers: Debit	78akd	−1	−3	−3	−5	−5	−14	−13	−21	−105	−143	−278	−394
Capital Account, n.i.e.	78bcd	....	....	....	....	....	14	14	13	30	45	18	34
Capital Account, n.i.e.: Credit	78bad	....	....	....	....	....	14	14	13	39	56	25	39
Capital Account: Debit	78bbd	....	....	....	....	....	−	−	−	−9	−11	−7	−5
Financial Account, n.i.e.	78bjd	−110	67	363	636	537	347	601	768	494	954	699	917
Direct Investment Abroad	78bdd	−2	5	65	65	−3	−6	−54	−17	−9	−12	−8	−32
Dir. Invest. in Rep. Econ., n.i.e.	78bed	29	45	214	180	382	521	357	348	410	164	382	359
Portfolio Investment Assets	78bfd	−	−	−22	−37	−165	−539	−33	58	−346	−57	−220	−286
Equity Securities	78bkd	....	−	−12	−7	12	−113	7	77	−40	7	−2	6
Debt Securities	78bld	−	−	−10	−30	−177	−426	−40	−19	−306	−64	−218	−292
Portfolio Investment Liab., n.i.e.	78bgd	....	....	....	−	24	−32	27	215	25	184	−10	62
Equity Securities	78bmd	....	....	....	−	−2	6	30	7	−7	1	22	29
Debt Securities	78bnd	....	....	....	....	26	−39	−3	209	32	183	−32	32
Financial Derivatives Assets	78bwd	....	....	....	....	....	−	−	−	2	3	−7	−5
Financial Derivatives Liabilities	78bxd	....	....	....	....	....	....	....	....	−	−3	20	11
Other Investment Assets	78bhd	−371	−129	−387	−31	−214	−326	75	−214	−361	−67	−476	−666
Monetary Authorities	78bod	−24	39	5	1	−1	−	−	36	−	−	−	−
General Government	78bpd	3	....	....	....	....	−	−	−	−	−7	6	−
Banks	78bqd	−59	−119	−400	99	−261	−253	67	−275	−370	−107	−484	−635
Other Sectors	78brd	−291	−50	8	−130	48	−73	9	25	10	46	2	−32
Other Investment Liab., n.i.e.	78bid	234	146	493	458	513	730	229	379	773	741	1,017	1,474
Monetary Authorities	78bsd	10	−4	−5	−	−	−	−	6	−	1	−1	−
General Government	78btd	22	99	54	55	45	20	45	14	−8	7	−3	−112
Banks	78bud	5	76	272	88	385	558	69	354	719	529	984	1,479
Other Sectors	78bvd	198	−25	172	315	84	152	115	4	62	204	37	106
Net Errors and Omissions	78cad	−44	−186	−508	−653	−46	87	97	38	−26	47	−57	85
Overall Balance	78cbd	37	298	57	−33	211	102	63	165	3	314	12	80
Reserves and Related Items	79dad	−37	−298	−57	33	−211	−102	−63	−165	−3	−314	−12	−80
Reserve Assets	79dbd	−73	−371	−103	36	−186	−65	−38	−150	7	−305	−2	−69
Use of Fund Credit and Loans	79dcd	36	74	47	−3	−25	−37	−25	−15	−10	−10	−10	−11
Exceptional Financing	79ded	....	....	....	....	....	....	....	....	−	−	−	−

Latvia 941

		1992	1993	1994	1995	1996	1997	1998	1999	2000	2001	2002	2003
International Investment Position						***Millions of US Dollars***							
Assets..	79aad	....	....	....	1,851	2,366	3,262	3,051	3,278	3,968	4,069	4,994	6,405
Direct Investment Abroad...............	79abd	....	....	....	231	209	222	281	244	242	47	66	105
Portfolio Investment......................	79acd	....	....	....	62	227	755	590	518	854	665	905	1,246
Equity Securities..........................	79add	....	....	....	21	9	123	113	22	63	56	58	54
Debt Securities............................	79aed	....	....	....	41	218	633	477	495	791	609	847	1,192
Financial Derivatives.....................	79ald	....	....	....	–	–	4	6	4	6	2	10	16
Other Investment.........................	79afd	....	....	....	972	1,158	1,447	1,301	1,568	1,947	2,136	2,686	3,502
Monetary Authorities...................	79agd	....	....	....	2	3	7	4	2	1	1	1	1
General Government.....................	79ahd	....	....	....	–	–	–	–	–	3	9	3	4
Banks..	79aid	....	....	....	542	800	1,047	872	1,135	1,515	1,616	2,120	2,843
Other Sectors.............................	79ajd	....	....	....	429	356	393	425	431	428	510	562	655
Reserve Assets..............................	79akd	....	....	....	586	772	833	873	944	919	1,219	1,327	1,535
Liabilities.....................................	79lad	....	....	....	1,932	2,717	3,710	4,252	5,110	6,109	7,157	9,026	11,589
Dir. Invest. in Rep. Economy...........	79lbd	....	....	....	616	936	1,272	1,558	1,794	2,084	2,331	2,751	3,320
Portfolio Investment......................	79lcd	....	....	....	23	46	13	42	248	245	419	475	636
Equity Securities..........................	79ldd	....	....	....	7	5	9	41	51	40	43	71	115
Debt Securities............................	79led	....	....	....	16	41	4	1	197	205	376	404	522
Financial Derivatives.....................	79lld	....	....	....	–	–	4	2	9	10	7	29	43
Other Investment.........................	79lfd	....	....	....	1,294	1,735	2,422	2,650	3,059	3,770	4,400	5,771	7,589
Monetary Authorities...................	79lgd	....	....	....	161	130	87	65	49	36	27	17	8
General Government.....................	79lhd	....	....	....	242	279	284	343	345	327	324	337	249
Banks..	79lid	....	....	....	399	782	1,332	1,278	1,619	2,328	2,616	3,688	5,380
Other Sectors.............................	79ljd	....	....	....	492	544	719	965	1,047	1,079	1,433	1,729	1,953
Government Finance						***Millions of Lats: Year Ending December 31***							
Deficit (-) or Surplus......................	80	....	....	....	....	†–44.13	†23.34	†5.32	–140.15	–118.96	–67.96	–98.27	–90.79
Total Revenue and Grants...............	81y	....	....	....	357.10	†874.92	1,174.54	†1,289.69	1,291.17	1,305.64	1,383.04	1,545.13	1,726.54
Revenue....................................	81	....	....	....	....	....	....	....	....	....	....	....	....
Grants.......................................	81z	....	....	....	....	....	....	....	....	....	....	....	....
Exp. & Lending Minus Repay...........	82z	....	....	....	....	†919.05	†1,151.20	†1,284.37	1,431.32	1,424.60	1,451.00	1,643.40	1,817.33
Expenditure................................	82	....	....	....	445.60	†907.14	†1,116.81	†1,283.65	1,419.29	1,412.14	1,442.07	1,648.65	1,830.97
Lending Minus Repayments..........	83	....	....	....	....	†11.91	34.39	†.72	12.03	12.46	8.93	–5.25	–13.64
Total Financing.............................	80h	....	....	....	....	†44.13	–23.34	†–5.32	140.15	118.96	67.96	98.27	90.79
Domestic....................................	84a	....	....	....	....	†31.81	–41.06	†–18.38	13.28	130.97	–37.57	86.96	135.84
Foreign......................................	85a	....	....	....	....	†12.32	17.72	†13.06	126.87	–12.01	105.53	11.31	–45.05
National Accounts						***Millions of Lats***							
Househ.Cons.Expend.,incl.NPISHs....	96f	400.2	779.0	1,206.1	1,470.5	1,902.9	2,181.1	2,316.0	2,445.5	2,693.5	2,989.0	3,259.3	3,985.5
Government Consumption Expend...	91f	120.0	294.6	410.6	630.4	731.1	742.7	917.3	961.2	1,009.6	1,065.2	1,150.2	1,317.1
Gross Fixed Capital Formation.........	93e	112.3	201.8	303.9	354.9	512.8	613.7	979.5	980.0	1,151.5	1,297.5	1,370.6	1,527.8
Changes in Inventories....................	93i	301.9	–67.2	86.9	14.2	–45.2	82.3	–39.7	.9	–52.7	91.9	154.5	295.9
Exports of Goods and Services.........	90c	803.1	1,074.4	948.8	1,101.0	1,440.1	1,669.1	1,841.4	1,708.1	1,983.8	2,138.3	2,361.6	2,680.5
Imports of Goods and Services (-)....	98c	734.0	835.9	906.8	1,157.8	1,668.8	1,947.3	2,326.8	2,109.8	2,360.0	2,676.0	2,912.6	3,484.2
Gross Domestic Product (GDP)........	99b	1,004.6	1,467.0	2,042.6	2,580.1	3,076.1	3,562.9	3,902.9	4,224.2	4,685.7	5,168.3	5,691.1	6,322.5
Net Primary Income from Abroad.....	98.n	1.1	–1.3	–4.0	11.5	22.9	32.1	31.9	–32.1	15.8	27.8	–4.8	–33.9
Gross National Income (GNI)...........	99a	1,005.7	1,465.7	2,038.5	2,591.6	3,099.1	3,594.9	3,934.8	4,192.1	4,701.5	5,196.1	5,686.3	6,288.6
Net Current Transf.from Abroad.......	98t	70.8	51.8	74.3	–214.9	–217.3	–248.4	–237.6	–280.3	–278.0	–306.4	....	....
Gross Nat'l Disposable Inc.(GNDI)....	99i	1,076.5	1,517.5	2,112.9	2,376.7	2,881.8	3,346.5	3,697.2	3,911.9	4,423.5	4,889.7	....	....
Gross Saving.................................	99s	556.2	443.9	496.2	384.4	366.6	552.5	613.2	667.9	873.0	971.9	1,082.3	....
Consumption of Fixed Capital..........	99cf	14.9	143.4	254.7	286.9	304.3	344.5	469.5	490.0	528.5	611.1	644.7	....
GDP Volume 1995 Prices.................	99b.p	2,764.2	2,353.2	2,368.4	2,349.2	....	....	....	....	....	....	....	....
GDP Volume 2000 Prices.................	99b.p	....	....	....	3,606.0	3,742.7	4,052.7	4,244.1	4,383.6	4,685.7	5,061.0	5,387.3	5,348.9
GDP Volume (2000=100)................	99bvp	90.6	77.1	77.6	†77.0	79.9	86.5	90.6	93.6	100.0	108.0	115.0	114.2
GDP Deflator (2000=100)................	99bip	23.7	40.6	56.2	71.6	82.2	87.9	92.0	96.4	100.0	102.1	105.6	118.2
						Millions: Midyear Estimates							
Population....................................	99z	2.65	2.60	2.54	2.50	2.46	2.43	2.41	2.39	2.37	2.35	2.33	2.31

Lebanon 446

		1992	1993	1994	1995	1996	1997	1998	1999	2000	2001	2002	2003
Exchange Rates		*Pounds per SDR: End of Period*											
Market Rate	aa	2,527.3	2,350.2	2,404.4	2,372.4	2,231.7	2,060.3	2,123.3	2,069.1	1,964.1	1,894.5	2,049.5	2,240.1
		Pounds per US Dollar: End of Period (ae) Period Average (rf)											
Market Rate	ae	1,838.0	1,711.0	1,647.0	1,596.0	1,552.0	1,527.0	1,508.0	1,507.5	1,507.5	1,507.5	1,507.5	1,507.5
Market Rate	rf	1,712.8	1,741.4	1,680.1	1,621.4	1,571.4	1,539.5	1,516.1	1,507.8	1,507.5	1,507.5	1,507.5	1,507.5
		Index Numbers (2000=100): Period Averages											
Market Rate	ahx	98.48	86.62	89.76	92.98	95.94	97.95	99.42	99.97	100.00	100.07	100.13	100.13
Nominal Effective Exchange Rate	nec	62.88	63.56	69.99	69.38	74.00	83.53	88.51	91.43	100.00	105.22	102.62	91.12
Fund Position		*Millions of SDRs: End of Period*											
Quota	2f.s	78.7	78.7	146.0	146.0	146.0	146.0	146.0	203.0	203.0	203.0	203.0	203.0
SDRs	1b.s	9.5	10.5	11.4	12.3	13.3	14.3	15.4	16.4	18.2	19.4	20.1	20.6
Reserve Position in the Fund	1c.s	18.8	18.8	18.8	18.8	18.8	18.8	18.8	18.8	18.8	18.8	18.8	18.8
Total Fund Cred.&Loans Outstg.	2tl	–	–	–	–	–	–	–	–	–	–	–	–
International Liquidity		*Millions of US Dollars Unless Otherwise Indicated: End of Period*											
Total Reserves minus Gold	1l.d	1,496.4	2,260.3	3,884.2	4,533.3	5,931.9	5,976.4	6,556.3	7,775.6	5,943.7	5,013.8	7,243.8	12,519.4
SDRs	1b.d	13.0	14.4	16.6	18.3	19.2	19.3	21.7	22.5	23.7	24.3	27.3	30.7
Reserve Position in the Fund	1c.d	25.9	25.9	27.5	28.0	27.1	25.4	26.5	25.8	24.5	23.7	25.6	28.0
Foreign Exchange	1d.d	1,457.5	2,220.0	3,840.1	4,487.0	5,885.6	5,931.6	6,508.0	7,727.3	5,895.4	4,965.8	7,190.9	12,460.8
Gold (Million Fine Troy Ounces)	1ad	9.222	9.222	9.222	9.222	9.222	9.222	9.222	9.222	9.222	9.222	9.222	9.222
Gold (National Valuation)	1and	3,066.4	3,603.6	3,534.5	3,571.8	3,410.0	2,670.3	2,651.0	2,678.0	2,524.6	2,561.1	3,216.3	3,833.5
Monetary Authorities: Other Liab.	4..d	3.3	5.6	29.5	71.3	54.4	72.9	174.0	156.3	138.4	152.0	158.0	134.7
Deposit Money Banks: Assets	7a.d	3,169.1	4,114.9	3,806.5	3,970.7	4,329.2	6,014.1	6,620.8	5,910.8	8,159.3	8,615.7	9,503.2	9,906.7
Liabilities	7b.d	950.5	1,198.6	1,579.7	2,063.4	2,989.5	4,189.3	5,908.2	6,392.5	7,190.2	7,347.2	7,339.9	9,300.8
Monetary Authorities		*Billions of Pounds: End of Period*											
Foreign Assets	11	8,362.5	10,025.9	12,208.7	12,923.9	14,486.2	13,191.4	13,851.8	15,725.0	12,730.1	10,531.7	12,566.0	21,216.7
Claims on Central Government	12a	236.3	427.8	31.6	57.2	63.6	354.8	113.0	147.5	2,060.8	6,835.9	3,829.0	12,064.4
Claims on Private Sector	12d	95.1	44.4	73.1	120.0	338.7	587.7	640.3	578.7	628.8	696.1	914.4	973.4
Claims on Deposit Money Banks	12e	163.9	187.1	166.8	289.9	105.1	96.8	346.1	405.9	734.8	781.0	1,719.6	1,826.8
Reserve Money	14	1,521.9	2,159.8	3,816.7	4,624.5	5,604.4	8,404.0	7,944.3	8,378.2	8,927.4	12,246.5	13,487.7	29,908.7
of which: Currency Outside DMBs	14a	798.0	714.7	938.8	1,046.2	1,160.7	1,210.1	1,241.3	1,369.3	1,423.4	1,381.7	1,375.3	1,530.6
Foreign Liabilities	16c	6.0	9.6	48.6	113.8	84.4	111.3	262.3	235.6	208.7	229.1	238.3	203.1
Long-Term Foreign Liabilities	16cl	....	....	....	....	....	....	1,068.1	1,068.1	1,068.1	1,386.2	1,418.9	1,342.6
Central Government Deposits	16d	927.4	1,237.3	2,383.5	2,440.5	3,585.5	1,189.3	1,795.8	3,304.4	1,910.2	1,401.9	2,373.2	1,693.3
Capital Accounts	17a	79.9	95.7	88.5	134.1	312.7	328.1	796.7	883.1	911.9	1,049.2	1,255.5	1,913.9
Other Items (Net)	17r	6,322.6	7,182.8	6,142.7	6,078.2	5,406.6	4,197.8	3,084.2	2,987.8	3,128.2	2,531.7	255.4	1,019.8
of which: Valuation Adjustment	17rv	6,252.5	6,630.3	6,094.0	5,912.1	5,222.7	3,616.3	3,046.4	2,918.3	2,521.6	2,742.2	102.5	645.9
Deposit Money Banks		*Billions of Pounds: End of Period*											
Reserves	20	669.2	1,434.9	2,786.4	3,541.5	4,377.9	6,224.6	6,513.4	6,826.7	7,330.8	10,655.9	11,959.8	28,332.5
Foreign Assets	21	5,824.9	7,040.6	6,269.3	6,337.3	6,718.9	9,184.0	9,984.2	8,910.5	12,300.2	12,988.2	14,326.0	14,934.4
Claims on Central Government	22a	3,098.4	4,013.3	6,908.6	7,948.9	12,060.3	13,234.2	17,942.1	21,840.8	23,271.3	23,066.8	26,577.4	21,005.8
Claims on Private Sector	22d	4,804.1	5,897.9	7,799.8	10,320.0	12,687.0	15,451.3	18,681.5	20,994.3	22,243.2	22,192.0	22,757.8	22,506.5
Demand Deposits	24	393.5	422.4	492.7	508.0	568.7	685.5	758.3	845.8	862.2	889.6	1,072.3	1,258.1
Time & Foreign Currency Deposits	25	10,574.9	13,986.8	18,193.7	21,297.8	26,935.9	32,621.4	38,067.1	42,458.0	46,720.0	50,344.6	53,995.7	60,207.3
Foreign Liabilities	26c	1,746.9	2,050.9	2,601.7	3,293.1	4,639.8	6,397.1	8,909.6	9,636.7	10,839.2	11,075.9	11,064.9	14,020.9
Central Government Deposits	26d	106.5	151.7	255.4	261.0	285.1	216.6	346.1	701.7	720.9	525.5	591.0	1,325.3
Credit from Monetary Authorities	26g	163.9	187.1	166.8	289.9	105.1	96.8	346.1	405.9	734.8	781.0	1,719.6	1,826.8
Capital Accounts	27a	215.4	444.1	675.8	1,145.9	1,943.5	2,990.1	3,619.9	4,019.3	4,376.3	4,463.2	5,023.5	5,498.6
Other Items (Net)	27r	1,195.3	1,143.6	1,378.0	1,351.9	1,366.1	1,086.5	1,074.0	504.8	892.1	823.1	2,154.0	2,642.2
Monetary Survey		*Billions of Pounds: End of Period*											
Foreign Assets (Net)	31n	12,434.4	15,006.0	15,827.6	15,854.3	16,481.0	15,866.9	13,596.1	13,695.1	12,914.3	10,828.7	14,170.0	20,584.5
Domestic Credit	32	7,199.9	8,994.3	12,174.1	15,744.6	21,279.0	28,222.0	35,235.0	39,555.2	45,573.0	50,863.4	51,114.3	53,531.5
Claims on Central Govt. (Net)	32an	2,300.8	3,052.0	4,301.3	5,304.6	8,253.3	12,183.0	15,913.2	17,982.2	22,701.0	27,975.3	27,442.2	30,051.6
Claims on Private Sector	32d	4,899.2	5,942.3	7,872.9	10,440.0	13,025.7	16,039.0	19,321.8	21,573.0	22,872.0	22,888.1	23,672.1	23,479.9
Money	34	1,199.4	1,143.2	1,436.8	1,560.6	1,753.4	1,929.4	2,051.5	2,260.8	2,389.3	2,365.3	2,544.4	2,827.8
Quasi-Money	35	10,576.4	14,535.2	18,214.5	21,322.7	27,161.6	32,640.2	38,087.2	42,564.3	46,845.5	50,545.1	54,250.4	61,481.9
Other Items (Net)	37r	7,858.5	8,321.8	8,350.4	8,715.5	8,844.9	9,519.2	8,692.3	8,425.2	9,252.5	8,781.6	8,489.4	9,806.3
Money plus Quasi-Money	35l	11,775.8	15,678.5	19,651.3	22,883.3	28,915.1	34,569.6	40,138.8	44,825.1	49,234.8	52,910.4	56,794.9	64,309.7
Interest Rates		*Percent Per Annum*											
Discount Rate (End of Period)	60	16.00	20.22	16.49	19.01	25.00	30.00	30.00	25.00	20.00	20.00	20.00	20.00
Treasury Bill Rate	60c	22.40	18.27	15.09	19.40	15.19	13.42	12.70	11.57	11.18	11.18	10.90	....
Deposit Rate	60l	17.09	15.56	14.80	16.30	15.54	13.37	13.61	12.50	11.21	10.85	11.03	8.69
Lending Rate	60p	40.21	28.53	23.88	24.69	25.21	20.29	....	19.48	18.15	17.19	16.58	13.43
International Transactions		*Millions of US Dollars*											
Exports	70..d	560	452	470	656	736	643	662	677	715	870	1,046	1,524
Imports, c.i.f.	71..d	4,202	† 2,215	2,598	5,480	7,540	7,467	7,070	6,207	6,230	7,293	6,447	7,171

Lebanon 446

		1992	1993	1994	1995	1996	1997	1998	1999	2000	2001	2002	2003
Government Finance		\multicolumn{12}{c}{***Billions of Pounds: Year Ending December 31***}
Deficit (-) or Surplus	80	....	–1,017.0	–2,631.0	–3,309.3	–4,198.3	–5,902.8	–3,936.1	–4,029.8	....	....	....	....
Revenue	81	....	1,855.0	2,241.0	3,032.7	3,533.7	3,753.2	4,449.4	4,868.2	....	....	....	....
Grants Received	81z	....	197.0	507.0	–	–	72.0	–	12.0	....	....	....	....
Expenditure	82	....	3,069.0	5,379.0	6,342.0	7,732.0	9,728.0	8,385.5	8,910.0	....	....	....	....
Lending Minus Repayments	83	....	–	–	–	–	–	–	–	....	....	....	....
Financing													
Domestic	84a	....	868.0	1,946.0	2,452.3	3,334.3	5,158.3	1,468.8	2,008.3	....	....	....	....
Foreign	85a	....	149.0	685.0	857.0	864.0	744.5	2,467.3	2,021.5	....	....	....	....
Debt: Domestic	88a	....	6,089.4	9,347.5	11,997.2	17,228.8	19,797.1	21,685.7	25,382.8	....	....	....	....
Debt: Foreign	89a	....	563.6	1,286.0	2,157.8	2,958.5	3,713.3	6,282.5	8,350.8	....	....	....	....
		\multicolumn{12}{c}{***Millions: Midyear Estimates***}
Population	99z	2.86	2.96	3.06	3.15	3.23	3.30	3.36	3.42	3.48	3.54	3.60	3.65

2004, International Monetary Fund : *International Financial Statistics Yearbook*

Lesotho 666

		1992	1993	1994	1995	1996	1997	1998	1999	2000	2001	2002	2003
Exchange Rates													
		\multicolumn{12}{c}{*Loti per SDR: End of Period*}
Principal Rate	aa	4.19788	4.66667	5.17298	5.42197	6.73325	6.56747	8.25106	8.44711	9.86107	15.23974	11.74625	9.86684
		\multicolumn{12}{c}{*Loti per US Dollar: End of Period (ae) Period Average (rf)*}
Principal Rate	ae	3.05300	3.39750	3.54350	3.64750	4.68250	4.86750	5.86000	6.15450	7.56850	12.12650	8.64000	6.64000
Principal Rate	rf	2.85201	3.26774	3.55080	3.62709	4.29935	4.60796	5.52828	6.10948	6.93983	8.60918	10.54075	7.56475
		\multicolumn{12}{c}{*Index Numbers (2000=100): Period Averages*}
Principal Rate	ahx	242.3	211.6	194.6	190.4	161.7	150.0	126.0	113.0	100.0	81.3	66.7	91.6
Nominal Effective Exchange Rate	nec	203.4	186.6	171.5	162.1	140.1	136.5	117.3	107.6	100.0	83.1	66.2	88.5
Real Effective Exchange Rate	rec	132.1	131.2	124.9	124.9	113.7	117.1	106.4	104.2	100.0	86.7	75.9	105.5
Fund Position													
		\multicolumn{12}{c}{*Millions of SDRs: End of Period*}
Quota	2f.s	23.90	23.90	23.90	23.90	23.90	23.90	23.90	34.90	34.90	34.90	34.90	34.90
SDRs	1b.s	.48	.41	.33	.24	.92	.89	.86	.85	.51	.46	.44	.42
Reserve Position in the Fund	1c.s	3.51	3.51	3.51	3.51	3.51	3.52	3.53	3.53	3.54	3.54	3.54	3.54
Total Fund Cred.&Loans Outstg.	2tl	18.12	24.92	27.63	25.82	23.48	20.39	16.76	12.46	8.53	12.13	16.19	17.88
International Liquidity													
		\multicolumn{12}{c}{*Millions of US Dollars Unless Otherwise Indicated: End of Period*}
Total Reserves minus Gold	1l.d	157.49	252.69	372.62	456.74	460.51	571.74	575.08	499.56	417.89	386.49	406.37	460.33
SDRs	1b.d	.66	.56	.47	.35	1.33	1.20	1.22	1.17	.66	.58	.60	.63
Reserve Position in the Fund	1c.d	4.83	4.82	5.13	5.22	5.05	4.75	4.98	4.85	4.61	4.45	4.82	5.26
Foreign Exchange	1d.d	152.00	247.30	367.02	451.17	454.13	565.78	568.89	493.54	412.62	381.46	400.95	454.44
Monetary Authorities: Other Liab.	4..d	1.80	1.63	1.85	33.39	28.73	26.79	24.79	42.72	37.78	27.16	52.98	47.33
Deposit Money Banks: Assets	7a.d	95.26	65.84	48.52	65.04	58.36	41.80	72.97	80.37	80.48	65.11	76.28	126.11
Liabilities	7b.d	7.99	9.64	10.29	16.51	12.83	11.69	8.05	6.48	18.50	8.48	11.53	34.58
Monetary Authorities													
		\multicolumn{12}{c}{*Millions of Maloti: End of Period*}
Foreign Assets	11	483.08	869.28	1,337.58	1,802.01	2,310.26	2,929.82	3,549.85	3,349.33	3,486.14	5,138.38	3,858.43	3,341.55
Claims on Central Government	12a	213.38	375.85	381.63	287.92	318.78	166.39	145.88	110.39	105.04	250.96	192.44	176.44
Claims on Private Sector	12d	—	—	—	8.91	8.69	10.52	11.54	12.20	13.90	13.56	13.53	14.99
Claims on Deposit Money Banks	12e	6.25	.39	.44	—	—	—	—	—	—	—	—	—
Reserve Money	14	191.77	233.68	249.15	329.83	346.37	388.95	540.13	717.32	669.79	499.36	500.91	533.95
of which: Currency Outside DMBs.	14a	39.86	43.75	52.57	74.11	84.09	92.51	134.50	122.66	139.34	147.14	179.68	183.52
Foreign Liabilities	16c	81.55	121.82	149.49	261.78	292.62	264.26	283.56	368.13	370.06	514.22	647.88	490.68
Central Government Deposits	16d	349.19	790.87	1,134.25	1,350.19	1,659.50	2,062.82	2,125.51	1,602.59	1,356.38	1,502.35	1,257.31	1,263.91
Capital Accounts	17a	54.30	77.86	82.34	185.68	368.79	409.22	735.54	805.41	1,208.99	2,858.28	1,772.05	1,393.50
Other Items (Net)	17r	25.90	21.30	104.42	−28.64	−29.55	−18.54	22.52	−21.54	−.14	28.69	−113.75	−149.06
Deposit Money Banks													
		\multicolumn{12}{c}{*Millions of Maloti: End of Period*}
Reserves	20	135.95	179.47	180.45	165.68	245.58	245.22	490.59	573.72	506.81	127.06	159.15	181.10
Foreign Assets	21	290.84	223.69	171.94	237.24	273.27	203.46	427.59	494.65	609.09	789.61	659.10	837.34
Claims on Central Government	22a	108.45	99.72	103.95	74.91	74.35	74.23	51.53	586.38	586.20	691.32	812.38	991.45
Claims on Nonfin.Pub.Enterprises	22c	28.91	29.31	30.92	80.53	141.33	127.62	225.53	105.28	79.22	46.39	42.75	38.94
Claims on Private Sector	22d	316.37	502.61	699.24	665.46	667.27	979.29	829.70	845.29	869.11	927.44	1,062.83	493.73
Claims on Other Banking Insts.	22f	2.77	10.00	10.39	—	—	—	—	—	—	—	—	—
Demand Deposits	24	311.29	389.43	434.02	445.91	548.00	686.57	836.92	821.27	873.73	939.04	1,099.15	1,185.21
Time and Savings Deposits	25	371.62	501.99	550.42	601.05	692.40	743.97	785.67	720.52	664.94	700.44	727.24	760.10
Foreign Liabilities	26c	24.40	32.74	36.47	60.23	60.06	56.89	47.20	39.89	140.01	102.82	99.63	229.64
Central Government Deposits	26d	39.85	48.30	39.59	37.53	43.66	46.04	76.77	77.12	68.38	63.31	63.89	68.35
Capital Accounts	27a	160.67	189.51	233.51	119.12	56.11	−74.15	−38.31	209.92	318.90	279.18	286.81	303.43
Other Items (Net)	27r	−24.54	−117.17	−97.12	−40.02	1.56	170.50	316.70	736.60	584.47	497.04	459.49	−4.16
Monetary Survey													
		\multicolumn{12}{c}{*Millions of Maloti: End of Period*}
Foreign Assets (Net)	31n	667.97	938.41	1,323.56	1,717.24	2,230.85	2,812.12	3,646.68	3,435.95	3,585.17	5,310.96	3,770.03	3,458.57
Domestic Credit	32	280.84	178.33	52.29	−270.00	−492.76	−750.82	−938.11	−20.17	228.70	364.01	802.72	383.30
Claims on Central Govt. (Net)	32an	−67.21	−363.59	−688.26	−1,024.89	−1,310.03	−1,868.24	−2,004.88	−982.95	−733.52	−623.38	−316.38	−164.36
Claims on Nonfin.Pub.Enterprises	32c	28.91	29.31	30.92	80.53	141.33	127.62	225.53	105.28	79.22	46.39	42.75	38.94
Claims on Private Sector	32d	316.37	502.61	699.24	674.37	675.95	989.81	841.24	857.49	883.00	941.00	1,076.35	508.72
Claims on Other Banking Insts.	32f	2.77	10.00	10.39	—	—	—	—	—	—	—	—	—
Money	34	351.15	433.18	486.59	537.70	641.62	787.03	983.17	957.32	1,035.96	1,292.27	1,440.94	1,537.75
Quasi-Money	35	371.62	501.99	550.42	601.05	692.40	743.97	785.67	720.52	664.94	700.44	727.24	760.10
Capital Accounts	37a	214.97	267.37	315.85	304.80	424.89	335.07	697.22	1,015.34	1,527.89	3,137.46	2,058.86	1,696.93
Other Items (Net)	37r	11.07	−85.81	23.00	3.70	−20.83	195.23	242.51	722.60	585.07	544.80	345.71	−152.91
Money plus Quasi-Money	35l	722.77	935.17	1,037.01	1,138.74	1,334.02	1,531.00	1,768.83	1,677.84	1,700.90	1,992.71	2,168.18	2,297.85
Other Banking Institutions													
		\multicolumn{12}{c}{*Millions of Maloti: End of Period*}
Cash	40	8.00	....	....	....	....	....	....	....	....	....	....	....
Claims on Private Sector	42d	64.91	....	....	....	....	....	....	....	....	....	....	....
Time and Savings Deposits	45	41.52	....	....	....	....	....	....	....	....	....	....	....
Capital Accounts	47a	9.23	....	....	....	....	....	....	....	....	....	....	....
Other Items (Net)	47r	22.16	....	....	....	....	....	....	....	....	....	....	....

Lesotho 666

		1992	1993	1994	1995	1996	1997	1998	1999	2000	2001	2002	2003
Interest Rates		\multicolumn{12}{c}{*Percent Per Annum*}
Discount Rate (End of Period)	60	15.00	13.50	13.50	15.50	17.00	15.60	19.50	19.00	15.00	13.00	16.19	15.00
Treasury Bill Rate	60c	14.20	†10.01	9.44	12.40	13.89	14.83	15.47	12.45	9.06	9.49	11.34	11.96
Deposit Rate	60l	10.63	8.06	8.43	13.34	12.73	11.81	10.73	7.45	4.92	4.83	5.19	5.16
Lending Rate	60p	18.25	15.83	14.25	16.38	17.71	18.03	20.06	19.06	17.11	16.55	17.11	16.02
Prices		\multicolumn{12}{c}{*Index Numbers (2000=100): Period Averages*}
Consumer Prices	64	51.1	57.8	62.5	68.3	74.7	....	....	†94.2	100.0	90.4	120.9	129.0
International Transactions		\multicolumn{12}{c}{*Millions of Maloti*}
Exports	70	310.0	438.0	509.0	581.0	812.0	904.0	1,071.0	1,053.3	1,528.0	2,426.2	3,852.0	3,604.9
Imports, c.i.f.	71	2,564.0	2,839.0	3,000.0	3,576.0	4,303.0	4,722.0	4,699.0	4,773.2	5,048.0	5,823.8	8,120.0	7,693.3
Balance of Payments		\multicolumn{12}{c}{*Millions of US Dollars: Minus Sign Indicates Debit*}
Current Account, n.i.e.	78ald	37.6	29.3	108.1	−323.0	−302.5	−269.2	−280.2	−220.8	−151.4	−95.1	−118.8	....
Goods: Exports f.o.b.	78aad	109.2	134.0	143.5	160.0	186.9	196.1	193.4	172.5	211.1	278.6	354.8	....
Goods: Imports f.o.b.	78abd	−932.6	−868.1	−810.2	−985.2	−998.6	−1,024.4	−866.0	−779.2	−727.6	−678.6	−736.0	....
Trade Balance	78acd	−823.4	−734.1	−666.7	−825.2	−811.8	−828.3	−672.5	−606.7	−516.5	−400.0	−381.2	....
Services: Credit	78add	41.3	37.0	37.8	39.0	42.6	86.9	53.6	43.7	42.7	40.5	35.4	....
Services: Debit	78aed	−82.8	−70.5	−64.2	−61.1	−55.9	−67.6	−52.2	−50.1	−42.5	−49.0	−55.5	....
Balance on Goods & Services	78afd	−864.9	−767.6	−693.2	−847.3	−825.1	−809.0	−671.2	−613.1	−516.4	−408.5	−401.4	....
Income: Credit	78agd	496.3	444.5	369.6	471.6	453.0	447.4	357.7	325.0	288.8	235.3	177.8	....
Income: Debit	78ahd	−32.6	−22.8	−39.4	−157.4	−119.5	−110.0	−123.6	−80.6	−62.6	−56.7	−16.4	....
Balance on Gds, Serv. & Inc.	78aid	−401.1	−345.9	−363.0	−533.2	−491.6	−471.6	−437.1	−368.6	−290.2	−229.9	−240.0	....
Current Transfers, n.i.e.: Credit	78ajd	542.1	376.5	472.1	211.3	190.2	202.9	158.0	149.4	139.8	137.2	123.0	....
Current Transfers: Debit	78akd	−103.3	−1.3	−.9	−1.2	−1.1	−.5	−1.2	−1.6	−1.0	−2.5	−1.7	....
Capital Account, n.i.e.	78bcd	−	−	−	43.7	45.5	44.5	22.9	15.2	22.0	16.8	23.4	....
Capital Account, n.i.e.: Credit	78bad	−	−	−	43.7	45.5	44.5	22.9	15.2	22.0	16.8	23.4	....
Capital Account: Debit	78bbd	−	−	−	....	....	....	....	....	....	....	....	....
Financial Account, n.i.e.	78bjd	−67.0	55.2	33.0	349.1	350.6	323.7	316.1	135.8	85.2	88.6	85.7	....
Direct Investment Abroad	78bdd	−	−	....	....	....	....	....	....	....	....	−	....
Dir. Invest. in Rep. Econ., n.i.e.	78bed	2.7	15.0	18.7	275.3	287.5	268.1	264.8	163.3	117.8	117.0	80.8	....
Portfolio Investment Assets	78bfd	−	−	−	....	....	....	....	....	....	....	....	....
Equity Securities	78bkd	−	−	−	....	....	....	....	....	....	....	−	....
Debt Securities	78bld	−	−	−	....	....	....	....	....	....	....	....	....
Portfolio Investment Liab., n.i.e.	78bgd	−	−	−	....	....	....	....	....	....	....	....	....
Equity Securities	78bmd	−	−	−	....	....	....	....	....	....	....	....	....
Debt Securities	78bnd	−	−	−	....	....	....	....	....	....	....	....	....
Financial Derivatives Assets	78bwd	....	....	....	....	....	....	....	....	....	....	....	....
Financial Derivatives Liabilities	78bxd	....	....	....	....	....	....	....	....	....	....	....	....
Other Investment Assets	78bhd	−106.4	8.9	−13.4	18.8	−7.0	−5.0	−1.7	−11.0	−19.1	−20.2	.7	....
Monetary Authorities	78bod	....	....	....	....	....	....	....	....	....	....	....	....
General Government	78bpd	−73.2	−	−	....	....	....	....	....	....	....	....	....
Banks	78bqd	−33.3	8.9	−13.4	18.8	−7.0	−5.0	−1.7	−11.0	−19.1	−20.2	.7	....
Other Sectors	78brd	−	−	−	....	....	....	....	....	....	....	....	....
Other Investment Liab., n.i.e.	78bid	36.8	31.3	27.6	55.0	70.1	60.5	53.0	−16.6	−13.5	−8.2	4.0	....
Monetary Authorities	78bsd	−.1	−	.3	6.3	−.2	−	.1	−5.4	−3.5	16.0	4.8	....
General Government	78btd	37.1	27.7	26.0	49.2	71.8	68.6	59.8	−9.3	−15.1	−19.0	....	....
Banks	78bud	.5	1.5	1.9	....	....	−7.2	−6.7	−1.2	5.2	−4.8	−.3	....
Other Sectors	78bvd	−.7	2.1	−.5	−.5	−1.4	−.9	−.1	−.6	−.1	−.5	−.5	....
Net Errors and Omissions	78cad	79.2	17.8	−20.3	28.1	23.3	42.1	56.8	29.0	62.1	155.4	−115.7	....
Overall Balance	78cbd	49.9	102.3	120.9	97.8	116.9	141.0	115.6	−40.8	17.8	165.7	−125.3	....
Reserves and Related Items	79dad	−49.9	−102.3	−120.9	−97.8	−116.9	−141.0	−115.6	40.8	−17.8	−165.7	125.3	....
Reserve Assets	79dbd	−57.3	−111.7	−124.6	−95.1	−113.5	−136.8	−110.7	46.7	−12.6	−170.2	120.1	....
Use of Fund Credit and Loans	79dcd	7.5	9.5	3.8	−2.7	−3.4	−4.3	−4.9	−5.9	−5.2	4.5	5.2	....
Exceptional Financing	79ded	....	....	....	....	....	....	....	....	....	....	....	....

Lesotho 666

		1992	1993	1994	1995	1996	1997	1998	1999	2000	2001	2002	2003
International Investment Position					*Millions of US Dollars*								
Assets	79aad	....	....	....	....	....	....	....	....	....	....	....	....
Direct Investment Abroad	79abd	....	....	....	—	—	—	—	—	—	—	—	....
Portfolio Investment	79acd	....	....	....	—	—	—	—	—	—	—	—	....
Equity Securities	79add	....	....	....	—	—	—	—	—	—	—	—	....
Debt Securities	79aed	....	....	....	—	—	—	—	—	—	—	—	....
Financial Derivatives	79ald	....	....	....	....	....	....	....	....	....	....	....	....
Other Investment	79afd	....	....	....	71.8	61.9	114.5	83.8	79.6	80.5	65.1	89.4	....
Monetary Authorities	79agd	....	....	....	—	—	—	—	—	—	—	—	....
General Government	79ahd	....	....	....	—	—	—	—	—	—	—	—	....
Banks	79aid	....	....	....	71.8	61.9	114.5	83.8	79.6	80.5	65.1	89.4	....
Other Sectors	79ajd	....	....	....	—	—	—	—	—	—	—	—	....
Reserve Assets	79akd	....	....	....	456.7	460.5	571.7	575.1	499.8	419.8	423.7	446.6	....
Liabilities	79lad	....	....	....	....	....	....	....	....	....	....	....	....
Dir. Invest. in Rep. Economy	79lbd	....	....	....	—	—	—	—	—	—	—	—	....
Portfolio Investment	79lcd	....	....	....	—	—	—	—	—	—	—	—	....
Equity Securities	79ldd	....	....	....	—	—	—	—	—	—	—	—	....
Debt Securities	79led	....	....	....	—	—	—	—	—	—	—	—	....
Financial Derivatives	79lld	....	....	....	....	....	....	....	....	....	....	....	....
Other Investment	79lfd	....	....	....	566.8	535.6	512.6	590.7	559.5	600.9	580.9	702.2	....
Monetary Authorities	79lgd	....	....	....	39.9	35.1	28.8	24.7	18.2	11.7	57.3	96.9	....
General Government	79lhd	....	....	....	510.3	487.7	475.3	543.5	534.8	570.7	515.1	593.8	....
Banks	79lid	....	....	....	16.5	12.8	8.5	22.4	6.5	18.5	8.5	11.5	....
Other Sectors	79ljd	....	....	....	—	—	—	—	—	—	—	—	....
Government Finance					*Millions of Maloti: Year Beginning April 1*								
Deficit (-) or Surplus	80	81.5	147.2	149.3	108.6	137.4	88.8	−188.8	−286.8	−204.8	153.6	....	....
Revenue	81	1,003.1	1,269.4	1,438.5	1,681.6	2,034.6	2,353.4	2,158.7	2,275.7	2,626.6	2,864.9	....	....
Grants Received	81z	141.8	137.4	143.6	163.2	203.4	178.7	120.0	130.0	125.6	257.6	....	....
Exp. & Lending Minus Repay	82z	1,063.4	1,259.6	1,432.8	1,736.2	2,100.6	2,443.3	2,467.5	2,692.5	2,957.0	2,968.9	....	....
Expenditure	82	1,050.9	1,169.4	994.1	1,118.1	1,179.0	1,537.6	1,971.7	2,311.5	2,457.9	2,342.3	....	....
Lending Minus Repayments	83	12.6	90.2	438.7	618.1	921.6	905.7	495.8	381.0	499.1	626.6	....	....
Financing													
Domestic	84a	−253.6	−298.9	−252.5	−319.5	−537.3	−559.8	155.1	386.3	426.5	−130.7	....	....
Foreign	85a	172.1	151.7	103.2	210.9	399.9	471.0	33.7	−99.8	−221.7	−22.9	....	....
Debt: Domestic	88a	....	....	....	....	....	190.2	160.1	730.1	724.0	763.3	....	....
Debt: Foreign	89a	1,345.7	....	1,704.4	1,861.5	2,255.1	2,313.4	3,185.1	3,121.9	4,317.1	6,246.2	....	....
National Accounts					*Millions of Maloti: Year Beginning April 1*								
Househ.Cons.Expend.,incl.NPISHs	96f	2,811.0	3,472.3	3,544.9	4,075.3	4,834.8	5,399.5	5,543.7	5,730.1	6,041.3	6,468.4	7,345.2	....
Government Consumption Expend	91f	346.4	403.6	486.5	607.2	658.6	800.0	1,023.4	1,080.8	1,139.8	1,188.2	1,323.0	....
Gross Fixed Capital Formation	93e	1,533.1	1,476.5	1,693.1	2,071.2	2,360.2	2,593.5	2,411.0	2,651.0	2,657.1	2,810.0	3,254.6	3,287.1
Changes in Inventories	93i	22.2	−16.1	−44.6	−24.3	7.8	−47.1	−93.4	−56.2	−178.2	−171.1	−135.4	—
Exports of Goods and Services	90c	430.7	559.6	642.8	720.4	965.6	1,261.3	1,320.7	1,322.4	1,775.6	2,771.7	4,112.9	4,195.3
Imports of Goods and Services (-)	98c	2,800.3	3,231.9	3,357.4	4,066.1	4,801.8	5,287.7	5,284.6	5,275.6	5,511.9	6,458.3	8,039.7	8,284.6
Gross Domestic Product (GDP)	99b	2,343.0	2,664.1	2,965.3	3,383.7	4,053.7	4,719.5	4,920.7	5,564.9	5,964.0	6,608.8	7,773.1	8,617.8
Net Primary Income from Abroad	98.n	1,215.1	1,325.2	1,348.5	1,410.9	1,421.5	1,538.9	1,384.7	1,492.5	1,522.3	1,509.9	1,700.5	1,823.2
Gross National Income (GNI)	99a	3,558.1	3,989.3	4,310.8	4,794.6	5,475.1	6,258.5	6,305.4	7,057.4	7,485.8	8,117.6	9,473.6	10,441.0
Net National Income	99e	4,190.8	4,664.4	5,103.1	5,713.2	6,473.4	7,396.3	7,272.9	8,055.5	8,529.8	9,402.4	10,751.3	11,714.7
GDP Volume 1995 Prices	99b.p	3,029.5	3,134.8	3,241.5	3,383.7	3,720.6	4,023.8	3,837.0	3,846.4	3,897.1	4,022.2	4,175.2	....
GDP Volume (2000=100)	99bvp	77.7	80.4	83.2	86.8	95.5	103.3	98.5	98.7	100.0	103.2	107.1	....
GDP Deflator (2000=100)	99bip	50.5	55.5	59.8	65.3	71.2	76.6	83.8	94.5	100.0	107.4	121.7	....
					Millions: Midyear Estimates								
Population	99z	1.62	1.64	1.66	1.68	1.71	1.73	1.75	1.77	1.78	1.79	1.80	1.80

Liberia 668

		1992	1993	1994	1995	1996	1997	1998	1999	2000	2001	2002	2003
Exchange Rates						*Liberian Dollars per SDR: End of Period*							
Market Rate	aa	1.3750	1.3736	1.4599	1.4865	1.4380	1.3493	†60.8973	54.2141	55.6994	62.2081	88.3688	75.0415
					Liberian Dollars per US Dollar: End of Period (ae) Period Average (rf)								
Market Rate	ae	1.0000	1.0000	1.0000	1.0000	1.0000	1.0000	†43.2500	39.5000	42.7500	49.5000	65.0000	50.5000
Market Rate	rf	1.0000	1.0000	1.0000	1.0000	1.0000	1.0000	†41.5075	41.9025	40.9525	48.5833	61.7542	59.3788
Fund Position						*Millions of SDRs: End of Period*							
Quota	2f.s	71.30	71.30	71.30	71.30	71.30	71.30	71.30	71.30	71.30	71.30	71.30	71.30
SDRs	1b.s	–	–	–	–	–	–	–	–	–	–	–	–
Reserve Position in the Fund	1c.s	.03	.03	.03	.03	.03	.03	.03	.03	.03	.03	.03	.03
Total Fund Cred.&Loans Outstg	2tl	226.52	226.52	225.83	225.74	225.74	225.70	225.26	224.82	224.36	223.91	223.67	223.67
International Liquidity						*Millions of US Dollars: End of Period*							
Total Reserves minus Gold	1l.d	.98	2.36	5.07	28.09	.38	.42	.62	.43	.27	.48	3.30	7.88
SDRs	1b.d	–	–	–	–	–	–	–	–	–	–	–	–
Reserve Position in the Fund	1c.d	.04	.04	.04	.04	.04	.04	.04	.04	.04	.04	.04	.04
Foreign Exchange	1d.d	.94	2.32	5.03	28.05	.34	.38	.58	.39	.23	.44	3.26	7.84
Monetary Authorities: Other Liab.	4..d	3.13	9.45	9.08	9.68	12.40	12.56	10.87	10.48	9.78	6.38	7.16	7.16
Banking Institutions: Assets	7a.d	13.78	49.05	9.46	12.04	9.49	15.59	10.36	16.71	12.39	11.04	10.30	17.73
Liabilities	7b.d	36.97	17.86	46.33	15.35	5.12	8.44	2.47	3.01	10.01	11.87	9.65	1.09
Monetary Authorities						*Millions of Liberian Dollars: End of Period*							
Foreign Assets	11	1.0	2.4	5.1	28.1	.4	.4	26.7	17.0	†11.4	23.8	214.4	397.8
Claims on Central Government	12a	1,072.9	1,264.1	1,284.9	1,513.0	1,803.1	1,916.2	35,687.0	32,605.1	†36,643.0	41,690.6	59,003.5	49,822.1
Claims on Nonfin.Pub.Enterprises	12c	4.8	4.8	4.8	4.8	5.6	5.6	5.8	5.5	†–	–	.8	.5
Claims on Private Sector	12d	12.0	17.8	15.5	15.4	20.5	20.2	25.5	24.6	†48.9	16.5	44.7	55.0
Claims on Banking Institutions	12e	23.8	23.4	51.4	61.5	2.5	2.3	4.3	1.7	†77.3	134.9	162.1	65.9
Claims on Nonbank Financial Insts	12g	3.8	.7	.7	–	.2	.2	1.5	1.5	†–	–	–	–
Reserve Money	14	411.0	522.9	551.1	723.4	852.6	920.5	938.4	979.9	†1,384.7	1,548.2	1,645.9	1,732.7
of which: Currency Outside Banks	14a	154.9	274.1	302.9	485.8	568.4	576.6	565.5	556.9	†698.3	845.1	1,045.0	1,303.6
Time Deposits	15	1.4	2.2	2.1	2.7	3.9	4.8	3.0	1.7	†533.2	716.9	–	–
Foreign Liabilities	16c	543.9	571.5	622.4	651.1	646.9	622.4	28,629.2	25,893.0	†27,242.9	30,922.3	44,487.4	38,133.7
Central Government Deposits	16d	7.8	71.6	74.2	15.1	18.6	20.0	137.4	71.0	†–	34.0	46.2	294.4
Capital Accounts	17a	73.2	69.6	60.8	12.7	42.3	61.8	9,259.2	7,735.2	†7,675.1	8,876.7	14,414.5	11,336.4
Other Items (Net)	17r	81.1	75.4	51.8	217.7	267.8	315.3	–3,216.4	–2,025.2	†–55.2	–232.4	–1,168.6	–1,155.7
Banking Institutions						*Millions of Liberian Dollars: End of Period*							
Reserves	20	143.9	217.3	215.4	201.8	188.4	240.0	768.5	815.2	†1,174.5	1,402.8	1,532.3	1,225.2
Foreign Assets	21	13.8	49.1	9.5	12.0	9.5	15.6	447.9	660.2	†529.8	546.7	669.5	895.4
Claims on Central Government	22a	3.1	8.8	5.4	5.1	3.5	–	306.2	358.1	†425.3	580.9	921.3	732.2
Claims on Nonfin.Pub.Enterprises	22c	55.6	82.7	63.1	21.0	5.7	7.9	12.2	44.5	†39.5	64.6	64.3	42.1
Claims on Private Sector	22d	152.8	127.2	222.7	176.0	55.4	82.7	1,148.1	900.9	†663.2	877.0	1,064.4	1,005.2
Claims on Nonbank Financial Insts	22g	.3	.3	–	2.1	5.3	–	–	–	†123.6	181.2	14.1	164.2
Demand Deposits	24	111.4	151.6	155.3	167.0	127.4	110.0	1,005.5	1,247.9	†898.8	851.6	1,318.2	1,203.2
Time and Savings Deposits	25	156.3	274.5	324.4	360.9	195.5	235.5	335.8	324.7	†391.5	422.4	535.4	433.9
Foreign Liabilities	26c	37.0	17.9	46.3	15.3	5.1	8.4	106.9	119.0	†427.9	587.4	627.2	55.1
Central Government Deposits	26d	29.9	30.5	35.3	30.3	10.6	51.1	112.0	165.4	†134.1	122.8	80.3	39.6
Credit from Monetary Authorities	26g	20.7	20.0	23.7	16.9	–	–	1.9	2.0	†104.3	115.8	37.0	44.3
Capital Accounts	27a	48.3	22.7	33.5	3.8	3.4	–5.5	36.3	685.6	†889.9	1,247.7	1,342.1	1,242.4
Other Items (Net)	27r	–33.9	–31.7	–102.4	–176.3	–74.1	–53.4	1,084.5	234.3	†–42.8	153.4	325.7	1,045.7
Banking Survey						*Millions of Liberian Dollars: End of Period*							
Foreign Assets (Net)	31n	–566.1	–538.0	–654.2	–626.3	–642.2	–614.9	–28,261.6	–25,334.9	†–27,129.6	–30,939.3	–44,230.7	–36,895.6
Domestic Credit	32	1,267.8	1,404.4	1,487.6	1,692.0	1,870.1	1,961.7	36,936.9	33,703.9	†37,809.3	43,253.9	60,986.5	51,487.4
Claims on Central Govt. (Net)	32an	1,038.4	1,170.8	1,180.7	1,472.6	1,777.4	1,845.0	35,743.8	32,726.8	†36,934.3	42,114.7	59,798.2	50,220.4
Claims on Nonfin.Pub.Enterprises	32c	60.4	87.5	68.0	25.8	11.3	13.5	18.0	50.1	†39.5	64.6	65.1	42.6
Claims on Private Sector	32d	164.9	145.1	238.2	191.5	75.8	102.9	1,173.6	925.5	†712.1	893.5	1,109.1	1,060.2
Claims on Nonbank Fin. Insts	32g	4.1	1.0	.7	2.1	5.5	.2	1.5	1.5	†123.6	181.2	14.1	164.2
Money	34	266.4	425.8	458.3	652.8	696.2	686.8	1,571.0	1,804.8	†1,597.0	1,703.4	2,363.5	2,507.0
Quasi-Money	35	157.7	276.7	326.5	363.6	199.4	240.3	338.8	326.4	†924.7	1,139.3	535.4	433.9
Capital Accounts	37a	121.5	92.2	94.3	16.6	45.7	56.3	9,295.6	8,420.7	†8,565.0	10,124.4	15,756.6	12,578.8
Other Items (Net)	37r	156.1	71.7	–45.7	32.7	286.6	363.5	–2,530.0	–2,182.9	†–559.1	–804.6	–1,899.7	–927.9
Money plus Quasi-Money	35l	424.1	702.5	784.8	1,016.4	895.6	927.0	1,909.8	2,131.2	†2,521.8	2,842.7	2,898.9	2,940.9
Interest Rates						*Percent Per Annum*							
Savings Rate	60k	....	....	6.16	6.12	....	6.08	6.00	6.02	5.83	5.63	5.43	4.50
Deposit Rate	60l	....	....	6.34	6.37	....	6.43	6.22	6.25	6.18	5.94	6.25	5.29
Lending Rate	60p	....	....	14.53	15.57	....	16.83	†21.74	16.72	20.53	22.14	20.21	17.06
						Millions: Midyear Estimates							
Population	99z	2.08	2.06	2.07	2.13	2.24	2.40	Ü 2.58	2.77	2.94	3.10	3.24	3.37

2004, International Monetary Fund : *International Financial Statistics Yearbook*

Libya 672

		1992	1993	1994	1995	1996	1997	1998	1999	2000	2001	2002	2003
Exchange Rates			*SDRs per Dinar: End of Period (ac) US Dollars per Dinar: End of Period (ag)*
Official Rate	ac	2.4138	2.2400	1.5770	1.5770	1.5770	1.5770	1.5770	1.5770	1.4204	1.2240	.6080	.5175
Official Rate	ag	3.3190	3.0768	2.3022	2.3442	2.2677	2.1278	2.2205	2.1645	1.8507	1.5382	.8266	.7690
Fund Position			*Millions of SDRs: End of Period*
Quota	2f.s	818	818	818	818	818	818	818	1,124	1,124	1,124	1,124	1,124
SDRs	1b.s	278	303	325	350	374	398	426	373	413	441	449	462
Reserve Position in the Fund	1c.s	319	319	319	319	319	319	319	396	396	396	396	396
Total Fund Cred.&Loans Outstg.	2tl	–	–	–	–	–	–	–	–	–	–	–	–
International Liquidity			*Millions of US Dollars Unless Otherwise Indicated: End of Period*
Total Reserves minus Gold	1l.d	6,182e	....	....	....	....	....	7,270	7,280	12,461	14,800	14,307	19,584
SDRs	1b.d	383	417	474	520	538	538	600	511	538	554	610	686
Reserve Position in the Fund	1c.d	439	438	466	474	459	430	449	543	515	497	538	588
Foreign Exchange	1d.d	5,361e	....	....	....	....	....	6,221	6,226	11,408	13,749	13,159	18,310
Gold (Million Fine Troy Ounces)	1ad	3.600	....	....	....	....	....	4.616	4.624	4.624	4.624	4.624	4.624
Gold (National Valuation)	1and	152	....	....	....	....	....	194	194	194	194	194	194
Deposit Money Banks: Assets	7a.d	435	401	319	380	483	979	619	735	937	928	637	606
Liabilities	7b.d	694	171	169	109	207	2,965	2,165	1,834	1,461	2,484	1,476	1,224
Monetary Authorities			*Millions of Dinars: End of Period*
Foreign Assets	11	2,037.8	1,435.5	1,745.0	2,487.4	2,815.9	3,658.5	3,658.5	3,813.4	7,295.9	9,489.2	19,192.3	27,757.4
Claims on Central Government	12a	4,726.5	4,740	4,815.0	5,064.6	5,107.4	5,406.7	5,927.2	5,320.1	6,832.6	6,789.0	6,789.5	6,791.9
Claims on Nonfin.Pub.Enterprises	12c	1,168.0	1,230.0	1,890.1	2,208.3	2,336.3	1,671.4	1,559.2	1,704.0	2,567.9	2,694.2	4,063.2	5,695.9
Claims on Private Sector	12d	6.3	6.3	6.7	6.6	6.4	6.4	6.4	7.1	8.0	9.5	11.1	12.8
Claims on Deposit Money Banks	12e	298.8	298.8	283.5	283.5	200.0	144.4	144.4	144.4	115.5	86.6	57.8	28.9
Reserve Money	14	4,092.3	3,992.6	4,627.4	4,985.7	5,434.8	†5,821.2	5,760.4	5,455.4	5,404.8	5,946.9	6,100.7	6,782.3
of which: Currency Outside DMBs	14a	1,982.2	2,216.8	1,989.8	2,035.4	2,419.8	2,534.2	2,698.6	2,657.5	2,711.0	2,577.4	2,630.5	2,780.1
Nonfin.Pub.Enterp.Dep.	14e	312.0	264.3	478.8	603.9	414.5	536.2	176.3	133.7	200.8	297.8	349.3	240.8
Time & Foreign Currency Deposits	15	419.8	529.5	615.0	701.4	522.8	†62.6	65.3	19.4	38.9	245.2	204.3	200.0
Restricted Deposits	16b	175.6	248.6	988.1	344.8	414.2	414.2	332.0	428.1	561.9	738.2	1,185.0	1,702.2
Foreign Liabilities	16c	–	–	–	–	–	618.3	476.9	623.8	1,501.5	1,673.2	3,297.6	4,920.5
Central Government Deposits	16d	694.1	676.6	678.2	708.3	741.2	†3,368.6	3,696.4	4,450.6	6,941.0	7,439.1	7,936.3	12,199.9
Capital Accounts	17a	354.3	356.2	367.3	367.3	367.3	†1,214.3	1,250.0	1,076.6	1,520.0	2,634.6	9,919.5	13,991.0
Other Items (Net)	17r	2,501.3	1,907.1	1,464.3	2,942.9	2,985.8	–611.4	–285.3	–1,064.9	851.9	391.3	1,470.3	491.1
Deposit Money Banks			*Millions of Dinars: End of Period*
Reserves	20	1,786.3	1,506.6	2,204.6	2,336.6	2,606.1	2,705.8	2,776.1	2,428.4	2,357.2	2,346.1	2,458.7	3,192.1
Foreign Assets	21	131.1	130.3	138.6	162.2	212.8	460.3	278.6	339.7	506.4	603.1	770.1	787.5
Claims on Central Government	22a	1,444.1	1,444.1	1,451.1	1,451.1	1,436.5	1,387.5	1,387.5	1,387.5	1,392.5	1,810.5	1,810.5	1,810.5
Claims on Nonfin. Pub. Enterprises	22c	109.1	127.1	146.2	153.2	328.8	†1,440.7	1,491.9	1,866.4	1,776.5	3,163.7	3,649.9	3,257.1
Claims on Private Sector	22d	2,737.3	3,001.2	3,223.6	3,468.1	2,878.4	3,109.1	3,123.4	3,989.1	4,004.0	4,039.0	4,004.9	4,450.2
Claims on Other Banking Insts	22f	....	....	....	....	....	....	....	40.3	49.7	27.3	29.1	27.6
Claims on Nonbank Financial Insts	22g	....	....	....	....	....	....	....	124.2	506.7	75.6	69.8	123.0
Demand Deposits	24	2,693.0	2,728.2	3,417.3	3,612.1	3,489.4	3,556.5	3,753.4	4,162.8	4,363.1	4,370.1	4,753.6	5,209.9
Time & Foreign Currency Deposits	25	1,019.3	1,069.4	1,260.5	1,550.4	1,744.0	1,555.2	1,838.0	†2,202.1	2,156.7	2,271.6	1,983.7	2,369.5
Restricted Deposits	26b	236.9	208.7	173.9	271.7	277.3	368.1	331.0	266.5	341.0	709.1	633.9	768.2
Foreign Liabilities	26c	209.0	55.7	60.8	38.5	75.7	†1,393.3	975.0	847.4	789.5	1,614.8	1,785.2	1,592.0
Central Government Deposits	26d	181.0	175.5	171.5	114.3	340.0	385.0	354.9	284.6	267.9	259.0	609.3	566.0
Credit from Monetary Authorities	26g	291.5	299.9	283.5	283.5	203.6	147.9	147.9	147.9	119.1	90.2	61.3	32.4
Capital Accounts	27a	373.3	391.2	405.2	411.8	491.5	601.3	659.7	728.5	793.9	962.4	1,202.1	1,362.5
Other Items (Net)	27r	1,204.0	1,280.6	1,391.7	1,289.9	841.1	1,096.3	997.9	1,535.8	1,761.8	1,787.8	1,763.9	1,747.5
Monetary Survey			*Millions of Dinars: End of Period*
Foreign Assets (Net)	31n	1,960.0	1,510.1	1,822.8	2,611.1	2,953.0	2,107.2	2,485.2	2,681.9	5,511.3	6,804.3	14,879.4	22,032.4
Domestic Credit	32	9,316.2	9,696.7	10,683.0	11,529.3	11,012.6	†9,268.2	9,444.3	9,703.5	9,929.0	10,910.7	11,882.4	9,403.1
Claims on Central Govt. (Net)	32an	5,295.5	5,332.1	5,416.4	5,693.1	5,462.7	†3,040.6	3,263.4	1,972.4	1,016.2	901.4	54.4	–4,163.5
Claims on Nonfin.Pub.Enterprises	32c	1,277.1	1,357.1	2,036.3	2,361.5	2,665.1	†3,112.1	3,051.1	3,570.4	4,344.4	5,857.9	7,713.1	8,953.0
Claims on Private Sector	32d	2,743.7	3,007.5	3,230.3	3,474.7	2,884.8	3,115.5	3,129.8	3,996.2	4,012.0	4,048.5	4,016.0	4,463.0
Claims on Other Banking Insts	32f	....	....	....	....	....	–	–	40.3	49.7	27.3	29.1	27.6
Claims on Nonbank Fin. Insts	32g	....	....	....	....	....	....	....	124.2	506.7	75.6	69.8	123.0
Money	34	4,987.2	5,209.3	5,885.9	6,251.4	6,323.7	6,654.5	6,683.8	7,001.2	7,313.5	7,402.7	7,843.4	8,340.9
Quasi-Money	35	1,439.0	1,598.9	1,875.5	2,251.8	2,266.8	1,617.8	1,903.3	2,221.5	2,195.6	2,516.8	2,188.0	2,569.5
Restricted Deposits	36b	412.5	457.3	1,162.0	616.5	691.5	782.3	663.0	694.6	902.9	1,447.3	1,818.9	2,470.4
Capital Accounts	37a	727.6	747.4	766.1	772.7	852.4	1,815.6	1,909.7	1,805.1	2,313.9	3,597.0	11,121.6	15,353.5
Other Items (Net)	37r	3,709.9	3,193.7	2,810.1	4,242.6	3,824.9	505.8	770	663.0	2,714.5	2,750.9	3,789.9	2,701.3
Money plus Quasi-Money	35l	6,426.2	6,808.2	7,761.4	8,503.2	8,590.5	8,272.3	8,587.1	9,222.7	9,509.1	9,919.5	10,031.4	10,910.4
Other Banking Institutions			*Millions of Dinars: End of Period*
Cash	40	75.70	73.10	53.60	41.40	40.80	54.40	29.40	85.50	96.40	269.20	187.60	....
Claims on Private Sector	42d	43.40	40.30	38.80	48.90	51.00	63.90	63.50	97.40	118.70	201.60	350.60	....
Capital Accounts	47a	80.20	82.80	84.70	85.50	86.40	89.60	90.70	84.40	88.40	89.10	92.20	....
Other Items (Net)	47r	38.90	30.60	7.60	4.80	5.40	28.70	2.20	98.50	126.70	381.70	445.90	....

Libya 672

		1992	1993	1994	1995	1996	1997	1998	1999	2000	2001	2002	2003
Interest Rates						*Percent Per Annum*							
Discount Rate (End of Period)	60	5.0	5.0	....	....	....	....	3.0	5.0	5.0	5.0	5.0	5.0
Money Market Rate	60b	4.0	4.0	....	....	....	....	4.0	4.0	4.0	4.0	4.0	4.0
Deposit Rate	60l	5.5	5.5	....	....	....	....	....	3.2	3.0	3.0	3.0	3.0
Lending Rate	60p	7.0	7.0	....	....	....	....	....	7.0	7.0	7.0	7.0	7.0
Production						*Index Numbers (2000=100): Period Averages*							
Consumer Prices	64	71.7	79.7	83.7	89.8	93.4	96.7	100.3	†103.0	100.0	91.2	82.3	....
Crude Petroleum Production	66aa	107.4	99.4	99.6	100.4	101.4	102.1	99.4	95.3	100.0	98.5	95.3	103.7
International Transactions						*Millions of Dinars*							
Exports	70	3,038.8	2,477.6	3,177.2	3,222.1	3,578.7	3,455.6	2,374.1	3,682.2	5,221.5	5,394.0	10,177.0	....
Imports, c.i.f.	71	1,422.1	1,711.3	1,487.9	1,728.5	1,914.8	2,138.6	2,203.8	1,928.6	1,911.4	2,660.4	5,585.7	....
						2000=100							
Volume of Exports	72	132.5	126.6	133.3	†132.5	122.6	129.0	94.2	107.9	100.0	110.5	94.6	....
Volume of Imports	73	165.9	188.6	162.9	†170.9	184.8	208.4	156.1	146.8	100.0	173.2	213.8	....
Unit Value of Exports	74	47.1	41.2	49.4	†52.1	63.6	57.4	48.3	65.3	100.0	102.6	216.9	....
Unit Value of Imports	75	66.2	67.3	71.5	†79.7	82.1	83.3	87.5	103.1	100.0	98.1	116.7	....
Balance of Payments						*Millions of US Dollars: Minus Sign Indicates Debit*							
Current Account, n.i.e.	78ald	1,407	−1,366	26	1,650	1,220	1,550	−351	2,136	....	....	....	....
Goods: Exports f.o.b.	78aad	10,191	8,544	7,704	7,483	7,930	8,177	5,326	7,276	....	....	....	....
Goods: Imports f.o.b.	78abd	−7,545	−8,431	−6,760	−5,181	−5,845	−5,928	−4,930	−4,302	....	....	....	....
Trade Balance	78acd	2,647	113	945	2,302	2,085	2,249	396	2,974	....	....	....	....
Services: Credit	78add	100	55	37	31	26	28	40	59	....	....	....	....
Services: Debit	78aed	−1,206	−1,174	−718	−597	−790	−765	−877	−989	....	....	....	....
Balance on Goods & Services	78afd	1,541	−1,006	263	1,736	1,321	1,512	−441	2,044	....	....	....	....
Income: Credit	78agd	776	571	448	435	474	530	533	546	....	....	....	....
Income: Debit	78ahd	−452	−602	−403	−302	−295	−293	−218	−235	....	....	....	....
Balance on Gds, Serv. & Inc.	78aid	1,865	−1,037	308	1,870	1,500	1,748	−127	2,355	....	....	....	....
Current Transfers, n.i.e.: Credit	78ajd	7	8	5	4	3	3	4	7	....	....	....	....
Current Transfers: Debit	78akd	−465	−337	−286	−224	−283	−202	−229	−226	....	....	....	....
Capital Account, n.i.e.	78bcd	−	−	−	....	....	....	....	....	....	....	....	....
Capital Account, n.i.e.: Credit	78bad	−	−	−	....	....	....	....	....	....	....	....	....
Capital Account: Debit	78bbd	−	−	−	....	....	....	....	....	....	....	....	....
Financial Account, n.i.e.	78bjd	333	−202	147	−207	186	−732	−467	−1,045	....	....	....	....
Direct Investment Abroad	78bdd	151	479	−26	−69	−52	−233	−256	−226	....	....	....	....
Dir. Invest. in Rep. Econ., n.i.e.	78bed	99	58	−73	−88	−112	−68	−128	−128	....	....	....	....
Portfolio Investment Assets	78bfd	−55	−62	−126	−106	−	−641	−178	−3	....	....	....	....
Equity Securities	78bkd	−55	−62	−126	−106	−	−641	−178	−3	....	....	....	....
Debt Securities	78bld	−	−	−	....	....	....	....	....	....	....	....	....
Portfolio Investment Liab., n.i.e.	78bgd	−	−	−	....	....	....	....	....	....	....	....	....
Equity Securities	78bmd	−	−	−	....	....	....	....	....	....	....	....	....
Debt Securities	78bnd	−	−	−	....	....	....	....	....	....	....	....	....
Financial Derivatives Assets	78bwd	....	....	....	....	....	....	....	....	....	....	....	....
Financial Derivatives Liabilities	78bxd	....	....	....	....	....	....	....	....	....	....	....	....
Other Investment Assets	78bhd	188	−487	−1,754	−1,363	−1,435	−861	−138	−315	....	....	....	....
Monetary Authorities	78bod	2	241	−9	38	−27	38	−6	−650	....	....	....	....
General Government	78bpd	−35	−731	−1,728	−1,372	−1,275	−561	−497	496	....	....	....	....
Banks	78bqd	221	3	−17	−29	−133	−338	365	−161	....	....	....	....
Other Sectors	78brd	....	....	....	....	....	....	....	....	....	....	....	....
Other Investment Liab., n.i.e.	78bid	−50	−191	2,126	1,419	1,785	1,071	233	−373	....	....	....	....
Monetary Authorities	78bsd	−31	96	169	171	367	−181	−5	−78	....	....	....	....
General Government	78btd	82	213	1,942	1,301	1,392	1,305	221	−230	....	....	....	....
Banks	78bud	−100	−499	14	−53	27	−52	17	−65	....	....	....	....
Other Sectors	78bvd	....	....	....	....	....	....	....	....	....	....	....	....
Net Errors and Omissions	78cad	38	−149	100	258	−185	735	392	−403	....	....	....	....
Overall Balance	78cbd	1,778	−1,716	274	1,701	1,221	1,553	−426	688	....	....	....	....
Reserves and Related Items	79dad	−1,778	1,716	−274	−1,701	−1,221	−1,553	426	−688	....	....	....	....
Reserve Assets	79dbd	−1,778	1,716	−274	−1,701	−1,221	−1,553	426	−688	....	....	....	....
Use of Fund Credit and Loans	79dcd	−	−	−	−	−	−	−	−	....	....	....	....
Exceptional Financing	79ded	....	....	....	....	....	....	....	....	....	....	....	....
National Accounts						*Millions of Dinars*							
Househ.Cons.Expend.,incl.NPISHs	96f	5,137	5,989	5,993	6,276	6,809	8,368	8,072	8,514	8,150	8,994	13,939	....
Government Consumption Expend.	91f	2,755	2,132	2,254	2,383	2,903	3,333	3,339	3,102	3,616	3,925	4,077	....
Gross Fixed Capital Formation	93e	1,008	1,504	1,622	1,245	1,640	1,685	1,397	1,536	2,214	2,158	3,366	....
Changes in Inventories	93i	152	15	6	54	248	64	127	46	74	74	150	....
Exports of Goods and Services	90c	2,919	2,636	2,695	3,116	3,490	3,790	2,468	3,374	6,186	5,478	11,645	....
Imports of Goods and Services (-)	98c	2,430	2,944	2,603	2,394	2,910	3,091	2,661	2,433	2,690	3,433	8,868	....
Gross Domestic Product (GDP)	99b	9,541	9,332	9,967	10,680	12,180	14,149	12,742	14,139	17,550	17,196	24,309	....
Net Primary Income from Abroad	98.n	−222	−91	−114	−146	−202	−201	−248	−243	−341	−445	−672	....
Gross National Income (GNI)	99a	9,319	9,241	9,853	10,534	11,978	13,948	12,494	13,896	17,209	16,751	23,637	....
						Millions: Midyear Estimates							
Population	99z	4.48	4.57	4.66	Ü 4.75	4.84	4.94	5.04	5.14	5.24	5.34	5.44	5.55

2004, International Monetary Fund : *International Financial Statistics Yearbook*

Lithuania 946

		1992	1993	1994	1995	1996	1997	1998	1999	2000	2001	2002	2003
Exchange Rates		\multicolumn{12}{c}{*Litai per SDR: End of Period*}
Official Rate	aa	5.211	5.357	5.839	5.946	5.752	5.397	5.632	5.490	5.212	5.027	4.502	4.104
		\multicolumn{12}{c}{*Litai per US Dollar: End of Period (ae) Period Average (rf)*}
Official Rate	ae	3.790	3.900	4.000	4.000	4.000	4.000	4.000	4.000	4.000	4.000	3.311	2.762
Official Rate	rf	1.773	4.344	3.978	4.000	4.000	4.000	4.000	4.000	4.000	4.000	3.677	3.061
Fund Position		\multicolumn{12}{c}{*Millions of SDRs: End of Period*}
Quota	2f.s	103.50	103.50	103.50	103.50	103.50	103.50	103.50	144.20	144.20	144.20	144.20	144.20
SDRs	1b.s	.94	54.71	10.38	12.22	7.09	7.95	11.50	3.19	1.01	14.67	39.31	.04
Reserve Position in the Fund	1c.s	.01	.01	.01	.01	.01	.01	.02	.02	.02	.02	.02	.02
Total Fund Cred.&Loans Outstg	2tl	17.25	87.98	134.55	175.95	190.11	200.46	179.83	167.76	147.06	120.32	89.27	30.19
International Liquidity		\multicolumn{12}{c}{*Millions of US Dollars Unless Otherwise Indicated: End of Period*}
Total Reserves minus Gold	1l.d	45.34	350.32	525.48	757.05	772.25	1,009.95	1,409.13	1,195.01	1,311.55	1,617.72	2,349.32	3,371.98
SDRs	1b.d	1.29	75.14	15.15	18.16	10.20	10.73	16.19	4.38	1.32	18.43	53.44	.06
Reserve Position in the Fund	1c.d	.01	.01	.01	.01	.01	.01	.02	.02	.02	.02	.02	.02
Foreign Exchange	1d.d	44.03	275.17	510.33	738.88	762.04	999.21	1,392.92	1,190.61	1,310.21	1,599.27	2,295.86	3,371.89
Gold (Million Fine Troy Ounces)	1ad	.1859	.1859	.1858	.1860	.1863	.1864	.1861	.1863	.1863	.1861	.1862	.1862
Gold (National Valuation)	1and	61.90	61.90	61.86	61.95	62.04	52.74	50.87	47.10	47.10	51.47	63.82	77.69
Monetary Authorities: Other Liab	4..d	106.17	28.05	26.38	.28	1.30	.35	.33	.25	.18	51.85	58.65	67.27
Banking Institutions: Assets	7a.d	....	77.77	96.68	123.35	293.60	370.63	302.15	423.30	693.30	751.85	723.77	926.83
Liabilities	7b.d	....	9.54	82.70	88.45	195.83	292.48	438.15	522.70	503.05	599.83	827.32	1,816.55
Monetary Authorities		\multicolumn{12}{c}{*Millions of Litai: End of Period*}
Foreign Assets	11	1,004.7	1,904.6	2,618.1	3,284.7	3,345.3	4,258.6	5,847.7	4,976.2	5,375.7	6,629.3	7,933.5	9,448.3
Claims on Central Government	12a	–	–	–	19.2	–	–	–	6.8	6.8	6.8	6.8	5.4
Claims on Private Sector	12d	–	1.4	5.9	12.1	9.9	7.6	6.9	6.1	5.5	6.4	7.8	9.6
Claims on Banking Institutions	12e	270.2	292.1	157.0	168.1	142.4	70.4	52.3	30.1	23.7	15.3	15.9	10.0
Claims on Nonbank Financial Insts	12g	–	–	–	.3	3.1	19.4	6.9	20.0	–	–	–	–
Reserve Money	14	413.8	1,256.8	1,812.4	2,446.2	2,499.3	3,308.8	4,260.4	4,088.3	3,952.4	4,279.6	5,168.0	6,540.2
of which: Currency Outside Banks	14a	....	791.3	1,334.3	1,907.0	1,899.3	2,535.5	2,800.4	2,738.7	2,658.3	2,919.9	3,756.4	4,632.0
Foreign Currency Deposits	15	–	–	1.9	43.8	19.8	8.2	6.5	1.5	.1	.1	.1	.1
Foreign Liabilities	16c	492.3	580.7	891.2	1,047.3	1,098.7	1,083.3	1,014.1	922.0	767.1	812.2	596.1	309.7
Central Government Deposits	16d	17.1	93.1	45.0	111.0	66.0	268.7	904.4	302.1	781.8	1,488.2	1,950.3	2,213.7
Counterpart Funds	16e	–	–	14.7	37.5	41.9	38.1	40.8	30.8	29.2	28.2	28.5	29.0
Central Government Lending Funds	16f	–	–	.6	.7	–	.6	1.5	–	–	–	–	–
Capital Accounts	17a	373.5	1,029.6	54.8	–77.8	–48.4	–247.3	–111.8	–90.4	117.2	270.4	453.2	612.6
Other Items (Net)	17r	–21.8	–762.1	–39.6	–124.3	–176.6	–104.3	–202.1	–215.1	–236.1	–220.9	–232.2	–232.0
Banking Institutions		\multicolumn{12}{c}{*Millions of Litai: End of Period*}
Reserves	20	....	469.0	464.1	522.7	583.6	742.1	1,447.5	1,342.3	1,282.4	1,343.1	1,391.8	1,897.1
Foreign Assets	21	....	303.3	386.7	493.4	1,174.4	1,482.5	1,208.6	1,693.2	2,773.2	3,007.4	2,396.7	2,560.0
Claims on Central Government	22a	....	–	240.8	505.2	860.7	1,890.0	1,965.5	1,665.9	2,151.1	2,637.3	2,950.8	2,691.3
Claims on State and Local Govts	22b	....	–	2.0	7.7	37.1	51.9	123.8	212.3	273.5	279.6	302.5	397.1
Claims on Nonfin.Pub.Enterprises	22c	....	409.3	398.6	237.5	134.4	109.4	272.7	276.9	304.5	253.1	197.8	148.0
Claims on Private Sector	22d	....	1,603.5	† 2,974.6	3,654.8	3,496.2	4,161.9	4,866.7	5,538.7	5,203.2	5,531.7	7,213.5	11,460.2
Claims on Nonbank Financial Insts	22g	....	5.0	20.6	49.5	44.7	150.2	462.8	448.3	513.5	791.3	980.5	1,358.0
Demand Deposits	24	....	954.4	1,134.8	1,566.5	1,694.3	2,543.1	2,757.9	2,528.9	3,002.6	3,808.0	4,553.0	5,891.9
Time, Savings,& Fgn.Currency Dep	25	....	926.8	1,879.5	2,086.2	1,793.3	2,153.8	2,750.0	3,695.5	4,782.8	5,946.2	6,505.4	7,001.5
Foreign Liabilities	26c	....	37.2	330.8	353.8	783.3	1,169.9	1,752.6	2,090.8	2,012.2	2,399.3	2,739.6	5,017.5
Central Government Deposits	26d	....	122.5	357.6	683.7	779.3	1,008.1	792.0	778.4	740.7	438.9	439.4	652.4
Counterpart Funds	26e	....	16.4	28.2	52.6	59.3	50.7	22.8	19.5	23.3	2.0	10.0	1.4
Central Government Lending Funds	26f	....	174.5	337.7	480.3	473.3	615.4	754.1	555.5	287.3	19.6	23.8	37.9
Credit from Monetary Authorities	26g	....	285.5	157.0	168.1	142.0	70.3	52.3	30.2	23.8	15.4	15.8	9.9
Capital Accounts	27a	....	467.7	936.1	996.7	1,448.1	2,021.4	2,690.4	2,849.7	2,928.6	1,992.6	2,226.6	2,484.5
Other Items (Net)	27r	....	–194.9	† –674.3	–917.1	–841.8	–1,044.7	–1,224.5	–1,370.9	–1,299.9	–778.5	–1,080.0	–585.3
Banking Survey		\multicolumn{12}{c}{*Millions of Litai: End of Period*}
Foreign Assets (Net)	31n	....	1,590.0	1,782.8	2,377.0	2,637.7	3,488.0	4,289.6	3,656.6	5,369.6	6,425.2	6,994.5	6,681.1
Domestic Credit	32	....	1,803.6	† 3,239.9	3,691.6	3,740.8	5,113.6	6,008.9	7,094.5	6,935.6	7,579.1	9,270.0	13,203.5
Claims on Central Govt. (Net)	32an	....	–215.6	–161.8	–270.3	15.4	613.2	269.1	592.2	635.4	717.0	567.9	–169.4
Claims on State and Local Govts	32b	....	–	2.0	7.7	37.1	51.9	123.8	212.3	273.5	279.6	302.5	397.1
Claims on Nonfin.Pub.Enterprises	32c	....	409.3	398.6	237.5	134.4	109.4	272.7	276.9	304.5	253.1	197.8	148.0
Claims on Private Sector	32d	....	1,604.9	† 2,980.5	3,666.9	3,506.1	4,169.5	4,873.6	5,544.8	5,208.7	5,538.1	7,221.3	11,469.8
Claims on Nonbank Fin. Insts	32g	....	5.0	20.6	49.8	47.8	169.6	469.7	468.3	513.5	791.3	980.5	1,358.0
Money	34	....	1,746.4	2,475.7	3,488.4	3,610.9	5,109.9	5,570.8	5,275.0	5,672.6	6,744.5	8,329.2	10,535.1
Quasi-Money	35	....	926.8	1,881.4	2,130.0	1,813.1	2,162.0	2,756.5	3,697.0	4,782.9	5,946.3	6,505.5	7,001.6
of which: Fgn. Currency Deposits	35b	....	681.4	1,169.6	1,462.9	1,325.4	1,539.0	2,006.8	2,724.6	3,554.5	4,181.5	3,613.8	3,427.0
Counterpart Funds	36e	....	16.4	42.9	90.1	101.2	88.8	63.6	50.3	52.5	30.2	38.5	30.4
Central Government Lending Funds	36f	....	174.5	338.3	481.0	473.3	616.0	755.6	555.5	287.3	19.6	23.8	37.9
Capital Accounts	37a	....	1,497.3	990.9	918.9	1,399.7	1,774.1	2,578.6	2,759.3	3,045.8	2,263.0	2,679.8	3,097.1
Other Items (Net)	37r	....	–967.8	† –706.5	–1,039.8	–1,019.7	–1,149.2	–1,426.6	–1,586.0	–1,535.9	–999.3	–1,312.3	–817.5
Money plus Quasi-Money	35l	....	2,673.2	4,357.1	5,618.4	5,424.0	7,271.9	8,327.3	8,972.0	10,455.5	12,690.8	14,834.7	17,536.7

Lithuania 946

		1992	1993	1994	1995	1996	1997	1998	1999	2000	2001	2002	2003
Interest Rates		\multicolumn{12}{c}{*Percent Per Annum*}
Money Market Rate	60b	....	....	69.48	26.73	20.26	9.55	†6.12	6.26	3.60	3.37	2.21	1.79
Treasury Bill Rate	60c	....	....	....	26.82	20.95	8.64	10.69	11.14	†9.27	5.68	3.72	2.61
Deposit Rate	60l	....	88.29	48.43	20.05	13.95	7.89	5.98	4.94	3.86	3.00	1.70	1.27
Lending Rate	60p	....	91.84	62.30	27.08	21.56	14.39	12.21	13.09	12.14	9.63	6.84	5.84
Prices, Production, Labor		\multicolumn{12}{c}{*Index Numbers (2000=100): Period Averages*}
Producer Prices	63	8.11	39.90	57.75	74.11	86.90	90.60	83.90	85.10	100.00	96.30	92.80	92.50
Consumer Prices	64	5.6	†28.7	49.4	68.9	85.9	93.5	98.3	†99.0	100.0	101.3	101.6	100.4
Wages: Average Earnings	65	6.6	21.5	35.4	50.7	68.5	84.5	95.2	100.7	100.0	100.9	103.0	106.5
Manufacturing Production	66	....	....	....	84.2	87.1	†94.1	107.3	94.9	100.0	116.1	119.2	135.9
Manufacturing Employment	67	203.1	159.4	127.2	†109.1	104.5	104.7	103.6	102.1	100.0	97.1	....	....
		\multicolumn{12}{c}{*Number in Thousands: Period Averages*}
Labor Force	67d	1,879	1,859	1,741	1,753	1,784	1,820	1,843	1,862	1,820	1,760	1,630	....
Employment	67e	1,855	1,778	1,656	1,632	1,620	1,571	1,489	1,457	1,398	1,352	1,406	1,438
Unemployment	67c	67	66	78	128	109	120	123	177	226	224	....	168
Unemployment Rate (%)	67r	3.5	3.5	4.5	7.3	6.2	6.7	6.5	10.0	12.6	12.9	....	11.3
International Transactions		\multicolumn{12}{c}{*Millions of Litai*}
Exports	70	....	8,707	8,077	10,820	13,420	15,441	14,842	12,015	14,193	17,117	19,117	21,263
Imports, c.i.f.	71	....	9,798	9,355	14,594	18,235	22,577	23,174	19,338	20,877	24,241	27,479	29,438
Balance of Payments		\multicolumn{12}{c}{*Millions of US Dollars: Minus Sign Indicates Debit*}
Current Account, n.i.e.	78ald	....	−85.7	−94.0	−614.4	−722.6	−981.3	−1,298.2	−1,194.0	−674.9	−573.6	−720.7	−1,278.4
Goods: Exports f.o.b.	78aad	....	2,025.8	2,029.2	2,706.1	3,413.2	4,192.4	3,961.6	3,146.7	4,050.4	4,889.0	6,028.4	7,657.8
Goods: Imports f.o.b.	78abd	....	−2,180.5	−2,234.1	−3,404.0	−4,309.3	−5,339.9	−5,479.9	−4,551.2	−5,154.1	−5,997.0	−7,343.3	−9,362.0
Trade Balance	78acd	....	−154.7	−204.9	−697.9	−896.2	−1,147.5	−1,518.3	−1,404.6	−1,103.8	−1,108.0	−1,314.9	−1,704.2
Services: Credit	78add	....	197.8	321.9	485.2	797.5	1,031.8	1,109.0	1,091.5	1,058.8	1,157.0	1,463.7	1,878.0
Services: Debit	78aed	....	−252.9	−376.5	−498.1	−676.7	−897.4	−868.5	−786.1	−678.7	−700.3	−915.0	−1,263.6
Balance on Goods & Services	78afd	....	−209.8	−259.4	−710.8	−775.4	−1,013.0	−1,277.8	−1,099.1	−723.7	−651.4	−766.1	−1,089.8
Income: Credit	78agd	....	12.5	21.4	50.9	52.0	80.4	124.6	114.8	185.5	205.7	191.6	235.2
Income: Debit	78ahd	....	−4.3	−12.8	−63.7	−143.0	−278.8	−380.0	−372.6	−379.3	−385.5	−375.0	−717.4
Balance on Gds, Serv. & Inc.	78aid	....	−201.5	−250.8	−723.7	−866.4	−1,211.4	−1,533.2	−1,356.8	−917.5	−831.1	−949.5	−1,572.0
Current Transfers, n.i.e.: Credit	78ajd	....	115.9	161.6	112.3	149.4	237.0	240.4	167.4	246.8	262.0	231.7	301.5
Current Transfers: Debit	78akd	....	−	−4.8	−3.0	−5.6	−7.0	−5.4	−4.6	−4.3	−4.5	−2.9	−7.8
Capital Account, n.i.e.	78bcd	....	−	12.9	−39.0	5.5	4.1	−1.7	−3.3	2.1	1.4	56.5	67.5
Capital Account, n.i.e.: Credit	78bad	....	−	12.9	3.3	5.5	4.5	.9	2.7	2.6	1.5	56.8	68.3
Capital Account: Debit	78bbd	....	−	−	−42.3	−	−.4	−2.6	−6.0	−.4	−.1	−.4	−.8
Financial Account, n.i.e.	78bjd	....	301.5	240.9	534.5	645.6	1,005.6	1,443.9	1,060.7	702.4	777.6	1,048.4	1,642.3
Direct Investment Abroad	78bdd	....	....	....	−1.0	−.1	−26.9	−4.2	−8.6	−3.7	−7.1	−17.7	−37.2
Dir. Invest. in Rep. Econ., n.i.e.	78bed	....	30.2	31.3	72.6	152.4	354.5	925.5	486.5	378.9	445.8	712.5	179.2
Portfolio Investment Assets	78bfd	....	−.9	−.2	−10.5	−26.9	7.7	−10.1	−1.9	−141.4	26.2	−124.5	29.8
Equity Securities	78bkd	....	−.9	−.2	−3.0	.8	.1	−.3	−3.0	−1.4	1.1	−3.7	−1.8
Debt Securities	78bld	....	....	....	−7.5	−27.7	7.6	−9.8	1.1	−140.0	25.1	−120.9	31.6
Portfolio Investment Liab., n.i.e.	78bgd	....	.6	4.6	26.6	89.6	180.5	−42.7	507.5	405.9	238.0	148.8	222.3
Equity Securities	78bmd	....	.6	4.6	6.2	15.9	30.5	11.4	8.9	121.5	−16.3	5.6	4.2
Debt Securities	78bnd	....	....	−	20.4	73.7	150.1	−54.1	498.6	284.4	254.3	143.2	218.0
Financial Derivatives Assets	78bwd	....	....	....	....	....	....	−	−	−	18.3	19.6	28.1
Financial Derivatives Liabilities	78bxd	....	....	....	....	....	....	−	−	−	−19.6	−22.7	−56.2
Other Investment Assets	78bhd	....	95.3	−26.4	−36.1	−170.4	−219.3	−24.0	−182.5	39.9	−225.0	154.7	−100.9
Monetary Authorities	78bod	....	....	....	67.0	.2	.1	−	−	−	−	−	−
General Government	78bpd	....	....	....	....	....	....	−	−	−	−2.6	−	−
Banks	78bqd	....	108.9	−17.3	−18.0	−139.5	−88.1	57.2	−125.7	−142.2	−158.2	212.7	−161.0
Other Sectors	78brd	....	−13.6	−9.2	−85.0	−31.1	−131.3	−81.2	−56.7	182.1	−64.2	−58.0	60.1
Other Investment Liab., n.i.e.	78bid	....	176.5	231.6	482.8	601.0	709.1	599.3	259.7	22.8	300.9	177.7	1,377.2
Monetary Authorities	78bsd	....	−	−.9	−25.1	1.0	−1.0	−	−.1	−102.0	51.7	−3.6	−8.0
General Government	78btd	....	255.7	85.5	178.5	228.5	42.9	129.3	212.0	−	−53.7	−70.6	−9.4
Banks	78bud	....	−62.9	75.8	10.8	108.5	104.3	177.9	99.9	53.1	169.4	111.8	737.6
Other Sectors	78bvd	....	−16.3	71.2	318.5	263.1	562.8	292.1	−52.1	71.7	133.5	140.0	657.0
Net Errors and Omissions	78cad	....	−7.4	−46.9	287.2	66.7	195.8	282.9	−42.2	128.3	153.6	78.5	181.2
Overall Balance	78cbd	....	208.5	112.8	168.3	−4.8	224.2	426.8	−178.7	158.0	359.0	462.7	612.7
Reserves and Related Items	79dad	....	−208.5	−112.8	−168.3	4.8	−224.2	−426.8	178.7	−158.0	−359.0	−462.7	−612.7
Reserve Assets	79dbd	....	−308.0	−179.7	−231.3	−15.9	−238.2	−398.8	195.3	−130.7	−325.0	−422.5	−531.2
Use of Fund Credit and Loans	79dcd	....	99.5	66.9	63.0	20.7	14.1	−28.0	−16.6	−27.3	−34.0	−40.2	−81.4
Exceptional Financing	79ded	....	....	−	−	−	−	−	−	−	−	−	−

2004, International Monetary Fund: *International Financial Statistics Yearbook*

Lithuania 946

		1992	1993	1994	1995	1996	1997	1998	1999	2000	2001	2002	2003
International Investment Position							*Millions of US Dollars*						
Assets	79aad	....	....	997.6	1,274.6	1,692.7	2,148.6	2,472.2	2,452.7	2,677.7	3,126.3	4,225.5	5,717.0
Direct Investment Abroad	79abd	....	....	.2	1.2	2.8	26.0	16.5	25.9	29.3	47.9	59.5	119.7
Portfolio Investment	79acd	....	....	.6	11.1	38.1	29.7	38.0	32.5	172.3	138.2	286.3	268.8
Equity Securities	79add	....	....	.2	3.1	2.6	2.9	2.9	5.9	6.0	4.9	10.5	11.8
Debt Securities	79aed	....	....	.5	7.9	35.5	26.8	35.1	26.7	166.4	133.2	275.8	257.0
Financial Derivatives	79ald	....	....	–	–	–	–	–	–	–	–	–	.2
Other Investment	79afd	....	....	409.4	443.4	817.5	1,030.2	957.7	1,152.1	1,117.4	1,271.1	1,459.7	1,878.7
Monetary Authorities	79agd	....	....	67.2	.2	.1	–	–	–	–	–	–	–
General Government	79ahd	....	....	–	–	–	–	–	–	–	–	–	–
Banks	79aid	....	....	103.3	119.2	243.3	331.3	273.7	390.5	539.7	636.5	504.0	736.3
Other Sectors	79ajd	....	....	238.9	323.9	574.1	699.0	684.0	761.7	577.7	634.5	955.6	1,142.4
Reserve Assets	79akd	....	....	587.4	819.0	834.3	1,062.7	1,460.0	1,242.1	1,358.7	1,669.2	2,420.0	3,449.7
Liabilities	79lad	....	....	1,115.8	1,795.8	2,813.2	3,964.8	4,928.8	6,114.1	6,693.3	7,331.4	9,373.3	12,575.8
Dir. Invest. in Rep. Economy	79lbd	....	....	262.2	353.9	700.3	1,040.6	1,625.3	2,063.0	2,334.3	2,665.5	3,981.3	4,959.8
Portfolio Investment	79lcd	....	....	12.9	40.5	306.8	416.1	368.2	833.6	1,140.4	1,312.6	1,511.2	2,077.3
Equity Securities	79ldd	....	....	5.8	12.4	31.5	61.3	67.1	62.0	128.1	95.6	111.0	144.0
Debt Securities	79led	....	....	7.2	28.1	275.3	354.7	301.1	771.6	1,012.3	1,217.1	1,400.3	1,933.3
Financial Derivatives	79lld	....	....	–	–	–	–	–	–	–	–	10.1	10.2
Other Investment	79lfd	....	....	840.7	1,401.4	1,806.1	2,508.1	2,935.3	3,217.5	3,218.6	3,353.3	3,870.5	5,528.6
Monetary Authorities	79lgd	....	....	221.6	261.6	275.1	270.8	253.5	230.5	191.8	203.1	180.0	112.1
General Government	79lhd	....	....	235.2	424.0	447.4	549.2	694.2	881.3	767.0	694.1	669.2	717.7
Banks	79lid	....	....	86.1	99.2	182.3	282.8	463.3	539.8	568.2	691.1	933.4	1,910.2
Other Sectors	79ljd	....	....	297.8	616.7	901.3	1,405.4	1,524.3	1,566.0	1,691.6	1,765.0	2,087.9	2,788.5
Government Finance						*Millions of Litai: Year Ending December 31*							
Deficit (-) or Surplus	80	....	−694.2	−797.0	−1,151.5	−1,145.1	†−735.8	−183.6	−3,006.6	−584.7	−171.8	−593.3	....
Total Revenue and Grants	81y	....	2,693.6	4,034.1	5,661.1	7,157.3	†10,198.6	11,474.9	11,051.0	11,135.3	11,999.1	14,180.0	....
Revenue	81	....	2,688.1	4,031.9	5,661.1	7,128.8	†10,198.3	11,474.9	11,051.0	11,135.3	11,759.2	13,846.8	....
Grants	81z	....	5.5	2.2	–	28.5	.3	–	–	–	239.9	333.2	....
Exp.& Lending Minus Repayments	82z	....	3,387.8	4,831.1	6,812.6	8,302.4	†10,934.4	11,658.5	14,057.6	11,720.0	12,170.9	14,773.3	....
Expenditure	82	....	2,475.3	4,292.1	6,079.1	7,894.1	†10,515.0	13,037.6	13,260.8	12,447.3	12,616.8	15,098.8	....
Lending Minus Repayments	83	....	912.5	539.0	733.5	408.3	419.4	−1,379.1	796.8	−727.3	−445.9	−325.5	....
Total Financing													
Domestic	84a	....	71.4	518.2	417.9	138.7	†451.6	−574.1	129.1	−334.2	−307.2	178.8	....
Foreign	85a	....	622.8	278.8	733.6	1,006.4	†284.2	757.7	2,877.5	918.9	479.0	414.5	....
Total Debt by Currency	88z	....	1,749.4	2,639.1	4,470.6	4,749.9	8,077.4	9,613.6	12,069.3	12,729.9	12,903.6	13,161.5	13,137.3
National	88b	....	514.6	654.3	1,111.4	2,024.0	2,470.1	2,876.1	2,354.1	2,827.4	3,047.4	3,983.7	4,267.0
Foreign	89b	....	1,234.8	1,984.8	3,359.2	2,725.9	5,607.3	6,737.5	9,715.2	9,902.5	9,856.2	9,177.8	8,870.3
National Accounts							*Millions of Litai*						
Househ.Cons.Expend.,incl.NPISHs	96f	2,309	8,474	11,489	16,240	20,611	23,812	26,431	27,513	28,713	30,540	33,303	36,081
Government Consumption Expend	91f	445	1,800	3,319	5,602	7,201	8,967	10,767	9,634	9,854	9,598	10,002	10,507
Gross Fixed Capital Formation	93e	783	2,677	3,905	5,460	6,902	9,049	10,723	9,614	8,565	9,785	10,549	11,569
Changes in Inventories	93i	−247	−455	−792	274	−214	619	605	107	327	122	664	632
Exports of Goods and Services	90c	795	9,567	9,361	12,765	16,843	20,897	20,282	16,953	20,437	24,182	27,411	28,867
Imports of Goods and Services (-)	98c	679	10,472	10,378	15,609	19,944	24,949	25,393	21,350	23,331	26,789	30,291	31,934
Gross Domestic Product (GDP)	99b	3,406	11,590	16,904	25,568	32,290	39,378	44,377	43,359	45,526	48,379	51,633	55,737
Net Primary Income from Abroad	98.n	....	34	34	−51	−364	−794	−1,022	−1,031	−775	−719	−642	−1,494
Gross National Income (GNI)	99a	....	11,624	16,938	25,516	31,926	38,584	43,356	42,328	44,751	47,660	50,991	54,243
Net Current Transf.from Abroad	98t	....	508	624	437	575	920	940	651	970	1,030	814	....
Gross Nat'l Disposable Inc.(GNDI)	99i	....	12,132	17,562	25,302	31,872	38,763	43,597	42,323	44,969	47,878	50,984	....
Gross Saving	99s	....	1,859	2,754	3,276	3,801	5,748	6,148	4,959	6,204	7,621	8,537	8,544
Consumption of Fixed Capital	99cf	....	1,040	1,496	2,861	4,219	5,067	5,649	6,020	6,301	6,667	6,834	7,007
GDP Volume 2000 Prices	99b.p	....	....	....	37,086	38,821	41,541	44,565	43,810	45,526	48,429	51,701	56,335
GDP Volume (2000=100)	99bvp	104.3	87.4	78.9	†81.5	85.3	91.2	97.9	96.2	100.0	106.4	113.6	123.7
GDP Deflator (2000=100)	99bip	7.2	29.1	47.1	68.9	83.2	94.8	99.6	99.0	100.0	99.9	99.9	98.9
						Millions: Midyear Estimates							
Population	99z	3.69	3.65	3.60	3.56	3.54	3.53	3.52	3.51	3.50	3.48	3.47	3.44

Luxembourg 137

		1992	1993	1994	1995	1996	1997	1998	1999	2000	2001	2002	2003
Exchange Rates		\multicolumn{12}{c}{*Francs per SDR through 1998, Euros per SDR Thereafter: End of Period*}
Market Rate..................................	aa	45.623	49.599	46.478	43.725	46.022	49.814	48.682	1.3662	1.4002	1.4260	1.2964	1.1765
		\multicolumn{12}{c}{*Francs per US Dollar through 1998, Euros per US Dollar Thereafter: End of Period (ae) Period Average (rf)*}
Market Rate..................................	ae	33.180	36.110	31.838	29.415	32.005	36.920	34.575	.9954	1.0747	1.1347	.9536	.7918
Market Rate..................................	rf	32.150	34.597	33.456	29.480	30.962	35.774	36.299	.9386	1.0854	1.1175	1.0626	.8860
		\multicolumn{12}{c}{*Francs per ECU: End of Period (ea) Period Average (eb)*}
ECU Rate......................................	ea	40.178	40.266	39.161	38.697	40.102	40.781	40.340	....	....	....	....	....
ECU Rate......................................	eb	41.604	40.468	39.661	38.548	39.295	40.529	40.621	....	....	....	....	....
		\multicolumn{12}{c}{*Index Numbers (2000=100): Period Averages*}
Market Rate (1995=100)................	ahx	91.8	85.2	88.2	100.0	95.1	82.4	81.2	....	....	....	....	....
Nominal Effective Exchange Rate.....	nec	101.7	101.6	102.8	104.7	103.5	101.5	101.3	101.0	100.0	99.9	100.1	101.4
Real Effective Exchange Rate...........	rec	101.7	101.9	102.8	104.8	102.9	100.6	100.3	100.0	100.0	100.3	100.9	102.6
Fund Position		\multicolumn{12}{c}{*Millions of SDRs: End of Period*}
Quota...	2f.s	135.50	135.50	135.50	135.50	135.50	135.50	135.50	279.10	279.10	279.10	279.10	279.10
SDRs...	1b.s	6.62	6.98	7.22	7.46	7.75	8.04	8.72	1.78	3.22	5.00	6.72	8.29
Reserve Position in the Fund...........	1c.s	25.85	23.58	23.61	22.94	23.56	21.75	59.37	54.37	55.47	78.95	104.75	120.26
of which: Outstg.Fund Borrowing...	2c	–	–	–	–	–	–	31.34	–	–	–	–	–
International Liquidity		\multicolumn{12}{c}{*Millions of US Dollars Unless Otherwise Indicated: End of Period*}
Total Res.Min.Gold (Eurosys.Def).....	1l.d	74.13	67.38	75.73	74.98	73.68	64.07	....	†77.40	76.61	105.62	151.72	279.91
SDRs...	1b.d	9.10	9.59	10.54	11.09	11.14	10.85	12.28	2.45	4.19	6.28	9.14	12.32
Reserve Position in the Fund.........	1c.d	35.54	32.38	34.46	34.10	33.87	29.35	83.60	74.62	72.27	99.21	142.41	178.70
Foreign Exchange........................	1d.d	29.48	25.40	30.73	29.79	28.67	23.87	....	.33	.15	.13	.18	88.89
o/w:Fin.Deriv.Rel.to Reserves......	1ddd	....	....	....	....	....	....	....	–	–	–	–	–
Other Reserve Assets....................	1e.d	....	....	....	....	....	....	....	–	–	–	–	–
Gold (Million Fine Troy Ounces).....	1ad	.343	.305	.305	.305	.305	.305	....	.076	.076	.076	.076	.075
Gold (Eurosystem Valuation)..........	1and	19.25	14.90	16.90	18.28	16.81	14.44	....	22.16	20.96	21.11	26.05	31.29
Memo:Euro Cl. on Non-EA Res.....	1dgd	....	....	....	....	....	....	....	....	....	....	....	....
Non-Euro Cl. on EA Res.............	1dhd	....	....	....	....	....	....	....	–	–	–	–	–
Mon. Auth.: Other Foreign Assets....	3..d	....	....	....	....	....	....	....	–	–	–	–	–
Foreign Liabilities......................	4..d	26.22	25.48	30.78	29.58	28.43	24.11	....	†2,171.54	47.73	56.03	56.59	90.59
Banking Insts.: Foreign Assets..........	7a.d	376,499	....	451,135	504,838	496,510	471,904	....	†178,653	174,954	207,513	237,001	301,437
Foreign Liab....................	7b.d	320,644	....	386,770	434,105	415,569	389,816	....	†164,243	159,292	163,497	173,268	198,972
Monetary Authorities		\multicolumn{12}{c}{*Billions of Francs through 1998; Millions of Euros Beginning 1999: End of Period*}
Fgn. Assets (Cl.on Non-EA Ctys)......	11	7.0	8.3	8.5	8.3	7.5	6.2	....	952	156	333	436	762
Claims on General Government........	12a.u	....	....	....	....	....	....	....	97	45	20	46	113
o/w: Claims on Gen.Govt.in Cty...	12a	3.2	5.5	5.5	4.9	4.8	4.7	....	....	....	....	....	....
Claims on Banking Institutions.........	12e.u	....	....	....	....	....	....	....	13,038	19,495	16,751	23,568	26,306
o/w: Claims on Bank.Inst.in Cty...	12e	.3	.1	.1	.2	1.0	2.6	....	9,000	19,282	16,511	23,371	23,423
Claims on Other Resident Sectors.....	12d.u	....	....	....	....	....	....	....	163	242	217	342	502
o/w: Cl. on Oth.Res.Sect.in Cty...	12d	....	....	....	....	....	....	....	–	–	–	–	93
Currency Issued...............................	14a	3.2	5.5	5.5	4.9	5.7	5.7	....	585	661	647	677	821
Liabilities to Banking Insts................	14c.u	....	....	....	....	....	....	....	11,509	19,272	16,555	23,197	25,845
o/w: Liabs to Bank.Inst.in Cty.........	14c	....	....	....	....	....	....	....	4,183	4,912	5,981	4,638	6,766
Demand Dep. of Other Res.Sect......	14d.u	....	....	....	....	....	....	....	18	16	15	–	–
o/w:D.Dep.of Oth.Res.Sect.in Cty...	14d	....	....	....	....	....	....	....	3	–	–	–	–
Other Dep. of Other Res.Sect...........	15..u	....	....	....	....	....	....	....	–	–	–	–	–
o/w:O.Dep.of Oth.Res.Sect.in Cty...	15	....	....	....	....	....	....	....	–	–	–	–	–
Bonds & Money Mkt. Instruments....	16n.u	....	....	....	....	....	....	....	–	–	–	–	–
o/w: Held by Resid.of Cty.............	16n	....	....	....	....	....	....	....	–	–	–	–	–
Foreign Liab. (to Non-EA Ctys).........	16c	.9	.9	1.0	.9	.9	.9	....	2,162	51	64	54	72
Central Government Deposits...........	16d.u	....	....	....	....	....	....	....	485	569	581	526	592
o/w: Cent.Govt.Dep. in Cty...........	16d	2.9	3.2	3.4	3.4	3.3	3.4	....	485	569	581	526	592
Capital Accounts.............................	17a	3.3	4.1	4.2	4.2	4.3	4.5	....	199	203	188	205	192
Other Items (Net)............................	17r	.2	.2	.1	–	–.9	–1.1	....	–709	–833	–730	–268	161
Memo: Net Claims on Eurosystem....	12e.s	....	....	....	....	....	....	....	–3,376	–14,211	–10,425	–18,408	–16,583
Currency Put into Circ................	14m	....	....	....	....	....	....	....	....	....	....	9,932	19,900

2004, International Monetary Fund : *International Financial Statistics Yearbook*

Luxembourg 137

		1992	1993	1994	1995	1996	1997	1998	1999	2000	2001	2002	2003
Banking Institutions		*Billions of Francs through 1998; Millions of Euros Beginning 1999: End of Period*											
Claims on Monetary Authorities	20	4.0	....	3.0	3.7	19.1	13.6	....	4,183	4,912	5,981	4,638	6,766
Claims on Bk.Inst.in Oth.EA Ctys	20b.u	....	....	....	....	....	....	....	228,490	254,464	283,512	291,098	307,198
Fgn. Assets (Cl.on Non-EA Ctys)	21	12,492.3	....	14,363.0	14,849.8	15,890.8	17,422.7	....	177,835	188,021	235,462	225,995	238,667
Claims on General Government	22a.u	....	....	....	....	....	....	....	53,469	46,551	49,303	48,921	60,573
o/w: Claims on Gen.Govt.in Cty	22a	3.1	....	12.2	54.3	22.1	19.9	....	733	1,078	1,050	1,027	1,291
Claims on Other Resident Sectors	22d.u	....	....	....	....	....	....	....	82,554	98,232	107,910	105,621	108,296
o/w: Cl. on Oth.Res.Sect.in Cty	22d	578.5	....	489.7	525.4	552.9	616.0	....	19,778	22,495	29,128	24,879	26,537
Demand Deposits	24..u	....	....	....	....	....	....	....	42,610	50,376	50,708	48,161	50,277
o/w:D.Dep.of Oth.Res.Sect. in Cty	24	101.8	....	78.5	72.7	79.5	81.5	....	26,687	34,188	31,842	31,519	33,777
Other Deposits	25..u	....	....	....	....	....	....	....	89,947	99,507	104,401	102,256	104,507
o/w:O.Dep.of Oth.Res.Sect. in Cty	25	1,384.6	....	1,674.0	1,677.1	1,933.2	2,155.8	....	32,027	34,711	38,855	39,367	41,854
Money Market Fund Shares	26m.u	....	....	....	....	....	....	....	65,940	76,337	119,162	138,406	161,713
Bonds & Money Mkt. Instruments	26n.u	....	....	....	....	....	....	....	38,771	44,774	52,322	54,359	74,347
o/w: Held by Resid.of Cty	26n	....	....	293.8	453.3	599.1	797.7	....	....	....	....	....	....
Foreign Liab. (to Non-EA Ctys)	26c	10,639.0	....	12,313.8	12,769.2	13,300.3	14,392.0	....	163,491	171,190	185,518	165,222	157,539
Central Government Deposits	26d.u	....	....	....	....	....	....	....	4,595	12,745	8,819	3,178	5,686
o/w: Cent.Govt.Dep. in Cty	26d	....	....	53.8	59.8	72.1	79.6	....	3,377	3,213	2,118	1,915	2,965
Credit from Monetary Authorities	26g	....	....	3.8	35.5	3.8	4.6	....	9,000	19,282	16,511	23,371	23,423
Liab. to Bk.Inst.in Oth. EA Ctys	26h.u	....	....	....	....	....	....	....	105,620	93,339	119,350	116,015	116,903
Capital Accounts	27a	860.3	....	486.3	526.5	549.0	562.0	....	16,551	34,090	37,432	39,962	39,712
Other Items (Net)	27r	88.2	....	†−36.2	−161.0	−51.9	−1.0	....	10,005	−9,459	−12,056	−14,657	−12,605
Central Govt. Monetary Liabilities	25.iu	....	....	....	....	....	12,008	12,778	327	344	438	502	694
Banking Survey (Nat'l Residency)		*Billions of Francs through 1998; Millions of Euros Beginning 1999: End of Period*											
Foreign Assets (Net)	31n	1,859.4	....	2,056.7	2,088.0	2,597.1	3,036.0	....	164,333	185,959	209,704	237,495	256,351
Domestic Credit	32	581.9	....	†450.2	521.4	504.4	557.6	....	16,649	19,791	27,479	23,465	24,364
Claims on General Govt. (Net)	32an	3.4	....	†−39.5	−4.0	−48.5	−58.4	....	−3,129	−2,704	−1,649	−1,414	−2,266
Claims on Other Resident Sectors	32d	578.5	....	489.7	525.4	552.9	616.0	....	19,778	22,495	29,128	24,879	26,630
Currency Issued	34a.n	3.2	5.5	5.5	4.9	5.7	5.7	....	585	661	647	677	821
Demand Deposits	34b.n	101.8	....	78.5	72.7	79.5	81.5	....	26,690	34,188	31,842	31,519	33,777
Other Deposits	35..n	1,384.6	....	1,674.0	1,677.1	1,933.2	2,155.8	....	32,027	34,711	38,855	39,367	41,854
Money Market Fund Shares	36m	....	....	....	....	....	....	....	35,981	40,002	55,128	274,685	80,299
Bonds & Money Mkt. Instruments	36n	....	....	293.8	453.3	599.1	797.7	....	55,678	66,598	79,848	78,841	74,399
o/w: Over Two Years	36na	....	....	....	....	....	....	....	31,161	34,014	40,999	45,217	
Capital Accounts	37a	863.7	....	490.5	530.7	553.3	566.5	....	16,750	34,292	37,620	40,168	39,904
Other Items (Net)	37r	84.1	....	†−35.4	−129.4	−69.0	−13.7	....	13,271	−4,703	−6,707	90	9,661
Banking Survey (EA-Wide Residency)						*Millions of Euros: End of Period*							
Foreign Assets (Net)	31n.u	....	....	....	....	....	....	....	13,134	16,937	50,213	61,155	81,819
Domestic Credit	32..u	....	....	....	....	....	....	....	131,203	131,756	148,048	151,226	163,206
Claims on General Govt. (Net)	32anu	....	....	....	....	....	....	....	48,486	33,281	39,922	45,264	54,408
Claims on Other Resident Sect	32d.u	....	....	....	....	....	....	....	82,717	98,474	108,127	105,962	108,798
Currency Issued	34a.u	....	....	....	....	....	....	....	585	661	647	677	821
Demand Deposits	34b.u	....	....	....	....	....	....	....	42,628	50,391	50,723	48,161	50,277
Other Deposits	35..u	....	....	....	....	....	....	....	89,947	99,507	104,401	102,256	104,507
o/w: Other Dep. Over Two Yrs	35abu	....	....	....	....	....	....	....	6,926	3,823	5,371	5,038	7,839
Money Market Fund Shares	36m.u	....	....	....	....	....	....	....	65,940	76,337	119,162	138,406	161,713
Bonds & Money Mkt. Instruments	36n.u	....	....	....	....	....	....	....	38,771	44,774	52,322	54,359	74,347
o/w: Over Two Years	36nau	....	....	....	....	....	....	....	31,161	34,014	38,011	41,048	45,127
Capital Accounts	37a	....	....	....	....	....	....	....	16,750	34,292	37,620	40,168	39,904
Other Items (Net)	37r.u	....	....	....	....	....	....	....	−110,285	−157,271	−166,615	−171,646	−186,544
Money (National Definitions)						*Billions of Francs: End of Period*							
Money	39ma	81.8	....	104.5	....	111.4	115.0	....	....	....	....	....	....
Quasi-Money	39mb	406.8	....	399.6	....	423.5	396.0	....	....	....	....	....	....
Broad Money	39mc	488.6	....	504.1	....	534.9	511.0	....	....	....	....	....	....
Interest Rates						*Percent Per Annum*							
Money Market Rate	60b	8.93	8.09	5.16	4.26	3.29	3.36	3.48	....	....	....	....	....
Deposit Rate	60l	6.00	5.33	5.00	5.00	3.54	3.46	3.31	....	....	....	....	....
Lending Rate	60p	8.75	7.65	6.58	6.50	5.50	5.50	5.27	....	....	....	....	....
Government Bond Yield	61	7.90	6.93	6.38	6.05	5.21	5.39	5.29	....	....	....	....	....
Prices, Production, Labor						*Index Numbers (2000=100): Period Averages*							
Share Prices (1995=100)	62	55.7	78.3	110.4	100.0	117.5	152.5	194.2	....	....	....	....	....
Producer Prices in Industry	63a	93.9	92.7	†94.1	97.8	94.7	96.1	98.5	†95.4	100.0	101.0	100.0	101.5
Consumer Prices	64	85.7	88.8	90.8	92.5	†93.8	95.1	96.0	96.9	100.0	102.7	104.8	106.9
Harmonized CPI	64h	....	....	....	92.1	93.2	94.5	95.4	96.4	100.0	102.4	104.5	107.2
Industrial Production	66	78.6	75.2	79.7	81.3	81.4	86.1	86.0	95.9	100.0	101.8	102.8	105.4
Employment	67	....	....	....	....	....	....	....	94.7	100.0	105.6	109.0	111.1
						Number in Thousands: Period Averages							
Labor Force	67d	....	....	....	....	172	175	179	181	....	189	194	....
Employment	67e	....	....	....	214	220	227	237	248	265	280	288	294
Unemployment	67c	3	4	5	5	6	6	6	5	5	5	6	8
Unemployment Rate (%)	67r	1.6	2.1	2.8	3.0	3.3	3.6	3.1	2.9	2.7	2.6	2.9	3.8

2004, International Monetary Fund: *International Financial Statistics Yearbook*

Luxembourg 137

		1992	1993	1994	1995	1996	1997	1998	1999	2000	2001	2002	2003
International Transactions					Billions of Francs through 1998; Millions of Euros Beginning 1999								
Exports................................	70	207.96	203.60	219.10	228.40	223.20	250.10	287.30	†7.42	8.62	9.21	9.10	9.02
Imports, c.i.f.........................	71	264.31	265.90	280.00	287.30	299.20	335.70	370.60	†10.38	11.65	12.47	12.23	12.01
Balance of Payments					Millions of US Dollars: Minus Sign Indicates Debit								
Current Account, n.i.e..............	78ald	....	....	....	2,426	2,219	1,834	1,626	1,650	2,562	1,674	1,636	2,492
Goods: Exports f.o.b..............	78aad	....	....	....	8,578	7,944	7,745	8,557	8,565	8,635	8,996	9,668	11,233
Goods: Imports f.o.b..............	78abd	....	....	....	−10,269	−9,872	−9,770	−10,881	−11,151	−11,056	−11,395	−11,741	−13,696
Trade Balance.....................	78acd	....	....	....	−1,690	−1,928	−2,025	−2,324	−2,586	−2,420	−2,399	−2,073	−2,463
Services: Credit.......................	78add	....	....	....	10,619	11,930	12,583	14,084	17,134	20,301	19,945	20,415	25,451
Services: Debit........................	78aed	....	....	....	−7,519	−8,483	−8,683	−9,947	−11,840	−13,581	−13,708	−13,640	−16,916
Balance on Goods & Services.......	78afd	....	....	....	1,410	1,519	1,874	1,813	2,708	4,300	3,838	4,702	6,073
Income: Credit........................	78agd	....	....	....	48,798	40,476	38,439	46,814	47,931	50,400	52,302	49,841	52,092
Income: Debit.........................	78ahd	....	....	....	−47,209	−39,220	−37,971	−46,578	−48,413	−51,678	−53,941	−52,206	−55,117
Balance on Gds, Serv. & Inc.........	78aid	....	....	....	2,999	2,774	2,342	2,049	2,227	3,022	2,199	2,337	3,048
Current Transfers, n.i.e.: Credit......	78ajd	....	....	....	1,791	2,186	1,985	2,185	2,282	2,750	2,269	2,680	3,884
Current Transfers: Debit...............	78akd	....	....	....	−2,364	−2,741	−2,493	−2,608	−2,859	−3,211	−2,793	−3,381	−4,440
Capital Account, n.i.e...............	78bcd	....	....	....	....	....	....	....	....	....	....	−166	−176
Capital Account, n.i.e.: Credit........	78bad	....	....	....	....	....	....	....	....	....	....	60	54
Capital Account: Debit................	78bbd	....	....	....	....	....	....	....	....	....	....	−226	−231
Financial Account, n.i.e.............	78bjd	....	....	....	....	....	....	....	....	....	....	−275	−1,790
Direct Investment Abroad............	78bdd	....	....	....	....	....	....	....	....	....	....	−154,425	−96,428
Dir. Invest. in Rep. Econ., n.i.e.......	78bed	....	....	....	....	....	....	....	....	....	....	130,051	87,871
Portfolio Investment Assets...........	78bfd	....	....	....	....	....	....	....	....	....	....	7,478	−78,423
Equity Securities....................	78bkd	....	....	....	....	....	....	....	....	....	....	4,330	−35,857
Debt Securities......................	78bld	....	....	....	....	....	....	....	....	....	....	3,148	−42,566
Portfolio Investment Liab., n.i.e......	78bgd	....	....	....	....	....	....	....	....	....	....	63,289	99,152
Equity Securities....................	78bmd	....	....	....	....	....	....	....	....	....	....	36,113	70,450
Debt Securities......................	78bnd	....	....	....	....	....	....	....	....	....	....	27,176	28,703
Financial Derivatives Assets...........	78bwd	....	....	....	....	....	....	....	....	....	....	....	7,366
Financial Derivatives Liabilities.......	78bxd	....	....	....	....	....	....	....	....	....	....	−41	−530
Other Investment Assets..............	78bhd	....	....	....	....	....	....	....	....	....	....	−19,493	−30,035
Monetary Authorities..............	78bod	....	....	....	....	....	....	....	....	....	....	−	−
General Government................	78bpd	....	....	....	....	....	....	....	....	....	....	−50	−18
Banks...............................	78bqd	....	....	....	....	....	....	....	....	....	....	20,185	−3,623
Other Sectors.......................	78brd	....	....	....	....	....	....	....	....	....	....	−39,629	−26,393
Other Investment Liab., n.i.e.........	78bid	....	....	....	....	....	....	....	....	....	....	−27,133	9,236
Monetary Authorities................	78bsd	....	....	....	....	....	....	....	....	....	....	−887	−13,465
General Government................	78btd	....	....	....	....	....	....	....	....	....	....	3	−2
Banks...............................	78bud	....	....	....	....	....	....	....	....	....	....	−26,505	17,866
Other Sectors......................	78bvd	....	....	....	....	....	....	....	....	....	....	255	4,837
Net Errors and Omissions.............	78cad	....	....	....	....	....	....	....	....	....	....	−1,160	−417
Overall Balance.....................	78cbd	....	....	....	....	....	....	....	....	....	....	35	108
Reserves and Related Items...........	79dad	....	....	....	....	....	....	....	....	....	....	−35	−108
Reserve Assets.....................	79dbd	....	....	....	−	....	−	....	....	....	....	−35	−108
Use of Fund Credit and Loans........	79dcd	....	....	....	....	....	....	....	....	....	....	−	−
Exceptional Financing...............	79ded	....	....	....	....	....	....	....	....	....	....	−	....
Government Finance														
Central Government					Millions of Francs through 1998; Millions of Euros Beginning 1999: Year Ending December 31								
Deficit (-) or Surplus.................	80	....	....	2,656	12,573	25,846	12,609	....	....	....	....	....	....
Revenue............................	81	184,524	202,183	217,830	220,074	239,082	261,696	....	....	....	....	....	....
Grants Received...................	81z	525	944	596	797	507	7,037	....	....	....	....	....	....
Expenditure........................	82	177,525	192,807	205,656	211,557	222,710	240,847	....	....	....	....	....	....
Lending Minus Repayments...........	83	1,385	603	700	613	641	−5,563	....	....	....	....	....	....
Adjustment for Complem. Period....	80x	....	....	−9,414	3,872	9,608	−20,840	....	....	....	....	....	....
Financing														
Total Financing....................	84	....	....	−2,656	−11,810	−25,846	−12,609	....	....	....	....	....	....
Domestic...........................	84a	....	....	−2,300	−11,776	−25,598	−12,455	....	....	....	....	....	....
Foreign............................	85a	....	....	−356	−34	−248	−154	....	....	....	....	....	....
Debt: Domestic......................	88a	12,181	15,473	....	....	....	24,616	....	....	....	....	....	....
Foreign...........................	89a	902	512	....	....	....	6,311	....	....	....	....	....	....
General Government					As Percent of Gross Domestic Product								
Deficit (-) or Surplus.................	80g	.8	1.7	2.8	1.8	2.7	3.6	3.2	3.8	5.8	5.0	....	....
Debt................................	88g	5.1	6.1	5.7	5.8	6.2	6.0	6.3	6.0	5.6	5.5	....	....

Luxembourg 137

National Accounts		1992	1993	1994	1995	1996	1997	1998	1999	2000	2001	2002	2003
		Billions of Francs through 1998; Billions of Euros Beginning 1999
Househ.Cons.Expend.,incl.NPISHs....	96f	240.2	254.4	269.7	†256.5	271.3	286.5	312.4	†7.9	8.5	9.2	9.6	10.0
Government Consumption Expend...	91f	53.2	57.5	60.0	†98.4	106.3	112.1	115.1	†3.1	3.3	3.7	4.0	4.4
Gross Fixed Capital Formation.........	93e	98.5	114.7	107.2	†115.0	119.9	139.1	155.2	†4.5	4.4	5.0	5.0	5.0
Changes in Inventories....................	93i	1.7	.5	1.9	†.2	.2	.2	.2	†.1	.3	.2	-.2	....
Exports of Goods and Services.........	90c	427.2	456.3	425.0	†578.2	625.6	748.1	874.2	†25.5	32.2	33.7	32.7	33.5
Imports of Goods and Services (-)....	98c	361.8	377.8	383.4	†520.4	566.5	666.5	776.2	†22.4	27.7	29.9	28.8	29.5
Gross Domestic Product (GDP)........	99b	417.8	456.8	498.6	†533.1	561.9	625.1	686.2	†18.7	21.3	22.0	22.4	23.3
Net Primary Income from Abroad.....	98.n	....	....	48.2	†32.2	30.1	14.0	-11.5	†-.6	-2.0	....	....	....
Net Primary Income from Abroad.....	98.n	40.1	34.4	17.3	35.0	37.4	9.9	1.0	†-.4	-1.9	-1.4	-2.2	-2.4
Gross National Income (GNI)............	99a	....	....	528.0	†570.6	593.6	638.6	654.3	†18.4	19.3	20.5	20.2	20.9
Net Current Transf.from Abroad......	98t	....	....	....	....	....	....	....	†-.5	-.9	-2.4	....	....
Gross Nat'l Disposable Inc.(GNDI)....	99i	....	....	....	....	....	....	....	†17.8	18.4	18.1	....	....
Consumption of Fixed Capital..........	99cf	71.3	74.8	79.2	82.7	86.9	87.9	92.6	†2.4	2.6	2.9	2.9	....
GDP Volume 1985 Prices.................	99b.p	270.30	....	....	....	....	....	....	....	....	....	....	....
GDP Volume (2000=100)................	99bvp	....	....	....	71.1	73.7	80.4	85.1	†91.7	100.0	101.3	103.1	105.3
GDP Deflator (1990=100)................	99bip	110.9	....	....	....	....	....	....	....	....	....	....	....
GDP Deflator (2000=100)................	99bip	....	....	....	†87.4	89.0	90.7	94.0	†96.1	100.0	102.1	102.2	104.0
		Millions: Midyear Estimates
Population...............................	99z	.39	.39	.40	.41	.41	.42	.42	.43	.44	.44	.45	.45

Macedonia, FYR 962

		1992	1993	1994	1995	1996	1997	1998	1999	2000	2001	2002	2003
Exchange Rates						*Denar per SDR: End of Period*							
Market Rate	aa	....	61.062	59.264	56.456	59.547	74.776	72.987	82.816	86.420	86.930	79.665	72.887
				Denar per US Dollar: End of Period (ae) Period Average (rf)									
Market Rate	ae	....	44.456	40.596	37.980	41.411	55.421	51.836	60.339	66.328	69.172	58.598	49.050
Market Rate	rf	....	....	43.263	37.882	39.981	50.004	54.462	56.902	65.904	68.037	64.350	54.322
				Index Numbers (2000=100): Period Averages									
Nominal Effective Exchange Rate	nec	417.20	70.63	44.44	54.39	64.19	89.03	88.11	99.67	100.00	102.70	105.65	109.42
Real Effective Exchange Rate	rec	139.58	123.13	127.43	138.57	133.90	114.69	100.99	101.54	100.00	100.33	99.50	99.90
Fund Position						*Millions of SDRs: End of Period*							
Quota	2f.s	–	49.6	49.6	49.6	49.6	49.6	49.6	68.9	68.9	68.9	68.9	68.9
SDRs	1b.s	–	–	–	.2	–	.3	.8	.9	.5	1.8	4.5	.2
Reserve Position in the Fund	1c.s	–	–	–	–	–	–	–	–	–	–	–	–
Total Fund Cred.&Loans Outstg	2tl	–	2.8	14.0	38.1	47.4	65.3	72.7	74.1	62.3	56.3	49.6	46.0
International Liquidity					*Millions of US Dollars Unless Otherwise Indicated: End of Period*								
Total Reserves minus Gold	1l.d	....	104.59	149.05	257.49	239.55	257.00	306.11	429.92	429.38	745.17	722.03	898.06
SDRs	1b.d	–	–	–	.2	–	.4	1.1	1.2	.7	2.2	6.1	.3
Reserve Position in the Fund	1c.d	–	–	–	–	–	–	–	–	–	–	–	–
Foreign Exchange	1d.d	....	104.57	149.04	257.26	239.51	256.61	305.04	428.73	428.73	742.94	715.91	897.78
Gold (Million Fine Troy Ounces)	1ad	.021	.041	.045	.046	.076	.081	.100	.102	.112	.194	.198	.089
Gold (National Valuation)	1and	7.07	14.66	16.36	17.61	27.98	23.45	28.50	29.69	30.66	53.68	67.81	37.08
Other Liab	4..d	....	–	–	–	–	–	–	–	14.01	–	–	–
Deposit Money Banks: Assets	7a.d	....	158.20	232.98	254.61	229.70	286.84	337.78	404.22	430.92	643.02	560.34	674.80
Liabilities	7b.d	....	579.43	528.30	84.62	138.39	185.76	250.00	262.28	233.08	195.31	205.59	199.65
Monetary Authorities						*Millions of Denar: End of Period*							
Foreign Assets	11	....	5,303	6,715	10,732	11,453	15,894	18,977	30,072	47,910	70,945	45,560	45,835
Claims on Central Government	12a	....	749	2,400	2,395	3,049	8,706	8,675	8,116	5,869	8,796	8,275	3,878
Claims on Deposit Money Banks	12e	....	1,830	2,333	4,673	5,642	3,672	3,538	1,918	1,259	394	410	240
Reserve Money	14	....	3,705	6,360	†8,306	8,044	9,872	10,421	13,508	19,804	21,402	22,209	23,944
of which: Currency Outside DMBs	14a	....	2,703	4,786	5,965	6,401	6,846	6,964	8,271	9,522	14,134	14,136	14,177
Restricted Deposits	16b	....	–	–	114	136	9	56	271	135	588	560	648
Foreign Liabilities	16c	....	172	831	2,150	2,822	4,882	5,308	6,137	6,314	4,897	3,949	3,353
Central Government Deposits	16d	....	14	31	2,633	3,695	5,070	6,152	9,465	16,759	24,926	17,318	11,667
Capital Accounts	17a	....	4,754	4,682	5,059	5,771	8,398	8,130	9,547	11,076	12,348	9,984	7,729
Other Items (Net)	17r	....	–911	–360	–462	–325	41	1,123	1,178	950	15,974	225	2,612
Deposit Money Banks						*Millions of Denar: End of Period*							
Reserves	20	....	678	1,470	1,836	1,125	2,158	2,379	3,861	6,192	6,195	6,364	8,098
Foreign Assets	21	....	7,033	9,458	9,670	9,512	15,897	17,509	24,390	28,582	44,479	32,835	33,099
Claims on Central Government	22a	....	52,503	48,954	5,624	6,311	1,782	1,288	1,289	7,337	7,744	8,257	6,745
Claims on Local Government	22b	....	–	–	2	12	27	20	14	44	7	11	2
Claims on Nonfin.Pub.Enterprises	22c	....	–	–	528	121	208	293	237	515	755	814	458
Claims on Private Sector	22d	....	35,107	66,392	39,181	46,826	50,711	34,531	43,611	42,157	41,151	43,104	49,704
Demand Deposits	24	....	2,853	5,080	5,567	4,854	6,281	7,336	10,458	11,896	11,168	12,255	12,800
Time, Savings,& Fgn.Currency Dep	25	....	38,138	9,726	8,417	8,652	11,537	13,573	17,846	23,294	49,200	42,096	52,584
Restricted Deposits	26b	....	9,613	38,938	1,039	1,111	1,006	1,099	1,185	1,373	1,708	692	567
Foreign Liabilities	26c	....	25,759	21,447	3,214	5,731	10,295	12,959	15,826	15,460	13,510	12,047	9,793
Central Government Deposits	26d	....	445	2,411	1,481	1,345	1,678	2,181	2,904	5,214	4,150	2,692	2,034
Credit from Monetary Authorities	26g	....	1,310	1,961	4,016	4,395	2,388	2,303	1,287	805	427	398	374
Capital Accounts	27a	....	10,520	15,567	17,483	23,799	23,157	23,651	29,046	33,120	30,105	30,102	31,723
Other Items (Net)	27r	....	6,687	31,132	15,624	14,021	14,441	–7,082	–5,150	–6,335	–9,937	–8,897	–11,769
Monetary Survey						*Millions of Denar: End of Period*							
Foreign Assets (Net)	31n	....	–13,595	–6,106	15,038	12,412	16,614	18,219	32,499	54,718	30,969	66,617	66,014
Domestic Credit	32	....	87,900	115,304	43,635	51,406	54,797	36,637	41,075	34,027	45,516	38,805	45,307
Claims on Central Govt. (Net)	32an	....	52,793	48,912	3,905	4,320	3,740	1,630	–2,964	–8,767	3,594	–5,124	–4,859
Claims on Local Government	32b	....	–	–	2	12	27	20	14	44	7	11	2
Claims on Nonfin.Pub.Enterprises	32c	....	–	–	528	121	208	293	237	515	755	814	458
Claims on Private Sector	32d	....	35,107	66,392	39,181	46,826	50,711	34,531	43,611	42,157	41,151	43,104	49,704
Money	34	....	5,590	9,965	†12,223	11,788	13,702	14,952	19,795	22,392	11,168	27,722	27,152
Quasi-Money	35	....	37,510	8,507	†8,417	8,652	11,537	13,573	17,846	23,294	49,200	42,096	52,584
Restricted Deposits	36b	....	9,613	38,938	1,153	1,247	1,015	1,155	1,456	1,508	1,708	1,381	815
Capital Accounts	37a	....	15,274	20,249	22,542	29,570	31,555	31,781	38,593	44,196	30,105	40,994	40,118
Other Items (Net)	37r	....	6,174	31,624	14,338	12,561	13,602	–6,605	–4,116	–2,645	–15,696	–6,771	–9,348
Money plus Quasi-Money	35l	....	43,100	18,472	†20,640	20,440	25,239	28,525	37,641	45,686	60,368	69,818	79,736
Interest Rates						*Percent Per Annum*							
Bank Rate (End of Period)	60	....	295.00	33.00	15.00	9.20	8.90	8.90	8.90	7.90	10.70	10.70	6.50
Deposit Rate	60l	....	....	117.56	24.07	12.75	11.64	11.68	11.40	11.18	9.97	9.56	7.97
Lending Rate	60p	....	....	159.82	45.95	21.58	21.42	21.03	20.45	18.93	19.35	18.36	16.00

2004, International Monetary Fund: *International Financial Statistics Yearbook*

Macedonia, FYR 962

		1992	1993	1994	1995	1996	1997	1998	1999	2000	2001	2002	2003
Prices, Production, Labor						*Index Numbers (2000=100): Period Averages*							
Consumer Prices	64	....	36.6	82.8	96.4	99.0	100.0	100.6	†99.3	100.0	99.3	99.3	99.4
Wages: Average Monthly	65	....	....	76.2	84.2	86.5	88.9	92.1	94.7	100.0	103.6	110.7	116.0
Industrial Production	66	....	113.2	101.8	90.6	93.5	95.0	99.3	96.6	100.0	89.8	85.0	88.9
						Number in Thousands: Period Averages							
Employment	67e	446	421	396	357	340	319	310	316	312	292	280	....
Unemployment	67c	172	175	186	216	238	253	....	....	....	....	....	....
International Transactions						*Millions of US Dollars*							
Exports	70..d	....	1,055.3	1,086.3	1,204.0	1,148.0	1,236.8	1,310.7	1,192.0	1,318.8	1,154.0	1,112.0	1,351.0
Imports, c.i.f.	71..d	....	1,199.4	1,484.1	1,718.9	1,627.0	1,778.5	1,914.7	1,795.8	2,085.0	1,676.0	1,928.0	2,241.1
Balance of Payments						*Millions of US Dollars: Minus Sign Indicates Debit*							
Current Account, n.i.e.	78ald	....	....	....	....	−288.1	−275.5	−269.7	−32.4	−72.4	−243.6	−325.3	....
Goods: Exports f.o.b.	78aad	....	....	....	....	1,147.4	1,201.4	1,291.5	1,190.0	1,320.7	1,155.4	1,110.5	....
Goods: Imports f.o.b.	78abd	....	....	....	....	−1,464.0	−1,589.1	−1,806.6	−1,685.8	−2,011.1	−1,681.8	−1,878.1	....
Trade Balance	78acd	....	....	....	....	−316.5	−387.6	−515.1	−495.8	−690.4	−526.4	−767.6	....
Services: Credit	78add	....	....	....	....	154.3	128.3	149.3	272.8	316.7	244.6	253.0	....
Services: Debit	78aed	....	....	....	....	−309.3	−272.9	−209.1	−230.9	−268.0	−263.8	−277.8	....
Balance on Goods & Services	78afd	....	....	....	....	−471.5	−532.2	−574.9	−453.8	−641.7	−545.6	−792.3	....
Income: Credit	78agd	....	....	....	....	45.3	39.0	23.5	24.2	41.6	52.6	51.0	....
Income: Debit	78ahd	....	....	....	....	−75.0	−72.6	−68.5	−66.5	−87.3	−93.3	−82.4	....
Balance on Gds, Serv. & Inc.	78aid	....	....	....	....	−501.2	−565.8	−619.9	−496.1	−687.3	−586.3	−823.6	....
Current Transfers, n.i.e.: Credit	78ajd	....	....	....	....	475.4	535.0	542.7	618.5	788.2	725.7	655.3	....
Current Transfers: Debit	78akd	....	....	....	....	−262.3	−244.8	−192.5	−154.8	−173.3	−383.0	−157.0	....
Capital Account, n.i.e.	78bcd	....	....	....	....	....	....	−1.8	−	.3	1.3	8.3	....
Capital Account, n.i.e.: Credit	78bad	....	....	....	....	....	....	−	−	.3	3.6	9.9	....
Capital Account: Debit	78bbd	....	....	....	....	....	....	−1.8	−	−	−2.3	−1.7	....
Financial Account, n.i.e.	78bjd	....	....	....	....	174.3	186.8	329.9	14.2	290.3	325.7	207.2	....
Direct Investment Abroad	78bdd	....	....	....	....	....	....	−	−.3	.6	−.9	−.1	....
Dir. Invest. in Rep. Econ., n.i.e.	78bed	....	....	....	....	11.2	15.7	127.7	32.7	174.5	441.5	77.2	....
Portfolio Investment Assets	78bfd	....	....	....	....	−.5	−2.5	.2	.1	−.8	3.2	1.1	....
Equity Securities	78bkd	....	....	....	....	−.5	−2.5	−	−	−	−	.3	....
Debt Securities	78bld	....	....	....	....	....	....	.2	.1	−.8	3.2	.8	....
Portfolio Investment Liab., n.i.e.	78bgd	....	....	....	....	.8	4.6	.1	−	−.1	.4	.1	....
Equity Securities	78bmd	....	....	....	....	.8	4.6	−	−	−	−	−	....
Debt Securities	78bnd	....	....	....	....	....	....	.1	−	−.1	.4	−	....
Financial Derivatives Assets	78bwd	....	....	....	....	....	....	−	....	....	....	....	....
Financial Derivatives Liabilities	78bxd	....	....	....	....	....	....	−	....	....	....	....	....
Other Investment Assets	78bhd	....	....	....	....	−133.2	−73.0	−58.9	−184.1	−77.7	−98.1	245.4	....
Monetary Authorities	78bod	....	....	....	....	....	....	−15.2	−6.2	14.1	−236.8	223.0	....
General Government	78bpd	....	....	....	....	....	....	−	−	−	−	−	....
Banks	78bqd	....	....	....	....	25.3	−57.5	−31.3	−114.9	−62.1	−237.6	158.7	....
Other Sectors	78brd	....	....	....	....	−158.5	−15.6	−12.3	−62.9	−29.6	376.2	−136.3	....
Other Investment Liab., n.i.e.	78bid	....	....	....	....	295.9	242.0	260.9	165.8	193.7	−20.4	−116.4	....
Monetary Authorities	78bsd	....	....	....	....	....	....	−	−	14.7	140.1	−154.2	....
General Government	78btd	....	....	....	....	59.9	−71.6	109.2	89.4	77.3	−65.4	−25.2	....
Banks	78bud	....	....	....	....	−1.2	29.8	105.1	68.1	−44.0	−38.3	−6.1	....
Other Sectors	78bvd	....	....	....	....	237.3	283.8	46.5	8.2	145.7	−56.8	69.1	....
Net Errors and Omissions	78cad	....	....	....	....	18.8	−29.9	−15.1	159.9	61.0	2.3	−12.2	....
Overall Balance	78cbd	....	....	....	....	−95.1	−118.6	43.3	141.7	279.2	85.6	−122.1	....
Reserves and Related Items	79dad	....	....	....	....	95.1	118.6	−43.3	−141.7	−279.2	−85.6	122.1	....
Reserve Assets	79dbd	....	....	....	....	7.6	−35.1	−53.2	−143.5	−263.6	−78.0	130.9	....
Use of Fund Credit and Loans	79dcd	....	....	....	....	13.5	24.6	9.9	1.8	−15.6	−7.6	−8.8	....
Exceptional Financing	79ded	....	....	....	....	73.9	129.2	−	−	−	−	−	....

Macedonia, FYR 962

		1992	1993	1994	1995	1996	1997	1998	1999	2000	2001	2002	2003
International Investment Position						*Millions of US Dollars*							
Assets...	79aad	....	....	....	....	....	....	....	....	....	....	....	....
Direct Investment Abroad...............	79abd	....	....	....	....	−	−	−	−	−	−	−	....
Portfolio Investment......................	79acd	....	....	....	....	−	−	−	−	−	−	−	....
Equity Securities..........................	79add	....	....	....	....	−	−	−	−	−	−	−	....
Debt Securities............................	79aed	....	....	....	....	−	−	−	−	−	−	−	....
Financial Derivatives.....................	79ald	....	....	....	....	....	....	....	....	....	....	....	....
Other Investment.........................	79afd	....	....	....	....	229.3	286.8	337.8	425.4	458.8	895.7	614.2	....
Monetary Authorities...................	79agd	....	....	....	....	−	−	−	21.2	21.4	252.7	49.2	....
General Government....................	79ahd	....	....	....	....	−	−	−	−	−	−	−	....
Banks...	79aid	....	....	....	....	229.3	286.8	337.8	404.2	437.4	643.0	565.0	....
Other Sectors.............................	79ajd	....	....	....	....	−	−	−	−	−	−	−	....
Reserve Assets.............................	79akd	....	....	....	....	267.5	280.4	367.2	478.3	712.6	775.2	734.4	....
Liabilities.....................................	79lad	....	....	....	....	....	....	....	....	....	....	....	....
Dir. Invest. in Rep. Economy...........	79lbd	....	....	....	....	−	−	−	−	−	−	−	....
Portfolio Investment......................	79lcd	....	....	....	....	−	−	−	−	−	−	−	....
Equity Securities..........................	79ldd	....	....	....	....	−	−	−	−	−	−	−	....
Debt Securities............................	79led	....	....	....	....	−	−	−	−	−	−	−	....
Financial Derivatives.....................	79lld	....	....	....	....	....	....	....	....	....	....	....	....
Other Investment.........................	79lfd	....	....	....	....	1,243.1	1,259.7	1,545.0	1,603.7	1,603.0	1,654.3	1,611.1	....
Monetary Authorities...................	79lgd	....	....	....	....	68.2	88.1	102.4	101.7	95.4	225.0	67.4	....
General Government....................	79lhd	....	....	....	....	1,041.2	999.3	1,126.2	1,156.3	1,216.3	1,147.8	1,250.3	....
Banks...	79lid	....	....	....	....	121.3	156.3	289.7	321.2	217.4	177.3	177.9	....
Other Sectors.............................	79ljd	....	....	....	....	12.4	16.0	26.8	24.5	73.9	104.2	115.6	....
Government Finance						*Millions of Denar: Year Ending December 31*							
Deficit (-) or Surplus........................	80	....	....	....	2,267.6	175.3	....	....	....	....	....	....	....
Total Revenue and Grants...............	81y	....	....	....	40,437.0	39,865.2	....	....	....	....	....	....	....
Revenue......................................	81	....	....	....	39,775.8	39,766.1	....	....	....	....	....	....	....
Grants...	81z	....	....	....	661.2	99.1	....	....	....	....	....	....	....
Exp. & Lending Minus Repay...........	82z	....	....	....	38,169.4	39,689.9	....	....	....	....	....	....	....
Expenditure.................................	82	....	....	....	36,511.0	37,423.3	....	....	....	....	....	....	....
Lending Minus Repayments...........	83	....	....	....	1,658.4	2,266.6	....	....	....	....	....	....	....
Total Financing..............................	80h	....	....	....	−2,267.6	−175.3	....	....	....	....	....	....	....
Total Net Borrowing.......................	84	....	....	....	−3,445.2	−175.5	....	....	....	....	....	....	....
Net Domestic...............................	84a	....	....	....	−3,334.1	−1,200.0	....	....	....	....	....	....	....
Net Foreign.................................	85a	....	....	....	−111.1	1,024.5	....	....	....	....	....	....	....
Use of Cash Balances.....................	87	....	....	....	1,177.6	.2	....	....	....	....	....	....	....
National Accounts						*Millions of Denar*							
Househ.Cons.Expend.,incl.NPISHs....	96f	....	47,182	110,847	119,381	127,253	135,487	141,078	145,693	175,965	163,788	188,179	....
Government Consumption Expend...	91f	....	12,472	27,875	31,491	31,985	36,700	39,504	43,009	43,021	57,983	54,616	....
Gross Fixed Capital Formation..........	93e	....	10,994	22,461	28,027	30,654	32,236	33,982	34,710	38,332	34,716	40,448	....
Changes in Inventories....................	93i	....	−416	182	7,162	4,790	6,778	9,426	6,461	14,274	9,902	9,991	....
Exports of Goods and Services..........	90c	....	27,660	55,920	55,961	49,722	69,408	80,343	88,143	114,958	99,833	92,791	....
Imports of Goods and Services (-).....	98c	....	32,360	70,876	72,501	67,961	94,590	109,355	109,007	150,161	132,381	142,055	....
GDP, Production Based...................	99bp	....	59,165	146,409	169,521	176,444	186,019	194,979	209,010	236,389	233,841	243,970	....
Statistical Discrepancy.....................	99bs	....	−6,368	−	−	−	−	−	−	−	−	−	....
						Millions: Midyear Estimates							
Population.............................	99z	....	2	2	2	2	2	2	2	2	2	2	2

Madagascar 674

		1992	1993	1994	1995	1996	1997	1998	1999	2000	2001	2002	2003
Exchange Rates		\multicolumn{12}{c}{*Francs per SDR: End of Period*}
Official Rate	aa	2,626.5	2,695.8	5,651.2	5,088.2	6,224.2	7,130.3	7,606.5	8,980.6	8,534.6	8,333.6	8,748.2	9,061.6
		\multicolumn{12}{c}{*Francs per US Dollar: End of Period (ae) Period Average (rf)*}
Official Rate	ae	1,910.2	1,962.7	3,871.1	3,423.0	4,328.5	5,284.7	5,402.2	6,543.2	6,550.4	6,631.2	6,434.8	6,098.1
Official Rate	rf	1,864.0	1,913.8	3,067.3	4,265.6	4,061.3	5,090.9	5,441.4	6,283.8	6,767.5	6,588.5	6,832.0	6,191.6
Fund Position		\multicolumn{12}{c}{*Millions of SDRs: End of Period*}
Quota	2f.s	90.4	90.4	90.4	90.4	90.4	90.4	90.4	122.2	122.2	122.2	122.2	122.2
SDRs	1b.s	–	.1	–	–	–	–	–	.1	–	.1	–	–
Reserve Position in the Fund	1c.s	–	–	–	–	–	–	–	–	–	–	–	–
Total Fund Cred.&Loans Outstg	2tl	77.1	67.0	58.6	48.9	50.8	51.5	41.2	45.8	80.0	101.4	110.0	115.9
International Liquidity		\multicolumn{12}{c}{*Millions of US Dollars Unless Otherwise Indicated: End of Period*}
Total Reserves minus Gold	1l.d	84.4	80.6	71.6	109.0	240.9	281.6	171.4	227.2	285.2	398.3	363.3	414.3
SDRs	1b.d	–	.1	–	–	.1	.1	–	.1	–	.1	–	–
Reserve Position in the Fund	1c.d	–	–	–	–	–	–	–	–	–	–	–	–
Foreign Exchange	1d.d	84.4	80.5	71.6	108.9	240.8	281.5	171.3	227.0	285.1	398.2	363.2	414.2
Deposit Money Banks: Assets	7a.d	102.8	126.7	157.7	176.6	137.9	151.7	142.0	140.5	180.4	158.4	188.5	230.4
Liabilities	7b.d	22.9	22.2	38.6	33.5	37.3	32.0	40.0	50.9	62.2	57.7	50.8	57.3
Monetary Authorities		\multicolumn{12}{c}{*Billions of Francs: End of Period*}
Foreign Assets	11	159.8	156.8	238.1	374.6	1,043.6	1,492.9	926.8	1,487.2	1,953.8	2,632.3	2,293.1	2,540.4
Claims on Central Government	12a	1,246.9	1,252.9	1,412.3	1,445.8	1,437.0	1,360.2	1,752.2	1,881.0	2,028.4	2,096.3	2,137.1	2,372.1
Claims on Nonfin.Pub.Enterprises	12c	9.3	8.1	7.0	12.6	14.1	15.1	15.9	15.8	111.1	276.4	364.1	17.7
Claims on Deposit Money Banks	12e	46.4	49.5	134.7	175.1	127.5	107.3	102.7	75.1	59.5	40.4	27.2	17.2
Reserve Money	14	556.5	519.9	893.9	1,159.0	1,723.1	1,741.8	1,855.0	2,339.0	2,614.2	3,385.1	3,535.6	3,527.3
of which: Currency Outside DMBs	14a	317.2	378.7	614.5	758.7	829.4	1,020.3	1,169.9	1,434.9	1,789.1	2,159.6	2,330.1	2,570.0
Time, Savings,& Fgn. Currency Dep	15	....	....	....	7.5	1.5	3.0	3.4	5.2	.1	.2	.3	.5
Foreign Liabilities	16c	452.1	378.8	719.6	568.0	642.4	669.4	582.1	647.8	871.0	1,010.3	1,048.9	1,121.2
Central Government Deposits	16d	327.3	389.7	283.4	552.8	609.4	871.4	658.2	636.7	860.3	888.7	552.1	674.9
Counterpart Funds	16e	–	–	–	–	–	–	–	–	–	–	–	–
Capital Accounts	17a	42.7	42.2	43.8	122.6	33.5	93.9	94.1	107.2	93.0	121.5	240.0	244.8
Other Items (Net)	17r	83.8	136.7	–148.6	–401.3	–387.7	–404.1	–395.0	–276.8	–285.8	–360.4	–555.5	–621.3
Deposit Money Banks		\multicolumn{12}{c}{*Billions of Francs: End of Period*}
Reserves	20	239.2	141.1	279.3	400.2	893.7	721.5	678.7	887.1	823.4	1,225.3	1,204.9	954.6
Foreign Assets	21	196.3	248.6	610.3	604.4	597.0	801.5	766.9	919.1	1,181.8	1,050.5	1,212.8	1,404.9
Claims on Central Government	22a	19.0	220.1	250.6	174.0	206.3	356.5	436.4	481.0	606.5	1,182.4	1,526.6	1,798.7
Claims on Private Sector	22d	918.5	1,061.6	1,338.5	1,550.4	1,573.6	1,797.6	1,811.8	1,937.5	2,303.3	2,500.8	2,434.5	2,974.5
Demand Deposits	24	598.1	645.7	989.0	1,089.3	1,338.3	1,643.7	1,783.1	2,115.4	2,228.9	3,074.1	3,297.8	3,292.3
Time Deposits	25	277.1	456.8	656.1	770.6	875.8	1,012.0	950.2	1,100.6	1,436.7	1,520.6	1,663.7	2,071.9
Bonds	26ab	36.5	39.7	42.6	58.5	95.5	70.4	129.8	151.8	169.3	172.7	177.4	177.2
Foreign Liabilities	26c	37.4	37.4	128.1	94.9	136.7	135.7	191.0	262.9	346.0	267.1	263.1	263.1
Long-Term Foreign Liabilities	26cl	6.3	6.3	21.2	19.9	24.9	33.3	25.1	70.2	61.7	115.2	63.6	86.5
Central Government Deposits	26d	137.9	155.5	141.3	123.9	160.4	157.5	141.2	134.9	200.5	335.2	394.1	403.2
Central Govt. Lending Funds	26f	1.2	1.1	1.4	.9	2.9	2.4	.8	6.1	5.4	7.2	10.9	14.5
Credit from Monetary Authorities	26g	46.4	49.5	134.7	174.4	127.5	107.3	102.7	75.1	59.5	40.4	27.2	17.2
Capital Accounts	27a	226.9	106.6	97.6	207.0	535.6	645.9	399.5	445.8	517.9	620.7	726.3	791.5
Other Items (Net)	27r	5.2	173.1	266.9	189.8	–27.0	–131.0	–29.6	–138.0	–110.8	–194.2	–245.3	15.4
Treasury Claims: Private Sector	22d.i	9.2	10.0	10.2	14.0	13.3	1.4	.5	2.1	.5	1.2	3.1	1.3
Post Office: Checking Deposits	24..i	5.7	5.3	4.5	5.8	11.5	15.0	11.9	12.3	76.1	196.4	134.7	21.8
Treasury: Checking Deposits	24..r	9.7	9.7	9.7	9.7	9.7	9.7	9.7	9.7	9.7	9.7	9.7	9.7
Monetary Survey		\multicolumn{12}{c}{*Billions of Francs: End of Period*}
Foreign Assets (Net)	31n	–133.5	–10.7	.8	316.1	861.4	1,489.3	920.6	1,495.6	1,918.6	2,405.4	2,193.9	2,561.0
Domestic Credit	32	1,728.4	1,997.5	2,583.7	2,506.2	2,461.3	2,500.4	3,216.9	3,543.7	3,988.4	4,832.0	5,516.1	6,084.9
Claims on Central Govt. (Net)	32an	800.6	927.8	1,238.2	943.2	873.5	687.7	1,389.2	1,590.4	1,574.1	2,054.9	2,717.5	3,092.7
Claims on Private Sector	32d	927.8	1,069.7	1,345.5	1,563.0	1,587.8	1,812.7	1,827.6	1,953.3	2,414.3	2,777.2	2,798.6	2,992.2
Money	34	915.3	1,024.4	1,603.5	1,848.0	2,167.7	2,663.9	2,953.2	3,550.3	4,018.0	5,233.7	5,627.9	5,862.3
Quasi-Money	35	277.1	456.8	656.1	778.1	877.3	1,015.0	953.6	1,105.8	1,436.8	1,520.8	1,664.1	2,072.4
Bonds	36ab	36.5	39.7	42.6	58.5	95.5	70.4	129.8	151.8	169.3	172.7	177.4	177.2
Long-Term Foreign Liabilities	36cl	6.3	6.3	21.2	19.9	24.9	33.3	25.1	70.2	61.7	115.2	63.6	86.5
Other Items (Net)	37r	359.8	459.6	261.0	118.3	157.3	207.2	76.1	161.2	221.3	195.0	177.0	447.5
Money plus Quasi-Money	35l	1,192.4	1,481.3	2,259.7	2,626.1	3,045.0	3,678.9	3,906.8	4,656.1	5,454.8	6,754.5	7,292.0	7,934.7
Liquid Liabilities	55l	1,266.7	1,636.3	2,473.2	2,901.4	3,608.0	4,501.2	5,070.9	6,089.6	7,027.4	....	....	....
Interest Rates		\multicolumn{12}{c}{*Percent Per Annum*}
Discount Rate (End of Period)	60	....	....	....	....	....	....	....	15.00	....	....	....	....
Base Rate (End of Period)	60a	12.0	12.0	15.6	31.3	26.4	12.8	9.3	....	....	11.0	9.0	7.0
Money Market Rate	60b	15.0	....	–	29.0	10.0	....	11.2	....	16.0	....	....	10.5
Treasury Bill Rate	60c	....	....	....	....	....	....	....	....	....	10.3	....	11.9
Deposit Rate	60l	20.5	19.5	19.5	18.5	19.0	14.4	8.0	15.3	15.0	12.0	12.0	11.5
Lending Rate	60p	25.0	26.0	30.5	37.5	32.8	30.0	27.0	28.0	26.5	25.3	25.3	24.3

Madagascar 674

		1992	1993	1994	1995	1996	1997	1998	1999	2000	2001	2002	2003
Prices and Labor						*Index Numbers (2000=100): Period Averages*							
Consumer Prices	64	26.8	29.5	41.0	61.1	73.2	76.5	81.2	89.3	†100.0	106.9	124.0	122.5
						Number in Thousands: Period Averages							
Labor Force	67d	....	5,300	....	....	....	....	....	....	....	....	....	....
Employment	67e	....	315	322	337	....	....	....	....	....	....	....	....
Unemployment	67c	6	5	4	3	....	....	....	....	....	....	....	....
International Transactions						*Billions of Francs*							
Exports	70	516.82	499.00	1,246.72	1,569.39	1,850.09	2,109.63	3,007.23	3,769.72	5,578.12	4,563.17	3,423.22	....
Imports, c.i.f.	71	833.77	895.69	1,408.62	2,333.89	2,114.82	2,534.76	2,953.22	3,696.30	4,953.41	4,894.02	3,458.01	....
Balance of Payments						*Millions of US Dollars: Minus Sign Indicates Debit*							
Current Account, n.i.e.	78ald	−198	−258	−277	−276	−291	−266	−301	−252	−283	−170	−298	....
Goods: Exports f.o.b.	78aad	327	335	450	507	509	516	538	584	824	928	486	....
Goods: Imports f.o.b.	78abd	−471	−514	−546	−628	−629	−694	−693	−742	−997	−955	−603	....
Trade Balance	78acd	−144	−180	−96	−122	−120	−178	−154	−158	−174	−27	−117	....
Services: Credit	78add	174	187	206	242	293	272	291	326	364	351	224	....
Services: Debit	78aed	−260	−302	−328	−359	−373	−386	−436	−456	−522	−511	−398	....
Balance on Goods & Services	78afd	−230	−295	−218	−238	−200	−292	−299	−289	−332	−187	−291	....
Income: Credit	78agd	6	3	2	7	6	20	25	21	22	24	26	....
Income: Debit	78ahd	−153	−154	−158	−174	−169	−115	−103	−63	−64	−106	−101	....
Balance on Gds, Serv. & Inc.	78aid	−377	−446	−374	−405	−363	−387	−377	−331	−373	−270	−366	....
Current Transfers, n.i.e.: Credit	78ajd	197	202	114	141	94	156	109	111	122	114	88	....
Current Transfers: Debit	78akd	−17	−14	−17	−12	−23	−35	−33	−32	−31	−15	−21	....
Capital Account, n.i.e.	78bcd	50	78	62	45	5	115	103	129	115	113	58	....
Capital Account, n.i.e.: Credit	78bad	50	78	62	45	5	115	103	129	115	113	58	....
Capital Account: Debit	78bbd	−	−	−	−	....	....	....	....	....	....	−	....
Financial Account, n.i.e.	78bjd	−100	−158	−122	−198	133	110	−76	−14	−31	−139	−54	....
Direct Investment Abroad	78bdd	−	−	−	−	....	....	....	....	....	−	−	....
Dir. Invest. in Rep. Econ., n.i.e.	78bed	21	15	6	10	10	14	17	58	83	93	8	....
Portfolio Investment Assets	78bfd	−	−	−	....	....	....	....	....	....	−	−	....
Equity Securities	78bkd	....	....	....	....	....	....	....	....	....	−	−	....
Debt Securities	78bld	....	....	....	....	....	....	....	....	....	−	−	....
Portfolio Investment Liab., n.i.e.	78bgd	....	....	....	....	....	....	....	....	....	−	−	....
Equity Securities	78bmd	....	....	....	....	....	....	....	....	....	−	−	....
Debt Securities	78bnd	....	....	....	....	....	....	....	....	....	−	−	....
Financial Derivatives Assets	78bwd	....	....	....	....	....	....	....	....	....	....	....	....
Financial Derivatives Liabilities	78bxd	....	....	....	....	....	....	....	....	....	....	....	....
Other Investment Assets	78bhd	−3	−47	19	−62	37	135	−68	−73	−87	−128	42	....
Monetary Authorities	78bod	9	−19	38	−45	....	157	−84	−71	−40	−144	58	....
General Government	78bpd	....	....	....	....	....	....	....	....	....	−	−	....
Banks	78bqd	−13	−28	−18	−12	37	−22	16	−2	−48	15	−16	....
Other Sectors	78brd	....	....	−1	−5	....	....	....	....	....	....	....	....
Other Investment Liab., n.i.e.	78bid	−117	−126	−147	−145	86	−39	−25	1	−26	−103	−104	....
Monetary Authorities	78bsd	−238	−254	−235	−230	−	−	−	−	−1	−	2	....
General Government	78btd	124	123	79	91	−167	−28	−26	−3	−28	−84	−93	....
Banks	78bud	−3	5	6	−8	....	−4	9	6	15	−11	−3	....
Other Sectors	78bvd	....	−	3	3	253	−8	−7	−2	−12	−8	−10	....
Net Errors and Omissions	78cad	−31	4	61	98	59	25	−25	32	39	−57	11	....
Overall Balance	78cbd	−278	−334	−276	−330	−94	−16	−299	−104	−160	−253	−283	....
Reserves and Related Items	79dad	278	334	276	330	94	16	299	104	160	253	283	....
Reserve Assets	79dbd	−8	23	−14	−2	−137	−214	205	11	−30	18	8	....
Use of Fund Credit and Loans	79dcd	−16	−14	−12	−15	3	1	−14	6	45	27	12	....
Exceptional Financing	79ded	303	326	303	347	228	229	108	88	145	208	264	....
Government Finance						*Billions of Francs: Year Ending December 31*							
Deficit (−) or Surplus	80	−346.4	−307.5	−367.6	−212.8	−217.4	−428.5	−646.9	−624.7	−625.6	−1,203.1	....	....
Revenue	81	557.2	633.6	762.0	1,149.6	1,407.0	1,746.8	2,076.9	2,666.8	3,067.8	3,029.0	....	....
Grants Received	81z	195.4	225.4	274.0	392.1	683.5	735.4	707.9	770.1	946.7	1,003.7	....	....
Expenditure	82	1,049.7	1,267.6	1,734.3	2,344.2	2,817.1	2,879.4	3,477.5	4,068.9	4,550.8	5,182.2	....	....
Lending Minus Repayments	83	71.1	55.2	44.3	29.7	66.2	8.8	−38.8	51.2	26.5	26.8	....	....
Adjustment to Cash Basis	80x	21.8	156.3	375.0	619.4	575.4	−22.5	7.0	58.5	−62.8	−26.8	....	....
Financing													
Domestic	84a	194.9	121.8	213.3	−38.1	−15.0	−145.5	760.9	126.0	121.4	580.9	....	....
Foreign	85a	151.5	185.7	154.3	250.9	232.5	574.0	−114.0	446.8	457.3	518.1	....	....
Adjustment to Total Financing	84x	....	....	....	....	−	−	−	51.8	46.3	104.1	....	....
Debt: Domestic	88a	805.5	934.8	1,124.0	1,076.7	895.4	....	....	....	....	....	....	....
Debt: Foreign	89a	6,610.6	7,169.1	15,646.3	15,072.4	....	....	....	....	....	....	....	....

2004, International Monetary Fund : *International Financial Statistics Yearbook*

Madagascar 674

		1992	1993	1994	1995	1996	1997	1998	1999	2000	2001	2002	2003
National Accounts							**Billions of Francs**						
Househ.Cons.Expend.,incl.NPISHs	96f	4,929.9	5,751.0	8,102.8	12,120.8	14,462.9	16,294.7	17,726.0	20,032.0	22,483.0	24,001.0	26,221.0	28,147.0
Government Consumption Expend	91f	498.3	561.2	723.9	904.2	731.9	1,097.7	1,621.0	1,741.1	2,063.8	2,639.0	2,510.0	3,551.0
Gross Fixed Capital Formation	93e	631.9	738.5	995.6	1,474.9	1,888.0	2,139.6	2,678.0	3,374.0	4,250.0	5,340.0	4,019.0	5,844.0
Exports of Goods and Services	90c	923.6	988.1	2,011.8	3,418.0	3,325.8	3,938.3	4,358.1	5,867.0	7,984.0	8,627.0	4,893.0	7,277.0
Imports of Goods and Services (-)	98c	1,390.6	1,587.9	2,702.8	4,274.3	4,184.3	5,419.4	6,034.4	7,629.4	10,539.0	10,746.0	7,502.0	10,876.0
Gross Domestic Product (GDP)	99b	5,593.1	6,450.9	9,131.1	13,478.7	16,224.3	18,050.9	20,349.5	23,384.0	26,242.0	29,843.0	30,042.0	33,893.0
GDP Volume 1984 Prices	99b.p	1,861.1	1,900.1	1,898.8	1,931.3	1,972.8	2,045.5	2,126.1	2,225.5	2,331.0	2,471.0	2,158.0	2,369.0
GDP Volume (2000=100)	99bvp	79.8	81.5	81.5	82.9	84.6	87.8	91.2	95.5	100.0	106.0	92.6	101.6
GDP Deflator (2000=100)	99bip	26.7	30.2	42.7	62.0	73.1	78.4	85.0	93.3	100.0	107.3	123.7	127.1
							Millions: Midyear Estimates						
Population	99z	Ü 12.65	13.02	13.39	13.79	14.20	14.62	15.06	15.51	15.97	16.44	16.92	17.40

Malawi 676

		1992	1993	1994	1995	1996	1997	1998	1999	2000	2001	2002	2003
Exchange Rates						*Kwacha per SDR: End of Period*							
Official Rate	aa	6.0442	6.1733	22.3337	22.7479	22.0340	28.6416	61.7894	63.7362	104.3318	84.5705	118.4665	161.3258
					Kwacha per US Dollar: End of Period (ae) Period Average (rf)								
Official Rate	ae	4.3958	4.4944	15.2986	15.3031	15.3231	21.2278	43.8836	46.4377	80.0760	67.2941	87.1385	108.5660
Official Rate	rf	3.6033	4.4028	8.7364	15.2837	15.3085	16.4442	31.0727	44.0881	59.5438	72.1973	76.6866	97.4325
					Index Numbers (2000=100): Period Averages								
Official Rate	ahx	1,626.0	1,292.9	743.2	373.0	372.3	348.8	195.9	129.3	100.0	79.7	74.7	58.9
Nominal Effective Exchange Rate	nec	965.1	906.0	575.5	277.8	288.9	290.8	173.0	121.0	100.0	84.4	77.8	63.7
Real Effective Exchange Rate	rec	140.5	143.4	101.8	88.8	122.3	136.6	99.3	99.7	100.0	103.4	102.2	79.7
Fund Position						*Millions of SDRs: End of Period*							
Quota	2f.s	50.90	50.90	50.90	50.90	50.90	50.90	50.90	69.40	69.40	69.40	69.40	69.40
SDRs	1b.s	.06	.17	4.25	.59	.94	.07	4.84	.29	.36	.67	.07	.32
Reserve Position in the Fund	1c.s	2.22	2.22	2.22	2.22	2.22	2.22	2.24	2.24	2.24	2.27	2.28	2.29
Total Fund Cred.&Loans Outstg	2tl	66.86	62.62	76.90	78.02	83.06	78.42	72.57	63.79	63.35	57.90	69.55	68.77
International Liquidity					*Millions of US Dollars Unless Otherwise Indicated: End of Period*								
Total Reserves minus Gold	1l.d	39.95	56.88	42.80	110.01	225.72	162.25	269.73	250.62	246.91	206.74	165.17	126.46
SDRs	1b.d	.08	.23	6.20	.88	1.36	.09	6.82	.39	.47	.84	.09	.47
Reserve Position in the Fund	1c.d	3.05	3.05	3.25	3.31	3.20	3.00	3.15	3.07	2.91	2.85	3.11	3.40
Foreign Exchange	1d.d	36.82	53.59	33.35	105.82	221.16	159.16	259.76	247.15	243.52	203.05	161.98	122.58
Gold (Million Fine Troy Ounces)	1ad	.013	.013	.013	.013	.013	.013	.013	.013	.013	.013	.013	.013
Gold (National Valuation)	1and	.54	.54	.55	.54	.54	.54	.54	.54	.54	.54	.51	.54
Monetary Authorities: Other Liab.	4..d	55.42	36.81	21.92	.02	.02	.09	.06	.59	19.86	.06	50.00	7.55
Deposit Money Banks: Assets	7a.d	10.06	17.34	25.61	29.39	36.17	41.63	61.64	49.74	58.27	76.10	49.31	51.71
Liabilities	7b.d	29.15	24.47	27.22	9.80	10.37	10.67	13.75	16.03	16.86	15.09	12.83	14.76
Other Banking Institutions: Assets	7e.d	–	–	–	–	–	–	–	9.84	4.06	5.59	7.09	11.05
Liabilities	7f.d	–	–	–	–	–	.06	–	8.87	10.64	10.87	18.38	12.88
Monetary Authorities						*Millions of Kwacha: End of Period*							
Foreign Assets	11	215.7	255.6	613.6	1,670.0	3,387.7	3,342.4	11,327.9	11,468.6	19,500.3	13,663.9	14,115.5	14,127.8
Claims on Central Government	12a	803.3	958.7	1,309.5	1,266.2	710.8	877.0	3,727.9	2,559.3	445.8	5,846.3	13,407.4	14,707.0
Claims on Nonfin.Pub.Enterprises	12c	119.7	117.5	115.5	127.0	159.3	187.5	191.4	274.6	313.7	313.7	–	–
Claims on Deposit Money Banks	12e	–	–	–	–	140.0	–	–	–	–	–	–	–
Claims on Other Banking Insts	12f	–	36.6	28.2	13.4	10.5	9.8	9.4	8.2	112.2	3.5	3.3	2.9
Reserve Money	14	541.8	880.7	1,244.8	2,360.6	3,269.7	3,277.1	4,542.6	6,001.4	6,349.2	8,497.7	10,767.2	13,742.9
of which: Currency Outside DMBs	14a	289.8	414.2	624.7	987.5	1,223.8	1,375.3	1,986.5	2,959.3	4,023.7	4,066.3	5,964.0	7,838.1
Liabs. of Central Bank: Securities	16ac	–	–	–	–	–	–	–	–	1,713.3	8,519.2	6,425.0	2,914.0
Restricted Deposits	16b	–	–	–	–	–	–	–	–	–	–	–	–
Foreign Liabilities	16c	647.7	552.0	2,052.7	1,775.2	1,830.5	2,247.9	4,486.2	4,093.5	8,200.3	4,900.3	12,596.9	11,914.2
Central Government Deposits	16d	235.0	351.7	349.5	591.8	883.3	291.3	4,564.6	3,035.3	1,513.5	2,182.9	3,655.9	6,461.6
Capital Accounts	17a	95.1	153.0	330.3	280.7	476.8	653.9	1,072.0	1,101.6	1,547.2	1,269.9	1,641.9	2,076.6
Other Items (Net)	17r	–380.8	–569.0	–1,910.6	–1,931.6	–2,052.0	–2,053.3	591.2	78.9	1,048.6	–5,542.5	–7,560.8	–8,271.6
Deposit Money Banks						*Millions of Kwacha: End of Period*							
Reserves	20	209.5	380.2	591.4	1,311.7	1,814.5	1,803.6	2,273.6	2,877.1	2,290.1	4,158.7	4,837.7	5,350.5
Claims on Mon.Author.:Securities	20c	–	–	–	–	–	–	–	–	250.0	1,419.6	1,342.1	340.0
Foreign Assets	21	44.2	77.9	391.7	449.8	554.2	883.7	2,705.0	2,310.0	4,666.1	5,121.3	4,296.4	5,613.5
Claims on Central Government	22a	153.5	335.3	387.9	867.3	1,746.3	1,206.7	1,388.0	1,412.7	2,418.9	2,731.4	6,748.3	10,967.5
Claims on Nonfin.Pub.Enterprises	22c	22.5	154.3	47.6	183.0	398.0	413.6	185.8	1,442.9	1,218.2	575.1	676.5	277.4
Claims on Private Sector	22d	884.4	764.9	1,178.1	1,252.6	1,406.8	1,603.3	3,478.8	3,717.1	5,817.5	6,454.0	7,363.5	9,808.7
Demand Deposits	24	444.9	560.2	895.9	1,218.1	1,518.0	1,824.4	2,996.3	3,976.2	5,594.0	6,649.4	7,929.3	9,925.2
Time, Savings,& Fgn. Currency Dep	25	633.5	924.4	1,119.5	1,936.4	3,048.1	2,712.4	4,692.1	5,715.7	8,779.5	11,860.7	14,114.1	18,048.4
Foreign Liabilities	26c	128.1	110.0	416.5	150.0	158.8	226.4	603.5	744.4	1,349.7	1,015.7	1,118.0	1,602.9
Central Government Deposits	26d	4.8	1.2	2.7	471.8	469.7	557.2	1,016.1	1,349.9	783.9	565.8	788.6	518.9
Credit from Monetary Authorities	26g	3.2	6.0	6.8	9.5	7.7	3.9	3.0	–	–	–	–	–
Capital Accounts	27a	184.5	214.2	410.5	598.2	845.2	1,113.4	1,497.8	2,284.9	3,238.9	3,730.4	4,902.6	6,563.9
Other Items (Net)	27r	–85.0	–103.4	–255.2	–319.6	–127.7	–526.9	–777.6	–2,311.4	–3,085.2	–3,361.9	–3,588.1	–4,301.8
Monetary Survey						*Millions of Kwacha: End of Period*							
Foreign Assets (Net)	31n	–515.9	–328.4	–1,463.8	194.6	1,952.6	1,751.8	8,943.1	8,940.7	14,616.5	12,869.2	4,697.0	6,224.2
Domestic Credit	32	1,743.6	2,014.4	2,714.5	2,645.9	3,078.7	3,449.4	3,400.7	5,029.5	8,029.0	13,175.5	23,754.5	28,782.9
Claims on Central Govt. (Net)	32an	717.0	941.0	1,345.1	1,069.8	1,104.1	1,235.2	–464.8	–413.2	567.3	5,829.0	15,711.2	18,693.9
Claims on Nonfin.Pub.Enterprises	32c	142.3	271.9	163.1	310.0	557.3	601.0	377.2	1,717.5	1,532.0	888.9	676.5	277.4
Claims on Private Sector	32d	884.4	764.9	1,178.1	1,252.6	1,406.8	1,603.3	3,478.8	3,717.1	5,817.5	6,454.0	7,363.5	9,808.7
Claims on Other Banking Insts	32f	–	36.6	28.2	13.4	10.5	9.8	9.4	8.2	112.2	3.5	3.3	2.9
Money	34	756.7	1,019.9	1,535.4	2,211.2	2,756.8	3,213.0	5,248.4	7,007.3	9,736.5	11,048.7	13,979.0	17,763.4
Quasi-Money	35	633.5	924.4	1,119.5	1,936.4	3,048.1	2,712.4	4,692.1	5,715.7	8,779.5	11,860.7	14,114.1	18,048.4
Liabs. of Central Bank: Securities	36ac	–	–	–	–	–	–	–	–	1,463.3	7,099.6	5,082.9	2,574.0
Restricted Deposits	36b	–	–	–	–	–	–	–	–	–	–	–	–
Capital Accounts	37a	279.6	367.2	740.8	878.9	1,322.0	1,767.2	2,569.9	3,386.6	4,786.1	5,000.4	6,544.5	8,640.5
Other Items (Net)	37r	–442.1	–625.6	–2,145.0	–2,186.0	–2,095.7	–2,491.4	–166.6	–2,139.2	–2,119.9	–8,964.7	–11,269.1	–12,019.1
Money plus Quasi-Money	35l	1,390.2	1,944.3	2,654.9	4,147.6	5,805.0	5,925.4	9,940.6	12,722.9	18,516.0	22,909.4	28,093.1	35,811.8

2004, International Monetary Fund : *International Financial Statistics Yearbook*

Malawi 676

		1992	1993	1994	1995	1996	1997	1998	1999	2000	2001	2002	2003
Other Banking Institutions		\multicolumn{12}{c}{*Millions of Kwacha: End of Period*}
Reserves	40	31.1	10.7	7.9	45.3	3.1	23.4	19.6	45.1	152.7	278.6	334.9	746.2
Claims on Mon.Author.:Securities	40c	–	–	–	–	–	–	–	–	–	706.6	457.7	654.2
Foreign Assets	41	–	–	–	–	–	–	–	457.1	324.9	376.4	617.4	1,199.2
Claims on Central Government	42a	204.0	262.3	284.7	351.3	414.3	648.9	1,086.5	752.7	1,415.2	2,369.2	3,225.0	5,910.5
Claims on Nonfin.Pub.Enterprises	42c	6.3	5.3	5.7	9.8	11.2	–	–	75.2	29.9	48.2	31.8	40.0
Claims on Private Sector	42d	68.5	91.5	118.8	134.8	167.9	275.3	388.1	2,515.8	3,604.6	3,981.4	4,494.9	3,091.7
Claims on Deposit Money Banks	42e	1.5	19.6	8.4	4.8	18.8	19.8	31.4	563.6	887.1	648.6	482.4	536.7
Demand Deposits	44	19.3	17.6	19.5	22.0	29.8	39.5	504.7	–	157.1	822.6	364.4	1,196.7
Time, Savings,& Fgn. Currency Dep	45	187.4	263.0	319.8	404.3	580.1	612.5	663.9	3,271.6	4,083.3	5,329.6	5,580.7	7,015.6
Foreign Liabilities	46c	–	–	–	–	–	–	–	391.5	701.3	706.8	1,575.1	1,381.4
Long-Term Foreign Liabilities	46cl	–	–	–	–	–	1.3	–	20.6	151.0	24.6	26.9	16.7
Credit from Monetary Authorities	46g	–	–	–	–	–	–	–	10.7	102.0	.9	–	–
Credit from Deposit Money Banks	46h	.3	–	–	–	–	–	–	84.0	250.5	195.0	281.5	834.6
Capital Accounts	47a	74.6	103.9	124.0	152.3	216.6	308.2	429.9	569.5	905.7	1,121.3	1,607.5	2,074.4
Other Items (Net)	47r	29.7	4.8	–37.9	–32.6	–211.3	6.0	–73.0	61.6	63.5	208.2	208.1	–340.8
Banking Survey		\multicolumn{12}{c}{*Millions of Kwacha: End of Period*}
Foreign Assets (Net)	51n	–515.9	–328.4	–1,463.8	194.6	1,952.6	1,751.8	8,943.1	9,006.3	14,240.1	12,538.7	3,739.2	6,042.0
Domestic Credit	52	2,022.4	2,336.8	3,095.4	3,128.4	3,661.6	4,363.7	4,865.8	8,365.1	12,966.5	19,570.8	31,502.9	37,822.2
Claims on Central Govt. (Net)	52an	920.9	1,203.3	1,629.8	1,421.1	1,518.4	1,884.1	621.7	339.5	1,982.5	8,198.3	18,936.2	24,604.4
Claims on Nonfin.Pub.Enterprises	52c	148.6	277.2	168.8	319.8	568.5	601.0	377.2	1,792.6	1,561.9	937.1	708.3	317.4
Claims on Private Sector	52d	952.8	856.4	1,296.8	1,387.5	1,574.7	1,878.6	3,866.9	6,232.9	9,422.1	10,435.4	11,858.4	12,900.4
Liquid Liabilities	55l	1,565.9	2,214.3	2,986.3	4,528.6	6,411.8	6,554.0	11,089.6	15,949.4	22,603.6	28,783.0	33,703.3	43,277.8
Liabs.of Central Bank: Securities	56ac	–	–	–	–	–	–	–	–	1,463.3	6,393.0	4,625.1	1,919.8
Restricted Deposits	56b	–	–	–	–	–	–	–	–	–	–	–	–
Long-Term Foreign Liabilities	56cl	–	–	–	–	–	1.3	–	20.6	151.0	24.6	26.9	16.7
Capital Accounts	57a	354.2	471.0	864.8	1,031.2	1,538.7	2,075.4	2,999.8	3,956.1	5,691.9	6,121.6	8,152.0	10,714.9
Other Items (Net)	57r	–413.6	–676.9	–2,219.5	–2,236.8	–2,336.3	–2,515.1	–280.5	–2,554.8	–2,703.2	–9,212.7	–11,265.2	–12,064.9
Nonbank Financial Institutions		\multicolumn{12}{c}{*Millions of Kwacha: End of Period*}
Claims on Central Government	42a.s	84.91	71.06	93.51	172.57	216.19	232.89	437.70	575.90	202.47	393.05	463.81	547.24
Claims on Private Sector	42d.s	138.82	208.70	269.01	377.83	584.02	230.34	332.00	352.89	176.86	301.35	125.74	121.43
of which: Policy Loans	42dxs	12.34	11.05	12.48	15.25	16.38	22.30	33.31	23.59	31.50	133.28	24.26	24.65
Incr.in Total Assets(Within Per.)	49z.s	45.49	70.20	103.28	242.14	296.06	–247.43	416.41	168.14	–120.83	876.12	–56.81	136.69
Interest Rates		\multicolumn{12}{c}{*Percent Per Annum*}
Discount Rate (End of Period)	60	20.00	25.00	40.00	50.00	27.00	23.00	43.00	47.00	50.23	46.80	40.00	35.00
Treasury Bill Rate	60c	15.62	23.54	27.68	46.30	30.83	18.31	32.98	42.85	39.52	42.41	41.75	39.32
Deposit Rate	60l	16.50	21.75	25.00	37.27	26.33	10.21	19.06	33.21	33.25	34.96	28.08	25.13
Lending Rate	60p	22.00	29.50	31.00	47.33	45.33	28.25	37.67	53.58	53.13	56.17	50.54	48.92
Government Bond Yield	61	....	....	23.50	38.58	42.67	39.25	....	....	....	....	....	....
Prices, Production, Labor		\multicolumn{12}{c}{*Index Numbers (2000=100): Period Averages*}
Consumer Prices	64	9.0	11.1	14.9	27.4	37.6	41.1	53.3	77.2	†100.0	122.7	140.8	154.3
Industrial Production	66	122.3	115.4	109.8	111.2	115.2	113.5	110.3	98.0	100.0	91.0	91.3	....
		\multicolumn{12}{c}{*Number in Thousands: Period Averages*}
Employment	67e	546	583	653	701	....	....	....	....	....	....	....	....
International Transactions		\multicolumn{12}{c}{*Millions of Kwacha*}
Exports	70	1,489	1,411	2,954	6,193	7,359	8,827	13,861	19,907	23,630	31,817	31,417	....
Imports, c.i.f	71	2,654	2,405	4,214	7,255	9,545	12,848	16,431	29,696	32,252	39,480	53,657	....
Imports, f.o.b	71.v	1,592	1,440	2,793	4,353	5,727	7,709	10,799	18,455	28,389	....	....	....

Malawi 676

		1992	1993	1994	1995	1996	1997	1998	1999	2000	2001	2002	2003
Balance of Payments						*Millions of US Dollars: Minus Sign Indicates Debit*							
Current Account, n.i.e.	78ald	−284.9	−165.6	−180.7	−78.0	−147.4	−276.2	−4.4	−157.5	−73.5	−60.0	−200.7	....
Goods: Exports f.o.b.	78aad	399.9	317.5	323.1	445.5	509.6	540.2	539.6	448.4	403.1	427.9	422.4	....
Goods: Imports f.o.b.	78abd	−415.0	−340.2	−483.1	−508.8	−587.5	−698.7	−500.6	−575.0	−462.0	−472.2	−573.2	....
Trade Balance	78acd	−15.0	−22.8	−160.1	−63.3	−77.9	−158.4	39.0	−126.6	−58.8	−44.3	−150.8	....
Services: Credit	78add	28.5	30.0	26.1	24.2	36.6	38.8	31.5	49.2	34.3	43.6	49.4	....
Services: Debit	78aed	−338.8	−260.1	−147.7	−151.4	−185.7	−219.2	−161.5	−184.7	−167.1	−171.4	−221.9	....
Balance on Goods & Services	78afd	−325.4	−252.9	−281.7	−190.6	−227.0	−338.8	−91.1	−262.1	−191.7	−172.1	−323.3	....
Income: Credit	78agd	6.3	2.2	4.9	3.7	9.5	12.2	11.5	25.5	33.3	12.2	6.0	....
Income: Debit	78ahd	−83.4	−70.9	−47.2	−48.0	−44.8	−40.9	−48.1	−50.5	−50.5	−42.6	−44.5	....
Balance on Gds, Serv. & Inc.	78aid	−402.5	−321.6	−324.1	−234.9	−262.3	−367.6	−127.7	−287.0	−209.0	−202.5	−361.8	....
Current Transfers, n.i.e.: Credit	78ajd	155.2	167.9	154.0	171.0	138.0	116.2	134.1	137.7	143.1	148.8	170.0	....
Current Transfers: Debit	78akd	−37.7	−11.9	−10.6	−14.2	−23.0	−24.9	−10.8	−8.2	−7.6	−6.2	−8.9	....
Capital Account, n.i.e.	78bcd	−	−	....	....	....	....	....	....	....	....	....	....
Capital Account, n.i.e.: Credit	78bad	−	−	....	....	....	....	....	....	....	....	....	....
Capital Account: Debit	78bbd	−	−	....	....	....	....	....	....	....	....	....	....
Financial Account, n.i.e.	78bjd	93.6	188.9	200.5	87.6	170.5	146.5	237.8	219.6	188.8	213.4	134.0	....
Direct Investment Abroad	78bdd			....	....	....	....	....	....	....	....	....	....
Dir. Invest. in Rep. Econ., n.i.e.	78bed	−	−	25.0	5.6	15.8	14.9	12.1	58.5	26.0	19.3	5.9	....
Portfolio Investment Assets	78bfd			....	....	....	....	....	....	....	....	....	....
Equity Securities	78bkd	−	−	....	....	....	....	....	....	....	....	....	....
Debt Securities	78bld	−	−	....	....	....	....	....	....	....	....	....	....
Portfolio Investment Liab., n.i.e.	78bgd	−	−	....	....	....	....	....	....	....	....	....	....
Equity Securities	78bmd	−	−	....	....	....	....	....	....	....	....	....	....
Debt Securities	78bnd	−	−	....	....	....	....	....	....	....	....	....	....
Financial Derivatives Assets	78bwd	....	....	....	....	....	....	....	....	....	....	....	....
Financial Derivatives Liabilities	78bxd	....	....	....	....	....	....	....	....	....	....	....	....
Other Investment Assets	78bhd	11.9	−11.8	....	....	....	....	....	....	....	....	....	....
Monetary Authorities	78bod	....	....	....	....	....	....	....	....	....	....	....	....
General Government	78bpd	−	−	....	....	....	....	....	....	....	....	....	....
Banks	78bqd	11.9	−11.8	....	....	....	....	....	....	....	....	....	....
Other Sectors	78brd	−	−	....	....	....	....	....	....	....	....	....	....
Other Investment Liab., n.i.e.	78bid	81.7	200.6	175.6	81.9	154.7	131.7	225.7	161.1	162.8	194.1	128.1	....
Monetary Authorities	78bsd	−	−	−	−	−	−	−	−	−	−	−	....
General Government	78btd	41.4	150.9	130.1	49.9	131.5	128.1	169.4	106.2	107.9	139.2	73.3	....
Banks	78bud	−	−	−	−	−	−	−	−	−	−	−	....
Other Sectors	78bvd	40.3	49.7	45.4	32.0	23.2	3.6	56.3	54.8	54.8	54.8	54.8	....
Net Errors and Omissions	78cad	144.8	.7	−6.0	−84.3	−144.6	145.2	−407.6	−28.8	−23.9	−221.5	156.7	....
Overall Balance	78cbd	−46.5	24.0	13.9	−74.8	−121.6	15.5	−174.1	33.3	91.4	−68.0	90.0	....
Reserves and Related Items	79dad	46.5	−24.0	−13.9	74.8	121.6	−15.5	174.1	−33.3	−91.4	68.0	−90.0	....
Reserve Assets	79dbd	65.7	−18.1	−34.7	73.1	114.5	−9.1	181.4	−21.4	−90.6	75.0	−105.5	....
Use of Fund Credit and Loans	79dcd	−19.2	−5.9	20.8	1.6	7.1	−6.5	−7.3	−11.9	−.8	−7.0	15.5	....
Exceptional Financing	79ded	−	−	....	....	....	....	....	....	....	....	....	....
National Accounts							*Millions of Kwacha*							
Househ.Cons.Expend.,incl.NPISHs	96f	5,340.4	7,677.6	7,715.8	18,380.8	34,395.9	36,873.9	46,301.9	69,784.2	80,064.2	....	....	....
Government Consumption Expend	91f	1,240.9	1,423.5	3,257.9	4,068.7	4,635.8	5,241.8	6,399.2	9,676.3	12,933.2	....	....	....
Gross Fixed Capital Formation	93e	1,077.0	1,098.1	2,764.3	3,164.7	3,404.5	4,079.7	6,035.8	9,870.5	13,563.4	....	....	....
Changes in Inventories	93i	180.0	200.0	240.0	550.0	900.0	1,000.0	1,288.6	1,600.0	1,290.0	....	....	....
Exports of Goods and Services	90c	1,504.3	1,470.7	3,033.2	7,093.9	8,321.5	9,658.2	18,022.1	21,569.2	26,276.6	....	....	....
Imports of Goods and Services (-)	98c	2,858.4	2,900.9	6,784.8	11,318.1	15,203.7	14,543.3	20,728.6	33,878.4	36,968.4	....	....	....
Gross Domestic Product (GDP)	99b	6,484.2	8,968.9	10,227.4	21,940.0	36,454.0	42,310.4	57,319.0	78,621.9	97,159.0	....	....	....
Net Primary Income from Abroad	98.n	−140.5	−184.0	−375.3	−725.1	−596.7	−589.7	−1,230.4	−1,185.5	−1,437.0	....	....	....
Gross National Income (GNI)	99a	6,343.7	8,784.9	9,852.1	21,214.9	35,857.3	41,720.7	56,088.6	77,436.4	95,722.0	....	....	....
GDP Volume 1978 Prices	99b.p	972.1	1,077.1	952.1	....	....	....	....	....	....	....	....	....
GDP Volume 1994 Prices	99b.p	....	....	9,148.8	10,410.5	11,497.9	12,302.5	12,567.9	13,022.6	13,316.2	....	....	....
GDP Volume (2000=100)	99bvp	70.1	77.7	†68.7	78.2	86.3	92.4	94.4	97.8	100.0	....	....	....
GDP Deflator (2000=100)	99bip	9.5	11.9	15.3	28.9	43.5	47.1	62.5	82.7	100.0	....	....	....
						Millions: Midyear Estimates							
Population	99z	9.80	9.85	9.92	10.05	10.25	10.50	10.79	11.09	11.37	11.63	11.87	12.11

2004, International Monetary Fund : *International Financial Statistics Yearbook*

Malaysia 548

		1992	1993	1994	1995	1996	1997	1998	1999	2000	2001	2002	2003
Exchange Rates						*Ringgit per SDR: End of Period*							
Official Rate	aa	3.5915	3.7107	3.7372	3.7787	3.6366	5.2511	5.3505	5.2155	4.9511	4.7756	5.1662	5.6467
					Ringgit per US Dollar: End of Period (ae) Period Average (rf)								
Official Rate	ae	2.6120	2.7015	2.5600	2.5420	2.5290	3.8919	3.8000	3.8000	3.8000	3.8000	3.8000	3.8000
Official Rate	rf	2.5474	2.5741	2.6243	2.5044	2.5159	2.8132	3.9244	3.8000	3.8000	3.8000	3.8000	3.8000
					Index Numbers (2000=100): Period Averages								
Official Rate	ahx	149.2	147.6	144.9	151.5	151.0	137.8	97.1	100.0	100.0	100.0	100.0	100.0
Nominal Effective Exchange Rate	nec	121.3	125.9	125.0	124.9	128.9	125.3	96.4	97.4	100.0	105.8	105.0	98.0
Real Effective Exchange Rate	rec	119.2	120.5	115.8	115.7	121.1	119.4	94.9	97.6	100.0	105.5	105.6	97.1
Fund Position						*Millions of SDRs: End of Period*							
Quota	2f.s	833	833	833	833	833	833	833	1,487	1,487	1,487	1,487	1,487
SDRs	1b.s	82	88	93	102	115	130	146	61	81	100	111	120
Reserve Position in the Fund	1c.s	240	229	274	456	478	445	445	608	608	608	581	586
of which: Outstg.Fund Borrowing	2c	–	–	–	–	–	–	–	–	–	–	–	–
Total Fund Cred.&Loans Outstg	2tl	–	–	–	–	–	–	–	–	–	–	–	–
International Liquidity						*Millions of US Dollars Unless Otherwise Indicated: End of Period*							
Total Reserves minus Gold	1l.d	17,228	27,249	25,423	23,774	27,009	20,788	25,559	30,588	29,523	30,474	34,222	44,515
SDRs	1b.d	113	121	135	151	166	175	205	83	105	125	151	178
Reserve Position in the Fund	1c.d	330	315	400	678	688	600	626	835	792	764	790	871
Foreign Exchange	1d.d	16,784	26,814	24,888	22,945	26,156	20,013	24,728	29,670	28,625	29,585	33,280	43,466
Gold (Million Fine Troy Ounces)	1ad	2.390	2.390	2.390	2.390	2.390	2.350	2.350	1.180	1.170	1.170	1.170	1.170
Gold (National Valuation)	1and	115	115	122	124	120	111	116	57	53	51	56	61
Monetary Authorities: Other Liab.	4..d	8.5	14.5	11.7	10.5	6.3	.7	.8	.5	1.3	.7	.9	.8
Deposit Money Banks: Assets	7a.d	2,008.6	3,893.0	4,168.0	4,178.0	4,357.3	6,003.2	5,517.3	6,519.0	7,470.4	7,161.5	7,460.5	6,213.2
Liabilities	7b.d	7,153.1	13,956.0	8,161.0	8,242.0	11,240.9	12,339.4	9,160.5	7,296.3	6,772.2	6,079.6	8,343.4	9,367.7
Other Banking Insts.: Assets	7e.d	49.5	50.8	65.4	82.1	147.0	274.6	266.9	245.4	382.6	278.6	393.0	458.6
Liabilities	7f.d	–	–	11.9	24.3	346.0	445.7	348.6	244.6	201.0	136.9	308.9	243.9
Monetary Authorities						*Millions of Ringgit: End of Period*							
Foreign Assets	11	†47,233	76,485	68,200	63,790	†70,737	60,369	99,427	117,255	113,247	116,922	131,093	170,127
Claims on Central Government	12a	†561	454	980	2,155	†7,113	7,153	3,926	2,377	1,838	1,422	600	99
Claims on Private Sector	12d	410	1,296	601	566	†8,270	9,843	16,018	22,517	29,476	27,403	25,029	25,118
Claims on Deposit Money Banks	12e	3,860	3,597	3,443	3,250	†3,676	27,451	2,512	2,135	1,616	1,193	2,902	2,894
Claims on Nonbank Financial Insts	12g	698	1,104	2,718	3,505	†634	508	2,114	2,282	2,157	2,219	1,983	1,968
Reserve Money	14	†40,732	28,253	38,482	47,970	†64,559	82,896	36,178	45,675	41,372	40,022	42,582	45,534
of which: Currency Outside DMBs	14a	†12,124	13,506	15,884	17,433	†18,979	21,360	18,162	24,757	22,263	22,148	23,897	26,101
Other Liabilities to DMBs	14n	†–	–	–	–	†6,036	7,030	19,014	46,152	43,509	38,688	53,280	82,410
Time and Savings Deposits	15	†5	25	16	5	†5,790	2,320	9,079	2,043	9,171	10,637	5,601	5,379
Liabs. of Central Bank: Securities	16ac	–	–	–	–	†4,968	909	4	379	7,085	7,477	12,281	13,385
Foreign Liabilities	16c	22	39	30	27	†16	3	3	2	5	3	3	3
Central Government Deposits	16d	†5,679	2,912	8,469	8,379	†11,401	10,545	25,281	18,514	17,845	25,237	13,827	4,905
Capital Accounts	17a	4,155	4,172	3,507	3,513	†3,633	4,085	4,099	31,413	27,384	24,092	30,960	43,192
Other Items (Net)	17r	†2,168	47,535	25,438	13,374	†–5,974	–2,466	30,339	2,389	1,962	3,003	3,073	5,397
Deposit Money Banks						*Millions of Ringgit: End of Period*							
Reserves	20	†23,850	51,493	35,670	32,421	†30,729	42,266	13,679	16,918	14,902	13,978	14,664	15,169
Claims on Mon.Author.:Securities	20c	–	–	–	–	†3,096	–	–	9	4,822	5,112	7,464	7,661
Other Claims on Monetary Author	20n	–	–	–	–	†2,183	2,931	17,135	41,231	38,366	29,137	39,094	62,631
Foreign Assets	21	†5,247	10,482	10,542	10,320	†11,020	23,364	20,966	24,772	28,387	27,214	28,350	23,610
Claims on Central Government	22a	†11,324	10,683	11,127	10,182	†10,270	12,605	17,719	15,292	19,108	21,100	21,256	27,121
Claims on State & Local Govts	22b	–	–	–	–	†556	744	721	552	639	786	518	544
Claims on Nonfin.Pub.Enterprises	22c	–	–	–	–	†864	4,008	4,416	4,839	4,951	2,638	3,135	3,634
Claims on Private Sector	22d	†110,418	122,344	141,965	185,472	†234,484	289,853	298,162	303,657	322,206	336,825	359,802	380,799
Claims on Other Banking Insts	22f	†8,252	8,770	14,463	18,631	†29,358	43,220	25,383	12,887	15,393	18,330	18,099	29,210
Claims on Nonbank Financial Insts	22g	....	....	....	....	8,921	16,051	23,672	21,227	22,519	22,490	20,565	20,283
Demand Deposits	24	†18,931	29,128	31,724	36,191	†40,466	41,970	36,032	46,841	54,520	57,791	63,892	75,083
Time, Savings,& Fgn.Currency Dep	25	†73,682	90,184	99,776	124,935	†154,338	189,878	203,465	239,207	258,524	262,450	270,641	291,307
Money Market Instruments	26aa	21,741	23,196	35,731	48,266	†39,026	50,121	50,465	28,565	30,487	32,760	38,189	45,430
Bonds	26ab	....	....	....	....	561	1,878	1,267	1,704	1,594	2,083	667	667
Foreign Liabilities	26c	†18,684	31,488	17,000	15,873	†28,428	48,024	34,810	27,726	25,734	23,103	31,705	35,597
Central Government Deposits	26d	†1,495	1,903	2,795	4,149	†5,887	7,182	10,069	12,238	11,819	10,829	10,077	9,892
Credit from Central Bank	26g	2,304	2,171	1,781	1,772	†1,710	18,055	12	4	82	55	12	4
Liabilities to Other Banking Insts	26i	435	742	2,116	2,813	†6,723	15,148	8,474	9,386	8,218	7,167	7,115	13,221
Capital Accounts	27a	†14,843	16,884	23,813	29,478	†35,933	52,930	63,061	64,329	65,172	69,998	73,116	77,142
Other Items (Net)	27r	†6,976	8,076	–970	–6,452	†18,467	9,856	14,198	11,384	15,144	11,374	17,534	22,319

2004, International Monetary Fund : *International Financial Statistics Yearbook*

Malaysia 548

		1992	1993	1994	1995	1996	1997	1998	1999	2000	2001	2002	2003
Monetary Survey		\multicolumn{12}{c}{*Millions of Ringgit: End of Period*}
Foreign Assets (Net)	31n	†33,773	55,440	61,712	58,210	†53,313	35,706	85,579	114,299	115,895	121,030	127,734	158,137
Domestic Credit	32	†124,488	139,837	160,591	207,985	†283,180	366,257	356,783	354,878	388,623	397,148	427,083	473,979
Claims on Central Govt. (Net)	32an	†4,710	6,323	844	−190	†93	2,031	−13,705	−13,083	−8,719	−13,544	−2,048	12,422
Claims on State & Local Govts	32b	†–	–	–	–	†556	744	721	552	639	786	518	544
Claims on Nonfin.Pub.Enterprises	32c	–	–	–	–	†864	4,008	4,416	4,839	4,951	2,638	3,135	3,634
Claims on Private Sector	32d	†110,828	123,640	142,566	186,038	†242,754	299,695	314,181	326,174	351,682	364,228	384,831	405,918
Claims on Other Banking Insts	32f	†8,252	8,770	14,463	18,631	†29,358	43,220	25,383	12,887	15,393	18,330	18,099	29,210
Claims on Nonbank Financial Inst	32g	698	1,104	2,718	3,505	†9,555	16,559	25,786	23,509	24,676	24,710	22,548	22,251
Money	34	†35,544	48,077	56,175	63,594	†74,182	82,840	58,522	75,602	80,656	83,882	91,932	105,602
Quasi-Money	35	†73,687	90,209	99,791	124,940	†160,127	192,198	212,544	241,249	267,695	273,088	276,241	296,686
Money Market Instruments	36aa	21,741	23,196	35,731	48,266	†39,026	50,121	50,465	28,565	30,487	32,760	38,189	45,430
Bonds	36ab	….	….	….	….	561	1,878	1,267	1,704	1,594	2,083	667	667
Liabs. of Central Bank: Securities	36ac	–	–	–	–	†1,872	909	4	370	2,263	2,365	4,817	5,724
Liabilities to Other Banking Insts	36i	435	742	2,116	2,813	†6,723	15,148	8,474	9,386	8,218	7,167	7,115	13,221
Capital Accounts	37a	†18,998	21,056	27,321	32,991	†39,565	57,016	67,160	95,741	92,556	94,090	104,076	120,334
Other Items (Net)	37r	†7,856	11,996	1,168	−6,409	†14,436	1,854	43,925	16,559	21,049	22,742	31,781	44,450
Money plus Quasi-Money	35l	†109,231	138,286	155,966	188,533	†234,309	275,038	271,066	316,852	348,351	356,970	368,173	402,288
Other Banking Institutions		\multicolumn{12}{c}{*Millions of Ringgit: End of Period*}
Reserves	40	†4,436	8,421	10,394	12,259	†14,865	19,711	4,516	4,795	4,116	4,136	4,335	4,582
Claims on Mon.Author.:Securities	40c	†–	–	–	–	†539	–	–	–	1,503	2,086	2,403	2,167
Other Claims on Monetary Author	40n	†–	–	–	–	†113	2	1,887	4,921	5,093	9,584	13,757	18,681
Foreign Assets	41	†129	137	167	209	†372	1,069	1,014	933	1,454	1,059	1,493	1,743
Claims on Central Government	42a	†4,209	3,703	3,010	2,997	†4,239	3,003	5,747	6,437	5,830	7,708	7,223	5,271
Claims on State & Local Govts	42b	–	–	–	–	†36	55	42	17	9	55	7	9
Claims on Nonfin.Pub.Enterprises	42c	–	–	–	–	†79	593	828	660	320	375	298	676
Claims on Private Sector	42d	†52,706	59,678	70,911	90,750	†116,616	146,626	134,775	122,425	129,459	134,845	142,128	151,012
Claims on Deposit Money Banks	42e	5,482	7,020	9,136	9,149	†5,599	10,740	9,681	10,231	8,351	6,176	6,951	13,950
Claims on Nonbank Financial Insts	42g	….	….	….	….	3,820	3,698	3,102	2,024	1,647	1,174	1,049	817
Time, Savings,& Fgn.Currency Dep	45	†44,801	56,353	61,072	68,712	†85,518	93,802	98,003	101,224	103,873	105,837	113,418	117,517
Money Market Instruments	46aa	7,685	7,343	10,883	16,166	†2,625	5,548	5,890	226	–	531	340	6,048
Bonds	46ab	….	….	….	….	212	1,022	892	820	787	787	120	120
Foreign Liabilities	46c	†–	–	31	62	†875	1,735	1,325	929	764	520	1,174	927
Central Government Deposits	46d	†453	722	707	1,213	†2,365	1,711	2,274	2,167	2,621	3,215	3,386	3,069
Credit from Monetary Authorities	46g	†–	–	–	–	†510	11,788	989	553	–	132	20	21
Credit from Deposit Money Banks	46h	6,085	6,981	13,267	19,094	†31,981	43,720	22,470	19,126	15,347	18,510	17,778	29,288
Capital Accounts	47a	†5,934	6,834	8,588	10,746	†14,721	19,572	20,446	20,523	21,638	24,108	25,281	26,200
Other Items (Net)	47r	†2,006	726	−930	−630	†7,469	6,600	9,303	6,876	12,752	13,557	18,126	15,716
Banking Survey		\multicolumn{12}{c}{*Millions of Ringgit: End of Period*}
Foreign Assets (Net)	51n	†33,902	55,577	61,849	58,357	†52,809	35,040	85,269	114,303	116,585	121,569	128,054	158,952
Domestic Credit	52	†172,698	193,725	219,341	281,887	†376,247	475,302	473,619	471,387	507,873	519,760	556,302	599,483
Claims on Central Govt. (Net)	52an	†8,466	9,304	3,146	1,594	†1,967	3,323	−10,232	−8,812	−5,510	−9,050	1,789	14,623
Claims on State & Local Govts	52b	†–	–	–	–	†593	799	763	569	649	841	525	553
Claims on Nonfin.Pub.Enterprises	52c	–	–	–	–	†943	4,602	5,244	5,499	5,271	3,013	3,433	4,310
Claims on Private Sector	52d	†163,534	183,317	213,477	276,788	†359,370	446,321	448,955	448,598	481,141	499,073	526,959	556,929
Claims on Nonbank Financial Inst	52g	698	1,104	2,718	3,505	†13,375	20,257	28,889	25,533	26,323	25,883	23,596	23,068
Liquid Liabilities	55l	†149,596	186,218	206,644	244,986	†304,962	349,129	364,552	413,280	448,108	458,670	477,255	515,223
Money Market Instruments	56aa	29,426	30,539	46,614	64,432	†41,651	55,669	56,356	28,792	30,487	33,292	38,529	51,478
Bonds	56ab	….	….	….	….	773	2,900	2,159	2,523	2,380	2,870	787	787
Liabs. of Central Bank: Securities	56ac	–	–	–	–	†1,334	909	4	370	760	279	2,414	3,557
Capital Accounts	57a	†24,932	27,890	35,908	43,737	†54,287	76,587	87,607	116,264	114,194	118,198	129,358	146,534
Other Items (Net)	57r	†2,647	4,655	−7,976	−12,911	†26,049	25,148	48,210	24,461	28,529	28,019	36,013	40,855
Money (National Definitions)		\multicolumn{12}{c}{*Millions of Ringgit: End of Period*}
Reserve Money	19ma	24,745	27,564	39,445	47,331	64,559	82,896	36,178	45,675	41,372	40,023	42,582	45,534
M1	59ma	30,395	41,792	46,471	51,924	60,585	63,365	54,135	73,447	78,216	80,728	89,072	102,081
M2	59mb	114,481	139,800	160,366	198,873	238,209	292,217	296,472	337,138	354,702	362,512	383,542	426,039
M3	59mc	159,178	196,611	222,330	271,948	329,708	390,809	401,459	434,590	456,496	469,519	501,125	549,627
Nonbank Financial Institutions		\multicolumn{12}{c}{*Millions of Ringgit: End of Period*}
Claims on Central Government	42a.s	3,170.2	4,546.6	6,050.1	….	….	….	….	….	….	….	….	….
Claims on Private Sector	42d.s	3,527.9	4,108.5	6,555.5	….	….	….	….	….	….	….	….	….
Real Estate	42h.s	372.8	382.4	834.7	….	….	….	….	….	….	….	….	….
Interest Rates		\multicolumn{12}{c}{*Percent Per Annum*}
Discount Rate (End of Period)	60	7.10	5.24	4.51	6.47	7.28	….	….	….	….	….	….	….
Money Market Rate	60b	7.92	7.10	4.20	5.60	6.92	7.61	8.46	3.38	2.66	2.79	2.73	2.74
Treasury Bill Rate	60c	7.66	6.48	3.68	5.50	6.41	6.41	6.86	3.53	2.86	2.79	2.73	2.79
Savings Rate	60k	3.35	4.21	3.67	3.61	3.87	4.18	4.26	3.10	2.73	2.55	2.25	1.95
Deposit Rate	60l	7.94	7.03	4.89	5.93	7.09	7.78	8.51	4.12	3.36	3.37	3.21	3.07
Lending Rate	60p	10.16	10.03	8.76	8.73	9.94	10.63	12.13	8.56	7.67	7.13	6.53	6.30
Government Bond Yield	61	….	6.35	5.11	6.51	6.39	6.87	7.66	5.63	5.11	3.54	3.47	3.60

Malaysia 548

		1992	1993	1994	1995	1996	1997	1998	1999	2000	2001	2002	2003
Prices, Production, Labor						*Index Numbers (2000=100): Period Averages*							
Share Prices	62	71.3	93.0	125.7	117.1	134.9	116.3	61.6	82.4	100.0	76.0	84.5	83.8
Producer Prices	63	76.8	77.9	81.7	86.2	88.2	90.5	100.3	97.0	100.0	95.0	99.2	104.8
Consumer Prices	64	77.1	79.9	†82.8	85.7	88.7	91.1	95.9	98.5	†100.0	101.4	103.3	104.3
Industrial Production	66	48.6	53.3	†59.7	67.5	74.9	82.9	77.0	83.9	100.0	95.9	100.3	109.6
Total Employment	67	74.3	77.4	79.7	84.0	88.1	90.0	93.0	95.8	100.0	101.5	103.5	107.2
						Number in Thousands: Period Averages							
Labor Force	67d	7,319	7,700	....	7,893	8,616	8,784	8,890	9,145	9,591	9,877	9,910	10,304
Employment	67e	7,048	7,383	....	7,645	8,400	8,569	8,603	8,831	9,291	9,517	9,564	9,935
Unemployment	67c	271	317	231	248	217	215	287	314	299	360	346	369
Unemployment Rate (%)	67r	3.7	3.0	2.9	2.8	2.5	2.5	3.2	3.5	3.1	3.7	3.5	3.6
International Transactions						*Millions of Ringgit*							
Exports	70	103,657	121,238	153,921	184,987	197,026	220,890	286,563	321,560	373,270	334,420	354,407	377,602
Rubber	70l	2,357	2,132	2,927	4,038	3,510	2,971	2,829	2,344	2,571	1,886	2,492	3,583
Palm Oil	70dg	5,436	5,799	8,365	10,395	9,435	10,817	17,779	14,475	9,948	9,876	14,861	20,286
Tin	70q	721	489	507	545	533	477	485	491	435	461	426	284
Imports, c.i.f.	71	101,441	117,405	155,921	194,345	197,280	220,936	228,124	248,478	311,459	280,691	303,502	311,402
Volume of Exports						*2000=100*							
Rubber	72l	105.8	95.8	104.0	103.6	100.2	104.1	101.1	98.5	100.0	84.0	93.0	96.7
Palm Oil	72dg	63.0	66.4	74.3	75.1	83.1	85.6	84.8	101.1	100.0	118.1	122.7	141.5
Tin	72q	219.0	172.4	176.2	170.8	166.6	154.2	108.6	116.5	100.0	132.3	131.3	73.5
Export Prices													
Rubber (Wholesale Price)	76l	86.6	86.5	109.5	151.6	136.2	111.0	108.8	90.6	100.0	87.3	103.8	143.9
Palm Oil (Unit Value)	74dg	86.8	87.9	113.2	139.2	114.2	127.0	210.8	143.9	100.0	84.1	121.7	144.2
Tin (Unit Value)	76q	75.7	65.2	65.3	73.4	73.6	71.5	102.7	96.9	100.0	80.1	74.9	87.0
Balance of Payments						*Millions of US Dollars: Minus Sign Indicates Debit*							
Current Account, n.i.e.	78ald	−2,167	−2,991	−4,520	−8,644	−4,462	−5,935	9,529	12,604	8,488	7,287	7,190	....
Goods: Exports f.o.b.	78aad	39,823	46,238	56,897	71,767	76,985	77,538	71,883	84,097	98,429	87,981	93,383	....
Goods: Imports f.o.b.	78abd	−36,673	−43,201	−55,320	−71,871	−73,137	−74,029	−54,378	−61,453	−77,602	−69,597	−75,248	....
Trade Balance	78acd	3,150	3,037	1,577	−103	3,848	3,510	17,505	22,644	20,827	18,383	18,135	....
Services: Credit	78add	4,989	6,412	9,320	11,602	15,135	15,727	11,517	11,919	13,941	14,455	14,878	....
Services: Debit	78aed	−7,336	−9,516	−12,052	−14,981	−17,573	−18,297	−13,127	−14,735	−16,747	−16,657	−16,448	....
Balance on Goods & Services	78afd	804	−68	−1,155	−3,483	1,411	940	15,895	19,828	18,020	16,182	16,565	....
Income: Credit	78agd	1,609	2,007	2,308	2,623	2,693	2,485	1,542	2,003	1,986	1,847	2,139	....
Income: Debit	78ahd	−4,752	−5,218	−5,903	−6,767	−7,383	−7,851	−5,446	−7,499	−9,594	−8,590	−8,734	....
Balance on Gds, Serv. & Inc.	78aid	−2,339	−3,278	−4,750	−7,626	−3,279	−4,426	11,991	14,332	10,412	9,439	9,970	....
Current Transfers, n.i.e.: Credit	78ajd	296	469	411	700	766	944	728	801	756	537	661	....
Current Transfers: Debit	78akd	−124	−181	−182	−1,717	−1,948	−2,453	−3,190	−2,529	−2,680	−2,689	−3,442	....
Capital Account, n.i.e.	78bcd	−40	−88	−82	–	–	–	–	....	....	....	–	....
Capital Account, n.i.e.: Credit	78bad	–	–	–	–	–	–	–	....	....	....	–	....
Capital Account: Debit	78bbd	−40	−88	−82	–	–	–	–	....	....	....	–	....
Financial Account, n.i.e.	78bjd	8,746	10,805	1,288	7,643	9,477	2,198	−2,550	−6,619	−6,276	−3,063	−3,142	....
Direct Investment Abroad	78bdd	–	–	–	–	–	–	–	−1,422	−2,026	−267	−1,905	....
Dir. Invest. in Rep. Econ., n.i.e.	78bed	5,183	5,006	4,342	4,178	5,078	5,137	2,163	3,895	3,788	554	3,203	....
Portfolio Investment Assets	78bfd	–	–	–	–	–	–	–	−133	−387	254	−563	....
Equity Securities	78bkd	–	–	–	–	–	–	–	....	....	....	−43	....
Debt Securities	78bld	–	–	–	–	–	–	–	....	....	....	−520	....
Portfolio Investment Liab., n.i.e.	78bgd	−1,122	−709	−1,649	−436	−268	−248	283	−892	−2,145	−666	−836	....
Equity Securities	78bmd	–	–	–	–	–	–	–	....	....	....	−55	....
Debt Securities	78bnd	−1,122	−709	−1,649	−436	−268	−248	283	....	....	....	−781	....
Financial Derivatives Assets	78bwd	....	....	....	....	....	....	....	160	279	−234	−174	....
Financial Derivatives Liabilities	78bxd	....	....	....	....	....	....	....	−291	−220	−3	−139	....
Other Investment Assets	78bhd	1,502	−934	504	1,015	4,134	−4,604	−5,269	−7,936	−5,565	−2,702	−4,597	....
Monetary Authorities	78bod	....	....	....	....	....	....	....	....	....	....	....	....
General Government	78bpd	−42	−64	−52	5	33	−14	−11	....	....	....	−3	....
Banks	78bqd	481	−2,057	−1,281	28	3,339	−979	−2,677	....	....	....	−96	....
Other Sectors	78brd	1,063	1,187	1,837	982	762	−3,611	−2,581	....	....	....	−4,497	....
Other Investment Liab., n.i.e.	78bid	3,183	7,441	−1,909	2,885	533	1,912	272	–	–	–	1,868	....
Monetary Authorities	78bsd	3	7	−3	–	–	–	–	–	–	–	–	....
General Government	78btd	−122	−509	−163	−216	−597	−350	180	....	....	....	1,245	....
Banks	78bud	3,150	6,282	−3,789	–	–	–	–	....	....	....	862	....
Other Sectors	78bvd	153	1,662	2,047	3,102	1,130	2,263	92	....	....	....	−239	....
Net Errors and Omissions	78cad	79	3,624	154	−762	−2,502	−137	3,039	−1,273	−3,221	−2,394	−391	....
Overall Balance	78cbd	6,618	11,350	−3,160	−1,763	2,513	−3,875	10,018	4,712	−1,009	1,829	3,657	....
Reserves and Related Items	79dad	−6,618	−11,350	3,160	1,763	−2,513	3,875	−10,018	−4,712	1,009	−1,000	−3,657	....
Reserve Assets	79dbd	−6,618	−11,350	3,160	1,763	−2,513	3,875	−10,018	−4,712	1,009	−1,000	−3,657	....
Use of Fund Credit and Loans	79dcd	–	–	–	–	–	–	–	–	–	–	–	....
Exceptional Financing	79ded	....	....	....	....	....	....	....	....	....	....	–	....

Malaysia 548

		1992	1993	1994	1995	1996	1997	1998	1999	2000	2001	2002	2003
International Investment Position						*Millions of US Dollars*							
Assets..................................	79aad	21,600	34,063	34,122	....	....	....	....	....	....	61,389	....	....
Direct Investment Abroad...............	79abd	1,058	1,437	2,635	....	....	....	....	....	....	8,982	....	....
Portfolio Investment.....................	79acd	429	391	650	....	....	....	....	....	....	1,792	....	....
Equity Securities........................	79add	429	391	650	....	....	....	....	....	....	1,261	....	....
Debt Securities.........................	79aed	–	–	–	....	....	....	....	....	....	531	....	....
Financial Derivatives.....................	79ald	–	–	–	....	....	....	....	....	....	617	....	....
Other Investment.........................	79afd	1,999	3,892	4,164	....	....	....	....	....	....	19,229	....	....
Monetary Authorities...................	79agd	–	–	–	....	....	....	....	....	....	....	....	....
General Government.....................	79ahd	–	–	–	....	....	....	....	....	....	....	....	....
Banks.....................................	79aid	1,999	3,892	4,164	....	....	....	....	....	....	....	....	....
Other Sectors............................	79ajd	–	–	–	....	....	....	....	....	....	....	....	....
Reserve Assets...........................	79akd	18,115	28,343	26,673	....	....	....	....	....	....	30,769	....	....
Liabilities..................................	79lad	35,247	42,898	39,757	....	....	....	....	....	....	77,002	....	....
Dir. Invest. in Rep. Economy...........	79lbd	16,860	20,591	22,916	....	....	....	....	....	....	20,760	....	....
Portfolio Investment.....................	79lcd	8,136	7,777	7,238	....	....	....	....	....	....	12,790	....	....
Equity Securities........................	79ldd	3,223	3,485	4,300	....	....	....	....	....	....	10,702	....	....
Debt Securities.........................	79led	4,913	4,292	2,938	....	....	....	....	....	....	2,088	....	....
Financial Derivatives.....................	79lld	–	–	–	....	....	....	....	....	....	568	....	....
Other Investment.........................	79lfd	10,252	14,530	9,604	....	....	....	....	....	....	42,884	....	....
Monetary Authorities...................	79lgd	–	–	–	....	....	....	....	....	....	....	....	....
General Government.....................	79lhd	3,097	2,875	2,956	....	....	....	....	....	....	....	....	....
Banks.....................................	79lid	7,155	11,656	6,647	....	....	....	....	....	....	....	....	....
Other Sectors............................	79ljd	–	–	–	....	....	....	....	....	....	....	....	....
Government Finance						*Millions of Ringgit: Year Ending December 31*							
Deficit (–) or Surplus.....................	80	–1,243	354	4,408	1,861	1,815	6,627	–5,002	–9,488	....	....	....	....
Revenue...................................	81	39,250	41,691	49,446	50,954	58,279	65,736	56,710	58,675	....	....	....	....
Expenditure...............................	82	40,493	41,337	45,038	49,093	56,464	59,109	60,371	68,210	....	....	....	....
Lending Minus Repayments............	83	....	....	....	....	....	....	1,341	–47	....	....	....	....
Financing													
Net Borrowing: Domestic...............	84a	1,480	375	1,751	–	1,291	–2,048	11,040	5,423	....	....	....	....
Net borrowing: Foreign.................	85a	–3,170	–3,134	–4,757	–1,635	–2,177	–1,682	1,819	2,923	....	....	....	....
Special Receipts..........................	86	201	126	519	166	475	....	....	....	....	....	....	....
Use of Cash Balances...................	87	2,732	2,279	–1,921	–392	–1,404	†–2,897	–7,857	1,142	....	....	....	....
Debt: Domestic............................	88b	76,083	76,536	78,260	78,038	79,211	76,968	88,197	93,750	....	....	....	....
Debt: Foreign..............................	89b	20,922	19,362	14,818	13,331	10,471	12,951	14,924	18,369	....	....	....	....
National Accounts						*Millions of Ringgit*							
Househ.Cons.Expend.,incl.NPISHs....	96f	75,749	83,144	94,088	106,613	116,794	127,783	117,718	125,056	145,355	150,644	159,506	169,813
Government Consumption Expend...	91f	19,604	21,750	23,973	27,527	28,178	30,341	27,670	33,044	35,676	42,097	50,015	53,892
Gross Fixed Capital Formation.........	93e	55,191	66,937	78,664	96,967	107,825	121,494	75,982	65,841	87,729	83,345	83,764	87,089
Changes in Inventories.....................	93i	–1,906	535	1,870	120	–2,579	–398	–427	1,476	5,378	–3,268	4,425	–1,456
Exports of Goods and Services.........	90c	114,494	135,896	174,255	209,323	232,358	262,885	327,836	364,861	427,004	389,256	411,391	450,592
Imports of Goods and Services (–).....	98c	112,450	136,068	177,389	218,077	228,843	260,310	265,536	289,514	358,530	327,765	348,443	367,917
Gross Domestic Product (GDP)........	99b	150,682	172,194	195,461	222,473	253,732	281,795	283,243	300,764	342,612	334,309	360,658	392,012
Net Primary Income from Abroad.....	98.n	–8,006	–8,265	–9,412	–10,377	–11,801	–15,095	–15,321	–20,886	–28,909	–25,623	–25,061	....
Gross National Income (GNI)...........	99a	142,676	163,928	186,049	212,095	241,931	266,699	267,923	279,878	313,703	308,686	335,597	....
GDP Volume 1987 Prices................	99b.p	126,408	138,916	151,713	166,625	183,292	196,714	182,237	193,422	209,538	210,480	208,975	230,710
GDP Volume (2000=100)................	99bvp	60.3	66.3	72.4	79.5	87.5	93.9	87.0	92.3	100.0	100.4	99.7	110.1
GDP Deflator (2000=100)................	99bip	72.9	75.8	78.8	81.7	84.7	87.6	95.1	95.1	100.0	97.1	105.6	103.9
						Millions: Midyear Estimates							
Population..............................	99z	18.82	19.32	19.84	20.36	20.89	21.43	21.97	22.49	23.00	23.49	23.97	24.42

2004, International Monetary Fund: *International Financial Statistics Yearbook*

Maldives 556

		1992	1993	1994	1995	1996	1997	1998	1999	2000	2001	2002	2003
Exchange Rates													
			*Rufiyaa per SDR: End of Period*
Market Rate	aa	14.486	15.253	17.182	17.496	16.925	15.881	16.573	16.154	15.335	16.086	17.402	19.020
						Rufiyaa per US Dollar: End of Period (ae) Period Average (rf)							
Market Rate	ae	10.535	11.105	11.770	11.770	11.770	11.770	11.770	11.770	11.770	12.800	12.800	12.800
Market Rate	rf	10.569	10.957	11.586	11.770	11.770	11.770	11.770	11.770	11.770	12.242	12.800	12.800
Fund Position						*Millions of SDRs: End of Period*							
Quota	2f.s	5.5	5.5	5.5	5.5	5.5	5.5	5.5	8.2	8.2	8.2	8.2	8.2
SDRs	1b.s	–	–	–	–	.1	.1	.1	.1	.2	.2	.3	.3
Reserve Position in the Fund	1c.s	.9	.9	.9	.9	.9	.9	.9	1.6	1.6	1.6	1.6	1.6
Total Fund Cred.&Loans Outstg.	2tl	–	–	–	–	–	–	–	–	–	–	–	–
International Liquidity						*Millions of US Dollars Unless Otherwise Indicated: End of Period*							
Total Reserves minus Gold	1l.d	28.19	26.15	31.22	47.95	76.17	98.31	118.54	127.12	122.80	93.07	133.14	159.49
SDRs	1b.d	.01	.03	.05	.07	.09	.11	.14	.19	.26	.31	.38	.45
Reserve Position in the Fund	1c.d	1.21	1.21	1.28	1.31	1.26	1.19	1.24	2.13	2.02	1.95	2.11	2.31
Foreign Exchange	1d.d	26.97	24.92	29.89	46.57	74.81	97.01	117.15	124.80	120.52	90.80	130.65	156.73
Gold (Million Fine Troy Ounces)	1ad	.001	.001	.001	.001	.002	.002	.002	.002	.002	.002	.002	.002
Gold (National Valuation)	1and	.042	.042	.042	....	....	....	....	....	....	....	.587	.705
Monetary Authorities: Other Liab.	4..d	.17	15.39	16.13	16.21	16.20	.86	.86	.86	.86	.79	.79	.79
Deposit Money Banks: Assets	7a.d	14.62	10.30	10.23	14.02	22.35	11.50	23.65	19.09	21.87	24.88	32.13	60.60
Liabilities	7b.d	22.08	18.37	13.61	19.03	12.83	12.20	15.06	26.90	32.42	27.58	35.02	16.61
Monetary Authorities						*Millions of Rufiyaa: End of Period*							
Foreign Assets	11	292.60	293.92	376.86	580.10	912.94	1,173.55	1,411.67	1,512.69	1,460.53	1,207.23	1,722.66	2,060.46
Claims on Central Government	12a	618.97	910.65	999.33	1,076.06	987.57	920.12	1,024.38	1,156.15	1,409.01	1,584.47	1,704.26	1,517.24
Claims on Nonfin.Pub.Enterprises	12c	8.86	9.75	6.16	8.42	7.86	–	3.20	2.48	1.57	1.48	1.48	1.48
Claims on Deposit Money Banks	12e	8.80	7.91	6.57	5.62	1.37	1.41	1.42	1.43	–	–	–	–
Reserve Money	14	730.74	869.86	993.09	1,008.87	1,187.93	1,371.25	1,520.08	1,624.79	1,696.13	1,861.31	2,209.09	2,171.67
of which: Currency Outside DMBs	14a	300.91	330.38	382.27	405.83	425.85	489.68	524.92	593.34	618.14	566.52	569.88	624.90
Foreign Currency Deposits	15	1.63	.63	5.50	17.00	26.64	32.70	20.69	26.51	37.35	10.16	14.88	10.00
Foreign Liabilities	16c	1.81	170.90	189.90	190.76	190.65	10.10	10.13	10.15	10.16	10.15	10.15	10.16
Central Government Deposits	16d	93.65	70.28	66.47	180.22	148.50	163.00	225.18	235.02	231.83	283.81	310.58	338.72
Capital Accounts	17a	46.61	74.45	90.55	62.72	105.60	130.39	105.82	118.28	179.30	185.61	89.11	183.52
Other Items (Net)	17r	54.80	36.11	43.41	210.63	250.42	387.63	559.19	658.00	716.34	442.13	794.59	865.11
Deposit Money Banks						*Millions of Rufiyaa: End of Period*							
Reserves	20	383.00	454.02	498.55	612.78	859.80	1,173.97	1,346.56	1,553.30	1,695.24	1,563.42	2,094.32	2,062.01
Foreign Assets	21	154.02	114.43	120.46	165.04	263.03	135.34	278.39	224.66	257.46	318.49	411.23	775.67
Claims on Central Government	22a	9.95	4.21	–	–	–	–	–	–	–	–	–	25.60
Claims on Nonfin.Pub.Enterprises	22c	154.31	177.04	137.24	160.98	147.32	103.78	161.89	193.80	183.15	182.55	209.55	88.88
Claims on Private Sector	22d	256.75	398.53	507.38	655.09	717.40	996.79	1,253.18	1,302.81	1,407.08	1,827.24	2,100.78	2,244.42
Demand Deposits	24	117.02	281.13	356.06	393.70	552.92	619.23	725.45	935.95	1,074.43	1,022.15	1,252.96	1,398.76
Time, Savings,& Fgn. Currency Dep.	25	293.80	340.13	429.26	569.91	785.77	1,075.30	1,423.72	1,318.10	1,252.06	1,658.63	2,064.84	2,428.39
Foreign Liabilities	26c	232.62	203.95	160.22	224.00	150.98	143.65	177.25	316.60	381.62	353.07	448.23	212.59
Central Government Deposits	26d	51.06	60.40	31.52	58.43	90.24	93.48	126.08	160.95	182.16	222.09	259.80	292.26
Credit from Monetary Authorities	26g	8.67	7.64	6.63	5.15	1.34	.89	.89	.14	–	–	–	–
Capital Accounts	27a	91.72	122.32	143.77	157.69	281.00	358.92	486.96	496.18	610.86	572.11	646.51	685.56
Other Items (Net)	27r	163.14	132.66	136.17	185.01	125.30	118.41	99.67	46.65	41.80	63.65	143.55	179.01
Monetary Survey						*Millions of Rufiyaa: End of Period*							
Foreign Assets (Net)	31n	212.19	33.50	147.20	330.38	834.34	1,155.14	1,502.68	1,410.60	1,326.21	1,162.50	1,675.52	2,613.38
Domestic Credit	32	904.13	1,369.50	1,552.12	1,661.90	1,621.41	1,764.21	2,091.39	2,259.27	2,586.82	3,089.84	3,445.69	3,246.63
Claims on Central Govt. (Net)	32an	484.21	784.18	901.34	837.41	748.83	663.64	673.12	760.18	995.02	1,078.57	1,133.88	911.85
Claims on Nonfin.Pub.Enterprises	32c	163.17	186.79	143.40	169.40	155.18	103.78	165.09	196.28	184.72	184.03	211.03	90.37
Claims on Private Sector	32d	256.75	398.53	507.38	655.09	717.40	996.79	1,253.18	1,302.81	1,407.08	1,827.24	2,100.78	2,244.42
Money	34	463.88	694.54	850.87	899.06	1,059.35	1,195.60	1,384.24	1,585.18	1,760.44	1,655.91	1,886.71	2,105.35
Quasi-Money	35	295.43	340.76	434.76	586.91	812.41	1,108.00	1,444.41	1,344.61	1,289.41	1,668.79	2,079.71	2,438.39
Capital Accounts	37a	138.33	196.77	234.32	220.41	386.60	489.31	592.35	614.46	790.16	757.72	735.62	869.08
Other Items (Net)	37r	218.69	170.93	179.37	285.90	197.39	126.43	173.06	125.62	73.02	169.91	419.16	447.19
Money plus Quasi-Money	35l	759.31	1,035.30	1,285.63	1,485.97	1,871.76	2,303.60	2,828.65	2,929.79	3,049.85	3,324.70	3,966.42	4,543.75
Interest Rates						*Percent Per Annum*							
Money Market Rate	60b	7.00	5.00	5.00	6.80	6.80	6.80	6.80	6.80	6.80	....	....	....
Savings Rate	60k	....	....	....	....	6.00	6.00	6.00	6.00	6.00	6.00	5.50	5.25
Deposit Rate	60l	....	....	....	....	6.80	6.80	6.80	6.93	6.88	6.97	7.50	7.50
Lending Rate	60p	....	....	....	15.00	15.00	15.00	15.00	12.50	13.00	13.00	13.54	14.00
Prices, Production, Labor						*Index Numbers (2000=100): Period Averages*							
Consumer Prices	64	66.6	80.0	82.7	87.2	92.7	99.7	98.3	101.2	100.0	100.7	101.6	98.7
Total Fish Catch	66al	71.1	77.9	90.1	90.5	91.3	88.2	99.7	106.8	100.0	108.3	138.8	131.9
Tourist Bed Night Index	66.t	50.2	53.1	59.7	69.2	77.2	83.1	88.1	94.4	100.0	99.9	103.3	119.5
						Number in Thousands: Period Averages							
Labor Force	67d	....	....	....	67	....	....	....	....	86	....	....	....

Maldives 556

		1992	1993	1994	1995	1996	1997	1998	1999	2000	2001	2002	2003
International Transactions							*Millions of US Dollars*						
Exports	70..d	39.7	34.6	47.9	49.6	59.2	69.9	74.3	63.7	75.9	76.2	90.4	112.5
Imports, c.i.f.	71..d	189.3	191.3	221.7	267.9	301.7	348.8	354.0	402.2	388.6	393.5	391.7	470.8
Imports, f.o.b.	71.vd	166.6	168.3	195.1	235.8	265.5	307.0	311.5	353.9	342.0	346.3	344.7	414.3
Balance of Payments						*Millions of US Dollars: Minus Sign Indicates Debit*							
Current Account, n.i.e.	78ald	−19.6	−53.8	−11.1	−18.1	−7.4	−34.7	−21.9	−78.9	−51.5	−57.3	−44.0	....
Goods: Exports f.o.b.	78aad	65.1	52.7	75.4	85.0	79.9	89.7	95.6	91.5	108.7	110.2	133.6	....
Goods: Imports f.o.b.	78abd	−167.9	−177.7	−195.1	−235.8	−265.5	−307.0	−311.5	−353.9	−342.0	−346.3	−344.7	....
Trade Balance	78acd	−102.8	−125.0	−119.6	−150.8	−185.6	−217.3	−215.9	−262.4	−233.3	−236.0	−211.1	....
Services: Credit	78add	154.3	160.7	197.4	232.8	289.0	312.2	331.3	342.8	348.5	354.1	355.5	....
Services: Debit	78aed	−49.4	−57.2	−62.8	−76.7	−87.9	−94.2	−98.9	−108.1	−109.7	−109.2	−111.2	....
Balance on Goods & Services	78afd	2.1	−21.5	15.0	5.4	15.5	.6	16.6	−27.8	5.5	8.8	33.2	....
Income: Credit	78agd	2.9	3.0	3.8	4.5	6.0	7.5	8.6	9.0	10.3	6.8	4.1	....
Income: Debit	78ahd	−20.0	−22.0	−24.0	−24.5	−27.8	−34.9	−36.8	−40.1	−40.3	−45.3	−40.7	....
Balance on Gds, Serv. & Inc.	78aid	−15.0	−40.5	−5.3	−14.6	−6.3	−26.8	−11.6	−58.8	−24.5	−29.7	−3.4	....
Current Transfers, n.i.e.: Credit	78ajd	14.3	13.3	16.3	23.0	26.2	20.0	20.3	20.4	19.3	22.0	9.6	....
Current Transfers: Debit	78akd	−18.9	−26.5	−22.2	−26.6	−27.3	−27.9	−30.6	−40.5	−46.2	−49.6	−50.2	....
Capital Account, n.i.e.	78bcd	−	−	−	−	−	−	−	−	−	−	−	....
Capital Account, n.i.e.: Credit	78bad	−	−	−	−	−	−	−	−	−	−	−	....
Capital Account: Debit	78bbd	−	−	−	−	−	−	−	−	−	−	−	....
Financial Account, n.i.e.	78bjd	44.6	46.3	27.5	67.6	52.2	71.0	60.2	76.2	40.2	35.5	78.9	....
Direct Investment Abroad	78bdd	−	−	−	−	−	−	−	−	−	−	−	....
Dir. Invest. in Rep. Econ., n.i.e.	78bed	6.6	6.9	8.7	7.2	9.3	11.4	11.5	12.3	13.0	11.7	11.7	....
Portfolio Investment Assets	78bfd	−	−	−	−	−	−	−	−	−	−	−	....
Equity Securities	78bkd	−	−	−	−	−	−	−	−	−	−	−	....
Debt Securities	78bld	−	−	−	−	−	−	−	−	−	−	−	....
Portfolio Investment Liab., n.i.e.	78bgd	−	−	−	−	−	−	−	−	−	−	−	....
Equity Securities	78bmd	−	−	−	−	−	−	−	−	−	−	−	....
Debt Securities	78bnd	....	....	....	....	....	....	....	....	....	....	....	....
Financial Derivatives Assets	78bwd	....	....	....	....	....	....	....	....	....	....	....	
Financial Derivatives Liabilities	78bxd	....	....	....	....	....	....	....	....	....	....	....	
Other Investment Assets	78bhd	15.7	25.0	13.2	29.8	32.6	53.8	30.8	47.5	22.8	21.3	36.0	....
Monetary Authorities	78bod	....	....	....	....	....	....	....	....	....	....	....	
General Government	78bpd	−	−	−	−	−	−	−	−	−	−	−	
Banks	78bqd	−1.8	4.3	.1	−3.8	−8.3	10.8	−12.2	4.6	−2.8	−3.0	2.2	....
Other Sectors	78brd	17.5	20.7	13.1	33.6	41.0	42.9	42.9	42.9	25.6	24.3	33.8	....
Other Investment Liab., n.i.e.	78bid	22.3	14.4	5.5	30.5	10.2	5.8	17.9	16.4	4.4	2.4	31.2	....
Monetary Authorities	78bsd	−	15.2	.7	.1	−	−15.3	−	−	−	−.1	−	
General Government	78btd	17.1	3.8	8.2	24.8	17.3	21.9	14.6	5.2	−1.9	7.8	37.0	....
Banks	78bud	5.2	−4.6	−3.4	5.7	−7.1	−.8	3.3	11.2	6.3	−5.3	−5.8	....
Other Sectors	78bvd	−	−	−	−	−	−	−	−	....	....	....	
Net Errors and Omissions	78cad	−20.2	6.1	−10.9	−32.2	−16.4	−14.0	−18.2	11.4	6.9	−7.9	−27.1	....
Overall Balance	78cbd	4.8	−1.3	5.5	17.2	28.3	22.2	20.2	8.6	−4.3	−29.7	7.8	....
Reserves and Related Items	79dad	−4.8	1.3	−5.5	−17.2	−28.3	−22.2	−20.2	−8.6	4.3	29.7	−7.8	....
Reserve Assets	79dbd	−4.8	1.3	−5.5	−17.2	−28.3	−22.2	−20.2	−8.6	4.3	29.7	−7.8	....
Use of Fund Credit and Loans	79dcd	−	−	−	−	−	−	−	−	−	−	−	
Exceptional Financing	79ded	−	−	−	−	−	−	−	−	....	....	....	....
International Investment Position							*Millions of US Dollars*						
Assets	79aad	....	....	....	....	....	....	....	....	....	....	....	
Direct Investment Abroad	79abd	−	−	−	−	−	−	−	−	−	−	−	
Portfolio Investment	79acd	−	−	−	−	−	−	−	−	−	−	−	
Equity Securities	79add	−	−	−	−	−	−	−	−	−	−	−	
Debt Securities	79aed	−	−	−	−	−	−	−	−	−	−	−	
Financial Derivatives	79ald	....	....	....	....	....	....	....	....	....	....	....	
Other Investment	79afd	14.6	10.3	10.2	14.0	22.3	11.5	23.7	19.1	21.9	24.9	32.1	....
Monetary Authorities	79agd	−	−	−	−	−	−	−	−	−	−	−	
General Government	79ahd	−	−	−	−	−	−	−	−	−	−	−	
Banks	79aid	14.6	10.3	10.2	14.0	22.3	11.5	23.7	19.1	21.9	24.9	32.1	....
Other Sectors	79ajd	−	−	−	−	−	−	−	−	−	−	−	
Reserve Assets	79akd	27.8	26.5	32.0	49.3	77.6	99.7	119.9	128.5	124.1	94.3	134.6	....
Liabilities	79lad	....	....	....	....	....	....	....	....	....	....	....	
Dir. Invest. in Rep. Economy	79lbd	....	....	....	....	....	....	....	....	....	....	....	
Portfolio Investment	79lcd	−	−	−	−	−	−	−	−	−	−	−	
Equity Securities	79ldd	−	−	−	−	−	−	−	−	−	−	−	
Debt Securities	79led	−	−	−	−	−	−	−	−	−	−	−	
Financial Derivatives	79lld	....	....	....	....	....	....	....	....	....	....	....	
Other Investment	79lfd	116.5	130.4	141.9	173.1	178.1	178.9	201.6	213.8	212.4	210.6	257.9	....
Monetary Authorities	79lgd	.2	15.4	16.1	16.2	16.2	.9	.9	.9	.9	.8	.8	....
General Government	79lhd	93.3	96.7	110.8	136.2	148.4	165.3	184.7	185.6	178.0	181.5	221.2	....
Banks	79lid	23.0	18.4	15.0	20.6	13.5	12.8	16.1	27.3	33.6	28.3	35.9	....
Other Sectors	79ljd	−	−	−	−	−	−	−	−	−	−	−	

2004, International Monetary Fund : *International Financial Statistics Yearbook*

Maldives   556

		1992	1993	1994	1995	1996	1997	1998	1999	2000	2001	2002	2003
Government Finance			*Millions of Rufiyaa: Year Ending December 31*
Deficit (-) or Surplus	80	−356.9	−412.6	−206.6	−300.1	−133.8	−81.3	−123.1	−281.1	−321.5	−363.3	−402.4	−366.6f
Revenue	81	684.2	765.2	981.7	1,209.5	1,324.9	1,656.5	1,765.7	2,062.6	2,206.8	2,310.9	2,582.4	2,939.4f
Grants Received	81z	151.4	153.3	162.6	199.2	242.9	168.2	164.5	162.7	165.9	211.7	132.5	122.4f
Expenditure	82	1,166.9	1,317.4	1,357.5	1,717.8	1,692.6	1,936.9	2,113.9	2,494.9	2,739.9	2,912.1	3,135.5	3,529.2f
Lending Minus Repayments	83	25.6	13.7	−6.6	−9.0	9.0	−30.9	−60.6	11.5	−45.7	−26.2	−18.2	−100.8f
Financing													
Domestic	84a	189.9	377.0	106.4	2.1	−29.2	−90.9	−6.2	224.4	317.9	217.5	30.0	−104.3f
Foreign	85a	167.0	35.6	100.2	298.0	163.0	172.2	129.3	56.7	3.6	145.8	372.4	470.9f
Debt: Domestic	88a	526.1	846.5	960.9	1,063.0	957.6	877.1	980.3	1,101.0	1,317.4	1,495.1	1,653.2	1,464.7f
Debt: Foreign	89a	726.9	762.5	862.7	1,160.7	1,323.7	1,495.9	1,625.2	1,681.9	1,685.5	1,831.3	2,203.7	2,674.6f
National Accounts			*Millions of Rufiyaa*
Government Consumption Expend	91f	....	....	....	788	859	1,060	1,184	1,386	1,599	1,619	....	....
Gross Fixed Capital Formation	93e	....	....	....	1,479	1,053	2,087	2,042	2,400	1,727	2,079	....	....
Changes in Inventories	93i	....	....	....	....	....	....	....	....	....	....	....	....
Exports of Goods and Services	90c	417	377	555	4,961	4,954	5,476	5,859	6,107	6,796	6,817	....	....
Imports of Goods and Services (-)	98c	2,002	2,097	2,571	3,153	3,361	4,774	4,961	5,604	5,809	6,022	....	....
GDP Volume 1995 Prices	99b.p	3,510	3,700	3,978	4,272	4,660	5,145	5,648	6,057	6,345	6,564	6,993	7,586
GDP Volume (2000=100)	99bvp	55.3	58.3	62.7	67.3	73.4	81.1	89.0	95.4	100.0	103.5	110.2	119.5
GDP Deflator (2000=100)	99bip	73.1	81.4	88.4	93.3	96.6	98.9	97.2	98.7	100.0	102.0	....	....
			*Millions: Midyear Estimates*
Population	99z	.23	.24	.24	.25	.26	.27	.27	.28	.29	.30	.31	.32

Mali 678

		1992	1993	1994	1995	1996	1997	1998	1999	2000	2001	2002	2003
Exchange Rates						*Francs per SDR: End of Period*							
Official Rate	aa	378.57	404.89	†780.44	728.38	753.06	807.94	791.61	†896.19	918.49	935.39	850.37	771.76
					Francs per US Dollar: End of Period (ae) Period Average (rf)								
Official Rate	ae	275.32	294.77	†534.60	490.00	523.70	598.81	562.21	†652.95	704.95	744.31	625.50	519.36
Official Rate	rf	264.69	283.16	†555.20	499.15	511.55	583.67	589.95	†615.70	711.98	733.04	696.99	581.20
Fund Position						*Millions of SDRs: End of Period*							
Quota	2f.s	68.9	68.9	68.9	68.9	68.9	68.9	68.9	93.3	93.3	93.3	93.3	93.3
SDRs	1b.s	.1	.1	.1	.3	.2	–	.1	.4	.1	.3	–	.6
Reserve Position in the Fund	1c.s	8.7	8.7	8.7	8.7	8.8	8.8	8.8	8.8	8.8	8.8	8.8	8.9
Total Fund Cred.&Loans Outstg.	2tl	47.5	51.4	74.1	99.0	114.6	130.2	132.4	140.9	134.7	136.0	121.8	113.6
International Liquidity						*Millions of US Dollars Unless Otherwise Indicated: End of Period*							
Total Reserves minus Gold	1l.d	307.9	332.4	†221.4	323.0	431.5	414.9	402.9	349.7	381.3	348.9	594.5	908.7
SDRs	1b.d	.1	.1	.2	.5	.3	.1	.1	.6	.1	.4	–	.9
Reserve Position in the Fund	1c.d	11.9	12.0	12.7	13.0	12.6	11.8	12.4	12.1	11.4	11.1	12.0	13.2
Foreign Exchange	1d.d	295.9	320.3	†208.5	309.5	418.6	403.0	390.4	337.1	369.7	337.4	582.4	894.6
Gold (Million Fine Troy Ounces)	1ad	.019	.019	.019	–	–	–	–	–	–	–	–	–
Gold (National Valuation)	1and	6.5	7.0	7.0	–	–	–	–	–	–	–	–	–
Monetary Authorities: Other Liab.	4..d	2.5	6.0	9.7	1.9	–6.9	3.7	1.8	3.1	2.0	2.7	5.7	6.9
Deposit Money Banks: Assets	7a.d	40.4	26.3	118.7	163.6	136.7	117.6	125.2	116.6	140.1	195.0	189.9	218.8
Liabilities	7b.d	47.3	42.2	34.3	102.1	70.0	28.2	49.1	87.9	79.6	83.9	115.2	146.8
Monetary Authorities						*Billions of Francs: End of Period*							
Foreign Assets	11	84.8	98.0	118.4	158.2	226.0	248.4	226.5	228.3	268.8	259.7	371.8	471.9
Claims on Central Government	12a	37.2	41.0	58.7	65.1	77.0	99.8	105.9	112.9	108.9	135.9	125.3	117.6
Claims on Deposit Money Banks	12e	23.9	23.9	–	–	–	–	–	–	–	–	–	–
Claims on Other Financial Insts.	12f	–	–	–	–	–	–	–	–	–	–	–	–
Reserve Money	14	131.7	143.8	115.9	127.7	151.1	162.8	153.7	173.1	219.0	245.2	359.3	451.5
of which: Currency Outside DMBs	14a	60.9	65.1	91.1	107.5	120.3	129.5	135.3	123.4	146.9	179.0	247.5	318.2
Foreign Liabilities	16c	18.7	22.6	63.0	73.1	82.7	107.5	105.9	128.4	125.2	129.2	107.1	91.3
Central Government Deposits	16d	5.9	5.5	12.8	27.1	63.0	70.6	63.7	41.5	34.7	17.2	17.8	25.8
Other Items (Net)	17r	–10.4	–9.1	–14.6	–4.6	6.2	7.4	9.2	–1.8	–1.2	4.1	12.9	21.0
Deposit Money Banks						*Billions of Francs: End of Period*							
Reserves	20	70.5	79.4	25.3	17.1	29.5	32.1	16.5	47.7	70.7	59.2	99.7	132.4
Foreign Assets	21	11.1	7.8	63.4	80.2	71.6	70.4	70.4	76.2	98.8	145.2	118.8	113.6
Claims on Central Government	22a	3.4	3.4	28.0	19.4	24.0	21.1	13.6	14.0	17.8	27.7	23.3	14.3
Claims on Private Sector	22d	91.9	93.8	84.9	130.3	171.2	195.9	251.0	286.5	283.6	342.2	412.2	482.3
Claims on Other Financial Insts.	22f	–	–	–	–	–	–	–	–	–	–	–	–
Demand Deposits	24	47.4	52.7	83.0	90.5	119.5	126.2	131.8	142.3	143.6	197.8	238.2	272.8
Time Deposits	25	49.0	52.6	63.1	56.4	76.4	89.0	91.9	97.0	116.1	110.0	137.0	173.4
Foreign Liabilities	26c	8.7	8.8	11.5	45.3	30.5	5.9	19.5	50.3	45.2	52.4	59.7	60.2
Long-Term Foreign Liabilities	26cl	4.3	3.6	6.9	4.7	6.1	10.9	8.1	7.1	10.9	10.1	12.4	16.0
Central Government Deposits	26d	37.1	33.0	39.3	50.8	71.5	68.2	78.0	102.3	129.8	159.2	158.5	178.7
Credit from Monetary Authorities	26g	24.1	23.9	–	–	.1	–	–	–	–	–	–	–
Other Items (Net)	27	6.3	9.8	–2.1	–.7	–8.0	19.3	22.2	25.3	25.3	44.8	48.3	41.6
Treasury Claims: Private Sector	22d.i	.7	1.5	2.1	1.5	2.0	4.5	3.9	5.2	2.7	1.3	–	.6
Post Office: Checking Deposits	24..i	–	–	–	–	–	–	–	–	–	–	–	–
Monetary Survey						*Billions of Francs: End of Period*							
Foreign Assets (Net)	31n	68.5	74.3	107.3	120.0	184.3	205.5	171.5	125.9	197.2	223.2	323.8	434.1
Domestic Credit	32	89.4	99.7	119.5	136.9	137.6	178.0	228.8	269.5	245.8	329.4	384.4	409.8
Claims on Central Govt. (Net)	32an	–3.2	4.4	32.6	5.1	–35.6	–22.4	–26.1	–22.2	–40.5	–14.0	–27.8	–73.1
Claims on Private Sector	32d	92.6	95.3	86.9	131.8	173.2	200.4	254.9	291.7	286.3	343.5	412.2	482.9
Claims on Other Financial Insts.	32f	–	–	–	–	–	–	–	–	–	–	–	–
Money	34	108.3	117.8	174.2	198.2	240.4	256.0	267.6	266.0	291.2	377.2	486.1	591.4
Quasi-Money	35	49.0	52.6	63.1	56.4	76.4	89.0	91.9	97.0	116.1	110.0	137.0	173.4
Long-Term Foreign Liabilities	36cl	4.3	3.6	6.9	4.7	6.1	10.9	8.1	7.1	10.9	10.1	12.4	16.0
Other Items (Net)	37r	–3.7	–	–17.3	–2.4	–1.0	27.5	32.8	25.2	24.9	55.4	72.8	63.1
Money plus Quasi-Money	35l	157.2	170.4	237.2	254.6	316.8	345.0	359.5	363.1	407.2	487.2	623.1	764.8
Interest Rates						*Percent Per Annum*							
Bank Rate (End of Period)	60	12.50	†6.00	6.00	6.00	6.00	6.00	6.00	6.00	6.00	6.00	6.00	4.50
Money Market Rate	60b	11.44	....	....	....	....	....	4.81	4.95	4.95	4.95	4.95	4.95
Deposit Rate	60l	7.75	....	....	....	....	....	3.50	3.50	3.50	3.50	3.50	3.50
Lending Rate	60p	16.75	....	....	....	....	....	....	....	....	....	....	....
Prices						*Index Numbers (2000=100): Period Averages*							
Consumer Prices	64	66.0	65.9	81.1	92.0	98.3	†98.0	101.9	100.7	100.0	105.2	110.5	109.0
International Transactions						*Billions of Francs*							
Exports	70	90.72	135.30	185.95	220.50	221.41	327.70	331.10	351.57	391.95	531.60	617.60	541.60
Imports, c.i.f.	71	160.81	179.43	327.22	385.40	395.17	431.20	448.80	372.80	421.50	538.60	520.00	657.50

2004, International Monetary Fund : *International Financial Statistics Yearbook*

Mali 678

		1992	1993	1994	1995	1996	1997	1998	1999	2000	2001	2002	2003
Balance of Payments		*Millions of US Dollars: Minus Sign Indicates Debit*
Current Account, n.i.e.	78ald	−240.5	−188.6	−162.6	−283.8	−260.8	−178.4	−163.6	−252.4	−236.8	−310.0	−148.8	....
Goods: Exports f.o.b.	78aad	364.0	371.9	334.9	441.8	432.8	561.5	556.2	571.0	545.1	725.2	875.1	....
Goods: Imports f.o.b.	78abd	−526.8	−492.4	−449.2	−556.8	−551.5	−545.7	−558.2	−605.5	−592.1	−734.7	−712.5	....
Trade Balance	78acd	−162.8	−120.4	−114.3	−115.0	−118.6	15.7	−2.0	−34.5	−46.9	−9.6	162.7	....
Services: Credit	78add	78.3	74.8	69.0	87.6	91.9	81.2	79.0	103.9	94.1	151.2	169.4	....
Services: Debit	78aed	−428.6	−360.8	−317.0	−434.5	−383.4	−350.0	−304.3	−365.3	−312.2	−421.4	−387.0	....
Balance on Goods & Services	78afd	−513.0	−406.4	−362.3	−461.9	−410.2	−253.1	−227.4	−295.9	−265.0	−279.7	−54.9	....
Income: Credit	78agd	27.8	30.2	9.3	8.3	26.5	19.0	29.3	31.3	20.6	22.1	36.1	....
Income: Debit	78ahd	−56.1	−43.2	−49.7	−48.9	−69.5	−70.7	−80.1	−101.4	−118.7	−188.2	−276.3	....
Balance on Gds, Serv. & Inc.	78aid	−541.2	−419.4	−402.7	−502.6	−453.2	−304.8	−278.2	−366.0	−363.2	−445.8	−295.1	....
Current Transfers, n.i.e.: Credit	78ajd	380.0	294.6	281.3	266.8	218.3	151.9	151.6	145.8	157.2	160.7	182.1	....
Current Transfers: Debit	78akd	−79.3	−63.7	−41.2	−48.0	−25.9	−25.5	−37.1	−32.2	−30.8	−25.0	−35.7	....
Capital Account, n.i.e.	78bcd	143.6	111.9	99.1	126.2	138.0	111.4	124.0	113.3	101.6	107.4	104.2	....
Capital Account, n.i.e.: Credit	78bad	143.6	111.9	99.1	126.2	138.1	112.5	124.0	113.4	101.6	107.5	104.4	....
Capital Account: Debit	78bbd	−	−	....	....	−	−1.1	−	−.1	−	−.1	−.2	....
Financial Account, n.i.e.	78bjd	−5.6	−14.5	−7.0	118.6	138.0	53.1	48.0	116.9	201.1	92.0	188.6	....
Direct Investment Abroad	78bdd	−	−	−	−	−1.6	6.8	−	−.8	−4.0	−17.3	−1.6	....
Dir. Invest. in Rep. Econ., n.i.e.	78bed	−21.9	4.1	17.4	111.4	44.8	63.0	8.9	2.2	82.4	121.7	243.8	....
Portfolio Investment Assets	78bfd	−	−	−	−	−1.1	−4.2	−4.5	−21.1	15.5	−.8	−.5	....
Equity Securities	78bkd	−	−	−	−	−.1	−.1	3.9	−	−.1	−.1	−.6	....
Debt Securities	78bld	−	−	−	....	−1.0	−4.1	−8.4	−21.1	15.6	−.7	.1	....
Portfolio Investment Liab., n.i.e.	78bgd	−	−	−	....	1.6	−3.6	−.4	22.0	1.0	12.4	54.1	....
Equity Securities	78bmd	−	−	−	....	−	.2	−.1	22.9	.4	13.5	−2.1	....
Debt Securities	78bnd	−	−	−	....	1.6	−3.8	−.3	−1.0	.6	−1.1	56.2	....
Financial Derivatives Assets	78bwd	....	....	....	....	−	−	−	−	−	−	−	....
Financial Derivatives Liabilities	78bxd	....	....	....	....	.1	.1	−	−	−	−	−	....
Other Investment Assets	78bhd	5.8	−21.4	−104.0	−52.3	22.3	−85.4	−33.8	−45.4	−87.0	−87.7	−248.4	....
Monetary Authorities	78bod	−	−	−	−	−	−	−	−	−	−	−	....
General Government	78bpd	−	−	−	....	−	−	−	−	−1.4	−	−	....
Banks	78bqd	17.5	11.9	−100.3	−33.2	32.3	1.8	1.4	3.9	−42.5	−64.2	30.4	....
Other Sectors	78brd	−11.7	−33.3	−3.7	−19.2	−10.0	−87.2	−35.2	−49.3	−43.1	−23.5	−278.7	....
Other Investment Liab., n.i.e.	78bid	10.5	2.8	79.6	59.6	71.9	76.4	77.9	160.1	193.2	63.7	141.1	....
Monetary Authorities	78bsd	−	−	−	−	−9.3	10.2	−2.2	1.7	−.6	.7	2.6	....
General Government	78btd	12.8	−18.0	33.1	89.8	80.5	57.7	98.3	97.9	69.1	57.3	87.5	....
Banks	78bud	−19.8	.4	11.9	−1.4	−40.5	7.0	18.9	48.1	−1.9	8.4	25.9	....
Other Sectors	78bvd	17.4	20.4	34.5	−28.7	41.2	1.5	−37.2	12.5	126.6	−2.7	25.1	....
Net Errors and Omissions	78cad	−35.3	−6.0	5.6	−13.0	14.2	4.1	−54.3	8.8	−3.3	63.5	−6.1	....
Overall Balance	78cbd	−137.9	−97.2	−65.0	−52.0	29.4	−9.9	−45.9	−13.4	62.6	−47.0	137.8	....
Reserves and Related Items	79dad	137.9	97.2	65.0	52.0	−29.4	9.9	45.9	13.4	−62.6	47.0	−137.8	....
Reserve Assets	79dbd	−7.2	−45.8	−37.6	−80.2	−132.0	−37.6	33.7	1.6	−57.9	14.0	−159.0	....
Use of Fund Credit and Loans	79dcd	8.4	5.6	32.7	38.4	22.4	21.3	2.7	11.7	−8.3	1.5	−18.3	....
Exceptional Financing	79ded	136.8	137.4	69.9	93.8	80.1	26.2	9.4	−	3.7	31.5	39.5	....
International Investment Position						*Millions of US Dollars*
Assets	79aad	....	....	....	....	673.4	598.1	628.6	673.9	596.7	671.1	1,223.5	....
Direct Investment Abroad	79abd	....	....	....	....	1.8	−6.9	−.1	.7	.6	15.9	2.1	....
Portfolio Investment	79acd	....	....	....	....	60.1	4.5	7.4	49.3	28.4	35.0	41.1	....
Equity Securities	79add	....	....	....	....	.9	.5	.3	.2	1.7	.4	1.5	....
Debt Securities	79aed	....	....	....	....	59.2	4.0	7.1	49.1	26.6	34.6	39.7	....
Financial Derivatives	79afd	....	....	....	....	−	.1	−	−	−	.1	.1	....
Other Investment	79afd	....	....	....	....	179.9	185.5	214.9	274.2	185.0	271.5	589.5	....
Monetary Authorities	79agd	....	....	....	....	−	−	−	−	−	−	−	....
General Government	79ahd	....	....	....	....	−	−	−	−	1.4	−	−	....
Banks	79aid	....	....	....	....	136.7	117.6	123.9	103.0	100.7	187.3	182.7	....
Other Sectors	79ajd	....	....	....	....	43.2	67.9	91.0	171.3	82.9	84.2	406.8	....
Reserve Assets	79akd	....	....	....	....	431.5	414.9	406.2	349.7	382.7	348.7	590.8	....
Liabilities	79lad	....	....	....	....	2,716.8	3,297.0	3,415.8	3,252.6	3,059.8	3,021.8	3,781.1	....
Dir. Invest. in Rep. Economy	79lbd	....	....	....	....	64.1	454.8	309.9	228.1	132.4	210.4	524.2	....
Portfolio Investment	79lcd	....	....	....	....	5.3	4.5	10.4	41.0	4.7	16.7	76.4	....
Equity Securities	79ldd	....	....	....	....	.9	.9	.5	37.0	.8	14.0	13.8	....
Debt Securities	79led	....	....	....	....	4.4	3.7	9.9	4.0	4.0	2.7	62.6	....
Financial Derivatives	79lld	....	....	....	....	.1	.2	−	−	−	−	−	....
Other Investment	79lfd	....	....	....	....	2,647.2	2,837.3	3,095.6	2,983.5	2,922.7	2,794.7	3,180.5	....
Monetary Authorities	79lgd	....	....	....	....	157.5	176.8	192.8	183.7	184.4	173.6	185.8	....
General Government	79lhd	....	....	....	....	2,391.6	2,569.2	2,804.9	2,509.2	2,295.1	2,238.5	2,576.0	....
Banks	79lid	....	....	....	....	25.6	28.2	49.9	88.2	79.9	89.5	154.3	....
Other Sectors	79ljd	....	....	....	....	72.5	63.2	48.0	202.3	363.4	293.1	264.3	....

Mali 678

		1992	1993	1994	1995	1996	1997	1998	1999	2000	2001	2002	2003
Government Finance		\multicolumn{12}{c}{*Billions of Francs; Year Ending December 31*}
Deficit (-) or Surplus....................	80	−29.1	−30.6	−43.4	−36.7	−11.1	−29.9	†−38.6	−61.4	−69.1	−112.2	−84.8	−89.6p
Total Revenue and Grants...........	81y	154.3	146.7	236.7	269.7	314.0	320.5	†344.8	356.1	371.1p	420.4	474.2	542.7
Revenue..................................	81	100.7	104.7	138.9	177.3	217.5	236.3	†254.9	272.7	269.9	320.1	388.4	434.4p
Grants.....................................	81z	53.6	42.0	97.8	92.4	96.5	84.2	†89.9	83.4	101.2	100.3	85.8	108.3p
Exp.& Lending Minus Repay........	82z	....	....	....	....	....	....	†383.4	417.5	440.2	532.6	559.0	632.3p
Expenditure.............................	82	183.4	177.3	280.1	306.4	325.1	350.4	†387.0	419.7	442.7	543.2	563.9	634.6p
Lending Minus Repay................	83	....	....	....	....	....	....	†−3.6	−2.2	−2.5	−10.6	−4.9	−2.3p
Statistical Discrepancy...............	80xx	4.9	8.1	−29.7	−14.0	−18.9	−8.5	−10.0	2.4	1.6	–	–	–p
Total Financing...........................	80h	24.2	22.5	73.1	50.7	30.0	38.4	48.5	59.1	67.4	112.2	85.1	89.5p
Domestic..................................	84a	−8.6	−3.0	−3.6	−40.1	−52.1	−10.6	−9.5	−1.2	3.0	6.1	−3.4	−36.4p
Foreign....................................	85a	32.8	25.5	76.7	90.8	82.1	49.0	58.0	60.3	64.4	106.1	88.5	125.9p
Debt													
Total Debt...................................	88	....	....	....	....	....	....	....	....	....	....	....	....
Domestic..................................	88a	....	....	....	....	....	....	....	....	....	....	....	....
Foreign....................................	89a	730.3	773.9	1,576.6	1,395.2	1,498.4	1,614.8	1,684.3	1,618.0	1,701.6	1,731.7	1,776.1	1,825.7p
National Accounts		\multicolumn{12}{c}{*Billions of Francs*}
Househ.Cons.Expend.,incl.NPISHs....	96f	546.3	560.5	749.0	928.3	1,055.4	1,051.7	1,191.0	1,324.3	1,393.5	1,509.7	1,550.1	....
Government Consumption Expend...	91f	130.2	123.4	187.9	204.4	210.5	290.6	322.9	308.5	310.8	346.8	369.0	....
Gross Fixed Capital Formation.........	93e	143.7	144.7	249.3	299.7	316.8	348.1	305.4	313.0	362.8	433.2	438.3	....
Changes in Inventories.....................	93i	12.6	−21.1	−10.8	−14.2	−41.3	8.8	36.3	24.8	17.3	119.2	48.4	....
Exports of Goods and Services.........	90c	116.7	129.9	224.7	259.9	264.7	361.6	366.2	376.4	458.6	642.4	746.3	....
Imports of Goods and Services (-).....	98c	229.5	226.6	421.2	491.8	487.2	486.2	498.3	544.3	659.9	847.5	792.8	....
Gross Domestic Product (GDP)........	99b	721.4	712.1	978.7	1,187.1	1,319.3	1,574.6	1,723.5	1,802.7	1,883.1	2,203.8	2,359.3	....
GDP Volume 1987 Prices................	99b.p	713.3	690.6	708.9	755.9	783.0	....	....	....	....	....	....	....
GDP Volume (1995=100)................	99bvp	94.4	91.4	93.8	100.0	103.6	....	....	....	....	....	....	....
GDP Deflator (1995=100)................	99bip	64.4	65.7	87.9	100.0	107.3	....	....	....	....	....	....	....
		\multicolumn{12}{c}{*Millions: Midyear Estimates*}
Population.............................	99z	9.54	9.81	10.08	10.36	10.64	10.94	11.25	11.57	11.90	12.26	12.62	13.01

2004, International Monetary Fund : *International Financial Statistics Yearbook*

Malta 181

		1992	1993	1994	1995	1996	1997	1998	1999	2000	2001	2002	2003
Exchange Rates													
		SDRs per Lira: End of Period											
Official Rate	ac	1.9436	1.8426	1.8609	1.9090	1.9338	1.8969	1.8818	1.7681	1.7532	1.7602	1.8443	1.9648
		US Dollars per Lira: End of Period (ag) Period Average (rh)											
Official Rate	ag	2.6725	2.5309	2.7166	2.8377	2.7807	2.5594	2.6496	2.4268	2.2843	2.2121	2.5074	2.9197
Official Rate	rh	3.1462	2.6171	2.6486	2.8333	2.7745	2.5924	2.5743	2.5039	2.2851	2.2226	2.3100	2.6544
		Index Numbers (2000=100): Period Averages											
Official Rate	ahx	137.7	114.5	115.9	124.0	121.4	113.4	112.7	109.6	100.0	97.3	101.1	116.2
Nominal Effective Exchange Rate	nec	101.7	95.5	95.9	97.1	95.9	97.4	98.4	98.4	100.0	100.9	100.4	100.1
Real Effective Exchange Rate	rec	97.4	92.1	93.6	94.6	93.4	96.1	98.6	98.4	100.0	102.5	102.8	100.9
Fund Position													
		Millions of SDRs: End of Period											
Quota	2f.s	67.5	67.5	67.5	67.5	67.5	67.5	67.5	102.0	102.0	102.0	102.0	102.0
SDRs	1b.s	33.1	35.3	35.6	37.6	39.7	41.9	44.4	22.5	24.5	26.4	28.9	29.8
Reserve Position in the Fund	1c.s	25.3	25.3	25.4	27.3	30.7	31.6	31.6	40.3	40.3	40.3	40.3	40.3
International Liquidity													
		Millions of US Dollars Unless Otherwise Indicated: End of Period											
Total Reserves minus Gold	1l.d	1,268.3	1,362.4	1,849.6	1,604.5	1,619.8	1,487.6	1,662.7	1,788.0	1,470.2	1,666.2	2,209.3	....
SDRs	1b.d	45.5	48.4	52.0	56.0	57.2	56.6	62.5	30.9	31.9	33.2	39.3	44.3
Reserve Position in the Fund	1c.d	34.8	34.7	37.1	40.5	44.1	42.7	44.5	55.3	52.5	50.6	54.7	59.8
Foreign Exchange	1d.d	1,188.0	1,279.3	1,760.5	1,508.0	1,518.6	1,388.3	1,555.7	1,701.9	1,385.8	1,582.4	2,115.2	....
Gold (Million Fine Troy Ounces)	1ad	.120	.100	.105	.041	.044	.011	.006	.006	.004	.005	.004	....
Gold (National Valuation)	1and	40.3	38.5	40.0	15.9	7.2	3.3	1.8	1.8	1.0	1.4	1.2	....
Monetary Authorities:Other Assets	3..d	29.6	26.8	27.2	.1	.1	–	.1	....	....	....	....	....
Other Official Insts.: Assets	3b.d	29.6	26.8	27.2	.1	.1	–	.1	–	....	....	....	....
Deposit Money Banks: Assets	7a.d	1,163.1	1,233.9	1,129.8	† 2,235.5	2,875.5	3,415.0	5,850.0	6,815.0	8,595.6	6,890.9	9,416.4	....
Liabilities	7b.d	632.0	758.9	621.5	† 1,576.0	2,333.9	2,972.8	5,242.4	6,339.0	7,905.0	6,164.1	8,361.4	....
Other Banking Insts.: Assets	7e.d	303.1	294.0	13.7	11.0	9.1	18.0	18.6	15.9	15.6	....	....	....
Liabilities	7f.d	467.8	496.3	366.3	–	–	–	–	.5	–	....	....	....
Monetary Authorities													
		Millions of Liri: End of Period											
Foreign Assets	11	494.46	559.11	698.01	593.74	568.12	575.53	639.77	740.30	644.17	753.93	880.86	....
Claims on Central Government	12a	62.30	18.08	39.22	67.73	74.28	59.16	24.32	6.15	9.18	5.80	4.29	....
Reserve Money	14	442.60	443.58	584.20	512.98	491.66	498.99	514.05	549.32	568.41	589.40	614.28	....
of which: Currency Outside DMBs	14a	337.64	353.26	365.91	352.47	362.97	364.42	368.97	385.57	397.36	419.14	436.83	....
Central Government Deposits	16d	17.00	21.04	22.25	42.01	33.53	35.70	47.61	96.21	56.18	69.08	146.96	....
Other Items (Net)	17r	97.17	112.56	130.78	106.48	117.22	100.01	102.44	100.92	28.76	101.25	123.90	....
Banking Institutions													
		Millions of Liri: End of Period											
Reserves	20	93.82	83.26	194.50	† 101.31	97.78	126.14	141.73	172.17	153.63	173.57	295.92	....
Foreign Assets	21	435.23	487.52	415.89	† 787.78	1,034.11	1,334.30	2,207.90	2,808.27	3,762.92	3,115.08	3,755.44	....
Claims on Central Government	22a	78.25	142.65	135.88	† 149.80	196.50	297.01	391.72	463.02	466.15	550.96	550.82	....
Claims on Private Sector	22d	772.21	879.53	985.51	† 1,097.10	1,261.33	1,350.46	1,492.26	1,658.93	1,822.57	1,976.37	2,015.43	....
Demand Deposits	24	57.43	59.42	72.15	† 80.93	87.31	111.39	146.77	190.52	194.40	215.70	241.81	....
Time and Savings Deposits	25	827.13	940.86	1,105.35	† 1,254.60	1,414.07	1,567.09	1,698.96	1,860.65	1,944.22	2,117.15	2,357.95	....
Foreign Liabilities	26c	236.47	299.86	228.78	† 555.36	839.34	1,161.54	1,978.55	2,612.12	3,460.58	2,786.53	3,334.70	....
Capital Accounts	27a	37.21	39.09	40.98	† 128.61	147.62	198.02	299.97	336.14	372.76	447.91	430.77	....
Other Items (Net)	27r	221.26	253.73	284.51	† 116.48	101.40	69.86	109.36	102.95	233.31	248.67	252.37	....
Banking Survey													
		Millions of Liri: End of Period											
Foreign Assets (Net)	31n	693.22	746.77	885.12	† 826.16	762.89	748.29	869.13	936.44	946.51	1,082.47	1,294.62	....
Domestic Credit	32	893.80	1,016.85	1,136.14	† 1,265.87	1,489.64	1,660.93	1,848.85	2,017.02	2,228.28	2,451.52	2,409.38	....
Claims on Central Govt. (Net)	32an	121.59	137.33	150.63	† 168.77	228.31	310.47	356.59	358.09	405.71	475.16	393.95	....
Claims on Private Sector	32d	772.21	879.53	985.51	† 1,097.10	1,261.33	1,350.46	1,492.26	1,658.93	1,822.57	1,976.37	2,015.43	....
Money	34	408.56	425.07	463.55	† 498.91	489.66	489.63	525.09	580.70	595.72	635.61	680.12	....
Quasi-Money	35	827.13	940.86	1,105.35	† 1,254.60	1,414.07	1,567.09	1,698.96	1,860.65	1,944.22	2,117.15	2,357.95	....
Other Items (Net)	37r	351.33	397.70	452.35	† 338.52	348.80	352.50	493.93	512.11	634.85	781.24	665.93	....
Money plus Quasi-Money	35l	1,235.69	1,365.93	1,568.90	† 1,753.51	1,903.73	2,056.72	2,224.05	2,441.35	2,539.94	2,752.76	3,038.07	....
Interest Rates													
		Percent Per Annum											
Discount Rate (End of Period)	60	5.50	5.50	5.50	5.50	5.50	5.50	5.50	4.75	4.75	4.25	3.75	....
Treasury Bill Rate	60c	4.58	4.60	4.29	4.65	4.99	5.08	5.41	5.15	4.89	4.93	4.03	....
Deposit Rate	60l	4.50	4.50	4.50	4.50	4.50	4.56	4.64	4.66	4.86	4.84	4.30	....
Lending Rate	60p	8.50	8.50	8.50	† 7.38	7.77	7.99	8.09	7.70	7.28	6.90	6.04	....
Prices and Labor													
		Index Numbers (2000=100): Period Averages											
Consumer Prices	64	78.4	81.6	85.0	88.8	90.6	93.4	95.6	97.7	100.0	102.9	† 105.2	105.7
Industrial Production	66	55.0	56.9	† 64.1	64.5	65.1	64.8	71.2	76.6	100.0	85.2	85.3	88.5
		Number in Thousands: Period Averages											
Labor Force	67d	136	138	136	140	142	144	144	146	147	....	....	....
Employment	67e	132	132	134	149	140	137	137	138	145	146	148	147
Unemployment	67c	6	6	6	5	6	7	7	8	7	7	7	8
Unemployment Rate (%)	67r	4.0	4.5	4.1	3.7	4.4	5.0	5.1	5.3	4.5	4.7	4.7	5.7

Malta 181

		1992	1993	1994	1995	1996	1997	1998	1999	2000	2001	2002	2003
International Transactions							*Millions of Liri*						
Exports	70	490.91	518.33	592.42	674.94	624.15	628.93	711.99	791.14	1,072.44	880.68	961.15	....
Imports, c.i.f.	71	747.77	830.92	918.77	1,037.65	1,007.80	984.23	1,034.92	1,136.23	1,492.37	1,226.42	1,227.53	....
Balance of Payments						*Millions of US Dollars: Minus Sign Indicates Debit*							
Current Account, n.i.e.	78ald	30.2	−84.3	−131.5	−360.9	−406.1	−202.0	−221.4	−121.8	−469.6	−165.1	−45.5	−270.7
Goods: Exports f.o.b.	78aad	1,609.8	1,408.1	1,618.5	1,949.4	1,772.8	1,663.4	1,824.5	2,017.3	2,478.5	2,002.2	2,254.2	2,504.9
Goods: Imports f.o.b.	78abd	−2,122.9	−1,976.4	−2,221.0	−2,759.3	−2,611.1	−2,384.6	−2,497.5	−2,680.2	−3,232.0	−2,568.2	−2,667.8	−3,194.1
Trade Balance	78acd	−513.0	−568.3	−602.5	−810.0	−838.4	−721.2	−673.0	−662.9	−753.5	−566.0	−413.6	−689.2
Services: Credit	78add	883.8	912.4	994.6	1,048.0	1,069.7	1,111.3	1,181.2	1,219.8	1,105.0	1,105.8	1,144.4	1,269.2
Services: Debit	78aed	−588.6	−604.2	−686.5	−664.5	−679.9	−656.5	−720.3	−755.0	−733.1	−738.1	−740.5	−833.6
Balance on Goods & Services	78afd	−217.8	−260.2	−294.5	−426.4	−448.5	−266.4	−212.1	−198.0	−381.6	−198.3	−9.7	−253.6
Income: Credit	78agd	271.2	241.8	219.4	287.4	309.8	360.7	511.0	1,234.9	895.2	824.1	834.1	880.1
Income: Debit	78ahd	−116.9	−126.8	−150.6	−247.6	−298.0	−351.6	−578.1	−1,201.2	−1,008.6	−799.1	−832.0	−842.8
Balance on Gds, Serv. & Inc.	78aid	−63.5	−145.2	−225.7	−386.7	−436.8	−257.2	−279.2	−164.3	−495.0	−173.4	−7.5	−216.3
Current Transfers, n.i.e.: Credit	78ajd	98.6	64.9	101.2	80.3	86.7	122.4	115.0	120.4	101.8	190.5	249.2	190.6
Current Transfers: Debit	78akd	−4.8	−4.1	−7.1	−54.6	−56.0	−67.2	−57.2	−77.9	−76.4	−182.3	−287.2	−244.9
Capital Account, n.i.e.	78bcd	−	13.1	−	12.9	58.4	8.4	28.6	25.7	18.6	1.5	6.6	6.3
Capital Account, n.i.e.: Credit	78bad	−	13.1	−	16.8	64.4	32.9	33.3	31.1	24.1	4.4	8.5	7.7
Capital Account: Debit	78bbd	−	−	−	−3.9	−6.0	−24.4	−4.7	−5.4	−5.5	−2.9	−1.9	−1.4
Financial Account, n.i.e.	78bjd	27.0	188.7	480.9	25.3	206.1	106.6	293.5	402.6	156.2	267.4	203.7	256.9
Direct Investment Abroad	78bdd	−	−.9	1.0	−4.7	−6.4	−16.5	−14.5	−44.7	−25.7	−23.8	3.2	−23.9
Dir. Invest. in Rep. Econ., n.i.e.	78bed	39.5	56.4	151.7	131.6	276.8	81.0	272.9	814.2	604.4	270.1	−415.9	394.6
Portfolio Investment Assets	78bfd	−214.1	−266.6	304.4	−459.9	−120.2	107.6	−141.5	−470.7	−745.1	−445.2	−411.3	−1,553.8
Equity Securities	78bkd	4.7	13.2	247.2	−.1	−1.1	−10.1	6.2	−11.8	−17.5	−37.0	−18.8	−42.2
Debt Securities	78bld	−218.8	−279.8	57.2	−459.8	−119.1	117.7	−147.7	−458.9	−727.6	−408.2	−392.5	−1,511.6
Portfolio Investment Liab., n.i.e.	78bgd	−	−	−	1.9	3.0	.4	58.7	−33.0	−8.5	.3	−1.5	−12.3
Equity Securities	78bmd	−	−	−	−4.1	2.8	.5	−1.5	−7.7	1.3	.8	8.9	−5.2
Debt Securities	78bnd	−	−	−	6.0	.2	−	60.3	−25.3	−9.8	−.4	−10.5	−7.1
Financial Derivatives Assets	78bwd	−	−	−	−	−	−	−	−	−	−	−	−5.0
Financial Derivatives Liabilities	78bxd	−	−	−	−	−	−	−	−	−	−	−	30.0
Other Investment Assets	78bhd	−96.1	131.1	103.4	−285.6	−618.7	−1,003.5	−2,052.3	−1,593.0	−928.6	1,844.7	−543.4	−24.0
Monetary Authorities	78bod	−	−	−	−	−	−	−	−	−	−	−	−
General Government	78bpd	−	−	−.5	−	−	−	−	−	−	−	−	−
Banks	78bqd	−99.7	146.4	79.6	−280.5	−581.2	−934.5	−2,077.1	−1,605.6	−965.5	1,835.0	−634.6	−87.3
Other Sectors	78brd	3.6	−15.3	24.4	−5.1	−37.5	−69.0	24.9	12.6	37.0	9.7	91.2	63.4
Other Investment Liab., n.i.e.	78bid	297.7	268.7	−79.7	642.0	671.5	937.6	2,170.1	1,729.8	1,259.8	−1,378.7	1,572.6	1,451.1
Monetary Authorities	78bsd	−	−	−	−	−	−	−	−	−	−	−	−
General Government	78btd	102.8	35.3	6.0	−41.2	51.5	−26.4	−9.4	222.7	−23.0	12.7	8.0	68.4
Banks	78bud	48.5	111.2	−274.6	680.9	597.7	903.5	2,183.7	1,807.8	1,267.6	−1,415.9	1,596.7	1,292.1
Other Sectors	78bvd	146.4	122.2	188.8	2.3	22.3	60.5	−4.2	−300.8	15.2	24.5	−32.1	90.7
Net Errors and Omissions	78cad	−12.7	17.4	33.4	15.9	56.3	93.7	90.2	−68.2	73.0	151.3	123.0	151.4
Overall Balance	78cbd	44.6	134.8	382.8	−306.8	−85.4	6.7	190.9	238.3	−221.8	255.0	287.9	144.0
Reserves and Related Items	79dad	−44.6	−134.8	−382.8	306.8	85.4	−6.7	−190.9	−238.3	221.8	−255.0	−287.9	−144.0
Reserve Assets	79dbd	−44.6	−134.8	−382.8	306.8	85.4	−6.7	−190.9	−238.3	221.8	−255.0	−287.9	−144.0
Use of Fund Credit and Loans	79dcd	−	−	−	−	−	−	−	−	−	−	−	−
Exceptional Financing	79ded	−	−	−	−	−	−	−	−	−	−	−	−
International Investment Position						*Millions of US Dollars*							
Assets	79aad	....	....	3,479.5	4,102.2	4,754.5	5,296.6	8,018.2	9,726.1	10,729.7	9,380.3	....	....
Direct Investment Abroad	79abd	....	....	28.3	32.3	107.6	140.0	170.4	185.2	203.1	250.2	....	....
Portfolio Investment	79acd	....	....	886.4	1,394.4	1,505.2	1,286.1	1,496.0	1,911.3	2,595.2	2,967.5	....	....
Equity Securities	79add	....	....	2.4	4.0	4.7	15.1	6.6	24.5	40.4	76.3	....	....
Debt Securities	79aed	....	....	884.0	1,390.5	1,500.5	1,271.0	1,489.3	1,886.8	2,554.8	2,891.2	....	....
Financial Derivatives	79ald	....	....	−	−	−	−	−	−	−	−	....	....
Other Investment	79afd	....	....	689.2	1,027.5	1,600.8	2,433.5	4,656.1	5,833.2	6,459.8	4,480.5	....	....
Monetary Authorities	79agd	....	....	−	−	−	−	−	−	−	−	....	....
General Government	79ahd	....	....	2.7	2.0	2.5	2.6	2.6	2.4	2.3	2.7	....	....
Banks	79aid	....	....	396.1	694.1	1,262.4	2,073.1	4,299.2	5,491.0	6,186.3	4,205.1	....	....
Other Sectors	79ajd	....	....	290.4	331.4	335.9	357.8	354.3	339.7	271.1	272.7	....	....
Reserve Assets	79akd	....	....	1,875.6	1,647.8	1,540.8	1,437.0	1,695.7	1,796.5	1,471.6	1,682.2	....	....
Liabilities	79lad	....	....	2,126.0	2,947.2	3,877.4	4,578.3	7,295.4	9,139.9	10,554.8	9,102.5	....	....
Dir. Invest. in Rep. Economy	79lbd	....	....	415.9	562.1	844.2	857.9	1,174.3	1,860.6	2,373.8	2,538.6	....	....
Portfolio Investment	79lcd	....	....	17.4	24.1	23.9	65.0	129.8	94.4	95.5	91.8	....	....
Equity Securities	79ldd	....	....	−	−	−	−	−	−	−	.5	....	....
Debt Securities	79led	....	....	17.4	24.1	23.9	65.0	129.8	94.4	95.5	91.3	....	....
Financial Derivatives	79lld	....	....	−	−	−	−	−	−	−	−	....	....
Other Investment	79lfd	....	....	1,692.7	2,361.0	3,009.3	3,655.3	5,991.3	7,184.9	8,085.5	6,472.2	....	....
Monetary Authorities	79lgd	....	....	−	−	−	−	−	−	−	−	....	....
General Government	79lhd	....	....	152.9	151.5	144.0	129.0	123.2	107.5	89.8	89.6	....	....
Banks	79lid	....	....	702.0	1,376.0	1,947.9	2,626.7	4,955.0	6,256.6	7,222.0	5,595.2	....	....
Other Sectors	79ljd	....	....	837.8	833.4	917.4	899.6	913.1	820.7	773.7	787.4	....	....

2004, International Monetary Fund : *International Financial Statistics Yearbook*

Malta 181

		1992	1993	1994	1995	1996	1997	1998	1999	2000	2001	2002	2003
Government Finance		\multicolumn{12}{c}{*Millions of Liri: Year Ending December 31*}
Deficit (-) or Surplus...............	80	−27.19	−27.56	−37.57	−30.87	−92.92	−125.99	−76.49	....	....	....	....	....
Total Revenue and Grants...........	81y	309.30	335.53	358.31	406.84	407.43	450.75	460.30	....	....	....	....	....
Revenue...........................	81	292.91	327.10	345.46	402.32	386.63	440.94	450.26	....	....	....	....	....
Grants.............................	81z	16.39	8.43	12.85	4.52	20.80	9.81	10.04	....	....	....	....	....
Exp. & Lending Minus Repay........	82z	336.49	363.09	395.88	437.71	500.35	576.74	536.79	....	....	....	....	....
Expenditure......................	82	333.79	367.78	402.47	447.46	500.00	535.42	576.32	....	....	....	....	....
Lending Minus Repayments.........	83	2.70	−4.69	−6.59	−9.75	.35	41.32	−39.53	....	....	....	....	....
Total Financing.....................	80h	27.19	27.56	37.57	30.87	92.92	125.99	76.49	....	....	....	....	....
Total Net Borrowing.................	84	25.72	28.17	35.61	32.89	104.04	145.16	95.87	....	....	....	....	....
Net Domestic.....................	84b	29.78	28.66	28.70	35.44	105.44	146.70	100.01	....	....	....	....	....
Net Foreign.......................	85b	−4.06	−.49	6.91	−2.55	−1.40	−1.54	−4.14	....	....	....	....	....
Use of Cash Balances...............	87	1.47	−.61	1.96	−2.02	−11.12	−19.17	−19.38	....	....	....	....	....
Total Debt by Residence.............	88	235.33	296.30	339.59	410.79	514.47	661.35	761.59	....	....	....	....	....
Domestic..........................	88a	186.93	245.82	283.33	357.36	462.68	610.90	715.08	....	....	....	....	....
Foreign...........................	89a	48.40	50.48	56.26	53.43	51.79	50.45	46.51	....	....	....	....	....
National Accounts		\multicolumn{12}{c}{*Millions of Liri*}
Househ.Cons.Expend.,incl.NPISHs.....	96f	531.5	561.5	608.3	700.4	764.9	803.5	846.0	915.0	994.3	1,041.9	1,079.4	1,092.8
Government Consumption Expend...	91f	164.3	188.9	209.5	235.2	259.8	264.1	269.0	272.6	289.4	326.6	339.9	366.9
Gross Fixed Capital Formation.........	93e	240.9	276.8	305.4	365.2	345.3	326.4	333.6	340.0	409.5	379.5	350.7	419.2
Changes in Inventories...............	93i	.1	3.7	10.0	1.2	−1.4	3.0	−10.7	9.4	33.4	−39.3	−75.0	−69.9
Exports of Goods and Services........	90c	804.1	896.3	994.4	1,074.7	1,045.6	1,095.8	1,194.7	1,321.3	1,604.3	1,428.1	1,497.7	1,446.7
Imports of Goods and Services (-).....	98c	866.0	987.2	1,099.0	1,231.2	1,212.8	1,204.6	1,270.3	1,402.2	1,772.6	1,506.5	1,507.0	1,543.6
Gross Domestic Product (GDP).........	99b	874.8	940.0	1,028.5	1,145.5	1,201.3	1,288.2	1,362.3	1,456.1	1,558.2	1,630.4	1,685.6	1,712.2
Net Primary Income from Abroad.....	98.n	41.7	35.5	19.3	12.0	3.2	4.1	−27.4	12.4	−54.3	11.7	2.6	13.9
Gross National Income (GNI)...........	99a	916.5	975.5	1,047.9	1,157.5	1,204.5	1,292.3	1,334.9	1,468.5	1,504.0	1,642.1	1,688.2	1,726.1
Consumption of Fixed Capital.........	99cf	42.2	53.4	60.0	77.2	86.9	95.7	98.7	104.2	118.6	126.2	128.8	....
Net National Income...................	99e	874.3	922.1	987.9	1,080.3	1,117.5	1,196.6	1,236.2	1,364.3	1,389.9	1,519.9	1,558.1	....
GDP Volume 1995 Prices................	99b.p	976.2	1,017.2	1,047.8	1,145.5	1,191.2	1,249.0	1,291.8	1,344.2	1,428.9	1,413.0	1,444.8	1,419.6
GDP Volume (2000=100)...............	99bvp	68.3	71.2	73.3	80.2	83.4	87.4	90.4	94.1	100.0	98.9	101.1	99.3
GDP Deflator (2000=100)...............	99bip	82.2	84.7	90.0	91.7	92.5	94.6	96.7	99.3	100.0	105.8	107.0	110.6
		\multicolumn{12}{c}{*Millions: Midyear Estimates*}
Population.............................	99z	.37	.37	.37	.38	.38	.38	.39	.39	.39	.39	.39	.39

Mauritania 682

		1992	1993	1994	1995	1996	1997	1998	1999	2000	2001	2002	2003
Exchange Rates		\multicolumn{12}{c}{*Ouguiyas per SDR: End of Period*}
Official Rate	aa	158.263	170.541	187.401	203.813	204.837	227.146	289.744	308.815	328.724	331.928	365.317	394.674
		\multicolumn{12}{c}{*Ouguiyas per US Dollar End of Period (ae) Period Average (rf)*}
Official Rate	ae	115.100	124.160	128.370	137.110	142.450	168.350	205.780	225.000	252.300	264.120	268.710	265.600
Official Rate	rf	87.027	120.806	123.575	129.768	137.222	151.853	188.476	209.514	238.923	255.629	271.739	263.030
Fund Position		\multicolumn{12}{c}{*Millions of SDRs: End of Period*}
Quota	2f.s	47.5	47.5	47.5	47.5	47.5	47.5	47.5	64.4	64.4	64.4	64.4	64.4
SDRs	1b.s	.1	.1	–	–	1.0	.3	–	–	.3	.2	.2	.1
Reserve Position in the Fund	1c.s	–	–	–	–	–	–	–	–	–	–	–	–
Total Fund Cred.&Loans Outstg	2tl	42.0	46.1	58.8	67.1	74.6	83.4	78.3	77.6	75.4	83.2	82.9	70.2
International Liquidity		\multicolumn{12}{c}{*Millions of US Dollars Unless Otherwise Indicated: End of Period*}
Total Reserves minus Gold	1l.d	61.2	44.6	39.7	85.5	141.2	200.8	202.9	224.3	279.9	284.5	396.2	415.3
SDRs	1b.d	.1	.1	–	.1	1.4	.4	–	–	.4	.2	.2	.1
Reserve Position in the Fund	1c.d	–	–	–	–	–	–	–	–	–	–	–	–
Foreign Exchange	1d.d	61.1	44.4	39.7	85.4	139.8	200.4	202.8	224.3	279.5	284.3	396.0	415.2
Gold (Million Fine Troy Ounces)	1ad	.012	.012	.012	.012	.012	.012	.012	.012	.012	.012	.012	.012
Gold (National Valuation)	1and	3.8	4.5	4.3	4.4	4.2	3.3	3.3	3.3	3.1	3.1	3.1	4.0
Monetary Authorities: Other Liab	4..d	216.0	187.1	199.2	212.0	205.3	209.7	209.6	202.0	195.0	195.2	197.2	184.1
Deposit Money Banks: Assets	7a.d	15.7	25.8	27.7	25.9	27.0	24.7	24.1	22.1	21.6	19.0	19.4	18.5
Liabilities	7b.d	110.0	106.4	105.8	67.4	35.5	26.4	15.0	13.6	12.5	12.1	12.1	17.5
Monetary Authorities		\multicolumn{12}{c}{*Millions of Ouguiyas: End of Period*}
Foreign Assets	11	7,598	6,218	5,746	12,425	21,030	34,425	42,546	51,335	71,429	76,028	107,383	111,024
Claims on Central Government	12a	14,057	18,979	17,949	17,109	17,109	17,102	17,012	16,912	16,912	16,912	16,912	22,130
Claims on Nonfin.Pub.Enterprises	12c	60	60	60	60	60	60	60	60	60	60	60	60
Claims on Private Sector	12d	450	516	581	695	755	1,023	1,003	1,065	1,185	869	889	1,090
Claims on Deposit Money Banks	12e	5,980	2,353	2,571	1,872	2,334	2,793	2,789	2,232	1,539	1,539	1,539	21,400
Claims on Nonbank Financial Insts	12g	49	49	49	49	49	49	49	49	49	49	49	49
Reserve Money	14	14,706	22,810	21,966	20,724	10,462	9,089	8,406	8,788	9,222	9,723	10,038	10,009
of which: Currency Outside DMBs	14a	7,898	9,097	8,598	7,383	5,093	5,854	5,801	5,963	6,402	6,688	6,282	6,412
Restricted Deposits	16b	86	29	91	147	91	82	55	154	225	49	49	49
Foreign Liabilities	16c	13,533	10,813	12,093	14,649	15,543	19,232	23,096	23,968	24,848	27,905	30,301	27,845
Long-Term Foreign Liabilities	16cl	15,031	15,663	16,342	16,702	15,160	17,069	20,923	22,108	24,794	23,873	22,684	21,041
Central Government Deposits	16d	4,200	7,573	8,024	13,342	30,844	42,765	51,300	55,512	68,516	68,413	96,974	128,029
Capital Accounts	17a	4,496	4,946	4,888	4,415	4,059	4,821	5,161	5,594	6,339	6,912	7,181	7,126
Other Items (Net)	17r	–23,858	–33,659	–36,448	–37,769	–34,822	–37,606	–46,075	–44,471	–42,770	–41,418	–40,395	–38,353
Deposit Money Banks		\multicolumn{12}{c}{*Millions of Ouguiyas: End of Period*}
Reserves	20	5,191	10,799	12,775	12,486	5,355	3,083	2,390	2,984	2,887	3,105	3,884	3,521
Foreign Assets	21	1,809	3,201	3,561	3,556	3,853	4,165	4,962	4,964	5,450	5,022	5,224	4,901
Claims on Central Government	22a	193	1,083	916	782	2,742	4,302	4,202	4,637	3,882	6,152	8,602	5,479
Claims on Nonfin.Pub.Enterprises	22c	–	–	–	–	–	–	–	–	–	–	–	–
Claims on Private Sector	22d	40,101	41,191	42,500	30,722	34,634	37,279	39,835	46,942	58,486	68,939	82,534	90,197
Claims on Nonbank Financial Insts	22g	–	–	–	–	–	–	–	–	–	–	–	–
Demand Deposits	24	11,986	11,508	11,145	10,674	11,015	11,629	12,467	13,697	17,749	21,033	22,628	25,790
Time Deposits	25	7,187	6,635	7,612	7,817	8,476	9,101	9,282	8,708	8,800	10,929	13,192	14,313
Foreign Liabilities	26c	12,656	13,216	13,583	9,246	5,054	4,451	3,078	3,058	3,164	3,195	3,255	4,646
Long-Term Foreign Liabilities	26cl	–	–	–	–	–	–	–	–	–	–	–	–
Central Government Deposits	26d	1,093	1,330	1,552	3,198	3,428	4,058	6,487	13,596	18,085	23,365	34,050	11,757
Central Govt. Lending Funds	26f	1,179	1,208	1,208	–	–	–	–	–	–	–	–	–
Credit from Monetary Authorities	26g	4,380	3,351	3,358	7	7	7	7	7	7	7	7	20,477
Capital Accounts	27a	14,018	20,802	21,972	20,709	22,359	23,260	24,203	25,169	28,636	29,923	32,358	33,243
Other Items (Net)	27r	–5,205	–1,776	–678	–4,105	–3,755	–3,677	–4,135	–4,708	–5,736	–5,233	–5,246	–6,126
Monetary Survey		\multicolumn{12}{c}{*Millions of Ouguiyas: End of Period*}
Foreign Assets (Net)	31n	–31,813	–30,273	–32,711	–24,616	–10,874	–2,162	411	7,165	24,073	26,077	56,367	62,393
Domestic Credit	32	49,617	52,975	52,479	32,877	21,077	12,992	4,374	557	–6,027	1,203	–21,978	–20,781
Claims on Central Govt. (Net)	32an	8,957	11,159	9,289	1,351	–14,421	–25,419	–36,573	–47,559	–65,807	–68,714	–105,510	–112,177
Claims on Nonfin.Pub.Enterprises	32c	60	60	60	60	60	60	60	60	60	60	60	60
Claims on Private Sector	32d	40,551	41,707	43,081	31,417	35,389	38,302	40,838	48,007	59,671	69,808	83,423	91,287
Claims on Nonbank Financial Inst	32g	49	49	49	49	49	49	49	49	49	49	49	49
Money	34	20,202	20,938	19,816	18,202	16,227	17,579	18,504	19,675	24,151	27,721	28,910	32,202
Quasi-Money	35	7,187	6,635	7,612	7,817	8,476	9,101	9,282	8,708	8,800	10,929	13,192	14,313
Restricted Deposits	36b	86	29	91	147	91	82	55	154	225	49	49	49
Central Govt. Lending Funds	36f	1,179	1,208	1,208	–	–	–	–	–	–	–	–	–
Other Items (Net)	37r	–10,850	–6,108	–8,959	–17,905	–14,591	–15,932	–23,649	–20,815	–15,130	–11,418	–7,762	–4,957
Money plus Quasi-Money	35l	27,389	27,573	27,428	26,019	24,703	26,680	27,786	28,383	32,951	38,650	42,102	46,515
Interest Rates		\multicolumn{12}{c}{*Percent Per Annum*}
Discount Rate (End of Period)	60	7.00	....	....	....	....	....	....	....	....	....	....	11.00
Deposit Rate	60l	5.00	....	....	....	....	....	....	....	....	....	....	8.00
Lending Rate	60p	10.00	....	....	....	....	....	....	....	....	....	....	21.00

Mauritania 682

		1992	1993	1994	1995	1996	1997	1998	1999	2000	2001	2002	2003
Prices		\multicolumn{12}{c}{*Index Numbers (2000=100): Period Averages*}
Consumer Prices................	64	64.8	70.9	73.8	78.6	82.3	86.1	93.1	96.8	100.0	104.7	108.8	114.4
International Transactions													
Balance of Payments		\multicolumn{12}{c}{*Millions of US Dollars: Minus Sign Indicates Debit*}
Current Account, n.i.e..............	78ald	−118.3	−174.0	−69.9	22.1	91.3	47.8	77.2	....	....	....	....	....
Goods: Exports f.o.b.............	78aad	406.8	403.0	399.7	476.4	480.0	423.6	358.6	....	....	....	....	....
Goods: Imports f.o.b.............	78abd	−461.3	−400.4	−352.3	−292.6	−346.1	−316.5	−318.7	....	....	....	....	....
Trade Balance..................	78acd	−54.5	2.6	47.4	183.8	133.9	107.2	40.0	....	....	....	....	....
Services: Credit.................	78add	20.2	21.4	26.0	27.9	31.6	34.9	34.0	....	....	....	....	....
Services: Debit..................	78aed	−179.1	−184.9	−181.1	−217.0	−231.3	−200.0	−152.5	....	....	....	....	....
Balance on Goods & Services......	78afd	−213.4	−160.9	−107.7	−5.3	−65.8	−57.9	−78.6	....	....	....	....	....
Income: Credit...................	78agd	1.1	.8	1.1	1.3	.9	1.4	2.5	....	....	....	....	....
Income: Debit...................	78ahd	−29.9	−97.6	−47.7	−49.5	−45.9	−40.3	−34.0	....	....	....	....	....
Balance on Gds, Serv. & Inc......	78aid	−242.2	−257.8	−154.3	−53.5	−110.8	−96.8	−110.2	....	....	....	....	....
Current Transfers, n.i.e.: Credit......	78ajd	157.4	110.3	113.3	94.7	217.5	157.9	198.3	....	....	....	....	....
Current Transfers: Debit..............	78akd	−33.4	−26.5	−28.9	−19.2	−15.5	−13.3	−10.8	....	....	....	....	....
Capital Account, n.i.e..................	78bcd	−	−	−	−	−	−	−	....	....	....	....	....
Capital Account, n.i.e.: Credit.........	78bad	−	−	−	−	−	−	−	....	....	....	....	....
Capital Account: Debit................	78bbd	−	−	−	−	−	−	−	....	....	....	....	....
Financial Account, n.i.e................	78bjd	77.9	−134.8	−11.4	−10.2	−86.1	−17.3	−25.9	....	....	....	....	....
Direct Investment Abroad...........	78bdd	−	−	−	−	−	−	−	....	....	....	....	....
Dir. Invest. in Rep. Econ., n.i.e......	78bed	7.5	16.1	2.1	7.0	−	−	.1	....	....	....	....	....
Portfolio Investment Assets.........	78bfd	−	−	−	−	−	−	−	....	....	....	....	....
Equity Securities.................	78bkd	−	−	−	−	−	−	−	....	....	....	....	....
Debt Securities.................	78bld	−	−	−	−	−	−	−	....	....	....	....	....
Portfolio Investment Liab., n.i.e......	78bgd	−	−.1	−.2	−.5	−.4	−	−.4	....	....	....	....	....
Equity Securities.................	78bmd	−	−	−	−	−	−	−	....	....	....	....	....
Debt Securities.................	78bnd	−	−.1	−.2	−.5	−.4	−	−.4	....	....	....	....	....
Financial Derivatives Assets.........	78bwd	....	....	....	....	....	....	....	....	....	....	....	....
Financial Derivatives Liabilities.......	78bxd	....	....	....	....	....	....	....	....	....	....	....	....
Other Investment Assets............	78bhd	168.7	170.5	169.3	211.5	236.0	191.1	190.1	....	....	....	....	....
Monetary Authorities.............	78bod	....	....	....	....	....	....	....	....	....	....	....	....
General Government.............	78bpd	−	−.8	−2.2	−.4	−.2	−	−	....	....	....	....	....
Banks..........................	78bqd	−	−	−	−	−	−	−	....	....	....	....	....
Other Sectors....................	78brd	168.7	171.3	171.5	211.9	236.2	191.1	190.1	....	....	....	....	....
Other Investment Liab., n.i.e.......	78bid	−98.3	−321.3	−182.6	−228.2	−321.6	−208.4	−215.7	....	....	....	....	....
Monetary Authorities.............	78bsd	−	−	−	−	−	−	−	....	....	....	....	....
General Government.............	78btd	35.6	−137.6	−7.0	.2	−.2	5.3	.7	....	....	....	....	....
Banks..........................	78bud	−.8	−18.8	−	−	−	−	−	....	....	....	....	....
Other Sectors....................	78bvd	−133.1	−164.9	−175.5	−228.4	−321.4	−213.7	−216.4	....	....	....	....	....
Net Errors and Omissions............	78cad	57.4	26.7	−23.5	−18.1	−1.0	−3.0	−8.1	....	....	....	....	....
Overall Balance....................	78cbd	17.0	−282.1	−104.7	−6.2	4.2	27.6	43.2	....	....	....	....	....
Reserves and Related Items............	79dad	−17.0	282.1	104.7	6.2	−4.2	−27.6	−43.2	....	....	....	....	....
Reserve Assets....................	79dbd	−20.4	69.0	46.9	−42.9	−58.3	−58.8	−46.3	....	....	....	....	....
Use of Fund Credit and Loans........	79dcd	3.4	5.6	17.9	12.2	10.9	12.0	−6.9	....	....	....	....	....
Exceptional Financing...............	79ded	−	207.5	40.0	36.9	43.3	19.3	10.0	....	....	....	....	....
Government Finance		\multicolumn{12}{c}{*Billions of Ouguiyas: Year Ending December 31*}
Deficit (-) or Surplus...............	80	−2.85	−8.86	−3.19	1.58	11.26	....	....	....	....	....	....	....
Revenue........................	81	20.15	29.32	29.46	33.21	44.72	....	....	....	....	....	....	....
Grants Received.................	81z	2.73	3.72	2.55	2.75	3.28	....	....	....	....	....	....	....
Exp. & Lending Minus Repay.........	82z	25.73	41.90	35.20	34.38	36.74	....	....	....	....	....	....	....
Financing													
Domestic.......................	84a	−1.35	3.24	−1.47	−7.52	−15.81	....	....	....	....	....	....	....
Foreign........................	85a	4.22	5.62	4.66	5.94	4.55	....	....	....	....	....	....	....
National Accounts		\multicolumn{12}{c}{*Millions of Ouguiyas*}
Househ.Cons.Expend.,incl.NPISHs.....	96f	76,200	87,887	87,863	79,984	99,913	111,297	113,422	....	....	....	....	....
Government Consumption Expend...	91f	17,545	24,814	25,883	30,072	31,111	32,456	23,525	....	....	....	....	....
Gross Fixed Capital Formation.........	93e	18,080	17,314	20,147	23,684	17,326	25,094	....	....	....	....	....	....
Changes in Inventories..............	93i	6,170	3,963	3,590	4,308	9,015	2,626	....	....	....	....	....	....
Exports of Goods and Services.........	90c	38,021	51,167	52,479	65,306	70,066	67,477	52,795	....	....	....	....	....
Imports of Goods and Services (-).....	98c	59,425	70,601	65,800	66,015	79,113	78,332	46,562	....	....	....	....	....
Gross Domestic Product (GDP).........	99b	96,591	114,544	124,162	137,339	148,318	160,618	....	....	....	....	....	....
		\multicolumn{12}{c}{*Millions: Midyear Estimates*}
Population..........................	99z	2.13	2.18	2.24	2.30	2.36	2.43	2.50	2.57	2.64	2.72	2.81	2.89

Mauritius 684

		1992	1993	1994	1995	1996	1997	1998	1999	2000	2001	2002	2003
Exchange Rates		\multicolumn{12}{c}{*Rupees per SDR: End of Period*}
Market Rate	aa	23.372	25.625	26.077	26.258	25.842	30.041	34.896	34.955	36.327	38.197	39.694	38.766
		\multicolumn{12}{c}{*Rupees per US Dollar: End of Period (ae) Period Average (rf)*}
Market Rate	ae	16.998	18.656	17.863	17.664	17.972	22.265	24.784	25.468	27.882	30.394	29.197	26.088
Market Rate	rf	15.563	17.648	17.960	17.386	17.948	21.057	23.993	25.186	26.250	29.129	29.962	27.901
Fund Position		\multicolumn{12}{c}{*Millions of SDRs: End of Period*}
Quota	2f.s	73.3	73.3	73.3	73.3	73.3	73.3	73.3	101.6	101.6	101.6	101.6	101.6
SDRs	1b.s	17.6	21.0	21.3	21.7	22.2	22.5	22.8	16.1	16.5	16.8	17.0	17.2
Reserve Position in the Fund	1c.s	6.2	7.3	7.3	7.3	7.4	7.4	7.4	14.5	14.5	14.5	14.5	21.9
Total Fund Cred.&Loans Outstg.	2tl	–	–	–	–	–	–	–	–	–	–	–	–
International Liquidity		\multicolumn{12}{c}{*Millions of US Dollars Unless Otherwise Indicated: End of Period*}
Total Reserves minus Gold	1l.d	820.1	757.0	747.6	863.3	896.1	693.3	559.0	731.0	897.4	835.6	1,227.4	1,577.3
SDRs	1b.d	24.3	28.9	31.2	32.2	31.9	30.3	32.2	22.1	21.4	21.1	23.2	25.6
Reserve Position in the Fund	1c.d	8.6	10.1	10.7	10.9	10.6	9.9	10.4	19.9	18.9	18.2	19.7	32.5
Foreign Exchange	1d.d	787.3	718.1	705.7	820.2	853.7	653.0	516.5	689.1	857.1	796.3	1,184.5	1,519.2
Gold (Million Fine Troy Ounces)	1ad	.061	.062	.062	.062	.062	.062	.062	.062	.062	.062	.062	.062
Gold (National Valuation)	1and	4.2	3.9	4.0	4.1	4.0	6.1	11.9	12.3	12.3	12.3	12.3	21.1
Government Assets	3bad	.1	.1	.1	...	...	...	...	...	...	...	...	...
Monetary Authorities: Other Liab.	4..d	4.4	.6	1.9	.7	1.1	.9	.6	.2	.7	.3	.6	2.8
Deposit Money Banks: Assets	7a.d	124.2	160.4	178.3	264.2	263.6	327.4	361.0	383.8	400.2	427.0	465.5	503.1
Liabilities	7b.d	3.3	28.2	39.8	67.5	59.5	38.4	127.9	104.3	106.6	98.3	196.7	225.3
Monetary Authorities		\multicolumn{12}{c}{*Millions of Rupees: End of Period*}
Foreign Assets	11	14,011.5	14,194.9	13,425.7	15,322.0	16,176.8	15,571.8	14,150.3	18,930.9	25,366.1	25,772.9	36,195.4	41,698.1
Claims on Central Government	12a	1,351.4	1,021.4	1,741.9	654.7	914.5	1,662.5	4,994.9	2,223.5	2,196.1	2,210.7	1,743.9	551.8
Claims on Deposit Money Banks	12e	411.2	523.5	291.0	672.8	446.2	410.8	707.8	375.1	328.3	726.6	2,222.7	2,188.6
Reserve Money	14	6,767.2	7,992.6	8,403.1	9,628.3	9,123.0	8,923.4	9,759.6	10,522.3	11,763.5	12,989.7	14,920.7	16,314.1
of which: Currency Outside DMBs	14a	3,820.1	4,230.9	4,412.2	4,847.2	5,050.7	5,410.4	5,832.9	6,126.7	6,647.6	7,329.0	8,286.0	9,347.0
Liabs. of Central Bank: Securities	16ac	3,888.9	1,579.0	434.0	649.9	2,955.1	430.2	–	–	–	–	–	8,499.0
Foreign Liabilities	16c	74.7	11.1	33.2	12.1	19.9	20.7	14.8	5.7	19.2	10.4	17.9	72.1
Central Government Deposits	16d	17.5	12.0	6.2	452.7	251.2	3.1	13.6	3.4	3,421.0	757.7	9,394.2	5,734.0
Capital Accounts	17a	400.9	436.3	443.6	446.4	439.7	506.0	582.4	583.3	604.9	634.4	657.9	643.3
Other Items (Net)	17r	4,624.9	5,708.8	6,138.6	5,460.1	4,748.5	7,761.8	9,482.6	10,414.7	12,081.9	14,318.1	15,171.3	13,176.0
Deposit Money Banks		\multicolumn{12}{c}{*Millions of Rupees: End of Period*}
Reserves	20	2,941.4	3,757.8	3,982.4	4,740.9	4,067.2	3,506.9	3,899.8	4,365.3	5,030.0	5,512.9	6,523.1	6,853.5
Claims on Mon.Author.: Securities	20c	3,440.3	1,517.7	434.0	490.9	2,237.4	190.2	–	–	–	–	–	5,595.3
Foreign Assets	21	2,110.8	2,991.6	3,185.7	4,667.7	4,736.9	7,289.0	8,947.3	9,775.5	11,159.4	12,978.1	13,591.6	13,124.9
Claims on Central Government	22a	6,451.2	8,329.5	10,344.5	14,623.7	14,219.6	17,025.7	13,318.5	15,759.0	15,001.3	18,286.5	28,648.0	32,361.7
Claims on Private Sector	22d	18,684.9	23,923.9	28,714.4	32,878.6	34,467.6	43,360.3	56,653.0	62,520.7	70,569.6	77,891.5	83,976.7	88,424.2
Claims on Other Banking Insts.	22f	304.9	238.0	146.5	132.3	163.1	160.5	424.6	1,766.2	1,817.2	1,283.0	894.0	1,918.7
Demand Deposits	24	3,383.4	3,188.3	4,443.3	4,685.4	4,774.0	5,194.5	5,730.2	5,844.8	6,563.6	7,974.9	9,759.0	10,940.5
Time, Savings,& Fgn.Currency Dep.	25	27,501.1	33,198.5	36,754.5	44,574.4	48,406.8	57,201.3	63,819.9	74,851.6	81,573.9	89,789.2	100,200.4	110,821.6
Foreign Liabilities	26c	56.7	525.7	710.7	1,192.9	1,068.8	855.5	3,169.0	2,655.5	2,971.7	2,986.4	5,741.7	5,877.6
Central Government Deposits	26d	224.8	277.9	84.2	1,468.0	319.6	277.0	132.0	264.4	190.9	225.0	234.1	207.7
Credit from Monetary Authorities	26g	267.5	329.0	156.2	550.0	–	250.0	475.0	250.0	250.0	660.3	2,171.0	2,157.0
Capital Accounts	27a	3,439.0	4,758.6	5,144.4	5,447.8	6,620.4	7,842.4	9,092.1	10,848.6	11,953.6	12,037.2	14,477.0	15,602.8
Other Items (Net)	27r	–939.0	–1,519.5	–485.8	–384.4	–1,297.8	–88.1	825.0	–528.2	73.8	2,279.0	1,050.2	2,671.1
Monetary Survey		\multicolumn{12}{c}{*Millions of Rupees: End of Period*}
Foreign Assets (Net)	31n	15,990.9	16,649.7	15,867.5	18,784.7	19,825.0	21,984.6	19,913.8	26,045.2	33,534.6	35,754.2	44,027.4	48,873.3
Domestic Credit	32	26,550.1	33,222.9	40,856.9	46,368.6	49,194.0	61,928.9	75,245.4	82,001.6	85,972.3	98,689.0	105,634.3	117,314.7
Claims on Central Govt. (Net)	32an	7,560.3	9,061.0	11,996.0	13,357.7	14,563.3	18,408.1	18,167.8	17,714.7	13,585.5	19,514.5	20,763.6	26,971.8
Claims on Private Sector	32d	18,684.9	23,923.9	28,714.4	32,878.6	34,467.6	43,360.3	56,653.0	62,520.7	70,569.6	77,891.5	83,976.7	88,424.2
Claims on Other Banking Insts.	32f	304.9	238.0	146.5	132.3	163.1	160.5	424.6	1,766.2	1,817.2	1,283.0	894.0	1,918.7
Money	34	7,209.2	7,423.2	8,864.0	9,572.8	9,829.8	10,611.0	11,590.0	12,001.8	13,297.1	15,451.7	18,156.6	20,401.1
Quasi-Money	35	27,501.1	33,198.5	36,754.5	44,574.4	48,406.8	57,201.3	63,819.9	74,851.6	81,573.9	89,789.2	100,200.4	110,821.6
Liabs. of Central Bank: Securities	36ac	448.6	61.3	–	159.0	717.7	240.0	–	–	–	–	–	2,903.7
Capital Accounts	37a	3,839.9	5,194.9	5,588.0	5,894.2	7,060.3	8,348.4	9,674.5	11,431.9	12,558.5	12,671.6	15,134.9	16,246.1
Other Items (Net)	37r	3,542.2	3,994.7	5,518.0	4,952.9	3,004.5	7,512.9	10,074.8	9,761.4	12,077.4	16,530.8	16,169.8	15,815.5
Money plus Quasi-Money	35l	34,710.3	40,621.7	45,618.5	54,147.2	58,236.6	67,812.3	75,409.9	86,853.4	94,871.0	105,240.9	118,357.0	131,222.7
Other Banking Institutions		\multicolumn{12}{c}{*Millions of Rupees: End of Period*}
Deposits	45	346.3	373.8	397.0	420.4	448.2	494.8	557.3	611.0	670.9	762.6	1,105.5	....
Liquid Liabilities	55l	35,056.6	40,995.5	46,015.5	54,567.6	58,684.8	68,307.1	75,967.2	87,464.4	95,541.9	106,003.5	119,462.5	....
Interest Rates		\multicolumn{12}{c}{*Percent Per Annum*}
Discount Rate (End of Period)	60	8.30	8.30	13.80	11.40	11.82	10.46	17.19	....	....	....	....	....
Money Market Rate	60b	9.05	7.73	10.23	10.35	9.96	9.43	8.99	10.01	7.66	7.25	6.20	3.22
Deposit Rate	60l	10.07	8.40	11.04	12.23	10.77	9.08	9.28	10.92	9.61	9.78	9.88	9.53
Lending Rate	60p	17.13	16.58	18.92	20.81	20.81	18.92	19.92	21.63	20.77	21.10	21.00	21.00

2004, International Monetary Fund : *International Financial Statistics Yearbook*

Mauritius 684

		1992	1993	1994	1995	1996	1997	1998	1999	2000	2001	2002	2003
Prices and Labor						*Index Numbers (2000=100): Period Averages*							
Share Prices	62	39.8	63.2	96.2	92.5	81.6	92.6	110.4	101.5	100.0	91.3	90.0	115.6
Consumer Prices	64	58.7	64.9	69.6	73.8	78.7	†84.0	89.8	96.0	100.0	†105.4	112.5	117.2
						Number in Thousands: Period Averages							
Labor Force	67d	474	485	499	484	482	491	499	507	514	522	524	531
Employment	67e	292	290	292	290	287	288	295	297	298	301	296	296
Unemployment	67c	....	....	....	....	28	32	34	39	45	48	51	54
International Transactions						*Millions of Rupees*							
Exports	70	20,244	22,992	24,097	26,756	32,312	33,694	39,634	40,025	40,882	47,511	53,893	54,164
Imports, c.i.f.	71	25,280	30,319	34,548	34,363	41,082	46,093	49,811	56,629	54,928	57,940	64,888	66,429
Imports, f.o.b.	71.v	22,931	27,507	31,601	31,508	38,073	42,570	46,015	....	....	....	....	....
						2000=100							
Unit Value of Exports	74	†64.2	70.0	73.2	77.7	86.4	†89.3	101.8	101.1	100.0	101.8	110.3	116.7
Unit Value of Imports	75	†61.9	68.7	73.7	78.0	83.5	†85.5	90.6	96.2	100.0	107.7	112.8	120.5
Balance of Payments						*Millions of US Dollars: Minus Sign Indicates Debit*							
Current Account, n.i.e.	78ald	–.1	–92.0	–232.1	–21.9	34.0	–88.9	3.3	–124.2	–36.9	276.1	259.2	....
Goods: Exports f.o.b.	78aad	1,334.7	1,334.4	1,376.9	1,571.7	1,810.6	1,600.1	1,669.3	1,589.2	1,552.2	1,628.2	1,830.2	....
Goods: Imports f.o.b.	78abd	–1,493.9	–1,576.0	–1,773.9	–1,812.2	–2,136.3	–2,036.1	–1,933.3	–2,107.9	–1,944.4	–1,846.0	–2,018.3	....
Trade Balance	78acd	–159.2	–241.6	–397.0	–240.5	–325.7	–436.0	–264.0	–518.7	–392.1	–217.7	–188.1	....
Services: Credit	78add	577.5	566.2	632.7	777.7	960.8	893.7	916.9	1,035.6	1,070.2	1,222.0	1,134.8	....
Services: Debit	78aed	–522.8	–521.7	–546.4	–641.3	–672.9	–656.3	–718.0	–728.2	–762.5	–810.1	–786.5	....
Balance on Goods & Services	78afd	–104.5	–197.1	–310.6	–104.2	–37.9	–198.6	–65.1	–211.3	–84.5	194.1	160.2	....
Income: Credit	78agd	91.0	70.0	31.7	52.2	31.1	47.0	47.8	43.0	48.7	75.2	74.8	....
Income: Debit	78ahd	–80.1	–66.5	–56.4	–71.3	–75.1	–64.6	–74.4	–59.5	–64.9	–60.9	–65.1	....
Balance on Gds, Serv. & Inc.	78aid	–93.6	–193.6	–335.3	–123.3	–81.8	–216.3	–91.7	–227.8	–100.7	208.4	169.9	....
Current Transfers, n.i.e.: Credit	78ajd	109.9	115.9	129.6	146.8	182.8	206.4	186.8	196.4	167.6	193.1	188.3	....
Current Transfers: Debit	78akd	–16.4	–14.4	–26.3	–45.4	–67.0	–79.0	–91.8	–92.8	–103.8	–125.4	–98.9	....
Capital Account, n.i.e.	78bcd	–1.4	–1.5	–1.3	–1.1	–.8	–.5	–.8	–.5	–.6	–1.4	–1.9	....
Capital Account, n.i.e.: Credit	78bad	–	–	–	–	–	–	–	–	–	.4	–	....
Capital Account: Debit	78bbd	–1.4	–1.5	–1.3	–1.1	–.8	–.5	–.8	–.5	–.6	–1.8	–1.9	....
Financial Account, n.i.e.	78bjd	–14.8	19.3	41.4	25.1	91.9	–18.6	–26.0	180.5	258.0	–247.8	123.4	....
Direct Investment Abroad	78bdd	–43.3	–33.2	–1.1	–3.6	–2.7	–3.2	–13.7	–6.4	–13.0	–2.9	–1.2	....
Dir. Invest. in Rep. Econ., n.i.e.	78bed	14.7	14.7	20.0	18.7	36.7	55.3	12.2	49.4	265.6	–27.7	27.6	....
Portfolio Investment Assets	78bfd	–	–2.2	–.3	–	–2.0	–96.8	43.6	59.5	–18.8	–17.7	–18.3	....
Equity Securities	78bkd	–	–	–	–	–	–	–3.3	59.5	–18.8	–17.7	–18.3	....
Debt Securities	78bld	–	–2.2	–.3	–	–2.0	–96.8	46.9	–	–	–	–	....
Portfolio Investment Liab., n.i.e.	78bgd	–	–	2.1	175.9	36.8	30.6	–28.7	–15.3	–120.4	–1.6	.9	....
Equity Securities	78bmd	–	–	2.1	22.0	36.8	30.6	5.0	–15.3	–3.5	–8.7	–.7	....
Debt Securities	78bnd	–	–	–	154.0	–	–	–33.7	–	–116.8	7.1	1.6	....
Financial Derivatives Assets	78bwd	....	....	....	–	–	–	–	–	–	....	....	....
Financial Derivatives Liabilities	78bxd	....	....	....	–	–	–	–	–	–	....	....	....
Other Investment Assets	78bhd	14.3	–26.7	–64.6	–136.4	17.9	–115.7	–66.7	–245.9	–307.6	–336.9	–440.5	....
Monetary Authorities	78bod	....	....	....	....	....	....	....	....	....	....	....	....
General Government	78bpd	–	–	–	–	–	–	–	–	–	–	–	....
Banks	78bqd	33.0	–49.0	–11.5	–85.2	–3.9	–121.2	–69.1	–32.9	–51.5	–61.7	–20.4	....
Other Sectors	78brd	–18.7	22.3	–53.1	–51.2	21.8	5.5	2.4	–213.0	–256.1	–275.2	–420.0	....
Other Investment Liab., n.i.e.	78bid	–.5	66.6	85.2	–29.5	5.1	111.2	27.3	339.4	452.1	138.9	554.9	....
Monetary Authorities	78bsd	–	–	–	–	–	–	–	–	–	–	–	....
General Government	78btd	–34.7	1.4	–14.1	–18.8	–20.4	9.0	–14.2	–11.4	91.6	–118.7	34.5	....
Banks	78bud	–5.8	26.6	9.2	27.7	–6.9	–10.1	96.4	–20.4	13.7	.4	93.1	....
Other Sectors	78bvd	40.0	38.6	90.1	–38.5	32.5	112.3	–54.9	371.2	346.8	257.2	427.3	....
Net Errors and Omissions	78cad	59.6	81.2	148.5	106.7	–76.8	73.4	–41.9	133.9	10.1	–78.6	–39.6	....
Overall Balance	78cbd	43.3	7.0	–43.5	108.8	48.3	–34.6	–65.4	189.7	230.6	–51.8	341.1	....
Reserves and Related Items	79dad	–43.3	–7.0	43.5	–108.8	–48.3	34.6	65.4	–189.7	–230.6	51.8	–341.1	....
Reserve Assets	79dbd	–43.3	–7.0	43.5	–108.8	–48.3	34.6	65.4	–189.7	–230.6	51.8	–341.1	....
Use of Fund Credit and Loans	79dcd	–	–	–	–	–	–	–	–	–	–	–	....
Exceptional Financing	79ded	–	–	–	–	–	–	–	–	–	–	–	....

Mauritius 684

		1992	1993	1994	1995	1996	1997	1998	1999	2000	2001	2002	2003
International Investment Position						*Millions of US Dollars*							
Assets..	79aad	....	....	....	....	....	....	....	....	....	....	....	....
Direct Investment Abroad..............	79abd	–	–	–	–	–	–	–	–	–	–	–	....
Portfolio Investment......................	79acd	–	–	–	–	–	–	–	–	–	–	–	....
Equity Securities......................	79add	....	....	....	–	–	–	–	–	–	–	–	....
Debt Securities........................	79aed	....	....	....	–	–	–	–	–	–	–	–	....
Financial Derivatives....................	79ald	....	....	....	....	....	....	....	....	....	....	....	....
Other Investment.........................	79afd	177.5	187.0	243.0	364.8	342.9	386.1	394.7	652.3	887.2	1,138.1	1,636.3	....
Monetary Authorities.................	79agd	–	–	–	–	–	–	–	–	–	–	–	....
General Government..................	79ahd	–	–	–	–	–	–	–	–	–	–	–	....
Banks......................................	79aid	87.9	126.4	142.5	227.9	228.4	298.8	335.1	383.8	400.2	427.0	465.5	....
Other Sectors............................	79ajd	89.6	60.6	100.5	136.9	114.6	87.3	59.6	268.5	487.0	711.1	1,170.7	....
Reserve Assets............................	79akd	824.4	760.9	751.8	867.5	900.2	699.5	571.0	743.3	909.8	848.0	1,239.8	....
Liabilities...................................	79lad	....	....	....	....	....	....	....	....	....	....	....	....
Dir. Invest. in Rep. Economy..........	79lbd	–	–	–	–	–	–	–	–	–	–	–	....
Portfolio Investment......................	79lcd	–	–	–	156.3	167.2	150.9	117.7	117.8	–	–	–	....
Equity Securities......................	79ldd	....	....	....	–	–	–	–	–	–	–	–	....
Debt Securities........................	79led	....	....	....	156.3	167.2	150.9	117.7	117.8	–	–	–	....
Financial Derivatives....................	79lld	....	....	....	....	....	....	....	....	....	....	....	....
Other Investment.........................	79lfd	922.5	937.5	1,128.3	1,189.2	1,259.9	1,167.2	1,202.3	1,483.6	1,831.0	1,886.1	2,585.9	....
Monetary Authorities.................	79lgd	–	–	–	–	–	–	–	–	–	–	–	....
General Government..................	79lhd	316.2	316.6	324.8	328.3	352.6	300.1	294.1	273.4	358.3	230.2	285.6	....
Banks......................................	79lid	3.4	28.2	39.8	67.5	59.5	38.4	127.9	104.3	106.6	98.2	196.7	....
Other Sectors............................	79ljd	603.0	592.7	763.7	793.4	847.9	828.7	780.3	1,105.9	1,366.1	1,557.7	2,103.7	....
Government Finance					*Millions of Rupees: Year Ending June 30*								
Deficit (-) or Surplus........................	80	†–358	†19	†–167	–812	–3,083	–3,427	858	†–1,559	–1,458	†1,171	–5,608	–6,012
Revenue.....................................	81	†11,378	12,364	14,076	14,398	14,469	18,277	20,327	†23,082	25,587	†25,374	27,418	32,447
Grants Received...........................	81z	†25	78	130	262	221	63	216	†135	161	†199	317	363
Expenditure.................................	82	†11,518	12,148	14,271	15,502	17,280	20,260	21,446	†25,479	27,032	†30,592	32,843	37,863
Lending Minus Repayments...........	83	†244	275	102	–31	493	1,506	–1,761	†–703	174	†–6,190	500	959
Financing													
Net Borrowing: Domestic...............	84a	†–2,739	†725	†1,737	2,059	1,544	3,228	3,010	†1,191	3,560	†2,241	9,419	12,822
Net borrowing: Foreign.................	85a	†–331	†–313	†–113	–371	2,374	198	–274	†–1,170	–510	†–3,584	1,030	87
Use of Cash Balances....................	87	†3,428	†–431	†–1,458	–874	–834	2	–3,594	†1,538	–1,592	†172	–4,841	–6,897
Debt: Domestic............................	88a	†10,560	11,696	14,149	17,311	19,215	21,921	22,857	†24,326	29,424	†33,764	48,973	63,531
Debt: Foreign..............................	89a	†5,476	5,712	5,766	5,778	9,159	9,666	10,752	†10,037	9,891	†6,816	8,785	9,074
National Accounts						*Millions of Rupees*							
Househ.Cons.Expend.,incl.NPISHs....	96f	30,999	35,996	40,524	44,768	49,759	55,056	62,436	68,710	73,939	80,112	88,038	96,541
Government Consumption Expend...	91f	6,223	7,486	8,658	9,212	10,565	11,508	12,648	14,193	15,582	16,751	18,292	20,365
Gross Fixed Capital Formation.........	93e	13,848	16,101	19,400	16,798	20,181	23,481	23,082	29,676	28,069	29,798	31,369	35,550
Changes in Inventories..................	93i	807	1,532	1,050	1,208	–874	2,358	2,230	–1,373	2,576	–2,396	–133	1,591
Exports of Goods and Services.........	90c	29,759	33,543	36,249	41,205	50,465	54,194	65,711	69,099	73,841	90,463	88,301	89,812
Imports of Goods and Services (-).....	98c	31,386	37,021	41,833	42,908	51,010	58,498	66,543	72,861	74,513	82,636	83,964	86,953
Gross Domestic Product (GDP).........	99b	50,250	57,637	64,048	70,283	79,086	88,099	99,564	107,444	119,494	132,092	141,903	156,906
Net Primary Income from Abroad.....	98.n	171	63	–443	–332	–789	–372	–637	–594	–783	393	396	–793
Gross National Income (GNI)...........	99a	50,421	57,700	63,605	69,951	78,297	87,727	98,927	106,850	118,711	132,485	142,299	156,113
GDP Volume 1992 Prices................	99b.p	50,250	52,779	55,016	57,446	60,638	64,133	67,996	69,970	76,378	80,408	81,953	85,482
GDP Volume (2000=100)...............	99bvp	†65.8	69.1	72.0	75.2	79.4	84.0	89.0	91.6	100.0	105.3	107.3	111.9
GDP Deflator (2000=100)...............	99bip	63.9	69.8	74.4	78.2	83.4	87.8	93.6	98.2	100.0	105.0	110.7	117.3
						Millions: Midyear Estimates							
Population...............................	99z	1.08	1.10	1.11	1.12	1.14	1.15	1.16	1.17	1.19	1.20	1.21	1.22

Mexico 273

		1992	1993	1994	1995	1996	1997	1998	1999	2000	2001	2002	2003
Exchange Rates		*Pesos per SDR: End of Period*
Market Rate......aa=	wa	4.2837	4.2661	7.7737	11.3605	11.2893	10.9064	13.8902	13.0585	12.4717	11.4894	14.0201	16.6964
		Pesos per US Dollar: End of Period (we) Period Average (wf)
Market Rate......ae=	we	3.1154	3.1059	5.3250	7.6425	7.8509	8.0833	9.8650	9.5143	9.5722	9.1423	10.3125	11.2360
Market Rate......rf=	wf	3.0949	3.1156	3.3751	6.4194	7.5994	7.9185	9.1360	9.5604	9.4556	9.3423	9.6560	10.7890
Fund Position		*Millions of SDRs: End of Period*
Quota	2f.s	1,753	1,753	1,753	1,753	1,753	1,753	1,753	2,586	2,586	2,586	2,586	2,586
SDRs	1b.s	399	163	121	1,074	179	490	240	575	281	283	288	292
Reserve Position in the Fund	1c.s	–	–	–	–	–	–	–	–	–	–	226	527
Total Fund Cred.&Loans Outstg	2tl	4,327	3,485	2,644	10,648	9,234	6,735	5,952	3,259	–	–	–	–
International Liquidity		*Millions of US Dollars Unless Otherwise Indicated: End of Period*
Total Reserves minus Gold	1l.d	18,942	25,110	6,278	16,847	19,433	28,797	31,799	31,782	35,509	44,741	50,594	58,956
SDRs	1b.d	548	223	177	1,597	257	661	337	790	366	356	392	433
Reserve Position in the Fund	1c.d	–	–	–	–	–	–	–	–	–	–	308	782
Foreign Exchange	1d.d	18,394	24,886	6,101	15,250	19,176	28,136	31,461	30,992	35,142	44,384	49,895	57,740
Gold (Million Fine Troy Ounces)	1ad	.688	.484	.426	.514	.255	.190	.223	.159	.249	.231	.225	.170
Monetary Authorities: Other Liab.	4..d	94	75	66	91	84	560	552	377	226	214	170	153
Banking Institutions: Assets	7a.d	2,007	1,721	2,829	4,089	4,825	12,612	14,954	20,292	35,890	46,342	50,913	86,593
Liabilities	7b.d	30,205	36,580	43,800	44,355	38,029	41,380	39,852	40,010	50,627	51,847	59,493	105,391
Nonbank Financial Insts.: Assets	7e.d	....	....	....	....	....	–	–	–	–	–	–	–
Liabilities	7f.d	....	....	....	....	....	–	–	–	–	–	–	–
Monetary Authorities		*Millions of Pesos: End of Period*
Foreign Assets	11	60,940	79,710	34,490	122,814	140,217	† 239,470	323,604	310,238	349,523	418,139	537,194	672,107
Claims on Central Government	12a	30,123	9,864	2,000	13,211	10,488	† –	–	–	–	–	–	–
Claims on Nonbank Pub.Fin.Insts.	12cg	14,623	21,227	38,043	78,001	70,327	† 43,023	55,753	63,827	69,722	73,290	69,642	67,006
Claims on Banking Institutions	12e	2,418	3,641	102,100	45,021	11,883	† 2,430	699	96,326	95,120	83,533	110,132	89,564
Claims on Nonbank Financial Insts.	12g	–	–	–	–	–	† 38,043	38,043	36,099	33,033	30,527	27,558	25,053
Reserve Money	14	45,535	50,274	60,923	81,274	100,069	† 150,907	206,943	286,280	267,505	329,252	416,947	487,103
of which: Currency Outside Banks	14a	38,116	43,351	52,035	60,839	74,338	† 94,185	115,917	164,158	181,938	198,849	232,082	263,399
Time & Foreign Currency Deposits	15	528	592	10	6	12	† 4,795	3,736	7,756	13,151	4,567	14,034	16,707
Liabs. of Central Bank: Securities	16ac	–	–	–	–	–	† –	–	–	21,834	156,725	225,051	231,806
Foreign Liabilities	16c	18,826	15,101	20,906	121,665	104,910	† 77,835	88,390	46,072	2,169	1,964	1,772	1,716
Central Government Deposits	16d	14,145	18,678	71,270	26,195	16,124	† 82,330	95,005	185,941	274,351	180,545	102,723	112,492
Liab. to Nonbank Pub.Fin.Insts	16dg	3,484	5,801	8,884	23,420	18,732	† 21,159	12,936	5,387	5	6	6	–
Capital Accounts	17a	1,313	1,309	2,327	3,367	3,346	† 30,030	49,767	35,949	30,163	–4,447	24,470	24,712
Other Items (Net)	17r	24,273	22,686	12,313	3,120	–10,279	† –44,090	–38,676	–60,893	–61,781	–63,123	–40,475	–20,806
Banking Institutions		*Millions of Pesos: End of Period*
Reserves	20	8,611	7,679	10,879	117,373	241,398	† 55,773	72,038	115,255	72,543	116,266	183,561	223,646
Claims on Mon.Author.:Securities	20c	–	–	–	–	–	† –	–	–	845	90,707	136,235	154,509
Foreign Assets	21	6,251	5,344	15,065	31,250	37,877	† 102,614	147,522	193,066	344,894	424,932	531,501	973,060
Claims on Central Government	22a	74,099	56,659	106,267	185,036	176,293	† 545,296	601,093	759,777	901,439	846,699	886,741	917,899
Claims on State and Local Govts	22b	9,728	14,620	23,773	16,574	13,032	† 20,902	24,641	25,908	31,249	36,075	42,485	54,323
Claims on Nonfin.Pub.Enterprises	22c	4,419	4,650	8,083	8,868	7,629	† 12,454	15,137	12,860	19,645	18,461	21,048	34,917
Claims on Nonbank Pub.Fin.Insts	22cg	1,675	1,841	3,388	69,246	210,476	† 290,335	401,741	560,901	561,681	677,210	721,755	662,662
Claims on Private Sector	22d	315,510	398,519	550,204	537,611	474,757	† 801,971	866,844	883,086	943,328	850,201	1,059,796	1,101,242
Claims on Nonbank Financial Insts	22g	23,998	33,413	45,092	47,955	25,187	† 38,250	61,835	81,761	45,229	111,340	59,509	77,133
Demand Deposits	24	83,964	100,549	93,080	87,695	131,732	† 173,026	193,564	233,478	273,265	324,282	364,664	415,908
Time, Savings,& Fgn.Currency Dep	25	182,411	212,074	283,140	416,152	511,140	† 852,953	993,605	1,153,602	1,019,917	1,153,339	1,224,671	1,270,805
Money Market Instruments	26aa	14,885	24,283	30,693	50,762	52,031	† 241,844	255,835	324,367	320,638	501,203	514,256	494,021
Foreign Liabilities	26c	832	737	1,532	2,574	4,332	† 55,886	62,575	90,612	207,999	228,980	357,019	909,711
Long-Term Foreign Liabilities	26cl	93,257	112,877	231,703	336,412	294,229	† 280,783	330,566	290,050	278,520	246,432	264,049	274,588
Central Government Deposits	26d	5,162	5,653	8,510	18,349	27,075	† 22,031	29,454	21,358	19,915	25,877	47,947	33,581
Liab. to Nonbank Pub.Fin.Insts	26dg	22,112	27,322	39,508	76,040	119,675	† 126,365	211,436	200,383	186,809	230,096	285,062	297,603
Credit from Monetary Authorities	26g	2,249	5,873	46,223	48,184	16,769	† 7,021	6,361	101,918	102,149	85,208	110,949	98,889
Liab. to Nonbank Financial Insts	26j	–	–	–	–	–	† 117,448	137,863	165,720	142,822	153,105	136,985	140,091
Capital Accounts	27a	29,416	34,919	44,014	21,911	20,970	† 26,784	41,678	42,913	38,862	9,833	43,560	41,717
Other Items (Net)	27r	10,003	–1,562	–15,652	–44,166	8,696	† –36,546	–72,087	8,213	329,958	213,536	293,470	222,477

Mexico 273

		1992	1993	1994	1995	1996	1997	1998	1999	2000	2001	2002	2003
Banking Survey						*Millions of Pesos: End of Period*							
Foreign Assets (Net)	31n	47,533	69,216	27,117	29,825	68,852	†208,364	320,161	366,621	484,249	612,127	709,904	733,740
Domestic Credit	32	438,949	493,844	655,639	764,711	664,187	†1,352,555	1,483,134	1,592,192	1,679,657	1,686,882	1,946,468	2,064,494
Claims on Central Govt. (Net)	32an	84,915	42,192	28,487	153,703	143,582	†440,935	476,633	552,478	607,173	640,276	736,071	771,826
Claims on State and Local Govts.	32b	9,728	14,620	23,773	16,574	13,032	†20,902	24,641	25,908	31,249	36,075	42,485	54,323
Claims on Nonfin.Pub.Enterprises	32c	4,419	4,650	8,083	8,868	7,629	†12,454	15,137	12,860	19,645	18,461	21,048	34,917
Claims on Private Sector	32d	315,889	398,969	550,204	537,611	474,757	†801,971	866,844	883,086	943,328	850,201	1,059,796	1,101,242
Claims on Nonbank Financial Inst.	32g	23,998	33,413	45,092	47,955	25,187	†76,294	99,878	117,861	78,262	141,868	87,068	102,186
Money	34	122,080	143,900	145,115	148,534	206,070	†267,211	323,912	407,601	465,485	527,513	596,746	679,307
Quasi-Money	35	182,939	212,666	283,150	416,158	511,152	†857,749	997,340	1,161,358	1,033,068	1,157,906	1,238,705	1,287,512
Money Market Instruments	36aa	14,885	24,283	30,693	50,762	52,031	†241,844	255,835	324,367	320,638	501,203	514,256	494,021
Liabs. of Central Bank: Securities	36ac	–	–	–	–	–	† –	–	–	20,989	66,018	88,816	77,297
Long-Term Foreign Liabilities	36cl	93,257	112,877	231,703	336,412	294,229	†280,783	330,566	290,050	278,520	246,432	264,049	274,588
Liab. to Nonbank Financial Insts.	36j	–	–	–	–	–	†117,448	137,863	165,720	142,822	153,105	136,985	140,091
Capital Accounts	37a	30,729	36,228	46,341	25,278	24,316	†56,813	91,445	78,862	69,025	5,386	68,030	66,429
Other Items (Net)	37r	42,592	33,105	−54,246	−182,608	−354,760	†−260,930	−333,667	−469,147	−166,642	−358,555	−251,213	−221,010
Money plus Quasi-Money	35l	305,019	356,566	428,265	564,692	717,222	†1,124,959	1,321,252	1,568,960	1,498,554	1,685,419	1,835,451	1,966,819
Nonbank Financial Institutions						*Millions of Pesos End of Period*							
Reserves	40	....	....	....	....	....	86	14,568	10,418	10,648	4,035	72	220
Claims on Mon.Author.:Securities	40c	....	....	....	....	....	–	–	–	680	4,546	10,721	14,843
Foreign Assets	41	....	....	....	....	....	–	–	–	–	–	–	–
Claims on Central Government	42a	....	....	....	....	....	25,866	77,863	145,919	210,305	316,713	400,162	491,097
Claims on State and Local Govts	42b	....	....	....	....	....	793	901	979	1,002	992	972	405
Claims on Nonfin.Pub.Enterprises	42c	....	....	....	....	....	–	–	–	–	–	–	–
Claims on Private Sector	42d	....	....	....	....	....	39,982	46,419	54,664	63,399	82,886	118,860	146,328
Claims on Banking Institutions	42e	....	....	....	....	....	149,809	159,688	183,637	150,659	143,735	135,919	134,225
Foreign Liabilities	46c	....	....	....	....	....	–	–	–	–	–	–	–
Central Government Deposits	46d	....	....	....	....	....	4,139	7,072	7,324	361	308	193	162
Credit from Monetary Authorities	46g	....	....	....	....	....	86,892	104,060	116,901	118,479	118,316	113,485	106,962
Credit from Banking Institutions	46h	....	....	....	....	....	6,662	6,912	5,779	6,577	9,298	7,199	7,528
Capital Accounts	47a	....	....	....	....	....	117,831	200,830	299,582	361,997	475,557	585,509	701,529
Other Items (Net)	47r	....	....	....	....	....	1,012	−19,435	−33,969	−50,721	−50,572	−39,680	−29,063
Financial Survey						*Millions of Pesos: End of Period*							
Foreign Assets (Net)	51n	....	....	....	....	....	208,364	320,161	366,621	484,249	612,127	709,904	733,740
Domestic Credit	52	....	....	....	....	....	1,338,763	1,501,367	1,668,570	1,875,740	1,945,297	2,379,202	2,599,976
Claims on Central Govt. (Net)	52an	....	....	....	....	....	462,662	547,424	691,073	817,117	956,681	1,136,040	1,262,761
Claims on State and Local Govts.	52b	....	....	....	....	....	21,695	25,542	26,887	32,251	37,067	43,457	54,728
Claims on Nonfin.Pub.Enterprises	52c	....	....	....	....	....	12,454	15,137	12,860	19,645	18,461	21,048	34,917
Claims on Private Sector	52d	....	....	....	....	....	841,953	913,263	937,750	1,006,727	933,087	1,178,656	1,247,570
Liquid Liabilities	55l	....	....	....	....	....	1,124,873	1,306,684	1,558,542	1,487,906	1,681,384	1,835,379	1,966,599
Money Market Instruments	56aa	....	....	....	....	....	241,844	255,835	324,367	320,638	501,203	514,256	494,021
Liabs. of Central Bank: Securities	56ac	....	....	....	....	....	–	–	–	20,309	61,472	78,095	62,454
Long-Term Foreign Liabilities	56cl	....	....	....	....	....	280,783	330,566	290,050	278,520	246,432	264,049	274,588
Capital Accounts	57a	....	....	....	....	....	174,644	292,275	378,444	431,022	480,943	653,539	767,958
Other Items (Net)	57r	....	....	....	....	....	−275,018	−363,833	−516,213	−178,405	−414,011	−256,211	−231,903
Money (National Definitions)						*Millions of Pesos: End of Period*							
Reserve Money	19ma	43,972	47,193	56,935	66,809	83,991	108,891	131,528	188,718	208,943	225,580	263,937	303,614
M1	59ma	131,732	157,044	163,828	171,638	245,260	325,389	387,896	489,133	564,191	679,660	765,206	856,216
M2	59mb	380,487	469,738	554,930	754,407	995,166	1,286,542	1,658,914	2,024,168	2,363,045	2,766,088	3,082,245	3,494,391
M3	59mc	426,852	540,845	657,102	784,495	1,025,835	1,317,019	1,685,449	2,041,049	2,391,423	2,794,502	3,107,499	3,528,227
M4	59md	458,384	580,326	724,203	869,209	1,116,079	1,396,850	1,771,338	2,114,744	2,447,804	2,843,330	3,151,273	3,559,576
M4a	59mda	468,036	590,378	737,608	898,115	1,183,256	1,518,386	1,899,491	2,272,111	2,566,246	2,976,623	3,294,771	3,731,811
M4 National Currency	59mdn	417,073	527,218	530,328	754,710	985,566	1,274,956	1,629,335	1,970,540	2,310,999	2,687,988	3,003,968	3,435,777
M4 Foreign Currency	59mdf	41,311	53,108	193,876	114,498	130,512	121,895	142,004	144,204	136,805	155,342	147,305	123,799
Interest Rates						*Percent Per Annum*							
Money Market Rate	60b	18.87	17.39	16.47	†60.92	33.61	21.91	26.89	24.10	16.96	12.89	8.17	6.83
Treasury Bill Rate	60c	15.62	14.99	14.10	48.44	31.39	19.80	24.76	21.41	15.24	11.31	7.09	6.23
Savings Rate	60k	....	8.41	5.38	6.67	6.58	7.57	6.38	5.85	4.86	3.26	2.00	1.72
Deposit Rate	60l	15.88	16.69	15.03	39.82	26.40	16.36	15.45	11.60	8.26	6.23	3.76	3.09
Average Cost of Funds	60n	18.78	18.56	15.50	45.12	†31.57	20.04	22.39	20.89	14.59	10.95	6.17	5.15
Lending Rate	60p	....	17.73	19.30	59.43	36.39	22.14	26.36	23.74	16.93	12.80	8.20	6.91
Government Bond Yield	61	....	....	....	51.74	32.81	21.44	....	20.11	†15.81	†10.28	10.13	8.98

Mexico 273

		1992	1993	1994	1995	1996	1997	1998	1999	2000	2001	2002	2003
Prices, Production, Labor		\multicolumn{12}{c}{*Index Numbers (2000=100): Period Averages*}
Share Prices	62	25.5	28.5	38.7	34.1	48.5	68.2	65.1	81.8	100.0	93.9	100.0	110.3
Wholesale Prices	63	28.1	30.2	32.1	44.5	59.5	70.0	81.2	92.7	100.0	105.0	110.4	118.6
Consumer Prices	64	†26.3	28.9	30.9	41.7	56.0	67.6	78.3	91.3	100.0	†106.4	111.7	116.8
Wages, Monthly	65	102.0	†110.8	115.4	100.9	90.9	90.4	93.0	94.4	100.0	106.7	108.7	110.0
Industrial Production	66	73.0	73.3	76.8	70.8	77.9	85.1	90.5	94.3	100.0	96.6	96.3	95.6
Manufacturing Production	66ey	70.8	†69.4	72.2	68.7	76.2	83.6	89.8	93.5	100.0	96.2	95.5	93.6
Mining Production	66zx	84.1	†85.0	87.1	84.8	91.8	95.8	98.4	96.3	100.0	101.5	101.9	105.6
Crude Petroleum	66aa	†86.8	86.9	87.3	85.9	94.2	99.3	101.6	97.1	100.0	102.4	103.3	108.9
		\multicolumn{12}{c}{*Number in Thousands: Period Averages*}
Labor Force	67d	....	....	....	34,309	35,444	37,217	39,507	39,751	39,634	39,683	41,086	....
Employment	67e	....	32,833	....	33,881	35,226	37,360	38,659	38,953	39,502	39,386	40,302	....
Unemployment	67c	....	819	....	1,677	1,355	985	890	682	650	679	....	....
Unemployment Rate (%)	67r	....	2.4	....	4.7	3.7	2.6	2.3	1.7	1.6	1.7	....	....
International Transactions		\multicolumn{12}{c}{*Millions of US Dollars*}
Excluding Maquiladoras													
Exports	70n.d	27,529	30,003	34,318	46,864	59,084	65,266	64,376	72,954	86,987	81,562	82,641	87,561
Imports, f.o.b	71nvd	48,180	49,054	58,362	44,893	58,961	73,475	82,816	91,655	112,749	110,798	109,383	111,933
Including Maquiladoras													
Exports	70..d	46,196	51,886	60,882	79,542	96,000	110,431	117,460	136,391	166,368	158,547	160,682	165,396
Imports, f.o.b	71.vd	62,129	65,367	79,346	72,453	89,469	109,808	125,373	141,975	174,501	168,276	168,679	170,490
Balance of Payments		\multicolumn{12}{c}{*Millions of US Dollars: Minus Sign Indicates Debit*}
Current Account, n.i.e	78ald	−24,442	−23,400	−29,662	−1,576	−2,529	−7,696	−16,097	−14,038	−18,212	−18,218	−14,099	−9,247
Goods: Exports f.o.b	78aad	46,196	51,885	60,882	79,542	96,002	110,431	117,459	136,391	166,455	158,443	160,763	164,922
Goods: Imports f.o.b	78abd	−62,130	−65,366	−79,346	−72,453	−89,469	−109,808	−125,373	−141,975	−174,458	−168,397	−168,679	−170,546
Trade Balance	78acd	−15,934	−13,481	−18,464	7,089	6,533	623	−7,914	−5,584	−8,003	−9,954	−7,916	−5,624
Services: Credit	78add	9,275	9,517	10,321	9,780	10,723	11,182	11,661	11,734	13,756	12,701	12,740	12,712
Services: Debit	78aed	−11,959	−12,046	−13,043	−9,715	−10,817	−12,615	−13,008	−14,471	−17,360	−17,194	−17,660	−18,233
Balance on Goods & Services	78afd	−18,618	−16,010	−21,185	7,153	6,439	−810	−9,261	−8,321	−11,608	−14,446	−12,836	−11,144
Income: Credit	78agd	2,789	2,694	3,347	3,713	4,033	4,431	4,909	4,475	6,048	5,098	4,050	3,672
Income: Debit	78ahd	−11,998	−13,724	−15,605	−16,402	−17,506	−16,537	−17,733	−16,479	−19,622	−18,184	−15,565	−15,486
Balance on Gds, Serv. & Inc	78aid	−27,827	−27,040	−33,444	−5,536	−7,034	−12,916	−22,085	−20,325	−25,182	−27,533	−24,351	−22,959
Current Transfers, n.i.e.: Credit	78ajd	3,404	3,656	3,822	3,995	4,535	5,245	6,015	6,313	6,999	9,336	10,287	13,749
Current Transfers: Debit	78akd	−19	−16	−40	−35	−30	−25	−27	−27	−30	−22	−35	−37
Capital Account, n.i.e	78bcd	−	−	....	....	....	....	−	−	−	−	−	−
Capital Account, n.i.e.: Credit	78bad	−	−	....	....	....	....	−	−	−	−	−	−
Capital Account: Debit	78bbd	−	−	....	....	....	....	−	−	−	−	−	−
Financial Account, n.i.e	78bjd	27,039	33,760	15,787	−10,487	4,248	25,745	19,794	17,603	22,748	25,609	22,570	17,683
Direct Investment Abroad	78bdd	−	−	−	−	−	−	−	−	−	−4,404	−930	−1,390
Dir. Invest. in Rep. Econ., n.i.e	78bed	4,393	4,389	10,973	9,526	9,186	12,831	12,332	13,206	16,586	26,776	14,774	10,784
Portfolio Investment Assets	78bfd	1,165	−564	−767	−662	544	−708	−769	−836	1,290	3,857	1,134	91
Equity Securities	78bkd	−	−	−	−	−	−	−	−	−	−	−	−
Debt Securities	78bld	1,165	−564	−767	−662	544	−708	−769	−836	1,290	3,857	1,134	91
Portfolio Investment Liab., n.i.e	78bgd	18,041	28,919	8,182	−9,715	3,537	6,002	1,027	12,005	−1,134	3,882	−632	3,864
Equity Securities	78bmd	4,783	10,716	4,084	519	2,801	3,215	−666	3,769	447	151	−104	−123
Debt Securities	78bnd	13,258	18,203	4,099	−10,234	736	2,787	1,693	8,236	−1,581	3,731	−528	3,987
Financial Derivatives Assets	78bwd	....	....	....	....	....	....	....	....	....	....	....	....
Financial Derivatives Liabilities	78bxd	....	....	....	....	....	....	....	....	....	....	....	....
Other Investment Assets	78bhd	4,387	−3,038	−4,903	−6,694	−6,886	7,425	1,200	−3,169	5,809	−3,287	11,601	8,266
Monetary Authorities	78bod	....	....	....	....	....	....	−	−	−	−	−	−
General Government	78bpd	−	−	−1,400	−3,619	−22	57	25	−	−	−	−	−
Banks	78bqd	22	−1,683	−885	−1,510	−1,018	5,112	−1,208	−1,894	45	−5,423	7,401	4,456
Other Sectors	78brd	4,365	−1,355	−2,618	−1,565	−5,846	2,256	2,384	−1,275	5,764	2,136	4,199	3,810
Other Investment Liab., n.i.e	78bid	−947	4,054	2,302	−2,942	−2,133	195	6,004	−3,603	198	−1,214	−3,377	−3,931
Monetary Authorities	78bsd	−	−	−	−788	−1,459	−	−	−	−	−	−	−
General Government	78btd	−5,867	−1,136	−986	210	−659	206	1,355	−4,294	−2,896	−603	316	832
Banks	78bud	1,626	3,622	2,799	−5,297	−	−	97	−2,312	−883	−4,222	−2,861	−850
Other Sectors	78bvd	3,294	1,568	488	2,933	−15	−11	4,552	3,003	3,977	3,611	−832	−3,913
Net Errors and Omissions	78cad	−852	−3,128	−3,323	−4,248	229	2,411	−527	685	2,590	−76	−1,112	1,381
Overall Balance	78cbd	1,745	7,232	−17,199	−16,312	1,948	20,460	3,170	4,250	7,126	7,314	7,359	9,817
Reserves and Related Items	79dad	−1,745	−7,232	17,199	16,312	−1,948	−20,460	−3,170	−4,250	−7,126	−7,314	−7,359	−9,817
Reserve Assets	79dbd	−1,173	−6,057	18,398	−9,648	−1,805	−10,513	−2,120	−596	−2,862	−7,338	−7,376	−9,833
Use of Fund Credit and Loans	79dcd	−572	−1,175	−1,199	11,950	−2,057	−3,485	−1,075	−3,681	−4,288	−	−	−
Exceptional Financing	79ded	−	−	−	14,010	1,913	−6,463	24	27	24	24	16	16

Mexico 273

		1992	1993	1994	1995	1996	1997	1998	1999	2000	2001	2002	2003
International Investment Position							*Millions of US Dollars*						
Assets..	79aad	....	....	....	....	....	....	....	....	....	110,255	104,349	....
Direct Investment Abroad...............	79abd	....	....	....	....	....	....	....	....	....	13,187	14,156	....
Portfolio Investment......................	79acd	....	....	....	....	....	....	....	....	....	6,237	4,296	....
Equity Securities.........................	79add	....	....	....	....	....	....	....	....	....	....	....	....
Debt Securities...........................	79aed	....	....	....	....	....	....	....	....	....	....	....	....
Financial Derivatives......................	79ald	....	....	....	....	....	....	....	....	....	–	–	....
Other Investment...........................	79afd	....	....	....	....	....	....	....	....	....	46,016	35,223	....
Monetary Authorities..................	79agd	....	....	....	....	....	....	....	....	....	....	....	....
General Government...................	79ahd	....	....	....	....	....	....	....	....	....	....	....	....
Banks..	79aid	....	....	....	....	....	....	....	....	....	....	....	....
Other Sectors.............................	79ajd	....	....	....	....	....	....	....	....	....	....	....	....
Reserve Assets...............................	79akd	....	....	....	....	....	....	....	....	....	44,814	50,674	....
Liabilities.......................................	79lad	....	....	....	....	....	....	....	....	....	352,575	353,612	....
Dir. Invest. in Rep. Economy...........	79lbd	....	....	....	....	....	....	....	....	....	140,376	154,344	....
Portfolio Investment......................	79lcd	....	....	....	....	....	....	....	....	....	135,298	124,917	....
Equity Securities.........................	79ldd	....	....	....	....	....	....	....	....	....	53,162	42,786	....
Debt Securities...........................	79led	....	....	....	....	....	....	....	....	....	82,136	82,131	....
Financial Derivatives......................	79lld	....	....	....	....	....	....	....	....	....	–	–	....
Other Investment...........................	79lfd	....	....	....	....	....	....	....	....	....	76,901	74,351	....
Monetary Authorities..................	79lgd	....	....	....	....	....	....	....	....	....	....	....	....
General Government...................	79lhd	....	....	....	....	....	....	....	....	....	....	....	....
Banks..	79lid	....	....	....	....	....	....	....	....	....	....	....	....
Other Sectors.............................	79ljd	....	....	....	....	....	....	....	....	....	....	....	....
Government Finance						*Millions of Pesos: Year Ending December 31*							
Deficit (-) or Surplus......................	80	46,921	6,451	–386	–9,784	–5,546	–34,161	–55,591	–71,289	–69,256	–42,377	–111,592	–72,154
Total Revenue and Grants..............	81y	174,278	186,644	211,434	278,626	379,573	459,047	488,959	620,135	791,040	859,998	875,710	1,048,263
Revenue.....................................	81	174,278	186,644	211,434	278,626	379,573	459,047	488,959	620,135	791,040	859,998	875,710	1,048,263
Grants...	81z	–	–	–	–	–	–	–	–	–	–	–	–
Exp.& Lending Minus Repayments..	82z	127,357	180,193	211,820	288,410	385,119	493,208	544,550	691,424	860,296	902,375	987,302	1,120,417
Expenditure.................................	82	158,189	183,876	217,249	285,147	382,499	505,902	556,079	689,921	848,502	897,049	1,009,733	1,119,138
Lending Minus Repayments.........	83	–30,832	–3,683	–5,429	3,263	2,620	–12,694	–11,529	1,503	11,794	5,326	–22,431	1,279
Total Financing...............................	80h	–46,921	–6,451	386	9,784	5,546	34,161	55,591	71,289	69,256	42,377	111,592	72,190
Domestic......................................	84a	–42,888	–1,397	4,934	–90,101	24,233	56,387	35,073	64,994	117,589	46,922	125,971	76,910
Foreign...	85a	–4,033	–5,054	–4,548	99,885	–18,687	–22,226	20,518	6,295	–48,333	–4,545	–14,379	–4,720
Total Debt by Residence..................	88	316,514	317,977	417,115	751,601	787,822	821,777	1,073,220	1,175,528	1,276,451	1,306,415	1,504,286	1,667,603
Domestic......................................	88a	133,478	134,769	178,960	155,360	192,162	273,656	378,256	506,389	675,107	763,559	907,408	1,011,889
Foreign...	89a	183,036	183,208	238,155	596,241	595,660	548,121	694,964	669,139	601,344	542,856	596,878	655,714
National Accounts							*Billions of Pesos*						
Househ.Cons.Expend.,incl.NPISHs....	96f.c	808.12	† 903.17	1,016.13	1,232.00	1,646.26	2,042.08	2,593.35	3,084.14	3,682.55	4,044.88	4,319.87	4,672.27
Government Consumption Expend...	91f.c	111.75	† 138.56	164.16	191.98	243.71	314.62	399.96	506.46	612.62	683.38	758.49	855.87
Gross Fixed Capital Formation..........	93e.c	220.55	† 233.18	274.86	296.71	451.08	619.49	804.00	973.80	1,174.30	1,161.95	1,209.68	1,304.29
Changes in Inventories.....................	93i.c	41.56	† 30.60	33.54	67.39	132.48	201.46	131.41	103.51	127.79	53.01	85.72	35.10
Exports of Goods and Services.........	90c.c	171.48	† 191.54	238.96	558.80	811.51	962.22	1,180.39	1,414.34	1,704.08	1,598.52	1,677.56	1,920.55
Imports of Goods and Services (-).....	98c.c	228.12	† 240.86	307.49	509.86	759.45	965.61	1,262.76	1,488.56	1,810.58	1,730.39	1,794.95	2,033.31
Gross Domestic Product (GDP).........	99b.c	1,125.33	† 1,256.20	1,420.16	1,837.02	2,525.58	3,174.28	3,846.35	4,593.69	5,490.76	5,811.35	6,256.38	6,754.77
Net Primary Income from Abroad.....	98.nc	–29	–36	–42	–84	–104	–99	–121	–120	–131	–124	–116	....
Gross National Income (GNI)...........	99a.c	1,096	1,220	1,378	1,753	2,421	3,075	3,726	4,474	5,359	5,687	6,140	....
GDP Volume 1993 Prices..................	99b.r	1,232.16	1,256.20	1,311.66	1,230.77	1,294.20	1,381.84	1,451.35	1,503.93	1,602.64	1,602.71	1,613.21	1,633.08
GDP Volume (2000=100).................	99bvr	76.9	78.4	81.8	76.8	80.8	86.2	90.6	93.8	100.0	100.0	100.7	101.9
GDP Deflator (2000=100)................	99bir	26.7	† 29.2	31.6	43.6	57.0	67.0	77.4	89.2	100.0	105.8	113.2	120.7
						Millions: Midyear Estimates							
Population...............................	99z	86.38	87.97	89.56	91.14	92.72	94.29	95.85	97.40	98.93	100.46	101.97	103.46

Micronesia, Fed.Sts. 868

		1992	1993	1994	1995	1996	1997	1998	1999	2000	2001	2002	2003
Exchange Rates						*US Dollars per SDR: End of Period*							
Market Rate	aa	1.3750	1.3736	1.4599	1.4865	1.4380	1.3493	1.4080	1.3725	1.3029	1.2567	1.3595	1.4860
Fund Position						*Millions of SDRs: End of Period*							
Quota	2f.s	–	3.5	3.5	3.5	3.5	3.5	3.5	5.1	5.1	5.1	5.1	5.1
SDRs	1b.s	–	.8	.9	.9	.9	1.0	1.0	1.1	1.1	1.1	1.2	1.2
Reserve Position in the Fund	1c.s	–	–	–	–	–	–	–	–	–	–	–	–
Total Fund Cred.&Loans Outstg	2tl												
International Liquidity					*Millions of US Dollars Unless Otherwise Indicated: End of Period*								
Total Reserves minus Gold	1l.d	....	....	....	69.500	89.600	85.801	101.602	92.669	113.047	98.330	117.391	89.607
SDRs	1b.d	–	1.141	1.264	1.349	1.357	1.325	1.442	1.455	1.442	1.445	1.598	1.777
Reserve Position in the Fund	1c.d	–	–	.001	.001	.001	.001	.001	.001	.001	.001	.001	.001
Foreign Exchange	1d.d	....	....	....	68.150	88.242	84.475	100.159	91.213	111.605	96.885	115.792	87.829
Gold (Million Fine Troy Ounces)	1ad	....	....	....	–	–	–	–	–	–	–	–	–
Gold (National Valuation)	1and	....	....	....	–	–	–	–	–	–	–	–	–
Monetary Authorities:Other Assets	3..d	....	....	....	60.7	54.0	51.5	55.6	55.3	47.4	37.0	33.5	41.8
Monetary Authorities: Other Liab.	4..d	....	....	....	–	–	–	–	–	–	–	–	–
Banking Institutions: Assets	7a.d	....	....	....	82.200	97.210	96.273	93.042	93.472	91.259	97.967	112.961	117.521
Liabilities	7b.d	....	....	....	1.962	1.332	.948	.131	.107	–	–	5.226	1.604
Monetary Authorities						*Millions of US Dollars: End of Period*							
Foreign Assets	11	....	....	....	130.249	143.635	137.338	157.181	147.952	160.455	135.319	150.894	131.399
Foreign Liabilities	16c												
Central Government Deposits	16d	....	....	....	130.249	143.635	137.338	157.181	147.952	160.456	135.319	150.893	131.399
Other Items (Net)	17r				–	–	–	–	–	–.001	–	.001	–
Banking Institutions						*Millions of US Dollars: End of Period*							
Foreign Assets	21	....	....	....	82.200	97.210	96.273	93.042	93.472	91.259	97.967	112.961	117.521
Claims on Central Government	22a	....	....	....	–	–	–	–	–	–	.173	–	–
Claims on State & Local Govts	22b	....	....	....	–	–	–	–	.787	.442	–	.117	–
Claims on Nonfin.Pub.Enterprises	22c	....	....	....	.699	.106	–	–	.001	–	–	–	–
Claims on Private Sector	22d	....	....	....	65.572	60.141	58.129	65.618	70.749	71.595	69.907	50.558	40.048
Demand Deposits	24	....	....	....	19.863	19.528	21.514	21.284	19.891	18.802	21.245	19.697	22.476
Time, Savings,& Fgn. Currency Dep.	25	....	....	....	87.971	82.067	83.947	84.933	89.926	89.965	94.015	81.766	75.187
Foreign Liabilities	26c	....	....	....	1.962	1.332	.948	.131	.107	–	–	5.226	1.604
Central Government Deposits	26d	....	....	....	4.949	14.976	11.745	11.736	11.351	10.336	7.727	12.754	12.659
Liab. to Nonbank Financial Insts	26j	....	....	....	.365	2.836	1.446	.587	2.007	.958	1.827	3.268	3.643
Capital Accounts	27a	....	....	....	39.137	43.175	44.506	46.739	46.152	47.017	49.433	48.543	50.472
Other Items (Net)	27r	....	....	....	–5.776	–6.457	–9.704	–6.750	–4.425	–3.782	–6.200	–7.618	–8.472
Banking Survey						*Millions of US Dollars: End of Period*							
Foreign Assets (Net)	31n	....	....	....	210.487	239.513	232.663	250.092	241.317	251.714	233.286	258.629	247.316
Domestic Credit	32	....	....	....	–68.927	–98.364	–90.954	–103.299	–87.766	–98.755	–72.966	–112.972	–104.010
Claims on Central Govt. (Net)	32an	....	....	....	–135.198	–158.611	–149.083	–168.917	–159.303	–170.792	–142.873	–163.647	–144.058
Claims on Local Government	32b	....	....	....	–	–	–	–	.787	.442	–	.117	–
Claims on Nonfin.Pub.Enterprises	32c	....	....	....	.699	.106	–	–	.001	–	–	–	–
Claims on Private Sector	32d	....	....	....	65.572	60.141	58.129	65.618	70.749	71.595	69.907	50.558	40.048
Money	34	....	....	....	19.863	19.528	21.514	21.284	19.891	18.802	21.245	19.697	22.476
Quasi-Money	35	....	....	....	87.971	82.067	83.947	84.933	89.926	89.965	94.015	81.766	75.187
Liab. to Nonbank Financial Insts	36j	....	....	....	.365	2.836	1.446	.587	2.007	.958	1.827	3.268	3.643
Capital Accounts	37a	....	....	....	39.137	43.175	44.506	46.739	46.152	47.017	49.433	48.543	50.472
Other Items (Net)	37r	....	....	....	–5.776	–6.457	–9.704	–6.750	–4.425	–3.783	–6.200	–7.617	–8.472
Money plus Quasi-Money	35l	....	....	....	107.834	101.595	105.461	106.217	109.817	108.767	115.260	101.463	97.663
Interest Rates						*Percent Per Annum*							
Savings Rate	60k	....	....	....	3.17	3.01	3.00	2.90	2.72	2.67	2.47	1.33	.95
Deposit Rate	60l	....	....	....	5.33	4.58	4.21	3.98	3.72	4.59	3.17	1.47	1.02
Lending Rate	60p	....	....	....	15.00	15.00	15.00	15.00	15.17	15.33	15.33	15.28	15.00
						Millions: Midyear Estimates							
Population	99z	.10	.10	Ü .11	.11	.11	.11	.11	.11	.11	.11	.11	.11

Moldova 921

		1992	1993	1994	1995	1996	1997	1998	1999	2000	2001	2002	2003
Exchange Rates			*Lei per SDR: End of Period*
Official Rate	aa	.5699	4.9998	6.2336	6.6877	6.7215	6.2882	11.7185	15.9077	16.1343	16.4517	18.7913	19.6445
					Lei per US Dollar: End of Period (ae) Period Average (rf)
Official Rate	ae	.4145	3.6400	4.2700	4.4990	4.6743	4.6605	8.3226	11.5902	12.3833	13.0909	13.8220	13.2200
Official Rate	rf	....	....	....	4.4958	4.6045	4.6236	5.3707	10.5158	12.4342	12.8651	13.5705	13.9449
					Index Numbers (2000=100): Period Averages
Nominal Effective Exchange Rate	nec	....	....	27.67	48.97	57.48	75.90	89.88	94.52	100.00	106.71	107.30	102.18
Real Effective Exchange Rate	rec	....	....	105.38	91.15	89.18	96.34	97.59	91.43	100.00	97.52	91.41	87.52
Fund Position						*Millions of SDRs: End of Period*
Quota	2f.s	90.00	90.00	90.00	90.00	90.00	90.00	90.00	123.20	123.20	123.20	123.20	123.20
SDRs	1b.s	–	25.05	14.62	8.81	5.45	.89	.50	.23	.26	.59	.20	.03
Reserve Position in the Fund	1c.s	.01	.01	.01	.01	.01	.01	.01	.01	.01	.01	–	.01
Total Fund Cred.&Loans Outstg	2tl	–	63.00	112.45	154.85	172.29	172.73	125.56	127.69	118.30	116.29	111.78	95.95
International Liquidity					*Millions of US Dollars Unless Otherwise Indicated: End of Period*
Total Reserves minus Gold	1l.d	2.45	76.34	179.92	257.01	311.96	365.99	143.56	185.70	222.49	228.53	268.86	302.27
SDRs	1b.d	–	34.41	21.34	13.10	7.84	1.21	.70	.32	.34	.74	.27	.04
Reserve Position in the Fund	1c.d	.01	.01	.01	.01	.01	.01	.01	.01	.01	.01	.01	.01
Foreign Exchange	1d.d	2.44	41.92	158.57	243.90	304.11	364.77	142.85	185.37	222.15	227.78	268.58	302.22
Gold (Million Fine Troy Ounces)	1ad	–	–	–	–	–	–	–	–	–	–	–	–
Gold (National Valuation)	1and	–	–	–	–	–	–	–	–	–	–	–	–
Monetary Authorities: Other Liab	4..d	138.12	12.02	10.10	7.42	4.94	4.00	2.77	10.06	9.66	1.30	.83	1.53
Dep.Money Banks: Assets Conv	7axd	2.19	14.92	18.86	32.71	37.41	23.78	32.33	53.42	67.22	59.77	70.05	103.79
Assets Nonconv	7ayd	.20	2.14	7.79	5.24	5.55	9.25	3.44	2.23	5.16	4.92	7.15	8.06
Dep.Money Banks: Liab. Conv	7bxd	–	.51	1.42	10.60	50.70	58.10	67.27	41.78	44.42	41.70	44.51	54.58
Liab. Nonconv	7byd	–	1.51	.41	3.10	1.55	4.91	7.62	3.33	5.80	5.45	9.00	5.20
Monetary Authorities						*Millions of Lei: End of Period*
Foreign Assets	11	49.32	345.41	825.14	1,198.42	†1,486.91	1,716.60	1,199.82	2,207.49	2,876.49	3,008.38	3,727.14	4,010.31
Claims on Central Government	12a	52.24	236.21	284.01	452.92	†496.12	524.83	1,409.21	1,737.46	1,730.79	1,899.28	2,158.18	2,175.41
Claims on Private Sector	12d	–	–	–	1.79	†2.88	3.92	5.10	6.03	7.28	7.10	6.37	6.11
Claims on Deposit Money Banks	12e	3.37	98.68	274.67	366.55	†362.63	286.02	233.02	130.27	105.44	91.15	81.40	72.29
Reserve Money	14	49.04	241.14	551.94	779.85	†854.28	1,138.64	1,063.45	1,506.63	1,988.86	2,504.44	3,285.81	3,896.88
of which: Currency Outside DMB	14a	9.75	119.45	345.55	640.15	†731.06	972.10	†855.45	1,122.07	1,469.26	1,834.20	2,288.56	2,740.52
Foreign Liabilities	16c	57.25	358.73	744.09	1,068.96	†1,181.13	1,104.75	1,494.36	2,147.89	2,028.31	1,930.21	2,112.02	1,905.15
Central Government Deposits	16d	.20	90.12	17.45	21.38	†126.37	9.99	60.00	85.72	277.93	100.52	71.91	3.81
Capital Accounts	17a	.06	1.72	24.72	79.11	†95.26	91.92	161.36	215.21	296.22	416.61	385.22	477.32
Other Items (Net)	17r	–1.62	–11.40	45.63	70.37	†91.49	186.07	67.97	125.81	128.69	54.13	118.12	–19.04
Deposit Money Banks						*Millions of Lei: End of Period*
Reserves	20	10.60	48.87	52.44	54.38	36.54	52.05	†200.66	360.92	465.22	652.38	979.20	1,154.08
Foreign Assets	21	.99	62.11	113.76	171.03	200.79	153.90	†297.69	644.99	896.23	846.80	1,067.07	1,478.66
Claims on Central Government	22a	28.16	122.13	31.56	10.31	13.68	67.58	†184.46	267.81	335.33	571.44	668.42	598.05
Claims on Local Government	22b	4.03	10.21	22.82	2.59	13.19	23.68	†33.01	14.98	17.24	25.45	105.86	70.48
Claims on Nonfin.Pub.Enterprises	22c	32.81	243.28	493.91	692.37	852.27	1,120.82	†144.17	146.32	230.71	293.61	315.16	449.14
Claims on Private Sector	22d	11.23	91.06	174.79	433.62	600.88	617.05	†1,265.65	1,453.15	2,025.31	2,804.49	3,867.39	5,605.06
Claims on Nonbank Financial Insts	22g	–	–	–	–	–	–	†23.06	37.30	28.36	5.65	9.47	1.01
Demand Deposits	24	49.94	121.24	173.69	244.57	263.13	326.49	†210.00	357.76	553.75	665.76	1,271.14	1,674.28
Time, Savings,& Fgn.Currency Dep	25	23.61	106.02	228.68	358.18	435.57	624.02	†698.48	1,040.18	1,548.25	2,350.96	3,165.91	4,357.36
Money Market Instruments	26aa	–	–	–	–	–	–	†1.21	2.10	.20	.29	.28	.86
Foreign Liabilities	26c	–	7.36	7.80	61.64	244.21	293.67	†623.24	522.87	621.93	617.29	739.57	790.40
Central Government Deposits	26d	21.67	149.65	56.54	35.81	27.84	33.55	†13.51	44.72	57.11	270.93	502.38	753.60
Credit from Monetary Authorities	26g	6.47	104.70	292.23	389.12	368.12	285.91	†229.83	130.27	106.44	93.15	85.31	72.31
Liabs. to Nonbank Financial Insts	26j	–	–	–	–	–	–	†.77	1.55	2.22	2.45	26.48	13.71
Capital Accounts	27a	9.57	136.65	333.05	569.03	731.41	839.27	†756.20	1,242.83	1,692.04	1,896.54	2,099.43	2,506.26
Other Items (Net)	27r	–23.44	–47.96	–202.72	–294.04	–352.93	–367.84	†–384.56	–416.81	–583.56	–697.56	–877.92	–812.30
Monetary Survey						*Millions of Lei: End of Period*
Foreign Assets (Net)	31n	–6.94	41.44	187.01	238.85	†262.37	472.08	†–620.10	181.71	1,122.48	1,307.68	1,942.62	2,793.42
Domestic Credit	32	107.39	463.12	933.10	1,536.40	†1,824.80	2,314.34	†2,991.14	3,532.62	4,039.97	5,235.57	6,556.57	8,147.84
Claims on Central Govt. (Net)	32an	58.53	118.57	241.58	406.04	†355.59	548.88	†1,520.16	1,874.84	1,731.07	2,099.27	2,252.32	2,016.06
Claims on Local Government	32b	4.03	10.21	22.82	2.59	†13.19	23.68	†33.01	14.98	17.24	25.45	105.86	70.48
Claims on Nonfin.Pub.Enterprises	32c	33.60	243.28	493.91	692.37	†852.27	1,120.82	†144.17	146.32	230.71	293.61	315.16	449.14
Claims on Private Sector	32d	11.23	91.06	174.79	435.41	†603.76	620.97	†1,270.75	1,459.19	2,032.59	2,811.59	3,873.76	5,611.17
Claims on Nonbank Financial Inst.	32g	–	–	–	–	†–	–	†23.06	37.30	28.36	5.65	9.47	1.01
Money	34	59.79	242.07	524.20	885.04	†994.51	1,298.83	†1,065.46	1,479.84	2,023.22	2,500.00	3,559.80	4,415.07
Quasi-Money	35	23.61	107.17	229.01	360.18	†435.57	624.02	†698.48	1,040.18	1,548.25	2,350.96	3,165.91	4,357.36
Money Market Instruments	36aa	–	–	–	–	†–	–	†1.21	2.10	.20	.29	.28	.86
Liabs. to Nonbank Financial Insts	36j	–	–	–	–	†–	–	†.77	1.55	2.22	2.45	26.48	13.71
Capital Accounts	37a	9.63	138.37	357.77	648.15	†826.67	931.20	†917.56	1,458.04	1,988.26	2,313.16	2,484.65	2,983.58
Other Items (Net)	37r	7.42	16.94	9.13	–118.10	†–169.58	–67.63	†–312.44	–267.37	–399.70	–623.60	–737.93	–829.30
Money plus Quasi-Money	35l	83.39	349.24	753.21	1,245.22	†1,430.08	1,922.86	†1,763.94	2,520.02	3,571.47	4,850.95	6,725.71	8,772.43

Moldova 921

		1992	1993	1994	1995	1996	1997	1998	1999	2000	2001	2002	2003
Interest Rates						*Percent Per Annum*							
Refinancing Rate	60a	....	....	143.94	28.25	20.15	19.03	....	....	....	....	....	....
Money Market Rate	60b	....	....	....	....	....	28.10	30.91	32.60	20.77	11.04	5.13	11.51
Money Market Rate (Fgn. Cur.)	60b.f	....	....	....	....	....	....	....	11.88	6.86	9.06	4.80	2.51
Treasury Bill Rate	60c	....	....	....	52.90	39.01	23.63	30.54	28.49	22.20	14.24	5.89	15.08
Deposit Rate	60l	....	....	....	....	25.43	23.47	21.68	27.54	24.87	20.93	14.20	12.55
Deposit Rate (Foreign Currency)	60l.f	....	....	....	....	....	....	9.86	5.27	5.12	4.09	3.22	3.13
Lending Rate	60p	....	....	....	....	36.67	33.33	30.83	35.54	33.78	28.69	23.52	19.29
Lending Rate (Foreign Currency)	60p.f	....	....	....	....	....	....	22.03	20.37	17.12	14.22	12.32	10.98
Prices and Labor						*Index Numbers (2000=100): Period Averages*							
Consumer Prices	64	....	....	33.4	37.5	45.3	48.9	52.2	76.2	100.0	109.8	115.6	129.2
						Number in Thousands: Period Averages							
Labor Force	67d	2,065	....	....	....	1,686	....	1,659	1,682	1,655	1,617	1,615	....
Employment	67e	2,050	1,688	1,681	1,673	1,660	1,646	1,642	1,494	1,515	1,499	1,501	1,357
Unemployment	67c	15	14	21	25	23	28	32	187	140	118	110	....
Unemployment Rate (%)	67r	.7	.7	1.1	1.0	1.5	1.5	1.9	11.2	8.5	7.3	6.8	....
International Transactions						*Millions of US Dollars*							
Exports	70..d	470	483	558	739	823	890	644	474	477	567	660	806
Imports, c.i.f.	71..d	640	628	703	841	1,072	1,171	1,024	586	776	897	....	....
Imports, f.o.b.	71.vd	....	....	672	809	1,083	1,238	1,032	611	770	880	1,038	1,429
Balance of Payments						*Millions of US Dollars: Minus Sign Indicates Debit*							
Current Account, n.i.e.	78ald	....	....	−82.0	−87.8	−194.8	−274.9	−334.7	−78.6	−125.3	−77.9	−56.4	−142.3
Goods: Exports f.o.b.	78aad	....	....	618.5	739.0	822.9	889.6	643.6	474.3	476.8	567.2	659.8	806.3
Goods: Imports f.o.b.	78abd	....	....	−672.4	−809.2	−1,082.5	−1,237.6	−1,031.7	−611.5	−770.5	−880.3	−1,038.0	−1,428.6
Trade Balance	78acd	....	....	−53.9	−70.2	−259.7	−348.0	−388.1	−137.2	−293.6	−313.0	−378.2	−622.3
Services: Credit	78add	....	....	32.8	144.5	106.0	167.7	152.0	135.7	164.5	170.7	215.3	250.5
Services: Debit	78aed	....	....	−79.0	−196.3	−166.4	−196.1	−198.6	−177.9	−201.7	−203.3	−246.3	−290.0
Balance on Goods & Services	78afd	....	....	−100.0	−122.0	−320.0	−376.4	−434.6	−179.4	−330.8	−345.7	−409.2	−661.8
Income: Credit	78agd	....	....	10.8	14.2	99.3	132.7	136.8	120.5	173.3	165.0	216.5	325.8
Income: Debit	78ahd	....	....	−26.1	−32.4	−44.2	−85.3	−102.3	−95.8	−123.3	−124.4	−109.4	−110.8
Balance on Gds, Serv. & Inc.	78aid	....	....	−115.4	−140.2	−264.9	−329.0	−400.1	−154.7	−280.9	−305.1	−302.1	−446.7
Current Transfers, n.i.e.: Credit	78ajd	....	....	36.9	66.6	72.9	104.1	110.9	111.5	164.7	240.5	261.5	326.3
Current Transfers: Debit	78akd	....	....	−3.6	−14.1	−2.8	−50.0	−45.5	−35.4	−9.1	−13.3	−15.8	−21.8
Capital Account, n.i.e.	78bcd	....	....	−1.0	−.4	−.1	−.2	−.4	1.1	−14.4	−20.7	−15.3	−12.8
Capital Account, n.i.e.: Credit	78bad	....	....	−	−	.1	.1	2.1	1.5	2.8	1.1	.8	3.5
Capital Account: Debit	78bbd	....	....	−1.0	−.4	−.1	−.3	−2.5	−.4	−17.1	−21.8	−16.1	−16.3
Financial Account, n.i.e.	78bjd	....	....	211.1	−68.8	76.6	95.2	5.2	−34.6	144.6	75.4	31.3	22.6
Direct Investment Abroad	78bdd	....	....	....	−.5	−.6	−.5	.7	−.1	−.1	−.1	−.4	−.1
Dir. Invest. in Rep. Econ., n.i.e.	78bed	....	....	11.6	25.9	23.7	78.7	75.5	37.9	136.1	97.2	116.6	58.5
Portfolio Investment Assets	78bfd	....	....	−.4	−	−	−	−	−	−	−3.2	−1.0	2.0
Equity Securities	78bkd	....	....	−.4	....	....	....	....	....	....	....	....	−.1
Debt Securities	78bld	....	....	....	....	....	....	....	−	−	−3.2	−1.0	2.1
Portfolio Investment Liab., n.i.e.	78bgd	....	....	.6	−.5	30.8	18.6	−59.1	−7.3	−4.2	−3.5	−26.5	−23.9
Equity Securities	78bmd	....	....	.6	−.5	.8	3.7	6.5	5.2	2.7	3.2	1.8	1.0
Debt Securities	78bnd	....	....	....	−	30.0	14.9	−65.6	−12.5	−6.9	−6.8	−28.2	−24.9
Financial Derivatives Assets	78bwd	....	....	....	....	....	....	....	....	....	....	....	....
Financial Derivatives Liabilities	78bxd	....	....	....	....	....	....	....	....	....	....	....	....
Other Investment Assets	78bhd	....	....	−81.7	−116.4	−51.4	1.8	−86.8	−107.4	−28.7	−8.6	−58.4	−49.7
Monetary Authorities	78bod	....	....	−1.3	2.9	.3	3.7	2.9	−	.1	−	−	−
General Government	78bpd	....	....	−4.1	11.9	12.2	1.6	−.6	−4.3	−	8.3	.5	−.2
Banks	78bqd	....	....	−10.1	−13.5	−6.5	10.6	−10.9	−15.4	−16.5	1.2	−15.7	−19.6
Other Sectors	78brd	....	....	−66.2	−117.7	−57.4	−14.2	−78.2	−87.8	−12.4	−18.1	−43.2	−29.9
Other Investment Liab., n.i.e.	78bid	....	....	281.0	22.7	74.0	−3.4	74.8	42.3	41.5	−6.5	1.0	35.8
Monetary Authorities	78bsd	....	....	3.1	1.8	−1.9	−2.7	5.2	−2.4	1.6	−1.0	.1	.5
General Government	78btd	....	....	147.0	−19.7	43.2	−59.2	9.7	−22.4	−11.6	−14.2	−13.4	−25.1
Banks	78bud	....	....	−.8	11.4	21.9	11.8	6.9	−21.2	2.4	−1.3	10.8	13.6
Other Sectors	78bvd	....	....	131.6	29.2	10.7	46.6	53.1	88.3	49.0	10.0	3.4	46.8
Net Errors and Omissions	78cad	....	....	−115.2	−18.4	15.5	−7.9	−22.8	−3.8	−6.7	−3.4	−8.4	89.5
Overall Balance	78cbd	....	....	12.9	−175.4	−102.7	−187.8	−352.8	−115.9	−1.8	−26.7	−48.8	−43.0
Reserves and Related Items	79dad	....	....	−12.9	175.4	102.7	187.8	352.8	115.9	1.8	26.7	48.8	43.0
Reserve Assets	79dbd	....	....	−103.1	−76.7	−56.9	−50.2	225.7	−48.8	−47.4	−9.5	−27.0	−14.1
Use of Fund Credit and Loans	79dcd	....	....	71.5	64.8	25.2	.8	−64.4	4.0	−12.7	−2.3	−5.6	−22.2
Exceptional Financing	79ded	....	....	18.7	187.3	134.4	237.2	191.4	160.6	61.9	38.5	81.3	79.3

Moldova 921

		1992	1993	1994	1995	1996	1997	1998	1999	2000	2001	2002	2003
International Investment Position						*Millions of US Dollars*							
Assets...............................	79aad	....	....	303.2	499.7	616.8	661.9	468.0	594.8	658.2	667.8	766.8	911.5
Direct Investment Abroad.........	79abd	....	....	17.8	18.3	23.1	23.5	22.8	22.9	23.0	23.0	23.5	23.5
Portfolio Investment.............	79acd	....	....	.4	.4	.4	.4	.4	.4	.4	3.6	4.6	2.5
Equity Securities..............	79add	....	....	.4	.4	.4	.4	.4	.4	.4	.4	.4	.5
Debt Securities................	79aed	....	....	–	–	–	–	–	–	–	3.2	4.2	2.1
Financial Derivatives............	79ald	....	....	–	–	–	–	–	–	–	–	–	–
Other Investment.................	79afd	....	....	105.3	224.0	279.8	275.8	308.0	391.2	412.2	412.7	469.9	583.2
Monetary Authorities..........	79agd	....	....	9.9	7.1	6.8	3.1	.1	.1	–	–	–	–
General Government...........	79ahd	....	....	31.7	19.9	7.9	6.2	6.8	10.1	9.9	1.6	1.1	1.4
Banks..........................	79aid	....	....	27.4	40.8	47.3	36.7	44.9	58.1	74.4	72.7	89.6	115.2
Other Sectors..................	79ajd	....	....	36.3	156.3	217.9	229.9	256.2	323.0	328.0	338.4	379.2	466.6
Reserve Assets....................	79akd	....	....	179.8	257.0	313.5	362.2	136.9	180.4	222.6	228.5	268.9	302.3
Liabilities........................	79lad	....	....	723.1	1,029.8	1,282.9	1,608.5	1,841.3	1,959.1	2,131.6	2,203.8	2,417.0	2,606.5
Dir. Invest. in Rep. Economy......	79lbd	....	....	28.6	94.2	116.9	195.8	257.6	323.2	458.7	600.1	726.6	788.9
Portfolio Investment.............	79lcd	....	....	.7	.4	60.7	296.3	232.5	86.8	201.2	161.1	133.3	110.8
Equity Securities..............	79ldd	....	....	.7	.4	.8	6.0	10.6	11.6	11.7	13.7	14.1	16.5
Debt Securities................	79led	....	....	–	.1	59.9	290.3	221.9	75.1	189.5	147.4	119.2	94.3
Financial Derivatives............	79lld	....	....	–	–	–	–	–	–	–	–	–	–
Other Investment.................	79lfd	....	....	693.9	935.2	1,105.3	1,116.4	1,351.2	1,549.1	1,471.7	1,442.7	1,557.1	1,706.9
Monetary Authorities..........	79lgd	....	....	170.6	238.5	254.1	236.7	181.2	176.4	156.7	147.7	153.5	144.7
General Government...........	79lhd	....	....	345.5	425.8	479.0	468.7	578.4	636.6	631.5	608.4	663.3	713.9
Banks..........................	79lid	....	....	1.1	12.4	32.7	42.1	51.4	29.3	31.4	31.1	42.1	55.5
Other Sectors..................	79ljd	....	....	176.6	258.5	339.5	368.8	540.3	706.9	652.1	655.5	698.2	792.9
Government Finance						*Millions of Lei: Year Ending December 31*							
Deficit(-) or Surplus.............	80	....	....	....	–412	–443	–679	–288	–420	–206	208	–320	....
Total Revenue and Grants.........	81y	....	....	....	1,903	2,022	3,150	2,946	3,300	4,500	4,519	5,422	....
Revenue........................	81	....	....	....	1,858	1,976	2,844	2,809	3,064	4,034	4,078	4,978	....
Grants.........................	81z	....	....	....	45	46	306	137	236	466	441	445	....
Exp. & Lending Minus Repayments.	82z	....	....	....	2,315	2,465	3,828	3,234	3,721	4,706	4,311	5,742	....
Expenditure....................	82	....	....	....	2,315	2,217	3,710	3,272	3,660	4,739	4,336	5,757	....
Lending Minus Repayments.....	83	....	....	....	–	248	119	–38	60	–33	–25	–14	....
Financing: Domestic..............	84a	....	....	....	....	236	302	591	224	238	313	884	....
Financing: Foreign...............	85a	....	....	....	....	208	376	–302	196	–32	–520	–564	....
National Accounts						*Millions of Lei*							
Househ.Cons.Expend.,incl.NPISHs....	96f	80	728	2,486	3,616	5,243	6,017	6,876	9,137	14,031	17,037	....	....
Government Consumption Expend...	91f	31	290	1,087	1,755	2,113	2,663	2,327	1,954	2,472	2,812	....	....
Gross Fixed Capital Formation.........	93e	31	283	914	1,034	1,540	1,774	2,012	2,272	2,473	2,575	....	....
Changes in Inventories................	93i	84	734	451	578	351	349	349	548	1,364	1,241	....	....
Exports (Net)...................	90n	–33	–213	–202	–503	–1,449	–1,887	–2,441	–1,588	–4,319	–4,646	....	....
Gross Domestic Product (GDP)......	99b	192	1,821	4,737	6,480	7,798	8,917	9,122	12,322	16,020	19,019	....	....
Net Primary Income from Abroad.....	98.n	....	–12	–24	....	–114	–209	–365	....	....	....	....	....
Gross National Income (GNI)...........	99a	....	1,809	4,713	6,480	8,070	9,207	9,279	12,678	16,814	....	....	....
Net Current Transf.from Abroad.......	98t	....	26	125	97	317	403	438	798	1,795	....	....	....
Gross Nat'l Disposable Inc.(GNDI)....	99i	....	1,836	4,838	6,577	8,387	9,610	9,717	13,476	18,609	....	....	....
Gross Saving.....................	99s	....	818	1,265	1,206	1,031	930	513	2,385	2,106	....	....	....
						Millions: Midyear Estimates							
Population.......................	99z	4.37	4.36	4.35	4.34	4.33	Ü 4.31	4.30	4.29	4.28	4.28	4.27	4.27

2004, International Monetary Fund : *International Financial Statistics Yearbook*

Mongolia 948

		1992	1993	1994	1995	1996	1997	1998	1999	2000	2001	2002	2003
Exchange Rates						*Togrogs per SDR: End of Period*							
Market Rate	aa	55.00	†544.63	604.51	704.03	997.24	1,097.16	1,270.04	1,471.84	1,429.29	1,384.92	1,529.46	1,735.61
					Togrogs per US Dollar: End of Period (ae) Period Average (rf)								
Market Rate	ae	40.00	†396.51	414.09	473.62	693.51	813.16	902.00	1,072.37	1,097.00	1,102.00	1,125.00	1,168.00
Market Rate	rf	35.83	†295.01	412.72	448.61	548.40	789.99	840.83	1,021.87	1,076.67	1,097.70	1,110.31	1,146.54
Fund Position						*Millions of SDRs: End of Period*							
Quota	2f.s	37.10	37.10	37.10	37.10	37.10	37.10	37.10	51.10	51.10	51.10	51.10	51.10
SDRs	1b.s	.01	.02	1.98	1.70	.30	.52	.34	.12	.01	.01	.03	.03
Reserve Position in the Fund	1c.s	.01	.01	–	–	–	–	–	.02	.04	.06	.08	.10
Total Fund Cred.&Loans Outstg.	2tl	13.75	23.03	37.87	31.62	30.31	35.25	34.32	37.47	38.58	37.27	31.34	33.36
International Liquidity					*Millions of US Dollars Unless Otherwise Indicated: End of Period*								
Total Reserves Minus Gold	1l.d	16.35	59.74	81.39	117.03	107.44	175.71	94.09	136.49	178.77	205.70	349.65	236.08
SDRs	1b.d	.01	.03	2.89	2.52	.43	.70	.48	.16	.01	.02	.04	.04
Reserve Position in the Fund	1c.d	.01	.01	.01	.01	.01	.01	.01	.03	.05	.08	.12	.14
Foreign Exchange	1d.d	16.33	59.70	78.49	114.50	107.00	175.00	93.60	136.30	178.70	205.60	349.50	235.90
Gold (Million Fine Troy Ounces)	1ad	.02	.02	.03	.10	.15	.08	.03	–	.08	.18	.14	.02
Gold (National Valuation)	1and	24.20	5.31	11.00	34.50	53.60	24.60	9.10	.40	23.31	50.91	49.79	6.65
Monetary Authorities: Other Liab.	4..d	.35	26.13	28.77	30.17	16.04	4.50	–	5.30	–	–	–	25.03
Deposit Money Banks: Assets	7a.d	52.26	41.17	41.71	53.66	60.86	81.68	28.95	38.90	48.85	47.50	62.87	113.27
Liabilities	7b.d	162.92	11.67	11.90	14.06	12.38	15.06	22.14	9.13	10.20	11.58	14.65	44.03
Monetary Authorities						*Millions of Togrogs: End of Period*							
Foreign Assets	11	1,031	25,630	40,380	60,836	67,814	113,878	114,319	174,385	210,591	227,812	302,920	252,482
Claims on Central Government	12a	945	7,477	13,661	4,520	38,953	23,980	26,111	24,136	21,443	13,570	–	164,482
Claims on Deposit Money Banks	12e	5,964	6,637	10,375	7,740	1,712	3,093	5,631	6,651	4,777	7,348	8,038	12,689
Reserve Money	14	5,015	14,266	29,081	37,508	51,167	62,967	74,491	112,062	134,689	143,780	175,292	200,789
of which: Currency Outside DMBs	14a	1,839	8,751	18,946	25,591	40,136	49,768	56,446	87,281	100,910	109,131	120,755	131,482
Liabs. of Central Bank: Securities	16ac	–	1,500	2,106	830	–	19,296	11,715	21,200	21,080	50,000	61,000	76,000
Foreign Liabilities	16c	770	22,899	34,804	36,548	41,343	42,328	43,585	60,832	55,148	51,622	47,931	87,126
Central Government Deposits	16d	1,202	580	2,465	9,500	8,388	14,417	3,673	4,833	19,289	16,930	33,517	91,714
Capital Accounts	17a	3,700	2,980	4,998	7,998	24,004	37,082	41,049	37,921	44,431	41,992	33,160	41,084
Other Items (Net)	17r	−2,748	−2,481	−9,039	−19,289	−16,422	−35,140	−28,452	−31,676	−37,826	−55,594	−39,941	−67,060
Deposit Money Banks						*Millions of Togrogs: End of Period*							
Reserves	20	3,023	5,690	10,319	12,531	17,848	13,457	17,921	24,171	33,858	34,637	54,530	73,480
Claims on Mon.Author.:Securities	20c	–	1,500	2,106	830	–	19,055	11,697	21,200	21,080	49,651	60,768	75,487
Foreign Assets	21	2,091	16,325	17,272	25,412	42,207	66,416	26,116	41,711	53,591	52,341	70,730	132,295
Claims on Central Government	22a	2,793	513	737	643	10,472	35,451	38,328	39,269	43,371	32,458	30,743	46,905
Claims on Nonfin.Pub.Enterprises	22c	11,789	16,938	12,193	10,883	8,660	7,963	10,151	4,661	5,929	9,823	11,492	16,022
Claims on Private Sector	22d	7,340	14,675	40,763	51,838	59,763	44,256	77,293	75,821	83,959	139,989	232,768	441,515
Demand Deposits	24	5,790	9,756	14,104	17,045	20,702	26,341	26,136	27,544	29,842	46,995	66,944	81,337
Time, Savings,& Fgn.Currency Dep	25	5,412	24,216	43,906	59,408	58,757	93,957	84,668	105,341	128,068	174,909	282,398	490,463
Money Market Instruments	26aa	–	–	–	–	287	29	26	24	–	–	173	4,036
Restricted Deposits	26b	–	–	–	–	15,821	6,430	6,938	3,604	5,814	7,699	11,580	13,193
Foreign Liabilities	26c	6,517	4,629	4,926	6,660	8,585	12,246	19,973	9,794	11,193	12,758	16,477	51,429
Central Government Deposits	26d	1,950	7,498	8,451	16,655	21,768	33,258	20,081	24,126	26,732	35,927	29,665	22,720
Credit from Monetary Authorities	26g	6,288	5,391	10,152	7,402	18,574	763	4,459	1,900	1,647	4,094	4,327	12,839
Capital Accounts	27a	3,782	11,460	15,892	18,725	4,789	28,518	34,167	41,568	50,527	62,730	79,596	131,959
Other Items (Net)	27r	−2,702	−7,307	−14,041	−23,758	−10,334	−14,944	−14,943	−7,070	−12,034	−26,214	−30,131	−22,270
Monetary Survey						*Millions of Togrogs: End of Period*							
Foreign Assets (Net)	31n	−4,165	14,427	17,920	43,040	60,093	125,718	76,876	145,470	197,841	215,773	309,242	246,222
Domestic Credit	32	19,716	31,535	56,446	41,730	93,206	67,882	137,089	119,493	109,584	144,015	212,851	555,047
Claims on Central Govt. (Net)	32an	586	−87	3,483	−20,992	19,270	11,755	40,685	34,446	18,793	−6,829	−32,439	96,953
Claims on Nonfin.Pub.Enterprises	32c	11,789	16,938	12,193	10,883	8,660	7,963	10,151	4,661	5,929	9,823	11,492	16,022
Claims on Private Sector	32d	7,341	14,684	40,770	51,839	65,277	48,164	86,253	80,386	84,862	141,021	233,799	442,072
Money	34	7,641	18,547	33,050	42,637	60,838	76,109	82,582	114,826	130,751	156,126	187,699	212,819
Quasi-Money	35	5,412	24,216	43,906	59,408	58,757	93,957	84,668	105,341	128,068	174,909	282,398	490,463
Money Market Instruments	36aa	–	–	–	–	287	29	26	24	–	–	173	4,036
Liabs. of Central Bank: Securities	36ac	–	–	–	–	–	241	18	–	–	349	232	513
Restricted Deposits	36b	–	–	–	–	15,821	6,430	6,938	3,604	5,814	7,699	11,580	13,193
Capital Accounts	37a	7,483	14,440	20,891	26,723	28,794	65,599	75,216	79,489	94,958	104,722	112,756	173,043
Other Items (Net)	37r	−4,984	−11,241	−23,480	−43,998	−11,198	−48,764	−35,483	−38,322	−52,165	−84,017	−72,745	−92,796
Money plus Quasi-Money	35l	13,053	42,763	76,956	102,045	119,595	170,066	167,250	220,167	258,819	331,035	470,097	703,282
Interest Rates						*Percent per Annum*							
Bank Rate (End of Period)	60	....	628.80	180.00	150.00	109.00	45.50	23.30	11.40	8.65	8.60	9.90	11.50
Deposit Rate (End of Period)	60l	362.50	280.20	115.71	74.62	44.75	36.37	27.51	23.42	16.80	14.30	13.22	14.00
Lending Rate (End of Period)	60p	....	300.00	279.22	134.37	87.91	82.05	46.77	39.29	32.75	30.24	28.38	26.31

Mongolia 948

		1992	1993	1994	1995	1996	1997	1998	1999	2000	2001	2002	2003
Prices, Production, Labor			*Index Numbers (2000=100): Period Averages*										
Consumer Prices	64	3.5	12.9	24.2	†38.0	55.8	76.2	83.3	89.6	100.0	106.3	107.3	112.8
Wages: Avg. Earnings ('90=100)	65	348.7	....	....	....	....	....	....	....	....	....	....	....
Industrial Production ('90=100)	66	72.4	63.0	65.3	....	....	....	....	....	....	....	....	....
Industrial Employment ('90=100)	67	97.9	....	....	....	....	....	....	....	....	....	....	....
International Transactions						*Millions of US Dollars*							
Exports	70..d	388.4	382.7	356.1	473.3	424.3	451.5	345.2	358.3	466.1	448.5	....	....
Imports, c.i.f.	71..d	418.3	379.0	258.4	415.3	450.9	468.3	503.3	512.8	614.5	630.1	....	....
Balance of Payments					*Millions of US Dollars: Minus Sign Indicates Debit*								
Current Account, n.i.e.	78ald	−55.7	31.1	46.4	38.9	−100.5	55.2	−128.5	−112.2	−156.1	−154.2	−158.0	....
Goods: Exports f.o.b.	78aad	355.8	365.8	367.0	451.0	423.4	568.5	462.4	454.3	535.8	523.2	524.0	....
Goods: Imports f.o.b.	78abd	−384.9	−344.5	−333.3	−425.7	−459.7	−453.1	−524.2	−510.7	−608.4	−623.8	−680.2	....
Trade Balance	78acd	−29.1	21.3	33.7	25.3	−36.3	115.4	−61.8	−56.4	−72.6	−100.6	−156.2	....
Services: Credit	78add	34.8	26.0	45.4	57.3	55.7	52.7	77.8	75.8	77.7	113.5	183.9	....
Services: Debit	78aed	−69.7	−66.9	−91.2	−95.4	−112.8	−105.1	−146.8	−145.7	−162.8	−205.4	−265.8	....
Balance on Goods & Services	78afd	−64.0	−19.6	−12.1	−12.8	−93.4	63.0	−130.8	−126.3	−157.7	−192.5	−238.1	....
Income: Credit	78agd	.2	.8	3.2	3.0	13.4	6.1	10.1	6.7	13.0	14.8	14.1	....
Income: Debit	78ahd	−27.1	−21.0	−22.5	−28.4	−26.7	−18.1	−9.7	−6.6	−19.5	−16.8	−18.6	....
Balance on Gds, Serv. & Inc.	78aid	−90.9	−39.8	−31.4	−38.2	−106.7	51.0	−130.4	−126.2	−164.2	−194.5	−242.6	....
Current Transfers, n.i.e.: Credit	78ajd	38.7	66.7	77.8	77.1	6.2	4.2	5.5	17.6	25.0	40.3	126.9	....
Current Transfers: Debit	78akd	−3.5	4.2	−	−	−	−	−3.6	−3.6	−16.9	−	−42.3	....
Capital Account, n.i.e.	78bcd	−	−	−	−	−	−	−	−	....	−	−	....
Capital Account, n.i.e.: Credit	78bad	−	−	−	−	−	−	−	−	....	−	−	....
Capital Account: Debit	78bbd	−	−	−	−	−	−	−	−	....	−	−	....
Financial Account, n.i.e.	78bjd	−44.0	−11.8	−39.0	−15.9	41.3	27.0	126.2	69.6	89.9	107.0	157.4	....
Direct Investment Abroad	78bdd	−	−	−	−	−	−	−	−	−	−	−	....
Dir. Invest. in Rep. Econ., n.i.e.	78bed	2.0	7.7	6.9	9.8	15.9	25.0	18.9	30.4	53.7	43.0	77.8	....
Portfolio Investment Assets	78bfd	−	−	−	−	−	−	−	−	....	....	....	....
Equity Securities	78bkd	−	−	−	−	−	−	−	−	−	−	−	....
Debt Securities	78bld	−	−	−	−	−	−	−	−	....	....	....	....
Portfolio Investment Liab., n.i.e.	78bgd	−	−	−	−	1.0	−	−	−	....	....	....	....
Equity Securities	78bmd	−	−	−	−	−	−	−	−	−	−	−	....
Debt Securities	78bnd	−	−	−	−	1.0	−	−	−	....	....	....	....
Financial Derivatives Assets	78bwd	....	....	....	....	....	....	....	....	....	....	....	....
Financial Derivatives Liabilities	78bxd	−	−	−	....	....	....	....	....	....	....	....	....
Other Investment Assets	78bhd	−64.0	−35.4	−51.0	−49.2	−76.4	−108.1	−54.8	−51.8	−44.3	−5.2	−32.1	....
Monetary Authorities	78bod	−	−	−	−	−	−	−	−	....	....	−	....
General Government	78bpd	−	−	−	−	−	−	−	−	....	−	−	....
Banks	78bqd	−11.6	−24.9	−15.3	−15.3	−9.3	−18.1	−	−14.8	−10.7	1.1	−24.4	....
Other Sectors	78brd	−52.4	−10.5	−35.7	−33.9	−67.1	−90.0	−54.8	−37.0	−33.6	−6.3	−7.8	....
Other Investment Liab., n.i.e.	78bid	18.0	15.9	5.1	22.5	101.8	110.1	162.1	91.0	80.5	69.2	111.7	....
Monetary Authorities	78bsd	−69.8	−11.2	−	−	−	−	−5.2	−	−	−	−	....
General Government	78btd	45.6	32.5	7.9	22.5	56.1	79.3	80.8	91.4	60.5	66.2	72.5	....
Banks	78bud	−	3.6	−	−	−	−	40.0	−4.8	−2.3	.6	6.9	....
Other Sectors	78bvd	42.2	−9.0	−2.8	−	45.7	30.8	46.5	4.4	22.3	2.4	32.3	....
Net Errors and Omissions	78cad	17.4	−4.8	−1.0	9.1	−28.1	−75.6	−50.2	23.6	−19.3	−32.2	14.1	....
Overall Balance	78cbd	−82.3	14.5	6.4	32.1	−87.3	6.6	−52.5	−19.0	−85.5	−79.4	13.4	....
Reserves and Related Items	79dad	82.3	−14.5	−6.4	−32.1	87.3	−6.6	52.5	19.0	85.5	79.4	−13.4	....
Reserve Assets	79dbd	72.3	−23.5	−27.4	−22.6	19.6	−61.2	−6.3	−40.6	−2.5	−15.8	−58.1	....
Use of Fund Credit and Loans	79dcd	3.5	13.1	21.1	−9.5	−1.8	6.7	−1.3	4.2	1.8	−1.6	−7.7	....
Exceptional Financing	79ded	6.5	−4.1	−	−	69.5	47.9	60.2	55.5	86.2	96.9	52.3	....
Government Finance					*Millions of Togrogs: Year Ending December 31*								
Deficit (-) or Surplus	80	†−2,840	−27,706	−23,647	−29,185	−49,679	†−65,909	−94,913	−99,816	−63,227	−45,824	....	....
Total Revenue and Grants	81y	†9,896	48,637	65,267	113,568	126,725	†176,152	192,103	203,452	308,283	367,420	....	....
Revenue	81	†8,672	45,610	62,002	108,483	122,316	†171,744	183,552	196,561	303,215	358,244	....	....
Grants	81z	†1,224	3,027	3,265	5,085	4,409	†4,408	8,551	6,891	5,068	9,176	....	....
Exp. & Lending Minus Repay	82z	†12,736	76,343	88,914	142,753	176,404	†242,061	287,016	303,268	371,510	413,244	....	....
Expenditure	82	†10,187	42,468	63,824	97,656	121,233	†176,436	201,279	232,795	306,037	353,580	....	....
Lending Minus Repayments	83	†2,549	33,875	25,090	45,097	55,171	†65,625	85,737	70,473	65,473	59,664	....	....
Total Financing	80h	†2,840	27,707	23,648	29,185	49,679	†65,909	94,913	99,816	63,227	45,824	....	....
Domestic	84a	†−470	−4,650	5,010	5,271	14,804	†−24,989	26,319	−6,020	−3,346	−26,166	....	....
Foreign	85a	†3,310	32,357	18,638	23,914	34,875	†90,898	68,594	105,836	66,573	71,990	....	....
Total Debt by Residence	88	11,575	94,353	196,533	241,503	365,158	†509,635	676,717	906,723	959,889	961,785	....	....
Domestic	88a	1,063	233	5,281	233	41,206	†69,151	82,158	90,039	104,192	82,865	....	....
Foreign	89a	10,512	94,120	191,252	241,270	323,952	†440,484	594,559	816,684	855,697	878,920	....	....
National Accounts						*Millions of Togrogs*							
Gross Domestic Product (GDP)	99b	47,298	166,219	283,263	550,254	646,559	832,636	817,393	925,300	1,018,900	1,115,600	1,225,300	1,362,200
GDP Volume 1995 Prices	99b.p	406,865	394,646	403,723	550,254	563,201	585,720	606,410	625,910	632,976	639,013	664,253	697,465
GDP Volume (2000=100)	99bvp	64.3	62.3	63.8	86.9	89.0	92.5	95.8	98.9	100.0	101.0	104.9	110.2
GDP Deflator (2000=100)	99bip	7.2	26.2	43.6	62.1	71.3	88.3	83.7	91.8	100.0	108.5	114.6	121.3
						Millions: Midyear Estimates							
Population	99z	2.30	2.34	2.37	2.39	2.42	2.44	2.46	2.48	2.50	2.53	2.56	2.59

Montserrat 351

		1992	1993	1994	1995	1996	1997	1998	1999	2000	2001	2002	2003
Exchange Rates		\multicolumn{12}{l}{E. Caribbean Dollars per SDR: End of Period (aa) E. Caribbean Dollars per US Dollar: End of Period (ae)}
Official Rate	aa	3.7125	3.7086	3.9416	4.0135	3.8825	3.6430	3.8017	3.7058	3.5179	3.3932	3.6707	4.0121
Official Rate	ae	2.7000	2.7000	2.7000	2.7000	2.7000	2.7000	2.7000	2.7000	2.7000	2.7000	2.7000	2.7000
International Liquidity		\multicolumn{12}{c}{Millions of US Dollars: End of Period}
Total Reserves minus Gold	1l.d	6.52	6.16	7.62	8.81	8.66	11.30	24.78	14.02	10.40	12.50	14.40	15.24
Foreign Exchange	1d.d	6.52	6.16	7.62	8.81	8.66	11.30	24.78	14.02	10.40	12.50	14.40	15.24
Monetary Authorities: Other Liab.	4..d	–	–	–	–	–	–	–	–	–	–	–	–
Deposit Money Banks: Assets	7a.d	4.75	12.63	15.45	19.09	23.50	32.75	33.01	44.27	44.99	44.94	45.93	55.71
Liabilities	7b.d	10.06	9.64	6.80	10.06	9.04	7.29	9.20	8.86	11.29	9.23	9.85	10.35
Monetary Authorities		\multicolumn{12}{c}{Millions of E. Caribbean Dollars: End of Period}
Foreign Assets	11	17.62	16.65	20.18	23.87	23.52	30.69	67.35	38.39	28.63	33.99	38.89	41.11
Claims on Central Government	12a	1.00	1.83	1.83	1.83	1.83	1.89	1.83	1.93	1.71	.88	.86	.87
Claims on Deposit Money Banks	12e	.02	.01	.02	.01	.01	.02	.02	.03	.02	.01	.01	.01
Reserve Money	14	18.61	18.37	21.95	23.92	24.65	31.08	66.90	37.47	28.15	32.33	36.65	38.89
of which: Currency Outside DMBs	14a	7.91	6.63	7.44	7.72	9.03	17.55	13.27	13.36	9.66	11.83	10.81	12.55
Foreign Liabilities	16c	–	–	–	–	–	–	–	–	–	–	–	–
Central Government Deposits	16d	.03	.12	.08	1.79	.71	1.52	2.29	2.87	2.21	2.55	3.10	3.10
Other Items (Net)	17r	–	–	–	–	–	–	–	–	–	–	–	–
Deposit Money Banks		\multicolumn{12}{c}{Millions of E. Caribbean Dollars: End of Period}
Reserves	20	10.61	10.97	13.28	17.85	13.73	20.03	67.15	23.99	18.61	21.60	26.33	29.24
Foreign Assets	21	12.84	34.09	41.71	51.55	63.45	88.42	89.14	119.52	121.47	121.34	124.02	150.41
Claims on Central Government	22a	.60	.62	.50	.25	.50	.50	.25	2.17	2.33	.87	2.27	1.18
Claims on Local Government	22b	–	–	–	.52	–	–	–	–	–	.10	–	–
Claims on Nonfin.Pub.Enterprises	22c	.29	.06	.09	2.80	3.12	2.68	–	–	–	–	–	–
Claims on Private Sector	22d	97.98	78.81	74.97	70.24	65.39	57.41	32.78	22.72	23.12	23.88	22.24	22.94
Claims on Nonbank Financial Insts.	22g	.59	.34	.31	.62	.50	.40	.36	.33	.25	1.79	.12	.39
Demand Deposits	24	13.67	16.16	20.02	19.64	16.47	23.75	29.55	23.32	20.41	20.51	22.09	29.66
Time, Savings,& Fgn.Currency Dep	25	69.13	65.89	79.27	78.58	71.48	71.51	82.33	83.05	79.19	81.02	79.57	83.36
Foreign Liabilities	26c	27.18	26.02	18.36	27.17	24.41	19.68	24.84	23.92	30.49	24.93	26.60	27.96
Central Government Deposits	26d	5.38	6.35	1.97	5.17	11.72	28.97	22.12	18.08	14.94	19.15	29.04	39.44
Credit from Monetary Authorities	26g	.01	.01	.01	–	.01	–	.01	1.03	–	.01	.01	.12
Capital Accounts	27a	4.17	5.62	5.07	4.69	2.14	4.59	5.44	6.89	8.20	9.80	11.32	13.75
Other Items (Net)	27r	3.38	4.83	6.16	8.59	20.47	20.92	25.39	12.44	12.56	14.17	6.35	9.86
Monetary Survey		\multicolumn{12}{c}{Millions of E. Caribbean Dollars: End of Period}
Foreign Assets (Net)	31n	3.28	24.72	43.53	48.26	62.56	99.43	131.65	133.99	119.62	130.41	136.31	163.57
Domestic Credit	32	95.06	75.18	75.64	69.29	58.91	32.38	10.80	6.18	10.26	5.81	–6.65	–17.17
Claims on Central Govt. (Net)	32an	–3.80	–4.02	.28	–4.88	–10.10	–28.10	–22.34	–16.86	–13.11	–19.96	–29.02	–40.50
Claims on Local Government	32b	–	–	–	.52	–	–	–	–	–	.10	–	–
Claims on Nonfin.Pub.Enterprises	32c	.29	.06	.09	2.80	3.12	2.68	–	–	–	–	–	–
Claims on Private Sector	32d	97.98	78.81	74.97	70.24	65.39	57.41	32.78	22.72	23.12	23.88	22.24	22.94
Claims on Nonbank Financial Inst.	32g	.59	.34	.31	.62	.50	.40	.36	.33	.25	1.79	.12	.39
Money	34	21.59	22.80	27.45	27.36	25.51	41.30	42.82	36.68	31.07	32.34	32.90	42.22
Quasi-Money	35	69.13	65.89	79.27	78.58	71.48	71.51	82.33	83.05	79.19	81.02	79.57	83.36
Capital Accounts	37a	4.17	5.62	5.07	4.69	2.14	4.59	5.44	6.89	8.20	9.80	11.32	13.75
Other Items (Net)	37r	3.45	5.59	7.37	6.92	22.35	14.41	11.87	13.56	11.42	13.06	5.87	7.07
Money plus Quasi-Money	35l	90.72	88.69	106.72	105.94	96.98	112.81	125.14	119.73	110.26	113.36	112.46	125.57
Money (National Definitions)		\multicolumn{12}{c}{Millions of E. Caribbean Dollars: End of Period}
M1	39ma	19.57	17.03	20.34	20.88	22.94	34.29	37.41	31.44	26.11	25.45	26.33	32.73
M2	39mb	80.78	73.14	85.49	81.42	84.08	98.84	117.44	111.30	101.05	102.03	99.80	108.26
Interest Rates		\multicolumn{12}{c}{Percent Per Annum}
Discount Rate (End of Period)	60	....	....	9.00	9.00	9.00	8.00	8.00	8.00	8.00	7.00	7.00	6.50
Money Market Rate	60b	5.25	5.25	5.25	5.25	5.25	5.25	5.25	5.25	5.25	†5.64	6.32	6.07
Savings Rate	60k	5.00	4.54	4.00	4.00	4.00	4.00	4.00	4.21	4.50	4.50	4.50	†4.20
Deposit Rate	60l	3.49	3.44	3.25	3.24	3.29	3.02	2.74	3.14	3.35	3.35	3.08	3.06
Deposit Rate (Fgn. Currency)	60l.f	....	....	....	....	....	....	....	....	....	....	....	5.70
Lending Rate	60p	11.95	13.12	13.06	12.63	12.37	12.37	12.15	11.52	11.52	11.52	11.34	12.10

Montserrat 351

		1992	1993	1994	1995	1996	1997	1998	1999	2000	2001	2002	2003
Balance of Payments		\multicolumn{12}{c}{*Millions of US Dollars: Minus Sign Indicates Debit*}
Current Account, n.i.e.	78ald	−13.10	−7.89	−12.24	−1.96	15.71	−1.97	3.41	−1.41	−6.51	−5.62	−8.16	....
Goods: Exports f.o.b.	78aad	1.58	2.27	2.92	12.14	41.34	8.20	1.20	1.26	1.12	.73	1.47	....
Goods: Imports f.o.b.	78abd	−29.83	−24.23	−30.04	−33.90	−35.97	−28.11	−19.35	−19.27	−19.02	−17.05	−22.38	....
Trade Balance	78acd	−28.25	−21.96	−27.12	−21.76	5.38	−19.91	−18.15	−18.00	−17.90	−16.33	−20.91	....
Services: Credit	78add	19.79	23.34	27.16	24.61	15.54	13.88	13.00	20.26	15.83	14.21	14.13	....
Services: Debit	78aed	−12.33	−11.34	−14.32	−14.77	−17.39	−12.92	−20.71	−21.53	−18.73	−24.03	−23.22	....
Balance on Goods & Services	78afd	−20.79	−9.96	−14.28	−11.92	3.53	−18.95	−25.87	−19.28	−20.81	−26.15	−30.01	....
Income: Credit	78agd	.53	.42	−.01	.66	.54	.97	.77	1.19	1.48	1.28	1.45	....
Income: Debit	78ahd	−1.62	−3.90	−4.44	−2.93	−2.00	−3.29	−2.55	−7.13	−4.17	−1.94	−4.54	....
Balance on Gds, Serv. & Inc.	78aid	−21.88	−13.44	−18.73	−14.19	2.08	−21.27	−27.64	−25.22	−23.50	−26.81	−33.10	....
Current Transfers, n.i.e.: Credit	78ajd	12.15	9.71	10.61	13.55	14.90	20.38	33.24	26.49	18.90	23.66	28.13	....
Current Transfers: Debit	78akd	−3.36	−4.16	−4.12	−1.33	−1.26	−1.08	−2.19	−2.69	−1.91	−2.47	−3.19	....
Capital Account, n.i.e.	78bcd	2.07	5.41	10.10	5.16	−12.50	3.56	3.59	1.33	4.43	7.70	12.55	....
Capital Account, n.i.e.: Credit	78bad	2.07	5.41	10.10	6.67	2.32	7.19	7.22	4.96	7.32	9.66	14.64	....
Capital Account: Debit	78bbd	−	−	−	−1.51	−14.81	−3.63	−3.63	−3.63	−2.89	−1.96	−2.09	....
Financial Account, n.i.e.	78bjd	4.87	1.40	.73	1.93	−6.00	−9.07	3.92	−5.90	3.59	−3.16	−.14	....
Direct Investment Abroad	78bdd	−	−	−	−	−	−	−	−	−	−	−	....
Dir. Invest. in Rep. Econ., n.i.e.	78bed	4.61	4.86	7.16	3.03	−.32	2.57	2.57	8.21	3.46	.96	2.09	....
Portfolio Investment Assets	78bfd	−	−	−.03	−.03	−	−	−	−	−	−	−	....
Equity Securities	78bkd	....	....	....	....	....	....	....	....	....	....	....	....
Debt Securities	78bld	....	....	....	....	....	....	....	....	....	....	....	....
Portfolio Investment Liab., n.i.e.	78bgd	−	.10	−	.06	−	.06	.09	−.03	.55	−.60	−.22	....
Equity Securities	78bmd	....	....	....	....	....	....	....	....	....	....	....	....
Debt Securities	78bnd	....	....	....	....	....	....	....	....	....	....	....	....
Financial Derivatives Assets	78bwd	....	....	....	....	....	....	....	....	....	....	....	....
Financial Derivatives Liabilities	78bxd	....	....	....	....	....	....	....	....	....	....	....	....
Other Investment Assets	78bhd	−.51	−8.23	−3.60	−4.20	−.84	−1.23	−1.09	−.93	−4.61	−.83	−.25	....
Monetary Authorities	78bod	....	....	....	....	....	....	....	....	....	....	....	....
General Government	78bpd	....	....	....	....	....	....	....	....	....	....	....	....
Banks	78bqd	....	....	....	....	....	....	....	....	....	....	....	....
Other Sectors	78brd	....	....	....	....	....	....	....	....	....	....	....	....
Other Investment Liab., n.i.e.	78bid	.77	4.67	−2.81	3.06	−4.84	−10.47	2.35	−13.16	4.19	−2.69	−1.77	....
Monetary Authorities	78bsd	....	....	....	....	....	....	....	....	....	....	....	....
General Government	78btd	....	....	....	....	....	....	....	....	....	....	....	....
Banks	78bud	....	....	....	....	....	....	....	....	....	....	....	....
Other Sectors	78bvd	....	....	....	....	....	....	....	....	....	....	....	....
Net Errors and Omissions	78cad	6.24	.73	2.97	−3.94	2.63	10.11	2.61	−4.71	−5.06	3.20	−2.57	....
Overall Balance	78cbd	.09	−.35	1.57	1.19	−.15	2.63	13.53	−10.69	−3.55	2.12	1.67	....
Reserves and Related Items	79dad	−.09	.36	−1.57	−1.19	.15	−2.63	−13.53	10.69	3.55	−2.12	−1.67	....
Reserve Assets	79dbd	−.09	.36	−1.57	−1.19	.15	−2.63	−13.53	10.69	3.55	−2.12	−1.67	....
Use of Fund Credit and Loans	79dcd	....	....	....	....	....	....	....	....	....	....	....	....
Exceptional Financing	79ded	....	....	....	....	....	....	....	....	....	....	....	....
National Accounts		\multicolumn{12}{c}{*Millions of E. Caribbean Dollars*}
Gross Domestic Product (GDP)	99b	132.8	140.0	147.3	139.2	113.1	95.8	88.6	80.3	79.3	82.6	88.0	....
GDP Volume 1990 Prices	99b.p	127.8	131.0	132.1	122.1	95.9	76.7	69.0	60.3	58.5	56.9	59.5	....
GDP Volume (2000=100)	99bvp	218.3	223.8	225.8	208.6	163.9	131.2	117.9	103.1	100.0	97.2	101.6	....
GDP Deflator (2000=100)	99bip	76.6	78.8	82.2	84.1	87.0	92.0	94.7	98.2	100.0	107.1	109.1	....
		\multicolumn{12}{c}{*Millions: Midyear Estimates*}
Population	99z	.0109	.0110	.0108	.0102	.0092	.0078	.0062	.0049	.0039	.0034	.0033	.0035

2004, International Monetary Fund : *International Financial Statistics Yearbook*

Morocco 686

		1992	1993	1994	1995	1996	1997	1998	1999	2000	2001	2002	2003
Exchange Rates						*Dirhams per SDR: End of Period*							
Official Rate	aa	12.442	13.257	13.080	12.589	12.653	13.107	13.031	13.845	13.836	14.528	13.822	13.002
					Dirhams per US Dollar: End of Period (ae) Period Average (rf)								
Official Rate	ae	9.049	9.651	8.960	8.469	8.800	9.714	9.255	10.087	10.619	11.560	10.167	8.750
Official Rate	rf	8.538	9.299	9.203	8.540	8.716	9.527	9.604	9.804	10.626	11.303	11.021	9.574
					Index Numbers (2000=100): Period Averages								
Official Rate	ahx	124.5	114.2	115.5	124.4	121.8	111.5	110.6	108.3	100.0	94.0	96.5	111.0
Nominal Effective Exchange Rate	nec	80.3	84.9	90.5	91.8	92.5	94.2	95.3	96.9	100.0	97.7	96.7	96.2
Real Effective Exchange Rate	rec	84.4	86.8	89.5	92.4	93.2	94.0	96.3	97.3	100.0	95.9	95.6	94.3
Fund Position						*Millions of SDRs: End of Period*							
Quota	2f.s	428	428	428	428	428	428	428	588	588	588	588	588
SDRs	1b.s	56	25	18	17	5	1	2	62	92	98	90	76
Reserve Position in the Fund	1c.s	30	30	30	30	30	30	30	70	70	70	70	70
Total Fund Cred.&Loans Outstg	2tl	319	207	101	35	2	—	—	—	—	—	—	—
International Liquidity						*Millions of US Dollars Unless Otherwise Indicated: End of Period*							
Total Reserves minus Gold	1l.d	3,584	3,655	4,352	3,601	3,794	3,993	4,435	5,689	4,823	8,474	10,133	13,851
SDRs	1b.d	77	34	26	26	7	1	3	85	119	123	122	112
Reserve Position in the Fund	1c.d	42	42	44	45	44	41	43	97	92	89	96	105
Foreign Exchange	1d.d	3,465	3,579	4,281	3,530	3,743	3,951	4,389	5,507	4,612	8,262	9,915	13,634
Gold (Million Fine Troy Ounces)	1ad	.704	.704	.704	.704	.704	.704	.704	.704	.706	.707	.708	.708
Gold (National Valuation)	1and	14	202	218	230	222	201	211	193	184	169	193	224
Monetary Authorities:Other Assets	3..d	....	....	....	....	....	....	....	....	....	....	....	....
Monetary Authorities: Other Liab	4..d	139	53	47	41	62	84	78	82	84	80	80	135
Deposit Money Banks: Assets	7a.d	598	518	755	653	665	†381	496	477	599	568	888	996
Liabilities	7b.d	354	386	672	442	520	†351	462	457	407	336	269	412
Other Banking Insts.: Liabilities	7f.d	1,523	1,450	1,534	1,589	1,452	....	....	....	....	....	....	....
Monetary Authorities						*Millions of Dirhams: End of Period*							
Foreign Assets	11	32,570	37,243	41,001	32,509	35,402	40,808	43,070	59,392	53,224	99,920	104,979	123,156
Claims on Central Government	12a	9,861	8,752	8,305	18,389	19,179	†27,860	27,459	21,129	24,310	15,993	16,485	18,093
Claims on Private Sector	12d	7,611	8,803	8,416	9,129	9,075	†1,250	3,495	1,393	7,243	71	66	73
Claims on Deposit Money Banks	12e	1,828	599	512	500	1,250	†—	—	—	—	—	—	—
Reserve Money	14	44,023	47,796	50,746	53,384	57,467	†62,557	66,999	75,912	78,356	95,151	98,581	114,594
of which: Currency Outside DMBs	14a	35,745	37,202	41,107	43,261	46,581	48,662	50,644	56,713	58,169	66,025	69,565	74,893
Foreign Liabilities	16c	5,227	3,256	1,745	787	577	†817	725	826	893	927	809	1,183
Central Government Deposits	16d	498	523	605	633	816	†786	826	532	806	10,806	11,322	13,801
Capital Accounts	17a	....	....	....	....	....	4,799	4,877	4,977	5,107	5,252	5,410	5,455
Other Items (Net)	17r	2,122	3,822	5,139	5,722	6,046	†959	597	−332	−384	3,848	5,408	6,289
Deposit Money Banks						*Millions of Dirhams: End of Period*							
Reserves	20	7,109	8,671	8,293	9,018	9,419	†11,936	13,380	17,100	18,980	27,466	27,535	39,446
Foreign Assets	21	5,408	5,002	6,765	5,533	5,855	†3,703	4,592	4,812	6,356	6,566	9,030	8,713
Claims on Central Government	22a	39,545	44,652	50,746	49,633	50,048	58,616	58,614	54,917	61,729	73,161	76,923	77,123
Claims on Private Sector	22d	56,581	62,351	70,408	81,777	90,545	†151,203	167,602	183,531	199,576	208,026	214,949	232,159
Claims on Other Financial Insts	22f	994	355	1,409	1,637	627	†25,580	29,834	32,884	34,309	35,883	39,075	40,004
Demand Deposits	24	66,636	70,033	79,099	84,606	87,323	†116,054	126,767	140,895	156,545	181,099	199,374	222,896
Time Deposits	25	36,425	42,687	45,958	50,552	54,962	†64,121	65,114	69,389	76,281	84,294	83,337	87,360
Foreign Liabilities	26c	3,205	3,729	6,020	3,745	4,579	†3,409	4,276	4,605	4,322	3,881	2,740	3,603
Credit from Monetary Authorities	26g	2,566	965	1,108	1,232	2,508	†1,209	3,381	1,346	7,161	7	1	—
Capital Accounts	27a	....	....	....	....	....	38,743	44,973	47,759	48,890	57,568	59,850	66,685
Other Items (Net)	27r	805	3,617	5,436	7,463	7,122	†27,502	29,511	29,383	27,751	24,253	22,210	16,901
Post Office: Checking Deposits	24..i	1,520	1,625	1,833	1,701	1,721	1,871	....	....	....	....	....	....
Treasury: Checking Deposits	24..r	5,041	4,906	4,950	5,088	6,311	6,202	....	....	....	....	....	....
Monetary Survey						*Millions of Dirhams: End of Period*							
Foreign Assets (Net)	31n	29,546	35,260	40,002	33,509	36,101	†40,285	42,661	58,773	54,365	101,678	110,460	127,083
Domestic Credit	32	120,655	130,921	145,462	166,721	176,690	†263,723	286,178	293,322	326,361	322,328	336,176	353,651
Claims on Central Govt. (Net)	32an	55,469	59,412	65,229	74,178	76,443	†85,690	85,247	75,514	85,233	78,348	82,086	81,415
Claims on Private Sector	32d	64,192	71,154	78,824	90,906	99,620	†153,279	171,990	187,165	207,796	208,718	216,540	234,604
Claims on Other Financial Insts	32f	994	355	1,409	1,637	627	†24,754	28,941	30,643	33,332	35,262	37,550	37,632
Money	34	110,082	115,458	128,284	135,964	143,818	†166,843	179,795	200,597	216,503	249,693	272,184	298,983
Quasi-Money	35	36,425	42,687	45,958	50,552	54,962	†64,121	65,114	69,389	76,281	84,294	83,337	87,360
Other Items (Net)	37r	3,694	8,036	11,222	13,714	14,011	†73,044	83,930	82,242	87,942	90,019	91,115	94,391
Money plus Quasi-Money	35l	146,507	158,145	174,242	186,516	198,780	†230,964	244,909	269,986	292,784	333,987	355,521	386,343

Morocco 686

		1992	1993	1994	1995	1996	1997	1998	1999	2000	2001	2002	2003
Other Banking Institutions					*Millions of Dirhams: End of Period*								
Reserves	40	1,428	1,938	1,383	1,301	1,469	....	....	....	....	....	....	....
Claims on Central Government	42a	7,191	7,980	10,966	13,063	16,164	....	....	....	....	....	....	....
Claims on Official Entities	42bx	–	–	–	–	–	....	....	....	....	....	....	....
Claims on Private Sector	42d	37,601	39,365	41,311	44,167	47,249	....	....	....	....	....	....	....
Time Deposits	45	19,670	21,836	24,606	28,574	32,745	....	....	....	....	....	....	....
Bonds	46ab	9,663	10,134	10,628	10,987	11,848	....	....	....	....	....	....	....
Long-Term Foreign Liabilities	46cl	13,779	13,997	13,744	13,461	12,776	....	....	....	....	....	....	....
Central Govt. Lending Funds	46f	617	547	393	277	271	....	....	....	....	....	....	....
Credit from Monetary Authorities	46g	14	5	8	–	–	....	....	....	....	....	....	....
Credit from Deposit Money Banks	46h	515	508	604	623	683	....	....	....	....	....	....	....
Capital Accounts	47a	5,958	6,911	8,093	9,122	10,068	....	....	....	....	....	....	....
Other Items (Net)	47r	–3,996	–4,655	–4,416	–4,513	–3,509	....	....	....	....	....	....	....
Liquid Liabilities	55l	166,177	179,981	198,848	215,090	231,525	....	....	....	....	....	....	....
Interest Rates					*Percent Per Annum*								
Discount Rate (End of Period)	60	....	....	7.17	....	....	....	6.04	5.42	5.00	4.71	3.79	3.25
Money Market Rate	60b	....	....	12.29	10.06	8.42	7.89	6.30	5.64	5.41	4.44	2.99	3.22
Treasury Bill Rate	60c	....	....	....	....	....	....	....	....	....	....	....	....
Deposit Rate	60l	....	....	....	....	....	....	7.3	6.4	5.2	5.0	4.5	3.8
Lending Rate	60p	....	....	10.0	....	....	....	13.5	13.5	13.3	13.3	13.1	12.6
Govt.Bond Yield: Long-Term	61	....	....	....	....	....	....	....	....	....	....	....	....
Med.-Term	61a	....	....	....	....	....	....	....	....	....	....	5.6	....
Prices, Production, Labor					*Index Numbers (2000=100): Period Averages*								
Wholesale Prices	63	80.7	84.3	86.2	91.8	95.9	94.4	97.6	96.0	100.0	99.6	101.8	97.2
Consumer Prices	64	77.7	81.7	85.9	91.2	93.9	94.9	97.5	98.1	100.0	100.6	103.4	104.6
Manufacturing Production	66ey	82.8	†81.5	86.2	85.8	89.3	92.2	94.5	96.7	100.0	103.3	106.3	....
Mining Production	66zx	87.2	†88.7	95.6	96.4	98.7	107.5	107.0	103.6	100.0	102.4	105.0	....
Energy Production	66ze	83.4	†85.0	92.8	91.8	91.8	97.7	97.1	103.4	100.0	107.3	106.9	....
					Number in Thousands: Period Averages								
Labor Force	67d	....	....	....	4,863	4,875	....	5,138	....	....	10,605	10,379	....
Employment	67e	3,494	3,660	....	3,870	4,034	4,224	4,168	4,175	4,199	4,372	4,541	....
Unemployment	67c	650	681	....	1,112	871	845	969	1,162	1,146	1,061	1,017	....
Unemployment Rate (%)	67r	16.0	15.9	....	22.9	18.1	16.9	19.1	22.0	21.5	19.5	....	....
International Transactions					*Millions of Dirhams*								
Exports	70	33,960	28,446	50,965	58,673	60,013	67,057	68,608	72,283	73,869	80,667	86,389	....
Imports, c.i.f.	71	62,805	62,606	76,059	85,493	84,612	90,712	98,676	97,454	122,527	124,718	130,410	....
Imports, f.o.b.	71.v	57,146	60,579	60,168	78,654	77,843	83,455	90,782	97,457	122,527	114,744	....	....
					2000=100								
Volume of Exports	72	70.0	72.7	†79.5	78.9	76.7	82.0	†84.0	91.8	100.0	101.9	105.6	....
Volume of Imports	73	77.7	72.7	†58.4	65.7	61.3	66.1	†81.7	89.2	100.0	98.3	103.8	....
Unit Value of Imports	75	96.5	105.9	†119.8	117.5	124.3	120.1	†104.9	104.8	100.0	96.9	101.0	....

Morocco 686

		1992	1993	1994	1995	1996	1997	1998	1999	2000	2001	2002	2003
Balance of Payments		*Millions of US Dollars: Minus Sign Indicates Debit*										
Current Account, n.i.e.	78ald	−433	−521	−723	−1,296	−58	−169	−146	−171	−501	1,606	1,472	1,603
Goods: Exports f.o.b.	78aad	5,010	4,936	5,541	6,871	6,886	7,039	7,144	7,509	7,419	7,142	7,839	8,729
Goods: Imports f.o.b.	78abd	−7,473	−7,001	−7,648	−9,353	−9,080	−8,903	−9,463	−9,957	−10,654	−10,164	−10,900	−13,039
Trade Balance	78acd	−2,463	−2,065	−2,107	−2,482	−2,193	−1,864	−2,319	−2,448	−3,235	−3,022	−3,061	−4,310
Services: Credit	78add	2,125	2,050	2,014	2,173	2,743	2,471	2,827	3,115	3,034	4,029	4,360	5,412
Services: Debit	78aed	−1,571	−1,593	−1,730	−1,890	−1,782	−1,724	−1,963	−2,003	−1,892	−2,118	−2,413	−2,874
Balance on Goods & Services	78afd	−1,909	−1,608	−1,822	−2,199	−1,233	−1,117	−1,455	−1,335	−2,093	−1,111	−1,115	−1,773
Income: Credit	78agd	292	224	224	251	189	172	194	187	276	326	377	428
Income: Debit	78ahd	−1,349	−1,431	−1,394	−1,569	−1,498	−1,348	−1,227	−1,172	−1,140	−1,159	−1,115	−1,157
Balance on Gds, Serv. & Inc.	78aid	−2,966	−2,816	−2,992	−3,516	−2,541	−2,292	−2,489	−2,321	−2,958	−1,944	−1,853	−2,501
Current Transfers, n.i.e.: Credit	78ajd	2,614	2,361	2,355	2,298	2,565	2,204	2,438	2,246	2,574	3,670	3,441	4,250
Current Transfers: Debit	78akd	−81	−66	−86	−78	−82	−81	−95	−96	−118	−120	−115	−147
Capital Account, n.i.e.	78bcd	−6	−3	−3	−6	73	−5	−10	−9	−6	−9	−6	−10
Capital Account, n.i.e.: Credit	78bad	—	—	—	—	78	1	—	—	—	—	—	—
Capital Account: Debit	78bbd	−6	−3	−4	−6	−5	−5	−10	−9	−6	−9	−6	−10
Financial Account, n.i.e.	78bjd	1,239	966	1,248	−984	−897	−990	−644	−13	−774	−966	−1,336	−2,612
Direct Investment Abroad	78bdd	−32	−23	−24	−15	−30	−9	−20	−18	−59	−97	−28	−12
Dir. Invest. in Rep. Econ., n.i.e.	78bed	422	491	551	92	76	4	12	3	221	144	79	79
Portfolio Investment Assets	78bfd	—	—	—	—	—	—	—	—	—	—	—	—
Equity Securities	78bkd	—	—	—	—	—	—	—	—	—	—	—	—
Debt Securities	78bld	—	—	—	—	—	—	—	—	—	—	—	—
Portfolio Investment Liab., n.i.e.	78bgd	1	24	238	20	142	38	24	6	18	−7	−8	6
Equity Securities	78bmd	—	24	238	20	142	38	24	6	18	−7	−8	6
Debt Securities	78bnd	1	1	—	—	—	—	—	—	—	—	—	—
Financial Derivatives Assets	78bwd	….	….	….	….	….	….	….	….	….	….	….	….
Financial Derivatives Liabilities	78bxd	….	….	….	….	….	….	….	….	….	….	….	….
Other Investment Assets	78bhd	—	—	344	—	—	—	—	—	—	—	—	−776
Monetary Authorities	78bod	….	….	….	….	….	….	….	….	….	—	—	—
General Government	78bpd	—	—	—	—	—	—	—	—	—	—	—	—
Banks	78bqd	—	—	—	—	—	….	….	….	—	—	—	−522
Other Sectors	78brd	—	—	344	—	….	….	….	….	—	—	—	−254
Other Investment Liab., n.i.e.	78bid	848	473	139	−1,083	−1,085	−1,022	−660	−4	−953	−1,006	−1,380	−1,909
Monetary Authorities	78bsd	−11	−7	19	—	—	—	—	—	—	—	—	—
General Government	78btd	157	59	−421	−967	−867	−1,232	−954	−1,293	−1,208	−1,215	−1,465	−1,843
Banks	78bud	—	—	−48	−132	−167	−123	−197	−152	−80	−93	−128	−207
Other Sectors	78bvd	702	422	588	16	−50	333	492	1,441	335	302	214	141
Net Errors and Omissions	78cad	−10	−5	−39	391	209	175	160	123	114	230	−182	−377
Overall Balance	78cbd	791	436	483	−1,895	−673	−988	−640	−69	−1,166	861	−52	−1,396
Reserves and Related Items	79dad	−791	−436	−483	1,895	673	988	640	69	1,166	−861	52	1,396
Reserve Assets	79dbd	−675	−280	−362	984	−274	−553	−248	−1,636	416	−3,842	−644	−1,660
Use of Fund Credit and Loans	79dcd	−116	−156	−152	−101	−47	−3	—	—	—	—	—	—
Exceptional Financing	79ded	—	—	31	1,013	995	1,544	887	1,705	751	2,982	696	3,056
Government Finance		*Millions of Dirhams: Year Ending December 31*										
Deficit (-) or Surplus	80	−3,368	−6,509	−8,915	†−12,365	−9,485	−4,778	−13,226	3,065	−20,776	−10,042	−17,251	−15,332
Revenue	81	69,907	78,653	81,442	†82,018	79,180	88,845	91,160	111,425	100,904	127,444	104,723	117,550
Expenditure	82	73,008	84,832	90,072	†93,889	88,667	96,461	105,539	109,424	122,019	137,887	122,242	132,637
Lending Minus Repayments	83	267	330	285	†494	−2	−2,838	−1,153	−1,064	−339	−401	−268	245
Financing													
Net Borrowing: Domestic	84a	5,816	5,682	13,949	†14,843	12,914	18,069	10,722	12,973	15,038	28,699	28,680	26,176
Net borrowing: Foreign	85a	−445	−958	−4,428	†−2,111	−2,666	−8,398	−4,738	−4,394	−6,320	−9,861	−11,199	−8,746
Use of Cash Balances	87	−2,003	1,785	−606	†−367	−763	−4,893	7,213	−11,625	12,062	−8,796	−231	−2,098
Debt: Domestic	88a	67,225	76,847	93,843	†93,843	110,461	121,526	131,034	136,668	149,388	175,899	191,554	211,590
Debt: Foreign	89a	136,952	141,345	134,952	†129,766	131,038	130,377	125,864	123,955	118,646	110,597	92,800	78,800
National Accounts		*Billions of Dirhams*										
Househ.Cons.Expend.,incl.NPISHs	96f	170.14	170.67	197.17	201.70	227.34	218.61	234.26	229.09	242.97	257.97	264.87	273.82
Government Consumption Expend	91f	40.85	45.05	47.85	48.99	53.82	56.61	62.00	66.15	67.69	75.82	79.96	88.12
Gross Fixed Capital Formation	93e	54.36	56.72	57.90	60.39	61.94	65.79	75.74	81.90	85.42	85.37	91.14	98.38
Changes in Inventories	93i	2.01	−.74	1.72	−1.99	.60	.11	.48	−1.98	−1.48	2.35	−.83	1.14
Exports of Goods and Services	90c	54.64	56.76	69.53	77.63	69.64	73.55	77.72	84.66	92.95	106.95	115.15	116.86
Imports of Goods and Services (-)	98c	69.30	69.69	74.56	96.02	82.02	85.55	93.50	99.54	116.20	120.48	128.25	134.07
Gross Domestic Product (GDP)	99b	242.91	249.22	279.32	281.70	319.34	318.34	344.00	345.59	354.21	383.18	397.78	418.66
Net Primary Income from Abroad	98.n	11.94	9.06	10.11	8.70	12.68	11.17	14.40	13.24	18.20	31.74	29.38	32.74
Gross National Income (GNI)	99a	254.85	258.29	289.44	290.40	332.02	329.51	358.41	358.84	372.41	414.93	427.16	451.40
GDP Volume 1980 Prices	99b.p	110.92	109.80	121.17	113.62	127.05	124.20	133.73	133.62	134.90	143.39	147.97	155.73
GDP Volume (2000=100)	99bvp	82.2	81.4	89.8	84.2	94.2	92.1	99.1	99.1	100.0	106.3	109.7	115.4
GDP Deflator (2000=100)	99bip	83.4	86.4	87.8	94.4	95.7	97.6	98.0	98.5	100.0	101.8	102.4	102.4
		Millions: Midyear Estimates										
Population	99z	25.50	25.95	26.39	26.84	27.28	27.73	28.18	28.64	29.11	29.59	30.07	30.57

Mozambique 688

		1992	1993	1994	1995	1996	1997	1998	1999	2000	2001	2002	2003
Exchange Rates						*Meticais per SDR: End of Period*							
Market Rate	aa	†4,058.2	7,339.2	9,709.5	16,187.9	16,359.7	15,574.4	17,411.7	18,254.4	†22,332.5	29,307.5	32,430.4	35,450.3
				Meticais per US Dollar: End of Period (ae) Period Average (rf)									
Market Rate	ae	†2,951.4	5,343.2	6,651.0	10,890.0	11,377.0	11,543.0	12,366.0	13,300.0	†17,140.5	23,320.4	23,854.3	23,856.7
Market Rate	rf	†2,516.6	3,874.2	6,038.6	9,024.3	11,293.7	11,543.6	11,874.6	12,775.1	15,227.2	20,703.6	23,678.0	23,782.3
Fund Position						*Millions of SDRs: End of Period*							
Quota	2f.s	84.00	84.00	84.00	84.00	84.00	84.00	84.00	113.60	113.60	113.60	113.60	113.60
SDRs	1b.s	.03	.03	.03	.03	.04	.04	.04	.05	.05	.05	.05	.05
Reserve Position in the Fund	1c.s	.01	.01	.01	.01	.01	.01	.01	.01	.01	.01	.01	.01
Total Fund Cred.&Loans Outstg	2tl	126.88	137.86	145.24	135.79	125.89	140.11	147.24	145.42	168.47	155.89	147.16	140.75
International Liquidity						*Millions of US Dollars Unless Otherwise Indicated: End of Period*							
Total Reserves minus Gold	1l.d	233.37	187.24	177.51	195.32	344.06	517.35	608.50	651.60	725.11	715.57	819.19	998.45
SDRs	1b.d	.04	.04	.05	.05	.05	.05	.06	.06	.06	.06	.07	.08
Reserve Position in the Fund	1c.d	.01	.01	.01	.01	.01	.01	.01	.01	.01	.01	.01	.01
Foreign Exchange	1d.d	233.31	187.19	177.45	195.26	344.00	517.29	608.43	651.53	725.04	715.50	819.11	998.36
Monetary Authorities: Other Liab	4..d	1,058.99	1,185.63	645.60	551.40	537.91	591.66	593.36	587.88	545.92	470.15	480.28	494.89
Banking Institutions: Assets	7a.d	96.80	148.34	220.79	274.47	250.19	242.10	204.66	192.08	315.88	341.14	382.98	364.05
Liabilities	7b.d	41.78	55.75	56.24	76.77	60.68	95.78	80.14	41.92	72.64	83.70	42.03	57.71
Monetary Authorities						*Billions of Meticais: End of Period*							
Foreign Assets	11	769.6	1,175.2	1,367.2	2,424.4	4,359.3	6,359.0	7,928.0	9,089.9	13,018.5	17,297.2	20,164.1	23,900.1
Claims on Central Government	12a	250.1	545.5	578.4	663.2	496.9	369.8	82.7	6.9	6.8	6.8	10.0	.7
Claims on Local Government	12b	3.8	.3	.3	.2	1.5	.2	.2	.2	.2	.2	.2	.2
Claims on Nonfin.Pub.Enterprises	12c	—	—	.5	50.5	34.0	.5	.5	.5	.5	.5	.5	.5
Claims on Private Sector	12d	—	.9	2.2	.9	14.3	54.7	74.7	73.9				
Claims on Banking Institutions	12e	94.0	478.1	781.5	734.9	768.6	566.7	589.5	552.8	682.8	491.3	598.8	399.6
Reserve Money	14	506.4	890.1	1,481.4	1,951.1	2,469.5	2,866.6	2,760.2	3,244.5	4,078.8	6,239.4	7,317.3	8,917.4
of which: Currency Outside Banks	14a	257.5	469.5	762.4	1,130.2	1,394.4	1,544.1	1,649.7	2,174.2	2,425.3	2,970.4	3,485.8	4,258.8
Time & Foreign Currency Deposits	15	.1	30.7	27.9	84.3	14.8	52.0	72.2	66.0	31.5	46.2		
Liabs. of Central Bank: Securities	16ac	—	—	—	—	—	—	135.0	145.0	200.0	5.0	2,821.3	3,607.1
Foreign Liabilities	16c	514.9	1,011.8	1,410.2	2,198.1	2,059.5	2,182.1	2,563.7	2,654.6	3,762.2	4,568.7	4,772.5	4,989.6
Long-Term Foreign Liabilities	16cl	3,125.5	6,335.0	4,293.9	6,004.8	6,119.8	6,829.6	7,337.5	7,818.8	9,357.4	10,964.2	11,456.7	11,806.4
Central Government Deposits	16d	548.0	1,105.4	1,295.4	1,711.8	3,006.9	4,145.1	4,909.8	5,051.4	5,301.0	4,405.0	4,314.3	5,726.3
o/w: Cent.Govt.Earmarked Funds	16df	467.8	907.9	960.6	1,125.3	2,151.5	2,900.6	3,735.6	4,118.1	3,319.7	1,807.9	1,937.2	1,280.5
Capital Accounts	17a	346.1	579.0	896.8	969.7	1,201.4	1,294.0	1,363.9	1,581.6	1,679.9	4,741.0	4,685.2	5,002.4
Other Items (Net)	17r	−3,923.5	−7,752.0	−6,675.5	−9,045.6	−9,197.3	−10,018.5	−10,466.7	−10,837.7	−10,702.0	−13,173.6	−14,593.5	−15,748.1
of which: Valuation Adjustment	17rv	−1,621.2	−3,257.9	−5,663.9	−8,339.7	−8,683.2	−8,762.3	−9,192.1	−9,675.9	−10,916.7	−13,841.8	−15,036.7	−15,616.8
Banking Institutions						*Billions of Meticais: End of Period*							
Reserves	20	278.6	433.1	744.6	838.6	1,111.4	1,389.9	1,310.0	1,013.1	1,545.2	3,306.8	3,773.6	4,862.1
Claims on Mon.Author.:Securities	20c	—	—	—	—	—	—	135.0	145.0	—	—	2,684.0	3,607.1
Foreign Assets	21	285.7	792.6	1,468.5	2,989.0	2,846.4	2,794.5	2,530.8	2,554.7	5,414.3	7,955.6	9,135.8	8,685.1
Claims on Central Government	22a	42.7	6.6	—	.1	65.2	.1	8.3	232.7	1,610.6	2,274.1	2,834.7	4,880.0
Claims on Local Government	22b	19.7	—	.6	1.1	1.2	103.9	1.9	149.7	1.5	—		
Claims on Nonfin.Pub.Enterprises	22c	42.2	121.2	170.4	111.0	65.0	223.0	181.1	46.2	85.9	12,050.1	12,756.5	12,012.8
Claims on Private Sector	22d	856.2	971.3	1,538.2	2,373.3	3,440.3	5,114.8	6,467.0	8,552.7	10,987.7	1,893.1	1,768.9	2,306.8
Claims on Nonbank Financial Insts	22g	—	—	—	.7	11.4	12.5	1.3	46.4	269.7			
Demand Deposits	24	794.9	1,132.2	1,653.2	2,130.4	2,486.7	3,283.0	3,894.7	4,693.0	5,992.9	6,912.7	7,850.1	9,768.8
Time & Foreign Currency Deposits	25	465.8	906.9	1,380.7	2,303.3	2,800.9	3,388.4	4,144.1	5,893.5	9,328.8	12,860.0	16,287.4	18,631.0
Foreign Liabilities	26c	123.3	295.2	298.9	752.0	660.4	730.8	748.3	368.9	746.3	1,835.5	845.5	1,232.0
Long-Term Foreign Liabilities	26cl	—	2.7	75.2	84.1	30.0	374.8	242.8	188.6	498.8	116.5	157.1	144.9
Central Government Deposits	26d	179.5	238.7	228.7	375.0	430.9	350.0	313.1	356.4	588.0	1,780.4	1,638.9	2,137.1
o/w: Cent.Govt.Earmarked Funds	26df	23.6	23.0	22.5	141.3	204.1	95.9	92.7	91.4	37.8	513.3	273.2	434.5
Credit from Central Bank	26g	92.5	.8	581.2	671.0	691.1	560.6	477.4	458.3	965.5	637.5	560.8	134.8
Capital Accounts	27a	302.4	555.2	770.4	1,415.7	1,934.5	2,723.9	3,146.1	3,809.6	5,367.7	7,175.9	8,914.3	7,888.6
Other Items (Net)	27r	−433.3	−806.9	−1,066.0	−1,417.7	−1,493.5	−1,772.7	−2,331.2	−3,028.0	−3,573.2	−3,838.8	−3,300.6	−3,583.3
Banking Survey						*Billions of Meticais: End of Period*							
Foreign Assets (Net)	31n	−2,708.4	−5,676.9	−3,242.5	−3,625.5	−1,663.9	−963.8	−433.4	613.7	4,068.1	7,767.9	12,068.2	14,412.3
Domestic Credit	32	487.2	302.3	766.5	1,114.2	691.9	1,384.6	1,594.7	3,701.5	7,073.8	10,039.4	11,417.6	11,337.7
Claims on Central Govt.(Net)	32an	−434.7	−792.0	−945.7	−1,423.5	−2,875.8	−4,125.2	−5,132.0	−5,168.1	−4,271.6	−3,904.6	−3,108.5	−2,982.7
Claims on Local Government	32b	23.5	.3	.9	1.3	2.7	104.1	2.1	149.9	1.7	.2	.2	.2
Claims on Nonfin.Pub.Enterprises	32c	42.2	121.2	170.9	161.5	99.0	223.6	181.6	46.8	86.4	12,050.6	12,757.0	12,013.3
Claims on Private Sector	32d	856.2	972.2	1,540.4	2,374.2	3,454.6	5,169.5	6,541.6	8,626.6	10,987.7	1,893.1	1,768.9	2,306.8
Claims on Nonbank Financial Inst	32g	—	.6	—	.7	11.4	12.5	1.3	46.4	269.7			
Money	34	1,056.6	1,606.1	2,417.9	3,264.0	3,917.2	4,901.7	5,613.0	6,994.4	8,557.2	10,066.0	11,520.8	14,263.4
Quasi-Money	35	465.9	937.6	1,408.6	2,387.6	2,815.6	3,440.4	4,216.3	5,959.5	9,360.3	12,906.2	16,287.4	18,631.0
Liabs. of Central Bank: Securities	36ac	—	—	—	—	—	—	—	—	200.0	5.0	137.3	—
Capital Accounts	37a	648.5	1,134.2	1,667.2	2,385.4	3,135.9	4,017.9	4,510.0	5,391.4	7,047.7	11,916.9	13,599.5	12,891.0
Other Items (Net)	37r	−4,392.2	−9,052.5	−7,969.7	−10,548.3	−10,840.7	−11,939.2	−13,178.0	−14,030.1	−14,023.2	−17,086.8	−18,059.1	−20,035.5
Money plus Quasi-Money	35l	1,522.5	2,543.7	3,826.5	5,651.6	6,732.9	8,342.0	9,829.2	12,953.9	17,917.5	22,972.2	27,808.2	32,894.4

2004, International Monetary Fund : *International Financial Statistics Yearbook*

Mozambique 688

		1992	1993	1994	1995	1996	1997	1998	1999	2000	2001	2002	2003
Money (National Definitions)					*Billions of Meticais: End of Period*								
Reserve Money	19ma	....	....	....	....	....	2,792.1	2,691.7	3,117.3	3,939.8	6,056.5	7,133.7	8,681.5
M1	59ma	....	....	....	....	....	6,123.1	7,019.2	9,410.7	13,199.8	17,002.7	19,852.7	23,155.8
M2	59mb	....	....	....	....	....	7,413.5	8,720.0	11,721.6	16,778.7	21,814.1	26,145.0	32,256.9
Interest Rates						*Percent Per Annum*								
Discount Rate (End of Period)	60	....	....	69.70	57.75	32.00	12.95	9.95	9.95	9.95	9.95	9.95	9.95
Money Market Rate	60b	....	....	....	....	....	....	....	9.92	16.12	†25.00	20.40	13.34
Treasury Bill Rate	60c	....	....	....	....	....	....	....	....	16.97	24.77	29.55	15.31
Deposit Rate	60l	....	....	33.38	38.84	18.14	25.43	8.22	7.86	9.70	†15.01	17.99	12.15
Lending Rate	60p	....	....	....	....	....	....	24.35	19.63	19.04	†22.73	26.71	24.69
Prices					*Index Numbers (2000=100): Period Averages*									
Consumer Prices	64	14.9	21.2	34.5	†53.3	79.2	85.0	86.2	88.7	100.0	109.0	127.4	144.4
International Transactions						*Billions of Meticais*								
Exports	70	....	....	979.3	1,573.2	2,509.2	2,614.4	2,783.1	3,429.0	....	....	....	....
Imports, c.i.f.	71	....	....	3,279.0	6,527.1	8,733.7	8,704.7	9,575.9	14,859.3	....	....	....	....
Balance of Payments					*Millions of US Dollars: Minus Sign Indicates Debit*									
Current Account, n.i.e.	78ald	−352.3	−446.3	−467.2	−444.7	−420.5	−295.6	−429.3	−912.0	−763.6	−657.2	−711.6	−515.6
Goods: Exports f.o.b.	78aad	139.3	131.8	149.5	168.9	226.1	230.0	244.6	283.8	364.0	726.0	679.3	880.2
Goods: Imports f.o.b.	78abd	−769.5	−859.2	−916.7	−705.2	−704.4	−684.0	−735.6	−1,090.0	−1,046.0	−997.3	−1,215.7	−1,228.2
Trade Balance	78acd	−630.2	−727.4	−767.2	−536.3	−478.3	−454.0	−491.0	−806.2	−682.0	−271.3	−536.4	−347.9
Services: Credit	78add	164.6	180.2	191.1	242.4	253.2	278.7	286.2	295.2	325.4	249.7	339.4	304.0
Services: Debit	78aed	−246.4	−270.6	−323.3	−350.0	−319.0	−328.6	−396.2	−405.7	−445.8	−618.4	−549.6	−548.3
Balance on Goods & Services	78afd	−712.0	−817.8	−899.4	−643.9	−544.1	−503.9	−601.0	−916.7	−802.4	−640.0	−746.7	−592.3
Income: Credit	78agd	58.0	59.6	54.8	59.1	61.0	63.6	46.3	57.8	79.3	56.0	52.1	55.7
Income: Debit	78ahd	−197.7	−191.4	−187.2	−199.1	−162.1	−168.2	−187.8	−214.8	−271.4	−290.7	−655.3	−221.4
Balance on Gds, Serv. & Inc.	78aid	−851.7	−949.6	−1,031.8	−783.9	−645.2	−608.5	−742.5	−1,073.7	−994.5	−874.7	−1,349.8	−758.0
Current Transfers, n.i.e.: Credit	78ajd	499.4	503.3	564.6	339.2	224.7	312.9	313.2	256.3	337.3	254.6	827.0	293.2
Current Transfers: Debit	78akd	−	−	−	−	−	−	−	−94.6	−106.4	−37.1	−188.7	−50.8
Capital Account, n.i.e.	78bcd	−	−	−	−	−	−	−	180.3	226.8	256.7	222.0	270.7
Capital Account, n.i.e.: Credit	78bad	−	−	−	−	−	−	−	180.3	226.8	256.7	222.5	271.2
Capital Account: Debit	78bbd	−	−	−	−	−	−	−	−	−	−	−.4	−.5
Financial Account, n.i.e.	78bjd	513.7	246.9	344.4	366.7	235.0	182.2	300.4	403.9	83.2	−24.8	−731.7	372.8
Direct Investment Abroad	78bdd	−	−	−	−	−	−	−	−	−	−	−	−
Dir. Invest. in Rep. Econ., n.i.e.	78bed	25.3	32.0	35.0	45.0	72.5	64.4	212.7	381.7	139.2	255.4	347.6	336.7
Portfolio Investment Assets	78bfd	−	−	−	−	−	−	−	−	−	−	32.2	5.0
Equity Securities	78bkd	−	−	−	−	−	−	−	−	−	−	32.2	5.0
Debt Securities	78bld	−	−	−	−	−	−	−	−	−	−	....	....
Portfolio Investment Liab., n.i.e.	78bgd	−	−	−	−	−	−	−	−	−	−	....	....
Equity Securities	78bmd	−	−	−	−	−	−	−	−	−	−	....	....
Debt Securities	78bnd	−	−	−	−	−	−	−	−	−	−	....	....
Financial Derivatives Assets	78bwd	....	....	....	....	....	....	....	....	....	....	....	....
Financial Derivatives Liabilities	78bxd	....	....	....	....	....	....	....	....	....	....	....	....
Other Investment Assets	78bhd	−	−	−	−	−	−	19.0	2.6	−145.0	−33.8	−207.7	−77.1
Monetary Authorities	78bod	−	−	−	−	−	−	1.3	1.7	−	−.8	−5.6	6.9
General Government	78bpd	−	−	−	−	−	−	−	−	−	−	−	−
Banks	78bqd	−	−	−	−	−	−	17.7	13.9	−124.0	−23.9	−74.6	13.1
Other Sectors	78brd	−	−	−	−	−	−	−	−13.0	−21.0	−9.1	−127.5	−97.1
Other Investment Liab., n.i.e.	78bid	488.4	214.9	309.4	321.7	162.5	117.8	68.7	19.6	89.0	−246.4	−903.8	108.2
Monetary Authorities	78bsd	−	−	−	−	−	−	−	−5.8	−40.8	−	10.1	22.3
General Government	78btd	488.4	214.9	309.4	321.7	86.2	48.8	−.8	−261.7	−171.4	−263.1	−1,302.9	53.0
Banks	78bud	−	−	−	−	−	−	20.3	−33.6	16.6	35.1	−43.0	15.7
Other Sectors	78bvd	−	−	−	−	76.3	69.0	49.2	320.7	284.6	−18.4	432.0	17.3
Net Errors and Omissions	78cad	−684.2	−447.4	−443.2	−308.6	−238.3	−364.8	−263.8	1.5	37.5	−59.6	−217.6	−92.6
Overall Balance	78cbd	−522.8	−646.8	−566.0	−386.6	−423.8	−478.2	−392.7	−326.3	−416.1	−484.9	−1,438.8	35.3
Reserves and Related Items	79dad	522.8	646.8	566.0	386.6	423.8	478.2	392.7	326.3	416.1	484.9	1,438.8	−35.3
Reserve Assets	79dbd	13.9	63.6	−12.0	16.4	161.0	162.3	91.5	−44.0	−76.8	18.8	−97.8	−181.5
Use of Fund Credit and Loans	79dcd	62.5	15.4	10.4	−14.4	−14.4	19.9	9.6	−2.9	31.1	−15.8	−11.5	−9.1
Exceptional Financing	79ded	446.4	567.8	567.6	384.6	277.1	296.0	291.6	373.2	461.8	481.9	1,548.2	155.3
National Accounts						*Billions of Meticais*								
Househ.Cons.Expend.,incl.NPISHs	96f	5,270	8,012	12,295	20,564	30,692	35,735	38,822	40,823	44,678	51,708	61,420	....
Government Consumption Expend.	91f	666	1,203	2,588	2,009	2,625	3,655	4,892	6,401	7,730	10,326	16,178	....
Gross Fixed Capital Formation	93e	999	1,637	2,976	5,578	6,617	8,197	8,602	10,378	28,746	15,956	17,696	....
Changes in Inventories	93i	167	267	330	755	524	−3	2,758	8,663	−9,423	2,890	....	....
Exports of Goods and Services	90c	531	757	1,547	2,601	3,982	4,510	4,923	5,256	7,326	15,472	20,030	....
Imports of Goods and Services (-)	98c	2,580	3,867	6,416	10,830	11,722	12,276	13,085	19,607	22,139	25,217	32,577	....
Gross Domestic Product (GDP)	99b	5,053	8,012	13,319	20,678	32,719	39,819	46,912	51,913	56,917	71,135	82,747	....
Gross National Income (GNI)	99a	4,164	7,136	11,665	16,128	....	....	....	....	....	....	....	....
GDP Volume 1996 Prices	99b.p	25,967	27,729	29,665	30,646	32,719	36,340	40,932	44,018	44,686	50,484	54,668	....
GDP Volume (2000=100)	99bvp	58.1	62.1	66.4	68.6	73.2	81.3	91.6	98.5	100.0	113.0	122.3	....
GDP Deflator (2000=100)	99bip	15.3	22.7	35.2	53.0	78.5	86.0	90.0	92.6	100.0	110.6	118.8	....
						Millions: Midyear Estimates								
Population	99z	14.29	14.86	15.43	15.95	16.40	16.81	17.17	17.52	17.86	18.20	18.54	18.86

Myanmar 518

		1992	1993	1994	1995	1996	1997	1998	1999	2000	2001	2002	2003
Exchange Rates		\multicolumn{12}{c}{*Kyats per SDR: End of Period*}
Official Rate	aa	8.5085	8.5085	8.5085	8.5085	8.5085	8.5085	8.5085	8.5085	8.5085	8.5085	8.5085	8.5085
		\multicolumn{12}{c}{*Kyats per US Dollar: End of Period (ae) Period Average (rf)*}
Official Rate	ae	6.1880	6.1945	5.8283	5.7239	5.9171	6.3061	6.0428	6.1992	6.5303	6.7704	6.2584	5.7259
Official Rate	rf	6.0428	6.0938	5.9446	5.6106	5.8609	6.1838	6.2738	6.2233	6.4257	6.6841	6.5734	6.0764
Fund Position		\multicolumn{12}{c}{*Millions of SDRs: End of Period*}
Quota	2f.s	184.9	184.9	184.9	184.9	184.9	184.9	184.9	258.4	258.4	258.4	258.4	258.4
SDRs	1b.s	–	.2	.1	.1	.1	.1	.2	.1	.1	.4	.1	.1
Reserve Position in the Fund	1c.s	–	–	–	–	–	–	–	–	–	–	–	–
Total Fund Cred.&Loans Outstg.	2tl	–	–	–	–	–	–	–	–	–	–	–	–
International Liquidity		\multicolumn{12}{c}{*Millions of US Dollars Unless Otherwise Indicated: End of Period*}
Total Reserves minus Gold	1l.d	280.1	302.9	422.0	561.1	229.2	249.8	314.9	265.5	223.0	400.5	470.0	550.2
SDRs	1b.d	–	.3	.1	.1	.1	.1	.3	.2	.1	.6	.1	.1
Reserve Position in the Fund	1c.d	–	–	–	–	–	–	–	–	–	–	–	–
Foreign Exchange	1d.d	280.1	302.6	421.9	561.1	229.1	249.7	314.6	265.3	222.8	399.9	469.9	550.1
Gold (Million Fine Troy Ounces)	1ad	.251	.251	.251	.231	.231	.231	.231	.231	.231	.231	.231	.231
Gold (National Valuation)	1and	12.1	12.1	12.8	12.0	11.6	10.9	11.4	11.1	10.6	10.2	11.0	12.0
Monetary Authorities:Other Assets	3..d	....	....	....	....	....	....	....	....	....	....	....	....
Monetary Authorities: Other Liab.	4..d	321.5	336.4	346.0	328.6	335.3	343.0	337.5	338.8	336.3	531.3	542.1	368.0
Deposit Money Banks: Assets	7a.d	116.7	132.1	161.7	195.4	122.0	144.6	232.3	223.5	184.8	173.3	236.0	285.3
Liabilities	7b.d	172.6	1,765.7	1,972.9	2,119.6	1,961.2	1,706.0	1,640.0	1,705.2	1,698.9	1,645.1	1,606.6	1,858.0
Monetary Authorities		\multicolumn{12}{c}{*Millions of Kyats: End of Period*}
Foreign Assets	11	2,259	2,030	2,656	3,587	2,119	1,690	3,663	2,494	2,933	4,149	5,136	4,410
Claims on Central Government	12a	74,710	91,399	116,131	142,023	182,431	214,392	281,383	331,425	447,581	675,040	892,581	1,262,588
Claims on Deposit Money Banks	12e	14,138	10,375	3,639	5,191	5,923	23,785	15,553	19,602	15,918	21,576	38,732	93,952
Reserve Money	14	65,698	79,275	97,584	124,675	164,513	213,025	270,104	320,579	431,085	653,723	882,043	1,289,016
of which: Currency Outside DMBs	14a	53,724	67,611	89,084	114,524	152,789	194,129	237,098	272,769	344,728	494,521	718,633	1,102,937
Other Liabilities to DMBs	14n	22,798	22,662	23,320	24,284	22,904	22,624	24,435	23,402	23,847	23,850	24,916	24,285
Foreign Liabilities	16c	1,942	2,050	2,056	1,843	1,965	2,121	2,117	2,108	2,170	3,551	3,562	2,239
Capital Accounts	17a	666	787	788	1,086	1,082	1,681	2,882	4,874	5,282	8,952	10,083	18,911
Other Items (Net)	17r	3	–969	–1,317	–1,086	9	414	1,062	2,559	4,048	10,690	15,846	26,500
Deposit Money Banks		\multicolumn{12}{c}{*Millions of Kyats: End of Period*}
Reserves	20	1,074	5,300	–11,374	–17,511	–12,258	14,570	44,356	57,339	70,591	99,973	113,696	104,837
Other Claims on Monetary Author.	20n	22,798	22,662	23,320	24,284	22,904	22,624	24,435	23,402	23,847	23,850	24,916	24,285
Foreign Assets	21	–	–	–	1	3	8	20	1	369	3	13	9	–
Claims on Central Govt. (Net)	22an	3,367	2,751	–727	–305	–2,402	2,312	–30,179	11,960	35,659	40,485	42,548	34,546
Claims on Local Government	22b	545	449	511	310	184	61	61	–	–	–	–	–
Claims on Nonfin.Pub.Enterprises	22c	4,571	6,459	11,343	8,351	10,631	11,419	46,688	53,960	69,158	72,338	69,162	68,107
Claims on Private Sector	22d	19,173	23,076	28,262	45,956	75,346	115,505	155,761	188,649	266,966	416,676	609,101	342,547
Demand Deposits	24	4,963	5,827	9,183	11,241	14,961	25,600	44,782	72,707	119,746	206,349	290,520	82,948
Time, Savings,& Fgn.Currency Dep.	25	18,120	24,024	33,942	54,572	82,786	102,944	151,363	216,459	335,574	450,560	541,307	386,298
Restricted Deposits	26b	808	1,039	1,179	1,814	2,349	1,739	1,549	1,635	1,703	1,760	2,661	2,812
Foreign Liabilities	26c	10,355	10,759	11,725	11,889	11,494	10,549	10,287	10,611	10,961	10,995	10,557	11,306
Credit from Monetary Authorities	26g	1,250	1,823	1,777	5,038	3,835	10,119	5,762	5,030	7,439	15,601	44,251	96,692
Capital Accounts	27a	2,074	2,402	3,228	4,128	7,790	10,733	12,546	17,908	24,094	32,285	47,881	62,272
Other Items (Net)	27r	13,957	14,803	–9,696	–27,593	–28,802	4,827	14,829	11,329	–33,294	–64,216	–77,742	–67,995
Monetary Survey		\multicolumn{12}{c}{*Millions of Kyats: End of Period*}
Foreign Assets (Net)	31n	–10,038	–10,779	–11,124	–10,143	–11,332	–10,960	–8,740	–9,856	–10,195	–10,384	–8,974	–9,135
Domestic Credit	32	102,366	124,134	155,520	196,335	266,191	343,714	453,714	585,994	819,364	1,204,539	1,613,392	1,707,788
Claims on Central Govt. (Net)	32an	78,077	94,150	115,404	141,718	180,029	216,704	251,204	343,385	483,240	715,525	935,129	1,297,134
Claims on Local Government	32b	545	449	511	310	184	61	61	–	–	–	–	–
Claims on Nonfin.Pub.Enterprises	32c	4,571	6,459	11,343	8,351	10,631	11,419	46,688	53,960	69,158	72,338	69,162	68,107
Claims on Private Sector	32d	19,173	23,076	28,262	45,956	75,346	115,505	155,761	188,649	266,966	416,676	609,101	342,547
Money	34	58,688	73,457	98,289	125,956	167,971	219,983	282,087	345,765	464,968	701,153	1,009,471	1,186,104
Quasi-Money	35	18,120	24,024	33,942	54,572	82,786	102,944	151,363	216,459	335,574	450,560	541,307	386,298
Restricted Deposits	36b	808	1,039	1,179	1,814	2,349	1,739	1,549	1,635	1,703	1,760	2,661	2,812
Capital Accounts	37a	2,740	3,189	4,016	5,213	8,871	12,413	15,428	22,782	29,376	41,237	57,964	81,183
Other Items (Net)	37r	11,971	11,627	6,977	–1,361	–7,120	–4,354	–5,457	–10,502	–22,453	–555	–6,981	42,268
Money plus Quasi-Money	35l	76,808	97,480	132,231	180,528	250,758	322,927	433,451	562,224	800,542	1,151,713	1,550,778	1,572,402
Interest Rates		\multicolumn{12}{c}{*Percent Per Annum*}
Central Bank Rate (End of Per.)	60	11.00	11.00	11.00	12.50	15.00	15.00	15.00	12.00	10.00	10.00	10.00	9.00
Deposit Rate	60l	9.00	9.00	9.00	9.75	12.50	12.50	12.50	11.00	9.75	9.50	9.50	9.50
Lending Rate	60p	8.00	....	16.50	16.50	16.50	16.50	16.50	16.13	15.25	15.00	15.00	15.00
Government Bond Yield	61	....	....	10.50	10.50	13.13	14.00	14.00	†11.00	9.00	9.00	9.00	9.00

2004, International Monetary Fund : *International Financial Statistics Yearbook*

Myanmar 518

		1992	1993	1994	1995	1996	1997	1998	1999	2000	2001	2002	2003
Prices		*Index Numbers (2000=100): Period Averages*											
Consumer Prices................	64	18.1	23.8	29.6	37.0	43.0	55.8	84.6	†100.1	100.0	121.1	190.2	259.8
		*Number in Thousands: Period Averages*											
Employment...............	67e	15,737	16,469	16,817	....	....	17,964	18,359	....	....	....	....	....
Unemployment............	67c	503	518	541	....	....	535	452	425	382	398	....	....
International Transactions								*Millions of Kyats*						
Exports..................	70	3,241.1	3,609.4	4,776.7	4,825.8	4,419.5	5,415.8	6,737.2	7,073.5	10,600.5	15,929.4	19,980.3	15,123.0
Imports, c.i.f..........	71	3,971.0	5,007.0	5,285.9	7,564.2	8,032.0	12,735.9	16,920.7	14,463.9	15,426.3	19,248.3	15,373.2	12,720.7
Balance of Payments						*Millions of US Dollars: Minus Sign Indicates Debit*								
Current Account, n.i.e........	78ald	−115.6	−230.2	−130.3	−261.0	−282.6	−415.9	−499.1	−284.7	−211.7	−308.5	....	....
Goods: Exports f.o.b........	78aad	536.7	637.4	861.6	942.6	946.9	983.7	1,077.3	1,293.9	1,661.6	2,316.9	....	....
Goods: Imports f.o.b........	78abd	−642.7	−1,273.9	−1,474.2	−1,773.9	−1,887.2	−2,126.4	−2,478.2	−2,181.3	−2,165.4	−2,587.9	....	....
Trade Balance.................	78acd	−106.0	−636.5	−612.6	−831.3	−940.2	−1,142.7	−1,400.9	−887.3	−503.8	−271.1	....	....
Services: Credit...............	78add	113.5	249.1	272.2	364.6	431.9	526.6	633.2	512.2	477.9	423.6	....	....
Services: Debit.................	78aed	−42.9	−131.6	−129.5	−246.2	−304.9	−447.5	−368.8	−291.1	−328.1	−380.2	....	....
Balance on Goods & Services..	78afd	−35.4	−518.9	−470.0	−712.9	−813.2	−1,063.6	−1,136.5	−666.3	−354.0	−227.7	....	....
Income: Credit.................	78agd	3.5	4.8	7.2	15.5	9.1	6.6	11.0	51.6	35.5	35.9	....	....
Income: Debit..................	78ahd	−152.9	−63.7	−74.5	−125.4	−53.6	−20.4	−11.4	−54.6	−168.8	−402.6	....	....
Balance on Gds, Serv. & Inc.	78aid	−184.8	−577.8	−537.3	−822.8	−857.7	−1,077.5	−1,137.0	−669.2	−487.3	−594.3	....	....
Current Transfers, n.i.e.: Credit.	78ajd	71.0	348.2	407.6	569.9	604.1	691.6	638.1	384.8	289.7	298.5	....	....
Current Transfers: Debit......	78akd	−1.8	−.5	−.6	−8.1	−29.1	−30.0	−.3	−.3	−14.1	−12.8	....	....
Capital Account, n.i.e........	78bcd	−	−	−	−	−	....	....	....	....	....	....	....
Capital Account, n.i.e.: Credit...	78bad	−	−	−	−	−	....	....	....	....	....	....	....
Capital Account: Debit........	78bbd	−	−	−	−	−	....	....	....	....	....	....	....
Financial Account, n.i.e.......	78bjd	193.0	162.4	186.4	245.2	269.4	473.5	540.9	251.2	212.8	399.1	....	....
Direct Investment Abroad.....	78bdd	....	....	....	....	....	....	....	....	....	....	....	....
Dir. Invest. in Rep. Econ., n.i.e..	78bed	173.3	105.7	126.9	279.9	313.4	390.8	317.8	255.6	258.3	210.3	....	....
Portfolio Investment Assets....	78bfd	....	....	....	....	....	....	....	....	....	....	....	....
Equity Securities...............	78bkd	....	....	....	....	....	....	....	....	....	....	....	....
Debt Securities................	78bld	....	....	....	....	....	....	....	....	....	....	....	....
Portfolio Investment Liab., n.i.e..	78bgd	....	....	....	....	....	....	....	....	....	....	....	....
Equity Securities...............	78bmd	....	....	....	....	....	....	....	....	....	....	....	....
Debt Securities................	78bnd	....	....	....	....	....	....	....	....	....	....	....	....
Financial Derivatives Assets....	78bwd	....	....	....	....	....	....	....	....	....	....	....	....
Financial Derivatives Liabilities...	78bxd	....	....	....	....	....	....	....	....	....	....	....	....
Other Investment Assets......	78bhd	−	....	....	....	....	....	....	....	....	....	....	....
Monetary Authorities........	78bod	....	....	....	....	....	....	....	....	....	....	....	....
General Government.........	78bpd	−	....	....	....	....	....	....	....	....	....	....	....
Banks...........................	78bqd	−	....	....	....	....	....	....	....	....	....	....	....
Other Sectors.................	78brd	−	....	....	....	....	....	....	....	....	....	....	....
Other Investment Liab., n.i.e...	78bid	19.7	56.7	59.5	−34.7	−44.0	82.7	223.0	−4.4	−45.4	188.8	....	....
Monetary Authorities........	78bsd	−.8	−	2.6	2.4	−3.1	−5.6	−2.7	1.1	7.2	200.8	....	....
General Government.........	78btd	20.4	56.7	56.8	−37.1	−40.9	88.3	229.3	−4.1	−56.8	−11.9	....	....
Banks...........................	78bud	....	....	....	....	....	....	−3.6	−1.3	4.1	−.1	....	....
Other Sectors.................	78bvd	....	....	....	....	....	....	....	....	....	....	....	....
Net Errors and Omissions.....	78cad	17.9	−10.1	−10.4	−16.3	−11.8	−26.3	18.7	−12.4	−24.5	89.3	....	....
Overall Balance................	78cbd	95.3	−77.8	45.8	−32.2	−25.0	31.3	60.4	−45.9	−23.4	179.8	....	....
Reserves and Related Items.....	79dad	−95.3	77.8	−45.8	32.2	25.0	−31.3	−60.4	45.9	23.4	−179.8	....	....
Reserve Assets.................	79dbd	−95.3	77.8	−45.8	32.2	25.0	−31.3	−60.4	45.9	23.4	−179.8	....	....
Use of Fund Credit and Loans...	79dcd	−	−	−	−	−	....	....	....	....	....	....	....
Exceptional Financing.........	79ded	....	....	....	....	....	....	....	....	....	....	....	....
International Investment Position								*Millions of US Dollars*						
Assets.............................	79aad	....	....	....	....	....	....	....	....	....	....	....	....
Direct Investment Abroad.....	79abd	....	....	....	....	....	....	....	....	....	....	....	....
Portfolio Investment...........	79acd	....	....	....	....	....	....	....	....	−	−	−	....
Equity Securities...............	79add	....	....	....	....	....	....	....	....	−	−	−	....
Debt Securities................	79aed	....	....	....	....	....	....	....	....	−	−	−	....
Financial Derivatives...........	79ald	....	....	....	....	....	....	....	....	....	....	....	....
Other Investment..............	79afd	....	....	....	....	....	....	....	....	....	....	....	....
Monetary Authorities........	79agd	....	....	....	....	....	....	....	....	....	....	....	....
General Government.........	79ahd	....	....	....	....	....	....	....	....	....	....	....	....
Banks...........................	79aid	....	....	....	....	....	....	....	....	....	....	....	....
Other Sectors.................	79ajd	....	....	....	....	....	....	....	....	....	....	....	....
Reserve Assets.................	79akd	....	....	....	....	....	....	....	....	331.7	290.4	460.4	....
Liabilities........................	79lad	....	....	....	....	....	....	....	....	....	....	....	....
Dir. Invest. in Rep. Economy...	79lbd	....	....	....	....	....	....	....	....	3,130.7	3,211.0	3,304.8	....
Portfolio Investment...........	79lcd	....	....	....	....	....	....	....	....	−	−	−	....
Equity Securities...............	79ldd	....	....	....	....	....	....	....	....	−	−	−	....
Debt Securities................	79led	....	....	....	....	....	....	....	....	−	−	−	....
Financial Derivatives...........	79lld	....	....	....	....	....	....	....	....	....	....	....	....
Other Investment..............	79lfd	....	....	....	....	....	....	....	....	5,430.3	5,109.9	5,115.8	....
Monetary Authorities........	79lgd	....	....	....	....	....	....	....	....	....	....	....	....
General Government.........	79lhd	....	....	....	....	....	....	....	....	....	....	....	....
Banks...........................	79lid	....	....	....	....	....	....	....	....	....	....	....	....
Other Sectors.................	79ljd	....	....	....	....	....	....	....	....	....	....	....	....

Myanmar 518

		1992	1993	1994	1995	1996	1997	1998	1999	2000	2001	2002	2003
Government Finance		\multicolumn{12}{c}{*Millions of Kyats: Year Beginning April 1*}
Deficit (-) or Surplus...............	80	†−7,054	−7,761	−15,757	−24,924	−25,052	−10,343	−6,946	−30,444	−86,578	....	....	....
Revenue................................	81	†20,313	27,329	32,029	39,429	54,726	86,690	116,066	122,895	134,308	....	....	....
Grants Received..................	81z	†358	456	429	744	421	1,548	524	221	242	....	....	....
Expenditure..........................	82	†27,931	35,696	48,021	64,884	80,120	98,426	124,064	153,497	221,255	....	....	....
Lending Minus Repayments......	83	†−206	−150	194	213	79	155	−528	63	−127	....	....	....
Financing													
Domestic.............................	84a	†7,038	7,738	15,749	25,201	25,230	9,833	5,680	30,311	86,661	....	....	....
Foreign................................	85a	†16	23	8	−277	−178	510	1,266	133	−83	....	....	....
National Accounts		\multicolumn{12}{c}{*Millions of Kyats: Year Beginning April 1*}
Househ.Cons.Expend.,incl.NPISHs....	96f	217,384	319,191	417,230	523,876	701,220	987,513	1,419,709	1,906,136	....	....	....	....
Gross Fixed Capital Formation...........	93e	31,184	37,466	54,596	82,582	118,313	150,240	206,912	241,694	....	....	....	....
Changes in Inventories...................	93i	2,601	7,360	3,875	3,540	−21,262	−10,276	−7,604	48,325	....	....	....	....
Exports of Goods and Services..........	90c	3,590	4,228	5,405	5,033	5,488	6,290	7,700	9,394	....	....	....	....
Imports of Goods and Services (-).....	98c	5,365	7,923	8,332	10,302	11,779	14,258	16,941	15,248	....	....	....	....
Gross Domestic Product (GDP).........	99b	249,395	360,321	472,774	604,729	791,980	1,119,509	1,609,776	2,190,301	....	....	....	....
Net Primary Income from Abroad.....	98.n	−153	−429	−396	−689	−116	−69	34	−118	....	....	....	....
Gross National Income (GNI).............	99a	249,242	359,892	472,378	604,040	791,864	1,119,440	1,609,810	2,190,183	....	....	....	....
GDP Volume 1985/86 Prices............	99b.p	54,757	58,064	62,406	66,742	71,042	75,123	79,460	88,134	93,629	....	....	....
GDP Volume (2000=100).................	99bvp	58.5	62.0	66.7	71.3	75.9	80.2	84.9	94.1	100.0	....	....	....
GDP Deflator (1995=100)................	99bip	50.3	68.5	83.6	100.0	123.0	164.5	223.6	274.3	....	....	....	....
		\multicolumn{12}{c}{*Millions: Midyear Estimates*}
Population...............................	99z	41.93	42.65	43.38	44.09	44.80	45.50	46.19	46.87	47.54	48.20	48.85	49.49

Namibia 728

		1992	1993	1994	1995	1996	1997	1998	1999	2000	2001	2002	2003
Exchange Rates													
Market Rate	aa	4.19788	4.66667	5.17298	5.42197	6.73325	6.56747	8.25106	8.44711	9.86107	15.23974	11.74625	9.86684
		Namibia Dollars per SDR: End of Period											
		Namibia Dollars per US Dollar: End of Period (ae) Period Average (rf)											
Market Rate	ae	3.05300	3.39750	3.54350	3.64750	4.68250	4.86750	5.86000	6.15450	7.56850	12.12650	8.64000	6.64000
Market Rate	rf	2.85201	3.26774	3.55080	3.62709	4.29935	4.60796	5.52828	6.10948	6.93983	8.60918	10.54075	7.56475
Fund Position													
		Millions of SDRs: End of Period											
Quota	2f.s	100	100	100	100	100	100	100	137	137	137	137	137
SDRs	1b.s	–	–	–	–	–	–	–	–	–	–	–	–
Reserve Position in the Fund	1c.s	–	–	–	–	–	–	–	–	–	–	–	–
Total Fund Cred.&Loans Outstg	2tl	–	–	–	–	–	–	–	–	–	–	–	–
International Liquidity													
		Millions of US Dollars Unless Otherwise Indicated: End of Period											
Total Reserves minus Gold	1l.d	49.72	133.70	202.62	220.98	193.87	250.53	260.25	305.49	260.01	234.25	323.13	325.22
SDRs	1b.d	.01	.02	.02	.02	.02	.02	.02	.02	.02	.02	.02	.03
Reserve Position in the Fund	1c.d	.01	.01	.01	.03	.04	.04	.05	.05	.05	.05	.06	.08
Foreign Exchange	1d.d	49.69	133.67	202.59	220.94	193.81	250.47	260.18	305.42	259.94	234.18	323.05	325.11
Gold (Million Fine Troy Ounces)	1ad	–	–	–	–	–	–	–	–	–	–	–	–
Gold (National Valuation)	1and	–	–	–	–	–	–	–	–	–	–	–	–
Monetary Authorities: Other Liab	4..d	166.66	179.93	200.87	212.20	181.89	4.96	6.63	7.70	8.48	5.87	6.66	23.75
Deposit Money Banks: Assets	7a.d	123.05	57.38	54.87	38.58	74.70	110.33	93.58	142.63	231.65	121.40	130.62	165.56
Liabilities	7b.d	32.53	47.35	110.49	137.26	63.00	172.31	116.20	67.99	129.63	129.09	255.33	382.21
Other Banking Insts.: Liabilities	7f.d	2.80	3.01	5.15	2.80	2.11	3.07	4.01	4.17	11.04	12.47	23.26	21.58
Monetary Authorities													
		Millions of Namibia Dollars: End of Period											
Foreign Assets	11	346.8	465.9	725.8	818.1	918.0	1,236.0	1,550.1	1,885.6	2,032.0	2,715.9	2,904.7	2,132.4
Claims on Central Government	12a	510.3	619.6	720.0	783.7	856.9							
Reserve Money	14	221.8	233.3	373.6	415.6	508.3	609.3	631.4	906.7	849.6	919.7	991.7	1,187.5
Foreign Liabilities	16c	508.8	611.3	711.8	774.0	851.7	24.1	38.8	47.4	64.2	71.2	57.5	157.7
Central Government Deposits	16d	143.5	221.7	291.2	280.8	162.4	374.4	416.1	471.8	446.3	360.5	1,044.6	251.7
Capital Accounts	17a	31.9	40.6	71.2	119.5	303.8	316.5	513.4	562.9	783.9	1,587.9	1,076.3	725.8
Other Items (Net)	17r	–48.9	–21.4	–2.0	11.9	–51.3	–88.4	–49.8	–103.2	–112.0	–223.3	–265.3	–190.3
Deposit Money Banks													
		Millions of Namibia Dollars: End of Period											
Reserves	20	83.4	99.5	156.2	175.4	226.4	275.7	265.7	510.5	368.5	412.3	425.8	603.5
Foreign Assets	21	375.7	195.0	194.4	140.7	349.8	537.0	548.4	877.8	1,753.3	1,472.2	1,128.5	1,099.3
Claims on Central Government	22a	171.6	279.2	238.8	256.2	460.9	659.8	701.7	1,020.0	949.1	904.2	1,183.0	1,696.9
Claims on Local Government	22b	15.2	15.0	17.2	19.2	18.6	17.4	18.8	16.3	12.4	32.8	5.7	14.6
Claims on Nonfin.Pub.Enterprises	22c	42.1	42.2	42.1	72.1	72.2	148.8	142.7	136.6	234.0	119.1	158.1	144.3
Claims on Private Sector	22d	2,079.2	2,705.5	3,542.6	4,742.8	5,663.2	6,553.5	7,129.3	7,434.2	8,699.8	10,115.5	12,161.2	15,405.8
Claims on Other Banking Insts	22f	21.0	10.1	95.1	74.6	7.0	23.6	14.6	.6	.4	19.7	–	–
Claims on Nonbank Financial Insts	22g					10.1	–	–	10.1	45.6	2.3	1.3	–
Demand Deposits	24	1,002.4	1,333.1	1,465.3	1,581.9	2,516.7	2,562.5	3,315.9	4,073.6	5,284.8	5,805.2	6,152.4	7,266.8
Time, Savings,& Fgn.Currency Dep	25	1,375.1	1,521.9	2,081.0	2,851.6	3,229.9	3,535.8	3,479.6	3,979.9	3,808.7	3,691.0	3,999.9	5,062.0
Money Market Instruments	26aa	–	–	–	–	–	–	–	–	–	103.3	258.9	158.2
Bonds	26ab	2.4	3.9	4.1	4.1	8.9	7.0	5.5	–	–	–	–	–
Foreign Liabilities	26c	99.3	160.9	391.5	500.6	295.0	838.7	680.9	418.4	981.1	1,565.4	2,206.1	2,537.9
Central Government Deposits	26d	109.9	113.3	83.1	73.5	77.9	217.6	173.2	89.2	227.5	258.6	380.6	671.2
Credit from Monetary Authorities	26g	–	–	–	–	–	–	7.7	120.3	18.5	124.2	19.5	14.4
Liabilities to Other Banking Insts	26i	45.1	7.6	5.1	74.0	20.9	67.2	45.2	56.8	50.0	–	–	20.4
Capital Accounts	27a	204.5	273.2	293.8	432.5	644.0	782.7	919.0	1,080.7	1,291.0	1,537.1	1,604.0	2,536.3
Other Items (Net)	27r	–50.5	–67.4	–37.6	–37.2	14.8	204.4	194.0	187.3	401.5	–6.9	442.2	697.2
Monetary Survey													
		Millions of Namibia Dollars: End of Period											
Foreign Assets (Net)	31n	114.3	–111.3	–183.0	–315.8	121.1	910.1	1,378.7	2,297.7	2,740.0	2,551.5	1,769.6	536.1
Domestic Credit	32	2,586.3	3,336.9	4,282.1	5,595.0	6,849.1	6,811.9	7,418.2	8,057.5	9,268.2	10,575.6	12,085.5	16,340.2
Claims on Central Govt. (Net)	32an	428.5	563.8	584.5	685.6	1,077.4	67.8	112.3	459.0	275.3	285.1	–242.1	774.0
Claims on Local Government	32b	15.2	15.0	17.2	19.2	18.6	17.5	18.8	16.3	12.4	32.8	5.7	14.6
Claims on Nonfin.Pub.Enterprises	32c	42.1	42.2	42.1	72.1	72.2	148.8	142.7	136.6	234.0	119.1	158.1	144.3
Claims on Private Sector	32d	2,079.2	2,705.5	3,542.6	4,742.8	5,663.2	6,553.5	7,129.3	7,434.2	8,699.8	10,115.5	12,161.2	15,405.8
Claims on Other Banking Insts	32f	21.3	10.5	95.6	75.3	7.7	24.3	15.1	1.3	1.0	20.8	1.3	1.5
Claims on Nonbank Financial Inst.	32g								10.1	45.6	2.3	1.3	–
Money	34	1,002.4	1,466.8	1,682.8	1,822.2	2,799.5	2,898.1	3,680.9	4,496.3	5,766.0	6,312.7	6,698.2	7,851.4
Quasi-Money	35	1,375.1	1,521.9	2,081.0	2,851.6	3,229.9	3,535.8	3,479.6	3,979.9	3,808.7	3,691.0	3,999.9	5,062.0
Money Market Instruments	36aa	–	–	–	–	–	–	–	–	–	103.3	258.9	158.2
Bonds	36ab	2.4	3.9	4.1	4.1	8.9	7.0	5.5	–	–	–	–	–
Liabilities to Other Banking Insts	36i	45.1	7.6	5.1	74.0	20.9	67.2	45.2	56.8	50.0	–	–	20.4
Capital Accounts	37a	236.4	313.8	365.0	552.0	947.8	1,099.3	1,432.4	1,643.6	2,074.9	3,125.0	2,680.3	3,262.1
Other Items (Net)	37r	39.3	–88.4	–39.0	–24.5	–36.7	114.6	153.3	178.6	308.6	–104.9	217.9	522.2
Money plus Quasi-Money	35l	2,377.5	2,988.8	3,763.8	4,673.7	6,029.4	6,433.9	7,160.5	8,476.2	9,574.7	10,003.7	10,698.1	12,913.3

Namibia 728

		1992	1993	1994	1995	1996	1997	1998	1999	2000	2001	2002	2003
Other Banking Institutions					*Millions of Namibia Dollars: End of Period*								
Reserves...........................	40	138.4	43.1	.6	6.9	1.1	1.2	1.4	1.9	2.0	2.2	2.1	—
Claims on Central Government........	42a	3.0	6.0	31.0	5.1	140.0	166.4	151.9	209.5	34.3	138.5	164.0	—
Claims on Local Government...........	42b	5.8	6.1	5.5	5.3	5.3	5.2	5.1	5.0	4.9	4.6	4.6	4.7
Claims on Nonfin.Pub.Enterprises.....	42c	2.4	7.7	16.7	7.8	4.6	4.7	7.5	8.6	211.6	63.4	66.9	—
Claims on Private Sector.................	42d	1,003.8	1,148.7	1,374.3	1,519.6	1,352.9	1,402.5	1,623.6	1,799.5	2,091.8	2,498.7	2,656.5	1,659.6
Claims on Deposit Money Banks......	42e	—	95.8	116.8	164.1	91.3	160.6	118.8	167.6	121.5	151.6	90.9	125.3
Claims on Nonbank Financial Insts...	42g	7.0	16.6	8.7	9.7	8.0	17.7	18.1	14.6	12.9	12.9	12.7	16.2
Time, Savings,& Fgn.Currency Dep...	45	479.8	499.4	701.7	795.1	718.1	845.4	868.8	1,123.3	1,284.2	1,531.5	1,613.3	524.6
Money Market Instruments...............	46aa	153.1	223.8	190.9	180.3	234.6	197.8	182.5	45.8	45.4	44.4	34.9	189.0
Foreign Liabilities...............	46c	8.6	10.2	18.3	10.2	9.9	15.0	23.5	25.7	83.6	151.2	201.0	143.3
Central Government Deposits...........	46d	10.9	21.8	16.4	18.0	7.1	3.4	3.7	3.6	27.5	3.4	2.5	—
Credit from Deposit Money Banks....	46h	21.0	20.0	24.0	68.5	35.6	36.3	41.0	38.0	74.4	82.4	72.8	60.2
Capital Accounts...............	47a	563.2	634.2	763.1	821.2	792.2	894.7	960.2	1,099.9	1,237.3	1,325.0	1,349.3	1,118.7
Other Items (Net)...............	47r	−76.3	−85.6	−160.8	−174.9	−194.4	−234.3	−153.3	−129.5	−273.4	−266.0	−276.1	−230.0
Banking Survey					*Millions of Namibia Dollars: End of Period*								
Foreign Assets (Net)...............	51n	106.4	−120.8	−200.7	−325.5	111.2	895.2	1,355.2	2,272.0	2,656.4	2,400.4	1,568.6	392.8
Domestic Credit...............	52	3,576.0	4,489.6	5,606.2	7,049.1	8,345.1	8,380.8	9,205.5	10,089.8	11,595.1	13,269.5	14,986.4	18,019.2
Claims on Central Govt. (Net)...	52an	420.6	548.0	599.1	672.7	1,210.3	230.8	260.5	664.8	282.1	420.2	−80.6	774.0
Claims on Local Government..........	52b	20.9	21.1	22.7	24.5	23.9	22.6	23.9	21.3	17.2	37.4	10.3	19.3
Claims on Nonfin.Pub.Enterprises...	52c	44.5	49.8	58.8	79.9	76.7	153.6	150.2	145.2	445.7	182.4	225.0	144.3
Claims on Private Sector...............	52d	3,082.9	3,854.2	4,917.0	6,262.4	7,016.1	7,956.1	8,752.8	9,233.8	10,791.7	12,614.2	14,817.7	17,065.4
Claims on Nonbank Financial Inst..	52g	7.0	16.6	8.7	9.7	18.1	17.7	18.1	24.7	58.4	15.2	14.0	16.2
Liquid Liabilities...............	55l	2,718.9	3,445.1	4,464.9	5,461.9	6,746.4	7,278.2	8,027.9	9,597.6	10,856.9	11,533.0	12,309.3	13,437.9
Money Market Instruments...............	56aa	153.1	223.8	190.9	180.3	234.6	197.8	182.5	45.8	45.4	147.7	293.7	347.2
Bonds...............	56ab	2.4	3.9	4.1	4.1	8.9	7.0	5.5	—	—	—	—	—
Capital Accounts...............	57a	799.6	948.0	1,128.1	1,373.2	1,740.0	1,994.0	2,392.6	2,743.5	3,312.2	4,450.1	4,029.6	4,380.8
Other Items (Net)...............	57r	8.4	−252.0	−382.5	−295.9	−273.5	−201.0	−47.7	−25.1	37.0	−460.9	−77.5	246.1
Interest Rates							*Percent Per Annum*						
BoN Overdraft Rate...............	60	16.50	14.50	15.50	17.50	17.75	16.00	18.75	11.50	11.25	9.25	12.75	7.75
Money Market Rate...............	60b	13.87	10.83	10.25	13.08	15.00	15.41	17.14	13.17	9.19	9.53	10.46	10.03
Treasury Bill Rate...............	60c	13.88	12.16	11.35	13.91	15.25	15.69	17.24	13.28	10.26	9.29	11.00	10.51
Deposit Rate...............	60l	11.36	9.61	9.18	10.84	12.56	12.70	12.94	10.82	7.39	6.79	7.81	8.76
Lending Rate...............	60p	20.21	18.02	17.05	18.51	19.16	20.18	20.72	18.48	15.28	14.53	13.84	14.70
Government Bond Yield...............	61	15.44	13.94	14.63	16.11	15.48	14.70	15.10	14.90	13.81	11.39	12.86	12.72
Prices						*Index Numbers (2000=100): Period Averages*							
Consumer Prices...............	64	51.2	55.6	61.5	67.7	73.1	79.5	84.5	91.7	100.0	109.5	122.0	130.7
International Transactions							*Millions of Namibia Dollars*						
Exports...............	70	3,826	4,052	4,646	5,112	6,095	6,167	6,812	7,539	9,164	10,148	....	....
Imports, c.i.f..............	71	3,659	4,332	5,015	5,860	7,182	8,077	9,112	9,834	10,755	13,319	....	....
Imports, f.o.b...............	71.v	3,551	4,002	4,555	5,311	6,589	7,399	8,374	8,992	9,851	12,281	....	....

Namibia 728

		1992	1993	1994	1995	1996	1997	1998	1999	2000	2001	2002	2003
Balance of Payments		*Millions of US Dollars: Minus Sign Indicates Debit*											
Current Account, n.i.e.	78ald	49.8	110.2	85.3	175.9	115.8	90.4	161.8	159.0	254.8	16.7	79.1	270.6
Goods: Exports f.o.b.	78aad	1,311.3	1,293.1	1,320.4	1,418.4	1,403.7	1,343.3	1,278.3	1,196.8	1,309.5	1,147.0	1,071.6	1,260.2
Goods: Imports f.o.b.	78abd	−1,389.1	−1,335.0	−1,406.3	−1,548.2	−1,530.9	−1,615.0	−1,450.9	−1,401.3	−1,310.0	−1,349.0	−1,282.5	−1,726.0
Trade Balance	78acd	−77.8	−41.8	−85.8	−129.7	−127.1	−271.7	−172.6	−204.5	−.5	−202.0	−210.9	−465.9
Services: Credit	78add	169.8	228.1	259.0	315.3	337.4	380.1	327.0	323.5	184.4	257.0	236.6	360.4
Services: Debit	78aed	−510.5	−485.4	−468.3	−551.5	−580.9	−533.7	−456.9	−445.7	−332.6	−275.6	−223.8	−249.3
Balance on Goods & Services	78afd	−418.4	−299.0	−295.1	−365.9	−370.7	−425.2	−302.4	−326.7	−148.7	−220.7	−198.0	−354.7
Income: Credit	78agd	201.9	212.7	213.8	374.0	319.2	252.0	226.7	271.6	247.1	195.5	170.6	280.3
Income: Debit	78ahd	−185.4	−154.7	−159.8	−235.1	−249.0	−180.6	−165.9	−108.4	−226.3	−269.2	−133.9	−54.0
Balance on Gds, Serv. & Inc.	78aid	−402.0	−241.1	−241.1	−227.1	−300.5	−353.8	−241.6	−163.5	−127.9	−294.3	−161.4	−128.4
Current Transfers, n.i.e.: Credit	78ajd	476.6	373.2	349.2	426.9	437.3	462.2	418.2	380.9	419.6	346.7	270.4	426.2
Current Transfers: Debit	78akd	−24.9	−21.9	−22.7	−23.9	−21.0	−18.0	−14.7	−58.4	−37.0	−35.6	−29.9	−27.2
Capital Account, n.i.e.	78bcd	32.0	27.0	43.2	40.1	42.1	33.5	23.8	22.9	112.6	95.8	111.4	57.0
Capital Account, n.i.e.: Credit	78bad	32.7	27.6	43.8	40.7	42.5	33.9	24.2	23.2	112.9	96.0	111.6	57.3
Capital Account: Debit	78bbd	−.7	−.6	−.6	−.6	−.5	−.4	−.4	−.3	−.3	−.2	−.2	−.4
Financial Account, n.i.e.	78bjd	−121.2	−62.1	−102.1	−205.3	−174.0	−71.4	−145.6	−342.6	−498.8	−533.9	−369.0	−653.3
Direct Investment Abroad	78bdd	1.6	−8.7	6.1	3.5	21.7	−.7	2.2	.7	−1.7	12.5	4.7	10.8
Dir. Invest. in Rep. Econ., n.i.e.	78bed	118.2	55.3	98.0	153.0	128.7	91.0	96.2	1.6	118.9	36.1	51.2	33.3
Portfolio Investment Assets	78bfd	.9	15.5	−17.0	−5.1	−8.1	−14.6	−11.1	−26.8	−118.4	−180.2	−144.1	−217.4
Equity Securities	78bkd	−6.9	−4.9	−5.0	−3.8	−7.9	−14.6	−7.4	−18.6	−104.7	−173.2	−138.1	−208.9
Debt Securities	78bld	7.8	20.4	−12.0	−1.3	−.3	−	−3.6	−8.2	−13.7	−7.0	−6.0	−8.4
Portfolio Investment Liab., n.i.e.	78bgd	15.1	60.0	64.2	82.2	31.2	26.0	−4.4	40.7	34.7	25.9	8.2	3.9
Equity Securities	78bmd	6.0	1.1	37.5	45.7	51.2	28.8	18.1	40.7	34.7	25.9	8.2	3.9
Debt Securities	78bnd	9.0	58.9	26.7	36.5	−20.0	−2.8	−22.4	−	−	−	−	−
Financial Derivatives Assets	78bwd	....	....	....	....	....	....	....	....	....	....	....	....
Financial Derivatives Liabilities	78bxd	....	....	....	....	....	....	....	....	....	....	....	....
Other Investment Assets	78bhd	−231.9	−180.9	−301.0	−428.0	−411.2	−289.9	−175.5	−304.7	−502.3	−378.4	−247.2	−451.1
Monetary Authorities	78bod	....	....	....	....	....	....	....	....	....	....	....	....
General Government	78bpd	−6.0	−9.4	9.5	−1.4	−1.2	−1.1	−.9	−.8	−3.4	−2.8	−2.3	−3.9
Banks	78bqd	76.4	56.5	.1	14.8	−48.6	−40.6	−2.1	−54.2	−118.7	34.4	47.7	28.5
Other Sectors	78brd	−302.3	−228.0	−310.7	−441.5	−361.4	−248.2	−172.6	−249.7	−380.2	−410.0	−292.6	−475.7
Other Investment Liab., n.i.e.	78bid	−25.0	−3.3	47.6	−10.9	63.8	116.7	−53.1	−54.1	−30.1	−49.8	−41.8	−32.7
Monetary Authorities	78bsd	−	−	−	−	−	−	−	−	−	−	−	−
General Government	78btd	3.5	18.5	4.9	21.8	27.7	17.4	16.9	−.4	−2.1	−2.0	−2.4	−6.9
Banks	78bud	−14.5	18.4	66.8	4.9	−49.0	116.5	−28.5	−46.5	−6.3	−33.9	−13.9	−
Other Sectors	78bvd	−14.0	−40.2	−24.1	−37.7	85.0	−17.1	−41.4	−7.3	−21.7	−13.9	−25.5	−25.9
Net Errors and Omissions	78cad	32.8	16.2	48.5	13.4	39.1	15.3	15.7	−42.4	−62.8	28.6	−54.0	.2
Overall Balance	78cbd	−6.6	91.3	75.0	24.2	22.9	67.8	55.8	−203.0	−194.3	−392.8	−232.5	−325.5
Reserves and Related Items	79dad	6.6	−91.3	−75.0	−24.2	−22.9	−67.8	−55.8	203.0	194.3	392.8	232.5	325.5
Reserve Assets	79dbd	6.6	−91.3	−75.0	−24.2	−22.9	−67.8	−55.8	−57.1	−10.6	−70.7	−17.9	95.1
Use of Fund Credit and Loans	79dcd	−	−	−	−	−	−	−	−	−	−	−	−
Exceptional Financing	79ded	....	....	....	....	....	....	....	260.1	204.9	463.4	250.4	230.4
International Investment Position						*Millions of US Dollars*								
Assets	79aad	2,264.7	2,579.9	2,788.0	2,692.6	2,095.9	....	....	....	1,213.5	....	....	....
Direct Investment Abroad	79abd	81.6	79.2	15.8	14.8	13.0	....	....	....	44.9	....	....	....
Portfolio Investment	79acd	145.1	117.4	165.1	164.8	128.8	....	....	....	610.5	....	....	....
Equity Securities	79add	43.6	45.6	85.2	90.2	72.8	....	....	....	603.7	....	....	....
Debt Securities	79aed	101.5	71.8	79.9	74.6	56.0	....	....	....	6.8	....	....	....
Financial Derivatives	79ald	−	−	−	−	−	....	....	....	−	....	....	....
Other Investment	79afd	1,988.2	2,249.6	2,404.1	2,291.4	1,760.6	....	....	....	295.1	....	....	....
Monetary Authorities	79agd	−	−	−	−	−	....	....	....	−	....	....	....
General Government	79ahd	9.5	17.7	7.3	8.5	7.7	....	....	....	−	....	....	....
Banks	79aid	106.8	46.8	38.1	29.9	67.5	....	....	....	51.7	....	....	....
Other Sectors	79ajd	1,871.9	2,185.1	2,358.7	2,253.1	1,685.4	....	....	....	243.4	....	....	....
Reserve Assets	79akd	49.8	133.7	202.9	221.6	193.5	....	....	....	262.9	....	....	....
Liabilities	79lad	2,811.0	2,201.0	2,420.2	2,685.1	2,355.2	....	....	....	1,807.3	....	....	....
Dir. Invest. in Rep. Economy	79lbd	2,141.8	1,490.8	1,601.2	1,707.7	1,492.2	....	....	....	1,276.3	....	....	....
Portfolio Investment	79lcd	183.8	221.3	289.8	390.4	334.9	....	....	....	75.0	....	....	....
Equity Securities	79ldd	22.6	19.1	69.1	119.0	141.8	....	....	....	1.7	....	....	....
Debt Securities	79led	161.2	202.2	220.7	271.4	193.1	....	....	....	73.3	....	....	....
Financial Derivatives	79lld	−	−	−	−	−	....	....	....	−	....	....	....
Other Investment	79lfd	485.4	488.9	529.1	587.0	528.1	....	....	....	455.9	....	....	....
Monetary Authorities	79lgd	164.4	181.9	203.2	214.9	183.0	....	....	....	−	....	....	....
General Government	79lhd	8.5	25.3	29.9	51.5	46.8	....	....	....	129.2	....	....	....
Banks	79lid	70.8	82.7	143.9	134.1	136.0	....	....	....	70.1	....	....	....
Other Sectors	79ljd	241.7	199.0	152.1	186.4	162.3	....	....	....	256.6	....	....	....
Government Finance				*Millions of Namibia Dollars: Year Beginning April 1*									
Deficit (-) or Surplus	80	−435.0	−333.1	−195.3	−476.1	−891.1	−439.4	−749.2	−679.3	−849.7p	....	....	....
Revenue	81	2,855.4	3,039.8	3,610.8	4,028.7	4,611.5	5,591.7	6,094.7	7,184.9	7,765.3p	....	....	....
Grants Received	81z	73.5	54.9	38.4	44.9	50.3	54.0	37.4	68.4	128.7p	....	....	....
Expenditure	82	3,333.6	3,410.0	3,812.7	4,502.3	5,461.6	6,041.5	6,839.7	7,831.8	8,610.0p	....	....	....
Lending Minus Repayments	83	30.3	17.8	31.8	47.4	91.3	43.6	41.6	101.3	133.7p	....	....	....

Namibia 728

		1992	1993	1994	1995	1996	1997	1998	1999	2000	2001	2002	2003
National Accounts		\multicolumn{12}{c}{*Millions of Namibia Dollars*}
Househ.Cons.Expend.,incl.NPISHs	96f	4,476	5,493	6,355	7,189	8,653	10,160	11,185	12,239	14,120	15,829	....	....
Government Consumption Expend...	91f	2,868	2,938	3,267	3,839	4,551	5,064	5,556	6,265	6,819	7,562	....	....
Gross Fixed Capital Formation	93e	1,689	1,967	2,255	2,817	3,535	3,288	4,321	4,760	4,464	5,932	....	....
Changes in Inventories	93i	80	–436	252	–60	–65	92	518	57	171	418	....	....
Exports of Goods and Services	90c	4,317	4,828	5,599	6,288	7,593	7,961	8,637	9,548	10,680	11,462	....	....
Imports of Goods and Services (-)	98c	5,071	5,273	5,926	7,073	8,796	9,638	10,900	11,773	12,354	14,243	....	....
Gross Domestic Product (GDP)	99b	8,358	9,302	11,549	12,706	15,011	16,754	18,790	20,693	23,264	26,689	....	....
Statistical Discrepancy	99bs	....	–213	–253	–294	–459	–174	–528	–402	–634	–271	....	....
Net Primary Income from Abroad	98.n	42	184	182	569	310	305	484	–105	–356	2	....	....
Gross National Income (GNI)	99a	8,400	9,486	11,731	13,275	15,321	17,059	19,274	20,588	22,908	26,691	....	....
Net Current Transf.from Abroad	98t	....	1,104	1,099	1,393	1,750	1,929	2,243	2,543	3,006	3,026	....	....
Gross Nat'l Disposable Inc.(GNDI)	99i	....	10,590	12,830	14,669	17,071	18,988	21,516	23,130	25,914	29,718	....	....
Gross Saving	99s	....	2,159	3,208	3,641	3,867	3,764	4,775	4,626	4,975	6,327	....	....
Consumption of Fixed Capital	99cf	....	....	....	1,721	1,945	2,191	2,482	2,851	3,104	3,558	....	....
GDP Volume 1990 Prices	99b.p	7,274	7,128	....	....	....	....	....	....	....	....	....	....
GDP Volume 1995 Prices	99b.p	....	11,372	12,204	12,706	13,111	13,665	14,114	14,597	15,074	....	....	....
GDP Volume (2000=100)	99bvp	77.0	†75.4	81.0	84.3	87.0	90.7	93.6	96.8	100.0	....	....	....
GDP Deflator (2000=100)	99bip	46.7	53.0	61.3	64.8	74.2	79.4	86.3	91.9	100.0	....	....	....
		\multicolumn{12}{c}{*Millions: Midyear Estimates*}
Population	99z	1.51	1.55	1.60	1.65	1.70	1.75	1.80	1.85	1.89	1.93	1.96	1.99

2004, International Monetary Fund : *International Financial Statistics Yearbook*

Nepal 558

		1992	1993	1994	1995	1996	1997	1998	1999	2000	2001	2002	2003
Exchange Rates						**Rupees per SDR: End of Period**							
Market Rate	aa	59.400	67.634	72.817	83.243	82.007	85.408	95.288	94.326	96.806	96.108	106.450	110.021
						Rupees per US Dollar: End of Period (ae) Period Average (rf)							
Market Rate	ae	43.200	49.240	49.880	56.000	57.030	63.300	67.675	68.725	74.300	76.475	78.300	74.040
Market Rate	rf	42.718	48.607	49.398	51.890	56.692	58.010	65.976	68.239	71.094	74.949	77.877	76.141
Fund Position						**Millions of SDRs: End of Period**							
Quota	2f.s	52.0	52.0	52.0	52.0	52.0	52.0	52.0	71.3	71.3	71.3	71.3	71.3
SDRs	1b.s	.1	–	.1	–	–	.1	–	.2	–	.1	–	.5
Reserve Position in the Fund	1c.s	5.7	5.7	5.7	5.7	5.7	5.7	5.7	5.7	5.7	5.7	5.7	5.8
Total Fund Cred.&Loans Outstg	2tl	31.7	35.8	37.7	32.5	27.2	22.0	17.2	12.9	9.5	6.2	2.8	7.7
International Liquidity					**Millions of US Dollars Unless Otherwise Indicated: Data as of Middle of Month**								
Total Reserves minus Gold	1l.d	467.4	640.2	693.6	586.4	571.4	626.2	756.3	845.1	945.4	1,037.7	1,017.6	1,222.5
SDRs	1b.d	.2	–	.1	–	–	.1	–	.3	–	.1	–	.8
Reserve Position in the Fund	1c.d	7.9	7.9	8.4	8.5	8.2	7.7	8.1	7.9	7.5	7.2	7.8	8.6
Foreign Exchange	1d.d	459.4	632.3	685.1	577.9	563.1	618.4	748.2	836.9	937.9	1,030.4	1,009.8	1,213.1
Gold (Million Fine Troy Ounces)	1ad	.153	.153	.153	.153	.153	.153	.153	.153	.153	.153	.153	.153
Gold (National Valuation)	1and	6.5	6.5	6.5	6.5	6.5	6.5	6.5	6.5	6.5	6.5	6.5	6.5
Monetary Authorities: Other Liab	4..d	51.6	55.3	62.1	54.0	45.0	20.1	27.8	18.5	16.8	8.8	7.4	14.8
Deposit Money Banks: Assets	7a.d	151.0	129.9	161.6	208.9	218.1	246.1	299.0	345.3	459.9	335.8	324.8	284.5
Liabilities	7b.d	57.8	68.6	66.1	67.4	87.7	111.3	149.7	174.9	206.8	224.9	242.8	248.5
Monetary Authorities					**Millions of Rupees: Data as of Middle of Month**								
Foreign Assets	11	21,320	32,721	35,627	33,960	33,883	59,104	52,331	59,155	71,427	80,535	80,842	91,702
Claims on Central Government	12a	17,907	19,032	19,439	24,001	24,714	30,590	29,805	30,539	34,366	32,612	37,834	30,028
Claims on Private Sector	12d	501	544	503	547	895	1,460	1,356	1,460	1,478	1,856	2,569	1,751
Claims on Deposit Money Banks	12e	49	39	21	12	646	5	6	5	5	6	928	25
Claims on Other Financial Insts	12f	690	499	484	844	1,122	1,613	1,631	1,613	1,560	1,666	1,512	1,488
Reserve Money	14	19,817	25,783	28,792	31,266	34,368	55,371	50,203	55,371	66,062	74,012	73,924	76,063
of which: Currency Outside DMBs	14a	14,201	17,390	21,005	23,230	25,428	37,829	32,244	36,929	44,526	51,699	56,022	58,076
Private Sector Deposits	14d	897	1,307	1,097	1,396	1,358	4,346	2,287	4,346	3,160	3,570	2,350	2,557
Foreign Liabilities	16c	4,113	5,145	5,840	5,725	4,798	3,154	3,516	2,488	2,167	1,267	879	1,944
Central Government Deposits	16d	7,845	7,870	7,782	7,459	7,447	11,473	10,474	11,473	13,081	13,247	15,646	18,595
Capital Accounts	17a	8,259	10,633	12,077	15,982	16,128	22,881	21,545	22,953	25,752	27,982	31,650	31,331
Other Items (Net)	17r	433	3,403	1,584	−1,069	−1,481	−122	−610	472	1,759	167	1,587	−2,939
Deposit Money Banks					**Millions of Rupees: Data as of Middle of Month**								
Reserves	20	3,943	5,837	7,321	8,488	7,583	9,972	15,673	14,096	18,376	18,742	15,552	15,430
Foreign Assets	21	6,525	6,397	8,060	11,698	12,438	15,577	20,238	23,729	34,174	25,679	25,429	21,063
Claims on Central Government	22a	9,677	10,734	8,776	6,497	7,610	8,621	8,957	13,330	15,471	28,318	36,045	44,678
Claims on Nonfin.Pub.Enterprises	22c	1,144	1,954	1,621	1,721	1,713	1,459	993	1,438	1,909	1,911	3,573	2,704
Claims on Private Sector	22d	19,991	25,059	36,462	49,494	56,848	65,541	84,875	97,306	114,913	....	....	....
Claims on Other Financial Insts	22f	29	29	29	211	4,023	4,668	530	5,915	7,419	8,144	8,673	9,667
Demand Deposits	24	5,331	6,622	8,422	8,927	8,758	9,090	10,979	13,832	15,343	....	....	....
Time and Savings Deposits	25	28,888	36,218	42,172	50,490	58,744	70,555	89,850	109,521	132,550	145,946	152,019	171,641
Foreign Liabilities	26c	2,498	3,380	3,297	3,776	5,003	7,048	10,134	12,020	15,367	17,202	19,015	18,398
Credit from Monetary Authorities	26g	49	39	21	12	646	6	6	6	45	6	928	25
Other Items (Net)	27r	4,543	3,749	8,356	14,906	17,063	19,138	20,297	20,435	28,958	....	....	....
Monetary Survey					**Millions of Rupees: Data as of Middle of Month**								
Foreign Assets (Net)	31n	21,234	30,592	34,550	36,158	36,519	64,479	58,918	68,376	88,067	87,745	86,377	92,423
Domestic Credit	32	42,101	49,986	59,539	75,863	89,486	102,486	117,680	140,135	164,043	....	....	....
Claims on Central Govt. (Net)	32an	19,739	21,895	20,433	23,039	24,877	27,738	28,287	32,396	36,757	47,682	58,234	56,111
Claims on Nonfin.Pub.Enterprises	32c	1,152	1,961	1,628	1,729	1,720	1,466	1,000	1,446	1,917	1,918	3,581	2,712
Claims on Private Sector	32d	20,492	25,602	36,965	50,041	57,742	67,001	86,231	98,766	116,391	....	....	....
Claims on Other Financial Insts	32f	719	527	513	1,054	5,145	6,281	2,161	7,528	8,978	9,810	10,185	11,155
Money	34	20,428	25,320	30,524	33,553	35,544	51,265	45,509	55,107	63,028	....	....	....
Quasi-Money	35	28,888	36,218	42,172	50,490	58,744	70,555	89,850	109,521	132,550	145,946	152,019	171,641
Other Items (Net)	37r	14,019	19,041	21,393	27,979	31,717	45,130	41,239	43,868	56,517	....	....	....
Money plus Quasi-Money	35l	49,316	61,538	72,696	84,043	94,288	121,820	135,359	164,628	195,578	....	....	....
Interest Rates					**Percent Per Annum: Data as of Middle of Month**								
Discount Rate	60	13.00	11.00	11.00	11.00	11.00	9.00	9.00	9.00	7.50	6.50	5.50	5.50
Treasury Bill Rate	60c	9.00	4.50	6.50	9.90	11.51	2.52	3.70	4.30	5.30	5.00	3.80	3.85
Deposit Rate	60l	....	....	8.75	....	9.63	9.79	8.92	7.31	5.96	4.75	....	....
Lending Rate	60p	....	....	....	....	12.88	14.54	14.00	11.33	9.46	7.67	....	....
Government Bond Yield	61	13.33	....	9.00	3.00	9.00	9.00	9.00	8.75	8.50	8.50	8.25	7.50
Prices					**Index Numbers (2000=100): Period Averages**								
Consumer Prices	64	57.3	61.6	66.8	71.9	78.5	†81.6	90.8	97.6	100.0	102.7	105.8	111.8
International Transactions					**Millions of Rupees**								
Exports	70	15,706	18,676	17,896	17,895	21,830	23,555	31,288	41,088	57,231	55,221	44,184	50,450
Imports, c.i.f	71	33,157	43,267	57,072	69,028	79,247	97,974	81,901	97,057	111,800	110,362	110,552	133,539

2004, International Monetary Fund: *International Financial Statistics Yearbook*

Nepal 558

		1992	1993	1994	1995	1996	1997	1998	1999	2000	2001	2002	2003
Balance of Payments		*Millions of US Dollars: Minus Sign Indicates Debit*											
Current Account, n.i.e.	78ald	−181.3	−222.5	−351.9	−356.4	−326.6	−388.1	−67.2	−256.5	−298.7	−339.3	....	....
Goods: Exports f.o.b.	78aad	376.3	397.0	368.7	349.9	388.7	413.8	482.0	612.3	776.1	720.5	....	....
Goods: Imports f.o.b.	78abd	−752.1	−858.6	−1,158.9	−1,310.8	−1,494.7	−1,691.9	−1,239.1	−1,494.2	−1,590.1	−1,485.7	....	....
Trade Balance	78acd	−375.8	−461.6	−790.3	−961.0	−1,105.9	−1,278.1	−757.1	−881.9	−814.0	−765.2	....	....
Services: Credit	78add	273.8	333.2	579.2	679.0	757.5	865.7	565.1	655.1	505.9	413.3	....	....
Services: Debit	78aed	−225.0	−251.8	−296.6	−313.3	−242.8	−224.5	−196.2	−212.5	−199.9	−214.7	....	....
Balance on Goods & Services	78afd	−327.0	−380.2	−507.6	−595.2	−591.3	−637.0	−388.1	−439.2	−508.0	−566.6	....	....
Income: Credit	78agd	33.5	28.9	34.6	43.6	33.1	31.9	45.4	55.8	72.2	70.3	....	....
Income: Debit	78ahd	−16.8	−23.7	−30.8	−34.9	−32.0	−28.6	−26.5	−28.4	−35.2	−58.8	....	....
Balance on Gds, Serv. & Inc.	78aid	−310.3	−375.0	−503.9	−586.5	−590.2	−633.7	−369.2	−411.9	−471.0	−555.2	....	....
Current Transfers, n.i.e.: Credit	78ajd	133.6	155.5	160.7	239.2	281.6	267.4	326.0	182.3	189.0	240.2	....	....
Current Transfers: Debit	78akd	−4.6	−3.0	−8.7	−9.1	−18.0	−21.8	−24.1	−26.9	−16.7	−24.3	....	....
Capital Account, n.i.e.	78bcd	−	−	−	−	−	−	−	−	−	−	....	....
Capital Account, n.i.e.: Credit	78bad	−	−	−	−	−	−	−	−	−	−	....	....
Capital Account: Debit	78bbd	−	−	−	−	−	−	−	−	−	−	....	....
Financial Account, n.i.e.	78bjd	335.9	283.5	407.3	368.5	275.2	340.3	212.9	−24.5	76.1	−216.9	....	....
Direct Investment Abroad	78bdd	−	−	−	−	−	−	−	−	−	−	....	....
Dir. Invest. in Rep. Econ., n.i.e.	78bed	−	−	−	−	19.2	23.1	12.0	−	−	−	....	....
Portfolio Investment Assets	78bfd	−	−	−	−	−	−	−	−	−	−	....	....
Equity Securities	78bkd	−	−	−	−	−	−	−	−	−	−	....	....
Debt Securities	78bld	−	−	−	−	−	−	−	−	−	−	....	....
Portfolio Investment Liab., n.i.e.	78bgd	−	−	−	−	−	−	−	−	−	−	....	....
Equity Securities	78bmd	−	−	−	−	−	−	−	−	−	−	....	....
Debt Securities	78bnd	−	−	−	−	−	−	−	−	−	−	....	....
Financial Derivatives Assets	78bwd	....	....	....	....	....	....	....	....	....	....	....	....
Financial Derivatives Liabilities	78bxd	....	....	....	....	....	....	....	....	....	....	....	....
Other Investment Assets	78bhd	182.3	149.6	159.2	264.4	91.6	89.4	90.8	48.2	128.6	11.2	....	....
Monetary Authorities	78bod	....	....	....	....	....	....	....	−	−	....	....	....
General Government	78bpd	−	−	−	−	−	−	−	−	−	−	....	....
Banks	78bqd	−	−	−	−	−	−	−	−	−	−	....	....
Other Sectors	78brd	182.3	149.6	159.2	264.4	91.6	89.4	90.8	48.2	128.6	11.2	....	....
Other Investment Liab., n.i.e.	78bid	153.7	133.9	248.0	104.1	164.5	227.8	110.0	−72.8	−52.6	−228.0	....	....
Monetary Authorities	78bsd	1.5	−4.0	4.3	.1	−3.3	1.0	.4	−2.0	4.5	−3.5	....	....
General Government	78btd	130.1	125.7	237.5	106.8	128.4	165.9	151.8	−56.2	−61.0	−63.5	....	....
Banks	78bud	22.1	11.7	5.4	−4.5	38.2	68.8	17.0	13.2	67.4	3.2	....	....
Other Sectors	78bvd	−	.4	.8	1.7	1.2	−7.8	−59.1	−27.8	−63.5	−164.3	....	....
Net Errors and Omissions	78cad	.8	4.6	7.1	2.8	82.3	216.6	134.0	58.3	145.7	256.5	....	....
Overall Balance	78cbd	155.4	65.6	62.5	15.0	30.9	168.8	279.7	−222.7	−77.0	−299.6	....	....
Reserves and Related Items	79dad	−155.4	−65.6	−62.5	−15.0	−30.9	−168.8	−279.7	222.7	77.0	299.6	....	....
Reserve Assets	79dbd	−162.3	−71.4	−65.0	−7.0	−23.4	−161.7	−273.0	−144.4	−291.0	−5.2	....	....
Use of Fund Credit and Loans	79dcd	6.9	5.8	2.5	−8.0	−7.5	−7.2	−6.6	−5.9	−4.4	−4.3	....	....
Exceptional Financing	79ded	−	−	−	....	....	....	....	373.0	372.4	309.1	....	....
Government Finance		*Millions of Rupees: Year Ending July 15*											
Deficit (−) or Surplus	80	−10,054	−10,359	−7,463	−7,894	−10,976	−10,908	−13,846	−13,349	−12,454	−18,498	−16,506	−11,391
Revenue	81	13,012	14,316	18,862	23,206	26,643	29,346	31,494	34,814	40,491	46,607	48,326	53,657
Grants Received	81z	1,644	3,793	2,394	3,937	4,825	5,988	5,403	4,337	5,712	6,753	6,686	8,372
Expenditure	82	25,134	29,180	29,309	36,242	43,520	47,073	51,963	54,720	60,794	73,905	73,394	74,715
Lending Minus Repayments	83	−424	−712	−590	−1,205	−1,076	−831	−1,220	−2,220	−2,137	−2,047	−1,876	−1,295
Financing													
Net Borrowing: Domestic	84a	4,179	4,691	−233	2,410	3,500	3,967	5,572	4,693	4,323	10,954	10,558	7,937
Foreign	85a	5,875	5,668	7,696	5,484	7,476	6,941	8,274	8,656	8,131	7,544	2,948	3,454
Use of Cash Balances	87	−	−	−	−	−	−	−	−	−	−	−	−
Debt: Domestic	88a	23,235	24,456	30,631	32,058	34,242	35,891	38,407	49,670	54,357	60,044	73,621	81,703
Foreign	89a	70,924	87,421	101,967	113,000	128,044	132,087	161,208	173,861	190,691	201,551	220,126	221,992
National Accounts		*Millions of Rupees: Year Ending July 15*											
Househ.Cons.Expend.,incl.NPISHs	96f	121,370	133,314	154,009	166,443	191,469	216,364	231,392	264,944	287,947	309,107	329,199	355,535
Government Consumption Expend	91f	11,908	14,900	15,987	20,267	23,018	24,987	28,015	30,529	33,964	40,150	42,327	46,653
Gross Fixed Capital Formation	93e	29,277	37,278	42,032	48,370	56,081	60,794	65,375	65,269	73,324	78,013	81,613	86,963
Changes in Inventories	93i	2,342	2,375	2,612	6,861	11,936	10,290	9,353	4,792	18,948	20,784	20,056	30,542
Exports of Goods and Services	90c	23,909	30,948	47,548	53,084	55,405	73,853	68,659	78,150	88,360	91,821	77,068	75,764
Imports of Goods and Services (−)	98c	39,321	47,429	62,972	75,850	88,996	105,775	101,949	101,648	123,055	129,104	127,961	140,522
Gross Domestic Product (GDP)	99b	149,485	171,386	199,216	219,175	248,913	280,513	300,845	342,036	379,488	410,789	422,301	454,934
GDP Volume 1994/95 Prices	99b.p	183,371	188,780	204,397	209,976	221,930	233,040	240,816	251,758	267,096	279,750	278,848	286,480
GDP Volume (2000=100)	99bvp	68.7	70.7	76.5	78.6	83.1	87.2	90.2	94.3	100.0	104.7	104.4	107.3
GDP Deflator (2000=100)	99bip	57.4	63.9	68.6	73.5	78.9	84.7	87.9	95.6	100.0	103.4	106.6	111.8
		Millions: Midyear Estimates											
Population	99z	19.52	19.98	20.45	20.94	21.43	21.94	22.46	22.98	23.52	24.06	24.61	25.16

2004, International Monetary Fund : *International Financial Statistics Yearbook*

Netherlands 138

		1992	1993	1994	1995	1996	1997	1998	1999	2000	2001	2002	2003
Exchange Rates													
		Guilders per SDR through 1998, Euros per SDR Thereafter: End of Period											
Market Rate	aa	2.4944	2.6659	2.5330	2.3849	2.5072	2.7217	2.6595	1.3662	1.4002	1.4260	1.2964	1.1765
		Guilders per US Dollar through 1998, Euros per US Dollar Thereafter: End of Period (ae) Period Average (rf)											
Market Rate	ae	1.8141	1.9409	1.7351	1.6044	1.7436	2.0172	1.8888	.9954	1.0747	1.1347	.9536	.7918
Market Rate	rf	1.7585	1.8573	1.8200	1.6057	1.6859	1.9513	1.9837	.9386	1.0854	1.1175	1.0626	.8860
		Guilders per ECU: End of Period (ea) Period Average (eb)											
ECU Rate	ea	2.1925	2.1670	2.1280	2.0554	2.1665	2.2280	2.2037	....	....	....	....	....
ECU Rate	eb	2.2725	2.1723	2.1528	2.0774	2.1113	2.2048	2.2227	....	....	....	....	....
		Index Numbers (2000=100): Period Averages											
Market Rate (1995=100)	ahx	91.4	86.4	88.3	100.0	95.2	82.3	81.0	....	....	....	....	....
Nominal Effective Exchange Rate	neu	104.4	107.6	108.0	112.3	110.1	105.0	104.9	103.5	100.0	100.6	101.4	104.9
Real Effective Exchange Rate	reu	103.6	106.0	107.0	109.6	106.4	101.6	102.9	102.3	100.0	102.0	104.9	108.5
Fund Position													
		Millions of SDRs: End of Period											
Quota	2f.s	3,444	3,444	3,444	3,444	3,444	3,444	3,444	5,162	5,162	5,162	5,162	5,162
SDRs	1b.s	403	424	442	616	566	586	644	742	501	598	513	523
Reserve Position in the Fund	1c.s	834	795	802	1,169	1,275	1,625	2,113	1,880	1,524	1,872	2,095	2,055
of which: Outstg.Fund Borrowing	2c	–	–	–	–	–	–	193	–	–	–	–	–
International Liquidity													
		Millions of US Dollars Unless Otherwise Indicated: End of Period											
Total Res.Min.Gold (Eurosys.Def)	1l.d	21,937	31,344	34,532	33,714	26,767	24,865	21,418	†9,886	9,643	9,034	9,563	11,012
SDRs	1b.d	554	583	645	916	814	791	907	1,019	653	752	697	778
Reserve Position in the Fund	1c.d	1,147	1,092	1,171	1,738	1,834	2,193	2,975	2,580	1,986	2,352	2,849	3,054
Foreign Exchange	1d.d	20,237	29,669	32,716	31,060	24,119	21,881	17,536	6,287	7,004	5,930	6,017	7,180
o/w:Fin.Deriv.Rel.to Reserves	1ddd	....	....	....	....	....	....	....	−319.46	10.24	79.32	−45.09	−174.29
Other Reserve Assets	1e.d	....	....	....	....	....	....	....	–	–	–	–	–
Gold (Million Fine Troy Ounces)	1ad	43.94	35.05	34.77	34.77	34.77	27.07	33.83	31.57	29.32	28.44	27.38	25.00
Gold (Eurosystem Valuation)	1and	13,712	7,639	8,477	9,168	8,622	5,801	7,299	9,164	8,046	7,863	9,385	10,430
Memo:Euro Cl. on Non-EA Res	1dgd	....	....	....	....	....	....	....	817	135	170	500	346
Non-Euro Cl. on EA Res	1dhd	....	....	....	....	....	....	....	1,195	491	1,355	1,516	1,465
Mon. Auth.: Other Foreign Assets	3..d	....	....	....	....	....	....	....	–	–	–	–	–
Foreign Liabilities	4..d	38	152	263	141	79	64	725	†542	115	45	737	1,221
Banking Insts.: Foreign Assets	7a.d	190,591	195,752	200,374	234,141	238,726	263,592	....	†155,624	163,895	211,400	256,244	308,245
Foreign Liab.	7b.d	165,530	169,204	186,977	220,964	245,746	290,784	....	†194,072	206,125	250,057	305,752	328,222
Monetary Authorities													
		Billions of Guilders through 1998; Billions of Euros Beginning 1999: End of Period											
Fgn. Assets (Cl.on Non-EA Ctys)	11	65.61	76.24	75.69	69.77	62.72	62.96	55.75	20.63	19.64	20.18	19.46	17.94
Claims on General Government	12a.u	....	....	....	....	....	....	....	7.58	8.63	7.71	7.41	7.97
o/w: Claims on Gen.Govt.in Cty	12a	6.15	4.14	4.12	4.20	4.47	4.74	4.90	1.73	1.53	1.90	.72	.41
Claims on Banking Institutions	12e.u	....	....	....	....	....	....	....	22.76	11.98	7.96	16.18	20.71
o/w: Claims on Bank.Inst.in Cty	12e	5.35	4.46	8.26	9.97	16.05	11.37	18.68	9.88	9.20	3.71	10.07	15.80
Claims on Other Resident Sectors	12d.u	....	....	....	....	....	....	....	.31	.40	.49	.52	.46
o/w: Cl. on Oth.Res.Sect.in Cty	12d	1.25	.60	.35	.35	.28	.22	.22	.12	.09	.10	.07	.04
Currency Issued	14a	39.89	40.41	40.93	41.30	41.67	42.10	40.90	18.98	18.73	11.39	19.36	21.90
Liabilities to Banking Insts	14c.u	....	....	....	....	....	....	....	20.70	9.40	12.05	12.43	13.69
o/w: Liabs to Bank.Inst.in Cty	14c	12.52	15.82	18.74	11.09	8.39	13.06	17.16	7.52	9.38	10.21	8.47	12.67
Demand Dep. of Other Res.Sect	14d.u	....	....	....	....	....	....	....	–	–	.01	.01	–
o/w:D.Dep.of Oth.Res.Sect.in Cty	14d	.08	.13	.10	.02	.06	.06	.14	–	–	.01	.01	–
Other Dep. of Other Res.Sect	15..u	....	....	....	....	....	....	....	–	–	–	–	–
o/w:O.Dep.of Oth.Res.Sect.in Cty	15	....	....	....	....	....	....	....	–	–	–	–	–
Bonds & Money Mkt. Instruments	16n.u	....	....	....	....	....	....	....	....	....	....	....	....
o/w: Held by Resid.of Cty	16n	....	....	....	....	....	....	....	....	....	....	....	....
Foreign Liab. (to Non-EA Ctys)	16c	.07	.30	.46	.23	.14	.13	1.37	.54	.12	.05	.70	.97
Central Government Deposits	16d.u	....	....	....	....	....	....	....	.01	.04	.02	–	.04
o/w: Cent.Govt.Dep. in Cty	16d	3.13	7.99	9.61	14.84	14.44	.09	5.10	.01	.04	.02	–	.04
Capital Accounts	17a	23.53	21.79	20.06	17.21	19.65	24.96	17.09	12.99	14.53	15.02	13.22	12.48
Other Items (Net)	17r	−.85	−1.00	−1.47	−.39	−.83	−1.10	−2.21	−1.95	−2.18	−2.20	−2.14	−1.28
Memo: Net Claims on Eurosystem	12e.s	....	....	....	....	....	....	....	−1.25	2.16	.32	.14	2.03
Currency Put into Circ.	14m	....	....	....	....	....	....	....	....	....	....	17.47	21.04

Netherlands 138

		1992	1993	1994	1995	1996	1997	1998	1999	2000	2001	2002	2003
Banking Institutions		\multicolumn{12}{c}{*Billions of Guilders through 1998; Billions of Euros Beginning 1999: End of Period*}
Claims on Monetary Authorities	20	2.88	2.81	2.80	3.09	3.38	3.36	....	7.14	9.24	9.68	8.37	12.54
Claims on Bk.Inst.in Oth.EA Ctys	20b.u	....	....	....	....	....	....	....	64.46	65.38	76.53	75.42	95.89
Fgn. Assets (Cl.on Non-EA Ctys)	21	345.75	379.94	347.67	375.66	416.24	531.72	....	154.91	176.14	239.87	244.34	244.06
Claims on General Government	22a.u	....	....	....	....	....	....	....	110.03	106.62	105.40	119.55	127.46
o/w: Claims on Gen.Govt.in Cty	22a	119.36	124.93	129.20	133.64	136.46	140.36	....	65.24	56.43	53.75	55.91	58.90
Claims on Other Resident Sectors	22d.u	....	....	....	....	....	....	....	496.17	577.35	627.59	679.84	737.66
o/w: Cl. on Oth.Res.Sect.in Cty	22d	485.59	518.79	559.34	626.83	698.86	788.56	....	484.02	560.82	605.67	656.64	705.80
Demand Deposits	24..u	....	....	....	....	....	....	....	118.42	131.89	150.97	152.52	156.22
o/w:D.Dep.of Oth.Res.Sect.in Cty	24	98.00	111.92	114.04	134.71	155.58	170.49	....	115.67	128.40	147.78	148.89	151.96
Other Deposits	25..u	....	....	....	....	....	....	....	242.68	270.83	295.28	307.65	342.17
o/w:O.Dep.of Oth.Res.Sect.in Cty	25	342.32	355.15	353.92	363.23	372.14	395.16	....	228.50	257.67	278.65	292.82	327.29
Money Market Fund Shares	26m.u	....	....	....	....	....	....	....	–	–	–	–	–
Bonds & Money Mkt. Instruments	26n.u	....	....	....	....	....	....	....	154.93	172.70	207.03	225.67	250.25
o/w: Held by Resid.of Cty	26n	150.11	154.41	169.53	187.19	193.55	196.41	....	....	....	....	....	....
Foreign Liab. (to Non-EA Ctys)	26c	300.29	328.41	324.42	354.51	428.48	586.57	....	193.18	221.52	283.74	291.55	259.88
Central Government Deposits	26d.u	....	....	....	....	....	....	....	1.93	.96	1.30	1.18	2.06
o/w: Cent.Govt.Dep. in Cty	26d	1.14	1.32	.79	1.02	1.51	1.82	....	1.92	.94	1.23	1.18	1.04
Credit from Monetary Authorities	26g	6.65	4.06	7.92	10.15	13.10	14.69	....	10.21	9.97	4.19	10.60	16.66
Liab. to Bk.Inst.in Oth. EA Ctys	26h.u	....	....	....	....	....	....	....	54.32	50.71	55.98	74.46	110.67
Capital Accounts	27a	48.84	54.30	57.52	61.65	78.17	86.89	....	47.70	58.33	60.75	63.73	63.28
Other Items (Net)	27r	6.24	16.90	10.88	26.74	12.40	11.97	....	9.34	17.81	–.16	.17	16.43
Banking Survey (Nat'l Residency)		\multicolumn{12}{c}{*Billions of Guilders through 1998; Billions of Euros Beginning 1999: End of Period*}
Foreign Assets (Net)	31n	111.01	127.48	98.48	90.68	50.34	7.98	....	43.19	54.60	64.91	57.26	86.68
Domestic Credit	32	608.08	639.15	682.62	749.16	824.11	931.97	....	549.19	617.88	660.17	712.16	764.08
Claims on General Govt. (Net)	32an	121.24	119.75	122.92	121.98	124.98	143.19	....	65.05	56.97	54.40	55.45	58.23
Claims on Other Resident Sectors	32d	486.84	519.40	559.69	627.18	699.13	788.78	....	484.14	560.91	605.77	656.71	705.84
Currency Issued	34a.n	39.89	40.41	40.93	41.30	41.67	42.10	40.90	18.98	18.73	11.39	19.36	21.90
Demand Deposits	34b.n	98.08	112.05	114.14	134.74	155.65	170.50	....	115.67	128.40	147.78	148.90	151.96
Other Deposits	35..n	342.32	355.15	353.92	363.23	372.14	395.16	....	228.50	257.67	278.65	292.82	327.29
Money Market Fund Shares	36m	....	....	....	....	....	....	....	–	–	–	–	–
Bonds & Money Mkt. Instruments	36n	150.11	154.41	169.53	187.19	193.55	196.41	....	154.93	172.70	207.03	225.67	250.25
o/w: Over Two Years	36na								134.74	152.76	175.59	188.59	216.71
Capital Accounts	37a	72.37	76.09	77.58	78.86	97.82	111.85	17.09	60.69	72.86	75.77	76.94	75.75
Other Items (Net)	37r	16.33	28.51	25.01	34.52	13.62	23.88	....	13.59	22.10	4.45	5.74	24.31
Banking Survey (EA-Wide Residency)		\multicolumn{12}{c}{*Billions of Euros: End of Period*}
Foreign Assets (Net)	31n.u	....	....	....	....	....	....	....	–18.19	–25.87	–23.74	–28.45	1.15
Domestic Credit	32..u	....	....	....	....	....	....	....	612.15	692.00	739.87	806.14	871.45
Claims on General Govt. (Net)	32anu	....	....	....	....	....	....	....	115.67	114.25	111.79	125.78	133.33
Claims on Other Resident Sect.	32d.u	....	....	....	....	....	....	....	496.48	577.75	628.09	680.36	738.12
Currency Issued	34a.u	....	....	....	....	....	....	....	18.98	18.73	11.39	19.36	21.90
Demand Deposits	34b.u	....	....	....	....	....	....	....	118.42	131.89	150.98	152.53	156.22
Other Deposits	35..u	....	....	....	....	....	....	....	242.68	270.83	295.28	307.65	342.17
o/w: Other Dep. Over Two Yrs.	35abu	....	....	....	....	....	....	....	57.62	66.15	62.84	62.99	63.58
Money Market Fund Shares	36m.u	....	....	....	....	....	....	....	–	–	–	–	–
Bonds & Money Mkt. Instruments	36n.u	....	....	....	....	....	....	....	154.93	172.70	207.03	225.67	250.25
o/w: Over Two Years	36nau								134.74	152.76	175.59	188.59	216.71
Capital Accounts	37a	....	....	....	....	....	....	....	60.69	72.86	75.77	76.94	75.75
Other Items (Net)	37r.u	....	....	....	....	....	....	....	–1.74	–.89	–24.31	–4.45	27.01
Money (National Definitions)		\multicolumn{12}{c}{*Billions of Guilders: End of Period*}
M3H	39m	432.15	465.08	466.02	486.57	514.99	553.24	....	....	....	....	....	....
M3H, Seasonally Adjusted	39m.c	434.02	474.64	469.75	489.45	515.51	553.72	....	....	....	....	....	....
Nonbank Financial Institutions		\multicolumn{12}{c}{*Billions of Guilders: End of Period*}
Cash	40..l	10.06	13.77	10.87	10.99	11.58	11.90	11.81	....	....	....	....	....
Foreign Assets	41..l	83.26	108.54	115.34	145.81	188.36	271.83	380.97	....	....	....	....	....
Claims on Central Government	42a.l	151.57	153.09	161.40	175.66	190.88	192.82	181.40	....	....	....	....	....
Claims on Local Government	42b.l	28.49	30.88	31.81	31.55	30.19	27.52	25.53	....	....	....	....	....
Claims on Private Sector	42d.l	291.20	326.30	346.67	369.32	411.29	457.37	501.60	....	....	....	....	....
Real Estate	42h.l	58.34	59.45	59.78	60.40	63.96	64.18	66.41	....	....	....	....	....
Capital Accounts	47a.l	604.65	673.25	702.32	767.87	871.78	994.43	1,138.09	....	....	....	....	....
Other Items (Net)	47r.l	18.27	18.79	23.56	25.85	24.49	31.19	29.64	....	....	....	....	....
Interest Rates		\multicolumn{12}{c}{*Percent Per Annum*}
Discount Rate (End of Period)	60	7.75	5.00	....	....	....	....	....	....	....	....	....	....
Rate on Advances	60a	8.33	5.52	4.50	2.98	2.00	2.75	2.75	....	....	....	....	....
Money Market Rate	60b	9.27	7.10	5.14	4.22	2.89	3.07	3.21	....	....	....	....	....
Treasury Bill Rate	60c	....	....	....	....	....	....	....	....	....	....	....	....
Deposit Rate	60l	3.20	3.11	†4.70	4.40	3.54	3.18	3.10	2.74	2.89	3.10	2.77	2.49
Lending Rate	60p	12.75	10.40	8.29	7.21	5.90	6.13	6.50	†3.46	4.79	5.00	3.96	3.00
Government Bond Yield	61	8.10	6.51	7.20	7.20	6.49	5.81	4.87	4.92	5.51	5.17	5.00	4.18

Netherlands 138

		1992	1993	1994	1995	1996	1997	1998	1999	2000	2001	2002	2003
Prices, Production, Labor					*Index Numbers (2000=100): Period Averages*								
Share Prices: General..................	62	20.1	22.9	28.1	29.9	38.0	56.7	74.5	84.7	100.0	81.9	63.1	45.7
Manufacturing..................	62a	20.7	24.2	29.4	31.3	39.4	60.1	75.9	82.7	100.0	82.3	63.2	....
Prices: Final Products..................	63	89.2	89.3	89.7	91.1	92.9	94.6	94.4	95.4	100.0	103.0	103.8	105.3
Consumer Prices..................	64	83.4	85.5	87.9	†89.8	91.6	93.6	95.4	97.5	100.0	104.5	†108.2	110.4
Harmonized CPI..................	64h	....	....	....	91.1	92.4	94.1	95.8	97.7	100.0	105.1	109.2	111.6
Wages: Hourly Rates..................	65	81.5	84.2	85.7	86.6	88.1	90.8	93.7	96.4	100.0	104.2	108.0	110.8
Industrial Production..................	66	87.3	86.3	90.5	90.9	93.1	93.3	95.3	96.6	100.0	100.5	99.5	97.5
					*Number in Thousands: Period Averages*								
Labor Force..................	67d	6,296	6,406	6,466	6,596	6,686	6,832	6,941	7,069	7,187	7,314	7,427	7,510
Employment..................	67e	†5,574	5,567	5,591	6,288	6,441	6,638	6,881	7,113	7,286	7,451	7,505	7,462
Unemployment..................	67c	336	415	486	464	440	375	286	221	188	146	174	251
Unemployment Rate (%)..................	67r	5.3	6.5	7.6	†7.0	6.6	5.5	4.1	3.1	2.6	2.0	2.3	3.4
International Transactions					*Millions of Guilders through 1998; Millions of Euros Beginning 1999*								
Exports..................	70	246,541	258,343	282,209	314,693	332,920	380,018	398,686	†188,046	226,903	241,300	235,383	228,745
Imports, c.i.f..................	71	236,597	231,637	256,442	283,538	304,559	347,286	371,760	†176,115	215,459	217,631	205,154	205,525
					*2000=100*								
Volume of Exports..................	72	55.8	59.8	†66.3	72.0	†75.2	81.9	87.9	92.0	100.0	100.2	101.9	105.1
Volume of Imports..................	73	56.9	59.4	†65.1	72.9	†76.4	81.4	89.2	95.7	100.0	101.0	94.5	100.4
Unit Value of Exports..................	74	88.2	85.4	†85.7	87.3	†87.5	93.0	89.9	87.6	100.0	103.4	97.1	93.2
Unit Value of Imports..................	75	91.1	85.5	†85.5	85.7	†86.5	91.7	89.4	89.3	100.0	102.6	100.8	95.1
Balance of Payments					*Millions of US Dollars: Minus Sign Indicates Debit*								
Current Account, n.i.e..................	78ald	6,847	13,203	17,294	25,773	21,502	25,077	13,031	12,996	6,817	7,830	10,116	16,467
Goods: Exports f.o.b..................	78aad	137,332	127,876	141,810	195,600	195,079	188,988	196,041	195,691	204,410	204,507	206,887	253,110
Goods: Imports f.o.b..................	78abd	−125,024	−110,972	−123,124	−171,788	−172,312	−168,051	−175,611	−179,657	−186,983	−183,667	−186,943	−226,540
Trade Balance..................	78acd	12,309	16,904	18,686	23,812	22,767	20,937	20,430	16,034	17,427	20,840	19,944	26,570
Services: Credit..................	78add	38,274	37,923	41,523	45,917	47,237	48,975	49,760	49,210	49,318	51,211	56,011	64,958
Services: Debit..................	78aed	−38,451	−38,004	−41,303	−44,770	−45,278	−45,699	−47,285	−49,471	−51,337	−53,717	−57,190	−65,966
Balance on Goods & Services.......	78afd	12,131	16,823	18,905	24,959	24,726	24,213	22,906	15,772	15,408	18,335	18,765	25,563
Income: Credit..................	78agd	27,230	28,117	29,466	35,755	36,297	39,176	35,287	43,584	45,497	39,901	40,054	48,288
Income: Debit..................	78ahd	−28,159	−27,236	−25,799	−28,508	−32,750	−32,193	−37,980	−40,008	−47,869	−43,667	−42,495	−49,641
Balance on Gds, Serv. & Inc......	78aid	11,202	17,704	22,571	32,206	28,272	31,196	20,213	19,348	13,035	14,569	16,324	24,210
Current Transfers, n.i.e.: Credit.....	78ajd	4,642	4,359	4,197	4,725	4,319	4,346	3,799	4,566	4,399	4,475	5,540	6,332
Current Transfers: Debit..................	78akd	−8,997	−8,860	−9,474	−11,159	−11,089	−10,465	−10,981	−10,918	−10,618	−11,214	−11,749	−14,074
Capital Account, n.i.e..................	78bcd	−631	−715	−1,006	−1,099	−2,024	−1,297	−420	−214	−97	−3,200	−545	−2,028
Capital Account, n.i.e.: Credit........	78bad	369	579	564	856	1,267	1,099	1,037	1,688	2,216	1,118	857	449
Capital Account: Debit..................	78bbd	−1,000	−1,294	−1,569	−1,955	−3,291	−2,396	−1,457	−1,902	−2,314	−4,317	−1,402	−2,477
Financial Account, n.i.e..................	78bjd	−7,279	−11,136	−9,969	−18,839	−5,474	−14,304	−14,398	−9,905	−7,484	504	−12,550	−23,430
Direct Investment Abroad..................	78bdd	−12,776	−9,954	−17,581	−20,188	−31,937	−24,499	−36,938	−57,166	−74,489	−47,137	−33,951	−36,619
Dir. Invest. in Rep. Econ., n.i.e......	78bed	6,187	6,380	7,127	12,206	16,604	11,033	37,619	41,148	63,229	51,716	28,534	19,197
Portfolio Investment Assets..................	78bfd	−13,398	−10,702	−9,570	−16,498	−25,013	−38,942	−69,294	−94,489	−65,634	−60,994	−64,293	−56,769
Equity Securities..................	78bkd	−2,703	−4,235	−6,595	−8,730	−2,895	−12,140	−19,890	−52,668	−23,447	−29,565	−7,917	−10,528
Debt Securities..................	78bld	−10,696	−6,467	−2,975	−7,768	−22,119	−26,802	−49,404	−41,821	−42,187	−31,429	−56,375	−46,241
Portfolio Investment Liab., n.i.e......	78bgd	3,847	12,344	−834	6,123	13,432	17,752	30,074	100,103	55,242	74,193	49,954	81,272
Equity Securities..................	78bmd	−1,512	3,503	−1,385	−743	3,280	774	3,825	30,491	16,970	12,947	−193	4,830
Debt Securities..................	78bnd	5,359	8,841	551	6,865	10,152	16,979	26,248	69,611	38,272	61,246	50,147	76,442
Financial Derivatives Assets..................	78bwd	5,695	7,271	11,888	18,454	23,385	31,899	53,364	63,425	82,999	87,517	70,419	126,753
Financial Derivatives Liabilities.......	78bxd	−5,613	−7,361	−12,256	−20,198	−24,134	−32,346	−52,388	−59,240	−86,979	−93,354	−77,263	−127,208
Other Investment Assets..................	78bhd	−7,819	−12,803	7,270	−8,127	1,582	−37,217	−56,475	354	−28,390	−69,787	−40,263	−64,038
Monetary Authorities..................	78bod	−	−	−	−	−	−	−235	107	675	−1,175	360	277
General Government..................	78bpd	−324	−189	−44	7	−270	146	181	−1,442	534	−837	−1,621	−1,730
Banks..................	78bqd	−4,200	−7,884	9,437	−3,474	2,926	−31,241	−49,373	9,488	−18,042	−60,706	−20,574	−55,675
Other Sectors..................	78brd	−3,295	−4,730	−2,124	−4,660	−1,075	−6,122	−7,047	−7,800	−11,557	−7,069	−18,428	−6,910
Other Investment Liab., n.i.e..................	78bid	16,599	3,688	3,988	9,389	20,607	58,015	79,641	−4,039	46,538	58,349	54,313	33,983
Monetary Authorities..................	78bsd	−309	99	91	−137	−42	41	930	−410	−3,542	1,977	2,279	−3,552
General Government..................	78btd	−183	166	1,151	24	−131	−536	284	640	329	2,828	4	−133
Banks..................	78bud	17,023	3,122	−493	4,174	15,697	52,519	60,697	−1,541	18,367	57,759	52,159	41,207
Other Sectors..................	78bvd	68	301	3,239	5,327	5,083	5,990	17,730	−2,728	31,384	−4,214	−129	−3,540
Net Errors and Omissions..................	78cad	7,181	5,288	−5,819	−7,745	−19,700	−12,185	−553	−7,488	984	−5,485	2,848	8,070
Overall Balance..................	78cbd	6,118	6,641	500	−1,911	−5,695	−2,709	−2,339	−4,611	219	−351	−132	−920
Reserves and Related Items..................	79dad	−6,118	−6,641	−500	1,911	5,695	2,709	2,339	4,611	−219	351	132	920
Reserve Assets..................	79dbd	−6,118	−6,641	−500	1,911	5,695	2,709	2,339	4,611	−219	351	132	920
Use of Fund Credit and Loans........	79dcd	−	−	−	−	−	−	−	−	−	−	−	−
Exceptional Financing..................	79ded	....	....	....	....	....	....	....	....	....	....	....	....

Netherlands 138

		1992	1993	1994	1995	1996	1997	1998	1999	2000	2001	2002	2003
International Investment Position						*Millions of US Dollars*							
Assets	79aad	464,334	498,632	547,618	651,021	696,815	746,981	957,871	1,072,804	1,135,519	1,239,029	1,481,118	....
Direct Investment Abroad	79abd	121,061	120,123	142,953	172,672	194,026	198,554	229,000	263,756	305,461	332,018	388,123	....
Portfolio Investment	79acd	84,500	106,470	119,467	164,012	204,757	242,157	363,140	453,076	478,298	485,696	570,003	....
Equity Securities	79add	44,209	59,663	67,258	91,747	107,708	124,066	173,149	249,426	253,589	235,023	217,387	....
Debt Securities	79aed	40,291	46,807	52,209	72,265	97,049	118,091	189,991	203,649	224,709	250,673	352,616	....
Financial Derivatives	79ald	–	–	–	–	–	–	–	39,731	29,220	44,606	71,813	....
Other Investment	79afd	221,845	227,612	237,294	267,155	258,384	273,551	336,184	297,172	304,903	359,780	432,231	....
Monetary Authorities	79agd	–	–	–	–	–	–	252	3,230	2,528	3,245	3,545	....
General Government	79ahd	20,804	20,492	22,441	23,984	23,124	21,255	22,597	22,292	20,918	19,908	23,438	....
Banks	79aid	154,179	158,773	159,052	179,830	174,050	190,892	241,262	197,320	203,784	255,851	302,652	....
Other Sectors	79ajd	46,861	48,348	55,801	63,342	61,210	61,404	72,072	74,330	77,673	80,776	102,596	....
Reserve Assets	79akd	36,927	44,427	47,903	47,182	39,648	32,719	29,547	19,070	17,636	16,929	18,948	....
Liabilities	79lad	405,198	435,686	484,362	586,113	658,739	721,135	973,050	1,098,446	1,194,747	1,291,941	1,610,722	....
Dir. Invest. in Rep. Economy	79lbd	74,440	74,478	93,409	116,049	126,543	122,193	164,473	192,588	243,732	282,882	352,646	....
Portfolio Investment	79lcd	132,135	164,632	176,410	225,266	276,532	318,336	445,573	536,599	567,014	547,592	647,363	....
Equity Securities	79ldd	65,817	92,380	105,239	129,955	179,628	224,692	308,671	363,796	350,571	283,978	262,251	....
Debt Securities	79led	66,318	72,252	71,171	95,311	96,903	93,645	136,902	172,803	216,443	263,614	385,112	....
Financial Derivatives	79lld	–	–	–	–	–	–	–	30,543	24,440	49,469	86,573	....
Other Investment	79lfd	198,623	196,576	214,543	244,798	255,665	280,606	363,003	338,716	359,561	411,997	524,140	....
Monetary Authorities	79lgd	38	152	263	141	80	64	725	3,271	115	1,666	4,889	....
General Government	79lhd	9,300	9,504	10,864	11,536	10,971	9,891	10,232	13,090	12,785	14,629	17,838	....
Banks	79lid	151,112	149,117	158,290	184,237	195,974	223,451	297,011	265,713	268,848	316,907	403,206	....
Other Sectors	79ljd	38,173	37,802	45,126	48,883	48,640	47,200	55,035	56,642	77,812	78,796	98,207	....
Government Finance													
Central Government			*Millions of Guilders through 1998; Millions of Euros Beginning 1999: Year Ending December 31*											
Deficit (-) or Surplus	80	−20,843	−8,343	2,763	−23,018	−9,626	−10,921	−3,177	†−5,815	−372	−3,500	−6,902	−10,718
Total Revenue and Grants	81y	182,845	204,088	199,517	204,769	189,159	197,347	210,688	†105,280	108,309	115,142	120,325	122,592
Revenue	81	182,843	204,066	199,508	204,611	188,965	196,930	210,397	†105,177	108,111	115,044	120,315	122,440
Grants	81z	2	22	9	158	194	417	291	†103	198	98	10	152
Exp. & Lending Minus Repay	82z	203,688	212,431	196,754	227,787	198,785	208,268	213,865	†111,095	108,681	118,642	127,227	133,310
Total Financing	80h	20,843	8,343	−2,763	23,018	9,626	10,921	3,177	†5,815	372	3,500	6,902	10,718
Total Net Borrowing	84	20,088	13,220	−1,685	28,816	9,885	−4,072	13,348	†2,254	−1,032	3,521	9,183	12,289
Net Domestic	84a	20,088	13,220	−1,685	28,816	9,885	−4,072	13,348	†2,254	−1,032	3,521	9,183	12,289
Net Foreign	85a	–	–	–	–	–	–	–	†–	–	–	–	–
Use of Cash Balances	87	755	−4,877	−1,078	−5,798	−259	14,993	−10,171	†3,561	1,404	−21	−2,281	−1,571
Total Debt by Currency	88z	358,007	371,209	374,645	399,825	410,989	417,467	431,383	†200,984	204,476	211,675	226,756	256,388
National	88b	358,007	371,209	374,645	399,825	410,989	417,467	431,383	†200,984	204,476	211,675	226,756	256,388
Foreign	89b	–	–	–	–	–	–	–	†–	–	–	–	–
General Government						*As Percent of Gross Domestic Product*							
Deficit (-) or Surplus	80g	−3.9	−3.2	−3.8	−4.0	−1.8	−1.1	−.8	.4	2.2	.2	....	....
Debt	88g	79.9	81.1	77.9	79.0	75.3	70.0	66.8	63.1	56.0	53.2	....	....
National Accounts			*Billions of Guilders through 1998; Billions of Euros Beginning 1999:*											
Househ.Cons.Expend.,incl.NPISHs	96f.c	340.9	352.0	368.1	379.6	398.5	419.4	445.3	†187.6	200.6	213.1	221.7	223.3
Government Consumption Expend	91f.c	83.0	84.7	86.5	89.1	92.4	97.4	102.2	†85.5	91.3	100.3	109.1	115.1
Gross Fixed Capital Formation	93e.c	113.3	111.7	117.3	124.8	131.6	142.4	149.9	†84.2	89.0	93.0	92.2	91.0
Changes in Inventories	93i.c	3.1	−2.4	4.3	3.8	−3.5	1.0	2.0	†.5	−.8	−.1	−2.7	3.0
Exports of Goods and Services	90c.c	294.9	292.7	312.1	336.3	354.9	384.7	414.7	†225.4	271.4	280.3	278.4	278.0
Imports of Goods and Services (-)	98c.c	269.2	259.7	279.8	298.9	318.7	346.5	364.4	†209.1	250.4	257.8	255.7	254.1
Gross Domestic Product (GDP)	99b.c	589.4	605.4	639.6	666.0	694.3	734.9	776.2	†374.1	402.3	429.1	444.6	453.8
Net Primary Income from Abroad	98.n	−2.3	−.6	1.7	8.0	3.5	13.1	8.6	†.7	1.7	−3.9	−9.1	−12.5
Gross National Income (GNI)	99a	563.8	580.9	616.0	674.0	697.8	748.0	784.8	†374.8	404.0	425.2	435.5	441.3
Net Current Transf.from Abroad	98t.c	....	....	....	....	....	....	....	†−2.2	−3.3	−3.7	−4.3	....
Gross Nat'l Disposable Inc.(GNDI)	99i.c	....	....	....	....	....	....	....	†372.6	403.4	420.6	429.6	....
Gross Saving	99s.c	....	....	....	....	....	....	....	†99.7	111.3	108.4	100.0	....
Consumption of Fixed Capital	99cfc	....	....	....	....	....	....	....	†56.5	61.3	66.2	71.4	....
GDP Volume 1995 Ref., Chained	99b.r	601.9	605.8	646.4	666.0	686.3	712.6	734.6	†350.9	363.1	367.5	368.4	365.7
GDP Volume (2000=100)	99bvr	75.2	75.7	80.8	83.2	85.8	89.1	91.8	†96.6	100.0	101.2	101.5	100.7
GDP Deflator (2000=100)	99bir	88.4	90.2	89.3	90.3	91.3	93.1	95.4	†96.2	100.0	105.4	108.9	112.0
						Millions: Midyear Estimates							
Population	99z	15.16	15.26	15.36	15.46	15.55	15.64	15.73	15.81	15.90	15.98	16.07	16.15

2004, International Monetary Fund : *International Financial Statistics Yearbook*

Netherlands Antilles 353

		1992	1993	1994	1995	1996	1997	1998	1999	2000	2001	2002	2003
Exchange Rates		*Guilders per SDR: End of Period (aa) Guilders per US Dollar: End of Period (ae)*											
Official Rate	aa	2.461	2.459	2.613	2.661	2.574	2.415	2.520	2.457	2.332	2.250	2.434	2.660
Official Rate	ae	1.790	1.790	1.790	1.790	1.790	1.790	1.790	1.790	1.790	1.790	1.790	1.790
		Index Numbers (2000=100): Period Averages											
Official Rate	ahx	100.0	100.0	100.0	100.0	100.0	100.0	100.0	100.0	100.0	100.0	100.0	100.0
Nominal Effective Exchange Rate	nec	70.1	76.8	81.3	80.2	84.6	90.1	92.6	94.4	100.0	103.0	103.1	97.6
Real Effective Exchange Rate	rec	93.5	96.3	94.6	90.6	93.7	98.9	99.6	97.6	100.0	100.0	97.5	89.4
International Liquidity		*Millions of US Dollars Unless Otherwise Indicated: End of Period*											
Total Reserves minus Gold	1l.d	220	234	179	203	189	214	248	265	261	301	406	373
Foreign Exchange	1d.d	220	234	179	203	189	214	248	265	261	301	406	373
Gold (Million Fine Troy Ounces)	1ad	.548	.548	.548	.548	.548	.548	.421	.421	.421	.421	.421	.421
Gold (National Valuation)	1and	38	38	38	117	106	106	100	100	78	78	78	132
Monetary Authorities: Other Liab	4..d	–	2	26	32	10	8	1	1	2	–	1	–
Deposit Money Banks: Assets	7a.d	749	825	748	442	400	396	471	473	552	862	653	709
Liabilities	7b.d	722	780	720	391	402	392	421	455	568	664	496	476
OBU: Assets	7k.d	†22,952	29,155	29,152	26,085	28,106	31,393	36,430	32,792	34,466	38,254	42,584	39,961
Liabilities	7m.d	†21,717	27,619	28,315	15,256	26,263	29,437	33,772	30,029	31,423	34,567	38,954	36,472
Monetary Authorities		*Millions of Guilders End of Period*											
Foreign Assets	11	461.8	490.1	435.2	683.3	546.5	591.5	625.9	655.1	608.7	678.7	867.9	905.3
Claims on Central Government	12a	71.0	66.2	59.9	69.2	68.6	82.0	79.1	117.5	94.8	150.5	124.4	119.9
Reserve Money	14	380.2	401.0	375.0	449.6	385.2	445.2	489.1	460.0	497.9	678.6	847.8	796.8
of which: Currency Outside DMBs	14a	178.6	184.5	198.2	209.6	195.6	188.0	186.6	197.0	188.9	218.2	235.2	232.9
Time Deposits	15	2.9	11.0	13.2	30.3	–	–	–	–	–	–	–	–
Foreign Liabilities	16c	.7	3.1	47.0	58.0	18.7	15.1	2.5	.9	3.1	.8	1.7	.8
Central Government Deposits	16d	40.0	71.2	13.0	46.0	38.7	45.1	55.5	164.7	170.7	168.1	123.0	94.9
Capital Accounts	17a	65.8	65.8	65.8	201.6	185.4	185.4	182.4	182.4	141.5	141.6	141.4	240.2
Other Items (Net)	17r	43.2	4.2	–18.9	–33.0	–12.9	–17.3	–24.5	–35.4	–109.7	–159.9	–121.6	–107.5
Deposit Money Banks		*Millions of Guilders: End of Period*											
Reserves	20	122.2	176.9	128.5	209.7	164.4	232.1	263.0	251.3	304.7	432.1	596.3	557.7
Foreign Assets	21	1,339.9	1,476.6	1,339.5	791.7	715.9	709.7	843.6	846.0	987.5	1,542.1	1,168.3	1,268.8
Claims on Local Government	22b	94.7	125.1	126.5	103.1	158.5	142.8	121.5	126.9	101.1	122.7	181.8	207.2
Claims on Private Sector	22d	1,716.6	1,796.9	2,034.4	2,130.2	2,275.8	2,262.8	2,299.8	2,529.3	2,677.4	2,686.9	2,782.5	2,834.4
Demand Deposits	24	424.8	501.8	560.7	653.6	702.9	710.7	721.7	770.3	806.8	896.4	1,064.9	1,007.7
Time and Savings Deposits	25a	1,018.6	1,136.5	1,201.7	1,231.4	1,266.4	1,325.7	1,417.1	1,484.6	1,552.9	1,743.7	1,921.2	2,195.4
Foreign Currency Deposits	25b	350.8	375.5	399.7	470.4	413.5	409.4	399.5	456.7	449.2	558.4	603.4	677.9
Foreign Liabilities	26c	1,292.9	1,396.8	1,289.6	699.0	719.1	701.5	752.9	813.6	1,017.5	1,188.7	888.2	852.9
Central Government Deposits	26d	47.5	39.0	36.0	22.6	36.5	45.7	46.2	30.0	34.5	41.8	39.3	34.9
Capital Accounts	27a	236.6	249.9	274.4	245.7	301.5	301.0	318.4	332.5	332.2	390.1	421.7	394.3
Other Items (Net)	27r	–97.8	–124.0	–133.2	–88.0	–125.3	–146.6	–127.9	–134.2	–122.4	–35.3	–209.8	–295.0
Girosystem Curacao													
Private Sector Deposits	24..i	55.5	60.1	87.1	71.4	–	....	....	....	....	....	....	....
Central Government Deposits	26d.i	34.5	34.3	34.9	1.5	–	....	....	....	....	....	....	....
Monetary Survey		*Millions of Guilders End of Period*											
Foreign Assets (Net)	31n	508.1	566.8	438.1	718.0	524.6	584.6	714.1	686.6	575.6	1,031.3	1,146.3	1,320.4
Domestic Credit	32	1,962.3	2,055.9	2,377.5	2,423.3	2,510.7	2,485.9	2,503.4	2,664.6	2,812.9	2,906.7	3,198.3	3,331.7
Claims on Central Govt. (Net)	32an	59.0	39.0	86.1	87.0	76.4	80.1	67.1	–6.6	–36.4	8.1	189.5	272.4
Claims on Local Government	32b	186.2	219.5	256.5	206.0	158.5	142.8	136.5	141.9	171.9	211.7	226.3	224.9
Claims on Private Sector	32d	1,717.1	1,797.4	2,034.9	2,130.3	2,275.8	2,263.0	2,299.8	2,529.3	2,677.4	2,686.9	2,782.5	2,834.4
Money	34	738.3	786.0	894.3	964.9	923.7	923.8	947.8	979.0	1,000.0	1,142.9	1,316.4	1,246.8
Quasi-Money	35	1,372.3	1,523.0	1,614.6	1,732.1	1,679.9	1,735.1	1,816.6	1,941.3	2,002.1	2,302.1	2,524.6	2,873.3
Other Items (Net)	37r	359.8	313.7	306.7	444.3	431.7	411.6	453.1	430.9	386.4	493.0	503.6	532.0
Money plus Quasi-Money	35l	2,110.6	2,309.0	2,508.9	2,697.0	2,603.6	2,658.9	2,764.4	2,920.3	3,002.1	3,445.0	3,841.0	4,120.1
Interest Rates		*Percent Per Annum*											
Discount Rate (End of Period)	60	6.00	5.00	5.00	6.00	6.00	6.00	6.00	6.00	6.00	6.00	6.00	....
Treasury Bill Rate	60c	....	4.83	4.48	5.46	5.66	5.77	5.82	6.15	6.15	6.15	4.96	2.80
Deposit Rate	60l	....	4.33	4.05	3.75	3.67	3.66	3.58	3.59	3.63	3.65	3.62	3.48
Lending Rate	60p	....	12.59	12.73	12.93	13.21	13.29	13.58	13.60	9.98	10.44	10.14	11.26
Government Bond Yield	61	....	8.14	7.48	8.02	8.25	8.67	8.60	8.75	8.77	9.00	8.20	6.72
Prices and Labor		*Index Numbers (2000=100): Period Averages*											
Consumer Prices	64	81.5	83.2	84.7	87.0	†90.2	93.1	94.2	94.5	100.0	101.8	102.2	104.3
		Number in Thousands: Period Averages											
Labor Force	67d	....	....	....	62	66	66	65	61	....	....	....	....
Employment	67e	51	52	55	54	57	56	54	....	52	....	....	....
Unemployment	67c	8	8	8	8	9	10	11	....	9	....	....	....
Unemployment Rate (%)	67r	13.9	13.6	12.8	13.1	14.2	15.2	16.2	14.1	12.9	14.5	14.2	....

Netherlands Antilles 353

		1992	1993	1994	1995	1996	1997	1998	1999	2000	2001	2002	2003
International Transactions						*Millions of Guilders*							
Exports	70	2,790	2,297	2,462	....	....	....	....	....	....	....	....	....
Imports, c.i.f.	71	3,344	3,485	3,146	....	....	....	....	....	....	....	....	....
Imports, f.o.b.	71.v	2,986	3,112	2,809	....	....	....	....	....	....	....	....	....
Balance of Payments					*Millions of US Dollars: Minus Sign Indicates Debit*								
Current Account, n.i.e.	78ald	9.9	1.2	−97.9	127.6	−253.8	−65.1	−136.9	−277.1	−50.7	−205.6	32.3	....
Goods: Exports f.o.b.	78aad	332.3	306.0	351.1	586.5	614.6	501.4	465.6	467.0	676.1	638.2	575.5	....
Goods: Imports f.o.b.	78abd	−1,168.4	−1,143.8	−1,271.6	−1,621.5	−1,743.7	−1,476.6	−1,513.2	−1,584.2	−1,661.7	−1,752.5	−1,602.4	....
Trade Balance	78acd	−836.1	−837.8	−920.5	−1,034.9	−1,129.1	−975.3	−1,047.7	−1,117.2	−985.6	−1,114.3	−1,026.8	....
Services: Credit	78add	1,339.6	1,346.0	1,414.2	1,491.6	1,405.9	1,425.0	1,508.9	1,518.7	1,613.4	1,649.4	1,716.0	....
Services: Debit	78aed	−606.9	−596.0	−670.5	−563.3	−624.0	−574.7	−611.3	−661.9	−733.5	−767.0	−769.6	....
Balance on Goods & Services	78afd	−103.5	−87.8	−176.8	−106.6	−347.3	−125.0	−150.0	−260.4	−105.8	−231.8	−80.4	....
Income: Credit	78agd	158.1	122.7	133.7	117.4	135.4	100.8	146.2	101.0	126.0	103.8	91.0	....
Income: Debit	78ahd	−146.6	−140.3	−99.4	−99.4	−71.7	−54.1	−109.3	−121.4	−103.2	−83.8	−90.3	....
Balance on Gds, Serv. & Inc.	78aid	−92.0	−105.4	−142.5	−88.5	−283.5	−78.3	−113.1	−280.8	−83.0	−211.9	−79.7	....
Current Transfers, n.i.e.: Credit	78ajd	217.4	250.3	217.9	365.8	174.7	165.3	137.2	179.6	246.6	222.4	368.8	....
Current Transfers: Debit	78akd	−115.5	−143.7	−173.3	−149.6	−145.0	−152.1	−160.9	−175.8	−214.3	−216.2	−256.8	....
Capital Account, n.i.e.	78bcd	−.6	−.8	−.7	61.9	71.3	75.1	86.9	108.4	29.8	37.2	27.7	....
Capital Account, n.i.e.: Credit	78bad	1.7	.8	1.0	66.8	71.9	76.9	91.3	109.8	31.3	37.9	29.3	....
Capital Account: Debit	78bbd	−2.3	−1.7	−1.7	−4.9	−.6	−1.7	−4.4	−1.5	−1.4	−.6	−1.6	....
Financial Account, n.i.e.	78bjd	41.7	32.2	−2.3	−142.5	95.8	−31.2	58.0	69.5	−122.2	359.4	8.7	....
Direct Investment Abroad	78bdd	−1.5	2.2	−1.0	−1.3	.8	6.5	2.0	1.2	2.3	−.5	−1.1	....
Dir. Invest. in Rep. Econ., n.i.e.	78bed	40.1	11.0	21.5	−150.0	−59.8	−88.5	−52.6	−21.8	−62.6	−4.7	7.9	....
Portfolio Investment Assets	78bfd	−21.6	−13.9	−69.1	−18.0	−22.3	9.2	−21.2	−7.1	−38.0	−31.6	−38.4	....
Equity Securities	78bkd	−	−	−	−15.7	−19.2	−5.4	−3.9	−3.0	−33.9	−7.2	−8.5	....
Debt Securities	78bld	−21.6	−13.9	−69.1	−2.3	−3.1	14.6	−17.3	−4.1	−4.1	−24.4	−29.9	....
Portfolio Investment Liab., n.i.e.	78bgd	2.8	1.5	10.9	1.1	−8.2	−.2	−.2	−3.1	.1	−.2	.9	....
Equity Securities	78bmd	−	−	−	−	....	−	−	−	−	−	−	....
Debt Securities	78bnd	2.8	1.5	10.9	1.1	−8.2	−.2	−.2	−3.1	.1	−.2	.9	....
Financial Derivatives Assets	78bwd	....	....	....	....	....	....	....	....	−	.1	−	....
Financial Derivatives Liabilities	78bxd	....	....	....	....	....	....	....	....	−	−	−	....
Other Investment Assets	78bhd	−68.7	−38.4	15.3	67.1	84.6	46.1	111.7	34.1	−40.8	83.7	.2	....
Monetary Authorities	78bod	....	....	....	−.8	5.1	2.8	3.9	2.6	−.1	−1.2	.4	....
General Government	78bpd	−	−	−	2.2	7.2	2.0	4.4	−	−.9	−.8	−	....
Banks	78bqd	−61.0	−46.9	−55.8	−3.4	42.8	19.3	21.7	57.2	5.2	1.5	28.9	....
Other Sectors	78brd	−7.7	8.5	71.1	69.1	29.4	21.9	81.7	−25.7	−45.0	84.2	−29.2	....
Other Investment Liab., n.i.e.	78bid	90.6	69.8	20.1	−41.3	100.7	−4.4	18.4	66.2	16.8	312.5	39.3	....
Monetary Authorities	78bsd	−	−	−	−	....	−	....	−	1.3	−	−	....
General Government	78btd	.4	−9.5	−38.3	−19.9	−19.9	−38.2	−51.2	−67.8	−33.3	−12.9	−20.6	....
Banks	78bud	60.6	59.7	59.7	−5.8	45.8	−5.7	−.1	3.0	40.0	91.8	−2.7	....
Other Sectors	78bvd	29.7	19.6	−1.3	−15.6	74.8	39.5	69.7	131.1	8.8	233.7	62.5	....
Net Errors and Omissions	78cad	8.2	11.5	24.9	13.4	14.8	14.9	17.4	24.5	13.4	26.8	−9.1	....
Overall Balance	78cbd	59.2	44.0	−75.9	60.4	−71.9	−6.3	25.5	−74.7	−129.6	217.7	59.5	....
Reserves and Related Items	79dad	−59.2	−44.0	75.9	−60.4	71.9	6.3	−25.5	74.7	129.6	−217.7	−59.5	....
Reserve Assets	79dbd	−59.2	−44.0	75.9	−60.4	53.8	−27.8	−75.6	8.3	47.8	−231.9	−75.5	....
Use of Fund Credit and Loans	79dcd	−	−	−	....	....	....	....	....	....	....	....	....
Exceptional Financing	79ded	−	−	−	....	18.1	34.1	50.2	66.5	81.8	14.2	15.9	....
Government Finance					*Millions of Guilders: Year Ending December 31*								
Deficit (−) or Surplus	80	−62.0	−25.2	−40.6p	† −100.2	....	....	....	....	....	....	....	....
Revenue	81	517.0	587.8	663.3p	† 462.2	....	....	....	....	....	....	....	....
Grants Received	81z	67.0	105.0	91.9p	† 92.8	....	....	....	....	....	....	....	....
Expenditure	82	638.0	719.4	795.4p	† 655.1	....	....	....	....	....	....	....	....
Lending Minus Repayments	83	8.0	−1.4	.4p	† .1	....	....	....	....	....	....	....	....
Financing													
Domestic	84a	62.0	25.2	40.6p	† 100.2	....	....	....	....	....	....	....	....
Foreign	85a	−	−	−p	† −	....	....	....	....	....	....	....	....
Debt: Domestic	88a	458.4	616.3	618.5p	† 704.6	....	....	....	....	....	....	....	....
Foreign	89a	187.8	170.9	−p	† −	....	....	....	....	....	....	....	....
					Millions: Midyear Estimates								
Population	99z	.19	.20	.20	.20	.21	.21	.21	.21	.22	.22	.22	.22

New Zealand 196

		1992	1993	1994	1995	1996	1997	1998	1999	2000	2001	2002	2003
Exchange Rates						*SDRs per New Zealand Dollar: End of Period*							
Market Rate	ac	.3740	.4068	.4401	.4395	.4910	.4311	.3742	.3793	.3379	.3306	.3873	.4408
				US Dollars per New Zealand Dollar: End of Period (ag) Period Average (rh)									
Market Rate	ag	.5143	.5588	.6425	.6533	.7060	.5817	.5269	.5206	.4402	.4155	.5265	.6550
Market Rate	rh	.5381	.5407	.5937	.6564	.6876	.6630	.5367	.5295	.4574	.4206	.4642	.5820
				Index Numbers (2000=100): Period Averages									
Market Rate	ahx	117.7	118.2	129.8	143.5	150.3	145.0	117.3	115.8	100.0	92.0	101.5	127.3
Nominal Effective Exchange Rate	nec	100.2	105.6	112.8	118.5	127.3	131.4	112.6	109.7	100.0	97.5	105.1	118.3
Real Effective Exchange Rate	rec	102.4	106.3	113.6	120.2	129.1	132.5	113.4	109.2	100.0	98.1	107.0	120.5
Fund Position				*Millions of SDRs: End of Period*									
Quota	2f.s	650	650	650	650	650	650	650	895	895	895	895	895
SDRs	1b.s	–	–	–	1	–	–	1	5	10	13	16	19
Reserve Position in the Fund	1c.s	109	104	101	110	127	132	253	309	246	308	338	433
Total Fund Cred.&Loans Outstg.	2tl	–	–	–	–	–	–	–	–	–	–	–	–
International Liquidity				*Millions of US Dollars Unless Otherwise Indicated: End of Period*									
Total Reserves minus Gold	1l.d	3,079	3,337	3,709	4,410	5,953	4,451	4,204	4,455	3,330	3,009	3,739	4,910
SDRs	1b.d	–	–	–	1	–	–	2	7	13	16	22	28
Reserve Position in the Fund	1c.d	150	142	147	164	182	178	356	424	320	387	459	644
Foreign Exchange	1d.d	2,929	3,195	3,561	4,245	5,771	4,273	3,846	4,025	2,997	2,605	3,258	4,238
Monetary Authorities	1dad	2,366	2,378	2,351	2,575	2,714	2,751	2,461	2,804	1,690	1,523	1,734	2,368
Government	1dbd	563	817	1,210	1,670	3,057	1,522	1,385	1,221	1,306	1,082	1,524	1,870
Gold (Million Fine Troy Ounces)	1ad	.001	–	–	–	–	–	–	–	–	–	–	–
Gold (National Valuation)	1and	–	–	–	–	–	–	–	–	–	–	–	–
Monetary Authorities: Other Liab.	4..d	100	96	–	178	299	461	383	379	605	302	501	477
Banking Institutions: Assets	7a.d	1,190	1,159	1,559	1,955	3,552	1,915	2,829	4,786	6,953	8,963	11,786	13,886
Liabilities	7b.d	8,838	9,249	12,319	14,439	17,197	17,024	20,031	25,261	25,554	27,632	33,990	41,884
Monetary Authorities				*Millions of New Zealand Dollars: End of Period*									
Foreign Assets	11	5,967	5,974	5,772	7,024	8,856	8,544	8,799	9,077	10,330	9,310	10,410	10,147
Claims on Central Government	12a	2,142	2,271	2,918	3,065	3,118	3,097	3,119	1,892	2,489	2,373	2,677	2,682
Claims on Banking Institutions	12e	789	796	301	476	1,305	1,079	451	2,178	1,802	2,247	2,931	2,829
Reserve Money	14	1,648	1,695	1,891	2,026	1,972	2,068	2,198	3,870	2,925	3,196	3,472	3,546
of which: Currency Outside DMBs	14a	1,173	1,199	1,367	1,489	1,497	1,633	1,724	2,077	2,069	2,241	2,451	2,597
Liabs.of Central Bank: Securities	16ac	1,056	1,149	1,185	1,218	1,242	1,250	1,076	–	–	–	–	–
Foreign Liabilities	16c	194	172	–	273	424	793	726	728	1,374	727	952	728
Central Government Deposits	16d	5,297	5,342	5,219	6,319	8,959	7,871	7,574	7,751	9,463	9,129	10,756	10,578
Capital Accounts	17a	783	734	748	769	745	801	853	843	893	914	868	836
Other Items (Net)	17r	–80	–52	–53	–39	–62	–63	–58	–45	–34	–36	–31	–30
Banking Institutions				*Millions of New Zealand Dollars: End of Period*									
Reserves	20	506	491	467	606	532	409	448	1,592	818	908	944	909
Claims on Mon.Author.:Securities	20c	1,056	1,149	1,185	1,218	1,242	1,250	1,076	–	–	–	–	–
Foreign Assets	21	2,314	2,074	2,427	2,993	5,031	3,292	5,369	9,194	15,794	21,572	22,386	21,200
Claims on Central Government	22a	8,448	7,079	5,932	4,249	3,302	3,572	4,384	6,921	7,149	5,818	8,183	7,920
Claims on Private Sector	22d	63,842	67,549	74,588	85,150	94,647	105,190	112,124	121,884	129,301	138,805	149,070	162,542
Demand Deposits	24	7,197	7,781	8,155	8,865	9,094	9,728	10,633	12,528	13,593	16,506	17,487	19,068
Time, Savings,Fgn.Currency Dep.	25	49,773	53,223	57,423	62,850	74,458	78,117	78,762	81,043	82,164	85,727	92,559	102,782
of which: Fgn Currency Deposits	25b	1,970	2,535	1,849	2,030	3,764	2,806	4,198	2,521	3,296	3,194	2,638	4,667
Foreign Liabilities	26c	17,184	16,552	19,174	22,101	24,359	29,267	38,016	48,523	58,051	66,504	64,559	63,945
Central Government Deposits	26d	12	–	9	19	25	33	29	61	52	53	48	57
Capital Accounts	27a	6,111	5,255	5,158	5,798	5,547	7,262	8,224	9,348	9,685	10,790	13,065	16,883
Other Items (Net)	27r	–4,110	–4,470	–5,320	–5,418	–8,727	–10,693	–12,263	–11,911	–10,483	–12,477	–7,135	–10,164
Banking Survey				*Millions per New Zealand Dollars: End of Period*									
Foreign Assets (Net)	31n	–9,097	–8,676	–10,976	–12,357	–10,896	–18,224	–24,575	–30,980	–33,300	–36,349	–32,716	–33,326
Domestic Credit	32	69,123	71,557	78,210	86,126	92,084	103,955	112,023	122,884	129,423	137,813	149,125	162,509
Claims on Central Govt. (Net)	32an	5,281	4,007	3,622	976	–2,564	–1,234	–101	1,001	122	–991	55	–32
Claims on Private Sector	32d	63,842	67,549	74,588	85,150	94,647	105,190	112,124	121,884	129,301	138,805	149,070	162,542
Money	34	8,429	9,044	9,594	10,398	10,619	11,386	12,378	14,649	15,700	18,795	20,019	21,705
Quasi-Money	35	49,773	53,223	57,423	62,850	74,458	78,117	78,762	81,043	82,164	85,727	92,559	102,782
Capital Accounts	37a	6,893	5,990	5,906	6,567	6,292	8,062	9,077	10,190	10,578	11,704	13,932	17,719
Other Items (Net)	37r	–5,069	–5,376	–5,688	–6,045	–10,180	–11,834	–12,767	–13,977	–12,319	–14,762	–10,100	–13,023
Money plus Quasi-Money	35l	58,202	62,267	67,017	73,247	85,076	89,503	91,140	95,692	97,865	104,522	112,577	124,487
Money (National Definitions)				*Millions of New Zealand Dollars: End of Period*									
M1	39ma	....	....	10,948	10,334	10,565	11,327	12,888	14,880	15,932	19,094	20,312	22,135
M2	39mb	....	....	27,840	31,990	32,836	33,336	37,873	40,964	41,319	47,412	51,193	53,293
M3R	39mc	....	....	58,385	65,515	73,469	78,652	78,786	84,669	86,644	92,732	103,352	113,171
M3	39md	64,239	65,873	67,948	77,854	87,719	91,411	92,383	98,748	105,179	117,213	130,720	138,100

New Zealand 196

		1992	1993	1994	1995	1996	1997	1998	1999	2000	2001	2002	2003
Nonbank Financial Institutions		*Millions of New Zealand Dollars: End of Period*											
Claims on Central Government	42a.s	2,349.7	2,328.6	2,435.4	....	....	....	....	....	....	....	....	....
Claims on Local Government	42b.s	738.6	782.3	546.4	526.9	624.7	551.3	....	....	....	....	....	....
Claims on Private Sector	42d.s	4,545.8	5,369.7	4,507.9	986.8	934.2	636.5	....	....	....	....	....	....
Real Estate	42h.s	1,740.6	1,488.7	1,590.9	....	....	....	....	....	....	....	....	....
Incr.in Total Assets(Within Per.)	49z.s	765.3	2,178.4	−618.4	....	....	....	....	....	....	....	....	....
Interest Rates		*Percent Per Annum*											
Discount Rate (End of Period)	60	9.15	5.70	9.75	9.80	8.80	9.70	5.60	5.00	6.50	4.75	5.75	5.00
Money Market Rate	60b	6.63	6.25	6.13	8.91	9.38	7.38	6.86	4.33	6.12	5.76	5.40	5.33
Treasury Bill Rate	60c	6.72	6.21	6.69	8.82	9.09	7.53	7.10	4.58	6.39	5.56	5.52	5.21
Deposit Rate	60l	6.58	6.24	6.38	8.49	8.49	7.26	6.78	4.56	6.36	5.35	5.33	5.10
Lending Rate	60p	11.39	10.34	9.69	12.09	12.27	11.35	11.22	8.49	10.22	9.88	9.81	9.80
Government Bond Yield	61	7.87	6.69	7.48	7.94	8.04	7.21	6.47	6.13	6.85	6.12	6.28	5.51
Prices, Production, Labor		*Index Numbers (2000=100): Period Averages*											
Share Prices	62	40.9	53.7	68.0	71.7	80.5	93.7	109.9	97.7	100.0	105.3	115.8	128.6
Input Prices: All Industry	63	86.5	88.7	89.9	90.6	91.1	91.4	92.1	93.0	100.0	106.0	106.3	105.3
Consumer Prices	64	86.4	87.6	†89.7	93.1	95.2	96.3	97.6	97.4	100.0	102.6	105.4	107.2
Wages: Weekly Rates (1990=100)	65	103.5	....	....	....	....	....	....	....	....	....	....	....
Labor Cost Index	65a	....	89.1	†90.0	91.4	93.1	95.3	97.1	98.5	100.0	101.9	104.2	106.5
Manufacturing Prod	66ey	67.6	71.8	76.2	95.6	97.5	98.1	94.8	96.4	100.0	99.9	104.0	105.4
Manufacturing Employment	67ey	90.4	90.4	100.8	104.7	103.6	98.2	102.8	99.2	100.0	103.1	103.2	99.1
		Number in Thousands: Period Averages											
Labor Force	67d	1,636	1,653	1,698	1,742	1,797	†1,817	1,864	1,878	1,892	1,922	1,980	2,015
Employment	67e	1,467	1,496	1,559	1,633	1,688	†1,693	1,725	1,750	1,779	1,819	1,877	1,921
Unemployment	67c	169	157	138	110	110	†123	139	128	113	103	103	94
Unemployment Rate (%)	67r	10.3	9.5	8.2	6.3	6.1	†6.6	7.5	6.8	6.0	5.3	5.2	4.7
International Transactions		*Millions of New Zealand Dollars*											
Exports	70	18,208.0	19,492.0	20,519.0	20,787.0	20,876.0	21,458.0	22,416.0	23,583.0	29,257.0	32,670.0	31,028.0	28,360.0
Butter	70fl	677.3	828.4	790.5	777.9	907.7	919.3	985.8	885.7	1,052.3	1,039.8	1,052.3	933.4
Imports, c.i.f.	71	17,131.0	17,781.0	19,981.0	21,251.0	21,399.0	21,964.0	23,348.0	27,114.0	30,736.0	31,682.0	32,339.0	31,792.0
Imports, f.o.b.	71.v	15,804.0	16,375.1	18,491.4	19,718.9	19,848.1	20,441.1	21,680.4p	25,438.2	28,854.0	29,668.0	....	....
		2000=100											
Volume of Exports	72	70.9	73.9	81.3	83.7	87.7	92.9	92.4	94.8	†100.0	103.2	108.9	111.9
Butter	72fl	53.2	73.4	74.3	68.8	80.9	97.2	87.8	91.0	100.0	86.3	114.2	107.6
Volume of Imports	73	63.8	66.6	77.5	82.6	85.4	88.5	90.6	102.8	†100.0	101.8	111.2	123.8
Unit Value of Exports	74	88.1	90.4	86.8	85.3	82.3	80.0	83.6	84.8	†100.0	108.9	97.6	86.9
Butter (Unit Value)	74fl	111.8	108.9	98.1	†100.0	114.8	90.2	98.4	86.9	100.0	114.8	90.2	83.2
Butter (Wholesale Price)	76fl	120.3	112.0	101.8	107.7	....	95.9	116.0	107.5	100.0	....	....	....
Unit Value of Imports	75	87.6	87.1	84.1	84.1	81.9	80.9	84.1	85.8	†100.0	101.5	95.2	84.1

2004, International Monetary Fund : *International Financial Statistics Yearbook*

New Zealand 196

		1992	1993	1994	1995	1996	1997	1998	1999	2000	2001	2002	2003
Balance of Payments						*Millions of US Dollars: Minus Sign Indicates Debit*							
Current Account, n.i.e..............	78ald	−1,071	−746	−2,384	−3,003	−3,891	−4,304	−2,157	−3,515	−15,994	−1,252	−1,939	−3,344
Goods: Exports f.o.b................	78aad	9,735	10,468	12,176	13,554	14,338	14,282	12,246	12,657	—	13,920	14,517	16,828
Goods: Imports f.o.b................	78abd	−8,108	−8,749	−10,769	−12,584	−13,815	−13,380	−11,333	−13,028	−12,850	−12,448	−14,014	−17,219
Trade Balance.......................	78acd	1,627	1,719	1,408	971	523	903	912	−371	−12,850	1,471	503	−391
Services: Credit.....................	78add	2,634	2,854	3,667	4,481	4,653	4,254	3,763	4,386	4,414	4,374	5,161	6,440
Services: Debit......................	78aed	−3,582	−3,505	−4,101	−4,694	−4,897	−4,903	−4,499	−4,581	−4,546	−4,286	−4,764	−5,643
Balance on Goods & Services......	78afd	679	1,068	973	757	279	254	176	−567	−12,982	1,559	900	405
Income: Credit.......................	78agd	117	394	358	940	372	393	880	919	710	596	1,077	1,379
Income: Debit........................	78ahd	−1,995	−2,340	−4,045	−4,895	−5,085	−5,249	−3,493	−4,036	−3,959	−3,594	−4,037	−5,274
Balance on Gds, Serv. & Inc......	78aid	−1,199	−877	−2,713	−3,198	−4,434	−4,601	−2,437	−3,684	−16,231	−1,439	−2,059	−3,489
Current Transfers, n.i.e.: Credit......	78ajd	310	310	638	558	897	680	681	609	634	578	616	792
Current Transfers: Debit.............	78akd	−182	−178	−309	−363	−354	−383	−401	−440	−398	−390	−496	−647
Capital Account, n.i.e..............	78bcd	292	542	617	1,224	1,336	242	−181	−217	−180	443	765	508
Capital Account, n.i.e.: Credit........	78bad	602	833	995	1,652	1,838	783	263	260	238	821	1,122	965
Capital Account: Debit...............	78bbd	−311	−291	−379	−427	−502	−541	−444	−477	−418	−378	−357	−458
Financial Account, n.i.e............	78bjd	3,229	2,825	2,220	4,665	3,571	4,045	1,580	1,974	1,199	2,894	834	2,106
Direct Investment Abroad............	78bdd	806	−1,276	−1,725	337	1,533	45	−928	−803	−1,300	1,144	−185	−299
Dir. Invest. in Rep. Econ., n.i.e......	78bed	2,095	2,350	2,543	3,659	2,231	2,624	1,191	1,412	3,370	1,911	739	1,611
Portfolio Investment Assets.........	78bfd	−7	−283	−72	−284	−430	−1,612	−467	−666	−2,284	−1,219	−935	−835
Equity Securities....................	78bkd	−11	−187	−152	−216	−339	−925	114	−893	−1,763	−941	−944	−919
Debt Securities......................	78bld	4	−97	81	−68	−90	−687	−581	227	−521	−279	10	84
Portfolio Investment Liab., n.i.e......	78bgd	−135	1,940	614	96	−104	403	425	−2,285	1,457	1,527	2,403	1,690
Equity Securities....................	78bmd	53	116	23	−100	175	88	22	172	−551	24	771	723
Debt Securities......................	78bnd	−188	1,823	591	197	−279	315	402	−2,458	2,008	1,502	1,632	968
Financial Derivatives Assets........	78bwd	....	....	....	....	....	....	....	....	....	....	....	....
Financial Derivatives Liabilities......	78bxd	....	....	....	....	....	....	....	....	....	....	....	....
Other Investment Assets...........	78bhd	328	−739	−78	−392	−920	991	−305	−1,282	−476	−3,537	−1,086	318
Monetary Authorities................	78bod	....	—	—	—	—	....	....	....	....	....	....	....
General Government................	78bpd	−11	−62	−82	−57	−94	238	55	212	....	....	....	....
Banks................................	78bqd	124	−747	66	−346	−932	819	−285	−1,591	....	....	....	....
Other Sectors.......................	78brd	215	71	−61	11	106	−65	−75	97	....	....	....	....
Other Investment Liab., n.i.e......	78bid	142	833	937	1,249	1,262	1,595	1,665	5,597	431	3,068	−103	−379
Monetary Authorities................	78bsd	—	—	—	—	—	—	—	—	....	....	....	....
General Government................	78btd	222	−117	−290	−144	−135	−73	68	13	....	....	....	....
Banks................................	78bud	1,365	573	767	1,096	964	1,131	1,559	5,446	....	....	....	....
Other Sectors.......................	78bvd	−1,445	377	460	297	432	537	38	138	....	....	....	....
Net Errors and Omissions.........	78cad	−2,319	−2,695	281	−2,502	756	−1,426	271	1,947	14,832	−2,273	1,426	1,511
Overall Balance....................	78cbd	131	−74	733	384	1,772	−1,442	−486	188	−143	−187	1,086	782
Reserves and Related Items.........	79dad	−131	74	−733	−384	−1,772	1,442	486	−188	143	187	−1,086	−782
Reserve Assets.....................	79dbd	−131	74	−733	−384	−1,772	1,442	486	−188	143	187	−1,086	−782
Use of Fund Credit and Loans.......	79dcd	—	—	—	—	—	—	—	—	....	....	....	....
Exceptional Financing...............	79ded	....	....	....	....	....	....	....	....	....	....	....	....
IIP:End-March Stocks Through 1999						*Millions of US Dollars*							
Assets................................	79aad	12,393	10,118	13,206	16,201	23,573	23,023	19,348	21,320	31,689	31,806	41,152	53,640
Direct Investment Abroad............	79abd	6,282	4,234	5,163	7,630	8,928	6,749	5,775	7,155	7,229	5,862	7,353	8,813
Portfolio Investment.................	79acd	882	952	1,362	1,707	5,815	6,434	6,476	6,760	11,264	11,766	13,644	19,970
Equity Securities....................	79add	503	602	834	1,226	4,407	4,895	4,620	4,447	6,721	7,114	7,652	13,527
Debt Securities......................	79aed	380	350	529	481	1,408	1,539	1,855	2,313	4,543	4,652	5,992	6,443
Financial Derivatives................	79ald	—	—	—	—	—	—	—	—	4,289	2,462	3,484	4,710
Other Investment...................	79afd	1,989	1,644	2,793	2,898	4,245	5,313	2,804	3,555	4,955	8,151	11,709	14,062
Monetary Authorities................	79agd	....	....	....	....	....	....	....	....	....	....	....	....
General Government................	79ahd	....	....	....	....	....	....	....	198	....	....	....	....
Banks................................	79aid	....	....	....	....	....	....	....	2,100	....	....	....	....
Other Sectors.......................	79ajd	....	....	....	....	....	....	....	1,257	....	....	....	....
Reserve Assets.....................	79akd	3,240	3,288	3,888	3,967	4,584	4,528	4,293	3,850	3,952	3,566	4,963	6,085
Liabilities...........................	79lad	40,971	44,240	51,100	62,339	71,631	78,547	68,752	67,651	72,412	70,118	93,638	122,805
Dir. Invest. in Rep. Economy.........	79lbd	12,545	14,849	19,315	25,574	33,381	37,491	34,889	33,555	23,098	19,564	28,255	42,062
Portfolio Investment.................	79lcd	14,273	15,290	17,595	19,809	19,361	20,166	17,581	17,710	25,591	25,859	33,942	43,879
Equity Securities....................	79ldd	468	1,320	816	1,483	288	1,045	208	241	4,582	4,170	5,670	9,056
Debt Securities......................	79led	13,805	13,970	16,779	18,327	19,072	19,121	17,373	17,469	21,009	21,689	28,272	34,823
Financial Derivatives................	79lld	—	—	—	—	—	—	—	—	3,256	2,640	4,139	5,513
Other Investment...................	79lfd	14,153	14,101	14,189	16,955	18,889	20,890	16,282	16,387	20,467	22,054	27,303	31,351
Monetary Authorities................	79lgd	....	....	....	....	....	....	....	....	....	....	....	....
General Government................	79lhd	....	....	....	....	....	....	....	428	....	....	....	....
Banks................................	79lid	....	....	....	....	....	....	....	10,924	....	....	....	....
Other Sectors.......................	79ljd	....	....	....	....	....	....	....	5,034	....	....	....	....
Government Finance						*Millions of New Zealand Dollars: Fiscal Year (see note)*							
Deficit (-) or Surplus................	80	−1,677	84	679	396	4,932	3,913	484	2,049	−385	....	....	....
Revenue............................	81	26,616	26,742	30,236	32,861	33,975	33,285	33,827	33,359	34,440	....	....	....
Expenditure........................	82	28,598	28,440	29,662	29,954	30,593	31,465	33,005	33,869	34,386	....	....	....
Lending Minus Repayments...........	83	−305	−1,782	−105	2,511	−1,550	−2,093	338	−2,559	439	....	....	....
Debt: Domestic.....................	88a	....	24,206	20,194	21,060	19,866	15,688	18,307	19,440	20,041	....	....	....
Foreign............................	89a	....	23,523	26,289	23,418	21,896	20,649	19,969	17,384	16,368	....	....	....

New Zealand 196

		1992	1993	1994	1995	1996	1997	1998	1999	2000	2001	2002	2003
National Accounts		*Millions of New Zealand Dollars; Year Beginning April 1*											
Househ.Cons.Expend.,incl.NPISHs....	96f.c	45,351	47,435	51,177	54,521	58,048	60,520	63,107	65,667	68,439	71,869	76,509	79,533
Government Consumption Expend...	91f.c	14,865	15,109	15,337	16,378	16,983	18,440	18,664	20,268	20,464	21,953	23,080	24,064
Gross Fixed Capital Formation.........	93e.c	12,571	15,035	17,747	19,890	20,877	20,610	19,713	21,068	21,541	23,481	25,521	27,806
Changes in Inventories....................	93i.c	624	1,432	1,166	1,182	809	817	120	1,373	1,242	1,919	731	1,085
Exports of Goods and Services.........	90c.c	23,700	25,085	26,951	27,125	27,528	28,531	30,468	33,488	41,442	43,595	41,836	39,606
Imports of Goods and Services (-)....	98c.c	21,865	22,708	25,326	26,417	27,006	28,179	30,135	34,462	39,252	39,913	39,907	39,184
Gross Domestic Product (GDP)........	99b.c	75,246	81,387	87,052	92,679	97,239	100,739	101,937	107,403	113,875	122,904	127,769	133,021
Net Primary Income from Abroad.....	98.nc	−4,675	−5,638	−5,686	−5,999	−7,263	−6,399	−4,968	−6,940	−7,281	−6,795	−6,210	−360
Gross National Income (GNI)...........	99a.c	70,571	75,749	81,366	86,680	89,976	94,340	96,969	100,463	106,594	116,109	121,559	132,661
Consumption of Fixed Capital..........	99cfc	11,322	11,527	11,932	12,407	13,094	13,425	13,877	14,328	15,294	16,344	17,202	....
GDP Volume 1995/96 Prices...........	99b.r	79,957	84,968	89,332	92,679	95,667	98,433	98,531	103,622	105,882	110,155	114,673	116,927
GDP Volume (2000=100)................	99bvr	75.5	80.2	84.4	87.5	90.4	93.0	93.1	97.9	100.0	104.0	108.3	110.4
GDP Deflator (2000=100)...............	99bir	87.5	89.1	90.6	93.0	94.5	95.2	96.2	96.4	100.0	103.7	103.6	105.8
						Millions: Midyear Estimates							
Population...............................	99z	3.45	3.50	3.56	3.60	3.65	3.68	3.72	3.75	3.78	3.82	3.85	3.88

Nicaragua 278

		1992	1993	1994	1995	1996	1997	1998	1999	2000	2001	2002	2003
Exchange Rates						*Córdobas per SDR: End of Period*							
Principal Rate........................	aam	6.88	8.72	10.38	11.84	12.83	13.49	15.76	16.91	17.01	17.39	19.95	23.11
						Córdobas per US Dollar: End of Period (ae) Period Average (rf)							
Principal Rate........................	aem	5.00	6.35	7.11	7.97	8.92	10.00	11.19	12.32	13.06	13.84	14.67	15.55
Principal Rate........................	rfm	5.00	5.62	6.72	7.55	8.44	9.45	10.58	11.81	12.69	13.37	14.25	15.10
						Index Numbers (2000=100): Period Averages							
Principal Rate........................	ahx	253.56	240.16	188.78	169.05	150.47	133.96	120.10	107.34	100.00	94.85	88.99	83.99
Nominal Effective Exchange Rate.....	nec	138.75	138.26	145.97	130.29	120.45	115.55	107.93	99.91	100.00	98.89	93.63	81.38
Real Effective Exchange Rate........	rec	101.50	102.87	96.42	88.56	87.01	89.14	91.63	92.28	100.00	103.00	98.80	87.29
Fund Position						*Millions of SDRs: End of Period*							
Quota..................................	2f.s	96.10	96.10	96.10	96.10	96.10	96.10	96.10	130.00	130.00	130.00	130.00	130.00
SDRs...................................	1b.s	.06	.03	.01	–	.02	.03	.15	.16	.05	.26	.02	.04
Reserve Position in the Fund........	1c.s	–	–	–	–	–	–	–	–	–	–	–	–
Total Fund Cred.&Loans Outstg......	2tl	17.03	17.03	34.92	26.41	20.02	20.02	36.84	113.15	129.33	125.33	128.29	143.50
International Liquidity						*Millions of US Dollars Unless Otherwise Indicated: End of Period*							
Total Reserves minus Gold...........	1l.d	130.48	55.04	141.01	136.20	197.32	377.94	350.41	509.71	488.46	379.93	448.13	502.06
SDRs...............................	1b.d	.08	.04	.01	–	.02	.04	.21	.21	.06	.33	.03	.06
Reserve Position in the Fund......	1c.d	–	–	–	–	–	–	–	–	–	–	–	–
Foreign Exchange..................	1d.d	130.40	55.00	141.00	136.20	197.30	377.90	350.20	509.50	488.40	379.60	448.10	502.00
Gold (Million Fine Troy Ounces).....	1ad	.475	.010	.013	.015	.015	.015	.015	.015	.015	.015	.015	.015
Gold (National Valuation)...........	1and	20.06	.42	.55	.63	.63	.63	.63	.63	.62	.62	.62	.62
Monetary Authorities: Other Liab.....	4..d	4,340.22	3,586.21	3,470.70	2,936.22	2,113.12	2,086.84	2,046.56	1,993.95	2,134.78	1,949.70	1,980.56	2,016.25
Deposit Money Banks: Assets.......	7a.d	43.30	47.36	53.56	45.00	146.65	211.27	162.15	143.98	65.66	88.39	92.50	97.15
Liabilities................	7b.d	24.38	18.74	31.62	31.34	44.61	54.65	55.09	109.86	90.42	102.58	107.00	109.01
Nonbank Financial Insts.: Assets.....	7e.d	....	....	....	....	.18	.16	–	–	–	–	–	–
Liabilities................	7f.d	....	....	....	....	33.90	36.76	.06	8.97	9.32	21.56	3.31	8.51
Monetary Authorities						*Millions of Córdobas: End of Period*							
Foreign Assets.......................	11	895.5	557.9	1,226.6	1,283.5	†2,197.5	4,034.7	4,199.5	6,466.0	6,620.8	†7,729.4	9,438.3	11,072.7
Claims on Central Government........	12a	20,497.8	21,646.0	23,256.5	22,469.2	†18,132.0	21,451.1	23,769.1	26,884.0	28,400.1	†43,259.2	44,737.7	46,467.6
Claims on Nonfin.Pub.Enterprises.....	12c	170.4	168.6	380.9	468.4	†98.3	101.0	113.1	124.4	77.4	†124.6	134.7	50.4
Claims on Private Sector............	12d	–	–	–	12.7	†206.0	260.4	314.7	303.4	307.3	†42.7	45.1	39.1
Claims on Deposit Money Banks......	12e	766.5	797.8	824.4	743.4	†152.3	806.5	99.1	326.8	2,012.8	†461.8	40.4	118.6
Claims on Nonbank Financial Insts...	12g	1,106.7	1,704.6	1,206.1	1,151.2	†3,168.2	3,003.9	4,028.3	4,203.4	4,453.3	†.9	.9	.9
Reserve Money......................	14	932.6	1,005.7	1,533.3	1,894.5	†2,545.9	3,372.6	4,038.1	4,267.6	4,468.1	†6,071.7	6,741.4	8,018.1
of which: Currency Outside DMBs..	14a	468.0	508.9	688.3	771.0	†864.1	1,096.1	1,339.6	1,734.8	1,760.5	†1,949.4	2,085.8	2,506.6
Time, Savings,& Fgn.Currency Dep...	15	49.7	18.3	17.6	11.6	†46.2	48.3	60.1	66.6	468.6	†.4	.4	.6
Liabs. of Central Bank: Securities.....	16ac	–	–	–	–	†436.4	3,643.5	2,250.3	2,302.9	3,658.1	†8,732.8	9,640.6	7,953.3
Foreign Liabilities...................	16c	21,818.2	22,919.9	25,045.1	23,699.6	†19,114.4	21,128.0	23,489.4	26,475.1	30,074.8	†29,165.4	31,616.1	34,668.5
Central Government Deposits.........	16d	1,252.8	396.6	329.6	198.5	†276.3	190.0	745.4	1,695.4	1,997.8	†742.4	2,066.9	3,450.6
Liab. to Nonbank Financial Insts......	16j	28.5	44.3	184.3	122.0	†118.6	13.4	.1	–	–	†–	–	–
Capital Accounts....................	17a	182.9	188.0	212.8	299.3	†1,494.2	1,838.3	2,498.0	4,303.8	3,315.9	†370.6	420.3	481.9
Other Items (Net)....................	17r	–827.8	302.1	–428.2	–97.1	†–77.6	–576.4	–557.5	–803.3	–2,111.5	†6,535.3	3,911.3	3,176.2
of which: Valuation Adjustment.....	17rv	–	–	–	–	†–	–	–	–	–1,280.3	†–	–	–
Deposit Money Banks						*Millions of Córdobas: End of Period*							
Reserves.............................	20	462.9	490.9	773.6	1,112.0	†1,680.9	2,324.5	2,752.8	2,627.3	2,728.5	†4,114.0	4,643.9	5,502.9
Claims on Mon.Author.:Securities....	20c	–	–	–	–	†158.2	1,365.2	1,367.0	1,506.2	2,885.4	†7,407.8	8,690.9	6,612.0
Foreign Assets......................	21	216.5	300.7	380.9	358.4	†1,308.7	2,111.7	1,815.1	1,773.5	857.3	†1,223.4	1,357.0	1,510.7
Claims on Central Government.......	22a	3.0	–	–	–	†513.7	372.5	356.8	1,107.1	1,400.3	†1,659.4	2,326.0	3,194.5
Claims on Local Government.........	22b	2.1	7.6	5.2	–	†34.5	6.7	6.7	210.3	243.0	†6.0	23.1	57.5
Claims on Nonfin.Pub.Enterprises.....	22c	17.3	11.8	41.4	10.0	†24.0	5.5	5.5	26.1	23.7	†111.0	110.5	439.3
Claims on Private Sector............	22d	2,035.2	3,049.5	4,075.5	5,159.0	†4,675.7	6,707.4	9,715.5	13,270.5	15,240.8	†9,783.2	11,228.2	15,048.0
Claims on Nonbank Financial Insts...	22g	–	–	–	–	†–	–	–	–	–	†115.7	67.3	149.6
Demand Deposits....................	24	373.2	295.1	407.6	471.4	†787.4	958.7	1,195.6	1,406.0	1,565.5	†1,316.2	1,280.5	1,696.0
Time, Savings,& Fgn.Currency Dep...	25	846.3	1,355.5	2,500.7	3,629.5	†5,747.6	9,249.8	12,404.3	14,622.3	15,632.1	†17,046.0	19,647.4	21,717.0
Money Market Instruments...........	26aa	–	–	–	–	†365.1	508.9	360.3	320.1	270.2	†–	–	–
Foreign Liabilities...................	26c	121.9	119.0	224.9	249.6	†398.1	546.2	616.7	1,353.5	1,180.7	†1,419.8	1,569.9	1,695.0
Central Government Deposits.........	26d	268.2	421.2	539.9	654.9	†755.7	1,098.8	798.2	1,662.2	1,381.8	†2,270.9	2,363.1	3,193.7
Credit from Monetary Authorities.....	26g	698.1	759.4	779.0	752.1	†35.5	743.4	34.7	27.5	2,340.9	†476.2	8.0	214.1
Liab. to Nonbank Financial Insts......	26j	266.6	714.4	1,198.1	1,389.6	†273.8	483.6	676.2	879.2	970.6	†1,175.6	1,311.7	1,274.7
Capital Accounts....................	27a	–	502.9	648.8	406.0	†825.0	222.4	1,201.4	1,998.5	2,696.9	†1,654.6	2,135.1	2,593.8
Other Items (Net)....................	27r	162.7	–307.0	–1,022.4	–913.7	†–792.5	–918.4	–1,267.9	–1,748.2	–2,659.7	†–939.0	131.3	130.2

Nicaragua 278

		1992	1993	1994	1995	1996	1997	1998	1999	2000	2001	2002	2003
Monetary Survey						*Millions of Córdobas: End of Period*							
Foreign Assets (Net)	31n	−20,828.1	−22,180.3	−23,662.5	−22,307.3	†−16,006.2	−15,527.8	−18,091.5	−19,588.9	−23,777.3	†−21,632.4	−22,390.7	−23,780.1
Domestic Credit	32	22,311.5	25,770.3	28,096.1	28,417.1	†25,820.5	30,619.7	36,766.2	42,771.5	46,766.3	†52,089.4	54,243.6	58,802.6
Claims on Central Govt. (Net)	32an	18,979.8	20,828.2	22,387.0	21,615.8	†17,613.8	20,534.7	22,582.4	24,633.4	26,420.8	†41,905.4	42,633.7	43,017.8
Claims on Local Government	32b	2.1	7.6	5.2	—	†34.5	6.7	6.7	210.5	243.0	†6.0	23.1	57.5
Claims on Nonfin.Pub.Enterprises	32c	187.7	180.4	422.3	478.4	†122.3	106.5	118.5	150.5	101.1	†235.6	245.2	489.6
Claims on Private Sector	32d	2,035.2	3,049.5	4,075.5	5,171.7	†4,881.7	6,967.9	10,030.2	13,573.9	15,548.1	†9,825.9	11,273.3	15,087.1
Claims on Nonbank Financial Inst.	32g	1,106.7	1,704.6	1,206.1	1,151.2	†3,168.2	3,003.9	4,028.3	4,203.4	4,453.3	†116.6	68.2	150.5
Money	34	844.7	805.5	1,097.2	1,242.4	†1,654.9	2,064.4	2,551.2	3,151.0	3,411.7	†3,267.1	3,368.1	4,208.3
Quasi-Money	35	896.0	1,373.8	2,518.3	3,641.1	†5,793.8	9,298.1	12,464.3	14,688.9	16,100.7	†17,046.4	19,647.8	21,717.6
Money Market Instruments	36aa	—	—	—	—	†365.1	508.9	360.3	320.1	270.2	†—	—	—
Liabs. of Central Bank: Securities	36ac	—	—	—	—	†278.2	2,278.3	883.3	796.6	772.7	†1,325.0	949.8	1,341.3
Liab. to Nonbank Financial Insts.	36j	295.1	758.7	1,382.4	1,511.6	†392.4	497.1	676.3	879.3	970.6	†1,175.7	1,311.8	1,274.8
Capital Accounts	37a	182.9	690.9	861.6	705.3	†2,319.2	2,060.7	3,699.4	6,302.3	6,012.8	†2,025.2	2,555.4	3,075.8
Other Items (Net)	37r	−735.3	−38.9	−1,425.9	−990.6	†−989.4	−1,615.5	−1,960.1	−2,955.6	−4,549.7	†5,617.5	4,020.2	3,404.8
Money plus Quasi-Money	35l	1,740.7	2,179.3	3,615.5	4,883.5	†7,448.6	11,362.5	15,015.5	17,839.9	19,512.4	†20,313.5	23,015.9	25,925.9
Nonbank Financial Institutions						*Millions of Córdobas: End of Period*							
Reserves	40	24	39	182	122	†122	4	—	—	—	—	1	1
Foreign Assets	41	13	20	40	15	†2	2	—	—	—	—	—	—
Claims on Central Government	42a	—	—	—	—	†319	367	—	—	—	—	—	—
Claims on Private Sector	42d	1,014	1,285	—	—	†442	504	690	906	1,028	1,291	1,046	1,175
Claims on Deposit Money Banks	42e	354	742	1,199	1,391	†4	113	14	32	14	75	176	159
Foreign Liabilities	46c	—	—	—	—	†303	367	1	111	122	298	49	132
Central Government Deposits	46d	—	—	—	—	†—	—	19	125	226	316	334	285
Credit from Monetary Authorities	46g	1,086	1,705	1,206	1,151	†90	100	80	48	26	—	—	—
Capital Accounts	47a	117	23	134	160	†517	563	579	668	754	800	857	937
Other Items (Net)	47r	201	359	81	217	†−21	−40	25	−13	−85	−48	−16	−20
Financial Survey						*Millions of Córdobas: End of Period*							
Foreign Assets (Net)	51n	−20,816	−22,161	−23,622	−22,292	†−16,307	−15,894	−18,092	−19,699	−23,899	†−21,931	−22,439	−23,912
Domestic Credit	52	22,219	25,351	26,890	27,266	†23,413	28,487	33,409	39,349	43,115	†52,948	54,888	59,542
Claims on Central Govt. (Net)	52an	18,980	20,828	22,387	21,616	†17,933	20,902	22,563	24,508	26,195	†41,590	42,300	42,733
Claims on Local Government	52b	2	8	5	—	†35	7	7	210	243	†6	23	58
Claims on Nonfin.Pub.Enterprises	52c	188	180	422	478	†122	106	119	150	101	†236	245	490
Claims on Private Sector	52d	3,049	4,335	4,076	5,172	†5,323	7,472	10,720	14,480	16,576	†11,116	12,319	16,262
Liquid Liabilities	55l	1,717	2,140	3,434	4,762	†7,326	11,358	15,015	17,840	19,512	†20,313	23,015	25,925
Money Market Instruments	56aa	—	—	—	—	†365	509	360	320	270	†—	—	—
Liabs. of Central Bank: Securities	56ac	—	—	—	—	†278	2,278	883	797	773	†1,325	950	1,341
Capital Accounts	57a	300	714	995	865	†2,837	2,624	4,278	6,970	6,766	†2,825	3,413	4,013
Other Items (Net)	57r	−613	336	−1,162	−653	†−3,700	−4,176	−5,221	−6,277	−8,105	†6,553	5,071	4,350
Interest Rates						*Percent Per Annum*							
Discount Rate (End of period)	60	15.00	11.75	10.50	….	….	….	….	….	….	….	….	….
Savings Rate	60k	8.12	8.53	8.81	8.87	9.04	8.87	8.59	†8.39	8.71	8.55	6.23	4.23
Savings Rate (Foreign Currency)	60k.f	3.78	4.30	4.64	5.07	5.51	5.28	5.19	†5.81	5.37	5.49	4.11	3.19
Deposit Rate	60l	12.01	11.61	11.70	11.15	12.35	12.41	10.77	†11.83	10.80	11.56	7.79	5.55
Deposit Rate (Foreign Currency)	60l.f	4.85	5.26	5.67	6.03	7.25	7.55	7.22	†7.95	8.86	9.01	6.94	5.08
Lending Rate	60p	19.32	20.23	20.14	19.89	20.72	21.02	21.63	†17.57	18.14	18.55	18.30	15.55
Lending Rate (Foreign Currency)	60p.f	….	….	….	15.50	16.89	17.63	17.90	†15.50	15.39	15.87	14.28	12.05
Prices and Labor						*Index Numbers (2000=100): Period Averages*							
Consumer Prices	64.c	41.0	49.4	52.7	58.5	65.3	71.3	80.6	89.6	100.0	107.4	111.6	117.4
						Number in Thousands: Period Averages							
Labor Force	67d	1,313	1,365	1,419	1,478	1,537	1,598	1,661	1,729	1,815	1,900	….	….
Employment	67e	1,124	1,122	1,177	1,228	1,292	1,370	1,442	1,544	1,637	1,702	….	….
Unemployment	67c	189	244	243	250	245	228	220	185	178	203	….	….
Unemployment Rate (%)	67r	14.4	17.8	17.1	16.9	16.0	14.3	13.2	10.7	9.8	10.7	….	….
International Transactions						*Millions of US Dollars*							
Exports	70..d	223.1	267.0	334.7	456.8	466.4	576.8	573.2	545.3	645.1	592.4	596.3	….
Imports, c.i.f.	71..d	855.1	744.0	870.3	992.7	1,153.9	1,449.7	1,491.6	1,861.9	1,805.5	1,779.3	1,795.5	….
Imports, f.o.b.	71.vd	770.9	669.6	783.8	897.1	1,043.5	1,370.7	1,396.9	1,698.8	1,653.2	1,620.4	1,636.4	….

Nicaragua 278

		1992	1993	1994	1995	1996	1997	1998	1999	2000	2001	2002	2003
Balance of Payments			*Millions of US Dollars: Minus Sign Indicates Debit*
Current Account, n.i.e.	78ald	−834.0	−644.3	−910.9	−722.5	−824.8	−840.8	−686.6	−928.4	−791.9	−784.8	−783.7	−779.5
Goods: Exports f.o.b.	78aad	223.1	267.0	375.9	545.0	595.2	744.8	761.0	748.6	880.6	910.9	916.7	1,049.1
Goods: Imports f.o.b.	78abd	−770.8	−659.4	−804.4	−929.5	−1,121.7	−1,473.1	−1,509.6	−1,819.8	−1,801.5	−1,808.2	−1,853.1	−2,021.2
Trade Balance	78acd	−547.7	−392.4	−428.5	−384.5	−526.5	−728.3	−748.6	−1,071.2	−920.9	−897.3	−936.4	−972.1
Services: Credit	78add	86.2	100.2	112.7	116.6	128.8	156.8	183.7	214.2	221.3	223.4	226.2	249.0
Services: Debit	78aed	−148.3	−156.6	−172.9	−220.5	−252.8	−239.4	−267.8	−334.7	−343.4	−353.1	−335.5	−372.1
Balance on Goods & Services	78afd	−609.8	−448.8	−488.7	−488.4	−650.5	−810.9	−832.7	−1,191.7	−1,043.0	−1,027.0	−1,045.7	−1,095.2
Income: Credit	78agd	7.5	5.4	6.7	7.1	10.5	14.7	26.0	30.7	30.7	14.7	9.2	6.7
Income: Debit	78ahd	−502.3	−434.5	−478.9	−379.2	−334.8	−279.4	−211.2	−227.5	−232.5	−255.0	−209.6	−209.9
Balance on Gds, Serv. & Inc.	78aid	−1,104.6	−877.9	−960.9	−860.5	−974.8	−1,075.6	−1,017.9	−1,388.5	−1,244.8	−1,267.3	−1,246.1	−1,298.4
Current Transfers, n.i.e.: Credit	78ajd	270.6	233.6	50.0	138.0	150.0	234.8	331.3	460.1	452.9	482.5	462.4	518.9
Current Transfers: Debit	78akd	−	−	−	−	−	−	−	−	−	−	−	−
Capital Account, n.i.e.	78bcd	−	−	244.6	227.0	262.1	194.1	194.4	307.2	308.9	294.7	248.2	261.6
Capital Account, n.i.e.: Credit	78bad	−	−	244.6	227.0	262.1	194.1	194.4	307.2	308.9	294.7	248.2	261.6
Capital Account: Debit	78bbd	−	−	−	−	−	−	−	−	−	−	−	−
Financial Account, n.i.e.	78bjd	−538.3	−502.8	−895.2	−611.5	−332.0	33.5	231.6	525.5	62.7	58.3	−13.8	−9.2
Direct Investment Abroad	78bdd	−	−	−	−	−	−	−	−	−	−	−	−
Dir. Invest. in Rep. Econ., n.i.e.	78bed	15.0	38.8	46.7	88.9	120.0	203.4	218.2	337.3	266.9	150.2	203.9	201.3
Portfolio Investment Assets	78bfd	−	−	−	−	−	−	−	−	−	−	−	−
Equity Securities	78bkd	−	−	−	−	−	−	−	−	−	−	−	−
Debt Securities	78bld	−	−	−	−	−	−	−	−	−	−	−	−
Portfolio Investment Liab., n.i.e.	78bgd	−	−	−	−	−	−	−	−	−	−	−	−
Equity Securities	78bmd	−	−	−	−	−	−	−	−	−	−	−	−
Debt Securities	78bnd	−	−	−	−	−	−	−	−	−	−	−	−
Financial Derivatives Assets	78bwd	....	....										
Financial Derivatives Liabilities	78bxd	....	....										
Other Investment Assets	78bhd	−5.9	−10.1	−1.3	−32.0	−54.3	−70.8	55.2	22.2	79.9	−60.4	2.9	−16.0
Monetary Authorities	78bod	....	....										
General Government	78bpd	−	−										
Banks	78bqd	−6.4	−10.1	−1.3	−32.0	−54.3	−70.8	55.2	22.2	79.9	−60.4	2.9	−16.0
Other Sectors	78brd	.5											
Other Investment Liab., n.i.e.	78bid	−547.4	−531.5	−940.6	−668.4	−397.7	−99.1	−41.8	166.0	−284.1	−31.5	−220.6	−194.5
Monetary Authorities	78bsd	−88.0	−94.9	−544.3	−221.7	−126.1	−106.0	−18.1	62.4	−39.4	−19.5	−24.7	2.4
General Government	78btd	−459.7	−390.7	−418.7	−381.2	−295.4	−103.1	−154.8	−63.9	−73.6	−83.1	−184.4	−183.4
Banks	78bud	−1.7	−16.6	14.3	5.8	6.0	25.1	.3	63.6	−19.2	38.4	−35.9	−10.7
Other Sectors	78bvd	2.0	−29.3	8.1	−71.3	17.8	84.9	130.8	103.9	−151.9	32.7	24.4	−2.8
Net Errors and Omissions	78cad	60.2	128.1	42.7	142.7	146.5	320.1	−141.3	−299.5	−35.5	−61.2	135.1	26.4
Overall Balance	78cbd	−1,312.0	−1,019.0	−1,518.8	−964.3	−748.2	−293.1	−401.9	−395.2	−455.8	−493.0	−414.2	−500.7
Reserves and Related Items	79dad	1,312.0	1,019.0	1,518.8	964.3	748.2	293.1	401.9	395.2	455.8	493.0	414.2	500.7
Reserve Assets	79dbd	−.5	79.4	−84.6	11.5	−53.1	−173.2	30.3	−156.5	16.8	113.9	−71.5	−45.4
Use of Fund Credit and Loans	79dcd	−	−	26.1	−12.9	−9.3	−	22.6	105.3	20.9	−5.0	4.0	21.6
Exceptional Financing	79ded	1,312.5	939.6	1,577.3	965.7	810.6	466.3	349.0	446.4	418.1	384.1	481.6	524.6
Government Finance			*Millions of Córdobas: Year Ending December 31*
Deficit (-) or Surplus	80	−302	−4	−4	−68	−254	−243	−415	−1,282	−2,357p	−3,900p	....	....
Revenue	81	1,892	2,222	2,222	3,134	3,654	4,660	5,906	6,739	7,541p	7,654p	....	....
Grants Received	81z	400	806	806	1,191	1,149	822	675	1,935	1,874p	1,712p	....	....
Expenditure	82	2,578	3,009	3,009	4,246	5,055	5,719	6,995	9,774	11,755p	13,136p	....	....
Lending Minus Repayments	83	16	23	23	147	2	6	−	182	17p	130p	....	....
Financing													
Domestic	84a	−568	−	−	100	−598	−22	−1,266	−1,304	619p	2,375p	....	....
Foreign	85a	870	4	4	−32	852	265	1,680	2,586	1,738p	1,525p	....	....
National Accounts			*Millions of Córdobas*
Househ.Cons.Expend.,incl.NPISHs	96f	8,553.0	9,715.0	16,269.9	18,890.7	22,089.7	25,541.1	29,708.1	33,856.8	38,550.3	41,238.9	44,919.7	49,290.4
Government Consumption Expend.	91f	1,763.0	1,891.0	2,978.5	3,589.3	4,088.3	4,393.0	5,353.7	7,226.6	8,610.4	9,723.4	8,872.4	9,963.6
Gross Fixed Capital Formation	93e	1,848.0	2,134.0	4,062.4	4,855.2	6,093.1	7,762.5	9,574.4	14,734.8	14,847.0	15,940.6	16,369.4	17,313.7
Changes in Inventories	93i	28.0	−41.0	14.0	430.8	1,125.4	2,199.4	2,158.1	2,782.0	1,596.6	775.8	1,970.2	2,330.3
Exports of Goods and Services	90c	1,546.0	2,196.0	3,123.2	4,594.5	5,605.7	7,374.7	8,683.2	9,729.4	11,932.4	12,832.2	12,931.7	15,064.8
Imports of Goods and Services (-)	98c	4,775.0	5,145.0	6,439.7	8,331.1	10,993.4	15,303.7	17,673.0	24,131.8	25,417.9	26,510.8	27,964.7	31,504.6
Gross Domestic Product (GDP)	99b	8,964.0	10,750.0	20,008.4	24,029.3	28,008.7	31,967.1	37,804.5	44,197.8	50,118.9	54,000.1	57,098.7	62,458.3
Net Primary Income from Abroad	98.n	−2,436.5	−2,593.2	−3,174.5	−2,801.2	−2,735.6	−2,500.9	−1,960.5	−2,324.0	−2,559.7	−3,230.7	−2,856.0	−3,069.6
Gross National Income (GNI)	99a	6,527.5	8,156.8	16,833.8	21,228.1	25,273.1	29,466.1	35,844.0	41,873.7	47,559.1	50,769.3	54,242.7	59,388.7
GDP Vol. 1980 Prices	99b.p	18,178.0	18,107.0	18,711.0	19,518.0	20,450.0	21,494.0	22,368.0	24,031.0	25,449.0	26,251.0	26,526.7	....
GDP Volume (2000=100)	99bvp	71.7	71.4	†73.8	78.2	83.1	86.4	89.6	95.9	100.0	103.0	104.0	106.4
GDP Deflator (2000=100)	99bip	24.9	30.0	54.1	61.3	67.2	73.8	84.2	91.9	100.0	104.7	109.5	117.1
			*Millions: Midyear Estimates*
Population	99z	4.05	4.17	4.30	4.43	4.55	4.68	4.81	4.94	5.07	5.20	5.34	5.47

Niger 692

		1992	1993	1994	1995	1996	1997	1998	1999	2000	2001	2002	2003
Exchange Rates		\multicolumn{12}{c}{*Francs per SDR: End of Period*}
Official Rate	aa	378.57	404.89	†780.44	728.38	753.06	807.94	791.61	†896.19	918.49	935.39	850.37	771.76
		\multicolumn{12}{c}{*Francs per US Dollar: End of Period (ae) Period Average (rf)*}
Official Rate	ae	275.32	294.77	†534.60	490.00	523.70	598.81	562.21	†652.95	704.95	744.31	625.50	519.36
Official Rate	rf	264.69	283.16	†555.20	499.15	511.55	583.67	589.95	†615.70	711.98	733.04	696.99	581.20
Fund Position		\multicolumn{12}{c}{*Millions of SDRs: End of Period*}
Quota	2f.s	48.3	48.3	48.3	48.3	48.3	48.3	48.3	65.8	65.8	65.8	65.8	65.8
SDRs	1b.s	–	.4	.3	.2	1.3	.1	.1	1.0	–	.3	.5	1.8
Reserve Position in the Fund	1c.s	8.6	8.6	8.6	8.6	8.6	8.6	8.6	8.6	8.6	8.6	8.6	8.6
Total Fund Cred.&Loans Outstg	2tl	44.6	37.7	41.8	35.0	36.6	45.0	54.1	49.6	56.8	64.3	78.3	88.4
International Liquidity		\multicolumn{12}{c}{*Millions of US Dollars Unless Otherwise Indicated: End of Period*}
Total Reserves minus Gold	1l.d	225.0	192.0	110.3	94.7	78.5	53.3	53.1	39.2	80.4	107.0	133.9	114.1
SDRs	1b.d	–	.6	.4	.3	1.9	.2	.2	1.3	–	.3	.7	2.7
Reserve Position in the Fund	1c.d	11.8	11.8	12.5	12.7	12.3	11.6	12.1	11.7	11.2	10.8	11.6	12.7
Foreign Exchange	1d.d	213.2	179.7	97.4	81.7	64.3	41.5	40.8	26.1	69.2	95.9	121.6	98.7
Gold (Million Fine Troy Ounces)	1ad	.011	.011	.011	–	–	–	–	–	–	–	–	–
Gold (National Valuation)	1and	3.8	4.1	4.1	–	–	–	–	–	–	–	–	–
Monetary Authorities: Other Liab	4..d	45.7	49.8	2.9	1.5	2.2	.4	1.1	2.2	1.6	1.3	3.2	–3.4
Deposit Money Banks: Assets	7a.d	26.7	23.8	40.6	41.5	35.1	40.9	37.9	44.2	41.3	53.7	48.4	65.4
Liabilities	7b.d	130.0	55.5	49.9	44.9	41.7	32.9	30.5	39.5	42.0	35.7	26.2	50.5
Monetary Authorities		\multicolumn{12}{c}{*Billions of Francs: End of Period*}
Foreign Assets	11	61.9	56.6	58.9	46.4	41.1	31.9	29.8	25.6	56.7	79.6	83.8	59.2
Claims on Central Government	12a	31.0	33.0	47.3	52.5	57.2	67.7	74.3	69.5	79.9	85.6	99.7	109.2
Claims on Deposit Money Banks	12e	27.0	27.0	1.1	4.9	4.6	3.2	3.9	1.2	1.2	1.2	1.2	1.2
Claims on Other Financial Insts	12f	–	–	–	–	–	–	–	–	–	–	–	–
Reserve Money	14	83.2	79.6	60.5	68.4	64.4	50.7	32.5	43.0	44.6	66.3	63.2	40.3
of which: Currency Outside DMBs	14a	39.5	48.3	48.7	59.6	57.7	41.7	24.5	34.1	32.2	49.3	39.3	9.1
Foreign Liabilities	16c	29.4	30.0	34.2	26.3	28.7	36.6	43.4	45.9	53.3	61.0	68.6	66.5
Central Government Deposits	16d	3.0	3.3	15.6	8.3	8.1	8.5	16.4	4.1	30.4	38.0	45.2	46.4
Other Items (Net)	17r	4.2	3.6	–3.0	.9	1.7	7.1	15.7	3.3	9.5	1.1	7.7	16.5
Deposit Money Banks		\multicolumn{12}{c}{*Billions of Francs: End of Period*}
Reserves	20	43.5	29.9	9.7	8.3	5.9	8.1	7.7	8.8	10.5	15.2	22.1	30.1
Foreign Assets	21	7.3	7.0	21.7	20.3	18.4	24.5	21.3	28.9	29.1	39.9	30.3	34.0
Claims on Central Government	22a	16.0	2.9	13.4	12.4	14.1	16.7	12.9	12.1	15.3	10.7	10.4	10.9
Claims on Private Sector	22d	72.4	64.9	71.4	42.0	43.3	35.5	49.4	47.7	61.4	66.0	75.8	83.0
Claims on Other Financial Insts	22f	–	–	–	–	–	–	–	–	–	–	–	–
Demand Deposits	24	30.5	28.8	40.3	38.4	30.2	28.8	32.0	33.9	43.3	52.4	54.2	61.6
Time Deposits	25	49.2	41.4	37.2	33.6	34.3	25.3	20.6	23.8	27.2	32.7	40.5	44.4
Foreign Liabilities	26c	12.2	10.0	23.3	18.4	18.5	19.7	17.2	25.8	29.6	26.6	16.1	26.0
Long-Term Foreign Liabilities	26cl	23.6	6.4	3.3	3.6	3.3	–	–	–	–	–	.3	.3
Central Government Deposits	26d	24.1	21.5	21.0	19.3	19.8	3.9	9.8	8.8	10.2	12.0	13.5	12.8
Credit from Monetary Authorities	26g	27.0	27.0	27.8	4.9	4.6	2.0	3.9	1.2	1.2	1.2	1.2	1.2
Other Items (Net)	27r	–27.4	–30.3	–36.8	–35.1	–29.0	5.2	7.7	4.0	4.9	7.0	12.7	11.6
Treasury Claims: Private Sector	22d.i	–	.1	–	–	–	–	–	–	–	–	–	–
Post Office: Checking Deposits	24..i	1.5	1.9	2.1	1.8	2.6	2.5	2.7	.3	1.2	1.9	1.7	2.4
Monetary Survey		\multicolumn{12}{c}{*Billions of Francs: End of Period*}
Foreign Assets (Net)	31n	27.6	23.7	23.2	22.1	12.2	–	–9.4	–17.2	2.9	31.9	29.4	.8
Domestic Credit	32	93.8	77.9	97.6	81.2	89.3	110.1	113.1	116.9	117.3	114.3	128.9	146.3
Claims on Central Govt. (Net)	32an	21.4	12.9	26.1	39.2	46.0	74.5	63.7	68.9	55.8	48.3	53.1	63.3
Claims on Private Sector	32d	72.4	64.9	71.4	42.0	43.3	35.6	49.4	47.7	61.4	66.0	75.8	83.0
Claims on Other Financial Insts	32f	–	–	–	–	–	–	–	–	–	–	–	–
Money	34	71.6	79.5	91.8	100.2	90.7	73.1	59.6	68.8	76.9	104.0	95.6	73.6
Quasi-Money	35	49.2	41.4	37.2	33.6	34.3	25.3	20.6	23.8	27.2	32.7	40.5	44.4
Long-Term Foreign Liabilities	36cl	23.6	6.4	3.3	3.6	3.3	–	–	–	–	–	.3	.3
Other Items (Net)	37r	–23.0	–25.7	–11.6	–34.1	–26.8	11.7	23.4	6.9	16.1	9.5	21.8	28.8
Money plus Quasi-Money	35l	120.8	120.9	129.0	133.8	125.0	98.4	80.2	92.6	104.1	136.8	136.1	118.1
Interest Rates		\multicolumn{12}{c}{*Percent Per Annum*}
Bank Rate (End of Period)	60	12.50	†6.00	6.00	6.00	6.00	6.00	6.00	6.00	6.00	6.00	6.00	4.50
Money Market Rate	60b	11.44	....	....	....	....	....	4.81	4.95	4.95	4.95	4.95	4.95
Deposit Rate	60l	7.75	....	....	....	....	....	3.50	3.50	3.50	3.50	3.50	3.50
Lending Rate	60p	16.75	....	....	....	....	....	....	....	....	....	....	....
Prices		\multicolumn{12}{c}{*Index Numbers (2000=100): Period Averages*}
Consumer Prices	64	59.1	58.4	79.4	87.8	92.4	†95.1	99.5	97.2	100.0	104.0	106.7	105.0
		\multicolumn{12}{c}{*Number in Thousands: Period Averages*}
International Transactions		\multicolumn{12}{c}{*Millions of Francs*}
Exports	70	88,200	81,200	125,100	143,800	166,300	158,500	197,000	176,600	201,500	199,700	194,800	196,800
Imports, c.i.f	71	126,684	106,123	182,097	186,501	229,271	218,067	277,886	206,500	230,400	242,800	258,700	265,700

2004, International Monetary Fund : *International Financial Statistics Yearbook*

Niger 692

		1992	1993	1994	1995	1996	1997	1998	1999	2000	2001	2002	2003
Balance of Payments		*Millions of US Dollars: Minus Sign Indicates Debit*											
Current Account, n.i.e.	78ald	−159.2	−97.2	−126.1	−151.7	....	....	....	....	....	....	....	....
Goods: Exports f.o.b.	78aad	347.3	300.4	226.8	288.1	....	....	....	....	....	....	....	....
Goods: Imports f.o.b.	78abd	−396.5	−312.1	−271.3	−305.6	....	....	....	....	....	....	....	....
Trade Balance	78acd	−49.2	−11.7	−44.5	−17.6	....	....	....	....	....	....	....	....
Services: Credit	78add	57.7	36.5	30.4	33.3	....	....	....	....	....	....	....	....
Services: Debit	78aed	−201.0	−185.6	−149.1	−151.8	....	....	....	....	....	....	....	....
Balance on Goods & Services	78afd	−192.6	−160.9	−163.2	−136.0	....	....	....	....	....	....	....	....
Income: Credit	78agd	19.7	19.3	15.6	5.8	....	....	....	....	....	....	....	....
Income: Debit	78ahd	−54.1	−30.2	−45.2	−52.9	....	....	....	....	....	....	....	....
Balance on Gds, Serv. & Inc	78aid	−227.0	−171.7	−192.8	−183.2	....	....	....	....	....	....	....	....
Current Transfers, n.i.e.: Credit	78ajd	133.6	139.5	115.1	60.6	....	....	....	....	....	....	....	....
Current Transfers: Debit	78akd	−65.7	−65.0	−48.5	−29.1	....	....	....	....	....	....	....	....
Capital Account, n.i.e.	78bcd	109.0	109.3	88.2	65.3	....	....	....	....	....	....	....	....
Capital Account, n.i.e.: Credit	78bad	109.0	109.3	88.2	65.3	....	....	....	....	....	....	....	....
Capital Account: Debit	78bbd	....	....	....	....	....	....	....	....	....	....	....	....
Financial Account, n.i.e.	78bjd	50.8	−123.3	29.9	−46.1	....	....	....	....	....	....	....	....
Direct Investment Abroad	78bdd	−40.7	−5.8	1.8	−7.1	....	....	....	....	....	....	....	....
Dir. Invest. in Rep. Econ., n.i.e.	78bed	56.4	−34.4	−11.3	7.2	....	....	....	....	....	....	....	....
Portfolio Investment Assets	78bfd	....	....	....	....	....	....	....	....	....	....	....	....
Equity Securities	78bkd	....	....	....	....	....	....	....	....	....	....	....	....
Debt Securities	78bld	....	....	....	....	....	....	....	....	....	....	....	....
Portfolio Investment Liab., n.i.e.	78bgd	....	....	....	....	....	....	....	....	....	....	....	....
Equity Securities	78bmd	....	....	....	....	....	....	....	....	....	....	....	....
Debt Securities	78bnd	....	....	....	....	....	....	....	....	....	....	....	....
Financial Derivatives Assets	78bwd	....	....	....	....	....	....	....	....	....	....	....	....
Financial Derivatives Liabilities	78bxd	....	....	....	....	....	....	....	....	....	....	....	....
Other Investment Assets	78bhd	10.4	11.2	22.3	−18.4	....	....	....	....	....	....	....	....
Monetary Authorities	78bod	....	....	....	....	....	....	....	....	....	....	....	....
General Government	78bpd	.1	.1	.3	−	....	....	....	....	....	....	....	....
Banks	78bqd	....	....	....	....	....	....	....	....	....	....	....	....
Other Sectors	78brd	10.2	11.1	22.0	−18.4	....	....	....	....	....	....	....	....
Other Investment Liab., n.i.e.	78bid	24.8	−94.4	17.1	−27.8	....	....	....	....	....	....	....	....
Monetary Authorities	78bsd	34.6	7.7	−22.3	−2.3	....	....	....	....	....	....	....	....
General Government	78btd	31.4	−10.8	6.7	−14.8	....	....	....	....	....	....	....	....
Banks	78bud	6.2	−65.0	19.4	−10.8	....	....	....	....	....	....	....	....
Other Sectors	78bvd	−47.4	−26.3	13.3	.1	....	....	....	....	....	....	....	....
Net Errors and Omissions	78cad	−95.5	87.2	−67.8	114.4	....	....	....	....	....	....	....	....
Overall Balance	78cbd	−94.9	−23.9	−75.8	−18.1	....	....	....	....	....	....	....	....
Reserves and Related Items	79dad	94.9	23.9	75.8	18.1	....	....	....	....	....	....	....	....
Reserve Assets	79dbd	31.0	−19.9	28.7	−25.8	....	....	....	....	....	....	....	....
Use of Fund Credit and Loans	79dcd	−9.4	−9.6	5.4	−10.2	....	....	....	....	....	....	....	....
Exceptional Financing	79ded	73.3	53.3	41.7	54.1	....	....	....	....	....	....	....	....
National Accounts		*Billions of Francs*											
Househ.Cons.Expend.,incl.NPISHs	96f	526.2	520.1	604.5	648.8	808.1	853.7	997.1	1,011.1	874.0	926.9	1,020.6	....
Government Consumption Expend	91f	106.0	111.6	127.4	131.9	137.5	138.8	139.8	199.3	172.3	182.7	200.6	....
Gross Fixed Capital Formation	93e	63.0	75.3	102.3	98.5	122.3	129.3	181.2	124.0	146.4	146.2	176.7	....
Changes in Inventories	93i	9.9	−22.6	32.0	20.9	38.6	42.7	17.2	3.0	78.2	131.7	85.0	....
Exports of Goods and Services	90c	105.6	94.3	141.4	167.1	188.2	181.0	217.9	197.6	228.2	224.7	239.6	....
Imports of Goods and Services (-)	98c	151.7	131.3	220.6	232.6	261.5	262.5	328.2	292.4	324.3	334.1	367.6	....
Gross Domestic Product (GDP)	99b	620.6	647.3	787.1	834.6	1,033.2	1,083.0	1,225.0	1,242.6	1,174.8	1,278.1	1,354.9	....
GDP Volume 1987 Prices	99b.p	693.4	700.5	718.1	731.9	760.6	778.6	855.3	841.6	839.6	889.5	....	....
GDP Volume (2000=100)	99bvp	82.6	83.4	85.5	87.2	90.6	92.7	101.9	100.2	100.0	105.9	....	....
GDP Deflator (2000=100)	99bip	64.0	66.0	78.3	81.5	97.1	99.4	102.4	105.5	100.0	102.7	....	....
		Millions: Midyear Estimates											
Population	99z	8.17	8.45	8.74	9.04	9.35	9.67	10.01	10.37	10.74	11.13	11.54	11.97

Nigeria 694

		1992	1993	1994	1995	1996	1997	1998	1999	2000	2001	2002	2003
Exchange Rates						*Naira per SDR: End of Period*							
Principal Rate..................	aa	27.014	30.056	32.113	32.534	31.471	29.530	†30.816	134.437	142.734	141.948	171.843	202.835
					Naira per US Dollar: End of Period (ae) Period Average (rf)								
Principal Rate..................	ae	19.646	21.882	21.997	21.887	21.886	21.886	†21.886	97.950	109.550	112.950	126.400	136.500
Principal Rate..................	rf	17.298	22.065	21.996	21.895	21.884	21.886	†21.886	92.338	101.697	111.231	120.578	129.222
					Index Numbers (2000=100): Period Averages								
Principal Rate..................	ahx	623.0	461.1	462.5	464.3	464.5	464.5	464.5	112.0	100.0	91.4	84.5	78.7
Nominal Effective Exchange Rate.....	nec	385.0	293.4	386.3	200.2	193.1	208.8	212.4	102.1	100.0	95.5	85.8	72.3
Real Effective Exchange Rate..........	rec	71.7	78.5	145.8	123.6	152.9	175.5	192.5	97.6	100.0	111.0	111.6	104.1
Fund Position						*Millions of SDRs: End of Period*							
Quota................................	2f.s	1,282	1,282	1,282	1,282	1,282	1,282	1,282	1,753	1,753	1,753	1,753	1,753
SDRs.................................	1b.s	–	–	–	–	–	–	1	–	–	1	–	–
Reserve Position in the Fund..........	1c.s	–	–	–	–	–	–	–	–	–	–	–	–
of which: Outstg.Fund Borrowing...	2c	–	–	–	–	–	–	–	–	–	–	–	–
Total Fund Cred.&Loans Outstg........	2tl	–	–	–	–	–	–	–	–	–	–	–	–
International Liquidity					*Millions of US Dollars Unless Otherwise Indicated: End of Period*								
Total Reserves minus Gold.............	1l.d	967	1,372	1,386	1,443	4,076	7,582	7,101	5,450	9,911	10,457	7,331	7,128
SDRs.................................	1b.d	–	–	–	1	1	1	1	–	–	1	–	–
Reserve Position in the Fund..........	1c.d	–	–	–	–	–	–	–	–	–	–	–	–
Foreign Exchange.....................	1d.d	967	1,372	1,386	1,443	4,075	7,581	7,100	5,450	9,910	10,456	7,331	7,128
Gold (Million Fine Troy Ounces).......	1ad	.687	.687	.687	.687	.687	.687	.687	.687	.687	.687	.687	.687
Gold (National Valuation)..............	1and	1	1	1	1	1	1	1	–	–	–	–	–
Monetary Authorities: Other Liab.....	4..d	2,993	2,539	2,747	2,450	2,162	2,313	1,630	172	1,224	1,080	875	685
Deposit Money Banks: Assets.........	7a.d	1,424	1,539	1,157	3,490	2,899	3,180	4,395	1,651	2,035	2,701	3,150	3,206
Liabilities...................	7b.d	122	64	130	137	148	137	299	56	138	152	150	154
Monetary Authorities						*Millions of Naira: End of Period*							
Foreign Assets.......................	11	†42,401	31,869	33,467	41,426	180,799	173,665	149,268	506,794	1,091,108	1,156,578	1,013,516	1,065,099
Claims on Central Government.......	12a	†139,847	211,409	308,858	438,481	313,849	406,053	456,985	532,292	513,003	716,769	532,453	552,859
Claims on State & Local Govts.......	12b	†94	12	124	25	2	7	7	7	7	–	–	–
Claims on Nonfin.Pub.Enterprises.....	12c	†2,347	2,747	3,655	3,480	1,525	1,453	926	692	951	1,080	164	212
Claims on Private Sector..............	12d	†570	850	763	604	967	778	517	884	2,163	3,103	1,646	1,705
Claims on Deposit Money Banks......	12e	†3,855	7,802	12,987	24,222	27,697	21,282	21,818	22,070	36,176	20,604	5,554	15,572
Claims on Nonbank Financial Insts...	12g	†1,492	3,100	2,941	3,160	3,267	5,916	4,580	4,568	4,881	6,330	5,488	6,878
Reserve Money......................	14	†77,326	115,542	151,737	182,795	193,953	202,667	236,470	287,893	426,610	571,928	646,876	924,393
of which: Currency Outside DMBs..	14a	†36,756	57,845	90,601	106,843	116,121	130,668	156,716	186,457	274,011	338,671	386,942	412,155
Foreign Liabilities.....................	16c	†33,151	945	187	7,060	3,651	11,751	3,957	567	23,924	11,394	5,575	5,982
Long-Term Foreign Liabilities...........	16cl	†25,652	54,611	60,230	46,558	43,672	38,881	31,728	16,304	110,141	110,546	104,982	87,455
Central Government Deposits..........	16d	†54,284	63,478	66,740	194,599	253,754	394,740	362,429	516,967	856,007	895,751	573,700	298,730
Capital Accounts.....................	17a	†34,589	66,251	77,543	76,542	69,618	73,083	85,212	259,537	344,995	325,030	97,559	345,698
Other Items (Net).....................	17r	†−34,397	−43,039	6,358	3,843	−36,542	−111,968	−85,695	−13,960	−113,389	−10,186	130,129	−19,935
Deposit Money Banks						*Millions of Naira: End of Period*							
Reserves............................	20	†32,141	44,488	53,441	60,281	64,343	64,903	65,895	120,585	170,099	318,986	321,495	362,400
Foreign Assets.......................	21	†27,968	33,680	25,449	76,390	63,440	69,590	96,184	161,754	222,988	305,029	398,210	437,659
Claims on Central Government........	22a	†6,908	39,292	47,829	22,894	56,469	46,187	58,881	202,253	292,975	182,116	467,522	378,205
Claims on State & Local Govts.........	22b	†1,419	1,532	2,117	2,909	3,528	1,475	935	2,095	7,558	26,796	17,327	20,235
Claims on Private Sector..............	22d	†74,037	87,249	141,400	201,181	251,325	309,883	365,609	446,959	580,442	817,690	931,138	1,182,964
Demand Deposits....................	24	†36,567	55,592	74,398	85,564	104,017	131,887	150,977	209,899	356,954	448,021	503,870	577,664
Time, Savings,& Fgn.Currency Dep...	25	†49,812	74,058	88,505	111,255	134,756	154,633	198,337	298,908	386,396	499,162	653,241	759,633
Money Market Instruments.............	26aa	†489	653	329	283	692	130	285	74	572	627	877	1,138
Bonds..............................	26ab	†290	302	3,030	9,002	9,899	14,488	10,929	18,100	18,212	25,610	24,533	30,657
Foreign Liabilities.....................	26c	†2,393	1,409	2,860	2,988	3,229	3,009	6,540	5,474	15,099	17,185	18,951	21,081
Central Government Deposits..........	26d	†1,360	2,055	1,834	3,773	6,098	11,143	13,521	40,773	73,961	28,342	52,636	79,764
Credit from Monetary Authorities.....	26g	†233	825	10,526	15,172	17,377	8,434	7,762	6,554	5,360	14,547	22,159	44,303
Capital Accounts.....................	27a	†56,084	65,727	71,598	88,854	116,729	136,368	169,117	222,146	249,211	364,259	500,751	537,208
Other Items (Net).....................	27r	†−4,753	5,621	17,158	46,766	46,308	31,946	30,038	131,719	168,296	252,864	358,672	330,015

2004, International Monetary Fund : International Financial Statistics Yearbook

Nigeria 694

		1992	1993	1994	1995	1996	1997	1998	1999	2000	2001	2002	2003
Monetary Survey						*Millions of Naira: End of Period*							
Foreign Assets (Net)	31n	†34,824	63,195	55,869	107,768	237,359	228,494	234,954	662,507	1,275,072	1,433,027	1,387,199	1,475,694
Domestic Credit	32	†171,071	280,658	439,114	474,361	371,079	365,871	512,490	632,010	472,012	829,791	1,329,401	1,764,563
Claims on Central Govt. (Net)	32an	†91,112	185,168	288,114	263,003	110,466	46,358	139,916	176,805	−123,990	−25,209	373,639	552,569
Claims on State & Local Govts	32b	†1,513	1,544	2,241	2,934	3,530	1,482	941	2,102	7,564	26,796	17,327	20,235
Claims on Nonfin.Pub.Enterprises	32c	†2,347	2,747	3,655	3,480	1,525	1,453	926	692	951	1,080	164	212
Claims on Private Sector	32d	†74,607	88,099	142,163	201,785	252,292	310,661	366,127	447,843	582,606	820,793	932,783	1,184,669
Claims on Nonbank Fin. Insts	32g	†1,492	3,100	2,941	3,160	3,267	5,916	4,580	4,568	4,881	6,330	5,488	6,878
Money	34	†79,273	124,422	178,440	207,509	235,577	275,098	327,300	400,826	649,684	816,708	946,253	1,225,559
Quasi-Money	35	†49,812	74,058	88,505	111,255	134,756	154,633	198,337	298,908	386,396	499,162	653,241	759,633
Money Market Instruments	36aa	†489	653	329	283	692	130	285	74	572	627	877	1,138
Bonds	36ab	†290	302	3,030	9,002	9,899	14,488	10,929	18,100	18,212	25,610	24,533	30,657
Long-Term Foreign Liabilities	36cl	†25,652	54,611	60,230	46,558	43,672	38,881	31,728	16,304	110,141	110,546	104,982	87,455
Capital Accounts	37a	†90,672	131,979	149,141	165,396	186,347	209,452	254,328	481,682	594,207	689,289	598,310	882,906
Other Items (Net)	37r	†−40,293	−42,171	15,307	42,127	−2,505	−98,317	−75,462	78,622	−12,127	120,876	388,403	252,909
Money plus Quasi-Money	35l	†129,085	198,479	266,945	318,763	370,334	429,731	525,638	699,735	1,036,080	1,315,869	1,599,495	1,985,192
Other Banking Institutions						*Millions of Naira: End of Period*							
Reserves	40..m	3,697	....	....	....	....	....	....	....	....	....	....	....
Foreign Assets	41..m	8,582	....	....	....	....	....	....	....	....	....	....	....
Claims on Central Government	42a.m	1,189	....	....	....	....	....	....	....	....	....	....	....
Claims on Private Sector	42d.m	11,761	....	....	....	....	....	....	....	....	....	....	....
Demand Deposits	44..m	3,303	....	....	....	....	....	....	....	....	....	....	....
Time and Savings Deposits	45..m	8,362	....	....	....	....	....	....	....	....	....	....	....
Foreign Liabilities	46c.m	1,259	....	....	....	....	....	....	....	....	....	....	....
Cred.from Deposit Money Banks	46h.m	6,551	....	....	....	....	....	....	....	....	....	....	....
Capital Accounts	47a.m	3,534	....	....	....	....	....	....	....	....	....	....	....
Other Items (Net)	47r.m	2,221	....	....	....	....	....	....	....	....	....	....	....
Interest Rates						*Percent Per Annum*							
Discount Rate (End of Period)	60	17.50	26.00	13.50	13.50	13.50	13.50	13.50	18.00	14.00	20.50	16.50	15.00
Treasury Bill Rate	60c	17.89	24.50	12.87	12.50	12.25	12.00	12.26	17.82	15.50	17.50	19.03	14.79
Deposit Rate	60l	18.04	23.24	13.09	13.53	13.06	7.17	10.11	12.81	11.69	15.26	16.67	14.22
Lending Rate	60p	24.76	31.65	20.48	20.23	19.84	17.80	18.18	20.29	21.27	23.44	24.77	20.71
Prices and Production						*Index Numbers (2000=100): Period Averages*							
Consumer Prices	64	12.7	19.9	31.2	54.0	69.8	75.6	83.3	87.3	100.0	113.0	127.5	†145.4
Industrial Production	66	98.5	92.7	90.9	90.6	93.2	93.9	94.0	91.3	100.0	101.4	102.6	102.6
Crude Petroleum Production	66aa	84.0	83.3	83.9	86.2	89.2	91.6	93.5	93.9	100.0	100.0	85.1	96.7
Manufacturing Production	66ey	130.9	105.3	104.3	98.6	100.4	100.1	96.3	99.6	100.0	102.9	105.8	105.6
International Transactions						*Millions of US Dollars*							
Exports	70..d	11,886	9,908	9,415	†12,342	16,154	15,207	9,855	13,856	20,975	17,261	15,107	19,887
Crude Petroleum (Naira)	70aa	201,384	213,779	9,171	†11,449	15,866	14,850	8,565	12,665	18,897	17,769	14,855	19,596
Imports, c.i.f.	71..d	8,275	5,537	6,613	†8,222	6,438	9,501	9,211	8,588	8,721	11,586	7,547	10,853
Volume of Exports						*2000=100*							
Crude Petroleum	72aa	95	92	92	91	103	106	122	101	100	106	85	98

Nigeria 694

		1992	1993	1994	1995	1996	1997	1998	1999	2000	2001	2002	2003
Balance of Payments					*Millions of US Dollars: Minus Sign Indicates Debit*								
Current Account, n.i.e.	78ald	2,268	−780	−2,128	−2,578	3,507	552	−4,244	506	....	....	....	....
Goods: Exports f.o.b.	78aad	11,791	9,910	9,459	11,734	16,117	15,207	8,971	12,876	....	....	....	....
Goods: Imports f.o.b.	78abd	−7,181	−6,662	−6,511	−8,222	−6,438	−9,501	−9,211	−8,588	....	....	....	....
Trade Balance	78acd	4,611	3,248	2,948	3,513	9,679	5,706	−240	4,288	....	....	....	....
Services: Credit	78add	1,053	1,163	371	608	733	786	884	980	....	....	....	....
Services: Debit	78aed	−1,810	−2,726	−3,007	−4,619	−4,827	−4,712	−4,166	−3,476	....	....	....	....
Balance on Goods & Services	78afd	3,853	1,685	312	−499	5,584	1,781	−3,522	1,792	....	....	....	....
Income: Credit	78agd	156	58	49	101	115	258	333	240	....	....	....	....
Income: Debit	78ahd	−2,494	−3,335	−2,986	−2,979	−3,137	−3,404	−2,624	−2,818	....	....	....	....
Balance on Gds, Serv. & Inc.	78aid	1,515	−1,593	−2,626	−3,377	2,562	−1,365	−5,813	−786	....	....	....	....
Current Transfers, n.i.e.: Credit	78ajd	817	857	550	804	947	1,920	1,574	1,301	....	....	....	....
Current Transfers: Debit	78akd	−64	−44	−52	−5	−2	−4	−5	−9	....	....	....	....
Capital Account, n.i.e.	78bcd	−	−	−	−66	−68	−49	−54	−48	....	....	....	....
Capital Account, n.i.e.: Credit	78bad	−	−	−	−	−	−	−	−	....	....	....	....
Capital Account: Debit	78bbd	−	−	−	−66	−68	−49	−54	−48	....	....	....	....
Financial Account, n.i.e.	78bjd	−7,784	−1,043	329	−46	−4,155	−425	1,502	−4,002	....	....	....	....
Direct Investment Abroad	78bdd	−	−	−	−	−	....	....	....	....	....	....	....
Dir. Invest. in Rep. Econ., n.i.e.	78bed	897	1,345	1,959	1,079	1,593	1,539	1,051	1,005	....	....	....	....
Portfolio Investment Assets	78bfd	−	−	−	−	−	9	51	50	....	....	....	....
Equity Securities	78bkd	−	−	−	−	−	−	−	−	....	....	....	....
Debt Securities	78bld	−	−	−	−	−	9	51	50	....	....	....	....
Portfolio Investment Liab., n.i.e.	78bgd	1,884	−18	−27	−82	−173	−76	−59	−39	....	....	....	....
Equity Securities	78bmd	−	−	−	−	−	....	....	....	....	....	....	....
Debt Securities	78bnd	1,884	−18	−27	−82	−173	−76	−59	−39	....	....	....	....
Financial Derivatives Assets	78bwd	....	....	....	....	....	....	....	....	....	....	....	....
Financial Derivatives Liabilities	78bxd	....	....	....	....	....	....	....	....	....	....	....	....
Other Investment Assets	78bhd	−5,840	−1,345	−1,286	−3,295	−4,320	−2,183	−332	−3,319	....	....	....	....
Monetary Authorities	78bod	−	−	−	−	−	....	....	....	....	....	....	....
General Government	78bpd	−2,168	−1,087	−969	−1,030	−	....	....	....	....	....	....	....
Banks	78bqd	−746	−249	320	−560	138	−80	−284	−651	....	....	....	....
Other Sectors	78brd	−2,926	−8	−637	−1,705	−4,458	−2,103	−48	−2,668	....	....	....	....
Other Investment Liab., n.i.e.	78bid	−4,725	−1,026	−317	2,251	−1,256	286	792	−1,699	....	....	....	....
Monetary Authorities	78bsd	−	−	−	−	−	−	−	−	....	....	....	....
General Government	78btd	−5,180	−1,736	−1,885	−1,535	−3,039	−2,883	−1,637	−1,659	....	....	....	....
Banks	78bud	33	−28	−1	−	−4	1	21	34	....	....	....	....
Other Sectors	78bvd	423	738	1,570	3,787	1,787	3,167	2,407	−74	....	....	....	....
Net Errors and Omissions	78cad	−122	−88	−139	−83	−45	−62	−77	7	....	....	....	....
Overall Balance	78cbd	−5,638	−1,911	−1,938	−2,774	−761	15	−2,873	−3,538	....	....	....	....
Reserves and Related Items	79dad	5,638	1,911	1,938	2,774	761	−15	2,873	3,538	....	....	....	....
Reserve Assets	79dbd	3,727	−611	−327	217	−2,634	−3,507	481	1,650	....	....	....	....
Use of Fund Credit and Loans	79dcd	−	−	−	−	−	−	−	−	....	....	....	....
Exceptional Financing	79ded	1,911	2,522	2,265	2,557	3,395	3,491	2,392	1,887	....	....	....	....
Government Finance					*Millions of Naira: Year Ending December 31*								
Deficit (-) or Surplus	80	−39,532	−107,735	−70,270	1,000	37,049	−5,000	−133,389	−285,105	−103,777	−221,049	−301,402	−202,725
Revenue	81	53,265	83,494	90,623	249,768	325,144	351,262	310,174	662,585	597,282	796,977	716,754	1,023,241
Grants Received	81z												
Expenditure	82	92,797	191,229	160,893	248,768	288,095	356,262	443,563	947,690	701,059	1,018,026	1,018,156	1,225,966
Lending Minus Repayments	83	−	−	−	−	−	−	−	−				
Financing													
Net Borrowing: Domestic	84a	46,716	91,136	60,248	7,102	−143,190	−60,637	103,886	264,064	103,777	194,053	149,027	163,692
Foreign	85a	−11,860	16,964	8,391	22,455	7,825	13,383	16,605	21,041	....	....	....	....
Use of Cash Balances	87	4,676	−364	1,632	−30,558	98,315	52,254	12,898					
Debt: Domestic	88a	161,900	261,093	299,361	248,774	343,674	359,028	537,489				149,027	167,852
Central Bank	88aa	122,028	189,773	199,662	187,509	247,461	264,229	435,131				−206,132	154,234
Commercial Banks	88ab	6,908	38,798	47,829	20,113	45,107	41,450	54,114				260,968	11,537
Other	88ac	32,964	32,522	51,870	41,152	51,106	53,349	48,244	−18,561	103,777	95,271	94,191	2,080
Debt: Foreign	89a	544,264	633,144	648,813	716,775	617,320	595,932	633,017	....	....	....	....	....
National Accounts					*Billions of Naira*								
Househ.Cons.Expend.,incl.NPISHs	96f	404	537	694	†1,543	2,368	2,435	2,757	1,970	2,447	3,466	4,674	4,980
Government Consumption Expend.	91f	20	28	89	†123	143	171	204	253	260	275	344	286
Gross Capital Formation	93	59	81	85	†115	172	206	194	178	191	393	408	431
Exports of Goods and Services	90c	197	229	217	†679	853	1,148	754	1,650	2,932	2,163	1,567	1,638
Imports of Goods and Services (-)	98c	131	174	170	†482	712	1,020	1,027	728	927	1,553	1,232	1,079
Gross Domestic Product (GDP)	99b	550	701	915	†1,978	2,824	2,940	2,881	3,322	4,903	5,703	5,928	6,255
Net Primary Income from Abroad	98.n	−64	−74	−66	†−204	−211	−226	−176	−238	−362	−391	−432	−400
Gross National Income (GNI)	99a	485	628	849	†1,774	2,613	2,714	2,705	3,084	4,540	5,311	5,496	5,855
Consumption of Fixed Capital	99cf	16	17	19	†20	22	24	26	29	32	36	40	....
GDP at Fact.Cost,Vol.'84 Prices	99bap	98	100	101	†104	108	111	114	117	121	126	....	....
GDP Volume (2000=100)	99bvp	80.4	82.5	83.6	85.4	88.7	91.5	93.7	96.3	100.0	104.2	....	....
GDP Deflator (2000=100)	99bip	13.9	17.3	22.3	†47.2	64.9	65.5	62.7	70.4	100.0	111.6	....	....
					Millions: Midyear Estimates								
Population	99z	91.31	94.05	96.85	99.72	102.64	105.62	108.63	111.68	114.75	117.82	120.91	124.01

2004, International Monetary Fund : *International Financial Statistics Yearbook*

Norway 142

		1992	1993	1994	1995	1996	1997	1998	1999	2000	2001	2002	2003
Exchange Rates						*Kroner per SDR: End of Period*							
Official Rate	aa	9.5212	10.3264	9.8715	9.3931	9.2641	9.8707	10.7010	11.0343	11.5288	11.3251	9.4700	9.9263
						Kroner per US Dollar: End of Period (ae) Period Average (rf)							
Official Rate	ae	6.9245	7.5180	6.7620	6.3190	6.4425	7.3157	7.6000	8.0395	8.8485	9.0116	6.9657	6.6800
Official Rate	rf	6.2145	7.0941	7.0576	6.3352	6.4498	7.0734	7.5451	7.7992	8.8018	8.9917	7.9838	7.0802
				Kroner per ECU through 1998; Kroner per Euro Beginning 1999; End of Period (ea) Period Average (eb)									
Euro Rate	ea	8.3848	8.3878	8.3175	8.3067	8.0615	8.0867	8.8708	†8.0765	8.2335	7.9735	7.2900	8.4200
Euro Rate	ag	....	....	....	....	....	....	....	1.0046	.9305	.8813	1.0487	1.2630
Euro Rate	eb	8.0398	8.3505	8.3760	8.2859	8.1971	8.0131	8.4541	†8.3140	8.1133	8.0493	7.5099	7.9992
Euro Rate	rh	....	....	....	....	....	....	....	1.0668	.9240	.8956	.9444	1.1308
						Index Numbers (2000=100): Period Averages							
Official Rate	ahx	141.7	123.6	124.6	138.7	136.2	124.4	116.4	112.6	100.0	97.7	110.7	123.5
Nominal Effective Exchange Rate	neu	107.4	105.9	104.5	107.1	106.9	107.4	102.5	101.8	100.0	102.8	111.3	108.1
Real Effective Exchange Rate	reu	83.8	82.2	82.0	86.6	88.8	92.6	93.6	98.1	100.0	105.6	118.2	118.1
Fund Position						*Millions of SDRs: End of Period*							
Quota	2f.s	1,104.6	1,104.6	1,104.6	1,104.6	1,104.6	1,104.6	1,104.6	1,671.7	1,671.7	1,671.7	1,671.7	1,671.7
SDRs	1b.s	139.1	288.4	266.7	311.5	247.2	257.9	294.1	298.0	235.4	282.1	232.1	225.4
Reserve Position in the Fund	1c.s	471.4	425.5	440.9	636.2	643.8	725.5	899.1	621.2	448.1	577.3	729.8	669.5
of which: Outstg.Fund Borrowing	2c	–	–	–	–	–	–	35.3	–	–	–	–	–
International Liquidity					*Millions of US Dollars Unless Otherwise Indicated: End of Period*								
Total Reserves minus Gold	1l.d	11,940.4	19,622.4	19,025.5	22,517.8	26,516.7	23,400.3	18,606.7	20,400.4	20,164.1	15,488.0	20,681.9	22,996.6
SDRs	1b.d	191.2	396.2	389.4	463.0	355.5	347.9	414.1	409.0	306.6	354.5	315.5	335.0
Reserve Position in the Fund	1c.d	648.1	584.4	643.7	945.6	925.8	978.9	1,266.0	852.6	583.8	725.6	992.2	994.9
Foreign Exchange	1d.d	11,101.0	18,641.8	17,992.4	21,109.2	25,235.5	22,073.5	16,926.7	19,138.7	19,273.7	14,408.0	19,374.2	21,666.7
Gold (Million Fine Troy Ounces)	1ad	1.184	1.184	1.184	1.184	1.184	1.184	1.184	1.184	1.184	1.184	1.184	1.184
Gold (National Valuation)	1and	41.2	37.9	42.1	45.1	44.2	38.8	37.5	274.5	257.1	260.3	402.8	....
Deposit Money Banks: Assets	7a.d	11,398.8	6,597.1	7,267.4	7,473.0	9,087.8	9,781.4	12,324.9	12,418.4	15,280.1	15,092.7	17,642.0	28,587.7
Liabilities	7b.d	11,049.5	9,637.4	9,241.3	9,617.3	19,885.4	25,617.0	29,849.7	31,818.9	37,022.4	39,759.2	52,761.4	69,457.7
Other Banking Insts.: Liabilities	7f.d	5,946.3	5,731.3	6,040.1	6,434.6	6,198.7	7,081.2	8,179.1	8,774.8	10,659.0	13,445.0	19,430.1	25,815.8
Monetary Authorities						*Billions of Kroner: End of Period*							
Foreign Assets	11	82.50	151.43	143.58	142.78	225.37	284.17	312.96	408.32	620.51	812.09	809.17	....
Claims on Central Government	12a	12.58	29.25	13.69	18.06	12.41	10.65	9.43	10.77	13.83	11.88	17.84	....
Claims on Deposit Money Banks	12e	55.40	17.48	5.86	10.09	.23	7.50	16.47	25.63	23.94	16.64	7.71	....
Reserve Money	14	38.52	42.66	44.09	46.39	70.96	62.79	55.89	83.95	70.29	69.75	104.09	....
of which: Currency Outside DMBs	14a	32.45	35.74	37.95	39.08	39.87	42.22	42.14	43.37	42.52	42.04	40.28	....
Central Government Deposits	16d	67.62	106.76	87.24	98.39	131.24	201.16	222.73	290.18	482.50	696.87	661.24	....
Other Items (Net)	17r	44.40	48.75	31.80	26.15	35.81	38.37	60.24	70.59	105.49	73.99	69.40	....
Deposit Money Banks						*Billions of Kroner: End of Period*							
Reserves	20	4.57	2.88	4.32	5.15	28.06	17.28	14.07	38.36	27.82	29.75	65.87	39.49
Foreign Assets	21	78.93	49.60	49.14	47.22	58.55	71.56	93.67	99.84	135.21	136.01	122.89	190.97
Claims on Central Government	22a	76.98	87.32	73.87	70.56	78.49	60.79	87.04	45.42	38.58	9.60	8.11	13.02
Claims on Local Government	22b	9.84	11.62	11.31	12.78	15.16	15.71	26.89	17.38	11.93	10.39	6.53	6.28
Claims on Nonfin.Pub.Enterprises	22c	6.31	9.05	9.24	5.80	8.04	9.19	12.03	11.21	14.05	13.96	17.07	16.02
Claims on Private Sector	22d	447.36	457.14	479.68	527.46	599.82	708.01	801.58	849.70	969.64	1,075.45	1,144.61	1,232.53
Claims on Other Financial Insts	22f	44.52	34.92	37.11	34.04	40.46	50.13	75.74	72.54	82.55	92.65	108.23	119.24
Demand Deposits	24	288.79	300.43	314.80	316.29	349.70	371.96	453.20	479.34	521.01	616.02	671.85	706.25
Time, Savings,& Fgn.Currency Dep	25	159.95	139.95	149.24	164.57	166.71	150.52	157.80	141.03	159.08	128.06	133.64	127.91
Foreign Liabilities	26c	76.51	72.45	62.49	60.77	128.11	187.41	226.86	255.81	327.59	358.29	367.52	463.98
Central Government Deposits	26d	31.67	36.55	33.02	34.00	37.62	32.09	57.40	25.90	24.64	6.71	7.63	11.29
Credit from Bank of Norway	26g	56.08	17.03	5.30	10.47	.45	7.88	18.79	25.94	24.70	16.72	8.81	19.99
Other Items (Net)	27r	56.09	86.13	99.57	115.92	145.98	182.80	196.97	206.44	222.75	242.00	283.86	288.13
Monetary Survey						*Billions of Kroner: End of Period*							
Foreign Assets (Net)	31n	80.32	123.14	123.81	125.01	142.13	159.34	169.03	224.99	367.23	545.97	510.65	....
Domestic Credit	32	499.07	486.63	505.25	536.90	586.05	621.74	735.92	691.51	624.01	511.00	634.23	....
Claims on Central Govt. (Net)	32an	–9.72	–26.74	–32.71	–43.77	–77.96	–161.81	–183.66	–259.89	–454.74	–682.09	–642.91	....
Claims on Local Government	32b	9.84	11.62	11.31	12.78	15.16	15.71	26.89	17.38	11.93	10.39	6.53	....
Claims on Nonfin.Pub.Enterprises	32c	6.31	9.05	9.24	5.80	8.04	9.19	12.03	11.21	14.05	13.96	17.07	....
Claims on Private Sector	32d	448.01	457.77	480.30	528.05	600.35	708.52	802.11	850.26	970.21	1,076.09	1,145.30	....
Claims on Other Financial Insts	32f	44.63	34.92	37.11	34.04	40.46	50.13	78.55	72.54	82.55	92.65	108.23	....
Money	34	323.33	340.12	354.96	358.71	392.72	416.99	497.51	525.30	565.22	659.56	713.64	....
Quasi-Money	35	160.02	139.99	149.27	164.59	166.73	150.53	157.81	141.04	159.08	128.06	133.64	....
Other Items (Net)	37r	96.66	129.66	124.58	137.62	168.72	213.56	249.62	250.17	266.94	269.35	297.60	....
Money plus Quasi-Money	35l	483.35	480.11	504.23	523.30	559.45	567.52	655.32	666.33	724.30	787.62	847.28	....
Money (National Definitions)						*Billions of Kroner: End of Period*							
Broad Money	39m	470.9	469.0	491.1	530.3	564.4	578.8	605.6	671.6	732.1	795.0	855.4	....
Broad Money, Seasonally Adj	39m.c	466.2	465.3	488.5	528.9	563.4	577.8	603.9	667.3	731.4	795.5	854.7	....

Norway 142

		1992	1993	1994	1995	1996	1997	1998	1999	2000	2001	2002	2003
Other Banking Institutions													
State Lending Institutions						*Billions of Kroner: End of Period*							
Claims on State and Local Govts......	42b	33.41	34.53	35.40	36.68	37.90	41.84	42.36	46.17	18.28	18.74	20.82	20.95
Claims on Private Sector...............	42d	149.31	145.34	139.53	138.56	135.69	131.73	140.96	146.46	152.02	161.47	166.59	167.91
Bonds (Net)...............................	46ab	20.81	21.39	16.68	10.39	11.81	16.01	20.16	28.65	.06	.05	.03	.02
Foreign Liabilities......................	46c	5.27	3.69	1.81	1.14	1.17	.33	1.39	–	–	–	–	–
Central Govt. Lending Funds..........	46f	162.13	160.22	155.32	154.28	153.78	152.38	158.75	162.43	168.96	177.87	187.59	189.79
Capital Accounts........................	47a	9.00	12.23	10.30	10.39	8.61	8.45	8.25	6.74	5.46	6.88	4.50	3.52
Other Items (Net).......................	47r	−14.50	−17.67	−9.18	−.95	−1.79	−3.61	−5.23	−5.19	−4.17	−4.57	−4.72	−4.47
Mortgage Institutions						*Billions of Kroner: End of Period*							
Foreign Assets..........................	41..l	23.61	19.67	23.95	24.02	22.11	19.36	29.99	33.39	30.32	39.59	56.61	60.68
Claims on Central Government.......	42a.l	1.37	2.85	1.48	1.94	1.55	1.22	1.53	1.09	1.16	1.26	.68	.91
Claims on State and Local Govt......	42b.l	1.82	2.00	1.91	2.64	4.33	5.60	5.55	8.08	49.83	60.37	65.25	79.40
Claims on Nonfin.Pub.Enterprises.....	42c.l	2.11	1.65	1.32	1.34	1.70	1.37	1.90	4.68	2.78	5.69	5.98	7.70
Claims on Private Sector...............	42d.l	80.73	72.15	62.34	60.05	55.55	66.33	88.87	82.04	93.61	103.07	112.08	124.20
Credit Market Instruments.............	46aal	3.77	5.45	6.97	7.40	5.49	3.70	3.13	8.21	4.81	5.57	1.75	5.81
Bonds (net)...............................	46abl	55.87	42.16	35.01	36.46	37.21	33.14	36.46	36.63	58.57	58.89	62.41	51.39
Foreign Liabilities......................	46c.l	35.91	39.40	39.04	39.52	38.76	51.47	60.77	70.55	94.32	121.16	135.34	172.45
Capital Accounts........................	47a.l	6.38	8.00	7.76	7.59	6.64	6.51	8.31	8.73	11.04	11.23	11.57	12.23
Other Items (Net).......................	47r.l	7.72	3.30	2.23	−.99	−2.87	−.93	1.17	5.16	8.97	13.13	29.52	30.99
Nonbank Financial Institutions						*Billions of Kroner: End of Period*							
Claims on Central Government.......	42a.s	18.16	32.36	40.47	42.34	42.83	49.16	35.95	34.07	31.34	43.74	46.25	67.33
Claims on Local Government.........	42b.s	30.54	31.29	32.27	30.85	29.55	27.42	28.61	35.07	38.14	43.52	39.08	48.29
Claims on Private Sector...............	42d.s	73.54	75.78	65.71	73.90	77.07	71.55	75.08	80.43	92.75	103.63	105.19	132.10
Claims on Other Financial Insts.......	42f.s	28.44	24.30	28.05	32.58	38.85	42.54	48.10	46.36	36.98	50.38	58.03	59.07
Incr.in Total Assets(Within Per.)......	49z.s	12.61	14.67	7.94	10.92	6.91	3.02	−.86	5.77	5.74	45.69	−28.21	100.19
Interest Rates						*Percent Per Annum*							
Discount Rate (End of Period)..........	60	11.00	7.00	6.75	6.75	6.00	5.50	10.00	7.50	9.00	8.50	8.50	4.25
Avg.Cost for Centr.Bank Funding.....	60.a	7.65	5.70	6.46	5.40	4.96	4.80	6.18	6.86	7.31	7.45	8.22	5.60
Deposit Rate..............................	60l	10.69	5.51	5.21	4.95	4.15	3.63	7.24	5.38	6.73	†6.43	6.46	2.12
Lending Rate.............................	60p	14.16	10.97	8.40	7.78	7.10	5.95	7.91	8.16	8.22	8.86	8.54	6.15
Three Month Interbank Rate...........	60zb	11.83	7.27	5.85	5.48	4.90	3.73	5.79	6.54	6.75	7.23	6.91	4.10
Government Bond Yield................	61	9.78	6.52	7.13	6.82	5.94	5.13	5.35	5.38	6.38	6.31	6.33	4.50
Prices, Production, Labor						*Index Numbers (2000=100): Period Averages*							
Industrial Share Prices..................	62	26.8	34.5	44.1	47.0	56.4	79.9	78.7	80.3	100.0	....	....	....
Producer Prices..........................	63	84.7	83.8	84.9	87.1	89.0	90.2	90.7	93.5	100.0	95.3	90.0	93.2
Consumer Prices........................	64	84.0	85.9	87.1	89.2	90.4	92.7	†94.8	97.0	100.0	103.0	104.3	106.9
Wages: Monthly Earnings.............	65	....	....	....	....	....	....	91.3	96.1	100.0	104.5	110.0	115.2
Industrial Production....................	66	76.9	79.6	85.2	90.3	95.1	98.5	97.3	97.1	100.0	98.7	99.7	95.6
Crude Petroleum Production..........	66aa	67.3	72.2	81.5	87.7	98.8	98.5	94.6	93.8	100.0	102.8	99.1	95.7
						Number in Thousands: Period Averages							
Labor Force...............................	67d	2,130	2,131	2,151	2,186	2,240	2,287	2,323	2,333	2,350	2,362	2,379	2,375
Employment..............................	67e	2,004	2,004	2,035	2,079	2,132	2,195	2,248	2,258	2,269	2,278	2,286	2,269
Unemployment..........................	67c	126	127	117	107	108	93	74	75	81	84	93	107
Unemployment Rate (%)...............	67r	5.9	6.0	5.4	4.9	4.8	4.1	3.2	3.2	3.5	3.6	3.9	4.3
International Transactions						*Millions of Kroner*							
Exports.....................................	70	218,474	225,714	243,809	265,883	320,130	342,421	304,653	355,172	529,814	532,042	473,265	476,981
Imports, c.i.f..............................	71	160,821	170,069	192,073	208,627	229,720	252,232	282,638	266,677	302,852	296,135	276,563	279,240
						2000=100							
Volume of Exports......................	72	62.7	66.0	73.8	78.0	88.0	92.8	93.0	95.1	100.0	104.6	107.1	107.4
Volume of Imports......................	73	54.7	54.9	63.5	69.0	75.9	82.8	93.5	93.9	100.0	101.3	102.6	105.7
Unit Value of Exports...................	74	62.8	63.0	61.0	62.9	67.9	68.8	61.0	69.1	100.0	95.2	84.6	83.9
Unit Value of Imports...................	75	101.1	102.8	103.7	104.3	103.5	101.7	100.8	96.6	100.0	100.3	93.3	93.4

2004, International Monetary Fund: *International Financial Statistics Yearbook*

Norway 142

		1992	1993	1994	1995	1996	1997	1998	1999	2000	2001	2002	2003
Balance of Payments		\multicolumn{12}{c}{*Millions of US Dollars: Minus Sign Indicates Debit*}
Current Account, n.i.e.	78ald	4,471	3,522	3,760	5,233	10,969	10,036	6	8,378	25,851	26,171	24,769	28,444
Goods: Exports f.o.b.	78aad	35,459	32,278	35,016	42,385	50,081	49,375	40,888	46,224	60,463	59,527	59,917	69,071
Goods: Imports f.o.b.	78abd	−27,205	−25,312	−27,520	−33,701	−37,109	−37,727	−38,827	−35,501	−34,488	−33,055	−35,578	−41,162
Trade Balance	78acd	8,254	6,966	7,496	8,685	12,972	11,648	2,061	10,723	25,975	26,472	24,339	27,910
Services: Credit	78add	12,692	12,159	12,247	13,672	14,819	15,708	15,542	15,878	17,263	17,603	18,598	21,789
Services: Debit	78aed	−12,210	−11,472	−12,065	−13,147	−13,435	−14,233	−14,820	−14,882	−14,465	−15,104	−16,520	−19,545
Balance on Goods & Services	78afd	8,736	7,653	7,678	9,210	14,356	13,123	2,783	11,719	28,773	28,971	26,416	30,154
Income: Credit	78agd	2,689	2,380	3,415	4,590	5,164	5,590	6,809	6,100	6,641	7,556	8,733	10,497
Income: Debit	78ahd	−5,501	−5,167	−5,589	−6,509	−7,046	−7,284	−8,053	−7,998	−8,278	−8,737	−7,986	−9,130
Balance on Gds, Serv. & Inc.	78aid	5,924	4,866	5,504	7,291	12,475	11,429	1,539	9,821	27,136	27,790	27,163	31,521
Current Transfers, n.i.e.: Credit	78ajd	1,678	1,533	1,291	1,280	1,329	1,468	1,500	1,681	1,605	1,760	1,614	1,747
Current Transfers: Debit	78akd	−3,131	−2,877	−3,035	−3,339	−2,835	−2,861	−3,034	−3,124	−2,890	−3,379	−4,008	−4,823
Capital Account, n.i.e.	78bcd	−172	−31	−157	−170	−127	−184	−116	−116	−91	−4	−75	680
Capital Account, n.i.e.: Credit	78bad	143	306	93	86	65	30	44	40	135	113	44	964
Capital Account: Debit	78bbd	−315	−337	−250	−255	−192	−214	−160	−156	−225	−118	−119	−284
Financial Account, n.i.e.	78bjd	−1,044	6,568	−1,363	−542	−1,462	−6,607	61	431	−13,395	−27,393	−7,810	−20,121
Direct Investment Abroad	78bdd	120	−718	−2,166	−2,859	−5,886	−5,003	−3,200	−6,018	−8,511	859	−3,680	−2,226
Dir. Invest. in Rep. Econ., n.i.e.	78bed	−668	992	2,736	2,393	3,179	3,886	4,354	8,056	5,806	2,109	502	1,958
Portfolio Investment Assets	78bfd	−1,972	2,088	992	−3,531	−9,833	−12,618	−9,348	−7,228	−25,143	−29,674	−22,988	−19,290
Equity Securities	78bkd	−446	−124	213	−379	−1,177	−2,644	−9,066	−2,378	−11,034	−12,342	−6,829	−8,504
Debt Securities	78bld	−1,526	2,212	780	−3,151	−8,657	−9,974	−282	−4,850	−14,109	−17,333	−16,159	−10,786
Portfolio Investment Liab., n.i.e.	78bgd	865	−1,175	−518	655	100	2,500	7,289	4,238	9,843	2,590	5,412	12,629
Equity Securities	78bmd	782	385	654	636	−237	−1,190	—	−1,033	1,630	2,698	352	1,997
Debt Securities	78bnd	83	−1,560	−1,172	19	337	3,691	7,289	5,271	8,213	−108	5,060	10,632
Financial Derivatives Assets	78bwd	....	....	....	....	−43	17	−162	152	−329	−1,228	−4,270	35
Financial Derivatives Liabilities	78bxd	....	....	....	....	101	125	74	92	−131	91	−556	−161
Other Investment Assets	78bhd	369	6,198	154	961	−67	−1,403	−3,632	−7,663	−14,100	−3,931	−10,205	−23,171
Monetary Authorities	78bod	....	....	....	....	....	....	....	....	....	....	....	....
General Government	78bpd	−46	−65	−13	−156	71	91	−1,167	−1,099	−2,072	1,379	457	−1,321
Banks	78bqd	−741	3,997	−638	435	−1,216	−1,465	−1,062	−969	−1,806	505	674	−4,286
Other Sectors	78brd	1,156	2,266	804	682	1,077	−29	−1,403	−5,595	−10,223	−5,816	−11,335	−17,564
Other Investment Liab., n.i.e.	78bid	242	−816	−2,562	1,840	10,987	5,888	4,685	8,802	19,171	1,791	27,975	10,106
Monetary Authorities	78bsd	1,282	217	139	−624	1,505	−803	19	−19	3	44	410	−322
General Government	78btd	−15	−7	−164	3	—	94	1,346	3,460	9,657	−96	15,678	9,872
Banks	78bud	−3,622	−302	−604	247	8,677	4,126	−856	1,789	1,321	2,320	8,549	408
Other Sectors	78bvd	2,597	−724	−1,933	2,214	806	2,472	4,176	3,573	8,190	−477	3,338	149
Net Errors and Omissions	78cad	−3,986	−1,806	−1,987	−3,947	−2,910	−4,443	−6,335	−2,710	−8,680	−1,120	−11,160	−8,706
Overall Balance	78cbd	−732	8,253	253	575	6,470	−1,198	−6,384	5,984	3,686	−2,346	5,723	297
Reserves and Related Items	79dad	732	−8,253	−253	−575	−6,470	1,198	6,384	−5,984	−3,686	2,346	−5,723	−297
Reserve Assets	79dbd	732	−8,253	−253	−575	−6,470	1,198	6,384	−5,984	−3,686	2,346	−5,723	−297
Use of Fund Credit and Loans	79dcd	—	—	—	—	—	—	—	—	—	—	—	—
Exceptional Financing	79ded	....	....	....	....	....	....	....	....	....	....	....	....
International Investment Position		\multicolumn{12}{c}{*Millions of US Dollars*}
Assets	79aad	48,393	46,433	....	....	....	....	....	....	....	....	....	....
Direct Investment Abroad	79abd	4,234	5,080	....	....	....	....	....	....	....	....	....	....
Portfolio Investment	79acd	5,607	5,762	....	....	....	....	....	....	....	....	....	....
Equity Securities	79add	—	—	....	....	....	....	....	....	....	....	....	....
Debt Securities	79aed	5,607	5,762	....	....	....	....	....	....	....	....	....	....
Financial Derivatives	79ald	—	—	....	....	....	....	....	....	....	....	....	....
Other Investment	79afd	26,673	19,910	....	....	....	....	....	....	....	....	....	....
Monetary Authorities	79agd	—	—	....	....	....	....	....	....	....	....	....	....
General Government	79ahd	1,697	1,868	....	....	....	....	....	....	....	....	....	....
Banks	79aid	9,325	5,813	....	....	....	....	....	....	....	....	....	....
Other Sectors	79ajd	15,651	12,228	....	....	....	....	....	....	....	....	....	....
Reserve Assets	79akd	11,880	15,680	....	....	....	....	....	....	....	....	....	....
Liabilities	79lad	58,399	57,536	....	....	....	....	....	....	....	....	....	....
Dir. Invest. in Rep. Economy	79lbd	3,969	3,880	....	....	....	....	....	....	....	....	....	....
Portfolio Investment	79lcd	24,400	22,449	....	....	....	....	....	....	....	....	....	....
Equity Securities	79ldd	—	—	....	....	....	....	....	....	....	....	....	....
Debt Securities	79led	24,400	22,449	....	....	....	....	....	....	....	....	....	....
Financial Derivatives	79lld	—	—	....	....	....	....	....	....	....	....	....	....
Other Investment	79lfd	30,030	31,207	....	....	....	....	....	....	....	....	....	....
Monetary Authorities	79lgd	705	101	....	....	....	....	....	....	....	....	....	....
General Government	79lhd	1,692	2,238	....	....	....	....	....	....	....	....	....	....
Banks	79lid	5,902	6,179	....	....	....	....	....	....	....	....	....	....
Other Sectors	79ljd	21,732	22,688	....	....	....	....	....	....	....	....	....	....

Norway 142

		1992	1993	1994	1995	1996	1997	1998	1999	2000	2001	2002	2003
Government Finance		*Millions of Kroner: Year Ending December 31*
Deficit (-) or Surplus...............	80	−51,912	−45,556	−14,774	14,487	6,519	8,816	−32,427	−47,230	92,791	95,927	37,213	....
Revenue..............................	81	318,151	326,507	348,841	383,106	425,506	469,040	464,460	495,055	643,173	712,019	698,126	....
Grants Received.................	81z	1,892	1,490	1,423	1,345	1,299	1,322	1,087	938	1,273	1,329	1,243	....
Expenditure........................	82	339,451	347,962	357,877	361,579	375,265	387,218	412,173	436,850	474,405	492,707	570,404	....
Lending Minus Repayments.........	83	32,504	25,591	7,161	8,385	45,021	74,328	85,801	106,373	77,250	124,714	91,752	....
Financing													
Domestic...........................	84a	28,073	25,189	20,459	−18,296	11,276	14,516	38,579	1,692	−198,292	−82,176	−124,112	....
Foreign............................	85a	23,839	20,368	−5,684	3,809	−17,795	−23,332	−6,152	45,538	105,500	−13,750	86,900	....
Debt: Domestic...................	88a	127,348	189,953	201,763	198,384	186,071	195,983	184,220	149,470	149,553	142,977	152,887	....
Foreign............................	89a	54,320	80,018	74,157	77,901	62,527	42,400	37,180	92,881	197,401	182,483	271,257	....
National Accounts		*Billions of Kroner*
House.Cons.Expend.,incl.NPISHs....	96f	396.79	416.23	435.35	462.26	498.97	527.14	554.54	584.27	625.50	651.34	679.96	721.91
Government Consumption Expend...	91f	179.71	187.47	193.83	202.14	214.68	227.49	247.44	263.73	281.12	314.80	336.84	353.25
Gross Fixed Capital Formation.........	93e	151.09	164.13	174.38	186.55	208.60	245.70	284.91	271.83	272.77	278.94	269.33	261.30
Changes in Inventories..................	93i	8.43	8.30	15.84	28.04	12.08	18.87	23.79	20.73	35.04	20.68	26.34	14.29
Exports of Goods and Services.........	90c	300.10	315.96	333.20	355.95	419.40	460.86	427.08	486.23	685.95	697.30	626.41	646.43
Imports of Goods and Services (-).....	98c	245.81	261.67	279.18	297.50	326.80	368.70	405.62	393.76	431.30	436.81	416.70	433.50
Gross Domestic Product (GDP)........	99b	790.30	830.42	873.41	937.44	1,026.93	1,111.35	1,132.13	1,233.04	1,469.08	1,526.23	1,522.18	1,563.69
Net Primary Income from Abroad.....	98.n	−17.48	−19.77	−15.42	−12.18	−12.18	−11.83	−9.37	−14.82	−14.42	−10.77	5.04	9.94
Gross National Income (GNI)...........	99a	772.83	810.64	857.99	925.27	1,014.74	1,099.52	1,122.77	1,218.22	1,454.66	1,515.46	1,527.22	1,573.63
Net Current Transf.from Abroad.......	98t	−9.03	−9.53	−12.23	−13.03	−9.71	−9.87	−11.55	−11.28	−11.36	−14.55	−18.67	−21.67
Gross Nat'l Disposable Inc.(GNDI)....	99i	763.80	801.11	845.76	912.24	1,005.03	1,089.65	1,111.21	1,206.94	1,443.30	1,500.91	1,508.55	1,551.96
Gross Saving........................	99s	187.30	197.41	216.58	247.84	291.39	335.03	309.24	358.94	536.68	534.78	491.75	476.80
Consumption of Fixed Capital.........	99cf	131.75	139.84	143.16	149.05	154.78	164.11	175.62	188.55	204.86	216.39	....	....
GDP Volume 2001 Prices................	99b.p	1,103.30	1,133.37	1,192.94	1,244.92	1,310.33	1,378.32	1,414.56	1,444.74	1,485.73	1,526.23	1,547.25	1,551.88
GDP Volume (2000=100)................	99bvp	74.3	76.3	80.3	83.8	88.2	92.8	95.2	97.2	100.0	102.7	104.1	104.5
GDP Deflator (2000=100)...............	99bip	72.4	74.1	74.0	76.2	79.3	81.5	80.9	86.3	100.0	101.1	99.5	101.9
		Millions: Midyear Estimates
Population.............................	99z	4.29	4.31	4.34	4.36	4.38	4.41	4.43	4.45	4.47	4.49	4.51	4.53

2004, International Monetary Fund : *International Financial Statistics Yearbook*

Oman 449

		1992	1993	1994	1995	1996	1997	1998	1999	2000	2001	2002	2003
Exchange Rates		*Rials Omani per SDR: End of Period (aa) Rials Omani per US Dollar: End of Period (ae)*											
Official Rate	aa	.5287	.5281	.5613	.5716	.5529	.5188	.5414	.5277	.5010	.4832	.5227	.5714
Official Rate	ae	.3845	.3845	.3845	.3845	.3845	.3845	.3845	.3845	.3845	.3845	.3845	.3845
		Index Numbers (2000=100): Period Averages											
Official Rate	ahx	100.0	100.0	100.0	100.0	100.0	100.0	100.0	100.0	100.0	100.0	100.0	100.0
Nominal Effective Exchange Rate	nec	88.2	92.7	90.1	85.1	89.0	93.5	96.2	95.1	100.0	105.4	103.2	93.8
Fund Position		*Millions of SDRs: End of Period*											
Quota	2f.s	119.4	119.4	119.4	119.4	119.4	119.4	119.4	194.0	194.0	194.0	194.0	194.0
SDRs	1b.s	3.4	5.0	6.2	7.5	8.8	10.1	11.5	1.3	3.1	5.0	6.5	7.8
Reserve Position in the Fund	1c.s	39.4	37.8	36.0	34.5	34.0	31.1	31.1	49.8	49.8	65.0	73.4	77.6
of which: Outstg.Fund Borrowing	2c	—	—	—	—	—	—	—	—	—	—	—	—
International Liquidity		*Millions of US Dollars Unless Otherwise Indicated: End of Period*											
Total Reserves minus Gold	1l.d	2,324.7	1,803.9	1,646.2	1,830.7	1,961.6	2,069.6	1,937.7	2,767.5	2,379.9	2,364.9	3,173.5	3,593.5
SDRs	1b.d	4.7	6.8	9.0	11.1	12.7	13.6	16.2	1.8	4.1	6.3	8.9	11.6
Reserve Position in the Fund	1c.d	54.1	52.0	52.5	51.2	48.8	42.0	43.9	68.3	64.9	81.6	99.8	115.3
Foreign Exchange	1d.d	2,265.9	1,745.1	1,584.7	1,768.3	1,900.1	2,014.0	1,877.7	2,697.3	2,310.9	2,277.0	3,064.8	3,466.6
Gold (Million Fine Troy Ounces)	1ad	.289	.289	.289	.291	.291	.291	.291	.291	.291	.001	.001	.001
Gold (National Valuation)	1and	68.3	68.3	68.3	68.3	68.3	68.3	68.3	68.3	68.3	80.5	.2	.3
Monetary Authorities:Other Assets	3..d	662.3	162.2	38.4	....	80.6	120.3	147.8	555.9	39.7	50.4	41.7	42.1
Other Liab.	4.d	1.0	1.0	1.2	1.7	1.0	1.7	1.2	1.1	1.0	1.0	1.1	1.1
Deposit Money Banks: Assets	7a.d	532.4	780.1	863.5	999.1	944.1	1,776.8	1,222.7	992.3	1,215.5	997.9	1,241.9	1,290.3
Liabilities	7b.d	105.8	167.1	239.5	441.4	652.4	1,326.5	1,522.2	1,662.4	1,641.8	1,532.5	1,401.8	1,176.1
Monetary Authorities		*Millions of Rials Omani: End of Period*											
Foreign Assets	11	920.5	720.1	635.0	730.4	780.8	822.5	771.6	1,090.4	941.4	940.3	1,220.3	1,382.2
Claims on Central Government	12a	38.9	49.3	97.0	89.4	47.0	32.7	159.6	4.1	5.0	79.5	25.7	4.3
Reserve Money	14	299.1	284.7	296.3	306.9	326.5	354.3	379.5	375.3	408.3	444.3	578.7	612.5
of which: Currency Outside DMBs	14a	226.7	232.9	245.5	235.9	231.2	242.2	244.2	273.5	276.8	275.9	289.6	303.8
Foreign Liabilities	16c	.4	.4	.5	.6	.4	.6	.5	.4	.4	.4	.4	.4
Central Government Deposits	16d	255.0	62.4	14.8	41.0	31.1	46.6	57.0	242.6	26.0	19.4	16.1	68.5
Capital Accounts	17a	213.7	219.9	235.2	251.9	268.3	283.1	297.9	312.4	342.8	373.5	406.8	403.4
Other Items (Net)	17r	191.2	201.9	185.3	219.5	201.5	170.4	196.3	163.8	168.8	182.2	243.9	301.7
Deposit Money Banks		*Millions of Rials Omani: End of Period*											
Reserves	20	72.3	49.4	51.6	67.8	86.9	116.0	132.2	99.2	129.7	136.2	164.2	129.0
Foreign Assets	21	204.7	299.9	332.0	384.2	363.0	683.2	470.1	381.5	467.4	383.7	477.5	496.1
Claims on Central Government	22a	190.7	154.1	97.9	91.9	175.8	157.4	198.0	334.7	323.0	427.0	357.2	417.7
Claims on Nonfin.Pub.Enterprises	22c	8.4	16.8	3.0	3.1	4.8	.6	—	4.1	16.3	28.1	46.0	69.0
Claims on Private Sector	22d	1,029.9	1,088.0	1,227.3	1,357.5	1,564.9	2,170.9	2,563.1	2,783.9	2,809.7	3,001.4	3,012.7	3,060.1
Demand Deposits	24	206.3	218.7	227.4	235.4	272.1	307.5	261.6	237.7	272.5	425.7	482.0	504.2
Quasi-Monetary Deposits	25	841.1	863.9	931.1	1,040.5	1,130.5	1,484.5	1,625.4	1,756.2	1,854.7	1,924.0	1,991.3	2,024.3
Foreign Liabilities	26c	40.7	64.2	92.1	169.7	250.9	510.0	585.3	639.2	631.3	589.3	539.0	452.2
Central Government Deposits	26d	138.6	153.4	148.9	140.7	211.3	289.8	292.4	316.1	306.0	285.5	276.4	300.0
Capital Accounts	27a	129.0	165.8	167.6	174.9	193.8	304.2	425.6	454.2	433.3	425.8	432.8	509.3
Other Items (Net)	27r	150.3	142.3	144.7	143.3	136.9	232.0	173.1	200.0	248.3	326.2	336.2	381.9
Monetary Survey		*Millions of Rials Omani: End of Period*											
Foreign Assets (Net)	31n	1,084.1	955.4	874.5	944.2	892.6	994.9	656.0	832.3	777.1	734.4	1,158.4	1,425.7
Domestic Credit	32	874.4	1,092.3	1,261.5	1,360.3	1,550.2	2,025.2	2,571.2	2,568.1	2,822.0	3,231.1	3,149.1	3,182.6
Claims on Central Govt. (Net)	32an	−164.0	−12.5	31.2	−.4	−19.6	−146.3	8.1	−219.9	−4.1	201.6	90.4	53.5
Claims on Nonfin.Pub.Enterprises	32c	8.4	16.8	3.0	3.1	4.8	.6	—	4.1	16.3	28.1	46.0	69.0
Claims on Private Sector	32d	1,029.9	1,088.0	1,227.3	1,357.5	1,564.9	2,170.9	2,563.1	2,783.9	2,809.7	3,001.4	3,012.7	3,060.1
Money	34	433.0	451.5	472.9	471.3	503.4	549.7	505.8	511.2	549.3	701.6	771.7	808.0
Quasi-Money	35	841.1	863.9	931.1	1,040.5	1,130.5	1,484.5	1,625.4	1,756.2	1,854.7	1,924.0	1,991.3	2,024.3
Other Items (Net)	37r	684.4	732.3	731.9	792.7	808.9	985.9	1,096.0	1,132.9	1,195.0	1,339.9	1,544.6	1,776.0
Money plus Quasi-Money	35l	1,274.1	1,315.5	1,404.1	1,511.8	1,633.9	2,034.2	2,131.2	2,267.5	2,404.1	2,625.6	2,762.9	2,832.3
Interest Rates		*Percent Per Annum*											
Deposit Rate	60l	6.29	4.17	4.34	6.53	6.85	7.30	8.46	8.12	7.63	4.50	2.89	2.37
Lending Rate	60p	9.24	8.49	8.57	9.38	9.23	9.30	10.09	10.32	10.06	9.23	8.55	8.23
Prices and Production		*Index Numbers (2000=100): Period Averages*											
Consumer Prices	64	†98.7	98.4	98.8	101.2	102.1	101.6	100.7	101.2	100.0	98.9	98.3	97.9
Crude Petroleum	66aa	77.5	81.4	84.6	89.3	93.1	93.9	92.8	93.9	100.0	99.7	93.7	85.6
International Transactions		*Millions of Rials Omani*											
Exports	70	2,135.3	2,064.9	2,132.0	2,333.2	2,824.5	2,933.8	2,118.0	2,783.0	4,352.0	4,258.0	4,295.5	4,486.6
Crude Petroleum	70aa	887.1	814.2	802.5	908.0	1,118.1	1,111.3	697.8	1,050.4	1,702.9	1,489.4	1,450.3	1,514.5
Imports, c.i.f.	71	1,449.3	1,581.8	1,505.3	1,633.2	1,760.1	1,932.5	2,184.6	1,797.1	1,937.7	2,229.3	2,309.1	2,527.0
Volume of Exports		*2000=100*											
Crude Petroleum	72aa	77.3	81.8	82.8	87.1	90.1	93.6	91.9	94.4	100.0	101.4	93.7	85.2
Export Prices		*2000=100: Index of Prices in US Dollars*											
Crude Petroleum	76aad	67.4	58.4	56.9	61.3	72.7	69.7	44.6	64.9	100.0	86.1	90.9	104.2

Oman 449

		1992	1993	1994	1995	1996	1997	1998	1999	2000	2001	2002	2003
Balance of Payments		\multicolumn{12}{c}{*Millions of US Dollars: Minus Sign Indicates Debit*}
Current Account, n.i.e.	78ald	−598	−1,190	−805	−801	338	−78	−2,950	−291	3,423	2,315	...	...
Goods: Exports f.o.b.	78aad	5,555	5,365	5,542	6,065	7,373	7,657	5,521	7,238	11,319	11,074	...	...
Goods: Imports f.o.b.	78abd	−3,627	−4,030	−3,693	−4,050	−4,231	−4,645	−5,215	−4,299	−4,593	−5,311	...	...
Trade Balance	78acd	1,928	1,336	1,849	2,015	3,142	3,012	307	2,939	6,726	5,763	...	...
Services: Credit	78add	13	13	13	13	237	268	369	401	424	349	...	...
Services: Debit	78aed	−932	−906	−900	−985	−1,233	−1,467	−1,683	−1,511	−1,566	−1,678	...	...
Balance on Goods & Services	78afd	1,009	442	962	1,043	2,146	1,813	−1,007	1,828	5,584	4,434	...	...
Income: Credit	78agd	328	421	257	325	257	385	338	187	291	309	...	...
Income: Debit	78ahd	−739	−688	−724	−699	−694	−775	−814	−869	−1,001	−897	...	...
Balance on Gds, Serv. & Inc.	78aid	598	175	495	669	1,709	1,423	−1,483	1,147	4,874	3,847	...	...
Current Transfers, n.i.e.: Credit	78ajd	39	57	65	68	−	−	−	−	−	−	...	...
Current Transfers: Debit	78akd	−1,235	−1,423	−1,365	−1,537	−1,371	−1,501	−1,467	−1,438	−1,451	−1,532	...	...
Capital Account, n.i.e.	78bcd	−	−	−	−	10	31	−5	−3	8	−10	...	...
Capital Account, n.i.e.: Credit	78bad	−	−	−	−	29	55	21	16	34	8	...	...
Capital Account: Debit	78bbd	−	−	−	−	−18	−23	−26	−18	−26	−18	...	...
Financial Account, n.i.e.	78bjd	497	−79	230	−19	260	52	1,488	109	−494	−887	...	...
Direct Investment Abroad	78bdd	−	−	−	−	−	−	−	−	−	−	...	...
Dir. Invest. in Rep. Econ., n.i.e.	78bed	104	142	76	46	60	65	101	21	70	42	...	...
Portfolio Investment Assets	78bfd	−	−	−	−	−	−	−	−	−	−	...	...
Equity Securities	78bkd	−	−	...	...	...	...	...	...	...	...	...	...
Debt Securities	78bld	−	−	...	...	...	...	...	...	...	...	...	...
Portfolio Investment Liab., n.i.e.	78bgd	−	−	...	...	8	18	185	26	−36	13	...	...
Equity Securities	78bmd	−	−	...	...	10	86	239	13	−10	−3	...	...
Debt Securities	78bnd	−	−	...	...	−3	−68	−55	13	−26	16	...	...
Financial Derivatives Assets	78bwd	...	...	...	...	...	...	...	...	...	...	...	...
Financial Derivatives Liabilities	78bxd	...	...	...	...	...	...	...	...	...	...	...	...
Other Investment Assets	78bhd	120	−187	−174	−52	−237	−715	642	−307	−356	229	...	...
Monetary Authorities	78bod	...	...	...	...	...	...	...	...	...	...	...	...
General Government	78bpd	−	−31	−104	−88	−291	117	88	−538	−133	10	...	...
Banks	78bqd	169	−187	−10	62	55	−832	554	231	−224	218	...	...
Other Sectors	78brd	−49	31	−60	−26	−	−	−	−	...	...	...	...
Other Investment Liab., n.i.e.	78bid	273	−34	328	−13	429	684	559	369	−172	−1,170	...	...
Monetary Authorities	78bsd	−	−	−	−	−	−	−	−	−	−	...	...
General Government	78btd	260	−91	325	−18	140	−112	−26	101	−114	−447	...	...
Banks	78bud	13	57	3	5	213	676	195	143	−21	−112	...	...
Other Sectors	78bvd	−	−	...	...	75	120	390	125	−36	−611	...	...
Net Errors and Omissions	78cad	401	211	−86	388	−420	526	702	399	−674	−384	...	...
Overall Balance	78cbd	300	−1,058	−661	−432	189	531	−765	215	2,262	1,034	...	...
Reserves and Related Items	79dad	−300	1,058	661	432	−189	−531	765	−215	−2,262	−1,034	...	...
Reserve Assets	79dbd	−300	1,058	661	432	−189	−531	765	−215	−2,262	−1,034	...	...
Use of Fund Credit and Loans	79dcd	−	−	−	−	−	−	−	−	−	−	...	...
Exceptional Financing	79ded	...	...	...	...	...	...	...	...	...	...	...	...
Government Finance		\multicolumn{12}{c}{*Millions of Rials Omani: Year Ending December 31*}
Deficit (-) or Surplus	80	−584.5	−511.1	−485.9	−468.1	−259.7	−28.3	−376.9	−474.1	−363.2	−324.1	...	...
Revenue	81	1,338.1	1,357.7	1,386.7	1,487.9	1,602.8	1,867.4	1,426.6	1,401.8	1,831.2	2,077.2	...	...
Grants Received	81z	.9	19.2	29.9	13.2	10.8	20.7	8.8	5.6	13.2	2.9	...	...
Expenditure	82	1,900.3	1,871.4	1,912.7	1,971.2	1,879.4	1,848.0	1,820.1	1,859.4	2,179.5	2,295.1	...	...
Lending Minus Repayments	83	23.2	16.6	−10.2	−2.0	−6.1	68.4	−7.8	22.1	28.1	109.1	...	...
Financing													
Domestic	84a	413.5	211.2	141.8	46.4	−250.6	35.5	9.1	105.7	76.6	86.4	...	...
Foreign	85a	171.0	299.9	344.1	421.7	510.3	−7.2	367.8	368.4	286.6	237.7	...	...
Debt: Domestic	88a	410.2	291.0	313.9	306.7	325.2	314.1	471.0	493.1	392.1	623.4	...	...
Foreign	89a	1,036.3	1,020.8	1,148.8	1,148.0	1,201.1	1,132.5	1,086.1	1,118.4	1,064.8	900.5	...	...
National Accounts		\multicolumn{12}{c}{*Millions of Rials Omani*}
Househ.Cons.Expend.,incl.NPISHs	96f	2,263	2,389	2,349	2,600	2,799	2,901	3,120	3,001	3,000	3,174	3,365	...
Government Consumption Expend.	91f	1,303	1,333	1,429	1,462	1,446	1,415	1,402	1,440	1,580	1,823	1,800	...
Gross Capital Formation	93	783	842	782	795	805	1,075	1,299	897	912	967	997	...
Exports of Goods and Services	90c	2,141	2,068	2,136	2,337	2,926	3,047	2,229	2,937	4,515	4,392	4,455	...
Imports of Goods and Services (-)	98c	1,702	1,828	1,728	1,887	2,101	2,348	2,633	2,234	2,368	2,687	2,808	...
Gross Domestic Product (GDP)	99b	4,788	4,804	4,967	5,307	5,874	6,090	5,416	6,041	7,639	7,668	7,809	...
Net Primary Income from Abroad	98.n	−608	−634	−683	−713	−695	−727	−747	−815	−831	−815	−898	...
Gross National Income (GNI)	99a	4,180	4,154	4,121	4,594	5,179	5,363	4,669	5,226	6,808	6,853	7,512	...
GDP Volume 1988 Prices	99b.p	4,141	4,395	4,564	4,784	4,923	5,227	5,368	5,356	5,650	6,175	6,177	...
GDP Volume (2000=100)	99bvp	73.3	77.8	80.8	84.7	87.1	92.5	95.0	94.8	100.0	109.3	109.3	...
GDP Deflator (2000=100)	99bip	85.5	†80.8	80.5	82.0	88.2	86.2	74.6	83.4	100.0	91.8	93.5	...
		\multicolumn{12}{c}{*Millions: Midyear Estimates*}
Population	99z	2.00	2.08	2.16	2.24	2.31	2.39	2.46	2.53	2.61	2.69	2.77	2.85

2004, International Monetary Fund : *International Financial Statistics Yearbook*

Pakistan 564

		1992	1993	1994	1995	1996	1997	1998	1999	2000	2001	2002	2003
Exchange Rates						*Rupees per SDR: End of Period (aa)*							
Market Rate	aa	35.338	41.372	44.963	50.912	57.691	59.434	64.608	†71.075	75.607	76.489	79.578	85.020
					Rupees per US Dollar: End of Period (ae) Period Average (rf)								
Market Rate	ae	25.700	30.120	30.800	34.250	40.120	44.050	45.885	†51.785	58.029	60.864	58.534	57.215
Market Rate	rf	25.083	28.107	30.567	31.643	36.079	41.112	45.047	†49.501	53.648	61.927	59.724	57.752
					Index Numbers (2000=100): Period Averages								
Nominal Effective Exchange Rate	nec	166.19	161.54	151.64	139.37	127.03	119.93	110.96	100.95	100.00	91.76	93.48	87.61
Real Effective Exchange Rate	rec	111.81	111.42	108.91	108.20	106.07	109.34	104.83	98.84	100.00	93.05	96.73	92.52
Fund Position						*Millions of SDRs: End of Period*							
Quota	2f.s	758	758	758	758	758	758	758	1,034	1,034	1,034	1,034	1,034
SDRs	1b.s	–	1	–	10	9	8	1	–	11	3	2	167
Reserve Position in the Fund	1c.s	–	–	–	–	–	–	–	–	–	–	–	–
Total Fund Cred.&Loans Outstg.	2tl	820	817	1,097	1,115	1,001	980	996	1,271	1,198	1,456	1,506	1,425
International Liquidity				*Millions of US Dollars Unless Otherwise Indicated: Last Thursday of Period*									
Total Reserves minus Gold	1l.d	850	1,197	2,929	1,733	548	1,195	1,028	1,511	1,513	3,640	8,078	10,941
SDRs	1b.d	–	1	–	15	13	11	1	–	14	4	2	248
Reserve Position in the Fund	1c.d	–	–	–	–	–	–	–	–	–	–	–	–
Foreign Exchange	1d.d	850	1,196	2,929	1,718	535	1,184	1,027	1,511	1,499	3,636	8,076	10,693
Gold (Million Fine Troy Ounces)	1ad	2.021	2.044	2.052	2.055	2.056	2.066	2.077	2.088	2.091	2.091	2.093	2.096
Gold (National Valuation)	1and	681	692	792	721	689	635	618	543	543	595	684	733
Monetary Authorities: Other Liab.	4..d	690	552	271	226	689	615	856	890	973	950	705	713
Deposit Money Banks: Assets	7a.d	1,384	1,405	1,582	1,605	1,546	1,406	1,281	1,365	1,440	1,771	1,574	1,582
Liabilities	7b.d	3,956	2,490	2,380	3,007	3,373	2,330	2,091	1,614	1,331	898	585	478
Monetary Authorities					*Millions of Rupees: Last Thursday of Period*								
Foreign Assets	11	39,544	56,923	115,577	86,701	61,805	93,159	77,768	104,870	115,554	249,986	511,539	676,336
Claims on General Government	12a	181,038	210,037	202,251	254,327	303,324	274,745	347,900	502,118	551,497	403,433	193,576	32,541
of which: Provincial Government	12ax	8,136	5,524	2,258	5,184	15,931	12,700	12,657	8,050	3,388	874	874	37,067
Claims on Deposit Money Banks	12e	71,593	78,137	89,110	98,220	67,864	119,962	171,286	192,862	195,646	184,842	160,603	194,671
Reserve Money	14	213,817	244,175	282,541	333,207	321,058	367,082	414,627	468,491	458,843	588,677	640,534	746,510
of which: Currency Outside DMBs	14a	162,316	177,856	195,827	234,011	252,069	272,052	301,146	341,024	410,469	429,360	487,745	567,519
Restricted Deposits	16b	....	....	....	....	....	....	....	8,115	11,124	13,187	18,049	19,315
Foreign Liabilities	16c	46,697	50,415	48,580	54,219	73,717	66,552	75,892	103,921	115,481	133,768	106,954	81,064
General Government Deposits	16d	15,355	37,304	37,682	34,365	28,502	30,603	63,742	138,006	199,021	43,203	96,550	71,757
Counterpart Funds	16e	539	671	614	644	686	644	585	660	532	589	562	607
Other Items (Net)	17r	15,766	12,533	37,524	16,813	9,030	22,985	42,110	80,659	77,694	58,836	3,068	−15,706
Deposit Money Banks					*Millions of Rupees: Last Thursday of Period*								
Reserves	20	51,207	68,030	93,268	109,689	80,122	100,518	119,696	145,480	81,205	169,195	150,861	172,747
Foreign Assets	21	35,563	42,306	48,721	54,958	62,022	61,940	58,800	70,682	83,534	107,789	92,157	90,535
Claims on General Government	22a	191,287	208,114	251,172	263,013	333,162	396,083	395,218	321,548	355,499	325,670	601,005	689,873
of which: Provincial Government	22ax	10,395	10,870	11,488	13,387	11,657	13,081	16,355	19,846	44,262	43,617	35,485	22,854
Claims on Private Sector	22d	290,851	337,082	385,463	464,913	538,370	613,944	686,932	761,793	868,069	929,064	978,492	1,215,181
Demand Deposits	24	203,653	191,613	235,265	253,189	269,947	420,823	423,091	447,919	457,773	524,429	628,531	816,587
Time Deposits	25	143,406	230,515	278,960	322,037	448,144	470,719	530,230	521,619	600,662	685,205	809,592	878,563
Foreign Liabilities	26c	101,680	74,987	73,295	102,995	135,309	102,617	95,936	83,579	77,248	54,662	34,230	27,330
General Government Deposits	26d	4,378	19,224	41,168	47,719	47,800	47,799	66,536	96,763	84,259	102,692	131,705	165,510
Counterpart Funds	26e	−20	−196	−181	−8	–	–	–	–	–	–	–	–
Central Government Lending Funds	26f	12,198	13,074	12,235	11,853	11,788	11,634	11,676	11,493	11,244	11,148	11,071	16,154
Credit from Monetary Authorities	26g	61,263	66,564	77,758	86,766	57,795	108,583	126,448	148,604	144,839	120,372	136,900	155,270
Other Items (Net)	27r	42,350	59,751	60,123	68,023	42,896	10,310	6,729	−10,474	12,282	33,210	70,487	108,922
Monetary Survey					*Millions of Rupees: Last Thursday of Period*								
Foreign Assets (Net)	31n	−73,269	−26,173	42,424	−15,555	−85,199	−14,070	−35,260	−11,948	6,358	169,345	462,512	658,478
Domestic Credit	32	673,944	731,780	797,149	941,758	1,140,771	1,246,771	1,349,909	1,411,041	1,560,180	1,553,264	1,577,662	1,726,304
Claims on General Govt. (Net)	32an	352,592	361,623	374,573	435,256	560,184	592,426	612,840	588,897	623,716	583,208	566,326	485,147
Claims on Private Sector	32d	321,352	370,157	422,576	506,502	580,587	654,345	737,069	822,144	936,464	970,056	1,011,336	1,241,157
Money	34	371,796	378,111	435,388	490,961	528,011	699,806	732,291	795,370	876,014	964,921	1,118,403	1,387,601
Quasi-Money	35	143,406	230,515	278,960	322,037	448,144	470,719	530,230	521,619	600,662	685,205	809,592	878,563
Restricted Deposits	36b	....	....	....	....	....	....	....	8,115	11,124	13,187	18,049	19,315
Counterpart Funds	36e	520	475	433	636	686	644	585	660	532	589	562	607
Central Government Lending Funds	36f	12,198	13,074	12,235	11,853	11,788	11,634	11,676	11,493	11,244	11,148	11,071	16,154
Other Items (Net)	37r	72,755	83,433	112,558	100,717	66,946	49,898	39,869	61,838	66,961	47,558	82,497	82,540
Money plus Quasi-Money	35l	515,202	608,626	714,348	812,998	976,155	1,170,525	1,262,521	1,316,989	1,476,676	1,650,126	1,927,995	2,266,163
Other Banking Institutions					*Millions of Rupees: Last Thursday of Period*								
Post Office: Savings Deposits	45..i	8,612	8,586	9,891	12,370	14,189	18,622	22,473	27,603	36,022	39,638	59,445	76,193
Liquid Liabilities	55l	523,814	617,212	724,239	825,368	990,344	1,189,147	1,284,994	1,344,592	1,512,698	1,689,764	1,987,440	2,342,356

Pakistan 564

		1992	1993	1994	1995	1996	1997	1998	1999	2000	2001	2002	2003
Interest Rates		\multicolumn{12}{c}{*Percent Per Annum*}											
Discount Rate (End of Period)	60	10.00	10.00	†15.00	17.00	20.00	18.00	16.50	13.00	13.00	10.00	7.50	7.50
Money Market Rate	60b	7.51	11.00	8.36	11.52	11.40	12.10	10.76	9.04	8.57	8.49	5.53	2.14
Treasury Bill Rate	60c	12.47	13.03	11.26	12.49	13.61	†15.74	....	....	8.38	10.71	6.08	....
Government Bond Yield	61	7.67	7.40	7.07	6.63	6.06	5.43	4.79	4.16	....	....	....	....
Prices, Production, Labor		\multicolumn{12}{c}{*Index Numbers (2000=100): Period Averages*}											
Share Prices	62	†127.2	125.5	204.1	145.2	119.2	111.2	80.2	79.2	100.0	75.6	82.2	140.9
Wholesale Prices	63	47.6	52.5	62.9	70.9	78.7	87.6	89.6	96.2	100.0	104.6	107.7	114.6
Consumer Prices	64	†50.7	55.8	62.7	70.5	77.8	86.6	92.0	95.8	100.0	†103.1	106.5	109.6
Manufacturing Production	66ey	82.0	84.7	87.0	90.5	89.9	89.5	95.8	102.9	100.0	110.3	115.9	....
		\multicolumn{12}{c}{*Number in Thousands: Period Averages*}											
Labor Force	67d	....	34,726	33,324	33,191	....	36,407	38,174	39,400	38,005	....	42,388	....
Employment	67e	29,694	30,534	31,288	31,407	32,491	34,597	36,419	37,296	36,847	37,481	38,882	....
Unemployment	67c	1,845	1,516	1,591	1,783	1,845	2,254	2,279	2,334	3,127	3,181	3,506	....
Unemployment Rate (%)	67r	5.9	4.7	4.8	5.4	5.4	6.1	5.9	5.9	7.8	7.8	8.3	....
International Transactions		\multicolumn{12}{c}{*Millions of Rupees*}											
Exports	70	183,599	187,787	225,200	252,714	335,313	359,046	382,477	417,322	484,476	572,471	591,714	688,882
Imports, c.i.f.	71	235,296	265,142	271,744	362,686	437,769	476,346	419,311	505,451	582,681	631,005	670,575	752,788
		\multicolumn{12}{c}{*2000=100*}											
Volume of Exports	72	82.6	75.0	92.6	73.4	87.0	†81.9	79.5	89.3	100.0	102.1	109.3	109.9
Volume of Imports	73	88.5	89.5	86.4	93.6	91.6	†94.3	89.5	101.3	100.0	112.1	123.0	122.7
Unit Value of Exports	74	43.1	47.0	55.1	69.4	76.8	†88.1	98.4	101.0	100.0	108.4	100.0	103.6
Unit Value of Imports	75	41.1	43.9	51.4	58.1	64.2	†74.2	72.1	85.5	100.0	108.5	105.5	116.8
Balance of Payments		\multicolumn{12}{c}{*Millions of US Dollars: Minus Sign Indicates Debit*}											
Current Account, n.i.e.	78ald	−1,877	−2,901	−1,812	−3,349	−4,436	−1,712	−2,248	−920	−85	1,878	3,854	3,597
Goods: Exports f.o.b.	78aad	6,913	6,793	7,117	8,356	8,507	8,351	7,850	7,673	8,739	9,131	9,832	11,869
Goods: Imports f.o.b.	78abd	−9,717	−9,380	−9,355	−11,248	−12,164	−10,750	−9,834	−9,520	−9,896	−9,741	−10,428	−11,969
Trade Balance	78acd	−2,803	−2,586	−2,239	−2,891	−3,656	−2,399	−1,984	−1,847	−1,157	−610	−596	−100
Services: Credit	78add	1,559	1,573	1,753	1,857	2,016	1,625	1,404	1,373	1,380	1,459	2,429	2,977
Services: Debit	78aed	−2,683	−2,639	−2,529	−2,938	−3,459	−2,658	−2,261	−2,146	−2,252	−2,330	−2,241	−3,288
Balance on Goods & Services	78afd	−3,927	−3,652	−3,015	−3,972	−5,099	−3,433	−2,841	−2,620	−2,029	−1,481	−408	−411
Income: Credit	78agd	73	63	149	187	175	147	83	119	118	113	128	180
Income: Debit	78ahd	−1,485	−1,610	−1,830	−2,125	−2,198	−2,366	−2,263	−1,959	−2,336	−2,189	−2,414	−2,397
Balance on Gds, Serv. & Inc.	78aid	−5,339	−5,199	−4,695	−5,910	−7,121	−5,652	−5,021	−4,460	−4,247	−3,557	−2,694	−2,628
Current Transfers, n.i.e.: Credit	78ajd	3,502	2,337	2,919	2,611	2,739	3,981	2,801	3,582	4,200	5,496	6,593	6,293
Current Transfers: Debit	78akd	−40	−38	−35	−49	−54	−40	−28	−42	−38	−61	−45	−68
Capital Account, n.i.e.	78bcd	−1	−	−	−	−	−	....	....	....	....	40	1,131
Capital Account, n.i.e.: Credit	78bad	−	−	−	−	−	−	....	....	....	....	40	1,133
Capital Account: Debit	78bbd	−1	−	−	−	−	−	....	....	....	....	−	−2
Financial Account, n.i.e.	78bjd	2,147	3,334	2,977	2,449	3,496	2,321	−1,873	−2,364	−3,099	−389	−784	−1,626
Direct Investment Abroad	78bdd	12	2	−1	−	−7	24	−50	−21	−11	−31	−28	−19
Dir. Invest. in Rep. Econ., n.i.e.	78bed	336	349	421	723	922	716	506	532	308	383	823	534
Portfolio Investment Assets	78bfd	−	−	−	−	−	−	....	....	....	....	....	−2
Equity Securities	78bkd	−	−	−	−	−	−	....	....	....	....	....	−2
Debt Securities	78bld	−	....	−	−	−	−	....	....	....	....	....	....
Portfolio Investment Liab., n.i.e.	78bgd	372	293	1,471	4	261	279	−57	46	−451	−192	−567	−119
Equity Securities	78bmd	241	225	1,254	10	285	330	−22	66	35	−130	79	−26
Debt Securities	78bnd	131	68	217	−6	−24	−51	−35	−20	−486	−62	−646	−93
Financial Derivatives Assets	78bwd	....	....	....	....	....	....	....	....	....	....	....	....
Financial Derivatives Liabilities	78bxd	....	....	....	....	....	....	....	....	....	....	....	....
Other Investment Assets	78bhd	−568	−286	−283	−196	−164	−21	44	−523	−437	53	−64	−395
Monetary Authorities	78bod	....	....	....	....	....	....	....	....	....	....	....	−
General Government	78bpd	−456	46	−19	6	116	96	247	−358	−15	44	−5	17
Banks	78bqd	173	−86	−108	−116	8	−40	172	−25	−18	−17	−6	−77
Other Sectors	78brd	−285	−246	−157	−85	−288	−77	−375	−140	−404	26	−53	−335
Other Investment Liab., n.i.e.	78bid	1,995	2,976	1,369	1,919	2,484	1,323	−2,316	−2,398	−2,508	−602	−948	−1,625
Monetary Authorities	78bsd	383	−140	−282	−50	474	−71	91	−262	−168	−13	−254	1
General Government	78btd	1,292	1,260	1,132	1,034	700	1,878	−795	2	−729	−37	−162	−1,577
Banks	78bud	−360	613	313	613	310	−1,044	−663	−1,292	−1,160	−14	−81	12
Other Sectors	78bvd	680	1,244	205	321	1,000	559	−949	−846	−451	−538	−451	−61
Net Errors and Omissions	78cad	122	−6	178	−304	160	−72	1,011	768	557	708	974	−108
Overall Balance	78cbd	392	428	1,343	−1,204	−780	538	−3,110	−2,516	−2,627	2,197	4,084	2,994
Reserves and Related Items	79dad	−392	−428	−1,343	1,204	780	−538	3,110	2,516	2,627	−2,197	−4,084	−2,994
Reserve Assets	79dbd	−496	−426	−1,744	1,180	946	−511	222	−842	7	−2,716	−4,525	−3,089
Use of Fund Credit and Loans	79dcd	100	−4	401	23	−166	−27	20	391	−101	328	68	−112
Exceptional Financing	79ded	5	2	−	−	−	−	2,868	2,966	2,721	192	373	207

2004, International Monetary Fund: *International Financial Statistics Yearbook*

Pakistan 564

		1992	1993	1994	1995	1996	1997	1998	1999	2000	2001	2002	2003
Government Finance		\multicolumn{12}{c}{*Millions of Rupees: Year Ending June 30*}
Deficit (-) or Surplus	80	−95,418	−118,999	−113,462	−123,742	−169,477	−189,788	−171,925	−202,024	−172,117	−160,994	−176,274p	−140,442
Revenue	81	216,586	242,812	273,238	321,323	370,510	384,263	433,636	464,372	531,300	535,091	619,069p	701,576
Grants Received	81z	7,511	—	—	5,665	5,513	4,804	—	—	—	37,991	46,779	91,136p	57,450
Expenditure	82	294,370	330,509	362,891	425,418	515,219	547,768	584,624	627,147	725,642	739,662	837,396p	899,611
Lending Minus Repayments	83	25,145	31,302	29,474	25,160	29,572	26,283	20,937	39,249	15,766	3,202	49,083p	−143
Financing													
Domestic	84a	73,110	86,815	78,040	82,235	128,717	142,159	129,295	91,750	143,408	85,878	142,272p	93,029
Foreign	85a	22,308	32,184	35,422	41,507	40,760	47,629	42,630	110,274	28,709	75,116	34,002p	47,413
Use of Cash Balances	87	....	....	....	....	....	....	....	....	....	....	....	....
Debt	88	902,828	1,058,682	....	....	....	....	2,117,616	....	2,832,571	....	....	....
Domestic	88a	527,595	612,642	....	....	....	....	1,183,232	....	1,659,121	....	....	....
Foreign	89a	375,233	446,040	....	....	....	....	934,384	....	1,173,450	....	....	....
National Accounts		\multicolumn{12}{c}{*Billions of Rupees: Year Ending June 30*}
Househ.Cons.Expend.,incl.NPISHs	96f	843.90	962.40	1,109.90	1,351.40	1,545.20	1,818.20	1,929.70	2,224.00	2,372.40	2,586.80	2,699.00	2,923.04
Government Consumption Expend	91f	155.57	174.68	189.10	219.12	268.10	288.81	301.61	304.40	351.60	350.40	408.90	470.00
Gross Fixed Capital Formation	93e	225.20	256.40	280.50	317.80	368.10	396.90	402.80	409.40	452.28	476.00	476.10	526.30
Changes in Inventories	93i	18.70	21.10	24.60	28.20	34.34	38.28	71.40	48.00	51.70	56.20	58.00	94.60
Exports of Goods and Services	90c	209.22	217.37	254.18	311.80	358.37	390.52	441.41	451.10	514.40	615.40	678.00	823.00
Imports of Goods and Services (-)	98c	247.41	299.15	297.30	362.41	454.29	504.37	469.31	498.50	656.24	661.20	691.15	818.30
Gross Domestic Product (GDP)	99b	1,205.20	1,332.80	1,561.10	1,865.90	2,120.20	2,428.30	2,677.70	2,938.40	3,177.20	3,423.10	3,628.73	4,018.11
Net Primary Income from Abroad	98.n	12.54	9.96	4.00	14.04	−7.14	−19.35	−24.36	−25.55	−44.91	−50.71	31.99	180.63
Gross National Income (GNI)	99a	1,217.70	1,342.80	1,565.10	1,880.00	2,113.00	2,409.00	2,653.30	2,912.80	3,132.26	3,372.37	3,660.72	4,198.74
Consumption of Fixed Capital	99cf	80.80	86.30	100.10	119.40	136.20	159.20	180.70	188.50	206.55	227.34	245.47	272.86
GDP Volume 1981 Prices	99b.p	539.13	549.45	570.86	600.19	630.15	629.55	645.61	669.24	697.75	714.71	735.92	778.72
GDP Volume (2000=100)	99bvp	77.3	78.7	81.8	86.0	90.3	90.2	92.5	95.9	100.0	102.4	105.5	111.6
GDP Deflator (2000=100)	99bip	49.1	53.3	60.1	68.3	73.9	84.7	91.1	96.4	100.0	105.2	108.3	113.3
		\multicolumn{12}{c}{*Millions: Midyear Estimates*}
Population	99z	116.54	119.28	122.11	125.13	128.37	131.80	Ü 135.38	139.02	142.65	146.28	149.91	153.58

Panama 283

		1992	1993	1994	1995	1996	1997	1998	1999	2000	2001	2002	2003
Exchange Rates						*Balboas per SDR: End of Period*							
Official Rate	aa	1.3750	1.3736	1.4599	1.4865	1.4380	1.3493	1.4080	1.3725	1.3029	1.2567	1.3595	1.4860
						Balboas per US Dollar: End of Period							
Official Rate	ae	1.0000	1.0000	1.0000	1.0000	1.0000	1.0000	1.0000	1.0000	1.0000	1.0000	1.0000	1.0000
Fund Position						*Millions of SDRs: End of Period*							
Quota	2f.s	149.6	149.6	149.6	149.6	149.6	149.6	149.6	206.6	206.6	206.6	206.6	206.6
SDRs	1b.s	3.3	.1	–	.6	–	.4	.1	1.2	.3	1.1	.8	.6
Reserve Position in the Fund	1c.s	11.9	11.9	11.9	11.9	11.9	11.9	11.9	11.9	11.9	11.9	11.9	11.9
Total Fund Cred.&Loans Outstg	2tl	79.8	82.3	91.3	74.4	91.0	105.4	125.5	108.3	69.1	42.9	36.7	30.0
International Liquidity					*Millions of US Dollars Unless Otherwise Indicated: End of Period*								
Total Reserves minus Gold	1l.d	504.4	597.4	704.3	781.4	866.5	1,147.8	954.5	822.9	722.6	1,091.8	1,182.8	1,011.0
SDRs	1b.d	4.6	.1	–	.8	–	.5	.1	1.6	.3	1.4	1.1	.8
Reserve Position in the Fund	1c.d	16.3	16.3	17.3	17.6	17.1	16.0	16.7	16.3	15.5	14.9	16.1	17.6
Foreign Exchange	1d.d	483.5	581.0	686.9	762.9	849.4	1,131.3	937.7	805.0	706.8	1,075.5	1,165.6	992.5
Gold (National Valuation)	1and	–	–	–	–	–	–	–	–	–	–	–	–
Monetary Authorities: Other Liab	4..d	352	334	292	343	158	149	123	118	108	104	90	74
Deposit Money Banks: Assets	7a.d	9,714	12,735	16,617	15,664	15,484	16,595	13,209	12,362	12,620	12,521	10,061	9,887
Liabilities	7b.d	8,522	11,336	14,846	13,930	13,954	14,825	11,745	11,845	11,776	12,081	9,568	8,428
Monetary Authorities						*Millions of Balboas: End of Period*							
Foreign Assets	11	504.4	597.4	704.3	781.4	866.5	1,147.8	954.5	822.9	722.6	1,091.8	1,182.8	1,011.0
Claims on Central Government	12a	1,019.4	1,050.1	1,014.0	945.6	1,280.9	1,080.7	1,099.7	1,047.3	839.2	791.9	806.6	759.3
Claims on Official Entities	12bx	106.8	–	–	–	–	–	–	–	–	–	–	–
Claims on Private Sector	12d	288.0	322.8	300.6	318.8	301.0	292.7	403.2	583.8	747.8	976.0	1,118.9	1,228.3
Claims on Deposit Money Banks	12e	464.3	633.0	732.8	948.8	615.4	765.2	949.4	999.8	908.6	607.1	264.2	103.6
Bankers Deposits	14c	175.6	184.4	167.4	172.7	266.0	252.7	272.6	284.1	301.8	280.0	276.6	278.2
Demand Deposits	14d	62.1	63.0	75.4	77.0	83.0	105.8	97.8	80.6	80.7	104.0	99.5	96.7
Time, Savings,& Fgn.Currency Dep	15	172.9	187.3	192.5	205.0	227.2	240.8	283.4	296.5	367.4	474.0	594.0	619.1
Foreign Liabilities	16c	254.8	244.7	225.5	182.2	195.1	207.2	224.8	195.1	138.5	93.9	94.4	75.5
Long-Term Foreign Liabilities	16cl	207.1	202.3	199.5	271.5	93.8	84.5	74.8	71.4	59.9	63.7	45.9	42.7
Central Government Deposits	16d	1,358.8	1,550.6	1,716.2	1,857.8	1,871.5	2,025.2	2,039.7	2,094.5	1,883.8	2,061.0	1,918.7	1,664.0
Capital Accounts	17a	157.7	196.0	228.3	297.7	424.9	471.5	543.9	536.1	534.3	533.1	535.8	539.1
Other Items (Net)	17r	–6.1	–24.9	–53.2	–69.4	–97.8	–101.4	–130.1	–104.5	–148.2	–142.8	–192.3	–213.1
Deposit Money Banks						*Millions of Balboas: End of Period*							
Foreign Assets	21	9,713.6	12,735.2	16,616.6	15,663.9	15,483.8	16,595.2	13,208.7	12,362.1	12,620.5	12,521.1	10,061.4	9,887.0
Claims on Central Government	22a	165.8	104.8	74.3	62.3	79.4	73.2	86.2	143.0	160.9	135.9	269.1	371.0
Claims on Private Sector	22d	3,458.9	4,332.5	5,118.6	5,852.4	6,347.6	7,294.0	9,010.2	10,507.1	11,092.3	11,842.8	10,881.9	10,631.0
Demand Deposits	24	577.1	645.2	728.6	737.7	758.3	889.7	1,027.5	1,062.2	1,095.0	1,193.0	1,224.0	1,354.0
Time and Savings Deposits	25	2,765.4	3,296.0	3,845.5	4,204.2	4,476.5	5,138.6	5,795.3	6,376.7	7,054.9	7,653.6	7,478.0	7,771.0
Foreign Liabilities	26c	8,521.8	11,336.5	14,845.9	13,929.8	13,954.3	14,825.0	11,744.9	11,844.5	11,775.8	12,081.2	9,568.0	8,428.0
Capital Accounts	27a	898.0	1,008.0	1,321.3	1,431.8	1,660.8	1,945.1	2,171.5	2,257.8	2,551.9	2,561.3	2,356.0	2,745.0
Other Items (Net)	27r	576.0	886.9	1,068.2	1,275.1	1,060.9	1,164.1	1,566.1	1,471.0	1,396.1	1,010.7	586.4	591.0
Monetary Survey						*Millions of Balboas: End of Period*							
Foreign Assets (Net)	31n	1,441.4	1,751.5	2,249.5	2,333.2	2,200.8	2,710.8	2,193.7	1,145.4	1,428.8	1,437.8	1,581.8	2,394.5
Domestic Credit	32	3,680.1	4,259.6	4,791.3	5,321.3	6,137.3	6,715.5	8,559.6	10,186.7	10,956.4	11,685.6	11,157.9	11,325.6
Claims on Central Govt. (Net)	32an	–173.6	–395.7	–627.9	–849.9	–511.3	–871.2	–853.8	–904.2	–883.6	–1,133.2	–842.9	–533.7
Claims on Private Sector	32d	3,746.9	4,655.3	5,419.2	6,171.2	6,648.6	7,586.7	9,413.4	11,090.9	11,840.1	12,818.8	12,000.8	11,859.3
Deposit Money	34	639.2	708.2	804.1	814.7	841.3	995.5	1,125.2	1,142.7	1,175.0	1,296.9	1,323.5	1,450.7
Quasi-Money	35	2,938.3	3,483.3	4,038.0	4,409.2	4,703.7	5,379.4	6,078.7	6,673.2	7,422.3	8,127.6	8,072.0	8,390.1
Long-Term Foreign Liabilities	36cl	207.1	202.3	199.5	271.5	93.8	84.5	74.8	71.4	59.9	63.7	45.9	42.7
Capital Accounts	37a	1,055.7	1,203.9	1,549.6	1,729.6	2,085.7	2,416.6	2,715.4	2,794.0	3,086.2	3,094.4	2,891.8	3,284.1
Other Items (Net)	37r	281.2	413.4	449.6	429.6	613.7	550.3	759.1	650.8	641.1	540.7	406.5	552.4
Money plus Quasi-Money	35l	3,577.5	4,191.5	4,842.1	5,223.9	5,544.9	6,374.9	7,203.9	7,815.9	8,598.0	9,424.6	9,395.6	9,840.9
Interest Rates						*Percent Per Annum*							
Money Market Rate	60b	....	....	....	....	....	....	....	....	....	....	2.22	1.50
Savings Rate	60k	....	....	....	....	....	....	....	....	....	2.83	2.23	1.55
Deposit Rate	60l	† 5.67	5.90	6.11	7.18	7.20	7.03	6.76	6.92	7.07	6.83	4.97	3.98
Lending Rate	60p	10.61	10.06	10.15	11.10	10.62	10.63	10.82	10.05	† 10.48	10.97	10.58	9.93
Prices, Production and Labor						*Index Numbers (2000=100): Period Averages*							
Wholesale Prices	63	89.1	88.8	90.7	93.4	95.3	93.2	89.6	92.0	100.0	96.8	93.9	96.0
Consumer Prices	64	91.8	92.2	93.4	94.3	95.5	96.8	97.3	98.5	100.0	100.3	101.3	102.7
Manufacturing Production (1995)	66ey	90.1	96.1	99.3	100.0	99.9	105.6	109.8	105.3	....	....	....	....
						Number in Thousands: Period Averages							
Labor Force	67d	....	940	967	1,008	....	1,049	1,049	1,089	....	....	....	....
Employment	67e	782	816	832	867	867	909	937	961	940	984	1,050	1,081
Unemployment	67c	134	125	135	141	145	140	147	128	....	....	....	....
Unemployment Rate (%)	67r	14.7	13.3	14.0	14.0	14.3	13.4	13.6	11.8	....	....	....	....

2004, International Monetary Fund: *International Financial Statistics Yearbook*

Panama 283

		1992	1993	1994	1995	1996	1997	1998	1999	2000	2001	2002	2003
International Transactions							*Millions of Balboas*						
Exports	70	501.5	553.2	583.3	625.2	....	722.8	784.1	822.1	859.5	910.5	846.4	864.2
Imports, c.i.f.	71	2,023.6	2,187.8	2,404.1	2,510.7	2,779.9	3,002.0	3,398.3	3,515.8	3,378.7	2,963.5	2,982.0	3,086.1
Imports, f.o.b.	71.v	1,830.6	1,979.6	2,177.5	2,280.2	2,548.1	2,738.5	2,806.4	3,214.7	3,097.7	2,714.5	....	....
							2000=100						
Volume of Exports	72	93.7	127.6	....	....	....	....	133.6	107.1	100.0	....	81.0	84.5
Balance of Payments						*Millions of US Dollars: Minus Sign Indicates Debit*							
Current Account, n.i.e.	78ald	−267.2	−95.7	15.9	−470.6	−200.6	−506.7	−1,182.3	−1,320.2	−715.5	−173.5	−92.3	−408.0
Goods: Exports f.o.b.	78aad	5,104.2	5,416.9	6,044.8	6,090.9	5,822.9	6,669.7	6,350.1	5,303.3	5,838.5	5,992.4	5,315.1	5,051.3
Goods: Imports f.o.b.	78abd	−5,479.7	−5,751.1	−6,294.9	−6,679.8	−6,467.0	−7,354.9	−7,714.6	−6,689.4	−6,981.4	−6,688.6	−6,352.2	−6,143.3
Trade Balance	78acd	−375.5	−334.2	−250.1	−588.9	−644.1	−685.2	−1,364.5	−1,386.1	−1,142.9	−696.2	−1,037.1	−1,092.0
Services: Credit	78add	1,225.4	1,297.4	1,403.7	1,519.4	1,592.0	1,720.7	1,836.8	1,793.2	1,981.5	2,004.5	2,251.8	2,556.6
Services: Debit	78aed	−917.1	−976.4	−1,064.3	−1,087.8	−1,034.0	−1,293.2	−1,222.5	−1,143.1	−1,117.6	−1,105.5	−1,272.6	−1,294.0
Balance on Goods & Services	78afd	−67.2	−13.2	89.3	−157.3	−86.1	−257.7	−750.2	−736.0	−279.0	202.8	−57.9	170.6
Income: Credit	78agd	1,138.9	1,054.7	1,202.9	1,644.1	1,422.1	1,436.0	1,679.7	1,503.3	1,579.2	1,384.0	936.5	769.5
Income: Debit	78ahd	−1,539.9	−1,340.3	−1,425.2	−2,110.0	−1,671.3	−1,835.6	−2,270.4	−2,258.6	−2,192.7	−1,986.4	−1,220.5	−1,589.4
Balance on Gds, Serv. & Inc.	78aid	−468.2	−298.8	−133.0	−623.2	−335.3	−657.3	−1,340.9	−1,491.3	−892.5	−399.6	−341.9	−649.3
Current Transfers, n.i.e.: Credit	78ajd	230.0	236.5	185.5	184.1	167.7	185.2	195.2	202.7	208.7	277.9	304.6	301.8
Current Transfers: Debit	78akd	−29.0	−33.4	−36.6	−31.5	−33.0	−34.6	−36.6	−31.6	−31.7	−51.8	−55.0	−60.5
Capital Account, n.i.e.	78bcd	130.0	....	....	8.5	2.5	72.7	50.9	3.0	1.7	1.6	–	–
Capital Account, n.i.e.: Credit	78bad	130.0	....	....	8.5	2.5	72.7	50.9	3.0	1.7	1.6	–	–
Capital Account: Debit	78bbd	....	....	....	....	....	....	....	....	....	....	–	–
Financial Account, n.i.e.	78bjd	−440.1	−521.4	−288.2	115.6	561.2	972.3	1,076.8	1,398.2	−11.4	1,278.8	−76.3	29.7
Direct Investment Abroad	78bdd	....	....	....	....	....	....	–	–	–	–	–	–
Dir. Invest. in Rep. Econ., n.i.e.	78bed	144.5	169.6	401.5	223.0	415.5	1,299.3	1,296.0	652.4	603.4	404.6	77.9	791.5
Portfolio Investment Assets	78bfd	−46.3	−754.6	−48.4	318.5	487.8	−1,036.5	431.7	−550.2	−100.2	−747.7	10.0	−59.3
Equity Securities	78bkd	....	....	....	.2	−10.2	−.8	−5.1	−28.7	−.6	−.2	3.9	3.0
Debt Securities	78bld	−46.3	−754.6	−48.4	318.3	498.0	−1,035.7	436.8	−521.5	−99.6	−747.5	6.1	−62.3
Portfolio Investment Liab., n.i.e.	78bgd	−71.1	−54.7	−.4	−.3	−67.1	−80.3	−65.5	−99.2	−86.8	727.1	102.2	139.6
Equity Securities	78bmd	−1.4	−.1	.4	.2	−.1	−.1	–	–	–	–	–	–
Debt Securities	78bnd	−69.7	−54.6	−.8	−.5	−67.0	−80.2	−65.5	−99.2	−86.8	727.1	102.2	139.6
Financial Derivatives Assets	78bwd	....	....	....	....	....	....	....	....	–	–	–	–
Financial Derivatives Liabilities	78bxd	....	....	....	....	....	....	....	....	–	–	–	–
Other Investment Assets	78bhd	−1,491.8	−1,281.4	−5,277.7	−371.3	406.2	−478.7	776.7	1,983.0	354.7	875.9	3,145.6	464.1
Monetary Authorities	78bod	....	....	....	....	....	....	....	−5.2	5.2	–	–	–
General Government	78bpd	−.9	−.9	....	−1.0	−38.2	−2.3	−263.3	266.6	−4.0	−2.1	−.9	10.4
Banks	78bqd	−1,442.9	−1,186.6	−5,254.4	−176.3	533.1	−276.1	1,284.6	1,968.7	185.4	1,016.2	3,231.9	588.2
Other Sectors	78brd	−48.0	−93.9	−23.3	−194.0	−88.7	−200.3	−244.6	−247.1	168.1	−138.2	−85.4	−134.5
Other Investment Liab., n.i.e.	78bid	1,024.6	1,399.7	4,636.8	−54.3	−681.2	1,268.5	−1,362.1	−587.8	−782.5	18.9	−3,412.0	−1,306.2
Monetary Authorities	78bsd	11.2	.8	−1.3	54.6	−1.7	6.8	−1.0	−.7	−6.4	3.7	−.9	1.6
General Government	78btd	−155.8	−117.5	−198.8	−36.1	−50.5	130.4	85.6	33.7	−2.6	3.5	46.1	10.2
Banks	78bud	1,199.7	1,606.7	4,915.5	−122.8	−793.7	1,033.2	−1,446.8	−550.8	−425.5	−3.3	−3,351.2	−1,325.0
Other Sectors	78bvd	−30.5	−90.3	−78.6	50.0	164.7	98.1	.1	−70.0	−348.0	15.0	−106.0	7.0
Net Errors and Omissions	78cad	390.2	309.0	−89.5	15.2	−96.3	−195.0	−325.1	−228.7	398.2	−462.4	398.1	223.8
Overall Balance	78cbd	−187.1	−308.1	−361.8	−331.3	266.8	343.3	−379.7	−147.7	−327.0	644.5	229.5	−154.5
Reserves and Related Items	79dad	187.1	308.1	361.8	331.3	−266.8	−343.3	379.7	147.7	327.0	−644.5	−229.5	154.5
Reserve Assets	79bdd	116.2	−93.0	−105.7	−77.7	−297.7	−611.1	19.8	−184.5	108.1	−634.1	−221.4	164.1
Use of Fund Credit and Loans	79dcd	−98.6	3.4	12.5	−25.9	24.2	19.6	27.3	−23.5	−51.7	−33.3	−8.1	−9.5
Exceptional Financing	79ded	169.5	397.7	454.9	434.9	6.8	248.2	332.6	355.7	270.6	22.9	–	–
International Investment Position						*Millions of US Dollars*							
Assets	79aad	....	....	....	25,275.7	24,677.0	26,871.0	25,643.3	24,394.5	24,036.1	24,441.9	20,997.9	....
Direct Investment Abroad	79abd	....	....	....	–	–	–	–	–	–	–	–	....
Portfolio Investment	79acd	....	....	....	1,889.4	1,401.6	2,438.1	2,006.4	2,556.6	2,665.9	3,444.2	3,216.1	....
Equity Securities	79add	....	....	....	7.6	17.8	18.6	23.7	52.4	53.0	53.2	49.3	....
Debt Securities	79aed	....	....	....	1,881.8	1,383.8	2,419.5	1,982.7	2,504.2	2,612.9	3,391.0	3,166.8	....
Financial Derivatives	79afd	....	....	....	....	....	....	....	....	....	....	....	....
Other Investment	79afd	....	....	....	22,605.0	22,196.8	22,675.5	21,898.7	19,915.7	19,557.1	18,700.7	15,355.0	....
Monetary Authorities	79agd	....	....	....	–	–	–	–	5.2	–	–	–	....
General Government	79ahd	....	....	....	27.7	63.9	66.2	329.5	62.9	66.9	69.0	69.9	....
Banks	79aid	....	....	....	20,768.8	20,235.7	20,511.8	19,227.2	17,258.5	17,069.4	16,048.6	12,615.7	....
Other Sectors	79ajd	....	....	....	1,808.5	1,897.2	2,097.5	2,342.0	2,589.1	2,420.8	2,583.1	2,669.4	....
Reserve Assets	79akd	....	....	....	781.3	1,078.6	1,757.4	1,738.2	1,922.2	1,813.1	2,297.0	2,426.8	....
Liabilities	79lad	....	....	....	31,056.1	30,081.7	32,548.8	32,766.1	33,029.9	32,098.5	33,337.7	29,657.0	....
Dir. Invest. in Rep. Economy	79lbd	....	....	....	3,244.6	3,660.1	4,959.4	6,308.0	6,960.4	6,744.0	7,256.6	7,313.6	....
Portfolio Investement	79lcd	....	....	....	432.7	3,593.9	3,528.5	3,733.8	3,948.2	4,097.6	4,820.6	4,833.7	....
Equity Securities	79ldd	....	....	....	.1	–	–	–	–	–	–	–	....
Debt Securities	79led	....	....	....	432.6	3,593.9	3,528.5	3,733.8	3,948.2	4,097.6	4,820.6	4,833.7	....
Financial Derivatives	79lld	....	....	....	....	....	....	....	....	....	....	....	....
Other Investment	79lfd	....	....	....	27,378.8	22,827.7	24,060.9	22,724.3	22,121.3	21,256.9	21,260.5	17,509.7	....
Monetary Authorities	79lgd	....	....	....	271.5	290.1	309.9	343.5	314.7	249.6	217.2	208.9	....
General Government	79lhd	....	....	....	4,637.4	1,086.8	1,178.0	1,339.3	1,398.1	1,353.6	1,334.1	1,417.2	....
Banks	79lid	....	....	....	20,710.4	19,916.7	20,949.9	19,503.1	18,952.3	18,533.9	18,591.0	14,877.4	....
Other Sectors	79ljd	....	....	....	1,759.5	1,534.1	1,623.1	1,538.4	1,456.2	1,119.8	1,118.2	1,006.2	....

Panama 283

		1992	1993	1994	1995	1996	1997	1998	1999	2000	2001	2002	2003
Government Finance						*Millions of Balboas: Year Ending December 31*							
Deficit (-) or Surplus	80	321.2	284.7	146.0	230.5	−60.9	17.9	−64.2	34.4	30.2	....	....	....
Revenue	81	1,692.8	1,950.8	2,010.5	2,065.1	2,140.3	2,202.8	2,331.2	2,664.5	2,688.4	....	....	....
Grants Received	81z	26.1	27.8	15.5	8.5	4.6	63.5	72.3	6.8	17.8	....	....	....
Expenditure	82	1,657.8	1,768.6	1,958.7	1,953.3	2,255.3	2,341.3	2,606.8	2,650.9	2,803.9	....	....	....
Lending Minus Repayments	83	−260.1	−74.7	−78.7	−110.2	−49.5	−92.9	−139.1	−14.0	−127.9	....	....	....
Financing													
Total Financing	84	−321.2	−284.7	−146.0	−230.5	60.9	−17.9	64.2	−34.4	−30.2	....	....	....
Domestic	84a	−277.6	−226.2	−135.2	−253.2	3.7	−133.6	−297.9	−237.2	−200.7	....	....	....
Foreign	85a	−43.6	−58.5	−10.8	22.7	57.2	115.7	362.1	202.8	170.5	....	....	....
Debt: Domestic	88a	999.5	1,810.1	1,805.6	1,681.4	1,794.2	1,737.5	1,737.6	2,108.8	2,090.4	2,089.0	2,122.1	2,094.3
Debt: Foreign	89a	2,624.9	2,600.2	2,812.9	3,001.5	4,542.2	4,659.6	5,042.5	5,457.6	5,552.3	6,243.3	6,298.0	6,420.8
National Accounts						*Millions of Balboas*							
Househ.Cons.Expend.,incl.NPISHs	96f	3,745.2	4,063.4	4,150.7	4,090.0	5,324.9	4,699.1	5,283.4	5,331.8	5,672.8	....	....	....
Government Consumption Expend	91f	1,055.9	1,098.3	1,144.8	1,194.1	1,256.9	1,402.6	1,507.6	1,500.0	1,605.3	....	....	....
Gross Fixed Capital Formation	93e	1,227.9	1,681.3	1,828.8	2,057.9	1,871.5	2,295.0	2,624.9	2,908.1	2,634.1	....	....	....
Changes in Inventories	93i	345.3	111.9	244.8	336.3	559.3	396.1	372.3	278.0	239.4	....	....	....
Exports of Goods and Services	90c	6,653.8	7,014.6	7,711.6	7,979.4	7,807.5	8,494.6	8,396.4	7,390.4	7,941.1	....	....	....
Imports of Goods and Services (-)	98c	6,386.7	6,716.8	7,346.8	7,751.6	7,666.6	8,629.9	8,839.9	7,771.7	8,073.7	....	....	....
Gross Domestic Product (GDP)	99b	7,272.9	7,942.3	8,469.2	8,657.8	9,322.1	10,084.0	10,932.5	11,456.3	11,620.5	11,807.5	12,215.6	....
Net Primary Income from Abroad	98.n	−447.1	−338.6	−272.3	−421.5	−319.6	−451.4	−608.8	−790.7	−700.5	....	....	....
Gross National Income (GNI)	99a	6,194.3	6,914.1	7,461.6	7,484.6	8,606.5	8,206.1	8,735.9	8,845.9	9,318.5	....	....	....
Consumption of Fixed Capital	99cf	375.3	497.0	533.3	558.9	472.9	601.1	667.8	723.2	747.2	....	....	....
GDP Volume 1996 Prices	99b.p	7,867.0	8,296.2	8,532.6	8,682.1	9,322.1	9,916.8	10,648.8	11,071.4	11,374.8	11,439.9	11,697.1	12,172.1
GDP Volume (2000=100)	99bvp	69.2	72.9	75.0	76.3	82.0	87.2	93.6	97.3	100.0	100.6	102.8	107.0
GDP Deflator (2000=100)	99bip	90.5	93.7	97.2	97.6	97.9	99.5	100.5	101.3	100.0	101.0	102.2	....
						Millions: Midyear Estimates							
Population	99z	2.51	2.56	2.62	2.67	2.73	2.78	2.84	2.89	2.95	3.01	3.06	3.12

2004, International Monetary Fund: *International Financial Statistics Yearbook*

Papua New Guinea 853

		1992	1993	1994	1995	1996	1997	1998	1999	2000	2001	2002	2003
Exchange Rates													
			*SDRs per Kina: End of Period*
Official Rate	ac	.7365	.7419	.5812	.5039	.5164	.4232	.3388	.2703	.2498	.2115	.1830	.2019
			*US Dollars per Kina: End of Period (ag) Period Average (rh)*
Official Rate	ag	1.0127	1.0190	.8485	.7490	.7425	.5710	.4770	.3710	.3255	.2658	.2488	.3000
Official Rate	rh	1.0367	1.0221	.9950	.7835	.7588	.6975	.4859	.3939	.3617	.2964	.2573	.2814
			*Index Numbers (2000=100): Period Averages*
Official Rate	ahx	286.6	282.6	275.1	216.6	209.8	192.8	134.3	108.9	100.0	81.9	71.2	77.8
Nominal Effective Exchange Rate	nec	196.9	217.9	224.9	171.3	168.9	166.3	128.2	103.0	100.0	88.0	75.2	73.8
Real Effective Exchange Rate	rec	128.9	134.8	127.5	108.3	116.5	116.7	99.6	91.0	100.0	93.6	87.6	97.1
Fund Position													
			*Millions of SDRs: End of Period*
Quota	2f.s	95.30	95.30	95.30	95.30	95.30	95.30	95.30	131.60	131.60	131.60	131.60	131.60
SDRs	1b.s	.10	.03	.07	.47	.04	.06	.04	.53	9.34	6.93	4.46	2.48
Reserve Position in the Fund	1c.s	.04	.05	.05	.05	.05	.05	.05	.05	.18	.30	.36	.40
Total Fund Cred.&Loans Outstg	2tl	42.84	32.13	10.71	33.34	35.34	35.34	32.35	15.68	29.89	85.54	85.54	81.79
International Liquidity													
			*Millions of US Dollars Unless Otherwise Indicated: Approximately End of Period*
Total Reserves minus Gold	1l.d	238.58	141.45	96.06	261.35	583.89	362.68	192.88	205.14	286.87	422.65	321.51	494.18
SDRs	1b.d	.14	.05	.11	.69	.06	.08	.05	.72	12.17	8.71	6.06	3.68
Reserve Position in the Fund	1c.d	.06	.07	.08	.08	.08	.07	.07	.07	.23	.38	.49	.59
Foreign Exchange	1d.d	238.39	141.34	95.88	260.58	583.75	362.53	192.76	204.35	274.46	413.56	314.96	489.90
Gold (Million Fine Troy Ounces)	1ad	.063	.063	.063	.014	.063	.063	.063	.063	.063	.063	.063	.063
Gold (National Valuation)	1and	11.23	11.30	2.39	2.11	21.02	16.17	13.31	10.35	9.08	7.42	21.89	25.83
Monetary Authorities: Other Liab.	4..d	115.27	87.35	109.58	161.71	106.44	84.50	61.30	6.90	52.64	180.70	197.46	228.37
Deposit Money Banks: Assets	7a.d	61.61	160.59	175.61	100.11	119.12	117.38	136.34	103.23	95.83	112.18	153.11	106.67
Liabilities	7b.d	118.34	88.07	120.46	41.39	23.07	7.99	54.53	37.44	18.13	24.24	25.99	16.88
Monetary Authorities													
			*Millions of Kina: Last Wednesday of Period*
Foreign Assets	11	242.31	138.61	112.51	357.55	789.20	666.07	391.06	552.92	909.24	1,617.94	1,380.18	1,733.33
Claims on Central Government	12a	284.20	421.02	776.65	592.62	587.28	880.81	1,284.96	599.66	163.60	160.19	790.21	705.98
Claims on Nonfin.Pub.Enterprises	12c	–	–	–	–	–	–	–	–	–	–	–	3.83
Claims on Deposit Money Banks	12e	127.74	239.43	282.50	233.80	228.94	216.27	121.10	53.63	53.27	52.15	52.09	50.06
Reserve Money	14	168.93	199.20	221.65	255.66	488.98	321.12	387.47	671.55	561.51	592.26	699.02	789.05
of which: Currency Outside DMBs	14a	141.17	160.70	179.00	194.21	216.40	234.85	278.09	357.49	306.93	308.98	379.94	417.93
Time Deposits	15	.50	.50	.50	.50	.50	.50	.50	.50	.50	.50	.42	.41
Foreign Liabilities	16c	171.99	129.04	147.57	282.07	211.79	231.49	224.00	76.61	281.34	1,084.29	1,261.05	1,166.37
Central Government Deposits	16d	224.57	369.66	663.01	623.10	840.32	977.77	916.71	100.24	30.76	274.50	242.49	505.65
Capital Accounts	17a	218.31	204.45	140.20	122.57	122.13	245.05	254.78	261.74	329.89	506.68	589.51	434.00
Other Items (Net)	17r	–130.04	–103.79	–1.29	–99.93	–58.30	–12.77	13.65	95.56	–77.91	–627.96	–569.99	–402.28
Deposit Money Banks													
			*Millions of Kina: Last Wednesday of Period*
Reserves	20	24.61	36.68	40.67	56.20	116.43	67.21	106.03	310.37	250.67	279.48	310.49	367.21
Foreign Assets	21	60.84	157.59	206.97	133.66	160.44	205.57	285.83	278.26	294.40	422.06	615.40	355.55
Claims on Central Government	22a	364.57	502.65	446.27	727.57	1,105.13	1,107.80	888.60	791.57	1,065.24	1,121.02	991.41	1,163.57
Claims on Local Governments	22b	3.96	6.22	5.95	1.58	1.91	1.29	5.05	5.46	1.05	.94	2.38	6.04
Claims on Nonfin.Pub.Enterprises	22c	233.52	294.69	374.70	329.25	315.00	297.71	202.94	153.06	123.02	113.64	125.69	95.04
Claims on Private Sector	22d	890.55	820.27	897.99	900.78	908.93	1,223.08	1,577.98	1,554.88	1,668.15	1,601.47	1,503.57	1,480.27
Demand Deposits	24	293.10	431.77	433.46	501.18	692.31	752.74	829.35	982.38	1,061.86	1,104.17	1,241.13	1,474.95
Time, Savings,& Fgn. Currency Dep.	25	993.78	1,091.68	1,049.85	1,192.55	1,410.43	1,659.12	1,620.62	1,638.32	1,758.57	1,765.73	1,681.63	1,401.10
Foreign Liabilities	26c	116.85	86.43	141.97	55.26	31.07	14.00	114.33	100.91	55.70	91.19	104.48	56.27
Central Government Deposits	26d	43.46	51.45	73.13	122.48	167.22	170.65	287.49	211.71	255.06	309.80	282.60	240.36
Credit from Monetary Authorities	26g	127.74	239.43	282.50	233.80	228.94	216.28	121.10	53.63	53.39	52.15	52.09	50.06
Capital Accounts	27a	65.21	60.63	78.36	92.65	114.78	139.25	212.80	332.05	284.09	374.62	426.13	537.28
Other Items (Net)	27r	–62.10	–143.29	–86.72	–48.88	–36.92	–49.39	–119.26	–225.40	–66.14	–159.07	–239.12	–292.33
Monetary Survey													
			*Millions of Kina: Last Wednesday of Period*
Foreign Assets (Net)	31n	14.31	80.73	29.94	153.88	706.78	626.15	338.56	653.65	866.60	864.52	630.05	866.24
Domestic Credit	32	1,517.69	1,630.57	1,765.41	1,806.21	1,910.71	2,362.27	2,755.32	2,792.67	2,735.23	2,412.94	2,888.18	2,708.72
Claims on Central Govt. (Net)	32an	380.74	502.55	486.77	574.60	684.87	840.19	969.35	1,079.27	943.01	696.90	1,256.53	1,123.54
Claims on Local Government	32b	3.96	6.22	5.95	1.58	1.91	1.29	5.05	5.46	1.05	.94	2.38	6.04
Claims on Nonfin.Pub.Enterprises	32c	233.52	294.69	374.70	329.25	315.00	297.71	202.94	153.06	123.02	113.64	125.69	98.87
Claims on Private Sector	32d	890.55	820.27	897.99	900.78	908.93	1,223.08	1,577.98	1,554.88	1,668.15	1,601.47	1,503.57	1,480.27
Claims on Other Financial Insts	32f	8.91	6.84	–	–	–	–	–	–	–	–	–	–
Money	34	437.42	594.29	614.48	700.64	1,064.87	1,006.66	1,110.79	1,343.56	1,372.69	1,416.95	1,629.66	1,896.79
Quasi-Money	35	994.28	1,092.18	1,050.35	1,193.05	1,410.93	1,659.62	1,621.12	1,638.82	1,759.07	1,766.23	1,682.05	1,401.52
Capital Accounts	37a	283.52	265.09	218.56	215.22	236.91	384.30	467.58	593.78	613.99	881.31	1,015.64	971.27
Other Items (Net)	37r	–183.23	–240.24	–88.05	–148.81	–95.22	–62.16	–105.61	–129.83	–143.92	–787.02	–809.12	–694.61
Money plus Quasi-Money	35l	1,431.70	1,686.46	1,664.83	1,893.69	2,475.80	2,666.29	2,731.91	2,982.37	3,131.76	3,183.18	3,311.71	3,298.30
Interest Rates													
			*Percent Per Annum*
Discount Rate (End of Period)	60	7.12	† 6.30	6.55	18.00	10.30	10.20	18.15	12.80	4.41	11.25	13.25	....
Treasury Bill Rate	60c	8.88	6.25	6.85	17.40	14.44	9.94	21.18	22.70	17.00	12.36	10.93	18.68
Deposit Rate	60l	7.85	5.03	5.09	12.18	12.19	7.31	13.73	15.46	14.54	8.91	5.80	8.16
Lending Rate	60p	14.53	11.29	9.16	13.14	13.30	10.45	17.70	18.90	17.54	16.21	13.89	13.36

Papua New Guinea 853

		1992	1993	1994	1995	1996	1997	1998	1999	2000	2001	2002	2003
Prices and Labor						*Index Numbers (2000=100): Period Averages*							
Consumer Prices	64	45.1	47.3	48.7	57.1	63.7	66.3	75.3	86.5	100.0	109.3	122.2	140.2
Total Employment	67	92.2	89.6	96.2	91.7	98.5	98.3	96.1	98.5	†100.0	94.5	91.2	98.9
International Transactions							*Millions of Kina*						
Exports	70	1,862.6	2,527.3	2,662.0	3,400.0	3,334.0	3,079.0	3,707.0	5,006.7	5,813.0	6,104.9	6,028.7	7,729.2
Imports, c.i.f.	71	1,431.2	1,270.5	1,534.1	1,862.9	2,296.0	2,448.4	2,565.7	3,174.0	3,195.8	3,637.9	4,826.3	4,616.9
Imports, f.o.b.	71.v	1,275.0	1,110.4	1,336.0	1,620.0	1,996.0	2,129.0	2,231.0	2,760.0	2,779.0	3,164.3	....	....
							2000=100						
Volume of Exports	72	107.2	108.5	†108.3	101.1	95.8	85.4	94.9	102.7	100.0	†94.4	88.1	....
Unit Value of Exports	74	24.3	27.2	†31.7	45.5	47.1	50.3	60.5	74.2	100.0	†108.9	119.7	....
Balance of Payments						*Millions of US Dollars: Minus Sign Indicates Debit*							
Current Account, n.i.e.	78ald	−159.9	474.1	402.1	491.9	188.9	−192.2	−28.9	94.7	345.4	282.1	....	....
Goods: Exports f.o.b.	78aad	1,947.7	2,604.4	2,651.0	2,670.4	2,529.8	2,160.1	1,773.3	1,927.4	2,094.1	1,812.9	....	....
Goods: Imports f.o.b.	78abd	−1,322.9	−1,134.7	−1,324.9	−1,262.4	−1,513.3	−1,483.3	−1,078.3	−1,071.4	−998.8	−932.4	....	....
Trade Balance	78acd	624.9	1,469.7	1,326.1	1,408.0	1,016.6	676.8	695.0	856.0	1,095.3	880.5	....	....
Services: Credit	78add	329.2	306.7	235.4	321.3	432.2	396.9	318.0	247.5	242.7	285.1	....	....
Services: Debit	78aed	−685.8	−804.6	−608.0	−642.1	−778.5	−923.6	−793.8	−727.9	−772.3	−662.0	....	....
Balance on Goods & Services	78afd	268.2	971.8	953.5	1,087.2	670.2	150.1	219.2	375.6	565.7	503.7	....	....
Income: Credit	78agd	59.7	31.3	22.4	22.5	32.1	35.1	20.9	18.6	32.0	20.0	....	....
Income: Debit	78ahd	−425.3	−400.2	−423.4	−510.7	−461.2	−344.8	−279.7	−291.1	−242.1	−250.2	....	....
Balance on Gds, Serv. & Inc.	78aid	−97.5	603.0	552.5	599.1	241.1	−159.5	−39.6	103.1	355.6	273.4	....	....
Current Transfers, n.i.e.: Credit	78ajd	48.6	49.0	58.8	66.7	252.1	69.9	82.4	60.3	62.4	75.9	....	....
Current Transfers: Debit	78akd	−111.1	−178.0	−209.3	−173.9	−304.2	−102.6	−71.6	−68.7	−72.7	−67.3	....	....
Capital Account, n.i.e.	78bcd	−	−	−	−	−	−	−	−	−	−	....	....
Capital Account, n.i.e.: Credit	78bad	20.7	20.4	19.9	15.7	15.2	13.9	9.7	7.8	7.2	5.9	....	....
Capital Account: Debit	78bbd	−20.7	−20.4	−19.9	−15.7	−15.2	−13.9	−9.7	−7.8	−7.2	−5.9	....	....
Financial Account, n.i.e.	78bjd	−149.0	−716.2	−609.2	−444.7	46.6	8.0	−179.7	16.0	−254.1	−151.9	....	....
Direct Investment Abroad	78bdd	−	−	−	−	−	−	−	−	....	....	....	....
Dir. invest. in Rep. Econ., n.i.e.	78bed	104.3	62.0	57.0	454.6	111.3	28.6	109.6	296.5	95.9	62.5	....	....
Portfolio Investment Assets	78bfd	18.5	−50.9	−2.1	−48.7	69.9	−25.5	87.0	89.0	−123.8	−72.7	....	....
Equity Securities	78bkd	−	−	−	....	....	....	....	....	....	....	....	....
Debt Securities	78bld	18.5	−50.9	−2.1	−48.7	69.9	−25.5	87.0	89.0	−123.8	−72.7	....	....
Portfolio Investment Liab., n.i.e.	78bgd	....	....	....	....	....	....	....	....	−	−	....	....
Equity Securities	78bmd	....	....	....	....	....	....	....	....	−	−	....	....
Debt Securities	78bnd	....	....	....	....	....	....	....	....	−	−	....	....
Financial Derivatives Assets	78bwd	....	....	....	....	....	....	....	....	....	....	....	....
Financial Derivatives Liabilities	78bxd	....	....	....	....	....	....	....	....	....	....	....	....
Other Investment Assets	78bhd	7.0	17.3	58.8	−283.8	180.0	29.6	−55.0	10.7	−41.0	−66.9	....	....
Monetary Authorities	78bod	....	....	....	....	....	....	....	....	....	....	....	....
General Government	78bpd	−	−	−	....	....	....	....	....	−2.1	−21.2	−26.7	....
Banks	78bqd	....	....	....	....	....	....	....	....	−2.1	−21.2	−26.7	....
Other Sectors	78brd	7.0	17.3	58.8	−283.8	180.0	29.6	−55.0	12.8	−19.8	−40.2	....	....
Other Investment Liab., n.i.e.	78bid	−278.8	−744.5	−722.9	−566.8	−314.6	−24.7	−321.2	−380.2	−185.2	−74.7	....	....
Monetary Authorities	78bsd	−	−	−	−	−68.2	−	−	−	−	−	....	....
General Government	78btd	59.6	66.5	−102.1	−23.5	10.0	−62.7	−44.2	39.4	.2	49.0	....	....
Banks	78bud	−36.1	−110.3	−26.9	27.4	−34.0	−42.3	16.4	−	....	....	....	....
Other Sectors	78bvd	−302.3	−700.8	−593.9	−570.7	−222.4	80.3	−293.4	−419.6	−185.4	−123.7	....	....
Net Errors and Omissions	78cad	−17.2	−11.3	37.1	−86.6	−33.1	7.3	−12.5	14.3	13.1	−1.6	....	....
Overall Balance	78cbd	−326.1	−253.4	−170.1	−39.5	202.5	−177.0	−221.0	125.0	104.5	128.6	....	....
Reserves and Related Items	79dad	326.1	253.4	170.1	39.5	−202.5	177.0	221.0	−125.0	−104.5	−128.6	....	....
Reserve Assets	79dbd	71.1	96.6	33.8	−177.4	−329.7	83.7	149.1	−49.7	−127.9	−203.6	....	....
Use of Fund Credit and Loans	79dcd	−	−15.0	−30.6	35.0	2.9	−	−4.2	−22.8	18.1	70.9	....	....
Exceptional Financing	79ded	255.0	171.8	166.8	181.9	124.4	93.2	76.1	−52.5	5.3	4.1	....	....
Government Finance						*Millions of Kina: Year Ending December 31*							
Deficit (-) or Surplus	80	−220.38	−283.55	†−136.78	−31.77	35.39	15.41	−137.40	−241.79	....	....	....	....
Total Revenue and Grants	81y	1,117.64	1,310.65	†1,443.43	1,692.95	1,896.12	2,024.01	1,991.20	2,216.11	....	....	....	....
Revenue	81	921.32	1,128.95	†1,278.62	1,499.84	1,730.67	1,711.98	1,686.46	1,750.59	....	....	....	....
Grants	81z	196.32	181.70	†164.81	193.11	165.45	312.03	304.74	465.52	....	....	....	....
Exp. & Lending Minus Repay	82z	1,338.02	1,594.20	†1,580.21	1,724.72	1,860.73	2,008.60	2,128.60	2,457.90	....	....	....	....
Expenditure	82	1,348.69	1,588.71	1,580.99	1,721.93	1,857.29	2,003.70	2,127.26	2,457.83	....	....	....	....
Lending Minus Repayments	83	−10.67	5.49	†−.78	2.79	3.44	4.90	1.34	.07	....	....	....	....
Total Financing	80h	220.38	283.55	†136.78	31.77	−35.39	−15.40	137.40	241.80	....	....	....	....
Domestic	84a	181.52	237.83	†255.22	75.30	−45.49	57.90	253.72	304.29	....	....	....	....
Foreign	85a	38.86	45.72	†−118.44	−43.53	10.10	−73.30	−116.32	−62.49	....	....	....	....
Total Debt by Residence	88	1,894.62	2,157.40	†2,961.20	3,324.20	3,780.80	4,418.00	5,177.70	5,609.20	....	....	....	....
Domestic	88a	676.41	1,036.60	†1,424.30	1,605.70	1,969.50	2,251.70	2,473.00	2,021.40	....	....	....	....
Foreign	89a	1,218.21	1,120.80	†1,536.90	1,718.50	1,811.30	2,166.30	2,704.70	3,587.80	....	....	....	....

2004, International Monetary Fund: *International Financial Statistics Yearbook*

Papua New Guinea 853

		1992	1993	1994	1995	1996	1997	1998	1999	2000	2001	2002	2003
National Accounts							*Millions of Kina*						
Househ.Cons.Expend.,incl.NPISHs	96f	2,144	2,046	2,240	2,454	3,375	4,119	4,620	6,123	....	....	....	....
Government Consumption Expend...	91f	1,005	1,199	1,001	1,006	1,370	1,361	1,407	1,488	....	....	....	....
Gross Fixed Capital Formation	93e	914	901	1,012	1,150	1,186	1,079	1,089	1,063	....	....	....	....
Changes in Inventories	93i	70	−43	142	149	375	409	307	377	....	....	....	....
Exports of Goods and Services	90c	2,021	2,562	3,031	3,675	3,575	3,312	3,942	4,153	....	....	....	....
Imports of Goods and Services (-)	98c	1,930	1,798	2,044	2,545	3,000	3,217	3,575	4,423	....	....	....	....
Gross Domestic Product (GDP)	99b	4,223	4,867	5,381	5,888	6,881	7,064	7,789	8,781	....	....	....	....
Net Primary Income from Abroad	98.n	336	−330	−246	−208	−307	−310	−343	−360	....	....	....	....
Gross National Income (GNI)	99a	3,887	4,537	5,136	5,681	6,574	6,754	7,445	8,421	....	....	....	....
Consumption of Fixed Capital	99cf	439	433	502	571	589	535	540	527	....	....	....	....
GDP Volume 1983 Prices	99b.p	2,931	3,465	3,671	3,549	3,824	3,675	3,635	3,804	....	....	....	....
GDP Volume (1995=100)	99bvp	82.6	97.6	103.4	100.0	107.7	103.5	102.4	107.2	....	....	....	....
GDP Deflator (1995=100)	99bip	86.8	84.7	88.4	100.0	108.5	115.9	129.2	139.2	....	....	....	....
						Millions: Midyear Estimates							
Population	99z	4.34	4.46	4.58	4.70	4.83	Ü 4.95	5.08	5.21	5.33	5.46	5.59	5.71

Paraguay 288

		1992	1993	1994	1995	1996	1997	1998	1999	2000	2001	2002	2003
Exchange Rates						*Guaranies per SDR: End of Period*							
Market Rate......aa=......	wa	2,241.3	2,582.3	2,809.8	2,942.7	3,033.6	3,184.2	3,999.1	4,568.9	4,595.2	5,884.0	9,657.5	9,086.6
				Guaranies per US Dollar: End of Period (we) Period Average (wf)									
Market Rate......ae=......	we	1,630.0	1,880.0	1,924.7	1,979.7	2,109.7	2,360.0	2,840.2	3,328.9	3,526.9	4,682.0	7,103.6	6,115.0
Market Rate......rf=......	wf	1,500.3	1,744.3	1,904.8	1,963.0	2,056.8	2,177.9	2,726.5	3,119.1	3,486.4	4,105.9	5,716.3	6,424.3
				Index Numbers (2000=100): Period Averages									
Market Rate.........	ahx	225.6	200.1	183.0	177.6	169.5	160.1	128.1	112.2	100.0	85.6	62.1	54.5
Nominal Effective Exchange Rate.....	nec	67.5	91.6	133.8	136.0	135.6	137.5	115.7	107.1	100.0	91.9	70.0	57.7
Real Effective Exchange Rate.........	rec	95.5	96.8	101.2	102.7	107.0	112.8	103.5	100.7	100.0	95.7	78.1	71.1
Fund Position						*Millions of SDRs: End of Period*							
Quota.........	2f.s	72.10	72.10	72.10	72.10	72.10	72.10	72.10	99.90	99.90	99.90	99.90	99.90
SDRs.........	1b.s	62.12	65.08	67.63	70.58	73.30	76.08	79.14	74.81	78.49	81.33	83.25	84.63
Reserve Position in the Fund.........	1c.s	16.94	16.48	14.53	14.53	14.53	14.53	14.53	21.48	21.48	21.48	21.48	21.48
Total Fund Cred.&Loans Outstg......	2tl	–	–	–	–	–	–	–	–	–	–	–	–
International Liquidity					*Millions of US Dollars Unless Otherwise Indicated: End of Period*								
Total Reserves minus Gold.........	1l.d	561.53	631.18	1,030.73	1,092.91	1,049.29	835.68	864.74	978.05	762.83	713.51	629.19	968.86
SDRs.........	1b.d	85.42	89.39	98.73	104.92	105.40	102.65	111.44	102.68	102.26	102.21	113.18	125.75
Reserve Position in the Fund.........	1c.d	23.29	22.63	21.20	21.59	20.89	19.60	20.45	29.48	27.98	26.99	29.20	31.91
Foreign Exchange.........	1d.d	452.82	519.16	910.80	966.40	923.00	713.42	732.85	845.89	632.58	584.32	486.82	811.19
of which: US Dollars.........	1dxd	329.34	416.00	583.80	602.40	415.53	521.25	561.87	736.13	525.20	467.98	353.95	674.97
Gold (Million Fine Troy Ounces)........	1ad	.035	.035	.035	.035	.035	.035	.035	.035	.035	.035	.035	.035
Gold (National Valuation).............	1and	11.60	13.70	13.40	13.50	12.90	10.10	10.03	10.15	9.60	9.66	12.14	14.51
Monetary Authorities:Other Assets...	3..d	–	39.40	3.98	3.45	3.44	3.40	7.07	9.80	14.14	12.28	3.20	8.96
Other Liab.........	4..d	83.31	86.91	86.60	85.11	76.47	67.87	60.76	53.37	44.88	93.88	115.11	63.96
Deposit Money Banks: Assets.........	7a.d	240.30	300.39	298.21	502.97	474.74	378.52	416.19	402.43	498.84	447.92	288.26	389.83
Liabilities.........	7b.d	89.18	147.37	124.57	453.01	256.93	304.67	232.03	119.86	105.33	96.63	69.12	46.44
Other Banking Insts.: Assets.........	7e.d	–	–	–	.34	.67	12.91	11.01	9.63	15.76	18.88	4.30	3.64
Liabilities.........	7f.d	41.51	36.40	32.78	–	–	8.54	2.12	.60	2.01	1.79	.72	4.32
Monetary Authorities						*Billions of Guaranies: End of Period*							
Foreign Assets.........	11	993.43	1,289.15	2,016.58	†2,239.16	2,263.63	1,993.00	2,521.04	3,341.31	2,804.01	3,420.08	4,528.71	6,038.97
Claims on Central Government.........	12a	794.81	916.73	1,047.15	†1,038.99	1,088.06	695.48	928.81	1,113.16	1,063.78	1,477.66	2,240.39	2,159.88
Claims on Local Government.........	12b	.83	.82	.82	†.67	.62	1.06	1.11	1.16	1.21	1.26	1.31	1.36
Claims on Nonfin.Pub.Enterprises.....	12c	242.74	266.79	222.35	†239.15	268.00	303.76	329.42	358.39	381.19	216.23	283.50	291.82
Claims on Private Sector.........	12d	6.30	6.29	6.58	†7.24	11.90	14.73	18.41	22.28	25.61	28.05	32.57	34.23
Claims on Deposit Money Banks.........	12e	170.29	102.77	98.07	†580.74	840.71	528.45	45.40	4.57	7.19	6.64	4.26	1.66
Claims on Other Banking Insts.........	12f	16.53	16.21	15.65	†21.31	104.20	20.03	33.85	26.94	35.98	44.16	58.07	27.04
Claims on Nonbank Financial Insts...	12g	–	–	–	†23.14	21.34	86.65	96.05	103.46	113.11	123.08	133.01	142.87
Reserve Money.........	14	954.56	1,083.20	1,378.91	†1,738.50	1,704.98	1,829.88	1,949.68	2,127.14	2,105.35	2,234.23	2,293.74	3,461.11
of which: Currency Outside DMBs..	14a	531.26	635.77	800.46	†956.00	961.77	1,122.90	1,264.08	1,398.68	1,327.19	1,377.21	1,451.20	1,814.57
Time & Foreign Currency Deposits.....	15	281.81	406.51	455.51	†448.56	648.47	635.95	833.43	1,040.74	1,090.23	1,366.33	1,577.06	1,599.30
Liabs. of Central Bank: Securities......	16ac	–	8.53	35.50	†201.90	250.79	319.05	381.75	75.88	45.93	284.47	578.50	1,070.96
Restricted Deposits.........	16b	10.12	17.11	26.47	†26.01	51.75	54.55	58.21	72.21	80.31	87.29	124.18	131.52
Foreign Liabilities.........	16c	7.49	17.36	16.21	†18.17	.98	.28	.28	.04	1.64	.85	3.47	2.98
Long-Term Foreign Liabilities.........	16cl	127.06	141.68	150.41	†150.77	160.30	157.86	172.29	176.87	157.47	434.29	802.32	385.28
Central Government Deposits.........	16d	228.31	134.37	414.23	†580.16	572.39	469.51	553.16	1,327.51	813.38	723.61	730.01	1,120.48
Capital Accounts.........	17a	286.94	303.95	332.20	†519.10	611.14	2,381.56	1,619.77	2,138.81	2,151.12	2,589.63	4,076.37	2,708.77
Other Items (Net).........	17r	328.66	486.04	597.76	†467.22	597.65	–2,205.47	–1,594.49	–1,987.93	–2,013.36	–2,403.53	–2,903.84	–1,782.57
Deposit Money Banks						*Billions of Guaranies: End of Period*							
Reserves.........	20	588.19	743.99	913.28	†1,032.56	1,173.75	1,189.09	1,421.92	1,636.09	1,740.62	2,106.19	2,250.36	3,085.37
Claims on Mon.Author.:Securities.....	20c	–	8.53	35.50	†173.67	238.76	287.18	209.91	60.79	39.94	172.61	324.57	642.36
Foreign Assets.........	21	388.08	549.71	573.75	†998.40	1,001.22	881.95	1,181.98	1,334.07	1,768.39	2,076.09	2,017.85	2,366.29
Claims on Central Government.........	22a	–	.18	–	†46.59	98.35	187.73	286.85	454.60	356.87	294.61	534.58	656.78
Claims on Local Government.........	22b	.30	.55	.01	†22.00	1.57	7.07	36.64	5.55	8.98	4.35	.95	1.78
Claims on Nonfin.Pub.Enterprises.....	22c	1.79	1.45	1.46	†–	–	–	.79	1.27	–	.02	–	–
Claims on Private Sector.........	22d	1,705.83	2,315.36	3,164.92	†3,795.04	4,660.78	5,217.41	5,093.49	5,654.33	5,937.32	6,757.09	6,777.93	5,054.30
Claims on Other Banking Insts.........	22f	4.93	11.08	11.58	†15.57	8.99	29.18	20.03	16.63	37.90	29.44	26.52	28.72
Claims on Nonbank Financial Insts...	22g	–	–	–	†39.39	25.98	33.45	25.52	40.35	45.80	63.21	3.21	.09
Demand Deposits.........	24	306.57	367.48	499.43	†594.40	681.90	698.08	678.97	730.19	1,192.53	1,326.51	1,273.39	1,918.52
Time, Savings,& Fgn.Currency Dep...	25	1,628.79	2,170.28	2,663.58	†3,286.94	3,844.68	4,156.49	4,522.84	5,470.17	5,444.15	6,477.35	6,582.20	6,362.06
Money Market Instruments.........	26aa	–	–	–	†50.16	36.98	49.11	13.11	9.42	39.32	12.13	17.09	9.17
Bonds.........	26ab	2.21	4.00	3.76	†1.94	4.13	5.85	15.72	12.97	14.17	37.05	144.60	30.35
Restricted Deposits.........	26b	–	–	–	†3.29	15.01	3.03	18.71	23.10	60.16	51.18	92.43	98.49
Foreign Liabilities.........	26c	71.07	149.61	211.29	†717.45	336.56	535.44	614.56	345.84	264.56	326.42	377.70	206.73
Long-Term Foreign Liabilities.........	26cl	72.96	120.08	28.39	†181.77	205.30	174.44	44.40	51.51	108.85	121.45	106.11	75.14
Central Government Deposits.........	26d	97.40	209.98	432.74	†324.39	886.07	758.05	721.32	728.42	777.54	895.15	919.28	901.47
Credit from Monetary Authorities.........	26g	169.18	102.45	94.01	†156.36	346.59	321.61	33.27	68.68	86.49	89.30	131.15	78.52
Liabilities to Other Banking Insts......	26i	2.85	.86	.01	†19.24	31.45	31.02	50.11	68.47	102.10	235.49	215.34	396.44
Capital Accounts.........	27a	342.21	483.01	719.50	†1,020.67	1,347.22	1,627.12	1,609.57	1,715.53	1,890.09	2,132.39	2,372.02	2,147.99
Other Items (Net).........	27r	–4.12	23.11	47.82	†–233.45	–526.49	–527.15	–45.45	–20.59	–44.14	–200.81	–295.34	–389.19

2004, International Monetary Fund : *International Financial Statistics Yearbook*

Paraguay 288

		1992	1993	1994	1995	1996	1997	1998	1999	2000	2001	2002	2003
Monetary Survey						*Billions of Guaranies: End of Period*							
Foreign Assets (Net)	31n	1,302.95	1,671.89	2,362.84	† 2,501.93	2,927.32	2,339.23	3,088.18	4,329.50	4,306.20	5,168.90	6,165.39	8,195.55
Domestic Credit	32	2,448.35	3,191.11	3,623.54	† 4,344.52	4,831.32	5,369.00	5,596.47	5,742.22	6,416.82	7,420.40	8,442.74	6,376.91
Claims on Central Govt. (Net)	32an	469.10	572.56	200.17	† 181.02	−272.06	−344.34	−58.82	−488.16	−170.27	153.51	1,125.66	794.70
Claims on Local Government	32b	1.13	1.37	.83	† 22.67	2.18	8.13	37.75	6.71	10.19	5.61	2.26	3.14
Claims on Nonfin.Pub.Enterprises	32c	244.53	268.23	223.81	† 239.15	268.00	303.76	330.20	359.66	381.19	216.25	283.50	291.82
Claims on Private Sector	32d	1,712.14	2,321.65	3,171.50	† 3,802.28	4,672.68	5,232.14	5,111.89	5,676.61	5,962.93	6,785.14	6,810.51	5,088.53
Claims on Other Banking Insts.	32f	21.46	27.29	27.23	† 36.87	113.19	49.21	53.88	43.58	73.88	73.60	84.59	55.76
Claims on Nonbank Fin. Insts.	32g	−	−	−	† 62.53	47.32	120.10	121.57	143.81	158.91	186.29	136.22	142.95
Money	34	905.03	1,054.01	1,370.31	† 1,699.93	1,708.85	1,886.18	1,984.45	2,166.89	2,562.25	2,743.15	2,759.53	3,788.14
Quasi-Money	35	1,910.60	2,576.79	3,119.08	† 3,735.50	4,493.15	4,792.44	5,356.27	6,510.91	6,534.39	7,843.68	8,159.26	7,961.37
Money Market Instruments	36aa	−	−	−	† 50.16	36.98	49.11	13.11	9.42	39.32	12.13	17.09	9.17
Bonds	36ab	2.21	4.00	3.76	† 1.94	4.13	5.85	15.72	12.97	14.17	37.05	144.60	30.35
Liabs. of Central Bank: Securities	36ac	−	−	−	† 28.23	12.03	31.87	171.84	15.09	5.99	111.85	253.93	428.59
Restricted Deposits	36b	10.12	17.11	26.47	† 29.30	66.76	57.58	76.92	95.31	140.47	138.48	216.61	230.01
Long-Term Foreign Liabilities	36cl	200.02	261.76	178.80	† 332.54	365.60	332.29	216.69	228.37	266.32	555.74	908.43	460.41
Liabilities to Other Banking Insts.	36i	2.85	.86	.01	† 19.24	31.45	31.02	50.11	68.47	102.10	235.49	215.34	396.44
Capital Accounts	37a	629.14	786.96	1,051.70	† 1,539.78	1,958.36	4,008.68	3,229.34	3,854.34	4,041.20	4,722.02	6,448.39	4,856.76
Other Items (Net)	37r	91.33	161.52	236.25	† −590.17	−918.67	−3,486.79	−2,429.78	−2,890.06	−2,983.19	−3,810.29	−4,515.04	−3,588.79
Money plus Quasi-Money	35l	2,815.63	3,630.80	4,489.40	† 5,435.43	6,202.01	6,678.62	7,340.72	8,677.80	9,096.64	10,586.83	10,918.78	11,749.51
Other Banking Institutions						*Billions of Guaranies: End of Period*							
Reserves	40	26.85	30.25	51.64	† 47.07	52.55	69.01	73.66	72.99	92.44	105.47	100.84	117.62
Claims on Mon.Author.: Securities	40c	−	−	−	† 1.29	.46	.02	3.36	5.08	5.99	2.17	6.26	−
Foreign Assets	41	−	−	−	† .68	1.41	30.08	31.26	31.92	55.87	87.53	30.13	22.07
Claims on Central Government	42a	−	−	−	† 2.11	3.65	4.30	3.58	5.79	6.52	5.28	36.86	34.92
Claims on Local Government	42b	−	−	−	† −	−	.01	.03	.04	.12	.03	.09	−
Claims on Nonfin.Pub.Enterprises	42c	−	−	−	† −	−	−	−	.08	−	−	−	−
Claims on Private Sector	42d	432.03	600.11	858.31	† 447.38	505.38	655.57	662.12	626.43	773.75	888.45	820.28	932.02
Claims on Deposit Money Banks	42e	59.07	68.59	122.40	† 30.14	38.50	39.56	57.90	87.07	74.99	92.86	95.22	148.65
Claims on Nonbank Financial Insts.	42g	−	−	−	† 4.24	6.59	7.46	.12	1.80	4.17	18.63	4.74	2.21
Time, Savings,& Fgn.Currency Dep.	45	179.67	201.09	270.97	† 352.02	401.87	501.74	491.48	475.48	615.14	766.92	747.24	931.67
Bonds	46ab	58.71	119.50	222.27	† 6.76	6.76	8.36	7.25	6.42	7.81	7.77	5.02	4.62
Foreign Liabilities	46c	−	−	−	† −	−	19.91	5.92	.21	7.11	8.22	5.03	26.21
Long-Term Foreign Liabilities	46cl	67.03	66.62	63.06	† −	−	−	.11	1.77	.03	.06	−	−
Credit from Monetary Authorities	46g	11.57	11.57	11.89	† 12.15	11.84	19.81	32.52	26.77	36.27	52.80	64.76	32.96
Credit from Deposit Money Banks	46h	1.41	2.31	1.77	† 15.86	17.52	36.28	41.58	42.75	69.07	43.87	13.96	18.78
Capital Accounts	47a	234.45	273.00	422.30	† 193.46	227.94	274.99	307.21	324.11	349.50	382.56	337.58	311.64
Other Items (Net)	47r	−34.89	24.87	40.09	† −47.34	−57.40	−55.07	−54.05	−46.33	−71.07	−61.78	−79.17	−68.38
Banking Survey						*Billions of Guaranies: End of Period*							
Foreign Assets (Net)	51n	1,302.95	1,671.89	2,362.84	† 2,502.61	2,928.72	2,349.40	3,113.52	4,361.20	4,354.97	5,248.21	6,190.49	8,191.40
Domestic Credit	52	2,858.92	3,763.93	4,454.62	† 4,759.09	5,233.74	5,987.13	6,208.44	6,332.78	7,127.51	8,259.19	9,220.12	7,290.30
Claims on Central Govt. (Net)	52an	469.10	572.56	200.17	† 180.85	−268.41	−340.05	−55.25	−482.37	−163.75	158.80	1,162.52	829.62
Claims on Local Government	52b	1.13	1.37	.83	† 22.67	2.18	8.14	37.78	6.75	10.31	5.64	2.35	3.14
Claims on Nonfin.Pub.Enterprises	52c	244.53	268.23	223.81	† 239.15	268.00	303.76	330.20	359.66	381.19	216.25	283.50	291.82
Claims on Private Sector	52d	2,144.16	2,921.76	4,029.80	† 4,249.65	5,178.06	5,887.71	5,774.01	6,303.04	6,736.68	7,673.59	7,630.78	6,020.56
Claims on Nonbank Fin. Insts.	52g	−	−	−	† 66.77	53.91	127.56	121.69	145.62	163.08	204.92	140.96	145.16
Liquid Liabilities	55l	2,968.45	3,801.63	4,708.73	† 5,740.38	6,551.33	7,111.35	7,758.54	9,080.29	9,619.33	11,248.29	11,565.22	12,563.58
Money Market Instruments	56aa	−	−	−	† 50.16	36.98	49.11	13.11	9.42	39.32	12.13	17.09	9.17
Bonds	56ab	60.92	123.49	226.03	† 8.70	10.89	14.21	22.97	19.39	21.97	44.82	149.62	34.97
Liabs. of Central Bank: Securities	56ac	−	−	−	† 26.94	11.56	31.84	168.48	10.01	−	109.69	247.68	428.59
Restricted Deposits	56b	10.12	17.11	26.47	† 29.40	66.76	57.58	76.92	95.31	140.47	138.48	216.61	230.01
Long-Term Foreign Liabilities	56cl	267.05	328.38	241.86	† 332.54	365.60	332.29	216.79	230.14	266.35	555.80	908.43	460.41
Capital Accounts	57a	863.59	1,059.96	1,474.00	† 1,733.23	2,186.30	4,283.67	3,536.55	4,178.45	4,390.71	5,104.58	6,785.96	5,168.40
Other Items (Net)	57r	−8.26	105.24	140.37	† −659.65	−1,066.95	−3,543.53	−2,471.40	−2,929.04	−2,995.69	−3,706.39	−4,480.00	−3,413.44
Money (National Definitions)						*Billions of Guaranies: End of Period*							
Reserve Money	19ma	901.98	1,053.31	1,342.25	1,650.91	1,703.49	1,831.80	1,987.33	2,138.55	2,106.94	2,227.57	2,193.18	3,461.74
M1	59ma	803.58	958.33	1,272.60	1,539.36	1,570.67	1,789.14	1,922.27	2,103.85	2,478.22	2,700.36	2,728.70	3,788.88
M2	59mb	1,356.55	1,563.47	2,166.15	2,827.35	3,204.72	3,437.43	3,341.82	3,706.11	3,824.42	4,068.44	3,914.07	5,079.18
M3	59mc	2,112.67	2,720.04	3,499.99	4,201.08	5,121.65	5,848.77	6,383.03	7,532.20	7,833.10	9,332.98	9,275.38	10,362.82
M4	59md	2,114.88	2,725.30	3,503.75	4,204.77	5,122.88	5,848.77	6,385.00	7,541.01	7,850.33	9,363.84	9,411.11	10,402.64
M5	59me	2,320.51	2,970.03	3,693.60	4,381.96	5,262.52	5,849.76	6,385.00	7,541.01	7,850.33	9,363.84	9,411.11	10,402.64
Interest Rates						*Percent Per Annum*							
Discount Rate (End of Period)	60	24.00	27.17	19.15	20.50	15.00	20.00	20.00	20.00	20.00	20.00	20.00	20.00
Money Market Rate	60b	21.59	22.55	18.64	20.18	16.35	12.48	20.74	17.26	10.70	13.45	13.19	13.02
Savings Rate	60k	10.37	10.60	† 12.00	11.53	9.92	6.93	5.12	6.06	6.43	5.67	9.42	6.90
Savings Rate (Fgn.Currency)	60k.f	....	....	4.27	4.68	4.08	3.22	2.74	2.40	2.35	2.07	1.40	.59
Deposit Rate	60l	20.15	22.10	23.12	21.16	17.16	13.00	15.95	† 19.75	15.72	16.22	22.86	15.83
Deposit Rate (Fgn.Currency)	60l.f	....	....	....	....	....	....	5.44	5.02	4.56	3.46	1.66	1.27
Lending Rate	60p	27.96	30.78	† 35.47	33.94	31.88	27.79	30.49	30.21	26.78	28.25	38.66	49.99
Lending Rate (Fgn.Currency)	60p.f	....	....	12.68	14.03	14.35	13.53	13.03	12.17	11.87	11.16	9.31	10.35

Paraguay 288

		1992	1993	1994	1995	1996	1997	1998	1999	2000	2001	2002	2003
Prices and Labor		\multicolumn{12}{c}{*Index Numbers (2000=100): Period Averages*}
Producer Prices............	63	....	....	....	....	71.2	72.1	82.8	87.2	100.0	105.8	126.9	160.4
Consumer Prices...........	64	40.6	48.0	57.8	65.6	72.0	77.1	86.0	91.8	100.0	107.3	118.5	135.4
		\multicolumn{12}{c}{*Number in Thousands: Period Averages*}
Labor Force.................	67d	....	587	†1,053	....	....	....	....	....	....	....	....	....
Employment.................	67e	523	570	†1,050	†1,160	1,190	1,771	2,151	2,196	2,558	2,373	2,260	....
Unemployment.............	67c	29	30	†48	....	106	....	....	....	....	....	....	....
Unemployment Rate (%).....	67r	5.3	5.1	†4.4	....	8.2	....	....	....	....	....	....	....
International Transactions		\multicolumn{12}{c}{*Millions of U.S. Dollars*}
Exports.......................	70..d	656.6	725.2	816.8	919.2	1,043.5	1,088.6	1,014.0	740.9	869.0	990.0	....	....
Imports, c.i.f.................	71..d	1,421.6	1,688.8	2,140.4	2,782.2	2,850.5	3,099.2	2,470.8	1,725.1	2,050.0	1,989.0	....	....
		\multicolumn{12}{c}{*1990=100*}
Volume of Exports.........	72	52.8	75.1	66.6	....	....	....	....	....	....	....	....	....
Balance of Payments		\multicolumn{12}{c}{*Millions of US Dollars: Minus Sign Indicates Debit*}
Current Account, n.i.e......	78ald	−57.3	59.1	−274.1	−92.3	−352.9	−650.4	−160.0	−165.4	−290.5	−266.4	73.2	146.0
Goods: Exports f.o.b.......	78aad	1,997.1	2,859.0	3,360.1	4,218.6	3,796.9	3,327.5	3,548.6	2,312.4	2,225.8	1,889.7	1,858.0	2,260.5
Goods: Imports f.o.b.......	78abd	−1,988.0	−2,779.6	−3,603.5	−4,489.0	−4,383.4	−4,192.4	−3,941.5	−2,752.9	−2,904.0	−2,503.6	−2,137.9	−2,520.7
Trade Balance..............	78acd	9.1	79.4	−243.4	−270.4	−586.5	−864.9	−392.9	−440.5	−678.2	−613.9	−279.9	−260.2
Services: Credit.............	78add	364.6	438.6	426.2	583.8	600.5	655.0	625.5	575.4	618.5	555.2	568.4	589.8
Services: Debit..............	78aed	−464.5	−592.8	−593.4	−710.7	−658.8	−654.6	−575.9	−493.0	−436.1	−390.0	−349.8	−348.1
Balance on Goods & Services.......	78afd	−90.8	−74.8	−410.6	−397.3	−644.8	−864.5	−343.3	−358.1	−495.8	−448.7	−61.3	−18.5
Income: Credit..............	78agd	157.4	198.3	247.9	272.6	280.9	278.1	266.3	212.5	247.9	255.9	193.5	165.1
Income: Debit...............	78ahd	−185.7	−142.6	−134.1	−162.9	−171.2	−244.9	−260.3	−195.0	−219.4	−240.1	−174.9	−165.2
Balance on Gds, Serv. & Inc........	78aid	−119.1	−19.1	−296.8	−287.6	−535.1	−831.3	−337.3	−340.6	−467.3	−432.9	−42.7	−18.6
Current Transfers, n.i.e.: Credit......	78ajd	62.1	78.6	25.6	199.7	183.0	182.2	178.3	176.7	178.3	168.0	117.5	166.1
Current Transfers: Debit...........	78akd	−.3	−.4	−2.9	−4.4	−.8	−1.3	−1.0	−1.5	−1.5	−1.5	−1.6	−1.5
Capital Account, n.i.e.....	78bcd	10.4	22.1	8.8	10.6	14.2	7.5	5.4	19.6	3.0	15.0	4.0	15.0
Capital Account, n.i.e.: Credit........	78bad	10.4	22.1	8.8	10.6	14.2	7.5	5.4	19.6	3.0	15.0	4.0	15.0
Capital Account: Debit........	78bbd	−	....	....	−	−	−	−	−	−	−	−	−
Financial Account, n.i.e...	78bjd	16.1	8.5	212.9	232.5	152.4	421.3	312.9	89.2	27.4	148.2	55.0	217.6
Direct Investment Abroad......	78bdd	−	....	....	−5.1	−5.2	−5.7	−5.6	−5.6	−5.7	−5.8	−5.5	−5.5
Dir. Invest. in Rep. Econ., n.i.e........	78bed	117.5	75.0	137.1	103.2	149.4	235.8	341.9	94.5	118.6	84.2	9.3	90.8
Portfolio Investment Assets.....	78bfd	−	....	....	−.8	−3.6	−4.3	9.0	−9.0	2.0	.7	−	−
Equity Securities...........	78bkd	−	....	....	−	−	−	−	−.7	−6.8	1.4	.2	−
Debt Securities.............	78bld	−	....	....	−.8	−3.6	−4.3	9.7	−2.2	.6	.5	−	−
Portfolio Investment Liab., n.i.e......	78bgd	−	....	....	−	−.1	−	−	−	−	.5	−.1	−.4
Equity Securities...........	78bmd	−	....	....	−	−	−	−	−	−	....	−	−
Debt Securities.............	78bnd	−	....	....	−	−.1	−	−	−	−	.5	−.1	−.4
Financial Derivatives Assets...........	78bwd	....	....	....	−	−	−	−	−	−	−	−	−
Financial Derivatives Liabilities.......	78bxd	....	....	....	−	−	−	−	−	−	−	−	−
Other Investment Assets......	78bhd	−48.4	−65.4	−89.8	−58.5	−31.9	72.9	−5.0	−117.7	−209.1	64.4	−9.5	202.3
Monetary Authorities.....	78bod	1.6	....	.1	−	−	−	−	−	−	....	−	−
General Government.....	78bpd	27.6	1.6	23.1	−43.1	−59.0	−45.8	60.7	−63.6	−81.2	78.8	−77.7	−38.0
Banks.........................	78bqd	−85.2	−75.2	−1.5	−169.7	3.5	100.5	−42.7	−1.9	−69.3	68.2	122.5	−108.7
Other Sectors..............	78brd	7.6	8.2	−111.5	154.3	23.6	18.2	−23.0	−52.2	−58.6	−82.6	−54.3	349.0
Other Investment Liab., n.i.e.....	78bid	−53.0	−1.1	165.6	193.7	43.8	122.6	−27.4	127.0	121.1	4.8	60.8	−69.6
Monetary Authorities.....	78bsd	1.8	2.1	−1.6	−8.7	−3.5	−5.0	−4.3	−3.8	−3.3	−3.2	−4.4	−4.4
General Government.....	78btd	−4.1	−2.6	29.8	101.6	122.5	137.1	112.3	97.6	90.4	41.9	23.0	53.1
Banks.........................	78bud	20.5	−94.2	97.3	118.6	−188.4	71.6	−50.7	−101.5	−8.9	−30.5	6.3	−23.9
Other Sectors..............	78bvd	−71.2	93.6	40.1	−17.8	113.2	−81.1	−84.7	134.7	42.9	−3.4	35.9	−94.4
Net Errors and Omissions........	78cad	11.9	−46.4	353.0	−106.0	139.8	5.8	−141.6	−244.3	−79.3	52.9	−257.9	−145.8
Overall Balance............	78cbd	−18.9	43.3	300.6	44.8	−46.5	−215.8	16.7	−300.9	−339.4	−50.2	−125.7	232.8
Reserves and Related Items........	79dad	18.9	−43.3	−300.6	−44.8	46.5	215.8	−16.7	300.9	339.4	50.2	125.7	−232.8
Reserve Assets.............	79dbd	360.2	−87.2	−339.3	−60.2	39.4	205.8	−23.4	−116.7	210.2	45.4	85.6	−303.2
Use of Fund Credit and Loans........	79dcd	−	−	−	−	−	−	−	−	−	−	−	−
Exceptional Financing.....	79ded	−341.3	43.9	38.7	15.4	7.1	10.0	6.7	417.6	129.2	4.8	40.1	70.4

2004, International Monetary Fund : *International Financial Statistics Yearbook*

Paraguay 288

		1992	1993	1994	1995	1996	1997	1998	1999	2000	2001	2002	2003
International Investment Position						*Millions of US Dollars*							
Assets	79aad	....	....	....	2,569.4	2,566.7	2,284.6	2,311.9	2,576.7	2,596.5	3,216.3	3,143.9	2,507.8
Direct Investment Abroad	79abd	....	....	....	178.6	186.0	194.1	201.3	208.2	213.9	139.7	137.7	143.2
Portfolio Investment	79acd	....	....	....	6.3	9.9	14.2	8.9	20.1	11.9	15.0	13.3	4.7
Equity Securities	79add	....	....	....	3.4	3.4	3.4	7.8	16.8	10.3	14.3	12.6	4.0
Debt Securities	79aed	....	....	....	2.9	6.5	10.8	1.1	3.3	1.6	.7	.7	.7
Financial Derivatives	79ald	....	....	....	–	–	–	–	–	–	–	–	–
Other Investment	79afd	....	....	....	1,278.1	1,308.5	1,230.5	1,226.9	1,360.2	1,598.9	2,338.5	2,342.7	1,367.4
Monetary Authorities	79agd	....	....	....	–	–	–	–	–	–	–	–	–
General Government	79ahd	....	....	....	188.3	247.3	293.1	232.6	296.2	377.4	332.7	410.4	448.4
Banks	79aid	....	....	....	511.6	507.6	404.2	442.5	443.4	512.8	444.6	280.5	389.2
Other Sectors	79ajd	....	....	....	578.2	553.6	533.2	551.8	620.6	708.7	1,561.2	1,651.8	529.7
Reserve Assets	79akd	....	....	....	1,106.4	1,062.3	845.8	874.8	988.2	771.8	723.1	650.2	992.5
Liabilities	79lad	....	....	....	2,877.1	2,954.2	3,132.1	3,385.5	3,982.3	4,340.1	4,057.2	3,996.0	4,290.6
Dir. Invest. in Rep. Economy	79lbd	....	....	....	705.2	829.3	977.7	1,196.1	1,215.7	1,311.2	1,135.4	893.2	1,087.6
Portfolio Investment	79lcd	....	....	....	.1	–	–	–	–	.5	.4	.3	–
Equity Securities	79ldd	....	....	....	–	–	–	–	–	–	–	–	–
Debt Securities	79led	....	....	....	.1	–	–	–	–	.5	.4	.3	–
Financial Derivatives	79lld	....	....	....	–	–	–	–	–	–	–	–	–
Other Investment	79lfd	....	....	....	2,171.8	2,124.9	2,154.4	2,189.4	2,766.6	3,028.4	2,921.4	3,102.5	3,203.0
Monetary Authorities	79lgd	....	....	....	50.8	47.3	42.3	38.0	34.3	32.7	31.2	28.6	22.3
General Government	79lhd	....	....	....	1,004.6	1,054.8	1,146.0	1,318.1	1,854.3	2,001.8	1,963.6	2,090.4	2,302.8
Banks	79lid	....	....	....	406.5	218.1	289.5	238.4	136.6	127.6	97.0	100.5	76.5
Other Sectors	79ljd	....	....	....	709.9	804.7	676.6	594.9	741.4	866.3	829.6	883.1	801.5
Government Finance						*Billions of Guaranies: Year Ending December 31*							
Deficit (-) or Surplus	80	77.7	138.7	294.8	–10.2	–183.3	–251.6	–81.3	–806.2	–1,080.5	–229.7	....	....
Revenue	81	1,391.6	1,688.0	2,196.7	2,724.1	2,919.5	3,192.9	3,715.7	4,004.0	4,201.7	4,838.7	....	....
Grants	81z	3.0	4.0	25.8	28.8	35.4	68.4	44.7	49.7	46.1	135.9	....	....
Expenditure	82	1,307.4	1,559.4	1,953.7	2,726.9	3,116.6	3,469.6	3,811.7	4,687.3	5,216.3	5,201.4	....	....
Lending Minus Repayments	83	9.4	–6.0	–25.9	36.1	21.5	43.2	30.0	172.6	112.0	2.8	....	....
Exch.Rate Adj.to Overall Def./Sur.	80x	–	–	....	....	....	....	....	....	....	....	....	....
Total Financing	80h	–77.7	–138.7	–294.8	10.2	183.3	251.6	81.3	806.2	1,080.5	229.7	....	....
Domestic Financing	84a	–2.1	–2.0	....	....	....	....	....	....	....	....	....	....
Foreign Financing	85a	20.3	–96.2	....	....	....	....	....	....	....	....	....	....
Use of Cash Balances	87	–95.9	–40.5	....	....	....	....	....	....	....	....	....	....
Total Debt	88	1,228.3	1,530.1	....	....	....	....	....	....	....	....	....	....
Domestic	88a	45.4	100.0	....	....	....	....	....	....	....	....	....	....
Foreign	89a	1,182.9	1,430.1	....	....	....	....	....	....	....	....	....	....
National Accounts						*Billions of Guaranies*							
Housh.Cons.Expend.,incl.NPISHs	96f	7,843.3	9,749.8	13,231.8	15,089.2	16,853.3	17,704.3	20,101.4	19,762.5	22,406.8	24,604.3	27,527.0	....
Government Consumption Expend	91f	629.1	801.9	1,012.5	1,275.9	1,528.5	1,693.0	1,928.3	2,135.4	2,601.6	2,479.9	2,470.2	....
Gross Fixed Capital Formation	93e	2,117.4	2,642.1	3,366.5	4,082.8	4,478.4	4,749.1	5,168.2	5,342.1	5,638.6	5,295.0	5,812.5	....
Changes in Inventories	93i	97.6	109.6	127.7	151.8	156.7	181.0	205.6	221.7	242.5	265.5	292.3	....
Exports of Goods and Services	90c	2,714.6	4,428.6	5,120.9	6,163.8	5,707.7	5,696.2	6,613.4	5,548.6	5,260.1	6,170.1	9,822.8	....
Imports of Goods and Services (-)	98c	3,731.1	5,740.2	7,899.3	9,064.9	8,919.8	9,089.3	10,580.0	8,866.1	9,228.7	10,696.0	13,948.0	....
Gross Domestic Product (GDP)	99b	9,670.8	11,991.7	14,960.1	17,698.6	19,804.8	20,934.3	23,436.9	24,144.3	26,921.0	28,118.8	31,977.0	....
Net Primary Income from Abroad	98.n	22.1	42.9	78.8	158.8	145.1	221.7	304.5	132.2	380.7	164.2	629.4	....
Gross National Income (GNI)	99a	9,692.9	12,034.7	15,039.0	17,857.4	19,949.9	21,156.0	23,741.4	24,276.5	27,301.7	28,283.0	32,606.3	....
Consumption of Fixed Capital	99cf	769.1	930.7	1,161.0	1,378.1	1,549.9	1,639.2	1,835.0	1,889.6	2,051.6	2,142.8	2,407.0	....
GDP Volume 1982 Prices	99b.p	967.3	1,007.4	1,038.5	1,087.4	1,101.2	1,129.7	1,125.0	1,130.4	1,126.4	1,157.0	1,130.1	....
GDP Volume (2000=100)	99bvp	85.9	89.4	92.2	96.5	97.8	100.3	99.9	100.4	100.0	102.7	100.3	....
GDP Deflator (2000=100)	99bip	41.8	49.8	60.3	68.1	75.2	77.5	87.2	89.4	100.0	101.7	118.4	....
						Millions: Midyear Estimates							
Population	99z	4.46	4.58	4.71	4.83	4.95	5.08	5.21	5.34	5.47	5.60	5.74	5.88

Peru 293

		1992	1993	1994	1995	1996	1997	1998	1999	2000	2001	2002	2003
Exchange Rates						*Nuevos Soles per SDRs: End of Period*							
Market Rate	aa	2.2413	2.9669	3.1825	3.4338	3.7387	3.6835	4.4494	4.8175	4.5954	4.3282	4.7774	5.1459
					Nuevos Soles per US$: End of Period(ae) Period Avg.(rf)									
Market Rate	ae	1.6300	2.1600	2.1800	2.3100	2.6000	2.7300	3.1600	3.5100	3.5270	3.4440	3.5140	3.4630
Market Rate	rf	1.2458	1.9883	2.1950	2.2533	2.4533	2.6642	2.9300	3.3833	3.4900	3.5068	3.5165	3.4785
Fund Position						*Millions of SDRs: End of Period*							
Quota	2f.s	330.9	466.1	466.1	466.1	466.1	466.1	466.1	638.4	638.4	638.4	638.4	638.4
SDRs	1b.s	–	.7	.3	.5	.2	.2	.2	.3	1.1	1.4	.5	.3
Reserve Position in the Fund	1c.s	–	–	–	–	–	–	1.5	.3	1.1	1.4	.5	.3
Total Fund Cred.&Loans Outstg	2tl	458.7	642.7	642.7	642.7	642.7	749.6	642.5	535.4	428.3	307.8	173.9	93.6
International Liquidity					*Millions of US Dollars Unless Otherwise Indicated: End of Period*									
Total Reserves minus Gold	1l.d	2,849.0	3,407.9	6,992.4	8,221.7	10,578.3	10,982.2	9,565.5	8,730.5	8,374.0	8,671.8	9,339.0	9,776.8
SDRs	1b.d	–	.9	.4	.7	.3	.2	2.1	.4	1.5	1.7	.7	.4
Reserve Position in the Fund	1c.d	–	–	–	–	–	–	–	–	–	–	–	–
Foreign Exchange	1d.d	2,849.0	3,407.0	6,992.0	8,221.0	10,578.0	10,982.0	9,563.4	8,730.1	8,372.5	8,670.1	9,338.3	9,776.4
Gold (Million Fine Troy Ounces)	1ad	1.822	1.305	1.116	1.116	1.115	1.115	1.100	1.100	1.100	1.115	1.115	1.115
Gold (National Valuation)	1and	515.6	434.0	362.9	366.6	349.7	272.0	268.8	270.9	254.1	261.6	386.7	462.7
Monetary Authorities: Other Liab.	4..d	549.8	517.7	540.6	573.4	494.2	497.8	446.6	693.8	831.6	842.0	791.0	884.1
Deposit Money Banks: Assets	7a.d	991.2	871.8	1,183.8	1,544.9	2,047.2	1,215.7	1,245.8	1,388.6	1,298.7	1,365.7	1,218.1	1,290.6
Liabilities	7b.d	396.9	415.3	765.8	1,566.1	1,812.4	3,473.6	3,291.0	2,286.3	2,029.9	1,562.9	1,002.1	913.7
Other Banking Insts.: Assets	7e.d	16.4	11.1	12.7	12.7	12.7	12.7	1.0	–	–	–	–	–
Liabilities	7f.d	108.7	107.3	71.0	71.0	71.1	71.0	10.3	–	–	–	–	–
Monetary Authorities					*Millions of Nuevos Soles: End of Period*									
Foreign Assets	11	5,461	9,335	16,001	19,093	25,933	31,208	32,399	33,548	33,200	33,344	36,836	38,410
Claims on Central Government	12a	90	55	614	614	614	614	614	538	425	396	350	237
Claims on Deposit Money Banks	12e	197	149	64	4	107	–	203	263	97	–	170	–
Claims on Other Banking Insts	12f	173	209	–	–	–	–	–	–	–	–	–	–
Reserve Money	14	3,586	5,715	7,487	9,823	13,536	18,773	19,847	22,952	23,405	24,474	26,510	24,865
of which: Currency Outside DMBs	14a	1,101	1,591	2,385	3,043	3,245	3,827	3,950	4,609	4,537	4,945	5,615	6,370
Time, Savings,& Fgn.Currency Dep	15	194	194	202	78	118	77	83	75	78	114	148	179
Restricted Deposits	16b	7	1	1	1	1	1	–	1	–	–	–	–
Foreign Liabilities	16c	1,419	1,907	2,045	2,207	2,403	2,761	2,859	2,579	1,968	1,332	831	482
Long-Term Foreign Liabilities	16cl	505	1,104	1,179	1,325	1,285	1,344	1,398	2,435	2,937	2,900	2,780	3,058
Central Government Deposits	16d	55	96	3,684	5,384	8,498	7,989	7,558	4,057	2,454	1,447	2,430	3,188
Capital Accounts	17a	224	254	377	457	592	735	867	871	854	962	1,146	1,272
Other Items (Net)	17r	−70	477	1,705	437	221	141	604	1,379	2,025	2,511	3,511	5,603
Deposit Money Banks					*Millions of Nuevos Soles: End of Period*									
Reserves	20	2,040	3,519	5,326	6,846	10,240	12,135	11,126	11,897	12,382	13,252	14,353	14,573
Foreign Assets	21	1,616	1,874	2,581	3,569	5,323	3,307	3,924	4,874	4,584	4,704	4,280	4,466
Claims on Central Government	22a	1,422	1,913	1,607	1,028	924	2,437	3,764	4,954	4,778	6,506	6,908	6,631
Claims on Local Government	22b	19	35	50	31	170	244	94	380	433	337	205	340
Claims on Official Entities	22bx	331	369	270	204	264	376	968	398	464	419	493	294
Claims on Private Sector	22d	4,076	7,694	13,095	19,090	28,512	37,812	45,835	49,221	47,569	45,464	45,229	43,123
Claims on Other Banking Insts	22f	7	7	3	3	3	–	–	–	–	–	–	–
Demand Deposits	24	1,298	2,142	3,193	4,357	5,633	7,950	10,174	11,018	9,110	8,977	8,359	8,193
Time, Savings,& Fgn.Currency Dep	25	5,148	9,528	13,501	17,362	25,136	29,510	33,269	37,779	38,737	39,589	42,065	41,187
Bonds	26ab	12	55	102	251	539	806	933	969	871	783	952	457
Foreign Liabilities	26c	590	796	1,462	3,127	4,023	8,196	9,160	6,540	5,459	4,178	2,677	2,428
Long-Term Foreign Liabilities	26cl	57	97	208	490	690	1,252	1,206	1,485	1,707	1,204	844	734
Central Government Deposits	26d	1,041	1,248	2,367	1,561	4,808	3,710	3,849	3,718	3,635	3,510	4,065	4,350
Credit from Monetary Authorities	26g	207	149	64	4	107	–	203	263	97	–	170	–
Capital Accounts	27a	2,096	3,181	4,792	6,261	8,514	11,045	14,309	18,857	20,518	22,616	23,701	21,540
Other Items (Net)	27r	−939	−1,785	−2,757	−2,643	−4,013	−6,157	−7,392	−8,904	−9,925	−10,177	−11,366	−9,462
Monetary Survey					*Millions of Nuevos Soles: End of Period*									
Foreign Assets (Net)	31n	5,067	8,507	15,074	17,327	24,831	23,557	24,304	29,303	30,358	32,537	37,608	39,966
Domestic Credit	32	5,029	8,947	9,588	14,025	17,181	29,784	39,869	47,717	47,579	48,165	46,690	43,088
Claims on Central Govt. (Net)	32an	416	625	−3,830	−5,303	−11,768	−8,648	−7,028	−2,282	−887	1,945	763	−669
Claims on Local Government	32b	19	35	50	31	170	244	94	380	433	337	205	340
Claims on Official Entities	32bx	331	369	270	204	264	376	968	398	464	419	493	294
Claims on Private Sector	32d	4,083	7,702	13,095	19,090	28,512	37,812	45,835	49,221	47,569	45,464	45,229	43,123
Claims on Other Banking Insts	32f	179	216	3	3	3	–	–	–	–	–	–	–
Money	34	2,843	4,337	5,589	7,498	8,972	15,175	19,165	22,273	21,072	21,445	22,049	21,351
Quasi-Money	35	5,341	9,722	13,703	17,440	25,254	29,587	33,352	37,854	38,815	39,703	42,213	41,366
Bonds	36ab	12	55	102	251	539	806	933	969	871	783	952	457
Restricted Deposits	36b	7	1	1	1	1	1	–	1	–	–	–	–
Long-Term Foreign Liabilities	36cl	562	1,201	1,386	1,815	1,975	2,596	2,604	3,921	4,644	4,104	3,624	3,792
Capital Accounts	37a	2,320	3,435	5,169	6,718	9,106	11,780	15,176	19,728	21,373	23,578	24,846	22,812
Other Items (Net)	37r	−989	−1,299	−1,288	−2,370	−3,835	−6,603	−7,058	−7,726	−8,839	−8,913	−9,387	−6,724
Money plus Quasi-Money	35l	8,184	14,060	19,292	24,938	34,226	44,762	52,518	60,127	59,887	61,148	64,262	62,717

Peru 293

		1992	1993	1994	1995	1996	1997	1998	1999	2000	2001	2002	2003
Other Banking Institutions						*Millions of Nuevos Soles: End of Period*							
Reserves	40	5	4	–	–	–	–	–	–	–	–	–	–
Foreign Assets	41	27	24	28	29	33	35	3	–	–	–	–	–
Claims on Central Government	42a	49	54	55	58	65	69	–	–	–	–	–	8
Claims on Official Entities	42bx	45	20	20	21	24	25	–	–	–	–	–	–
Claims on Private Sector	42d	769	743	718	744	803	828	910	809	761	644	657	686
Claims on Deposit Money Banks	42e	11	1	2	2	2	2	–	–	–	–	90	35
Demand Deposits	44	32	9	9	9	9	9	21	21	20	20	20	–
Time, Savings,& Fgn.Currency Dep	45	78	44	42	43	46	47	37	10	9	8	8	28
Bonds	46ab	17	11	6	6	6	6	–	–	–	–	–	–
Foreign Liabilities	46c	125	162	85	90	101	106	–	–	–	–	–	–
Long-Term Foreign Liabilities	46cl	52	69	70	74	84	87	33	–	–	–	–	–
Central Government Deposits	46d	5	5	5	6	6	6	–	–	–	–	–	–
Credit from Monetary Authorities	46g	168	209	–	–	–	–	–	–	–	–	–	–
Credit from Deposit Money Banks	46h	14	13	4	4	5	5	–	–	–	–	–	–
Capital Accounts	47a	506	709	671	698	757	782	865	939	975	1,023	1,132	1,111
Other Items (Net)	47r	–91	–385	–70	–76	–87	–92	–42	–160	–244	–406	–413	–410
Banking Survey						*Millions of Nuevos Soles: End of Period*							
Foreign Assets (Net)	51n	4,969	8,369	15,017	17,267	24,762	23,486	24,308	29,303	30,358	32,537	37,608	39,966
Domestic Credit	52	5,708	9,543	10,373	14,840	18,063	30,698	40,778	48,526	48,340	48,809	47,346	43,782
Claims on Central Govt. (Net)	52an	459	674	–3,780	–5,250	–11,708	–8,586	–7,028	–2,282	–887	1,945	763	–661
Claims on Local Government	52b	19	35	50	31	170	244	94	380	433	337	205	340
Claims on Official Entities	52bx	377	389	290	225	287	400	968	398	464	419	493	294
Claims on Private Sector	52d	4,852	8,445	13,812	19,834	29,314	38,640	46,745	50,030	48,330	46,108	45,886	43,810
Liquid Liabilities	55l	8,289	14,108	19,343	24,990	34,281	44,818	52,575	60,158	59,917	61,176	64,290	62,745
Bonds	56ab	29	66	108	257	545	812	933	969	871	783	952	457
Restricted Deposits	56b	7	1	1	1	1	1	–	1	–	–	–	–
Long-Term Foreign Liabilities	56cl	614	1,270	1,456	1,889	2,058	2,683	2,637	3,921	4,644	4,104	3,624	3,792
Capital Accounts	57a	2,826	4,144	5,840	7,416	9,863	12,562	16,041	20,667	22,348	24,601	25,978	23,923
Other Items (Net)	57r	–1,088	–1,679	–1,358	–2,446	–3,922	–6,691	–7,100	–7,886	–9,082	–9,319	–9,890	–7,169
Money (National Definitions)						*Millions of Nuevos Soles: End of Period*							
Monetary Base	19ma	1,349	1,803	2,672	3,658	3,996	4,761	5,023	5,876	5,642	6,087	6,759	7,441
Money	59ma	1,577	2,338	3,723	4,595	5,409	6,464	6,482	7,311	7,087	7,509	8,197	9,312
Quasi-Money in National Currency	59mb	1,221	1,394	2,412	3,299	4,200	5,552	5,217	5,342	5,732	6,643	7,102	7,477
Quasi-Money in Foreign Currency	59mbf	4,804	8,335	11,518	14,410	21,200	24,485	28,165	31,601	32,430	32,007	33,491	34,018
Interest Rates						*Percent Per Annum*							
Discount Rate (End of Period)	60	48.50	28.63	16.08	18.44	18.16	15.94	18.72	17.80	14.00	14.00	4.75	4.25
Savings Rate	60k	47.84	34.83	17.99	11.80	10.99	10.70	10.12	9.54	7.75	5.88	1.78	1.48
Deposit Rate	60l	59.65	44.14	22.35	15.70	14.90	15.01	15.11	16.27	13.29	9.92	4.19	3.83
Lending Rate	60p	173.80	97.37	53.56	27.16	26.07	29.96	30.80	30.79	27.91	20.43	14.73	14.21
Prices, Production, Labor						*Index Numbers (2000=100): Period Averages*							
Share Prices	62	11.6	45.6	83.6	87.9	92.8	126.3	105.3	111.9	100.0	85.2	84.8	126.9
Wholesale Prices	63	37.70	55.62	65.57	72.47	79.31	85.17	91.36	95.85	100.00	101.38	100.32	102.03
Consumer Prices	64	35.1	†52.2	64.5	71.7	80.0	86.9	93.1	96.4	100.0	†102.0	102.2	104.5
Manufacturing Production	66ey	72.5	74.9	87.4	92.2	93.6	98.6	95.1	94.4	100.0	100.3	104.5	106.7
Industrial Employment	67	123.7	113.7	112.2	109.4	†106.9	108.7	106.2	100.5	100.0	100.5	100.6	102.5
						Number in Thousands: Period Averages							
Labor Force	67d	....	....	2,930	3,103	....	....	7,407	7,512	7,695	8,271	12,892	....
Employment	67e	2,411	2,610	2,682	2,901	6,131	6,745	6,929	7,211	7,128	7,620	....	....
Unemployment	67c	251	286	263	221	†462	565	582	625	566	651	....	....
Unemployment Rate (%)	67r	9.4	9.9	8.9	7.1	†7.0	7.7	7.8	8.0	7.4	7.9	....	....
International Transactions						*Millions of US Dollars*							
Exports	70..d	3,484.4	3,384.5	4,424.9	5,492.4	5,877.4	6,824.4	5,756.8	6,087.3	6,950.8	7,006.8	7,647.0	8,979.1
Imports, c.i.f.	71..d	4,861.3	4,947.3	6,701.1	9,299.8	9,442.2	10,280.6	9,914.7	8,152.0	8,887.9	....	....	....
Imports, f.o.b.	71.vd	4,051.1	4,122.8	5,584.2	7,749.8	7,868.5	8,567.2	8,262.2	6,793.3	7,406.6	7,273.4	7,439.9	8,244.4
						2000=100							
Volume of Exports	72	66.6	73.0	82.0	82.1	85.9	94.1	81.7	88.8	100.0	114.1	126.4	122.5
						2000=100: Indexes of Unit Values in US Dollars							
Unit Value of Exports	74..d	88.9	75.0	88.5	107.2	106.8	103.6	83.9	82.7	100.0	83.6	86.6	97.2

Peru 293

		1992	1993	1994	1995	1996	1997	1998	1999	2000	2001	2002	2003
Balance of Payments						*Millions of US Dollars: Minus Sign Indicates Debit*							
Current Account, n.i.e.	78ald	−1,886	−2,464	−2,701	−4,625	−3,646	−3,367	−3,321	−1,464	−1,559	−1,159	−1,127	−1,061
Goods: Exports f.o.b.	78aad	3,662	3,385	4,424	5,491	5,878	6,825	5,757	6,088	6,955	7,026	7,723	8,986
Goods: Imports f.o.b.	78abd	−4,002	−4,160	−5,499	−7,733	−7,869	−8,503	−8,194	−6,743	−7,366	−7,221	−7,417	−8,255
Trade Balance	78acd	−340	−776	−1,075	−2,241	−1,991	−1,678	−2,437	−655	−411	−195	306	731
Services: Credit	78add	838	837	1,064	1,131	1,414	1,553	1,775	1,594	1,604	1,510	1,544	1,679
Services: Debit	78aed	−1,412	−1,387	−1,534	−1,864	−2,085	−2,339	−2,432	−2,256	−2,341	−2,391	−2,530	−2,609
Balance on Goods & Services	78afd	−914	−1,326	−1,545	−2,975	−2,662	−2,465	−3,094	−1,318	−1,148	−1,077	−680	−200
Income: Credit	78agd	199	205	338	574	610	720	786	655	737	647	337	282
Income: Debit	78ahd	−1,613	−1,876	−2,282	−3,056	−2,508	−2,542	−1,990	−1,767	−2,146	−1,771	−1,827	−2,364
Balance on Gds, Serv. & Inc.	78aid	−2,328	−2,996	−3,489	−5,457	−4,560	−4,287	−4,298	−2,430	−2,558	−2,201	−2,170	−2,281
Current Transfers, n.i.e.: Credit	78ajd	450	538	795	837	922	928	989	992	1,008	1,050	1,052	1,227
Current Transfers: Debit	78akd	−8	−6	−7	−5	−8	−8	−12	−27	−9	−8	−8	−6
Capital Account, n.i.e.	78bcd	−33	−45	−58	32	22	−50	−57	−54	−67	−68	−95	−93
Capital Account, n.i.e.: Credit	78bad	40	48	31	65	51	24	21	25	24	32	14	12
Capital Account: Debit	78bbd	−73	−92	−89	−34	−29	−74	−78	−79	−91	−100	−110	−105
Financial Account, n.i.e.	78bjd	498	919	3,870	3,719	3,802	5,479	1,779	548	1,016	1,590	2,024	1,061
Direct Investment Abroad	78bdd	–	–	–	−8	17	−85	−62	−128	–	−74	–	−60
Dir. Invest. in Rep. Econ., n.i.e.	78bed	−79	761	3,289	2,557	3,471	2,139	1,644	1,940	810	1,144	2,156	1,377
Portfolio Investment Assets	78bfd	−39	−26	−56	−4	−113	−252	−188	−223	−538	−269	−280	−1,435
Equity Securities	78bkd	−20	−6	−32	14	−98	−92	−184	−167	−374	−237	−310	−1,179
Debt Securities	78bld	−19	−20	−24	−18	−15	−160	−4	−56	−164	−32	30	−255
Portfolio Investment Liab., n.i.e.	78bgd	–	228	548	163	286	406	−224	−125	75	−54	1,724	1,211
Equity Securities	78bmd	–	222	465	171	294	156	−346	−107	123	43	−9	1
Debt Securities	78bnd	–	6	83	−8	−8	250	122	−18	−48	−97	1,733	1,210
Financial Derivatives Assets	78bwd	....	....	....	....	....	....	....	....	....	....	....	....
Financial Derivatives Liabilities	78bxd	....	....	....	....	....	....	....	....	....	....	....	....
Other Investment Assets	78bhd	290	375	−564	−274	−499	391	64	126	248	671	5	328
Monetary Authorities	78bod	−19	84	−2	−6	−33	−104	20	−5	−34	−15	153	118
General Government	78bpd	–	–	–	–	–	–	–	–	–	–	–	–
Banks	78bqd	81	121	−272	−425	−464	869	25	−102	233	48	35	186
Other Sectors	78brd	228	170	−290	157	−2	−374	19	233	49	638	−183	25
Other Investment Liab., n.i.e.	78bid	326	−418	653	1,285	640	2,880	545	−1,041	421	171	−1,581	−361
Monetary Authorities	78bsd	−106	−943	37	−23	−87	−8	−38	−33	24	−11	−4	−8
General Government	78btd	−450	325	98	−213	−438	491	−22	−69	666	599	−781	−294
Banks	78bud	169	146	−247	704	224	1,667	−225	−1,001	−168	−499	−513	−84
Other Sectors	78bvd	713	54	765	817	941	730	830	62	−101	82	−284	26
Net Errors and Omissions	78cad	499	1,231	443	284	703	−8	358	108	480	69	208	655
Overall Balance	78cbd	−922	−359	1,553	−590	880	2,055	−1,241	−862	−130	432	1,010	561
Reserves and Related Items	79dad	922	359	−1,553	590	−880	−2,055	1,241	862	130	−432	−1,010	−561
Reserve Assets	79dbd	−520	−663	−3,059	−921	−1,784	−1,493	1,142	985	329	−276	−851	−515
Use of Fund Credit and Loans	79dcd	−49	254	–	–	–	149	−145	−147	−141	−154	−172	−110
Exceptional Financing	79ded	1,491	768	1,506	1,512	904	−711	244	24	−58	−1	14	64
International Investment Position						*Millions of US Dollars*							
Assets	79aad	6,692	7,074	10,712	12,338	14,686	16,032	14,976	14,285	14,183	14,190	15,444	17,714
Direct Investment Abroad	79abd	122	109	109	567	543	602	438	651	505	649	666	814
Portfolio Investment	79acd	246	283	313	294	416	720	1,013	1,224	1,884	2,157	2,442	4,258
Equity Securities	79add	246	283	313	294	416	582	867	1,070	1,661	1,948	2,293	3,896
Debt Securities	79aed	–	–	–	–	–	138	146	154	223	209	149	362
Financial Derivatives	79ald	–	–	–	–	–	–	–	–	–	–	–	–
Other Investment	79afd	3,233	2,928	3,477	3,742	4,208	3,699	3,656	3,526	3,240	2,555	2,654	2,445
Monetary Authorities	79agd	92	77	64	62	62	48	49	50	46	47	−2	–
General Government	79ahd	–	–	–	–	–	–	–	–	–	–	–	–
Banks	79aid	911	791	1,062	1,487	1,951	1,082	1,057	1,159	926	878	843	657
Other Sectors	79ajd	2,230	2,060	2,350	2,193	2,195	2,569	2,550	2,317	2,268	1,630	1,813	1,788
Reserve Assets	79akd	3,091	3,754	6,813	7,735	9,518	11,011	9,869	8,883	8,553	8,829	9,682	10,197
Liabilities	79lad	28,113	29,707	36,200	40,390	43,533	40,228	41,099	41,162	41,321	41,456	43,322	46,276
Dir. Invest. in Rep. Economy	79lbd	1,504	1,642	4,451	5,510	6,720	7,753	8,297	9,791	11,062	11,835	12,460	12,745
Portfolio Investment	79lcd	27	695	1,636	1,681	3,185	8,138	7,312	7,013	6,384	6,436	7,544	9,523
Equity Securities	79ldd	27	689	1,547	1,599	3,111	3,685	2,737	2,859	2,278	2,427	2,990	3,799
Debt Securities	79led	–	6	89	81	73	4,453	4,575	4,154	4,106	4,010	4,554	5,724
Financial Derivatives	79lld	–	–	–	–	–	–	–	–	–	–	–	–
Other Investment	79lfd	26,582	27,370	30,113	33,199	33,629	24,336	25,490	24,357	23,874	23,185	23,318	24,008
Monetary Authorities	79lgd	1,124	1,045	1,137	1,131	1,013	1,092	947	745	592	410	256	151
General Government	79lhd	22,082	22,765	24,978	26,612	25,661	13,969	14,663	14,743	14,758	14,681	15,754	16,593
Banks	79lid	884	1,036	797	1,501	1,728	3,398	3,174	2,173	2,005	1,506	993	909
Other Sectors	79ljd	2,492	2,524	3,200	3,954	5,226	5,876	6,705	6,696	6,520	6,589	6,315	6,356
Government Finance						*Millions of Nuevos Soles: Year Ending December 31*							
Deficit (-) or Surplus	80	†−1,662	−2,077	2,144	−1,345	3,818	924	−324	−3,966	−3,410	−3,480	....	....
Revenue	81	†6,782	10,476	16,186	20,420	24,054	27,693	29,287	28,706	30,807	29,788	....	....
Grants Received	81z	49	62	201	111	325	325	405	445	635	702	....	....
Expenditure	82	8,385	12,559	18,259	23,053	24,725	27,264	30,123	34,203	36,053	34,754	....	....
Lending Minus Repayments	83	108	57	−4,016	−1,178	−4,164	−170	−107	−1,087	−1,201	−784	....	....
Financing													
Domestic	84a	†236	−63	−4,597	−1,534	−4,895	−935	−239	4,284	1,308	1,416	....	....
Foreign	85a	1,426	2,141	2,453	2,878	1,077	12	561	−319	2,103	2,064	....	....

Peru   293

		1992	1993	1994	1995	1996	1997	1998	1999	2000	2001	2002	2003
National Accounts						*Millions of Nuevos Soles*							
Househ.Cons.Expend.,incl.NPISHs	96f	34,934	52,996	71,306	85,933	98,598	110,782	118,269	122,261	131,565	136,040	142,960	....
Government Consumption Expend...	91f	3,566	5,568	8,672	11,786	13,827	15,487	17,296	18,854	19,717	20,290	20,703	....
Gross Fixed Capital Formation.........	93e	7,405	12,697	20,901	29,095	30,747	37,472	39,163	37,867	37,610	34,862	35,128	....
Changes in Inventories....................	93i	375	679	1,030	918	537	479	159	−973	−66	220	1,436	....
Exports of Goods and Services.........	90c	5,628	8,627	12,590	15,118	17,975	22,272	22,076	25,855	29,851	30,020	32,612	....
Imports of Goods and Services (-)....	98c	6,954	11,304	15,922	21,991	24,754	29,219	31,014	29,907	33,396	33,260	34,402	....
Gross Domestic Product (GDP)........	99b	44,953	69,262	98,577	120,858	136,929	157,274	165,949	173,957	185,281	188,172	198,437	....
Net Primary Income from Abroad.....	98.n	−1,083	−1,930	....	....	....	....	....	....	....	....	....	
Gross National Income (GNI)...........	99a	50,977	78,598	....	....	....	....	....	....	....	....	....	
GDP Volume 1994 Prices.................	99b.p	83,401	87,375	98,577	107,039	109,709	117,214	116,453	117,507	120,825	121,132	127,007	....
GDP Volume (2000=100)................	99bvp	69.0	72.3	81.6	88.6	90.8	97.0	96.4	97.3	100.0	100.3	105.1	....
GDP Deflator (2000=100)...............	99bip	35.1	51.7	65.2	73.6	81.4	87.5	92.9	96.5	100.0	101.3	101.9	....
						Millions: Midyear Estimates							
Population...............................	99z	22.60	23.01	23.42	23.84	24.26	24.68	25.11	25.53	25.95	26.36	26.77	27.17

Philippines 566

		1992	1993	1994	1995	1996	1997	1998	1999	2000	2001	2002	2003
Exchange Rates		\multicolumn{12}{c}{*Pesos per SDR: End of Period*}
Market Rate	aa	34.507	38.046	35.647	38.967	37.801	53.936	54.996	55.330	65.143	64.601	72.185	82.574
		\multicolumn{12}{c}{*Pesos per US Dollar: End of Period (ae) Period Average (rf)*}
Market Rate	ae	25.096	27.699	24.418	26.214	26.288	39.975	39.059	40.313	49.998	51.404	53.096	55.569
Market Rate	rf	25.512	27.120	26.417	25.714	26.216	29.471	40.893	39.089	44.192	50.993	51.604	54.203
		\multicolumn{12}{c}{*Index Numbers (2000=100): Period Averages*}
Market Rate	ahx	172.4	162.4	166.7	170.8	167.6	151.6	107.7	112.5	100.0	86.2	85.2	81.1
Nominal Effective Exchange Rate	nec	134.6	135.4	144.9	143.3	146.2	141.0	107.1	109.9	100.0	91.1	89.6	79.5
Real Effective Exchange Rate	rec	103.5	103.2	108.6	111.4	121.2	120.6	98.6	107.2	100.0	95.1	95.5	85.9
Fund Position		\multicolumn{12}{c}{*Millions of SDRs: End of Period*}
Quota	2f.s	633	633	633	633	633	633	633	880	880	880	880	880
SDRs	1b.s	–	7	17	5	2	1	1	5	1	11	7	1
Reserve Position in the Fund	1c.s	87	87	87	87	87	87	87	87	87	87	87	87
Total Fund Cred.&Loans Outstg	2tl	800	881	729	489	282	634	1,114	1,328	1,559	1,553	1,240	806
International Liquidity		\multicolumn{12}{c}{*Millions of US Dollars Unless Otherwise Indicated: End of Period*}
Total Reserves minus Gold	1l.d	4,403	4,676	6,017	6,372	10,030	7,266	9,226	13,230	13,047	13,429	13,135	13,457
SDRs	1b.d	1	10	24	8	2	2	2	7	2	14	10	2
Reserve Position in the Fund	1c.d	120	120	127	129	125	118	123	120	113	110	119	130
Foreign Exchange	1d.d	4,283	4,546	5,866	6,235	9,902	7,147	9,101	13,103	12,931	13,305	13,007	13,326
Gold (Million Fine Troy Ounces)	1ad	2.798	3.221	2.892	3.580	4.651	4.988	5.432	6.199	7.228	7.980	8.729	8.217
Gold (National Valuation)	1and	935	1,245	1,104	1,403	1,715	1,472	1,555	1,782	1,973	2,216	3,036	3,408
Monetary Authorities: Other Liab.	4..d	4,531	2,653	2,295	2,523	2,489	2,578	3,272	4,423	4,826	6,029	5,555	6,011
Deposit Money Banks: Assets	7a.d	4,691	4,778	6,036	6,402	8,185	8,878	9,153	10,114	8,181	7,468	8,074	8,239
Liabilities	7b.d	2,995	2,913	4,640	6,420	14,364	15,406	12,751	11,978	10,302	8,730	8,009	7,582
Other Banking Insts.: Liabilities	7f.d	480	911	963	1,080	49	62	64	46	45	47	312	44
OBU: Foreign Assets	7k.d	483	508	485	283	174	203	123	121	137	304	313	291
Foreign Liabilities	7m.d	1,418	1,055	1,674	1,545	1,647	1,826	1,296	1,167	928	987	807	819
Monetary Authorities		\multicolumn{12}{c}{*Billions of Pesos: End of Period*}
Foreign Assets	11	133.46	†164.01	173.78	203.60	308.76	349.29	422.13	605.18	751.29	804.92	861.63	937.49
Claims on Central Government	12a	76.24	†293.48	233.87	227.85	240.26	226.57	194.18	237.91	165.80	132.96	149.43	125.10
Claims on Local Government	12b	–	†–	–	–	–	–	–	–	–	–	–	–
Claims on Nonfin.Pub.Enterprises	12c	3.45	†2.31	1.97	1.93	1.82	2.98	4.26	17.76	38.33	30.12	56.04	83.45
Claims on Deposit Money Banks	12e	15.38	†7.27	6.17	7.31	7.68	26.43	18.20	12.69	48.98	40.94	17.46	27.83
Claims on Other Financial Insts	12f	6.45	†5.91	4.60	6.26	6.48	8.02	13.51	14.18	15.10	10.87	9.85	9.14
Claims on Nonbank Financial Insts	12g	–	†–	–	–	–	–	–	–	–	–	–	–
Reserve Money	14	178.15	†210.25	226.93	255.17	338.17	317.63	323.83	442.74	395.88	351.91	409.34	447.56
of which: Currency Outside DMBs	14a	74.30	†84.08	95.68	110.89	122.95	143.64	146.06	218.47	192.30	194.67	220.04	238.61
Time Deposits	15	2.24	†8.12	24.69	28.37	39.89	13.61	15.47	31.12	52.36	26.65	49.80	33.30
Liabs. of Central Bank: Securities	16ac	67.52	†24.79	4.57	.63	.25	.03	.03	.03	.03	–	–	–
Restricted Deposits	16b	.18	†6.51	4.92	2.12	1.68	1.68	1.69	.39	.04	.04	.32	.22
Foreign Liabilities	16c	141.32	†107.00	82.01	85.22	76.10	137.26	189.08	251.76	342.86	410.25	384.47	400.54
o/w:Med.&Long-Term Fgn Liabs.	16cl	53.38	†42.84	37.47	37.15	31.13	54.79	80.42	124.57	159.04	190.68	206.30	233.83
Central Government Deposits	16d	168.23	†113.80	84.54	73.43	106.54	78.35	59.49	90.74	95.42	86.52	78.89	104.23
Capital Accounts	17a	6.61	†21.06	26.49	30.15	30.08	71.98	88.15	100.23	159.45	188.96	197.81	222.77
Other Items (Net)	17r	–329.25	†–18.56	–33.76	–28.16	–27.71	–7.24	–25.44	–29.28	–26.54	–44.50	–26.23	–25.61
Deposit Money Banks		\multicolumn{12}{c}{*Billions of Pesos: End of Period*}
Reserves	20	102.17	114.55	123.30	123.93	142.84	161.06	168.17	190.99	178.09	181.18	216.57	206.93
Claims on Mon.Author.:Securities	20c	3.76	2.31	.94	.08	.08	.03	.03	.03	.03	–	–	–
Foreign Assets	21	117.73	132.35	147.38	167.83	215.16	354.90	357.52	407.73	409.03	383.90	428.72	457.81
Claims on Central Government	22a	84.34	98.89	147.56	177.21	237.53	304.31	300.34	332.42	432.55	534.56	563.11	635.41
Claims on Local Government	22b	.36	.80	2.37	4.68	6.95	9.07	10.34	12.20	15.52	17.15	18.41	20.27
Claims on Nonfin.Pub.Enterprises	22c	21.50	22.84	17.07	14.87	16.37	25.65	40.56	47.68	59.18	82.78	99.18	168.77
Claims on Private Sector	22d	276.30	388.87	491.98	715.32	1,063.80	1,370.07	1,279.19	1,249.58	1,316.59	1,293.29	1,303.35	1,317.66
Claims on Other Financial Insts	22f	10.17	11.50	24.61	27.09	60.26	76.61	117.98	130.68	175.13	157.71	166.94	179.86
Demand Deposits	24	34.72	49.10	55.08	72.04	96.41	111.92	134.09	172.87	192.98	191.94	252.77	274.92
Time, Savings,& Fgn.Currency Dep	25	371.44	477.63	613.16	765.20	949.71	1,225.32	1,332.79	1,483.42	1,622.30	1,720.15	1,833.30	1,893.55
Money Market Instruments	26aa	3.51	4.61	4.61	6.24	6.64	12.07	6.11	7.19	4.21	3.98	3.37	3.46
Restricted Deposits	26b	3.87	4.25	3.42	3.55	2.99	3.28	7.05	4.03	5.16	4.76	3.86	3.68
Foreign Liabilities	26c	75.17	80.70	113.29	168.29	377.59	615.86	498.05	482.86	515.10	448.75	425.22	421.30
Central Government Deposits	26d	26.55	41.76	26.62	39.41	51.73	38.90	32.43	39.86	33.97	42.39	39.87	33.91
Credit from Monetary Authorities	26g	22.35	22.17	17.06	16.67	15.26	15.02	10.38	8.47	38.09	26.73	16.31	19.63
Capital Accounts	27a	91.07	107.10	132.36	184.71	243.17	327.28	376.53	440.89	467.48	479.22	511.74	539.22
Other Items (Net)	27r	–12.34	–15.21	–10.40	–25.10	–.51	–47.95	–123.31	–268.28	–293.17	–267.36	–290.14	–202.97

Philippines 566

		1992	1993	1994	1995	1996	1997	1998	1999	2000	2001	2002	2003
Monetary Survey						**Billions of Pesos: End of Period**							
Foreign Assets (Net)	31n	34.70	†108.66	125.86	117.92	70.23	−48.93	92.51	278.29	302.37	329.81	480.66	573.46
Domestic Credit	32	286.82	†669.63	813.42	1,062.38	1,475.20	1,906.05	1,868.45	1,911.82	2,088.82	2,130.52	2,247.55	2,401.52
Claims on Central Govt. (Net)	32an	−34.20	†236.81	270.27	292.21	319.53	413.64	402.61	439.74	468.97	538.61	593.77	622.37
Claims on Local Government	32b	.36	†.80	2.37	4.68	6.95	9.07	10.34	12.20	15.52	17.15	18.41	20.27
Claims on Nonfin.Pub.Enterprises	32c	24.96	†25.14	19.04	16.80	18.19	28.63	44.82	65.44	97.51	112.90	155.23	252.22
Claims on Private Sector	32d	279.08	†389.47	492.53	715.34	1,063.80	1,370.08	1,279.19	1,249.59	1,316.59	1,293.29	1,303.35	1,317.66
Claims on Other Financial Insts.	32f	16.62	†17.41	29.21	33.35	66.73	84.63	131.49	144.86	190.22	168.58	176.79	188.99
Claims on Nonbank Financial Insts.	32g	–	†–										
Money	34	117.54	†143.71	159.90	194.63	233.12	266.33	285.95	395.56	390.55	392.25	478.48	519.84
Quasi-Money	35	373.67	†485.75	637.85	793.58	989.60	1,238.93	1,348.25	1,514.53	1,674.66	1,746.80	1,883.10	1,926.86
Money Market Instruments	36aa	3.51	†4.61	4.61	6.24	6.64	12.07	6.11	7.19	4.21	3.98	3.37	3.46
Liabs. of Central Bank: Securities	36ac	63.75	†22.48	3.63	.55	.17	–	–	–	–	–	–	–
Restricted Deposits	36b	4.05	†10.76	8.34	5.67	4.67	4.96	8.73	4.42	5.20	4.80	4.17	3.90
Capital Accounts	37a	97.67	†128.16	158.84	214.86	273.25	399.26	464.68	541.12	626.94	668.17	709.55	761.99
Other Items (Net)	37r	−338.68	†−17.18	−33.90	−35.22	37.98	−64.42	−152.77	−272.71	−310.36	−355.66	−350.46	−241.08
Money plus Quasi-Money	35l	491.21	†629.46	797.75	988.20	1,222.72	1,505.26	1,634.20	1,910.09	2,065.21	2,139.05	2,361.58	2,446.70
Other Banking Institutions						**Billions of Pesos: End of Period**							
Reserves	40	13.93	20.33	15.51	18.57	18.50	19.78	15.34	14.92	23.56	18.68	20.87	21.65
Claims on Central Government	42a	11.41	10.82	12.93	19.09	3.38	3.95	2.35	1.74	3.46	1.91	24.35	4.60
Claims on Private Sector	42d	61.24	82.32	115.93	143.41	127.55	139.92	144.74	145.55	152.43	166.17	161.22	189.60
Time and Savings Deposits	45	51.30	63.19	69.09	93.73	106.89	120.70	119.08	120.58	131.77	151.64	171.99	187.29
Bonds	46ab	–	.15	2.28	3.65	4.22	5.39	6.38	6.29	6.38	5.49	5.14	2.76
Foreign Liabilities	46c	12.04	25.23	23.51	28.31	1.29	2.49	2.49	1.87	2.23	2.44	16.56	2.44
Credit from Monetary Authorities	46g	3.72	3.53	3.56	3.65	3.67	5.08	10.59	10.74	11.95	8.40	7.34	7.54
Capital Accounts	47a	16.11	18.97	27.08	32.99	27.33	35.93	40.73	48.63	49.27	48.26	49.40	46.22
Other Items (Net)	47r	3.41	2.41	18.85	18.74	6.04	−5.95	−16.84	−25.89	−22.15	−29.48	−43.98	−30.41
Interest Rates						**Percent Per Annum**							
Discount Rate (End of Period)	60	14.300	9.400	8.300	10.830	11.700	14.640	12.400	7.894	13.806	8.298	4.193	5.532
Money Market Rate	60b	16.581	13.765	13.989	11.925	12.770	16.155	13.900	10.165	10.835	9.751	7.149	6.969
Treasury Bill Rate	60c	16.018	12.448	12.714	11.761	12.338	12.893	15.004	9.996	9.913	9.734	5.494	5.872
Savings Rate	60k	10.139	8.279	8.068	8.044	7.945	8.951	10.952	7.640	7.308	7.655	4.240	4.214
Savings Rate (Foreign Currency)	60k.f	2.593	2.213	2.268	2.275	2.200	2.200	2.200	2.200	2.200	2.004	1.288	.885
Deposit Rate	60l	14.275	9.606	10.539	8.392	9.683	10.194	12.106	8.167	8.305	8.744	4.608	5.221
Deposit Rate (Foreign Currency)	60l.f	3.394	3.212	4.203	5.295	5.097	5.322	5.441	5.037	5.207	3.804	2.322	1.908
Lending Rate	60p	19.479	14.683	15.057	14.682	14.840	16.276	16.777	11.776	10.907	12.402	9.139	9.472
Government Bond Yield	61	....	....	13.250	14.250	13.990	13.008	†17.985	12.332	11.767	13.399	8.688	8.715
Prices, Production, Labor						**Index Numbers (2000=100): Period Averages**							
Share Prices	62	92.5	109.7	137.3	122.4	119.3	103.9	69.1	106.7	100.0	64.4	48.4	40.8
Wholesale Prices	63	66.4	66.3	72.0	76.0	82.8	83.2	92.9	98.2	100.0	102.4	106.1	111.5
Consumer Prices	64	56.7	60.6	65.7	70.9	77.3	81.8	89.8	95.8	100.0	106.1	109.3	112.5
Manufacturing Production	66ey	†144.8	169.8	192.3	227.3	246.8	268.5	80.1	86.7	100.0	108.3	106.5	115.1
Manufacturing Empl. (1990=100)	67ey	88.3	87.0	85.8	....	....	....	....	....	....	....	....	....
						Number in Thousands: Period Averages							
Labor Force	67d	26,290	26,879	27,654	28,380	29,732	30,355	31,055	30,759	30,912	32,809	33,936	34,571
Employment	67e	23,696	24,382	25,032	25,676	27,186	27,715	27,912	27,742	27,453	29,156	30,062	30,635
Unemployment	67c	†2,594	2,497	2,622	2,704	2,546	2,640	3,143	3,017	3,459	3,653	3,874	3,936
Unemployment Rate (%)	67r	†9.8	9.3	9.5	9.5	8.6	8.7	10.1	9.8	11.2	11.1	11.4	11.4
International Transactions						**Millions of Pesos**							
Exports	70	248,359	302,998	350,078	450,487	535,054	738,415	1,206,197	1,432,594	1,773,137	1,665,023	1,884,323	2,008,842
Sugar	70i	2,212	2,740	1,629	1,713	3,544	2,864	3,200	2,597	2,227	1,124	1,830	3,122
Coconut Oil	70ai	12,275	9,698	12,552	21,242	14,960	19,846	28,857	13,379	20,450	21,292	18,196	27,365
Imports, c.i.f.	71	394,536	509,035	596,611	729,960	894,665	1,139,830	1,290,274	1,273,001	1,636,810	1,780,531	1,919,156	2,141,226
Imports, f.o.b.	71.v	369,635	479,296	562,163	679,701	835,863	1,060,815	1,213,859	1,201,519	1,526,636	1,684,742	1,827,806	2,030,102
						2000=100							
Volume of Exports	72	63.6	73.1	86.2	56.1	62.2	73.6	79.7	86.9	100.0	88.6	104.9	....
Sugar	72i	146.9	229.0	128.6	108.2	224.4	139.7	130.5	100.7	100.0	40.0	62.6	97.2
Coconut Oil	72ai	85.0	82.8	81.8	129.2	76.4	104.1	113.6	46.1	100.0	136.6	91.0	114.3
Volume of Imports	73	100.3	119.5	143.3	83.4	97.9	106.4	84.9	94.8	100.0	113.6	115.6	....
Export Prices	76	79.7	80.3	80.7	81.3	86.2	89.4	96.7	106.3	100.0	95.5	88.6	....
Sugar (Wholesale Price)	76i	62.2	49.3	53.3	65.3	65.1	67.0	98.0	10.8	100.0	116.2	120.9	211.9
Coconut Oil (W'sale price)	76ai	66.0	53.5	68.7	76.1	92.1	89.5	111.2	138.2	100.0	73.0	95.6	110.9
Import Prices	76.x	101.1	102.9	104.0	101.0	106.1	108.1	111.1	103.8	100.0	92.2	97.3	....

Philippines 566

		1992	1993	1994	1995	1996	1997	1998	1999	2000	2001	2002	2003
Balance of Payments		*Millions of US Dollars: Minus Sign Indicates Debit*											
Current Account, n.i.e.	78ald	−1,000	−3,016	−2,950	−1,980	−3,953	−4,351	1,546	7,219	6,258	1,323	4,383	3,347
Goods: Exports f.o.b.	78aad	9,824	11,375	13,483	17,447	20,543	25,228	29,496	34,211	37,295	31,243	34,377	34,842
Goods: Imports f.o.b.	78abd	−14,519	−17,597	−21,333	−26,391	−31,885	−36,355	−29,524	−29,252	−33,481	−31,986	−33,970	−36,095
Trade Balance	78acd	−4,695	−6,222	−7,850	−8,944	−11,342	−11,127	−28	4,959	3,814	−743	407	−1,253
Services: Credit	78add	4,742	4,673	6,768	9,348	12,947	15,137	7,477	4,803	3,972	3,148	3,055	2,970
Services: Debit	78aed	−2,308	−3,090	−4,654	−6,926	−9,429	−14,122	−10,107	−7,515	−6,402	−5,198	−4,072	−4,197
Balance on Goods & Services	78afd	−2,261	−4,639	−5,736	−6,522	−7,824	−10,112	−2,658	2,247	1,384	−2,793	−610	−2,480
Income: Credit	78agd	2,755	2,824	3,782	6,067	6,059	7,698	6,440	8,082	7,804	7,152	7,946	8,415
Income: Debit	78ahd	−2,310	−1,900	−1,932	−2,405	−2,777	−3,017	−2,671	−3,622	−3,367	−3,483	−3,456	−3,200
Balance on Gds, Serv. & Inc.	78aid	−1,816	−3,715	−3,886	−2,860	−4,542	−5,431	1,111	6,707	5,821	876	3,880	2,735
Current Transfers, n.i.e.: Credit	78ajd	825	746	1,041	1,147	1,185	1,670	758	607	552	517	594	682
Current Transfers: Debit	78akd	−9	−47	−105	−267	−596	−590	−323	−95	−115	−70	−91	−70
Capital Account, n.i.e.	78bcd	1	—	—	—	—	—	—	−8	38	−12	−19	21
Capital Account, n.i.e.: Credit	78bad	1	—	—	—	—	—	—	44	74	12	2	40
Capital Account: Debit	78bbd	—	—	—	—	—	—	—	−52	−36	−24	−21	−19
Financial Account, n.i.e.	78bjd	3,208	3,267	5,120	5,309	11,277	6,498	483	−2,250	−4,042	−745	−2,399	−5,533
Direct Investment Abroad	78bdd	—	−374	−302	−399	−182	−136	−160	29	108	160	−59	−158
Dir. Invest. in Rep. Econ., n.i.e.	78bed	228	1,238	1,591	1,478	1,517	1,222	2,287	1,725	1,345	989	1,792	319
Portfolio Investment Assets	78bfd	−115	−949	−632	−1,429	191	−9	−603	−807	−812	−457	−449	−1,586
Equity Securities	78bkd	—	....	....	....	21	30	−184	−55	−42	−4	−26	−43
Debt Securities	78bld	−115	−949	−632	−1,429	170	−39	−419	−752	−770	−453	−423	−1,543
Portfolio Investment Liab., n.i.e.	78bgd	155	897	901	2,619	5,126	600	−325	7,681	1,019	997	1,571	880
Equity Securities	78bmd	....	....	....	....	2,101	−406	264	1,410	−183	383	404	457
Debt Securities	78bnd	155	897	901	2,619	3,025	1,006	−589	6,271	1,202	614	1,167	423
Financial Derivatives Assets	78bwd	....	....	....	....	....	....	....	....	....	....	....	....
Financial Derivatives Liabilities	78bxd	....	....	....	....	....	....	....	....	....	....	....	....
Other Investment Assets	78bhd	—	—	—	—	−1,745	425	809	−18,639	−15,313	−14,034	−13,165	−13,307
Monetary Authorities	78bod	....	....	....	....	....	....	—	—	....	....	....	....
General Government	78bpd	—	....	....	....	....	....	—	—	....	....	....	....
Banks	78bqd	—	....	....	....	−1,745	425	809	−941	2,265	465	374	492
Other Sectors	78brd	—	—	—	—	—	—	—	−17,698	−17,578	−14,499	−13,539	−13,799
Other Investment Liab., n.i.e.	78bid	2,940	2,455	3,562	3,040	6,370	4,396	−1,525	7,761	9,611	11,600	7,911	8,319
Monetary Authorities	78bsd	—	—	—	—	199	−98	5	75	166	621	−814	8
General Government	78btd	2,731	1,065	−1,121	−408	−808	−218	−207	340	−125	16	−131	−154
Banks	78bud	1,921	−229	1,694	1,648	5,036	1,668	−1,118	−2,221	−1,368	−723	50	−392
Other Sectors	78bvd	−1,712	1,619	2,989	1,800	1,943	3,044	−205	9,567	10,938	11,686	8,806	8,857
Net Errors and Omissions	78cad	−520	85	157	−2,094	−2,986	−5,241	−750	−1,311	−2,630	−270	−2,076	2,081
Overall Balance	78cbd	1,689	336	2,327	1,235	4,338	−3,094	1,279	3,650	−376	296	−111	−84
Reserves and Related Items	79dad	−1,689	−336	−2,327	−1,235	−4,338	3,094	−1,279	−3,650	376	−296	111	84
Reserve Assets	79dbd	−1,746	−447	−2,107	−873	−4,037	2,610	−1,938	−3,938	73	−465	399	360
Use of Fund Credit and Loans	79dcd	58	111	−220	−362	−301	485	659	288	303	−8	−407	−607
Exceptional Financing	79ded	—	—	—	—	—	—	—	—	—	177	118	331
International Investment Position		*Millions of US Dollars*											
Assets	79aad	....	....	....	....	....	....	....	....	....	30,186	31,196	....
Direct Investment Abroad	79abd	....	....	....	....	....	....	....	....	....	729	815	....
Portfolio Investment	79acd	....	....	....	....	....	....	....	....	....	2,526	3,243	....
Equity Securities	79add	....	....	....	....	....	....	....	....	....	111	118	....
Debt Securities	79aed	....	....	....	....	....	....	....	....	....	2,415	3,125	....
Financial Derivatives	79ald	....	....	....	....	....	....	....	....	....	....	....	....
Other Investment	79afd	....	....	....	....	....	....	....	....	....	11,272	10,957	....
Monetary Authorities	79agd	....	....	....	....	....	....	....	....	....	—	—	....
General Government	79ahd	....	....	....	....	....	....	....	....	....	....	....	....
Banks	79aid	....	....	....	....	....	....	....	....	....	7,007	6,361	....
Other Sectors	79ajd	....	....	....	....	....	....	....	....	....	4,265	4,596	....
Reserve Assets	79akd	....	....	....	....	....	....	....	....	....	15,659	16,181	....
Liabilities	79lad	....	....	....	....	....	....	....	....	....	66,782	69,045	....
Dir. Invest. in Rep. Economy	79lbd	....	....	....	....	....	....	....	....	....	10,433	11,148	....
Portfolio Investment	79lcd	....	....	....	....	....	....	....	....	....	16,288	18,289	....
Equity Securities	79ldd	....	....	....	....	....	....	....	....	....	1,922	2,302	....
Debt Securities	79led	....	....	....	....	....	....	....	....	....	14,366	15,987	....
Financial Derivatives	79lld	....	....	....	....	....	....	....	....	....	....	....	....
Other Investment	79lfd	....	....	....	....	....	....	....	....	....	40,061	39,608	....
Monetary Authorities	79lgd	....	....	....	....	....	....	....	....	....	4,664	3,738	....
General Government	79lhd	....	....	....	....	....	....	....	....	....	13,209	14,065	....
Banks	79lid	....	....	....	....	....	....	....	....	....	5,067	5,642	....
Other Sectors	79ljd	....	....	....	....	....	....	....	....	....	17,121	16,163	....

2004, International Monetary Fund: *International Financial Statistics Yearbook*

Philippines 566

		1992	1993	1994	1995	1996	1997	1998	1999	2000	2001	2002	2003
Government Finance		\multicolumn{12}{c}{*Millions of Pesos: Year Ending December 31*}
Deficit (-) or Surplus	80	−15,965	−21,891	18,114	11,074	6,256	1,564	−49,981	−111,658	−136,110	−147,023	−210,741	−199,868
Revenue	81	240,570	258,855	334,488	360,232	409,880	470,087	462,119	478,210	504,349	561,857	566,089	625,432
Grants Received	81z	2,145	1,550	739	988	569	1,756	396	292	1,376	1,991	1,052	1,198
Expenditure	82	265,629	272,391	309,942	341,726	401,017	466,690	511,078	585,425	638,665	706,443	775,256	818,422
Lending Minus Repayments	83	−6,949	9,905	7,171	8,420	3,176	3,589	1,418	4,735	3,170	4,428	2,626	8,076
Financing													
Domestic	84a	1,576	8,979	−4,408	2,272	−348	5,254	37,635	28,858	90,927	124,108	101,628	56,006
Foreign	85a	14,390	12,912	−13,706	−13,346	−5,908	−6,818	12,346	82,800	45,183	22,915	109,113	143,862
Debt: Domestic	88a	435,110	640,867	638,025	....	....	....	....	....	....	....	....	....
Foreign	89a	278,150	348,955	317,068	....	....	....	....	....	....	....	....	....
National Accounts		\multicolumn{12}{c}{*Billions of Pesos*}
Househ.Cons.Expend.,incl.NPISHs	96f	1,019.2	1,122.5	1,258.8	1,411.9	1,595.3	1,762.0	1,980.1	2,161.6	2,335.5	2,565.0	2,750.9	2,988.1
Government Consumption Expend	91f	130.5	149.1	182.8	217.0	259.5	319.9	354.4	389.2	438.9	444.8	457.5	471.4
Gross Fixed Capital Formation	93e	282.8	350.5	400.1	423.2	508.7	592.6	563.6	568.2	710.5	651.3	693.0	715.2
Changes in Inventories	93i	5.6	3.1	7.2	4.7	12.9	8.7	−21.5	−10.0	−.4	37.8	2.1	.1
Exports of Goods and Services	90c	393.7	462.4	572.6	693.0	879.8	1,188.0	1,389.9	1,532.2	1,858.6	1,785.2	1,968.5	2,109.4
Imports of Goods and Services (-)	98c	459.9	586.9	679.4	842.1	1,070.6	1,438.9	1,566.6	1,527.4	1,794.7	1,899.4	1,988.5	2,221.3
Gross Domestic Product (GDP)	99b	1,351.6	1,474.5	1,692.9	1,906.0	2,171.9	2,426.7	2,665.1	2,976.9	3,354.7	3,631.5	3,959.6	4,299.9
Net Primary Income from Abroad	98.n	23.3	35.1	43.5	52.6	89.4	101.6	137.1	159.3	211.3	245.1	263.7	318.4
Gross National Income (GNI)	99a	1,374.8	1,509.5	1,736.4	1,958.6	2,261.3	2,528.3	2,802.1	3,136.2	3,566.1	3,876.6	4,223.3	4,618.3
Consumption of Fixed Capital	99cf	109.1	131.6	151.5	172.0	190.5	....	....	....	....	....	....	....
GDP Volume 1985 Prices	99b.p	718.9	734.2	766.4	802.2	849.1	893.2	888.0	918.2	955.0	987.4	1,042.1	1,093.3
GDP Volume (2000=100)	99bvp	75.3	76.9	80.3	84.0	88.9	93.5	93.0	96.1	100.0	103.4	109.1	114.5
GDP Deflator (2000=100)	99bip	53.5	57.2	62.9	67.6	72.8	77.3	85.4	92.3	100.0	104.7	108.2	112.0
		\multicolumn{12}{c}{*Millions: Midyear Estimates*}
Population	99z	63.99	65.45	66.92	68.40	69.87	71.34	72.80	74.26	75.71	77.15	78.58	80.00

Poland 964

		1992	1993	1994	1995	1996	1997	1998	1999	2000	2001	2002	2003
Exchange Rates						*Zlotys per SDR: End of Period*							
Market Rate	aa	2.1680	2.9317	3.5579	3.6687	4.1349	4.7467	4.9337	5.6936	5.3982	5.0097	5.2189	5.5587
				Zlotys per US Dollar: End of Period (ae) Period Average (rf)									
Market Rate	ae	1.5767	2.1344	2.4372	2.4680	2.8755	3.5180	3.5040	4.1483	4.1432	3.9863	3.8388	3.7408
Market Rate	rf	1.3626	1.8115	2.2723	2.4250	2.6961	3.2793	3.4754	3.9671	4.3461	4.0939	4.0800	3.8891
				Index Numbers (2000=100): Period Averages									
Market Rate	ahx	320.8	241.8	191.2	179.0	161.2	132.8	125.0	109.6	100.0	106.0	106.4	111.6
Nominal Effective Exchange Rate	nec	225.3	187.6	149.4	130.5	122.3	113.0	108.5	98.9	100.0	110.9	107.4	97.9
Real Effective Exchange Rate	rec	70.5	75.6	76.2	81.2	88.2	91.7	96.2	92.3	100.0	111.8	108.2	98.9
Fund Position						*Millions of SDRs: End of Period*							
Quota	2f.s	989	989	989	989	989	989	989	1,369	1,369	1,369	1,369	1,369
SDRs	1b.s	1	1	1	2	3	4	5	8	14	21	29	37
Reserve Position in the Fund	1c.s	77	77	77	77	77	77	77	172	172	367	479	538
Total Fund Cred.&Loans Outstg	2tl	597	498	919	–	–	–	–	–	–	–	–	–
International Liquidity					*Millions of US Dollars Unless Otherwise Indicated: End of Period*								
Total Reserves minus Gold	1l.d	4,099.1	4,091.9	5,841.8	14,774.1	17,844.0	20,407.2	27,325.2	26,354.7	26,562.0	25,648.4	28,649.7	32,579.1
SDRs	1b.d	1.1	.7	1.5	2.2	4.4	5.4	7.1	11.2	17.7	25.8	39.5	54.8
Reserve Position in the Fund	1c.d	106.1	105.9	112.6	114.6	110.9	104.1	108.6	236.4	224.4	461.0	651.0	799.4
Foreign Exchange	1d.d	3,992.0	3,985.3	5,727.7	14,657.2	17,728.7	20,297.7	27,209.5	26,107.1	26,319.9	25,161.6	27,959.2	31,724.9
Gold (Million Fine Troy Ounces)	1ad	.473	.473	.473	.473	.473	.904	3.305	3.306	3.306	3.308	3.309	3.307
Gold (National Valuation)	1and	189.0	189.0	189.0	189.0	189.0	262.4	950.0	959.4	901.5	914.7	1,134.0	1,380.5
Monetary Authorities: Other Liab.	4..d	423.5	446.2	355.6	363.5	246.4	914.3	1,028.2	1,939.3	498.6	588.2	145.6	233.4
Deposit Money Banks: Assets	7a.d	6,648.3	5,925.5	7,742.2	7,154.4	6,132.1	7,275.5	5,405.3	7,874.7	11,323.1	15,307.2	13,707.8	14,920.9
Liabilities	7b.d	1,921.0	1,469.8	1,543.2	2,070.1	2,746.5	4,284.0	5,213.8	6,745.7	6,608.9	7,766.1	9,069.2	12,638.8
Monetary Authorities						*Millions of Zlotys: End of Period*							
Foreign Assets	11	7,912	10,113	15,475	37,532	52,498	75,500	99,213	113,910	114,258	106,183	114,772	128,207
Claims on General Government	12a	12,170	15,729	19,530	11,534	12,761	16,792	17,765	18,803	16,745	18,426	6,579	384
Claims on Other Resident Sectors	12d	23	27	23	22	59	66	60	71	68	23	23	24
Claims on Deposit Money Banks	12e	4,848	6,362	7,450	8,244	11,246	9,710	8,044	7,394	7,121	6,033	5,421	4,833
Reserve Money	14	14,860	15,993	19,615	28,441	34,262	45,919	53,656	52,957	48,818	63,704	62,066	66,337
of which: Currency Outside DMBs	14a	7,798	9,982	12,274	19,530	23,563	27,256	30,225	38,083	34,113	38,213	42,193	49,417
Nonreserve Liabilities to Banks	16b	757	1,406	3,462	9,465	14,660	15,662	28,576	24,694	33,738	24,167	20,953	14,202
Foreign Liabilities	16c	1,961	2,411	4,135	897	708	3,216	3,603	8,045	2,066	2,345	559	873
General Government Deposits	16d	1,285	2,272	2,773	3,440	6,127	4,285	4,010	7,040	9,774	7,689	7,414	11,429
Capital Accounts	17a	150	210	300	400	400	400	1,548	1,548	1,594	1,694	1,748	1,845
Other Items (Net)	17r	5,939	9,939	12,193	14,689	20,406	32,586	33,688	45,894	42,202	31,064	34,055	38,761
Deposit Money Banks						*Millions of Zlotys: End of Period*							
Reserves	20	5,816	6,045	7,343	8,806	10,633	15,049	23,336	14,867	14,661	21,485	19,857	16,903
Claims on Mon.Author.:Securities	20c	757	732	1,879	4,585	11,018	13,927	28,321	24,539	33,507	24,133	20,735	14,225
Other Claims on Monetary Author.	20n	–	674	998	3,528	2,739	1,288	–	–	–	4,000	8	12
Foreign Assets	21	10,482	12,647	18,869	17,657	17,633	25,595	18,940	32,666	46,914	61,019	52,622	55,816
Claims on General Government	22a	12,013	19,201	27,204	38,920	48,638	50,980	57,431	63,792	54,591	65,668	78,040	96,008
Claims on Other Resident Sectors	22d	24,879	33,274	41,908	56,946	81,194	107,294	135,498	169,828	197,759	212,575	221,809	236,650
Demand Deposits	24	7,096	9,654	15,175	17,817	28,702	34,425	41,438	49,970	48,420	51,941	70,683	84,142
Time, Savings,& Fgn.Currency Dep	25	25,041	36,268	49,844	66,913	84,186	111,084	149,104	175,302	211,926	244,644	216,524	214,605
Foreign Liabilities	26c	3,029	3,137	3,761	5,109	7,898	15,071	18,269	27,983	27,382	30,958	34,815	47,229
General Government Deposits	26d	3,921	2,706	3,688	5,506	7,942	9,857	12,515	14,113	16,152	16,966	19,991	20,125
of which: Local Govt. Dep.	26db	860	1,149	1,503	2,523	3,401	4,395	5,551	7,146	7,472	7,313	8,434	8,818
Credit from Monetary Authorities	26g	4,848	6,338	7,020	7,788	10,685	9,180	7,565	7,010	6,800	5,763	4,023	3,636
Capital Accounts	27a	4,323	7,129	9,990	12,999	18,534	24,715	30,049	34,294	39,562	46,441	45,695	47,181
Other Items (Net)	27r	5,690	7,342	8,724	14,310	13,907	9,801	4,586	–2,980	–2,809	–7,832	1,339	2,648
Monetary Survey						*Millions of Zlotys: End of Period*							
Foreign Assets (Net)	31n	13,405	17,212	26,448	49,183	61,524	82,808	96,281	110,548	131,725	133,899	132,020	135,871
Domestic Credit	32	43,878	63,253	82,205	98,476	128,583	160,990	194,228	231,341	243,237	272,037	279,045	301,512
Claims on General Govt. (Net)	32an	18,977	29,952	40,274	41,508	47,330	53,630	58,671	61,442	45,409	59,439	57,214	64,838
Claims on Other Resident Sectors	32d	24,902	33,300	41,932	56,968	81,253	107,360	135,558	169,899	197,827	212,598	221,831	236,674
Money	34	14,963	19,646	27,450	37,439	52,331	61,686	71,670	88,201	82,574	94,158	112,889	133,576
Quasi-Money	35	26,145	36,278	49,852	66,913	84,331	114,705	149,110	175,307	211,930	244,647	216,527	214,608
Capital Accounts	37a	4,473	7,339	10,290	13,399	18,934	25,115	31,598	35,842	41,156	48,135	47,443	49,026
Other Items (Net)	37r	11,702	17,201	21,062	29,908	34,511	42,291	38,132	42,539	39,301	18,996	34,206	40,174
Money plus Quasi-Money	35l	41,108	55,924	77,302	104,352	136,662	176,392	220,780	263,508	294,505	338,805	329,416	348,183
Interest Rates						*Percent Per Annum*							
Discount Rate (End of Period)	60	32.0	29.0	28.0	25.0	22.0	24.5	18.3	19.0	21.5	14.0	7.8	5.8
Money Market Rate	60b	† 29.5	24.5	23.3	25.8	20.6	22.4	20.6	13.6	18.2	16.2	9.4	5.8
Treasury Bill Rate	60c	44.0	33.2	28.8	25.6	20.3	21.6	19.1	13.1	16.6	....	....	....
Deposit Rate	60l	37.8	34.0	† 33.4	26.8	20.0	19.4	18.2	11.2	14.2	11.8	6.2	3.7
Lending Rate	60p	39.0	35.3	32.8	† 33.5	26.1	25.0	24.5	16.9	20.0	18.4	12.0	7.3

2004, International Monetary Fund : *International Financial Statistics Yearbook*

Poland 964

		1992	1993	1994	1995	1996	1997	1998	1999	2000	2001	2002	2003
Prices, Production, Labor		\multicolumn{12}{c}{*Index Numbers (2000=100): Period Averages*}
Share Prices (1995=100)	62	....	....	....	100.0	168.9	....	....	....	....	....	....	....
Producer Prices: Industry	63	29.91	39.55	51.45	64.59	73.12	82.03	87.97	92.84	100.00	101.66	102.84	105.60
Consumer Prices	64	23.5	32.2	42.9	54.9	65.8	75.7	84.6	90.8	100.0	105.5	107.5	108.3
Wages: Average Earnings	65	18.3	25.6	33.7	47.7	60.3	72.3	83.1	90.6	100.0	106.9	111.0	114.2
Industrial Production	66	76.3	80.0	90.4	†69.7	76.2	84.8	88.8	93.0	100.0	100.4	101.8	110.7
Industrial Employment	67	121.7	115.5	113.5	114.5	113.0	112.4	111.2	106.2	100.0	94.9	89.6	87.1
		\multicolumn{12}{c}{*Number in Thousands: Period Averages*}
Labor Force	67d	17,526	17,367	17,122	17,004	17,076	17,100	17,162	....	17,311	17,376	17,213	....
Employment	67e	15,462	†14,894	14,658	14,791	14,969	15,177	15,354	14,747	14,526	14,207	13,782	13,617
Unemployment	67c	2,509	†2,890	2,838	2,629	2,360	1,826	1,831	2,350	2,703	2,912	3,162	3,238
Unemployment Rate (%)	67r	13.6	†16.4	16.0	15.2	13.2	10.5	10.4	13.0	13.9	16.2	17.8	19.9
International Transactions		\multicolumn{12}{c}{*Millions of Zlotys*}
Exports	70	17,969	25,757	39,246	55,515	65,819	84,480	95,015	108,706	137,909	148,115	167,338	208,944
Imports, c.i.f.	71	21,995	34,018	49,072	70,502	100,231	138,898	162,458	182,362	213,072	206,253	224,816	265,134
Imports, f.o.b.	71.v	19,126	29,581	42,287	61,306	87,157	120,781	141,268	....	....	....	....	....
		\multicolumn{12}{c}{*2000=100*}
Volume of Exports	72	42.0	41.5	49.1	57.4	62.9	71.5	76.4	80.9	100.0	111.8	121.1	143.7
Volume of Imports	73	29.9	35.4	40.1	48.3	61.8	75.4	90.0	93.5	100.0	103.2	110.7	119.8
Export Prices	76	35.8	44.9	57.8	70.1	75.7	85.6	92.0	98.5	100.0	96.0	100.2	105.5
Import Prices	76.x	38.8	45.2	57.5	65.0	76.1	86.5	91.0	97.0	100.0	93.8	95.3	103.9
Balance of Payments		\multicolumn{12}{c}{*Millions of US Dollars: Minus Sign Indicates Debit*}
Current Account, n.i.e.	78ald	−3,104	−5,788	954	854	−3,264	−5,744	−6,901	−12,487	−9,980	−5,371	−5,007	−4,085
Goods: Exports f.o.b.	78aad	13,929	13,582	18,355	25,041	27,557	30,731	32,467	30,060	35,902	41,663	46,742	61,007
Goods: Imports f.o.b.	78abd	−14,060	−17,087	−18,930	−26,687	−34,844	−40,553	−45,303	−45,132	−48,209	−49,324	−53,991	−66,732
Trade Balance	78acd	−131	−3,505	−575	−1,646	−7,287	−9,822	−12,836	−15,072	−12,307	−7,661	−7,249	−5,725
Services: Credit	78add	4,773	4,201	6,699	10,675	9,747	8,915	10,840	8,363	10,398	9,753	10,035	11,166
Services: Debit	78aed	−4,045	−3,631	−3,859	−7,138	−6,343	−5,743	−6,624	−6,982	−8,993	−8,960	−9,186	−10,647
Balance on Goods & Services	78afd	597	−2,935	2,265	1,891	−3,883	−6,650	−8,620	−13,691	−10,902	−6,868	−6,400	−5,206
Income: Credit	78agd	728	579	546	1,089	1,527	1,467	2,226	1,837	2,251	2,624	1,950	2,125
Income: Debit	78ahd	−4,895	−4,192	−3,109	−3,084	−2,602	−2,596	−3,404	−2,847	−3,709	−4,015	−3,837	−5,237
Balance on Gds, Serv. & Inc.	78aid	−3,570	−6,548	−298	−104	−4,958	−7,779	−9,798	−14,701	−12,360	−8,259	−8,287	−8,318
Current Transfers, n.i.e.: Credit	78ajd	6,214	5,840	2,174	2,459	2,825	2,700	3,520	2,898	3,007	3,737	4,182	5,314
Current Transfers: Debit	78akd	−5,748	−5,080	−922	−1,501	−1,131	−665	−623	−684	−627	−849	−902	−1,081
Capital Account, n.i.e.	78bcd	−	−	9,215	285	94	66	63	55	34	76	−7	−46
Capital Account, n.i.e.: Credit	78bad	−	−	9,215	285	5,833	91	117	95	110	113	46	60
Capital Account: Debit	78bbd	−	−	−	−	−5,739	−25	−54	−40	−76	−37	−53	−106
Financial Account, n.i.e.	78bjd	−1,045	2,341	−9,065	9,260	6,673	7,410	13,282	10,462	10,221	3,169	6,955	8,061
Direct Investment Abroad	78bdd	−13	−18	−29	−42	−53	−45	−316	−31	−16	86	−230	−386
Dir. Invest. in Rep. Econ., n.i.e.	78bed	678	1,715	1,875	3,659	4,498	4,908	6,365	7,270	9,343	5,714	4,131	4,225
Portfolio Investment Assets	78bfd	−	−	−624	1	282	815	−130	−548	−84	48	−1,157	−1,296
Equity Securities	78bkd	−	−	−	127	−17	56	1	−172	−20	−67	−268	183
Debt Securities	78bld	−	−	−624	−126	299	759	−131	−376	−64	115	−889	−1,479
Portfolio Investment Liab., n.i.e.	78bgd	−	−	−	1,176	22	1,295	1,827	691	3,423	1,067	2,826	3,740
Equity Securities	78bmd	−	−	−	219	749	599	1,734	14	447	−307	−545	−837
Debt Securities	78bnd	−	−	−	957	−727	696	93	677	2,976	1,374	3,371	4,577
Financial Derivatives Assets	78bwd	....	....	−	−	−	−	−	579	−	−	−	−
Financial Derivatives Liabilities	78bxd	....	....	−	−	−3	−12	−	−10	269	−336	−898	−869
Other Investment Assets	78bhd	−958	848	−1,841	3,356	6,191	−754	2,107	−3,339	−3,870	−4,072	1,887	−1,700
Monetary Authorities	78bod	....	....	194	65	37	−	1	1	2	3	−	−
General Government	78bpd	26	16	34	46	5,767	41	53	−6	−48	−38	−37	−47
Banks	78bqd	−823	649	−1,718	1,057	453	−1,076	2,207	−2,694	−3,015	−3,398	3,107	346
Other Sectors	78brd	−161	183	−351	2,188	−66	281	−154	−640	−809	−639	−1,183	−1,999
Other Investment Liab., n.i.e.	78bid	−752	−204	−8,446	1,110	−4,264	1,203	3,429	5,850	1,156	662	396	4,347
Monetary Authorities	78bsd	−	−	15	14	102	−561	199	380	−1,393	118	−473	−68
General Government	78btd	−1,439	−570	−8,709	−3	−6,033	−52	−370	−224	−290	−3,047	−503	−1,236
Banks	78bud	437	114	170	575	314	719	1,483	2,013	−474	283	−550	2,063
Other Sectors	78bvd	250	252	78	524	1,353	1,097	2,117	3,681	3,313	3,308	1,922	3,588
Net Errors and Omissions	78cad	−181	219	−98	−564	321	1,309	−520	2,126	349	1,699	−1,293	−2,724
Overall Balance	78cbd	−4,330	−3,228	1,006	9,835	3,824	3,041	5,924	156	624	−427	648	1,206
Reserves and Related Items	79dad	4,330	3,228	−1,006	−9,835	−3,824	−3,041	−5,924	−156	−624	427	−648	−1,206
Reserve Assets	79dbd	−616	−100	−1,514	−8,431	−3,828	−3,044	−5,926	−156	−624	427	−648	−1,206
Use of Fund Credit and Loans	79dcd	−	−138	603	−1,408	−	−	−	−	−	−	−	−
Exceptional Financing	79ded	4,946	3,466	−96	4	4	3	2	−	−	−	−	−

Poland 964

		1992	1993	1994	1995	1996	1997	1998	1999	2000	2001	2002	2003
International Investment Position							*Millions of US Dollars*						
Assets...	79aad	....	....	23,506	31,966	28,746	31,908	38,399	40,101	44,672	49,299	51,016	....
Direct Investment Abroad...............	79abd	....	....	461	539	735	678	1,165	1,024	1,018	1,156	1,453	....
Portfolio Investment.......................	79acd	....	....	1,287	1,937	1,338	839	1,093	1,143	1,575	1,311	2,175	....
Equity Securities...........................	79add	....	....	–	–	–	2	9	28	47	108	245	....
Debt Securities.............................	79aed	....	....	–	–	–	837	1,084	1,115	1,528	1,203	1,930	....
Financial Derivatives.....................	79ald	....	....	–	–	–	–	–	–	–	–	–	....
Other Investment...........................	79afd	....	....	15,727	14,527	8,454	8,988	7,866	10,619	14,615	20,275	17,604	....
Monetary Authorities.....................	79agd	....	....	252	187	150	5	4	2	1	–	–	....
General Government......................	79ahd	....	....	6,970	6,720	881	829	801	1,031	1,076	1,173	1,106	....
Banks...	79aid	....	....	6,672	5,678	4,997	6,161	4,419	6,697	9,758	14,507	10,593	....
Other Sectors.................................	79ajd	....	....	1,833	1,942	2,426	1,993	2,642	2,889	3,780	4,595	5,905	....
Reserve Assets................................	79akd	....	....	6,031	14,963	18,219	21,403	28,275	27,315	27,464	26,557	29,784	....
Liabilities..	79lad	....	....	53,075	59,304	58,515	62,439	80,205	89,257	99,999	107,128	123,542	....
Dir. Invest. in Rep. Economy...........	79lbd	....	....	3,789	7,843	11,463	14,587	22,479	26,075	34,227	41,247	47,900	....
Portfolio Investment.......................	79lcd	....	....	8,431	9,375	10,148	11,325	13,658	14,617	18,057	18,895	23,765	....
Equity Securities...........................	79ldd	....	....	443	663	2,279	2,672	4,969	4,980	5,350	4,301	4,398	....
Debt Securities.............................	79led	....	....	7,988	8,712	7,869	8,653	8,689	9,637	12,707	14,594	19,367	....
Financial Derivatives.....................	79lld	....	....	–	–	–	–	–	–	–	–	–	....
Other Investment...........................	79lfd	....	....	40,855	42,086	36,904	36,527	44,068	48,565	47,715	46,986	51,877	....
Monetary Authorities.....................	79lgd	....	....	1,493	174	265	791	925	1,844	436	428	110	....
General Government......................	79lhd	....	....	34,507	35,955	28,709	26,584	27,061	25,199	23,749	19,006	20,775	....
Banks...	79lid	....	....	1,394	1,834	2,231	3,054	4,735	6,404	5,812	6,437	6,916	....
Other Sectors.................................	79ljd	....	....	3,461	4,123	5,699	6,098	11,347	15,118	17,718	21,115	24,076	....
Government Finance							*Millions of Zlotys: Year Ending December 31*						
Deficit (-) or Surplus........................	80	....	....	–4,812	–5,762	–7,826	–8,304	–5,382	–5,021	1,935	–32,025	....	....
Total Revenue and Grants...............	81y	....	....	88,153	117,946	144,462	172,519	196,964	201,250	214,345	224,184	....	....
Revenue...	81	....	....	88,153	117,946	144,454	172,507	196,952	201,131	213,865	223,758	....	....
Grants...	81z	....	....	–	–	8	12	12	119	480	426	....	....
Exp. & Lending Minus Repay..........	82z	....	....	92,965	123,708	152,288	180,823	202,346	206,271	212,410	256,209	....	....
Expenditure....................................	82	....	....	93,039	124,322	153,047	185,431	207,370	216,912	236,865	263,580	....	....
Lending Minus Repayments..........	83	....	....	–74	–614	–759	–4,608	–5,024	–10,641	–24,455	–7,371	....	....
Total Financing...............................	80h	....	....	4,812	5,762	7,826	8,304	5,382	5,021	–1,935	32,025	....	....
Domestic..	84a	....	....	5,855	2,604	8,695	8,393	4,379	4,445	–2,200	42,976	....	....
Foreign...	85a	....	....	–1,043	3,158	–869	–89	1,003	576	265	–10,951	....	....
Total Debt by Residence.................	88	....	....	152,238	167,267	185,603	221,650	237,400	266,750	270,980	291,524	....	....
Domestic..	88a	....	....	55,611	63,083	76,919	97,635	109,647	123,519	134,477	174,705	....	....
Foreign...	89a	....	....	96,627	104,184	108,684	124,015	127,753	143,231	136,503	116,819	....	....
National Accounts							*Millions of Zlotys*						
Househ.Cons.Expend.,incl.NPISHs....	96f	71,925	99,627	142,746	188,416	245,560	301,069	352,063	402,341	454,206	486,375	511,888	....
Government Consumption Expend...	91f	23,819	30,407	37,853	51,747	63,480	75,653	85,497	114,868	127,943	134,667	138,084	....
Gross Fixed Capital Formation..........	93e	19,297	24,749	40,385	57,405	80,390	110,853	139,205	156,690	170,430	157,209	148,338	....
Changes in Inventories....................	93i	–1,860	–520	–715	3,300	4,428	5,150	5,801	5,595	8,132	512	259	....
Exports of Goods and Services.........	90c	27,242	35,733	53,218	78,172	94,192	120,408	155,874	160,787	201,548	210,585	231,409	....
Imports of Goods and Services (-).....	98c	25,479	34,215	48,389	70,935	100,224	140,782	184,879	199,904	248,867	238,562	257,535	....
Gross Domestic Product (GDP).........	99b	114,944	155,780	225,098	308,104	387,827	472,350	553,560	640,378	713,391	750,786	771,113	....
GDP Volume 1995 Prices.................	99b.p	263,635	273,653	287,883	308,104	326,679	348,982	365,882	380,701	440,876	445,065	452,320	....
GDP Volume (2000=100).................	99bvp	59.8	62.1	65.3	69.9	74.1	79.2	83.0	86.4	100.0	101.0	102.6	....
GDP Deflator (2000=100)................	99bip	26.9	35.2	48.3	61.8	73.4	83.6	93.5	104.0	100.0	104.3	105.4	....
							Millions: Midyear Estimates						
Population................................	99z	38.35	38.45	38.53	38.59	38.64	38.67	38.68	38.68	38.67	38.65	38.62	38.59

2004, International Monetary Fund : *International Financial Statistics Yearbook*

Portugal 182

		1992	1993	1994	1995	1996	1997	1998	1999	2000	2001	2002	2003
Exchange Rates		*Escudos per SDR through 1998, Euros per SDR Thereafter: End of Period*											
Market Rate	aa	201.7923	242.8619	232.2519	222.1009	224.8754	247.3526	241.9404	1.3662	1.4002	1.4260	1.2964	1.1765
		Escudos per US Dollar through 1998, Euros per US Dollar Thereafter: End of Period (ae) Period Average (rf)											
Market Rate	ae	146.7580	176.8120	159.0930	149.4130	156.3850	183.3260	171.8290	.9954	1.0747	1.1347	.9536	.7918
Market Rate	rf	134.9978	160.8002	165.9928	151.1055	154.2437	175.3124	180.1045	.9386	1.0854	1.1175	1.0626	.8860
		Escudos per ECU: End of Period (ea) Period Average (eb)											
ECU Rate	ea	177.35	197.20	195.17	191.58	194.27	202.13	201.22	....	....	....	....	....
ECU Rate	eb	174.44	187.80	196.37	194.12	193.18	197.96	201.99	....	....	....	....	....
		Index Numbers (2000=100): Period Averages											
Market Rate (1995=100)	ahx	112.1	94.3	91.2	100.0	97.9	86.3	84.0	....	....	....	....	....
Nominal Effective Exchange Rate	nec	116.3	109.7	105.9	107.7	107.9	105.7	104.5	103.0	100.0	100.6	101.4	104.2
Real Effective Exchange Rate	rec	104.5	101.4	100.2	103.1	104.1	102.2	102.6	102.5	100.0	102.5	105.0	109.1
Fund Position		*Millions of SDRs: End of Period*											
Quota	2f.s	558	558	558	558	558	558	558	867	867	867	867	867
SDRs	1b.s	34	42	48	57	68	79	96	32	41	49	56	61
Reserve Position in the Fund	1c.s	228	219	231	303	320	313	442	275	242	299	329	361
Total Fund Cred.&Loans Outstg.	2tl	–	–	–	–	–	–	–	–	–	–	–	–
International Liquidity		*Millions of US Dollars Unless Otherwise Indicated: End of Period*											
Total Res.Min.Gold (Eurosys.Def)	1l.d	19,129	15,840	15,513	15,850	15,918	15,660	15,825	†8,427	8,909	9,667	11,179	5,876
SDRs	1b.d	46	58	71	85	98	107	135	44	54	62	76	91
Reserve Position in the Fund	1c.d	314	301	337	450	461	423	623	377	316	376	447	536
Foreign Exchange	1d.d	18,769	15,481	15,106	15,315	15,359	15,130	15,067	†8,006	8,539	9,228	10,656	5,249
o/w:Fin.Deriv.Rel.to Reserves	1ddd	....	....	....	....	....	....	....	111.51	271.71	322.42	99.63	29.77
Other Reserve Assets	1e.d	....	....	....	....	....	....	....	–	–	–	–	–
Gold (Million Fine Troy Ounces)	1ad	16.06	16.06	16.07	16.07	16.07	16.07	20.09	19.51	19.51	19.51	19.03	16.63
Gold (Eurosystem Valuation)	1and	5,188	5,189	5,185	5,189	4,993	3,265	3,389	5,661	5,353	5,394	6,522	6,938
Memo:Euro Cl. on Non-EA Res.	1dgd	....	....	....	....	....	....	....	2,795	....	....	....	....
Non-Euro Cl. on EA Res.	1dhd	....	....	....	....	....	....	....	871	978	594	380	424
Mon. Auth.: Other Foreign Assets	3..d	....	....	....	....	....	....	....	3,666	....	....	....	....
Foreign Liabilities	4..d	20	18	122	48	44	144	6	†3,737	3,035	2,885	2,959	2,237
Banking Insts.: Foreign Assets	7a.d	13,903	20,042	28,500	35,922	37,500	47,451	54,669	†25,168	29,902	26,870	28,932	34,875
Foreign Liab.	7b.d	12,270	13,875	21,527	32,432	36,975	48,282	60,976	†31,352	47,626	50,007	62,151	84,365
Monetary Authorities		*Billions of Escudos through 1998; Billions of Euros Beginning 1999: End of Period*											
Fgn. Assets (Cl.on Non-EA Ctys)	11	3,568.2	3,706.7	3,294.8	3,142.8	3,250.5	3,469.8	3,324.6	16.70	15.71	19.77	17.85	11.29
Claims on General Government	12a.u	....	....	....	....	....	....	....	3.48	5.22	2.96	4.83	9.62
o/w: Claims on Gen.Govt.in Cty.	12a	336.2	313.0	289.9	267.6	248.2	217.6	94.6	.39	–	–	–	–
Claims on Banking Institutions	12e.u	....	....	....	....	....	....	....	11.92	4.98	3.58	4.93	7.99
o/w: Claims on Bank.Inst.in Cty.	12e	9.7	266.3	560.1	631.9	261.8	112.5	246.4	2.58	3.30	2.24	1.03	2.54
Claims on Other Resident Sectors	12d.u	....	....	....	....	....	....	....	.30	.58	.43	.23	.24
o/w: Cl. on Oth.Res.Sect.in Cty.	12d	35.0	36.3	45.7	38.2	39.8	41.0	42.6	.22	.22	.23	.23	.24
Currency Issued	14a	708.2	752.9	795.8	841.0	880.9	776.1	923.6	7.25	6.53	5.92	8.46	9.87
Liabilities to Banking Insts	14c.u	....	....	....	....	....	....	....	10.92	8.65	9.80	10.41	12.54
o/w: Liabs to Bank.Inst.in Cty.	14c	2,071.5	2,277.0	432.3	376.8	473.5	558.8	421.1	4.02	3.88	4.81	4.62	11.71
Demand Dep. of Other Res.Sect.	14d.u	....	....	....	....	....	....	....	–	.02	–	–	–
o/w:D.Dep.of Oth.Res.Sect.in Cty.	14d	2.0	1.1	21.6	.6	.2	1.9	.4	–	.02	–	–	–
Other Dep. of Other Res.Sect.	15..u	....	....	....	....	....	....	....	–	–	–	–	–
o/w:O.Dep.of Oth.Res.Sect.in Cty.	15	....	....	....	....	....	....	....	–	–	–	–	–
Bonds & Money Mkt. Instruments	16n.u	....	....	....	....	....	....	....	4.57	3.78	2.94	2.03	1.05
o/w: Held by Resid.of Cty.	16n	....	....	....	....	....	....	....	....	....	....	....	....
Foreign Liab. (to Non-EA Ctys)	16c	2.9	3.1	19.4	7.2	6.9	26.4	1.1	3.72	3.26	3.27	2.82	1.77
Central Government Deposits	16d.u	....	....	....	....	....	....	....	2.24	.01	.01	–	–
o/w: Cent.Govt.Dep. in Cty.	16d	573.9	539.8	510.6	693.0	524.0	486.7	465.1	2.24	.01	.01	–	–
Capital Accounts	17a	184.0	493.9	446.7	303.7	310.3	693.0	588.3	3.85	4.64	5.29	4.78	4.33
Other Items (Net)	17r	406.6	254.5	1,964.1	1,858.4	1,604.5	1,299.0	1,308.6	–.16	–.40	–.49	–.66	–.43
Memo: Net Claims on Eurosystem	12e.s	....	....	....	....	....	....	....	2.45	–3.35	–3.44	–1.65	4.68
Currency Put into Circ.	14m	....	....	....	....	....	....	....	....	....	....	5.97	5.71

Portugal 182

		1992	1993	1994	1995	1996	1997	1998	1999	2000	2001	2002	2003
Banking Institutions		*Billions of Escudos through 1998; Billions of Euros Beginning 1999: End of Period*											
Claims on Monetary Authorities	20	2,325.8	2,188.6	2,158.1	2,090.4	1,891.3	1,648.1	1,617.9	8.26	7.33	7.57	6.51	.96
Claims on Bk.Inst.in Oth.EA Ctys	20b.u	....	....	....	....	....	....	....	18.39	17.30	24.44	25.33	32.03
Fgn. Assets (Cl.on Non-EA Ctys)	21	2,040.3	3,543.7	4,534.1	5,367.2	5,864.5	8,698.9	9,393.7	25.05	32.14	30.49	27.59	27.61
Claims on General Government	22a.u	....	....	....	....	....	....	....	9.53	8.90	10.13	9.54	9.65
o/w: Claims on Gen.Govt.in Cty	22a	3,387.7	3,548.4	4,126.9	4,194.3	3,983.1	3,139.5	2,383.9	8.37	8.50	9.08	8.07	7.92
Claims on Other Resident Sectors	22d.u	....	....	....	....	....	....	....	133.68	168.25	184.23	195.86	202.72
o/w: Cl. on Oth.Res.Sect.in Cty	22d	7,599.2	8,465.2	9,369.0	11,137.5	13,084.8	15,771.6	19,705.1	129.36	160.56	179.18	190.81	193.89
Demand Deposits	24..u	....	....	....	....	....	....	....	40.03	42.50	46.93	46.12	49.00
o/w:D.Dep.of Oth.Res.Sect.in Cty	24	2,556.7	2,861.6	3,038.7	3,435.0	3,914.6	4,637.9	5,411.6	39.68	42.12	46.59	45.70	48.44
Other Deposits	25..u	....	....	....	....	....	....	....	71.25	75.32	78.58	77.80	78.93
o/w:O.Dep.of Oth.Res.Sect.in Cty	25	8,503.4	9,414.9	10,360.4	11,116.5	11,465.1	11,956.0	12,064.7	67.51	71.56	72.37	71.57	71.30
Money Market Fund Shares	26m.u	....	....	....	....	....	....	....	–	.12	.17	.66	1.06
Bonds & Money Mkt. Instruments	26n.u	....	....	....	....	....	....	....	16.91	21.97	25.76	26.48	29.43
o/w: Held by Resid.of Cty	26n	106.7	197.1	169.0	125.7	257.7	331.5	599.5	....	....	....	....	....
Foreign Liab. (to Non-EA Ctys)	26c	1,800.7	2,453.2	3,424.8	4,845.8	5,782.4	8,851.3	10,477.5	31.21	51.18	56.74	59.27	66.80
Central Government Deposits	26d.u	....	....	....	....	....	....	....	5.08	6.42	4.29	5.41	4.07
o/w: Cent.Govt.Dep. in Cty	26d	451.8	454.4	541.2	701.2	800.3	906.7	1,017.4	5.07	6.42	4.27	5.39	4.05
Credit from Monetary Authorities	26g	50.8	296.0	560.3	631.9	261.8	112.5	246.4	2.58	3.30	2.24	1.03	2.54
Liab. to Bk.Inst.in Oth. EA Ctys	26h.u	....	....	....	....	....	....	....	22.51	23.30	32.35	36.07	41.17
Capital Accounts	27a	1,945.7	2,251.7	2,430.8	2,500.8	2,782.6	2,978.4	4,117.9	20.21	22.91	24.57	25.73	30.78
Other Items (Net)	27r	–65.3	–183.6	–338.0	–573.1	–443.1	–515.9	–834.3	–14.87	–13.12	–14.77	–13.74	–30.82
Banking Survey (Nat'l Residency)		*Billions of Escudos through 1998; Billions of Euros Beginning 1999: End of Period*											
Foreign Assets (Net)	31n	3,804.9	4,794.2	4,384.7	3,657.0	3,325.6	3,291.0	2,239.7	10.67	–5.59	–17.74	–23.47	–21.03
Domestic Credit	32	10,332.5	11,368.7	12,779.7	14,243.5	16,031.6	17,776.3	20,743.7	131.03	162.85	184.20	193.72	198.01
Claims on General Govt. (Net)	32an	2,698.3	2,867.2	3,365.0	3,067.8	2,907.0	1,963.7	996.0	1.45	2.07	4.80	2.68	3.88
Claims on Other Resident Sectors	32d	7,634.3	8,501.5	9,414.7	11,175.7	13,124.6	15,812.6	19,747.7	129.58	160.78	179.40	191.04	194.13
Currency Issued	34a.n	708.2	752.9	795.8	841.0	880.9	776.1	923.6	7.25	6.53	5.92	8.46	9.87
Demand Deposits	34b.n	2,558.7	2,862.7	3,060.2	3,435.5	3,914.7	4,639.7	5,412.0	39.69	42.14	46.59	45.70	48.44
Other Deposits	35..n	8,503.4	9,414.9	10,360.4	11,116.5	11,465.1	11,956.0	12,064.7	67.51	71.56	72.37	71.57	71.30
Money Market Fund Shares	36m	....	....	....	....	....	....	....	–	.12	.17	.66	1.06
Bonds & Money Mkt. Instruments	36n	106.7	197.1	169.0	125.7	257.7	331.5	599.5	21.49	25.76	28.69	28.51	30.49
o/w: Over Two Years	36na	....	....	....	....	....	....	....	19.87	23.24	25.79	27.06	28.92
Capital Accounts	37a	2,129.7	2,745.6	2,877.5	2,804.5	3,093.0	3,671.4	4,706.2	24.06	27.55	29.86	30.51	35.12
Other Items (Net)	37r	128.1	189.1	–99.4	–428.4	–256.4	–306.3	–722.4	–18.29	–16.39	–17.13	–15.16	–19.30
Banking Survey (EA-Wide Residency)		*Billions of Euros: End of Period*											
Foreign Assets (Net)	31n.u	....	....	....	....	....	....	....	6.83	–6.60	–9.75	–16.65	–29.67
Domestic Credit	32..u	....	....	....	....	....	....	....	139.67	176.51	193.44	205.05	218.16
Claims on General Govt. (Net)	32anu	....	....	....	....	....	....	....	5.70	7.69	8.78	8.96	15.20
Claims on Other Resident Sect.	32d.u	....	....	....	....	....	....	....	133.97	168.82	184.66	196.09	202.96
Currency Issued	34a.u	....	....	....	....	....	....	....	7.25	6.53	5.92	8.46	9.87
Demand Deposits	34b.u	....	....	....	....	....	....	....	40.03	42.52	46.93	46.13	49.00
Other Deposits	35..u	....	....	....	....	....	....	....	71.25	75.32	78.58	77.80	78.93
o/w: Other Dep. Over Two Yrs	35abu	....	....	....	....	....	....	....	4.03	3.84	3.57	4.43	4.34
Money Market Fund Shares	36m.u	....	....	....	....	....	....	....	–	.12	.17	.66	1.06
Bonds & Money Mkt. Instruments	36n.u	....	....	....	....	....	....	....	21.49	25.76	28.69	28.51	30.49
o/w: Over Two Years	36nau	....	....	....	....	....	....	....	19.87	23.24	25.79	27.06	28.92
Capital Accounts	37a	....	....	....	....	....	....	....	24.06	27.55	29.86	30.51	35.12
Other Items (Net)	37r.u	....	....	....	....	....	....	....	–17.58	–7.87	–6.46	–3.66	–15.98
Money (National Definitions)		*Billions of Escudos: End of Period*											
M1	39ma	3,116.4	3,354.5	3,589.4	3,901.2	4,302.2	4,882.1	5,757.4	....	....	....	....	....
M2	39mb	9,054.3	9,701.9	10,586.2	11,434.5	12,468.2	13,316.2	14,401.3	....	....	....	....	....
L	39mc	8,601.4	9,376.2	10,020.3	11,102.1	11,907.3	12,825.5	13,667.5	....	....	....	....	....
Interest Rates		*Percent Per Annum*											
Banco de Portugal Rate(End of Per)	60	21.96	11.00	8.88	8.50	6.70	5.31	3.00	....	....	....	....	....
Money Market Rate	60b	†17.48	13.25	10.62	8.91	7.38	5.78	4.34	2.71	....	....	....	....
Treasury Bill Rate	60c	12.88	....	....	7.75	5.75	4.43	....	....	....	....	....	....
Deposit Rate	60l	14.59	11.06	8.37	8.38	6.32	4.56	3.37	2.40	....	....	....	....
Lending Rate	60p	20.43	16.48	15.01	13.80	11.73	9.15	7.24	5.19	....	....	....	....
Government Bond Yield	61	15.38	12.45	10.83	10.34	7.25	5.48	4.09	....	....	....	....	....
Prices, Production, Labor		*Index Numbers (2000=100): Period Averages*											
Share Prices (1995=100)	62	67.3	79.3	104.1	100.0	117.3	183.4	287.7	....	....	....	....	....
Producer Prices	63	....	....	....	....	....	....	....	....	100.0	102.8	103.2	104.0
Consumer Prices	64	75.3	80.2	84.4	87.8	90.6	†92.5	95.0	97.2	100.0	104.4	†108.1	111.6
Harmonized CPI	64h	....	....	....	....	....	....	95.2	97.3	100.0	104.4	108.3	111.8
Industrial Production	66	82.1	77.8	77.7	84.7	89.1	91.4	96.6	99.5	100.0	103.1	102.7	102.6
		Number in Thousands: Period Averages											
Labor Force	67d	4,781	4,708	4,799	4,777	4,809	4,645	5,117	5,155	5,235	5,314	5,379	5,460
Employment	67e	†4,587	4,493	4,482	4,442	4,467	4,307	†4,863	4,929	5,024	5,098	5,107	5,079
Unemployment	67c	194	248	396	430	468	443	254	227	206	216	272	342
Unemployment Rate (%)	67r	†4.2	5.6	6.9	7.2	7.3	6.8	5.0	4.4	3.9	4.1	5.1	6.3

Portugal 182

		1992	1993	1994	1995	1996	1997	1998	1999	2000	2001	2002	2003
International Transactions						*Billions of Escudos through 1998; Millions of Euros Beginning 1999*							
Exports	70	2,475.2	2,474.4	2,975.6	3,501.8	3,795.9	4,195.1	4,461.0	†23,715.6	25,241.2	27,322.8	27,089.8	27,101.9
Imports, c.i.f.	71	4,087.6	3,883.8	4,514.3	5,028.7	5,427.1	6,139.7	6,914.8	†37,505.6	41,425.2	44,054.0	40,655.9	36,146.2
Imports, f.o.b.	71.v	3,705.9	3,521.1	4,092.7	4,559.1	4,920.3	....	....	....	....	....	....	....
							2000=100						
Volume of Exports	72	100.5	88.3	101.2	97.9	101.6	100.5	94.4	92.8	100.0	94.6	95.3	97.1
Volume of Imports	73	111.3	87.6	101.6	97.6	101.5	105.7	103.9	100.5	100.0	96.5	93.6	94.5
Export Prices	76	90.6	99.7	101.3	100.1	93.3	96.0	96.2	94.6	100.0	95.7	94.3	91.5
Import Prices	76.x	85.0	94.7	95.1	95.6	92.2	92.7	90.5	91.7	100.0	91.5	89.1	90.0
Balance of Payments						*Millions of US Dollars: Minus Sign Indicates Debit*							
Current Account, n.i.e.	78ald	−184	233	−2,196	−132	−5,216	−6,465	−7,833	−9,733	−11,114	−10,403	−8,118	−7,549
Goods: Exports f.o.b.	78aad	18,348	15,931	18,645	24,024	25,623	25,379	25,618	25,474	25,225	25,251	27,358	33,534
Goods: Imports f.o.b.	78abd	−27,735	−23,981	−26,966	−32,934	−35,345	−35,721	−37,829	−39,187	−39,078	−38,552	−39,240	−45,978
Trade Balance	78acd	−9,387	−8,050	−8,321	−8,910	−9,722	−10,342	−12,211	−13,714	−13,853	−13,301	−11,882	−12,444
Services: Credit	78add	5,497	6,846	6,755	8,236	8,040	8,002	8,829	8,680	8,490	8,840	9,755	11,866
Services: Debit	78aed	−4,732	−5,481	−5,486	−6,611	−6,636	−6,572	−6,903	−6,814	−6,605	−6,343	−6,733	−7,930
Balance on Goods & Services	78afd	−8,621	−6,685	−7,052	−7,285	−8,317	−8,912	−10,285	−11,848	−11,967	−10,804	−8,860	−8,508
Income: Credit	78agd	2,067	2,455	2,232	4,095	4,250	4,238	4,496	4,261	4,570	5,321	5,205	5,544
Income: Debit	78ahd	−1,456	−2,236	−2,797	−4,074	−5,420	−5,744	−6,135	−6,029	−7,101	−8,304	−7,250	−7,993
Balance on Gds, Serv. & Inc.	78aid	−8,010	−6,466	−7,616	−7,264	−9,488	−10,418	−11,924	−13,616	−14,498	−13,786	−10,905	−10,957
Current Transfers, n.i.e.: Credit	78ajd	9,344	8,395	7,410	9,046	6,515	5,985	6,170	6,048	5,386	5,556	5,525	6,401
Current Transfers: Debit	78akd	−1,518	−1,696	−1,989	−1,914	−2,243	−2,031	−2,080	−2,164	−2,001	−2,173	−2,738	−2,993
Capital Account, n.i.e.	78bcd	−	−	−	−	2,695	2,704	2,546	2,459	1,512	1,067	1,917	3,081
Capital Account, n.i.e.: Credit	78bad	−	−	−	−	2,836	2,893	2,724	2,642	1,681	1,278	2,114	3,314
Capital Account: Debit	78bbd	−	−	−	−	−141	−189	−179	−183	−169	−210	−197	−234
Financial Account, n.i.e.	78bjd	−950	−3,032	1,052	3,025	3,835	6,662	5,980	9,107	10,728	10,330	7,343	−1,445
Direct Investment Abroad	78bdd	−687	−147	−287	−688	−972	−2,187	−3,851	−3,019	−7,655	−7,597	−3,462	−125
Dir. Invest. in Rep. Econ., n.i.e.	78bed	1,873	1,534	1,270	685	1,703	2,542	3,151	1,235	6,836	5,822	1,790	969
Portfolio Investment Assets	78bfd	−379	−2,382	−3,456	−3,148	−5,549	−8,697	−5,997	−6,737	−4,583	−7,504	−7,539	−19,272
Equity Securities	78bkd	−9	−168	−66	−159	−602	−568	−975	−2,110	−1,044	−1,644	−1,318	−943
Debt Securities	78bld	−370	−2,214	−3,390	−2,989	−4,947	−8,129	−5,022	−4,626	−3,539	−5,860	−6,221	−18,329
Portfolio Investment Liab., n.i.e.	78bgd	−2,685	4,214	3,934	2,066	2,383	8,790	5,385	9,945	2,792	9,738	10,173	15,430
Equity Securities	78bmd	570	579	562	−179	1,669	3,821	2,165	691	415	2,371	3,212	9,642
Debt Securities	78bnd	−3,255	3,634	3,372	2,244	714	4,970	3,221	9,254	2,376	7,367	6,962	5,787
Financial Derivatives Assets	78bwd	....	−5	−	−	93	341	1,116	2,682	3,673	3,088	3,796	4,740
Financial Derivatives Liabilities	78bxd	....	−	−	−	−130	−360	−985	−2,485	−3,351	−2,831	−3,802	−4,666
Other Investment Assets	78bhd	−1,923	−8,424	−7,098	−7,568	−3,368	−5,346	−7,100	429	−10,873	−4,623	−1,726	−10,676
Monetary Authorities	78bod	−	9	−	−26	−3	1	−94	−1,005	11	21	−295	351
General Government	78bpd	−40	....	....	....	1	11	−	−12	−12	−47	15	6
Banks	78bqd	−2,207	−7,024	−4,741	−6,679	−2,945	−3,116	−3,813	973	−7,201	−1,033	−29	−8,256
Other Sectors	78brd	324	−1,409	−2,358	−863	−422	−2,241	−3,192	473	−3,670	−3,564	−1,417	−2,776
Other Investment Liab., n.i.e.	78bid	2,851	2,178	6,689	11,678	9,675	11,579	14,260	7,055	23,888	14,236	8,113	12,156
Monetary Authorities	78bsd	−24	−32	299	−99	731	1,343	837	−3	4,862	87	699	−6,725
General Government	78btd	−	−146	−139	144	−312	−40	−73	−43	−179	−191	211	−140
Banks	78bud	1,757	1,327	7,069	11,189	8,595	8,936	12,245	6,999	17,715	14,058	8,460	19,470
Other Sectors	78bvd	1,117	1,028	−540	444	661	1,339	1,250	102	1,490	283	−1,258	−449
Net Errors and Omissions	78cad	978	−48	−287	−3,193	−767	−1,928	−184	−1,616	−756	−141	−125	−543
Overall Balance	78cbd	−156	−2,848	−1,430	−300	547	974	508	216	371	852	1,017	−6,455
Reserves and Related Items	79dad	156	2,848	1,430	300	−547	−974	−508	−216	−371	−852	−1,017	6,455
Reserve Assets	79dbd	156	2,848	1,430	300	−547	−974	−508	−216	−371	−852	−1,017	6,455
Use of Fund Credit and Loans	79dcd	−	−	−	−	−	−	−	−	−	−	−	−
Exceptional Financing	79ded	−	....	....	....	−	−	−	−	−	−	−	−
International Investment Position						*Millions of US Dollars*							
Assets	79aad	....	....	....	....	86,425	99,344	128,461	122,341	141,915	154,866	195,759	257,356
Direct Investment Abroad	79abd	....	−	−	−	4,726	5,932	9,622	10,331	17,170	23,491	31,872	38,543
Portfolio Investment	79acd	....	−	−	−	17,502	20,368	28,489	36,459	40,662	45,917	62,100	97,317
Equity Securities	79add	....	....	....	....	4,997	4,765	6,008	7,226	7,624	7,556	8,319	11,453
Debt Securities	79aed	....	....	....	....	12,505	15,602	22,480	29,233	33,038	38,361	53,781	85,864
Financial Derivatives	79ald	....	....	....	....	422	381	355	2,055	2,758	1,929	2,121	2,376
Other Investment	79afd	....	24,170	32,543	37,810	42,030	52,341	68,409	59,396	67,099	68,448	81,966	106,307
Monetary Authorities	79agd	....	−	−	−	47	28	127	1,479	1,367	1,280	1,806	1,717
General Government	79ahd	....	15	15	28	80	78	47	66	74	118	137	171
Banks	79aid	....	18,016	25,149	30,288	29,900	38,718	44,389	39,688	45,084	44,495	51,027	67,724
Other Sectors	79ajd	....	6,139	7,379	7,494	12,003	13,516	23,846	18,163	20,574	22,554	28,995	36,695
Reserve Assets	79akd	....	21,819	21,669	21,954	21,745	20,321	21,586	14,100	14,227	15,082	17,701	12,813
Liabilities	79lad	....	....	....	....	93,951	113,075	154,894	158,378	183,799	202,252	257,295	341,723
Dir. Invest. in Rep. Economy	79lbd	....	....	....	....	18,947	18,605	24,465	24,148	29,040	34,573	43,197	53,527
Portfolio Investment	79lcd	....	8,907	13,656	16,430	21,327	36,207	46,933	51,718	52,413	56,564	74,857	108,726
Equity Securities	79ldd	....	2,929	3,597	3,651	6,573	12,663	18,806	19,487	18,873	15,605	17,411	34,301
Debt Securities	79led	....	5,978	10,059	12,779	14,755	23,544	28,127	32,230	33,541	40,958	57,446	74,425
Financial Derivatives	79lld	....	....	....	....	−	−	63	1,412	2,223	1,185	1,662	2,892
Other Investment	79lfd	....	29,166	37,266	49,532	53,677	58,263	83,432	81,100	100,122	109,931	137,579	176,578
Monetary Authorities	79lgd	....	48	362	278	440	2,084	3,049	2,732	7,470	7,282	9,025	3,286
General Government	79lhd	....	2,099	1,973	2,229	1,676	1,614	2,057	2,114	1,926	1,650	2,140	2,342
Banks	79lid	....	13,875	21,527	32,432	36,320	42,261	56,578	57,823	72,364	83,133	105,593	145,118
Other Sectors	79ljd	....	13,144	13,403	14,592	15,241	12,305	21,748	18,431	18,362	17,866	20,820	25,832

2004, International Monetary Fund : *International Financial Statistics Yearbook*

Portugal 182

		1992	1993	1994	1995	1996	1997	1998	1999	2000	2001	2002	2003
Government Finance													
Central Government		*Billions of Escudos through 1998; Millions of Euros Beginning 1999: Year Ending December 31*											
Deficit (-) or Surplus.........	80	−289.8	−932.7	−708.1	−795.8	−379.9	−372.2	−247.6	....	....	....	....	....
Revenue.........................	81	4,594.7	4,624.9	5,016.5	5,456.7	5,759.9	6,391.8	6,984.7	....	....	....	....	....
Grants Received...............	81z	429.8	446.6	411.6	525.6	662.2	649.9	649.1	....	....	....	....	....
Expenditure.....................	82	5,527.0	6,012.0	6,137.9	6,613.6	6,974.5	7,242.2	7,795.1	....	....	....	....	....
Lending Minus Repayments..	83	−212.7	−7.8	−1.7	164.5	−172.5	171.7	86.3	....	....	....	....	....
Financing													
Domestic.........................	84a	296.5	656.5	659.0	218.2	2.7	−12.1	669.1	....	....	....	....	....
Foreign...........................	85a	−6.7	276.2	49.1	577.6	377.2	384.3	−421.5	....	....	....	....	....
General Government		*As Percent of Gross Domestic Product*											
Deficit (-) or Surplus.........	80g	−3.0	−6.1	−6.0	−5.7	−3.8	−2.7	−2.3	−2.2	−1.5	−2.2	....	....
Debt..............................	88g	60.1	63.1	63.8	65.9	63.6	59.1	54.8	54.2	53.2	55.6	....	....
National Accounts		*Billions of Escudos through 1998; Millions of Euros Beginning 1999*											
Househ.Cons.Expend.,incl.NPISHs....	96f	8,600	9,133	9,870	10,456	11,052	11,639	12,646	†67,394	71,116	74,968	78,125	80,433
Government Consumption Expend...	91f	2,363	2,596	2,781	3,019	3,298	3,546	3,896	†21,254	23,697	25,569	27,450	27,649
Gross Fixed Capital Formation.........	93e	3,194	3,142	3,439	3,743	4,005	4,498	4,992	†30,585	33,703	34,552	33,407	29,791
Changes in Inventories.................	93i	112	−18	56	115	95	101	108	†1,123	1,047	1,082	1,139	167
Exports of Goods and Services.........	90c	2,960	3,050	3,583	4,168	4,482	4,891	5,301	†32,089	36,536	38,097	38,957	40,076
Imports of Goods and Services (-).....	98c	4,485	4,458	5,111	5,698	6,123	6,798	7,698	†43,293	49,505	50,136	48,704	47,502
Gross Domestic Product (GDP).........	99b	12,743	13,445	14,617	15,802	16,809	17,876	19,246	†108,030	115,546	123,054	129,280	130,448
Net Primary Income from Abroad.....	98.n	145	141	178	412	568	624	....	....	....	....	....	....
Gross National Income (GNI)...........	99a	12,704	13,436	14,541	15,660	16,513	17,558	....	....	....	....	....	....
GDP Volume 1995 Prices................	99b.p	15,192	14,983	15,353	15,802	16,306	16,871	17,460	†94,450	97,933	99,540	99,973	98,577
GDP Volume (2000=100)................	99bvp	77.4	76.3	78.2	80.5	83.0	85.9	88.9	†96.4	100.0	101.6	102.1	100.7
GDP Deflator (2000=100)................	99bip	71.1	76.1	80.7	84.8	87.4	89.8	93.4	†96.9	100.0	104.8	109.6	112.2
		Millions: Midyear Estimates											
Population...............................	99z	9.88	9.89	9.90	9.92	9.93	9.95	9.97	10.00	10.02	10.03	10.05	10.06

2004, International Monetary Fund : *International Financial Statistics Yearbook*

Qatar 453

		1992	1993	1994	1995	1996	1997	1998	1999	2000	2001	2002	2003
Exchange Rates		\multicolumn{12}{c}{*Riyals per SDR: End of Period*}
Official Rate	aa	5.0050	4.9998	5.3139	5.4108	5.2342	4.9113	5.1252	4.9959	4.7426	4.5745	4.9487	5.4089
		\multicolumn{12}{c}{*Riyals per US Dollar: End of Period (ae) Period Average (rf)*}
Official Rate	ae	3.6400	3.6400	3.6400	3.6400	3.6400	3.6400	3.6400	3.6400	3.6400	3.6400	3.6400	3.6400
Official Rate	rf	3.6400	3.6400	3.6400	3.6400	3.6400	3.6400	3.6400	3.6400	3.6400	3.6400	3.6400	3.6400
		\multicolumn{12}{c}{*Index Numbers (2000=100): Period Averages*}
Official Rate	ahx	100.0	100.0	100.0	100.0	100.0	100.0	100.0	100.0	100.0	100.0	100.0	100.0
Nominal Effective Exchange Rate	nec	75.4	82.8	85.4	81.6	84.7	91.1	95.1	94.8	100.0	105.1	103.2	93.9
Fund Position		\multicolumn{12}{c}{*Millions of SDRs: End of Period*}
Quota	2f.s	190.5	190.5	190.5	190.5	190.5	190.5	190.5	263.8	263.8	263.8	263.8	263.8
SDRs	1b.s	17.1	18.7	19.9	21.2	22.5	23.8	25.1	10.7	15.8	17.9	20.0	21.7
Reserve Position in the Fund	1c.s	36.4	33.8	30.7	29.7	29.2	26.4	26.4	44.7	44.7	79.1	99.6	103.5
International Liquidity		\multicolumn{12}{c}{*Millions of US Dollars Unless Otherwise Indicated: End of Period*}
Total Reserves minus Gold	1l.d	683.3	693.7	657.7	743.8	686.2	820.6	1,043.3	1,304.2	1,158.0	1,312.7	1,566.8	2,944.2
SDRs	1b.d	23.4	25.6	29.0	31.5	32.4	32.1	35.3	14.6	20.6	22.5	27.2	32.3
Reserve Position in the Fund	1c.d	50.1	46.4	44.7	44.2	42.0	35.6	37.2	61.4	58.3	99.4	135.4	153.7
Foreign Exchange	1d.d	609.8	621.7	584.0	668.1	611.8	752.9	970.8	1,228.2	1,079.1	1,190.8	1,404.2	2,758.1
Gold (Million Fine Troy Ounces)	1ad	.861	.862	.814	.268	.268	.054	.054	.019	.019	.019	.019	.019
Gold (National Valuation)	1and	41.5	41.5	41.6	41.6	41.6	15.7	15.5	5.5	5.2	5.3	6.7	7.9
Deposit Money Banks: Assets	7a.d	2,195.0	†2,264.3	2,648.0	3,093.7	2,396.3	2,643.4	2,324.3	2,455.5	3,193.1	3,163.5	4,102.9	5,347.5
Liabilities	7b.d	58.2	†1,370.4	1,381.3	1,768.2	1,026.6	1,274.4	1,497.6	1,605.5	611.3	586.9	655.0	1,050.9
Monetary Authorities		\multicolumn{12}{c}{*Millions of Riyals: End of Period*}
Foreign Assets	11	2,638	†2,686	2,546	2,859	2,649	3,044	3,854	4,767	4,234	4,798	5,727	10,746
Claims on Central Government	12a	....	....	....	437	546	437	—	1,467	—	124	135	16
Claims on Deposit Money Banks	12e	151	†150	260	205	212	194	1,589	82	124	97	28	3
Reserve Money	14	2,086	2,181	2,030	2,131	2,261	2,481	2,557	2,868	3,061	3,416	3,995	4,590
of which: Currency Outside DMBs	14a	1,321	1,350	1,350	1,407	1,404	1,555	1,499	1,714	1,673	1,741	1,921	2,148
Central Government Deposits	16d	138	†33	42	381	116	120	145	30	41	26	38	51
Capital Accounts	17a	94	†576	705	1,178	1,242	1,339	1,466	1,536	1,456	1,402	1,848	6,112
Other Items (Net)	17r	470	†46	30	−188	−212	−265	1,275	1,881	−202	174	8	11
Deposit Money Banks		\multicolumn{12}{c}{*Millions of Riyals: End of Period*}
Reserves	20	768	830	680	739	852	919	1,064	1,169	1,368	1,678	2,068	2,435
Foreign Assets	21	7,990	†8,242	9,639	11,261	8,723	9,622	8,460	8,938	11,623	11,515	14,934	19,465
Claims on Central Government	22a	....	9,031	10,050	10,028	11,873	12,863	16,151	19,064	17,225	23,882	22,319	23,518
Claims on Nonfin.Pub.Enterprises	22c	....	232	228	384	728	878	609	537	621	790	1,789	3,343
Claims on Private Sector	22d	18,113	†10,948	9,544	10,267	10,251	12,548	14,451	15,664	17,338	17,614	19,374	23,865
Demand Deposits	24	2,669	†2,904	2,561	2,313	2,481	2,575	2,717	2,465	2,776	3,479	4,368	9,130
Time, Savings,& Fgn.Currency Dep.	25	11,036	†12,635	14,509	14,901	15,772	17,466	19,117	21,804	24,307	23,535	25,858	25,945
Foreign Liabilities	26c	212	†4,988	5,028	6,436	3,737	4,639	5,451	5,844	2,225	2,136	2,384	3,825
Central Government Deposits	26d	5,020	†3,394	1,903	2,671	3,795	4,601	5,248	6,540	9,262	15,504	15,544	17,610
Credit from Monetary Authorities	26g	43	18	91	69	60	140	72	94	140	115	22	98
Capital Accounts	27a	2,762	†4,659	5,049	5,473	5,702	6,249	6,821	7,467	8,070	8,925	10,189	10,618
Other Items (Net)	27r	5,129	†685	1,001	815	880	1,160	1,309	1,157	1,394	1,785	2,120	5,399
Monetary Survey		\multicolumn{12}{c}{*Millions of Riyals: End of Period*}
Foreign Assets (Net)	31n	10,416	†5,940	7,156	7,682	7,635	8,026	6,862	7,861	13,631	14,174	18,274	26,378
Domestic Credit	32	12,955	†16,785	17,879	18,064	19,488	22,007	25,819	30,162	25,881	26,883	28,038	33,083
Claims on Central Govt. (Net)	32an	−5,158	†5,604	8,105	7,413	8,508	8,579	10,757	13,960	7,922	8,475	6,872	5,872
Claims on Nonfin.Pub.Enterprises	32c	....	232	228	384	728	878	609	537	621	790	1,789	3,343
Claims on Private Sector	32d	18,113	†10,949	9,545	10,268	10,252	12,550	14,453	15,665	17,338	17,617	19,377	23,868
Money	34	3,990	†4,254	3,910	3,720	3,885	4,131	4,216	4,179	4,449	5,219	6,289	11,278
Quasi-Money	35	11,036	†12,635	14,509	14,901	15,772	17,466	19,117	21,804	24,307	23,535	25,858	25,945
Other Items (Net)	37r	8,345	†5,836	6,616	7,125	7,467	8,437	9,348	12,041	10,755	12,303	14,165	22,238
Money plus Quasi-Money	35l	15,026	†16,889	18,419	18,622	19,657	21,596	23,333	25,982	28,756	28,755	32,147	37,223
Interest Rates		\multicolumn{12}{c}{*Percent Per Annum*}
Deposit Rate	60l	4.8	4.1	4.8	6.2	6.5	6.6	6.6	6.5	....	....	....	....
Lending Rate	60p	8.1	7.2	8.9	....	....	....	....	....	....	....	....	....
Prices and Production		\multicolumn{12}{c}{*Index Numbers (2000=100): Period Averages*}
Consumer Prices	64	82.2	81.5	82.6	85.0	91.3	93.8	96.3	98.3	100.0	†101.4	101.7	104.0
Crude Petroleum	66aa	56.3	58.6	57.6	63.6	67.6	87.4	94.9	93.3	100.0	95.4	90.9	108.0
International Transactions		\multicolumn{12}{c}{*Millions of Riyals*}
Exports	70	....	....	11,453	12,672	13,659	13,801	17,763	25,703	....	....	....	....
Imports, c.i.f	71	7,336	6,882	7,016	12,369	10,441	12,091	12,407	9,098	11,838	13,678	14,749	....

Qatar 453

		1992	1993	1994	1995	1996	1997	1998	1999	2000	2001	2002	2003
National Accounts							*Millions of Riyals*						
Househ.Cons.Expend.,incl.NPISHs....	96f	8,519	8,557	8,030	9,497	8,996	9,335	9,450	9,525	9,843	10,176	....	....
Government Consumption Expend...	91f	9,258	9,370	9,250	9,436	10,886	12,236	11,789	11,573	12,715	12,910	....	....
Gross Fixed Capital Formation..........	93e	5,159	4,849	6,575	8,895	11,532	14,226	11,540	8,273	12,584	14,100	....	....
Changes in Inventories.....................	93i	583	300	8	1,495	262	345	395	245	443	550	....	....
Exports of Goods and Services..........	90c	14,203	12,011	12,046	13,134	14,419	19,855	19,074	27,085	43,496	40,884	....	....
Imports of Goods and Services (-).....	98c	9,890	9,037	9,066	12,835	13,119	14,873	14,918	11,590	14,435	16,279	....	....
Gross Domestic Product (GDP).........	99b	27,832	26,050	26,843	29,622	32,976	41,124	37,330	45,111	64,646	64,579	65,088	70,828
						Millions: Midyear Estimates							
Population...............................	99z	.49	.50	.51	Ü .52	.53	.55	.56	.57	.58	.59	.60	.61

2004, International Monetary Fund : *International Financial Statistics Yearbook*

Romania 968

		1992	1993	1994	1995	1996	1997	1998	1999	2000	2001	2002	2003
Exchange Rates						*Lei per SDR: End of Period*							
Market Rate	aa	632.5	1,752.7	2,579.6	3,832.2	5,802.2	10,825.0	15,419.3	25,055.2	33,779.2	39,708.9	45,543.9	48,435.2
					Lei per US Dollar: End of Period (ae) Period Average (rf)								
Market Rate	ae	460.0	1,276.0	1,767.0	2,578.0	4,035.0	8,023.0	10,951.0	18,255.0	25,926.0	31,597.0	33,500.0	32,595.0
Market Rate	rf	308.0	760.1	1,655.1	2,033.3	3,084.2	7,167.9	8,875.6	15,332.8	21,708.7	29,060.8	33,055.4	33,200.1
					Index Numbers (2000=100): Period Averages								
Nominal Effective Exchange Rate	nec	5,206.49	2,240.54	992.97	781.08	538.38	258.38	215.68	129.73	100.00	77.84	67.03	58.92
Real Effective Exchange Rate	rec	54.35	75.29	80.78	78.90	71.21	82.82	107.58	91.46	100.00	101.48	104.20	105.27
Fund Position						*Millions of SDRs: End of Period*							
Quota	2f.s	754	754	754	754	754	754	754	1,030	1,030	1,030	1,030	1,030
SDRs	1b.s	8	1	38	38	3	77	1	7	1	5	2	—
Reserve Position in the Fund	1c.s	—	—	—	—	—	—	—	—	—	—	—	—
Total Fund Cred.&Loans Outstg	2tl	751	751	906	698	453	475	383	334	348	308	315	401
International Liquidity						*Millions of US Dollars Unless Otherwise Indicated: End of Period*							
Total Reserves minus Gold	1l.d	826	995	2,086	1,579	2,103	3,803	2,867	2,687	3,922	5,442	7,211	9,002
SDRs	1b.d	11	2	56	56	4	104	1	10	1	7	2	—
Reserve Position in the Fund	1c.d	—	—	—	—	—	—	—	—	—	—	—	—
Foreign Exchange	1d.d	815	994	2,031	1,523	2,099	3,700	2,866	2,677	3,921	5,435	7,209	9,002
o/w: Held by Dep.Money Banks	1e.d	730	....	....	....	....	....	....	....	....	....	....	....
Gold (Million Fine Troy Ounces)	1ad	2.307	2.370	2.625	2.703	2.818	3.019	3.224	3.323	3.374	3.382	3.386	3.378
Gold (National Valuation)	1and	780	924	965	780	520	458	358	967	920	939	1,180	1,410
Deposit Money Banks: Assets	7a.d	132	223	129	73	72	79	87	91	95	94	105	126
Liabilities	7b.d	461	560	687	823	1,238	1,148	933	611	508	661	1,004	2,214
Monetary Authorities						*Billions of Lei: End of Period*							
Foreign Assets	11	405	†1,234	2,796	2,942	6,432	24,849	25,182	45,581	88,067	153,654	244,776	308,037
Claims on Government	12a	263	†336	1,771	3,562	—	3,271	9,142	21,412	16,176	8,415	2,484	5
Claims on Deposit Money Banks	12e	353	†1,880	2,395	4,724	8,822	3,367	3,618	2,433	2,296	1,148	—	—
Reserve Money	14	859	†2,031	3,809	5,952	9,008	21,305	25,738	49,520	76,598	122,483	189,463	227,272
of which: Currency Outside DMBs	14a	460	1,049	2,201	3,764	5,383	9,200	11,525	17,372	25,742	35,635	45,577	57,978
Transit Accounts	14x	−36	27	21	14	—	—	27	264	294	—	15	—
Foreign Liabilities	16c	475	†1,317	2,444	3,502	7,810	15,167	17,639	15,885	22,028	12,235	14,348	19,410
Central Government Deposits	16d	163	†496	1,354	2,660	−275	701	163	5,947	3,360	8,899	10,672	12,722
Other Items (Net)	17r	−441	†−421	−666	−899	−1,290	−5,686	−5,624	−2,190	4,261	19,600	32,763	48,639
Deposit Money Banks						*Billions of Lei: End of Period*							
Reserves	20	443	†1,462	2,416	3,293	3,632	5,347	13,050	35,014	51,038	87,125	143,956	169,128
Foreign Assets	21	298	†1,312	2,746	3,723	6,554	13,551	17,301	22,904	40,131	50,967	39,898	35,360
Claims on Central Government	22a	—	398	584	1,839	5,469	11,099	18,833	29,850	31,718	37,994	42,896	26,234
Claims on Nonfin.Pub.Enterprises	22c	1,912	4,902	9,485	16,099	13,202	12,749	11,734	9,223	10,854	16,633	24,169	30,924
Claims on Private Sector	22d	....	†−	—	—	12,516	21,146	43,180	44,031	57,624	90,242	126,250	179,964
Claims on Nonbank Financial Insts	22g	....	—	—	—	1,124	1,986	4,172	4,511	6,529	11,380	29,208	94,594
Demand Deposits	24	600	1,018	2,094	3,007	5,366	8,742	9,590	11,059	18,579	25,968	38,329	49,620
Transit Accounts	24x	153	159	212	354	615	110	328	364	682	1,421	671	1,127
Savings Deposits	25	376	890	3,605	6,939	11,901	25,625	40,219	53,973	63,873	90,419	138,599	176,323
Other Term Deposits	25a	121	219	390	444	580	898	994	1,238	2,011	2,706	4,397	5,662
Foreign Currency Deposits	25b	281	1,296	2,358	3,953	7,086	17,681	30,202	50,473	74,856	115,784	146,812	171,169
Foreign Liabilities	26c	212	715	1,213	2,121	4,996	9,213	10,213	11,158	13,181	20,897	33,642	72,160
Government Deposits	26d	237	885	1,303	1,810	1,135	2,167	5,749	5,638	7,024	13,030	14,691	18,755
Credit from Monetary Authorities	26g	343	1,568	2,316	3,179	8,024	632	556	1,930	2,296	1,148	—	—
Capital Accounts	27a	254	565	896	2,505	5,064	9,681	10,888	17,549	24,731	49,502	64,511	80,573
Other Items (Net)	27r	154	†758	843	643	−2,270	−8,869	−477	−7,849	−9,338	−26,534	−35,272	−39,183
Monetary Survey						*Billions of Lei: End of Period*							
Foreign Assets (Net)	31n	15	†514	1,884	1,043	181	14,020	14,632	41,442	92,989	171,489	236,685	251,828
Domestic Credit	32	1,912	4,255	9,183	17,030	31,450	47,384	81,150	97,442	112,517	142,734	199,644	300,245
Claims on Central Govt. (Net)	32an	....	†−647	−301	931	4,609	11,503	22,063	39,677	37,510	24,479	20,018	−5,237
Claims on Nonfin.Pub.Enterprises	32c	1,912	4,902	9,485	16,099	13,202	12,749	11,734	9,223	10,854	16,633	24,169	30,924
Claims on Private Sector	32d	....	—	—	—	12,516	21,146	43,180	44,031	57,624	90,242	126,250	179,964
Claims on Nonbank Financial Inst.	32g	....	—	—	—	1,124	1,986	4,172	4,511	6,529	11,380	29,208	94,594
Money	34	1,060	2,067	4,294	6,771	10,749	17,942	21,115	28,431	44,320	61,603	83,907	107,598
Transit Accounts	34x	117	185	233	368	615	110	355	628	975	1,421	685	1,127
Quasi-Money	35	778	2,405	6,353	11,336	19,567	44,203	71,415	105,684	140,740	208,909	289,808	353,153
Other Items (Net)	37r	−28	†111	187	−403	700	−852	2,888	4,141	19,471	42,290	61,932	90,195
Money plus Quasi-Money	35l	1,838	4,472	10,648	18,107	30,316	62,145	92,530	134,114	185,060	270,512	373,714	460,751
Interest Rates						*Percent Per Annum*							
Bank Rate (End of Period)	60a	....	....	66.9	41.3	35.1	45.0	37.9	35.0	35.0	35.0	29.0	18.8
Treasury Bill Rate	60c	....	....	....	....	51.1	85.7	64.0	74.2	51.9	42.2	27.0	....

Romania 968

		1992	1993	1994	1995	1996	1997	1998	1999	2000	2001	2002	2003
Prices, Production, Labor							*Index Numbers (2000=100): Period Averages*						
Producer Prices	63	1.0	2.7	6.5	8.8	13.2	33.9	45.1	65.2	100.0	141.0	175.8	210.1
Consumer Prices	64	.8	2.7	6.3	8.4	11.6	29.6	47.1	68.6	100.0	134.5	164.8	189.9
Wages: Avg. Earnings	65	.9	2.8	6.4	9.9	14.8	29.1	48.0	71.5	100.0	138.9	178.6	224.0
Industrial Production	66	101.9	†102.4	105.6	115.6	†127.0	118.7	†98.4	93.3	100.0	108.5	†115.0	118.8
Industrial Employment (1990=100)	67	78.2	....	....	....	....	....	....	....	....	....	....	....
						Number in Thousands: Period Averages								
Labor Force	67d	10,465	....	....	12,120	11,726	11,756	11,577	....	11,585	11,447	10,079	....
Employment	67e	†10,458	10,062	†10,914	11,152	10,936	11,050	10,845	10,776	10,764	10,697	9,673	....
Unemployment	67c	929	1,165	†1,224	998	658	706	733	1,119	1,067	867	955	704
Unemployment Rate (%)	67r	8.2	10.4	†11.0	10.0	7.8	7.5	9.3	11.3	11.2	9.0	10.0	7.5
International Transactions							*Millions of US Dollars*							
Exports	70..d	4,363.4	4,892.2	6,151.3	7,910.0	8,084.5	8,431.1	8,299.6	8,504.7	10,366.5	11,390.7	13,875.7	17,618.5
Imports, c.i.f	71..d	6,259.6	6,521.7	7,109.0	10,277.9	11,435.3	11,279.7	11,821.0	10,392.1	13,054.5	15,560.9	17,861.7	24,002.7
Imports, f.o.b	71.vd	5,784.1	6,020.1	6,562.4	9,486.7	10,555.0	10,411.4	10,911.0	9,592.1	12,049.6	14,362.9	16,486.7	22,155.1
Balance of Payments						*Millions of US Dollars: Minus Sign Indicates Debit*								
Current Account, n.i.e.	78ald	−1,506	−1,231	−455	−1,780	−2,579	−2,104	−2,917	−1,297	−1,355	−2,229	−1,525	−3,311
Goods: Exports f.o.b	78aad	4,364	4,892	6,151	7,910	8,085	8,431	8,302	8,503	10,366	11,385	13,876	17,618
Goods: Imports f.o.b	78abd	−5,558	−6,020	−6,562	−9,487	−10,555	−10,411	−10,927	−9,595	−12,050	−14,354	−16,487	−22,155
Trade Balance	78acd	−1,194	−1,128	−411	−1,577	−2,470	−1,980	−2,625	−1,092	−1,684	−2,969	−2,611	−4,537
Services: Credit	78add	659	799	1,044	1,494	1,563	1,523	1,226	1,365	1,747	2,032	2,347	3,028
Services: Debit	78aed	−946	−914	−1,215	−1,819	−1,948	−1,904	−1,829	−1,785	−1,993	−2,153	−2,338	−2,958
Balance on Goods & Services	78afd	−1,481	−1,243	−582	−1,902	−2,855	−2,361	−3,228	−1,512	−1,930	−3,090	−2,602	−4,467
Income: Credit	78agd	54	63	116	81	78	204	263	152	325	455	413	372
Income: Debit	78ahd	−144	−208	−245	−322	−387	−526	−705	−563	−610	−737	−872	−1,077
Balance on Gds, Serv. & Inc.	78aid	−1,571	−1,388	−711	−2,143	−3,164	−2,683	−3,670	−1,923	−2,215	−3,372	−3,061	−5,172
Current Transfers, n.i.e.: Credit	78ajd	136	174	317	473	667	731	886	804	1,079	1,417	1,808	2,200
Current Transfers: Debit	78akd	−71	−17	−61	−110	−82	−152	−133	−178	−219	−274	−272	−339
Capital Account, n.i.e	78bcd	−	−	−	32	152	43	39	45	36	95	93	213
Capital Account, n.i.e.: Credit	78bad	−	−	−	32	152	43	39	46	37	108	100	223
Capital Account: Debit	78bbd	−	−	−	−	−	−	−	−1	−1	−13	−7	−10
Financial Account, n.i.e	78bjd	1,380	640	535	812	1,486	2,458	2,042	697	2,102	2,938	4,079	4,400
Direct Investment Abroad	78bdd	−4	−7	−	−2	−	9	9	−16	11	17	−16	−39
Dir. Invest. in Rep. Econ., n.i.e	78bed	77	94	341	419	263	1,215	2,031	1,041	1,037	1,157	1,144	1,844
Portfolio Investment Assets	78bfd	−	−73	75	−22	−	−6	1	9	28	−8	−	9
Equity Securities	78bkd	−	−	−	−4	−	−6	1	9	31	−7	−	14
Debt Securities	78bld	−	−73	75	−18	−	−	−	−	−3	−1	−	−5
Portfolio Investment Liab., n.i.e	78bgd	−	−	−	54	193	540	129	−724	73	583	382	569
Equity Securities	78bmd	−	−	−	−	−	195	95	68	58	8	21	69
Debt Securities	78bnd	−	−	−	54	193	345	34	−792	15	575	361	500
Financial Derivatives Assets	78bwd	....	....	....	−	−	−	−	−	....	....	....	....
Financial Derivatives Liabilities	78bxd	....	....	....	−	−	−	−	−	....	....	....	....
Other Investment Assets	78bhd	94	−45	−671	186	−271	−6	208	246	−407	−44	692	72
Monetary Authorities	78bod	....	−	−	−	−	−	−	−	....	−	−	−1
General Government	78bpd	112	−49	−24	−62	−9	10	−10	9	−82	−44	−41	−36
Banks	78bqd	−	−168	−621	254	−315	−140	179	236	−354	−102	536	229
Other Sectors	78brd	−18	172	−26	−6	53	124	39	1	29	102	197	−120
Other Investment Liab., n.i.e	78bid	1,213	671	790	177	1,301	706	−336	141	1,360	1,233	1,877	1,945
Monetary Authorities	78bsd	−159	−	−	−	−150	−	−	73	−14	−	−100	−
General Government	78btd	812	68	75	−27	209	547	−7	40	681	320	465	889
Banks	78bud	−73	19	190	−57	536	−132	−260	−54	−107	159	309	918
Other Sectors	78bvd	633	584	525	261	706	291	−69	82	800	754	1,203	138
Net Errors and Omissions	78cad	−12	152	91	456	359	1,062	193	794	125	731	−856	−289
Overall Balance	78cbd	−138	−439	171	−480	−582	1,459	−643	239	908	1,535	1,791	1,013
Reserves and Related Items	79dad	138	439	−171	480	582	−1,459	643	−239	−908	−1,535	−1,791	−1,013
Reserve Assets	79dbd	−124	54	−616	259	−218	−1,664	844	−173	−928	−1,484	−1,802	−1,134
Use of Fund Credit and Loans	79dcd	262	−	217	−316	−356	29	−126	−66	20	−51	11	120
Exceptional Financing	79ded	−	385	228	536	1,157	176	−75	−	....	−	....	....

Romania 968

		1992	1993	1994	1995	1996	1997	1998	1999	2000	2001	2002	2003
International Investment Position						*Millions of US Dollars*							
Assets	79aad	7,249	7,483	8,847	8,492	7,832	9,046	8,365	8,216	9,494	11,418	13,292	15,574
Direct Investment Abroad	79abd	79	104	107	121	120	114	123	103	136	117	144	211
Portfolio Investment	79acd	1,124	1,208	1,179	1,224	13	11	23	34	6	11	11	9
Equity Securities	79add	1,113	1,124	1,176	1,211	–	–	–	30	5	10	10	–
Debt Securities	79aed	11	84	3	13	13	11	23	4	–	–	1	9
Financial Derivatives	79ald	–	–	–	–	–	–	–	–	–	–	–	–
Other Investment	79afd	5,187	5,215	5,964	5,768	6,107	5,860	5,921	5,587	5,963	6,430	5,831	5,904
Monetary Authorities	79agd	–	–	–	–	10	10	10	10	10	10	10	10
General Government	79ahd	2,929	2,990	3,004	3,006	3,109	2,926	3,058	3,727	3,807	3,873	3,921	3,970
Banks	79aid	730	871	1,491	1,244	1,556	1,637	1,472	1,178	1,487	1,552	1,099	978
Other Sectors	79ajd	1,529	1,355	1,468	1,517	1,432	1,288	1,382	672	659	995	801	945
Reserve Assets	79akd	858	956	1,598	1,380	1,592	3,061	2,299	2,493	3,390	4,861	7,306	9,450
Liabilities	79lad	5,276	6,196	7,500	7,976	10,318	12,846	15,097	15,360	17,957	20,878	25,523	33,919
Dir. Invest. in Rep. Economy	79lbd	122	216	402	421	1,097	2,352	4,418	5,469	6,480	7,638	9,369	13,051
Portfolio Investment	79lcd	943	858	719	785	1,229	2,023	2,249	1,605	1,654	2,187	3,234	4,451
Equity Securities	79ldd	943	858	719	732	–	266	361	429	487	495	516	700
Debt Securities	79led	–	–	–	54	1,229	1,757	1,888	1,176	1,167	1,692	2,718	3,751
Financial Derivatives	79lld	–	–	–	–	–	–	–	–	–	–	–	–
Other Investment	79lfd	4,212	5,123	6,379	6,770	7,991	8,471	8,430	8,286	9,823	11,053	12,920	16,417
Monetary Authorities	79lgd	1,032	1,031	1,383	1,358	941	958	580	572	553	487	428	595
General Government	79lhd	1,944	2,388	2,298	2,335	2,512	2,916	3,000	3,111	3,748	4,281	4,999	6,353
Banks	79lid	447	504	682	743	1,268	832	679	567	506	654	1,003	2,174
Other Sectors	79ljd	789	1,200	2,016	2,334	3,270	3,765	4,170	4,036	5,016	5,631	6,491	7,295
Government Finance						*Billions of Lei: Year Ending December 31*							
Deficit (-) or Surplus	80	−282	−94	−1,248	−2,133	−4,377	−9,755	−11,033	−9,230	−31,769	−35,410	....	....
Revenue	81	2,200	6,389	14,884	21,327	30,194	68,394	107,051	171,135	237,161	311,320	....	....
Grants	81z	–	–	–	–	–	–	695	4,235	880	1,345	....	....
Expenditure	82	2,406	6,312	15,913	22,927	34,033	79,734	124,595	191,341	273,990	354,837	....	....
Lending Minus Repayments	83	77	171	220	533	538	−1,585	−5,816	−6,741	−4,180	−6,762	....	....
Financing													
Domestic	84a	282	94	1,248	....	....	7,524	....	....	23,976	25,670	....	....
Foreign	85a	–	–	–	....	....	2,232	....	....	7,794	9,740	....	....
National Accounts						*Billions of Lei*							
Househ.Cons.Expend.,incl.NPISHs	96f	3,781	12,763	31,601	48,785	75,665	187,620	283,142	405,322	563,182	817,809	1,041,810	1,303,314
Government Consumption Expend	91f	861	2,473	6,852	9,877	14,274	31,000	54,327	79,040	129,351	176,928	201,297	271,223
Gross Fixed Capital Formation	93e	1,157	3,584	10,096	15,425	24,999	53,540	67,920	96,630	151,947	241,154	322,383	425,917
Changes in Inventories	93i	737	2,212	2,253	2,085	3,161	−1,369	−1,586	−8,890	4,544	22,295	33,432	40,063
Exports of Goods and Services	90c	1,676	4,612	12,394	19,921	30,651	73,796	84,559	152,903	264,187	389,147	536,758	685,002
Imports of Goods and Services (-)	98c	2,182	5,608	13,422	23,958	39,831	91,661	114,563	179,275	309,437	479,646	623,063	834,739
Gross Domestic Product (GDP)	99b	6,029	20,036	49,773	72,136	108,920	252,926	373,798	545,730	803,773	1,167,687	1,512,617	1,890,778
GDP Volume 1995 Prices	99b.p	63,809	64,780	67,329	72,136	74,984	70,445	67,051	66,280	67,704	71,594	75,140	78,785
GDP Volume (2000=100)	99bvp	94.2	95.7	99.4	106.5	110.8	104.0	99.0	97.9	100.0	105.7	111.0	116.4
GDP Deflator (2000=100)	99bip	.8	2.6	6.2	8.4	12.2	30.2	47.0	69.4	100.0	137.4	169.6	202.2
						Millions: Midyear Estimates							
Population	99z	23.06	22.92	22.79	22.68	22.61	22.56	22.54	22.51	22.48	22.44	22.39	22.33

Russia 922

		1992	1993	1994	1995	1996	1997	1998	1999	2000	2001	2002	2003
Exchange Rates							*Rubles per SDR: End of Period*						
Official Rate	aa	.5706	1.7128	5.1825	6.8973	7.9951	8.0415	†29.0758	37.0578	36.6899	37.8778	43.2115	43.7685
						Rubles per US Dollar: End of Period (ae) Period Average (rf)								
Official Rate	ae	.4150	1.2470	3.5500	4.6400	5.5600	5.9600	†20.6500	27.0000	28.1600	30.1400	31.7844	29.4545
Official Rate	rf	....	.9917	2.1908	4.5592	5.1208	5.7848	†9.7051	24.6199	28.1292	29.1685	31.3485	30.6920
					Index Numbers (2000=100): Period Averages									
Nominal Effective Exchange Rate	nec	....	....	472.81	290.15	281.62	286.92	233.02	94.33	100.00	105.73	99.64	94.87
Real Effective Exchange Rate	rec	....	....	102.96	112.86	137.62	145.18	128.47	90.53	100.00	118.72	123.12	127.40
Fund Position						*Millions of SDRs: End of Period*								
Quota	2f.s	4,313.1	4,313.1	4,313.1	4,313.1	4,313.1	4,313.1	4,313.1	5,945.4	5,945.4	5,945.4	5,945.4	5,945.4
SDRs	1b.s	.6	3.7	2.1	78.5	3.1	90.7	.1	.4	.4	2.3	.9	.5
Reserve Position in the Fund	1c.s	.5	1.0	.8	.8	.9	.9	.9	.9	.9	1.1	1.2	1.4
Total Fund Cred.&Loans Outstg	2tl	719.0	1,797.3	2,875.6	6,469.8	8,698.2	9,805.9	13,732.0	11,102.3	8,912.8	5,914.8	4,767.3	3,411.2
International Liquidity					*Millions of US Dollars Unless Otherwise Indicated: End of Period*									
Total Reserves minus Gold	1l.d	....	5,835.0	3,980.4	14,382.8	11,276.4	12,894.7	7,801.4	8,457.2	24,264.3	32,542.4	44,053.6	73,174.9
SDRs	1b.d	.8	5.0	3.1	116.7	4.5	122.4	.1	.6	.5	2.9	1.2	.7
Reserve Position in the Fund	1c.d	.7	1.4	1.1	1.2	1.2	1.3	1.3	1.3	1.2	1.4	1.6	2.1
Foreign Exchange	1d.d	....	5,828.6	3,976.1	14,264.9	11,270.6	12,771.1	7,800.0	8,455.4	24,262.6	32,538.1	44,050.8	73,172.1
Gold (Million Fine Troy Ounces)	1ad	....	10.195	8.417	9.414	13.490	16.297	14.738	13.326	12.359	13.599	12.464	12.545
Gold (National Valuation)	1and	....	3,058.5	2,525.1	2,824.1	4,047.1	4,889.2	4,421.6	3,998.3	3,707.8	4,079.8	3,739.3	3,763.4
Monetary Authorities:Other Assets	3..d	....	9,074.6	5,768.2	3,458.8	3,176.8	2,911.2	1,937.8	2,010.8	2,177.2	2,385.5	3,039.5	4,241.0
Other Liab	4..d	....	943.1	477.3	303.0	311.2	149.2	110.5	473.1	143.7	2,102.6	850.4	2,421.9
Deposit Money Banks: Assets	7a.d	....	12,669.3	13,891.6	9,946.1	13,107.0	12,513.8	11,251.1	14,281.9	17,435.3	18,146.2	19,033.0	20,660.0
Liabilities	7b.d	....	3,773.4	4,076.8	6,459.1	10,592.3	18,030.0	10,727.0	9,408.3	10,113.9	11,355.2	12,892.6	23,158.9
Monetary Authorities						*Millions of Rubles: End of Period*								
Foreign Assets	11	....	21,737	41,082	95,890	102,861	123,344	292,420	390,590	849,009	1,175,689	1,615,677	2,391,096
Claims on General Government	12a	....	16,802	84,498	138,578	187,365	226,049	525,374	572,030	504,702	488,102	551,547	477,640
Claims on Nonfin.Pub.Enterprises	12c	....	123	251	85	67	46	150	114	103	80	58	55
Claims on Private Sector	12d	....	21	72	237	813	281	412	316	264	168	2,181	2,264
Claims on Deposit Money Banks	12e	....	8,889	16,177	17,450	11,377	11,119	76,438	202,944	206,501	250,187	223,991	198,742
Reserve Money	14	....	20,544	62,357	129,601	164,929	210,450	269,665	446,432	746,252	963,137	1,263,728	1,947,711
of which: Currency Outside DMBs	14a	....	10,730	34,493	80,815	103,795	130,474	187,679	266,146	418,871	583,839	763,245	1,147,039
Time & Foreign Currency Deposits	15	....	1	4	17	23	240	1,828	1,575	7	2	29	5
Foreign Liabilities	16c	....	4,254	16,538	46,030	71,272	79,744	401,551	424,201	331,056	287,413	233,030	220,638
General Government Deposits	16d	....	7,003	17,096	24,898	15,062	21,313	41,863	75,871	240,488	294,914	357,878	446,001
of which: Local Govt. Deposits	16db	....	847	3,273	2,117	2,068	3,564	2,863	10,515	29,511	27,729	33,993	43,804
Capital Accounts	17a	....	638	17,014	27,530	54,179	69,552	118,113	151,844	166,048	242,312	364,731	298,234
Other Items (Net)	17r	....	15,132	29,071	24,164	−2,982	−20,460	61,775	66,072	76,728	126,448	174,058	157,208
Deposit Money Banks						*Millions of Rubles: End of Period*								
Reserves	20	....	7,914	24,151	36,712	48,301	74,981	77,728	168,180	310,781	356,771	471,563	768,914
Foreign Assets	21	....	15,798	49,316	46,150	72,875	74,582	232,336	385,611	490,977	546,926	604,953	608,529
Claims on General Government	22a	....	776	10,639	62,639	150,945	194,899	263,695	445,321	532,569	588,703	696,007	742,776
of which: Claims on Local Govts	22ab	....	–	–	722	2,796	18,699	26,174	22,080	20,538	27,612	52,314	98,844
Claims on Nonfin.Pub.Enterprises	22c	....	15,639	48,173	62,460	80,211	51,687	38,099	52,131	78,963	83,238	122,938	142,968
Claims on Private Sector	22d	....	20,208	74,017	133,786	166,517	250,134	410,691	631,137	969,413	1,473,097	1,915,108	2,772,461
Claims on Other Financial Insts	22f	....	–	–	525	242	8,077	7,526	13,738	15,378	23,232	32,948	55,561
Demand Deposits	24	....	12,519	32,589	69,332	87,303	163,658	150,931	250,927	444,625	586,721	706,693	1,003,198
Time, Savings,& Fgn.Currency Dep	25	....	17,101	61,183	124,497	164,899	160,771	287,686	463,999	688,453	944,814	1,361,495	1,780,146
of which: Fgn. Currency Deposits	25b	....	12,086	37,309	55,256	69,448	80,822	191,412	292,023	422,874	523,929	726,443	748,240
Money Market Instruments	26aa	....	211	3,516	11,858	26,653	31,485	42,062	113,089	199,080	263,885	399,866	545,464
Restricted Deposits	26b	....	–	–	–	9,929	17,423	65,596	100,849	90,509	77,582	43,759	30,360
Foreign Liabilities	26c	....	4,705	14,473	29,970	58,893	107,459	221,512	254,025	284,808	342,246	409,783	682,134
General Government Deposits	26d	....	2,117	6,914	9,741	12,142	19,105	22,723	31,272	58,923	73,538	67,892	85,484
of which: Local Govt. Deposits	26db	....	919	2,246	4,252	4,493	9,598	10,638	16,440	37,277	44,875	36,787	56,057
Credit from Monetary Authorities	26g	....	8,464	17,181	8,006	12,769	15,430	79,872	206,887	208,109	250,918	226,103	200,868
Capital Accounts	27a	....	12,031	26,211	56,810	106,684	124,005	102,678	166,259	234,223	352,141	491,277	686,650
Other Items (Net)	27r	....	3,187	44,229	32,058	39,819	15,024	57,015	108,811	189,351	180,122	136,649	76,905

Russia 922

		1992	1993	1994	1995	1996	1997	1998	1999	2000	2001	2002	2003
Monetary Survey						*Millions of Rubles: End of Period*							
Foreign Assets (Net)	31n	....	28,576	59,387	66,040	45,571	10,723	−98,306	97,976	724,122	1,092,956	1,577,817	2,096,853
Domestic Credit	32	....	44,449	193,640	363,671	558,956	690,755	1,181,361	1,607,644	1,801,981	2,288,168	2,895,017	3,662,240
Claims on General Govt. (Net)	32an	....	8,458	71,127	166,578	311,106	380,530	724,483	910,208	737,860	708,353	821,784	688,931
Claims on Nonfin.Pub.Enterprises	32c	....	15,762	48,424	62,545	80,278	51,733	38,249	52,245	79,066	83,318	122,996	143,023
Claims on Private Sector	32d	....	20,229	74,089	134,023	167,330	250,415	411,103	631,453	969,677	1,473,265	1,917,289	2,774,725
Claims on Other Financial Insts.	32f	....	–	–	525	242	8,077	7,526	13,738	15,378	23,232	32,948	55,561
Money	34	....	23,881	68,544	151,267	192,373	299,349	344,113	527,627	880,524	1,193,395	1,498,463	2,181,933
Quasi-Money	35	....	17,102	61,187	124,514	164,922	161,011	289,514	465,574	688,460	944,816	1,361,524	1,780,151
Money Market Instruments	36aa	....	211	3,516	11,858	26,653	31,485	42,062	113,089	199,080	263,885	399,866	545,464
Restricted Deposits	36b	....	–	–	–	9,929	17,423	65,596	100,849	90,509	77,582	43,759	30,360
Capital Accounts	37a	....	12,669	43,225	84,340	160,863	193,557	220,791	318,103	400,271	594,453	856,008	984,884
Other Items (Net)	37r	....	19,162	76,555	57,732	49,787	−1,347	120,979	180,378	267,259	306,993	313,214	236,301
Money plus Quasi-Money	35l	....	40,983	129,731	275,781	357,295	460,360	633,627	993,201	1,568,984	2,138,211	2,859,987	3,962,084
Interest Rates						*Percent Per Annum*							
Refinancing Rate (End of Period)	60	....	....	....	160.00	48.00	28.00	60.00	55.00	25.00	25.00	21.00	16.00
Money Market Rate	60b	....	....	....	190.43	47.65	20.97	50.56	14.79	7.14	10.10	8.19	3.77
Treasury Bill Rate	60c	....	....	....	168.04	86.07	23.43	....	....	12.12	12.45	12.72	5.35
Deposit Rate	60l	....	....	....	101.96	55.05	†16.77	17.05	13.68	6.51	4.85	4.96	4.48
Lending Rate	60p	....	....	....	320.31	146.81	†32.04	41.79	39.72	24.43	17.91	15.71	12.98
Prices, Production, Labor					*Percent Change over Previous Period Unless Otherwise indicated*									
Producer Prices	63.xx	....	943.76	337.00	236.46	50.81	15.00	7.03	58.95	46.53	19.17	11.55	15.49
Consumer Prices (2000=100)	64	.2	1.7	6.9	†20.6	30.4	34.9	44.6	82.8	100.0	121.5	140.6	159.9
Wages	65.xx	....	822.1	255.9	142.2	64.8	23.7	15.3	54.7	52.5	43.3	27.3	26.1
					Index Numbers (2000=100): Period Averages									
Industrial Employment	67	165.1	151.9	134.5	125.6	115.4	105.5	101.4	102.3	100.0	99.3	95.7	89.9
					Number in Thousands: Period Averages									
Labor Force	67d	73,008	....	....	69,469	68,264	....	66,736	69,731	....	....	71,919	....
Employment	67e	71,068	68,642	64,785	64,149	62,928	60,021	63,575	64,400	62,675	64,412	66,071	....
Unemployment	67c	578	†836	1,637	2,327	2,506	1,990	1,875	1,675	1,244	1,050	1,331	1,554
Unemployment Rate (%)	67r	.8	5.7	†7.5	8.9	9.9	11.3	13.3	12.7	10.6	9.0	....	....
International Transactions						*Millions of US Dollars*							
Exports	70..d	42,039	44,297	†67,826	82,913	90,563	89,008	74,884	75,665	105,565	103,139	107,110	134,377
Imports, c.i.f.	71..d	40,682	36,086	†55,497	68,863	74,879	79,076	63,817	43,588	49,125	58,992	66,243	81,654
Imports, f.o.b.	71.vd	....	....	....	....	....	....	....	....	....	53,629	60,221	74,231

Russia 922

		1992	1993	1994	1995	1996	1997	1998	1999	2000	2001	2002	2003
Balance of Payments					*Millions of US Dollars: Minus Sign Indicates Debit*								
Current Account, n.i.e.	78ald	....	....	7,844	6,965	10,847	−80	216	24,611	46,840	33,795	29,116	35,845
Goods: Exports f.o.b.	78aad	....	....	67,379	82,419	89,684	86,895	74,443	75,549	105,034	101,884	107,301	135,929
Goods: Imports f.o.b.	78abd	....	....	−50,451	−62,603	−68,093	−71,982	−58,014	−39,537	−44,862	−53,764	−60,966	−75,436
Trade Balance	78acd	....	....	16,928	19,816	21,591	14,913	16,429	36,012	60,172	48,121	46,335	60,493
Services: Credit	78add	....	....	8,425	10,568	13,283	14,079	12,375	9,071	9,565	11,441	13,611	16,030
Services: Debit	78aed	....	....	−15,435	−20,206	−18,665	−20,025	−16,456	−13,352	−16,229	−20,712	−23,497	−27,122
Balance on Goods & Services	78afd	....	....	9,918	10,178	16,209	8,967	12,348	31,731	53,508	38,850	36,449	49,401
Income: Credit	78agd	....	....	3,499	4,281	4,336	4,367	4,299	3,878	4,752	6,800	5,677	11,057
Income: Debit	78ahd	....	....	−5,342	−7,650	−9,768	−13,058	−16,094	−11,599	−11,491	−11,038	−12,260	−24,228
Balance on Gds, Serv. & Inc.	78aid	....	....	8,075	6,809	10,777	276	553	24,010	46,769	34,612	29,866	36,230
Current Transfers, n.i.e.: Credit	78ajd	....	....	311	894	771	410	308	1,183	808	744	1,352	2,537
Current Transfers: Debit	78akd	....	....	−542	−738	−701	−766	−645	−582	−737	−1,561	−2,103	−2,922
Capital Account, n.i.e.	78bcd	....	....	2,408	−348	−463	−796	−382	−326	10,675	−9,378	−12,396	−995
Capital Account, n.i.e.: Credit	78bad	....	....	5,882	3,122	3,066	2,138	1,705	887	11,543	2,125	7,528	614
Capital Account: Debit	78bbd	....	....	−3,474	−3,470	−3,529	−2,934	−2,087	−1,213	−868	−11,503	−19,924	−1,609
Financial Account, n.i.e.	78bjd	....	....	−29,340	−5,828	−19,890	3,164	−11,404	−17,434	−34,435	−3,802	1,346	342
Direct Investment Abroad	78bdd	....	....	−281	−605	−922	−3,186	−1,268	−2,206	−3,177	−2,533	−3,533	−9,727
Dir. Invest. in Rep. Econ., n.i.e.	78bed	....	....	690	2,065	2,579	4,864	2,764	3,309	2,713	2,748	3,461	6,725
Portfolio Investment Assets	78bfd	....	....	114	−1,704	−173	−157	−258	254	−411	77	−796	−2,543
Equity Securities	78bkd	....	....	−19	−42	−117	32	−11	5	−39	−60	85	−13
Debt Securities	78bld	....	....	133	−1,662	−56	−189	−247	249	−372	137	−880	−2,529
Portfolio Investment Liab., n.i.e.	78bgd	....	....	−93	−739	4,584	17,796	6,293	−1,881	−12,809	−730	3,756	−2,338
Equity Securities	78bmd	....	....	44	46	2,154	1,266	714	−287	150	542	2,626	413
Debt Securities	78bnd	....	....	−137	−785	2,430	16,530	5,579	−1,594	−12,959	−1,272	1,130	−2,750
Financial Derivatives Assets	78bwd	....	....	....	....	....	....	....	....	....	−	80	1,017
Financial Derivatives Liabilities	78bxd	....	....	....	....	....	....	....	....	....	−	−67	−377
Other Investment Assets	78bhd	....	....	−19,557	−150	−27,666	−20,637	−14,462	−13,218	−17,662	80	2,120	−16,472
Monetary Authorities	78bod	....	....	−	−	−	−	−	−	−	−266	971	467
General Government	78bpd	....	....	−3,119	−1,040	−319	7,156	−1,149	−1,349	−1,618	10,099	16,990	−299
Banks	78bqd	....	....	−3,117	4,318	−1,972	−1,084	502	−3,623	−3,332	−1,652	−675	−837
Other Sectors	78brd	....	....	−13,321	−3,428	−25,375	−26,709	−13,815	−8,246	−12,712	−8,102	−15,167	−15,802
Other Investment Liab., n.i.e.	78bid	....	....	−10,213	−4,695	1,708	4,484	−4,473	−3,692	−3,089	−3,444	−3,676	24,056
Monetary Authorities	78bsd	....	....	−325	391	−230	−38	66	3	155	1,908	−1,273	1,636
General Government	78btd	....	....	−11,744	−8,716	−6,034	−10,762	−3,175	−1,975	−2,876	−7,480	−13,341	−4,197
Banks	78bud	....	....	1,305	2,448	4,258	8,647	−6,361	−1,272	568	1,839	2,584	11,546
Other Sectors	78bvd	....	....	551	1,182	3,714	6,637	4,997	−448	−936	289	8,354	15,070
Net Errors and Omissions	78cad	....	....	−25	−9,115	−7,712	−8,808	−9,808	−8,555	−9,158	−9,350	−6,502	−7,430
Overall Balance	78cbd	....	....	−19,113	−8,326	−17,218	−6,520	−21,378	−1,704	13,922	11,266	11,563	27,762
Reserves and Related Items	79dad	....	....	19,113	8,326	17,218	6,520	21,378	1,704	−13,922	−11,266	−11,563	−27,762
Reserve Assets	79dbd	....	....	1,935	−10,382	2,840	−1,930	5,306	−1,772	−16,009	−8,210	−11,375	−26,365
Use of Fund Credit and Loans	79dcd	....	....	1,514	5,473	3,237	1,526	5,206	−3,603	−2,899	−3,829	−1,493	−1,897
Exceptional Financing	79ded	....	....	15,663	13,235	11,141	6,924	10,866	7,079	4,986	773	1,305	500
International Investment Position						*Millions of US Dollars*							
Assets	79aad	....	23,408	22,245	28,645	29,041	33,440	25,557	28,392	239,247	241,419	274,591	315,130
Direct Investment Abroad	79abd	....	2,277	2,272	2,420	2,685	2,789	2,703	1,076	20,141	32,437	54,608	72,273
Portfolio Investment	79acd	....	590	486	764	1,230	1,383	1,308	861	1,268	1,342	2,539	4,778
Equity Securities	79add	....	−	7	27	43	12	18	6	46	132	82	125
Debt Securities	79aed	....	590	479	737	1,187	1,371	1,290	855	1,222	1,210	2,456	4,653
Financial Derivatives	79afd	....	....	....	....	....	....	....	....	....	....	....	55
Other Investment	79afd	....	11,647	12,982	8,254	9,802	11,484	9,323	14,000	189,866	171,018	169,652	161,086
Monetary Authorities	79agd	....	−	−	−	−	−	−	−	1,436	1,677	1,518	1,095
General Government	79ahd	....	−	−	−	−	−	−	−	122,275	100,210	94,953	84,790
Banks	79aid	....	11,647	12,982	8,254	9,802	11,484	9,323	14,000	15,585	16,946	17,796	18,961
Other Sectors	79ajd	....	−	−	−	−	−	−	−	50,570	52,184	55,385	56,240
Reserve Assets	79akd	....	8,894	6,505	17,207	15,324	17,784	12,223	12,455	27,972	36,622	47,793	76,938
Liabilities	79lad	....	5,519	7,380	15,492	22,162	32,829	29,925	24,087	183,679	211,479	248,049	322,014
Dir. Invest. in Rep. Economy	79lbd	....	183	332	345	426	970	373	731	32,204	55,445	72,424	85,539
Portfolio Investment	79lcd	....	380	369	437	567	1,032	495	346	32,132	46,500	62,387	93,912
Equity Securities	79ldd	....	90	79	132	122	241	36	40	11,109	21,537	31,238	58,536
Debt Securities	79led	....	290	290	305	445	791	459	306	21,023	24,964	31,149	35,376
Financial Derivatives	79lld	....	....	....	....	....	....	....	....	....	....	....	31
Other Investment	79lfd	....	4,956	6,679	14,710	21,169	30,827	29,057	23,010	119,344	109,534	113,238	142,532
Monetary Authorities	79lgd	....	2,469	4,198	9,617	12,508	13,231	19,335	15,238	11,939	9,741	7,531	7,807
General Government	79lhd	....	−	−	−	−	−	−	−	81,864	72,577	67,114	69,385
Banks	79lid	....	2,487	2,481	5,093	8,661	17,596	9,722	7,772	7,990	9,702	12,326	23,525
Other Sectors	79ljd	....	−	−	−	−	−	−	−	17,552	17,515	26,267	41,815

2004, International Monetary Fund : *International Financial Statistics Yearbook*

Russia 922

		1992	1993	1994	1995	1996	1997	1998	1999	2000	2001	2002	2003
Government Finance					*Millions of Rubles: Year Ending December 31*								
Deficit (-) or Surplus...	80	....	....	....	−69,508	−147,607	−150,415	−126,958	−56,641	173,468	275,321	179,220	314,251
Total Revenue and Grants...	81y	....	....	....	226,071	281,770	322,690	299,403	608,033	1,127,571	1,598,482	2,219,266	2,577,933
Revenue...	81	....	....	....	....	....	....	....	....	....	....	2,218,389	2,577,031
Grants...	81z	....	....	....	....	....	....	....	....	....	....	877	902
Exp. & Lending Minus Repay...	82z	....	....	....	295,579	429,377	473,105	426,361	664,674	954,103	1,323,161	2,040,046	2,263,682
Expenditure...	82	....	....	....	277,744	409,792	454,768	416,872	655,391	1,004,265	1,376,552	2,042,943	2,351,111
Lending Minus Repayments...	83	....	....	....	17,835	19,585	18,337	9,489	9,283	−50,162	−53,391	−2,897	−87,429
Total Financing...	80h	....	....	....	69,508	147,607	150,415	126,958	56,641	−173,468	−275,321	−179,220	−314,251
Total Net Borrowing...	84	....	....	....	72,248	137,224	159,722	154,733	101,063	−173,468	−275,321	−179,220	−314,251
Net Domestic...	84a	....	....	....	48,814	103,968	106,253	64,545	53,644	−40,331	−50,068	−9,210	−81,435
Net Foreign...	85a	....	....	....	23,434	33,256	53,469	90,188	47,419	−133,137	−225,253	−170,010	−232,816
Use of Cash Balances...	87	....	....	....	−2,740	10,383	−9,307	−27,775	−44,422	−	−	−	−
Total Debt by Currency...	88z	....	....	....	787,689	1,122,323	1,302,052	3,786,106	....	....	....	4,550,774	4,004,304
Debt: Domestic...	88b	....	....	....	226,505	427,323	565,992	750,556	....	801,530	755,896	886,249	830,798
Debt: Foreign...	89b	....	....	....	561,184	695,000	736,060	3,035,550	....	....	....	3,664,525	3,173,506
National Accounts						*Billions of Rubles*							
Househ.Cons.Expend.,incl.NPISHs...	96f	7	77	285	744	1,044	1,283	1,511	2,582	3,374	4,417	5,545	6,723
Government Consumption Expend...	91f	3	30	137	273	391	494	493	703	1,102	1,470	1,916	2,247
Gross Fixed Capital Formation...	93e	5	35	133	301	402	429	425	694	1,232	1,689	1,943	2,418
Changes in Inventories...	93i	2	11	23	62	74	86	−31	21	134	274	243	320
Exports of Goods and Services...	90c	12	66	170	418	523	579	821	2,085	3,219	3,300	3,790	4,649
Imports of Goods and Services (-)...	98c	9	52	142	370	439	528	646	1,262	1,756	2,166	2,646	3,134
GDP, Production Based...	99bp	19	172	611	1,429	2,008	2,343	2,630	4,823	7,306	8,944	10,834	13,285
Statistical Discrepancy...	99bs	1	5	5	−	12	−	57	−	−	−40	43	63
						Millions: Midyear Estimates							
Population...	99z	148.79	148.69	148.45	148.14	147.78	147.35	146.85	146.27	145.61	144.88	144.08	143.25

Rwanda 714

		1992	1993	1994	1995	1996	1997	1998	1999	2000	2001	2002	2003
Exchange Rates						*Francs per SDR: End of Period*							
Official Rate	aa	201.39	201.39	201.39	445.67	437.37	411.31	450.75	479.24	560.67	572.84	695.88	849.07
						Francs per US Dollar: End of Period (ae) Period Average (rf)							
Official Rate	ae	146.46	146.62	137.95	299.81	304.16	304.84	320.13	349.17	430.32	455.82	511.85	571.39
Official Rate	rf	133.94	144.24	140.70	262.18	306.10	301.32	313.72	337.83	393.43	442.80	476.33	537.66
Fund Position						*Millions of SDRs: End of Period*							
Quota	2f.s	59.50	59.50	59.50	59.50	59.50	59.50	59.50	80.10	80.10	80.10	80.10	80.10
SDRs	1b.s	2.43	2.11	1.75	13.65	12.71	19.64	17.36	10.54	.87	9.82	7.48	20.03
Reserve Position in the Fund	1c.s	10.40	9.79	9.79	–	–	–	–	–	–	–	–	–
Total Fund Cred.&Loans Outstg	2tl	8.76	8.76	8.76	17.69	16.81	29.93	40.08	55.29	65.88	67.09	62.45	61.84
International Liquidity						*Millions of US Dollars Unless Otherwise Indicated: End of Period*							
Total Reserves minus Gold	1l.d	78.72	47.46	51.25	99.10	106.74	153.34	168.75	174.18	190.64	212.11	243.73	214.70
SDRs	1b.d	3.34	2.90	2.55	20.29	18.28	26.50	24.44	14.46	1.14	12.34	10.17	29.77
Reserve Position in the Fund	1c.d	14.30	13.45	14.29	–	–	–	–	–	–	–	–	–
Foreign Exchange	1d.d	61.08	31.11	34.40	78.80	88.47	126.84	144.31	159.72	189.50	199.77	233.55	184.93
Monetary Authorities: Other Liab	4..d	29.15	28.52	40.45	28.36	20.62	21.89	50.05	21.13	17.89	15.69	17.82	8.29
Deposit Money Banks: Assets	7a.d	41.66	31.68	26.63	51.92	66.27	73.17	75.22	56.23	76.54	74.87	76.17	85.77
Liabilities	7b.d	8.76	6.07	5.61	4.09	4.53	12.63	11.91	5.31	8.24	10.37	15.41	22.26
Other Banking Insts.: Liabilities	7f.d	15.59	14.73	8.67	7.96	7.41	4.70	2.99	2.92	2.39	8.09	8.09	13.39
Monetary Authorities						*Millions of Francs: End of Period*							
Foreign Assets	11	11,514	6,946	7,089	29,710	32,469	46,720	54,058	60,882	82,068	97,124	124,753	124,585
Claims on Central Government	12a	29,127	34,915	32,834	34,359	35,125	42,125	44,447	50,716	43,469	43,469	43,050	43,917
Claims on Official Entities	12bx	–	–	680	762	730	729	729	219	149	129	129	128
Claims on Private Sector	12d	115	123	151	157	253	220	342	561	1,112	1,682	2,091	2,306
Claims on Deposit Money Banks	12e	917	1,321	846	1,725	153	301	908	1,793	2,646	1,522	2,236	1,369
Claims on Other Financial Insts.	12f	32	20	11	9	9	9	426	431	314	207	121	72
Reserve Money	14	14,097	18,024	19,708	27,340	33,507	37,314	34,016	39,051	35,803	43,767	43,358	48,331
of which: Currency Outside DMBs	14a	10,321	11,522	11,924	17,257	19,908	20,635	22,865	21,510	24,609	24,380	23,953	29,246
Time Deposits	15	913	346	291	207	201	181	142	855	434	1,630	1,648	1,374
Foreign Liabilities	16c	6,026	5,935	7,365	16,383	13,624	18,974	34,112	33,907	44,654	45,789	52,580	58,128
Central Government Deposits	16d	7,527	4,492	4,430	19,156	15,753	15,032	16,276	20,929	24,681	29,115	49,599	32,257
Counterpart Funds	16e	4,098	4,157	4,596	2,304	3,231	4,174	3,408	1,620	1,311	770	569	658
Capital Accounts	17a	8,631	12,310	13,981	20,238	13,149	11,680	12,589	15,613	15,373	18,080	23,169	29,061
Other Items (Net)	17r	414	–1,939	–8,758	–18,904	–10,726	2,749	367	2,627	7,500	4,984	1,458	2,568
Deposit Money Banks						*Millions of Francs: End of Period*							
Reserves	20	3,117	5,778	6,618	8,590	13,816	16,035	11,835	15,845	10,823	15,496	13,511	13,055
Foreign Assets	21	6,093	4,637	3,683	15,566	20,157	22,293	24,095	19,652	32,949	34,281	38,990	49,769
Claims on Central Government	22a	6,667	4,495	4,311	4,528	4,968	5,573	6,995	7,747	7,265	7,345	14,408	14,862
Claims on Official Entities	22bx	298	679	581	354	205	15	421	587	678	1,010	3,533	4,952
Claims on Private Sector	22d	15,308	17,875	16,234	28,381	28,615	44,948	54,079	59,686	69,289	75,264	82,906	94,658
Demand Deposits	24	11,571	12,876	16,165	22,586	24,979	34,523	31,509	36,936	37,575	38,522	45,346	52,220
Time and Savings Deposits	25	14,249	13,356	8,084	22,181	22,851	32,445	36,051	38,680	50,588	61,622	70,974	81,352
Foreign Liabilities	26c	1,281	889	776	1,226	1,378	3,847	3,816	1,856	3,546	4,749	7,887	12,919
Central Government Deposits	26d	2,953	2,854	3,370	5,482	10,944	9,072	12,322	9,705	9,442	5,401	5,235	6,298
Credit from Monetary Authorities	26g	469	719	287	1,624	63	63	61	1,550	2,358	1,352	2,080	1,216
Capital Accounts	27a	3,535	3,778	3,745	6,908	7,683	11,832	16,749	20,059	23,749	26,097	23,427	27,937
Other Items (Net)	27r	–2,575	–1,008	–998	–2,589	–136	–2,919	–3,083	–5,269	–6,252	–4,542	–1,599	–4,648
Monetary Survey						*Millions of Francs: End of Period*							
Foreign Assets (Net)	31n	10,300	4,760	2,632	27,666	37,624	46,191	40,225	44,771	66,817	80,867	103,276	103,307
Domestic Credit	32	41,349	50,926	47,175	44,016	43,307	69,621	78,951	89,482	88,263	94,857	91,816	122,615
Claims on Central Govt. (Net)	32an	25,314	32,064	29,346	14,249	13,396	23,594	22,844	27,829	16,611	16,298	2,623	20,224
Claims on Official Entities	32bx	298	679	1,261	1,116	935	744	1,150	806	827	1,139	3,662	5,080
Claims on Private Sector	32d	15,423	17,998	16,385	28,538	28,868	45,168	54,421	60,248	70,401	76,946	84,997	96,963
Claims on Other Financial Insts.	32f	314	185	184	113	108	115	536	599	424	474	534	348
Money	34	22,509	24,919	28,810	40,658	45,423	55,746	55,291	59,172	63,110	63,718	70,373	82,305
Quasi-Money	35	15,162	13,701	8,375	22,388	23,052	32,626	36,193	39,535	51,022	63,252	72,621	82,726
Other Items (Net)	37r	13,981	17,069	12,625	8,637	12,457	27,440	27,692	35,547	40,948	48,562	52,102	60,891
Money plus Quasi-Money	35l	37,671	38,621	37,185	63,046	68,475	88,372	91,484	98,707	114,132	126,970	142,994	165,032
Other Banking Institutions						*Millions of Francs: End of Period*							
Cash	40..k	887	1,332	1,340	1,363	1,559	1,495	862	1,445	1,090	1,638	1,261	427
Claims on Official Entities	42bxk	108	83	–	52	491	21	316	298	–	–	–	–
Claims on Private Sector	42d.k	3,038	2,732	3,024	3,835	3,126	4,152	5,161	5,807	6,224	6,371	7,078	9,748
Long Term Foreign Liabilities	46clk	2,281	2,155	1,199	2,386	2,253	1,433	957	1,021	1,027	3,706	4,140	7,772
Credit from Monetary Authorities	46g.k	10	9	9	9	9	9	9	431	314	207	121	–
Cred.from Deposit Money Banks	46h.k	–	–	–	–	–	–	–	–	–	–	–	768
Capital Accounts	47a.k	2,208	2,310	3,996	3,736	4,228	4,067	4,986	6,074	6,319	6,380	6,135	6,779
Other Items (Net)	47r.k	–466	–327	–763	–881	–1,314	159	386	24	–345	–2,367	–2,378	–5,144

2004, International Monetary Fund : *International Financial Statistics Yearbook*

Rwanda 714

		1992	1993	1994	1995	1996	1997	1998	1999	2000	2001	2002	2003
Interest Rates							*Percent Per Annum*						
Discount Rate (End of Period)	60	11.00	11.00	11.00	16.00	16.00	10.75	11.38	11.19	11.69	13.00	13.00	14.50
Deposit Rate	60l	7.73	5.00	....	....	10.92	9.46	8.50	7.95	8.94	9.22	8.00	8.14
Lending Rate	60p	16.67	15.00	....	....	....	....	....	....	....	....	....	....
Prices						*Index Numbers (2000=100): Period Averages*							
Consumer Prices	64	34.4	38.6	....	76.9	82.6	92.5	98.2	95.9	100.0	103.0	105.5	112.8
International Transactions							*Millions of Francs*						
Exports	70	8,917	9,427	4,056	14,731	18,569	26,190	18,696	20,388	20,521	37,314	26,339	30,916
Imports, c.i.f.	71	38,263	47,907	17,270	62,193	78,837	89,694	89,218	84,508	82,586	110,488	96,460	132,134
						1995=100							
Volume of Exports	72	484	432	190	100	98	238	255	....	....	....	....	....
Export Prices	74	135	86	31	100	106	117	58	....	....	....	....	....
Balance of Payments						*Millions of US Dollars: Minus Sign Indicates Debit*							
Current Account, n.i.e.	78ald	−82.9	−129.1	−72.2	57.5	−8.5	−62.3	−82.7	−141.4	−94.4	−102.5	−126.2	....
Goods: Exports f.o.b.	78aad	68.2	67.7	50.4	56.7	61.8	93.2	64.2	61.5	68.4	93.3	67.2	....
Goods: Imports f.o.b.	78abd	−239.4	−267.9	−574.5	−219.1	−219.0	−278.4	−233.0	−246.9	−223.2	−245.2	−233.3	....
Trade Balance	78acd	−171.2	−200.2	−524.1	−162.5	−157.2	−185.1	−168.7	−185.3	−154.7	−151.9	−166.1	....
Services: Credit	78add	31.3	34.3	−	17.9	21.6	51.2	48.2	50.7	59.3	65.9	65.2	....
Services: Debit	78aed	−114.1	−136.5	−171.4	−154.7	−150.0	−198.5	−189.7	−193.3	−200.1	−189.2	−201.5	....
Balance on Goods & Services	78afd	−254.0	−302.4	−695.5	−299.3	−285.6	−332.4	−310.2	−327.9	−295.6	−275.1	−302.4	....
Income: Credit	78agd	4.7	3.0	−	24.3	5.5	8.0	8.7	7.8	13.7	14.1	8.4	....
Income: Debit	78ahd	−16.0	−18.2	−	−17.5	−18.9	−24.8	−15.9	−18.5	−28.4	−34.0	−27.2	....
Balance on Gds, Serv. & Inc.	78aid	−265.3	−317.6	−695.5	−292.5	−299.0	−349.2	−317.3	−338.6	−310.2	−295.1	−321.1	....
Current Transfers, n.i.e.: Credit	78ajd	212.7	208.6	623.2	355.0	294.6	311.9	251.4	209.9	232.9	210.5	215.3	....
Current Transfers: Debit	78akd	−30.3	−20.1	−	−4.9	−4.1	−25.0	−16.8	−12.7	−17.0	−17.9	−20.4	....
Capital Account, n.i.e.	78bcd	.1	−1.3	−	−	−	−	−	70.2	62.1	50.2	65.9	....
Capital Account, n.i.e.: Credit	78bad	1.8	1.0	−	−	−	−	−	70.2	62.1	50.2	66.2	....
Capital Account: Debit	78bbd	−1.7	−2.4	−	−	−	−	−	−	−	−	−.3	....
Financial Account, n.i.e.	78bjd	62.1	88.6	−19.6	−10.7	24.8	46.8	−16.7	−33.2	10.7	−44.1	75.5	....
Direct Investment Abroad	78bdd	−	−	−	−	−	−	−	−	−	−	−	....
Dir. Invest. in Rep. Econ., n.i.e.	78bed	2.2	5.9	−	2.2	2.2	2.6	7.1	1.7	8.3	4.6	2.6	....
Portfolio Investment Assets	78bfd	−	−	−	−	−.1	−	−.1	.8	.1	−	−	....
Equity Securities	78bkd	−	−	−	−	−.1	−	−.1	.8	.1	−	−	....
Debt Securities	78bld	−	−	−	−	−	−	−	−	−	−	−	....
Portfolio Investment Liab., n.i.e.	78bgd	−	−	−	−	−	−	−	−	−	−	−	....
Equity Securities	78bmd	−	−	−	−	−	−	−	−	−	−	−	....
Debt Securities	78bnd	−	−	−	−	−	−	−	−	−	−	−	....
Financial Derivatives Assets	78bwd	....	....	....	....	....	....	−	....	....	....	....	....
Financial Derivatives Liabilities	78bxd	....	....	....	....	....	....	−	....	....	....	....	....
Other Investment Assets	78bhd	19.2	−	−	−52.0	−13.6	1.2	−.8	−10.2	23.1	−.5	8.0	....
Monetary Authorities	78bod	....	....	....	....	....	−	−	−	−	−	−	....
General Government	78bpd	−	−	−	−	−	−	−	−	−	−	−	....
Banks	78bqd	−	−	−	−38.6	−13.6	1.2	−.8	−10.2	17.1	−4.9	−1.4	....
Other Sectors	78brd	19.2	−	−	−13.4	−	−	−	−	6.0	4.4	9.4	....
Other Investment Liab., n.i.e.	78bid	40.8	82.8	−19.6	39.1	36.4	43.1	−22.9	−25.4	−20.8	−48.2	64.9	....
Monetary Authorities	78bsd	4.5	3.9	−	−	−	−	−	−	−	−	−	....
General Government	78btd	34.4	61.9	−19.6	39.1	37.3	43.1	−22.4	−23.8	−22.8	−50.3	62.3	....
Banks	78bud	1.9	7.4	−	−	−	−	−	−	−	−	−	....
Other Sectors	78bvd	−	9.6	−	−	−.9	−	−.5	−1.6	2.0	2.1	2.6	....
Net Errors and Omissions	78cad	16.7	−8.1	97.9	5.8	4.1	46.0	92.3	32.3	−109.6	26.0	−36.0	....
Overall Balance	78cbd	−4.0	−50.0	6.0	52.6	20.4	30.6	−7.1	−72.1	−131.1	−70.3	−20.8	....
Reserves and Related Items	79dad	4.0	50.0	−6.0	−52.6	−20.4	−30.6	7.1	72.1	131.1	70.3	20.8	....
Reserve Assets	79dbd	4.0	25.4	−6.0	−66.0	−19.1	−48.5	−21.0	37.8	78.2	10.9	19.7	....
Use of Fund Credit and Loans	79dcd	−	−	−	13.3	−1.3	17.9	13.5	20.8	13.6	1.6	−5.9	....
Exceptional Financing	79ded	−	24.5	−	−	−	−	14.7	13.5	39.2	57.8	7.0	....

Rwanda 714

		1992	1993	1994	1995	1996	1997	1998	1999	2000	2001	2002	2003
International Investment Position							*Millions of US Dollars*						
Assets.............................	79aad	....	....	....	....	....	....	244.2	231.5	267.9	287.7	320.1	....
Direct Investment Abroad.......	79abd	....	....	....	....	....	....	–	–	–	–	–	....
Portfolio Investment..............	79acd	....	....	....	....	....	....	.1	.8	.7	.6	–	....
Equity Securities...............	79add	....	....	....	....	....	....	.1	.8	.7	.6	–	....
Debt Securities.................	79aed	....	....	....	....	....	....	–	–	–	–	–	....
Financial Derivatives.............	79ald	....	....	....	....	....	....	–	–	–	–	–	....
Other Investment..................	79afd	....	....	....	....	....	....	75.3	56.4	76.6	74.1	76.4	....
Monetary Authorities..........	79agd	....	....	....	....	....	....	....	....	....	....	....	....
General Government...........	79ahd	....	....	....	....	....	....	....	....	....	....	....	....
Banks.............................	79aid	....	....	....	....	....	....	....	....	....	....	....	....
Other Sectors....................	79ajd	....	....	....	....	....	....	....	....	....	....	....	....
Reserve Assets.....................	79akd	....	....	....	....	....	....	168.8	174.3	190.7	213.0	243.7	....
Liabilities............................	79lad	....	....	....	....	....	....	1,373.9	1,374.4	1,355.3	1,353.4	1,584.0	....
Dir. Invest. in Rep. Economy....	79lbd	....	....	....	....	....	....	62.6	59.0	55.2	56.6	52.9	....
Portfolio Investment..............	79lcd	....	....	....	....	....	....	.1	.1	.1	.1	.1	....
Equity Securities...............	79ldd	....	....	....	....	....	....	.1	.1	.1	.1	.1	....
Debt Securities.................	79led	....	....	....	....	....	....	–	–	–	–	–	....
Financial Derivatives.............	79lld	....	....	....	....	....	....	–	–	–	–	–	....
Other Investment..................	79lfd	....	....	....	....	....	....	1,311.2	1,315.3	1,300.0	1,296.7	1,531.1	....
Monetary Authorities..........	79lgd	....	....	....	....	....	....	....	....	....	....	....	....
General Government...........	79lhd	....	....	....	....	....	....	....	....	....	....	....	....
Banks.............................	79lid	....	....	....	....	....	....	....	....	....	....	....	....
Other Sectors....................	79ljd	....	....	....	....	....	....	....	....	....	....	....	....
Government Finance							*Millions of Francs: Year Ending December 31*						
Deficit (-) or Surplus.............	80	–17,234	–13,192	–3,194	5,300	–15,101	–12,275	–41,473	–41,161	–10,285	–41,307	–17,741	....
Total Revenue and Grants......	81y	44,289	44,005	7,547	61,528	70,828	95,768	99,019	103,803	132,809	150,370	172,000	....
Revenue...........................	81	27,563	25,865	6,032	23,128	39,428	58,037	66,019	65,996	68,664	86,206	101,200	....
Grants.............................	81z	16,726	18,140	1,515	38,400	31,400	37,731	33,000	37,807	64,145	64,164	70,800	....
Exp. & Lending Minus Repay..	82z	65,661	67,186	26,550	69,528	95,335	109,608	117,471	140,458	136,772	160,978	191,573	....
Expenditure.....................	82	65,796	65,152	26,550	69,528	95,335	110,157	117,632	138,858	136,298	160,350	191,000	....
Lending Minus Repayments...	83	–135	2,034	–	–	–	–549	–161	1,600	474	628	573	....
Statistical Discrepancy...........	80xx	4,138	9,989	15,809	13,300	9,406	1,565	–23,021	–4,506	–6,322	–30,699	1,832	....
Total Financing....................	80h	17,234	13,192	3,194	–5,300	15,101	12,275	41,473	41,161	10,285	41,307	17,741	....
Total Net Borrowing..............	84	17,234	13,192	3,194	–5,300	15,101	12,275	41,473	41,161	10,285	41,307	17,741	....
Net Domestic....................	84a	6,612	4,643	5,636	–12,742	4,464	645	–173	7,461	–8,650	–4,602	–17,937	....
Net Foreign......................	85a	10,622	8,549	–2,442	7,442	10,637	11,630	41,646	33,700	18,935	45,909	35,678	....
Total Debt by Residence........	88	147,890	163,882	171,065	353,894	370,697	403,971	469,522	537,278	630,670	607,500	756,100	....
Domestic.........................	88a	48,407	52,485	56,138	55,296	58,360	81,533	85,338	87,294	82,477	80,200	87,300	....
Foreign...........................	89a	99,483	111,397	114,927	298,598	312,337	322,438	384,184	449,984	548,193	527,300	668,800	....
National Accounts							*Billions of Francs*						
Housh.Cons.Expend.,incl.NPISHs....	96f	222.5	241.2	229.7	338.6	408.6	536.0	577.7	571.1	641.9	696.3	781.2	868.6
Government Consumption Expend...	91f	35.2	32.9	13.6	30.9	44.1	49.9	54.5	61.2	60.9	69.6	75.8	82.6
Gross Fixed Capital Formation........	93e	45.8	51.4	19.4	45.5	60.9	77.0	92.0	111.1	122.7	127.8	146.2	173.7
Changes in Inventories..........	93i	–.1	–1.9	–2.0	–1.3	....	....	....	....	....	....	....	....
Exports of Goods and Services........	90c	15.1	14.7	10.5	....	....	....	....	....	....	....	....	61.1
Imports of Goods and Services (-).....	98c	49.5	58.3	107.4	98.0	113.0	142.9	131.5	147.9	159.6	....	....	235.9
Gross Domestic Product (GDP)........	99b	269.0	281.9	165.8	336.5	426.2	563.4	627.3	633.3	708.9	766.3	838.5	950.1
Net Primary Income from Abroad.....	98.n	–1.5	–1.7	–.9	1.6	–4.5	–4.3	–2.1	–3.8	–6.7	–	–	....
Gross National Income (GNI)..........	99a	267.5	280.2	164.9	338.1	421.7	559.1	625.2	629.5	702.2	756.5	828.3	936.9
Net Current Transf.from Abroad.......	98t	57.9	99.5	391.7	223.0	200.1	171.7	163.0	200.3	204.6	....	....	....
Gross Saving.....................	99s	12.6	9.3	–68.7	–26.9	–22.7	–19.3	–1.2	1.8	18.3	....	....	....
GDP Volume 1995 Prices.......	99b.p	543.7	498.1	250.7	336.5	386.6	442.0	482.7	513.9	548.1	580.2	635.6	650.8
GDP Volume (2000=100)........	99bvp	99.2	90.9	45.7	61.4	70.5	80.6	88.1	93.8	100.0	105.9	116.0	118.7
GDP Deflator (2000=100)........	99bip	38.3	43.8	51.1	77.3	85.2	98.6	100.5	95.3	100.0	102.1	102.0	112.9
							Millions: Midyear Estimates						
Population........................	99z	6.06	5.57	5.22	5.14	5.38	5.89	6.56	7.21	7.72	8.07	8.27	8.39

St. Kitts and Nevis 361

		1992	1993	1994	1995	1996	1997	1998	1999	2000	2001	2002	2003
Exchange Rates		E. Caribbean Dollars per SDR: End of Period (aa) E. Caribbean Dollars per US Dollar: End of Period (ae)											
Official Rate	aa	3.7125	3.7086	3.9416	4.0135	3.8825	3.6430	3.8017	3.7058	3.5179	3.3932	3.6707	4.0121
Official Rate	ae	2.7000	2.7000	2.7000	2.7000	2.7000	2.7000	2.7000	2.7000	2.7000	2.7000	2.7000	2.7000
		Index Numbers (2000=100): Period Averages											
Nominal Effective Exchange Rate	nec	91.16	94.82	94.74	92.54	93.78	96.00	96.91	97.17	100.00	101.97	100.88	95.92
Real Effective Exchange Rate	rec	85.45	87.86	86.95	85.03	85.71	93.16	95.65	97.77	100.00	101.08	100.61	94.77
Fund Position		Millions of SDRs: End of Period											
Quota	2f.s	6.50	6.50	6.50	6.50	6.50	6.50	6.50	8.90	8.90	8.90	8.90	8.90
SDRs	1b.s	–	–	–	–	–	–	–	–	–	.01	–	–
Reserve Position in the Fund	1c.s	.01	.02	.01	.01	.01	.01	.01	.07	.08	.08	.08	.08
Total Fund Cred.&Loans Outstg	2tl	–	–	–	–	–	–	–	1.63	1.63	1.63	.81	–
International Liquidity		Millions of US Dollars Unless Otherwise Indicated: End of Period											
Total Reserves minus Gold	1l.d	26.24	29.42	31.82	33.47	32.73	36.07	46.80	49.58	45.20	56.43	65.75	64.80
SDRs	1b.d	–	–	–	–	–	–	–	–	–	.02	–	–
Reserve Position in the Fund	1c.d	.01	.02	.02	.02	.02	.02	.02	.10	.11	.10	.11	.12
Foreign Exchange	1d.d	26.23	29.40	31.80	33.45	32.71	36.05	46.78	49.48	45.09	56.31	65.64	64.68
Monetary Authorities: Other Liab	4..d	–	–	–	–	–	–	–	–	–	–	–	–
Deposit Money Banks: Assets	7a.d	45.57	59.65	73.44	76.69	88.78	121.88	123.28	112.59	148.52	165.58	222.11	288.85
Liabilities	7b.d	45.10	58.96	73.35	77.53	90.28	106.08	105.06	125.20	137.15	133.73	171.05	194.52
Monetary Authorities		Millions of E. Caribbean Dollars: End of Period											
Foreign Assets	11	75.82	79.66	85.89	90.55	88.42	97.45	126.44	134.09	122.18	153.84	178.15	175.93
Claims on Central Government	12a	7.80	8.34	4.95	4.42	4.01	3.20	8.73	8.56	10.65	11.29	9.74	3.88
Claims on Deposit Money Banks	12e	.03	.01	3.52	.01	–	.01	–	–	15.09	–	.02	.07
Reserve Money	14	83.59	88.01	94.35	92.97	89.90	95.82	114.73	129.56	139.86	154.44	179.84	174.91
of which: Currency Outside DMBs	14a	23.04	28.08	28.28	30.29	32.38	31.85	35.84	41.45	40.59	36.10	37.69	39.93
Foreign Liabilities	16c	–	–	–	–	–	–	6.18	6.02	5.72	5.51	2.98	–
Central Government Deposits	16d	.06	–	–	2.00	2.52	4.84	13.26	6.07	1.34	4.17	4.08	4.97
Other Items (Net)	17r	–	–	–	–	–	–	1.00	.99	1.00	1.02	1.00	–
Deposit Money Banks		Millions of E. Caribbean Dollars: End of Period											
Reserves	20	57.09	63.95	65.79	65.14	58.01	65.65	78.64	89.69	98.90	113.29	139.89	123.00
Foreign Assets	21	123.05	161.06	198.28	207.07	239.71	329.07	332.85	303.98	401.01	447.07	599.70	779.88
Claims on Central Government	22a	70.63	57.69	52.69	84.07	118.44	89.62	128.11	154.16	249.73	257.75	234.84	176.46
Claims on Local Government	22b	6.57	7.52	6.97	8.50	7.34	6.41	12.29	18.18	30.90	37.40	44.67	56.95
Claims on Nonfin.Pub.Enterprises	22c	30.17	32.46	52.51	87.13	105.75	117.67	135.32	160.45	158.26	191.67	225.42	252.13
Claims on Private Sector	22d	334.29	375.78	416.36	440.86	464.92	521.06	563.67	610.17	680.54	675.62	659.25	687.40
Claims on Nonbank Financial Insts	22g	1.00	1.18	.03	.50	1.10	1.69	3.34	5.77	5.95	6.39	6.44	41.99
Demand Deposits	24	46.37	46.81	44.09	52.21	56.26	53.11	70.57	69.08	70.38	66.86	87.42	98.37
Time, Savings,& Fgn. Currency Dep	25	302.55	332.09	339.43	390.56	395.15	465.57	506.96	524.01	694.68	711.30	758.65	857.75
Foreign Liabilities	26c	121.76	159.18	198.05	209.32	243.75	286.42	283.67	338.05	370.30	361.07	461.84	525.22
Central Government Deposits	26d	100.42	112.65	141.79	169.22	194.81	202.28	225.67	256.83	292.30	338.94	345.50	339.58
Credit from Monetary Authorities	26g	–	3.50	3.50	4.87	11.71	4.65	10.60	7.67	20.53	7.43	9.61	15.96
Capital Accounts	27a	43.28	46.87	49.79	60.03	70.40	81.09	84.98	96.50	103.25	123.29	175.76	206.65
Other Items (Net)	27r	8.42	−1.46	15.98	7.06	23.20	38.04	71.78	50.28	73.84	120.31	71.43	74.30
Monetary Survey		Millions of E. Caribbean Dollars: End of Period											
Foreign Assets (Net)	31n	77.11	81.54	86.12	88.29	84.38	140.11	169.44	94.00	147.17	234.32	313.03	430.60
Domestic Credit	32	349.97	370.31	391.72	454.26	504.23	532.52	612.53	694.41	842.37	837.03	830.77	874.26
Claims on Central Govt. (Net)	32an	−22.06	−46.62	−84.15	−82.74	−74.88	−114.30	−102.09	−100.17	−33.26	−74.06	−105.00	−164.21
Claims on Local Government	32b	6.57	7.52	6.97	8.50	7.34	6.41	12.29	18.18	30.90	37.40	44.67	56.95
Claims on Nonfin.Pub.Enterprises	32c	30.17	32.46	52.51	87.13	105.75	117.67	135.32	160.46	158.26	191.67	225.42	252.13
Claims on Private Sector	32d	334.29	375.78	416.36	440.86	464.92	521.06	563.67	610.17	680.54	675.62	659.25	687.40
Claims on Nonbank Financial Inst.	32g	1.00	1.18	.03	.50	1.10	1.69	3.34	5.77	5.95	6.39	6.44	41.99
Money	34	69.42	74.90	72.38	82.52	88.67	85.20	106.42	110.63	111.06	103.49	125.14	149.29
Quasi-Money	35	302.55	332.09	339.43	390.56	395.15	465.57	507.96	525.01	695.68	712.31	759.65	857.75
Capital Accounts	37a	43.28	46.87	49.79	60.03	70.40	81.09	84.98	96.50	103.25	123.29	175.76	206.65
Other Items (Net)	37r	11.83	−2.01	16.23	9.44	34.39	40.78	82.62	56.26	79.56	132.26	83.25	91.17
Money plus Quasi-Money	35l	371.97	406.99	411.81	473.07	483.83	550.77	614.38	635.65	806.74	815.80	884.79	1,007.04
Money (National Definitions)		Millions of E. Caribbean Dollars: End of Period											
M1	39ma	60.30	69.78	68.47	75.30	83.93	82.17	91.40	106.09	110.10	106.17	119.91	133.13
M2	39mb	333.17	374.93	390.12	438.38	462.66	525.05	545.92	607.38	776.67	794.23	844.80	903.05

St. Kitts and Nevis 361

		1992	1993	1994	1995	1996	1997	1998	1999	2000	2001	2002	2003
Interest Rates							*Percent Per Annum*						
Discount Rate (End of Period)	60	....	....	9.00	9.00	9.00	8.00	8.00	8.00	8.00	7.00	7.00	6.50
Money Market Rate	60b	5.25	5.25	5.25	5.25	5.25	5.25	5.25	5.25	5.25	†5.64	6.32	6.07
Treasury Bill Rate	60c	6.50	6.50	6.50	6.50	6.50	6.50	6.50	6.50	6.50	7.50	7.50	7.17
Savings Rate	60k	5.46	5.00	5.00	5.00	5.00	5.00	6.00	6.00	6.00	6.00	5.83	†3.59
Deposit Rate	60l	4.35	4.39	3.99	4.52	4.27	4.27	4.22	4.31	4.32	4.23	4.01	4.49
Deposit Rate (Fgn. Currency)	60l.f	....	....	....	....	....	....	....	....	....	....	....	3.05
Lending Rate	60p	10.76	10.28	10.94	10.89	10.92	11.16	11.42	11.21	11.10	11.08	10.89	12.22
Prices						*Index Numbers (2000=100): Period Averages*							
Consumer Prices	64	77.1	78.5	79.6	82.0	83.7	91.1	94.3	97.9	100.0	101.5	103.6	....
International Transactions						*Millions of E. Caribbean Dollars*							
Exports	70	71	73	61	51	103	120	113	120	133	142	150	....
Imports, c.i.f.	71	257	319	345	359	356	353	353	365	466	450	479	....
Balance of Payments						*Millions of US Dollars: Minus Sign Indicates Debit*							
Current Account, n.i.e.	78ald	−15.00	−29.29	−24.30	−45.46	−65.07	−61.66	−46.31	−82.47	−66.16	−105.94	−124.02	....
Goods: Exports f.o.b.	78aad	33.02	31.99	28.57	36.56	39.08	45.49	44.40	44.96	51.46	55.02	64.42	....
Goods: Imports f.o.b.	78abd	−84.15	−94.57	−98.27	−117.12	−131.93	−130.96	−130.99	−135.19	−172.67	−166.58	−177.59	....
Trade Balance	78acd	−51.13	−62.58	−69.70	−80.56	−92.84	−85.47	−86.59	−90.23	−121.21	−111.56	−113.17	....
Services: Credit	78add	79.77	83.43	92.38	81.95	88.54	94.75	100.58	101.06	98.53	99.00	90.56	....
Services: Debit	78aed	−40.97	−46.21	−44.86	−55.07	−61.31	−65.20	−62.03	−85.34	−76.01	−74.91	−79.65	....
Balance on Goods & Services	78afd	−12.33	−25.37	−22.18	−53.68	−65.61	−55.92	−48.03	−74.51	−98.70	−87.47	−102.26	....
Income: Credit	78agd	2.39	2.04	2.91	6.77	3.14	2.89	4.84	6.45	5.53	4.67	5.51	....
Income: Debit	78ahd	−13.08	−13.94	−15.91	−17.73	−18.76	−23.71	−30.19	−34.90	−35.64	−39.19	−43.68	....
Balance on Gds, Serv. & Inc.	78aid	−23.02	−37.27	−35.19	−64.64	−81.24	−76.74	−73.39	−102.97	−128.81	−122.00	−140.43	....
Current Transfers, n.i.e.: Credit	78ajd	13.74	14.16	16.56	23.26	20.80	21.76	33.66	24.05	69.90	26.61	28.30	....
Current Transfers: Debit	78akd	−5.72	−6.18	−5.67	−4.08	−4.63	−6.67	−6.58	−3.56	−7.25	−10.55	−11.89	....
Capital Account, n.i.e.	78bcd	4.07	3.33	1.73	7.26	5.45	4.17	8.25	5.81	5.99	10.31	14.59	....
Capital Account, n.i.e.: Credit	78bad	4.24	3.53	2.61	7.41	5.63	4.36	8.43	5.99	6.17	10.50	14.77	....
Capital Account: Debit	78bbd	−.17	−.20	−.88	−.16	−.19	−.19	−.19	−.19	−.19	−.19	−.19	....
Financial Account, n.i.e.	78bjd	19.39	25.53	23.74	24.79	49.10	48.19	45.67	95.48	70.20	103.95	106.92	....
Direct Investment Abroad	78bdd	−	−	−	−	−	−	−	−	−	−.13	−	....
Dir. Invest. in Rep. Econ., n.i.e.	78bed	12.53	13.76	15.35	20.47	35.17	19.67	31.93	57.74	96.21	88.23	80.41	....
Portfolio Investment Assets	78bfd	−	2.22	−	2.59	.88	.01	.01	.02	−.03	−1.09	−	....
Equity Securities	78bkd	....	....	....	....	....	....	....	....	....	....	....	....
Debt Securities	78bld	....	....	....	....	....	....	....	....	....	....	....	....
Portfolio Investment Liab., n.i.e.	78bgd	.01	−	.23	.15	7.09	15.44	2.22	14.14	5.06	35.64	31.47	....
Equity Securities	78bmd	....	....	....	....	....	....	....	....	....	....	....	....
Debt Securities	78bnd	....	....	....	....	....	....	....	....	....	....	....	....
Financial Derivatives Assets	78bwd	....	....	....	....	....	....	....	....	....	....	....	....
Financial Derivatives Liabilities	78bxd	....	....	....	....	....	....	....	....	....	....	....	....
Other Investment Assets	78bhd	−12.35	−13.50	−10.04	−3.70	−1.01	−3.30	−3.59	−9.22	−10.74	−7.71	.64	....
Monetary Authorities	78bod	....	....	....	....	....	....	....	....	....	....	....	....
General Government	78bpd	....	....	....	....	....	....	....	....	....	....	....	....
Banks	78bqd	....	....	....	....	....	....	....	....	....	....	....	....
Other Sectors	78brd	....	....	....	....	....	....	....	....	....	....	....	....
Other Investment Liab., n.i.e.	78bid	19.20	23.04	18.20	5.28	6.97	16.37	15.10	32.80	−20.30	−11.00	−5.60	....
Monetary Authorities	78bsd	−	−	−	−	−	−	−	−	−	−	−	....
General Government	78btd	....	....	....	....	....	....	....	....	....	....	....	....
Banks	78bud	....	....	....	....	....	....	....	....	....	....	....	....
Other Sectors	78bvd	....	....	....	....	....	....	....	....	....	....	....	....
Net Errors and Omissions	78cad	1.33	3.36	−1.77	15.71	9.63	12.96	3.38	−16.02	−14.40	3.28	12.19	....
Overall Balance	78cbd	9.80	2.93	−.61	2.29	−.89	3.66	10.99	2.79	−4.37	11.61	9.68	....
Reserves and Related Items	79dad	−9.80	−2.93	.61	−2.29	.89	−3.66	−10.99	−2.79	4.37	−11.61	−9.68	....
Reserve Assets	79dbd	−9.80	−2.93	.61	−2.29	.89	−3.66	−13.27	−2.79	4.37	−11.61	−8.62	....
Use of Fund Credit and Loans	79dcd	−	−	−	−	−	−	2.28	−	−	−	−1.06	....
Exceptional Financing	79ded	....	....	....	....	....	....	....	....	....	....	....	....
Government Finance					*Millions of E. Caribbean Dollars: Year Ending December 31*								
Deficit (−) or Surplus	80	6.61	9.90	6.77p	....	....	....	....	....	....	....	....	....
Revenue	81	137.42	165.33	181.84p	....	....	....	....	....	....	....	....	....
Grants Received	81z	2.79	.59	1.64p	....	....	....	....	....	....	....	....	....
Expenditure	82	134.97	155.98	176.49p	....	....	....	....	....	....	....	....	....
Lending Minus Repayments	83	−1.37	.04	.22p	....	....	....	....	....	....	....	....	....
Financing													
Domestic	84a	−5.37	−14.20	−10.88p	....	....	....	....	....	....	....	....	....
Foreign	85a	−1.24	4.30	4.11p	....	....	....	....	....	....	....	....	....

St. Kitts and Nevis 361

		1992	1993	1994	1995	1996	1997	1998	1999	2000	2001	2002	2003
National Accounts						*Millions of E. Caribbean Dollars*							
Househ.Cons.Expend.,incl.NPISHs	96f	234.2	248.0	295.3	351.7	401.9	425.0	410.7	559.7	556.1	475.6	540.9	....
Government Consumption Expend	91f	82.0	92.2	111.1	126.5	132.1	143.2	148.3	174.6	187.8	191.5	181.8	....
Gross Fixed Capital Formation	93e	191.6	242.8	227.9	288.4	304.1	326.7	333.0	293.3	406.5	466.5	457.3	....
Exports of Goods and Services	90c	302.7	312.3	327.2	317.9	344.6	378.7	404.2	390.1	404.8	431.3	430.7	....
Imports of Goods and Services (-)	98c	338.6	380.8	386.4	464.9	521.7	529.6	520.9	595.4	667.8	642.2	657.9	....
Gross Domestic Product (GDP)	99b	471.9	514.6	575.1	619.5	661.0	743.9	775.4	822.3	887.3	922.6	952.7	995.7
Net Primary Income from Abroad	98.n	−27.6	−32.2	−35.3	−29.6	−42.2	−56.2	−68.5	−76.7	−78.7	−90.8	....	....
Gross National Income (GNI)	99a	463.3	503.3	563.5	593.1	621.3	686.1	706.7	745.9	812.4	836.7	....	....
Net Current Transf.from Abroad	98t	21.7	21.5	29.4	53.9	43.7	40.7	73.1	55.3	169.2	53.3	....	....
Gross Nat'l Disposable Inc.(GNDI)	99i	485.0	524.9	592.9	647.0	665.0	726.8	779.9	801.3	981.6	890.0	....	....
Gross Saving	99s	149.7	163.7	162.8	165.7	128.4	160.2	221.0	66.6	271.2	249.0	....	....
GDP Volume 1990 Prices	99b.p	445.8	475.5	499.8	518.1	552.0	589.4	596.1	617.1	638.1	652.1	....	....
GDP Volume (2000=100)	99bvp	69.9	74.5	78.3	81.2	86.5	92.4	93.4	96.7	100.0	102.2	....	....
GDP Deflator (2000=100)	99bip	76.1	77.8	82.8	86.0	86.1	90.8	93.5	95.8	100.0	101.7	....	....
						Millions: Midyear Estimates							
Population	99z	.04	.04	.04	.04	.04	.04	.04	.04	.04	.04	.04	.04

St. Lucia 362

		1992	1993	1994	1995	1996	1997	1998	1999	2000	2001	2002	2003
Exchange Rates		\multicolumn{12}{c}{*E.Caribbean Dollars per SDR: End of Period (aa) E.Caribbean Dollars per US Dollar: End of Period (ae)*}
Official Rate................	aa	3.7125	3.7086	3.9416	4.0135	3.8825	3.6430	3.8017	3.7058	3.5179	3.3932	3.6707	4.0121
Official Rate................	ae	2.7000	2.7000	2.7000	2.7000	2.7000	2.7000	2.7000	2.7000	2.7000	2.7000	2.7000	2.7000
		\multicolumn{12}{c}{***Index Numbers (2000=100): Period Averages***}
Official Rate................	ahx	100.0	100.0	100.0	100.0	100.0	100.0	100.0	100.0	100.0	100.0	100.0	100.0
Nominal Effective Exchange Rate.....	nec	76.7	84.9	88.8	86.0	87.8	92.0	93.8	95.0	100.0	103.3	101.6	93.7
Real Effective Exchange Rate..........	rec	84.1	87.4	86.5	85.4	86.5	88.5	91.4	94.2	100.0	100.8	98.9	89.3
Fund Position		\multicolumn{12}{c}{*Millions of SDRs: End of Period*}
Quota................	2f.s	11.00	11.00	11.00	11.00	11.00	11.00	11.00	15.30	15.30	15.30	15.30	15.30
SDRs................	1b.s	1.31	1.34	1.36	1.39	1.42	1.45	1.48	1.50	1.43	1.46	1.48	1.49
Reserve Position in the Fund............	1c.s	–	–	–	–	–	–	–	–	–	–	–	.01
Total Fund Cred.&Loans Outstg........	2tl	–	–	–	–	–	–	–	–	–	–	–	–
International Liquidity		\multicolumn{12}{c}{*Millions of US Dollars Unless Otherwise Indicated: End of Period*}
Total Reserves minus Gold...............	1l.d	55.46	60.04	57.79	63.09	56.14	60.98	70.61	74.52	78.83	88.94	93.89	106.90
SDRs................	1b.d	1.80	1.84	1.99	2.07	2.04	1.95	2.08	2.06	1.87	1.84	2.01	2.22
Reserve Position in the Fund..........	1c.d	–	–	–	–	–	–	–	–	–	–	–	.01
Foreign Exchange................	1d.d	53.66	58.20	55.80	61.02	54.10	59.03	68.54	72.45	76.96	87.10	91.88	104.68
Monetary Authorities: Other Liab.....	4..d	–	–	–	–	–	–	–	–	–	–	–	–
Deposit Money Banks: Assets...........	7a.d	48.11	34.94	25.22	30.03	30.28	32.55	53.05	54.27	50.37	65.21	86.16	158.82
Liabilities................	7b.d	36.37	50.57	53.33	56.32	80.02	95.28	88.39	97.68	85.24	109.92	138.48	139.36
Monetary Authorities		\multicolumn{12}{c}{*Millions of E. Caribbean Dollars: End of Period*}
Foreign Assets................	11	149.79	162.22	156.60	170.50	151.87	165.08	191.27	201.81	213.57	241.07	254.50	289.76
Claims on Central Government........	12a	13.82	11.85	9.70	12.94	23.74	13.78	12.77	12.83	11.83	6.08	5.44	3.35
Claims on Deposit Money Banks......	12e	.81	.02	.02	.02	.02	.03	.09	.08	.02	.06	.05	.04
Reserve Money................	14	160.52	168.12	160.39	178.76	170.95	173.81	197.97	204.43	212.27	247.18	252.34	283.31
of which: Currency Outside DMBs..	14a	64.26	67.15	66.85	75.13	70.30	69.61	77.52	84.06	84.60	82.09	83.59	91.30
Foreign Liabilities................	16c	–	–	–	–	–	–	–	–	–	–	–	–
Central Government Deposits...........	16d	3.90	5.97	6.06	4.70	4.67	5.08	6.15	10.29	13.15	.04	7.65	9.83
Other Items (Net)................	17r	–	–	–.13	–	–	–	–	–	–	–	–	–
Deposit Money Banks		\multicolumn{12}{c}{*Millions of E. Caribbean Dollars: End of Period*}
Reserves................	20	97.73	106.58	103.66	97.02	101.94	105.33	108.52	129.00	121.03	152.42	173.87	194.13
Foreign Assets................	21	129.89	94.34	68.09	81.07	81.77	87.89	143.24	146.52	135.99	176.07	232.64	428.81
Claims on Central Government........	22a	47.91	52.12	47.49	43.65	48.13	63.06	109.65	119.95	128.28	129.64	142.29	129.75
Claims on Local Government............	22b	6.44	1.88	2.09	1.57	1.47	2.31	2.19	1.76	2.39	.25	.38	1.27
Claims on Nonfin.Pub.Enterprises.....	22c	34.50	49.25	57.48	72.67	67.82	64.61	46.72	47.09	65.51	64.56	65.30	96.04
Claims on Private Sector................	22d	680.14	806.47	860.41	946.42	1,071.26	1,171.82	1,258.19	1,394.19	1,481.69	1,541.82	1,553.47	1,498.20
Claims on Nonbank Financial Insts...	22g	9.59	1.78	8.72	8.28	13.60	14.50	14.11	30.47	30.66	25.91	28.27	31.66
Demand Deposits................	24	156.16	164.42	164.03	173.43	166.21	185.02	196.45	216.22	213.36	220.68	230.83	296.48
Time, Savings,& Fgn.Currency Dep...	25	546.91	568.10	618.95	673.13	731.81	756.03	848.10	912.16	978.34	1,046.25	1,070.30	1,113.29
Foreign Liabilities................	26c	98.20	136.53	143.99	152.07	216.05	257.26	238.64	263.73	230.14	296.78	373.90	376.28
Central Government Deposits...........	26d	158.49	174.24	170.92	195.35	213.77	235.09	318.57	354.53	400.96	432.67	413.57	460.62
Credit from Monetary Authorities.....	26g	.70	9.03	9.60	2.00	.09	2.10	–	.45	.93	63.23	48.53	4.07
Capital Accounts................	27a	55.16	60.25	62.76	74.05	67.37	66.25	76.86	119.14	132.32	167.30	159.56	159.34
Other Items (Net)................	27r	–9.43	–.15	–22.32	–19.35	–9.31	7.76	4.01	2.74	9.49	–136.25	–100.47	–30.22
Monetary Survey		\multicolumn{12}{c}{*Millions of E. Caribbean Dollars: End of Period*}
Foreign Assets (Net)................	31n	181.48	120.03	80.70	99.51	17.58	–4.29	95.87	84.61	119.42	120.35	113.24	342.28
Domestic Credit................	32	630.00	743.14	809.04	885.49	1,007.58	1,089.91	1,118.90	1,241.45	1,306.24	1,335.56	1,373.93	1,289.81
Claims on Central Govt. (Net)........	32an	–100.66	–116.24	–119.78	–143.45	–146.57	–163.33	–202.30	–232.05	–274.00	–296.98	–273.49	–337.36
Claims on Local Government............	32b	6.44	1.88	2.09	1.57	1.47	2.31	2.19	1.76	2.39	.25	.38	1.27
Claims on Nonfin.Pub.Enterprises...	32c	34.50	49.25	57.61	72.67	67.82	64.61	46.72	47.09	65.51	64.56	65.30	96.04
Claims on Private Sector................	32d	680.14	806.47	860.41	946.42	1,071.26	1,171.82	1,258.19	1,394.19	1,481.69	1,541.82	1,553.47	1,498.20
Claims on Nonbank Financial Inst..	32g	9.59	1.78	8.72	8.28	13.60	14.50	14.11	30.47	30.66	25.91	28.27	31.66
Money................	34	221.01	231.92	231.51	249.48	237.03	255.01	275.27	302.29	299.20	302.77	314.42	387.78
Quasi-Money................	35	546.91	568.10	618.95	673.13	731.81	756.03	848.10	912.16	978.34	1,046.25	1,070.30	1,113.29
Capital Accounts................	37a	57.91	62.99	65.69	77.02	70.24	68.95	79.68	121.89	134.93	169.82	162.28	162.31
Other Items (Net)................	37r	–14.36	.16	–26.40	–14.64	–13.92	5.62	11.72	–10.28	13.19	–62.92	–59.84	–31.28
Money plus Quasi-Money................	35l	767.92	800.02	850.46	922.62	968.83	1,011.04	1,123.37	1,214.45	1,277.54	1,349.02	1,384.72	1,501.07
Money (National Definitions)		\multicolumn{12}{c}{*Millions of E. Caribbean Dollars: End of Period*}
M1................	39ma	199.03	214.35	211.86	239.75	225.68	239.26	247.90	267.62	286.05	283.83	287.62	343.13
M2................	39mb	640.49	707.31	748.78	818.41	832.50	888.56	996.44	1,093.27	1,179.39	1,234.33	1,273.32	1,370.41

2004, International Monetary Fund : *International Financial Statistics Yearbook*

St. Lucia 362

		1992	1993	1994	1995	1996	1997	1998	1999	2000	2001	2002	2003
Interest Rates							*Percent Per Annum*						
Discount Rate (End of Period)	60	....	....	9.00	9.00	9.00	8.00	8.00	8.00	8.00	7.00	7.00	6.50
Money Market Rate	60b	5.25	5.25	5.25	5.25	5.25	5.25	5.25	5.25	5.25	†5.64	6.32	6.07
Treasury Bill Rate	60c	7.00	7.00	7.00	7.00	7.00	7.00	7.00	7.00	7.00	6.80	6.80	6.33
Savings Rate	60k	6.29	5.04	6.00	6.00	6.00	6.00	6.00	6.00	6.00	5.96	5.83	†4.09
Deposit Rate	60l	4.31	4.04	3.83	4.43	4.50	4.65	4.80	4.76	4.80	4.88	4.27	5.47
Deposit Rate (Fgn. Currency)	60l.f	....	....	....	....	....	....	....	....	....	....	....	4.74
Lending Rate	60p	12.81	11.81	11.06	12.68	12.82	12.68	11.40	12.79	13.06	12.97	12.59	15.00
Prices						*Index Numbers (2000=100): Period Averages*							
Consumer Prices	64	81.7	82.6	84.7	89.4	90.3	90.3	93.2	96.3	100.0	100.1	101.7	102.7
International Transactions						*Millions of E. Caribbean Dollars*							
Exports	70	334.90	323.00	254.80	294.30	214.70	165.38	167.92	150.33	117.09	119.75	120.03	....
Imports, c.i.f.	71	827.10	810.50	817.10	827.30	846.10	897.36	905.10	957.29	958.66	958.66	834.24	....
Balance of Payments						*Millions of US Dollars: Minus Sign Indicates Debit*							
Current Account, n.i.e.	78ald	−56.04	−50.17	−48.38	−33.09	−57.84	−78.32	−60.16	−96.85	−78.80	−74.99	−103.89	....
Goods: Exports f.o.b.	78aad	128.55	124.97	99.92	114.65	86.33	70.25	70.37	60.93	63.06	54.37	69.97	
Goods: Imports f.o.b.	78abd	−270.84	−264.00	−265.62	−269.38	−267.40	−292.37	−295.06	−312.01	−312.46	−272.07	−277.00	
Trade Balance	78acd	−142.29	−139.03	−165.70	−154.73	−181.08	−222.12	−224.69	−251.08	−249.40	−217.71	−207.03	
Services: Credit	78add	195.30	203.00	237.69	265.03	266.79	288.42	319.50	306.26	321.11	283.41	258.12	
Services: Debit	78aed	−89.30	−89.91	−104.16	−123.55	−122.44	−121.92	−132.18	−136.33	−124.20	−113.36	−124.51	
Balance on Goods & Services	78afd	−36.29	−25.95	−32.18	−13.24	−36.72	−55.62	−37.36	−81.15	−52.48	−47.66	−73.42	
Income: Credit	78agd	5.46	4.33	4.97	5.75	3.36	3.29	3.39	2.38	3.90	2.62	2.56	
Income: Debit	78ahd	−34.23	−38.11	−38.33	−44.53	−37.66	−38.97	−45.68	−40.50	−47.77	−44.02	−46.06	
Balance on Gds, Serv. & Inc.	78aid	−65.06	−59.73	−65.54	−52.02	−71.02	−91.30	−79.66	−119.27	−96.35	−89.06	−116.91	
Current Transfers, n.i.e.: Credit	78ajd	16.38	22.20	25.46	28.42	28.53	24.60	29.56	32.06	28.93	27.51	28.58	
Current Transfers: Debit	78akd	−7.36	−12.63	−8.30	−9.50	−15.35	−11.61	−10.06	−9.63	−11.38	−13.44	−15.56	
Capital Account, n.i.e.	78bcd	8.95	2.63	10.71	13.21	10.40	9.59	24.65	25.11	14.18	26.40	21.44	
Capital Account, n.i.e.: Credit	78bad	9.13	2.97	11.83	13.58	11.14	10.34	25.43	25.85	16.51	27.51	22.55	
Capital Account: Debit	78bbd	−.19	−.34	−1.12	−.37	−.74	−.76	−.78	−.74	−2.33	−1.11	−1.11	
Financial Account, n.i.e.	78bjd	65.32	62.29	41.71	27.62	49.21	85.12	58.51	66.25	70.88	43.73	68.40	
Direct Investment Abroad	78bdd	−	−	−	−	−	−	−	−	−	−	−	
Dir. Invest. in Rep. Econ., n.i.e.	78bed	40.94	34.16	32.52	32.75	18.41	47.83	83.40	82.81	54.90	23.57	48.05	
Portfolio Investment Assets	78bfd	−	−	−.47	−.47	−.06	−.06	−.11	−	−.64	−4.29	−16.54	
Equity Securities	78bkd	....	....	....	....	....	....	....	....	....	....	....	
Debt Securities	78bld	....	....	....	....	....	....	....	....	....	....	....	
Portfolio Investment Liab., n.i.e.	78bgd	.37	−.19	.77	.71	1.74	3.00	3.44	1.66	29.03	17.40	35.19	
Equity Securities	78bmd	....	....	....	....	....	....	....	....	....	....	....	
Debt Securities	78bnd	....	....	....	....	....	....	....	....	....	....	....	
Financial Derivatives Assets	78bwd	....	....	....	....	....	....	....	....	....	....	....	
Financial Derivatives Liabilities	78bxd	....	....	....	....	....	....	....	....	....	....	....	
Other Investment Assets	78bhd	−5.44	6.83	1.47	−15.34	−9.06	3.26	−11.46	−19.33	−15.00	−17.46	−16.43	
Monetary Authorities	78bod	....	....	....	....	....	....	....	....	....	....	....	
General Government	78bpd	....	....	....	....	....	....	....	....	....	....	....	
Banks	78bqd	....	....	....	....	....	....	....	....	....	....	....	
Other Sectors	78brd	....	....	....	....	....	....	....	....	....	....	....	
Other Investment Liab., n.i.e.	78bid	29.45	21.49	7.41	9.97	38.17	31.09	−16.75	1.11	2.60	24.51	18.13	
Monetary Authorities	78bsd	−	−	−	−	−	−	−	−	−	−	−	
General Government	78btd	....	....	....	....	....	....	....	....	....	....	....	
Banks	78bud	....	....	....	....	....	....	....	....	....	....	....	
Other Sectors	78bvd	....	....	....	....	....	....	....	....	....	....	....	
Net Errors and Omissions	78cad	−20.17	−10.13	−7.49	−2.01	−8.04	−11.42	−13.16	9.47	−1.45	16.92	19.22	
Overall Balance	78cbd	−1.94	4.62	−3.45	5.72	−6.28	4.97	9.84	3.97	4.81	12.06	5.17	
Reserves and Related Items	79dad	1.94	−4.62	3.45	−5.72	6.28	−4.97	−9.84	−3.97	−4.81	−12.06	−5.17	
Reserve Assets	79dbd	1.94	−4.62	3.45	−5.72	6.28	−4.97	−9.84	−3.97	−4.81	−12.06	−5.17	
Use of Fund Credit and Loans	79dcd	−	−	−	−	−	−	−	−	−	−	−	....
Exceptional Financing	79ded	....	....	....	....	....	....	....	....	....	....	....	
National Accounts						*Millions of E. Caribbean Dollars*							
Housek.Cons.Expend.,incl.NPISHs	96f	904.3	840.0	872.1	879.3	994.7	1,027.1	988.8	1,057.4	1,085.1	977.8	1,015.6	....
Government Consumption Expend.	91f	191.4	195.4	217.1	259.7	261.2	284.1	390.8	408.7	430.1	489.5	492.1	....
Gross Fixed Capital Formation	93e	346.2	376.9	389.9	367.2	381.5	417.7	433.1	500.5	490.7	459.4	415.9	....
Exports of Goods and Services	90c	889.7	909.1	918.2	1,038.7	953.3	968.3	1,037.3	1,031.4	980.9	961.2	884.7	....
Imports of Goods and Services (-)	98c	988.3	977.4	997.4	1,049.1	1,047.6	1,130.8	1,145.7	1,201.9	1,150.8	1,130.7	953.5	....
Gross Domestic Product (GDP)	99b	1,343.3	1,343.7	1,399.9	1,495.8	1,543.2	1,566.4	1,704.3	1,796.0	1,836.0	1,757.2	1,814.8	....
Net Primary Income from Abroad	98.n	−77.7	−91.1	−90.1	−104.7	−113.6	−119.7	−122.1	−130.1	−133.0	−142.0	−126.8	....
Gross National Income (GNI)	99a	1,265.3	1,252.6	1,310.1	1,391.1	1,429.6	1,446.7	1,582.2	1,665.9	1,703.0	1,615.2	1,688.0	....
Net Current Transf.from Abroad	98t	24.4	25.0	48.2	51.1	55.0	56.3	52.7	28.4	49.5	50.6	48.7	....
Gross Nat'l Disposable Inc.(GNDI)	99i	1,289.7	1,277.5	1,358.3	1,442.2	1,484.5	1,503.0	1,634.9	1,694.3	1,752.5	1,665.8	1,736.8	....
Gross Saving	99s	198.1	243.7	258.8	277.8	228.9	191.9	255.3	228.2	237.2	198.5	229.1	....
GDP Volume 1990 Prices	99b.p	1,189.9	1,220.6	1,236.7	1,249.8	1,288.3	1,273.1	1,332.5	1,394.5	1,392.8	1,316.1	....	....
GDP Volume (2000=100)	99bvp	85.4	87.6	88.8	89.7	92.5	91.4	95.7	100.1	100.0	94.5	....	....
GDP Deflator (2000=100)	99bip	85.6	83.5	85.9	90.8	90.9	93.3	97.0	97.7	100.0	101.3	....	....
						Millions: Midyear Estimates							
Population	99z	.14	.14	.14	.14	.14	.14	.14	.14	.15	.15	.15	.15

St. Vincent & Grens. 364

		1992	1993	1994	1995	1996	1997	1998	1999	2000	2001	2002	2003
Exchange Rates		*E. Caribbean Dollars per SDR: End of Period (aa) E.Caribbean Dollars per US Dollar: End of Period (ae)*
Official Rate	aa	3.7125	3.7086	3.9416	4.0135	3.8825	3.6430	3.8017	3.7058	3.5179	3.3932	3.6707	4.0121
Official Rate	ae	2.7000	2.7000	2.7000	2.7000	2.7000	2.7000	2.7000	2.7000	2.7000	2.7000	2.7000	2.7000
		Index Numbers (2000=100): Period Averages
Official Rate	ahx	100.0	100.0	100.0	100.0	100.0	100.0	100.0	100.0	100.0	100.0	100.0	100.0
Nominal Effective Exchange Rate	nec	73.8	82.1	86.6	83.7	86.0	91.0	94.1	95.1	100.0	103.8	102.2	94.4
Real Effective Exchange Rate	rec	88.4	94.5	92.0	87.5	91.3	94.4	97.8	98.1	100.0	102.5	99.1	90.5
Fund Position		*Millions of SDRs: End of Period*
Quota	2f.s	6.00	6.00	6.00	6.00	6.00	6.00	6.00	6.00	8.30	8.30	8.30	8.30
SDRs	1b.s	.09	.09	.09	.08	.07	.07	.07	.06	.06	.03	.02	—
Reserve Position in the Fund	1c.s	.50	.50	.50	.50	.50	.50	.50	.50	.50	.50	.50	.50
Total Fund Cred.&Loans Outstg.	2tl	—	—	—	—	—	—	—	—	—	—	—	—
International Liquidity		*Millions of US Dollars Unless Otherwise Indicated: End of Period*
Total Reserves minus Gold	1l.d	33.38	31.51	31.25	29.83	30.19	31.19	38.77	42.58	55.18	61.44	53.20	51.19
SDRs	1b.d	.12	.12	.12	.12	.11	.09	.09	.09	.08	.04	.02	.01
Reserve Position in the Fund	1c.d	.69	.69	.73	.74	.72	.67	.70	.69	.65	.63	.68	.74
Foreign Exchange	1d.d	32.57	30.70	30.40	28.97	29.36	30.42	37.97	41.81	54.45	60.77	52.49	50.44
Monetary Authorities: Other Liab.	4..d	—	—	—	—	—	—	—	—	—	—	—	—
Deposit Money Banks: Assets	7a.d	42.03	42.62	49.54	45.76	45.09	47.82	53.50	89.92	106.04	105.22	116.15	144.24
Liabilities	7b.d	27.38	27.95	26.77	32.13	35.35	29.73	24.98	51.95	56.70	71.93	67.59	78.61
Monetary Authorities		*Millions of E. Caribbean Dollars: End of Period*
Foreign Assets	11	103.69	85.10	84.41	80.64	81.54	84.27	104.78	114.95	148.93	165.79	143.65	138.25
Claims on Central Government	12a	9.04	9.94	9.25	8.68	8.94	9.05	7.61	16.22	9.05	9.39	9.97	22.08
Claims on Deposit Money Banks	12e	.01	.01	.01	.01	—	.01	.01	.01	.03	.01	.02	—
Reserve Money	14	106.12	94.73	91.59	86.68	84.45	92.10	111.29	129.99	156.75	171.71	153.57	160.21
of which: Currency Outside DMBs	14a	30.30	28.22	32.02	28.59	27.01	33.49	36.43	57.49	52.11	51.51	54.02	56.65
Foreign Liabilities	16c	—	—	—	—	—	—	—	—	—	—	—	—
Central Government Deposits	16d	6.62	.32	2.19	2.65	6.03	1.23	1.12	1.20	1.27	3.48	.07	.13
Other Items (Net)	17r	—	—	−.11	—	—	—	—	—	—	—	—	—
Deposit Money Banks		*Millions of E. Caribbean Dollars: End of Period*
Reserves	20	65.36	73.06	60.14	54.30	50.67	60.73	87.28	73.08	111.03	140.46	107.60	102.41
Foreign Assets	21	113.47	115.09	133.75	123.56	121.75	129.13	144.44	242.78	286.30	284.10	313.60	389.45
Claims on Central Government	22a	38.72	42.34	44.25	75.60	74.22	79.23	84.23	95.93	115.31	119.82	162.99	140.60
Claims on Local Government	22b	—	—	.26	.11	.06	.18	.16	—	—	.05	1.89	2.41
Claims on Nonfin.Pub.Enterprises	22c	33.24	38.39	47.55	22.03	24.94	21.04	18.71	19.98	22.06	34.10	24.50	28.73
Claims on Private Sector	22d	258.45	265.98	285.12	347.02	398.83	447.16	486.42	545.63	592.09	605.45	633.38	637.47
Claims on Nonbank Financial Insts.	22g	.61	2.65	5.85	6.12	13.50	14.45	14.80	14.69	10.71	9.41	8.14	10.28
Demand Deposits	24	59.91	64.85	78.50	76.57	86.07	111.55	125.99	142.23	177.18	199.42	201.34	224.99
Time, Savings,& Fgn.Currency Dep.	25	249.83	279.28	282.14	303.39	321.29	344.21	397.65	453.14	459.71	491.56	523.17	531.71
Foreign Liabilities	26c	73.93	75.46	72.28	86.75	95.43	80.28	67.44	140.26	153.10	194.22	182.50	212.26
Central Government Deposits	26d	95.88	101.95	110.64	124.38	141.22	165.25	196.62	203.79	214.38	212.01	230.42	246.26
Credit from Monetary Authorities	26g	—	—	—	.01	—	.63	.50	.01	7.68	3.15	3.47	1.86
Capital Accounts	27a	23.99	27.01	41.56	43.25	41.29	57.16	61.07	76.41	83.90	91.81	95.85	94.02
Other Items (Net)	27r	6.30	−11.04	−8.23	−5.62	−1.35	−7.17	−13.24	−23.75	41.56	1.21	15.34	.24
Monetary Survey		*Millions of E. Caribbean Dollars: End of Period*
Foreign Assets (Net)	31n	143.23	124.72	145.87	117.45	107.85	133.11	181.78	217.46	282.13	255.67	274.75	315.44
Domestic Credit	32	237.56	257.04	279.55	332.52	373.23	404.63	414.18	487.47	533.57	562.73	610.37	595.18
Claims on Central Govt. (Net)	32an	−54.74	−49.98	−59.34	−42.75	−64.09	−78.20	−105.90	−92.83	−91.28	−86.29	−57.53	−83.71
Claims on Local Government	32b	—	—	.26	.11	.06	.18	.16	—	—	.05	1.89	2.41
Claims on Nonfin.Pub.Enterprises	32c	33.24	38.39	47.66	22.03	24.94	21.04	18.71	19.98	22.06	34.10	24.50	28.73
Claims on Private Sector	32d	258.45	265.98	285.12	347.02	398.83	447.16	486.42	545.63	592.09	605.45	633.38	637.47
Claims on Nonbank Financial Inst.	32g	.61	2.65	5.85	6.12	13.50	14.45	14.80	14.69	10.71	9.41	8.14	10.28
Money	34	90.21	93.09	110.53	105.43	113.68	145.54	162.50	199.75	229.42	250.94	255.37	281.65
Quasi-Money	35	249.83	279.28	282.14	303.39	321.29	344.21	397.65	453.14	459.71	491.56	523.17	531.71
Capital Accounts	37a	25.29	28.31	42.95	44.67	42.66	58.45	62.42	77.72	85.14	93.01	97.15	95.44
Other Items (Net)	37r	15.46	−18.91	−10.21	−3.52	3.45	−10.46	−26.60	−25.67	41.44	−17.12	9.44	1.81
Money plus Quasi-Money	35l	340.04	372.36	392.68	408.82	434.97	489.75	560.14	652.89	689.12	742.50	778.53	813.36
Money (National Definitions)		*Millions of E. Caribbean Dollars: End of Period*
M1	39ma	85.01	84.93	96.19	95.21	96.25	129.25	150.75	182.73	212.25	219.16	239.16	253.70
M2	39mb	296.84	326.34	346.28	373.68	390.05	444.59	516.06	580.48	635.54	654.87	709.26	722.43

St. Vincent & Grens. 364

		1992	1993	1994	1995	1996	1997	1998	1999	2000	2001	2002	2003
Interest Rates						*Percent Per Annum*							
Discount Rate (End of Period)...........	60	....	....	9.00	9.00	9.00	8.00	8.00	8.00	8.00	7.00	7.00	6.50
Money Market Rate.....................	60b	5.25	5.25	5.25	5.25	5.25	5.25	5.25	5.25	5.25	†5.64	6.32	6.07
Treasury Bill Rate......................	60c	6.50	6.50	6.50	6.50	6.50	6.50	6.50	6.50	6.50	7.00	7.00	....
Savings Rate...........................	60k	5.63	5.71	6.00	6.00	5.50	5.08	5.00	5.00	5.00	4.96	5.00	†4.24
Deposit Rate..........................	60l	3.94	3.90	3.89	4.34	4.14	4.21	4.27	4.46	4.54	4.56	4.35	4.56
Deposit Rate (Fgn. Currency)............	60l.f	....	....	....	....	....	....	....	....	....	....	....	3.72
Lending Rate...........................	60p	11.30	11.92	11.73	11.07	11.23	11.29	11.31	11.55	11.46	11.63	11.56	11.83
Prices						*Index Numbers (2000=100): Period Averages*							
Consumer Prices.......................	64	86.0	89.7	90.6	92.2	96.3	96.7	98.8	99.8	100.0	†100.8	101.6	101.9
International Transactions						*Millions of E. Caribbean Dollars*							
Exports.................................	70	210.9	156.1	136.1	115.2	125.2	125.0	134.0	131.4	128.0	112.0	103.0	103.0
Imports, c.i.f...........................	71	356.6	362.7	351.0	367.0	356.0	491.0	520.0	543.0	440.0	502.0	471.0	541.0
Balance of Payments						*Millions of US Dollars: Minus Sign Indicates Debit*							
Current Account, n.i.e..................	78ald	−24.17	−43.87	−57.43	−40.68	−35.52	−84.18	−92.29	−72.52	−29.38	−41.29	−42.27	....
Goods: Exports f.o.b...................	78aad	79.03	57.13	48.86	61.94	52.59	47.30	50.10	49.61	51.75	42.76	40.45	....
Goods: Imports f.o.b...................	78abd	−116.87	−118.11	−115.43	−119.37	−128.07	−152.63	−169.96	−177.05	−144.36	−151.97	−157.22	....
Trade Balance.......................	78acd	−37.84	−60.99	−66.57	−57.43	−75.48	−105.33	−119.86	−127.44	−92.60	−109.21	−116.77	....
Services: Credit.......................	78add	58.93	62.36	63.40	74.37	96.67	99.44	107.32	125.92	126.23	131.38	136.52	....
Services: Debit.......................	78aed	−44.82	−44.81	−54.64	−55.14	−58.19	−76.37	−79.06	−65.96	−60.04	−59.58	−60.14	....
Balance on Goods & Services......	78afd	−23.72	−43.44	−57.81	−38.20	−37.00	−82.26	−91.60	−67.47	−26.41	−37.41	−40.39	....
Income: Credit........................	78agd	4.83	2.89	3.46	4.01	4.04	2.67	3.04	3.16	3.14	2.37	3.37	....
Income: Debit.........................	78ahd	−13.10	−11.11	−15.27	−15.67	−13.04	−15.33	−16.76	−22.62	−22.43	−18.85	−17.40	....
Balance on Gds, Serv. & Inc.....	78aid	−31.99	−51.66	−69.63	−49.86	−46.00	−94.92	−105.31	−86.93	−45.70	−53.90	−54.41	....
Current Transfers, n.i.e.: Credit......	78ajd	16.21	16.37	19.42	16.81	19.74	20.81	21.60	23.40	24.70	23.24	23.74	....
Current Transfers: Debit..............	78akd	−8.39	−8.59	−7.23	−7.63	−9.26	−10.07	−8.57	−8.99	−8.38	−10.63	−11.60	....
Capital Account, n.i.e..................	78bcd	13.70	6.31	4.01	5.87	3.83	5.91	13.56	7.86	5.60	8.76	10.61	....
Capital Account, n.i.e.: Credit........	78bad	14.32	7.00	5.37	6.92	4.94	7.02	14.82	9.13	6.86	10.03	11.87	....
Capital Account: Debit................	78bbd	−.62	−.69	−1.36	−1.05	−1.11	−1.11	−1.27	−1.27	−1.27	−1.27	−1.27	....
Financial Account, n.i.e................	78bjd	26.58	32.24	39.90	35.11	41.82	81.46	92.08	54.38	24.57	49.74	12.74	....
Direct Investment Abroad.............	78bdd	....	....	....	....	....	....	....	....	....	....	....	....
Dir. Invest. in Rep. Econ., n.i.e.......	78bed	13.90	31.40	46.91	30.64	42.67	92.48	88.95	56.80	37.75	21.04	32.49	....
Portfolio Investment Assets...........	78bfd	−	.03	.24	−	−.37	.07	−.37	−.22	−.52	.17	−5.40	....
Equity Securities.....................	78bkd	....	....	....	....	....	....	....	....	....	....	....	....
Debt Securities......................	78bld	....	....	....	....	....	....	....	....	....	....	....	....
Portfolio Investment Liab., n.i.e......	78bgd	.35	.66	.06	−	−2.37	1.61	.26	.11	1.96	3.32	6.41	....
Equity Securities.....................	78bmd	....	....	....	....	....	....	....	....	....	....	....	....
Debt Securities......................	78bnd	....	....	....	....	....	....	....	....	....	....	....	....
Financial Derivatives Assets...........	78bwd	....	....	....	....	....	....	....	....	....	....	....	....
Financial Derivatives Liabilities.......	78bxd	....	....	....	....	....	....	....	....	....	....	....	....
Other Investment Assets..............	78bhd	.25	−4.79	−8.92	2.06	−3.00	−3.04	−2.87	−8.42	−8.84	−10.71	−7.74	....
Monetary Authorities................	78bod	....	....	....	....	....	....	....	....	....	....	....	....
General Government.................	78bpd	....	....	....	....	....	....	....	....	....	....	....	....
Banks................................	78bqd	....	....	....	....	....	....	....	....	....	....	....	....
Other Sectors.......................	78brd	....	....	....	....	....	....	....	....	....	....	....	....
Other Investment Liab., n.i.e.........	78bid	12.08	4.94	1.60	2.41	4.89	−9.67	6.11	6.11	−5.78	35.93	−13.02	....
Monetary Authorities................	78bsd	−	−	−	−	−	−	−	−	−	−	−	....
General Government.................	78btd	....	....	....	....	....	....	....	....	....	....	....	....
Banks................................	78bud	....	....	....	....	....	....	....	....	....	....	....	....
Other Sectors.......................	78bvd	....	....	....	....	....	....	....	....	....	....	....	....
Net Errors and Omissions..............	78cad	−6.57	4.03	13.71	−1.68	−9.76	−2.12	−5.34	14.69	13.24	−8.14	12.98	....
Overall Balance........................	78cbd	9.55	−1.29	.18	−1.38	.36	1.07	8.00	4.40	14.02	9.07	−5.96	....
Reserves and Related Items...........	79dad	−9.55	1.29	−.18	1.38	−.36	−1.07	−8.00	−4.40	−14.02	−9.07	5.96	....
Reserve Assets.......................	79dbd	−9.55	1.29	−.18	1.38	−.36	−1.07	−8.00	−4.40	−14.02	−9.07	5.96	....
Use of Fund Credit and Loans........	79dcd	−	−	−	−	−	−	−	−	−	−	−	....
Exceptional Financing..................	79ded	....	....	....	....	....	....	....	....	....	....	....	....
Government Finance						*Millions of E. Caribbean Dollars: Year Ending December 31*							
Deficit (−) or Surplus...................	80	−27.2	−22.3	−6.7	−2.2	−15.4	−83.7	−28.0	−26.4	−20.4	−8.7	....	....
Revenue..............................	81	175.9	185.1	195.6	204.1	220.1	240.5	260.3	276.1	278.9	294.0	....	....
Grants Received.....................	81z	14.5	.9	2.1	1.5	1.4	12.8	32.6	12.6	9.7	50.5	....	....
Expenditure...........................	82	217.6	208.3	204.4	207.8	236.9	337.0	320.9	315.1	309.0	353.2	....	....
Lending Minus Repayments...........	83	−	−	−	−	−	−	−	−	−	−	....	....
Debt: Domestic......................	88a	70.9	117.4	124.5	133.7	139.4	144.0	147.1	167.4	195.0	212.6	....	....
Debt: Foreign.........................	89a	181.5	197.3	213.6	236.2	233.0	225.8	256.8	380.6	378.6	376.1	....	....

St. Vincent & Grens. 364

		1992	1993	1994	1995	1996	1997	1998	1999	2000	2001	2002	2003
National Accounts						*Millions of E. Caribbean Dollars*							
Househ.Cons.Expend.,incl.NPISHs....	96f	384.0	465.2	484.1	460.5	490.6	619.3	639.8	601.7	557.5	572.8	604.7	....
Government Consumption Expend....	91f	149.8	129.3	138.8	144.2	152.4	150.2	156.8	166.6	175.8	184.6	199.6	....
Gross Fixed Capital Formation..........	93e	152.8	165.3	185.4	215.4	212.8	243.8	306.2	308.4	247.1	277.8	292.8	....
Exports of Goods and Services..........	90c	373.5	322.4	303.9	368.0	402.9	396.1	424.7	473.5	480.6	469.7	469.8	....
Imports of Goods and Services (-).....	98c	430.4	437.4	461.8	471.2	503.0	618.2	672.3	657.5	555.3	569.7	591.8	....
Gross Domestic Product (GDP).........	99b	629.6	644.7	650.4	716.9	755.7	791.3	855.1	892.6	905.7	935.2	975.0	....
Net Primary Income from Abroad.....	98.n	−20.8	−22.2	−31.3	−31.5	−24.3	−34.1	−37.1	−52.5	−52.1	−50.5	−45.5	....
Gross National Income (GNI)............	99a	608.9	622.5	619.1	685.5	731.4	757.2	818.0	840.1	853.6	884.7	929.4	....
Net Current Transf.from Abroad.......	98t	21.1	18.9	31.9	24.8	28.2	29.1	29.6	41.7	50.7	41.3	41.7	....
Gross Nat'l Disposable Inc.(GNDI)....	99i	630.0	641.4	651.0	710.2	759.6	786.2	847.6	881.7	904.2	925.9	971.2	....
Gross Saving................................	99s	96.2	47.0	28.2	105.6	116.7	16.7	51.1	113.5	170.9	168.5	166.9	....
GDP Volume 1990 Prices.................	99b.p	575.0	588.6	576.8	620.5	629.5	652.5	686.0	714.0	727.2	736.2	....	....
GDP Volume (2000=100)...............	99bvp	79.1	80.9	79.3	85.3	86.6	89.7	94.3	98.2	100.0	101.2	....	....
GDP Deflator (2000=100)...............	99bip	87.9	87.9	90.5	92.8	96.4	97.4	100.1	100.4	100.0	102.0	....	....
						Millions: Midyear Estimates							
Population...............................	99z	.11	.11	.11	.11	.11	.12	.12	.12	.12	.12	.12	.12

2004, International Monetary Fund : *International Financial Statistics Yearbook*

Samoa 862

		1992	1993	1994	1995	1996	1997	1998	1999	2000	2001	2002	2003
Exchange Rates						*SDRs per Tala: End of Period*							
Official Rate............	ac	.2844	.2792	.2794	.2662	.2857	.2679	.2359	.2414	.2297	.2241	.2287	.2423
					US Dollars per Tala: End of Period (ag) Period Average (rh)								
Official Rate............	ag	.3910	.3835	.4079	.3957	.4108	.3615	.3322	.3313	.2993	.2816	.3109	.3600
Official Rate............	rh	.4056	.3894	.3945	.4045	.4062	.3912	.3398	.3320	.3057	.2880	.2963	.3336
					Index Numbers (2000=100): Period Averages								
Official Rate............	ahx	132.7	127.4	129.1	132.3	132.9	128.0	111.2	108.6	100.0	94.2	96.9	109.1
Nominal Effective Exchange Rate.....	nec	101.2	104.4	107.0	104.4	106.7	109.0	104.4	101.5	100.0	100.2	100.1	99.9
Real Effective Exchange Rate...........	rec	103.6	101.6	108.1	98.4	103.3	110.6	106.5	102.6	100.0	101.7	107.9	105.7
Fund Position						*Millions of SDRs: End of Period*							
Quota............	2f.s	8.50	8.50	8.50	8.50	8.50	8.50	8.50	11.60	11.60	11.60	11.60	11.60
SDRs............	1b.s	1.89	1.95	1.99	2.04	2.10	2.14	2.19	2.24	2.29	2.34	2.38	2.40
Reserve Position in the Fund............	1c.s	.66	.66	.66	.67	.67	.68	.68	.68	.68	.68	.69	.69
Total Fund Cred.&Loans Outstg........	2tl	–	–	–	–	–	–	–	–	–	–	–	–
International Liquidity					*Millions of US Dollars Unless Otherwise Indicated: End of Period*								
Total Reserves minus Gold...............	1l.d	57.65	50.71	50.80	55.31	60.80	64.21	61.42	68.20	63.66	56.64	62.49	83.91
SDRs............	1b.d	2.60	2.68	2.91	3.03	3.02	2.89	3.09	3.07	2.99	2.95	3.23	3.57
Reserve Position in the Fund............	1c.d	.91	.91	.97	1.00	.97	.92	.96	.94	.89	.86	.94	1.03
Foreign Exchange...................	1d.d	54.14	47.11	46.92	51.28	56.82	60.39	57.37	64.19	59.78	52.83	58.32	79.31
Monetary Authorities: Other Liab.....	4..d	–	–	–	–	–	.01	.05	.03	.50	.05	.23	.09
Deposit Money Banks: Assets..........	7a.d	3.76	3.11	6.26	4.66	5.38	6.98	8.00	11.41	14.61	12.29	7.45	13.74
Liabilities.................	7b.d	.22	.50	2.86	.30	.94	2.36	1.40	6.80	6.62	6.77	5.04	9.30
Monetary Authorities						*Millions of Tala: End of Period*							
Foreign Assets...............	11	135.99	112.38	109.39	119.13	134.91	158.30	166.00	171.41	163.89	157.48	174.81	194.92
Claims on Central Government.........	12a	1.69	1.69	.07	.07	–	–	–	–	–	–	–	–
Claims on Private Sector............	12d	–	–	–	–	1.39	1.68	1.67	1.69	1.80	2.16	2.34	2.38
Claims on Deposit Money Banks......	12e	5.85	6.00	6.23	.06	.03	.06	.09	.06	.83	.33	.38	.72
Reserve Money............	14	63.29	58.25	60.11	62.73	75.57	90.03	48.86	59.31	64.52	61.40	73.85	81.76
of which: Currency Outside DMBs..	14a	12.31	13.95	16.82	21.60	20.96	30.39	24.82	29.09	28.87	29.97	32.57	35.73
Liabs. of Central Bank: Securities.......	16ac	–	–	–	–	–	–	25.51	27.39	15.66	7.74	15.96	33.54
Foreign Liabilities.................	16c	–	–	–	–	–	.03	.14	.10	1.66	.18	.73	.24
Central Government Deposits............	16d	79.89	64.54	49.07	48.36	56.78	69.60	90.21	83.37	78.12	85.59	79.89	74.92
Capital Accounts............	17a	24.94	26.58	28.30	27.61	27.52	28.47	30.30	30.30	30.26	31.29	31.33	32.59
Other Items (Net)............	17r	−24.59	−29.31	−21.78	−19.44	−23.54	−28.10	−27.26	−27.31	−23.70	−26.22	−24.23	−25.04
Deposit Money Banks						*Millions of Tala: End of Period*							
Reserves............	20	50.98	44.30	43.29	41.13	54.41	59.64	24.04	30.22	35.65	31.43	41.28	46.03
Claims on Mon.Author.:Securities.....	20c	–	–	–	–	–	–	25.51	27.39	15.66	7.74	15.96	33.54
Foreign Assets............	21	9.61	8.10	15.34	11.78	13.09	19.30	24.09	34.45	48.83	43.66	23.96	38.17
Claims on Central Government.........	22a	2.99	3.62	3.67	1.30	.66	–	–	9.41	1.59	9.68	–	8.52
Claims on Nonfin.Pub.Enterprises.....	22c	2.37	.56	3.16	3.70	4.08	3.24	3.26	13.61	18.79	16.77	18.59	15.05
Claims on Private Sector............	22d	70.91	81.29	75.49	97.38	115.15	137.69	163.84	192.91	231.17	264.43	292.36	316.09
Demand Deposits............	24	25.73	29.70	30.38	39.34	39.86	44.14	41.71	51.23	64.41	56.87	63.04	82.48
Time, Savings,& Fgn.Currency Dep...	25	81.52	77.63	90.88	110.77	121.68	135.62	148.84	168.92	196.65	220.78	243.43	268.16
Foreign Liabilities.................	26c	.57	1.30	7.00	.76	2.30	6.52	4.20	20.53	22.13	24.05	16.22	25.82
Central Government Deposits............	26d	1.96	3.01	2.32	3.36	8.31	16.56	14.09	23.79	19.10	17.76	12.35	11.14
Credit from Monetary Authorities.....	26g	5.85	5.99	6.23	.06	.03	.10	.09	.05	.77	.30	.53	2.74
Capital Accounts............	27a	22.72	27.26	21.72	22.48	34.61	31.97	37.34	56.52	54.50	60.23	61.23	57.56
Other Items (Net)............	27r	−1.49	−7.02	−17.58	−21.48	−19.40	−15.04	−5.53	−13.05	−5.87	−6.28	−4.65	9.50
Monetary Survey						*Millions of Tala: End of Period*							
Foreign Assets (Net)............	31n	145.03	119.18	117.73	130.15	145.70	171.05	185.75	185.23	188.93	176.91	181.82	207.03
Domestic Credit............	32	−3.89	19.61	31.00	50.73	56.19	56.45	64.47	110.46	156.13	189.69	221.05	255.98
Claims on Central Govt. (Net)........	32an	−77.17	−62.24	−47.65	−50.35	−64.43	−86.16	−104.30	−97.75	−95.63	−93.67	−92.24	−77.54
Claims on Nonfin.Pub.Enterprises...	32c	2.37	.56	3.16	3.70	4.08	3.24	3.26	13.61	18.79	16.77	18.59	15.05
Claims on Private Sector............	32d	70.91	81.29	75.49	97.38	116.54	139.37	165.51	194.60	232.97	266.59	294.70	318.47
Money............	34	38.04	43.65	47.20	60.94	60.82	74.53	66.53	80.32	93.28	86.84	95.61	118.21
Quasi-Money............	35	81.52	77.63	90.88	110.77	121.68	135.62	148.84	168.92	196.65	220.78	243.43	268.16
Capital Accounts............	37a	47.66	53.84	50.02	50.09	62.13	60.44	67.64	86.82	84.76	91.52	92.56	90.15
Other Items (Net)............	37r	−26.08	−36.34	−39.36	−40.92	−42.74	−43.10	−32.79	−40.37	−29.63	−32.53	−28.73	−13.52
Money plus Quasi-Money............	35l	119.56	121.28	138.08	171.71	182.50	210.15	215.37	249.24	289.93	307.62	339.04	386.37
Other Banking Institutions						*Millions of Tala: End of Period*							
Deposits............	45	6.60	2.56	2.63	....	....	....	....	....	....	....	....	....
Liquid Liabilities............	55l	126.16	123.84	140.71	....	....	....	....	....	....	....	....	....

Samoa 862

		1992	1993	1994	1995	1996	1997	1998	1999	2000	2001	2002	2003
Interest Rates						*Percent Per Annum*							
Deposit Rate	60l	6.38	5.50	5.50	5.50	5.50	5.50	6.50	6.50	6.46	5.53	5.10	5.10
Lending Rate	60p	12.88	12.00	12.00	12.00	12.00	12.00	11.50	11.50	11.00	9.93	9.75	9.75
Government Bond Yield	61	13.50	13.50	13.50	13.50	13.50	13.50	13.50	13.50	13.50	13.50	13.50	13.50
Prices and Production						*Index Numbers (2000=100): Period Averages*							
Consumer Prices	64	77.5	78.9	88.4	85.8	90.4	†96.6	98.8	99.0	100.0	†103.8	112.2	112.3
Manufacturing Prod.(1995=100)	66ey	....	....	80.4	100.0	111.5	101.8	98.1	....	....	....	....	....
International Transactions						*Thousands of Tala Thousands of Tala*							
Exports	70	14,349	16,522	9,121	21,859	24,868	38,531	43,243	61,695	46,833	54,049	46,201	44,261
Imports, c.i.f.	71	271,325	269,079	206,347	235,353	247,126	247,377	285,652	346,765	348,607	453,066	381,035	406,970
Balance of Payments						*Millions of US Dollars: Minus Sign Indicates Debit*							
Current Account, n.i.e.	78ald	−52.50	−38.69	5.76	9.33	12.28	9.13	20.09	−18.79	....	....	....	....
Goods: Exports f.o.b.	78aad	5.82	6.44	3.52	8.76	10.08	14.63	20.40	18.15	....	....	....	....
Goods: Imports f.o.b.	78abd	−89.90	−87.41	−68.81	−80.29	−90.76	−100.11	−96.91	−115.66	....	....	....	....
Trade Balance	78acd	−84.07	−80.98	−65.29	−71.53	−80.67	−85.48	−76.51	−97.51	....	....	....	....
Services: Credit	78add	36.65	35.80	43.00	55.70	65.15	65.24	62.56	61.31	....	....	....	....
Services: Debit	78aed	−43.43	−38.24	−28.17	−35.19	−34.33	−40.08	−29.09	−24.55	....	....	....	....
Balance on Goods & Services	78afd	−90.85	−83.42	−50.46	−51.02	−49.85	−60.32	−43.04	−60.74	....	....	....	....
Income: Credit	78agd	6.15	4.33	4.03	4.66	5.45	5.52	5.97	2.75	....	....	....	....
Income: Debit	78ahd	−2.55	−4.42	−4.45	−4.42	−2.43	−4.14	−2.39	−2.36	....	....	....	....
Balance on Gds, Serv. & Inc	78aid	−87.25	−83.51	−50.88	−50.79	−46.84	−58.94	−39.47	−60.34	....	....	....	....
Current Transfers, n.i.e.: Credit	78ajd	39.07	49.93	62.75	66.74	66.89	73.71	64.12	44.67	....	....	....	....
Current Transfers: Debit	78akd	−4.32	−5.11	−6.11	−6.62	−7.77	−5.65	−4.56	−3.12	....	....	....	....
Capital Account, n.i.e.	78bcd	−	−	−	−	−	−	−	24.46	....	....	....	....
Capital Account, n.i.e.: Credit	78bad	−	−	−	−	−	−	−	27.11	....	....	....	....
Capital Account: Debit	78bbd	−	−	−	−	−	−	−	−2.66	....	....	....	....
Financial Account, n.i.e.	78bjd	15.94	15.55	−5.46	−5.60	−3.60	−5.93	−4.99	−.73	....	....	....	....
Direct Investment Abroad	78bdd	−	−	−	−	−	−	−	−	....	....	....	....
Dir. Invest. in Rep. Econ., n.i.e.	78bed	−	−	−	−	−	−	−	−	....	....	....	....
Portfolio Investment Assets	78bfd	−	−	−	−	−	−	−	−	....	....	....	....
Equity Securities	78bkd	−	−	−	−	−	−	−	−	....	....	....	....
Debt Securities	78bld	−	−	−	−	−	−	−	−	....	....	....	....
Portfolio Investment Liab., n.i.e.	78bgd	−	−	....	....	....	....	....	....	....	....	....	....
Equity Securities	78bmd	−	−	....	....	....	....	....	....	....	....	....	....
Debt Securities	78bnd	−	−	....	....	....	....	....	....	....	....	....	....
Financial Derivatives Assets	78bwd	....	....	....	....	....	....	....	....	....	....	....	....
Financial Derivatives Liabilities	78bxd	....	....	....	....	....	....	....	....	....	....	....	....
Other Investment Assets	78bhd	−	−	−	−	−	−	−	−	....	....	....	....
Monetary Authorities	78bod	....	....	....	....	....	....	....	....	....	....	....	....
General Government	78bpd	−	−	−	−	−	−	−	−	....	....	....	....
Banks	78bqd	−	−	−	−	−	−	−	−	....	....	....	....
Other Sectors	78brd	−	−	−	−	−	−	−	−	....	....	....	....
Other Investment Liab., n.i.e.	78bid	15.94	15.55	−5.46	−5.60	−3.60	−5.93	−4.99	−.73	....	....	....	....
Monetary Authorities	78bsd	−	−	−.13	.01	−.01	−.01	.16	−	....	....	....	....
General Government	78btd	16.54	15.26	6.82	3.80	.20	−1.48	−1.04	−2.79	....	....	....	....
Banks	78bud	−.24	.56	.03	−1.12	1.65	1.05	−.54	5.42	....	....	....	....
Other Sectors	78bvd	−.36	−.27	−12.18	−8.29	−5.44	−5.49	−3.57	−3.36	....	....	....	....
Net Errors and Omissions	78cad	23.83	13.83	−4.17	−1.70	−1.30	7.89	−9.59	2.10	....	....	....	....
Overall Balance	78cbd	−12.72	−9.31	−3.86	2.04	7.38	11.09	5.51	7.04	....	....	....	....
Reserves and Related Items	79dad	12.72	9.31	3.86	−2.04	−7.38	−11.09	−5.51	−7.04	....	....	....	....
Reserve Assets	79dbd	12.95	8.30	3.86	−2.04	−7.38	−11.09	−5.51	−7.04	....	....	....	....
Use of Fund Credit and Loans	79dcd	−.22	−	−	−	−	−	−	−	....	....	....	....
Exceptional Financing	79ded	−	1.01	−	−	−	−	....	−	....	....	....	....
National Accounts						*Millions of Tala*							
GDP Volume 1984 Prices	99b.p	128.6	131.7	126.8	....	....	....	....	....	....	....	....	....
GDP Volume 1994 prices	99b.p	....	....	468.8	500.7	531.4	539.9	....	....	....	....	....	....
GDP Volume (1995=100)	99bvp	95.0	97.2	†93.6	100.0	106.1	107.8	....	....	....	....	....	....
GDP Deflator (1995=100)	99bip	....	....	105.5	100.0	103.9	116.2	....	....	....	....	....	....
						Millions: Midyear Estimates							
Population	99z	.16	.16	.16	.17	.17	.17	.17	.17	.17	.17	.18	.18

San Marino 135

		1992	1993	1994	1995	1996	1997	1998	1999	2000	2001	2002	2003
Exchange Rates						*Lire per SDR through 1998, Euros per SDR Thereafter: End of Period*							
Market Rate	aa	2,022.4	2,340.5	2,379.2	2,355.7	2,200.9	2,373.6	2,327.6	1.3662	1.4002	1.4260	1.2964	1.1765
				Lire per US Dollar through 1998, Euros per US Dollar Thereafter: End of Period (ae) Period Average (rf)									
Market Rate	ae	1,470.9	1,704.0	1,629.7	1,584.7	1,530.6	1,759.2	1,653.1	.9954	1.0747	1.1347	.9536	.7918
Market Rate	rf	1,232.4	1,573.7	1,612.4	1,628.9	1,542.9	1,703.1	1,736.2	.9386	1.0854	1.1175	1.0626	.8860
Fund Position						*Millions of SDRs: End of Period*							
Quota	2f.s	6.50	10.00	10.00	10.00	10.00	10.00	10.00	17.00	17.00	17.00	17.00	17.00
SDRs	1b.s	–	.04	.11	.18	.25	.33	.42	.08	.20	.34	.43	.49
Reserve Position in the Fund	1c.s	–	2.35	2.35	2.35	2.35	2.35	2.35	4.10	4.10	4.10	4.10	4.10
Total Fund Cred.&Loans Outstg.	2tl	–	–	–	–	–	–	–	–	–	–	–	–
International Liquidity					*Millions of US Dollars Unless Otherwise Indicated: End of Period*								
Total Reserves Minus Gold	1l.d	....	119.86	176.31	198.55	215.02	182.94	170.67	144.13	135.16	133.51	183.41	252.69
SDRs	1b.d	–	.06	.16	.27	.36	.45	.59	.11	.26	.42	.58	.73
Reserve Position in the Fund	1c.d	–	3.23	3.43	3.50	3.38	3.17	3.31	5.63	5.34	5.15	5.58	6.09
Foreign Exchange	1d.d	....	116.57	172.72	194.78	211.27	179.32	166.77	138.39	129.56	127.93	177.25	245.87
Deposit Money Banks: Assets	7a.d	....	2,886.10	3,013.69	4,001.98	4,703.92	4,408.36	4,382.88	4,465.55	4,289.46	4,452.91	4,793.09	5,530.87
Liabilities	7b.d	....	2,094.00	2,248.21	3,156.34	4,048.64	3,793.34	3,817.43	3,870.92	3,839.12	3,968.26	3,428.61	4,259.72
Monetary Authorities					*Millions of Lire through 1998; Thousands of Euros Beginning 1999: End of Period*								
Foreign Assets	11	....	204,242	287,334	314,640	329,096	321,834	282,139	143,466	145,257	151,490	174,889	200,071
Claims on General Government	12a	....	877	4,242	1,233	1,855	16,966	28,514	14,559	14,851	14,259	15,310	15,427
Claims on Other Resident Sectors	12d	....	–	3,300	–	–	–	–	1,222	336	417	633	298
Claims on Deposit Money Banks	12e	....	85,905	30,273	34,373	40,896	18,542	1,855	745	4,012	9,845	3,093	7,343
Bankers Deposits	14c	....	–	–	–	–	–	3,255	294	2,288	12,867	1,911	6,764
Demand Deposits	14d	....	25,143	14,363	20,123	21,274	21,458	23,144	11,877	26,735	26,770	21,717	19,676
Time, Savings,& Fgn.Currency Dep.	15	....	63	18,496	25,382	26,593	16,889	16,255	9,872	271	171	18,144	29,184
Foreign Liabilities	16c	....	1,131	–	–	–	2	191	1	1	12,867	14,732	800
General Government Deposits	16d	....	231,436	256,504	263,412	269,709	267,432	215,854	108,059	100,494	88,707	99,587	122,925
Capital Accounts	17a	....	33,494	36,014	41,630	54,185	62,912	67,261	36,544	38,912	40,624	41,169	46,829
Other Items (Net)	17r	....	–246	–230	–301	85	–11,352	–13,452	–6,655	–4,247	–5,995	–3,335	–3,040
Deposit Money Banks					*Millions of Lire through 1998; Thousands of Euros Beginning 1999: End of Period*								
Claims on Monetary Authorities	20	....	–	–	–	–	–	3,255	294	2,288	12,867	1,911	6,681
Foreign Assets	21	....	4,917,835	4,911,532	6,342,022	7,199,683	7,755,149	7,245,343	4,445,099	4,609,849	5,052,656	4,570,506	4,379,154
Claims on Other Resident Sectors	22d	....	922,700	1,118,058	1,225,826	1,303,523	1,593,667	1,865,082	1,038,224	1,289,841	1,450,709	1,641,906	1,961,168
Claims on Nonbank Fin. Insts.	22g	....	126,524	143,263	167,394	172,262	189,366	236,356	131,490	165,072	199,835	327,016	380,835
Demand Deposits	24	....	692,456	795,744	565,206	415,528	420,685	464,148	274,054	272,388	317,164	618,910	634,108
Time, Savings,& Fgn.Currency Dep.	25	....	1,151,241	1,092,784	1,473,536	1,264,306	1,537,896	1,486,230	884,782	984,725	1,222,172	1,845,299	1,891,256
Foreign Liabilities	26c	....	3,568,115	3,663,998	5,001,919	6,196,728	6,673,202	6,310,594	3,853,200	4,125,871	4,502,736	3,269,389	3,372,699
Credit from Monetary Authorities	26g	....	85,629	30,273	34,373	40,896	18,325	1,854	743	4,012	9,845	3,093	7,343
Capital Accounts	27a	....	482,060	575,336	701,667	814,326	857,474	1,033,915	583,206	670,996	790,635	807,930	878,385
Other Items (Net)	27r	....	–12,442	14,718	–41,459	–56,316	30,600	53,294	19,121	9,057	–126,485	–3,282	–55,954
Monetary Survey					*Millions of Lire through 1998; Thousands of Euros Beginning 1999: End of Period*								
Foreign Assets (Net)	31n	....	1,552,831	1,534,868	1,654,743	1,332,051	1,403,779	1,216,697	735,364	629,234	688,543	1,461,274	1,205,725
Domestic Credit	32	....	818,665	1,012,359	1,131,041	1,207,931	1,532,567	1,914,098	1,077,436	1,369,605	1,576,513	1,885,278	2,234,802
Claims on General Govt. (Net)	32an	....	–230,559	–252,262	–262,179	–267,854	–250,466	–187,340	–93,500	–85,643	–74,448	–84,277	–107,498
Claims on Other Resident Sectors	32d	....	922,700	1,121,358	1,225,826	1,303,523	1,593,667	1,865,082	1,039,446	1,290,176	1,451,126	1,642,539	1,961,466
Claims on Nonbank Fin. Insts.	32g	....	126,524	143,263	167,394	172,262	189,366	236,356	131,490	165,072	199,835	327,016	380,835
Deposit Money	34	....	717,599	810,107	585,329	436,802	442,143	487,292	285,930	299,124	343,934	640,627	653,785
Quasi-Money	35	....	1,151,304	1,111,280	1,498,918	1,290,899	1,554,785	1,502,485	894,653	984,996	1,222,343	1,863,443	1,920,440
Capital Accounts	37a	....	515,554	611,350	743,297	868,511	920,386	1,101,176	619,751	709,908	831,260	849,099	925,213
Other Items (Net)	37r	....	–12,964	14,488	–41,760	–56,231	19,031	39,841	12,464	4,810	–132,480	–6,616	–58,912
Interest Rates						*Percent Per Annum*							
Deposit Rate	60l	10.00	9.00	7.50	7.35	6.18	4.65	3.70	2.45	2.63	2.88	2.68	1.64
Lending Rate	60p	17.90	16.00	15.00	15.23	14.45	11.43	9.53	7.93	9.20	8.80	7.95	7.49
Production						*Index Numbers (2000=100): Period Averages*							
Tourist Arrivals	66ta	104.5	100.0	101.1	109.7	108.9	107.7	106.3	102.5	100.0	98.8	101.0	93.9

San Marino 135

		1992	1993	1994	1995	1996	1997	1998	1999	2000	2001	2002	2003
National Accounts						*Billions of Lire through 1998; Millions of Euros Beginning 1999*							
Househ.Cons.Expend.,incl.NPISHs....	96f	....	....	....	....	....	795.41	834.22	†447.82	465.30	475.09	479.96	....
Government Consumption Expend...	91f	....	....	....	....	....	219.79	227.51	†132.99	135.44	124.50	127.75	....
Changes in Inventories...................	93i	....	....	....	....	....	40.74	69.00	†42.64	62.59	22.56	−11.56	....
Exports of Goods and Services..........	90c	....	....	....	....	....	3,002.40	2,834.65	†1,581.15	1,627.05	1,682.77	1,660.20	....
Imports of Goods and Services (-)....	98c	....	....	....	....	....	3,049.92	2,854.78	†1,602.18	1,675.01	1,744.28	1,756.40	....
Gross Domestic Product (GDP).........	99b	....	....	....	....	....	1,279.9	1,400.8	†801.03	839.65	929.02	934.94	....
Net Primary Income from Abroad.....	98.n	....	....	....	....	....	−234.38	−267.59	†−158.52	−178.31	−229.13	−206.28	....
Gross National Income (GNI)............	99a	....	....	....	....	....	1,045.48	1,133.25	†642.51	661.34	699.89	728.66	....
Net Current Transf.from Abroad.......	98t	....	....	....	....	....	9.37	7.51	†3.20	3.47	3.65	3.76	....
Gross Nat'l Disposable Inc.(GNDI) Gı	99i	....	....	....	....	....	964.99	1,026.75	†584.02	613.16	649.79	697.73	....
Gross Saving...................................	99s	....	....	....	....	....	183.68	209.00	†133.09	141.97	189.82	215.24	....
GDP Volume 1995 Prices.................	99b.p	....	....	....	....	....	1,210.84	1,301.90	†732.87	749.00	806.44	793.00	....
GDP Volume (2000=100)................	99bvp	....	....	....	....	....	83.5	89.8	†97.8	100.0	107.7	105.9	....
GDP Deflator (2000=100)................	99bip	....	....	....	....	....	94.3	96.0	†97.5	100.0	102.8	105.2	....
						Millions: Midyear Estimates							
Population.................................	99z	.024	.024	.025	.025	.025	.026	.026	.026	.027	.027	.027	.028

2004, International Monetary Fund : *International Financial Statistics Yearbook*

São Tomé & Príncipe 716

		1992	1993	1994	1995	1996	1997	1998	1999	2000	2001	2002	2003
Exchange Rates			*Dobras per SDR: End of Period*
Market Rate...........	aa	516.4	709.7	1,730.4	2,611.6	4,074.0	9,403.9	9,694.3	10,019.3	11,218.9	11,335.3	12,496.5	14,051.2
			*Dobras per US Dollar: End of Period (ae) Period Average (rf)*
Market Rate...........	ae	375.5	516.7	1,185.3	1,756.9	2,833.2	6,969.7	6,885.0	7,300.0	8,610.7	9,019.7	9,191.8	9,455.9
Market Rate...........	rf	321.3	429.9	732.6	1,420.3	2,203.2	4,552.5	6,883.2	7,119.0	7,978.2	8,842.1	9,088.3	9,347.6
Fund Position			*Millions of SDRs: End of Period*
Quota...........	2f.s	5.50	5.50	5.50	5.50	5.50	5.50	5.50	7.40	7.40	7.40	7.40	7.40
SDRs...........	1b.s	–	.01	.01	.03	.01	–	–	–	–	–	.01	.02
Reserve Position in the Fund...........	1c.s	–	–	–	–	–	–	–	–	–	–	–	–
Total Fund Cred.&Loans Outstg........	2tl	.80	.80	.72	.56	.40	.24	.08	–	1.90	1.90	1.90	1.90
International Liquidity			*Millions of US Dollars Unless Otherwise Indicated: End of Period*
Total Reserves minus Gold...........	1l.d	....	....	....	5.14	5.03	12.43	9.68	10.88	11.64	15.48	17.35	25.46
SDRs...........	1b.d	–	.01	.01	.04	.02	–	–	–	–	–	.01	.02
Reserve Position in the Fund...........	1c.d	–	–	–	–	–	–	–	–	–	–	–	–
Foreign Exchange...........	1d.d	....	....	....	5.09	5.01	12.43	9.68	10.88	11.64	15.48	17.34	25.44
Monetary Authorities: Other Liab.....	4..d	....	....	....	5.05	4.94	5.31	–	–	–	2.52	2.55	2.79
Banking Institutions: Assets...........	7a.d	....	....	....	7.11	8.08	8.03	6.85	6.14	5.45	6.09	7.98	9.91
Liabilities...........	7b.d	....	....	....	1.49	.77	.37	1.34	.34	.43	.30	.32	.50
Monetary Authorities			*Millions of Dobras: End of Period*
Foreign Assets...........	11	....	....	....	9,026	14,252	86,611	101,965	114,071	147,576	192,855	217,780	287,243
Claims on Central Government...........	12a	....	....	....	10,290	28,743	28,939	28,831	34,535	32,653	56,425	57,432	61,309
Claims on Nonfin.Pub.Enterprises.....	12c	....	....	....	7,837	–	–	–	–	–	–	–	–
Claims on Private Sector...........	12d	....	....	....	80	204	50	44	38	36	–	–	4,571
Claims on Banking Institutions...........	12e	....	....	....	2,375	1,757	1,839	1,839			762	1,672	1,137
Reserve Money...........	14	....	....	....	10,462	18,945	46,401	51,085	43,332	56,046	97,885	111,903	184,470
of which: Currency Outside Banks..	14a	....	....	....	4,794	6,845	14,818	18,652	20,945	25,048	35,763	39,424	55,854
Foreign Liabilities...........	16c	....	....	....	10,331	15,614	39,258	795	–	21,338	44,256	47,224	53,104
Central Government Deposits...........	16d	....	....	....	–	6,868	41,985	30,994	41,716	47,805	44,046	53,905	27,716
Counterpart Funds...........	16e	....	....	....	10,333	9,091	11,197	24,271	26,178	21,338	22,335	12,387	11,504
Capital Accounts...........	17a	....	....	....	1,887	−2,356	−13,966	46,025	54,327	57,154	64,493	76,544	100,236
of which: Valuation Adjustment.....	17rv	....	....	....	−2,018	−5,432	−21,841	29,394	34,783	–	–	–	–
Other Items (Net)...........	17r	....	....	....	−3,405	−3,207	−7,436	−20,491	−16,909	−23,415	−22,973	−25,078	−22,770
Banking Institutions			*Millions of Dobras: End of Period*
Reserves...........	20	....	....	....	5,488	12,730	30,646	30,485	26,620	35,474	62,633	75,299	129,769
Foreign Assets...........	21	....	....	....	12,491	22,880	55,935	47,139	44,819	46,923	54,919	73,357	93,662
Claims on Private Sector...........	22d	....	....	....	6,614	8,599	11,897	22,429	24,969	26,569	29,346	45,155	91,897
Demand Deposits...........	24	....	....	....	9,431	16,837	34,384	27,731	29,178	36,756	57,388	69,112	105,276
Time, Savings,& Fgn.Currency Dep...	25	....	....	....	6,110	13,830	31,992	35,892	39,793	50,401	61,815	88,046	138,483
of which: Fgn. Currency Deposits...	25b	....	....	....	6,011	13,086	30,803	32,763	35,266	43,260	52,932	75,839	123,164
Foreign Liabilities...........	26c	....	....	....	2,626	2,173	2,562	9,205	2,485	3,679	2,721	2,901	4,709
Central Government Deposits...........	26d	....	....	....	2,462	3,313	1,516	2,447	1,251	2,295	529	1,295	1,002
Counterpart Funds...........	26e	....	....	....	609	105	105	105	2,134	2,134	2,134	2,134	2,134
Credit from Monetary Authorities.....	26g	....	....	....	250	1,150	3,700	1,200	–	–	–	–	–
Capital Accounts...........	27a	....	....	....	3,687	11,828	30,722	36,555	36,038	33,934	34,964	41,841	72,895
Other Items (Net)...........	27r	....	....	....	−582	−5,028	−6,503	−13,082	−14,470	−20,233	−12,651	−11,517	−9,171
Banking Survey			*Millions of Dobras: End of Period*
Foreign Assets (Net)...........	31n	....	....	....	8,559	19,345	100,726	139,104	156,406	169,482	200,798	241,013	323,090
Domestic Credit...........	32	....	....	....	22,359	27,365	−2,615	17,863	16,574	9,159	41,196	47,387	129,059
Claims on Central Govt.(Net)...........	32an	....	....	....	7,829	18,562	−14,561	−4,610	−8,432	−17,446	11,850	2,232	32,591
Claims on Nonfin.Pub.Enterprises...	32c	....	....	....	7,837	–	–	–	–	–	–	–	–
Claims on Private Sector...........	32d	....	....	....	6,694	8,803	11,947	22,473	25,007	26,605	29,346	45,155	96,468
Money...........	34	....	....	....	14,225	23,683	49,202	47,584	50,123	61,885	95,483	108,597	161,230
Quasi-Money...........	35	....	....	....	6,110	13,830	31,992	35,892	39,793	50,401	61,815	88,046	138,483
Counterpart Funds...........	36e	....	....	....	10,942	9,196	11,302	24,375	28,311	23,472	24,469	14,521	13,637
Capital Accounts...........	37a	....	....	....	5,574	9,473	16,757	82,580	90,365	91,089	99,456	118,385	173,130
Other Items (Net)...........	37r	....	....	....	−5,932	−9,472	−11,142	−33,464	−35,613	−48,204	−39,229	−41,149	−34,331
Money plus Quasi-Money...........	35l	....	....	....	20,335	37,513	81,195	83,476	89,916	112,286	157,298	196,643	299,713
Interest Rates			*Percent Per Annum*
Discount Rate (End of Period)...........	60	45.00	30.00	32.00	50.00	35.00	55.00	29.50	17.00	17.00	15.50	15.50	14.50
Deposit Rate...........	60l	35.00	35.00	35.00	35.00	31.00	36.75	38.29	27.00	† 21.00	15.00	15.00	12.29
Lending Rate...........	60p	37.00	37.00	30.00	52.00	38.00	51.50	55.58	40.33	† 39.67	37.00	37.08	33.79

São Tomé & Príncipe 716

		1992	1993	1994	1995	1996	1997	1998	1999	2000	2001	2002	2003
Balance of Payments						*Millions of US Dollars: Minus Sign Indicates Debit*							
Current Account, n.i.e.	78ald	....	....	....	....	....	....	−10.47	−16.28	−19.13	−21.01	−22.77	....
Goods: Exports f.o.b.	78aad	....	....	....	....	....	....	4.74	3.90	2.69	3.28	5.12	....
Goods: Imports f.o.b.	78abd	....	....	....	....	....	....	−16.88	−21.94	−25.13	−24.43	−28.00	....
Trade Balance	78acd	....	....	....	....	....	....	−12.14	−18.04	−22.44	−21.14	−22.88	....
Services: Credit	78add	....	....	....	....	....	....	6.56	12.48	13.56	12.78	13.41	....
Services: Debit	78aed	....	....	....	....	....	....	−10.35	−11.83	−10.99	−12.07	−13.44	....
Balance on Goods & Services	78afd	....	....	....	....	....	....	−15.92	−17.40	−19.87	−20.43	−22.91	....
Income: Credit	78agd	....	....	....	....	....	....	....	....	....	−	....	....
Income: Debit	78ahd	....	....	....	....	....	....	−5.21	−5.32	−3.62	−4.62	−4.71	....
Balance on Gds, Serv. & Inc	78aid	....	....	....	....	....	....	−21.13	−22.71	−23.49	−25.05	−27.62	....
Current Transfers, n.i.e.: Credit	78ajd	....	....	....	....	....	....	10.66	6.44	4.36	4.05	4.85	....
Current Transfers: Debit	78akd	....	....	....	....	....	....	....	....	....	....	....	....
Capital Account, n.i.e.	78bcd	....	....	....	....	....	....	3.90	9.27	12.00	15.20	12.14	....
Capital Account, n.i.e.: Credit	78bad	....	....	....	....	....	....	3.90	9.27	12.00	15.20	12.14	....
Capital Account: Debit	78bbd	....	....	....	....	....	....	....	....	....	....	....	....
Financial Account, n.i.e.	78bjd	....	....	....	....	....	....	.27	4.36	3.32	1.67	3.69	....
Direct Investment Abroad	78bdd	....	....	....	....	....	....	....	....	....	−	....	....
Dir. Invest. in Rep. Econ., n.i.e.	78bed	....	....	....	....	....	....	4.20	3.04	3.80	3.47	3.04	....
Portfolio Investment Assets	78bfd	....	....	....	....	....	....	....	....	....	....	....	....
Equity Securities	78bkd	....	....	....	....	....	....	....	....	....	−	....	....
Debt Securities	78bld	....	....	....	....	....	....	....	....	....	....	....	....
Portfolio Investment Liab., n.i.e.	78bgd	....	....	....	....	....	....	....	....	....	−	....	....
Equity Securities	78bmd	....	....	....	....	....	....	....	....	....	−	....	....
Debt Securities	78bnd	....	....	....	....	....	....	....	....	....	−	....	....
Financial Derivatives Assets	78bwd	....	....	....	....	....	....	....	....	....	....	....	....
Financial Derivatives Liabilities	78bxd	....	....	....	....	....	....	....	....	....	....	....	....
Other Investment Assets	78bhd	....	....	....	....	....	....	−5.23	−5.18	−4.81	−4.82	−.25	....
Monetary Authorities	78bod	....	....	....	....	....	....	....	....	....	−	....	....
General Government	78bpd	....	....	....	....	....	....	....	....	....	....	....	....
Banks	78bqd	....	....	....	....	....	....	−5.23	−5.18	−4.81	−4.82	−.25	....
Other Sectors	78brd	....	....	....	....	....	....	....	....	....	−	....	....
Other Investment Liab., n.i.e.	78bid	....	....	....	....	....	....	1.30	6.50	4.33	3.01	.90	....
Monetary Authorities	78bsd	....	....	....	....	....	....	−	−	−	−	....	....
General Government	78btd	....	....	....	....	....	....	1.30	6.50	4.33	3.01	.90	....
Banks	78bud	....	....	....	....	....	....	....	....	....	−	....	....
Other Sectors	78bvd	....	....	....	....	....	....	....	....	....	−	....	....
Net Errors and Omissions	78cad	....	....	....	....	....	....	.26	.09	−1.66	2.66	−.04	....
Overall Balance	78cbd	....	....	....	....	....	....	−6.04	−2.56	−5.46	−1.48	−6.97	....
Reserves and Related Items	79dad	....	....	....	....	....	....	6.04	2.56	5.46	1.48	6.97	....
Reserve Assets	79dbd	....	....	....	....	....	....	2.70	−1.19	−1.50	−4.33	−2.37	....
Use of Fund Credit and Loans	79dcd	....	....	....	....	....	....	−.22	−.11	2.48	−	−	....
Exceptional Financing	79ded	....	....	....	....	....	....	3.56	3.86	4.49	5.80	9.34	....
						Millions: Midyear Estimates							
Population	99z	.12	.12	.13	.13	.13	.14	.14	.15	.15	.15	.16	.16

2004, International Monetary Fund : *International Financial Statistics Yearbook*

Saudi Arabia 456

		1992	1993	1994	1995	1996	1997	1998	1999	2000	2001	2002	2003
Exchange Rates						*Riyals per SDR: End of Period*							
Official Rate....................	aa	5.1494	5.1440	5.4671	5.5669	5.3852	5.0529	5.2731	5.1400	4.8794	4.7065	5.0914	5.5650
					Riyals per US Dollar: End of Period (ae) Period Average (rf)								
Official Rate....................	ae	3.7450	3.7450	3.7450	3.7450	3.7450	3.7450	3.7450	3.7450	3.7450	3.7450	3.7450	3.7450
Official Rate....................	rf	3.7450	3.7450	3.7450	3.7450	3.7450	3.7450	3.7450	3.7450	3.7450	3.7450	3.7450	3.7450
					Index Numbers (2000=100): Period Averages								
Official Rate....................	ahx	100.0	100.0	100.0	100.0	100.0	100.0	100.0	100.0	100.0	100.0	100.0	100.0
Nominal Effective Exchange Rate.....	nec	83.8	88.3	86.6	82.2	85.1	91.2	97.0	95.3	100.0	105.3	103.1	93.9
Real Effective Exchange Rate...........	rec	96.3	99.4	95.3	92.2	94.5	99.1	102.6	98.3	100.0	102.3	99.0	89.1
Fund Position					*Millions of SDRs: End of Period*								
Quota.............................	2f.s	3,202	5,131	5,131	5,131	5,131	5,131	5,131	6,986	6,986	6,986	6,986	6,986
SDRs...............................	1b.s	202	403	416	448	481	512	546	110	147	192	244	290
Reserve Position in the Fund...........	1c.s	797	869	604	575	561	532	524	987	1,043	2,036	2,621	3,047
of which: Outstg.Fund Borrowing...	2c	525	175	—	—	—	—	—	—	—	—	—	—
International Liquidity				*Millions of US Dollars Unless Otherwise Indicated: Approximately End of Period*									
Total Reserves minus Gold..............	1l.d	5,935	7,428	7,378	8,622	†14,321	14,876	14,220	16,997	19,585	17,596	20,610	22,620
SDRs................................	1b.d	278	553	607	666	692	691	769	152	191	242	332	431
Reserve Position in the Fund.........	1c.d	1,096	1,193	882	854	807	718	737	1,355	1,359	2,558	3,564	4,527
Foreign Exchange......................	1d.d	4,561	5,682	5,888	7,101	†12,822	13,467	12,714	15,490	18,036	14,796	16,715	17,662
Gold (Million Fine Troy Ounces).......	1ad	4.596	4.596	4.596	4.596	4.596	4.596	4.596	4.596	4.596	4.596	4.596	4.596
Gold (National Valuation).............	1and	221	221	235	239	231	217	226	221	210	202	219	239
Monetary Authorities:Other Assets...	3..d	....	....	....	....	....	....	....	....	....	....	....	....
Deposit Money Banks: Assets...........	7a.d	27,147	29,796	26,208	26,160	28,350	26,573	22,949	24,429	27,024	26,526	25,498	21,651
Liabilities.....................	7b.d	7,660	9,958	10,454	10,595	10,321	12,295	11,510	13,659	17,208	15,918	11,482	10,698
Other Banking Insts.: Assets............	7e.d	1,148	1,153	1,150	1,017	1,024	1,042	1,042	1,042	998	1,002	1,006	1,016
Monetary Authorities					*Billions of Riyals: Approximately End of Period*								
Foreign Assets......................	11	214.89	193.08	185.56	174.04	196.07	219.03	175.60	147.39	183.54	181.80	157.46	223.77
Reserve Money.....................	14	53.89	53.79	56.23	54.93	54.15	58.24	57.53	71.04	68.20	65.42	71.50	75.17
of which: Currency Outside DMBs..	14a	43.77	42.62	44.97	43.89	43.04	45.82	45.02	55.06	51.02	49.25	52.33	55.44
Central Government Deposits...........	16d	41.97	42.48	35.53	34.63	45.52	48.51	48.74	30.99	51.47	51.60	51.72	56.55
Other Items (Net)....................	17r	119.04	96.81	93.80	84.48	96.40	112.28	69.33	45.35	63.87	64.79	34.23	92.05
Deposit Money Banks					*Billions of Riyals: Approximately End of Period*								
Reserves............................	20	10.65	11.53	11.65	11.18	11.21	12.55	12.57	16.55	18.88	19.15	43.86	26.66
Foreign Assets......................	21	†101.67	111.59	98.15	97.97	106.17	99.52	85.94	91.49	101.20	99.34	95.49	81.08
Claims on Central Government........	22a	†37.92	43.46	50.03	52.28	65.27	83.21	89.37	102.27	112.27	123.83	123.43	150.72
Claims on Public Enterprises............	22c	24.67	22.60	26.93	24.45	16.70	20.86	23.60	14.35	12.44	10.82	11.96	25.84
Claims on Private Sector................	22d	†86.04	101.93	113.19	121.15	123.55	133.68	160.66	162.19	172.24	187.06	205.83	228.49
Demand Deposits.....................	24	†79.69	78.89	80.73	81.52	90.08	95.47	95.39	101.76	114.69	130.45	150.24	167.78
Quasi-Monetary Deposits...............	25a	†53.72	56.89	60.60	69.70	81.73	86.27	91.31	95.09	100.09	100.85	118.49	125.06
Foreign Currency Deposits.............	25b	†42.22	48.41	47.29	46.32	44.10	44.88	50.61	49.72	49.29	50.57	60.39	65.56
Foreign Liabilities....................	26c	†28.69	37.29	39.15	39.68	38.65	46.04	43.11	51.15	64.44	59.61	43.00	40.06
Credit from Monetary Authorities.....	26g	13.37	19.80	21.42	18.63	13.57	18.33	29.44	20.58	10.95	7.46	6.44	8.69
Capital Accounts.....................	27a	†28.17	34.48	36.96	39.25	42.65	44.87	47.60	48.69	52.38	53.85	57.85	59.18
Other Items (Net)....................	27r	†15.10	15.34	13.80	11.94	12.11	13.96	14.68	19.84	25.20	37.41	44.16	46.46
Monetary Survey					*Billions of Riyals: Approximately End of Period*								
Foreign Assets (Net)...................	31n	†287.87	267.37	244.55	232.33	263.59	272.50	218.44	187.72	220.30	221.53	209.95	264.79
Domestic Credit......................	32	†106.66	125.52	154.62	163.26	160.00	189.24	224.88	247.81	245.48	270.12	289.50	348.50
Claims on Central Govt. (Net)........	32an	†−4.05	.98	14.50	17.66	19.75	34.69	40.63	71.27	60.80	72.24	71.71	94.17
Claims on Public Enterprises..........	32c	24.67	22.60	26.93	24.45	16.70	20.86	23.60	14.35	12.44	10.82	11.96	25.84
Claims on Private Sector...............	32d	†86.04	101.93	113.19	121.15	123.55	133.68	160.66	162.19	172.24	187.06	205.83	228.49
Money.............................	34	†123.46	121.51	125.69	125.41	133.11	141.29	140.41	156.82	165.71	179.70	202.57	223.22
Quasi-Money.......................	35	†95.94	105.30	107.89	116.02	125.83	131.15	141.92	144.81	149.38	151.42	178.88	190.62
Other Items (Net)....................	37r	†175.13	166.08	165.59	154.17	164.64	189.30	160.99	133.90	150.69	160.52	118.00	199.45
Money plus Quasi-Money.............	35l	†219.40	226.81	233.58	241.43	258.95	272.44	282.33	301.62	315.09	331.12	381.45	413.84
Other Banking Institutions					*Billions of Riyals: Approximately End of Period*								
Cash...............................	40	18.60	21.88	17.21	14.34	21.92	28.20	21.62	13.00	15.42	20.95	15.07	18.49
Foreign Assets......................	41	4.30	4.32	4.31	3.81	3.84	3.90	3.90	3.90	3.74	3.75	3.77	3.81
Claims on Private Sector...............	42d	171.36	168.81	172.90	178.07	181.43	178.96	188.18	199.56	198.54	196.77	204.98	216.71
Capital Accounts.....................	47a	190.66	190.66	190.46	190.46	190.46	190.46	190.46	191.33	191.19	191.19	191.19	201.89
Other Items (Net)....................	47r	3.61	4.35	3.95	5.76	16.73	20.61	23.25	25.13	26.50	30.28	32.64	37.12
Interest Rates					*Percent per Annum*								
Deposit Rate........................	60l	3.649	3.521	5.100	6.178	5.469	5.790	6.211	6.137	6.667	3.922	2.234	1.631

Saudi Arabia 456

		1992	1993	1994	1995	1996	1997	1998	1999	2000	2001	2002	2003
Prices, Production, Labor						*Index Numbers (2000=100): Period Averages*							
Share Prices	62	83.6	79.4	56.8	60.6	67.8	86.7	62.6	89.8	100.0	107.6	111.5	196.5
Wholesale Prices	63	92.3	92.8	94.5	101.4	101.1	101.1	99.2	99.6	100.0	99.9	99.9	100.7
Consumer Prices	64	95.3	96.3	96.9	101.6	102.8	102.9	102.5	†101.1	100.0	98.9	99.1	99.7
Crude Petroleum	66aa	102.4	98.7	98.7	98.4	99.6	98.2	100.6	93.2	100.0	94.8	89.5	103.5
						Number in Thousands: Period Averages							
Employment	67e	3,140	2,495	2,496	2,495	....	....	....	....	....	....	....	....
International Transactions						*Billions of Riyals*							
Exports	70	188.32	158.77	159.59	187.40	227.43	227.44	145.39	190.10	290.55	254.90	271.70	....
Petroleum	70a	174.24	144.64	142.83	163.08	203.25	199.77	121.97	168.30	265.75	219.13	238.99	....
Crude Petroleum	70aa	148.31	119.91	117.20	132.99	163.28	163.02	98.84	138.34	232.21	190.56	206.22	....
Refined Petroleum	70ab	25.93	24.73	25.63	30.09	39.97	36.76	23.13	29.96	33.53	28.57	32.77	....
Imports, c.i.f.	71	124.60	105.60	87.40	105.20	103.90	107.60	112.40	104.90	113.24	116.93	121.01	137.17
Volume of Exports						*2000=100*							
Petroleum	72a	105.6	103.3	101.8	101.9	102.4	101.6	103.9	93.8	100.0	97.8	....	....
Crude Petroleum	72aa	105.5	100.6	99.7	100.6	98.0	98.9	102.2	91.5	100.0	100.0	....	....
Refined Petroleum	72ab	105.7	115.1	111.2	107.6	121.8	113.4	111.5	104.2	100.0	88.2	....	....
Export Prices						*2000=100: Index of Prices in US Dollars*							
Crude Petroleum	76aad	64.5	56.0	56.3	62.3	73.6	69.6	44.9	65.1	100.0	86.5	....	....
Balance of Payments						*Millions of US Dollars: Minus Sign Indicates Debit*							
Current Account, n.i.e.	78ald	−17,740	−17,268	−10,487	−5,325	680	305	−13,150	412	14,336	9,366	11,889	29,701
Goods: Exports f.o.b.	78aad	50,287	42,395	42,614	50,041	60,729	60,732	38,822	50,757	77,584	68,064	72,561	95,369
Goods: Imports f.o.b.	78abd	−30,248	−25,873	−21,325	−25,650	−25,358	−26,370	−27,535	−25,717	−27,741	−28,645	−29,664	−33,913
Trade Balance	78acd	20,039	16,522	21,289	24,390	35,370	34,362	11,287	25,039	49,843	39,418	42,897	61,456
Services: Credit	78add	3,466	3,283	3,347	3,480	2,772	4,257	4,730	5,380	4,785	5,014	5,184	5,346
Services: Debit	78aed	−32,282	−24,464	−17,893	−19,283	−24,295	−25,964	−16,881	−18,855	−25,262	−19,307	−20,006	−20,799
Balance on Goods & Services	78afd	−8,777	−4,659	6,743	8,587	13,847	12,655	−864	11,564	29,367	25,126	28,075	46,002
Income: Credit	78agd	7,378	6,208	4,032	4,987	5,127	5,756	5,810	5,811	3,349	4,130	3,719	2,998
Income: Debit	78ahd	−1,944	−2,300	−2,560	−2,184	−2,681	−2,971	−3,041	−2,887	−2,869	−4,650	−3,930	−4,283
Balance on Gds, Serv. & Inc.	78aid	−3,343	−751	8,215	11,391	16,294	15,440	1,905	14,488	29,847	24,606	27,864	44,718
Current Transfers, n.i.e.: Credit	78ajd	−	−	−	−	−	−	−	−	−	−	−	−
Current Transfers: Debit	78akd	−14,397	−16,517	−18,702	−16,716	−15,613	−15,134	−15,054	−14,077	−15,511	−15,240	−15,975	−15,016
Capital Account, n.i.e.	78bcd												
Capital Account, n.i.e.: Credit	78bad	−	−	−	−	−	−	−	−	−	−	−	−
Capital Account: Debit	78bbd	−	−	−	−	−	−	−	−	−	−	−	−
Financial Account, n.i.e.	78bjd	12,075	18,763	10,341	6,542	5,069	343	12,431	2,403	−11,671	−11,275	−9,153	−28,093
Direct Investment Abroad	78bdd												
Dir. Invest. in Rep. Econ., n.i.e.	78bed	−79	1,369	350	−1,877	−1,129	3,044	4,289	−780	−1,884	20	−615	−587
Portfolio Investment Assets	78bfd	−6,500	8,213	−2,527	4,057	−2,642	−7,362	6,941	11,712	−9,394	−2,798	7,558	−18,765
Equity Securities	78bkd	−	−	−	−	−	−	−	−	−	−	−	−
Debt Securities	78bld	−6,500	8,213	−2,527	4,057	−2,642	−7,362	6,941	11,712	−9,394	−2,798	7,558	−18,765
Portfolio Investment Liab., n.i.e.	78bgd	−	−	−	−	−	−	−	−	−	−	−	−
Equity Securities	78bmd	−	−	−	−	−	−	−	−	−	−	−	−
Debt Securities	78bnd	−	−	−	−	−	−	−	−	−	−	−	−
Financial Derivatives Assets	78bwd	....	....	....	....	....	....	....	....	....	....	....	....
Financial Derivatives Liabilities	78bxd	....	....	....	....	....	....	....	....	....	....	....	....
Other Investment Assets	78bhd	18,446	6,885	12,022	4,222	9,113	2,687	1,985	−10,678	−3,942	−7,206	−11,660	−7,957
Monetary Authorities	78bod	−	−	−	−	−	−	−	−	−	−	−	−
General Government	78bpd	−	−	−	−	−	−	−	−	−	−	−	−
Banks	78bqd	4,621	−2,661	3,588	47	−2,190	1,777	3,624	−1,480	−2,595	491	1,035	3,895
Other Sectors	78brd	13,825	9,545	8,434	4,175	11,303	910	−1,639	−9,198	−1,348	−7,697	−12,694	−11,852
Other Investment Liab., n.i.e.	78bid	208	2,296	497	141	−274	1,973	−785	2,149	3,549	−1,290	−4,437	−784
Monetary Authorities	78bsd	−	−	−	−	−	−	−	−	−	−	−	−
General Government	78btd	−	−	−	−	−	−	−	−	−	−	−	−
Banks	78bud	208	2,296	497	141	−274	1,973	−785	2,149	3,549	−1,290	−4,437	−784
Other Sectors	78bvd	−	−	−	−	−	−	−	−	−	−	−	−
Net Errors and Omissions	78cad	−	−	−	−	−	−	−	−	−	−	−	−
Overall Balance	78cbd	−5,664	1,495	−146	1,217	5,749	648	−719	2,815	2,665	−1,909	2,736	1,608
Reserves and Related Items	79dad	5,664	−1,495	146	−1,217	−5,749	−648	719	−2,815	−2,665	1,909	−2,736	−1,608
Reserve Assets	79dbd	5,664	−1,495	146	−1,217	−5,749	−648	719	−2,815	−2,665	1,909	−2,736	−1,608
Use of Fund Credit and Loans	79dcd	−	−	−	−	−	−	−	−	−	−	−	−
Exceptional Financing	79ded	....	....	....	....	....	....	....	....	....	....	....	....
Government Finance						*Billions of Riyals*							
Deficit (−) or Surplus	80	....	....	....	....	−18.50	−17.00	−18.00	−44.00	−28.00	....	....	....
Total Revenue and Grants	81y	....	....	....	....	131.50	164.00	178.00	121.00	157.00	....	....	....
Revenue	81	....	....	....	....	131.50	164.00	178.00	121.00	157.00	....	....	....
Grants	81z	....	....	....	....	−	−	−	−	−	....	....	....
Exp. & Lending Minus Repay.	82z	....	....	....	....	150.00	181.00	196.00	165.00	185.00	....	....	....
Expenditure	82	....	....	....	....	150.00	181.00	196.00	165.00	185.00	....	....	....
Lending Minus Repayments	83	....	....	....	....	−	−	−	−	−	....	....	....

2004, International Monetary Fund : *International Financial Statistics Yearbook*

Saudi Arabia 456

		1992	1993	1994	1995	1996	1997	1998	1999	2000	2001	2002	2003
National Accounts							*Billions of Riyals*						
Househ.Cons.Expend.,incl.NPISHs	96f	226.78	237.75	240.48	250.28	259.49	261.43	251.42	252.22	258.13	259.55	260.40	266.50
Government Consumption Expend	91f	152.69	130.98	122.55	125.92	144.78	161.80	155.19	154.09	183.80	188.70	184.52	198.15
Gross Fixed Capital Formation	93e	103.96	108.82	93.00	103.32	102.85	109.24	112.96	118.20	123.32	126.10	128.07	141.27
Changes in Inventories	93i	11.00	12.88	6.88	2.27	4.06	3.84	9.60	9.42	8.90	3.50	11.04	14.84
Exports of Goods and Services	90c	200.77	171.07	172.12	200.44	237.81	243.38	163.10	210.23	308.47	273.68	291.16	377.18
Imports of Goods and Services (-)	98c	184.75	166.59	131.98	148.72	158.24	161.78	145.62	140.57	175.97	165.22	168.11	193.71
Gross Domestic Product (GDP)	99b	510.46	494.91	503.05	533.50	590.75	617.90	546.65	603.59	706.66	686.30	707.07	804.23
Net Primary Income from Abroad	98.n	5.76	9.76	2.82	8.21	.11	−.23	4.87	7.97	3.35	6.65	—	—
Gross National Income (GNI)	99a	516.22	504.67	505.87	541.71	590.86	617.67	551.52	611.56	710.00	692.95	707.07	804.23
GDP Volume 1970 Prices	99b.p	62.66	62.26	62.58	62.88	63.76	....	....	....	....	....	....	....
GDP Volume 1999 Prices	99b.p	....	....	....	....	576.43	591.38	608.14	603.59	632.95	636.42	637.23	682.98
GDP Volume (2000=100)	99bvp	89.5	88.9	89.4	89.8	†91.1	93.4	96.1	95.4	100.0	100.5	100.7	107.9
GDP Deflator (2000=100)	99bip	80.7	78.7	79.6	84.1	91.8	93.6	80.5	89.6	100.0	96.6	99.4	105.5
						Millions: Midyear Estimates							
Population	99z	17.58	18.02	18.47	18.97	19.53	20.14	20.80	21.47	22.15	22.83	23.52	24.22

2004, International Monetary Fund : *International Financial Statistics Yearbook*

Senegal 722

		1992	1993	1994	1995	1996	1997	1998	1999	2000	2001	2002	2003
Exchange Rates						*Francs per SDR: End of Period*							
Official Rate	aa	378.57	404.89	†780.44	728.38	753.06	807.94	791.61	†896.19	918.49	935.39	850.37	771.76
					Francs per US Dollar: End of Period (ae) Period Average (rf)								
Official Rate	ae	275.32	294.77	†534.60	490.00	523.70	598.81	562.21	†652.95	704.95	744.31	625.50	519.36
Official Rate	rf	264.69	283.16	†555.20	499.15	511.55	583.67	589.95	†615.70	711.98	733.04	696.99	581.20
Fund Position						*Millions of SDRs: End of Period*							
Quota	2f.s	118.9	118.9	118.9	118.9	118.9	118.9	118.9	161.8	161.8	161.8	161.8	161.8
SDRs	1b.s	–	.3	.7	2.6	1.2	.3	.4	1.8	.7	6.0	6.7	7.1
Reserve Position in the Fund	1c.s	1.1	1.1	1.1	1.2	1.3	1.3	1.4	1.4	1.4	1.4	1.5	1.5
Total Fund Cred.&Loans Outstg	2tl	197.4	177.8	205.4	233.3	226.5	216.5	207.8	198.2	195.4	197.6	185.8	161.3
International Liquidity					*Millions of US Dollars Unless Otherwise Indicated: End of Period*								
Total Reserves minus Gold	1l.d	12.4	3.4	179.6	271.8	288.3	386.2	430.8	403.0	384.0	447.3	637.4	794.5
SDRs	1b.d	–	.4	1.1	3.8	1.7	.5	.5	2.5	.9	7.5	9.1	10.6
Reserve Position in the Fund	1c.d	1.4	1.5	1.7	1.8	1.8	1.8	1.8	1.9	1.9	1.8	2.0	2.2
Foreign Exchange	1d.d	10.9	1.5	176.9	266.2	284.8	383.9	428.4	398.6	381.2	438.0	626.3	781.8
Gold (Million Fine Troy Ounces)	1ad	.029	.029	.029	–	–	–	–	–	–	–	–	–
Gold (National Valuation)	1and	10.1	10.8	10.8	–	–	–	–	–	–	–	–	–
Monetary Authorities: Other Liab	4..d	298.2	408.2	144.4	122.8	116.9	101.6	109.2	96.6	97.2	86.3	107.4	143.0
Deposit Money Banks: Assets	7a.d	72.8	68.6	131.4	159.9	146.7	151.3	220.4	258.2	220.8	239.9	361.6	490.6
Liabilities	7b.d	171.8	154.7	134.0	131.7	105.0	94.0	117.5	119.9	86.9	101.6	107.2	107.0
Monetary Authorities						*Billions of Francs: End of Period*							
Foreign Assets	11	3.4	1.0	96.0	133.2	151.0	231.3	242.2	263.1	270.7	332.9	398.7	412.7
Claims on Central Government	12a	163.6	158.4	265.5	271.4	229.7	293.7	296.4	279.1	256.6	301.0	292.0	262.2
Claims on Deposit Money Banks	12e	189.0	172.3	11.5	–	2.6	31.7	26.9	12.6	2.0	–	–	–
Claims on Other Financial Insts	12f	.6	.6	.6	.7	.5	.5	.4	–	–	–	–	–
Reserve Money	14	181.7	126.6	188.9	196.6	168.7	174.2	186.0	215.7	228.1	306.4	343.9	360.2
of which: Currency Outside DMBs	14a	107.2	93.0	145.6	152.1	141.9	142.3	158.5	179.4	171.5	211.7	191.9	173.2
Foreign Liabilities	16c	156.8	192.3	237.5	230.1	231.7	235.7	225.9	240.6	248.0	249.1	225.2	198.7
Central Government Deposits	16d	4.0	5.7	13.8	19.2	26.8	142.1	137.4	105.0	55.9	80.2	104.1	86.6
Other Items (Net)	17r	14.0	7.6	–66.5	–40.7	–43.5	5.0	16.6	–6.6	–2.7	–1.8	17.5	29.3
Deposit Money Banks						*Billions of Francs: End of Period*							
Reserves	20	74.1	34.1	31.8	31.1	24.9	32.4	27.1	35.7	55.9	93.4	153.8	185.5
Foreign Assets	21	20.1	20.2	70.2	78.4	76.8	90.6	123.9	168.6	155.6	178.5	226.2	254.8
Claims on Central Government	22a	22.8	28.6	57.9	61.5	120.0	109.6	122.4	110.6	94.0	101.8	60.6	69.1
Claims on Private Sector	22d	417.5	424.3	349.9	355.6	411.0	428.3	437.1	483.0	619.5	651.8	682.0	782.1
Claims on Other Financial Insts	22f	2.1	1.6	1.3	.2	–	–	–	–	–	–	–	–
Demand Deposits	24	106.6	101.4	155.3	160.2	198.5	196.3	234.0	255.9	287.7	315.3	366.1	484.7
Time Deposits	25	167.6	138.8	161.4	184.6	216.4	237.7	233.2	273.2	325.3	363.8	406.4	444.1
Foreign Liabilities	26c	38.3	36.4	58.3	51.4	42.4	50.0	62.5	72.5	56.4	65.2	54.3	36.1
Long-Term Foreign Liabilities	26cl	9.0	9.2	13.4	13.2	12.6	6.3	3.5	5.8	4.9	10.4	12.8	19.5
Central Government Deposits	26d	100.8	118.1	136.4	136.3	161.7	109.5	101.5	97.6	136.5	143.8	143.5	186.3
Credit from Monetary Authorities	26g	190.2	176.8	11.5	–	3.6	31.7	26.9	12.6	2.0	–	–	–
Other Items (Net)	27r	–75.8	–71.9	–25.1	–18.9	–2.5	29.4	48.9	80.5	112.3	127.0	139.5	120.8
Treasury Claims: Private Sector	22d.i	2.4	2.3	2.3	2.2	3.0	2.8	2.9	3.2	2.6	4.5	5.6	2.5
Post Office: Checking Deposits	24..i	3.4	3.0	3.9	4.3	2.8	4.0	4.1	3.9	4.1	4.7	5.3	8.5
Monetary Survey						*Billions of Francs: End of Period*							
Foreign Assets (Net)	31n	–171.6	–207.4	–129.5	–69.9	–46.3	36.1	77.7	118.7	121.9	197.1	345.4	432.6
Domestic Credit	32	505.2	492.7	529.0	538.1	575.5	584.5	621.5	674.1	781.9	835.3	792.2	848.8
Claims on Central Govt. (Net)	32an	82.6	63.9	174.9	179.5	161.0	152.9	181.1	187.8	159.7	179.0	104.7	64.2
Claims on Private Sector	32d	419.9	426.6	352.2	357.8	414.1	431.1	439.9	486.2	622.2	656.3	687.6	784.6
Claims on Other Financial Insts	32f	2.7	2.2	1.9	.8	.5	.5	.4	–	–	–	–	–
Money	34	217.4	197.7	305.3	316.8	343.6	343.2	397.0	439.8	464.0	533.0	563.9	667.9
Quasi-Money	35	167.6	138.8	161.4	184.6	216.4	237.7	233.2	273.2	325.3	363.8	406.4	444.1
Long-Term Foreign Liabilities	36cl	9.0	9.2	13.4	13.2	12.6	6.3	3.5	5.8	4.9	10.4	12.8	19.5
Other Items (Net)	37r	–60.4	–60.5	–80.7	–46.4	–43.4	33.4	65.5	73.9	109.6	125.3	154.5	150.0
Money plus Quasi-Money	35l	385.0	336.5	466.7	501.4	560.0	580.9	630.2	713.0	789.3	896.8	970.3	1,111.9
Interest Rates						*Percent Per Annum*							
Bank Rate (End of Period)	60	12.50	†6.00	6.00	6.00	6.00	6.00	6.00	6.00	6.00	6.00	6.00	4.50
Money Market Rate	60b	11.44	....	....	....	....	....	4.81	4.95	4.95	4.95	4.95	4.95
Deposit Rate	60l	7.75	....	....	....	....	....	3.50	3.50	3.50	3.50	3.50	3.50
Lending Rate	60p	16.75	....	....	....	....	....	....	....	....	....	....	....
Prices and Production						*Index Numbers (2000=100): Period Averages*							
Consumer Prices	64	65.7	65.4	86.5	93.3	†95.8	97.3	98.5	99.3	100.0	103.1	105.4	105.3
Industrial Production	66	89.3	83.6	91.7	98.3	94.9	96.5	116.2	103.6	100.0	100.3	105.8	106.7
						Number in Thousands: Period Averages							
Unemployment	67c	12	10	....	....	....	....	....	....	....	....	....	....

2004, International Monetary Fund : *International Financial Statistics Yearbook*

Senegal 722

		1992	1993	1994	1995	1996	1997	1998	1999	2000	2001	2002	2003
International Transactions						*Billions of Francs*							
Exports	70	178.08	200.20	439.10	495.80	505.40	528.00	570.90	632.40	654.90	735.30	743.40	773.30
Imports, c.i.f.	71	273.72	307.70	567.40	704.90	734.60	779.00	858.50	845.30	951.60	1,047.10	1,117.90	1,178.40
Balance of Payments					*Millions of US Dollars: Minus Sign Indicates Debit*								
Current Account, n.i.e.	78ald	−401.3	−433.0	−187.5	−244.5	−199.4	−184.8	−247.5	−320.2	−332.4	−245.5	−317.0	....
Goods: Exports f.o.b.	78aad	860.6	736.8	818.8	993.3	988.0	904.6	967.7	1,027.1	919.8	1,003.1	1,066.5	....
Goods: Imports f.o.b.	78abd	−1,191.8	−1,086.7	−1,022.0	−1,242.9	−1,264.0	−1,176.0	−1,280.6	−1,372.8	−1,336.6	−1,428.4	−1,603.9	....
Trade Balance	78acd	−331.1	−349.9	−203.2	−249.6	−275.9	−271.5	−312.9	−345.8	−416.7	−425.3	−537.4	....
Services: Credit	78add	481.4	413.9	412.3	512.5	378.7	371.7	425.1	416.1	386.9	398.1	456.2	....
Services: Debit	78aed	−654.2	−581.3	−492.7	−578.2	−395.8	−391.7	−442.9	−430.4	−405.0	−413.6	−474.4	....
Balance on Goods & Services	78afd	−503.9	−517.3	−283.6	−315.3	−293.0	−291.5	−330.7	−360.0	−434.8	−440.8	−555.6	....
Income: Credit	78agd	96.5	82.8	63.3	87.2	81.3	67.9	76.6	83.3	85.2	67.1	67.4	....
Income: Debit	78ahd	−173.0	−162.3	−164.5	−211.5	−154.1	−139.8	−164.6	−202.5	−196.7	−171.9	−197.3	....
Balance on Gds, Serv. & Inc.	78aid	−580.5	−596.8	−384.7	−439.6	−365.9	−363.4	−418.6	−479.2	−546.3	−545.6	−685.6	....
Current Transfers, n.i.e.: Credit	78ajd	290.8	267.0	267.0	284.7	244.3	258.8	254.7	225.4	274.9	353.6	414.4	....
Current Transfers: Debit	78akd	−111.6	−103.2	−69.7	−89.6	−77.8	−80.3	−83.6	−66.3	−61.0	−53.4	−45.8	....
Capital Account, n.i.e.	78bcd	182.8	153.7	190.6	187.0	169.2	96.0	98.3	98.6	83.4	146.1	126.8	....
Capital Account, n.i.e.: Credit	78bad	198.3	165.9	200.5	201.2	169.3	96.3	98.8	99.0	83.6	146.1	127.1	....
Capital Account: Debit	78bbd	−15.5	−12.2	−9.9	−14.2	−.1	−.3	−.4	−.5	−.3	−.1	−.2	....
Financial Account, n.i.e.	78bjd	113.2	129.4	48.5	44.2	−179.0	3.5	−109.7	−54.8	27.1	−102.6	−88.2	....
Direct Investment Abroad	78bdd	−51.3	−.3	−17.4	3.3	−3.0	.5	−10.5	−14.5	−9.6	1.5	−36.2	....
Dir. Invest. in Rep. Econ., n.i.e.	78bed	21.4	−.8	66.9	31.7	8.4	176.4	70.8	156.6	71.9	37.5	80.3	....
Portfolio Investment Assets	78bfd	−	−	−1.5	−.4	−25.8	−18.9	−21.9	−31.3	11.0	15.9	−25.0	....
Equity Securities	78bkd	−	−	−1.5	−.4	−2.4	.9	−9.8	−6.2	−.2	7.0	.5	....
Debt Securities	78bld	−	−	−	−	−23.4	−19.9	−12.1	−25.1	11.3	8.9	−25.5	....
Portfolio Investment Liab., n.i.e.	78bgd	.7	5.8	.5	4.0	−4.8	−8.1	−3.9	−	11.9	−8.3	−13.1	....
Equity Securities	78bmd	.9	6.1	.5	4.1	−	8.4	2.6	3.4	−2.2	−5.2	3.2	....
Debt Securities	78bnd	−.2	−.3	−	−.1	−4.8	−16.4	−6.5	−3.4	14.1	−3.2	−16.4	....
Financial Derivatives Assets	78bwd	−	−	−	−	−	−.7	−	−.7	−	−.4	−1.9	....
Financial Derivatives Liabilities	78bxd	−	−	−	−	−	−	.1	−	−	.4	−.4	....
Other Investment Assets	78bhd	−24.9	4.1	−92.5	−6.2	−70.7	−22.1	−58.8	−62.3	−4.4	−3.9	11.9	....
Monetary Authorities	78bod	....	....										....
General Government	78bpd	−.7	−.6	−	−	−3.1	−.9	−.4	−	−	−	−1.5	....
Banks	78bqd	−24.4	−2.6	−108.8	10.9	31.0	−24.5	−42.4	−54.8	17.2	−33.0	−16.4	....
Other Sectors	78brd	.2	7.4	16.3	−17.1	−98.5	3.3	−15.9	−7.6	−21.6	29.2	29.8	....
Other Investment Liab., n.i.e.	78bid	167.4	120.7	92.6	11.8	−83.1	−123.7	−85.5	−102.6	−53.8	−145.3	−103.8	....
Monetary Authorities	78bsd	34.3	135.3	−76.2	−35.7	1.6	.3	.7	2.5	8.9	−6.7	10.7	....
General Government	78btd	173.0	69.0	90.7	83.9	−140.0	−132.6	−112.9	−114.8	−132.7	−136.1	−161.6	....
Banks	78bud	−23.4	−6.6	9.8	−27.1	−4.6	23.6	23.5	5.9	−6.1	7.8	−6.5	....
Other Sectors	78bvd	−16.5	−77.0	68.3	−9.3	60.0	−14.9	3.3	3.7	76.0	−10.4	53.7	....
Net Errors and Omissions	78cad	−19.6	8.4	−28.9	−19.6	7.7	−9.3	10.7	8.2	−9.0	7.9	30.9	....
Overall Balance	78cbd	−124.9	−141.5	22.8	−32.9	−201.4	−94.7	−248.1	−268.2	−231.0	−194.1	−247.3	....
Reserves and Related Items	79dad	124.9	141.5	−22.8	32.9	201.4	94.7	248.1	268.2	231.0	194.1	247.3	....
Reserve Assets	79dbd	.1	8.5	−170.1	−74.8	−34.8	−137.4	−20.7	−31.6	−14.1	−90.3	−92.5	....
Use of Fund Credit and Loans	79dcd	−44.2	−27.4	38.9	42.9	−9.8	−12.8	−11.6	−13.4	−3.3	3.4	−15.9	....
Exceptional Financing	79ded	169.0	160.3	108.4	64.9	246.0	244.8	280.4	313.2	248.4	281.0	355.8	....
International Investment Position						*Millions of US Dollars*							
Assets	79aad	....	....	....	561.4	640.7	711.7	860.1	889.8	....	....	....	....
Direct Investment Abroad	79abd	−	−	−	9.9	10.2	2.6	8.9	18.3				
Portfolio Investment	79acd	−	−	−	8.6	33.2	52.2	78.2	93.7				
Equity Securities	79add	....	....	....	.9	3.2	.7	20.8	14.2				
Debt Securities	79aed	....	....	....	7.6	30.0	51.5	57.4	79.5				
Financial Derivatives	79ald				.1	.1	.8	−	.7				
Other Investment	79afd	160.4	152.3	197.0	271.0	308.9	269.8	339.9	374.1				
Monetary Authorities	79agd	−											
General Government	79ahd				....	....	....	....	....				
Banks	79aid	160.4	152.3	197.0	144.4	104.9	115.6	167.5	195.9				
Other Sectors	79ajd	....	....	....									
Reserve Assets	79akd	12.4	3.4	179.6	271.8	288.3	386.2	433.1	403.0				
Liabilities	79lad	....	....	....	4,261.8	4,100.6	4,072.1	4,721.1	4,223.1	....	....	....	....
Dir. Invest. in Rep. Economy	79lbd	−	−	−	78.6	76.4	256.2	372.1	329.4				
Portfolio Investment	79lcd	−	−	−	83.3	73.0	56.8	96.2	92.9				
Equity Securities	79ldd	....	....	....	10.3	9.4	17.2	66.8	63.5				
Debt Securities	79led	....	....	....	73.0	63.6	39.6	29.4	29.4				
Financial Derivatives	79lld								.1				
Other Investment	79lfd	3,951.1	3,643.7	3,443.6	4,099.9	3,951.2	3,759.1	4,252.7	3,800.8				
Monetary Authorities	79lgd	569.8	652.9	446.1	470.1	442.5	394.6	402.4	369.0				
General Government	79lhd	3,171.5	2,801.1	2,882.7	3,323.6	3,035.5	2,864.5	3,232.7	2,852.3				
Banks	79lid	209.8	189.7	114.8	184.9	171.3	176.4	210.1	218.3				
Other Sectors	79ljd	−	−	−	121.3	302.0	323.7	407.4	361.2				

Senegal 722

		1992	1993	1994	1995	1996	1997	1998	1999	2000	2001	2002	2003
National Accounts							*Billions of Francs*						
Househ.Cons.Expend.,incl.NPISHs	96f	1,220.4	1,191.5	1,450.6	1,763.9	1,769.3	1,871.5	2,029.7	2,224.3	2,384.8	2,620.7	2,756.3	....
Government Consumption Expend...	91f	239.9	227.7	258.4	276.1	286.0	303.0	324.2	308.6	365.7	493.7	....	....
Gross Fixed Capital Formation..........	93e	222.9	207.1	295.1	327.7	362.9	381.4	455.0	567.0	538.7	598.2	728.1	....
Changes in Inventories.....................	93i	6.9	3.0	49.0	45.7	52.5	–	–	14.8	134.4	−2.4	−35.2	....
Exports of Goods and Services..........	90c	357.5	341.2	652.0	718.2	728.0	868.4	924.4	888.6	949.5	1,011.3	....	....
Imports of Goods and Services (-).....	98c	452.2	432.9	683.1	897.6	849.1	915.0	1,016.8	1,110.3	1,240.0	1,350.0	1,397.4	....
Gross Domestic Product (GDP)..........	99b	1,578.7	1,521.9	1,864.9	2,222.7	2,349.5	2,509.3	2,716.5	2,893.1	3,114.0	3,379.6	3,551.8	....
Net Primary Income from Abroad.....	98.n	86.3	79.3	179.2	86.2	217.0	209.0	192.0	164.0	161.0	338.0	....	....
Gross National Income (GNI)............	99a	1,681.7	1,617.1	2,201.4	2,320.3	2,669.0	2,785.0	2,989.0	3,164.0	3,353.0	3,681.0	....	....
GDP Volume 1987 Prices.................	99b.p	1,514.6	1,481.0	1,523.5	1,602.2	1,684.7	....	....	....	....	....	....	....
GDP Volume 1999 Prices.................	99b.p	....	....	....	....	2,619.0	2,705.0	2,825.0	3,000.0	3,089.0	3,235.0	....	....
GDP Volume (2000=100).................	99bvp	76.2	74.5	76.7	80.6	†84.8	87.6	91.5	97.1	100.0	104.7	....	....
GDP Deflator (2000=100)................	99bip	66.5	65.6	78.1	88.5	89.0	92.0	95.4	95.7	100.0	103.6	....	....
						Millions: Midyear Estimates							
Population...............................	99z	7.74	7.94	8.14	8.34	8.54	8.75	8.96	9.17	9.39	9.62	9.85	10.09

2004, International Monetary Fund : *International Financial Statistics Yearbook*

Seychelles 718

		1992	1993	1994	1995	1996	1997	1998	1999	2000	2001	2002	2003
Exchange Rates						*Rupees per SDR: End of Period*							
Official Rate	aa	7.2345	7.2345	7.2345	7.2345	7.2345	6.9218	7.6699	7.3671	8.1642	7.2226	6.8474	8.1434
					Rupees per US Dollar: End of Period (ae) Period Average (rf)								
Official Rate	ae	5.2545	5.2579	4.9695	4.8639	4.9946	5.1249	5.4521	5.3676	6.2689	5.7522	5.0550	5.5000
Official Rate	rf	5.1220	5.1815	5.0559	4.7620	4.9700	5.0263	5.2622	5.3426	5.7138	5.8575	5.4800	5.4007
Fund Position						*Millions of SDRs: End of Period*							
Quota	2f.s	6.00	6.00	6.00	6.00	6.00	6.00	6.00	8.80	8.80	8.80	8.80	8.80
SDRs	1b.s	.01	.01	.02	.02	.02	.03	.03	.03	.01	.02	.01	–
Reserve Position in the Fund	1c.s	.80	.80	.80	.80	.80	.80	–	–	–	–	–	–
Total Fund Cred.&Loans Outstg.	2tl	–	–	–	–	–	–	–	–	–	–	–	–
International Liquidity					*Millions of US Dollars Unless Otherwise Indicated: End of Period*								
Total Reserves minus Gold	1l.d	31.26	35.65	30.15	27.10	21.76	26.32	21.59	30.35	43.75	37.13	69.79	67.39
SDRs	1b.d	.01	.02	.02	.03	.03	.04	.04	.04	.01	.02	.01	–
Reserve Position in the Fund	1c.d	1.10	1.10	1.17	1.20	1.16	1.09	–	–	–	–	–	–
Foreign Exchange	1d.d	30.14	34.53	28.96	25.87	20.57	25.20	21.55	30.31	43.74	37.11	69.78	67.38
Monetary Authorities: Other Liab.	4..d	–	–	–	–	–	–	–	–	–	–	–	–
Deposit Money Banks: Assets	7a.d	9.44	7.66	5.03	9.91	19.28	30.97	29.36	43.72	51.43	51.11	59.25	62.89
Liabilities	7b.d	6.76	7.32	6.42	10.36	17.96	33.41	34.72	47.05	61.37	55.94	48.13	62.25
Monetary Authorities						*Millions of Rupees: End of Period*							
Foreign Assets	11	157.6	180.5	142.8	126.8	99.1	127.2	115.1	160.2	271.1	210.6	352.3	369.2
Claims on Central Government	12a	241.4	302.0	529.2	663.3	790.5	926.8	575.1	640.2	698.8	774.0	1,293.2	1,011.7
Claims on Deposit Money Banks	12e	4.0	21.5	7.0	1.8	–	–	10.0	–	22.0	–	–	19.0
Reserve Money	14	311.8	383.8	566.7	684.8	778.7	924.0	468.7	512.8	528.7	566.8	717.9	578.7
of which: Currency Outside DMBs	14a	122.5	134.5	141.6	148.1	165.7	192.2	206.4	248.0	264.4	279.8	301.0	305.9
Foreign Liabilities	16c	–	–	–	–	–	–	–	–	–	–	–	–
Central Government Deposits	16d	64.3	58.8	30.9	21.4	15.4	18.1	18.2	49.0	21.5	18.9	22.4	16.1
Capital Accounts	17a	14.0	14.0	13.9	13.9	13.9	13.8	14.1	25.9	43.2	51.4	56.7	68.7
Other Items (Net)	17r	12.9	47.4	67.4	71.7	81.6	98.0	199.2	212.7	398.4	347.5	848.5	736.2
Deposit Money Banks						*Millions of Rupees: End of Period*							
Reserves	20	188.5	248.7	424.5	536.0	612.3	731.1	261.6	264.1	263.5	286.1	416.0	271.9
Foreign Assets	21	49.6	40.3	25.0	48.2	96.3	158.7	160.1	234.7	322.4	294.0	299.5	345.9
Claims on Central Government	22a	632.9	779.0	692.3	747.8	843.1	1,086.9	2,106.7	2,526.6	2,805.7	3,101.6	3,182.4	3,268.2
Claims on Nonfin.Pub.Enterprises	22c	54.1	80.9	118.9	92.4	68.7	71.8	55.9	42.6	20.2	10.8	5.4	79.0
Claims on Private Sector	22d	157.8	172.8	209.0	245.1	269.6	387.6	460.0	503.5	565.6	643.5	753.5	944.4
Demand Deposits	24	170.0	200.7	184.4	186.2	284.0	456.5	574.2	823.3	873.0	1,010.7	1,275.9	1,350.4
Time and Savings Deposits	25	620.3	768.5	768.7	875.1	939.0	1,339.2	1,608.8	1,837.9	2,036.7	2,264.2	2,485.2	2,425.4
Restricted Deposits	26b	–	–	198.2	301.4	317.1	218.0	178.3	148.0	132.3	127.7	103.3	102.1
Foreign Liabilities	26c	35.5	38.5	31.9	50.4	89.7	171.2	189.3	252.6	384.7	321.8	243.3	342.4
Central Government Deposits	26d	83.9	107.7	118.8	112.8	88.5	163.2	180.9	203.5	204.5	230.1	247.0	241.1
Credit from Monetary Authorities	26g	4.0	21.5	7.0	1.8	–	–	10.0	–	22.0	–	–	19.0
Capital Accounts	27a	71.8	74.7	76.0	76.0	80.8	96.5	103.9	110.8	110.8	110.8	110.8	110.8
Other Items (Net)	27r	97.4	110.1	84.7	65.8	90.9	–8.5	198.9	195.7	213.4	270.7	191.4	318.2
Monetary Survey						*Millions of Rupees: End of Period*							
Foreign Assets (Net)	31n	171.7	182.3	135.9	124.6	105.7	114.7	85.9	142.3	208.8	182.8	408.5	372.7
Domestic Credit	32	939.0	1,169.2	1,400.7	1,615.4	1,869.0	2,292.8	2,999.6	3,461.4	3,865.3	4,281.9	4,966.1	5,047.0
Claims on Central Govt. (Net)	32an	726.1	914.5	1,071.8	1,276.9	1,529.7	1,832.4	2,482.7	2,914.4	3,278.5	3,626.6	4,206.2	4,022.6
Claims on Nonfin.Pub.Enterprises	32c	54.1	80.9	118.9	92.4	68.7	71.8	55.9	42.6	20.2	10.8	5.4	79.0
Claims on Private Sector	32d	157.8	172.8	209.0	245.1	269.6	387.6	460.0	503.5	565.6	643.5	753.5	944.4
Money	34	293.3	335.8	326.6	335.0	450.4	649.4	781.3	1,071.9	1,138.2	1,291.4	1,577.8	1,657.2
Quasi-Money	35	620.3	768.5	768.7	875.1	939.0	1,339.2	1,608.8	1,837.9	2,036.7	2,264.2	2,485.2	2,425.4
Restricted Deposits	36b	–	–	198.2	301.4	317.1	218.0	178.3	148.0	132.3	127.7	103.3	102.1
Capital Accounts	37a	85.8	88.7	89.9	89.9	94.7	110.3	118.0	136.6	154.0	162.2	167.4	179.5
Other Items (Net)	37r	111.3	158.5	153.1	138.5	173.5	90.5	399.1	409.5	612.9	619.2	1,040.9	1,055.4
Money plus Quasi-Money	35l	913.6	1,104.3	1,095.3	1,210.1	1,389.4	1,988.6	2,390.1	2,909.7	3,174.9	3,555.6	4,063.0	4,082.6
Other Banking Institutions						*Millions of Rupees: End of Period*							
Reserves	40	4.0	3.5	2.4	3.6	1.9	–	–	–	–	–	–	–
Claims on Central Government	42a	86.9	121.9	121.3	93.2	115.8	–	–	–	–	–	–	–
Claims on Nonfin.Pub.Enterprises	42c	77.5	65.1	78.1	55.1	49.1	34.5	28.0	20.7	13.6	7.9	4.1	.8
Claims on Private Sector	42d	76.3	99.3	124.9	152.4	186.6	163.8	176.2	184.7	202.1	217.9	252.3	267.4
Claims on Deposit Money Banks	42e	1.7	4.3	4.1	12.1	10.0	9.9	17.8	24.5	31.3	30.6	25.2	36.6
Time and Savings Deposits	45	92.7	138.2	182.8	176.1	197.0	–	–	–	–	–	–	–
Capital Accounts	47a	77.0	85.6	92.9	93.9	100.6	115	129.2	151.0	153.6	170.1	183.1	196.9
Other Items (Net)	47r	76.7	70.3	55.1	46.5	65.8	93.2	92.8	78.9	93.3	86.3	98.6	108.0

Seychelles 718

		1992	1993	1994	1995	1996	1997	1998	1999	2000	2001	2002	2003
Banking Survey						*Millions of Rupees: End of Period*							
Foreign Assets (Net)	51n	171.7	182.3	135.9	124.6	105.7	114.7	85.9	142.3	208.8	182.8	408.5	372.7
Domestic Credit	52	1,178.7	1,454.5	1,724.0	1,915.1	2,219.5	2,490.1	3,202.8	3,665.8	4,080.0	4,506.7	5,221.6	5,314.2
Claims on Central Govt. (Net)	52an	813.0	1,036.4	1,193.1	1,370.1	1,645.5	1,832.4	2,482.7	2,914.4	3,278.5	3,626.6	4,206.2	4,022.6
Claims on Nonfin.Pub.Enterprises	52c	131.6	146.0	197.0	147.5	117.8	106.3	83.9	63.3	33.8	18.7	9.5	79.8
Claims on Private Sector	52d	234.1	272.1	333.9	397.5	456.2	551.4	636.2	688.2	767.7	861.4	1,005.8	1,211.8
Liquid Liabilities	55l	1,002.3	1,239.0	1,275.7	1,382.5	1,584.4	1,988.6	2,390.1	2,909.7	3,174.9	3,555.6	4,063.0	4,082.6
Restricted Deposits	56b			198.2	301.4	317.1	218.0	178.3	148.0	132.3	127.7	103.3	102.1
Capital Accounts	57a	162.8	174.3	182.8	183.9	195.3	225.3	247.2	287.6	307.7	332.4	350.6	376.4
Other Items (Net)	57r	185.3	223.5	203.1	171.9	228.3	172.8	473.1	462.9	673.9	673.9	1,113.3	1,125.8
Money (National Definitions)						*Millions of Rupees: End of Period*							
M1	59ma	289.2	345.4	326.0	334.3	449.6	648.7	715.4	1,071.2	1,137.5	1,290.6	1,576.9	1,656.4
M2	59mb	1,002.2	1,183.0	1,094.7	1,209.3	1,388.6	1,987.8	2,112.9	2,908.9	3,174.2	3,554.8	4,062.1	4,081.8
M2(p)	59mc	1,002.2	1,183.0	1,292.8	1,510.8	1,705.7	2,205.9	2,291.2	3,056.9	3,306.5	3,682.5	4,165.4	4,183.9
Interest Rates						*Percent Per Annum*							
Discount Rate (End of Period)	60	13.53	13.08	12.50	12.83	11.00	11.00	5.50	5.50	5.50	5.50	5.50	4.67
Treasury Bill Rate	60c	13.40	13.25	12.50	12.28	11.55	10.50	8.13	5.00	5.00	5.00	5.00	4.61
Savings Rate	60k	9.07	8.61	8.00	8.00	8.00	8.00	5.75	3.00	3.02	3.03	3.03	2.85
Deposit Rate	60l	9.56	9.37	8.85	9.22	9.90	9.20	7.53	5.13	4.77	4.92	4.93	3.99
Lending Rate	60p	15.56	15.71	15.72	15.76	16.22	14.88	14.39	12.01	11.45	11.14	11.09	11.08
Government Bond Yield	61	14.80	14.40	14.38	13.25	13.25	11.63	8.96	8.58	8.22	8.13	8.25	5.96
Prices and Labor						*Index Numbers (2000=100): Period Averages*							
Consumer Prices	64	84.2	85.4	86.9	86.7	85.7	86.3	88.5	94.1	100.0	106.0	106.2	109.7
Employment	67	75.9	78.3	78.7	79.9	81.5	87.8	91.2	96.5	100.0	103.1	105.6	102.7
						Number in Thousands: Period Averages							
Employment	67e	24	25	25	26	26	28	29	31	32	33	34	....
International Transactions						*Millions of Rupees*							
Exports	70	245.66	265.02	262.15	253.50	693.43	569.23	643.67	775.12	1,108.48	1,263.20	1,249.04	1,506.37
Imports, c.i.f.	71	980.87	1,234.86	1,042.38	1,109.20	1,881.88	1,711.22	2,015.52	2,317.17	1,949.86	2,776.04	2,294.92	2,324.45
Balance of Payments						*Millions of US Dollars: Minus Sign Indicates Debit*							
Current Account, n.i.e.	78ald	–6.90	–7.33	23.83	–2.95	–59.25	–72.78	–118.03	–127.33	–51.33	–123.24	–130.64	....
Goods: Exports f.o.b	78aad	48.07	50.33	52.99	53.51	96.66	113.56	122.84	145.66	194.77	216.44	236.70	....
Goods: Imports f.o.b	78abd	–180.50	–215.73	–188.06	–214.26	–266.98	–303.50	–334.63	–369.75	–311.60	–421.93	–376.26	....
Trade Balance	78acd	–132.42	–165.40	–135.07	–160.75	–170.32	–189.94	–211.79	–224.09	–116.82	–205.50	–139.57	....
Services: Credit	78add	194.07	261.72	250.34	278.69	237.06	255.86	247.48	277.30	294.23	296.38	306.52	....
Services: Debit	78aed	–76.59	–87.27	–80.19	–103.48	–114.07	–127.61	–132.17	–155.98	–174.66	–169.20	–201.28	....
Balance on Goods & Services	78afd	–14.94	9.05	35.08	14.46	–47.33	–61.70	–96.49	–102.78	2.75	–78.31	–34.33	....
Income: Credit	78agd	5.24	1.99	8.09	12.56	10.48	9.65	5.43	8.46	9.24	8.25	7.44	....
Income: Debit	78ahd	–14.46	–19.09	–19.84	–32.21	–25.52	–21.92	–25.31	–32.29	–57.66	–52.19	–99.98	....
Balance on Gds, Serv. & Inc.	78aid	–24.16	–8.05	23.34	–5.20	–62.37	–73.97	–116.36	–126.61	–45.67	–122.25	–126.87	....
Current Transfers, n.i.e.: Credit	78ajd	31.10	15.84	13.85	13.52	15.20	14.24	9.77	10.09	4.34	7.90	7.82	....
Current Transfers: Debit	78akd	–13.84	–15.13	–13.35	–11.28	–12.07	–13.05	–11.44	–10.81	–9.99	–8.90	–11.59	....
Capital Account, n.i.e.	78bcd	....	1.74	4.27	1.05	5.65	6.76	21.66	16.47	.89	9.44	5.03	....
Capital Account, n.i.e.: Credit	78bad	....	1.74	4.27	1.05	5.65	6.76	21.66	16.47	.89	9.44	5.03	....
Capital Account: Debit	78bbd		–	–	–	–	–	–	–	–	–	–	....
Financial Account, n.i.e.	78bjd	–2.49	5.53	–.20	–1.18	–15.95	9.52	27.08	13.91	–32.07	52.33	–63.97	....
Direct Investment Abroad	78bdd	–1.17	–1.00	–13.33	–16.97	–12.47	–9.89	–3.00	–8.98	–6.86	–8.54	–8.90	....
Dir. Invest. in Rep. Econ., n.i.e.	78bed	9.01	18.84	30.74	45.88	28.81	53.40	53.21	55.22	24.33	59.43	61.43	....
Portfolio Investment Assets	78bfd	–.14	–.35	–.93	–5.76	6.65	.09	–.78	–.02	–.09	.07	.07	....
Equity Securities	78bkd	....	....	....	....	....	....	....	....	....	....	....	....
Debt Securities	78bld	–.14	–.35	–.93	–5.76	6.65	.09	–.78	–.02	–.09	.07	.07	....
Portfolio Investment Liab., n.i.e.	78bgd	–.02	.04	.16	–.17	–	2.94	2.83	.56	1.05	1.09	1.11	....
Equity Securities	78bmd	....	....	....	....	....	....	....	....	....	....	....	....
Debt Securities	78bnd	–.02	.04	.16	–.17	–	2.94	2.83	.56	1.05	1.09	1.11	....
Financial Derivatives Assets	78bwd	....	....	....	....	....	....	....	....	....	....	....	....
Financial Derivatives Liabilities	78bxd	....	....	....	....	....	....	....	....	....	....	....	....
Other Investment Assets	78bhd	.13	2.05	1.60	–2.56	–11.79	–12.73	–5.66	–12.97	–14.86	–8.76	–9.84	....
Monetary Authorities	78bod	....	....	....	....	....	....	....	....	....	....	....	....
General Government	78bpd	....	....	....	....	....	....	....	....	....	....	....	....
Banks	78bqd	2.09	....	....	....	....	....	....	....	....	....	....	....
Other Sectors	78brd	–1.95	2.05	1.60	–2.56	–11.79	–12.73	–5.66	–12.97	–14.86	–8.76	–9.84	....
Other Investment Liab., n.i.e.	78bid	–10.31	–14.04	–18.44	–21.61	–27.14	–24.29	–19.52	–19.90	–35.64	9.03	–107.84	....
Monetary Authorities	78bsd	–.86	–	–2.06	–2.86	–3.14	–10.19	–	–	–3.39	–15.94	–68.09	....
General Government	78btd	–6.48	–12.85	–14.22	–16.23	–21.33	–12.83	–16.02	–18.27	–13.56	–31.94	–7.03	....
Banks	78bud	–7.10	–	–	–	–	–	–	–	–	–4.30	–5.70	....
Other Sectors	78bvd	4.13	–1.20	–2.16	–2.52	–2.68	–1.27	–3.50	–1.63	–18.68	61.21	–27.03	....
Net Errors and Omissions	78cad	5.44	–30.41	–55.41	–28.70	7.04	11.65	–4.35	–2.14	–20.79	14.42	.51	....
Overall Balance	78cbd	–3.95	–30.48	–27.51	–31.78	–62.50	–44.84	–73.64	–99.09	–103.30	–47.06	–189.07	....
Reserves and Related Items	79dad	3.95	30.48	27.51	31.78	62.50	44.84	73.64	99.09	103.30	47.06	189.07	....
Reserve Assets	79dbd	–5.43	–4.47	7.43	3.42	4.86	–5.12	3.26	–8.42	–19.39	10.32	–25.84	....
Use of Fund Credit and Loans	79dcd	–	–	–	–	–	–	–	–	–	–	–	....
Exceptional Financing	79ded	9.38	34.95	20.09	28.36	57.63	49.96	70.38	107.51	122.69	36.74	214.92	....

2004, International Monetary Fund: *International Financial Statistics Yearbook*

Seychelles 718

		1992	1993	1994	1995	1996	1997	1998	1999	2000	2001	2002	2003
Government Finance		\multicolumn{12}{c}{*Millions of Rupees: Year Ending December 31*}
Deficit (-) or Surplus	80	−88.3	−769.2	−54.0	−200.5	−365.4	107.6	38.6	−385.5	−496.5	....	....	270.4
Total Revenue and Grants	81y	1,174.9	1,323.4	1,288.9	1,172.2	1,164.1	1,288.8	1,400.7	1,533.6	1,426.7	....	....	1,867.6
Revenue	81	1,135.7	1,260.4	1,271.1	1,158.4	1,151.1	1,273.5	1,372.9	1,491.9	1,377.1	....	....	1,856.8
Grants	81z	39.2	63.0	17.8	13.8	13.0	15.3	27.8	41.7	49.6	....	....	10.8
Exp. & Lending Minus Repay	82z	1,263.2	2,092.6	1,342.9	1,372.7	1,529.5	1,181.2	1,362.1	1,919.1	1,923.2	....	....	1,597.2
Expenditure	82	1,234.5	1,443.0	1,325.9	1,276.5	1,495.2	1,680.9	1,879.7	1,905.0	1,969.8	....	....	1,596.1
Lending Minus Repayments	83	28.7	649.6	17.0	96.2	34.3	−499.7	−517.6	14.1	−46.6	....	....	1.2
Total Financing	80h	88.3	769.2	54.0	200.5	365.4	−107.6	−38.6	385.5	496.5	....	....	−270.4
Domestic	84a	117.1	749.6	63.8	246.0	324.1	−128.6	−4.3	433.6	−19.3	....	....	−283.0
Foreign	85a	−28.8	19.6	−9.8	−45.5	41.3	21.0	−34.3	−48.1	515.8	....	....	12.6
National Accounts		\multicolumn{12}{c}{*Millions of Rupees*}
Househ.Cons.Expend.,incl.NPISHs	96f	1,207.4	1,241.6	1,129.8	1,179.4	1,191.0	1,465.8	1,603.9	....	....	....	....	....
Government Consumption Expend	91f	674.6	714.7	722.2	669.1	736.0	733.0	847.0	....	....	....	....	....
Gross Fixed Capital Formation	93e	465.4	651.2	648.5	733.9	822.6	863.1	1,100.0	....	....	....	....	....
Changes in Inventories	93i	6.2	46.0	17.4	.2	−19.0	109.1	56.0	....	....	....	....	....
Exports of Goods and Services	90c	1,207.4	1,319.2	1,250.5	1,292.0	1,592.9	1,896.9	2,045.5	....	....	....	....	....
Imports of Goods and Services (-)	98c	1,315.4	1,544.2	1,326.0	1,454.8	1,841.4	2,159.7	2,525.8	....	....	....	....	....
Gross Domestic Product (GDP)	99b	2,221.1	2,431.5	2,459.4	2,419.8	2,500.3	2,829.5	3,201.3	3,323.2	3,531.7	3,617.8	3,829.9	....
Net Primary Income from Abroad	98.n	−47.3	−31.6	9.6	−91.9	−73.6	−62.1	−110.1	−128.2	−151.5	....	....	....
Gross National Income (GNI)	99a	2,173.6	2,399.9	2,469.0	2,328.0	2,426.7	2,767.5	3,091.2	3,195.1	3,380.2	3,617.8	3,829.9	....
Consumption of Fixed Capital	99cf	181.9	202.3	211.5	210.2	240.5	276.9	291.3	318.5	....	....	....	....
GDP Volume 1986 Prices	99b.p	1,851.4	1,965.9	1,950.0	1,933.9	2,029.0	2,122.1	2,238.8	2,303.7	2,336.0	2,358.2	....	....
GDP Volume (2000=100)	99bvp	79.3	84.2	83.5	82.8	86.9	90.8	95.8	98.6	100.0	101.0	....	....
GDP Deflator (2000=100)	99bip	79.4	81.8	83.4	82.8	81.5	88.2	94.6	95.4	100.0	101.5	....	....
		\multicolumn{12}{c}{*Millions: Midyear Estimates*}
Population	99z	.07	.07	.07	.07	.08	.08	.08	.08	.08	.08	.08	.08

Sierra Leone 724

		1992	1993	1994	1995	1996	1997	1998	1999	2000	2001	2002	2003
Exchange Rates						Leones per SDR: End of Period							
Market Rate	aa	723.68	793.41	894.90	1,402.35	1,307.24	1,799.00	2,239.84	3,123.90	2,171.52	2,716.13	2,979.70	3,807.32
					Leones per US Dollar: End of Period (ae) Period Average (rf)								
Market Rate	ae	526.32	577.63	613.01	943.40	909.09	1,333.33	1,590.76	2,276.05	1,666.67	2,161.27	2,191.73	2,562.18
Market Rate	rf	499.44	567.46	586.74	755.22	920.73	981.48	1,563.62	1,804.20	2,092.13	1,986.15	2,099.03	2,347.94
					Index Numbers (2000=100): Period Averages								
Market Rate	ahx	418.2	366.3	354.3	282.8	226.2	217.8	132.9	116.5	100.0	105.4	99.0	88.7
Nominal Effective Exchange Rate	nec	272.0	278.7	293.7	223.7	184.9	192.6	121.8	107.5	100.0	111.0	102.1	81.7
Real Effective Exchange Rate	rec	83.4	92.6	106.7	96.4	97.2	111.5	95.0	110.9	100.0	110.7	90.1	82.4
Fund Position						Millions of SDRs: End of Period							
Quota	2f.s	57.9	57.9	77.2	77.2	77.2	77.2	77.2	103.7	103.7	103.7	103.7	103.7
SDRs	1b.s	1.2	2.8	6.2	11.5	5.3	8.3	7.4	15.2	4.0	.3	17.7	23.2
Reserve Position in the Fund	1c.s	–	–	–	–	–	–	–	–	–	–	–	–
Total Fund Cred.&Loans Outstg.	2tl	67.0	61.0	100.2	110.9	118.8	123.9	135.4	142.0	133.2	120.8	124.5	113.8
International Liquidity					Millions of US Dollars Unless Otherwise Indicated: End of Period								
Total Reserves minus Gold	1l.d	18.9	29.0	40.6	34.6	26.6	38.5	43.9	39.5	49.2	51.3	84.7	66.6
SDRs	1b.d	1.7	3.8	9.0	17.1	7.6	11.2	10.4	20.8	5.2	.4	24.0	34.5
Reserve Position in the Fund	1c.d	–	–	–	–	–	–	–	–	–	–	–	–
Foreign Exchange	1d.d	17.2	25.1	31.6	17.5	18.9	27.3	33.5	18.6	43.9	50.9	60.6	32.1
Monetary Authorities: Other Liab.	4..d	302.4	322.2	470.2	326.2	53.5	14.8	19.2	7.7	10.6	17.1	8.7	4.0
Deposit Money Banks: Assets	7a.d	16.1	22.5	16.9	22.5	19.9	15.6	19.2	17.9	24.4	21.9	26.6	30.8
Liabilities	7b.d	–	2.7	2.9	3.1	–	–	–	–	–	–	–	–
Monetary Authorities						Millions of Leones: End of Period							
Foreign Assets	11	11,143	18,943	30,443	48,695	†27,262	53,008	83,128	98,035	86,385	115,454	191,477	168,696
Claims on Central Government	12a	30,009	25,328	462,872	408,928	†415,564	470,930	475,265	524,834	633,405	650,358	655,133	685,472
Claims on Nonfin.Pub.Enterprises	12c	....	....	....	....	203	203	13	66	13	13	13	13
Claims on Private Sector	12d	112	126	160	324	†1,031	2,577	1,749	788	1,008	1,969	6,161	1,911
Claims on Deposit Money Banks	12e	–	–	–	–	†1,173	495	1,049	1,736	606	969	278	59
Claims on Other Banking Insts.	12f	....	....	....	....	33	34	–	4	–	–	–	–
Claims on Nonbank Financial Insts.	12g	....	....	....	....	302	85	6	26	853	520	102	334
Reserve Money	14	24,095	24,995	31,352	35,148	†43,548	91,008	72,415	100,627	109,843	142,103	177,441	217,217
of which: Currency Outside DMBs	14a	18,270	21,882	23,604	30,023	†36,186	57,260	61,492	82,815	88,854	116,153	148,015	188,448
Time, Savings,& Fgn.Currency Dep.	15	....	....	....	....	812	5,397	259	1,394	4,975	3,363	4,526	4,628
Restricted Deposits	16b	....	....	....	....	3	213	24	34	54	31	103	94
Foreign Liabilities	16c	207,647	234,495	377,912	463,327	†203,964	242,632	334,003	460,925	306,984	365,027	390,082	443,415
Long-Term Foreign Liabilities	16cl	....	....	....	....	19,421	22,120	31,180	44,973	32,536	43,533	42,959	51,239
Central Government Deposits	16d	1,974	6,598	5,936	10,955	†2,042	4,528	4,615	5,472	8,415	13,195	42,510	14,849
Capital Accounts	17a	147	149	24,151	24,156	†190,151	227,926	153,376	156,239	222,527	261,467	261,538	226,182
of which: Valuation Adjustment	17rv	–47,145	–90,274	–108,690	–111,158	†832	–40,714	–57,997	–135,494	8,177	–9,614	–54,187	–116,625
Other Items (Net)	17r	–192,599	–221,840	54,124	–75,639	†–14,373	–66,491	–34,661	–144,178	36,937	–59,436	–65,996	–101,140
Deposit Money Banks						Millions of Leones: End of Period							
Reserves	20	5,707	2,855	7,523	4,701	†5,926	26,240	8,088	23,229	20,543	17,047	21,696	20,099
Foreign Assets	21	8,462	12,986	10,378	21,232	†18,079	20,852	30,555	40,852	40,611	47,295	58,383	78,839
Claims on Central Government	22a	2,795	8,589	9,921	12,763	†18,470	10,311	41,161	72,209	71,752	100,748	130,035	121,829
Claims on Nonfin.Pub.Enterprises	22c	50	26	81	21	†30	335	63	66	622	486	950	3,647
Claims on Private Sector	22d	10,257	14,847	16,576	17,276	†20,705	24,506	26,895	24,234	27,035	32,974	50,559	91,406
Claims on Nonbank Financial Insts.	22g	....	....	....	....	598	594	2,094	2,165	10,803	11,649	16,732	14,397
Demand Deposits	24	13,005	12,753	14,719	19,462	†15,616	24,494	25,875	47,800	48,447	67,452	90,808	94,415
Time, Savings,& Fgn.Currency Dep.	25	10,446	15,951	16,955	16,481	†32,044	37,625	50,896	58,686	72,674	98,064	124,834	161,754
Foreign Liabilities	26c	11	1,551	1,761	2,896	†–	–	–	–	–	–	–	–
Central Government Deposits	26d	634	1,356	1,916	2,172	†2,102	3,190	5,059	14,107	13,266	10,894	21,244	23,196
Credit from Monetary Authorities	26g	–	–	–	–	†74	74	42	21	–	–	–	–
Capital Accounts	27a	1,025	1,292	5,483	8,961	†20,564	18,607	22,994	34,664	48,899	60,975	76,176	84,301
Other Items (Net)	27r	2,150	6,399	3,645	6,021	†–6,591	–1,153	3,990	7,480	–11,920	–27,186	–34,706	–33,450
Monetary Survey						Millions of Leones: End of Period							
Foreign Assets (Net)	31n	–188,052	–204,117	–338,852	–396,296	†–158,623	–168,771	–220,319	–322,038	–179,988	–202,278	–140,223	–195,880
Domestic Credit	32	40,615	40,961	481,758	426,184	†452,793	501,856	537,572	604,813	723,811	774,627	795,931	880,963
Claims on Central Govt. (Net)	32an	30,196	25,963	464,940	408,563	†429,891	473,523	506,752	577,463	683,477	727,016	721,414	769,255
Claims on Nonfin.Pub.Enterprises	32c	50	26	81	21	†233	538	76	134	635	499	963	3,661
Claims on Private Sector	32d	10,369	14,973	16,736	17,600	†21,736	27,083	28,644	25,022	28,043	34,943	56,719	93,317
Claims on Other Banking Insts.	32f	....	....	....	....	33	34	–	4	–	–	–	–
Claims on Nonbank Financial Inst.	32g	....	....	....	....	900	679	2,100	2,190	11,656	12,169	16,834	14,730
Money	34	31,387	35,053	38,542	49,902	†53,208	83,611	89,744	134,078	139,957	189,437	247,478	292,950
Quasi-Money	35	10,446	15,951	16,955	16,481	†32,856	43,022	51,155	60,080	77,649	101,427	129,360	166,383
Restricted Deposits	36b	....	....	....	....	3	213	24	34	54	31	103	94
Long-Term Foreign Liabilities	36cl	....	....	....	....	19,421	22,120	31,180	44,973	32,536	43,533	42,959	51,239
Capital Accounts	37a	1,172	1,441	29,633	33,116	†210,715	246,533	176,370	190,903	271,426	322,443	337,714	310,483
Other Items (Net)	37r	–190,442	–215,601	57,775	–69,611	†–22,033	–62,414	–31,221	–147,294	22,201	–84,521	–101,905	–136,066
Money plus Quasi-Money	35l	41,834	51,004	55,497	66,383	†86,064	126,633	140,899	194,159	217,605	290,864	376,838	459,333

Sierra Leone 724

		1992	1993	1994	1995	1996	1997	1998	1999	2000	2001	2002	2003
Interest Rates		\multicolumn{12}{c}{*Percent Per Annum*}
Treasury Bill Rate	60c	78.63	28.64	12.19	14.73	29.25	12.71	22.10	32.42	26.22	13.74	15.15	15.68
Deposit Rate	60l	54.67	27.00	11.63	7.03	13.96	9.91	7.12	9.50	9.25	7.67	8.23	8.42
Lending Rate	60p	62.83	50.46	27.33	28.83	32.12	23.87	23.83	26.83	26.25	24.27	22.17	20.00
Prices		\multicolumn{12}{c}{*Index Numbers (2000=100): Period Averages*}
Consumer Prices	64	20.5	†25.1	31.1	39.2	48.3	55.5	75.2	100.8	100.0	102.1	98.7	106.2
International Transactions		\multicolumn{12}{c}{*Millions of Leones*}
Exports	70	74,918	67,094	68,010	30,148	43,004	15,412	10,482	11,347	26,771	57,897	102,010	217,742
Imports, c.i.f.	71	72,776	83,460	88,492	102,488	193,628	80,010	148,226	153,856	314,639	368,323	554,838	707,909
Balance of Payments		\multicolumn{12}{c}{*Millions of US Dollars: Minus Sign Indicates Debit*}
Current Account, n.i.e.	78ald	−5.5	−57.8	−89.1	−118.1	−150.5	−54.9	−33.2	−99.3	−112.3	−97.9	−73.2	….
Goods: Exports f.o.b.	78aad	150.4	118.3	116.0	41.5	46.8	15.7	31.6	6.3	12.8	29.2	59.8	….
Goods: Imports f.o.b.	78abd	−139.0	−187.1	−188.7	−168.1	−226.5	−71.9	−88.8	−86.8	−136.9	−165.1	−254.9	….
Trade Balance	78acd	11.4	−68.8	−72.7	−126.7	−179.7	−56.2	−57.2	−80.5	−124.1	−136.0	−195.1	….
Services: Credit	78add	47.0	58.5	100.2	86.8	62.9	31.9	19.1	22.3	42.2	52.0	38.3	….
Services: Debit	78aed	−62.9	−61.5	−107.6	−91.8	−107.7	−47.8	−39.2	−100.9	−112.8	−110.9	−80.8	….
Balance on Goods & Services	78afd	−4.5	−71.9	−80.1	−131.7	−224.5	−72.1	−77.4	−159.1	−194.7	−194.9	−237.5	….
Income: Credit	78agd	6.8	2.3	1.5	.7	.8	1.5	6.8	6.2	7.4	4.3	18.3	….
Income: Debit	78ahd	−15.1	−5.6	−57.0	−30.3	−12.4	−9.4	−27.3	−14.1	−12.6	−14.8	−21.1	….
Balance on Gds, Serv. & Inc.	78aid	−12.8	−75.2	−135.7	−161.3	−236.1	−80.0	−97.8	−167.0	−199.9	−205.4	−240.4	….
Current Transfers, n.i.e.: Credit	78ajd	8.2	19.1	47.5	44.0	87.2	25.9	65.2	68.6	92.3	120.7	170.8	….
Current Transfers: Debit	78akd	−.8	−1.7	−.9	−.8	−1.6	−.8	−.6	−1.0	−4.7	−13.2	−3.6	….
Capital Account, n.i.e.	78bcd	.1	.1	.1	−	.1	.1	−	−	−	.2	50.6	….
Capital Account, n.i.e.: Credit	78bad	.1	.1	.1	−	.1	.1	−	−	−	.4	50.6	….
Capital Account: Debit	78bbd	−	−	−	−	−	−	−	−	−	−.1	−	….
Financial Account, n.i.e.	78bjd	−18.2	49.1	−25.5	97.9	31.2	15.4	10.6	−27.3	124.6	30.1	−.8	….
Direct Investment Abroad	78bdd	−	−	−	−	….	….	….	….	….	….	….	….
Dir. Invest. in Rep. Econ., n.i.e.	78bed	−5.6	−7.5	−2.9	7.3	.7	1.8	.1	.5	39.0	9.8	1.6	….
Portfolio Investment Assets	78bfd	−	−	−	−	….	….	….	….	….	….	.1	….
Equity Securities	78bkd	−	−	−	−	….	….	….	….	….	….	.1	….
Debt Securities	78bld	−	−	−	−	….	….	….	….	….	….	−	….
Portfolio Investment Liab., n.i.e.	78bgd	−	−	−	−	….	….	….	….	….	….	….	….
Equity Securities	78bmd	−	−	−	−	….	….	….	….	….	….	….	….
Debt Securities	78bnd	−	−	−	−	….	….	….	….	….	….	….	….
Financial Derivatives Assets	78bwd	….	….	….	….	….	….	….	….	….	….	….	….
Financial Derivatives Liabilities	78bxd	….	….	….	….	….	….	….	….	….	….	….	….
Other Investment Assets	78bhd	−31.2	−14.6	−.8	15.6	1.8	−.9	−50.8	−31.3	44.2	−3.5	8.1	….
Monetary Authorities	78bod	….	….	….	….	….	….	….	….	….	….	.8	….
General Government	78bpd	−	−	−	−	−	−	−	−	−	−	−	….
Banks	78bqd	−7.8	−10.0	4.4	15.9	3.5	−.9	−6.3	−5.7	.1	−3.4	1.9	….
Other Sectors	78brd	−23.4	−4.6	−5.2	−.4	−1.6	−	−44.4	−25.6	44.1	−.1	5.4	….
Other Investment Liab., n.i.e.	78bid	18.6	71.2	−21.8	75.1	28.7	14.5	61.3	3.4	41.3	23.7	−10.5	….
Monetary Authorities	78bsd	−	44.5	−	−	−	−	−	−	−	−	−	….
General Government	78btd	16.6	31.1	−15.2	69.2	30.7	14.6	62.4	30.3	43.4	45.7	−10.5	….
Banks	78bud	3.1	−2.6	2.8	−1.5	−	−	−	−	−	−	−	….
Other Sectors	78bvd	−1.1	−1.8	−9.5	7.4	−1.9	−.1	−1.1	−26.9	−2.1	−22.1	−	….
Net Errors and Omissions	78cad	39.8	16.1	55.1	21.5	97.1	59.1	24.7	110.5	−2.5	97.2	−28.8	….
Overall Balance	78cbd	16.2	7.5	−59.5	1.3	−22.2	19.7	2.1	−16.1	9.8	29.6	−52.2	….
Reserves and Related Items	79dad	−16.2	−7.5	59.5	−1.3	22.2	−19.7	−2.1	16.1	−9.8	−29.6	52.2	….
Reserve Assets	79dbd	−14.0	−13.6	−18.6	−17.2	10.9	−26.7	−18.2	7.2	2.0	−13.9	−32.3	….
Use of Fund Credit and Loans	79dcd	−5.2	−8.4	55.1	15.9	11.3	7.0	16.1	8.9	−11.8	−15.8	5.0	….
Exceptional Financing	79ded	3.0	14.4	22.9	−	….	….	….	….	….	….	79.5	….

Sierra Leone 724

		1992	1993	1994	1995	1996	1997	1998	1999	2000	2001	2002	2003
International Investment Position							*Millions of US Dollars*						
Assets...	79aad	....	....	....	....	....	....	....	....	....	....	....	....
Direct Investment Abroad...............	79abd	....	....	....	....	....	....	....	....	....	—	—	....
Portfolio Investment......................	79acd	....	....	....	....	....	....	....	....	....	.2	.9	....
Equity Securities........................	79add	....	....	....	....	....	....	....	....	....	—	—	....
Debt Securities..........................	79aed	....	....	....	....	....	....	....	....	....	.2	.9	....
Financial Derivatives......................	79ald	....	....	....	....	....	....	....	....	....	....	....	....
Other Investment...........................	79afd	....	....	....	....	....	....	....	....	....	9.4	8.6	....
Monetary Authorities..................	79agd	....	....	....	....	....	....	....	....	....	9.4	8.6	....
General Government..................	79ahd	....	....	....	....	....	....	....	....	....			....
Banks...	79aid	....	....	....	....	....	....	....	....	....	—	—	....
Other Sectors.............................	79ajd	....	....	....	....	....	....	....	....	....			....
Reserve Assets..............................	79akd	....	....	....	....	....	....	....	....	....	41.2	76.3	....
Liabilities...	79lad	....	....	....	....	....	....	....	....	....	....	....	....
Dir. Invest. in Rep. Economy............	79lbd	....	....	....	....	....	....	....	....	....			....
Portfolio Investment......................	79lcd	....	....	....	....	....	....	....	....	....	—	—	....
Equity Securities........................	79ldd	....	....	....	....	....	....	....	....	....	—	—	....
Debt Securities..........................	79led	....	....	....	....	....	....	....	....	....			....
Financial Derivatives......................	79lld	....	....	....	....	....	....	....	....	....	....	....	....
Other Investment...........................	79lfd	....	....	....	....	....	....	....	....	....	1,265.9	1,383.9	....
Monetary Authorities..................	79lgd	....	....	....	....	....	....	....	....	....	151.8	169.3	....
General Government..................	79lhd	....	....	....	....	....	....	....	....	....	1,114.1	1,214.6	....
Banks...	79lid	....	....	....	....	....	....	....	....	....	—	—	....
Other Sectors.............................	79ljd	....	....	....	....	....	....	....	....	....			....
Government Finance						*Millions of Leones: Year Ending December 31*							
Deficit (-) or Surplus........................	80	−16,502	−17,099	−26,123	−39,835	−49,925	−48,300	†−47,724	−102,373	−124,064	....	....	....
Revenue...	81	35,384	54,294	67,414	61,743	69,713	85,498	†77,199	85,819	152,174	....	....	....
Grants Received...............................	81z	5,107	7,302	11,117	5,734	8,529	9,495	†22,456	65,391	106,107	....	....	....
Expenditure.....................................	82	56,993	78,695	104,654	107,312	128,167	143,293	†147,052	252,884	370,697	....	....	....
Lending Minus Repayments............	83	—	—	—	—	—	—	†327	699	11,648	....	....	....
Financing													
Domestic.......................................	84a	356	61	−1,681	2,431	25,270	7,488	†47,784	88,807	11,679	....	....	....
Foreign..	85a	16,146	17,037	27,804	37,404	24,655	40,812	†−60	13,566	112,385	....	....	....
Debt: Domestic................................	88a	16,508	18,164	24,311	26,007	41,613	52,368	†133,201	231,666	232,663	....	....	....
Debt: Foreign...................................	89a	367,739	408,626	444,894	656,205	966,326	941,853	†1,840,991	2,755,965	2,153,630	....	....	....
National Accounts						*Millions of Leones: Year Ending December 31*							
Househ.Cons.Expend.,incl.NPISHs....	96f	278,714	372,562	436,876	566,824	709,799	734,139	887,613	1,040,868	1,142,681	1,398,461	1,528,299	1,713,929
Government Consumption Expend...	91f	28,867	44,067	54,247	57,869	84,973	85,954	107,236	119,746	134,374	255,265	325,223	353,541
Gross Fixed Capital Formation..........	93e	35,128	21,475	43,901	37,011	78,163	41,765	59,204	52,885	84,761	90,091	114,690	322,945
Changes in Inventories.....................	93i	8,826	−3,687	2,507	−914	8,689	−5,460	−1,427	−10,856	1,143	....	....	....
Exports of Goods and Services.........	90c	76,274	93,754	106,848	129,878	171,391	165,415	203,345	225,868	230,179	228,694	293,879	323,534
Imports of Goods and Services (-).....	98c	79,374	95,254	109,853	133,973	177,254	192,770	206,062	229,815	261,561	484,986	618,709	850,982
Gross Domestic Product (GDP).........	99b	339,609	436,304	535,019	657,604	867,072	834,502	1,051,336	1,209,552	1,330,433	1,487,724	1,658,729	1,852,477
Net Primary Income from Abroad.....	98.n	−45,119	−61,324	−70,868	−78,196	−81,853	−92,289	−110,746	−144,985	−165,955	−129,157	−187,167	−194,998
Gross National Income (GNI)...........	99a	285,566	400,273	473,474	626,173	773,754	725,680	817,068	1,128,867	....	....	....	....
Consumption of Fixed Capital..........	99cf	20,624	27,206	34,212	37,470	39,424	71,392	59,226	69,422	49,047	....	....	....
GDP Volume 1989/90 Prices............	99b.p	81,555	82,677	81,066	74,583	79,128	65,205	64,629	59,407	61,670	64,999	69,267	74,090
GDP Volume (2000=100).................	99bvp	132.2	134.1	131.5	120.9	128.3	105.7	104.8	96.3	100.0	105.4	112.3	120.1
GDP Deflator (2000=100)................	99bip	19.3	24.5	30.6	40.9	50.8	59.3	75.4	94.4	100.0	106.1	111.0	115.9
						Millions: Midyear Estimates							
Population.......................................	99z	4.09	4.08	4.07	4.08	4.11	4.14	4.20	4.29	4.41	4.57	4.76	4.97

Singapore 576

		1992	1993	1994	1995	1996	1997	1998	1999	2000	2001	2002	2003
Exchange Rates						*Singapore Dollars per SDR: End of Period*							
Market Rate	aa	2.2617	2.2087	2.1324	2.1023	2.0129	2.2607	2.3380	2.2866	2.2560	2.3262	2.3608	2.5273
					Singapore Dollars per US Dollar: End of Period (ae) Period Average (rf)									
Market Rate	ae	1.6449	1.6080	1.4607	1.4143	1.3998	1.6755	1.6605	1.6660	1.7315	1.8510	1.7365	1.7008
Market Rate	rf	1.6290	1.6158	1.5274	1.4174	1.4100	1.4848	1.6736	1.6950	1.7240	1.7917	1.7906	1.7422
					Index Numbers (2000=100): Period Averages									
Market Rate	ahx	105.8	106.7	113.0	121.6	122.2	116.4	103.1	101.7	100.0	96.2	96.3	98.9
Nominal Effective Exchange Rate	nec	90.3	92.0	95.6	98.5	103.1	105.7	105.0	99.7	100.0	101.4	100.5	96.8
Real Effective Exchange Rate	rec	98.6	99.4	103.2	104.9	108.6	110.7	106.5	99.7	100.0	100.8	98.0	93.9
Fund Position						*Millions of SDRs: End of Period*							
Quota	2f.s	357.6	357.6	357.6	357.6	357.6	357.6	357.6	862.5	862.5	862.5	862.5	862.5
SDRs	1b.s	49.4	56.9	24.1	33.1	42.5	52.2	64.9	89.2	105.3	119.6	130.2	139.6
Reserve Position in the Fund	1c.s	113.4	157.4	172.8	199.8	204.7	248.4	297.6	303.4	237.7	297.5	351.3	379.3
of which: Outstg.Fund Borrowing	2c	–	–	–	–	–	–	31.3	–	–	–	–	–
Total Fund Cred.&Loans Outstg	2tl	–	–	–	–	–	–	–	–	–	–	–	–
International Liquidity						*Millions of US Dollars Unless Otherwise Indicated: End of Period*							
Total Reserves (see notes)	1l.d	39,885	48,361	58,177	68,695	76,847	71,289	74,928	76,843	80,132	75,375	82,021	95,746
SDRs	1b.d	68	78	35	49	61	70	91	122	137	150	177	207
Reserve Position in the Fund	1c.d	156	216	252	297	294	335	419	416	310	374	478	564
Foreign Exchange	1d.d	39,661	48,066	57,890	68,349	76,491	70,883	74,418	76,304	79,685	74,851	81,367	94,975
Monetary Authorities: Other Liab	4..d	360	299	298	262	247	164	150	792	834	731	714	741
Deposit Money Banks: Assets	7a.d	31,396	31,345	38,992	39,115	43,079	46,963	44,434	52,703	47,567	52,976	53,501	52,827
Liabilities	7b.d	29,450	32,085	40,976	46,753	55,327	62,784	49,747	50,414	54,193	56,062	58,287	59,840
Other Banking Insts.: Assets	7e.d	129	124	163	168	154	124	107	80	75	51	43	16
Liabilities	7f.d	6	10	27	19	12	11	5	8	4	2	2	1
ACU: Foreign Assets	7k.d	292,475	306,703	326,698	373,774	396,655	425,242	394,550	364,733	360,440	339,255	346,865	359,009
Foreign Liabilities	7m.d	298,497	321,390	340,295	391,907	419,343	447,032	417,127	384,962	386,812	375,951	387,285	404,383
Monetary Authorities						*Millions of Singapore Dollars: End of Period*							
Foreign Assets	11	65,788	77,867	85,166	97,337	107,751	119,617	124,584	128,457	139,260	139,942	142,721	163,190
Claims on Central Government	12a	–	–	–	–	–	–	–	–	5,250	6,251	5,808	6,395
Reserve Money	14	13,531	14,669	15,577	17,040	18,189	19,200	16,641	21,395	18,471	20,032	19,964	20,653
of which: Currency Outside DMBs	14a	8,279	8,942	9,420	9,907	10,293	10,704	10,146	11,315	11,289	11,868	12,360	12,838
Foreign Liabilities	16c	592	481	435	371	346	274	249	1,319	1,444	1,353	1,240	1,261
Central Government Deposits	16d	25,077	30,080	35,669	44,471	51,554	57,520	57,484	58,994	69,958	85,106	94,404	94,391
Other Items (Net)	17r	26,588	32,637	33,485	35,455	37,662	42,623	50,210	46,749	54,637	39,702	32,921	53,280
Deposit Money Banks						*Millions of Singapore Dollars: End of Period*							
Reserves	20	5,301	5,770	6,150	7,152	7,900	8,498	6,423	10,076	7,174	8,199	7,633	7,798
Foreign Assets	21	51,644	50,402	56,956	55,321	60,302	78,687	73,782	87,803	82,363	98,058	92,905	89,848
Claims on Central Government	22a	11,587	12,758	13,568	15,754	17,538	18,883	26,477	30,949	33,719	40,512	42,621	45,556
Claims on Private Sector	22d	68,851	79,282	91,375	109,885	127,272	143,409	154,844	150,199	159,083	185,048	169,048	178,253
Demand Deposits	24	10,236	13,940	13,991	15,443	16,747	16,807	17,093	19,794	21,973	24,215	23,468	25,884
Time and Savings Deposits	25	57,213	59,248	70,569	76,618	84,911	95,933	133,545	143,365	137,636	144,826	144,480	156,106
Foreign Liabilities	26c	48,443	51,592	59,854	66,123	77,447	105,194	82,605	83,990	93,836	103,771	101,215	101,776
Central Government Deposits	26d	5,744	6,385	6,584	7,538	6,896	1,529	1,766	1,632	1,465	2,089	1,768	1,813
Other Items (Net)	27r	15,747	17,047	17,051	22,390	27,011	30,014	25,517	30,246	27,429	56,916	41,276	35,876
Monetary Survey						*Millions of Singapore Dollars: End of Period*							
Foreign Assets (Net)	31n	68,397	76,196	81,833	86,164	90,260	92,836	115,512	130,951	126,343	132,876	133,172	150,001
Domestic Credit	32	49,624	55,583	62,699	73,638	86,368	103,251	122,081	120,535	126,640	144,625	121,310	134,001
Claims on Central Govt. (Net)	32an	–19,234	–23,707	–28,685	–36,255	–40,912	–40,166	–32,773	–29,677	–32,454	–40,432	–47,743	–44,253
Claims on Private Sector	32d	68,858	79,290	91,384	109,893	127,280	143,417	154,854	150,212	159,094	185,057	169,052	178,254
Money	34	18,515	22,882	23,411	25,350	27,040	27,511	27,239	31,109	33,262	36,083	35,828	38,722
Quasi-Money	35	57,213	59,248	70,569	76,618	84,911	95,933	133,545	143,365	137,636	144,826	144,480	156,106
Other Items (Net)	37r	42,293	49,649	50,552	57,834	64,677	72,643	76,809	77,012	82,085	96,592	74,173	89,173
Money plus Quasi-Money	35l	75,728	82,130	93,980	101,968	111,951	123,444	160,784	174,474	170,898	180,909	180,308	194,828
Other Banking Institutions													
Finance Companies						*Millions of Singapore Dollars: End of Period*							
Cash	40	1,953	1,788	2,574	2,848	2,561	2,513	2,822	3,046	2,017	1,514	1,608	475
Foreign Assets	41	212	200	238	237	215	208	179	133	130	95	75	27
Claims on Private Sector	42d	10,251	12,047	15,110	16,717	17,073	18,034	16,891	15,751	15,880	11,919	10,752	6,632
Time and Savings Deposits	45	9,552	10,558	13,753	15,435	15,058	15,734	15,421	14,387	13,653	10,638	9,853	5,528
Foreign Liabilities	46c	10	17	39	26	16	18	9	14	6	4	3	2
Capital Accounts	47a	1,679	1,850	2,203	2,621	3,015	3,269	3,371	3,408	3,165	2,426	2,111	1,406
Other Items (Net)	47r	1,176	1,611	1,927	1,720	1,760	1,734	1,091	1,121	1,203	461	468	198
Post Office: Savings Deposits	45..i	18,007	20,085	20,127	22,188	24,734	25,130	....	....	....	....	....	....

Singapore 576

		1992	1993	1994	1995	1996	1997	1998	1999	2000	2001	2002	2003
Nonbank Financial Institutions		\multicolumn{12}{c}{*Millions of Singapore Dollars: End of Period*}
Cash..	40..s	761	1,160	1,772	2,269	2,657	3,041	3,809	4,036	3,796	4,057	4,081	4,049
Foreign Assets.........................	41..s	830	1,160	1,090	1,546	2,082	2,055	2,696	3,574	7,254	10,926	12,880	16,809
Claims on Central Government....	42a.s	1,337	1,190	918	901	746	815	933	2,417	3,169	6,100	8,280	10,247
Claims on Private Sector...........	42d.s	2,919	4,270	5,488	6,715	8,261	10,095	10,392	16,333	18,555	24,525	25,592	29,354
Fixed Assets.............................	42h.s	237	313	335	657	1,173	1,377	1,861	1,874	1,868	1,891	2,342	2,344
Incr.in Total Assets(Within Per.)..	49z.s	1,375	1,944	1,682	2,481	2,996	2,379	2,564	8,170	6,244	13,148	6,098	9,595
Money (National Definitions)		\multicolumn{12}{c}{*Millions of Singapore Dollars: End of Period*}
M1..	59ma	18,516	22,882	23,412	25,349	27,040	27,511	27,239	31,109	33,262	36,083	35,828	38,723
M2..	59mb	75,729	82,130	93,981	101,967	111,951	123,443	160,784	174,474	170,898	180,909	180,308	194,829
M3..	59mc	101,482	111,369	125,835	136,737	148,495	160,766	173,581	186,184	182,913	190,317	188,815	200,044
Interest Rates		\multicolumn{12}{c}{*Percent Per Annum*}
Money Market Rate...................	60b	2.74	2.50	3.68	2.56	2.93	4.35	5.00	2.04	2.57	1.99	.96	.74
Treasury Bill Rate......................	60c	1.73	.92	1.94	1.05	1.38	2.32	2.12	1.12	2.18	1.69	.81	.64
Eurodollar Rate in Singapore......	60d	3.88	3.33	4.86	6.04	5.52	5.75	5.53	5.42	6.55	3.66	1.80	1.22
Savings Rate.............................	60k	2.14	1.62	2.31	2.81	2.72	2.75	3.11	1.37	1.33	1.16	.61	.28
Deposit Rate.............................	60l	2.86	2.30	3.00	3.50	3.41	3.47	4.60	1.68	1.71	1.54	.91	.51
Lending Rate............................	60p	5.95	5.39	5.88	6.37	6.26	6.32	7.44	5.80	5.83	5.66	5.37	5.31
Prices, Production, Labor		\multicolumn{12}{c}{*Index Numbers (2000=100): Period Averages*}
Share Prices.............................	62	58.2	74.7	92.3	87.2	96.5	89.1	59.6	95.2	100.0	80.7	76.6	73.0
Wholesale Prices......................	63	97.3	93.1	92.7	92.7	92.8	91.8	89.0	90.8	100.0	98.4	97.0	98.9
Consumer Prices.......................	64	89.2	91.2	94.0	95.6	97.0	98.9	†98.6	98.7	100.0	101.0	100.6	101.1
Manufacturing Production........	66ey	51.5	56.7	64.1	†70.7	73.0	76.4	†76.1	86.7	100.0	88.4	95.9	†98.6
		\multicolumn{12}{c}{*Number in Thousands: Period Averages*}
Labor Force..............................	67d	1,620	1,636	1,693	1,748	1,801	1,876	1,932	1,976	2,196	2,120	2,129	2,152
Employment.............................	67e	1,576	1,592	1,649	1,702	1,748	1,831	1,870	1,886	2,095	2,047	2,017	2,034
Unemployment.........................	67c	43	44	44	74	54	46	62	90	98	73	111	116
Unemployment Rate (%).............	67r	2.7	2.7	2.6	2.7	3.0	2.4	3.2	4.6	4.4	3.4	5.2	5.4
International Transactions		\multicolumn{12}{c}{*Millions of Singapore Dollars*}
Exports.....................................	70	103,351	119,475	147,327	167,515	176,271	185,613	183,763	194,290	237,826	218,029	223,901	251,096
Imports, c.i.f.............................	71	117,530	137,602	156,397	176,317	185,183	196,606	174,867	188,143	232,176	207,694	208,312	222,811
		\multicolumn{12}{c}{*2000=100*}
Volume of Exports.....................	72	40.6	48.0	61.7	71.4	75.9	81.1	†81.9	86.4	100.0	95.3	†100.1	116.5
Volume of Imports....................	73	51.9	62.0	71.2	80.4	85.4	92.0	†83.5	88.3	100.0	89.2	....	....
Export Prices (Survey)..............	76	107.0	104.6	100.3	98.6	97.7	96.2	†94.4	94.6	100.0	96.2	†94.0	90.6
Import Prices (Survey)..............	76.x	97.5	95.5	94.5	94.5	93.4	92.0	†90.3	91.8	100.0	100.3	†99.6	100.0

2004, International Monetary Fund : *International Financial Statistics Yearbook*

Singapore 576

		1992	1993	1994	1995	1996	1997	1998	1999	2000	2001	2002	2003
Balance of Payments		*Millions of US Dollars: Minus Sign Indicates Debit*											
Current Account, n.i.e.	78ald	5,915	4,211	11,400	14,800	13,977	14,908	18,544	15,184	13,280	16,137	18,704	....
Goods: Exports f.o.b.	78aad	66,565	77,858	97,919	122,612	129,547	129,780	110,264	116,546	139,861	124,443	128,374	....
Goods: Imports f.o.b.	78abd	−68,387	−80,582	−96,565	−117,705	−123,894	−125,099	−95,917	−104,570	−127,563	−109,675	−109,825	....
Trade Balance	78acd	−1,821	−2,724	1,354	4,907	5,653	4,681	14,347	11,976	12,298	14,768	18,549	....
Services: Credit	78add	16,200	18,597	23,044	29,160	30,453	29,579	22,192	26,362	29,098	28,855	29,701	....
Services: Debit	78aed	−9,537	−11,321	−13,898	−20,587	−22,101	−22,085	−19,320	−23,937	−26,938	−26,886	−27,298	....
Balance on Goods & Services	78afd	4,842	4,552	10,500	13,480	14,004	12,175	17,219	14,401	14,459	16,737	20,953	....
Income: Credit	78agd	8,214	8,075	9,783	12,591	12,067	13,334	12,304	16,264	16,291	15,566	14,367	....
Income: Debit	78ahd	−6,666	−7,880	−8,222	−10,382	−11,036	−9,441	−9,878	−14,470	−16,349	−15,020	−15,512	....
Balance on Gds, Serv. & Inc.	78aid	6,390	4,747	12,061	15,690	15,035	16,067	19,645	16,195	14,401	17,283	19,808	....
Current Transfers, n.i.e.: Credit	78ajd	172	140	145	160	161	153	131	135	127	122	122	....
Current Transfers: Debit	78akd	−647	−676	−806	−1,050	−1,220	−1,312	−1,231	−1,146	−1,248	−1,268	−1,227	....
Capital Account, n.i.e.	78bcd	−38	−71	−84	−73	−139	−190	−226	−191	−163	−161	−160	....
Capital Account, n.i.e.: Credit	78bad	−	−	−	−	−	−	−	−	−	−	−	....
Capital Account: Debit	78bbd	−38	−71	−84	−73	−139	−190	−226	−191	−163	−161	−160	....
Financial Account, n.i.e.	78bjd	1,793	−1,212	−8,841	−1,550	−9,343	−12,535	−18,663	−12,747	−1,926	−15,389	−15,655	....
Direct Investment Abroad	78bdd	−1,317	−2,152	−4,577	−2,995	−6,234	−8,955	−380	−5,397	−6,061	−9,548	−4,082	....
Dir. Invest. in Rep. Econ., n.i.e.	78bed	2,204	4,686	8,550	11,503	9,303	13,532	7,594	13,245	12,463	10,949	6,097	....
Portfolio Investment Assets	78bfd	1,091	−7,833	−7,840	−7,283	−15,137	−13,872	−10,149	−12,036	−11,482	−11,284	−11,374	....
Equity Securities	78bkd	165	−7,555	−7,414	−7,861	−12,024	−11,610	−5,752	−12,863	−8,909	−6,619	−7,879	....
Debt Securities	78bld	926	−278	−426	578	−3,112	−2,263	−4,397	827	−2,574	−4,665	−3,495	....
Portfolio Investment Liab., n.i.e.	78bgd	1,398	2,867	114	−242	980	−489	702	3,159	−2,036	187	−1,272	....
Equity Securities	78bmd	1,398	2,759	169	−189	992	−496	697	3,173	−2,039	161	−1,301	....
Debt Securities	78bnd	−	108	−55	−52	−12	8	5	−14	4	25	29	....
Financial Derivatives Assets	78bwd	....	....	....	....	....	....	....	....	....	....	....	....
Financial Derivatives Liabilities	78bxd	....	....	....	....	....	....	....	....	....	....	....	....
Other Investment Assets	78bhd	−6,685	−7,104	−10,999	−12,738	−13,417	−43,979	−6,634	−23,942	−8,452	−11,183	−289	....
Monetary Authorities	78bod	−	−	−	−	−	−	−	−	−	−	−	....
General Government	78bpd	−	−	−	−	−	−	−	−	−	−	−	....
Banks	78bqd	−5,866	769	−4,291	1,163	−3,359	−12,289	2,200	−9,859	1,969	−9,822	1,073	....
Other Sectors	78brd	−819	−7,872	−6,708	−13,900	−10,058	−31,690	−8,834	−14,083	−10,420	−1,361	−1,361	....
Other Investment Liab., n.i.e.	78bid	5,101	8,324	5,911	10,204	15,162	41,227	−9,796	12,224	13,642	5,490	−4,735	....
Monetary Authorities	78bsd	−	−	−	−	−	−	−	−	−	−	−	....
General Government	78btd	−9	−9	−4	−	−	−	−	−	−	−	−	....
Banks	78bud	5,146	1,949	5,409	3,970	8,102	18,878	−11,260	3,155	7,702	7,923	2,485	....
Other Sectors	78bvd	−36	6,384	506	6,235	7,060	22,349	1,464	9,069	5,940	−2,433	−7,220	....
Net Errors and Omissions	78cad	−1,570	4,650	2,261	−4,578	2,901	5,757	3,310	1,947	−4,386	−1,448	−1,546	....
Overall Balance	78cbd	6,100	7,578	4,736	8,599	7,396	7,940	2,965	4,194	6,806	−861	1,342	....
Reserves and Related Items	79dad	−6,100	−7,578	−4,736	−8,599	−7,396	−7,940	−2,965	−4,194	−6,806	861	−1,342	....
Reserve Assets	79dbd	−6,100	−7,578	−4,736	−8,599	−7,396	−7,940	−2,965	−4,194	−6,806	861	−1,342	....
Use of Fund Credit and Loans	79dcd	−	−	−	−	−	−	−	−	−	−	−	....
Exceptional Financing	79ded	....	....	....	−	−	−	−	−	−	−	−	....
International Investment Position		*Millions of US Dollars*											
Assets	79aad	....	....	....	....	....	....	....	....	355,213	384,199		....
Direct Investment Abroad	79abd	....	....	....	....	....	....	....	....	73,025	81,392		....
Portfolio Investment	79acd	....	....	....	....	....	....	....	....	56,859	64,705		....
Equity Securities	79add	....	....	....	....	....	....	....	....	30,491	33,243		....
Debt Securities	79aed	....	....	....	....	....	....	....	....	26,368	31,462		....
Financial Derivatives	79ald	....	....	....	....	....	....	....	....	−	−		....
Other Investment	79afd	....	....	....	....	....	....	....	....	149,725	155,913		....
Monetary Authorities	79agd	....	....	....	....	....	....	....	....	....	....		....
General Government	79ahd	....	....	....	....	....	....	....	....	....	....		....
Banks	79aid	....	....	....	....	....	....	....	....	....	....		....
Other Sectors	79ajd	....	....	....	....	....	....	....	....	....	....		....
Reserve Assets	79akd	....	....	....	....	....	....	....	....	75,604	82,189		....
Liabilities	79lad	....	....	....	....	....	....	....	....	314,774	339,147		....
Dir. Invest. in Rep. Economy	79lbd	....	....	....	....	....	....	....	....	135,630	150,164		....
Portfolio Investment	79lcd	....	....	....	....	....	....	....	....	45,793	45,330		....
Equity Securities	79ldd	....	....	....	....	....	....	....	....	35,781	33,206		....
Debt Securities	79led	....	....	....	....	....	....	....	....	10,012	12,124		....
Financial Derivatives	79ljd	....	....	....	....	....	....	....	....	....	....		....
Other Investment	79lfd	....	....	....	....	....	....	....	....	133,351	143,652		....
Monetary Authorities	79lgd	....	....	....	....	....	....	....	....	....	....		....
General Government	79lhd	....	....	....	....	....	....	....	....	....	....		....
Banks	79lid	....	....	....	....	....	....	....	....	....	....		....
Other Sectors	79ljd	....	....	....	....	....	....	....	....	....	....		....

Singapore 576

		1992	1993	1994	1995	1996	1997	1998	1999	2000	2001	2002	2003
Government Finance		\multicolumn{12}{c}{*Millions of Singapore Dollars: Year Ending December 31*}
Deficit (-) or Surplus............	80	9,537	12,998	13,086	15,870	18,868	13,612	23,163	14,577	18,094	−467	−2,595	10,422
Total Revenue and Grants......	81y	25,355	29,488	33,094	40,026	47,617	57,048	59,724	49,950	52,255	35,393	27,703	33,108
Revenue............................	81	25,355	29,488	33,094	40,026	47,617	57,048	59,724	49,950	52,255	35,393	27,703	33,108
Grants..............................	81z	−	−	−	−	−	−	−	−	−	−	−	−
Exp. & Lending Minus Repay...	82z	15,818	16,490	20,008	24,156	28,749	43,436	36,561	35,373	34,161	35,860	30,298	22,686
Expenditure.......................	82	14,804	14,339	15,670	17,419	20,681	29,222	25,586	26,665	30,068	34,957	30,985	28,635
Lending Minus Repayments....	83	1,014	2,151	4,338	6,737	8,068	14,214	10,975	8,708	4,093	903	−687	−5,948
Total Financing......................	80h	−9,537	−12,998	−13,086	−15,870	−18,868	−13,612	−23,163	−14,577	−18,093	467	2,595	−10,422
Total Net Borrowing.............	84	−7,731	5,309	12,552	16,402	10,159	12,215	22,540	17,148	16,487	8,084	137	13,170
Use of Cash Balances...........	87	−1,806	−18,307	−25,638	−32,272	−29,027	−25,827	−45,703	−31,725	−34,580	−7,617	2,458	−23,592
Total Debt by Currency...........	88z	67,376	69,944	75,467	86,630	94,831	102,372	115,183	125,777	134,370	146,996	156,751	169,332
National............................	88b	....	....	....	....	94,831	102,372	115,183	125,777	134,370	146,996	156,751	169,332
Foreign.............................	89b	....	....	....	....	−	−	−	−	−	−	−	−
National Accounts		\multicolumn{12}{c}{*Millions of Singapore Dollars*}
Househ.Cons.Expend.,incl.NPISHs....	96f	36,415	42,232	47,183	49,085	52,336	56,077	52,604	56,826	65,120	67,473	69,213	68,652
Government Consumption Expend...	91f	7,459	8,723	9,008	10,124	12,208	13,180	13,883	14,007	17,410	18,684	19,052	18,996
Gross Fixed Capital Formation.........	93e	28,806	32,753	36,202	39,782	49,378	54,826	51,535	47,092	47,538	45,586	40,705	39,573
Changes in Inventories.....................	93i	269	2,505	−500	865	−2,850	760	−7,219	−2,352	3,612	−7,290	−7,261	−18,328
Exports (Net)................................	90n	7,887	7,356	16,039	19,107	19,747	18,077	28,818	24,618	25,331	29,463	35,988	53,060
Gross Domestic Product (GDP).........	99b	81,224	94,289	107,851	118,963	130,035	141,641	137,085	139,616	159,662	154,078	158,064	159,135
Net Primary Income from Abroad.....	98.n	2,522	315	2,384	3,131	1,454	5,780	4,060	3,042	−100	978	−2,050	....
Gross National Income (GNI)............	99a	83,746	94,604	110,235	122,094	131,488	147,421	141,144	140,977	157,600	153,044	153,677	....
GDP Volume 1995 Prices.................	99b.p	88,047	98,838	110,109	118,963	128,653	139,599	138,399	147,834	162,162	159,073	162,493	164,266
GDP Volume (2000=100)................	99bvp	54.3	61.0	67.9	73.4	79.3	86.1	85.3	91.2	100.0	98.1	100.2	101.3
GDP Deflator (2000=100)...............	99bip	93.7	96.9	99.5	101.6	102.7	103.1	100.6	95.9	100.0	98.4	98.8	98.4
		\multicolumn{12}{c}{*Millions: Midyear Estimates*}
Population...............................	99z	3.18	3.28	3.37	3.48	3.59	3.70	3.81	3.92	4.02	4.10	4.18	4.25

2004, International Monetary Fund : *International Financial Statistics Yearbook*

Slovak Republic 936

		1992	1993	1994	1995	1996	1997	1998	1999	2000	2001	2002	2003
Exchange Rates						*Koruny per SDR: End of Period*							
Official Rate	aa	....	45.605	45.660	43.954	45.864	46.930	51.975	58.011	61.744	60.910	54.430	49.000
						Koruny per US Dollar: End of Period (ae) Period Average (rf)							
Official Rate	ae	....	33.202	31.277	29.569	31.895	34.782	36.913	42.266	47.389	48.467	40.036	32.975
Official Rate	rf	....	30.770	32.045	29.713	30.654	33.616	35.233	41.363	46.035	48.355	45.327	36.773
						Index Numbers (2000=100): Period Averages							
Nominal Effective Exchange Rate	nec	111.93	109.64	105.19	105.90	106.60	111.99	109.66	98.86	100.00	95.54	92.26	86.81
Real Effective Exchange Rate	rec	83.70	88.28	89.14	91.66	91.36	95.88	93.80	91.60	100.00	99.00	96.97	98.02
Fund Position						*Millions of SDRs: End of Period*							
Quota	2f.s	–	257.4	257.4	257.4	257.4	257.4	257.4	357.5	357.5	357.5	357.5	357.5
SDRs	1b.s	–	.3	58.9	39.0	11.2	19.6	1.2	.6	.4	.5	.8	.9
Reserve Position in the Fund	1c.s	–	–	–	–	–	–	–	–	–	–	–	–
Total Fund Cred.&Loans Outstg	2tl	–	405.2	439.8	307.5	222.0	184.4	134.6	96.5	–	–	–	–
International Liquidity						*Millions of US Dollars Unless Otherwise Indicated: End of Period*							
Total Reserves minus Gold	1l.d	....	416	1,691	3,364	3,419	3,230	2,869	3,371	4,022	4,141	8,809	11,678
SDRs	1b.d	–	–	86	58	16	26	2	1	–	1	1	1
Reserve Position in the Fund	1c.d	–	–	–	–	–	–	–	–	–	–	–	–
Foreign Exchange	1d.d	....	415	1,605	3,306	3,403	3,204	2,867	3,370	4,022	4,140	8,808	11,677
Gold (Million Fine Troy Ounces)	1ad	....	1.290	1.290	1.290	1.290	1.290	1.290	1.290	1.290	1.129	1.129	1.129
Gold (National Valuation)	1and	....	76	80	85	79	72	68	59	53	45	55	67
Monetary Authorities:Other Assets	3..d	....	98	153	171	129	202	609	564	203	762	657	367
Other Liab.	4..d	....	1,040	1,355	1,428	1,351	659	1,578	760	355	463	299	† 1,100
Deposit Money Banks: Assets	7a.d	....	987	1,427	1,823	2,514	3,618	3,794	1,618	2,346	2,390	2,053	† 2,324
Liabilities	7b.d	....	425	499	979	2,160	2,851	2,628	643	644	845	1,498	† 3,141
Monetary Authorities						*Millions of Koruny: End of Period*							
Foreign Assets	11	....	19,557	60,184	107,032	115,665	121,904	130,881	168,820	202,763	239,806	381,180	† 399,377
Claims on Central Government	12a	....	46,476	46,456	25,743	30,068	5,495	9,067	1,778	–	–	–	† 7,700
Claims on Other Resident Sectors	12d	....	355	305	189	327	416	509	481	382	346	286	† 10,617
Claims on Banking Institutions	12e	....	40,654	36,143	36,485	36,585	41,340	55,242	40,225	36,236	37,802	15,073	† 8,067
Reserve Money	14	....	39,006	48,319	63,208	81,339	96,134	90,768	108,925	113,310	138,902	141,201	† 130,898
of which: Currency Outside BIs	14a	....	25,122	28,101	34,536	43,505	48,740	49,759	57,472	67,048	80,963	84,211	† 91,826
Other Liabilities to Banking Insts.	14n	....	488	225	13,324	1,833	2,682	3,369	15,191	118,534	56,572	126,826	† 105,684
Other Deposits	15	....	9	25	60	131	117	86	364	545	739	1,636	† 1,465
Foreign Liabilities	16c	....	52,997	62,454	55,736	53,259	31,559	65,244	37,727	16,813	22,427	11,979	† 36,277
Central Government Deposits	16d	....	6,458	11,726	16,152	18,060	16,558	11,650	25,526	27,725	31,162	115,434	† 116,379
Bonds	16n	....	....	....	....	....	....	....	....	....	....	....	55,760
Capital Accounts	17a	....	4,151	7,977	8,239	9,244	9,316	10,322	10,580	10,573	14,787	10,802	† –16,105
Other Items (Net)	17r	....	3,933	12,362	12,730	18,779	12,791	14,261	12,991	–48,119	13,365	–11,340	† –4,596
Banking Institutions						*Millions of Koruny: End of Period*							
Reserves	20	....	† 3,401	3,445	7,607	10,830	12,541	10,335	12,222	51,141	45,042	48,677	† 37,378
Other Claims on Monetary Author.	20n	....	10,560	16,211	21,433	28,798	37,564	32,406	41,428	† 26,320	51,366	84,719	† 161,470
Foreign Assets	21	....	† 32,773	44,634	53,916	80,189	125,842	140,045	68,402	111,169	115,818	82,200	† 76,619
Claims on Central Government	22a	....	28,798	50,693	74,653	89,709	112,716	93,002	76,936	113,360	301,964	289,192	† 258,052
Claims on Other General Govt	22b	....	....	....	....	....	....	....	....	....	....	....	† 7,577
Claims on Other Resident Sectors	22d	....	234,292	201,643	211,839	280,307	† 399,242	420,986	460,428	479,203	379,653	435,123	† 379,002
Demand Deposits	24	....	† 90,742	94,931	113,179	129,528	116,651	96,863	95,586	118,916	144,603	160,560	† 261,072
Other Deposits	25	....	137,344	174,427	203,328	236,632	† 279,996	320,891	368,800	414,933	446,841	454,399	† 413,032
Bonds	26n	....	–	–	5,228	5,906	5,217	3,968	7,045	8,196	6,172	11,212	† 12,239
Foreign Liabilities	26c	....	† 13,762	14,909	28,342	68,212	98,410	95,367	25,815	28,616	39,167	54,736	† 103,565
Central Government Deposits	26d	....	9,458	12,151	25,436	33,197	31,917	28,018	23,248	34,230	41,446	42,246	† 12,117
Credit from Monetary Authorities	26g	....	† 41,204	37,705	38,406	40,224	51,606	61,528	40,741	37,402	30,661	13,016	† 7,913
Money Market Fund Shares	26m	....	....	....	....	....	....	....	....	....	....	....	–
Capital Accounts	27a	....	† 48,722	63,813	66,953	76,526	82,642	95,243	93,704	103,940	115,301	100,459	† 136,024
Other Items (Net)	27r	....	–32,313	–82,948	–116,453	–113,127	† 7,453	–18,724	–5,567	25,943	62,414	98,066	† –25,865
Banking Survey						*Millions of Koruny: End of Period*							
Foreign Assets (Net)	31n	....	† –14,429	27,455	76,870	74,383	117,778	110,315	173,679	268,503	294,030	396,665	† 336,154
Domestic Credit	32	....	294,005	275,220	270,836	349,154	† 469,394	483,896	490,849	530,990	609,355	566,921	† 534,452
Claims on Central Govt. (Net)	32an	....	59,358	73,272	58,808	68,520	69,736	62,401	29,940	51,405	229,356	131,512	† 137,256
Claims on Other General Govt	32b	....	....	....	....	....	....	....	....	....	....	....	† 7,577
Claims on Other Resident Sectors	32d	....	234,647	201,948	212,028	280,634	† 399,658	421,495	460,909	479,585	379,999	435,409	† 389,619
Money	34	....	† 116,615	123,820	149,657	173,350	165,658	146,833	153,058	185,964	225,566	244,771	† 353,971
Quasi-Money	35	....	137,353	174,452	203,388	236,763	† 280,113	320,977	369,164	415,478	447,580	456,035	† 414,497
Money Market Fund Shares	36m	....	....	....	....	....	....	....	....	....	....	....	–
Bonds	36n	....	564	952	9,642	17,952	18,474	15,939	15,709	15,319	11,645	11,212	† 67,999
Capital Accounts	37a	....	† 52,873	71,790	75,192	85,770	91,958	105,565	104,284	114,513	130,088	111,261	† 119,919
Other Items (Net)	37r	....	–28,170	–69,025	–90,788	–90,987	† 30,214	3,249	20,934	66,325	86,741	135,089	† –85,780
Money plus Quasi-Money	35l	....	253,968	298,272	353,045	410,113	† 445,771	467,810	522,222	601,442	673,146	700,806	† 768,468

Slovak Republic   936

		1992	1993	1994	1995	1996	1997	1998	1999	2000	2001	2002	2003
Interest Rates						*Percent Per Annum*							
Bank Rate (End of Period)	60	....	12.00	12.00	9.75	8.80	8.80	8.80	8.80	8.80	†7.75	6.50	6.00
Money Market Rate	60b	....	...	...	...	...	...	...	...	8.08	7.76	6.33	6.08
Deposit Rate	60l	....	8.02	9.32	9.01	9.30	13.44	16.25	14.37	8.45	6.46	6.65	5.33
Lending Rate	60p	....	14.41	14.56	16.85	13.92	18.65	21.17	21.07	14.89	11.24	10.25	8.46
Government Bond Yield	61	....	....	....	....	....	....	....	....	8.34	8.06	6.91	4.99
Prices, Production, Labor						*Index Numbers (2000=100): Period Averages*							
Producer Prices	63	55.58	65.14	71.64	78.10	81.32	84.97	87.73	91.08	100.00	106.60	108.81	117.85
Consumer Prices	64	....	54.1	61.3	67.4	†71.3	75.7	80.7	89.3	100.0	†107.3	110.9	120.4
Wages	65	....	47.1	55.1	62.9	71.3	80.7	87.5	93.9	100.0	108.2	118.2	125.7
Industrial Production	66	77.2	74.4	78.0	85.9	88.0	89.1	94.0	92.1	100.0	107.3	114.5	120.8
Employment	67	....	101.6	100.0	102.2	103.0	102.6	102.8	100.6	100.0	107.4	107.6	109.5
						Number in Thousands: Period Averages							
Labor Force	67d	....	2,509	2,511	2,481	....	2,473	....	2,558	2,594	2,634	2,623	....
Employment	67e	....	2,196	2,110	2,147	2,225	2,206	2,199	2,132	2,102	2,124	2,127	2,165
Unemployment	67c	....	369	334	325	278	297	317	417	485	508	487	459
Unemployment Rate (%)	67r	....	....	13.7	13.1	11.3	11.8	12.5	16.2	18.6	19.2	18.5	17.5
International Transactions						*Millions of Koruny*							
Exports	70	....	168,114	214,375	255,096	270,643	277,434	377,807	423,648	548,527	611,325	652,018	803,037
Imports, c.i.f.	71	....	204,786	218,638	273,831	350,847	361,833	483,773	492,337	619,789	749,775	785,374	867,956
Imports, f.o.b.	71.v	110,212	195,034	211,811	260,791	340,903	345,006	460,736	468,892	590,275	714,071	747,975	826,625
Balance of Payments						*Millions of US Dollars: Minus Sign Indicates Debit*							
Current Account, n.i.e.	78ald	....	−580	671	390	−2,090	−1,961	−2,126	−1,155	−694	....	....	....
Goods: Exports f.o.b.	78aad	....	5,452	6,706	8,591	8,824	9,641	10,720	10,201	11,896	....	....	....
Goods: Imports f.o.b.	78abd	....	−6,365	−6,645	−8,820	−11,106	−11,725	−13,071	−11,310	−12,791	....	....	....
Trade Balance	78acd	....	−912	61	−229	−2,283	−2,084	−2,351	−1,109	−895	....	....	....
Services: Credit	78add	....	1,939	2,261	2,378	2,066	2,167	2,292	1,899	2,241	....	....	....
Services: Debit	78aed	....	−1,666	−1,600	−1,838	−2,028	−2,094	−2,276	−1,844	−1,805	....	....	....
Balance on Goods & Services	78afd	....	−640	722	311	−2,245	−2,011	−2,334	−1,054	−459	....	....	....
Income: Credit	78agd	....	185	155	250	224	315	437	268	268	....	....	....
Income: Debit	78ahd	....	−224	−275	−263	−270	−438	−595	−568	−623	....	....	....
Balance on Gds, Serv. & Inc.	78aid	....	−678	602	297	−2,291	−2,135	−2,492	−1,353	−814	....	....	....
Current Transfers, n.i.e.: Credit	78ajd	....	216	166	243	483	540	645	466	344	....	....	....
Current Transfers: Debit	78akd	....	−118	−98	−150	−282	−367	−279	−268	−224	....	....	....
Capital Account, n.i.e.	78bcd	....	564	84	46	30	−	70	158	91	....	....	....
Capital Account, n.i.e.: Credit	78bad	....	771	84	46	30	−	83	171	106	....	....	....
Capital Account: Debit	78bbd	....	−208	−	−	−	−	−12	−13	−15	....	....	....
Financial Account, n.i.e.	78bjd	....	−153	71	1,211	2,268	1,780	1,912	1,789	1,472	....	....	....
Direct Investment Abroad	78bdd	....	−61	−14	−10	−48	−95	−145	376	−22	....	....	....
Dir. Invest. in Rep. Econ., n.i.e.	78bed	....	199	270	236	351	174	562	354	2,052	....	....	....
Portfolio Investment Assets	78bfd	....	−774	−26	157	−12	−81	−57	247	−195	....	....	....
Equity Securities	78bkd	....	−774	−26	174	69	86	33	2	11	....	....	....
Debt Securities	78bld	....	....	−	−17	−81	−167	−91	246	−206	....	....	....
Portfolio Investment Liab., n.i.e.	78bgd	....	465	304	53	29	93	841	405	1,016	....	....	....
Equity Securities	78bmd	....	465	111	−16	28	102	−35	47	−53	....	....	....
Debt Securities	78bnd	....	....	193	69	1	−10	876	358	1,069	....	....	....
Financial Derivatives Assets	78bwd	....	....	−	−	−	−	−	....	....	....	....	....
Financial Derivatives Liabilities	78bxd	....	....	−	−	−	−	−	....	1	....	....	....
Other Investment Assets	78bhd	....	−412	−548	−116	−334	−1,028	190	1,713	−973	....	....	....
Monetary Authorities	78bod	....	....	....	....	....	....	−	....	....	....	....	....
General Government	78bpd	....	232	−211	140	337	61	117	9	1	....	....	....
Banks	78bqd	....	−530	−344	−248	−662	−1,122	110	1,878	−748	....	....	....
Other Sectors	78brd	....	−114	7	−8	−10	33	−37	−174	−226	....	....	....
Other Investment Liab., n.i.e.	78bid	....	430	84	891	2,282	2,718	520	−1,307	−407	....	....	....
Monetary Authorities	78bsd	....	−	38	42	52	153	55	14	−26	....	....	....
General Government	78btd	....	145	−52	−173	−124	184	−321	55	149	....	....	....
Banks	78bud	....	99	38	463	1,440	1,084	−138	−1,882	30	....	....	....
Other Sectors	78bvd	....	186	60	559	914	1,298	924	506	−561	....	....	....
Net Errors and Omissions	78cad	....	183	380	144	162	280	−333	−14	51	....	....	....
Overall Balance	78cbd	....	14	1,205	1,791	370	99	−478	777	920	....	....	....
Reserves and Related Items	79dad	....	−14	−1,205	−1,791	−370	−99	478	−777	−920	....	....	....
Reserve Assets	79dbd	....	−104	−1,256	−1,590	−245	−47	545	−725	−794	....	....	....
Use of Fund Credit and Loans	79dcd	....	89	51	−201	−125	−52	−67	−52	−125	....	....	....
Exceptional Financing	79ded	....	....	....	....	....	....	....	....	....	....	....	....

Slovak Republic 936

		1992	1993	1994	1995	1996	1997	1998	1999	2000	2001	2002	2003
International Investment Position							*Millions of US Dollars*						
Assets	79aad	....	....	8,421	10,156	10,311	10,648	10,322	8,652	10,089	....	14,686	....
Direct Investment Abroad	79abd	....	....	166	139	182	234	404	342	364	....	491	....
Portfolio Investment	79acd	....	....	429	259	282	330	406	146	336	....	686	....
Equity Securities	79add	....	....	424	234	171	71	35	28	15	....	42	....
Debt Securities	79aed	....	....	5	25	111	259	371	118	321	....	644	....
Financial Derivatives	79ald	....	....	–	–	–	–	–	–	–	....	....	....
Other Investment	79afd	....	....	5,633	5,896	5,948	6,461	6,267	4,419	5,006	....	4,313	....
Monetary Authorities	79agd	....	....	–	–	–	–	–	–	–	....	–	....
General Government	79ahd	....	....	2,947	2,928	2,393	2,136	1,897	1,657	1,484	....	1,101	....
Banks	79aid	....	....	1,451	1,676	2,276	3,141	3,203	1,526	2,186	....	1,660	....
Other Sectors	79ajd	....	....	1,234	1,291	1,280	1,185	1,167	1,236	1,335	....	1,552	....
Reserve Assets	79akd	....	....	2,192	3,862	3,898	3,623	3,244	3,745	4,384	....	9,196	....
Liabilities	79lad	....	....	6,137	7,316	9,769	11,848	14,656	13,200	14,368	....	22,448	....
Dir. Invest. in Rep. Economy	79lbd	....	....	897	1,297	2,046	2,083	2,890	3,188	4,504	....	10,465	....
Portfolio Investment	79lcd	....	....	583	608	563	595	1,549	2,039	2,830	....	3,323	....
Equity Securities	79ldd	....	....	56	43	62	157	102	341	260	....	509	....
Debt Securities	79led	....	....	527	565	500	438	1,447	1,698	2,570	....	2,814	....
Financial Derivatives	79lld	....	....	–	–	–	–	–	–	–	....	17	....
Other Investment	79lfd	....	....	4,657	5,411	7,161	9,170	10,217	7,974	7,034	....	8,644	....
Monetary Authorities	79lgd	....	....	682	537	442	507	536	522	324	....	435	....
General Government	79lhd	....	....	1,101	958	786	912	621	671	788	....	944	....
Banks	79lid	....	....	537	901	2,290	3,109	2,950	680	687	....	1,534	....
Other Sectors	79ljd	....	....	2,338	3,015	3,642	4,642	6,109	6,100	5,235	....	5,732	....
Government Finance						*Millions of Koruny: Year Ending December 31*							
Deficit (-) or Surplus	80	....	....	....	....	–8,540	–28,430	–28,663	–26,637	–27,464	–32,012	110,172	–33,537
Total Revenue and Grants	81y	....	....	....	....	254,769	265,402	274,888	315,683	325,614	331,821	366,636	387,288
Revenue	81	....	....	....	....	254,510	265,146	274,677	315,436	325,402	331,649	366,552	387,242
Grants	81z	....	....	....	....	259	256	211	247	212	172	84	46
Exp. & Lending Minus Repay	82z	....	....	....	....	263,309	293,832	303,551	342,320	353,078	363,833	256,464	420,825
Expenditure	82	....	....	....	....	266,814	290,026	303,952	317,447	368,407	366,901	434,127	438,960
Lending Minus Repayments	83	....	....	....	....	–3,505	3,806	–401	24,873	–15,329	–3,068	–177,663	–18,135
Total Financing	80h	....	....	....	....	8,540	28,430	28,663	26,637	27,464	32,012	–110,172	33,537
Domestic	84a	....	....	....	....	12,761	21,518	–6,057	–2,112	–681	24,080	–104,078	36,489
Foreign	85a	....	....	....	....	–4,221	6,912	34,720	28,749	28,145	7,932	....	–2,952
Total Debt by Residence	88	....	....	....	....	153,910	194,125	215,605	238,061	274,870	417,450	399,947	439,097
Domestic	88a	....	....	....	....	120,741	144,581	141,813	133,625	137,849	293,003	289,132	335,130
Foreign	89a	....	....	....	....	33,169	49,544	73,792	104,436	137,021	124,447	110,815	103,967
National Accounts							*Millions of Koruny*						
Househ.Cons.Expend.,incl.NPISHs	96f	....	227,835	260,998	300,439	340,419	380,935	429,243	480,727	528,000	585,900	632,096	678,075
Government Consumption Expend	91f	....	99,877	102,846	118,427	143,290	153,250	169,808	167,358	184,796	203,416	219,855	239,588
Gross Fixed Capital Formation	93e	....	123,374	131,819	144,248	205,846	243,539	281,774	249,792	242,277	291,027	300,560	308,404
Changes in Inventories	93i	....	–22,000	–27,900	–1,100	16,000	2,600	–16,100	–17,094	1,900	11,950	20,423	–6,379
Exports of Goods and Services	90c	....	233,214	296,372	336,007	345,557	405,319	466,740	518,078	661,511	741,008	787,349	933,235
Imports of Goods and Services (-)	98c	....	250,964	268,502	321,590	412,667	472,995	550,048	554,821	684,402	823,451	865,126	951,121
Gross Domestic Product (GDP)	99b	....	411,366	495,649	576,502	638,449	712,679	781,437	844,108	934,079	1,009,839	1,096,384	1,195,812
GDP Volume 1995 Prices	99b.p	....	512,849	544,674	576,502	611,935	640,151	667,107	676,919	690,697	716,845	748,385	779,875
GDP Volume (2000=100)	99bvp	....	74.3	78.9	83.5	88.6	92.7	96.6	98.0	100.0	103.8	108.4	112.9
GDP Deflator (2000=100)	99bip	....	59.3	67.3	73.9	77.1	82.3	86.6	92.2	100.0	104.2	108.3	113.4
						Millions: Midyear Estimates							
Population	99z	5.30	5.33	5.35	5.36	5.37	5.38	5.39	5.39	5.39	5.39	5.40	5.40

Slovenia 961

		1992	1993	1994	1995	1996	1997	1998	1999	2000	2001	2002	2003
Exchange Rates					*Tolars per SDR: End of Period*								
Official Rate	aa	135.71	181.09	184.61	187.28	203.44	228.27	226.97	270.07	296.25	315.37	300.55	281.39
					Tolars per US Dollar: End of Period (ae) Period Average (rf)								
Official Rate	ae	98.70	131.84	126.46	125.99	141.48	169.18	161.20	196.77	227.38	250.95	221.07	189.37
Official Rate	rf	81.29	113.24	128.81	118.52	135.36	159.69	166.13	181.77	222.66	242.75	240.25	207.11
Fund Position					*Millions of SDRs: End of Period*								
Quota	2f.s	–	150.50	150.50	150.50	150.50	150.50	150.50	231.70	231.70	231.70	231.70	231.70
SDRs	1b.s	–	.03	.04	.04	.09	.05	.17	1.17	2.83	4.00	5.13	6.18
Reserve Position in the Fund	1c.s	–	12.88	12.87	12.88	12.88	12.88	46.46	78.40	63.19	64.16	88.77	97.34
Total Fund Cred.&Loans Outstg	2tl	–	8.53	4.94	2.69	.90	–	–	–	–	–	–	–
International Liquidity					*Millions of US Dollars Unless Otherwise Indicated: End of Period*								
Total Reserves minus Gold	1l.d	715.54	787.80	1,498.98	1,820.79	2,297.36	3,314.67	3,638.52	3,168.00	3,196.01	4,329.99	6,980.23	8,496.91
SDRs	1b.d	–	.05	.06	.06	.13	.07	.24	1.60	3.69	5.03	6.98	9.18
Reserve Position in the Fund	1c.d	–	17.68	18.80	19.14	18.51	17.37	65.41	107.61	82.33	80.63	120.69	144.65
Foreign Exchange	1d.d	715.54	770.07	1,480.12	1,801.59	2,278.71	3,297.22	3,572.87	3,058.79	3,110.00	4,244.33	6,852.57	8,343.09
Gold (Million Fine Troy Ounces)	1ad	.0003	.0003	.0003	.0003	.0003	.0003	.0003	.0003	.0003	.2431	.2429	.2429
Gold (National Valuation)	1and	.11	.13	.12	.13	.12	.09	.09	.09	.09	67.22	83.25	101.09
Monetary Authorities:Other Assets	3..d	1.35	1.08	103.28	170.14	33.70	41.27	46.83	51.95	58.05	76.11	84.72	87.22
Other Liab	4..d	–	.06	.09	.14	.42	.34	1.05	.63	.48	1.11	.19	.13
Deposit Money Banks: Assets	7a.d	2,065.82	1,431.92	2,301.70	2,395.17	2,581.52	1,869.71	2,003.17	1,807.96	2,006.24	3,266.75	2,258.44	2,578.94
Liabilities	7b.d	1,183.47	1,058.95	1,258.55	1,483.20	1,458.57	1,219.38	1,333.58	1,440.06	1,570.22	1,760.66	2,794.88	4,586.06
Monetary Authorities					*Billions of Tolars: End of Period*								
Foreign Assets	11	70.77	104.02	190.06	250.85	329.81	559.27	594.10	629.76	724.66	861.63	1,580.26	1,644.70
Claims on Central Government	12a	8.88	18.78	15.65	15.28	15.52	15.67	16.01	16.61	17.75	9.81	9.22	26.98
Claims on Private Sector	12d	.05	.08	.10	.11	.15	.19	.21	.22	.25	.26	.28	.27
Claims on Deposit Money Banks	12e	16.29	16.00	29.90	43.06	15.72	18.08	3.91	25.82	22.25	261.38	1.29	.09
Reserve Money	14	37.11	51.29	80.49	100.79	116.55	143.36	171.63	208.23	212.18	287.44	282.27	297.48
of which: Currency Outside DMBs	14a	24.18	32.72	47.28	59.96	66.84	78.12	93.65	125.01	119.82	142.11	143.05	156.04
Liabs.of Central Bank: Securities	16ac	40.76	50.39	99.77	126.67	178.45	364.97	362.48	337.76	365.27	584.69	926.77	1,027.59
Restricted Deposits	16b	.04	.37	1.82	1.91	.86	2.29	4.30	4.30	4.58	4.91	4.76	8.22
Foreign Liabilities	16c	–	1.55	.92	.52	.24	.06	.17	.12	.11	.28	.04	.02
Central Government Deposits	16d	5.78	5.99	27.41	47.51	22.30	23.12	18.50	26.25	39.08	60.01	164.77	146.72
Capital Accounts	17a	12.40	29.33	27.17	31.82	43.31	58.65	55.45	96.59	134.96	182.30	191.37	153.70
Other Items (Net)	17r	–.10	–.03	–1.88	.08	–.51	.77	1.69	–.83	8.73	13.45	21.03	38.29
Deposit Money Banks					*Billions of Tolars: End of Period*								
Reserves	20	7.76	12.67	31.07	38.13	48.11	63.09	74.44	79.37	87.42	138.59	130.57	130.65
Claims on Mon.Author.:Securities	20c	36.17	42.74	† 82.42	106.96	160.92	345.08	344.49	327.91	365.32	584.16	919.96	1,027.18
Foreign Assets	21	203.90	188.79	291.07	301.77	365.23	316.32	322.91	355.75	456.17	819.78	499.28	488.37
Claims on General Government	22a	24.18	208.08	257.88	315.96	319.59	372.50	407.79	428.33	479.56	548.89	606.08	638.58
Claims on Private Sector	22d	236.86	316.45	427.04	609.72	736.01	829.98	1,066.35	1,313.36	1,538.76	1,828.26	2,067.20	2,385.56
Claims on Other Financial Insts	22f	.91	2.03	5.53	12.75	9.38	12.36	20.36	37.82	51.56	59.05	81.10	106.70
Demand Deposits	24	44.48	64.36	84.15	104.10	127.42	151.36	191.99	237.01	263.47	317.30	533.30	608.48
Time, Savings,& Fgn.Currency Dep	25	197.72	334.95	494.13	647.77	807.04	1,005.28	1,188.44	1,334.29	1,618.56	2,152.14	2,255.13	2,348.74
Money Market Instruments	26aa	10.00	16.44	12.51	26.97	13.24	18.47	21.37	13.56	24.64	52.56	92.46	115.59
Bonds	26ab	.66	2.57	8.27	18.09	23.84	33.95	36.28	40.80	53.96	66.30	92.64	114.68
Restricted Deposits	26b	6.04	9.51	10.28	10.98	17.04	17.63	14.93	10.80	15.09	23.08	19.80	18.78
Foreign Liabilities	26c	116.81	139.61	159.15	186.87	206.36	206.29	214.97	283.36	357.03	441.83	617.87	868.45
General Government Deposits	26d	33.55	57.93	87.22	94.87	140.69	167.98	191.06	190.17	147.10	124.77	173.63	144.60
of which: Local Govt. Deposits	26db	5.31	7.59	8.04	11.43	6.53	6.53	6.91	10.88	11.21	5.46	9.13	10.55
Central Govt. Lending Funds	26f	.91	2.43	4.87	8.29	12.34	14.04	24.35	27.88	34.35	36.75	46.03	22.93
Credit from Monetary Authorities	26g	15.61	15.48	29.64	41.66	15.28	17.83	3.53	25.47	22.08	260.98	1.17	.01
Liabilities to Other Financ. Insts	26i	6.00	9.92	5.53	10.39	15.43	23.33	33.20	41.84	57.15	71.15	87.67	120.80
Capital Accounts	27a	104.77	151.07	209.53	248.29	273.20	303.74	335.79	372.56	418.82	452.19	499.86	539.31
Other Items (Net)	27r	–26.77	–33.54	–10.29	–13.00	–12.64	–20.58	–19.57	–35.19	–33.47	–20.34	–115.38	–125.33

Slovenia 961

		1992	1993	1994	1995	1996	1997	1998	1999	2000	2001	2002	2003
Monetary Survey						*Billions of Tolars: End of Period*							
Foreign Assets (Net)	31n	157.86	151.64	321.05	365.23	488.45	669.24	701.86	702.03	823.69	1,239.30	1,461.62	1,264.59
Domestic Credit	32	231.54	481.50	591.57	811.45	917.66	1,039.61	1,301.17	1,579.92	1,901.71	2,261.48	2,425.47	2,866.77
Claims on General Govt. (Net)	32an	−6.27	162.93	158.89	188.87	172.13	197.08	214.24	228.52	311.14	373.91	276.89	374.23
Claims on Private Sector	32d	236.91	316.53	427.14	609.83	736.16	830.17	1,066.56	1,313.58	1,539.01	1,828.52	2,067.48	2,385.84
Claims on Other Financial Insts.	32f	.91	2.03	5.53	12.75	9.38	12.36	20.36	37.82	51.56	59.05	81.10	106.70
Money	34	68.77	97.28	131.44	164.06	194.29	229.48	287.26	363.70	385.88	462.53	680.49	767.70
Quasi-Money	35	197.72	334.95	494.13	647.77	807.04	1,005.28	1,188.44	1,334.29	1,618.56	2,152.14	2,255.13	2,348.74
Money Market Instruments	36aa	10.00	16.44	12.51	26.97	13.24	18.47	21.37	13.56	24.64	52.56	92.46	115.59
Bonds	36ab	.66	2.57	8.27	18.09	23.84	33.95	36.28	40.80	53.96	66.30	92.64	114.68
Liabs. of Central Bank: Securities	36ac	4.59	7.65	†17.35	19.71	17.53	19.89	18.00	9.85	−.05	.52	6.81	.41
Restricted Deposits	36b	6.08	9.88	12.10	12.90	17.90	19.92	19.23	15.10	19.68	27.99	24.56	27.00
Central Govt. Lending Funds	36f	.91	2.43	4.87	8.29	12.34	14.04	24.35	27.88	34.35	36.75	46.03	22.93
Liabilities to Other Financ. Insts.	36i	6.00	9.92	5.53	10.39	15.43	23.33	33.20	41.84	57.15	71.15	87.67	120.80
Capital Accounts	37a	117.17	180.40	236.70	280.11	316.51	362.39	391.24	469.15	553.78	634.50	691.24	693.00
Other Items (Net)	37r	−22.51	−28.39	†−11.34	−13.12	−12.02	−17.90	−16.34	−34.21	−22.55	−3.67	−89.96	−79.51
Money plus Quasi-Money	35l	266.50	432.23	625.56	811.83	1,001.33	1,234.76	1,475.70	1,697.99	2,004.44	2,614.67	2,935.62	3,116.45
Interest Rates						*Percent Per Annum*							
Central Bank Rate (End of Per.)	60	†26.00	19.00	17.00	11.00	11.00	11.00	11.00	9.00	11.00	12.00	10.50	7.25
Money Market Rate	60b	67.58	39.15	29.08	12.18	13.98	9.71	7.45	6.87	6.95	6.90	4.93	5.59
Treasury Bill Rate	60c	....	....	....	....	....	....	....	8.63	10.94	10.88	8.73	6.53
Deposit Rate	60l	153.02	33.04	28.10	15.38	15.08	13.19	10.54	7.24	10.05	9.81	8.24	5.95
Lending Rate	60p	195.11	48.61	38.87	23.36	22.60	20.02	16.09	12.38	15.77	15.05	13.17	10.75
Prices, Production, Labor						*Index Numbers (2000=100): Period Averages*							
Producer Prices	63	46.9	57.1	67.2	75.8	80.9	85.8	90.9	92.9	100.0	108.9	114.5	117.4
Consumer Prices	64	36.9	49.1	59.4	†67.4	74.0	80.2	86.6	91.9	100.0	108.4	116.5	123.0
Wages	65	26.6	39.4	49.4	58.4	67.4	75.3	82.5	90.4	100.0	111.9	122.9	132.1
Industrial Production, Seas. Adj.	66..c	83.7	81.4	87.4	89.7	90.4	91.1	93.7	93.1	100.0	103.3	105.5	106.5
Employment	67	102.1	98.4	97.1	97.0	96.6	96.8	97.0	98.7	100.0	101.4	102.0	101.2
						Number in Thousands: Period Averages							
Labor Force	67d	887	885	873	867	862	869	871	877	875	881	886	875
Employment	67e	784	756	746	745	742	743	745	758	768	779	783	777
Unemployment	67c	103	†129	127	121	120	125	126	119	107	102	103	98
Unemployment Rate (%)	67r	11.5	†14.6	14.5	14.0	13.9	14.4	14.5	13.6	12.2	11.6	11.6	11.2
International Transactions						*Millions of US Dollars*							
Exports	70..d	†6,681	6,083	6,828	8,316	8,310	8,369	9,051	8,546	8,732	9,252	10,357	12,767
Imports, c.i.f.	71..d	†6,141	6,501	7,304	9,492	9,421	9,366	10,111	10,083	10,116	10,148	10,932	13,854

Slovenia 961

		1992	1993	1994	1995	1996	1997	1998	1999	2000	2001	2002	2003
Balance of Payments		\multicolumn{12}{c}{*Millions of US Dollars: Minus Sign Indicates Debit*}
Current Account, n.i.e.	78ald	978.3	191.0	574.8	−74.8	55.4	50.4	−118.0	−698.3	−547.7	30.9	374.8	15.0
Goods: Exports f.o.b.	78aad	6,680.9	6,082.9	6,831.7	8,350.2	8,352.6	8,405.9	9,090.9	8,623.2	8,807.9	9,342.8	10,472.6	12,928.0
Goods: Imports f.o.b.	78abd	−5,891.8	−6,237.1	−7,168.2	−9,304.2	−9,178.7	−9,180.7	−9,882.9	−9,858.3	−9,946.9	−9,962.3	−10,715.7	−13,551.8
Trade Balance	78acd	789.1	−154.2	−336.5	−953.9	−826.1	−774.8	−792.0	−1,235.1	−1,138.9	−619.5	−243.0	−623.8
Services: Credit	78add	1,219.3	1,392.1	1,808.1	2,026.9	2,134.7	2,040.5	2,024.6	1,875.3	1,887.6	1,959.6	2,291.5	2,791.1
Services: Debit	78aed	−1,037.8	−1,017.4	−1,164.7	−1,444.2	−1,494.2	−1,404.8	−1,523.8	−1,521.8	−1,437.9	−1,457.5	−1,736.1	−2,180.8
Balance on Goods & Services	78afd	970.6	220.5	306.9	−371.3	−185.6	−139.2	−291.2	−881.6	−689.2	−117.4	312.4	−13.5
Income: Credit	78agd	111.7	114.5	324.7	405.6	413.1	391.8	412.9	426.9	434.0	462.6	487.8	592.0
Income: Debit	78ahd	−150.1	−166.0	−153.3	−204.3	−259.9	−316.4	−357.0	−363.2	−407.8	−443.4	−559.1	−669.5
Balance on Gds, Serv. & Inc.	78aid	932.2	169.0	478.2	−170.0	−32.4	−63.8	−235.4	−817.9	−663.0	−98.2	241.1	−91.1
Current Transfers, n.i.e.: Credit	78ajd	93.0	154.9	237.2	247.7	250.9	259.5	299.8	334.9	340.8	390.0	451.4	506.3
Current Transfers: Debit	78akd	−46.9	−132.9	−140.6	−152.4	−163.1	−145.3	−182.4	−215.3	−225.4	−260.8	−317.7	−400.2
Capital Account, n.i.e.	78bcd	−	4.1	−3.2	−7.0	−1.9	1.1	−1.5	−.7	3.5	−3.6	1.6	4.3
Capital Account, n.i.e.: Credit	78bad	−	6.7	2.7	3.1	5.5	5.0	3.5	3.3	6.8	3.3	4.9	7.8
Capital Account: Debit	78bbd	−	−2.6	−5.8	−10.1	−7.4	−3.9	−5.0	−4.0	−3.3	−6.9	−3.3	−3.5
Financial Account, n.i.e.	78bjd	−13.3	−80.9	138.6	516.3	534.5	1,162.9	215.8	576.1	680.4	1,204.3	1,456.8	264.5
Direct Investment Abroad	78bdd	1.8	−1.3	12.7	10.0	−7.0	−31.0	5.5	−47.6	−65.3	−132.8	−117.0	−305.6
Dir. Invest. in Rep. Econ., n.i.e.	78bed	111.0	112.6	116.7	150.5	173.5	334.3	215.5	106.5	135.9	503.3	1,865.3	179.6
Portfolio Investment Assets	78bfd	−8.9	−1.5	−32.5	−28.9	6.4	−.2	−30.2	−7.8	−58.4	−107.5	−94.1	−221.0
Equity Securities	78bkd	−	−	....	....	....	....	....	−.5	−14.5	−23.3	−73.1	−104.1
Debt Securities	78bld	−8.9	−1.5	−32.5	−28.9	6.4	−.2	−30.2	−7.3	−43.9	−84.2	−21.0	−116.8
Portfolio Investment Liab., n.i.e.	78bgd	−	4.5	....	15.5	630.5	236.1	119.8	361.6	246.0	188.9	27.0	−31.0
Equity Securities	78bmd	−	−	....	....	....	52.2	7.2	−3.2	25.4	−2.3	10.7	15.4
Debt Securities	78bnd	−	4.5	....	15.5	630.5	184.0	112.6	364.8	220.6	191.2	16.2	−46.3
Financial Derivatives Assets	78bwd	....	....	....	....	....	....	....	....	....	....	....	....
Financial Derivatives Liabilities	78bxd	....	....	....	....	....	....	....	....	....	....	....	....
Other Investment Assets	78bhd	−157.6	−313.5	−211.5	−242.8	−442.0	262.3	−464.6	−568.5	−519.2	206.6	−887.2	−1,089.7
Monetary Authorities	78bod	.5	−	−98.3	−66.8	131.4	−7.6	−5.4	−5.6	−5.9	−6.2	−6.2	.5
General Government	78bpd	−.1	−.3	−.4	−2.2	−1.4	−1.3	−1.8	−1.6	−1.1	−.5	−.6	−.9
Banks	78bqd	−173.8	−473.6	−353.1	−302.3	−321.8	479.2	−51.8	−7.8	−253.7	−303.1	160.1	21.2
Other Sectors	78brd	15.8	160.4	240.3	128.4	−250.2	−208.0	−405.6	−553.5	−258.5	516.4	−1,040.4	−1,110.5
Other Investment Liab., n.i.e.	78bid	40.4	118.3	253.1	612.1	173.1	361.4	369.8	732.0	941.3	545.7	662.8	1,732.2
Monetary Authorities	78bsd	−	−	.1	.1	.2	−	.1	−.4	.1	−	−	−
General Government	78btd	−18.3	80.2	92.2	137.6	−67.6	−25.7	−18.3	−3.2	79.6	−27.8	−.9	−77.9
Banks	78bud	11.3	−41.9	40.6	267.3	−19.8	4.7	90.6	260.5	290.8	230.6	375.1	1,221.7
Other Sectors	78bvd	47.4	80.0	120.3	207.1	260.4	382.5	297.3	474.9	570.9	343.0	288.6	588.3
Net Errors and Omissions	78cad	−332.4	10.7	−63.7	−194.6	2.0	74.0	61.4	41.5	42.1	53.0	33.6	58.0
Overall Balance	78cbd	632.6	124.9	646.5	240.0	590.0	1,288.4	157.8	−81.4	178.3	1,284.6	1,866.9	341.8
Reserves and Related Items	79dad	−632.6	−124.9	−646.5	−240.0	−590.0	−1,288.4	−157.8	81.4	−178.3	−1,284.6	−1,866.9	−341.8
Reserve Assets	79dbd	−632.6	−111.0	−641.3	−236.5	−587.4	−1,287.2	−157.8	81.4	−178.3	−1,284.6	−1,866.9	−341.8
Use of Fund Credit and Loans	79dcd	−	−13.8	−5.2	−3.4	−2.6	−1.2	−	−	−	−	−	−
Exceptional Financing	79ded	....	....	....	....	....	....	....	....	....	....	....	....
International Investment Position		\multicolumn{12}{c}{*Millions of US Dollars*}
Assets	79aad	....	....	5,925.6	6,841.5	7,155.4	7,668.1	8,450.3	7,856.1	8,300.2	9,939.0	13,627.9	....
Direct Investment Abroad	79abd	....	....	354.0	489.9	459.5	459.4	636.2	626.5	767.6	1,005.1	1,475.9	....
Portfolio Investment	79acd	....	....	62.1	106.4	93.9	55.9	39.7	130.4	175.4	251.4	323.5	....
Equity Securities	79add	....	....	15.0	17.1	15.8	15.4	16.7	32.4	36.8	21.8	35.9	....
Debt Securities	79aed	....	....	47.0	89.3	78.1	40.4	22.9	98.0	138.6	229.6	287.6	....
Financial Derivatives	79ald	....	....	−	−	−	−	−	−	−	−	−	....
Other Investment	79afd	....	....	4,010.4	4,424.3	4,304.6	3,838.1	4,135.9	3,931.1	4,161.1	4,285.3	4,765.0	....
Monetary Authorities	79agd	....	....	103.3	170.1	33.3	40.7	46.3	51.8	57.9	76.0	84.7	....
General Government	79ahd	....	....	−	−	−	−	−	−	−	−	−	....
Banks	79aid	....	....	1,709.2	1,909.3	2,066.3	1,397.6	1,510.8	1,342.3	1,516.7	1,770.1	1,778.4	....
Other Sectors	79ajd	....	....	2,197.9	2,344.9	2,205.0	2,399.7	2,578.8	2,537.0	2,586.5	2,439.2	2,901.9	....
Reserve Assets	79akd	....	....	1,499.1	1,820.9	2,297.5	3,314.8	3,638.6	3,168.1	3,196.1	4,397.2	7,063.5	....
Liabilities	79lad	....	....	5,189.2	6,379.7	7,674.7	8,067.0	9,437.4	9,832.1	10,668.0	11,223.1	15,098.3	....
Dir. Invest. in Rep. Economy	79lbd	....	....	1,325.9	1,763.4	1,998.1	2,207.4	2,777.0	2,682.4	2,892.7	2,604.9	4,081.1	....
Portfolio Investment	79lcd	....	....	88.9	104.1	1,138.2	1,276.6	1,421.5	1,661.0	1,793.4	1,893.3	2,197.1	....
Equity Securities	79ldd	....	....	45.9	62.7	133.8	156.7	139.4	163.0	167.8	170.5	108.6	....
Debt Securities	79led	....	....	43.0	41.4	1,004.4	1,119.9	1,282.1	1,497.9	1,625.6	1,722.8	2,088.5	....
Financial Derivatives	79lld	....	....	−	−	−	−	−	−	−	−	−	....
Other Investment	79lfd	....	....	3,774.4	4,512.2	4,538.5	4,583.0	5,238.9	5,488.7	5,981.9	6,724.9	8,820.2	....
Monetary Authorities	79lgd	....	....	7.3	4.2	1.6	.2	.4	.3	−	−	−	....
General Government	79lhd	....	....	577.5	786.9	734.0	686.8	823.4	702.1	752.9	528.6	493.7	....
Banks	79lid	....	....	561.4	686.1	1,045.9	980.7	1,017.8	1,178.4	1,298.3	1,762.8	2,549.4	....
Other Sectors	79ljd	....	....	2,628.3	3,035.1	2,757.0	2,915.3	3,397.4	3,608.0	3,930.7	4,433.5	5,777.0	....

Slovenia 961

		1992	1993	1994	1995	1996	1997	1998	1999	2000	2001	2002	2003
Government Finance		\multicolumn{12}{c}{*Billions of Tolars: Year Ending December 31*}
Deficit (-) or Surplus	80	....	5.37	−5.06	−6.45	1.62	−43.20	−25.04	−29.63	−38.90	−49.73	−45.91	−77.33
Revenue	81	....	611.44	768.50	926.42	1,041.64	1,163.38	1,332.10	1,445.54	1,563.30	1,772.31	1,862.38	2,137.97
Grants Received	81z	....	–	–	.49	.96	1.76	2.45	3.18	6.44	10.06	13.23	12.18
Expenditure	82	....	606.07	773.56	933.36	1,040.98	1,208.34	1,366.47	1,477.07	1,613.39	1,844.07	2,023.89	2,225.91
Lending Minus Repayments	83	....	–	–	–	–	–	−6.88	1.28	−4.75	−11.97	−102.37	1.57
Financing													
Net Borrowing: Domestic	84a	....	−3.10	−5.41	−10.53	−11.65	12.32	22.95	−19.80	−19.18	52.61	184.99	46.35
Foreign	85a	....	6.83	3.82	6.27	23.08	20.10	13.30	61.04	69.87	19.81	−21.30	−11.70
Use of Cash Balances	87	....	−9.10	6.65	10.70	−13.05	10.78	−11.21	−11.61	−11.79	−22.69	−117.78	42.67
National Accounts		\multicolumn{12}{c}{*Billions of Tolars*}
Househ.Cons.Expend.,incl.NPISHs	96f	....	839.2	1,050.2	1,414.9	1,605.5	1,793.8	1,986.7	2,231.4	2,426.0	2,682.0	2,896.5	3,144.4
Government Consumption Expend	91f	207.0	302.6	374.3	467.7	537.7	602.5	671.0	748.3	843.5	974.7	1,080.5	1,163.0
Gross Fixed Capital Formation	93e	189.6	270.2	372.7	489.5	591.6	709.7	823.2	1,019.5	1,066.8	1,164.4	1,234.8	1,350.0
Changes in Inventories	93i	−10.6	7.4	15.3	45.1	19.1	26.9	32.9	37.0	66.9	−27.3	20.9	69.9
Exports of Goods and Services	90c	642.8	843.1	1,111.3	1,226.0	1,424.6	1,668.8	1,842.5	1,912.2	2,387.3	2,744.5	3,062.3	3,247.4
Imports of Goods and Services (-)	98c	572.0	827.5	1,070.8	1,270.6	1,450.3	1,691.5	1,891.3	2,073.6	2,538.1	2,776.5	2,980.5	3,248.3
Gross Domestic Product (GDP)	99b	1,018.0	1,435.1	1,853.0	2,372.7	2,728.2	3,110.1	3,464.9	3,874.7	4,252.3	4,761.8	5,314.5	5,726.5
Net Primary Income from Abroad	98.n	....	4.1	13.9	23.7	20.5	11.9	9.2	11.2	6.0	9.3	−39.4	−16.0
Gross National Income (GNI)	99a	1,016.1	1,439.2	1,866.9	2,396.4	2,748.7	3,121.9	3,474.0	3,885.9	4,258.3	4,771.1	5,275.1	5,710.5
Net Current Transf.from Abroad	98t	5.6	11.3	17.1	11.2	11.2	18.9	20.1	22.2	25.7	31.2	32.1	21.7
Gross Nat'l Disposable Inc.(GNDI)	99i	....	1,450.5	1,884.0	2,407.6	2,759.9	3,140.8	3,494.1	3,908.1	4,284.1	4,802.3	5,307.4	5,732.3
Gross Saving	99s	253.6	308.6	459.6	512.6	607.4	723.7	820.8	924.3	1,019.3	1,152.9	1,326.7	1,424.9
GDP Volume 1995 Prices	99b.p	2,104.0	2,163.8	2,279.1	2,372.7	2,459.1	2,576.2	2,668.0	2,816.2	2,925.8	3,004.1	3,107.2	3,177.6
GDP Volume (2000=100)	99bvp	71.9	74.0	77.9	81.1	84.0	88.1	91.2	96.3	100.0	102.7	106.2	108.6
GDP Deflator (2000=100)	99bip	33.3	45.6	55.9	68.8	76.3	83.1	89.4	94.7	100.0	109.1	117.7	124.0
		\multicolumn{12}{c}{*Millions: Midyear Estimates*}
Population	99z	1.95	1.96	1.98	1.99	2.00	2.00	2.00	1.99	1.99	1.99	1.99	1.98

Solomon Islands 813

		1992	1993	1994	1995	1996	1997	1998	1999	2000	2001	2002	2003
Exchange Rates		\multicolumn{12}{c}{*Solomon Islands Dollars per SDR: End of Period*}
Official Rate	aa	4.2622	4.4611	4.8597	5.1668	5.2081	6.4067	6.8417	6.9671	6.6441	6.9935	10.1381	11.1309
		\multicolumn{12}{c}{*Solomon Islands Dollars per US Dollar: End of Period (ae) Period Average (rf)*}
Official Rate	ae	3.0998	3.2478	3.3289	3.4758	3.6219	4.7483	4.8591	5.0761	5.0994	5.5648	7.4571	7.4906
Official Rate	rf	2.9281	3.1877	3.2914	3.4059	3.5664	3.7169	4.8156	4.8381	5.0889	5.2780	6.7488	7.5059
		\multicolumn{12}{c}{*Index Numbers (2000=100): Period Averages*}
Official Rate	ahx	173.7	159.7	154.6	149.5	142.8	136.3	105.7	103.2	100.0	93.9	76.1	67.8
Nominal Effective Exchange Rate	nec	136.8	134.3	131.0	121.0	118.3	121.1	102.3	98.2	100.0	103.2	80.1	64.0
Real Effective Exchange Rate	rec	83.0	83.7	86.6	84.7	90.4	98.0	91.7	94.3	100.0	109.2	90.8	78.5
Fund Position		\multicolumn{12}{c}{*Millions of SDRs: End of Period*}
Quota	2f.s	7.50	7.50	7.50	7.50	7.50	7.50	7.50	10.40	10.40	10.40	10.40	10.40
SDRs	1b.s	.04	.03	.01	–	.01	–	–	.01	–	.01	–	–
Reserve Position in the Fund	1c.s	.54	.54	.54	.54	.54	.54	.54	.54	.54	.54	.55	.55
Total Fund Cred.&Loans Outstg.	2tl	–	–	–	–	–	–	–	–	–	–	–	–
International Liquidity		\multicolumn{12}{c}{*Millions of US Dollars Unless Otherwise Indicated: End of Period*}
Total Reserves minus Gold	1l.d	23.50	20.07	17.42	15.91	32.58	36.34	49.03	51.14	32.04	19.34	18.25	37.20
SDRs	1b.d	.06	.04	.01	.01	.01	–	–	.01	–	.01	.01	–
Reserve Position in the Fund	1c.d	.74	.74	.79	.80	.77	.73	.76	.74	.71	.68	.75	.82
Foreign Exchange	1d.d	22.70	19.29	16.62	15.10	31.80	35.61	48.27	50.39	31.34	18.66	17.49	36.39
Monetary Authorities: Other Liab.	4..d	.54	1.75	.42	.36	.63	.12	.44	.32	.25	–	–	1.05
Deposit Money Banks: Assets	7a.d	2.13	2.13	3.57	1.30	3.27	3.94	1.29	6.06	2.43	5.51	5.36	7.37
Liabilities	7b.d	1.71	1.75	4.82	1.82	4.00	2.56	2.58	5.56	3.13	4.35	3.97	8.17
Monetary Authorities		\multicolumn{12}{c}{*Millions of Solomon Islands Dollars: End of Period*}
Foreign Assets	11	73.45	65.07	58.21	55.39	117.71	153.90	237.13	261.57	163.40	106.81	136.03	277.21
Claims on Central Government	12a	37.92	45.39	64.47	77.98	73.06	76.36	76.15	46.56	44.47	174.96	173.47	173.01
Claims on Nonfin.Pub.Enterprises	12c	11.92	4.22	4.20	4.20	4.20	4.20	4.20	4.01	4.20	3.28	2.02	1.35
Claims on Deposit Money Banks	12e	–	–	–	–	–	–	–	–	–	–	–	–
Reserve Money	14	42.06	46.97	61.48	75.63	98.60	92.47	134.96	134.61	154.30	149.22	173.85	221.28
of which: Currency Outside DMBs	14a	30.83	42.11	50.23	54.93	59.67	70.79	81.28	100.07	88.15	84.57	91.39	101.43
Restricted Deposits	16b	.14	1.02	.83	1.10	1.71	1.28	3.51	1.46	.66	5.70	6.01	.23
Foreign Liabilities	16c	1.67	5.70	1.39	1.24	2.28	.59	2.13	1.64	1.29	–	.01	7.86
Central Government Deposits	16d	4.88	5.98	11.11	4.28	3.84	6.55	59.75	56.00	3.61	6.82	6.99	61.13
Capital Accounts	17a	50.99	52.31	57.39	59.41	68.82	103.81	108.23	109.93	104.45	108.91	–45.85	–20.36
Other Items (Net)	17r	23.56	2.70	–5.32	–4.10	19.71	29.77	8.89	8.51	–52.24	14.39	170.50	181.42
Deposit Money Banks		\multicolumn{12}{c}{*Millions of Solomon Islands Dollars: End of Period*}
Reserves	20	6.64	4.86	12.50	22.04	39.90	21.64	51.50	52.34	60.95	64.59	81.33	115.34
Foreign Assets	21	6.61	6.91	11.88	4.51	11.85	18.69	6.29	30.78	12.41	30.65	39.95	55.17
Claims on Central Government	22a	105.47	130.86	152.14	159.00	160.33	162.70	165.53	180.30	185.25	149.84	149.84	164.21
Claims on Local Government	22b	.48	.41	1.24	.22	.60	.31	.21	.22	.16	.16	.78	.72
Claims on Nonfin.Pub.Enterprises	22c	1.46	2.71	.91	1.22	2.71	.75	.78	2.58	3.59	2.00	1.97	1.36
Claims on Private Sector	22d	72.22	84.22	107.06	121.96	128.20	141.27	176.99	191.74	195.22	152.73	171.32	215.99
Claims on Other Banking Insts.	22f	.32	–	–	–	–	–	–	–	–	–	–	–
Demand Deposits	24	74.08	81.82	112.65	116.02	138.08	141.66	130.82	166.48	162.85	162.63	164.51	230.09
Time and Savings Deposits	25	111.12	125.88	149.70	170.41	195.89	207.49	218.50	194.08	212.21	152.95	168.09	200.15
Money Market Instruments	26aa	.13	.49	.54	–	–	.31	–	.61	.56	.48	3.78	3.17
Foreign Liabilities	26c	5.32	5.67	16.05	6.33	14.49	12.16	12.54	28.21	15.94	24.23	29.59	61.22
Central Government Deposits	26d	4.31	5.17	5.24	9.32	7.83	8.22	4.35	12.88	2.35	1.10	2.89	3.93
Credit from Monetary Authorities	26g	–	–	–	–	–	–	–	–	–	–	–	–
Capital Accounts	27a	22.72	32.30	30.87	28.80	32.54	38.35	62.39	72.19	76.35	87.88	95.84	99.57
Other Items (Net)	27r	–24.50	–21.36	–29.31	–21.93	–45.25	–62.82	–27.31	–16.49	–12.68	–29.29	–19.53	–45.36
Monetary Survey		\multicolumn{12}{c}{*Millions of Solomon Islands Dollars: End of Period*}
Foreign Assets (Net)	31n	73.08	60.61	52.64	52.33	112.79	159.84	228.74	262.49	158.58	113.23	146.36	263.30
Domestic Credit	32	220.60	256.67	313.68	350.97	357.41	370.82	359.75	356.53	426.93	475.05	489.51	491.56
Claims on Central Govt. (Net)	32an	134.20	165.10	200.27	223.37	221.72	224.29	177.57	157.98	223.76	316.88	313.44	272.16
Claims on Local Government	32b	.48	.41	1.24	.22	.60	.31	.21	.22	.16	.16	.78	.72
Claims on Nonfin.Pub.Enterprises	32c	13.38	6.94	5.11	5.42	6.90	4.95	4.98	6.60	7.78	5.28	3.98	2.70
Claims on Private Sector	32d	72.22	84.22	107.06	121.96	128.20	141.27	176.99	191.74	195.22	152.73	171.32	215.99
Claims on Other Banking Insts.	32f	.32	–	–	–	–	–	–	–	–	–	–	–
Money	34	104.91	123.93	162.88	170.96	197.75	212.45	212.10	266.54	251.00	247.20	255.90	331.52
Quasi-Money	35	111.12	125.88	149.70	170.41	195.89	207.49	218.50	194.08	212.21	152.95	168.09	200.15
Money Market Instruments	36aa	.13	.49	.54	–	–	.31	–	.61	.56	.48	3.78	3.17
Restricted Deposits	36b	.14	1.02	.83	1.10	1.71	1.28	3.51	1.46	.66	5.70	6.01	.23
Capital Accounts	37a	73.71	84.61	88.26	88.21	101.36	142.16	170.63	182.11	180.79	196.79	49.99	79.21
Other Items (Net)	37r	3.66	–18.65	–35.88	–27.37	–26.51	–33.02	–16.25	–25.78	–59.72	–14.83	152.09	140.57
Money plus Quasi-Money	35l	216.03	249.81	312.58	341.37	393.64	419.93	430.60	460.62	463.21	400.15	424.00	531.67

Solomon Islands 813

		1992	1993	1994	1995	1996	1997	1998	1999	2000	2001	2002	2003
Other Banking Institutions					*Millions of Solomon Islands Dollars: End of Period*								
Reserves	40	17.05	11.35	....	....	68.17	71.50	18.56	14.56	12.56	12.16	15.28	....
Claims on Private Sector	42d	54.50	65.65	....	....	113.32	125.99	139.13	140.53	142.24	143.89	144.60	....
Quasi-Monetary Liabilities	45	5.96	9.12	10.00	11.76	13.90	16.48	17.18	19.31	19.32	25.64	25.92	....
Central Govt. Lending Funds	46f	6.47	12.22	7.44	2.43	1.88	1.35	1.32	1.32	7.15	7.15	7.15	....
Credit from Monetary Authorities	46g	9.26	6.81	–	–	11.77	11.35	6.13	6.44	6.13	6.13	6.13	....
Credit from Deposit Money Banks	46h	.12	.04	....	....	–	–	–	–	–	–	–	....
Liabs. to Nonbank Financial Insts	46j	9.22	8.31	....	....	3.47	1.67	7.40	7.33	7.27	7.24	7.24	....
Capital Accounts	47a	13.79	16.58	....	....	18.03	26.77	34.82	29.98	12.22	12.35	12.59	....
Other Items (Net)	47r	26.74	23.93	....	....	132.44	139.88	90.84	90.70	102.71	97.54	100.84	....
Banking Survey					*Millions of Solomon Islands Dollars: End of Period*								
Foreign Assets (Net)	51n	73.08	60.61	52.64	52.33	112.79	159.84	228.74	262.49	158.58	113.23	146.36	263.30
Domestic Credit	52	274.78	322.32	....	....	470.73	496.81	498.88	497.06	569.17	618.94	634.11	....
Claims on Central Govt. (Net)	52an	134.20	165.10	200.27	223.37	221.72	224.29	177.57	157.98	223.76	316.88	313.44	272.16
Claims on Local Government	52b	.48	.41	1.24	.22	.60	.31	.21	.22	.16	.16	.78	....
Claims on Nonfin.Pub.Enterprises	52c	13.38	6.94	5.11	5.42	6.90	4.95	4.98	6.60	7.78	5.28	3.98	....
Claims on Private Sector	52d	126.72	149.88	....	....	241.52	267.26	316.12	332.26	337.46	296.61	315.91	....
Liquid Liabilities	55l	204.95	247.58	....	....	339.37	364.91	429.22	465.37	469.97	413.63	434.64	....
Money Market Instruments	56aa	.13	.49	.54	–	–	.31	–	.61	.56	.48	3.78	....
Restricted Deposits	56b	.14	1.02	.83	1.10	1.71	1.28	3.51	1.46	.66	5.70	6.01	....
Central Govt. Lending Funds	56f	6.47	12.22	7.44	2.43	1.88	1.35	1.32	1.32	7.15	7.15	7.15	....
Liabs. to Nonbank Financial Insts	56j	9.22	8.31	....	....	3.47	1.67	7.40	7.33	7.27	7.24	7.24	....
Capital Accounts	57a	87.49	101.19	....	....	119.39	168.92	205.45	212.10	193.02	209.14	62.58	....
Other Items (Net)	57r	39.45	12.13	....	....	117.70	118.21	80.72	71.36	49.12	88.83	259.06	....
Nonbank Financial Institutions					*Millions of Solomon Islands Dollars: End of Period*								
Reserves	40..m	22.79	21.61	26.98	....	....	38.85	47.24	45.73	59.08	13.99	31.99	48.40
Claims on Central Government	42a.m	49.14	68.00	73.98	....	....	83.78	125.30	118.73	104.86	112.67	94.27	94.27
Claims on Nonfin.Pub.Enterprises	42c.m	17.75	23.72	39.95	....	....	44.44	49.24	44.70	46.68	53.02	58.31	62.96
Claims on Private Sector	42d.m	15.24	24.69	31.83	....	....	53.47	59.76	61.66	59.01	55.56	54.89	51.52
Claims on Other Banking Insts	42f.m	8.07	8.43	7.37	....	....	25.10	7.62	3.09	3.17	3.64	4.11	4.48
Capital Accounts	47a.m	153.64	187.03	223.57	....	....	317.28	359.00	384.31	380.05	356.73	369.87	402.34
Other Items (Net)	47r.m	−40.65	−40.58	−43.46	....	....	−71.64	−69.84	−110.39	−107.26	−117.85	−126.30	−140.70
Interest Rates							*Percent Per Annum*						
Treasury Bill Rate	60c	13.50	12.15	11.25	12.50	12.75	12.88	6.00	6.00	7.05	8.23	6.87	5.85
Deposit Rate	60l	12.00	9.77	9.00	8.38	6.46	2.42	2.33	2.88	2.54	1.35	.75	.75
Lending Rate	60p	19.75	17.80	15.72	16.59	17.78	15.71	14.84	14.50	15.49	15.72	16.42	16.33
Government Bond Yield	61	13.00	13.00	13.00	13.00	11.50	11.75	12.50	12.88	13.00	13.00	13.00	13.00
Prices, Production, Labor					*Index Numbers (2000=100): Period Averages*								
Consumer Prices	64	47.0	51.3	58.1	63.7	71.2	76.9	86.5	93.4	100.0	106.9	117.7	129.5
Copra Production (1995=100)	66ag	83.8	81.7	76.2	100.0	105.7	132.9	....	....	....	....	....	....
Fish Catch (1995=100)	66al	76.4	57.1	69.6	100.0	73.2	73.2	87.5	....	....	....	....	....
					Number in Thousands: Period Averages								
Employment	67e	27	30	33	33	34	....	....	57				
International Transactions					*Millions of Solomon Islands Dollars*								
Exports	70	301.18	411.44	467.88	573.15	576.65	581.53	568.75	....	....	....	390.00	....
Imports, c.i.f	71	326.61	436.29	459.51	526.27	536.87	682.68	722.18	....	473.64	....	321.00	....
						1990=100							
Volume of Exports	72	136.3	....	....	....	....	....	....	....	....	....	....	....
Unit Value of Exports	74	102.8	....	....	....	....	....	....	....	....	....	....	....

Solomon Islands 813

		1992	1993	1994	1995	1996	1997	1998	1999	2000	2001	2002	2003
Balance of Payments		\multicolumn{8}{c}{*Millions of US Dollars: Minus Sign Indicates Debit*}								
Current Account, n.i.e.	78ald	−1.43	−7.65	−3.43	8.34	14.58	−37.91	8.12	21.48	….	….	….	….
Goods: Exports f.o.b.	78aad	101.74	129.06	142.16	168.30	161.51	156.45	141.83	164.57	….	….	….	….
Goods: Imports f.o.b.	78abd	−87.43	−136.87	−142.22	−154.53	−150.55	−184.53	−159.90	−110.04	….	….	….	….
Trade Balance	78acd	14.31	−7.81	−.06	13.77	10.96	−28.09	−18.07	54.53	….	….	….	….
Services: Credit	78add	36.03	42.44	49.95	41.81	53.14	70.35	55.07	56.30	….	….	….	….
Services: Debit	78aed	−78.04	−80.68	−105.94	−76.93	−85.47	−107.18	−54.53	−87.49	….	….	….	….
Balance on Goods & Services	78afd	−27.70	−46.05	−56.06	−21.35	−21.37	−64.92	−17.53	23.34	….	….	….	….
Income: Credit	78agd	.99	.69	1.52	1.20	2.36	2.69	2.12	5.46	….	….	….	….
Income: Debit	78ahd	−10.89	−4.61	−4.44	−7.96	−9.42	−11.17	−10.01	−22.38	….	….	….	….
Balance on Gds, Serv. & Inc.	78aid	−37.60	−49.97	−58.97	−28.10	−28.43	−73.39	−25.42	6.41	….	….	….	….
Current Transfers, n.i.e.: Credit	78ajd	43.78	47.84	66.60	53.17	57.48	52.57	56.44	41.54	….	….	….	….
Current Transfers: Debit	78akd	−7.62	−5.52	−11.06	−16.74	−14.47	−17.08	−22.90	−26.48	….	….	….	….
Capital Account, n.i.e.	78bcd	−.44	.85	2.70	.65	−2.19	−1.00	6.65	9.16	….	….	….	….
Capital Account, n.i.e.: Credit	78bad	−	.94	2.86	1.50	.50	.30	6.91	9.16	….	….	….	….
Capital Account: Debit	78bbd	−.44	−.09	−.15	−.85	−2.69	−1.29	−.27	−	….	….	….	….
Financial Account, n.i.e.	78bjd	22.44	8.22	1.49	−8.31	−1.37	45.68	16.88	−33.77	….	….	….	….
Direct Investment Abroad	78bdd	−	−	−	−	−	−	−	−	….	….	….	….
Dir. Invest. in Rep. Econ., n.i.e.	78bed	14.17	23.37	2.10	2.03	5.94	33.85	8.80	9.90	….	….	….	….
Portfolio Investment Assets	78bfd	−	−	−	−	−	−	−	−	….	….	….	….
Equity Securities	78bkd	−	−	−	−	−	−	−	−	….	….	….	….
Debt Securities	78bld	−	−	−	−	−	−	−	−	….	….	….	….
Portfolio Investment Liab., n.i.e.	78bgd	−	−	−	−	−	−	−	−	….	….	….	….
Equity Securities	78bmd	−	−	−	−	−	−	−	−	….	….	….	….
Debt Securities	78bnd	−	−	−	−	−	−	−	−	….	….	….	….
Financial Derivatives Assets	78bwd	….	−	−	−	−	−	−	….	….	….	….	….
Financial Derivatives Liabilities	78bxd	….	−	−	−	−	−	−	….	….	….	….	….
Other Investment Assets	78bhd	−.07	−	−	−	−	−	−	.04	….	….	….	….
Monetary Authorities	78bod	….	−	−	−	−	−	−	−	….	….	….	….
General Government	78bpd	−	−	−	−	−	−	−	−	….	….	….	….
Banks	78bqd	−.07	−	−	−	−	−	−	−	….	….	….	….
Other Sectors	78brd	−	−	−	−	−	−	−	.04	….	….	….	….
Other Investment Liab., n.i.e.	78bid	8.33	−15.15	−.61	−10.34	−7.32	11.84	8.08	−43.72	….	….	….	….
Monetary Authorities	78bsd	.41	1.32	−1.25	.03	.08	−.62	−.37	−	….	….	….	….
General Government	78btd	1.57	.94	−1.34	6.20	5.72	5.17	8.60	−11.02	….	….	….	….
Banks	78bud	−.82	.03	3.31	−2.85	2.30	−.62	−1.23	−.27	….	….	….	….
Other Sectors	78bvd	7.17	−17.44	−1.34	−13.71	−15.42	7.91	1.08	−32.43	….	….	….	….
Net Errors and Omissions	78cad	−6.16	−3.16	−2.80	−1.45	6.96	2.31	−14.41	−1.58	….	….	….	….
Overall Balance	78cbd	14.40	−1.74	−2.04	−.77	17.98	9.09	17.24	−4.72	….	….	….	….
Reserves and Related Items	79dad	−14.40	1.74	2.04	.77	−17.98	−9.09	−17.24	4.72	….	….	….	….
Reserve Assets	79dbd	−17.14	1.74	2.04	.77	−17.98	−9.09	−17.24	4.72	….	….	….	….
Use of Fund Credit and Loans	79dcd	−	−	−	−	−	−	−	−	….	….	….	….
Exceptional Financing	79ded	2.73	−	−	−	−	−	−	….	….	….	….	….
Government Finance		\multicolumn{8}{c}{*Millions of Solomon Islands Dollars: Year Ending December 31*}								
Deficit (-) or Surplus	80	2.31	−44.10	−30.91	−4.56	−2.32	−54.71	−171.55	−66.02	….	….	….	….
Revenue	81	140.31	206.00	272.89	309.54	336.58	314.69	347.35	397.58	277.77	….	….	….
Grants Received	81z	84.10	43.90	35.20	45.90	52.10	−	38.30	60.00	1.00	….	….	….
Expenditure	82	224.00	294.00	339.00	360.00	391.00	365.00	490.00	479.00	….	….	….	….
Lending Minus Repayments	83	−1.90	−	−	−	−	4.40	67.20	44.60	….	….	….	….
Total Debt	88	….	….	….	….	….	….	….	913.00	978.70	….	….	….
Domestic	88a	….	….	….	….	….	….	….	316.10	385.00	….	….	….
Foreign	89a	….	….	….	….	358.30	463.70	622.00	596.90	593.70	….	….	….
National Accounts		\multicolumn{8}{c}{*Millions of Solomon Islands Dollars*}								
Gross Domestic Product (GDP)	99b	829.4	1,250.0	1,390.8	1,250.0	1,293.1	1,390.8	1,448.7	1,585.2	1,453.4	1,453.9	1,527.6	….
		\multicolumn{8}{c}{*Millions: Midyear Estimates*}								
Population	99z	.34	.35	.36	.37	.39	.40	.41	.42	.44	.45	.46	.48

South Africa 199

		1992	1993	1994	1995	1996	1997	1998	1999	2000	2001	2002	2003
Exchange Rates						*Rand per SDR: End of Period*							
Principal Rate......aa=	wa	4.19788	4.66667	5.17298	5.42197	6.73325	6.56747	8.25106	8.44711	9.86107	15.23974	11.74625	9.86684
						Rand per US Dollar: End of Period (we) Period Average (wf)							
Principal Rate......ae=	we	3.05300	3.39750	3.54350	3.64750	4.68250	4.86750	5.86000	6.15450	7.56850	12.12650	8.64000	6.64000
Principal Rate......rf=	wf	2.85201	3.26774	3.55080	3.62709	4.29935	4.60796	5.52828	6.10948	6.93983	8.60918	10.54075	7.56475
						Index Numbers (2000=100): Period Averages							
Principal Rate	ahx	242.3	211.6	194.6	190.4	161.7	150.0	126.0	113.0	100.0	81.3	65.9	91.9
Nominal Effective Exchange Rate	nec	180.4	173.9	165.0	152.7	134.3	135.0	116.4	105.4	100.0	85.2	67.5	83.8
Real Effective Exchange Rate	rec	133.8	131.3	125.7	122.2	112.7	120.6	107.9	102.1	100.0	88.3	75.5	98.0
Fund Position						*Millions of SDRs: End of Period*							
Quota	2f.s	1,365	1,365	1,365	1,365	1,365	1,365	1,365	1,869	1,869	1,869	1,869	1,869
SDRs	1b.s	–	9	1	3	1	7	132	210	222	223	223	223
Reserve Position in the Fund	1c.s	–	–	–	–	–	–	–	–	–	–	–	1
Total Fund Cred.&Loans Outstg.	2tl	–	614	614	614	614	307	–	–	–	–	–	–
International Liquidity						*Millions of US Dollars Unless Otherwise Indicated: End of Period*							
Total Reserves minus Gold	1l.d	992	1,020	1,685	2,820	942	4,799	4,357	6,353	6,083	6,045	5,904	6,496
SDRs	1b.d	–	12	1	5	1	9	185	288	290	280	303	331
Reserve Position in the Fund	1c.d	–	–	–	–	–	–	–	–	–	–	1	1
Foreign Exchange	1d.d	991	1,008	1,684	2,815	940	4,790	4,171	6,065	5,793	5,765	5,601	6,164
Gold (Million Fine Troy Ounces)	1ad	6.65	4.76	4.20	4.25	3.79	3.99	4.00	3.94	5.90	5.72	5.58	3.98
Gold (National Valuation)	1and	1,992	1,658	1,445	1,481	1,261	1,048	1,034	1,020	1,451	1,427	1,735	1,476
Monetary Authorities:Other Assets	3..d	478	453	392	306	227	24	19	12	10	6	8	9
Other Liab.	4..d	385	1,812	1,633	225	93	2,161	3,177	3,254	2,683	4,028	2,647	3,136
Banking Institutions: Assets	7a.d	873	811	1,042	799	1,412	1,603	2,874	5,122	5,432	7,341	10,267	21,435
Liabilities	7b.d	7,418	6,135	7,854	9,184	9,489	9,676	10,483	8,878	8,885	8,148	6,691	10,082
Monetary Authorities						*Millions of Rand: End of Period*							
Foreign Assets	11	10,570	10,637	12,479	16,801	11,375	28,579	31,701	45,450	57,094	90,685	66,072	52,991
Claims on Central Government	12a	4,935	8,844	13,531	10,274	16,254	13,067	12,578	10,943	10,378	9,007	16,995	18,635
Claims on Private Sector	12d	2,414	2,978	4,296	3,003	2,055	2,502	704	603	598	574	12	14
Claims on Banking Institutions	12e	4,901	6,219	5,995	6,513	11,975	10,939	6,362	6,572	10,356	13,347	12,415	13,146
Reserve Money	14	17,952	16,428	19,347	25,091	28,517	31,771	33,500	47,346	61,883	76,428	101,685	69,829
of which: Currency Outside Banks	14a	9,536	10,490	12,237	14,332	15,954	17,327	18,510	22,663	23,724	25,286	29,219	33,718
Foreign Liabilities	16c	1,176	9,023	8,966	4,151	4,572	12,535	18,617	20,029	20,307	48,840	22,873	20,821
Central Government Deposits	16d	9,419	12,180	10,962	10,963	9,770	8,334	6,623	5,084	4,009	2,611	2,884	8,238
Capital Accounts	17a	1,021	1,148	1,270	1,339	1,637	1,646	2,059	2,157	2,476	2,242	2,917	2,524
Other Items (Net)	17r	–6,749	–10,101	–4,245	–4,953	–2,837	802	–9,451	–11,048	–10,249	–16,508	–34,864	–16,625
Banking Institutions						*Millions of Rand: End of Period*							
Reserves	20	†6,112	4,773	6,586	10,356	11,702	13,514	14,726	17,969	19,761	23,757	26,304	28,507
Foreign Assets	21	†2,666	2,757	3,693	2,913	6,610	7,805	16,844	31,522	41,115	89,019	88,709	142,327
Claims on Central Government	22a	†13,515	20,788	21,501	24,813	27,437	37,011	46,206	50,100	53,546	58,386	68,369	85,979
Claims on Private Sector	22d	†211,881	235,544	278,079	324,111	380,493	434,884	506,140	553,159	637,212	779,931	818,971	1,035,583
Demand Deposits	24	†58,977	63,902	81,736	97,050	130,858	155,065	194,873	237,083	242,244	286,776	320,393	341,694
Time and Savings Deposits	25	†117,031	124,142	141,757	162,301	165,626	195,762	205,958	205,309	232,628	269,562	341,373	401,943
Money Market Instruments	26aa	†4,791	4,858	3,922	4,920	5,531	3,374	2,657	7,576	5,869	8,395	16,652	15,467
Foreign Liabilities	26c	†22,648	20,843	27,829	33,497	44,431	47,097	61,431	54,642	67,243	98,810	57,810	66,945
Central Government Deposits	26d	†4,039	9,937	8,173	17,748	22,387	21,137	21,158	27,027	30,158	42,993	40,613	73,667
Capital Accounts	27a	†16,021	20,065	23,998	29,302	34,470	41,664	51,920	63,470	75,581	96,032	104,453	112,845
Other Items (Net)	27r	†10,667	20,114	22,444	17,375	22,939	29,115	45,919	57,643	97,911	148,525	121,059	279,836
Banking Survey						*Millions of Rand: End of Period*							
Foreign Assets (Net)	31n	†–10,588	–16,472	–20,624	–17,934	–31,018	–23,247	–31,502	2,301	10,658	32,054	74,099	107,553
Domestic Credit	32	†219,287	246,036	298,272	333,490	394,082	457,993	537,847	582,694	667,567	802,294	860,850	1,058,305
Claims on Central Govt. (Net)	32an	†4,992	7,514	15,897	6,376	11,534	20,607	31,004	28,932	29,757	21,789	41,867	22,709
Claims on Private Sector	32d	†214,295	238,522	282,375	327,114	382,548	437,386	506,844	553,762	637,810	780,505	818,983	1,035,590
Money	34	†70,809	75,550	94,511	111,844	147,664	173,335	213,532	259,935	266,184	312,364	349,817	375,748
Quasi-Money	35	†117,031	124,142	141,757	162,301	165,626	195,762	205,958	205,309	232,628	269,562	341,373	401,943
Money Market Instruments	36aa	†4,791	4,858	3,922	4,920	5,531	3,374	2,657	7,576	5,869	8,395	16,652	15,467
Capital Accounts	37a	†17,042	21,213	25,268	30,641	36,107	43,310	53,979	65,627	78,057	98,274	107,370	115,369
Other Items (Net)	37r	†–975	3,801	12,190	5,850	8,136	18,965	30,220	46,547	95,487	145,752	119,737	257,332
Money plus Quasi-Money	35l	†187,840	199,692	236,268	274,145	313,290	369,097	419,490	465,244	498,812	581,926	691,190	777,691
Nonbank Financial Institutions						*Millions of Rand: End of Period*							
Cash	40..s	32,026	35,931	43,655	60,144	58,805	68,998	80,453	98,868	92,396	106,932	116,047	126,285
Claims on Central Government	42a.s	41,076	59,428	66,880	84,992	93,588	106,149	103,428	103,059	122,381	132,408	140,650	142,505
Claims on Official Entities	42b.s	18,473	24,813	22,889	22,765	20,969	24,130	21,204	21,553	20,541	25,255	24,751	31,694
Claims on Private Sector	42d.s	167,034	222,407	268,488	326,976	358,163	359,677	370,342	540,167	595,366	667,385	627,435	680,244
Real Estate	42h.s	32,354	35,735	38,868	44,064	47,459	53,403	52,261	63,514	57,507	53,761	50,131	51,941
Incr.in Total Assets(Within Per.)	49z.s	35,316	87,351	62,466	98,161	40,043	33,373	15,331	199,473	61,030	97,550	–26,727	73,655

South Africa 199

		1992	1993	1994	1995	1996	1997	1998	1999	2000	2001	2002	2003
Financial Survey						*Millions of Rand: End of Period*							
Foreign Assets (Net)....................	51n	† –10,588	–16,472	–20,624	–17,934	–31,018	–23,247	–31,502	2,301	10,658	32,054	74,099	107,553
Domestic Credit...........................	52	† 445,870	552,684	656,529	768,223	866,802	947,949	1,032,821	1,247,473	1,405,855	1,627,342	1,653,686	1,912,748
Claims on Central Govt. (Net)........	52an	† 46,068	66,942	82,777	91,368	105,122	126,756	134,432	131,991	152,138	154,197	182,517	165,214
Claims on Official Entities.............	52b	† 18,473	24,813	22,889	22,765	20,969	24,130	21,204	21,553	20,541	25,255	24,751	31,694
Claims on Private Sector................	52d	† 381,329	460,929	550,863	654,090	740,711	797,063	877,186	1,093,929	1,233,176	1,447,890	1,446,418	1,715,840
Liquid Liabilities...........................	55l	† 155,814	163,761	192,613	214,001	254,485	300,099	339,037	366,376	406,416	474,994	575,143	651,406
Money Market Instruments.............	56aa	† 4,791	4,858	3,922	4,920	5,531	3,374	2,657	7,576	5,869	8,395	16,652	15,467
Other Items (Net).........................	57r	† 274,677	367,593	439,370	531,368	575,768	621,229	659,626	875,822	1,004,229	1,176,006	1,135,990	1,353,429
Money (National Definitions)						*Millions of Rand: End of Period*							
M0..	19ma	15,655	15,270	18,810	24,629	27,665	30,828	33,210	40,784	43,036	48,904	55,939	61,995
M1A...	39maa	39,727	46,332	57,810	67,503	82,270	101,174	114,813	145,146	147,583	175,326	190,951	210,962
M1..	39ma	71,571	76,398	94,538	112,745	147,580	173,092	213,921	258,282	266,924	313,211	350,598	376,855
M2..	39mb	172,149	178,947	215,823	245,722	284,423	337,547	383,366	435,526	462,509	535,085	618,685	712,687
M3..	39mc	197,156	210,978	244,150	281,156	319,428	374,218	428,672	472,177	507,591	595,473	698,001	783,558
M3 Seasonally Adjusted.................	39mcs	196,698	211,342	243,770	280,377	317,097	370,584	428,663	472,508	502,804	583,354	684,166	775,800
Interest Rates						*Percent Per Annum*							
Discount Rate (End of Period)..........	60	14.00	12.00	13.00	15.00	17.00	16.00	† 19.32	12.00	12.00	9.50	13.50	8.00
Money Market Rate.......................	60b	14.11	10.83	10.24	13.07	15.54	15.59	17.11	13.06	9.54	† 8.49	11.11	10.93
Treasury Bill Rate.........................	60c	13.77	11.31	10.93	13.53	15.04	15.26	16.53	12.85	10.11	9.68	11.16	10.67
Savings Rate................................	60k	....	....	....	....	....	....	....	....	1.27	3.44	4.76	4.30
Deposit Rate................................	60l	13.78	11.50	11.11	13.54	14.91	15.38	16.50	12.24	9.20	† 9.37	10.77	9.76
Lending Rate...............................	60p	18.91	16.16	15.58	17.90	19.52	20.00	21.79	18.00	14.50	13.77	15.75	14.96
Government Bond Yield.................	61	15.44	13.97	14.83	16.11	15.48	14.70	15.12	14.90	13.79	11.41	11.50	9.62
Prices, Production, Labor						*Index Numbers (2000=100): Period Averages*							
Share Prices: All Shares.................	62	42.1	48.2	67.7	69.5	83.9	86.8	82.1	86.7	100.0	108.4	123.9	108.2
Industrial..........................	62a	51.3	53.8	73.0	80.1	95.4	99.4	89.9	87.6	100.0	85.4	85.5	79.3
Gold Mining.....................	62b	84.7	130.7	187.7	136.9	164.1	117.3	95.5	99.5	100.0	118.3	277.0	253.2
Producer Prices.............................	63	57.8	61.6	66.7	73.1	78.1	83.7	86.6	91.6	100.0	108.5	123.9	125.9
Consumer Prices...........................	64	55.8	61.2	66.6	72.4	77.8	84.4	90.3	94.9	100.0	105.7	115.4	122.1
Manufacturing Prod, Seas Adj..........	66eyc	82.3	84.2	87.2	94.3	97.8	100.3	96.9	96.4	100.0	102.8	108.2	105.8
Mining Production, Seas Adj............	66zxc	103.7	106.7	105.2	104.4	102.6	104.7	103.6	101.5	100.0	101.4	102.2	106.6
Gold Production, Seas Adj...........	66krc	140.3	141.7	132.6	119.0	114.0	† 113.4	† 108.0	104.8	100.0	91.7	92.8	....
Mfg. Employment, Seas. Adj...........	67eyc	† 117.5	115.1	116.0	116.7	112.4	107.7	104.2	101.5	100.0	97.4	96.8	96.5
Mining Employment, Seas Adj..........	67zxc	† 158.8	148.1	146.0	142.8	136.1	131.5	110.4	103.9	100.0	97.7	99.0	102.2
						Number in Thousands: Period Averages							
Unemployment.............................	67c	288	313	271	273	296	310	....	....	4,208	4,383	4,788	....
Unemployment Rate (%).................	67r	....	....	4.4	4.5	5.1	5.4	....	23.3	26.3	28.0	30.0	....
International Transactions						*Millions of Rand*							
Exports...	70	66,774	79,279	89,907	101,051	126,101	142,937	† 145,518	163,182	208,476	249,348	311,679	274,505
Gold Output (Net).......................	70kr	19,391	22,449	23,671	22,537	26,300	25,818	25,907	23,289	27,159	30,909	42,344	34,749
Imports, c.i.f................................	71	56,358	65,411	83,042	110,826	129,522	151,779	† 161,802	163,092	206,620	241,311	307,312	307,611
Imports, f.o.b...............................	71.v	52,857	58,779	76,154	98,039	115,524	129,735	143,326	147,091	186,382	213,763	272,682	256,833
						2000=100							
Volume of Exports.........................	72	68.4	69.6	73.4	† 76.1	83.2	87.7	89.7	90.9	100.0	101.3	99.9	....
Volume of Imports........................	73	65.7	68.9	80.0	† 86.8	94.3	99.4	100.6	93.3	100.0	100.3	103.5	....
Unit Value of Exports.....................	74	44.5	48.8	55.0	† 64.3	70.9	74.6	82.6	88.0	100.0	115.9	145.2	....
Unit Value of Imports.....................	75	44.9	48.4	53.5	† 60.9	66.2	70.5	78.7	86.4	100.0	115.8	141.5	....

2004, International Monetary Fund: *International Financial Statistics Yearbook*

South Africa 199

Balance of Payments

Millions of US Dollars: Minus Sign Indicates Debit

		1992	1993	1994	1995	1996	1997	1998	1999	2000	2001	2002	2003
Current Account, n.i.e.	78ald	1,967	1,503	112	−2,206	−1,842	−2,223	−2,134	−528	−295	56	610	−1,456
Goods: Exports f.o.b.	78aad	24,527	24,717	26,333	30,071	30,263	31,171	29,264	28,681	31,845	30,989	31,422	38,703
Goods: Imports f.o.b.	78abd	−18,248	−18,485	−21,852	−27,404	−27,568	−28,848	−27,208	−24,526	−27,252	−25,809	−26,791	−35,002
Trade Balance	78acd	6,279	6,232	4,481	2,667	2,695	2,324	2,056	4,156	4,593	5,180	4,631	3,701
Services: Credit	78add	3,352	3,276	3,749	4,619	5,069	5,394	5,396	5,210	5,046	4,653	4,672	6,602
Services: Debit	78aed	−4,357	−4,706	−5,087	−5,971	−5,735	−6,003	−5,658	−5,759	−5,823	−5,251	−5,340	−7,554
Balance on Goods & Services	78afd	5,273	4,802	3,143	1,315	2,028	1,715	1,794	3,607	3,816	4,582	3,963	2,748
Income: Credit	78agd	930	696	972	1,136	1,077	1,399	1,474	1,791	2,511	2,480	2,179	2,751
Income: Debit	78ahd	−3,871	−3,352	−3,394	−4,011	−4,194	−4,612	−4,659	−5,000	−5,696	−6,267	−4,975	−6,137
Balance on Gds, Serv. & Inc.	78aid	2,332	2,145	721	−1,560	−1,089	−1,499	−1,391	399	631	795	1,167	−637
Current Transfers, n.i.e.: Credit	78ajd	123	127	143	196	54	138	60	66	106	126	139	252
Current Transfers: Debit	78akd	−488	−769	−752	−841	−807	−862	−804	−993	−1,033	−865	−695	−1,070
Capital Account, n.i.e.	78bcd	−42	−57	−67	−40	−47	−193	−56	−62	−52	−31	−15	2
Capital Account, n.i.e.: Credit	78bad	28	18	20	23	27	30	24	20	19	16	20	45
Capital Account: Debit	78bbd	−70	−75	−87	−63	−74	−223	−80	−82	−71	−47	−35	−43
Financial Account, n.i.e.	78bjd	−243	−344	1,087	4,003	3,018	8,131	4,852	5,305	99	1,172	597	6,289
Direct Investment Abroad	78bdd	−1,939	−292	−1,261	−2,494	−1,048	−2,324	−1,634	−1,584	−277	3,515	402	−721
Dir. Invest. in Rep. Econ., n.i.e.	78bed	3	11	374	1,248	816	3,811	550	1,503	969	7,270	735	820
Portfolio Investment Assets	78bfd	−98	−3	−82	−447	−2,000	−4,587	−5,575	−5,113	−3,672	−5,331	−875	−132
Equity Securities	78bkd	−32	−15	−29	−387	−1,698	−3,891	−4,768	−4,050	−3,019	−4,864	−572	−43
Debt Securities	78bld	−66	11	−53	−61	−302	−696	−807	−1,064	−652	−467	−303	−89
Portfolio Investment Liab., n.i.e.	78bgd	1,841	751	2,918	2,937	4,446	11,274	9,869	13,799	1,807	−2,971	457	893
Equity Securities	78bmd	−188	895	88	2,914	2,318	5,473	8,632	9,001	4,169	−962	−388	685
Debt Securities	78bnd	2,029	−145	2,830	23	2,127	5,802	1,237	4,798	−2,361	−2,009	845	207
Financial Derivatives Assets	78bwd	....	....	....	....	....	−	−	−46	−144	−	−	−
Financial Derivatives Liabilities	78bxd	....	....	....	....	....	53	97	−76	2	−	−	−
Other Investment Assets	78bhd	−321	−269	−298	−525	−599	−1,983	−694	−1,644	59	−1,561	1,761	3,216
Monetary Authorities	78bod	−266	−24	44	75	12	206	−	6	−	−	−	1
General Government	78bpd	−2	−	−1	1	−	2	1	−	−	−407	−424	−376
Banks	78bqd	−23	15	−85	62	−127	−122	−135	−61	−244	−334	−406	−57
Other Sectors	78brd	−30	−259	−255	−663	−484	−2,069	−560	−1,589	303	−819	2,591	3,648
Other Investment Liab., n.i.e.	78bid	271	−542	−565	3,285	1,403	1,887	2,237	−1,535	1,354	249	−1,884	2,214
Monetary Authorities	78bsd	279	1,495	−105	−1,414	−89	2,186	1,172	105	−410	1,582	−1,688	169
General Government	78btd	266	−617	−467	118	469	−120	−73	−270	6	134	1,944	−277
Banks	78bud	−11	−359	360	2,945	1,044	−283	784	−945	1,196	−787	−1,568	209
Other Sectors	78bvd	−263	−1,061	−353	1,636	−21	105	355	−425	563	−680	−572	2,113
Net Errors and Omissions	78cad	−1,179	−2,443	−449	−851	−2,401	−1,120	−1,742	−446	713	1,408	466	2,927
Overall Balance	78cbd	503	−1,341	683	907	−1,272	4,595	920	4,270	464	2,606	1,659	7,762
Reserves and Related Items	79dad	−503	1,341	−683	−907	1,272	−4,595	−920	−4,270	−464	−2,606	−1,659	−7,762
Reserve Assets	79dbd	−503	491	−683	−907	1,272	−4,174	−502	−4,270	−464	−2,606	−1,659	−7,762
Use of Fund Credit and Loans	79dcd	−	850	−	−	−	−421	−418	−	−	−	−	−
Exceptional Financing	79ded	−	−	−	−	−	−	−	−	−	−	−	−

International Investment Position

Millions of US Dollars

		1992	1993	1994	1995	1996	1997	1998	1999	2000	2001	2002	2003
Assets	79aad	25,834	25,743	27,559	33,893	35,056	47,869	56,855	92,532	95,596	65,228	73,000	....
Direct Investment Abroad	79abd	17,795	17,960	19,105	23,301	24,349	23,250	26,858	32,990	32,325	19,083	23,475	....
Portfolio Investment	79acd	216	145	98	632	2,605	12,060	18,231	41,961	45,264	29,793	28,720	....
Equity Securities	79add	177	109	61	569	2,237	10,895	15,833	38,349	41,675	28,461	26,700	....
Debt Securities	79aed	39	36	38	63	368	1,164	2,398	3,612	3,589	1,331	2,020	....
Financial Derivatives	79afd	−	−	−	−	−	−	−	−	−	−	−	....
Other Investment	79afd	4,005	4,171	4,349	4,985	4,657	5,297	4,565	6,308	6,720	8,881	13,167	....
Monetary Authorities	79agd	475	453	392	306	227	24	19	12	10	6	8	....
General Government	79ahd	1,839	1,838	2,040	2,371	2,148	1,839	1,596	2,512	2,703	703	1	....
Banks	79aid	37	19	104	39	150	258	300	338	496	5,554	9,263	....
Other Sectors	79ajd	1,653	1,862	1,813	2,269	2,132	3,176	2,650	3,447	3,511	2,618	3,895	....
Reserve Assets	79akd	3,818	3,467	4,008	4,975	3,445	7,262	7,201	11,273	11,287	7,471	7,638	....
Liabilities	79lad	40,898	44,022	52,197	62,610	60,449	68,546	69,835	116,962	102,231	75,105	82,654	....
Dir. Invest. in Rep. Economy	79lbd	10,662	10,694	12,615	15,014	13,236	16,736	15,676	51,772	43,451	30,569	29,611	....
Portfolio Investment	79lcd	12,549	13,470	18,998	23,446	23,804	28,143	30,547	42,249	36,529	26,402	35,677	....
Equity Securities	79ldd	5,359	6,027	9,246	12,492	13,366	13,144	17,519	26,461	22,599	16,577	23,308	....
Debt Securities	79led	7,190	7,443	9,752	10,953	10,439	14,999	13,028	15,789	13,930	9,825	12,369	....
Financial Derivatives	79lld	5	2	4	10	14	66	119	43	35	−	−	....
Other Investment	79lfd	17,683	19,855	20,580	24,140	23,395	23,601	23,492	22,898	22,216	18,134	17,366	....
Monetary Authorities	79lgd	390	2,660	2,534	1,142	979	2,578	3,181	3,261	2,681	4,026	2,646	....
General Government	79lhd	3,920	3,512	3,108	3,072	3,244	2,776	2,537	3,125	3,023	717	2,805	....
Banks	79lid	5,131	4,968	5,944	9,038	9,310	8,861	9,154	7,997	8,627	6,911	5,675	....
Other Sectors	79ljd	8,242	8,715	8,993	10,889	9,861	9,386	8,620	8,515	7,885	6,480	6,240	....

South Africa 199

		1992	1993	1994	1995	1996	1997	1998	1999	2000	2001	2002	2003
Government Finance						*Millions of Rand: Year Ending December 31*							
Deficit (-) or Surplus....................	80	−26,423	−28,342	−38,690	−23,465	−28,563	−28,129	−19,464	−14,759	−16,428	−9,975	−6,031	−26,040
Total Revenue and Grants.............	81y	83,464	95,710	111,916	125,470	147,738	162,983	181,749	202,330	211,984	245,952	279,922	295,661
Expenditure..................................	82	109,887	124,052	150,606	148,935	176,301	191,112	201,213	217,089	228,412	255,927	285,953	321,701
Total Financing.............................	80h	26,423	28,342	38,690	23,465	28,563	28,129	19,465	14,778	16,428	9,975	6,031	26,040
Total Net Borrowing.....................	84	21,223	31,469	37,928	25,504	24,224	26,507	21,647	13,269	17,790	19,348	7,777	45,884
Net Domestic............................	84a	20,649	31,632	35,317	24,323	21,596	23,553	21,591	7,651	10,299	6,489	−26,476	42,955
Net Foreign..............................	85a	574	−163	2,611	1,181	2,628	2,954	56	5,618	7,491	12,859	34,253	2,929
Use of Cash Balances..................	87	5,200	−3,127	762	−2,039	4,339	1,622	−2,182	1,509	−1,362	−9,373	−1,746	−19,844
Total Debt by Currency..................	88z	147,327	185,538	†239,714	275,489	302,608	†336,133	361,401	391,420	409,363	462,446	454,365	499,806
National.......................................	88b	144,960	180,542	†231,656	265,879	288,349	†320,981	345,559	371,395	378,245	395,827	374,488	427,190
Foreign..	89b	2,367	4,996	8,058	9,610	14,259	15,152	15,842	20,025	31,118	66,619	79,877	72,616
National Accounts						*Millions of Rand*							
Househ.Cons.Expend.,incl.NPISHs....	96f.c	234,167	†263,427	298,173	343,037	384,624	431,403	466,552	504,289	556,652	612,349	690,949	750,096
Government Consumption Expend...	91f.c	75,257	†85,551	96,503	100,424	118,013	131,903	140,170	149,393	166,469	185,704	209,353	230,475
Gross Fixed Capital Formation.........	93e.c	58,255	†62,601	73,045	87,042	100,632	113,221	125,333	122,162	131,984	143,048	167,662	190,256
Changes in Inventories..................	93i.c	−3,319	†2,603	8,013	11,517	7,089	841	−2,740	3,903	5,808	586	10,388	12,733
Exports of Goods and Services.........	90c.c	79,398	†91,578	106,842	125,870	151,967	168,693	190,811	207,057	256,448	304,874	378,534	340,963
Imports of Goods and Services (-).....	98c.c	64,403	†75,919	95,747	121,093	143,340	160,718	181,972	185,037	229,757	266,122	336,631	319,357
Gross Domestic Product (GDP)........	99b.c	372,225	†426,133	482,120	548,100	617,954	685,730	738,926	800,769	888,454	983,450	1,120,895	1,209,497
Net Primary Income from Abroad.....	98.nc	−8,401	†−8,700	−8,599	−10,427	−13,380	−14,844	−17,488	−19,601	−22,024	−32,175	−29,400	−25,532
Gross National Income (GNI)...........	99a.c	363,824	†417,433	473,521	537,673	604,574	670,886	721,438	781,168	866,430	951,275	1,091,495	1,183,965
Consumption of Fixed Capital.........	99cf	54,227	†58,575	64,500	71,827	78,817	87,188	96,582	107,858	118,573	129,455	147,913	159,847
GDP Volume 1995 Prices.................	99b.r	508,613	†514,887	531,539	548,100	571,705	586,837	591,267	603,291	624,485	641,243	664,075	676,384
GDP Volume (2000=100)................	99bvr	81.4	†82.4	85.1	87.8	91.5	94.0	94.7	96.6	100.0	102.7	106.3	108.3
GDP Deflator (2000=100)................	99bir	51.4	†58.2	63.8	70.3	76.0	82.1	87.8	93.3	100.0	107.8	118.6	125.7
						Millions: Midyear Estimates							
Population.................................	99z	38.51	39.34	40.16	40.93	41.66	42.33	42.96	43.51	44.00	44.42	44.76	45.03

2004, International Monetary Fund: *International Financial Statistics Yearbook*

Spain 184

		1992	1993	1994	1995	1996	1997	1998	1999	2000	2001	2002	2003
Exchange Rates		\multicolumn{12}{c}{*Pesetas per SDR through 1998, Euros per SDR Thereafter: End of Period*}
Market Rate........	aa	157.61	195.34	192.32	180.47	188.77	204.68	200.79	1.3662	1.4002	1.4260	1.2964	1.1765
		\multicolumn{12}{c}{*Pesetas per US Dollar through 1998, Euros per US Dollar Thereafter: End of Period (ae) Period Average (rf)*}
Market Rate........	ae	114.62	142.21	131.74	121.41	131.28	151.70	142.61	.9954	1.0747	1.1347	.9536	.7918
Market Rate........	rf	102.38	127.26	133.96	124.69	126.66	146.41	149.40	.9386	1.0854	1.1175	1.0626	.8860
		\multicolumn{12}{c}{*Pesetas per ECU: End of Period (ea) Period Average (eb)*}
ECU Rate........	ea	138.3730	159.2800	161.5520	155.5610	162.6500	167.3270	166.3860	....	....	....	....	....
ECU Rate........	eb	132.2572	148.6617	158.4871	161.1758	158.6182	165.3915	167.4876	....	....	....	....	....
		\multicolumn{12}{c}{*Index Numbers (2000=100): Period Averages*}
Market Rate (1995=100)....	ahx	122.1	98.4	93.1	100.0	98.4	85.2	83.5	....	....	....	....	....
Nominal Effective Exchange Rate.....	neu	132.6	117.6	109.8	108.9	109.6	104.9	104.3	102.9	100.0	100.5	101.2	104.1
Real Effective Exchange Rate........	reu	114.1	106.3	99.8	98.9	101.5	99.0	101.0	101.2	100.0	102.2	104.9	109.6
Fund Position		\multicolumn{12}{c}{*Millions of SDRs: End of Period*}
Quota........	2f.s	1,935	1,935	1,935	1,935	1,935	1,935	1,935	3,049	3,049	3,049	3,049	3,049
SDRs........	1b.s	134	157	174	277	314	351	408	190	223	279	260	278
Reserve Position in the Fund........	1c.s	832	751	760	1,065	1,110	1,409	1,558	1,111	908	1,055	1,171	1,253
of which: Outstg.Fund Borrowing...	2c	–	–	–	–	–	–	62	–	–	–	–	–
Total Fund Cred.&Loans Outstg....	2tl	–	–	–	–	–	–	–	–	–	–	–	–
International Liquidity		\multicolumn{12}{c}{*Millions of US Dollars Unless Otherwise Indicated: End of Period*}
Total Res.Min.Gold (Eurosys.Def).....	1l.d	45,504	41,045	41,546	34,485	57,927	68,398	55,258	†33,115	30,989	29,582	34,536	19,788
SDRs........	1b.d	184	216	255	411	451	474	575	260	290	351	354	413
Reserve Position in the Fund........	1c.d	1,144	1,031	1,109	1,583	1,597	1,902	2,193	1,525	1,182	1,326	1,592	1,862
Foreign Exchange........	1d.d	44,176	39,798	40,182	32,491	55,879	66,023	52,490	31,329	29,516	27,905	32,590	17,513
o/w:Fin.Deriv.Rel.to Reserves.......	1ddd	....	....	....	....	....	....	....	–1.01	162.84	–55.52	400.60	1,001.56
Other Reserve Assets........	1e.d	....	....	....	....	....	....	....	....	....	....	....	....
Gold (Million Fine Troy Ounces).....	1ad	15.62	15.62	15.62	15.63	15.63	15.63	19.54	16.83	16.83	16.83	16.83	16.83
Gold (Eurosystem Valuation)........	1and	4,217	4,217	4,217	4,221	4,221	4,139	5,617	4,885	4,619	4,653	5,768	7,021
Memo:Euro Cl. on Non-EA Res.......	1dgd	....	....	....	....	....	....	....	4,134	36	–	–	–
Non-Euro Cl. on EA Res........	1dhd	....	....	....	....	....	....	....	....	–	–	–	–
Mon. Auth.: Other Foreign Assets.....	3..d	....	....	....	....	....	....	....	....	....	....	....	....
Foreign Liabilities........	4..d	457	462	515	551	983	454	480	†1,004	445	317	1,488	143
Banking Insts.: Foreign Assets........	7a.d	68,542	117,311	110,693	146,061	129,727	111,176	126,792	†66,435	82,631	87,327	100,813	107,259
Foreign Liab........	7b.d	81,501	87,093	100,658	109,245	123,359	135,020	179,175	†125,663	147,328	157,560	176,270	231,737
Monetary Authorities		\multicolumn{12}{c}{*Billions of Pesetas through 1998; Billions of Euros Beginning 1999: End of Period*}
Fgn. Assets (Cl.on Non-EA Ctys)......	11	5,604	6,152	5,796	4,566	7,960	10,708	8,751	41.49	37.54	38.60	38.26	21.84
Claims on General Government.......	12a.u	....	....	....	....	....	....	....	15.17	14.45	13.95	14.17	30.28
o/w: Claims on Gen.Govt.in Cty......	12a	1,881	–219	2,981	3,074	3,056	2,984	3,023	15.17	14.45	13.95	14.17	16.32
Claims on Banking Institutions.........	12e.u	....	....	....	....	....	....	....	60.01	61.42	39.71	40.86	51.46
o/w: Claims on Bank.Inst.in Cty......	12e	4,296	6,525	5,949	6,641	4,439	2,267	4,471	24.18	16.14	10.55	18.20	33.19
Claims on Other Resident Sectors.....	12d.u	....	....	....	....	....	....	....	–	–	–	–	.06
o/w: Cl. on Oth.Res.Sect.in Cty......	12d	36	22	21	20	21	21	22	–	–	–	–	.06
Currency Issued.......	14a	6,025	6,509	7,165	7,535	7,942	8,378	8,437	61.35	59.79	48.75	40.50	46.38
Liabilities to Banking Insts........	14c.u	....	....	....	....	....	....	....	15.94	8.39	14.73	27.88	33.82
o/w: Liabs to Bank.Inst.in Cty.......	14c	1,728	1,283	1,430	1,394	1,310	1,484	1,788	12.49	8.39	14.73	9.29	14.41
Demand Dep. of Other Res.Sect.......	14d.u	....	....	....	....	....	....	....	5.22	7.34	10.52	12.43	13.92
o/w:D.Dep.of Oth.Res.Sect.in Cty...	14d	106	131	132	193	175	207	190	5.22	7.34	10.52	12.43	13.92
Other Dep. of Other Res.Sect........	15..u	....	....	....	....	....	....	....	–	–	–	–	–
o/w:O.Dep.of Oth.Res.Sect.in Cty...	15	....	....	....	....	....	....	....	–	–	–	–	–
Bonds & Money Mkt. Instruments.....	16n.u	....	....	....	....	....	....	....	3.30	–	–	–	–
o/w: Held by Resid.of Cty........	16n	3,314	3,067	2,860	2,334	1,947	1,613	1,219	....	....	....	....	....
Foreign Liab. (to Non-EA Ctys)........	16c	52	66	68	67	129	69	69	1.00	.48	.36	1.42	.11
Central Government Deposits........	16d.u	....	....	....	....	....	....	....	16.87	22.91	2.79	2.80	3.32
o/w: Cent.Govt.Dep. in Cty........	16d	95	193	2,058	1,752	2,742	1,890	2,120	16.87	22.91	2.79	2.80	3.32
Capital Accounts.......	17a	1,506	2,207	1,166	1,267	1,594	2,752	2,870	16.01	17.25	17.51	12.26	8.67
Other Items (Net)........	17r	–1,010	–975	–132	–243	–363	–412	–426	–3.01	–2.73	–2.39	–3.99	–2.59
Memo: Net Claims on Eurosystem....	12e.s	....	....	....	....	....	....	....	32.38	45.28	29.16	4.06	–1.14
Currency Put into Circ........	14m	....	....	....	....	....	....	....	....	....	....	59.09	65.79

Spain 184

		1992	1993	1994	1995	1996	1997	1998	1999	2000	2001	2002	2003
Banking Institutions		*Billions of Pesetas through 1998; Billions of Euros Beginning 1999: End of Period*
Claims on Monetary Authorities	20	5,043	4,348	4,328	3,725	3,262	3,093	2,992	15.79	8.39	14.73	9.29	14.41
Claims on Bk.Inst.in Oth.EA Ctys	20b.u	....	....	....	....	....	....	....	50.08	53.56	53.52	67.72	78.66
Fgn. Assets (Cl.on Non-EA Ctys)	21	7,868	16,690	14,565	17,737	17,057	16,909	18,155	66.13	88.80	99.09	96.13	84.92
Claims on General Government	22a.u	....	....	....	....	....	....	....	146.00	129.59	151.68	164.17	189.34
o/w: Claims on Gen.Govt.in Cty.	22a	14,585	16,114	20,853	22,358	24,083	22,400	21,258	136.21	124.10	133.84	138.22	147.75
Claims on Other Resident Sectors	22d.u	....	....	....	....	....	....	....	529.64	631.12	712.26	794.56	915.35
o/w: Cl. on Oth.Res.Sect.in Cty.	22d	49,059	49,600	50,345	53,764	57,682	65,592	76,417	519.57	615.88	688.45	770.91	886.18
Demand Deposits	24..u	....	....	....	....	....	....	....	127.47	140.23	159.67	175.19	191.06
o/w:D.Dep.of Oth.Res.Sect.in Cty	24	9,584	9,657	10,159	10,291	11,144	13,391	16,768	125.54	137.52	157.23	173.08	187.93
Other Deposits	25..u	....	....	....	....	....	....	....	319.89	368.97	408.74	440.18	490.00
o/w:O.Dep.of Oth.Res.Sect.in Cty	25	28,416	32,208	34,492	37,397	37,579	35,679	36,346	310.68	359.38	396.10	424.87	460.72
Money Market Fund Shares	26m.u	....	....	....	....	....	....	....	42.34	33.11	43.44	52.92	57.65
Bonds & Money Mkt. Instruments	26n.u	....	....	....	....	....	....	....	53.63	51.91	65.19	77.65	118.49
o/w: Held by Resid.of Cty.	26n	1,449	1,906	2,214	2,316	2,394	2,693	3,025	....	....	....	....	....
Foreign Liab. (to Non-EA Ctys)	26c	9,497	12,459	13,303	13,316	16,436	20,741	25,889	125.09	158.33	178.78	168.08	183.48
Central Government Deposits	26d.u	....	....	....	....	....	....	....	5.65	5.54	19.06	21.41	16.40
o/w: Cent.Govt.Dep. in Cty.	26d	2,890	2,866	2,706	2,954	3,063	3,352	3,882	5.62	5.52	19.06	21.40	16.27
Credit from Monetary Authorities	26g	4,282	6,525	6,063	6,643	4,447	2,265	4,450	24.18	16.14	10.55	18.20	33.19
Liab. to Bk.Inst.in Oth. EA Ctys.	26h.u	....	....	....	....	....	....	....	54.22	64.81	63.22	86.99	101.55
Capital Accounts	27a	9,424	10,234	10,709	10,807	11,261	12,026	12,668	80.53	98.56	108.50	119.24	126.90
Other Items (Net)	27r	11,015	10,897	10,445	13,860	15,761	17,847	15,794	−25.36	−26.13	−25.88	−27.99	−36.02
Banking Survey (Nat'l Residency)		*Billions of Pesetas through 1998; Billions of Euros Beginning 1999: End of Period*
Foreign Assets (Net)	31n	3,923	10,317	6,990	8,921	8,452	6,808	949	21.99	14.54	9.17	−12.10	−43.59
Domestic Credit	32	62,576	62,460	69,435	74,510	79,037	85,755	94,718	648.46	726.00	814.39	899.10	1,030.71
Claims on General Govt. (Net)	32an	13,481	12,837	19,069	20,726	21,334	20,142	18,279	128.89	110.12	125.94	128.19	144.48
Claims on Other Resident Sectors	32d	49,095	49,622	50,366	53,784	57,703	65,613	76,439	519.57	615.88	688.45	770.91	886.24
Currency Issued	34a.n	6,025	6,509	7,165	7,535	7,942	8,378	8,437	61.35	59.79	48.75	40.50	46.38
Demand Deposits	34b.n	9,690	9,788	10,291	10,484	11,319	13,598	16,959	130.76	144.86	167.74	185.51	201.85
Other Deposits	35..n	28,416	32,208	34,492	37,397	37,579	35,679	36,346	310.68	359.38	396.10	424.87	460.72
Money Market Fund Shares	36m	....	....	....	....	....	....	....	42.34	33.11	43.44	52.92	57.65
Bonds & Money Mkt. Instruments	36n	4,763	4,973	5,075	4,651	4,341	4,306	4,244	56.93	51.91	65.19	77.65	118.49
o/w: Over Two Years	36na	....	....	....	....	....	....	....	40.79	39.77	49.28	61.63	87.40
Capital Accounts	37a	10,930	12,441	11,875	12,074	12,855	14,778	15,538	96.54	115.81	126.01	131.50	135.56
Other Items (Net)	37r	6,675	6,857	7,529	11,289	13,454	15,824	14,143	−28.15	−24.32	−23.68	−25.95	−33.51
Banking Survey (EA-Wide Residency)		*Billions of Euros: End of Period*
Foreign Assets (Net)	31n.u	....	....	....	....	....	....	....	−18.46	−32.46	−41.45	−35.11	−76.83
Domestic Credit	32..u	....	....	....	....	....	....	....	668.28	746.72	856.03	948.69	1,115.31
Claims on General Govt. (Net)	32anu	....	....	....	....	....	....	....	138.64	115.60	143.78	154.13	199.90
Claims on Other Resident Sect.	32d.u	....	....	....	....	....	....	....	529.64	631.12	712.26	794.56	915.41
Currency Issued	34a.u	....	....	....	....	....	....	....	61.35	59.79	48.75	40.50	46.38
Demand Deposits	34b.u	....	....	....	....	....	....	....	132.68	147.56	170.19	187.61	204.98
Other Deposits	35..u	....	....	....	....	....	....	....	319.89	368.97	408.74	440.18	490.00
o/w: Other Dep. Over Two Yrs.	35abu	....	....	....	....	....	....	....	32.17	44.32	49.80	64.14	88.74
Money Market Fund Shares	36m.u	....	....	....	....	....	....	....	42.34	33.11	43.44	52.92	57.65
Bonds & Money Mkt. Instruments	36n.u	....	....	....	....	....	....	....	56.93	51.91	65.19	77.65	118.49
o/w: Over Two Years	36nau	....	....	....	....	....	....	....	40.79	39.77	49.28	61.63	87.40
Capital Accounts	37a	....	....	....	....	....	....	....	96.54	115.81	126.01	131.50	135.56
Other Items (Net)	37r.u	....	....	....	....	....	....	....	−59.91	−62.89	−47.73	−16.78	−14.58
Money (National Definitions)		*Billions of Pesetas: End of Period*
M1	59ma	15,631.3	16,180.5	17,337.6	17,887.8	19,116.1	21,834.9	25,270.6	....	....	....	....	....
M2	59mb	25,690.3	26,966.7	28,753.4	29,637.5	31,717.5	35,483.7	40,616.5	....	....	....	....	....
M3	59mc	54,237.5	59,260.7	63,675.8	70,439.4	73,819.5	77,136.6	78,665.1	....	....	....	....	....
ALP	59md	59,449.7	65,429.1	70,045.8	76,479.0	82,118.8	85,674.3	86,588.1	....	....	....	....	....
Interest Rates		*Percent Per Annum*
Bank of Spain Rate(End of Period)	60	13.25	9.00	7.38	9.00	6.25	4.75	3.00	....	....	....	....	....
Money Market Rate	60b	13.01	12.33	7.81	8.98	7.65	5.49	4.34	2.72	4.11	4.36	3.28	2.31
Treasury Bill Rate	60c	12.44	10.53	8.11	9.79	7.23	5.02	3.79	3.01	4.61	3.92	3.34	2.21
Deposit Rate	60l	10.43	9.63	6.70	7.68	6.12	3.96	2.92	1.85	2.95	3.08	2.50	....
Lending Rate	60p	14.23	12.78	8.95	10.05	8.50	6.08	5.01	3.95	5.18	5.16	4.31	....
Government Bond Yield	61	12.17	10.16	9.69	11.04	8.18	5.84	4.55	4.30	5.36	4.87	4.62	3.52

Spain 184

		1992	1993	1994	1995	1996	1997	1998	1999	2000	2001	2002	2003
Prices, Production, Labor		\multicolumn{12}{c}{*Index Numbers (2000=100): Period Averages*}
Share Prices	62	23.2	27.2	31.6	29.8	36.9	55.9	82.2	89.9	100.0	85.8	72.7	71.0
Industrial Prices	63	81.19	83.24	86.79	92.32	93.87	94.83	94.20	94.85	100.00	101.71	102.41	103.87
Consumer Prices	64	76.7	80.2	84.0	87.9	91.0	92.8	94.5	96.7	100.0	103.6	106.8	110.0
Harmonized CPI	64h	....	....	....	88.0	91.2	92.9	94.5	96.6	100.0	102.8	106.5	109.8
Wages	65	72.4	77.3	80.7	84.6	89.1	92.7	95.3	97.7	100.0	103.8	108.1	112.7
Industrial Production	66	77.9	74.3	80.0	83.9	82.8	88.5	93.4	95.7	100.0	98.5	98.7	100.1
Employment	67	83	80	79	81	84	86	90	95	100	104	106	109
		\multicolumn{12}{c}{*Number in Thousands: Period Averages*}
Labor Force	67d	....	15,319	....	15,625	15,936	16,121	16,265	16,423	16,844	17,815	18,340	....
Employment	67e	12,366.2	11,837.4	12,207.0	12,512.0	12,835.0	13,259.5	13,807.6	14,568.0	15,369.7	15,945.6	16,257.6	16,694.6
Unemployment	67c	2,789	3,481	3,738	3,584	3,540	3,356	3,060	2,606	2,370	2,213	1,621	1,658
Unemployment Rate (%)	67r	18.4	22.7	24.2	22.9	22.2	20.8	18.8	15.9	14.1	13.1	11.4	8.8
International Transactions		\multicolumn{12}{c}{*Billions of Pesetas through 1998; Millions of Euros Beginning 1999*}
Exports	70	6,657.6	7,754.6	9,746.6	11,339.6	12,931.2	15,266.9	16,290.8†	103,343.2	123,099.5	128,671.8	130,814.1	137,814.8
Imports, c.i.f.	71	10,204.5	10,131.0	12,306.3	14,106.7	15,435.7	17,966.0	19,837.9†	135,866.3	166,138.4	171,690.8	172,788.6	184,094.8
		\multicolumn{12}{c}{*2000=100*}
Volume of Exports	72	41.1	46.0	56.0	61.2	63.3	78.0	83.6	88.7	100.0	102.0	103.6	109.6
Volume of Imports	73	49.2	46.5	53.5	59.5	63.8	71.1	81.1	92.1	100.0	104.1	108.3	115.6
Unit Value of Exports	74	78.1	81.9	85.5	91.1	92.0	95.0	95.1	94.2	100.0	102.7	102.9	102.0
Unit Value of Imports	75	75.1	79.0	83.6	87.3	87.6	90.7	88.7	88.6	100.0	99.5	96.3	95.9
Export Prices (1975=100)	76	....	....	....	....	....	....	....	....	....	....	....	....
Balance of Payments		\multicolumn{12}{c}{*Millions of US Dollars: Minus Sign Indicates Debit*}
Current Account, n.i.e.	78ald	−21,537	−5,804	−6,389	792	407	2,512	−3,135	−13,761	−19,237	−16,404	−16,044	−23,676
Goods: Exports f.o.b.	78aad	65,826	62,021	73,925	93,439	102,735	106,926	111,986	112,664	116,205	117,935	127,949	159,545
Goods: Imports f.o.b.	78abd	−96,247	−77,020	−88,817	−111,854	−119,017	−120,333	−132,744	−143,002	−151,025	−150,474	−160,790	−202,468
Trade Balance	78acd	−30,420	−14,999	−14,892	−18,415	−16,283	−13,407	−20,758	−30,339	−34,820	−32,539	−32,841	−42,923
Services: Credit	78add	33,921	30,446	33,859	40,209	44,387	44,161	49,308	53,418	53,540	58,201	62,682	76,881
Services: Debit	78aed	−21,314	−18,902	−18,865	−21,509	−23,979	−24,315	−27,421	−30,532	−31,283	−33,988	−37,365	−45,959
Balance on Goods & Services	78afd	−17,813	−3,454	102	284	4,126	6,439	1,129	−7,452	−12,564	−8,325	−7,524	−12,001
Income: Credit	78agd	14,084	11,845	8,687	13,689	14,095	13,162	14,621	12,636	15,017	19,829	20,234	24,654
Income: Debit	78ahd	−19,874	−15,456	−16,457	−17,817	−20,207	−19,911	−22,134	−22,087	−23,268	−29,576	−30,922	−36,573
Balance on Gds, Serv. & Inc.	78aid	−23,603	−7,066	−7,668	−3,843	−1,986	−310	−6,385	−16,903	−20,815	−18,073	−18,212	−23,920
Current Transfers, n.i.e.: Credit	78ajd	10,771	8,821	9,171	12,055	11,112	11,738	12,690	13,435	11,629	12,569	14,074	17,506
Current Transfers: Debit	78akd	−8,705	−7,558	−7,893	−7,420	−8,718	−8,916	−9,441	−10,292	−10,050	−10,900	−11,905	−17,262
Capital Account, n.i.e.	78bcd	3,726	2,872	2,305	6,004	6,589	6,437	6,330	6,967	4,792	4,970	7,309	9,982
Capital Account, n.i.e.: Credit	78bad	4,219	3,997	3,571	7,374	7,713	7,275	7,160	8,060	5,806	5,864	8,192	11,040
Capital Account: Debit	78bbd	−493	−1,125	−1,266	−1,370	−1,124	−837	−830	−1,094	−1,014	−895	−884	−1,058
Financial Account, n.i.e.	78bjd	5,959	−434	4,491	−7,951	20,138	8,547	−14,156	−10,997	16,942	16,602	17,483	4,444
Direct Investment Abroad	78bdd	−2,192	−3,188	−4,051	−4,206	−5,577	−12,423	−19,065	−41,754	−53,865	−32,875	−32,410	−23,350
Dir. Invest. in Rep. Econ., n.i.e.	78bed	13,276	9,681	9,216	6,297	6,796	6,384	11,905	15,541	36,931	27,741	36,727	25,513
Portfolio Investment Assets	78bfd	−2,829	−6,567	−1,492	−490	−3,653	−16,450	−44,193	−47,397	−59,320	−45,042	−28,983	−91,061
Equity Securities	78bkd	−145	−728	−1,039	−534	−776	−5,272	−10,120	−17,279	−36,136	−260	283	−12,239
Debt Securities	78bld	−2,684	−5,839	−453	44	−2,877	−11,178	−34,073	−30,118	−23,185	−44,783	−29,267	−78,822
Portfolio Investment Liab., n.i.e.	78bgd	12,098	55,314	−20,856	21,653	3,128	11,772	16,736	45,549	58,146	27,246	34,849	40,908
Equity Securities	78bmd	3,648	6,600	1,154	4,215	147	−294	10,072	9,975	19,692	7,233	3,550	−8,558
Debt Securities	78bnd	8,450	48,714	−22,010	17,438	2,981	12,066	6,664	35,574	38,455	20,013	31,299	49,466
Financial Derivatives Assets	78bwd	18	−	−	−	−	−	−	−	....	....	....	....
Financial Derivatives Liabilities	78bxd	71	−2,791	158	−557	−875	41	−2,776	260	2,025	−274	−4,712	−3,699
Other Investment Assets	78bhd	−40,441	−71,940	9,152	−36,816	2,469	−1,415	−21,604	−24,624	−18,640	10,362	−22,610	−14,437
Monetary Authorities	78bod	....	−3	3	−71	−4	8	−422	−39,311	−7,837	14,992	6,115	5,211
General Government	78bpd	−897	−663	−620	−402	−502	−377	−427	−209	−253	−283	−332	−384
Banks	78bqd	−28,758	−63,178	14,437	−26,899	9,969	13,175	−1,960	5,298	−7,588	−3,873	−17,417	−12,051
Other Sectors	78brd	−10,786	−8,097	−4,668	−9,446	−6,993	−14,220	−18,795	9,599	−2,962	−474	−10,976	−7,212
Other Investment Liab., n.i.e.	78bid	25,958	19,058	12,363	6,168	17,849	20,638	44,841	41,427	51,666	29,445	34,623	70,570
Monetary Authorities	78bsd	−	−121	27	23	461	−466	−2	−11	−141	−185	1,119	−1,331
General Government	78btd	3,418	938	3,007	1,493	−226	4	1,043	−296	902	575	437	−1,669
Banks	78bud	13,609	13,242	10,572	4,049	18,646	20,490	38,957	26,039	36,510	15,501	26,183	62,628
Other Sectors	78bvd	8,932	4,999	−1,242	604	−1,032	611	4,843	15,695	14,395	13,553	6,883	10,942
Net Errors and Omissions	78cad	−5,957	−1,838	−371	−5,260	−2,856	−5,741	−3,395	−5,059	−5,379	−6,507	−5,058	−6,237
Overall Balance	78cbd	−17,809	−5,203	36	−6,414	24,279	11,756	−14,355	−22,850	−2,881	−1,340	3,690	−15,487
Reserves and Related Items	79dad	17,809	5,203	−36	6,414	−24,279	−11,756	14,355	22,850	2,881	1,340	−3,690	15,487
Reserve Assets	79dbd	17,809	5,203	−36	6,414	−24,279	−11,756	14,355	22,850	2,881	1,340	−3,690	15,487
Use of Fund Credit and Loans	79dcd	−	−	−	−	−	−	−	−	−	−	−	−
Exceptional Financing	79ded	−	−	−	−	−	−	−	−	....	....	....	....

Spain 184

		1992	1993	1994	1995	1996	1997	1998	1999	2000	2001	2002	2003
International Investment Position						*Millions of US Dollars*							
Assets	79aad	165,640	213,491	221,860	268,762	289,787	311,244	397,987	464,207	566,745	594,340	755,440	997,725
Direct Investment Abroad	79abd	22,010	24,027	30,052	36,225	40,548	50,322	70,130	112,802	159,959	184,462	224,364	279,818
Portfolio Investment	79acd	9,710	14,802	17,284	18,244	21,108	34,858	81,237	127,994	180,256	205,136	272,397	432,696
Equity Securities	79add	1,972	2,285	3,454	3,764	4,441	9,235	19,978	42,482	78,094	65,765	53,180	83,402
Debt Securities	79aed	7,738	12,516	13,830	14,480	16,667	25,623	61,259	85,513	102,161	139,371	219,217	349,294
Financial Derivatives	79ald	–	–	–	–	–	–	–	–	–	–	–	–
Other Investment	79afd	85,198	131,562	130,690	176,931	167,717	155,680	185,832	185,401	190,953	170,488	218,376	258,402
Monetary Authorities	79agd	–	148	159	247	229	198	582	36,652	42,557	26,059	24,206	23,648
General Government	79ahd	–	4,662	5,465	6,029	6,323	6,328	6,872	6,706	6,781	6,882	7,723	8,720
Banks	79aid	62,880	105,292	97,086	130,872	116,763	94,956	100,738	84,840	87,836	86,771	117,944	143,128
Other Sectors	79ajd	22,317	21,461	27,980	39,783	44,403	54,198	77,640	57,203	53,779	50,776	68,503	82,906
Reserve Assets	79akd	48,722	43,100	43,834	37,362	60,414	70,384	60,788	38,010	35,576	34,254	40,304	26,809
Liabilities	79lad	258,566	305,835	322,228	383,415	400,206	410,687	528,172	630,123	718,800	762,749	997,006	1,360,919
Dir. Invest. in Rep. Economy	79lbd	86,230	80,287	96,312	109,185	107,880	100,025	118,115	116,230	144,850	165,291	236,606	313,267
Portfolio Investment	79lcd	54,163	103,393	83,764	118,426	126,696	137,322	183,995	269,359	288,813	293,324	375,309	520,592
Equity Securities	79ldd	18,577	22,818	24,146	32,461	39,162	46,974	75,775	146,619	137,268	127,040	122,687	186,788
Debt Securities	79led	35,585	80,576	59,618	85,966	87,534	90,348	108,221	122,740	151,545	166,284	252,621	333,805
Financial Derivatives	79lld	–	–	–	–	–	–	–	–	–	–	–	–
Other Investment	79lfd	118,173	122,154	142,152	155,804	165,629	173,340	226,062	244,534	285,137	304,134	385,092	527,060
Monetary Authorities	79lgd	–	49	76	107	556	53	63	34	422	263	1,438	116
General Government	79lhd	4,491	6,546	9,989	12,355	11,503	10,158	11,725	9,939	10,343	10,125	11,972	12,888
Banks	79lid	88,167	89,991	104,912	114,506	127,770	138,350	183,084	191,090	219,207	225,809	286,551	400,933
Other Sectors	79ljd	25,515	25,567	27,175	28,836	25,801	24,779	31,191	43,471	55,165	67,937	85,131	113,123
Government Finance													
Central Government		*Billions of Pesetas through 1998; Millions of Euros Beginning 1999: Year Ending December 31*											
Deficit (-) or Surplus	80	–2,100.5	–3,738.0	–4,147.6	–3,606.3	–4,003.5	–1,909.4	–800.0	† –6,054	–787	–2,261	–4,055	–7,199
Total Revenue and Grants	81y	12,286.5	12,683.7	12,960.3	14,077.2	14,629.7	16,636.5	17,519.0	† 110,370	118,693	125,193	108,456	109,655
Revenue	81	12,286.5	12,683.7	12,960.3	14,077.2	14,629.7	16,636.5	17,519.0	† 110,370	118,693	125,193	108,456	109,655
Grants	81z	–	–	–	–	–	–	–	† –	–	–	–	–
Exp. & Lending Minus Repay	82z	14,387.0	16,421.7	17,107.9	17,683.5	18,633.2	18,545.9	18,319.0	† 116,424	119,480	127,455	112,511	116,854
Expenditure	82	14,160.0	16,465.8	16,438.3	17,241.5	18,322.2	18,694.0	18,633.4	† 116,724	121,124	128,077	111,082	113,787
Lending Minus Repayments	83	227.0	–44.1	669.6	442.0	311.0	–148.1	–314.4	† –299	–1,644	–623	1,429	3,066
Total Financing	80h	2,100.5	3,737.5	4,147.2	3,605.7	4,003.0	1,908.8	800.2	† 6,054	787	2,261	4,055	7,199
Total Net Borrowing	84	2,177.0	6,238.6	2,317.7	3,324.5	5,039.2	973.4	910.7	† 11,187	6,788	–2,640	6,481	656
Use of Cash Balances	87	76.5	2,501.1	–1,829.5	–281.2	1,036.2	–935.4	110.5	† 5,092	6,001	–4,901	2,426	–6,543
Total Debt by Residence	88	23,911.0	31,236.7	34,266.0	38,678.1	43,922.0	45,616.6	47,243.4	† 298,378	308,212	307,434	308,792	302,968
Domestic	88a	20,371.5	21,751.8	27,389.8	29,951.8	34,934.4	35,121.6	35,756.1	† 207,308	187,787	177,644	171,913	182,945
Foreign	89a	3,539.5	9,484.9	6,876.2	8,726.3	8,987.6	10,495.0	11,487.3	† 91,070	120,424	129,791	136,880	120,023
General Government						*As Percent of Gross Domestic Product*							
Deficit (-) or Surplus	80g	–4.1	–7.0	–6.3	–7.1	–5.0	–3.2	–2.6	–1.1	–.3	–	....	....
Debt	88g	48.0	60.0	62.6	64.2	68.0	66.7	64.6	63.1	60.4	57.2	....	....
National Accounts					*Billions of Pesetas: through 1998; Billions of Euros Beginning 1999*								
Househ.Cons.Expend.,incl.NPISHs	96f.c	37,277	38,482	40,724	43,554	46,064	48,771	52,072	† 335	359	382	405	430
Government Consumption Expend	91f.c	10,093	10,701	10,963	13,159	13,864	14,415	15,332	† 99	107	115	124	133
Gross Fixed Capital Formation	93e.c	12,889	12,100	12,860	16,015	16,703	17,983	20,054	† 136	155	166	175	190
Changes in Inventories	93i.c	488	10	154	249	216	213	346	† 3	2	2	4	3
Exports of Goods and Services	90c.c	10,420	11,841	14,443	16,465	18,454	21,991	23,936	† 156	184	195	198	208
Imports of Goods and Services (-)	98c.c	12,063	12,180	14,331	16,601	18,055	21,155	23,895	† 163	197	206	208	221
Gross Domestic Product (GDP)	99b.c	59,105	60,953	64,812	72,842	77,245	82,218	87,845	† 565	610	653	696	743
Net Primary Income from Abroad	98.n	–708	–526	–1,182	–607	–890	–1,135	–1,013	† –6	–6	–9	–9	–8
Gross National Income (GNI)	99a	58,397	60,426	63,630	72,660	76,766	81,409	86,780	† 560	603	644	688	735
Net Current Transf.from Abroad	98t	....	....	....	295	197	209	192	† 1	–	–	–	625
Gross Nat'l Disposable Inc.(GNDI)	99i	....	....	....	72,954	76,963	81,618	86,972	† 561	604	644	688	625
Gross Saving	99s	....	....	....	16,241	17,036	18,576	19,816	† 127	137	148	159	62
Consumption of Fixed Capital	99cf	6,452	6,980	7,428	7,951	8,363	8,851	11,430	† 74	83	90	98	–
GDP Volume 1986 Prices	99b.r	40,177	39,710	40,604	41,707	42,715	44,224	45,901	....	....	....	....	....
GDP Volume 1995 Prices	99b.r								80,468	† 507.3	528.7	543.7	554.9	568.3
GDP Volume (2000=100)	99bvr	80.1	79.1	80.9	83.1	85.1	88.1	† 91.5	† 96.0	100.0	102.8	104.9	107.5
GDP Deflator (2000=100)	99bir	72.8	75.9	79.0	86.4	89.4	92.0	94.7	† 96.6	100.0	104.2	108.8	113.4
						Millions: Midyear Estimates							
Population	99z	39.56	39.67	39.80	39.93	40.09	40.26	40.44	40.61	40.75	40.88	40.98	41.06

Sri Lanka 524

		1992	1993	1994	1995	1996	1997	1998	1999	2000	2001	2002	2003
Exchange Rates						*Rupees per SDR: End of Period*							
Market Rate	aa	63.250	68.076	72.963	80.341	81.540	82.689	96.164	99.054	107.594	117.075	131.500	143.750
					Rupees per US Dollar: End of Period (ae) Period Average (rf)								
Market Rate	ae	46.000	49.562	49.980	54.048	56.705	61.285	68.297	72.170	82.580	93.159	96.725	96.738
Market Rate	rf	43.830	48.322	49.415	51.252	55.271	58.995	64.450	70.635	77.005	89.383	95.662	96.521
Fund Position						*Millions of SDRs: End of Period*							
Quota	2f.s	304	304	304	304	304	304	304	413	413	413	413	413
SDRs	1b.s	–	–	–	1	1	–	1	1	–	1	2	–
Reserve Position in the Fund	1c.s	20	20	20	20	20	20	20	48	48	48	48	48
Total Fund Cred.&Loans Outstg	2tl	338	376	423	400	369	321	261	188	123	171	228	265
International Liquidity					*Millions of US Dollars Unless Otherwise Indicated: End of Period*								
Total Reserves minus Gold	1l.d	927	1,629	2,046	2,088	1,962	2,024	1,980	1,636	1,039	1,287	1,631	....
SDRs	1b.d	–	–	–	1	2	–	1	1	–	1	2	1
Reserve Position in the Fund	1c.d	28	28	30	30	29	27	29	65	62	60	65	71
Foreign Exchange	1d.d	899	1,601	2,016	2,057	1,931	1,996	1,950	1,569	976	1,226	1,564	....
Gold (Million Fine Troy Ounces)	1ad	.160	.063	.063	.063	.063	.063	.063	.063	.063	.063	.063	....
Gold (National Valuation)	1and	37	6	6	6	5	5	4	4	4	3	†74	....
Monetary Authorities: Other Liab.	4..d	187	416	505	575	859	820	728	833	707	636	671	....
Deposit Money Banks: Assets	7a.d	504	516	639	839	780	1,103	916	941	1,050	900	795	889
Liabilities	7b.d	464	547	615	1,004	964	1,094	859	764	909	1,009	865	863
FCBU: Assets	7k.d	539	456	540	574	504	682	479	439	429	422	330	424
Liabilities	7m.d	635	601	665	682	615	702	438	306	429	519	330	276
Monetary Authorities						*Millions of Rupees: End of Period*							
Foreign Assets	11	40,387	76,694	95,672	105,898	†104,899	120,675	133,128	116,796	82,334	117,507	160,499	225,879
Claims on Central Government	12a	40,611	26,563	29,335	37,224	37,799	26,776	29,018	49,179	94,708	88,969	83,893	64,387
Claims on Deposit Money Banks	12e	5,506	4,900	3,376	2,812	2,259	1,692	1,122	748	520	150	2,657	2,627
Reserve Money	14	44,868	56,469	68,055	78,587	85,509	83,736	92,866	100,444	105,163	112,522	126,410	141,446
of which: Currency Outside DMBs	14a	27,291	32,134	38,907	42,199	42,565	45,680	51,767	58,481	62,647	65,536	75,292	85,601
Other Liabilities to DMBs	14n	....	....	....	....	....	....	....	....	....	....	11,156	20,974
Foreign Liabilities	16c	19,339	30,969	35,658	40,748	†34,787	33,170	31,355	27,710	24,716	30,190	43,316	61,302
Central Government Deposits	16d	2,666	1,801	2,813	3,040	3,510	6,476	3,108	2,463	3,152	4,301	201	569
Capital Accounts	17a	23,619	22,737	25,358	30,829	28,343	35,547	47,532	49,043	59,866	71,449	72,920	74,331
Other Items (Net)	17r	–3,966	–3,817	–3,500	–7,269	†–7,191	–9,786	–11,594	–12,939	–15,335	–11,838	–6,953	–5,730
Deposit Money Banks						*Millions of Rupees: End of Period*							
Reserves	20	16,289	20,562	25,389	35,449	41,188	36,500	39,667	40,110	39,542	49,760	53,234	51,083
Other Claims on Monetary Author.	20n	....	....	....	....	–	–	–	–	–	–	11,156	20,974
Foreign Assets	21	23,162	25,567	31,918	†45,338	44,212	67,596	62,560	67,946	86,682	83,814	76,921	86,011
Claims on Central Government	22a	13,886	18,782	21,039	†23,808	29,579	42,469	53,514	60,618	69,336	143,109	125,439	129,523
Claims on Nonfin.Pub.Enterprises	22ca	9,010	3,966	3,118	13,305	15,491	14,658	10,836	13,715	38,254	40,811	43,031	36,192
Claims on Cooperatives	22cb	1,739	1,903	2,541	3,939	1,465	1,661	1,812	1,608	1,668	1,577	1,349	1,365
Claims on Private Sector	22d	38,470	49,052	62,676	206,783	228,992	261,359	291,969	323,374	362,435	395,216	452,054	527,079
Demand Deposits	24	22,741	27,169	31,415	32,970	35,516	40,108	44,470	50,059	55,788	56,665	64,052	76,014
Time and Savings Deposits	25	79,741	100,780	121,210	†184,224	210,454	247,817	281,473	319,765	364,944	426,927	483,135	556,220
Foreign Liabilities	26c	21,356	27,119	30,746	54,256	54,678	67,030	58,656	55,141	75,101	94,030	83,655	83,513
Central Government Deposits	26d	9,075	6,304	9,290	†9,483	12,947	13,765	11,646	13,122	13,292	26,333	14,535	16,436
Credit from Monetary Authorities	26g	5,603	5,843	4,054	3,625	4,050	4,775	4,813	5,171	5,886	4,811	4,858	6,577
Capital Accounts	27a	9,868	21,851	28,278	33,460	39,238	44,368	50,220	51,571	51,808	44,520	51,770	75,197
Other Items (Net)	27r	15,552	–932	1,877	10,603	4,045	6,380	9,081	12,543	31,098	61,001	61,180	38,269
Monetary Survey						*Millions of Rupees: End of Period*							
Foreign Assets (Net)	31n	22,854	44,174	61,186	56,232	†59,646	88,070	105,677	101,890	69,198	77,100	110,450	167,074
Domestic Credit	32	154,843	161,686	188,564	273,209	297,517	327,436	372,817	433,115	550,156	639,415	691,082	741,577
Claims on Central Govt. (Net)	32an	42,757	37,240	38,271	†48,509	50,922	49,004	67,778	94,212	147,600	201,444	194,596	176,905
Claims on Nonfin.Pub.Enterprises	32ca	15,032	7,775	5,163	13,305	15,491	14,658	10,836	13,715	38,254	40,811	43,031	36,192
Claims on Cooperatives	32cb	1,739	1,903	2,541	3,939	1,465	1,661	1,812	1,608	1,668	1,577	1,349	1,365
Claims on Private Sector	32d	38,516	49,124	63,453	207,456	229,640	262,113	292,392	323,580	362,634	395,583	452,106	527,116
Money	34	50,068	59,356	70,463	75,218	78,202	85,851	96,269	108,554	118,478	122,211	139,361	161,635
Quasi-Money	35	79,386	100,256	120,539	†184,224	210,454	247,817	281,473	319,765	364,944	426,927	483,135	556,220
Other Items (Net)	37r	45,534	43,722	56,278	68,364	†68,507	81,838	100,753	106,685	135,933	167,378	179,037	190,796
Money plus Quasi-Money	35l	129,442	159,611	191,002	259,442	288,656	333,668	377,741	428,319	483,421	549,138	622,496	717,855
Interest Rates						*Percent Per Annum*							
Bank Rate (End of Period)	60	17.00	17.00	17.00	17.00	17.00	17.00	17.00	16.00	25.00	....	18.00	15.00
Money Market Rate	60b	21.63	25.65	18.54	41.87	24.33	18.42	15.74	16.69	17.30	21.24	12.33	9.68
Treasury Bill Rate	60c	16.19	16.52	12.68	16.81	†17.40	....	12.59	12.51	14.02	17.57	12.47	8.09
Deposit Rate	60l	13.74	13.77	13.10	12.13	12.36	11.25	9.56	9.12	9.17	11.01	9.22	6.00
Lending Rate	60p	19.68	20.20	18.13	18.04	18.26	14.69	15.03	14.72	16.16	19.39	13.17	10.34
Government Bond Yield	61	16.00	16.25	....	....	....	....	....	....	....	....	....	....

Sri Lanka 524

		1992	1993	1994	1995	1996	1997	1998	1999	2000	2001	2002	2003
Prices and Labor						*Index Numbers (2000=100): Period Averages*							
Share Prices	62	147.0	139.9	....	148.8	124.4	135.9	123.7	111.4	100.0	91.6	143.2	203.1
Wholesale Prices	63	58.7	63.1	66.3	72.1	86.9	92.9	98.7	98.3	100.0	111.7	123.7	127.5
Consumer Prices	64	49.6	55.5	60.1	64.8	75.1	82.3	90.0	94.2	100.0	114.2	125.1	133.0
Wages: Agr. Minimum Rates	65	33.7	40.8	41.7	42.1	46.1	49.3	55.7	56.6	100.0	59.7	64.4	70.1
						Number in Thousands: Period Averages							
Labor Force	67d	5,808	6,032	6,079	6,106	6,242	6,266	6,661	6,673	6,827	6,773	7,145	....
Employment	67e	4,962	5,201	5,281	5,357	5,537	5,608	6,049	6,083	6,310	6,236	6,519	....
Unemployment	67c	846	831	798	749	705	658	611	591	517	537	626	....
Unemployment Rate (%)	67r	14.6	13.8	13.1	12.3	11.3	10.5	9.2	8.9	7.6	7.9	8.8	....
International Transactions						*Millions of Rupees*							
Exports	70	107,855	138,175	158,554	195,117	226,801	274,193	310,398	325,171	420,114	430,372	449,850	494,648
Tea	70s	14,893	19,911	20,964	24,638	34,068	42,533	50,280	43,727	53,133	61,602	63,105	68,063
Imports, c.i.f.	71	153,555	193,550	235,576	272,201	301,076	346,026	380,138	421,888	554,290	532,963	584,491	643,767
						2000=100							
Volume of Exports	72	52.9	60.5	66.2	†70.9	73.9	81.7	80.5	83.7	100.0	91.9	92.7	98.3
Tea	72s	63.0	75.8	79.7	83.6	84.7	93.2	94.4	93.4	100.0	102.3	101.2	102.8
Volume of Imports	73	54.1	63.2	71.1	†73.1	73.4	82.5	89.5	89.8	100.0	90.8	100.6	111.3
Unit Value of Exports	74	49.7	54.5	57.2	†65.7	73.3	80.1	92.0	92.3	100.0	111.7	112.7	120.6
Tea	74s	44.5	49.4	49.5	55.5	75.7	85.9	100.3	88.1	100.0	113.3	117.4	124.6
Unit Value of Imports (1995=100)	75	77.6	81.7	86.5	100.0	110.5	114.7	....	....	....	....	....	....
Balance of Payments						*Millions of US Dollars: Minus Sign Indicates Debit*							
Current Account, n.i.e.	78ald	−450.7	−382.2	−757.4	−769.9	−682.7	−394.7	−227.7	−561.3	−1,043.6	−264.8	−289.7	....
Goods: Exports f.o.b.	78aad	2,301.4	2,785.7	3,208.3	3,797.9	4,095.2	4,638.7	4,808.0	4,596.2	5,439.6	4,816.9	4,699.2	....
Goods: Imports f.o.b.	78abd	−3,016.5	−3,527.8	−4,293.4	−4,782.6	−4,895.0	−5,278.3	−5,313.4	−5,365.5	−6,483.6	−5,974.0	−6,105.6	....
Trade Balance	78acd	−715.1	−742.1	−1,085.0	−984.7	−799.7	−639.6	−505.4	−769.3	−1,044.0	−1,157.1	−1,406.5	....
Services: Credit	78add	621.4	634.4	753.9	819.2	765.5	875.3	916.6	964.3	938.7	1,355.5	1,268.3	....
Services: Debit	78aed	−823.2	−874.3	−1,052.1	−1,199.1	−1,204.3	−1,302.6	−1,361.6	−1,413.7	−1,621.4	−1,180.2	−997.0	....
Balance on Goods & Services	78afd	−916.9	−982.1	−1,383.4	−1,364.6	−1,238.6	−1,066.9	−950.5	−1,218.6	−1,726.7	−981.8	−1,135.2	....
Income: Credit	78agd	68.1	111.4	143.9	223.3	175.1	233.3	214.2	166.7	149.0	107.9	75.3	....
Income: Debit	78ahd	−246.2	−234.3	−312.0	−360.6	−378.2	−392.9	−394.5	−419.3	−448.9	−374.6	−326.7	....
Balance on Gds, Serv. & Inc.	78aid	−1,094.9	−1,105.0	−1,551.6	−1,501.9	−1,441.6	−1,226.5	−1,130.8	−1,471.2	−2,026.6	−1,248.5	−1,386.5	....
Current Transfers, n.i.e.: Credit	78ajd	730.4	795.4	882.3	846.7	881.4	966.5	1,054.5	1,078.1	1,165.7	1,155.4	1,287.1	....
Current Transfers: Debit	78akd	−86.1	−72.6	−88.1	−114.7	−122.4	−134.7	−151.3	−168.2	−182.7	−171.7	−190.2	....
Capital Account, n.i.e.	78bcd	−	−	−	120.6	95.9	87.1	79.9	80.0	49.4	49.9	55.4	....
Capital Account, n.i.e.: Credit	78bad	−	−	−	124.2	99.7	91.3	84.6	85.2	55.0	55.2	61.3	....
Capital Account: Debit	78bbd	−	−	−	−3.5	−3.8	−4.2	−4.7	−5.2	−5.7	−5.3	−5.9	....
Financial Account, n.i.e.	78bjd	479.0	1,022.1	958.8	730.1	452.2	466.7	345.1	413.4	447.2	−136.3	−200.2	....
Direct Investment Abroad	78bdd	−1.6	−6.9	−8.3	−	−	−	−	−	−	−	−11.5	....
Dir. Invest. in Rep. Econ., n.i.e.	78bed	122.6	194.5	166.4	56.0	119.9	430.1	193.4	176.4	173.0	171.8	241.5	....
Portfolio Investment Assets	78bfd	25.7	200.1	292.9	105.3	76.8	139.9	88.9	71.8	19.1	....	....	....
Equity Securities	78bkd	....	....	....	....	....	....	....	....	....	....	....	....
Debt Securities	78bld	25.7	200.1	292.9	105.3	76.8	139.9	88.9	71.8	19.1	−	−	....
Portfolio Investment Liab., n.i.e.	78bgd	−	−132.9	−265.9	−107.3	−70.2	−126.8	−112.9	−84.6	−63.4	−11.0	25.4	....
Equity Securities	78bmd	−	....	....	....	....	....	....	....	....	−11.0	25.4	....
Debt Securities	78bnd	−	−132.9	−265.9	−107.3	−70.2	−126.8	−112.9	−84.6	−63.4	−	−	....
Financial Derivatives Assets	78bwd	....	....	....	....	....	....	....	....	....	....	....	....
Financial Derivatives Liabilities	78bxd	....	....	....	....	....	....	....	....	....	....	....	....
Other Investment Assets	78bhd	−100.3	16.4	−134.0	41.7	−27.9	−392.9	75.9	23.2	−243.7	183.0	104.4	....
Monetary Authorities	78bod	....	−	−	....	−	−	....	....	....	....	....	....
General Government	78bpd	3.3	−2.4	9.4	3.6	−6.4	1.7	−2.9	−1.1	−4.4	....	....	....
Banks	78bqd	−103.6	18.8	−143.4	38.1	−21.5	−394.6	78.8	24.3	−239.4	183.0	104.4	....
Other Sectors	78brd	....	....	....	....	....	....	....	....	....	....	....	....
Other Investment Liab., n.i.e.	78bid	432.7	750.9	907.6	634.4	353.6	416.5	99.7	226.6	562.3	−480.0	−560.0	....
Monetary Authorities	78bsd	−22.2	25.9	9.6	14.4	11.6	30.3	17.5	65.8	75.8	−32.9	26.8	....
General Government	78btd	233.3	262.6	246.9	448.4	218.0	144.5	203.6	62.5	46.6	−174.4	−374.5	....
Banks	78bud	108.3	128.2	73.4	86.7	95.8	209.4	−130.7	−88.4	258.3	71.0	−144.5	....
Other Sectors	78bvd	113.3	334.3	577.7	85.0	28.2	32.3	9.3	186.8	181.5	−343.7	−67.8	....
Net Errors and Omissions	78cad	173.3	128.0	106.3	157.9	143.6	148.0	26.3	−27.3	186.2	92.6	103.0	....
Overall Balance	78cbd	201.7	767.9	307.7	238.7	9.0	307.2	223.6	−95.2	−360.8	−258.5	−331.5	....
Reserves and Related Items	79dad	−201.7	−767.9	−307.7	−238.7	−9.0	−307.2	−223.6	95.2	360.8	258.5	331.5	....
Reserve Assets	79dbd	−284.6	−820.7	−373.5	−204.7	36.3	−241.4	−141.0	194.8	446.5	−290.7	−394.4	....
Use of Fund Credit and Loans	79dcd	82.9	52.8	65.9	−34.1	−45.2	−65.7	−82.6	−99.7	−85.7	59.8	74.0	....
Exceptional Financing	79ded	−	−	−	....	−	−	....	....	....	489.4	651.8	....

Sri Lanka 524

		1992	1993	1994	1995	1996	1997	1998	1999	2000	2001	2002	2003
Government Finance						*Millions of Rupees: Year Ending December 31*							
Deficit (-) or Surplus	80	−22,912	−32,084	−49,474	−55,196	−59,913	−40,234	−81,559	−76,359	−118,995	−138,133p	....	....
Revenue	81	85,780	98,495	110,038	136,257	146,280	165,036	175,032	195,905	211,282	231,463p	....	....
Grants Received	81z	8,280	8,025	8,257	9,028	7,739	7,329	7,200	6,761	5,145	5,500p	....	....
Expenditure	82	114,586	134,728	157,476	195,880	212,787	228,732	253,808	267,611	322,048	367,966p	....	....
Lending Minus Repayments	83	2,386	3,876	10,293	4,601	1,145	−16,133	9,983	11,414	13,374	7,130p	....	....
Financing (by Residence of Lender)													
Domestic	84a	15,551	22,229	37,696	33,972	49,753	30,276	71,363	74,875	118,500	123,595p	....	....
Foreign	85a	7,361	9,855	11,778	21,224	10,160	9,958	10,196	1,484	495	14,538p	....	....
Debt: Domestic	88a	170,020	213,685	249,118	285,759	349,007	387,740	463,426	543,465	676,660p	....	....	....
Foreign	89a	235,538	269,883	300,174	346,286	360,313	376,331	461,273	507,866	542,040p	....	....	....
Debt (by Currency)													
Debt: Rupees	88b	170,020	213,685	249,118	285,759	349,007	382,962	446,547	543,465	676,660	815,965p	....	....
Intragovernmental Debt	88s	–	–	–	–	–	–	–	–	–	−p	....	....
Debt: Foreign Currency	89b	235,538	269,883	300,174	346,286	360,313	383,615	461,454	508,396	542,207	634,622p	....	....
National Accounts						*Millions of Rupees*							
Househ.Cons.Expend.,incl.NPISHs	96f	320,466	373,785	434,933	489,057	569,416	643,839	723,506	790,379	906,188	1,041,041	1,214,117	1,343,896
Government Consumption Expend	91f	40,972	45,791	56,002	76,604	81,021	92,196	99,145	99,851	132,189	144,441	139,311	139,268
Gross Fixed Capital Formation	93e	100,039	125,875	154,260	170,875	183,509	216,873	255,714	301,728	352,644	309,684	337,782	392,940
Changes in Inventories	93i	3,200	1,800	2,250	950	2,755	230	175	95	40	40	4,261	2,135
Exports of Goods and Services	90c	135,114	168,858	195,805	237,711	268,640	325,289	368,957	392,437	490,676	525,398	570,995	629,696
Imports of Goods and Services (-)	98c	174,508	216,544	264,166	307,425	337,213	388,154	430,111	478,526	624,048	613,167	679,550	745,520
Gross Domestic Product (GDP)	99b	425,283	499,565	579,084	667,772	768,133	890,272	1,017,986	1,105,985	1,257,682	1,407,398	1,582,655	1,760,280
Net Primary Income from Abroad	98.n	−7,820	−5,979	−8,310	−6,958	−11,258	−9,409	−11,556	−17,831	−23,083	−23,830	−25,159	−18,821
GDP at Factor Cost	99ba	386,999	453,092	523,300	598,327	695,934	803,698	912,839	994,730	1,125,259	1,245,598	1,403,310	1,560,806
Gross National Income (GNI)	99a	417,463	493,586	570,774	660,814	756,875	880,828	1,006,373	1,088,154	1,234,599	1,383,568	1,557,496	1,741,459
GDP at Fact.Cost,Vol.'82 Prices	99bap	140,990	150,783	159,269	167,953	174,261	....	....	....	....	....	....	....
GDP at Fact.Cost,Vol.'96 Prices	99bap	....	....	....	....	695,934	739,763	774,796	808,340	857,035	843,794	877,248	929,038
GDP Volume (2000=100)	99bvp	65.7	70.3	74.2	78.3	†81.2	86.3	90.4	94.3	100.0	98.5	102.4	108.4
GDP Deflator (2000=100)	99bip	52.3	57.3	62.7	67.9	76.2	82.7	89.7	93.7	100.0	112.4	121.8	128.0
						Millions: Midyear Estimates							
Population	99z	17.24	17.43	17.61	17.78	17.95	18.12	18.28	18.44	18.59	18.75	18.91	19.07

Sudan 732

		1992	1993	1994	1995	1996	1997	1998	1999	2000	2001	2002	2003
Exchange Rates						*Dinars per SDR: End of Period*							
Market Rate	aa	18.58	29.86	58.39	78.24	208.40	232.35	334.83	353.70	335.30	328.55	355.76	386.59
					Dinars per US Dollar: End of Period (ae) Period Average (rf)								
Market Rate	ae	13.51	21.74	40.00	52.63	144.93	172.21	237.80	257.70	257.35	261.43	261.68	260.16
Market Rate	rf	9.74	15.93	28.96	58.09	125.08	157.57	200.80	252.55	257.12	258.70	263.31	260.98
Fund Position						*Millions of SDRs: End of Period*							
Quota	2f.s	169.7	169.7	169.7	169.7	169.7	169.7	169.7	169.7	169.7	169.7	169.7	169.7
SDRs	1b.s	–	–	–	–	–	–	–	–	–	–	.1	.2
Reserve Position in the Fund	1c.s	–	–	–	–	–	–	–	–	–	–	–	–
Total Fund Cred.&Loans Outstg.	2tl	671.6	671.6	671.6	645.7	621.2	590.5	548.4	520.8	479.7	438.6	421.6	402.9
International Liquidity					*Millions of US Dollars Unless Otherwise Indicated: End of Period*								
Total Reserves minus Gold	1l.d	27.5	37.4	78.2	163.4	106.8	81.6	90.6	188.7	†247.3	117.8	440.9	847.5
SDRs	1b.d	–	–	–	–	–	–	–	–	–	–	.2	.3
Reserve Position in the Fund	1c.d	–	–	–	–	–	–	–	–	–	–	–	–
Foreign Exchange	1d.d	27.5	37.4	78.1	163.3	106.8	81.6	90.6	188.7	†247.3	117.8	440.7	847.2
Monetary Authorities: Other Liab.	4..d	2,165.8	2,288.0	2,471.8	3,407.1	2,549.9	2,464.4	2,538.9	2,618.8	2,640.2	2,654.1	2,793.2	3,005.8
Deposit Money Banks: Assets	7a.d	32.2	44.8	27.0	32.1	20.7	25.8	26.9	266.1	286.2	343.2	488.8	500.7
Liabilities	7b.d	7.0	6.9	3.8	5.3	3.0	2.6	2.0	13.4	14.8	34.8	52.4	56.9
Monetary Authorities						*Billions of Dinars: End of Period*							
Foreign Assets	11	†.37	.82	3.13	8.61	15.50	14.07	21.58	48.64	†73.11	41.25	119.85	229.81
Claims on Central Government	12a	†10.80	16.52	22.03	32.90	76.03	84.76	101.77	134.79	†168.95	195.46	230.35	277.93
of which:Accum. Interest Arrears.	12ag	....	....	....	....	....	....	....	....	52.69	64.09	76.09	88.68
Claims on Nonfin.Pub.Enterprises	12c	†.24	.22	.22	.22	.22	.22	.22	3.45	†17.14	14.81	5.74	17.34
Claims on Deposit Money Banks	12e	†.07	.52	.36	.36	.35	2.39	6.14	7.21	†8.82	12.58	17.15	33.49
Reserve Money	14	†8.78	14.45	20.21	35.72	64.94	87.18	112.81	152.42	†223.58	233.59	283.30	360.59
of which: Currency Outside DMBs	14a	†4.35	9.45	14.79	24.86	44.44	58.49	82.14	108.11	†142.08	153.84	193.58	240.21
Quasi-Monetary Deposits	15	†.62	.63	2.08	3.21	3.24	3.06	3.34	3.21	–	–	–	–
Cent. Bk. Liab.: Musharaka Certif.	16ac	....	....	....	....	....	....	4.85	4.20	†1.11	.64	.76	2.75
Foreign Liabilities	16c	†40.50	67.78	134.16	224.80	485.58	547.81	767.53	838.10	†820.43	818.50	859.84	914.84
Central Government Deposits	16d	†1.22	.91	.86	1.24	10.77	9.18	3.74	5.11	†8.44	9.62	27.27	64.78
Capital Accounts	17a	†.04	.13	.24	.43	1.24	1.16	2.05	2.61	†4.24	4.32	9.11	13.16
Valuation Adjustment	17rv	†–39.22	–63.09	–124.94	–206.55	–444.81	–514.97	–724.21	–772.02	†–776.69	–781.52	–783.05	–774.95
Other Items (Net)	17r	†–.45	–2.73	–6.88	–16.78	–28.85	–31.99	–40.39	–39.53	†–13.09	–21.04	–24.15	–22.62
Deposit Money Banks						*Billions of Dinars: End of Period*							
Reserves	20	†3.73	4.62	5.58	8.01	14.27	28.07	30.62	37.91	57.15	57.41	67.68	91.01
Claims on Mon.Author.:Securities	20c	....	....	....	....	....	....	4.85	4.20	1.11	.64	.76	2.75
Foreign Assets	21	†4.35	9.73	10.80	16.87	29.98	44.50	63.92	68.57	73.66	89.73	127.92	130.27
Claims on Central Government	22a	†.01	.45	.21	.16	.12	.03	.13	.16	4.22	7.33	20.88	35.04
Claims on State and Local Govt.	22b	–	.07	.03	.13	.16	.17	.05	.07	.01	.53	1.33	1.28
Claims on Nonfin.Pub.Enterprises	22c	.57	.70	1.22	1.19	1.67	1.68	2.57	4.72	5.65	9.06	11.56	11.30
Claims on Private Sector	22d	†2.67	4.51	8.82	13.07	31.90	39.35	44.34	43.58	71.48	101.14	178.43	279.63
Claims on Nonbank Financial Insts.	22f	.05	.08	.09	.12	.22	.36	.43	.35	2.09	.62	1.89	2.46
Demand Deposits	24	†4.57	6.25	9.49	15.60	30.92	41.35	46.94	56.90	84.13	109.14	147.46	194.63
Time and Savings Deposits	25	†3.44	10.13	13.65	25.41	35.82	55.13	73.62	85.35	107.26	158.54	210.53	271.88
Foreign Liabilities	26c	†.95	1.50	1.51	2.81	4.30	4.41	4.72	3.44	3.81	9.11	13.72	14.79
Central Government Deposits	26d	†.21	.26	.23	.31	.77	.40	.42	3.53	6.35	7.08	5.09	6.44
Credit from Monetary Authorities	26g	†.01	.07	.10	.75	.08	.11	.32	3.01	2.51	2.51	7.26	14.91
Capital Accounts	27a	†.63	1.69	3.86	5.47	11.14	14.77	20.34	24.47	32.20	47.64	73.69	110.31
Valuation Adjustment	27rv	†1.21	1.07	.70	1.08	1.39	2.81	2.36	–.39	–.78	–.17	–.69	–.40
Other Items (Net)	27r	†–.19	–1.58	–4.07	–13.51	–8.21	–6.53	–.93	–16.47	–19.62	–66.83	–46.63	–58.72
Monetary Survey						*Billions of Dinars: End of Period*							
Foreign Assets (Net)	31n	†–36.72	–58.73	–121.73	–202.14	–444.40	–493.66	–686.75	–724.34	†–677.49	–696.62	–625.80	–569.55
Domestic Credit	32	†12.92	21.36	31.52	46.24	98.78	116.99	145.34	178.50	†254.74	312.25	417.81	553.76
Claims on Central Govt. (Net)	32an	†9.39	15.79	21.14	31.51	64.61	75.22	97.74	126.32	†158.38	186.10	218.87	241.74
Claims on State and Local Govt.	32b	–	.07	.03	.13	.16	.17	.05	.07	.01	.53	1.33	1.28
Claims on Nonfin.Pub.Enterprises	32c	†.81	.92	1.44	1.41	1.88	1.89	2.78	8.18	†22.79	23.87	17.30	28.64
Claims on Private Sector	32d	†2.67	4.51	8.82	13.07	31.90	39.35	44.34	43.58	71.48	101.14	178.43	279.63
Claims on Nonbank Financial Inst.	32f	†.05	.08	.09	.12	.22	.36	.43	.35	2.09	.62	1.89	2.46
Money	34	†8.92	15.70	24.28	40.46	75.36	99.85	129.08	165.01	†234.59	271.39	352.26	458.48
Quasi-Money	35	†4.06	10.76	15.73	28.62	39.06	58.20	76.95	88.56	†112.60	161.39	211.00	275.61
Valuation Adjustment	37rv	†–38.01	–62.02	–124.24	–205.47	–443.42	–512.15	–721.85	–772.41	†–777.47	–781.68	–783.73	–775.35
Other Items (Net)	37r	†.25	–1.81	–6.00	–19.82	–16.90	–22.41	–24.72	–26.73	†8.06	–34.90	12.48	25.56
Money plus Quasi-Money	35l	†12.98	26.47	40.04	69.39	114.70	157.90	205.16	253.31	347.19	432.77	563.27	734.09
Prices and Labor					*Index Numbers (2000=100): Period Averages*								
Consumer Prices	64	2.8	5.6	12.1	20.4	47.5	69.7	81.6	†94.6	100.0	105.8	....	....
					Number in Thousands: Period Averages								
Labor Force	67d	....	5,841	....	....	7,415	....	....	....	....	....	....	....

2004, International Monetary Fund: *International Financial Statistics Yearbook*

Sudan 732

		1992	1993	1994	1995	1996	1997	1998	1999	2000	2001	2002	2003
International Transactions		\multicolumn{12}{c}{*Millions of US Dollars: Year Ending June 30 through 1994, Year Ending December 31 Thereafter*}
Exports	70..d	319.3	417.3	502.6	555.6	620.3	594.2	595.8	780.0	1,806.7	1,698.7	....	....
Imports, c.i.f.	71..d	820.9	944.9	1,227.4	†1,218.8	1,547.5	1,579.6	1,914.7	1,415.0	1,552.7	1,585.5	....	....
Balance of Payments		\multicolumn{12}{c}{*Millions of US Dollars: Minus Sign Indicates Debit*}
Current Account, n.i.e.	78ald	−506.2	−202.2	−601.7	−499.9	−826.8	−828.1	−956.5	−464.8	−556.8	−618.3	−1,008.1	−726.5
Goods: Exports f.o.b.	78aad	213.4	306.3	523.9	555.7	620.3	594.2	595.7	780.1	1,806.7	1,698.7	1,949.1	2,354.6
Goods: Imports f.o.b.	78abd	−810.2	−532.8	−1,045.4	−1,066.0	−1,339.5	−1,421.9	−1,732.2	−1,256.0	−1,366.3	−1,395.1	−2,293.8	−2,651.2
Trade Balance	78acd	−596.8	−226.5	−521.5	−510.3	−719.2	−827.7	−1,136.5	−475.9	440.4	303.6	−344.7	−296.6
Services: Credit	78add	155.5	69.4	76.2	125.3	50.7	31.5	15.8	81.6	27.4	14.6	132.2	136.9
Services: Debit	78aed	−204.1	−109.8	−223.7	−172.3	−200.8	−172.8	−204.0	−274.9	−647.6	−660.3	−818.2	−686.2
Balance on Goods & Services	78afd	−645.4	−266.9	−669.0	−557.3	−869.3	−969.0	−1,324.7	−669.2	−179.8	−342.1	−1,030.7	−845.9
Income: Credit	78agd	−	.7	1.6	1.9	6.3	16.9	13.7	19.1	4.6	17.8	29.2	10.0
Income: Debit	78ahd	−93.5	−20.9	−15.9	−4.9	−.7	−5.3	−10.6	−123.2	−579.6	−571.9	−638.0	−592.3
Balance on Gds, Serv. & Inc.	78aid	−738.9	−287.1	−683.3	−560.3	−863.7	−957.4	−1,321.6	−773.3	−754.8	−896.2	−1,639.5	−1,428.1
Current Transfers, n.i.e.: Credit	78ajd	232.7	84.9	120.1	346.2	236.3	439.1	731.8	702.2	651.3	730.4	1,085.9	1,218.4
Current Transfers: Debit	78akd	−	−	−38.5	−285.8	−199.4	−309.8	−366.7	−393.7	−453.3	−452.5	−454.5	−516.8
Capital Account, n.i.e.	78bcd	....	....	....	....	....	....	−54.2	−22.9	−119.3	−93.3	−	−
Capital Account, n.i.e.: Credit	78bad	−	....	....	....	....	....	13.0	45.8	16.5	11.9	−	−
Capital Account: Debit	78bbd	−	....	....	....	....	....	−67.2	−68.7	−135.8	−105.2	−	−
Financial Account, n.i.e.	78bjd	316.4	326.6	276.0	473.7	136.8	195.0	333.4	435.3	431.6	561.2	761.2	1,319.2
Direct Investment Abroad	78bdd	−	....	....	−	....	....	....	−	−	....	....	....
Dir. Invest. in Rep. Econ., n.i.e.	78bed	−	....	....	−	.4	97.9	370.7	370.8	392.2	574.0	713.2	1,349.2
Portfolio Investment Assets	78bfd	−	....	....	−	....	....	−	−	−	.7	14.8	35.3
Equity Securities	78bkd	−	....	....	−	....	....	−	−	−	....	....	35.3
Debt Securities	78bld	−	....	....	−	....	....	−	−	−	.7	14.8	−
Portfolio Investment Liab., n.i.e.	78bgd	−	−	−	−	....	....	−	−	−	−	−	−
Equity Securities	78bmd	−	−	−	−	....	....	−	−	−	−	−	−
Debt Securities	78bnd	−	−	−	−	....	....	−	−	−	....	....	....
Financial Derivatives Assets	78bwd	....	....	....	....	....	....	....	....	....	....	....	....
Financial Derivatives Liabilities	78bxd	....	....	....	....	....	....	....	....	....	....	....	....
Other Investment Assets	78bhd	−82.8	....	....	....	....	....	−78.5	−38.4	−53.4	−55.1	−148.0	296.5
Monetary Authorities	78bod	....	....	....	....	....	....	....	....	....	....	....	....
General Government	78bpd	−	....	....	....	....	....	....	....	....	....	−	56.8
Banks	78bqd	−82.8	....	....	....	....	....	−78.5	−38.4	−53.4	−55.1	−145.6	−9.0
Other Sectors	78brd	−	....	....	....	....	....	−	−	−	−	−2.4	248.9
Other Investment Liab., n.i.e.	78bid	399.2	326.6	276.0	473.7	136.4	97.1	41.2	102.9	92.8	41.6	181.2	−361.7
Monetary Authorities	78bsd	110.4	163.3	28.3	73.6	62.4	20.1	8.0	−3.7	14.0	40.6	64.2	119.8
General Government	78btd	268.5	200.8	−3.1	9.8	−22.5	−45.1	−1.0	−	−	−	−87.8	−262.2
Banks	78bud	20.3	−37.5	250.8	390.3	96.2	119.3	34.2	106.6	78.8	1.0	204.8	4.1
Other Sectors	78bvd	−	....	....	....	.3	2.8	−	−	−	−	....	−223.4
Net Errors and Omissions	78cad	31.0	−82.6	344.8	89.3	727.5	651.2	750.5	167.2	368.4	−.5	492.2	−231.0
Overall Balance	78cbd	−158.8	41.8	19.1	63.1	37.5	18.1	73.2	114.8	123.9	−150.9	245.3	361.7
Reserves and Related Items	79dad	158.8	−41.8	−19.1	−63.1	−37.5	−18.1	−73.2	−114.8	−123.9	150.9	−245.3	−361.7
Reserve Assets	79dbd	29.3	−41.8	−19.1	−23.6	−2.0	24.0	−16.0	−110.0	−108.0	127.6	−300.2	−422.7
Use of Fund Credit and Loans	79dcd	−	−	−	−39.5	−35.5	−42.1	−57.2	−37.8	−54.0	−52.3	−22.3	−26.3
Exceptional Financing	79ded	129.5	−	−	....	....	....	....	33.0	38.1	75.6	77.2	87.3
Government Finance		\multicolumn{12}{c}{*Millions of Dinars: Year Ending December 31*}
Deficit (−) or Surplus	80	−5	−7	−9	†−13,500	−34,600	−13,400	....	....	....	....	....	....
Revenue	81	4	8	13	†36,500	62,900	107,300	....	....	....	....	....	....
Grants Received	81z	−	−	−	†−	−	−	....	....	....	....	....	....
Expenditure	82	8	15	22	†50,000	97,500	120,700	....	....	....	....	....	....
Lending Minus Repayments	83	−	−	−	†−	−	−	....	....	....	....	....	....
Financing													
Domestic	84a	3	4	7	†9,300	32,400	10,800	....	....	....	....	....	....
Foreign	85a	1	3	2	†4,200	2,200	2,600	....	....	....	....	....	....
National Accounts		\multicolumn{12}{c}{*Billions of Dinars: Yr.End.June 30 through '94, December 31 Thereafter*}
Gross Domestic Product (GDP)	99b	41	84	168	†483	1,022	1,601	....	....	....	....	....	....
		\multicolumn{12}{c}{*Millions: Midyear Estimates*}
Population	99z	26.11	26.75	27.41	Ü 28.08	28.74	29.40	30.06	30.74	31.44	32.15	32.88	33.61

Suriname 366

		1992	1993	1994	1995	1996	1997	1998	1999	2000	2001	2002	2003
Exchange Rates		\multicolumn{12}{c}{*Surinamese Dollars per SDR: End of Period*}
Market Rate	aa	.0025	.0025	†.5978	.6050	.5766	.5410	.5646	1.3554	2.8384	2.7378	3.4192	†3.9007
		\multicolumn{12}{c}{*Surinamese Dollars per US Dollar: End of Period (ae) Period Average (rf)*}
Market Rate	ae	.0018	.0018	†.4095	.4070	.4010	.4010	.4010	.9875	2.1785	2.1785	2.5150	†2.6250
Market Rate	rf	.0018	.0018	†.1341	.4422	.4013	.4010	.4010	.8594	1.3225	2.1785	2.3468	†2.6013
Fund Position		\multicolumn{12}{c}{*Millions of SDRs: End of Period*}
Quota	2f.s	49.30	67.60	67.60	67.60	67.60	67.60	67.60	92.10	92.10	92.10	92.10	92.10
SDRs	1b.s	–	–	–	7.75	8.22	8.23	8.25	2.00	1.77	1.56	1.42	1.32
Reserve Position in the Fund	1c.s	–	–	–	–	–	–	–	6.13	6.13	6.13	6.13	6.12
Total Fund Cred.&Loans Outstg.	2tl	–	–	–	–	–	–	–	–	–	–	–	–
International Liquidity		\multicolumn{12}{c}{*Millions of US Dollars Unless Otherwise Indicated: End of Period*}
Total Reserves minus Gold	1l.d	17.30	17.70	39.70	132.92	96.32	109.11	106.14	38.46	62.99	119.25	106.16	105.76
SDRs	1b.d	–	–	–	11.52	11.82	11.11	11.62	2.75	2.31	1.95	1.93	1.96
Reserve Position in the Fund	1c.d	–	–	–	–	–	–	–	8.41	7.98	7.70	8.33	9.10
Foreign Exchange	1d.d	17.30	17.70	39.70	121.40	84.50	98.00	94.52	27.30	52.70	109.60	95.90	94.70
Gold (Million Fine Troy Ounces)	1ad	.054	.054	.054	.093	.134	.193	.128	.246	.256	.265	.021	.021
Gold (National Valuation)	1and	16.21	841.67	14.32	41.34	58.18	54.53	177.34	70.29	64.39	68.48	6.13	7.20
Monetary Authorities: Other Liab.	4..d	46.80	1,316.25	18.08	3.25	3.03	74.81	229.66	111.10	103.74	77.92	1.05	.84
Deposit Money Banks: Assets	7a.d	20.20	1,093.52	49.67	68.84	116.40	128.94	122.43	180.59	131.02	188.33	142.10	194.35
Liabilities	7b.d	89.01	374.71	28.62	45.71	75.09	86.00	96.29	160.52	128.08	181.12	5.36	8.62
Monetary Authorities		\multicolumn{12}{c}{*Thousands of Surinamese Dollars: End of Period*}
Foreign Assets	11	65	3,277	23,546	65,538	56,984	60,615	†127,893	123,498	253,498	386,507	257,282	266,374
Claims on Central Government	12a	3,512	5,224	5,307	4,909	6,768	6,376	†38,602	101,982	287,462	57,158	263,098	281,471
Claims on Nonfin.Pub.Enterprises	12c	....	....	....	....	....	....	4,052	3,783	6,564	1,293	1,523	1,450
Claims on Private Sector	12d	1	2	9	31	69	246	†1,669	4,018	5,677	12,886	8,573	7,318
Claims on Deposit Money Banks	12e	2	4	13	–	26	13,414	†19,077	38,249	43,064	44,884	21,721	22,838
Claims on Other Banking Insts.	12f	....	....	....	....	....	....	218	511	623	719	783	671
Reserve Money	14	3,317	5,640	17,361	56,775	50,953	50,740	†83,480	147,142	337,510	382,815	471,690	432,727
of which: Currency Outside DMBs	14a	1,347	2,638	10,486	25,199	27,404	32,256	†50,478	81,686	150,657	182,476	†203,804	209,008
Time & Fgn. Currency Deposits	15	2	–	–	–	–	–	†192	232	1,442	1,082	1,380	1,436
Foreign Liabilities	16c	84	2,349	7,403	1,321	1,214	29,997	†92,093	109,711	225,998	169,753	2,647	2,193
Central Government Deposits	16d	15	29	844	9,900	9,076	3,021	†8,317	22,493	60,746	45,963	55,730	83,121
Capital Accounts	17a	54	54	4,668	4,723	4,589	4,420	†13,191	29,404	19,905	–45,195	41,635	87,863
Other Items (Net)	17r	108	434	–1,401	–2,240	–1,985	–7,529	†–5,582	–12,606	–24,367	–26,626	–20,102	–27,217
Deposit Money Banks		\multicolumn{12}{c}{*Thousands of Surinamese Dollars: End of Period*}
Reserves	20	1,914	2,873	6,242	29,584	19,142	18,531	31,462	32,392	122,759	124,630	†220,338	228,082
Foreign Assets	21	36	1,952	20,341	28,016	46,675	51,705	49,095	178,333	285,419	410,276	†357,389	510,166
Claims on Central Government	22a	225	266	392	567	913	8,639	20,814	23,594	64,030	95,884	†98,779	99,032
Claims on Nonfin.Pub.Enterprises	22c	–	–	–	–	–	–	–	–	–	–	†1,944	10,821
Claims on Private Sector	22d	2,464	3,133	6,645	20,120	45,486	63,383	79,103	106,703	93,296	147,134	†401,942	566,365
Claims on Nonbank Financial Insts.	22g	–	–	–	–	–	–	–	–	–	–	†26	3,251
Demand Deposits	24	1,818	3,276	9,763	30,912	25,156	35,476	39,929	51,367	111,010	175,972	†279,407	324,681
Quasi-Monetary Liabilities	25	2,344	3,179	7,218	20,995	52,609	61,973	87,578	108,151	160,966	178,435	†696,805	921,143
Bonds	26ab	23	104	153	357	256	226	28	21	13	5	†–	–
Foreign Liabilities	26c	159	669	11,721	18,603	30,113	34,486	38,612	158,517	279,029	394,561	†13,475	22,635
Central Government Deposits	26d	25	103	956	1,273	371	885	167	542	525	840	†720	1,230
Credit from Monetary Authorities	26g	2	4	13	–	26	14,197	15,726	34,170	38,124	39,510	†16,508	54,110
Capital Accounts	27a	377	611	2,852	5,263	8,732	11,681	12,516	20,933	29,669	73,054	†75,037	82,159
Other Items (Net)	27r	–108	279	945	885	–5,048	–16,666	–14,082	–32,678	–53,833	–84,453	†–1,535	11,758
Monetary Survey		\multicolumn{12}{c}{*Thousands of Surinamese Dollars: End of Period*}
Foreign Assets (Net)	31n	–141	2,210	24,763	73,630	72,332	47,837	†46,283	33,603	33,889	232,469	†598,549	751,712
Domestic Credit	32	6,162	8,493	10,554	14,456	43,789	74,737	†135,975	217,555	396,382	268,272	†720,218	886,027
Claims on Central Govt. (Net)	32an	3,696	5,358	3,900	–5,696	–1,767	11,109	†50,932	102,541	290,222	106,240	†305,427	296,151
Claims on Nonfin.Pub.Enterprises	32c	–	–	–	–	–	–	†4,052	3,783	6,564	1,293	†3,467	12,271
Claims on Private Sector	32d	2,465	3,135	6,654	20,152	45,556	63,628	†80,773	110,720	98,973	160,020	†410,515	573,683
Claims on Other Banking Insts.	32f	–	–	–	–	–	–	†218	511	623	719	†783	671
Claims on Nonbank Financial Insts.	32g	–	–	–	–	–	–	†–	–	–	–	†26	3,251
Money	34	3,221	6,043	20,883	58,103	56,967	68,468	†92,428	164,115	309,941	418,962	†546,199	569,069
Quasi-Money	35	2,346	3,179	7,218	20,995	52,609	61,973	†87,770	108,383	162,409	179,517	†698,185	922,580
Bonds	36ab	23	104	153	357	256	226	†28	21	13	5	†–	–
Capital Accounts	37a	430	664	7,520	9,986	13,321	16,101	†25,706	50,337	49,574	27,860	†116,672	170,022
Other Items (Net)	37r	–	712	–456	–1,355	–7,033	–24,194	†–23,496	–47,361	–67,321	–101,257	†–42,289	–23,931
Money plus Quasi-Money	35l	5,567	9,222	28,101	79,098	109,576	130,442	†180,199	272,499	472,350	598,479	†1,244,384	1,491,648
Money (National Definitions)		\multicolumn{12}{c}{*Thousands of Surinamese Dollars: End of Period*}
M1	59ma	....	....	....	....	....	....	....	135,548	267,357	384,688	538,388	547,094
M2	59mb	....	....	....	....	....	....	....	159,755	306,019	426,711	596,375	621,610
M3	59mc	....	....	....	....	....	....	....	246,765	439,331	572,391	768,440	795,829

2004, International Monetary Fund : *International Financial Statistics Yearbook*

Suriname 366

		1992	1993	1994	1995	1996	1997	1998	1999	2000	2001	2002	2003
Interest Rates		\multicolumn{12}{c}{*Percent per Annum*}
Deposit Rate	60l	4.50	4.75	7.45	21.00	17.83	17.25	16.00	15.60	15.48	11.86	9.00	8.28
Lending Rate	60p	8.93	9.35	15.38	40.18	35.78	33.13	27.50	27.33	28.95	25.73	22.18	21.04
Prices and Labor		\multicolumn{12}{c}{*Index Numbers (2000=100): Period Averages*}
Consumer Prices	64	.7	1.6	7.4	24.9	24.7	26.5	31.5	†62.7	100.0	138.6	160.1	196.9
		\multicolumn{12}{c}{*Number in Thousands: Period Averages*}
Labor Force	67d	107	92	90	90	....	....	....	86	....	....	....	....
Employment	67e	89	83	78	82	87	83	88	73	....	....	....	....
Unemployment	67c	18	14	11	8	11	10	10	12	....	....	....	....
Unemployment Rate (%)	67r	17.2	14.7	12.7	8.4	11.0	....	....	....	....	....	....	....
International Transactions		\multicolumn{12}{c}{*Millions of Surinamese Dollars*}
Exports	70	.7	2.1	60.2	211.0	215.2	226.4	204.0	398.7	668.2	877.8	1,101.7	1,658.8
Imports, c.i.f.	71	1.0	1.8	56.7	258.9	200.8	227.2	221.4	485.1	685.1	1,003.2	1,154.6	1,830.4
Balance of Payments		\multicolumn{12}{c}{*Millions of US Dollars: Minus Sign Indicates Debit*}
Current Account, n.i.e.	78ald	25.4	44.0	58.6	73.4	−63.5	−67.7	−154.9	−29.1	32.3	−83.6	−131.0	−159.0
Goods: Exports f.o.b.	78aad	608.6	298.3	293.6	415.6	397.2	401.6	349.7	342.0	399.1	437.0	369.3	487.8
Goods: Imports f.o.b.	78abd	−486.5	−213.9	−194.3	−292.6	−398.8	−365.5	−376.9	−297.9	−246.1	−297.2	−321.9	−458.0
Trade Balance	78acd	122.1	84.4	99.3	123.0	−1.6	36.1	−27.2	44.1	153.0	139.8	47.4	29.8
Services: Credit	78add	40.4	46.5	72.6	104.1	103.8	91.6	72.0	79.1	90.9	59.4	38.5	59.0
Services: Debit	78aed	−176.1	−101.6	−113.5	−161.4	−169.5	−193.8	−196.9	−151.1	−215.5	−174.3	−166.1	−194.6
Balance on Goods & Services	78afd	−13.6	29.3	58.4	65.7	−67.3	−66.1	−152.1	−27.9	28.4	24.9	−80.2	−105.8
Income: Credit	78agd	1.3	.2	.9	2.7	7.0	7.4	6.5	7.9	13.2	5.4	8.4	11.7
Income: Debit	78ahd	−14.6	−6.4	−4.7	−5.3	−4.3	−10.0	−7.0	−7.6	−7.2	−113.0	−50.7	−60.2
Balance on Gds, Serv. & Inc.	78aid	−26.9	23.1	54.6	63.1	−64.6	−68.7	−152.6	−27.6	34.4	−82.7	−122.5	−154.3
Current Transfers, n.i.e.: Credit	78ajd	67.7	26.7	6.2	12.6	3.6	4.0	1.3	1.8	1.2	2.1	12.9	24.8
Current Transfers: Debit	78akd	−15.4	−5.8	−2.2	−2.3	−2.5	−3.0	−3.6	−3.3	−3.3	−3.0	−21.4	−29.5
Capital Account, n.i.e.	78bcd	−5.7	.5	−.2	22.1	41.6	14.6	6.6	3.5	2.3	1.5	5.9	9.0
Capital Account, n.i.e.: Credit	78bad	4.6	3.5	.2	22.1	41.6	14.6	6.6	3.5	2.3	1.5	5.9	9.2
Capital Account: Debit	78bbd	−10.3	−3.0	−.4	−	−	−	−	−	−	−	−	−.2
Financial Account, n.i.e.	78bjd	−86.6	−73.1	−84.1	−29.5	27.7	26.9	30.5	−21.6	−139.1	104.1	−38.1	−36.5
Direct Investment Abroad	78bdd	−	−	−	−	−	−	....	....	....	....	−	−
Dir. Invest. in Rep. Econ., n.i.e.	78bed	−54.3	−46.6	−30.2	−20.6	19.1	−9.2	9.1	−61.5	−148.0	−26.8	−73.6	−76.1
Portfolio Investment Assets	78bfd	−	−	−	−	−	−	....	....	....	....	−	−
Equity Securities	78bkd	−	−	−	−	−	−	−	−	−	−	−	−
Debt Securities	78bld	−	−	−	−	−	−	....	....	....	....	−	−
Portfolio Investment Liab., n.i.e.	78bgd	2.6	−	−	−	−	−	−	−	−	−	−	−
Equity Securities	78bmd	−	−	−	−	−	−	−	−	−	−	−	−
Debt Securities	78bnd	2.6	−	−	−	−	−	−	−	−	−	−	−
Financial Derivatives Assets	78bwd	....	....	....	....	....	....	....	....	....	....	....	....
Financial Derivatives Liabilities	78bxd	....	....	....	....	....	....	....	....	....	....	....	....
Other Investment Assets	78bhd	−.1	−4.4	−19.1	3.2	25.5	15.2	18.6	27.1	24.6	40.7	23.9	46.9
Monetary Authorities	78bod	....	....	....	....	....	....	....	....	....	....	....	....
General Government	78bpd	−	−	−	−	−	−	....	....	....	....	−	−
Banks	78bqd	−6.6	−14.5	−31.3	−10.0	−	−	−	−	−	−	−	−
Other Sectors	78brd	6.5	10.1	12.2	13.2	25.5	15.2	18.6	27.1	24.6	40.7	23.9	46.9
Other Investment Liab., n.i.e.	78bid	−34.8	−22.1	−34.8	−12.1	−16.9	20.9	2.8	12.8	−15.7	90.2	11.6	−7.3
Monetary Authorities	78bsd	.6	−	−	−	−	−	−	−	−	1.6	−.9	4.3
General Government	78btd	10.6	2.0	2.1	4.2	−15.0	1.3	19.3	16.1	−21.4	50.7	−30.8	−23.0
Banks	78bud	−41.8	−23.7	−29.6	−10.1	−	−	−	−	−	−.8	6.4	−9.1
Other Sectors	78bvd	−4.2	−.4	−7.3	−6.2	−1.9	19.6	−16.5	−3.3	5.7	38.7	36.9	20.5
Net Errors and Omissions	78cad	45.4	41.3	60.0	56.6	−7.5	45.3	125.9	42.8	114.3	56.1	144.1	193.7
Overall Balance	78cbd	−21.5	12.7	34.3	122.6	−1.7	19.1	8.1	−4.4	9.8	78.1	−19.1	7.2
Reserves and Related Items	79dad	21.5	−12.7	−34.3	−122.6	1.7	−19.1	−8.1	4.4	−9.8	−78.1	19.1	−7.2
Reserve Assets	79dbd	21.5	−12.7	−34.3	−122.6	1.7	−19.1	−8.1	4.4	−9.8	−78.1	19.1	−7.2
Use of Fund Credit and Loans	79dcd	−	−	−	−	−	−	−	−	−	−	−	−
Exceptional Financing	79ded	....	....	....	....	....	....	....	....	....	....	−	−
National Accounts		\multicolumn{12}{c}{*Millions of Surinamese Dollars*}
House.Cons.Expend.,incl.NPISHs	96f	3	3	18	37	162	213	....	....	....	....	....	....
Government Consumption Expend.	91f	1	2	7	45	48	51	....	....	....	....	....	....
Gross Capital Formation	93	1	3	28	119	116	127	....	....	....	....	....	....
Exports of Goods and Services	90c	1	15	76	229	199	195	....	....	....	....	....	....
Imports of Goods and Services (-)	98c	1	12	64	201	226	224	....	....	....	....	....	....
Gross Domestic Product (GDP)	99b	5	11	64	229	268	303	339	586	948	1,309	1,746	2,244
Net Primary Income from Abroad	98.n	−	−	−	−	−	1	....	....	....	....	....	....
Gross National Income (GNI)	99a	5	11	63	228	301	362	....	....	....	....	....	....
Net National Income	99e	4	9	57	206	272	328	....	....	....	....	....	....
GDP Volume 1980 Prices	99b.p	2	1	1	....	....	....	....	....	....	....	....	....
GDP Volume 1990 Prices	99b.p	....	....	....	....	3	3	3	3	4	3	4	4
GDP Volume	99bvp	109.5	104.5	103.7	....	87.1	88.3	90.9	88.6	100.0	96.4	98.6	101.9
GDP Deflator	99bip	147.2	332.1	1,954.2	....	32.5	36.2	39.3	69.8	100.0	143.2	186.8	232.5
		\multicolumn{12}{c}{*Millions: Midyear Estimates*}
Population	99z	.40	.41	.41	.41	.41	.41	.42	.42	.43	.43	.43	.44

Swaziland 734

		1992	1993	1994	1995	1996	1997	1998	1999	2000	2001	2002	2003
Exchange Rates					*SDRs per Lilangeni: End of Period*								
Official Rate	ac	.23822	.21429	.19331	.18443	.14852	.15227	.12120	.11838	.10141	.06562	.08513	.10135
					US Dollars per Lilangeni: End of Period (ag) Period Average (rh)								
Official Rate	ag	.32755	.29433	.28221	.27416	.21356	.20544	.17065	.16248	.13213	.08246	.11574	.15060
Official Rate	rh	.35092	.30641	.28177	.27574	.23416	.21724	.18246	.16370	.14481	.11774	.09539	.13315
Fund Position					*Millions of SDRs: End of Period*								
Quota	2f.s	36.50	36.50	36.50	36.50	36.50	36.50	36.50	50.70	50.70	50.70	50.70	50.70
SDRs	1b.s	5.84	5.88	5.89	5.90	5.93	5.94	5.96	2.42	2.44	2.45	2.46	2.47
Reserve Position in the Fund	1c.s	3.00	3.00	3.00	3.00	3.00	3.00	3.00	6.55	6.55	6.55	6.55	6.55
Total Fund Cred.&Loans Outstg.	2tl	—	—	—	—	—	—	—	—	—	—	—	—
International Liquidity					*Millions of US Dollars Unless Otherwise Indicated: End of Period*								
Total Reserves minus Gold	1l.d	309.06	264.29	296.97	298.20	254.00	294.84	358.61	375.93	351.79	271.78	275.84	277.51
SDRs	1b.d	8.03	8.08	8.60	8.77	8.52	8.02	8.39	3.33	3.18	3.08	3.35	3.67
Reserve Position in the Fund	1c.d	4.13	4.12	4.38	4.46	4.32	4.05	4.23	8.99	8.54	8.23	8.91	9.74
Foreign Exchange	1d.d	296.90	252.09	283.99	284.96	241.16	282.77	345.99	363.61	340.08	260.46	263.59	264.11
Monetary Authorities: Other Liab.	4..d	1.55	1.48	32.02	21.34	20.14	1.24	21.98	49.16	45.66	38.90	42.70	53.26
Deposit Money Banks: Assets	7a.d	52.01	52.43	43.59	47.52	107.45	91.79	99.16	135.46	84.13	71.89	89.29	76.46
Liabilities	7b.d	20.83	19.69	17.83	17.61	50.70	20.92	6.13	9.43	13.84	1.85	8.42	7.70
Monetary Authorities					*Millions of Emalangeni: End of Period*								
Foreign Assets	11	929.80	875.03	872.21	1,023.66	1,335.33	1,427.69	2,083.56	2,304.34	2,643.72	3,362.53	2,339.37	1,836.58
Claims on Central Government	12a	—	—	40.00	20.63	.06	—	—	—	—	—	57.32	82.64
Claims on Private Sector	12d	9.63	8.87	10.63	12.52	14.02	13.06	12.30	15.23	16.34	15.50	12.98	12.02
Claims on Deposit Money Banks	12e	9.60	6.82	5.65	30.00	36.76	43.19	42.55	44.31	41.95	41.95	—	—
Reserve Money	14	287.97	255.34	300.24	307.81	284.95	300.47	275.33	307.27	293.36	274.53	349.36	443.90
of which: Currency Outside DMBs	14a	56.09	75.19	69.59	80.33	90.85	109.00	107.23	136.95	148.06	134.93	155.44	213.45
Time Deposits	15	25.11	43.92	36.90	52.57	53.45	77.68	48.33	50.14	68.30	79.54	90.05	91.81
Foreign Liabilities	16c	4.74	5.02	113.47	77.82	94.32	6.04	128.81	302.53	345.57	471.70	368.96	353.67
Central Government Deposits	16d	500.48	508.49	386.14	555.97	771.74	995.41	1,471.42	1,552.66	1,765.98	2,113.64	1,358.69	1,114.71
Capital Accounts	17a	33.67	36.80	40.14	41.95	50.52	50.80	62.46	86.23	96.66	134.10	114.41	102.44
Other Items (Net)	17r	97.05	41.15	51.60	50.69	131.19	53.53	152.05	65.05	132.14	346.45	128.20	−175.30
Deposit Money Banks					*Millions of Emalangeni: End of Period*								
Reserves	20	217.80	185.65	227.46	232.42	199.22	193.84	151.48	176.57	145.07	130.86	196.02	207.23
Foreign Assets	21	158.78	178.14	154.45	173.32	503.13	446.80	581.07	833.68	636.74	871.83	771.46	507.70
Claims on Central Government	22a	—	30.00	38.00	49.79	68.35	52.17	52.73	50.21	59.49	60.00	215.43	286.68
Claims on Private Sector	22d	673.59	739.14	902.68	915.60	971.81	1,095.03	1,159.43	1,223.39	1,308.23	1,383.56	1,770.13	2,327.69
Demand Deposits	24	197.76	215.06	241.75	282.57	331.99	382.76	393.64	525.72	512.53	619.15	670.09	834.39
Time and Savings Deposits	25	659.16	731.45	833.28	811.70	951.43	1,135.61	1,375.32	1,512.47	1,349.40	1,467.33	1,686.86	1,829.35
Foreign Liabilities	26c	63.58	66.89	63.17	64.22	237.41	101.82	35.92	58.04	104.72	22.45	72.75	51.13
Central Government Deposits	26d	89.16	73.71	90.88	114.57	101.22	10.17	14.25	14.70	.22	.23	.23	.28
Capital Accounts	27a	74.36	96.20	92.33	97.61	75.09	127.53	114.39	139.44	157.73	292.70	378.31	487.94
Other Items (Net)	27r	−33.83	−50.38	1.17	.47	45.37	29.97	11.19	33.48	24.93	44.40	144.79	126.21
Monetary Survey					*Millions of Emalangeni: End of Period*								
Foreign Assets (Net)	31n	1,020.26	981.26	850.02	1,054.94	1,506.73	1,766.63	2,499.89	2,777.46	2,830.18	3,740.21	2,669.12	1,939.47
Domestic Credit	32	93.58	195.81	514.28	328.00	181.28	154.69	−261.20	−278.54	−382.14	−654.82	696.94	1,594.04
Claims on Central Govt. (Net)	32an	−589.64	−552.19	−399.02	−600.12	−804.55	−953.40	−1,432.94	−1,517.16	−1,706.71	−2,053.88	−1,086.18	−745.67
Claims on Private Sector	32d	683.22	748.00	913.30	928.12	985.83	1,108.09	1,171.74	1,238.62	1,324.58	1,399.06	1,783.11	2,339.71
Money	34	254.29	290.50	311.59	363.16	423.03	491.75	500.87	662.69	660.58	754.08	825.53	1,047.84
Quasi-Money	35	684.27	775.37	870.18	864.27	1,004.88	1,213.29	1,423.66	1,562.61	1,417.69	1,546.87	1,776.91	1,921.16
Capital Accounts	37a	108.03	132.99	132.47	139.56	125.61	178.33	176.85	225.67	254.40	426.80	492.72	590.38
Other Items (Net)	37r	67.25	−21.79	50.07	15.96	134.49	37.95	137.31	47.95	115.37	357.65	270.89	−25.87
Money plus Quasi-Money	35l	938.56	1,065.87	1,181.76	1,227.43	1,427.91	1,705.04	1,924.52	2,225.30	2,078.28	2,300.95	2,602.44	2,969.00
Interest Rates					*Percent Per Annum*								
Discount Rate (End of Period)	60	12.00	11.00	12.00	15.00	16.75	15.75	18.00	12.00	11.00	9.50	13.50	8.00
Money Market Rate	60b	10.25	9.73	7.01	8.52	9.77	10.35	10.63	8.86	5.54	5.06	7.31	6.98
Treasury Bill Rate	60c	12.34	8.25	8.35	10.87	13.68	14.37	13.09	11.19	8.30	7.16	8.59	10.61
Deposit Rate	60l	10.49	7.89	7.54	9.44	11.08	12.00	11.92	9.86	6.53	6.15	8.02	7.59
Lending Rate	60p	15.92	14.35	14.25	17.05	18.67	19.50	19.50	17.42	14.00	13.25	15.25	14.63
Prices and Labor					*Index Numbers (2000=100): Period Averages*								
Consumer Prices	64	47.6	53.4	60.7	68.2	72.5	77.7	84.0	89.1	100.0	105.9	118.7	127.3
					Number in Thousands: Period Averages								
Labor Force	67d	....	....	....	....	....	....	....	....	....	....	....	....
Employment	67e	92	93	87	87	90	....	....	....	....	....	....	....
International Transactions					*Millions of Emalangeni*								
Exports	70	1,820.2	2,237.3	2,808.5	3,147.6	3,656.7	4,429.7	5,330.5	5,722.6	6,280.7	8,950.6	9,827.4	....
Imports, c.i.f	71	2,468.0	2,576.8	2,986.3	3,660.7	4,533.4	4,908.8	5,936.4	6,525.8	7,225.2	9,586.6	10,302.3	....

2004, International Monetary Fund : *International Financial Statistics Yearbook*

Swaziland 734

		1992	1993	1994	1995	1996	1997	1998	1999	2000	2001	2002	2003
Balance of Payments						*Millions of US Dollars: Minus Sign Indicates Debit*							
Current Account, n.i.e.	78ald	−40.6	−63.7	1.8	−29.7	−52.0	−2.7	−93.3	−35.1	−65.2	−53.0	−46.3	....
Goods: Exports f.o.b.	78aad	638.5	684.7	790.9	867.8	850.5	961.3	967.8	936.7	905.0	1,039.7	955.2	....
Goods: Imports f.o.b.	78abd	−779.6	−788.6	−841.0	−1,064.4	−1,054.4	−1,065.5	−1,073.8	−1,068.1	−1,041.1	−1,116.4	−1,034.6	....
Trade Balance	78acd	−141.1	−103.9	−50.1	−196.6	−203.9	−104.2	−106.0	−131.5	−136.1	−76.7	−79.4	....
Services: Credit	78add	98.4	92.8	112.9	151.8	100.8	91.9	91.4	69.4	213.6	120.7	116.6	....
Services: Debit	78aed	−208.4	−256.4	−201.9	−209.5	−240.7	−244.8	−267.7	−192.0	−290.7	−185.9	−142.2	....
Balance on Goods & Services	78afd	−251.1	−267.5	−139.1	−254.2	−343.9	−257.1	−282.2	−254.0	−213.2	−141.8	−104.9	....
Income: Credit	78agd	196.8	155.2	138.5	162.6	200.8	182.7	167.8	164.0	153.5	160.1	141.4	....
Income: Debit	78ahd	−113.7	−107.3	−155.0	−82.0	−68.7	−44.6	−111.4	−76.3	−112.6	−105.6	−93.1	....
Balance on Gds, Serv. & Inc.	78aid	−168.0	−219.5	−155.7	−173.7	−211.8	−119.0	−225.8	−166.3	−172.2	−87.4	−56.6	....
Current Transfers, n.i.e.: Credit	78ajd	222.4	248.1	252.6	257.2	268.7	226.8	242.7	241.4	234.1	229.7	218.9	....
Current Transfers: Debit	78akd	−95.0	−92.3	−95.1	−113.3	−108.9	−110.5	−110.3	−110.2	−127.0	−195.3	−208.6	....
Capital Account, n.i.e.	78bcd	−.1	−	−.2	−	.1	.1	−	−	.1	−.2	.5	....
Capital Account, n.i.e.: Credit	78bad	.4	.3	.1	.3	.1	.1	−	−	.1	.2	.5	....
Capital Account: Debit	78bbd	−.5	−.3	−.3	−.3	−	−	−	−	−	−.4	−.1	....
Financial Account, n.i.e.	78bjd	38.3	−7.3	−54.1	−25.4	6.8	47.0	130.5	25.1	−9.6	−31.5	26.8	....
Direct Investment Abroad	78bdd	−33.2	−27.8	−64.7	−20.6	6.4	12.0	−23.9	−13.2	−17.2	17.8	9.2	....
Dir. Invest. in Rep. Econ., n.i.e.	78bed	87.3	71.9	63.3	51.8	21.7	−15.3	152.7	100.4	90.2	49.8	45.0	....
Portfolio Investment Assets	78bfd	−1.0	−.1	−3.9	−9.6	−2.0	−2.0	−2.8	3.2	−4.0	−3.9	.5	....
Equity Securities	78bkd	−.9	−	−	−1.9	−.2	−1.9	−1.3	1.5	−.1	−.1	−	....
Debt Securities	78bld	−.1	−.1	−3.9	−7.6	−1.7	−	−1.5	1.7	−3.9	−3.8	.5	....
Portfolio Investment Liab., n.i.e.	78bgd	−.1	−1.0	.1	.8	.4	−.1	3.4	2.7	1.4	−2.5	−.1	....
Equity Securities	78bmd	−.1	−1.0	.1	.8	.4	−.1	3.4	2.7	1.4	−2.5	−.1	....
Debt Securities	78bnd	....	....	....	....	....	....	....	....	....	....	....	....
Financial Derivatives Assets	78bwd	....	....	....	....	....	....	....	....	....	....	....	....
Financial Derivatives Liabilities	78bxd	....	....	....	....	....	....	....	....	....	....	....	....
Other Investment Assets	78bhd	−40.8	−78.2	−80.5	−31.0	−120.0	−12.3	1.6	−122.4	−98.5	−155.7	−50.4	....
Monetary Authorities	78bod	....	....	....	....	....	....	....	....	....	....	....	....
General Government	78bpd	−.6	−25.3	−18.0	−6.7	−2.7	13.4	−4.8	16.3	8.1	−31.7	−47.1	....
Banks	78bqd	−15.4	−6.9	5.7	−5.3	−77.0	11.1	−22.9	−41.7	27.7	−27.7	9.6	....
Other Sectors	78brd	−24.8	−46.1	−68.3	−19.0	−40.3	−36.8	29.2	−97.0	−134.4	−96.3	−12.9	....
Other Investment Liab., n.i.e.	78bid	26.1	27.9	31.6	−16.7	100.2	64.7	−.4	54.4	18.5	63.0	22.6	....
Monetary Authorities	78bsd	−1.1	.1	30.5	−9.8	3.8	−19.2	22.2	28.5	6.2	14.7	−9.8	....
General Government	78btd	−10.7	−	−	−	−	−	−	−	−	−	−	....
Banks	78bud	12.5	−.3	.7	.4	41.5	−25.9	−13.8	.3	6.4	−9.5	4.7	....
Other Sectors	78bvd	25.3	28.1	.4	−7.3	54.9	109.8	−8.8	25.6	5.8	57.8	27.6	....
Net Errors and Omissions	78cad	94.3	2.4	48.9	78.9	37.0	−16.8	4.1	13.4	46.7	41.6	18.9	....
Overall Balance	78cbd	91.9	−68.5	−3.6	23.8	−8.1	27.5	41.3	3.3	−28.0	−43.0	−.2	....
Reserves and Related Items	79dad	−91.9	68.5	3.6	−23.8	8.1	−27.5	−41.3	−3.3	28.0	43.0	.2	....
Reserve Assets	79dbd	−91.9	63.7	12.6	−29.8	−15.4	−25.3	−50.5	−26.3	6.5	56.5	29.1	....
Use of Fund Credit and Loans	79dcd	−	−	−	−	−	−	−	−	−	−	−	....
Exceptional Financing	79ded	....	4.8	−8.9	6.0	23.4	−2.2	9.2	23.0	21.6	−13.5	−28.9	....
International Investment Position						*Millions of US Dollars*							
Assets	79aad	754.0	721.2	838.2	982.9	965.1	977.2	958.5	1,151.8	1,151.9	894.5	1,286.9	....
Direct Investment Abroad	79abd	49.2	52.6	108.8	135.5	95.4	82.3	90.1	98.1	94.9	46.2	53.6	....
Portfolio Investment	79acd	3.9	3.6	7.3	16.6	14.8	16.1	16.0	12.0	13.4	11.2	15.0	....
Equity Securities	79add	.9	.8	.8	2.7	2.3	4.0	4.6	2.8	2.4	1.6	2.2	....
Debt Securities	79aed	3.0	2.8	6.6	14.0	12.5	12.0	11.4	9.2	11.1	9.6	12.9	....
Financial Derivatives	79ald	−	−	−	−	−	−	−	−	−	−	−	....
Other Investment	79afd	398.0	425.8	479.2	553.4	572.5	589.3	497.2	669.0	696.5	561.5	949.8	....
Monetary Authorities	79agd	−	−	−	−	−	−	−	−	−	−	−	....
General Government	79ahd	139.1	142.3	144.6	124.6	98.8	86.5	77.0	56.2	34.3	10.7	114.8	....
Banks	79aid	53.7	54.8	46.9	50.8	110.3	116.1	101.0	137.5	86.4	73.6	91.6	....
Other Sectors	79ajd	205.2	228.7	287.7	377.9	363.5	386.6	319.2	475.4	575.8	477.2	743.4	....
Reserve Assets	79akd	302.9	239.2	242.9	277.4	282.4	289.5	355.3	372.6	347.1	275.6	268.4	....
Liabilities	79lad	762.0	820.2	848.7	981.3	894.5	846.3	929.3	1,053.8	975.3	638.7	....	....
Dir. Invest. in Rep. Economy	79lbd	437.7	462.5	506.8	535.6	437.2	406.4	481.6	558.2	536.7	370.3	574.7	....
Portfolio Investment	79lcd	1.7	.6	.7	1.4	1.5	1.4	4.3	6.8	6.8	2.4	3.3	....
Equity Securities	79ldd	1.7	.6	.7	1.4	1.5	1.4	4.3	6.8	6.8	2.4	3.3	....
Debt Securities	79led	−	−	−	−	−	−	−	−	−	−	−	....
Financial Derivatives	79lld	−	−	−	−	−	−	−	−	−	−	−	....
Other Investment	79lfd	322.7	357.1	341.2	444.2	455.7	438.5	443.4	488.8	431.8	265.9	....	....
Monetary Authorities	79lgd	1.5	−.3	−.3	77.3	19.9	1.0	21.8	48.9	45.5	38.8	....	....
General Government	79lhd	184.7	192.1	175.3	194.5	194.4	177.4	243.3	262.5	210.0	136.7	....	....
Banks	79lid	24.7	21.9	21.7	21.5	54.9	28.2	10.4	10.3	14.3	2.2	....	....
Other Sectors	79ljd	111.7	143.5	144.5	150.9	186.5	231.8	167.9	167.1	162.1	88.3	56.7	....

Swaziland 734

		1992	1993	1994	1995	1996	1997	1998	1999	2000	2001	2002	2003
Government Finance		\multicolumn{12}{c}{*Millions of Emalangeni: Year Beginning April 1*}
Deficit (-) or Surplus	80	–42.2	–171.1	–197.5	68.3	–56.2	184.1	–7.1	–138.7	–141.4	–255.3	–593.1	–444.9
Revenue	81	844.1	953.0	1,168.7	1,447.7	1,684.0	2,020.5	2,230.3	2,536.1	2,713.2	2,922.7	3,262.8	3,681.6
Grants Received	81z	46.3	28.7	31.4	7.5	20.2	18.3	44.7	31.8	112.1	157.4	162.3	265.1
Expenditure	82	1,025.5	1,138.4	1,398.7	1,382.1	1,758.4	1,826.6	2,214.8	2,676.0	2,967.9	3,332.5	4,018.2	4,391.6
Lending Minus Repayments	83	–92.9	14.4	–1.1	4.8	2.0	28.1	67.3	30.6	–1.2	2.9	–	–
Financing													
Domestic	84a	50.4	196.4	235.5	–80.6	41.4	–226.1	–191.2	133.1	122.5	–52.2	480.5	318.5
Foreign	85a	–8.2	–25.3	–38.0	12.3	14.8	42.0	198.3	5.6	18.9	307.5	112.6	126.4
Debt: Domestic	88a	24.6	25.5	53.7	62.9	102.9	97.6	85.6	78.0	78.0	78.0	300.0	300.0
Foreign	89a	515.9	630.2	791.9	914.5	1,150.5	820.0	1,060.6	1,467.9	2,069.8	2,690.0	3,351.0	2,755.8
National Accounts		\multicolumn{12}{c}{*Millions of Emalangeni: Year Ending June 30*}
Househ.Cons.Expend.,incl.NPISHs	96f	2,303.0	2,649.0	3,052.1	3,932.6	4,801.5	4,752.6	5,403.2	6,214.1	7,273.1	8,425.9	....	....
Government Consumption Expend	91f	490.1	781.0	874.0	951.0	1,185.8	1,639.2	1,800.9	1,864.3	1,929.1	1,996.2	....	....
Gross Fixed Capital Formation	93e	697.6	771.8	840.7	950.0	1,125.4	1,308.1	1,665.4	1,577.1	1,916.7	1,984.5	....	....
Changes in Inventories	93i	24.9	29.0	33.9	37.4	51.2	53.9	–	–	–	–	....	....
Exports of Goods and Services	90c	2,101.4	2,540.6	2,970.6	3,698.4	4,090.0	5,003.2	5,917.4	6,116.1	6,141.0	7,699.4	....	....
Imports of Goods and Services (-)	98c	2,817.7	3,414.6	3,703.2	4,620.5	5,568.4	6,144.5	7,337.5	7,363.9	7,621.0	9,135.0	....	....
Gross Domestic Product (GDP)	99b	2,799.3	3,356.8	4,068.1	4,948.9	5,685.5	6,612.5	7,449.4	8,407.7	9,638.9	10,971.0	12,287.0	....
Net Primary Income from Abroad	98.n	237.2	156.6	–58.9	292.2	567.9	636.3	311.8	535.9	574.7	291.5	....	....
Gross National Income (GNI)	99a	3,036.5	3,513.4	4,009.2	5,244.1	6,253.4	7,248.8	7,761.2	8,943.6	10,213.6	11,262.5	....	....
Consumption of Fixed Capital	99cf	170.8	189.6	214.2	235.8	258.4	297.2	334.6	377.4	434.0	499.1	....	....
Net National Income	99e	2,865.7	3,323.8	3,795.0	5,005.3	5,995.0	6,951.6	7,426.6	8,566.3	9,779.6	10,763.4	....	....
GDP Volume 1985 Prices	99b.p	1,358.8	1,403.1	1,450.3	1,505.2	1,563.7	1,623.6	1,676.5	1,735.6	1,770.9	1,802.3	....	....
GDP Volume (2000=100)	99bvp	76.7	79.2	81.9	85.0	88.3	91.7	94.7	98.0	100.0	101.8	....	....
GDP Deflator (2000=100)	99bip	37.8	44.0	51.5	60.4	66.8	74.8	81.6	89.0	100.0	111.8	....	....
		\multicolumn{12}{c}{*Millions: Midyear Estimates*}
Population	99z	.89	.90	.92	.94	.96	Ü .98	1.01	1.03	1.04	1.06	1.07	1.08

Sweden 144

		1992	1993	1994	1995	1996	1997	1998	1999	2000	2001	2002	2003
Exchange Rates													
						Kronor per SDR: End of Period							
Official Rate	aa	9.6841	11.4054	10.8927	9.8973	9.8802	10.6280	11.3501	11.7006	12.4232	13.4062	11.9978	10.6829
					Kronor per US Dollar: End of Period (ae) Period Average (rf)								
Official Rate	ae	7.0430	8.3035	7.4615	6.6582	6.8710	7.8770	8.0610	8.5250	9.5350	10.6675	8.8250	7.1892
Official Rate	rf	5.8238	7.7834	7.7160	7.1333	6.7060	7.6349	7.9499	8.2624	9.1622	10.3291	9.7371	8.0863
			Kronor per ECU through 1998; Kronor per Euro Beginning 1999: End of Period (ea) Period Average (eb)										
Euro Rate	ea	8.5490	9.2963	9.1779	8.6973	8.6280	8.7323	9.4880	†8.5625	8.8313	9.4200	9.1925	9.0800
Euro Rate	ag	....	....	....	....	....	....	....	1.0046	.9305	.8813	1.0487	1.2630
Euro Rate	eb	7.5299	9.1146	9.1579	9.3337	8.5156	8.6551	8.9085	†8.8102	8.4459	9.2553	9.1603	9.1243
Euro Rate	rh	....	....	....	....	....	....	....	1.0668	.9240	.8956	.9444	1.1308
						Index Numbers (2000=100): Period Averages							
Official Rate	ahx	157.7	117.6	118.5	128.2	136.2	119.7	114.9	110.5	100.0	88.6	94.1	113.2
Nominal Effective Exchange Rate	neu	122.3	100.0	98.7	98.0	107.4	103.4	101.1	99.7	100.0	91.6	93.1	97.5
Real Effective Exchange Rate	reu	118.8	96.3	95.4	95.9	108.2	105.5	103.8	100.6	100.0	90.8	93.0	98.4
Fund Position						*Millions of SDRs: End of Period*							
Quota	2f.s	1,614	1,614	1,614	1,614	1,614	1,614	1,614	2,396	2,396	2,396	2,396	2,396
SDRs	1b.s	33	42	46	297	199	277	292	228	165	157	132	133
Reserve Position in the Fund	1c.s	451	451	451	451	451	589	900	863	683	827	1,050	988
of which: Outstg.Fund Borrowing	2c	–	–	–	–	–	–	112	–	–	–	–	–
International Liquidity					*Millions of US Dollars Unless Otherwise Indicated: End of Period*								
Total Reserves minus Gold	1l.d	22,624	19,050	23,254	24,051	19,107	10,825	14,098	15,019	14,863	13,977	17,127	19,681
SDRs	1b.d	45	58	68	441	286	373	412	313	215	197	179	198
Reserve Position in the Fund	1c.d	621	620	659	671	649	795	1,267	1,184	890	1,039	1,428	1,468
Foreign Exchange	1d.d	21,959	18,372	22,527	22,939	18,172	9,657	12,420	13,522	13,757	12,740	15,520	18,015
Gold (Million Fine Troy Ounces)	1ad	6.069	6.069	6.069	4.702	4.702	4.722	4.722	5.961	5.961	5.961	5.961	5.961
Gold (National Valuation)	1and	292	292	310	245	237	223	233	286	272	262	284	310
Deposit Money Banks: Assets	7a.d	32,056	26,261	24,727	36,158	44,707	44,943	50,853	53,087	67,355	....	....	....
Liabilities	7b.d	62,745	50,253	50,925	55,100	56,670	60,376	86,846	76,769	102,345	....	....	....
Other Banking Insts.: Assets	7e.d	4,395	3,743	4,661	5,734	8,834	11,116	12,171	13,226	....	....	....	....
Liabilities	7f.d	22,534	20,605	22,196	16,597	14,535	13,686	29,960	34,387	....	....	....	....
Monetary Authorities						*Billions of Kronor: End of Period*							
Foreign Assets	11	163.29	175.69	177.95	171.96	140.21	93.41	136.22	152.55	167.92	158.04	168.68	160.82
Claims on Central Government	12a	145.98	98.99	87.52	71.03	59.05	53.09	32.84	†27.69	20.23	–	–	–
Claims on Deposit Money Banks	12e	61.02	1.26	.01	2.61	9.64	40.33	43.85	†45.63	43.20	69.11	30.72	23.83
Claims on Other Financial Insts	12f	....	....	....	....	....	....	....	1.31	.50	–	–	–
Reserve Money	14	110.95	163.84	200.59	170.74	114.30	84.76	87.95	102.91	97.77	107.15	107.07	109.48
of which: Currency Outside DMBs	14a	64.30	67.05	68.81	68.55	70.71	72.97	74.63	78.64	89.16	....	....	....
Foreign Liabilities	16c	12.47	.08	.22	3.48	4.14	3.98	4.10	†5.26	4.11	3.29	.36	1.00
Central Government Deposits	16d	159.57	21.79	–	–	–	–	–	†2.17	1.59	2.39	.21	.13
Capital Accounts	17a	63.05	59.59	76.62	74.46	75.71	82.25	100.07	114.42	108.24	100.60	92.23	84.33
Other Items (Net)	17r	24.25	30.65	–11.95	–3.10	14.75	15.83	20.79	2.43	20.14	13.72	–.46	–10.29
Deposit Money Banks						*Billions of Kronor: End of Period*							
Reserves	20	35.40	21.25	8.75	9.42	11.13	10.17	13.52	30.67	9.80	....	....	....
Foreign Assets	21	328.95	329.24	281.57	408.71	†572.15	682.15	698.05	741.63	961.14	....	....	....
Claims on Central Government	22a	65.32	149.50	162.35	143.46	122.00	109.15	167.93	86.99	115.77	....	....	....
Claims on Local Government	22b	19.68	14.58	17.54	24.99	31.05	36.85	37.58	42.74	39.61	....	....	....
Claims on Private Sector	22d	784.30	631.41	605.08	596.72	†623.21	711.06	771.67	848.41	958.69	....	....	....
Claims on Other Financial Insts	22f	169.86	182.54	247.87	267.14	†310.92	359.86	448.69	467.02	550.81	....	....	....
Demand,Time,Savings,Fgn.Cur.Dep	25l	618.55	643.01	644.16	664.37	746.37	753.29	748.02	814.05	820.67	....	....	....
Bonds	26ab	28.91	27.77	27.00	22.83	11.25	25.12	30.81	31.96	25.81	....	....	....
Foreign Liabilities	26c	545.64	532.70	504.20	568.22	†639.64	788.10	985.59	924.94	1,256.78	....	....	....
Central Government Deposits	26d	.38	.34	.43	1.61	2.38	.86	12.24	31.02	31.51	....	....	....
Credit from Monetary Authorities	26g	82.15	.74	.02	.01	10.53	31.65	29.26	34.44	45.78	....	....	....
Credit from Other Financial Insts	26i	49.57	40.96	40.16	48.80	66.23	88.88	110.27	119.72	152.25	....	....	....
Capital Accounts	27a	57.71	78.31	83.63	100.76	61.74	74.37	82.99	88.53	95.95	....	....	....
Other Items (Net)	27r	20.60	4.68	23.55	43.85	†132.33	146.98	138.26	172.80	207.08	....	....	....
Monetary Survey						*Billions of Kronor: End of Period*							
Foreign Assets (Net)	31n	–65.87	–27.85	–44.90	8.97	†68.58	–16.52	–155.42	†–36.02	–131.83	....	....	....
Domestic Credit	32	1,025.20	1,054.89	1,119.92	1,101.73	†1,143.85	1,269.15	1,446.47	†1,440.97	1,652.52	....	....	....
Claims on Central Govt. (Net)	32an	51.35	226.37	249.43	212.88	178.67	161.37	188.54	†81.49	102.91	....	....	....
Claims on Local Government	32b	19.68	14.58	17.54	24.99	31.05	36.85	37.58	42.74	39.61	....	....	....
Claims on Private Sector	32d	784.30	631.41	605.08	596.72	†623.21	711.06	771.67	848.41	958.69	....	....	....
Claims on Other Financial Insts	32f	169.86	182.54	247.87	267.14	†310.92	359.86	448.69	468.33	551.31	....	....	....
Money plus Quasi-Money	35l	694.10	723.03	728.05	750.56	817.08	826.26	822.65	892.69	909.84	....	....	....
Bonds	36ab	28.91	27.77	27.00	22.83	11.25	25.12	30.81	31.96	25.81	....	....	....
Liabilities to Other Banking Inst	36i	49.57	40.96	40.16	48.80	66.23	88.88	110.27	119.72	152.25	....	....	....
Capital Accounts	37a	120.77	137.90	160.25	175.27	137.45	156.62	183.06	202.95	204.20	....	....	....
Other Items (Net)	37r	65.98	97.37	119.57	113.28	†180.42	155.76	144.27	†157.64	228.60	....	....	....
Money + Quasi-Money,Seas.Adj	35l.b	669.10	700.88	709.30	734.24	802.65	815.14	814.82	887.17	905.89	....	....	....
Unused Bank Credits	39b	166.20	173.66	184.13	197.97	....	....	....	....	....	....	....	....

Sweden 144

		1992	1993	1994	1995	1996	1997	1998	1999	2000	2001	2002	2003
Money (National Definitions)						*Billions of Kronor: End of Period*							
Broad Money	39m	682.85	710.06	712.33	731.81	815.53	826.24	843.42	926.95	946.12	....	....	....
Other Banking Institutions						*Billions of Kronor: End of Period*							
Cash	40	.08	.03	.64	.02	–	–	–	–	....	....	....	....
Foreign Assets	41	46.54	37.45	46.15	38.26	†60.70	87.56	98.11	112.75	....	....	....	....
Claims on Central Government	42a	18.01	17.40	28.84	23.98	16.02	16.26	18.53	18.67	....	....	....	....
Claims on Local Government	42b	.02	–	.02	.01	†35.70	39.04	40.72	42.16	....	....	....	....
Claims on Private Sector	42d	1,133.15	1,124.98	1,133.60	1,162.92	†1,154.15	1,161.62	1,200.06	1,249.53	....	....	....	....
Claims on Deposit Money Banks	42e	36.98	31.36	25.92	†28.69	39.90	46.18	59.23	54.60	....	....	....	....
Time, Savings, & Fgn. Currency Dep.	45	96.86	66.01	92.34	134.44	167.26	173.49	2.43	.52	....	....	....	....
Bonds	46ab	849.44	960.64	915.53	856.98	804.90	736.65	720.90	648.43	....	....	....	....
Foreign Liabilities	46c	42.10	26.57	41.49	24.08	†99.87	107.80	241.51	293.15	....	....	....	....
Central Govt. Lending Funds	46f	279.70	278.12	247.18	230.97	†189.15	184.74	211.22	155.66	....	....	....	....
Credit from Deposit Money Banks	46h	93.48	51.38	66.74	81.61	96.58	170.02	222.74	250.19	....	....	....	....
Capital Accounts	47a	47.15	66.72	73.35	82.26	60.74	65.24	68.36	73.71	....	....	....	....
Other Items (Net)	47r	–173.97	–238.24	–201.50	–156.47	–112.04	–87.29	–50.51	56.06	....	....	....	....
Banking Survey						*Billions of Kronor: End of Period*							
Foreign Assets (Net)	51n	–61.44	–16.98	–40.24	23.15	†29.41	–36.77	–298.81	†–216.41	....	....	....	....
Domestic Credit	52	2,006.51	2,014.73	2,034.50	2,021.48	†2,038.79	2,126.20	2,257.10	2,283.00	....	....	....	....
Claims on Central Govt. (Net)	52an	69.36	243.76	278.27	236.86	194.68	177.63	207.06	100.16	....	....	....	....
Claims on Local Government	52b	19.70	14.58	17.55	25.00	†66.75	75.89	78.30	84.90	....	....	....	....
Claims on Private Sector	52d	1,917.45	1,756.39	1,738.68	1,759.64	†1,777.36	1,872.68	1,971.73	2,097.94	....	....	....	....
Liquid Liabilities	55l	790.96	789.03	820.39	885.00	984.34	999.74	825.08	893.21	....	....	....	....
Bonds	56ab	878.35	988.42	942.53	879.81	816.16	761.77	751.71	680.39	....	....	....	....
Central Govt. Lending Funds	56f	279.70	278.12	247.18	230.97	†189.15	184.74	211.22	155.66	102.52	....	....	....
Capital Accounts	57a	167.92	204.63	233.60	257.48	198.19	221.86	251.42	276.66	....	....	....	....
Other Items (Net)	57r	–169.48	–261.00	–248.53	–208.62	†–119.51	–78.64	–81.13	†60.67	....	....	....	....
Nonbank Financial Institutions						*Billions of Kronor: End of Period*							
Cash	40..l	9.67	9.08	8.63	7.21	†6.76	–	–	–	–	–	–	–
Foreign Assets	41..l	77.98	100.48	102.79	131.88	†51.82	77.41	119.68	154.47	264.15	259.66	250.17	259.73
Claims on Central Government	42a.l	77.43	130.95	161.20	254.55	†247.21	259.93	290.98	341.92	285.64	306.40	370.19	390.28
Claims on Private Sector	42d.l	160.00	201.46	215.18	239.53	†424.12	546.83	656.76	897.16	910.81	877.10	604.87	730.31
Claims on Other Banking Insts.	42f.l	231.03	242.55	188.15	159.25	†211.54	230.24	239.02	217.46	226.92	242.72	313.38	341.54
Interest Rates						*Percent Per Annum*							
Discount Rate (End of Period)	60	†10.00	5.00	7.00	7.00	3.50	2.50	2.00	1.50	2.00	2.00	2.00	....
Repurchase Rate (End of Period)	60a	16.62	8.83	†7.51	8.91	4.27	4.19	3.50	3.25	3.89	3.75	3.75	2.75
Money Market Rate	60b	18.42	9.08	7.36	8.54	6.28	4.21	4.24	3.14	3.81	4.08	....	....
Treasury Bill Rate	60c	12.85	8.35	7.40	8.75	5.79	4.11	4.19	3.12	3.95	....	....	....
Deposit Rate (End of Period)	60l	†7.80	5.10	4.91	6.16	2.47	2.50	1.91	1.65	2.15	....	....	....
Lending Rate (End of Period)	60p	†15.20	11.40	10.64	11.11	7.38	7.01	5.94	5.53	5.82	....	....	....
Government Bond Yield	61	10.02	8.54	†9.41	....	....	....	....	....	....	....	....	....
Prices, Production, Labor						*Index Numbers (2000=100): Period Averages*							
Share Prices	62	15	20	26	29	....	50	59	69	100	71	54	....
Forest Industries	62a	48	59	72	76	....	97	94	101	100	127	154	....
Industrials	62b	25	37	48	†55	63	87	86	93	100	93	87	....
Prices: Domestic Supply	63	78.9	83.8	87.8	94.6	92.9	94.0	93.5	94.5	100.0	103.2	103.8	102.9
Consumer Prices	64	89.2	93.4	95.4	97.7	98.3	98.9	98.7	99.1	100.0	102.4	104.6	106.6
Harmonized CPI	64h	....	....	....	94.7	95.4	97.2	98.2	98.7	100.0	102.7	104.7	107.1
Wages: Hourly Earnings	65	72.7	75.0	78.2	82.4	87.8	91.7	95.0	96.7	100.0	102.9	106.4	109.4
Industrial Production	66	83.1	82.5	91.7	84.1	84.7	89.2	92.4	93.8	100.0	99.6	99.9	102.7
Industrial Employment	67	105.5	97.1	95.6	100.8	101.6	100.5	100.9	100.1	100.0	97.6	93.8	90.9
						Number in Thousands: Period Averages							
Labor Force	67d	4,464	4,320	4,266	4,319	4,310	4,264	4,255	4,308	4,362	4,415	4,421	4,450
Employment	67e	4,209	†3,964	3,928	3,986	3,963	3,922	3,979	4,068	4,159	4,239	4,244	4,234
Unemployment	67c	233	†356	340	332	346	342	276	241	203	175	176	184
Unemployment Rate (%)	67r	5.9	†8.2	8.0	7.7	8.0	8.0	6.5	5.6	4.7	4.0	4.0	4.9
International Transactions						*Millions of Kronor*							
Exports	70	326,040	388,300	471,600	567,700	569,200	632,800	675,300	700,800	796,900	781,900	789,900	816,300
Imports, c.i.f.	71	290,510	332,490	397,410	460,500	448,700	501,100	545,300	568,100	669,200	654,000	647,700	667,400
						2000=100							
Volume of Exports	72	45.9	50.1	58.9	65.9	69.6	77.0	84.0	89.1	100.0	98.5	101.2	106.1
Volume of Imports	73	54.0	55.8	64.0	69.3	71.1	78.7	86.3	89.3	100.0	94.9	94.4	100.4
Export Prices	76	79.3	86.8	91.2	101.6	96.6	97.5	97.0	96.1	100.0	101.6	99.7	97.4
Import Prices	76.x	73.5	83.2	87.1	92.8	89.5	91.3	90.4	92.6	100.0	104.5	104.8	102.6

2004, International Monetary Fund: *International Financial Statistics Yearbook*

Sweden 144

		1992	1993	1994	1995	1996	1997	1998	1999	2000	2001	2002	2003
Balance of Payments						*Millions of US Dollars: Minus Sign Indicates Debit*							
Current Account, n.i.e.	78ald	−8,827	−4,159	743	4,940	5,892	7,406	4,639	5,982	6,617	6,696	12,784	22,844
Goods: Exports f.o.b.	78aad	55,363	49,348	60,199	79,903	84,690	83,194	85,179	87,568	87,431	76,200	84,172	102,080
Goods: Imports f.o.b.	78abd	−48,642	−41,801	−50,641	−63,926	−66,053	−65,195	−67,547	−71,854	−72,216	−62,368	−67,541	−83,147
Trade Balance	78acd	6,720	7,548	9,558	15,978	18,636	17,999	17,632	15,714	15,215	13,832	16,631	18,933
Services: Credit	78add	16,195	12,589	13,674	15,622	16,930	17,769	17,952	19,904	20,252	21,997	24,009	30,654
Services: Debit	78aed	−19,090	−13,355	−14,690	−17,216	−18,755	−19,524	−21,721	−22,617	−23,440	−23,020	−23,958	−28,771
Balance on Goods & Services	78afd	3,826	6,782	8,542	14,384	16,811	16,245	13,862	13,001	12,027	12,809	16,682	20,816
Income: Credit	78agd	8,142	7,127	9,611	14,906	14,338	14,404	16,564	19,871	20,074	17,934	18,018	22,934
Income: Debit	78ahd	−18,181	−16,261	−15,530	−21,379	−22,641	−20,513	−22,349	−23,291	−22,137	−20,786	−19,044	−22,637
Balance on Gds, Serv. & Inc.	78aid	−6,213	−2,352	2,623	7,910	8,508	10,135	8,077	9,581	9,964	9,957	15,657	21,113
Current Transfers, n.i.e.: Credit	78ajd	405	456	544	1,555	2,524	2,319	2,266	2,341	2,602	2,578	3,345	3,577
Current Transfers: Debit	78akd	−3,019	−2,263	−2,424	−4,525	−5,140	−5,048	−5,704	−5,940	−5,950	−5,839	−6,218	−1,845
Capital Account, n.i.e.	78bcd	6	23	23	14	9	−228	868	−2,143	384	509	−79	−46
Capital Account, n.i.e.: Credit	78bad	37	37	37	32	31	211	1,502	1,289	1,226	1,111	529	552
Capital Account: Debit	78bbd	−31	−15	−14	−18	−22	−439	−634	−3,432	−841	−601	−609	−599
Financial Account, n.i.e.	78bjd	10,214	11,518	6,078	−5,052	−10,046	−10,121	5,961	−1,413	−3,297	1,824	−10,704	−20,163
Direct Investment Abroad	78bdd	−419	−1,471	−6,685	−11,399	−5,112	−12,119	−22,671	−19,554	−39,962	−6,959	−10,673	−17,341
Dir. Invest. in Rep. Econ., n.i.e.	78bed	−5	3,705	6,269	14,939	5,492	10,271	19,413	59,386	22,125	13,085	11,709	3,268
Portfolio Investment Assets	78bfd	−1,578	−94	−2,459	−10,765	−13,136	−13,818	−17,615	−36,749	−12,772	−23,041	−4,038	−13,701
Equity Securities	78bkd	−505	−76	−2,509	−9,378	−7,518	−10,179	−7,427	−29,766	758	−22,642	−124	−4,618
Debt Securities	78bld	−1,073	−18	51	−1,386	−5,618	−3,640	−10,188	−6,983	−13,530	−400	−3,914	−9,083
Portfolio Investment Liab., n.i.e.	78bgd	2,563	1,472	721	8,201	1,661	−2,384	2,023	1,882	9,017	10,338	−6,691	4,134
Equity Securities	78bmd	2,257	4,212	6,795	1,853	4,047	−1,687	−328	−3,895	17,997	−2,336	2,536	452
Debt Securities	78bnd	306	−2,741	−6,074	6,348	−2,386	−697	2,351	5,777	−8,980	12,674	−9,227	3,682
Financial Derivatives Assets	78bwd	….	….	….	20,264	24,800	31,244	30,125	22,982	31,481	33,678	37,720	40,045
Financial Derivatives Liabilities	78bxd	….	….	….	−21,096	−23,243	−29,280	−31,428	−22,923	−31,795	−38,894	−37,888	−38,964
Other Investment Assets	78bhd	1,633	1,159	−3,400	−12,197	−10,828	−9,670	−5,901	−10,333	−16,000	929	−998	−8,349
Monetary Authorities	78bod	….	….	….	—	—	—	—	—	—	—	—	—
General Government	78bpd	−337	−144	−290	−483	−303	−322	−244	−642	−150	37	−1,589	442
Banks	78bqd	1,083	4,682	2,902	−8,037	−10,239	−4,971	−1,135	−5,296	−13,279	1,672	697	−8,688
Other Sectors	78brd	887	−3,379	−6,012	−3,677	−287	−4,377	−4,522	−4,396	−2,571	−779	−106	−103
Other Investment Liab., n.i.e.	78bid	8,020	6,748	11,633	6,999	10,320	15,635	32,015	3,897	34,609	12,689	155	10,744
Monetary Authorities	78bsd	—	—	—	—	—	−39	88	−243	−556	−812	993	2,605
General Government	78btd	28,567	11,723	5,075	8,842	1,817	−1,583	578	1,047	129	−32	683	−941
Banks	78bud	−26,461	−10,851	−1,957	−1,055	2,935	9,269	20,205	−3,846	29,682	10,077	−1,299	1,905
Other Sectors	78bvd	5,914	5,876	8,515	−788	5,569	7,988	11,144	6,938	5,354	3,455	−222	7,175
Net Errors and Omissions	78cad	5,560	−4,852	−4,462	−1,566	−2,241	−3,769	−8,214	−545	−3,534	−10,078	−1,336	−558
Overall Balance	78cbd	6,953	2,530	2,381	−1,664	−6,386	−6,712	3,254	1,881	170	−1,048	665	2,076
Reserves and Related Items	79dad	−6,953	−2,530	−2,381	1,664	6,386	6,712	−3,254	−1,881	−170	1,048	−665	−2,076
Reserve Assets	79dbd	−6,953	−2,530	−2,381	1,664	6,386	6,712	−3,254	−1,881	−170	1,048	−665	−2,076
Use of Fund Credit and Loans	79dcd	—	—	—	—	—	—	—	—	—	—	—	—
Exceptional Financing	79ded	—	—	—	—	—	—	—	—	—	….	….	….
International Investment Position						*Millions of US Dollars*							
Assets	79aad	148,658	135,124	165,515	227,989	248,580	241,838	295,255	353,559	365,450	362,361	….	….
Direct Investment Abroad	79abd	47,707	44,560	59,237	69,088	71,751	79,099	94,674	104,948	115,582	122,032	….	….
Portfolio Investment	79acd	14,057	17,583	22,114	36,947	50,357	69,478	100,589	142,802	133,506	139,675	….	….
Equity Securities	79add	11,217	15,054	18,227	29,738	38,859	51,248	71,207	108,387	89,546	99,592	….	….
Debt Securities	79aed	2,840	2,529	3,887	7,209	11,498	18,230	29,382	34,415	43,960	40,083	….	….
Financial Derivatives	79ald	—	—	—	15,920	16,446	16,450	15,579	14,990	18,679	15,661	….	….
Other Investment	79afd	63,609	51,785	60,310	80,352	89,652	65,265	67,529	72,855	81,368	70,177	….	….
Monetary Authorities	79agd	—	—	—	—	—	—	—	—	—	—	….	….
General Government	79ahd	12,921	4,456	5,227	6,158	6,258	6,174	6,517	6,508	5,984	5,856	….	….
Banks	79aid	32,231	26,254	24,660	36,346	44,681	46,599	46,143	48,128	56,018	47,949	….	….
Other Sectors	79ajd	18,458	21,075	30,423	37,848	38,713	12,492	14,869	18,219	19,365	16,372	….	….
Reserve Assets	79akd	23,285	21,196	23,855	25,682	20,375	11,546	16,884	17,964	16,316	14,815	….	….
Liabilities	79lad	208,434	215,813	261,074	324,863	352,787	339,476	389,867	430,625	424,279	418,345	….	….
Dir. Invest. in Rep. Economy	79lbd	13,773	12,886	23,454	33,042	34,056	42,399	53,792	68,053	77,009	92,196	….	….
Portfolio Investment	79lcd	30,953	47,089	57,897	77,348	99,549	207,565	225,711	259,959	225,025	207,912	….	….
Equity Securities	79ldd	13,063	21,798	35,918	48,061	70,295	79,472	94,033	129,384	106,660	76,522	….	….
Debt Securities	79led	17,890	25,291	21,979	29,287	29,253	128,093	131,678	130,575	118,365	131,390	….	….
Financial Derivatives	79lld	—	—	—	16,821	17,610	16,420	15,936	14,095	15,276	14,240	….	….
Other Investment	79lfd	163,709	155,838	179,723	197,651	201,572	73,091	94,427	88,518	106,969	103,998	….	….
Monetary Authorities	79lgd	1,704	—	—	—	146	—	—	—	—	—	….	….
General Government	79lhd	37,200	47,089	57,227	65,934	64,328	1,836	2,238	2,857	1,922	1,556	….	….
Banks	79lid	62,757	50,340	50,928	55,270	56,615	51,247	68,238	59,978	80,756	81,744	….	….
Other Sectors	79ljd	62,047	58,409	71,567	76,447	80,483	20,009	23,951	25,683	24,291	20,698	….	….

Sweden 144

		1992	1993	1994	1995	1996	1997	1998	1999	2000	2001	2002	2003
Government Finance					*Billions of Kronor: Year Ending December 31*								
Deficit (-) or Surplus..................	80	−74.07	−231.41	† −133.63	−153.18	−58.02	† −16.66	6.84	64.01	125.82	....	† 1.11	−46.35
Revenue...............................	81	610.94	544.63	† 419.06	459.93	590.08	640.06	696.46	715.81	790.96	....	† 730.45	661.74
Grants Received......................	81z	–	–	† –	5.66	10.40	8.88	9.87	9.28	9.02	....	....	....
Expenditure...........................	82	665.96	747.15	† 552.69	618.77	658.50	† 665.60	699.49	661.08	674.16	....	† 729.34	708.09
Lending Minus Repayments...........	83	19.05	28.89	....	....	....	....	....	....	....	....	....	....
Financing													
Domestic.............................	84a	50.27	66.36	† 129.85	135.42	27.07	−11.34	−20.25	47.13	8.78	....	....	....
Foreign..............................	85a	23.80	165.05	† 3.78	17.76	30.95	28.01	13.43	−111.15	−135.30	....	....	....
Total Debt..............................	88	606.26	828.02	† 1,098.92	1,169.48	1,189.53	1,208.36	1,217.64	1,142.23	1,008.30	....	....	† 1,228.74
Debt: Domestic.......................	88a	461.90	518.61	† 585.96	638.76	627.85	618.69	614.53	650.28	598.86	....	....	† 898.31
Debt: Foreign.........................	89a	144.36	309.41	† 512.96	530.72	561.68	589.67	603.11	491.95	409.44	....	....	330.43
Intragovernmental Debt...............	88s	103.66	132.59	† 1,976.46	2,502.25	2,713.16	2,753.88	2,812.89	2,901.91	3,120.39	....	....	....
National Accounts						*Billions of Kronor*							
Househ.Cons.Expend.,incl.NPISHs....	96f	774.18	796.01	† 832.96	865.24	890.59	931.69	967.19	1,015.74	1,078.36	1,108.42	1,143.83	1,194.86
Government Consumption Expend...	91f	419.67	453.55	† 466.08	481.35	504.33	513.55	540.93	569.37	583.44	613.33	658.53	690.77
Gross Fixed Capital Formation.........	93e	267.28	241.85	† 255.00	282.85	293.47	296.63	324.50	358.33	389.01	395.62	391.38	383.22
Changes in Inventories................	93i	−2.48	−5.03	† 17.31	21.45	6.96	9.23	15.19	5.35	16.47	6.56	2.10	9.41
Exports of Goods and Services........	90c	417.35	492.99	† 582.93	695.38	688.32	781.87	838.23	885.30	1,012.09	1,039.54	1,031.90	1,069.98
Imports of Goods and Services (-)....	98c	390.88	435.42	508.33	† 576.06	568.70	644.88	714.29	757.56	884.40	897.08	880.34	908.95
Gross Domestic Product (GDP)........	99b	1,485.13	1,544.04	† 1,645.79	1,770.25	1,815.14	1,888.23	1,971.87	2,076.53	2,194.97	2,266.39	2,347.40	2,438.87
Net Primary Income from Abroad.....	98.n	−58.39	−68.13	−45.88	−45.90	−46.72	−43.08	−28.71	−19.69	−16.45	−18.99	−9.44	−3.89
Gross National Income (GNI)..........	99a	1,426.74	1,475.91	1,599.91	1,724.35	1,768.42	1,845.15	1,943.16	2,056.84	2,178.52	2,247.40	2,337.97	2,434.99
Net Current Transf.from Abroad......	98t	....	−9.79	−9.54	−6.97	−7.49	−12.19	−16.53	−20.27	−20.10	−24.24	−22.76	−19.95
Gross Nat'l Disposable Inc.(GNDI)....	99i	....	1,424.60	1,550.89	1,681.50	1,728.39	1,804.65	1,897.14	2,036.57	2,158.42	2,223.16	2,315.21	2,415.04
Gross Saving..........................	99s	....	173.59	250.06	333.13	331.46	357.45	387.04	451.45	496.62	501.41	512.84	529.41
Consumption of Fixed Capital.........	99cf	193.3	197.6	192.9	199.5	207.8	218.4	232.3	251.5	274.1	292.4	306.2	309.0
Net National Income..................	99e	1,388.69	1,236.76	1,367.56	1,488.96	1,528.06	1,598.39	1,681.41	1,805.38	1,904.42	1,954.98	2,031.80	2,126.03
GDP Volume 1995 Prices..............	99b.p	1,616.70	1,725.97	† 1,797.85	1,870.72	1,894.87	1,941.06	2,011.82	1,990.94	2,077.08	2,096.28	2,140.27	2,174.75
GDP Volume (2000=100)..............	99bvp	77.8	83.1	† 86.6	90.1	91.2	93.5	96.9	95.9	100.0	100.9	103.0	104.7
GDP Deflator (2000=100)..............	99bip	86.9	84.7	† 86.6	89.5	90.6	92.1	92.7	98.7	100.0	102.3	103.8	106.1
						Millions: Midyear Estimates							
Population.............................	99z	8.68	8.74	8.79	8.83	8.85	8.86	8.86	8.86	8.86	8.86	8.87	8.88

Switzerland 146

		1992	1993	1994	1995	1996	1997	1998	1999	2000	2001	2002	2003
Exchange Rates						*Francs per SDR: End of Period*							
Market Rate	aa	2.0020	2.0322	1.9146	1.7102	1.9361	1.9636	1.9382	2.1955	2.1322	2.1079	1.8854	1.8380
					Francs per US Dollar: End of Period (ae) Period Average (rf)								
Market Rate	ae	1.4560	1.4795	1.3115	1.1505	1.3464	1.4553	1.3765	1.5996	1.6365	1.6773	1.3868	1.2369
Market Rate	rf	1.4062	1.4776	1.3677	1.1825	1.2360	1.4513	1.4498	1.5022	1.6888	1.6876	1.5586	1.3467
					Index Numbers (2000=100): Period Averages								
Market Rate	ahx	120.4	114.2	123.7	142.9	136.6	116.3	116.6	112.4	100.0	100.1	108.6	125.4
Nominal Effective Exchange Rate	neu	91.9	94.9	101.1	107.8	106.1	100.0	101.9	100.8	100.0	103.8	108.1	107.7
Real Effective Exchange Rate	reu	84.5	84.9	92.1	97.9	98.1	95.1	100.6	100.3	100.0	105.1	110.9	112.0
Fund Position						*Millions of SDRs: End of Period*							
Quota	2f.s	2,470	2,470	2,470	2,470	2,470	2,470	2,470	3,459	3,459	3,459	3,459	3,459
SDRs	1b.s	12	113	162	181	88	170	192	345	125	225	54	25
Reserve Position in the Fund	1c.s	581	605	643	981	1,065	1,407	1,828	1,218	964	1,259	1,410	1,383
of which: Outstg.Fund Borrowing	2c	–	–	–	–	–	–	230	–	–	–	–	–
International Liquidity						*Millions of US Dollars Unless Otherwise Indicated: End of Period*							
Total Reserves minus Gold	1l.d	33,255	32,635	34,729	36,413	38,433	39,028	41,191	36,321	32,272	32,006	40,155	47,652
SDRs	1b.d	16	155	236	269	126	230	271	473	162	283	74	37
Reserve Position in the Fund	1c.d	799	830	939	1,459	1,531	1,899	2,574	1,672	1,256	1,582	1,917	2,056
Foreign Exchange	1d.d	32,440	31,650	33,554	34,685	36,775	36,899	38,346	34,176	30,854	30,141	38,164	45,560
Gold (Million Fine Troy Ounces)	1ad	83.28	83.28	83.28	83.28	83.28	83.28	83.28	83.28	77.79	70.68	61.62	52.51
Gold (National Valuation)	1and	8,176	8,046	9,077	10,347	8,841	8,182	8,667	7,464	21,219	19,664	21,156	21,932
Monetary Authorities: Other Liab.	4..d	–	–	–	–	–	33	119	134	124	375	401	393
Deposit Money Banks: Assets	7a.d	143,589	154,224	187,875	212,374	†263,362	314,438	369,712	463,670	465,833	446,488	557,850	616,287
Liabilities	7b.d	125,791	129,333	171,093	184,869	†223,836	268,969	300,777	395,023	440,005	415,253	498,607	546,820
Trustee Accounts: Assets	7k.d	268,344	235,558	271,584	288,831	†294,323	293,492	311,232	292,460	325,518	323,209	328,419	327,835
Liabilities	7m.d	204,428	182,470	213,280	232,765	†239,280	241,593	255,032	243,663	264,004	265,599	273,602	276,692
Monetary Authorities						*Billions of Francs: End of Period*							
Foreign Assets	11	59.22	60.94	59.98	56.30	63.13	69.04	69.34	71.05	88.14	87.52	85.45	86.42
Claims on Central Government	12a	4.99	5.02	5.13	5.19	5.26	7.12	7.22	7.14	7.71	8.32	9.36	10.04
Claims on Deposit Money Banks	12e	1.34	1.36	1.30	1.87	2.86	1.09	17.73	28.53	24.46	25.99	28.01	27.13
Reserve Money	14	39.60	39.10	39.33	38.40	40.35	39.43	42.47	49.67	44.41	49.96	46.56	50.24
of which: Currency Outside DMBs	14a	31.37	31.38	32.64	33.02	34.61	34.33	35.43	39.44	37.78	42.17	41.94	42.93
Central Government Deposits	16d	.42	.49	.75	1.12	1.08	†2.69	15.36	17.16	10.21	2.59	7.29	3.01
Other Items (Net)	17r	25.53	27.73	26.33	23.84	29.83	35.15	36.46	39.87	65.68	69.29	68.96	70.34
Deposit Money Banks						*Billions of Francs: End of Period*							
Reserves	20	7.82	8.01	7.64	8.27	†9.61	9.83	10.95	17.17	12.51	12.74	13.62	14.33
Foreign Assets	21	209.07	228.17	246.40	244.34	†354.59	457.60	508.91	741.69	762.34	748.90	773.63	762.29
Claims on Central Government	22a	36.17	47.40	49.57	†50.70	†52.66	52.44	51.68	53.46	59.29	56.88	61.84	59.05
Claims on Private Sector	22d	563.92	574.31	594.37	611.70	†608.17	625.65	635.67	676.49	668.94	660.94	662.90	686.97
Demand Deposits	24	54.86	59.86	62.22	67.63	†93.57	105.45	113.88	124.00	122.25	131.40	149.32	194.49
Time and Savings Deposits	25	300.34	329.73	343.60	358.01	†374.36	396.05	413.84	474.49	369.90	377.10	390.97	393.48
Bonds	26ab	183.49	173.22	164.72	161.13	†149.66	137.25	127.55	123.04	128.19	129.07	129.91	120.29
Foreign Liabilities	26c	183.15	191.35	224.39	212.69	†301.37	391.43	414.02	631.88	720.07	696.50	691.47	676.36
Other Items (Net)	27r	95.13	103.74	103.04	115.54	†106.06	115.34	137.93	135.39	162.68	145.39	150.31	138.02
Monetary Survey						*Billions of Francs: End of Period*							
Foreign Assets (Net)	31n	85.13	97.76	81.99	87.94	†116.35	135.17	164.06	180.64	130.21	139.28	167.05	171.86
Domestic Credit	32	604.67	626.24	648.31	†666.47	†665.01	†682.53	679.22	719.93	725.73	723.56	726.80	753.06
Claims on Central Govt. (Net)	32an	40.75	51.93	53.94	†54.77	†56.84	†56.88	43.54	43.44	56.78	62.61	63.91	66.09
Claims on Private Sector	32d	563.92	574.31	594.37	611.70	†608.17	625.65	635.67	676.49	668.94	660.94	662.90	686.97
Money	34	86.23	91.24	94.86	100.65	†128.18	139.78	149.31	163.44	160.03	173.57	191.26	237.41
Quasi-Money	35	300.34	329.73	343.60	358.01	†374.36	396.05	413.84	474.49	369.90	377.10	390.97	393.48
Bonds	36ab	183.49	173.22	164.72	161.13	†149.66	137.25	127.55	123.04	128.19	129.07	129.91	120.29
Other Items (Net)	37r	119.74	129.82	127.11	134.62	†129.16	144.62	152.58	139.59	197.82	183.11	181.71	173.73
Money plus Quasi-Money	35l	386.57	420.97	438.46	458.66	†502.54	535.83	563.15	637.93	529.93	550.66	582.23	630.90
Other Banking Institutions						*Billions of Francs: End of Period*							
Foreign Assets	41..x	390.71	348.51	356.18	332.30	†396.28	427.12	428.41	467.82	532.71	542.12	455.45	405.50
Domestic Liabilities	45..x	93.06	78.54	76.47	64.50	†74.11	75.53	77.36	78.06	100.67	96.63	76.02	63.26
Foreign Liabilities	46c.x	297.65	269.96	279.72	267.80	†322.17	351.59	351.05	389.76	432.04	445.49	379.43	342.24
Nonbank Financial Institutions						*Billions of Francs: End of Period*							
Claims on Central Government	42a.s	....	....	....	....	....	....	....	....	....	....	....	....
Claims on Priv.Sec.& Local Govt.	42d.s	127.21	139.24	152.91	163.99	180.80	200.00	227.30	250.10	254.80	264.20	263.20	....
Real Estate	42h.s	19.75	20.82	21.79	22.50	23.40	24.30	25.00	25.60	25.80	27.00	28.60	....
Incr.in Total Assets(Within Per.)	49z.s	13.54	13.09	14.64	11.79	24.11	20.50	28.10	24.60	7.30	8.50	1.00	....
Liquid Liabilities	55l	479.63	499.51	514.93	523.16	†576.65	611.36	640.51	715.99	630.59	647.29	658.25	694.16

Switzerland 146

		1992	1993	1994	1995	1996	1997	1998	1999	2000	2001	2002	2003
Interest Rates						*Percent Per Annum*							
Bank Rate (End of Period)	60	6.00	4.00	3.50	1.50	1.00	1.00	1.00	.50	†3.20	1.59	.50	.11
Money Market Rate	60b	7.47	4.94	3.85	2.89	1.78	1.35	1.22	.93	†3.50	1.65	.44	.09
Treasury Bill Rate	60c	7.76	4.75	3.97	2.78	1.72	1.45	1.32	1.17	2.93	2.68	.94	.16
Deposit Rate	60l	5.50	3.50	3.63	1.28	1.34	1.00	.69	1.24	†3.00	1.68	.43	.17
Lending Rate	60p	7.80	6.40	5.51	5.48	4.97	4.47	4.07	3.90	4.29	4.30	3.93	3.27
Government Bond Yield	61	5.48	4.05	5.23	3.73	3.63	3.08	†2.71	3.62	3.55	3.56	2.40	2.78
Prices, Production, Labor						*Index Numbers (2000=100): Period Averages*							
Share Prices	62	24.1	31.0	35.7	37.3	46.6	66.1	88.0	89.6	100.0	88.7	72.2	61.7
Producer Prices	63	104.00	104.45	103.97	103.88	102.05	101.31	100.06	99.06	100.00	100.49	100.00	100.00
Prices: Home & Imported Goods	63s	102.7	102.9	102.6	102.6	100.2	100.3	98.7	97.4	100.0	99.9	98.7	98.4
Consumer Prices	64	90.9	93.9	94.7	96.4	97.2	97.7	97.7	98.5	100.0	101.0	101.6	102.3
Wages: Hourly Earn	65	....	93.5	94.9	96.2	97.4	97.8	98.5	98.8	100.0	102.5	104.3	105.8
Industrial Production	66	78.7	77.3	80.6	82.2	82.2	86.0	89.1	92.2	100.0	99.3	94.2	94.2
Manufacturing Employment	67ey	†117.7	112.0	107.1	105.7	103.0	100.4	99.9	99.0	100.0	101.4	98.7	95.6
						Number in Thousands: Period Averages							
Labor Force	67d	....	3,873	....	3,871	3,925	3,928	3,975	3,984	3,985	4,039	4,079	4,120
Employment	67e	3,759	3,746	3,719	3,747	3,781	3,766	3,833	3,862	3,870	3,938	3,959	3,951
Unemployment	67c	92	163	171	153	169	188	140	99	72	67	101	144
Unemployment Rate (%)	67r	2.5	4.5	4.7	4.2	4.7	5.2	3.9	2.7	2.0	1.9	2.8	3.8
International Transactions						*Millions of Francs*							
Exports	70	†86,148	86,659	90,213	92,012	94,174	105,133	109,113	114,446	126,549	131,717	130,381	130,661
Imports, c.i.f.	71	†86,739	83,767	87,279	90,775	91,967	103,088	106,866	113,416	128,615	130,052	123,125	123,778
						2000=100							
Volume of Exports	72.a	71.8	72.2	75.8	78.9	80.0	86.1	90.3	93.4	100.0	102.1	....	....
Volume of Exports	72.b	....	....	....	....	....	87.0	90.1	93.0	100.0	102.8	104.7	104.8
Volume of Imports	73.a	64.5	63.6	69.6	74.1	75.1	79.9	86.4	93.5	100.0	99.6	....	....
Volume of Imports	73.b	....	....	....	....	....	80.5	85.7	93.1	100.0	101.1	98.6	99.5
Unit Value of Exports	74.a	94.8	94.8	94.1	92.1	93.0	96.4	95.5	96.8	100.0	102.0	....	....
Unit Value of Exports	74.b	....	....	....	....	....	95.4	95.7	97.3	100.0	101.2	98.4	98.6
Unit Value of Imports	75.a	104.6	102.3	97.5	95.2	95.2	100.3	96.1	94.3	100.0	101.6	....	....
Unit Value of Imports	75.b	....	....	....	....	....	99.6	96.9	94.8	100.0	100.0	97.1	96.7
Import Prices	76.x	99.9	99.6	99.5	99.7	96.0	97.9	95.8	93.7	100.0	98.4	95.6	94.7

Switzerland 146

		1992	1993	1994	1995	1996	1997	1998	1999	2000	2001	2002	2003
Balance of Payments		\multicolumn{12}{c}{*Millions of US Dollars: Minus Sign Indicates Debit*}
Current Account, n.i.e.	78ald	14,247	17,926	17,588	21,804	21,051	26,679	26,775	29,611	34,417	23,898	26,011	....
Goods: Exports f.o.b.	78aad	79,870	75,424	82,625	97,139	95,544	95,039	93,782	91,823	94,842	95,826	100,475	....
Goods: Imports f.o.b.	78abd	−80,135	−73,832	−79,279	−93,880	−93,676	−92,302	−92,849	−90,980	−92,738	−94,262	−94,043	....
Trade Balance	78acd	−265	1,592	3,346	3,258	1,868	2,738	933	843	2,104	1,563	6,432	....
Services: Credit	78add	21,064	21,476	22,619	26,027	26,250	25,301	26,731	28,459	28,881	27,697	29,378	....
Services: Debit	78aed	−11,935	−11,548	−12,768	−15,037	−15,691	−14,100	−15,085	−15,888	−15,573	−16,477	−17,106	....
Balance on Goods & Services	78afd	8,864	11,520	13,196	14,249	12,426	13,939	12,579	13,414	15,412	12,783	18,705	....
Income: Credit	78agd	26,239	25,152	26,747	31,575	32,997	35,066	45,926	50,110	61,612	53,147	41,429	....
Income: Debit	78ahd	−17,902	−16,006	−18,932	−19,778	−20,383	−18,923	−28,049	−29,799	−39,682	−38,049	−29,944	....
Balance on Gds, Serv. & Inc.	78aid	17,201	20,666	21,012	26,045	25,040	30,081	30,456	33,725	37,343	27,881	30,190	....
Current Transfers, n.i.e.: Credit	78ajd	2,530	2,484	2,526	2,995	2,961	2,625	2,786	7,638	6,854	9,731	10,696	....
Current Transfers: Debit	78akd	−5,484	−5,225	−5,949	−7,237	−6,949	−6,027	−6,467	−11,752	−9,780	−13,714	−14,875	....
Capital Account, n.i.e.	78bcd	−43	−134	−350	−462	−214	−167	139	−515	−3,539	1,522	−1,133	....
Capital Account, n.i.e.: Credit	78bad	−	−	31	10	19	36	755	52	489	2,313	272	....
Capital Account: Debit	78bbd	−43	−134	−380	−472	−233	−203	−616	−567	−4,028	−791	−1,405	....
Financial Account, n.i.e.	78bjd	−15,780	−18,984	−16,398	−12,711	−27,317	−24,712	−31,161	−34,077	−30,229	−37,038	−33,692	....
Direct Investment Abroad	78bdd	−6,057	−8,764	−10,793	−12,210	−16,152	−17,732	−18,767	−33,276	−44,673	−18,298	−10,069	....
Dir. Invest. in Rep. Econ., n.i.e.	78bed	1,249	899	4,104	3,599	4,373	7,306	9,649	12,341	19,878	9,529	3,599	....
Portfolio Investment Assets	78bfd	−9,716	−30,121	−19,112	−8,884	−22,731	−19,739	−14,882	−46,839	−22,309	−42,841	−29,914	....
Equity Securities	78bkd	−6,464	−16,650	−8,073	−4,064	−14,686	−9,159	−2,529	−17,500	−20,323	−14,958	−7,618	....
Debt Securities	78bld	−3,252	−13,470	−11,040	−4,820	−8,045	−10,580	−12,353	−29,339	−1,986	−27,882	−22,296	....
Portfolio Investment Liab., n.i.e.	78bgd	3,571	12,501	911	4,960	12,895	9,033	10,247	5,894	10,547	1,896	7,323	....
Equity Securities	78bmd	1,809	7,923	−1,573	5,851	11,677	6,945	8,632	5,489	9,080	1,847	5,640	....
Debt Securities	78bnd	1,761	4,578	2,484	−891	1,218	2,088	1,615	404	1,467	49	1,683	....
Financial Derivatives Assets	78bwd	....	....	....	....	....	....	....	....	....	....	....	....
Financial Derivatives Liabilities	78bxd	....	....	....	....	....	....	....	....	....	....	....	....
Other Investment Assets	78bhd	−8,477	7,188	−30,797	−368	−70,356	−55,265	−60,089	−80,612	−93,277	23,059	−43,832	....
Monetary Authorities	78bod	−	−	−	−	−	−	−	−	−	−	−	....
General Government	78bpd	−177	−133	−70	−15	39	197	204	203	36	49	64	....
Banks	78bqd	−4,794	−2,666	−19,166	−9,423	−59,915	−52,384	−45,489	−77,286	−83,137	27,526	−58,469	....
Other Sectors	78brd	−3,506	9,987	−11,562	9,070	−10,480	−3,078	−14,804	−3,528	−10,176	−4,515	14,574	....
Other Investment Liab., n.i.e.	78bid	3,651	−687	39,290	191	64,654	51,683	42,681	108,416	99,604	−10,382	39,200	....
Monetary Authorities	78bsd	−43	91	−104	−3	−9	11	80	34	38	846	−882	....
General Government	78btd	84	79	40	267	31	121	−4	−58	−59	−23	140	....
Banks	78bud	−733	4,074	30,261	1,608	49,121	51,563	34,000	95,594	89,669	−16,550	37,643	....
Other Sectors	78bvd	4,343	−4,932	9,093	−1,680	15,511	−11	8,606	12,846	9,955	5,344	2,299	....
Net Errors and Omissions	78cad	5,973	1,678	169	−8,601	9,001	354	5,427	2,496	−4,654	12,256	11,216	....
Overall Balance	78cbd	4,397	486	1,009	29	2,521	2,154	1,179	−2,484	−4,005	638	2,402	....
Reserves and Related Items	79dad	−4,397	−486	−1,009	−29	−2,521	−2,154	−1,179	2,484	4,005	−638	−2,402	....
Reserve Assets	79dbd	−4,397	−486	−1,009	−29	−2,521	−2,154	−1,179	2,484	4,005	−638	−2,402	....
Use of Fund Credit and Loans	79dcd	−	−	−	−	−	−	−	−	−	−	−	....
Exceptional Financing	79ded	−	−	−	−	−	−	−	−	−	−	−	....
International Investment Position		\multicolumn{12}{c}{*Millions of US Dollars*}
Assets	79aad	586,781	647,184	745,816	860,214	924,274	1,009,487	1,196,819	1,239,355	1,363,615	1,314,056	1,511,965	....
Direct Investment Abroad	79abd	74,413	91,571	112,586	142,479	141,591	165,364	184,232	194,585	233,370	247,807	293,865	....
Portfolio Investment	79acd	219,559	271,003	293,846	347,040	359,820	382,782	469,522	504,757	501,598	489,069	520,785	....
Equity Securities	79add	56,416	88,919	100,797	120,543	138,922	165,438	209,617	259,679	265,897	247,409	218,245	....
Debt Securities	79aed	163,144	182,084	193,049	226,497	220,898	217,344	259,905	245,078	235,701	241,660	302,540	....
Financial Derivatives	79ald	−	−	−	−	−	−	−	−	−	−	−	....
Other Investment	79afd	252,215	243,643	293,976	322,125	375,575	414,208	492,632	496,075	575,166	525,483	635,979	....
Monetary Authorities	79agd	−	−	−	−	−	−	−	−	−	−	−	....
General Government	79ahd	889	884	1,037	1,250	1,051	946	943	759	755	584	696	....
Banks	79aid	127,784	133,539	163,590	183,006	231,511	276,736	332,647	342,082	413,332	375,251	465,885	....
Other Sectors	79ajd	123,542	109,220	129,349	137,870	143,012	136,526	159,043	153,234	161,079	149,648	169,397	....
Reserve Assets	79akd	40,594	40,967	45,409	48,569	47,288	47,132	50,432	43,938	53,480	51,697	61,337	....
Liabilities	79lad	351,455	404,168	472,874	556,487	587,559	700,953	838,861	881,470	1,045,164	964,864	1,080,119	....
Dir. Invest. in Rep. Economy	79lbd	42,986	49,532	61,691	73,324	69,001	74,142	88,201	90,510	101,706	104,426	131,608	....
Portfolio Investment	79lcd	109,190	162,151	162,400	208,583	203,380	272,805	353,572	339,491	411,445	349,732	350,558	....
Equity Securities	79ldd	90,876	139,056	134,721	179,290	176,566	246,515	323,809	309,597	382,038	321,678	315,134	....
Debt Securities	79led	18,314	23,095	27,679	29,293	26,814	26,289	29,763	29,894	29,408	28,054	35,425	....
Financial Derivatives	79lld	−	−	−	−	−	−	−	−	−	−	−	....
Other Investment	79lfd	199,279	192,485	248,783	274,580	315,178	354,006	397,088	451,470	532,013	510,707	597,953	....
Monetary Authorities	79lgd	38	128	36	37	24	33	119	355	393	1,252	507	....
General Government	79lhd	114	192	258	568	514	596	626	484	413	380	616	....
Banks	79lid	126,124	128,116	170,567	180,873	218,606	258,708	290,465	344,836	423,106	398,719	468,764	....
Other Sectors	79ljd	73,003	64,049	77,923	93,102	96,034	94,669	105,879	105,794	108,101	110,356	128,066	....

Switzerland 146

		1992	1993	1994	1995	1996	1997	1998	1999	2000	2001	2002	2003
Government Finance		\multicolumn{12}{c}{*Millions of Francs: Year Ending December 31*}
Deficit (-) or Surplus	80	−2,437	−8,351	−4,443	−5,141	−4,404	−4,917	363	−2,399	3,820	1,367	−3,989	−2,950
Revenue	81	32,355	29,559	33,752	32,202	35,279	34,695	39,359	37,742	44,031	43,018	35,537	40,259
Expenditure	82	34,354	35,443	36,759	37,474	39,417	38,151	41,634	40,839	40,832	42,147	39,526	43,645
Lending Minus Repayments	83	438	2,467	1,436	−131	266	1,461	−2,638	−698	−621	−496	—	−436
Financing													
Net Domestic Borrowing	84a	8,801	14,923	7,399	6,472	5,706	8,486	13,860	−6,817	3,244	−2,419	14,277	1,886
Other Financing	86c	−1,810	−1,131	−1,598	−1,050	1,202	−596	−4,245	−10,960	−9,000	−5,401	−3,223	−2,204
Use of Cash Balances	87	−4,554	−5,441	−1,358	−281	−2,504	−2,973	−9,978	20,176	1,936	6,453	−7,065	3,268
Total Debt	88	55,297	67,513	75,714	82,152	88,418	97,050	109,620	102,254	108,108	106,813	122,366	123,711
National Accounts		\multicolumn{12}{c}{*Billions of Francs*}
Househ.Cons.Expend.,incl.NPISHs	96f.c	209.4	214.5	217.7	222.6	226.3	231.3	235.8	242.0	249.6	256.0	260.6	265.2
Government Consumption Expend	91f.c	42.4	42.4	43.0	43.5	44.3	44.0	44.0	44.3	46.2	49.1	50.1	50.9
Gross Fixed Capital Formation	93e.c	86.6	83.0	86.4	86.5	82.7	82.2	87.0	88.6	94.6	93.6	88.0	87.1
Changes in Inventories	93i.c	−2.8	−2.6	—	.5	1.5	1.9	4.3	.5	1.5	3.2	−2.3	−4.5
Exports of Goods and Services	90c.c	125.0	128.8	131.3	131.9	135.5	151.6	156.9	165.8	189.8	190.7	189.0	188.3
Imports of Goods and Services (-)	98c.c	109.7	107.7	110.8	112.8	116.4	130.5	137.8	143.4	165.8	169.7	157.7	156.6
Gross Domestic Product (GDP)	99b.c	350.8	358.3	367.7	372.3	374.0	380.6	390.2	397.9	415.9	422.8	427.8	430.5
Net Primary Income from Abroad	98.n	13.4	15.6	12.7	15.6	....	....	....	....	....	....	....	....
Gross National Income (GNI)	99a	352.2	358.4	365.6	377.6	....	....	....	....	....	....	....	....
Net National Income	99e	316.7	322.2	328.8	339.8	....	....	....	....	....	....	....	....
GDP Volume 2000 Ref., Chained	99b.r	371.5	370.6	374.6	376.0	378.0	385.2	396.0	401.2	415.9	420.1	420.8	418.5
GDP Volume (2000=100)	99bvr	89.3	89.1	90.1	90.4	90.9	92.6	95.2	96.5	100.0	101.0	101.2	100.6
GDP Deflator (2000=100)	99bir	94.4	96.7	98.2	99.0	98.9	98.8	98.5	99.2	100.0	100.6	101.7	102.9
		\multicolumn{12}{c}{*Millions: Midyear Estimates*}
Population	99z	6.96	7.02	7.08	7.12	7.15	7.16	7.17	7.17	7.17	7.17	7.17	7.17

2004, International Monetary Fund: *International Financial Statistics Yearbook*

Syrian Arab Republic 463

		1992	1993	1994	1995	1996	1997	1998	1999	2000	2001	2002	2003
Exchange Rates		*Pounds per SDR: End of Period (aa) Pounds per US Dollar: End of Period (ae)*
Principal Rate	aa	15.434	15.418	16.387	16.686	16.141	15.145	15.805	15.406	14.625	14.107	15.261	16.680
Principal Rate	ae	11.225	11.225	11.225	11.225	11.225	11.225	11.225	11.225	11.225	11.225	11.225	11.225
Fund Position		*Millions of SDRs: End of Period*
Quota	2f.s	139	210	210	210	210	210	210	294	294	294	294	294
SDRs	1b.s	–	–	–	–	–	–	–	–	–	–	–	–
Reserve Position in the Fund	1c.s	–	–	–	–	–	–	–	–	–	–	–	–
Total Fund Cred.&Loans Outstg	2tl	–	–	–	–	–	–	–	–	–	–	–	–
International Liquidity		*Millions of US Dollars Unless Otherwise Indicated: End of Period*
SDRs	1b.d	–	–	–	–	–	–	–	–	–	–	–	–
Reserve Position in the Fund	1c.d	–	–	–	–	–	–	–	–	–	–	–	–
Gold (Million Fine Troy Ounces)	1ad	.833	.833	.833	.833	.833	.833	.833	.833	.833	.833	.833	.833
Gold (National Valuation)	1and	29	29	29	29	29	29	29	29	29	29	29	29
Monetary Authorities:Other Assets	3..d	....	....	....	....	....	....	....	....	....	....	....	....
Other Liab	4..d	1,169	1,037	1,041	1,124	1,041	1,084	1,137	1,150	805	730	692	581
Monetary Authorities		*Millions of Pounds: End of Period*
Foreign Assets	11	23,544	24,368	28,568	37,206	49,156	52,376	55,216	67,512	88,391	101,503	115,018	130,666
Claims on Central Government	12a	136,064	153,089	178,802	203,998	241,730	265,783	270,370	270,369	274,877	301,278	321,202	304,929
Claims on Official Entities	12bx	106	106	106	106	106	106	106	106	106	106	106	106
Claims on Deposit Money Banks	12e	51,499	71,006	90,674	104,602	112,460	126,599	135,455	164,991	161,558	157,174	156,554	174,811
Reserve Money	14	132,508	151,867	164,996	172,711	185,864	194,799	204,513	219,475	252,814	295,442	342,625	377,685
of which: Currency Outside DMBs	14a	107,602	126,116	135,021	143,800	153,715	159,808	178,191	182,184	203,863	229,266	258,359	285,015
Foreign Liabilities	16c	13,117	11,640	11,683	12,614	11,686	12,168	12,768	12,911	9,040	8,196	7,773	6,520
Central Government Deposits	16d	76,633	93,898	126,027	156,479	213,995	256,253	272,085	314,414	355,693	374,313	391,594	391,924
Capital Accounts	17a	11,186	14,242	18,755	23,902	23,902	33,839	38,195	43,909	51,426	55,814	55,815	59,195
Other Items (Net)	17r	−22,230	−23,077	−23,311	−19,794	−31,995	−52,193	−66,415	−87,732	−144,041	−173,704	−204,927	−224,813
Deposit Money Banks		*Millions of Pounds: End of Period*
Reserves	20	23,773	24,854	31,556	29,366	38,771	25,946	21,403	23,716	31,419	42,242	71,788	85,910
Foreign Assets	21	26,105	111,872	126,639	150,020	180,547	222,465	255,655	285,762	398,681	502,229	581,672	591,826
Claims on Central Government	22a	12,118	21,992	26,252	30,931	35,560	41,573	48,639	58,275	69,385	100,656	127,428	154,462
Claims on Official Entities	22bx	89,540	160,109	120,667	140,439	147,202	164,580	160,381	179,711	187,356	191,020	157,802	173,976
Claims on Private Sector	22d	35,556	44,457	52,343	63,667	66,633	73,351	72,617	75,345	76,611	78,737	83,676	108,658
Demand Deposits	24	48,799	60,761	68,885	78,028	84,685	93,665	97,683	121,471	151,753	176,845	222,391	329,809
Time and Savings Deposits	25	41,505	67,156	83,113	91,775	104,624	116,939	135,636	160,346	194,800	276,181	330,155	261,080
Restricted Deposits	26b	18,659	30,119	24,411	26,708	27,182	33,235	22,776	20,327	28,394	40,542	50,451	73,208
Foreign Liabilities	26c	6,593	16,584	10,347	5,574	5,551	2,782	3,653	4,915	4,583	3,891	11,116	13,576
Central Government Deposits	26d	5,634	6,302	6,327	7,780	8,643	12,863	13,686	14,960	18,078	19,310	20,154	26,536
Credit from Monetary Authorities	26g	51,671	71,068	90,741	104,712	119,897	136,811	135,199	149,810	160,744	150,193	168,217	178,531
Capital Accounts	27a	10,344	13,529	17,546	23,065	29,908	34,666	40,576	48,878	47,799	50,598	52,098	44,622
Other Items (Net)	27r	3,888	97,765	56,087	76,780	88,224	96,955	109,485	102,102	157,300	197,322	167,784	187,469
Monetary Survey		*Millions of Pounds: End of Period*
Foreign Assets (Net)	31n	29,940	108,016	133,177	169,038	212,466	259,891	294,450	335,448	473,449	591,645	677,801	702,396
Domestic Credit	32	191,117	279,553	245,816	274,882	268,593	276,278	266,342	254,432	234,564	278,174	278,466	323,671
Claims on Central Govt. (Net)	32an	65,915	74,881	72,700	70,670	54,652	38,241	33,238	−730	−29,509	8,311	36,882	40,931
Claims on Official Entities	32bx	89,646	160,215	120,773	140,545	147,308	164,686	160,487	179,817	187,462	191,126	157,908	174,082
Claims on Private Sector	32d	35,556	44,457	52,343	63,667	66,633	73,351	72,617	75,345	76,611	78,737	83,676	108,658
Money	34	156,907	191,432	207,106	225,038	244,495	260,927	281,926	313,318	368,670	419,911	494,681	628,279
Quasi-Money	35	41,505	67,156	83,113	91,775	104,624	116,939	135,636	160,346	194,800	276,181	330,155	261,080
Restricted Deposits	36b	18,659	30,119	24,411	26,708	27,182	33,235	22,776	20,327	28,394	40,542	50,451	73,208
Other Items (Net)	37r	3,986	98,863	64,364	100,397	104,759	125,069	120,452	95,889	116,148	133,183	80,980	63,498
Money plus Quasi-Money	35l	198,412	258,588	290,219	316,813	349,119	377,866	417,562	473,663	563,470	696,092	824,836	889,359
Interest Rates		*Percent Per Annum*
Discount Rate (End of Period)	60	5.00	5.00	5.00	5.00	5.00	5.00	5.00	5.00	5.00	5.00	5.00	....
Deposit Rate	60l	4.0	4.0	4.0	4.0	4.0	4.0	4.0	4.0	4.0	4.0	4.0	....
Lending Rate	60p	9.0	9.0	9.0	9.0	9.0	9.0	9.0	9.0	9.0	9.0	9.0	....
Prices and Production		*Index Numbers (2000=100): Period Averages*
Wholesale Prices	63	77.5	84.1	96.1	102.7	106.0	108.7	108.0	106.0	100.0	95.0	102.0	....
Consumer Prices	64	70.0	79.3	91.4	98.7	106.9	108.9	†108.0	104.0	100.0	103.0	104.0	....
Industrial Production	66	†79.1	80.9	87.2	89.9	90.8	96.2	†98.0	100.0	100.0	103.0	109.0	....
		Number in Thousands: Period Averages
Labor Force	67d	....	....	....	....	....	....	4,411	4,527	4,937	....	....	....
Employment	67e	....	....	....	....	....	....	....	....	....	....	4,844	4,822	....
Unemployment	67c	....	....	....	....	....	....	....	....	....	348	....	....
Unemployment Rate (%)	67r	....	....	....	....	....	....	....	....	....	11.2	....	....

Syrian Arab Republic 463

		1992	1993	1994	1995	1996	1997	1998	1999	2000	2001	2002	2003
International Transactions						*Millions of Pounds*							
Exports...............................	70	34,720	35,319	34,200	40,000	44,890	43,960	32,440	38,880	†216,190	243,000	315,920	....
Imports, c.i.f.......................	71	39,178	46,468	61,370	52,860	60,390	45,210	43,720	43,010	†187,530	220,000	235,720	....
						1995=100							
Volume of Exports................	72	62.9	94.6	102.4	100.0	98.2	109.6	....	....	....	....	....	....
Volume of Imports................	73	57.7	90.7	111.3	100.0	100.8	87.9	....	....	....	....	....	....
Unit Value of Exports............	74	75.6	74.4	80.0	100.0	105.6	83.3	....	....	....	....	....	....
Unit Value of Imports............	75	83.1	78.8	89.0	100.0	105.9	90.7	....	....	....	....	....	....
Balance of Payments					*Millions of US Dollars: Minus Sign Indicates Debit*								
Current Account, n.i.e...........	78ald	55	−203	−791	263	40	461	58	201	1,061	1,221	1,440	....
Goods: Exports f.o.b..............	78aad	3,100	3,253	3,329	3,858	4,178	4,057	3,142	3,806	5,146	5,706	6,668	....
Goods: Imports f.o.b.............	78abd	−2,941	−3,512	−4,604	−4,004	−4,516	−3,603	−3,320	−3,590	−3,723	−4,282	−4,458	....
Trade Balance...................	78acd	159	−259	−1,275	−146	−338	454	−178	216	1,423	1,424	2,210	....
Services: Credit.....................	78add	1,281	1,595	1,863	1,899	1,792	1,582	1,666	1,651	1,699	1,781	1,559	....
Services: Debit......................	78aed	−1,102	−1,442	−1,611	−1,537	−1,555	−1,489	−1,491	−1,612	−1,667	−1,694	−1,883	....
Balance on Goods & Services......	78afd	338	−106	−1,023	216	−101	547	−3	255	1,455	1,511	1,886	....
Income: Credit......................	78agd	619	432	638	444	534	421	369	356	345	379	250	....
Income: Debit.......................	78ahd	−1,214	−1,064	−997	−1,004	−1,017	−1,006	−839	−899	−1,224	−1,162	−1,175	....
Balance on Gds, Serv. & Inc.........	78aid	−258	−738	−1,382	−344	−584	−38	−473	−288	576	728	961	....
Current Transfers, n.i.e.: Credit......	78ajd	321	543	597	610	630	504	533	491	495	512	499	....
Current Transfers: Debit................	78akd	−8	−8	−6	−3	−6	−5	−2	−2	−10	−19	−20	....
Capital Account, n.i.e............	78bcd	−	28	102	20	26	18	27	80	63	17	20	....
Capital Account, n.i.e.: Credit........	78bad	−	28	102	20	26	18	27	80	63	17	20	....
Capital Account: Debit..................	78bbd	−	−	−	−	−	−	−	....	....	....	....	....
Financial Account, n.i.e.........	78bjd	−50	598	1,159	521	782	65	196	173	−139	−244	−250	....
Direct Investment Abroad.......	78bdd	−	−	−	−	−	−	−	−	−	−	−	....
Dir. Invest. in Rep. Econ., n.i.e........	78bed	−	109	251	100	89	80	82	263	270	110	115	....
Portfolio Investment Assets............	78bfd	−	−	−	−	−	−	−	−	−	−	−	....
Equity Securities................	78bkd	−	−	−	−	−	−	−	−	−	−	−	....
Debt Securities..................	78bld	−	−	−	−	−	−	−	−	−	−	−	....
Portfolio Investment Liab., n.i.e.......	78bgd	−	−	−	−	−	−	−	−	−	−	−	....
Equity Securities................	78bmd	−	−	−	−	−	−	−	−	−	−	−	....
Debt Securities..................	78bnd	−	−	−	−	−	−	−	−	−	−	−	....
Financial Derivatives Assets.......	78bwd	....	....	....	....	....	....	....	....	....	....	....	....
Financial Derivatives Liabilities.....	78bxd	....	....	....	....	....	....	....	....	....	....	....	....
Other Investment Assets...............	78bhd	−1,175	−815	−718	1,510	1,660	1,496	1,422	1,332	1,206	1,136	1,180	....
Monetary Authorities...............	78bod	−	−	−	−	−	−	−	−	−	−	−	....
General Government...............	78bpd	−74	−	−	−	−	−	−	−	−	−	−	....
Banks................................	78bqd	−241	−	−	1,510	1,660	1,496	1,422	1,332	1,206	1,136	1,180	....
Other Sectors.......................	78brd	−860	−815	−718	−	−	−	−	−	−	−	−	....
Other Investment Liab., n.i.e........	78bid	1,126	1,304	1,626	−1,089	−967	−1,511	−1,308	−1,422	−1,615	−1,490	−1,545	....
Monetary Authorities...............	78bsd	28	11	20	−	−	−	−	−	−	−	−	....
General Government...............	78btd	173	−121	339	−	−	−	−	−	−	−	−	....
Banks................................	78bud	−226	−128	−147	−1,089	−967	−1,511	−1,308	−1,422	−1,615	−1,490	−1,545	....
Other Sectors.......................	78bvd	1,151	1,542	1,414	−	−	−	−	−	−	−	−	....
Net Errors and Omissions.................	78cad	70	−119	96	35	139	−95	153	−195	−171	26	−160	....
Overall Balance....................	78cbd	76	304	566	839	987	449	434	259	814	1,020	1,050	....
Reserves and Related Items..............	79dad	−76	−304	−566	−839	−987	−449	−434	−259	−814	−1,020	−1,050	....
Reserve Assets.....................	79dbd	−76	−304	−566	−839	−987	−449	−434	−259	−814	−1,020	−1,050	....
Use of Fund Credit and Loans........	79dcd	−	−	−	−	−	−	−	−	−	−	−	....
Exceptional Financing.................	79ded	−	−	−	−	−	−	−	....	....	....	....	....
Government Finance					*Millions of Pounds: Year Ending December 31*								
Deficit (-) or Surplus.............	80	6,273	115	−18,860	−10,059	−1,577	−1,723	−5,534	5,827	....	....	....	....
Revenue.............................	81	85,788	92,619	111,892	131,002	152,231	179,202	180,437	196,127	....	....	....	....
Grants Received................	81z	6,250	2,864	1,264	896	1,788	798	2	−	....	....	....	....
Expenditure........................	82	85,765	95,368	132,016	141,957	155,596	181,723	185,973	190,300	....	....	....	....
National Accounts						*Millions of Pounds*							
Househ.Cons.Expend.,incl.NPISHs.....	96f	274,195	303,988	348,865	378,143	489,728	515,411	542,374	575,866	572,761	570,781	594,487	....
Government Consumption Expend....	91f	53,588	56,239	68,019	76,709	81,316	84,994	88,521	86,857	112,244	121,723	125,007	....
Exports of Goods and Services..........	90c	97,577	115,294	167,327	177,229	219,872	241,719	241,316	264,704	326,715	359,278	404,102	....
Gross Capital Formation..................	93	86,120	107,466	151,622	155,504	163,076	155,464	162,446	153,706	156,092	199,162	200,031	....
Imports of Goods and Services (-).....	98c	139,850	169,242	229,732	216,610	263,135	252,019	244,213	262,041	263,868	296,893	324,176	....
Gross Domestic Product (GDP)........	99b	371,630	413,755	506,101	570,975	690,857	745,569	790,444	819,092	903,944	954,051	999,451	....
Consumption of Fixed Capital..........	99cf	15,958	14,492	17,674	20,344	26,257	30,151	31,668	34,282	38,551	38,499	40,313	....
GDP Volume 1995 Prices.................	99b.p	476,850	501,546	539,929	570,975	612,896	628,148	675,888	662,396	666,567	....	....	....
GDP Volume 2000 Prices.................	99b.p	....	....	....	....	....	....	....	....	903,944	934,409	964,574	....
GDP Volume (2000=100)................	99bvp	71.5	75.2	81.0	85.7	91.9	94.2	101.4	99.4	†100.0	103.4	106.7	....
GDP Deflator (2000=100)...............	99bip	57.5	60.8	69.1	73.7	83.1	87.5	86.2	91.2	100.0	102.1	103.6	....
						Millions: Midyear Estimates							
Population................................	99z	13.47	13.84	14.22	14.60	14.98	15.37	15.76	16.16	16.56	16.97	17.38	17.80

2004, International Monetary Fund : *International Financial Statistics Yearbook*

Tajikistan 923

		1992	1993	1994	1995	1996	1997	1998	1999	2000	2001	2002	2003
Exchange Rates						*Somoni per SDR: End of Period*							
Official Rate	aa	.006	.019	.058	.436	.472	1.008	1.377	1.971	† 2.866	3.205	4.079	4.393
					Somoni per US Dollar: End of Period (ae) Period Average (rf)								
Official Rate	ae	.005	.014	.039	.294	.328	.747	.978	1.436	† 2.200	2.550	3.000	2.957
Official Rate	rf	.002	.010	.024	.123	.296	.562	.777	1.238	2.076	2.372	2.764	3.061
Fund Position						*Millions of SDRs: End of Period*							
Quota	2f.s	–	60.00	60.00	60.00	60.00	60.00	60.00	87.00	87.00	87.00	87.00	87.00
SDRs	1b.s	–	–	–	–	2.21	9.06	2.05	.04	6.02	3.86	1.34	.57
Reserve Position in the Fund	1c.s	–	–	–	–	–	–	–	–	–	–	–	–
Total Fund Cred.&Loans Outstg	2tl	–	–	–	–	15.00	22.50	70.30	73.21	85.03	87.66	69.17	67.16
International Liquidity						*Millions of US Dollars Unless Otherwise Indicated: End of Period*							
Total Reserves minus Gold	1l.d	....	....	....	....	....	36.5	53.6	55.2	92.9	92.6	89.5	111.9
SDRs	1b.d	–	–	–	–	3.2	12.2	2.9	–	7.8	4.9	1.8	.9
Reserve Position in the Fund	1c.d	–	–	–	–	–	–	–	–	–	–	–	–
Foreign Exchange	1d.d	....	....	....	....	....	24.3	50.7	55.1	85.0	87.7	87.7	111.0
Gold (Million Fine Troy Ounces)	1ad	....	....	....	....	....	.01	.01	.01	.01	.01	–	.01
Gold (National Valuation)	1and	....	....	....	....	....	2.4	2.3	2.3	1.4	1.7	–	5.7
Monetary Authorities:Other Liab	4..d	....	....	....	....	....	....	2.22	.14	.09	.24	.31	.39
Deposit Money Banks: Assets	7a.d	....	....	....	....	....	....	1.04	1.10	1.44	2.44	2.82	9.67
Liabilities	7b.d	....	....	....	....	....	....	74.64	42.62	65.06	86.22	92.15	106.34
Monetary Authorities						*Millions of Somoni: End of Period*							
Foreign Assets	11	....	....	....	....	....	....	67.2	83.6	209.1	256.4	294.0	402.9
Claims on General Government	12a	....	....	....	....	....	....	102.4	64.9	131.9	92.8	156.8	153.8
Claims on Other Resident Sectors	12d	....	....	....	....	....	....	16.7	96.5	1.1	215.9	171.4	142.1
Claims on Deposit Money Banks	12e	....	....	....	....	....	....	26.3	49.0	150.0	37.6	34.1	42.1
Reserve Money	14	....	....	....	....	....	....	60.4	76.5	117.0	146.2	179.8	237.7
of which: Currency Outside Banks	14a	....	....	....	....	....	....	46.6	62.0	86.8	103.6	135.8	158.1
Foreign Liabilities	16c	....	....	....	....	....	....	99.0	144.5	243.9	281.5	283.0	296.2
General Government Deposits	16d	....	....	....	....	....	....	9.4	21.2	48.2	38.1	65.3	137.0
Counterpart Funds	16e	....	....	....	....	....	....	3.0	15.0	38.8	85.8	101.0	94.6
Capital Accounts	17a	....	....	....	....	....	....	36.3	41.5	11.5	64.8	47.4	18.4
Other Items (Net)	17r	....	....	....	....	....	....	4.5	–4.7	32.6	–13.8	–20.2	–42.9
Deposit Money Banks						*Millions of Somoni: End of Period*							
Reserves	20	....	....	....	....	....	....	12.0	13.5	34.6	49.8	51.4	86.7
Foreign Assets	21	....	....	....	....	....	....	1.0	1.6	3.2	6.2	8.5	28.6
Claims on General Government	22a	....	....	....	....	....	....	1.1	1.1	1.3	3.1	.7	.3
Claims on Other Resident Sectors	22d	....	....	....	....	....	....	115.7	142.1	245.0	359.5	456.1	523.7
Demand Deposits	24	....	....	....	....	....	....	12.7	7.8	15.7	23.8	36.3	61.8
Other Deposits	25	....	....	....	....	....	....	10.2	18.9	42.7	61.9	99.7	158.3
Foreign Liabilities	26c	....	....	....	....	....	....	73.0	61.2	143.1	219.9	276.5	314.4
General Government Deposits	26d	....	....	....	....	....	....	–	3.8	10.9	9.0	7.9	17.1
Credit from Monetary Authorities	26g	....	....	....	....	....	....	16.8	44.2	44.2	34.1	29.2	43.8
Capital Accounts	27a	....	....	....	....	....	....	22.0	29.4	39.9	50.4	85.5	133.5
Other Items (Net)	27r	....	....	....	....	....	....	–4.9	–7.1	–12.4	19.7	–18.4	–89.5
Monetary Survey						*Millions of Somoni: End of Period*							
Foreign Assets (Net)	31n	....	....	....	....	....	....	–103.8	–120.5	–174.8	–238.8	–257.0	–179.1
Domestic Credit	32	....	....	....	....	....	....	226.5	279.6	320.2	624.2	711.8	665.9
Claims on General Govt. (Net)	32an	....	....	....	....	....	....	94.1	41.0	74.1	48.8	84.3	.1
Claims on Other Resident Sectors	32d	....	....	....	....	....	....	132.4	238.6	246.0	575.4	627.5	665.8
Money	34	....	....	....	....	....	....	59.4	69.9	102.7	128.8	173.2	222.2
Quasi-Money	35	....	....	....	....	....	....	13.2	20.5	44.9	70.5	106.8	172.3
Counterpart Funds	36e	....	....	....	....	....	....	3.0	15.0	38.8	85.8	101.0	94.6
Capital Accounts	37a	....	....	....	....	....	....	58.2	70.9	51.4	115.2	132.9	151.9
Other Items (Net)	37r	....	....	....	....	....	....	–11.0	–17.3	–92.4	–14.9	–59.1	–154.1
Money plus Quasi-Money	35l	....	....	....	....	....	....	72.6	90.4	147.6	199.4	280.0	394.5
Interest Rates						*Percent Per Annum*							
Refinancing Rate	60	....	....	....	....	....	76.00	36.40	20.10	20.60	20.00	† 24.75	† 15.00
Deposit Rate	60l	....	....	....	....	....	23.93	9.82	5.24	1.26	5.19	† 9.21	9.67
Lending Rate	60p	....	....	....	....	....	75.52	50.89	26.24	25.59	21.05	† 14.20	16.57

Tajikistan 923

		1992	1993	1994	1995	1996	1997	1998	1999	2000	2001	2002	2003
Balance of Payments					*Millions of US Dollars: Minus Sign Indicates Debit*								
Current Account, n.i.e.	78ald	....	....	....	....	....	....	....	....	....	....	−15.13	−4.82
Goods: Exports f.o.b.	78aad	....	....	....	....	....	....	....	....	....	....	699.15	906.20
Goods: Imports f.o.b.	78abd	....	....	....	....	....	....	....	....	....	....	−822.90	−1,025.73
Trade Balance	78acd	....	....	....	....	....	....	....	....	....	....	−123.75	−119.53
Services: Credit	78add	....	....	....	....	....	....	....	....	....	....	68.99	88.51
Services: Debit	78aed	....	....	....	....	....	....	....	....	....	....	−104.88	−121.53
Balance on Goods & Services	78afd	....	....	....	....	....	....	....	....	....	....	−159.64	−152.56
Income: Credit	78agd	....	....	....	....	....	....	....	....	....	....	1.23	.88
Income: Debit	78ahd	....	....	....	....	....	....	....	....	....	....	−42.36	−71.22
Balance on Gds, Serv. & Inc.	78aid	....	....	....	....	....	....	....	....	....	....	−200.77	−222.90
Current Transfers, n.i.e.: Credit	78ajd	....	....	....	....	....	....	....	....	....	....	201.72	285.11
Current Transfers: Debit	78akd	....	....	....	....	....	....	....	....	....	....	−16.08	−67.03
Capital Account, n.i.e.	78bcd	....	....	....	....	....	....	....	....	....	....	−	−
Capital Account, n.i.e.: Credit	78bad	....	....	....	....	....	....	....	....	....	....	−	−
Capital Account: Debit	78bbd	....	....	....	....	....	....	....	....	....	....	....	−
Financial Account, n.i.e.	78bjd	....	....	....	....	....	....	....	....	....	....	72.39	62.69
Direct Investment Abroad	78bdd	....	....	....	....	....	....	....	....	....	....	−	−
Dir. Invest. in Rep. Econ., n.i.e.	78bed	....	....	....	....	....	....	....	....	....	....	36.07	31.65
Portfolio Investment Assets	78bfd	....	....	....	....	....	....	....	....	....	....	−	−
Equity Securities	78bkd	....	....	....	....	....	....	....	....	....	....	−	−
Debt Securities	78bld	....	....	....	....	....	....	....	....	....	....	....	....
Portfolio Investment Liab., n.i.e.	78bgd	....	....	....	....	....	....	....	....	....	....	1.51	.34
Equity Securities	78bmd	....	....	....	....	....	....	....	....	....	....	1.51	.34
Debt Securities	78bnd	....	....	....	....	....	....	....	....	....	....	−	−
Financial Derivatives Assets	78bwd	....	....	....	....	....	....	....	....	....	....	....	....
Financial Derivatives Liabilities	78bxd	....	....	....	....	....	....	....	....	....	....	....	....
Other Investment Assets	78bhd	....	....	....	....	....	....	....	....	....	....	−23.44	−15.63
Monetary Authorities	78bod	....	....	....	....	....	....	....	....	....	....	−	−
General Government	78bpd	....	....	....	....	....	....	....	....	....	....	.17	−.41
Banks	78bqd	....	....	....	....	....	....	....	....	....	....	−6.59	−14.39
Other Sectors	78brd	....	....	....	....	....	....	....	....	....	....	−17.03	−.83
Other Investment Liab., n.i.e.	78bid	....	....	....	....	....	....	....	....	....	....	58.25	46.33
Monetary Authorities	78bsd	....	....	....	....	....	....	....	....	....	....	−	−
General Government	78btd	....	....	....	....	....	....	....	....	....	....	−9.28	−2.12
Banks	78bud	....	....	....	....	....	....	....	....	....	....	1.19	3.72
Other Sectors	78bvd	....	....	....	....	....	....	....	....	....	....	66.34	44.74
Net Errors and Omissions	78cad	....	....	....	....	....	....	....	....	....	....	−55.60	−29.92
Overall Balance	78cbd	....	....	....	....	....	....	....	....	....	....	1.65	27.95
Reserves and Related Items	79dad	....	....	....	....	....	....	....	....	....	....	−1.65	−27.95
Reserve Assets	79dbd	....	....	....	....	....	....	....	....	....	....	.11	−40.46
Use of Fund Credit and Loans	79dcd	....	....	....	....	....	....	....	....	....	....	−23.95	−2.72
Exceptional Financing	79ded	....	....	....	....	....	....	....	....	....	....	22.19	15.24
Government Finance					*Millions of Somoni Year Ending December 31*								
Deficit (-) or Surplus	80	....	....	....	....	....	....	−25.78	−10.42	−3.75	1.42	....	....
Total Revenue and Grants	81y	....	....	....	....	....	....	97.20	140.57	189.88	288.66	....	....
Revenue	81	....	....	....	....	....	....	95.04	136.99	189.88	288.66	....	....
Grants Received	81z	....	....	....	....	....	....	2.16	3.58	−	−	....	....
Exp. & Lending Minus Repay	82z	....	....	....	....	....	....	122.98	150.99	193.63	287.24	....	....
Expenditure	82	....	....	....	....	....	....	130.56	166.97	204.30	292.54	....	....
Lending Minus Repayments	83	....	....	....	....	....	....	−7.58	−15.98	−10.67	−5.30	....	....
Total Financing	80h	....	....	....	....	....	....	25.78	10.42	3.75	−1.42	....	....
Domestic	84a	....	....	....	....	....	....	23.10	32.68	8.81	4.26	....	....
Foreign	85a	....	....	....	....	....	....	2.68	−22.26	−5.06	−5.68	....	....
Total Debt by Residence	88	....	....	....	....	....	....	1,014.60	....	2,038.20	2,046.02	....	....
Domestic	88a	....	....	....	....	....	....	44.67	....	131.92	155.32	....	....
Foreign	89a	....	....	....	....	....	....	969.93	....	1,906.28	1,890.70	....	....
					Millions: Midyear Estimates								
Population	99z	5.51	5.59	5.67	5.74	5.82	5.89	5.96	6.03	6.09	6.14	6.20	6.24

2004, International Monetary Fund : *International Financial Statistics Yearbook*

Tanzania 738

		1992	1993	1994	1995	1996	1997	1998	1999	2000	2001	2002	2003
Exchange Rates						*Shillings per SDR: End of Period*							
Official Rate	aa	460.63	659.13	764.16	818.10	856.51	842.70	958.87	1,094.34	1,046.58	1,151.54	1,327.30	1,580.51
					Shillings per US Dollar: End of Period (ae) Period Average (rf)								
Official Rate	ae	335.00	479.87	523.45	550.36	595.64	624.57	681.00	797.33	803.26	916.30	976.30	1,063.62
Official Rate	rf	297.71	405.27	509.63	574.76	579.98	612.12	664.67	744.76	800.41	876.41	966.58	1,038.42
Fund Position						*Millions of SDRs: End of Period*							
Quota	2f.s	146.9	146.9	146.9	146.9	146.9	146.9	146.9	198.9	198.9	198.9	198.9	198.9
SDRs	1b.s	–	–	–	.1	.1	.1	.3	.2	.1	.4	.1	.3
Reserve Position in the Fund	1c.s	10.0	10.0	10.0	10.0	10.0	10.0	10.0	10.0	10.0	10.0	10.0	10.0
Total Fund Cred.&Loans Outstg	2tl	160.5	156.2	145.5	132.7	143.4	182.4	190.2	227.6	248.3	271.2	293.9	294.3
International Liquidity						*Millions of US Dollars Unless Otherwise Indicated: End of Period*							
Total Reserves minus Gold	1l.d	327.3	203.3	332.1	270.2	440.1	622.1	599.2	775.5	974.2	1,156.6	1,528.8	2,038.4
SDRs	1b.d	–	–	–	.1	.1	.1	.4	.3	.1	.5	.1	.5
Reserve Position in the Fund	1c.d	13.7	13.7	14.6	14.8	14.3	13.5	14.0	13.7	13.0	12.5	13.6	14.9
Foreign Exchange	1d.d	313.6	189.6	317.5	255.3	425.6	608.5	584.8	761.5	961.1	1,143.6	1,515.2	2,023.0
Monetary Authorities: Other Liab	4..d	991.9	957.8	900.7	836.9	808.7	574.9	574.5	678.5	755.2	747.7	881.5	1,061.5
Deposit Money Banks: Assets	7a.d	103.0	145.4	146.6	309.2	304.8	373.9	392.4	377.6	511.7	588.3	585.4	644.5
Liabilities	7b.d	307.0	93.6	20.9	51.4	8.1	7.8	3.6	2.2	5.2	17.6	36.0	6.5
Monetary Authorities						*Billions of Shillings: End of Period*							
Foreign Assets	11	139.86	†97.56	173.82	150.65	264.72	390.09	407.27	618.47	782.42	1,059.85	1,492.78	2,167.75
Claims on Central Government	12a	179.07	†262.10	270.60	326.37	299.38	269.69	234.08	302.79	296.67	296.67	201.46	202.20
Claims on Deposit Money Banks	12e	2.30	†2.07	–	5.46	5.46	4.61	5.36	4.16	–	–	–	–
Reserve Money	14	112.75	†152.32	226.44	314.89	335.77	364.94	418.73	508.67	556.43	584.37	695.70	783.31
of which: Currency Outside DMBs	14a	95.45	†122.17	176.31	244.31	257.66	287.88	307.80	384.86	392.40	411.64	495.45	553.05
Foreign Liabilities	16c	366.80	†506.18	517.26	499.09	509.17	373.50	397.37	543.32	606.65	685.16	860.56	1,129.02
Central Government Deposits	16d	–	†25.35	29.56	39.67	82.66	87.32	83.03	84.01	137.32	161.98	198.65	357.82
Capital Accounts	17a	−184.66	†−278.34	−242.89	−266.81	−238.07	−16.35	−2.23	45.81	25.67	102.44	99.71	149.85
Other Items (Net)	17r	42.54	†−43.78	−85.94	−104.36	−119.97	−145.02	−250.20	−256.39	−246.98	−177.42	−160.39	−50.05
Deposit Money Banks						*Billions of Shillings: End of Period*							
Reserves	20	14.38	†30.13	49.91	66.03	72.80	59.71	113.20	123.20	172.10	177.33	195.15	226.87
Foreign Assets	21	34.39	†69.78	76.74	170.16	181.55	233.56	267.26	301.08	410.99	539.06	571.57	685.49
Claims on Central Government	22a	33.14	†93.39	124.41	181.09	261.94	247.39	312.75	331.26	403.76	295.70	364.64	322.41
Claims on Official Entities	22bx	44.71	†49.26	57.18	46.83	17.34	16.22	3.06	4.72	2.98	1.02	–	–
Claims on Private Sector	22d	133.49	†186.31	222.98	201.02	116.56	166.75	239.86	302.17	333.26	403.49	570.67	817.13
Demand Deposits	24	90.66	†125.16	153.32	183.97	191.55	205.99	237.72	247.72	302.60	354.38	463.34	560.33
Time, Savings,& Fgn.Currency Dep	25	116.24	†173.62	240.12	329.52	372.28	433.20	481.47	584.95	702.68	870.71	1,088.90	1,274.94
Foreign Liabilities	26c	102.75	†44.94	10.92	28.26	4.83	4.88	2.46	1.77	4.16	16.17	35.19	6.88
Central Government Deposits	26d	5.00	†4.82	22.52	21.75	20.96	28.43	25.33	21.56	26.09	29.32	30.82	81.83
Credit from Monetary Authorities	26g	73.99	†147.40	1.34	7.59	.16	12.76	–	5.43	–	–	.08	.05
Capital Accounts	27a	−12.45	†48.62	139.91	−29.91	75.62	43.11	61.64	27.26	113.33	133.74	142.09	207.97
Other Items (Net)	27r	−116.10	†−115.69	−36.90	123.95	−15.21	−4.74	127.52	173.73	174.23	12.28	−58.39	−80.11
Monetary Survey						*Billions of Shillings: End of Period*							
Foreign Assets (Net)	31n	−295.30	†−383.77	−277.62	−206.54	−67.72	245.27	274.70	374.46	582.60	897.58	1,168.60	1,717.35
Domestic Credit	32	401.60	†560.89	623.10	693.88	591.60	584.31	681.39	835.36	873.27	805.59	907.29	902.08
Claims on Central Govt. (Net)	32an	223.39	†325.32	342.94	446.03	457.70	401.34	438.47	528.48	537.03	401.08	336.62	84.95
Claims on Official Entities	32bx	44.71	†49.26	57.18	46.83	17.34	16.22	3.06	4.72	2.98	1.02	–	–
Claims on Private Sector	32d	133.49	†186.31	222.98	201.02	116.56	166.75	239.86	302.17	333.26	403.49	570.67	817.13
Money	34	186.12	†247.33	329.63	428.28	449.21	493.87	545.52	632.58	695.01	766.02	958.79	1,113.38
Quasi-Money	35	116.24	†173.62	240.12	329.52	372.28	433.20	481.47	584.95	702.68	870.71	1,088.90	1,274.94
Capital Accounts	37a	−197.11	†−229.73	−102.98	−296.72	−162.45	26.76	59.41	73.07	139.00	236.18	241.80	357.83
Other Items (Net)	37r	1.05	†−14.11	−121.28	26.26	−135.17	−124.25	−130.30	−80.78	−80.82	−169.74	−213.59	−126.72
Money plus Quasi-Money	35l	302.36	†420.95	569.74	757.81	821.50	927.07	1,026.98	1,217.53	1,397.69	1,636.73	2,047.68	2,388.32
Other Banking Institutions						*Billions of Shillings: End of Period*							
Deposits	45	.80	†1.12	1.67	16.82	16.60	17.56	17.88	24.38	28.44	34.15	37.42	34.73
Liquid Liabilities	55l	303.16	†422.07	571.42	774.63	838.09	944.63	1,044.87	1,241.91	1,426.13	1,670.88	2,085.11	2,423.05
Interest Rates						*Percent Per Annum*							
Discount Rate (End of Period)	60	14.50	14.50	67.50	47.90	19.00	16.20	17.60	20.20	10.70	8.70	9.18	12.34
Treasury Bill Rate	60c	....	34.00	35.09	40.33	15.30	9.59	11.83	10.05	9.78	4.14	3.55	6.26
Savings Rate	60k	....	24.00	23.98	22.70	14.25	8.79	8.29	8.27	†6.55	4.15	3.36	2.58
Deposit Rate	60l	....	....	....	24.63	13.59	7.83	7.75	7.75	†7.39	4.81	3.29	3.05
Lending Rate	60p	....	31.00	39.00	42.83	†33.97	26.27	22.89	21.89	†21.58	20.26	16.43	14.48
Prices and Production						*Index Numbers (2000=100): Period Averages*							
Consumer Prices	64	25.8	32.3	43.0	55.2	66.8	77.6	87.5	94.4	100.0	105.1	109.9	114.8
Manufacturing Production	66ey	77.5	77.5	70.4	73.2	73.9	78.2	84.5	87.3	100.0	104.2	119.0	....

Tanzania 738

		1992	1993	1994	1995	1996	1997	1998	1999	2000	2001	2002	2003
International Transactions		\multicolumn{12}{c}{*Millions of Shillings*}
Exports	70	123,966	181,147	265,177	390,378	455,519	459,549	391,805	412,204	531,058	681,186	847,200	681,186
Imports, c.i.f.	71	449,480	615,990	765,757	968,910	804,949	818,703	967,080	1,161,841	1,219,385	1,502,636	1,630,388	1,504,415
Balance of Payments		\multicolumn{12}{c}{*Millions of US Dollars: Minus Sign Indicates Debit*}
Current Account, n.i.e.	78ald	−714.2	−1,048.0	−710.9	−646.3	−510.9	−629.8	−919.7	−835.3	−498.6	−479.6	−251.3	....
Goods: Exports f.o.b.	78aad	406.4	446.9	519.4	682.5	764.1	715.3	589.5	543.3	663.3	776.4	902.5	....
Goods: Imports f.o.b.	78abd	−1,335.2	−1,304.0	−1,309.3	−1,340.0	−1,213.1	−1,164.4	−1,365.3	−1,415.4	−1,367.6	−1,560.3	−1,511.3	....
Trade Balance	78acd	−928.8	−857.1	−789.9	−657.5	−449.0	−449.1	−775.9	−872.1	−704.3	−783.9	−608.8	....
Services: Credit	78add	169.9	317.9	418.2	582.6	608.1	494.1	555.0	600.3	627.4	679.3	665.8	....
Services: Debit	78aed	−341.3	−717.0	−503.3	−799.4	−953.4	−797.3	−988.1	−795.0	−682.4	−689.3	−712.6	....
Balance on Goods & Services	78afd	−1,100.2	−1,256.2	−875.0	−874.2	−794.3	−752.4	−1,209.0	−1,066.8	−759.3	−793.9	−655.6	....
Income: Credit	78agd	8.2	21.9	30.9	31.8	50.3	44.9	35.0	43.1	50.3	55.4	74.5	....
Income: Debit	78ahd	−236.8	−172.9	−153.4	−142.0	−105.4	−168.2	−136.8	−148.2	−180.4	−140.6	−90.7	....
Balance on Gds, Serv. & Inc.	78aid	−1,328.9	−1,407.2	−997.5	−984.5	−849.4	−875.7	−1,310.8	−1,171.9	−889.4	−879.1	−671.8	....
Current Transfers, n.i.e.: Credit	78ajd	650.1	389.8	311.5	370.5	370.9	313.6	426.6	445.6	463.7	469.5	472.9	....
Current Transfers: Debit	78akd	−35.5	−30.7	−25.0	−32.3	−32.3	−67.7	−35.5	−109.0	−72.9	−70.0	−52.4	....
Capital Account, n.i.e.	78bcd	302.4	205.2	262.6	190.9	191.0	360.6	422.9	347.8	420.4	1,078.6	1,168.0	....
Capital Account, n.i.e.: Credit	78bad	302.4	205.2	262.6	190.9	191.0	360.6	422.9	347.8	420.4	1,078.6	1,168.0	....
Capital Account: Debit	78bbd	−	−	−	−	−	−	−	−	−	−	−	....
Financial Account, n.i.e.	78bjd	70.2	130.5	−91.7	66.7	−92.8	3.6	77.6	565.2	492.6	−483.7	−507.0	....
Direct Investment Abroad	78bdd	−	−	−	−	−	−	−	−	−	−	−	....
Dir. Invest. in Rep. Econ., n.i.e.	78bed	12.2	20.5	50.0	119.9	150.1	157.9	172.3	516.7	463.4	327.2	240.4	....
Portfolio Investment Assets	78bfd	−	−	−	−	−	−	−	−	−	−	−	....
Equity Securities	78bkd	−	−	−	−	−	−	−	−	−	−	−	....
Debt Securities	78bld	−	−	−	−	−	−	−	−	−	−	−	....
Portfolio Investment Liab., n.i.e.	78bgd	−	−	−	−	−	−	−	−	−	−	−	....
Equity Securities	78bmd	−	−	−	−	−	−	−	−	−	−	−	....
Debt Securities	78bnd	−	−	−	−	−	−	−	−	−	−	−	....
Financial Derivatives Assets	78bwd	−	−	−	−	−	−	−	....	....	....	....	....
Financial Derivatives Liabilities	78bxd	−	−	−	−	−	−	−	....	....	....	....	....
Other Investment Assets	78bhd	−	56.7	11.9	−75.1	20.1	−85.0	−50.7	14.8	−134.0	−76.7	2.9	....
Monetary Authorities	78bod	−	−	−	−	−	−	−	−	−	−	−	....
General Government	78bpd	−	−	−	−	−	−	−	−	−	−	−	....
Banks	78bqd	−	−68.6	−75.6	−162.5	−19.6	−85.0	−50.7	14.8	−134.0	−76.7	2.9	....
Other Sectors	78brd	−	125.3	87.5	87.4	39.7	−	−	−	−	−	−	....
Other Investment Liab., n.i.e.	78bid	58.1	53.3	−153.6	21.8	−262.9	−69.3	−44.0	33.7	163.2	−734.2	−750.3	....
Monetary Authorities	78bsd	8.8	.2	11.9	5.9	14.9	24.6	−48.7	9.8	49.7	−52.9	14.2	....
General Government	78btd	31.3	−56.5	−202.0	−71.2	−225.9	−32.4	−	52.0	145.4	−820.7	−750.5	....
Banks	78bud	.2	−1.4	6.7	22.9	−23.5	−67.6	−17.6	−1.4	3.0	12.5	18.4	....
Other Sectors	78bvd	17.7	111.0	29.8	64.2	−28.5	6.2	22.4	−26.7	−34.9	126.9	−32.4	....
Net Errors and Omissions	78cad	137.7	137.3	121.4	30.0	158.6	−31.9	−90.3	−156.7	−415.7	16.1	−83.8	....
Overall Balance	78cbd	−203.9	−575.1	−418.6	−358.7	−254.0	−297.5	−509.4	−79.0	−1.3	131.4	325.9	....
Reserves and Related Items	79dad	203.9	575.1	418.6	358.7	254.0	297.5	509.4	79.0	1.3	−131.4	−325.9	....
Reserve Assets	79dbd	−255.4	60.5	−122.8	43.3	−195.4	−206.9	22.3	−176.4	−199.2	−183.0	−371.2	....
Use of Fund Credit and Loans	79dcd	83.7	−6.0	−15.4	−19.6	15.7	53.2	9.6	51.5	27.6	29.5	29.1	....
Exceptional Financing	79ded	375.6	520.7	556.8	335.1	433.8	451.2	477.5	204.0	172.9	22.1	16.3	....
International Investment Position		\multicolumn{12}{c}{*Millions of US Dollars*}
Assets	79aad	497.3	370.2	477.0	578.8	744.4	995.6	991.4	1,153.0	1,485.6	1,744.9	2,114.5	....
Direct Investment Abroad	79abd	−	−	−	−	−	−	−	−	−	−	−	....
Portfolio Investment	79acd	−	−	−	−	−	−	−	−	−	−	−	....
Equity Securities	79add	−	−	−	−	−	−	−	−	−	−	−	....
Debt Securities	79aed	−	−	−	−	−	−	−	−	−	−	−	....
Financial Derivatives	79ald	−	−	−	−	−	−	−	−	−	−	−	....
Other Investment	79afd	103.0	145.4	146.6	309.2	304.8	373.9	392.4	377.6	511.6	588.3	585.4	....
Monetary Authorities	79agd	....	....	....	....	....	....	....	−	−	−	−	....
General Government	79ahd	....	....	....	....	....	....	....	−	−	−	−	....
Banks	79aid	....	....	....	....	304.8	373.9	392.4	377.6	511.6	588.3	585.4	....
Other Sectors	79ajd	....	....	....	....	....	....	....	....	−	−	−	....
Reserve Assets	79akd	394.3	224.8	330.4	269.6	439.6	621.7	599.0	775.4	974.0	1,156.6	1,529.1	....
Liabilities	79lad	8,485.8	8,679.4	9,037.5	9,645.7	9,965.9	7,271.3	7,229.0	7,648.1	9,540.3	9,208.3	9,922.3	....
Dir. Invest. in Rep. Economy	79lbd	10.7	24.3	71.0	224.2	351.7	490.2	619.0	700.0	1,310.1	1,637.3	1,877.7	....
Portfolio Investment	79lcd	−	−	−	−	−	−	−	−	−	−	−	....
Equity Securities	79ldd	−	−	−	−	−	−	−	−	−	−	−	....
Debt Securities	79led	−	−	−	−	−	−	−	−	−	−	−	....
Financial Derivatives	79lld	−	−	−	−	−	−	−	−	−	−	−	....
Other Investment	79lfd	8,475.1	8,655.1	8,966.5	9,421.5	9,614.2	6,781.1	6,610.0	6,948.1	8,230.2	7,571.0	8,044.6	....
Monetary Authorities	79lgd	220.7	214.6	212.4	197.2	206.2	246.0	315.9	370.3	431.3	395.7	468.5	....
General Government	79lhd	7,443.9	7,494.4	8,129.9	8,510.0	8,614.9	6,337.2	6,200.6	6,050.4	6,723.1	5,890.0	6,348.9	....
Banks	79lid	−	−	−	−	−	−	19.4	.9	5.2	17.6	36.0	....
Other Sectors	79ljd	810.5	946.1	624.2	714.3	793.0	197.8	74.1	526.4	1,070.6	1,267.7	1,191.2	....

2004, International Monetary Fund: *International Financial Statistics Yearbook*

Tanzania 738

		1992	1993	1994	1995	1996	1997	1998	1999	2000	2001	2002	2003
Government Finance		\multicolumn{12}{c}{*Millions of Shillings: Year Ending June 30*}
Deficit (-) or Surplus	80	9,601	−72,141	−104,515	−64,559	−21,269	77,143	−68,138	24,422	−114,472	−87,860	−38,191	....
Total Revenue and Grants	81y	206,364	222,422	349,234	389,743	495,255	653,446	738,443	859,268	1,057,952	1,215,930	1,401,774	....
Revenue	81	173,566	164,109	242,444	331,238	448,373	572,030	619,084	689,324	777,645	929,624	1,042,956	....
Grants	81z	32,798	58,313	106,790	58,505	46,882	81,416	119,359	169,944	280,307	286,306	358,818	....
Exp. & Lending Minus Repay.	82z	161,474	263,413	374,962	398,024	420,522	515,390	730,338	816,706	1,168,779	1,311,928	1,441,669	....
Expenditure	82	161,474	263,413	374,962	398,024	420,522	515,390	730,338	816,706	1,168,779	1,305,035	1,441,669	....
Lending Minus Repayments	83	−	−	−	−	−	−	−	−	−	6,893	−	....
Financing													
Overall Adjustment	80x	−35,289	−31,150	−78,787	−56,278	−96,002	−60,913	−76,243	−18,140	−3,644	8,139	1,704	....
Total Financing	80h	−9,601	72,141	104,515	64,559	21,269	−77,142	68,139	−24,424	114,472	87,860	38,191	....
Domestic	84a	−32,277	44,144	40,557	61,603	56,169	−28,074	3,670	−5,740	9,055	−2,494	−83,087	....
Foreign	85a	22,676	27,997	63,958	2,956	−34,900	−49,068	64,468	−18,684	105,417	90,354	121,278	....
National Accounts		\multicolumn{12}{c}{*Billions of Shillings*}
Househ.Cons.Expend.,incl.NPISHs	96f	1,133.19	1,445.37	1,931.98	2,532.84	3,130.07	3,968.07	4,909.25	5,667.44	6,069.58	6,917.58	7,499.65	....
Government Consumption Expend	91f	269.02	334.52	393.50	462.32	435.33	413.56	433.79	451.14	482.72	516.33	598.94	....
Gross Fixed Capital Formation	93e	369.37	429.55	561.82	591.94	620.60	692.40	892.70	989.34	1,266.68	1,390.64	1,789.90	....
Changes in Inventories	93i	3.68	4.00	4.84	5.86	6.64	8.40	9.91	10.31	14.37	15.66	17.85	....
Exports of Goods and Services	90c	170.44	310.31	473.89	727.18	751.16	762.81	748.97	885.94	1,064.77	1,284.71	1,561.06	....
Imports of Goods and Services (-)	98c	539.10	823.21	1,002.88	1,253.74	1,203.52	1,208.30	1,565.32	1,703.75	1,676.34	1,962.79	2,104.38	....
GDP, Production Based	99bp	1,369.87	1,725.54	2,298.87	3,020.50	3,767.64	4,703.46	5,571.26	6,432.91	7,268.38	8,274.61	9,363.67	....
Statistical Discrepancy	99bs	−36.72	25.01	−64.28	−45.89	27.36	93.04	142.34	132.50	46.61	112.47	.66	....
Net Primary Income from Abroad	98.n	−67.08	−61.19	−62.43	−63.38	−36.92	−75.78	−52.39	−55.19	−66.70	−74.93	−87.48	....
Gross National Income (GNI)	99a	1,302.79	1,664.35	2,236.44	2,957.12	3,730.72	4,654.22	5,519.25	6,377.72	7,201.68	8,199.67	9,276.19	....
Net National Income	99e	1,264.03	1,619.70	2,175.83	2,876.16	3,640.05	4,541.78	5,385.99	6,216.13	7,007.78	7,963.11	8,985.21	....
GDP, Prod. Based, 1992 Prices	99bpp	1,275.92	1,281.01	1,298.94	1,345.25	1,401.71	1,448.21	1,505.83	1,577.29	1,654.32	1,749.36	1,857.16	....
GDP Volume (2000=100)	99bvp	77.1	77.4	78.5	81.3	84.7	87.5	91.0	95.3	100.0	105.7	112.3	....
GDP Deflator (2000=100)	99bip	24.4	30.7	40.3	51.1	61.2	73.9	84.2	92.8	100.0	107.7	114.8	....
		\multicolumn{12}{c}{*Millions: Midyear Estimates*}
Population	99z	27.96	28.95	29.92	30.85	31.72	32.55	Ü 33.34	34.09	34.84	35.56	36.28	36.98

Thailand 578

		1992	1993	1994	1995	1996	1997	1998	1999	2000	2001	2002	2003
Exchange Rates			*Baht per SDR: End of Period*
Official Rate	aa	35.090	35.081	36.628	37.445	36.826	†63.748	51.662	51.428	56.374	55.575	58.665	58.831
			*Baht per US Dollar: End of Period (ae) Period Average (rf)*
Official Rate	ae	25.520	25.540	25.090	25.190	25.610	†47.247	36.691	37.470	43.268	44.222	43.152	39.591
Official Rate	rf	25.400	25.320	25.150	24.915	25.343	†31.364	41.359	37.814	40.112	44.432	42.960	41.485
Fund Position			*Millions of SDRs: End of Period*
Quota	2f.s	574	574	574	574	574	574	574	1,082	1,082	1,082	1,082	1,082
SDRs	1b.s	9	16	22	30	41	358	278	188	63	4	3	–
Reserve Position in the Fund	1c.s	243	272	285	319	333	–	–	–	–	–	–	75
of which: Outstg.Fund Borrowing	2c	–	–	–	–	–	–	–	–	–	–	–	–
Total Fund Cred.&Loans Outstg	2tl	–	–	–	–	–	1,800	2,300	2,500	2,350	1,338	288	–
International Liquidity			*Millions of US Dollars Unless Otherwise Indicated: End of Period*
Total Reserves minus Gold	1l.d	20,359	24,473	29,332	35,982	37,731	26,179	28,825	34,063	32,016	32,355	38,046	41,077
SDRs	1b.d	12	22	32	45	60	482	391	258	83	5	4	–
Reserve Position in the Fund	1c.d	335	373	416	474	480	–	–	–	–	–	–	111
Foreign Exchange	1d.d	20,012	24,078	28,884	35,463	37,192	25,697	28,434	33,805	31,933	32,350	38,042	40,965
Gold (Million Fine Troy Ounces)	1ad	2.474	2.474	2.474	2.474	2.474	2.474	2.474	2.474	2.367	2.480	2.500	2.600
Gold (National Valuation)	1and	823	967	947	963	914	713	711	718	645	686	869	1,071
Monetary Authorities: Other Liab	4..d	5	6	6	5	4	4,733	7,967	9,390	8,960	6,651	4,516	3
Deposit Money Banks: Assets	7a.d	3,046	6,165	6,739	9,365	7,028	8,665	12,605	15,158	16,642	16,923	14,683	15,604
Liabilities	7b.d	6,567	13,799	31,086	46,214	48,781	40,307	29,058	19,165	13,070	10,439	9,575	8,498
Other Banking Insts.: Assets	7e.d	–	–	27	34	72	100	407	403	403	332	413	336
Liabilities	7f.d	2,518	3,323	4,035	5,939	8,748	6,973	5,550	4,437	3,683	2,805	1,682	1,419
Monetary Authorities			*Billions of Baht: End of Period*
Foreign Assets	11	539.1	649.1	759.0	929.7	988.8	1,270.7	1,083.4	1,303.3	1,413.2	1,478.9	1,695.5	1,690.1
Claims on Central Government	12a	60.6	50.7	32.5	29.7	33.5	31.8	170.7	139.7	109.0	146.5	131.7	135.9
Claims on Nonfin.Pub.Enterprises	12c	–	–	–	8.4	17.9	71.5	75.0	64.0	48.3	33.4	23.0	14.8
Claims on Deposit Money Banks	12e	37.1	21.2	26.4	37.8	55.9	309.4	158.6	85.9	59.2	19.2	58.8	47.0
Claims on Other Financial Insts	12f	22.4	25.2	39.9	47.5	76.6	438.7	511.3	393.9	439.8	338.9	414.6	489.4
Reserve Money	14	248.0	288.1	329.9	404.3	458.9	531.4	507.6	785.8	684.5	727.3	744.7	941.7
of which: Currency Outside DMBs	14a	180.2	208.6	241.9	284.1	304.3	334.0	318.3	472.4	406.8	440.9	496.0	546.9
Money Market Instruments	16aa	–	–	18.1	16.9	28.5	330.5	541.6	172.9	217.9	220.5	194.0	376.2
Foreign Liabilities	16c	.1	.2	.1	.1	.1	338.4	411.1	480.4	537.6	439.6	227.9	25.8
Central Government Deposits	16d	201.6	213.7	235.8	328.5	341.7	283.3	96.6	81.5	45.8	38.3	76.0	60.9
Capital Accounts	17a	231.8	263.1	306.8	337.8	377.8	202.4	803.2	814.0	1,013.2	1,159.7	1,092.4	1,627.4	1,676.1
Other Items (Net)	17r	–22.5	–18.9	–33.0	–34.4	–34.4	–164.6	–371.9	–547.1	–576.0	–501.3	–546.5	–703.5
Deposit Money Banks			*Billions of Baht: End of Period*
Reserves	20	60.9	73.5	79.7	117.8	165.8	203.6	145.7	143.0	112.8	186.0	201.6	293.7
Other Claims on Monetary Author	20n	–	–	5.5	5.9	17.5	262.2	356.4	94.8	155.0	129.7	106.0	266.8
Foreign Assets	21	77.7	157.5	169.1	235.9	180.0	409.4	462.5	568.0	720.1	748.4	633.6	617.8
Claims on Central Government	22a	69.7	50.3	41.8	40.7	20.2	15.6	154.7	249.2	306.3	318.0	398.7	294.4
Claims on Nonfin.Pub.Enterprises	22c	53.2	76.5	94.2	108.4	112.7	99.9	108.5	135.1	123.9	150.0	150.0	149.3
Claims on Private Sector	22d	2,045.1	2,536.5	3,304.1	4,089.2	4,688.3	5,729.6	5,299.6	5,014.5	4,211.6	3,774.7	4,404.7	4,705.3
Claims on Other Financial Insts	22f	113.1	126.6	158.0	213.4	213.9	331.3	173.1	233.8	512.2	673.2	375.3	249.0
Demand Deposits	24	66.1	82.4	96.4	94.3	106.1	86.6	93.9	94.9	114.0	134.4	157.8	215.5
Time, Savings,& Fgn.Currency Dep	25	1,868.1	2,210.9	2,482.9	2,922.3	3,303.0	3,910.6	4,311.6	4,279.1	4,505.8	4,662.6	4,714.6	4,873.3
Foreign Liabilities	26c	167.6	352.4	780.0	1,164.1	1,249.3	1,904.4	1,066.2	718.1	565.5	461.6	413.2	336.4
Central Government Deposits	26d	76.5	92.7	122.5	135.5	178.1	190.5	229.8	242.3	239.6	252.6	278.0	286.1
Credit from Monetary Authorities	26g	36.3	21.2	24.9	36.2	53.8	313.1	154.5	48.3	25.5	17.1	18.9	19.6
Liabilities to Other Banking Insts	26i	14.9	20.0	55.9	86.3	85.7	118.2	56.9	152.8	142.9	126.4	100.8	200.0
Capital Accounts	27a	170.2	220.6	369.8	471.3	600.2	690.8	1,067.7	1,162.3	716.7	644.0	882.8	984.8
Other Items (Net)	27r	19.9	20.6	–80.2	–98.7	–177.6	–162.6	–280.0	–259.5	–168.3	–318.8	–296.3	–339.5
Monetary Survey			*Billions of Baht: End of Period*
Foreign Assets (Net)	31n	449.1	454.0	148.0	1.4	–80.7	–562.6	68.6	672.7	1,030.1	1,326.0	1,688.0	1,945.7
Domestic Credit	32	2,085.9	2,559.3	3,312.1	4,073.4	4,643.4	6,244.6	6,166.5	5,906.3	5,465.6	5,143.8	5,543.9	5,691.1
Claims on Central Govt. (Net)	32an	–147.8	–205.5	–284.1	–393.6	–466.1	–426.4	–1.0	65.1	130.0	173.7	176.4	83.3
Claims on Nonfin.Pub.Enterprises	32c	53.2	76.5	94.2	116.8	130.7	171.3	183.5	199.1	172.1	183.4	172.9	164.1
Claims on Private Sector	32d	2,045.1	2,536.5	3,304.1	4,089.2	4,688.3	5,729.6	5,299.6	5,014.5	4,211.6	3,774.7	4,404.7	4,705.3
Claims on Other Financial Insts	32f	135.5	151.8	197.9	261.0	290.5	770.1	684.4	627.6	951.9	1,012.1	789.9	738.4
Money	34	249.7	296.2	346.4	388.3	423.7	430.1	451.0	739.7	684.3	650.6	674.9	869.2
Quasi-Money	35	1,868.1	2,210.9	2,482.9	2,922.3	3,303.0	3,910.6	4,311.6	4,279.1	4,505.8	4,662.6	4,714.6	4,873.3
Money Market Instruments	36aa	–	–	12.7	11.0	11.1	68.4	185.2	78.1	62.9	90.8	88.0	109.4
Liabilities to Other Banking Insts	36i	14.9	20.0	55.9	86.3	85.7	118.2	56.9	152.8	142.9	126.4	100.8	200.0
Capital Accounts	37a	402.1	483.7	676.6	809.1	977.9	1,493.9	1,881.7	2,175.5	1,876.4	1,736.4	2,510.2	2,660.9
Other Items (Net)	37r	.2	2.4	–114.4	–142.3	–238.6	–339.2	–651.3	–846.1	–776.6	–797.0	–856.6	–1,076.1
Money plus Quasi-Money	35l	2,117.8	2,507.1	2,829.4	3,310.6	3,726.7	4,340.7	4,762.6	5,018.8	5,190.1	5,313.2	5,389.5	5,742.5

2004, International Monetary Fund: *International Financial Statistics Yearbook*

Thailand 578

		1992	1993	1994	1995	1996	1997	1998	1999	2000	2001	2002	2003
Other Banking Institutions													
Development Institutions						*Billions of Baht: End of Period*							
Cash	40	8.1	12.5	19.8	18.3	39.8	51.0	46.9	23.3	24.0	20.8	14.9	16.4
Other Claims on Monetary Author.	40n	–	–	–	–	–	17.4	43.0	17.3	38.4	47.5	55.7	72.3
Foreign Assets	41	–	–	–	–	1.0	4.0	14.4	15.0	16.1	14.5	17.7	13.2
Claims on Central Government	42a	.1	–	–	.3	.2	–	30.4	23.7	16.0	15.0	11.6	13.6
Claims on Nonfin.Pub.Enterprises	42c	–	–	–	–	.6	.1	.5	.4	1.2	8.2	9.3	3.4
Claims on Private Sector	42d	159.3	209.1	270.5	365.7	498.2	674.6	678.6	686.1	734.7	758.0	801.0	865.1
Demand Deposits	44	43.8	46.4	60.9	54.3	40.8	52.3	69.3	80.1	63.7	80.5	90.0	107.7
Time and Savings Deposits	45	28.0	44.9	56.1	100.7	88.3	189.8	233.7	190.9	261.3	281.4	313.0	338.3
Bonds	46ab	37.0	65.7	94.6	144.7	151.3	167.0	183.7	188.8	189.3	193.2	201.4	202.5
Long-Term Foreign Liabilities	46cl	23.1	26.0	29.9	33.1	91.4	206.1	160.6	139.6	130.5	98.0	71.8	55.7
Central Govt. Lending Funds	46f	1.4	3.0	1.7	4.2	100.9	56.4	89.6	88.0	97.1	110.6	136.1	171.4
Credit from Monetary Authorities	46g	8.6	9.2	9.0	8.5	32.2	32.0	19.8	18.3	20.4	22.6	12.5	17.0
Credit from Deposit Money Banks	46h	12.5	7.6	11.6	7.1	5.2	6.2	4.8	2.0	2.9	3.3	3.6	1.6
Capital Accounts	47a	17.0	25.7	35.3	41.7	49.9	60.6	79.0	110.3	119.0	135.6	150.4	166.9
Other Items (Net)	47r	–3.9	–6.8	–8.8	–9.9	–20.2	–23.4	–26.7	–52.3	–53.7	–61.2	–68.7	–76.8
Finance and Securities Companies						*Billions of Baht: End of Period*							
Reserves	40..f	22.7	31.2	40.2	51.8	51.5	37.4	79.6	195.1	210.2	102.3	18.4	17.1
Other Claims on Mon. Author.	40n.f	–	–	2.9	3.2	7.6	35.0	65.2	39.3	8.5	11.6	4.2	4.6
Claims on Central Government	42a.f	28.3	40.0	9.7	5.6	4.0	1.6	29.7	23.2	23.3	21.4	23.8	17.3
Claims on Nonfin.Pub.Enterprises	42c.f	4.4	10.6	36.3	32.8	45.0	26.5	8.0	2.7	3.2	1.0	5.3	7.5
Claims on Private Sector	42d.f	568.5	761.1	1,035.1	1,363.1	1,554.7	1,373.8	1,165.5	347.6	301.3	330.0	213.2	285.7
Bonds	46abf	415.4	559.0	763.2	931.8	1,081.1	549.8	499.8	388.0	343.7	360.8	182.6	220.9
Foreign Liabilities	46c.f	41.2	58.8	71.3	116.5	132.6	123.3	43.1	26.6	28.9	26.0	.7	.5
Credit from Monetary Authorities	46g.f	3.8	3.5	8.5	9.1	30.1	449.3	561.9	439.8	364.3	363.9	–	3.5
Cred. from Deposit Money Banks	46h.f	52.7	68.5	98.6	146.6	148.1	144.2	103.7	98.4	191.3	78.2	1.9	3.1
Capital Accounts	47a.f	76.6	101.0	145.6	196.7	226.2	197.4	158.6	–353.2	–418.7	–405.8	82.0	95.4
Other Items (Net)	47r.f	34.2	52.2	36.9	55.7	44.7	10.2	–19.0	8.3	37.0	43.1	–2.4	8.8
Government Savings Bank						*Billions of Baht: End of Period*							
Cash	40..g	25.0	29.6	52.9	77.8	82.4	62.6	62.4	51.3	42.4	23.5	18.6	18.4
Other Claims on Mon. Author.	40n.g	–	–	9.4	8.1	2.1	31.5	71.7	18.4	22.6	35.7	27.6	30.0
Claims on Central Government	42a.g	69.0	60.4	40.7	30.3	26.2	18.0	43.9	137.8	139.1	179.8	203.1	184.1
Claims on Nonfin.Pub.Enterprises	42c.g	18.9	31.5	26.8	29.6	47.2	67.4	87.6	121.1	167.8	176.1	157.5	149.8
Claims on Private Sector	42d.g	14.7	18.1	26.8	35.4	45.5	64.9	68.8	69.2	81.9	112.3	170.1	245.3
Demand Deposits	44..g	36.0	41.4	47.1	49.7	54.5	55.0	54.3	51.0	65.5	100.5	106.2	123.7
Time and Savings Deposits	45..g	75.6	100.7	109.8	131.3	153.0	188.4	276.4	310.2	339.3	360.4	393.4	406.4
Bonds	46abg	16.4	–	–	–	–	–	–	–	–	–	–	–
Central Government Deposits	46d.g	.8	1.5	1.2	1.1	1.2	3.5	3.3	16.3	17.5	22.3	22.9	23.9
Capital Accounts	47a.g	11.1	13.1	15.9	18.6	21.4	19.7	25.0	38.5	41.4	49.5	64.2	69.6
Other Items (Net)	47r.g	–12.3	–16.9	–17.3	–19.4	–26.8	–22.1	–24.5	–18.4	–10.0	–5.1	–9.7	4.0
Banking Survey						*Billions of Baht: End of Period*							
Foreign Assets (Net)	51n	407.9	395.1	77.3	–114.3	–211.4	–681.3	40.5	661.2	1,018.7	1,314.6	1,705.0	1,958.4
Domestic Credit	52	2,812.8	3,537.0	4,558.9	5,674.1	6,573.2	7,697.8	7,591.8	6,674.1	5,964.6	5,711.5	6,326.1	6,700.6
Claims on Central Govt. (Net)	52an	–51.3	–106.5	–234.9	–358.6	–437.0	–410.4	99.7	233.4	290.8	367.7	392.0	274.3
Claims on Nonfin.Pub.Enterprises	52c	76.5	118.6	157.3	179.2	223.4	265.4	279.6	323.3	344.3	368.7	345.1	324.9
Claims on Private Sector	52d	2,787.6	3,524.8	4,636.4	5,853.5	6,786.8	7,842.8	7,212.5	6,117.4	5,329.5	4,975.1	5,589.0	6,101.4
Liquid Liabilities	55l	2,245.4	2,667.1	2,990.2	3,498.5	3,889.6	4,675.0	5,207.4	5,381.3	5,643.3	5,989.4	6,240.1	6,666.7
Bonds	56ab	468.8	624.7	857.8	1,076.5	1,232.4	716.8	683.5	576.8	533.1	554.1	384.0	423.4
Long-Term Foreign Liabilities	56cl	23.1	26.0	29.9	33.1	91.4	206.1	160.6	139.6	130.5	98.0	71.8	55.7
Capital Accounts	57a	506.8	623.5	873.4	1,066.2	1,275.4	1,771.7	2,144.2	1,971.2	1,618.1	1,515.6	2,806.8	2,992.8
Other Items (Net)	57r	–23.3	–9.1	–115.2	–114.5	–127.0	–353.0	–563.4	–733.6	–941.6	–1,131.0	–1,471.7	–1,479.5
Interest Rates						*Percent Per Annum*							
Discount Rate (End of Period)	60	11.00	9.00	9.50	10.50	10.50	12.50	12.50	4.00	4.00	3.75	3.25	2.75
Money Market Rate	60b	6.93	6.54	7.25	10.96	9.23	14.59	13.02	1.77	1.95	2.00	1.76	1.31
Deposit Rate	60l	8.88	8.63	8.46	11.58	10.33	10.52	10.65	4.73	3.29	2.54	1.98	1.33
Lending Rate	60p	12.17	11.17	10.90	13.25	13.40	13.65	14.42	8.98	7.83	7.25	6.88	5.94
Government Bond Yield	61	10.75	10.75	10.75	10.75	10.75	10.75	10.25	6.69	6.95	5.82	5.07	3.76
Prices and Labor						*Index Numbers (2000=100): Period Averages*							
Share Prices	62	....	....	....	....	....	173.4	103.3	123.0	100.0	88.6	107.0	140.9
Producer Prices	63	75.1	74.8	77.8	84.1	85.7	90.0	101.0	96.2	100.0	102.5	104.2	108.4
Consumer Prices	64	70.7	73.1	76.8	†81.3	86.0	90.8	98.2	98.5	100.0	101.7	102.3	104.1
						Number in Thousands: Period Averages							
Labor Force	67d	32,839	32,644	32,515	32,887	32,543	33,339	33,352	33,209	33,799	33,815	34,228	34,881
Employment	67e	32,383	32,150	32,093	32,512	32,232	33,162	32,138	32,087	33,001	32,110	33,026	33,818
Unemployment	67c	456	494	423	375	354	293	1,138	986	813	1,119	826	761
Unemployment Rate (%)	67r	1.4	1.5	1.3	1.1	1.1	.9	3.4	3.0	2.4	3.3	2.4	2.2

Thailand 578

		1992	1993	1994	1995	1996	1997	1998	1999	2000	2001	2002	2003
International Transactions							*Billions of Baht*						
Exports	70	824.6	935.9	1,137.6	1,406.3	1,412.1	1,806.7	2,247.5	2,214.0	2,777.7	2,886.8	2,923.9	3,333.9
Rice	70n	36.2	32.6	59.3	48.6	50.7	65.1	86.9	68.3	65.5	70.1	70.0	76.7
Rubber	70l	28.9	30.4	41.8	61.3	63.4	57.5	55.4	40.3	60.7	58.7	74.6	115.8
Maize	70j	.5	.7	.6	.5	.4	.5	.9	.4	.4	2.5	1.2	1.6
Tin	70q	1.1	.5	.4	.4	.8	1.4	2.6	2.5	2.8	3.7	2.2	2.0
Imports, c.i.f.	71	1,033.2	1,166.6	1,369.0	1,763.6	1,832.8	1,924.3	1,774.1	1,907.1	2,494.2	2,752.4	2,774.8	3,138.1
							2000=100						
Volume of Exports	72	38.6	43.2	51.1	†70.1	63.2	68.0	73.3	82.1	100.0	94.5	107.3	116.9
Rice	72n	79.8	81.6	79.1	100.9	88.9	155.8	106.5	111.4	100.0	124.8	119.3	119.6
Rubber	72l	57.6	61.1	67.3	68.8	75.6	75.5	78.6	79.9	100.0	100.3	109.6	122.2
Maize	72j	466.9	633.2	460.5	348.6	182.3	195.1	438.1	258.1	100.0	1,612.2	509.8	669.8
Tin	72q	56.2	26.8	21.0	20.4	37.6	61.7	86.5	95.8	100.0	146.0	98.1	76.3
Volume of Imports	73	77.8	86.5	100.5	†112.8	102.2	91.4	66.6	82.2	100.0	89.3	99.0	108.2
Unit Value of Exports	74	64.4	65.0	66.8	†72.3	80.1	95.4	109.5	96.2	100.0	109.2	97.9	101.9
Rice (Unit Value)	74n	69.3	61.0	114.3	73.5	87.1	63.8	124.5	93.6	100.0	85.7	89.6	97.9
Rice (Wholesale Price)	76n	83.2	73.5	82.9	97.8	104.9	116.1	154.6	115.2	100.0	93.9	100.9	101.3
Rubber (Unit Value)	74l	82.7	81.9	102.3	146.7	138.1	125.3	116.0	83.0	100.0	96.4	112.1	156.0
Rubber (Wholesale Price)	76l	81.7	78.6	105.7	147.0	132.6	119.1	111.4	89.7	100.0	95.4	122.7	167.7
Maize (Unit Value)	74j	29.3	27.0	32.5	40.1	60.0	69.9	50.9	43.3	100.0	39.6	62.0	61.0
Tin (Unit Value)	74q	68.4	60.6	64.4	70.9	72.7	82.5	105.7	92.9	100.0	89.2	81.6	93.1
Unit Value of Imports	75	54.1	54.1	55.4	†62.0	70.0	83.0	100.7	89.6	100.0	120.2	109.5	113.3
Balance of Payments						*Millions of US Dollars: Minus Sign Indicates Debit*							
Current Account, n.i.e.	78ald	−6,303	−6,364	−8,085	−13,554	−14,691	−3,021	14,243	12,428	9,313	6,192	7,014	7,965
Goods: Exports f.o.b.	78aad	32,099	36,398	44,478	55,447	54,408	56,656	52,753	56,775	67,894	63,082	66,089	78,397
Goods: Imports f.o.b.	78abd	−36,260	−40,694	−48,204	−63,415	−63,897	−55,084	−36,515	−42,762	−56,193	−54,539	−57,008	−66,790
Trade Balance	78acd	−4,161	−4,297	−3,726	−7,968	−9,488	1,572	16,238	14,013	11,701	8,543	9,081	11,606
Services: Credit	78add	9,288	11,059	11,640	14,845	17,007	15,763	13,156	14,635	13,868	13,024	15,391	15,774
Services: Debit	78aed	−10,368	−12,469	−15,396	−18,804	−19,585	−17,355	−11,998	−13,583	−15,460	−14,610	−16,720	−18,503
Balance on Goods & Services	78afd	−5,241	−5,707	−7,482	−11,927	−12,066	−20	17,395	15,066	10,109	6,957	7,751	8,877
Income: Credit	78agd	1,532	2,140	2,562	3,801	3,969	3,742	3,324	3,092	4,235	3,833	3,356	2,988
Income: Debit	78ahd	−3,240	−3,546	−4,292	−5,915	−7,354	−7,223	−6,891	−6,083	−5,616	−5,200	−4,696	−4,790
Balance on Gds, Serv. & Inc.	78aid	−6,949	−7,113	−9,213	−14,040	−15,451	−3,500	13,828	12,075	8,727	5,591	6,411	7,075
Current Transfers, n.i.e.: Credit	78ajd	1,000	1,222	1,901	1,190	1,651	1,392	820	806	952	990	978	1,275
Current Transfers: Debit	78akd	−355	−473	−774	−704	−891	−913	−405	−452	−366	−389	−375	−385
Capital Account, n.i.e.	78bcd	−	−	−	....	....	....	....	....	....	....	....	....
Capital Account, n.i.e.: Credit	78bad	−	−	−	....	....	....	....	....	....	....	....	....
Capital Account: Debit	78bbd	−	−	−	....	....	....	....	....	....	....	....	....
Financial Account, n.i.e.	78bjd	9,475	10,500	12,167	21,909	19,486	−12,056	−14,110	−11,073	−10,434	−3,658	−2,887	−8,183
Direct Investment Abroad	78bdd	−147	−233	−493	−886	−931	−580	−130	−346	23	−344	−106	−558
Dir. Invest. in Rep. Econ., n.i.e.	78bed	2,113	1,804	1,366	2,068	2,336	3,895	7,315	6,103	3,366	3,892	953	1,866
Portfolio Investment Assets	78bfd	....	−	−5	−2	−41	−70	18	−2	−160	−360	−913	−937
Equity Securities	78bkd	....	−	−5	−2	−41	−	−	−	−	−	−9	−
Debt Securities	78bld	....	....	....	....	....	−70	18	−2	−160	−360	−905	−937
Portfolio Investment Liab., n.i.e.	78bgd	924	5,455	2,486	4,083	3,585	4,598	338	−109	−546	−525	−694	302
Equity Securities	78bmd	455	2,679	−389	2,123	1,164	3,868	289	945	900	352	539	585
Debt Securities	78bnd	469	2,776	2,875	1,960	2,421	730	48	−1,054	−1,446	−877	−1,233	−283
Financial Derivatives Assets	78bwd	....	....	....	....	....	....	....	....	....	....	−	−
Financial Derivatives Liabilities	78bxd	....	....	....	....	....	....	....	....	....	....	−	−
Other Investment Assets	78bhd	104	−3,265	−1,027	−2,738	2,661	−2,555	−3,407	−1,755	−2,203	577	4,135	−416
Monetary Authorities	78bod	−	−	−	....	....	....	....	....	....	−31	−	−3
General Government	78bpd	−	−	−	....	....	....	....	....	....	−31	−5	−3
Banks	78bqd	104	−3,265	−1,027	−2,737	2,741	−2,608	−3,460	−1,708	−2,189	743	4,235	−409
Other Sectors	78brd	−	−	−	−1	−80	53	53	−47	−14	−135	−94	−5
Other Investment Liab., n.i.e.	78bid	6,479	6,739	9,839	19,383	11,876	−17,343	−18,243	−14,964	−10,914	−6,897	−6,263	−8,441
Monetary Authorities	78bsd	−	−	−	−	−	−5,262	658	2,731	43	894	5,352	3,031
General Government	78btd	−611	−464	−705	46	−58	737	100	−70	93	80	−1,361	−609
Banks	78bud	1,758	6,589	14,295	13,218	2,909	−3,045	−11,783	−11,566	−4,799	−2,534	−1,761	−1,488
Other Sectors	78bvd	5,333	614	−3,751	6,118	9,025	−9,774	−7,218	−6,060	−6,251	−5,338	−8,493	−9,375
Net Errors and Omissions	78cad	−142	−230	87	−1,196	−2,627	−3,173	−2,828	33	−685	−258	1,410	736
Overall Balance	78cbd	3,029	3,907	4,169	7,159	2,167	−18,250	−2,696	1,388	−1,806	2,276	5,537	518
Reserves and Related Items	79dad	−3,029	−3,907	−4,169	−7,159	−2,167	18,250	2,696	−1,388	1,806	−2,276	−5,537	−518
Reserve Assets	79dbd	−3,029	−3,907	−4,169	−7,159	−2,167	9,900	−1,433	−4,556	1,608	−1,307	−4,197	−122
Use of Fund Credit and Loans	79dcd	−	−	−	−	−	2,437	679	269	−192	−1,288	−1,360	−398
Exceptional Financing	79ded	....	....	....	....	....	5,913	3,450	2,898	391	320	19	3

2004, International Monetary Fund: *International Financial Statistics Yearbook*

Thailand 578

		1992	1993	1994	1995	1996	1997	1998	1999	2000	2001	2002	2003
International Investment Position							*Millions of US Dollars*						
Assets	79aad	....	....	....	46,982	46,005	35,007	41,368	48,360	53,759	54,426	58,167	....
Direct Investment Abroad	79abd	....	....	....	365	481	401	410	418	2,165	2,735	2,321	....
Portfolio Investment	79acd	....	....	....	–	–	43	28	29	488	825	1,699	....
Equity Securities	79add	....	....	....	....	....	....	....	....	53	82	83	....
Debt Securities	79aed	....	....	....	....	....	....	....	....	435	743	1,616	....
Financial Derivatives	79ald	....	....	....	....	....	....	....	....	517	141	282	....
Other Investment	79afd	....	....	....	9,672	6,879	7,671	11,394	13,132	17,928	17,684	14,940	....
Monetary Authorities	79agd	....	....	....	–	–	–	–	–	–	–	–	....
General Government	79ahd	....	....	....	–	–	–	–	–	127	158	166	....
Banks	79aid	....	....	....	9,672	6,879	7,671	11,394	13,132	16,342	15,612	11,450	....
Other Sectors	79ajd	....	....	....	–	–	–	–	–	1,459	1,914	3,324	....
Reserve Assets	79akd	....	....	....	36,945	38,645	26,892	29,536	34,781	32,661	33,041	38,925	....
Liabilities	79lad	....	....	....	100,832	108,742	109,276	105,061	95,051	114,241	106,276	104,002	....
Dir. Invest. in Rep. Economy	79lbd	....	....	....	4,919	4,745	4,738	6,481	6,837	29,915	33,374	37,994	....
Portfolio Investment	79lcd	....	....	....	6,684	9,472	9,774	10,552	9,921	16,360	17,123	17,821	....
Equity Securities	79ldd	....	....	....	–	–	–	–	–	8,153	10,240	12,270	....
Debt Securities	79led	....	....	....	6,684	9,472	9,774	10,552	9,921	8,207	6,883	5,551	....
Financial Derivatives	79lld	....	....	....	–	–	–	–	–	684	506	519	....
Other Investment	79lfd	....	....	....	89,229	94,525	94,764	88,028	78,293	67,281	55,272	47,667	....
Monetary Authorities	79lgd	....	....	....	–	–	7,157	11,203	12,817	12,019	8,327	4,904	....
General Government	79lhd	....	....	....	3,126	2,994	3,672	4,768	7,102	7,347	7,297	6,315	....
Banks	79lid	....	....	....	41,346	41,410	38,898	28,083	17,450	13,656	10,434	9,298	....
Other Sectors	79ljd	....	....	....	44,757	50,121	45,037	43,974	40,924	34,259	29,214	27,150	....
Government Finance						*Millions of Baht: Year Ending December 31*							
Deficit (-) or Surplus	80	71,793	55,618	101,239	134,965	†43,303	–15,061	–128,951	–154,193	–108,065	–122,993	–76,815	23,998
Total Revenue and Grants	81y	....	....	....	....	....	....	....	....	....	....	....	....
Revenue	81	511,835	575,100	680,455	777,286	853,201	847,689	717,779	713,066	746,817	776,362	876,901	1,012,588
Grants	81z	....	....	....	....	....	....	....	....	....	....	....	....
Exp. & Lending Minus Repay	82z	....	....	....	....	....	....	....	....	....	....	....	....
Expenditure	82	440,042	519,482	579,216	642,321	819,083	875,714	842,581	833,042	853,067	908,613	955,492	996,198
Lending Minus Repayments	83	....	....	....	....	....	....	....	....	....	....	....	....
Extrabudgetary Deficits/Surpluses	80xz	....	....	....	....	†9,185	12,964	–4,149	–34,217	–1,815	9,258	1,776	7,608
Total Financing	80h	–71,793	–55,618	–101,239	–134,965	†–43,303	15,061	128,951	154,192	108,065	122,993	76,815	–23,998
Total Net Borrowing	84	–44,468	–44,605	–80,051	–44,147	†–28,788	–76,109	–7,764	135,204	65,101	113,520	113,439	–35,268
Net Domestic	84a	....	....	....	....	–25,123	–72,348	–3,361	84,566	48,967	112,595	145,487	3,579
Net Foreign	85a	....	....	....	....	–3,665	–3,761	–4,403	50,638	16,134	925	–32,048	–38,847
Use of Cash Balances	87	–27,325	–11,013	–21,188	–90,818	–14,515	91,170	136,715	18,988	42,964	9,473	–36,624	11,270
Total Debt by Currency	88z	300,261	271,406	219,829	193,630	175,594	299,547	674,032	991,104	1,104,586	1,263,856	1,691,215	1,630,838
National	88b	202,694	161,071	103,200	72,696	44,254	31,755	426,928	642,371	688,937	836,689	1,293,881	1,279,282
Foreign	89b	97,567	110,335	116,629	120,934	131,340	267,792	247,104	348,733	415,649	427,167	397,334	351,556
National Accounts							*Billions of Baht*						
Househ.Cons.Expend.,incl.NPISHs	96f	1,550.5	1,730.5	1,958.7	2,225.7	2,479.8	2,587.0	2,505.3	2,595.1	2,750.5	2,913.7	3,067.4	3,337.6
Government Consumption Expend	91f	280.2	316.0	354.4	414.4	469.5	476.7	511.7	533.0	559.8	592.7	609.8	629.2
Gross Fixed Capital Formation	93e	1,111.3	1,252.9	1,450.2	1,719.1	1,892.9	1,598.6	1,035.4	965.9	1,080.0	1,178.5	1,251.6	1,427.6
Changes in Inventories	93i	20.1	13.5	10.7	43.0	35.2	–5.5	–89.5	–15.3	37.6	46.7	43.7	71.3
Exports of Goods and Services	90c	1,046.7	1,201.5	1,410.8	1,751.7	1,809.9	2,272.1	2,724.0	2,703.3	3,287.3	3,386.1	3,516.9	3,898.9
Imports of Goods and Services (-)	98c	1,160.2	1,335.7	1,586.6	2,033.9	2,099.2	2,205.1	1,988.9	2,120.3	2,862.3	3,051.6	3,123.6	3,499.6
Statistical Discrepancy	99bs	–17.6	–13.5	31.1	66.1	22.9	8.8	–71.6	–24.6	63.6	57.3	67.4	74.0
Gross Domestic Product (GDP)	99b	2,830.9	3,165.2	3,629.3	4,186.2	4,611.0	4,732.6	4,626.4	4,637.1	4,916.5	5,123.4	5,433.3	5,938.9
Net Primary Income from Abroad	98.n	–63.0	–45.9	–55.8	–68.2	–102.1	–123.4	–160.0	–126.4	–76.9	–85.1	–89.5	–104.6
Gross National Income (GNI)	99a	2,768.0	3,119.3	3,573.6	4,118.0	4,509.0	4,609.2	4,466.4	4,510.6	4,839.6	5,038.3	5,343.8	5,834.3
Consumption of Fixed Capital	99cf	282.7	335.9	397.0	471.6	556.7	599.1	....	....	....	....	....	....
GDP Volume 1988 Prices	99b.p	2,282.6	2,470.9	2,693.0	2,941.7	3,115.3	3,072.6	2,749.7	2,871.5	3,004.7	3,058.7	3,224.6	3,457.7
GDP Volume (2000=100)	99bvp	76.0	82.2	89.6	97.9	103.7	102.3	91.5	95.6	100.0	101.8	107.3	115.1
GDP Deflator (2000=100)	99bip	75.8	78.3	82.4	87.0	90.5	94.1	102.8	98.7	100.0	102.4	103.0	105.0
						Millions: Midyear Estimates							
Population	99z	55.81	56.50	57.17	57.83	58.46	59.08	59.69	60.31	60.92	61.55	62.19	62.83

Togo 742

		1992	1993	1994	1995	1996	1997	1998	1999	2000	2001	2002	2003
Exchange Rates					*Francs per SDR: End of Period*								
Official Rate	aa	378.57	404.89	780.44	728.38	753.06	807.94	791.61	†896.19	918.49	935.39	850.37	771.76
				Francs per US Dollar: End of Period (ae) Period Average (rf)									
Official Rate	ae	275.32	294.77	534.60	490.00	523.70	598.81	562.21	†652.95	704.95	744.31	625.50	519.36
Official Rate	rf	264.69	283.16	†555.20	499.15	511.55	583.67	589.95	†615.70	711.98	733.04	696.99	581.20
				Index Numbers (2000=100): Period Averages									
Official Rate	ahx	268.8	250.9	128.1	142.3	138.8	121.8	120.5	115.5	100.0	96.9	102.2	122.4
Nominal Effective Exchange Rate	nec	183.1	191.9	103.9	108.7	109.4	105.6	109.3	106.3	100.0	101.7	104.1	110.5
Real Effective Exchange Rate	rec	136.2	131.5	87.6	101.6	104.0	106.4	110.7	106.5	100.0	103.3	107.1	110.3
Fund Position					*Millions of SDRs: End of Period*								
Quota	2f.s	54.3	54.3	54.3	54.3	54.3	54.3	54.3	73.4	73.4	73.4	73.4	73.4
SDRs	1b.s	.2	.1	—	.3	.2	—	.1	.2	—	.2	.2	.1
Reserve Position in the Fund	1c.s	.3	.2	.3	.3	.3	.3	.3	.3	.3	.3	.3	.3
Total Fund Cred.&Loans Outstg	2tl	55.8	49.9	56.0	70.4	62.5	64.9	67.4	60.4	53.3	45.3	38.0	28.2
International Liquidity					*Millions of US Dollars Unless Otherwise Indicated: End of Period*								
Total Reserves minus Gold	1l.d	272.5	156.3	94.4	130.4	88.5	118.6	117.7	122.1	152.3	126.4	205.1	182.5
SDRs	1b.d	.3	.1	.1	.4	.4	—	.1	.2	—	.2	.3	.2
Reserve Position in the Fund	1c.d	.3	.3	.4	.4	.4	.3	.4	.3	.4	.4	.4	.5
Foreign Exchange	1d.d	271.9	155.9	94.0	129.6	87.8	118.3	117.3	121.5	151.9	125.8	204.4	181.8
Gold (Million Fine Troy Ounces)	1ad	.013	.013	.013	—	—	—	—	—	—	—	—	—
Gold (National Valuation)	1and	4.3	4.7	4.7	—	—	—	—	—	—	—	—	—
Monetary Authorities: Other Liab.	4..d	−.1	10.3	5.5	1.1	2.8	2.7	8.9	3.1	6.5	6.8	40.5	31.5
Deposit Money Banks: Assets	7a.d	87.9	58.4	109.7	111.1	100.6	66.3	69.1	60.0	81.4	87.2	103.6	118.7
Liabilities	7b.d	95.1	64.8	40.6	76.1	77.8	71.8	71.5	64.1	64.9	62.1	73.3	91.9
Monetary Authorities					*Billions of Francs: End of Period*								
Foreign Assets	11	75.0	46.1	50.5	63.9	46.3	71.0	66.2	79.7	107.4	94.1	128.3	94.8
Claims on Central Government	12a	40.0	40.4	49.8	71.1	70.2	66.0	76.5	67.8	66.9	65.9	53.6	46.2
Claims on Deposit Money Banks	12e	6.4	6.4	7.2	2.0	7.5	4.2	8.5	5.0	2.6	1.8	—	—
Claims on Other Financial Insts.	12f	1.6	1.5	1.3	.3	.2	.3	.3	.3	.3	.3	.3	—
Reserve Money	14	90.4	61.3	62.8	80.9	70.7	71.2	79.0	90.3	109.4	102.3	108.4	74.0
of which: Currency Outside DMBs	14a	22.1	10.3	44.8	73.5	59.7	60.3	65.3	79.5	95.7	85.7	64.0	37.0
Foreign Liabilities	16c	21.1	23.2	46.7	51.8	48.6	54.1	58.3	56.2	53.6	47.5	57.6	38.1
Central Government Deposits	16d	6.5	6.6	9.6	8.1	8.4	9.9	5.8	3.8	3.7	8.6	7.6	18.1
Other Items (Net)	17r	5.1	3.3	−10.3	−3.6	−3.4	6.3	8.3	2.6	10.5	3.7	8.6	10.7
Deposit Money Banks					*Billions of Francs: End of Period*								
Reserves	20	69.0	54.1	15.1	12.5	14.9	17.7	7.9	9.0	13.4	12.8	33.7	38.0
Foreign Assets	21	24.2	17.2	58.6	54.4	52.7	39.7	38.8	39.2	57.4	64.9	64.8	61.6
Claims on Central Government	22a	2.1	1.9	12.4	12.3	16.5	17.4	16.7	14.1	10.8	7.9	6.6	6.4
Claims on Private Sector	22d	110.6	101.9	101.8	130.4	140.2	154.8	161.9	146.6	147.6	137.3	127.7	166.7
Claims on Other Financial Insts.	22f	.5	.6	.5	—	—	—	—	—	—	—	—	—
Demand Deposits	24	34.1	35.1	49.3	56.4	59.9	60.6	63.5	61.1	78.4	73.0	82.4	103.3
Time Deposits	25	78.1	66.7	68.2	68.7	66.2	73.8	65.4	68.9	69.4	78.2	86.1	105.3
Foreign Liabilities	26c	24.3	17.2	19.9	33.7	37.3	42.5	39.1	40.1	44.4	45.2	45.2	47.3
Long-Term Foreign Liabilities	26cl	1.9	1.9	1.7	3.5	3.4	.5	1.2	1.7	1.4	1.0	.7	.5
Central Government Deposits	26d	53.2	43.1	39.1	37.4	32.8	29.8	28.9	20.6	17.2	15.1	18.1	18.7
Credit from Monetary Authorities	26g	6.4	7.1	7.4	2.0	7.6	4.7	8.5	5.0	2.6	2.1	—	—
Other Items (Net)	27r	8.4	4.5	2.7	7.9	16.9	17.7	18.8	11.4	16.0	8.3	.3	−2.3
Treasury Claims: Private Sector	22d.i	1.5	1.4	.6	.9	.7	.7	.5	.3	.3	.3	.3	.3
Post Office: Checking Deposits	24..i	.9	1.0	1.0	1.3	1.2	1.7	1.2	1.9	1.5	1.2	1.5	1.3
Monetary Survey					*Billions of Francs: End of Period*								
Foreign Assets (Net)	31n	53.8	22.8	42.5	32.7	13.2	14.0	7.7	22.6	66.8	66.3	90.3	71.0
Domestic Credit	32	96.0	97.6	118.1	169.8	187.1	200.4	221.8	206.2	206.3	189.0	164.0	183.9
Claims on Central Govt. (Net)	32an	−18.2	−7.8	13.8	38.3	46.0	44.7	59.1	59.1	58.1	51.1	35.7	16.8
Claims on Private Sector	32d	112.1	103.3	102.5	131.2	140.9	155.5	162.4	146.8	147.8	137.6	127.9	167.0
Claims on Other Financial Insts.	32f	2.1	2.1	1.8	.3	.2	.3	.3	.3	.3	.3	.3	—
Money	34	57.1	46.6	95.3	131.2	121.0	123.3	131.8	144.8	176.9	161.5	148.4	143.1
Quasi-Money	35	78.1	66.7	68.2	68.7	66.2	73.8	65.4	68.9	69.4	78.2	86.1	105.3
Long-Term Foreign Liabilities	36cl	1.9	1.9	1.7	3.5	3.4	.5	1.2	1.7	1.4	1.0	.7	.5
Other Items (Net)	37r	12.8	5.3	−4.6	−.9	9.6	16.9	31.1	13.4	25.5	14.5	19.0	6.0
Money plus Quasi-Money	35l	135.2	113.3	163.5	199.9	187.2	197.0	197.2	213.7	246.3	239.7	234.6	248.4
Interest Rates					*Percent Per Annum*								
Bank Rate (End of Period)	60	12.50	†6.00	6.00	6.00	6.00	6.00	6.00	6.00	6.00	6.00	6.00	4.50
Money Market Rate	60b	11.44	....	....	....	....	....	4.81	4.95	4.95	4.95	4.95	4.95
Deposit Rate	60l	7.75	....	....	....	....	....	3.50	3.50	3.50	3.50	3.50	3.50
Lending Rate	60p	17.50	....	....	....	....	....	....	....	....	....	....	....

2004, International Monetary Fund: *International Financial Statistics Yearbook*

Togo 742

		1992	1993	1994	1995	1996	1997	1998	1999	2000	2001	2002	2003
Prices and Labor						*Index Numbers (2000=100): Period Averages*							
Consumer Prices	64	53.5	†53.0	73.7	85.8	89.9	†97.3	98.2	98.1	100.0	103.9	107.1	106.1
						Number in Thousands: Period Averages							
Employment	67e	61	60	56	54	50	49	....	....	....	....	....	....
International Transactions						*Millions of Francs*							
Exports	70	72,779	38,512	182,300	188,400	225,400	246,600	247,900	241,000	257,400	261,900	295,700	357,000
Imports, c.i.f.	71	104,461	50,810	123,265	295,700	339,900	376,400	346,700	301,300	345,100	378,300	401,200	490,200
						2000=100							
Export Prices	74	....	....	....	....	122.5	128.9	120.0	100.5	100.0	59.7	57.1	51.7
Unit Value of Imports	75	....	....	....	....	62.2	77.5	83.6	104.0	100.0	158.4	187.5	212.4
Balance of Payments						*Millions of US Dollars: Minus Sign Indicates Debit*							
Current Account, n.i.e.	78ald	−140.6	−82.4	−56.3	−122.0	−153.9	−116.9	−140.1	−127.1	−139.6	−169.1	....	....
Goods: Exports f.o.b.	78aad	419.7	264.0	328.4	377.4	440.6	422.5	420.3	391.5	361.8	357.2	....	....
Goods: Imports f.o.b.	78abd	−547.4	−375.3	−365.5	−506.5	−567.8	−530.6	−553.5	−489.4	−484.6	−516.1	....	....
Trade Balance	78acd	−127.7	−111.3	−37.1	−129.1	−127.2	−108.1	−133.2	−98.0	−122.8	−158.9	....	....
Services: Credit	78add	129.2	84.6	70.9	87.3	116.2	88.5	76.0	68.4	61.8	71.8	....	....
Services: Debit	78aed	−203.3	−128.2	−125.3	−164.3	−201.4	−167.8	−149.2	−130.6	−117.5	−129.9	....	....
Balance on Goods & Services	78afd	−201.8	−154.9	−91.6	−206.0	−212.3	−187.4	−206.4	−160.1	−178.5	−217.0	....	....
Income: Credit	78agd	31.4	26.8	9.1	8.8	45.6	35.0	44.4	40.2	32.9	25.9	....	....
Income: Debit	78ahd	−58.6	−17.7	−54.0	−42.4	−72.0	−63.9	−67.7	−78.6	−62.0	−55.2	....	....
Balance on Gds, Serv. & Inc.	78aid	−229.0	−145.7	−136.5	−239.6	−238.8	−216.3	−229.7	−198.5	−207.6	−246.3	....	....
Current Transfers, n.i.e.: Credit	78ajd	111.1	82.6	91.3	129.7	106.8	120.2	101.8	73.6	73.3	88.3	....	....
Current Transfers: Debit	78akd	−22.7	−19.3	−11.2	−12.1	−21.9	−20.8	−12.2	−2.2	−5.4	−11.1	....	....
Capital Account, n.i.e.	78bcd	−	−	−	−	5.6	5.8	6.1	6.9	8.7	21.4	....	....
Capital Account, n.i.e.: Credit	78bad	−	−	−	−	5.6	5.8	6.1	6.9	8.7	21.4	....	....
Capital Account: Debit	78bbd	−	−	−	−	....	....	....	....	....	....	....	....
Financial Account, n.i.e.	78bjd	−23.8	−105.1	−40.5	−52.8	151.3	126.9	114.1	155.5	162.8	151.2	....	....
Direct Investment Abroad	78bdd	−	−	−	5.8	−2.8	−2.5	−10.6	−2.9	−.4	7.3	....	....
Dir. Invest. in Rep. Econ., n.i.e.	78bed	−	−11.9	15.4	26.2	17.3	21.0	30.2	42.6	41.9	63.6	....	....
Portfolio Investment Assets	78bfd	−	−.7	.7	5.0	−16.1	6.7	−5.2	−1.3	.8	5.3	....	....
Equity Securities	78bkd	−	.3	1.1	5.0	−.3	7.0	−4.4	−2.8	.6	−	....	....
Debt Securities	78bld	−	−.9	−.4	−	−15.8	−.3	−.7	1.6	.2	5.3	....	....
Portfolio Investment Liab., n.i.e.	78bgd	−	.1	−	....	20.1	9.4	11.4	8.6	6.1	5.8	....	....
Equity Securities	78bmd	−	−	−	−	18.8	10.6	11.6	8.5	6.1	1.5	....	....
Debt Securities	78bnd	−	.1	−	....	1.3	−1.2	−.2	.1	−	4.3	....	....
Financial Derivatives Assets	78bwd	....	....	....	20.6	.3	2.1	−.1	−	−	−	....	....
Financial Derivatives Liabilities	78bxd	....	....	....	....	1.6	−7.0	−.2	−.3	−.1	−	....	....
Other Investment Assets	78bhd	.2	−3.2	−1.5	12.1	−19.2	−1.6	16.2	13.0	8.8	8.2	....	....
Monetary Authorities	78bod	....	....	....	....	....	....	....	−	....	....	....	....
General Government	78bpd	−	−	−	....	−3.7	12.2	5.3	7.8	7.5	4.8	....	....
Banks	78bqd	.2	−	−	....	4.6	....	−.7	.5	−16.8	−8.8	....	....
Other Sectors	78brd	−	−3.2	−1.5	12.1	−20.1	−13.8	11.6	4.7	18.1	12.3	....	....
Other Investment Liab., n.i.e.	78bid	−24.0	−89.5	−55.2	−122.4	150.1	98.9	72.3	95.8	105.7	61.0	....	....
Monetary Authorities	78bsd	−	−	−	−	3.8	4.8	5.8	−5.0	2.5	1.7	....	....
General Government	78btd	−53.3	−44.8	−19.3	−133.5	67.8	62.0	45.0	33.2	41.6	28.6	....	....
Banks	78bud	10.4	−.7	−66.2	....	13.1	....	−6.4	1.6	1.4	.4	....	....
Other Sectors	78bvd	18.9	−44.0	30.3	11.0	65.4	32.0	28.0	65.9	60.1	30.3	....	....
Net Errors and Omissions	78cad	4.0	−2.1	−.2	−19.3	−27.9	−2.7	2.7	−3.7	5.0	−5.4	....	....
Overall Balance	78cbd	−160.3	−189.6	−97.1	−194.0	−24.9	13.1	−17.2	31.6	36.8	−2.0	....	....
Reserves and Related Items	79dad	160.3	189.6	97.1	194.0	24.9	−13.1	17.2	−31.6	−36.8	2.0	....	....
Reserve Assets	79dbd	73.6	102.2	−7.7	−26.9	34.3	−26.2	8.8	−22.2	−27.5	7.4	....	....
Use of Fund Credit and Loans	79dcd	.6	−8.3	9.3	22.0	−11.4	3.4	3.0	−9.4	−9.3	−10.2	....	....
Exceptional Financing	79ded	86.1	95.7	95.5	199.0	2.0	9.7	5.4	−	−	4.8	....	....

Togo 742

		1992	1993	1994	1995	1996	1997	1998	1999	2000	2001	2002	2003
International Investment Position						*Millions of US Dollars*							
Assets....................................	79aad	....	....	....	....	....	....	....	394.9	367.7	336.5	....	....
Direct Investment Abroad............	79abd	....	....	....	....	....	....	....	20.8	17.4	17.6	....	....
Portfolio Investment....................	79acd	....	....	....	....	....	....	....	14.3	13.8	48.4	....	....
Equity Securities....................	79add	....	....	....	....	....	....	....	6.6	7.3	6.6	....	....
Debt Securities......................	79aed	....	....	....	....	....	....	....	7.7	6.5	41.8	....	....
Financial Derivatives..................	79ald	....	....	....	....	....	....	....	.1	.1	–	....	....
Other Investment......................	79afd	....	....	....	....	....	....	....	237.7	195.5	144.3	....	....
Monetary Authorities...............	79agd	....	....	....	....	....	....	....	–	–	–	....	....
General Government................	79ahd	....	....	....	....	....	....	....	35.8	21.3	–	....	....
Banks.................................	79aid	....	....	....	....	....	....	....	67.1	83.2	87.5	....	....
Other Sectors.......................	79ajd	....	....	....	....	....	....	....	134.8	91.0	56.8	....	....
Reserve Assets........................	79akd	....	....	....	....	....	....	....	122.1	140.9	126.2	....	....
Liabilities.................................	79lad	....	....	....	....	....	....	....	1,728.8	1,745.3	1,735.6	....	....
Dir. Invest. in Rep. Economy.........	79lbd	....	....	....	....	....	....	....	47.5	86.8	141.1	....	....
Portfolio Investment....................	79lcd	....	....	....	....	....	....	....	24.2	30.1	33.2	....	....
Equity Securities....................	79ldd	....	....	....	....	....	....	....	24.2	30.1	29.0	....	....
Debt Securities......................	79led	....	....	....	....	....	....	....	.1	–	4.2	....	....
Financial Derivatives..................	79lld	....	....	....	....	....	....	....	.7	–	–	....	....
Other Investment......................	79lfd	....	....	....	....	....	....	....	1,656.5	1,628.4	1,561.4	....	....
Monetary Authorities...............	79lgd	....	....	....	....	....	....	....	86.9	81.6	71.1	....	....
General Government................	79lhd	....	....	....	....	....	....	....	1,322.3	1,274.6	1,232.5	....	....
Banks.................................	79lid	....	....	....	....	....	....	....	56.0	76.7	51.2	....	....
Other Sectors.......................	79ljd	....	....	....	....	....	....	....	191.3	195.6	206.5	....	....
Government Finance					*Billions of Francs: Year Ending December 31*								
Deficit (-) or Surplus...................	80	–18	–53	–59	–35	–24	–17	–48	–27	–43	....	....	....
Total Revenue and Grants............	81y	81	39	77	109	127	140	141	142	121	....	....	....
Revenue...............................	81	73	38	67	97	110	129	127	127	117	....	....	....
Grants.................................	81z	8	1	10	12	16	12	14	15	4	....	....	....
Exp. & Lending Minus Repay.........	82z	99	92	136	144	151	157	188	169	164	....	....	....
Expenditure...........................	82	99	92	136	144	151	157	188	168	168	....	....	....
Lending Minus Repayments.........	83	–	–	–	–	–	–	1	1	–3	....	....	....
Statistical Discrepancy................	80xx	10	35	21	–4	–5	–30	–1	4	28	....	....	....
Total Financing													
Domestic................................	84a	5	16	19	19	7	13	10	1	–4	....	....	....
Foreign.................................	85a	3	2	19	20	22	34	39	23	20	....	....	....
National Accounts						*Billions of Francs*							
Househ.Cons.Expend.,incl.NPISHs....	96f	390.4	323.5	438.1	577.2	647.8	761.5	726.5	762.1	747.1	800.6	895.2	....
Government Consumption Expend...	91f	55.1	57.8	77.1	77.0	100.6	95.2	103.0	95.4	96.7	88.6	100.8	....
Gross Fixed Capital Formation.........	93e	57.7	25.4	63.1	84.4	99.1	118.2	128.3	120.7	137.4	153.4	181.8	....
Changes in Inventories................	93i	6.6	–10.4	18.2	17.8	10.7	9.3	–.6	–.8	4.9	8.1	6.2	....
Exports of Goods and Services.........	90c	140.8	98.7	221.7	232.0	284.9	298.2	292.7	283.1	301.6	325.0	365.2	....
Imports of Goods and Services (-).....	98c	200.5	142.6	272.5	334.8	393.5	407.6	414.4	381.7	428.7	472.1	527.8	....
Gross Domestic Product (GDP)........	99b	443.5	352.3	545.6	653.6	748.7	874.8	835.6	878.7	859.0	903.6	1,021.4	....
Net National Income....................	99e	398.6	321.5	468.3	574.8	664.3	775.3	742.2	764.2	829.7			
GDP Volume 1978 Prices................	99b.p	214.5	179.0	209.0	223.5	245.2	255.7	250.1	257.5	255.2	256.8	264.2	....
GDP Volume (2000=100)................	99bvp	84.1	70.1	81.9	87.6	96.1	100.2	98.0	100.9	100.0	100.6	103.5	....
GDP Deflator (2000=100)...............	99bip	61.4	58.5	77.6	86.9	90.7	101.6	99.3	101.4	100.0	104.5	114.9	....
						Millions: Midyear Estimates							
Population...............................	99z	3.73	3.84	3.93	4.06	4.17	4.28	4.40	4.51	4.53	....	....	....

2004, International Monetary Fund : *International Financial Statistics Yearbook*

Tonga 866

		1992	1993	1994	1995	1996	1997	1998	1999	2000	2001	2002	2003
Exchange Rates						*Pa'anga per SDR: End of Period*							
Official Rate	aa	1.9116	1.8946	1.8371	1.8883	1.7438	1.8377	2.2749	2.2066	2.5754	2.7736	3.0299	3.0020
					Pa'anga per US Dollar: End of Period (ae) Period Average (rf)								
Official Rate	ae	1.3902	1.3793	1.2584	1.2703	1.2127	1.3620	1.6156	1.6077	1.9767	2.2070	2.2287	2.0202
Official Rate	rf	1.3471	1.3840	1.3202	1.2709	1.2319	1.2635	1.4920	1.5991	1.7585	2.1236	2.1952	2.1420
Fund Position						*Millions of SDRs: End of Period*							
Quota	2f.s	5.00	5.00	5.00	5.00	5.00	5.00	5.00	6.90	6.90	6.90	6.90	6.90
SDRs	1b.s	.38	.44	.49	.04	.08	.11	.15	.03	.10	.15	.19	.22
Reserve Position in the Fund	1c.s	1.18	1.19	1.20	1.21	1.21	1.21	1.22	1.70	1.71	1.71	1.71	1.71
Total Fund Cred.&Loans Outstg.	2tl	–	–	–	–	–	–	–	–	–	–	–	–
International Liquidity					*Millions of US Dollars Unless Otherwise Indicated: End of Period*								
Total Reserves minus Gold	1l.d	31.77	37.06	35.54	28.71	30.62	27.49	28.66	26.78	26.99	26.10	27.70	42.63
SDRs	1b.d	.52	.60	.71	.06	.11	.14	.21	.05	.12	.19	.26	.32
Reserve Position in the Fund	1c.d	1.62	1.64	1.76	1.80	1.74	1.63	1.72	2.33	2.23	2.15	2.33	2.54
Foreign Exchange	1d.d	29.62	34.82	33.07	26.85	28.77	25.72	26.73	24.40	24.64	23.76	25.11	39.76
Monetary Authorities: Other Liab.	4..d	.13	.58	.36	.24	.10	.11	.39	.18	.26	.16	.18	.34
Deposit Money Banks: Assets	7a.d	.33	1.54	1.84	1.96	1.39	1.61	4.27	2.89	11.50	10.30	5.07	11.68
Liabilities	7b.d	.47	.64	.94	1.22	.63	4.34	4.86	4.36	6.92	5.06	5.76	10.55
Other Banking Insts.: Liabilities	7f.d	2.86	3.65	4.33	3.83	3.51	2.94	2.46	2.32	1.49	1.34	1.19	.90
Monetary Authorities						*Thousands of Pa'anga: End of Period*							
Foreign Assets	11	44,165	49,994	41,812	31,493	33,157	32,798	36,311	34,569	25,977	29,709	44,696	56,743
Claims on Central Government	12a	10,432	11,236	9,516	5,493	5,439	5,439	5,456	5,404	6,380	14,095	17,446	18,162
Claims on Deposit Money Banks	12e	–	–	–	–	–	–	–	–	9,078	5,447	1,816	–
Claims on Other Banking Insts.	12f	–	–	–	–	–	–	–	–	–	–	–	–
Reserve Money	14	51,698	19,226	18,368	15,125	21,629	24,300	26,805	28,804	32,437	42,087	50,818	46,047
of which: Currency Outside DMBs	14a	7,127	7,894	7,346	7,321	6,850	6,471	8,076	9,443	9,966	11,355	12,168	14,322
Liabs. of Central Bank: Securities	16ac	–	42,590	39,200	29,367	24,893	21,818	15,963	13,471	100	–	–	–
Foreign Liabilities	16c	184	803	455	306	122	155	623	295	517	356	412	687
Central Government Deposits	16d	1,091	3,432	2,142	1,814	1,577	1,366	6,358	7,126	5,777	6,715	15,149	31,168
Capital Accounts	17a	2,725	2,789	2,922	3,000	2,459	1,676	1,146	1,039	1,331	2,147	4,071	5,995
Other Items (Net)	17r	–1,101	–7,610	–11,759	–12,626	–12,084	–11,078	–9,128	–10,764	1,273	–2,054	–6,492	–8,992
Deposit Money Banks						*Thousands of Pa'anga: End of Period*							
Reserves	20	42,000	48,582	46,688	35,000	39,252	38,006	33,857	33,572	22,483	29,814	38,137	31,025
Foreign Assets	21	457	2,125	2,314	2,491	1,682	2,189	6,893	4,644	22,733	22,729	11,289	23,602
Claims on Central Government	22a	6,898	6,816	6,262	9,057	8,970	10,616	10,039	9,632	9,094	9,361	8,215	8,949
Claims on Nonfin.Pub.Enterprises	22c	413	55	152	103	497	164	1,551	1,392	3,068	6,111	8,571	12,071
Claims on Private Sector	22d	31,051	31,351	47,273	57,191	59,114	68,094	79,720	87,420	102,774	112,835	137,506	154,151
Claims on Other Banking Insts	22f	350	350	3,850	2,450	1,550	2,375	2,000	3,000	3,000	2,000	2,000	–
Demand Deposits	24	15,285	18,969	16,637	14,674	15,701	16,941	16,429	20,472	23,106	30,389	42,935	47,764
Time, Savings,& Fgn.Currency Dep.	25	30,173	38,730	44,553	48,567	51,483	56,684	67,350	72,854	89,042	98,505	96,094	110,814
Foreign Liabilities	26c	654	879	1,181	1,545	760	5,909	7,850	7,007	13,679	11,171	12,841	21,306
Central Government Deposits	26d	10,382	7,565	12,394	11,534	10,037	8,009	6,929	6,974	7,086	4,530	7,927	10,276
Credit from Monetary Authorities	26g	–	–	–	–	–	–	–	–	9,078	5,447	1,816	–
Liabilities to Other Banking Insts.	26i	–	744	5,225	2,764	4,741	4,399	4,216	5,003	2,604	1,378	4,591	875
Capital Accounts	27a	32,559	30,758	36,560	38,275	38,264	37,889	39,919	36,738	39,805	42,887	46,085	52,977
Other Items (Net)	27r	–7,884	–8,366	–10,011	–11,067	–9,921	–8,387	–8,633	–9,388	–21,248	–11,457	–6,571	–14,214
Monetary Survey						*Thousands of Pa'anga: End of Period*							
Foreign Assets (Net)	31n	43,784	50,437	42,490	32,133	33,957	28,923	34,731	31,910	34,514	40,912	42,732	58,352
Domestic Credit	32	37,671	38,811	52,517	60,946	63,956	77,313	85,479	92,748	111,453	133,157	150,662	151,889
Claims on Central Govt. (Net)	32an	5,857	7,055	1,242	1,202	2,795	6,680	2,208	936	2,611	12,211	2,585	–14,333
Claims on Nonfin.Pub.Enterprises	32c	413	55	152	103	497	164	1,551	1,392	3,068	6,111	8,571	12,071
Claims on Private Sector	32d	31,051	31,351	47,273	57,191	59,114	68,094	79,720	87,420	102,774	112,835	137,506	154,151
Claims on Other Banking Insts	32f	350	350	3,850	2,450	1,550	2,375	2,000	3,000	3,000	2,000	2,000	–
Money	34	22,412	27,016	25,535	21,995	22,826	23,412	24,505	29,915	33,072	41,744	55,103	62,086
Quasi-Money	35	30,173	38,730	44,553	48,567	51,483	56,684	67,350	72,854	89,042	98,505	96,094	110,814
Liabs.of Central Bank: Securities	36ac	–	42,590	39,200	29,367	24,893	21,818	15,963	13,471	100	–	–	–
Liabilities to Other Banking Insts.	36i	–	744	5,225	2,764	4,741	4,399	4,216	5,003	2,604	1,378	4,591	875
Capital Accounts	37a	35,284	33,547	39,482	41,275	40,723	39,565	41,065	37,777	41,136	45,034	50,156	58,972
Other Items (Net)	37r	–6,414	–53,379	–58,988	–50,889	–46,753	–39,642	–32,889	–34,362	–19,987	–12,593	–12,550	–22,506
Money plus Quasi-Money	35l	52,585	65,746	70,088	70,562	74,309	80,096	91,855	102,769	122,114	140,249	151,197	172,900

Tonga 866

		1992	1993	1994	1995	1996	1997	1998	1999	2000	2001	2002	2003
Other Banking Institutions						*Thousands of Pa'anga: End of Period*							
Reserves	40	2,997	4,277	6,695	4,290	834	475	1,247	1,734	1,607	1,815	1,818	1,824
Claims on Central Government	42a	1,553	1,651	2,000	2,000	1,700	1,700	1,700	2,000	1,500	200	200	1,200
Claims on Nonfin.Pub.Enterprises	42c	574	926	3,647	2,937	2,940	1,452	987	834	1,045	885	388	2,383
Claims on Private Sector	42d	24,569	29,380	31,176	37,063	38,270	41,669	41,055	31,939	33,247	35,412	40,175	43,870
Claims on Deposit Money Banks	42e	100	–	3,200	100	3,578	3,600	2,800	4,100	1,500	250	3,600	200
Bonds	46ab	–	2,476	9,189	1,823	2,005	3,908	4,604	5,022	5,696	9,133	13,915	17,516
Long-Term Foreign Liabilities	46cl	3,973	5,040	5,444	4,863	4,256	4,008	3,976	3,728	2,950	2,950	2,654	1,824
Central Government Deposits	46d	–	–	–	3,600	3,600	3,600	3,600	2,000	2,400	1,800	3,573	2,944
Central Govt. Lending Funds	46f	14,029	14,597	15,761	16,155	17,411	16,743	15,950	14,552	13,036	11,395	9,347	8,469
Credit from Monetary Authorities	46g	–	–	–	–	–	–	–	–	–	–	–	–
Credit from Deposit Money Banks	46h	–	–	–	2,100	1,200	2,200	2,000	2,000	3,000	2,000	2,000	–
Capital Accounts	47a	15,514	16,643	17,703	19,828	21,356	22,074	22,391	19,874	19,020	17,797	21,312	24,491
Other Items (Net)	47r	–3,723	–2,522	–1,379	–1,979	–2,506	–3,637	–4,732	–6,569	–7,203	–6,513	–6,620	–5,767
Banking Survey						*Thousands of Pa'anga: End of Period*							
Foreign Assets (Net)	51n	43,784	50,437	42,490	32,133	33,957	28,923	34,731	31,910	34,514	40,912	42,732	58,352
Domestic Credit	52	64,017	70,418	85,490	96,896	101,716	116,159	123,621	122,521	141,845	165,854	185,852	196,398
Claims on Central Govt. (Net)	52an	7,410	8,706	3,242	–398	895	4,780	308	936	1,711	10,611	–788	–16,077
Claims on Nonfin.Pub.Enterprises	52c	987	981	3,799	3,040	3,437	1,616	2,538	2,226	4,113	6,996	8,959	14,454
Claims on Private Sector	52d	55,620	60,731	78,449	94,254	97,384	109,763	120,775	119,359	136,021	148,247	177,681	198,021
Liquid Liabilities	55l	49,588	61,469	63,393	66,272	73,475	79,621	90,608	101,035	120,507	138,434	149,379	171,076
Bonds	56ab	–	2,476	9,189	1,823	2,005	3,908	4,604	5,022	5,696	9,133	13,915	17,516
Liabs.of Central Bank: Securities	56ac	–	42,590	39,200	29,367	24,893	21,818	15,963	13,471	100	–	–	–
Long-Term Foreign Liabilities	56cl	3,973	5,040	5,444	4,863	4,256	4,008	3,976	3,728	2,950	2,950	2,654	1,824
Central Govt. Lending Funds	56f	14,029	14,597	15,761	16,155	17,411	16,743	15,950	14,552	13,036	11,395	9,347	8,469
Capital Accounts	57a	50,798	50,190	57,185	61,103	62,079	61,639	63,456	57,651	60,156	62,831	71,468	83,463
Other Items (Net)	57r	–10,587	–55,507	–62,192	–50,554	–48,446	–42,655	–36,205	–41,028	–26,086	–17,978	–18,179	–27,598
Interest Rates						*Percent Per Annum*							
Deposit Rate	60l	5.50	4.25	4.64	4.72	5.53	5.57	5.63	5.42	5.36	5.47	5.47	5.47
Lending Rate	60p	13.50	†9.94	9.48	9.82	10.16	10.02	10.40	10.32	10.35	11.43	11.43	10.15
Prices and Labor						*Index Numbers (2000=100): Period Averages*							
Consumer Prices	64	80.1	80.9	81.7	†82.9	85.4	87.2	90.0	94.4	100.0	108.3	119.5	133.4
						Number in Thousands: Period Averages							
Labor Force	67d	....	35	35	....	34	....	....	....	....	....	....	....
International Transactions						*Thousands of Pa'anga Thousands of Pa'anga*							
Exports	70	17,402	23,430	18,367	18,443	16,263	12,800	11,600	20,000	16,000	14,600	32,300	....
Imports, c.i.f.	71	84,294	84,933	91,210	98,034	91,807	92,100	102,400	116,400	123,100	155,100	195,000	....

Tonga 866

		1992	1993	1994	1995	1996	1997	1998	1999	2000	2001	2002	2003
Balance of Payments		*Thousands of US Dollars: Minus Sign Indicates Debit*											
Current Account, n.i.e.	78ald	−468	−5,928	....	....	....	....	....	....	....	−12,858	....	....
Goods: Exports f.o.b.	78aad	12,306	16,083	....	....	....	....	....	....	....	6,657	....	....
Goods: Imports f.o.b.	78abd	−51,301	−56,608	....	....	....	....	....	....	....	−63,688	....	....
Trade Balance	78acd	−38,995	−40,525	....	....	....	....	....	....	....	−57,031	....	....
Services: Credit	78add	16,623	15,953	....	....	....	....	....	....	....	17,125	....	....
Services: Debit	78aed	−22,246	−21,146	....	....	....	....	....	....	....	−27,152	....	....
Balance on Goods & Services	78afd	−44,619	−45,718	....	....	....	....	....	....	....	−67,058	....	....
Income: Credit	78agd	4,244	5,557	....	....	....	....	....	....	....	5,675	....	....
Income: Debit	78ahd	−1,211	−2,383	....	....	....	....	....	....	....	−2,266	....	....
Balance on Gds, Serv. & Inc.	78aid	−41,586	−42,543	....	....	....	....	....	....	....	−63,650	....	....
Current Transfers, n.i.e.: Credit	78ajd	50,552	49,741	....	....	....	....	....	....	....	62,507	....	....
Current Transfers: Debit	78akd	−9,434	−13,126	....	....	....	....	....	....	....	−11,716	....	....
Capital Account, n.i.e.	78bcd	557	605	....	....	....	....	....	....	....	9,152	....	....
Capital Account, n.i.e.: Credit	78bad	732	1,340	....	....	....	....	....	....	....	11,727	....	....
Capital Account: Debit	78bbd	−176	−735	....	....	....	....	....	....	....	−2,575	....	....
Financial Account, n.i.e.	78bjd	4,421	3,189	....	....	....	....	....	....	....	823	....	....
Direct Investment Abroad	78bdd	−2	−1	....	....	....	....	....	....	....	....	....	....
Dir. Invest. in Rep. Econ., n.i.e.	78bed	1,224	2,178	....	....	....	....	....	....	....	....	....	....
Portfolio Investment Assets	78bfd	−	−	....	....	....	....	....	....	....	....	....	....
Equity Securities	78bkd	−	−	....	....	....	....	....	....	....	....	....	....
Debt Securities	78bld	−	−	....	....	....	....	....	....	....	....	....	....
Portfolio Investment Liab., n.i.e.	78bgd	−141	−64	....	....	....	....	....	....	....	....	....	....
Equity Securities	78bmd	−33	−	....	....	....	....	....	....	....	....	....	....
Debt Securities	78bnd	−109	−64	....	....	....	....	....	....	....	....	....	....
Financial Derivatives Assets	78bwd	....	....	....	....	....	....	....	....	....	....	....	....
Financial Derivatives Liabilities	78bxd	....	....	....	....	....	....	....	....	....	....	....	....
Other Investment Assets	78bhd	815	−	....	....	....	....	....	....	....	....	....	....
Monetary Authorities	78bod	....	....	....	....	....	....	....	....	....	....	....	....
General Government	78bpd	812	−	....	....	....	....	....	....	....	....	....	....
Banks	78bqd	−	−	....	....	....	....	....	....	....	....	....	....
Other Sectors	78brd	4	−	....	....	....	....	....	....	....	....	....	....
Other Investment Liab., n.i.e.	78bid	2,525	1,076	....	....	....	....	....	....	....	823	....	....
Monetary Authorities	78bsd	−68	−14	....	....	....	....	....	....	....	823	....	....
General Government	78btd	3,095	1,095	....	....	....	....	....	....	....	....	....	....
Banks	78bud	−208	−	....	....	....	....	....	....	....	....	....	....
Other Sectors	78bvd	−294	−4	....	....	....	....	....	....	....	....	....	....
Net Errors and Omissions	78cad	−3,437	−260	....	....	....	....	....	....	....	4,527	....	....
Overall Balance	78cbd	1,072	−2,394	....	....	....	....	....	....	....	1,645	....	....
Reserves and Related Items	79dad	−1,072	2,394	....	....	....	....	....	....	....	−1,645	....	....
Reserve Assets	79dbd	−1,072	2,394	....	....	....	....	....	....	....	−1,645	....	....
Use of Fund Credit and Loans	79dcd	−	−	....	....	....	....	....	....	....	−	....	....
Exceptional Financing	79ded	....	....	....	....	....	....	....	....	....	....	....	....
National Accounts					*Millions of Pa'anga: Year Ending June 30*								
Gross Domestic Product (GDP)	99b	198.2	201.0	214.8	....	....	....	....	....	....	....	....	....
GDP Volume (1990=100)	99bvp	101.9	101.8	106.7	....	....	....	....	....	....	....	....	....
GDP Deflator (1990=100)	99bip	122.8	124.6	127.1	....	....	....	....	....	....	....	....	....
					Millions: Midyear Estimates								
Population	99z	.10	.10	.10	.10	.10	.10	.10	.10	.10	.10	.10	.10

Trinidad and Tobago 369

		1992	1993	1994	1995	1996	1997	1998	1999	2000	2001	2002	2003
Exchange Rates													
		\multicolumn{12}{c}{TT Dollars per SDR: End of Period}												
Market Rate	aa	5.8438	7.9860	8.6616	8.9146	8.9074	8.5001	9.2881	8.6467	8.2078	7.9051	8.5648	9.3615
		\multicolumn{12}{c}{TT Dollars per US Dollar: End of Period (ae) Period Average (rf)}												
Market Rate	ae	4.2500	5.8141	5.9332	5.9971	6.1945	6.2999	6.5965	6.2999	6.2996	6.2902	6.2999	6.2999
Market Rate	rf	4.2500	5.3511	5.9249	5.9478	6.0051	6.2517	6.2983	6.2989	6.2998	6.2332	6.2487	6.2951
		\multicolumn{12}{c}{Index Numbers (2000=100): Period Averages}												
Nominal Effective Exchange Rate	nec	101.45	92.74	90.16	88.71	92.10	92.58	94.42	95.87	100.00	104.84	105.16	99.56
Real Effective Exchange Rate	rec	105.49	95.30	88.80	86.69	88.32	88.68	93.06	95.56	100.00	107.58	110.08	104.93
Fund Position													
		\multicolumn{12}{c}{Millions of SDRs: End of Period}												
Quota	2f.s	246.8	246.8	246.8	246.8	246.8	246.8	246.8	335.6	335.6	335.6	335.6	335.6
SDRs	1b.s	.2	.2	.1	.1	–	.1	.1	–	.1	.2	.3	.7
Reserve Position in the Fund	1c.s	–	–	–	–	–	–	–	–	–	24.6	76.4	129.3
of which: Outstg.Fund Borrowing	2c	–	–	–	–	–	–	–	–	–	–	–	–
Total Fund Cred.&Loans Outstg	2tl	205.3	112.8	62.4	33.8	16.5	3.1	–	–	–	–	–	–
International Liquidity													
		\multicolumn{12}{c}{Millions of US Dollars Unless Otherwise Indicated: End of Period}												
Total Reserves minus Gold	1l.d	172.2	206.3	352.4	358.2	543.9	706.4	783.1	945.4	1,386.3	1,907.1	2,027.7	2,451.1
SDRs	1b.d	.3	.3	.1	.2	–	.1	.1	–	.1	.2	.4	1.1
Reserve Position in the Fund	1c.d	–	–	–	–	–	–	–	–	–	30.9	103.8	192.2
Foreign Exchange	1d.d	171.9	206.0	352.3	358.0	543.8	706.2	783.0	945.4	1,386.2	1,876.0	1,923.5	2,257.8
Gold (Million Fine Troy Ounces)	1ad	.054	.056	.054	.054	.054	.058	.059	.060	.060	.061	.061	.061
Gold (National Valuation)	1and	2.0	1.4	1.4	1.4	1.3	16.8	16.1	17.4	16.4	16.8	20.9	25.5
Monetary Authorities: Other Liab.	4..d	86.9	99.8	55.0	33.7	32.2	29.3	31.8	37.7	32.3	38.5	37.9	38.2
Deposit Money Banks: Assets	7a.d	99.3	208.4	294.1	216.4	287.3	265.2	298.4	381.7	456.2	538.3	602.5	753.6
Liabilities	7b.d	60.8	66.5	50.5	98.7	137.6	154.1	182.2	239.8	256.0	549.9	596.3	962.9
Other Banking Insts.: Assets	7e.d	5.2	3.0	8.5	11.7	29.2	76.7	73.4	79.8	133.9	243.6	382.6	525.8
Liabilities	7f.d	53.5	53.2	62.4	62.2	58.2	30.2	41.2	37.6	58.2	115.5	221.8	268.8
Monetary Authorities													
		\multicolumn{12}{c}{Millions of TT Dollars: End of Period}												
Foreign Assets	11	2,180.4	3,610.2	4,602.3	4,577.1	†4,764.4	5,641.3	6,210.7	7,457.7	10,196.3	13,303.6	14,025.3	16,523.0
Claims on Central Government	12a	3,220.3	2,122.3	1,514.0	724.1	†93.6	752.4	709.8	899.8	765.4	961.3	1,104.7	1,129.9
Claims on Nonfin.Pub.Enterprises	12c	29.3	28.5	28.5	361.3	†346.6	345.0	336.0	334.0	328.7	310.3	300.1	280.0
Claims on Private Sector	12d	....	....	....	....	52.7	48.4	44.9	41.0	36.5	27.8	23.9	21.0
Claims on Deposit Money Banks	12e	260.1	250.0	507.2	384.7	†807.2	802.6	807.2	803.4	789.0	775.7	759.3	731.8
Claims on Other Banking Insts.	12f	23.5	21.7	18.7	18.7	†.5	.5	2.7	.6	.6	.6	.6	.1
Claims on Nonbank Financial Insts.	12g	....	....	....	....	56.9	48.1	36.7	31.8	23.4	15.1	6.4	6.1
Reserve Money	14	2,185.9	2,083.4	3,269.7	3,247.8	†3,538.0	4,106.4	4,963.7	5,146.5	5,305.4	5,872.7	5,788.6	6,156.4
of which: Currency Outside DMBs	14a	698.2	707.4	744.6	832.8	†909.8	1,063.0	1,046.8	1,292.4	1,271.0	1,373.5	1,501.8	1,708.6
Foreign Liabilities	16c	1,568.9	1,480.8	867.3	503.1	†346.3	211.2	209.9	237.6	203.8	242.1	238.5	240.6
Central Government Deposits	16d	927.1	526.8	780.1	579.3	†1,377.1	2,516.0	1,484.6	2,491.6	4,885.9	7,190.2	7,669.8	9,359.8
Capital Accounts	17a	1,564.3	2,513.8	2,651.5	2,648.5	†1,510.1	1,594.5	1,861.6	1,962.2	2,283.4	2,550.6	2,564.4	2,652.3
Other Items (Net)	17r	−532.6	−572.1	−897.8	−912.8	†−649.6	−789.8	−371.8	−269.7	−538.5	−461.3	−40.9	282.7
Deposit Money Banks													
		\multicolumn{12}{c}{Millions of TT Dollars: End of Period}												
Reserves	20	1,348.8	1,221.2	2,320.3	2,245.4	†2,370.0	2,772.7	3,058.6	3,021.7	3,214.3	3,935.6	3,534.6	3,541.4
Foreign Assets	21	421.9	1,211.6	1,745.0	1,297.7	†1,779.4	1,671.0	1,968.2	2,404.5	2,874.0	3,386.3	3,795.9	4,747.9
Claims on Central Government	22a	568.6	774.9	899.4	1,729.1	†2,084.6	3,823.1	2,293.1	2,728.1	2,411.9	3,411.6	3,566.4	3,616.4
Claims on Local Government	22b	–	.7	1.9	1.9	†–	54.4	2.1	16.4	83.0	65.7	19.2	1.4
Claims on Nonfin.Pub.Enterprises	22c	689.8	747.7	377.9	801.3	†779.5	773.8	904.0	562.1	265.7	802.7	1,149.5	1,030.7
Claims on Private Sector	22d	7,710.0	7,995.1	7,625.6	8,739.4	†9,741.0	11,835.3	13,433.3	14,498.6	16,353.1	16,922.7	17,645.6	18,073.5
Claims on Other Banking Insts.	22f	....	....	....	....	252.1	238.0	231.0	207.7	273.0	571.7	202.8	841.0
Claims on Nonbank Financial Insts.	22g	....	....	....	....	1,711.1	616.6	111.2	128.0	220.7	565.0	1,255.1	1,427.2
Demand Deposits	24	1,858.9	2,274.3	2,798.8	2,921.0	†2,524.6	3,130.4	2,819.7	3,182.0	3,722.4	4,829.4	5,620.0	5,108.0
Time, Savings,& Fgn.Currency Dep	25	6,525.9	7,492.1	8,651.1	8,966.8	†12,194.9	13,215.0	15,516.0	15,790.9	17,905.9	18,432.8	18,792.7	18,712.4
Foreign Liabilities	26c	258.4	386.6	299.8	591.7	†852.3	970.5	1,201.9	1,510.5	1,612.4	3,459.1	3,756.8	6,066.1
Central Government Deposits	26d	135.2	143.2	102.1	267.8	†364.6	204.9	203.2	281.9	231.4	1,011.3	452.6	568.7
Credit from Monetary Authorities	26g	260.1	288.7	507.1	384.9	†395.3	388.4	386.9	385.1	383.3	381.6	379.8	382.2
Liabilities to Other Banking Insts.	26i	....	....	....	....	455.7	312.8	681.7	410.6	333.5	431.8	447.3	520.8
Capital Accounts	27a	1,525.6	1,669.4	1,748.2	1,771.6	†2,513.5	3,093.9	3,443.9	4,017.6	4,867.3	5,486.0	6,208.5	6,791.2
Other Items (Net)	27r	175.0	−303.1	−1,137.0	−89.0	†−583.3	469.0	−2,251.8	−2,011.6	−3,360.5	−4,370.6	−4,488.7	−4,869.9

Trinidad and Tobago 369

		1992	1993	1994	1995	1996	1997	1998	1999	2000	2001	2002	2003
Monetary Survey		\multicolumn{12}{c}{*Millions of TT Dollars: End of Period*}
Foreign Assets (Net)	31n	774.9	2,954.4	5,180.3	4,780.0	†5,345.2	6,130.6	6,767.1	8,114.0	11,254.1	12,988.7	13,825.9	14,964.2
Domestic Credit	32	11,179.2	11,020.9	9,583.8	11,528.7	†13,376.9	15,814.6	16,417.0	16,674.6	15,644.8	15,452.9	17,151.8	16,498.6
Claims on Central Govt. (Net)	32an	2,726.6	2,227.2	1,531.2	1,606.1	†436.5	1,854.5	1,315.1	854.3	−1,940.0	−3,828.6	−3,451.3	−5,182.3
Claims on Local Government	32b	–	.7	1.9	1.9	†–	54.4	2.1	16.4	83.0	65.7	19.2	1.4
Claims on Nonfin.Pub.Enterprises	32c	719.1	776.2	406.4	1,162.6	†1,126.1	1,118.9	1,240.0	896.1	594.5	1,113.0	1,449.6	1,310.6
Claims on Private Sector	32d	7,710.0	7,995.1	7,625.6	8,739.4	†9,793.7	11,883.6	13,478.2	14,539.6	16,389.6	16,950.5	17,669.5	18,094.5
Claims on Other Banking Insts.	32f	23.5	21.7	18.7	18.7	†252.6	238.5	233.7	208.4	273.6	572.3	203.4	841.1
Claims on Nonbank Financial Inst.	32g	....	....	....	....	1,768.0	664.8	147.9	159.8	244.2	580.0	1,261.5	1,433.3
Money	34	2,696.0	3,136.5	3,748.2	3,923.4	†3,685.0	4,464.1	4,724.8	5,306.8	5,658.0	6,766.6	7,834.2	7,723.0
Quasi-Money	35	6,525.9	7,492.1	8,651.1	8,966.8	†12,194.9	13,215.0	15,516.0	15,790.9	17,905.9	18,432.8	18,792.7	18,712.4
Liabilities to Other Banking Insts.	36i	....	....	....	....	455.7	312.8	681.7	410.6	333.5	431.8	447.3	520.8
Capital Accounts	37a	3,089.9	4,183.2	4,399.7	4,420.1	†4,023.6	4,688.4	5,305.5	5,979.8	7,150.7	8,036.6	8,772.9	9,443.5
Other Items (Net)	37r	−357.6	−836.5	−2,034.9	−1,001.6	†−1,637.1	−735.0	−3,044.0	−2,699.5	−4,149.2	−5,226.1	−4,869.3	−4,936.7
Money plus Quasi-Money	35l	9,221.9	10,628.6	12,399.3	12,890.2	†15,880.0	17,679.0	20,240.8	21,097.8	23,563.9	25,199.3	26,626.9	26,435.3
Other Banking Institutions													
Other Banklike Institutions		\multicolumn{12}{c}{*Millions of TT Dollars: End of Period*}
Reserves	40	128.7	143.7	148.0	171.5	†241.5	272.7	409.8	485.3	534.1	513.2	510.2	661.5
Foreign Assets	41	22.3	17.5	50.3	70.4	†181.1	483.1	484.4	502.7	843.5	1,532.1	2,410.4	3,312.5
Claims on Central Government	42a	181.3	505.7	588.7	965.4	†1,190.0	1,437.1	1,075.4	1,098.9	1,471.6	672.5	925.5	1,513.7
Claims on Local Government	42b	....	....	....	....	–	4.1	4.7	5.1	–	–	–	15.0
Claims on Nonfin.Pub.Enterprises	42c	12.4	9.2	65.5	33.0	†147.5	137.0	80.3	196.2	291.2	562.1	418.9	550.8
Claims on Private Sector	42d	2,749.3	2,852.1	3,341.6	3,982.3	†2,770.0	3,141.9	3,358.5	3,903.7	4,697.0	4,878.9	5,524.5	6,174.9
Claims on Deposit Money Banks	42e	356.7	381.8	325.2	335.6	†786.2	645.4	1,195.6	1,418.3	1,824.6	1,787.6	2,046.1	2,148.8
Claims on Nonbank Financial Insts.	42g	....	....	....	....	47.4	37.8	201.3	526.1	627.8	571.1	479.4	469.6
Time, Savings,& Fgn.Currency Dep.	45	2,471.7	2,805.5	2,894.1	3,138.9	†2,993.9	3,180.3	4,017.2	4,792.5	4,746.5	5,704.3	4,858.3	5,176.4
Foreign Liabilities	46c	.3	.3	1.4	.3	†169.5	152.5	238.0	207.3	341.5	705.6	1,380.4	1,681.0
Central Government Deposits	46d	....	....	....	....	47.8	100.7	33.6	34.8	87.8	20.3	79.0	131.1
Credit from Monetary Authorities	46g	....	....	....	....	25.3	44.6	52.7	49.9	42.6	34.7	23.6	17.0
Credit from Deposit Money Banks	46h	147.0	138.9	30.3	48.5	†92.1	249.0	70.0	670.2	530.1	840.8	633.8	453.0
Capital Accounts	47a	464.4	470.6	512.2	690.3	†762.5	885.4	1,188.8	1,474.7	1,852.2	2,293.5	2,743.8	3,521.7
Other Items (Net)	47r	367.3	494.7	1,081.3	1,680.2	†1,272.7	1,546.5	1,209.6	906.9	2,689.2	918.3	2,596.0	3,866.7
Development Banks		\multicolumn{12}{c}{*Millions of TT Dollars: End of Period*}
Reserves	40..n	–	–	–	–	–	–	–	–	1.5	3.6	–	18.7
Claims on Central Government	42a.n	–	–	27.8	33.7	–	–	–	–	–	–	–	–
Claims on Private Sector	42d.n	1,126.5	1,165.7	1,011.9	1,031.3	845.5	852.8	927.5	975.6	1,007.7	1,063.2	1,125.5	1,524.0
Claims on Deposit Money Banks	42e.n	72.5	99.4	110.6	88.6	48.0	78.2	101.3	60.1	56.8	172.0	122.3	223.9
Foreign Liabilities	46c.n	226.9	309.1	368.9	373.0	190.9	37.9	33.6	29.4	25.3	21.0	16.8	12.6
Central Government Deposits	46d.n	419.2	401.6	517.4	500.8	446.8	440.3	430.7	418.1	418.2	532.7	514.8	505.4
Credit from Dep. Money Banks	46h.n	33.6	27.3	28.0	40.2	16.0	30.0	17.3	34.7	18.8	20.0	24.5	23.1
Capital Accounts	47a.n	389.9	389.2	282.4	275.0	204.4	356.0	377.7	409.3	428.0	304.4	321.8	358.0
Other Items (Net)	47r.n	129.4	137.9	−46.4	−35.4	35.4	66.8	169.5	144.2	175.7	360.7	369.9	867.5
Banking Survey		\multicolumn{12}{c}{*Millions of TT Dollars: End of Period*}
Foreign Assets (Net)	51n	570.0	2,662.5	4,860.3	4,477.1	†5,165.9	6,423.3	6,979.9	8,380.0	11,730.9	13,794.2	14,839.1	16,583.1
Domestic Credit	52	14,806.1	15,130.3	14,083.2	17,054.9	†17,630.1	20,645.8	21,366.6	22,718.9	22,960.4	22,075.3	24,828.5	25,269.1
Claims on Central Govt. (Net)	52an	2,488.7	2,331.3	1,630.3	2,104.4	†1,131.9	2,750.6	1,926.2	1,500.3	−974.4	−3,709.1	−3,119.6	−4,305.1
Claims on Local Government	52b	–	.7	1.9	1.9	†–	58.6	6.8	21.5	83.0	65.7	19.2	16.4
Claims on Nonfin.Pub.Enterprises	52c	731.5	785.4	471.9	1,195.6	†1,273.7	1,255.8	1,320.3	1,092.3	885.7	1,675.1	1,868.5	1,861.4
Claims on Private Sector	52d	11,585.8	12,012.9	11,979.1	13,753.0	†13,409.1	15,878.3	17,764.2	19,418.9	22,094.3	22,892.5	24,319.5	25,793.4
Claims on Nonbank Financial Inst.	52g	....	....	....	....	1,815.4	702.6	349.2	685.9	871.9	1,151.1	1,740.9	1,902.9
Liquid Liabilities	55l	11,564.9	13,290.4	15,145.4	15,857.6	†18,632.3	20,586.7	23,848.2	25,404.9	27,774.8	30,386.8	30,975.1	30,931.5
Capital Accounts	57a	3,944.2	5,043.0	5,194.3	5,385.4	†4,990.5	5,929.7	6,872.0	7,863.8	9,430.9	10,634.5	11,838.5	13,323.2
Other Items (Net)	57r	−133.0	−540.6	−1,396.2	289.0	†−826.8	552.7	−2,373.7	−2,169.8	−2,514.4	−5,151.7	−3,146.0	−2,402.5
Interest Rates		\multicolumn{12}{c}{*Percent Per Annum*}
Bank Rate (End of Period)	60	13.00	13.00	13.00	13.00	13.00	13.00	13.00	13.00	13.00	13.00	7.25	7.00
Treasury Bill Rate	60c	9.26	9.45	10.00	8.41	10.44	9.83	11.93	10.40	10.56	8.55	4.83	4.71
Savings Rate	60k	2.58	2.75	2.69	2.50	2.52	2.50	2.83	2.81	2.96	3.40	2.30	1.97
Deposit Rate	60l	6.99	7.06	6.91	....	....	6.91	7.95	8.51	8.15	7.66	4.76	2.91
Deposit Rate (Foreign Currency)	60l.f	....	....	....	....	....	6.35	6.69	6.41	6.74	7.07	4.13	2.62
Lending Rate	60p	15.33	15.50	15.98	15.17	15.79	15.33	17.33	17.04	16.50	15.67	12.48	11.17
Government Bond Yield	61	13.30	....	....	....	....	....	....	....	....	....	....	....

Trinidad and Tobago 369

		1992	1993	1994	1995	1996	1997	1998	1999	2000	2001	2002	2003
Prices, Production, Labor		\multicolumn{12}{c}{*Index Numbers (2000=100): Period Averages*}
Share Prices	62	....	....	18.8	26.2	35.0	53.0	91.7	87.4	100.0	93.2	105.0	128.8
Producer Prices	63	79.3	83.6	88.1	91.2	93.9	95.7	97.1	98.7	100.0	100.9	101.5	....
Consumer Prices	64	65.0	72.1	78.4	82.5	85.3	88.4	93.4	96.6	100.0	†105.5	109.9	114.1
Wages: Avg Weekly Earn.('90=100)	65	103.0	104.6	109.9	....	....	....	....	....	....	....	....	....
Industrial Production	66	59.5	55.7	†63.6	68.3	72.2	76.9	85.6	94.9	100.0	107.7	133.5	....
Crude Petroleum Production	66aa	113.4	103.5	109.5	109.2	108.0	103.5	102.8	104.6	100.0	95.1	109.2	....
Total Employment	67	89.6	87.9	91.8	†85.7	88.3	91.4	95.2	97.2	100.0	102.1	104.3	....
		\multicolumn{12}{c}{*Number in Thousands: Period Averages*}
Labor Force	67d	....	504	....	521	530	541	559	563	573	576	586	....
Employment	67e	406	405	416	432	444	460	479	489	503	514	525	....
Unemployment	67c	99	100	94	89	86	81	79	74	70	62	61	62
Unemployment Rate (%)	67r	19.6	19.8	18.4	17.2	16.3	15.0	14.2	13.2	12.2	10.8	10.4	10.5
International Transactions		\multicolumn{12}{c}{*Millions of TT Dollars*}
Exports	70	7,188.3	8,800.9	11,055.2	14,608.6	15,014.4	15,887.6	14,220.5	17,661.2	26,923.5	26,709.0	24,232.4	....
Imports, c.i.f.	71	4,693.5	7,495.3	6,700.9	10,191.1	12,866.8	18,705.9	18,886.8	17,263.0	20,841.9	22,199.6	22,762.0	....
Balance of Payments		\multicolumn{12}{c}{*Millions of US Dollars: Minus Sign Indicates Debit*}
Current Account, n.i.e.	78ald	138.9	113.1	217.8	293.8	105.1	−613.6	−643.5	30.6	544.3	416.0	....	....
Goods: Exports f.o.b.	78aad	1,691.4	1,500.1	1,777.6	2,456.1	2,354.1	2,448.0	2,258.0	2,815.8	4,290.3	4,304.2	....	....
Goods: Imports f.o.b.	78abd	−995.6	−952.9	−1,036.6	−1,868.5	−1,971.6	−2,976.6	−2,998.9	−2,752.2	−3,321.5	−3,586.1	....	....
Trade Balance	78acd	695.7	547.2	741.1	587.7	382.4	−528.6	−740.8	63.6	968.8	718.1	....	....
Services: Credit	78add	452.7	353.4	326.6	342.6	461.2	546.5	671.7	603.2	553.8	573.8	....	....
Services: Debit	78aed	−561.9	−466.4	−438.1	−241.9	−217.5	−254.1	−255.4	−274.0	−387.7	−370.0	....	....
Balance on Goods & Services	78afd	586.6	434.2	629.5	688.4	626.2	−236.2	−324.5	392.8	1,134.9	921.9	....	....
Income: Credit	78agd	29.8	40.2	56.7	76.6	39.1	63.8	64.0	68.3	80.9	108.7	....	....
Income: Debit	78ahd	−477.9	−366.0	−468.7	−466.7	−553.1	−445.0	−405.3	−468.2	−709.4	−648.0	....	....
Balance on Gds, Serv. & Inc.	78aid	138.5	108.4	217.5	298.3	112.2	−617.4	−665.8	−7.1	506.4	382.6	....	....
Current Transfers, n.i.e.: Credit	78ajd	11.1	23.7	28.3	34.0	34.2	37.0	58.4	68.9	63.9	64.0	....	....
Current Transfers: Debit	78akd	−10.7	−19.0	−27.9	−38.5	−41.3	−33.2	−36.2	−31.2	−26.0	−30.6	....	....
Capital Account, n.i.e.	78bcd	−16.5	−11.5	−6.4	−11.9	....	....	....	....	....	....	....	....
Capital Account, n.i.e.: Credit	78bad	.4	1.3	1.1	1.1	....	....	....	....	....	....	....	....
Capital Account: Debit	78bbd	−16.9	−12.8	−7.5	−13.0	....	....	....	....	....	....	....	....
Financial Account, n.i.e.	78bjd	−154.2	98.8	−32.2	−214.7	43.0	697.2	471.5	38.3	173.7	321.5	....	....
Direct Investment Abroad	78bdd	....	....	....	....	....	....	....	....	−264.1	−25.2	−150.0	....
Dir. Invest. in Rep. Econ., n.i.e.	78bed	177.9	379.2	516.2	298.9	355.4	999.3	729.8	643.3	679.5	834.9	....	....
Portfolio Investment Assets	78bfd	−	−	−	−7.9	−	−	−.4	....	....	....	....	....
Equity Securities	78bkd	−	−	−	−7.9	−	−	−.4	....	....	....	....	....
Debt Securities	78bld	....	....	....	....	....	....	....	....	....	....	....	....
Portfolio Investment Liab., n.i.e.	78bgd	−	−	−	16.7	....	....	....	−177.5	−30.0	−206.2	....	....
Equity Securities	78bmd	−	−	−	16.7	....	....	....	....	....	....	....	....
Debt Securities	78bnd	....	....	....	....	....	....	....	−177.5	−30.0	−206.2	....	....
Financial Derivatives Assets	78bwd	....	....	....	....	....	....	....	....	....	....	....	....
Financial Derivatives Liabilities	78bxd	....	....	....	....	....	....	....	....	....	....	....	....
Other Investment Assets	78bhd	−31.3	−76.2	−233.5	−57.3	3.0	32.6	1.0	512.3	397.7	285.0	....	....
Monetary Authorities	78bod	....	....	....	−	....	....	....	295.2	383.6	26.5	....	....
General Government	78bpd	−	−	−56.1	32.4	3.0	32.6	1.0	−	2.8	−	....	....
Banks	78bqd	−5.3	−105.6	−109.3	−23.7	....	....	....	73.7	−	257.1	....	....
Other Sectors	78brd	−26.0	29.3	−68.2	−66.0	....	....	....	143.4	11.3	1.4	....	....
Other Investment Liab., n.i.e.	78bid	−300.8	−204.2	−314.9	−465.1	−315.4	−334.7	−258.8	−675.7	−848.3	−442.2	....	....
Monetary Authorities	78bsd	−	−	−	−	−	−	−1.4	−170.8	−268.7	−61.2	....	....
General Government	78btd	−101.9	19.9	−7.2	−116.8	47.3	−245.4	−104.7	−4.9	−63.8	−14.7	....	....
Banks	78bud	16.5	20.4	−10.2	−51.3	−27.3	−21.9	−49.6	−	−86.1	−	....	....
Other Sectors	78bvd	−215.4	−244.4	−297.4	−297.0	−335.4	−67.4	−103.2	−500.0	−429.7	−366.3	....	....
Net Errors and Omissions	78cad	−72.6	−41.8	6.3	16.5	90.0	110.0	252.2	93.2	−276.9	−235.3	....	....
Overall Balance	78cbd	−104.4	158.6	185.5	83.7	238.1	193.6	80.2	162.1	441.1	502.2	....	....
Reserves and Related Items	79dad	104.4	−158.6	−185.5	−83.7	−238.1	−193.6	−80.2	−162.1	−441.1	−502.2	....	....
Reserve Assets	79dbd	124.4	−29.4	−113.6	−40.1	−213.0	−175.3	−76.0	−162.1	−441.1	−502.2	....	....
Use of Fund Credit and Loans	79dcd	−89.8	−129.2	−71.9	−43.6	−25.1	−18.4	−4.2	−	−	−	....	....
Exceptional Financing	79ded	69.8	−	−	....	....	....	....	....	....	....	....	....
Government Finance		\multicolumn{12}{c}{*Millions of TT Dollars: Year Ending December 31*}
Deficit (-) or Surplus	80	....	15.9	117.5	62.5	....	....	....	....	....	....	....	....
Revenue	81	....	7,116.1	7,905.1	8,847.3	....	....	....	....	....	....	....	....
Grants Received	81z	....	17.8	36.0	51.6	....	....	....	....	....	....	....	....
Expenditure	82	....	7,193.6	7,826.9	8,917.9	....	....	....	....	....	....	....	....
Lending Minus Repayments	83	....	−75.6	−3.3	−81.5	....	....	....	....	....	....	....	....
Financing													
Domestic	84a	....	582.8	218.1	−878.7	....	....	....	....	....	....	....	....
Foreign	85a	....	−598.7	−335.6	816.2	....	....	....	....	....	....	....	....
Use of Cash Balances	87	....	−	−	....	....	....	....	....	....	....	....	....

Trinidad and Tobago 369

		1992	1993	1994	1995	1996	1997	1998	1999	2000	2001	2002	2003
National Accounts						*Millions of TT Dollars*							
Househ.Cons.Expend.,incl.NPISHs....	96f	13,713	15,607	15,196	15,479	17,131	20,702	21,911	25,105	27,863	30,829	....	....
Government Consumption Expend...	91f	4,117	4,174	4,432	5,029	5,473	5,519	5,472	6,301	6,201	7,376	....	....
Gross Fixed Capital Formation..........	93e	3,152	3,407	5,799	5,932	7,984	10,494	11,945	8,833	10,116	12,470	....	....
Changes in Inventories.....................	93i	37	108	123	655	412	308	762	178	171	171	....	....
Exports of Goods and Services..........	90c	9,867	10,765	13,504	17,042	17,778	19,306	18,453	21,437	30,421	30,238	....	....
Imports of Goods and Services (-).....	98c	7,772	9,569	9,742	12,440	14,191	20,457	20,478	18,964	23,288	24,382	....	....
Gross Domestic Product (GDP).........	99b	23,118	24,491	29,312	31,697	34,587	35,871	38,065	42,889	51,485	56,700	58,200	....
Net Primary Income from Abroad.....	98.n	−1,931	−1,852	−2,595	−2,916	−3,136	−2,490	−2,527	−2,518	−3,953	−2,929	....	....
Gross National Income (GNI)............	99a	21,187	22,639	26,717	28,781	31,451	33,381	35,898	40,372	47,532	53,771	....	....
Consumption of Fixed Capital..........	99cf	2,613	2,643	3,046	2,839	3,761	3,885	4,310	5,237	5,511	5,823	....	....
GDP Volume 1985 Prices..................	99b.p	16,294	16,058	16,630	17,288	....	....	....	....	....	....	....	....
GDP Volume 2000 Prices..................	99b.p	....	....	....	34,558	36,339	38,835	41,817	46,268	51,485	52,822	....	....
GDP Volume (2000=100)................	99bvp	63.3	62.3	64.6	†67.1	70.6	75.4	81.2	89.9	100.0	102.6	....	....
GDP Deflator (2000=100)................	99bip	71.0	76.3	88.2	91.7	95.2	92.4	91.0	92.7	100.0	107.3	....	....
						Millions: Midyear Estimates							
Population.................................	99z	**1.23**	**1.24**	**1.25**	**1.26**	**1.27**	**1.27**	**1.28**	**1.28**	**1.29**	**1.29**	**1.30**	**1.30**

Tunisia 744

		1992	1993	1994	1995	1996	1997	1998	1999	2000	2001	2002	2003
Exchange Rates		*Dinars per SDR: End of Period*											
Market Rate	aa	1.3071	1.4376	1.4470	1.4134	1.4358	1.5483	1.5502	1.7191	1.8049	1.8453	1.8137	1.7955
		Dinars per US Dollar: End of Period (ae) Period Average (rf)											
Market Rate	ae	.9507	1.0466	.9912	.9508	.9985	1.1475	1.1010	1.2525	1.3853	1.4683	1.3341	1.2083
Market Rate	rf	.8844	1.0037	1.0116	.9458	.9734	1.1059	1.1387	1.1862	1.3707	1.4387	1.4217	1.2885
		Index Numbers (2000=100): Period Averages											
Nominal Effective Exchange Rate	nec	104.66	101.38	101.91	102.25	102.94	102.16	101.45	101.79	100.00	98.62	97.23	92.76
Real Effective Exchange Rate	rec	102.26	98.43	99.17	101.38	102.03	101.93	101.29	101.75	100.00	97.57	96.71	93.27
Fund Position		*Millions of SDRs: End of Period*											
Quota	2f.s	206.0	206.0	206.0	206.0	206.0	206.0	206.0	286.5	286.5	286.5	286.5	286.5
SDRs	1b.s	8.8	1.3	1.8	4.7	11.1	12.1	2.1	19.3	3.0	1.3	2.0	1.7
Reserve Position in the Fund	1c.s	–	–	–	–	–	–	–	20.2	20.2	20.2	20.2	20.2
Total Fund Cred.&Loans Outstg	2tl	211.1	207.3	207.3	197.1	165.0	128.4	91.8	55.2	24.7	–	–	–
International Liquidity		*Millions of US Dollars Unless Otherwise Indicated: End of Period*											
Total Reserves minus Gold	1l.d	852.0	853.8	1,461.5	1,605.3	1,897.6	1,978.1	1,850.1	2,261.5	1,811.0	1,989.2	2,290.3	2,945.4
SDRs	1b.d	12.1	1.8	2.7	7.0	15.9	16.3	2.9	26.5	3.9	1.7	2.7	2.5
Reserve Position in the Fund	1c.d	–	–	.1	.1	.1	.1	.1	27.7	26.3	25.3	27.4	30.0
Foreign Exchange	1d.d	839.9	852.0	1,458.8	1,598.2	1,881.7	1,961.7	1,847.1	2,207.3	1,780.9	1,962.2	2,260.2	2,912.9
Gold (Million Fine Troy Ounces)	1ad	.215	.215	.216	.217	.217	.217	.217	.217	.220	.218	.218	.218
Gold (National Valuation)	1and	4.6	4.2	4.4	4.8	4.4	3.8	4.0	3.5	3.2	3.0	3.3	3.6
Deposit Money Banks: Assets	7a.d	570.6	545.2	536.9	451.6	569.5	607.8	643.6	621.1	669.9	550.0	641.0	706.1
Liabilities	7b.d	1,461.9	1,374.3	1,729.3	1,740.8	1,938.4	1,845.2	1,979.9	2,091.4	2,618.5	2,608.8	3,198.6	3,703.5
Other Banking Insts.: Liabilities	7f.d	–	–	–	–	–	–	–	–	–	–	–	–
Monetary Authorities		*Millions of Dinars: End of Period*											
Foreign Assets	11	868	930	1,462	1,536	1,913	2,277	2,053	2,868	2,527	2,899	3,097	3,594
Claims on Central Government	12a	117	122	93	85	103	58	78	79	132	147	129	51
Claims on Private Sector	12d	....	....	....	....	....	....	21	23	25	26	25	25
Claims on Deposit Money Banks	12e	1,079	1,177	835	829	178	115	†93	93	449	854	503	435
Reserve Money	14	1,355	1,420	1,523	1,667	2,264	2,448	2,159	2,818	2,497	2,943	2,851	3,064
of which: Currency Outside DMBs	14a	1,156	1,179	1,196	1,315	1,473	1,594	1,695	1,994	2,229	2,378	2,518	2,664
Foreign Liabilities	16c	296	324	326	304	251	244	173	166	249	186	72	75
Central Government Deposits	16d	71	128	198	137	254	231	241	244	206	390	418	555
Capital Accounts	17a	99	109	119	128	134	143	151	103	116	125	150	146
Other Items (Net)	17r	243	248	224	214	−709	−616	−478	−268	66	281	263	265
Deposit Money Banks		*Millions of Dinars: End of Period*											
Reserves	20	129	181	294	275	760	816	356	853	468	749	700	695
Foreign Assets	21	542	571	532	429	569	697	709	778	928	808	855	853
Claims on Central Government	22a	535	536	544	341	291	682	556	942	1,561	1,487	1,543	1,655
Claims on Private Sector	22d	7,402	7,907	8,510	9,274	9,373	10,540	11,542	12,652	15,717	17,423	18,306	19,586
Demand Deposits	24	1,555	1,676	1,957	2,092	2,371	2,847	3,091	3,435	3,779	4,169	3,918	4,174
Quasi-Monetary Liabilities	25	3,490	3,777	4,003	4,166	4,736	5,660	5,871	7,122	8,372	9,304	10,149	10,868
Foreign Liabilities	26c	605	614	780	817	1,076	1,214	1,260	1,684	1,839	1,827	1,913	2,052
Long-Term Foreign Liabilities	26cl	785	824	934	839	859	904	919	936	1,788	2,004	2,355	2,423
Counterpart Funds	26e	–	–	–	–	–	–	–	–	–	–	–	–
Central Govt. Lending Funds	26f	–	–	–	–	–	–	–	–	–	–	–	–
Credit from Monetary Authorities	26g	1,485	1,494	1,175	1,119	206	153	127	113	470	870	514	444
Capital Accounts	27a	885	1,053	1,246	1,672	1,914	2,150	2,361	2,577	2,935	2,881	3,077	3,208
Other Items (Net)	27r	−196	−244	−214	−384	−171	−192	−467	−641	−510	−587	−522	−379
Post Office: Checking Deposits	24..i	157	110	122	184	230	162	164	321	328	430	416	402
Monetary Survey		*Millions of Dinars: End of Period*											
Foreign Assets (Net)	31n	509	562	888	846	1,154	1,516	1,328	1,796	1,367	1,694	1,968	2,320
Domestic Credit	32	8,141	8,546	9,072	9,746	9,743	11,212	†12,121	13,774	17,558	19,122	20,001	21,164
Claims on Central Govt. (Net)	32an	739	639	562	473	371	672	557	1,099	1,816	1,673	1,670	1,553
Claims on Private Sector	32d	7,402	7,907	8,510	9,274	9,373	10,540	†11,564	12,675	15,742	17,449	18,332	19,611
Money	34	2,894	2,998	3,319	3,637	4,109	4,645	4,994	5,794	6,369	7,014	6,892	7,261
Quasi-Money	35	3,490	3,777	4,003	4,166	4,736	5,660	5,871	7,122	8,372	9,304	10,149	10,868
Long-Term Foreign Liabilities	36cl	785	824	934	839	859	904	919	936	1,788	2,004	2,355	2,423
Counterpart Funds	36e	64	78	49	39	47	67	80	81	174	201	176	226
Central Govt. Lending Funds	36f	–	–	–	–	–	–	–	–	–	–	–	–
Other Items (Net)	37r	1,417	1,430	1,655	1,912	1,146	1,453	†1,584	1,637	2,221	2,293	2,396	2,706
Money plus Quasi-Money	35l	6,384	6,775	7,322	7,803	8,845	10,304	10,865	12,916	14,742	16,318	17,042	18,129

2004, International Monetary Fund : *International Financial Statistics Yearbook*

Tunisia 744

		1992	1993	1994	1995	1996	1997	1998	1999	2000	2001	2002	2003
Other Banking Institutions						*Millions of Dinars: End of Period*							
Foreign Assets (Net)	41n	21	25	29	18	7	37	28	41	36	−38	−29	−28
Claims on Central Govt. (Net)	42an	–	–	1	–	9	7	7	37	62	59	83	82
Claims on Private Sector	42d	1,667	1,943	2,171	2,395	2,684	2,984	3,311	3,510	1,915	2,079	2,167	1,971
Monetary Deposits	44	5	8	7	11	8	7	11	11	14	31	33	39
Time and Savings Deposits	45	327	393	418	443	489	507	674	791	657	763	874	898
Long-Term Foreign Liabilities	46cl	–	–	–	–	–	–	–	–	–	–	–	–
Central Govt. Lending Funds	46f	535	688	843	918	985	1,061	1,012	1,005	215	172	181	256
Capital Accounts	47a	846	906	952	1,049	1,115	1,192	1,246	1,296	1,086	1,039	1,078	827
Other Items (Net)	47r	−25	−27	−18	−7	104	260	402	486	41	95	55	6
Banking Survey						*Millions of Dinars: End of Period*							
Foreign Assets (Net)	51n	529	587	917	864	1,161	1,553	1,356	1,837	1,403	1,655	1,938	2,292
Domestic Credit	52	9,808	10,490	11,244	12,142	12,437	14,203	†15,439	17,321	19,535	21,260	22,251	23,218
Claims on Government (Net)	52an	739	639	563	473	380	679	564	1,136	1,878	1,732	1,753	1,636
Claims on Private Sector	52d	9,069	9,851	10,681	11,669	12,057	13,524	†14,875	16,185	17,657	19,528	20,499	21,582
Liquid Liabilities	55l	6,716	7,176	7,746	8,256	9,341	10,819	11,551	13,717	15,412	17,111	17,949	19,066
Long Term Foreign Liabilities	56cl	785	824	934	839	859	904	919	936	1,788	2,004	2,355	2,423
Other Items (Net)	57r	2,837	3,076	3,482	3,911	3,397	4,033	†4,325	4,505	3,737	3,800	3,886	4,021
Interest Rates						*Percent Per Annum*							
Discount Rate (End of Period)	60	11.38	8.88	8.88	8.88	7.88	....	....	....	....	....	....	....
Money Market Rate	60b	11.73	10.48	8.81	8.81	8.64	6.88	6.89	5.99	5.88	6.04	5.93	5.14
Prices, Production, Labor						*Index Numbers (2000=100): Period Averages*							
Producer Prices	63	76.9	80.5	83.2	88.0	91.2	93.4	96.4	96.8	100.0	101.8	104.3	106.8
Consumer Prices	64	73.8	76.7	80.3	85.3	88.5	91.7	94.6	97.2	†100.0	102.0	104.8	107.6
Industrial Production	66	71.9	72.1	75.6	78.0	80.1	83.6	89.3	94.1	100.0	105.3	105.9	105.7
Mining Production	66zx	69.8	60.2	64.8	81.9	86.4	76.3	93.2	99.6	100.0	96.6	93.5	98.2
Crude Petroleum Production	66aa	142.1	127.0	119.6	115.7	114.5	104.1	106.5	107.6	100.0	91.4	95.0	86.6
						Number in Thousands: Period Averages							
Labor Force	67d	....	....	2,772	....	....	2,978	....	3,144	3,216	3,293	3,376	3,461
Employment	67e	....	....	2,321	....	....	2,504	....	2,635	2,705	2,789	2,852	2,951
Unemployment	67c	137	142	160	190	181	225	278	278	76	72	74	78
International Transactions						*Millions of Dinars*							
Exports	70	3,549.7	3,759.5	4,696.6	5,172.9	5,372.0	6,148.1	6,518.3	6,966.9	8,004.8	9,536.2	9,748.6	10,342.6
Imports, c.i.f.	71	5,688.8	6,172.1	6,647.3	7,464.1	7,498.8	8,793.5	9,489.5	10,070.7	11,738.0	13,697.3	13,510.9	14,038.9
						1990=100							
Volume of Exports	72	111.3	120.8	137.1	....	....	....	....	....	....	....	....	....
Volume of Imports	73	103.8	115.5	119.8	....	....	....	....	....	....	....	....	....
Unit Value of Exports	74	95.3	96.2	100.8	....	....	....	....	....	....	....	....	....

Tunisia 744

		1992	1993	1994	1995	1996	1997	1998	1999	2000	2001	2002	2003
Balance of Payments					*Millions of US Dollars: Minus Sign Indicates Debit*								
Current Account, n.i.e.	78ald	−1,104	−1,323	−537	−774	−478	−595	−675	−442	−821	−840	−746	−730
Goods: Exports f.o.b.	78aad	4,041	3,746	4,643	5,470	5,519	5,559	5,724	5,873	5,840	6,628	6,857	8,027
Goods: Imports f.o.b.	78abd	−6,078	−5,810	−6,210	−7,459	−7,280	−7,514	−7,875	−8,014	−8,093	−8,997	−8,981	−10,297
Trade Balance	78acd	−2,037	−2,064	−1,567	−1,989	−1,761	−1,955	−2,152	−2,141	−2,253	−2,369	−2,123	−2,269
Services: Credit	78add	1,972	2,040	2,267	2,509	2,632	2,613	2,757	2,920	2,767	2,912	2,681	2,937
Services: Debit	78aed	−1,158	−1,356	−1,361	−1,352	−1,244	−1,182	−1,257	−1,234	−1,218	−1,425	−1,450	−1,612
Balance on Goods & Services	78afd	−1,223	−1,380	−661	−832	−373	−524	−651	−455	−705	−882	−893	−945
Income: Credit	78agd	101	73	71	119	66	77	90	89	94	95	72	81
Income: Debit	78ahd	−646	−629	−745	−835	−1,030	−939	−947	−978	−1,036	−1,036	−1,056	−1,173
Balance on Gds, Serv. & Inc.	78aid	−1,768	−1,936	−1,336	−1,548	−1,338	−1,386	−1,507	−1,344	−1,647	−1,822	−1,877	−2,037
Current Transfers, n.i.e.: Credit	78ajd	682	629	816	805	879	821	852	920	854	1,016	1,156	1,343
Current Transfers: Debit	78akd	−17	−16	−17	−31	−20	−30	−20	−18	−29	−34	−25	−36
Capital Account, n.i.e.	78bcd	−5	−2	−3	32	37	77	61	59	3	53	75	59
Capital Account, n.i.e.: Credit	78bad	−	5	5	47	46	95	83	72	9	56	83	66
Capital Account: Debit	78bbd	−5	−7	−8	−15	−9	−18	−22	−13	−6	−3	−8	−7
Financial Account, n.i.e.	78bjd	957	1,272	1,144	958	816	699	489	1,083	646	1,063	857	1,110
Direct Investment Abroad	78bdd	−5	−	−6	5	−1	−6	1	−3	−1	−1	−1	−2
Dir. Invest. in Rep. Econ., n.i.e.	78bed	526	562	432	264	238	339	650	350	752	457	795	541
Portfolio Investment Assets	78bfd	−3	−6	−1	2	−5	−1	−	−	−	−	−	....
Equity Securities	78bkd	−3	−	1	−	−	−	−	−	−	−	−	....
Debt Securities	78bld	−	−6	−2	2	−5	−1	−	−	−	−	−	....
Portfolio Investment Liab., n.i.e.	78bgd	50	24	16	23	67	109	33	10	−20	−15	6	14
Equity Securities	78bmd	47	20	6	12	29	55	58	−3	−18	−15	6	14
Debt Securities	78bnd	2	4	10	12	38	54	−25	13	−3	−	−	....
Financial Derivatives Assets	78bwd	−	−	−	−	−	−	−	−	−	−	−	....
Financial Derivatives Liabilities	78bxd	−	−	−	−	−	−	−	−	−	−	−	....
Other Investment Assets	78bhd	−369	−143	−326	−327	−705	−729	−508	−228	−624	−439	−886	−428
Monetary Authorities	78bod	35	15	86	88	95	14	−	−	−	−	−	....
General Government	78bpd	−	−	−	−	−	−	−	−	−	−	−	....
Banks	78bqd	−320	−12	67	150	−305	−250	10	8	−	−	−	....
Other Sectors	78brd	−84	−146	−479	−565	−494	−493	−517	−236	−624	−439	−886	−428
Other Investment Liab., n.i.e.	78bid	758	836	1,029	990	1,221	987	313	954	540	1,059	942	985
Monetary Authorities	78bsd	11	5	−	−1	−11	28	−	−	−	−	−	....
General Government	78btd	166	234	411	546	517	324	−49	314	128	752	392	649
Banks	78bud	122	75	168	44	189	90	−	−	−	−	−	....
Other Sectors	78bvd	458	522	450	401	527	544	362	640	412	307	549	336
Net Errors and Omissions	78cad	343	119	−78	−119	67	206	−12	38	−33	13	−47	−58
Overall Balance	78cbd	191	67	527	97	442	386	−138	738	−205	288	139	380
Reserves and Related Items	79dad	−191	−67	−527	−97	−442	−386	138	−738	205	−288	−139	−380
Reserve Assets	79dbd	−237	−61	−527	−82	−395	−336	187	−688	245	−257	−139	−380
Use of Fund Credit and Loans	79dcd	45	−5	−	−15	−47	−51	−50	−50	−40	−31	−	−
Exceptional Financing	79ded	....	....	....	....	....	....	....	....	....	....	....	....
International Investment Position					*Millions of US Dollars*								
Assets	79aad	....	....	....	2,953	3,112	3,175	3,313	3,359	3,276	3,303	4,129	4,496
Direct Investment Abroad	79abd	....	....	....	28	29	32	35	34	32	33	37	44
Portfolio Investment	79acd	....	....	....	48	53	50	54	49	45	45	51	58
Equity Securities	79add	....	....	....	48	53	50	54	49	45	45	51	58
Debt Securities	79aed	....	....	....	−	−	−	−	−	−	−	−	−
Financial Derivatives	79ald	....	....	....	−	−	−	−	−	−	−	−	−
Other Investment	79afd	....	....	....	1,195	1,043	1,039	1,278	911	1,300	1,184	1,646	1,341
Monetary Authorities	79agd	....	....	....	−	−	−	−	−	−	−	−	−
General Government	79ahd	....	....	....	−	−	−	−	−	−	−	−	−
Banks	79aid	....	....	....	447	562	621	665	646	696	547	711	701
Other Sectors	79ajd	....	....	....	748	481	417	613	265	604	637	935	640
Reserve Assets	79akd	....	....	....	1,681	1,987	2,054	1,947	2,366	1,898	2,042	2,395	3,053
Liabilities	79lad	....	....	....	23,341	23,399	21,212	23,731	21,983	24,043	24,408	28,899	34,131
Dir. Invest. in Rep. Economy	79lbd	....	....	....	11,534	11,218	9,263	11,114	9,152	11,545	11,667	14,060	16,567
Portfolio Investment	79lcd	....	....	....	947	1,012	1,035	1,161	1,065	993	950	1,083	1,246
Equity Securities	79ldd	....	....	....	947	1,012	1,035	1,161	1,065	993	950	1,083	1,246
Debt Securities	79led	....	....	....	−	−	−	−	−	−	−	−	−
Financial Derivatives	79lld	....	....	....	−	−	−	−	−	−	−	−	−
Other Investment	79lfd	....	....	....	10,860	11,170	10,914	11,456	11,766	11,506	11,791	13,755	16,317
Monetary Authorities	79lgd	....	....	....	−	−	−	−	−	32	−	−	−
General Government	79lhd	....	....	....	6,896	6,979	7,014	7,381	7,646	7,334	7,671	8,761	10,369
Banks	79lid	....	....	....	934	1,157	1,157	1,240	1,457	1,452	1,374	1,634	1,846
Other Sectors	79ljd	....	....	....	3,030	3,034	2,742	2,835	2,663	2,687	2,745	3,360	4,102

Tunisia 744

		1992	1993	1994	1995	1996	1997	1998	1999	2000	2001	2002	2003
Government Finance		\multicolumn{8}{c}{*Millions of Dinars: Year Ending December 31*}					
Deficit (-) or Surplus	80	−419.4	−475.4	−219.2	−543.6	−599.0	−855.2	−200.2	−646.2	....	....	....	....
Revenue	81	4,037.8	4,442.1	4,958.7	5,121.9	5,670.1	6,012.8	7,058.2	7,180.2	....	....	....	....
Grants Received	81z	56.7	53.3	63.4	44.6	42.3	–	–	–	....	....	....	....
Expenditure	82	4,393.6	4,850.6	5,101.2	5,584.2	6,208.3	6,677.4	7,160.2	7,864.8	....	....	....	....
Lending Minus Repayments	83	120.3	120.2	140.1	125.9	103.1	190.6	98.2	−38.4	....	....	....	....
Financing													
Domestic	84a	278.5	300.3	1.2	53.8	72.6	216.8	81.5	213.5	....	....	....	....
Foreign	85a	140.9	175.1	218.0	489.8	526.4	542.4	10.0	349.6	....	....	....	....
Debt: Domestic	88a	2,648.8	2,986.3	3,165.7	3,251.4	3,574.0	4,946.4	5,240.4	5,570.3	....	....	....	....
Foreign	89a	4,957.8	5,710.3	6,169.9	6,556.5	6,969.0	8,116.5	8,236.4	9,572.2	....	....	....	....
National Accounts		\multicolumn{12}{c}{*Millions of Dinars*}
House.Cons.Expend.,incl.NPISHs	96f	8,461	9,093	9,799	10,728	11,618	12,591	13,717	14,900	16,181	17,500	18,700	20,120
Government Consumption Expend	91f	2,193	2,385	2,582	2,778	2,965	3,296	3,530	3,840	4,170	4,530	4,930	5,360
Gross Fixed Capital Formation	93e	3,729	4,122	4,279	4,121	4,422	5,153	5,610	6,278	7,020	7,530	7,540	7,520
Changes in Inventories	93i	273	165	−382	91	347	372	459	210	260	480	−10	570
Exports of Goods and Services	90c	5,419	5,931	7,106	7,657	8,029	9,147	9,712	10,500	11,780	13,560	13,400	13,910
Imports of Goods and Services (-)	98c	6,368	7,033	7,570	8,323	8,315	9,660	10,467	11,050	12,720	14,860	14,670	15,220
Gross Domestic Product (GDP)	99b	13,706	14,663	15,814	17,052	19,066	20,898	22,561	24,672	26,685	28,740	29,890	32,260
Net Primary Income from Abroad	98.n	−628	−874	−918	−811	−1,004	−998	−988	−1,070	−1,300	−1,360	−1,420	−1,410
Gross National Income (GNI)	99a	13,078	13,789	14,896	16,241	18,062	19,900	21,574	23,602	25,385	27,380	28,470	30,850
Net Current Transf.from Abroad	98t	499	594	673	712	801	834	942	1,080	1,122	1,411	1,620	1,740
Gross Nat'l Disposable Inc.(GNDI)	99i	13,577	14,383	15,570	16,953	18,862	20,734	22,515	24,682	26,507	28,791	30,090	32,590
GDP Volume 1990 Prices	99b.p	12,115	12,380	12,774	13,074	14,009	14,771	15,477	16,415	17,181	18,020	18,320	19,340
GDP Volume (2000=100)	99bvp	70.5	72.1	74.3	76.1	81.5	86.0	90.1	95.5	100.0	104.9	106.6	112.6
GDP Deflator (2000=100)	99bip	72.8	76.3	79.7	84.0	87.6	91.1	93.9	96.8	100.0	102.7	105.0	107.4
		\multicolumn{12}{c}{*Millions: Midyear Estimates*}
Population	99z	8.52	8.67	8.82	8.95	9.08	9.19	9.30	9.41	9.52	9.62	9.73	9.83

Turkey 186

		1992	1993	1994	1995	1996	1997	1998	1999	2000	2001	2002	2003
Exchange Rates		\multicolumn{12}{c}{*Liras per SDR: End of Period*}
Market Rate	aa	11,776	19,879	56,534	88,669	154,976	277,413	442,775	743,077	877,360	1,822,418	2,234,642	2,075,362
		\multicolumn{12}{c}{*Liras per US Dollar: End of Period (ae) Period Average (rf)*}
Market Rate	ae	8,564	14,473	38,726	59,650	107,775	205,605	314,464	541,400	673,385	1,450,127	1,643,699	1,396,638
Market Rate	rf	6,872	10,985	29,609	45,845	81,405	151,865	260,724	418,783	625,219	1,225,588	1,507,226	1,500,885
Fund Position		\multicolumn{12}{c}{*Millions of SDRs: End of Period*}
Quota	2f.s	642	642	642	642	642	642	642	964	964	964	964	964
SDRs	1b.s	–	–	1	2	1	1	1	–	22	4	23	20
Reserve Position in the Fund	1c.s	32	32	32	32	32	32	32	113	113	113	113	113
Total Fund Cred.&Loans Outstg	2tl	–	–	236	461	461	440	276	649	3,205	11,233	16,246	16,213
International Liquidity		\multicolumn{12}{c}{*Millions of US Dollars Unless Otherwise Indicated: End of Period*}
Total Reserves minus Gold	1l.d	6,159	6,272	7,169	12,442	16,436	18,658	19,489	23,346	22,488	18,879	27,069	33,991
SDRs	1b.d	–	–	1	3	1	1	1	–	29	4	31	30
Reserve Position in the Fund	1c.d	44	44	47	48	46	44	45	155	147	142	153	168
Foreign Exchange	1d.d	6,115	6,227	7,121	12,391	16,388	18,614	19,442	23,191	22,313	18,733	26,884	33,793
Gold (Million Fine Troy Ounces)	1ad	4.047	4.031	3.820	3.747	3.747	3.748	3.748	3.744	3.739	3.733	3.733	3.733
Gold (National Valuation)	1and	1,494	1,488	1,410	1,383	1,383	1,384	1,125	1,011	1,010	992	1,032	1,558
Monetary Authorities: Other Liab	4..d	6,985	7,490	9,650	11,797	12,054	11,502	12,809	10,816	10,634	10,940	14,271	17,495
Deposit Money Banks: Assets	7a.d	8,540	10,708	8,655	9,951	9,400	10,474	11,616	14,896	17,072	12,218	12,559	13,554
Liabilities	7b.d	6,379	9,369	3,245	5,293	8,089	11,394	14,647	†18,078	22,968	9,919	9,602	13,642
Other Banking Insts.: Assets	7e.d	555	612	478	1,015	942	1,062	1,084	1,146	1,082	1,090	901	868
Liabilities	7f.d	928	937	799	816	839	765	864	†2,026	2,202	1,821	1,707	2,028
Monetary Authorities		\multicolumn{12}{c}{*Billions of Lira through 1995; Trillions of Lira Beginning 1996: End of Period*}
Foreign Assets	11	73,521	124,914	372,848	888,772	†2,029	4,260	6,896	13,864	16,627	30,790	48,273	51,101
Claims on Central Government	12a	53,229	109,813	216,484	531,546	†846	983	878	1,135	1,727	34,692	53,910	51,620
Claims on Nonfin.Pub.Enterprises	12c	11,601	12,515	25,930	1,203	†2	2	2	3	2	4	5	3
Claims on Deposit Money Banks	12e	8,655	16,866	20,503	28,677	†73	823	2,072	3,088	6,543	9,665	2,703	1,765
Claims on Other Banking Insts	12f	1,517	1,996	71	29	†–	–	9	–	–	–	–	–
Claims on Nonbank Financial Insts	12g	–	–	–	–	†–	–	–	–	500	750	250	–
Reserve Money	14	76,773	128,902	282,973	507,819	†972	1,943	3,506	6,923	10,118	18,064	21,250	25,193
of which: Currency Outside DMBs	14a	30,244	51,364	101,401	188,506	†316	599	1,031	1,887	3,197	4,463	6,899	9,775
Other Liabilities to DMBs	14n	14,948	15,021	8,503	20,974	†47	–	–	–	–	7,200	9,574	8,259
Time and Savings Deposits	15	1,982	2,942	6,773	12,425	†33	56	112	232	286	419	653	837
Foreign Currency Deposits	15.a	1,843	3,827	3,130	12,147	†39	111	135	23	142	530	33	28
Restricted Deposits	16b	14	11	12	15	†–	–	–	–	1	1	–	–
Foreign Liabilities	16c	59,826	108,401	387,018	744,534	†1,370	2,487	4,150	6,338	9,973	36,335	59,760	58,082
Central Government Deposits	16d	14,309	16,541	22,482	103,109	†225	875	833	1,812	1,478	3,473	5,800	7,425
Capital Accounts	17a	3,468	8,784	13,753	19,192	†114	204	436	1,327	2,233	9,410	5,017	3,192
Other Items (Net)	17r	–24,639	–18,324	–102,124	29,693	†149	391	685	1,435	1,168	470	3,054	1,472
Deposit Money Banks		\multicolumn{12}{c}{*Billions of Lira through 1995; Trillions of Lira Beginning 1996: End of Period*}
Reserves	20	44,839	74,625	172,477	314,480	†641	1,298	2,433	4,544	5,766	10,713	12,679	13,971
Other Claims on Monetary Auth	20n	14,954	15,027	8,509	19,879	†47	–	–	5	59	1,126	2,079	439
Foreign Assets	21	73,144	154,976	335,160	593,596	†1,016	2,161	3,662	8,078	11,514	17,746	20,667	19,042
Claims on Central Government	22a	55,478	99,892	224,733	411,849	†1,423	3,593	9,849	23,148	35,251	62,070	80,303	99,960
Claims on Local Government	22b	–	–	2,756	4,746	†6	8	20	22	48	112	74	151
Claims on Nonfin.Pub.Enterprises	22c	7,120	24,052	44,629	40,289	†49	217	290	625	541	390	51	193
Claims on Private Sector	22d	182,233	336,615	571,521	1,356,669	†3,203	7,252	11,493	16,565	28,515	34,995	38,574	55,757
Claims on Other Banking Insts	22f	2,489	4,856	17,848	28,032	†58	129	204	585	719	1,054	1,070	869
Claims on Nonbank Financial Insts	22g	992	1,893	2,192	4,827	†13	58	119	499	1,338	944	1,930	2,654
Demand Deposits	24	45,590	73,402	125,850	193,429	†562	887	1,387	2,802	4,187	6,339	7,860	11,357
Time and Savings Deposits	25	124,654	183,910	434,518	959,241	†2,098	4,237	9,138	17,651	24,519	35,910	50,706	67,235
Foreign Currency Deposits	25.a	101,391	186,790	561,875	1,145,819	†2,410	4,894	8,654	18,398	25,278	59,597	72,287	68,817
Money Market Instruments	26aa	3,709	3,064	4,633	6,919	†11	–	–	–	–	–	–	–
Bonds	26ab	6,192	24,524	15,757	36,690	†6	81	123	†–	–	–	–	–
Foreign Liabilities	26c	54,629	135,596	125,647	315,755	†872	2,343	4,606	†9,787	15,466	14,383	15,783	19,053
Central Government Deposits	26d	38,069	65,803	91,715	143,856	†393	838	1,495	2,961	5,053	6,163	9,478	14,094
Credit from Monetary Authorities	26g	8,652	17,903	12,661	11,470	†33	764	1,725	2,335	5,600	5,823	191	85
Capital Accounts	27a	50,209	99,670	182,053	383,839	†869	1,864	3,944	6,645	9,628	21,348	31,953	42,099
Other Items (Net)	27r	–51,846	–78,726	–174,883	–422,650	†–796	–1,192	–3,003	–6,509	–5,980	–20,415	–30,832	–29,703

2004, International Monetary Fund: *International Financial Statistics Yearbook*

Turkey 186

		1992	1993	1994	1995	1996	1997	1998	1999	2000	2001	2002	2003
Monetary Survey		*Billions of Lira through 1995; Trillions of Lira Beginning 1996: End of Period*												
Foreign Assets (Net)........................	31n	32,211	35,893	195,343	422,079	†803	1,591	1,802	†5,816	2,702	–2,182	–6,603	–6,991
Domestic Credit...............................	32	262,281	509,288	991,967	2,132,224	†4,984	10,529	20,534	37,807	62,110	125,375	160,889	189,689
Claims on Central Govt. (Net)........	32an	56,329	127,361	327,020	696,429	†1,652	2,863	8,398	19,509	30,447	87,126	118,935	130,061
Claims on Local Government.........	32b	–	–	2,756	4,746	†6	8	20	22	48	112	74	151
Claims on Nonfin.Pub.Enterprises...	32c	18,721	36,567	70,559	41,492	†51	219	291	627	543	394	56	196
Claims on Private Sector.................	32d	182,233	336,615	571,521	1,356,669	†3,203	7,252	11,493	16,565	28,515	34,995	38,574	55,757
Claims on Other Banking Insts.......	32f	4,007	6,852	17,918	28,061	†58	129	214	585	719	1,054	1,070	869
Claims on Nonbank Financial Inst...	32g	992	1,893	2,192	4,827	†13	58	119	499	1,838	1,694	2,180	2,654
Money...	34	76,373	125,868	228,413	384,391	†882	1,492	2,433	4,710	7,407	10,840	14,814	21,194
Quasi-Money....................................	35	229,870	377,469	1,006,296	2,129,632	†4,580	9,298	18,040	36,303	50,226	96,457	123,680	136,917
Money Market Instruments.............	36aa	3,709	3,064	4,633	6,919	†11	–	–	–	–	–	–	–
Bonds..	36ab	6,192	24,524	15,757	36,690	†6	81	123	†–	–	–	–	–
Restricted Deposits.........................	36b	14	11	12	15	†–	–	–	–	1	1	–	–
Other Items (Net).............................	37r	–21,665	14,245	–81,116	–3,662	†307	1,248	1,740	2,610	7,179	15,896	15,792	24,587
Money plus Quasi-Money................	35l	306,242	503,336	1,234,709	2,514,022	†5,462	10,790	20,473	41,013	57,633	107,296	138,494	158,110
Other Banking Institutions		*Billions of Lira through 1995; Trillions of Lira Beginning 1996: End of Period*												
Reserves..	40	10,381	19,738	52,327	84,106	†147	257	457	894	1,124	1,543	1,472	1,786
Foreign Assets.................................	41	4,757	8,859	18,513	60,545	†101	218	341	620	728	1,580	1,480	1,212
Claims on Central Government......	42a	1,202	3,254	4,639	7,856	†17	43	86	334	395	434	848	1,099
Claims on Local Government.........	42b	2,292	5,717	5,942	10,131	†24	45	93	387	715	920	1,205	1,644
Claims on Nonfin.Pub.Enterprises...	42c	1,320	1,713	1,272	9,222	†7	17	11	42	25	29	44	68
Claims on Private Sector.................	42d	13,931	22,562	45,137	78,314	†170	332	573	825	1,070	1,883	2,516	2,749
Claims on Nonbank Financial Insts.	42g	119	710	230	136	†1	5	7	35	36	56	86	116
Time and Savings Deposits.............	45	1,255	1,664	1,827	2,897	†2	3	3	330	359	1,070	750	653
Bonds..	46ab	8,856	16,545	39,255	50,758	†70	130	104	†–	–	–	–	–
Foreign Liabilities............................	46c	7,946	13,558	30,961	48,672	†90	157	272	†1,097	1,483	2,640	2,805	2,832
Central Government Deposits........	46d	5,309	13,202	23,550	44,215	†67	142	214	181	245	519	590	580
Credit from Monetary Authorities...	46g	753	829	71	30	†15	30	47	82	100	225	197	119
Credit from Deposit Money Banks...	46h	5,900	11,252	42,689	88,224	†160	284	502	690	878	891	1,145	937
Capital Accounts..............................	47a	7,495	12,058	13,174	33,010	†86	194	384	763	1,298	2,204	3,397	4,807
Other Items (Net).............................	47r	–4,278	–7,720	–23,527	–18,274	†–23	–23	42	–6	–269	–1,103	–1,233	–1,254
Banking Survey		*Billions of Lira through 1995; Trillions of Lira Beginning 1996: End of Period*												
Foreign Assets (Net)........................	51n	29,021	31,194	182,895	433,952	†814	1,652	1,871	†5,340	1,947	–3,242	–7,928	–8,612
Domestic Credit...............................	52	271,829	523,189	1,007,719	2,165,607	†5,077	10,700	20,877	38,664	63,388	127,124	163,928	193,915
Claims on Central Govt. (Net)........	52an	52,221	117,413	308,110	660,070	†1,602	2,764	8,270	19,662	30,597	87,042	119,193	130,580
Claims on Local Government.........	52b	2,292	5,717	8,698	14,876	†30	54	113	409	763	1,032	1,278	1,795
Claims on Nonfin.Pub.Enterprises...	52c	20,041	38,279	71,831	50,714	†58	236	303	670	567	423	100	264
Claims on Private Sector.................	52d	196,164	359,178	616,658	1,434,983	†3,372	7,584	12,066	17,389	29,585	36,878	41,090	58,507
Claims on Nonbank Financial Inst...	52g	1,110	2,602	2,422	4,963	†14	62	126	534	1,875	1,750	2,266	2,770
Liquid Liabilities..............................	55l	300,968	488,455	1,189,694	2,440,215	†5,330	10,541	20,026	40,460	56,890	106,974	137,799	157,017
Bonds..	56ab	15,048	41,069	55,012	87,448	†76	212	227	†–	–	–	–	–
Other Items (Net).............................	57r	–15,929	23,693	–67,467	70,800	†485	1,600	2,495	3,544	8,445	16,908	18,201	28,287
Interest Rates		*Percent Per Annum*												
Discount Rate (End of Period)........	60	48.00	48.00	55.00	50.00	50.00	67.00	67.00	60.00	60.00	60.00	55.00	43.00
Interbank Money Market Rate........	60b	65.35	62.83	136.47	72.30	76.24	70.32	74.60	73.53	56.72	91.95	49.51	36.16
Treasury Bill Rate............................	60c	72.17	....	....	....	....	....	....	....	25.18	85.33	59.50	34.90
Deposit Rate.....................................	60l	68.74	64.58	87.79	76.02	80.74	79.49	80.11	78.43	47.16	74.70	50.49	37.68
Prices, Production, Labor		*Index Numbers (2000=100): Period Averages*												
Wholesale Prices..............................	63	1.2	1.9	4.2	7.8	13.8	25.1	43.1	66.0	100.0	161.6	242.6	304.6
Consumer Prices..............................	64	1.0	1.6	†3.4	6.3	11.4	21.2	39.2	64.6	100.0	154.4	223.8	280.4
Industrial Production.......................	66	78.4	83.0	77.8	84.5	89.4	99.0	99.9	94.9	100.0	91.2	99.4	107.9
		Number in Thousands: Period Averages												
Labor Force......................................	67d	....	20,384	....	22,078	22,259	21,818	23,415	23,779	20,579	23,491	23,818	23,787
Employment.....................................	67e	19,959	19,905	20,396	21,378	21,698	20,815	21,958	22,049	22,031	21,524	21,354	21,291
Unemployment................................	67c	1,745	1,722	1,740	1,522	1,332	1,545	1,547	1,730	1,452	1,958	2,464	2,497
Unemployment Rate (%).................	67r	8.0	8.0	7.6	6.6	5.8	6.9	6.2	7.3	6.6	8.4	10.3	10.5
International Transactions		*Millions of US Dollars*												
Exports...	70..d	14,715	15,345	18,106	21,637	23,225	26,261	26,974	26,587	27,775	31,334	34,561	46,576
Imports, c.i.f.....................................	71..d	22,871	29,428	23,270	35,709	43,627	48,559	45,921	40,671	54,503	41,399	49,663	65,637
Imports, f.o.b....................................	71.vd	21,291	27,661	21,875	35,187	43,028	48,005	45,440	39,773	....	....	....	....
		2000=100												
Volume of Exports...........................	72..d	49.1	52.3	†60.0	63.8	70.0	79.4	87.1	89.9	100.0	122.2	141.5	172.5
Volume of Imports...........................	73..d	37.2	51.0	†37.8	48.9	63.3	78.2	76.3	75.4	100.0	75.2	90.8	121.0
Unit Value of Exports.....................	74..d	120.8	117.4	†113.9	128.3	122.6	116.8	112.1	104.5	100.0	97.4	95.7	105.3
Unit Value of Imports.....................	75..d	104.9	98.4	†105.3	123.0	115.6	105.6	101.2	95.7	100.0	99.7	98.5	106.3

Turkey 186

Balance of Payments

Millions of US Dollars: Minus Sign Indicates Debit

		1992	1993	1994	1995	1996	1997	1998	1999	2000	2001	2002	2003
Current Account, n.i.e.	78ald	−974	−6,433	2,631	−2,338	−2,437	−2,638	1,984	−1,344	−9,819	3,390	−1,521	−6,850
Goods: Exports f.o.b.	78aad	14,891	15,611	18,390	21,975	32,067	32,110	30,662	28,842	30,721	34,373	40,124	51,206
Goods: Imports f.o.b.	78abd	−23,081	−29,771	−22,606	−35,187	−42,681	−47,513	−44,926	−39,311	−53,131	−38,916	−48,461	−65,240
Trade Balance	78acd	−8,190	−14,160	−4,216	−13,212	−10,614	−15,403	−14,264	−10,469	−22,410	−4,543	−8,337	−14,034
Services: Credit	78add	9,407	10,652	10,801	14,606	13,430	19,910	23,879	16,881	20,429	16,059	14,785	19,086
Services: Debit	78aed	−3,625	−3,948	−3,782	−5,024	−6,773	−8,998	−10,373	−9,394	−9,061	−6,929	−6,905	−8,581
Balance on Goods & Services	78afd	−2,408	−7,456	2,803	−3,630	−3,957	−4,491	−758	−2,982	−11,042	4,587	−457	−3,529
Income: Credit	78agd	1,012	1,135	890	1,489	1,577	1,900	2,481	2,350	2,836	2,753	2,486	2,246
Income: Debit	78ahd	−3,637	−3,880	−4,154	−4,693	−4,504	−4,913	−5,466	−5,887	−6,838	−7,753	−7,040	−7,673
Balance on Gds, Serv. & Inc.	78aid	−5,033	−10,201	−461	−6,834	−6,884	−7,504	−3,743	−6,519	−15,044	−413	−5,011	−8,956
Current Transfers, n.i.e.: Credit	78ajd	4,075	3,800	3,113	4,512	4,466	4,909	5,861	5,295	5,317	3,861	3,536	2,167
Current Transfers: Debit	78akd	−16	−32	−21	−16	−19	−43	−134	−120	−92	−58	−46	−61
Capital Account, n.i.e.	78bcd	−	−	−	−	−	−	−	−	....	....	−	−
Capital Account, n.i.e.: Credit	78bad	−	−	−	−	−	−	−	−	....	....	−	−
Capital Account: Debit	78bbd	−	−	−	−	−	−	−	−	....	....	−	−
Financial Account, n.i.e.	78bjd	3,648	8,963	−4,194	4,643	5,483	6,969	−840	4,979	8,584	−14,644	1,328	6,959
Direct Investment Abroad	78bdd	−65	−14	−49	−113	−110	−251	−367	−645	−870	−498	−176	−499
Dir. Invest. in Rep. Econ., n.i.e.	78bed	844	636	608	885	722	805	940	783	982	3,266	1,038	1,562
Portfolio Investment Assets	78bfd	−754	−563	35	−466	−1,380	−710	−1,622	−759	−593	−788	−2,096	−1,386
Equity Securities	78bkd	−50	−139	5	−75	7	−50	−21	−46	−33	−36	−42	−33
Debt Securities	78bld	−704	−424	30	−391	−1,387	−660	−1,601	−713	−560	−752	−2,054	−1,353
Portfolio Investment Liab., n.i.e.	78bjd	3,165	4,480	1,123	703	1,950	2,344	−5,089	4,188	1,615	−3,727	1,503	3,955
Equity Securities	78bmd	350	570	989	195	191	8	−518	428	489	−79	−16	1,009
Debt Securities	78bnd	2,815	3,910	134	508	1,759	2,336	−4,571	3,760	1,126	−3,648	1,519	2,946
Financial Derivatives Assets	78bwd	....	....	....	....	....	....	−	−	....	−	−	−
Financial Derivatives Liabilities	78bxd	....	....	....	....	....	....	−	−	....	−	−	−
Other Investment Assets	78bhd	−2,438	−3,291	2,423	−383	331	−1,750	−1,464	−2,304	−1,939	−601	−777	−986
Monetary Authorities	78bod	36	−61	−18	−102	−117	−98	−95	−98	1	−39	−30	−28
General Government	78bpd	....	....	....	....	....	....	....	....	....	....	....	....
Banks	78bqd	−2,474	−3,230	2,441	−281	1,448	−976	−942	−1,839	−1,574	233	643	348
Other Sectors	78brd	....	....	....	....	−1,000	−676	−427	−367	−366	−795	−1,390	−1,306
Other Investment Liab., n.i.e.	78bid	2,896	7,715	−8,334	4,017	3,970	6,531	6,762	3,716	9,389	−12,296	1,836	4,313
Monetary Authorities	78bsd	300	1,085	1,415	1,734	1,380	1,245	760	−160	706	817	1,433	605
General Government	78btd	−1,310	−1,953	−2,516	−1,991	−2,108	−1,456	−1,655	−1,932	−883	−1,977	−669	−2,194
Banks	78bud	2,100	4,495	−7,053	1,973	3,046	2,232	3,195	2,655	3,736	−9,644	−2,016	2,846
Other Sectors	78bvd	1,806	4,088	−180	2,301	1,652	4,510	4,462	3,153	5,830	−1,492	3,088	3,056
Net Errors and Omissions	78cad	−1,190	−2,222	1,766	2,355	1,498	−988	−703	1,719	−2,699	−1,634	−21	3,978
Overall Balance	78cbd	1,484	308	203	4,660	4,544	3,343	441	5,354	−3,934	−12,888	−214	4,087
Reserves and Related Items	79dad	−1,484	−308	−203	−4,660	−4,544	−3,343	−441	−5,354	3,934	12,888	214	−4,087
Reserve Assets	79dbd	−1,484	−308	−547	−5,007	−4,544	−3,316	−217	−5,724	−383	2,718	−6,177	−4,030
Use of Fund Credit and Loans	79dcd	−	−	344	347	−	−27	−224	519	3,316	10,169	6,390	−57
Exceptional Financing	79ded	−	−	−	−	−	−	−	−150	1,000	−	−	−

International Investment Position

Millions of US Dollars

		1992	1993	1994	1995	1996	1997	1998	1999	2000	2001	2002	2003
Assets	79aad	....	....	....	....	....	....	....	....	53,222	52,783	62,809	74,515
Direct Investment Abroad	79abd	−	−	−	−	−	−	−	−	3,668	4,581	5,847	6,138
Portfolio Investment	79acd	−	−	−	−	5	5	5	4	4	550	810	1,956
Equity Securities	79add	....	....	....	....	5	5	5	4	4	53	45	61
Debt Securities	79aed	−	−	−	−	−	−	−	−	−	497	765	1,895
Financial Derivatives	79ald	....	....	....	....	....	....	....	....	−	−	−	−
Other Investment	79afd	10,901	13,545	11,624	13,571	9,911	10,450	13,709	25,041	26,197	27,687	28,035	31,217
Monetary Authorities	79agd	1,088	1,034	1,061	1,103	1,162	1,213	1,266	1,322	1,393	1,418	1,411	1,391
General Government	79ahd	−	−	−	−	−	−	−	−	598	584	643	762
Banks	79aid	9,813	12,511	10,563	12,468	8,749	9,237	10,446	11,564	12,862	13,159	12,196	12,492
Other Sectors	79ajd	−	−	−	−	−	−	1,997	12,155	11,344	12,526	13,785	16,572
Reserve Assets	79akd	7,654	7,746	8,570	13,825	17,704	19,587	20,780	24,343	23,353	19,965	28,117	35,204
Liabilities	79lad	....	....	....	....	....	....	....	....	152,414	137,656	164,088	202,569
Dir. Invest. in Rep. Economy	79lbd	−	−	−	−	−	−	−	−	19,209	19,677	18,846	32,334
Portfolio Investment	79lcd	9,316	12,623	13,788	14,186	16,166	19,749	17,734	38,408	36,168	25,018	24,132	33,609
Equity Securities	79ldd	−	−	−	−	3,085	6,018	3,700	15,358	7,404	5,635	3,450	8,954
Debt Securities	79led	9,316	12,623	13,788	14,186	13,081	13,731	14,034	23,050	28,764	19,383	20,682	24,655
Financial Derivatives	79lld	....	....	....	....	....	....	....	....	−	−	−	−
Other Investment	79lfd	46,420	54,829	52,239	59,829	66,142	70,506	82,380	86,744	97,037	92,961	121,110	136,626
Monetary Authorities	79lgd	6,680	7,208	9,658	12,216	12,374	11,758	12,982	11,501	14,561	24,825	36,021	41,193
General Government	79lhd	20,635	19,733	21,660	21,428	23,749	22,134	22,415	21,727	22,477	21,047	35,988	38,787
Banks	79lid	8,262	12,461	5,814	8,025	11,211	12,568	15,987	18,715	22,118	11,699	9,872	13,429
Other Sectors	79ljd	10,843	15,427	15,107	18,160	18,808	24,046	30,996	34,801	37,881	35,390	39,229	43,217

2004, International Monetary Fund: *International Financial Statistics Yearbook*

Turkey 186

		1992	1993	1994	1995	1996	1997	1998	1999	2000	2001	2002	2003
Government Finance		*Billions of Lira through 1995; Trillions of Lira Beginning 1996: Year Ending December 31*											
Deficit (-) or Surplus............	80	−47,328	−133,105	−150,838	−316,621	†−1,238	−2,444	−4,387	−10,076	−14,263	−34,963	....	....
Revenue........................	81	176,370	355,736	750,673	1,401,847	†2,726	6,327	12,657	19,798	35,426	54,433	....	....
Grants Received...............	81z	1,700	1,597	942	7,404	†2	2	−	8	−	−	....	....
Expenditure....................	82	225,256	490,129	902,077	1,725,514	†3,966	8,617	16,762	29,467	49,134	88,403	....	....
Lending Minus Repayments...	83	142	309	376	358	†−	156	282	414	554	993	....	....
Financing													
Domestic........................	84a	43,395	112,795	219,353	396,181	†1,373	2,828	5,158	9,180	10,769	38,295	....	....
Foreign.........................	85a	3,933	20,310	−68,515	−79,560	†−134	−384	−771	896	3,494	−3,332	....	....
Total Debt......................	88	371,934	667,854	1,702,786	2,782,173	†5,602	12,656	21,629	41,452	63,416	178,193	....	....
Domestic........................	88a	194,237	356,555	799,309	1,361,007	†3,149	6,283	11,613	22,920	36,421	122,157	....	....
Foreign.........................	89a	177,697	311,299	903,477	1,421,166	†2,453	6,373	10,016	18,532	26,996	56,036	....	....
National Accounts		*Billions of Lira through 1995; Trillions of Lira Beginning 1996*											
Househ.Cons.Expend.,incl.NPISHs....	96f	734,305	1,369,419	2,706,263	5,457,903	†9,938	19,619	36,123	55,928	88,978	128,513	184,036	239,586
Government Consumption Expend...	91f	140,584	258,084	450,605	837,243	†1,709	3,535	6,633	11,748	17,539	25,405	38,722	49,004
Gross Fixed Capital Formation.......	93e	258,406	525,506	952,322	1,850,288	†3,706	7,618	12,839	16,931	27,848	32,409	46,031	55,618
Changes in Inventories................	93i	2,454	21,619	−121,416	127,149	†−80	−377	−212	1,149	2,685	−2,475	12,869	26,329
Exports of Goods and Services.......	90c	157,360	270,997	826,379	1,544,077	†3,182	7,088	12,713	17,972	29,959	60,151	79,464	98,496
Imports of Goods and Services (-)....	98c	189,646	383,358	788,530	1,890,238	†4,111	8,763	14,573	20,801	39,285	55,862	84,151	110,334
Gross Domestic Product (GDP).......	99b	1,093,368	1,981,867	3,868,429	7,762,456	†14,772	28,836	52,225	77,415	124,583	178,412	276,003	359,763
Statistical Discrepancy...............	99bs	−36,046	−80,320	−157,193	−163,966	†427	115	−1,090	−5,510	−2,442	−9,729	−969	1,063
GDP Vol. 1987 Prices..................	99b.p	89,401	96,591	91,321	97,889	†105	113	116	111	119	110	118	125
GDP Volume (2000=100)...............	99bvp	75.4	81.5	77.0	82.6	88.3	95.0	97.9	93.3	100.0	92.7	99.9	105.8
GDP Deflator (2000=100)..............	99bip	1.2	2.0	4.0	7.5	13.4	24.4	42.8	66.6	100.0	154.5	221.8	272.8
						Millions: Midyear Estimates							
Population.............................	99z	59.82	60.91	62.00	63.07	64.13	65.18	66.22	67.25	68.28	69.30	70.32	71.33

Uganda 746

		1992	1993	1994	1995	1996	1997	1998	1999	2000	2001	2002	2003
Exchange Rates					*Shillings per SDR: End of Period*								
Principal Rate	aa	1,673.6	1,552.3	1,352.9	1,500.5	1,480.5	1,538.3	1,918.7	2,067.1	2,301.8	2,170.9	2,518.6	2,875.8
				Shillings per US Dollar: End of Period (ae) Period Average (rf)									
Principal Rate	ae	1,217.2	1,130.2	926.8	1,009.5	1,029.6	1,140.1	1,362.7	1,506.0	1,766.7	1,727.4	1,852.6	1,935.3
Principal Rate	rf	1,133.8	1,195.0	979.4	968.9	1,046.1	1,083.0	1,240.3	1,454.8	1,644.5	1,755.7	1,797.6	1,963.7
				Index Numbers (2000=100): Period Averages									
Principal Rate	ahx	145.05	136.90	167.65	169.08	156.31	151.25	132.31	112.55	100.00	93.17	91.00	83.32
Nominal Effective Exchange Rate	nec	78.70	95.90	130.83	127.18	123.57	127.86	116.23	104.10	100.00	98.23	94.48	78.91
Real Effective Exchange Rate	rec	91.67	97.89	121.74	119.07	118.74	127.30	112.56	104.54	100.00	97.18	91.34	80.37
Fund Position					*Millions of SDRs: End of Period*								
Quota	2f.s	133.9	133.9	133.9	133.9	133.9	133.9	133.9	180.5	180.5	180.5	180.5	180.5
SDRs	1b.s	6.6	—	2.1	.3	.7	4.0	3.5	1.7	2.7	1.5	2.2	3.2
Reserve Position in the Fund	1c.s	—	—	—	—	—	—	—	—	—	—	—	—
Total Fund Cred.&Loans Outstg	2tl	250.1	243.0	262.6	280.6	290.1	291.7	282.7	270.8	242.6	219.1	188.9	158.8
International Liquidity				*Millions of US Dollars Unless Otherwise Indicated: End of Period*									
Total Reserves minus Gold	1l.d	94.4	146.4	321.4	458.9	528.4	633.5	725.4	763.1	808.0	983.4	934.0	1,080.3
SDRs	1b.d	9.0	.1	3.1	.5	1.1	5.4	5.0	2.3	3.5	1.9	3.0	4.8
Reserve Position in the Fund	1c.d	—	—	—	—	—	—	—	—	—	—	—	—
Foreign Exchange	1d.d	85.4	146.3	318.3	458.4	527.3	628.1	720.4	760.8	804.5	981.5	931.1	1,075.5
Monetary Authorities: Other Liab.	4..d	2.6	1.8	7.7	2.7	3.0	1.4	7.5	2.0	2.3	2.4	2.8	2.6
Deposit Money Banks: Assets	7a.d	72.2	91.4	145.2	132.5	142.6	160.8	190.2	199.8	265.6	248.6	240.1	362.2
Liabilities	7b.d	21.6	.7	8.0	.1	—	2.0	2.1	25.5	41.7	32.1	38.7	25.8
Monetary Authorities					*Billions of Shillings: End of Period*								
Foreign Assets	11	†117.08	172.28	299.21	466.80	538.08	660.96	951.07	1,090.38	1,363.64	1,624.55	1,660.49	2,141.52
Claims on Central Government	12a	†792.17	791.08	963.06	1,152.68	1,227.76	1,348.13	1,591.13	1,801.56	1,911.39	1,678.33	2,022.48	1,900.14
Claims on Nonfin.Pub.Enterprises	12c	†24.26	20.75	23.19	24.18	24.47	25.13	25.56	3.50	4.15	4.17	3.86	4.24
Claims on Private Sector	12d	†4.77	4.36	1.47	.54	.54	.54	.45	27.35	52.43	85.64	82.98	60.03
Claims on Deposit Money Banks	12e	†10.13	6.27	3.86	1.88	7.72	13.06	31.82	61.84	61.76	58.04	77.50	104.71
Reserve Money	14	†138.59	170.97	253.14	287.89	321.37	350.61	420.77	484.14	589.68	668.44	739.76	820.95
of which: Currency Outside DMBs	14a	†98.33	132.64	176.52	204.52	221.09	240.46	285.88	330.76	362.25	393.43	466.61	546.23
Liabs. of Central Bank: Securities	16ac	†—	—	—	—	—	7.00	6.70	52.42	.02	20.02	38.71	38.21
Restricted Deposits	16b	†8.45	10.55	9.33	10.45	9.96	13.43	26.58	123.49	125.60	133.22	151.19	169.04
Foreign Liabilities	16c	†421.73	379.31	362.37	423.84	432.55	450.43	552.70	562.73	562.54	479.82	480.94	461.66
Central Government Deposits	16d	†464.83	550.28	830.12	1,247.93	1,319.14	1,457.69	1,688.73	1,925.47	1,727.99	1,824.37	2,022.31	2,102.12
Capital Accounts	17a	†80.79	61.50	20.49	56.71	140.81	215.89	408.85	492.39	433.31	305.79	494.48	556.95
Other Items (Net)	17r	†−166.01	−177.86	−184.65	−380.74	−425.26	−447.22	−504.29	−656.00	−45.76	19.05	−80.09	61.71
Deposit Money Banks					*Billions of Shillings: End of Period*								
Reserves	20	34.64	37.06	75.12	79.60	109.62	104.22	129.41	121.02	188.93	233.79	205.80	207.26
Claims on Mon.Author.:Securities	20c	—	—	—	—	—	7.00	6.70	52.42	—	20.00	26.50	38.20
Foreign Assets	21	87.88	103.30	134.55	133.77	146.80	183.34	259.23	300.95	469.23	429.43	444.76	701.05
Claims on Central Government	22a	5.85	14.27	34.74	41.75	65.67	182.64	199.24	286.12	404.25	586.78	868.01	890.35
Claims on State and Local Govts	22b	.30	—	—	—	—	—	—	1.41	1.04	.78	.88	.87
Claims on Nonfin.Pub.Enterprises	22c	27.91	32.53	51.21	56.63	65.85	65.83	63.59	70.66	115.36	141.41	192.47	212.51
Claims on Private Sector	22d	105.08	166.95	190.69	245.82	323.18	319.96	424.82	491.90	531.35	503.51	596.50	757.27
Demand Deposits	24	107.68	126.76	177.50	204.18	229.74	272.08	326.53	358.60	443.24	515.36	632.83	688.68
Time, Savings,& Fgn. Currency Dep.	25	57.88	155.49	209.41	233.30	315.37	402.46	512.42	588.01	703.62	739.40	961.11	1,193.75
Foreign Liabilities	26c	26.27	.75	7.44	.08	—	2.23	2.92	38.43	73.69	55.46	71.68	49.90
Central Government Deposits	26d	8.15	11.19	28.00	38.68	73.01	49.03	46.29	99.81	149.24	159.62	175.29	245.08
Central Government Lending Funds	26f	—	14.52	18.81	15.39	7.99	11.17	10.98	17.03	54.62	52.97	40.23	101.77
Credit from Monetary Authorities	26g	7.58	10.47	6.71	8.45	.15	7.24	23.40	27.22	22.22	20.30	21.48	20.30
Capital Accounts	27a	51.14	37.65	36.00	50.07	73.33	145.90	169.82	172.64	264.46	308.30	338.59	416.99
Other Items (Net)	27r	2.96	−2.72	2.44	7.42	11.52	−27.12	−9.40	22.74	−.94	64.29	93.72	91.05
Monetary Survey					*Billions of Shillings: End of Period*								
Foreign Assets (Net)	31n	†−243.04	−104.47	63.95	176.66	252.33	391.64	654.68	790.18	1,196.64	1,518.70	1,552.64	2,331.02
Domestic Credit	32	†487.34	468.47	406.25	234.99	315.32	435.51	569.77	657.22	1,142.75	1,016.62	1,569.57	1,478.20
Claims on Central Govt. (Net)	32an	†325.03	243.88	139.69	−92.18	−98.72	24.05	55.35	62.40	438.41	281.12	692.89	443.29
Claims on State and Local Govts	32b	†.30	—	—	—	—	—	—	1.41	1.04	.78	.88	.87
Claims on Nonfin.Pub. Enterprises	32c	†52.17	53.29	74.40	80.81	90.32	90.96	89.15	74.16	119.52	145.57	196.32	216.75
Claims on Private Sector	32d	†109.85	171.30	192.16	246.36	323.72	320.51	425.28	519.25	583.79	589.15	679.48	817.30
Money	34	†206.01	259.40	354.02	408.70	450.84	512.53	612.44	689.36	805.49	908.80	1,099.44	1,234.91
Quasi-Money	35	†57.88	155.49	209.41	233.30	315.37	402.46	512.42	588.01	703.62	739.40	961.11	1,193.75
Liabs. of Central Bank: Securities	36ac	†—	—	—	—	—	—	—	—	.02	.02	12.21	.01
Restricted Deposits	36b	†8.45	10.55	9.33	10.45	9.96	13.43	26.58	123.49	125.60	133.22	151.19	169.04
Central Government Lending Funds	36f	†—	14.52	18.81	15.39	7.99	11.17	10.98	17.03	54.62	52.97	40.23	101.77
Capital Accounts	37a	†131.93	99.16	56.48	106.77	214.14	361.79	578.66	665.03	697.77	614.10	833.07	973.94
Other Items (Net)	37r	†−159.97	−175.11	−177.86	−362.97	−430.65	−474.22	−516.63	−635.52	−47.73	86.82	24.96	135.80
Money plus Quasi-Money	35l	†263.89	414.89	563.43	642.00	766.21	914.99	1,124.86	1,277.37	1,509.11	1,648.20	2,060.55	2,428.66

2004, International Monetary Fund: *International Financial Statistics Yearbook*

Uganda 746

		1992	1993	1994	1995	1996	1997	1998	1999	2000	2001	2002	2003
Interest Rates		\multicolumn{12}{c}{*Percent Per Annum*}
Bank Rate (End of Period)	60	41.00	24.00	15.00	13.30	15.85	14.08	9.10	15.75	18.86	8.88	13.08	25.62
Treasury Bill Rate	60c	....	†21.30	12.52	8.75	11.71	10.59	7.77	7.43	13.19	11.00	5.85	16.87
Savings Rate	60k	32.67	12.28	5.95	2.76	3.18	3.76	4.14	3.95	3.99	3.72	1.81	2.38
Deposit Rate	60l	35.83	16.26	9.99	7.61	10.62	11.84	11.36	8.73	9.84	8.47	5.56	9.85
Lending Rate	60p	....	....	....	20.16	20.29	21.37	20.86	21.55	22.92	22.66	19.10	18.94
Government Bond Yield	61	43.50	....	....	....	....	....	....	....	....	....	....	....
Prices		\multicolumn{12}{c}{*Index Numbers (2000=100): Period Averages*}
Consumer Prices	64	63.1	66.9	73.5	79.8	85.5	91.5	91.4	†97.3	100.0	102.0	101.7	109.6
International Transactions		\multicolumn{12}{c}{*Millions of Shillings*}
Exports	70	159,387	213,846	393,960	446,086	613,598	594,804	624,509	748,862	759,273	802,296	795,511	1,102,401
Imports, c.i.f. (Cash Basis)	71	580,685	732,340	850,411	1,024,317	1,247,379	1,425,904	1,753,335	1,955,849	2,486,275	2,798,212	1,998,152	2,456,629
Balance of Payments		\multicolumn{12}{c}{*Millions of US Dollars: Minus Sign Indicates Debit*}
Current Account, n.i.e.	78ald	−99.6	−224.3	−207.5	−338.9	−252.3	−366.8	−502.6	−710.7	−825.4	−802.4	−389.6	−387.9
Goods: Exports f.o.b.	78aad	151.2	200.0	463.0	560.3	639.3	592.6	510.2	483.5	449.9	451.6	480.7	563.0
Goods: Imports f.o.b.	78abd	−421.9	−478.3	−714.2	−926.8	−986.9	−1,042.6	−1,166.3	−989.1	−949.7	−1,026.6	−1,073.5	−1,258.3
Trade Balance	78acd	−270.7	−278.3	−251.2	−366.5	−347.6	−449.9	−656.1	−505.6	−499.8	−575.0	−592.8	−695.3
Services: Credit	78add	34.5	93.6	64.1	104.0	144.7	164.6	176.3	196.0	213.2	221.0	232.8	289.8
Services: Debit	78aed	−247.7	−293.1	−436.3	−562.7	−674.6	−668.9	−728.1	−419.2	−458.8	−523.2	−519.4	−509.1
Balance on Goods & Services	78afd	−483.9	−477.8	−623.4	−825.2	−877.5	−954.2	−1,208.0	−728.8	−745.4	−877.2	−879.3	−914.6
Income: Credit	78agd	4.1	6.4	13.8	17.7	29.7	40.5	50.7	35.1	53.1	37.3	24.2	27.6
Income: Debit	78ahd	−88.3	−65.3	−71.0	−113.3	−79.2	−55.7	−59.9	−162.5	−165.5	−177.6	−189.5	−203.1
Balance on Gds, Serv. & Inc.	78aid	−568.1	−536.7	−680.6	−920.8	−927.0	−969.4	−1,217.2	−856.2	−857.8	−1,017.5	−1,044.6	−1,090.1
Current Transfers, n.i.e.: Credit	78ajd	468.5	312.4	473.1	581.9	674.7	602.6	714.6	329.7	340.0	583.0	979.5	927.0
Current Transfers: Debit	78akd	−	−	−	−	−	−	−	−184.2	−307.6	−367.9	−324.5	−224.8
Capital Account, n.i.e.	78bcd	−	42.4	36.1	48.3	61.4	31.9	49.5	−	−	−	−	−
Capital Account, n.i.e.: Credit	78bad	−	42.4	36.1	48.3	61.4	31.9	49.5	−	−	−	−	−
Capital Account: Debit	78bbd	−	−	−	−	−	−	−	−	−	−	−	−
Financial Account, n.i.e.	78bjd	114.8	56.6	76.8	210.7	140.5	298.8	372.8	253.3	320.5	499.7	258.1	435.1
Direct Investment Abroad	78bdd	−	−	−	−	−	−	−	−	−	−	−	−
Dir. Invest. in Rep. Econ., n.i.e.	78bed	3.0	54.6	88.2	121.2	121.0	175.0	210.0	140.2	160.7	144.7	186.6	194.2
Portfolio Investment Assets	78bfd	−	−	−	−	−	−	−	−	−	−	−	−
Equity Securities	78bkd	−	−	−	−	−	−	−	−	−	−	−	−
Debt Securities	78bld	−	−	−	−	−	−	−	−	−	−	−	−
Portfolio Investment Liab., n.i.e.	78bgd	−	−	−	−	−	−	−	−	−	−	.4	20.8
Equity Securities	78bmd	−	−	−	−	−	−	−	−	−	−	.4	.5
Debt Securities	78bnd	−	−	−	−	−	−	−	−	−	−	−	20.3
Financial Derivatives Assets	78bwd	....	....	....	....	....	....	....	....	....	....	....	....
Financial Derivatives Liabilities	78bxd	....	....	....	....	....	....	....	....	....	....	....	....
Other Investment Assets	78bhd	1.8	−5.0	−40.3	−9.9	−37.2	−14.0	5.3	−8.2	−.9	−15.0	−23.3	−39.7
Monetary Authorities	78bod	....	....	....	....	....	....	....	....	....	....	....	....
General Government	78bpd	−	−	−	−	−	−	−	−	−	−	−	−
Banks	78bqd	−	−8.7	−53.0	12.7	−10.1	−18.2	−29.4	−9.6	−65.8	17.0	8.5	−109.7
Other Sectors	78brd	1.8	3.7	12.7	−22.6	−27.1	4.2	34.7	1.4	64.9	−32.0	−31.8	70.0
Other Investment Liab., n.i.e.	78bid	110.0	7.0	28.9	99.4	56.7	137.9	157.5	121.3	160.7	370.0	94.3	259.8
Monetary Authorities	78bsd	−6.6	2.2	.9	1.7	1.1	.2	−	−	−	−	−	−
General Government	78btd	150.7	56.3	50.8	111.7	114.4	158.2	178.2	131.1	154.9	327.5	101.0	259.1
Banks	78bud	−22.8	−	−	−	−	−	−	−	−	−	9.0	2.2
Other Sectors	78bvd	−11.3	−51.5	−22.8	−14.0	−58.8	−20.5	−20.7	−9.8	5.8	42.5	−15.7	−1.4
Net Errors and Omissions	78cad	9.0	−.1	32.5	28.8	41.3	−4.8	39.7	2.0	40.6	63.8	2.5	.1
Overall Balance	78cbd	24.2	−125.4	−62.1	−51.2	−9.1	−40.9	−40.6	−455.4	−464.3	−238.9	−129.0	47.2
Reserves and Related Items	79dad	−24.2	125.4	62.1	51.2	9.1	40.9	40.6	455.4	464.3	238.9	129.0	−47.2
Reserve Assets	79dbd	−50.6	−49.4	−166.9	−140.7	−68.9	−105.2	−91.7	−37.8	−45.1	−175.4	102.4	−75.2
Use of Fund Credit and Loans	79dcd	26.4	−9.8	27.1	27.5	13.3	2.5	−12.2	−16.0	−37.4	−29.6	−39.4	−42.6
Exceptional Financing	79ded	−	184.7	201.9	164.3	64.8	143.6	144.4	509.2	546.8	444.0	66.1	70.5

Uganda 746

		1992	1993	1994	1995	1996	1997	1998	1999	2000	2001	2002	2003
International Investment Position						*Millions of US Dollars*							
Assets	79aad	....	....	....	....	....	....	....	....	....	....	....	....
Direct Investment Abroad	79abd	....	....	....	....	....	....	....	—	—	—	—	—
Portfolio Investment	79acd	....	....	....	....	....	....	....	—	—	—	—	—
Equity Securities	79add	....	....	....	....	....	....	....	—	—	—	—	—
Debt Securities	79aed	....	....	....	....	....	....	....	—	—	—	—	—
Financial Derivatives	79ald	....	....	....	....	....	....	....	....	....	....	....	....
Other Investment	79afd	....	....	....	....	....	....	....	199.8	265.6	248.6	240.1	362.7
Monetary Authorities	79agd	....	....	....	....	....	....	....	—	—	—	—	—
General Government	79ahd	....	....	....	....	....	....	....	—	—	—	—	—
Banks	79aid	....	....	....	....	....	....	....	199.8	265.6	248.6	240.1	362.7
Other Sectors	79ajd	....	....	....	....	....	....	....	—	—	—	—	—
Reserve Assets	79akd	....	....	....	....	....	....	....	763.1	808.1	983.3	934.0	1,080.3
Liabilities	79lad	....	....	....	....	....	....	....	....	....	....	....	....
Dir. Invest. in Rep. Economy	79lbd	....	....	....	....	....	....	....	666.9	807.1	962.3	1,148.9	1,343.1
Portfolio Investment	79lcd	....	....	....	....	....	....	....	—	—	—	—	22.4
Equity Securities	79ldd	....	....	....	....	....	....	....	—	—	—	—	—
Debt Securities	79led	....	....	....	....	....	....	....	—	—	—	—	22.4
Financial Derivatives	79lld	....	....	....	....	....	....	....	....	....	....	....	....
Other Investment	79lfd	....	....	....	....	....	....	....	4,106.6	3,587.5	3,821.2	4,126.1	4,697.6
Monetary Authorities	79lgd	....	....	....	....	....	....	....	371.7	316.1	275.4	256.8	236.0
General Government	79lhd	....	....	....	....	....	....	....	3,580.0	3,088.7	3,378.9	3,686.5	4,250.5
Banks	79lid	....	....	....	....	....	....	....	37.3	58.5	51.7	60.7	79.0
Other Sectors	79ljd	....	....	....	....	....	....	....	117.7	124.2	115.2	122.0	132.2
Government Finance						*Millions of Shillings: Year Ending June 30*							
Deficit (-) or Surplus	80	−263,572	−113,513	−169,806	−131,554	−112,872	−120,191f	−49,043	−109,033	−640,250	−218,703	−473,266	....
Revenue	81	185,381	291,075	399,152	531,194	622,790	744,344f	794,052	961,993	1,074,065	1,083,486	1,253,748	....
Grants Received	81z	94,635	313,754	282,487	253,876	325,023	351,091f	397,552	406,936	586,045	798,917	761,046	....
Expenditure	82	535,088	717,142	848,645	905,277	1,057,885	1,213,626f	1,237,646	1,475,643	1,817,223	2,127,236	2,483,210	....
Lending Minus Repayments	83	8,500	1,200	2,800	11,347	2,800	2,000f	3,000	2,319	483,137	−26,131	4,850	....
Financing													
Total Financing	84	263,572	113,513	169,806	131,554	112,872	120,191f	49,043	109,034	640,250	218,703	473,266	....
Net Borrowing: Domestic	84a	56,027	−23,826	−26,962	−86,701	−60,262	−51,990f	−87,500	−16,749	539,885	65,920	24,946	....
Net borrowing: Foreign	85a	140,433	200,816	243,227	211,719	209,432	231,400f	254,936	218,739	193,407	323,437	484,721	....
Use of Cash Balances	87	2,490	−72,868	−51,017	−22,182	−34,200	−30,001f	−67,117	−146,123	−67,593	−186,878	−164,915	....
Adj. to Total Financing	84x	64,622	9,391	4,558	28,718	−2,098	−29,218f	−51,276	53,167	−25,449	16,225	128,514	....
Debt													
Domestic	88a	....	....	....	....	....	....	143,248	214,480	325,442	503,462	857,474	....
Debt: Foreign	89a	3,096,200	3,162,800	2,908,300	3,271,300	3,721,500	3,907,200	4,469,957	5,064,691	5,599,887	5,994,951	6,803,726	....
National Accounts						*Millions of Shillings*							
Househ.Cons.Expend.,incl.NPISHs	96f	3,338,716	3,521,432	4,356,600	4,997,984	5,434,499	5,724,224	6,210,171	7,018,498	7,721,524	8,227,248	8,636,159	9,968,593
Government Consumption Expend	91f	321,603	424,897	476,591	577,183	660,574	915,724	1,011,850	1,134,457	1,301,776	1,483,822	1,691,744	1,855,560
Gross Fixed Capital Formation	93e	547,106	647,912	738,346	984,963	1,012,671	1,181,783	1,430,734	1,730,995	1,768,525	1,982,961	2,214,316	2,665,627
Changes in Inventories	93i	−5,460	3,107	−27,115	−5,190	−7,539	21,320	30,877	15,791	40,936	38,066	40,876	51,637
Exports of Goods and Services	90c	253,431	310,187	555,517	648,754	791,972	794,351	875,583	1,005,087	1,009,806	1,196,891	1,262,698	1,760,414
Imports of Goods and Services (-)	98c	754,349	803,611	945,341	1,240,509	1,374,620	1,423,095	1,783,874	2,050,909	2,308,889	2,677,308	2,945,476	3,536,338
Gross Domestic Product (GDP)	99b	3,687,704	4,024,186	5,171,744	5,977,762	6,636,521	7,214,306	7,775,341	8,853,919	9,533,678	10,251,680	10,900,317	12,765,492
GDP Volume 1991 Prices	99b.p	2,325,781	2,489,937	2,753,332	3,018,149	3,195,141	....	....	....	....	....	....	....
GDP Volume (1995=100)	99bvp	77.1	82.5	91.2	100.0	105.9	....	....	....	....	....	....	....
GDP Deflator (1995=100)	99bip	80.1	81.6	94.8	100.0	104.9	....	....	....	....	....	....	....
						Millions: Midyear Estimates							
Population	99z	18.52	19.10	19.68	20.27	20.88	21.49	22.13	22.79	23.49	24.22	25.00	25.83

2004, International Monetary Fund: *International Financial Statistics Yearbook*

Ukraine 926

		1992	1993	1994	1995	1996	1997	1998	1999	2000	2001	2002	2003
Exchange Rates						*Hryvnias per SDR: End of Period*							
Official Rate	aa	.0088	.1732	1.5212	2.6668	†2.7163	2.5622	4.8253	7.1594	7.0807	6.6588	7.2495	7.9224
					Hryvnias per US Dollar: End of Period (ae) Period Average (rf)								
Official Rate	ae	.0064	.1261	1.0420	1.7940	†1.8890	1.8990	3.4270	5.2163	5.4345	5.2985	5.3324	5.3315
Official Rate	rf	....	.0453	.3275	1.4731	†1.8295	1.8617	2.4495	4.1304	5.4402	5.3722	5.3266	5.3327
					Index Numbers (2000=100): Period Averages								
Nominal Effective Exchange Rate	nec	7,095.24	957.55	161.41	85.81	75.68	86.35	92.07	117.15	100.00	105.07	110.83	106.20
Real Effective Exchange Rate	rec	113.72	49.78	70.54	84.36	99.36	112.48	109.74	106.77	100.00	100.39	94.88	86.42
Fund Position						*Millions of SDRs: End of Period*							
Quota	2f.s	997.30	997.30	997.30	997.30	997.30	997.30	997.30	1,372.00	1,372.00	1,372.00	1,372.00	1,372.00
SDRs	1b.s	–	–	123.73	97.06	46.72	52.70	129.53	47.86	191.19	199.80	20.81	14.27
Reserve Position in the Fund	1c.s	.01	.01	.01	–	–	.01	.01	–	–	–	–	–
Total Fund Cred.&Loans Outstg.	2tl			249.33	1,037.30	1,573.30	1,780.56	1,985.05	2,044.62	1,591.19	1,520.74	1,379.99	1,235.48
International Liquidity					*Millions of US Dollars Unless Otherwise Indicated: End of Period*								
Total Reserves minus Gold	1l.d	468.8	161.6	650.7	1,050.6	1,960.0	2,341.1	761.3	1,046.4	1,352.7	2,955.3	4,241.4	6,730.7
SDRs	1b.d	–	–	180.6	144.3	67.2	71.1	182.4	65.7	249.1	251.1	28.3	21.2
Reserve Position in the Fund	1c.d	–	–	–	–	–	–	–	–	–	–	–	–
Foreign Exchange	1d.d	468.8	161.6	470.1	906.3	1,892.8	2,270.0	578.9	980.7	1,103.6	2,704.3	4,213.1	6,709.5
Gold (Million Fine Troy Ounces)	1ad	.0003	.0115	.0360	.0470	.0316	.0613	.1100	.1624	.4536	.4831	.5037	.4969
Gold (National Valuation)	1and	.1	4.4	13.7	18.3	11.6	17.7	31.6	47.2	123.7	134.1	175.4	206.5
Monetary Authorities:Other Assets	3..d	981.4	88.1	4.3	2.5	2.3	–	235.9	104.9	177.4	90.3	109.2	137.5
Other Liab.	4..d	2,398.5	279.9	7.3	22.1	36.6	67.6	175.6	172.4	122.4	92.2	78.9	93.0
Deposit Money Banks: Assets	7a.d	863.5	1,264.5	1,406.3	1,044.3	942.1	963.1	906.8	849.2	921.5	774.7	851.6	1,357.9
Liabilities	7b.d	896.3	570.4	724.8	302.0	334.4	949.9	507.2	338.7	462.6	650.9	807.8	1,718.8
Monetary Authorities						*Millions of Hryvnias: End of Period*							
Foreign Assets	11	9.2	32.0	696.8	2,027.1	3,729.0	4,479.4	†3,525.4	6,251.8	8,987.5	16,847.8	24,134.4	37,718.8
Claims on General Government	12a	17.5	131.2	1,410.7	4,393.1	6,211.3	7,430.1	†15,075.2	19,712.8	20,854.0	19,898.4	19,634.2	18,548.2
Claims on Nonfin.Pub.Enterprises	12c	–	.5	4.8	–	–	–	† –	–	–	–	–	–
Claims on Private Sector	12d	–	.2	.3	.1	1.2	35.0	†104.8	154.0	178.7	178.9	186.7	190.0
Claims on Banks	12e	18.7	147.7	336.3	665.2	859.6	1,555.0	†1,365.1	1,687.8	1,600.7	1,552.7	1,755.7	2,497.3
Reserve Money	14	18.1	301.2	1,528.2	3,557.1	4,974.9	7,410.5	†8,639.6	12,209.2	17,561.4	25,033.7	30,990.3	40,303.7
of which: Currency Outside Banks	14a	4.8	127.7	793.1	2,623.3	4,040.6	6,132.3	†7,157.3	9,583.3	12,799.0	19,464.8	26,433.8	33,119.3
Time, Savings,& Fgn.Currency Dep	15	–	2.5	2.1	3.1	158.4	21.8	†31.1	23.1	57.1	110.3	205.6	76.9
Foreign Liabilities	16c	15.3	35.3	386.9	2,805.9	4,342.8	4,690.6	†10,180.1	15,537.6	11,932.1	10,614.6	10,425.1	10,283.9
General Government Deposits	16d	–	18.6	166.7	97.7	216.0	334.0	†455.1	592.1	915.0	1,380.3	2,185.6	4,973.2
Capital Accounts	17a	.5	12.2	75.8	231.3	420.8	914.5	†2,230.7	1,185.4	2,691.9	3,238.8	3,640.8	5,665.5
Other Items (Net)	17r	11.5	–58.1	289.2	390.3	688.1	128.0	†–1,466.1	–1,741.0	–1,536.6	–1,900.1	–1,736.3	–2,348.9
Banking Institutions						*Millions of Hryvnias: End of Period*							
Reserves	20	16.5	182.4	762.9	960.3	848.6	925.5	†1,454.6	2,613.3	4,749.6	5,538.9	4,515.8	7,125.8
Foreign Assets	21	5.5	159.5	1,465.3	1,873.4	1,779.7	1,829.0	†3,107.6	4,429.7	5,007.8	4,104.5	4,540.9	7,239.4
Claims on General Government	22a	1.3	17.1	–	207.6	774.5	1,815.4	†1,530.5	1,133.3	804.5	1,412.7	2,577.2	2,620.2
Claims on Nonfin.Pub.Enterprises	22c	25.5	389.5	1,426.7	3,662.8	4,932.0	5,549.0	†1,440.9	1,782.4	1,916.1	2,876.7	3,688.9	5,654.7
Claims on Private Sector	22d	1.3	20.9	556.5	804.2	1,128.2	2,259.1	†7,922.1	11,046.0	18,816.3	26,430.0	39,614.8	64,894.3
Claims on Nonbank Financial Insts.	22g	–	–	–	4.1	5.5	–	†129.4	153.5	219.0	198.4	222.0	686.2
Demand Deposits	24	15.8	213.6	1,061.9	2,041.9	2,253.9	2,887.3	†3,205.0	4,568.9	8,013.5	10,301.5	13,806.8	19,968.3
Time, Savings,& Fgn.Currency Dep	25	4.5	137.1	1,353.7	2,244.9	2,890.6	3,468.6	†5,139.1	7,683.9	10,725.0	15,279.8	23,834.8	41,256.5
of which: Fgn. Currency Deposits	25b	2.1	87.6	1,019.5	1,576.8	1,562.0	1,641.6	†3,265.4	5,357.6	7,187.9	8,281.2	12,078.6	19,571.0
Bonds	26ab	–	–	–	–	–	–	†220.2	305.0	642.0	569.4	548.4	580.4
Foreign Liabilities	26c	5.7	71.9	755.2	541.8	631.6	1,803.8	†1,738.2	1,766.6	2,514.0	3,448.9	4,307.8	9,163.6
General Government Deposits	26d	3.7	87.0	323.7	514.4	795.5	805.0	†544.2	487.7	1,358.8	1,541.1	1,752.5	1,115.3
Credit from Monetary Authorities	26g	14.4	158.2	169.4	632.0	699.7	979.8	†1,237.0	1,569.4	1,604.9	1,125.8	1,305.5	2,377.3
Capital Accounts	27a	1.3	66.1	396.9	1,406.2	3,018.1	4,261.4	†5,462.2	7,497.7	9,182.9	11,044.4	13,859.2	18,169.2
Other Items (Net)	27r	4.6	35.3	150.7	131.1	–820.9	–1,827.9	†–1,961.1	–2,721.1	–2,527.8	–2,749.6	–4,255.4	–4,409.9
Banking Survey						*Millions of Hryvnias: End of Period*							
Foreign Assets (Net)	31n	–6.3	84.3	1,020.0	552.8	534.3	–186.0	†–5,285.3	–6,622.6	–450.7	6,888.8	13,942.4	25,510.7
Domestic Credit	32	41.9	453.7	2,908.6	8,459.8	12,041.1	15,949.6	†25,203.5	32,902.1	40,514.8	48,073.7	61,985.7	86,505.2
Claims on General Govt. (Net)	32an	15.0	42.6	920.3	3,988.6	5,974.2	8,106.5	†15,606.3	19,766.2	19,384.7	18,389.7	18,273.3	15,079.9
Claims on Nonfin.Pub.Enterprises	32c	25.5	390.0	1,431.5	3,662.8	4,932.0	5,549.0	†1,440.9	1,782.4	1,916.1	2,876.7	3,688.9	5,654.7
Claims on Private Sector	32d	1.3	21.1	556.7	804.3	1,129.4	2,294.1	†8,026.8	11,200.4	18,995.0	26,608.9	39,801.6	65,084.3
Claims on Nonbank Financial Inst.	32g	–	–	–	4.1	5.5	–	†129.4	153.5	219.0	198.4	222.0	686.2
Money	34	20.7	341.9	1,860.0	4,681.9	6,315.5	9,050.4	†10,386.0	14,161.8	20,825.3	29,795.6	40,281.1	53,129.4
Quasi-Money	35	4.5	139.5	1,355.7	2,248.1	3,048.9	3,490.4	†5,170.2	7,707.0	10,782.1	15,390.2	24,040.4	41,333.4
Bonds	36ab	–	–	–	–	–	–	†220.2	305.0	642.0	569.4	548.4	580.4
Capital Accounts	37a	1.8	78.4	472.7	1,637.5	3,438.9	5,176.0	†7,692.8	8,683.1	11,874.8	14,283.2	17,500.0	23,834.8
Other Items (Net)	37r	8.5	–21.9	240.1	445.1	–228.0	–1,953.1	†–3,551.1	–4,577.4	–4,060.2	–5,075.9	–6,441.8	–6,862.1
Money plus Quasi-Money	35l	25.2	481.5	3,215.7	6,930.0	9,364.4	12,540.8	†15,556.2	21,868.8	31,607.4	45,185.8	64,321.5	94,462.9

Ukraine 926

		1992	1993	1994	1995	1996	1997	1998	1999	2000	2001	2002	2003
Interest Rates							**Percent Per Annum**						
Refinancing Rate (End of Period)	60	80.00	240.00	252.00	110.00	40.00	35.00	60.00	45.00	27.00	12.50	7.00	7.00
Money Market Rate	60b	....	....	....	....	....	22.05	40.41	44.98	18.34	16.57	5.50	7.90
Money Market Rate (Fgn. Cur.)	60b.f	....	....	....	....	....	....	10.61	5.44	6.27	5.87	3.14	3.61
Deposit Rate	60l	....	148.63	208.63	70.29	33.63	18.21	22.25	20.70	13.72	10.99	7.93	6.98
Deposit Rate (Foreign Currency)	60l.f	....	....	....	....	....	....	10.70	9.68	6.10	5.60	6.09	5.94
Lending Rate	60p	....	184.25	250.28	122.70	79.88	49.12	54.50	54.95	41.53	32.28	25.35	17.89
Lending Rate (Foreign Currency)	60p.f	....	....	....	....	....	....	19.98	20.62	17.42	13.51	11.98	11.95
Prices and Labor						**Percent Change over Previous Period**							
Wholesale Prices	63.xx	....	4,619.3	1,143.8	487.9	51.9	7.7	13.2	31.1	20.9	8.6	3.1	7.8
Consumer Prices	64.xx	....	4,734.9	891.2	376.7	80.3	15.9	10.6	22.7	28.2	12.0	.8	5.2
Wages: Average Earnings	65.xx	....	2,331.9	786.6	†434.2	....	....	....	....	....	....	....	....
					Index Numbers (2000=100): Period Averages								
Industrial Employment	67	189.1	174.5	159.0	146.2	134.7	124.0	120.2	114.1	100.0	94.2	103.9	99.2
					Number in Thousands: Period Averages								
Labor Force	67d	....	....	....	25,562	....	....	25,936	22,747	23,127	22,755	22,702	....
Employment	67e	....	....	....	24,125	24,114	23,756	22,998	20,048	20,420	20,238	20,401	20,555
Unemployment	67c	....	....	....	1,437	1,998	2,330	2,937	2,699	2,708	2,517	2,301	2,008
Unemployment Rate (%)	67r	....	....	....	5.6	7.6	8.9	11.3	11.9	11.7	11.1	10.2	9.1
International Transactions						**Millions of US Dollars**							
Exports	70..d	8,045	7,817	10,305	13,128	14,401	14,232	12,637	11,582	14,573	16,265	17,957	23,080
Imports, c.i.f.	71..d	7,099	9,533	10,748	15,484	17,603	17,128	14,676	11,846	13,956	15,775	16,977	23,021
Imports, f.o.b.	71.vd	7,099	9,533	10,589	....	....	....	....	....	....	....	....	....
Balance of Payments					**Millions of US Dollars: Minus Sign Indicates Debit**								
Current Account, n.i.e.	78ald	....	....	–1,163	–1,152	–1,184	–1,335	–1,296	1,658	1,481	1,402	3,174	2,891
Goods: Exports f.o.b.	78aad	....	....	13,894	14,244	15,547	15,418	13,699	13,189	15,722	17,091	18,669	23,739
Goods: Imports f.o.b.	78abd	....	....	–16,469	–16,946	–19,843	–19,623	–16,283	–12,945	–14,943	–16,893	–17,959	–24,008
Trade Balance	78acd	....	....	–2,575	–2,702	–4,296	–4,205	–2,584	244	779	198	710	–269
Services: Credit	78add	....	....	2,747	2,846	4,799	4,937	3,922	3,869	3,800	3,995	4,682	5,214
Services: Debit	78aed	....	....	–1,538	–1,334	–1,625	–2,268	–2,545	–2,292	–3,004	–3,580	–3,535	–3,657
Balance on Goods & Services	78afd	....	....	–1,366	–1,190	–1,122	–1,536	–1,207	1,821	1,575	613	1,857	1,288
Income: Credit	78agd	....	....	56	247	102	158	122	98	143	167	165	254
Income: Debit	78ahd	....	....	–400	–681	–673	–802	–993	–967	–1,085	–834	–769	–835
Balance on Gds, Serv. & Inc.	78aid	....	....	–1,710	–1,624	–1,693	–2,180	–2,078	952	633	–54	1,253	707
Current Transfers, n.i.e.: Credit	78ajd	....	....	583	557	619	942	868	754	967	1,516	1,967	2,270
Current Transfers: Debit	78akd	....	....	–36	–85	–110	–97	–86	–48	–119	–60	–46	–86
Capital Account, n.i.e.	78bcd	....	....	97	6	5	–	–3	–10	–8	3	17	–17
Capital Account, n.i.e.: Credit	78bad	....	....	106	6	5	–	–	–	–	8	28	11
Capital Account: Debit	78bbd	....	....	–9	–	–	–	–3	–10	–8	–5	–11	–28
Financial Account, n.i.e.	78bjd	....	....	–557	–726	317	1,413	–1,340	–879	–752	–191	–1,065	264
Direct Investment Abroad	78bdd	....	....	–8	–10	5	–42	4	–7	–1	–23	5	–13
Dir. Invest. in Rep. Econ., n.i.e.	78bed	....	....	159	267	521	623	743	496	595	792	693	1,424
Portfolio Investment Assets	78bfd	....	....	–	–12	–1	–2	–2	–11	–4	1	2	1
Equity Securities	78bkd	....	....	....	....	–11	–14	–3	–5	–2	–1	....	–4
Debt Securities	78bld	....	....	....	–12	10	12	1	–6	–2	2	2	5
Portfolio Investment Liab., n.i.e.	78bgd	....	....	–	16	199	1,605	–1,379	–75	–197	–867	–1,718	–923
Equity Securities	78bmd	....	....	....	....	46	248	227	129	–193	–734	–1,958	–1,705
Debt Securities	78bnd	....	....	–	16	153	1,357	–1,606	–204	–4	–133	240	782
Financial Derivatives Assets	78bwd	....	....	....	....	....	....	....	....	....	....	....	....
Financial Derivatives Liabilities	78bxd	....	....	....	....	....	....	....	....	....	....	....	....
Other Investment Assets	78bhd	....	....	–3,026	–1,574	–821	–1,583	–1,321	–2,264	–449	–1,015	–781	–940
Monetary Authorities	78bod	....	....	....	....	....	....	....	....	–15	1	–23	–30
General Government	78bpd	....	....	....	....	....	....	....	....	1,002	–	....	–
Banks	78bqd	....	....	–779	–328	83	–536	–46	51	–64	137	–86	–455
Other Sectors	78brd	....	....	–2,247	–1,246	–904	–1,047	–1,275	–2,315	–1,372	–1,153	–672	–455
Other Investment Liab., n.i.e.	78bid	....	....	2,318	587	414	812	615	982	–696	921	734	715
Monetary Authorities	78bsd	....	....	–	–	–	–	–	–	–	–	–4	16
General Government	78btd	....	....	–1,097	–783	–477	–267	–857	–231	–1,457	–537	–384	–379
Banks	78bud	....	....	577	724	565	–51	–264	–16	113	180	76	779
Other Sectors	78bvd	....	....	2,838	646	326	1,130	1,736	1,229	648	1,278	1,046	299
Net Errors and Omissions	78cad	....	....	423	248	259	–781	–818	–953	–148	–221	–895	–965
Overall Balance	78cbd	....	....	–1,200	–1,624	–603	–703	–3,457	–184	573	993	1,231	2,173
Reserves and Related Items	79dad	....	....	1,200	1,624	603	703	3,457	184	–573	–993	–1,231	–2,173
Reserve Assets	79dbd	....	....	–549	–469	–894	–385	1,328	–281	–401	–1,609	–1,047	–2,045
Use of Fund Credit and Loans	79dcd	....	....	368	1,221	776	283	279	75	–603	–86	–181	–203
Exceptional Financing	79ded	....	....	1,380	871	721	805	1,850	390	431	702	–2	75

2004, International Monetary Fund: *International Financial Statistics Yearbook*

Ukraine 926

		1992	1993	1994	1995	1996	1997	1998	1999	2000	2001	2002	2003
International Investment Position						*Millions of US Dollars*							
Assets	79aad	....	....	....	....	....	....	....	....	....	6,220	7,676	11,035
Direct Investment Abroad	79abd	....	....	....	....	....	....	....	....	....	156	144	164
Portfolio Investment	79acd	....	....	....	....	....	....	....	....	....	30	28	26
Equity Securities	79add	....	....	....	....	....	....	....	....	....	20	19	23
Debt Securities	79aed	....	....	....	....	....	....	....	....	....	10	9	3
Financial Derivatives	79ald	....	....	....	....	....	....	....	....	....	–	–	–
Other Investment	79afd	....	....	....	....	....	....	....	....	....	2,945	3,087	3,908
Monetary Authorities	79agd	....	....	....	....	....	....	....	....	....	157	197	261
General Government	79ahd	....	....	....	....	....	....	....	....	....	–	–	–
Banks	79aid	....	....	....	....	....	....	....	....	....	731	840	1,355
Other Sectors	79ajd	....	....	....	....	....	....	....	....	....	2,057	2,050	2,292
Reserve Assets	79akd	....	....	....	....	....	....	....	....	....	3,089	4,417	6,937
Liabilities	79lad	....	....	....	....	....	....	....	....	....	25,968	28,003	31,314
Dir. Invest. in Rep. Economy	79lbd	....	....	....	....	....	....	....	....	....	4,801	5,924	7,502
Portfolio Investment	79lcd	....	....	....	....	....	....	....	....	....	2,980	3,293	4,016
Equity Securities	79ldd	....	....	....	....	....	....	....	....	....	763	668	415
Debt Securities	79led	....	....	....	....	....	....	....	....	....	2,217	2,625	3,601
Financial Derivatives	79lld	....	....	....	....	....	....	....	....	....	–	–	–
Other Investment	79lfd	....	....	....	....	....	....	....	....	....	18,187	18,786	19,796
Monetary Authorities	79lgd	....	....	....	....	....	....	....	....	....	1,972	1,933	1,909
General Government	79lhd	....	....	....	....	....	....	....	....	....	5,986	5,762	5,649
Banks	79lid	....	....	....	....	....	....	....	....	....	539	859	1,634
Other Sectors	79ljd	....	....	....	....	....	....	....	....	....	9,690	10,232	10,604
Government Finance						*Millions of Hryvnias: Year Ending December 31*							
Deficit (-) or Surplus	80								–2,747	–1,061	–1,800	....	....
Total Revenue and Grants	81y	....	....	....	....	....	....	....	31,172	47,062	57,354	....	....
Revenue	81	....	....	....	....	....	....	....	30,858	45,591	54,569	....	....
Grants	81z	....	....	....	....	....	....	....	314	1,470	2,785	....	....
Exp. & Lending Minus Repayments	82z	....	....	....	....	....	....	....	33,919	48,123	59,154	....	....
Expenditure	82	....	....	....	....	....	....	....	33,900	48,074	58,974	....	....
Lending Minus Repayments	83	....	....	....	....	....	....	....	19	49	181	....	....
Financing: Domestic	84a	....	....	....	....	....	....	....	2,829	1,645	1,333	....	....
Financing: Foreign	85a	....	....	....	....	....	....	....	–82	–584	467	....	....
National Accounts						*Billions of Hryvnias*							
Househ.Cons.Expend.,incl.NPISHs	96f	–	.7	5.8	30.1	58.0	67.1	74.8	91.1	115.9	140.0	151.0	182.6
Government Consumption Expend	91f	–	.2	2.3	11.6	7.1	9.1	8.8	9.4	12.1	16.4	17.9	20.8
Gross Fixed Capital Formation	93e	–	.4	2.9	12.8	17.0	18.7	20.2	25.3	33.6	40.3	44.8	52.4
Changes in Inventories	93i	–	.2	1.4	1.8	1.5	1.3	1.1	–2.5	–	4.2	–2.7	.4
Exports of Goods and Services	90c	–	.4	4.3	25.7	37.2	37.9	43.0	70.9	106.2	113.2	124.4	154.5
Imports of Goods and Services (-)	98c	–	.4	4.6	27.3	39.3	40.8	45.3	63.7	97.6	109.9	114.5	147.5
Gross Domestic Product (GDP)	99b	.1	1.5	12.0	54.5	81.5	93.4	102.6	130.4	170.1	204.2	220.9	263.4
Net Primary Income from Abroad	98.n	–	–	–.1	–.9	–1.0	–1.2	–2.1	–3.5	–5.1	–3.6	....	....
Gross National Income (GNI)	99a	.1	1.4	12.0	53.6	80.5	92.2	100.5	126.9	164.9	200.6	....	....
Net Current Transf.from Abroad	98t	–	–	.1	.7	.9	1.5	2.7	2.9	4.9	8.0	....	....
Gross Nat'l Disposable Inc.(GNDI)	99i	.1	1.4	12.0	54.3	81.4	93.7	103.2	129.8	169.9	208.6	....	....
Gross Saving	99s	–	.5	3.9	12.7	16.3	17.5	19.6	29.4	41.9	52.2	....	....
						Millions: Midyear Estimates							
Population	99z	51.94	51.88	51.74	51.53	51.25	50.90	50.51	50.10	49.69	49.29	48.90	48.52

United Arab Emirates 466

		1992	1993	1994	1995	1996	1997	1998	1999	2000	2001	2002	2003
Exchange Rates						*Dirhams per SDR: End of Period*							
Official Rate	aa	5.0476	5.0423	5.3591	5.4569	5.2788	4.9551	5.1710	5.0405	4.7849	4.6153	4.9928	5.4572
						Dirhams per US Dollar: End of Period (ae) Period Average (rf)							
Official Rate	ae	3.6710	3.6710	3.6710	3.6710	3.6725	3.6725	3.6725	3.6725	3.6725	3.6725	3.6725	3.6725
Official Rate	rf	3.6710	3.6710	3.6710	3.6710	3.6710	3.6711	3.6725	3.6725	3.6725	3.6725	3.6725	3.6725
						Index Numbers (2000=100): Period Averages							
Official Rate	ahx	100.0	100.0	100.0	100.0	100.0	100.0	100.0	100.0	100.0	100.0	100.0	100.0
Nominal Effective Exchange Rate	nec	81.8	85.8	84.3	80.0	83.1	89.9	96.9	95.2	100.0	105.7	103.6	94.4
Fund Position						*Millions of SDRs: End of Period*							
Quota	2f.s	392.1	392.1	392.1	392.1	392.1	392.1	392.1	611.7	611.7	611.7	611.7	611.7
SDRs	1b.s	52.4	54.1	55.0	55.9	57.6	58.4	59.2	4.5	3.1	1.8	1.1	.5
Reserve Position in the Fund	1c.s	158.3	162.8	149.1	185.8	204.4	197.4	233.9	212.6	164.8	179.8	235.8	239.3
of which: Outstg.Fund Borrowing	2c	–	–	–	–	–	–	–	–	–	–	–	–
International Liquidity						*Millions of US Dollars Unless Otherwise Indicated: End of Period*							
Total Reserves minus Gold	1l.d	5,711.8	6,103.7	6,658.8	7,470.9	8,055.5	8,372.3	9,077.1	10,675.1	13,522.7	14,146.4	15,219.4	15,087.8
SDRs	1b.d	72.1	74.4	80.3	83.1	82.8	78.7	83.3	6.2	4.0	2.2	1.5	.7
Reserve Position in the Fund	1c.d	217.6	223.6	217.7	276.2	293.9	266.3	329.3	291.7	214.7	225.9	320.6	355.6
Foreign Exchange	1d.d	5,422.1	5,805.7	6,360.8	7,111.6	7,678.8	8,027.3	8,664.4	10,377.1	13,303.9	13,918.2	14,897.2	14,731.5
Gold (Million Fine Troy Ounces)	1ad	.796	.798	.795	.795	.798	.795	.795	.397	.397	.397	.397	–
Gold (National Valuation)	1and	182.0	182.5	181.7	181.7	182.8	181.3	181.3	90.7	90.7	90.7	90.7	–
Monetary Authorities:Other Assets	3..d	....	....	....	....	....	....	....	....	....	....	....	....
Deposit Money Banks: Assets	7a.d	18,496.6	17,997.8	17,737.4	17,377.8	19,086.9	20,735.7	22,108.9	22,010.3	24,454.7	26,822.6	30,595.0	30,422.6
Liabilities	7b.d	7,157.7	7,221.7	8,997.8	7,653.5	10,053.4	12,351.5	14,446.6	14,577.8	14,133.4	8,137.0	8,136.7	8,248.9
RLB: Foreign Assets	7k.d	162.9	118.8	106.0	134.0	134.6	154.7	200.7	265.5	147.9	245.6	15.2	–
Foreign Liabilities	7m.d	79.0	60.2	35.4	59.1	112.8	101.3	75.4	281.0	138.6	216.5	13.6	–
Monetary Authorities						*Millions of Dirhams: End of Period*							
Foreign Assets	11	21,804	23,357	25,812	28,408	30,567	31,692	34,512	40,185	50,781	52,479	56,259	55,530
Claims on Central Government	12a	425	–	–	–	–	–	–	–	–	–	–	–
Claims on Official Entities	12bx	–	–	–	–	–	–	–	–	–	–	–	–
Claims on Deposit Money Banks	12e	50	50	50	50	50	50	50	50	50	50	50	50
Claims on Other Financial Insts	12f	–	–	–	–	–	–	–	–	–	–	–	–
Reserve Money	14	13,576	13,124	16,501	18,667	20,188	20,294	20,326	26,530	36,201	38,387	37,652	42,301
of which: Currency Outside DMBs	14a	5,108	5,667	6,031	6,404	6,767	7,366	8,195	10,272	10,017	10,537	11,938	13,785
Quasi-Monetary Deposits	15	–	–	–	–	–	–	–	–	–	–	–	–
Foreign Liabilities	16c	336	313	380	175	75	52	11	403	587	516	284	349
Central Government Deposits	16d	6,166	6,788	7,178	7,930	8,591	9,692	10,692	11,518	12,164	11,722	11,101	11,283
Capital Accounts	17a	1,696	1,695	1,708	1,711	1,704	1,692	1,700	1,755	1,745	1,739	1,753	1,771
Other Items (Net)	17r	505	1,486	96	−25	54	12	1,832	29	134	165	5,519	−125
Deposit Money Banks						*Millions of Dirhams: End of Period*							
Reserves	20	8,466	7,452	10,465	12,258	13,416	12,923	12,127	16,256	25,893	27,849	25,711	28,515
Foreign Assets	21	67,901	66,070	65,114	63,794	70,068	76,152	81,195	80,833	89,810	98,506	112,360	111,727
Claims on Central Government	22a	10,806	12,334	12,558	12,787	10,394	9,105	12,719	15,725	12,581	11,035	15,650	21,407
Claims on Official Entities	22bx	1,421	2,791	5,869	5,840	5,064	5,511	5,236	5,581	5,780	5,258	7,122	12,990
Claims on Private Sector	22d	53,713	57,691	63,836	71,759	78,927	89,925	102,416	110,276	119,828	130,549	145,592	165,143
Claims on Other Financial Insts	22f	2,193	3,014	2,656	2,526	2,330	2,689	3,443	3,075	3,317	3,415	3,692	4,251
Demand Deposits	24	9,873	12,507	13,152	14,420	15,499	18,002	19,589	19,980	24,050	28,927	35,116	44,477
Time and Savings Deposits	25	54,530	50,241	54,635	60,537	64,676	69,437	71,000	79,847	92,902	116,981	126,592	142,338
Foreign Liabilities	26c	26,276	26,511	33,031	28,096	36,906	45,361	53,055	53,537	51,905	29,883	29,882	30,294
Central Government Deposits	26d	11,008	14,830	12,550	15,156	9,962	6,948	10,920	11,671	18,441	27,382	36,972	40,133
Central Govt. Lending Funds	26f	282	243	184	113	95	92	77	62	41	37	28	23
Credit from Monetary Authorities	26g	51	50	51	54	55	50	51	54	52	55	61	101
Capital Accounts	27a	16,838	17,516	19,563	21,616	23,273	25,435	29,883	31,910	34,226	36,769	40,975	44,455
Other Items (Net)	27r	25,642	27,455	27,331	28,971	29,733	30,980	32,560	34,685	35,592	36,578	40,501	42,212
Monetary Survey						*Millions of Dirhams: End of Period*							
Foreign Assets (Net)	31n	63,093	62,603	57,515	63,931	63,654	62,431	62,641	67,078	88,099	120,586	138,453	136,614
Domestic Credit	32	51,400	54,229	65,207	69,841	78,178	90,607	102,221	111,489	110,925	111,182	124,045	152,450
Claims on Central Govt. (Net)	32an	−5,943	−9,284	−7,170	−10,299	−8,159	−7,535	−8,893	−7,464	−18,024	−28,069	−32,423	−30,009
Claims on Official Entities	32bx	1,421	2,791	5,869	5,840	5,064	5,511	5,236	5,581	5,780	5,258	7,122	12,990
Claims on Private Sector	32d	53,729	57,708	63,852	71,774	78,943	89,942	102,435	110,297	119,852	130,578	145,654	165,218
Claims on Other Financial Insts	32f	2,193	3,014	2,656	2,526	2,330	2,689	3,443	3,075	3,317	3,415	3,692	4,251
Money	34	14,981	18,174	19,183	20,824	22,266	25,368	27,784	30,252	34,067	39,464	47,054	58,262
Quasi-Money	35	54,530	50,241	54,635	60,537	64,676	69,437	71,000	79,847	92,902	116,981	126,592	142,338
Other Items (Net)	37r	44,982	48,417	48,904	52,410	54,885	58,233	66,076	68,468	72,055	75,323	88,852	88,463
Money plus Quasi-Money	35l	69,511	68,415	73,818	81,361	86,942	94,805	98,784	110,099	126,969	156,445	173,646	200,600
Production						*Index Numbers (2000=100): Period Averages*							
Crude Petroleum	66aa	99.3	95.3	94.8	95.5	95.8	97.8	96.3	98.9	100.0	94.4	86.9	87.5

2004, International Monetary Fund: *International Financial Statistics Yearbook*

United Arab Emirates 466

		1992	1993	1994	1995	1996	1997	1998	1999	2000	2001	2002	2003
International Transactions		\multicolumn{12}{c}{*Millions of US Dollars*}
Exports............................	70..d	24,756	....	....	....	....	....	....	....	....	....	....	....
Imports, c.i.f.....................	71..d	17,410	19,520	21,024	20,984	22,638	29,952	24,728	33,231	38,139	....	....	....
Government Finance		\multicolumn{12}{c}{*Millions of Dirhams: Year Ending December 31*}
Deficit (-) or Surplus...........	80	1,050	−323	74	−1,249	620	897	−532	57	....	....	....	....
Revenue.........................	81	4,110	2,975	3,316	3,876	5,017	5,609	5,938	6,863	....	....	....	....
Grants Received..............	81z	12,511	12,273	12,731	12,708	12,555	13,403	13,318	13,371	....	....	....	....
Expenditure...................	82	15,571	15,571	15,973	17,833	16,952	18,050	19,170	20,050	....	....	....	....
Lending Minus Repayments..	83	–	–	–	–	–	–	65	618	127	....	....	....
Financing													
Domestic........................	84a	−1,050	323	−73	1,249	−620	−897	532	−57	....	....	....	....
Foreign..........................	85a	–	–	–	–	–	–	–	–	....	....	....	....
National Accounts		\multicolumn{12}{c}{*Billions of Dirhams*}
Househ.Cons.Expend.,incl.NPISHs....	96f	57.9	57.7	60.7	69.3	74.4	86.2	90.7	....	....	....	....	....
Government Consumption Expend...	91f	22.8	23.4	24.2	25.4	26.2	28.1	28.6	....	....	....	....	....
Gross Fixed Capital Formation.........	93e	29.8	36.4	37.5	39.8	40.9	48.8	49.2	....	....	....	....	....
Changes in Inventories.................	93i	1.6	1.9	2.0	2.1	2.3	2.2	2.2	....	....	....	....	....
Exports of Goods and Services.........	90c	92.0	98.4	104.8	109.4	125.8	128.6	115.0	....	....	....	....	....
Imports of Goods and Services (-)....	98c	74.1	87.3	94.6	99.0	105.9	112.7	115.0	....	....	....	....	....
Gross Domestic Product (GDP).........	99b	130.0	130.4	134.6	147.0	163.8	181.2	170.7	....	....	....	....	....
		\multicolumn{12}{c}{*Millions: Midyear Estimates*}
Population.............................	99z	2.23	2.32	2.41	2.50	2.57	2.64	2.70	2.76	2.82	2.88	2.94	2.99

United Kingdom 112

		1992	1993	1994	1995	1996	1997	1998	1999	2000	2001	2002	2003
Exchange Rates		*SDRs per Pound: End of Period*
Market Rate	ac	1.0996	1.0784	1.0703	1.0427	1.1808	1.2257	1.1814	1.1777	1.1453	1.1541	1.1856	1.2010
		US Dollars per Pound: End of Period (ag) Period Average (rh)
Market Rate	ag	1.5120	1.4812	1.5625	1.5500	1.6980	1.6538	1.6635	1.6164	1.4922	1.4504	1.6118	1.7847
Market Rate	rh	1.7655	1.5020	1.5316	1.5785	1.5617	1.6377	1.6564	1.6182	1.5161	1.4400	1.5013	1.6344
		ECUs per Pound through 1998; Euros per Pound Beginning 1999: End of Period (ec) Period Average (ed)
Euro Rate	ec	1.2528	1.3225	1.2705	1.1832	1.3564	1.5011	1.4175	†1.6090	1.6037	1.6458	1.5370	1.4131
Euro Rate	ed	1.3607	1.2822	1.2897	1.2070	1.2304	1.4452	1.4796	†1.5189	1.6456	1.6092	1.5952	1.4481
		Index Numbers (2000=100): Period Averages
Market Rate	ahx	116.5	99.1	101.0	104.1	103.0	108.0	109.3	106.7	100.0	95.0	99.0	107.8
Nominal Effective Exchange Rate	neu	90.1	82.6	83.0	78.9	80.3	93.5	96.6	96.5	100.0	98.4	98.6	93.2
Real Effective Exchange Rate	reu	78.1	71.9	73.5	71.0	73.5	87.6	93.2	94.8	100.0	99.8	101.7	97.7
Fund Position		*Millions of SDRs: End of Period*
Quota	2f.s	7,415	7,415	7,415	7,415	7,415	7,415	7,415	10,739	10,739	10,739	10,739	10,739
SDRs	1b.s	393	210	335	279	239	350	332	374	250	234	267	255
Reserve Position in the Fund	1c.s	1,464	1,354	1,366	1,630	1,689	2,198	3,111	3,847	3,288	4,020	4,565	4,256
of which: Outstg.Fund Borrowing	2c	–	–	–	–	–	–	382	–	–	–	–	–
Total Fund Cred.&Loans Outstg	2tl	–	–	–	–	–	–	–	–	–	–	–	–
International Liquidity		*Billions of US Dollars Unless Otherwise Indicated: End of Period*
Total Reserves minus Gold	1l.d	36.64	36.78	41.01	42.02	39.90	32.32	32.21	†35.87	43.89	37.28	39.36	41.85
SDRs	1b.d	.54	.29	.49	.41	.34	.47	.47	.51	.33	.29	.36	.38
Reserve Position in the Fund	1c.d	2.01	1.86	1.99	2.42	2.43	2.97	4.38	5.28	4.28	5.05	6.21	6.32
Foreign Exchange	1d.d	34.09	34.63	38.53	39.18	37.12	28.88	27.36	†30.08	39.28	31.94	32.79	35.15
Other Liquid Foreign Assets	1e.d	....	....	....	....	....	....	....	7.80	8.68	10.52	14.72	16.37
Gold (Million Fine Troy Ounces)	1ad	18.61	18.45	18.44	18.43	18.43	18.42	23.00	20.55	15.67	11.42	10.09	10.07
Gold (National Valuation)	1and	4.77	4.56	5.31	5.24	5.48	4.81	5.08	†5.96	4.27	3.16	3.46	4.20
Banking Insts: Foreign Assets	7a.d	1,019.46	1,053.63	1,200.67	1,350.86	1,460.35	1,685.14	1,868.89	1,802.87	2,060.13	2,168.36	2,477.20	3,023.92
Foreign Liabs	7b.d	1,115.27	1,129.07	1,274.82	1,429.20	1,533.44	1,748.76	1,893.68	1,871.05	2,159.79	2,306.08	2,684.27	3,297.18
Monetary Authorities		*Billions of Pounds: End of Period*
Foreign Assets	11	28.84	30.22	28.33	31.89	27.40	22.92	†6.52	7.98	4.34	6.24	7.92	9.15
Claims on Central Govt. (Net)	12an	15.90	14.97	28.53	25.07	29.86	27.63	†14.45	20.56	14.30	16.07	16.27	15.87
Claims on Private Sector	12d	–	–	–	–	–	–	6.91	5.86	8.41	5.48	8.20	6.40
Reserve Money	14	23.58	25.19	26.53	28.37	29.36	31.45	†27.37	32.46	32.37	32.58	34.00	36.68
of which: Currency Outside DMBs	14a	17.76	18.87	19.94	21.21	22.10	23.44	†19.20	21.20	23.59	25.42	26.72	28.54
Foreign Liabilities	16c	20.22	25.99	31.86	31.16	28.36	23.60	†2.28	9.62	6.28	4.75	8.00	7.49
Other Items (Net)	17r	.94	–5.80	–1.52	–2.57	–.46	–4.49	†–1.77	–7.68	–11.60	–9.54	–9.61	–12.75
Banking Institutions		*Billions of Pounds: End of Period*
Reserves	20	6.28	6.78	7.04	7.56	7.71	8.26	8.39	11.54	9.75	8.56	8.92	9.73
Foreign Assets	21	†649.72	686.90	741.28	845.36	835.98	1,033.98	1,143.91	1,133.76	1,417.84	1,528.23	1,563.39	1,725.58
Claims on Central Govt. (Net)	22an	†1.55	2.66	11.80	19.72	14.92	10.59	10.74	†8.17	–8.05	–1.94	8.52	1.13
Claims on Official Entities	22bx	4.27	5.68	6.11	5.74	4.81	4.34	3.75	2.70	2.52	2.38	3.61	4.77
Claims on Private Sector	22d	†683.45	706.86	745.43	829.14	911.89	972.88	1,016.75	†1,094.16	1,254.50	1,368.03	1,479.66	1,624.69
Demand,Time,Savings,Fgn.Cur.Dep	25l	†361.77	378.48	407.82	493.35	567.10	716.32	764.84	912.81	1,014.28	1,101.68	1,157.24	1,257.29
Foreign Liabilities	26c	†685.76	711.50	763.74	866.18	843.63	1,050.25	1,120.59	1,128.39	1,411.50	1,547.90	1,621.14	1,797.96
Other Items (Net)	27r	†98.85	113.14	123.87	133.50	146.52	172.05	188.04	209.12	250.78	255.67	285.71	310.65
Banking Survey		*Billions of Pounds: End of Period*
Foreign Assets (Net)	31n	†–27.42	–20.38	–25.98	–20.09	–8.62	–16.94	†27.55	3.72	4.40	–18.18	–57.82	–70.72
Domestic Credit	32	†705.17	730.18	791.87	879.67	961.48	1,015.44	†1,052.60	†1,131.45	1,271.68	1,390.01	1,516.25	1,652.86
Claims on Central Govt. (Net)	32an	†17.45	17.64	40.34	44.79	44.78	38.22	†25.19	†28.73	6.26	14.13	24.79	17.00
Claims on Official Entities	32bx	4.27	5.68	6.11	5.74	4.81	4.34	3.75	2.70	2.52	2.38	3.61	4.77
Claims on Private Sector	32d	†683.45	706.86	745.43	829.14	911.89	972.88	1,023.66	†1,100.02	1,262.91	1,373.51	1,487.85	1,631.09
Money Plus Quasi-Money	35l	†379.52	397.34	427.76	514.56	589.20	739.76	†784.04	934.01	1,037.87	1,127.10	1,183.96	1,285.83
Other Items (Net)	37r	†99.33	106.70	121.90	130.53	145.60	167.31	†296.10	†201.17	238.21	244.73	274.46	296.32
Money (National Definitions)		*Billions of Pounds: End of Period*
M0	59mc	20.58	21.73	23.32	24.54	26.15	27.80	29.35	32.77	34.57	37.32	39.54	42.32
M4	59md	517.88	544.06	567.16	623.39	682.79	721.98	783.24	816.55	884.84	942.43	1,008.68	1,069.18
		Millions of Pounds: Period Change
M0, Seasonally Adjusted	59mcc	582	1,160	1,284	1,231	1,554	1,562	1,574	3,251	1,389	2,605	2,125	2,686
M4, Seasonally Adjusted	59mdc	18,611	24,001	25,860	55,741	59,909	79,983	60,429	33,640	67,219	58,204	68,009	68,163
Interest Rates		*Percent Per Annum*
Money Market Rate	60b	9.37	5.91	4.88	6.08	5.96	6.61	7.21	5.20	5.77	5.08	3.89	3.59
Treasury Bill Rate	60c	8.94	5.21	5.15	6.33	5.78	6.48	6.82	5.04	5.80	4.77	3.86	3.55
Treas. Bill Rate(Bond Equivalent)	60cs	9.21	5.35	5.18	6.40	5.89	6.62	7.23	5.14	5.83	4.79	3.96	3.55
Eurodollar Rate in London	60d	3.77	3.24	4.68	5.97	5.44	5.66	5.50	5.36	6.48	3.73	1.76	1.17
Deposit Rate	60l	7.46	3.97	3.66	4.11	3.05	3.63	4.48	....	....	....	....	....
Lending Rate	60p	9.42	5.92	5.48	6.69	5.96	6.58	7.21	5.33	5.98	5.08	4.00	3.69
Govt. Bond Yield: Short-Term	61a	8.94	6.65	7.83	7.93	7.28	6.98	5.77	5.38	5.79	5.03	4.82	4.24
Long-Term	61	9.12	7.87	8.05	8.26	8.10	7.09	5.45	4.70	4.68	4.78	4.83	4.64

United Kingdom 112

		1992	1993	1994	1995	1996	1997	1998	1999	2000	2001	2002	2003
Prices, Production, Labor			*Index Numbers (2000=100): Period Averages*
Industrial Share Prices (1995=100)..	62	77.9	89.4	96.1	100.0	113.3	128.3	150.5	....	....	....	....	....
Prices: Manufacturing Output..........	63	85.5	88.8	91.1	94.8	97.2	98.1	98.1	98.5	100.0	99.7	99.8	101.3
Consumer Prices................................	64	81.3	82.6	84.7	87.6	89.7	92.5	95.7	97.2	100.0	101.8	103.5	106.5
Harmonized CPI..................................	64h	86.1	88.3	90.0	92.4	94.7	96.4	97.9	99.2	100.0	101.2	102.5	103.9
Wages: Avg. Monthly Earnings........	65..c	73.0	75.2	77.9	80.4	83.2	86.8	91.3	95.7	100.0	104.4	108.1	....
Industrial Production.........................	66	85.4	87.2	91.8	†93.4	94.7	96.0	97.0	98.2	100.0	98.4	96.0	95.8
Employment, Seas. Adj.....................	67..c	90.2	89.6	90.2	91.3	92.8	94.9	96.7	98.3	100.0	101.1	101.4	101.6
			*Number in Thousands: Period Averages*
Labor Force..	67d	....	28,271	....	....	28,552	28,716	28,713	29,194	29,412	29,638	29,934	29,300
Employment..	67e	†25,812	25,511	25,717	26,026	26,323	26,814	27,116	27,442	27,793	28,225	28,415	27,821
Unemployment...................................	67c	2,779	2,919	2,637	2,442	2,300	1,986	1,786	1,724	1,584	1,486	1,520	1,479
Unemployment Rate (%)..................	67r	9.3	9.9	9.0	7.7	7.2	5.4	4.6	4.2	3.6	3.2	3.1	3.1
International Transactions			*Millions of Pounds*
Exports...	70	108,508	120,936	133,030	153,353	167,764	171,595	164,066	165,739	186,171	185,673	184,161	186,175
Imports, c.i.f......................................	71	125,867	137,404	147,564	168,055	184,113	187,135	189,532	196,504	221,027	222,944	223,433	232,868
Imports, f.o.b. (on a BOP basis)........	71.v	120,447	134,858	145,793	164,659	179,578	183,124	....	....	....	....	....	....
			*2000=100*
Volume of Exports............................	72	58.5	60.7	66.7	73.3	78.9	85.4	86.4	89.2	100.0	102.7	100.9	100.4
Volume of Imports...........................	73	57.1	59.3	61.9	65.7	71.9	79.0	85.7	91.5	100.0	105.4	109.8	111.4
Export Prices.....................................	76	91.0	102.2	104.3	107.6	108.3	102.6	97.2	96.3	100.0	100.2	106.4	....
Import Prices.....................................	76.x	91.9	101.2	104.6	111.0	110.8	103.4	97.2	95.9	100.0	99.7	107.0	....
Balance of Payments			*Billions of US Dollars: Minus Sign Indicates Debit*
Current Account, n.i.e.....................	78ald	−23.42	−17.97	−10.23	−14.29	−10.77	−1.56	−6.56	−39.55	−36.22	−32.14	−27.06	−33.46
Goods: Exports f.o.b........................	78aad	189.37	183.31	207.19	242.32	261.25	281.54	271.72	268.88	284.38	273.66	279.86	307.00
Goods: Imports f.o.b........................	78abd	−212.70	−202.96	−224.14	−261.32	−282.48	−301.74	−307.85	−315.90	−334.23	−332.14	−350.07	−384.30
Trade Balance................................	78acd	−23.33	−19.65	−16.95	−19.01	−21.23	−20.20	−36.13	−47.01	−49.85	−58.48	−70.21	−77.30
Services: Credit.................................	78add	64.02	62.14	69.54	78.78	88.73	100.02	109.78	117.48	119.54	118.49	131.13	146.50
Services: Debit..................................	78aed	−54.52	−52.31	−59.77	−65.41	−72.62	−78.04	−87.74	−96.20	−99.13	−99.43	−107.74	−122.62
Balance on Goods & Services.......	78afd	−13.84	−9.82	−7.18	−5.64	−5.12	1.77	−14.09	−25.74	−29.44	−39.43	−46.82	−53.42
Income: Credit...................................	78agd	117.27	109.38	113.97	138.87	144.49	157.74	173.11	162.87	204.72	204.84	188.65	206.36
Income: Debit....................................	78ahd	−116.99	−109.67	−108.86	−135.59	−142.72	−151.40	−151.70	−164.73	−196.78	−188.05	−156.04	−170.36
Balance on Gds, Serv. & Inc...........	78aid	−13.56	−10.11	−2.08	−2.35	−3.34	8.11	7.31	−27.59	−21.50	−22.63	−14.21	−17.41
Current Transfers, n.i.e.: Credit......	78ajd	21.98	18.59	17.71	19.70	31.08	21.28	20.35	21.56	16.38	20.96	18.38	21.53
Current Transfers: Debit..................	78akd	−31.84	−26.45	−25.86	−31.64	−38.51	−30.95	−34.23	−33.51	−31.09	−30.47	−31.22	−37.57
Capital Account, n.i.e......................	78bcd	.75	.46	.05	.84	1.97	1.61	.86	1.25	2.31	1.73	1.32	2.06
Capital Account, n.i.e.: Credit.........	78bad	2.16	1.67	1.93	1.84	3.01	3.06	2.51	2.63	3.94	4.79	3.51	4.47
Capital Account: Debit.....................	78bbd	−1.42	−1.21	−1.88	−.99	−1.04	−1.45	−1.65	−1.38	−1.63	−3.06	−2.18	−2.42
Financial Account, n.i.e...................	78bjd	1.91	22.68	4.71	7.47	5.55	−12.26	3.49	32.93	43.27	29.75	14.72	27.06
Direct Investment Abroad...............	78bdd	−19.70	−27.25	−34.90	−45.31	−34.82	−62.44	−122.06	−201.57	−245.38	−59.66	−34.20	−51.17
Dir. Invest. in Rep. Econ., n.i.e.......	78bed	16.56	16.52	10.73	21.73	27.39	37.38	74.65	89.53	122.16	53.84	29.18	15.53
Portfolio Investment Assets.............	78bfd	−49.27	−133.55	31.47	−61.69	−93.13	−85.09	−53.24	−34.21	−97.09	−124.68	1.17	−56.26
Equity Securities...........................	78bkd	7.43	−11.92	−1.47	−13.15	−16.30	7.04	−4.97	−23.76	−28.36	−63.59	7.40	−31.85
Debt Securities..............................	78bld	−56.70	−121.63	32.95	−48.55	−76.83	−92.13	−48.28	−10.45	−68.73	−61.10	−6.23	−24.42
Portfolio Investment Liab., n.i.e......	78bgd	16.19	43.63	47.01	58.79	67.98	43.53	35.16	183.94	255.65	69.57	76.57	149.32
Equity Securities...........................	78bmd	18.26	26.12	7.35	8.07	9.40	7.85	63.17	116.04	179.17	33.11	4.22	9.41
Debt Securities..............................	78bnd	−2.07	17.52	39.66	50.72	58.58	35.68	−28.02	67.90	76.48	36.47	72.35	139.90
Financial Derivatives Assets............	78bwd	....	....	....	....	....	....	....	....	....	....	....	....
Financial Derivatives Liabilities........	78bxd	2.25	.37	3.67	2.63	1.52	1.90	−5.07	4.41	2.26	12.18	1.35	−8.49
Other Investment Assets.................	78bhd	−60.51	−68.46	−42.45	−74.90	−217.75	−276.00	−29.83	−92.80	−417.55	−254.68	−150.48	−432.30
Monetary Authorities....................	78bod	....	....	....	....	....	....	....	....	....	....	....	....
General Government.....................	78bpd	−.71	−.71	−.69	−.74	−2.97	−.20	.12	−.51	−.40	.01	−1.16	−.92
Banks...	78bqd	−36.40	6.48	−72.66	−34.91	−102.10	−241.01	−31.23	19.86	−289.04	−124.85	−111.14	−258.67
Other Sectors.................................	78brd	−23.40	−74.23	30.90	−39.25	−112.68	−34.79	1.28	−112.14	−128.11	−129.84	−38.19	−172.72
Other Investment Liab., n.i.e..........	78bid	96.39	191.42	−10.81	106.22	254.36	328.47	103.87	83.62	423.22	333.18	91.13	410.45
Monetary Authorities....................	78bsd	–	–	–	–	–	–	–	–	–	–	–	–
General Government.....................	78btd	−.51	.34	.86	.59	−1.06	−1.74	.42	.54	–	.40	−1.01	.83
Banks...	78bud	55.95	59.49	76.62	41.95	111.45	243.12	84.79	20.33	308.95	182.41	141.42	279.05
Other Sectors.................................	78bvd	40.95	131.58	−88.29	63.68	143.97	87.09	18.67	62.75	114.27	150.37	−49.28	130.57
Net Errors and Omissions.................	78cad	14.10	.27	6.98	5.13	2.61	8.31	1.96	4.33	−4.06	−3.79	10.38	1.75
Overall Balance..................................	78cbd	−6.67	5.44	1.50	−.85	−.65	−3.90	−.26	−1.04	5.30	−4.46	−.63	−2.59
Reserves and Related Items..............	79dad	6.67	−5.44	−1.50	.85	.65	3.90	.26	1.04	−5.30	4.46	.63	2.59
Reserve Assets....................................	79dbd	2.43	−1.26	−1.48	.90	.65	3.90	.26	1.04	−5.30	4.46	.63	2.59
Use of Fund Credit and Loans.........	79dcd	–	–	–	–	–	–	–	–	–	–	–	–
Exceptional Financing.......................	79ded	4.24	−4.17	−.02	−.04	–	–	–	–	–	–	–	–

United Kingdom 112

		1992	1993	1994	1995	1996	1997	1998	1999	2000	2001	2002	2003
International Investment Position						*Billions of US Dollars*							
Assets	79aad	1,734.18	2,009.26	2,101.90	2,391.34	2,767.18	3,250.21	3,546.98	3,909.92	4,442.69	4,564.80	4,977.49	6,335.33
Direct Investment Abroad	79abd	229.45	255.64	275.23	315.74	342.31	369.24	498.36	691.91	906.40	875.03	928.62	1,128.02
Portfolio Investment	79acd	494.71	695.83	671.53	773.94	930.84	1,076.56	1,170.85	1,355.01	1,352.04	1,359.63	1,360.51	1,729.52
Equity Securities	79add	209.94	287.40	291.92	336.30	404.67	466.94	505.15	678.65	640.63	586.88	493.17	749.80
Debt Securities	79aed	284.78	408.43	379.62	437.63	526.17	609.62	665.70	676.35	711.41	772.75	867.35	979.72
Financial Derivatives	79ald	–	–	–	–	–	–	–	–	–	–	–	–
Other Investment	79afd	967.24	1,013.74	1,107.20	1,252.52	1,447.63	1,766.63	1,838.92	1,827.14	2,141.27	2,292.89	2,647.31	3,435.30
Monetary Authorities	79agd	–	–	–	–	–	–	–	–	–	–	–	–
General Government	79ahd	12.24	12.69	14.09	14.71	19.33	19.02	19.00	5.74	5.80	5.66	7.25	8.94
Banks	79aid	789.61	768.47	877.15	979.78	1,063.88	1,367.32	1,457.48	1,364.00	1,579.68	1,641.21	1,891.53	2,359.27
Other Sectors	79ajd	165.39	232.57	215.96	258.04	364.42	380.28	362.44	457.40	555.79	646.02	748.53	1,067.10
Reserve Assets	79akd	42.78	44.04	47.93	49.15	46.39	37.79	38.84	35.86	42.97	37.24	41.05	42.48
Liabilities	79lad	1,714.85	1,962.79	2,073.93	2,426.47	2,882.36	3,372.31	3,768.59	4,024.11	4,496.58	4,671.26	5,156.94	6,428.81
Dir. Invest. in Rep. Economy	79lbd	197.81	201.29	203.05	226.63	259.17	287.31	355.40	404.51	463.13	527.39	592.57	673.58
Portfolio Investment	79lcd	373.56	454.58	499.95	629.75	815.00	964.64	1,152.49	1,339.79	1,489.58	1,390.22	1,441.02	1,862.89
Equity Securities	79ldd	140.33	198.06	197.10	267.66	383.89	499.23	668.90	824.10	901.93	767.90	660.48	874.08
Debt Securities	79led	233.23	256.52	302.85	362.09	431.10	465.41	483.59	515.69	587.65	622.31	780.54	988.81
Financial Derivatives	79lld	–	–	–	–	–	–	–	–	–	–	–	–
Other Investment	79lfd	1,143.48	1,306.92	1,370.94	1,570.09	1,808.20	2,120.37	2,260.70	2,279.81	2,543.87	2,753.66	3,123.35	3,892.34
Monetary Authorities	79lgd	–	–	–	–	–	–	–	–	–	–	–	–
General Government	79lhd	9.54	5.60	6.70	7.31	6.68	4.78	5.39	5.81	5.90	6.13	5.57	7.00
Banks	79lid	948.64	982.44	1,114.40	1,242.42	1,327.38	1,577.98	1,729.58	1,669.18	1,888.52	1,992.89	2,321.90	2,866.53
Other Sectors	79ljd	185.30	318.88	249.84	320.36	474.13	537.60	525.73	604.82	649.45	754.64	795.88	1,018.81
Government Finance						*Millions of Pounds: Year Ending December 31*							
Deficit (-) or Surplus	80	−29,218	−46,447	−39,868	−38,922	−27,440	−16,136	4,853	295	....	....	....	....
Revenue	81	218,613	217,062	236,083	253,918	270,360	288,223	317,543	325,102	....	....	....	....
Grants Received	81z	1,907	2,558	1,752	1,233	2,424	1,739	1,384	3,176	....	....	....	....
Expenditure	82	261,542	272,600	284,051	295,172	307,310	306,579	313,836	324,393	....	....	....	....
Lending Minus Repayments	83	−11,804	−6,533	−6,348	−1,099	−7,086	−481	238	3,590	....	....	....	....
Financing													
Domestic Borrowing	84a	20,397	32,798	34,931	38,275	20,446	18,064	−2,908	2,984	....	....	....	....
Foreign Borrowing	85a	8,821	13,649	4,937	647	6,994	−1,928	−1,945	−3,279	....	....	....	....
Use of Cash Balances	87	....	....	....	....	....	....	....	....	....	....	....	....
Adj. to Total Financing	84x	875	....	....	....	....	....	....	....	....	....	....	....
						Millions of Pounds Year Beginning April 1							
Debt: Domestic	88a	169,660	201,928	243,394	277,476	314,021	341,171	....	....	....	....	....	....
Foreign	89a	34,678	47,998	58,262	56,234	58,691	60,213	....	....	....	....	....	....
National Accounts						*Billions of Pounds*							
Househ.Cons.Expend.,incl.NPISHs	96f.c	390.56	415.95	437.68	459.85	492.65	523.32	557.99	592.51	626.54	659.93	692.26	721.08
Government Consumption Expend	91f.c	129.20	131.53	136.26	141.03	146.19	148.18	153.96	165.64	177.09	189.72	208.87	229.89
Gross Fixed Capital Formation	93e.c	100.60	101.00	108.43	117.33	126.13	133.75	150.97	154.88	161.21	167.09	170.19	177.57
Changes in Inventories	93i.c	−1.94	.33	3.71	4.51	1.77	4.62	5.03	6.06	5.27	3.00	1.58	1.81
Exports of Goods and Services	90c.c	144.09	163.64	180.51	203.51	223.97	233.03	230.33	238.79	267.01	271.71	273.27	276.01
Imports of Goods and Services (-)	98c.c	151.66	170.13	185.26	207.05	227.42	231.95	238.84	254.71	286.56	299.33	304.72	308.41
Gross Domestic Product (GDP)	99b.c	610.85	642.33	681.33	719.18	763.29	810.94	859.44	903.17	950.56	994.31	1,044.15	1,099.90
Net Primary Income from Abroad	98.nc	−4.13	−4.70	.29	−2.83	−2.68	1.30	9.12	.28	5.53	9.36	19.15	20.90
Gross National Income (GNI)	99a.c	606.73	637.63	681.61	716.35	760.61	812.25	868.56	903.45	956.09	1,003.67	1,063.29	1,120.80
Net Current Transf.from Abroad	98t.c	−1.28	−.73	−2.31	−2.65	−1.90	−3.21	−4.79	−4.44	−6.25	−3.43	−6.76	−8.22
Gross Nat'l Disposable Inc.(GNDI)	99i.c	605.45	636.89	679.30	713.70	757.63	809.16	863.72	894.67	946.01	999.35	1,057.02	1,112.14
Gross Saving	99s.c	85.69	89.41	105.37	112.82	118.67	137.04	151.48	136.52	142.39	149.70	155.90	161.16
Consumption of Fixed Capital	99cfc	77.12	83.52	85.16	86.96	89.64	93.53	96.07	98.36	103.70	108.65	115.79	120.91
GDP Volume 2000 Ref., Chained	99b.r	741.86	759.14	792.72	815.23	837.16	864.71	891.68	916.64	951.27	971.57	988.34	1,009.38
GDP Volume (2000=100)	99bvr	78.0	79.8	83.3	85.7	88.0	90.9	93.7	96.4	100.0	102.1	103.9	106.1
GDP Deflator (2000=100)	99bir	82.4	84.7	86.0	88.3	91.2	93.9	96.5	98.6	100.0	102.4	105.7	109.0
						Millions: Midyear Estimates							
Population	99z	57.12	57.31	57.50	57.70	57.90	58.10	58.30	58.49	58.69	58.88	59.07	59.25

United States 111

Exchange Rates		1992	1993	1994	1995	1996	1997	1998	1999	2000	2001	2002	2003
		End of Period (sa and sc) Period Averages (sb and sd) End of Period (sa and sc) Period Averages (sb and sd)											
US Dollar/SDR Rate.........aa=.....	sa	1.3750	1.3736	1.4599	1.4865	1.4380	1.3493	1.4080	1.3725	1.3029	1.2567	1.3595	1.4860
US Dollar/SDR Rate..................	sb	1.4084	1.3963	1.4317	1.5170	1.4518	1.3760	1.3565	1.3673	1.3188	1.2730	1.2948	1.3988
SDR/US Dollar Rate........ac=.....	sc	.7273	.7280	.6850	.6727	.6954	.7412	.7102	.7286	.7675	.7957	.7356	.6730
SDR/US Dollar Rate..................	sd	.7100	.7162	.6985	.6592	.6888	.7267	.7372	.7314	.7583	.7855	.7723	.7152
		Dollars per ECU through 1998; Dollars per Euro Beginning 1999: End of Period (ea) Period Average (eb)											
Euro Rate...............................	ag	1.2109	1.1200	1.2300	1.3142	1.2530	1.1042	1.1668	1.0046	.9305	.8813	1.0487	1.2630
Euro Rate...............................	rh	1.2968	1.1723	1.1886	1.3081	1.2680	1.1341	1.1200	1.0668	.9240	.8956	.9444	1.1308
		Index Numbers (2000=100): Period Averages											
Nominal Effective Exchange Rate.....	neu	86.9	89.5	87.9	82.6	86.9	94.0	98.6	96.1	100.0	106.6	105.5	93.2
Real Effective Exchange Rate...........	reu	88.3	90.0	87.9	81.0	83.9	88.7	94.4	93.0	100.0	109.5	108.8	96.6
Fund Position		*Billions of SDRs: End of Period*											
Quota..................................	2f.s	26.53	26.53	26.53	26.53	26.53	26.53	26.53	37.15	37.15	37.15	37.15	37.15
SDRs....................................	1b.s	6.18	6.57	6.88	7.42	7.17	7.43	7.53	7.54	8.09	8.58	8.95	8.50
Reserve Position in the Fund............	1c.s	8.55	8.59	8.24	9.85	10.73	13.39	17.12	13.09	11.38	14.22	16.17	15.16
of which: Outstg.Fund Borrowing...	2c	–	–	–	–	–	–	.98	–	–	–	–	–
International Liquidity		*Billions of US Dollars Unless Otherwise Indicated: End of Period*											
Total Reserves minus Gold...............	1l.d	60.27	62.35	63.28	74.78	64.04	58.91	70.71	60.50	56.60	57.63	67.96	74.89
SDRs....................................	1b.d	8.50	9.02	10.04	11.04	10.31	10.03	10.60	10.35	10.54	10.78	12.17	12.64
Reserve Position in the Fund..........	1c.d	11.76	11.80	12.03	14.65	15.43	18.07	24.11	17.97	14.82	17.87	21.98	22.53
Foreign Exchange.....................	1d.d	40.01	41.53	41.22	49.10	38.29	30.81	36.00	32.18	31.24	28.98	33.82	39.72
Gold (Million Fine Troy Ounces).........	1ad	261.84	261.79	261.73	261.70	261.66	261.64	261.61	261.67	261.61	262.00	262.00	261.55
Gold (National Valuation)................	1and	11.06	11.05	11.05	11.05	11.05	11.05	11.05	11.05	11.05	11.05	11.04	11.04
Monetary Authorities: Other Liab.....	4..d	.21	.39	.25	.39	.17	.46	.17	.07	.22	.06	.14	.16
Deposit Money Banks: Assets...........	7a.d	562.24	552.33	546.14	606.46	665.94	791.26	813.16	860.50	961.55	1,126.71	1,257.17	1,297.96
Liabilities....................	7b.d	755.41	828.19	941.32	1,011.91	1,028.68	1,207.31	1,265.47	1,311.60	1,411.34	1,523.67	1,829.34	2,116.78
Nonbank Financial Insts.: Assets......	7e.d	–	–	–	–	–	–	–	–	–	–	–	–
Liabilities...................	7f.d	74.61	107.88	125.08	146.22	175.13	209.37	227.82	300.17	445.24	553.80	669.38	646.12
Monetary Authorities		*Billions of US Dollars: End of Period*											
Foreign Assets............................	11	72.0	73.4	74.3	85.8	75.1	70.0	81.8	71.5	67.6	68.7	79.0	85.9
Claims on Central Government........	12a	312.4	350.3	383.5	397.7	410.2	447.5	463.5	494.2	530.7	569.0	648.3	681.8
Claims on Banking Institutions........	12e	.7	.1	.2	.1	.1	2.0	–	.2	.1	–	–	.1
Claims on Nonbank Financial Insts...	12g	5.4	4.6	3.6	2.6	2.2	.7	.3	.2	.1	–	–	–
Federal Reserve Float.....................	13a	3.3	.9	–.7	.1	4.3	.7	1.6	–.2	.9	–	.4	–.3
Reserve Money............................	14	366.8	400.2	434.6	453.8	475.2	513.2	543.8	652.4	612.7	660.8	710.1	747.3
of which: Currency Outside Banks..	14a	298.5	327.5	363.5	381.9	406.1	437.6	473.2	567.7	578.5	599.4	644.2	680.1
Foreign Liabilities.........................	16c	.2	.4	.3	.4	.2	.5	.2	.1	.2	.1	.1	.2
Central Government Deposits.........	16d	28.0	36.3	29.2	37.7	30.0	22.6	26.0	48.1	24.9	25.7	26.8	30.9
Other Items (Net)........................	17r	–1.4	–7.5	–3.1	–5.5	–13.5	–15.4	–22.7	–134.6	–38.3	–48.8	–9.2	–10.9
Banking Institutions													
Commercial Banks		*Billions of US Dollars: End of Period*											
Reserves................................	20	60.9	64.2	67.3	67.5	67.5	74.1	66.5	86.1	61.8	62.5	67.4	67.6
Foreign Assets...........................	21	125.4	78.9	38.9	34.1	102.0	151.0	237.1	295.9	374.2	481.9	497.5	593.8
Claims on Central Government.........	22a	294.4	322.2	290.4	278.7	261.8	270.1	214.1	228.9	184.5	162.7	205.8	203.3
Claims on State and Local Govts......	22b	97.5	99.2	97.6	93.4	94.2	96.7	104.8	110.8	114.1	120.2	121.7	132.5
Claims on Private Sector................	22d	2,245.5	2,331.1	2,512.2	2,755.6	2,926.9	3,179.2	3,462.4	3,704.3	4,127.4	4,297.7	4,506.9	4,883.9
Claims on Nonbank Financial Insts....	22g	378.5	423.2	428.7	467.5	495.7	571.9	663.2	699.6	721.8	777.4	917.9	999.5
Demand Deposits........................	24	714.3	788.4	756.7	710.8	676.3	656.4	622.9	626.4	540.9	628.8	571.4	502.8
Time and Savings Deposits..............	25	1,389.2	1,377.2	1,376.2	1,490.1	1,613.2	1,761.5	1,945.2	2,017.1	2,228.7	2,478.1	2,747.8	2,978.3
Money Market Instruments..............	26aa	339.2	308.9	331.7	390.9	488.2	585.8	643.4	754.1	845.6	890.1	873.2	889.5
Bonds...................................	26ab	127.6	134.9	142.6	161.1	168.9	192.6	220.2	240.6	273.2	310.2	332.2	379.1
Foreign Liabilities.......................	26c	247.2	256.3	311.3	305.3	327.5	381.2	449.4	528.2	612.3	657.3	685.0	797.7
Central Government Deposits.........	26d	30.6	42.6	23.8	19.0	28.7	27.8	13.2	49.6	16.4	47.5	31.1	–
Credit from Monetary Authorities.....	26g	7.2	1.9	–	.3	8.7	3.5	3.3	–	1.9	–	.9	–
Liab. to Nonbank Financial Insts.......	26j	12.5	21.2	30.5	36.7	39.0	58.1	104.9	145.6	172.4	196.6	226.9	235.5
Other Items (Net).......................	27r	334.3	387.3	462.3	582.3	597.6	675.1	745.6	764.1	892.5	693.8	848.7	1,097.7
Credit Unions and Savings Insts		*Billions of US Dollars: End of Period*											
Reserves................................	20..t	52.7	54.0	41.2	43.8	41.7	43.0	54.2	66.5	64.4	85.2	93.1	98.7
Claims on Central Government.........	22a.t	53.9	50.8	49.2	36.7	34.8	30.2	23.3	19.8	17.0	18.8	17.0	21.2
Claims on State and Local Govts......	22b.t	2.1	2.1	2.0	2.0	2.1	2.1	2.5	3.0	3.2	4.5	5.5	6.3
Claims on Private Sector................	22d.t	918.0	908.9	926.0	941.6	995.8	1,018.4	1,085.5	1,176.8	1,271.0	1,315.2	1,363.9	1,496.5
Claims on Nonbank Financial Insts....	22g.t	171.7	183.6	200.8	210.3	206.7	206.3	202.0	208.4	201.4	242.0	273.5	314.2
Demand Deposits........................	24..t	109.0	115.1	111.8	128.0	154.9	186.1	228.6	267.7	317.0	371.2	430.6	495.7
Time and Savings Deposits..............	25..t	904.3	845.9	807.0	789.7	763.8	712.7	681.4	654.5	631.6	649.5	650.9	650.0
Money Market Instruments..............	26aat	101.0	106.1	122.8	133.6	141.5	154.2	183.5	216.5	233.8	275.5	313.4	376.6
Bonds...................................	26abt	5.5	3.9	3.1	3.1	2.7	2.8	2.6	2.7	6.3	3.6	3.4	5.1
Central Government Deposits..........	26d.t	74.0	87.3	100.0	97.4	121.9	138.0	180.1	243.7	260.0	268.5	250.8	261.8
Other Items (Net).......................	27r.t	4.6	41.2	74.5	82.6	96.4	106.3	91.4	89.4	108.2	97.4	103.7	147.5

United States 111

		1992	1993	1994	1995	1996	1997	1998	1999	2000	2001	2002	2003
Banking Institutions (Cont.)													
Money Market Funds						*Billions of US Dollars: End of Period*							
Foreign Assets	21..m	20.3	10.0	15.7	19.7	23.1	23.2	30.6	42.9	91.1	124.2	114.1	74.2
Claims on Central Government	22a.m	78.4	79.4	66.1	70.0	90.2	86.2	103.6	103.8	90.4	135.7	140.2	130.2
Claims on State and Local Govts	22b.m	96.0	105.6	113.4	127.7	144.5	167.0	193.0	210.4	244.7	281.0	282.8	297.3
Claims on Private Sector	22d.m	179.9	176.2	202.3	257.0	297.8	372.4	495.4	642.7	770.5	801.9	764.6	644.7
Claims on Banking Institutions	22e.m	32.0	30.7	28.9	48.9	81.6	112.8	126.0	158.1	144.6	224.0	203.4	155.0
Claims on Nonbank Financial Insts.	22g.m	54.3	67.8	77.2	90.8	101.8	96.3	173.8	190.9	185.2	318.4	324.1	326.2
Time Deposits	25..m	539.5	559.6	600.1	741.3	886.7	1,042.5	1,329.7	1,578.8	1,812.1	2,240.7	2,223.9	2,016.0
Other Items (Net)	27r.m	−78.7	−90.1	−96.6	−127.2	−147.6	−184.7	−207.2	−230.0	−285.5	−355.6	−394.8	−388.4
Banking Survey						*Billions of US Dollars: End of Period*							
Foreign Assets (Net)	31n	−29.8	−94.4	−182.6	−166.1	−127.5	−137.6	−100.2	−118.0	−79.5	17.4	5.5	−43.9
Domestic Credit	32	4,755.4	4,938.7	5,200.0	5,577.3	5,884.2	6,355.7	6,968.3	7,452.5	8,160.9	8,702.7	9,263.3	9,844.8
Claims on Central Govt. (Net)	32an	606.6	636.5	636.3	628.9	616.4	645.5	585.2	505.4	521.4	544.5	702.6	743.7
Claims on State and Local Govts.	32b	195.6	206.9	213.0	223.1	240.8	265.7	300.3	324.2	362.0	405.6	410.0	436.1
Claims on Private Sector	32d	3,343.4	3,416.1	3,640.5	3,954.2	4,220.5	4,570.0	5,043.4	5,523.8	6,168.9	6,414.8	6,635.4	7,025.1
Claims on Nonbank Financial Insts.	32g	609.9	679.2	710.3	771.2	806.4	874.5	1,039.4	1,099.1	1,108.5	1,337.8	1,515.4	1,639.9
Money	34	1,121.9	1,231.0	1,232.0	1,220.7	1,237.3	1,280.2	1,324.7	1,461.8	1,436.4	1,599.4	1,646.2	1,678.6
Quasi-Money	35	2,832.9	2,782.8	2,783.4	3,021.1	3,263.7	3,516.7	3,956.3	4,250.4	4,672.5	5,368.3	5,622.6	5,644.3
Money Market Instruments	36aa	440.2	414.9	454.5	524.5	629.7	740.1	826.9	970.6	1,079.4	1,165.6	1,186.6	1,266.1
Bonds	36ab	133.1	138.8	145.7	164.2	171.6	195.5	222.8	243.3	279.4	313.8	335.6	384.2
Liab. to Nonbank Financial Insts.	36j	12.5	21.2	30.5	36.7	39.0	58.1	104.9	145.6	172.4	196.6	226.9	235.5
Other Items (Net)	37r	184.9	255.6	371.3	444.1	415.4	427.6	432.5	262.8	441.2	76.3	250.8	592.1
Money plus Quasi-Money	35l	3,954.8	4,013.8	4,015.4	4,241.8	4,501.0	4,796.9	5,281.0	5,712.2	6,108.9	6,967.8	7,268.9	7,322.9
Nonbank Financial Institutions													
Other Financial Institutions						*Billions of US Dollars: End of Period*							
Foreign Assets	41	–	–	–	–	–	–	–	–	–	–	–	–
Claims on Central Government	42a	207.2	203.5	182.5	258.7	168.7	187.1	208.0	130.5	184.5	175.0	153.1	205.5
Claims on State and Local Govts.	42b	318.6	391.7	393.5	394.9	392.8	388.2	415.2	432.0	417.4	457.5	498.4	518.9
Claims on Private Sector	42d	3,250.2	3,715.7	4,019.3	4,706.7	5,565.5	6,628.5	7,810.4	9,487.0	9,941.2	10,160.9	10,027.4	12,195.8
Claims on Banking Institutions	42e	140.0	153.3	187.3	196.8	235.7	253.6	348.9	430.6	452.5	607.7	623.8	600.9
Credit Market Instruments	46aa	1,183.6	1,402.7	1,586.1	1,818.8	2,321.3	2,958.5	3,626.8	4,466.7	4,552.5	4,313.0	3,797.5	4,743.5
Bonds	46ab	695.6	812.9	924.3	1,094.4	1,247.5	1,362.8	1,623.2	1,789.4	1,946.6	2,174.6	2,485.9	2,883.5
Foreign Liabilities	46c	74.6	107.9	125.1	146.2	175.1	209.4	227.8	300.2	445.2	553.8	669.4	646.1
Credit from Monetary Authorities	46g	5.4	4.6	3.6	2.6	2.2	.7	.3	.2	.1	–	–	–
Credit from Banking Institutions	46h	1,340.5	1,428.1	1,450.2	1,613.5	1,729.2	1,884.7	2,128.9	2,321.7	2,291.0	2,404.8	2,457.6	2,679.6
Liabs. to Insur. Cos. & Pen. Funds	46j	546.5	637.8	762.2	929.4	1,023.2	1,223.7	1,330.3	1,659.5	1,700.2	1,617.9	1,564.2	1,823.4
Other Items (Net)	47r	69.7	70.3	−68.9	−47.9	−135.9	−182.5	−154.9	−57.7	59.9	336.9	328.1	745.0
Insurance Companies & Pension Funds						*Billions of US Dollars: End of Period*							
Claims on Central Government	42a.s	522.3	576.9	608.1	612.1	593.8	573.9	508.9	489.3	453.0	415.6	456.7	465.8
Claims on State and Local Govts.	42b.s	146.1	162.2	167.7	174.8	189.3	209.8	229.7	222.1	204.8	193.9	203.3	226.6
Claims on Private Sector	42d.s	3,166.3	3,542.6	3,652.6	4,330.2	4,894.3	5,759.9	6,549.1	7,198.3	7,132.5	6,798.5	6,216.9	7,432.7
Claims on Banking Institutions	42e.s	170.4	179.5	173.8	190.4	245.5	300.4	348.5	353.1	369.7	434.5	434.6	434.9
Claims on Nonbank Financial Insts.	42g.s	546.5	637.8	762.2	929.4	1,023.2	1,223.7	1,330.3	1,659.5	1,700.2	1,617.9	1,564.2	1,823.4
Insurance and Pension Reserves	47a.s	4,572.3	5,069.8	5,373.8	6,207.6	6,905.3	7,956.1	8,895.2	9,844.4	9,850.4	9,497.4	8,861.9	10,215.7
Other Items (Net)	47r.s	−20.7	29.3	−9.4	29.3	40.8	111.5	71.3	78.0	10.2	−36.9	13.9	167.6
Financial Survey						*Billions of US Dollars: End of Period*							
Foreign Assets (Net)	51n	−104.4	−202.3	−307.7	−312.3	−302.6	−347.0	−328.0	−418.1	−524.8	−536.4	−663.9	−690.0
Domestic Credit	52	11,751.4	12,847.4	13,513.5	15,283.5	16,882.0	19,228.5	21,650.1	24,312.5	25,385.8	25,566.4	25,303.7	29,250.1
Claims on Central Govt. (Net)	52an	1,331.2	1,412.2	1,426.9	1,499.7	1,378.9	1,406.4	1,302.1	1,125.1	1,158.9	1,135.2	1,312.4	1,415.0
Claims on State and Local Govts.	52b	660.3	760.8	774.3	792.7	822.9	863.7	945.2	978.3	984.2	1,057.1	1,111.7	1,181.6
Claims on Private Sector	52d	9,759.8	10,674.5	11,312.4	12,991.0	14,680.2	16,958.4	19,402.8	22,209.1	23,242.6	23,374.1	22,879.6	26,653.5
Liquid Liabilities	55l	3,954.8	4,013.8	4,015.4	4,241.8	4,501.0	4,796.9	5,281.0	5,712.2	6,108.9	6,967.8	7,268.9	7,322.9
Credit Market Instruments	56aa	1,623.9	1,817.7	2,040.6	2,343.3	2,950.9	3,698.5	4,453.7	5,437.3	5,631.9	5,478.6	4,984.1	6,009.6
Bonds	56ab	828.8	951.7	1,070.1	1,258.5	1,419.1	1,558.3	1,846.0	2,032.7	2,226.0	2,488.4	2,821.5	3,267.8
Other Items (Net)	57r	5,239.6	5,862.1	6,079.8	7,127.5	7,708.3	8,827.9	9,741.4	10,712.1	10,894.2	10,095.1	9,565.3	11,959.8
Money Stock, Liquid Assets, and Debt Measures (National Definitions)						*Billions of US Dollars: End of Period*							
M1	59ma	1,045.6	1,153.3	1,174.2	1,152.1	1,104.5	1,096.9	1,120.2	1,147.9	1,112.1	1,205.2	1,242.6	1,318.5
M1, Seasonally Adjusted	59mac	1,025.0	1,129.9	1,150.5	1,127.0	1,079.3	1,072.5	1,096.1	1,124.0	1,087.9	1,179.4	1,217.2	1,292.8
M2	59mb	3,449.2	3,504.9	3,519.2	3,664.8	3,838.0	4,054.1	4,407.8	4,677.5	4,967.7	5,487.2	5,833.8	6,102.9
M2, Seasonally Adjusted	59mbc	3,432.8	3,484.7	3,497.7	3,641.4	3,817.1	4,032.2	4,384.5	4,649.4	4,933.3	5,449.1	5,795.3	6,062.7
M3	59mc	4,234.9	4,300.8	4,384.4	4,653.4	5,001.5	5,481.6	6,079.4	6,588.0	7,166.1	8,091.7	8,616.8	8,895.5
M3, Seasonally Adjusted	59mcc	4,219.7	4,281.8	4,364.8	4,630.9	4,978.8	5,453.5	6,044.6	6,544.8	7,113.0	8,025.1	8,552.5	8,837.0
L	59md	5,108.3	5,201.9	5,344.6	5,732.8	6,111.6	6,636.7	….	….	….	….	….	….
L, Seasonally Adjusted	59mdc	5,081.4	5,173.3	5,315.8	5,702.3	6,083.6	6,611.3	….	….	….	….	….	….
Debt	59me	11,827.0	12,409.8	12,990.0	13,694.5	14,430.5	15,221.5	16,264.9	17,352.9	18,270.1	19,363.8	….	….
Debt, Seasonally Adjusted	59mec	11,823.7	12,407.6	12,988.5	13,694.9	14,433.5	15,227.3	16,277.3	17,360.8	18,278.3	19,375.5	….	….

2004, International Monetary Fund : *International Financial Statistics Yearbook*

United States 111

		1992	1993	1994	1995	1996	1997	1998	1999	2000	2001	2002	2003
Treasury Securities by Holders						*Billions of US Dollars: End of Period*							
Total...	59t	3,061.6	3,309.9	3,465.6	3,608.5	3,755.1	3,778.3	3,723.7	3,652.7	3,357.8	3,352.7	3,609.8	4,008.2
Nonresidents...........................	59ta	520.3	594.6	632.6	820.2	1,047.3	1,165.7	1,185.0	1,080.4	1,026.1	1,039.7	1,214.2	1,482.7
Residents................................	59tb	2,541.2	2,715.3	2,833.0	2,788.4	2,707.8	2,612.6	2,538.7	2,572.2	2,331.6	2,313.0	2,395.5	2,525.5
Monetary Authorities.............	59tba	295.0	332.0	364.5	378.2	390.9	430.7	452.1	478.0	511.7	551.7	629.4	666.7
Commercial Banks.................	59tbb	294.4	322.2	290.4	278.7	261.8	270.1	214.1	228.9	184.5	162.7	205.8	133.8
Govt. Sponsored Enterprises....	59tbc	58.7	51.6	51.9	58.0	18.8	25.9	25.2	30.9	41.2	31.8	7.2	7.4
Other Financial Institutions......	59tbd	863.7	907.9	904.8	976.6	915.8	878.2	842.3	731.7	721.8	729.8	793.0	850.9
Nonfinancial Sectors..............	59tbe	1,029.4	1,101.6	1,221.3	1,096.9	1,120.5	1,007.7	1,005.1	1,102.7	872.4	837.1	760.1	866.7
Interest Rates						*Percent Per Annum*							
Discount Rate (End of Period).........	60	3.00	3.00	4.75	5.25	5.00	5.00	4.50	5.00	6.00	1.25	.75	† 2.00
Federal Funds Rate........................	60b	3.52	3.02	4.20	5.84	5.30	5.46	5.35	4.97	6.24	3.89	1.67	1.13
Commercial Paper Rate..................	60bc	3.75	3.22	4.66	5.93	5.41	5.57	5.34	5.18	6.31	3.61	1.69	1.11
Treasury Bill Rate...........................	60c	3.46	3.02	4.27	5.51	5.02	5.07	4.82	4.66	5.84	3.45	1.61	1.01
Treas. Bill Rate(Bond Equivalent)......	60cs	3.51	3.06	4.35	5.65	5.14	5.20	4.90	4.77	6.00	3.48	1.63	1.02
Certificates of Deposit Rate.............	60lc	3.68	3.17	4.63	5.92	5.39	5.62	5.47	5.33	6.46	3.69	1.73	1.15
Lending Rate (Prime Rate)..............	60p	6.25	6.00	7.14	8.83	8.27	8.44	8.35	7.99	9.23	6.92	4.68	4.12
Govt. Bond Yield: Med.-Term...........	61a	5.31	4.44	6.26	6.26	5.99	6.10	5.14	5.49	6.22	4.08	3.10	2.11
Long-Term.............................	61	7.01	5.87	7.08	6.58	6.44	6.35	5.26	5.64	6.03	5.02	4.61	4.02
Prices, Production, Labor						*Index Numbers (2000=100): Period Averages*							
Industrial Share Prices...................	62	28.0	29.5	30.8	36.7	45.3	58.4	72.8	92.1	100.0	78.9	65.3	62.9
Producer Prices............................	63	88.3	89.6	90.8	94.0	96.2	96.1	93.8	94.5	100.0	101.1	98.8	104.1
Industrial Goods.......................	63a	87.1	88.3	89.5	93.1	94.5	94.8	92.6	93.9	100.0	100.7	98.3	103.2
Finished Goods........................	63b	89.3	90.4	91.0	92.7	95.1	95.5	94.7	96.4	100.0	102.0	100.6	103.8
Consumer Goods..................	63ba	88.0	89.0	89.2	90.9	93.7	94.2	93.3	95.5	100.0	102.4	100.8	105.1
Capital Equipment.................	63bb	93.0	94.6	96.6	98.5	99.6	99.6	99.1	99.1	100.0	100.6	100.2	100.5
Consumer Prices...........................	64	81.5	83.9	86.1	88.5	91.1	93.2	94.7	96.7	100.0	102.8	104.5	106.8
Wages: Hourly Earnings(Mfg)...........	65ey	79.6	81.7	84.0	86.2	89.0	91.7	93.9	96.7	100.0	103.1	106.8	109.9
Industrial Production......................	66	67.8	70.0	73.8	77.3	80.7	86.6	91.8	95.8	100.0	96.6	96.1	96.3
Crude Petroleum Production............	66aa	123.2	117.6	114.4	112.7	111.1	110.8	107.4	101.0	100.0	99.6	98.7	98.6
Nonagr.Employment, Seas.Adj.........	67..c	82.5	84.1	86.7	89.0	90.8	93.2	95.5	97.9	100.0	100.0	98.9	98.6
						Number in Thousands: Period Averages							
Labor Force..................................	67d	† 127,211	128,040	† 131,057	132,304	133,945	† 136,297	137,673	139,368	142,583	143,734	144,863	146,510
Employment..................................	67e	† 117,598	119,306	† 123,060	124,900	126,709	† 129,558	131,464	133,488	136,891	136,933	136,485	137,736
Unemployment..............................	67c	9,613	8,734	† 7,997	7,404	7,236	† 6,739	6,210	5,880	5,692	6,801	8,378	8,774
Unemployment Rate (%).................	67r	7.5	6.9	† 6.1	5.6	5.4	† 5.0	4.5	4.2	4.0	4.7	5.8	6.0
International Transactions						*Billions of US Dollars*							
Exports, f.a.s................................	70	448.16	464.77	512.63	584.74	625.07	688.70	682.14	702.10	781.13	730.80	693.86	723.81
Imports, c.i.f.................................	71	553.92	603.44	689.22	770.85	822.02	899.02	944.35	1,059.44	1,259.30	1,179.18	1,202.43	1,305.41
Imports, f.o.b................................	71.v	532.67	580.51	663.83	743.54	795.29	870.57	911.90	1,024.62	1,218.02	1,141.00	1,163.56	1,259.48
						2000=100							
Volume of Exports..........................	72	59.6	61.4	66.3	72.0	76.6	85.5	87.6	91.3	100.0	94.4	90.5	92.9
Volume of Imports.........................	73	46.4	50.6	56.9	60.9	64.3	72.1	80.5	89.6	100.0	97.1	101.5	107.0
Export Prices................................	76	† 96.3	96.9	98.9	103.9	104.5	103.1	99.7	98.4	100.0	99.2	98.2	99.7
Import Prices................................	76.x	† 94.9	94.6	96.2	100.6	101.6	99.1	93.1	93.9	100.0	96.5	94.1	96.9

United States 111

		1992	1993	1994	1995	1996	1997	1998	1999	2000	2001	2002	2003
Balance of Payments						*Billions of US Dollars: Minus Sign Indicates Debit*							
Current Account, n.i.e.	78ald	−48.00	−81.96	−118.06	−109.47	−120.17	−135.98	−209.53	−296.85	−413.44	−385.70	−473.94	−530.66
Goods: Exports f.o.b.	78aad	441.40	458.84	504.91	577.04	614.01	680.33	672.38	686.27	774.63	721.84	685.34	716.41
Goods: Imports f.o.b.	78abd	−536.53	−589.39	−668.69	−749.37	−803.11	−876.49	−917.11	−1,029.99	−1,224.42	−1,145.93	−1,164.75	−1,260.71
Trade Balance	78acd	−95.13	−130.55	−163.78	−172.33	−189.10	−196.16	−244.74	−343.72	−449.78	−424.09	−479.41	−544.30
Services: Credit	78add	175.47	184.01	198.35	217.35	237.62	254.32	261.13	280.17	296.35	284.81	290.60	304.09
Services: Debit	78aed	−119.44	−123.66	−132.96	−141.29	−152.43	−166.35	−181.25	−199.73	−224.91	−223.42	−232.93	−256.30
Balance on Goods & Services	78afd	−39.09	−70.20	−98.40	−96.27	−103.91	−108.19	−164.86	−263.28	−378.34	−362.69	−421.74	−496.51
Income: Credit	78agd	133.76	136.08	166.52	210.26	226.13	256.82	261.32	293.22	350.45	286.69	266.80	294.39
Income: Debit	78ahd	−109.52	−110.74	−149.38	−189.36	−203.81	−244.20	−257.55	−280.04	−329.86	−263.12	−259.63	−261.10
Balance on Gds, Serv. & Inc.		−14.86	−44.86	−81.26	−75.37	−81.59	−95.57	−161.09	−250.09	−357.76	−339.12	−414.56	−463.23
Current Transfers, n.i.e.: Credit	78ajd	6.54	6.67	7.99	8.63	10.40	9.89	9.64	8.85	10.78	8.51	11.83	14.80
Current Transfers: Debit	78akd	−39.68	−43.77	−44.78	−42.73	−48.98	−50.30	−58.08	−55.61	−66.46	−55.09	−71.21	−82.24
Capital Account, n.i.e.	78bcd	−.56	−1.30	−1.72	−.93	−.65	−1.04	−.74	−4.84	−.81	−1.08	−1.26	−3.08
Capital Account, n.i.e.: Credit	78bad	.85	.81	.82	1.03	.89	.83	.93	1.08	1.07	1.03	1.13	1.12
Capital Account: Debit	78bbd	−1.41	−2.11	−2.55	−1.96	−1.55	−1.87	−1.67	−5.92	−1.87	−2.11	−2.39	−4.20
Financial Account, n.i.e.	78bjd	92.34	82.91	121.72	96.02	131.05	222.30	82.51	227.82	477.39	421.00	573.91	544.24
Direct Investment Abroad	78bdd	−48.27	−83.95	−80.18	−98.78	−91.88	−104.82	−142.64	−224.93	−159.21	−142.35	−134.84	−173.80
Dir. Invest. in Rep. Econ., n.i.e.	78bed	19.81	51.38	46.13	57.80	86.52	105.59	179.03	289.44	321.27	167.02	72.41	39.89
Portfolio Investment Assets	78bfd	−49.17	−146.25	−63.19	−122.39	−149.32	−116.85	−124.20	−116.24	−121.91	−84.64	15.89	−72.34
Equity Securities	78bkd	−32.40	−63.37	−48.29	−65.51	−82.71	−57.29	−101.36	−114.31	−106.71	−109.12	−17.61	−100.43
Debt Securities	78bld	−16.77	−82.88	−14.90	−56.89	−66.61	−59.57	−22.84	−1.93	−15.19	24.48	33.50	28.09
Portfolio Investment Liab., n.i.e.	78bgd	71.98	111.00	139.41	210.35	332.78	333.11	187.56	285.60	436.57	428.34	427.88	544.49
Equity Securities	78bmd	−5.61	20.94	.89	16.52	11.06	67.03	41.96	112.29	193.60	121.46	54.22	36.89
Debt Securities	78bnd	77.59	90.06	138.52	193.83	321.72	266.08	145.61	173.31	242.97	306.88	373.66	507.60
Financial Derivatives Assets	78bwd	....	....	....	....	....	....	....	−	....	....	....	....
Financial Derivatives Liabilities	78bxd	....	....	....	....	....	....	....	−	....	....	....	....
Other Investment Assets	78bhd	19.13	31.02	−40.92	−121.38	−178.87	−262.82	−74.20	−171.22	−288.39	−134.86	−75.39	−38.80
Monetary Authorities	78bod	−	−	−	−	−	−	−	−	−	−	−	−
General Government	78bpd	−1.67	−.35	−.39	−.98	−.99	.07	−.42	2.75	−.94	−.49	.35	.54
Banks	78bqd	21.18	30.62	−4.20	−75.11	−91.56	−141.12	−35.57	−76.26	−148.66	−125.86	−30.31	−10.41
Other Sectors	78brd	−.38	.76	−36.33	−45.29	−86.33	−121.77	−38.20	−97.70	−138.79	−8.52	−45.43	−28.93
Other Investment Liab., n.i.e.	78bid	78.87	119.71	120.47	170.43	131.82	268.09	56.96	165.17	289.05	187.50	267.95	244.80
Monetary Authorities	78bsd	30.31	68.00	9.59	46.72	56.88	−18.85	6.88	24.59	−2.52	35.29	72.19	36.28
General Government	78btd	2.83	.56	2.77	.90	.73	−2.70	−3.25	−.98	−.39	−4.78	2.66	1.95
Banks	78bud	32.79	39.90	108.00	64.18	22.18	171.31	30.27	67.20	122.72	88.40	117.63	125.06
Other Sectors	78bvd	12.94	11.24	.10	58.63	52.03	118.33	23.07	74.37	169.24	68.58	75.47	81.50
Net Errors and Omissions	78cad	−47.72	1.72	−7.28	24.12	−16.89	−84.27	134.49	65.14	−62.84	−29.29	−95.02	−12.02
Overall Balance	78cbd	−3.93	1.38	−5.35	9.75	−6.67	1.01	6.73	−8.73	.29	4.93	3.69	−1.53
Reserves and Related Items	79dad	3.93	−1.38	5.35	−9.75	6.67	−1.01	−6.73	8.73	−.29	−4.93	−3.69	1.53
Reserve Assets	79dbd	3.93	−1.38	5.35	−9.75	6.67	−1.01	−6.73	8.73	−.29	−4.93	−3.69	1.53
Use of Fund Credit and Loans	79dcd	−	−	−	−	−	−	−	−	−	−	−	−
Exceptional Financing	79ded	−	−	−	−	−	−	−	−	−	−	−	−
International Investment Position						*Billions of US Dollars*							
Assets	79aad	2,466.46	3,091.40	3,315.13	3,964.56	4,650.84	5,379.13	6,174.52	7,390.46	7,393.64	6,898.71	6,613.32	7,863.97
Direct Investment Abroad	79abd	798.63	1,061.30	1,114.58	1,363.79	1,608.34	1,879.29	2,279.60	2,839.64	2,694.01	2,314.93	2,039.78	2,730.29
Portfolio Investment	79acd	515.04	853.53	937.15	1,203.93	1,487.55	1,751.18	2,053.00	2,525.34	2,385.35	2,114.73	1,846.88	2,474.37
Equity Securities	79add	314.23	543.86	626.76	790.62	1,006.14	1,207.79	1,474.98	2,003.72	1,852.84	1,612.67	1,345.12	1,972.24
Debt Securities	79aed	200.82	309.67	310.39	413.31	481.41	543.40	578.01	521.63	532.51	502.06	501.76	502.13
Financial Derivatives	79ald	−	−	−	−	−	−	−	−	−	−	−	−
Other Investment	79afd	1,005.35	1,011.66	1,100.01	1,220.78	1,394.21	1,613.82	1,695.92	1,889.03	2,185.88	2,339.08	2,568.06	2,475.73
Monetary Authorities	79agd	−	−	−	−	−	−	−	−	−	−	−	−
General Government	79ahd	83.02	83.38	83.91	85.06	86.12	86.20	86.77	84.23	85.17	85.65	85.31	84.77
Banks	79aid	668.02	686.25	693.12	768.15	857.51	982.10	1,020.83	1,100.29	1,264.15	1,414.12	1,574.73	1,776.28
Other Sectors	79ajd	254.30	242.03	322.98	367.57	450.58	545.52	588.32	704.52	836.56	839.30	908.02	614.67
Reserve Assets	79akd	147.44	164.91	163.39	176.06	160.74	134.84	146.01	136.45	128.40	129.96	158.60	183.58
Liabilities	79lad	2,918.79	3,235.71	3,450.39	4,270.39	5,010.86	6,201.86	7,249.90	8,437.12	8,982.20	9,206.87	9,166.73	10,514.96
Dir. Invest. in Rep. Economy	79lbd	696.18	768.42	757.85	1,005.73	1,229.12	1,637.41	2,179.04	2,798.19	2,783.24	2,560.29	2,025.35	2,435.54
Portfolio Investment	79lcd	1,158.68	1,335.54	1,413.54	1,848.75	2,284.15	2,767.48	3,198.67	3,583.08	3,862.63	4,121.72	4,295.25	5,200.57
Equity Securities	79ldd	328.99	373.52	397.72	549.51	672.40	952.89	1,250.34	1,611.53	1,643.21	1,572.68	1,260.84	1,632.03
Debt Securities	79led	829.69	962.02	1,015.82	1,299.24	1,611.75	1,814.59	1,948.33	1,971.54	2,219.43	2,549.04	3,034.41	3,568.55
Financial Derivatives	79lld	−	−	−	−	−	−	−	−	−	−	−	−
Other Investment	79lfd	1,063.94	1,131.75	1,278.99	1,415.92	1,497.59	1,796.97	1,872.19	2,055.85	2,336.33	2,524.86	2,846.13	2,878.85
Monetary Authorities	79lgd	114.80	133.73	157.19	169.48	186.85	211.63	228.25	250.66	255.97	279.76	301.27	317.91
General Government	79lhd	20.80	22.11	23.68	23.57	22.59	21.71	18.39	21.14	19.32	17.01	17.14	16.58
Banks	79lid	707.67	746.87	858.31	922.44	941.35	1,104.22	1,139.88	1,206.00	1,322.14	1,429.78	1,663.09	2,077.82
Other Sectors	79ljd	220.67	229.04	239.82	300.42	346.81	459.41	485.68	578.05	738.90	798.31	864.63	466.54

2004, International Monetary Fund: *International Financial Statistics Yearbook*

United States 111

		1992	1993	1994	1995	1996	1997	1998	1999	2000	2001	2002	2003
Government Finance		\multicolumn{12}{c}{*Billions of US Dollars: Year Ending December 31*}
Deficit (-) or Surplus	80	−326.8	−226.5	−184.6	−146.2	−110.8	−2.4	54.4	156.7	254.6	92.4	−230.5	−396.3
Total Revenue and Grants	81y	1,101.4	1,175.2	1,277.5	1,367.2	1,474.7	1,619.3	1,747.7	1,858.3	2,042.7	1,995.3	1,814.4	1,795.7
Revenue	81	....	....	1,277.5	1,367.2	1,474.7	1,619.3	1,747.7	1,858.3	2,042.7	1,995.3	1,814.4	1,795.7
Grants	81z	....	....	−	−	−	−	−	−	−	−	−	−
Exp. & Lending Minus Repay	82z	1,428.3	1,401.8	1,462.1	1,513.4	1,585.4	1,621.8	1,693.3	1,701.6	1,788.1	1,902.8	2,044.9	2,191.9
Expenditure	82	....	....	....	....	....	....	....	....	....	....	....	....
Lending Minus Repayments	83	....	....	....	....	....	....	....	....	....	....	....	....
Total Financing	80h	326.8	226.5	184.6	146.2	110.8	2.4	−54.4	−156.7	−254.6	−92.4	230.5	396.3
Total Net Borrowing	84	308.8	248.2	161.3	151.1	119.9	4.3	−62.2	−92.2	−316.7	−43.1	235.8	381.2
Net Domestic	84a	....	....	....	....	....	....	....	....	....	....	....	....
Net Foreign	85a	....	....	....	....	....	....	....	....	....	....	....	....
Use of Cash Balances	87	18.1	−21.7	23.3	−4.9	−9.1	−1.9	7.9	−64.4	62.1	−49.3	−5.2	15.0
Total Debt by Residence	88	3,149.8	3,403.8	3,551.7	3,698.7	3,842.1	3,866.5	3,805.7	3,711.6	3,413.2	3,394.4	3,647.9	4,042.9
Domestic	88a	2,573.1	2,753.5	2,884.4	2,863.5	2,740.0	2,624.9	2,527.0	2,442.9	2,379.0	2,343.2	2,401.1	2,504.9
Foreign	89a	576.7	650.3	667.3	835.2	1,102.1	1,241.6	1,278.7	1,268.7	1,034.2	1,051.2	1,246.8	1,538.0
National Accounts		\multicolumn{12}{c}{*Billions of US Dollars*}
Househ.Cons.Expend.,incl.NPISHs	96f.c	4,235.3	4,477.9	4,743.3	4,975.8	5,256.8	5,547.4	5,879.5	6,282.5	6,739.4	7,055.1	7,376.1	7,760.9
Government Consumption Expend	91f.c	1,047.9	1,072.2	1,104.1	1,136.5	1,171.1	1,216.6	1,256.0	1,334.0	1,417.1	1,501.7	1,609.2	1,717.1
Gross Fixed Capital Formation	93e.c	1,071.6	1,151.6	1,254.6	1,345.6	1,454.4	1,570.0	1,700.7	1,845.6	1,983.5	1,970.1	1,915.5	2,025.4
Changes in Inventories	93i.c	16.3	20.8	63.8	31.1	30.8	72.0	70.8	66.9	56.5	−31.7	11.2	−1.2
Exports of Goods and Services	90c.c	635.3	655.8	720.9	812.2	868.6	955.4	955.9	991.3	1,096.3	1,032.8	1,005.0	1,046.2
Imports of Goods and Services (-)	98c.c	668.6	720.9	814.5	903.6	964.8	1,056.9	1,115.9	1,251.8	1,475.8	1,399.9	1,429.9	1,544.3
Gross Domestic Product (GDP)	99b.c	6,337.8	6,657.4	7,072.2	7,397.7	7,816.8	8,304.3	8,747.0	9,268.4	9,817.0	10,128.0	10,487.0	11,004.1
Net Primary Income from Abroad	98.nc	29.7	32.0	26.2	35.8	35.0	33.0	21.4	33.8	39.0	43.7	27.1	55.2
Gross National Income (GNI)	99a.c	6,264.7	6,549.8	6,955.9	7,332.3	7,758.2	8,266.6	8,783.0	9,337.9	9,983.1	10,261.3	10,529.4	11,033.6
Net Current Transf. from Abroad	98t.c	33.4	37.3	37.8	35.4	39.1	41.6	48.8	47.2	56.1	47.0	59.9	68.0
Gross Saving	99s.c	948.2	962.5	1,070.7	1,184.6	1,291.2	1,461.1	1,598.7	1,674.3	1,770.5	1,657.6	1,484.3	1,487.7
Consumption of Fixed Capital	99cfc	751.9	776.4	833.7	878.4	918.1	974.5	1,030.2	1,101.3	1,187.8	1,281.5	1,304.0	1,354.0
GDP Volume 2000 Ref., Chained	99b.r	7,336.6	7,532.7	7,835.5	8,031.7	8,328.9	8,703.5	9,066.9	9,470.4	9,817.0	9,890.7	10,074.8	10,381.3
GDP Volume (2000=100)	99bvr	74.7	76.7	79.8	81.8	84.8	88.7	92.4	96.5	100.0	100.8	102.6	105.7
GDP Deflator (2000=100)	99bir	86.4	88.4	90.3	92.1	93.9	95.4	96.5	97.9	100.0	102.4	104.1	106.0
		\multicolumn{12}{c}{*Millions: Midyear Estimates*}
Population	99z	261.19	264.07	266.99	269.95	272.92	275.93	278.95	281.98	285.00	288.02	291.04	294.04

Uruguay 298

		1992	1993	1994	1995	1996	1997	1998	1999	2000	2001	2002	2003
Exchange Rates		\multicolumn{12}{c}{*Pesos per SDR: End of Period*}
Market Rate	aa	4.7850	†6.0656	8.1766	10.5704	12.5289	13.5465	15.2307	15.9417	16.3059	18.5594	36.9789	43.5389
		\multicolumn{12}{c}{*Pesos per US Dollar: End of Period (ae) Period Average (rf)*}
Market Rate	ae	3.4800	†4.4160	5.6010	7.1110	8.7130	10.0400	10.8170	11.6150	12.5150	14.7680	27.2000	29.3000
Market Rate	rf	3.0248	†3.9411	5.0439	6.3490	7.9718	9.4418	10.4719	11.3393	12.0996	13.3191	21.2570	28.2087
		\multicolumn{12}{c}{*Index Numbers (2000=100): Period Averages*}
Market Rate	ahx	403.6	308.3	241.3	191.3	152.2	128.3	115.5	106.7	100.0	90.9	61.1	42.9
Nominal Effective Exchange Rate	nec	106.6	134.3	175.1	146.3	120.9	109.0	102.1	101.5	100.0	97.4	71.3	47.3
Real Effective Exchange Rate	rec	67.2	79.9	86.3	89.2	90.4	95.0	96.8	99.7	100.0	98.8	78.3	60.3
Fund Position		\multicolumn{12}{c}{*Millions of SDRs: End of Period*}
Quota	2f.s	225	225	225	225	225	225	225	307	307	307	307	307
SDRs	1b.s	–	–	–	2	3	–	1	1	–	1	4	3
Reserve Position in the Fund	1c.s	15	15	15	15	15	15	15	36	36	36	–	–
Total Fund Cred.&Loans Outstg.	2tl	38	28	20	14	6	–	114	114	114	114	1,319	1,626
International Liquidity		\multicolumn{12}{c}{*Millions of US Dollars Unless Otherwise Indicated: End of Period*}
Total Reserves minus Gold	1l.d	509	758	969	1,150	1,251	1,556	2,073	2,081	2,479	3,097	769	2,083
SDRs	1b.d	–	–	–	4	4	–	1	1	–	2	6	4
Reserve Position in the Fund	1c.d	21	21	22	23	22	21	22	49	46	45	–	–
Foreign Exchange	1d.d	488	737	946	1,124	1,225	1,536	2,051	2,031	2,432	3,050	763	2,079
Gold (Million Fine Troy Ounces)	1ad	2.028	1.700	1.704	1.715	1.736	1.760	1.783	1.800	1.081	.008	.008	.008
Gold (National Valuation)	1and	541	454	497	525	672	651	517	518	295	2	3	3
Monetary Authorities: Other Assets	3..d	215	217	234	238	255	266	270	251	253	257	780	463
Monetary Authorities: Other Liab.	4..d	1,107	1,062	1,030	976	941	911	884	730	673	489	476	217
Banking Institutions: Assets	7a.d	3,797	3,790	3,499	3,479	4,179	4,758	5,015	5,803	6,252	7,271	4,138	3,725
Liabilities	7b.d	3,337	3,393	3,335	3,364	3,966	4,697	5,315	6,076	6,815	7,969	3,586	2,512
Nonbank Financial Insts.:Assets	7e.d	....	....	91	207	242	200	191	86	1,160	1,294	461	773
Nonbank Financial Insts.:Liabs.	7f.d	....	....	77	185	219	180	162	63	868	993	304	706
Monetary Authorities		\multicolumn{12}{c}{*Millions of Pesos: End of Period*}
Foreign Assets	11	4,524.9	6,452.5	9,847.2	14,662.8	18,854.9	23,437.0	†30,926.9	33,135.3	37,944.3	49,565.5	42,221.0	74,714.4
Claims on Central Government	12a	4,035.7	6,080.3	8,305.9	11,543.8	13,985.3	16,586.3	†22,043.9	25,926.4	33,860.7	8,160.5	72,765.2	75,217.1
Claims on Local Government	12b	.1	.1	.2	.2	.3	.3	†.3	.3	.3	.3	.7	.8
Claims on Nonfin.Pub.Enterprises	12c	2,537.6	2,567.7	3,226.9	3,984.7	4,694.5	5,334.5	†5,253.2	4,998.1	4,701.6	4,677.3	7,439.7	5,656.2
Claims on Private Sector	12d	61.7	145.0	130.2	150.5	114.9	163.0	†433.6	458.2	484.3	284.3	2,163.3	2,066.7
Claims on Banking Institutions	12e	2,371.8	3,272.0	4,070.7	5,385.7	6,769.6	8,927.5	†10,258.1	10,803.3	10,447.5	11,928.4	33,030.2	6,187.5
Reserve Money	14	5,988.8	8,542.6	11,314.0	14,760.9	19,563.8	24,455.0	†27,602.3	33,455.0	36,591.5	46,166.3	46,478.7	74,668.0
of which: Currency Outside Banks	14a	1,426.0	2,312.8	3,313.8	4,327.1	5,269.3	6,498.2	†7,084.0	7,639.0	7,284.0	7,095.1	7,673.4	9,440.5
Time, Savings,& Fgn.Currency Dep.	15	408.1	716.3	997.0	2,083.1	3,926.9	4,872.6	†6,298.9	7,247.2	5,131.6	5,844.2	7,727.1	7,866.5
Liabs. of Central Bank: Securities	16ac	192.4	–	–	1,341.9	533.3	803.2	†1,367.8	1,882.5	519.8	531.9	914.0	7,116.4
Foreign Liabilities	16c	370.3	372.4	471.0	398.8	294.6	25.3	†1,755.9	1,849.2	1,879.2	2,121.3	48,767.8	70,789.9
Long-Term Foreign Liabilities	16cl	3,663.5	4,486.1	5,465.0	6,690.6	7,980.5	9,121.7	†9,549.2	8,454.2	8,409.8	7,220.8	12,934.5	6,351.4
Central Government Deposits	16d	4,290.0	5,691.3	8,342.1	11,089.0	14,208.1	18,471.3	†26,237.6	26,300.6	38,629.3	16,040.6	38,167.3	8,263.0
Capital Accounts	17a	–3,489.8	–2,149.5	–2,490.5	682.8	363.4	–779.7	†508.4	596.1	–865.1	–334.2	2,100.1	–8,176.5
Other Items (Net)	17r	2,108.6	858.5	1,482.5	–1,319.3	–2,451.2	–2,520.7	†–4,404.1	–4,463.3	–2,857.4	–2,974.6	530.4	–3,036.2
Banking Institutions		\multicolumn{12}{c}{*Millions of Pesos: End of Period*}
Reserves	20	4,872.9	6,439.4	7,651.2	9,419.5	12,931.7	15,780.5	†17,771.7	21,389.5	23,776.6	37,789.7	39,548.8	63,422.8
Claims on Mon.Author.:Securities	20c	181.9	–	–	593.2	520.5	397.3	†911.4	1,735.1	477.7	531.9	806.4	172.3
Foreign Assets	21	13,215.2	16,737.6	19,599.6	24,741.8	36,409.7	47,774.0	†54,248.8	67,402.9	78,243.2	107,379.3	112,543.6	109,142.7
Claims on Central Government	22a	1,580.0	2,055.2	3,917.9	3,944.5	4,980.3	7,368.4	†9,239.7	6,207.5	7,677.1	11,414.2	29,319.8	27,677.1
Claims on Local Government	22b	57.7	71.2	115.9	194.0	248.9	302.6	†3,706.8	3,994.3	1,871.6	2,088.1	2,097.4	2,495.7
Claims on Nonfin.Pub.Enterprises	22c	96.6	161.4	284.7	535.1	712.6	820.2	†949.2	1,238.3	1,548.5	2,275.2	5,250.4	4,413.8
Claims on Private Sector	22d	9,801.4	14,555.5	20,896.4	32,241.8	43,728.0	58,466.5	†107,287.7	118,105.4	124,044.4	133,635.6	171,868.8	138,471.2
Demand Deposits	24	975.0	1,466.1	2,012.5	2,658.7	3,474.1	3,738.0	†7,314.2	7,216.6	7,053.7	6,641.0	6,556.6	9,706.8
Time, Savings,& Fgn.Currency Dep.	25	14,211.4	18,885.7	26,920.9	37,093.6	50,401.5	65,891.6	†82,057.8	94,100.1	105,053.1	128,569.9	167,909.3	186,530.5
Money Market Instruments	26aa	–	–	–	–	–	–	†3,531.2	4,640.4	4,905.9	5,890.4	10,211.1	11,540.9
Foreign Liabilities	26c	3,881.4	5,568.6	6,192.1	9,126.9	13,369.9	19,378.2	†53,736.6	66,428.5	78,801.3	108,925.1	85,166.1	64,258.3
Long-Term Foreign Liabilities	26cl	7,731.9	9,417.0	12,485.0	14,792.0	21,184.1	27,778.2	†3,752.4	4,148.4	6,491.9	8,767.1	12,382.6	9,337.0
Central Government Deposits	26d	1,014.0	1,093.2	1,570.0	1,844.5	2,655.0	4,522.6	†7,537.6	4,803.5	3,860.6	4,600.4	9,249.9	23,660.5
Credit from Monetary Authorities	26g	660.0	995.7	818.2	1,042.4	1,475.9	2,072.7	†10,135.3	10,162.5	10,602.5	11,941.2	35,542.2	5,669.6
Liab. to Nonbank Financial Insts.	26j	–	–	–	–	–	85.7	†215.4	183.1	227.6	144.9	–	–
Capital Accounts	27a	1,613.5	2,414.0	3,249.6	5,630.9	8,053.5	10,033.8	†32,788.5	36,132.5	31,353.1	26,216.6	–7,089.4	10,176.7
Other Items (Net)	27r	–281.5	180.0	–782.6	–518.9	–1,078.1	–2,591.3	†–6,953.9	–7,742.6	–10,710.5	–6,582.7	41,506.7	24,915.3

2004, International Monetary Fund : *International Financial Statistics Yearbook*

Uruguay 298

		1992	1993	1994	1995	1996	1997	1998	1999	2000	2001	2002	2003
Banking Survey						*Millions of Pesos: End of Period*							
Foreign Assets (Net)...............	31n	13,488.5	17,249.2	22,783.6	29,878.9	41,600.1	51,807.4	†29,683.2	32,260.5	35,507.0	45,898.4	20,830.7	48,809.0
Domestic Credit......................	32	12,866.8	18,851.9	26,966.0	39,661.2	51,601.6	66,048.1	†115,139.1	129,824.4	131,698.5	141,896.5	243,488.0	224,074.9
Claims on Central Govt. (Net)......	32an	311.7	1,351.0	2,311.7	2,554.8	2,102.4	960.9	†−2,491.7	1,029.9	−952.2	−1,066.3	54,667.8	70,970.6
Claims on Local Government......	32b	57.8	71.3	116.1	194.2	249.2	302.9	†3,707.1	3,994.6	1,871.9	2,088.4	2,098.1	2,496.5
Claims on Nonfin.Pub.Enterprises...	32c	2,634.2	2,729.1	3,511.7	4,519.8	5,407.1	6,154.8	†6,202.4	6,236.4	6,250.1	6,952.4	12,690.1	10,069.9
Claims on Private Sector..........	32d	9,863.1	14,700.5	21,026.6	32,392.3	43,842.9	58,629.5	†107,721.3	118,563.5	124,528.7	133,919.9	174,032.0	140,537.9
Money..................................	34	2,410.2	3,804.6	5,341.1	7,066.3	8,819.1	10,294.6	†14,420.3	14,873.9	14,355.8	13,755.2	14,278.4	19,177.4
Quasi-Money.........................	35	14,619.5	19,602.1	27,918.0	39,176.7	54,328.4	70,764.3	†88,356.7	101,347.2	110,184.6	134,414.2	175,636.4	194,397.0
Money Market Instruments........	36aa	–	–	–	–	–	–	†3,531.2	4,640.4	4,905.9	5,890.4	10,211.1	11,540.9
Liabs. of Central Bank: Securities...	36ac	10.5	–	–	748.7	8.8	405.9	†456.4	147.4	42.0	–	107.7	6,944.2
Long-Term Foreign Liabilities.....	36cl	11,395.4	13,903.1	17,950.0	21,482.6	29,164.5	36,899.9	†13,301.6	12,602.7	14,901.7	15,987.9	25,317.1	15,688.4
Liabs. to Nonbank Financial Insts.....	36j	–	–	–	–	–	85.7	†215.4	183.1	227.6	144.9	–	–
Capital Accounts....................	37a	−1,876.3	264.5	759.1	6,313.7	8,416.9	9,254.1	†33,296.9	36,728.6	30,488.0	25,882.5	−4,989.3	2,000.3
Other Items (Net)....................	37r	−204.0	−1,473.2	−2,218.5	−5,247.7	−7,535.9	−9,848.9	†−8,756.2	−8,438.4	−7,900.1	−8,280.1	43,757.3	23,135.8
Money plus Quasi-Money.........	35l	17,029.7	23,406.6	33,259.1	46,243.0	63,147.4	81,058.8	†102,777.1	116,221.1	124,540.4	148,169.3	189,914.8	213,574.4
Nonbank Financial Institutions						*Millions of Pesos: End of Period*							
Reserves...............................	40	....	....	3.1	5.6	7.0	4.5	5.2	9.3	72.7	101.4	99.7	80.6
Claims on Mon.Author.:Securities...	40c	....	....	2.5	2.1	2.7	2.7	2.4	2.1	22.6	22.7	4.4	3.6
Foreign Assets......................	41	....	....	510.0	1,469.4	2,109.7	2,011.3	2,066.0	994.3	14,513.2	19,110.9	12,531.9	22,635.1
Claims on Central Government.......	42a	....	....	2.6	3.7	4.3	4.3	4.2	2.1	20.4	15.8	13.7	23.1
Claims on Private Sector..........	42d	....	....	.2	1.3	1.8	2.0	.4	.1	3.4	7.0	25.8	18.0
Claims on Banking Institutions...	42e	....	....	2.5	5.2	3.0	3.4	2.8	2.4	17.1	34.8	9.9	25.4
Foreign Currency Deposits.......	45	....	....	.1	.2	.4	.2	.2	.1	1.7	1.6	1.1	.8
Foreign Liabilities...................	46c	....	....	421.8	1,285.6	1,846.7	1,747.1	1,681.9	589.8	10,281.7	11,947.4	4,351.2	18,306.4
Long-term Foreign Liabilities.....	46cl	....	....	10.0	29.6	63.4	60.2	71.6	146.8	582.8	2,710.4	3,913.7	2,367.6
Central Government Deposits.....	46d	....	....	.5	.6	.8	.4	.5	.3	3.8	5.1	14.1	9.6
Capital Accounts....................	47a	....	....	101.3	189.2	272.2	336.0	389.9	288.1	4,296.5	5,090.3	4,973.8	3,331.2
Other Items (Net)....................	47r	....	....	−12.9	−17.8	−55.1	−115.7	−63.0	−14.7	−517.1	−462.2	−568.3	−1,229.7
Money (National Definitions)						*Millions of Pesos: End of Period*							
Reserve Money......................	19ma	2,054.7	2,892.2	4,593.9	5,927.9	7,649.8	9,570.5	12,910.0	9,879.3	9,503.6	8,288.0	11,969.4	14,308.1
M1.......................................	59ma	2,453.0	4,399.1	6,226.1	8,273.3	10,712.5	12,577.3	14,500.8	15,000.7	14,237.2	13,729.4	14,206.0	19,444.6
M2.......................................	59mb	4,942.1	7,598.3	10,031.1	14,351.6	17,990.9	21,392.5	24,763.1	26,094.9	26,832.6	27,217.0	24,410.2	30,294.5
Interest Rates						*Percent Per Annum*							
Discount Rate (End of Period)....	60	162.40	164.30	182.30	178.70	160.30	95.50	73.70	66.39	57.26	71.66	316.01	....
Discount Rate (Fgn.Cur.)(End Per)...	60..f	14.40	14.30	17.40	17.60	17.50	17.30	15.30	15.68	16.73	14.06	16.96	....
Money Market Rate................	60b			39.82	36.81	28.47	23.43	20.48	13.96	14.82	22.10	89.37	....
Treasury Bill Rate...................	60c	....	....	44.60	39.40	29.20	23.18	....	....	....	....	....	....
Treasury Bill Rate (Fgn.Currency)...	60c.f	....	....	4.91	6.11	5.36	5.18	....	....	....	....	....	....
Savings Rate.........................	60k	24.52	17.18	16.12	15.98	15.00	11.50	7.15	5.40	4.25	4.00	....	....
Savings Rate (Fgn.Currency).....	60k.f	1.89	1.65	1.54	1.80	1.73	1.71	1.51	1.13	1.11	.76	.56	....
Deposit Rate.........................	60l	54.47	39.38	36.98	38.24	28.13	19.61	15.09	14.25	12.11	14.32	....	....
Deposit Rate (Fgn.Currency).....	60l.f	3.42	3.09	3.45	4.56	4.84	4.85	4.92	4.99	5.19	4.27	....	....
Lending Rate.........................	60p	117.77	97.33	95.08	99.10	91.52	71.55	57.93	53.28	49.05	51.71	126.07	....
Lending Rate (Fgn.Currency).....	60p.f	11.80	11.17	11.68	13.83	13.14	12.67	12.42	12.63	13.49	12.47	....	....
Prices, Production, Labor						*Index Numbers (2000=100): Period Averages*							
Wholesale Prices...................	63	24.10	32.14	43.13	59.39	74.25	86.40	94.43	93.60	100.00	106.58	140.61	195.32
Consumer Prices...................	64	16.7	25.8	37.3	53.0	68.0	81.5	90.3	95.5	100	104.4	118.9	142.0
Manufacturing Production.......	66ey	107.9	98.2	102.1	99.3	103.3	109.3	111.9	104.5	100.0	94.1	....	....
						Number in Thousands: Period Averages							
Labor Force..........................	67d	1,259	1,261	1,307	1,343	....	....	1,239		1,235	1,270		
Employment..........................	67e	1,146	1,156	1,188	1,206	....	....	1,104	1,082	1,068	1,076	1,038	1,032
Unemployment......................	67c	113	105	120	138	....	....	124	138	168	193	211	209
Unemployment Rate (%)..........	67r	9.0	8.3	9.2	10.2	....	....	10.1	11.3	13.6	15.3	17.0	16.9
International Transactions						*Millions of US Dollars*							
Exports................................	70..d	1,702.5	1,645.3	1,913.4	2,106.0	2,397.2	2,725.7	2,770.7	2,237.1	2,294.7	2,060.4	1,861.0	2,198.0
Imports, c.i.f.........................	71..d	2,045.1	2,325.7	2,786.1	2,866.9	3,322.8	3,726.8	3,810.5	3,356.8	3,465.8	3,060.8	1,964.3	2,190.4

Uruguay 298

		1992	1993	1994	1995	1996	1997	1998	1999	2000	2001	2002	2003
Balance of Payments		\multicolumn{12}{c}{*Millions of US Dollars: Minus Sign Indicates Debit*}
Current Account, n.i.e.	78ald	−8.8	−243.8	−438.3	−212.5	−233.4	−287.4	−475.5	−507.6	−566.2	−487.7	322.2	52.1
Goods: Exports f.o.b.	78aad	1,801.4	1,731.6	1,917.6	2,147.6	2,448.5	2,793.1	2,829.3	2,290.6	2,383.8	2,139.4	1,922.1	2,273.3
Goods: Imports f.o.b.	78abd	−1,923.2	−2,118.3	−2,623.6	−2,710.6	−3,135.4	−3,497.5	−3,601.4	−3,187.2	−3,311.1	−2,914.7	−1,873.8	−2,091.5
Trade Balance	78acd	−121.8	−386.7	−706.0	−563.0	−686.9	−704.4	−772.1	−896.6	−927.3	−775.3	48.3	181.8
Services: Credit	78add	830.3	1,028.4	1,330.7	1,359.2	1,398.7	1,424.1	1,319.1	1,261.6	1,275.7	1,122.5	753.7	777.9
Services: Debit	78aed	−558.8	−746.5	−861.6	−857.7	−839.0	−888.6	−883.6	−802.3	−881.8	−801.4	−600.3	−615.3
Balance on Goods & Services	78afd	149.7	−104.8	−236.9	−61.5	−127.2	−168.9	−336.6	−437.3	−533.4	−454.2	201.7	344.4
Income: Credit	78agd	225.0	250.1	282.5	404.3	460.5	547.3	608.0	735.5	781.5	832.0	453.4	237.8
Income: Debit	78ahd	−412.1	−442.5	−525.1	−631.3	−649.2	−740.0	−805.9	−879.3	−841.8	−895.2	−405.1	−601.7
Balance on Gds, Serv. & Inc.	78aid	−37.4	−297.2	−479.5	−288.5	−315.9	−361.6	−534.5	−581.1	−593.7	−517.4	250.0	−19.5
Current Transfers, n.i.e.: Credit	78ajd	36.0	61.2	49.2	84.0	90.7	83.0	75.0	78.4	48.0	48.0	83.7	79.8
Current Transfers: Debit	78akd	−7.4	−7.8	−8.0	−8.0	−8.2	−8.8	−16.0	−4.9	−20.5	−18.3	−11.5	−8.2
Capital Account, n.i.e.	78bcd	−	−	−	−	−	−	−	−	−	−	−	−
Capital Account, n.i.e.: Credit	78bad	−	−	−	−	−	−	−	−	−	−	−	−
Capital Account: Debit	78bbd	−	−	−	−	−	−	−	−	−	−	−	−
Financial Account, n.i.e.	78bjd	−91.5	228.0	537.2	421.7	233.6	608.7	545.1	147.1	779.3	457.3	−1,927.5	−342.6
Direct Investment Abroad	78bdd							−13.2	−9.3	.6	−6.2	−53.8	−3.7
Dir. Invest. in Rep. Econ., n.i.e.	78bed	−	101.5	154.5	156.6	136.8	126.4	164.1	235.3	273.5	271.0	174.6	274.6
Portfolio Investment Assets	78bfd	−	−	−	−	−	−	−	−44.3	−98.1	236.7	95.2	−521.7
Equity Securities	78bkd	−	−	−	−	−	−	−	−	−	10.2	−	−
Debt Securities	78bld	−	−	−	−	−	−	−	−44.3	−98.1	226.5	95.2	−521.7
Portfolio Investment Liab., n.i.e.	78bgd	83.4	29.3	158.1	288.8	179.9	209.6	419.4	128.2	289.5	264.4	204.5	22.9
Equity Securities	78bmd	−	−	−	−	−	−	−	−	−	28.1	−	−
Debt Securities	78bnd	83.4	29.3	158.1	288.8	179.9	209.6	419.4	128.2	289.5	236.3	204.5	22.9
Financial Derivatives Assets	78bwd	....	....	....	−	−	−	−	−	−	....	....	....
Financial Derivatives Liabilities	78bxd	....	....	....	−	−	−	−	−	−	....	....	....
Other Investment Assets	78bhd	−589.8	−19.3	−71.8	−961.9	−1,238.5	−626.6	−428.0	−119.3	−690.4	−2,275.2	1,825.5	−1,252.8
Monetary Authorities	78bod	....	−	−10.1	−	−	−	−	−	.9	−5.3	−522.6	272.4
General Government	78bpd	−	−	−	−	−	−	−	−	−	10.0	2.0	−
Banks	78bqd	−589.8	−18.6	−44.0	−961.3	−1,232.4	−636.4	−428.0	65.4	−549.3	−2,210.5	3,014.5	−1,400.8
Other Sectors	78brd	−	−.7	−17.7	−.6	−6.1	9.8	−	−184.7	−142.0	−69.4	−668.4	−124.4
Other Investment Liab., n.i.e.	78bid	414.9	116.5	296.4	938.2	1,155.4	912.5	398.9	−52.8	1,004.2	1,966.6	−4,173.5	1,138.1
Monetary Authorities	78bsd	−139.2	−23.7	5.7	−62.5	−10.3	−31.3	−37.2	−135.7	−38.8	−52.4	−13.1	−84.0
General Government	78btd	104.9	120.3	134.0	18.6	20.3	96.8	169.1	260.5	200.7	144.4	666.6	328.4
Banks	78bud	434.2	16.0	99.8	1,017.9	1,112.9	778.9	272.9	−161.3	862.5	1,780.5	−4,693.7	964.4
Other Sectors	78bvd	15.0	3.9	56.9	−35.8	32.5	68.1	−5.9	−16.3	−20.2	94.1	−133.3	−70.7
Net Errors and Omissions	78cad	238.3	208.7	10.2	18.6	152.2	78.8	285.5	250.9	−46.6	334.4	−2,291.8	1,248.5
Overall Balance	78cbd	138.0	192.9	109.1	227.8	152.4	400.1	355.1	−109.6	166.5	304.0	−3,897.1	957.9
Reserves and Related Items	79dad	−138.0	−192.9	−109.1	−227.8	−152.4	−400.1	−355.1	109.6	−166.5	−304.0	3,897.1	−957.9
Reserve Assets	79dbd	−186.2	−178.6	−98.5	−218.0	−140.8	−391.7	−515.2	109.6	−166.5	−304.0	2,331.2	−1,380.4
Use of Fund Credit and Loans	79dcd	−2.5	−14.4	−10.6	−9.8	−11.6	−8.3	160.1	−	−	−	1,565.9	422.5
Exceptional Financing	79ded	50.7	−	−	−	−	....	−	−	−	−	−	−
International Investment Position		\multicolumn{12}{c}{*Millions of US Dollars*}
Assets	79aad	....	....	....	....	....	....	....	12,747.3	13,789.1	16,986.1	10,271.8	13,324.8
Direct Investment Abroad	79abd	−	−	−	−	−	−	−	47.2	54.0	132.0	108.0	111.6
Portfolio Investment	79acd	48.1	48.1	50.4	52.4	56.9	61.7	66.9	842.3	799.0	1,203.4	999.3	1,479.9
Equity Securities	79add	−	−	−	−	−	−	−	−	−	−	−	−
Debt Securities	79aed	48.1	48.1	50.4	52.4	56.9	61.7	66.9	842.3	799.0	1,203.4	999.3	1,479.9
Financial Derivatives	79ald	....	....	....	....	....	....	....	−	−	−	−	−
Other Investment	79afd	3,232.4	3,270.3	3,892.6	4,805.5	6,060.9	6,718.3	7,276.9	8,691.9	10,158.3	12,550.7	8,392.1	9,646.6
Monetary Authorities	79agd	73.6	72.6	80.2	83.3	49.1	111.8	113.1	−	103.4	177.0	600.4	329.9
General Government	79ahd	−	−	−	−	−	−	−	−	−	−	−	−
Banks	79aid	3,119.2	3,161.4	3,758.3	4,667.5	5,951.0	6,555.5	7,108.0	5,457.5	6,607.2	8,804.8	3,197.6	4,598.2
Other Sectors	79ajd	39.6	36.3	54.1	54.7	60.8	51.0	55.8	3,234.4	3,447.7	3,568.8	4,594.1	4,718.5
Reserve Assets	79akd	1,990.8	2,201.2	2,292.9	2,490.6	2,600.2	2,776.8	3,320.6	3,165.9	2,777.8	3,100.0	772.4	2,086.7
Liabilities	79lad	....	....	....	....	....	....	....	14,511.7	15,583.1	18,800.6	12,034.9	14,232.1
Dir. Invest. in Rep. Economy	79lbd	−	−	−	−	−	−	−	1,790.3	2,088.0	2,406.2	1,402.5	1,677.1
Portfolio Investment	79lcd	1,472.4	1,512.6	1,668.6	1,954.9	2,136.7	2,187.3	2,606.7	2,340.2	2,721.1	3,053.0	2,433.9	2,561.2
Equity Securities	79ldd	−	−	−	−	−	−	−	−	−	−	−	−
Debt Securities	79led	1,472.4	1,512.6	1,668.6	1,954.9	2,136.7	2,187.3	2,606.7	2,340.2	2,721.1	3,053.0	2,433.9	2,561.2
Financial Derivatives	79lld	....	....	....	....	....	....	....	−	−	−	−	−
Other Investment	79lfd	6,277.1	6,440.5	7,501.7	8,436.9	9,467.3	10,297.2	11,055.7	10,381.2	10,774.0	13,341.4	8,198.5	9,993.8
Monetary Authorities	79lgd	204.3	165.6	150.2	68.0	50.3	77.4	232.0	218.9	518.5	550.8	2,093.1	2,632.2
General Government	79lhd	1,102.4	1,268.3	1,416.9	1,537.6	1,507.2	1,594.8	1,738.3	1,976.2	1,904.1	2,077.6	2,493.8	2,848.4
Banks	79lid	3,607.1	3,644.8	4,150.3	5,182.4	6,275.2	7,152.8	7,628.9	6,911.5	7,753.9	9,679.6	2,999.5	3,963.8
Other Sectors	79ljd	1,363.3	1,361.8	1,784.3	1,648.9	1,634.6	1,472.2	1,456.5	1,274.6	597.5	1,033.4	612.1	549.4

2004, International Monetary Fund : *International Financial Statistics Yearbook*

Uruguay 298

		1992	1993	1994	1995	1996	1997	1998	1999	2000	2001	2002	2003
Government Finance			***Millions of Pesos: Year Ending December 31***
Deficit (-) or Surplus............	80	222.0	−304.0	−2,308.0	−1,467.0	−2,379.0	−2,435.0	−1,817.0	† −8,882.0	−8,322.0	−11,554.0	....	....
Revenue............................	81	10,421.0	17,799.0	26,409.0	33,923.0	45,535.0	60,165.0	70,664.0	† 67,197.0	68,167.0	65,933.0	....	....
Expenditure.......................	82	10,165.0	18,103.0	28,717.0	35,390.0	47,914.0	62,363.0	72,673.0	† 76,079.0	76,489.0	77,487.0	....	....
Lending Minus Repayments...	83	34.0	−	−	−	−	−	237.0	−192.0	† −	−	....	....
Financing													
Net Borrowing...................	84	−222.0	304.0	2,308.0	....	....	....	....	....	....	....	....	....
Domestic..................	84a	−451.0	322.0	1,378.0	....	....	....	....	....	....	....	....	....
Foreign....................	85a	229.0	−18.0	930.0	....	....	....	....	....	....	....	....	....
Use of Cash Balances............	87	−	−	−	....	....	....	....	....	....	....	....	....
Debt: Domestic...................	88a	2,058.0	3,608.0	7,728.0	....	....	....	....	....	....	....	....	....
Foreign.......................	89a	7,137.0	9,328.0	13,893.0	....	....	....	....	....	....	....	....	....
National Accounts			***Millions of Pesos***
Househ.Cons.Expend.,incl.NPISHs...	96f	28,128	42,934	64,230	89,265	117,978	148,387	169,442	173,360	181,114	183,519	192,167	229,928
Government Consumption Expend...	91f	4,512	7,199	10,464	14,505	20,952	25,324	29,357	30,871	32,070	33,837	33,622	36,829
Gross Fixed Capital Formation........	93e	5,531	8,724	12,820	16,573	22,835	29,609	35,522	34,377	32,029	30,943	26,360	30,543
Changes in Inventories..............	93i	462	524	1,169	2,304	2,089	1,585	1,657	1,536	1,891	3,106	3,707	10,646
Exports of Goods and Services.......	90c	7,965	11,308	17,423	23,275	32,169	42,109	46,511	42,758	46,915	45,353	57,325	80,655
Imports of Goods and Services (-)...	98c	7,645	11,564	17,965	23,403	32,478	42,088	48,222	45,758	50,993	49,546	52,214	73,154
Gross Domestic Product (GDP).......	99b	38,954	59,125	88,140	122,521	163,546	204,926	234,267	237,143	243,027	247,211	260,967	315,446
Net Primary Income from Abroad.....	98.n	−700	−958	−1,617	−1,929	−2,265	−2,910	−3,168	−3,249	−3,386	−5,077	−2,595	−11,321
Gross National Income (GNI).........	99a	38,254	58,167	86,523	120,592	161,281	202,016	231,099	233,894	239,641	242,134	258,371	304,125
GDP Vol. 1983 Prices (Millions)......	99b.p	238	244	262	258	273	286	299	291	287	277	246	253
GDP Volume (2000=100)............	99bvp	83.0	85.2	91.4	90.1	95.1	99.9	104.4	101.5	100.0	96.6	86.0	88.1
GDP Deflator (2000=100)...........	99bip	19.3	28.6	39.7	56.0	70.8	84.4	92.3	96.2	100.0	105.3	124.9	147.3
			***Millions: Midyear Estimates***
Population..........................	99z	**3.15**	**3.17**	**3.19**	**3.22**	**3.24**	**3.27**	**3.29**	**3.32**	**3.34**	**3.37**	**3.39**	**3.42**

Vanuatu 846

		1992	1993	1994	1995	1996	1997	1998	1999	2000	2001	2002	2003
Exchange Rates		*Vatu per SDR: Unless Otherwise Indicated: End of Period*
Official Rate	aa	163.63	165.93	163.62	169.07	159.28	167.73	182.73	176.90	186.07	184.41	181.05	166.15
		Vatu per US Dollar: End of Period (ae) Period Average (rf)
Official Rate	ae	119.00	120.80	112.08	113.74	110.77	124.31	129.78	128.89	142.81	146.74	133.17	111.81
Official Rate	rf	113.39	121.58	116.41	112.11	111.72	115.87	127.52	129.08	137.64	145.31	139.20	122.19
Fund Position		*Millions of SDRs: Unless Otherwise Indicated: End of Period*
Quota	2f.s	9.00	12.50	12.50	12.50	12.50	12.50	12.50	17.00	17.00	17.00	17.00	17.00
SDRs	1b.s	.68	.15	.22	.29	.36	.44	.53	.60	.70	.79	.84	.89
Reserve Position in the Fund	1c.s	1.61	2.49	2.49	2.49	2.49	2.50	2.50	2.50	2.50	2.50	2.50	2.50
Total Fund Cred.&Loans Outstg.	2tl	–	–	–	–	–	–	–	–	–	–	–	–
International Liquidity		*Millions of US Dollars Unless Otherwise Indicated: End of Period*
Total Reserves minus Gold	1l.d	42.46	45.59	43.58	48.29	43.92	37.30	44.67	41.35	38.92	37.66	36.52	43.82
SDRs	1b.d	.94	.21	.31	.43	.52	.60	.74	.83	.91	.99	1.15	1.32
Reserve Position in the Fund	1c.d	2.21	3.42	3.63	3.70	3.58	3.37	3.51	3.43	3.25	3.14	3.39	3.71
Foreign Exchange	1d.d	39.31	41.96	39.63	44.16	39.82	33.34	40.41	37.10	34.76	33.53	31.98	38.79
Monetary Authorities	1dad	39.00	41.95	39.62	44.16	39.82	33.34	40.41	37.10	34.76	33.53	31.98	38.79
Government	1dbd	.31	.01	.01	–	–	–	–	–	–	–	–	–
Monetary Authorities: Other Liab.	4..d	.01	.17	.22	.04	.16	.04	.13	.18	.23	.52	.40	.18
Deposit Money Banks: Assets	7a.d	150.93	157.83	158.73	183.94	205.28	204.83	189.99	164.26	160.63	192.62	215.72	243.35
Liabilities	7b.d	20.07	29.48	26.54	32.05	28.42	47.97	25.01	33.92	26.15	28.47	65.22	65.00
Other Banking Insts.: Assets	7e.d	–	–	–	–	–	–	....	....	....	....	....	....
Liabilities	7f.d	2	2	6	4	4	4	....	....	....	....	....	....
Monetary Authorities		*Millions of Vatu: End of Period*
Foreign Assets	11	4,978	5,519	4,883	5,491	4,865	4,638	5,796	5,331	5,728	5,642	4,960	4,826
Claims on Central Government	12a	–	–	307	420	408	898	1,221	1,401	1,442	1,151	1,241	1,471
Claims on Nonfin.Pub.Enterprises	12c	....	....	310	327	353	260	36	32	58	294	320	–
Claims on Private Sector	12d	63	73	76	95	108	124	130	148	143	155	172	180
Claims on Deposit Money Banks	12e	–	4	1	3	98	257	–	316	2	–	2	100
of which: Fgn.Currency Claims	12ex	–	4	1	3	2	1	–	–	2	–	2	–
Reserve Money	14	1,956	3,005	2,801	3,654	3,500	3,493	3,674	4,493	4,579	4,563	4,561	4,924
of which: Currency Outside DMBs	14a	901	1,224	1,351	1,566	1,571	1,662	2,042	1,936	1,834	1,941	1,916	2,108
Liabs. of Central Bank: Securities	16ac	–	–	–	–	–	–	1,233	297	99	446	324	99
Foreign Liabilities	16c	1	21	25	5	18	4	17	23	33	77	53	20
Central Government Deposits	16d	2,594	2,315	2,102	1,962	1,739	2,104	1,679	1,902	1,898	1,377	965	833
Capital Accounts	17a	780	748	740	641	654	672	686	698	709	724	729	792
Valuation Adjustment	17rv	319	248	134	236	87	64	61	49	32	10	39	–
Other Items (Net)	17r	–610	–741	†–224	–162	–166	–161	–169	–233	23	45	22	–91
Deposit Money Banks		*Millions of Vatu: End of Period*
Reserves	20	1,070	1,821	1,397	2,033	1,829	1,742	1,238	2,215	2,547	2,496	2,563	2,720
Claims on Mon.Author.:Securities	20c	–	–	–	–	–	–	1,001	297	99	446	324	99
Foreign Assets	21	17,960	19,065	17,790	20,921	22,738	25,462	24,657	21,171	22,940	28,265	28,727	27,209
Claims on Central Government	22a	833	937	527	506	492	496	1,131	930	1,417	1,108	1,191	773
Claims on Local Government	22b	–	–	–	2	2	4	–	4	3	5	2	5
Claims on Nonfin.Pub.Enterprises	22c	20	6	105	62	30	134	108	53	100	28	15	16
Claims on Private Sector	22d	7,914	7,944	8,540	9,075	9,796	9,580	10,605	12,158	11,556	12,295	13,265	14,558
Claims on Other Financial Insts	22f	6	100	38	21	–	2	–	–	–	–	–	–
Demand Deposits	24	4,119	4,448	4,339	4,690	4,880	4,941	5,368	5,296	6,051	5,974	9,608	10,067
Time, Savings,& Fgn.Currency Dep.	25	18,248	18,778	19,443	22,225	24,879	24,645	27,626	24,377	25,686	27,643	23,485	22,553
of which: Nonreporting Bks' Deps.	25e	1,487	80	–	–	–	–	–	–	–	–	–	–
Foreign Liabilities	26c	2,388	3,561	2,975	3,645	3,148	5,963	3,246	4,372	3,735	4,177	8,685	7,268
Central Government Deposits	26d	376	709	296	161	10	52	140	141	157	292	244	282
Credit from Monetary Authorities	26g	–	3	1	3	1	3	–	316	–	–	–	–
Capital Accounts	27a	3,124	2,297	1,726	1,698	2,142	1,350	2,468	2,734	3,550	4,266	4,129	5,222
Other Items (Net)	27r	–452	76	–381	199	–174	464	–108	–409	–515	2,290	–64	–11
Monetary Survey		*Millions of Vatu: End of Period*
Foreign Assets (Net)	31n	20,549	21,003	19,674	22,763	24,438	24,132	27,189	22,107	24,901	29,653	24,948	24,748
Domestic Credit	32	5,865	6,036	†7,514	8,385	9,439	9,341	11,412	12,683	12,664	13,366	14,996	15,888
Claims on Central Govt. (Net)	32an	–2,137	–2,087	–1,564	–1,197	–849	–762	533	288	804	589	1,223	1,129
Claims on Local Government	32b	–	–	–	2	2	4	–	4	3	5	2	5
Claims on Nonfin.Pub.Enterprises	32c	20	6	†416	389	382	394	144	85	158	322	334	16
Claims on Private Sector	32d	7,976	8,017	8,616	9,170	9,904	9,703	10,735	12,306	11,699	12,451	13,437	14,738
Claims on Other Financial Insts	32f	6	100	†46	21	–	2	–	–	–	–	–	–
Money	34	5,056	5,679	5,728	6,306	6,528	6,642	7,600	7,616	8,082	8,041	11,606	12,271
Quasi-Money	35	18,248	18,778	19,443	22,225	24,879	24,645	27,626	24,377	25,686	27,643	23,485	22,553
Capital Accounts	37a	3,904	3,045	2,466	2,339	2,797	2,022	3,155	3,432	4,259	4,990	4,858	6,014
Other Items (Net)	37r	–793	–463	†–449	277	–327	163	221	–636	–462	2,344	–5	–202
Money plus Quasi-Money	35l	23,303	24,457	25,171	28,531	31,407	31,287	35,226	31,994	33,769	35,684	35,091	34,824

Vanuatu 846

		1992	1993	1994	1995	1996	1997	1998	1999	2000	2001	2002	2003
Other Banking Institutions							*Millions of Vatu: End of Period*						
Cash..	40	30	43	15	5	572	36	....	....	....	....	....	....
Foreign Assets...............................	41	41	42	45	51	–	–	....	....	....	....	....	....
Claims on Central Government........	42a	50	60	10	10	10	10	....	....	....	....	....	....
Claims on Private Sector.................	42d	507	608	598	691	40	548	....	....	....	....	....	....
Claims on Deposit Money Banks......	42e	–	–	–	–	–	–	....	....	....	....	....	....
Time and Savings Deposits.............	45	–	–	–	–	–	–	....	....	....	....	....	....
Foreign Liabilities...........................	46c	238	183	625	495	492	491	....	....	....	....	....	....
Capital Accounts............................	47a	450	450	450	535	535	535	....	....	....	....	....	....
Other Items (Net)...........................	47r	–60	120	–407	–273	–405	–432	....	....	....	....	....	....
Banking Survey							*Millions of Vatu: End of Period*						
Foreign Assets (Net).......................	51n	20,352	20,862	19,094	22,318	23,946	23,641	....	....	....	....	....	....
Domestic Credit..............................	52	6,417	6,604	8,076	9,065	9,488	9,897	....	....	....	....	....	....
Claims on Central Govt. (Net)........	52an	–2,087	–2,027	–1,554	–1,187	–839	–752	....	....	....	....	....	....
Claims on Nonfin.Pub.Enterprises...	52c	20	6	†416	389	382	394	....	....	....	....	....	....
Claims on Private Sector................	52d	8,484	8,625	9,214	9,861	9,944	10,251	....	....	....	....	....	....
Liquid Liabilities.............................	55l	23,273	24,414	25,156	28,526	30,835	31,251	....	....	....	....	....	....
Other Items (Net)...........................	57r	3,495	3,052	†2,014	2,857	2,599	2,287	....	....	....	....	....	....
Interest Rates							*Percent Per Annum*						
Discount Rate (End of Period).........	60	....	....	....	....	....	....	7.00	7.00	7.00	6.50	6.50	6.50
Money Market Rate........................	60b	5.92	6.00	6.00	6.00	6.00	6.00	8.65	6.99	5.58	5.50	5.50	5.50
Deposit Rate...................................	60l	4.69	5.00	5.06	3.00	4.50	3.73	3.29	1.60	1.27	1.25	1.00	1.21
Lending Rate..................................	60p	16.25	16.00	16.00	10.50	10.50	10.50	10.96	10.29	9.85	8.81	7.41	5.90
Government Bond Yield..................	61	8.00	8.00	8.00	8.00	8.00	8.00	8.00	8.50	8.50	8.50	8.50	8.50
Prices							*Index Numbers (2000=100): Period Averages*						
Consumer Prices.............................	64	82.4	85.4	87.3	89.3	90.1	92.6	95.7	†97.6	100.0	103.7	105.7	108.9
International Transactions							*Millions of Vatu*						
Exports...	70	2,677	2,758	2,911	3,173	3,368	4,087	4,323	3,327	3,214	2,267	2,126	2,598
Imports, c.i.f..................................	71	9,276	9,581	10,404	10,659	10,888	10,888	11,257	12,337	11,936	14,800	12,350	12,703
Balance of Payments							*Millions of US Dollars: Minus Sign Indicates Debit*						
Current Account, n.i.e....................	78ald	–13.07	–14.93	–19.78	–18.25	–26.94	–19.34	–9.41	–33.22	–13.65	–14.53	....	....
Goods: Exports f.o.b.....................	78aad	17.80	17.43	25.11	28.28	30.20	35.32	33.78	25.66	27.19	19.89	....	....
Goods: Imports f.o.b.....................	78abd	–66.79	–64.71	–74.68	–79.44	–81.11	–78.99	–76.23	–84.46	–76.94	–77.96	....	....
Trade Balance.............................	78acd	–48.99	–47.28	–49.58	–51.16	–50.91	–43.67	–42.44	–58.80	–49.74	–58.07	....	....
Services: Credit.............................	78add	69.93	68.88	78.14	81.65	92.75	87.79	113.95	114.80	129.81	119.26	....	....
Services: Debit..............................	78aed	–26.79	–29.97	–33.44	–35.27	–36.50	–35.95	–56.97	–72.09	–70.15	–72.99	....	....
Balance on Goods & Services.......	78afd	–5.85	–8.36	–4.88	–4.78	5.34	8.16	14.55	–16.09	9.91	–11.80	....	....
Income: Credit...............................	78agd	17.60	14.95	9.94	13.07	15.82	15.41	20.98	21.00	18.74	17.23	....	....
Income: Debit................................	78ahd	–47.55	–43.48	–47.36	–49.79	–47.55	–45.68	–29.26	–26.09	–31.71	–21.23	....	....
Balance on Gds, Serv. & Inc.........	78aid	–35.80	–36.89	–42.30	–41.49	–26.39	–22.11	6.26	–21.18	–3.06	–15.80	....	....
Current Transfers, n.i.e.: Credit.....	78ajd	23.28	22.54	23.24	23.81	22.39	21.77	15.55	18.72	27.41	39.53	....	....
Current Transfers: Debit................	78akd	–.55	–.58	–.72	–.56	–22.94	–19.00	–31.22	–30.76	–38.00	–38.26	....	....
Capital Account, n.i.e....................	78bcd	17.22	26.30	37.28	31.62	4.90	–5.46	–20.86	–49.72	–23.58	–16.03	....	....
Capital Account, n.i.e.: Credit........	78bad	26.59	32.04	41.45	38.33	43.38	23.75	25.44	23.94	31.88	46.07	....	....
Capital Account: Debit...................	78bbd	–9.37	–5.74	–4.17	–6.71	–38.48	–29.21	–46.29	–73.66	–55.46	–62.10	....	....
Financial Account, n.i.e..................	78bjd	23.71	14.53	–13.41	25.30	20.88	–16.73	17.37	56.17	19.33	12.75	....	....
Direct Investment Abroad..............	78bdd	–	–	–	–	....	....	....	....	....	....	....	....
Dir. Invest. in Rep. Econ., n.i.e......	78bed	26.45	25.97	29.79	31.04	32.73	30.23	20.38	13.40	20.26	18.00	....	....
Portfolio Investment Assets...........	78bfd	–	–	–	–	–	–	3.45	–1.01	.69	–4.33	....	....
Equity Securities.........................	78bkd	–	–	–	–	–	–	....	....	....	....	....	....
Debt Securities............................	78bld	–	–	–	–	–	–	....	....	....	....	....	....
Portfolio Investment Liab., n.i.e.....	78bgd	–	–	–	–	–	–	....	....	....	....	....	....
Equity Securities.........................	78bmd	–	–	–	–	–	–	....	....	....	....	....	....
Debt Securities............................	78bnd	–	–	–	–	–	–	....	....	....	....	....	....
Financial Derivatives Assets...........	78bwd	....	....	....	....	....	....	....	....	....	....	....	....
Financial Derivatives Liabilities.......	78bxd	....	....	....	....	....	....	....	....	....	....	....	....
Other Investment Assets...............	78bhd	–8.57	–27.50	–45.47	–1.59	–16.63	–23.53	5.12	29.63	–13.55	–11.41	....	....
Monetary Authorities..................	78bod	....	....	....	....	....	....	....	....	....	....	....	....
General Government....................	78bpd	–.38	–.43	–.45	–.30	–.39	–.46	....	....	....	....	....	....
Banks..	78bqd	21.22	–10.76	10.60	–2.18	–16.25	–23.07	5.89	27.05	–13.10	–14.81	....	....
Other Sectors..............................	78brd	–29.42	–16.31	–55.62	.89	....	....	–.77	2.59	–.45	3.40	....	....
Other Investment Liab., n.i.e.........	78bid	5.83	16.05	2.27	–4.15	4.78	–23.43	–11.58	14.15	11.93	10.48	....	....
Monetary Authorities..................	78bsd	–.36	.16	–.05	.18	–.12	.12	–.11	1.30	–.03	.53	....	....
General Government....................	78btd	7.03	6.60	2.17	2.21	.45	.68	10.52	5.12	16.36	3.20	....	....
Banks..	78bud	–.84	9.29	.16	–6.54	4.46	–24.23	–20.91	8.73	–4.79	3.05	....	....
Other Sectors..............................	78bvd	–	–	–	–	....	....	–1.09	–1.01	.39	3.70	....	....
Net Errors and Omissions................	78cad	–27.10	–22.44	–10.21	–33.38	–4.14	39.37	6.01	3.57	–.88	7.55	....	....
Overall Balance..............................	78cbd	.75	3.45	–6.12	5.30	–5.30	–2.16	–6.89	–23.19	–18.77	–10.27	....	....
Reserves and Related Items............	79dad	–.75	–3.45	6.12	–5.30	5.30	2.16	6.89	23.19	18.77	10.27	....	....
Reserve Assets................................	79dbd	–4.16	–6.70	4.86	–5.30	5.30	2.16	–8.06	3.48	.87	.62	....	....
Use of Fund Credit and Loans........	79dcd	–	–	–	–	–	–	–	–	–	–	....	....
Exceptional Financing.....................	79ded	3.41	3.26	1.26	....	....	....	14.95	19.71	17.90	9.64	....	....

Vanuatu 846

		1992	1993	1994	1995	1996	1997	1998	1999	2000	2001	2002	2003
International Investment Position							**Millions of US Dollars**						
Assets...	79aad	....	....	....	....	....	....	....	....	....	....	....	....
Direct Investment Abroad.............	79abd	....	....	....	....	....	....	—	—	....	....	....	....
Portfolio Investment......................	79acd	....	....	....	....	....	....	2.93	4.42	....	....	....	....
Equity Securities.......................	79add	....	....	....	....	....	....	2.00	3.49	....	....	....	....
Debt Securities.........................	79aed	....	....	....	....	....	....	.92	.93	....	....	....	....
Financial Derivatives.....................	79ald	....	....	....	....	....	....	....	....	....	....	....	....
Other Investment...........................	79afd	....	....	....	....	....	....	189.99	219.01	....	....	....	....
Monetary Authorities.................	79agd	....	....	....	....	....	....	—	—	....	....	....	....
General Government.................	79ahd	....	....	....	....	....	....	—	—	....	....	....	....
Banks.......................................	79aid	....	....	....	....	....	....	189.99	164.26	....	....	....	....
Other Sectors...........................	79ajd	....	....	....	....	....	....	—	54.74	....	....	....	....
Reserve Assets.............................	79akd	....	....	....	....	....	....	44.65	41.36	....	....	....	....
Liabilities......................................	79lad	....	....	....	....	....	....	....	....	....	....	....	....
Dir. Invest. in Rep. Economy...........	79lbd	....	....	....	....	....	....	47.62	66.53	....	....	....	....
Portfolio Investment......................	79lcd	....	....	....	....	....	....	—	—	....	....	....	....
Equity Securities.......................	79ldd	....	....	....	....	....	....	....	....	....	....	....	....
Debt Securities.........................	79led	....	....	....	....	....	....	....	....	....	....	....	....
Financial Derivatives.....................	79lld	....	....	....	....	....	....	....	....	....	....	....	....
Other Investment...........................	79lfd	....	....	....	....	....	....	217.52	214.19	....	....	....	....
Monetary Authorities.................	79lgd	....	....	....	....	....	....	.18	1.70	....	....	....	....
General Government.................	79lhd	....	....	....	....	....	....	51.93	56.98	....	....	....	....
Banks.......................................	79lid	....	....	....	....	....	....	162.17	153.25	....	....	....	....
Other Sectors...........................	79ljd	....	....	....	....	....	....	3.25	2.27	....	....	....	....
National Accounts							**Millions of Vatu**							
Housh.Cons.Expend.,incl.NPISHs....	96f	11,662	11,701	12,286	12,777	....	17,473	18,399	18,727	19,376	19,407	19,968	....
Government Consumption Expend...	91f	5,988	6,765	6,903	6,916	....	6,161	6,751	7,462	7,787	7,688	7,488	....
Gross Fixed Capital Formation.........	93e	5,645	6,075	6,618	8,128	....	5,343	5,606	6,418	7,181	6,880	6,890	....
Changes in Inventories....................	93i	520	540	580	570	....	242	129	152	275	−67	10	....
Exports of Goods and Services.........	90c	10,471	10,772	11,796	12,041	....	15,459	17,693	18,146	21,498	20,115	18,130	....
Imports of Goods and Services (-)....	98c	12,270	12,789	14,278	14,603	....	14,945	16,513	19,511	19,860	21,393	21,222	....
Gross Domestic Product (GDP)........	99b	21,541	23,779	24,962	26,633	27,393	29,650	32,423	32,399	33,662	34,121	32,956	....
Net Primary Income from Abroad.....	98.n	−2,133	−2,696	−3,021	−2,792	−2,027	−1,342	−1,055	−657	−1,784	−579	−704	....
Gross National Income (GNI)...........	99a	19,408	21,083	21,941	23,841	25,366	28,308	31,368	31,742	31,878	33,542	32,252	....
GDP Volume 1983 Prices................	99b.p	13,088	13,676	14,024	14,469	15,733	16,505	17,216	16,668	17,113	16,760	16,285	....
GDP Volume (2000=100)................	99bvp	76.5	79.9	82.0	84.6	91.9	96.5	100.6	97.4	100.0	97.9	95.2	....
GDP Deflator (2000=100)...............	99bip	83.7	88.4	90.5	93.6	88.5	91.3	95.7	98.8	100.0	103.5	102.9	....
						Millions: Midyear Estimates							
Population.....................................	99z	.16	.16	.17	.17	.18	.18	.19	.19	.20	.20	.21	.21

Venezuela, Rep. Bol. 299

		1992	1993	1994	1995	1996	1997	1998	1999	2000	2001	2002	2003
Exchange Rates					*Bolivares per SDR: End of Period*								
Official Rate	aa	109.244	145.102	†248.175	431.082	685.188	680.359	794.833	889.730	911.711	958.885	1,905.027	2,374.580
					Bolivares per US Dollar: End of Period (ae) Period Average (rf)								
Official Rate	ae	79.450	105.640	†170.000	290.000	476.500	504.250	564.500	648.250	699.750	763.000	1,401.250	1,598.000
Official Rate	rf	68.376	90.826	†148.503	176.843	417.333	488.635	547.556	605.717	679.960	723.666	1,160.953	1,606.962
					Index Numbers (2000=100): Period Averages								
Market Rate	ahx	999.5	753.2	477.0	388.9	170.4	139.3	124.4	112.4	100.0	94.0	61.5	42.3
Nominal Effective Exchange Rate	nec	624.2	548.8	392.6	319.4	144.3	124.6	115.2	106.6	100.0	97.8	63.6	40.6
Real Effective Exchange Rate	rec	49.3	51.5	49.4	61.9	52.2	68.4	83.8	94.3	100.0	107.2	82.7	68.8
Fund Position					*Millions of SDRs: End of Period*								
Quota	2f.s	1,951	1,951	1,951	1,951	1,951	1,951	1,951	2,659	2,659	2,659	2,659	2,659
SDRs	1b.s	55	354	317	255	317	135	74	93	28	8	8	7
Reserve Position in the Fund	1c.s	145	145	145	145	145	145	145	322	322	322	322	322
of which: Outstg.Fund Borrowing	2c	–	–	–	–	–	–	–	–	–	–	–	–
Total Fund Cred.&Loans Outstg	2tl	2,143	1,951	1,810	1,506	1,527	1,199	870	540	156	–	–	–
International Liquidity					*Millions of US Dollars Unless Otherwise Indicated: End of Period*								
Total Reserves minus Gold	1l.d	9,562	9,216	8,067	6,283	11,788	14,378	11,920	12,277	13,088	9,239	8,487	16,035
SDRs	1b.d	75	486	463	380	456	183	104	127	36	10	11	10
Reserve Position in the Fund	1c.d	199	199	212	215	208	196	204	442	419	405	438	478
Foreign Exchange	1d.d	9,288	8,531	7,393	5,688	11,124	14,000	11,612	11,708	12,633	8,825	8,038	15,546
Gold (Million Fine Troy Ounces)	1ad	11.46	11.46	11.46	11.46	11.46	11.46	9.76	9.76	10.24	10.94	10.56	11.47
Gold (National Valuation)	1and	3,439	3,440	3,440	3,440	3,440	3,440	2,929	2,887	2,794	3,056	3,515	4,632
Monetary Authorities: Other Liab.	4..d	1,461	2,180	2,142	1,784	1,875	1,006	270	228	214	194	159	140
Deposit Money Banks: Assets	7a.d	1,425	1,495	1,133	647	794	767	859	1,192	1,159	976	1,096	1,146
Liabilities	7b.d	613	634	261	181	212	209	170	131	316	433	228	101
Other Banking Insts.: Assets	7e.d	6	28	32	23	40	37	67	8	18	5	6	2
Liabilities	7f.d	4	1	1	–	–	–	–	–	–	–	1	–
Monetary Authorities					*Billions of Bolivares: End of Period*								
Foreign Assets	11	1,032.97	1,340.04	1,951.31	2,813.96	†7,242.40	9,609.67	8,850.62	9,863.17	11,148.95	9,459.92	16,937.94	33,153.73
Claims on Central Government	12a	276.47	359.09	632.06	1,038.12	†1,649.40	1,095.54	1,007.04	1,057.18	1,106.42	1,044.66	1,656.85	1,114.74
Claims on Nonfin.Pub.Enterprises	12c	10.35	10.05	10.05	22.18	†9.78	.55	.55	.55	.55	.50	.50	.50
Claims on Nonbank Pub. Fin. Inst	12cg	15.12	15.47	813.15	1,355.13	†1,372.75	1,384.14	1,386.24	1,385.64	1,389.73	1,389.34	1,391.71	1,387.85
Claims on Deposit Money Banks	12e	15.53	33.90	18.59	26.42	†10.95	10.23	.80	.90	17.58	42.61	36.18	.53
Claims on Other Banking Insts	12f	2.21	1.43	1.05	1.00	†.40	.34	.77	.77	.76	–	–	–
Reserve Money	14	390.66	431.28	707.13	931.36	†1,852.07	3,221.25	3,808.74	5,064.63	5,815.51	6,515.18	7,783.42	11,460.22
of which: Currency Outside DMBs	14a	108.63	136.55	278.53	355.23	†566.73	987.34	1,235.05	1,816.79	1,997.61	2,286.26	3,795.87	4,777.52
Time, Savings,& Fgn.Currency Dep	15	8.74	8.71	16.24	21.91	†20.33	36.58	16.28	13.01	11.44	11.47	15.98	27.06
Liabs. of Central Bank: Securities	16ac	54.89	70.88	744.71	609.34	†1,659.38	1,803.07	1,579.69	895.74	.76	.73	391.66	7,551.98
Foreign Liabilities	16c	299.93	455.52	718.66	1,026.71	†1,533.35	1,094.31	709.78	491.23	161.86	24.44	39.66	63.46
Long-Term Foreign Liabilities	16cl	50.45	59.11	92.72	139.77	†402.57	226.15	132.79	136.33	129.26	123.38	181.93	160.20
Central Government Deposits	16d	78.89	119.69	222.88	192.32	†991.45	1,739.49	727.67	684.87	2,119.13	1,081.89	786.23	3,614.10
Liab. to Nonbank Pub. Fin. Insts	16dg	96.30	21.96	59.60	70.09	†98.01	15.85	10.59	3.32	12.37	16.72	29.24	644.03
Capital Accounts	17a	103.29	117.36	311.91	325.79	†2,250.32	3,277.72	4,232.05	4,849.26	3,898.43	3,919.34	10,293.08	10,699.78
Other Items (Net)	17r	269.49	475.47	552.35	1,939.52	†1,478.21	686.03	28.44	169.81	1,515.25	243.88	501.99	1,436.51
Deposit Money Banks					*Billions of Bolivares: End of Period*								
Reserves	20	279.85	291.61	400.34	483.54	†1,077.68	1,874.69	2,392.37	2,921.31	3,566.15	4,031.12	3,827.13	6,004.15
Claims on Mon.Author.:Securities	20c	15.80	13.92	354.06	252.27	†1,043.96	783.22	802.00	390.76	–	–	380.93	7,468.14
Foreign Assets	21	113.19	157.92	192.57	187.51	†377.44	385.99	484.14	771.76	809.98	743.73	1,532.11	1,828.38
Claims on Central Government	22a	39.83	139.48	440.70	839.70	†721.61	765.20	777.96	1,220.47	2,511.38	2,904.51	4,364.02	5,372.99
Claims on State and Local Govts	22b	.53	–	1.20	4.92	†1.19	.12	.15	13.51	26.82	.07	.07	.07
Claims on Nonfin.Pub.Enterprises	22c	26.71	79.64	136.68	179.52	†7.76	8.21	2.79	16.04	88.69	3.34	.02	.83
Claims on Nonbank Pub. Fin. Inst	22cg	....	....	....	....	293.88	56.41	32.21	45.43	22.27	.01	–	–
Claims on Private Sector	22d	767.97	859.81	797.97	1,184.61	†2,392.28	5,287.72	6,021.81	6,655.06	8,350.97	10,310.04	10,406.55	11,494.47
Claims on Other Banking Insts	22f	.99	.80	.72	.18	†47.42	45.55	112.78	145.49	314.18	60.18	210.68	130.44
Claims on Nonbank Financial Insts	22g	–	–	10.75	12.79	†24.89	46.38	57.16	179.77	409.56	129.95	118.71	379.04
Demand Deposits	24	245.24	256.54	666.18	902.56	†2,010.16	3,616.46	3,683.59	4,211.88	5,743.23	6,821.99	7,029.87	13,651.21
Time, Savings,& Fgn.Currency Dep	25	817.46	1,077.76	1,532.33	2,079.16	†2,405.98	3,431.80	4,508.54	5,247.37	6,325.39	7,270.21	8,191.19	11,138.65
Money Market Instruments	26aa	....	....	....	....	32.43	63.76	15.43	50.72	94.92	103.94	80.97	44.93
Bonds	26ab	....	....	....	....	17.15	.51	3.48	8.96	10.69	28.01	6.95	14.38
Restricted Deposits	26b	....	....	....	....	47.98	63.17	68.21	94.91	168.57	226.77	259.17	306.46
Foreign Liabilities	26c	22.04	32.29	11.25	17.07	†65.89	95.33	69.11	76.59	204.09	308.57	284.17	150.32
Long-Term Foreign Liabilities	26cl	26.68	34.71	33.16	35.54	†35.01	9.68	26.54	7.98	16.45	21.26	34.16	10.86
Central Government Deposits	26d	24.68	27.81	47.20	57.95	†270.51	464.51	492.97	865.93	1,523.01	1,277.75	1,236.90	2,479.25
Liab. to Nonbank Pub. Fin. Insts	26dg	9.70	16.17	106.12	13.42	†41.70	51.53	52.57	109.29	138.83	64.36	87.46	88.69
Credit from Monetary Authorities	26g	14.82	33.04	17.73	25.57	†1.06	–	–	13.10	41.16	84.16	971.65	21.60
Liabilities to Other Banking Insts	26i	32.90	37.02	31.05	21.87	†208.18	287.70	283.77	267.04	400.01	297.94	94.83	52.92
Liab. to Nonbank Financial Insts	26j	....	....	....	....	38.83	105.51	195.18	160.53	164.28	296.23	253.09	204.48
Capital Accounts	27a	100.37	146.86	90.55	330.50	†848.76	1,271.61	1,665.67	1,877.47	2,364.81	2,937.11	3,863.99	5,175.24
Other Items (Net)	27r	–49.05	–119.04	–200.58	–338.59	†–35.51	–208.08	–381.70	–632.18	–1,095.43	–1,555.36	–1,554.15	–660.45

Venezuela, Rep. Bol. 299

		1992	1993	1994	1995	1996	1997	1998	1999	2000	2001	2002	2003
Monetary Survey		\multicolumn{12}{c}{*Billions of Bolivares: End of Period*}
Foreign Assets (Net)	31n	824.19	1,010.14	1,413.97	1,957.69	†6,020.60	8,806.02	8,555.87	10,067.11	11,592.98	9,870.64	18,146.21	34,768.34
Domestic Credit	32	1,036.60	1,318.27	2,574.26	4,387.89	†5,259.43	6,486.16	8,178.82	9,169.12	10,579.20	13,483.77	16,126.82	13,788.40
Claims on Central Govt. (Net)	32an	212.73	351.07	802.68	1,627.54	†1,109.07	−343.25	564.36	726.85	−24.34	1,589.53	3,997.74	394.38
Claims on State and Local Govts.	32b	.53	—	1.20	4.92	†1.19	.12	.15	13.51	26.82	.07	.07	.07
Claims on Nonfin.Pub.Enterprises.	32c	37.06	89.69	146.73	201.71	†17.53	8.76	3.34	16.59	89.24	3.84	.52	1.33
Claims on Nonbank Pub.Fin.Inst.	32cg	15.12	15.47	813.15	1,355.13	†1,666.63	1,440.54	1,418.45	1,431.07	1,412.00	1,389.34	1,391.71	1,387.85
Claims on Private Sector	32d	767.97	859.82	797.98	1,184.62	†2,392.29	5,287.73	6,021.82	6,655.07	8,350.98	10,310.86	10,407.37	11,495.29
Claims on Other Banking Insts.	32f	3.20	2.23	1.78	1.18	†47.83	45.89	113.55	146.26	314.95	60.18	210.68	130.44
Claims on Nonbank Financial Inst.	32g	—	—	10.75	12.79	†24.89	46.38	57.16	179.77	409.56	129.95	118.71	379.04
Money	34	363.53	407.22	974.12	1,343.96	†2,777.65	4,917.78	5,149.17	6,412.64	8,037.22	9,287.01	10,973.46	19,055.81
Quasi-Money	35	826.20	1,086.46	1,548.58	2,101.07	†2,426.31	3,468.38	4,524.82	5,260.38	6,336.83	7,281.68	8,207.17	11,165.71
Money Market Instruments	36aa	....	....	....	....	32.43	63.76	15.43	50.72	94.92	103.94	80.97	44.93
Bonds	36ab	....	....	....	....	17.15	.51	3.48	8.96	10.69	28.01	6.95	14.38
Liabs. of Central Bank: Securities	36ac	39.09	56.96	390.65	357.06	†615.43	1,019.85	777.68	504.98	.76	.73	10.73	83.84
Restricted Deposits	36b	....	....	....	....	47.98	63.17	68.21	94.91	168.57	226.77	259.17	306.46
Long-Term Foreign Liabilities	36cl	77.14	93.83	125.89	175.32	†437.58	235.84	159.33	144.31	145.71	144.64	216.10	171.06
Liab. to Nonbank Pub. Fin. Insts.	36dg	106.00	38.13	165.72	83.52	†139.70	67.39	63.16	112.62	151.20	81.08	116.69	732.72
Liabilities to Other Banking Insts.	36i	32.90	37.02	31.05	21.87	†208.18	287.70	283.77	267.04	400.01	297.94	94.83	52.92
Liab. to Nonbank Financial Insts.	36j	....	....	....	....	38.83	105.51	195.18	160.53	164.28	296.23	253.09	204.48
Capital Accounts	37a	203.66	264.22	402.46	656.29	†3,099.09	4,549.33	5,897.72	6,726.74	6,263.24	6,856.46	14,157.06	15,875.02
Other Items (Net)	37r	212.27	344.57	349.77	1,606.49	†1,439.71	512.97	−403.27	−507.59	398.77	−1,250.08	−103.17	849.43
Money plus Quasi-Money	35l	1,189.73	1,493.68	2,522.70	3,445.03	†5,203.96	8,386.16	9,674.00	11,673.02	14,374.05	16,568.69	19,180.62	30,221.51
Other Banking Institutions		\multicolumn{12}{c}{*Billions of Bolivares: End of Period*}
Reserves	40	7.87	12.34	22.69	27.57	†37.95	86.71	96.01	210.86	298.50	95.38	72.54	90.90
Claims on Mon.Author.:Securities	40c	.12	.07	1.39	2.06	†39.04	40.06	22.91	9.12	—	—	6.24	14.85
Foreign Assets	41	.50	2.99	5.42	6.55	†18.89	18.50	37.55	4.92	12.84	3.60	8.20	3.72
Claims on Central Government	42a	40.74	32.00	103.93	88.07	†24.77	18.34	23.50	97.10	238.45	63.42	100.84	273.92
Claims on Nonfin.Pub.Enterprises	42c	1.13	.81	1.71	.02	†27.96	5.07	2.31	—	—	—	—	—
Claims on Nonbank Pub. Fin. Inst.	42cg	....	....	....	....	16.39	10.74	4.61	5.26	5.07	.43	—	—
Claims on Private Sector	42d	341.90	361.62	326.46	430.61	†401.52	897.44	1,007.23	1,426.40	1,581.47	527.25	354.51	278.92
Claims on Deposit Money Banks	42e	44.89	81.30	47.11	44.77	†110.27	101.60	137.59	172.19	138.65	106.76	81.30	126.00
Claims on Nonbank Financial Insts.	42g	....	....	....	....	4.17	7.77	6.97	21.93	40.84	19.31	71.77	15.58
Demand Deposits	44	8.11	11.15	13.43	16.13	†29.88	46.95	109.68	156.41	276.51	92.19	108.58	135.51
Time, Savings,& Fgn.Currency Dep.	45	387.14	452.53	460.63	558.42	†300.16	613.32	686.24	1,019.00	1,155.61	260.23	265.99	353.10
Money Market Instruments	46aa	....	....	....	....	4.75	—	—	.05	1.06	13.01	—	—
Bonds	46ab	8.86	11.03	8.49	7.04	†.77	.94	18.89	50.31	48.66	28.97	15.89	2.55
Restricted Deposits	46b	....	....	....	....	.28	1.19	1.27	2.40	3.75	1.36	1.26	1.50
Foreign Liabilities	46c	—	—	—	—	†.06	—	—	—	—	—	1.21	—
Long-Term Foreign Liabilities	46cl	.29	.07	.12	—	†—	—	—	—	—	—	—	—
Central Government Deposits	46d	19.76	5.27	1.03	.76	†13.37	40.80	30.89	191.78	438.28	4.72	6.16	12.77
Liab. to Nonbank Pub. Fin. Insts.	46dg	1.36	.79	.64	.14	†2.18	2.71	.58	3.82	8.59	1.38	37.93	80.51
Credit from Monetary Authorities	46g	1.90	.56	.50	.18	†.11	.02	.01	.01	—	—	5.38	3.32
Credit from Deposit Money Banks	46h	6.08	8.40	8.17	7.36	†41.96	115.46	117.67	110.73	70.67	79.65	100.06	77.31
Liab. to Nonbank Financial Insts.	46j	....	....	....	....	10.10	20.54	7.50	49.85	89.34	13.19	11.06	8.16
Capital Accounts	47a	40.17	60.63	63.72	77.47	†174.41	198.62	242.89	296.05	362.53	112.07	86.74	102.82
Other Items (Net)	47r	−36.52	−59.30	−48.02	−67.82	†102.94	145.68	123.06	67.36	−139.18	209.37	55.16	26.35
Banking Survey		\multicolumn{12}{c}{*Billions of Bolivares: End of Period*}
Foreign Assets (Net)	51n	824.69	1,013.13	1,419.39	1,964.24	†6,039.43	8,824.52	8,593.42	10,072.03	11,605.83	9,874.24	18,153.21	34,772.06
Domestic Credit	52	1,397.41	1,705.20	3,003.55	4,904.65	†5,673.05	7,338.85	9,079.02	10,381.76	11,691.81	14,029.28	16,437.10	14,213.62
Claims on Central Govt. (Net)	52an	233.71	377.80	905.58	1,714.85	†1,120.47	−365.71	556.96	632.17	−224.17	1,648.24	4,092.42	655.53
Claims on State and Local Govts.	52b	.53	—	1.20	4.92	†1.19	.12	.15	13.51	26.82	.07	.07	.07
Claims on Nonfin.Pub.Enterprises.	52c	38.18	90.49	148.44	201.73	†45.50	13.83	5.66	16.59	89.24	3.84	.52	1.33
Claims on Nonbank Pub.Fin.Insts.	52cg	15.12	15.47	813.15	1,355.13	†1,683.03	1,451.28	1,423.07	1,436.33	1,417.07	1,389.71	1,391.71	1,387.85
Claims on Private Sector	52d	1,109.88	1,221.44	1,124.44	1,615.24	†2,793.81	6,185.17	7,029.05	8,081.47	9,932.45	10,838.11	10,761.88	11,774.21
Claims on Nonbank Financial Inst.	52g	—	—	10.75	12.79	†29.06	54.15	64.13	201.70	450.41	149.26	190.48	394.62
Liquid Liabilities	55l	1,577.11	1,945.02	2,974.06	3,992.00	†5,496.05	8,959.72	10,373.90	12,637.57	15,507.67	16,825.73	19,482.65	30,619.21
Money Market Instruments	56aa	....	....	....	....	37.18	63.77	15.43	50.76	95.98	116.95	80.97	44.93
Bonds	56ab	8.86	11.03	8.49	7.04	†17.92	1.46	22.37	59.27	59.35	56.99	22.84	16.93
Liabs. of Central Bank: Securities	56ac	38.97	56.89	389.27	355.00	†576.38	979.79	754.77	495.86	.76	.73	4.48	68.99
Restricted Deposits	56b	....	....	....	....	48.25	64.36	69.49	97.31	172.32	228.13	260.43	307.97
Long-Term Foreign Liabilities	56cl	77.43	93.90	126.00	175.32	†437.58	235.84	159.33	144.31	145.71	144.64	216.10	171.06
Liab. to Nonbank Pub. Fin. Insts.	56dg	107.36	38.92	166.36	83.65	†141.89	70.10	63.75	116.44	159.79	82.46	154.62	813.23
Liab. to Nonbank Financial Insts.	56j	....	....	....	....	48.93	126.05	202.68	210.39	253.62	309.42	264.14	212.64
Capital Accounts	57a	243.83	324.86	466.18	733.76	†3,273.50	4,747.95	6,140.61	7,022.79	6,625.76	6,968.53	14,243.80	15,977.84
Other Items (Net)	57r	168.54	247.72	292.58	1,522.12	†1,634.80	914.33	−129.89	−380.90	276.68	−830.05	−139.73	752.88
Interest Rates		\multicolumn{12}{c}{*Percent Per Annum*}
Discount Rate (End of Period)	60	52.20	71.25	48.00	49.00	45.00	45.00	60.00	38.00	38.00	37.00	40.00	28.50
Money Market Rate	60b	....	....	....	....	16.70	12.47	18.58	7.48	8.14	13.33	28.87	13.23
Savings Rate	60k	28.76	38.59	29.11	22.17	19.53	7.59	12.34	8.15	3.17	2.66	3.86	6.24
Deposit Rate	60l	35.43	53.75	39.02	24.72	27.58	14.70	34.84	21.28	16.30	15.51	29.00	17.21
Lending Rate	60p	41.33	59.90	54.66	39.74	39.41	23.69	46.35	32.13	25.20	22.45	36.58	25.19
Government Bond Yield	61	31.66	41.03	54.73	53.38	49.09	25.41	47.88	†31.12	21.03	22.12	38.51	32.15

2004, International Monetary Fund : *International Financial Statistics Yearbook*

Venezuela, Rep. Bol. 299

		1992	1993	1994	1995	1996	1997	1998	1999	2000	2001	2002	2003
Prices, Production, Labor						*Index Numbers (2000=100): Period Averages*							
Industrial Share Prices............	62	16.0	12.8	†23.0	24.5	73.6	130.8	79.2	76.5	100.0	112.6	100.1	208.5
Prices: Home & Import Goods......	63	6.11	8.25	14.70	23.19	47.13	61.15	74.71	86.82	100.0	113.28	155.50	235.44
Home Goods...................	63a	5.8	7.8	13.8	22.1	44.1	58.5	72.7	85.6	100.0	†114.8	152.5	228.9
Consumer Prices..................	64	4.8	6.6	10.7	17.1	34.2	51.3	69.6	†86.1	100.0	112.5	137.8	180.6
Crude Petroleum Production........	66aa	76.0	78.4	83.0	92.4	95.7	103.8	104.8	94.3	100.0	98.9	....	....
						Number in Thousands: Period Averages							
Labor Force.......................	67d	7,538	7,546	8,027	8,545	....	9,507	....	....	....	11,105	11,674	....
Employment.......................	67e	6,986	7,103	7,626	7,667	7,819	8,287	8,711	8,717	8,822	9,405	9,699	....
Unemployment.....................	67c	582	503	687	875	1,043	1,061	1,093	1,526	1,424	1,436	1,823	....
Unemployment Rate (%)............	67r	7.7	6.7	8.7	10.3	11.8	11.4	11.2	14.9	13.9	13.2	15.8	....
International Transactions						*Billions of Bolivares*							
Exports............................	70	975.4	1,311.8	2,409.8	3,332.6	9,803.1	10,295.6	9,393.5	12,751.4	21,602.2	17,568.9	32,525.7	8,419.5
Petroleum........................	70a	770.9	979.9	1,751.6	2,444.8	7,844.8	8,853.1	6,557.6	9,954.5	18,188.4	14,678.3	23,163.8	....
Crude Petroleum...............	70aa	492.4	637.6	1,197.8	1,641.7	5,346.6	5,934.9	4,220.1	6,592.4	12,390.9	10,297.9	16,645.5	....
Imports, c.i.f......................	71	961.9	1,107.2	1,324.0	2,202.0	4,179.9	7,145.5	8,604.0	8,380.5	10,997.3	13,221.1	....	....
Imports, f.o.b.....................	71.v	866.6	997.4	1,192.8	1,983.8	3,765.7	6,437.3	7,751.3	7,550.0	9,907.5	11,910.9	....	....
						Millions of US Dollars							
Exports............................	70..d	14,185	14,686	16,089	18,457	23,060	21,624	17,193	20,190	31,802	27,409	24,482	5,289
Petroleum........................	70a.d	11,208	11,030	11,473	13,739	18,520	18,186	12,021	16,295	26,772	22,112	18,887	....
Imports, f.o.b.....................	71.vd	12,672	11,271	8,277	11,396	8,901	13,159	14,250	12,670	14,606	16,236	10,667	8,068
Volume of Exports						*2000=100*							
Petroleum........................	72a	72.9	76.6	82.5	90.8	97.3	107.5	109.6	98.6	100.0	96.9	....	....
Crude Petroleum...............	72aa	71.5	76.8	84.5	92.2	98.9	110.3	112.8	96.0	100.0	103.0	....	....
Refined Pretroleum.............	72ab	75.7	76.1	78.4	87.8	93.9	101.7	103.0	104.0	100.0	84.3	....	....
Import Prices (Wholesale).........	76.x	7.4	10.0	18.0	27.1	58.0	70.7	81.7	91.0	100.0	†107.7	165.5	256.9
Balance of Payments						*Millions of US Dollars: Minus Sign Indicates Debit*							
Current Account, n.i.e.............	78a1d	−3,749	−1,993	2,541	2,014	8,914	3,732	−4,432	2,112	11,853	1,987	7,423	9,624
Goods: Exports f.o.b.............	78aad	14,202	14,779	16,105	19,082	23,707	23,871	17,707	20,963	33,529	26,667	26,656	25,750
Goods: Imports f.o.b.............	78abd	−12,880	−11,504	−8,480	−12,069	−9,937	−14,917	−16,755	−14,492	−16,865	−19,207	−13,622	−10,707
Trade Balance..................	78acd	1,322	3,275	7,625	7,013	13,770	8,954	952	6,471	16,664	7,460	13,034	15,043
Services: Credit..................	78add	1,312	1,340	1,576	1,671	1,573	1,314	1,423	1,352	1,182	1,376	1,060	877
Services: Debit...................	78aed	−4,263	−4,525	−4,672	−4,836	−4,842	−3,922	−4,072	−4,191	−4,435	−4,681	−3,852	−3,319
Balance on Goods & Services....	78afd	−1,629	90	4,529	3,848	10,501	6,346	−1,697	3,632	13,411	4,155	10,242	12,601
Income: Credit...................	78agd	1,607	1,599	1,626	1,867	1,579	2,421	2,479	2,272	3,049	2,603	1,587	1,121
Income: Debit....................	78ahd	−3,353	−3,314	−3,530	−3,810	−3,304	−4,938	−5,013	−3,725	−4,437	−4,623	−4,241	−4,096
Balance on Gds, Serv. & Inc....	78aid	−3,375	−1,625	2,625	1,905	8,776	3,829	−4,231	2,179	12,023	2,135	7,588	9,626
Current Transfers, n.i.e.: Credit...	78ajd	533	452	606	413	526	233	169	203	261	356	285	251
Current Transfers: Debit..........	78akd	−907	−820	−690	−304	−388	−330	−370	−270	−431	−504	−450	−253
Capital Account, n.i.e.............	78bcd	−	−	−	−	−	−	−	−	−	−	−	−
Capital Account, n.i.e.: Credit.....	78bad	−	−	−	−	−	−	−	−	−	−	−	−
Capital Account: Debit............	78bbd	−	−	−	−	−	−	−	−	−	−	−	−
Financial Account, n.i.e............	78bjd	3,386	2,656	−3,204	−2,964	−1,784	879	2,689	−516	−2,969	−211	−9,368	−3,160
Direct Investment Abroad.........	78bdd	−156	−886	−358	−91	−507	−557	−1,043	−872	−521	−204	−1,020	−1,143
Dir. Invest. in Rep. Econ., n.i.e...	78bed	629	372	813	985	2,183	6,202	4,985	2,890	4,701	3,683	779	2,531
Portfolio Investment Assets.......	78bfd	2	79	−22	−14	−41	−1,651	470	248	−954	397	−1,347	−175
Equity Securities................	78bkd	−44	−1	10	−3	−11	−47	−240	72	13	138	−165	−200
Debt Securities.................	78bld	46	80	−32	−11	−30	−1,604	710	176	−967	259	−1,182	25
Portfolio Investment Liab., n.i.e....	78bgd	1,001	542	275	−787	780	911	306	1,857	−2,180	710	−957	−885
Equity Securities................	78bmd	165	48	585	270	1,318	1,444	187	417	−574	31	−5	100
Debt Securities.................	78bnd	836	494	−310	−1,057	−538	−533	119	1,440	−1,606	679	−952	−985
Financial Derivatives Assets.......	78bwd	−	−	....	....	−	−	−	−	−	−	−	....
Financial Derivatives Liabilities.....	78bxd	−	−	−	−	−	−	−	−	−	−	−	....
Other Investment Assets..........	78bhd	−590	615	−4,173	−661	−1,592	−3,748	−3,325	−4,788	−4,839	−3,919	−7,407	−1,977
Monetary Authorities............	78bod	−	−	−	−	−	−2	28	128	18	42	20	11
General Government............	78bpd	−45	−16	−27	240	57	−264	391	64	−228	−1,016	65	−632
Banks.........................	78bqd	−58	−538	−932	216	−53	−17	−182	−262	−50	267	420	131
Other Sectors..................	78brd	−487	1,169	−3,214	−1,117	−1,596	−3,465	−3,562	−4,718	−4,579	−3,212	−7,912	−1,487
Other Investment Liab., n.i.e......	78bid	2,500	1,934	261	−2,396	−2,607	−278	1,296	149	824	−878	584	−1,511
Monetary Authorities............	78bsd	282	778	−51	−317	−289	−430	−561	−24	8	18	−22	16
General Government............	78btd	593	−210	128	−262	−543	162	986	272	36	−1	170	54
Banks.........................	78bud	86	113	−77	52	153	36	−69	−34	197	122	−256	−137
Other Sectors..................	78bvd	1,539	1,253	261	−1,869	−1,928	−46	940	−65	583	−1,017	692	−1,444
Net Errors and Omissions..........	78cad	−299	−539	−281	−494	−892	−1,517	−1,662	−538	−2,926	−3,605	−2,483	−1,010
Overall Balance....................	78cbd	−662	124	−944	−1,444	6,238	3,094	−3,405	1,058	5,958	−1,829	−4,428	5,454
Reserves and Related Items........	79dad	662	−124	944	1,444	−6,238	−3,094	3,405	−1,058	−5,958	1,829	4,428	−5,454
Reserve Assets....................	79dbd	845	144	1,145	1,907	−6,271	−2,643	3,853	−608	−5,449	2,027	4,428	−5,454
Use of Fund Credit and Loans......	79dcd	−183	−268	−201	−463	33	−452	−448	−450	−508	−198	−	−
Exceptional Financing..............	79ded	−	−	−	−	−	−	−	−	−	−	−	−

Venezuela, Rep. Bol. 299

		1992	1993	1994	1995	1996	1997	1998	1999	2000	2001	2002	2003
International Investment Position						**Millions of US Dollars**							
Assets	79aad	41,806	43,156	46,634	45,944	41,216	49,537	50,051	55,792	67,928	70,047	75,620	....
Direct Investment Abroad	79abd	1,568	2,447	3,124	3,427	4,595	5,209	6,176	7,143	7,676	7,894	8,914	....
Portfolio Investment	79acd	1,879	1,799	1,796	1,530	1,986	3,646	3,406	2,784	4,054	3,812	4,846	....
Equity Securities	79add	–	–	–	–	43	113	385	260	245	101	268	....
Debt Securities	79aed	1,879	1,799	1,796	1,530	1,943	3,533	3,021	2,524	3,809	3,711	4,578	....
Financial Derivatives	79ald	–	–	–	–	–	–	–	–	–	–	–	....
Other Investment	79afd	24,363	25,106	28,955	30,391	17,862	21,669	25,019	29,835	34,707	39,819	47,000	....
Monetary Authorities	79agd	–	–	–	–	205	340	313	186	167	125	105	....
General Government	79ahd	796	812	812	874	1,401	1,658	1,272	1,216	1,430	2,456	2,420	....
Banks	79aid	2,181	2,719	3,774	3,586	188	240	443	703	753	485	542	....
Other Sectors	79ajd	21,386	21,575	24,369	25,931	16,068	19,431	22,991	27,730	32,357	36,753	43,933	....
Reserve Assets	79akd	13,996	13,804	12,759	10,596	16,773	19,013	15,450	16,030	21,491	18,522	14,860	....
Liabilities	79lad	47,046	50,713	51,730	49,250	56,284	62,393	62,251	67,275	69,531	71,912	72,187	....
Dir. Invest. in Rep. Economy	79lbd	4,687	5,059	5,872	6,772	18,124	24,694	28,915	31,470	35,480	39,074	38,808	....
Portfolio Investment	79lcd	20,241	22,816	22,844	22,555	20,506	21,218	15,772	18,486	16,638	16,524	16,193	....
Equity Securities	79ldd	–	917	1,184	1,060	2,488	3,882	1,623	2,185	1,706	1,301	948	....
Debt Securities	79led	20,241	21,899	21,660	21,495	18,018	17,336	14,149	16,301	14,932	15,223	15,245	....
Financial Derivatives	79lld	–	–	–	–	–	–	–	–	–	–	–	....
Other Investment	79lfd	22,118	22,838	23,014	19,923	17,654	16,481	17,564	17,319	17,413	16,314	17,186	....
Monetary Authorities	79lgd	3,821	4,376	4,246	3,525	2,271	1,714	1,271	769	234	40	21	....
General Government	79lhd	8,975	8,459	8,454	8,009	3,960	3,978	5,055	5,362	5,242	5,214	5,793	....
Banks	79lid	1,335	1,447	1,394	1,451	294	327	253	220	347	540	284	....
Other Sectors	79ljd	7,987	8,556	8,920	6,938	11,129	10,462	10,985	10,968	11,590	10,520	11,088	....
Government Finance						**Billions of Bolivares: Year Ending December 31**							
Deficit (-) or Surplus	80	−128.2	−125.0	† −485.9	−493.8	456.5	955.5	−1,967.6	−999.8	−1,361.1	−3,941.1	....	....
Revenue	81	749.1	946.0	† 1,575.1	2,242.6	5,767.8	10,241.0	9,157.1	11,251.8	16,873.5	19,326.5	....	....
Grants Received	81z	–	–	–	–	–	–	–	–	–	–	....	....
Expenditure	82	824.7	1,013.8	1,666.3	2,541.5	4,964.2	8,894.3	11,014.0	12,170.0	17,860.2	22,883.8	....	....
Lending Minus Repayments	83	52.6	57.3	394.6	195.0	347.1	391.2	110.6	81.7	374.4	383.8	....	....
Financing													
Net Borrowing	84	128.2	125.0	485.9	493.8	−456.5	−955.5	1,967.6	999.8	1,361.1	3,941.1	....	....
Domestic	84a	79.0	131.8	530.6	476.2	−301.7	−1,359.9	1,378.4	1,623.4	3,207.4	3,640.4	....	....
Foreign	85a	49.1	−6.8	−44.8	17.7	−154.8	404.4	589.2	−623.6	−1,846.2	300.7	....	....
Use of Cash Balances	87	....	....	....	....	....	....	....	....	....	....	....	....
National Accounts						**Billions of Bolivares**							
Househ.Cons.Expend.,incl.NPISHs	96f	2,877.6	3,977.4	6,077.1	9,507.7	18,618.0	28,524.0	37,685.0	43,236.9	52,295.1	61,107.9	72,405.5	....
Government Consumption Expend	91f	379.4	466.0	627.0	974.8	1,475.6	2,807.7	3,957.6	4,700.3	5,958.9	7,846.7	8,924.5	....
Gross Fixed Capital Formation	93e	886.4	1,091.1	1,528.4	2,255.6	4,645.8	8,123.0	9,991.3	9,850.6	11,719.0	14,952.6	15,913.7	....
Changes in Inventories	93i	93.6	−68.5	−300.3	223.4	227.6	998.5	1,485.0	1,477.2	2,475.0	3,057.0	−602.0	....
Exports of Goods and Services	90c	1,088.8	1,470.3	2,677.5	3,709.8	10,748.9	12,312.5	10,441.8	13,546.0	23,457.0	20,320.2	32,429.4	....
Imports of Goods and Services (-)	98c	1,194.4	1,482.4	1,934.5	2,985.7	6,278.3	9,422.0	11,078.2	10,233.9	13,454.3	15,959.6	18,288.7	....
Gross Domestic Product (GDP)	99b	4,131.5	5,453.9	8,675.2	13,685.7	29,437.7	43,343.7	52,482.5	62,577.0	82,450.7	91,324.8	110,782.4	....
Net Primary Income from Abroad	98.n	−123.8	−162.4	−274.6	−322.9	−665.7	−1,178.2	−1,061.9	−928.8	−818.1	−1,092.0	−3,417.5	....
Gross National Income (GNI)	99a	4,007.7	5,291.5	8,400.6	13,362.8	28,772.0	42,165.5	51,420.6	61,648.2	81,632.6	90,232.8	107,364.8	....
Consumption of Fixed Capital	99cf	309.3	422.4	625.8	927.7	1,884.4	2,947.2	4,069.0	4,777.7	5,923.6	6,822.2	8,133.5	....
GDP Volume 1984 Prices	99b.p	556.7	558.2	545.1	566.6	565.5	601.5	602.6	565.9	584.2	600.5	547.2	....
GDP Volume (2000=100)	99bvp	95.3	95.5	93.3	97.0	96.8	103.0	103.1	96.9	100.0	102.8	93.7	....
GDP Deflator (2000=100)	99bip	5.3	6.9	11.3	17.1	36.9	51.1	61.7	78.4	100.0	107.8	143.5	....
						Millions: Midyear Estimates							
Population	99z	20.46	20.93	21.41	21.89	22.37	22.84	23.32	23.80	24.28	24.75	25.23	25.70

Vietnam 582

		1992	1993	1994	1995	1996	1997	1998	1999	2000	2001	2002	2003
Exchange Rates						Dong per SDR: End of Period							
Market Rate	aa	†14,527	14,893	16,133	16,374	16,032	16,585	19,558	19,254	18,910	18,957	20,941	23,249
					Dong per US Dollar: End of Period (ae) Period Average (rf)									
Market Rate	ae	†10,565	10,843	11,051	11,015	11,149	12,292	13,890	14,028	14,514	15,084	15,403	15,646
Market Rate	rf	†11,202	10,641	10,966	11,038	11,033	11,683	13,268	13,943	14,168	14,725	15,280	15,510
Fund Position						Millions of SDRs: End of Period							
Quota	2f.s	176.8	241.6	241.6	241.6	241.6	241.6	241.6	329.1	329.1	329.1	329.1	329.1
SDRs	1b.s	–	4.9	11.0	2.2	11.9	9.4	1.8	1.1	.3	11.6	–	1.5
Reserve Position in the Fund	1c.s	–	–	–	–	–	–	–	–	–	–	–	–
Total Fund Cred.&Loans Outstg	2tl	71.5	72.5	193.4	253.8	374.6	335.3	277.9	258.7	242.6	291.2	280.2	227.9
International Liquidity					Millions of US Dollars Unless Otherwise Indicated: End of Period								
Total Reserves minus Gold	1l.d	....	....	....	1,323.7	1,735.9	1,985.9	2,002.3	3,326.1	3,416.5	3,674.6	4,121.1	6,224.2
SDRs	1b.d	–	6.8	16.1	3.3	17.1	12.7	2.5	1.5	.3	14.6	–	2.2
Reserve Position in the Fund	1c.d	–	–	–	–	–	–	–	–	–	–	–	–
Foreign Exchange	1d.d	....	....	....	1,320.4	1,718.8	1,973.1	1,999.7	3,324.7	3,416.2	3,660.0	4,121.0	6,222.0
Gold (Market Valuation)	1and	....	....	....	55.4	77.9	112.3	98.2	97.3	93.1	90.6	110.8	135.0
Monetary Authorities: Other Liab	4..d	–	–	....	377.1	537.3	507.8	505.5	513.5	487.6	535.9	557.4	537.8
Deposit Money Banks: Assets	7a.d	877.9	538.3	....	869.2	1,004.2	999.2	1,347.0	2,119.0	4,221.8	5,261.4	4,589.2	3,264.2
Liabilities	7b.d	201.5	321.4	....	865.0	985.5	868.7	679.0	664.7	682.6	679.6	640.1	684.8
Monetary Authorities						Billions of Dong: End of Period							
Foreign Assets	11	4,897	4,381	....	15,153	20,031	25,633	29,147	48,004	50,934	56,586	65,177	99,460
Claims on General Government	12a	9,326	13,323	....	9,593	12,576	13,382	16,658	11,289	11,732	12,421	15,130	15,223
Claims on Banking Institutions	12e	5,004	6,792	....	6,779	7,693	6,776	6,521	10,312	14,234	17,776	19,182	13,565
Reserve Money	14	14,314	18,296	....	26,343	31,633	35,599	38,687	58,220	72,759	84,945	95,502	121,633
of which: Currency Outside DMBs	14a	10,579	14,218	....	19,370	22,639	25,101	26,965	41,254	52,208	66,320	74,263	90,584
Foreign Liabilities	16c	–	–	....	4,154	5,991	6,241	7,022	7,203	7,077	8,083	8,585	8,414
General Government Deposits	16d	4,273	4,883	....	6,575	7,383	9,348	10,340	11,089	7,410	4,390	4,005	4,553
Capital Accounts	17a	776	476	....	809	1,055	2,511	6,888	6,440	8,216	9,770	12,129	15,645
Other Items (Net)	17r	–283	750	....	–6,791	–6,245	–7,938	–10,611	–13,348	–18,562	–20,405	–20,731	–21,997
Banking Institutions						Billions of Dong: End of Period							
Reserves	20	3,451	3,709	....	7,409	9,323	9,451	9,920	16,881	20,390	18,426	20,166	30,778
Foreign Assets	21	9,275	5,836	....	9,574	11,196	12,282	18,710	29,725	61,276	79,364	70,687	51,071
Claims on General Government	22a	1,634	1,718	....	4,372	2,031	3,492	5,332	6,358	8,246	10,258	17,566	34,169
Claims on Rest of Economy	22d	2,743	7,669	....	18,199	23,942	31,220	34,889	112,730	155,720	189,103	231,078	296,737
Demand Deposits	24	3,971	4,796	....	6,870	10,213	14,682	18,241	27,106	38,781	46,089	51,066	66,441
Time and Savings Deposits	25a	3,822	3,250	....	9,622	12,445	15,194	20,091	36,191	47,462	60,251	77,387	133,617
Foreign Currency Deposits	25b	6,506	5,892	....	8,924	11,042	15,611	22,098	40,919	58,543	78,187	81,428	87,418
Bonds & Money Mkt. Instruments	26a	298	2,544	....	5,490	5,635	7,703	10,890	10,865	18,842	21,012	35,262	26,265
Restricted Deposits	26b	1,708	1,514	....	2,138	2,117	3,080	2,830	4,059	7,045	7,923	9,744	7,899
Foreign Liabilities	26c	2,128	3,485	....	9,528	10,987	10,678	9,432	9,324	9,908	10,251	9,860	10,715
General Government Deposits	26d	4,268	1,786	....	3,321	2,795	3,127	4,974	3,606	13,052	16,187	19,848	23,805
Credit from Central Bank	26g	4,752	6,621	....	5,793	6,133	5,565	4,249	11,576	14,427	17,753	19,250	14,491
Capital Accounts	27a	2,176	2,702	....	5,292	6,237	8,182	11,562	18,520	22,392	24,274	30,927	41,620
Other Items (Net)	27r	126	1,856	....	6,688	5,735	3,655	2,246	3,528	15,181	15,224	4,724	485
Banking Survey						Billions of Dong: End of Period							
Foreign Assets (Net)	31n	12,043	6,732	....	11,046	14,249	20,997	31,404	61,201	95,225	117,616	117,419	131,402
Domestic Credit	32	5,161	16,040	....	22,268	28,370	35,620	41,566	115,682	155,236	191,204	239,921	317,771
Claims on General Govt. (Net)	32an	2,418	8,371	....	4,069	4,428	4,400	6,677	2,952	–484	2,102	8,843	21,034
Claims on Rest of Economy	32d	2,743	7,669	....	18,199	23,942	31,220	34,889	112,730	155,720	189,103	231,078	296,737
Money	34	14,811	19,088	....	26,736	33,439	39,972	45,207	68,360	90,989	112,408	125,329	157,025
Quasi-Money	35	10,327	9,142	....	18,546	23,487	30,805	42,189	77,110	106,005	138,437	158,815	221,035
Bonds & Money Mkt. Instruments	36a	298	2,544	....	5,490	5,635	7,703	10,890	10,865	18,842	21,012	35,262	26,265
Restricted Deposits	36b	1,708	1,514	....	2,138	2,117	3,080	2,830	4,059	7,045	7,923	9,744	7,899
Capital Accounts	37a	2,953	3,178	....	6,101	7,292	10,693	18,450	24,961	30,608	34,044	43,056	57,264
Other Items (Net)	37r	–126	2,804	....	–1,525	–2,398	–4,447	–8,835	–8,471	–3,027	–5,006	–14,865	–20,315
Money plus Quasi-Money	35l	25,138	28,231	....	45,283	56,926	70,777	87,396	145,470	196,994	250,846	284,144	378,060
Interest Rates						Percent Per Annum							
Refinancing Rate (End of Period)	60	....	....	....	....	18.90	10.80	12.00	6.00	6.00	4.80	4.80	5.00
Treasury Bill Rate	60c	....	26.40	....	....	....	....	....	....	5.42	5.49	5.92	5.83
Deposit Rate	60l	....	22.04	....	....	....	8.51	9.23	7.37	3.65	5.30	6.45	6.62
Lending Rate	60p	....	32.18	....	....	20.10	14.42	14.40	12.70	10.55	9.42	9.06	9.48
Prices						Index Numbers (2000=100): Period Averages							
Consumer Prices	64	....	....	....	83.5	88.3	91.1	97.7	101.7	100.0	99.6	103.4	106.6
International Transactions							Billions of Dong						
Exports	70..d	....	....	....	7,256	9,185	9,361	11,540	14,449	15,100	16,530	20,176	
Imports, c.i.f.	71..d	....	....	....	11,144	11,592	11,500	11,742	15,638	15,999	19,000	24,863	

Vietnam 582

		1992	1993	1994	1995	1996	1997	1998	1999	2000	2001	2002	2003
Balance of Payments						*Millions of US Dollars: Minus Sign Indicates Debit*							
Current Account, n.i.e.	78ald	....	....	....	....	−2,020	−1,528	−1,074	1,177	1,106	682	−604	....
Goods: Exports f.o.b.	78aad	....	....	....	....	7,255	9,185	9,361	11,540	14,448	15,027	16,706	....
Goods: Imports f.o.b.	78abd	....	....	....	....	−10,030	−10,432	−10,350	−10,568	−14,073	−14,546	−17,760	....
Trade Balance	78acd	....	....	....	....	−2,775	−1,247	−989	972	375	481	−1,054	....
Services: Credit	78add	....	....	....	....	2,243	2,530	2,616	2,493	2,702	2,810	2,948	....
Services: Debit	78aed	....	....	....	....	−2,304	−3,153	−3,146	−3,040	−3,252	−3,382	−3,698	....
Balance on Goods & Services	78afd	....	....	....	....	−2,836	−1,870	−1,519	425	−175	−91	−1,804	....
Income: Credit	78agd	....	....	....	....	140	136	127	142	331	318	167	....
Income: Debit	78ahd	....	....	....	....	−524	−679	−804	−571	−782	−795	−888	....
Balance on Gds. Serv. & Inc.	78aid	....	....	....	....	−3,220	−2,413	−2,196	−4	−626	−568	−2,525	....
Current Transfers, n.i.e.: Credit	78ajd	....	....	....	....	1,200	885	1,122	1,181	1,732	1,250	1,921	....
Current Transfers: Debit	78akd	....	....	....	....	−	−	−	−	−	−	−	....
Capital Account, n.i.e.	78bcd	....	....	....	....	−	−	−	−	−	−	−	....
Capital Account, n.i.e.: Credit	78bad	....	....	....	....	−	−	−	−	−	−	−	....
Capital Account: Debit	78bbd	....	....	....	....	−	−	−	−	−	−	−	....
Financial Account, n.i.e.	78bjd	....	....	....	....	2,909	2,125	1,646	1,058	−316	371	2,090	....
Direct Investment Abroad	78bdd	....	....	....	....	−	−	−	−	−	−	−	....
Dir. Invest. in Rep. Econ., n.i.e.	78bed	....	....	....	....	2,395	2,220	1,671	1,412	1,298	1,300	1,400	....
Portfolio Investment Assets	78bfd	....	....	....	....	−	−	−	−	−	−	−	....
Equity Securities	78bkd	....	....	....	....	....	....	....	....	....	....	....	....
Debt Securities	78bld	....	....	....	....	....	....	....	....	....	....	....	....
Portfolio Investment Liab., n.i.e.	78bgd	....	....	....	....	−	−	−	−	−	−	−	....
Equity Securities	78bmd	....	....	....	....	....	....	....	....	....	....	....	....
Debt Securities	78bnd	....	....	....	....	....	....	....	....	....	....	....	....
Financial Derivatives Assets	78bwd	....	....	....	....	−	−	−	−	−	−	−	....
Financial Derivatives Liabilities	78bxd	....	....	....	....	−	−	−	−	−	−	−	....
Other Investment Assets	78bhd	....	....	....	....	−33	−112	−537	−786	−2,089	−1,197	624	....
Monetary Authorities	78bod	....	....	....	....	....	....	....	....	....	....	....	....
General Government	78bpd	....	....	....	....	....	....	....	....	....	....	....	....
Banks	78bqd	....	....	....	....	−33	−112	−537	−786	−2,089	−1,197	624	....
Other Sectors	78brd	....	....	....	....	−	....	....	....	....	....	....	....
Other Investment Liab., n.i.e.	78bid	....	....	....	....	547	17	512	432	475	268	66	....
Monetary Authorities	78bsd	....	....	....	....	−	−	−	−	−	−	−	....
General Government	78btd	....	....	....	....	....	....	....	....	....	....	....	....
Banks	78bud	....	....	....	....	....	....	....	....	....	....	....	....
Other Sectors	78bvd	....	....	....	....	547	17	512	432	475	268	66	....
Net Errors and Omissions	78cad	....	....	....	....	−611	−269	−535	−925	−680	−847	−1,038	....
Overall Balance	78cbd	....	....	....	....	278	328	37	1,310	110	206	448	....
Reserves and Related Items	79dad	....	....	....	....	−278	−328	−37	−1,310	−110	−206	−448	....
Reserve Assets	79dbd	....	....	....	....	−453	−274	41	−1,284	−89	−267	−435	....
Use of Fund Credit and Loans	79dcd	....	....	....	....	175	−54	−78	−26	−21	61	−13	....
Exceptional Financing	79ded	....	....	....	....	−	−	−	−	−	−	−	....
Government Finance						*Billions of Dong: Year Ending December 31*							
Deficit (-) or Surplus	80	−2,017p	−6,035p	−2,530	−1,219	−502	−5,397	462	−6,328	−12,402	−14,130	....	....
Total Revenue and Grants	81y	12,658p	19,265p	42,125	53,370	62,387	65,352	72,965	78,489	90,749	103,050	....	....
Revenue	81	11,849p	18,416p	40,925	51,750	60,844	62,766	70,822	76,128	88,721	97,750	....	....
Grants	81z	809p	849p	1,200	1,620	1,543	2,586	2,143	2,361	2,028p	5,300f	....	....
Exp. & Lending Minus Repay	82z	14,675p	25,300p	44,655	54,589	62,889	70,749	73,419	84,817	103,151	117,180	....	....
Expenditure	82	16,130p	27,021p	44,655	54,589	62,889	70,749	73,419	84,817	103,151	117,180	....	....
Lending Minus Repayments	83	−1,455p	−1,721p	−	−	−	−	−	−	−	−	....	....
Total Financing	80h	2,017p	6,035p	2,530	1,219	502	5,416	454	6,328	12,402	14,130	....	....
Domestic Financing	84a	−945p	4,449p	2,330	2,709	552	5,396	−2,814	1,491	6,110	9,086	....	....
Foreign Financing	85a	2,962p	1,586p	200	−1,490	−50	191	3,268	4,837	6,292	5,044	....	....
Debt: Domestic	88a	2,234p	4,709p	....	....	....	....	....	....	....	....	....	....
Foreign	89a	74,152p	72,680p	....	....	....	....	....	....	....	....	....	....
National Accounts								*Billions of Dong*					
Househ.Cons.Expend.,incl.NPISHs	96f	87,661	106,440	133,299	168,492	202,509	225,084	255,921	274,553	293,507	312,144	348,060	392,200
Government Consumption Expend.	91f	7,653	10,279	14,738	18,741	22,722	25,500	27,523	27,137	28,346	30,463	33,390	41,770
Gross Fixed Capital Formation	93e	18,406	30,635	43,325	58,187	71,597	83,734	97,551	102,799	122,101	140,301	160,840	199,600
Changes in Inventories	93i	1,092	3,385	2,153	3,944	4,853	5,020	7,324	7,704	8,670	9,732	11,155	12,800
Exports of Goods and Services	90c	38,405	40,285	60,725	75,106	111,177	135,180	161,910	199,836	243,049	262,864	297,546	358,040
Imports of Goods and Services (-)	98c	42,921	52,582	77,591	95,925	141,016	160,706	188,281	211,254	253,927	273,828	319,017	411,600
Gross Domestic Product (GDP)	99b	110,532	140,258	178,534	228,892	272,037	313,624	361,016	399,942	441,646	481,295	536,098	605,400
Net Primary Income from Abroad	98.n	−3,775.0	−5,345.0	−4,517.0	215.0	−2,383.0	−5,024.0	−8,180.0	−7,249.0	−6,328.0	−6,440.0	−8,711.0	....
Gross National Income (GNI)	99a	106,757	134,913	174,017	228,677	269,654	308,600	352,836	392,693	435,318	474,855	527,387	....
GDP Volume 1994 Prices	99b.p	151,782	164,043	178,534	195,567	213,833	231,264	244,596	256,272	273,666	292,535	313,135	335,800
GDP Volume (2000=100)	99bvp	55.5	59.9	65.2	71.5	78.1	84.5	89.4	93.6	100.0	106.9	114.4	122.7
GDP Deflator (2000=100)	99bip	45.1	53.0	62.0	72.5	78.8	84.0	91.5	96.7	100.0	101.9	106.1	111.7
						Millions: Midyear Estimates							
Population	99z	68.90	70.28	71.60	72.84	73.99	75.07	76.09	77.11	78.14	Ü 79.20	80.28	81.38

2004, International Monetary Fund: International Financial Statistics Yearbook

WAEMU 759

		1992	1993	1994	1995	1996	1997	1998	1999	2000	2001	2002	2003
Exchange Rates						*Francs per SDR: End of Period*							
Official Rate	aa	378.57	404.89	†780.44	728.38	753.06	807.94	791.61	896.19	918.49	935.39	850.37	771.76
				Francs per US Dollar: End of Period (ae) Period Average (rf)									
Official Rate	ae	275.32	294.77	†534.60	490.00	523.70	598.81	562.21	652.95	704.95	744.31	625.50	519.36
Official Rate	rf	264.69	283.16	†555.20	499.15	511.55	583.67	589.95	615.70	711.98	733.04	696.99	581.20
Fund Position						*Millions of SDRs: End of Period*							
Quota	2f.s	628.6	628.6	628.6	628.6	628.6	628.6	628.6	855.8	855.8	855.8	855.8	855.8
SDRs	1b.s	6.1	7.3	6.9	10.2	5.8	2.3	1.3	6.6	2.2	8.1	8.9	10.9
Reserve Position in the Fund	1c.s	27.8	28.0	28.1	28.2	28.3	28.5	28.5	28.6	28.7	28.9	29.0	29.3
Total Fund Cred.&Loans Outstg.	2tl	565.5	525.9	686.9	836.0	920.6	938.1	1,076.0	1,068.3	1,031.3	984.6	949.0	824.4
International Liquidity					*Millions of US Dollars Unless Otherwise Indicated: End of Period*								
Total Reserves minus Gold	1l.d	....	....	....	2,538.6	2,739.8	2,868.4	3,164.3	2,932.1	3,283.9	3,780.5	5,454.9	6,728.8
SDRs	1b.d	8.4	10.0	10.1	15.2	8.3	3.1	1.9	9.1	2.8	10.2	12.2	16.2
Reserve Position in the Fund	1c.d	38.3	38.5	41.0	41.9	40.7	38.4	40.2	39.3	37.4	36.3	39.5	43.5
Foreign Exchange	1d.d	....	....	....	2,481.5	2,690.7	2,826.9	3,122.3	2,883.7	3,243.6	3,734.0	5,403.2	6,669.0
Gold (Million Fine Troy Ounces)	1ad	....	....	....	.801	.859	.902	.959	1.012	1.058	1.117	1.172	1.172
Gold (National Valuation)	1and	....	....	....	308.3	322.8	276.1	281.4	298.9	284.4	310.6	377.8	458.4
Monetary Authorities: Other Liab.	4..d	....	415.4	313.1	264.1	256.5	252.9	242.0	239.9	203.6	144.1	220.3	276.6
Deposit Money Banks: Assets	7a.d	....	391.4	571.1	813.5	746.7	649.1	722.1	801.0	682.4	655.7	811.6	825.0
Liabilities	7b.d	....	699.5	461.2	641.1	527.9	438.7	565.4	659.7	478.3	438.8	405.9	507.0
Monetary Authorities						*Billions of Francs: End of Period*							
Foreign Assets	11	....	....	....	1,416	1,612	1,889	1,944	2,114	2,521	3,046	3,664	3,734
Claims on Central Government	12a	....	....	....	940	976	1,122	1,283	1,295	1,228	1,262	1,248	1,131
Claims on Deposit Money Banks	12e	....	....	....	150	146	159	179	123	91	43	16	2
Claims on Other Financial Insts.	12f	....	....	....	13	16	15	17	16	14	11	9	6
Reserve Money	14	....	....	....	1,251	1,284	1,428	1,534	1,589	1,773	2,194	2,647	2,596
of which: Currency Outside DMBs	14a	....	....	....	1,018	1,060	1,217	1,305	1,361	1,465	1,703	2,010	1,848
Foreign Liabilities	16c	....	....	....	738	828	909	988	1,114	1,091	1,028	945	780
Central Government Deposits	16d	....	....	....	158	231	325	352	328	252	343	392	430
Other Items (Net)	17r	....	....	....	372	407	523	547	517	739	797	954	1,066
Deposit Money Banks						*Billions of Francs: End of Period*							
Reserves	20	....	....	....	177	178	188	175	198	280	392	534	700
Foreign Assets	21	....	....	....	399	391	389	406	523	481	488	508	428
Claims on Central Government	22a	....	....	....	724	827	807	824	805	699	705	719	776
Claims on Private Sector	22d	....	....	....	1,819	1,998	2,204	2,377	2,407	2,665	2,835	3,010	3,223
Claims on Other Financial Insts.	22f	....	....	....	3	–	–	–	–	–	–	–	–
Demand Deposits	24	....	....	....	1,028	1,108	1,137	1,245	1,303	1,378	1,488	1,686	1,899
Time Deposits	25	....	....	....	995	1,101	1,157	1,090	1,160	1,264	1,369	1,598	1,718
Foreign Liabilities	26c	....	....	....	255	227	239	295	391	304	288	213	222
Long-Term Foreign Liabilities	26cl	....	....	....	59	49	24	23	40	33	39	41	41
Central Government Deposits	26d	....	....	....	524	624	599	663	606	706	765	778	778
Credit from Monetary Authorities	26g	....	....	....	162	148	159	180	114	96	44	16	2
Other Items (Net)	27r	....	....	....	98	136	274	285	320	343	426	439	468
Monetary Survey						*Billions of Francs: End of Period*							
Foreign Assets (Net)	31n	....	....	....	821	948	1,130	1,066	1,132	1,607	2,218	3,014	3,160
Domestic Credit	32	....	....	....	2,831	2,978	3,243	3,501	3,608	3,670	3,727	3,839	3,957
Claims on Central Govt. (Net)	32an	....	....	....	971	935	992	1,081	1,157	974	854	797	710
Claims on Private Sector	32d	....	....	....	1,844	2,028	2,236	2,404	2,435	2,682	2,862	3,033	3,241
Claims on Other Financial Insts.	32f	....	....	....	16	16	15	17	16	14	11	9	6
Money	34	....	....	....	2,101	2,229	2,415	2,607	2,721	2,896	3,281	3,775	3,816
Quasi-Money	35	....	....	....	995	1,101	1,157	1,090	1,160	1,264	1,369	1,598	1,718
Long-Term Foreign Liabilities	36cl	....	....	....	59	49	24	23	40	33	39	41	41
Other Items (Net)	37r	....	....	....	497	547	777	848	819	1,084	1,256	1,439	1,542
Money plus Quasi-Money	35l	....	....	....	3,096	3,330	3,573	3,697	3,881	4,160	4,650	5,374	5,534
Interest Rates						*Percent Per Annum*							
Bank Rate (End of Period)	60	....	....	....	6.00	6.00	6.00	6.00	6.00	6.00	6.00	6.00	4.50
Money Market Rate	60b	....	....	....	4.95	4.95	4.95	4.95	4.95	4.95	4.95	4.95	4.95
Deposit Rate	60l	....	....	....	3.50	3.50	3.50	3.50	3.50	3.50	3.50	3.50	3.50
Prices						*Index Numbers (2000=100): Period Averages*							
Share Price Index	62	....	....	....	....	....	....	112.4	100.0	89.0	92.3	93.5	
Consumer Prices	64	60.3	61.0	79.2	88.8	91.8	94.6	98.1	98.3	100.0	104.0	107.1	108.5

WAEMU 759

		1992	1993	1994	1995	1996	1997	1998	1999	2000	2001	2002	2003
National Accounts							*Billions of Francs*						
Househ.Cons.Expend.,incl.NPISHs.....	96f	....	....	....	....	9,714.3	11,206.6	12,185.5	12,687.5	13,103.6	13,910.0	14,657.1	....
Government Consumption Expend....	91f	....	....	....	....	1,689.8	1,860.7	2,321.6	2,421.3	2,387.8	2,681.5	2,911.3	....
Gross Fixed Capital Formation.........	93e	....	....	....	....	2,242.6	2,538.8	2,845.7	2,950.0	2,753.0	2,963.2	3,310.5	....
Changes in Inventories...................	93i	....	....	....	....	−47.1	93.3	214.0	−43.8	215.5	352.3	32.2	....
Exports of Goods and Services.........	90c	....	....	....	....	4,430.0	4,950.4	5,203.3	5,387.1	5,504.9	5,991.5	6,427.8	....
Imports of Goods and Services(-)......	98c	....	....	....	....	4,671.8	5,025.5	5,440.4	5,724.6	6,067.8	6,563.5	6,770.2	....
Gross Domestic Product (GDP)........	99b	....	....	....	....	13,357.7	15,623.9	17,007.0	17,677.6	17,896.9	19,334.4	20,568.0	....

Yemen, Republic of 474

		1992	1993	1994	1995	1996	1997	1998	1999	2000	2001	2002	2003
Exchange Rates						**Rial per SDR: End of Period**							
Market Rate	aa	16.514	16.496	17.533	†74.384	†182.492	176.023	199.447	218.366	215.749	217.754	243.368	273.879
						Rial per US Dollar: End of Period (ae) Period Average (rf)							
Market Rate	ae	12.010	12.010	12.010	†50.040	†126.910	130.460	141.650	159.100	165.590	173.270	179.010	184.310
Market Rate	rf	12.010	12.010	12.010	†40.839	†94.157	129.281	135.882	155.718	161.718	168.672	175.625	183.448
Fund Position						**Millions of SDRs: End of Period**							
Quota	2f.s	176.5	176.5	176.5	176.5	176.5	176.5	176.5	243.5	243.5	243.5	243.5	243.5
SDRs	1b.s	2.9	.5	33.5	37.0	33.3	124.1	131.6	128.5	65.0	14.7	33.0	3.3
Reserve Position in the Fund	1c.s	—	—	—	—	—	—	—	—	—	—	—	—
Total Fund Cred.&Loans Outstg.	2tl	—	—	—	—	84.0	185.4	238.4	297.6	243.5	297.3	283.8	270.1
International Liquidity						**Millions of US Dollars Unless Otherwise Indicated: End of Period**							
Total Reserves minus Gold	1l.d	320.5	145.3	254.8	619.0	1,017.2	1,203.1	995.5	1,471.5	2,900.3	3,658.1	4,410.5	4,986.9
SDRs	1b.d	4.0	.6	48.9	55.0	47.9	167.4	185.2	176.3	84.6	18.5	44.9	4.9
Reserve Position in the Fund	1c.d	—	—	—	—	—	—	—	—	—	—	—	—
Foreign Exchange	1d.d	316.5	144.6	205.9	564.0	969.3	1,035.7	810.3	1,295.1	2,815.6	3,639.6	4,365.6	4,982.0
Gold (Million Fine Troy Ounces)	1ad	.050	.050	.050	.050	.050	.050	.050	.050	.050	.050	.050	.050
Gold (National Valuation)	1and	2.4	2.4	2.6	2.6	18.6	18.5	15.3	15.3	14.4	14.6	18.4	21.9
Deposit Money Banks: Assets	7a.d	543.7	547.7	477.2	861.1	334.5	455.9	457.9	446.2	624.1	695.5	849.0	862.3
Liabilities	7b.d	590.4	549.4	548.1	479.1	209.8	60.8	50.2	45.6	56.5	26.9	18.7	21.7
Monetary Authorities						**Millions of Rial: End of Period**							
Foreign Assets	11	3,878	1,774	4,292	31,108	131,459	159,892	143,257	†237,502	482,436	636,331	792,193	923,080
Claims on Central Government	12a	104,818	135,664	180,586	209,342	199,058	171,234	196,702	†159,621	17,913	2,082	686	206
Claims on Nonfin.Pub.Enterprises	12c	92	76	57	—	10	50	1,108	†9,026	1,821	1,540	1,513	1,650
Claims on Deposit Money Banks	12e	—	5	40	94	54	49	—	—	—	—	—	—
Reserve Money	14	83,927	108,933	147,585	176,756	189,030	165,443	184,002	222,245	253,255	288,694	315,140	381,668
of which: Currency Outside Banks	14a	55,531	79,019	111,006	129,114	120,477	126,904	139,668	166,924	197,123	212,795	239,329	268,813
Other Liab. to Dep. Money Banks	14n	....	....	....	....	....	....	....	5,659	5,865	41,933	46,807	39,429
Time, Savings,& Fgn.Currency Dep.	15	316	2,352	3,881	9,440	19,966	22,193	18,978	11,932	18,531	22,112	20,267	31,902
Restricted Deposits	16b	....	....	....	....	....	....	....	8,388	7,935	19,858	15,090	42,623
Foreign Liabilities	16c	2,136	1,913	2,053	11,323	43,931	66,613	84,138	†101,159	89,094	100,821	103,187	108,094
Central Government Deposits	16d	14,063	16,326	18,294	27,011	41,003	46,106	18,171	†26,095	79,708	106,488	195,311	158,199
Capital Accounts	17a	1,075	1,077	1,100	2,738	5,835	5,673	6,323	†35,201	24,592	65,636	91,451	143,224
Other Items (Net)	17r	7,271	6,916	12,023	13,182	30,762	24,846	29,458	†−4,526	23,190	−5,589	7,138	19,796
Deposit Money Banks						**Millions of Rial: End of Period**							
Reserves	20	24,120	25,987	32,879	44,055	59,903	28,052	35,714	43,631	45,545	50,647	55,710	87,593
Other Claims on Monetary Author.	20n	....	....	....	....	....	....	....	5,659	5,865	31,790	46,207	38,779
Foreign Assets	21	6,530	6,578	5,731	43,088	42,453	59,472	64,857	70,991	103,340	120,511	151,981	158,925
Claims on Central Government	22a	352	281	336	1,295	6,963	34,873	36,267	39,972	63,173	54,814	75,215	112,467
Claims on Nonfin.Pub.Enterprises	22c	3,793	3,395	3,401	11,011	2,237	1,641	317	649	474	674	1,066	1,303
Claims on Private Sector	22d	10,040	12,653	14,143	23,865	22,358	34,380	45,957	62,426	75,747	95,318	108,949	137,553
Demand Deposits	24	18,237	21,489	25,390	22,985	27,353	28,875	31,490	29,649	41,004	49,458	49,819	56,346
Time, Savings,& Fgn.Currency Dep.	25	15,096	17,251	19,359	71,956	88,640	106,272	130,753	155,981	204,053	252,725	328,914	405,096
Restricted Deposits	26b	1,329	1,240	1,210	1,977	3,661	3,540	3,684	4,185	4,692	5,064	9,034	12,909
Foreign Liabilities	26c	7,091	6,599	6,582	23,973	26,624	7,932	7,114	7,248	9,358	4,652	3,351	3,991
Central Government Deposits	26d	1,272	1,543	1,863	1,127	171	474	52	30	46	62	38	101
Credit from Monetary Authorities	26g	—	—	14	4	5	26	23	32	—	—	—	—
Capital Accounts	27a	1,564	1,997	2,829	4,601	6,669	10,762	17,615	†22,688	23,439	28,074	32,724	36,424
Other Items (Net)	27r	247	−1,224	−745	−3,305	−19,203	564	−7,597	†3,515	11,552	13,718	15,249	21,754
Monetary Survey						**Millions of Rial: End of Period**							
Foreign Assets (Net)	31n	1,181	−160	1,388	38,900	103,358	144,820	116,863	†200,086	487,324	651,369	837,637	969,920
Domestic Credit	32	103,762	134,201	178,365	217,375	189,453	195,598	262,128	†245,568	79,373	47,878	−7,921	94,879
Claims on Central Govt. (Net)	32an	89,836	118,076	160,765	182,499	164,848	159,527	214,746	†173,468	1,331	−49,654	−119,449	−45,627
Claims on Nonfin.Pub.Enterprises	32c	3,886	3,472	3,457	11,011	2,247	1,691	1,425	†9,674	2,295	2,214	2,579	2,953
Claims on Private Sector	32d	10,040	12,653	14,143	23,865	22,358	34,380	45,957	62,426	75,747	95,318	108,949	137,553
Money	34	78,314	103,306	139,590	164,019	156,579	166,384	179,927	207,197	247,248	283,149	306,450	347,465
Quasi-Money	35	15,412	19,604	23,239	81,396	108,605	128,465	149,731	167,913	222,585	274,836	349,181	436,997
Restricted Deposits	36b	1,329	1,240	1,210	1,977	3,661	3,540	3,684	†12,573	12,627	24,922	24,123	55,532
Capital Accounts	37a	2,640	3,073	3,929	7,339	12,504	16,434	23,938	†57,889	48,030	93,711	124,176	179,648
Other Items (Net)	37r	7,248	6,821	11,784	1,544	11,461	25,292	21,712	†87	36,208	22,628	25,786	45,156
Money plus Quasi-Money	35l	93,726	122,909	162,829	245,415	265,184	294,849	329,658	375,109	469,833	557,985	655,631	784,463
Interest Rates						**Percent Per Annum**							
Discount Rate	60	....	....	....	27	29	15	20	19	16	15	13	....
Treasury Bill Rate	60c	....	....	....	....	25	16	13	21	14	13	12	13
Deposit Rate	60l	....	....	....	....	24	15	11	18	14	13	13	13
Lending Rate	60p	....	....	....	....	31	23	15	24	20	18	18	18
Prices						**Index Numbers (2000=100): Period Averages**							
Consumer Prices	64	†19.8	26.8	40.1	62.2	81.3	83.0	88.0	95.6	100.0	111.9	125.6	139.2

Yemen, Republic of 474

		1992	1993	1994	1995	1996	1997	1998	1999	2000	2001	2002	2003
International Transactions							*Millions of Rial*						
Exports	70	7,435	7,333	11,216	79,434	251,830	323,716	203,480	380,010	659,609	542,359	....	....
Imports, c.i.f.	71	31,076	33,883	25,070	64,591	191,862	260,331	294,510	312,749	375,783	389,638	....	....
Balance of Payments						*Millions of US Dollars: Minus Sign Indicates Debit*							
Current Account, n.i.e.	78ald	−1,126.1	−1,275.3	178.3	143.7	38.8	−68.8	−472.2	358.2	1,336.6	667.1	538.2	148.7
Goods: Exports f.o.b.	78aad	1,073.4	1,166.8	1,796.2	1,980.1	2,262.7	2,274.0	1,503.7	2,478.3	3,797.2	3,366.9	3,620.7	3,934.3
Goods: Imports f.o.b.	78abd	−1,935.5	−2,138.1	−1,522.0	−1,831.5	−2,293.5	−2,406.5	−2,288.8	−2,120.5	−2,484.4	−2,600.4	−2,932.0	−3,557.4
Trade Balance	78acd	−862.1	−971.3	274.2	148.6	−30.8	−132.5	−785.1	357.8	1,312.8	766.4	688.7	376.9
Services: Credit	78add	161.9	177.2	148.0	179.4	185.7	207.6	174.4	183.2	210.9	166.4	166.2	317.7
Services: Debit	78aed	−969.4	−1,043.4	−704.3	−639.3	−555.4	−677.4	−692.9	−718.7	−809.4	−847.8	−934.8	−1,003.6
Balance on Goods & Services	78afd	−1,669.6	−1,837.5	−282.1	−311.3	−400.5	−602.3	−1,303.6	−177.6	714.2	85.1	−79.9	−308.9
Income: Credit	78agd	38.1	22.0	22.0	37.4	46.8	69.6	69.0	56.7	149.6	178.5	135.0	98.9
Income: Debit	78ahd	−455.3	−430.2	−553.9	−598.4	−680.7	−670.6	−413.4	−752.3	−926.7	−869.4	−900.6	−1,008.3
Balance on Gds, Serv. & Inc.	78aid	−2,086.8	−2,245.7	−814.0	−872.3	−1,034.4	−1,203.3	−1,648.0	−873.2	−62.9	−605.8	−845.6	−1,218.3
Current Transfers, n.i.e.: Credit	78ajd	1,058.2	1,065.2	1,062.3	1,080.5	1,140.1	1,177.6	1,223.5	1,262.1	1,471.9	1,344.4	1,456.8	1,442.1
Current Transfers: Debit	78akd	−97.5	−94.8	−70.0	−64.5	−66.9	−43.1	−47.7	−30.7	−72.4	−71.4	−73.1	−75.0
Capital Account, n.i.e.	78bcd	....	....	....	....	....	4,236.2	2.2	1.5	338.9	49.5	−	86.3
Capital Account, n.i.e.: Credit	78bad	....	....	....	....	....	4,236.2	2.2	1.5	338.9	49.5	−	86.3
Capital Account: Debit	78bbd	....	....	....	....	....	....	−	−	−	−	−	−
Financial Account, n.i.e.	78bjd	−149.9	49.5	−710.7	−858.4	−367.8	−197.6	−418.0	−415.1	−376.2	−53.5	−156.8	−61.1
Direct Investment Abroad	78bdd	....	....	....	....	....	....	−	−	−	−	−	−
Dir. Invest. in Rep. Econ., n.i.e.	78bed	718.0	903.0	15.8	−217.7	−60.1	−138.5	−219.4	−307.6	6.4	155.1	114.3	−89.1
Portfolio Investment Assets	78bfd	....	1.6	2.8	−3.1	.9	5.0	4.9	4.1	.1	−1.4	−5.8	−.4
Equity Securities	78bkd	....	1.6	2.8	−3.1	.9	5.0	4.9	4.1	.1	−1.4	−5.8	−.4
Debt Securities	78bld	....	....	....	....	....	....	−	−	−	−	−	−
Portfolio Investment Liab., n.i.e.	78bpd	....	....	....	....	....	....						
Equity Securities	78bmd	....	....	....	....	....	....						
Debt Securities	78bnd	....	....	....	....	....	....						
Financial Derivatives Assets	78bwd	....	....	....	....	....	....	....	....	....	....	....	....
Financial Derivatives Liabilities	78bxd	....	....	....	....	....	....	....	....	....	....	....	....
Other Investment Assets	78bhd	82.3	−5.3	−130.9	158.8	24.0	196.3	60.1	−110.1	−177.9	5.6	−124.5	−31.7
Monetary Authorities	78bod	....	....	....	....	....	....						
General Government	78bpd	12.1	−51.3	1.3	−32.5	−63.7	63.5	70.7	−119.4	−	75.6	−57.6	−
Banks	78bqd	20.2	−4.0	67.8	141.3	7.7	−122.3	−10.6	9.3	−177.9	−70.0	−147.7	−12.8
Other Sectors	78brd	50.0	50.0	−200.0	50.0	80.0	255.1	−	−	−	−	80.8	−18.9
Other Investment Liab., n.i.e.	78bid	−950.2	−849.8	−598.4	−796.4	−332.6	−260.4	−263.6	−1.5	−204.8	−212.8	−140.8	60.2
Monetary Authorities	78bsd	−25.2	−31.5	61.1	4.4	−.6	34.3	−3.0	−23.7	−8.1	−11.5	−22.4	−10.9
General Government	78btd	−762.0	−771.4	−656.6	−626.1	−353.2	−145.7	−250.5	27.1	−207.7	−171.6	−110.3	68.1
Banks	78bud	−158.6	−41.0	−1.4	−174.7	21.2	−149.0	−10.1	−4.9	11.0	−29.7	−8.1	2.9
Other Sectors	78bvd	−4.4	−5.9	−1.5									
Net Errors and Omissions	78cad	−25.7	113.9	−189.2	186.5	−107.0	48.4	307.0	129.4	295.1	−110.0	43.3	156.4
Overall Balance	78cbd	−1,301.7	−1,111.9	−721.6	−528.2	−436.0	4,018.2	−580.9	74.0	1,594.4	553.2	424.7	330.3
Reserves and Related Items	79dad	1,301.7	1,111.9	721.6	528.2	436.0	−4,018.2	580.9	−74.0	−1,594.4	−553.2	−424.7	−330.3
Reserve Assets	79dbd	356.4	175.2	−207.9	−263.1	−415.7	−192.7	210.9	−482.2	−1,429.4	−761.3	−556.9	−326.3
Use of Fund Credit and Loans	79dcd	−	−	−	−	122.5	139.4	72.3	79.5	−71.0	69.0	−17.2	−19.3
Exceptional Financing	79ded	945.3	936.7	929.5	791.3	729.3	−3,964.9	297.7	328.7	−94.0	139.1	149.4	15.3
International Investment Position							*Millions of US Dollars*						
Assets	79aad	....	....	....	....	....	....	1,484.0	2,067.5	3,686.8	4,441.7	5,405.6	6,020.7
Direct Investment Abroad	79abd	....	....	....	....	....	....	−	−	−	−	−	−
Portfolio Investment	79acd	....	....	....	....	....	....	4.5	.4	.3	1.7	7.5	7.9
Equity Securities	79add	....	....	....	....	....	....	4.5	.4	.3	1.7	7.5	7.9
Debt Securities	79aed	....	....	....	....	....	....	−	−	−	−	−	−
Financial Derivatives	79ald	....	....	....	....	....	....	−	−	−	−	−	−
Other Investment	79afd	....	....	....	....	....	....	466.3	576.5	772.9	767.3	972.5	1,004.3
Monetary Authorities	79agd	....	....	....	....	....	....						
General Government	79ahd	....	....	....	....	....	....	12.0	131.4	149.1	73.5	131.0	149.9
Banks	79aid	....	....	....	....	....	....	454.3	445.1	623.8	693.8	841.5	854.4
Other Sectors	79ajd	....	....	....	....	....	....						
Reserve Assets	79akd	....	....	....	....	....	....	1,013.2	1,490.6	2,913.6	3,672.7	4,425.6	5,008.5
Liabilities	79lad	....	....	....	....	....	....	6,077.9	6,305.5	6,372.9	6,006.5	6,092.8	6,543.6
Dir. Invest. in Rep. Economy	79lbd	....	....	....	....	....	....	1,088.6	993.2	843.0	998.1	1,112.4	1,010.7
Portfolio Investment	79lcd	....	....	....	....	....	....	−	−	−	−	−	−
Equity Securities	79ldd	....	....	....	....	....	....	−	−	−	−	−	−
Debt Securities	79led	....	....	....	....	....	....	−	−	−	−	−	−
Financial Derivatives	79lld	....	....	....	....	....	....						
Other Investment	79lfd	....	....	....	....	....	....	4,989.3	5,312.3	5,529.9	5,008.4	4,980.3	5,532.9
Monetary Authorities	79lgd	....	....	....	....	....	....	624.6	664.0	538.0	596.3	576.4	586.5
General Government	79lhd	....	....	....	....	....	....	4,314.4	4,602.9	4,935.3	4,385.2	4,385.2	4,924.8
Banks	79lid	....	....	....	....	....	....	50.3	45.4	56.5	26.9	18.7	21.7
Other Sectors	79ljd	....	....	....	....	....	....	−	−	−	−	−	−

2004, International Monetary Fund : International Financial Statistics Yearbook

Yemen, Republic of 474

		1992	1993	1994	1995	1996	1997	1998	1999	2000	2001	2002	2003
Government Finance						*Millions of Rial: Year Ending December 31*							
Deficit (-) or Surplus	80	−23,428	−29,297	−44,788	−24,907	−17,428	−13,588	−19,116f	−40,278f	....	....	....	....
Revenue	81	32,911	36,720	41,384	89,646	216,053	287,347	300,791f	279,418f	....	....	....	....
Grants Received	81z	–	1,201	856	1,620	1,870	4,639	5,480f	4,219f	....	....	....	....
Expenditure	82	54,848	65,247	85,875	111,128	215,738	290,571	309,942f	310,702f	....	....	....	....
Lending Minus Repayments	83	1,491	1,971	1,153	5,045	19,613	15,003	15,445f	13,213f	....	....	....	....
Financing													
Domestic	84a	23,055	28,804	43,838	25,976	11,860	2,696p	−7,750f	25,283f	....	....	....	....
Foreign	85a	373	493	950	−1,069	5,568	16,572p	26,866f	14,995f	....	....	....	....
National Accounts						*Millions of Rial*							
Househ.Cons.Expend.,incl.NPISHs	96f	154,273	212,249	244,753	431,346	531,423	618,701	620,429	765,695p	965,294p	1,105,217p	1,258,531p	1,551,942p
Government Consumption Expend	91f	37,187	45,483	57,585	74,017	97,458	116,832	124,473	156,273p	193,322p	219,124p	244,560p	267,147p
Gross Fixed Capital Formation	93e	38,157	41,627	58,267	106,227	158,016	191,666	267,810	265,371p	251,684p	263,994p	277,593p	330,988p
Changes in Inventories	93i	4,869	6,622	6,123	6,486	12,863	29,549	8,655	13,122p	12,590p	13,894p	14,610p	19,541p
Exports of Goods and Services	90c	22,513	32,833	42,091	115,957	285,587	320,822	228,025	414,527p	645,230p	596,006p	659,824p	647,138p
Imports of Goods and Services (-)	98c	64,575	99,760	98,218	217,390	351,795	398,686	405,152	442,194p	528,485p	582,290p	651,728p	735,112p
Gross Domestic Product (GDP)	99b	192,424	239,054	310,601	516,643	733,552	878,884	844,240	1,172,794p	1,539,635p	1,615,945p	1,803,390p	2,081,644p
Net Primary Income from Abroad	98.n	−5,011	−4,901	−6,388	−22,535	−72,365	−77,697	−23,846	−74,262p	−125,746p	−113,566p	−130,484p	−113,898p
Gross National Income (GNI)	99a	187,413	234,153	304,213	494,108	661,187	801,187	820,394	1,098,532p	1,413,889p	1,502,379p	1,672,906p	1,967,746p
GDP Volume 1990 Prices	99b.p	132,314	142,818	147,106	165,040	178,293	189,450	202,393	207,320p	216,970p	227,086p	235,943p	245,411p
GDP Volume (2000=100)	99bvp	61.0	65.8	67.8	76.1	82.2	87.3	93.3	95.6	100.0	104.7	108.7	113.1
GDP Deflator (2000=100)	99bip	20.5	23.6	29.8	44.1	58.0	65.4	58.8	79.7	100.0	100.3	107.7	119.5
						Millions: Midyear Estimates							
Population	99z	13.16	13.82	Ü 14.49	15.12	15.72	16.29	16.85	17.42	18.02	18.65	19.32	20.01

Zambia 754

		1992	1993	1994	1995	1996	1997	1998	1999	2000	2001	2002	2003
Exchange Rates						*Kwacha per SDR: End of Period*							
Official Rate	aa	494.60	686.78	993.10	1,421.28	1,844.46	1,908.97	3,236.95	3,612.71	5,417.28	4,813.78	5,892.70	6,903.04
				Kwacha per US Dollar: End of Period (ae) Period Average (rf)									
Official Rate	ae	359.71	500.00	680.27	956.13	1,282.69	1,414.84	2,298.92	2,632.19	4,157.83	3,830.40	4,334.40	4,645.48
Official Rate	rf	172.21	452.76	669.37	864.12	1,207.90	1,314.50	1,862.07	2,388.02	3,110.84	3,610.94	4,398.60	4,733.27
				Index Numbers (2000=100): Period Averages									
Official Rate	ahx	1,960.5	693.3	408.0	357.9	255.9	233.3	167.1	128.5	100.0	85.3	71.6	64.8
Nominal Effective Exchange Rate	nec	1,496.3	572.2	370.5	272.7	204.4	200.9	152.6	119.7	100.0	92.4	74.5	64.0
Real Effective Exchange Rate	rec	84.5	95.8	92.2	88.3	92.4	110.7	101.1	98.8	100.0	108.7	103.1	101.3
Fund Position						*Millions of SDRs: End of Period*							
Quota	2f.s	270.3	270.3	270.3	363.5	363.5	363.5	363.5	489.1	489.1	489.1	489.1	489.1
SDRs	1b.s	–	–	–	8.2	1.4	.8	.6	.1	17.1	53.3	51.7	.3
Reserve Position in the Fund	1c.s	–	–	–	–	–	–	–	–	–	–	–	–
Total Fund Cred.&Loans Outstg	2tl	615.6	565.8	551.2	833.4	833.4	843.4	843.4	853.4	873.4	781.6	746.6	577.9
International Liquidity				*Millions of US Dollars Unless Otherwise Indicated: End of Period*									
Total Reserves minus Gold	1l.d	....	192.3	268.1	222.7	222.7	239.1	69.4	45.4	244.8	183.4	535.1	247.7
SDRs	1b.d	–	–	–	12.1	2.0	1.1	.8	.1	22.3	66.9	70.3	.5
Reserve Position in the Fund	1c.d	–	–	–	–	–	–	–	–	–	–	–	–
Foreign Exchange	1d.d	....	192.3	268.1	210.5	220.7	238.0	68.6	45.3	222.5	116.5	464.8	247.2
Gold (Million Fine Troy Ounces)	1ad	....	....	....	–	–	–	–	–	–	–	–	–
Gold (National Valuation)	1and	....	....	....	–	–	–	–	–	–	–	–	–
Monetary Authorities: Other Liab.	4..d	....	678.7	736.0	1,128.8	1,088.8	1,007.1	1,001.4	974.3	938.2	868.6	1,027.3	896.2
Deposit Money Banks: Assets	7a.d	120.7	205.5	84.3	116.5	148.7	155.0	198.9	201.4	239.5	233.3	293.5	235.3
Liabilities	7b.d	20.0	16.8	15.6	9.3	11.2	13.2	29.2	34.9	25.9	24.5	26.0	35.0
Monetary Authorities						*Billions of Kwacha: End of Period*							
Foreign Assets	11	....	137.7	213.7	208.1	268.4	338.4	103.0	211.2	336.8	432.6	1,337.2	1,196.3
Claims on Central Government	12a	....	611.9	1,114.7	2,017.5	2,636.7	2,659.5	4,670.2	5,584.5	8,605.1	7,816.2	9,320.4	9,318.6
Claims on Nonfin.Pub.Enterprises	12c	....	20.2	9.1	1.2	1.3	1.3	5.3	7.9	69.2	195.0	30.5	54.3
Claims on Private Sector	12d	....	2.1	4.4	14.0	23.6	25.1	30.7	31.4	35.7	42.6	50.9	46.9
Claims on Deposit Money Banks	12e	....	7.8	–	121.8	157.2	164.9	161.4	120.9	82.4	72.9	107.7	125.1
Reserve Money	14	....	102.3	151.4	129.2	175.0	259.3	303.0	389.2	597.0	870.0	1,258.7	1,438.5
of which: Currency Outside DMBs	14a	....	40.4	56.3	77.8	106.3	136.7	†169.7	212.2	287.8	373.6	422.4	592.5
Time, Savings,& Fgn.Currency Dep	15	....	5.4	–	1.5	2.3	.7	.8	1.6	2.2	3.5	6.1	5.9
Foreign Liabilities	16c	....	727.9	1,048.1	1,337.6	1,731.8	1,771.9	2,890.4	3,221.2	4,885.6	4,027.0	5,095.3	4,665.0
Central Government Deposits	16d	....	267.8	173.6	545.4	895.6	955.0	1,351.6	2,011.9	2,975.3	3,112.4	3,642.8	4,338.6
Capital Accounts	17a	....	–411.6	–52.7	286.0	329.8	421.6	444.8	493.0	1,063.7	990.5	479.9	793.1
Other Items (Net)	17r	....	87.9	21.6	62.9	–47.3	–219.2	–20.0	–160.9	–394.7	–444.1	363.8	–499.9
Deposit Money Banks						*Billions of Kwacha: End of Period*							
Reserves	20	20.8	49.8	96.1	34.6	62.8	87.8	†134.7	175.6	322.7	475.5	731.3	766.0
Foreign Assets	21	43.4	102.8	57.4	116.5	190.7	224.6	†457.3	530.2	995.7	893.6	1,272.1	1,093.2
Claims on Central Government	22a	38.3	71.4	84.7	202.8	216.4	222.7	†153.0	231.6	356.7	776.9	916.3	1,599.0
Claims on Local Government	22b	....	....	....	....	....	....	2.6	.4	.4	.4	–	.6
Claims on Nonfin.Pub.Enterprises	22c	13.4	29.1	16.8	35.6	49.7	40.9	†119.1	248.9	289.7	246.8	63.0	61.8
Claims on Private Sector	22d	29.2	68.9	136.0	240.0	350.2	386.1	†392.7	522.0	825.5	902.8	958.3	1,331.5
Claims on Other Banking Insts	22f	....	....	....	....	....	....	.4	.4	.4	.4	.5	1.4
Claims on Nonbank Financial Insts	22g	....	....	....	....	....	....	2.7	1.4	.5	.4	9.7	10.4
Demand Deposits	24	33.0	56.8	83.8	140.2	163.1	217.2	†243.7	299.0	472.0	637.1	912.6	1,121.3
Time, Savings,& Fgn.Currency Dep	25	45.1	105.8	191.0	287.6	423.4	515.6	†679.0	883.3	1,651.0	1,714.9	2,273.7	2,719.2
Money Market Instruments	26aa	10.7	15.0	14.9	23.3	31.1	29.8	†11.8	9.9	34.6	21.3	4.8	–
Foreign Liabilities	26c	7.2	8.4	10.6	9.3	14.4	19.1	†67.1	91.8	107.7	93.7	112.5	162.8
Central Government Deposits	26d	5.7	5.8	12.4	44.6	57.7	63.6	†61.3	125.2	43.2	94.4	112.4	202.1
Credit from Monetary Authorities	26g	–	.2	2.7	60.2	86.6	82.5	†21.4	78.5	39.1	30.3	23.1	32.9
Liabs. to Other Banking Insts	26i	....	....	....	....	....	....	.1	1.3	5.6	15.3	41.7	36.6
Capital Accounts	27a	17.8	44.2	58.5	74.5	112.7	138.1	†227.8	297.2	448.6	533.7	769.9	740.3
Other Items (Net)	27r	25.5	85.7	17.0	–10.1	–19.2	–103.8	†–49.7	–75.6	–10.2	156.0	–299.5	–151.4

Zambia 754

		1992	1993	1994	1995	1996	1997	1998	1999	2000	2001	2002	2003
Monetary Survey						**Billions of Kwacha: End of Period**							
Foreign Assets (Net)	31n	....	−495.9	−787.6	−1,022.4	−1,287.1	−1,228.0	†−2,397.2	−2,571.6	−3,660.9	−2,794.4	−2,598.6	−2,538.3
Domestic Credit	32	....	530.0	1,179.7	1,921.1	2,324.6	2,316.9	†3,963.7	4,491.7	7,164.8	6,774.6	7,594.5	7,883.8
Claims on Central Govt. (Net)	32an	....	409.7	1,013.4	1,630.3	1,899.7	1,863.6	†3,410.2	3,679.1	5,943.4	5,386.3	6,481.5	6,377.0
Claims on Local Government	32b	....	....	....	....	....	....	....	2.6	.4	.4	−	.6
Claims on Nonfin.Pub.Enterprises	32c	....	49.3	25.9	36.9	51.0	42.2	†124.4	256.9	358.8	441.7	93.5	116.1
Claims on Private Sector	32d	....	71.0	140.4	254.0	373.8	411.1	†423.5	553.5	861.3	945.4	1,009.2	1,378.4
Claims on Other Banking Insts	32f	....	....	....	....	....	....	.4	.4	.4	.4	.5	1.4
Claims on Nonbank Financial Inst.	32g	....	−	−	−	−	−	†2.7	1.4	.5	.4	9.7	10.4
Money	34	....	97.3	141.0	227.1	271.1	355.2	†414.9	513.0	775.9	1,041.4	1,339.3	1,715.7
Quasi-Money	35	....	111.2	191.0	289.1	425.7	516.3	†679.8	884.9	1,653.2	1,718.3	2,279.9	2,725.0
Money Market Instruments	36aa	10.7	15.0	14.9	23.3	31.1	29.8	†11.8	9.9	34.6	21.3	4.8	−
Liabs. to Other Banking Insts	36i	....	....	....	....	....	....	.1	1.3	5.6	15.3	41.7	36.6
Capital Accounts	37a	17.8	−367.4	5.8	360.5	442.5	559.7	†672.6	790.2	1,512.4	1,524.2	1,249.8	1,533.5
Other Items (Net)	37r	....	177.9	39.4	−1.1	−133.0	−372.1	†−212.8	−279.2	−477.7	−340.4	80.4	−665.5
Money plus Quasi-Money	35l	....	208.6	332.0	516.2	696.9	871.5	†1,094.7	1,397.9	2,429.1	2,759.7	3,619.2	4,440.8
Money (National Definitions)						**Billions of Kwacha: End of Period**							
M1	39ma	....	....	....	....	....	382.9	409.4	513.8	795.3	1,036.6	1,328.3	1,695.6
M2	39mb	....	....	....	....	....	889.7	1,049.5	1,352.0	2,404.6	2,718.6	3,515.2	4,340.4
M3	39mc	....	....	....	....	....	901.3	1,080.2	1,396.9	2,446.4	2,747.4	3,606.2	4,419.8
Interest Rates						**Percent Per Annum**							
Discount Rate (End of Period)	60	47.00	72.50	20.50	40.20	47.00	17.70	....	32.93	25.67	40.10	27.87	14.35
Treasury Bill Rate	60c	....	124.03	74.21	39.81	52.78	29.48	24.94	36.19	31.37	44.28	34.54	29.97
Deposit Rate	60l	48.50	....	46.14	30.24	42.13	34.48	13.08	20.27	20.24	23.41	23.33	21.95
Lending Rate	60p	54.57	113.31	70.56	45.53	53.78	46.69	31.80	40.52	38.80	46.23	45.20	40.57
Prices and Production						**Index Numbers (2000=100): Period Averages**							
Wholesale Prices (1995=100)	63	14.15	34.07	58.13	100.00	....	....	....	....	....	....	....	....
Home & Import Goods	63a	447.2	....	....	....	....	....	....	....	....	....	....	....
Consumer Prices	64	4.8	13.5	20.9	28.2	40.4	50.3	62.6	79.3	100.0	121.4	148.4	....
Cons.Prices (Low Inc.Househ)(1995	64a	16.6	48.1	73.6	100.0	143.8	....	....	....	....	....	....	....
Industrial Production (1995=100)	66	134.6	122.0	107.0	100.0	....	....	....	....	....	....	....	....
Mining Production (1990=100)	66zx	100.8	92.0	76.8	....	....	....	....	....	....	....	....	....
International Transactions						**Billions of Kwacha**							
Exports	70	129.5	374.1	620.5	898.6	1,252.7	1,203.0	....	....	....	....	....	....
Imports, c.i.f.	71	144.1	366.3	397.7	604.8	1,004.3	1,077.0	....	....	....	....	....	....

Zambia 754

		1992	1993	1994	1995	1996	1997	1998	1999	2000	2001	2002	2003
Balance of Payments		\multicolumn{12}{c}{*Millions of US Dollars: Minus Sign Indicates Debit*}
Current Account, n.i.e.	78ald	....	....	....	....	....	−353	−573	−447	−584	....	....	....
Goods: Exports f.o.b.	78aad	....	....	....	....	....	1,110	818	772	757	....	....	....
Goods: Imports f.o.b.	78abd	....	....	....	....	....	−1,056	−971	−870	−978	....	....	....
Trade Balance	78acd	....	....	....	....	....	54	−153	−98	−221	....	....	....
Services: Credit	78add	....	....	....	....	....	112	102	107	114	....	....	....
Services: Debit	78aed	....	....	....	....	....	−282	−282	−306	−340	....	....	....
Balance on Goods & Services	78afd	....	....	....	....	....	−115	−332	−297	−447	....	....	....
Income: Credit	78agd	....	....	....	....	....	77	44	44	46	....	....	....
Income: Debit	78ahd	....	....	....	....	....	−296	−258	−178	−166	....	....	....
Balance on Gds, Serv. & Inc.	78aid	....	....	....	....	....	−334	−546	−431	−566	....	....	....
Current Transfers, n.i.e.: Credit	78ajd	....	....	....	....	....	–	–	–	–	....	....	....
Current Transfers: Debit	78akd	....	....	....	....	....	−19	−27	−16	−18	....	....	....
Capital Account, n.i.e.	78bcd	....	....	....	....	....	–	203	196	153	....	....	....
Capital Account, n.i.e.: Credit	78bad	....	....	....	....	....	–	203	196	153	....	....	....
Capital Account: Debit	78bbd	....	....	....	....	....	–	–	–	–	....	....	....
Financial Account, n.i.e.	78bjd	....	....	....	....	....	−324	−264	−174	−274	....	....	....
Direct Investment Abroad	78bdd	....	....	....	....	....	–	–	–	–	....	....	....
Dir. Invest. in Rep. Econ., n.i.e.	78bed	....	....	....	....	....	207	198	162	122	....	....	....
Portfolio Investment Assets	78bfd	....	....	....	....	....	–	–	–	–	....	....	....
Equity Securities	78bkd	....	....	....	....	....	–	–	–	–	....	....	....
Debt Securities	78bld	....	....	....	....	....	–	–	–	–	....	....	....
Portfolio Investment Liab., n.i.e.	78bgd	....	....	....	....	....	1	1	13	−1	....	....	....
Equity Securities	78bmd	....	....	....	....	....	1	1	13	−1	....	....	....
Debt Securities	78bnd	....	....	....	....	....	....	....	....	....	....	....	....
Financial Derivatives Assets	78bwd	....	....	....	....	....	....	....	....	....	....	....	....
Financial Derivatives Liabilities	78bxd	....	....	....	....	....	....	....	....	....	....	....	....
Other Investment Assets	78bhd	....	....	....	....	....	−24	−40	−2	−85	....	....	....
Monetary Authorities	78bod	....	....	....	....	....	....	....	....	....	....	....	....
General Government	78bpd	....	....	....	....	....	....	....	....	....	....	....	....
Banks	78bqd	....	....	....	....	....	−24	−40	−2	−85	....	....	....
Other Sectors	78brd	....	....	....	....	....	....	....	....	....	....	....	....
Other Investment Liab., n.i.e.	78bid	....	....	....	....	....	−508	−422	−347	−309	....	....	....
Monetary Authorities	78bsd	....	....	....	....	....	–	–	–	−7	....	....	....
General Government	78btd	....	....	....	....	....	−192	−136	−259	−290	....	....	....
Banks	78bud	....	....	....	....	....	19	−2	–	–	....	....	....
Other Sectors	78bvd	....	....	....	....	....	−335	−284	−88	−12	....	....	....
Net Errors and Omissions	78cad	....	....	....	....	....	−255	−37	−229	185	....	....	....
Overall Balance	78cbd	....	....	....	....	....	−932	−671	−654	−520	....	....	....
Reserves and Related Items	79dad	....	....	....	....	....	932	671	654	520	....	....	....
Reserve Assets	79dbd	....	....	....	....	....	−25	194	−1	−90	....	....	....
Use of Fund Credit and Loans	79dcd	....	....	....	....	....	14	–	14	26	....	....	....
Exceptional Financing	79ded	....	....	....	....	....	944	477	642	584	....	....	....
Government Finance		\multicolumn{12}{c}{*Billions of Kwacha: Year Ending December 31*}
Deficit (−) or Surplus	80	−37.3	−115.6	−27.4	−136.9	−96.2	−488.5	−330.4p	−275.4f	....	....	....	....
Revenue	81	113.5	266.4	502.8	600.7	745.3	957.0	1,097.6p	1,430.4f	....	....	....	....
Grants Received	81z	....	....	.6	5.6	25.4	4.7	432.7	414.2	....	....	....	....
Expenditure	82	171.2	391.1	492.2	727.5	842.7	1,313.6	1,717.1p	1,874.3f	....	....	....	....
Lending Minus Repayments	83	9.4	26.6	38.6	15.7	24.2	136.6	143.6p	245.7f	....	....	....	....
Financing													
Net Borrowing: Domestic	84a	37.3	38.0	−46.5	−351.4	−91.2	−283.9	50.2	....	....	....	....	....
Net borrowing: Foreign	85a	.1	77.6	73.9	488.3	187.4	772.4	280.2	....	....	....	....	....
Use of Cash Balances	87	2.7	14.3	−674.3	....	....	....	....	....	....	....	....	....
Debt: Domestic	88a	.8	1.6	149.9	238.8	265.8	303.2	212.8p	....	....	....	....	....
Debt: Foreign	89a	937.3	2,396.3	3,502.4	4,869.4	7,378.7	8,185.9	10,408.4p	....	....	....	....	....
National Accounts		\multicolumn{12}{c}{*Billions of Kwacha*}
Househ.Cons.Expend.,incl.NPISHs	96f	447.6	1,015.7	1,602.7	1,775.9	2,033.2	3,006.0	....	....	....	....	....	....
Government Consumption Expend.	91f	85.5	273.2	293.6	464.0	676.5	792.3	....	....	....	....	....	....
Gross Fixed Capital Formation	93e	60.2	170.0	512.1	799.4	1,719.6	1,928.6	....	....	....	....	....	....
Changes in Inventories	93i	7.5	52.9	−69.1	104.8	63.1	73.9	....	....	....	....	....	....
Exports of Goods and Services	90c	147.1	420.9	806.5	1,082.3	1,237.4	1,552.0	....	....	....	....	....	....
Imports of Goods and Services (−)	98c	178.4	450.6	905.2	1,228.2	1,710.4	2,196.0	....	....	....	....	....	....
Gross Domestic Product (GDP)	99b	569.6	1,482.1	2,240.7	2,998.3	3,969.5	5,155.8	....	....	....	....	....	....
Net Primary Income from Abroad	98.n	−87.0	−377.2	69.0	−104.9	−13.2	−72.9	....	....	....	....	....	....
Gross National Income (GNI)	99a	482.6	1,104.9	2,309.7	2,893.4	3,956.3	5,082.9	....	....	....	....	....	....
Net National Income	99e	425.2	866.0	1,518.0	2,227.4	3,396.4	....	....	....	....	....	....	....
GDP Vol. 1977 Prices (Billions)	99b.p	2.174	2.322	2.241	2.190	2.332	2.414	....	....	....	....	....	....
GDP Volume (1995=100)	99bvp	99.3	106.0	102.3	100.0	106.5	110.2	....	....	....	....	....	....
GDP Deflator (1995=100)	99bip	19.1	46.5	73.0	100.0	124.3	156.0	....	....	....	....	....	....
		\multicolumn{12}{c}{*Millions: Midyear Estimates*}
Population	99z	8.67	8.91	9.14	9.37	9.60	9.83	10.04	10.24	10.42	10.57	10.70	10.81

Zimbabwe 698

		1992	1993	1994	1995	1996	1997	1998	1999	2000	2001	2002	2003
Exchange Rates		\multicolumn{12}{c}{*SDRs per Zimbabwe Dollar: End of Period*}
Official Rate	ac	.1327	.1050	.0817	.0723	.0642	.0398	.0190	.0191	.0139	.0145	.0134	.0008
		\multicolumn{12}{c}{*US Dollars per Zimbabwe Dollar: End of Period (ag) Period Average (rh)*}
Official Rate	ag	.1824	.1442	.1192	.1074	.0923	.0537	.0268	.0262	.0182	.0182	.0182	.0012
Official Rate	rh	.1963	.1545	.1227	.1155	.1008	.0841	.0467	.0261	.0231	.0182	.0182	.0040
Fund Position		\multicolumn{12}{c}{*Millions of SDRs: End of Period*}
Quota	2f.s	261.3	261.3	261.3	261.3	261.3	261.3	261.3	353.4	353.4	353.4	353.4	353.4
SDRs	1b.s	.3	.6	–	.5	6.8	.2	.3	.8	.2	–	–	–
Reserve Position in the Fund	1c.s	.1	.1	.1	.1	.1	.1	.2	.3	.3	.3	.3	.3
Total Fund Cred.&Loans Outstg.	2tl	157.2	205.0	257.5	310.0	304.1	285.5	289.2	268.8	215.4	208.4	206.1	202.9
International Liquidity		\multicolumn{12}{c}{*Millions of US Dollars Unless Otherwise Indicated: End of Period*}
Total Reserves minus Gold	1l.d	222.2	432.0	405.3	595.5	598.8	160.1	130.8	268.0	193.1	64.7	83.4	....
SDRs	1b.d	.4	.9	.1	.8	9.8	.3	.4	1.1	.2	–	–	....
Reserve Position in the Fund	1c.d	.1	.1	.1	.1	.2	.2	.3	.4	.4	.4	.4	.5
Foreign Exchange	1d.d	221.7	431.1	405.1	594.6	588.9	159.6	130.1	266.5	192.5	64.3	82.9	....
Gold (Million Fine Troy Ounces)	1ad	.55	.50	.47	.76	.64	.77	.62	.73	.47	.20	.14	....
Gold (National Valuation)	1and	88.1	79.1	89.7	139.7	117.2	56.0	82.6	105.4	45.4	27.5	22.7	....
Monetary Authorities: Other Liab.	4..d	435.2	291.1	76.1	36.5	28.5	224.6	335.6	229.9	99.5	59.0	82.9	119.7
Deposit Money Banks: Assets	7a.d	95.5	79.6	321.3	275.0	299.8	314.7	179.3	156.9	163.4	146.0	230.6	219.0
Liabilities	7b.d	220.6	518.6	579.3	814.4	827.8	623.8	458.3	245.0	169.2	126.6	186.6	97.0
Other Banking Insts.: Assets	7e.d	.4	1.5	1.0	3.9	6.4	1.3	.6	1.4	1.1	.7	–	–
Liabilities	7f.d	–	–	.2	17.0	15.4	6.8	2.4	2.6	4.0	3.0	1.8	.9
Monetary Authorities		\multicolumn{12}{c}{*Millions of Zimbabwe Dollars: End of Period*}
Foreign Assets	11	1,656	3,545	4,152	6,701	7,710	3,991	7,937	14,241	13,130	5,156	5,838	89,646
Claims on Central Government	12a	2,034	2,760	7,102	13,640	22,828	30,545	47,543	58,734	98,658	38,608	66,744	499,311
Claims on Nonfin.Pub.Enterprises	12c	177	99	134	131	160	188	674	653	651	2,034	645	117
Claims on Private Sector	12d	466	207	182	216	285	361	808	1,095	2,037	2,257	2,652	7,203
Claims on Deposit Money Banks	12e	266	311	448	1,330	1,337	1,403	4,373	3,232	8,066	26,621	62,846	423,734
Reserve Money	14	1,933	2,938	3,632	3,722	6,174	8,509	11,052	17,786	20,638	54,670	148,247	733,549
of which: Currency Outside DMBs	14a	861	1,191	1,467	1,823	2,440	3,558	4,468	7,256	9,943	25,642	79,664	441,710
Central Bank Bills Outstanding	16ad	–	–	2,050	917								
Foreign Liabilities	16c	3,571	3,971	3,791	4,631	5,048	11,349	27,758	22,839	20,935	17,664	19,986	347,027
Central Government Deposits	16d	2	1	3,311	14,737	22,833	18,043	26,064	43,773	80,055	–	9,617	1
Capital Accounts	17a	8	392	670	872	804	842	1,015	1,965	1,915	5,028	6,348	12,537
Other Items (Net)	17r	–916	–380	–1,436	–2,860	–2,541	–2,255	–4,553	–8,409	–1,002	–2,686	–45,475	–73,102
Deposit Money Banks		\multicolumn{12}{c}{*Millions of Zimbabwe Dollars: End of Period*}
Reserves	20	1,046	1,188	2,019	1,819	3,598	4,279	6,045	10,109	9,720	30,625	88,691	610,582
Claims on Mon.Author.:Securities	20c	–	–	2,052	579								
Foreign Assets	21	524	552	2,695	2,561	3,250	5,856	6,699	5,985	8,997	8,036	12,694	180,393
Claims on Central Government	22a	489	1,456	968	6,031	7,149	7,103	6,737	11,234	30,895	56,589	108,493	167,285
Claims on Local Government	22b	3	11	28	25	32	95	240	267	380	449	677	1,534
Claims on Nonfin.Pub.Enterprises	22c	406	1,120	732	630	957	1,084	1,834	2,645	7,521	17,375	47,098	227,323
Claims on Private Sector	22d	5,967	9,056	11,736	15,060	18,147	27,098	36,811	41,357	62,037	101,184	293,379	2,116,630
Claims on Other Banking Insts	22f	44	63	28	186	306	915	141	1,481	1,925	2,124	10,371	22,420
Claims on Nonbank Financial Insts	22g	–	31	58	8	56	40	186	95	735	5,992	6,230	52,523
Demand Deposits	24	2,294	4,550	5,791	9,352	11,290	17,102	21,424	27,804	44,169	106,000	275,397	1,636,450
Time and Savings Deposits	25	2,470	3,473	5,753	5,238	8,136	9,757	8,251	11,512	24,976	49,238	172,328	717,098
Money Market Instruments	26aa	30	592	691	479	314	891	1,274	2,548	4,101	16,661	18,653	145,074
Foreign Liabilities	26c	1,209	3,597	4,859	7,583	8,972	11,608	17,126	9,345	9,319	6,968	10,270	79,906
Central Government Deposits	26d	695	509	440	694	1,078	1,753	1,702	1,995	5,303	6,687	23,623	53,724
Credit from Monetary Authorities	26g	122	249	429	1,329	1,331	951	3,798	2,615	7,889	7,771	50,110	439,888
Capital Accounts	27a	1,017	1,435	1,920	2,054	2,515	4,412	6,445	9,510	15,166	31,443	79,872	406,160
Other Items (Net)	27r	644	–929	433	171	–142	–3	–1,326	7,847	11,289	–2,393	–62,619	–99,610
Monetary Survey		\multicolumn{12}{c}{*Millions of Zimbabwe Dollars: End of Period*}
Foreign Assets (Net)	31n	–2,601	–3,471	–1,803	–2,952	–3,061	–13,110	–30,247	–11,959	–8,126	–11,441	–11,724	–156,894
Domestic Credit	32	9,013	14,342	17,242	20,496	26,008	47,633	67,209	71,793	119,481	219,925	503,048	3,040,621
Claims on Central Govt. (Net)	32an	1,826	3,705	4,320	4,240	6,066	17,852	26,515	24,201	44,196	88,510	141,996	612,871
Claims on Local Government	32b	3	11	28	25	32	95	240	267	380	449	677	1,534
Claims on Nonfin.Pub.Enterprises	32c	583	1,219	866	761	1,117	1,272	2,509	3,298	8,171	19,409	47,743	227,441
Claims on Private Sector	32d	6,432	9,263	11,918	15,276	18,431	27,459	37,618	42,452	64,074	103,441	296,031	2,123,833
Claims on Other Banking Insts	32f	44	63	28	186	306	915	141	1,481	1,925	2,124	10,371	22,420
Claims on Nonbank Financial Inst.	32g	125	81	83	8	56	40	186	95	735	5,992	6,230	52,523
Money	34	3,211	6,259	7,396	11,270	13,874	21,320	26,332	35,473	54,396	132,093	356,644	2,086,702
Quasi-Money	35	2,470	3,473	5,753	5,238	8,136	9,757	8,251	11,512	24,976	49,238	172,328	717,098
Money Market Instruments	36aa	30	592	689	817	314	891	1,274	2,548	4,101	16,661	18,653	145,074
Capital Accounts	37a	1,025	1,827	2,589	2,926	3,319	5,253	7,459	11,475	17,081	36,470	86,220	418,697
Other Items (Net)	37r	–323	–1,280	–990	–2,706	–2,697	–2,698	–6,354	–1,173	10,801	–25,977	–142,521	–483,844
Money plus Quasi-Money	35l	5,681	9,731	13,149	16,507	22,011	31,077	34,583	46,985	79,371	181,330	528,972	2,803,800

Zimbabwe 698

		1992	1993	1994	1995	1996	1997	1998	1999	2000	2001	2002	2003
Other Banking Institutions		*Millions of Zimbabwe Dollars: End of Period*
Reserves	40	175	679	914	3,634	4,453	7,510	4,691	5,058	12,315	21,328	50,183	150,348
Foreign Assets	41	2	10	8	36	70	25	24	55	61	41	–	–
Claims on Central Government	42a	2,187	2,348	2,795	3,962	4,410	3,723	4,050	9,233	18,465	18,156	12,749	17,442
Claims on Local Government	42b	43	42	43	64	266	432	438	443	463	448	413	409
Claims on Nonfin.Pub.Enterprises	42c	126	182	404	2,147	590	857	1,075	1,468	1,703	2,010	2,248	1,622
Claims on Private Sector	42d	3,463	3,414	4,036	5,575	8,289	12,412	14,998	16,091	16,488	25,361	65,691	154,262
Claims on Nonbank Financial Insts	42g	–	–	–	5	2,486	741	30	3	3	3	50	2,588
Time and Savings Deposits	45	5,359	6,705	9,348	14,894	20,685	26,024	23,959	28,522	43,501	57,353	120,339	348,023
Money Market Instruments	46aa	192	208	386	481	459	1,356	2,742	1,878	1,628	4,892	15,236	5,286
Foreign Liabilities	46c	–	–	1	158	167	127	90	101	222	168	99	759
Credit from Deposit Money Banks	46h	20	157	25	113	70	423	322	907	435	1,282	3,375	10,196
Capital Accounts	47a	591	639	691	1,047	1,499	2,143	2,045	4,044	7,456	9,260	15,449	65,635
Other Items (Net)	47r	–166	–1,033	–2,251	–1,271	–2,316	–4,374	–3,851	–3,099	–3,742	–5,608	–23,166	–103,229
Banking Survey		*Millions of Zimbabwe Dollars: End of Period*
Foreign Assets (Net)	51n	–2,598	–3,461	–1,796	–3,074	–3,158	–13,212	–30,313	–12,004	–8,287	–11,567	–11,823	–157,653
Domestic Credit	52	14,787	20,265	24,492	32,064	41,743	64,883	87,659	97,551	154,678	263,779	573,828	3,194,524
Claims on Central Govt. (Net)	52an	4,012	6,053	7,115	8,201	10,476	21,575	30,565	33,434	62,661	106,666	154,745	630,313
Claims on Local Government	52b	46	53	70	89	298	527	678	710	843	897	1,090	1,942
Claims on Nonfin.Pub.Enterprises	52c	709	1,402	1,270	2,908	1,707	2,129	3,584	4,766	9,875	21,419	49,991	229,063
Claims on Private Sector	52d	9,895	12,677	15,954	20,852	26,720	39,871	52,617	58,543	80,562	128,802	361,722	2,278,095
Claims on Nonbank Financial Inst	52g	125	81	83	13	2,542	781	215	98	738	5,995	6,280	55,111
Liquid Liabilities	55l	10,865	15,758	21,583	27,768	38,243	49,591	53,850	70,449	110,557	217,355	599,128	3,001,475
Money Market Instruments	56aa	222	800	1,075	1,297	773	2,248	4,016	4,425	5,729	21,553	33,889	150,360
Capital Accounts	57a	1,616	2,466	3,280	3,974	4,819	7,396	9,504	15,519	24,537	45,730	101,669	484,332
Other Items (Net)	57r	–513	–2,219	–3,243	–4,050	–5,249	–7,564	–10,024	–4,846	5,569	–32,427	–172,682	–599,296
Interest Rates		*Percent Per Annum*
Bank Rate (End of Period)	60	29.50	28.50	29.50	29.50	27.00	31.50	†39.50	74.41	57.84	57.20	29.65	300.00
Money Market Rate	60b	34.77	34.18	30.90	29.64	26.18	25.15	37.22	53.13	64.98	21.52	32.35	110.05
Treasury Bill Rate	60c	26.16	33.04	29.22	27.98	24.53	22.07	32.78	50.48	64.78	17.60	28.51	52.73
Deposit Rate	60l	28.63	29.45	26.75	25.92	21.58	18.60	29.06	38.51	50.17	13.95	18.38	35.92
Lending Rate	60p	19.77	36.33	34.86	34.73	34.23	32.55	42.06	55.39	68.21	38.02	36.48	97.29
Government Bond Yield	61	17.40	....	....	....	....	....	....	....	....	....	....	....
Prices, Production, Labor		*Index Numbers (2000=100): Period Averages*
Consumer Prices	64	11.1	14.2	17.4	21.3	25.9	30.7	40.5	64.2	100.0	176.7	424.3	....
Manufacturing Prod.(1995=100)	66ey	115.1	105.7	115.8	100.0	103.6	106.9	....	....	....	....	....	....
		Number in Thousands: Period Averages
Labor Force	67d	3,502	....	....	....	....	4,921	....	4,963	....	....	....	....
Employment	67e	1,236	1,239	1,264	1,240	1,273	1,323	1,349	1,316	1,237	1,184	1,071	....
International Transactions		*Millions of Zimbabwe Dollars*
Exports	70	7,365.7	10,164.2	15,364.7	18,359.1	24,209.3	....	....	....	....	....	....	....
Imports, c.i.f.	71	11,232.3	11,798.4	18,270.6	23,048.1	28,095.1	....	....	....	....	....	....	....
Imports, f.o.b.	71.v	9,767.2	10,259.5	15,887.5	20,043.0	....	....	....	....	....	....	....	....

2004, International Monetary Fund: *International Financial Statistics Yearbook*

Zimbabwe 698

		1992	1993	1994	1995	1996	1997	1998	1999	2000	2001	2002	2003
Balance of Payments					*Millions of US Dollars: Minus Sign Indicates Debit*								
Current Account, n.i.e.	78ald	−603.7	−115.7	−424.9	....	....	....	....	....	....	....	....	....
Goods: Exports f.o.b.	78aad	1,527.6	1,609.1	1,961.1	....	....	....	....	....	....	....	....	....
Goods: Imports f.o.b.	78abd	−1,782.1	−1,487.0	−1,803.5	....	....	....	....	....	....	....	....	....
Trade Balance	78acd	−254.5	122.1	157.6	....	....	....	....	....	....	....	....	....
Services: Credit	78add	305.1	372.1	383.2	....	....	....	....	....	....	....	....	....
Services: Debit	78aed	−660.9	−563.8	−711.7	....	....	....	....	....	....	....	....	....
Balance on Goods & Services	78afd	−610.3	−69.6	−170.9	....	....	....	....	....	....	....	....	....
Income: Credit	78agd	26.0	35.0	27.5	....	....	....	....	....	....	....	....	....
Income: Debit	78ahd	−302.3	−287.1	−321.2	....	....	....	....	....	....	....	....	....
Balance on Gds, Serv. & Inc.	78aid	−886.6	−321.6	−464.5	....	....	....	....	....	....	....	....	....
Current Transfers, n.i.e.: Credit	78ajd	347.3	270.6	69.4	....	....	....	....	....	....	....	....	....
Current Transfers: Debit	78akd	−64.4	−64.7	−29.8	....	....	....	....	....	....	....	....	....
Capital Account, n.i.e.	78bcd	−1.4	−.4	284.4	....	....	....	....	....	....	....	....	....
Capital Account, n.i.e.: Credit	78bad	.2	.6	285.4	....	....	....	....	....	....	....	....	....
Capital Account: Debit	78bbd	−1.6	−1.0	−1.0	....	....	....	....	....	....	....	....	....
Financial Account, n.i.e.	78bjd	373.4	327.2	−25.5	....	....	....	....	....	....	....	....	....
Direct Investment Abroad	78bdd	—	—	−4.7	....	....	....	....	....	....	....	....	....
Dir. Invest. in Rep. Econ., n.i.e.	78bed	15.0	28.0	34.7	....	....	....	....	....	....	....	....	....
Portfolio Investment Assets	78bfd	27.6	—	—	....	....	....	....	....	....	....	....	....
Equity Securities	78bkd	—	—	—	....	....	....	....	....	....	....	....	....
Debt Securities	78bld	27.6	—	—	....	....	....	....	....	....	....	....	....
Portfolio Investment Liab., n.i.e.	78bgd	−37.1	−5.1	50.2	....	....	....	....	....	....	....	....	....
Equity Securities	78bmd	—	—	56.9	....	....	....	....	....	....	....	....	....
Debt Securities	78bnd	−37.1	−5.1	−6.7	....	....	....	....	....	....	....	....	....
Financial Derivatives Assets	78bwd	....	....	—	....	....	....	....	....	....	....	....	....
Financial Derivatives Liabilities	78bxd	....	....	—	....	....	....	....	....	....	....	....	....
Other Investment Assets	78bhd	15.9	99.9	−260.3	....	....	....	....	....	....	....	....	....
Monetary Authorities	78bod	....	....	—	....	....	....	....	....	....	....	....	....
General Government	78bpd	—	—	—	....	....	....	....	....	....	....	....	....
Banks	78bqd	15.9	99.9	−260.3	....	....	....	....	....	....	....	....	....
Other Sectors	78brd	—	—	—	....	....	....	....	....	....	....	....	....
Other Investment Liab., n.i.e.	78bid	352.0	204.4	154.7	....	....	....	....	....	....	....	....	....
Monetary Authorities	78bsd	−78.2	−7.8	−109.9	....	....	....	....	....	....	....	....	....
General Government	78btd	407.9	191.0	62.0	....	....	....	....	....	....	....	....	....
Banks	78bud	—	—	—	....	....	....	....	....	....	....	....	....
Other Sectors	78bvd	22.3	21.2	202.6	....	....	....	....	....	....	....	....	....
Net Errors and Omissions	78cad	37.2	14.9	80.2	....	....	....	....	....	....	....	....	....
Overall Balance	78cbd	−194.6	225.9	−85.8	....	....	....	....	....	....	....	....	....
Reserves and Related Items	79dad	194.6	−225.9	85.8	....	....	....	....	....	....	....	....	....
Reserve Assets	79dbd	−31.1	−293.6	12.9	....	....	....	....	....	....	....	....	....
Use of Fund Credit and Loans	79dcd	225.7	67.7	72.8	....	....	....	....	....	....	....	....	....
Exceptional Financing	79ded	....	....	....	....	....	....	....	....	....	....	....	....
Government Finance					*Millions of Zimbabwe Dollars: Year Ending June 30*								
Deficit (−) or Surplus	80	−3,861	−2,645	−2,092	−5,791	−5,147	−5,077	....	....	....	....	....	....
Total Revenue and Grants	81y	8,634	11,752	13,699	18,687	23,811	31,126	....	....	....	....	....	....
Revenue	81	8,285	11,152	12,776	16,998	22,808	30,670	....	....	....	....	....	....
Grants	81z	349	600	923	1,690	1,003	456	....	....	....	....	....	....
Exp. & Lending Minus Repay.	82z	12,495	14,396	15,790	24,479	28,958	36,202	....	....	....	....	....	....
Expenditure	82	11,217	12,390	14,538	22,000	29,691	36,454	....	....	....	....	....	....
Lending Minus Repayments	83	1,278	2,006	1,252	2,479	−733	−252	....	....	....	....	....	....
Total Financing	80h	3,860	2,645	2,092	5,791	5,147	5,077	....	....	....	....	....	....
Domestic	84a	1,321	1,279	1,733	4,802	3,973	5,168	....	....	....	....	....	....
Foreign	85a	2,539	1,366	359	990	1,175	−91	....	....	....	....	....	....
Total Debt by Residence	88	20,400	25,054	31,131	47,503	53,201	59,303	....	....	....	....	....	....
Domestic	88a	7,993	9,071	12,875	24,671	31,407	30,371	....	....	....	....	....	....
Foreign	89a	12,407	15,983	18,257	22,832	21,793	28,932	....	....	....	....	....	....
National Accounts					*Millions of Zimbabwe Dollars*								
Househ.Cons.Expend.,incl.NPISHs	96f	22,580	29,259	31,586	36,853	57,218	78,435	92,808	146,108	223,743	....	....	....
Government Consumption Expend.	91f	8,308	6,350	9,375	11,100	14,492	16,653	23,764	32,423	47,907	....	....	....
Gross Fixed Capital Formation	93e	7,691	10,022	12,002	15,265	15,434	18,424	31,122	33,550	41,554	....	....	....
Changes in Inventories	93i	−1,004	−2,416	4,274	410	−253	1,971	1,531	4,278	550	....	....	....
Exports of Goods and Services	90c	9,364	13,050	19,431	23,562	30,910	....	....	....	....	....	....	....
Imports of Goods and Services (−)	98c	12,548	13,784	20,509	25,216	30,747	....	....	....	....	....	....	....
Gross Domestic Product (GDP)	99b	34,392	42,481	56,159	61,974	87,055	108,323	146,744	221,588	311,890	....	....	....
Net Primary Income from Abroad	98.n	−1,407	−1,604	−2,405	−2,794	−2,931	−3,908	....	....	....	....	....	....
Gross National Income (GNI)	99a	32,889	40,877	53,375	58,951	84,144	....	....	....	....	....	....	....
GDP Volume 1990 Prices	99b.p	21,086	21,531	22,780	22,820	25,038	25,389	25,586	24,537	22,876	....	....	....
GDP Volume (2000=100)	99bvp	92.2	94.1	99.6	99.8	109.5	111.0	111.8	107.3	100.0	....	....	....
GDP Deflator (2000=100)	99bip	12.0	14.5	18.1	19.9	25.5	31.3	42.1	66.2	100.0	....	....	....
					Millions: Midyear Estimates								
Population	99z	11.03	11.27	11.51	11.73	11.95	12.15	12.35	12.51	12.65	12.76	12.84	12.89

International Financial Statistics
YEARBOOK
2004

1-58906-381-3